A Guide to Reviewing

World History: People and Nations

The world — in the context and color your students will appreciate!

The list below is a brief guide to key features of ***World History: People and Nations.*** Page references provide examples of these features.

◇ **Manageable, authoritative accounts** of significant historical events and personalities explore cause-and-effect relationships, helping students understand how people and nations have developed from early times to the present (pages 9, 858).

◇ **Geographical facts** consistently establish important connections to social, political, cultural, and economic developments — extending student understanding (pages 118, 143).

◇ An **invigorating writing style** (page 106), a **stunning graphic presentation** of maps, photographs, charts, and tables (pages 250, 847, 398), and an **abundance of primary sources** (pages 53, 731) add excitement and interest to history.

◇ **Clear, logical organization** provides a framework for learning, emphasizing place, time, and significance of historical events (pages 223, 711).

◇ **Motivating learning strategies** guide students to success in developing critical-thinking and social studies skills.

Developing Critical Thinking Skills (page 122)
Applying Critical Thinking Skills (page 176)
Building History Study Skills (page 683)
Applying History Study Skills (page 689)
Questions within the text (page 727)

◇ **Imaginative special features** intrigue students and creatively extend their understanding of history.

Connections: Now and Then (page 151)
What If? (page 193)
History Through the Arts (page 23)
Perspectives: Legacies of the Past (pages 308-309)
Linking Geography and History (page 623)

◇ **Concise, purposeful reviews** consistently reinforce important ideas, strengthen student understanding, and enhance skills development with an array of motivating exercises and activities.

Section Review (page 475)
Chapter Review (pages 688-689)
Unit Review (pages 740-741)

◇ An extensive **Reference Section** (pages R1-R64) assists students throughout their history study and includes an instructive **Atlas,** a complete **Glossary** of key terms, and a comprehensive **Index.**

HBJ Harcourt Brace Jovanovich, Inc.
School Department

World History
PEOPLE AND NATIONS

he world— in the context and color your students will appreciate!

With emphasis on *place, time,* and *significance,* **World History: People and Nations** blends social, political, economic, and cultural developments to help students understand people and their achievements from early times to the present. Vividly written, the textbook presents the fascinating story of historical events and incorporates the geographical facts that influenced them.

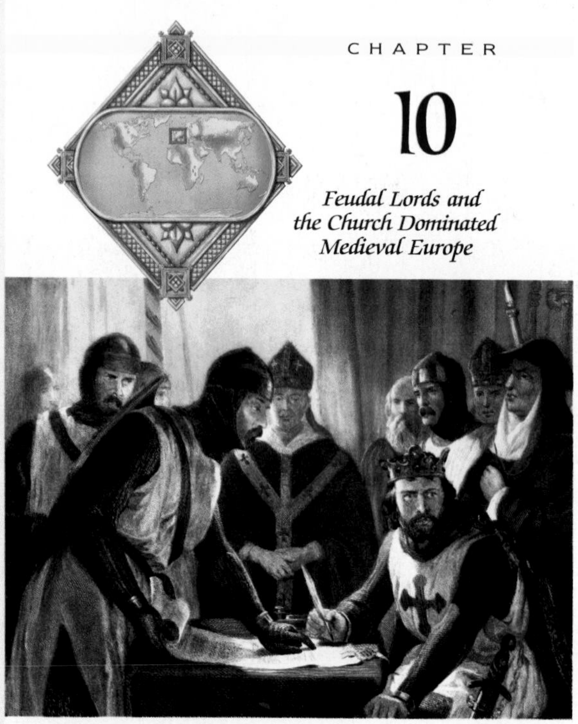

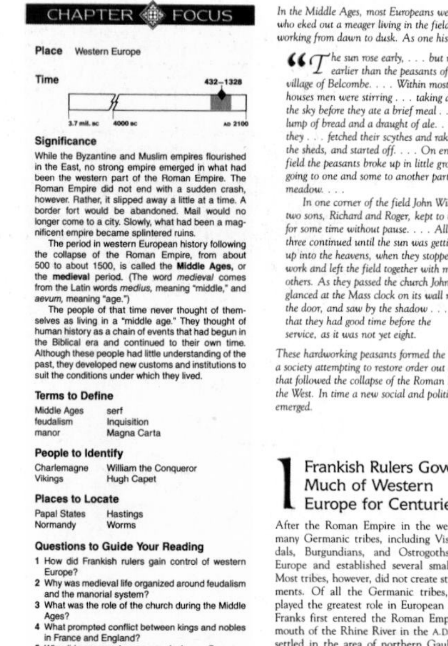

CHAPTER FOCUS

Place Western Europe

Time

432–1328

3.7 mil. BC 4000 BC AD 2100

Significance

While the Byzantine and Muslim empires flourished in the East, no strong empire emerged in what had been the western part of the Roman Empire. The Roman Empire did not end with a sudden crash, however. Rather, it slipped away a little at a time. A border fort would be abandoned. Mail would no longer come to a city. Slowly, what had been a magnificent empire became splintered ruins.

The period in western European history following the collapse of the Roman Empire, from about 500 to about 1500, is called the **Middle Ages,** or the **medieval** period. (The word *medieval* comes from the Latin words *medius,* meaning "middle," and *aevum,* meaning "age.")

The people of that time never thought of themselves as living in a "middle age." They thought of human history as a chain of events that had begun in the Biblical era and continued to their own time. Although these people had little understanding of the past, they developed new customs and institutions to suit the conditions under which they lived.

Terms to Define

Middle Ages serf
feudalism Inquisition
manor Magna Carta

People to Identify

Charlemagne William the Conqueror
Vikings Hugh Capet

Places to Locate

Papal States Hastings
Normandy Worms

Questions to Guide Your Reading

1 How did Frankish rulers gain control of western Europe?
2 Why was medieval life organized around feudalism and the manorial system?
3 What was the role of the church during the Middle Ages?
4 What prompted conflict between kings and nobles in France and England?
5 Why did popes and emperors clash over Germany and Italy?

◀ *King John signing the Magna Carta*

In the Middle Ages, most Europeans were peasants who eked out a meager living in the fields, often working from dawn to dusk. As one historian noted:

> *"The sun rose early, . . . but not much earlier than the peasants of the little village of Belcombe. . . . Within most of the houses men were stirring . . . taking a look at the sky before they ate a brief meal . . . of a lump of bread and a draught of ale. . . . Then they . . . fetched their scythes and rakes from the sheds, and started off. . . . On entering the field the peasants broke up in little groups, some going to one and some to another part of the meadow. . . .*
>
> *In one corner of the field John Wilde and his two sons, Richard and Roger, kept to their tasks for some time without pause. . . . All three continued until the sun was getting well up into the heavens, when they stopped their work and left the field together with many others. As they passed the church John glanced at the Mass clock on its wall near the door, and saw by the shadow . . . that they had good time before the service, as it was not yet eight."*

These hardworking peasants formed the backbone of a society attempting to restore order out of the chaos that followed the collapse of the Roman Empire in the West. In time a new social and political order emerged.

1 Frankish Rulers Governed Much of Western Europe for Centuries

After the Roman Empire in the west collapsed, many Germanic tribes, including Visigoths, Vandals, Burgundians, and Ostrogoths, plundered Europe and established several small kingdoms. Most tribes, however, did not create strong governments. Of all the Germanic tribes, the Franks played the greatest role in European history. The Franks first entered the Roman Empire near the mouth of the Rhine River in the A.D. 300s. They settled in the area of northern Gaul that corresponds roughly to the present-day nations of Belgium and the Netherlands.

223

Written and reviewed by both classroom teachers and distinguished scholars, ***World History*** presents manageable, authoritative accounts of significant historical events and personalities—with emphasis on cause-and-effect relationships.

The **Chapter Focus,** which introduces each chapter, prepares students for learning. At a glance, students can identify *Place, Time,* and *Significance* of important historical events.

In each chapter, well-organized, readable sections build interest and understanding. Each section concludes with a **Section Review** that allows students to monitor their progress and develop critical-thinking skills (not shown).

Throughout the text, insightful anecdotes and an upbeat, lively writing style make history enjoyable, as well as meaningful.

nlivened by graphics that inform!

Learning from Pictures *This copper mine is in Lubumbashi, Zaire. Zaire ranks as one of the top producers and exporters of copper and copper products.*

Tanzania was a vivid reminder of the economic problems that African nations still had to overcome.

Among these problems was a constant threat of famine. As the population of Africa continued to expand, many farmers overused the land. To grow more food, farmers planted crops in dry areas or on hills, where fierce winds often stripped away the topsoil. In addition, people in many parts of Africa cut down trees for firewood. As a result of these practices, **desertification**, or the spread of the
m 1984 to 1989, for
over an estimated
)0 square kilometers)
plain that stretches

d untold miseries for
ternational aid in the
elped people survive

re

political disappoint-
dence, the people of
one very important

area. They experienced a rebirth of cultural self-confidence.

During the colonial era, many Africans lost faith in their own culture as they adopted European attitudes toward Africa. African art and music were considered primitive and crude. Magnificent constructions like Great Zimbabwe, which you read about in Chapter 13, or exquisite artifacts like the bronze masks of Benin, were wrongly attributed to foreign influences. They were thought to be works of ancient Greeks or other people who had been shipwrecked on Africa's shores and had wandered into the interior. The literature of Africa—a treasury of oral traditions including myths, proverbs, and folk tales—was largely unknown to Europeans. Seeing the attitudes of Europeans, most Africans themselves turned away from their h
cultural heritage.

Not all Africans,
example. In East A
continued to be stud
dreds of years. The t
alive in the Islamic mo
The written records of
to the 1600s. The lang
evolve. James Mbotela's
(Freedom for the Slaves)
the modern form from w
Many plays and novels hav
the national language of

In West Africa, a new
oped, using the colonial l
French. Many African au
from French-speaking areas
tional recognition through
colonial oppression. In a ver
style, the poems of Léopold S
came president of independe
the hardships of colonialism.
the novels of Camara Laye of
pointed to the deep, spiritual
and its sense of social communi

In 1986 the Nigerian playwr
Soyinka won the Nobel Prize in
ing the the first African to win t
Soyinka accepted the award sayi
minute consider that the prize is ju
what I represent. I'm a part of th
tradition of Africa."

These African writers created a r
dition. The result was a remarkab

THE PERSIAN WARS 499 B.C.–479 B.C.

Persian Empire
Rebellious Ionian city-states
Greek city-states allied against the Persians
Neutral Greek city-states
Greek victory
Persian victory

Black Sea
THRACE
MACEDONIA
Mt. Olympus
Byzantium
Sea of Marmara
Wreck of Darius's fleet 492 B.C.
EPIRUS
THESSALY
Xerxes' fleet 480 B.C.
Xerxes' army 480 B.C.
Aegean Sea
Asia Minor
Thermopylae 480 B.C.
Delphi
Pergamum
Thebes
Eretria
Plataea 479 B.C.
ATTICA
Marathon 490 B.C.
Sardis
Olympia
Corinth
Athens
Salamis 480 B.C.
Ionian Sea
PELOPONNESUS
Sparta
Darius's fleet 490 B.C.
Samos
Ephesus
Delos
Miletus
Naxos
Cos
Darius's fleet (Mardonius) 492 B.C.
Rhodes
Crete
Mediterranean Sea
N
0 50 100 Miles
0 50 100 Kilometers

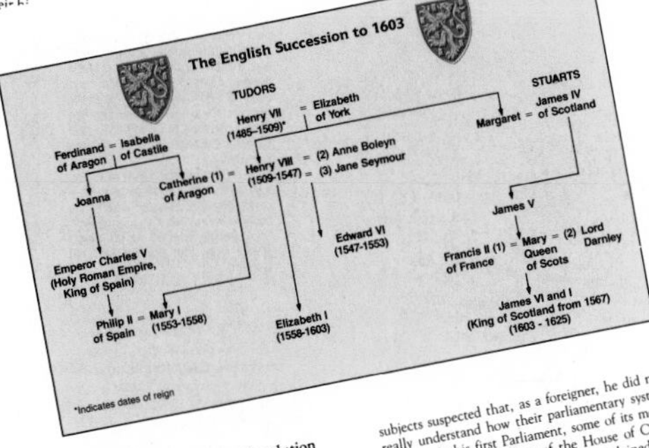

The Roots of the English Revolution

Between 1603, when Elizabeth died, and 1640, relations between the monarchy and its subjects deteriorated. The main stages in that deterioration suggest how and why it happened.

James I. The first problem arose almost immediately. King James VI of Scotland, a member of the Stuart family and the son of Mary Queen of Scots, succeeded Elizabeth to the English throne as James I of England.* He was tall and had blue eyes. At age 39, he had thin brown hair, a straggly beard, and spindly legs. The gangly king was also coarse in his habits. The French ambassador said that "where he wishes to assume the language of a king his tone is that of a tyrant, and where he condescends he is vulgar." But James had a taste for learning and was a man of considerable intelligence. Even so, he lacked common sense. According to Henry IV of France, he was "the wisest fool in Christendom."

James managed to rule in Scotland by pitting one faction against another and keeping the powerful church of Scotland under control. His English subjects suspected that, as a foreigner, he did not really understand how their parliamentary system worked. At his first Parliament, some of its members drew up an Apology of the House of Commons, a document that arrogantly explained the way its authors thought England ought to be ruled. James, who strongly believed in the divine right of kings, openly ignored their advice.

Finance and foreign policy occupied the attention of James I during much of his reign. He left the Puritans alone and even pleased them by ordering a new translation of the Bible into English. This Bible, known as the Authorized Version, or King James Version, is still one of the most widely used English translations.

James I's troubles came not from the Puritans but from Parliament. The 1600s was a time of inflation and growing government activity. James could never collect enough money in taxes to finance his policies. When the taxes passed by Parliament proved insufficient, he raised money by selling titles of nobility, granting monopoly rights to private companies, and increasing customs duties. Parliament objected to these methods. It also objected to James's attempt to create an alliance with England's old enemy, Spain.

*From this time on, England and Scotland were ruled by the same monarch.

398

More than 150 colorful, clearly labeled maps display the physical and cultural characteristics of world regions—enhancing content and developing practical map reading and interpretation skills. To boost comprehension, maps appear with related text and captions that incorporate questions.

Informative time lines help students put events in perspective, while colorful charts and tables visually clarify history.

Hundreds of striking photographs—including an 8-page introductory photo essay—with informative captions engage students, enrich the text, and reinforce key ideas.

Sample pages are reduced. Actual sizes are 8″ × 10″.

Features that enrich and excite!

In every chapter, **Connections: Then and Now** helps students discover how familiar places, customs, and traditions have developed and changed throughout time.

Brief, thought-provoking **What If?** features provide intriguing opportunities for students to strengthen their creative understanding of history—imagining what might have happened had events been different.

Linking Geography and History—at the beginning of the book and in each unit—allows students to explore the physical characteristics of regions and reinforces their understanding of cultures and history.

CONNECTIONS: THEN AND NOW

Baths

Ancient peoples were just as fond of taking a plunge into water as we are. The Romans were particularly fond of bathing and built many large public pools and baths. These pools and baths were often filled with water of different temperatures, heated either by natural hot springs or by furnaces. The Roman bather would go from one pool to the other, combining dips with exercises followed by massages with fine oils.

Some of the Roman bath houses also contained libraries, sports facilities, and shops. The public bath was a social gathering place where people could meet, gossip, and even do business. The largest public bath in Rome is credited as the main achievement of its builder, the Emperor Caracalla, who ruled in the A.D. 200s.

The Romans built baths wherever they settled. One such place in England, which had natural hot springs, became known as the city of Bath (top). People enjoyed its refreshing waters long after the Romans left England.

Today public baths are used as neighborhood gathering places and are extremely popular throughout Japan. There is also a very ornate public bath in Moscow, the capital of the Soviet Union, and in Budapest, Hungary (below). In the United States, outdoor and indoor public swimming pools provide the same enjoyment and recreation the ancient Romans knew.

71 B.C. the Roman army had crushed the uprising. The generals crucified Spartacus and 6,000 of his followers. **Crucifixion,** in which the accused was tied to a cross and left to die a slow and agonizing death from suffocation, was a common Roman method of execution.

SECTION 2 REVIEW

1. **Define** indemnity, latifundia, equites, crucifixion
2. **Identify** publican, Spartacus
3. **Locate** Carthage, Sicily, Zama
4. **Summarizing Ideas** **(a)** How were Rome and Carthage in competition with each other? **(b)** What were the final results of the Punic Wars?
5. **Determining Cause and Effect** **(a)** How did the government of Rome change as a result of the conquest of new territories? **(b)** What effect did the Punic Wars have on Roman agriculture?

3 The Roman Republic Was Transformed into an Empire

By 133 B.C. the Roman Republic faced many problems. Although courageous leaders attempted reform, the days of the republic were numbered.

The Gracchi

Two brothers, Tiberi… uhs), were among… Elected tribune in… senators used pub… therefore limite… could use. He… from the citie…

Despite such determined resistance, the Allies continued their intensive bombing of Japan. Japanese ports were effectively blockaded, and the Japanese navy was immobilized. Nevertheless, the Japanese government still refused to surrender.

Yalta and Potsdam

Roosevelt and Churchill had long hoped to pe… suade Stalin to enter the war in the Pacific. Befo… the defeat of Germany, however, the Soviet Uni… had been completely occupied in defending its… Moreover, it considered the war against Japan… business of the United States.

In February 1945 Roosevelt and Churchill… with Stalin at Yalta, in the Soviet Union. The… Three, as these Allied leaders were called, ag… that Germany should be temporarily divided… occupied by Allied troops including those of Fr… The liberated areas of Europe were to have d… cratically elected governments. The Soviet U… was to enter the war against Japan. As comp… tion it was to receive several Japanese territo… Another conference began on July 17, 19… Potsdam, near Berlin. Roosevelt had died in…

Learning from Pictures On the grounds of L… Palace located in Yalta in the Soviet Union, the… Three decide the fate of postwar Europe.

…declared war on Japan. Sovie… met little resistance. Manchuria, where they met little resistance. On August 9 an American plane dropped a second and even more powerful atomic bomb on the city of Nagasaki.

What If?

The Atomic Bomb

The atomic bomb had been tested earlier in the war, but in August 1945 only two atomic bombs existed. One bomb was dropped on Hiroshima, and a few days later the second bomb was dropped on Nagasaki. How do you think world history might have been different if the bombs had not detonated, or if the Japanese had known that the Allies had no more atomic bombs? Since Germany was also developing atomic weapons near the end of the war, how might history have been different if Germany had actually produced the atomic bomb first?

736

LINKING GEOGRAPHY TO HISTORY

The Berlin Conference: Making a New Map of Africa

The continent of Africa has a distinctive location. It sits directly on the equator and reaches almost as far north as it does south of the earth's mid-line. In addition, Africa occupies an amazingly central position in relation to the other landmasses of the world. The Americas lie to the west, Eurasia to the north and east, Australia to the southeast, and Antarctica to the south. Africa's central location, along with its huge size and vast stores of mineral wealth, made it a prime target for colonization by European nations during the 1800s. As you have read in this chapter, each of the European colonial powers created spheres of influence in Africa.

Among the most significant of these powers was Germany. Otto von Bismarck, the German imperial chancellor, planned not only to expand Germany's control in Africa but also to play his country's European rivals one against the other, thereby weakening their influence. By the 1880s Germany had begun to carry out these plans by establishing colonies in locations designed to obstruct the imperial designs of other European powers. For example, the Germans had taken Cameroon which lay between French colonies, and German East Africa separated two huge British colonies. Then in 1884 Bismarck called for a meeting in Berlin to complete the division of Africa among all interested parties.

At the time of this Berlin Conference, more than 80 percent of the African people still lived under traditional African tribal rule. With absolutely no regard for tribal boundaries, the representatives of the colonial powers carved up the entire African continent among themselves. These representatives argued over, drew, erased, and redrew the boundary lines of their new colonies. Huge parcels of land changed hands, sometimes simply at the whim of one representative. Often, people from the same tribe found themselves separated and ruled by different colonial powers. Conversely, the new boundaries frequently threw together tribes hostile to one another. Also, in drawing boundary lines the representatives ignored such natural boundaries as rivers and mountain ranges. Ignorant of the continent's geography, the representatives had no idea of the location of such natural dividing lines.

Probably no meeting in history has had the lasting impact on a continent that the Berlin Conference had on Africa. In many… sions made at… still…

Africa secured independence after 1950, but the colonial boundaries established by the Berlin Conference had acquired the legitimacy of time. Even though many of these boundaries were arbitrary and a possible cause for future trouble, the leaders of the new African nations feared that drawing new boundaries might result in… chaos. Yet at the… leaders found… the…

Victoria Falls, on the Zambia-Zimbabwe border

Engrossing **History Through the Arts** features display the cultural history of a civilization as reflected in its art, music, literature, religion, and philosophy.

In each unit, **Perspectives: Legacies of the Past** help students discover special people, events, and inventions that have changed history.

Excerpts from hundreds of primary sources add excitement and interest to **World History.** These eyewitness accounts and descriptions of people, places, and events weave fact with personal views.

Special sections at the back of the textbook—an instructive **Atlas,** a complete **Glossary** of key terms, and a comprehensive **Index**—are convenient reference tools for students (not shown).

History Through the Arts

PAINTING

Lady with a Unicorn

The work of the great Italian artist Raphael reflected the intellectual and artistic ideals of the Renaissance. His paintings combined spirituality and artistry with the search for realism and truth that characterized his age. Raphael studied and worked in Florence, in the schools of Michelangelo and Leonardo da Vinci. He became so accomplished that he was called to Rome to help decorate the Vatican. Each year millions of visitors to Rome marvel at some of his most famous works.

In his paintings Raphael conveyed a feeling of balanced space, giving the viewer a sensation of tranquility and joy. In this painting we see a Renaissance lady holding a baby unicorn. The unicorn is snugly enclosed in the lady's arms, yet relaxed in the spaciousness of her lap. The main figure takes up almost the entire canvas and the landscape stretches back into the distance; yet there is no sense of crowding. The glowing fabric of the lady's dress and the beauty of her pendant reveal the splendor of Renaissance taste.

Raphael's respect for antiquity are demonstrated in the little unicorn, a fabled animal that appeared in the art of ancient civilizations. During the

"THE GIRL HE LEFT BEHIND"
IS STILL BEHIND HIM
She's a WOW
WOMAN ORDNANCE WORKER

Learning from Pictures *In the United States, posters like this one encouraged civilians to take part in the war effort.*

were sunk; others were badly damaged. American dead totaled more than 2,300.

In an excerpt from his book *At Dawn We Slept,* historian Gordon Prange relates an eyewitness account of the attack on Pearl Harbor:

> "When the attack began, . . . the explosion of bombs, the whine of bullets, the roar of planes, the belching guns of aroused defenders, the acrid smell of fire and smoke—all blended into a nerve-racking [sound] of chaos. . . . Bombardiers still dropped their torpedoes, while dive bombers pounced like hawks. . . . Far above, high-level bombers rained their deadly missiles as fighters shuttled in and out, weaving together the fearful tapestry of destruction."

On December 8, 1941, Congress declared war on Japan, as did the British Parliament. Three days

731

PERSPECTIVES: LEGACIES OF THE PAST

The Calendar—Will We Ever Get It Straight?

The calendar is a mess. Some months have 31 days, some have 30, and February has 28—except, of course, in "leap years," when February has 29 days instead of 28. We are told that it's easy to remember that leap days always occur in years divisible by four—such as 1984, 1988, and 1992. But the year 1900, although it was divisible by four, was not a leap year. Neither were 1700 and 1800. The year 2000 will be a leap year, but 2100 (3 × 700 2100) will not be.

For thousands of years people have tried to make the calendar as accurate as possible. Yet we still don't have it quite right. Each year is still 26 seconds off. Fortunately, that's not a lot—it's off by one day out of every 3,323 years.

As imprecise as this is, our calendar is better than what our forefathers put up with. The year 46 B.C. had 445 days. In A.D. 1582, October had only 21 days. And in 1752, Americans went to bed the night of September 2nd and awoke the morning of September 14th.

People have kept track of time for their own survival. To know when to plant, or when to prepare for floods and storms, people learned to watch the movements of the sun, moon, and stars. Many early cultures worshiped these heavenly bodies and devised calendars to know when to hold religious festivals. A lunar month—from one full moon to the next—was one good measure of time everyone could *see*. But, because each solar year contains about 12.37 lunar months, the sun cycle and the moon cycle didn't fit together. People had to choose between the two, or try to harmonize them.

The Babylonians may have been the first to use a formal calendar. Following the moon cycle, they alternated between 29- and 30-day months, which only added up to 364 days—not a full year. The ancient Chinese and, later, the Hebrews and Muslims also used the lunar cycle.

The Egyptians counted 365 days between the *annual* rising of the Nile, and divided the year into 12 30-day months with 5 extra days. This was closer than the Babylonian calendar, but it compensated for the extra ¼ day each year has.

308

The ancestor of the calendar we use today was invented in Rome—although the early Romans were quite nonchalant about calendrical accuracy, and made do with a 10-month, 304-day year. About 700 B.C., two new months were added—Januarius and Februarius—making the year 355 days long. By the time Julius Caesar came to power in 59 B.C., the Roman calendar was more than two months behind—and the spring festival was ridiculously being celebrated in July. With the help of the Egyptian astronomer Sosigines, Caesar changed the calendar to 365 days, adding one extra day every fourth February. Caesar rewarded himself by changing the name of the month Quintilis to his own, Julius (July). His successor Augustus, not to be outdone, changed the next month, Sextilis, to Augustus.

Things went along pretty smoothly for the next 1,500 years until a pope in Rome noticed that the annual date for Easter—the first full moon after the spring equinox—was getting later and later in the year. He discovered that the Julian (Julius Caesar's) calendar was about 11 minutes too long. Over 1,500 years this had put an extra 10 days on the year. So in 1582 Pope Gregory XIII declared that the day after October 4 would be October 15. To prevent this problem from recurring, he had to find a way of eliminating three days about every 400 years. He did this by abolishing leap day in all turn-of-the-century years except those divisible by 400. Therefore, 1600 remained a leap year but 1700, 1800, and 1900 each lost the leap day. This made the calendar correct to within 26 seconds a year, or one day every 3,323 years.

Roman Catholic countries adopted the Gregorian calendar immediately. Protestant countries were reluctant. When England and its colonies, including America, finally adopted the calendar in 1752, they were 11 days behind. After Parliament announced that the day after September 2, 1752, would be September 14, angry people shouting "Give us back our 11 days!" mobbed the House of Commons. Landlords protested losing two weeks' rents, and everyone protested changing dates for holidays and birthdays. But in America, Ben Franklin advised people not to regret the lost time but to rejoice that one could "lie down in peace on the second of the month and not . . . awake till the morning of the 14th."

In Orthodox Christian countries—Greece, Russia, Romania, Serbia, Bulgaria, and others—the Julian Calendar continued. The Russian Orthodox church still follows the Julian calendar and celebrates Christmas 13 days later than western Christians. Russia kept the Julian calendar until the 1918 Communist takeover. The ensuing loss of 13 days led to the oddity that the Communist "October Revolution" had to be celebrated in November.

Some people argue for a "world calendar." Each 52-week year would begin with Sunday, and leap days would be tacked on at the end of the year wherever necessary. Such a change is hard to make, and many people would protest, but it has been done before. "Time stops for no man," but time has frequently been rearranged—on paper.

Photos *Page 308: Jewish omer calendar (top); Pope Gregory XII presenting calendar (bottom); Page 309: Stonehenge (top); Egyptian calendar (middle); Aztec calendar (bottom)*

309

Sample pages are reduced. Actual sizes are 8″ × 10″.

Motivating skills activities!

READ
WRITE
INTERPRET
●CONNECT
THINK

BUILDING HISTORY STUDY SKILLS

Making Connections With History: Linking History to Architec

Architecture often reflects the values of a culture. The skyscraper is both the triumphant symbol of, and at the same time, an unwelcome intruder into, the city. It shatters scale and steals light, yet it suggests the personality of the city of which it is a part. It has also made the city's character a reflection of its own quality. For example, the Sears Tower in Chicago and the Empire State Building in New York City are the symbols of these metropolitan areas just as the

Practicing the skill. Select se library that include photographs of b ies. Then write a brief explanation of relation to the culture and history of

To apply this skill, see Applying His page 895.

READ
●WRITE
INTERPRET
CONNECT
THINK

BUILDING HISTORY STUDY SKILLS

Writing About History: Paraphrasing Information

you study world history and perfect your writing skills, u will use many primary and secondary sources. You ight either quote or paraphrase th ... repeating exactly the words of t ... *Paraphrasing* is translating som words. Putting something into your you think about what you have rea understand and remember, espe writing a report, paraphrasing wil rizing, or copying the words an acknowledging the source.

How to Paraphrase

...hrase information, fol ...e main idea of the ... the details—bits ... to the main idea. ... main idea and de ... are your statement ... questions: ... you written a co ... es it make sense? ... es it have new ... eaning?

...loping the Skill

...ollowing documer ... African city of K ... e the main idea a ... sentences.

"The story goes that there was a Sultan of Shiraz named Hasan bin Ali. . . . One day he saw a vision of a rat with an iron snout nibbling and gnawing at the walls. From this he foreboded the ... country, and so, . . . the whole family, ... away from the doomed ... the sixth

Arab dhous

READ
WRITE
INTERPRET
CONNECT
●THINK

BUILDING HISTORY STUDY SKILLS

Thinking About History: Identifying Bias

Bias is a word that often has negative connotations. People often equate bias with *prejudice*, a negative (or posi-

Developing the Skill

Procopius, an official in Constantinople, wrote *The Secret*

●READ
WRITE
INTERPRET
CONNECT
THINK

BUILDING HISTORY STUDY SKILLS

Reading About History: Identifying Sources of Evidence

Identifying sources of evidence—information used to support an explanation of the past—helps us interpret historical events. Two basic categories of sources are used as evidence. Primary sources include items such as artifacts, original documents, letters, diaries, and eyewitness accounts of an event or a period of history. Secondary sources are accounts written after the events by people who played no part in them.

How to Identify Sources of Evidence

To identify sources of evidence, follow these steps.

1. Identify the document or artifact. For example, is it a letter, diary, government record, work of art, building, or photograph?
2. Review the definitions of primary and secondary sources to determine the category of the evidence you have labeled.
3. Determine and then record the usefulness of the evidence. What question will it help you answer? Is a primary source always more reliable as evidence than a secondary source? Why or why not? Support your opinion with facts.

Developing the Skill

The work of art "The Royal Standard of Ur" was found in a Sumerian grave dated about 2700 B.C. It is made of shell, lapis lazuli (a semiprecious stone), and red stone inlaid on the sides of a wooden box. In the panel, the fruits of victory are being celebrated by the court. From this artifact depicting domestic animals, the wheel, leisure activities such as listening to music, and the banquet itself, historians can determine the sophistication of Sumerian society.

"The Royal Standard of Ur" is classified as a primary source. Sometimes a piece of evidence, however, can be classified as both a primary source and a secondary source, depending on the purpose for its use and the question that historians wish to answer. For example, Howard Carter's description of the opening of Egyptian pharaoh Tutankhamen's tomb can be classified as a primary source when the question posed concerns the discovery of the tomb. However, this same description is considered a secondary source when it is used to answer questions about Egyptian life during ancient times. Can you see the two applications of sources of evidence from the excerpt below?

> "With suppressed excitement I carefully cut the cord, removed that precious seal, drew back the bolts, and opened the doors, when a fourth shrine was revealed . . . even more brilliant in workmanship than the last. . . . There, filling the entire area within . . . stood an immense yellow quartzite sarcophagus [stone coffin]. . . .
>
> The tackle for raising the lid was in position. I gave the word. Amid intense silence the huge slab . . . rose from its bed. . . . The lid being suspended in mid-air, we rolled back those covering shrouds, one by one. . . . So gorgeous was the sight that met our eyes: a golden effigy of the young boy king."

Practicing the skill. How might an account of the 1988 discovery of a Spanish galleon that sank off the coast of Florida in 1568 be considered both a primary and a secondary source?

To apply this skill, see Applying History Study Skills on page 47.

Sumerian Royal Standard of Ur

31

READ
WRITE
●INTERPRET
CONNECT
THINK

BUILDING HISTORY STUDY SKILLS

Interpreting Visuals: Using a Time Line to Understand B.C. and A.D.

To understand history you need to be aware of when events happened. In this book we will be using a system of dating years from the birth of Christ. Years following Christ's birth are identified in numerical order and start with the letters A.D. The letters A.D. stand for the Latin phrase *Anno Domini,* which means "in the year of our Lord," or "since the birth of Christ." The year A.D. 1900 thus stands for 1,900 years after Christ's birth. Years before Christ's birth are identified in reverse numerical order and are followed by the letters B.C., which stand for "Before the birth of Christ." Thus the date 2000 B.C. means 2,000 years before Christ's birth.

To calculate how many years separate events in modern times from events in ancient history requires using both B.C. and A.D. For example, 5000 B.C. was 6,990 years before A.D. 1990 (5,000 + 1,990 = 6,990), while 1000 B.C. was about 2,500 years before A.D. 1500 (1,000 + 1,500 = 2,500).

The method of dating events from the birth of Christ is only one of several ways of calculating time. Muslims, Chinese, Jews, and Hindus count the years in different ways. For example, the Christian year A.D. 1900 corresponds with the Muslim year 1318, the Hebrew year 5660, and the Chinese year 4597.

How to Use a Time Line to Understand B.C. and A.D.

To help you understand when important events occurred, the Chapter Review in each chapter in this book includes a time line that shows the order, or sequence, of important events discussed in the chapter. A time line can also help you see relationships between certain events. In order to use a time line to understand B.C. and A.D., follow these steps.

1. Determine the length of time shown on the time line. Be certain to calculate the years that are B.C. and those that are A.D.
2. Read the time line from left to right so that you can determine the sequence of events.
3. Identify the important events that the time line shows. Which events occurred in B.C.? Which events occurred in A.D.?
4. Identify relationships in time between the events on the time line. For example, how many years before A.D. 158 was 1350 B.C.?

Developing the Skill

The time line at the bottom of this page includes several important events that you will study in later chapters of this book. The time line documents events that occurred between 1200 B.C. and A.D. 1988, a period of 3,188 years (1,200 + 1,988 = 3,188).

As you read the time line from left to right, notice that 1000 B.C. is earlier in time than 100 B.C. and that 500 B.C. is later in time than 800 B.C. This is true because the years before the birth of Christ (B.C.) are numbered in reverse numerical order. Also note that A.D. 1900 is later in time than A.D. 100 because the years after the birth of Christ (A.D.) are numbered in numerical order.

The time line helps you to understand the order in which events occurred. For example, the Bronze Age began in southwestern Asia in 1200 B.C.—447 years before the legendary founding of Rome (753 B.C.) and 739 years before the Age of Pericles in Athens (461 B.C.). Also note that the Bronze Age began about 2,976 years before the signing of the Declaration of Independence. You know that this is true because from 1200 B.C. to the end of the B.C. period was 1,200 years, and from the beginning of A.D. to A.D. 1776 was 1776 years (1,200 + 1,776 = 2,976).

Practicing the skill. How many years after the beginning of the Bronze Age in southwestern Asia was George Bush elected President of the United States?

To apply this skill, see Applying History Study Skills on page 15.

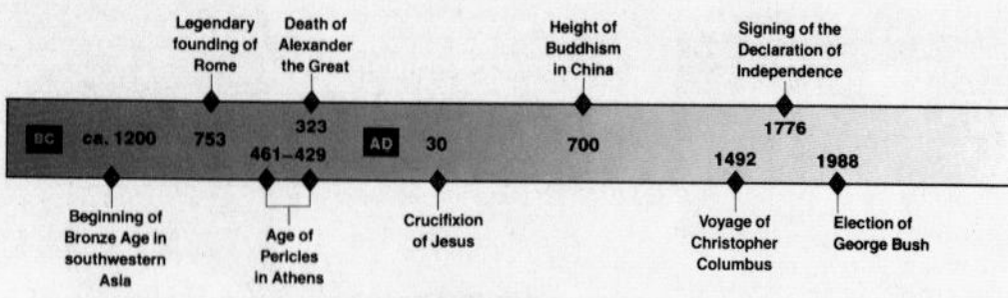

12

In each chapter, **Building History Study Skills** provides opportunities for students to develop skills in five important strands: "Reading About History," "Writing About History," "Interpreting Visuals," "Making Connections with History," or "Thinking About History." Students practice skills in **Applying History Study Skills** in each **Chapter Review.**

Sample pages are reduced. Actual sizes are 8″ × 10″.

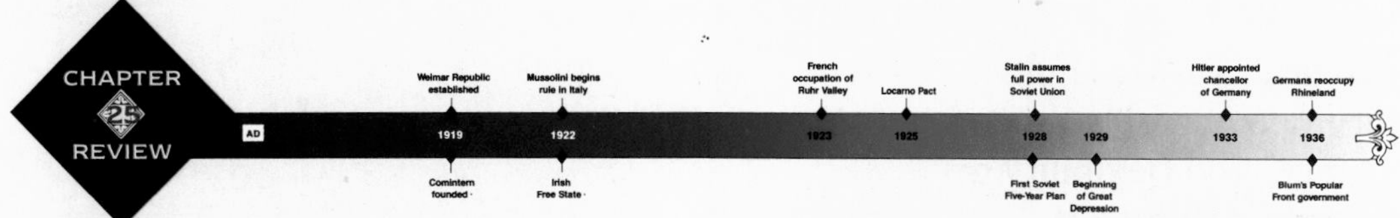

Chapter Summary

The following list contains the key concepts you have learned about political, social, and economic conditions in the United States and Europe following World War I.

1. The period following World War I was a time of major stresses and uncertainties.
2. The literature, music, art, and science of the time

Reviewing Important Terms

Supply the term that correctly completes each statement.

1. _______ _______ are formed when land is pooled into large farms on which people can work together.
2. Governmental regulation and direction of national resources to achieve economic stability occurs in a _______ _______.

5. **Comparing Ideas** **(a)** How did the economic situation in the United States compare with the economic situation in Europe during the postwar years? **(b)** What brought the boom years to an end?
6. **Interpreting Ideas** **(a)** How did the arts reflect the disillusionment of the postwar era? **(b)** How did popular culture reflect this disillusionment?

"It is sometimes asked whether it is not possible to slow down the tempo a bit, to put a check on the movement. No, comrades, it is not possible! The tempo must not be reduced! On the contrary, we must increase it as much as is within our powers and possibilities. . . .

To slacken the tempo would mean falling behind. And those who fall behind get beaten. . . . No, we refuse to be beaten! One feature of the history of old Russia was the continual beatings she suffered for falling behind, for her backwardness. She was beaten by the Mongol Khans. She was beaten by the Turkish beys. She was beaten by the Swedish feudal lords. She was beaten by the Polish and Lithuanian gentry. She was beaten by the British and French capitalists. . . . All beat her—for her backwardness: . . ."

The Five-Year Plans	First 5-Year Plan		Second 5-Year Plan
	1928	1932	1937
Industrial production (million rubles)	18.3	43.3	95.5
Electricity (million kilowatts)	5.05	13.4	36.2
Steel (million tons)	4.0	5.9	17.7
Grain harvest (million tons)	73.3	69.6	75.0
Cattle (million head)	70.5	40.7	63.2

Investigating Further

1. **Writing a Report** Using encyclopedias and books, prepare a brief biographical sketch of Benito Mussolini.
2. **Presenting an Oral Report** Prepare a report on the response of the United States and European nations to the Great Depression, explaining why the policy of economic nationalism created more problems than it solved.

689

UNIT 6 REVIEW 1882–1945

Unit Summary

The following list contains the key concepts you have learned about world war in the twentieth century.

1. The rivalries among European nations intensified in the early 1900s.
2. The 1914 assassination of Archduke Ferdinand in Sarajevo sparked World War I and within a few months, almost all the nations of Europe, plus Japan, were at war.
3. A dramatic upheaval took place in Russia, where in 1917 a revolution abolished the monarchy. Following the civil war in Russia, a government based on the principles of Marx and communism was created.
4. Although World War I ended in 1918, the problems it caused continued to plague governments.
5. Woodrow Wilson's Fourteen Points offered idealistic goals, but as the Allies sought to collect reparations for their wartime losses and to gain additional territory, many of Wilson's goals were forgotten.
6. In 1920, 42 nations founded the League of Nations. However, the United States did not join, and the League's efforts were thus crippled from the start.
7. The new outlook and the uncertainties of the stressful period following World War I were reflected by the science, literature, music, and art of the time.
8. In the United States, a sense of optimism and the influence of European contact brought about rapid change during the decade called the Roaring Twenties.
9. The stock market crash marked the beginning of the Great Depression in 1929, and in Europe instability due to the depression was widespread.
10. In Italy and Germany, dissatisfaction with the weakness and hesitations of democratic governments led to an extreme form of dictatorship, fascism.
11. In territories controlled by Great Britain, major political changes took place during the 1920s and 1930s. Political and social reforms were also attempted in Turkey, Persia, China, Japan, and Africa.
12. Developments in Latin America reflected the worldwide economic crisis.
13. In the 1930s the League of Nations failed to halt aggressions by the imperial government of Japan and the Fascists, which brought about World War II. In 1945 the Allies conquered Germany and Japan.

On a separate sheet of paper, complete the following review exercises.

Reviewing Concepts

Match each of the following items with the correct description in column 2.

a. Kellogg-Briand Pact
b. Balfour Declaration
c. Nazi-Soviet Pact
d. Atlantic Charter
e. Zimmerman telegram
f. Fourteen Points
g. Yalta Conference
h. *Mein Kampf*
i. Treaty of Portsmouth
j. Versailles Treaty

____ 1. Called for "peace with justice"
____ 2. Stated principles underlying Nazi movement
____ 3. Settled Russo-Japanese War
____ 4. Levied heavy reparations on Germany
____ 5. Outlawed war
____ 6. Announced war aims of the democracies
____ 7. Pledged Soviet Union's neutrality
____ 8. Temporarily divided Germany
____ 9. Favored creation of Jewish "national home"
____ 10. Invited Mexico to join the Central Powers

Applying Critical Thinking Skills

1. **Summarizing Ideas** **(a)** How did World War I help bring about a boom period in the United States? **(b)** What conditions brought this period to an end?
2. **Classifying Ideas** Choose two of the following and discuss how they reflected the uncertainties of the period following World War I: **(a)** literature, **(b)** music, **(c)** painting, **(d)** architecture, **(e)** film.
3. **Contrasting Ideas** How did Sun Yat-sen, Chiang Kai-shek, and Mao Zedong differ in their plans for China's future? Include the following topics in your answer: **(a)** the role of the people; **(b)** foreign interference in China; **(c)** economic reforms; **(d)** constitutional government; **(e)** the need for modernization.
4. **Evaluating Ideas** **(a)** What were the foreign policy objectives of Italy, Germany, and Japan in the 1930s? **(b)** How did these nations achieve their objectives?
5. **Determining Cause and Effect** **(a)** Compare the causes of World War I with the causes of World War II. **(b)** Why might the Versailles Treaty be considered a cause of World War II?
6. **Comparing Ideas** **(a)** Compare the principles expressed in the Atlantic Charter with those listed in the Fourteen Points. **(b)** How did each of these documents seek to establish "peace with justice"?
7. **Analyzing Ideas** **(a)** How did the United States assist the Allies before December 1941? **(b)** Why did the United States move away from its neutral status?
8. **Determining Cause and Effect** **(a)** How did the bombings of Hiroshima and Nagasaki change the nature of warfare? **(b)** What other technological developments grew out of World War II?

Relating Geography to History

Refer to maps in Chapter 24 and Chapter 27. How did the map of Europe change after the Versailles Peace Conference? How did it change after the end of World War II?

740

Writing About History

President Truman once declared, "Men make history and not the other way around." Use three of the following leaders as examples to explain Truman's statement: **(a)** Woodrow Wilson, **(b)** Sun Yat-sen, **(c)** Mustafa Kemal, **(d)** Mohandas Gandhi, **(e)** Winston Churchill.

Further Reading

Archer, Jules. *African Firebrand: Kenyatta of Kenya.* Julian Messner, New York. Tells the story of Kenya's struggle for independence during the turbulent 1950s and 1960s.

Feuerlicht, Roberta. *Desperate Act: The Assassination of Franz Ferdinand at Sarajevo.* McGraw-Hill, New York. Describes the events leading to war and the assassination of the archduke.

Marshall, S. L. A. *World War I*, McGraw-Hill, New York. Summarizes the war and its effects.

Richter, Hans Peter. *I Was There.* Dell, New York. Gives an eyewitness account of a boy who participated in German Youth.

Robertson, John R. *China: From Manchu to Mao.* Atheneum, New York. Chronicles twentieth-century China.

Sulzberger, C. L. *World War II.* McGraw-Hill, New York. Covers campaigns of World War II.

Unit Six Chronology

Date	Political and Social Developments	Technological and Scientific Advances	Visual Arts and Literature	Religious and Philosophical Thought
1880–1910	Triple Alliance and Triple Entente 24* Boxer Rebellion 26 Russo–Japanese War 24	Industrial Revolution continues 24 Einsteinian physics 25 Leon Sullivan 25	Picasso, cubism 25 Motion pictures 25	Freudian psychology 25 Zionism 26
1910–1920	Chinese Republic 26 Assassination of Franz Ferdinand 24 World War I 24 Lusitania sunk 24 Russian Revolution 24 Treaties of Brest–Litovsk and Versailles 24	U–boats 24 Machine guns 24 Poison gas 24 Tank 24	Proust 25 Stravinsky, Schoenberg, Berg, Webern 25	Gandhi 26
1920–1930	Weimar Republic 25 Chiang Kai-shek 26, Mussolini 25, Stalin 25, Kemal 26 Lenin's NEP 25 African and Asian nationalism 26 Fascism 25	Frank Lloyd Wright 25 Auto, phone, radio 25 Industrialization 24–26	Mann 25 Kafka and surrealism 25 Joyce *Ulysses* 25 T. S. Eliot 25 Jazz 25	Gandhi 26
1930–1939	Rise of Hitler 25 Great Depression 25 FDR's New Deal 25 Soviet purges 25 Kenyatta, Azikiwe 26 Long March 26	TVA 25 Autobahn 25 Corporate collectivism 25	*Grapes of Wrath* 25 Dali 25 Big Band Era 25	Spengler: *Decline of the West* 25
1939–1945	Germany invades Poland 27 Pearl Harbor 27 UN agreement 27 Yalta and Potsdam 27 Hiroshima 27	Blitzkrieg 27 Nuclear power 27 Panzer units 27 Radar 27		Meltzer *Never to Forget* 27

*Indicates chapter in which concept is discussed

741

Each **Chapter Review** reinforces ideas and enhances skills development with an array of motivating exercises and activities:

- Chapter Summary
- Reviewing Important Terms
- Developing Critical Thinking Skills
- Relating Geography to History
- Relating Past to Present
- Investigating Further

Each **Unit Review** further reinforces comprehension and extends skills development through:

- Unit Summary
- Reviewing Concepts
- Applying Critical Thinking Skills
- Relating Geography to History
- Writing About History
- Unit Chronology
- Further Reading

n abundance of teaching resources

Annotated Teacher's Edition

Our remarkable *Annotated Teacher's Edition* offers incomparable support, guidance, and flexibility to help you teach history effectively and creatively.

UNIT THREE SYNTHESIS

The World in Transition

I The Byzantine Empire Preserved the Heritage of Rome

In the West the collapse of the Roman Empire resulted in the disappearance of strong governments. However, the Roman Empire in the East—the Byzantine Empire—maintained its traditions and kept out barbarian invaders.

The Byzantine Empire

By the early 500s the empire in the West had broken down into a group of Germanic tribal kingdoms. The Eastern Roman Empire, on the other hand, had ousted the barbarians and ... great political, eco...

Kievan Rus

A vast, grassy, almost treeless plain called the steppe stretches across eastern Europe and central Asia. On the western portions of the steppe, another civilization—Kievan Rus—arose.

Kiev, one of many city-states in the region, prospered because of its strategic location astride rich trade routes. In time, Kiev became the most powerful city in a region that included many semi-independent principalities.

Religion dominated Kievan culture. Although authors wrote epic poems and historical chronicles about wars and the personal tragedies associated with war, religious hymns and sermons constituted the bulk of Kievan literature. Icon painting became the most distinctive Kievan art form.

The Mongols

fter the rule of Yaroslav the Wise ended in 1054, ev declined in power and wealth. By 1240 fierce ngol invaders from Central Asia had conquered burned almost every city in Kievan Rus. The ngols retained control of the Kievan region until 1400s.

n time, Mongol rule grew weaker and the es of the region became more independent. g the 1300s Moscow, or Muscovy, became rongest principality. By the late 1400s, Musad overthrown Mongol rule and become the of an independent state called Russia.

Islam Became a Powerful Force from Spain to India

the prophet Muhammad founded Islam, st of the world's major religions.

● Wilson was compassionate toward the defeated peoples. He had grown up in the Reconstruction South, where Southerners received a "peace of vengeance."

SECTION 5

Focus/Motivation
Write on the chalkboard or on an overhead projector the following quotation from one of the British delegates to the Paris Peace Conference:

"We arrived determined that a peace of justice and wisdom should be negotiated: we left it conscious that the Treaties imposed upon our enemies were neither just nor wise."

Have students hypothesize about the type of treaty that would cause a delegate to the peace conference to make such a statement. *(For example, the victors did not include the defeated in the negotiations; the defeated were forced to give up large amounts of territory; the defeated were forced to pay large indemnities; the defeated were forced to disarm beyond a reasonable point; the Allies received unequal benefits from the treaty.)* As students read the section, have them note the characteristics of the treaty that were "neither just nor wise."

Presentation
Identifying Ideas (Average/Group)
Have students review the map on page 659 and identify the nine new countries that were added to Europe as a result of World War I.

seizure of Chinese territory, Japan was to have the first choice and the largest share. A bitter fight and Japan's threat to leave the conference caused Wilson to give in on the Shandong Peninsula.

Reparations and peacekeeping. The destruction caused by the war brought up the problem of **reparations**—payment for war damages. Who should pay for restoring the land? Did war damages include damage to property only? Or should reparations also include pensions to wounded veterans, and to widows and orphans?

Finally, the conference had to consider the issue of a world organization to maintain peace. The formation of a League of Nations had widespread appeal, but many European leaders doubted its chances for success.

The Peace: Justice or Vengeance?

Early in the conference, two conflicting viewpoints surfaced. The British, French, and Italian governments had appeared to support the Fourteen Points. Yet they had never really given up the aims stated in the secret treaties—to divide the territories taken from the Central Powers among themselves after the war. The Fourteen Points represented a "peace of justice," whereas the terms of the secret treaties represented a "peace of vengeance." ●

Wilson believed that the conference must write a "peace of justice." Many people disagreed. The war had left bitterness, hatred, and a longing for revenge. Many of the victors believed that the defeated must be taught a lesson. Only harsh treatment could teach Germany and Austria the consequences of starting a war.

SECTION 4 REVIEW

1. **Define** Fourteen Points, armistice, reparations
2. **Identify** Ferdinand Foch, Paris Peace Conference, Big Four, Big Three, League of Nations
3. **Locate** Château-Thierry, St. Mihiel, Rhineland, Saar River valley, Tirol, Trieste, Fiume
4. **Summarizing Ideas** (a) What were the six general proposals of Wilson's Fourteen Points? (b) What effect did the Fourteen Points have?
5. **Interpreting Ideas** Describe the territorial demands the following nations made after World War I: (a) France (b) Italy (c) Great Britain (d) Belgium (e) Japan.
6. **Evaluating Ideas** (a) Why did Wilson believe in a "peace of justice"? (b) Why did others oppose this belief?

5 The Peace Treaties Created a "New Europe"

The victors made separate treaties with each of the five Central Powers. The most famous was the Versailles Treaty with Germany.

The Versailles Treaty

In May 1919 leaders of the new German Republic were called in, presented with a peace treaty, and told to sign it. The Germans complained bitterly that the treaty did not follow the Fourteen Points. They objected especially to two features. First, the treaty made Germany admit that it alone was guilty of starting the war and therefore must pay reparations. Second, the treaty did not specify the amount of reparations. In spite of their protest, the Germans had no choice but to sign.

Under the Versailles Treaty, Germany agreed to pay $5 billion in reparations within two years and an unspecified sum later. In 1921 the Allies set the total amount at $33 billion. The treaty also provided for the formation of the League of Nations and for numerous territorial adjustments.

Germany lost considerable territory along its northern, western, and eastern borders (see map, page 659) as well as its overseas colonies. Germany agreed not to fortify the Rhineland, which Allied troops would occupy for an unspecified period of time. The Saar Valley would fall under the administration of the League of Nations for 15 years. During that time all of the coal mined in the area would go to France in partial payment of reparations. At the end of 15 years, the people of the region were to vote on whether to continue under the League, to become part of France, or to rejoin Germany.

The restored nation of Poland received a large area of German land. This region included the Polish Corridor, which cut off East Prussia from the rest of Germany and gave Poland an outlet to the Baltic Sea. Danzig became a free city administered by the League of Nations.

Germany had to abolish conscription and could not maintain a reserve army. It was not allowed to manufacture heavy artillery, tanks, military airplanes, or poison gas. In addition, Germany could have no submarines, and no battleships larger

Learning from Maps *After World War I nine new countries were added to the continent of Europe. Which of these countries now had a coastline on the Mediterranean Sea?* Yugoslavia

than 10,000 tons. The authors of the treaties imposed these measures to ensure that Germany would be a peacekeeping nation. However, although the Allies made strict rules for Germany, they had weak means of enforcing them.

Austria-Hungary

The Dual Monarchy split in two as the war ended. Therefore, the victors arranged one treaty with Austria in September 1919 and a separate treaty with Hungary in June 1920. Austria, now recognized as an independent republic, lost the southern Tirol and the city of Trieste to Italy. The new republic could not grow enough food for its people ● or supply its industries with adequate raw materials. Austria rapidly sank into financial crisis and poverty.

Hungary lost a great deal of the territory it had governed under the Dual Monarchy to the new nation of Czechoslovakia that included Czechs, Slovaks, and Ruthenians. In the western Balkans, the new nation of Yugoslavia united the former independent kingdoms of Serbia and Montenegro, the former Hapsburg provinces of Bosnia and Herzegovina, and a section of the Adriatic coast.

659

SECTION 5

Closure
Ask students to review pages 660–661 and describe the organization of the League of Nations.

Review Answers
1. ***mandate:*** area to be administered by the government of an advanced nation; ***economic sanction:*** refusal to trade with an offending member nation of the League of Nations
2. ***Treaty of Versailles:*** Peace treaty signed with Germany to officially end World War I; ***World Court:*** the Permanent Court of International Justice that worked closely with the League of Nations and was located at the Hague
3. ***Polish Corridor:*** strip of land in the northern part of Poland; ***Czechoslovakia:*** formed in 1918 from territories formerly part of the Austro-Hungarian Empire—bordered by east Germany, Poland, the Soviet Union, Austria, and Hungary; ***Yugoslavia:*** bordered by Austria, Hungary, Romania, Bulgaria, Greece, Albania, Italy, and the Adriatic Sea; ***Finland:*** part of Russia until 1918—bordered by Norway, Russia, the Gulf of Finland, the Gulf of Bothnia, and Sweden; ***Estonia:*** formerly part of Russia—bordered by Russia, Latvia, and the Baltic Sea; ***Latvia:*** formerly part of Russia—bordered by Russia, Estonia, Lithuania, and the Baltic Sea; ***Lithuania:*** formerly part of Russia—bordered by Russia, Poland, Latvia, and

659

To simplify planning, pages at the beginning of each chapter provide chapter and section overviews, suggested lesson plans, annotated bibliographies, teaching strategies, enrichment activities, daily quizzes, and assignment ideas.

Margin notes include ideas for **Introducing the Unit** and **Chapter** and essential **Unit Goals** and **Chapter Objectives** (not shown).

These valuable notes also enhance instruction with **Focus/Motivation, Presentation,** and **Closure** activities, in addition to **Review Answers** for each section, chapter, and unit.

An innovative feature!

The six-page **Unit Synthesis**—in both the student's book and the *Annotated Teacher's Edition*—is a convenient resource to introduce, review, reteach, or summarize each unit. It also enables you to cover selected topics without presenting entire units or chapters!

For flexibility and convenience!

Teacher's ResourceBank™

The *Teacher's ResourceBank™* provides a wealth of supplements in a sturdy and accessible storage case. It includes:

- ◆Daily Lesson Planner
- ◆Vocabulary Worksheets
- ◆Building History Study Skills Worksheets
- ◆Basic Concepts Study Guide
- ◆Critical Thinking Study Guide
- ◆Profiles in History: People, Places, and Events
- ◆Geography Worksheets and Outline Maps
- ◆Writing About World History
- ◆Study Guide for Review
- ◆World and Regional Wall Maps
- ◆Unit Syntheses Transparencies with Student Worksheets, Tests, and Answer Key
- ◆Tests: Forms A and B
- ◆Daily Quizzes
- ◆Reteaching Worksheets

Also Available

A rich variety of ancillaries enhances instruction and boosts learning, including:

World and Regional Map Transparencies with Thematic Overlays
Readings in World History
Religions of the World Video Series
Art and History Transparencies
Everyday Life: Images of Social History Transparencies
Computer Test Generator

ANNOTATED TEACHER'S EDITION

World History

People and Nations

Texas Edition

HBJ
Harcourt Brace Jovanovich, Publishers
Orlando San Diego Chicago Dallas

An Annotated Teacher's Edition is not automatically included with each shipment of a classroom set of textbooks. However, an Annotated Teacher's Edition will be forwarded when requested by a teacher, an administrator, or a representative of Harcourt Brace Jovanovich, Inc.

The Annotated Teacher's Edition of *WORLD HISTORY: People and Nations,* Texas Edition, is complemented by the TEACHER'S RESOURCEBANK ™. When used with the Pupil's Edition, they provide a complete world history program.

Printed in the United States of America

ISBN 0-15-373460-4

CONTENTS

UNIT 4

The Emergence of Modern Nations

UNIT 5

The Development of Industrial Society

UNIT 6

World War in the Twentieth Century

UNIT 7

The World Since 1945

INTRODUCTION

World History: People and Nations is a comprehensive world history textbook designed to provide students with a vital understanding of the past in order to help them understand their own times. To meet this goal, ***World History: People and Nations*** presents history so that students can see the world in all its relationships, rather than as a composite of isolated nations and civilizations. Emphasizing *place, time,* and *significance,* the authors have tried to show the continuity of history, the sweeping forces that shaped events, and the influence of each era upon succeeding times. Great attention has been given to balancing political and economic developments with the growth of ideas, religions, education, the arts, and other aspects of intellectual and social history.

A careful reading of the introductory material in this **Annotated Teacher's Edition** will provide an orientation to the complete ***World History: People and Nations*** world history program: the **Pupil's Edition**, the **Annotated Teacher's Edition**, the **Teacher's ResourceBank™**, and other supplementary materials. The introductory notes contain comments on such important points as the organization of the textbook, its special features, the function of illustrations, the use of maps and geography skills, and the purpose and organization of the review materials.

The teacher support materials that comprise this **Annotated Teacher's Edition** complement and reinforce the strength of the **Pupil's Edition** of ***World History: People and Nations.*** Throughout this program, the authors have made every effort to ensure a successful learning experience in world history for today's high school students.

CHARACTERISTICS OF THE PUPIL'S EDITION

World History: People and Nations is designed to give teachers and students the widest panorama of world history, from the earliest times to the present. It is truly world history, covering traditional societies in the West as well as those of Asia, Africa, and the Middle East. The book brings world history up-to-date, with a fresh look at the world since 1945, including the pivotal trends of recent years and the key personalities on the world scene today. Its chronological presentation permits students to study parallel developments in different parts of the world during each major period of history.

World History: People and Nations draws on the most recent scholarship to give a balanced presentation of political, economic, social, and cultural history, taking particular care to describe in detail how people lived in other times and places. This outlook, coupled with the lively narrative style, the rich illustration program, the special features, and the numerous and varied learning resources, should appeal to today's high school students.

World History: People and Nations and its accompanying materials offer a complete educational package. The textbook and satellites provide techniques for motivating, reinforcing, and extending the learning experience for students of varying abilities. The wealth of teaching suggestions enables the program to be adapted to suit a variety of course requirements, teaching styles, and individual student needs.

ORGANIZATION OF THE PUPIL'S EDITION

World History: People and Nations is organized by units, chapters, and sections. There are 7 units and 33 chapters. Each chapter is divided into sections that deal with a specific period or topic. There are 151 sections of approximately equal length.

Introductory Features

The text begins with a five-page **Linking Geography to History** that emphasizes the many interconnections between geography and history. A highly motivational eight-page **Linking Past to Present** feature designed to enhance student interest in world history follows the geography feature. In the feature a series of dynamic illustrations juxtapose past and present achievements throughout the world and emphasize why the study of world history is both important and relevant in students' lives. The introductory series of high-interest features concludes with a two-page essay entitled **History and You**. In this feature the authors explain *why* the study of history is important and then detail how ***World History: People and Nations*** can help students understand the many complex historical processes that have molded life on our planet.

Units

Seven units divide the span of history into broad chronological periods. Within each unit, chapters deal with ideas and events involving civilization in specific areas, making reference wherever possible to events taking place elsewhere at the same time.

Each unit opens with a large, colorful illustration that highlights one of the themes to be explored in the unit (for example, see textbook pages xl–1 and 486–87). A list of the chapters, with their dates, provides an outline of the unit and enables you to plan your time and to identify those parts of the unit that best suit your course. This outline may also be used with the students to remind them of the global nature of their study.

Each unit ends with a two-page **Unit Review** and allows students to review important concepts, apply critical thinking skills, relate geography to history, and write about history; gives students a list of further readings; and contains a chronology chart that details the major events studied in the unit. (For more on **Unit Reviews**, see page ATE 9.)

Unit Syntheses

Each unit of ***World History: People and Nations*** concludes with a six-page **Unit Synthesis** divided into sections that correspond to each chapter in the textbook. For example, note that in the **Unit One Synthesis** Section 1 corresponds to Chapter 1; Section 2, to Chapter 2; Section 3, to Chapter 3; and Section 4, to Chapter 4 (see pages 92–97). Such an organization allows the teachers to conveniently use any section of the synthesis that they deem appropriate for their course.

The **Unit Syntheses** may be used for several purposes. First, they may be used as a preteaching tool. Teachers may wish to assign the **Unit Synthesis** before students study the unit so that students can familiarize themselves with the concepts to be studied. Or they may wish to assign the appropriate section of the synthesis before students study a chapter. Second, teachers may wish to use the **Unit Synthesis** as a review of specific chapters or the entire unit. Third, each synthesis may be used as a reteaching tool to help those students who have difficulty grasping the major concepts analyzed in the unit. Finally, the syntheses may be used to tailor the textbook to specific curricula that emphasize certain eras of history. For example, if the curriculum calls for a course in modern history, teachers may wish to use the syntheses for units one, two, and three to provide an overview of history before the Renaissance. Such an overview would give students the background necessary to understand developments in the modern world. Using the syntheses in this manner adds to the great flexibility of ***World History: People and Nations*** (see pages ATE 13–15.)

Chapters

Each of the 33 chapters in ***World History: People and Nations*** provides students with a thorough discussion of a particular topic in the study of world history. Each chapter opens with a dramatic picture, a locator map, and a section entitled **Chapter Focus** that gives students a brief preview of the chapter. By studying the **Chapter Focus**, students will be better prepared to understand the chapter. Each chapter concludes with a two-page **Chapter Review** that includes a dramatic time line and a summary and provides students opportunities to review important terms, develop critical thinking skills, relate geography to history, relate past to present, apply history study skills, and investigate further. (For more on **Chapter Reviews,** see pages ATE 8.)

Sections

Each chapter consists of two to six sections. Each section is sufficient for a daily lesson, but the material may be used in any way you find effective, either speeding up or slowing down the presentation (see pages ATE 13–15 for alternative course outlines). Sections also can be combined with special features, research projects, or field trips to enrich and vary the assignments.

The Reference Section

World History: People and Nations includes a valuable **Reference Section** (see pages R1–R64). The **Reference Section** begins with a 21-page **Atlas** that uses colorful and informative maps to familiarize the students with the physical and political features of the world. The **Reference Section** also includes a **Phonetic Respelling Guide**, a **Glossary**, and an **Index.** The **Phonetic Respelling Guide** explains the phonetic respellings used throughout the text to help students pronounce unfamiliar terms. It also explains the use of Pinyin for Chinese names. The **Glossary** includes definitions of every boldface term in the text, phonetic respellings of most terms, as well as a reference to the text page or pages on which the term is used in context. The **Index** provides thorough references and cross-references to the material in the text and indicates whether the information is presented in the narrative, or a map, or in a feature.

FEATURES OF THE PUPIL'S EDITION

As a world history textbook, ***World History: People and Nations*** concentrates on explaining history clearly by using a highly readable narrative style. Woven into the textbook are a number of skill and comprehension programs that accomplish essential goals in both the cognitive and affective learning areas.

The Learning Resources Program

World History: People and Nations provides students and teachers with a comprehensive learning resources program. Learning resources are located at the beginning of each chapter as well as at the end of each section, chapter, and unit.

Chapter Opener. The Chapter Opener contains a number of carefully planned learning resources to ensure comprehension and to engage student interest. Many students have trouble with three key concepts that are vital to a complete understanding of world history—geography, chronology, and relevance; or place, time, and significance. Therefore, special attention is given to help identify and reinforce the time and the area being studied as well as to answer the important question: Why study this part of history? A key element is a *locator map,* which appears at the top of the first page of the **Chapter Opener** and identifies the area or areas to be studied in the chapter. The dates of the chapter's *time span* are given in the **Chapter Focus**. These two resources, the locator map and the time span, focus the study in place and in time and help orient students to the chapter's content.

The right-hand page of each **Chapter Opener** begins with a **Chapter Focus**. The **Chapter Focus** includes the following components:

- **Place:** This section lists the places of the world to be studied in the chapter and reinforces the highlighted areas of the locator map on the previous page.

- **Time:** This section includes a schematic time line that highlights the dates that the chapter covers in relation to the history of the world and further reinforces the concept of chronology.
- **Significance:** This section explains to students the developments that they will be studying in the chapter and analyzes why these developments were important to the history of the world. In other words, it answers the important question: Why study this part of history?
- **Terms to Define:** This section is part of the textbook's comprehensive vocabulary program (see below). It provides a selected list of important terms that are discussed and defined in the chapter.
- **People to Identify:** This section lists some of the key people that the students will be learning about in the chapter.
- **Places to Locate:** This section lists some of the key places where the historical drama analyzed in the chapter takes place and emphasizes the link between geography and history so vital to a true understanding of world history.
- **Questions to Guide Your Reading:** This section provides students with a series of prereading questions that prepare them to study the chapter.

The last part of the **Chapter Opener**, which begins just before the first section, includes a motivational description or primary source that sets the tone for the chapter.

The vocabulary program. To ensure maximum usefulness of ***World History: People and Nations,*** the reading level has been carefully monitored. Much attention has been given to vocabulary development, and definitions and pronunciation guides are always included for new and for difficult terms. When a social studies term is introduced, it appears in **boldface** type and is defined in context. For example, the word "republic" is first used on page 145: "When the Romans overthrew the last Etruscan king in 509 B.C., they set up a republic. A **republic** is a form of government in which voters elect their leaders." On page 439, another social studies term is introduced and defined in this way: "A seizure of power by force is called a **coup d'état** (kood • ay • TAH), meaning literally a 'stroke of state.'" In addition, each term is defined in the **Glossary.**

Reinforcement of vocabulary development takes place in the **Chapter Focus, Section Reviews,** and **Chapter Reviews.** For the teacher's convenience, the **Sidetext** in this **Annotated Teacher's Edition** provides model answers to each **Section** and **Chapter Review** at point-of-use.

As in the example of coup d'état, words and places that are difficult to pronounce are followed, in parentheses, by phonetic respellings, with the accented syllable set in small capital letters. To help students fully utilize the phonetic respellings, the **Reference Section** includes an easy-to-use guide to the phonetic respellings. In addition, wherever possible, the authors give word derivations, as on page 145: "Each could **veto,** or refuse to approve, acts of the other. (The Latin word *veto* means 'I forbid.')"

Section Reviews. A **Section Review** concludes each section. Each **Section Review** may have as many as four parts. The first part, *Define,* asks the students to review the boldfaced terms that were discussed in the section. The second part, *Identify,* asks students to briefly identify key people, events, and documents discussed in the section. The third part, *Locate,* asks students to locate significant places mentioned in the section. The fourth part consists of questions to reinforce knowledge of key facts and main ideas. Each question is labeled with the critical thinking skill that the students need to apply in order to answer the question.

The **Section Reviews** serve three general purposes. First, the questions in a Review can serve as a detailed guide to reading if students are directed to familiarize themselves with the questions before beginning the study of the section. Taken as a whole, the **Section Reviews** help students organize the details that support the generalizations stated in the section titles. Second, the questions serve as a review of the section. The Reviews may be assigned as homework or used as the basis of an oral review before the next day's lesson begins. Finally, the **Section Reviews** can serve as a quiz or other evaluation instrument to assess students' comprehension of the section's material.

The **Sidetext** of this **Annotated Teacher's Edition** provides suggested, or model, answers to the questions in each **Section Review** at point-of-use.

Chapter Reviews. Each chapter concludes with a two-page **Chapter Review** designed to help students review and reinforce information in the text (see pages 174–75). Parts of the **Chapter Reviews,** too, can serve the same three purposes as the **Section Reviews.**

- **Time Line:** A time line appears at the top of each **Chapter Review.** The time line presents the sequence of the main events, ideas, and participants discussed in the chapter and provides chronological reference points in a clear and simple design.
- **Chapter Summary:** This numbered list provides a summary of the key concepts that students have learned in the chapter.
- **Reviewing Important Terms:** This part of the **Chapter Review** measures students' understanding of the historical terms introduced in the chapter.
- **Developing Critical Thinking Skills:** This section consists of questions that require the students to recall and interpret information presented in the chapter. Each question has a label that clearly indicates the skill students need to apply in answering the question.
- **Relating Geography to History:** This section includes a variety of questions designed to build geographic literacy, help students realize the vital interconnection between geography and history, and reinforce the theme of place.
- **Relating Past to Present:** This section includes exercises that ask students to trace developments analyzed in the chapter through the present. It reinforces the theme of time.
- **Applying History Study Skills:** This section gives students an opportunity to apply the skill they learned in the **Building History Study Skills** feature of the chapter.
- **Investigating Further:** The final section of the **Chapter Review** provides motivational activities designed to extend students' knowledge and to further build their understanding of history.

The **Sidetext** of this **Annotated Teacher's Edition** provides suggested, or model, answers to the questions in each **Chapter Review** at point-of-use.

Unit Reviews. At the conclusion of each unit there is a two-page **Unit Review**, designed to help evaluate what students have learned in the unit. Each **Unit Review** has seven parts.

- **Unit Summary:** This numbered list provides a summary of the key concepts that students have learned in the unit.
- **Reviewing Concepts:** This section consists of recall questions that review unit content.
- **Applying Critical Thinking Skills:** This part includes critical thinking questions that help students bring the ideas from the various chapters of the unit together in a needed synthesis. Each question has a label that clearly indicates the skill students need to apply in answering the question.
- **Relating Geography to History:** This section includes a variety of questions designed to build geographic literacy, help students realize the vital interconnection between geography and history, and reinforce the theme of place.
- **Writing About History:** This section includes a variety of writing assignments in which students are asked to investigate significant concepts discussed in the unit.
- **Further Readings:** This part provides a list of additional readings for students who wish to learn more about the material presented in the unit.
- **Unit Chronology:** The last section of each **Unit Review** consists of a chart listing the major developments in politics and society, technology and science, the visual arts and literature, and religion and philosophy. Each chart entry includes a reference to the chapter where it is discussed.

The **Sidetext** of this **Annotated Teacher's Edition** provides suggested, or model, answers to the questions in each **Unit Review** at point-of-use.

The Skills Program

Because successful skills instruction depends upon a systematic presentation, ***World History: People and Nations*** includes a comprehensive skills program. Each of the 33 chapters includes a skill lesson entitled **Building History Study Skills**. Each of these lessons promotes the mastery of a specific skill from one of five skill strands. For a list of the skills see the chart in the next column.

All skill lessons are closely tied to the content of the chapters in which they appear. Students are led through the various skills on a step-by-step basis, focusing on one learning operation at a time. After directed development of the skill, students are given an opportunity to practice the skill independently. Then, in the **Chapter Review**, the students are provided an opportunity to apply the skill in the section entitled "Applying History Study Skills." In addition, the supplementary material that precedes each chapter in this **Annotated Teacher's Edition** provides a strategy for reinforcing the skill.

BUILDING HISTORY STUDY SKILLS
Reading About History Identifying Sources of Evidence Classifying Information Analyzing a Statement Making Comparisons Understanding Sequence Making Inferences Identifying a Point of View Understanding Ideology Understanding a Biographical Account Identifying an Argument Identifying Fallacies in Reasoning
Writing About History Formulating a Thesis Statement Paraphrasing Information Writing a Comparison Essay Writing a Problem-Solution Essay
Interpreting Visuals Using a Time Line to Understand B.C. and A.D. Reading a Chart Determining Cause and Effect Using Art as a Historical Document Using a Map as a Historical Document Reading a Special-Purpose Map
Making Connections with History Identifying Cultural Diffusion Linking Literature to History Using Art to Understand Values Linking Economics to History Linking Architecture to History
Thinking About History Identifying Bias Distinguishing a Fact from a Value Statement Examining How Perspective Influences Viewpoints Analyzing Consequences Determining Relevancy Analyzing Documents Conducting a Debate

The Map and Graphics Program

The textbook includes 123 maps, which have been designed by leading cartographers, and 14 charts. Together, these colorful, highly motivational visuals help promote the textbook's goal of building a sense of place, time, and relevance. The narrative fully explains each graphic so that students may refer to it as they read the text. In addition, color photographs provide real-life examples of the concepts being studied. Most of these maps and photographs include an informative caption and a question. Many of these questions ask the students to study the visual or the information in the narrative to find the answer. Other questions ask the students to synthesize the information they have learned in earlier chapters with the subject presented in the visual. For your convenience, suggested, or model, answers to these questions appear in the **Annotations** in this **Annotated Teacher's Edition**.

The Enrichment Program

Six unique features are distributed throughout ***World History: People and Nations.*** These features are designed to motivate interest and to provide additional information by taking students into areas of study that extend and enhance the textbook's narrative.

History Through the Arts is a series of 50 illustrated features that reveal how civilizations are reflected in their arts and literature. Carefully chosen illustrations of paintings, sculpture, pottery, textiles, furniture, and architecture are accompanied by extended captions that describe the object shown and its relationship, both cultural and historical, to its creators and the times in which they lived. The literature features include excerpts from literature of the times accompanied by lively illustrations. The feature on page 107, for example, includes an excerpt from the *Odyssey*. On page 277 a rare ceramic camel from the Tang dynasty illuminates the grandeur of Chinese art during this period. The beautiful painting by Jan Vermeer on page 374 shows not only the artist's technique, but through the background objects of a world map, Oriental tapestry, and brass and copper ornaments, the results of Dutch exploration and trade in the 1600s. On page 668, a still photograph of Charlie Chaplin from *Modern Times* shows the comedian wrestling with bolts on an assembly line. It at once reveals the era's mixed feelings about mechanization and the fascination of the new art form—the movies. Finally, in Unit Seven, several **History Through the Arts** features focus on new expressions of traditional art forms—a modern chapel in France (page 766), stained-glass windows in Jerusalem (page 821), and the Opera House in Sydney, Australia (page 887).

You will find the **History Through the Arts** features useful in motivating lessons and in stimulating student interest in the arts and traditions of other peoples. Here is a complete list of the 50 **History Through the Arts** features:

	Page
Sculpture—Prehistoric Ivory Head	7
Metalworking—Funeral Mask of a Pharaoh	23
Sculpture—Sacred Sumerian Animal	29
Pottery—Seals from the Indus Valley	52
Literature—*Atharva-Veda*	56
Sculpture—The God Siva	59
Sculpture—Ancient Chinese Elephant	72
Literature—The *Odyssey*	107
Sculpture—Greek Funeral Stele	109
Sculpture—Etruscan Archers and Discus Thrower	145
Literature—The *Metamorphoses*	161
Weaving—Egyptian Christian Cloth	190
Painting—Sacred Icons	201
Weaving—Oriental Carpets	214
Print Design—Lindisfarne Gospel	235
Metal Sculpture—Reliquary of St. Faith	237
Weaving—Medieval Tapestry	256
Literature—*The Canterbury Tales*	260
Sculpture—Tang Camel	277
Sculpture—Royal Figure from West Africa	301
Literature—*The Book of the Courtier*	327
Painting—Realism and Perspective	329
Painting—*Lady with a Unicorn*	330
Technology— A Mariner's Astrolabe	357
Painting—*Young Woman with a Water Jug*	374
Painting—Rembrandt Self-portrait	376
Metalworking—Engraved Sons of Liberty Bowl	413
Painting—*The Death of Marat*	437
Painting—*Evening Squall at Ohashi*	466
Furniture—Thonet Rocker	497
Literature—*Hard Times*	505
Poster Art—Paris Exposition Poster	516
Literature—*Alice's Adventures in Wonderland*	532
Drawing—The Victorians and King Arthur	546
Painting—*The Gleaners*	559
Painting—*Two Men Looking at the Moon*	584
Jewelry Design—Fabergé Egg	589
Painting—The Influence of Japanese Art	613
Painted Glass—Duchamp and the Dadaists	656
Painting —*The City* by Fernand Léger	667
Films—Charlie Chaplin in *Modern Times*	668
Painting—Chinese Painting	698
Frescoes—Rivera's *Fruits of Labor*	705
Painting —*Guernica* by Pablo Picasso	715
Architecture —Chapel by Le Corbusier	766
Architecture—Japanese Ceremonial Gate	785
Weaving—Ikat Cloth	792
Stained Glass—Windows in Jerusalem	821
Painting—Georgia O'Keeffe	854
Architecture: Sydney Opera House	887

Connections: Then and Now is a series of 18 illustrated essays that relate past to present by showing how familiar customs and traditions have existed throughout history. Each **Connections: Then and Now** feature brings earlier times to life by discussing such commonly shared experiences as music, harvest festivals, medicine, the use of money, and theaters. In Chapter 3 (page 65), through an illustrated discussion of "Fairy Tales," students learn that some themes are universal and appear in the literature and traditions of many cultures. In Chapter 5 (page 85) the **Connections: Then and Now** feature is "Stadiums." Through pictures and text, students come to see that from the amphitheaters of ancient Greece to the Astrodome in Houston, people have gathered in arenas to enjoy sports, watch dramatic presentations, or attend religious or political ceremonies. A list of the **Connections: Then and Now** features follows:

What If? is a series of 15 features designed to stimulate student discussion and to develop critical thinking skills. The **What If?** feature on page 119, for example, asks students to speculate how history might have been different if the Persians rather than the Greeks had won the Persian Wars. Although there are certainly no concrete answers to such thought-provoking questions, suggested answers to the **What If?** features are included in **Annotations** in this **Annotated Teacher's Edition**. A list of the **What If?** features follows:

Perspectives: Legacies of the Past is a series of seven two-page features that trace specific developments or concepts through time and analyze how these developments or concepts affect our lives today. For example, the **Perspectives: Legacies of the Past** feature on page 308 entitled "The Calendar—Will We Ever Get it Straight?" provides a lively description of how peoples in various societies have tried to develop accurate calendars. These heavily illustrated features are designed to spark student interest and help students see the relevance of particular topics. A list of the **Perspectives: Legacies of the Past** follows:

Linking Geography to History is a series of eight features designed to build geographic literacy and reinforce the important theme of place. The first of these features on pages xxv–xxix introduces the connections between geography and history that are reinforced in the other **Linking Geography to History** features as well as throughout the narrative. Sections in the text that emphasize geography are highlighted by an antique compass rose (see pages 39, 101, and 123). A list of the **Linking Geography to History** features follows:

Primary Sources. The text also includes numerous primary sources that are interwoven throughout the narrative. This feature, set off by large burgundy quotation marks, allows students to catch a glimpse of the past as expressed by the people of the time and further applies, extends, and enriches the students' understanding of history.

FEATURES OF THE ANNOTATED TEACHER'S EDITION

The **Annotated Teacher's Edition** of ***World History: People and Nations*** includes all the **Pupil's Edition** pages, slightly reduced in size to create top and side margins. Each chapter of this **Annotated Teacher's Edition** includes a variety of resources and teaching suggestions. The **Annotated Teacher's Edition** is organized into three parts—an **Interleaf**, a **Sidetext**, and **Annotations**. The **Interleaf** is inserted at the beginning of each chapter and will help the teacher develop effective lesson plans and develop teaching strategies. The **Sidetext** is printed in the side-margins of the text at the appropriate point-of-use and will help the teacher develop effective presentation of chapter information. The **Annotations**, printed in blue, appear in the top margins and provide a wealth of supplementary information and activities designed to enhance student understanding of major concepts presented in each chapter.

	ABILITY GUIDELINES
BASIC	Strategy or activity requires full class participation, is basic to content comprehension, and should be within the ability range of all students.
AVERAGE/ GROUP	Strategy or activity often requires group participation, selective assignment, and teacher direction. It is expected that the majority of students will be able to handle successfully their assigned tasks. The activity may require the use of supplementary sources and the application of a variety of study and thinking skills.
CHALLENGING	These are challenging activities especially applicable to those students willing and able to work independently. Successful completion of these tasks will require the use of several sources other than the textbook and the integration of higher-level critical thinking skills and creativity.

Interleaf

The **Interleaf** provides teachers with several teaching resources.

- **Chapter Overview:** The **Chapter Overview** provides a brief synopsis of the chapter with emphasis on the main ideas, the sequence of historical events, and the relationship between the causes of these events and their results.
- **Suggested Lesson Plan:** The **Suggested Lesson Plan** consists of a chart that provides suggested time allotments for presentation of material within each section of the chapter, codes for applicable unit goals and chapter objectives, **Sidetext** page references for suggested activities coordinated with each section, and materials available to the teacher. Also included in the **Suggested Lesson Plan** for each chapter are references to the appropriate Form A Test, Reteaching Worksheet, and Form B Test.
- **Books for the Teacher:** This section consists of an annotated bibliography of appropriate reference materials.
- **Books for the Student:** This section includes a bibliography for students.
- **Multimedia Materials:** This section includes a list of materials to accompany the chapter. Planning for the use of these filmstrips and films may be required in order to ensure that they are available when the class is studying the chapter.

The **Interleaf** for each section of the chapter includes a **Section Overview, Suggested Teaching Strategies, Enrichment Activities,** a **Daily Quiz,** and **Suggested Assignments.**

- **Section Overview:** The **Section Overview** provides a concise summary of the major points of the section.
- **Suggested Teaching Strategies:** Each section includes at least two **Suggested Teaching Strategies** that offer a number of ways in which you can help students understand and interpret what they are learning. The varied activities are suitable for different achievement levels and the varying interests of students and are clearly labeled Basic, Average/Group, or Challenging (see Ability Guidelines above). Activities include matching exercises, word scrambles, panel discussions, debates, newscasts, research reports, and many others.

  At the same time that students are being encouraged to master the content, the variety of **Suggested Teaching Strategies** also reinforce skills development. For example, activities provide practice in such skills as outlining, classifying information, using maps, interpreting primary sources, and practicing expository writing. In addition, students are given an opportunity to reinforce the skill presented in **Building History Study Skills** where appropriate. These strategies are clearly marked with an * in the **Interleaf**.
- **Enrichment Activities:** These activities provide students with opportunities to extend the concepts presented in the textbook and often include conducting research, preparing interviews, and preparing oral or written reports. Like the **Suggested Teaching Strategies,** each **Enrichment Activity** is labeled Basic, Average/Group, or Challenging.
- **Daily Quiz: Daily Quizzes** enable the teacher to assess student understanding of each section. These quizzes provide numerous opportunities for daily grades. Teachers may wish to delay the daily quiz over a particular section until students have an opportunity to reread and study the information presented in the section. Each **Daily Quiz** may also be used as a pretest or as an assessment instrument to identify specific concepts to be included in reteaching activities and assignments.
- **Suggested Assignments:** Two or more **Suggested Assignments** conclude the **Interleaf** activities.

Sidetext

The **Sidetext** provides teachers with point-of-use teaching resources.

- **Introducing the Unit:** The introductory page of each unit includes a motivational activity designed to introduce the unit to the students.
- **Unit Goals:** The **Unit Goals** set forth the major goals that students should meet after they have studied the unit.
- **Introducing the Chapter:** The **Sidetext** for each chapter begins with a motivational activity designed to spark student interest in the topic about to be studied.
- **Chapter Objectives:** The **Chapter Objectives** set forth the major objectives that students should meet after they have studied the chapter.

The **Sidetext** for each section of each chapter contains a **Focus/ Motivation** strategy, a **Presentation** feature, a **Closure** activity, and **Review Answers.**

- **Focus/Motivation:** The **Focus/Motivation** for each section contains suggestions for introducing the lesson designed to be used either before the section is read or after students have been assigned the section as homework. A number of primary and secondary source excerpts are included along with strategies on how to use them.
- **Presentation:** The **Presentation** for each section contains a suggested strategy suitable to use with the entire class while studying the section.
- **Closure:** The **Closure** for each section contains a short activity designed to be used to assess student understanding of the major concepts studied in the section.
- **Review Answers:** Answers to each **Section Review** are included at point-of-use in the **Sidetext**.

An answer key to each **Chapter Review** concludes the **Sidetext** for each chapter and appears on the **Chapter Review** page. In addition, an answer key to each **Unit Review** appears on the **Unit Review** page.

Annotations

The **Annotated Teacher's Edition** contains **Annotations** printed in blue in the top margins. These **Annotations** provide background information for the teacher, suggest class activities and discussion, research, report, and critical thinking topics, and provide suggested, or model, answers for the questions contained in captions. Where appropriate, the **Annotations** provide cross-references to relevant sections of the **Interleaf**.

A system of coding helps teachers match specific **Annotations** to the content. Whenever a symbol appears in front of an **Annotation**, a similar symbol is placed next to the appropriate line in the content.

FLEXIBILITY OF THE TEXTBOOK

The remarkable completeness and distinctive organization of ***World History: People and Nations*** make it suitable for a variety of curriculum needs and teaching strategies. The textbook has been designed to allow great flexibility in teaching. Social studies teachers recognize that no single approach or method is adequate in all situations. Instead, creative teachers employ a whole set of different approaches that are best suited to the needs of their course and the abilities, interests, and backgrounds of their students.

World History: People and Nations allows you to pick and choose the textbook portions suitable to your course. The seven six-page **Unit Syntheses** that conclude each unit in the **Pupil's Edition** add to this flexibility. The syntheses allow teachers to substitute abbreviated discussions for certain chapters due to time or curricular constraints. At the same time, the **Unit Syntheses** provide students with needed background information. The following are some of the many ways in which the textbook can be used.

The Complete Course

For a complete course in world history from its beginnings to the present, the organization of ***World History: People and Nations*** is ideal. Students study parallel developments occurring in different places, and their awareness of the world as a whole is enriched. Within each chapter, the material is presented in sections—from two to six. Each section has been designed to serve as the basis for a reasonable assignment for one lesson. When review assignments or tests are added to the daily reading schedule, a full year's course would be presented. The Table of Contents provides a suitable outline for such a course.

Western Civilization

This alternative outline is ideal for a course in Western Civilization, while giving students an overview of non-Western history.

Chapter 1: Cultures and Civilizations Began in Prehistoric Times
Chapter 2: Great Civilizations Developed in the Middle East
Unit One Synthesis, Section 3: People Created Thriving Civilizations in India
Unit One Synthesis, Section 4: Ancient Chinese Civilization Developed Lasting Traditions
Chapter 5: Greek City-states Developed in the Mediterranean Region
Chapter 6: Greek Civilization Triumphed During the Golden Age and the Hellenistic Age
Chapter 7: Rome Ruled the Western World for Centuries
Unit Three Synthesis, Section 1: The Byzantine Empire Preserved the Heritage of Rome
Unit Three Synthesis, Section 2: Islam Became a Powerful Force from Spain to India
Chapter 10: Feudal Lords and the Church Dominated Medieval Europe
Chapter 11: Trade Revived and Nations Developed in Europe
Unit Three Synthesis, Section 5: Civilization in East Asia Reached New Heights
Unit Three Synthesis, Section 6: Africa and the Americas Produced Complex Civilizations
Chapter 14: The Renaissance, Reformation, and Scientific Revolution Changed Europe
Chapter 15: Strong Monarchies Helped European States Expand
Chapter 16: The English-speaking World Took a New Political Course
Chapter 17: The French Revolution Changed the Course of World History
Unit Four Synthesis, Section 5: The Countries of Asia Experienced a Transition
Chapter 19: The Industrial Revolution Transformed the Modern World
Chapter 20: The Industrial Age Revolutionized Science and Culture

Chapter 21, Section 1: Liberal Theories Affected Great Britain and its Empire
Chapter 21, Section 2: The United States Expanded and Changed
Chapter 21, Section 3: France Underwent Revolutions and Changes of Government
Chapter 22: Unification of New Nations Added to Rising Tensions in Europe
Chapter 23: Imperialist Powers Competed in Many Areas of the World
Chapter 24: World War I and the Russian Revolution Altered the Course of History
Chapter 25: The Great Depression Helped the Rise of Totalitarian Dictatorships
Unit Six Synthesis, Section 3: New Political Forces Emerged in Africa, Asia, and Latin America
Chapter 27: Local Aggressions Brought About World War II
Chapter 28: Challenges Faced Europe and North America in the Postwar Years
Unit Seven Synthesis, Section 2: Asian Nations Struggled to Gain Stability
Unit Seven Synthesis, Section 3: The Nations of Africa and the Middle East Became Independent
Unit Seven Synthesis, Section 4: Latin America Became the Focus of World Attention
Chapter 32: Challenges Faced the Superpowers in the Modern Era
Chapter 33: The Modern World Faced the Challenge of Rapid Change

Modern European History

This alternative outline is ideal for a course in Modern European History, while giving students a brief overview of ancient history, medieval history, and non-Western history.

Unit One Synthesis: The Beginnings of Civilization
Unit Two Synthesis: Civilizations of the Mediterranean World
Unit Three Synthesis: The World in Transition
Chapter 14: The Renaissance, Reformation, and Scientific Revolution Changed Europe
Chapter 15: Strong Monarchies Helped European States Expand
Chapter 16: The English-speaking World Took a New Political Course
Chapter 17: The French Revolution Changed the Course of World History
Unit Four Synthesis, Section 5: The Countries of Asia Experienced a Transition
Chapter 19: The Industrial Revolution Transformed the Modern World
Chapter 20: The Industrial Age Revolutionized Science and Culture
Chapter 21, Section 1: Liberal Theories Affected Great Britain and its Empire
Chapter 21, Section 2: The United States Expanded and Changed
Chapter 21, Section 3: France Underwent Revolutions and Changes of Government

Chapter 22: Unification of New Nations Added to Rising Tensions in Europe
Chapter 23: Imperialist Powers Competed in Many Areas of the World
Chapter 24: World War I and the Russian Revolution Altered the Course of History
Chapter 25: The Great Depression Helped the Rise of Totalitarian Dictatorships
Unit Six Synthesis, Section 3: New Political Forces Emerged in Africa, Asia, and Latin America
Chapter 27: Local Aggressions Brought About World War II
Chapter 28: Challenges Faced Europe and North America in the Postwar Years
Unit Seven Synthesis, Section 2: Asian Nations Struggled to Gain Stability
Unit Seven Synthesis, Section 3: The Nations of Africa and the Middle East Became Independent
Unit Seven Synthesis, Section 4: Latin America Became the Focus of World Attention
Chapter 32: Challenges Faced the Superpowers in the Modern Era
Chapter 33: The Modern World Faced the Challenge of Rapid Change

World Cultures

World History: People and Nations also is suitable for use as a textbook on World Cultures. The textbook pays special attention to the aspects of social history that define the lives of a people—family life, methods of earning a living, education, the rearing of children, and use of leisure time. Particular effort has been made to include abundant detail on the diverse societies of East Asia, the Middle East, Latin America, and Africa. The following alternative outline is designed to meet the curriculum requirements of a course in World Cultures.

Chapter 1: Cultures and Civilizations Began in Prehistoric Times
Unit One Synthesis, Section 2: Great Civilizations Developed in the Middle East
Chapter 3: People Created Thriving Civilizations in India
Chapter 4: Ancient Chinese Civilization Developed Lasting Traditions
Unit Two Synthesis: Civilizations of the Mediterranean World
Chapter 8: The Byzantine Empire Preserved the Heritage of Rome
Chapter 9: Islam Became a Powerful Force from Spain to India
Unit Three Synthesis, Section 3: Feudal Lords and the Church Dominated Medieval Europe
Unit Three Synthesis, Section 4: Trade Revived and Nations Developed in Europe
Chapter 12: Civilization in East Asia Reached New Heights
Chapter 13: Africa and the Americas Produced Complex Civilizations
Unit Four Synthesis, Section 1: The Renaissance; Reformation; and Scientific Revolution Changed Europe
Unit Four Synthesis, Section 2: Strong Monarchies Helped European States Expand

Unit Four Synthesis, Section 3: The English-speaking World Took a New Political Course

Unit Four Synthesis, Section 4: The French Revolution Changed the Course of World History

Chapter 18: The Countries of Asia Experienced a Transition

Unit Five Synthesis, Section 1: The Industrial Revolution Transformed the Modern World

Unit Five Synthesis, Section 2: The Industrial Age Revolutionized Science and Culture

Unit Five Synthesis, Section 3: Reforms Swept Through the British Empire, the United States, France, and Latin America

Chapter 21, Section 4: The Nations of Latin America Gained Independence

Unit Five Synthesis, Section 4: Unification of New Nations Added to Rising Tensions in Europe

Chapter 23: Imperialist Powers Competed in Many Areas of the World

Unit Six Synthesis, Section 1: World War I and the Russian Revolution Altered the Course of History

Unit Six Synthesis, Section 2: The Great Depression Helped the Rise of Totalitarian Dictatorships

Chapter 26: New Political Forces Emerged in Africa, Asia, and Latin America

Unit Six Synthesis, Section 4: Local Aggressions Brought About World War II

Unit Seven Synthesis, Section 1: Challenges Faced Europe and North America in the Postwar Years

Chapter 29: Asian Nations Struggled to Gain Stability

Chapter 30: The Nations of Africa and the Middle East Became Independent

Chapter 31: Latin America Became the Focus of World Attention

Unit Seven Synthesis, Section 5: Challenges Faced the Superpowers in the Modern Era

Chapter 33: The Modern World Faced the Challenge of Rapid Change

Humanities

Another approach to the teaching of history that has been adopted in some schools is the Humanities course. Organized around history and literature, with a lesser emphasis on art and music, this course stresses ideas and concepts. ***World History: People and Nations*** is an ideal basic text for such a course. It is rich in illustrations, and great effort has been made to relate art to history by means of the **History Through the Arts** features. In addition, much space is devoted to discussions of literature and culture, enhanced by the **Connections: Then and Now** and the **Perspectives: Legacies of the Past** features.

PLANNING THE COURSE

Planning is an important element of successful teaching. The **Annotated Teacher's Edition** of ***World History: People and Nations*** allows you to make long-range plans for reading assignments, written work, research, and activities and evaluation. The convenient **Suggested Lesson Plan** in the **Interleaf** pages for each chapter list time allotments and the teaching resources available for each section and chapter. Each chapter introduction and each section of the textbook can constitute a daily lesson. The features also lend themselves to daily lessons, while review, tests, and other activities can be scheduled to complete the year. Using your school calendar, you may want to block out the daily work for the year, or use the **Suggested Lesson Plan** to make your plans month by month.

In planning the daily lesson, examine in advance the teaching suggestions in the **Interleaf** and **Sidetext** of this **Annotated Teacher's Edition** and the materials in the **Teacher's ResourceBank**™. This will enable you to to assign student activities in advance and to secure books and multimedia materials as early as possible. Multimedia materials are listed in the **Interleaf** for each chapter. In addition, pages ATE 17–19 list books for use throughout the course and for use with each unit in the textbook.

Adapting Instruction to Varying Abilities. The authors of ***World History: People and Nations*** recognize that students of varying abilities learn best from activities suited to their particular levels. Therefore, activities in the textbook and in the **Annotated Teacher's Edition** offer a wide range of instructional strategies and procedures to enable you to adapt the course to meet the needs of students of varying abilities. Activities in the **Interleaf** and the **Sidetext** of the **Annotated Teacher's Edition** indicate whether the activity is Basic, Average/Group, or Challenging (see chart, page ATE 12.)

Of course, it is extremely difficult to designate an activity as suitable for a specific ability group. Some students learn best by reading or writing. For others, a visual presentation is more helpful. Because you can best estimate your students' potential and anticipate how they may respond to a particular activity, the decision of what to assign is best left to your own judgement. Therefore, the notes that follow are intended only as general guidelines to illustrate the many ways the ***World History: People and Nations*** program can be adapted for your students.

Learning resources in the textbook, for example, provide numerous opportunities for review, reinforcement, and enrichment. **Section Reviews, Chapter Reviews,** and **Unit Reviews** offer review questions that stress the acquisition of knowledge—important for all students. Critical thinking questions will challenge above average students. Furthermore, the time line and Chapter Summary in each **Chapter Review** provide handy references for average and below average students. In addition, the **Unit Syntheses** may be used to reteach certain key concepts.

All the features in ***World History: People and Nations*** are intended to motivate students at different levels. Below average students, for example, can often reinforce their learning by examining pictures. These students especially will be aided by the book's rich illustration program. The art accompanying the **Connections: Then and Now, History Through the Arts,** and **Perspectives: Legacies of the Past** features provides opportunities for average and below average students to analyze the details in pictures. More able students may be interested in doing additional research.

The worksheets and **Geography Supplement** in the **Teacher's ResourceBank™** contain activities of varying degrees of difficulty. Average and below average students can use worksheets that involve such activities as outlining, making charts, matching, identifying, etc. More able students can use worksheets on primary sources, interpreting cartoons, using graphs, etc. All students will benefit from the additional practice provided by the **Geography Supplement** in working with maps, locating places, reading legends, using map scales, etc. Especially useful for less able students is the Reviewing Map Skills section, which reviews such basic concepts as map projection, latitude and longitude, and map scales.

Studying Controversial Topics. The study of a subject as broad and comprehensive as world history introduces students to a number of issues on which there have been conflicting points of view. Controversial topics can provide excellent learning opportunities, especially opportunities for the development of critical thinking skills. It is important for students to recognize the difference between fact and opinion, and to be aware that throughout history opinions on many issues have differed.

There are various methods of approaching controversial issues in a world history course. However, all these methods generally include the following steps:

1. Defining the issue
2. Placing the issue in its historical context
3. Identifying different viewpoints on the issue
4. Collecting and examining evidence to support each viewpoint
5. Identifying other relevant information

The **Interleaf** and **Sidetext** provide a variety of activities and investigations to help students develop an understanding of controversial issues in their historical context. Additional research, analysis, discussion, and debate activities help students to seek concrete information, compare points of view on a particular issue, and deal with areas of agreement and disagreement. Because the gathering of evidence is essential in an exploration of controversial issues, ample bibliographic references are provided throughout the **Annotated Teacher's Edition.**

INTRODUCING THE COURSE

Because of the vastness of the subject, students frequently come to the study of world history with some apprehension. They may also be anxious about the need to learn dates, details about battles, and strange and hard-to-pronounce names of people and places. One way to help students approach the year's work with interest and anticipation is to emphasize the relevance of the study of world history to their own lives and to make them comfortable with their textbook.

To introduce students to ***World History: People and Nations,*** have them first leaf through the book for several minutes to get a feeling for the variety of illustrations. Then ask them what kinds of illustrations they would expect to find in a world history textbook. *(Possible answers: portraits of monarchs, battle scenes, maps, etc.)* Do they come across pictures that surprise them? You may want to list these on the chalkboard or an overhead projector. *(Possible answers: an Oriental rug, a rocking chair, Sleeping Beauty)*

Next, have each student look up in the **Index** an area of special interest, such as theater, sports, music, family. What do students notice about the listings for these entries? Lead students into a discussion of the scope of world history as it will be presented in ***World History: People and Nations,*** the study of events and ideas, but also the study of people and how they lived, what family life was like, the kinds of homes people had, what recreation they enjoyed, what work they did, etc.

Now have students read to themselves and then read aloud with the class the essay **History and You** on pages xxxviii–xxxix in the textbook. Point out to the class that although the questions may seem rather broad at the beginning of the course, the answers will really come together from the study of the many ideas, people, events, and special interests students have glimpsed in the illustrations and in the **Index**. Remind students that together these details form the rich story of the development of the world as they know it.

Now discuss with students each of the features described here. The following questions might be asked: What is the purpose of a **Chapter Focus**? How can the **Section Review** questions help you? What can be learned from the **Chapter Review** page? How can you make use of maps, charts, and illustrations? What is the purpose of the **Index**? How does it differ from the **Table of Contents**?

With the students, examine closely the different parts of the textbook. As each feature is studied, ask specific questions that can be answered by reference to the book. This will be a valuable class exercise.

Walking students through the textbook during the first periods in which the class meets will pay dividends throughout the course. Such a lesson will help students learn about the organization of the material, the learning resources, and the devices built into the textbook that will help them locate information they need. Making them comfortable with their textbook is one more way to help students toward success.

Multimedia Sources

Many of the materials listed in this **Annotated Teacher's Edition** may be obtained through local or regional film libraries. Although some of the materials may no longer be available from the publisher, information concerning them may be obtained from the following sources. (The names or abbreviations in italics are the shortened forms in which the sources are listed in the **Interleaf.**)

ACI Media, Inc., 35 West 45th St., New York, NY 10036

Atlantis Production, Inc., 1252 La Granada Drive, Thousand Oaks, CA 91360

BFA Educational Media, 2211 Michigan Ave., Santa Monica, CA 90404

Carousel Films, Inc., 1501 Broadway, New York, NY 10036

Centron Educational Films, P.O. Box 687, 1621 West 9th St., Lawrence, KS 66044

Chatsworth Film Distributors, Ltd., 97-99 Dean St., London W1V 5RA, England
Churchill Film, 662 North Robertson Blvd., Los Angeles, CA 90069
Classroom Film Distributors, Inc., 5610 Hollywood Blvd., Los Angeles, CA 90028
Coronet Instructional Films, 65 E.S. Water St., Chicago, IL 60601
Current Affairs Films, 24 Danbury Rd., Wilton, CT 06897
EBE, Encyclopedia Britannica Educational Corp., 425 North Michigan Ave., Chicago, IL 60611
Educational Audio-Visual, Inc., 17 Marble Ave., Pleasantville, NY 10570
Filmfare Communications, 10900 Ventura Blvd., Studio City, CA 91604
Films, Inc., 1144 Wilmette Ave., Wilmette, IL 60091
Guidance Associates, Box 3000, Communication Park Video, Mt. Kisco, NY 10549
Independent Film Producers Co., 180 East California, Pasadena, CA 91102
International Film Bureau, 332 South Michigan Ave., Chicago, IL 60604
International Film Foundation, Inc., 475 Fifth Ave., New York, NY 10017
Journal Films, 930 Pitner Ave., Evanston, IL 60201
Learning Corp. of America, 1350 Avenue of the Americas, New York, NY 10017
Life, Time-Life Broadcast, Inc., 9 Rockefeller Plaza, New York, NY 10020
McGraw-Hill Films, 1221 Avenue of the Americas, New York, NY 10020
Multimedia Productions, Inc., P.O. Box 5097, Stanford, CA 94305
National Geographic Society, Special Publications & Filmstrip Division, 17th and M Sts., N.W., Washington, D.C. 20036
NET Film Service, Indiana University, Audio-Visual Center, Bloomington, IN 47401
Newsreels, San Francisco Newsreels, 1232 Market St., San Francisco, CA 94102
Newsweek, 444 Madison Ave., New York, NY 10022
New York Times, 2 Kisco Plaza, Times Square, New York, NY 10549
Prentice-Hall Media, 150 White Plains Rd., Tarrytown, NY 10591
Screen News Digest, 235 East 45th Street, New York, NY 10017
Time-Life Multimedia, 1271 Avenue of the Americas, New York, NY 10020
Visual Publications, 197 Kensington High St., London W8, England
Young American Films, distributed by McGraw-Hill

BIBLIOGRAPHY

Books for Use Throughout the Course

Blom, Eric, ed. *Grove's Dictionary of Music and Musicians.* St. Martin's Press.
Bronowski, J. and Bruce Mazlish. *The Western Intellectual Tradition.* Harper & Row.
Clark, Leon E., ed. *Through African Eyes.* 6 vols., Praeger.
Durant, Will and Ariel. *The Story of Civilization.* 11 vols., Simon and Schuster.
Eisen, Sydney, and Maurice Filler, eds. *The Human Adventure: Readings in World History.* vols 1 and 2, Harcourt Brace Jovanovich.
Falls, Cyril. *Great Military Battles.* Macmillan.
Fenton, Edwin, ed. *Thirty-Two Problems in World History: Source Readings and Interpretations.* Scott Foresman.
Greer, Thomas H., gen. ed. *Classics of Western Thought.* 3 vols., Harcourt Brace Jovanovich.
Jones, W. T. *A History of Philosophy.* 5 vols., Harcourt Brace Jovanovich.
Knoles, G. H., and R. Snyder, eds. *Readings in Western Civilization.* Lippincott.
Russell, Bertrand. *A History of Western Philosophy.* Simon and Schuster.
Smith, Huston. *Religions of Man.* Harper & Row.
Stavrianos, Leften S., and others. *Readings in World History.* Allyn and Bacon.
Time-Life Books eds. and others. *Time-Life Library of Art.* 28 vols., Time-Life.
Warner, Oliver. *Great Sea Battles.* Macmillan.

Books for Use Unit by Unit

Unit One: The Beginnings of Civilization

Breasted, James. *Development of Religion and Thought in Ancient Egypt.* Harper & Row.
Cottrell, Leonard. *Life Under the Pharaohs.* Grosset & Dunlop.
_____. *The Horizon Book of Lost Worlds.* American Heritage.
Glubok, Shirley. *Discovering the Royal Tombs at Ur.* Macmillan.
_____. *Discovering Tutankhamen's Tomb.* Macmillan.
Knauth, Percy. *The Metalsmiths.* Time-Life.
Kramer, S. N. *History Begins at Sumer.* Doubleday.
_____. *Cradle of Civilization.* Time-Life.
Life eds. *The Epic of Man.* Time-Life.
Piggott, Stuart. *The Dawn of Civilization.* McGraw-Hill.
Reader's Digest eds. *The World's Last Mysteries.* Reader's Digest.
Rowland, Benjamin, ed. *The Ajanta Caves: Early Buddhist Painting from India.* New American Library.
Schafer, Edward H. *Ancient China.* Time-Life.
Wolf, J., and Z. Burian. *The Dawn of Man.* Abrams.

Unit Two: Civilizations of the Mediterranean World

Ariès, Philippe and Georges Duby, gen. eds. *A Hsitory of Private Life: From Pagan Rome to Byzantuim.* Belknap.
Bowra, C.M. *Classical Greece.* Time-Life.
Chambers, M. *The Fall of Rome.* Holt, Rinehart and Winston.
Grant, Michael. *The World of Rome.* Mentor.
_____, ed. *The Birth of Western Civilization.* McGraw-Hill.
Hadas, M. *Imperial Rome.* Time-Life.

Hale, William H., ed. *The Horizon Book of Ancient Greece*. American Heritage.
Kagan, D., ed. *The End of the Roman Empire*. Heath.
Kitto, H. D. F. *The Greeks*. Pelican.
Michell, H. *Sparta*. Cambridge.
National Geographic eds. *Greece and Rome: Builders of Our World*. National Geographic Society.
Plutarch. *Lives of the Noble Romans*. Dell.
_____. *Lives of the Noble Greeks*. Dell.

Unit Three: The World in Transition

Phillippe Ariès and Georges Duby, gen. eds. *A History of Private Life: Revelations of the Medieval World*. Belknap.
Carmichael, Joel. *An Illustrated History of Russia*. Reynal.
Caso, Alfonso. *The Aztecs: People of the Sun*. University of Oklahoma.
Clavell, James. *Shōgun*. Atheneum.
Coughlin, Robert. *Tropical Africa*. Time-Life.
Davidson, Basil. *A History of West Africa: 1000–1800*. Longman.
Hallett, Robin. *Africa to 1875*. University of Michigan.
Josephy, Jr. Alvin M. *The Indian Heritage of America*. Knopf.
Kotker, Norman. *The Horizon Book of the Middle Ages*. American Heritage.
Murasaki, Lady. *The Tale of Genji*. tr. Arthur Waley, Modern Library.
Needham, Joseph. *Science and Civilization in China*. Cambridge University.
Stewart, Desmond. *Early Islam*. Time-Life.
Stuart, George E. *Discovering Man's Past in the Americas*. National Geographic Society.
Thompson, J. Eric S. *The Rise and Fall of Mayan Civilization*. University of Oklahoma.
Wallace, Robert. *The Rise of Russia*. Time-Life.
Ziegler, Philip. *The Black Death: A Study of the Plague in 14th-Century Europe*. Harper & Row.

Unit Four: The Emergence of Modern Nations

Bohannon, Paul. *Africa and Africans*. Natural History Press.
Carter, Philip. *The Atlantic Slave Trade: A Census*. University of Wisconsin.
Church, William F., ed. *The Greatness of Louis XIV: Myth or Reality?*. Heath.
Clyde, P. H., and B. F. Beers. *A History of the Far East*. Prentice-Hall.
Crankshaw, Edward. *Maria Theresa*. Viking.
Elkins, Stanley M. *Slavery*. University of Chicago.
Fraser, Antonia. *Cromwell: The Lord Protector*. Knopf.
_____. *Royal Charles: Charles II and the Restoration*. Knopf.
Gentiles, Frederick, and Melvin Steinfield. *Hangups from Way Back*. vol. 2, Harper & Row.
Lefebvre, Georges. *Coming of the French Revolution*. Random House.
Morison, S. E. *The European Discovery of America*. Oxford University.
Palmer, R. R. *Twelve Who Ruled*. Atheneum.
Pratt, Fletcher. *The Battles That Changed History*. Doubleday.
Ross, James B., and Mary M. McLaughlin, eds. *The Portable Renaissance Reader*. Viking.
Thompson, J. M. *The French Revolution*. Oxford University.
Troyat, Henri. *Catherine the Great*. Dutton.

Unit Five: The Development of Industrial Society

American Heritage eds. *Men of Science and Invention*. American Heritage.
Ascherson, Neal. *The King Incorporated*. Doubleday.
Asimov, Isaac. *Asimov's Biographical Encyclopedia of Science and Technology*. Doubleday.
Bailey, Thomas A. *A Diplomatic History of the United States*. Appleton-Century-Crofts.
_____. *The American Pageant*. Heath.
Cornwell, E. L., ed. *The Pictorial Story of the Railways*. Hamlyn.
Dostoyevsky, Feodor. *The Brothers Karamazov*. Modern Library.
Drackett, Phil, ed. *The Encyclopedia of the Motorcar*. Crown.
Feldman, A., and P. Ford. *Scientists and Inventors*. Facts on File.
Fogel, Robert W., and Stanley Engerman. *Time on the Cross*. Little, Brown.
Genovese, Eugene D. *Roll Jordan Roll*. Vintage.
Hibbert, Christopher. *Daily Life in Victorian England*. American Heritage.
Hopkinson, T. *South Africa*. Time-Life.
Jablonski, Edward. *Man with Wings*. Doubleday.
Maddocks, Melvin. *The Great Liners*. Time-Life.
Manuel, Frank E. *The Prophets of Paris*. Harper Torchbooks.
Singletary, Otis. *The Mexican War*. University of Chicago.
Stampp, Kenneth. *The Peculiar Institution*. Random House.
Stein, Ralph. *The Treasury of the Automobile*. Golden Press.
Taylor, A. J. P., ed. *Purnell's History of the 20th Century*. vol. 2, Purnell & Sons.
Turgenev, Ivan. *Fathers and Sons*. Dutton.
Tryckare, Tre. *The Lore of Flight*. Cagner.
Weisberger, Bernard Al. *The Age of Steel and Steam*. Time-Life.
Wilson, Edmund. *To the Finland Station*. Doubleday.
Wilson, Mitchell. *American Science and Invention*. Simon and Schuster.
Untermeyer, Louis. *Makers of the Modern Mind*. Simon and Schuster.

Unit Six: World War in the Twentieth Century

Aberg, Sherill E. *Woodrow Wilson and the League of Nations*. Scholastic.
Arwas, Victor. *Art Deco*. Abrams.
Bailey, Thomas A. *Probing America's Past: A Critical Examination of Major Myths and Misconceptions*. vol. 2, Heath.
Bailey, Thomas A., and Paul B. Ryan. *Hitler vs. Roosevelt*. Macmillan.
Bullock, Alan. *Hitler: A Study in Tyranny*. Harper & Row.
Burns, James MacGregor. *Roosevelt: The Soldier of Fortune*. Harcourt Brace Jovanovich.

Cochran, Thomas C. *The Great Depression and World War II.* Scott Foresman.
Ewen, David. *All the Years of American Popular Music.* Prentice-Hall.
Feather, Leonard. *The New Edition of the Encyclopedia of Jazz.* Horizon.
Fenno, Jr., R. R., ed. *The Yalta Conference.* Heath.
Fermi, Laura. *Mussolini.* University of Chicago.
Ferro, M. *The Great War 1914–1918.* Routledge & Kegan.
Fessler, Loren. *China.* Time-Life.
Fitzsimmons, Bernard, ed. *Tanks and Weapons of World War I.* Beekman.
______. *Airplanes and Air Battles of World War I.* Beekman.
Fogelman, Edwin, ed. *Hiroshima: The Decision to Use the A-Bomb.* American Library.
Haslam, Malcolm. *The Real World of the Surrealists.* Rizzoli.
Hoag, Edwin and Joy. *Masters of Modern Architecture.* Bobbs-Merrill.
Leuchtenberg, William F. *Franklin D. Roosevelt: The New Deal 1932–1940.* Harper & Row.
Life eds. *Picture History of World War II.* Simon and Schuster.
Payne, Robert. *The Life and Death of Mahatma Gandhi.* Dutton.
Rozwenc, E. C., ed. *The New Deal.* Heath.
Rubin, William. *Pablo Picasso: A Retrospective.* Museum of Modern Art.
Shirer, William A. *The Rise and Fall of the Third Reich.* Simon and Schuster.
Stewart, Desmond. *Turkey.* Time-Life.
Toland, Jon. *Infamy: Pearl Harbor and Its Aftermath.* Doubleday.
Wolfe, Tom. *From Bauhaus to Our House.* Farrar, Straus & Giroux.

Unit Seven: The World Since 1945

Abboushi, F. *The Angry Arabs.* Westminster.
Beasley, W. G. *The Modern History of Japan.* St. Martin's Press.
Bonavia, David. *Peking.* Time-Life.
Bullock, Paul, ed. *Watts: The Aftermath.* Grove.
Caputo, Philip. *A Rumor of War.* Holt, Rinehart and Winston.
Council of Environmental Quality. *The Global 2000 Report to the President.* U.S. Government.
Dayan, M. *Story of My Life.* William Morrow.
Dean, John. *Blind Ambition.* Simon and Schuster.
Fisher, Lois. *A Peking Diary.* St. Martin's Press.
Fitzgerald, Frances. *Fire in the Lake.* Little, Brown.
Fraser, John. *The Chinese: Portrait of a People.* Summit.
Gate, Curtis. *The Ides of August: The Berlin Wall Crisis.* M. Evans.
Golston, R. *Next Year in Jerusalem.* Little, Brown.
Haber, E. *Menahem Begin: The Legend and the Man.* Delacorte.
Halberstam, David. *Making of a Quagmire.* Random House.
Heaps, W. A. *The Wall of Shame.* Duell, Sloan, & Pearce.
Laquer, W., ed. *The Israel-Arab Reader.* Bantam.
MacEoin, Gary. *What Happened at Rome.* Holt, Rinehart and Winston.
Phillips, Cabell. *The Truman Presidency.* Macmillan.
Prittie, Terrance. *Germany.* Time-Life.
Robinson, A. *Israel and the Arabs.* Pantheon.
Rynne, Xavier. *Letters from Vatican City.* Farrar, Straus, & Giroux.
Sadat, Anwar. *In Search of Identity.* Harper & Row.
Scheel, Orville. *In the People's Republic.* Random House.
Spanier, John. *Truman-MacArthur Controversy and Korean War.* Norton.
Terrill, Ross, ed. *The Chinese Difference.* Harper & Row.
______. *The Future of China,* Delacorte.
Watson, Andrew. *Living in China.* Rowman & Littlefield.
Windsor, P., and A. Roberts. *Czechoslovakia, 1968.* Columbia University.
Woodward, B., and C. Bernstein. *All the President's Men.* Warner.
Zeman, Z. A. B. *Prague Spring.* Hill & Wang.

FEATURES OF THE TEACHER'S RESOURCEBANK™

The **Teacher's ResourceBank™** of ***World History: People and Nations*** contains a variety of teaching resources designed to enhance instruction.

Transparencies

The **Teacher's ResourceBank™** includes seven synthesis transparencies, each of which details one of the major themes of each of the seven units in the **Pupil's Edition.**

Worksheets

The **Teacher's ResourceBank™** includes the following worksheets.

- **Critical Thinking:** These copying masters provide worksheets that build important critical thinking skills.
- **Building History Study Skills:** These copying masters provide worksheets to reinforce the Building History Study Skills features presented in the text.
- **Basic Concepts:** These copying masters provide study guides suitable for students who need extra help to grasp key concepts.
- **Profile:** These copying masters provide worksheets that analyze specific events in history in a highly readable narrative style.
- **Review:** These copying masters provide worksheets for further review of major concepts of each chapter and unit. They are designed to be used before students take Form A Tests.
- **Reteaching:** These copying masters provide worksheets for further review of chapter and unit concepts. They are designed for students whose Form A Tests indicate the need for reinforcement of key concepts. The Reteaching Worksheets may be used before students take Form B Tests.
- **Synthesis:** These copying masters provide worksheets reviewing the concepts presented in each of the seven Unit Syntheses.
- **Vocabulary:** These copying masters provide worksheets designed to enhance student understanding of basic social studies vocabulary terms.

Tests

The **Teacher's ResourceBank™** provides the following copying masters for a comprehensive evaluation program.

- **Daily Quizzes:** 151 **Daily Quizzes,** one for each section in the textbook.
- **Form A Tests:** 33 two-page Chapter **Form A Tests;** 7-two-page Unit **Form A Tests,** one four-page **Mid-Book Test,** and one four-page **End-of-Book Test.**
- **Form B Tests:** 40 **Form B Tests,** one for each chapter and unit.
- **Unit Synthesis Tests:** seven **Unit Synthesis Tests,** one for each Unit Synthesis.

Geography Worksheets and Outline Maps

A set of **Geography Worksheets and Outline Maps** is included as part of the ***World History: People and Nations*** program in an effort to expand students' knowledge of world geography as they study world history. A knowledge of world geography is essential to the study of world history. Unfortunately, in today's crowded curriculum, the study of the two subjects is often an either/or proposition—a student takes one or the other, but not both.

The **Geography Worksheets** consist of three parts: **Reviewing Map Skills, Geography Fact Sheets** that describe important geographic concepts, and **Geography Applications** that relate history and geography.

The set of **Geography Worksheets and Outline Maps** also contains seven reproducible outline maps—maps of the world, Europe, Asia, North and South America, Africa, and the waters and landforms of the Pacific. These maps may be reproduced and distributed for use with map activities suggested in the textbook, the **Annotated Teacher's Edition,** or the **Teacher's ResourceBank™.**

Daily Lesson Planner

A **Daily Lesson Planner** is included as part of the ***World History: People and Nations*** program to help teachers plan their presentation of world history.

ADDITIONAL COMPONENTS

World History: People and Nations includes a wealth of additional components, each designed to enhance the teaching of world history.

- **Workbook:** A separate **Workbook** for ***World History: People and Nations*** is available. The **Teacher's Edition Workbook** carries answers in place for each worksheet.
- **Test Booklet:** A separate booklet includes 33 two-page Chapter **Form A Tests,** 7 two-page Unit **Form A Tests,** one four-page **Mid-Book Test,** one four-page **End-of-Book Test,** and 40 one-page **Form B Tests** (one for each chapter and unit).
- **World and Regional Map Transparencies with Thematic Overlays:** A set of 10 transparencies accompanies ***World History: People and Nations.*** The set includes its own **Teacher's Manual.**
- **Readings in World History:** This collection offers a wealth of primary- and secondary-source historical readings. The selections discuss events of political, cultural, social, and intellectual significance in each of the major periods of world history.
- **50 World Biographies:** This collection details the lives of 50 important people in world history. The collection includes its own **Teacher's Manual.**

Teacher's Notes

Teacher's Notes

Essential Elements of Texas

PART A: World History Studies

ESSENTIAL ELEMENT		PUPIL'S EDITION
Relationships between geography and history. The student shall be provided opportunities to:		
1A	describe the physical and cultural geographic characteristics of places studied	5, 6, 9, 10, 15, 17, 18, 21, 27, 28, 32, 33, 34, 35, 36, 38, 39, 44, 47, 50, 51, 54, 61, 63, 67, 69, 70, 71, 73, 77, 78, 79, 89, 90, 92, 97, 101, 102, 106, 110, 118, 123, 134, 140, 143, 144, 145, 149, 159, 165, 169, 175, 176, 188, 189, 191, 196, 197, 203, 205, 206, 209, 218, 221, 225, 226, 227, 242, 247, 250, 251, 265, 267, 268, 273, 276, 278, 281, 289, 290, 294, 298, 303, 304, 307, 313, 314, 326, 340, 353, 360, 368, 378, 382, 385, 387, 390, 393, 407, 415, 416, 417, 418, 419, 431, 442, 446, 447, 448, 451, 454, 456, 465, 470, 474, 513, 541, 549, 551, 553, 555, 565, 568, 571, 577, 582, 592, 594, 596, 607, 615, 618, 623, 624, 627, 628, 644, 645, 648, 650, 657, 659, 663, 687, 689, 700, 709, 713, 717, 727, 728, 733, 761, 763, 773, 776, 781, 787, 795, 797, 805, 809, 820, 823, 829, 837, 848, 849, 864, 873, 894, R2, R4. R6. R8. R10, R11, R12, R14, R16, R17, R18
1B	understand the effects of the physical environment on the history of cultures and societies	5, 6, 7, 8, 10, 11, 13, 14, 19, 20, 21, 22, 23, 24, 26, 27, 28, 29, 30, 31, 32, 33, 34, 35, 36, 37, 38, 39, 40, 41, 42, 43, 45, 46, 52, 53, 54, 55, 56, 57, 59, 60, 61, 62, 63, 64, 65, 66, 71, 72, 73, 74, 75, 76, 77, 78, 80, 81, 82, 84, 85, 86, 87, 88, 90, 92, 94, 95, 96, 97, 102, 104, 105, 106, 109, 112, 114, 115, 116, 117, 122, 125, 126, 127, 128, 129, 130, 131, 132, 133, 135, 136, 137, 138, 140, 144, 145, 147, 151, 152, 153, 156, 157, 158, 159, 160, 161, 162, 168, 169, 171, 172, 174, 176, 178, 179, 180, 181, 182, 183, 187, 188, 189, 190, 191, 192, 193, 194, 195, 196, 197, 198, 199, 200, 201, 202, 206, 207, 208, 209, 210, 211, 212, 213, 214, 215, 216, 217, 218, 219, 220, 224, 225, 226, 227, 228, 229, 230, 231, 232, 233, 234, 235, 236, 237, 238, 239, 240, 241, 243, 244, 245, 246, 250, 251, 252, 253, 254, 255, 256, 258, 259, 260, 261, 262, 263, 264, 265, 266, 267, 268, 269, 271, 272, 275, 276, 277, 278, 279, 280, 281, 282, 283, 284, 285, 286, 287, 288, 289, 290, 294, 295, 296, 297, 298, 299, 300, 301, 302, 303, 304, 305, 306, 308, 310, 311, 312, 314, 315, 316, 317, 318, 319, 320, 321, 325, 326, 327, 328, 329, 330, 331, 332, 333, 334, 335, 336, 337, 338, 339, 340, 341, 342, 343, 344, 345, 346, 347, 348, 349, 350, 351, 352, 355, 356, 357, 358, 359, 362, 363, 364, 365, 366, 367, 370, 371, 372, 373, 374, 375, 376, 377, 378, 379, 380, 381, 382, 383, 384, 385, 386, 387, 388, 389, 390, 391, 392, 395, 396, 397, 398, 399, 400, 401, 402, 403, 404, 405, 406, 407, 408, 409, 418, 421, 422, 423, 424, 425, 426, 427, 428, 429, 430, 431, 432, 433, 434, 435, 436, 437, 438, 439, 440, 441, 442, 443, 444, 445, 446, 447, 448, 449, 450, 453, 454, 455, 456, 457, 458, 459, 460, 461, 462, 463, 464, 465, 466, 467, 468, 473, 474, 475, 476, 478, 480, 481, 482, 483, 484, 485, 489, 490, 491, 492, 493, 494, 495, 496, 497, 498, 499, 500, 502, 504, 505, 506, 507, 508, 509, 510, 511, 512, 515, 516, 517, 518, 519, 520, 521, 522, 523, 524, 525, 526, 527, 528, 529, 530, 531, 532, 533, 534, 535, 536, 537, 538, 539, 540, 543, 544, 545, 546, 547, 548, 549, 550, 551, 552, 553, 556, 558, 559, 560, 561, 562, 563, 564, 566, 567, 570, 573, 574, 575, 576, 577, 578, 579, 580, 581, 582, 583, 584,

Key correlations of the textbook's content with the Texas Essential Elements are included throughout this Annotated Teacher's Edition. Correlations with content are listed at the top of the page (for example, see page 3). For the Essential Element to which each notation refers, see the Texas Essential Elements chart on pages ATE23–35.

ESSENTIAL ELEMENT		PUPIL'S EDITION
Relationships between geography and history. The student shall be provided opportunities to:		
1B	understand the effects of the physical environment on the history of cultures and societies	585, 586, 587, 588, 589, 590, 591, 592, 593, 594, 595, 596, 599, 600, 601, 602, 603, 604, 605, 609, 610, 611, 613, 614, 616, 617, 618, 621, 622, 623, 624, 625, 626, 628, 630, 631, 632, 633, 634, 635, 662, 666, 667, 668, 669, 670, 671, 688, 691, 692, 694, 695, 696, 697, 698, 699, 700, 701, 702, 703, 704, 705, 706, 707, 708, 711, 712, 713, 714, 715, 717, 718, 719, 738, 740, 742, 743, 744, 745, 746, 747, 751, 752, 753, 754, 758, 759, 764, 766, 772, 775, 776, 777, 778, 779, 780, 781, 782, 783, 784, 785, 786, 788, 789, 790, 791, 792, 793, 794, 795, 796, 797, 800, 801, 803, 804, 815, 828, 832, 844, 845, 851, 852, 854, 856, 872, 884, 885, 886, 887, 888, 889, 890, 891, 892, 893, 894, 896, 898, 899, 900, 901, 902, 903
1C	examine the effects of human modifications of the physical environment in places and time periods studied	xxvi, 8, 10, 18, 20, 24, 28, 30, 43, 44, 54, 71, 80, 86, 89, 93, 105, 106, 111, 115, 118, 123, 126, 131, 135, 145, 149, 150, 157, 160, 166, 168, 172, 190, 193, 196, 197, 199, 205, 206, 210, 213, 216, 218, 219, 236, 251, 253, 255, 258, 259, 270, 275, 280, 282, 285, 295, 299, 301, 303, 305, 307, 310, 366, 408, 443, 455, 456, 490, 492, 493, 496, 497, 498, 504, 506, 508, 509, 517, 525, 526, 529, 551, 554, 556, 563, 584, 601, 602, 605, 606, 609, 610, 612, 613, 619, 621, 622, 623, 627, 630, 650, 674, 675, 695, 696, 702, 724, 737, 742, 763, 764, 780, 782, 784, 788, 797, 813, 819, 832, 838, 846, 847, 853, 854, 881, 882, 883, 892, 893
1D	explain the effects of new forms of transportation, trade, and communications on historical developments	9, 10, 13, 14, 38, 46, 52, 57, 63, 71, 72, 73, 74, 76, 78, 80, 86, 87, 88, 90, 102, 105, 106, 110, 112, 115, 120, 122, 138, 150, 157, 166, 167, 171, 172, 174, 176, 181, 182, 190, 195, 198, 202, 220, 253, 254, 255, 256, 257, 258, 272, 298, 300, 301, 303, 305, 306, 312, 314, 315, 318, 319, 331, 344, 345, 358, 359, 362, 363, 364, 365, 366, 375, 392, 410, 411, 412, 418, 455, 456, 460, 481, 490, 491, 492, 493, 494, 495, 496, 497, 498, 499, 500, 501, 508, 509, 512, 515, 516, 532, 533, 534, 540, 557, 602, 606, 608, 609, 610, 613, 616, 617, 619, 621, 626, 628, 630, 649, 651, 661, 704, 707, 766, 772, 777, 778, 780, 782, 784, 804, 814, 833, 834, 835, 853, 877, 878, 879
1E	compare the effects on the development of resources in countries where private property rights have been honored and where they have not	508, 509, 674, 675, 676, 677, 678, 685, 686, 688, 759, 762, 763, 764, 765, 766, 767, 768, 769, 772, 776, 777, 778, 779, 780, 782, 792, 793, 802, 804, 867, 868, 869, 871, 872, 892, 898, 899, 902
Early civilizations of Asia, Africa, and the Western Hemisphere and their contributions to world civilizations. The student shall be provided opportunities to:		
2A	analyze the river valley civilizations (Middle East, China, Indus Valley, Nile Valley)	9, 10, 11, 13, 14, 17, 18, 19, 20, 21, 22, 23, 24, 25, 26, 27, 29, 30, 31, 32, 33, 34, 35, 46, 90, 92, 93, 94, 95, 96, 97, 297, 298, 300, 301, 312, 321
2B	describe the kingdoms, societies, and cultures of Africa	4, 5, 6, 9, 19, 20, 21, 22, 23, 24, 25, 26, 27, 92, 93, 293, 294, 295, 297, 298, 299, 300, 301, 302, 303, 312, 313, 321, 322
2C	understand the cultures and societies of pre-Columbian North, Central, and South America	303, 304, 305, 306, 307, 310, 311, 312, 314, 315, 321, 635

ESSENTIAL ELEMENT		PUPIL'S EDITION
Early civilizations of Asia, Africa, and the Western Hemisphere and their contributions to world civilizations. The student shall be provided opportunities to:		
2D	trace the historical development, precepts, and influences of Buddhism, Hinduism, Confucianism	57, 58, 59, 60, 61, 62, 66, 67, 79, 81, 82, 84, 88, 89, 90, 91, 94, 97, 216, 218, 277, 283, 284, 287, 289, 291, 454, 455, 457, 466, 474, 475, 610, 611, 692, 782, 786, 787, 788
Foundations of Western Civilization. The student shall be provided opportunities to:		
3A	describe Greek and Roman societies and their contributions	41, 101, 102, 103, 104, 105, 106, 107, 108, 110, 111, 112, 113, 114, 115, 116, 117, 118, 119, 120, 121, 122, 125, 126, 127, 128, 129, 130, 131, 132, 133, 134, 135, 136, 137, 138, 139, 140, 143, 144, 145, 146, 147, 148, 149, 150, 151, 152, 153, 154, 155, 156, 157, 158, 159, 160, 161, 162, 163, 164, 165, 166, 167, 168, 169, 171, 172, 174, 176, 178, 179, 180, 181, 182, 183, 308, 882
3B	trace the historical development, precepts, and influences of Judaism, Christianity and Islam	12, 39, 42, 43, 45, 94, 162, 163, 164, 165, 166, 174, 176, 182, 183, 190, 191, 200, 201, 202, 205, 206, 207, 208, 209, 210, 211, 212, 214, 215, 216, 217, 218, 219, 220, 233, 234, 235, 236, 237, 244, 246, 249, 250, 251, 252, 269, 271, 272, 314, 315, 316, 317, 318, 319, 320, 471, 476, 478, 480, 485, 729, 730, 820, 821, 822, 824, 825, 827, 828, 833, 891, 901
3C	analyze the growth and impact of the Byzantine Empire	187, 188, 189, 190, 191, 192, 193, 194, 196, 197, 198, 199, 200, 201, 202, 214
Emergence of European predominance. The student shall be provided opportunities to:		
4A	trace the origins and basis for the concepts of liberty, individual freedom, property rights, and representative government	112, 113, 115, 145, 156, 257, 272, 308, 372, 373, 395, 396, 397, 398, 399, 400, 401, 402, 403, 404, 405, 407, 408, 409, 413, 414, 415, 416, 417, 418, 421, 422, 423, 424, 425, 426, 427, 428, 429, 430, 431, 432, 433, 434, 435, 436, 437, 438, 439, 440, 441, 442, 443, 444, 445, 446, 447, 448, 449, 450, 478, 482, 483, 484, 543, 544, 545, 546, 547, 556, 558, 570, 632
4B	describe the political, social, economic, and cultural aspects of Europe in the Middle Ages	223, 224, 225, 226, 227, 228, 229, 230, 231, 232, 233, 234, 235, 236, 237, 238, 239, 240, 241, 242, 243, 244, 245, 246, 249, 250, 251, 252, 253, 254, 255, 256, 257, 258, 259, 260, 261, 262, 263, 264, 265, 266, 267, 268, 269, 271, 272, 314, 315, 317, 318, 319, 320, 341, 342, 344, 345
4C	identify the causes, characteristics, and impact of the Reformation and Renaissance	325, 326, 327, 328, 329, 330, 331, 332, 333, 334, 335, 336, 337, 338, 339, 340, 341, 342, 343, 344, 345, 346, 347, 348, 349, 350, 351, 352, 478, 480, 481

ESSENTIAL ELEMENT		PUPIL'S EDITION
Emergence of European predominance. The student shall be provided opportunities to:		
4D	analyze the development of nationalism and the nation-state (with emphasis on England, France, Spain)	265, 266, 267, 268, 269, 272, 314, 319, 376, 377, 378, 379, 380, 381, 382, 383, 384, 385, 386, 387, 388, 389, 390, 391, 392, 395, 396, 397, 398, 399, 400, 401, 402, 403, 404, 405, 407, 408
4E	describe the causes and effects of European expansion (discovery, exploration, colonization, investment, mercantilism)	355, 356, 357, 358, 359, 362, 363, 364, 365, 366, 367, 370, 371, 374, 375, 376, 377, 378, 379, 380, 381, 382, 383, 384, 385, 386, 387, 388, 389, 390, 391, 392, 410, 411, 412, 459, 460, 473, 474, 476, 478, 481, 482, 483, 484, 508, 509, 549, 550, 551, 552, 557, 559, 560, 563, 564, 566, 567, 569, 691, 692, 693, 694, 695, 696, 697, 698, 699, 700, 701, 702, 786, 788, 789, 790, 791, 792, 793, 794, 795, 796, 797, 798, 800, 801, 802, 808, 809, 810, 811, 812, 816, 817, 818, 828
4F	identify the causes, characteristics, and effects of the Enlightenment	405, 421, 422, 423, 424, 450, 451, 478, 479, 483
4G	understand the causes and results of political revolutions (emphasis on 18th and 19th century North, Central, and South America; England; and France)	398, 399, 400, 401, 402, 403, 404, 405, 407, 408, 412, 413, 414, 415, 416, 417, 418, 419, 424, 425, 426, 427, 429, 430, 431, 432, 433, 434, 435, 436, 437, 438, 439, 449, 450, 451, 478, 479, 482, 483, 484, 543, 544, 545, 546, 547, 557, 558, 562, 563, 564, 565, 566, 567, 568, 569, 570, 571, 628, 629, 632
4H	analyze the causes, characteristics, and results fo the Industrial Revolution (including the increased productivity and prosperity resulting from the Industrial Revolution)	489, 490, 491, 492, 493, 494, 495, 496, 497, 498, 499, 500, 501, 502, 503, 504, 505, 506, 507, 508, 509, 510, 511, 512, 515, 516, 517, 518, 519, 520, 521, 522, 523, 524, 525, 526, 527, 528, 529, 530, 531, 532, 533, 534, 535, 536, 537, 538, 539, 540, 546, 547, 556, 583, 584, 599, 600, 613, 626, 628, 630, 631, 632, 705, 706, 833, 835, 836
4I	trace the development of capitalism, socialism, and communism	256, 266, 357, 358, 359, 490, 491, 492, 493, 494, 495, 496, 497, 498, 499, 500, 501, 502, 503, 504, 505, 506, 507, 508, 509, 510, 511, 512, 547, 548, 570, 583, 584, 585, 628, 630, 631, 632, 652, 653, 671, 672, 673, 674, 685, 686, 687, 688, 699, 700, 740, 743, 744, 746, 758, 759, 760, 761, 762, 765, 767, 768, 775, 776, 777, 778, 779, 780, 782, 783, 796, 800, 801, 802, 804, 842, 856, 860, 862, 870, 872, 898, 899, 900, 902
4J	describe the development of nationalism and completion of nation-building (emphasis on Germany, Italy, and Soviet Union)	441, 447, 448, 449, 450, 478, 479, 485, 573, 574, 575, 576, 577, 578, 579, 580, 581, 582, 583, 584, 585, 586, 587, 588, 589, 590, 591, 592, 593, 594, 595, 596, 597, 600, 626, 628, 629, 633, 634, 640

ESSENTIAL ELEMENT		PUPIL'S EDITION
Emergence of European predominance. The student shall be provided opportunities to:		
4K	explain the causes of and effects of Western imperialism	599, 600, 601, 602, 603, 604, 605, 606, 607, 608, 609, 610, 611, 612, 613, 614, 615, 616, 617, 618, 619, 620, 621, 622, 623, 624, 625, 626, 627, 628, 629, 634, 635, 640, 661, 691, 692, 693, 694, 696, 697, 712, 742, 745, 786, 787, 791, 792, 793, 794, 795, 807, 808, 809, 810, 811, 812, 813, 814, 815, 816, 817, 818, 819
Contemporary world developments. The student shall be provided opportunities to:		
5A	examine nationalism, anticolonial revolutions, and development of new states in Asia, Africa, and the Middle East noting economic and political perspectives	611, 612, 613, 614, 615, 616, 626, 628, 691, 692, 694, 695, 696, 697, 698, 699, 700, 701, 702, 703, 704, 708, 709, 740, 741, 745, 746, 786, 787, 788, 789, 790, 791, 792, 793, 794, 795, 797, 801, 802, 803, 804, 807, 808, 809, 810, 811, 812, 813, 814, 815, 816, 817, 818, 819, 820, 821, 822, 823, 824, 825, 826, 827, 828, 896, 899, 900, 901
5B	explain the causes and effects of limited and unlimited wars (WWI-II, Korea, Viet Nam, Afghanistan, Middle East, etc.)	639, 640, 641, 642, 643, 644, 645, 646, 648, 649, 650, 651, 652, 653, 654, 655, 656, 657, 658, 659, 660, 661, 662, 665, 666, 667, 668, 669, 670, 671, 672, 673, 674, 675, 676, 677, 678, 679, 680, 681, 682, 683, 685, 688, 695, 696, 711, 712, 713, 714, 715, 716, 717, 718, 719, 720, 721, 722, 723, 724, 725, 726, 727, 729, 730, 731, 732, 733, 734, 735, 736, 737, 738, 740, 742, 743, 744, 746, 747, 751, 752, 753, 754, 755, 757, 758, 759, 760, 761, 762, 763, 764, 765, 766, 767, 768, 769, 771, 772, 781, 782, 783, 784, 794, 795, 796, 797, 798, 799, 800, 804, 807, 808, 810, 818, 820, 821, 822, 824, 828, 831, 833, 838, 844, 848, 855, 856, 857, 867, 882, 891, 894, 896, 898, 899, 900, 901
5C	explain the causes and effects of Soviet expansion, imperialism, and the struggle for world domination based on the stated goal of world communism	687, 744, 745, 752, 758, 759, 760, 761, 762, 767, 768, 770, 771, 772, 780, 781, 782, 784, 794, 802, 803, 814, 816, 819, 820, 841, 842, 846, 848, 854, 855, 856, 860, 863, 866, 878, 896, 898
5D	analyze the impact of changing economic relations and economic interdependence among regions and nations	742, 744, 755, 756, 757, 761, 762, 764, 765, 766, 769, 814, 815, 819, 822, 826, 851, 853, 855, 856, 857, 858, 859, 860, 862, 863, 864, 865, 866, 867, 868, 870, 871, 872, 876, 877, 878, 879, 880, 881, 884, 885, 887, 889, 890, 891, 892, 894, 896, 898, 899, 900, 901, 902, 903
5E	trace the developments in and impact of science and technology (space, medicine, communications) noting the positive impact of individual freedom and incentives on technological advancement	519, 648, 649, 650, 732, 733, 734, 735, 736, 737, 742, 747, 755, 757, 761, 762, 764, 784, 854, 861, 872, 875, 876, 877, 878, 879, 880, 881, 896, 903

ESSENTIAL ELEMENT		PUPIL'S EDITION
Contemporary world developments. The student shall be provided opportunities to:		
5F	identify developments in the arts, literature, religion, and philosophy	639, 640, 656, 666, 667, 668, 669, 670, 703, 705, 715, 731, 741, 743, 766, 815, 816, 821, 824, 827, 854, 884, 885, 886, 887, 888, 889, 890, 891, 892, 893, 894, 895, 897, 901, 903
5G	describe the growth of authoritarian and totalitarian governments (communist, socialist, fascist) and their adverse effects on liberty, freedom, and human rights	679, 680, 681, 682, 683, 684, 685, 686, 687, 688, 699, 700, 711, 712, 715, 716, 717, 718, 719, 720, 721, 722, 723, 730, 731, 738, 740, 743, 744, 745, 746, 747, 751, 752, 753, 754, 755, 758, 760, 767, 768, 770, 771, 772, 777, 778, 793, 796, 839, 841, 842, 846, 855, 856, 860, 866, 867, 868, 870, 871, 872, 892, 898, 899, 900, 902
5H	contrast the effects on productivity and living standards of countries with similar resource bases but with market economies vs. restricted economies	508, 509, 674, 675, 676, 677, 678, 685, 686, 688, 759, 762, 763, 764, 765, 766, 767, 768, 769, 772, 776, 777, 778, 779, 780, 782, 792, 793, 802, 804, 867, 868, 869, 871, 872, 892, 898, 899, 902
5I	explain the positive aspects and effects of American capitalism upon the world	651, 747, 752, 762, 763, 765, 766, 769, 803, 821, 835, 840, 843, 848, 851, 854, 855, 856, 872, 892, 898, 902, 903
5J	describe democratic forms of government, their growth, and explain the positive effects of American democracy on liberty, freedom, and human rights	768, 801, 836, 840, 846, 847, 870, 871

ESSENTIAL ELEMENT	PUPIL'S EDITION
Respect for self and others	
a1A respect beliefs of other individuals, groups, and cultures	6, 8, 9, 10, 11, 13, 49, 53, 54, 55, 56, 57, 58, 59, 60, 61, 66, 72, 75, 81, 82, 83, 84, 85, 86, 88, 90, 95, 97, 102, 104, 105, 106, 108, 109, 110, 111, 112, 113, 114, 115, 116, 117, 121, 122, 126, 132, 135, 137, 140, 144, 147, 162, 163, 164, 165, 172, 182, 183, 187, 190, 191, 192, 193, 194, 196, 197, 198, 200, 201, 202, 205, 206, 207, 208, 210, 211, 213, 214, 215, 217, 218, 219, 220, 234, 235, 236, 261, 262, 263, 269, 271, 277, 278, 280, 283, 287, 289, 290, 295, 296, 302, 305, 306, 307, 308, 310, 311, 312, 314, 316, 317, 318, 326, 332, 333, 334, 335, 336, 337, 338, 339, 340, 341, 342, 343, 347, 348, 349, 350, 351, 352, 359, 372, 374, 375, 377, 378, 379, 385, 388, 392, 401, 403, 404, 405, 407, 408, 409, 414, 416, 417, 418, 421, 422, 423, 424, 425, 426, 427, 428, 429, 430, 431, 432, 433, 434, 435, 436, 437, 438, 439, 440, 441, 442, 443, 444, 445, 446, 447, 448, 449, 450, 453, 454, 455, 456, 457, 458, 459, 460, 461, 462, 463, 464, 465, 466, 467, 468, 469, 470, 471, 473, 474, 475, 476, 478, 498, 499, 510, 511, 512, 543, 544, 545, 546, 547, 548, 554, 555, 556, 557, 558, 559, 560, 561, 562, 563, 564, 566, 567, 569, 570, 574, 575, 581, 604, 611, 612, 666, 667, 693, 694, 729, 821, 827, 833, 889, 890, 891, 901
a1B be aware that some things are valued more in some groups and cultures than in others	58, 59, 62, 63, 74, 75, 103, 105, 106, 108, 109, 112, 113, 114, 115, 116, 117, 120, 122, 127, 128, 179, 180, 182, 194, 195, 197, 198, 199, 200, 201, 206, 207, 211, 214, 216, 218, 257, 259, 260, 265, 275, 276, 279, 281, 282, 284, 285, 288, 300, 301, 316, 317, 325, 327, 328, 329, 330, 331, 334, 345, 346, 387, 415, 432, 465, 466, 467, 481, 490, 508, 535, 536, 538, 539, 548, 549, 550, 554, 557, 558, 559, 564, 569, 570, 630, 631, 666, 667, 668, 669, 670, 699, 702, 705, 708, 711, 712, 718, 724, 725, 729, 738, 740, 769, 770, 771, 780, 782, 783, 784, 788, 790, 791, 792, 793, 794, 796, 797, 798, 800, 801, 802, 804, 807, 808, 810, 811, 812, 813, 814, 815, 816, 817, 818, 819, 820, 821, 822, 826, 828, 834, 835, 844, 845, 846, 847, 853, 854, 855, 856, 857, 858, 859, 862, 863, 867, 868, 884, 893, 894
a1C recognize how societal values affect individual beliefs and attitudes	64, 65, 79, 81, 82, 85, 92, 93, 94, 95, 96, 97, 107, 118, 119, 120, 131, 132, 135, 138, 158, 160, 172, 178, 179, 180, 181, 182, 183, 199, 210, 211, 215, 218, 219, 220, 229, 230, 231, 246, 251, 256, 258, 259, 260, 261, 277, 278, 279, 280, 281, 282, 283, 285, 286, 290, 295, 296, 297, 300, 301, 302, 304, 305, 306, 307, 308, 310, 311, 312, 314, 316, 317, 318, 319, 320, 321, 326, 327, 328, 329, 330, 331, 332, 333, 334, 335, 336, 337, 338, 339, 340, 341, 342, 344, 345, 346, 347, 348, 349, 350, 351, 352, 359, 372, 374, 375, 377, 378, 379, 385, 388, 392, 400, 401, 403, 406, 408, 409, 413, 414, 415, 416, 417, 418, 422, 423, 424, 425, 426, 427, 429, 430, 431, 432, 433, 434, 435, 436, 437, 445, 446, 447, 448, 449, 450, 454, 455, 456, 457, 458, 459, 460, 461, 463, 464, 465, 466, 467, 468, 469, 470, 471, 473, 474, 475, 476, 480, 481, 483, 484, 485, 490, 491, 492, 493, 494, 495, 496, 497, 498, 499, 500, 501, 502, 504, 505, 506, 507, 508, 510, 511, 512, 515, 516, 517, 518, 519, 520, 521, 522, 523, 524, 525, 526, 527, 528, 529, 530, 531, 532, 533, 534, 535, 536, 537, 538, 539, 540, 543, 544, 545, 546, 547, 548, 549, 550, 551, 552, 554, 555, 556, 557, 558, 559, 560, 561, 562, 563, 564, 566, 567, 569, 570, 579, 580, 583, 584, 585, 586, 587, 588, 589, 590, 591, 592, 593, 594, 595, 596, 604, 611, 612, 619, 623, 624, 625, 626, 628, 630, 631, 632, 633, 634, 635, 642, 649, 651, 652, 653, 654, 655, 658, 660, 666, 667, 668, 669, 670, 671, 673, 674, 675, 676, 677, 679, 680, 681, 684, 685, 686, 688, 691, 692, 695, 696, 697, 698, 700, 701, 702, 703, 704, 705, 706, 707, 708, 711, 712, 713, 714, 715, 716, 717, 718, 719, 720, 722, 723, 724, 725, 726, 727, 729, 730, 731, 738, 740, 742, 743, 744, 746, 747, 758, 759, 760, 761, 763, 764, 765, 766, 767, 768, 769, 770, 771, 772, 778, 779, 784, 786, 789, 792, 796, 798, 803, 804, 812, 815, 825, 827, 828, 834, 836, 843, 845, 846, 847, 853, 854, 855, 856, 857, 858, 859, 862, 863, 867, 868, 875, 876, 877, 878, 879, 880, 881, 884, 885, 887, 888, 889, 890, 891, 892, 893, 894, 898, 899, 900, 901, 902, 903

ESSENTIAL ELEMENT		PUPIL'S EDITION
Respect for self and others		
a1D	recognize that individuals must accept the consequences of their decisions	60, 110, 112, 113, 114, 115, 171, 240, 241, 257, 328, 370, 371, 377, 381, 382, 383, 384, 385, 386, 389, 390, 392, 395, 396, 397, 398, 399, 402, 404, 405, 407, 409, 413, 414, 415, 416, 417, 418, 423, 432, 435, 436, 440, 442, 443, 462, 482, 651, 718, 753, 754, 821, 824, 847, 853, 854, 855, 866, 867, 891, 893
Democratic beliefs and personal responsibility		
a2A	respect the principles that underlie the Texas and the United States Constitutions, the Bill of Rights, and the Declaration of independence	110, 112, 113, 114, 115, 145, 146, 241, 372, 404, 405, 407, 408, 414, 415, 416, 417, 418, 424, 425, 426, 427, 428, 429, 430, 431, 432, 433, 434, 483, 484, 544, 546, 547, 554, 556, 651, 660, 725, 852, 857
a2B	consider one's own values as well as those of others when making political decisions	241, 404, 405, 407, 408, 414, 415, 416, 417, 423, 424, 425, 426, 427, 428, 429, 430, 431, 432, 433, 434, 544, 546, 547, 554, 556, 651, 660, 770, 771
a2C	value open-mindedness, tolerance of differing opinions, and civic participation as important aspects of democratic behavior	110, 112, 113, 114, 115, 145, 146, 241, 404, 405, 407, 408, 414, 415, 416, 417, 424, 425, 426, 427, 428, 429, 430, 431, 432, 433, 434, 544, 546, 547, 554, 556, 558, 769, 770, 771, 852, 857, 867, 872
a2D	respect the laws of one's society and work responsibly to change laws that one judges to be unjust	112, 113, 114, 115, 145, 146, 241, 404, 405, 407, 408, 414, 415, 416, 417, 424, 425, 426, 427, 428, 429, 430, 431, 432, 433, 434, 544, 545, 546, 547, 554, 556, 558, 770, 771, 772, 852, 857, 859
a2E	understand the importance of individual participation in civic affairs	110, 112, 113, 114, 115, 145, 146, 241, 404, 405, 407, 408, 414, 415, 416, 417, 424, 425, 426, 427, 428, 429, 430, 431, 432, 433, 434, 499, 544, 545, 546, 547, 554, 556, 558, 770, 771, 852
a2F	understand that legal rights and protections must be balanced with civic responsibilities	145, 146, 241, 404, 405, 407, 408, 414, 415, 416, 417, 424, 425, 426, 427, 428, 429, 430, 431, 432, 433, 434, 482, 484, 499, 544, 545, 546, 547, 554, 556, 558, 770, 771, 772, 852
a2G	recognize the value of compromise in the democratic process	110, 112, 113, 114, 115, 121, 145, 146, 178, 179, 241, 318, 403, 404, 405, 407, 408, 409, 414, 415, 416, 417, 418, 423, 424, 425, 426, 427, 428, 429, 430, 431, 432, 433, 434, 436, 445, 446, 449, 450, 483, 484, 544, 545, 546, 547, 554, 556, 558, 620, 770, 771, 862, 868, 869, 870, 871, 872

ESSENTIAL ELEMENT		PUPIL'S EDITION
Democratic beliefs and personal responsibility		
a2H	examine reasons that participation and decision making in civic affairs require knowledge, time, and personal efforts	110, 112, 113, 114, 115, 145, 146, 241, 404, 405, 407, 408, 414, 415, 416, 417, 424, 425, 426, 427, 428, 429, 430, 431, 432, 433, 434, 544, 545, 546, 547, 554, 556, 558, 562, 563, 564, 566, 567, 770, 771, 857
a2I	identify legal rights, responsibilities, and protection afforded juveniles and adults	145, 146, 241, 318, 404, 405, 407, 408, 414, 415, 416, 417, 424, 425, 426, 427, 428, 429, 430, 431, 432, 433, 434, 482, 533, 544, 545, 546, 547, 556, 558, 753, 754, 770, 771, 843
a2J	support the democratic processes of the republican form of government	110, 112, 113, 114, 115, 145, 146, 178, 179, 241, 318, 400, 401, 402, 403, 404, 405, 407, 408, 414, 415, 416, 417, 418, 424, 434, 483, 484, 544, 545, 546, 547, 556, 725, 745, 769, 770, 771, 832, 833, 835, 843, 852, 853
a2K	support the basic values of American society (e.g., justice, responsibilities, freedom, respect for the law, diversity, privacy, private property rights, free enterprise, and voluntary exchange)	110, 112, 113, 114, 115, 145, 146, 241, 242, 404, 405, 407, 408, 414, 415, 416, 417, 424, 425, 426, 427, 428, 429, 430, 431, 432, 433, 434, 483, 484, 499, 525, 544, 545, 546, 547, 554, 556, 558, 651, 660, 725, 745, 747, 769, 770, 771, 852, 853, 854, 855, 856, 857, 862, 863, 865, 866, 870, 871, 872
a2L	support the rules and laws of one's school, community, state, and nation	110, 112, 113, 114, 115, 145, 146, 241, 404, 405, 407, 408, 414, 415, 416, 417, 424, 425, 426, 427, 428, 429, 430, 431, 432, 433, 434, 499, 544, 545, 546, 547, 554, 556, 562, 563, 564, 566, 567, 660, 770, 771, 852, 853, 855, 856, 859
Support for the American economic system		
a3A	recognize the contributions of the American economic system to the standard of living of Americans	493, 494, 495, 499, 500, 501, 506, 507, 516, 517, 526, 621, 622, 671, 673, 742, 853, 857, 872, 875, 876, 877, 878, 879, 880, 881, 884, 885, 886, 887, 888, 889, 890, 891, 892, 894
a3B	support the role of profit in the American market system	40, 255, 256, 257, 258, 357, 358, 359, 490, 491, 492, 493, 494, 495, 496, 499, 500, 501, 506, 507, 516, 517, 526, 619, 621, 622, 671, 673, 769, 780, 782, 784, 794, 802, 803, 853, 872, 875, 876, 877, 878, 879, 880, 881, 884
a3C	believe in the right of individuals to acquire, use, and dispose of property	40, 255, 256, 257, 258, 357, 358, 359, 490, 491, 492, 493, 494, 495, 496, 497, 498, 500, 501, 506, 507, 508, 526, 619, 671, 673, 725, 769, 780, 781, 782, 784, 794, 802, 803, 869, 870, 871
a3D	support the freedom of consumers to choose how to spend their income	255, 256, 257, 258, 357, 358, 359, 490, 491, 492, 493, 494, 495, 496, 497, 498, 500, 501, 506, 507, 619, 671, 673, 890, 891

ESSENTIAL ELEMENT		PUPIL'S EDITION
Support for the American economic system		
a3E	recognize that citizens, through legal political activities, can influence economic decisions made by government	257, 258, 357, 358, 359, 490, 491, 492, 494, 495, 496, 500, 501, 506, 507, 671, 673, 725, 870, 881
a3F	acknowledge the role of government in regulating unreasonable restraint on competition by either producers or consumers	377, 490, 495, 496, 500, 501, 506, 507, 526, 621, 622, 672, 673, 769, 865, 866, 872
a3G	support competition by either producers or consumers	255, 256, 257, 258, 357, 358, 359, 490, 491, 492, 493, 494, 495, 496, 497, 498, 499, 500, 501, 506, 507, 508, 516, 517, 619, 671, 673, 742, 743, 766, 780, 782, 784, 794, 802, 803, 875, 876, 878, 879, 880, 881
a3H	support competition as it affects the quantity and quality of goods and services produced	255, 256, 257, 258, 357, 358, 359, 490, 491, 492, 493, 494, 495, 496, 497, 498, 500, 501, 506, 507, 516, 517, 619, 671, 673, 742, 853, 875, 876, 878, 879, 880, 881
a3I	recognize that as individuals act in their own economic interest they may also serve the economic interest of others	255, 256, 257, 258, 357, 358, 490, 491, 492, 493, 494, 495, 496, 497, 498, 499, 500, 501, 506, 507, 508, 516, 517, 526, 619, 671, 673, 743, 780, 782, 784, 794, 802, 803, 853
a3J	compare the control and treatment of public and private property	490, 495, 501, 506, 507, 526, 621, 622, 673, 685, 686, 769, 770, 866, 869, 870, 871, 872

ESSENTIAL ELEMENT	PUPIL'S EDITION
Application of social studies skills	
a4A locate and gather information	3, 4, 6, 9, 12, 13, 14, 15, 17, 24, 26, 27, 30, 31, 32, 33, 37, 38, 45, 46, 47, 49, 50, 54, 55, 57, 61, 63, 65, 66, 67, 69, 70, 72, 73, 76, 79, 80, 84, 87, 88, 89, 90, 97, 101, 102, 105, 106, 110, 111, 114, 115, 117, 118, 121, 122, 123, 125, 128, 132, 136, 139, 140, 141, 143, 144, 148, 151, 154, 155, 162, 165, 166, 167, 171, 174, 175, 176, 177, 183, 187, 188, 191, 192, 193, 194, 199, 201, 202, 203, 205, 209, 210, 213, 215, 217, 219, 220, 221, 223, 226, 228, 229, 230, 232, 233, 237, 243, 244, 245, 246, 247, 249, 253, 257, 259, 262, 264, 265, 268, 269, 271, 272, 273, 275, 276, 280, 283, 287, 289, 290, 291, 293, 297, 303, 306, 307, 310, 311, 312, 313, 314, 321, 325, 326, 332, 336, 338, 341, 347, 351, 352, 353, 355, 356, 359, 362, 363, 366, 376, 380, 383, 390, 391, 392, 393, 395, 400, 402, 404, 408, 409, 412, 414, 416, 417, 418, 419, 421, 424, 429, 430, 432, 434, 439, 442, 444, 449, 450, 451, 453, 456, 457, 458, 461, 462, 463, 464, 469, 470, 471, 473, 475, 476, 477, 478, 485, 489, 495, 498, 499, 500, 501, 503, 507, 511, 512, 513, 515, 517, 518, 524, 527, 529, 533, 534, 537, 539, 540, 541, 543, 545, 548, 552, 557, 562, 565, 569, 570, 571, 573, 577, 582, 583, 586, 587, 591, 594, 595, 596, 597, 599, 601, 602, 604, 606, 609, 610, 615, 619, 624, 625, 626, 627, 628, 629, 635, 639, 643, 644, 645, 648, 650, 651, 652, 654, 657, 658, 661, 662, 663, 665, 670, 674, 678, 683, 685, 687, 688, 689, 691, 693, 694, 696, 701, 702, 704, 707, 708, 709, 711, 714, 716, 719, 720, 721, 724, 726, 727, 731, 733, 735, 737, 738, 739, 740, 744, 747, 751, 757, 760, 761, 762, 767, 769, 771, 772, 773, 775, 781, 782, 783, 786, 788, 791, 794, 799, 800, 803, 804, 805, 807, 811, 813, 816, 820, 823, 825, 827, 828, 829, 831, 834, 836, 837, 840, 843, 844, 847, 848, 849, 857, 864, 865, 869, 871, 872, 873, 875, 884, 886, 891, 893, 894, 895, 896, 903
a4B observe for detail	6, 12, 15, 18, 21, 28, 32, 34, 35, 36, 38, 47, 50, 54, 61, 63, 67, 70, 73, 77, 79, 88, 89, 91, 102, 106, 110, 118, 123, 134, 136, 141, 144, 149, 159, 165, 169, 175, 188, 189, 191, 197, 203, 209, 218, 221, 225, 226, 227, 242, 247, 250, 251, 265, 267, 268, 273, 276, 278, 281, 288, 289, 291, 294, 298, 304, 307, 313, 326, 338, 340, 353, 378, 382, 385, 387, 390, 393, 407, 415, 416, 417, 419, 431, 432, 442, 446, 451, 454, 456, 465, 470, 474, 477, 478, 513, 537, 541, 549, 551, 553, 555, 565, 568, 571, 577, 582, 592, 594, 597, 615, 618, 624, 627, 644, 645, 648, 650, 657, 659, 661, 662, 663, 687, 689, 700, 709, 713, 717, 727, 733, 739, 761, 763, 773, 776, 781, 787, 795, 797, 805, 809, 820, 823, 829, 837, 849, 864, 869, 873, 886, 895, 896
a4C translate information from one medium to another	6, 12, 14, 15, 21, 28, 32, 34, 35, 36, 38, 47, 50, 54, 61, 63, 67, 70, 73, 77, 79, 88, 89, 102, 106, 110, 116, 118, 123, 134, 136, 141, 144, 149, 159, 165, 169, 175, 188, 189, 191, 197, 203, 209, 217, 218, 221, 225, 226, 227, 242, 247, 250, 251, 265, 267, 268, 273, 276, 278, 281, 289, 291, 294, 298, 304, 307, 313, 326, 338, 340, 353, 378, 382, 385, 387, 390, 393, 407, 415, 416, 417, 419, 431, 442, 446, 451, 454, 456, 465, 470, 474, 477, 478, 513, 537, 541, 549, 551, 553, 555, 565, 568, 571, 577, 582, 592, 594, 597, 615, 618, 624, 627, 644, 645, 648, 650, 657, 659, 661, 662, 663, 687, 689, 700, 709, 713, 717, 727, 733, 739, 761, 763, 773, 776, 781, 787, 795, 797, 805, 809, 820, 823, 829, 837, 849, 864, 869, 873, 886, 895, 896
a4D organize and express ideas in written form	15, 31, 47, 67, 83, 89, 91, 123, 141, 154, 171, 175, 177, 203, 221, 247, 273, 291, 299, 313, 314, 353, 393, 419, 451, 477, 478, 513, 541, 571, 586, 597, 627, 629, 663. 689. 709, 724, 739, 741, 773, 805, 828, 829, 849, 873, 895, 896
a4E distinguish fact from opinion	15, 47, 67, 89, 123, 141, 175, 192, 210, 221, 232, 246, 247, 273, 291, 313, 314, 353, 393, 417, 419, 432, 451, 477, 478, 513, 537, 540, 541, 548, 571, 597, 604, 610, 625, 627, 628, 663, 683, 689, 696, 708, 709, 724, 731, 739, 740, 760, 772, 773, 804, 805, 828, 829, 849, 873, 894, 895, 896

ESSENTIAL ELEMENT	PUPIL'S EDITION
Application of social studies skills	
a4F analyze information	9, 13, 15, 17, 18, 21, 22, 24, 27, 32, 37, 45, 46, 47, 49, 51, 54, 57, 61, 63, 65, 67, 69, 72, 76, 77, 80, 83, 84, 87, 88, 89, 90, 97, 101, 106, 111, 113, 115, 117, 121, 122, 123, 125, 126, 128, 132, 137, 141, 143, 148, 151, 154, 155, 162, 166, 171, 175, 176, 177, 183, 187, 191, 194, 199, 201, 202, 203, 210, 215, 217, 218, 219, 220, 221, 223, 225, 228, 232, 233, 237, 243, 245, 246, 247, 249, 251, 253, 257, 259, 262, 264, 269, 271, 272, 273, 275, 278, 281, 283, 288, 289, 290, 291, 297, 299, 303, 304, 311, 313, 321, 325, 332, 336, 341, 347, 352, 353, 355, 359, 376, 383, 391, 392, 393, 395, 400, 408, 409, 415, 417, 418, 419, 421, 424, 429, 434, 439, 444, 446, 451, 462, 463, 469, 475, 476, 477, 478, 495, 501, 503, 512, 513, 534, 541, 552, 557, 562, 570, 571, 573, 577, 583, 586, 587, 591, 592, 596, 597, 599, 604, 619, 627, 628, 629, 635, 651, 654, 657, 663, 670, 674, 678, 683, 685, 687, 688, 689, 691, 694, 696, 701, 704, 707, 708, 709, 711, 713, 717, 724, 737, 738, 739, 740, 741, 757, 760, 762, 767, 769, 771, 772, 773, 775, 783, 786, 787, 791, 794, 799, 800, 803, 804, 805, 813, 823, 825, 828, 829, 834, 836, 840, 847, 848, 849, 857, 865, 869, 871, 872, 873, 875, 884, 886, 891, 894, 895, 896, 903
a4G draw conclusions	9, 13, 15, 24, 27, 37, 45, 46, 47, 54, 57, 61, 65, 67, 72, 76, 83, 87, 88, 89, 90, 104, 111, 117, 121, 123, 128, 132, 137, 140, 141, 148, 154, 155, 162, 166, 175, 176, 177, 192, 194, 199, 201, 203, 210, 215, 220, 221, 228, 232, 233, 237, 243, 245, 246, 247, 253, 259, 262, 273, 290, 291, 297, 299, 303, 306, 311, 313, 321, 353, 380, 383, 387, 391, 393, 408, 409, 412, 418, 419, 429, 432, 434, 439, 444, 451, 462, 465, 469, 475, 476, 477, 478, 495, 503, 507, 513, 534, 541, 548, 568, 571, 586, 597, 610, 625, 627, 628, 629, 654, 659, 663, 678, 683, 685, 689, 693, 700, 701, 708, 709, 716, 720, 724, 726, 739, 740, 741, 747, 757, 763, 767, 771, 773, 783, 786, 795, 799, 804, 805, 813, 823, 827, 828, 829, 834, 836, 840, 848, 849, 869, 872, 873, 886, 894, 895, 896, 903
a4H synthesize information	15, 24, 27, 32, 34, 35, 37, 45, 46, 47, 57, 61, 67, 72, 76, 80, 84, 89, 90, 97, 106, 115, 123, 128, 132, 136, 137, 139, 140, 141, 154, 162, 171, 175, 176, 177, 183, 189, 194, 199, 201, 203, 210, 215, 217, 219, 220, 221, 228, 232, 233, 237, 243, 245, 246, 247, 259, 264, 269, 271, 272, 273, 280, 283, 289, 290, 291, 297, 303, 306, 311, 312, 313, 314, 321, 332, 336, 347, 351, 352, 353, 359, 366, 383, 391, 392, 393, 400, 402, 412, 418, 419, 424, 444, 449, 451, 469, 475, 476, 477, 478, 485, 499, 501, 507, 513, 518, 524, 534, 539, 541, 548, 552, 557, 562, 569, 571, 577, 583, 586, 596, 597, 604, 606, 619, 625, 627, 628, 629, 635, 645, 651, 654, 657, 658, 661, 662, 663, 670, 674, 685, 687, 688, 689, 694, 701, 707, 708, 709, 716, 720, 726, 737, 738, 739, 740, 741, 747, 757, 760, 762, 767, 769, 772, 773, 783, 786, 791, 794, 797, 799, 800, 803, 804, 805, 809, 816, 820, 825, 828, 829, 836, 843, 847, 848, 849, 857, 865, 871, 872, 873, 884, 886, 891, 893, 894, 895, 896, 903
a4I develop criteria for making judgments	9, 15, 31, 47, 67, 89, 97, 123, 139, 141, 175, 183, 192, 199, 201, 202, 203, 217, 220, 221, 233, 243, 247, 273, 288, 290, 291, 294, 312, 313, 321, 338, 340, 341, 351, 353, 391, 393, 419, 450, 451, 454, 463, 477, 478, 485, 499, 501, 513, 534, 537, 541, 549, 551, 571, 591, 595, 596, 597, 602, 604, 610, 627, 628, 635, 645, 657, 658, 663, 674, 678, 687, 689, 693, 709, 724, 731, 739, 740, 747, 757, 760, 762, 771, 772, 773, 776, 794, 800, 804, 805, 813, 816, 820, 825, 828, 829, 849, 865, 869, 871, 872, 873, 894, 895, 896, 903

ESSENTIAL ELEMENT	PUPIL'S EDITION
Application of social studies skills	
a4J use problem-solving skills	9, 14, 15, 28, 31, 36, 47, 53, 67, 88, 89, 91, 113, 123, 140, 141, 175, 176, 192, 197, 199, 203, 217, 221, 227, 232, 247, 250, 273, 291, 313, 353, 380, 393, 402, 409, 419, 451, 477, 478, 495, 503, 511, 513, 537, 540, 541, 548, 552, 555, 571, 596, 597, 604, 627, 629, 651, 657, 663, 689, 693, 708, 709, 731, 739, 740, 760, 772, 773, 794, 804, 805, 823, 828, 829, 849, 869, 872, 873, 886, 891, 894, 895, 896
a4K sequence historical data and information	9, 12, 14, 15, 33, 47, 67, 89, 91, 97, 122, 123, 134, 139, 140, 141, 149, 159, 166, 169, 174, 175, 177, 203, 215, 217, 221, 228, 233, 237, 242, 243, 245, 246, 247, 264, 273, 280, 283, 291, 298, 313, 314, 315, 321, 353, 382, 393, 419, 434, 449, 451, 462, 463, 477, 478, 479, 485, 511, 513, 540, 541, 548, 552, 553, 571, 577, 583, 587, 591, 595, 597, 627, 629, 654, 657, 663, 674, 678, 688, 689, 704, 708, 709, 720, 724, 726, 737, 738, 739, 740, 741, 760, 767, 769, 772, 773, 791, 794, 800, 803, 804, 805, 828, 829, 840, 843, 848, 849, 857, 865, 872, 873, 884, 891, 893, 894, 895, 896, 897
a4L draw inferences	13, 14, 15, 38, 47, 54, 67, 72, 80, 89, 90, 97, 106, 119, 121, 123, 137, 139, 140, 141, 149, 155, 175, 176, 177, 193, 194, 199, 201, 203, 209, 210, 215, 219, 220, 221, 224, 233, 237, 243, 245, 246, 247, 259, 262, 264, 269, 271, 273, 280, 289, 290, 291, 297, 303, 306, 311, 313, 314, 321, 336, 352, 353, 359, 363, 366, 376, 380, 383, 388, 392, 393, 400, 408, 412, 417, 418, 419, 432, 434, 439, 444, 451, 463, 469, 476, 477, 478, 485, 501, 503, 507, 511, 513, 518, 524, 529, 537, 539, 541, 548, 557, 562, 569, 570, 571, 586, 587, 595, 596, 597, 606, 617, 618, 619, 625, 627, 628, 629, 635, 645, 651, 655, 657, 658, 661, 662, 663, 670, 674, 678, 683, 685, 688, 689, 694, 701, 707, 708, 709, 716, 720, 726, 736, 737, 738, 739, 740, 741, 747, 757, 760, 762, 767, 771, 772, 773, 786, 791, 794, 799, 800, 803, 804, 805, 813, 816, 827, 828, 829, 836, 848, 849, 857, 862, 865, 871, 872, 873, 884, 893, 894, 895, 896, 903
a4M perceive cause-effect relationships	14, 15, 46, 47, 63, 67, 76, 89, 90, 111, 117, 122, 123, 141, 151, 154, 162, 167, 175, 201, 202, 203, 217, 221, 228, 247, 257, 259, 273, 289, 290, 291, 311, 313, 321, 353, 393, 419, 451, 463, 477, 478, 485, 495, 503, 507, 512, 513, 534, 540, 541, 571, 597, 602, 610, 627, 628, 654, 663, 683, 689, 704, 708, 709, 739, 740, 760, 767, 769, 771, 772, 773, 783, 786, 799, 800, 804, 805, 813, 816, 820, 827, 828, 829, 834, 840, 843, 847, 848, 849, 865, 869, 871, 873, 894, 895, 896

A CORRELATION OF THE ANNOTATED TEACHER'S EDITION WITH THE TEXAS TEACHER APPRAISAL SYSTEM INSTRUMENT

The features of the **Annotated Teacher's Edition** of ***World History: People and Nations***, include information and suggested activities that help the teacher incorporate elements of the **TEXAS TEACHER APPRAISAL SYSTEM** into daily class instruction. The systematic arrangement of the features enables the teacher to present information and implement a variety of activities in an appropriate sequence (1a, 6b, 4b). The features included in the **Annotated Teacher's Edition** help prevent off-task behavior (5b) by supplying relevant activities that may be used to focus student attention on the study of the selection. These features also solicit student participation (1c) and implement student instruction at an appropriate level of difficulty (1f).

The **Annotated Teacher's Edition** is organized into three parts —an **Interleaf**, a **Sidetext**, and **Annotations**. The **Interleaf** is inserted at the beginning of each chapter and will help the teacher develop effective lesson plans (4a). The **Sidetext** is printed in the side-margins of the text at the appropriate point-of-use and will help the teacher develop effective sequential presentation of chapter information (4b). The **Annotations** are printed in blue in the top margins of this **Annotated Teacher's Edition.** In addition, special **Annotations** printed in red correlate the content of the **Pupil's Edition** with the Texas Essential Elements.

INTERLEAF

Chapter Overview

The **Chapter Overview** provides a brief synopsis of the chapter. This synopsis emphasize the chapter's main ideas, the sequence of historical events, and the relationship between the causes and results of these events (4b, 6b, 6c, 6d, 6f, 7d).

Suggested Lesson Plan

The **Suggested Lesson Plan** consists of a chart that provides recommended time allotments for presentation of material within each section of the chapter (4a). In addition, the chart lists applicable unit goals and chapter objectives and provides **Sidetext** page references for suggested activities and other materials for the teacher's use (1a). Also included in the **Suggested Lesson Plan** for each chapter are references to the appropriate **Form A Test, Reteaching Worksheet**, and **Form B Test** (2a, 2b, 2c, 2d, 2e, 2f).

Books for the Teacher

A bibliography of references that pertain to the chapter is located in the **Books for the Teacher** feature. This bibliography is organized alphabetically by author or editor. Each entry is accompanied by a brief description that helps the teacher determine at what point in the lesson these books may be used most effectively (4d, 4e).

Books for the Student

A bibliography of references suitable for use by students is located in each chapter's **Books for the Student** feature. The brief description that accompanies each entry will help the teacher determine how these books may be employed most effectively by students. These selections may be used to spark student interest and enhance research activities (4d, 4e).

Multimedia Materials

Selected **Multimedia Materials** appropriate for high school students are listed alphabetically by title. These materials include films, filmstrips, and videocassettes that are pertinent to the content of each chapter. The use of these materials may require planning in order to coordinate their availability with the presentation of each chapter (1a, 2f, 3e).

The **Interleaf** for each section of the chapter includes a **Section Overview, Suggested Teaching Strategies, Enrichment Activities,** a **Daily Quiz,** and **Suggested Assignments.**

Section Overview

The **Section Overview** provides a brief synopsis of the main points presented in the section. This information may be used to introduce the topic of the section or to provide a constructive transition from previously learned knowledge to new information (6a, 6c, 7d). The **Section Overview** also enables the teacher to help students in identifying the main ideas presented in each section and incorporating these ideas into the broader perspective of world history (6f).

Suggested Teaching Strategies

At least two **Suggested Teaching Strategies** are provided to help the teacher introduce the individual sections of each chapter (6a). These suggested teaching strategies also enable the teacher to enhance student participation in a wide range of specific skills, with emphasis on critical thinking (1a, 1b, 1c, 2b, 6d, 6e). In each suggested teaching strategy, the selected skill and the ability level of the skill are identified in boldface type (1f, 6d, 6e, 6f). **Basic** strategies are appropriate for all levels of ability. **Average/Group** strategies offer activities that involve the class as a whole or groups of students (1b). These activities are designed so that students of all ability levels may take part. **Challenging** strategies provide activities to stimulate advanced students in an individual or group setting (9d). The completion of these activities involves extra research and higher-level thinking skills. A suggested teaching strategy correlated to **Building History Study Skills** is included in the chapter section where the skill feature appears. The skill designated in the **Building History Study Skills** feature is identified in boldface type in the corresponding strategy (6d, 6e, 6f, 6g).

Enrichment Activities

One or more suggested **Enrichment Activities** provide opportunities for additional instruction or in-depth study (1a). The skill and the ability level of each enrichment activity are identified in boldface type (1a, 1b, 1c, 1f, 4d, 4e, 5b, 6c, 6d).

Daily Quiz

The **Interleaf** includes **Daily Quizzes** that enable the teacher to assess student understanding of each section. These quizzes provide numerous opportunities for daily grades (2b). Teachers may wish to delay administering the **Daily Quiz** for a particular section until students have had an opportunity to reread and study the information presented in that section. Each **Daily Quiz** may also be used as a pretest or as an assessment instrument to identify specific concepts that should be included in reteaching activities and assignments (2a, 2e, 2f, 7d).

Suggested Assignments

Two or more **Suggested Assignments** conclude the **Interleaf** activities. These assignments are designed to enhance or to test student understanding of the material presented in the section (2b). Each assignment includes a skill and a skill ability level identified in boldface type (1a, 1b, 1c, 6d, 6e, 6f, 7d). These assignments often include appropriate **Critical Thinking Worksheets, Profile Worksheets, Geography Supplement Worksheets, Skill Worksheets,** and **Review Worksheets** available in the **Teacher's ResourceBank™**.

SIDETEXT

Introducing the Unit

A brief summary of the topic of each unit and a strategy to focus student attention on the main idea of the unit is found in **Introducing the Unit** (3a, 4d, 4e, 6a, 6c, 7d). This feature is located at the beginning of each unit and may be used as a transition between historical periods or topics of study (3a).

Unit Goals

The **Unit Goals** feature may be used to direct student attention to the purpose of the unit (6a). This feature also may be used to communicate to students learning tasks (7b) and expectations (2a) and to emphasize the importance of the content of the unit (9b).

Introducing the Chapter

The study of each chapter may be initiated by using the **Introducing the Chapter** feature located at the beginning of the chapter (2a, 7d). This feature consists of a question or strategy that may be used to direct student attention to the new information to be studied (3a). Where appropriate, this question or strategy is accompanied by an answer (2b, 2c).

Chapter Objectives

The **Chapter Objectives** may be used to direct student attention to the purpose of the chapter (6a). This feature also may be used to communicate to students learning tasks (7b) and expectations (2a) and to emphasize the importance of the content of the chapter (9b).

The **Sidetext** for each section of each chapter contains **Focus/Motivation, Presentation,** and **Closure** features. The strategies and activities included in these features use current instructional methodology (10c). The **Sidetext** also contains **Review Answers** for each section of each chapter.

Focus/Motivation

Each section begins with a **Focus/Motivation** feature that may be used to direct student attention to the main idea of the section or to challenge students to apply map skills or critical thinking skills to the topic of study (7d, 9d). This feature provides a variety of activities (1a) that involve teacher interaction with the class (1b) and relate the content of the section to student interests and experiences (9a). These activities are designed to both secure student attention (3a) and elicit student participation (1c).

Presentation

A task-centered activity designed to engage student interest and elicit student participation is incorporated into the **Presentation** feature (1c, 3a, 4e). The specific skill and ability level of the skill being presented are identified in boldface type (1f). This feature provides a variety of activities (1a) to help the teacher explain content and/or tasks clearly (7b). It also offers teachers an opportunity to help students apply newly learned information to a specific assignment or class activity (6d, 6e, 6f, 6g).

Closure

An opportunity to close instruction appropriately (6h) is provided by the **Closure** feature incorporated into the **Sidetext** for each section. **Closure** features provide a variety of strategies (1a) designed to enhance student discussion of information relevant to the section and encourage application of critical thinking skills (1c, 3a, 4d, 6e, 6f). Teachers may also use **Closure** features to relate to prior or future learning (6c), to stress important points and dimensions of a section's content (7d), or to emphasize the importance of the content (9b).

Review Answers

Definitions of terms; identifications of important people, documents, and events; geographical locations of historical sites; and answers to recall and critical thinking questions presented in the **Section Review** are incorporated into the **Review Answers** feature. These answers appear near the **Section Review** and provide ready access to information that forms the basis of test material (4b, 6b, 6c, 6d). The **Review Answers** feature may be used to assess student understanding of the material (2b, 2c, 2d, 6e, 6f, 6g, 9c), to identify subjects to be incorporated into reteaching strategies (2e, 2f, 7e, 9c), and as an effective closure technique.

An answer key to each **Chapter Review** is provided in the **Sidetext** that accompanies the **Chapter Review**. Sections of the answer key are designated by boldface type and correspond to the sections of the **Chapter Review** (4b). These sections, which include **Reviewing Important Terms, Developing Critical Thinking Skills, Relating Geography to History, Relating Past to Present,** and **Applying History Study Skills** may be used to assess student understanding, (2b, 2c, 2d, 6e, 6f, 6g, 9c), to identify subjects to be incorporated into reteaching strategies (2e, 2f, 7e, 9c), and as an effective closure technique (6h).

An answer key to each **Unit Review** is provided in the **Sidetext** that accompanies the **Unit Review**. Sections of the answer key are designated by boldface type and correspond to the sections of the **Unit Review** (4b). These sections, which include **Reviewing Concepts, Applying Critical Thinking Skills, Relating Geography to History,** and **Writing about History,** may be used to test student understanding (2b, 2c, 2d, 6e, 6f, 6g, 9c), or to provide challenging exercises for students (9d). Each unit concludes with a chronology chart that features significant dates, political and social developments, technological and scientific advances, visual arts and literature, and religious and philosophical thought emphasized in the unit. The number of the chapter where these topics are presented is printed in boldface type for ready reference (4b).

ANNOTATIONS

In addition to the features incorporated into the **Interleaf** and the **Sidetext,** answers to questions presented in picture captions, map captions, and ***What If?*** features appear in blue type as an on-page **Annotations** (4b). These may be used to test student understanding (2b, 2c, 2d, 6e, 6f, 6g, 9c), or as a starting point for further discussion (6c, 6e, 6f, 6g). Additional **Annotations** supply interesting information or provide a variety of suggested topics for discussion, class activities, and research assignments (1a, 1d, 2c, 4e, 6d, 6f, 6g, 7c, 7d, 9c, 9d).

Special **Annotations** printed in red correlate the content of the **Pupil's Edition** with the Texas Essential Elements.

Complete LESSON CYCLE format

BEGINNING THE LESSON
FOCUS
INTRODUCING THE CHAPTER
CHAPTER OBJECTIVES
CHAPTER FOCUS
PRETEACHING VOCABULARY
FOCUS/MOTIVATION

PRESENTING THE LESSON
GUIDED PRACTICE
PRESENTATION
ANNOTATIONS
SUGGESTED TEACHING STRATEGIES

REVIEW
REVIEW WORKSHEETS
SECTION REVIEWS
CHAPTER REVIEWS
BASIC CONCEPTS STUDY GUIDE WORKSHEETS

CHECKING FOR MASTERY
DAILY QUIZZES
FORM A TESTS

RETEACHING
RETEACHING WORKSHEETS
FORM B TESTS
UNIT SYNTHESIS

INDEPENDENT PRACTICE
CRITICAL THINKING WORKSHEETS
SKILL WORKSHEETS
ENRICHMENT ACTIVITIES
SUGGESTED ASSIGNMENTS

EVALUATION
ANSWERS TO QUESTIONS AND EXERCISES

ENDING THE LESSON
CLOSURE

World History

People and Nations

World History

People and Nations

Anatole G. Mazour
John M. Peoples

Harcourt Brace Jovanovich, Publishers
Orlando San Diego Chicago Dallas

AUTHORS **Anatole G. Mazour** was Professor of History at Stanford University for 25 years. He received an M.A. from Yale University and a Ph.D. from the University of California. His other books include *Russia: Past and Present; Finland Between East and West; The Rise and Fall of the Romanovs;* and *Russia: Tsarist and Communist.*

John M. Peoples taught world history and other social studies courses at Alameda High School in California for 35 years. Dr. Peoples received both an M.A. and a Ph.D. from the University of California.

Cover: Funeral mask of the Egyptian pharaoh Tutankhamen

Acknowledgments: For permission to reprint copyrighted material, grateful acknowledgment is made to the following sources:
American Heritage, a division of Forbes Inc.: From pp. 179 and 184 in *The Horizon History of Africa,* edited by Alvin M. Josephy, Jr. Copyright © 1971 by American Heritage Publishing Co., Inc. From p. 606 in *The American Heritage Picture Book of World War II* by C. L. Sulzberger. Copyright © 1966 by American Heritage Publishing Co., Inc. *Apt Books, Inc., on behalf of Asia Publishing House:* "The War Drum" from *Hymns from the Vedas,* English translation by Abinash Chandra Bose. © 1966 by Abinash Chandra Bose. *Atheneum Publishers, an imprint of Macmillan Publishing Company:* From pp. 135–136 in *Florence Nightingale* by Cecil Woodham-Smith. Copyright 1951 by Cecil Woodham-Smith; copyright renewed 1979 by Charles Woodham-Smith and Mrs. John Bonython. *British Crown Copyright and Hansard:* From Prime Minister Winston Churchill's speech to the House of Commons, May 1940 in *Hansard. Cambridge University Press:* From "The Ten Commandments" in *The New English Bible.* Copyright © 1961, 1970 by the Delegates of the Oxford University Press and the Syndics of the Cambridge University Press. From *Life on an English Manor: A Study of Peasant Conditions, 1150–1400* by H. S. Bennett. Published by Cambridge University Press, 1937. From p. 33 in *The Stages of Economic Growth* by W. W. Rostow. © 1960 by Cambridge University Press. *Carnegie Endowment for International Peace:* From "The Political and Social Doctrines of Fascism" by Benito Mussolini in *International Conciliation* No. 306, January 1935. *Lionel Casson:* From pp. 64–73 in *Smithsonian,* June 1984. *Leon E. Clark and Richard H. Minear:* From "A Closed Society: 1600–1853" in *Through Japanese Eyes* by Richard H. Minear, edited by Leon E. Clark. © 1974, 1981 by Leon E. Clark and Richard H. Minear. *Columbia University Press:* From pp. 129–130 in *CHUANG TZU: Basic Writings,* translated by Burton Watson. Copyright © 1964 by Columbia University Press. From p. 115 in *Sources of Chinese Tradition,* Volume I, compiled by Wm. Theodore de Bary, Wing-tsit Chan, and Burton Watson. Copyright © 1960 by Columbia University Press. *Robert Lloyd Davis:* From "We Lose the Next War" by Elmer Davis. Originally published in *Harper's* Magazine, March 1938. *Dembner Books, a division of Red Dembner Enterprises Corporation:* From "About Kings" in *Isaac Asimov's Book of Facts* by Isaac Asimov. Copyright © 1979 by Red Dembner Enterprises Corp. *Doubleday, a division of Bantam, Doubleday, Dell Publishing Group, Inc.*: From p. 30 in *An Introduction to Haiku* by Harold G. Henderson. Copyright © 1958 by Harold G. Henderson. From *The Odyssey* by Homer, translated by Robert Fitzgerald. Copyright © 1961 by Robert Fitzgerald. *E. P. Dutton, a division of Penguin Books USA Inc.*: From the Preface and from pp. 152–154 in *Lost City of the Incas* by Hiram Bingham. Copyright 1948 by Duell Sloan and Pearce, renewed 1976 by Alfred Bingham. *Egypt Exploration Society:* From "The Hyksos Rule in Egypt" by Torgny Säve-Soderbergh in *Journal of Egyptian Archaeology,* Volume 37, 1951. *Kathleen Schmidgall Floria and Audrey A. Tursam:* From p. 13 in *Sparks from the Anvil* by Carl Schmidgall. Copyright 1953 by Carl Henry Schmidgall. *Harcourt Brace Jovanovich, Inc.*: From pp. 16–17 in *Elizabeth and Essex: A Tragic History* by Lytton Strachey. Copyright 1928 by Lytton Strachey and the Curtis Publishing Company, renewed 1956 by James Strachey. *Harper & Row, Publishers, Inc.*: From pp. 145–146 in *A History of Their Own: Women in Europe from Prehistory to the Present,* Volume I, by Bonnie S. Anderson and Judith P. Zinsser. Copyright © 1988 by Bonnie S. Anderson and Judith P. Zinsser. From p. 307 in *Not In God's Image,* edited by Julia O'Faolain and Lauro Martines. Copyright © 1973 by Julia O'Faolain and Lauro Martines. From pp. 45, 172, and 193 in *DELIVERED FROM EVIL: The Saga of World War II* by Robert Leckie. Copyright © 1987 by Robert Leckie. From SS First Lieutenant Kurt Gerstein's handwritten account in *Never to Forget: The Jews of the Holocaust* by Milton Meltzer. Copyright © 1976 by Milton Meltzer. From pp. 78 and 79 in *Documents in World History, Volume I, The Great Traditions: From Ancient Times to 1500,* edited by Peter N. Stearns, et al. Copyright © 1988 by Harper & Row, Publishers, Inc. *D. C. Heath, a division of Raytheon Co.*: From Chapter 2, "Early India and China" in *World Civilizations* by F. Roy Willis. Copyright © 1982 by D. C. Heath and Company. *Heinemann Educational Books, Ltd.*: "The Election Results" (chart) from *History Broadsheets: Hitler & Germany 1919–1939* by Tony Edwards. © 1972 by Tony Edwards. *David Higham Associates Limited and Macmillan Press, Ltd.*: From "The Vietnam War: A Reporter with the Vietcong, near Hanoi, 10 December 1965" in *What a Way to Run the Tribe* by James Cameron. Published in 1968 by Macmillan & Co. Ltd. *Holt, Rinehart and Winston, Inc.*: From p. 68 in *Source Problems in World Civilization: China's Cultural Tradition* by Derk Bodde. Copyright © 1957 by Derk Bodde. From p. 188 in *The Quest for a Principal Authority in Europe, 1715–Present* by Thomas C. Mendenhall, Basil O. Henning, and Archibald S. Foord. Copyright 1948 by Holt, Rinehart and Winston, Inc. *Houghton Mifflin Company:* From pp. 15–16, 72–73, 86, 98, 218, 261, 352–353, 412–413 in *Sources of the Western Tradition, Vol. 1: From Ancient Times to the Enlightenment* by Perry, Peden and Von Laue. Copyright © 1987 by Houghton Mifflin. From p. 180 in *Sources of the Western Tradition, Vol. II: From the Scientific Revolution to the Present* by Perry, Peden and Von Laue. Copyright © 1987 by Houghton Mifflin. *Indiana University Press:* From "The Story of Daedalus and Icarus" in *Metamorphoses* by Ovid, translated by Rolfe Humphries. *Jean Kistler Kendall, Executrix of the Estates of Elizabeth Bothwell Kistler and Jean Bothwell:* From pp. 40–41 in *The Story of India* by Jean Bothwell. Copyright 1952 by Harcourt Brace Jovanovich, Inc. *Alfred A. Knopf, Inc.*: From pp. 80–81 and 220 in *Ten Keys to Latin America* by Frank Tannenbaum. Copyright © 1959 by The American Assembly; copyright © 1960 by the Council on Foreign Relations, Inc; copyright © 1960, 1962 by Frank Tannenbaum. *Longman Group Limited:* From "The Breakneck Speed of Industrialisation" in *Stalin and Stalinism* by Martin McCauley. © 1983 by Longman Group Limited. Table from *The Modern World* by L. E. Snellgrove. © 1984 by Longman Group Limited. *Macmillan Publishing Company:* From *A Short History of the Near East, From the Founding of Constantinople (330 A.D. to 1922)* by William Stearns Davis. Copyright 1922 by the Macmillan Publishing Company, renewed 1953 by Alice R. Davis. From p. 1 in *The Guns of August* by Barbara W. Tuchman. © 1962 by Barbara W. Tuchman. From "Garibaldi's Report on the Conquest of Naples" in *Prologue: A Documentary History of Europe: 1846–1960,* edited by Christine Walsh. Originally published by Cassell, Australia, 1968. *David McKay Company, Inc., a division of Random House, Inc.*: From p. 5 in *Germany and the East-West Crisis: The Decisive Challenge to American Policy* by William S. Schlamm. Copyright © 1959 by William S. Schlamm. *National Geographic Society:* From "La Navidad, 1462: Searching for Columbus's Lost Colony" by Kathleen A. Deagan in *National Geographic* Magazine, November 1987. Copyright © 1987 by National Geographic Society. From "Viking Trail East" by R. P. Jordan in *National Geographic* Magazine, March 1985. *(Acknowledgments continued on page R63)*

Printed in the United States of America
ISBN 0–15–373458–2

iv

EDITORIAL REVIEW BOARD

v

EDITORIAL REVIEW BOARD

Curriculum Specialists and Field Test Teachers

vi

C◆O◆N◆T◆E◆N◆T◆S

vii

3

People Created Thriving Civilizations in India *ca. 2500 B.C.–A.D. 535* **48**

4

Ancient Chinese Civilization Developed Lasting Traditions *1500 B.C.–A.D. 589* **68**

viii

UNIT TWO

CIVILIZATIONS OF THE MEDITERRANEAN WORLD 98

5

6

ix

7

UNIT THREE

8

x

9

10

11

xi

12

Civilization in East Asia Reached New Heights *100–1644* **274**

13

Africa and the Americas Produced Complex Civilizations *1800 B.C.–A.D. 1500* **292**

xii

UNIT FOUR

THE EMERGENCE OF MODERN NATIONS 322

14

15

xiii

xiv

UNIT FIVE

THE DEVELOPMENT OF INDUSTRIAL SOCIETY 486

19

20

xv

21

22

23

UNIT SIX

24

xvii

25

The Great Depression Helped the Rise of Totalitarian Dictators *1919–1936* **664**

26

New Political Forces Emerged in Africa, Asia, and Latin America *1900–1938* **690**

xviii

27

UNIT SEVEN

28

xix

29

30

xx

31

32

33

REFERENCE SECTION

xxi

FEATURES

History Through the Arts

Connections: Then and Now

What If?

Building History Study Skills

Reading About History

xxii

Perspectives: Legacies of the Past

Linking Geography to History

MAPS

xxiii

Atlas

CHARTS

xxiv

LINKING GEOGRAPHY TO HISTORY

Geography and World History: An Introduction

World History: People and Nations focuses on the story of the world's people from the very earliest times to the present. *History* describes the events that make up this story, while *geography* describes the places in which the events take place. History, then, represents the unfolding drama of people and events through the ages. Geography describes the stage on which this drama is played out.

History and geography are so intertwined that to separate them would leave the story only partially told. More than 350 years ago, English historian Peter Heylyn wrote some lines that beautifully describe the interconnection between these two disciplines. The language that Heylyn used was quite different from modern English, yet the message rings as true today as it did in the early 1600s.

> "As Geography without History, hath life and motion, but at randome, & unstable: So History without Geography, like a dead carkasse hath neither life nor motion at all &: as the exact notice of the place addeth a satisfactorie delight to the action: so the mention of the action, beautifieth the notice of the place."

Time and Space

Even though history and geography are closely related, they are still two distinct subjects. The basic difference between them may be stated quite simply. As you study history, you acquire an orientation to time; as you study geography, you acquire an orientation to space. Geographers, then, organize their thoughts with respect to spatial arrangements and distributions over the earth's surface. Historians, on the other hand, organize their ideas with respect to time.

Although history is mostly concerned with time, and geography mostly with space, each subject employs aspects of the other as analytical tools. Historians know full well that events occur in place as well as in time. Events, like people, are widely distributed across the earth. In other words, events have a spatial, or geographic, dimension. And geographers, in examining distributions and arrangements throughout the world today, find that they often must look back in time in order to explain these current patterns.

World History: People and Nations tells the story of world history. Geography helps bring this story into focus. Therefore, understanding the special themes and tools of geography will be of great value to you as you read and think about the great personalities and events of the past.

The Five Basic Themes in Geography

Modern geography focuses on five basic themes, or topics: location, place, relationships within places, movement, and regions. Each of these five basic themes helps to clarify the relationship between the world's physical landscape and its human occupants. These relationships, of course, have a time as well as a spatial context.

Location. The first theme, location, has two aspects. Absolute location deals with the exact, or precise, spot on the earth that a place occupies. Relative location, on the other hand, describes the position of a place in relation to other places.

The latitude and longitude of a place best describe its absolute location. To calculate latitude and longitude, geographers use a grid formed by a series of imaginary lines drawn around the earth (see map, this page). The equator, an imaginary line that circles the earth halfway

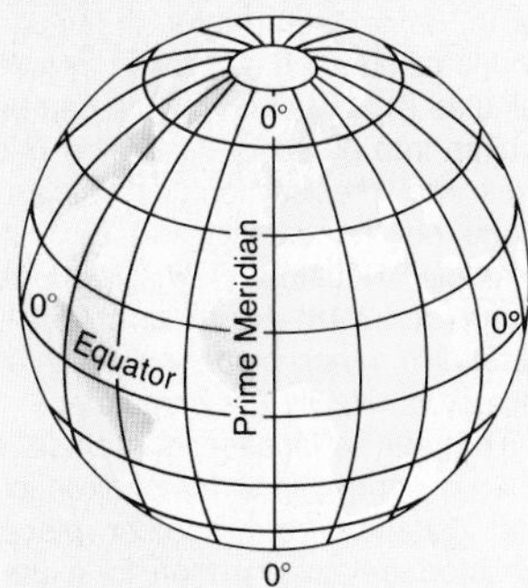

Lines of latitude and longitude circling the earth

between the North and South poles, divides the earth into two halves, or hemispheres. Geographers call these hemispheres the Northern Hemisphere and the Southern Hemisphere. Several shorter imaginary lines—called parallels, or lines of latitude—circle the earth, parallel to the equator.

Geographers identify different parallels through a special numbering system based on degrees. In the Northern Hemisphere, the parallels number from zero degrees (0°) at the equator to ninety degrees north (90° N) at the North Pole. Similarly, in the Southern Hemisphere they run from 0° at the equator to 90° south (S) at the South Pole.

Another set of imaginary lines, called meridians, or lines of longitude, circle the earth from pole to pole. The prime meridian, which runs through the Royal Observatory, in Greenwich, England, serves as 0° longitude. The meridian directly opposite the prime meridian, on the other side of the globe, is the 180° meridian. The prime meridian and the 180° meridian together divide the earth into the Eastern and Western hemispheres. The Eastern Hemisphere includes the half of the earth that extends east of the prime meridian to the 180° meridian. The Western Hemisphere includes the half of the earth west of the prime meridian to the 180° meridian.

Together, parallels and meridians form an imaginary grid over the earth. Since each degree of latitude and longitude can be broken into 60 minutes (′), and each minute can be broken into 60 seconds (″), the grid fixes the precise location of any place on the earth's surface. For example, Houston, Texas, can be found at 33°46′ North and 95°21′ West. No other place on earth is located at exactly this same place.

The relative location of a place is often described in terms of direction and distance from another place. Houston's relative location, for example, might be expressed as 1,221 air miles southwest of Washington, D.C. Other ways of describing relative location include nearness to resources and accessibility to trade routes.

Place. The second basic theme of geography, place, grows directly out of location. Every location on earth has its own unique, or distinctive, physical and human characteristics. These physical characteristics include the shape of the land, climate, soils, vegetation, and animal life. Land use, street layout, architecture, and population distribution all constitute a location's human characteristics. Together, these physical and human characteristics make up a location's place identity. This identity changes through time and, therefore, is very important to an understanding of history.

Relationships within places. Throughout time, people have adapted their way of life to accommodate their environment. For example, people who live in hot climates often use pungent spices in their cooking. These spices cover the rancid taste of meat, which quickly becomes tainted in hot weather. People also have made changes to their physical environment. They have cleared forests, dug irrigation ditches, and built huge cities. Geographers define relationships within places as all the ways in which people interact with their natural environment.

The theme of relationships within places is of great importance to historians, for it includes not only how people interact with their physical surroundings but also the consequences of such interactions. For example, the decision to mine and use fossil fuels to produce energy had the negative consequence of polluting the environment. This consequence, in turn, gave rise to a movement to protect the environment. Such movements are of great interest to historians.

Skyline of Houston, Texas

Tea fields in Sri Lanka

Movement. The fourth theme of modern geography, movement, concerns the interactions of people with one another as they travel, communicate, and exchange goods and services on a worldwide basis. Movement also includes an examination of the spread of ideas and the great human migrations that have occurred through the centuries—two vital themes in the study of history.

Regions. In order to better study and understand the earth, geographers divide it into smaller units called regions. The fifth theme of geography concerns these regions. Geographical regions vary in size from those that cover an entire continent to those that include only a small part of a city, such as its retail shopping area. The particular features that characterize a region set it apart from other regions. A vast number of different characteristics may be used to define the regions of the world. As a result, any given area might be part of a great number of regions, and the boundaries of one region might overlap the boundaries of others. To make the study of regions less complex, however, the defining characteristics used include such physical features as climate or vegetation and such cultural features as economic activities or dominant religion or language.

xxvi

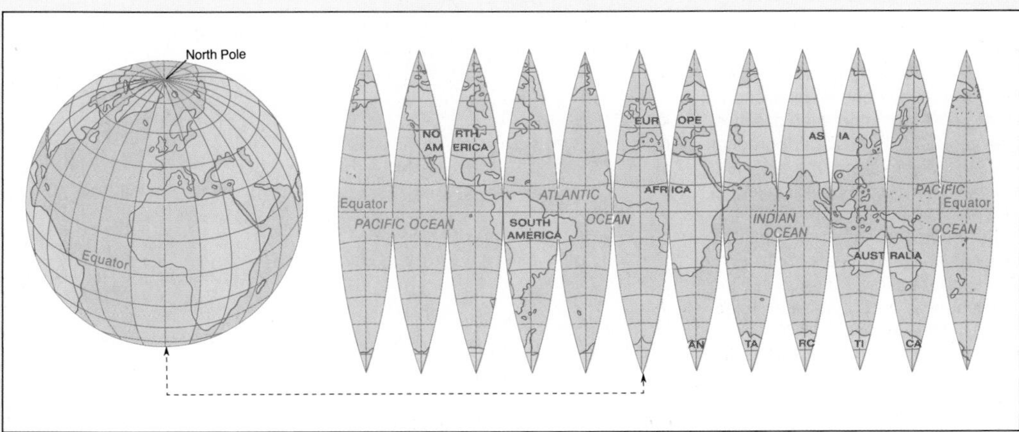

The making of a map projection

The Tools of Geography

To develop these five basic themes, geographers use a wide variety of tools. These tools include such modern and sophisticated items as aerial photographs, satellite images, and extremely intricate computer programs. However, the geographers' most basic and essential tools—globes and maps—have been used for centuries. Globes and maps, of course, are very familiar objects. Undoubtedly you have seen them in your classroom or school library and, perhaps, even in your home. Nevertheless, globes and maps are essential to the study of geography because they provide fairly accurate representations of the earth. However, globes and maps are not perfect models of the earth, and each has advantages and disadvantages as a geographical tool.

The most important advantage of a globe is its shape. It is the only model of the earth that is spherical like the earth. Because a globe's shape follows the spherical shape of the earth, the landmasses and bodies of water shown on it are correct in terms of shape and area. A globe also accurately shows distance and direction from one place to another.

In spite of its accuracy, the globe has some limitations. To begin with, a globe is bulky and awkward to carry. In addition, it makes it impossible to see the entire earth at once. For example, if you focus on South America, Australia is hidden from your view. When you turn the globe to find Australia, South America disappears. A globe's greatest problem, however, is that it lacks detail. Even the largest globes could not show the detailed features of the ancient Nile Valley. There would be no way to indicate the location of each of the 80 or more pyramids, the huge stone figure of the Sphinx, or the thousands of irrigation channels and reservoirs used by the farmers of the region.

In contrast, the intricate details shown on maps make them useful to geographers. Through the use of symbols and colors, a huge range of information can be shown clearly on a map. By comparing maps, geographers can see movements, relationships within places, and the locations of various physical and cultural regions. In addition, maps are far more manageable than globes. They can be rolled or folded and, therefore, are easy to carry.

Yet maps do have one serious drawback—they are never totally accurate. Regardless of the skill of the cartographer, or mapmaker, no map can accurately show the qualities of shape, area, distance, and direction at the same time. This is because mapmaking involves the difficult task of transferring the curved surface of the earth onto a flat piece of paper (see map, this page).

To appreciate the problems faced by cartographers, place a piece of paper directly over one of the Great Lakes of North America on a globe. Now trace the outline of the lake onto your paper. You should be able to trace its outline accurately without once bending or twisting your paper. Next, try tracing the outline of the entire North American continent. You can see immediately that some cutting or folding of the paper is required. Otherwise, you are going to have to drastically distort the outline of the continent. Yet in cutting or folding the map, you create other distortions.

Distortion, then, is a major problem for cartographers when transferring large areas of the earth's curved surface onto a flat map. Since maps cannot accurately show all four map qualities—shape, area, distance, and direction—at the same time, cartographers must decide which quality they want their maps to distort least. A variety of projections—methods by which the earth's surface is transferred, or projected, onto paper to create flat maps—enables them to do this.

Map Projections

Literally thousands of map projections exist. Each one distorts one or more of the four major map qualities. The projection that a cartographer chooses depends on the size and location of the area being projected and on the purpose of the map.

Cartographers often choose the Robinson projection (see map, right). The Robinson projection is unique because it is a compromise projection. It maintains no single property but minimizes overall distortion.

If true shape is the most important objective of the cartographer, he or she will select a conformal projection, such as the Mercator projection (see map, below). On a map using such a projection, the shapes of the land and water areas conform to, or look like, the shapes shown on a globe. If the purpose of the map is to show correct relative area, an equal-area projection, such as the Molleweide projection (see map, page xxix) or the Peters projection

The Robinson projection

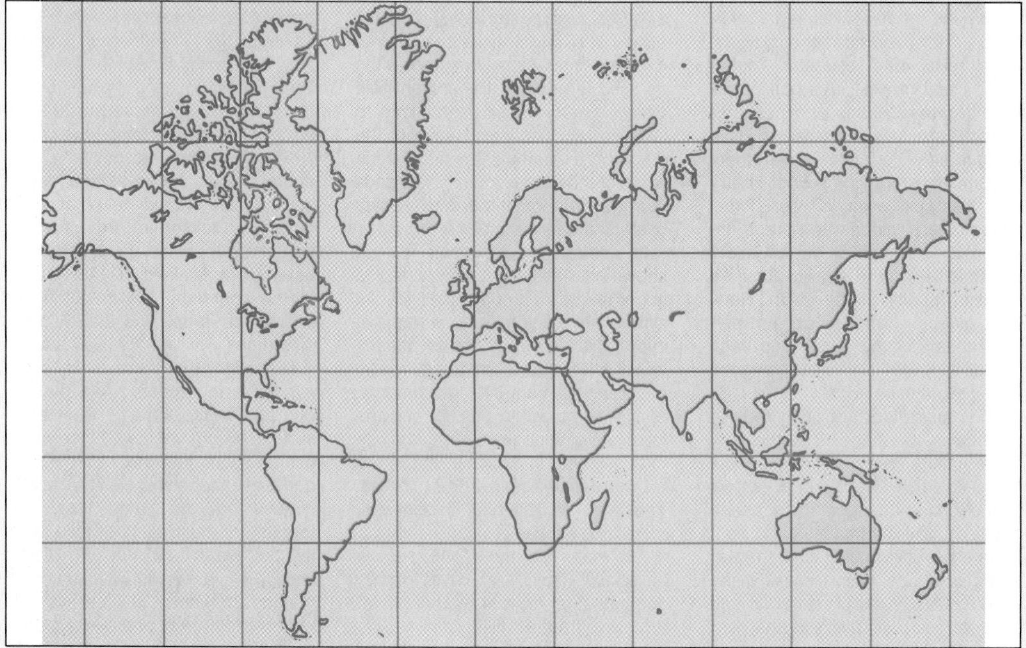

The Mercator projection

xxviii

(see map, below), will be used. Maps using projections that show correct distances between places are called equidistant maps. Equidistant maps work well for projecting areas of limited size, such as a city or a state. There is no way, however, that maps of the entire world can be equidistant, because it is impossible to show the lengths of lines of latitude and longitude on a flat map as accurately as they appear on a globe. Finally, maps using projections that show accurate compass directions are called azimuthal maps (see map at the bottom of this page).

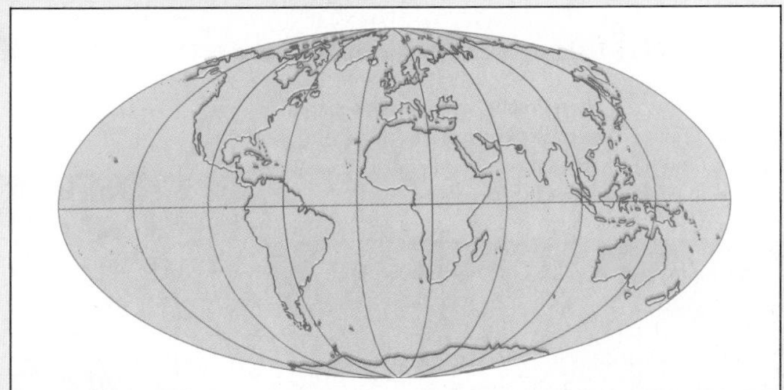

The Molleweide projection

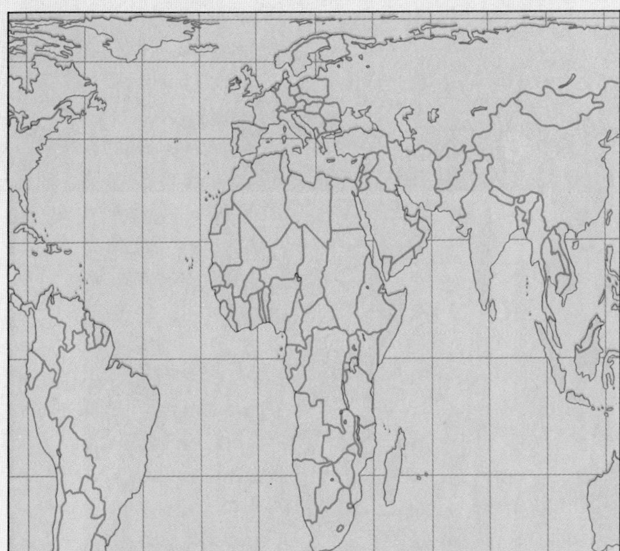

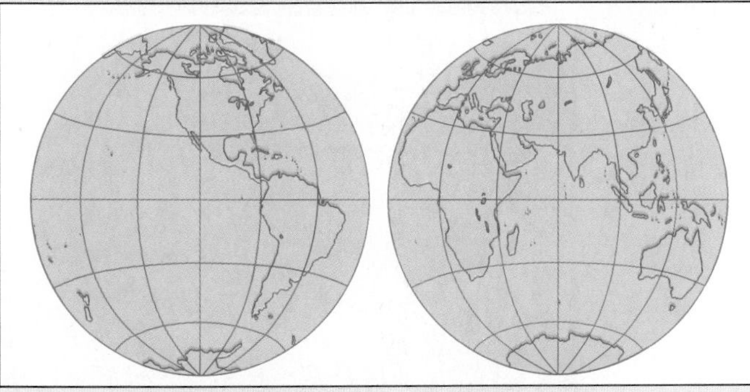

The Peters projection (top) and an azimuthal projection (bottom)

If you think about the types of projections described in the paragraphs above, you may see how and why each of them is used. Many people like to use a conformal map, for example, because the shapes of the continents and oceans look familiar and are, therefore, easy to recognize. Unfortunately, conformal maps often greatly distort distance and area.

Equal-area maps, on the other hand, are especially useful for comparing factors that may be affected by an area's size, such as temperature patterns, population size, or mineral production. The greatest drawback of equal-area maps is that they distort the shapes of the areas shown.

Equidistant projections are used for road maps because they allow the driver to get a clear and accurate picture of the distances to be traveled. Azimuthal maps, in contrast, are especially useful to navigators who must plot their courses along exact compass directions.

In spite of their drawbacks, then, there is indeed a map projection to meet every need. In studying maps, however, always remember to note the type of projection being used so that you will be aware of exactly how it is different from a globe, the one precise model of the earth. To aid you in this task, each of the maps in this book identifies the map projection being used.

xxix

Using the Photo Essay
You may wish to use the Photo Essay to introduce students to the course. Ask students to study the photos in the Essay. Point out that all of the photos emphasize the continuity of world history. That is, many of the inventions, customs, and works of art that are a part of our lives today have their roots in the distant past. For example, Christianity developed in the Roman province of Judea almost 2,000 years ago, and scientists have been struggling to conquer disease throughout history. Then tell students that their study of world history will help them understand the powerful forces that have molded the world into what it is today.

LINKING PAST TO PRESENT

As you study the photographs on pages xxx-xxxvii of this Linking Past to Present feature, think of how understanding what went on thousands of years ago will help you understand the world today.

Photos: 1. *Renaissance festival in Italy*
2. *concert for human rights in Los Angeles*
3. *opening ceremonies at the 1980 Winter Olympics in Lake Placid, New York*
4. *college football game*
5. *early baseball game*
6. *festival in Chile*
7. *Sudanese dancers*
8. *Nigerian wedding festival*
9. *Alvin Ailey dancers perform* Orozo
10. *Indian at the Inca Sun Festival in Peru*
11. *traditional stylized No drama in Japan*
12. *Mardi Gras celebration in Venice*
13. *Kabuki performance in modern-day Japan*

PEOPLE AND SOCIETY

Our world is divided into more than 160 nations, each with its own traditions, government, and ways of life. Yet in many ways people throughout the world are very similar. They celebrate joyous events such as weddings and festivals. Actors and singers entertain audiences. Sports enthusiasts cheer their favorite team on to victory. Many of these pastimes have their roots in the distant past. The Olympics, for example, began in ancient Greece, while the Inca Sun Festival predates the arrival of Europeans in the Americas. No matter what their origins or nationality, people value their traditions—traditions that have their roots in thousands of years of history.

xxxi

SCIENCE AND TECHNOLOGY

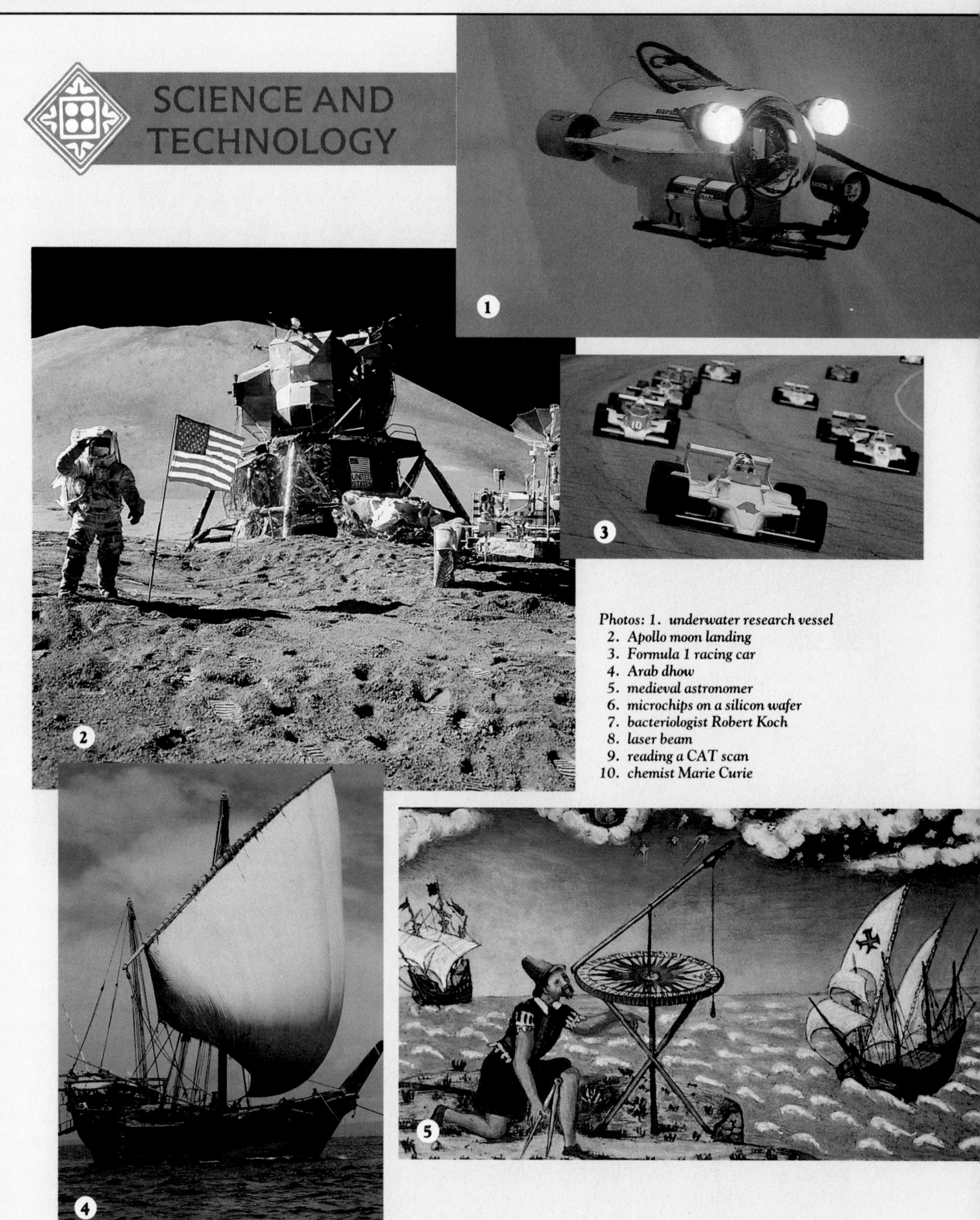

Photos: 1. *underwater research vessel*
2. *Apollo moon landing*
3. *Formula 1 racing car*
4. *Arab dhow*
5. *medieval astronomer*
6. *microchips on a silicon wafer*
7. *bacteriologist Robert Koch*
8. *laser beam*
9. *reading a CAT scan*
10. *chemist Marie Curie*

xxxii

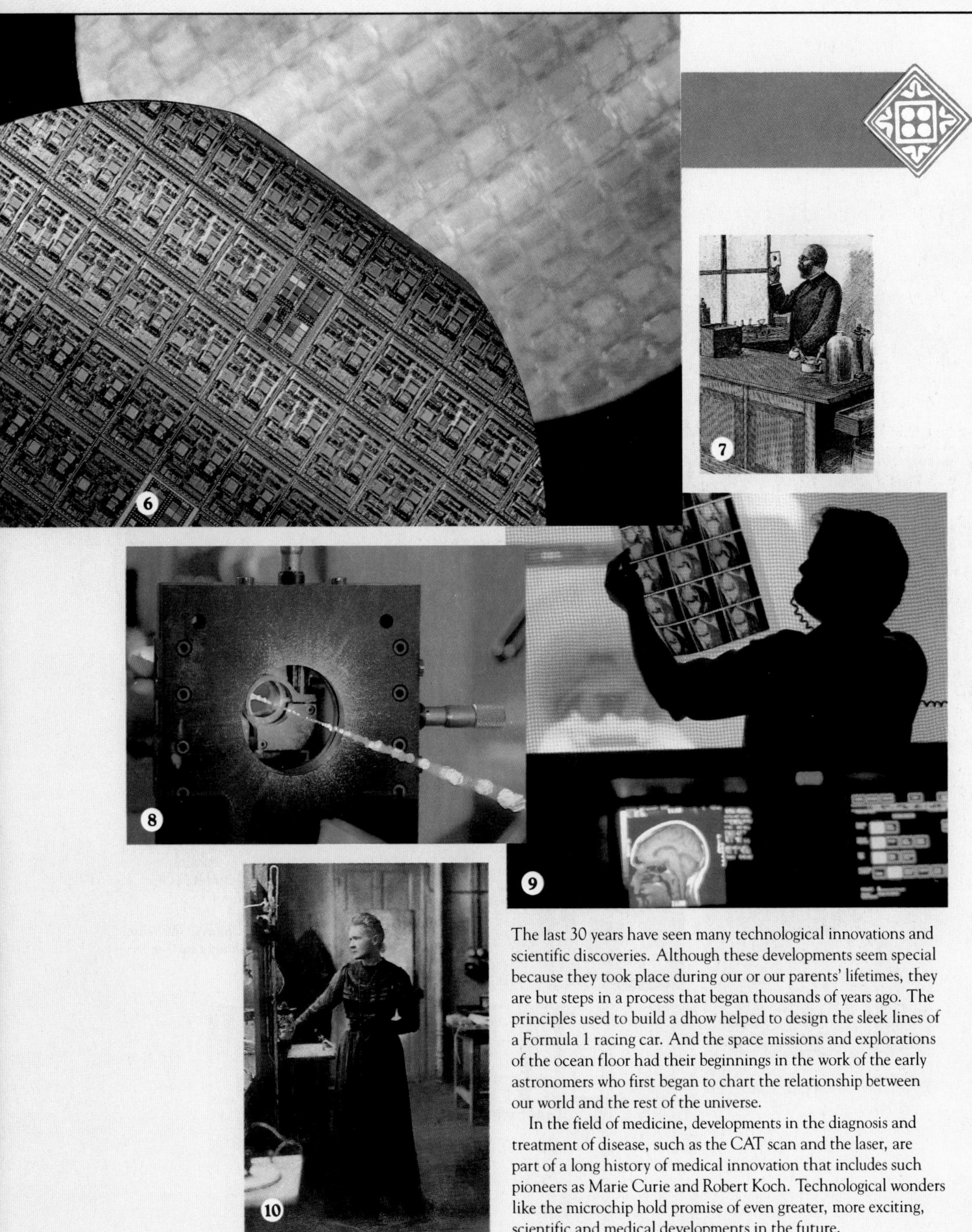

The last 30 years have seen many technological innovations and scientific discoveries. Although these developments seem special because they took place during our or our parents' lifetimes, they are but steps in a process that began thousands of years ago. The principles used to build a dhow helped to design the sleek lines of a Formula 1 racing car. And the space missions and explorations of the ocean floor had their beginnings in the work of the early astronomers who first began to chart the relationship between our world and the rest of the universe.

In the field of medicine, developments in the diagnosis and treatment of disease, such as the CAT scan and the laser, are part of a long history of medical innovation that includes such pioneers as Marie Curie and Robert Koch. Technological wonders like the microchip hold promise of even greater, more exciting, scientific and medical developments in the future.

xxxiii

Photos: 1. *Japanese painting*
2. *prehistoric cave painting*
3. *Chinese print*
4. *Islamic art*
5. Madonna and Child *by Raphael*
6. *Russian icon*
7. The Three Musicians *by Picasso*
8. The Room of Van Gogh at Arles *by Van Gogh;* 9. *the Sphinx*
10. *Transamerica Building*
11. *Buddhist temple;* 12. *Chartres Cathedral*
13. *African mask;* 14. *Chinese carving*
15. *Picasso sculpture*
16. *Pieta by Michelangelo*

xxxiv

From the beginnings of time people have used art to express themselves. And in many cases, artists have drawn upon inspirations from the past as they crafted new works of art. The Transamerica Building in San Francisco, for example, reflects the towering elegance of the pyramids of ancient Egypt. A modern Picasso sculpture reflects the majesty of the Sphinx. A madonna by Raphael deals with the same subject as a pieta by Michelangelo and a Russian icon. In other ways, however, the art of a society reflects that society's unique contributions and ways of life and helps us understand societies at various points in time and place.

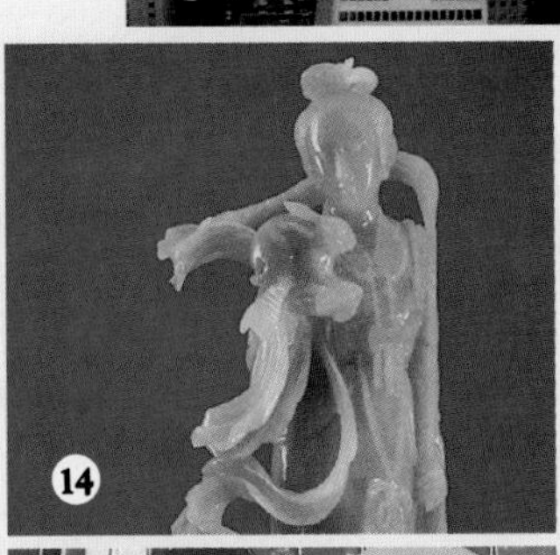

xxxv

CUSTOMS AND BELIEFS

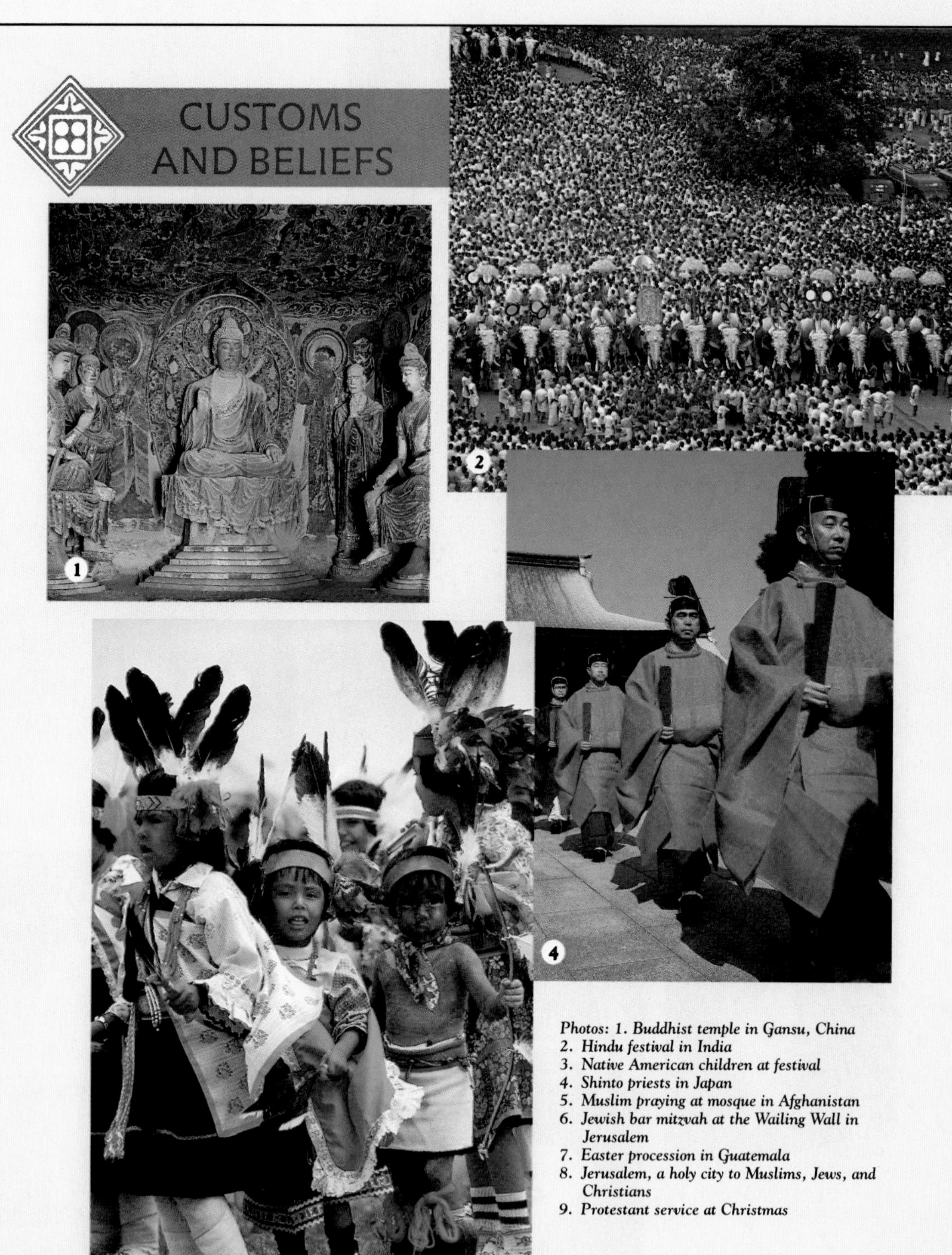

Photos: 1. Buddhist temple in Gansu, China
2. Hindu festival in India
3. Native American children at festival
4. Shinto priests in Japan
5. Muslim praying at mosque in Afghanistan
6. Jewish bar mitzvah at the Wailing Wall in Jerusalem
7. Easter procession in Guatemala
8. Jerusalem, a holy city to Muslims, Jews, and Christians
9. Protestant service at Christmas

xxxvi

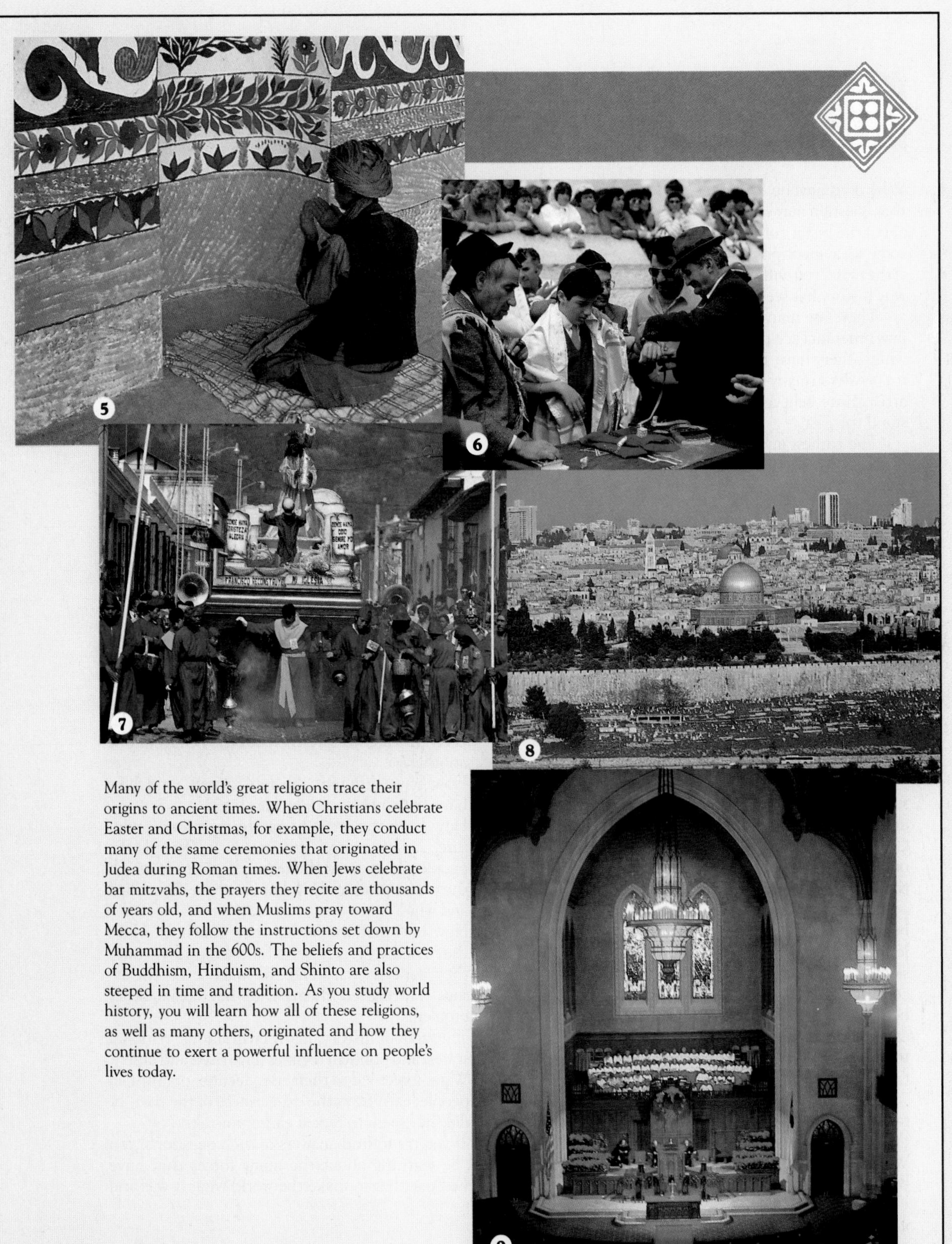

Many of the world's great religions trace their origins to ancient times. When Christians celebrate Easter and Christmas, for example, they conduct many of the same ceremonies that originated in Judea during Roman times. When Jews celebrate bar mitzvahs, the prayers they recite are thousands of years old, and when Muslims pray toward Mecca, they follow the instructions set down by Muhammad in the 600s. The beliefs and practices of Buddhism, Hinduism, and Shinto are also steeped in time and tradition. As you study world history, you will learn how all of these religions, as well as many others, originated and how they continue to exert a powerful influence on people's lives today.

HISTORY AND YOU

Why does anyone bother to study history? Asking that question may seem a strange way to start a book about the history of the world, but you ought to have some idea about possible answers before you begin. Otherwise, you will have no idea what to look for, or why history has seemed important to all peoples.

There are many answers to the question. They may differ for each person. It is useful, though, to see what others have thought about the value of history—why so many writers, politicians, teachers, and artists have believed that it is important to understand the past.

The earliest audience for history consisted simply of people who liked a good story. The two words, story and history, are essentially the same, and the appeal of history for many was that it brought to life real people and events, rather than invented ones. Before long, though, these real-life stories came to have a moral purpose—they taught lessons about how one should behave. The brave and the good usually succeeded; the cowardly or evil did not.

History was also considered important because it could explain—even without moral teachings—how or why things turned out as they did. It could show how a war happened, why one side won, and what the results were. By studying the past, people could thus learn what mistakes to avoid and what good examples to follow.

Finally, history came to be seen as a way of understanding ourselves and our own world. We cannot understand why Americans place such faith in their Constitution, why Islam is so important to Iranians, or why the Chinese think their revolution is still continuing, if we do not understand their history.

These different reasons for studying the past can be contradictory. Someone who looks for the moral lessons of history may not reach the same conclusions as someone who wants to explain the success of certain policies. Sometimes, for example, immoral behavior has proved successful. The historian has to assess these matters, try to reach conclusions about them, and thus determine their significance for our times.

As you read this book, think of yourself as a historian. Try to figure out why some people or events of the past seem more interesting to you than others. What do they tell you about yourself and your times? By keeping such questions in mind, you will be able to form your own answer about the reasons for studying history.

It may also help you to realize that a number of powerful forces have helped shape history in all periods. If you read thoughtfully and critically, you can learn what these forces are by asking yourself questions like these:

1. How has geography influenced the course of history? Have people simply adjusted to their environment, or have they tried to modify it?
2. How have people worked and earned their living? In other words, how have they organized their economy? What roles have farming, trade, and manufacturing played? How has income been distributed?
3. How have people been governed? Has political power been held by a few, or by many? Have individuals had rights and liberties? How have rights and liberties been gained, protected, or lost? In what way were laws made and enforced? How have they worked in practice, and for whose benefit? Why and how have people changed their form of government?
4. How have people gained knowledge, and how have they passed it on to their descendants? Have they had a formal system of education? Who has been educated? Have societies learned from one another?
5. How have different religions arisen, and how have they influenced people's lives?
6. How have the arts—literature, painting, sculpture, architecture, and music—reflected the people who created them and the times in which they were produced? What arts have flourished and why?
7. How have nations settled their conflicts? Have they tried to reach peaceful solutions, or have they gone to war? Did the wars settle the issues that caused them? Did they create other problems?
8. Throughout history, many civilizations, national states, and political regimes have risen and fallen. What forces led to their rise, decline, or fall? Did people learn from the experiences of the past, or did they seem to repeat earlier mistakes?

If you try to find answers to such questions, you will be learning about the many forces that have worked together to make the world what it was and

xxxviii

what it is. You will learn about the power of ideas, such as the belief that every human being has worth and dignity that must be respected. You can watch ideas like this appear, develop gradually, become strong, and finally be accepted by enough people to be put into practice. You will see other ideas decline and die out.

People have been pondering questions and ideas like these since earliest times. As you seek your own answers, you will be discovering what kind of person you are and want to be; you will be shaping your own role in the world of the future.

World History: People and Nations has been organized to help you seek the answers to these many questions.

Units. There are seven units, which group the chapters into broad historical periods. Each unit opens with a large illustration, symbolizing its contents, and with a list of the chapters it contains. Each chapter title is accompanied by the dates covered in the chapter so that you will easily recognize the time period. (See, for example, page 1.)

Unit Syntheses. Each unit of ***World History: People and Nations*** concludes with a six-page **Unit Synthesis** that highlights the major themes of the unit. You may use these syntheses to preview a unit or as a quick review before taking the unit test. (See pages 92–97.)

Chapters. The 33 chapters of ***World History: People and Nations*** are organized around definite periods or topics. Like the units, each begins with a single illustration symbolic of its contents. Above the illustration is a map of the world that locates the area or areas discussed in the chapter. The **Chapter Focus** allows you to briefly understand the place, time, and significance of what you are about to study and lists important terms, people, and places that you will be studying. The **Chapter Focus** concludes with a series of questions designed to guide your reading. (See pages 2–3.)

Chapter Sections. A chapter may contain from two to six sections, each numbered. At the end of each section is a **Section Review** to help you review and check your understanding of the material you have just read. (See page 13.)

Chapter Reviews. Every chapter ends with a two-page review. First there is a **Time Line,** which presents in graphic form the most important events—with their dates—discussed in the chapter. It is followed by a **Chapter Summary,** which traces the main ideas of the chapter. The questions, activities, and research projects that complete the Chapter Review are divided into six parts: **Reviewing Important Terms, Developing Critical Thinking Skills, Relating Geography to History, Relating Past to Present, Applying History Study Skills,** and **Investigating Further.** (See pages 14–15.)

Unit Reviews. Each of the seven units ends with a two-page **Unit Review.** Here you will find a number of questions that will help you review what you learned in the unit. (See pages 90–91.)

Graphics. The 123 maps will give you the location of every place mentioned in the text as well as show you topography, the size of empires, the thrust of invasions, and the extent of alliances. Each map is placed as close as possible to the relevant text. (See page 18.) Important sequences of events or ideas are summarized in chart form. (See page 43.) The hundreds of illustrations show you how people and places looked throughout the history of the world.

Features. You will find six kinds of special features running throughout the book. Combining text and illustrations, they will give you additional insights into world history:

- **Building History Study Skills** Each of the 33 chapters includes a skill lesson designed to help you master a specific skill. (See page 12.)
- **History Through the Arts** is a series of 50 illustrated features that reveal how civilizations are reflected in their arts and literature. (See page 23.)
- **Connections: Then and Now** is a series of 18 illustrated essays that relate past to present by showing how familiar customs and traditions have existed throughout history. (See page 25.)
- **What If?** is a series of 15 features designed to stimulate discussion and to develop critical thinking skills. (See page 38.)
- **Perspectives: Legacies of the Past** is a series of seven two-page features that trace specific developments or concepts through time and analyze how these developments or concepts affect our lives today. (See pages 40–41.)
- **Linking Geography to History** is a series of eight features designed to build your understanding of geography. (See page 44.)

Reference Section. The **Reference Section** at the back of the book includes an **Atlas,** a **Glossary,** and an **Index.**

xxxix

UNIT ONE

The Beginnings of Civilization

◀ *Egyptian wall painting in Luxor*

Unit Goals

After studying Unit One, students will be able to:

1. Describe how scientists learn about prehistory.
2. Summarize the achievements that prehistoric peoples made.
3. List the five characteristics of civilizations.
4. Compare the physical settings of the Nile Valley and the Fertile Crescent.
5. Compare Egyptian civilization with that of the empires of the Fertile Crescent.
6. Analyze the major components of early Indian civilization.
7. Describe the beliefs of Judaism, Hinduism, Buddhism, Confucianism, and Daoism.
8. List the major Chinese river civilizations and their unique characteristics.
9. Describe the cultural, economic, social, and political developments in China during the Shang, Zhou, Qin, and Han dynasties.

UNIT ONE THE BEGINNINGS OF CIVILIZATION

CHAPTER (pages 2-15)

1 Cultures and Civilizations Began in Prehistoric Times

(ca. 3,700,000 B.C.–1200 B.C.)

CHAPTER OVERVIEW

Prehistoric people left no written records, but their bones and artifacts provide us with clues to their existence. In studying their remains, we see that prehistoric people invented tools and weapons, created works of art, used fire, and buried their dead.

The earliest people were hunters who wandered from place to place. With the discovery of agriculture, they abandoned hunting and began to farm and raise animals. Agriculture allowed people to live in permanent settlements. This change in life style is called the Neolithic Revolution.

In four river valleys, Neolithic people developed civilizations that made use of advanced technical skills, established cities and governments, and were marked by intellectual achievements such as the invention of writing.

SUGGESTED LESSON PLAN			
Day	**Objec-tives**	**Suggested Activities**	**Materials**
1	U1-3,* C1-7	Introducing the Unit (page xxxx), Introducing the Chapter (page 2) Section 1 (pages 3-8), Focus/Motivation (page 3-4), Presentation (page 4), Closure (page 7), Suggested Teaching Strategies, Enrichment Activities, Daily Quiz, Suggested Assignments (page 1B)	ATE, Pupil's Edition, Teacher's Resource-Bank™
2	U3, C7-10	Section 2 (pages 9-13), Focus/Motivation (page 9), Presentation (page 9), Closure (page 14), Suggested Teaching Strategies, Enrichment Activities, Daily Quiz, Suggested Assignments (page 1B)	ATE, Pupil's Edition, Teacher's Resource-Bank™
3	U1-3, C1-10	Chapter 1 Form A Test, Reteaching Worksheet, Chapter 1 Form B Test	Teacher's Resource-Bank™ or Workbook and Test Booklet

*C refers to applicable Chapter Objective, U refers to applicable Unit Goal

BOOKS FOR THE TEACHER

Hoebel, E. Adamson. *Anthropology: The Study of Man.* McGraw-Hill. Analyzes the study of anthropology.

Leakey, Richard S., and Roger Lewin. *Origins.* Dutton. Discusses human origins based on discoveries in Africa.

Simak, Clifford D. *Prehistoric Man.* St. Martin's. Describes prehistoric people and the development of skills and social habits.

Starr, Chester G. *Early Man.* Oxford University Press. Recounts the history of prehistoric people and early civilizations of the Middle East.

BOOKS FOR THE STUDENT

Freed, Stanley A., and Ruth S. Freed. *Man from the Beginning.* Creative Science Series. Describes early people and their ancient cultures.

Howell, Charles F. *Early Man.* Time-Life. Illustrates the story of early peoples.

Pfeiffer, John E., and C. S. Coon. *The Search for Early Man.* Harper & Row. Describes the search for early people in the caves at Lascaux, France, and other areas. Includes numerous pictures, graphs, and charts.

Weisgard, Leonard. *The First Farmers.* Coward, McCann. Reconstructs life in the New Stone Age through pictures and text.

Wibberley, Leonard. *Attar of the Ice Valley.* Farrar, Straus & Giroux. Tells the story of a Neanderthal boy who reaches manhood and leads his tribe to better hunting grounds.

MULTIMEDIA MATERIALS

Cave People of the Philippines (mp, 2 parts, 38 min.), Films. Part 1 depicts a small group of Stone Age people, discovered in 1971, living in a Philippine rain forest. Part 2 shows how they were affected by contact with modern culture.

Dr. Leakey and the Dawn of Man (mp, 28 min.), Films. Traces the development of theories about the earliest humans and their place of origin.

The Epic of Man (17 fs), Life. Studies human development from the Stone Age through the first great civilizations of the Fertile Crescent.

Man Hunters (mp, 2 parts, 52 min.), Films. Traces the search for human origins from France to China, and from Israel to South Africa.

Search for Fossil Man (mp, 24 min.), National Geographic. Follows the activities of a renowned paleontologist and a team of amateur anthropologists at a fossil site.

Section (pages 3-9)

1 Prehistoric People Made Important Discoveries

SECTION OVERVIEW

Evidence of the existence of prehistoric people has been found in several areas of the world. This evidence indicates that prehistoric people made important discoveries that equipped them for survival. With the discovery of agriculture, prehistoric people changed from food gatherers to food producers.

SUGGESTED TEACHING STRATEGIES

1. **Preteaching Vocabulary (Basic)** You may wish to preteach the following important vocabulary terms: history, prehistory, civilization, anthropologist, archaeologist, artifact *(page 3)*; culture, radiocarbon dating *(page 4)*; migrate, glacier, Ice Age *(page 5)*; agriculture, domesticate, nomad, Neolithic Revolution *(page 8)*. List the terms above that an archaeologist could study easily or would aid in that study. *(artifact, culture, radiocarbon dating, agriculture, domesticate, Neolithic Revolution)* Then ask students to look up the meanings of these words in the Glossary.
2. **Identifying Concepts (Basic)** One way to demonstrate the concept of historical time is to draw a 50-inch (125-centimeter) line across the chalkboard on which 1 inch (2.5 centimeters) equals 100 years. Put the scale and the following basic facts on the chalkboard:

5,000 years	historic time
1,750,000 years	earliest appearance of humans
1,000,000,000 years	early forms of life
4,500,000,000 years	age of the earth

   Mark off historic time and ask students how far the line must be extended for the remaining number of years.
3. Relating Past to Present (Basic) An excellent way of studying early people is to investigate present-day Stone Age cultures. Show the film, *Cave People of the Philippines* (38 minutes, Films Inc.). Appropriate readings for discussion are "Stone Age Cultures Today" and "Neolithic Life of the Present" in *The Epic of Man* (Time-Life).

ENRICHMENT ACTIVITIES

1. **Preparing a Report (Average/Group)** The illustration at the top of page 11 is only one of several prehistoric ruins found in Great Britain. One or more students might prepare an oral report on Stonehenge, discussing the theories of its purpose. Students should use encyclopedias or library books as sources.
2. **Local Research (Challenging)** Assign groups of students to research the following topic: Did prehistoric people live in your region? Students should examine sources such as the local newspaper, museum, or historical society.

DAILY QUIZ

To assess student understanding of Section 1, give the class the following quiz. (Each item is worth 10 points.)

1. _______ study the skeletal remains of humanlike creatures and people to determine physical features and how long they lived. *(Anthropologists)*
2. Buildings, furniture, clothing, tools, coins, and toys are examples of _______, or objects shaped by human beings. *(artifacts)*
3. (T or F) In 1974 Donald Johanson discovered "Lucy" in Ethiopia, and calculated that she walked on two legs. *(T)*
4. (T or F) Archaeologists have uncovered the remains of Neanderthal people in caves in the Middle East, Asia, and particularly in the Neander Valley of Germany. *(T)*
5. (T or F) Early humans migrated in search of food and to flee from the adverse living conditions caused by the Ice Age. *(T)*
6. _______ people, named after a cave where their remains were found in southern France, were probably the first real artists because they covered the cave interiors with paintings of animals and outlines of human hands and faces. *(Cro-Magnon)*
7. A _______ wanders or travels from place to place in search of food. *(nomad)*
8. List three crops early people cultivated or harvested. *(wheat, barley, rice, millet, corn)*
9. What was the Neolithic Revolution? *(The Neolithic Revolution was the shift from food gathering to food producing.)*
10. How did the Neolithic Revolution affect people? *(Instead of spending time gathering food, people settled in agricultural villages and developed tools, made furniture, and wove cloth.)*

SUGGESTED ASSIGNMENTS

1. **Critical Thinking Worksheet (Average/Group)** Have students complete Critical Thinking Worksheet 1 in the TEACHER'S RESOURCEBANK™.
2. **Profile Worksheet (Basic)** Have students complete Profile Worksheet 1 in the TEACHER'S RESOURCEBANK™. Have them write brief reports on the hoax, stressing how paleoanthropology is not an exact science.

Section (pages 9-13)

2 The First Civilizations Began in Four Great River Valleys

SECTION OVERVIEW

In Neolithic times farmers developed civilizations in four river valleys. The characteristics of these civilizations were highly advanced technical skills, cities with some form of government, division of labor, the development of writing systems, and calendars.

SUGGESTED TEACHING STRATEGIES

1. **Preteaching Vocabulary (Basic)** You may wish to preteach the following important vocabulary terms: division of labor *(page 9)*; irrigation, artisan *(page 10)*; cultural diffusion *(page 11)*. Ask students to make a chart showing the *division of labor* in their home, a local place of employment, or in their state.
2. **Finding the Main Idea (Average/Group)** Finding the main idea in a paragraph is an important skill. Have students read the section "Learning to Use Metals" on pages 9-10. Then have them write the main idea of each paragraph on a sheet of paper. Collect the work to be corrected or ask for volunteers to read their answers.

   *(**Answers: Paragraph 1:** The discovery of metals was probably accidental. **Paragraph 2:** Copper tools and weapons were used for several thousand years but later were replaced by a harder alloy, bronze. **Paragraph 3:** Iron is a stronger material than copper or bronze, but because of difficulties in separating the iron from the ore it came into use much later. **Paragraph 4:** The Iron Age began when people learned how to make iron weapons and tools.)*

*3. **Interpreting Visuals: Using a Time Line to Understand B.C. and A.D. (Basic)** Have students reread "Building History Study Skills" on page 12. Then have them construct a time line for the years from 1960 to the present. Have them mark each year on the bottom of the line. Have them mark the year of their birth and label that on the time line. Then they should add other events that are important (1) in their own lives and (2) in the world at large *(the election of a pope or president, a favorite team winning the World Series or the Super Bowl, the Olympics)*.

ENRICHMENT ACTIVITIES

1. **Discussing Ideas (Challenging)** Select four to six students to conduct a panel discussion on the following topic: In early civilizations women made major cultural advance. Students should review the subsection "The Family in Early Civilizations" on page 13. Information on the role of women in early civilizations can be found in Jacquetta Hawkes's *The First Great Civilization* (Knopf). A discussion of women in various occupations, with numerous drawings, can be found in Leonard Weisgard's *The First Farmers* (Coward, McCann).
2. **Understanding Research Methods (Challenging)** Radiocarbon dating is one of several scientific methods used to determine the age of ancient artifacts and the dates of ancient civilizations. Have interested students prepare written reports on other procedures such as amino acid racemization, the study of fossils, the potassium-argon method, and recent tree-ring research. A member of the physical science department might provide information on these methods. Read and discuss the reports in class.

DAILY QUIZ

To assess student understanding of Section 2, give the class the following quiz. (Each item is worth 10 points.)

1. List three of the four great river valley civilizations. *(Nile, Tigris-Euphrates, Indus, Hwang He)*
2. List three of the five characteristics of a civilization. *(advanced technical skills; cities/government; division of labor; calendar; writing)*
3. What kind of metal did people make weapons from in the Nile and Tigris-Euphrates river valleys 6,000 years ago? *(copper)*
4. What is the mixture of copper and tin called? *(bronze)*
5. How did valley farmers water their crops during the dry season? *(Irrigation canals/ditches)*
6. Name a class of skilled workers in river valley communities that either made handicrafts or exchanged goods. *(artisans; traders; merchants)*
7. People developed a lunar ________ as a timetable to measure the beginning and end of the yearly floods. *(calendar)*
8. The letters that designate all years before the birth of Christ in most Western civilizations are ________. *(B.C.)*
9. List the steps in the development of an alphabet. *(The representation of things and ideas in pictures and the representation of a sound with a sign, consonant, or vowel)*
10. List the duties of man or woman in the prehistoric family and community. *(Answers will vary. See pages 8 and 13.)*

SUGGESTED ASSIGNMENTS

1. **Geography Worksheet (Basic)** Have students complete "Understanding Map Projections" in the Geography Supplement of the TEACHER'S RESOURCEBANK™.
2. **Critical Thinking Worksheet (Average/Group)** Have students complete Critical Thinking Worksheet 2 in the TEACHER'S RESOURCEBANK™.
3. **Skill Worksheet (Basic)** Have students complete Skill Worksheet 1 in the TEACHER'S RESOURCEBANK™.
4. **Review Worksheet (Basic)** Have students complete Review Worksheet 1 in the TEACHER'S RESOURCEBANK™.

Teacher's Notes

For suggested lesson plan, additional teaching strategies, enrichment activities, daily quizzes, and suggested assignments, see pages 1A–1D.

Introducing the Chapter
Have students turn to the pictures on pages 7, 9, and 11. Ask them not to read the captions but to study the pictures for clues about the lives of prehistoric people. What tools did they use? What skills might they have possessed? What did their art tell about them? What were some of their beliefs and values? Next gather four or five objects within the classroom or from students—for example, stapler, pencil, photograph, jewelry, wallet. Have students imagine they are visitors from another planet who have uncovered these artifacts. What can they infer about our civilization from them? How complete or accurate would these inferences be? Students should conclude that though much can be learned about the lives of prehistoric peoples, we will never have complete knowledge about the prehistoric era.

Chapter Objectives
After studying Chapter 1, students will be able to:

1. Describe the work that archaeologists and anthropologists do.
2. Name one method of dating prehistoric culture.
3. Identify Donald Johanson and Mary Leakey, and state why these scientists are important.
4. Summarize the difficulties faced by prehistoric peoples during the Ice Age.
5. Compare the activities

CHAPTER 1

Cultures and Civilizations Began in Prehistoric Times

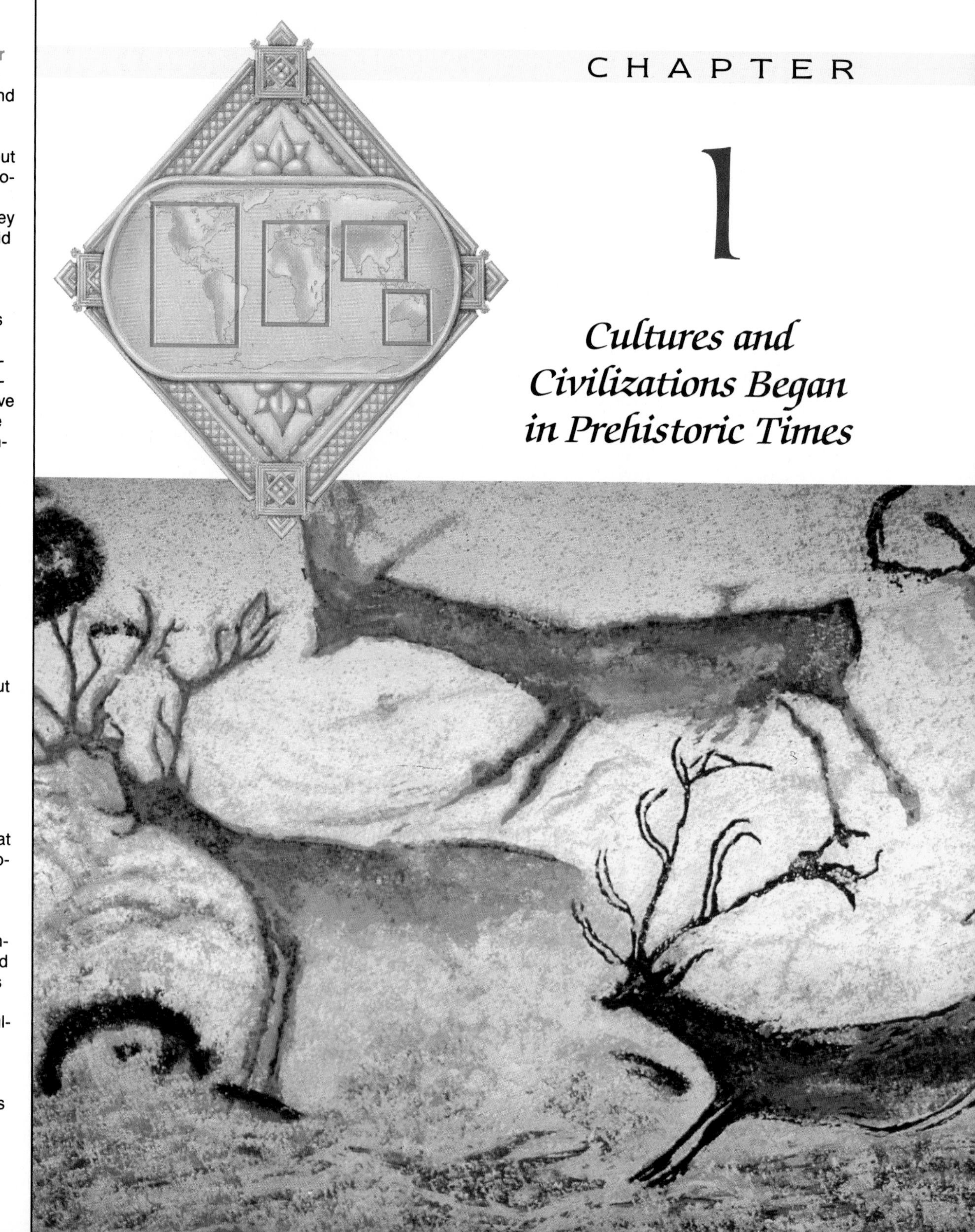

CHAPTER FOCUS

Place Africa, Asia, Europe, the Americas, and Australia

Time ca.*3,700,000 B.C.–1200 B.C.

3.7 mil. BC 4000 BC AD 2100

Significance

This book deals primarily with **history**—the record of events since people first developed writing, about 5,000 years ago. Writing allowed people to leave permanent information, facts, descriptions, opinions, ideas, and literature. But evidence indicates that people lived on earth long before the development of writing, during the period known as **prehistory.**

Since we have no written records of prehistoric times, many of the events of that remote past remain cloaked in mystery. Nevertheless, we know that the lives of prehistoric people resembled ours in several important ways. For example, prehistoric people invented tools, produced beautiful art, built cities, and developed forms of government. They gradually created what we call **civilizations**—highly organized societies with complex institutions and attitudes that link a large number of people together.

With civilizations came the first forms of writing and thus the end of prehistory. Our main story, the story of history, could begin.

Terms to Define

history	culture
prehistory	migrate
civilization	glacier
anthropologist	agriculture
archaeologist	nomad
artifact	irrigation

People to Identify

Mary Leakey — Donald C. Johanson

Places to Locate

Laetoli	Nile River
Neander Valley	Tigris River
Jarmo	Euphrates River
Çatal Hüyük	Indus River

Questions to Guide Your Reading

1 What important discoveries did prehistoric people make?
2 In what great river valleys did civilization first develop?

*ca. stands for *circa* and means "about."

In 1978 in a remote, almost inaccessible region of northern Tanzania, the noted scientist Mary D. Leakey made a remarkable discovery. As she stared down into the rugged terrain, she was amazed to see that a simple series of footprints lay imbedded in the volcanic rock. What fascinated her was that these footprints had not been left earlier that day or even earlier that week. Instead, they were millions of years old. Made in the soft ash of a volcanic eruption, the prints had been preserved as the ash had hardened.

Although we will never know exactly who made these prints, Leakey believes that they belonged to one of the humanlike creatures who, according to her theory, preceded us on earth.

> *"Following the path produces, at least for me, a kind of poignant time wrench. At one point, and you need not be an expert tracker to discern this, the traveler stops, pauses, turns to the left to glance at some possible threat or irregularity, then continues to the north. This motion, so intensely human, transcends time. Three million seven hundred thousand years ago, a remote ancestor—just as you or I—experienced a moment of doubt."*

Leakey is only one of many dedicated scholars who have tried to piece together the distant past.

1 Prehistoric People Made Important Discoveries

How can we learn anything about what happened on the earth before people learned to keep written records? Surprisingly enough, we can find out a great deal.

Examining Prehistory

Researchers called **anthropologists** (an • thruh • PAHL • uh • jists) and **archaeologists** (ahr • kee • AHL • uh • jists) have discovered many things about prehistory, often by using scientific methods. Anthropologists study the skeletal remains of early humanlike creatures and people to determine how they looked, how long they lived, and other physical characteristics. Archaeologists excavate ancient settlements and study **artifacts**—material objects

◀ *Animal painting from Lascaux Cave in France*

of Neanderthal and Cro-Magnon people.
6. Describe how the Neolithic Revolution affected the way people lived during the New Stone Age.
7. List the four great river valley civilizations and the characteristics that made them civilizations.
8. Describe how the discovery of bronze and iron influenced the people who lived in the early river valley civilizations.
9. Discuss how government and the division of labor developed.
10. Summarize the formation and function of calendars and alphabets in the early river valley civilizations.

SECTION 1

Focus/Motivation

Write the following quotation on the chalkboard or an overhead projector: "Time has changed but not basic problems." Ask students what they consider the basic problems facing the United States today. Write these in one column under the heading *Modern Problems.* Then ask students to speculate about the problems faced by prehistoric people. Write the responses under a second column entitled *Prehistoric Problems. (Answers should include food, clothing, shelter, and protection.)* Then ask: What are the differences between the two lists? Ask students to account for these differences. *(Answers should include the fact that prehistoric people faced*

2B, a4A

● radiocarbon dating and amino acid racemization

■ The technical term for anthropologists who study the remains of such skeletons is *paleoanthropologist.* Note the correlation with the word *paleolithic.*

problems of basic survival while modern humans are, for the most part, confronted by problems caused by the complexity of their society.)

Presentation
Illustrating Ideas (Average/Group)

To illustrate the concept of historical time, draw the face of a clock on the chalkboard or an overhead projector. Let one hour represent the total age of the earth. Point out that the earliest forms of life appeared only 13 minutes before the end of the hour and only within the last minute have humans been on the earth. The last second of the hour represents all recorded history.

shaped by human beings. Examples of artifacts include buildings, furniture, clothing, tools, weapons, works of art, coins, and toys. By studying these objects, archaeologists can piece together information on the cultures of early people. **Culture** is what a human group acquires through living together, and includes language, knowledge, skills, art, literature, law, and life styles.

To assign a date to prehistoric remains, scientists use a variety of scientific techniques, including **radiocarbon dating.** Each living thing contains radiocarbon atoms that begin to decay when the organism dies. Radiocarbon dating measures the rate of this decay for organic matter up to about 100,000 years old. For remains more than 100,000 years old, scientists usually use other methods that record the rate of decay of certain key elements and compounds. For example, the *amino acid racemization* method can be used to date items up to 1 million years old.

Despite these sophisticated methods, scientists still must rely on guesses. However, scientists usually are quite confident about the conclusions they reach. They can tell us when important changes took place thousands of years ago. They can also describe some of the ways the first human beings spent their lives.

Learning from Pictures *In Egypt an archaeologist traces an artifact for further study. What methods do* ● *archaeologists use to date prehistoric remains?*

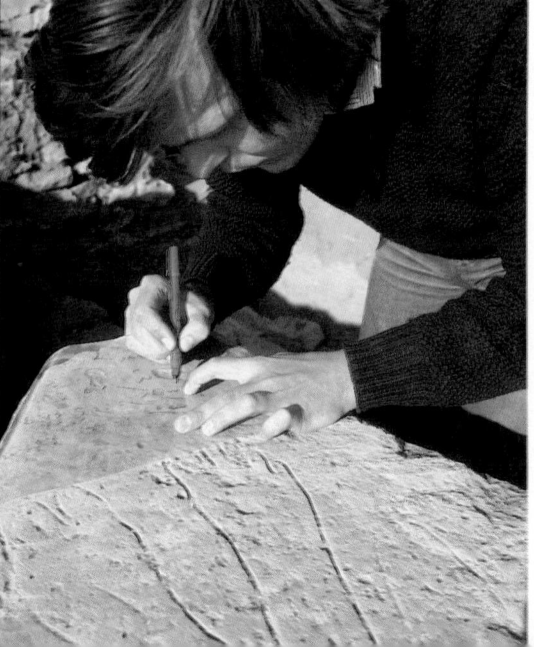

Early Humanlike Creatures

Anthropologists now know that humanlike creatures appeared on the earth millions of years ago. That period of prehistory is called the Old Stone Age, or Paleolithic (pay • lee • oh • LITH • ik) Age. The word *paleolithic* comes from the Greek words *palaios,* meaning "old," and *lithos,* meaning "stone." We call this period the Stone Age because almost all of the artifacts that have survived were made of stone. ■

In 1974 in Ethiopia, anthropologist Donald C. Johanson discovered female skeletal remains that may be 3 million years old. Although Johanson named his find Australopithecus (aw • struh • loh • PITH • uh • kuhs), the skeleton became known as "Lucy," after the Beatles' song "Lucy in the Sky with Diamonds," which was popular at the time of the discovery.

After examining the bones found at the excavation site, particularly fragments of her leg and foot, Johanson concluded that Lucy walked on two legs. In 1978 at Laetoli (lay • TOH • lee) in Tanzania (tan • zuh • NEE • uh), Mary Leakey unearthed the skeletons of other Australopithecines dating back 3.7 million years. These creatures also walked on two legs.

Creatures similar to the Australopithecines lived in eastern Africa 2 million years ago. In 1986, for example, Donald Johanson discovered the skeleton of a female who probably lived about 1.8 million years ago in Olduvai (OHL • duh • way) Gorge in Tanzania. Scientists also uncovered tools made of chipped stone when they found the bones.

Anthropologists are still not certain whether a relationship exists between these Australopithecines and the humans of today. But many believe that upright posture and the ability to make tools occurred very early in human development.

The First People

Despite the many findings of anthropologists, knowledge of early humans and of the humanlike creatures that preceded them on earth millions of years ago is based on fragmentary remains. Because these remains are very difficult to study, scientists often disagree on the significance of the bones and other materials found at excavation sites. Future discoveries may lead to theories different from those commonly held today.

● Research topic: How the "greenhouse effect"—the warming of the earth's surface and atmosphere—compares with the Ice Age in its effect on the world's people

■ Discussion topic: How the "land bridge" affected the movement of peoples between Asia and the Americas and between Australia and Asia

1A, 1B, 2B

Anthropologists have used the excavated bones to describe how the first people looked. These individuals were very strong and had powerful jaws, sharply receding chins, low foreheads, and heavy eyebrow ridges.

Scientists believe these early people sometimes used caves as shelters and probably ate vegetables and gathered seeds, fruits, nuts, and other edible plants. Later, people added meat to their diets as they began to hunt small animals. Eventually, humans hunted large animals. In order to hunt successfully, people had to work together, communicate with one another, and make tools. Inquiring minds—and hands freed by an upright posture—helped make these developments possible.

As humans became successful hunters, they moved, or **migrated,** over great distances in search of food. Their populations expanded from Africa to Asia. Paleolithic people lived in Asia as early as 1 to 1.5 million years ago. Archaeologists discovered the remains of prehistoric people on the Indonesian island of Java in 1891 and near Beijing (BAY • JING), China, in 1929. Scientists named these people Java people and Beijing people.

More recently, scientists have discovered the remains of Paleolithic people in other parts of Asia as well as in Europe and Africa. For thousands of years, however, periods of extremely cold weather limited the areas to which early people could migrate.

The Ice Age

Extremes of climate have greatly influenced human history and the history of the earth itself. Four times within the last 1.5 million years, the earth has had periods of extremely cold weather. Each time, the northern polar icecap (a permanent ice sheet near the North Pole) moved south and joined **glaciers**—large, slowly moving masses of snow and ice—that formed in the mountain ranges. Each of these four cold-weather periods lasted from 10,000 to 50,000 years. Together they are known as the **Ice Age.** Scientists believe that we now live in a warm era that began after the fourth period of the Ice Age, which ended between 10,000 and 25,000 years ago.

It is difficult to imagine the vastness of the great ice sheets of the Ice Age. Today ice covers about one-twelfth of the earth's land surface. During the third and longest period of the Ice Age, ice covered about one-third of the earth's surface. In some places the ice was several miles thick. Large areas of northern North America, Europe, and Asia lay engulfed in ice.

The Ice Age affected the earth in various ways. ● Some humans and animals migrated to warmer, ice-free areas. Many kinds of animals and plants disappeared completely. The grinding, chiseling effect of the moving ice changed the surface of the earth greatly. While ice covered much of the northern half of the earth, the rest of the earth received unusually large amounts of rainfall. Rivers and lakes rose. Inland seas formed. Former desert regions began to produce vegetation and support animal life.

On the other hand, the sea level dropped because so much water was frozen in the icecaps. As the sea level fell, underwater ridges became uncovered and formed "land bridges." These bridges linked certain continents and islands that are today separated by water. To escape the ice, ■ many people and animals walked over some of these land bridges.

The icecap and glaciers gradually melted between glacial advances. Only when prehistoric peoples learned to use fire and craft warm clothing could they successfully settle in the colder regions of the earth.

Neanderthal People

In caves located in many parts of Europe, the Middle East, and Asia, anthropologists have found the remains of the Neanderthal (nee • AN • duhr • thawl) people—humans who lived some 30,000 to 100,000 years ago. These people were named after the Neander Valley in Germany, where Neanderthal remains were first found in 1856. Neanderthal skulls reveal that these people had powerful builds, heavy jaws, thick eyebrow ridges, and large noses.

Neanderthal people made more efficient tools than did the humans who preceded them. They lived in caves, wore clothing made of animal skins, and used fire.

Since the Neanderthals lived in cold regions, some anthropologists believe they were the first people to cook food. According to this theory, Neanderthals placed frozen meat on hot coals to thaw. When they discovered that the cooked meat tasted better than raw meat, they adopted cooking.

1A, 1B, 2B, a1A, a4A, a4B, a4C

Neanderthal people differed from earlier humans in another very significant way—they buried their dead. What is more, they buried them with tools, weapons, and even food. Many scientists believe this practice shows that the Neanderthals expected these items to be useful to the dead person after his or her death. If the theories of these scientists are correct, this practice shows a belief in some form of life after death—a belief basic to many of the world's religions. Perhaps the Neanderthals were the first people to believe in a god or gods.

Many scientists also think that the Neanderthals nursed their sick instead of abandoning them to die as earlier humans apparently did. One Neanderthal skeleton is that of a man who was about 40 years old. Analyses of this skeleton show that the man suffered from severe arthritis and had lost most of his teeth. It would have been almost impossible for him to survive unless someone had cared for him.

Like earlier humans, Neanderthal people disappeared. We do not know why. Massive glaciers had again advanced southward and covered much of Europe and North America, and Neanderthal people may have perished because of the cold, hostile environment. Perhaps physically stronger or more mentally alert people overwhelmed and destroyed the Neanderthals.

Learning from Maps *This map indicates where remains of prehistoric people have been discovered. In what four river valleys did prehistoric people settle?* **Nile, Tigris-Euphrates, Indus, Huang He**

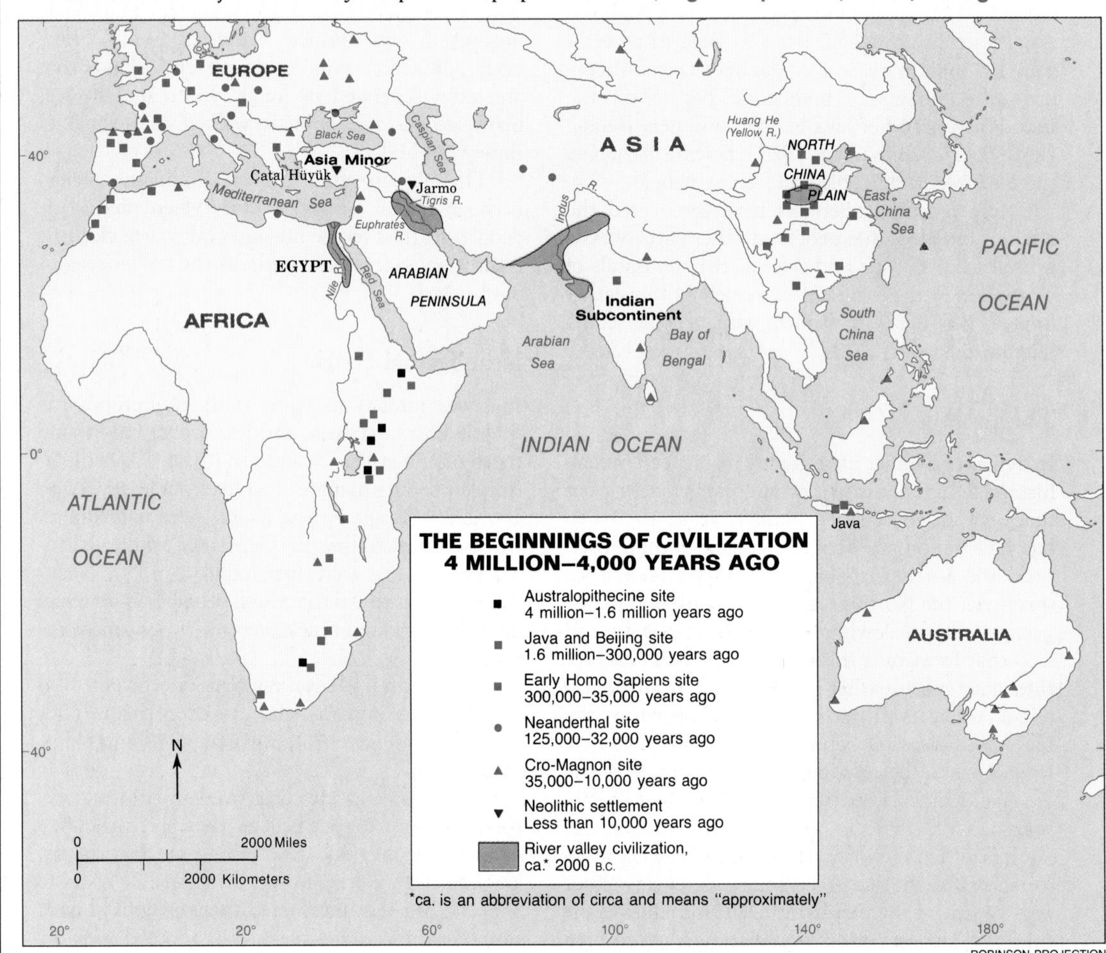

6

● Critical thinking activity: Ask students how the ivory head shows that the people were beginning to develop civilization.

SCULPTURE

Prehistoric Ivory Head

A Cro-Magnon artist carved this ivory head of a woman about 20,000 years ago, during the Old Stone Age. Found in France, it is small enough to hold in the palm of your hand. From works like this, we learn that some prehistoric peoples had an appreciation of beauty similar to our own. Such artifacts also tell us that some prehistoric groups had time for activities other than looking for food and making tools. This carving is one of the earliest known attempts to create a portrait. It may have been an object of worship that the owner could easily carry from place to place as he or ● she searched for food.

Cro-Magnon People

At just about the time Neanderthal people disappeared—some 30,000 to 35,000 years ago—a new kind of people appeared in Europe, perhaps having come from Africa or Asia. These new people were better equipped to survive than Neanderthal people were, for the new arrivals made better tools and weapons. Their invention of the spear, for example, made them more effective hunters. This new group of humans—Cro-Magnon people—are named for a cave in southern France where remains were first found in 1868 (see map, page 6).

By 20,000 years ago, humans had migrated to northeastern Europe, northern Asia, North America, and Australia. Scientists theorize that people crossed land bridges to reach the Americas and Australia.

We know much more about Cro-Magnon people than we do about any of the other early humans. For one thing, more Cro-Magnon remains have been found. Then, too, the Cro-Magnons themselves have "told" us more about themselves. They could not write, but they could draw and paint and were probably the first real artists. In Spain and southern France where Cro-Magnon people lived, paintings of the animals they hunted cover the walls of caves. There, in limestone caverns, hundreds of feet from the entrance, we can see paintings of bulls tossing their heads, wounded bison charging a hunter, herds of fleeing reindeer, and schools of swimming salmon and trout. Paintings of red and black horses six feet (1.8 meters) long leap majestically out of the darkness. And faint drawings of human hands and faces appear and disappear depending on the angle of light.

Scientists are uncertain about why the Cro-Magnons created these artworks. The art may have been a chronicle of the hunt or a means not only of teaching hunting techniques to the younger people but also of passing on tales about how the world began and how people and animals were created.

With high foreheads, well-defined chins, and small brow ridges, Cro-Magnon people looked almost the same as men and women living today. The Cro-Magnons lived on earth for many thousands of years. By the end of the Old Stone Age, however, the Cro-Magnon as a distinct type of people no longer existed. In appearance, people had become as they are today.

SECTION 1

Closure

Ask students to list the major achievements that prehistoric humans made.

Review Answers

1. ***history:*** record of events since people first developed writing about 5,000 years ago; ***prehistory:*** long period of time before people kept written records; ***civilization:*** highly organized society with complex institutions and attitudes that link a large number of people together; ***anthropologist:*** scientist who studies the skeletal remains of early humanlike creatures and people to determine how they looked and lived; ***archaeologist:*** scientist who excavates ancient settlements to study material objects made by human beings; ***artifact:*** human-made material object including tools, weapons, and coins; ***culture:*** what humans acquire by living together—language, knowledge, skills, art, literature, and life styles; ***radiocarbon dating:*** technique that measures the rate of decay for organic matter; ***migrate:*** to move from place to place; ***glacier:*** large, slowly moving mass of snow and ice; ***Ice Age:*** one of four time periods in the last 1.5 million years of the earth's history, during which a polar icecap covered much of the Northern Hemisphere; ***agriculture:*** the raising of crops for

● Research topic: One of several types of animals that people have domesticated, when they were domesticated, and what purpose each animal served

food; ***domesticate:*** to tame animals such as the goat for a source of milk and meat; ***nomad:*** a wanderer who travels from place to place in search of food; ***Neolithic Revolution:*** shift from food gathering to food production
2. ***Mary Leakey:*** anthropologist who unearthed in Tanzania the skeletons of Australopithecines dating back 3.7 million years; ***Donald C. Johanson:*** anthropologist who discovered the remains of a 3-million-year-old female in Ethiopia in 1974
3. ***Laetoli:*** area in Tanzania where Mary Leakey unearthed Australopithecines; ***Neander Valley:*** location in Germany where first Neanderthal remains were found in 1856; ***Jarmo:*** site of Iraqi town 8,750 years old; ***Çatal Hüyük:*** Neolithic town in Turkey
4. buildings, furniture, clothing, tools, weapons, art, coins, and toys
5. (a) ***Paleolithic:*** use of stone tools, gathering and hunting food, use of fire, wearing of clothing, burying the dead, possible practice of religious ceremonies; **(b)** ***Mesolithic:*** domestication of animals, invention of bow and arrow, fishhooks, spears, harpoons, and dugout canoes; **(c)** ***Neolithic:*** use of polished stone tools; creation of special tools such as awls, wedges, saws, drills, and needles; development of settled agriculture and permanent villages; domestication of additional animals.

The Middle Stone Age

The period lasting from the end of the last Ice Age until the development of **agriculture,** or the raising of crops for food, is called the Middle Stone Age. Since people in different parts of the world developed agriculture at different times, the dates of the Middle Stone Age vary according to region. For example, the Middle Stone Age lasted from about 12,000 to about 10,000 years ago in Africa and Asia. In most of northern Europe, however, the era lasted until about 5,000 years ago. The era is also often called the Mesolithic Age, from the Greek words *mesos,* meaning "middle," and *lithos,* meaning "stone."

People made much progress during this short ● period. They **domesticated,** or tamed, the goat as a source of milk and meat. They also domesticated the dog, which proved valuable in hunting smaller animals. They invented the bow and arrow, as well as fishhooks, fish spears, and harpoons made from bones and antlers. By hollowing out logs, they made dugout canoes so that they could fish in deep water and cross rivers.

The New Stone Age

About 10,000 years ago, in certain parts of the world, basic changes occurred in the way people lived. The period that began then is called the New Stone Age, or Neolithic Age. Its scientific name comes from the Greek words *neos,* meaning "new," and *lithos,* meaning "stone."

In the Old Stone Age and Middle Stone Age, people chipped stone to produce an edge or a point. In the New Stone Age, people discovered a better way to make tools and weapons. They learned how to use a flat piece of sandstone to polish stones to a fine edge or a sharp point. They learned to make tools from wood and from many kinds of stone. With these new methods and materials, they could make special tools—awls, wedges, saws, drills, chisels, and needles.

But other far more important changes occurred during the New Stone Age. Earlier people had been **nomads,** or wanderers who travel from place to place in search of food. Neolithic people, however, began settling in permanent villages because of two important developments: (1) the taming of several additional kinds of animals, and (2) the development of agriculture.

Paleolithic and Mesolithic hunters never knew whether enough food would be available. They might have bad luck in hunting, or animals might starve or migrate. The food supply became much more certain once people domesticated animals. Mesolithic people had tamed dogs and goats, but Neolithic people also learned to raise cattle, horses, sheep, and pigs. They used the flesh of these animals for food and the hides for clothing.

The greatest advance Neolithic people made was agriculture, though exactly how people learned that seeds could be planted and made to grow year after year remains a mystery. In prehistoric times men went out in search of animals, while women remained near the campsite to care for the children. Women and children gathered plants and fruit from nearby areas for food. Perhaps a woman first noticed that seeds could be planted and grown. In any case, people somehow learned to plant wheat, barley, rice, and millet, a grass cultivated for grain. They also learned to use fertilizer and invented the plow.

Certain areas of the world became centers from which new domesticated plant species spread to other parts of the world. Wheat and barley originated in the Middle East, rice developed in southwestern Asia, and corn was first cultivated in the Americas. Other domesticated plants included bananas and yams in Southeast Asia and potatoes in South America.

The important shift from food gathering to food producing has often been called the **Neolithic Revolution.** (Although the word *revolution* is most often used to mean the overthrow of a government, it may also mean a very important change in people's lives.)

Having new sources of food permitted Neolithic people to build homes and settle permanently in one region. By 9,000 years ago, agricultural villages numbering up to about 200 inhabitants dotted the hills and valleys of many parts of the world. In Iraq, for example, archaeologists have unearthed the remains of a town called Jarmo that existed about 8,750 years ago. And in Turkey, scientists have excavated Çatal Hüyük (chah • TUHL hoo • YOOK), a town that had almost 3,000 residents 8,000 years ago. Evidence shows that the people of Çatal Hüyük built shrines to many gods and probably offered them food and other forms of wealth to win their favor or to express gratitude for past favors.

Learning from Pictures *Archaeologists discovered kitchen utensils (right) in the burial mounds (far right) of Çatal Hüyük.*

SECTION 1 REVIEW

1. **Define** history, prehistory, civilization, anthropologist, archaeologist, artifact, culture, radiocarbon dating, migrate, glacier, Ice Age, agriculture, domesticate, nomad, Neolithic Revolution
2. **Identify** Mary Leakey, Donald C. Johanson
3. **Locate** Laetoli, Neander Valley, Jarmo, Çatal Hüyük
4. **Understanding Ideas** What evidence left by prehistoric people tells us about their daily life?
5. **Identifying Ideas** List the advances made in the following periods: **(a)** Paleolithic, **(b)** Mesolithic, **(c)** Neolithic.
6. **Analyzing Ideas** Why is the development of agriculture considered a "revolution"?

2 The First Civilizations Began in Four Great River Valleys

By the end of the Stone Age, people had learned to make tools and weapons, use fire, create works of art, tame animals, grow their own food, and establish permanent settlements. However, not everyone developed this way of life during the Neolithic Age. For example, not all areas of the world had soil and climate suitable for farming. In some regions with grassy pasture lands, people maintained a herding culture in which they moved their flocks from one place to another to graze. They continued as nomads, wandering about in small groups or tribes and never settling down.

Moving into the River Valleys

Although Neolithic people settled in many areas, the settlements in four specific regions had particular importance in later human development. These four regions were: (1) the Nile River valley in Egypt, (2) the valley of the Tigris and Euphrates (yoo • FRAY • teez) rivers in southwestern Asia, (3) the Indus River valley in southern Asia, and (4) the Huang He (HWANG HOOH) valley in eastern Asia (see map, page 6).

In these four river valleys, people first developed the advanced form of culture known as civilization. All people have some sort of culture. Only when a culture becomes highly developed do we call it a civilization.

Most civilizations have at least five characteristics: (1) The people have advanced technical skills, such as the ability to use metals. (2) People have created cities with some form of government. (3) A **division of labor** exists, in which different people perform different jobs, instead of one person doing all kinds of work. (4) People have developed a calendar. (5) People have developed a form of writing.

Learning to Use Metals

People probably discovered metals by accident. It may have happened when someone built a fire over an area that contained the metal copper. Later, the fire builder might have noticed lumps of this metal in the ashes. People may then have learned how to shape the heated metal.

6. People no longer wandered to gather food but settled in one place.

SECTION 2

Focus/Motivation
Ask students to name characteristics of a civilization. List these on the chalkboard or an overhead projector. When the students have agreed on a list, have them read the subsection "Moving into the River Valleys" on page 9. Compare the class list of the elements with those listed in this section. The class list should be longer and might include such items as art forms, law, science, distinct groups such as the military and priesthood, and buildings.

Presentation
Interpreting Ideas (Average/Group)
Because it is believed that women made many of the major cultural advances in early civilization, ask the students to review the subsection "The Family in Early Civilizations" on page 13. Discuss the major contributions of women and the impact these contributions had on civilization. Information on this topic can be found in Jacquetta Hawkes's *The First Great Civilization* (Knopf). A discussion of women in various occupations can be found in Leonard Weisgard's *The First Farmers* (Coward, McCann).

1A, 1B, 1C, 1D, 2A, a1A

● **Ask: What advantage would warriors from a civilization using iron weapons have over those using bronze weapons?**

■ **Discussion topic: Advantages that people living in settled agricultural communities have over nomadic herders and gatherers**

About 6,000 years ago, people in both the Nile and Tigris-Euphrates River valleys knew how to make copper weapons, tools, utensils, and jewelry. Copper tools and weapons proved unsatisfactory, however, mainly because the soft metal could not keep a sharp edge or be used in heavy work. In time, people learned to make a better metal—bronze. An alloy, or mixture, of copper and tin, bronze is harder than copper. People in Egypt and in the Tigris-Euphrates River valley knew how to make bronze jewelry and weapons as early as 5,000 years ago. People in India and China also used bronze at an early date. The invention of bronze tools marked the end of the Stone Age and the beginning of the Bronze Age.

A stronger metal than either copper or bronze, iron ore—the iron as it exists in the earth mixed with other minerals—exists in more places and in larger amounts than either copper or tin. Yet its use came much later, because separating the iron from the ore required an extremely long and difficult process. The invention of the forge, a kind of furnace in which forcing air through fire produces great heat, helped make the use of iron possible. After the extreme heat of the forge had softened the iron ore, the hot metal had to be hammered to eliminate impurities that would weaken the iron and render it useless.

We do not know when people discovered the process of making iron or who invented it. It may have originated separately in several different areas. We do know, however, that about 3,200 years ago people in southwestern Asia learned to make iron and craft it into stronger tools and weapons, more durable than those made of copper or bronze. The
● Iron Age had begun.

Irrigation, Government, and Cities

The valleys of the Nile, Tigris-Euphrates, Indus, and Huang He have a common feature that greatly influenced their early histories. Once a year their rivers rise and flood the valleys. Except for this rainy period, however, little if any rain falls. Hot, dry conditions prevail throughout the rest of the year.

This climate challenged the farmers of these valleys; somehow they had to get water to their crops during the dry season. Carrying water proved difficult, time-consuming, and backbreaking. At some point in the distant past, however, the farmers in these valleys learned to dig ditches and canals to transport needed water to their fields. Thus they developed the first systems of **irrigation.**

Violent floods occurred during the rainy season in three of the river valleys—the Tigris-Euphrates, the Indus, and the Huang He. Therefore, farmers in these valleys also had to build dikes to keep the rivers within their banks.

Farming in these river valleys, then, depended on irrigation and the ability to control floods. Because individuals working alone could not build large irrigation and flood-control projects, people had to learn to work together.

Governments may have developed gradually as a result of such cooperation. As people worked together, they needed rules to govern their behavior and to plan, direct, and regulate their work.

The first valley dwellers moved into their valleys in tribes. Each tribe settled in a village along the river. People lived together in the villages and worked the surrounding land. In time more and more people banded together to work on group projects and to defend their villages. Some of these village communities grew to become cities.

An increase in population, made possible by improved farming methods such as irrigation and better tools, also led to the growth of cities. Improved farming meant more and better food and, therefore, a healthier and more comfortable life for each person. The large number of people living in cities also provided the labor to create great palaces, temples, and other public buildings.

Division of Labor

As methods of farming improved, fewer people had to work in the fields in order to produce enough food for all. Some people could specialize in work other than farming. Expert toolmakers and weaponmakers could devote all their time to this type of work. They would then trade their products for food. Thus a class of skilled craftworkers called **artisans** appeared. ■

Other people became merchants and traders. They made their living by buying goods from farmers or artisans and then selling the goods for a profit to anyone who needed them, especially to people in the cities. Traders not only transported goods to be sold but also passed along ideas. For example, these early traders spread their systems of counting that

10

Research topic: Prehistoric monuments or burial sites in different areas of the world

Learning from Pictures *These prehistoric monuments in Outer Hebrides, Scotland, are believed to be grave markers called dolmens.*

showed the number of articles bought and sold. Today we call the spread of certain parts of cultures from one area of the world to another **cultural diffusion.**

Developing a Calendar

The people in the great river valleys developed calendars early in their history. Because these people farmed, they carefully observed the changes of the seasons. They had to know, for example, when the yearly floods would start and stop. One way was to regard the time from flood to flood as a year and to divide the interval according to the phases of the moon. These changes in the moon's appearance were the most regular repetitions that early people could see in the sky.

The time from one new moon to the next new moon would be a month. Twelve of these lunar months would equal a year. But this system presented a major problem. A month based on the movement of the moon—on the time it takes the moon to revolve once completely around the earth—lasts only about 29 1/2 days. Twelve "moon" months thus equal 354 days. But by measuring the time it takes the earth to revolve once completely around the sun, we know a year has approximately 365 1/4 days. A calendar based on the moon, therefore, fell about 11 days short. As a result, the months came earlier each year, and 12 months did not fill the time until the next flood. As you read more about river-valley civilizations, you will see how early people coped with this problem. In addition to discussing the many ways early people used to identify the months of the year, in this book we will be using a system of dating years with the letters B.C. and A.D. (see *Building History Study Skills,* page 12).

11

READ
WRITE
● INTERPRET
CONNECT
THINK

BUILDING HISTORY STUDY SKILLS

Interpreting Visuals: Using a Time Line to Understand B.C. and A.D.

To understand history you need to be aware of when events happened. In this book we will be using a system of dating years from the birth of Christ. Years following Christ's birth are identified in numerical order and start with the letters A.D. The letters A.D. stand for the Latin phrase ***Anno Domini,*** which means "in the year of our Lord," or "since the birth of Christ." The year A.D. 1900 thus stands for 1,900 years after Christ's birth. Years before Christ's birth are identified in reverse numerical order and are followed by the letters B.C., which stand for "***B***efore the birth of **C**hrist." Thus the date 2000 B.C. means 2,000 years before Christ's birth.

To calculate how many years separate events in modern times from events in ancient history requires using both B.C. and A.D. For example, 5000 B.C. was 6,990 years before A.D. 1990 (5,000 + 1,990 = 6,990), while 1000 B.C. was about 2,500 years before A.D. 1500 (1,000 + 1,500 = 2,500).

The method of dating events from the birth of Christ is only one of several ways of calculating time. Muslims, Chinese, Jews, and Hindus count the years in different ways. For example, the Christian year A.D. 1900 corresponds with the Muslim year 1318, the Hebrew year 5660, and the Chinese year 4597.

How to Use a Time Line to Understand B.C. and A.D.

To help you understand when important events occurred, the Chapter Review in each chapter in this book includes a time line that shows the order, or sequence, of important events discussed in the chapter. A time line can also help you see relationships between certain events. In order to use a time line to understand B.C. and A.D., follow these steps.

1. Determine the length of time shown on the time line. Be certain to calculate the years that are B.C. and those that are A.D.
2. Read the time line from left to right so that you can determine the sequence of events.
3. Identify the important events that the time line shows. Which events occurred in B.C.? Which events occurred in A.D.?
4. Identify relationships in time between the events on the time line. For example, how many years before A.D. 158 was 1350 B.C.?

Developing the Skill

The time line at the bottom of this page includes several important events that you will study in later chapters of this book. The time line documents events that occurred between 1200 B.C. and A.D. 1988, a period of 3,188 years (1,200 + 1,988 = 3,188).

As you read the time line from left to right, notice that 1000 B.C. is earlier in time than 100 B.C. and that 500 B.C. is later in time than 800 B.C. This is true because the years before the birth of Christ (B.C.) are numbered in reverse numerical order. Also note that A.D. 1900 is later in time than A.D. 100 because the years after the birth of Christ (A.D.) are numbered in numerical order.

The time line helps you to understand the order in which events occurred. For example, the Bronze Age began in southwestern Asia in 1200 B.C.–447 years before the legendary founding of Rome (753 B.C.) and 739 years before the Age of Pericles in Athens (461 B.C.). Also note that the Bronze Age began about 2,976 years before the signing of the Declaration of Independence. You know that this is true because from 1200 B.C. to the end of the B.C. period was 1,200 years, and from the beginning of A.D. to A.D. 1776 was 1,776 years (1,200 + 1,776 = 2,976).

Practicing the skill. How many years after the beginning of the Bronze Age in southwestern Asia was George Bush elected President of the United States? **3,188**

To apply this skill, see Applying History Study Skills on page 15.

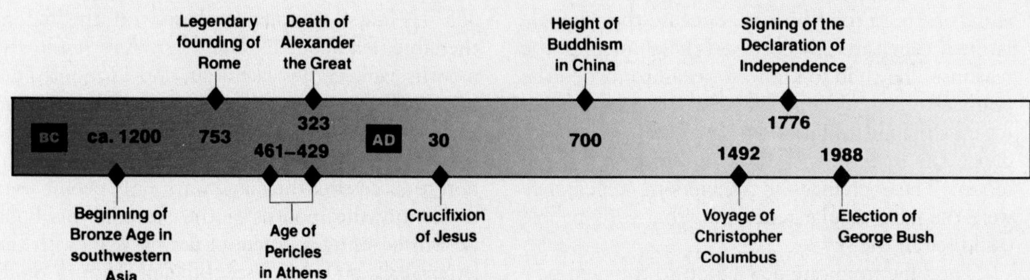

12

● Put examples of pictograms, ideograms, and phonograms on the chalkboard or an overhead projector. Have students suggest additions to each type.

■ Ask: In what ways do peoples of the world today live in the same way as the peoples of early civilizations?

1B, 1D, 2A, a1A, a4A, a4F, a4G, a4L

Inventing Writing

With the many changes of late Neolithic times, life became increasingly complex. People in settled communities developed rules for living together and for protecting property. They also developed agreements for working together. Governments were established and with them taxes to pay the costs of government. Trade also developed between various communities.

Speech no longer sufficed as the only means of communication. People needed a written language to preserve and pass on ideas and information. Rulers wished to keep a permanent record of the events of their reigns and to keep tax records; parents wished to hand down lasting instruction to their children. The long and complex process of the development of writing may be summarized in four chief steps:

● (1) A *picture represents a thing.* For example, a picture of a tree stands for the word *tree.* Picture signs of this sort are called *pictograms.* Pictograms have disadvantages, however. It is easy to show a tree or a person. But how would you represent an idea, such as "truth," "honesty," "liberty," or "life after death"?

(2) A *picture stands for an idea.* As time went on, people used symbols to stand for ideas. Suppose a farmer had orchards. In this case the farmer might use the drawing of a tree to represent the idea of "wealth." We call picture signs of this sort *ideograms.*

(3) A *picture stands for a sound, usually a syllable.* In using pictograms and ideograms, a great many pictures are needed. Fewer are required if a certain symbol can represent a sound, not just one meaning. Thus the tree symbol could stand not only for *tree* but also for the syllable *trea* in the word *treason.* We call signs of this sort *phonograms.*

(4) A *sign represents a single consonant or vowel.* These signs, or letters, form an alphabet. An alphabet marks the final step in the development of writing. Over the years two things happened to the tree symbol. First, it was simplified so that it became easier to draw. Second, it came to stand for the beginning sound of the phonogram, not the whole sound. Thus a simplified version of the picture—the letter *T*—came to represent just the first sound of *tree.* This story of the development of the letter *T* is an imaginary and simplified one, but it illustrates how people invented alphabets.

The Family in Early Civilizations

When civilization developed, men hunted less, and many became farmers. Women also continued to do some of the farming, such as planting and harvesting crops. In the early river-valley civilizations, men farmed and made metal products, such as weapons. Women managed the family, cared for the children, and made items necessary for survival. They prepared food, made clothing, and probably invented pottery and weaving.

Religion also played an important part in the lives of early families. Early people believed in many gods and in the unseen forces of nature. They believed that the gods and these forces controlled all aspects of their lives. People feared that the rains would not come and that their crops would not grow. Since crop failure would mean starvation, they begged their gods to provide water and to make seeds grow. Often these people offered sacrifices to their gods in order to ensure good harvests and offered thanks when they believed their prayers had been answered.

People in early civilizations lived in large families. In addition to mothers, fathers, and children, families included grandparents, aunts and uncles, and cousins. However, because of limited medical knowledge, many children died as infants. When people grew old, they expected their children to take care of them. People of all ages began to depend on their relatives for help in everyday affairs.

In most early civilizations, the father headed the family. But because the mother played a key role in running the family's daily life, she also had great authority. However, women's authority often did not extend into politics or religion. ■

SECTION 2 REVIEW

1. **Define** division of labor, irrigation, artisan, cultural diffusion
2. **Locate** Nile River, Tigris River, Euphrates River, Indus River, Huang He
3. **Seeing Relationships** How did the need for irrigation and flood control lead to the development of governments?
4. **Analyzing Ideas** Why were calendars important to people of early civilizations?
5. **Understanding Ideas** **(a)** Why was written language needed? **(b)** What were the four chief steps in developing a written language?

SECTION 2

Closure

Ask students to list the five characteristics of civilizations. *(advanced technical skills, cities with some form of government, division of labor, calendar, writing)*

Review Answers

1. ***division of labor:*** different people perform different tasks; ***irrigation:*** using ditches and canals to supply water for crops; ***artisan:*** skilled craftsworker; ***cultural diffusion:*** spread of culture from one area of the world to another

2. ***Nile River:*** site in Egypt of one of the world's four early river valley civilizations; ***Tigris River:*** southwestern Asian river that flows into Persian Gulf; ***Euphrates River:*** with the Tigris, the site of early river valley civilization; ***Indus River:*** center of early civilization in western India; ***Huang He:*** site of river valley civilization in northern China

3. Governments developed to encourage cooperation and direct and regulate the building of large irrigation and flood-control projects.

4. Farmers needed calendars to predict the time of the yearly floods.

5. **(a)** As society became more complex, written language enabled people to preserve and pass on ideas and information; **(b)** pictograms, ideograms, phonograms, alphabet

Reviewing Important Terms
1. d; **2.** b; **3.** a; **4.** g; **5.** h; **6.** j; **7.** c; **8.** e; **9.** f; **10.** i

Developing Critical Thinking Skills
1. (a) because no written records exist and many artifacts remain undiscovered; **(b)** They examine artifacts to find out how people lived and use scientific methods such as radiocarbon dating to find out the age of things.
2. (a) upright posture, meat eaters, use of fire, plow; **(b)** Austrolopithecus, Beijing people, Neanderthal people, Cro-Magnon people; **(c)** gathering of fruits and seeds, hunting, herding of animals, farming
3. People became farmers rather than hunters, developed technical skills that led to a variety of jobs, settled in permanent communities, and formed governments.
4. (a) Neolithic people obtained food by developing agriculture and domesticating animals; Paleolithic people gathered and hunted. **(b)** Neolithic people made special tools by polishing stones; Paleolithic people chipped stones to create simple tools and weapons. **(c)** Neolithic people created the first organized governments; Paleolithic people did not have any government.
5. (a) the development of technical skills, the creation of cities and government, division of labor, development of a calendar, and writing; **(b)** Answers will vary. Students might mention technology, the many large cities, complex labor structure of modern society, and government at many levels.

1B, 1D, 2A, a4A, a4C, a4J, a4K, a4L, a4M

Reteaching
Have students review the Chapter Summary and the appropriate section and questions in the Unit Synthesis. Discuss the concepts until students demonstrate a clear understanding of the material.

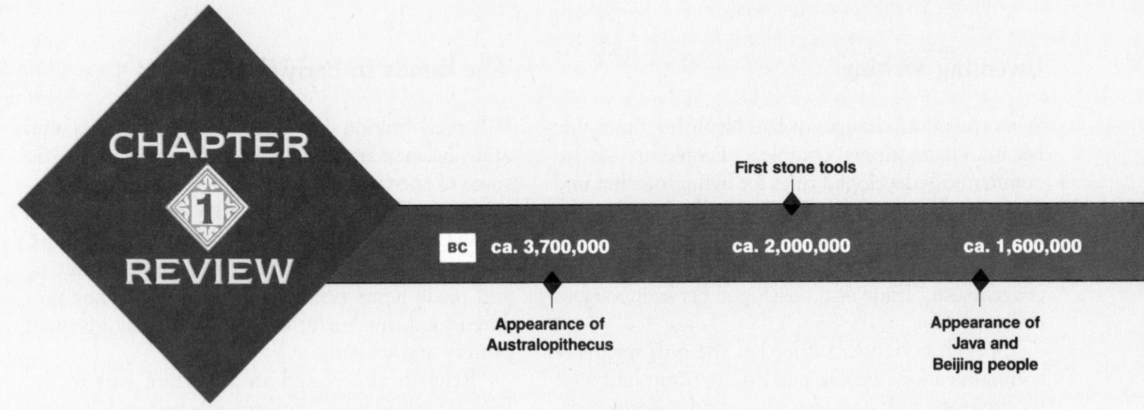

Chapter Summary

The following list contains the key concepts you have learned about the cultures and civilizations that began during prehistoric times.

1. The first humans left behind bones, artifacts, and pictures. From these, anthropologists have been able to determine what the first human beings looked like, what they ate, where they lived, and what some of their customs were.
2. Many scientists believe that during prehistoric times people gradually developed greater skills, such as producing more effective tools, learning to hunt more efficiently, and creating the earliest works of art.
3. Eventually, people learned to domesticate animals and to farm. As a result, they began settling in villages and gave up their nomadic life styles.
4. Changes during Neolithic times brought about one of the most important turning points in human history—the development of civilization.
5. People developed the first civilizations in four great river valleys in Africa and Asia. There, people learned how to use metals, build cities, promote economic activity, and establish governments.
6. One of the most significant developments was writing. The ability to keep written records gave civilizations continuity. It also allows us, for the first time, to find out what early people thought about their own times. With the development of writing, prehistory ended and history began.

On a separate sheet of paper, complete the following review exercises.

Reviewing Important Terms

Match each of the following terms with the correct definition in column two.

a. prehistory
b. civilization
c. artifact
d. history
e. division of labor
f. anthropologist
g. radiocarbon dating
h. glacier
i. agriculture
j. Neolithic Revolution

___ **1.** Record of what has taken place in the world since the invention of writing
___ **2.** Highly organized society with complex institutions and attitudes that link a large number of people together
___ **3.** Period before the invention of writing
___ **4.** Technique that measures the rate of decay of certain atoms present in organic matter
___ **5.** Large, slowly moving mass of snow and ice
___ **6.** The shift from food gathering to food producing
___ **7.** Material object shaped by a human being
___ **8.** System in which different people perform different jobs, instead of one person having to do all kinds of work
___ **9.** Scientist who studies the skeletal remains of early humans to determine how they looked, how tall they were, how long they lived, and other physical characteristics
___ **10.** The raising of crops for food

Developing Critical Thinking Skills

1. **Understanding Ideas** **(a)** Why do the events of prehistory remain cloaked in mystery? **(b)** What methods do archaeologists and anthropologists use to unlock these mysteries?
2. **Understanding Chronology** Place the items in each of the following three lists in chronological order from most ancient to most recent: **(a)** plow, upright posture, meat eaters, use of fire; **(b)** Beijing people, Australopithecus, Cro-Magnon people, Neanderthal people; **(c)** farming, hunting, herding of animals, gathering of fruits and seeds
3. **Seeing Relationships** How did the lives of early people change after they learned to domesticate animals and raise food crops?
4. **Contrasting Ideas** How did the people of the Neolithic Age differ from those of the Paleolithic Age in these categories: **(a)** method of obtaining food; **(b)** tools; **(c)** government?
5. **Synthesizing Ideas** **(a)** What are the five major characteristics of civilizations? **(b)** How does life in the United States today meet each of these five characteristics?

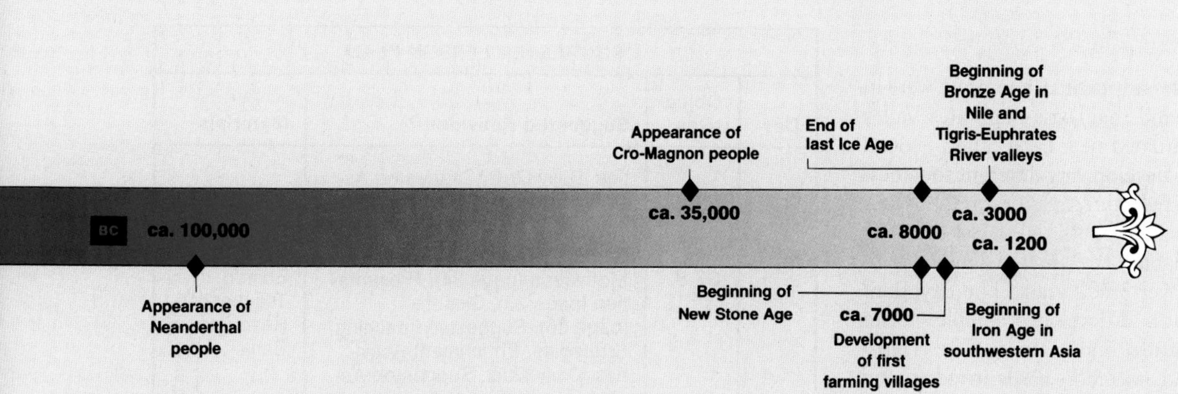

Relating Geography to History

Study the map of the sites of early human remains and the four river-valley civilizations on page 6. **(a)** List the large bodies of water that are closest to the four major river-valley civilizations. **(b)** Which two of these civilizations were most likely, because of their location, to have some trading contact with each other? **(c)** Which civilization seems the most isolated from the others?

Relating Past to Present

1. **(a)** What was the role of women in Neolithic society? **(b)** On what can we base this view? **(c)** How have the roles of women in the United States changed in the past 25 years? **(d)** What new inventions, developments, and attitudes have helped bring about these changes?
2. What do you think a civilization from outer space would learn of the culture of the United States today from investigating the contents of our garbage dumps, cemeteries, and junkyards?
3. Over thousands of years, prehistoric people discovered new skills and inventions that greatly changed their lives. Among these were methods of agriculture, the use of metals, and the calendar. **(a)** Choose a modern skill or invention and explain how it has changed our lives today. **(b)** Why do you think it took prehistoric people thousands of years to make a few important discoveries?

Applying History Study Skills

Before completing this activity, review Building History Study Skills on page 12.

Look again at the events shown on the time line in Building History Study Skills on page 12. Notice that some events occurred during B.C. and some during A.D. Remember that B.C. years are numbered in reverse numerical order before the birth of Christ. A.D. (***A***nno ***D***omini) years are numbered in numerical order after the birth of Christ. Then use the time line to help you place the events in column two in the order in which they happened.

(a) Crucifixion of Jesus
(b) Election of George Bush as President of the United States
(c) Beginning of Bronze Age in southwestern Asia
(d) Legendary founding of Rome
(e) Age of Pericles in Athens
(f) Height of Buddhism in China
(g) Death of Alexander the Great
(h) Signing of the Declaration of Independence
(i) Voyage of Christopher Columbus

Investigating Further

1. **Writing a Report** In your school or local library, locate information about hunting and gathering societies in the world today. For example, you might read Elizabeth M. Thomas's *The Harmless People* (Random House), which is about the Bush people of southern Africa. Or you might choose to read about the Pygmies of Central Africa, who are described in Colin M. Turnbull's *The Forest People* (Simon and Schuster). Other groups that you might read about are New Guinea tribes, Amazon tribes, or Philippine tribes. Periodicals such as *National Geographic* and *Explorer* would be good sources for your research. Then write a report describing: **(a)** how the group is organized and governed; **(b)** the roles of men and women; **(c)** how food is obtained and distributed within the group; **(d)** the group's religious practices; **(e)** the physical environment and how it affects the way the people live; **(f)** the types of tools made and used.
2. **Making Comparisons** Use encyclopedias to locate information about one of these calendars—the Chinese, Hebrew, Muslim, or Hindu calendar. **(a)** How does each calendar calculate a one-month period? **(b)** How does this period compare with one month on the Christian calendar? **(c)** Why does each calendar have a different beginning of the year?
3. **Making Charts** Reread the information on inventing writing on page 13. Then use resources in your school or public library to find more information on the systems of writing that early people developed. Use the information you find to help you construct a chart illustrating the four major steps in the development of writing.

Relating Geography to History

(a) *Nile:* Mediterranean Sea and Red Sea; *Tigris-Euphrates rivers:* Persian Gulf; *Indus River Valley:* Indian Ocean; *Huang He:* Pacific Ocean; **(b)** The Tigris-Euphrates and Nile civilizations seem most likely to have had trading contacts. **(c)** Huang He civilization

Relating Past to Present

1. (a) Neolithic women cared for children, gathered plants for food, and made clothing. **(b)** We examine artifacts and the roles of women in their historic social settings. **(c)** More women work outside the home. **(d)** Answers will vary. Students might say that microwaves and frozen foods make it possible to eliminate lengthy food preparation. Day-care centers eliminate the need for mothers to stay at home. Many women are now guaranteed equal wages for equal work.
2. Answers will vary. Students could mention the dependence upon the car, eating and drinking habits, use of plastics, and burial customs and attitudes toward death.
3. (a) Students might discuss the effects automobiles, airplanes, telephones, and computers have on our lives. **(b)** Answers will vary. Prehistoric people discovered skills or inventions by trial and error, and communication between cultures was minimal, so cultural diffusion was slow.

Applying History Study Skills:
c, d, e, g, a, f, i, h, b

CHAPTER (pages 16-47)

2 Great Civilizations Developed in the Middle East

(ca. 6000 B.C.-586 B.C.)

CHAPTER OVERVIEW

Two of the four river valleys in which early civilizations arose were in the Middle East—the Nile Valley and the Tigris-Euphrates Valley (the Fertile Crescent). Although situated near each other, geography and climate helped the areas to develop very different societies.

The Nile Valley was well protected from invasion, and the predictable flooding of the river deposited fertile soil along the river banks each year. These factors enabled the ancient Egyptians to create a stable society that lasted over 2,000 years. The Egyptians established an effective government and developed complex forms of art, religion, writing, mathematics, and science. The Tigris-Euphrates Valley, on the other hand, was more easily invaded, and the flooding of its rivers was unpredictable. The societies that developed there were less stable. A succession of different peoples invaded the valley and the surrounding region.

In the western end of the Fertile Crescent, three peoples made important contributions to Western civilization. The Phoenicians were seafarers who carried their alphabet throughout the Mediterranean. The Lydians developed a money economy, using coins. The Hebrews contributed ethical monotheism and the Old Testament.

SUGGESTED LESSON PLAN

Day	Objectives	Suggested Activities	Materials
1	U4-5,* C1-4	Introducing the Chapter (page 16) Section 1 (pages 17-24), Focus/Motivation (page 17), Presentation (page 17), Closure (page 23), Suggested Teaching Strategies, Enrichment Activity, Daily Quiz, Suggested Assignments (page 15B)	ATE, Pupil's Edition, Teacher's Resource-Bank™
2	U4-5, C1-4	Section 2 (pages 24-27), Focus/Motivation (page 25), Presentation (page 25), Closure (page 26), Suggested Teaching Strategies, Enrichment Activities, Daily Quiz, Suggested Assignments (page 15C)	ATE, Pupil's Edition
3	U4-5, C5-6	Section 3 (pages 27-32), Focus/Motivation (page 27), Presentation (page 28), Closure (page 32), Suggested Teaching Strategies, Enrichment Activities, Daily Quiz, Suggested Assignments (page 15C)	ATE, Pupil's Edition, Teacher's Resource-Bank™
4	U4-5, C7-8	Section 4 (pages 32-37), Focus/Motivation (page 34), Presentation (page 33), Closure (page 36), Suggested Teaching Strategies, Enrichment Activities, Daily Quiz, Suggested Assignments (page 15D)	ATE, Pupil's Edition, Teacher's Resource-Bank™
5	U4-5, C9	Section 5 (pages 38-45), Focus/Motivation (page 38), Presentation (pages 38-39), Closure (page 44), Suggested Teaching Strategies, Enrichment Activities, Daily Quiz, Suggested Assignments (page 15E)	ATE, Pupil's Edition, Teacher's Resource-Bank™
6	U4-5, C1-9	Chapter 2 Form A Test, Reteaching Worksheet, Chapter 2 Form B Test	Teacher's Resource-Bank™ or Workbook and Test Booklet

*C refers to applicable Chapter Objective, U refers to applicable Unit Goal

BOOKS FOR THE TEACHER

Carson, Lionel. *Ancient Egypt* (Great Ages of Man Series). Time-Life. Provides scholarly text with excellent illustrations.

Edey, Maitland A. *The Sea-Traders* (Emergence of Man Series). Time-Life. Brings Phoenicians to life in this informative text with vivid picture and photographs.

Hawkes, Jacquetta. *The First Great Civilizations.* Knopf. Presents the societies of Mesopotamia, the Indus Valley, and ancient Egypt.

Hicks, Jim. *The Empire Builders* (Emergence of Man Series). Time-Life. Presents recent research on the Hittites in a well-written, illustrated text.

Kramer, Samuel. *The Sumerians.* University of Chicago Press. Examines Sumerian society.

BOOKS FOR THE STUDENT

Baumann, Hans. *In the Land of Ur, The Discovery of Ancient Mesopotamia.* Pantheon Books. Analyzes social history of ancient Mesopotamia.

Cottrell, Leonard. *Five Queens of Ancient Egypt.* Bobbs-Merrill. Gives substance to the lives of five Egyptian queens from the scant sources available.

________. *The Warrior Pharaohs.* Putnam. Provides interesting reading on the great warrior kings of Egypt.

Millard, H. W. F. *Everyday Life in Babylonia and Assyria.* Putnam. Examines the social and cultural life of these empires, with numerous illustrations.

MULTIMEDIA MATERIALS

Ancient Civilizations (fs), National Geographic. A series of 6 filmstrips. Titles appropriate for Chapter 2: "Mesopotamia," "Egypt."

Ancient Persia (mp, 11 min.), Coronet. Shows the empire of Cyrus and Darius through ruins, excavations, and other remains.

Ancient Phoenicia and Her Contributions (mp, 14 min.), Atlantis. Highlights the many cultural achievements of the ancient Phoenicians.

The Epic of Man (17 fs), Life. Titles appropriate for Chapter 2: "Sumer: First Great Civilization," "Oldest Nation: Egypt," "Egypt's Eras of Splendor."

Hatshepsut: The First Woman of History (fs), Multi-Media. Tells the story of the only Egyptian woman to rule as pharaoh.

Section (pages 17-24)

1 The Egyptians Built a Civilization Along the Nile River

SECTION OVERVIEW

Geography played an important role in the development of Egypt. Fertile soil, a frost-free climate, mineral deposits, and surrounding deserts and seas as protection from invaders provided the conditions for a flourishing and long-lasting civilization. Rulers known as pharaohs reigned over Egypt for more than 2,000 years. This span of time is divided into four periods: Old Kingdom, Middle Kingdom, New Kingdom, and Decline. In the 300s B.C., native rule in Egypt finally came to an end.

SUGGESTED TEACHING STRATEGIES

1. **Preteaching Vocabulary (Basic)** You may wish to preteach the following important vocabulary terms: oasis (*page 17*); silt (*page 18*); hieroglyphics, papyrus (*page 19*); kingdom, monarchy, pharaoh, dynasty (*page 20*); empire, polytheism, monotheism (*page 22*). Have students name countries today that are monarchies. What religions are monotheistic?
2. **Understanding Words (Average/Group)** Reproduce the following scrambled words and their clues and distribute copies to the class.

1. gphicloyehrsi	A system of writing that uses pictures or symbols to indicate words or sounds
2. gdikonm	Another name for a monarchy
3. ymahnorc	A government headed by a king or queen
4. raphaoh	Title given to the ruler of Egypt
5. ynaydst	A family of rulers
6. premei	A form of government that unites different territories and peoples under one ruler
7. mthepoiyls	Belief in many gods

(Answers: 1-hieroglyphics, 2-kingdom, 3-monarchy, 4-pharaoh, 5-dynasty, 6-empire, 7-polytheism)

ENRICHMENT ACTIVITY

Researching Biography (Average/Group) Accounts of the lives of pharaohs and queens of Egypt provide students with an additional perspective on the era. Assign written or oral reports on one or more ancient Egyptian rulers. Leonard Cottrell's books, *Five Queens of Ancient Egypt* (Bobbs-Merrill) and *The Warrior Pharaohs* (Putnam), will be helpful. The exhibition of artifacts from Tutankhamen's tomb that toured the United States in 1980 and the Ramses exhibit that toured in 1987 stimulated many new books on the subject.

DAILY QUIZ

To assess student understanding of Section 1, give the class the following quiz. (Each item is worth 10 points.)

1. The silt left behind that provided the soil's fertility was referred to by Herodotus as the gift of what river? *(Nile)*
2. State three natural advantages enjoyed by the Nile Valley inhabitants. *(climate; flooding/natural resource; ore deposit/geographical location; barriers)*
3. What is the Egyptian word that describes the "sacred writings?" *(hieroglyphics)*
4. What did papyrus form when picked, sliced, and woven into a mat? *(the first paper)*
5. What is the title of the Egyptian king that literally means "great house?" *(pharaoh)*
6. (T or F) A dynasty is a family of rulers, with the right of rule passing normally from father to son or daughter. *(T)*
7. What were the two social classes of the Old Kingdom? *(upper class; pharaoh, nobility, priests/lower class; everyone else)*
8. Who utilized horses, chariots, and superior equipment to conquer and rule the Egyptians in 1730 B.C.? *(Hyksos)*
9. (T or F) Amenhotep IV moved the capital from Thebes to Tell el Amarna and changed the legal religion from polytheism to monotheism to limit the priests' influence on government. *(T)*
10. (T or F) The Egyptian barrier states along the eastern Mediterranean shore were difficult to rule and contributed to the erosion of the pharaoh's power. *(T)*

SUGGESTED ASSIGNMENTS

1. **Critical Thinking Worksheet (Basic)** Have students complete Critical Thinking Worksheet 3 in the TEACHER'S RESOURCEBANK™

2. **Geography Supplement (Basic)** Have students complete "Map Skills Worksheet: Using Latitude and Longitude" in the Geography Supplement of the TEACHER'S RESOURCEBANK™

Section (pages 24-27)

2 The Culture of Ancient Egypt Reached Impressive Heights

SECTION OVERVIEW

The Egyptians produced a stable culture in which agriculture and trade flourished. They produced outstanding art and architecture, and made discoveries in science and mathematics. Religion was important to the polytheistic Egyptians, who had great concern for the afterlife.

SUGGESTED TEACHING STRATEGIES

1. **Preteaching Vocabulary (Basic)** You may wish to preteach the following important vocabulary terms: caravan (*page 24*); scribe (*page 26*); mummification (*page 27*). Ask students how important they believe a scribe's tasks were.
2. **Classifying Information (Basic)** Have students list in their notebooks the advances in science, mathematics, and medicine of ancient Egypt. The list should include the following: 365-day calendar; numbering of years; number system based on 10; use of fractions; use of geometry for measurement; classification of diseases according to symptoms and prescribed treatments; use of herbs and drugs for treatment of disease.

ENRICHMENT ACTIVITIES

1. **Explaining Relationships (Basic)** Ask students to write a short paragraph explaining the relationship between the pyramids and the Egyptian belief in an afterlife. Ask for volunteers to read their papers to the class.
2. **Building a Model (Challenging)** Some students might enjoy making a model or drawing a diagram of a pyramid, a tomb, a temple, a public building, or the house of a noble or commoner. Several books with excellent illustrations include: Lionel Casson's *Ancient Egypt* (Time-Life); Helen and Richard Leacraft's *The Buildings of Ancient Egypt* (William R. Scott); Anne Millard's *Ancient Egypt* (Warwick Press); R. J. Unstead's *An Egyptian Town* (Warwick Press); and John Weeks's *The Pyramids* (Cambridge University Press).

DAILY QUIZ

To assess student understanding of Section 2, give the class the following quiz. (Each item is worth 10 points.)

1. List the crops grown by the Egyptians. (*cotton, flax, wheat, barley*)
2. (T or F) Merchants traveled individually from place to place across Middle Eastern deserts, riding mules and horses. (*F*)
3. The pharaohs built huge tombs called ________. (*pyramids*)
4. The Egyptians initiated each year with the appearance of the ________ to maintain the accuracy of their calendar. (*Sirius or the Dog Star*)
5. The Egyptians developed ________ to reestablish boundaries of fields after the floods and to construct pyramids and irrigation canals. (*geometry*)
6. (T or F) The scribes served as clerks, or record keepers. (*T*)
7. Name the Egyptian sacred animals/insect. (*cat, bull, crocodile, scarab, or beetle*)
8. This book was placed in the tomb with the dead to guard them from serpents, demons, and other dangers lurking in the afterlife. (*Book of the Dead*)
9. (T or F) Osiris was the despised Egyptian god who threatened the dead with eternal punishment. (*F*)
10. This pharaoh's tomb, discovered in 1922, taught us much about Egyptian life because it was untouched since the 1300s B.C. (*Tutankhamen*)

SUGGESTED ASSIGNMENTS

1. **Writing a Diary (Average/Group)** Have students prepare diary entries for a day in the life of a member of the royal family, a government official, a priest, a scribe, or a farmer in ancient Egypt. Call upon students to read their entries to the class. Students might choose to investigate issues such as class structure or the status of women.
2. **Researching a Topic (Challenging)** Have students interested in ancient Egyptian religion do further research. The results of their research may be presented in different ways: an essay, an oral report, paintings, or a bulletin board display. Some available sources are James Henry Breasted's *Development of Religion and Thought in Ancient Egypt* (Harper & Row) and Lionel Casson's *Ancient Egypt* (Time-Life).

Section (pages 27–32)

3 Sumerian Civilization Arose Along the Tigris and Euphrates Rivers

SECTION OVERVIEW

The earliest civilization in the Fertile Crescent arose in Sumer. The Sumerians developed a government organized around city-states. They engaged in farming and trade, developed educational and religious systems, produced cuneiform writing, and invented new architectural forms.

SUGGESTED TEACHING STRATEGIES

Preteaching Vocabulary (Basic) You may wish to preteach the following important vocabulary terms: city-state, cuneiform (*page 29*); arch, ziggurat (*page 30*). Ask students to compare the ziggurat and the pyramid. Ask: Do buildings exist in our modern cities that use these ancient forms of architecture? (*Transamerica Building pyramid in San Francisco; setbacks on many modern skyscrapers resemble ziggurats*)

2. **Organizing Information (Basic)** Have students list in their notebooks the Sumerian contributions in architecture, engineering, and science. After they have finished the assignment ask for volunteers to write the items on the chalkboard or an overhead projector. The list should include the arch, domes or vaults, use of the ramp, possible invention of the wheel, number system based on 60, circle divided into 360 degrees, 12-month calendar.

*3. **READING ABOUT HISTORY: Identifying Sources of Evidence (Basic)** To reinforce the skill lesson presented on page 31, have students describe how the ruins of a Sumerian ziggurat can be considered both a primary and a secondary source.

ENRICHMENT ACTIVITIES

1. **Creating a Model (Basic)** One way to increase students' appreciation of cuneiform writing is to let students try it themselves. Clay should be provided so that students can make their own tablets. Write numerous cuneiform signs on the chalkboard or an overhead projector. Many of the signs and samples of cuneiform tablets can be found in *History Begins at Sumer* (Doubleday), *The Sumerians* (University of Chicago Press), and *Cradle of Civilization* (Time-Life), all by Samuel Kramer. The clay must be flattened and the marks should be made with a pointed stick. Afterwards the clay should be dried in a kiln if possible, or left undisturbed for a few days until it hardens. You may choose to let students try to compose letters to each other using cuneiform writing. The receiver of the letter can then attempt to read it to the class.
2. **Oral Report (Average/Group)** Have students research and present oral reports on various aspects of Sumerian life. Some suggested topics include: Sumerian temples, gods and goddesses, burial ritual, warfare, farming, schools, social life, and status of women. Sources include: Jacquetta Hawkes's *The First Great Civilizations*, (Knopf); *The Epic of Man* (Time-Life); Elizabeth Lansing's *The Sumerians, Inventors and Builders* (McGraw-Hill). A fascinating story about the discovery of the many royal tombs at Ur can be found in Shirley Glubok's *Discovering the Royal Tombs at Ur* (Macmillan).
3. **Researching a Topic (Challenging)** Some students may choose to engage in further study of the development of writing. Zdenek Saltzmann's *Anthropology* (Harcourt Brace Jovanovich) provides an overview. More detailed sources include David Diringer's *Writing: Its Origins and Early History* (Praeger) and Gerd Fraenkel's *Writing Systems* (Ginn).

DAILY QUIZ

To assess student understanding of Section 3, give the class the following quiz. (Each item is worth 10 points.)

1. This region stretched in a crescent-shaped arc from Canaan to Sumer. (*Fertile Crescent*)
2. Name the two primary rivers located in the fertile region northeast of Sumer. (*Tigris and Euphrates*)
3. The Greek name for the northern section of the land between the two primary rivers of the Fertile Crescent is ________. (*Mesopotamia*)
4. List the three Sumerian city-state classes from upper to lower class. (*upper class: nobles, priests, government officials/middle class: merchants, artisans/lower class: peasants, slaves*)
5. Cuneiform, using wedge-shaped characters imprinted in a clay tablet with a stylus, is a form of ________. (*writing*)
6. List the crops or the domesticated animals Sumerians grew and raised in their culture. (*grain, vegetables, dates, flax; cows, sheep, goats, oxen, donkeys*)
7. (T or F) The Sumerians used sun-dried clay to build their structures, sometimes highlighted with the arch. (*T*)
8. The most striking Sumerian buildings were temples made in layers called ________. (*ziggurats*)
9. Name one important discovery Sumerians made. (*arch, ramp, sewers, numbers based on 60, 12-month calendar*)
10. Sumerians were polytheistic. How many gods did they believe in—one, a few, many, or none? (*many*)

SUGGESTED ASSIGNMENTS

1. **Critical Thinking Worksheet (Basic)** Have students complete Critical Thinking Worksheet 4 in the TEACHER'S RESOURCEBANK™.
2. **Geography Worksheet (Basic)** Have students complete "Using Maps for Different Purposes" in the Geography Supplement in the TEACHER'S RESOURCEBANK™.
3. **Skill Worksheet (Basic)** Have students complete Skill Worksheet 2 in the TEACHER'S RESOURCEBANK™.

Section 4 (pages 32–37)
Several Empires Were Established in the Fertile Crescent

SECTION OVERVIEW

After the downfall of the Sumerians, a succession of invading peoples settled in the Fertile Crescent. The first were the Babylonians, who lived under Hammurabi's code of laws. Next were the Hittites, the first to use iron extensively for weapons. The Assyrians followed. The Chaldeans overthrew the Assyrians but ruled briefly. The Persians established a great empire reaching from Egypt to the Indus River. They contributed Zoroastrianism to civilization.

SUGGESTED TEACHING STRATEGIES

1. **Preteaching Vocabulary (Basic)** You may wish to preteach the following important vocabulary terms: cavalry (*page 34*); mercenary (*page 35*). Ask: In what context do you hear the word

mercenary today? (*soldiers of fortune who fight in revolutionary situations*)

2. **Organizing a Class Discussion (Average/Group)** Organize the class into groups to discuss the following questions: Why was religion so important to early people? Why did people worship the forces of nature? Why do you think polytheism developed before monotheism? How do you explain the rise of priesthoods and temples? Have the groups share their findings with the rest of the class.

   (*Students' answers should include the following: People were trying to understand the forces of nature, sickness, death, and disasters—events that probably frightened them and over which they had no control. Thus the forces of nature were the first to be made deities. This accounts for the worship of many gods. The people who seemed able to influence the forces of nature, such as rulers and priests, were held in great esteem. Temples became important as places for worship and homes for the gods.*)

ENRICHMENT ACTIVITIES

1. **Illustrating Ideas (Basic)** Have each student prepare a letter from a ruler of Assyria or Persia to a governor in a distant part of the empire. The letter should contain instructions in one or more of the following areas: collection of taxes, care of the army, administration of justice, repair of roads, supervision of postal service, dealing with conquered people.
2. **Researching Ideas (Average/Group)** Have interested students prepare written reports on the Hittites or the Persians. Have them examine as sources two volumes in the "Emergence of Man" series (Time-Life): *The Empire Builders* is about the Hittites. A student could present a report on Hattusa, the Hittite capital, or on the battle of Kadesh, in which Rameses II fought the Hittites. *The Persians* contains accounts of the Persian government, social life, and the Zoroastrian religion.

DAILY QUIZ

To assess student understanding of Section 4, give the class the following quiz. (Each item is worth 10 points.)

1. This great Babylonian king devised a code of laws and conquered Mesopotamia. (*Hammurabi*)
2. (T or F) Babylonian women could own property and work as merchants and traders much like the Egyptian women. (*T*)
3. These nomadic people were the first to make use of iron for weapons and a code of laws. (*Hittites*)
4. (T or F) The Assyrians used chariots, treated conquered people kindly and permitted limited self-government in conquered lands. (*F*)
5. (T or F) The Assyrians built roads, established a postal system, hired mercenaries, and built Nineveh. (*T*)
6. (T or F) Nineveh included a huge defensive wall and a large library. (*T*)
7. (T or F) The Persians, led by Nebuchadnezzar, built the Hanging Gardens. (*F*)
8. This group conquered the Assyrians and developed a kingdom in present-day Iran. (*Medes/Persians*)
9. (T or F) Cyrus, Darius, and Xerxes were all great Zoroastrian rulers who conquered the Hittites. (*F*)
10. List three things the Persians developed during their empire period. (*wise administration that heeded customs of local peoples, fair system of justice, cultural diffusion over royal roads, Zoroastrian religion*)

SUGGESTED ASSIGNMENTS

1. **Critical Thinking Worksheet (Basic)** Have students complete Critical Thinking Worksheet 5 in the TEACHER'S RESOURCEBANK™
2. **Profile Worksheet (Basic)** Have students complete Profile Worksheet 2 in the TEACHER'S RESOURCEBANK™

Section 5 (pages 38–45)

Phoenicians, Lydians, and Hebrews Made Lasting Contributions

SECTION OVERVIEW

Three peoples in the Fertile Crescent, the Phoenicians, Lydians, and Hebrews, had great impact on future civilization. The Phoenicians were seafaring traders who developed an alphabet that became the model for later Western alphabets. The Lydians, a trading people, first used coined money instead of barter in the exchange of goods and services. The Hebrews maintained their identity throughout years of slavery and conquest. Ethical monotheism was their greatest contribution to Western civilization

SUGGESTED TEACHING STRATEGIES

1. **Preteaching Vocabulary (Basic)** You may wish to preteach the following important vocabulary terms: barter, money economy (*page* 39); Ten Commandments (*page* 42); prophet (*page* 43); ethical monotheism (*page* 45). Ask students if they can think of uses of barter today.
2. **Analyzing Ideas (Basic)** The prophet Ezekiel described the wealth of Phoenicia in glowing terms. Distribute copies of this reading (Ezekiel 27:12-19) to students.

   "Tarshis traded with you, so great was your wealth, exchanging silver, iron, tin, and lead for your wares. Javan, Tubal, and Meschech were also traders with you, exchanging slaves and articles of bronze for your goods. From Beth-togamah horses, steeds, and mules were exchanged for your wares.

   The Rhodanites trafficked with you; many coastlands traded with you; ivory tusks and ebony wood they gave you for payment.

   Edom traded with you, so many were your products, exchanging garments, purple, embroidered cloth, fine linen, coral, and rubies for your wares.

Judah and the land of Israel trafficked with you, exchanging Minnith wheat, figs, honey, oil, and balm for your goods.

Damascus traded with you, so great was your wealth, exchanging Helbon wine and Zahar wood."

Ask students to name the items traded, and write them on the chalkboard or an overhead projector. Ask: Why did the Phoenicians rely so heavily on trade? What did they export in return?

ENRICHMENT ACTIVITIES

1. **Writing an Essay (Average/Group)** Have students write a paragraph describing why the Hebrews changed their idea of God. How did the Hebrew concept of the nature of God differ from other ancient religions? Students may want to reread the subsection "Judaism" on page 45 before writing.
2. **Researching (Challenging)** An important archaeological find of recent times was the discovery of the Dead Sea Scrolls. Have interested students prepare an oral report on the Dead Sea Scrolls, summarizing their contents and the information they convey about life in ancient Palestine. Suggest that students use encyclopedias or other books in the library for sources.

DAILY QUIZ

To assess student understanding of Section 5, give the class the following quiz. (Each item is worth 10 points.)

1. The people who built seagoing ships and established city-states along the eastern Mediterranean were called ________ . (*Phoenicians*)
2. (T or F) The Phoenicians had many natural resources to help the farmers and craftsworkers. (*F*)
3. The Phoenicians became ________ because the region from which they came had little fertile land. (*traders, merchants, sailors, artisans*)
4. (T or F) The Phoenicians established many colonies throughout the Mediterranean. (*T*)
5. What was the most important Phoenician contribution to Western culture? (*alphabet*)
6. Name the two parts of Canaan after the Hebrews conquered it. (*Israel and Judah*)
7. ________ was a Hebrew leader who led the Israelites out of Egyptian slavery into Canaan. (*Moses*)
8. (T or F) The Jews followed the Mosaic laws, or the Ten Commandments, which they had received on Mt. Sinai. (*T*)
9. Name the great Hebrew literary work which contains 39 books composed of history, poetry, law, religion, and prophecy. (*Old Testament*)
10. (T or F) The Jewish religion emphasized ethics, or proper conduct, and could be called ethical monotheism. (*T*)

SUGGESTED ASSIGNMENTS

1. **Geography Worksheet (Basic)** Have students complete "Map Skills Worksheet: Identifying Direction, Scale, and Legend" in the TEACHER'S RESOURCEBANK™.
2. **Review Worksheet (Basic)** Have students complete Review Worksheet 2 in the TEACHER'S RESOURCEBANK™.

For suggested lesson plan, additional teaching strategies, enrichment activities, daily quizzes, and suggested assignments, see pages 15A–15F.

Introducing the Chapter
Geography played a key role in the appearance of the river valley civilizations. To illustrate this importance, have the class speculate on the kind of geography best suited for the development of a civilization. First, ask students to review the basic needs people must fulfill in order to survive *(food, shelter, clothing)*. List these on the chalkboard or an overhead projector. Then discuss the resources available in various geographic areas, such as river valleys, forests, and deserts, that would enable people to meet these needs. Could civilization have started in places other than the river areas? Ask students to suggest why this did not occur. *(Reasons might include land barriers, scarcity of game, and lack of arable land.)*

Chapter Objectives
After studying Chapter 2, students will be able to:

1. List the Nile Valley's geographic advantages for settlement.
2. Summarize ancient Egyptian cultural and social developments.
3. Name the crops the Egyptians harvested.
4. Describe Egyptian developments in archaeology, art, science, mathematics, education, and religion.
5. Locate the Fertile Crescent and state why it was important to several ancient civilizations.

CHAPTER 2

Great Civilizations Developed in the Middle East

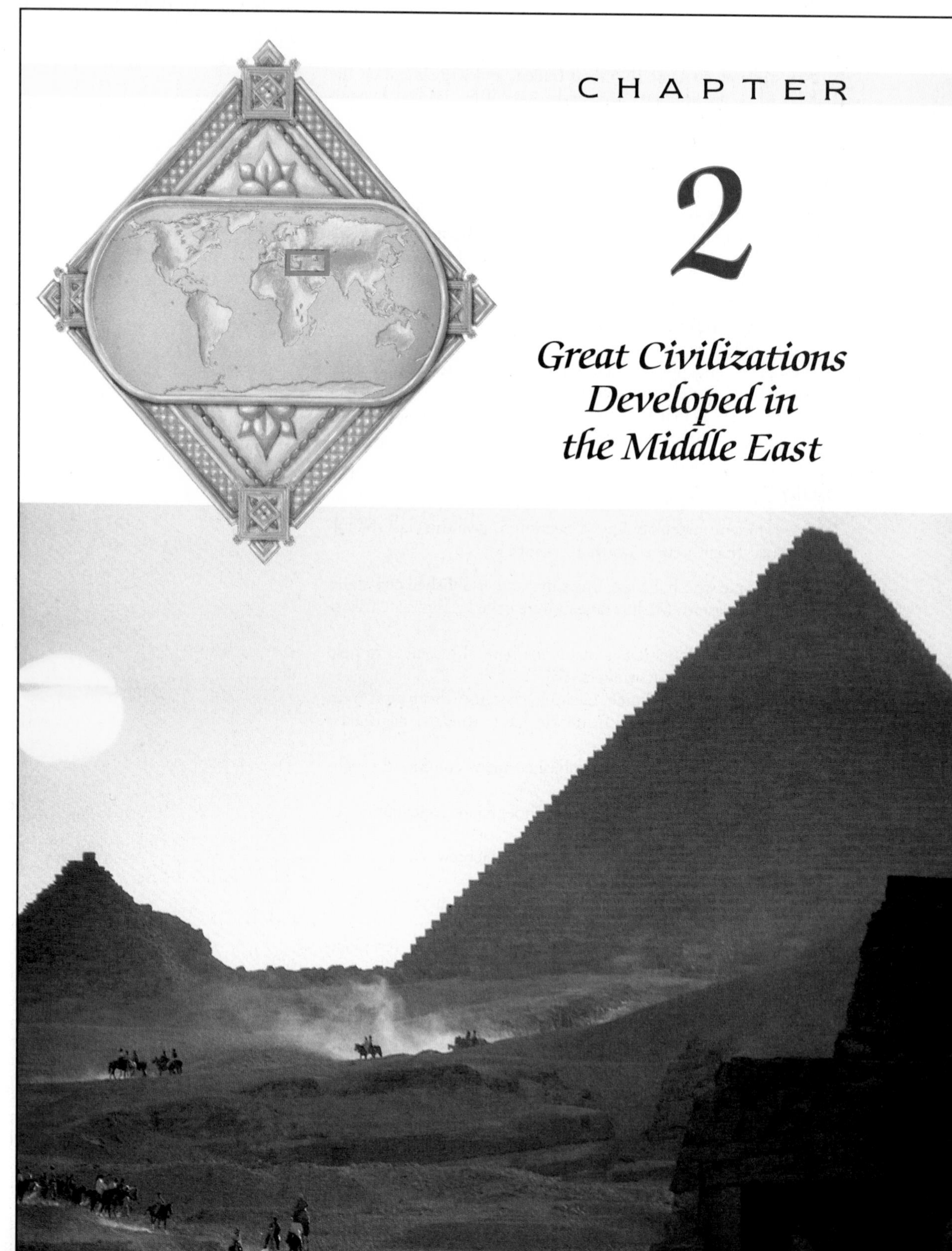

● Point out that the top inscriptions are written in hieroglyphics, the middle inscriptions are written in demotic, and the bottom inscriptions are written in Greek.

■ An ancient Egyptian "book" is actually a roll of paper. Some papyrus rolls were over 100 feet (31 meters) long.

1B, 2A, 2B

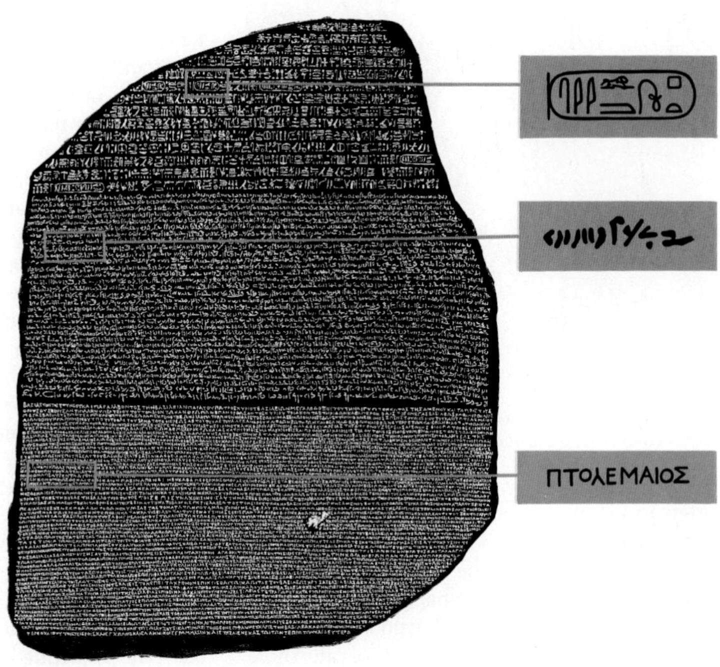

Learning from Pictures *Scholars translated the Rosetta Stone and discovered that the way the birds in the script faced determined whether the symbols should be read from left to right or right to left.* ●

Early Steps Toward Civilization

People have lived in the long valley of the Nile River since earliest times. Archaeologists have discovered Paleolithic remains in the Nile Valley, and a Neolithic culture probably developed there about 6000 B.C.

By about 3800 B.C. the people of the Nile Valley began to take important steps along the road to civilization. They learned to use copper to make needles, chisels, and jewelry. They discovered how to make bronze, the strong alloy of copper and tin. Evidence indicates that they invented the potter's wheel, a rotating disk that made it easier to make round pots and jars.

Egyptian writing. Writing developed along with the other major achievements of Egyptian civilization. By about 3000 B.C. the Egyptians had worked out a system of writing called **hieroglyphics** (hy • ruh • GLIF • iks). The word comes from the Greek words *hieros,* meaning "sacred," and *glyphe,* meaning "carving." Hieroglyphic writing used more than 600 hieroglyphic signs, pictures, or symbols to indicate words or sounds. The Egyptians did not develop a true alphabet, but they did progress toward one. They developed 24 signs that each stood for only one sound—all consonants. In addition, about 80 signs contained two consonants. They developed no signs for vowels.

At first Egyptians carved hieroglyphics on slate and ivory, but this involved a long and difficult process. Searching for a better material on which to write, they discovered how to use the papyrus plant that grew in the marshes near the Nile. The Egyptians cut the stem of the plant into long, thin slices. They then placed the slices together and ■ moistened and pounded them to form a mat with a smooth surface. The Egyptians called this product **papyrus,** from which we get our word *paper.*

Egyptians wrote on papyrus with ink made from soot, water, and vegetable gum, a sticky juice from certain trees and plants. The Egyptians diluted the gum with water before mixing it with soot. They used a sharpened reed as a pen.

Solving the hieroglyphic puzzle. Modern scholars learned to read the language of the ancient Egyptians through a clever bit of detective work. In A.D. 1798 a French army commanded by Napoleon Bonaparte invaded Egypt. The next year a French officer discovered a large stone with inscriptions

1B, 1C, 2A, 2B

Learning from Pictures *The ancient Egyptians used many symbols to reflect their beliefs. The ankh above symbolizes life and immortality.*

written in Greek, hieroglyphics, and an Egyptian writing called *demotic.* The Rosetta Stone, named for the Rosetta branch of the Nile Delta where the officer stumbled upon the stone, provided the key to the language of the ancient Egyptians.

Scholars guessed that the text of all three kinds of writing had the same meaning. Almost 23 years after the discovery of the Rosetta Stone, a French language expert, Jean François Champollion (shan • paw • LYAWN), solved the mystery. Beginning with the Greek, which he could read, he deciphered the hieroglyphic inscription that described honors granted by the priesthood to the ruler Ptolemy (TAHL • uh • mee) V in 196 B.C. Champollion went on to translate the hieroglyphic symbols and establish the principles by which all other hieroglyphics could be read. Because scholars could now decipher hieroglyphics, they could read eyewitness accounts of Egypt's glorious history.

A United Kingdom

Over the centuries strong leaders united early Egyptian settlements to form two kingdoms—Upper Egypt and Lower Egypt. (A king or queen heads a **kingdom,** one of the earliest forms of government. Another name for *kingdom* is **monarchy.**) Upper Egypt lay farther south from the Mediterranean Sea, along the upper Nile River. Lower Egypt lay to the north, nearer the sea (see map, page 18).

Then, about 3100 B.C., a ruler known as Menes (MEE • neez) united all Egypt into one kingdom. Menes and his successors crushed rebellions, gained new territory, regulated irrigation, and encouraged trade and prosperity.

Much of the power of these rulers came from their roles as religious as well as political leaders. The people regarded them as gods. In later years rulers took the title **pharaoh,** which means "great house," after the palace in which they lived.

The pharaohs' position as gods placed them far above ordinary people. They led the government and served as judges, high priests, and generals of the armies. Although the pharaohs had absolute, or unlimited, power, their duties included protecting and caring for their people.

Menes founded a **dynasty,** or family of rulers in which the right to rule passes on within the family, usually from father to son or daughter. This hereditary rule ends only when a family is overthrown, or when it dies out so that there is no one left to become ruler. In more than 2,500 years, beginning with the time of Menes and continuing to about 300 B.C., about 30 Egyptian dynasties rose and fell. Historians divide this span of time into four periods—the Old Kingdom, the Middle Kingdom, the New Kingdom, and the Late Period.

The Old Kingdom

The Old Kingdom—probably the greatest period of Egyptian history—existed from about 2700 B.C. to 2181 B.C. Many important discoveries in science and the arts took place during this time. For example, Egyptians of the Old Kingdom built the largest pyramids, which still stand as symbols of the glory of Egyptian civilization. For this reason historians sometimes call the period of the Old Kingdom the Pyramid Age.

In the early dynasties of the Old Kingdom, Egyptian society included only two main groups of people: (1) an upper class—the pharaoh, the royal family, and the priests and officials who helped govern the country—and (2) a lower class—everyone else. The majority of this lower class consisted of peasants, or farmers. They owed the pharaoh their services, such as duty in the army or work on the irrigation system or on the pyramids and public buildings.

As time passed, officials in the upper class gradually became a hereditary group of nobles. Toward the end of the Old Kingdom, the pharaohs grew weaker and the nobles grew stronger. For 125 years

20

after the end of this period, civil wars divided the country as rivals claimed the throne.

The Middle Kingdom

In about 2000 B.C. a strong new line of pharaohs united Egypt again, beginning a period known as the Middle Kingdom. These pharaohs restored order and prosperity for a while. However, the difficulty of making and carrying out all decisions by themselves defeated all but the strongest rulers. Meanwhile, other officials became more powerful in the government. They also became wealthy. Once again the rise of a hereditary class of nobles and priests weakened the power of the pharaoh.

The Middle Kingdom ended in disorder around 1780 B.C., the victim of rivalries, conflicts, and the division of power. Then, about 1730 B.C., much of Egypt fell under the rule of an Asiatic people—the Hyksos (HIHK • sohs)—whose horse-drawn chariots overwhelmed the donkey carts the Egyptians used.

The story of the Hyksos' rule in Egypt provides an excellent example of differing interpretations of history. Historians investigate past events and interpret these events based on the evidence they find. Often, historians disagree as to exactly what happened.

According to Egyptian records written hundreds of years later, the brutal, warlike Hyksos savagely invaded Lower Egypt. As the Egyptian priest Manetho recorded in about 200 B.C.:

> "Unexpectedly from the regions of the East invaders of obscure race marched in confidence of victory against our land. By main force they seized it without striking a blow; and having overpowered the rulers of the land, they then burned our cities ruthlessly, razed to the ground the temples of the gods, and treated all the natives with a cruel hostility, massacring some and leading into slavery the wives and children of others."

Based on this account and others from ancient Egyptian sources, some scholars believe that the Hyksos invaded and conquered Egypt.

Other scholars, however, point out that little evidence confirms the destruction of Egyptian temples during this period. They discount Egyptian stories of the Hyksos' brutality as explanations for why the Hyksos were able to conquer Egypt. After all, how could a land ruled by a god fall under foreign rule unless those foreigners had mighty armies?

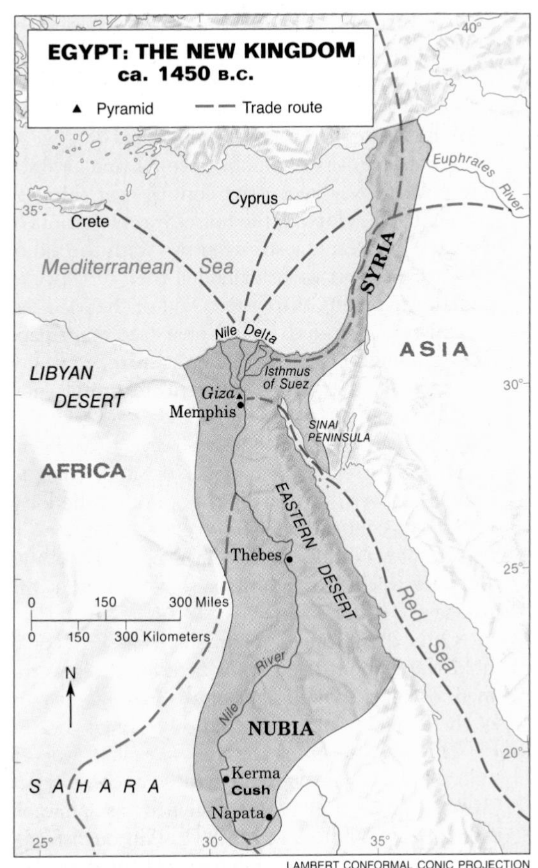

Learning from Maps *The New Kingdom expanded Egypt's borders. Why did the New Kingdom expand to the northeast rather than to the west?*

because of deserts

These scholars believe nomadic Hyksos migrated into the Nile Delta about 1800 B.C. In the confusion following the collapse of the Middle Kingdom, the Hyksos emerged as the most powerful people in the region and ruled most of Lower Egypt for about 150 years.

The New Kingdom

Although historians disagree about how the Hyksos came to rule Egypt, all agree that the proud Egyptians despised their foreign—and in Egyptian eyes, inferior—rulers. Eventually, rulers of Upper Egypt forged an army, rebelled against the Hyksos,

21

1B, 2A, 2B, a4F

Priests of Amon became infuriated, and people's religious beliefs could not be changed on command.

and drove them from the country. A number of strong pharaohs who lived in the city of Thebes far up the Nile ruled a reunited Egypt. The period in which they ruled—from about 1550 B.C. to about 1085 B.C.—is called the New Kingdom.

For a time, the pharaohs once more had absolute power. They kept strict control over the government and, adopting the horse-drawn chariots of the Hyksos, created a strong army. With the aid of this army, the pharaohs extended their territory to include land along the eastern end of the Mediterranean Sea and south into Nubia (see map, page 21). In doing so, they created an **empire,** a form of government that unites different territories and peoples under one ruler.

Like many other peoples, however, the Egyptians found it easier to conquer territory than to keep and govern it. Usually they allowed the local prince of a conquered region to act as governor. To be sure of his loyalty and obedience, they took his son back to Egypt as a hostage to be trained at the palace of Thebes.

Only the strongest pharaohs, however, could hold the empire together. Whenever the government of Egypt showed signs of weakness, some part of the empire would revolt and try to break away.

Hatshepsut rules Egypt. The first woman ruler about whom we have written records, Hatshepsut (hat • SHEP • soot), reigned as pharaoh from about 1500 B.C. to 1480 B.C. Although Egyptian queens often gained fame as wives of kings, few ever became pharaoh. Hatshepsut, however, proved an able ruler. More interested in the welfare of her country than in war and conquest, she ordered the construction of temples to the gods and other public buildings.

Hatshepsut first ruled with her husband, Thutmose (thoot • MOH • suh) II, who was also her half-brother. This marriage illustrates a unique custom of Egyptian rulers. As a god, the pharaoh could not marry an ordinary human being. Instead, he usually married his sister or half-sister. After Thutmose II died, his son, Thutmose III, took his place, but Hatshepsut continued to rule. Angry at Hatshepsut for refusing to give him power, Thutmose III had her name removed from all public monuments after she died.

Amenhotep and religious revolution. The pharaoh Amenhotep (ah • muhn • HOH • tep) IV ruled from about 1379 B.C. to 1362 B.C. Neither a famous conqueror nor a good ruler, Amenhotep is remembered because he brought about a social and religious revolution.

Learning from Pictures *Nefertiti supported her husband, Akhenaton, in his social and religious revolution. Why did their religious reforms fail?*

Before Amenhotep became pharaoh, Egyptians believed in the existence of many gods. We call such a belief **polytheism** (PAHL • i • thee • iz • uhm), from the Greek words *polys,* meaning "many," and *theos,* meaning "god." The greatest of the Egyptian gods was Amon.

Amenhotep tried to change Egyptian religion. He believed in only one god—the sun, symbolized by a sun disk called the Aton—and that the pharaoh was the god's earthly son. We call this belief in only one god **monotheism** (MAHN • uh • thee • iz • uhm), from the Greek word *monos,* meaning "one," plus *theos.* To honor the Aton, pharaoh Amenhotep changed his own name to Akhenaton (ahk • uh • NAHT • uhn), which means "he who is beneficial to Aton."

The priests of Amon had become so powerful that they interfered in all affairs. To help break

22

● Bacteria has destroyed many of the paintings in the tomb. Although scientists can kill the bacteria, they cannot restore the paintings.

History Through the Arts

METALWORKING

Funeral Mask of a Pharaoh

One of the most beautiful treasures in the world is this life-sized funeral mask of the pharaoh Tutankhamen. The discovery of his tomb in 1922 captured the imagination of people around the world. What was extraordinary about the find was that the tomb's treasures had not been stolen. The tomb contained more than 5,000 works of art that revealed many aspects of Egyptian life.

● The mask is made of beaten gold inlaid with jewels and colored glass. It shows Tutankhamen as the handsome youth he was when he died more than 3,200 years ago at the age of 18. The decorative beard on the mask is a symbol of Osiris, the god of the dead. On the headdress are symbols of the vulture and cobra goddesses. They represent Upper and Lower Egypt.

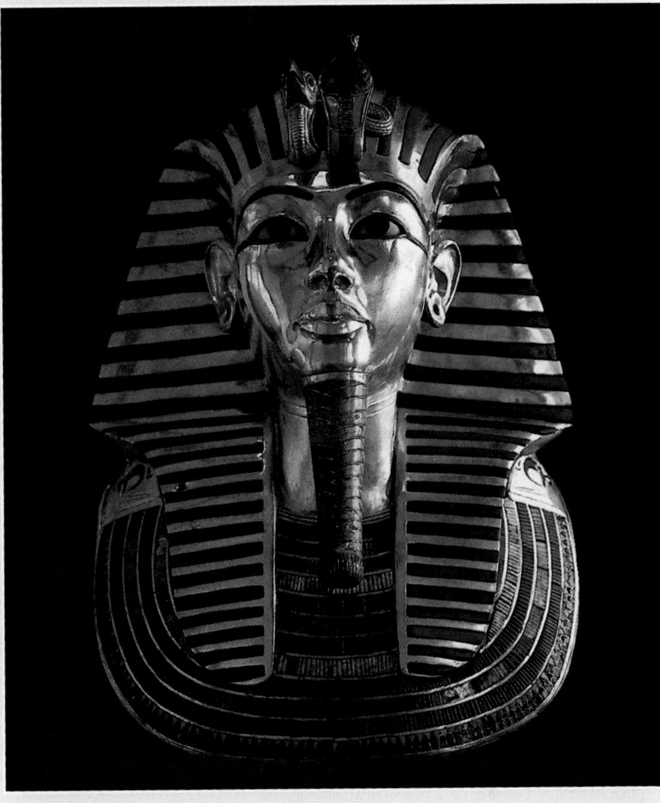

their power, Akhenaton moved his capital from Thebes, the site of the great temple of Amon, to a new city, Tell el Amarna. At Tell el Amarna, Akhenaton devoted his time to religion and neglected the ruling of the empire.

Akhenaton's actions infuriated the priests of Amon. The wealth that formerly came to them at their great temple of Thebes now went to the temple of the new god in the new capital. Their easy life suddenly ended. Appointments to high positions, which formerly went to the priests of Amon, now went to followers of Aton.

Akhenaton learned that he could not change all his people's religious beliefs by command. A bitter struggle between pharaoh and priests disrupted Egypt during the later years of his reign. When Akhenaton died, the priests of Amon reestablished their power, and the religious and cultural upheaval that Akhenaton had begun ended. His successor, Tutankhamen (too • tahn • KAHM • uhn), moved the capital back to Thebes. Polytheism was reinstated and the priests of Amon regained their influence.

After the death of Akhenaton, few strong pharaohs ruled Egypt. Ramses II, however, was a powerful leader who ruled from about 1304 B.C. to 1237 B.C. and held Egypt and the empire intact. His successors could not maintain the empire or prevent corruption in the government. Slowly Egypt slipped into the Late Period, a period of decline.

The Late Period

Beginning about 1100 B.C., Egypt grew steadily weaker. The empire crumbled, and foreign invaders, including the Nubians, the Assyrians, and the Persians, ravaged Egypt. Even during these times, however, dynasties of Egyptian pharaohs continued to reign. It was not until the 300s B.C. that native rule in Egypt finally came to an end.

SECTION 1

Closure

Of all the ancient civilizations of the Middle East, that of Egypt survived the longest and under the most peaceable conditions. Ask students what the Egyptian government did to change the lives of many Egyptian peasants, who had previously lived much as their ancestors had 5,000 years earlier.

Review Answers

1. ***oasis:*** place in the desert with irrigation or an underground spring; ***silt:*** fertile soil carried as sediment in river water; ***hieroglyphics:*** Egyptian system of writing that uses signs, pictures, and symbols to indicate words or sounds; ***papyrus:*** Egyptians made paper from this reed plant that grew in Nile marshes; ***kingdom:*** one of earliest forms of government, headed by king or queen; ***monarchy:*** another name for kingdom; ***pharaoh:*** Egyptian ruler's title, which means "great house"; ***dynasty:*** family of rulers; ***empire:*** form of government that unites different territories and people under one ruler; ***polytheism:*** belief in the existence of many gods; ***monotheism:*** belief in the existence of one god
2. ***Menes:*** ruler who united Upper and Lower Egypt; ***Hyksos:*** Asiatic invaders who ruled Lower Egypt for more than a century; ***Hatshepsut:*** first Egyptian female ruler of historic times; ***Amenhotep IV:*** began

1B, 1C, 2A, 2B, a4A, A4F, a4G, a4H

social and religious revolution in Egypt; changed own name to Akhenaton; ***Tutankhamen:*** successor to Akhenaton who reintroduced polytheism; ***Ramses II:*** one of the last powerful pharaohs to maintain the Egyptian empire
3. ***Egypt:*** area in northeast Africa that was site of ancient civilization; ***Nile River:*** flows through Egypt and empties into the Mediterranean; ***Isthmus of Suez:*** land bridge between Asia and Africa; ***Upper Egypt:*** southern section of Egypt, farthest away from the Mediterranean; ***Lower Egypt:*** northern Egypt near Mediterranean Sea; ***Nubia:*** region located along the Nile in present-day Ethiopia; ***Thebes:*** Egyptian capital located in Upper Egypt
4. Without the Nile, civilization in Egypt would have been impossible. The silt left behind by the yearly floods renewed the soil so the farmers could continue producing many crops.
5. A sunny, frost-free climate; prevailing winds for sailing up and down the Nile; deposits of clay, granite, sandstone, and limestone for building; deserts and seas for natural protection against invaders
6. (a) Akhenaton introduced the idea of monotheism based on the sun god Aton. He may have wanted to break the influence of the priests in all affairs. **(b)** The priests of Amon objected because they lost their power and because the worship of Aton denied the existence of other deities.

SECTION 1 REVIEW

1. **Define** oasis, silt, hieroglyphics, papyrus, kingdom, monarchy, pharaoh, dynasty, empire, polytheism, monotheism
2. **Identify** Menes, Hyksos, Hatshepsut, Amenhotep IV, Tutankhamen, Ramses II
3. **Locate** Egypt, Nile River, Isthmus of Suez, Upper Egypt, Lower Egypt, Nubia, Thebes
4. **Interpreting Ideas** Why is Herodotus' statement "All Egypt is the gift of the Nile" an accurate description?
5. **Understanding Ideas** In addition to the Nile River, what are the natural advantages of the Nile Valley?
6. **Summarizing Ideas** **(a)** What were the new ideas taught by Akhenaton? **(b)** Why was there opposition to Akhenaton's religious reforms?

2 The Culture of Ancient Egypt Reached Impressive Heights

Although dynasties rose and fell, the remarkably stable Egyptian culture extended over many centuries. This stability resulted partly from favorable conditions, particularly the regular Nile floods and Egypt's protected geographic location.

Farming and Trade

Farmland in Egypt was divided into large estates. Peasants did most of the farming, using crude hoes or wooden plows. The peasants, however, kept only part of the crop. The rest went to the pharaoh for rents and taxes.

Wheat and barley ranked as the chief grain crops. Farmers grew flax to be spun and woven into linen. They also raised cotton, as important an Egyptian crop in ancient times as it is today, to be woven into cloth.

Ancient Egypt produced more food than its people required. The Egyptians traded the surplus with other peoples for products that Egypt needed. Egyptians were among the first to build seagoing ships. These ships sailed into the Mediterranean and Aegean seas, the Red Sea, and along the African coast. On land, merchants riding donkeys and camels joined **caravans**—groups of people traveling together for safety over long distances—into western Asia and deep into Africa (see map, page 21).

Social Classes

For the most part, rigid divisions separated Egyptian social classes. Although people in the lower

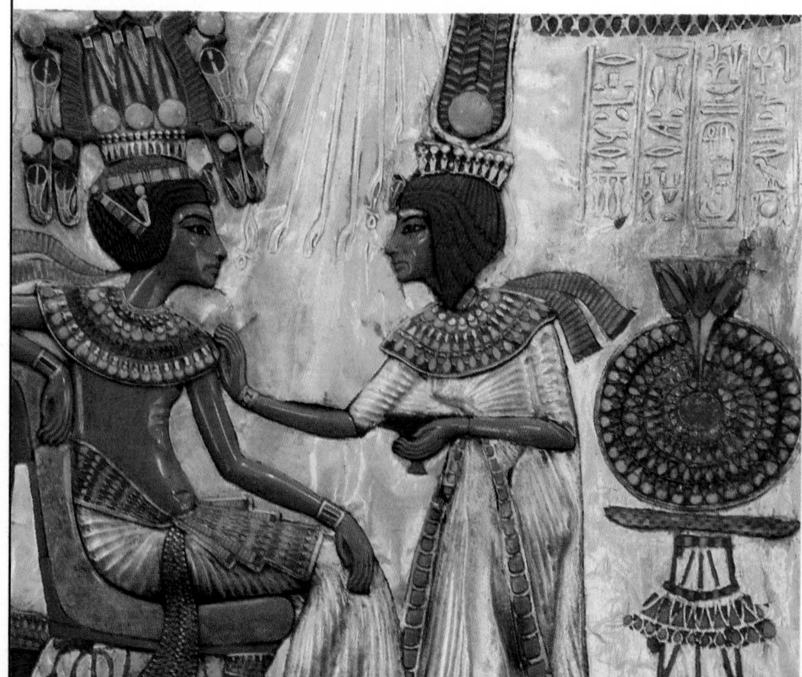

Learning from Pictures
The upper class, or nobles, in ancient Egypt followed many rituals. This painting depicts a wife anointing her husband.

● Pollution is rapidly destroying the Sphinx. Although scientists are trying to solve the problem, they have yet to find a solution.

CONNECTIONS: THEN AND NOW

Cotton

The painted figures on ancient Egyptian temple walls (below and right) and mummy cases wear draped garments of woven cotton cloth. Egypt has long been a major source of cotton, which is second only to food as the most important agricultural product in the world today. Egypt's warm climate and the irrigation provided by the Nile River combine to produce a highly desirable type of cotton. Because of its high quality, Egyptian cotton is exported throughout the world.

Cotton probably appeared first in India around 3000 B.C. Evidence also indicates that it existed long ago in Peru and in what is now Arizona. Some kinds of cotton are named after the places where they originated. For example, the cotton we know as madras is named after the port of Madras in India.

The fabric woven from the fluffy blossoms of the cotton plant absorbs moisture and remains cool even in hot weather. It is so comfortable that manufacturers today use it in clothing of all kinds, from pajamas to jeans. Cotton is used in many other products, too, such as bandages, life vests, and the stuffing for sofas. Its popularity spans thousands of years, and the demand for cotton is now greater than it has ever been.

class sometimes could improve their status, they almost never entered the ranks of the upper class.

Women, however, enjoyed many rights and ranked as the equals of their husbands in social and business affairs. An Egyptian woman could own property in her own right and could leave it to her daughter. In many ways, Egyptian women at that time had more privileges than women in other cultures of the Middle East.

Architecture and the Arts

When you think of Egypt, you probably first think of the huge stone figure of the Sphinx and the majestic pyramids, all of which still stand after nearly 5,000 years. Early Greek travelers named the huge limestone beast crouched in the sand near the present-day village of Giza the Great Sphinx. The statue has the 240-foot (73-meter) body of a lion, stands 66 feet (20 meters) tall, and has a human face measuring 13 feet (4 meters) across. Thought to be about 4,500 years old, the Great Sphinx represents the ancient Egyptian sun god. ●

The Egyptians built the pyramids as tombs for the pharaohs. Most of the 80 or so pyramids that still stand are clustered in groups along the west bank of the Nile. The best known soar above the scorching sands at Giza and include the Great Pyramid, which dates from about 2600 B.C. This gigantic structure measures more than half a mile (800 meters) in circumference at the base and is 450 feet (137 meters) high. It consists of more than 2 million blocks of stone, each of which weighs about 2.5 tons (2.3 metric tons).

SECTION 2

Focus/Motivation
Paintings and other forms of art can tell us a great deal about civilization. The pictures on pages 24 and 25 provide a glimpse of Egyptian life. Before students read the captions, have them identify the various aspects of Egyptian life portrayed in the pictures. Point out that they will learn more about Egyptian life as they study this section.

Presentation
Summarizing Ideas (Average/Group)
The ancient Egyptians made many contributions to civilization. Have the students list in their notebooks some of these major contributions. This list should include advances in medicine, art, architecture, education, and religion. Ask students to volunteer to read their list to the class and have a class discussion on each of these lists.

1B, 2A, 2B, a4A

SECTION 2

Closure

Other ancient civilizations believed in an afterlife, but none surpassed the Egyptians in making such elaborate preparations for it. Ask: What did Egyptians do for their dead? *(embalmed)*

Review Answers

1. *caravan:* groups of people with pack animals who traveled together for safety over long distances; ***scribe:*** clerk who would read or write. training of whom was focus of education in Egypt; ***mummification:*** treating the body with substances so it would remain dry and preserved for centuries
2. *Giza:* site of the Great Sphinx and pyramids
3. The Egyptians developed a base-10 number system, used fractions, whole numbers, and geometry. The Egyptians also invented the lunar calendar, studied the human body, treated illness with herbs and drugs, and preserved bodies.
4. (a) Egyptians built pyramids as tombs for the pharaohs. **(b)** Egyptians believed in life after death for everyone, including animals. They mummified the body so its soul could travel to the Realm of the Dead. Osiris judged the soul and placed it on a great scale to be weighed against the feather of truth. If the scales balanced, the soul could live in eternal happiness. If the scales did not balance,

The building of these pyramids obviously required skillful engineering. Egyptian architects and engineers ranked among the best in the ancient world. They built ramps, or sloping walkways, along which thousands of slaves pushed or pulled enormous stones into place. They also used levers for moving heavy objects.

The Egyptians perfected other art forms as well. In addition to large-scale works, sculptors also made small, lifelike statues of kings and sacred animals from copper, bronze, stone, or wood.

Egyptians decorated many of their buildings with paintings showing everyday life. Scenes included artisans at work, farmers harvesting grain, and people enjoying banquets. Egyptians developed a distinctive way of drawing the human figure. They showed the head in profile, the shoulders facing forward, and the feet in profile. Despite this angular, somewhat stiff interpretation, the surviving paintings provide colorful examples of the Egyptian enjoyment of life.

Science and Mathematics

Early in their history the Egyptians invented a lunar calendar, that is, one based on the moon's movements. Such a calendar caused difficulties because it did not fill the entire year. Then, somewhere in the Nile Valley, someone noticed that a very bright star began to appear above the horizon just before the floods came. The time between one rising of this star, which we now call Sirius, the Dog Star, and the next was 365 days, almost exactly a full year. The ancient Egyptians based their year on this cycle, dividing it into 12 months of 30 days each. This system left them with five extra days, which they used for holidays and feasting.

Numbering the years posed no great problem. At first, the Egyptians named years for an outstanding event—the year of the great flood or the year the locusts swarmed over the fields. Later, people used the years of the reigns of pharaohs to classify years; for example, the first, second, or twentieth year of the reign of a certain pharaoh. Using this method, we can trace the yearly record in Egypt to about 2780 B.C. Some historians believe that this is the earliest recorded date that can be firmly established in terms of our own system of dating.

The Egyptians developed a number system based on 10, similar to the decimal system we use today, and used fractions as well as whole numbers. They also used geometry to calculate how to restore the boundaries of fields after floods and to determine how to lay out canals and irrigation ditches.

The Egyptians also made discoveries in medicine. They knew a great deal about the human body and used this knowledge in treating illnesses and in preserving bodies. *The Book of Healing Diseases,* written during the Old Kingdom, classified diseases according to symptoms and also prescribed treatments. Although the treatments included some "magic spells," many scientifically specified the use of herbs and medicine.

Education and Religion

The Egyptians could not have gathered and passed on their knowledge without a system of education. Religious instruction formed an important part of Egyptian education, and schools were usually in temples. Most education, however, focused on training clerks, or **scribes,** for the government.

Learning from Pictures *These papyrus-shaped pillars form the Great Hall of Pillars at the Temple of Amon in Luxor.*

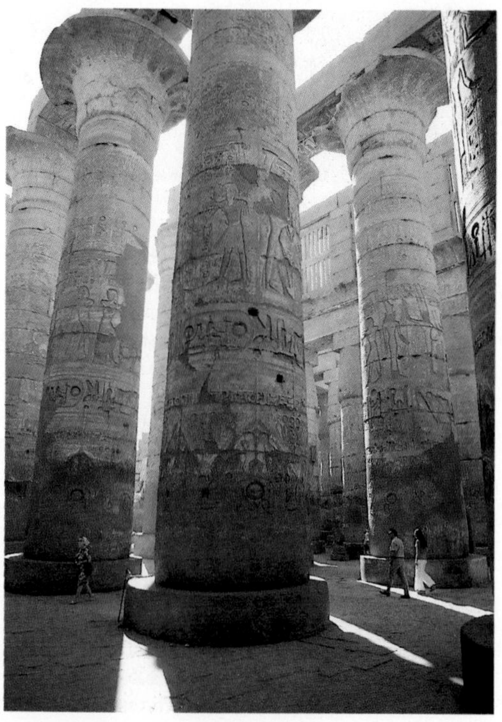

● Have students construct a chart showing the Egyptian gods and each of the god's symbols.

■ The pharaoh's inner coffin was made of solid gold.

Religion formed an extremely important part of Egyptian life, specifically the worship of the sun and moon. The most important god of ancient Egypt was Amon, whose priests fought Akhenaton's attempt to replace Amon with Aton, the sun god. The people loved Osiris, god of the Nile River and lord of the Realm of the Dead, the most. His wife, Isis, the moon goddess, was also mother of the universe and queen of the world and the heavens. In early days each village and district had its local god or gods. In time people throughout the country accepted and worshiped some of these gods. Each god had an animal symbol that people considered sacred. Sacred animals included the cat, the bull, the crocodile, and the scarab (beetle). ●

The afterlife. At first Egyptians believed that only the pharaohs and a few others chosen by the pharaohs had an afterlife, or a life after death. Later, Egyptians believed that everyone, including animals, had a life after death. They thought that the spirit would be happier if the body were preserved. To do this, they developed a process called **mummification,** which involved treating the body with chemicals so that it would dry and remain preserved for centuries.

Workers placed the mummy in a tomb stocked with clothing, food, jewelry, tools, weapons, and even servants in the form of sculptured or painted figures. The number and richness of the articles in the tomb depended on the importance of the dead person. The Egyptians considered these articles necessary for the long journey to a place called "the Realm of the Dead." To guard the soul against attacks from vicious serpents and demons, the Egyptians placed in the tomb *The Book of the Dead*—a collection of hymns, prayers, and magic chants that formed a kind of guide to the afterlife.

When the soul reached the Realm of the Dead, it entered the Hall of Truth, where the god Osiris sat in judgment. Here the soul had to testify to the kind of life it had lived on earth. It had to take an oath that it had not lied, murdered, or been excessively proud.

When the soul had testified and had taken the oath, Osiris weighed it on a great scale against a feather, the symbol of truth. If the scales balanced, the soul had spoken the truth. It could then enter into the presence of the sun god and enjoy eternal happiness. But if it outweighed the feather, the soul was thrown to a horrible monster called "the Eater of the Dead." Ancient Egyptians emphasized the importance of having a good character and living a morally pure life because these qualities led to rewards in the afterlife.

Egyptian tombs. Because of the precious articles buried inside Egyptian graves, robbers constantly plundered them. Looters opened the pyramids built during the Old Kingdom and stole their contents. During the Middle Kingdom and New Kingdom, the Egyptians cut elaborate secret tombs into cliff walls. But thieves robbed most of these tombs also. In A.D. 1922, however, archaeologists discovered the previously unopened grave of Tutankhamen. This tomb, cut into rock, dated from the 1300s B.C. and contained gold, objects decorated with jewels, furniture, and household items that have taught us much about life in ancient Egypt. ■

SECTION 2 REVIEW

1. **Define** caravan, scribe, mummification
2. **Locate** Giza
3. **Understanding Ideas** What mathematical and scientific contributions did the ancient Egyptians make?
4. **Interpreting Ideas** **(a)** Why did the Egyptians build the pyramids? **(b)** What did the ancient Egyptians believe about life after death?
5. **Evaluating Ideas** How did the Egyptians apply their understanding of mathematics to both agriculture and construction?

3 Sumerian Civilization Arose Along the Tigris and Euphrates Rivers

The story of ancient Egypt described one people living in one place for generations. A very different story developed in the area of western Asia called the Fertile Crescent. Here, wave upon wave of invaders crisscrossed the land.

The Physical Setting

Look at the map of the Fertile Crescent on page 28. Note the green strip of land that begins at the Isthmus of Suez and arcs through the Middle East before dipping to the Persian Gulf. Much fertile land lies within this crescent-shaped area known as the Fertile Crescent.

Osiris threw the soul to the Eater of the Dead.
5. The Egyptians used geometry to reestablish boundaries of fields, canal routes, and irrigation ditches after the annual flooding. They used mathematics and geometry in the construction of the massive pyramids.

SECTION 3

Focus/Motivation

Ask students to turn to the map on page 28. Then ask the following questions: Where is Mesopotamia? Babylonia? Sumer? *(Mesopotamia refers to the northern part of the Tigris-Euphrates Valley; Babylonia lies to the south. Sumer is the southern part of Babylonia.)* Where do the Tigris and Euphrates rivers originate? *(in the hills of Armenia)* What natural boundaries surround the Fertile Crescent? *(deserts, mountains, Mediterranean Sea, Persian Gulf)* Could they protect the Fertile Crescent from invasion? *(Unlike the mountains and deserts surrounding Egypt, those in the Fertile Crescent supported wandering peoples who envied and attacked the people living in the rich river valleys.)* What effect might these invasions have had on the political development of the Tigris-Euphrates Valley? *(Less stable societies developed.)*

1A, 1B, 1C, a4B, a4C, a4J

● Despite the difference in flooding patterns between the Tigris-Euphrates and Nile rivers, both ensured an ample supply of water and fertile silt.

Presentation
Organizing Ideas (Average/Group)
Have students list in their notebooks the Sumerian contributions in architecture, engineering, and science. After they have finished the assignment call upon individual students to write the items on the chalkboard or an overhead projector. *(Answers should include the arch, domes or vaults, use of the ramp, possible invention of the wheel, number based on 60, circle divided into 360 degrees, calendar divided into 12 months.)*

As in Egypt, deserts and mountains surrounded the Fertile Crescent. One great difference in geography, however, made the history of the two areas quite different. The deserts and hills around the Fertile Crescent were not as barren as those around Egypt. Thus, grass and other plant life sustained tribes of wandering herders. Their way of life toughened these wild, fierce people. They envied the richer, easier life of the people who lived in the river valleys. At various times the people of the Fertile Crescent became less powerful and could not defend themselves. During these periods the herders came into the region, conquered it, and established empires. In time, these invaders, too, grew weak, and new waves of invaders conquered them. Thus the history of the Fertile Crescent provides a story of migration into the fertile valleys of the Tigris and Euphrates rivers.

The Tigris and Euphrates rivers both begin in the hills of Armenia. The Tigris flows about 1,100 miles (1,770 kilometers) to the Persian Gulf. The Euphrates, to the west, flows about 1,700 miles (2,740 kilometers) before reaching the Persian Gulf. At one point the two rivers come within 20 miles (30 kilometers) of each other and then spread apart until the valley between them—the Tigris-Euphrates Valley—widens to more than 150 miles (240 kilometers). They then flow together to form the Shatt-al-Arab near the Persian Gulf (see map, this page).

Shatt-al-Arab

Learning from Maps *The people of the Tigris and Euphrates River valleys used the rivers' waters for irrigation. Where do the Tigris and Euphrates meet?*

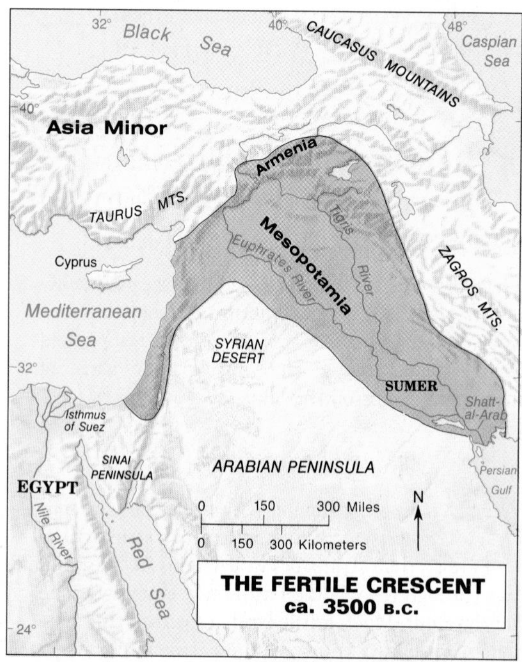

LAMBERT CONFORMAL CONIC PROJECTION

The Tigris has the greater amount of water. It cuts a deep path in the earth, lowering the water level below that of the land and making irrigation difficult. The Euphrates, too, creates problems for those who live along its banks. Its treacherous current carries five times the amount of silt the Nile does. Because this silt builds up at the bottom of the river, the Euphrates often overflows and sends floodwaters swirling across the surrounding land. Valley dwellers must dig canals and dikes to bring water to the fields and also to carry excess water back to the river after floods.

The flood of the Tigris and the Euphrates, unlike that of the Nile, cannot be predicted. It may ● come anytime between the beginning of April and the early part of June. Not only is the exact time of year unpredictable, but the extent of the flood cannot be estimated. Not surprisingly, the people of the valley viewed nature and the gods as angry and unreasonable. Their world differed greatly from that of the Egyptians, who generally saw only goodness in nature.

Various names have been given to certain regions of the Tigris-Euphrates Valley. The Greeks called the northern part Mesopotamia (meaning "between rivers"). The southern part of the valley has usually been known as Babylonia. Today, the nation of Iraq controls the entire valley.

Sumer and Its People

The lowest part of the Tigris-Euphrates Valley contains the rich soil the rivers carry as they pour into the Persian Gulf. In ancient times especially fertile soil covered this area, called Sumer (SOO • muhr). Here Neolithic people settled and grew crops. Joined by two groups of people from the east, the inhabitants created what we call Sumerian culture. We do not know much about the Sumerians except that a group of nomadic people probably migrated to Sumer and mingled with the original inhabitants. By 3000 B.C. these people knew how to use metal and had developed a kind of writing.

SCULPTURE

Sacred Sumerian Animal

This beautiful statue of an animal peering through the branches of a flowering tree was crafted in Sumer about 4,500 years ago. It is made of wood decorated with gold, lapis lazuli, silver, and mother-of-pearl. Scholars think the animal may be a goat or a ram. The combination of the flowering tree and the animal leads some scholars to believe that the statue had an agricultural meaning. Sumer was located in an area of sparse rainfall and depended on water from the unpredictable flooding of the Tigris and Euphrates rivers. The animal may have been used in ceremonies to ensure the fertility of the fields.

The Sumerian culture was at least as rich and as advanced as that of Egypt. In many ways the Sumerians were even more original than the Egyptians. In fact, some historians believe that civilization first began in Sumer.

City-states

Early in their history the Sumerians developed a form of government called the **city-state,** which included a town or city and the surrounding land it controlled. The major city-states, including Ur, Erech, and Kish, had thousands of residents.

The people believed that much of the land in each of these early city-states belonged to a god or gods, while other land belonged to the palace, the temple, the nobles, or private citizens. Priests managed the gods' land, interpreted the gods' will to the people, and directed worship. Evidence indicates that kings ruled these city-states.

The many Sumerian city-states seldom united under a single government. Instead, the city-states competed, particularly over land boundaries and water rights.

Social Classes

The Sumerians had three distinct social classes. At the top stood a privileged class of nobles, including priests and government officials. Next came a group of merchants and artisans. Peasants and slaves made up the lowest class.

Sumerian Writing

Sumerian writing looked quite different from Egyptian writing. While Egyptian hieroglyphics consisted of symbols carved on slate or ivory or scribed on papyrus, Sumerian writing began mostly as marks pressed into clay tablets. Because the writers used a pointed stick called a stylus, most of the signs were combinations of wedge shapes. Today we call Sumerian writing **cuneiform** (kyoo • NEE • uh • fawrm) from the Latin word for "wedge," *cuneus.* The Sumerians had about 600 cuneiform signs.

The papyrus reed, which the Egyptians used to make paper, did not grow in Sumer, so the Sumerians did not learn to make paper. Instead, throughout their history, they wrote primarily on clay.

29

1B, 1C, 2A, a4A

● The Sumerian lack of stone for building made it more difficult for archaeologists to tell us how their buildings looked.

Learning from Pictures *Khuzistan Ziggurat is located in Choga Zanbil, Iran, and was built about 1250 B.C. What important architectural designs did the Sumerians invent?*
the arch, use of the ramp, sewers

They rolled out a lump of soft clay, made their wedge-shaped marks on it, and then allowed the clay tablet to dry until hard. Hardened clay would last for many years. It might shatter, but the pieces could usually be fitted together.

Farming and Trade

Most Sumerians farmed, growing grains, vegetables, and dates. Their domestic animals included cows, sheep, and goats, as well as oxen to pull plows and donkeys to pull carts and chariots. The Sumerians also developed a dairy industry, wove fine woolen goods, and raised flax for linen.

Sumer produced enough food to allow many people to work as traders and artisans. Before about 3000 B.C., Sumerians had begun trading with other peoples of the Middle East. Some merchants had agents in faraway places, while others traveled from city to city to sell Sumerian products.

Architecture, Engineering, and Science

The Sumerians used sun-dried clay bricks to build houses. Their brick structures did not last as long as the stone buildings of the Egyptians, but they were ● nonetheless well planned and well built.

The Sumerians may have invented several important architectural designs, including one of the strongest forms in building—the **arch,** a curved structure over an opening. By combining several arches, the Sumerians built rounded roofs in the shape of domes or vaults. They also knew how to use the ramp and even built sewers beneath their buildings.

The most striking Sumerian buildings were the temples, known as **ziggurats,** built on hills specially created on the flat land of the valley. Builders erected a ziggurat in layers, each one smaller than the one below, so that it looked somewhat like a wedding cake. They sometimes painted each story a different color. Usually a ziggurat soared seven stories, with the top one serving as the shrine of one of the gods.

Sumerian engineers and scientists made many important discoveries. Some scholars think that Sumerians were the first Neolithic people to develop and use the wheel. Later the Sumerians developed some of the principles of algebra. In mathematics they used a system of numbers based on 60. They stated large numbers in 60s—for example, they expressed 120 as two 60s and 180 as three 60s. They divided a circle into 360 degrees (six 60s), each degree into 60 minutes, each minute

● It would be a primary source when the question asked concerns the discovery of the ship. It would be a secondary source when the discovery is used to answer questions about Spanish life.

READ
WRITE
INTERPRET
CONNECT
THINK

BUILDING HISTORY STUDY SKILLS

Reading About History: Identifying Sources of Evidence

Identifying sources of evidence—information used to support an explanation of the past—helps us interpret historical events. Two basic categories of sources are used as evidence. Primary sources include items such as artifacts, original documents, letters, diaries, and eyewitness accounts of an event or a period of history. Secondary sources are accounts written after the events by people who played no part in them.

How to Identify Sources of Evidence

To identify sources of evidence, follow these steps.

1. Identify the document or artifact. For example, is it a letter, diary, government record, work of art, building, or photograph?
2. Review the definitions of primary and secondary sources to determine the category of the evidence you have labeled.
3. Determine and then record the usefulness of the evidence. What question will it help you answer? Is a primary source always more reliable as evidence than a secondary source? Why or why not? Support your opinion with facts.

Developing the Skill

The work of art "The Royal Standard of Ur" was found in a Sumerian grave dated about 2700 B.C. It is made of shell, lapis lazuli (a semiprecious stone), and red stone inlaid on the sides of a wooden box. In the panel, the fruits of victory are being celebrated by the court. From this artifact depicting domestic animals, the wheel, leisure activities such as listening to music, and the banquet itself, historians can determine the sophistication of Sumerian society.

"The Royal Standard of Ur" is classified as a primary source. Sometimes a piece of evidence, however, can be classified as both a primary source and a secondary source, depending on the purpose for its use and the question that historians wish to answer. For example, Howard Carter's description of the opening of Egyptian pharaoh Tutankhamen's tomb can be classified as a primary source when the question posed concerns the discovery of the tomb. However, this same description is considered a secondary source when it is used to answer questions about Egyptian life during ancient times. Can you see the two applications of sources of evidence from the excerpt below?

> "With suppressed excitement I carefully cut the cord, removed that precious seal, drew back the bolts, and opened the doors, when a fourth shrine was revealed . . . even more brilliant in workmanship than the last. . . . There, filling the entire area within . . . stood an immense yellow quartzite sarcophagus [stone coffin]. . . .
>
> The tackle for raising the lid was in position. I gave the word. Amid intense silence the huge slab . . . rose from its bed. . . . The lid being suspended in mid-air, we rolled back those covering shrouds, one by one. . . . So gorgeous was the sight that met our eyes: a golden effigy of the young boy king."

Practicing the skill. How might an account of the 1988 discovery of a Spanish galleon that sank off the coast of Florida in 1568 be considered both a primary and a secondary source? ●

To apply this skill, see Applying History Study Skills on page 47.

Sumerian Royal Standard of Ur

31

1A, 1B, 2A, a4A, a4B, a4C, a4F, a4H

SECTION 3

Closure

Ask students to compare the Sumerian civilization with that of Egypt. Ask: How important was geography in contributing to any differences? *(Sumer was not as well protected from invaders as Egypt was.)*

Review Answers

1. ***city-state:*** government that included a town or a city and the surrounding land; ***cuneiform:*** wedge-shaped Sumerian writing; ***arch:*** curved structure over an opening; ***ziggurat:*** temple built in layers to look like a wedding cake
2. ***Sumerians:*** people who lived in lower section of the Tigris-Euphrates Valley
3. ***Fertile Crescent:*** fertile area in the Middle East that arcs between the Isthmus of Suez and the Persian Gulf; ***Tigris-Euphrates Valley:*** valley between major rivers that begin in Armenia and flow to the Persian Gulf; ***Persian Gulf:*** body of water between Arabia and Persia; ***Mesopotamia:*** land between Tigris and Euphrates; ***Babylonia:*** south-central Mesopotamia; ***Sumer:*** lowest section of the Mesopotamian valley
4. because the river floods were so unpredictable and destructive
5. The Sumerians probably invented the arch. They also combined arches to form dome- or vault-shaped roofs. They used ramps in construction and built sewers.

into 60 seconds. Today, when you look at a compass or a watch, you are seeing a principle the Sumerians developed thousands of years ago.

The Sumerians also developed a 12-month lunar calendar. When the passage of years made their calendar inaccurate, they added a thirteenth month to bring it back into line with the seasons.

Education and Religion

The Sumerians considered education very important, although only upper-class boys attended schools. Students learned to write and spell by copying religious books and songs. They also studied reading, history, mathematics, foreign languages, and mapmaking. Advanced education included law, medicine, and surgery. Students also spent much time trying to predict the future.

Like the Egyptians, the Sumerians practiced polytheism. They associated their gods with the forces of nature and with heavenly bodies, such as the sun and moon. Sumerians believed the gods had the same habits and feelings as ordinary humans but had much more power. Anu, lord of heaven, Enlil, god of air and storms, and Ea, god of the waters, ranked as the most important Sumerian gods.

Unlike the Egyptians, the Sumerians did not have a firm set of beliefs about an afterlife. They did not believe in reward in heaven or punishment in hell, but they did believe in some form of life after death. They also feared ghosts. They thought, for example, that if they did not bury personal objects such as jewelry with the dead, the spirits of the dead person would be displeased and would return to haunt the homes and families of the living.

SECTION 3 REVIEW

1. **Define** city-state, cuneiform, arch, ziggurat
2. **Identify** Sumerians
3. **Locate** Fertile Crescent, Tigris-Euphrates Valley, Persian Gulf, Mesopotamia, Babylonia, Sumer
4. **Understanding Ideas** Why did the inhabitants of the Tigris-Euphrates Valley regard nature as a hostile force?
5. **Summarizing Ideas** Describe the Sumerian contributions to architecture.
6. **Interpreting Ideas** Explain the mathematical ideas that originated in the Sumerian culture.
7. **Synthesizing Ideas** **(a)** How did the religious beliefs of the Sumerians resemble those of the Egyptians? **(b)** How were they different? **(c)** How do you account for the differences?

4 Several Empires Were Established in the Fertile Crescent

Sumerian city-states did not unite under one government. This lack of unity proved to be a fatal weakness.

The Akkadians Under Sargon

After 2400 B.C. the Akkadians (uh • KAYD • ee • uhnz), a people who also lived in Mesopotamia, conquered the Sumerians. Unlike the Sumerians, the Akkadians spoke a Semitic language closely related to modern Hebrew and Arabic. The most powerful of the Semitic kings, Sargon of Akkad, established a great empire that extended as far west as the Mediterranean (see map, this page). The Akkadian empire lasted about 100 years. When it ended, Sumerian city-states once again became prosperous, but new waves of invaders soon swept through the eastern Fertile Crescent. Another powerful

Learning from Maps *The Akkadian Empire had its capital at the magnificent city of Akkad. What was the southernmost city in the Akkadian Empire?* **Ur**

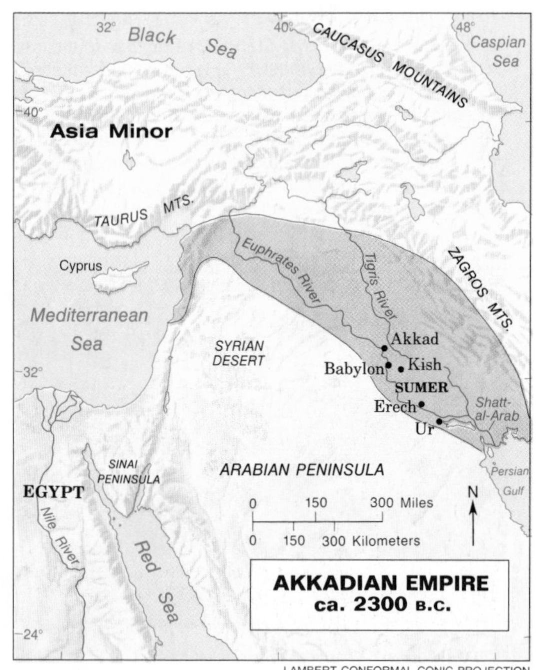

LAMBERT CONFORMAL CONIC PROJECTION

Semitic state arose, this time centered at the large new city of Babylon.

The Lawgiving Babylonians

About 1792 B.C. a strong ruler named Hammurabi (ham • uh • RAHB • ee) came to power in Babylon and conquered most of the upper Tigris-Euphrates Valley (see map, this page). More than a great military leader, Hammurabi was a just political leader as well. He is best known for the Code of Hammurabi, a collection of laws passed under his direction.

The Code of Hammurabi consisted of 282 laws that controlled all aspects of life in Babylon. For example, the code carefully regulated agriculture. Farmers who failed to cultivate their fields or keep the irrigation canals and ditches in good condition were punished. Some laws concerned commerce and industry and included provisions regarding wages, hours, and working conditions. Other laws dealt with property rights, contracts, and bankruptcy. Still others dealt with marriage and divorce. Judges enforced the laws under the supervision of the king's advisers and officials.

The Code of Hammurabi provided for harsh punishments. For example:

> "If a man has accused another man and has brought a charge of murder against him, but has not proved it, his accuser shall be put to death. 22–23 If a man has committed robbery and is caught, that man shall be put to death. If the robber is not caught, the man who has been robbed shall formally declare whatever he has lost before a god, and the city and mayor in whose territory or district the robbery was committed shall make good to him his lost property. 229–30 If a builder has constructed a house for an *awilum* [man] but has not made his work strong, with the result that the house which he built collapsed and so caused the death of the owner of the house, that builder shall be put to death. If it has caused the death of the son of the owner of the house, they shall put to death the son of the builder."

The concept of "an eye for an eye, a tooth for a tooth" provided the basis of punishment. If a man caused another to lose an eye, then his own eye was put out.

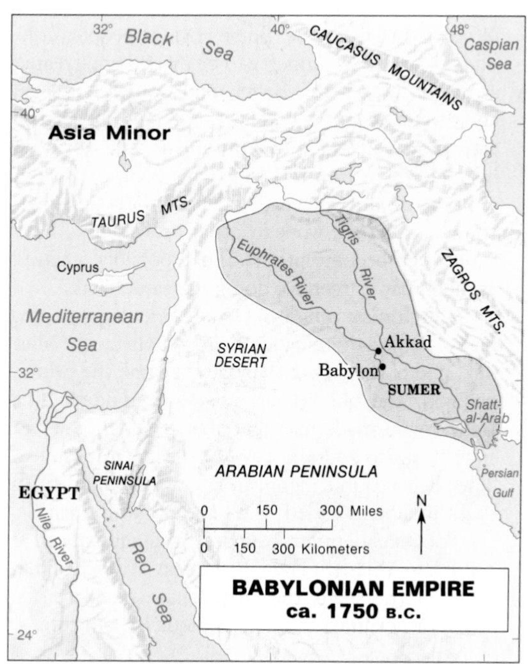

Learning from Maps *A Hittite king eventually overthrew the Babylonian Empire, encountering little opposition. Who was Babylon's first strong military ruler?* **Hammurabi**

Punishment often varied according to wealth, however. If a wealthy man destroyed the eye of a poor man, the wealthy man did not lose his eye but merely paid a fine. A thief who could not repay what was stolen was put to death. If the thief had money, however, the only punishment was to repay more than had been stolen.

Babylonian culture. Like the Sumerians, most Babylonians farmed. They domesticated animals, grew large amounts of food, and also wove textiles. As traders, however, the Babylonians surpassed the Sumerians. They traded with merchants from distant parts of the Fertile Crescent as well as from Egypt and even India.

The social organization of the Babylonians also resembled that of the Sumerians. A nobility including priests and government officials made up the upper class. Next came a middle class of artisans and merchants and a lower class of peasants and slaves.

Babylonian women probably had fewer privileges than Egyptian women, but they enjoyed a higher position in society than that of most women

6. Sumerians developed some of the principles of algebra, including a number system based on 60.
7. (a) The Egyptians and Sumerians were both polytheists. **(b)** The Sumerians, unlike the Egyptians, did not believe in an afterlife complete with rewards or penalties. **(c)** Answers will vary. Students may speculate that Sumerian polytheism was less sophisticated than that of the Egyptians.

SECTION 4

Focus/Motivation

Be sure the students understand the definition of an empire: a government that unites different territories and people under one rule. Ask students to answer the following questions: What system and skill are necessary for running an empire? *(a strong army, an efficient bureaucracy, a legal system, good transportation and communication, and skill in organization)* What are some advantages of an empire? *(helps create stable societies, spread cultural achievements, and bring economic prosperity)* Some disadvantages? *(It can be cruel and oppressive, exploit people economically, and disregard the culture of conquered peoples.)* Close the discussion by asking whether any empires exist today.

1A, 1B, 2A, a4B, a4C, a4H

- **Little was known about the Assyrians until the mid-1800s, when the Assyrian cities of Dur Sharrukin and Nineveh were discovered. Have students report on the findings of Paul Emile Botta and Sir Austen Layard.**

Presentation
Analyzing Ideas (Average/Group)
Organize the class into groups to discuss the following questions: Why was religion so important to early people? *(Answers will vary. Students might say that people were trying to understand the forces of nature, sickness, death, and disastrous events over which they had no control.)* Why did people worship the forces of nature? Why do you think polytheism developed before monotheism? *(People worshiped the forces of nature because they could not be controlled and needed to be appeased. This accounts for the worship of many gods.)* How do you explain the rise of priesthoods and temples? *(The people who seemed able to influence the forces of nature, such as rulers and priests, were held in great esteem. Temples became important as places for worship and homes for the gods.)* Have the groups share their findings with the rest of the class.

in ancient civilizations. Some ancient peoples considered women as property to be owned and treated as slaves. In contrast, Babylonian women had legal and economic rights, and laws protected their property. However, a man might sell his wife—or even his children or himself—to pay his debts.

Babylonian women could be traders and merchants and could work in other professions. They could even become priests. They possibly received as much pay as men for doing the same work.

Babylonian religion. The Babylonians adopted many Sumerian religious beliefs. Although Marduk, god of the city of Babylon, became the principal god, the old Sumerian gods remained. The Babylonians made many sacrifices to their gods for such things as good harvests or success in business. They believed in a gloomy, hopeless life after death spent in a place called "the Land of No Return."

Babylonian priests wielded as much power as Sumerian priests. They had great influence because of the spells they used against evil spirits. They also claimed they could predict the future.

The Invading Hittites

Many times in history, you will read of conquerors who adopted the culture of the people they conquered. This was certainly true of the Babylonians after they conquered the Sumerians. However, it was definitely not true of the Hittites, a warlike people who invaded the Tigris-Euphrates Valley from Asia Minor about 1600 B.C.

The Hittites were the first people to make extensive use of iron weapons. Their most important achievement, however, lay in their laws, which were less brutal than the Code of Hammurabi. Only major crimes, such as rebellion, warranted execution. Hittite law called for a person to pay a fine for causing damage or injury. For example, if you broke someone's arm, you paid 20 pieces of silver rather than having your own arm broken. In determining the punishment, the law also considered such factors as premeditation—whether a person intended beforehand to commit the crime.

When the Hittites invaded the Tigris-Euphrates Valley, they conquered and looted Babylon itself. The Hittites were too far from their homeland to control Babylonia permanently, however, and soon withdrew to the western part of the Fertile Crescent. They remained a powerful force in the west until about 1200 B.C.

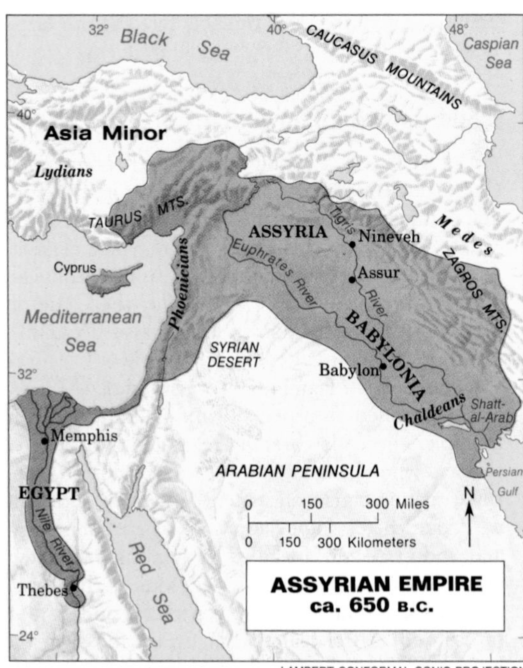

Learning from Maps *The last Assyrian army was defeated six years after Nineveh was destroyed. What city survived the changing empires of the Fertile Crescent?*
Babylon

The Conquering Assyrians

Following the decline of the Hittites, Babylon suffered further invasions by mountain peoples. Then about 900 B.C., the fiercest, cruelest, and most warlike of all ancient peoples—the Assyrians—overwhelmed Mesopotamia.

The Assyrians first settled along the Tigris River, northwest of Babylonia. There they built the city-state Assur, named for their chief god. Both the region, Assyria, and the people took their name from the word *Assur.* From Assur they spread throughout the region until they controlled Syria, Babylonia, and even Egypt (see map, this page).

The Assyrians excelled in warfare. Instead of chariots they used **cavalry**—a military unit of riders on horses. They also used many iron weapons and invented the battering ram to break through the brick walls of cities they attacked.

And how cruel they were! Often using savage methods, the Assyrians killed the enemies they captured in battle. They enslaved conquered peoples and deported them to other areas, replacing them with Assyrian colonists. In this way the Assyrians easily controlled conquered lands and gained many slaves. About 700 B.C. the Assyrians captured Babylon, looted it, and finally destroyed it completely. They even changed the course of the Euphrates River to flow over the site. Such acts of destruction earned the Assyrians the hatred and fear of people throughout the ancient world.

Assyrian government. The Assyrian king had total power. Priests and government officials took orders from him and answered to him. The monarch was responsible only to the god Assur, whose representative on earth he claimed to be.

The Assyrians created an extremely efficient government, building roads so that troops could move about quickly and establishing a postal service to speed news of rebellions to the army. Governors ruled conquered lands, collected high taxes, and made regular and frequent reports to the king. To ensure loyalty, inspectors checked on the governors' activities. The king always stationed an army in a conquered area to keep the people under control. This army sometimes consisted of large groups of **mercenaries**—professional soldiers paid to serve in a foreign army.

The Assyrians were the first people to develop an effective method of governing an empire, and all other empires of the ancient Middle East modeled their governments after it. In other fields, however, the Assyrians contributed little to civilization.

Assyrian greatness and decline. After the Assyrians became powerful, they made the city of Nineveh (NIN • uh • vuh) their capital. Nineveh symbolized the pride and cruelty of the Assyrians. Attempting to make it the most fortified city in the world, the Assyrians constructed a huge double wall, 50 feet (15 meters) thick and 100 feet (30 meters) high, that stretched for seven miles (11.2 kilometers) around the city. The wall had 15 gates, each beautifully decorated and strongly defended. To assure a supply of water, the Assyrians diverted 18 mountain streams to flow through Nineveh. Within the city the Assyrians built a large library in which scholars collected clay tablets from all over Assyria and Babylonia, preserving these literary works for future generations.

Powerful Nineveh was not powerful enough to resist Assyria's many enemies, however. Finally, in 612 B.C., a group of opponents led by the Chaldeans (kal • DEE • uhnz) and the Medes (MEEDZ) captured and destroyed Nineveh.

The Chaldeans

The Chaldeans took control of much of the territory that the Assyrians had ruled. Under the leadership of a wise ruler named Nebuchadnezzar (neb • uh • kuhd • NEZ • uhr), who ruled from the rebuilt capital city of Babylon between 605 B.C. and 562 B.C., the Chaldeans conquered most of the Fertile Crescent (see map, this page).

The Chaldeans of Babylon enjoyed a high standard of living and surrounded themselves with beautiful buildings. The enormous palace of Nebuchadnezzar, perhaps the most impressive building in the city, contained a very unusual feature—the Hanging Gardens. According to legend, Nebuchadnezzar's wife had lived in the mountains and was homesick on the flat plains of Babylonia. To please her, the king planted thousands of brightly colored tropical plants and flowers on the roof of the palace. The Greeks and other peoples of the ancient world regarded the Hanging Gardens of Babylon as one of the Seven Wonders of the World.

Learning from Maps *Under the Chaldeans, Babylon once again became the center of civilization in the Fertile Crescent. What was the other major city of the Chaldean Empire?* **Jerusalem**

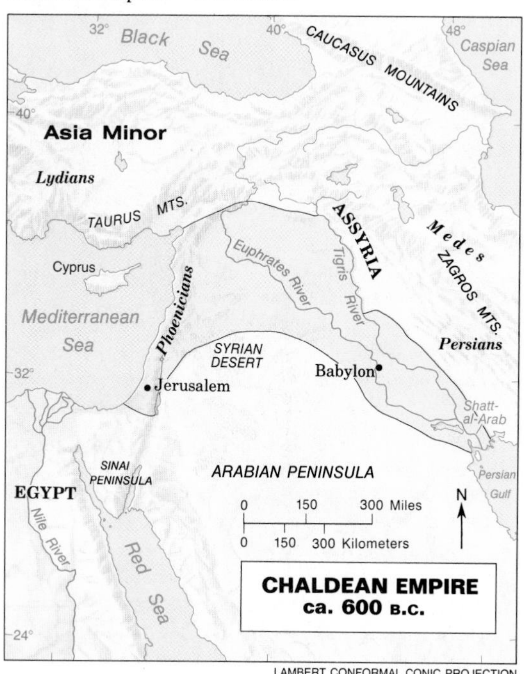

35

SECTION 4

Closure

Ancient Egypt had native dynasties ruling the country throughout most of its history. Ask: How did the Fertile Crescent differ? *(It was subject to succeeding groups of peoples competing for the same region.)*

Review Answers

1. ***cavalry:*** military unit of riders on horses; ***mercenary:*** professional soldier paid to serve in a foreign army

2. ***Sargon of Akkad:*** Akkadian king who established an empire that extended west to Syria; ***Hammurabi:*** Babylonian ruler who codified law; ***Babylonians:*** Semitic people who lived in Mesopotamia; ***Chaldeans:*** conquered Assyrians and eventually most of the Fertile Crescent; ***Nebuchadnezzar:*** Chaldean ruler who built Hanging Gardens for wife; ***Cyrus:*** Persian who led a successful revolt against the Medes and conquered the Fertile Crescent and Asia Minor; ***Darius:*** Persian ruler who added regions south and east of Persia as far as the Indus River; ***Xerxes:*** Persian ruler who tried and failed to conquer Greece; ***Zoroaster:*** Persian religious reformer who saw world as a battleground between good and evil, and where humans trained for future life.

3. ***Syria:*** western part of Fertile Crescent and boundary for Akkadians; ***Babylon:*** capital of Babylonian and Chaldean em-

All the strength of the Chaldeans seemed to lie in the leadership ability of Nebuchadnezzar. One of his successors, a religious fanatic, opposed the priests, who then betrayed the city to the Persians. Within 30 years after Nebuchadnezzar's death, the Chaldean Empire fell.

Like the Assyrians, the Chaldeans contributed little to civilization. An exception was their deep interest in astronomy, which enabled them to calculate the length of a year to within seven minutes.

The Mighty Persians

The Persians who conquered Babylon in 539 B.C. spoke an Indo-European language and, like the Medes, had migrated into what is today Iran about 1800 B.C.* The region became known as Persia and Media after these two tribes.

*The Indo-Europeans originally lived in the region north of the Caspian and Black seas. Other Indo-European peoples included the Hittites and the ancestors of the Greeks and Romans.

Cyrus, Darius, and Xerxes. About 550 B.C. Cyrus, a Persian and one of the greatest leaders in all history, led a successful revolt against the Medes. Cyrus then began a series of conquests, capturing Babylon and conquering the rest of the Fertile Crescent and Asia Minor.

A later Persian ruler, Darius the Great, added regions south and east of Persia as far as the Indus River in India as well as parts of southeastern Europe (see map, this page). Both Darius and his son Xerxes (ZUHRK • seez) invaded Greece in the 400s B.C. but failed to conquer it. Nevertheless, the Persians ruled the mightiest empire known up to that time.

Persian government. The early Persian kings distinguished themselves not only as great generals but also as wise rulers. Although all-powerful in government, they showed great concern for justice. They collected taxes and administered justice fairly.

Persian rulers chose the best officials they could find, often from among the conquered peoples, to govern their huge empire. They paid close attention to local customs and allowed the conquered peoples

Learning from Maps *Persian emperors relied on the corps of Persian soldiers called the "10,000 Immortals" to protect the huge empire. How far was Susa from Persepolis?* **250 mi./375 km.**

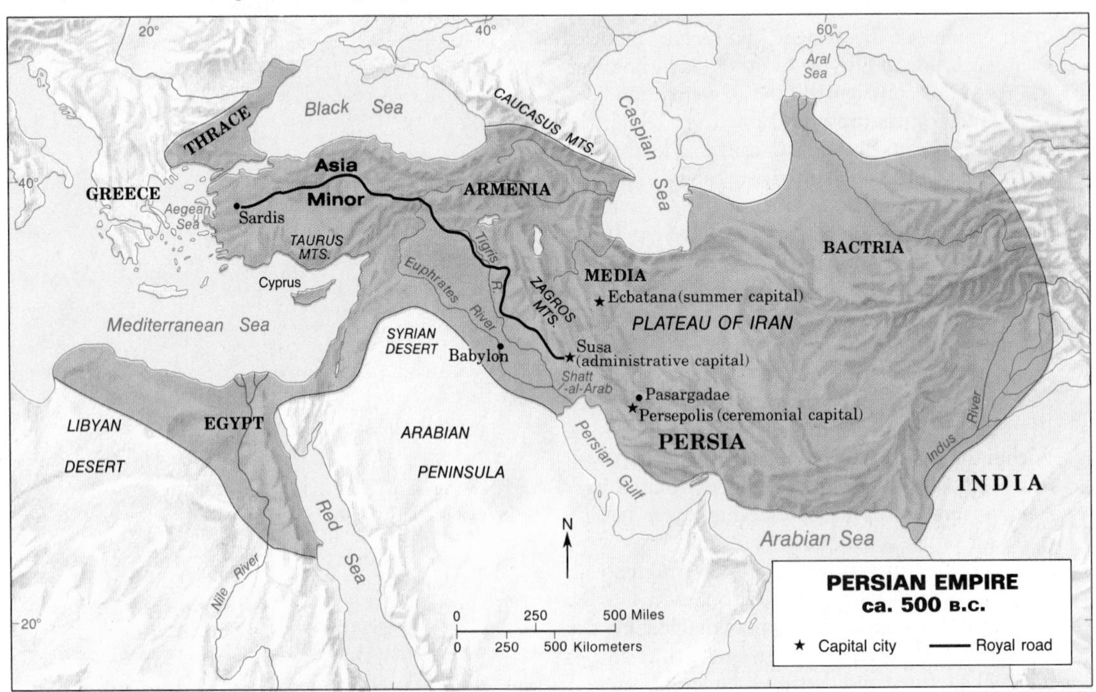

● Research topic: Zoroastrianism today

Learning from Pictures Darius the Great is shown here in a stone carving receiving homage in his palace at Persepolis.

to keep their own religions and laws. This tolerant practice won the favor of the priests and the loyalty of the people.

The Persians copied some things from the Assyrians, especially the kinds of officials used to govern the empire. Inspectors called "the King's Eyes and Ears" helped Persian rulers. The Persians also extended the Assyrian road system. The most famous road, the Royal Road, extended from Sardis, in Asia Minor, to Susa, one of the capitals of the empire. The Persians built these roads mainly for the army and postal riders, but merchants also used them. As a result, these roads aided the process of cultural diffusion in the empire by promoting the exchange of customs and ideas.

Persian religion. The greatest cultural contribution of the Persians concerned religion. At first, like other early peoples, the Persians worshiped many gods. Then about 600 B.C. a great prophet and religious reformer named Zoroaster (ZOHR • uh • was • tuhr) completely changed their religious ideas.

Zoroaster taught that on earth people received training for a future life. In the world the forces of good and evil struggled savagely, and people could choose between good and evil. Those who chose good (symbolized by light) would be rewarded with eternal life. Those who chose evil would face darkness and misery after death. In the distant future, the forces of good would triumph. Then the earth would disappear, having served its purpose as the stage on which the great conflict had taken place.

The ideas of Zoroaster, called Zoroastrianism, strongly influenced the lives of the Persians. According to this prophet, nothing was more shameful than lying. The Persians taught their children that they must always tell the truth. They also considered getting into debt a form of lying and therefore a disgrace.

Zoroaster's idea of a struggle between good and evil is similar to that of the Hebrews and, later, of the Christians. Zoroastrian ideas also taught that final judgment was based on reward or punishment and, according to what some people believed, depended on human choice. ●

The decline of the Persians. The Persian kings who followed Darius and Xerxes lacked strength and wisdom. Therefore, both the government and the army grew weak. In 331 B.C., more than 200 years after Cyrus led the revolt against the Medes, Alexander the Great led his army out of Greece and conquered the Persian Empire.

SECTION 4 REVIEW

1. **Define** cavalry, mercenary
2. **Identify** Sargon of Akkad, Hammurabi, Babylonians, Chaldeans, Nebuchadnezzar, Cyrus, Darius, Xerxes, Zoroaster
3. **Locate** Syria, Babylon, Asia Minor, Nineveh, Persia, Caspian Sea, Black Sea, Royal Road, Sardis, Susa
4. **Summarizing Ideas** **(a)** List five laws in the Code of Hammurabi. **(b)** How did the Hittite laws vary from the Code of Hammurabi?
5. **Understanding Ideas** Describe the treatment of women in Babylonian society.
6. **Evaluating Ideas** **(a)** List briefly the accomplishments of the Babylonians, the Hittites, the Assyrians, the Chaldeans, and the Persians. **(b)** Which accomplishment do you believe was the most important? **(c)** Why?

pires; ***Asia Minor:*** located between Mediterranean and Black seas; ***Nineveh:*** Assyrian capital; ***Persia:*** largest empire of the ancient Middle East; ***Caspian Sea:*** large inland sea located east of Black Sea; ***Black Sea:*** located north of Asia Minor; ***Royal Road:*** Persian road extending from Susa to Sardis; ***Sardis:*** city in western Asia Minor; ***Susa:*** one of Persian capitals
4. (a) Answers will vary. Students may include (1) Men who accuse others falsely of murder shall be executed; (2) Robbers will be executed; (3) Builders of faulty homes shall lose whatever the occupant loses if the home collapses; (4) Maintain irrigation canals and ditches; (5) Limited specific types of labor to so many hours; **(b)** Hittite laws were less brutal, the death penalty being used only for major crimes. A person also could pay with money for damages or injury done. The law considered premeditation in determining punishment.
5. Women had legal and economic rights. Their property was protected, and they could engage in business and other professions or even become priests.
6. (a) The Babylonians codified law; the Hittites used iron and less brutal laws. The Assyrians specialized in warfare and created the first efficient imperial government. The Chaldeans studied the stars and built the Hanging Gardens. The Persians

1A, 1B, 1D, a4A, a4B, a4C, a4L

● **Students might suggest that our alphabet would reflect other cultural influences such as those of the Arabs or the Chinese.**

created an empire noted for toleration of local customs, and developed Zoroastrianism. **(b)** Answers will vary. **(c)** Answers will vary.

SECTION 5

Focus/Motivation
Have students refer to the map of the Eastern Mediterranean on this page. Ask students why the area between Syria and the Mediterranean Sea would be of interest to an aggressive nation. *(Answers should include its use as a land bridge between Asia and Africa for trade and troop movements, its use as a fertile area for farming, and its access to the Mediterranean Sea.)*

Next refer students to the continuing conflict in that area. Are the reasons for interest in the area today the same as in ancient times? *(Students should recognize that the reasons are not quite the same. Other complex social, religious, and political issues are involved.)*

Presentation
Comparing Ideas (Average/Group)
Students will enjoy comparing the account of the flood in the Old Testament with the Babylonian story of the flood. Call upon students to read passages from the Biblical account in

5 Phoenicians, Lydians, and Hebrews Made Lasting Contributions

The peoples who lived in the western end of the Fertile Crescent and in western Asia Minor did not create large empires, but they had a great influence on the modern world. This narrow strip of land along the Mediterranean Sea today forms portions of the nations of Egypt, Israel, Jordan, Lebanon, Syria, and Turkey. In ancient times, however, people called the northern part Phoenicia (fi • NEESH • ee • uh) and Lydia (LID • ee • uh). The southern section had different names during the course of history, including Canaan, Israel, and Palestine. Between about 1200 B.C. and 500 B.C. the peoples of this region—the Phoenicians, Lydians, and Hebrews—made important contributions in economics and religion.

The Phoenicians

Phoenicia consisted of a loose union of city-states, each governed by a different king. Although Phoenicia had hills and mountains, its lack of fertile land made large-scale farming impossible. Blocked by the high ridges of the Lebanon Mountains, the Phoenicians did not migrate eastward. Instead, they turned to the sea and to commerce for their living. On the map on this page, notice the cities of Tyre (TYR) and Sidon (SYD • uhn). Both of these seaports became world famous.

The Phoenicians built seagoing ships that today would seem small and frail, but the Phoenicians proved skillful and fearless sailors. Propelled by sails and oars, Phoenician ships plied the Mediterranean Sea. Some historians believe that the Phoenicians sailed as far as Britain in search of tin and may also have sailed around Africa. In time the Phoenicians became the greatest traders in the ancient world.

Articles of trade. Phoenicia had only one important natural resource—lumber taken from the beautiful cedar trees of the Lebanon Mountains. Many ancient peoples used this lumber for building.

Because of the lack of local mineral resources, the Phoenicians bought metals from other regions. They became highly skilled in creating beautiful objects of gold, silver, copper, and bronze. They also learned how to make exquisite glass.

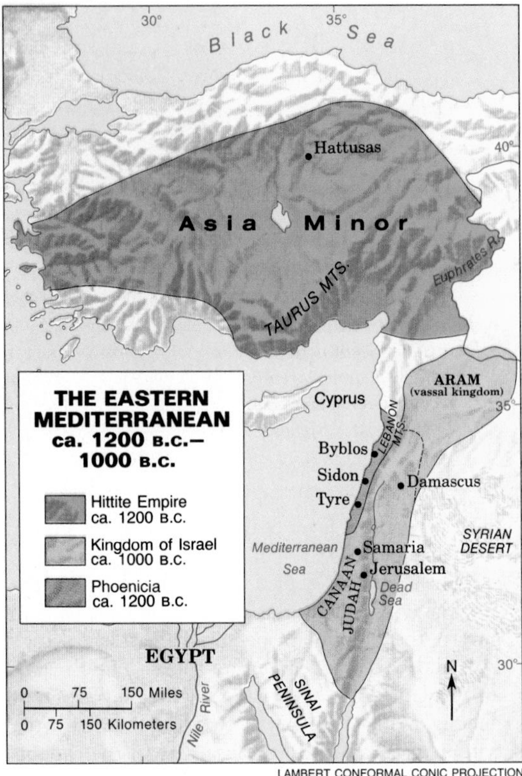

Learning from Maps *Because of their location along the sea, the territories of the eastern Mediterranean depended on trade. Which region had the most centers of trade?* **Phoenicia**

Along their seacoast the Phoenicians found a shellfish called murex, which they used to make purple dye. People throughout the ancient world prized Phoenician woolen cloth, dyed purple. So expensive that only the wealthy could afford it, purple—the royal purple—became the color worn by kings and queens.

Phoenician colonies. Between 1000 and 700 B.C., conditions favored the Phoenician traders. The Hittite Empire had disintegrated, and Egypt

What If?
The Phoenician Alphabet

Phoenician trade helped spread the alphabet throughout the Mediterranean region. How might the history of writing have been different if the Phoenicians had not been traders? ●

The most famous Phoenician colony was the North African city of Carthage, which became the great rival of Rome in the Mediterranean.

was in decline. Tyre united the Phoenician city-states under its leadership, and the Phoenicians began to establish colonies throughout the Mediterranean region.

These new colonies, on the islands of Sicily, Sardinia, and Malta and throughout the Mediterranean Sea, served as centers for trade. Farther west, beyond the Mediterranean Sea, the Phoenicians also established a colony on the site of the modern city of Cádiz, Spain.

Phoenician culture. The Phoenicians imitated the cultures of other peoples. They patterned their government and most of their customs after the Egyptians and the Babylonians. Through trading the Phoenicians indirectly spread Egyptian and Babylonian culture throughout the Mediterranean area.

Phoenician religion offered the people few comforts. Phoenicians did not believe in an afterlife and sometimes sacrificed their own children to win favor from the many gods they worshiped.

The Phoenicians made one very important contribution to Western civilization—the alphabet. Earlier alphabets had been developed in Canaan, the Sinai Peninsula, and northern Syria, but the Phoenicians developed the alphabet that became the model for later Western alphabets.

The spread of the alphabet provides a good example of how commerce can speed the process of cultural diffusion. The practical Phoenicians used writing in their businesses for recording contracts and drawing up bills. Phoenician commerce made it possible for the knowledge of alphabetical writing to spread throughout the Mediterranean world.

The Greeks adopted and improved the Phoenician alphabet by adding signs for vowel sounds. Later, the Romans copied this alphabet from the Greeks and developed the Roman alphabet we use.

The Lydians

Like the Phoenicians, the Lydians of Asia Minor made a significant contribution to civilization based on trade. About 600 B.C., the Lydians became the first people in history to use coined money. Before this invention, traders had to rely on **barter,** or exchanging one good or service for another. Barter, however, limited trade because two people could strike a bargain only if each had a good or service that the other wanted. The use of money allowed traders to set prices for various goods and services and to develop a **money economy,** an economic system based on the use of money rather than on barter.

Like the Phoenicians, the Lydians did not rule an empire. Through trade, however, they passed on the concept of a money economy to the Greeks and the Persians, who in turn helped spread this concept to other parts of the world.

The Physical Setting

To the south of Phoenicia lay a small strip of land known as Canaan that had no forests and few minerals or other natural resources. As you can see on the map on page 38, Canaan consisted of two regions. The Jordan River watered the northern valley. There the fertile soil helped farmers grow grains, olives, figs, and grapes. Desert covered most of the southern region, around and south of the Dead Sea. (The sea was called *dead* because the high salt content of the water killed all marine life.) This arid plateau had poor and rocky soil.

Canaan lay along the great land bridge between Asia and Africa. In one way, this location gave the people an advantage, because the merchants who carried goods and ideas between Egypt and the Fertile Crescent traveled this route.

In another way, however, Canaan's location was a disadvantage, because armies also passed along the route. The people of Canaan lacked powerful armies, and at one time or another the Egyptians, Hittites, Assyrians, Chaldeans, and Persians conquered Canaan.

The Hebrews

Just as in the eastern part of the Fertile Crescent, a series of peoples inhabited Canaan. The Hebrews, or Jews, however, had the greatest influence on their own times and on all of later history. The Hebrews did not always live in Canaan. Abraham, the leader of the Hebrew people according to the Bible, once lived in Sumer. After leaving there, he led his nomadic people through the desert to the borders of northern Canaan and farther south across the Isthmus of Suez into Egypt. They settled in the "Land of Goshen," east of the Nile Delta, where the Nile flows into the Mediterranean Sea.

These Hebrews lived peacefully in Egypt for some time, but eventually they fell from favor. Some scholars believe that one group of Hebrews

Text continues on page 42.

Genesis 6:8 and the Babylonian version in Nels M. Bailey's *Readings in Ancient History: From Gilgamesh to Diocletian* (D. C. Heath). Discuss with students the similarities and differences between the two accounts. The similarities should be evident. *(Differences include the following: In the Hebrew version the flood is sent because of sin, and Noah is saved because he is good. In the Babylonian version the hero is saved out of favoritism. The Hebrews have one supreme God in contrast to the many Babylonian gods.)*

1B, a3B, a3C

PERSPECTIVES: LEGACIES OF THE PAST

What is money? Quite simply, it is any object that people are willing to accept as payment for goods or services.

Throughout history, money has taken many different forms, but its definition has changed in only one way: Today money is accepted as payment by all people; in the past it was accepted only by some.

Early societies—people who hunted, fished, and farmed for their own needs—used a barter system. One family might trade a basket of fish for another family's extra vegetables. This system was extremely burdensome, however. If the farmer did not want fish that day, the fisher would have to make several trades to get the needed vegetables.

To make trade easier, people began to look for objects with a common value. To work well, the object had to be useful to everyone, rare enough to be valuable, and small and light enough to be carried. One of the first kinds of this "commodity money" people tried was salt. In the ancient Middle East, people carried salt in small containers and traded it for other objects. Early Roman emperors gave salt to their soldiers as a type of travel allowance. In fact, our word "salary" comes from the Roman word "salarium" or "salt place." Salt was also used in Africa, Abyssinia and parts of Asia. But this money was useful only in areas where salt was rare. The ancient Greeks, Romans, Egyptians, and early Europeans also used cattle as money.

A most impractical form of money was employed on the island of Yap in the South Pacific. People there used wheel-shaped boulders as money until the mid-1900s. To carry their money, two people had to pass a pole through a hole in the middle and rest it on their shoulders. Unlike cattle, the stones had no other practical use, but because they came from the distant islands of Guam and Peleu, they were greatly prized. Even today, many Yaps place these large stones in front of their houses, and smaller stones are still used as currency.

Seashells were another widely accepted form of money. In southern Asia, the Pacific Islands, and parts of the Middle East and Africa, people used the colorful cowrie shell. But the shell money with which Americans are most familiar is "wampum." These carefully cut and highly polished black and white shells were both beautiful and rare.

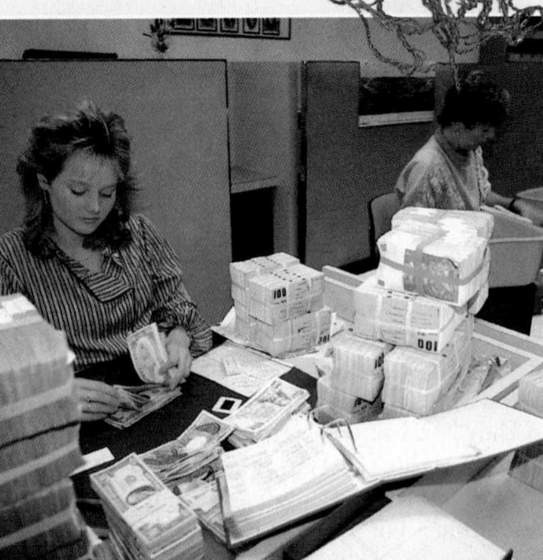

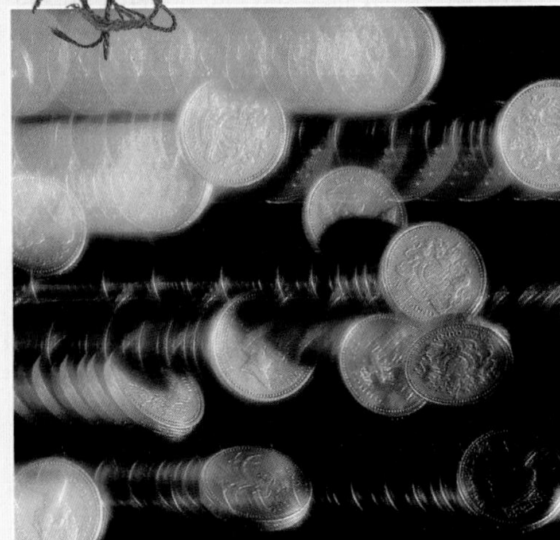

40

The Rich History of Money

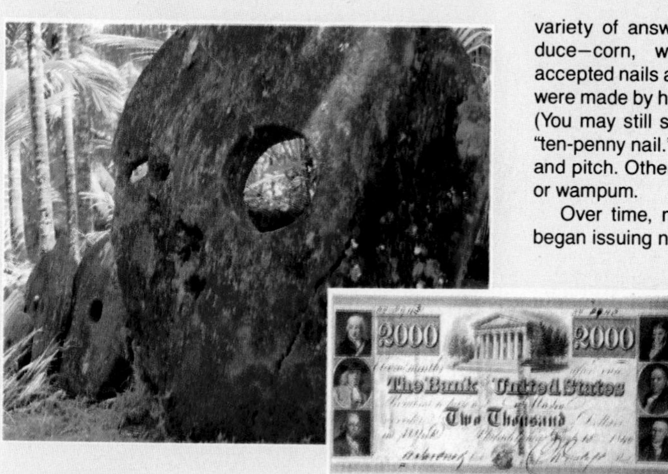

For hundreds of years, Indians in what is today the northeastern United States used these tiny, hard objects, strung together on their belts and jewelry, as their only money.

Easy to carry, durable, and scarce, shells made excellent money. But in other parts of the world, another object—metal—met these requirements. By 800 B.C., parts of China and the Middle East were using gold, silver, and copper shaped as long bars or even lumps. Farmers of early Rome used crude copper or bronze bars. Since the metal was exchanged for its actual value, it was weighed at every transaction, and eventually merchants began to mark the weight on each bar.

As the countries around the Mediterranean Sea began to trade with one another, they needed to find a kind of money that was guaranteed in value and was light enough to be carried on ships without sinking them. About 700 B.C., the king of Lydia, in what is now called Turkey, came up with the idea of stamping his personal mark on small kidney-bean-shaped pieces of electrum (a mixture of gold and silver). These "staters" are usually considered to be the first coins. Within 100 years, Greece began minting coins. About 200 B.C., Rome came out with the silver "denarius," which became one of the most widely accepted coins in the world.

The early American colonists were unable to use coins. Few of the settlers who first arrived in the British colonies were wealthy, and the money they had brought with them soon flowed back to Europe to buy supplies. When the colonists tried to mint their own money, such as the Massachusetts Pine-tree Shilling, the British government stopped them.

Faced with these problems, what were the colonists to use for money? The inventive colonists came up with a variety of answers to this question. In addition to produce—corn, wheat, peas, and rye—many colonies accepted nails as money. Scarce and costly because they were made by hand, nails were valued in terms of a penny. (You may still sometimes hear the terms "two-penny" or "ten-penny nail.") The Carolinas accepted rice, indigo, tar, and pitch. Other colonies used Indian corn, beaver skins, or wampum.

Over time, many governments throughout the world began issuing notes or IOUs for their coins. Unlike earlier forms of money, the notes had no value themselves. The government simply agreed to pay the owner the face value of the note in gold or silver. These early forms of paper money, first used in China more than 1,000 years ago, became common all over the world by the 1700s. But the value of paper money depended on the confidence people had in the government that issued it. After the Civil War, for example, Confederate "scrip" issued by the South became totally worthless.

Coins today are little more than symbols themselves. The face value stamped on the coin is far more than the coin's metal is worth. Beginning in 1965 dimes and quarters minted by the United States contained no silver at all.

Today, with automated banking and computerized checking, we think little about the problems of storing, handling, and transporting our money. However, not so long ago a cow would have gotten you a lot further than a credit card.

Photos Page 40: wampum belt (top), Swiss bank worker (bottom left), manufacturing coins (bottom right); Page 41: Yap money (top), early United States paper money (middle), ancient coins (bottom)

1B, 3B

Learning from Pictures *In their siege on the Canaanite city of Jericho, the Hebrews carry the ark of the covenant containing the Ten Commandments around the walls of the city.*

entered Egypt along with the Hyksos in the 1700s B.C. When the Egyptians finally expelled the Hyksos in the 1500s B.C., the pharaohs enslaved the Hebrews.

Establishing a homeland. A great leader, Moses, later arose among the Hebrews and led his people out of slavery and into the deserts of the Sinai Peninsula. The books of Exodus, Numbers, and Deuteronomy in the Bible describe Moses and the escape from Egypt.

According to the Bible, Moses climbed to the top of Mount Sinai and returned to the Hebrews bearing the **Ten Commandments**—the moral laws the Hebrew god Yahweh (YAH • way) revealed to him. These commandments emphasize the Hebrew principles of self-restraint; the importance of the family, human life, and formal worship; and the nature of the monotheistic religion. As the Bible records:

"God spoke, and these were his words:
I am the LORD your God who brought you out of Egypt, out of the land of slavery.

[1] You shall have no other god to set against me.

[2] You shall not make a carved image for yourself nor the likeness of anything in the heavens above, or on the earth below, or in the waters under the earth. . . .

[3] You shall not make wrong use of the name of the LORD your God; the LORD will not leave unpunished the man who misuses his name.

[4] Remember to keep the sabbath day holy. You have six days to labour and do all your work. But the seventh day is a sabbath of the LORD your God; that day you shall not do any work. . . .

42

[5] Honour your father and your mother. . . .
[6] You shall not commit murder.
[7] You shall not commit adultery.
[8] You shall not steal.
[9] You shall not give false evidence against your neighbour.
[10] You shall not covet your neighbour's house; you shall not covet your neighbour's wife . . . or anything that belongs to him. ”

Moses claimed that Canaan was a promised land and that Yahweh had commissioned him to found a holy nation. Inspired by his words, the Hebrews set out for Canaan. According to the Bible, Moses and his followers wandered in the desert for many years. Finally, a new generation of Hebrews entered Canaan.

The Hebrews who had come from Egypt joined those who had lived for so long on the borders of northern Canaan. By this time the harsh desert life had hardened the Hebrews into tough desert tribes. But establishing a homeland in Canaan proved difficult. A people known as the Canaanites held the northern Jordan Valley, while the Philistines lived along the southern coast. Both groups vigorously defended their land in a struggle that lasted more than 100 years. The Hebrews first conquered the Canaanites, making it possible for some of the Hebrews to settle in the Jordan Valley. The Philistines proved fiercer opponents. The Hebrews drove them closer to the seacoast but never conquered them completely.

A new government and new customs. As nomads the Hebrews had been divided into 12 tribes. During the long years of fighting, the tribes united under the rule of one king. The first king of this united kingdom called Israel was Saul. David, and then Solomon, succeeded Saul.

David occupied the city of Jerusalem and made it a capital and a religious center. His son, Solomon, built palaces there and a great temple for Yahweh, but the enormous cost overburdened the poor country. The government levied high taxes and forced many people to work on these great buildings without pay.

At the end of Solomon's reign in 922 B.C., the 10 northern tribes revolted, and the kingdom divided into two parts. The northern part became the kingdom of Israel, with its capital at Samaria. The southern part, situated around the Dead Sea, became the kingdom of Judah, with Jerusalem as its capital (see map, page 38).

These two Hebrew kingdoms lacked the strength to withstand invasions from the east. About 722 B.C. the Assyrians ravaged Samaria and conquered Israel, capturing many Hebrews and deporting them as slaves. Later, in 586 B.C., the Chaldeans captured Judah and its capital, Jerusalem (see chart, this page). They destroyed Solomon's temple and took the southern Hebrews into captivity. Cyrus, the Persian king, conquered the Chaldeans and allowed the Hebrews to return to their homeland to rebuild the temple at Jerusalem. Thereafter, however, one people after another conquered the Hebrews.

Kingdoms and Empires of the Fertile Crescent

ca. 3000 B.C. – 2400 B.C.	Sumerians
ca. 2400 B.C. – 2300 B.C.	Akkadians
ca. 1800 B.C. – 1600 B.C.	Babylonians
ca. 1600 B.C. – 1200 B.C.	Hittites
ca. 1200 B.C. – 586 B.C.	Hebrews
ca. 1000 B.C. – 700 B.C.	Phoenicians
ca. 900 B.C. – 612 B.C.	Assyrians
ca. 700 B.C. – 547 B.C.	Lydians
612 B.C. – 539 B.C.	Chaldeans
550 B.C. – 331 B.C.	Persians

The Old Testament and Jewish Law

The great Hebrew work of literature is the Old Testament of the Bible. Its 39 books tell the story of the creation of the world, the special mission of the Hebrews, their escape from slavery in Egypt, and the progress of their history and beliefs over 1,000 years. About one-third of the books tell the history. The remainder includes poetry, religious instruction, prophecy, and laws.

The Hebrews did not think of **prophets** as people who predicted the future, though some prophets claimed that they could. Rather, they viewed the prophets as great religious and moral thinkers—the nagging conscience of the people. The messages that prophets conveyed in such phrases as "A soft answer turneth away wrath," "There is no peace unto the wicked," and "Thou shalt love thy neighbor as thyself" have remained the foundation for moral and ethical behavior.

43

1A, 1C

SECTION 5

Closure

The peoples of the western Fertile Crescent—the Phoenicians, Lydians, and Hebrews—did not form large and powerful empires. Ask: What were their contributions that had a more lasting impact on world history? *(alphabet, money economy, ethical monotheism)*

Review Answers

1. ***barter:*** trading one good or service for another without money; ***money economy:*** economic system based on the use of money; ***Ten Commandments:*** moral laws revealed to Moses by the Hebrew God Yahweh; ***prophet:*** religious and moral thinker; ***ethical monotheism:*** Hebrew form of monotheism based on ethics, or proper conduct
2. ***Phoenicians:*** people who lived in western part of Fertile Crescent and were noted for skillful sailing and contributing alphabet to Western civilization; ***Hebrews:*** another name for Jews; ***Abraham:*** Biblical ancestor of Hebrews; ***Moses:*** led Jews out of Egypt to Canaan, the Biblical promised land; ***Saul:*** first king of Israel; ***David:*** Saul's successor, moved capital to Jerusalem; ***Solomon:*** Son of David, built great temple
3. ***Phoenicia:*** area north of Canaan; ***Lydia:*** area in Asia Minor; ***Tyre:*** seaport in Phoenicia; ***Sidon:*** seaport in Phoenicia; ***Israel:*** northern area of Canaan;

LINKING GEOGRAPHY TO HISTORY

The Amazing Variety of the Earth's Surface

Plains, plateaus, hills, mountains, canyons, valleys, and ridges are but a few of our planet's amazing variety of landforms, or shapes on the earth's surface. As you read about these landforms, think about the ones that can be seen in the area where you live.

Types of Landforms

By and large, geographers recognize four general types of landforms—plains, plateaus, hills, and mountains. Geographers categorize these landforms in terms of such characteristics as slope and local relief. Slope refers to the slant of the land. Local relief refers to a landform's elevation. Elevation is a place's distance above or below sea level. The difference in elevation between the highest and lowest points in an area is that area's local relief.

Plains. Geographers classify landforms with nearly level or gently rolling land as plains. This type of landform has little slope and, by definition, a local relief of less than 500 feet (150 meters). Most plains occur at low elevations—less than 1,000 feet (305 meters) above sea level. The Gulf Coastal Plain of the United States, for example, stretches from the Gulf of Mexico to southern Illinois, but no part of it rises higher than 500 feet (150 meters) above sea level. A few plains, such as the western Great Plains of the United States, however, are located at higher elevations.

Plateaus. A plateau is a generally flat area that rises far above the surrounding land on at least one side. Tableland—another name for plateau—provides a helpful image of the characteristics of this landform. Like a table, a plateau has a flat surface high off the ground.

Among the most distinguishing feature of plateaus is their high elevation. The Colorado Plateau of the western United States, for example, lies 7,000 to 8,000 feet (2,135 to 2,440 meters) above sea level. The Plateau of Tibet in China rises more than 15,000 feet (4,572 meters) above sea level. Some plateaus, however, occur at relatively low elevations.

The land at the top of a plateau is usually broad and flat. On some plateaus, deep canyons break up this pattern. These canyons have high slope and high local relief. For example, the Grand Canyon, which the Colorado River carved into the Colorado Plateau, has a local relief of more than 5,000 feet (1,525 meters).

Hills. Geographers classify as a hill any generally rounded landform that rises at least 500 feet (152 meters) above the surrounding area. The slope of hills varies from very gentle to very steep. By definition, however, the local relief of a hill must be less than 2,000 feet (610 meters).

Mountains. A dramatic type of landform that rises sharply from the surrounding land to heights thousands of feet above sea level is called a mountain. Mountains have steep slope and local relief of at least 2,000 feet (610 meters). The summit, or highest point, of a mountain typically appears smaller and sharper than the summit of a hill. High elevations also distinguish mountains from other landforms. For example, the highest mountain in the world, Mount Everest in the Himalayas in Asia, soars to an elevation of 29,028 feet (8,848 meters) above sea level.

Landforms and History

Throughout history landforms have had an important impact on human activity. For example, the fertile plains areas of North Africa and the Middle East nurtured the growth of the early civilizations you have read about in this chapter. In addition, huge mountain barriers have isolated some civilizations from outside influence for thousands of years. However, you should note that landforms only influence history, they do not determine it. In fact, one of the most important themes of history concerns the ways in which people have altered their physical environment to suit their way of life.

The majestic Austrian Alps

Learning from Pictures *At the Synagogue of the Home for the Aged in Tel-Aviv, this elderly man reads about the teachings of Judaism.*

The first five books of the Old Testament, known as the Torah, listed the Hebrew, or Jewish, code of laws. This code of laws, named for Moses, was called Mosaic law and included the Ten Commandments and laws developed during later periods. Mosaic law, like the Code of Hammurabi, demanded "an eye for an eye," but it set a much higher value on human life. Although Mosaic law accepted slavery as the custom of the ancient world, the law demanded kindness for slaves. Mosaic law also preached kindness toward the poor and toward strangers, as did Babylonian law. Mosaic law reserved the most severe punishments for witchcraft and sacrifices to idols, crimes punished by death.

Mosaic law reflected the belief that all people, regardless of their station in life, deserved kindness and respect. This belief was based on the idea that Yahweh had created each person in his image. In later centuries, Christians adopted this same belief as part of their religion.

Judaism

Judaism, the religion of the Hebrews, survived partly because it changed throughout history. The early Hebrews worshiped Yahweh as a god who belonged to them alone and believed that people needed only to trust in Yahweh. They believed that Yahweh protected them from their enemies, took their side in battle, and provided them with food and water. According to the Ten Commandments, Yahweh was a jealous god. If people sinned against Yahweh, not only would they be punished but also their children and succeeding generations would suffer. The Hebrews therefore viewed Yahweh not only as their protector and provider but also as a god to fear.

This concept of Yahweh slowly changed, partly because of the Hebrews' many sufferings and partly because of the teachings and writings of their prophets. In general, the prophets insisted that Yahweh was more concerned with a person's moral behavior than with religious rituals. Like the Zoroastrians, the Hebrews believed that people had a choice between good and evil. The Hebrews also believed that Yahweh held them responsible for their choices.

These ideas led the Hebrews to think of Yahweh as a loving father—a god who lived in the hearts of his worshipers and the god of all peoples. Other ancient peoples thought of their gods as having human qualities, but as being more powerful than humans. The Hebrews viewed Yahweh as a spiritual force rather than as a human being. The kings of other ancient peoples claimed to be gods or the representatives of gods in order to gain power. Hebrew kings were not gods. Only Yahweh was divine.

Because of its emphasis on ethics, or proper conduct, the Hebrew form of monotheism is often called **ethical monotheism.** It ranks as the most important contribution of the ancient Jews to Western civilization.

SECTION 5 REVIEW

1. **Define** barter, money economy, Ten Commandments, prophet, ethical monotheism
2. **Identify** Phoenicians, Hebrews, Abraham, Moses, Saul, David, Solomon
3. **Locate** Phoenicia, Lydia, Tyre, Sidon, Israel, Canaan, Sinai Peninsula, Jordan River, Samaria, Judah, Jerusalem
4. **Evaluating Ideas** **(a)** How did Phoenician sea trade benefit the peoples of the Mediterranean? **(b)** How did the invention of coined money make trade easier?
5. **Analyzing Ideas** **(a)** Why did the Hebrews leave Egypt? **(b)** Why was it difficult for the Hebrews to conquer Canaan?
6. **Summarizing Ideas** What were three of the most important contributions of the Hebrews to our civilization?

Canaan: coastal strip of land south of Phoenicia; ***Sinai Peninsula:*** northern boundary of Red Sea and desert home of Moses; ***Jordan River:*** river in Canaan that empties into Dead Sea; ***Samaria:*** capital of Israel; ***Judah:*** southern section of Canaan along Dead Sea; ***Jerusalem:*** capital of Israel and then Judah

4. (a) The trade helped Mediterranean peoples to exchange goods and ideas. **(b)** Coined money allowed traders to set prices for goods and services.

5. (a) The Hebrews left Egypt to escape slavery. **(b)** Neither the Canaanites nor the Philistines desired to give up their land and fought against the Hebrews.

6. Mosaic law, the Old Testament, and ethical monotheism

Reviewing Important Terms
1. c; **2.** g; **3.** h; **4.** j; **5.** b; **6.** d; **7.** a; **8.** f; **9.** i; **10.** e

Developing Critical Thinking Skills
1. In Egypt people settled in permanent locations and generally lived in their ancestors' lands. In the Fertile Crescent, many different cultures invaded the surrounding regions and, in turn, were overthrown by new invaders.
2. (a) and **(b)** ***Sumerians:*** cuneiform writing, arch, dome, wheel, sewers, ramps, ziggurats, base-60 number system; ***Babylonians:*** Hammurabi's code, trade with other regions; ***Hittites:*** iron weapons, less brutal code of law; ***Assyrians:*** skilled warriors, imperial administration, road building, and postal service; ***Chaldeans:*** Hanging Gardens, astrology; ***Persians:*** efficient system of ruling an empire, road system, Zoroastrianism; ***Phoenicians:*** Mediterranean colonies; alphabet; ***Hebrews:*** Mosiac law, Old Testament, ethical monotheism
3. (a) The Red and Mediterranean seas and Persian Gulf are effective barriers, while deserts and mountains also separate civilizations and cultures. **(b)** People built ships, searched for mountain passes, and constructed roads.
4. (a) Jewish and Babylonian law demanded an "eye for an eye," although Jewish law set a higher value on human life. The Hittites accepted money payments (fines) for damages. Wealthy Babylonians could sometimes escape punishment by paying a fine. All three codes accepted slavery, but Jewish law demanded kindness.

1B, 1D, 2A, a4A, a4F, a4G, a4H, a4M

Reteaching
Have students review the Chapter Summary and the appropriate section and questions in the Unit Synthesis. Discuss the concepts until students demonstrate a clear understanding of the material.

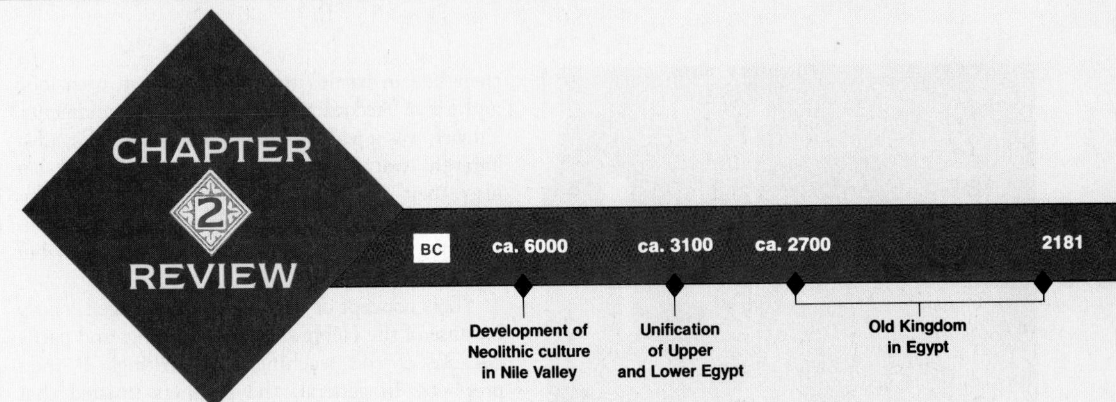

Chapter Summary

The following list contains the key concepts you have learned about the great civilizations that developed in the Middle East.

1. Because of its geography and climate, Egypt created a long-lasting and distinctive civilization whose monuments have endured to this day.
2. About 3100 B.C. Upper and Lower Egypt were united into a single kingdom ruled by pharaohs. The successive dynasties of pharaohs made Egypt a considerable power for some 2,000 years.
3. The Egyptians developed a remarkable society and culture. The arts, literature, science, and religion became sophisticated, and a complex and effective agricultural system evolved. At the same time, strict divisions were maintained between social classes. It was a very rigid but also an extremely inventive society.
4. In the Fertile Crescent a succession of conquests and empires led to a variety of societies and cultures.
5. The Sumerians organized city-states, invented a new form of writing, and made many discoveries in architecture and engineering.
6. The Babylonians were famous for their laws, written in the Code of Hammurabi.
7. The Assyrians were fierce warriors and extended their conquests farther than any previous empire.
8. The Persians developed a complex and effective government for their empire. They also adopted an influential new religion called Zoroastrianism.
9. The Phoenicians were the world's first great sea traders. They organized a loose union of cities and colonies around the Mediterranean that were linked by the sea. The alphabet that the Phoenicians developed became the model for later Western alphabets.
10. The Lydians of Asia Minor were the first to use coined money.
11. The Hebrews developed Judaism—a system of laws and a religious faith that has had a major influence on Western civilization. The great written work of Judaism, the Old Testament, introduced the concept of ethical monotheism, which has shaped Western history ever since.

On a separate sheet of paper, complete the following review exercises.

Reviewing Important Terms

Match each of the following terms with the correct definition below.

a. hieroglyphics
b. pharaoh
c. dynasty
d. monotheism
e. caravan
f. scribe
g. barter
h. ziggurat
i. Ten Commandments
j. prophet

___ **1.** family of rulers
___ **2.** exchange of a good or service for another good or service
___ **3.** Sumerian temple
___ **4.** great religious and moral thinker
___ **5.** leader of Egyptian government
___ **6.** belief in one god
___ **7.** writing that uses pictures or symbols to indicate words or sounds
___ **8.** clerk who read or wrote for those who could not
___ **9.** moral laws revealed to Moses
___ **10.** group of people traveling together for safety over long distances

Developing Critical Thinking Skills

1. **Contrasting Ideas** How did the civilization that arose along the banks of the Nile in Egypt differ from that of the Fertile Crescent?
2. **Understanding Ideas** **(a)** List the peoples of the Fertile Crescent. **(b)** Next to the name of each group, write down that group's most important achievements.
3. **Analyzing Maps** **(a)** Using the maps in Chapter 2, name the geographic barriers between the ancient civilizations of the Middle East. **(b)** How do you think the peoples of these early civilizations overcame these geographic barriers?
4. **Comparing Ideas** **(a)** Compare the legal systems of the Babylonians, the Hittites, and the Hebrews. **(b)** Under which system would you have preferred to live? Explain your choice.

Generally, Hittite and Jewish laws were less harsh than Babylonian. **(b)** Answers will vary.

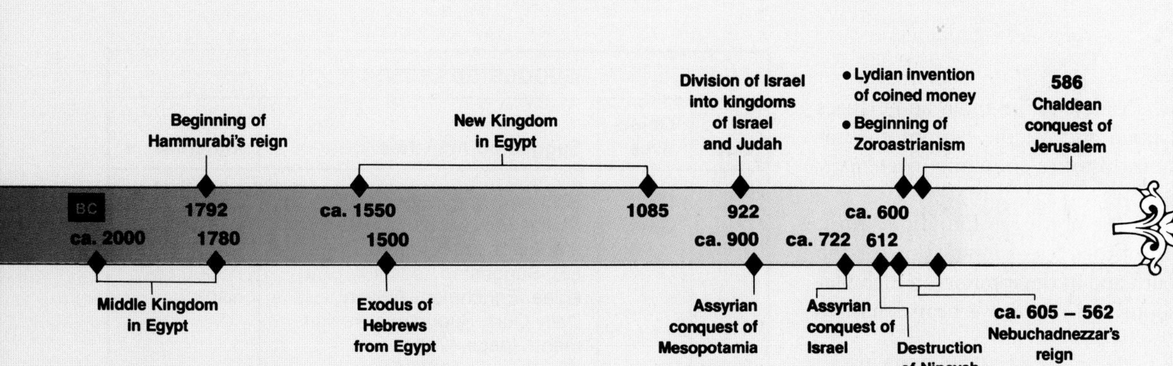

Relating Geography to History

The environment has an enormous impact on how a group of people lives and on the ideas and attitudes it holds. Choose two groups of people in this chapter and show how the environment affected **(a)** their ways of life, **(b)** their ways of making a living, and **(c)** their ideas and attitudes.

Relating Past to Present

1. **(a)** Look up the word *justice* in a dictionary. How would you define it? **(b)** How does the concept of justice in the United States today compare with the concept of justice shown in Hammurabi's code? **(c)** Which concept of justice do you think would be more effective in combating crime?
2. **(a)** Throughout history, trade has been an important source for the spread of ideas from one culture to another. How does trade in the world today help the spread of ideas from one culture to another? **(b)** What effects do you think movies and records from the United States might have on other cultures? **(c)** Can you give other examples of cultural diffusion?
3. In this chapter you read about the pharaoh Akhenaton's conflict with the priests of the god Amon. This was an early example in history of a conflict between governmental authority and religion. Review how the First Amendment to the United States Constitution deals with the relationship between church and state in the United States.
4. Economic power is an important part of being a major empire. **(a)** Explain the basis of the economic power of ancient Egypt. **(b)** What was the basis of the economic power of the Fertile Crescent? **(c)** Explain the economic power of oil-producing countries today. How does this affect the political and military power of the United States and the Soviet Union?
5. **(a)** Cotton continues to be an important crop in Egypt and many other parts of the world, including the southeastern United States. Using encyclopedias and statistical abstracts, find out about the size and nature of the cotton industry in the United States. **(b)** What are some of the items produced from the cotton crop in the United States?

Applying History Study Skills

Before completing this activity, review Building History Study Skills on page 31.

Look again at the definitions of a primary source and a secondary source. Then review the guidelines for identifying sources of evidence.

Select a historical event that occurred in the last 100 years. For example, you may be interested in a particular aspect of the Great Depression, World War II, or the Vietnam War. If possible, interview a person who experienced that event. You may wish to prepare a list of questions ahead of time.

After you have discussed the historical event with an "eyewitness," locate a secondary source, such as a magazine article, on the same topic. Then compare the information you have available. Did both sources present a similar point of view? What advantages or disadvantages can you identify regarding the use of primary sources and secondary sources? Which type of evidence is more useful?

Investigating Further

1. **Making Comparisons** Use encyclopedias in your school or public library to write a report comparing Judaism, Christianity, Zoroastrianism, and the religion of ancient Egypt. You should write about the beliefs each religion has regarding the struggle between good and evil. Conclude your report by discussing why the conflict between good and evil is a persistent theme in most religions.
2. **Writing a Report** The pyramids are among the most impressive structures left by any civilization. Research and write a report on the techniques of Egyptian building. You might use the following books as sources: Ahmed Fakhry's *The Pyramids* (University of Chicago Press), and James Finch's *The Story of Engineering* (Doubleday), which has a chapter titled "The Chief Works of Ancient Egypt."
3. **Contrasting Ideas** Find pictures of modern Egyptian cities that also show ancient Egyptian structures. Write a paragraph contrasting the modern structures with the ancient structures.

Relating Geography to History
Answers will vary.

Relating Past to Present
1. (a) Answers will vary. Students should include a sense of "to treat fairly" or "administer the law impartially." **(b)** Hammurabi's "eye-for-an-eye" code versus our society's concern for a fair, impartially-administered trial by jury **(c)** Answers will vary.
2. (a) As trade between countries increases, international contacts become more frequent and extend beyond pure commerce. **(b)** American movies and records influence music and life styles. **(c)** Answers will vary.
3. The First Amendment guarantees freedom of worship to individuals but separates church and state.
4. (a) Agriculture was the basis of the economic power of ancient Egypt. **(b)** Agriculture and trade were the basis of the economic power of the Fertile Crescent. **(c)** Answers will vary.
5. (a) Answers will vary. Students could also research the value of the cotton industry for several individual states in the United States. **(b)** Answers will vary. Students will probably center their research on the textile industry, particularly clothing.

Applying History Study Skills
Answers will vary.

CHAPTER (pages 48-67)

3 People Created Thriving Civilizations in India

(ca. 2500 B.C.–A.D. 535)

CHAPTER OVERVIEW

Civilization developed early in the valleys of the Indus and Ganges rivers in India. Unlike the Egyptian and Middle Eastern civilizations, they had nearly continuous histories stretching over many centuries into the present.

India's geography is varied. In the north are the Hindu Kush and Himalaya mountains. South of these great mountains lies the Indo-Gangetic Plain. Farther south and in the interior is a high plateau called the Deccan. Monsoons and oppressive heat dominate the climate.

The earliest civilization in India appeared about 2500 B.C., centered in the cities of Harappa and Mohenjo-Daro. Indus Valley people had a written language and an animistic religion. About 1500 B.C. a nomadic people from the north, the Aryans, invaded India. They brought with them their religion, which was based on the Vedas, their sacred collections of knowledge.

In India two important influences emerged—the caste system and Hinduism. The classes developed by the early Aryans eventually developed into some 3,000 hereditary castes. Each caste had a fixed social position and rules governing all aspects of life. Hinduism taught that the world of the senses is an illusion. Humans can escape only through many lifetimes of reincarnation.

A second religion to develop in India was Buddhism. Gautama Buddha stressed ethics rather than ceremonies. Buddhism gained many followers in India and elsewhere in Asia, although it later declined in India.

The Maurya and Gupta empires united most of India. Under the Guptas, particularly, outstanding achievements were made in literature, art, education, mathematics, astronomy, and medicine.

Southern India developed quite differently. Many of its people became traders.

SUGGESTED LESSON PLAN

Day	Objec-tives	Suggested Activities	Materials
1	U6* C1-2,	Introducing the Chapter (page 48) Section 1 (pages 49-54), Focus/Motivation (page 49), Presentation (pages 49-50), Closure (page 54), Suggested Teaching Strategies, Enrichment Activity, Daily Quiz, Suggested Assignments (pages 47B-47C)	ATE, Pupil's Edition, Teacher's Resource-Bank™

*C refers to applicable Chapter Objective, U refers to applicable Unit Goal

SUGGESTED LESSON PLAN

Day	Objec-tives	Suggested Activities	Materials
2	U6, C3-4	Section 2 (pages 54-57), Focus/Motivation (page 55), Presentation (page 55), Closure (page 56), Suggested Teaching Strategies, Enrichment Activity, Daily Quiz, Suggested Assignments (page 47C)	ATE, Pupil's Edition, Teacher's Resource-Bank™
3	U7, C5-9	Section 3 (pages 57-61), Focus/Motivation (page 57), Presentation (pages 57-58), Closure (page 60), Suggested Teaching Strategies, Enrichment Activities, Daily Quiz, Suggested Assignments (page 47D)	ATE, Pupil's Edition, Teacher's Resource-Bank™
4	U6, C10-11	Section 4 (pages 62-63), Focus/Motivation (page 62), Presentation (page 62), Closure (page 62), Suggested Teaching Strategies, Enrichment Activity Daily Quiz, Suggested Assignments (pages 47D-47E)	ATE, Pupil's Edition, Teacher's Resource-Bank™
5	U6, C12	Section 5 (pages 63-65), Focus/Motivation (page 63), Presentation (page 64), Closure (page 64), Suggested Teaching Strategies, Enrichment Activity, Daily Quiz, Suggested Assignments (pages 47E-47F)	ATE, Pupil's Edition, Teacher's Resource-Bank™
6	U6-7 C1-12	Chapter 3 Form A Test, Reteaching Worksheet, Chapter 3 Form B Test	Teacher's Resource-Bank™ or Workbook and Test Booklet

BOOKS FOR THE TEACHER

Auboyer, Jeanine. *Daily Life in Ancient India.* Macmillan. Describes the social life of India from 200 B.C. to A.D. 700.

Schulberg, Lucille. *Historic India.* Time-Life. Examines the historical, social, political, and cultural aspects of India. Includes illustrations.

Smith, Huston. *The Religions of Man.* Harper & Row. Compares Hinduism, Buddhism, Daoism, and Confucianism.

Welty, Paul. *The Asians.* Lippincott. Introduces traditional Asian societies.

Wolpert, Stanley. *India.* Prentice-Hall. Presents a short history of India. Also useful for later chapters.

BOOKS FOR THE STUDENT

Kelen, Betty. *Gautama Buddha.* Lothrop, Lee & Shepard. Explains the life and teachings of Gautama Buddha.

Wirsing, Robert, and Nancy Wirsing. *Ancient India and Its Influence in Modern Times.* Franklin Watts. Focuses on early Indian civilizations, with good coverage of both the Harappan and Aryan civilizations.

MULTIMEDIA MATERIALS

Ancient Orient (mp, 14 min.), Coronet. Portrays the religions, philosophies, and arts of ancient India, China, and Japan.

Buddhist World (mp, 11 min.). Coronet. Presents the life and teachings of Gautama Buddha and the growth of Buddhism.

Hindu World (mp, 11 min.), Coronet. Surveys the history and culture of the Hindu world against a background of ancient temples and scenes of Hindu religious rites.

India: Greece of the Orient (fs), Multi-Media. Examines the culture and philosophy of India.

Men Who Made History: Gautama Buddha (fs), EBE. Presents the life, teachings, and influence of Buddha.

Pakistan: The Mound of the Dead (mp, 27 min.), Centron. Examines the ruins of Mohenjo-Daro and Harappa and offers explanations for the decline of Indus Valley civilization.

World's Great Religions (fs), Life. Includes two titles appropriate for Chapter 7: "Buddhism," "Hinduism."

Section 1 (pages 49-54) The First Indian Civilization Arose in the Indus Valley

SECTION OVERVIEW

The subcontinent of India has four main geographical regions: the northern mountains, the Indo-Gangetic Plain, the Deccan, and the Coastal Plain. Monsoons and oppressive heat are dominant features of the Indian climate. An impressive civilization appeared in the Indus River Valley about 2500 B.C. The ruins of Mohenjo-Daro and Harappa show that the Indus Valley people were skilled city planners and builders who lived by industry and trade. The civilization lasted for about 1,000 years. However, the reason for the decline of this civilization has not been determined

SUGGESTED TEACHING STRATEGIES

1. **Preteaching Vocabulary (Basic)** You may wish to preteach the following important vocabulary terms: monsoon *(page 51)*; citadel, animism *(page 52)*. Ask students where the heaviest monsoon rains fall. *(Ganges Valley and eastern Himalayas)*
2. **Presenting a Report (Average/Group)** Have two or three students give oral reports and show pictures on some aspect of Mohenjo-Daran and Harappan civilization. Several books with excellent illustrations and photographs include: Leonard Cottrell's *Horizon Book of Lost Worlds* (American Heritage); Stuart Piggott's *The Dawn of Civilization* (McGraw-Hill); and *The World's Last Mysteries* (Reader's Digest).

*3. **Reading About History: Classifying Information (Basic)** To reinforce the skill presented on page 53, have students construct a chart that illustrates the achievements of Indian civilization from the Epic Age to the Gupta Empire.

ENRICHMENT ACTIVITY

Understanding Climate (Average/Group) Have students do research on the monsoons. India of course has river valleys—the Indus and Ganges. In addition, India is affected by the monsoons. Have students explain how monsoons make Indian civilization different than the Nile River valley civilization. Have them then make a general statement about the importance of climate in determining how a civilization will develop.

DAILY QUIZ

To assess student understanding of Section 1, give the class the following quiz. (Each item is worth 10 points.)

1. List the four geographic regions of India. *(the northern mountains; Indo-Gangetic Plain; Deccan; Coastal Plain)*
2. (T or F) The northern mountains, particularly the Hindu Kush, effectively isolated India from northern invaders and protected those who lived on the river plain. *(F)*
3. (T or F) Of the two great rivers, the Ganges is the most important, flowing to the southeast and creating a very broad, fertile valley. *(F)*
4. (T or F) The Deccan is an area of rapid cultural assimilation, its people borrowing from those who settled on the other side of the Vindhya Mountains. *(F)*
5. (T or F) The people who lived along the Costal Plain frequently traded with those people who lived on the Indo-Gangetic Plain. *(F)*
6. Name the two features that dominate the climate of India. *(monsoons; heat)*
7. (T or F) The ruins of Mohenjo-Daro and Harappa reveal well-planned cities, complete with water system, public baths, and sewers. *(T)*
8. Name the products crafted by those who lived in Mohenjo-Daro and Harappa. *(bronze sculptures; copper and bronze tools; oven-baked bricks; gold and silver jewelry; cotton cloth)*
9. Indus River valley artifacts indicate the people believed in a type of religion called ______, in which spirits inhabited everything. *(animism)*

10. Name possible causes of the collapse of Harappan civilization. *(earthquakes; floods; salt-water intrusion; invasion)*

SUGGESTED ASSIGNMENTS

1. **Applying Geography Skills (Basic)** Have students complete "Geography Fact Sheet: World Physical Features," in the TEACHER'S RESOURCEBANK™.
2. **Skill Worksheet (Basic)** Have students complete Skill Worksheet 3 in the TEACHER'S RESOURCEBANK™

Section 2 (pages 54-57)

Aryan Invaders Ruled India's Northern Plain During the Vedic Age

SECTION OVERVIEW

Aryan warriors entered northwestern India about 1500 B.C. and destroyed the urban civilization of the Indus Valley. They established a simple form of government and engaged in agriculture and the production of handicrafts. Aryan religion was based on the Vedas—their collections of sacred knowledge. Most of our information on the Aryans comes from the Vedas, which were written down long after the Vedic Age.

SUGGESTED TEACHING STRATEGIES

1. **Preteaching Vocabulary (Basic)** You may wish to preteach the following important vocabulary terms: Brahman (*page* 55); rajah (*page* 57). Ask students why the Brahmans became important in Aryan society.
2. **Understanding Words (Basic)** Reproduce the following scrambled words and their clues and distribute copies to the class.

a. yanars	Indo-European warrior tribes that forced their way into northwestern India
b. avanur	God who began as the heavens and evolved into the enforcer of right and wrong
c. haajr	A prince who ruled each city-state
d. desav	The great literature of the Aryan religion
e. tsinaskr	Language spoken by the Aryans
f. mabnshar	Priests in the Aryan religion
g. tabrer	Exchange of one item for another without the use of money

(Answers: a. Aryans, b. Varuna, c. rajah, d. Vedas, e. Sanskrit, f. Brahmans, g. barter)

3. **Classifying Information (Basic)** Have students make a chart of the characteristics of Aryan society in their notebooks. The headings should be: Government, Social Life, and Economy. Completed charts should be similar to the following one.

CHARACTERISTICS OF ARYAN SOCIETY		
Government	**Social Life**	**Economy**
Tribes formed small city-states Each state ruled by rajah and council of friends and relatives	Aryans looked down on conquered people Laws against marriage of Aryans with original valley dwellers Men permitted more than one wife Men owned wives and children Sons expected to be warriors and perform ritual at father's funeral	Mostly farmers Barley major crop Most owned their land Handicrafts in villages System of barter for goods Cattle traded for goods

ENRICHMENT ACTIVITY

Comparing Past and Present (Average/Group) Modern society has challenged traditional Indian views on marriage. Have students check newspapers and the *Readers' Guide to Periodical Literature* for current articles. Ask students to share their articles with the class.

DAILY QUIZ

To assess student understanding of Section 2, give the class the following quiz. (Each item is worth 10 points.)

1. What language did the Indo-Aryans speak? *(Sanskrit)*
2. What was the primary Indo-Aryan occupation? *(herding)*
3. What are the Vedas? *(Hindu books of sacred knowledge, religious rituals, and hymns)*
4. How were the Vedas originally preserved and passed on from generation to generation like other cultures? *(word of mouth)*
5. (T or F) Unlike the Persians, the Aryans did not believe in immortality. *(F)*
6. (T or F) The Vedic religion, full of references to many gods, had one chief god, Varuna. *(F)*
7. What were Brahmans? *(Priests)*
8. (T or F) The Aryans initiated rules prohibiting marriage between the darker-complected, Indus Valley city dwellers and light-skinned Aryans. *(T)*
9. List a crop raised on the Indo-Gangetic Plain. *(barley)*

10. (T or F) The rajah, or prince, rules each city-state, acting as military leader, chief priest, lawmaker, and judge. *(T)*

SUGGESTED ASSIGNMENTS

1. **Critical Thinking Worksheet (Average/Group)** Have students complete Critical Thinking Worksheet 6 in the TEACHER'S RESOURCEBANK™.
2. **Comparing World Climates (Basic)** Have students complete "Geography Fact Sheet: World Climates," in the TEACHER'S RESOURCEBANK™.

Section (pages 57-61)

3 Buddhism and Hinduism Took Hold in India

SECTION OVERVIEW

The Epic Age lasted from about 1000 to 500 B.C. and took its name from the religious literature of the period. From this literature and the Vedas, scholars have gained information about the origins and development of Hinduism and the caste system. Buddhism, founded in India by Gautama Buddha, taught that salvation comes from knowing the Four Noble Truths and following the Eightfold Path. Buddhism spread throughout many parts of Asia and split into two branches: Hinayana, which regards Buddha as a teacher, and Mahayana, which regards Buddha as a god. Buddhism gained many followers, but it later declined in India.

SUGGESTED TEACHING STRATEGIES

1. **Preteaching Vocabulary (Basic)** You may wish to preteach the following important vocabulary terms: Epic Age *(page 57)*; epic, caste system, monism, reincarnation, dharma, karma *(page 58)*; yoga *(page 59)*; nirvana *(page 60)*. Ask students to list the four castes in their early order from top to bottom. *(Kshatriyas, Brahmans, Vaisyas, Sudras)* Which two castes later switched in order of importance? *(Brahmans and Kshatriyas)*
2. **Organizing Ideas (Basic)** Have students study the Aryan caste system on page 58. Then put the following chart on the chalkboard or an overhead projector. Ask students to copy it into their notebooks.

CLASS SYSTEM IN EARLY INDIA	
Upper class	Brahman: priests, scholars
	Kshatriyas: ruler, warriors
Middle class	Vaisyas: merchants, traders, farmers
Lower class	Sudras: peasants bound to land
	outcastes: untouchables

3. **Making an Outline (Basic)** Put the outline of the following chart on the chalkboard or an overhead projector. Have students complete the chart in their notebooks. The finished chart should resemble the following:

	HINAYANA	MAHAYANA
View of Buddha	Teacher	God and savior
Religious trappings	None	Priests, temples, creeds, and rituals
Areas of influence	Burma, Thailand, and Cambodia	Afghanistan, central China, Korea, and Japan

ENRICHMENT ACTIVITIES

1. **Interpreting a Reading (Average/Group)** Organize the class into four groups. Ask students to read "A Hindu View of Life" in Edwin Fenton's *Thirty-two Problems in World History* (Scott, Foresman). This reading contains selections from the *Upanishads.* Appoint a student in each group to lead a discussion on one of the questions provided with the reading. After the topic has been discussed in groups, call the students together to share ideas.
2. **Comparing Ideas (Average/Group)** Ask the students to review pages 58 to 61. Conduct a classroom discussion comparing Buddhism and Hinduism. The discussion should cover the origins of each religion; their teachings, practices, and rituals; and the similarities and differences between the two. Sources for an in-depth discussion include Paul Welty's *The Asians* (Lippincott); Lucille Shulberg's *Historic India* (Time-Life); and Elizabeth Seeger's *Eastern Religions* (Crowell).

DAILY QUIZ

To assess student understanding of Section 3, give the class the following quiz. (Each item is worth 10 points.)

1. (T or F) In poetic story form, the *Mahabharata* and the *Ramayana* summarize the tenets of the Vedic religion for the common people. *(T)*
2. The ______ system is a form of social organization, initiated by Aryans as they gained control of the northern plain. *(caste)*
3. List the four major Indian castes. *(Kshatriyas: rulers, warriors; Brahmans: priests, scholars; Vaisyas: merchants, traders; Sudras: peasants)*
4. Approximately how many castes evolved from the Aryan system? 1,000; 2,000; 3,000; 4,000 *(3,000)*
5. The lifetimes of experience needed to identify Maya is provided by ______, or the transmigration of souls in which the soul enters another body when the host dies. *(reincarnation)*

6. List the ways of following the Eightfold Path. *(right views; right intentions; right speech; right action; right living; right effort; right mindfulness; right concentration)*
7. (T or F) Hinayana, or Lesser Vehicle, kept the traditional beliefs of Buddhism and regarded Buddha as a teacher. *(T)*
8. (T or F) The Brahmans embraced Buddhism because it gave people, especially the untouchables, a chance to reach nirvana by avoiding reincarnation. *(F)*
9. (T or F) Gautama, the son of an Indian prince, renounced his wealth and position to search for the truth. *(T)*
10. Name the Hindu trinity. *(Brahma/Creator; Vishnu/Preserver; Siva/Destroyer)*

SUGGESTED ASSIGNMENTS

1. **Writing Assignment (Average/Group)** Have students write a letter from a Hindu student to a Western student explaining the Hindu religion. The letter should include five basic beliefs of Hinduism. Call upon volunteers to read their letters to the class.
2. **Profile Worksheet (Basic)** Have students complete Profile Worksheet 3 in the TEACHER'S RESOURCEBANK™.

Section (pages 62-63)

4 Dynasties and Empires Rose and Fell in Ancient India

SECTION OVERVIEW

Indian civilization reached great heights under Maurya and Gupta rulers. Literature and drama were popular, a distinctive style of architecture for the Hindu temple was developed, and murals were painted to decorate caves. Nalanda became a center of learning, and Indians made important discoveries in mathematics and medicine. In southern India people became seafarers and merchants who traded with Arabia and the Roman Empire.

SUGGESTED TEACHING STRATEGIES

1. **Relating Ideas (Basic)** Have students write short essays describing the reign of Chandragupta Maurya and the reign of Asoka. Ask for volunteers to read their essays to the class.
2. **Interpreting Ideas (Average/Group)** Ask: How did Asoka's military campaigns affect his outlook on life? *(War sickened Asoka and he became a devout Buddhist; urged religious toleration, relaxed harsh laws, and forbade animal sacrifices.)*

ENRICHMENT ACTIVITY

Researching Ideas (Challenging) Have interested students study and write a report on the Gupta Empire in India, A.D 320-A.D. 535. Ask them to answer the following questions in their reports: (1) How did the Guptas come to power? (2) What achievements took place during their years in power that caused people to call it a golden age in Indian history? (3) Why did the Guptas decline?

DAILY QUIZ

To assess student understanding of Section 4, give the class the following quiz. (Each item is worth 10 points.)

1. The Gupta rulers claimed they ruled because of their selection by the gods and supported the Brahmans and which religion? *(Hinduism)*
2. (T or F) The Maurya empire controlled only the Deccan and collapsed right before Mahaputra took over. *(F)*
3. One of the greatest rulers of the Maurya Empire was ________, who conquered almost all of India, converted to Buddhism and urged religious toleration. *(Asoka)*
4. (T or F) After the Maurya Empire collapsed, India entered a new period of cultural growth and economic success. *(F)*
5. What were the two major influences that played the primary role in southern Indian history? *(location, natural resources)*
6. (T or F) The golden age in Indian history occurred under the Maurya Empire. *(F)*
7. (T or F) Pataliputra on the Ganges River was the capital city of the Maurya rulers. *(T)*
8. The Persian ruler ________ conquered part of the Indus Valley in the 500s B.C. *(Darius)*
9. The ________ ________ have served as an effective barrier in separating the cultures of northern India from the south. *(Vindhya Mountains)*
10. (T or F) Asoka sent Hindu missionaries into the Deccan in 250 B.C. *(F)*

SUGGESTED ASSIGNMENT

Critical Thinking Worksheet (Average/Group) Have students complete Critical Thinking Worksheet 7 in the TEACHER'S RESOURCEBANK™.

Section (pages 63-65)

5 Civilization Flourished in Ancient India

SECTION OVERVIEW

Early Indian civilization left its mark upon Indian society. India was a land rich in products—silks, spices, jewels—that it could trade throughout the known world. Yet most Indians only eked out a meager existence on the soil while their rulers lived in great luxury. Nevertheless, the Epic Age and the Golden Age of the Gupta Empire were rich in literature, the arts, and architecture. Mathematicians invented the "Arabic" numeral system—1 through 9 and zero—that we use today, and astronomers understood many things about the earth and the planets that took the West much longer to discover.

SUGGESTED TEACHING STRATEGIES

1. **Preteaching Vocabulary (Basic)** You may wish to preteach the following important vocabulary terms: polygamy, suttee, stupa *(page 64)*. Ask students to compare the stupa with styles of other ancient civilizations. *(the pyramids in Egypt, the Ziggurats in Mesopotamia)*
2. **Relating Ideas (Basic)** Have students read about the *Panchatantra* in the subsection "Literature" on page 64. Then ask them to list a number of stories children read today. Have students investigate further the origins of these stories to discover which stories come from India and which come from other countries

ENRICHMENT ACTIVITY

Illustrating Ideas (Average/Group) Have interested students make oral presentations on the art and architecture of India. The Ajanta caves, Hindu tower temples, or Buddhist stupas make excellent topics for reports. Sources include Lucille Shulberg's *Historic India* (Time-Life); Benjamin Rowland's *The Ajanta Caves: Early Buddhist Paintings From India* (New American Library); and Benjamin Rowland's *The Art and Architecture of India* (Penguin).

DAILY QUIZ

To assess student understanding of Section 5, give the class the following quiz. (Each item is worth 10 points.)

1. (T or F) In Gupta India, a woman was man's truest friend, and equal to him in all respects. *(F)*
2. ________ is the marriage of a person to more than one spouse. *(Polygamy)*
3. (T or F) The *Panchatantra,* one of the most popularly translated books in the world, included stories about Sinbad the Sailor, Jack the Giant Killer, and the Seven League Boots. *(T)*
4. Asoka ordered construction of many ________, hemispheric-like buildings with ornate carvings containing the artifacts of Buddhism. *(stupas)*
5. In Gupta India, formal education of upper-class children began at the age of ________. *(nine)*
6. ________ mathematicians actually invented the "Arabic" digit 0 (zero), greatly aiding the development of the Arabic numeral system. *(Indian)*
7. Name the developments in Indian medicine. *(inoculation; plastic surgery; free hospitals)*
8. (T or F) Like the civilizations of Mesopotamia, the Gupta empire also faced the threat of outside invasion. *(T)*
9. (T or F) Indian astronomers identified only five of the seven planets that can be seen without the aid of a telescope. *(F)*
10. The ritual suicide of a widow who throws herself on top of her husband's funeral pyre is called ________. *(suttee)*

SUGGESTED ASSIGNMENTS

1. **Research (Average/Group)** Musicians were frequently portrayed in early Indian art. Have students work in groups to research music in early India, Egypt, or the civilizations of the Fertile Crescent. Reports should include the following topics: the function of music in society, the instruments used, and the occasions on which music was played. Have students compare the music in their selected society and the music in the United States.
2. **Critical Thinking Worksheet (Average/Group)** Have students complete Critical Thinking Worksheet 8 in the TEACHER'S RESOURCEBANK™.
3. **Chart (Basic)** Have students make a chart, similar to the one below, of Gupta accomplishments in mathematics, astronomy, and medicine. Ask students to compile items from their charts on the chalkboard or an overhead projector.

GUPTA ACCOMPLISHMENTS		
Mathematics	**Astronomy**	**Medicine**
Invented a numeral system. Developed concept of negative numbers. Calculated square root of 2. Developed table of sines. Computed value of pi.	Identified seven planets. Determined that planets and moon reflect sun's light. Understood daily rotation of earth on its axis. Predicted eclipses. Developted theory of gravity. Calculated diameter of earth.	Understood importance of spinal cord. Knew how to set bones. Performed plastic surgery. Perfected inoculation technique. Practiced sterilization of wounds.

The students' chart could serve as the basis for a class discussion comparing Gupta accomplishments with those made by the peoples of the Nile and Tigris-Euphrates valleys.

4. **Review Worksheet (Basic)** Have students complete Review Worksheet 3 in the TEACHER'S RESOURCEBANK™.

For suggested lesson plan, additional teaching strategies, enrichment activities, daily quizzes, and suggested assignments, see pages 47A–47F.

Introducing the Chapter
India has retained many of its customs and traditions mainly because of its relative isolation. Students will understand this concept more clearly if they look at the maps on pages 50 and 61. Ask students what geographic features contributed to the isolation of India. *(Responses should include the Himalaya, Karakorum, and Hindu Kush mountains. The people along the coastal rim traded with other regions, but their influence did not penetrate into the Deccan.)*

Chapter Objectives
After studying Chapter 3, students will be able to:

1. Locate on a map of India the four Indian geographical regions and describe the dominating climatic features.
2. Summarize the developments of the Indus River Valley civilization during the Mohenjo-Daro period.
3. Describe the Indo-Aryan invasion.
4. Summarize the contributions of the Aryans to the Indian cultural development and the importance of the Vedic Age.
5. Summarize the important literary contributions of the Epic Age.
6. Describe the evolution of the Indian caste system.
7. Define Hinduism and list the major Hindu deities and their duties.
8. Identify Buddha's creation of an ethical system.
9. Compare Buddhism and Hinduism and detail how these ideas spread

CHAPTER 3

People Created Thriving Civilizations in India

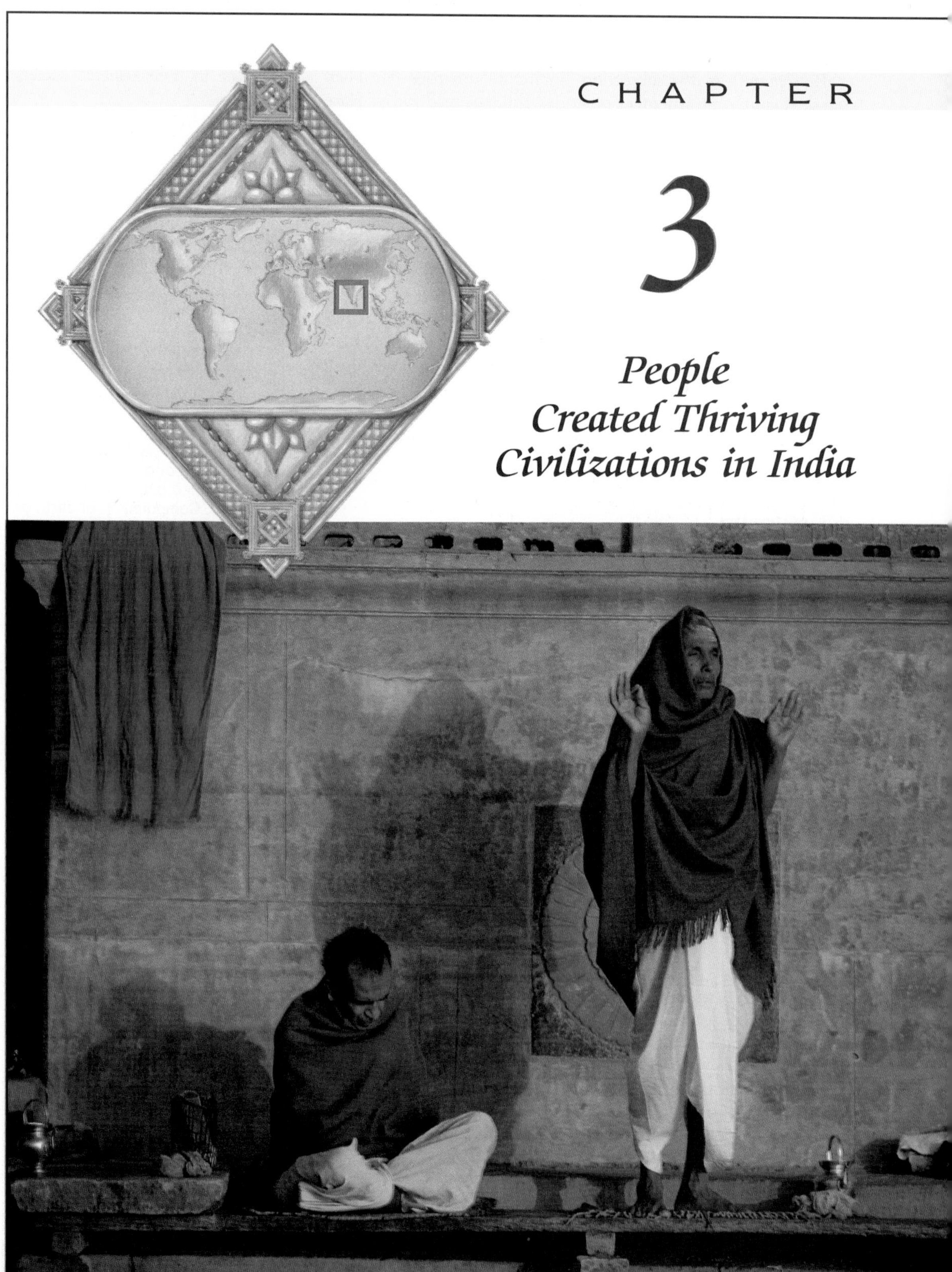

CHAPTER FOCUS

Place India

Time

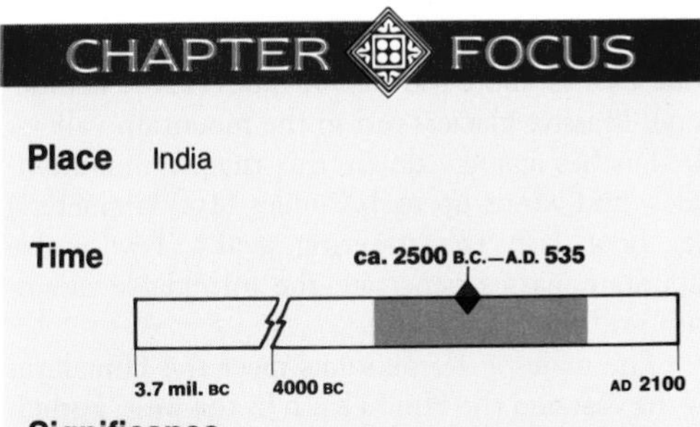

Significance

In some ways the Indus River valley civilization that developed in India resembled the early civilizations of the Nile and Tigris-Euphrates valleys. For example, the early people of India learned to farm, developed a written language and calendars, and created a complex civilization that included trade, cities, and a sophisticated government. Through philosophy and religion they tried to understand the mysterious forces of nature, the mind, and the soul.

Important differences existed between Eastern, or Oriental, civilizations and those of the West, however. For example, the ideals and beliefs of the Egyptians, Sumerians, and Babylonians vanished long ago. In contrast, the customs and traditions developed in the East in ancient India remain a part of Indian life today. Hindu priests still recite the same prayers that their ancestors did. Cows are still sacred, and people continue to practice the specialized crafts common 4,000 years ago. While the problems of East and West have often been similar, the people of the two regions have frequently found different ways to solve them.

Terms to Define

monsoon	monism
citadel	reincarnation
caste system	yoga

People to Identify

Aryans	Chandragupta I
Buddha	Guptas

Places to Locate

Ganges River	Mohenjo-Daro
Indus River	Harappa

Questions to Guide Your Reading

1. How did the geographic features of India affect the civilization that arose in the Indus Valley?
2. What contributions did the Aryans make to Indian civilization during the Vedic Age?
3. How did Buddhism and Hinduism influence the structure of Indian society during the Epic Age?
4. What cultural imprint did the dynasties and empires of ancient India leave on Indian society?
5. Why did ancient Indian civilization flourish from the Epic Age to the Golden Age of the Gupta Empire?

The Hindu religion of India contains many unique practices and rituals. One of these is the practice of yoga in which an individual or yogi attempts to make contact with the divine spirit. To succeed the yogi must first concentrate on ignoring everything going on around him. Only then can the yogi continue his search for the divine spirit. The following is an excerpt from the famous Hindu sacred text, the Bhagavad-Gita (*Song of the Lord*)*. Here the Lord Krishna, a Hindu god, discusses the practice and meaning of yoga.*

> *"A yogi should always try to concentrate his mind in absolute solitude, having retired to a secret place. . . . Having in a clean place firmly fixed his seat neither too high nor too low, and having spread over it the sacred grass, and then a deerskin, and then a cloth, he should practice yoga . . . restraining his thoughts and senses, and bringing his mind to a point. Sitting firm he should hold his body, head, and neck erect and still, and gaze steadfastly on the point of his nose, without looking around. Serene and fearless, steadfast in the vow of celibacy, and subdued in mind, he should sit in yoga, thinking on me and intent on me alone."*

Although many Hindu rituals no longer exist in India, some, such as walking across a bed of hot coals or lying on a bed of nails, are still practiced to gain forgiveness of sins or to build spiritual control. They continue to intrigue outsiders who have never experienced the rich cultural diversity of India.

1 The First Indian Civilization Arose in the Indus Valley

The first Indian civilization developed in the Indus Valley of northern India about 4,500 years ago. In time people settled throughout the entire subcontinent* of India, a region that includes the modern countries of India, Pakistan, Bangladesh (bahn • gluh • DESH), Nepal, Bhutan, and Sri Lanka (SREE LAHNG • kuh).

*A subcontinent is a large landmass that is smaller than a continent.

◀ *Hindus praying on the banks of the Ganges River*

throughout Asia.
10. Identify the Maurya Empire and describe its development.
11. Outline the development of Southern India.
12. Recognize the social, literary, artistic, architectural, and educational contributions made during the Gupta period.

SECTION 1

Focus/Motivation
Have students read the subsection "Early Civilization in the Indus Valley" on page 52 and enumerate the advances in civilization made by the people of this region. *(These advances should include a systematic plan of building villages, centralized government, the development of trade, industry, and written language.)* Organize a class discussion comparing this civilization with the civilizations of Egypt, the Fertile Crescent, and the eastern Mediterranean area. *(Answers should include their laws, governments, and religion as well as many lasting contributions to civilization.)*

Presentation
Illustrating Ideas (Average/Group)
A good way for students to learn map skills is by drawing schematic maps. Have students draw only the diamond-shaped outline of India by referring to the map on page 50. Point out that the top point lies in the mountains to the north. The bottom point lies to

● Brahmaputra
■ India got its name from the Indus River. Later the name "India" was given to the entire region.
▲ *Ghat* means "steppe" in Hindi. A steppe is a level, often arid, treeless plain.

the south, in the Indian Ocean. The point on the left lies in the Arabian Sea. Instruct the students to draw the shape in their notebooks and put the four regions as well as the four boundaries in the proper location. Information can be added as the lesson proceeds.

The Physical Setting

The northern border of the Indian subcontinent nestles in the Himalayas (him • uh • LAY • uhz), the tallest mountains on earth. Half as large as the United States, India has a wide diversity of both terrain and climate. Dense rain forests, great fertile plains, high plateaus, dry deserts, narrow coastal plains, and vast rivers sprawl across this subcontinent of timeless beauty in South Asia.

Physical regions. Geographically, the Indian subcontinent can be divided into four main regions. Each region has its own geographic features, climate, and natural resources. While reading about each region, look carefully at the map of India on this page.

(1) *The northern mountains.* Three mountain ranges, the Himalayas, the Karakorums (kar • uh • KOHR • uhms), and the Hindu Kush, loom in the north. The Himalayas, named for the Hindi word meaning "place of the snow," consist of a series of parallel mountain ranges that stretch east and southeast for more than 1,500 miles (2,400 kilometers). Massive glaciers rest in the mountain valleys. Avalanches careen down the rugged mountainsides, and winds up to 100 miles (160 kilometers) per hour lash the towering peaks. Few usable mountain passes penetrate the formidable mountain walls.

Learning from Maps *Heavy flooding accompanies the monsoon season in the Ganges River valley. What* ● *other river empties into the Bay of Bengal?*

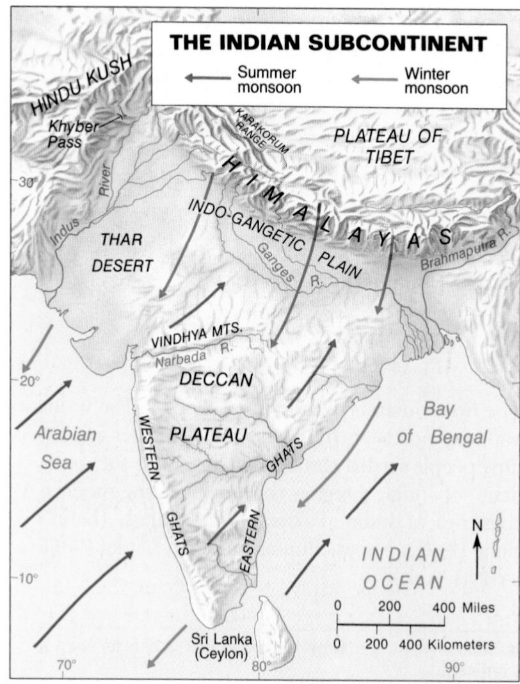

LAMBERT CONFORMAL CONIC PROJECTION

The majestic Karakorums meet the Himalayas in the east and the Hindu Kush in the west. Forbidding peaks, many as high as 22,000 feet (6,600 meters), jut boldly to the sky. The Karakorums compose part of the mountain chain that forms a wall between the Indian subcontinent and the rest of Asia.

Not quite as rugged as the other mountain ranges of northern India, the Hindu Kush lie to the northwest of the Karakorums. Several usable passes, including the famous Khyber (KY • buhr) Pass, provided migrating and invading tribes access to India.

(2) *The Indo-Gangetic Plain.* Two great rivers lie south of the three mountain ranges. The Ganges (GAN • jeez) River flows to the southeast through an immensely fertile valley, while the Indus River ■ flows southwest through drier lands. Only a low divide, or ridge, separates the northern ends of the two river valleys. Think of the two valleys as one broad plain stretching more than 1,500 miles (2,400 kilometers) from west to east. After immigrants and invaders traveled through the narrow mountain passes, they spread out along this broad plain and established contact with the earlier settlers in this area.

(3) *The Deccan.* The interior region of the vast Indian subcontinent lies south of the Indo-Gangetic Plain. This high plateau is called the Deccan, meaning "southland." A range of hills—the Vindhya (VIN • dyah) Mountains—separates the Deccan from the Indo-Gangetic Plain. Historically this mountain range has formed a cultural barrier between northern and southern India.

At the western edge of the Deccan lie the Western Ghats, a low mountain range that slopes ▲ gradually eastward to the inland plateau. A lower mountain range called the Eastern Ghats marks the eastern edge of the Deccan.

(4) *The Coastal Plain.* The Coastal Plain extends around southern India, facing the Arabian Sea on the west and the Bay of Bengal on the east. Not far from the sea, the abrupt rise of the Western

50

● crops wither and starvation threatens
■ The word *monsoon* comes from an Arabic word, *mawsin,* meaning "season."

Learning from Pictures *Mount Everest and Mount Kala Paltar in the Himalayas rise above the clouds. What happens when the monsoon arrives late in India?* ●

Ghats isolates the Coastal Plain's narrow western rim. The broader eastern rim slopes gradually upward toward the Eastern Ghats.

The people of the Coastal Plain turned to the sea very early in their history. Those in the west traded with the people of the Fertile Crescent, Egypt, and the Mediterranean region. Those in the east traded with the people living in what is now Sri Lanka (Ceylon) and Southeast Asia. The coastal people had more contacts with people overseas than they did with the people of the Indo-Gangetic Plain.

The climate. Two features dominate India's climate—the monsoons and the high temperatures. ■ **Monsoons** are seasonal winds named for the direction in which they blow or the season in which they occur. From late September until the end of the following March, the monsoon blows from the north and northeast. Any moisture it carries falls onto the northern slopes of the Himalayas before reaching the rest of India.

Beginning in late May or early June, the monsoon swings around and blows from the southwest. As the southwest monsoon crosses the Indian Ocean, it picks up moisture, which drops unevenly throughout India in the form of rain. Heavy rains fall along the Coastal Plain, while sparse rainfall is typical of the land behind the Western Ghats. The lower Ganges Valley and the eastern Himalayas receive the heaviest rainfall because they lie directly in the path of these winds.

In most of India, the rainfall for the entire year comes during the four months when the monsoon comes out of the southwest. The timing of the monsoon is critical. If the monsoon arrives late, or if little rain falls, crops wither and starvation threatens India. If the monsoon brings too much rain, destructive floods rage across the countryside. When the monsoon brings the right amount of rain, however, farmers can grow two or more crops in one year.

The second important feature of India's climate is the high temperature. Although temperatures seldom soar on the Coastal Plain or on the Deccan, scorching heat plagues the Indo-Gangetic Plain. Here, temperatures in the winter months of December, January, and February remain cool, but during the rest of the year they become stifling, with many days in May and early June averaging 120°F (49°C).

51

1B, 1D

● Research topic: How archaeologists first discovered evidence of Harappan civilization

History Through the Arts

POTTERY

Seals from the Indus Valley

Much of our knowledge of Harappan civilization comes from tantalizing bits and pieces. Seals like the ones shown here are the most puzzling of the remains that archaeologists have unearthed. Such objects are the only known examples of the picture writing of the Harappans. Scholars have been unable to translate this writing, but a widely held opinion is that the Harappans used the seals to stamp property or to identify their owners.

Many of the pictures on the seals seem to have a religious meaning. The most common carving is that of a bull, an object of worship throughout the ancient world. Many seals also show seated figures that may represent gods. Because Harappan seals have been found in the Tigris-Euphrates region near the site of Sumerian civilization, scholars think that the people of the Indus Valley traded with the people of the Middle East.

Early Civilization in the Indus Valley

● An impressive civilization appeared in the Indus River valley about 2500 B.C., not long after Egypt and Sumer developed civilizations. Although our knowledge of this early civilization is incomplete, archaeologists have unearthed much information in the past 100 years. Scholars now believe that this civilization flourished until about 1500 B.C.

The twin cities. The ruins of two cities, Mohenjo-Daro (moh • hen • joh-DAHR • oh) and Harappa (huh • RAP • uh), provide the most complete evidence of this early Indus Valley civilization. Harappa became so important to this civilization that historians often call it the Harappan civilization.

For their day, Harappa and Mohenjo-Daro represented miracles of city planning and design. Wide streets, laid out in a regular pattern, intersected at right angles. Each city had a water system, complete with public baths, and a covered brick sewer system for private homes. The brick homes of the wealthy appear to have been two stories tall, equipped with bathrooms and garbage chutes.

The people of Harappa and Mohenjo-Daro designed their buildings for use, not beauty. In many of these buildings, they used bricks superior to those used in Sumer. Many of the bricks, baked in kilns, or ovens, instead of being sun-dried, have remained intact over the centuries.

The two cities seem to have been twin capitals and not rivals. Each had a strong central fortress, or **citadel,** built on a platform of bricks. At Harappa, farmers stored enough grain in large storehouses to feed the city's population of about 35,000 people.

Indus Valley culture. Agricultural regions surrounded Harappa and Mohenjo-Daro. The Indus River, with its swift current of heavy silt, probably made irrigation difficult. But archaeologists do not know how the Indus Valley people solved these problems, because since then silt deposits have raised the level of the plain around the two cities as much as 12 feet (3.66 meters).

City dwellers worked primarily in industry or trade. As early as 2300 B.C., they traded with people of the Tigris-Euphrates Valley. Indus Valley artisans produced fine articles, including cotton cloth, pottery, bronze items, and gold and silver jewelry.

These early Indus Valley people also developed a written language. Pictograms dating from about 2300 B.C. have been found, but scholars have not yet deciphered the language, partly because most are personal seals believed to be signatures. Although additional writing has been found on clay pots and fragments, scholars have established no connection with any other language.

Scholars know little about Indus Valley religion, but studies indicate that it was a form of **animism,** a belief that spirits inhabit everything —trees and other natural objects, animals, and even

52

READ
WRITE
INTERPRET
CONNECT
THINK

BUILDING HISTORY STUDY SKILLS

Reading About History: Classifying Information

Classifying information involves grouping ideas, objects, or people according to the things they have in common. Grouping ideas or events within a category enables you to organize and understand large amounts of information and give added meaning to isolated bits of information. When data are organized, conclusions can be drawn and comparisons can be made.

How to Classify Information

To classify information, follow these steps:

1. Read the information or items.
2. Sort the information into similar groups.
3. Assign a category to each group.
4. Place the information within broader categories.
5. Formulate a statement clarifying the meaning of the information.

Developing the Skill

Read the following description of Mohenjo-Daro and Harappa to determine the characteristics of Harappan society.

> "Innumerable artifacts of this civilization have been found, including copper, bronze, gold and jeweled tools. . . . Sculpted figures . . . depicted gods and priest-kings. More than a thousand carved seals, possibly used as signatures on clay tablets, depict the humped bull, rhinoceros, and sometimes a three headed god. . . . Mohenjo-Daro was laid out in strict rectangular blocks, in a north-south direction that took advantage of prevailing winds. Its houses were usually composed of a first floor of furnace baked bricks . . . with an upper floor of wood. Almost every house had a bathroom, in which the family would shower by pouring water over themselves with jugs. The runoff was funneled through drainpipes in the floor into the city drainage system that ran through all the streets. Chutes in the wall provided an outlet for garbage to bins in the streets, where it was presumably collected by the city authorities. The houses were topped by waterproof roofs built from mud spread over layers of bamboo and rush mats. The government buildings were clustered on a mud-brick mound, thirty feet in height and twelve hundred feet in length. Grain, mostly barley, was stored in a government granary. An open colonnaded courtyard may have been a kind of college. A vast bath or swimming pool, forty feet long and eight feet deep, was probably used for sacred absolutions [remission of sins] or bathing. Elaborate palace buildings suggest the presence of powerful rulers, who . . . were also religious leaders."

Study the chart below to learn how the characteristics of the Harappan civilization can be grouped into four major categories.

Government	Religion	Technology	Economy
government buildings	seals	drainage systems	grain production
city services	sacred pool	bathrooms	grain storage
elaborate palaces	sacred animals	sewer systems	public works

Studying the chart enables you to draw conclusions about the civilization of Mohenjo-Daro. The civilization was concerned with cleanliness. This is evident in the elaborate technology devoted to cleanliness—bathrooms, sewers, the drainage system, and the swimming pool for sacred washing. In addition, we know that the government protected the people's welfare because it performed extensive public services. A connection between religion and politics seems to exist. The government seals were religious, and the government buildings seem to have been connected to powerful religious leaders. This was a highly developed urban civilization, as evidenced by the technology, the city services, and the layout of the city.

Practicing the skill. Use the categories in the chart to list the major characteristics of society in your town or city.

To apply this skill, see Applying History Study Skills on page 67.

The excavation site at Mohenjo-Daro

53

1A, 1B, 1C, a1A, a4A, a4B, a4C, a4F, a4G, a4L

● Stress the theme that throughout history less civilized peoples often invaded agricultural societies.

SECTION 1

Closure

Ask students to describe the physical setting of India and then explain its impact on the history of the subcontinent.

Review Answers

1. ***monsoon:*** seasonal winds named for the direction in which they blow or the season in which they occur; ***citadel:*** strong fortress built on a platform of bricks; ***animism:*** a belief that spirits inhabit everything

2. ***Himalayas:*** mountain range that stretches across northern India and Tibet; ***Indo-Gangetic Plain:*** plains of Indus and Ganges rivers; ***Indus River:*** great river in western India; ***Deccan:*** high plateau located south of Indo-Gangetic Plain; ***Coastal Plain:*** extends around southern India; ***Harappa:*** partner city of Mohenjo-Daro

3. ***Northern mountains:*** three great ranges, the Himalayas, Karakorums, and the Hindu Kush; ***Indo-Gangetic Plain:*** broad plain formed by valleys of Indus and Ganges; ***Deccan:*** high plateau south of the Indo-Gangetic Plain; ***Coastal Plain:*** narrow plain extending around southern India

4. Archaeologists believe the layout of the cities and uniform size of bricks used in construction indicate a strong, centralized government. City dwellers earned their living by industry and trade. They produced cloth, pottery, and articles of copper and bronze.

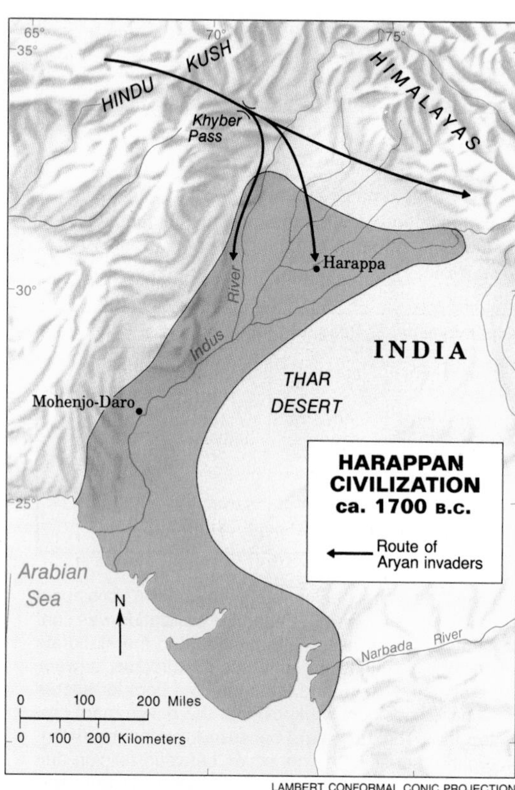

Learning from Maps *Natural river highways encouraged exchange as well as unity in Harappan civilization. Where did the Aryan invaders cross into India?*
the Khyber Pass

people. The Harappans believed these spirits influenced a person's life; therefore, they tried to control them and please them.

Although archaeologists have found no temples, shrines, or religious writings, they believe that the people of the Indus Valley also worshiped animals associated with physical power and fertility, such as bulls, crocodiles, and snakes. One of the most important symbols was the unicorn, a fabled animal with a single long horn jutting from its forehead. Other evidence indicates that a sacred tree and a mother goddess symbolized fertility.

Scholars do not know why the Indus Valley civilization declined. They speculate that tribes from outside lands conquered the valley. More recent evidence indicates that the salt content of underground water increased. Such an increase probably made agriculture impossible and may have disintegrated the baked bricks of the buildings.

Some evidence suggests that major earthquakes and floods struck the region about 1700 B.C. The discovery of several unburied skeletons, together with homes and personal belongings hastily abandoned, seems to indicate some disastrous event at Mohenjo-Daro. The evidence needed to verify this theory, however, remains incomplete.

SECTION 1 REVIEW

1. **Define** monsoon, citadel, animism
2. **Locate** Himalayas, Indo-Gangetic Plain, Indus River, Deccan, Coastal Plain, Harappa
3. **Summarizing Ideas** Name and briefly describe the four main geographical regions of India.
4. **Interpreting Ideas** What do archaeological findings in the Indus Valley suggest about the political, economic, and social aspects of city life?

2 Aryan Invaders Ruled India's Northern Plain During the Vedic Age

About 1500 B.C. a new group of people flooded through the Khyber Pass into India. They came from the region north of the Black and Caspian seas and spoke an Indo-European language.

The Conquering Aryans

We call the many Indo-European tribes that forced their way into northwestern India, one after another, Indo-Aryans, or Aryans (see map, this page). As one historian observed: ●

> "There is no ancient record of that first successful trip to India. We do not know how difficult the journey was when the Aryan invaders first led their people down . . . beyond the snowline to the hot, rock-strewn [narrow passage] and out onto the broad grasslands which they had come seeking. We have no way of knowing how the animals felt, and whether or not their owners knew that horses would die unless their noses bled at the top of the Pass, to relieve the pressure of the height. We know only that enough people and animals survived that rugged experience to change the course of Indian history."

● priests who celebrated almost all occasions of Aryan life

The nomadic Aryans herded sheep and cows. In fact, their word for "war" meant "a desire for more cows." Many strong and brave Aryan archers followed horse-drawn chariots into battle. Skillful fighters, they conquered the Indus Valley and then moved eastward along the Ganges until they controlled the entire northern plain.

Aryan Civilization During the Vedic Age

Neither traders nor builders, the Aryans did nothing to improve the cities they conquered. They simply left the ruins of the cities to decay. Their early history remains vague because they had no written language. What we do know of the Aryans comes from the Vedas (VAY • duhz), the great literature of the Aryan religion. For centuries people memorized the Vedas and handed them down by word of mouth. Later, with the development of writing, scholars wrote them in the Aryan language, Sanskrit. So important are the Vedas to Indian history that we call the period from 1500 B.C. to 1000 B.C. the Vedic Age.

Aryan religion. The earliest gods mentioned in the Vedas include elements of nature, such as the sky, sun, earth, light, fire, wind, storms, water, and rain. The Vedas personified these natural objects and forces—that is, they regarded or represented them as people. Thus, the sky became a father, the earth a mother. Although the Vedas mention gods and goddesses, a very important hymn celebrating the creation of the universe suggests a concept of a supreme god, called "That One," who created universal order out of the original chaos.

The Vedic religion constantly changed and developed, as shown in the story of the god Varuna. He began as the heavens. His garment was the sky, his breath the storm. As the spiritual beliefs of his worshipers changed, so did Varuna. He watched over the world through his eye, the sun. He rewarded good and punished evil. Thus he became the guardian and enforcer of an eternal law of morality—of right and wrong.

Like the Persians, the early Aryans believed in immortality. After death Varuna either thrust the soul into a dark pit of eternal punishment or raised it into a heaven filled with earthly joy. Through repeated ritual sacrifices and correct ritual action, a person reached this heaven free of his or her earthly body.

Apparently, no temples or images characterized the early Vedic religion. Rituals consisted of building fires on newly constructed altars and pouring the juice of the soma plant and liquid butter into the sacred fire. The important point was to perform the ceremony properly. The good qualities of the person performing it did not matter.

As time passed, the rituals of sacrifice became more complicated. The spoken language of the Indian people also changed, until it became quite different from the Sanskrit of the first Aryan invaders. Since they emphasized the importance of proper observance, priests who knew the proper forms and could read and write Sanskrit also became more important. These priests, called **Brahmans,** prepared the proper ceremony for almost every occasion in life and charged heavily for their services.

Early Aryan society. The Aryans had the habits and customs of wanderers. They eventually settled in the Indo-Gangetic Plain, however, where they found one of the richest and most fertile areas

Learning from Pictures *In this relief from Ghandara, two young Brahmans raise their hands in a gesture meaning "do not fear." What did Brahmans do in Aryan society?* ●

They used pictograms in writing.

SECTION 2

Focus/Motivation
Explain to the students that every society gives status to certain occupations it considers important. Ask each student to list the 10 occupations that appear to have the highest status in the United States today. Call upon students to read their lists. *(Many lists will probably include doctors, dentists, judges, ministers, college professors, lawyers, artists, and perhaps athletes and entertainers.)* Point out that these occupations are in the service field. Ask students to hypothesize about occupations important in Aryan society. On what did they base their hypotheses? Have students read the fourth paragraph in the subsection, "Early Aryan society," on this page. Ask them to explain why warriors and priests were held in high esteem in Aryan society.

Presentation
Classifying Information (Average/Group)
Have the students make a chart of the characteristics of Aryan society in their notebook. The headings should be: *Government, Social Life,* and *Economy.* Completed charts should include the following items. *Government:* tribes and their rulers, villages and their rulers. *Social Life:* treatment of conquered

people, marriage, and family laws. *Economy:* types of work, system of exchange.

SECTION 2

Closure

Have students list the contributions of the Aryan invaders to the civilization of India. *(language, religion, and caste)*

Review Answers

1. ***Brahman:*** priest in Vedic religion; ***rajah:*** prince who ruled an Aryan city-state
2. ***Aryans:*** warrior society that invaded Indus River valley and initiated Vedic Age; ***Varuna:*** changeable god in Vedic religion
3. ***Black Sea:*** sea north of present-day Turkey around which Aryans originated; ***Caspian Sea:*** sea east of Black Sea
4. The Aryans contributed new social classes, a new language, and a new religion.
5. The Aryans memorized the Vedas and used word of mouth to pass on their traditions and history to new generations.
6. The Aryans personified the forces of nature. The beliefs changed and developed with time. The god Varuna was first thought of as heaven, but later became the enforcer of right and wrong. The early Aryans believed in immortality. There were apparently no temples or images. Great stress was placed on proper performance of the many religious ceremonies.
7. Warriors were the most

History Through the Arts

LITERATURE

Atharva-Veda

The Aryans who surged through the Khyber Pass (right) later developed literary works called the Vedas. The word *veda* means "knowledge" or "wisdom" in Sanskrit. The Vedas—books of sacred knowledge that make up the body of Hindu scripture—consist of collections of religious rituals and hymns to the gods.

Only four major collections have survived: (1) the *Rig-Veda,* hymns of praise; (2) the *Sama-Veda,* melodies or chants; (3) the *Yajur-Veda,* rituals of sacrifice; and (4) the *Atharva-Veda,* chants and magic spells.

The Vedas cover an amazing variety of subjects. The *Rig-Veda,* the greatest of the Vedas as literature, contains more than 1,000 hymns of praise to all the objects of Aryan worship. Some are straightforward prayers for good crops or long life. Some show a simple, childlike wonder: Why doesn't the sun fall very rapidly once it begins to slip downward? Still others are as eloquent and beautiful as the Psalms of the Bible.

The *Atharva-Veda* has chants for a variety of purposes—to obtain children, to ward off evil, to prolong life, and to destroy enemies. The excerpt below is a chant to bring victory on the battlefield.

"Speak to our enemies, O Drum,
faintheartedness and discord of minds;
We bring upon our adversaries
hatred, division, and panic.

Trembling in the mind, in the eye,
in the heart, let our enemies
flee in fright, in consternation,
as soon as our oblation is made.

Wrought out of wood, compact
with leather-straps, dear to the whole clan,
besprinkled with molten butter,
speak thou terror to our enemies.

As animals of the forest flee,
panic-stricken, from a man,
so do thou, Drum, roar out to our enemies,
and frighten them, and then confound their minds.

As from a wolf goats and sheep
run away greatly terrified,
so do thou, Drum, roar out to our enemies,
and frighten them and then confound their minds.

As from a hawk birds in the sky fly in terror
day by day, as if from the roaring of a lion,
so do thou, Drum, roar out to the enemies,
and frighten them and then confound their minds.

May all the Devas who control
the fortunes of the battle-field,
frighten away our foes with the Drum
and the skin of the antelope.

Let those our enemies who go
in battalions be terrified
with the sound of feet and the shadows
with which Indra makes his sport.

May the clang of bowstrings and Drums
cry out to the direction where
the defeated hosts of our enemies
flee in full battalions.

O Sun, take away their sight!
Beams of Light, follow them close:
Let these cling to foot-bound hosts
when their valour has ebbed away.

You mighty Maruts, Sons of Prishni,
allied with Indra, crush our enemies!
May King Soma, King Varuna,
Mahādeva, Mrityu, and Indra,

may these embattled Devas
bright as the sun, united in mind,
conquer our enemies. All hail!"

1B, 1D, 2D, a1A, a4A, a4F, a4G, a4H

● The peoples of ancient India, and especially southern India, are sometimes called Dravidians.

in the world. Here, along with farming and a settled life style, they also developed simple forms of government.

In time Aryan tribes joined to form small city-states. A **rajah,** or prince, ruled each city-state. He acted as military leader, chief priest, lawmaker, and judge. A royal council of friends and relatives assisted the rajah. For hundreds of years, the city-states enjoyed peace and independence.

Several physical and social differences existed between conquerors and conquered. The light-skinned Aryans had been nomads. The dark-skinned Indus Valley people had been city dwellers. Although the original Indus Valley people outnumbered them, the Aryans believed in maintaining their separate identity. To do so they passed laws prohibiting marriages between Aryans and the valley dwellers.

Class divisions began to form during the Vedic Age, but not until later did fixed hereditary classes appear. The early Aryans considered warriors to be among the most admirable and important members of society. But when peace came, and farmers needed to ask religious leaders for help against the hostile forces of nature, Brahman priests gained importance.

In addition to providing information about Aryan religion, the Vedas provide a great deal of information about family life in the Vedic Age. Marriages took place by kidnapping, by purchase, or by mutual consent. A woman considered it a great compliment to be stolen. To be bought and paid for was more flattering than to be married by consent. Men could marry more than one woman and owned their wives and children.

The wife had a primary duty to produce sons who would help the father care for their herds of cattle and other animals. Fathers also expected their sons to go to battle to bring honor to their families, and to perform the correct rituals at their fathers' funerals.

The Aryan economy. When the Aryans began farming the Indo-Gangetic Plain, they raised barley as their principal crop. Rice, the most important food in India today, was apparently unknown in Vedic times. Each village divided its land among its families, but the whole village shared the responsibility for irrigation. Land could not be sold to outsiders and could be willed only to male heirs. Most Aryans owned their land. They considered working for someone else a disgrace.

Although poor transportation and trading methods limited trade, handicrafts gradually appeared in the villages. Early traders bartered, often exchanging cattle for goods.

The Aryan invaders made significant contributions to the civilization of the Indian subcontinent. These contributions included a new social order of classes, a new language, and new religious interpretations of how the world works. In time Aryan contributions blended with the previous civilization of Indus Valley people. Farmers gradually displaced herders. Religious values changed, and social classes became more rigid and closely identified with ritual purity.

SECTION 2 REVIEW

1. **Define** Brahman, rajah
2. **Identify** Aryans, Varuna
3. **Locate** Black Sea, Caspian Sea
4. **Interpreting Ideas** What did the Aryans contribute to Indian civilization?
5. **Evaluating Ideas** How were the Vedas used in Aryan society?
6. **Summarizing Ideas** What were the most important beliefs and rituals of the Aryan religion?
7. **Classifying Ideas** Describe the class divisions that began in Aryan society.

3 Buddhism and Hinduism Took Hold in India

During the Vedic Age, a new social structure appeared in India. In time this system formed the foundation of Indian society.

The Great Epics

The Vedic Age was named after the Vedas, collections of religious rituals and hymns to the gods. The **Epic Age,** the period from 1000 to 500 B.C., also takes its name from religious literature.

Brahman priests interpreted the rituals and hymns of the Vedas and became increasingly influential in Aryan society. During the Epic Age, the Brahman priests gained even more importance when they composed the *Upanishads* (oo • PAHN • i • shahdz), complex philosophical explanations of the Vedic religion.

admirable members of society, but Brahmans became important for helping against the hostile forces of nature.

SECTION 3

Focus/Motivation

The caste system in India emerged from the five groups named on page 58. These groups roughly correspond to upper, middle, and lower classes. The original five groups were later subdivided many times into smaller groups (castes), and eventually some 3,000 hereditary castes developed.

Ask students if American society has social classes. How is membership in these classes determined? Can an individual pass from one class to another?

(Students should recognize that class in the United States is determined by such factors as wealth, occupation, education, and birth, but that it is possible for individuals to move from class to class. This should be contrasted with the fixed caste system in which an individual inherits a caste and remains in it.)

Presentation
Analyzing Ideas (Average/Group)

Begin a discussion on Hindu veneration of animals by reading to the class "The Sacred Cow" in L. S. Stavrianos's *Readings in World History* (Allyn and Bacon).

Ask students what practical reasons may have

2D, a1A, a1B

From an early date, the Aryans kept their dominant position by permitting only their own people to become priests, warriors, and craftsworkers.

influenced the Hindu attitude toward cows. *(Students should mention that cattle were used as currency in early India, that they provided food [milk and butter], dung for fuel, and power for the plow and the cart.)* Explain to the class the relationship between respect for animals and reincarnation. Point out that Hindus regarded all forms of life as important and as part of a single life force. When a creature died, it was reincarnated in some other form. Therefore, in killing an animal, one might be killing a creature with the soul of an ancestor.

Ordinary people did not understand the *Upanishads* any more than they could the Vedas. But they could understand simple stories that made these ideas about Vedic religion clearer. These stories, retold from generation to generation, were eventually combined into two **epics,** or long poems describing heroes and great events. These epics are the *Mahabharata* (muh • HAH • bah • ruh • tuh) and the *Ramayana* (rah • MAH • yuh • nuh).

Sacred Hindu scripture includes the longest epic poem in literature, the *Mahabharata,* or "Great War." It tells the story of a great civil war in a kingdom near Delhi, in what is today northern India. The last 18 chapters of this epic, known as the *Bhagavad-Gita,* or "Lord's Song," stress that doing one's moral duty according to one's responsibilities marks the highest fulfillment in life. In the *Bhagavad-Gita,* Krishna, a human incarnation of the god Vishnu, also explains that love and devotion to Vishnu can lead to salvation in the afterlife.

The *Ramayana* tells the story of two royal heroic figures—Rama (another human incarnation of the god Vishnu) and his devoted wife, Sita. Because of their faithfulness to duty and their devotion to each other and the people of their kingdom, Rama and Sita symbolize the ideals of Indian manhood and womanhood.

From the *Mahabharata* and the *Ramayana,* and from the *Upanishads* and the Vedas themselves, scholars have pieced together the origins of the two most important influences in Indian history—the caste system and Hinduism.

The Caste System

The **caste system,** a form of social organization unlike any developed elsewhere in the world, began in northern India when the invading Aryans laid down rules prohibiting marriages between themselves and the peoples they had conquered. During the Epic Age, four distinct classes emerged in Indian society. At the top of the social scale stood the rulers and warriors called Kshatriyas (kuh • SHA • tree • yuhz). Next came the priests, scholars, and wise men called Brahmans. During the Epic Age, the Brahmans and the Kshatriyas changed positions within society, with the Brahmans becoming most important. The class of Vaisyas (VYSH • yuhz), which included merchants, traders, and owners of small farms, came third. The Sudras—peasants bound to work the fields of large landowners—stood at the foot of the social ladder.

A fifth group of people in Indian society did not even appear on the ladder. These people were called "untouchables" because the other people in Indian society thought that merely touching them would make one impure. Indians considered many of the conquered peoples untouchables.

As time passed, the caste system emerged as the original four groups divided into smaller groups called castes. Eventually, some 3,000 hereditary castes developed. Each had its own fixed social position and rules about eating, marriage, labor, and worship. For example, people could not eat or drink with someone of a lower caste, but they could perform services that were consistent with the duties of their caste for other people. They could work only at those occupations recognized as fitting for members of their caste, and they could not marry outside their caste.

Hinduism

Hinduism, India's major religion, developed through Brahman priests' interpretations of the Vedas. According to the *Upanishads,* a basic divine essence known as Brahman fills everything in the world. Atman, or self, refers to the essence of an individual person. When Hindus say that Brahma and Atman are one and indivisible, they mean that God and human beings are one. We call this idea **monism.**

According to Hinduism, the world known to our senses is merely an illusion called Maya, which betrays people, giving them sorrow and pain. People can be delivered from their suffering if they can identify Maya. However, this requires lifetimes of experience. Hinduism explains that **reincarnation**—the transmigration or rebirth of the soul—provides this experience. According to this belief, the soul does not die with the body but enters the body of another being, either human or animal, and thus lives again and again.

Two major elements in the theory of reincarnation are known as dharma and karma. **Dharma** is fulfillment of one's moral duty in this life so that the soul can make progress toward deliverance from punishment in the next life. **Karma** is the belief that the present condition of a person's life reflects what a person did or did not do during a previous

History Through the Arts

SCULPTURE

The God Siva

Along with Brahma and Vishnu, Siva is one of the three great gods of Hinduism. Siva had many roles but is best known as the destroyer whose actions bring forth new life. The god is also worshiped as time, justice, and the sun. This bronze statue emphasizes the role of destroyer. Around the edge of the circular frame and in one left hand are the flames of destruction. The other left hand points to a dwarf, an enemy overcome by Siva as the lord of death.

Another of Siva's roles is shown by a hand raised in a gesture that means "do not fear." It represents the god's kindliness. A fourth hand holds a drum, the instrument that made the first sound in the universe. The power of meditation is symbolized by a third eye, engraved on the forehead. Siva is often shown dancing and is worshiped as the god of dancers.

life. Ultimately, each person hopes to end the repeated transmigrations and enable the soul to reunite with the soul of Brahma.

According to Hinduism, good persons are rewarded and evil ones are punished. Reward means that the soul enters the body of someone of a higher caste. Punishment occurs when the souls of evil people are reborn in the bodies of people of lower castes or of insects. Since Hindus believe that all souls make up part of the Universal Soul, or Brahman, Hindus respect the sacredness of life in all forms. Members of the Brahman, or highest caste, have to be particularly careful not to bring injury or violence to any living thing.

Hindu religious practices. Hindus commonly practice **yoga,** a physical and mental discipline harmonizing body with soul. A Hindu practicing one form of yoga might, for example, sit for many hours in a certain position in order to free the mind of bodily concerns.

The Brahman priests teach that people can achieve salvation by fulfilling one's dharma and uniting with the Universal Soul or Brahman. Brahman's characteristics include a basic trinity, or three closely related persons or things. The Brahman trinity includes (1) Brahma the Creator, (2) Vishnu the Preserver, and (3) Siva the Destroyer. Below these come many other gods, represented in the spirits of trees, animals, and people.

Some Hindus pay special reverence to certain animals. For example, they consider cows especially sacred because cows provide the power for the plow and the cart and produce food (milk and butter) and fuel (dung). For these reasons most Hindus will not eat beef.

To Westerners this religion of many gods sounds polytheistic. However, Hindus insist that it is

59

SECTION 3

Closure

Have students review the major ideas of Hinduism. Then ask them to explain how Buddhism developed. Ask: Why did Buddhism later decline in India? *(Students might suggest that the Brahmans, who opposed Buddhism, grew stronger.*

Review Answers

1. ***Epic Age:*** period in Indian history from 1000 B.C. to 500 B.C., also takes name from religious literature; ***epic:*** long poem describing heroes and great events; ***caste system:*** form of social organization unique to India; ***monism:*** Hindu belief that Brahma and Atman are one and indivisible, and that God and humans are one; ***reincarnation:*** transmigration of the soul; ***dharma:*** fulfillment of moral duty so that soul can progress toward deliverance from punishment in the next life; ***karma:*** present condition of a person's life reflects what a person did during a previous life; ***yoga:*** physical and mental discipline harmonizing body with soul; ***nirvana:*** Buddhist belief of attaining the perfect peace by freeing soul from endless cycle of reincarnation
2. ***Krishna:*** human incarnation of Vishnu; ***Rama:*** human incarnation of Vishnu; ***Sita:*** devoted wife of Rama in *Ramayana;* ***Universal Soul:*** basic divine essence all souls are part of; ***Enlightened One:*** Buddha

monistic—that the basic trinity and all the other gods are merely different representations of the oneness of the universe.

Establishment of the caste system and Hinduism ranked as the most important developments of Indian history during the Epic Age—or of any other age in Indian history. These two ideas became interwoven in the fabric of Indian society.

The Early Life of Buddha

Another of the world's great religions—Buddhism—also arose in India. Buddhism's founder, Gautama, who became known as Buddha, or the "Enlightened One," was born about 563 B.C. and died about 483 B.C. The son of an Indian prince, he lived in luxury, shielded from the ordinary people of his native city. At the age of 29, he ventured into the city streets. What he saw—an old decrepit man, a very sick man covered with boils, and a corpse about to be cremated—profoundly disturbed him. He wondered about the great problems of life and asked "Why does suffering exist? What is the value of life and death?"

Gautama decided to spend the rest of his life seeking answers to these questions. In what is called the Great Renunciation, he put aside all his possessions, left his wife and infant son, and set out to search for the truth.

Gautama followed all the practices recommended to attain wisdom. He lived as a hermit and a scholar and practiced the mental and physical discipline of yoga so strictly that he almost died. He tried fasting—not eating for a specified amount of time—and self-torture. But none of these practices gave him the answers he longed for so much.

One day, after six years of searching, as Gautama meditated under a fig tree, he felt that he understood the truth which formed the basis of life. In that moment, according to his followers, he became Buddha—the "Enlightened One." He spent the remainder of his life teaching the Enlightenment, the Way of Life.

Buddha's Teachings

Buddha accepted the Hindu belief that the progress of the soul depends on the life a person leads and that good is rewarded and evil punished. Departing from Hindu beliefs, however, Buddha said that since only deeds, good or bad, count, salvation cannot come through self-torture or from the sacrifice of animals. According to Buddha, salvation comes from knowing the Four Noble Truths and following the Eightfold Path.

The Four Noble Truths. The Four Noble Truths were as follows: (1) all human life contains suffering and sorrow; (2) a greedy desire for only pleasure and material things causes suffering and sorrow; (3) renouncing desire frees people from suffering and helps their souls attain **nirvana,** or the perfect peace, which frees the soul from the endless cycle of reincarnation; and (4) following the Eightfold Path leads to renunciation, or denial of desire and attainment of nirvana.

The Eightfold Path. The Eightfold Path consists of eight guides to thought and conduct. It includes (1) right views, or seeing life as it really is, with all its imperfections; (2) right intentions; (3) right speech, or avoiding lying and gossiping; (4) right action, or avoiding committing crimes and instead, seeking to be honest; (5) right living, by which Buddha meant working at a job that did not harm others; (6) right effort, or working to prevent evil; (7) right mindfulness, or constant awareness of one's self; and (8) right concentration to direct the mind in meditation.

Buddha stressed ethics, a code of morals and conduct, rather than ceremonies. Unselfishness formed the key to his ethics, and he gave definite rules for unselfish behavior. A person should not kill, steal, lie, gossip, find fault with others, use profanity, or become greedy.

Buddha did not accept the Hindu gods. According to Buddha, only people could change good to evil and evil to good. They did not need the help of gods, priests, temples, or idols to follow the Eightfold Path. Buddha taught that only two kinds of people exist—the good and the bad. Although he did not attack the Hindu caste system openly, he did not accept it.

The Spread of Buddhism

Buddha gained some followers in his lifetime, but not many. Over several centuries, however, his teachings won wide acceptance (see map, page 61).

By the 100s B.C., Buddhism had split into two branches—Hinayana (HEE • nuh • yahn • uh) and Mahayana (MAH • huh • yahn • uh). Hinayana followed the traditional beliefs of Buddhism and regarded Buddha simply as a teacher. In time this

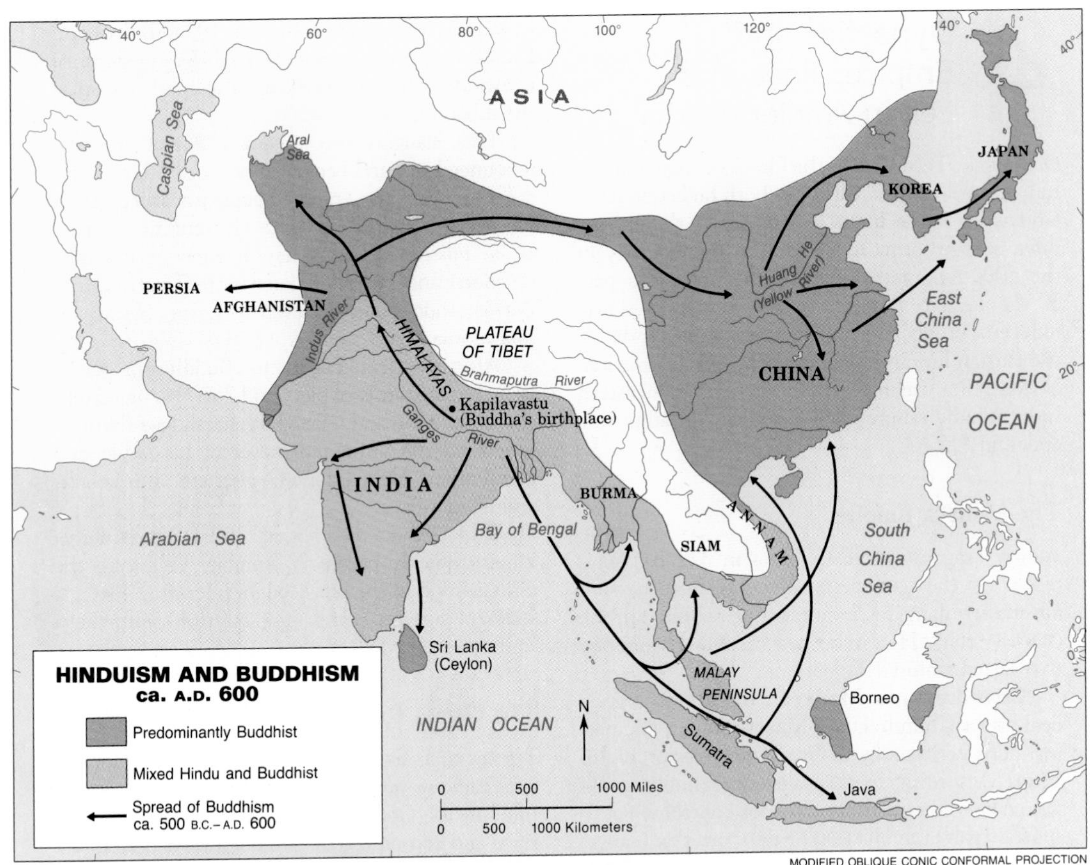

Learning from Maps *Buddhism spread to China over major trade routes about A.D. 250. According to the map, how long did it take for Buddhism to spread?* **1,100 years**

form of Buddhism spread to countries outside India, including Burma, Thailand, and Cambodia.

Believers in the Mahayana form of Buddhism regarded Buddha as a god and savior. They developed Buddhism into a religion with priests, temples, creeds, and rituals. Mahayana Buddhism spread over a wide area, including Afghanistan, central Asia, China, Korea, and Japan.

In India itself the priestly Brahmans opposed Buddhism. Their high position depended on people's acceptance of their role in performing rituals. The Brahmans opposed any religion that taught that people, regardless of caste, could reach nirvana without help if only they were good.

Despite the strong opposition of the Brahmans, Buddhism gained many followers in India over several centuries and then slowly declined. Buddhism achieved greater acceptance in other areas of Asia.

SECTION 3 REVIEW

1. **Define** Epic Age, epic, caste system, monism, reincarnation, dharma, karma, yoga, nirvana
2. **Identify** Krishna, Rama, Sita, Universal Soul, Enlightened One
3. **Locate** Afghanistan, China, Korea, Japan
4. **Identifying Ideas** **(a)** What was the origin of the caste system? **(b)** What five groups had emerged in India by the beginning of the Epic Age?
5. **Analyzing Ideas** According to Hindus, how can a soul reach salvation?
6. **Comparing Ideas** **(a)** Which Hindu ideas did Buddha accept? **(b)** Which did he reject?
7. **Summarizing Ideas** Explain the Four Noble Truths and the principles of the Eightfold Path.

3. ***Afghanistan:*** northwest of India, Pakistan; ***China:*** north and east of India; ***Korea:*** peninsula off coast of northern China; ***Japan:*** island nation off coast of Korea
4. (a) Invading Aryans established rules to prevent intermarriage between themselves and peoples they had conquered.
(b) Kshatriyas, Brahmans, Vaisyas, Sudras, and untouchables
5. Hindus believe that salvation can be achieved by fulfilling one's dharma and uniting with Brahman.
6. (a) Buddha accepted Hindu beliefs that the progress of the soul depends on the life a person leads and good is rewarded while evil is punished.
(b) He rejected the ideas that salvation could come through self-torture or animal sacrifice. He also rejected the Hindu gods and the caste system.
7. ***Four Noble Truths:*** (1) Life is full of suffering and sorrow; (2) Suffering and sorrow are caused by desire for pleasure and material things; (3) By renouncing desire, people are freed from suffering and souls attain nirvana; (4) Renunciation of desire and attainment of nirvana may be gained by following the Eightfold Path; ***Eightfold Path:*** right views, right intentions, right speech, right action, right living, right effort, right mindfulness, and right concentration

61

SECTION 4

Focus/Motivation
Ask students to suggest why the powerful Persian Empire did not conquer all of India, considering that the Persians had the means, and the route of conquest—the Khyber Pass—was open. *(The students might answer that the Persians had a large empire and control of India would have vastly overextended their resources.)*

Presentation
Analyzing Maps (Average/Group)
Have students study the map of the Gupta Empire on page 63. Ask: What geographic barrier prevented the Guptas from conquering more land to the north? *(the Himalayas)* Why would it have been easier for the Guptas to expand south than north? *(The Vindhya Mountains are lower than the Himalayas.)*

SECTION 4

Closure
Ask students if they see any similarity in the rise and fall of the Maurya and Gupta empires with that of the empires in the Fertile Crescent. *(Both civilizations fell to foreigners.)*

Review Answers
1. *Asoka:* Chandragupta's grandson who enlarged Maurya Empire to include all of northern and central India; ***Guptas:*** Hindu dynasty that claimed gods

4 Dynasties and Empires Rose and Fell in Ancient India

Neither the Persians nor the Greeks conquered the Indian subcontinent, although both had conquered land as far as the Indus River. Darius, the Persian ruler, sent an army to invade the Indus Valley in the 500s B.C. and organized the area as a part of the Persian Empire. Indian kingdoms slowly reduced Persian control of northwestern India as the Persian Empire began to decline. The kingdom of Magadha (mah • GAH • duh), in northeastern India, finally absorbed this region. Magadha rule ended in 322 B.C.

The Maurya Empire

A new kingdom arose in India in 322 B.C. as a result of the conquests of a powerful young adventurer named Chandragupta (chuhn • druh • GOOHP • tuh). He established the Maurya Empire that lasted almost 150 years.

Chandragupta Maurya. We know a good deal about Chandragupta Maurya from a fascinating book written by a Greek ambassador to his court. According to this account, Chandragupta was an able administrator. He took control of Pataliputra (pah • tah • li • POOT • rah) on the Ganges River and made it a magnificent and beautiful city. He learned the science of government and methods of warfare from the Macedonians who had conquered Persia. Chandragupta raised a huge army of 700,000 soldiers, with 10,000 chariots and 9,000 elephants. He maintained an efficient postal service that moved swiftly over the empire's excellent roads, and he united northern India from the delta of the Ganges to the region west of the Indus. Eventually, he conquered all of northwestern India up to the Hindu Kush.

An able but harsh ruler, Chandragupta made many enemies. Some of these enemies dug tunnels under his palace in their attempts to kill him. To avoid assassination, he slept in a different room each night and employed food tasters as protection against poisoning. Finally, Chandragupta abdicated the throne in favor of his son.

Asoka. Perhaps one of India's greatest rulers was Asoka (uh • SHOH • kuh), Chandragupta's grandson, who came to the throne about 270 B.C. In military campaigns that took 100,000 lives and 150,000 captives, Asoka enlarged the empire until it included all of India except the southern tip of the subcontinent.

This slaughter so sickened Asoka that he renounced war and became a devout Buddhist. He did not force the Indian people to accept Buddhism, although many did. He sent his brother as a missionary to what is now Sri Lanka (Ceylon) and other missionaries to Tibet, China, Burma, Indonesia, and even to Egypt, Syria, and Macedonia.

After his conversion to Buddhism, Asoka thought constantly of piety and duty. He urged religious toleration and relaxed the harsh laws that had supported the unlimited power of his father and grandfather. He pardoned prisoners and forbade animal sacrifices.

When Asoka died about 230 B.C., the Maurya Empire quickly began to crumble. Following the assassination of the last Maurya ruler in 184 B.C., a series of foreign rulers took control of northern India.

The Gupta Rulers

The next great rulers of India were the Guptas, who came to power in A.D. 320. The Guptas first ruled in the Ganges Valley, but through intermarriage and conquest they extended their power over a wide area of India (see map, page 63). The first three Gupta rulers—Chandragupta I (no relation to the earlier Chandragupta of the Maurya dynasty), Samudragupta (sam • oo • drah • GOOHP • tah), and Chandragupta II—used their great powers for the good of society.

The Guptas, believing the gods had appointed them to rule, favored Hinduism over Buddhism, because Hinduism stressed the gods and Buddhism did not. By the end of the Gupta period, Buddhism had declined in India, while it gained strength in many other parts of Asia. Hinduism, now somewhat influenced by Buddhism, again became the dominant religion of India and remains so today.

The time during which the Guptas ruled has been called a golden age because of the brilliant civilization that flourished then. Gupta rule ended in A.D. 535, however, when once again invaders stormed into the subcontinent and brutally ravaged northern India.

● Arabian Sea and the Bay of Bengal

Southern India

Because few of the Indian empires controlled southern India, its history developed quite differently from that of northern India. Location and natural resources played a major role in this history. Separated from the north by the Vindhya Mountains, southern Indians, particularly those along the coast, turned to trade and commerce. As traders they became wealthy because they had products, such as cotton, spices, ivory, and gold, that brought high prices.

Hinduism penetrated the region sometime after the 600s B.C. The first recorded date in the history of southern India is 250 B.C., when Asoka sent Buddhist missionaries to the Deccan. During the period of Maurya decline, beginning around 230 B.C., the Andhra dynasty arose in the south. The Andhras created an empire that eventually included a large part of southern India. When the empire declined, about A.D. 225, the south broke up into a number of small, warring states.

Learning from Maps *The Gupta rulers made Pataliputra their capital. What bodies of water border* ● *the Gupta Empire?*

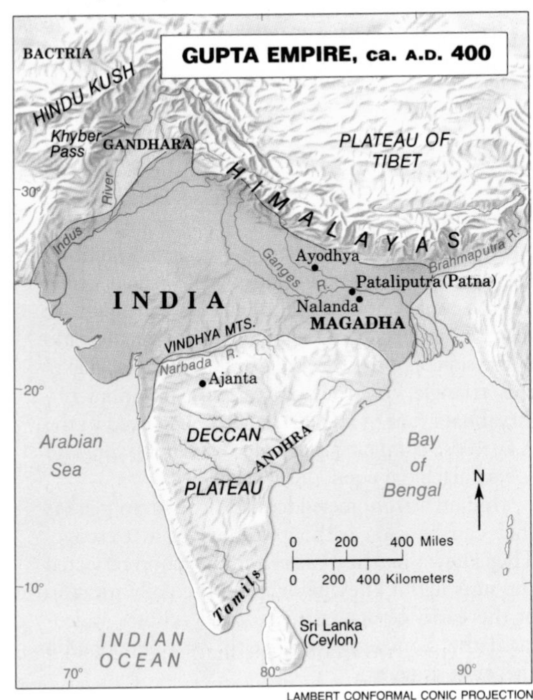

SECTION 4 REVIEW

1. **Identify** Asoka, Guptas, Chandragupta I
2. **Locate** Ganges River
3. **Summarizing Ideas** What did Chandragupta Maurya and Asoka accomplish as rulers?
4. **Analyzing Ideas** Why did the Guptas favor Hinduism over Buddhism?
5. **Determining Cause and Effect** Why did northern and southern India develop differently?

5 Civilization Flourished in Ancient India

Indian civilization reached new heights from the Epic Age to the Golden Age of the Gupta Empire. India has indeed left the world a rich legacy in the areas of art, literature, mathematics, and science. These ancient societies also established the cultural traditions of India. Their impact reached beyond the borders of India, endured through the centuries, and still influences Indian society today.

Economy and Social Life

From ancient times the land had provided a living for nearly all the people of northern India. For a limited few at the top of the caste system, the land provided great luxury. Nevertheless, most people eked out a meager existence. During the Epic Age, the rajahs in theory owned all the land and took what they wanted from the farmers. By the time of the Guptas, the rulers claimed one-sixth of the agricultural produce as their share.

Many people in southern India made their living from commerce or trade with foreign nations. Foreign trade also flourished in northern India under the Guptas. In the ancient world, Indian goods such as silks, spices, precious gems, muslins, and cashmere could be found in areas as widely scattered as the Far East, the Middle East, and Europe.

Women's freedom in India became more restricted as empires rose and fell. Women enjoyed some measure of freedom in Aryan society, and Hindu laws allowed women certain rights. However, in Gupta India a woman's status was lower than a man's. The *Mahabharata* called a man's wife

appointed them to rule; ***Chandragupta I:*** first Gupta king
2. *Ganges River:* major river of India
3. Chandragupta Maurya united northern India from the delta of the Ganges to the Indus, eventually conquering all of northwestern India; Asoka enlarged the empire by conquest until it included all of India except the southern tip.
4. Gupta rulers claimed they had been divinely appointed to rule, so they favored Hinduism because it stressed the gods and Buddhism did not.
5. The Vindhya Mountains separated the Indo-Gangetic Plain from the Deccan, or southern plateau, and provided a natural barrier to invaders.

SECTION 5

Focus/Motivation
Point out to students that one Gupta ruler supported the educational system of Nalanda much as federal and state governments support education in the United States. Then hold a class discussion on the following topic: educational aid in America should be total—that is, the government should provide free higher education for all students.

Presentation
Summarizing Ideas (Average/Group)
Have students make a chart in their notebooks of Gupta accomplishments. There should be three columns labeled *Mathematics, Astronomy*, and *Medicine*. *(The list in the column under* ***Mathematics*** *should include the following: invented a numeral system; developed concept of negative numbers; calculated square root of 2; developed table of sines; computed value of π. The list under* ***Astronomy*** *should include the following: identified seven planets; determined that planets and moon reflect sun's light; understood daily rotation of earth on its axis; predicted eclipses; developed theory of gravity; calculated diameter of earth. The column under* ***Medicine*** *should include the following: understood importance of spinal cord; knew how to set bones; performed plastic surgery; perfected inoculation technique; practiced sterilization of wounds.)*

Have one student put his or her chart on the chalkboard or an overhead projector. From this, conduct a class discussion.

Closure
Have students list some of the achievements made by peoples of early India that were not discovered or passed on in the West until much later. *(inoculation, numeral system)*

his "truest friend," but a Gupta legal treatise recommended that the wife worship her husband as a god. **Polygamy,** or marriage to more than one person, became common in the Epic Age and widespread under the Guptas. Another practice that became common during the Gupta period, especially among the upper castes, was **suttee.** In this practice a widow would commit suicide by throwing herself on top of her husband's flaming funeral pyre.

Literature

In addition to the *Mahabharata* and *Ramayana*, people enjoyed the stories of the *Panchatantra* (pahn • chah • TAN • trah), a series of fables from the Gupta period. These stories contained underlying morals and emphasized desirable traits such as adaptability, shrewdness, and determination. The *Panchatantra* includes stories about Sinbad the Sailor, Jack the Giant Killer, the Magic Mirror, and the Seven League Boots—stories known throughout the world today. Next to the Bible, the *Panchatantra* is the most widely translated book in the world today.

Indian drama developed greatly under the Guptas. Indian plays, which always had happy endings, offered little action and used different dialects, or regional variations of language, for different characters. Actors, who formed a distinct caste, performed these plays in a courtyard, using only simple scenery.

Art and Architecture

We know little about Indian art before the reign of Asoka in the 200s B.C. because these artists used perishable materials such as wood. Asoka, however, set up pillars with his laws carved on them throughout his empire and possibly built 84,000 stupas. A **stupa** was a hemisphere or dome-shaped shrine that held artifacts and objects associated with Buddha.

Early images of Buddha showed foreign influence. However, during the rule of the Guptas, Indian sculptors developed their own more rigid and formal style, which still characterizes Indian art. As Hinduism increased in importance, Indians also created a distinctive style of Hindu temple—a square building with heavy walls enclosing the statue of a god.

Mural paintings in caves tell us something about the artistic style of early Indian painters. However, we know most about mural painting in the time of the Guptas. Today people continue to visit the caves at Ajanta in central India to admire the paintings of Buddha and his followers. These paintings provide a valuable source of information about the daily life of Indian people under the Gupta rulers.

Education

In India formal schooling began at the age of nine. Although poor children learned only crafts or trades, upper-class Indian children received a formal education. Indian children read the *Upanishads*, the *Mahabharata*, and the *Ramayana*.

By the time of the Guptas, Nalanda, a famous Buddhist monastic university, had become the chief center of Indian education. Located in the lower Ganges Valley, it attracted students from as far away as Tibet, China, and Korea. Nalanda had more than 100 lecture halls, 3 large library buildings, dormitories, a model dairy, and an observatory. The curriculum included religion, philosophy, medicine, art, architecture, and agriculture.

Mathematics and Astronomy

Indian mathematicians learned to deal with abstract numbers. Indians actually invented the numeral system we call Arabic—1 through 9 and the zero. Arab traders brought it to the West from India. People in India used these so-called Arabic numerals as early as A.D. 595.

Indians also understood negative numbers (numbers preceded by a minus sign), without which algebra could not exist. They calculated the square root of 2 and prepared a table of sines, or the ratio of the side opposite the angle and the longest side of the triangle, used extensively in trigonometry. Aryabhata (ahr • yuh • BUHT • uh), who lived in the A.D. 400s, computed the value of π (pi) and also solved algebraic equations.

Indian astronomers identified the seven planets that can be seen without the aid of a telescope. They knew that the planets and the moon reflected the sun's light. They understood the daily rotation of the earth on its axis, predicted eclipses, calculated the diameter of the earth, and developed a theory of gravity.

CONNECTIONS: THEN AND NOW

Fairy Tales

"Once upon a time . . ." is a phrase we all recognize from fairy tales we heard as children. These stories occur in every culture, and a number of them are familiar to us all.

The Jataka Tales, ancient Indian stories taken from Buddhist writings, tell of animal and human kindness (top). Their theme is good versus evil. The same theme underlies the story of Cinderella (bottom). Her fairy godmother represents good; the wicked stepmother and stepsisters represent evil. In the Chinese version of this tale, a talking fish plays the fairy godmother's role, but the slipper, the prince, and the wedding are all there. In the Algonquin Indian version, the gods, rather than the prince, search for the true Cinderella. One collector of fairy tales estimates that there may be almost 300 different versions of the Cinderella story.

Another worldwide theme is that of the sleeper and the awakening. A wicked witch or fairy gives a curse, and the sleeper sleeps until awakened by a person of good will. We know this theme in Sleeping Beauty. In an Indian story, the Lord Krishna awakens the Hindu king Muchukunda.

A third universal theme is that of magical transformation, usually brought about by love. Pinocchio turns from a wooden puppet into a donkey, and finally into a real boy. In a Chinese fairy tale, Mrs. Number Three is turned into a donkey.

Psychologists see fairy tales as a way in which societies pass their values along to their young. Such tales also provide vivid examples of different kinds of human character. And they communicate eternal human concerns, dreams, and fears—the triumph of good, the power of nature, and the chance of success even for the most unlikely people.

Medicine

Indian physicians understood the importance of the spinal cord, and their surgery included bone setting and plastic surgery. They perfected the technique of inoculation—infecting a person with a mild form of a disease so that he or she will not fall ill with the more serious form. For example, Indian physicians used relatively harmless cowpox germs to inoculate against deadly smallpox, a method unknown in the Western world until the end of the 1700s.

Indian rulers built free hospitals in the early 400s. Susruta (suhs • ROO • tuh), a great Indian doctor, practiced strict cleanliness before an operation and also sterilized wounds, a procedure unknown in the West until modern times.

SECTION 5 REVIEW

1. **Define** polygamy, suttee, stupa
2. **Identify** Aryabhata, Susruta
3. **Locate** Ajanta, Nalanda
4. **Summarizing Ideas** **(a)** From what books did Indian children learn to read? **(b)** What subjects were studied at Nalanda?
5. **Classifying Ideas** What contributions did the early Indians make in the fields of mathematics, astronomy, and medicine?

Review Answers

1. ***polygamy:*** marriage to more than one person; ***suttee:*** ritual suicide by a widow; ***stupa:*** hemisphere or dome-shaped shrine that held objects associated with Buddha
2. ***Aryabhata:*** Indian mathematician who computed the value of π; ***Susruta:*** Indian doctor who practiced strict cleanliness before operations and sterilized wounds
3. ***Ajanta:*** cave in central India famous for mural paintings of Buddha and followers; ***Nalanda:*** chief center of Indian scholarship under Guptas
4. (a) Indian children learned to read the *Upanishads, Mahabharata*, and *Ramayana.* **(b)** The curriculum at Nalanda included religion, philosophy, medicine, art, architecture, and agriculture.
5. Indians invented the "Arabic" numeral system, negative numbers, and a table of sines. Aryabhata computed the value of π. Astronomers identified seven planets, knew planets and moon reflected light, and understood the daily rotation of the earth. They also predicted eclipses, calculated the diameter of the earth, and developed a theory of gravity. In medicine, Indians set bones, performed plastic surgery, and inoculated against smallpox.

65

Reviewing Important Terms

1. monsoon; 2. citadel; 3. Animism; 4. Brahmans; 5. rajahs; 6. Epic Age; 7. monism; 8. polygamy; 9. reincarnation; 10. Karma; 11. yoga

Developing Critical Thinking Skills

1. language, religious beliefs, and caste system
2. The Himalayas, Karakorum, and Hindu Kush ranges slowed the spread of Indian culture elsewhere. The Vindhya Mountains formed a barrier between northern and southern India. Deserts and vast distances also slowed cultural diffusion.
3. The monsoon brings a light rain in the Deccan, heavier rain along the coastal rim and lower Ganges Valley, and the heaviest rain in the eastern Himalayas. If enough moisture is available, crops can be grown. If the monsoon is late or rainfall is light, crops are lost. If there is too much rain, destructive floods result.
4. ***Indus Valley:*** systematically planned cities with water and sewer system; fine articles for trade; written language; ***Aryan:*** Vedas; social order of classes; Sanskrit; religion
5. **(a)** Answers will vary. Students might mention they all had writing, engaged in industry and trade, and were based on agriculture. They all began in river valleys and had many similar characteristics. Egyptians and Indo-Aryans worshiped animals. However, Indo-Aryans included animism. **(b)** The climate, natural barriers to cultural diffusion, and difficulty in traversing regions isolated the regions.

1B, 2D, a1A, a4A

Reteaching

Have students review the Chapter Summary and the appropriate section and questions in the Unit Synthesis. Discuss the concepts until students demonstrate a clear understanding of the material.

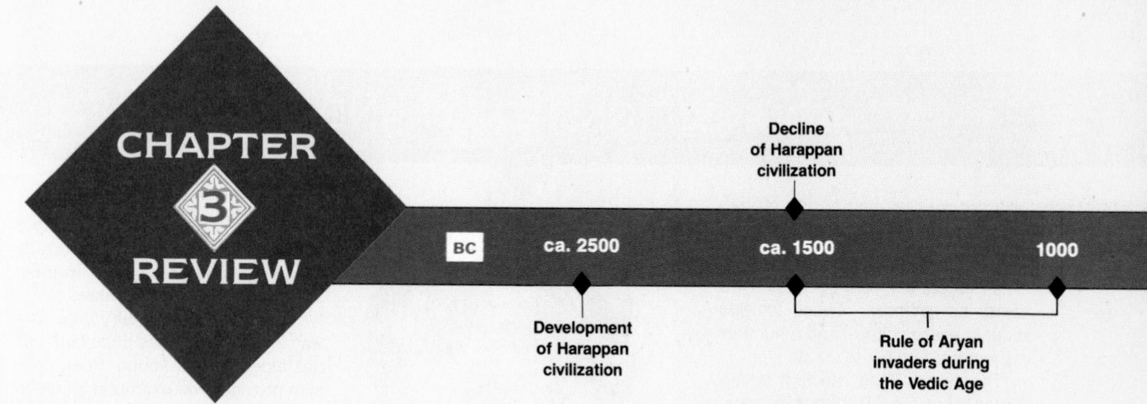

Chapter Summary

The following list contains the key concepts you have learned about the ancient civilizations of India.

1. The Indian subcontinent is divided roughly into four geographical regions–the northern mountains, the Indo-Gangetic Plain, the Deccan, and the Coastal Plain.
2. Monsoons and oppressive heat dominate India's climate.
3. About 2500 B.C. an impressive civilization, the Harappan civilization, appeared in the Indus Valley. Industry and trade were centered in such cities as Harappa and Mohenjo-Daro. The Harappans developed a written language and a form of animistic religion.
4. About 1500 B.C. the Aryans began to enter the Indus Valley. Because the Aryans lacked a written language, knowledge of their early history comes mainly from the Vedas, their sacred books, which describe their religious beliefs. Originally herders and nomads, the Aryans became farmers and founded small tribal states. Intermarriage with the original Indus Valley people was prohibited, and class divisions began to form during the Vedic Age.
5. The Aryans of India developed a caste system. Each caste had its own fixed position in society and its own rules about eating, marriage, labor, and worship. Caste remains an important part of social organization in India today.
6. Brahman scholars composed the *Upanishads* to explain the Vedic religion. From these explanations grew a complex set of ideas known as Hinduism, which remains the major Indian religion.
7. Hinduism teaches that the world of the senses is an illusion. Only through reincarnation can a person gain the experience needed to escape suffering and be reunited with the Universal Soul.
8. Gautama, an Indian prince who became known as Buddha, taught that people could attain salvation by accepting the Four Noble Truths and following the Eightfold Path. These teachings, which became known as Buddhism, exerted an even more powerful influence on the rest of Asia than on India itself.
9. From 322 B.C. to 184 B.C., the Maurya Empire ruled India. Asoka, a Mauryan emperor, was one of India's greatest rulers. He embraced Buddhism, relaxed harsh laws, and urged toleration for the many religions of India.
10. The Gupta dynasty lasted from A.D. 320 to A.D. 535. This period is known as the "Golden Age" in India. The first three Gupta rulers, Chandragupta I, Samudragupta, and Chandragupta II, used their great powers for the good of society. It was during this period that Hinduism became the major religion of India.
11. Indian culture reached new heights during ancient times. Great epics, such as the *Mahabharata* and the *Ramayana,* and the famous fables of the *Panchatantra* were written at this time. Many of India's greatest dramatists and poets wrote plays and poems during this time. Great advances were made in the areas of mathematics, astronomy, and medicine. Indians invented Arabic numerals, computed the value of π (pi), identified seven planets, and practiced surgery and inoculation.

On a separate sheet of paper, complete the following review exercises.

Reviewing Important Terms

Supply the term that correctly completes each sentence.

1. A ________ is a seasonal wind named for the direction in which it blows.
2. A ________ is a strong central fortress.
3. ________ is a belief that spirits inhabit everything, even people.
4. Indian priests were called ________ .
5. In Aryan times princes, or ________ , ruled each city-state.
6. The ________ ________ in Indian history lasted from 1000 B.C. to 500 B.C. and takes its name from religious literature.
7. The Hindu belief that God and human beings are one and indivisible is called ________ .
8. Marriage to more than one person is called ________ .
9. The Hindu belief in the transmigration or rebirth of the soul is called ________ .
10. ________ is the belief that the present condition of a person's life is wholly the result of what was done or not done during a previous life.

Relating Geography to History
Have students check an atlas for rainfall statistics and monsoons.

Relating Past to Present
1. (a) They believed spirits inhabited everything and could influence a person's life. They are similar to superstitions. **(b)** Symbols considered "lucky" today include rabbits' feet, four-leaf clovers, rainbows, and horseshoes. "Unlucky symbols" include black cats.
2. (a) sewage disposal and water supply; **(b)** Answers will vary. Students might include traffic congestion; water, noise, and air pollution; decaying housing and overcrowding. **(c)** Answers will vary. Students may say cities are encouraging urban planning.

Applying History Study Skills
Charts and answers will vary, but accept all reasonable classifications.

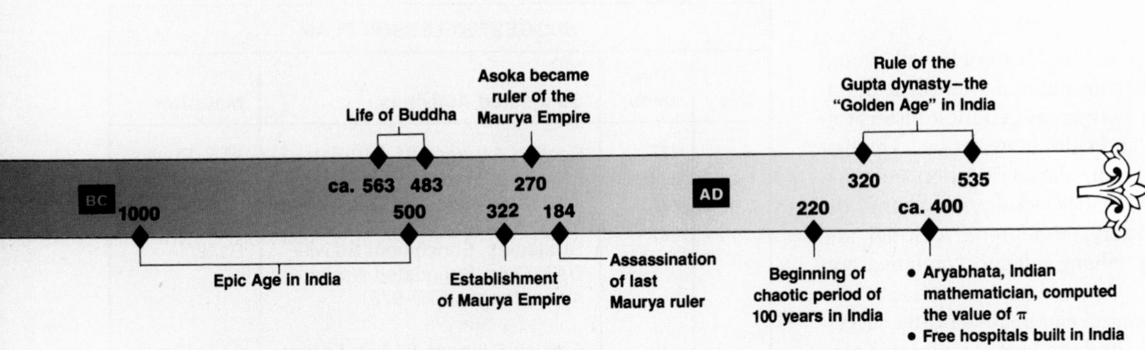

11. Hindus commonly practice ________, a physical and mental discipline designed to harmonize the body with the soul.

Developing Critical Thinking Skills

1. **Summarizing Ideas** What changes did the Aryans bring to the Indus Valley civilization?
2. **Describing Ideas** Describe the geographical features of India that were barriers to the spread of Indian culture.
3. **Determining Cause and Effect** How does climate influence agricultural production in the four geographic regions of India?
4. **Making Charts** Make a chart showing the major accomplishments of the Indus Valley civilization and the Aryans.
5. **Analyzing Information** **(a)** What differences and similarities can you find between the civilizations of the Indus Valley and the civilizations that you read about in Chapter 2? **(b)** How would you account for these differences?

Relating Geography to History

(a) Trace a map of India. **(b)** Indicate the areas that have heavy rainfall. **(c)** Indicate the areas that need irrigation in order to grow crops. **(d)** Show the desert areas that might be used for grazing. **(e)** Indicate the wind direction for summer and fall monsoons and for winter winds.

Relating Past to Present

1. Animism is the term used to describe the ancient religious beliefs of the Harappan civilization. **(a)** List some of their ideas and practices and compare them with what people today call "superstitions." **(b)** What are some of the symbols considered "lucky" and "unlucky" today?
2. **(a)** What city-planning problems did the people of Harappa and Mohenjo-Daro solve? **(b)** What are some modern city-planning problems that were unknown to the people of these ancient civilizations? **(c)** How are these city-planning problems being solved?

Applying History Study Skills

Before completing this activity, review Building History Study Skills on page 53.

The *Rig-Veda,* the Aryan collection of hymns, consists of stanzas of praise to the Aryan gods. This literature helps us to understand the religious beliefs and the society of the early Indian people. Study the names and functions of the gods listed below. Then construct a chart in which you classify the gods according to the characteristics they share.

Varuna–directed the cosmos; god of justice and order
Soma–god of immortality
Indra–victorious war god
Rudra–storm god
Agni–god of fire, healing, and the home
Ushas–god of the dawn
Surya–god of the sun
Vac–goddess of speech
Tad Ekam–"That One," the source of all creation

Investigating Further

1. **Presenting an Oral Report** Present an oral report on the achievements, mysterious beginnings, and sudden end of the Harappan civilization. Good sources for your report are "The Valley of the Indus" in *The Horizon Book of Lost Worlds* by Leonard Cottrell (American Heritage) and "India's Forgotten Civilization" in *Readings in World History* by Leften S. Stavrianos et al. (Allyn and Bacon).
2. **Writing a Report** Using encyclopedias, find out more about Chandragupta Maurya and Asoka. Prepare a written report on the life and accomplishments of one of these Indian rulers.
3. **Constructing a Model** Use resources in your school or public library to find more information on the architecture of Mohenjo-Daro or Harappa. Then construct a model showing what the city might have looked like.

67

CHAPTER (pages 68-89)

4 Ancient Chinese Civilization Developed Lasting Traditions

(1500 B.C.–A.D. 589)

CHAPTER OVERVIEW

Chinese civilization developed first in the Huang He valley, and like that of India, has had a nearly continuous existence. It developed in relative isolation from other civilizations. Chinese history followed a pattern of dynastic cycles and cultural evolution. The first historic dynasty, the Shang dynasty, introduced irrigation and flood control systems in the Yellow River valley. Under the Shang, the Chinese produced silk cloth, pottery, and bronze castings and developed a calendar and writing. Shang religion combined animism and ancestor worship.

China grew into a large and powerful empire under three successive dynasties—the Zhou, the Qin, and the Han. During this period a number of important philosophies appeared in China. Confucius taught that the family was important to the state and that only educated and virtuous people should enter government service. Daoism taught that people should withdraw from the world and try to achieve harmony with nature. Naturalist philosophers were concerned with the dualism of nature. Legalism stressed political power and harsh laws.

SUGGESTED LESSON PLAN

Day	Objectives	Suggested Activities	Materials
1	U8,* C1-3	Introducing the Chapter (page 68) Section 1 (pages 69-72), Focus/Motivation (pages 69-70), Presentation (page 72), Closure (page 70), Suggested Teaching Strategies, Enrichment Activity, Daily Quiz, Suggested Assignments (page 67B)	ATE, Pupil's Edition, Teacher's Resource-Bank™
2	U9, C4-5	Section 2 (pages 73-76), Focus/Motivation (page 73), Presentation (page 74), Closure (page 76), Suggested Teaching Strategies, Enrichment Activity, Daily Quiz, Suggested Assignments (page 67C)	ATE, Pupil's Edition, Teacher's Resource-Bank™
3	U9, C6	Section 3 (pages 76-80), Focus/Motivation (page 77), Presentation (pages 77-78), Closure (page 80), Suggested Teaching Strategies, Enrichment Activity, Daily Quiz, Suggested Assignments (pages 67C-67D)	ATE, Pupil's Edition, Teacher's Resource-Bank™
4	U7, U9, C7	Section 4 (pages 81-84), Focus/Motivation (pages 81-82), Presentation (page 82), Closure (page 84), Suggested Teaching Strategies, Enrichment Activity, Daily Quiz, Suggested Assignments (pages 67D-67E)	ATE, Pupil's Edition, Teacher's Resource-Bank™
5	U9, C8	Section 5 (pages 84-87), Focus/Motivation (page 85), Presentation (page 86), Closure (page 86), Suggested Teaching Strategies, Enrichment Activity, Daily Quiz, Suggested Assignments (pages 67E-67F)	ATE, Pupil's Edition, Teacher's Resource-Bank™
6	U7-9, C1-8	Chapter 4 Form A Test, Reteaching Worksheet, Chapter 4 Form B Test	Teacher's Resource-Bank™ or Workbook and Test Booklet
7	U1-9	Unit One Review Worksheet, Unit One Test	Teacher's Resource-Bank™ or Test Booklet

*C refers to applicable Chapter Objective, U refers to applicable Unit Goal

BOOKS FOR THE TEACHER

Fitzgerald, C. P. *Horizon History of China.* American Heritage. Covers all aspects of Chinese life.

Latourette, Kenneth S. *China.* Prentice-Hall. Analyzes Chinese history.

Schafer, Edward. *Ancient China.* Time-Life. Discusses the history and culture of ancient China, with illustrations.

Smith, Huston. *The Religions of Man.* Harper & Row. Contains chapters on Hinduism, Buddhism, Daoism, and Confucianism.

Welty, Paul. *The Asians.* Lippincott. Introduces Asian societies.

Yap, Yong, and Arthur Cottrell. *The Early Civilization of China.* Putnam. Analyzes political, social, and cultural history.

BOOKS FOR THE STUDENT

Hay, John. *Ancient China.* Henry Z. Walck. Discusses Chinese history from Peking people to the Tang dynasty.

Kublin, Hyman. *China.* Houghton Mifflin. Gives a concise history of China. Also useful for later chapters.

Silverberg, Robert. *The Long Rampart.* Chilton. Examines the Great Wall and the dynasties involved in its creation.

Sims, Bennett. *Confucius.* Franklin Watts. Describes the life and philosophy of Confucius.

Spencer, Cornelia. *Ancient China.* John Day. Examines the history of China to 1840. Also useful for later chapters.

MULTIMEDIA MATERIALS

Ancient Chinese (mp, 24 min.), Independent Film. Shows how China's history and deeply rooted traditions have continued longer than those of any other civilization.

Ancient Civilizations (fs), National Geographic. A series of 6 filmstrips. Title appropriate for Chapter 4: "China."

Ancient Orient (mp, 14 min.), Coronet. Portrays the religions, philosophies, and arts of ancient India, China, and Japan.

Past and Present China (fs), Visual. Describes Chinese life during several dynasties. Titles appropriate for Chapter 8: "The Han and T'ang Dynasties," "The Sung and Yüan Dynasties," "The Home in Imperial China."

World's Great Religions (fs), Life. Titles appropriate for Chapter 4: "Buddhism," "Confucianism and Daoism," "Hinduism."

Section 1 (pages 69-72) Geographic and Cultural Features Helped Shape Chinese History

SECTION OVERVIEW

China is divided, both physically and politically, into two main parts. The smaller and more important parts are in China Proper, which stretches inland up the valleys of the Huang He and Chang Jiang rivers. China has remained isolated from the rest of the world for centuries, both because of geographic barriers and because the Chinese considered other peoples to be inferior. China's history has been marked by two basic patterns: the dynastic cycle and cultural evolution.

SUGGESTED TEACHING STRATEGIES

1. **Preteaching Vocabulary (Basic)** You may wish to preteach the following important vocabulary terms: loess, silt (*page 71*). Ask students to look up the definitions to these terms in the glossary and find where they are boldfaced in the chapter.
2. **Writing a Letter (Average/Group)** Have students pretend they are the ruler of China writing to an imaginary ruler in Europe. The Chinese ruler is telling the Western monarch that the Chinese want nothing to do with the West. The letter should illustrate the Chinese sense of superiority, list the achievements of the Chinese, and explain why the Chinese feel the West has nothing to offer China.

ENRICHMENT ACTIVITY

Making a Diagram (Average/Group) Have interested students reread pages 71-72 about the dynastic cycle. Then have them prepare a diagram detailing the steps in the cycle.

DAILY QUIZ

To assess student understanding of Section 1, give the class the following quiz. (Each item is worth 10 points.)

1. ________ separate China into many distinct, separate regions. *(Mountains)*
2. Name the two great rivers that people based their civilizations upon in ancient China. *(Huang He, Chang Jiang)*
3. What is the principal crop in North China? *(wheat)*
4. What is the principal crop in South China? *(rice)*
5. (T or F) Politically, China was divided into two parts, China Proper and the surrounding regions of Tibet, Xinjiang, Mongolia, Manchuria, and Korea. *(T)*
6. Why is the Huang He called "China's Sorrow"? *(periodic destructive flooding)*
7. What did the Chinese construct to try and control the Huang He? *(dikes)*
8. (T or F) Isolated from the West by deserts, distance, and mountains, the Chinese formed the opinion that their land was the only civilization and the center of the world. *(T)*
9. A dynastic cycle includes all of the following except: establishing the dynasty, period of great power, period of decline, period of renewal, overthrow of the dynasty. *(period of renewal)*
10. (T or F) Chinese civilization developed steadily. *(T)*

SUGGESTED ASSIGNMENTS

1. **Understanding Geography (Basic)** Have students complete "Geography Fact Sheet: World Resources" in the TEACHER'S RESOURCEBANK™.
2. **Outlining (Basic)** Have students outline Section 1.
3. **Critical Thinking Worksheet (Average/Group)** Have students complete Critical Thinking Worksheet 9 in the TEACHER'S RESOURCEBANK™.

Section 2 (pages 73-76) Chinese Civilization Flourished Under the Shang Dynasty

SECTION OVERVIEW

The Shang dynasty began along the Huang He and controlled China for about 500 years. Chinese monarchs ruled by the Mandate of Heaven. If they failed to win wars or see that harvests were plentiful, the people had the right to change their rulers. Shang artisans produced kaolin pottery and impressive bronze castings. A calendar and an original written language were devised, and a religion combining animism and ancestor worship was developed.

SUGGESTED TEACHING STRATEGIES

1. **Preteaching Vocabulary (Basic)** You may wish to preteach the following important vocabulary terms: Mandate of Heaven (*page 73*); calligraphy, oracle bones (*page 75*). You may wish to provide students with examples of Chinese calligraphy before they study this section.
2. **Illustrating Ideas (Average/Group)** You might have an interested student give a demonstration to the class on calligraphy, or you might involve the entire class. Sources include: Kurt Weise's *You Can Write Chinese* (Viking) and Yee Chiang's *Chinese Calligraphy* (Harvard University Press). An effective way to demonstrate the strokes is to draw them on the chalkboard, using a brush and plain water.
3. **Analyzing Ideas (Average/Group)** Hold a class discussion on the role of the ruler in the Shang dynasty. What geographic factor made a strong ruler necessary? What were the ruler's functions? Compare his role with those of the rulers of Egypt and the Fertile Crescent. *(Students should state that the need for controlling the Huang He led to the development of a strong ruler. The king was a leader in battle and in certain religious ceremonies. As opposed to rulers of the Middle East, the Shang king was not considered a god or in any way divine.)*

ENRICHMENT ACTIVITY

Making a Report (Average/Group) Students may want to learn more about religion in the Shang period and make oral presentations to the class. One student might describe the practice of divination with bones and tortoise shells. Another might describe the burial rituals for a Shang ruler. Both topics can be found in *Epic of Man* (Time-Life). Another interesting topic for research is bronze casting. An excellent article in Percy Knauth's *The Metalsmiths* (Time-Life) illustrates the process for Shang bronze casting. A worthwhile book about other Chinese achievements is Frank Ross's *Oracle Bones, Stars, and Wheelbarrows: Ancient Chinese Science and Technology* (Houghton Mifflin).

DAILY QUIZ

To assess student understanding of Section 2, give the class the following quiz. (Each item is worth 10 points.)

1. (T or F) Pan Gu, the first Shang king, controlled the Xi River Valley and, as a religious ruler, formed the first real Chinese culture in the 200s B.C. *(F)*
2. The first major Chinese dynasty existed in the ________ valley. *(Huang He)*
3. Summarize why irrigation and the building of dikes were so important in China and led to the creation of the Shang dynasty. *(The Shang government began the regulation of irrigation, drainage, and flood control.)*
4. (T or F) If the Chinese had a poor harvest or were defeated in battle, the people believed the king had lost favor with the gods. *(T)*
5. List the crops and products the Chinese grew and produced during the Shang dynasty. *(millet, barley, rice; silk, cord from hemp)*
6. (T or F) The Chinese calendar included 6 cycles of 60 days making a year. *(T)*
7. (T or F) Astronomers became the first Chinese historians because of their expertise in record keeping. *(T)*
8. List the characteristics of the Chinese written and oral language. *(one-syllable words; lack of inflection; pictograms; idea sign; sound sign)*
9. The art of writing is called ________ . *(calligraphy)*
10. During the Shang dynasty, Chinese religion became a combination of animism and ________ worship. *(ancestor)*

SUGGESTED ASSIGNMENTS

1. **Analyzing Maps (Basic)** Have students compare the map of the Shang dynasty on page 73 with a map of modern China. How do the territories under Chinese control today differ from those under the control of the Shang rulers? *(They are much larger today.)*
2. **Understanding Geography (Basic)** Have students complete "Geography Fact Sheet: World Population" in the TEACHER'S RESOURCEBANK™.

Section 3 (pages 76-80)

Chinese Civilization Evolved Through Changing Dynasties

SECTION OVERVIEW

Under three successive dynasties—the Zhou, the Qin, and the Han—China grew into a large and powerful empire. Under the Zhou, the longest dynasty in China's history, agriculture expanded and China's population grew steadily. The Qin dynasty lasted only a short time but unified China under a strong central government. During the Han dynasty the civil service system was established and the Silk Route was opened. After the Han dynasty fell in A.D. 220, China suffered from constant war for over 350 years.

SUGGESTED TEACHING STRATEGIES

1. **Preteaching Vocabulary (Basic)** You may wish to preteach the following important vocabulary terms: autocracy (*page 78*), civil service (*page 79*). Point out to the students that even though the word *autocracy* as defined in this chapter applies to ancient China, autocracies still exist in the world today.
2. **Comparing Ideas (Average/Group)** Have selected students compare the Chinese and American civil service systems and make a written or oral report. They should examine the kinds of jobs requiring an examination, the content of the tests, and the

numbers of applicants who pass the tests. Students should visit the Post Office for information on the United States Civil Service. For information on China, students can begin with "The Civil Service Examination" in L. S. Stavrianos's *Readings in World History* (Allyn and Bacon).

ENRICHMENT ACTIVITY

Preparing a Written Report (Average/Group) Have students report on the Silk Route opened during the Han dynasty. A recommended source is Robert Collins's *East to Cathay: The Silk Road* (McGraw-Hill). Other sources may be found in the *Reader's Guide to Periodical Literature*. Select some reports to read to the class. Then begin a class discussion on how trade brings civilizations together. Ask what products—food, clothing, the fine and performing arts—enrich American lives today as a result of foreign contacts and trade.

DAILY QUIZ

To assess student understanding of Section 3, give the class the following quiz. (Each item is worth 10 points.)

1. (T or F) The Zhou established the most enduring dynasty in Chinese history. *(T)*
2. The Zhou introduced agricultural tools and plows made of ________, which transformed Chinese agriculture and allowed the peasants to cultivate more land and produce more grain. *(iron)*
3. (T or F) Many rebellious city-states created their own independent provinces as the Zhou dynasty lost power. *(T)*
4. Who was the most important ruler in the Qin dynasty, and whose name means "first emperor"? *(Shi Huangdi)*
5. (T or F) The Qin dynasty used cavalry armed with bows and arrows to conquer the remnants of the Zhou dynasty. *(T)*
6. What great structure did Shi Huangdi complete during his reign? *(Great Wall)*
7. (T or F) As in most autocratic governments, Shi Huangdi burned books and persecuted scholars to stop the discussion of his policies. *(T)*
8. ________, the most famous Han ruler, extended the Chinese borders to Manchuria and Korea. *(Wu Di)*
9. During the Han dynasty, the Chinese established the ________. *(civil service)*
10. Under the Han dynasty, the Chinese had a time of peace called the ________. *(Pax Sinica)*

SUGGESTED ASSIGNMENT

Classifying Ideas (Basic) Have students make a chart comparing and contrasting the accomplishments of the Zhou, Qin, and Han dynasties.

Section (pages 81-84)

The Ancient Chinese Created Unique Philosophies

SECTION OVERVIEW

Under the early dynasties, the Chinese developed patterns of thinking and living that had a lasting impact. Naturalism, Confucianism, Legalism, and Daoism each contributed to Chinese thought. The most important social unit was the family, and the father was the source of authority

SUGGESTED TEACHING STRATEGIES

1. **Leading a Panel Discussion (Average/Group)** The entire class can become involved in a panel discussion of the themes and relative merits of the Chinese philosophies. One student can act as moderator; four other students can represent Confucianism, Daoism, Naturalism, and Legalism. The rest of the class should prepare questions to ask the panel. Panel members may wish to do additional reading. Two sources are Paul Welty's *The Asians* (Lippincott) and Elizabeth Seeger's *Eastern Religions* (T. Y. Crowell).
2. **Writing a Biography (Average/Group)** Have students do research on the lives of Confucius and Laozi and write a three-page report to present to the class. Students should indicate in their reports how the two philosphers differed. Use the material presented in the reports for a class discussion comparing Confucianism and Daoism.

*3. **Reading About History: Analyzing a Statement (Basic)** To reinforce the skill presented on page 83, have students reread "Building History Study Skills" on page 83. Then have them analyze the following: "China is a sea which salts all rivers that run into it."

ENRICHMENT ACTIVITY

Learning Through Art (Challenging) Students interested in art could draw Chinese landscape paintings for the bulletin board. Others could make oral reports on Chinese art of this period, using an opaque projector or slides. Sources include Edward H. Schafer's, *Ancient China* (Time-Life).

DAILY QUIZ

To assess student understanding of Section 4, give the class the following quiz. (Each item is worth 10 points.)

1. (T or F) During the collapse of the Zhou dynasty, Chinese education, thought, and religion failed to develop any new scholars or ethical systems. *(F)*
2. Identify the two words that describe the Chinese dualism of nature. *(yin; yang)*
3. Which of these would *not* be yin? night, winter, male *(male)*

4. (T or F) Confucius believed that every person should accept his or her assigned position and perform expected duties. *(T)*
5. (T or F) The Legalists believed government should be very powerful and centralized to limit the selfish, untrustworthy desires of people. *(T)*
6. ________ founded Daoism during the sixth century B.C. *(Laozi)*
7. (T or F) According to Daoism, people should withdraw from public affairs to better bring themselves into harmony with nature, becoming quiet, thoughtful, and humble. *(T)*
8. What faith came from outside to influence Chinese thought during the Han dynasty? *(Buddhism)*
9. According to Confucian ideals, which became the most important in Chinese society? family, country, individual, foreigners *(family)*
10. The founder of the Han dynasty ordered schools in China to make sacrifices to which phiolosopher? *(Confucius)*

SUGGESTED ASSIGNMENTS

1. **Critical Thinking Worksheet (Average/Group)** Have students complete Critical Thinking Worksheet 10 in the TEACHER'S RESOURCEBANK™.
2. **Skill Worksheet (Basic)** Have students complete Skill Worksheet 4 in the TEACHER'S RESOURCEBANK™.
3. **Profile Worksheet (Basic)** Have students complete Profile Worksheet 4 in the TEACHER'S RESOURCEBANK™.

Section (pages 84-87)

5 Culture Reached New Heights During the Zhou, Qin, and Han Dynasties

SECTION OVERVIEW

Confucianism taught that the family was the most important unit in Chinese society. The values of the family applied as well to national life. While the cities of China grew and trade increased, the vast majority of Chinese continued to work the soil. Despite this relative changelessness, the Chinese made great strides in science and technology. They further refined the calendar and observed sunspots. They built instruments to register earthquakes and to observe what they believed to be the orbit of the sun. The Chinese also invented paper, which eventually spread westward to replace papyrus. In medicine they contributed acupuncture therapy.

SUGGESTED TEACHING STRATEGIES

1. **Preteaching Vocabulary (Basic)** You may wish to preteach the following important vocabulary term: acupuncture (*page 87*). Point out that acupuncture has become very popular in the United States in recent years.
2. **Understanding Ideas (Basic)** Put the following quotation on the chalkboard or an overhead projector.

"Obedience and respect, rather than affection, are required of the Chinese child . . . . The child is early taught to walk respectfully behind his superiors, to sit only when he is bidden, to speak only when questions are asked him, and to salute his superiors by the correct designations . . . . He must rise from his seat when they approach him. If he is taken to task for anything he has done, he must never contradict, never seek to explain. Such an offense is not easily forgiven and double punishment is likely to immediately overtake the offender."

Then have students read the subsection, "Family and Social Life," on pages 84 and 86. Ask them to relate the quotation to the material in the text. Use the quotation as the basis for a class discussion on Chinese ideas concerning obedience, respect, and affection. How do these ideas compare to contemporary American values?

ENRICHMENT ACTIVITY

Writing a Report (Average/Group) Assign interested students to examine the role and importance of the family in ancient society. Have each student write a report on one country—China, India, Egypt, or any one of the peoples of the Fertile Crescent. They should examine the role of the father and the mother, the duties of the children, attitudes toward other members of the family, and the importance given the family by the state or religion. After students have completed their reports, have them read them to the class. Use the material presented as the basis of a class discussion. You might wish to make a chart for the chalkboard or overhead projector that shows how each ancient civilization viewed particular roles of family members.

DAILY QUIZ

To assess student understanding of Section 5, give the class the following quiz. (Each item is worth 10 points.)

1. (T or F) The values that governed family life in ancient China were of little importance to national life. *(F)*
2. (T or F) The individual, not the family, constituted the most important unit in Chinese society. *(F)*
3. (T or F) Each family in China consisted of the father and mother, the sons with their wives and children, and the unmarried daughters. *(T)*
4. (T or F) Women in China were subordinate to men and had no property rights of their own. *(T)*
5. (T or F) In China, children could marry without their parents' permission. *(F)*
6. (T or F) The low rate of literacy in China occurred because learning to read the Chinese language was difficult and tutors were expensive. *(T)*
7. (T or F) Local government was responsible for educating children in China. *(F)*
8. and **9.** A well-educated young man in China had to learn the ________ of Confucius and the ________ ________. *(Analects, Five Classics)*

10. The therapy whereby the doctor inserts needles into certain points of the body is called ________ . *(acupuncture)*

SUGGESTED ASSIGNMENTS

1. **Geography Fact Sheet (Basic)** Have students complete "Geography Fact Sheet: Using Earth's Land" in the TEACHER'S RESOURCEBANK™.
2. **Review Worksheet (Basic)** Have students complete Review Worksheet 4 in the TEACHER'S RESOURCEBANK™.

For suggested lesson plan, additional teaching strategies, enrichment activities, daily quizzes, and suggested assignments, see pages 67A–67F.

Introducing the Chapter
Distribute copies of the following quotations to use as the basis of discussion.

"Confucius:
When one cultivates to the utmost the principles of his nature, and exercises them on the principle of reciprocity, he is not far from the path. What you do not like when done to yourself, do not do to others.
Buddha:
Monks, these two extremes should not be followed . . . (on the one hand); and (on the other) devotion of self-mortification, which is painful, unworthy, and unprofitable. By avoiding these two extremes, the (holy man) has gained knowledge of that middle path . . . which causeth calm, special knowledge, enlightenment."

Ask: What do these writers stress, religious beliefs or ethical behavior? What basic principle does Confucius propose? To what other teaching is this similar? What seems to be the focus of Confucian teaching? of Buddhism?
(Confucius stressed ethical behavior. Buddha stressed both ethical behavior and religious beliefs. Confucius proposed that people not do to others what they would not like to have done to themselves. This is similar to the teachings of Jesus. Confucius was concerned with people's relationships to other people. Buddhism seems to

CHAPTER

4

Ancient Chinese Civilization Developed Lasting Traditions

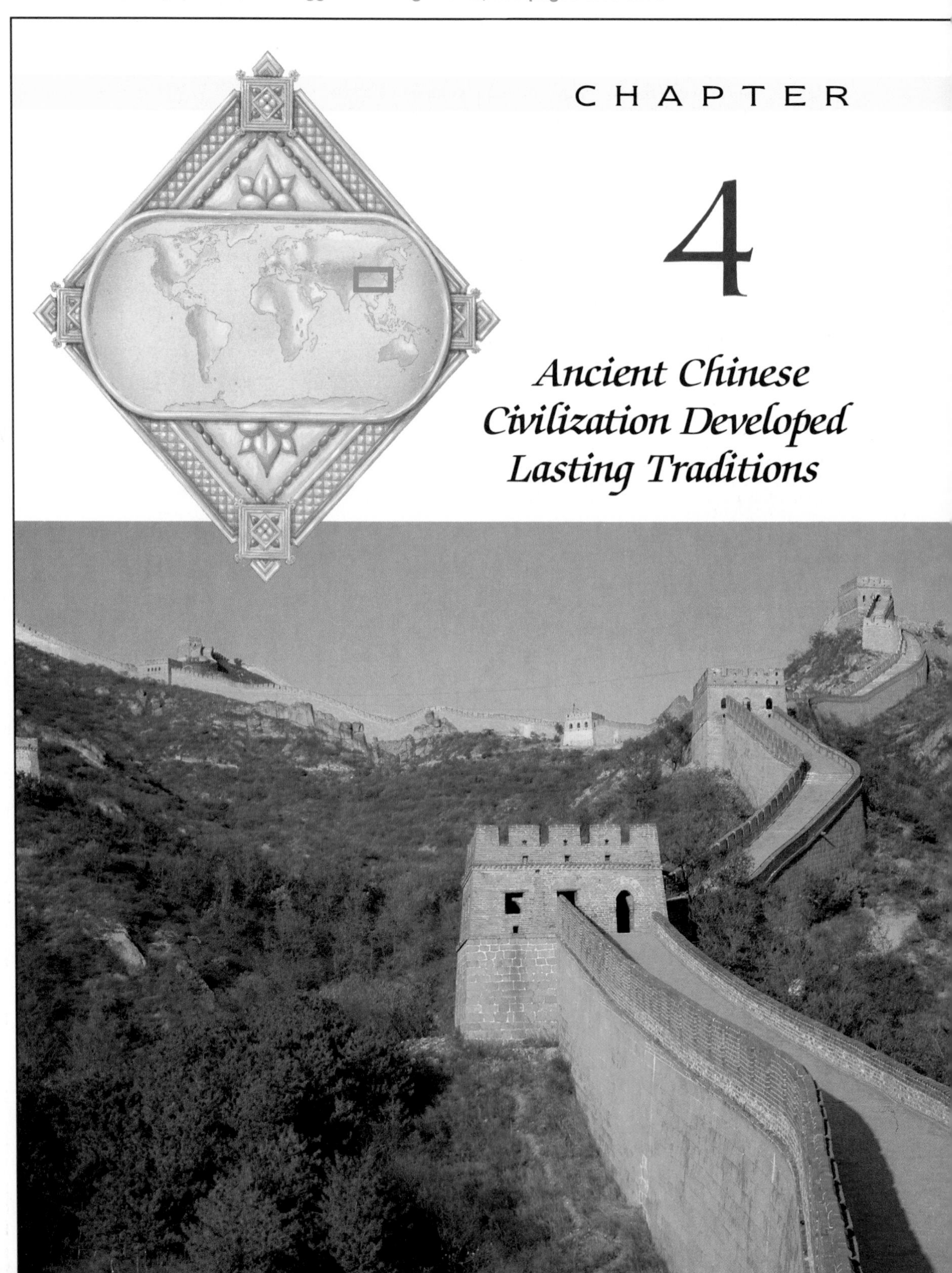

CHAPTER FOCUS

Place China

Time 1500 B.C.–A.D. 589

3.7 mil. BC 4000 BC AD 2100

Significance

Throughout much of the world in the 500s B.C., many great civilizations struggled in the first stages of development. Some of these civilizations would survive, and some would not. In all of them, people tested ideas and created traditions that most of the nations of the world today still share.

Chinese civilization began in the vastness of the North China Plain, to the northeast of the rugged, snowcapped peaks of the Himalayas. As in India, many of the customs and traditions developed in ancient China remain a part of Chinese life today. One reason for this continuity is the enduring influence of two great leaders, Gautama Buddha and Confucius, on Chinese life. In one of the great coincidences of history, both leaders lived at about the same time, in the 500s B.C. As you have read, Buddhism, the religion founded by Gautama Buddha, began in India and spread throughout Asia. Confucius, on the other hand, lived and taught in China. Both leaders influenced the lives of millions of people in China, the Middle East, and other parts of Asia.

Terms to Define

loess	calligraphy
silt	oracle bones
Mandate of Heaven	civil service

People to Identify

Shang	Wu Di
Zhou	Kongzi
Qin	Laozi

Places to Locate

Huang He	China Proper
Chang Jiang	Xi Jiang

Questions to Guide Your Reading

1 What geographic and cultural features helped shape Chinese history?
2 How did the first Chinese civilization flourish under the Shang dynasty?
3 How did Chinese civilization evolve through changing dynasties?
4 What philosophies emerged in ancient China?
5 How did China develop under the rule of the Zhou, Qin, and Han dynasties?

Not long ago, in 1974, some modern Chinese farmers near the ancient city of Xian made a momentous discovery. As the farmers were digging new wells to bring badly needed water to their village, they uncovered a life-sized figure of an ancient Chinese knight. Soon the farmers began to uncover other life-sized figures lined up in a vast underground cavern.

News of this discovery spread quickly, and archaeologists launched a large-scale excavation. As work progressed, they found row after row of knights, horses, servants, chariots, and weapons—thousands in all. But who had created these sculptures? And why were there so many? Although scholars still cannot answer these questions, many believe that an early Chinese emperor, Shi Huangdi (SHUHR HWAHNG • DEE), had them made to help him in his conquests in the afterlife. These sculptures provide just one example of the magnificent accomplishments of the ancient Chinese civilization.

1 Geographic and Cultural Features Helped Shape Chinese History

Paleolithic people lived near what is today the city of Beijing (BAY • JING). Later Neolithic developments along the Yellow River, or Huang He* (HWANG HOOH), resembled those in other parts of the world. The people domesticated many kinds of animals, improved their tools and weapons, developed agriculture, and eventually settled in permanent communities.

Before continuing the story of China, however, it is helpful to do two things. First, we must examine the geography of China. Second, we must learn about the basic patterns of Chinese history.

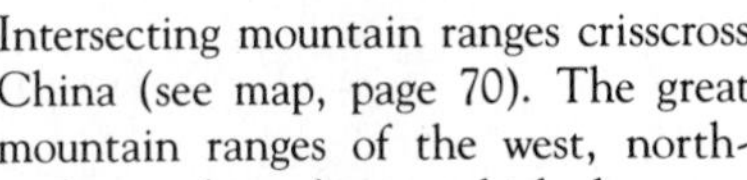

The Physical Setting

Intersecting mountain ranges crisscross China (see map, page 70). The great mountain ranges of the west, northwest, and southwest slope down to high desert or semi-desert plateaus. In the south the plateaus give way to a region of many low hills and valleys. In

*The words *He* and *Jiang* are Chinese for "river." Throughout this book we will be using the Pinyin system of spelling Chinese names. For an explanation of the Pinyin system, see page R22.

◀ *The Great Wall of China*

focus on individual enlightenment.

Chapter Objectives
After studying Chapter 4, students will be able to:

1. Locate on a map the major geographical features of China.
2. List the major Chinese river civilizations and their unique characteristics.
3. Summarize the major reasons for Chinese isolation, its dynastic cycles, and its cultural evolution.
4. Describe the cultural, economic, social, and political developments in China during the Shang dynasty.
5. Discuss how the Shang dynasty fit into the dynastic and cultural evolutionary patterns.
6. Describe the accomplishments as well as the failures of the Zhou, Qin, and Han dynasties.
7. Explain the ideas of naturalism, Confucianism, Daoism, and Legalism and understand the influence of Buddhism in China.
8. Describe social, cultural, and economic life during the rule of the Zhou, Qin, and Han dynasties.

SECTION 1

Focus/Motivation
Since earliest times the Chinese have regarded their land as the only civilized land. They called it the Middle Kingdom (see page 71). Ask students to speculate why the Chinese might have thought they were superior to other peoples. *(Answers might*

1A, a4A, a4B, a4C

include the following: China's geographic isolation, its rare contacts with other peoples, the vastness of China's population, and China's ability to absorb invading people into its magnificent culture.)

Presentation Summarizing Ideas (Average/Group)

Have students outline the subsection "The Physical Setting" on pages 69-71. Have students use their outline to discuss the physical geography of China and how it has affected the Chinese people politically and culturally. *(Answers might include a description of the natural boundary of the Qin Ling which lies between North and South China, as well as other chains of mountains that separate China into distinct regions.)*

the north the plateaus slope gradually down to the North China Plain, a coastal plain along the Pacific Ocean. Much smaller than the plain that stretches across northern India, the North China Plain became the center of early Chinese civilization.

Look again at the map on this page. Notice the range of mountains that cuts from west to east across the center of China. This range separates the valleys of the two greatest rivers of China—the Huang He and the Chang Jiang, or Yangtze River. Known as the Qin Ling (CHIN LING), it marks the boundary between North and South China. The range also marks the boundary between the two major agricultural areas of China. In the north, where relatively little rain falls, wheat is the principal crop. In the center and south, where rainfall is more plentiful, rice is the leading farm product.

Throughout its history China has also been divided politically into two main sections. The smaller and more important section lies along the seacoast and stretches inland up the valleys of the Huang He and Chang Jiang. We call this region China Proper—the heart of China.

The second section surrounds China Proper with a great semicircle of regions, including Tibet, Xinjiang (SHIN • JAHNG), Mongolia, Manchuria, and Korea. At various times throughout their history, the Chinese conquered and ruled these regions, usually to protect themselves from attack. On a few occasions, nomads from one or another of these outlying regions conquered and ruled China's heartland.

The rivers of China. China has many rivers, but the Huang He, the Chang Jiang, and the Xi (SHEE) Jiang have played particularly important roles in its history. The Huang He meanders for more than 2,900 miles (4,600 kilometers) across China before emptying into the Gulf of Chihli. The climate in the Huang He valley includes long, cold winters and short, hot summers. Duststorms

Learning from Maps *The Chang Jiang flows 3,434 miles (5,494 km) from west to east, emptying into the East China Sea. What river in China crosses the Tropic of Cancer?* **Xi Jiang**

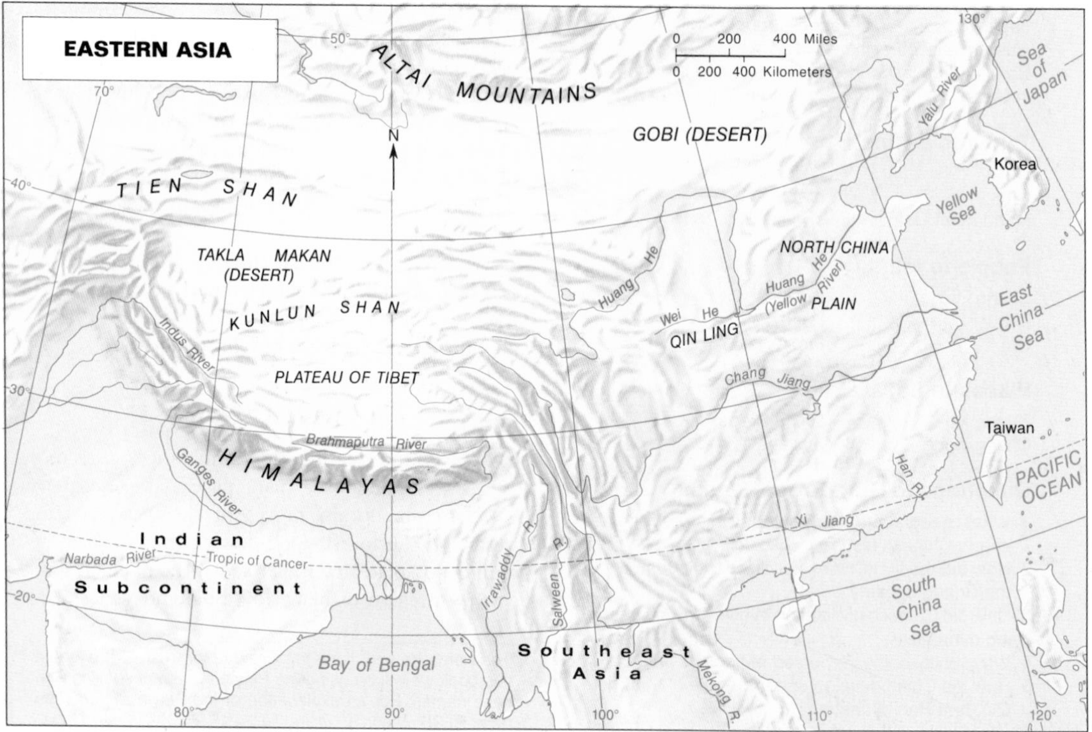

● Ask: How did the building of dikes make flooding worse in the Huang He valley? *(Silt raised river level and flooding occurred even after moderate rains)*

sweep across the valley in the spring. Yet enough rain falls to nourish most crops. More importantly, the region has extraordinarily fertile yellow soil called **loess** (LES).

Most rivers carry only 2 to 3 percent of their weight as **silt,** or moist soil carried as sediment in a river's waters. In contrast the Huang He carries between 10 and 40 percent. The Chinese often call the Huang He the Yellow River because the loess gives the water a yellowish tint.

Early Chinese farmers in the Huang He valley built earthen dikes to protect their crops from periodic floods. These dikes, however, caused the ● Huang He to deposit loess on the river bottom. Over the years so much silt accumulated that the river level reached the tops of the dikes. Even moderate rains brought the Huang He to flood stage, sending torrents of water raging over the dikes and into the fields. Successive generations of Chinese farmers responded to the threat of floods by building higher dikes. As a result, today the Huang He flows from 10 to 40 feet (3 to 12 meters) above the land outside the dikes.

The higher dikes did not end the flooding, however. Every few years the Huang He still broke through the dikes, and the rampaging floodwater destroyed everything in its path. The floodwater remained on the land until it evaporated—sometimes for as long as three years—because it could not drain back into the higher riverbed. Such devastating floods led the ancient Chinese to nickname the river "China's Sorrow."

The Chang Jiang, in central China, flows for 3,400 miles (5,400 kilometers) and cuts a deep channel. In modern times large oceangoing ships have been able to navigate 600 miles (960 kilometers) upstream to the great city of Wuhan (WOO • HAHN). Smaller ships can travel as far as Chongqing (CHOOHNG • CHING), about 1,300 miles (2,000 kilometers) from the sea.

The Xi Jiang, in southern China, is more than 1,200 miles (1,900 kilometers) long. Like the Chang Jiang, it forms an important commercial waterway. Large ships can navigate the Xi Jiang as far as Zangwu (ZAHNG • WOO), about 220 miles (350 kilometers) inland.

China's isolation. Civilization in China developed in relative isolation from the civilizations of India and the West. Great distances, the towering mountains of central Asia, and formidable deserts such as the Gobi (GOH • BEE) made China almost inaccessible. As a result, China developed and retained its own distinctive culture. Although the Chinese did adopt some of the ideas and skills of other peoples, they probably owed less to outside influence than any other people in ancient times.

Until modern times China's only regular contact with foreigners was with the nomads from the dry lands to the north and northwest. These peoples spoke their own languages and had their own tribal religions. Usually they traded peacefully with the Chinese, exchanging livestock for grain and other agricultural products. Sometimes, however, they organized bands of mounted warriors and attacked Chinese settlements. The Chinese called these nomadic peoples "barbarians" and considered them culturally inferior.

Lack of contact with foreigners helped give the Chinese a strong sense of identity and superiority. They regarded their land as the only civilized land and called it *zhongguo* (JOOHNG • GWAH), or the Middle Kingdom. To the Chinese it represented the center of the world. In their eyes other people could become civilized only by learning the Chinese language and adopting Chinese customs. Even when outsiders overran China, as sometimes happened, the Chinese believed that the strangers would in time lose their identity and be absorbed into China's vast population. "China," they said, "is a sea which salts all rivers that run into it."

Patterns of Chinese History

In reading about Chinese civilization, you will encounter many ideas and customs that differ from those of your own civilization. These differences exist because of two basic patterns of Chinese history—the dynastic cycle and cultural evolution.

The dynastic cycle. From the beginning of its recorded history until the early A.D. 1900s, a succession of dynasties ruled China. The first dynasty, the Shang, came to power about 1500 B.C. The last dynasty, the Qing (CHING), ruled China from A.D. 1644 to A.D. 1912. Some dynasties lasted only a few years; others held power for centuries. No matter how long they lasted, however, all went through a dynastic cycle consisting of several stages.

The first stage involved the founding of the dynasty. By defeating military rivals in war, an individual leader gained control of China. The right to rule the country then became hereditary within the leader's family, and a new dynasty emerged. Next

71

1B, 1D, a1A, a4A, a4F,
a4G, a4H, a4L

SECTION 1

Closure

Ask students to compare the geography of China's river valley civilizations with those of other ancient peoples. For example, was the Huang He more like the Tigris-Euphrates or the Nile? *(Tigris-Euphrates, with unpredictable flooding)* What other ancient civilization gave great importance to dynasties? *(Egypt)*

Review Answers

1. ***loess:*** fertile soil of Huang He valley; ***silt:*** sediment carried in a river's waters
2. ***Huang He:*** shallow river, 2,900 miles long, important, for irrigation in northern China; ***Chang Jiang:*** important river in central China; ***Qin Ling:*** mountains that mark boundary between northern and southern China; ***China Proper:*** heart of China along seacoast and inland up Huang He and Chang Jiang valleys; ***Tibet:*** region west of China; ***Xinjiang:*** region west of China Proper; ***Mongolia:*** northwest region of China Proper; ***Manchuria:*** northeast region of China Proper; ***Korea:*** peninsula east of northern China; ***Xi Jiang:*** southern China's important commercial river; ***Gobi Desert:*** northern China
3. The Huang He was called "China's Sorrow" because it was destructive and difficult to control.
4. The Chinese considered foreigners barbarians and their culture inferior because only the Chinese

SCULPTURE

Ancient Chinese Elephant

This small, boldly decorated bronze elephant is a container that probably once held food. It was buried as an offering to the spirit of a river or mountain near where it was found in Hunan Province in China.

Containers such as this one give us an idea of the importance of nature to the Chinese. Spiral designs representing clouds and rain cover the elephant. Use of these symbols was widespread during the Shang dynasty, when the container was made. Real and imaginary animals also decorate the container. The animals stood for the spirits of nature or for particular families. These ceremonial containers are extraordinary examples of bronze casting, a craft the Chinese developed into a great art.

came a period of internal peace, expansion, and great power. The new dynasty collected taxes and labor services from the people. The dynasty used its wealth to improve roads and irrigation systems, to support education and the arts, and to build splendid palaces to enhance its prestige.

A period of regression marked by decline followed the period of great power. During this stage the rulers thought less of the people and more about living in luxury. It raised taxes whenever it could, creating hardship among the people. The government stopped maintaining dikes and irrigation systems, increasing the risk of floods. The ruling dynasty gradually became unable to defend the frontiers of China, and nomadic invasions increased. When its decline reached a low point, with chaos and rebellion in many parts of the land, the dynasty collapsed. A new leader emerged, and another dynastic cycle began.

Cultural evolution. The dynastic cycle describes the political history of China, but it does not explain many other aspects of China's history. Beneath the recurring pattern of events in politics was a continuous evolution, or development, of culture over the centuries. For example, structures such as the family, the farm, and the village developed their own patterns of change. During some stages of the dynastic cycle, the pace of cultural evolution quickened; during others, it slowed. Over the centuries, however, civilization in China maintained a steady pattern of growth as institutions and ideas became more complex.

SECTION 1 REVIEW

1. **Define** loess, silt
2. **Locate** Huang He, Chang Jiang, Qin Ling, China Proper, Tibet, Xinjiang, Mongolia, Manchuria, Korea, Xi Jiang, Gobi Desert
3. **Interpreting Ideas** Explain why the Huang He has been called "China's Sorrow."
4. **Evaluating Ideas** Why did the Chinese consider all other people to be "barbarians"?
5. **Analyzing Ideas** What was meant by the statement, "China is a sea which salts all rivers that run into it"?
6. **Summarizing Ideas** Describe the stages of China's dynastic cycle.

72

● Zheng-Zhou

2 Chinese Civilization Flourished Under the Shang Dynasty

The Chinese placed great importance on explanations of the distant past and on China's role in history. Many legends about the beginnings of the world and about ancient China and its people lend vivid illustrations to centuries of Chinese history.

Legends of Ancient China

The legends of ancient China tell of Pan Gu (BAHN GOO), the first man, who worked for 18,000 years to create the universe. They tell of hero-kings who ruled for more than 100 years each and personally created such institutions and inventions as marriage, music, painting, and the wheel. The legends also tell of the Xia (SHAH) dynasty, which ruled the Huang He region from about 2000 B.C. to about 1500 B.C.

Unfortunately, these legends contain very few proven facts. Whether or not the Xia dynasty existed, however, scholars do not doubt that the people of the Huang He valley made great advances during those 500 years. The Chinese improved their methods of agriculture, and some evidence indicates they began to use written symbols. With the development of writing, the history of China became more concrete.

China's first historic dynasty, the Shang, began about 1500 B.C. along the Huang He. Although scholars do not know how the Shang rulers established power, legend tells us that the Shang were immigrants, not natives. Before the Shang dynasty, the people of the valley had no government to regulate irrigation, drainage, or flood control. They lived well in good years but starved when droughts or floods struck. Many scholars believe that the Shang introduced simple irrigation and flood control systems to their people. Control of these systems meant control of the region.

Government During the Shang Dynasty

The first Shang rulers probably conquered 1,800 city-states. Apparently the Shang moved their capital many times, either because it was difficult to defend or because of floods. During the last centuries of Shang rule, the capital was situated near what is today the city of Anyang (AHN • YAHNG).

Shang rulers created a relatively simple government. A hereditary king gave land to his principal followers. In return the followers pledged loyalty, performed certain services, and paid dues. Less advanced peoples lived on the borders of the kingdom. The Shang used war chariots and bronze weapons to maintain their power over these peoples. Shang military force enabled them to gain territory and to spread the knowledge of their more advanced civilization. At one point, they ruled most of northern and central China (see map, this page).

The Chinese believed that their ruler symbolized the direct link between the people and heaven, where the gods of nature and fertility lived. The gods gave the monarch the right to rule, a right known as the **Mandate of Heaven.** People believed that the gods helped their ruler in war and in planning for good crops. However, the ruler had to produce results, and rebellions broke out when he failed. Poor crops or defeat in battle meant the ruler had lost the Mandate of Heaven and thus the right to rule. Throughout Chinese history, when rebels overthrew a dynasty, they justified their actions by saying the old dynasty had lost the Mandate of Heaven.

Learning from Maps *Shang rulers interpreted the calendar to predict the best times for planting and harvesting. Which city on the map is closest to the Huang He?* ●

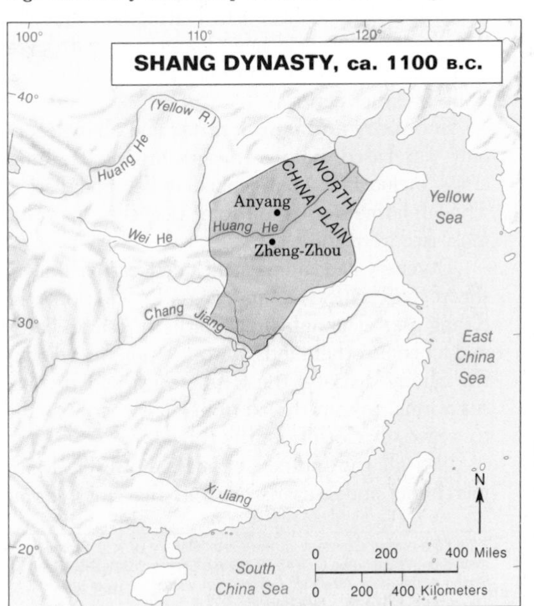

language and customs were civilized.
5. The Chinese believed outsiders who invaded China would lose their identity and be absorbed into the Chinese population.
6. The dynastic cycle has four stages: founding the dynasty, period of power and prosperity, period of decline, overthrow of the dynasty.

SECTION 2

Focus/Motivation
Ask the students to read the subsections "Legends of Ancient China" and "Government During the Shang Dynasty" on this page. Then hold a class discussion on the role of the ruler in the Shang dynasty. What geographic factor made a strong ruler necessary? What were the ruler's functions? Compare his rule with those of the rulers of Egypt and the empires of the Fertile Crescent.

(Students should answer that the need for controlling the Huang He River led to the development of a strong ruler. Chinese rulers symbolized the link between the gods and people. They had to see that crops were good and lead China successfully in war, or they would lose their right to rule—the Mandate of Heaven. Unlike Middle Eastern rulers, Shang rulers were not in any way considered divine.)

Presentation Illustrating Ideas (Average/Group)
Have students make two columns in their notebooks, one headed *Chinese Farmers* and the other headed *Chinese Artisans.* Students are to list the activities of each group. Suggest that they refer to the subsection "Economy and handicrafts" on this page. Call upon students to volunteer to suggest items as you write them on the chalkboard or an overhead projector. The list should include the following:

Farmers	Artisans
Grew millet, barley, rice; Domesticated cattle, horses, sheep pigs, chickens, dogs; Raised silkworms	Made silk cloth, cord from hemp; Carved jade, ivory, bone objects; Made pottery of kaolin, bronze castings

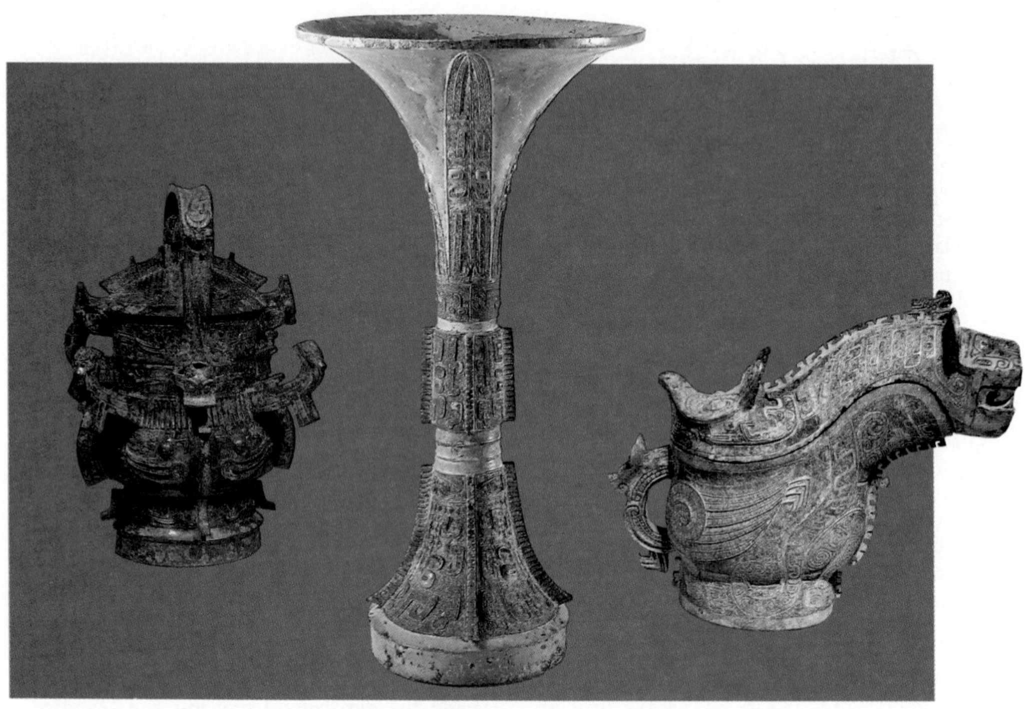

Learning from Pictures *Bronze castings of the Shang dynasty are considered some of the most remarkable achievements in metal craft of ancient history.* †

Culture During the Shang Dynasty

Shang rulers held the Mandate of Heaven from about 1500 B.C. to 1122 B.C. During this time the Chinese people made new discoveries and developed new skills while refining the discoveries and skills of earlier periods.

Economy and handicrafts. The Shang economy was based mainly on agriculture. The chief crops included a grain called millet and barley. Though farmers also grew some rice, they imported most rice from the south.

Domesticated animals included cattle, horses, sheep, pigs, chickens, and dogs. In addition, the Shang used elephants from southern Asia in battle and for some other kinds of work. Sometime during the Shang dynasty, the Chinese learned to raise silkworms, to spin thread from their cocoons, and to weave silk cloth from the thread.

Not all the Chinese farmed, however. Many merchants and artisans lived in the cities. Some merchants made clothing from silk, and others made cord from hemp. Artisans crafted jewelry by carving jade and also inlaid turquoise in ivory and bone.

Shang artisans established the foundation for all later Chinese ceramic art, including every form and shape used in Chinese ceremonial vases. Shang potters learned to use kaolin (KAY • uh • luhn), a fine white clay, and to shape items on a potter's wheel. They also glazed some of their pottery to give it a shiny, durable finish.

Today people throughout the world regard the bronze castings of Shang artisans as outstanding works of art. The Chinese may have learned the technique of casting from the Middle East, possibly Sumer. However, the forms of the vessels and the designs of the decorations were uniquely Chinese. Chinese artisans probably imported copper and tin ores and mixed the bronze themselves. They cast small figures as well as large ceremonial vessels whose surfaces featured delicate relief work characterized by elevations in the metal.

Astronomy and the calendar. An accurate calendar meant as much to Shang farmers and their

† (middle photo) Courtesy of the *Freer Gallery of Art,* Smithsonian Institution, Washington D.C. 43.9 Chinese Bronze: 12th–11th Cent. B.C. Shang Middle-late An-yang. Ceremonial vessel of type ku. 29.3 × 16.7 overall (11-9/16 × 6-9/16)

● **Ask students to list words in English that have new meanings when compounded. *(Examples: afternoon, anchorwoman, carpetbagger, checkbook, greenhouse, loudspeaker, shipwreck, sweatshirt, wastebasket, wiretapping)***

rulers as it did to the peoples of Egypt and the Fertile Crescent. The Chinese based their calendar on the movement of the moon. The shortest period in the calendar consisted of 10 days. Three such periods, sometimes shortened by a day, made a month. Six 10-day periods made a "cycle." Six cycles made a year of up to 360 days. To provide enough days for a full 365-day year, responsible and skilled priest-astronomers employed by the government added days as needed. Since the king's popularity depended on the success of the harvest, which in part depended on the time of planting as determined by the calendar, the priest-astronomers played a very important role.

Shang astronomers predicted eclipses of the moon so accurately that even an error of 24 hours alarmed the authorities. Because of their skill with the calendar, the astronomers were given the duty of keeping other records. Thus the Chinese had "official historians" very early in their history.

Language and writing. The Chinese rank as one of the few peoples who developed an original written language. To understand the ancient Chinese writing system, one must first understand some characteristics of spoken Chinese.

First, almost all ancient Chinese words consisted of one syllable. To express a new or more complicated meaning, the Chinese would combine ● two or more simple words. Thus the word for *magnet* was made up of three one-syllable words meaning "pull-iron-stone." Each word-syllable kept just as much of its original meaning as was needed to accurately define the compound word. This compound word was something new, not just a collection of the three things named.

Second, the ancient Chinese language did not include as many variations or uses of the same word as some other languages. For example, the same noun could be either singular or plural.

Because of the characteristics of their language, the Chinese did not need a phonetic system of writing. Instead they assigned a special symbol, or character, to every word in their language. At first these characters were pictograms, or drawings of objects. Later, as their culture and therefore their language became more complex, the Chinese developed ideograms and phonograms. Many written characters then consisted of two parts. One was a signific, or "idea sign." It gave a clue to the meaning of the character. The other was a phonetic, or "sound sign." It told how to pronounce the character.

The Chinese developed their system of writing in an effective way, and they could combine signs to invent new characters. However, because each character had to be memorized, it took years of painstaking study to learn to read and write. For centuries a well-educated Chinese person had to know more than 10,000 characters. Thus, until the Chinese developed a simplified version of the language in recent times, only a small percentage of Chinese people could read and write.

Unlike the Aryans of India, the early Chinese used writing to compose and preserve literary works. They used a brush to write characters in lines that ran from the top to the bottom of a page, beginning on the right side. Writing itself became an art, called **calligraphy** (kuh • LIG • ruh • fee). Even today the Chinese admire beautiful calligraphy as much as they admire beautiful paintings.

Religion in the Shang period. The religion that developed during the Shang dynasty combined animism and ancestor worship. People believed in an all-powerful and kindly dragon that lived in the seas and rivers and could rise into the clouds. They believed that dragons fighting in the heavens caused the summer thunderstorms that brought rain. In time this good dragon became the symbol of Chinese rulers.

The Chinese held great religious festivals in the spring and autumn. In spring, the planting season, the ruler plowed the first furrow to ensure good crops. In autumn the people thanked the gods for the harvest.

In addition to animistic beliefs, the Chinese revered the elders and ancestors of their families. They regarded the family as both earth-dwelling and spirit-dwelling, believing that all members of the family—the living and the dead—were united forever through their religion. A child's obligation to a parent was most important. In Chinese writing the character that symbolizes the honor and reverence owed to parents shows a son supporting his aged father as he walks.

Priests played an important role in Chinese religion. Some worked as priest-astronomers. Others foretold the future in order to learn the wishes of the spirits, especially of the spirits of ancestors. The priests wrote questions on **oracle bones,** the shoulder bones of cattle or the bottoms of tortoise shells, into which they thrust a heated metal rod. They used the pattern of cracks that formed to interpret the answers, which the priests then inscribed on

1B, 1D, a4A, a4F, a4G, a4H, a4M

● The Zhou did not rule China singlehandedly. The Zhou period was part of a multistate system with many competing and unstable states. The Qin and Han began China's first real empires.

SECTION 2

Closure

Ask students to explain how the Mandate of Heaven functioned in the selection of the emperors of China.

Review Answers

1. ***Mandate of Heaven:*** ruler received his power from the gods of nature, but poor crops and military defeat meant loss of the mandate; ***calligraphy:*** writing as an art; ***oracle bones:*** shoulder bones of cattle or the bottom of tortoise shells, used by priests to interpret answers from patterns of cracks formed by heating
2. ***Xia dynasty:*** legendary dynasty that ruled Huang He region from 2000 B.C. to 1500 B.C.; ***Zhou:*** dynasty that conquered the Shang
3. The Shang introduced and controlled irrigation and flood control systems in the Huang He valley. Control of these systems meant control of the entire country.
4. It predicted the time of planting and thus determined whether harvest would be bountiful.
5. Religion combined animism and ancestor worship. Many of their religious festivals concerned planting and the harvest. They stressed proper behavior and reverence toward elders in this life.

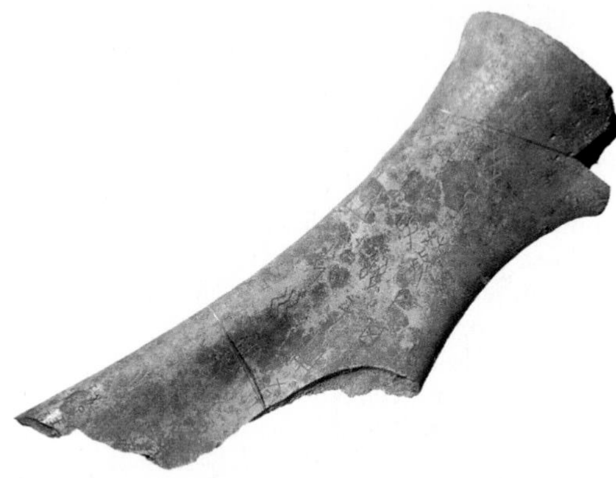

Learning from Pictures *Some oracle bones, unlike the one above, were never burned with rods. They contain written records of receipts and historical events dealing with the Shang royal court.*

the bone or shell. The inscriptions often included the name of the ruler who asked the questions. These recorded questions and answers have helped scholars solve many of the historical and cultural mysteries of the Shang dynasty.

Fall of the Shang Dynasty

The Shang kingdom collapsed in 1122 B.C., apparently because the last king was busy trying to expand his boundaries south to the Chang Jiang. He failed to guard the northwest frontier, where a tribe of soldier-farmers called the Zhou (JOH) led a rebellion. The Zhou ultimately conquered the Shang, claiming that the last Shang king had lost the Mandate of Heaven because he was a monster of corrupt wickedness and cruelty. Yet another dynastic cycle had begun.

SECTION 2 REVIEW

1. **Define** Mandate of Heaven, calligraphy, oracle bones
2. **Identify** Xia dynasty, Zhou
3. **Determining Cause and Effect** What was the relationship between flood control in the Huang He valley and the establishment of the Shang dynasty?
4. **Interpreting Ideas** Why was the calendar important to the development of Chinese civilization?
5. **Summarizing Ideas** What were the religious beliefs of the Chinese during the Shang dynasty?

3 Chinese Civilization Evolved Through Changing Dynasties

The Zhou conquest of China in 1122 B.C. marked the beginning of a dynamic era in Chinese history. Under the rule of three successive dynasties—the Zhou (JOH), the Qin (CHIN), and the Han—China gradually became a large and powerful empire. Great technological and economic growth occurred in China during this first imperial age, or age of an empire. Tremendous philosophical activity also took place, as the Chinese formulated ideas and theories of lasting importance to their civilization. Eventually, internal weaknesses and foreign invasions brought this imperial age to an end.

The Zhou Dynasty

The most enduring Chinese dynasty—the Zhou—lasted almost 800 years, from 1122 B.C. to 256 B.C. Originally less advanced than the Shang, the Zhou quickly adopted many aspects of Shang culture and later developed some of their own.

Zhou rulers called themselves Sons of Heaven. Like the Shang rulers, they claimed to rule by the Mandate of Heaven, which obligated them to keep the gods contented, perform rites to ensure the fertility of the soil, and control the rivers.

During the many years of Zhou rule, internal trade expanded, and copper coins came into use as money. The introduction of iron, which helped transform Chinese agriculture, probably ranks as the most important development. Using iron farm tools and plows pulled by oxen, Chinese peasants cultivated new lands and produced more grain than ever before. They built canals, dikes, and reservoirs for irrigation, among them the Grand Canal, which irrigated approximately 1,000 square miles (2,600 square kilometers) of land. As a result, China's population grew steadily. By the 700s B.C., China probably ranked as the most densely populated land in the world.

The Zhou rulers did not create a unified empire. ● They established a central government first in the capital city of Hao and later in Luoyang (LOH • YAHNG), but many independent city-states also existed. Although they owed certain obligations to the Zhou, these city-states could also act on their own.

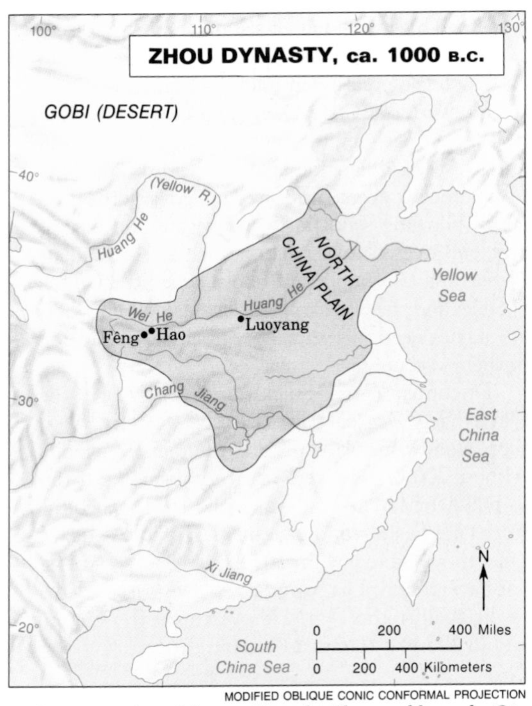

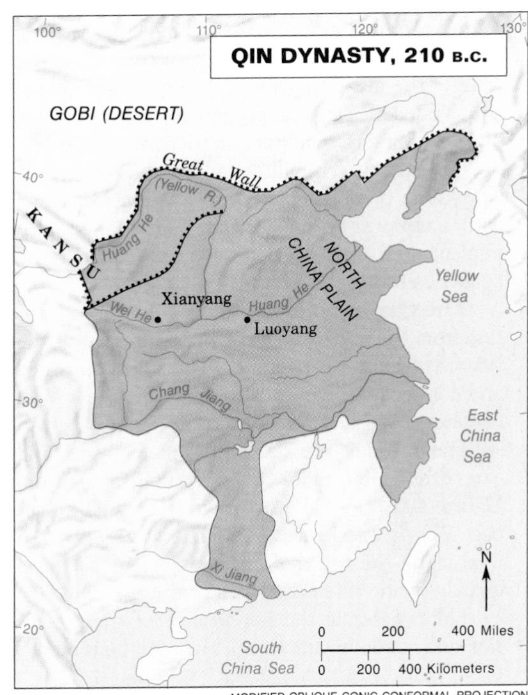

Learning from Maps *First the Zhou and later the Qin dynasties lost the Mandate of Heaven after their rulers put personal interests before those of the kingdom. In what part of China did the emperors have the Great Wall built? Why?* **north/keep invading nomads from the Gobi out of China**

In the early days of the Zhou dynasty, the heads of the city-states sent military and financial assistance to the Zhou rulers whenever requested to do so. Crisis struck the Zhou, however, in 771 B.C. The frivolous King You (YOO) had entertained his favorite princess by lighting the warning fires which signaled the nobles that nomadic raiders were attacking. The princess and the king enjoyed watching the powerful nobles gallop into town to protect the capital. But the false alarms had infuriated the nobles. When an army of nomads really appeared, the nobles ignored the warning fires. The nomads killed King You and then ransacked the capital.

After You's death the city-states grew rebellious. The warring states, as they were called, began to fight among themselves to expand their territories. By the 400s B.C., the Zhou rulers had no real power outside their own city-state. Instead, local rulers wielded great power. Zhou rulers continued to hold the Mandate of Heaven, however, until a new dynasty, the Qin, replaced them.

The Qin Dynasty

The Qin dynasty came to power in 221 B.C. by using cavalry armed with bows and arrows, a military technique new to the Chinese. Shi Huangdi, which means "first emperor," founded this new dynasty.

From its beautiful capital at Xianyang (SHEE • EN • YAHNG), the Qin dynasty ruled a larger area than did either of the preceding dynasties and controlled it more firmly. Although the Qin dynasty lasted only a short time, until 207 B.C., it unified China under a strong central government for the first time in history. This dynasty, from whose name the Western name for China comes, created the first Chinese empire, standardized weights, measures, and coinage, and established a uniform system of writing.

Not satisfied with ruling northern China and parts of the Chang Jiang valley, Shi Huangdi sent his armies far to the south. In a brilliant military campaign, he soon conquered the central part of

SECTION 3

Focus/Motivation

Have students review the definition of civil service on page 79. Then base a discussion on the following questions: How did China's civil service system test its candidates? What advantages do you see in this form of testing? What disadvantages? Do we have a civil service in the United States? Name some civil service jobs. How are these jobs filled?

(The test was based on the Chinese classics of law and literature. It produced administrators who were also scholars. Some students might suggest that the study of literature would have little relevance for solving practical problems. A postal worker is one example of a civil service employee in the United States. Candidates for these jobs are chosen on the basis of competitive examinations. Students should note that examinations in the United States have a more direct relationship to the job than they did in China.)

Presentation
Summarizing Ideas (Average/Group)

Write the following items on the chalkboard or an overhead projector: Zhou dynasty, Qin dynasty, Han dynasty. After reading the subsections "The Zhou Dynasty," "The Qin Dynasty," and "The Han Dynasty," ask the students to list three major accomplishments of each dynasty. Write these under the

● Discussion topic: How the building of the Great Wall compared to the building of the pyramids in Egypt

appropriate dynasty. *(The list under the Zhou dynasty should include: introduced the use of iron farm tools, used copper coins as currency, agriculture expanded, built Grand Canal, and population increased. The Qin dynasty should include: completed the Great Wall of China, made a uniform law code, standardized weights and measures. The Han dynasty should include: established the civil service system, instituted the economic policy of leveling, and established the Pax Sinica.)*

Ask for a volunteer to put his or her chart on the chalkboard or an overhead projector. You might use the chart as the basis for a class discussion.

southern China as far as the delta of the Xi Jiang River (see map, page 77). He also tore down the walls of the many city-states, disarmed their rulers, and ended their independence. The emperor divided China into military districts ruled by governors who used stern military and civilian authority. The Code of Qin replaced conflicting local laws with a uniform system of laws. Shi Huangdi also implemented a single tax system throughout the country, ending chaos in tax collecting.

The Qin as builders. To guard against invasion from the north and west, the Chinese over the years had built several walls. The Qin completed and connected these walls to form the Great Wall of China. This massive structure, much of which still stands today, was 25 feet (7.5 meters) high and extended 1,400 miles (2,250 kilometers) from Gansu (GAHN • SOO) province to the sea (see map, page 77). It was 15 feet (4.5 meters) wide, with a road along the top that enabled soldiers to travel quickly to any threatened area of the frontier.

Understanding the importance of transportation and communication, Shi Huangdi built broad, tree-lined highways. He set a standard width for the axles of carts and other vehicles so that they could pass each other easily on roads and bridges.

Harshness of the Qin. The Qin maintained order in their empire, but they established an **autocracy** in which the emperor held total power. Like autocrats ever since, Shi Huangdi saw the danger of allowing scholars to investigate and discuss problems freely. He began his attack on the scholars by burning two important books called the *Classic of Songs* and the *Classic of Documents.* When scholars did not heed this warning, Shi Huangdi had 460 of them executed.

Discontent spread quickly under the rule of the Qin dynasty. A great gap existed between the ruler, supported by his warriors, and the mass of people. Almost 700,000 workers had been brutally driven to build the Great Wall—it is said that each of its stones cost a life—and peasants resented the heavy taxes they had to pay. In 207 B.C. a general of peasant background, Liu Bang (LEE • OO BAHNG), led a revolt against the Qin. He overthrew the empire and in 202 B.C. founded the Han dynasty. ●

Learning from Pictures *The imperial tomb of Shi Huangdi is housed in the Army Vault Museum and contains terra-cotta statues of warriors, horses, and the emperor's royal guards.*

1A, 2D, a1C, a4A, a4B, a4C

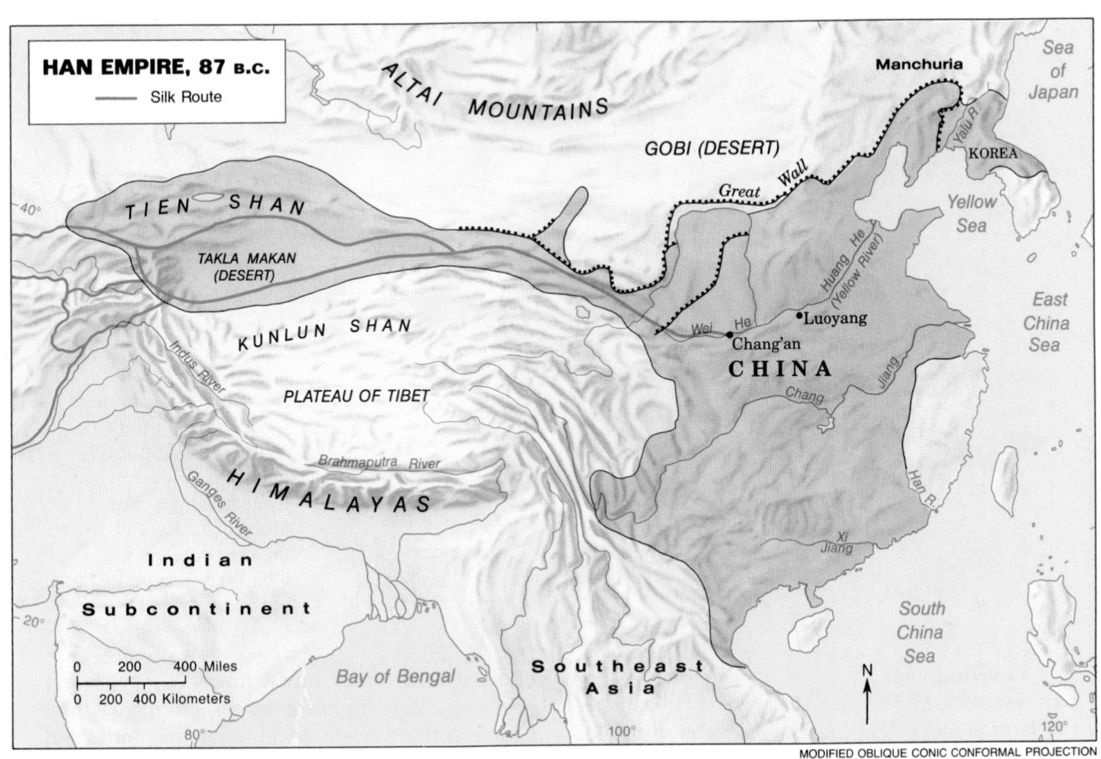

Learning from Maps *By appointing friends and family as administrators of the empire, Liu Bang almost caused its breakup. What is the easternmost point of the Silk Route?* **Chang'an**

The Han Dynasty

The new dynasty took its name from the Han River, where Liu Bang had been stationed as a general for several years. Like the Qin, the Han dynasty ruled a centralized and expanding empire. Unlike the Qin, however, it was less autocratic and succeeded in maintaining its power for almost 400 years. Han rulers so influenced China that even today many Chinese refer to themselves as "Sons of Han."

The most famous Han emperor, Wu Di (WOO DEE), ruled from 140 B.C. to 87 B.C. He established his capital at Chang'an (CHAHNG • AHN), now called Xian (SHEE • AHN), and extended Chinese territory north into Manchuria and Korea, south into Indochina, and west into central Asia (see map, this page).

The civil service system. The Han dynasty established the Chinese civil service system. A **civil service** administers the day-to-day business of government, and its members usually receive their appointments based on the results of competitive examinations. The philosopher Confucius, who believed that only educated and virtuous people should enter government service, originated the idea for civil service examinations. These long and difficult examinations tested candidates for civil service positions on their knowledge of the great classics of Chinese literature and law. As a result, the best scholars in the country became government officials. Civil service examinations remained important to the Chinese government until the early A.D. 1900s.

In theory anyone could take the examinations, and cases in which a poor boy rose to great heights in the civil service were not unknown. Since education cost a great deal of money, however, few peasant families could afford to send their sons to school. Generally, only the sons of wealthy landowning families had a chance to become civil servants.

1B, 1C, 1D, a4A, a4F, a4H, a4L

● The Silk Route was extremely important in linking the world of Europe with the Far East.

■ The Han were also important as preservers of the great literature of earlier dynasties. During the Han dynasty, sun dials, water clocks, and simple scientific instruments were developed.

SECTION 3

Closure

Ask students why the Qin rulers completed the building of the Great Wall of China. *(to protect China from invasion)* Tell students that later the Romans would use this same means of guarding the frontiers in their large empire.

Review Answers

1. ***autocracy:*** form of government established by Qin dynasty in which emperor held total power; ***civil service:*** government members usually appointed after competitive examination
2. ***Liu Bang:*** general of peasant background who overthrew Qin dynasty and founded Han dynasty; ***"Sons of Han":*** name many Chinese call themselves, indicating great influence of Han dynasty; ***Wu Di:*** most famous of the Han emperors
3. ***Chang'an:*** capital city (now Xian) of Han emperor Wu Di
4. The Qin government was autocratic. It divided China into military districts ruled by military governors. It introduced a uniform code of laws and imposed a single tax system.
5. Shi Huangdi brilliantly led military conquests, centralized the government and imposed a tax system and a uniform code of laws. He completed the Great Wall, encouraged construction to aid transportation and communication, and standardized currency, weights, and

Learning from Pictures *Under the Han Empire, education and the arts flourished. This bronze flying horse was made around 150 B.C., at about the same time the first Chinese dictionary was published.*

Leveling. Wu Di began an economic policy known as leveling because the rise and fall of prices of farm products had caused endless hardships for peasants. Under this policy, in years of good harvests government agents bought and stored surpluses to keep prices from falling. In years of poor harvests, the agents sold the stored food to prevent scarcity and high prices.

The Pax Sinica. Wu Di fought vigorous battles with the nomadic Huns of central and eastern Asia who threatened the frontiers of his empire. He later established what historians call the *Pax Sinica,* or "Chinese Peace," through much of Asia.

During this period of peace, merchants opened the famous Silk Route from China across central Asia to the Mediterranean region (see map, page 79). Long camel caravans carried silk, jade, and other valuable Chinese goods to be sold to wealthy ● Greeks and Romans. They returned with glass, amber, asbestos, and wool and linen textiles.

China's population grew to more than 60 million during the Han dynasty. The imperial capital at Chang'an became a huge city, with imposing palaces and broad avenues and a population of 250,000. On its many side streets stood the shops of merchants and artisans. There one could find luxury goods from lands throughout the world as well as many products from China, including two of the greatest of all Chinese inventions, paper and porcelain. Both of these inventions spread from China to the Western world in later centuries and had a profound impact on Western life. Even today we call porcelain, or highly glazed ceramic ware, china. ■

None of Wu Di's successors in the Han dynasty matched his leadership abilities. Still, with the exception of one brief interruption, the Han dynasty ruled China until A.D. 220, when a revolt overthrew the last Han emperor.

For hundreds of years, countless nomadic tribes swept across China, ravaging the countryside and terrorizing the people. Not until A.D. 589 did a Chinese general unify China once again.

SECTION 3 REVIEW

1. **Define** autocracy, civil service
2. **Identify** Liu Bang, "Sons of Han," Wu Di
3. **Locate** Chang'an
4. **Summarizing Ideas** Describe the government under the rule of the Qin dynasty.
5. **Contrasting Ideas** Two emperors, Shi Huangdi and Wu Di, are considered among China's greatest. What did each do to earn his reputation?
6. **Classifying Ideas** How were Chinese government officials chosen during the Han dynasty?

4 The Ancient Chinese Created Unique Philosophies

Although political disunity and almost constant warfare marked the last years of the Zhou dynasty, this period marked one of the most creative in the history of Chinese philosophy. As in other ancient civilizations of the same period, new political, economic, and social problems prompted many new ideas and theories. Scholars classify these theories into four important groups—Naturalism, Confucianism, Legalism, and Daoism.

Naturalism

Like all other Chinese philosophers of the period, the Naturalists were far more interested in human beings and the real world than in divine or spiritual matters. They tried to explain the workings of nature by certain cosmic principles—principles that applied to the whole universe. One of their basic ideas concerned the dualism, or two-sidedness, of nature. Naturalists defined this dualism of nature as its *yin* and *yang*. *Yin* was female, dark, cold, and passive. *Yang* was male, light, hot, and active.

Yin and *yang* did not conflict with each other, however, as did the concepts of good and evil in Western civilization. Rather they depended on one another and constantly maintained a balance. Day, which was *yang*, gave way to night, which was *yin*. Summer gave way to winter.

The Naturalists also believed that balance in human affairs was inevitable. For example, extremes such as a harsh government or an anarchy (no government) could not exist for long.

Confucianism

Westerners know Kongzi (KOOHNG • ZUH), meaning "Kong the Philosopher," or "Reverend Master Kong," as Confucius. Left in poverty at the age of three when his father died, Confucius, who lived from about 551 B.C. to 478 B.C., still managed to receive a good education. At age 22, Confucius began teaching and soon gained many followers. In time his ideas and teachings, as written by his followers in a collection of writings called *Analects*, became known as Confucianism. The philosophy of Confucianism exerted a more powerful influence on later Chinese beliefs and life styles than did any other philosophy.

Confucius was not a religious prophet and had little to say about the gods, the meaning of death, or the idea of life after death. Instead, he taught about the importance of the family, respect for one's elders, and reverence for the past and one's ancestors. These three concepts formed the basis of Confucian philosophy.

Confucius had a primary interest in politics and wanted to end the political disorder of his time. He believed this could be accomplished in two ways. First, every person should accept an assigned role in society and perform the duties of that role. Second, government should be virtuous. Instead of relying

Learning from Pictures *This Chinese pagoda in Kunming in southern China emphasizes the Chinese ideal of harmony with nature—an ideal that was part of the Chinese philosophy of naturalism.*

measures. Wu Di also expanded China's territory and introduced changes in government. He established the civil service system exams and an economic policy of leveling, or the storing of crop surpluses to keep prices steady. He also established the Pax Sinica throughout Asia and opened the Silk Route to trade with the West.

6. Government officials were chosen through competitive exams on Chinese literature and law.

SECTION 4

Focus/Motivation

Write the following quotations on the chalkboard or an overhead projector.

"What a man dislikes in his superiors, let him not display in the treatment of his inferiors, let him not display in the service of his superiors." (Confucianism)

"He who overcomes others is strong,
He who overcomes himself is mighty."
(Daoism)

"When the guiding principles of the people become unsuited to the circumstances, their standards of value must change. As conditions in the world change, different principles are practiced." (Legalism)

Have students discuss the meaning of the three quotations. *(Students should bring out the following points in the discussion:*

● Research topic: The status of Confucianism and Daoism in the world today

The Confucian philosophy resembles the Golden Rule: Do unto others as you would have them do unto you. Daoism stresses the need for personal discipline. The Legalist quote indicates a belief in expediency; permanent moral standards have no place.)

Presentation
Comparing Ideas (Average/Group)
Involve the entire class in a panel discussion of the themes and relative merits of the Chinese philosophies. One student can act as moderator; four other students can represent Confucianism, Daoism, Naturalism, and Legalism. The rest of the class should prepare questions to ask the panel. Ask the students to reread pages 81-84 to prepare their questions. Panel members may wish to do additional reading. Two sources are Paul Wetly's *The Asians* (Lippincott), and Elizabeth Seeger's *Eastern Religions* (Crowell).

on military power, rulers should be honest and have concern for others. Only well-educated and extremely virtuous officials should be appointed to run the government.

Confucius taught that government should set a good example, believing that the people would willingly obey a ruler who lived and governed virtuously. Virtue, in Confucian teaching, consists of correct behavior toward others. This basic principle resembled the Christian Golden Rule, although stated negatively: "What you do not like when done unto yourself, do not do unto others."

Confucius hoped to put his ideas into practice by becoming adviser to a local ruler. According to legend, he worked as minister of crime in his native province of Shandong (SHAHN • DOOHNG), and within a year crime had almost disappeared. Neighboring rulers became jealous, however, and forced Confucius to retire. He spent the rest of his life teaching, and eventually his teachings took on religious significance. In 195 B.C., for example, Liu Bang, founder of the Han dynasty, visited the tomb of Confucius and offered a sacrifice to his spirit. In A.D. 58 the emperor of China ordered schools to offer sacrifices to Confucius.

● Daoism

Laozi (LOW • ZUH), thought to have lived in the 500s B.C., founded a philosophy called Daoism (DOW • iz • um). Daoism got its name from its central idea, Dao, which can be defined as the "Way of Nature." Laozi saw Dao as an indescribable force that governed the universe and all nature. Only by withdrawing from the world and contemplating nature could people understand Dao and live in harmony with it.

According to Laozi, people should not strive for learning, riches, or power. Rather they should try to bring themselves into harmony with Dao by being quiet, thoughtful, and humble. As Laozi said, "He who overcomes others is strong; he who overcomes himself is mighty." Unlike Confucius, Laozi shunned politics and advised people not to participate in public affairs.

Daoism became second only to Confucianism in its importance to the Chinese. Daoism appealed to the masses of peasants because of its concern with nature and natural forces. It also appealed to many artists and poets because it encouraged artistic expression as a means of understanding Dao.

Daoism appealed to many Confucianists as well because it added balance to their lives. Some Confucianists believed that being concerned only with politics and social problems was too restrictive. Even officials and the emperor needed a temporary escape from governing the country. They found the escape they desired within the Daoist contemplation of nature.

Like *yin* and *yang,* Daoism and Confucianism came to be complementary parts in Chinese culture. Each supplied what the other lacked.

Legalism

Like Confucianism, the school of philosophy known as Legalism concerned itself with politics. Its teachings, however, differed greatly from the teachings of Confucianism. The Legalists believed in power, not virtue, and in harsh laws. In their view, people were by nature selfish and untrustworthy. Peace and prosperity could be achieved only by threatening severe punishment if people failed to do what the laws expected of them.

The first Qin emperor, Shi Huangdi, followed the ideas of Legalism. He succeeded in creating a powerful empire, but his dynasty ruled for a very short period. Later Chinese philosophers believed that the Qin dynasty failed because of its extremely cruel methods. The Qin failed to maintain a proper balance between *yin* and *yang.*

The government of the Han dynasty was Legalist in structure—that is, it was highly centralized and powerful. However, it was Confucian in operation, since educated officials who believed in the ethical principles of righteousness and compassion controlled it. The Han dynasty lasted as long as it did because it achieved a balance.

Buddhism in China

Another great influence on Chinese thought and religious belief came not from China but from India—from the teachings of Buddha. Missionaries from India first brought Buddhism to China during the Han dynasty.

As the Han dynasty collapsed and nomads from the north raided China, Buddhism found many converts, especially among the peasants. People looking for consolation in this time of crisis found it in Mahayana Buddhism, with its worship of Buddha as a savior and its promise of an eventual

READ
WRITE
INTERPRET
CONNECT
THINK

BUILDING HISTORY STUDY SKILLS

Reading About History: Analyzing a Statement

To analyze a statement, you must take it apart in order to find its meaning, identify the main idea, see relationships, or determine the importance of the information. Analysis has a specific goal. For example, you would analyze a statement so that you could understand the author's thoughts and relate them to a movement, idea, or situation. You may tie together the various parts of a theory by analyzing the statements.

How to Analyze a Statement

To analyze a statement, follow these steps.

1. Determine the goal or purpose of the analysis.
2. Read the statement carefully.
3. Identify the key words in the statement.
4. Explain what the statement means.
5. Determine how the statement relates to other ideas.

Developing the Skill

Read the following statements. The first is attributed to Laozi and the second to Zhuan Zu. Both were founders of Daoist thought in the 500s B.C. By analyzing both statements, you will be able to understand the meaning of Daoism and its impact on Chinese thought and institutions.

> "He who knows others is learned;
> He who knows himself is wise.
> He who conquers others has power of muscles;
> He who conquers himself is strong.
> He who is contented is rich.
> He who is determined has strength of will.
> He who does not loose his center endures;
> He who dies yet (his power) remains has long life."
> (Laozi)

> "Once long ago a bird alighted in the suburbs of the Lu capital. The ruler of Lu was delighted with it, had a . . . sacrifice prepared for it to feast on, and . . . music performed for its enjoyment. But the bird immediately began to look unhappy, and dazed, and did not dare to eat or drink. This is what is called trying to nourish a bird with what would nourish you. If you want to nourish a bird with what will nourish a bird, you had best let it roost in the deep forest, float on the rivers and lakes, and live on snakes—then it can feel at ease."
> (Zhuan Zu)

The key words in Laozi's statement are *learned, wise, strong, strength of will, endures,* and *long life.* These are desired virtues or states of being that Laozi believes people will acquire when they learn self-mastery. One develops this self-mastery through knowledge and determination.

The key words in Zhuan Zu's statement are *unhappy, nourish, roost,* and *float.* These words refer to being natural and finding happiness through discovering one's own nature. Zhuan Zu is pointing out that every person must realize his or her own human nature in order to be healthy, creative, and happy.

Both statements illustrate one of the key beliefs of Daoism—the importance of internal harmony or peace, which can only be reached through self-realization, or knowledge of one's self.

Practicing the skill. Using the steps for analyzing a statement, find and analyze a statement or quote made by a famous person in the 1900s.

To apply this skill, see Applying History Study Skills on page 89.

Miniature house from the Han Dynasty

83

1B, 2D, a1A, a4A, a4F, a4H

● Each person in a Chinese family had a specific role based on age and sex. Such rules of behavior were based on the teachings of Confucius. The theme of the wicked stepmother is a favorite in Chinese literature.

SECTION 4

Closure

Ask students how Confucianism differed from the religions they have studied in the text. *(Confucianism is a philosophy concerned with the family, respect for one's elders, and reverence for the past; Confucius was not concerned with the gods or an afterlife.)*

Review Answers

1. ***Kongzi:*** Kong the Philosopher, also known as Confucius; ***Laozi:*** founder of Daoism
2. *Yin* and *yang* represent the two-sidedness of nature. Yin is female, dark, cold, and passive. Yang is male, light, hot, and active. They do not conflict but depend on and balance one another.
3. **(a)** Confucius taught that each person should accept his or her assigned role in society and perform the duties of that role. Government should be virtuous. **(b)** Daoism appealed to many Confucianists because it added balance to their lives by offering an escape from worldly concerns to the contemplation of nature.
4. Legalists believed in power and harsh laws. People were selfish and untrustworthy. Peace and prosperity was best achieved by threats and punishment.

Learning from Pictures
These three jade Buddhas are in a temple in Shanghai, China. What other philosophies had the greatest influence in ancient China?
Confucianism and Daoism

escape from the miseries of the world in nirvana. Buddhist temples and ceremonies also offered a sense of comfort and tranquillity in turbulent times.

Of all the philosophies of ancient China, those of Confucius, Laozi, and Buddha had the greatest influence on Chinese attitudes. Confucianism, with its reverence for the past and emphasis on the family, won the most followers. The Chinese had always revered their ancestors and worshiped the emperor as almost a divine being, and these practices continued. Other ideas contained in Daoism and Buddhism—humility, contentment, loyalty, justice, wisdom, and obedience—were absorbed into Chinese culture and helped make the Chinese a patient and enduring people.

SECTION 4 REVIEW

1. **Identify** Kongzi, Laozi
2. **Comparing Ideas** Explain the concept of *yin* and *yang.*
3. **Analyzing Ideas** **(a)** What are the basic teachings of Confucianism? **(b)** How did the ideas of Daoism complement the ideas of Confucianism?
4. **Classifying Ideas** List the ideas of Legalism.

5 Culture Reached New Heights During the Zhou, Qin, and Han Dynasties

Chinese society rested on the Confucian principle that the family was of key importance to the welfare of the state. The values that governed family life—reverence for one's family, respect for age, and acceptance of the decisions made by one's superiors—governed national life as well as Chinese social and cultural life, including the economy, education, literature, and science. ●

Family and Social Life

The family, not the individual, constituted the most important unit in Chinese society. A man rose or fell in the social system not because of wealth or personal accomplishments but because of his family's position. Each family consisted of the father, his wife, the sons with their wives and children, and the unmarried daughters. Often all members of a family lived in the same house and shared day-to-day tasks.

CONNECTIONS: THEN AND NOW

Harvest Festivals

When Americans sit down for Thanksgiving dinner each year, they are repeating a celebration found in almost every society in the world. All peoples find a way to give thanks when they have finished gathering the harvest. The summer is over, and the food has been grown. There is a feeling of gratitude that the earth has once again provided grain, vegetables, and fruits, such as at the Irish strawberry festival (right).

Long ago the ancient Hebrews celebrated a fall thanksgiving, a holiday called *Succoth* that Jews today still celebrate.

As early as the Shang dynasty, there were harvest gods in China (below). Later the Chinese celebrated the Harvest Moon Festival, and they saw a rabbit's form in the moon. They ate cakes in the shape of rabbits and moons, and gave thanks at altars adorned with wheat. In Japan today the harvest is honored by placing the produce of the earth on altars. The Japanese also hold large parades and carry giant fish to thank the ocean for the food it provides.

Among the early American Indians there were many rituals of planting and harvest (above). The ancient wish to give thanks when the farmer's work is done, and when the earth gives up its harvest, continues. The forms differ from place to place, but the importance of the land is the same for people all over the world.

SECTION 5

Focus/Motivation

Write the following quotation on the chalkboard or an overhead projector:

"A mellow understanding of life and of human nature is . . . the Chinese ideal of character, and from that understanding other qualities are derived, such as pacifism, contentment, calm and strength of endurance . . . ."

Then ask students what the word *character* means to them. Compare our modern idea of character with that of the Chinese peoples they have studied in this chapter. Ask the students if they believe the Chinese are peaceful, contented, and have great endurance. *(Students may answer that the series of rebellions that overthrew dynasties showed that the Chinese were not always peaceful or contented, the cruel rulers forced them to rebel. At the same time, they seem to have great endurance: they contended with the labor on the Great Wall and a hard life on the land, facing bad weather, floods, and tax collectors.)*

Then have students read the subsection "Family and Social Life" on pages 84–86, and discuss character in relation to the Chinese family.

1B, 1C, 1D, a1A

● The major purpose of marriage was to continue the family line. If a wife bore no child, her husband could return her to her family.

Presentation
Comparing Ideas (Average/Group)
Have the students read the subsection "Science and Technology" on page 87. Ask them to note the work Chinese astronomers did on a calendar. *(Chinese astronomers calculated the year at 365 1/4 days.)* Ask students to compare the Chinese calendar with the calendar made by the Egyptians *(page 26)*. Assign interested students to do research on the calendars of other ancient peoples—the Babylonians, Assyrians, Persians, Indians—and make reports to the class on their findings.

SECTION 5

Closure
During the Zhou, Qin, and Han dynasties, towns and cities grew. Ask students to name the features of Chinese life that endured despite these changes. *(family structure and life; majority of people still worked the land)*

Review Answers
1. ***acupuncture:*** Chinese medicinal practice in which doctor inserts needles into body to enable life-force energy to move properly **2.** The Chinese father ruled an extended family and arranged marriages, education, and careers of his children and grandchildren. Fathers played the role of an autocrat in the family, and the emphasis upon genealogy helped

The Chinese father ruled the family. The older he was, the more authority he had, for the Chinese respected age as a source of wisdom. Respect for one's aged parents and especially for one's father was an important virtue. Each family kept a careful genealogy, or record of their family tree, even including third cousins. When family members died, they became honored ancestors. Most families constructed altars where they worshiped their ancestors as links between the family's past, present, and future.

The Chinese father arranged his children's and his grandchildren's marriages, decided how much education his sons would receive, and even chose his sons' careers. Women were subordinate to men and had no property rights of their own. After marriage a young wife became almost a servant in the household of her husband's family. Before her wedding she often cried, not because she did not yet know her husband but because she did not know how her new family would treat her. With motherhood and age, however, the wife became an important figure in the family. ●

The Economy

Despite the growth of cities and towns, the vast majority of Chinese people continued to eke out meager existences as farmers in small villages. On the one hand, they had to contend with nature. If too much or too little rain fell, their crops might be ruined and they would starve. On the other hand, they had to contend with government. In addition to paying taxes, peasants also had to perform labor. For about one month each year, they left their farms and worked on roads, canals, or other local construction projects.

Just as during the Shang dynasty, farmers grew millet and wheat in the north and rice in the south. In both northern and southern China, about eight families worked fields in common. They used ox-drawn plows and complex systems of irrigation and flood control. These systems were so well constructed that Chinese farmers still use some built in the 200s B.C.

Although trade was never very important to the Chinese economy, it increased early in the

Learning from Pictures *The ancient Chinese used sailboats called junks to trade throughout East Asia. Even today junks ply the rivers of China.*

Zhou dynasty, when the northern Chinese began migrating into southern China. Items of trade between northern and southern China included leather goods, silk, jade, jewelry, screens, and couches. Trade improved when the Qin dynasty standardized the currency system and weights and measures. Trade increased further when the Silk Route linked China with the Mediterranean region during the Han dynasty.

Education

The Chinese did not consider education the responsibility of government, on either the national or the local level. Instead, families hired private tutors. If a family could not afford to do so, the children went uneducated. Even as late as the year 1900, not more than 5 percent of the Chinese people could read or write. Both the expense of paying a tutor and the difficulty of learning Chinese reading and writing caused this low rate of literacy.

Literature

The most important works of Chinese literature and the basis for all Chinese education were the Five Classics. We do not know who wrote these works or when they were written, but we do know that they were already important by the time of the Zhou dynasty. Officials used two of the Five Classics in civil service examinations: the *Classic of Songs,* containing more than 300 songs about love, joy, politics, and domestic life; and the *Classic of Documents,* containing semihistorical speeches and documents about government. The other three classics included the *Classic of Changes,* about the art of foretelling the future; *Spring and Autumn Annals,* a record of events in the important city-state of Lu from 722 B.C. to 481 B.C.; and *Ceremonies and Rituals,* about etiquette and ceremonies.

Shi Huangdi ordered the burning of the *Classic of Songs* and the *Classic of Documents* and tried to ban the reading of the other three. Toward the end of the Qin dynasty, this ban was lifted and the texts restored to their present form. In A.D. 175 the Five Classics were carved in stone to ensure that they would never again be destroyed.

Learning the Five Classics became essential for every well-brought-up young man of China. The Chinese also expected such young men to know many of the *Analects* of Confucius.

Science and Technology

As early as 444 B.C., Chinese astronomers had computed the year at 365 1/4 days. During the Han dynasty, scientists refined these calculations even further. In 28 B.C. astronomers in China first observed sunspots, which Europeans did not discover until the A.D. 1600s.

Sometime before A.D. 100, Chinese astronomers built special instruments to observe the orbit they believed the sun followed. Using these instruments, an early astronomer estimated the number of stars at 11,520. Other scientific achievements included the invention of a primitive seismograph that registered earthquakes so faint that royal officials did not even notice them.

The Chinese also invented paper. First produced in A.D. 105 from hemp, old rags, fishing nets, and the bark of mulberry trees, the paper was a bright yellow. The use of paper had spread throughout Asia by A.D. 700 and also to Europe, where it replaced papyrus as the main writing material. The Chinese also invented the sun dial, the water clock, and printing.

Perhaps the most widely known Chinese contribution to medicine is the therapy known as **acupuncture.** Its development stemmed from the Daoist belief that good health depends on the movement of a life-force energy through the body and that illness or pain results when something interferes with that movement.

In acupuncture the doctor inserts needles into certain points of the body to enable the life-force energy to move properly. Some modern researchers believe that these needle-insertion points have less electrical resistance than other parts of the body and thus may affect the nervous system. Today the Chinese use acupuncture as a general anesthetic in most types of surgery. Many Americans use it to relieve the pain of arthritis, cancer, and neuralgia.

SECTION 5 REVIEW

1. **Define** acupuncture
2. **Understanding Ideas** Explain the important role that the family played in Chinese government and social life.
3. **Interpreting Ideas (a)** What were the Five Classics? **(b)** the *Analects?*
4. **Analyzing Ideas (a)** How did the Chinese educate their children? **(b)** Why did so few Chinese learn to read and write?

incorporate ancestor worship as part of Chinese culture.
3. (a) The Five Classics were the *Classic of Songs:* 300 songs about love, joy, politics, and domestic life; *Classic of Documents:* semihistorical speeches and documents about government; *Classic of Changes:* art of foretelling the future; *Spring and Autumn Annals:* record of events in city-state of Lu from 722 B.C.–481 B.C.; *Ceremonies and Rituals:* etiquette and ceremonies. **(b)** The *Analects* were the most important works by Confucius.
4. (a) Families hired private tutors. **(b)** Children went uneducated if a family could not afford to pay a tutor. The complexity of Chinese characters discouraged developing reading and writing skills.

Reviewing Important Terms
1. autocracy; **2.** Calligraphy; **3.** Civil service; **4.** loess; **5.** Mandate of Heaven; **6.** oracle bones; **7.** Acupuncture; **8.** Silt

Developing Critical Thinking Skills
1. deserts, mountain ranges, and vast distances
2. silk cloth, carved jade jewelry, ivory and bone objects inlaid with turquoise, kaolin, pottery, bronze castings, calendar, written language, calligraphy
3. literature: h, j; technology; e, f, i, k; philosophy: d, h, l; government: a, b, c, g, i
4. Answers will vary. Students should be able to support their selection with evidence from pages 76 to 80 in the chapter.
5. (a) Confucius believed society should be changed by education and virtuous living. Legalists believed people were selfish and untrustworthy and had to be ruled by harsh laws. **(b)** Answers will vary. Western democracies tend to follow the Confucian view. Dictatorships use repressive laws to control people.
6. (a) The Chinese people developed a strong sense of identity and superiority, and they regarded China as the center of the world; hence the "Middle" Kingdom. **(b)** Answers will vary. The Chinese attitude toward foreigners and their belief in the superiority of all things Chinese kept them isolated from changes elsewhere, which delayed domestic development. **(c)** Answers will vary. Students should emphasize that the Chinese people are attempting to catch up in Western technological ideas.

1B, 1D, 2D, a1A, a4A, a4B, a4C, a4F, a4G, a4J

Reteaching
Have students review the Chapter Summary and the appropriate section and questions in the Unit Synthesis. Discuss the concepts until students demonstrate a clear understanding of the material.

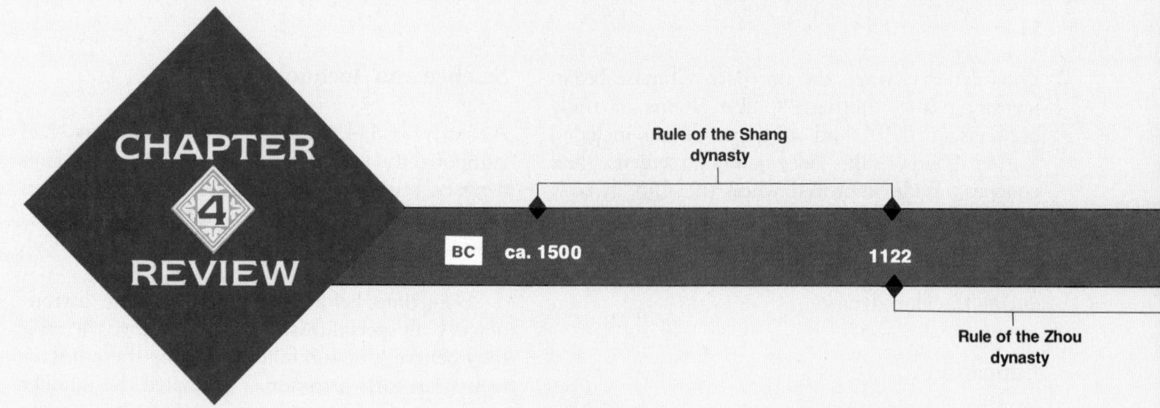

Chapter Summary

The following list contains the key concepts you have learned about the great civilization of China.

1. China is divided into two main sections–China Proper and the vast semicircle of regions that surround it. These regions include Tibet, Xinjiang, Mongolia, Manchuria, and Korea.
2. The major rivers of China include the Chang Jiang, the Huang He, and the Xi Jiang. Because of devastating floods, the Huang He is often referred to as "China's Sorrow."
3. China's political history involves a succession of ruling dynasties that rose and fell in a recognizable pattern or cycle. China's cultural history concerns the gradual evolution of civilization over the centuries.
4. The Shang was the first historic Chinese dynasty. During their rule simple irrigation and flood control systems, a calendar, and an original written language were developed.
5. The Zhou, Qin, and Han dynasties had an important and enduring influence on the development of Chinese government and thought.
6. China's most influential philosopher was Confucius, who taught that emphasizing family and choosing virtuous rulers led to a healthy society. Confucianism became the most important philosophy in China. It later evolved into a religion.
7. Laozi, the founder of Daoism, taught that people should withdraw from the world and try to achieve harmony with nature. In time Daoism became the second most important philosophy in China.
8. Two other significant schools of Chinese philosophy were Naturalism and Legalism. Naturalism explained nature through the principles of *yin* and *yang*. Legalism stressed political power and harsh laws.
9. The most important unit in Chinese society was the family. Age was highly respected, and fathers had great authority.
10. Many cultural and technological advances occurred during the Zhou, Qin, and Han dynasties. The Five Classics became the most important works of Chinese literature. Technological advances included the invention of paper as well as scientific instruments and the medical technique of acupuncture.

On a separate sheet of paper, complete the following review exercises.

Reviewing Important Terms

Supply the term that correctly completes each sentence.

1. In an ______ the ruler wields unlimited power.
2. ______ is the art of beautiful writing.
3. ______ ______ administers the government on a day-to-day basis, and its members are usually appointed based on the results of highly competitive examinations.
4. The yellowish silt carried in the waters of the Huang He is called ______.
5. The gods gave the Chinese monarch the right to rule, a right known as the ______ ______ ______.
6. During the Shang dynasty, priests wrote questions on ______ ______, the shoulder bones of cattle or the bottoms of tortoise shells.
7. ______ is a Chinese therapy in which doctors insert needles into certain points of the body to enable life-force energy to move properly.
8. ______ is moist soil carried as sediment in a river's waters.

Developing Critical Thinking Skills

1. **Seeing Relationships** Describe the geographical barriers of China that limited the spread of Chinese culture.
2. **Making Charts** Make a chart listing the accomplishments of the Shang dynasty.
3. **Classifying Ideas** Put each of the following names or ideas in one of these four categories: literature, technology, philosophy, government.
   (a) leveling
   (b) Pax Sinica
   (c) civil service examinations
   (d) *yin* and *yang*
   (e) standard width of axle for carts
   (f) Great Wall
   (g) uniform law code
   (h) teachings of Confucius

1A, 1C, 2D, a4A, a4B, a4C, a4D, a4E, a4F, a4G, a4H, a4I, a4J, a4K, a4L, a4M

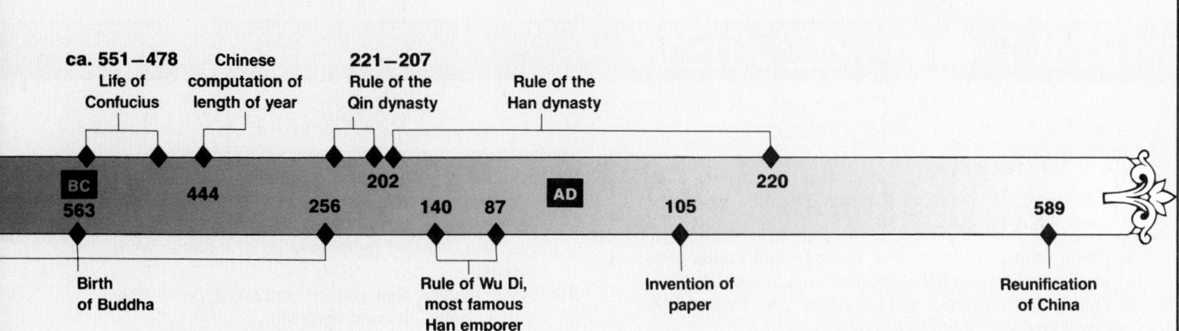

(i) large-scale irrigation and flood control
(j) *Classic of Songs* and *Classic of Documents*
(k) acupuncture
(l) Naturalism

4. **Evaluating Ideas** Which dynasty—the Zhou, the Qin, or the Han—did the most to advance Chinese culture? Give evidence to support your answer.
5. **Analyzing Ideas** **(a)** Compare the ideas of Confucianism and Legalism regarding how society should be changed. **(b)** Are any of these ideas or values used in our society today? Give examples from newspapers to support your opinion.
6. **Synthesizing Ideas** **(a)** Why did the Chinese call their country the Middle Kingdom? **(b)** How do you think the attitude the Chinese held toward foreigners might have affected ancient Chinese history? **(c)** How might it affect China today?

Relating Geography to History

(a) Trace the map of eastern Asia on page 70. Then use atlases to complete the following activities. **(b)** Indicate the areas that have heavy rainfall. **(c)** Indicate the areas that need irrigation in order to grow crops. **(d)** Show the desert area (the Gobi Desert) that might be used for grazing.

Relating Past to Present

1. Animism is the belief that spirits inhabit everything—rocks, plants, animals, and even people. Scholars believe that the people who lived in China during the Shang dynasty were animists. **(a)** List some of these animistic ideas and practices and compare them with what people today call "superstitions." **(b)** What are some of the symbols considered "lucky" and "unlucky" today?
2. It is sometimes said that a culture can be judged by the people to whom the greatest honor is paid. **(a)** Which people were most honored in ancient China? **(b)** Which people do you think people in the United States today respect or honor most? **(c)** What qualities make people in the United States regard these people so highly?

Applying History Study Skills

Before completing this activity, review Building History Study Skills on page 83.

Look again at the steps for analyzing statements. Then complete the following exercise.

Read the following statement from the Confucian book *The Great Learning.* Then analyze the statement by answering the questions below.

> "The ancients who wished clearly to exemplify . . . virtue throughout the world would first set up good government in their states. Wishing to govern well their states, they would first regulate their families. Wishing to regulate their families, they would first cultivate their persons. Wishing to cultivate their persons, they would first rectify their minds. Wishing to rectify their minds, they would first seek sincerity in their thoughts. Wishing for sincerity in their thoughts, they would first extend their knowledge."

1. What is the purpose of the statement?
2. One of the key words in the statement is *cultivate.* **(a)** What does the word mean? **(b)** What are the other key words in the statement?
3. **(a)** According to Confucius, how is harmony in society achieved? **(b)** Do you agree? Why or why not?

Investigating Further

1. **Presenting an Oral Report** Learn how to write 10 characters of the Chinese language as an art form. You may use *Chinese Calligraphy* by Chiang Yee (Harvard University Press) as a source. Report to the class the skills learned in the use of the brush.
2. **Writing a Report** Find pictures of bronze items from the Shang dynasty in reference books in your school or public library. Study the pictures to determine the religious functions and the aesthetic value of the bronzes. Write a report describing your findings.
3. **Interviewing** Visit a Chinese restaurant in your community and interview one of the employees to find what types of food are typically Chinese. How do these foods differ from American food? How are they prepared differently than American foods?

Relating Geography to History
Check any atlas or encyclopedia to supplement materials in the text.

Relating Past to Present
1. (a) In Shang China, people believed dragons fighting caused thunderstorms. Ceremonies were held in spring to bring good crops and in autumn to give thanks for the harvest. Modern people might call these beliefs superstitions because we have scientific reasons for natural occurrences. **(b)** "Lucky" symbols are considered rabbits' feet, four-leaf clovers, rainbows, and horseshoes. "Unlucky" include broken mirrors, walking under ladders, and black cats.
2. (a) In China scholar-officials had the highest status, next to the imperial family. **(b)** Answers will vary. Students will probably state that in our society doctors, judges, lawyers, engineers, athletes, and entertainers are honored. **(c)** They have special skills or charismatic qualities.

Applying History Study Skills
1. The statement describes the ideal self and self-improvement.
2. (a) Cultivate means "to encourage" or "develop." **(b)** rectify, seek, extend
3. (a) Social harmony is achieved as individuals study to extend their knowledge to improve their thoughts and minds.
(b) Answers will vary.

89

Reviewing Concepts

1. (a) polytheism; (b) Vedas; (c) artisans; (d) City-state; (e) Cuneiform

2. (a) Egyptians; (b) Indians; (c) Sumerians; (d) Egyptians; (e) Chinese; (f) Persians; (g) Phoenicians; (h) Hebrews

3. (a) They worshiped sun and moon, animals like cat, bull, crocodile, insects like scarab. They believed in life after death, and that the soul, judged against the feather of truth, would be sent to eternal happiness or to the Eater of the Dead. (b) These polytheists matched their gods with the forces of nature. They did not believe in a future life or in heaven but that there was some life after death. (c) They were monotheists who believed in Yahweh. If the people rejected God, they and their descendants would be punished. (d) These teachings include knowing the Four Noble Truths and following the Eightfold Path to nirvana. (e) They believed gods were forces of nature. (f) They combined animism and ancestor worship. They were not interested in life after death. (g) Zoroaster taught there were good and evil gods from which people could choose. Those who chose good would be rewarded with eternal life, while those who chose evil faced darkness and misery after death.

Applying Critical Thinking Skills

1. Answers will vary. Various cultures conquered the region and succeeding generations were exposed to new cultures, social and governmental systems.

1A, 1B, 1D, 2A, 2D, a1A, a4A, a4F, a4G, a4H, a4L, a4M

Reteaching

Have students review the Chapter Summary and the appropriate section and questions in the Unit Synthesis. Discuss the concepts until students demonstrate a clear understanding of the material.

UNIT 1 REVIEW

Unit Summary

The following list contains the key concepts you have learned about ancient civilizations.

1. Using bones, artifacts, and pictures, anthropologists study early human behavior, customs, and skills.
2. During Neolithic times, people in four great river valleys developed the first civilizations.
3. Protected by geographic barriers, the Egyptians developed a remarkable culture that included literature, science, art, complex agricultural practices, hieroglyphics, and elaborate religious rituals.
4. In the Fertile Crescent, a succession of empire builders formed societies and cultures. Major developments included cuneiform (Sumerians), codification of law (Babylonians), effective methods of government (Persians), the alphabet (Phoenicians), invention of money (Lydians), and ethical monotheism (Hebrews).
5. About 2500 B.C. people in the Indus Valley cities of Harappa and Mohenjo-Daro developed a complex civilization. In 1500 B.C. nomadic Aryans swept through the Khyber Pass and settled in India. By 1000 B.C. they had developed the rigid caste system that regulated everyday contacts between more than 3,000 hereditary classes.
6. The religious books of Hinduism, the *Upanishads,* outline the path of reincarnation each soul must take to be reunited with the Universal Soul.
7. Gautama founded Buddhism. According to this religion, people can reach salvation by accepting the Four Noble Truths and following the Eightfold Path.
8. Geographical barriers isolated China as its civilization evolved along the Huang He. The Chinese built irrigation ditches and dikes and developed a lunar calendar and written language.
9. During the Zhou, Qin, and Han dynasties, philosophy flourished, with Naturalists, Confucianists, Legalists, and Daoists developing systems of thought.

On a separate sheet of paper, complete the following review exercises.

Reviewing Concepts

1. Supply the term that correctly completes each sentence.
   (a) Belief in many gods is ________.
   (b) ________ are books of sacred knowledge in India.
   (c) Skilled craftworkers are called ________.
   (d) A ________ is a town or city and the surrounding land it controlled.
   (e) ________ is the Sumerian form of writing.
2. Identify the specific society or culture with which each of the following ideas or facts is associated:
   (a) Constructed pyramids as royal tombs
   (b) Built large granaries to store food for city-state
   (c) Worshiped in seven-story temples called *ziggurats*
   (d) Permitted women to own property in their own right
   (e) Lacked direct contact with other great civilizations and believed peoples of other cultures were barbarians
   (f) Had a religion that placed emphasis on earthly struggle between good and evil
   (g) Developed the alphabet that became the model for later Western alphabets
   (h) Believed that Canaan was their promised land
3. Explain the beliefs about God (or gods) and an afterlife in three of the following civilizations: (a) Egyptian, (b) Sumerian, (c) Hebrew, (d) Buddhist, (e) Aryan, (f) Shang, (g) Persian

Applying Critical Thinking Skills

1. **Understanding Ideas** Discuss how cultural diffusion took place in the Fertile Crescent.
2. **Analyzing Ideas** (a) Describe some of the laws included in the Code of Hammurabi and in Mosaic law. (b) Explain why such codes of law became important as people began living together in groups.
3. **Evaluating Ideas** Choose two of the following leaders: Akhenaton, Hammurabi, Moses, Darius, Buddha, Asoka, Shi Huangdi, Wu Di, or Confucius. (a) Describe each person's accomplishments. (b) Do you think that these leaders achieved their goals? Why or why not?
4. **Synthesizing Ideas** Using evidence from the civilizations explained in Unit One, discuss the following statement: "Cultures obtain more ideas and ways of doing things from other cultures, rather than creating ideas and methods that are unique to themselves."

Relating Geography to History

The earliest civilizations developed in four great river valleys—the Huang He, the Nile, the Indus, and the Tigris-Euphrates. Almost all other civilizations also originally developed in river valleys. (a) Why do you think this was so? (b) What advantages did rivers provide to the people of early civilizations?

Writing About History

1. Write a dialogue to take place within one of the following groups of people:
   (a) the pharaoh of Egypt and his advisers, deciding which countries they wish to be allies with and which countries they wish to attack. The dialogue should be taking place in the year 1000 B.C.
   (b) a Hebrew prophet, a follower of Zoroastrianism, a Buddhist priest, and a Brahman, arguing about the

role of religion in shaping the values of their particular societies.

2. Write a newspaper story dated A.D. 536, summarizing the great accomplishments of the Gupta rulers.

Further Readings

Bothwell, Jean. *Dancing Princess.* San Diego: Harcourt Brace Jovanovich. Describes the life of a young woman in ancient India.

Casson, Lionel. *Daily Life in Ancient Egypt.* New York: American Heritage. Describes daily life during the New Kingdom.

Everyday Life in Bible Times. Washington, D.C.: National Geographic Society. Describes the history of Judaism.

Hall, Alice J. "Special Treasures from a Chinese Tomb." *National Geographic,* May 1974: 661–681. Describes life during the Han dynasty.

The World's Last Mysteries. Pleasantville, New York: Reader's Digest Association. Analyzes mythical ancient kingdoms and peoples that mysteriously vanished.

Weaver, Kenneth F. "The Search for Our Ancestors." *National Geographic,* May 1975: 560–629. Describes the recent discoveries that anthropologists and archaeologists have made.

Unit One Chronology

Date	Political and Social Developments	Technological and Scientific Advances	Visual Arts and Literature	Religious and Philosophical Thought
6000 B.C.–3000 B.C.	Prehistoric times 1* River valley civilizations 1	Neolithic culture 1	Cave paintings 1	
3000 B.C.–2000 B.C.	Sumerian civilization 2 Egyptian Old Kingdom 2 Mohenjo-Daro 3	Egyptian irrigation 2 Egyptian pyramids 2 Sumerian ziggurats 2 Hieroglyphics 2 Cuneiform 2 Sumerian arch 2	Egyptian calendar 2 *The Book of the Dead* 2	Polytheism in Egypt 2 Animism in India and China 3, 4
2000 B.C.–1000 B.C.	Egyptian Middle Kingdom 2 Hammurabi's Code 2 Aryan invasions 3 Xia dynasty 4 Shang dynasty 4	Hittites use iron weapons 2	Chinese bronze casting 4 Chinese pottery 4 Chinese calendar 4	Amenhotep; Israelites develop monotheism 2 Indian Vedic religion 3 Chinese ancestor worship 4
1000 B.C.–500 B.C.	Phoenicians and trade 2 Solomon in Israel 2 Indian caste system 3 Chinese Zhou dynasty 4	Assyrians use cavalry 2 Iron in China 4 Chaldean math and astronomy 2	Nineveh library 2 Phoenician alphabet 2 *Upanishads* 3	Zoroaster in Persia 2 Jewish ethical monotheism 2 Hinduism 3
500 B.C.–0	Qin dynasty 4 Pax Sinica 4 Han dynasty 4 Persian Empire 2 Maurya Empire and Asoka 3	Great Wall 4 Chinese civil service 4 Chinese calendar 4 Chinese astronomy 4	Ajanta cave painting 3 Stupas constructed 3	Buddhism in India 3 Confucius 4 Laozi 4
0–A.D. 500	Gupta rulers 3 Huns invade China 4	Indian numeral system 3 Chinese paper 4	Indian *Sakuntala* 3	

* Indicates chapter in which development is discussed

2. (a) Hammurabi's code develops the idea of "eye for an eye" justice. Moses' code of commandments places much more value on human institutions like the family and interpersonal relationships. **(b)** Law codes helped maintain stability in societies often beset by famine, drought, or invasion.

3. Answers will vary. **(a) Akhenaton:** introduced monotheism in Egypt; **Hammurabi:** Babylonian law code; **Moses,** Hebraic law code; **Darius,** created large, well-administered empire in Persia; **Buddha:** religious code of law to attain nirvana and govern relations between individuals; **Asoka:** conquered most of India and supported spread of Buddhism; **Shi Huangdi:** Qin emperor who built Great Wall; **Wu Di:** instituted Pax Sinica and civil service; **Confucius:** encouraged development of virtue to maintain order. **(b)** Answers will vary.

4. Answers will vary. Students might suggest that many early civilizations developed in relative isolation and borrowed little from other peoples. Some people, as those who lived in the Fertile Crescent, absorbed economic, cultural, and technological ideas from neighboring or conquering peoples.

Relating Geography to History

(a) People used the rivers for water, for themselves and their crops, and for transportation. **(b)** Rivers guaranteed the basic necessities of life and eliminated the need for a nomadic life style.

Focus/Motivation
On a wall map of the world, point out the sites of the earliest civilizations *(Egypt, Mesopotamia, the Indus Valley, and the valley of the Huang He)*. Ask: Why do you think that the earliest civilizations began in river valleys? *(Students might suggest that river valleys were ideal sites for the development of agriculture.)* Then ask them why agriculture is so important to the development of civilization. *(It ensures a steady food supply.)*

UNIT ONE SYNTHESIS

The Beginnings of Civilization

1 Cultures and Civilizations Began in Prehistoric Times

Scholars believe that people lived on earth long before the development of writing, during the period known as prehistory. Although unable to write, prehistoric people made significant discoveries and advances.

Prehistoric Discoveries

Based on scientific studies, researchers have concluded that humanlike creatures appeared on the earth millions of years ago during a period of prehistory called the Old Stone Age, or Paleolithic (pay • lee • oh • LITH • ik) Age. Centuries later, the first prehistoric people migrated to many parts of the world. Long periods of extremely cold weather known as the Ice Age, however, prevented these early people from moving into the colder regions of the earth. It was only when prehistoric peoples such as the Neanderthals and later the Cro-Magnons learned to use fire and to craft warm clothing, that they could successfully settle in the colder regions of the earth.

Both the Neanderthals and the Cro-Magnons had been nomads who traveled from place to place in search of food. About 10,000 years ago, in the period called the New Stone Age or Neolithic Age, however, people began to settle in villages. Two important developments—the domestication, or taming, of several kinds of animals and the development of agriculture—helped make permanent settlements possible.

The First Civilizations

Although Neolithic people settled in many regions, the settlements in the Nile River valley in Egypt, the valley of the Tigris and Euphrates (yoo • FRAY • teez) rivers in southwestern Asia, the Indus River valley in southern Asia, and the Huang He (HWANG HOOH) valley in eastern Asia had particular significance. In these four river valleys, people first developed civilizations.

The people of these civilizations became the first in the world to develop advanced technical skills, such as the ability to use metals. In addition, an increase in population, made possible by improved farming methods, encouraged the growth of cities. Eventually the people of these communities developed calendars to predict when crops should be planted and harvested.

With the many changes of late Neolithic times, life became increasingly complex. People in settled communities developed rules for living together and for protecting property. They also developed governments and traded with other communities. To keep government records and to better communicate with one another, the people of these civilizations developed the first forms of writing. The development of writing marked the end of prehistory and the beginning of history.

2 Great Civilizations Developed in the Middle East

Civilizations first appeared along the Nile River and along the Tigris and Euphrates rivers.

The Egyptians

Along the narrow ribbon of fertile land that straddles the Nile River in Egypt in northeastern Africa, people created a thriving civilization. Each year the river swept over its banks and deposited a layer of fertile silt in the valley. This fertile silt enabled the early inhabitants of the valley to establish agriculture.

The people of the Nile Valley learned to use copper to make needles, chisels, and jewelry. They discovered how to make bronze, the strong alloy of copper and tin. They also developed a system of writing known as hieroglyphics about 3000 B.C.

Over the centuries early Egyptian settlements were united to form the two kingdoms of Upper Egypt and Lower Egypt. Then, about 3100 B.C., a ruler known as Menes (MEE • neez) united all Egypt into one kingdom and took the title pharaoh.

In more than 2,500 years, beginning with the time of Menes and continuing to about 300 B.C., there were about 30 Egyptian dynasties. This span of time is divided into four periods—the Old Kingdom, the Middle Kingdom, the New Kingdom, and the Late Period.

Egyptian Culture

The Egyptians created great monuments to their gods and rulers. These monuments included the great Sphinx near Giza and the pyramids, designed as tombs for the pharaohs. In addition to large-scale works, sculptors also made small, lifelike statues of kings and sacred animals from copper, bronze, stone, or wood.

The Egyptians developed an accurate calendar with 12 months of 30 days each. This system left them with five extra days, which they used for holidays and feasting. The Egyptians also developed a number system based on 10, used geometry, made significant advances in medicine, and developed an excellent educational system.

Sumerian Civilization

To the east of Egypt, the fertile valley of the Tigris and Euphrates rivers nurtured equally brilliant civilizations. There, in a region known as the Fertile Crescent that stretches from the Mediterranean Sea to the Persian Gulf, many civilizations rose and fell. The earliest was that of Sumer.

Early in their history the Sumerians developed a form of government called the city-state, which included a town or city and the surrounding land it controlled. Unlike Egypt, the many Sumerian city-states were seldom united.

The Sumerians used sun-dried clay bricks to build houses and may have invented several important architectural designs. These included the arch, the ramp, and the dome. The most striking Sumerian buildings were the temples known as ziggurats. Built on hills that were specially created on the flat land of the valley, a ziggurat was constructed in layers, each one smaller than the one below.

The pyramids

The Sumerians developed a form of writing known as cuneiform and considered education very important, although only upper-class boys were educated. Students learned to write and spell by copying religious books and songs. They also studied reading, history, mathematics, foreign languages, and mapmaking.

Empires of the Fertile Crescent

The disunity of the Sumerian city-states proved to be a fatal weakness.

The Akkadians. After 2400 B.C. the Akkadians (uh • KAYD • ee • uhnz) conquered the Sumerians and established a great empire that lasted about 100 years. When it ended, new waves of invaders swept through the region.

The Babylonians. About 1792 B.C. a strong ruler named Hammurabi (ham • uh • RAHB • ee) came to power in Babylon and conquered the upper Tigris-Euphrates Valley. Hammurabi's greatest accomplishment was the Code of Hammurabi, a collection of 282 harsh laws that controlled all aspects of life in Babylon.

The Hittites. About 1600 B.C. the Hittites invaded the Tigris-Euphrates Valley from Asia Minor. The Hittites were the first people to make extensive use of iron for weapons. Their most important achievement, however, was their laws, which were less brutal than the Code of Hammurabi. The Hittites were too far from their homeland to control

1B, 2A, 2D, 3B, a1C

Presentation
Comparing Ideas
(Average/Group)
Write the following headings on the chalkboard or an overhead projector: *Egypt, Mesopotamia, India, China.* Then ask students to work in groups of two to write the major accomplishments of the early civilizations in each of the four regions. Use the completed charts as the basis for a class discussion on these brilliant civilizations.

Babylonia permanently, however, and soon withdrew to the western part of the Fertile Crescent.

The Assyrians. Following the decline of the Hittites, Babylon suffered further invasions. Then about 900 B.C., the fiercest, cruelest, and most warlike of all ancient peoples—the Assyrians—overwhelmed the region.

The Assyrians were specialists in warfare. Often using savage methods, the Assyrians killed the enemies they captured in battle, enslaved conquered peoples, and deported them to other areas.

The Assyrians were the first people to develop an effective method of governing an empire, and all other empires of the ancient Middle East were modeled after it. In other fields, however, the Assyrians contributed few new ideas to civilization. And in 612 B.C., a group of opponents captured and destroyed the Assyrian capital of Nineveh.

The Chaldeans. A people known as the Chaldeans took control of much of the territory that the Assyrians had ruled. Under the leadership of a wise ruler named Nebuchadnezzar (neb • uh • kuhd • NEZ • uhr), who ruled from the rebuilt capital city of Babylon between 605 and 562 B.C., the Chaldeans conquered most of the Fertile Crescent.

All the strength of the Chaldeans seemed to lie in the ability of Nebuchadnezzar. Within 30 years of Nebuchadnezzar's death, the empire fell.

The Persians. About 550 B.C. Cyrus, a Persian and one of the greatest leaders in all history, began a series of conquests, capturing Babylon, and conquering the rest of the Fertile Crescent and Asia Minor. A later Persian ruler, Darius the Great, added regions south and east of Persia as far as the Indus River in India, as well as parts of Europe.

The Persians ruled the mightiest empire known up to that time. Although all-powerful in government, Persian rulers showed great concern for justice. Tax collection and the administration of justice were fair. And rulers chose the best officials they could find, often from among the conquered peoples, to govern their huge empire.

The Phoenicians, Lydians, and Hebrews

The peoples who lived in the western end of the Fertile Crescent and in western Asia Minor did not create large empires, but they made important contributions in economics and religion.

Because of a lack of good farmland, the Phoenicians turned to the sea and to commerce for their living. The most important contribution of the Phoenicians was the alphabet upon which our alphabet is patterned.

The Lydians of Asia Minor made a significant contribution to civilization that was based on trade. About 600 B.C., they became the first people in history to use coined money.

Just as in the eastern part of the Fertile Crescent, a series of peoples inhabited Canaan to the south of Phoenicia. The people who had the greatest influence on their own times and on all later history were the Hebrews, or Jews.

Judaism, the religion of the Hebrews, is the Hebrews' most important contribution. Judaism was the first major example of monotheism—the belief in one supreme god. To the Hebrews, their god, Yahweh, was not like a human being but was a spiritual force. The kings of many other ancient peoples claimed to be gods, but Hebrew kings were not gods. Other ancient peoples worshiped statues or idols. To the Hebrews, only Yahweh was divine. Because of its emphasis on ethics, or proper conduct, the Hebrew form of monotheism is often called ethical monotheism.

3 People Created Thriving Civilizations in India

In India early people learned to farm, developed a written language and calendars, and created a complex civilization.

Harappan Civilization

The first Indian civilization developed in the Indus Valley about 2500 B.C., not long after Egypt and Sumer developed civilizations. This early Indus Valley civilization is best seen in the ruins of two cities, Mohenjo-Daro (moh • hen • joh-DAHR • oh) and Harappa (huh • RAP • uh). Harappa was so important to this civilization that historians often call it Harappan civilization.

The areas surrounding Harappa and Mohenjo-Daro were agricultural regions. City dwellers worked primarily in industry or trade. These early Indus Valley people also developed a written language before the civilization's mysterious collapse about 1700 B.C.

Aryan Invaders

About 1500 B.C. a new group of people, the Aryans, invaded the Indus Valley. Although outnumbered by the original Indus Valley people, the Aryans believed they had to maintain their identity. To do so they passed laws prohibiting marriages between Aryans and the valley dwellers. In later centuries, this class system evolved into a rigid social organization known as the caste system.

Hinduism and Buddhism

Two of the world's great religions—Hinduism and Buddhism developed in ancient India.

Hinduism. According to Hinduism, the world known to our senses is an illusion called Maya, which betrays people, giving them sorrow and pain. People can be delivered from their suffering if they can identify Maya, but this requires lifetimes of experience. Hinduism explains that this experience is provided through reincarnation—the transmigration or rebirth of the soul. According to this belief, the soul does not die with the body but enters the body of another being, either human or animal, and thus lives second, third, and more lives. Ultimately each person hopes to be the one who ends the repeated reincarnations and enables the soul to be reunited with the soul of Brahma.

Buddhism. The other great religion of India, Buddhism, was founded by an Indian prince named Gautama and known as Buddha, or the "Enlightened One." Buddha accepted the Hindu belief that the progress of the soul depends on the life a person leads and that good is rewarded and evil punished. Departing from Hindu beliefs, however,

Religious pilgrims in India

Buddha said that salvation came from following the guidelines for conduct embodied in the Four Noble Truths and the Eightfold Path.

Empires in Ancient India

The subcontinent of India was never conquered by the Persians or Greeks, although both had conquered land as far as the Indus River.

The Maurya Empire. A kingdom arose in India in 322 B.C. as a result of the conquests of a powerful young adventurer named Chandragupta (chuhn • druh • GOOHP • tuh). He established what is called the Maurya Empire. Chandragupta's grandson Asoka (uh • SHOH • kuh), who came to the throne about 270 B.C., enlarged the empire until it included all of India except the southern tip.

The Gupta rulers. The next great rulers of India were the Guptas, who came to power in A.D. 320. The time during which the Guptas ruled has been called a golden age because of the brilliant civilization that flourished then. Gupta rule ended in A.D. 535, however, when once again invaders stormed into the subcontinent and brutally ravaged northern India.

Indian Culture

India has indeed left the world a rich legacy in the areas of art, literature, mathematics, and science.

Economy and social life. From ancient times the land had provided a living for nearly all the people of India. For a limited few at the top of the caste system, the land provided great luxury. Nevertheless, most people were poor.

Literature. Throughout Indian history the most popular writings were the two great epics, the *Mahabharata* and *Ramayana.* People also enjoyed the stories of the *Panchatantra* (pahn • chah • TAN • trah), a series of fables from the Gupta period.

Architecture and art. Much Indian architecture and art reflects religious influences. For example, stupas, hemispheres or dome-shaped shrines, held artifacts and objects associated with Buddha. Indians also created a distinctive style of Hindu temple—a square building with heavy walls that enclosed the statue of a god.

Mathematics and astronomy. Indians actually invented the numeral system we call Arabic—1 through 9 and the zero. Arab traders brought it to

95

Closure
Ask: Which of the early civilizations have the most impact on our lives today? *(Students should give reasons for their choices.)*

the West from India. Indians also understood negative numbers and prepared a table of sines, or the ratio of the side opposite the angle and the longest side of the triangle, used extensively in trigonometry.

Indian astronomers identified the seven planets that can be seen without the aid of a telescope. They knew that the planets and the moon reflected the sun's light. They understood the daily rotation of the earth on its axis. They also predicted eclipses, calculated the diameter of the earth, and developed a theory of gravity.

Medicine. Indian physicians understood the importance of the spinal cord, and their surgery included bone setting and plastic surgery on ears, noses, and lips. They perfected the technique of inoculation.

4 Ancient Chinese Civilization Developed Lasting Traditions

Great distances, the towering mountains of central Asia, and such formidable deserts as the Gobi (GOH • BEE) made China almost inaccessible. As a result, China developed and retained its own distinctive culture in relative isolation.

The Shaping of Chinese History

From the beginning of its recorded history until the early 1900s, a succession of dynasties ruled China. Each dynasty went through a dynastic cycle consisting of four major stages. The first stage involved the founding of the dynasty. Next came a period of internal peace, expansion, and great power. A period of regression marked by decline followed the period of great power. When its decline reached a low point, with chaos and rebellion engulfing many parts of the land, the dynasty collapsed. A new leader emerged, and another dynastic cycle then began.

Beneath the recurring pattern of the dynastic cycle lay a continuous evolution, or development, of culture over the centuries. For example, structures such as the family, the farm, and the village developed their own pattern of change. During some stages of the dynastic cycle the pace of cultural evolution quickened; during others it slowed.

The Shang Dynasty

China's first historic dynasty, the Shang, began about 1500 B.C. along the Huang He. Shang government was relatively simple. A hereditary king granted land to his principal followers. In return they pledged loyalty, performed certain services, and paid dues. Although the Shang economy was based mainly on agriculture, Shang artisans established the foundation for all later Chinese ceramic art, including the development of every form and shape used in Chinese ceremonial vases.

Changing Dynasties

In 1122 B.C. a new dynasty—the Zhou (JOH) overthrew the Shang. The Zhou dynasty was the most enduring Chinese dynasty, lasting almost 800 years, from 1122 B.C. to 256 B.C. During the many years of Zhou rule, internal trade expanded, and copper coins came into use as money. But probably the most important development was the introduction of iron, which helped transform Chinese agriculture. Using iron farm tools and plows pulled by oxen, Chinese peasants cultivated new lands and produced more grain than ever before.

The Qin dynasty. The Qin (CHIN) dynasty came to power in 221 B.C. by using cavalry armed with bows and arrows, a military technique new to the Chinese. The dynasty's founder was Shi Huangdi (SHUHR HWAHNG • DEE), which means "first emperor." Although the Qin dynasty lasted only a short time, until 207 B.C., it succeeded in unifying China under a strong central government for the very first time. It was also noted for standardizing weights, measures, and coinage, and for establishing a uniform system of writing. To guard against invasion from the north and west, the Qin completed the Great Wall of China, much of which still stands today.

The Han dynasty. In 202 B.C. a general of peasant background, Liu Bang (LEE • OO BAHNG), founded the Han dynasty. Like the Qin, the Han dynasty ruled a centralized and expanding empire. Unlike the Qin, however, it succeeded in maintaining its power for almost 400 years. Han influence was so great that even today many Chinese refer to themselves as "Sons of Han."

The Han dynasty established the Chinese civil service system to administer the government on a day-to-day basis. Candidates for civil service

Question 1 of the Synthesis Review corresponds to Section 1; Question 2, to Section 2; Question 3, to Section 3; Question 4, to Section 4. Question 5 asks students to synthesize information from various sections of the synthesis.

1A, 1B, 2A, 2D, a1A, a1C, a4A, a4F, a4H, a4I, a4K, a4L

The Great Wall of China

positions had to pass rigorous tests based on their knowledge of the great classics of Chinese literature and law. As a result, the best scholars in the country became government officials.

Chinese Philosophies

Although political disunity and almost constant warfare marked the last years of the Zhou dynasty, this period was one of the most creative in the history of Chinese philosophy.

Naturalism. Like other Chinese philosophers, the Naturalists were far more interested in human beings and the real world than in divine or spiritual matters. One of their basic ideas concerned the dualism, or two-sidedness, of nature. The Naturalists defined this dualism of nature as its *yin* and *yang*. *Yin* was female, dark, cold, and passive. *Yang* was male, light, hot, and active.

Confucianism. Kongzi, (KOOHNG • ZUH), meaning "Kong the Philosopher," or "Reverend Master Kong," is known to Westerners as Confucius. Confucius was not a religious prophet and had little to say about the gods, the meaning of death, or the idea of life after death. Instead, he taught about the importance of the family, respect for one's elders, and reverence for the past. These three concepts formed the basis of Confucian philosophy.

Daoism. Daoism (DOW • iz • um) got its name from its central idea, Dao, which can be defined as the Way of Nature. Laozi (LOW • ZUH), the founder of Daoism, believed that only by withdrawing from the world and contemplating nature could people live in harmony with nature.

Legalism. Like Confucianism, the school of philosophy known as Legalism was concerned with politics. Its teachings, however, were very different from the teachings of Confucianism. The Legalists believed in power, not virtue. They also believed in harsh laws. In their view, people were by nature selfish and untrustworthy. Peace and prosperity could only be achieved by threatening severe punishment if people failed to do what was expected.

Chinese Culture

The family, not the individual, was the most important unit in Chinese society. The Chinese father was the source of all family authority. He arranged his children's and his grandchildren's marriages, decided how much education his sons would receive, and even chose his sons' careers. Women were subordinate to men and had no property rights of their own.

The most important works of Chinese literature and the basis for all Chinese education were the Five Classics. Two of the Five Classics were used in civil service examinations: the *Classic of Songs,* containing more than 300 songs about love, joy, politics, and domestic life; and the *Classic of Documents,* containing semihistorical speeches and documents about government.

As early as 444 B.C., Chinese astronomers had computed the year at 365 1/4 days. During the Han dynasty these calculations were refined even further. Sometime before A.D. 100, Chinese astronomers built special instruments to observe the orbit they believed the sun followed. Using these instruments, an early astronomer estimated the number of stars at 11,520. Other achievements included the invention of a primitive seismograph that registered earthquakes so faint they were unnoticed by the royal court, and the invention of paper in A.D. 105.

SYNTHESIS REVIEW

1. **Classifying Ideas** What advances were made by the people of the earliest civilizations?
2. **Contrasting Ideas** How was Egyptian civilization different from that of the Fertile Crescent?
3. **Understanding Ideas** What were the major beliefs of Hinduism and Buddhism?
4. **Analyzing Ideas** Why did Chinese civilization develop in relative isolation?
5. **Synthesizing Ideas** What characteristics of Indian, Chinese, and Egyptian cultures made them civilizations?

Review Answers

1. People of these civilizations became the first in the world to develop advanced technical skills, such as the ability to use metals. In addition, an increase in population encouraged the growth of cities. Eventually the people of these communities developed calendars to predict when crops should be planted and harvested. They later developed governments.

2. Egypt developed a single, stable society, while invaders crisscrossed the Fertile Crescent.

3. Hindus believed that the world known to our senses is an illusion called Maya, which betrays people, giving them sorrow and pain. People can be delivered from their suffering if they can identify Maya, but this requires lifetimes of experience acquired through the process of reincarnation. Ultimately people hope to escape this cycle and be reunited with the soul of Brahma. Buddhists believed that salvation came from following the guidelines for conduct embodied in the Four Noble Truths and the Eightfold Path.

4. Great distances, the towering mountains of central Asia, and such formidable deserts as the Gobi made China almost inaccessible.

5. All three had agriculture, cities, calendars, and writing.

Introducing the Unit

Ask students to study the map on page 102. Point out that the map shows the major geographic features of the Mediterranean Region and that they will be studying early developments in this region in Unit Two. Ask for volunteers to locate the sites of Rome and Athens on the map. Then point out that Unit Two will deal with these two civilizations as well as others that developed in the Mediterranean Region.

UNIT TWO

Civilizations of the Mediterranean World

A panoramic Roman mosaic of the Nile

Unit Goals

After studying Unit Two, students will be able to:

1. Trace the development and achievements of ancient Greek civilization.
2. List the four primary physical characteristics of Greek city-states.
3. Describe how Athens evolved into a democracy.
4. Compare Sparta, Athens, and Rome.
5. Evaluate the Greek achievements of the Golden Age.
6. Analyze the achievements of Alexander the Great and of the Hellenistic Age.
7. Summarize the evolution of Roman government as it changed from a republic to an empire.
8. Evaluate how Greek and Roman civilization continues to influence us today.
9. Assess the reasons for Rome's decline.

CHAPTER (pages 100–123)

5 Greek City-states Developed in the Mediterranean Region

(2000 B.C.–404 B.C.)

CHAPTER OVERVIEW

In Greece and Asia Minor and on nearby islands, the Greeks created one of the world's greatest civilizations. Western civilization is largely based on the Greek experience in government, philosophy, and other fields.

The earliest civilization of the region began on the island of Crete. The mainland Mycenaeans became the dominant power.

The social and political unit of ancient Greece was the *polis*, or city-state. The governments of the city-states passed through four stages: monarchy, aristocracy, tyranny, and self-government.

Sparta and Athens, the two most important city-states, developed quite different ways of life. Sparta became a highly militaristic state. Athens developed into a democracy, although the majority of its people could not take part in politics. Between 492 B.C. and 479 B.C., the Persians made several attempts to conquer the Greek mainland. The Greeks were able to thwart these invasions, thus preserving their independence.

After the Persian defeat, Athens led an alliance of Greek city-states. However, Athens' imperial ambitions led to a prolonged and disastrous conflict with Sparta in the Peloponnesian War.

SUGGESTED LESSON PLAN

Day	Objectives	Suggested Activities	Materials
1	U1-2,* C1-3	Introducing the Unit (page 98) Introducing the Chapter (page 100) Section 1 (pages 101-06), Focus/Motivation (page 101), Presentation (page 102), Closure (page 106), Suggested Teaching Strategies, Enrichment Activity, Daily Quiz, Suggested Assignments (page 99B)	ATE, Pupil's Edition, Teacher's Resource-Bank™
2	U3, C4-7	Section 2 (pages 106-11), Focus/Motivation (page 107), Presentation (page 108), Closure (page 110), Suggested Teaching Strategies, Enrichment Activity, Daily Quiz, Suggested Assignments (page 99C)	ATE, Pupil's Edition, Teacher's Resource-Bank™

*C refers to applicable Chapter Objective, U refers to applicable Unit Goal

SUGGESTED LESSON PLAN

Day	Objectives	Suggested Activities	Materials
3	U3-4, C5-9	Section 3 (pages 111-15), Focus/Motivation (page 111), Presentation (page 111), Closure (page 114), Suggested Teaching Strategies, Enrichment Activity, Daily Quiz, Suggested Assignments (page 99D)	ATE, Pupil's Edition, Teacher's Resource-Bank™
4	U4, C10	Section 4 (pages 115-17), Focus/Motivation (page 115), Presentation (page 116), Closure (page 116), Suggested Teaching Strategies, Enrichment Activities, Daily Quiz, Suggested Assignments (page 99E)	ATE, Pupil's Edition, Teacher's Resource-Bank™
5	U4, C11-14	Section 5 (pages 117-21), Focus/Motivation (page 117), Presentation (page 118), Closure (page 120), Suggested Teaching Strategies, Enrichment Activity, Daily Quiz, Suggested Assignments (page 99E)	ATE, Pupil's Edition, Teacher's Resource-Bank™
6	U1-5 C1-14	Chapter 5 Form A Test, Reteaching Worksheet, Chapter 5 Form B Test	Teacher's Resource-Bank™ or Workbook and Test Booklet

BOOKS FOR THE TEACHER

Durant, Will. *The Life of Greece.* Simon and Schuster. Touches on most aspects of Greek history.

Edey, Maitland. *Lost World of the Aegean.* Time-Life. Provides an informative account of Minoan and Mycenaean society.

Ferguson, John. *The Heritage of Hellenism.* Neale Watson. Gives a short cultural history of the Hellenistic Period.

Flaceliere, Robert. *Daily Life in Greece at the Time of Pericles.* Macmillan. Portrays Greek life during the Golden Age.

Frost, Frank J. *Greek Society.* D. C. Heath. Analyzes the social history of Greece.

Green, Peter. *Armada from Athens.* Doubleday. Details the Athenian defeat in Sicily during the Peloponnesian War.

Hamilton, Edith. *The Greek Way.* Norton. Summarizes the achievements of Greek culture.

Hignett, Charles. *Xerxes' Invasion of Greece.* Oxford University Press. Gives a scholarly account of the Persian Wars.

BOOKS FOR THE STUDENT

Asimov, Isaac. *The Greeks: A Great Adventure.* Houghton Mifflin. Analyzes the history of Greece in a readable style.

Connolly, Peter. *The Greek Armies.* Silver Burdett. Details armor, tactics, formations, and numerous other military topics.

Cottrell, Leonard. *The Bull of Minos.* Grosset and Dunlop. Examines the archaeological discoveries at Troy, Mycenae, and Crete.

Robinson, Charles A. *Ancient Crete and Mycenae.* Franklin Watts. Provides pictures of archaeological digs and floor plans of ancient buildings in an illustrated and easily readable text.

Warner, Rex. *Athens at War.* Dutton. Retells Thucydides' account of the Peloponnesian War.

MULTIMEDIA MATERIALS

The Aegean Age (mp, 14 min.), Coronet. Studies the advances made by the Minoans and the Mycenaeans in architecture, engineering, commerce, and the arts.

Greek Civilization (2 fs), Educational Audio-Visual. Part 1 considers the political and social life of ancient Greece. Part 2 examines Greek art and architecture.

Odyssey: Return of Odysseus (mp, 26 min.), EBE. Dramatizes Odysseus's return from Ithaca.

Section (pages 101–106)

1 Early Greeks Settled in City-states

SECTION OVERVIEW

Neolithic culture developed before 3000 B.C. on Crete and the Aegean islands. The Minoan civilization on Crete flourished between 2000 B.C. and 1400 B.C. During this time invaders from the north entered the Greek mainland. The Mycenaeans, a warlike people, swept through the entire Greek mainland and conquered Crete. After the collapse of Mycenaean society, a more barbaric people, the Dorians, occupied the Peloponnesus and Crete. Influenced by geography, the early Greeks lived in an organization that is called the polis, or city-state.

SUGGESTED TEACHING STRATEGIES

1. **Preteaching Vocabulary (Basic)** You may wish to preteach the following important vocabulary terms: Western civilization *(page 101)*; fresco *(page 104)*; polis, chora *(page 105)*; acropolis, agora *(page 106)*. Ask students to look up the definition of polis on page 105. Explain that our word *metropolis* is based on the Greek word *polis.*
2. **Understanding Maps (Basic)** Have students examine the map of Greece on page 102 and explain the statement in the text: "In many ways, nature did not smile kindly on the Greeks."
3. **Relating Cause and Effect (Average/Group)** Write the following statements on the chalkboard or an overhead projector and have students copy them in their notebooks. Tell students that each statement is to be considered a cause for which they must determine an effect. Ask for volunteers to read their lists.

   a. Many islands in the Aegean Sea were close together. *(This made trade and cultural exchange easier.)*
   b. Short mountain ranges divided the country. *(They prevented the development of a sense of Greek unity.)*
   c. The Greeks could not produce enough food for their own needs. *(They had to become traders.)*
   d. The long coastline brought every part of the mainland close to the sea. *(Greeks became fishers, sailors, and traders.)*

ENRICHMENT ACTIVITY

Conducting Research (Challenging) Have interested students find information on what one of the cities that evolved from the ancient Greek city-states is like today. Possible choices include Athens, Sparta, Corinth, or Mycenae. Ask for volunteers to share their findings with the class.

DAILY QUIZ

To assess student understanding of Section 1, give the class the following quiz. (Each item is worth 10 points.)

1. (T or F) The several finger-like peninsulas that extend from the Balkans into the Mediterranean and Aegean seas form the region of the early Greek settlements. *(T)*
2. (T or F) Many of those who lived on the Peloponnesus limited agricultural activities to growing grapes, olives, and grain. *(T)*
3. (T or F) The short, even coastline along the Mediterranean Sea discouraged Greeks from trading, fishing, or taking part in other seafaring activities. *(F)*
4. (T or F) Recent archaeological work indicates the Minoans developed a seafaring culture that included colonies on many Aegean islands. *(T)*
5. List Minoan accomplishments. *(Answers will vary, but will probably include the following: running water in homes of nobility; frescoes; carvings of ivory, stone, gold, silver and bronze; women's rights)*
6. About 2000 B.C., people called ______ invaded from the northern Balkans while Minoan civilization was developing. *(Mycenaeans)*
7. (T or F) Families of these northern invaders developed clans and selected clan chieftains who helped the tribal chief govern the group. They later began to develop city-states. *(T)*

8. Define *acropolis* or *agora*. *(Acropolis is the fortified hill and site of public buildings; agora is the public meeting place or marketplace.)*
9. Name one modern English word that evolved from *polis*, and define it. *(police, politics, policy)*
10. List the physical features common to Greek city-states. *(Answers will vary and should include the following: small size; small population; original polis, or hill fortress; public meeting place, or agora)*

SUGGESTED ASSIGNMENTS

1. **Applying Geography Skills (Basic)** Have students complete Geography Application Worksheet 1, "The End of an Island Civilization," in the TEACHER'S RESOURCEBANK™.
2. **Outlining (Average/Group)** Haves students prepare an outline of Section 1.

Section (pages 106–111)

2 Greek Government and Society Became More Varied

SECTION OVERVIEW

The early Greeks settled in small city-states. Between 1000 B.C. and 500 B.C., the form of government changed from monarchy to aristocracy to tyranny to self-government.

SUGGESTED TEACHING STRATEGIES

1. **Preteaching Vocabulary (Basic)** You may wish to preteach the following important vocabulary terms: epic *(page 106)*; myth *(page 108)*; import, export, aristocracy, tyrant, popular government, democracy *(page 110)*. Ask students to list the political terms from ancient Greece that are used to describe political or social systems today. *(aristocracy, democracy)*
2. **Analyzing Information (Challenging)** On the chalkboard or an overhead projector, draw a chart with the headings *Factors Encouraging Greek Unity* and *Factors Discouraging Greek Unity*. Then have students complete the chart. Completed charts should be similar to the following one.

FACTORS ENCOURAGING GREEK UNITY	FACTORS DISCOURAGING GREEK UNITY
Common language, religion, and festivals	Rugged mountains separating the valleys
Belief that all Greeks were descended from the same ancestor	Fierce spirit of independence

ENRICHMENT ACTIVITY

Writing a Report (Average/Group) A great deal has been written about Troy, Mycenae, and Crete. Have students present either oral or written reports on one of these sites. Books that describe the adventure in digging at these sites are Hans Baumann's *Lion Gate and Labyrinth* (Pantheon Books); Charles A. Robinson's *Ancient Crete and Mycenae* (Franklin Watts); and Leonard Cottrell's *The Bull of Minos* (Grosset and Dunlop). Excellent photographs and illustrations of Mycenaean and Minoan cultures can be found in *The Birth of Western Civilization* (McGraw-Hill), edited by Michael Grant; *Greece and Rome: Builders of Our World* (National Geographic Society); and Maitland Edey's *Lost World of the Aegean* (Time-Life). These books can be used as visual aids in an oral report on religion, burial tombs, social life, art, or architecture.

DAILY QUIZ

To assess student understanding of Section 2, give the class the following quiz. (Each item is worth 10 points.)

1. ________ was the blind poet who wrote the *Iliad* and the *Odyssey*. *(Homer)*
2. What epic described Odysseus' 10-year journey home after his trickery with the wooden horse at Troy? *(Odyssey)*
3. Why did the Greeks develop myths? *(The Greeks developed myths to explain events in everyday life.)*
4. ________ was the god of the sky, king of the gods, and the father of some humans. *(Zeus)*
5. ________ was the daughter of Zeus, the goddess of wisdom, womanly virtue, and technical skill. *(Athena)*
6. ________ was the goddess of love and beauty. *(Aphrodite)*
7. Describe the events of the Olympic Games. *(footraces, jumping, javelin and discus throwing, boxing, wrestling, and horse and chariot racing)*
8. Compare the Greek system of monarchy, aristocracy, tyranny, and democracy. *(Monarchy is a government by a royal family—in ancient Greece, a king. The aristocracy was comprised of the nobility, or landowning class, that ruled the city-state. The tyrant seized power, gaining popular support by promising to defend the poor from the aristocracy. In Greek democracy, the council of citizens helped form laws and limited the power of rulers.)*
9. List the factors that provided the impetus for Greek unification. *(Answers will vary. Students should include some of the following: common language; common origins; common religion; cooperative supervision of certain temples; occasional participation in various religious practices.)*
10. Describe the factors that kept the Greeks from unifying their city-states into nations. *(Geography; rivalries between city-states; separate legal systems; independent city-state calendars, money, or weights and measures.)*

SUGGESTED ASSIGNMENTS

1. **Understanding Research (Average/Group)** Have students work individually or in small groups to do additional research on

Greek religion. Students can write reports on some aspect of Greek religion, such as the oracle of Delphi, or make charts listing the gods and goddesses. More ambitious projects might include the construction of a miniature temple. Students should share their projects with the class.

2. **Comparing Past and Present (Average/Group)** Have students prepare reports comparing the Olympic games of the ancient Greeks with today's Olympics. What were the origins of the ancient games? Which sports were included? Which sports are included today? Who could participate in the ancient games? Who participates today? Which traditions are still performed? For information on the Greek games, students can use C. M. Bowra's *Classical Greece* (Time-Life). Students should consult the *Readers' Guide to Periodical Literature* for some articles on recent Olympics.

Section (pages 111–115)

3 Sparta and Athens Developed Different Ways of Life

SECTION OVERVIEW

Sparta developed into a militaristic state. Athens developed a democratic form of government. Although more than half the population was denied citizenship, those who participated enjoyed the full benefits of democracy.

SUGGESTED TEACHING STRATEGIES

1. **Preteaching Vocabulary (Basic)** You may wish to preteach the following important vocabulary terms: helot *(page 111)*; ephor *(page 112)*; metic, archon *(page 114)*; direct democracy, representative democracy *(page 115)*. Ask students to name other forms of government they have studied so far in this chapter *(aristocracy, tyranny)*.
2. **Organizing a Discussion (Average/Group)** The following quotation from the writings of Xenophon could serve as the basis for discussion. Explain to students that Lycurgus was the legendary lawgiver of Sparta.

   "In Sparta nothing was left without regulation, but with all the necessary acts of life Lycurgus mingled some ceremony which might enkindle virtue or discourage vice . . . . He would not allow citizens to leave the country at pleasure to wander in foreign lands, where they would contact strange habits and learn to imitate the untrained lives and ill-regulated institutions to be found abroad. Also, he banished . . . all strangers who were there for no useful purpose . . . . Strangers introduce strange ideas, and these could lead to subversive discussions and political views which would jar with the established constitution . . . . Therefore he thought it was more important to keep bad habits from entering the city than it was to keep out the plague."

   Ask students the following questions: What advantages can be gained from a system like this one? What are the disadvantages? *(Accept all reasonable answers. The system produced obedient citizens and good warriors, but personal initiative and the arts suffered.)* Do you agree or disagree with the statement, "It was more important to keep bad habits from entering the city than it was to keep out the plague"? *(Accept all reasonable answers.)*

*3. **Reading About History: Making Comparisons (Basic)** Ask students to reread "Building History Study Skills" on page 113. Then have them locate information to help them prepare a comparison of life in the United States today with life in the Soviet Union.

ENRICHMENT ACTIVITY

Dramatizing History (Challenging) Some students might enjoy preparing a class play in which representatives from Persia, Egypt, Assyria, Babylonia, and Greece discuss the merits of their particular civilizations.

DAILY QUIZ

To assess student understanding of Section 3, give the class the following quiz. (Each item is worth 10 points.)

1. When the ______ conquered Sparta, they forced the local inhabitants to serve as agricultural laborers. *(Dorians)*
2. List the three Spartan social groups. *(Spartans/Dorians/citizens; "neighbors"; helots)*
3. The Spartans frequently killed any ______ who might show signs of defiance or rebellion. *(helot)*
4. The ______, selected by the Spartan Assembly for one-year terms, possessed unlimited political power, and regulated Spartan contacts with foreigners. *(ephors)*
5. (T or F) Spartans trained their young males in the virtues of courage, strength, endurance, and cunning to develop an elite military force. *(T)*
6. (T or F) Many Athenians became traders, sailors, or merchants because of their city-state's poor soil. *(T)*
7. Which of these was *not* an Athenian social class? citizens, solons, metics, slaves *(solons)*
8. (T or F) In Athens, Draco, Solon, and Pisistratus served as archons who gradually prepared Athenians for Cleisthenes' democratic reforms. *(T)*
9. List two of the three qualifications which an Athenian had to fulfill to qualify as a member of the Council of 500. *(male; citizen; 30 years or older)*
10. Define direct democracy. *(government in which all citizens participate directly in making decisions)*

SUGGESTED ASSIGNMENTS

1. **Writing a Diary (Average/Group)** Have students write a diary entry for one day in the life of a Spartan boy or girl. Call upon

volunteers to read their entries to the class. Use the entries as the basis of a class discussion.

2. **Writing Editorials (Challenging)** Have students write editorials defending the militaristic life of Sparta. They should discuss the threat of the helots, training of boys and girls, absence of luxury, and avoidance of travel. Have other students write letters disagreeing with the editorials.
3. **Skill Worksheet (Basic)** Have students complete Skill Worksheet 5 in the TEACHER'S RESOURCEBANK™.

Section (pages 115–117)

4 Daily Life in Athens Combined Recreation and Public Duties

SECTION OVERVIEW

More than half the citizens of Athens were farmers. Manufacturing was carried on in small shops and was of an extraordinarily high quality. Athenians valued simple homes, strong family life, and education that would produce a sound mind in a sound body. Most boys received an elementary education, studying grammar, music, and gymnastics. Higher education was conducted by Sophists. Women had few legal rights and were expected to do little more than bear and rear children.

SUGGESTED TEACHING STRATEGIES

1. **Preteaching Vocabulary (Basic)** You may wish to preteach the following important vocabulary terms: terracing (*page 115*); pedagogue (*page 116*); rhetoric (*page 117*). Ask students to name one crop often associated with terracing (*rice, especially in Southeast Asia*).
2. **Comparing Past and Present (Average/Group)** Ask students to compare Greek architecture with contemporary American architecture. Then begin a class discussion with the following questions: Are our public buildings beautiful? Do we stress beauty in our private homes or city apartment houses? Do Americans consider architectural design important?

ENRICHMENT ACTIVITIES

1. **Researching Ideas (Challenging)** Students may do oral or written reports on some aspect of Athenian life. Possible topics include occupations, marriage, slavery, dress, living quarters, food, or entertainment. A student might prepare a floor plan of a Greek house or public building. Some available sources are Jonathan Rutland's *An Ancient Greek Town* (Warwick Press); Frank J. Frost's *Greek Society* (D. C. Heath); Marjorie and C. H. B. Quennell's *Everyday Life in Ancient Greece* (Putnam); and Robert Flaceliere's *Daily Life in Greece at the Time of Pericles* (Macmillan).
2. **Debating Ideas (Average/Group)** Organize the class into two groups and conduct an informal discussion on government in the major city-states of ancient Greece. One group will defend the militaristic state of Sparta. The other group will defend the democratic life of Athens.

DAILY QUIZ

To assess student understanding of Section 4, give the class the following quiz. (Each item is worth 10 points.)

1. List the Athenian agricultural products exchanged for grain. (*olives, olive oil, grapes, wine, figs*)
2. What important agricultural product did the Athenians need to import? (*grain*)
3. (T or F) Most Athenians constructed their plain, single-story homes of sun-dried brick. (*T*)
4. Athenian mothers raised both male and female children until the age of six, when they placed the small boys under the care and instruction of a slave, or ________. (*pedagogue*)
5. List the three primary subjects taught in elementary schools. (*grammar: reading, writing, arithmetic; music; gymnastics*)
6. (T or F) An Athenian boy attending elementary school studies Homeric epics, wrote on wooden tablets covered with wax, but avoided gymnastics because that type of activity was reserved for the "lower class." (*F*)
7. List the subjects taught by the Sophists. (*poetry, government, ethics, geography, astronomy, rhetoric*)
8. At what age did the Athenian male become a citizen? (*19*)
9. List two Greek terms used today in discussions about government. (*politics, democracy, aristocracy, monarchy, tyranny*)
10. During this period, what language became the Mediterranean region's language of commerce, trade, and education? (*Greek*)

SUGGESTED ASSIGNMENTS

1. **Building Vocabulary (Basic)** Have students prepare a list of political terms that they have learned in Sections 1 through 4.
2. **Writing a Diary (Average/Group)** Have students write a diary entry for one day in the life of an Athenian boy or girl. Ask volunteers to read their entries to the class. Then have students compare these entries to the diary entries for Spartan children that they prepared for Section 3.

Section (pages 117–121)

5 Greek Civilization Defended Itself and Expanded

Greece and Persia clashed over colonies in Asia Minor, and the Persians decided to invade Greece itself. However, the Greeks were able to stop the Persian advances and thus preserve their independence. Although badly damaged in the war, Athens was still the most powerful Greek city-state. Determined to unify Greece, Athens formed the Delian League and soon gained complete control of it. With Pericles as leader, Athens achieved great power.

SUGGESTED TEACHING STRATEGIES

1. **Practicing Map Skills (Basic)** Distribute outline maps of Greece and Asia Minor to the class. Have students complete the maps according the following instructions: **(a)** Identify by different colors the Persian Empire and allied states, patriotic Greek city-states, and neutral Greek city-states. **(b)** Draw the routes of Darius' fleets and Xerxes' army and fleet. **(c)** Locate the Hellespont, Thermopylae, Plataea, Marathon, Athens, Salamis, Sparta, Delos, Thebes, Corinth, and The Peloponnesus. Students should refer to the map on page 118.
2. **Relating Cause and Effect (Average/Group)** Organize the class into several small groups. Then write the following lists on the chalkboard or an overhear projector. In each of the sets of three statements, have students identify the cause and the effects.

   a. Athens creates an empire.
   Greeks become arrogant.
   Greeks defeat the Persians. *(cause)*

   b. Athens forms Delian League.
   Persian threat continues as long as Xerxes lives. *(cause)*
   Sparta tries to unite city-states.

   c. Corinth becomes ally of Sparta.
   Athens makes alliance with nearby city-states.
   Athens wants to weaken Corinth, its commercial rival. *(cause)*

ENRICHMENT ACTIVITY

Writing a Report: Biography (Challenging) Have students prepare written or oral reports on such individuals as Pericles, Themistocles, Xerxes, Darius, King Leonidas, or Herodotus. Reports should include a discussion of the reasons the individual rose to power as well as biographical material. Students may work individually or in small groups

DAILY QUIZ

To assess student understanding of Section 5, give the class the following quiz. (Each item is worth 10 points.)

1. Which Persian ruler attempted to crush the Athenians for supporting the revolts in Asia Minor? *(Darius)*
2. Name two major battles in which the Greeks defeated the Persians. *(Marathon, Salamis, Plataea)*
3. How did Athens benefit by defeating the Persians. *(Athenian victory promoted traditions and culture and helped Athens create the Aegean Sea Empire.)*
4. What league, led and controlled by Athens, included almost 140 city-states and functioned as an alliance and Athenian colonial empire? *(Delian League)*
5. This important leader broadened Athenian democratic traditions to include poor citizens in the Assembly and ensured payment of officeholders. *(Pericles)*
6. (T or F) All Athenian males over the age of 30 participated in the Assembly. *(F)*
7. (T or F) Athenian dominance of the Delian League and commercial rivalry with Corinth and Sparta led to the Peloponnesian War. *(T)*
8. (T or F) Corinth defeated the Persian air force, Athenian navy, and Spartan army to win the first portion of the Peloponnesian War. *(F)*
9. Which city-state defeated Athens in the Peloponnesian War? *(Sparta)*
10. (T or F) After the Athenians surrendered to their conquerors in 404 B.C., the Greeks successfully created a new "league of city-states" and initiated an era of cooperation and democratic self-government. *(F)*

SUGGESTED ASSIGNMENTS

1. **Review Worksheet (Basic)** Have students complete Review Worksheet 5 in the TEACHER'S RESOURCEBANK™.
2. **Critical Thinking Worksheet (Basic)** Have students complete Critical Thinking Worksheet 11 in the TEACHER'S RESOURCEBANK™.
3. **Critical Thinking Worksheet (Average/Group)** Have students complete Critical Thinking Worksheet 12 in the TEACHER'S RESOURCEBANK™.
4. **Profile Worksheet (Average/Group)** Have students complete Profile Worksheet 5 in the TEACHER'S RESOURCEBANK™.

For suggested lesson plan, additional teaching strategies, enrichment activities, daily quizzes, and suggested assignments, see pages 99A-99F.

Introducing the Chapter
An important historical concept in the process of cultural diffusion is the migration and borrowing of cultural traits. Have students suggest contributions made by other cultures to life in the United States. To provide a framework for students' suggestions write the following categories on the chalkboard or an overhead projector: food, words, music, art, architecture, literature, theater, athletics, philosophy and religion, mathematics and science, government. Ask students to compare the way in which cultural diffusion would have taken place in the time of the ancient Greeks *(through travel and trade)* to the ways in which it can occur today *(through television and movies, for example)*.

Explain to students that as they read the chapter they will become familiar with Greek contributions in many of the categories mentioned. The epilogue in Will Durant's *The Life of Greece* (Simon and Schuster) provides an exhaustive list of Greek contributions.

Chapter Objectives
After studying Chapter 5, students will be able to:

1. Describe how the geographical characteristics of the Balkan Peninsula influenced the ancient Greeks.
2. Briefly trace the development and achievements of the Minoans and the Mycenaeans.

CHAPTER 5

Greek City-states Developed in the Mediterranean Region

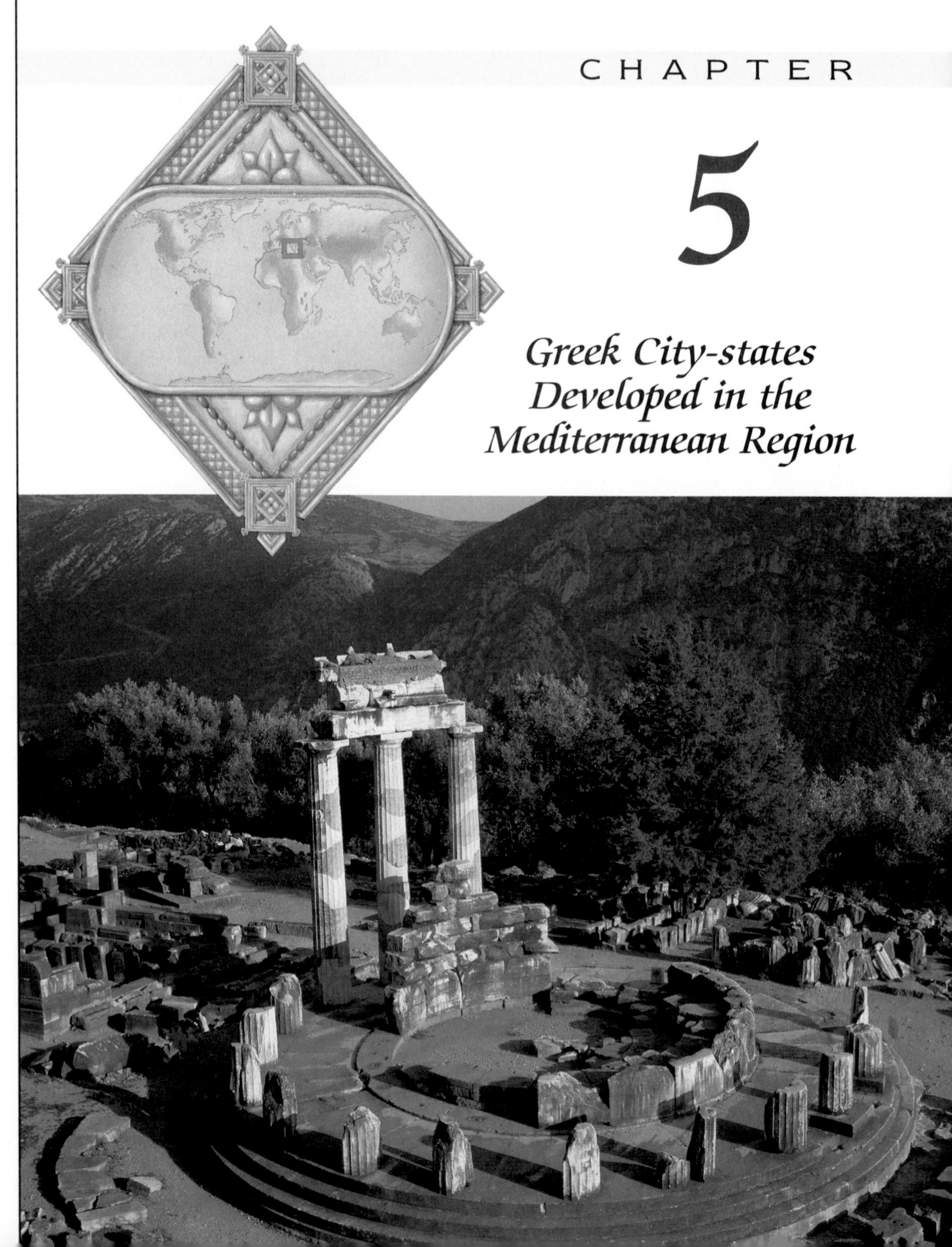

CHAPTER FOCUS

Place Greece and Asia Minor

Time

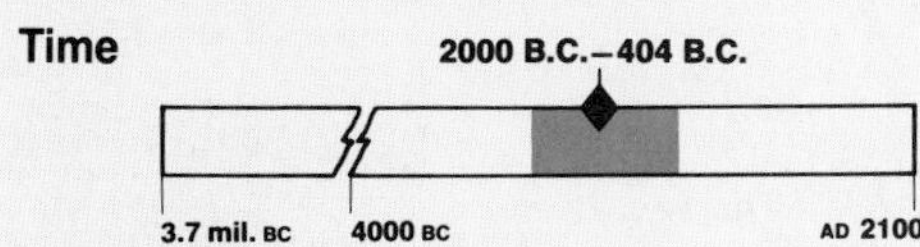

Significance

The rugged Balkan Peninsula juts crooked fingers southward from Europe into the northeastern part of the Mediterranean Sea. On the southern end of this peninsula, as well as in Asia Minor and on the nearby islands, one of the greatest civilizations the world has known–Greek civilization–developed.

At first glance it might seem puzzling that the people of this region, the ancient Greeks, created such an important civilization. A quarrelsome people, they could never agree among themselves for any length of time. Nor were they great empire-builders. We take a special interest in them, however, because much of **Western civilization**–the civilization that in later centuries evolved in Europe and spread to the Americas–had its foundations in early Greece. For example, the Greeks were the first people to experiment successfully with the idea that citizens could govern themselves, an idea that the United States and many other countries have since adopted and refined.

Terms to Define

Western civilization	popular government
polis	democracy
chora	helot
myth	metic
aristocracy	rhetoric

People to Identify

Mycenaeans	Solon
Homer	Pericles

Places to Locate

Crete	Sparta
Athens	Peloponnesus

Questions to Guide Your Reading

1 Why did early Greeks settle in city-states?
2 How did Greek government and society become more varied?
3 How did the city-states of Sparta and Athens develop differently?
4 What were the major features of daily life in Athens?
5 What challenges did Greek civilization face during the 400s B.C.?

When the world's best athletes test their skills at the Olympic Games every four years, they repeat a tradition that began thousands of years ago among the rocky hills of Greece. As historian Lionel Casson noted:

> *"One midsummer day in the year we calculate to have been 776 B.C., a 200-meter dash was run in a rural backwater in southwestern Greece, and a young local named Coroebus won it. It was an obscure event in an obscure spot but it earned him immortality: he is the first Olympic victor on record."*

Over time, the ancient Olympics became a ritual of Greek life with ceremonies honoring the winners.

> *"Winners formed a procession and marched to the Temple of Zeus [the chief Greek god]. . . . At the temple, each was handed what ancient athletes considered the most precious object in the world, the victor's olive wreath. . . .*
>
> *Winning was everything; there were no seconds or thirds, no Greek equivalents of silver or bronze medals. . . . Losers were jeered and, hiding their heads in shame, slunk away. Even their mothers treated them with scorn. 'The wreath or death' was their motto."*

The Olympic Games are only one of the many traditions we owe to the people of ancient Greece.

1 Early Greeks Settled in City-states

Geography influences history. This has certainly been true in Greece, where the location and surroundings of each city influenced its growth, development, and ultimate fate.

The Physical Setting

At the extreme northeastern end of the Mediterranean, the Aegean (i•JEE•uhn) Sea separates the Balkan Peninsula from Asia Minor. The southern tip of the Balkan Peninsula consists of many small peninsulas that form the mainland of Greece. In addition,

◀ *The Temple of Athena at Delphi*

3. List the four primary physical characteristics of city-states.
4. Define the epic literary form and briefly summarize the *Iliad* and the *Odyssey*.
5. Summarize the three traits of Greek religion.
6. Summarize the problems that led the Greeks to form a monarchy, an aristocracy, a tyranny, and a democracy.
7. Compare the factors that might have provided Greek unity with those that maintained the traditions of independent city-states.
8. Compare Spartan and Athenian educational, social, cultural, economic, and political activities and traditions.
9. Summarize the evolution of Athenian democracy during the rule of Draco, Solon, Pisistratus, and Cleisthenes.
10. Describe the importance of Athenian manufacturing and trade.
11. Summarize the causes, events, and effects of the Persian War.
12. Compare the Spartan and Athenian efforts in building empires.
13. Identify Pericles' contributions to the Athenian democratic tradition.
14. Describe the causes, events, and effects of the Peloponnesian War.

SECTION 1

Focus/Motivation
Display a topographical wall map of Greece and the Mediterranean region or ask the class to turn to the map on page 102.

1A, 1B, 1D, 3A, a1A, a4A, a4B, a4C

● Ask: Besides the Greeks, what other early peoples in the Mediterranean region turned to overseas trade for a livelihood? *(Phoenicians)*

Have students identify Greece's major geographical features: mountains, a long, irregular coastline, and some plains. Ask students the following questions: What are the advantages of a long, irregular coastline? How do you think the Greeks made a living? How might the mountains have affected the relationships among the Greek settlements? *(Answers should include the following: the coastline brings every part of the mainland close to the sea and provides many good harbors; the location of Greece in the Mediterranean is advantageous for trade, and the mountains would make communication difficult and tend to create small, politically and socially independent units.)*

Presentation
Studying Cause and Effect (Average/Group)
The Greek city-state was small in size and population. Ask students if small size and population have any impact on the role of the citizen and the laws of the state. Then ask: Does small size allow greater individual participation in government? *(Some students might suggest that the larger the state, the greater the need for laws and law enforcement. Others might say that the impact of an individual's vote diminishes as the number of votes gets larger.)*

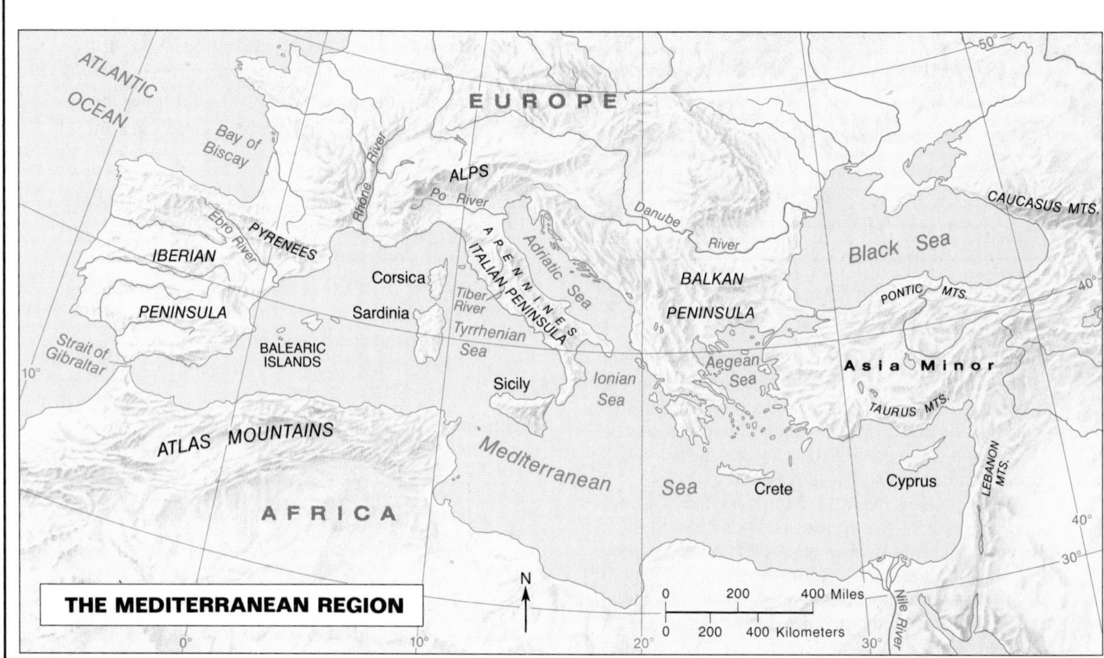

Learning from Maps *Ancient Greek civilization developed on the Balkan Peninsula. What other two peninsulas extend southward into the Mediterranean Sea?* **Italian Peninsula, Iberian Peninsula**

many small islands dot the Aegean Sea and are considered part of Greece.

In many ways nature did not smile kindly on the Greeks. Look at the map of the Mediterranean region on this page. Notice that short mountain ranges cut up the Greek mainland. These mountains separated communities and prevented them from developing a sense of unity. Also notice that Greece had no important rivers such as those along which the ancient civilizations of Egypt and Mesopotamia developed. Despite these disadvantages Greece had a mild climate, enough good soil, and sufficient rainfall to grow grain, grapes, and olives in the small valleys and in the foothills of the mountains. The foothills also provided pasture for sheep and goats. Still Greece could not produce the amount or the variety of food that its increasing population needed. Many Greeks became traders, both to improve their quality of life and to make their fortunes. The invention of coined money in the 500s B.C. also stimulated trade by making it easier to buy and sell goods.

● Greece's geography encouraged the development of trade. The long, irregular coastline allowed every part of the mainland to be close to the sea, and both the mainland and the islands had many good harbors. With the sea so much a part of their lives, the Greeks became fishers, sailors, traders, and eventually colonizers of new lands.

These early sailors and traders traveled throughout the eastern Mediterranean. From Egypt and the Fertile Crescent, people brought knowledge and ideas to the Aegean Islands, to the mainland of Greece, and to the Aegean shores of Asia Minor.

Minoan Civilization

Look again at the map on this page and locate the long, narrow island of Crete in the Aegean Sea. For centuries Greek myths told of a great and powerful civilization that had existed there before about 1500 B.C. Many scholars, however, doubted that the barren, sandy soil of the island could have supported a great civilization. Then in 1898 British archaeologist Arthur Evans discovered the ruins of a great palace with more than 800 rooms. Evans believed he had unearthed Knossos (kuh • NAHS • uhs), the palace of Minos (MY • nuhs), the legendary king of Crete. Evans named this civilization Minoan (mi • NOH • uhn) in honor of its king, who

CONNECTIONS: THEN AND NOW

Stadiums

Millions of sports fans jam stadiums each year to watch their favorite teams compete. The idea of a big "bowl" with terraced steps on which people can sit goes back nearly 3,000 years, to the time of the ancient Greeks. When the first Olympic Games were held, the events took place in a magnificent stadium built for the occasion in the city-state of Olympia. Many ancient stadiums still stand, such as the one in Tunisia (top).

The Greeks, and later the Romans, erected many of these arenas, which often were used for other entertainments. Circuses were held there, and plays were performed on a stage at one end.

Today stadiums continue to have various uses. Yankee Stadium in New York City, for example, is mainly a place to play baseball. Yet it has also held huge crowds attending a concert or seeing the pope during his visit to the United States.

Ancient stadiums were smaller than modern stadiums. One of the largest, the Colosseum in Rome, could hold perhaps 40,000 people. Modern stadiums have room for many more. For example, the soccer stadium in Rio de Janeiro, Brazil, can hold 200,000 people, and one in Prague, Czechoslovakia, has a capacity of 240,000.

In the United States, the football stadium in Los Angeles, California (center), has room for 100,000, and the Astrodome (bottom), the indoor stadium in Houston, Texas, can hold 60,000. Putting a roof over a stadium is a modern innovation. It solves the one problem that makes scheduling events in the open air so difficult: bad weather.

The appeal of sports thus goes back thousands of years. So, too, does the need to provide a place where a large number of people can watch an event at the same time. The stadium remains the best way of meeting that need.

103

allegedly protected a giant creature—half human and half bull—called the *Minotaur.*

Since Evans's discovery, other archaeologists have unearthed artifacts showing that a great civilization did indeed flourish on the island. Although the Minoans developed writing, scholars have not been able to decipher all of the script. As a result, much of what we believe about this civilization is theory.

Evidence indicates that Minoan civilization reached its height between 2000 B.C. and 1400 B.C. Although the great civilizations of nearby Egypt and the Fertile Crescent influenced Minoan civilization, the Minoans added ideas of their own. Ruins excavated in Knossos show that the royal palace and the homes of the nobles had running water and walls decorated with colorful **frescoes**—paintings made on wet plaster walls. Minoan artisans made beautiful, delicately carved figures from ivory, stone, gold, silver, and bronze. These artifacts show the Minoans as a cheerful people who enjoyed festivals, who worshiped the bull and an earth goddess, and who accorded women many rights.

Since the soil of Crete was unsuitable for growing many kinds of crops, the Minoans turned to the sea for their livelihood. They controlled the Aegean Islands and probably founded colonies both there and in Asia Minor. Excellent sailors, they built ships powered by both oars and sails. The Minoans also traded widely, bringing much of the art and civilization of Egypt and the Fertile Crescent back to Crete. The kings of Crete had so much confidence in the strength of their navy that they did not bother to fortify their cities. They overlooked the forces of nature, however.

About 1500 B.C. a volcanic explosion on a nearby island sent giant tidal waves crashing across Crete, causing great destruction and loss of life. Soon after, warriors from Greece conquered the weakened civilization. The glory of the Minoans was soon forgotten, but through trade they had influenced the peoples of mainland Greece.

Early Migrations into Greece

At the same time that the Minoan civilization developed, important changes took place on the Greek mainland. Beginning about 2000 B.C., new people entered Greece from the north. They spoke an Indo-European language that was an early form of Greek.

Learning from Pictures *The dangerous ritual of leaping over bulls was popular among young Minoans. How was the bull perceived in Minoan society?* **Minoans worshiped the bull.**

● Ask: What other civilization you read about earlier in this chapter perished through natural disaster? *(Minoan civilization on Crete)* How do historians believe this happened? *(volcanic explosion that created a tidal wave)*

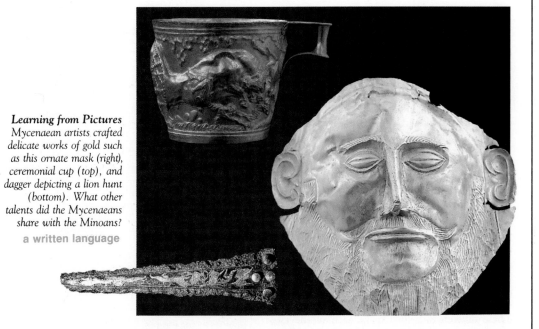

Learning from Pictures *Mycenaean artists crafted delicate works of gold such as this ornate mask (right), ceremonial cup (top), and dagger depicting a lion hunt (bottom). What other talents did the Mycenaeans share with the Minoans?*
a written language

The invaders were organized into clans and tribes. Several related families formed a clan headed by a chief. A number of clans made up a tribe, which had its own chief. The clan chiefs formed a council to help in governing. In Greece these wandering people learned how to grow grain, grapes, and olives. They also learned how to sail and often became pirates.

The Mycenaeans (my • suh • NEE • uhnz)* dominated the Greek mainland from about 1600 B.C. to 1200 B.C. They built fortified cities in the Peloponnesus (pel • uh • puh • NEE • suhs), the southern part of Greece. These included Mycenae (my • SEE • nee), Tiryns, and Pylos (see map, page 106). A warlike people who carried out raids throughout the eastern Mediterranean, the Mycenaeans conquered Crete and, in turn, adopted many elements of Minoan civilization.

Like the Minoans, the Mycenaeans had a written language. However, only a few of their documents have survived. Continual warfare probably weakened the Mycenaeans. By 1200 B.C. most of their major cities, including Mycenae, had been destroyed. According to tradition, the destruction of the city of Troy in Asia Minor also took place about this time. Perhaps these cities perished in the general upheaval caused by other migrating tribes, the legendary Sea Peoples. ●

After the collapse of Mycenaean society about 1200 B.C., more-primitive Greeks—the Dorians—moved into the fertile areas of the Peloponnesus, Crete, and southwestern Asia Minor. The newcomers were illiterate, and knowledge of writing disappeared when the Mycenaeans fell. A dark age descended on Greece until Phoenician traders introduced an alphabet about 750 B.C.

The City-states of Greece

Influenced by the geography of Greece and their own tribal organization, the early Greeks established city-states, such as Athens and Sparta (see map, page 110), in the 800s B.C. and 700s B.C. The Greek word for city-state—**polis**—originally meant a fort, a refuge in time of danger. As a village or city grew up around the fort, *polis* came to mean not only the fort but also the city, its surrounding region including the **chora,** or land outside the city walls, and the government. Our words *police, politics,* and *policy* all come from the Greek word *polis.*

*The Mycenaeans were part of the Achaean (uh • KEE • uhn) tribe. We call them Mycenaeans after Mycenae (my • SEE • nee), one of their principal cities.

105

1A, 1B, 1C, 1D, 3A, a1A, a1B, a4A, a4B, a4C, a4F, a4H, a4L

SECTION 1

Closure

Ask students how they think the polis of Greece served as a model to political writers and influenced later peoples such as the Romans. Tell students as they read the chapter that they should look for reasons why the polis failed politically.

Review Answers

1. ***Western civilization:*** the civilization that in later centuries evolved in Europe and spread to the Americas; ***polis:*** city-state, originally meant a fort, a refuge in time of danger; ***chora:*** land outside the city walls; ***acropolis:*** a hill or mountain on which stood the fort and public buildings of the polis; ***agora:*** a public meeting place
2. ***Mycenaeans:*** dominated the Greek mainland from about 1600 B.C. to 1200 B.C., built fortified cities in the Peloponnesus; ***Dorians:*** moved into the Peloponnesus, Crete, and southwestern Asia Minor after the Mycenaeans fell
3. ***Balkan Peninsula:*** rugged land in southeastern Europe; ***Aegean Sea:*** body of water separating Greece from Asia Minor; ***Crete:*** long, narrow island in the Aegean Sea, home of the Minoans; ***Mycenae:*** fortified city on the Peloponnesus; ***Troy:*** Greek city in Asia Minor; ***Athens:*** city-state in Greece; ***Sparta:*** largest city-state in Greece
4. Mild climate, good soil, and adequate rain provided

All Greek city-states shared certain physical features: (1) *Small size.* Athens at its greatest extent was smaller than Rhode Island. Sparta, the largest city-state, was only three-fourths the size of Connecticut. (2) *Small population.* The Greeks considered the ideal city-state population to be 5,000 to 10,000 citizens, not including slaves and other noncitizens. Only adult males had all the rights of citizenship because the Greeks did not count women or children. A few city-states had populations of more than 10,000 citizens, but most had fewer. One exception was Athens, which at its height had approximately 40,000 citizens. (3) *The original polis.* In most city-states the fort stood on an **acropolis** (uh•CRAHP•uh•luhs), a hill or mountain, together with temples and other public buildings. (4) *A public meeting place,* or **agora** (AG•uh•ruh), where all citizens could gather. In almost all city-states the agora was the city marketplace.

Although physically similar, the Greek city-states developed different forms of government. These differences helped make each of the city-states unique as they developed between 1000 B.C. and 500 B.C.

SECTION 1 REVIEW

1. **Define** Western civilization, polis, chora, acropolis, agora
2. **Identify** Mycenaeans, Dorians
3. **Locate** Balkan Peninsula, Aegean Sea, Crete, Mycenae, Troy, Athens, Sparta
4. **Interpreting Ideas** How did geography influence the way of life of the early Greeks?
5. **Summarizing Ideas** What were the accomplishments of Minoan civilization?
6. **Comparing Ideas** **(a)** What four things did all Greek city-states have in common? **(b)** How do these characteristics compare to those of modern cities in the United States?

2 Greek Government and Society Became More Varied

Between about 1000 B.C. and 700 B.C., chiefs ruled the tribal systems of Greece. Later, as the independent Greek city-states emerged, a variety of governments developed throughout Greece.

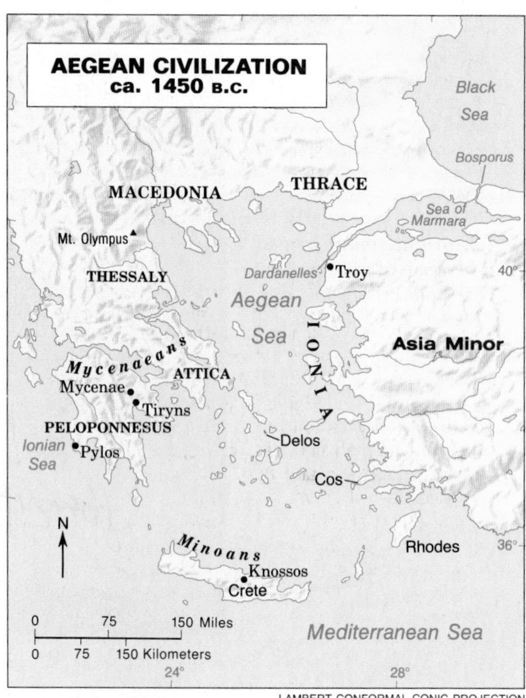

Learning from Maps *Mycenae was the center of Aegean civilization. What other fortified cities did the Mycenaeans build?* **Tiryns, Pylos**

The Age of Kings

Little is known about Greek civilization between 1000 B.C. and 700 B.C. We do know that the city-states had similar forms of government based on the tribal systems introduced during the early migrations. These tribal systems gradually developed into small kingdoms, or monarchies, during a period often called the *Age of Kings.* The city-states constantly waged war among themselves, and as a result little trade took place.

The Greeks of this period did not have a very advanced civilization. Few people could write. Most communication was oral, with poets wandering from village to village, singing or reciting folk songs, ballads, and **epics**—long poems describing heroes and great events.

Sometime during the 700s B.C., much of this oral poetry was gathered together and woven into two great epics—the *Iliad* (IL•ee•uhd) and the *Odyssey* (AHD•uh•see). According to tradition the blind poet Homer composed them. Scholars

History Through the Arts

LITERATURE

The *Odyssey*

Homer's *Odyssey* details the many adventures of Odysseus and his crew as they made their way home from the Trojan Wars. In one adventure they landed on the island of the Cyclopes, legendary one-eyed giants known for their cruelty. A Cyclops named Polyphemus (pahl • uh • FEE • muhs) captured Odysseus and part of his crew and viciously devoured some of the men. Through a clever trick, however, Odysseus saved the remaining crew members.

" Three bowls I brought him, and he poured them down.
I saw the fuddle and flush come over him, then I
sang out in cordial tones:
'Cyclops,
you ask my honorable name? Remember
the gift you promised me, and I shall tell you.
My name is Nohbdy: mother, father, and friends,
everyone calls me Nohbdy,'
And he said:
'Nohbdy's my meat, then, after I eat his friends.
Others come first. There's a noble gift, now.'

Even as he spoke, he reeled and tumbled backward,
his great head lolling to one side; and sleep
took him like any creature. Drunk, hiccuping,
he dribbled streams of liquor and bits of men.

Now, by the gods, I drove my big hand spike
deep in the embers, charring it again,
and cheered my men along with battle talk
to keep their courage up: no quitting now.
The pike of olive, green though it had been,
reddened and glowed as if about to catch.
I drew it from the coals and my four fellows
gave me a hand, lugging it near the Cyclops
as more than natural force nerved them; straight
forward they sprinted, lifted it, and rammed it deep
in his crater eye, and I leaned on it
turning it as a shipwright turns a drill
in planking, having men below to swing
the two-handled strap that spins it in the groove.
So with our brand we bored that great eye socket
while blood ran out around the red-hot bar.
Eyelid and lash were seared; the pierced ball
hissed broiling, and the roots popped. . . .
The Cyclops bellowed and the rock roared round him,
and we fell back in fear. Clawing his face
he tugged the bloody spike out of his eye,
threw it away, and his wild hands went groping;
then he set up a howl for Cyclopes
who lived in caves on windy peaks nearby.
Some heard him; and they came by divers ways
to clump around outside and call:
'What ails you,
Polyphemus? Why do you cry so sore
in the starry night? You will not let us sleep.
Sure no man's driving off your flock? No man
has tricked you, ruined you?'
Out of the cave
the mammoth Polyphemus roared in answer:

'Nohbdy, Nohbdy's tricked me, Nohbdy's ruined me!'

To this rough shout they made a sage reply:

'Ah well, if nobody has played you foul
there in your lonely bed, we are not use in pain
given by great Zeus. Let it be your father,
Poseidon Lord, to whom you pray.'
So saying
they trailed away. And I was filled with laughter
to see how like a charm
the name deceived them. . . . "

good conditions for herding and some agriculture, although Greece could not produce enough food for its growing population. Because every part of the Greek mainland was close to the sea, the Greeks became fishers, sailors, traders, and colonizers. Greece's Mediterranean location facilitated the exchange of knowledge and ideas.

5. Minoan civilization had running water and frescoes in the royal palace and homes of Minoan nobles. Artisans made carved objects of ivory, stone, gold, silver, and bronze. The Minoans were excellent sailors, who built ships powered by both oars and sails. Minoan traders brought the art and civilization of Egypt and the Fertile Crescent to Crete.

6. (a) small size; small population; the original polis, usually a fort, on an acropolis; and public meeting place; **(b)** Answers will vary. Students might include central business district, shopping districts or malls, government buildings.

SECTION 2

Focus/Motivation

Many students are fascinated by the story of the Trojan War. (You might choose to read a selection from the *Iliad* to the class.) Ask students what reason the Greeks gave for starting the war. *(The mythological reason is that Paris, the son of the king of Troy, stole Helen from the king of*

3A, a1A, a1B

● Critical thinking activity: Have students compare Greek religious beliefs with those of the Hebrews (see Chapter 2, Section 5).

■ The Romans adopted the Greek gods and goddesses but gave them different names. Have interested students make a comparative study of the Greek and Roman dieties.

Sparta. The real issue was probably control of the Hellespont and the Black Sea area.) Ask the students to relate the story of the Trojan Horse. Inform the class that Troy was destroyed and rebuilt at least nine times on the same site. A chart of the nine cities can be found in *Greece and Rome: Builders of Our World* (National Geographic Society). The same book contains an article, "The World of Odysseus," summarizing the Trojan War.

Presentation Comparing Ideas (Average/Group)

Draw on the chalkboard or an overhead projector a chart with four vertical columns. Place one of the following titles at the head of each column: *Egyptians, Persians, Hebrews,* and *Greeks.* Next make four horizontal columns on the left-hand side of the chart. Label the columns: *moral beliefs, belief in the after-life, belief in God or gods, religious practices.* Have the students fill in the columns by reviewing the textbook pages 26-27, 37, and 42-45 in Chapter 2. After listing these characteristics, conduct a class discussion on the similarities and differences among these people.

often refer to this period as the *Homeric Age* because of Homer's magnificent description of it.

The Trojan* War provided a backdrop for the Homeric epics. Legends told how Paris, a Trojan prince, stole Helen, the beautiful wife of a Mycenaean king. The Mycenaeans then sent a great sea expedition against Troy. After years of fighting, Troy was defeated by a clever trick. The Mycenaeans built a giant wooden horse outside Troy's walls. Then, after secretly filling the horse with soldiers, they broke camp and left. Thinking the Mycenaeans had given up the fight, the unsuspecting Trojans dragged the horse into the city as a trophy. But when night fell, the soldiers inside the horse burst out and threw open the city gates. The rest of the Mycenaean forces poured into Troy and destroyed it.

The *Iliad* describes incidents in the tenth year of the Trojan War. The *Odyssey* relates the many adventures of the Mycenaean hero Odysseus on his long journey home from the war. According to legend several gods, angered by Odysseus' trickery, condemned him to wander for 10 years before finally arriving home.

The *Iliad* and the *Odyssey* supposedly describe the Mycenaeans of the 1200s B.C. But they actually provide our best and richest source of information about the life, customs, and ideals of the Greeks between 1000 B.C. and 700 B.C.

Religious and moral beliefs. The religion that developed among the Greeks during the Homeric Age differed greatly from the religions of the Egyptians, Persians, and Hebrews. The Greeks asked three things of their religion: (1) an explanation for such mysteries of the physical world as thunder, lightning, and the change of the seasons; (2) an explanation of the passions that could make people lose the self-control that the Greeks considered necessary; and (3) a way to gain such benefits as long life, good fortune, and abundant harvests.

● Greek religion did not focus on morality. The Greeks did not expect their religion to save them from sin, to bring them any spiritual blessings, or to ensure a life after death. Their religion contained no commandments.

Greeks of the Homeric Age were not as concerned, for example, as the Egyptians were about what happened to them after death. Often they cremated, or burned, their dead with only a simple ritual. They thought that with few exceptions the spirits of all people went to a gray and gloomy place—the underworld—ruled by the god Hades (HAY • deez). The "house of Hades" was not a place of punishment except for extremely evil people.

The Greek gods. The Egyptians worshiped the sun and the moon, attributed both human and animal characteristics to many of their gods, and believed their pharaoh represented these gods. In contrast the Greeks attributed human qualities and personal characteristics to all of their gods and goddesses.

The Greeks thought of gods as having weaknesses and wants much like their own but on a larger scale. Greek gods lived not in some remote heaven but on the top of Mount Olympus, a peak in northern Greece (see map, page 106).

To explain their world, the Greeks developed **myths**—traditional stories about the deeds and misdeeds of gods, goddesses, and heroes. The Greeks ■ believed in many gods and goddesses, all more or less equal to one another. Zeus (ZOOS), god of the sky, was the king of the gods and the father of some humans. Hera, his sister and wife, protected women and marriage. Poseidon (poh • SY • duhn), brother of Zeus, was god of the sea—a particularly important god to the seafaring Greeks. Hades ruled the underworld.

Athena, daughter of Zeus, was the goddess of wisdom, womanly virtue, and technical skill—the special protector of the great city-states, especially Athens, which was named in her honor. Aphrodite (af • ruh • DYT • ee), another daughter, reigned as goddess of love and beauty. Apollo was god of light, music, and poetry, as well as the symbol of manly beauty. Dionysus (dy • uh • NY • suhs) was the god of fertility and wine.

Religious practices. At special sanctuaries called *oracles,* the Greeks believed that the gods spoke through priests or priestesses, usually in answer to questions about the future. The most famous oracle was that of Apollo at Delphi in the rugged mountains north of the Gulf of Corinth (see map, page 110).

Because displays of strength and courage supposedly pleased the gods, the Greeks held athletic

*For centuries scholars believed Homer's epics were mere legend. Then in 1870 the German archaeologist Heinrich Schliemann unearthed the ruins of a city in Asia Minor that scholars determined was Troy. Schliemann later discovered the ruins of Mycenae, Troy's chief enemy.

History Through the Arts

SCULPTURE

Greek Funeral Stele

By the time of the sculptor Phidias, in the 400s B.C., the Greeks did not have a very religious attitude about death. The Greeks held funerals without priests, hymns, or prayers. They emphasized the memory of the deceased. The Greeks erected steles (STEE • leez), or stone slabs, to commemorate their dead permanently and publicly. The earliest steles were rough pillars used only to mark grave sites. In time steles became more elaborate, with stylized figures symbolizing how the dead person had lived and worked—for example, as a soldier, a farmer, or a politician. By 400 B.C. simple scenes showing the deceased with their families, in courageous feats, or preparing for death decorated steles.

This grave stele of Hegeso was done in the late 400s B.C. It captures the lovely Athenian woman as she carefully selects a precious jewel from a jewelry box held by her servant. Perhaps Hegeso is planning to wear the jewel on her journey to the next world. The stele is set inside an architectural frame, typical of the classic style. Symmetry and balance, so important in Greek art, are evident in this stele. Hegeso's right hand is located precisely in the center of the relief. In keeping with the Greek idealization of human beings, the unknown sculptor suggests that Hegeso was beautiful in spirit as well as in body.

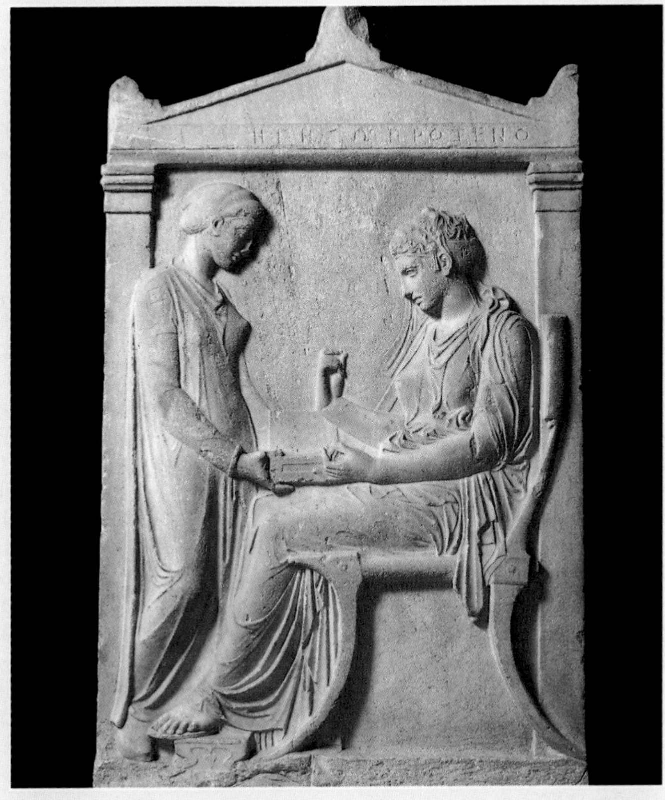

contests in their honor. Most famous were the games at Olympia, held every fourth year in honor of Zeus. Only men, however, could compete in and attend the Olympic Games. Women had their own events, dedicated to the goddess Hera.

At first the Olympic Games consisted only of footraces. Later the Greeks added jumping, javelin and discus throwing, boxing, wrestling, and horse and chariot racing. At the games winners received only wreaths of wild olive branches, but when they returned home their fellow citizens showered them with honors, money, and valuable gifts. The games became so important that the Greeks used them as the basis for dating events. Beginning in 776 B.C., they figured time in four-year periods called *Olympiads*.

Rise of the Nobles

About 700 B.C. the nobles—the chief landowners—began to have more influence on the kings. One reason for the nobles' importance was that they supplied cavalry to the military forces. Another reason was that although the population steadily increased, the amount of land that could be farmed did not. Farmers with small plots of land had trouble providing their families with enough food. When the harvest was meager, these farmers frequently had to mortgage or sell their land to a noble. Nobles often sold farmers who could not pay their debts into slavery.

Some of the unemployed farmers and laborers moved to the cities, where a commercial class of

109

1A, 1D, 3A, a1A, a1D, a2A, a2C, a2E, a2G, a2H, a2J, a2K, a2L, a4A, a4B, a4C

● Note that the Greeks made significant settlements on the Italian Peninsula. They came into contact with the Latin peoples there and had a great influence on Roman culture.

SECTION 2

Closure

Ask: How does the Greek city-state differ from the United States? *(Students might mention size, great loyalty to the local unit rather than the national state, distrust of others)*

Review Answers

1. ***epic:*** long poem describing heroes and great events; ***myth:*** traditional story about the deeds of gods, goddesses, and heroes; ***import:*** good or service brought into a country from another country; ***export:*** good or service sold to another country; ***aristocracy:*** city-state governed by nobles; ***tyrant:*** person who seizes power by force; ***popular government:*** rule by the people; ***democracy:*** government in which all citizens take part
2. ***Homer:*** author of *Iliad* and *Odyssey*; ***Zeus:*** Greek king of the gods; ***Athena:*** daughter of Zeus, goddess of wisdom and Athens
3. ***Mount Olympus:*** a peak in northern Greece where Greek gods lived
4. The Greeks believed that there was little connection between moral behavior and religion, that the spirits of all people went to Hades after death, and that gods and goddesses had human weaknesses.
5. **(a)** Nobles won power because they supplied cavalry to the military; **(b)** They lost power because foot soldiers became more important, the nobles fought among themselves,

merchants developed. Although the merchants could become wealthy, they always remained beneath the nobles in social position.

The nobles encouraged discontented peasants and laborers to establish colonies outside Greece. This drive to colonize proved very successful because the Greeks usually chose leaders, laws, and forms of government in advance. Greek colonies, set up as city-states like those on the mainland, were established on islands and shorelines throughout the Black, Aegean, and Mediterranean seas (see map, this page). In this manner Greek culture ● spread throughout the Mediterranean region.

Colonization also promoted trade. The new colonies often imported goods from and exported grain and other products to the mainland. An **import** is a good or service brought from another country or region. An **export** is a good or service sold to another country or region.

The nobles controlled many Greek city-states called **aristocracies.** (Today the word *aristocracy* often means a privileged social class.) Eventually, changes took place that weakened the nobles' power. Foot soldiers became more important in war, eliminating the need for the nobles' cavalry. Nobles fought among themselves. Many people became discontented with the rule of the nobles and looked for leaders who could promise them a better life.

Learning from Maps *The ancient Greek city-states established colonies to relieve overcrowding on the mainland and to increase the food supply. Where were the Greek colonies located?* **Ionia, Asia Minor**

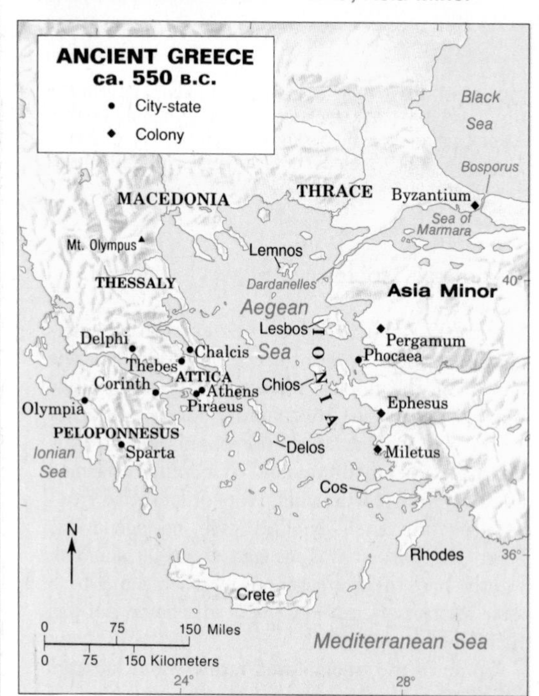

The Age of Tyrants

The leaders who appeared with those promises were called **tyrants.** The ancient Greeks defined a tyrant as someone who seized power by force and ruled alone. Tyrants always promised to bring peace and prosperity and to defend the poor against the nobles and officials. Many of the tyrants governed well because their interest in commerce made them want peace. They put an end to the nobles' struggles for political power, encouraged trade, and passed laws that were just.

The height of tyranny, or rule by tyrants, occurred in many of the Greek city-states between 650 B.C. and 500 B.C. As time went on, some of these leaders became harsh and unjust, giving the word *tyrant* its present meaning—a ruler who exercises absolute power brutally and oppressively.

Popular Government

As Greek government changed first from monarchy to aristocracy and then to tyranny, the idea of **popular government**—that people could and should rule themselves rather than be ruled by others—began to take root in many city-states. Some cities that ousted their tyrants restored the old monarchies or aristocracies. Others developed the form of government called **democracy**—a government in which all citizens take part. Even in monarchies and aristocracies, however, a council of citizens limited the power of the rulers.

At this time many factors might have led the Greeks to unite. All spoke the same language, which they regarded as a common tie. They referred to peoples who did not speak Greek as "barbarians." The ancient Greeks also believed they all were descended from the same ancestor, the hero Hellen. They called themselves Hellenes and their country Hellas. They also shared a common religion, and great festivals such as the Olympic Games brought them together. They joined in common management of certain temples, such as those of Zeus at Olympia and Apollo at Delphi.

However, other factors kept the Greeks apart. One factor was geography. The rugged mountains separated the small valleys and their populations from one another. Another factor was the fierce spirit of independence that made Greeks so proud of their own city-states and so distrustful of others. Each city-state had its own laws, calendar, money, and system of weights and measures. Citizens loved their city-state and would willingly give up their lives for it.

SECTION 2 REVIEW

1. **Define** epic, myth, import, export, aristocracy, tyrant, popular government, democracy
2. **Identify** Homer, Zeus, Athena
3. **Locate** Mount Olympus
4. **Understanding Ideas** List three religious beliefs of the Greeks.
5. **Interpreting Ideas** **(a)** How did the nobles win power in Greece? **(b)** Why did they lose power? **(c)** What parts did tyrants play in the process?
6. **Evaluating Ideas** Name and discuss the many factors that might have led the Greeks to unite.

3 Sparta and Athens Developed Different Ways of Life

Greek city-states had both similarities and differences. The wide range of differences shows clearly in a comparison of the two city-states that became most important, Sparta and Athens.

Sparta: The Military Ideal

The Dorians moved south to the Peloponnesus about 1200 B.C. They conquered the city of Sparta and made it their capital (see map, page 110). The conquerors maintained their separate societies but forced the agricultural laborers, known as **helots** (HEL • uhts), to work for them. The Spartans constantly had to use force to control the rebellious helots, who outnumbered them by about five to one.

In spite of this danger, the Spartans built their city-state in a valley, without a wall to surround it. Spartans were boastful people, and one of their leaders said, "A city is well fortified which has a wall of men instead of brick." The Spartans

Learning from Pictures
The rugged mountains of Greece created a geographical barrier that hindered communication among the city-states, allowing each to develop its own unique way of life.

and people became discontented with their rule. **(c)** Tyrants promised peace and prosperity and defense of the poor against the nobles and high officials.
6. The Greeks shared a common language, religion, and festivals, and they believed they descended from a common ancestor.

SECTION 3
Focus/Motivation
Ask students the following questions to stimulate a discussion on the comparative virtues of Athens and Sparta. Would you agree with the Spartans that luxury is bad for society? Is it true, as the Spartans believed, that foreign influence weakens a society? Do you think that the "Spartan virtues" of courage, strength, cunning, and devotion to country should be fostered today? Do you approve of the Athenian practice of choosing government officials by lot? Why or why not?

Presentation
Summarizing Ideas (Average/Group)
Write the following items on the chalkboard or an overhead projector:

1. Cancelled debts of the poor
2. Determined that all male citizens over age 20 could be in the Assembly
3. Wrote harsh code of laws
4. Created a following among lower classes

111

1B, 1D, 3A, 4A, a1A, a1B, a1D, a2A, a2C, a2D, a2E, a2G, a2H, a2J, a2K, a2L

● The word *spartan* is today defined as something marked by simplicity, frugality, or avoidance of luxury and comfort. Ask students to relate this to what they have read about ancient Spartans.

5. Stopped debt slavery
6. Set up the Council of 500
7. Exiled nobles who disagreed with his policies
8. Set up a court of appeals for citizens

After reading the subsection "Four reformers" on pages 114-15, ask the students to give you the correct name of the ruler which corresponds to the policy carried out under his rule. Write this name next to the correct policy. The names of the four rulers are; Draco, Solon, Pisistratus, Cleisthenes. *(Answers:* 1. *Solon* 2. *Cleisthenes* 3. *Draco* 4. *Pisistratus* 5. *Solon* 6. *Cleisthenes* 7. *Pisistratus* 8. *Solon)*

devoted their culture to this militaristic idea—this "wall of men."

Social groups. Three groups lived in Sparta. The first group consisted of citizens descended from the Dorian invaders; they controlled the government. To support these citizens and their families, the government in Sparta divided land equally among them. With each allotment of land went helots to work it.

The Spartans called the second group of people "neighbors." Although free, they did not have citizenship. They lived in the towns, and most of them worked in commerce and industry. Some "neighbors" became rich, but they could never be citizens.

The third group, the helots, ranked at the bottom of the social scale. Because the Spartans lived in constant fear of a helot revolt, they tried to prevent the helots from developing any leaders. Sometimes the Spartans killed helots who defied the government.

Government in Sparta. Sparta had an Assembly elected by all citizens, a Council of Elders that proposed laws, and two ceremonial kings. However, five **ephors,** or overseers, elected by the Assembly for one-year terms controlled the government. The ephors had unlimited power to act as guardians of the state, and they used that power harshly. For example, fearing the people would come to love money and luxuries, the ephors prohibited the use of gold and silver. Money was made of iron bars, which were too heavy to carry around and would not buy much. Fearing also that contact with outside peoples and ideas would weaken discipline and obedience, the ephors forbade citizens to travel and did not welcome foreign visitors.

The military machine. Sparta regulated the lives of its citizens from birth to death. All the rules had the same basic aim: to make every adult male citizen part of an efficient military machine designed to control the helots and extend Spartan power.

The development of Spartan fighting men, and of women fit to marry them, began at birth when a group of officials examined newborn babies. Any child who seemed weak, unhealthy, or deformed in any way was abandoned in the countryside to die. At the age of seven, boys went to live in military barracks. Although they learned to read and write, military training formed the basis of their education.

It was a harsh education. To develop endurance, boys wore only a single garment, summer and winter. They never wore shoes. Often they were beaten publicly so they would learn to bear pain without crying out. To teach them to feed themselves in wartime, the authorities provided coarse and scanty food. The boys had to steal food to keep from starving. Anyone caught received a severe punishment. The punishment, however, was not for stealing but for being clumsy enough to get caught.

The citizen began his military service at the age of 20, remaining in the army until the age of 60. At 30 a Spartan was expected to marry, but he had little family life. He devoted most of his time to military training, eating his meals and spending his leisure time in a military club. The authorities did not allow him to engage in any trade or business because business activities and love of money interfered with military discipline.

Spartan girls, as the future mothers of soldiers, had to be healthy, too. They received strict physical training to develop strength and endurance. They also had training in patriotic devotion.

The strict discipline of Sparta did lead to efficient government and an almost unconquerable army. The Spartans paid heavily for this military might, however. First, they sacrificed individual freedom to the state. Second, their society produced nothing in art, literature, philosophy, or science.

Athens: The Birth of Democracy

The early history of Athens differed greatly from that of Sparta. To begin with, Athens had no military class of conquering invaders imposing its rule upon a conquered people, as did Sparta.

Because Athens had rocky and unproductive soil, the Athenians became sea traders. They built their city inland to protect it against pirates and constructed Piraeus (py • REE • uhs) as its special port (see map, page 110). Athens itself was a typical polis built around the rocky, fortified hill of the Acropolis. In time of war, people from all the surrounding region took refuge within the city's strong walls.

Social groups. As in Sparta, three groups lived in Athens. At the top stood the citizens. In Athens, as a rule, one could be a citizen only if both parents were citizens. If only one parent had been a citizen, a person might become a citizen by decree.

READ
WRITE
INTERPRET
CONNECT
THINK

BUILDING HISTORY STUDY SKILLS

Reading About History: Making Comparisons

Making comparisons helps you organize information. It helps you to remember ideas and facts because you are able to place the details in a historical context. Making comparisons means identifying the similarities and differences between events, ideas, and actions in order to understand them.

How to Make Comparisons

To make comparisons, follow these guidelines.

1. Identify the purpose of the comparison.
2. Select the categories to be compared, such as government, family life, or education.
3. Identify similarities and differences by asking questions about the categories.
4. Draw a conclusion based on the similarities and differences.

Developing the Skill

Read the following excerpts to make a comparison between life in ancient Athens and Sparta. The first excerpt, about Athens, is from Thucydides' account of a funeral oration that Pericles made. The second excerpt, which describes the Spartan system, is from a biography of the Spartan lawmaker Lycurgus (ly • KUHR • guhs) by Plutarch.

"Our constitution is called a democracy because power is in the hands not of a minority but of the whole people. When it is a question of settling private disputes, everyone is equal before the law, when it is a question of putting one person before another in positions of public responsibility, what counts is not membership of a particular class, but the actual ability which the man possesses. . . . And, just as our political life is free and open, so is our day-to-day life in our relations with each other. We do not get into a state with our next door neighbour if he enjoys himself in his own way. . . . We are free and tolerant in our private lives; but in public affairs we keep to the law. This is because it commands our deep respect. . . . When our work is over, we are in a position to enjoy all kinds of recreation for our spirits. . . . Our love of what is beautiful does not lead to extravagance; our love of the things of the mind does not make us soft."

"Nor was it lawful, indeed, for the father himself to breed up the children after his own fancy; but soon as they were seven years old, they were to be enrolled in certain companies . . . where they lived under the same order and discipline. . . . Reading and writing they gave them, just enough to serve their term; their chief care was to make them good subjects, and to teach them to endure pain and conquer in battle. To this end, as they grew in years, their discipline was proportionately increased. . . . No one was allowed to live after his own fancy; but the city was sort of a camp, in which every man had his share . . . of businesses set out, and looked upon himself not so much born to serve his own ends as the interest of his country."

The first step in comparing life in ancient Athens with life in Sparta is to establish categories for analysis. The categories here are the relationship of the citizen to the government, and the value system.

You can discover the similarities between Athens and Sparta by asking questions. For example: What was the purpose of government in each city-state? The purposes were similar in that the good of the group and the strength of the state were important to both societies. Both valued obedience to the law and loyalty to the government. The relationship of the citizen to the state, however, was different. Individuals in Athens could pursue their own interests freely as long as they obeyed the law. Sparta allowed no private interest apart from the state. Individuals were trained to think of the city-state above themselves. In addition, the Spartans valued the body over the mind; the strong body better protected the state. The Athenians felt that the mind should be cultivated so that the individual initiative could develop and the state would be stronger.

What conclusion can you draw about Sparta and Athens by comparing the two societies? Sparta denied the individual full development, while the Athenian was encouraged to be creative and develop the mind.

Practicing the skill. What other conclusion can you draw about life in Athens and life in Sparta?

To apply this skill, see Applying History Study Skills on page 123.

Greek cavalry

113

1B, 3A, a1A, a1B, a1D, a2A, a2C, a2D, a2E, a2G, a2H, a2J, a2K, a2L, a4A

● Critical thinking activity: How do you think the Athenians reconciled their belief in democracy with the existence of slavery?

■ Solon canceled their debts, outlawed debt slavery, and freed those already enslaved for debt.

SECTION 3

Closure

Ask: Which Greek city-state most resembled the United States politically? *(Athens)* Which was the most different? *(Sparta)*

Review Answers

1. ***helot:*** Spartan agricultural laborer; ***ephor:*** "overseers" and real rulers of Sparta; ***metic:*** alien inhabitant of Athens who was free but not a citizen; ***archon:*** one of nine elected rulers who appointed all officials and made all laws in early Athens; ***direct democracy:*** government in which all citizens participate in making decisions; ***representative democracy:*** government in which elected representatives run the government
2. ***Solon:*** Athenian archon who limited power of judges, canceled debts of poor, and forbade enslavement for debt, freeing those who had been enslaved for nonpayment; ***Cleisthenes:*** archon whose reforms moved Athens closer to democracy
3. ***Piraeus:*** port city for Athens
4. **(a)** citizens elected the Assembly, which in turn chose 5 ephors to govern; a Council of Elders proposed laws; two ceremonial kings; **(b)** Spartans kept the helots from developing leaders and sometimes killed defiant helots.
5. **(a)** Early Athenian government was an aristocracy. Only citizens owning a certain amount of land

The government rarely issued such decrees, however. Although women could have citizenship, they could not vote or hold office and were regarded legally as minors.

Next came the aliens—non-Athenians—called **metics.** Most metics worked as merchants or artisans. Although free they could not own land or take part in government, even though they paid the same taxes as citizens.

At the bottom stood the slaves, whom the Athenians—just as all Greeks—considered a necessity and part of the natural order of things. At the time of Athens' greatest glory, more than half its population consisted of metics and slaves. In Athens, as in all of Greece, people regarded slaves as property, dependent on their master's will. An Athenian master could not treat his slaves brutally, nor did he have the power of life and death over them. However, if a slave complained or was killed, the court accepted the word of the master. If the master agreed, the slave might acquire property and even become wealthy. A freed slave became a metic.

Early government in Athens. After the Age of Kings, Athens had an aristocratic government. Only those citizens who had a certain amount of land could vote.

The voters met in an Assembly and elected nine **archons,** or rulers, each of whom served a one-year term. The archons appointed all officials and made all the laws, but they did not write these laws down. The judges, always a group of nobles, interpreted the laws and applied them in each case. The laws, by the way, always seemed to favor the nobles.

Four reformers. Four rulers—Draco, Solon, Pisistratus (pi • SIS • truht • uhs), and Cleisthenes (KLYS • thuh • neez)—strongly influenced the political development of Athens. Each ruler helped Athens move closer to democracy.

Draco, who served as archon in 621 B.C., is known for his code of laws. Although harsh and severe, these laws were written down so that everyone could know them. Today we call a harsh law a Draconian law.

Overall, conditions in Athens remained unsatisfactory under Draco. Nobles and metics became wealthy from trade, but small farmers grew poorer. More and more citizens were sold into slavery to pay off their debts. The poor began to demand that their debts be canceled and that the land be divided

Learning from Pictures *Solon was a poet as well as a political leader. What economic reform did Solon make to settle the debts of the poor?* ■

equally. Creditors and landowners opposed both demands.

In this emergency Solon, a trusted business leader, took control of Athens. Solon, who served as archon about 594 B.C., took a moderate position in the dispute between debtors and creditors. He canceled the debts of the poor, outlawed enslavement for debt, and freed those who had been enslaved for nonpayment.

Most citizens could vote, although only wealthier citizens could hold office. To limit the power of the judges, Solon set up a court, composed of a large number of citizens, to which a citizen could appeal an unfavorable decision.

Under Solon's rule, however, Athens still suffered much unrest. The nobles formed rival political groups and struggled for control of the government. Then Pisistratus, a wealthy aristocrat and a relative of Solon, developed a following

1B, 1C, 1D, 3A, 4A, a1A, a1B, a1D, a2A, a2C, a2D, a2E, a2G, a2H, a2J, a2K, a2L, a4A, a4F, a4H

among the lower classes. About 560 B.C. he became a tyrant and remained one off and on until 527 B.C. Pisistratus lessened opposition by exiling nobles who disagreed with him, seizing their estates and dividing the estates among peasants.

About 510 B.C. Cleisthenes seized power in Athens. Although a man of wealth and high social position, Cleisthenes cared about the welfare of the common people. He opposed class divisions based on wealth and instead divided citizens into 10 tribes based on where they lived. All male citizens over 20 years of age became members of the Assembly. Cleisthenes set up the Council of 500 with 50 members from each tribe, selected from all male citizens over 30 years of age. The council took over many of the powers and duties the archons formerly held.

A democratic state. Cleisthenes' reforms moved Athens even closer to democracy. The Assembly had much power. It chose archons and generals and could punish them for wrongdoing. The Council of 500 proposed laws to the Assembly.

Athens even had democratic courts. Jurors and some officials were chosen by lot, in keeping with the Athenian belief in the equality and fitness of all citizens for government service. Each man could plead his own case, and no judge presided. The jury of citizens made up the entire court, and each juror voted by secret ballot.

Athenian democracy under Cleisthenes was what we call **direct democracy.** That is, all citizens participated directly in making decisions. In contrast, present-day democratic nations such as the United States are **representative democracies,** in which the citizens elect representatives to run the government for them.

SECTION 3 REVIEW

1. **Define** helot, ephor, metic, archon, direct democracy, representative democracy
2. **Identify** Solon, Cleisthenes
3. **Locate** Piraeus
4. **Summarizing Ideas** **(a)** How was Sparta governed? **(b)** How did Spartans try to prevent helot revolts?
5. **Analyzing Ideas** **(a)** Describe the features of Athens' early government. **(b)** What reforms occurred to transform this government into a democracy?
6. **Synthesizing Ideas** Why would direct democracy be impractical in the United States today?

4 Daily Life in Athens Combined Recreation and Public Duties

The citizens of Athens and the other Greek city-states lived in much the same way. Their lives consisted of work, recreation, and the fulfillment of their responsibilities to the city-state.

Farming

Farming was the most honored occupation for an Athenian citizen. More than half of all citizens farmed, including many who owned the small plots of land that they worked. Unlike small farmers and peasants in most other societies, however, Athenian citizens could vote and hold public office.

Although some areas of Greece had good farmland, the soil around Athens was poor, and fields had to lie unplanted every second year so the soil could regain fertility. To make matters worse, much of the level land proved unsuitable for raising grain. Thus farmers concentrated instead on growing olives, grapes, and figs on terraced hillsides. (**Terracing** means creating small, flat plots of land by building low walls around the hillsides and filling the space behind them with soil.) Athens exported olive oil and wine and imported much of the grain needed to feed its people.

The principal domestic animals were sheep and goats. People used goat's milk for making cheese, and they valued sheep for their wool and meat. However, Athenians did not eat much meat. Fish and cheese made up most of their diet.

Manufacturing and Trade

Athenian manufacturing took place in small workshops. The largest shop was a shield factory, owned by a metic, which employed 120 workers. However, Athenians considered a shop with 20 workers large. Many artisans worked in their homes, where family members labored side by side with slaves and free employees. Today people throughout the world value Athenian vases and household utensils for their simple grace and beauty and their extraordinarily high quality. Yet ordinary citizens rather than famous artists made most of these objects.

The Athenian economy depended on trade. The desire to increase the food supply influenced

could vote in the Assembly. Nine archons appointed all officials and made all laws. **(b)** Draco had laws written down so everyone could know them. Solon checked the power of the judges. Cleisthenes divided citizens into 10 tribes based on geographic location rather than wealth.
6. Answers will vary. Students might suggest that the United States is too large both in size and population to have direct democracy.

SECTION 4

Focus/Motivation

Begin a class discussion by asking students why the Athenian ideal, "A sound mind in a healthy body," is a valid concept. Ask them why the democratic city-state of Athens would place great emphasis on education. Why is it important for democracies to do so today? How would educating people help to spread their culture? *(Answers might include the following: The Athenians realized that if their democracy was to be successful, it needed educated leaders. Greek became the major language of trade throughout the Mediterranean world and became the second language of educated non-Greeks everywhere. Culture spread through the language.)*

Presentation
Comparing Ideas (Average/Group)
Ask the students to reread the subsection "Family Life" on this page. Ask the students to describe the type of life led by most Athenian women. Ask them to describe what they think life may have been like for the typical American woman in 1900. *(Answers will vary. Students should include women's legal rights, social life, position and responsibilities within the family as well as within society.)*

SECTION 4

Closure
Point out that although Athens' economy depended on foreign trade, farming was the most honored occupation. Most Athenians worked hard and led simple lives, but they also recognized the importance in a democracy of education and physical fitness for their youth.

Review Answers
1. ***terracing:*** creating small, flat plots of land by building low walls around the hillsides and filling the space behind them with soil; ***pedagogue:*** slave used as a tutor for Greek boys: ***rhetoric:*** study of oratory, or public speaking **2. (a)** Athens depended on trade because it could not produce enough food to feed its population. **(b)** Colonies could provide the necessary increases in the food supply.

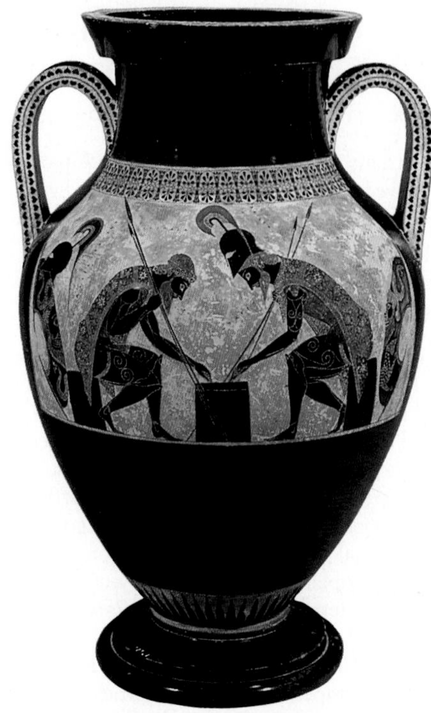

Learning from Pictures *Highly valued Athenian pottery was often exported. In what kind of activity might these Greeks be engaged?* **Playing a game**

all government policy. It made foreign trade a necessity and led to the building of the Athenian fleet and the establishment of colonies. Athenian ships went everywhere in the Mediterranean world, from the Black Sea in the east to Spain in the west.

Homes and Streets

Although the Athenians built magnificent temples and other public buildings, they lived in simple homes. Athenians believed money should be spent on buildings to benefit the whole community, not on private homes.

Houses made of sun-dried brick sat close to the street and usually were one story high. The street wall was plain except for a door leading into an open court. From the court other doors opened into the living room, dining room, bedrooms, storerooms, and kitchen. Athenians paid little attention to the appearance of the house itself, and it contained simple furnishings. The only heat came from open pans that held burning coals. Lamps that burned olive oil furnished a dim light. Houses had neither plumbing nor running water. Instead residents carried water in large jars from wells or springs.

The narrow, crooked streets were usually dirty because people threw rubbish into them. The city had neither sidewalks nor paving, no sewage system, and no services such as garbage collection and street cleaning.

Family Life

Athenians considered marriage a very important institution. Its main purpose was the bearing and rearing of children. The parents always arranged the marriages. A girl married early, typically at age 13 or 14 and to a man who was at least twice her age. Many women died in childbirth because of poor medical knowledge. And if a family could not afford to raise a baby, they abandoned it to die. More females than males were abandoned.

A married woman had few legal rights. She could not make a contract or bring a suit in court. Also, when a man died, his wife did not inherit his property. In social life, too, Athenians considered women inferior to men. Their duties included managing the household and the slaves and raising the children. They rarely appeared in public, and then only with the permission of their husbands. During banquets or entertainment in the home, the wife stayed out of sight.

In many Athenian households, the mother, aided by a woman slave, took care of both the boys and the girls until they were six. At the age of six, a boy was placed in the care of a male slave, or **pedagogue,** who taught the boy manners and went everywhere with him, including to school. Girls stayed at home, where they learned how to run a household but received no other schooling.

Education and Recreation

Most Greeks were poor and hardworking. They toiled long hours at monotonous work, with little time off. The rich did no work with their hands, preferring the pursuit of intellectual and physical excellence. They spent most of their time engaging in politics, gossip in the marketplace, conversations with friends, and athletic activities.

1B, 3A, a1A, a1B, a4A, a4F, a4G, a4M

Discussion topic: How army service for a young man in Athens compared with that of a young Spartan

Learning from Pictures *Greek artists depicted scenes from everyday life, such as baking bread (bottom) and hunting (top). What was the Athenian ideal of life?*

a sound mind in a healthy body

The citizens of Athens knew that for their democracy to succeed, its leaders had to receive an education. Boys therefore attended elementary schools, which charged fees.

Students in these elementary schools studied grammar, music, and gymnastics. Grammar included arithmetic, reading, and writing, done on a wax-covered wooden tablet. Much of the reading consisted of Homer's *Iliad* and *Odyssey.* Boys also learned to sing and to play musical instruments.

The Athenian ideal stressed a sound mind in a healthy body. Grammar and music developed the mind and the emotions. Gymnastics developed the body. In open fields at the edge of the city, boys practiced running, jumping, boxing, and throwing the discus and the javelin.

Men who called themselves Sophists, from the Greek word *sophos,* meaning "wise," conducted schools for older boys. Here the boys studied poetry, government, ethics, geometry, astronomy, and rhetoric (RET • uh • rik). **Rhetoric** was the study of oratory, or public speaking, and debating. Today the term *rhetoric* means the art of speaking or writing effectively.

At the age of 18, a boy received a year of military training. At 19, in an impressive public ceremony, he became a full citizen. After becoming a citizen, a young man who could afford to pay for weapons and armor served in the army for a year. The poor served the city by rowing the warships of the Athenian fleet.

Education played an important role in the spread of both the Greek language and Greek civilization throughout the Mediterranean world. Traders commonly spoke Greek, which was a second language for educated non-Greeks everywhere. Even today we use many words derived from Greek. We can hardly write or talk about government without using such Greek terms as *politics, democracy,* and *aristocracy.* Most terms used in medicine come from Greek. For example, the Greek ending *-itis* means "an inflammation" and is part of the words *appendicitis* and *tonsillitis,* among many others.

SECTION 4 REVIEW

1. **Define** terracing, pedagogue, rhetoric
2. **Analyzing Ideas** **(a)** Why was the Athenian economy so dependent on trade? **(b)** How did this dependence on trade lead the Greeks to found colonies?
3. **Understanding Ideas** **(a)** Describe a typical home in ancient Athens. **(b)** Why were the homes not more elaborate?
4. **Interpreting Ideas** Describe Greek attitudes toward women, as shown in marriage customs, the rights of citizenship, and social life.

5 Greek Civilization Defended Itself and Expanded

The Greek city-states and their colonies around the Aegean, Black, and Mediterranean seas developed for a long time without interference from the empires of the Middle East. Then the powerful Persian Empire intervened in Greek affairs, leading to war between the city-states and the Persians. Once they defeated the Persians, however, the Greeks warred among themselves.

3. (a) Athenians lived in simple, one-story, sun-dried brick houses built close to the street. There was an inner court, with living quarters opening on to it. Heat came from coals in open pans. Light was furnished by oil lamps. There was no plumbing or running water. **(b)** Athenians preferred to spend money on public buildings that could beautify and benefit the community.
4. Marriages were arranged by parents. Girls married at age 13 or 14 to men twice their age. Greek women had few legal rights; they could not make a contract, bring suit in court, or inherit property. Socially women were inferior to men. They rarely appeared in public and took little part in social life.

SECTION 5

Focus/Motivation

The theme of Herodotus' history of the Persian Wars is the clash of two cultures, East and West. Explore this idea with the students. Have students review Chapters 2 and 5 for characteristics of Greek and Persian culture in such areas as government, religion, and occupations. *(A comparison of the two cultures might include the following: The Greeks had a variety of governments in which the citizens generally could participate. In Persia the ruler was absolute. The Greeks were traders, fishers, and farmers. The Persians were mostly farmers.)*

117

1A, 1C, 3A, a1C, a4A, a4B, a4C

Have students look at the map on this page. What reason does the map suggest for an inevitable clash between Greeks and Persians? *(Answers might include the following: The Persians controlled former Greek city-states in Asia Minor; they blocked the entrance to the Hellespont, keeping Athens from trading in the Black Sea area; and they competed with the Greeks for trade in the Aegean.)*

Presentation
Organizing Ideas (Average/Group)
The following is a list of events in the Persian Wars. Write these events on the chalkboard or an overhead projector and have the students copy the list in their notebooks. Then have them arrange the events in chronological order by writing *1* before the event that took place first, 2 before the event that took place second, and so on.

- *(3)* Spartans fight delaying action at Thermopylae
- *(4)* Persian soldiers occupy Athens
- *(7)* Remaining Persian army is defeated at Plataea
- *(1)* City-states in Asia Minor revolt
- *(5)* Persian fleet is defeated at Salamis
- *(2)* Greeks defeat Persians at Marathon
- *(6)* Emperor Xerxes returns to Persia

The Persian Wars

In 546 B.C. Cyrus of Persia conquered the Greek city-states on the western shores of Asia Minor. The Persians did not treat the Greeks cruelly and permitted the Greeks to keep their own local governments. Nevertheless, the conquered Greeks had to pay tribute to Persia and consequently resented Persian rule. In 499 B.C. revolts broke out in several city-states of Asia Minor (see map, this page). These rebellions, which Athens aided, began a series of conflicts that lasted until 479 B.C. Together these conflicts are known as the Persian Wars.

Darius, Cyrus' son, easily crushed the revolts. However, he wanted to punish Athens for its support of the Greek rebels and to control the city-states on the Greek mainland as well as those of Asia Minor.

With this goal in mind, Darius sent a Persian army and a fleet toward Greece in 492 B.C. (see map, this page). Fortunately for the Greeks, a violent storm destroyed the fleet and the invasion attempt failed. Still determined to defeat the Greeks, Darius launched another invasion in 490 B.C. The Persians landed on the coast of Attica and set up camp on the plain of Marathon, some 20 miles (32 kilometers) from Athens.

Learning from Maps *Thebes remained neutral during the Persian Wars. What city-states revolted against the Persians in 499 B.C.?* **Miletus, Ephesus, Byzantium**

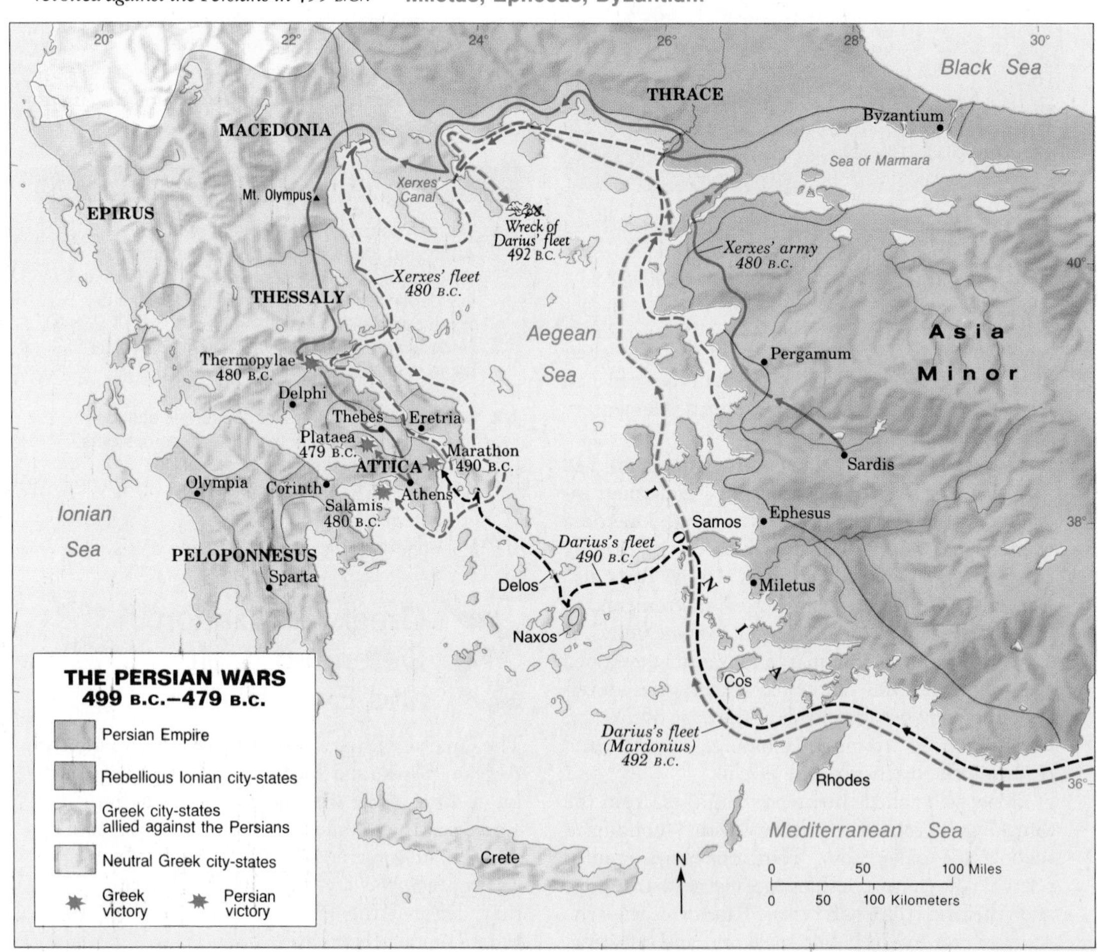

● Answers will vary. Students might suggest that rule by an absolute monarch would become the accepted form of government everywhere, and that many of the Greek ideals associated with democracy may have disappeared.

The Greek historian Herodotus wrote that the Persians outnumbered the Athenians 10 to 1. Although he may have exaggerated, it is certain that the smaller Athenian army attacked bravely and drove out the Persians.

For 10 years an uneasy peace existed. Then in 480 B.C., the dreaded news spread throughout Greece—Darius' son Xerxes was coming with a vast army and fleet from every part of the Persian Empire. Herodotus, who loved a good story, wrote that the Persian army was so large that when it drank water, whole rivers ran dry. The exaggeration pointed to the truth—Xerxes was marching with little opposition through Thrace and Macedonia toward northern Greece.

To advance from northern Greece into central Greece, the Persians had to march through the narrow mountain pass of Thermopylae (thur • MAHP • uh • lee). There King Leonidas of Sparta, with a force of 300 Spartans and about 6,000 allies, met the 200,000 Persians.

Aware that the Greek forces could not possibly survive the attack, Leonidas allowed only soldiers who had sons to carry on the family line to remain at Thermopylae. It was these soldiers who valiantly held the narrow pass against the entire Persian army for three days. Finally a Greek traitor showed the Persians a secret pass through the mountains. Surrounded, the Spartans and their allies refused to surrender and fought until every one of their soldiers was killed.

With the pass cleared, the Persians had an unobstructed route to Athens, which itself was in turmoil. The able Greek general Themistocles (thuh • MIS • tuh • kleez) persuaded the Athenians to abandon their city and to sail to the island of Salamis. With Athens evacuated, Xerxes' army entered the city and destroyed it.

Themistocles next tricked Xerxes into attacking the Athenian fleet in the Strait of Salamis. The narrow waters of the strait gave the light, maneuverable Greek ships an advantage over the lumbering Persian ships. From his throne high atop the coastal plain, Xerxes watched in horror as the Athenian ships rammed and sank many of the Persian ships.

After abandoning the naval attack, Xerxes withdrew most of his army and returned home. The next year, 479 B.C., a combined Greek army defeated the remnants of the Persian army at Plataea (pluh • TEE • uh). The Persian Wars were over.

Importance of the Greek Victories

Winning the Persian Wars did not immediately seem like a great victory for Greece. The Persian Empire remained powerful, and its rulers continued to meddle in Greek affairs. The Greek cities of Asia Minor fell under Persian rule again, and the Persians actively worked to prevent any unity in Greece.

From a long-range viewpoint, however, the battles of Marathon, Salamis, and Plataea are considered important and decisive in history. Success against the Persians gave the Greeks confidence and made them believe that their way of life was superior to that of others. Athens took credit for the defeat of Persia and created an empire in the Aegean. The wealth of this empire helped usher in an unprecedented Golden Age for Athens.

Athens as Leader

After these destructive wars, the Athenians completely rebuilt their city with even more magnificent temples and public buildings. Although the remnants of Xerxes' army had been defeated, the threat of invasion from the Persian Empire continued as long as Xerxes lived. Unity among the Greek city-states seemed necessary for survival.

Sparta wanted Greek unity under its own leadership. The Spartans tried conquest, but fear of helot revolt kept them from sending expeditions far from home. Even their strong army could not extend Spartan power beyond the Peloponnesus.

Athens was much more successful, using diplomacy to form the Delian League, a system of alliances among some 140 other city-states. Each city-state contributed either ships or money to the alliance. No city-state could withdraw from the league without unanimous consent. The league's

What If?
The Persian Wars

The Greek victory over Persia ensured the survival of the Greek way of life and government. As a result the Greek ideal of democracy, rather than the Persian concept of rule by an absolute monarch, was passed on to the Western world. How do you think a Persian victory in the war would have affected the course of world history? ●

119

1D, 3A, a1B, a1C

● Political turmoil in Athens centered on avoiding rule by tyrants. To avoid tyranny Athenians used ostracism, by which a person had to leave the city for 10 years.

Closure

Ask students how the rival interests of the Greek city-states prevented any one of them from unifying Greece. *(The cities were always jealous of one another.)* Tell them that this lack of unity, over the long run, caused the city-states to lose their independence altogether.

Review Answers

1. ***Darius:*** Persian ruler who failed to conquer Greece in 492 B.C. and 490 B.C.; ***Xerxes:*** son of Darius who destroyed Athens but was defeated by the Greeks at Salamis and Plataea; ***Themistocles:*** Greek general who tricked Xerxes into attacking the Athenian fleet at Salamis; ***Pericles:*** leader of Athens during the time of its greatest power and prosperity
2. ***Thrace:*** region east of Macedonia where Xerxes marched with little opposition; ***Thermopylae:*** mountain pass where Spartans refused to surrender to the Persians; ***Salamis:*** Athenian naval victory over Persian fleet; ***Delos:*** island where funds of Delian League were deposited
3. Marathon, Salamis, and Plataea are decisive because success against the Persians gave the Greeks confidence and made them believe their way of life was superior to that of others. Athens took credit for the Persian defeat and created an empire in the Aegean.

funds were deposited on the island of Delos (from which the name *Delian* is derived). As the league's leading city-state, Athens had the power to decide how many ships and how much money other city-states would contribute.

With the death of Xerxes in 465 B.C., the threat of Persian invasion ended. The Delian League, however, continued under Athens' domination. By the 450s B.C., it had become an Athenian empire.

The Age of Pericles

During this time Pericles (PER • uh • kleez), the ● greatest of Athenian leaders, rose to power. His ability and reputation for honesty commanded such awe that he was chosen general for 16 successive years. Even when he did not hold this official position, he was the most influential speaker in the Assembly.

Pericles led Athens for more than 30 years—from 461 B.C. to 429 B.C.—the time of its greatest power and prosperity. So significant was his rule that this period of Athenian history is called the *Age of Pericles.*

Under Pericles, Athenian democracy reached its height. (The chart below shows the major steps in the growth of Athenian democracy.) All citizens could hold public office, and officeholders received salaries, ensuring that even poor citizens could take an active role in government. For those allowed to participate, Athens was probably the most completely democratic government in history. However, more than half of the residents did not hold citizenship. And many Athenians could contribute so much time and service to government because slaves supported them.

Democracy in Athens

621 B.C.	Draco drew up code of laws.
594 B.C.	Solon abolished enslavement for debt, permitted most citizens to vote, established court of appeals.
560 B.C.–527 B.C.	Pisistratus abolished landowning requirement for citizenship, divided estates among landless peasants.
510 B.C.–508 B.C.	Cleisthenes abolished class divisions based on wealth, broadened Assembly membership, established Council of 500.
461 B.C.–429 B.C.	Pericles opened offices to all citizens, provided that officeholders be paid.

The Empire Under Pericles

In foreign affairs Pericles enlarged the Delian League by forcing more city-states to join. He moved the league treasury from Delos to Athens, openly using the money to benefit Athens. Athenian forces crushed revolts by other city-states against these policies. Although Athenian government within the city-state was democratic, the Athenians did not extend these rights to others. As the historian Thucydides (thoo • SID • uh • deez) warned:

> "You entirely forget that your empire is a despotism and your subjects disaffected conspirators, whose obedience is insured not by your suicidal concessions, but by the superiority given you by your own strength and not their loyalty."

Even Athens could not unify the Greek city-states, however. Quarrels with Athens' commercial rival, Corinth, as well as with Sparta increased tensions in the region, until a devastating war broke out in 431 B.C. The war is called the *Peloponnesian War* because much of the fighting took place in the Peloponnesus, where Sparta and Corinth are located.

The Peloponnesian War

Athens and Sparta shared responsibility for the Peloponnesian War. There was, of course, economic and commercial rivalry among a number of city-states. But Athens and Sparta had a long-standing social and cultural rivalry. Athens was progressive, commercial, and culturally advanced; Sparta was conservative, agricultural, and culturally backward. Athenians considered Spartans rude and ill-mannered; Spartans considered Athenians money-mad.

The Spartans started the fighting, but the Athenians had provoked them into action. Neither side tried very hard to avoid war. Thucydides wrote:

3A, a1A, a2G, a4A, a4F, a4G, a4L

Syracuse was the most important of the Greek colonies on the island of Sicily in Italy.

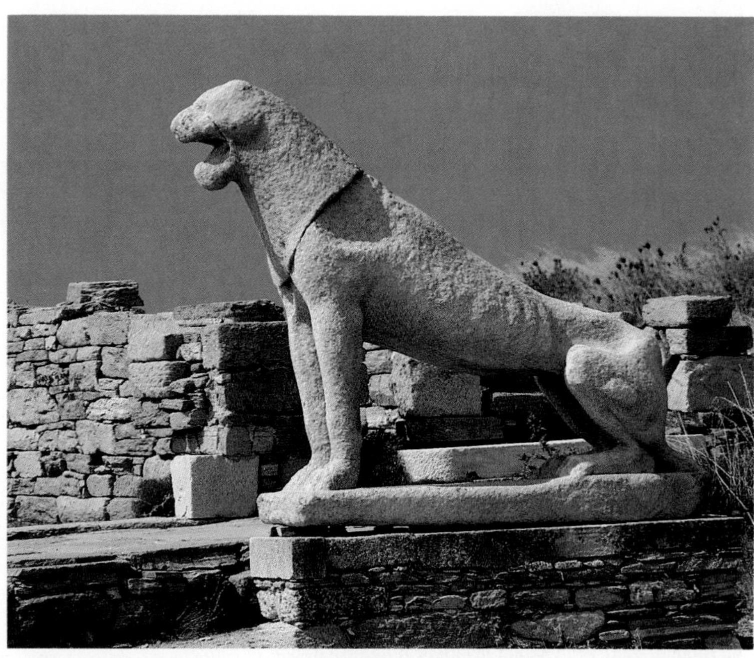

Learning from Pictures Many lions like the one here guard the temples on the island of Delos. The Greeks carved them from rough marble.

"The Peloponnesus and Athens were both full of young men whose inexperience made them eager to take up arms."

The Spartans invaded Attica, the region surrounding Athens, and destroyed fields and villages. The Athenian army and the entire population of the city withdrew behind the walls and the fortifications of Athens. The Spartans and their allies could not starve them out because Athens controlled the sea. However, a terrible plague broke out among the Athenians, killing many people, including Pericles.

The war went on for a generation, with great loss of life. Even during a period of peace, Athens could not resist the temptation to attack the great city of Syracuse in Sicily. There, however, Athens suffered a great defeat. After that some Athenians lost faith in democracy and allowed aristocrats to seize power in the city. They were soon overthrown and democracy was restored, but Athens' prestige was shaken. Athens finally surrendered to the Spartans in 404 B.C.

Greek Disunity

After the defeat of Athens, first Sparta and then Thebes tried to dominate Greece. The Spartans proved even harsher than the Athenians. Thebes then defeated Sparta and tried to control all of Greece. But Theban rule was not successful, and the ruinous wars continued.

All the city-states realized that unity was necessary, but each wanted to dominate any union that might be formed. Some promised democratic rule, others aristocracy, but all practiced tyranny. Some Greeks believed union could come only under a foreign power, and Persia seemed the logical choice. The power that brought unity, however, was not to appear for more than a generation. In the meantime, as you will read in Chapter 6, Greek civilization reached new heights.

SECTION 5 REVIEW

1. **Identify** Darius, Xerxes, Themistocles, Pericles
2. **Locate** Thrace, Thermopylae, Salamis, Delos
3. **Interpreting Ideas** Why are the battles of Marathon, Salamis, and Plataea considered decisive in the history of the world?
4. **Analyzing Ideas** **(a)** What was the Delian League? **(b)** How did Athens use it? **(c)** Why did other Greek city-states fear Athens?
5. **Understanding Ideas** What qualities gave Pericles his great hold over the people of Athens?

4. (a) The Delian League was a system of alliances of Greek city-states. **(b)** Athens dominated it for trade and political purposes. **(c)** Athenians crushed revolts.
5. Pericles was able, honest, and an influential speaker.

121

Reviewing Important Terms
1. Western civilization; **2.** polis; **3.** aristocracies; **4.** tyrant; **5.** popular government; **6.** democracy; **7.** representative democracy; **8.** Terracing.

Developing Critical Thinking Skills
1. (c), (a), (b), (e), (d)
2. (a) The Mediterranean borders on Asia, Africa, and Europe; The Mediterranean was a pathway for trade and ideas; The Mediterranean became the center of early Western civilization. **(b)** Nobles proved to be poor leaders; People became discontented with the rule of the nobles; Tyrants promised to bring peace and prosperity.
(c) Poor soil made the growing of grain difficult; Athens exported olive oil and wine; Athens built a large navy and established colonies throughout the Mediterranean.
3. (a) Sparta was militaristic; Athens was democratic. **(b)** The Spartans were soldiers. The Athenians were farmers.
4. (a) Four reformers developed democracy in Athens because they were interested in the welfare of the average citizens.
(b) Slaves were not considered citizens.
5. (a) Answers will vary. Athenians probably viewed their allies as colonies to be used for the benefit of Athens. **(b)** The allies resented Athens.

Relating Geography to History
Short mountain ranges separated communities and prevented them from developing a sense of unity.

1B, 1D, 3A, a1A, a1B, a4A, a4F, a4K, a4M

Reteaching
Have students review the Chapter Summary and the appropriate section and questions in the Unit Synthesis. Discuss the concepts until students demonstrate a clear understanding of the material.

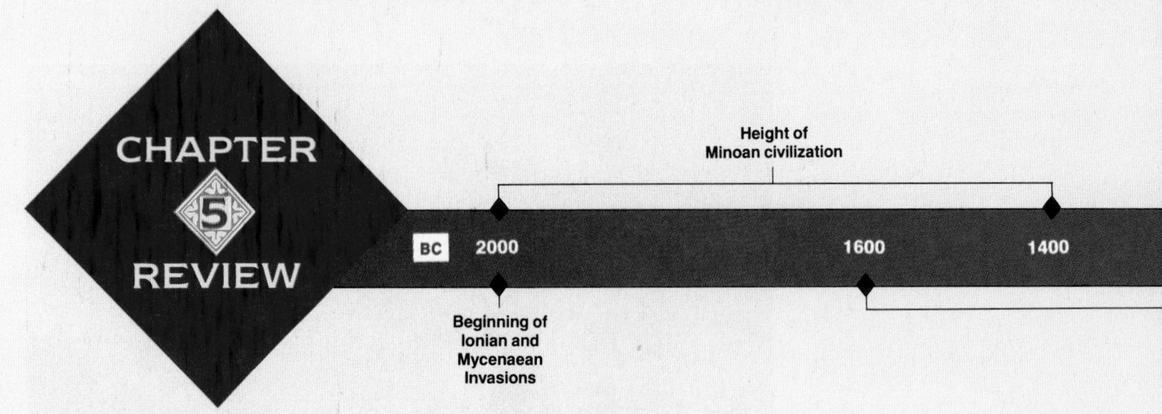

Chapter Summary

The following list contains the key concepts you have learned about the Greek city-states.

1. The geography of Greece was not as favorable to settlement as that of the great river valleys.
2. The Greeks became traders to increase their food supply and to improve the quality of their lives.
3. The Minoan culture of Crete was an important early influence on the Greeks.
4. Around 2000 B.C. various invaders entered Greece. The period during which these invaders dominated Greece is called the Mycenaean Age.
5. The polis was the basic political unit of ancient Greece.
6. After being ruled by kings, nobles, and tyrants for hundreds of years, many cities adopted popular governments, or democracies.
7. Sparta was a powerful militaristic state in which a select few inhabitants were considered citizens and ran the government.
8. Athens gradually adopted a democratic government.
9. The Athenian economy depended on farming, manufacturing, and trade.
10. After the Greeks defeated the Persian invaders, Athens became the leader of the Delian League.
11. Athens enjoyed a Golden Age under the rule of Pericles. Although more than half of its population could not participate in government, those who did participate enjoyed one of the most complete democracies the world has ever seen.
12. Rivalries among the city-states led to the disastrous Peloponnesian War, which lasted from 431 B.C. to 404 B.C. and left much of Greece in ruins.

On a separate sheet of paper, complete the following review exercises.

Reviewing Important Terms

Supply the term that correctly completes each statement.

1. The civilization that evolved in Europe and spread to the Americas is called ______ ______.
2. The Greek word for city-state was ______.
3. City-states governed by nobles were ______.
4. To the ancient Greeks, a ______ was someone who seized power by force rather than inheriting it.
5. The idea that people could and should rule themselves rather than be ruled by others is called ______ ______.
6. A government in which all citizens take part is a ______.
7. A system in which people select representatives to run the government is a ______ ______.
8. ______ means creating small, flat plots of land by building walls and filling the space behind them with soil.

Developing Critical Thinking Skills

1. **Understanding Chronology** Place the following events in the correct chronological order: **(a)** Mycenaean civilization, **(b)** early aristocratic city-states, **(c)** Minoan civilization, **(d)** early age of democracy, **(e)** Age of Tyrants.
2. **Determining Cause and Effect** In each of the following sets of three statements, one statement may be considered the cause and the other two the results. List the cause first and then the results:
   (a) The Mediterranean became the center of early Western civilization.
   The Mediterranean borders on Asia, Africa, and Europe.
   The Mediterranean was a pathway for trade and ideas.
   (b) Tyrants promised to bring peace and prosperity.
   Nobles proved to be poor leaders.
   People became discontented with the rule of the nobles.
   (c) Athens exported olive oil and wine.
   Poor soil made the growing of grain difficult.
   Athens built a large navy and established colonies throughout the Mediterranean.
3. **Comparing Ideas (a)** Compare the government in Sparta with the government in Athens in the 400s B.C. **(b)** How do you account for the differences?
4. **Interpreting Ideas (a)** How did democracy develop in Athens? **(b)** How did slavery fit into Athenian democracy?

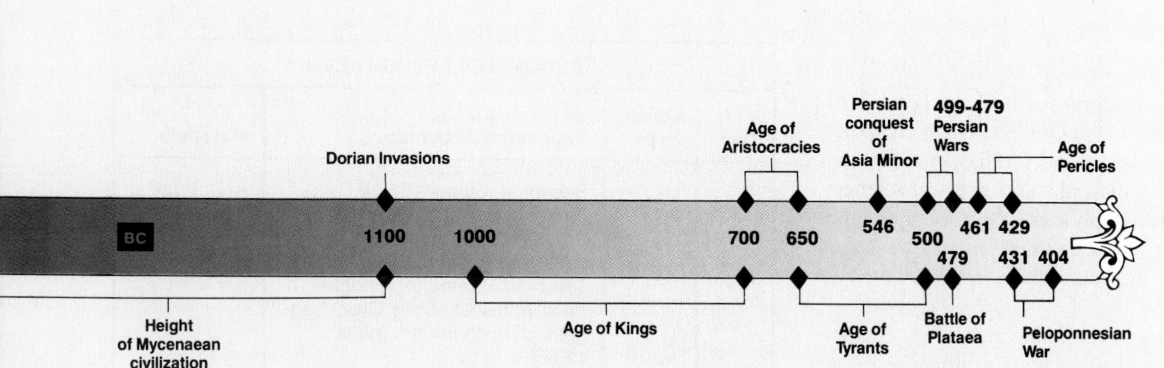

5. **Analyzing Primary Sources** Reread the excerpt from Thucydides on page 120. **(a)** Why do you think the Athenians championed democratic ideals in their city-state but denied them to other members of the Delian League? **(b)** How might this have contributed to the eventual defeat of Athens?

Relating Geography to History

Study the maps on pages 102, 106, 110, and 118. How did the geography of Greece influence the patterns of settlement and the types of government that the ancient Greeks developed?

Relating Past to Present

1. Sports were important in the culture of ancient Greece, where the Olympic Games originated. The modern Olympics trace their origins to these ancient Greek games. **(a)** How does the importance of sports and physical fitness in our society compare with that in ancient Greece? **(b)** In what ways do the modern Olympics differ from the ancient Greek Olympics?
2. Compare the ideas and practices of Greek democracy with the democratic ideals of American government in the following areas: **(a)** right of citizenship, **(b)** right to hold public office, **(c)** right to vote, **(d)** passage and review of laws.

Applying History Study Skills

Before completing this activity, review Building History Study Skills on page 113.

Read the following descriptions of the treatment of women in Athens and Sparta. Then answer the questions below to compare the two societies' views of the status and role of women.

Athens

"Since the indoor and outdoor tasks demand labour and attention, God from the first adapted the woman's nature . . . to the indoor and man's to the outdoor tasks and cares. . . . To the woman, since he had made her body less capable of such endurance . . . God has imposed on her the nourishment of the infants . . . the protection of the stores. . . . And besides, the law declares those tasks to be honourable for each of them wherein God had made them to excel the other. Thus, to the woman, it is more honourable to stay indoors. . . . "

(Xenophon, *Oeconomicus*)

Sparta

"The truth is, he [Lycurgus] took in their case, also, all the care that was possible; he ordered the maidens to exercise themselves with wrestling, running, throwing the quoit, and casting the dart. . . . Hence it was natural for them to think and speak as Gorgo, for example, the wife of Leonidas, is said to have done, when some foreign lady . . . told her that the women of Lacedaemon were the only women of the world who could rule men; 'With good reason,' she said, 'for we are the only women who bring forth men.' "

(Plutarch, *The Library of Original Sources*)

1. **(a)** What are the similarities between the role and status of women in Athens and the role and status of women in Sparta? **(b)** What are the differences?
2. Do you think Spartan women were more respected than Athenian women? Why or why not?
3. How does the status of women in Athens and in Sparta compare with that of women in the United States today?

Investigating Further

1. **Writing a Report** In your school or public library, use the card catalog or the *Readers' Guide to Periodical Literature* to find books or magazine articles about the excavations at Mycenae. Then write a report on this important archaeological site. Be certain to discuss what archaeologists were involved.
2. **Making Comparisons** Compare Greek religion with the religions of the Egyptians, Persians, and Hebrews that you studied in Chapter 2. What are the differences and similarities?

Because of the geography, the early Greeks established city-states.

Relating Past to Present
1. (a) Answers will vary. Students may say that today the emphasis is on winning and performance for glory for the individual or one's country. **(b)** Answers will vary. Students might state that there are many different competitions today, and winners are rewarded by nations.
2. (a) Answers will vary. Not every Greek had the right of citizenship.
(b) Unless one is a convicted criminal, one can hold public office in the United States; only those with the right of citizenship could hold public office in Greece. **(c)** In Greece only male citizens could vote. **(d)** In Athens all citizens voted on laws. Legislative bodies make our laws.

Applying History Study Skills
1. (a) supervising child-rearing and home life;
(b) Spartan women engaged in athletic and physical skills for themselves and their offspring; women in Athens managed the household.
2. Answers will vary. Some students might argue that Spartan women had more respect because of their important role in a military society.
3. Answers will vary. Students might point out that today women can own property, vote, govern, and own their business.

123

CHAPTER (pages 124–41)

6 Greek Civilization Triumphed During the Golden Age and the Hellenistic Age

(478 B.C.–146 B.C.)

CHAPTER OVERVIEW

After the Greeks under Athenian leadership forced the Persians to withdraw, Athens became the center for a Golden Age of creativity in art, philosophy, and science. Myron and Phidias in sculpture; Plato, Socrates, and Aristotle in philosophy and political science; Thucydides in history; Aeschylus, Sophocles, Aristophanes, and Euripides in drama; Phythagoras and Democritis in mathematics and science; and Hippocrates in medicine made lasting contributions to civilization.

Despite cultural achievements and economic prosperity, Athens and the other Greek city-states could not achieve political peace or unity. The Peloponnesian War weakened Athens and Sparta. After additional wars erupted, Greece became easy prey for the armies of Philip of Macedon. His son, Alexander the Great, became master of Greece and conquered the Persian Empire.

As a result of Alexander's conquest, Greek culture spread as far as Egypt and the borders of India. At the same time, Greek culture was modified by ideas from other lands. This mingled culture became known as Hellenistic.

SUGGESTED LESSON PLAN

Day	Objectives	Suggested Activities	Materials
1	U1,* C1-2	Introducing The Chapter (pages 124-25) Section 1 (pages 125-28), Focus/Motivation (page 125), Presentation (page 126), Closure (page 127), Suggested Teaching Strategies, Enrichment Activity, Daily Quiz, Suggested Assignments (page 123B)	ATE, Pupil's Edition, Teacher's Resource-Bank™
2	U5, C3-5	Section 2 (pages 128-32), Focus/Motivation (page 128), Presentation (page 129), Closure (page 131), Suggested Teaching Strategies, Enrichment Activities, Daily Quiz, Suggested Assignments (page 123C)	ATE, Pupil's Edition, Teacher's Resource-Bank™
3	U6, C6-7	Section 3 (pages 133-37), Focus/Motivation (page 133), Presentation (page 133), Closure (page 136), Suggested Teaching Strategies, Enrichment Activities, Daily Quiz, Suggested Assignments (page 123D)	ATE, Pupil's Edition, Teacher's Resource-Bank™
4	U1, U5-6, C8-11	Section 4 (pages 137-39, Focus/Motivation (page 137), Presentation (page 138), Closure (page 138), Suggested Teaching Strategies, Enrichment Activities, Daily Quiz, Suggested Assignments (page 123E)	ATE, Pupil's Edition, Teacher's Resource-Bank™
5	U1, U5-6 C1-11	Chapter 6 Form A Test, Reteaching Worksheet, Chapter 6 Form B Test	Teacher's Resource-Bank™ or Workbook and Test Booklet

*C refers to applicable Chapter Objective, U refers to applicable Unit Goal

BOOKS FOR THE TEACHER

Ferguson, John. *The Heritage of Hellenism.* Neale Watson. Features a short and informative cultural and social history of the Hellenistic period.

Hamilton, Edith. *The Greek Way.* Norton. Includes a popular account of Greek culture. Many scholars consider this one of the standard works.

Hamilton, J. R. *Alexander the Great.* University of Pittsburgh Press. Presents challenges of some of the traditional interpretations of Alexander's life and career.

Renault, Mary. *The Nature of Alexander.* Pantheon. Examines the career and character of Alexander through the eyes of a master storyteller.

BOOKS FOR THE STUDENT

Connolly, Peter. *The Greek Armies.* Silver Burdett. Discusses armor, tactics, formations, and numerous other military topics; includes many illustrations.

Coolidge, Olivia. *Men of Athens.* Houghton Mifflin. Features historical tales of outstanding Athenian individuals during the Golden Age.

Mercer, Charles. *Alexander the Great.* American Heritage. Details the major tragedies and triumphs of the life of Alexander the Great. Text includes many colorful illustrations.

Warner, Rex. *Athens at War.* Dutton. Presents retelling of Thucydides' account of the Peloponnesian War.

Warner, Rex, ed. *The Greek Philosophers.* New American Library. Introduces Greek philosophy.

MULTIMEDIA MATERIALS

Alexander the Great and the Hellenistic Age (mp, 14 min.), Coronet. Follows Alexander's campaigns and the spread of Greek culture.

Aristotle's Ethics: The Theory of Happiness (mp, 29 min.), EBE. Considers the factors that contribute to Aristotle's conception of a good life.

Athens: The Golden Age (mp, 30 min.), EBE. Focuses on the accomplishments of Athens in the 400s B.C.

The Death of Socrates (27 min., b&w), McGraw-Hill. Describes the last days of Socrates.

Greek Civilization (2 fs), Educational Audio-Visual. Part 1 considers the political and social life of ancient Greece. Part 2 examines Greek art and architecture.

Men Who Made History: God and Man (fs), EBE. Examines Alexander's career and his influential role in history.

Plato's Apology: The Life and Teaching of Socrates (30 min., color), EBE. Discusses Socrates through Plato's eyes.

Triumph of Alexander the Great (mp, 25 min.), Young American Films. Describes Alexander's exploits.

Section (pages 125–28)

1 Greek Art Represented the Ideals of Greek Civilization

SECTION OVERVIEW

Greek art reached a peak of excellence during the 400s B.C., a period called the Golden Age. The Greeks excelled in architecture, painting, and sculpture. In their art the Greeks glorified humans; showed pride in their city-states; expressed the Greek ideals of harmony, balance, order, and moderation; and combined beauty and usefulness.

SUGGESTED TEACHING STRATEGIES

1. **Preteaching Vocabulary (Basic)** You may wish to preteach the following important vocabulary term: Hellenistic culture *(page 125)*. Have students make a list of fields in which the Greeks excelled. *(philosophy, science, mathematics, art, drama, architecture, medicine)*
2. **Contrasting Ideas (Basic)** Place the following statements on the chalkboard. Students are to match the artist with the characteristics that apply to him.

   a. Phidias **b.** Praxiteles

   1. He created two statues of Athena.
   2. He expressed the beauty of the human body.
   3. His greatest statue was of Zeus.
   4. His statues were human and lifelike.
   5. His works were large, formal, and dignified.
   6. His statues were the more graceful.

   (Answers: 1-a, 2-b, 3-a, 4-b, 5-a, 6-b)

ENRICHMENT ACTIVITY

Comparing Art (Basic) Have the students refer to the picture on page 127. How does the sculpture differ from that of other civilizations the class has studied so far? *(Students may observe that the figures have become more lifelike and less rigid.)* To illustrate this development, show pictures and slides of Greek sculptures from all periods of ancient Greece. Numerous pictures can be found in *The Dawn of Civilization* (McGraw-Hill), edited by Michael Grant, or in the art section of the library. Students should observe that the statues of early Greek civilization resemble Egyptian statues. Ask them to identify characteristics of the Classical style. *(Answers should include idealization of the human body, proportion, and controlled movement.)* Ask students to make some generalizations about Greek art and architecture.

DAILY QUIZ

To assess student understanding of Section 1, give the class the following quiz. (Each item is worth 10 points.)

1. Name the hill in the center of Athens that became the scene of special artistic creations and temples. *(Acropolis)*
2. Name the temple dedicated to Athena. *(Parthenon)*
3. The architectural design of the temple dedicated to Athena represents a Greek ideal known as the ______ ______. *(Golden Mean)*
4. From which of these objects do we obtain most of our illustrations of everyday life in Greece? mosaics, paintings, murals, vases *(vases)*
5. Name the famous Greek sculptors during this era and one of their works or types of work. *(Myron/Discus Thrower; Phidias/Athena, Zeus; Praxiteles/lifelike figures)*
6. Name the topics the Golden Age artists illustrated. *(everyday life, myths, athletic events, epics)*
7. Because many of the early Greek paintings and sculptures were destroyed, we depend on copies made by the ______ to learn of their techniques. *(Romans)*
8. (T or F) Greek artists glorified humans as the most important creatures in the universe, idealizing subjects and omitting any blemishes. *(T)*
9. (T or F) Greek artists did not honor the gods or demonstrate any loyalty to their city-states. *(F)*
10. (T or F) Greek art expressed the Greek ideals of harmony, balance, order, moderation, and usefulness. *(T)*

SUGGESTED ASSIGNMENTS

1. **Slide Presentation (Average/Group)** An interested student may choose to make a slide presentation on Greek architecture, vase painting, or sculpture. Or a student might select a theme, such as daily life, or sports and entertainment, and show how it is expressed in Greek art. You might ask a member of the art department to make such a presentation or to help the students prepare one.
2. **Art Projects (Challenging)** Students may do one or more of

the following projects: construct a model of the Parthenon, make copies of vase paintings, fashion small figures out of clay, or prepare a collage on Greek art. Students may work individually or in groups. Have students refer to C. M. Bowra's *Classical Greece* (Time-Life) and Jonathan Rutland's *An Ancient Greek Town* (Warwich Press).

Section (pages 128–132)

2 Philosophers and Writers Added to the Heritage of Greece

SECTION OVERVIEW

Greek philosophers, scientists, and writers made lasting contributions to civilization. Socrates, Plato, and Aristotle were great philosophers. Pythagoras made advances in mathematics, and Hippocrates and Thucydides wrote the first objective histories. Aeschylus, Sophocles, Euripides, and Aristophanes wrote the first dramas—both tragedies and comedies.

SUGGESTED TEACHING STRATEGIES

1. **Preteaching Vocabulary (Basic)** You may wish to preteach the following important vocabulary terms: philosophy *(page 128)*; drama *(page 131)*; tragedy, hubris, comedy *(page 132)*. Ask students to name a number of Greek dramas. Ask if they have seen any staged. If so, how were these accomplished? in modern dress or ancient Greek style?
2. **Learning from Charts (Basic)** Ask students to make a chart in their notebooks of Greek scientists and their contributions. Charts should be similar to the following

SCIENTIST	CONTRIBUTIONS
Pythagoras	Developed the Pythagorean theorem
Aristotle	Laid the foundations of botany, zoology, and anatomy
Democritus	Theorized that all matter is composed of atoms
Hippocrates	Taught that disease comes from natural causes; Hippocratic Oath is based on his teachings

3. **Contrasting Past and Present (Challenging)** Have interested students read selections by Hippocrates. One source is "Hippocrates Advances the Science of Medicine" in Sydney Eisen's and Maurice Filler's *The Human Adventure,* vol. 1 (Harcourt Brace Jovanovich). Then have students prepare oral or written reports on medical training and ethics today. Students could interview physicians or use the *Readers' Guide to Periodical Literature* to find the articles on medicine today.

ENRICHMENT ACTIVITIES

1. **Presenting a Drama (Average/Group)** Organize the class into groups. Have each group select a short scene from one of the plays mentioned on page 132 *(Oedipus the Tyrant, The Trojan Women, The Clouds)* and present it to the rest of the class. The presentation should include a short summary of the play and an introduction to the scene.
2. **Understanding Ideas (Challenging)** Students may want to read accounts of other important events in ancient Greece as described by early Greek historians. Abridged translations of the writings of Herodotus, Thucydides, and others should be available in the library. Students may want to choose one event from these works and read it to the class. Use the reports as the basis for a class discussion.

DAILY QUIZ

To assess student understanding of Section 2, give the class the following quiz. (Each item is worth 10 points.)

1. _______ trained as a sculptor, became a teacher, and criticized Sophist philosophy. *(Socrates)*
2. What was Socrates' basic motto? *("Know thyself")*
3. Who recorded Socrates' writings in the form of dialogues while teaching in his own academy? *(Plato)*
4. What is the primary governmental system espoused in the *Republic*—aristocracy, monarchy, or democracy? *(aristocracy)*
5. _______ wrote *Ethics, Politics, Logic,* and *Poetics. (Aristotle)*
6. (T or F) According to *Politics,* the best government included a powerful leader, aristocratic advisors, and a democratic assembly to ensure the total control of the individual for the benefit of the state. *(F)*
7. Whose work resulted in laying the foundations of modern medicine? *(Hippocrates)*
8. Name the first two historians. *(Herodotus and Thucydides)*
9. Name four famous Greek playwrights. *(Aristophanes, Euripides, Sophocles, Aeschylus)*
10. (T or F) In a Greek drama, the orchestra is the area where the chorus changed and the actors performed. *(T)*

SUGGESTED ASSIGNMENTS

1. **Applying Ideas (Average/Group)** Although Socrates criticized democracy, he believed that people should think for themselves. Have the students write a paragraph that explains why this philosophy is important to the success of many of the present-day democratic governments.
2. **Reports (Average/Group)** A student might give a report on the structure and function of Greek theater, including the staging of Greek plays. Another student might make a model of a Greek theater. Two sources are C. M. Bowra's *Classical Greece* (Time-Life); and *The Birth of Western Civilization* (McGraw-Hill), edited by Michael Grant.
3. **Profile Worksheet (Basic)** Have students complete Profile Worksheet 6 in the TEACHER'S RESOURCEBANK™.

Section (pages 133–37)

3 Alexander the Great Created a Huge Empire

SECTION OVERVIEW

Alexander the Great carried out his father's dream of conquering the Persian Empire. His plans included founding new cities, merging the Macedonians and Persians into one ruling group, and being considered a god-king by his subjects. After Alexander's death, his empire was divided among three of his generals.

SUGGESTED TEACHING STRATEGIES

1. **Preteaching Vocabulary (Basic)** You may wish to preteach the following important vocabulary terms: infantry, phalanx *(page 133)*; orator *(page 134)*. Have students read the pages indicated and define the terms.
2. **Interpreting Ideas (Basic)** In Will Durant's book, *The Life of Greece* (Simon and Schuster), the author describes Alexander the Great as physically handsome and a good athlete, with great energy and a strong will. He had an inquisitive mind, but was also superstitious. Alexander was truthful, warm-hearted, generous, and kind, yet he could have moments of cruelty. He could control men, but not his temper. Ambition was his most outstanding characteristic.

   Ask students to reread the subsection "Alexander the Great" on pages 134-37. Next have them discuss how these contrasting qualities affected the soldiers he led and the people he ruled. *(Answers will vary. Students might point out that Alexander's ambitions led him to push the limits, but when his soldiers refused to fight any further, he accepted this and turned back.*
3. **Identifying Results (Average/Group)** Write Alexander's three goals for himself and his empire on the chalkboard or an overhead projector. Have students copy these goals in their notebooks. Then have them list two outcomes of Alexander's attempts to reach each goal.

   Goal: To create new cities and rebuild old ones as cultural centers
   Outcomes: *(More than 70 cities were built. Groups of Greeks and Macedonians settled in each.)*
   Goal: To merge Macedonians and Persians into one ruling group
   Outcomes: *(He married a Persian princess and made his generals do the same.)*
   Goal: To be considered a god-king
   Outcomes: *(He insisted that all subjects honor him as being part human and part divine. Not all of his subjects believed he was a god-king.)*

*4. **Making Connections with History: Identifying Cultural Diffusion (Challenging)** Have students compare the fusion of Greek cultures and Oriental cultures that resulted from the conquests of Alexander the Great with the fusion of European and Latin American cultures in the United States from about 1500 to the present. Students should focus on the methods and extent of diffusion and the similarities and differences between the cultures at these different times in world history.

ENRICHMENT ACTIVITIES

1. **Presenting a Drama (Average/Group)** Terence Rattigan has written an absorbing play about Alexander the Great entitled *Adventure Story*. Have a group of students present a short scene from this play to the rest of the class.
2. **Writing a Research Report (Average/Group)** Give students the option of doing either an oral or written book report on Alexander. Mary Renault's *Fire from Heaven* (Pantheon) is a novel about the life of Alexander. Two nonfiction works are Mary Renault's *The Nature of Alexander* (Pantheon) and Charles Mercer's *Alexander the Great* (American Heritage), which includes several illustrations.

DAILY QUIZ

To assess student understanding of Section 3, give the class the following quiz. (Each item is worth 10 points.)

1. Philip of Macedon was held as a hostage for three years in this city, and he developed an admiration for its military organization. *(Thebes)*
2. Who served in the cavalry in Philip's army? *(landowners)*
3. Describe a phalanx. *(16 rows of tightly spaced lancers)*
4. (T or F) The infantry in the Macedonian army were hunters and peasants also trained to fight on horseback. *(F)*
5. The great orator who warned Athenians of the danger to Greek liberty from Philip of Macedon was ______. *(Demosthenes)*
6. (T or F) Philip defeated the Athenians at the battle of Chaeronea. *(T)*
7. Under which Greek philosopher did Alexander receive his education? *(Aristotle)*
8. (T or F) Alexander and his army reached the Ganges River and established it as the eastern border of Persia. *(F)*
9. Of what illness do historians think that Alexander died? *(cholera or malaria)*
10. (T or F) After Alexander's death his generals fought for control of his empire, but Alexander's son succeeded in becoming ruler of the united empire. *(F)*

SUGGESTED ASSIGNMENTS

1. **Understanding Geography (Basic)** Have students complete "Geography Application Sheet: Stopping Alexander the Great" in the TEACHER'S RESOURCEBANK™.
2. **Research Report (Challenging)** Have students do research on the military organization of the phalanx, which served so successfully under Philip of Macedon and Alexander the Great. Have students include in their reports (1) how the phalanx was organized, (2) what weapons it carried, (3) what uniforms its soldiers wore, and (4) what advantages it had that allowed the pha-

lanx to overcome its enemies. Select the best reports to read to the class. Use these reports as a basis for a class discussion on military units and weapons used by other ancient civilizations.

3. **Skill Worksheet (Basic)** Have students complete Skill Worksheet 6 in the TEACHER'S RESOURCEBANK™.

Section (pages 137–39)

4 Hellenistic Culture Spread Throughout the Mediterranean Region

SECTION OVERVIEW

After the death of Alexander the Great, the Greeks spread their culture over the lands of his former empire. At the same time, the Greeks absorbed much of the culture from the conquered peoples. The mixture was called Hellenistic culture. The Hellenistic Age was a period of prosperity for the new middle class. Education became more widespread, and philosophers discussed problems of ethics. Great advances were made in mathematics, physics, medicine, astronomy, and geography.

SUGGESTED TEACHING STRATEGIES

1. **Organizing a Panel Discussion (Average/Group)** Ask for three volunteers and have each take the point of view of one of the Hellenistic philosophies. Each student should present arguments in favor of Stoicism, Cynicism, or Epicureanism, and then the group should debate the merits of each philosophy. Invite comments from the class. Finally, the class should identify groups of individuals in our society that seem to live according to one of these philosophies. Rex Warner's *The Greek Philosophers* (New American Library) has selections written in a style that high school students will understand. Bertrand Russell's *A History of Western Philosophy* (Simon and Schuster) is a popular account of philosophy.
2. **Writing Assignment (Basic)** Have students write a letter from a teenager living in ancient Alexandria, Egypt, to a friend in Babylon, describing life in Alexandria. Before students start writing, you might want them to read the description of Alexandria in *Greece and Rome: Builders of Our World* (National Geographic Society). After the assignment has been completed, ask for volunteers to read their letters to the class.
3. **Contrasting Ideas (Average/Group)** Ask students to reread the subsection "Changing Attitudes" on page 138. Then have them compare the role of Hellenistic women with women in earlier Greek city-states. You might ask students to do further research comparing the Classical Greek civilization with Hellenistic civilization.

ENRICHMENT ACTIVITY

Writing a Report (Average/Group) Hellenistic culture offers several opportunities for oral or written reports. Students could make oral presentations on some form of Hellenistic art. Reports can be written on some aspect of social life in a Hellenistic city or advances in medicine during this period. Biographical sketches could be made of Euclid, Archimedes, Aristarchus of Samos, Hipparchus of Rhodes, and Eratosthenes. Sources include Frank Frost's *Greek Society* (Heath); John Ferguson's *The Heritage of Hellenism* (Neale Watson); and the *Harper Encyclopedia of Science.*

DAILY QUIZ

To assess student understanding of Section 4, give the class the following quiz. (Each item is worth 10 points.)

1. (T or F) After the division of Alexander's kingdom among the three dynastic families, Greek culture spread rapidly. *(T)*
2. (T or F) Hellenistic culture did not incorporate any ideas outside of the original Greek traditions. *(F)*
3. Which of these was *not* a major Hellenistic trade center? Rhodes, Madrid, Alexandria, Antioch *(Madrid)*
4. ________ taught that people should seek virtue only, scorning pleasure, wealth, and social position. Today the word denotes sarcasm. *(Cynics)*
5. (T or F) Zeno's philosophy of Stoicism encouraged people to quietly accept the status quo and also influenced Roman and Christian thought. *(T)*
6. ________ shaped geometry into a system by showing how theorems developed logically from one another. *(Euclid)*
7. ________ is credited with discovering the relation between the diameter and the circumference of a circle. *(Archimedes)*
8. (T or F) Most Hellenistic scientists did not use math to calculate the daily positions of the stars and planets, but still believed the planets did revolve around the sun. *(F)*
9. (T or F) Most Hellenistic geographers knew the earth was round. *(T)*
10. (T or F) The Greeks frequently applied their scientific knowledge in practical ways, creating many labor-saving devices particularly to aid the slave. *(F)*

SUGGESTED ASSIGNMENTS

1. **Critical Thinking Worksheet (Basic)** Have students complete Critical Thinking Worksheet 13 in the TEACHER'S RESOURCEBANK™.
2. **Critical Thinking Worksheet (Basic)** Have students complete Critical Thinking Worksheet 14 in the TEACHER'S RESOURCEBANK™.
3. **Review Worksheet (Basic)** Have students complete Review Worksheet 6 in the TEACHER'S RESOURCEBANK™.
4. **Report (Challenging)** Have interested students do research on a number of the cities founded by and named for Alexander the Great. The most obvious is Alexandria in Egypt. Ask them to describe the history of the cities, what kind of people lived there and how they made a living, and what the cities are called today. Have them find out how many cities are still in existence and, if so, what are their populations and current names.

Teacher's Notes

For suggested lesson plan, additional teaching strategies, enrichment activities, daily quizzes, and suggested assignments, see pages 123A-123F.

Introducing the Chapter
Have students refer to the map on page 134. Use the map as a basis for discussing Alexander's plans for creating a world empire. Some questions to ask are: What areas did Alexander control? What problems would occur in ruling such a large kingdom? What would be the advantages of such an empire? *(Answers should include the following: Alexander conquered almost all of the world known to him. He occupied Greece, Asia Minor, Syria, Palestine, Egypt, Mesopotamia, and Persia, and entered India. The size of the empire would make it difficult to govern. Transportation and communication from one end of the empire to the other would be difficult and would take time. Administering people with diverse laws, customs, and religions might pose problems. However, uniting the various peoples would encourage the exchange of ideas and cultures. New markets would cause trade and industry to prosper. The possibility of uniform weights, measures, and coinage would make buying and selling easier.)*

Chapter Objectives
After studying Chapter 6, students will be able to:

1. Evaluate architecture, painting, sculpture, and other developments in art during Greece's "golden age."
2. State why the Greek artistic expressions were so

CHAPTER 6

Greek Civilization Triumphed During the Golden Age and the Hellenistic Age

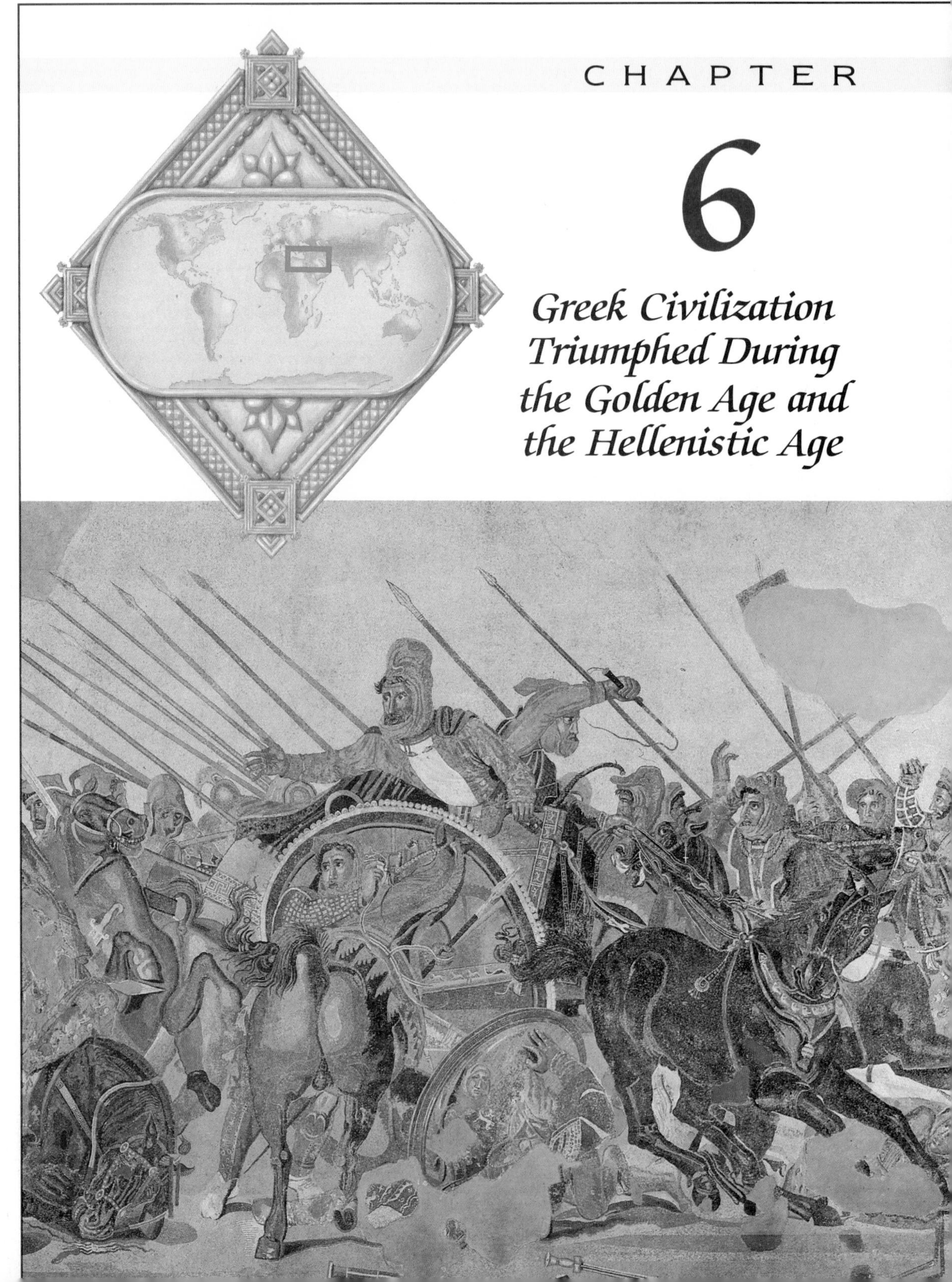

CHAPTER FOCUS

Place Greece, the Middle East, Egypt, and Persia

Time

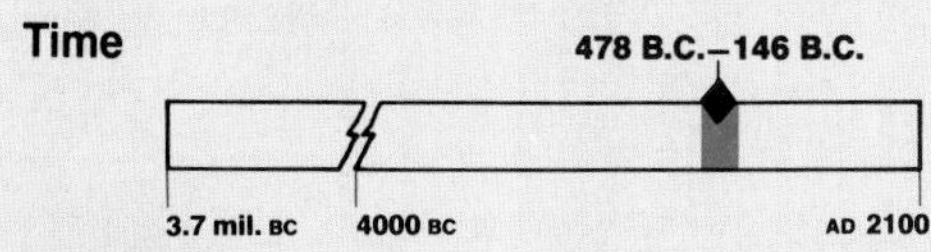

Significance

Greek culture reached new heights during the 400s B.C., a period so magnificent we call it the *Golden Age.* It may seem astonishing that in such a short time one group of people created so many enduring contributions in art, thought, and politics. Their achievements appear even more remarkable if we consider that they took place when the Greek city-states were engaged in fierce military struggles among themselves and also faced serious danger from enemies outside Greece.

In the 300s B.C. an outside power, Macedonia, conquered the Greek city-states. An extraordinary commander, Alexander the Great, established a vast empire. By creating a much larger area within which Greek ideas and art could thrive, Alexander made possible the development of the **Hellenistic culture,** a new culture founded on Greek ideas and features from other cultures of the Mediterranean region. Remarkable advances in philosophy, science, mathematics, medicine, and astronomy dramatically changed the way people thought. These achievements molded ideas about the physical universe and influenced Western civilization for centuries.

Terms to Define

Hellenistic culture	infantry
philosophy	phalanx
drama	orator

People to Identify

Socrates	Demosthenes
Plato	Alexander the Great
Aristotle	

Places to Locate

Macedonia	Susa
Thebes	Syria

Questions to Guide Your Reading

1. How did Greek art represent the ideals of Greek civilization?
2. In what ways did philosophers and writers add to the heritage of Greece?
3. How did Alexander the Great create an empire?
4. How did Hellenistic culture spread throughout the Mediterranean region?

History records the feats of the Macedonian conqueror known as Alexander the Great primarily in terms of military conquest. But those who knew Alexander witnessed more than history in the making. They saw the soul of the man, the melting eyes, the emotion inspired by poetry and music, the uncontrollable temper, the grief he bore when his army suffered, and the frenzied excitement of victory.

A natural athlete, Alexander became a swift runner, an agile fencer, an accomplished archer, and a fearless hunter. He also exhibited an uncanny ability as a horseman. Alexander's prowess emerged when, as a young boy, he tamed a horse that reared, thrashed its hooves, and shied away from everyone. Alexander watched the horse and noticed that it was afraid of its own shadow. Soothing the spirited animal, Alexander turned it to face the sun and quickly mounted the horse, called Bucephalas (byoo • SEF • uh • luhs).

Seeing his young son's success, Philip of Macedon turned proudly to Alexander and said "My son, Macedonia is too small for you; seek out a larger empire, worthier of you." Philip saw something in the young prince that day that historians can write about but never define—the elements of greatness that shape human history. These qualities in Alexander the Great sparked the spread of Greek culture throughout the Mediterranean world.

1 Greek Art Represented the Ideals of Greek Civilization

After the Persian Wars, the wealth and power of Athens attracted artists and teachers from throughout Greece to the city. As Greece's center of art and culture, Athens inspired many people whose artistic and literary contributions exerted a lasting impact on Western civilization. The peak of cultural activity in Athens occurred during the 400s B.C.—a period called the Golden Age.

Architecture

The Athenians surrounded themselves with beauty. They showed their love of Athens and their pride in it by erecting impressive temples, gymnasiums, and theaters. They decorated these structures with their finest works of art, especially sculpture.

◀ *The Battle of Issus*

revolutionary when compared to Egyptian, Minoan, and Middle Eastern art forms.
3. Describe the lives. teachings, and significant contributions of Socrates, Aristotle, and Plato.
4. Summarize the Greek contributions and major developments in math, science, history, and drama.
5. Sketch a model of a Greek theater and describe the characteristics of a Greek play—both tragedy and comedy.
6. Describe Philip of Macedon's army and the methods he used to conquer the Greeks.
7. Outline Alexander the Great's goals, the major actions he took to carry them out, and the changes in Mediterranean society that developed after the division of his empire.
8. Categorize the economic classes and their respective roles in society during the Hellenistic Age.
9. Provide examples of how "Hellenization" of the Mediterranean world changed both Greek and non-Greek traditions and culture.
10. Compare Cynic, Stoic, and Epicurean founders and their philosophies.
11. Describe Hellenistic developments in mathematics, medicine, geography, and science.

SECTION 1

Focus/Motivation
Students should understand the differences between Hellenistic and Classical art. Have them study

1B, 1C, 3A, a1A, a4F

the picture on page 127. Bring in additional examples of Classical and Hellenistic art. *The Birth of Western Civilization* (McGraw-Hill), edited by Michael Grant, has numerous examples. Other examples are readily available in art books or illustrated books on Greek history.

Use the following to help students distinguish between the two artistic periods: Which style portrays the ideal beauty of gods and heroes? *(Classical)* Which appears to show human emotions and capture fleeting moments? *(Hellenistic)* The art of which period is more elaborate? more emotional? more active in appearance? *(Hellenistic)* Which appears to strive for complete balance and harmony? *(Classical)* Which appears to be more individualistic? *(Hellenistic)*

Presentation Analyzing Ideas (Average/Group)

Write the following list on the chalkboard or an overhead projector, or distribute copies of the list. Students are to identify the four major characteristics of Greek art.

(X) **1.** Expressed ideals of harmony, balance, order and moderation
___ **2.** Concerned with death
(X) **3.** Glorified humans

● It symbolizes graceful design and balanced proportion instead of size.

Learning from Pictures *Athenians built their major temples on the easily defended and centrally located Acropolis. Why is the Parthenon the finest example of Greek architecture?*

The Acropolis, the location of the original polis, provided the backdrop for special artistic creations. A magnificent gate graced the entrance to the path up the hill. Inside the gate towered a huge bronze statue of the goddess Athena that stood 70 feet (21 meters) high. As the special protector of the city of Athens, she bore a shield and a spear.

At the top of the Acropolis stood the Parthenon, a white marble temple built in honor of Athena. Begun in 447 B.C. and completed about 14 years later, it is considered the finest example of Greek architecture. This splendid structure measures 230 feet (69 meters) long, 100 feet (30 meters) wide, and 65 feet (19.5 meters) high. Its exquisite beauty lay not in its great size but in its graceful design and balanced proportions—the relation of length to width, and of length and width to height. The structure represents a Greek ideal known as the Golden Mean—a midpoint between two extremes—"Nothing in excess, and everything in proportion."

Like most Greek temples, built as shrines rather than meeting places for worshipers, the Parthenon had doors but no windows. A series of columns, or a colonnade, encircled the structure. Sculptured figures painted in a variety of vivid colors adorned the slabs of marble above the columns. Inside the Parthenon stood a large statue of Athena, with a surface delicately carved of ivory and draped in gold studded with jewels. Today people consider this type of sculpture and architecture one of the greatest gifts of the Greeks to Western civilization.

Painting

Because many of the originals have been lost or severely damaged, our knowledge of Greek painting comes mainly from literary descriptions and from later Roman copies. The best-preserved Greek paintings are those found on vases. Greek vase painters illustrated scenes from everyday life as well as mythological events. These artists delighted in showing the graceful and natural movements of their subjects. Some of these vase painters could depict light and shade on the pottery, a technique used to show contour and depth.

Other Greek painters decorated public buildings with murals, or wall paintings. Mural painters often chose to illustrate scenes from the *Iliad* or the *Odyssey*. On one of the public buildings of Athens, for example, an artist painted *The Sack of Troy*. With a true sense of tragedy, he did not depict the massacre at the moment of the Greek victory but the silence of the following day, with the bodies of the defeated lying amid the ruins of the once magnificent city.

Sculpture

As with Greek painting, few original works of Greek sculpture still exist. What we know about Greek sculpture has come chiefly from studying the copies made during Roman times.

Myron and Phidias (FID • ee • uhs), two of history's greatest sculptors, lived during the Golden Age. Myron sculpted the famous figure called *The Discus Thrower*. Phidias created the two exquisite statues of Athena in the Parthenon. His greatest work, however, was the statue of Zeus at the Temple of Olympia. Greeks who attended the Olympic Games viewed the statue with awe. In ancient times people considered this statue one of the Seven Wonders of the World.

Praxiteles (prak • SIT • uh • leez), who lived about 100 years after Phidias, from 385 B.C. to 320 B.C., created quite a different kind of sculpture. While Phidias created large, formal, dignified works appropriate for the gods, Praxiteles created more delicate, lifelike, often life-sized figures. Though more graceful than those of Phidias, these figures did not inspire awe and reverence, as had the works of the earlier master. Above all, the works of Praxiteles expressed the Greek admiration for the beauty of the human body.

Learning from Pictures *Praxiteles' admiration for the beauty of the human body is seen here in his statue of the god Hermes holding the god Dionysus as a child.*

___ **4.** Depicted mostly animals
___ **5.** Highly emotional
(X) **6.** Symbolized pride of people in their city-states
___ **7.** Abstract and geometric designs
(X) **8.** Combined beauty and usefulness

Have the students reread page 127 and write a short comparison of the sculpture of Phidias with that of Praxiteles. They may find works about these two sculptors in your school or local library. Ask some of the students to read their comparisons to the class.

SECTION 1

Closure
The Greeks provided some of the greatest art and architecture the world has ever seen. Ask students to give examples in architecture, painting, and sculpture. *(Parthenon, Hermes)*

Review Answers
1. ***Hellenistic culture:*** a new culture founded on Greek ideas and features from other cultures of the Mediterranean region
2. ***Myron:*** Greek sculptor, *Discus Thrower;* ***Phidias:*** Greek sculptor, created statues of Athena in the Parthenon and Zeus at Temple of Olympia; ***Praxiteles:*** his graceful statues expressed the Greek admiration for the beauty of human body
3. ***Athens:*** center of Greek art and culture
4. It means we should do

1B, 3A, a1B, a4A, a4F, a4G, a4H

everything moderately as the ideal of the Golden Mean. For example, the beauty of the Parthenon lay not in its great size but in its pleasing proportions. **5. (a)** Vase painters illustrated everyday life and myths. **(b)** Sculptors carved statues of athletes, gods, and goddesses. **6.** Phidias' sculptures were large, formal and dignified, but Praxiteles' work was more human and graceful. **7. (a)** Greek art glorified humans as the most important creatures in the universe; symbolized the pride of the Greeks in their city-states and gods; expressed their ideals of harmony, balance, order and moderation; and combined beauty and usefulness. **(b)** Statues suggested ideal traits admired by the Greeks—strength, intelligence, pride, grace, and courage. They also helped show their love for their city and their hope for its continuing good fortune. They expressed harmony, balance, order and moderation in all things. They believed that usefulness and beauty should be combined.

SECTION 2

Focus/Motivation

A discussion on the nature of philosophy would be helpful to the students. Begin by asking for a definition of the term *philosophy (inquiring into the fundamental questions of reality and human existence).* Then ask students the following questions:

The Nature of Greek Art

Throughout Greek history architecture, painting, and sculpture reflected the Greeks' view of themselves and the world. Four characteristics in particular helped establish the style of this great art.

First, Greek art glorified humans as the most important creatures in the universe. Much of the painting and sculpture portrayed gods and goddesses, but the Greeks thought the gods existed for the benefit of the people. When humans glorified the gods, then, they glorified themselves. To gain this effect, the Greek painter or sculptor idealized the subject, omitting any blemishes. The faces and figures of men and women represented the Greek ideal of beauty. The statues also suggested other ideal traits admired by the Greeks—strength, intelligence, pride, grace, and courage.

Second, Greek art symbolized the peoples' pride in their city-states. At the same time, it honored the gods, thanked them for life and fortune, and tried to win their favor. Thus, in giving Athena a beautiful shrine in the Parthenon, the Athenians showed their love for their city and their hope for its continuing good fortune.

Third, all Greek art expressed Greek ideals of harmony, balance, order, and moderation. By moderation the Greeks meant simplicity and restraint—qualities that they emphasized in their day-to-day lives.

Finally, the Greeks believed in combining beauty and usefulness. To them, the useful, the beautiful, and the good were closely bound together. They wanted their art and even their furniture and kitchen utensils to be both serviceable and beautiful.

SECTION 1 REVIEW

1. **Define** Hellenistic culture
2. **Identify** Myron, Phidias, Praxiteles
3. **Locate** Athens
4. **Interpreting Ideas** Briefly explain the meaning of the following quotation: "Nothing in excess, and everything in proportion."
5. **Understanding Ideas** **(a)** What do the paintings on Greek vases depict? **(b)** How is the subject matter different from that of sculpture?
6. **Comparing Ideas** How did the style of Phidias differ from that of Praxiteles?
7. **Analyzing Ideas** **(a)** List the four main characteristics of Greek art. **(b)** How did each reflect Greek ideals?

2 Philosophers and Writers Added to the Heritage of Greece

The Greeks have been honored through the ages for their artistic and intellectual achievements. No people before them—and few since—have demonstrated so clearly the capacity of the human hand and mind.

Socrates

Socrates (SAHK • ruh • teez), one of history's greatest thinkers and teachers, lived in Athens from 469 B.C. to 399 B.C. Trained as a sculptor, Socrates left that profession to become a teacher.

Socrates criticized Athenian education, especially the teachings of the Sophists, who taught in most Athenian schools. He believed that they boasted of their wisdom, too often inspiring conceit in their pupils. He would not allow himself to be called a Sophist, preferring the term *philosopher,* a Greek word that means "lover of wisdom." From this term comes our word **philosophy,** or the study of the most fundamental questions of reality and human existence.

Socrates wanted people to think for themselves and not imitate their elders. Only then could they acquire wisdom, which would lead to "right living." According to Socrates, only evil could result from ignorance. People should depend on reason and logic to guide their lives.

Unlike the Sophists Socrates did not use the teaching method of memorizing. Instead he asked questions of anyone he met, anywhere. His purpose was not to receive information but to make people think in order to answer the questions. Constantly repeating his motto "know thyself," Socrates tried to teach people to understand what love, friendship, duty, patriotism, honor, and justice really meant. He urged each person to find his or her own answers to these and other questions. This way of teaching became known as the "Socratic method."

Although greatly loved because of his wisdom, honesty, and kindness, Socrates also had enemies. His questions often made public officials look foolish. He also criticized democracy. He believed it unwise to elect unskilled people to positions of power, and he distrusted the wisdom of the Assembly. After all, he said, we do not elect doctors or

Learning from Pictures *This mosaic named the* School of Plato *depicts the Academy, where Plato taught students to systematically pursue philosophical knowledge.*

ship pilots—why should we elect rulers? Crowds of young followers gathered to hear Socrates mock democracy and its leaders, who did not find him so amusing.

Though Socrates honored the gods of Athens, his enemies accused him of denying the existence of many Greek gods. The Athenian leaders brought him to trial on charges of teaching false religion and corrupting the minds of Athenian youth.

At his trial Socrates said that his conscience made him teach. If allowed to live, he would continue to teach because his conscience would compel him to do so. Found guilty and condemned to die by drinking a poison made from the hemlock plant, Socrates faced his fate cheerfully. He believed in the immortality of his soul and persisted in his search for truth until his death.

Plato

Although Socrates never recorded his ideas, later generations learned of them from the writings of Plato, a wealthy young aristocrat and the greatest of his students. After the death of Socrates, Plato traveled throughout the Mediterranean region. He then returned to Athens and began to teach philosophy on the grounds of the Academy, a public park and athletic field.

Plato wrote dialogues, or imaginary conversations among several people, covering such topics as government, education, justice, virtue, and religion. In each dialogue Socrates usually appeared as the primary speaker and asked questions of the others. The dialogues, however, expressed many of Plato's theories as well.

In one such dialogue, Socrates asked "What is justice?" To answer the question, Plato wrote the *Republic,* a long dialogue describing his concept of the ideal form of government. People, he said, should do the work for which they are best suited. For example, those noted for their bravery should be in the army. People interested in material things such as food, clothing, and luxuries should conduct the business and perform the labor. Plato's ideal

What is the difference between philosophy and religion? Between philosophy and science? With what questions is the philosopher concerned?

In conducting this activity you will be using the Socratic method. Mention this to the class and ask them to describe Socrates' method of education. For information on the nature of philosophy, you may wish to consult the introduction in Bertrand Russell's *A History of Western Philosophy* (Simon and Schuster).

Presentation
Summarizing Ideas
(Average/Group)

Ask students to make a chart in their notebooks of Greek scientists and their contributions. Charts should have two columns with the heading *Scientist* at the top of the first column, and *Contributions* at the top of the second. The list should include Pythagoras, developed the Pythagorean theorem in geometry; Aristotle, laid the foundations of botany, zoology, and anatomy; Democritus, theorized that all matter is composed of atoms; Hippocrates, taught that disease comes from natural causes—the Hippocratic Oath is based on his teachings. After the students have compiled their lists, conduct a class discussion on how these contributions affected their particular field of science.

government was an aristocracy—a government ruled by an upper class. However, it was not an aristocracy of birth or of wealth but one based on intelligence, reasoning, education, and high ideals. Plato's ideal "aristocrats" were philosophers, chosen for their wisdom, ability, and "correct" ideas about justice.

Aristotle

Among Plato's students in the Academy was a young man named Aristotle, who founded his own school at Athens in 335 B.C. An accomplished scientist as well as a great philosopher, Aristotle vigorously embarked upon the task of investigating every kind of knowledge and collected as many facts as possible. He then organized these facts into systems, comparing one fact with another to find what each meant or showed. Aristotle demonstrated a special skill for defining words and grouping similar or related facts. This process of organization forms an important part of modern scientific thinking.

Aristotle almost accomplished his goal of investigating every known field of knowledge in his time. He collected, described, and classified plants and animals. For his book *Ethics,* Aristotle examined the acts and beliefs of individuals to learn what brought them the greatest happiness. He concluded that the Greek ideal of style in the arts—balance, order, and restraint—also represented the ideal in terms of human behavior. In his work *Poetics,* he studied Greek drama to show the differences between a good play and a bad one. In his *Logic* he attempted to define the principles of correct reasoning. Aristotle studied the political organization of 150 city-states in order to describe the principles of government, and he recorded his conclusions in a book called *Politics.* He concluded that the best type of government contained a middle class—those people neither wealthy nor poor—who played an important role. He wrote:

> "The middle class is least likely to shrink from rule, or to be overambitious for it; both of which are injuries to the state. . . . But a city ought to be composed, as far as possible, of equals and similars; and these are generally the middle classes. . . .
>
> Thus it is manifest that the best political community is formed by citizens of the middle class, and that those states are likely to be well administered in which the middle class is large, and stronger if possible than both the other classes, or at any rate than either singly; for the addition of the middle class turns the scale, and prevents either of the extremes from being dominant."

Aristotle's political writings, like those of other great philosophers of the Golden Age, reflected his study of Greek culture and his experiences in public life. Aristotle believed that although pure monarchy, aristocracy, and democracy were equally good forms of government, each could easily be corrupted. For example, he believed that the power of the people in a democracy could easily lead to a dictatorship of the "mob." Therefore, the best government should include aspects of each form of government—a powerful leader, aristocratic advisers, and a democratic assembly.

Aristotle's belief in division of power among different levels of government contrasted with Plato's belief that one level of government should control a person's life for the benefit of the whole state. According to Plato, people of the lower classes could never rise above their position in society and achieve success in life without the guidance of intellectual leaders who represented a higher level of authority.

Mathematics and Science

In the 500s B.C., the philosopher and mathematician Pythagoras (puh • THAG • uh • ruhs), who was born on the island of Samos in the Aegean Sea, wrote that everything could be explained or expressed with numbers. He is probably best known for the Pythagorean theorem, the geometric theory that states that the square of the hypotenuse of a right triangle equals the sum of the squares of the other two sides.

The Greeks of the Golden Age also made some advances in science. However, Greek scientific achievements did not develop fully until a later period. Aristotle laid the foundations for the development of botany, zoology, and anatomy. The Greek philosopher Democritus (di • MAHK • ruht • uhs) believed that moving atoms—small particles that could not be divided—compose all matter. Scientists have since proved that the atom can be divided, but they still accept the theory that all matter consists of atoms.

130

One of the greatest scientists of the Golden Age was Hippocrates (hip • AHK • ruh • teez). Considered the founder of medicine, he taught that all disease comes from natural causes, not as punishment from the gods. He believed that rest, fresh air, and a proper diet made the best cures. Hippocrates recorded his ideas in his *Regimen of Health.* He wrote:

> "In winter it is beneficial to counteract the cold and congealed season by living according to the following regimen. First, a man should have one meal a day only, unless he have a very dry belly; in that case let him take a light luncheon. The articles of diet to be used are such as are of a drying nature, of a warming character, assorted and undiluted; wheaten bread is to be preferred to barley cake, and roasted to boiled meats . . . vegetables should be reduced to a minimum, except such as are warming and dry."

Hippocrates had high ideals for physicians. Today physicians still take the Hippocratic oath, a pledge to follow the code of medical ethics based on Hippocrates' teachings.

History

The Greeks became the first people to take the writing of history seriously. Herodotus, an enthusiastic traveler and the first great historian of the western world, visited Babylonia, Phoenicia, and Egypt. He included his impressions of these countries and their people in his histories.

A fascinating writer and a wonderful storyteller, Herodotus exaggerated at times, but always carefully distinguished between the things he had personally seen or investigated and those he had been told. He often expressed doubt about legends but reported them for whatever they were worth. Historians still consult his writings for information about the world during his time, and he is often called the "Father of History."

Another Greek historian, Thucydides (thoo • SID • uh • deez), became famous for his *History of the Peloponnesian War* (see Chapter 5). Thucydides wanted his account of history to reflect his belief that studying the past yields an understanding of human nature. He also hoped that his scientific approach to history would serve as a guide for future political leaders.

Learning from Pictures *During the Festival of Dionysus, plays were held in this well-preserved theater at Epidaurus.*

Greek Drama

Greeks living in Athens during the Golden Age wrote a surprising number of the world's greatest works of literature. A tremendous flood of creative writing occurred during that brief period. Greek literature still endures today because of its simple, beautiful, and realistic portrayal of people.

The Greeks were the first people to write **dramas,** or plays containing action or dialogue and usually involving conflict and emotion. They excelled in this form of literature. They always wrote plays in poetic form, and two or three actors and a chorus, or a group of singers and dancers who described the scenes, spoke or sang the lines in front of an audience.

Reflecting the idea of harmony with nature, the Greeks carved outdoor theaters into hillsides noted for beauty and serenity. The Greeks frequently built seats for the audience into the slopes of these hillsides. The base contained the *orchestra,* the area where the chorus changed and the actors performed. Greek theaters did not have raised stages as the Romans would use for plays. Also, unlike the "sets" of many plays today, sets for Greek dramas featured little scenery. Audiences relied on choral descriptions to set the time and place of various scenes.

The male actors, their voices trained to produce variety in tone and pitch, also played women's roles. They wore elaborate padded costumes and thick-soled boots to make them look larger than life. Actors also used masks to indicate the characters and emotions they portrayed.

SECTION 2

Closure

Ask students to explain how Socrates, Plato, and Aristotle carried out their search for knowledge—their methodology. What kind of government would each have established?

Review Answers

1. ***philosophy:*** inquiry into the most fundamental questions of reality and human existence; ***drama:*** play usually involving conflict and emotion through action and dialogue; ***tragedy:*** drama that showed the major character struggling against fate; ***hubris:*** assumption a person had knowledge or ability equal to that of the gods; ***comedy:*** Greek play that mocked ideas and peoples, but in which the central characters solved their problems

2. ***Socrates:*** Greek philosopher who wanted people to think for themselves; ***Plato:*** wrote Socrates' philosophies in a dialogue called the *Republic;* ***Aristotle:*** student of Plato who grouped facts into a process important to modern scientific thinking; ***Pythagoras:*** philosopher and mathematician; ***Democritus:*** believed all matter is composed of moving atoms; ***Hippocrates:*** considered the founder of medicine; ***Thucydides:*** historian famous for *History of the Peloponnesian War;* ***Aeschylus:*** playwright whose tragedies described the relationships between gods

1B, 3A, a1C, a4A, a4F, a4G, a4H

● to indicate the characters and emotions they portrayed
■ The word *hubris* is often used today to mean exaggerated pride or self-esteem.

and people; ***Sophocles:*** author of *Oedipus the Tyrant,* his plays defended traditional values; ***Euripides:*** realist playwright, who questioned old beliefs and ideas; ***Aristophanes:*** greatest Greek writer of comedies
3. (a) Socrates thought the Sophists boasted too much and taught boys to live by memorization instead of reasoning for themselves; **(b)** He taught by the Socratic method—asking questions so people could find their own answers; **(c)** so people could learn to think for themselves
4. Plato's ideal government was an aristocracy based on intelligence, ability, and high ideals.
5. (a) As a scientist, Aristotle collected, described and classified plants and animals. **(b)** He also studied political organization in *Politics*. *Ethics* dealt with virtue and happiness. *Poetics* was a study of Greek drama. *Logic* defined the principles of reasoning.
6. Aristotle's ideas of the best government would include aspects of each form of government—a powerful leader, aristocratic advisors, and a democratic assembly. Plato's ideal government was an aristocracy of an intelligent, educated, idealistic upper class.
7. Spartans did not allow criticism.

Learning from Pictures *This comic mask belonged to a Greek actor around 300 B.C. Why did actors use* ● *masks in their performances?*

Performed in connection with religious festivals, the plays often focused on a religious theme. Each spring and winter, such festivals were held in honor of Dionysus (dy • uh • NY • suhs), the god of fertility and wine. At the winter Festival of Dionysus, three plays were presented each day for three successive days. Each day the audience selected the best play, judging it by the beauty of the language and the wisdom of its ideas. The winning author received a crown of ivy, the traditional Greek symbol of victory.

Tragedies. In Greek **tragedies** the main character struggled against fate. Often a combination of outside forces overcame this central character, who assumed that he or she had the same knowledge or ability as the gods. Such an assumption, known ■ as **hubris** (HYOO • bruhs), insulted the gods and doomed the character to a tragic fate.

Three great writers of tragedy lived during the 400s B.C. One writer, Aeschylus (ES • kuh • luhs), wrote of the old religious beliefs concerning the relationship between gods and people. His three most famous plays centered on the murder of Agamemnon, the king who led the Greeks against Troy, and the revenge that followed.

Another writer of tragedies, Sophocles (SAHF • uh • kleez), defended traditional values. Aristotle called Sophocles' most famous play, *Oedipus the Tyrant,* a perfect example of tragedy.

Euripides (yoo • RIP • uh • deez), the third playwright, was more of a realist than Aeschylus or Sophocles. Like Socrates he questioned many old beliefs and ideas. Earlier writers often glorified war for its deeds of courage and heroism. In *The Trojan Women,* Euripides showed the reality of war, exposing all its pain and misery.

Comedies. Greek **comedies,** which also originated at the festival honoring Dionysus, mocked ideas and people. The comedies usually introduced both tragic and comic figures. Unlike their counterparts in tragedies, however, the central characters in comedies succeeded in solving their problems.

No person or institution could escape the wit of Aristophanes (ar • uh • STAHF • uh • neez), the greatest Greek writer of comedies. In *The Clouds* he poked fun at Socrates for his theories about educating the youth of Athens. Aristophanes also disliked war and used comedy to make Athenians think about its causes and consequences. In some of his plays, women controlled the government or persuaded their husbands to make peace during war. This amused the Athenians because of their low opinion of women.

SECTION 2 REVIEW

1. **Define** philosophy, drama, tragedy, hubris, comedy
2. **Identify** Socrates, Plato, Aristotle, Pythagoras, Democritus, Hippocrates, Thucydides, Aeschylus, Sophocles, Euripides, Aristophanes
3. **Understanding Ideas** **(a)** Why did Socrates criticize the Sophists? **(b)** What teaching method did Socrates use? **(c)** What was its purpose?
4. **Summarizing Ideas** What were the main characteristics of the ideal government described in Plato's *Republic?*
5. **Interpreting Ideas** **(a)** Why is Aristotle considered a scientist as well as a philosopher? **(b)** List the major ideas presented in *Politics, Ethics, Poetics,* and *Logic.*
6. **Contrasting Ideas** In what ways did Aristotle's view of government differ from Plato's view of government?
7. **Synthesizing Ideas** Why would the comedies of Aristophanes have been impossible to perform in Sparta?

3 Alexander the Great Created a Huge Empire

Between 404 B.C. and 362 B.C., Sparta and then Thebes attempted to dominate Greece. However, unsuccessful leadership and continuous Persian interference in Greek affairs prevented unity. Wars raged, and although Persia seemed the most logical victor, another foreign power—Macedonia—brought unity to Greece.

Philip of Macedon

The power that finally unified Greece came from an unexpected direction. Look at the map on page 134. A mountainous land called Macedonia lies north of Greece. In the 300s B.C., the Macedonians, a hardy, warlike people closely related to Greeks, inhabited this land. The Macedonians lived in small villages, each ruled by a powerful noble. Macedonia also had a king, but the extent of his power depended on his own leadership abilities and on the help of the nobles.

In 359 B.C. a remarkable young man known as Philip of Macedon became king. Captured by the Thebans in his youth, Philip remained a hostage in Thebes for three years. During that time he came to admire both the Greek life style and the organization of the Theban military.

Philip wanted to be a strong king and to control the unruly Macedonian nobles and people. Instead of depending on the nobles to supply troops for an army, Philip recruited the first regular paid army in Macedonian history.

He drilled his force of 10,000 soldiers into the most powerful army Europe had ever known. Landowners, serving as cavalry, rode massive horses and underwent extensive training that taught them to fight in close formation. In addition, Philip organized hunters and peasants into an **infantry**—a group of soldiers trained and equipped to fight on foot. Philip organized part of the infantry into phalanxes (fuh • LAN • jeez) similar to those used by the armies of the Greek city-states. A **phalanx** (FAY • langks) consisted of 16 rows of tightly spaced soldiers equipped with lances 21 feet (6.4 meters) long. Weighted at the back, each lance became a deadly weapon when hurled.

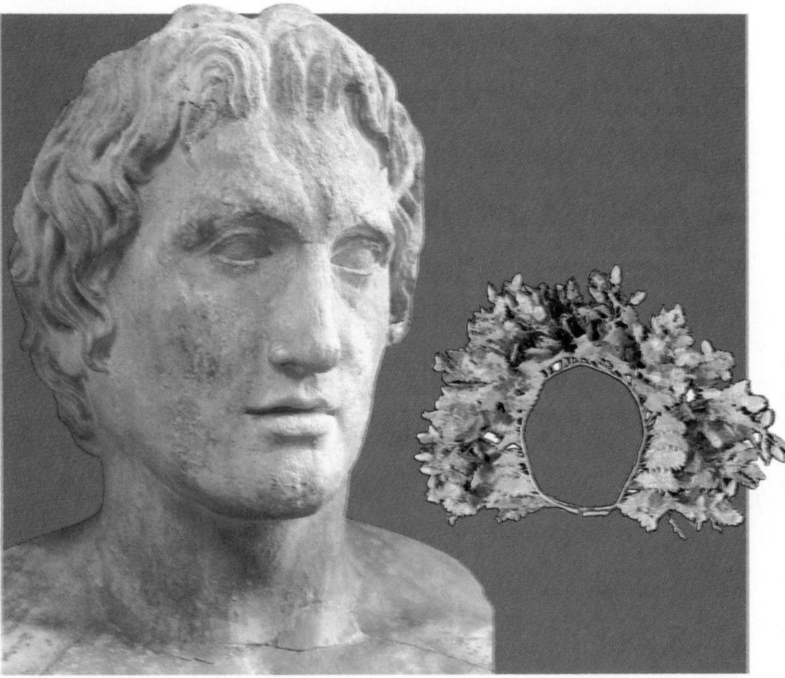

Learning from Pictures *The gold crown (far right) found in the city of Vergina in Macedonia may have belonged to Alexander the Great (right). Alexander had his own silver coin minted (above) since traders in the empire accepted silver as the medium of exchange.*

SECTION 3

Focus/Motivation

In this section the students will learn that a strong leader, Philip of Macedon, invaded Greece and took control of the Greek city-states. Quarreling among the Greek city-states caused the Peloponnesian War. This war so devastated Greece that it left the city-states open to foreign invasion. Ask the students to speculate on what might be some of the causes of the Peloponnesian War. *(Answers might include economic and commercial rivalry, social differences, and cultural differences.)* Ask students how this type of bitter rivalry might lead to a takeover by a powerful outside leader. *(Answers will vary. Students might argue that wars occur when one faction attempts to dominate the others. Then an outsider or third party is seen as an objective observer who would be impartial to all sides. Therefore, these quarreling parties are more willing to accept leadership and be dominated by this outsider.)*

Presentation
Evaluating Ideas (Average/Group)

Write the following statements on the chalkboard or an overhead projector:

There is always a power struggle among states to dominate a union.

A strong leader can take over easily when a power vacuum exists.

1A, 3A, a4B, a4C, a4K

● Demosthenes' attacks on Philip were so violent that today we call such a speech a philippic.

People are in danger of giving up their freedoms when they turn the power of government over to a strong leader.

Lead a discussion in which students try to determine which statement had the most decisive effect on the Greek city-states. Students should support their choice with evidence. Some students may not be able to evaluate the degree of impact, but through the discussion they should become knowledgeable about factors affecting a nation with internal problems.

After unifying his own kingdom, Philip used his army to conquer surrounding peoples. He first gained control of some towns in northern Greece that Athens claimed as colonies. He then turned south and began unifying the Greek city-states under his rule.

The Greeks had varying opinions of Philip. Some people regarded him as a savior who could bring unity to Greece. Others opposed him as a menace to liberty. Demosthenes (di • MAHS • thuh • neez), one of the greatest **orators,** or public speakers, in all Athenian history, led the opposition to Philip in Athens.

Demosthenes tried to make Athenians aware of the danger he believed Philip of Macedon posed. ● He bitterly attacked Philip in a series of speeches to the Assembly and tried to get Athens to lead the Greeks once more in a fight for liberty. Demosthenes did spur the Athenians to action. As so often happened in Greek history, however, the city-states failed to present a unified defense. As Philip and his army relentlessly marched south, traitors betrayed some city-states, supporting Philip's belief that "No fortress is inaccessible if one can only introduce within it a mule laden with gold." One by one, other city-states fell to Philip's army. Finally it defeated the forces of Thebes and Athens at the battle of Chaeronea (ker • uh • NEE • uh) in 338 B.C. (see map, this page), and Philip became master of Greece.

The Greeks were at last united, but they had lost their freedom. Although Philip organized the cities into a league to support his plans for an invasion of Persia, he never achieved his goal. At his daughter's wedding in the summer of 336 B.C., an army officer whom Philip had refused to help with a dispute assassinated him. His 20-year-old son Alexander, known to history as Alexander the Great, succeeded him.

Alexander the Great

Alexander proved to be even more remarkable than his father. Although very much alike, Alexander

Learning from Maps *Alexander conquered Persepolis before turning north to conquer the rest of Persia. Which city did he conquer first, Susa or Persepolis?* Susa

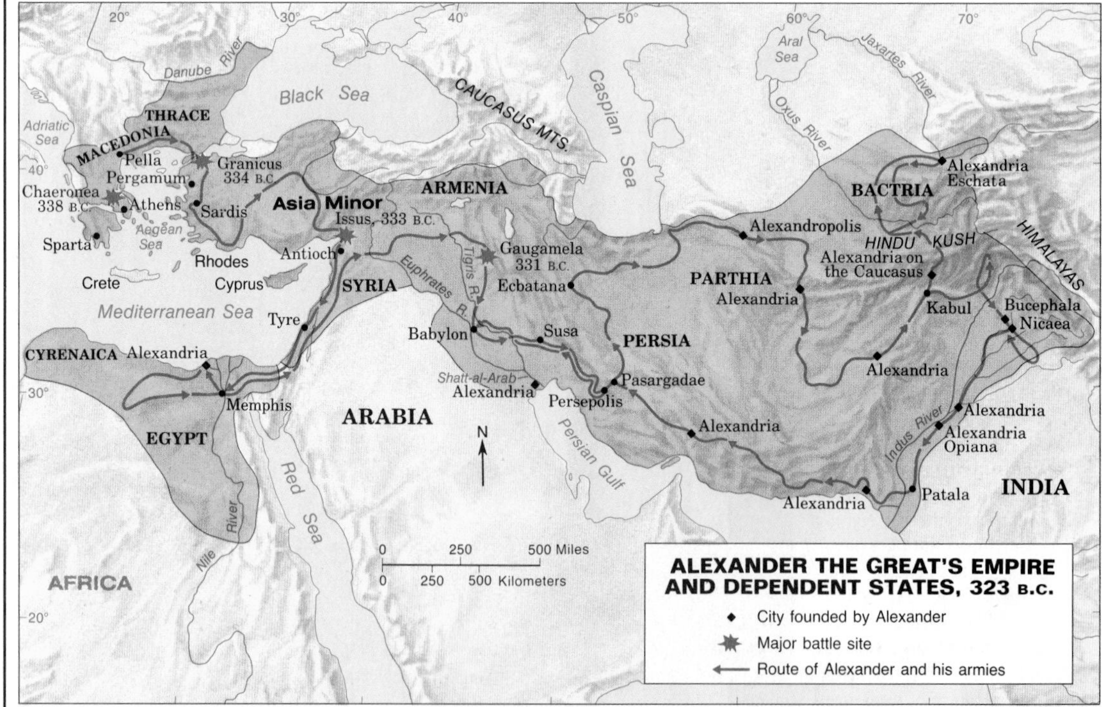

CONNECTIONS: THEN AND NOW

Memorials

What is the name of your school? Many schools, libraries, colleges, and towns are named for famous people. In this way we remember individuals and honor their contributions long after they have died. In the United States, our two most famous leaders are honored by the Washington and Lincoln Memorials in Washington, D.C., in the state and cities called Washington, and in the 19 American cities and towns named Lincoln.

In all history Alexander the Great probably has been memorialized more than anyone else. As he conquered cities and towns, he gave many of them his name (right). Beginning in Alexandria, Egypt, his route can be traced eastward by following the towns having his name or that of *Iskander,* his name in Arabic.

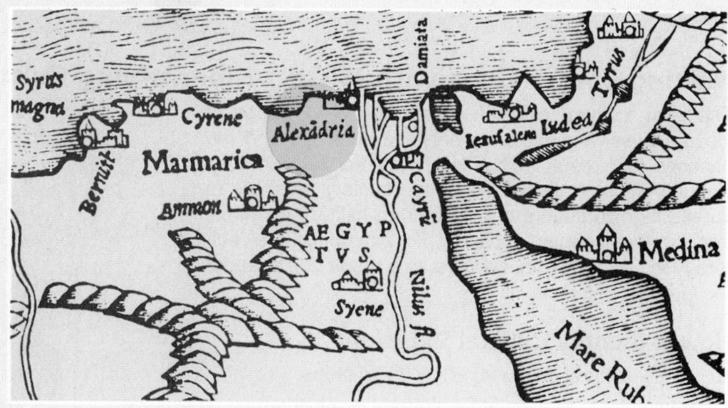

Although in the ancient world cities were generally named after living people, the cities memorialized that person after his or her death.

Names sometimes change with history. For example, Idlewild Airport in New York was renamed Kennedy Airport in honor of John F. Kennedy.

Notice the names of places in your town. Perhaps you can think of other people who have been memorialized in this way.

and Philip rarely agreed and often quarreled bitterly. Despite their differences, however, Philip did everything to give his son the best training and education possible. Alexander received his military training in the Macedonian army and his formal education from the great Greek philosopher Aristotle. The opportunity to cultivate both military skills and an appreciation for his cultural heritage prepared Alexander for leadership and made him a lifelong admirer of Greek culture.

As a military commander, Alexander was even more skilled than his father. His military campaigns rank among the greatest in history. Physically strong and brave to the point of rashness, Alexander's dramatic acts in battle so captured the imagination of his troops that they willingly followed him into unknown lands.

Alexander's plan. Alexander dreamed of a Hellenistic empire—a world empire that would connect East and West and blend the best features of the Greek and Persian cultures into a new culture. He planned to create his vast empire in three ways. First, he wanted to found new cities and rebuild old ones as cultural centers of his empire. He actually established more than 70 cities, many of them named Alexandria in his honor. Groups of Greeks and Macedonians settled in each one.

Second, Alexander planned to merge the Macedonians and the Persians into one ruling group in order to run his empire more efficiently. He married the Persian princess Roxana and also required his generals to marry Persian royalty.

Third, Alexander wanted his subjects to consider him a divine monarch, a god-king. He became convinced that his real father was not Philip but the god Zeus-Ammon. Alexander insisted that all of his subjects honor him as being part human and part divine. The Persians did not believe in god-kings, but the Egyptians did; and the Greeks thought that some heroes became gods.

Alexander's conquests. Having developed a plan to create his empire, Alexander put his plan into action by crushing rebellions in the Greek city-states and declaring himself master of Greece. He then set out to conquer the world. By 331 B.C. he had conquered Asia Minor, Syria, Egypt, Mesopotamia, and the once mighty Persian Empire (see map, page 134).

135

1B, 3A, a4A, a4B, a4C, a4H

SECTION 3

Closure

Ask: What was Alexander the Great's dream? *(world empire)* Ask students why they believe Alexander had such a driving ambition. What forced him to pull back? Have students evaluate Alexander's achievements.

Review Answers

1. ***infantry:*** soldiers trained and equipped to fight on foot; ***phalanx:*** formation consisting of 16 rows of tightly spaced soldiers equipped with lances 21 feet long; ***orator:*** public speaker
2. ***Philip:*** Macedonian king; ***Demosthenes:*** one of greatest Athenian orators; ***Alexander the Great:*** conqueror of the Mediterranean world
3. ***Macedonia:*** mountainous land north of Greece; ***Indus River:*** eastern boundary of Alexander's empire; ***Ganges River:*** river in India; ***Susa:*** Persian city; ***Egypt:*** site of Alexander's great city; ***Syria:*** one of three kingdoms formed from Alexander's empire
4. He was a menace to liberty.
5. Alexander wanted to create new cities in his empire, blending the best of Greek and Persian culture into a new Hellenistic culture; merge Macedonian and Persian ruling families; develop a divine monarchy.
6. into three main kingdoms

READ
WRITE
INTERPRET
● CONNECT
THINK

BUILDING HISTORY STUDY SKILLS

Making Connections with History: Identifying Cultural Diffusion

The term "cultural diffusion" refers to the exchange of ideas, values, and products between societies and the changes that result from such cross-cultural contacts. Cultural diffusion occurs when one society attempts to spread its own culture or results from military ventures, trade, or the migration of people. For example, Greek culture fused with Oriental cultures as a result of Alexander the Great's conquests.

How to Identify Cultural Diffusion

To identify cultural diffusion, follow these steps.

1. Identify the cultures and the method of diffusion.
2. Identify the subject.
3. Compare the cultures by stating similarities and differences.
4. Determine the connection between the cultures.

Developing the Skill

Study the sculptures in the photographs on this page and note their similarities and differences. The statue on the left illustrates classic Greek sculpture. The statues above reveal the cultural diffusion Alexander the Great promoted through military conquests.

Sculpted by Myron in the 400s B.C., "The Discus Thrower" mixes idealism and realism. The human body is depicted as it appears to the human eye, but the sculpture stresses the Greek ideals of perfection and self-restraint. The artist captures the athlete at the moment before he makes his supreme effort. He appears dynamically poised and in full control. Yet he represents the Greek ideal rather than an individual. He symbolizes the balance between the individual and the community so characteristic of the Greeks.

The product of cultural diffusion, the Hellenistic statues of a woman and a boy reflect the Greek ideal in that the proportions of the figures are correct. But these statues take realism a step further and represent particular people.

How do the Hellenistic statues show cultural diffusion? First, the statues retain the technical excellence and emphasis on proportions that characterize the Greek ideals. But they also emphasize the individual by focusing on the material aspects of life rather than on perfection.

Practicing the skill. Locate photographs of sculptures and paintings depicting ancient Egyptian culture and ancient Sumerian and Babylonian culture about 2000 B.C. Explain how the statues of Babylon show the influence of Egyptian and Sumerian cultures.

To apply this skill, see Applying History Study Skills on page 141.

1B, 3A, a1A, a4F, a4G, a4H, a4L

● The major successor empires of Alexander are often named after the generals who ruled there: Antigonus in Asia Minor, Seleucus in Syria, and Ptolemy in Egypt. Cleopatra was one of the last descendants of Ptolemy.

Although Alexander now ruled a huge territory, he longed to acquire more. Beyond Persia lay India, the "end of the world," as the people around the Mediterranean Sea then called it. For almost four years he led his troops east, meeting little resistance and going as far as the Indus River. From there he wanted to march on to the Ganges River and so control the entire vast plain of northern India. After four years, however, Alexander's long-suffering army had finally had enough fighting. For three days he pleaded with them, but his exhausted soldiers would not follow. Reluctantly, Alexander turned back in 326 B.C.

Alexander led his army to the Indian Ocean, where he divided his troops. Half of them traveled west by sea, explored the shores of the Persian Gulf as far as the mouth of the Euphrates, and sailed inland to meet Alexander at Susa. Alexander led the rest of his army through the desert, where many of his troops died from scorching heat and searing thirst. Throughout this ordeal Alexander shared the hardships with his troops. At one point a soldier brought him water in a helmet, but Alexander poured the water on the ground, refusing to drink it because his soldiers had none. According to Arrian, a second-century Greek historian, "So extraordinary was the effect of this action that the water wasted by Alexander was as good as a drink for every man in the army."

The tattered remnants of his forces finally reached Susa in the spring of 324 B.C. Although Alexander's fleet suffered only minor losses and joined the king at Susa, the great army would never be reassembled. Alexander and his soldiers had spent years in Asia and had suffered greatly. Amid the growing discontent in his army, Alexander withdrew to a lonely life dominated by suspicions of his soldiers' disloyalty.

One night shortly after his return to Babylon in 323 B.C., Alexander became ill with a fever now thought to be cholera or malaria. In the early evening of the eleventh day of his raging fever, Alexander the Great died at the age of 33.

In 13 years Alexander had never lost a battle and had conquered much of the world known to him. Although his dream of ruling the entire world remained unfulfilled and his empire soon crumbled, Alexander's reign spread Hellenistic culture throughout much of the world. So great was the influence of this culture that we refer to the time between Alexander's death and the Roman conquest of Greece in 146 B.C. as the Hellenistic Age.

The Breakup of Alexander's Empire

After Alexander's death his generals murdered his family and divided the "one world" that composed his empire. A fierce power struggle raged until 301 B.C., when the last attempt to hold the empire together under one ambitious general failed. The three surviving generals, honored as god-kings, divided Alexander's empire into three main kingdoms—Macedonia, Egypt, and Syria. The three ● kingdoms, often at war with one another, used the cities of Greece as pawns in their struggles. They wasted much wealth and energy on war. After 200 B.C. a new people, the Romans, filtered into Greece, and over a span of more than 150 years they conquered the three kingdoms.

SECTION 3 REVIEW

1. **Define** infantry, phalanx, orator
2. **Identify** Philip, Demosthenes, Alexander the Great
3. **Locate** Macedonia, Indus River, Ganges River, Susa, Egypt, Syria
4. **Evaluating Ideas** Why did Demosthenes and other Athenians oppose Philip of Macedon?
5. **Summarizing Ideas** Describe Alexander's three goals for his empire.
6. **Analyzing Ideas** How did Alexander's generals divide his empire after his death?

4 Hellenistic Culture Spread Throughout the Mediterranean Region

The conquests of Alexander the Great brought Greek culture to Egypt and other lands of the Middle East, up to the border of India. Greek culture continued to influence these areas long after Alexander's death. At the same time, the ideas that Alexander's followers brought from other lands modified Greek culture at home. Although the greatest achievements of Hellenistic culture included new advances in philosophy and science, writers also made important contributions that influenced Western thought for centuries.

SECTION 4

Focus/Motivation
The civilization of the Greek city-states passed into the larger world through Alexander's conquests. Greek settlers, traders, and administrators carried Greek ideas and material culture throughout the Middle East. Tell students that this cultural diffusion was a two-way street. Much of Persian and other Eastern cultures got absorbed and metamorphosed into the old Greek culture. This is an example of synthesis on a grand level. Ask students to write in their notebooks that Eastern autocracy predominated over Greek democracy, that the god-kings of the East replaced the citizen rulers of Greece, that mystical Eastern religions began to influence and replace the civic religions of Greece and, later, Rome. Tell students to note that the synthesized Hellenistic world would influence the Romans, about whom they will read in Chapter 7.

Then ask students to give modern examples of cultural diffusion. *(Answers will vary. Students might mention the Westernization of African and Asian nations once ruled by European powers, or the Japanese adoption of Western technology and economic systems; Eastern religions have influenced people in the West.)*

1B, 1D, 3A, a1C

● The middle class is a social and economic group between the upper and lower classes. This class consisted chiefly of people who lived in cities and were engaged in trade.

■ Students may have heard the perhaps apocryphal story of Diogenes wandering about in the daylight with a lantern looking for an honest man.

Presentation
Evaluating Ideas (Average/Group)
Ask the class for three volunteers and have each take the point of view of one of the Hellenistic philosophies. Each student should present arguments in favor of Stoicism, Cynicism, or Epicureanism, and then the group should debate the merits of each philosophy. Invite comments from the class. Finally, the class should identify groups or individuals in our society that seem to live according to one of these philosophies. Rex Warner's *The Greek Philosophers* (New American Library) has selections written in a style that high school students will understand. Bertrand Russell's *A History of Western Philosophy* (Simon and Schuster) is a popular account of philosophy with several chapters on Hellenistic philosophy.

SECTION 4

Closure
Ask students to state Eratosthenes' contributions to geographical knowledge *(calculation of diameter of earth; claimed people could sail around the world)* Why did no one do so during the Hellenistic Age? *(No ships then built could risk a long ocean voyage.)*

Review Answers
1. ***Diogenes:*** most famous Cynic philosopher; ***Zeno:*** established the Stoic philosophy; ***Epicurus:*** founder

The Economy

● Throughout the Hellenistic world, rulers or governments owned much land. Wealthy aristocrats usually held most of the privately owned land, while slaves or poorly paid free laborers did the work. Hellenistic society included a small class of very wealthy people and a large class of miserably poor people. Still the middle class thrived because of the many opportunities for acquiring wealth.

Trade, the most profitable activity, originated from the main trading centers in the cities of Alexandria, in Egypt; Rhodes, on the island of Rhodes, off the coast of Asia Minor; and Antioch, in Syria. Trade routes now connected the entire Mediterranean world, reaching as far east as India. Bigger and better ships contributed greatly to this increase in trade.

The cities Alexander had built or rebuilt became the wonders of the Hellenistic world. Carefully planned and laid out, these cities included market squares and large public buildings such as theaters, schools, or gymnasiums, where men exercised and discussed important issues. Homes of the wealthy included elaborate furniture, running water, and drain pipes. Alexandria, in Egypt, with a population of almost 1 million, became the largest city. Its museum and its library, which housed 750,000 papyrus rolls, made Alexandria a great center of learning and an important center of commerce.

Changing Attitudes

As the middle class expanded, education became widespread. Novels gained popularity. The old and now less respected values of Greece faded. The status of women improved. Hellenistic women appeared more often in public and acquired more rights regarding property and divorce.

Another major change centered on a new definition of what it meant to be a Greek. A Hellenized Egyptian or Syrian was considered a "Greek." Nevertheless, tensions still surfaced when Greeks, Hellenized Greeks, and non-Greeks lived side by side, because the old Greek bias against "barbarians" did not actually decrease; more of the world became Greek.

Philosophy

Hellenistic philosophers concerned themselves more with ethics than with the basic questions of reality and human existence. Three chief schools of philosophy existed—the Cynic, the Stoic, and the Epicurean schools.

The Cynics taught that people should seek virtue only. They scorned pleasure, wealth, and social position. Many stories exist about the best known Cynic, Diogenes (dy • AHJ • uh • neez). One story concerns the meeting of Diogenes and Alexander the Great. "If I were not Alexander, I would prefer to be Diogenes," the conqueror said. But Diogenes growled in reply, "If I were not Diogenes, I would prefer to be any man except Alexander." ■ Today the word *cynic* means a sarcastic person who believes that selfish and insincere motives underlie people's actions.

Zeno established the Stoic philosophy in Athens in the late 300s B.C. He and his followers believed that divine reason directed the world. For example, they believed that whatever fate dictated was right. In their opinion, people should not complain but should learn to accept whatever nature might bring. They should be indifferent to grief, fear, pain, and pleasure.

The Stoics greatly influenced Roman and Christian thinking. Today the word *stoic* means much the same as it meant in Hellenistic times—one who remains outwardly unaffected by pain or pleasure.

Epicurus, founder of the Epicurean philosophy, taught that the aim of life focused on seeking pleasure and avoiding pain. Pleasure to him was intellectual, not physical. After his death, however, his followers sought physical pleasures as well. Their motto became "Eat, drink, and be merry, for tomorrow may bring pain or death." Today the word *epicure* means a person who enjoys the pleasures of the senses, particularly someone who enjoys fine food and chooses to postpone worry.

Mathematics and Physics

Greeks of the Hellenistic Age became outstanding scientists and mathematicians. Euclid contributed extremely important work to the field of mathematics. He developed geometry into a system by showing how geometric statements of truth, or theorems, develop logically from one another. His *Elements* textbook, used for more than 1,000 years, is the basis for many of today's geometry books.

Archimedes (ahr • kuh • MEED • eez), considered the greatest scientist of the Hellenistic period, used

3A, a4A, a4H, a4I, a4K, a4L

geometry to measure spheres, cones, and cylinders. He also calculated the value of pi (π)—the ratio of the circumference of a circle to its diameter—and used mathematics to explain the principle of the lever, building many machines that employed levers. His inventions included the compound pulley (or block and tackle) and cogged wheels used as gears.

Medicine

Hellenistic scientists greatly enhanced the medical knowledge of the Greeks. Alexandria became the center for the study of medicine and surgery. By dissecting the bodies of executed criminals physicians learned much about human anatomy. Studies by Alexandrian physicians revealed that the brain is the center of the nervous system. These and other advances in medicine allowed Hellenistic physicians to perform delicate surgery on patients, using anesthetics (painkillers).

Astronomy and Geography

Hellenistic scientists added to the knowledge of astronomy. They used mathematics to calculate the daily position of stars and planets. Aristarchus (ar • uh • STAHR • kuhs) of Samos believed that the earth and other planets moved around the sun, but he failed to convince other scientists of his day. Hipparchus (hip • AHR • kuhs) of Rhodes, the first scientist to systematically use trigonometry, calculated the times of eclipses of the sun and the moon and the length of the year according to both the sun and the moon.

Hellenistic geographers knew that the earth was round. At Alexandria Eratosthenes (er • uh • TAHS • thuh • neez) calculated the diameter of the earth to within 50 miles (70 kilometers) of the actual figure. He also claimed that people could reach India by sailing west around the world. However, no ship built then could risk so long an ocean voyage.

Characteristics of Hellenistic Science

Two characteristics of Hellenistic science remain particularly remarkable. First, scientists learned so much using simple instruments. They had no microscopes, telescopes, compasses, or delicate balances for weighing small quantities.

Second, the Hellenistic Greeks made little effort to apply their scientific knowledge in practical ways, except perhaps in the field of geography. They valued knowledge for its own sake and had no interest in inventions or mechanical progress. For example, an Alexandrian scientist named Hero invented a steam engine, but people regarded it only as an interesting toy. One explanation for this attitude stems from the fact that slavery served as the basis for Hellenistic civilization. These labor-saving inventions would have helped the slaves, and the Greeks did not think it necessary or fitting to improve the slaves' situation.

Learning from Pictures *An unknown sculptor carved* Winged Victory *on the island of Samothrace to commemorate a successful Greek naval battle.*

SECTION 4 REVIEW

1. **Identify** Diogenes, Zeno, Epicurus, Euclid, Archimedes, Aristarchus, Hipparchus, Eratosthenes
2. **Summarizing Ideas** What people were considered Greek during the Hellenistic Age?
3. **Classifying Ideas** What were the main ideas of the three major Hellenistic philosophies?
4. **Evaluating Ideas** Why did Hellenistic Greeks have relatively little interest in the practical application of science?

of Epicurean philosophy; ***Euclid:*** mathematician who developed geometry into a system by showing how theorems develop logically from each other; ***Archimedes:*** greatest scientist of Hellenistic era, calculated the value of π; ***Aristarchus:*** scientist who believed the earth and other planets moved around the sun; ***Hipparchus:*** calculated eclipses of sun and moon, and length of year according to the sun and moon, and was first scientist to make systematic use of trigonometry; ***Eratosthenes:*** calculated the diameter of the earth

2. During the Hellenistic Age anyone who accepted Hellenistic culture and values was considered to be Greek.

3. The Cynics taught people should seek virtue. They scorned pleasure, wealth, and social position. Stoics believed the world was directed by divine reason. People should accept their fate and be indifferent to grief, fear, pain, or pleasure. Epicureans taught the aim of life was to seek pleasure and avoid pain. Epicurus taught pleasure was primarily intellectual, but some followers sought pleasure of the senses.

4. Hellenistic scientists valued knowledge for its own sake and were not interested in inventions or mechanical progress. One explanation is that Hellenistic civilization was based on slavery so labor-saving inventions were not necessary.

139

Reviewing Important Terms
1. Hellenistic culture; 2. Philosophy; 3. drama; 4. hubris; 5. tragedy; 6. comedy; 7. Infantry.

Developing Critical Thinking Skills
1. Greek art symbolized the pride of the people. At the same time, it honored the gods, thanking them for life and fortune, and attempted to win their favor.
2. Plato's ideal form of government according to the *Republic* was an aristocracy—a government ruled by an upper class. Modern democratic government calls for rule by the people.
3. Answers will vary. Students might suggest that dictators or small groups of people are running today's nondemocratic nations. Contrary to Aristotle's view, the middle class has little power.
4. The Hellenistic world had divine monarchs, prosperous new cities, and a blend of Greek and Persian customs.
5. As the middle class grew, education became more widespread. The old, and now less respected, Greek values faded and the conditions of women in society improved.
6. The Greek philosophers of the Hellenistic Age were more concerned with ethics than with fundamental questions of reality and human existence.
7. Thucydides wanted his history to reflect his belief that explanations of human nature are revealed in studies of the past.

1A, 1B, 3A, a1A, a4A, a4G, a4H, a4J, a4K, a4L

Reteaching
Have students review the Chapter Summary and the appropriate section and questions in the Unit Synthesis. Discuss the concepts until students demonstrate a clear understanding of the material.

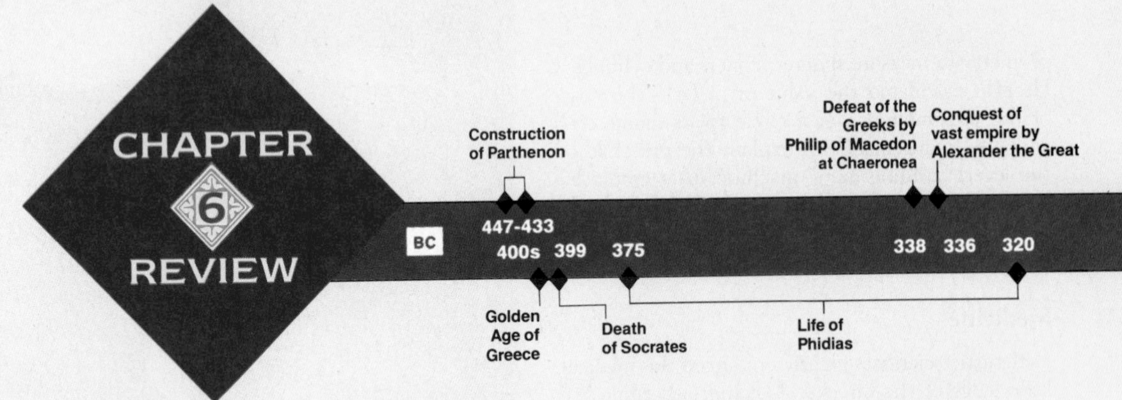

Chapter Summary

The following list contains the key concepts you have learned about Greek civilization and the Hellenistic Age.

1. The peak of cultural activity in Athens occurred in the 400s B.C.—a period known as the Golden Age.
2. Athenians surrounded themselves with beauty and showed their love for Athens by building temples, gymnasiums, and public theaters adorned with sculpture and other fine works of art.
3. The Parthenon, a shrine constructed in honor of the goddess Athena, still stands atop the Acropolis, the hill where the original polis was located.
4. Greek art glorified humans, symbolized the pride of Greeks, honored the gods, expressed the ideals of balance and order, and combined beauty with usefulness.
5. The works of Greek philosophers and writers, such as Aristotle and Plato, remain among the world's greatest works of literature.
6. Philip of Macedon invaded Greece, conquered all the city-states, and united them under his rule.
7. Philip's son, Alexander the Great, went on to conquer the entire Persian Empire and more. He hoped to rule the world, but he died before he could accomplish his goal. In time his empire was divided into three separate kingdoms.
8. As a result of Alexander's conquests, Greek culture, known as Hellenistic culture, spread throughout the Mediterranean area.
9. Hellenistic contributions to our understanding of ethics, mathematics, and science—especially geometry, physics, medicine, and astronomy—remained influential for more than 1,000 years.

On a separate sheet of paper, complete the following review exercises.

Reviewing Important Terms

Supply the term that correctly completes each statement.

1. The new culture founded on Greek ideas and features from other cultures of the Mediterranean is known as ________ ________.
2. ________ is the inquiry into the most fundamental questions of reality and human existence.
3. A play containing action and dialogue and usually involving conflict and emotion is called a ________.
4. The Greeks called an assumption that a person had the same knowledge or ability as the gods ________.
5. A Greek ________ showed the main character struggling against a fate that resulted in a sad ending.
6. A ________ is a form of Greek drama that mocks ideas and people.
7. ________ is a term for soldiers trained and equipped to fight on foot.

Developing Critical Thinking Skills

1. **Evaluating Ideas** How did the architecture and art of the Golden Age in Athens reflect the values of Greek culture? Include specific examples to support your answer.
2. **Contrasting Ideas** How does Socrates' concept of the ideal form of government, as described in Plato's *Republic*, differ from modern democratic governments?
3. **Applying Ideas** How might Aristotle's views of the importance of the middle class be reflected in the governments of many nondemocratic nations today?
4. **Classifying Ideas** In what ways did the Hellenistic world follow the models set by Alexander?
5. **Interpreting Ideas** How did middle-class expansion change Greek attitudes during the Hellenistic Age?
6. **Comparing Ideas** How did the views of Greek philosophers of the Golden Age differ from the views of philosophers of the Hellenistic Age?
7. **Relating Ideas** How might Thucydides' approach to history apply to other contributions of Greek culture?

Relating Geography to History

Compare the map on page 134 with a modern map of the same area. **(a)** What countries now lie in the land that once formed Alexander's empire? **(b)** What geographic barriers prevented Alexander from conquering the Indian subcontinent?

Relating Past to Present

1. The architects of many of the public buildings in our nation's capital, Washington, D.C., were influenced by

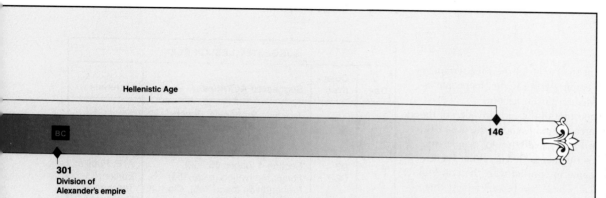

the architecture of ancient Greece. In your school or local library, find a book with photographs of buildings located in Washington, D.C. Find another book with photographs of ancient buildings still standing in Greece today. Compare the buildings shown in each book. **(a)** List the ways in which the buildings shown are similar and the ways in which they are different. **(b)** What functions did the ancient Greek buildings serve? **(c)** What functions do the modern buildings in Washington, D.C. serve?

2. Explore the history of your town or city to find streets, parks, or buildings named after people. Which of these people have been memorialized in other parts of the United States?
3. Give examples of how Hellenistic culture influenced the governments and economies of the regions with which it came in contact. What aspects of American culture have spread to other countries today?

Applying History Study Skills

Before completing this activity, review Building History Study Skills on page 136.

Look again at the steps explaining how to identify cultural diffusion. Then read the following selections from Plato's *Republic* and Epicurus' *The Prudent Pursuit of Pleasure* to answer the questions below.

“Unless either philosophers become kings in their countries or those who are now called kings and rulers come to be sufficiently inspired with a genuine desire for wisdom; unless, that is to say, political power and philosophy meet together . . . there can be no rest from troubles . . . for states, nor yet, as I believe, for all mankind.”

(Plato)

“When, therefore, we maintain that pleasure is the end, we do not mean . . . continuous drinkings and revellings, . . . but sober reasoning, searching out the motives for all choice and avoidance, and banishing mere opinions, to which are due the greatest disturbance of the spirit.

Of all this the beginning and the greatest good is prudence [self-discipline] . . . for from prudence are sprung all the other virtues, and it teaches us that it is not possible to live pleasantly without living prudently and honourably and justly.”

(Epicurus)

1. **(a)** How are the purposes of these two writers similar? **(b)** How do their goals differ?
2. How does Plato's philosophy represent a response to a polis or city-state?
3. How does Epicurus' philosophy represent a response to a society that is multiracial and a center of trade?
4. What evidence of cultural diffusion is present in the quotes by these two philosophers?

Investigating Further

1. **Preparing an Oral Presentation** Read selections from Plato's *Republic.* Then choose one idea from his work on each of the following subjects: **(a)** education, **(b)** the role of women, **(c)** the organization of society, **(d)** the definition of a state. Prepare an oral report on the ways these ideas were reflected in the city-state governments of ancient Greece.
2. **Conducting an Interview** Choose one of the mathematicians or scientists, such as Hippocrates or Aristarchus, mentioned in this chapter. Interview a math or science teacher to learn how the ideas of these ancient scholars were developed and are used today. Investigate the work of other mathematicians or scientists who may have tried to prove them wrong.
3. **Writing a Report** Report on the speeches that Demosthenes made in defense of Athens and discuss the arguments that he advanced against Philip of Macedon. You can locate the appropriate speeches in Lewis Copeland and Lawrence Lamm's *The World's Great Speeches* (Dover), or in the book by Houston Peterson, *Treasury of the World's Great Speeches* (Simon and Schuster).
4. **Studying Literature** During the Golden Age in Athens, women were subordinate to men in matters of education, legal rights, government participation, and business affairs. Yet during this same period Euripides composed great plays about strong women (for example, *Medea*), and Sophocles wrote *Antigone.* What role did these women play in Greek tradition?

Relating Geography to History
(a) Greece, India, Turkey, Egypt, Israel, Lebanon, Syria, Iran, Iraq, Pakistan, Afghanistan, Libya, Cyprus **(b)** distance, climate, aridity

Relating Past to Present
1. **(a)** *Similarities:* columns, rectangular shapes, steps, and pediments; *Differences:* use of windows, more walls, and fewer columns in the buildings; **(b)** religious and governmental purposes; **(c)** governmental
2. Answers will vary.
3. Throughout the Hellenistic world, the city-state disappeared and strong rulers took control. Students might state that American rock music, fashions, fast-food restaurants, weapons, machinery, and computers are copied or used worldwide.

Applying History Study Skills
1. **(a)** Plato wanted kings to control their desires, while Epicurus hoped all individuals would do the same. **(b)** Plato deals with the public good, while Epicurus wanted the individual to exercise self-control.
2. Plato encourages rulers to exercise caution and philosophical principles.
3. Epicurus encourages using prudence and living honorably and justly, which would include tolerance of other groups.
4. Both Plato and Epicurus emphasize stability during times of change brought on by cultural diffusion.

141

CHAPTER (pages 142–175)

7 Rome Ruled the Western World for Centuries

(1000 B.C.–A.D. 476)

CHAPTER OVERVIEW

The Italian Peninsula, situated at the center of the Mediterranean area, became the base of a vast empire. From Rome, its people established control of the entire Mediterranean region.

The Latins were the most important of the early invaders of Italy. The Etruscans captured the area around Rome in the 600s B.C., but they were eventually absorbed into the mixture of peoples that came to be known as Romans. By the mid-200s B.C., Rome had expanded to the tip of Italy and came in conflict with the powerful city of Carthage in North Africa. These two powers fought three wars in which Rome was victorious.

After much political turmoil, Octavian established the Roman Empire and ruled as Augustus. From his reign until his death of the emperor Marcus Aurelius, Rome was at peace.

During this period the new Christian religion, based on the teachings of Jesus, spread throughout the Roman Empire. At first the Romans persecuted the Christians, but by the A.D. 300s Christianity had become the dominant religion of the Roman Empire.

The Roman Empire gradually declined and then collapsed in the West owing in part to internal problems and invasions by Germanic tribes.

SUGGESTED LESSON PLAN

Day	Objectives	Suggested Activities	Materials
1	U8* C1-2	Introducing the Chapter (page 142) Section 1 (pages 143-48), Focus/Motivation (page 143), Presentation (page 144), Closure (page 147), Suggested Teaching Strategies, Enrichment Activity, Daily Quiz, Suggested Assignments (page 141B)	ATE, Pupil's Edition, Teacher's Resource-Bank™
2	U7, C3-4	Section 2 (pages 148-51), Focus/Motivation (page 148), Presentation (page 149), Closure (page 150), Suggested Teaching Strategies, Enrichment Activities, Daily Quiz, Suggested Assignments (page 141C)	ATE, Pupil's Edition, Teacher's Resource-Bank™
3	U7, C5	Section 3 (pages 151-55), Focus/Motivation (page 151), Presentation (page 152), Closure (page 154), Suggested Teaching Strategies, Enrichment Activity, Daily Quiz, Suggested Assignments (page 141D)	ATE, Pupil's Edition, Teacher's Resource-Bank™
4	U8, C6-7	Section 4 (pages 155-62), Focus/Motivation (page 155), Presentation (page 156), Closure (page 162), Suggested Teaching Strategies, Enrichment Activity, Daily Quiz, Suggested Assignments (page 141E)	ATE, Pupil's Edition, Teacher's Resource-Bank™
5	U8, C8-9	Section 5 (pages 162-66), Focus/Motivation (page 163), Presentation (page 164), Closure (page 166), Suggested Teaching Strategies, Enrichment Activity, Daily Quiz, Suggested Assignments (page 141F)	ATE, Pupil's Edition, Teacher's Resource-Bank™
6	U8-9, C10	Section 6 (pages 166-71), Focus/Motivation (page 167), Presentation (page 168), Closure (page 170), Suggested Teaching Strategies, Enrichment Activity, Daily Quiz, Suggested Assignments (page 141G)	ATE, Pupil's Edition, Teacher's Resource-Bank™
7	U7-9, C1-10	Chapter 7 Form A Test, Reteaching Worksheet, Chapter 7 Form B Test	Teacher's Resource-Bank™ or Workbook and Test Booklet
8	U1-9	Unit Two Review Worksheet, Unit Two Test	Teacher's Resource-Bank™ or Workbook and Test Booklet

*C refers to applicable Chapter Objective, U refers to applicable Unit Goal.

BOOKS FOR THE TEACHER

Boren, Henry C. *Roman Society.* D. D. Heath. Describes the social, economic, and cultural history of Rome.

Carcopino, Jerome. *Daily Life in Ancient Rome.* Yale University Press. Examines almost every aspect of Roman daily life.

Durant, Will. *Caesar and Christ.* Simon and Schuster. Gives an account of Roman history and Christianity.

Hamblin, Dora Jane. *The Etruscans.* Time-Life. Reconstructs the life of the Etruscans from archeological finds.

Johnson, Paul. *A History of Christianity.* Atheneum. Provides a useful background on Christianity.

BOOKS FOR THE STUDENT

Armstrong, Donald. *The Reluctant Warriors.* Crowell. Examines the history and social life of Carthage.

Asimov, Isaac. *The Roman Republic.* Houghton Mifflin. Gives an account of the history of Rome from the early kings to the assassination of Julius Caesar.

Coolidge, Olivia. *Lives of Famous Romans.* Houghton Mifflin. Profiles the lives of famous Romans.

Dillon, Ellis. *Rome Under the Emperors.* Describes the lives of various Roman citizens and their families.

Honnes, Elizabeth. *The Etruscans: An Unsolved Mystery.* Lippincott. Describes the Etruscan civilization.

MULTIMEDIA MATERIALS

Christianity in World History (mp, 14 min.), Coronet. Provides a survey of Christianity.

Greek and Roman Sports (2 fs), Educational Audio-Visual. Contrasts Roman and Greek sports; gladiator fights, contests between men and animals, and chariot races are featured.

Julius Caesar: Rise of the Roman Empire (mp, 22 min.), EBE. Explores the political and cultural significance of Caesar's career.

Roman Civilization (2 fs), Educational Audio-Visual. Part 1 examines social classes and daily life. Part 2 deals with the military, administration of the empire, art, and literature.

World's Great Religions (fs), Life. The section on Christianity provides information appropriate for Chapter 7.

Section 1 (pages 143–148)
The Romans Founded a Republic on the Italian Peninsula

SECTION OVERVIEW

Latins, Etruscans, and Greeks were early settlers of Italy. Those settling in and around Rome gradually began to think of themselves as Romans. They established a republican form of government and had a highly disciplined citizen army. The family, the most important social unit in early Roman society, was the center of religion and education.

SUGGESTED TEACHING STRATEGIES

1. **Preteaching Vocabulary (Basic)** You may wish to preteach the following important vocabulary terms: republic, consul, veto *(page 145)*; checks and balances, praetor, censor, tribune, dictator, patrician, plebeian, legion *(page 146)*; paterfamilias *(page 147)*. Ask students to explain checks and balances in the United States system of government.
2. **Relating Past to Present (Average/Group)** Ask students to study the picture on page 147. Have them make a chart listing in the first column the characteristics of the Roman army (who served, whether it was professional or volunteer, and its equipment.) In a second column, have them make another list comparing the characteristics of the Roman army to today's American army. Students should consult the *Readers' Guide to Periodical Literature* to find articles on the status of the American army today.
3. **Understanding Ideas (Basic)** Discuss with the class the role of the family in Rome, using the following questions as a guide. Did the family of ancient Rome differ from a family of today? In what ways? Has the role of the father changed? How? Compare the role of a Roman woman with an ancient Greek woman or a modern woman. What role did education play in the family? How did religion tie the family together?

ENRICHMENT ACTIVITY

Preparing a Report (Average/Group) Interested students may enjoy working individually or in small groups to prepare and present oral reports on the Etruscans. If possible, students should show pictures or slides of Etruscan tombs and art. Sources include Leonard Cottrell's *The Horizon Book of Lost Worlds* (American Heritage); *Life* eds., *The Epic of Man* (Time-Life); Dora Jane Hamblin's *The Etruscans* (Time-Life); and Ellen MacNamara's *The Everyday Life of the Etruscans* (Putnam).

DAILY QUIZ

To assess student understanding of Section 1, give the class the following quiz. (Each item is worth 10 points.)

1. What people greatly influenced the Latins, wrote an alphabet based on Greek characters, made fine clothing and jewelry, became skilled in metallurgy and pottery, developed woodworking, and learned how to pave roads, drain marshes, and build sewers? *(Etruscans)*
2. Give the reasons why Rome was ideally located. *(center of land trade routes on a shallow river crossing; close to sea but protected from invasions by sea)*
3. What were the qualifications for voting in the early Roman Republic? *(adult, male, citizen)*
4. The powerful aristocratic class of landowners that could hold office was called ______ . *(patricians)*
5. Officials called ______ , elected from the Assembly of Tribes, could veto measures they believed contrary to public interest. *(tribunes)*
6. This was the most important body in the Roman government and consisted of 300 men. It controlled public funds and political appointments. *(Senate)*

7. (T or F) The censors registered people according to their wealth to determine how much they should pay in taxes. *(T)*
8. (T or F) The dictator, nominated by the consuls and elected by the Assembly of Centuries, held office for two years. *(F)*
9. The ________ was the most important military unit in the citizen army and was comprised of 4,500 to 6,000 men. *(legion)*
10. (T or F) The Romans borrowed many of their religious practices, especially the roles of the gods and goddesses, from the Greeks. *(T)*

SUGGESTED ASSIGNMENTS

1. **Critical Thinking Worksheet (Average/Group)** Have students complete Critical Thinking Worksheet 15 in the TEACHER'S RESOURCEBANK™.
2. **Comparing Ideas (Average/Group)** Have interested students prepare reports comparing the Roman pantheon of gods with that of the Greeks. Ask them to read about Greek and Roman gods in encyclopedias or secondary works in their school or public libraries. They should include in their reports the different names of the gods and goddesses in Greece and Rome, which were ranked as most important, and how important they were to the people. Students should determine whether the Romans had gods or spirits that the Greeks did not, and vice versa. Select the best reports for the students to read to the class. Use the reports as the basis for a class discussion on the significance of a state or official religion to Rome and to modern nations.

Section (pages 148–151)

2 The Roman Republic Expanded into the Entire Mediterranean Region

SECTION OVERVIEW

The growth of Rome's power brought it into conflict with Carthage, and the three Punic Wars resulted. With the defeat of Carthage, Rome grew into a great Mediterranean power. Along with expansion came a number of problems: corruption in the administration of the provinces; changes in agriculture with small farmers in Italy forced off the land because they could not compete with cheaper grain from the provinces; and a weakening of discipline and devotion to the state.

SUGGESTED TEACHING STRATEGIES

1. **Preteaching Vocabulary (Basic)** You may wish to preteach the following important vocabulary terms: indemnity *(page 148)*; latifundia, equites *(page 150)*; crucifixion *(page 151)*. Ask the students to compare the political power of the equites with the political power of the business class in the United States today.
2. **Identifying Results (Basic)** Draw the outline of the following chart on the chalkboard or an overhead projector. Have students fill in the causes and results of each of the Punic Wars. (Refer the students to pages 148-149.) The completed chart should be similar to the one that follows.

PUNIC WARS		
	Causes	**Results**
First Punic War	Carthage was afraid Rome would take Sicily; Rome was afraid Carthage would close the Adriatic Sea and the Strait of Messina.	Carthage asked for peace; had to pay indemnity and give up control of Sicily.
Second Punic War	Hannibal invaded Italy.	Carthage asked for peace; paid an indemnity and lost the Spanish colonies.
Third Punic War	Some Romans passionately hated Carthage; Rome declared war.	Carthage was destroyed.

3. **Interpreting Ideas (Average/Group)** Organize the class into two groups, one representing Roman historians and the other Carthaginian historians. Ask students to write short histories of the Punic Wars from their respective viewpoints. They can base their histories on the textbook and on outside readings such as *Greece and Rome: Builders of Our World* (National Geographic Society). Several students from both groups may wish to read their accounts to the class. Discuss with the class why a difference exists between the two points of view.

ENRICHMENT ACTIVITIES

1. **Comparing Past and Present (Average/Group)** Have interested students examine encyclopedias and secondary works on crime and punishment in ancient Rome. Ask them to determine whether a person's social status affected the punishment received —for example, a slave versus a free citizen. Which crimes did ancient Romans regard as the worst and thus deserving of the most severe punishment? Which criminals received crucifixion? Then have students prepare a short report to present to the class. Use their findings as the basis for a class discussion on capital punishment.
2. **Analyzing Ideas (Average/Group)** Have students reread the subsection "Social Change" on pages 150-151. Have them prepare a short oral report answering the following questions about slavery in ancient Rome. How important were slaves to Rome's economy? Where did the slaves come from? Did race play an important role in the selection of slaves? What caused slave revolts? Were they frequent? Use the reports as the basis for a class discussion comparing slavery in the United States before 1865 with slavery in Rome.

DAILY QUIZ

To assess student understanding of Section 2, give the class the following quiz. (Each item is worth 10 points.)

1. The city of Carthage originally had been a colony of ________. *(Phoenicia)*
2. (T or F) Rome feared the Carthaginian navy would close the Straits of Messina. *(T)*
3. (T or F) Carthaginians feared Rome would invade its colonies, especially in Sicily. *(T)*
4. (T or F) The first two Punic Wars resulted in Rome paying Carthage an indemnity and giving up its colonies in North Africa, Spain, and Gaul. *(F)*
5. ________ led the Carthaginian army through Spain, France, and over the Alps and dominated, but did not destroy, the Roman army in Italy. *(Hannibal)*
6. The Roman general who finally defeated the Carthaginians at the Battle of Zama in the Second Punic War was ________. *(Scipio)*
7. The system of allowing a publican to pay a fixed amount to the Roman treasury and keep any excess amount is called ________ ________. *(tax farming)*
8. (T or F) The Roman proconsul governed colonies. *(T)*
9. (T or F) Rome's annexation of distant territories increased the power of the citizen-farmer in Roman life. *(F)*
10. (T or F) A freed Roman slave became a citizen. *(T)*

SUGGESTED ASSIGNMENTS

1. **Oral Reports (Average/Group)** Interested students may give reports on important leaders or battles of the period. Sources include Peter Connolly's *Hannibal and the Enemies of Rome* (Silver Burdett).
2. **Interpreting Ideas (Average/Group)** Have interested students do research on Roman agriculture before and after the Punic Wars. They first should describe the size of the farms, what kinds of implements the farmer had, free or slave labor, and the products from the land. Then after the citizen-soldier returns to his land, what does he find has happened to the farm? What are the latifundia and what role did they have in changes made to the citizen-farmer's life? Finally, what does the farmer do? Students wish to write their reports in a diary form, as entries over a period of time by the citizen-farmer. Have students read their reports to the class. Use the material they have gathered as the basis for a class discussion on the effects of war on the land.

Section 3 (pages 151–155)

The Roman Republic Was Transformed into an Empire

SECTION OVERVIEW

The many problems in the Roman Republic caused internal strife. Tiberius and Gaius Gracchus tried and failed to reform the republic. They were followed by military leaders who often forced their will on the Roman people. Julius Caesar made himself dictator and secured a number of reforms. After Julius Caesar's assassination, the scramble for power ended in the sole rule of his grandnephew as Augustus Caesar. Although Augustus retained the outward forms of the republic, his rule marked the beginning of the Roman Empire.

SUGGESTED TEACHING STRATEGIES

1. **Comparing Ideas (Basic)** Have students compare the First Triumvirate and the Second Triumvirate. They should reread the subsections "The First Triumvirate," "Caesar in Power," "The Second Triumvirate," and "Octavian: The First Augustus," on pages 152-153. They should compare the individuals in each triumvirate, their goals, and the results. Use the comparisons as the basis for a class discussion focusing on why the Roman Republic failed. How were a handful of men able to assume total control of so large a territory? What conditions made this likely? How might the results have been changed?
2. **Writing Biographical Sketches (Average/Group)** Many important people in the history of Rome are discussed in this section. Have students prepare a biographical sketch of one of the following: Tiberius Gracchus, Gaius Gracchus, Marius, Sulla, Pompey, Julius Caesar, Augustus, Marc Antony, Cleopatra, or one of the Julian or Good Emperors. The sketch should include a description of the individual's personality, life, and role in history. Some recommended sources are: Olivia Coolidge's *Lives of Famous Romans* (Houghton Mifflin); Monroe Stearns's *Julius Caesar* (Franklin Watts); and Irwin Isenberg's *Caesar* (American Heritage).

*3. **Writing About History: Writing a Thesis Statement (Average/Group)** To reinforce the skill presented on page 154, have students collect data on significant events covering a particular period of Ancient Roman history. From the data they collect, have students formulate a thesis statement.

ENRICHMENT ACTIVITY

Presenting a Drama (Average/Group) Interested students may enjoy staging a television newscast on the assassination of Julius Caesar. A student playing the role of a newscaster could interview two or three conspirators and Marc Antony. Another student could portray a commentator summarizing the incident and making an evaluation. Participants may want to read "The Deified Julius" in Suetonius, *The Lives of the Caesars,* and "Julius Caesar" in Plutarch, *Parallel Lives,* for help in preparing the skit.

DAILY QUIZ

To assess student understanding of Section 3, give the class the following quiz. (Each item is worth 10 points.)

1. These two brothers attempted the earliest reform measures but met violent deaths because of powerful opponents. *(Tiberius and Gaius Gracchus)*
2. Name two reforms implemented by the Gracchus brothers. *(limiting the amount of public land that senators could use; distributing land to the poor; providing grain at low prices for the unemployed)*

3. Which body did Marius, Sulla, Pompey, and Crassus use to control Rome—army, navy, poor, or Senate? *(army)*
4. ______ had been a member of the First Triumvirate. He later eliminated Pompey as a competitor for power and ruled as a dictator for life until his friends, fearing his power, stabbed him to death. *(Julius Caesar)*
5. Who wrote *Commentaries on the Gallic Wars* and made the irreversible decision to cross the Rubicon River? *(Julius Caesar)*
6. Name the three men in the Second Triumvirate. *(Octavian; Marc Antony; Lepidus)*
7. What does the word Augustus mean? *(set aside for religious purposes, or sacred)*
8. (T or F) Augustus was really the first emperor. *(T)*
9. Which of these was *not* a "good emperor"? Nero, Nerva, Trajan, Hadrian *(Nero)*
10. (T or F) The "good emperors" protected landowners, law and order, and "Romanized" the provinces. *(T)*

SUGGESTED ASSIGNMENTS

1. **Geography Fact Sheet (Basic)** Have students complete "Geography Fact Sheet: Urbanization Around the World" in the TEACHER'S RESOURCEBANK™.
2. **Book Report (Challenging)** Have interested students read Robert Graves's *I, Claudius* (Modern Library). Then ask them to write a book report contrasting the fictional account of the times of the emperor Claudius with what they know of Rome. Ask for volunteers to read their reports to the class. Then use the reports as the basis for a class discussion about the usefulness of historical fiction. Ask: Does historical fiction provide accurate accounts of the past? How biased are the authors? Ask students to tell the class about books they have read that helped in their understanding of the subject and the period covered. If possible, obtain copies of *I, Claudius* filmed for public broadcasting and show them to the class.
3. **Skill Worksheet (Basic)** Have students complete Skill Worksheet 7 in the TEACHER'S RESOURCEBANK ™.

Section (pages 155–162)

4 The Romans Developed a Distinctive Society and Culture

SECTION OVERVIEW

The Pax Romana was a period of peace and prosperity that lasted more than 200 years. Efficient government and law, military organization, and widespread trade and transportation united the empire. Romans enjoyed theater, chariot racing, and spectacles in the Colosseum. Roman science, engineering, and architecture reached great heights, and many emperors encouraged art and literature in the Empire.

SUGGESTED TEACHING STRATEGIES

1. **Preteaching Vocabulary (Basic)** You may wish to preteach the following important vocabulary terms: Pax Romana *(page 155)*; aqueduct (*page 156*); colonus (*page 157*). Ask students to identify and explain how Roman fortifications helped to preserve the Pax Romana.
2. **Understanding Ideas (Basic)** The film *The Emperor and Slave: Philosophy of Roman Stoicism* can serve as a basis for studying the philosophy that was popular among the Roman upper classes. Have students take notes during the film to use as a basis for discussion. Students should recognize the concept of natural law, the assumption that certain basic legal principles are common to all humans.
3. **Reporting for a Newspaper (Average/Group)** Organize the class into groups of five. Each group is to prepare a Roman newspaper. The newspaper can cover a particular day, a particular era, or the reign of one emperor. (Approximately two weeks should be given to this project.) When the newspapers have been completed, you might pass them around the class and display them on the bulletin board.

ENRICHMENT ACTIVITY

Presenting a Report (Average/Group) Organize the class into groups of three to five students for oral presentations. Suggested topics are: the Roman army, family life, towns, sports and entertainment, travel, architecture, and religion. Students should be encouraged to use models, pictures, slides, charts, and diagrams in their presentations. Sources include: *Aspects of Roman Life* Series (Longman), edited by Peter Hodge; J. Carcopino's *Daily Life in Ancient Rome* (Yale University Press); F. R. Cowell's *Everyday Life in Ancient Rome* (Putnam); Ian Andrews's *Pompeii* and *The Roman Army* (Cambridge University Press); and Jonathan Rutland's *A Roman Town* (Warwick Press).

DAILY QUIZ

To assess student understanding of Section 4, give the class the following quiz. (Each item is worth 10 points.)

1. Pax Romana means ______ ______, and designates the period from the reign of Caesar Augustus to the death of Marcus Aurelius. *(Roman Peace)*
2. (T or F) During the Pax Romana, judges had to rigidly maintain the standards of the Twelve Tables for the agrarian society in Rome and its few provinces. *(F)*
3. (T or F) Romans built many roads to link provincial capitals with Rome itself. *(T)*
4. A ______, a tenant farmer that replaced slaves as labor on larger farms, received a small plot of land from the owner. *(colonus)*
5. The part of the Roman network of fortifications that crosses Britain is called ______ ______. *(Hadrian's Wall)*
6. (T or F) During the Pax Romana, most Romans fell into three classes, the slaves, the poor, and the wealthy. *(T)*

7. All but one of the following were favorite leisure pastimes of Romans—performances by mimes, jugglers, and acrobats; boxing; soccer; chariot racing; gladiator combat. *(soccer)*
8. Ptolemy studied ______ (medicine, engineering, astronomy, livestock breeding). *(astronomy)*
9. ______ wrote the *Aeneid. (Virgil)*
10. This language utilized the Greek alphabet, formed the basis for modern scientific terminology, and served as the language for the Christian Church. *(Latin)*

SUGGESTED ASSIGNMENTS

1. **Profile Worksheet (Basic)** Have students complete Profile Worksheet 7 in the TEACHER'S RESOURCEBANK™.
2. **Writing a Diary (Average/Group)** Have students write a diary entry for a day in the life of a member of Roman society, such as a soldier, senator, student, gladiator, slave, housewife, or poor city dweller. Use the diary entries as the basis for a class discussion on the Roman social system.

Section (pages 162–166)

5 Christianity Took Root in Judea

SECTION OVERVIEW

Although the Romans tolerated Judaism, many Jews were discontented with Roman rule and hoped for a Messiah who would restore their independence. In this setting, Jesus was born. His teachings, which formed the basis of the new religion of Christianity, spread among all peoples within the empire, not Jews alone. The Romans persecuted the early Christians because they refused to worship the emperor. Nevertheless, Christianity gained many followers, and during the 300s it became the official religion of the Roman Empire. As the Church grew in size and strength, it developed an organization of priests and bishops. Church councils clarifed Christian doctrines.

SUGGESTED TEACHING STRATEGIES

1. **Preteaching Vocabulary (Basic)** You may wish to preteach the following important vocabulary terms: rabbi *(page 162)*; martyr *(page 164)*; patriarch, pope *(page 166)*. Have students rank the Christian Church clergy from bottom to top. *(priest, bishop, patriarch, pope)* Ask them to name other church positions added later. *(archbishop, cardinal)*
2. **Understanding Ideas (Basic)** The following excerpts were taken from correspondence between Pliny the Younger, governor of a Roman province, and the Emperor Trajan. Distribute copies of these excerpts to the class.

   "Pliny to Trajan:

   This is the plan which I have adopted in the case of those Christians who have been brought before me. I ask them whether they are Christians, if they say 'Yes,' then I repeat the question a second time, and also a third—warning them of the penalties involved; and if they persist, I order them away to prison . . . . Those who denied that they were or had been Christians and called upon the gods with the usual formula, reciting the words after me, and those who offered incense and wine before your image . . . all such I considered acquitted. . . .

   Trajan to Pliny:

   You have adopted the right course, my dear Pliny . . . Christians are not be be hunted out. If brought before you, and the offense is proved, they are to be punished, but . . . if any denies he is a Christian . . . then he is to pardoned on his recantation. . . ."

   Use these letters as the basis for a class discussion, using the following questions as a guide. What kind of evidence is being used in court? What does Pliny's letter imply some Christians are doing? What does Trajan reply?

   Both Jews and Christians suffered for their religious beliefs during this period. Ask the class if they can think of any religious groups in the United States or the world who are suffering persecution. Is it similar to the situation of the Jews and Christians under the Romans?
3. **Interpreting Diagrams (Average/Group)** Draw the outline of the following diagram on the chalkboard or an overhead projector. Have students complete the pyramid to represent the organization of the early Church.

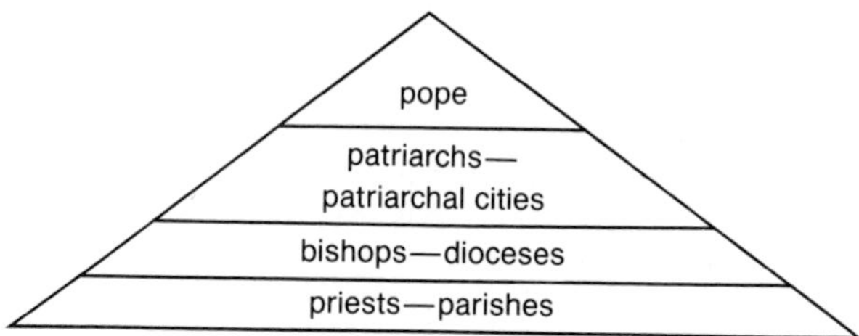

ENRICHMENT ACTIVITY

Discussing Ideas (Basic) To familiarize students with the teachings of Paul, reproduce the First Epistle to the Corinthians (13:1-13) and distribute copies to the class. Discuss with the class how important love is to Paul and what he considers to be the characteristics of this love.

DAILY QUIZ

To assess student understanding of Section 5, give the class the following quiz. (Each item is worth 10 points.)

1. As the Roman Empire expanded, it required people to worship the ______ as divine. *(emperor)*
2. (T or F) The Jews hoped for a Messiah who could lead them to political independence and return to them a government in the tradition of King David's. *(T)*
3. List three things that Jesus taught. *(God cares more for people than for laws; Jesus saw himself as the link that reestablished the*

loving relationship God desires; God will forgive people's sins.)

4. (T or F) We have learned most of what we know about Jesus from the four Gospels of the New Testament. *(T)*
5. ______, a Jew from the town of Tarsus, became a great Christian missionary and helped spread Jesus' teachings throughout the Mediterranean region. *(Paul)*
6. (T or F) The religious cults of Mithras, Cybele, and Isis excluded certain people or were very expensive to join, but Christianity accepted everyone and charged nothing. *(T)*
7. ______ legalized Christianity after seeing a vision of a cross in the sky and winning a battle. *(Constantine)*
8. A ______ served members of the Christian parish, conducting services and performing baptisms and marriages. *(priest)*
9. Bishops in most important administrative centers of the Christian Church were called ______, or "fathers." *(patriarchs)*
10. The Council of Nicaea proclaimed the Christian doctrine of the ______. *(Trinity)*

SUGGESTED ASSIGNMENTS

1. **Critical Thinking Worksheet (Basic)** Have students complete Critical Thinking Worksheet 16 in the TEACHER'S RESOURCEBANK™.
2. **Commentary (Challenging)** Have three to five interested students organize a Roman "talk show" on the topic "Should everyone worship the emperor for the greater good of the state?" One student should serve as moderator and two students should argue in favor and two should argue against the question. The two against the question may represent the Christian or Jewish faiths, or one of the Eastern cults of Isis, Cybele, or Mithras. The students should do research on the principles of their selected faith, so that they are well prepared to answer those favoring emperor worship. Those students in favor of the proposal should have a clear understanding of the reasons why Rome developed divinity for the emperor. Following the panel discussion, ask members of the class to ask the panelists questions about the proposal. Then ask students to discuss freedom of religion as a concept in ancient civilizations.

Section (pages 166–171)

6 A Weakened Roman Empire in the West Declined and Fell

SECTION OVERVIEW

After the reign of Marcus Aurelius, the Pax Romana ended and the Roman Empire fell into a long period of decline. There was great confusion and civil war during the A.D. 200s. Two able emperors, Diocletian and Constantine, prevented the empire's collapse for nearly 200 years. By the year 400 there were two empires, one in the east and one in the west. The Western Roman Empire suffered from a number of internal weaknesses, and Germanic tribes invaded. Its ultimate collapse resulted from a combination of factors. However, two key ideas did survive: the Roman heritage and Christianity.

SUGGESTED TEACHING STRATEGIES

1. **Preteaching Vocabulary (Basic)** inflation *(page 166)*; collegia *(page 167)*; anarchy *(page 168)*. Ask students to describe how inflation affects people today.
2. **Writing Letters (Basic)** Have students write letters from officials in the provinces to the Roman emperor, telling him of the problems they face.
3. **Organizing a Panel Discussion (Average/Group)** You might organize a panel discussion on the reasons for the decline of the Roman Empire. Each panelist should read an essay on the breakdown of Rome and present the point of view of that essay. Sources might include *The Fall of Rome* (Holt, Rhinehart and Winston), edited by Mortimer Chambers, and D. Kagan's *The End of the Roman Empire* (D. C. Heath). Welcome questions from the class and encourage discussion of what contributed to Rome's decline. During the discussion it should become clear that the collapse of the Roman Empire was the result of many causes.

ENRICHMENT ACTIVITY

Forming Hypotheses (Average/Group) Have students hypothesize about the reasons barbarians entered the Roman Empire. Write their hypotheses on the chalkboard or an overhead projector. These should include population pressure, search for better farmland, wealth of the Roman Empire, use of barbarians as soldiers in the Roman army. Ask students to provide you with the evidence on which they based their hypotheses.

DAILY QUIZ

To assess student understanding of Section 6, give the class the following quiz. (Each item is worth 10 points.)

1. (T or F) A major problem faced by Roman emperors after A.D. 180 was how to protect the frontiers. *(T)*
2. The government assigned ______ to collegia, or workers' trade associations, to force the people to remain at their jobs in the city. *(artisans; workers)*
3. Name the two emperors who successfully reorganized the empire and postponed its collapse. *(Diocletian; Constantine)*
4. Name the Roman Empire's new administrative center in the East. *(Constantinople/Byzantium/Istanbul)*
5. The Germanic tribe, ______, invaded Italy and sacked Rome in 410. *(Visigoths)*
6. The ______ swept into Europe during the late 300s, pushing many Germans into the empire. *(Huns)*
7. The collapse of the Roman government resulted in ______, or the absence of any government at all. *(anarchy)*
8. (T or F) The economy of the Roman Empire did not produce enough wealth to support a great civilization permanently. *(T)*

9. (T or F) Despite the decline, most Romans remained hard-working, patriotic, and politically uncorrupted. *(F)*
10. Name the two key Roman ideas that survived the collapse of the empire. *(Roman heritage, culture/civilization; Christianity)*

SUGGESTED ASSIGNMENTS

1. **Critical Thinking Worksheet (Basic)** Have students complete Critical Thinking Worksheet 17 in the TEACHER'S RESOURCEBANK™.
2. **Review Worksheet (Basic)** Have students complete Review Worksheet 7 in the TEACHER'S RESOURCEBANK™.

For suggested lesson plan, additional teaching strategies, enrichment activities, daily quizzes, and suggested assignments, see pages 141A–141H.

CHAPTER

7

Rome Ruled the Western World for Centuries

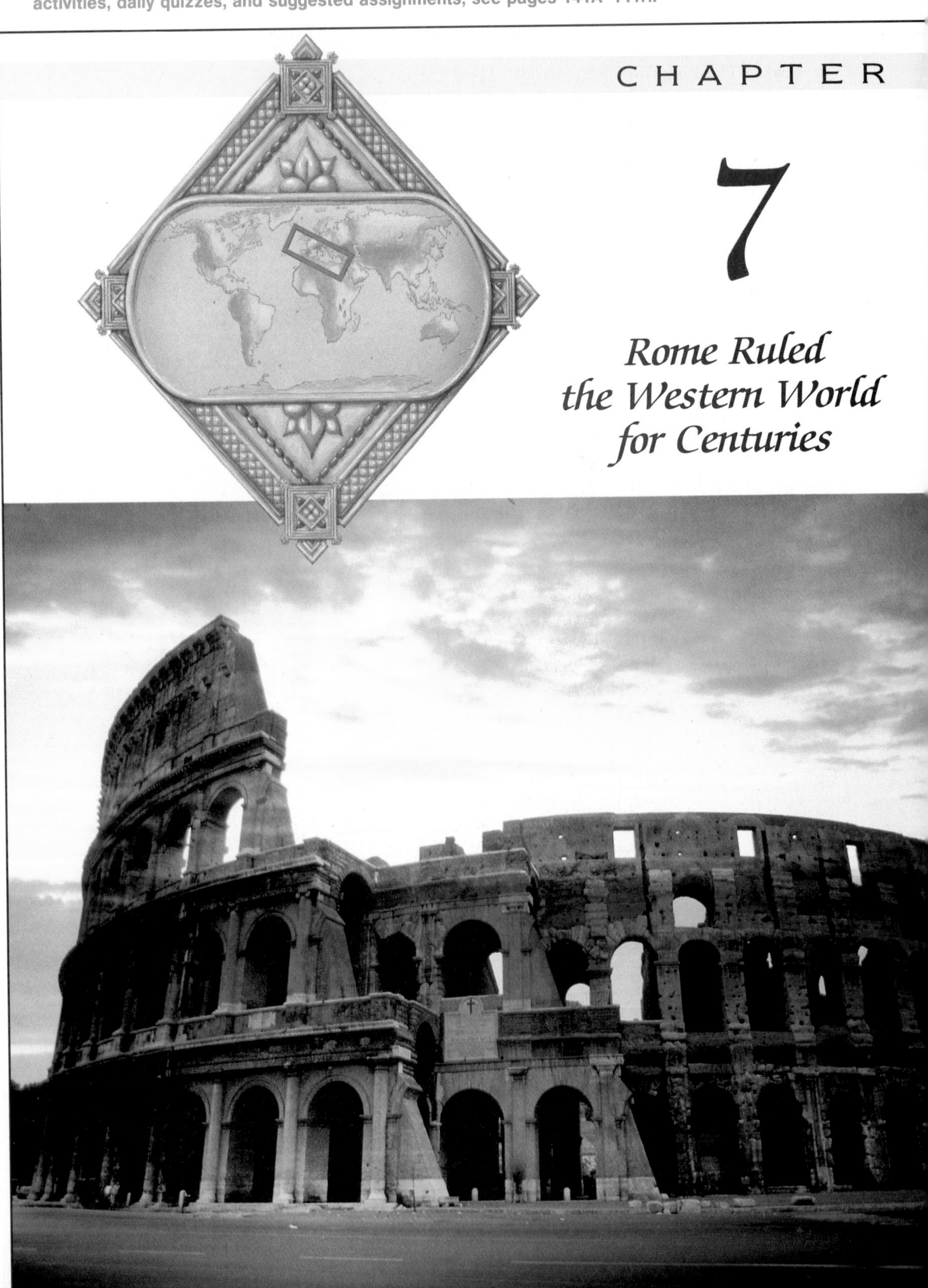

Introducing the Chapter
Have students turn to the map on page 144 or refer to a large topographical map of Italy. Hold a discussion on the influence of geography on the development of Italy, using the following questions as a guide. What are the most noticeable geographical features of Italy? How safe does Italy appear to be from invasions? Does its geography appear to encourage or discourage unity? Why did the Romans not become seafarers like the Greeks? How might Italy's geographic position have contributed to its ability to expand into the Mediterranean?

(Answers should include the following: Italy is a peninsula jutting into the Mediterranean and has a mountain range — the Apennines — running down its spine. Invaders could enter through several passes in the Alps and anywhere along Italy's long seacoast. The Apennines are not very rugged and thus did not prevent trade or travel. Italy has few good harbors, so its people did not become seafarers like the Greeks. Because the peninsula is situated in the center of the Mediterranean area, the empire could expand in any direction.)

Chapter Objectives
After studying Chapter 7, students will be able to:

1. Summarize the Latin and Etruscan cultural advances that led to the formation of Roman culture.

CHAPTER FOCUS

Place Italy and the Mediterranean region

Time

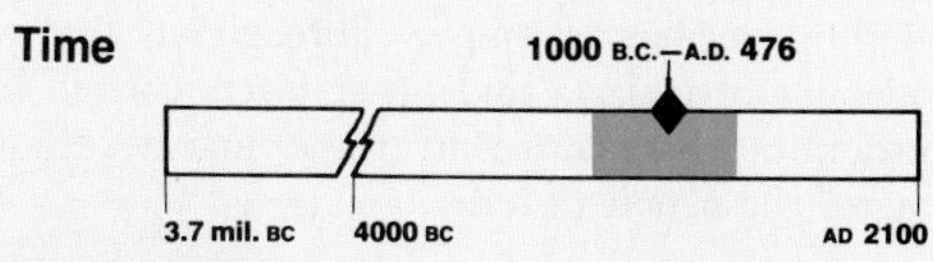

Significance

The date 146 B.C. is often given as the end of the Hellenistic Age because by that year the Romans had extended their power over a large part of the eastern Mediterranean. But who were the Romans? How did they become powerful enough to gain control of the Mediterranean region and much of Europe as well? And why are they important to us today?

To answer these questions, we must look west of Greece to the shores of the Tiber River, on the rugged Italian Peninsula. There the settlement that would in time become the imperial city of Rome was founded about 750 B.C. In contrast to the genius of the Greeks, which lay in the development of philosophy, the genius of the Romans lay in politics and law. Even today we trace the origins of many of our legal and political institutions to those of ancient Rome.

Terms to Define

republic, consul, veto, patrician, plebeian, indemnity, latifundia, Pax Romana, inflation, anarchy

People to Identify

Julius Caesar, Octavian, Cicero, Jesus, Constantine, Diocletian

Places to Locate

Italian Peninsula, Rome, Carthage, Judea, Nicaea, Constantinople

Questions to Guide Your Reading

1 How did the geography of Italy influence the rise of Roman power?
2 How did the Roman Republic expand its territory to include the entire Mediterranean region?
3 How was the Roman Republic transformed into an empire?
4 What features of Roman society and culture helped the Romans build and maintain their empire?
5 Why did Christianity take root in Judea?
6 What problems led to the decline and fall of the Roman Empire in the west?

No one knows exactly when the city of Rome was founded, but several colorful legends exist. The most famous legend holds that Romulus, the son of a priestess and Mars—the god of war—founded the city. Romulus and his twin brother, Remus, were allegedly abandoned by their mother and left to die. Good fortune saved the infants, a wolf mothered them, and a shepherd raised them. As adults the brothers founded villages on separate hills—the Palatine and the Aventine. The brothers soon quarreled, and Remus—to show how little he thought of Romulus' village—jumped over its unfinished wall. Furious, Romulus killed his brother and swore to do the same to "whoever else shall leap over my walls." Rome, the city formed when the two villages eventually united, was named after Romulus.

1 The Romans Founded a Republic on the Italian Peninsula

The geography of Italy and the location of Rome itself had a great deal to do with the rise of Roman power. In time Rome became the heart of a vast empire. Like most empires, it took shape gradually.

The Physical Setting

Italy is the central peninsula of the three great peninsulas in the Mediterranean region. On the map on page 144, note that Italy resembles a boot, with its top nestled in the Alps to the north and its toe and heel jutting into the Mediterranean Sea to the south. The toe of Italy rests only about 2 miles (3 kilometers) from Sicily, which is only 80 miles (128 kilometers) from Africa. Italy lies at the center of the Mediterranean region, slicing the sea nearly in half. Because of its location, Italy is also the obvious base from which to control both the eastern and the western halves of the region.

At first glance the snowcapped Alps separating Italy from the rest of Europe seem to be good protection against invasion. However, for centuries invaders have streamed through several passes that cut through the jagged mountains. Italy's location also makes it vulnerable to sea invasion, for invaders can land anywhere along the peninsula's long, rugged seacoast.

◀ *The Roman Colosseum*

2. Describe the form of government in the Roman Republic and the duties of Roman citizens.
3. List three reasons for and effects of the Punic wars.
4. Explain why Rome expanded and what political, economic, and social problems this expansion caused.
5. State the problems that forced many to believe an empire (instead of a republic) would better serve Rome's needs and describe the activities of those who attempted to solve these problems.
6. Describe Roman government and law during the Pax Romana.
7. Describe living conditions in Rome and its colonies during the Pax Romana.
8. Summarize the problems in Judea and why Christianity appealed to many as a religion.
9. Describe the governmental organization of the Roman Empire.
10. List problems that led to the Roman Empire's collapse and describe the results of this decline.

SECTION 1

Focus/Motivation

Ask students to name the type of government the United States has. *(representative democracy)* Ask them to name the form of government mentioned in the Pledge of Allegiance. *(republic)* Point out that the United States is called a democratic republic. Arrive

143

1A, 1B, 3A, a1A, a4A, a4B, a4C

at a definition of these terms. Explain that the founders of our country were influenced by the Roman Republic. Ask them to keep this in mind as they read the section.

Presentation
Illustrating Ideas (Average/Group)
Working with the class, develop a diagram on the chalkboard or an overhead projector showing the organization of the Roman Republic's government. Include all governing bodies (Senate, Assembly of Centuries, Assembly of Tribes) and officials (consuls, praetors, censors, dictator, tribunes) in the organization. Students should copy the diagram into their notebooks. Then ask students what terms used in the government of the Roman Republic are commonly used today? *(senate, consuls, dictators)* Ask them if they have the same meaning today. *(Answers will vary. A senate is similar but may have less influence in the whole government. Consuls today are a nation's commercial representatives in foreign cities. Dictators have absolute powers but are not limited to the term they may serve.)*

Geographical factors made unity possible in Italy, whereas in Greece the geography prevented it. Notice on the map that the Apennine Mountains, which run the full length of the boot, divide the peninsula. Because the Apennines are less rugged than the mountains of Greece, they did not hinder trade and travel. In addition, although Italy has a long coastline, it has fewer good harbors than Greece has. For these reasons the people living in the early coastal settlements turned inland for trade and growth rather than toward the sea as the Greeks had done.

Except for the long coastal plain to the west and the great valley of the Po River to the north, mountains dominate the landscape of Italy. Heavy rains easily wash away the sandy soil, and most land can be used only for grazing. Nevertheless, Italy's pleasant climate and plentiful winter rains enable farmers to raise vegetables, olives, grapes, and citrus fruits.

Italy's rivers are short and shallow. Soil that washes down from higher land partially blocks the mouths of most of these rivers, making the surrounding regions swampy. Throughout history epidemics of malaria and other fevers carried by mosquitoes that thrive in these marshes have plagued the people of Italy.

Learning from Maps *Rome was in an ideal location to become the leading city and the center of power on the Italian Peninsula. On what island did the Greeks establish a colony?* Sicily

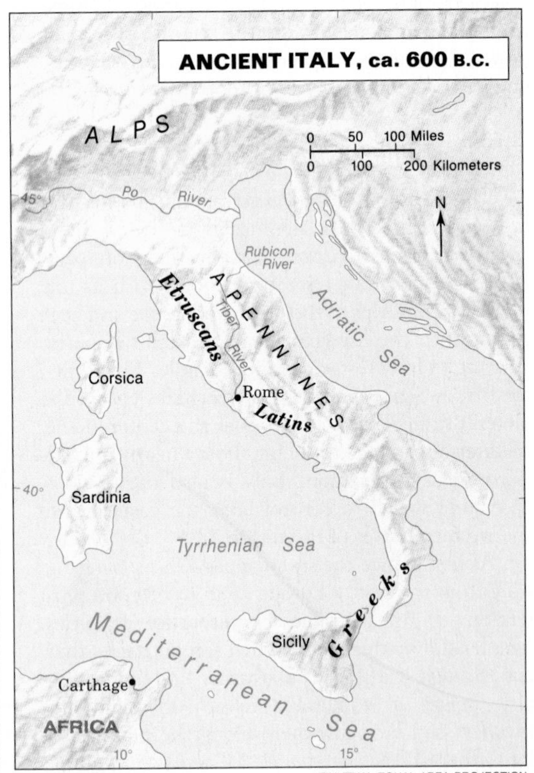

Early Peoples in Italy

People lived in Italy as early as the Old Stone Age, and a Neolithic culture had developed there before 3000 B.C. After 2000 B.C. waves of invaders swept through the mountain passes and overran the peninsula. As in Greece these invaders came from north of the Black and Caspian seas.

About 1000 B.C. the Latins entered the peninsula and settled in the west-central plains region called Latium (LAY • shee • uhm). Some of the Latin settlers built villages along the Tiber River. In time these villages united to form the city of Rome (see map, this page).

In the late 600s B.C., Etruscans (ih • TRUHS • kuhnz) from north of the Tiber River captured the plains of Latium, including Rome, and controlled the area for about 100 years. They were later absorbed into the mixture of peoples who came to be known as Romans.

Although the Etruscans disappeared as a people, their culture continued to influence the Latins. The Etruscans had developed a written language using an alphabet based on Greek characters. Although scholars have not yet deciphered the script, many believe that the Romans patterned their alphabet after the Etruscan alphabet.

The Etruscans also made fine clothing and jewelry and were skilled workers in metal, pottery, and wood. From the Etruscans the early farmers of Latium learned how to pave roads, drain unhealthy marshes, and build sewers.

The Etruscans introduced to the people of Rome the triumph, a splendid parade held for a conquering military leader returning victorious from battle. Preceded by the spoils and prisoners of war, the leader rode in a special chariot at the head of the troops. To keep the leader from being completely carried away by the cheers of the people, a servant rode in the chariot and constantly repeated, "Remember that you are mortal."

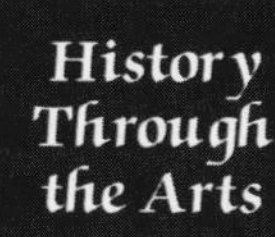

History Through the Arts

SCULPTURE

Etruscan Archers and Discus Thrower

The Etruscans were a powerful people of ancient Italy. Skilled fighters and merchants whose wealth came from shipping, the Etruscans traded across the Mediterranean, especially with the Greeks and Egyptians.

Wealthy Etruscans built magnificent tombs for their dead. They filled the tombs with items they thought the dead might need in their future life. Much of our knowledge of Etruscan customs comes from objects found in these tombs. They tell us that Etruscans loved music, games, wrestling, horseback riding, and chariot races.

Metropolitan Museum of Art, Purchase, John Pulitzer Bequest, 1940. (40.11.3)

Sometimes the Etruscans cremated, or burned, their dead. The bronze funeral urn shown here was used to hold ashes. Etruscan funeral urns were decorated with scenes of real life. The discus thrower and four mounted archers may have been placed on the lid to represent pleasures the dead person had once enjoyed.

Some Greeks also settled in ancient Italy. Greek colonies in Sicily and southern Italy became city-states, as disunited and quarrelsome as those of the homeland. The Greek culture of these colonies strongly influenced the Romans.

A Strategic Location

Latins, Etruscans, and other peoples living around Rome gradually began to call themselves Romans. At first Rome was only one of many city-states on the plains of Latium. Rome's location, however, gave it an advantage over other city-states on the Italian Peninsula.

Locate Rome on the map on page 144. Built on seven hills along the Tiber River, Rome lies about 15 miles (24 kilometers) inland from the western coast of Italy. This location protected the Romans from sea invasions.

Rome's location gave the city economic advantages as well. The city lay along one of the shallowest parts of the Tiber, near a small island in the river. This location at the easiest river crossing for many miles put the city at the center of land trade routes that spread out in all directions.

Roman Government

When the Romans overthrew the last Etruscan king in 509 B.C., they set up a republic to govern Rome. A **republic** is a form of government in which voters elect their leaders. In the early Roman Republic, only adult male citizens were entitled to vote and participate in government.

Three groups of citizens helped govern Rome: the Assembly of Centuries, the Assembly of Tribes, and the Senate.

The Assembly of Centuries took its name from a military formation of 100 men. The formation was called a "century" after the Latin word *centum,* which means "hundred." The Assembly declared war and peace and elected three kinds of magistrates, or public officials, to oversee the daily affairs of government.

First, two **consuls** were elected for one-year terms. They served as the chief executives who ran the government and as army commanders. Each could **veto,** or refuse to approve, acts of the other. (The Latin word *veto* means "I forbid.") Although powerful, the consuls governed with the advice of the Senate. This division of power was an example

145

3A, a2A, a2C, a2D, a2E, a2F, a2G, a2H, a2I, a2J, a2K, a2L

● **Point out that the word *patrician* today means a person of the upper class.**

of the principle of **checks and balances** that prevented any one part of the government from becoming too powerful. Many nations of the modern world, including the United States, later adopted the principle of checks and balances as well as the veto.

Second, **praetors** (PREET • uhrz) served as military commanders and judges. They became very important because they actually created most of the laws of Rome through their decisions in court cases.

Third, **censors** registered people according to their wealth to determine how much they should pay in taxes.

The Assembly of Tribes. Citizens grouped into 35 tribes according to where they lived made up the Assembly of Tribes. The Assembly elected 10 officials called **tribunes.** Although they did not take part in day-to-day government, the 10 tribunes became the most important officials without administrative authority in Rome. They could veto Senate bills and the actions of public officials if they believed that the acts were contrary to the public interest.

The Senate. The most important and powerful of the three governing bodies—the Senate—included 300 men. The Senate controlled public funds, determined foreign policy, and sometimes acted as a court. In times of emergency, the Senate could propose that a citizen be named **dictator.** If the consuls agreed, the Senate gave the dictator absolute power for a term limited to six months.

The composition of the assemblies and responsibilities of the elected officials changed throughout the life of the republic. The changes stemmed from the common people's attempts to win more rights, conflicts known as "the struggle of the orders."

The Struggle of the Orders

In the earliest days of Rome, most men farmed. No one was very rich, and no one was miserably poor. As time passed, however, the distinctions among social classes became greater. A powerful aristocratic class, the **patricians,** gained control of the government. All other citizens were **plebeians** (pli • BEE • yuhnz).

Plebeians suffered discrimination for many years. Laws prevented them from holding public office or marrying patricians. They could not even know what the laws said because the laws were not written down. In court, a judge stated and applied all laws, and only patricians served as judges.

Gradually the plebeians increased their power by making demands and by leading strikes. They gained the right to marry patricians and to hold office in the government. In one of their greatest victories, they forced the government to write the laws down. About 450 B.C. the Romans engraved these laws on tablets known as the Twelve Tables and placed them in the Forum—the chief public square—for all to view.

Over the years the plebeians won additional rights. Laws banned debt slavery and permitted plebeians to fill public offices, including that of consul.

By about 300 B.C. wealthy and powerful plebeians had joined with the patricians to form the Roman nobility. From that time on, the distinction between patricians and plebeians was of little importance. Although the common people had the right to elect officials and make laws, they did not exert much influence. Since no official received a salary, only the wealthy nobles could afford to hold office. The nobles controlled the Assembly of Centuries and the Senate. The Senate overshadowed the magistrates. And ambitious tribunes, hoping for higher office, sometimes cooperated with the Senate in using their veto power. Therefore, through skillful political maneuvering, the nobles dominated the republic.

Roman Expansion

For more than 200 years after the founding of the republic, the Romans fought many wars against neighboring peoples in Italy. By 265 B.C. the Romans controlled all of Italy south of the Rubicon River on the northeast coast. Both military organization and wise policies helped the Romans achieve their victories.

The army. Roman law obligated every adult male citizen to serve in the army. Discipline was strict, and the soldiers themselves enforced it. No man could be a candidate for high office until he had served at least 10 years in the army, and for many centuries only citizens could serve.

The most important military unit of the Roman army was the **legion,** consisting of 4,500 to 6,000 men called legionnaries. Because of excellent organization, training, and high morale, the Roman legions eventually defeated even the great Macedonian army.

146

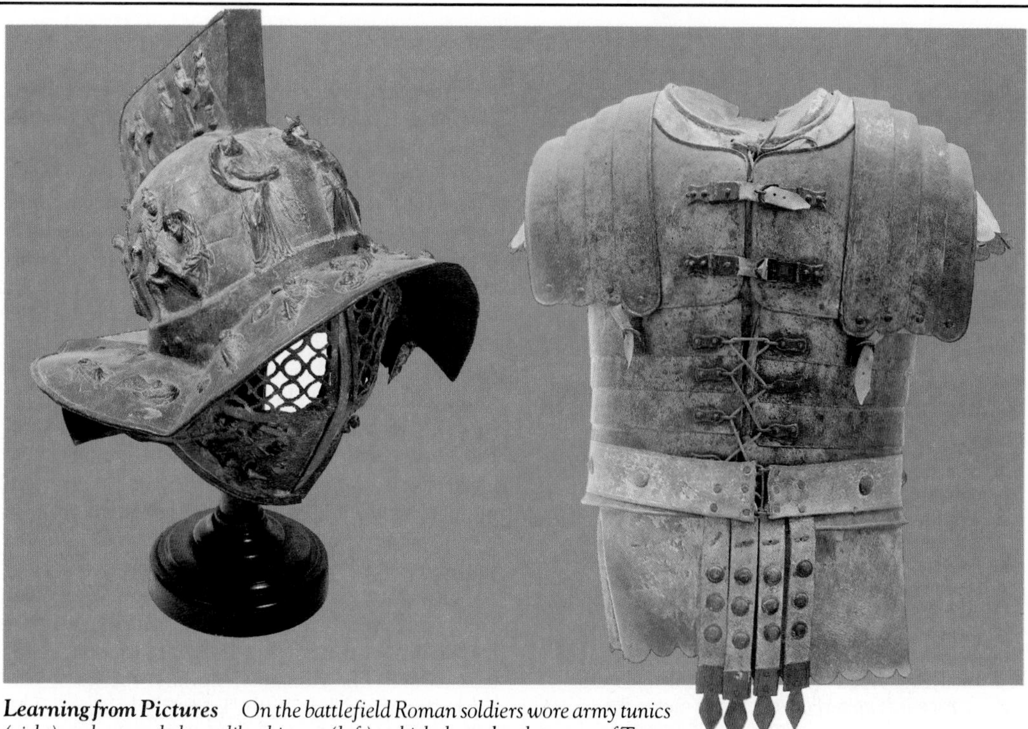

Learning from Pictures *On the battlefield Roman soldiers wore army tunics (right) and ornate helmets like this one (left), which shows battle scenes of Troy.*

Wise policies. To ensure the loyalty of their subjects, the Romans shared citizenship and political power with the people they conquered. The Romans granted full citizenship to the inhabitants of nearby Italian cities and partial citizenship to the inhabitants of more distant cities, including the Greek city-states in Italy. Partial citizens could own property and marry under Roman law, but they could not vote. The Romans also made treaties of alliance with more distant cities. The allies remained independent, but they promised to provide military assistance to the Romans and to support Rome's foreign policy.

The early Romans did not care to obtain tribute or slaves, but did expect subject peoples to provide land for Roman farmers' resettlement. This land settlement policy enabled the Romans to maintain military control over their conquests and to spread the Latin language, Roman law, and other aspects of Roman culture throughout Italy.

The Family

As the center of religion, morals, and education, the family became the most important unit in Roman society during the days of the republic. A Roman family included all unmarried children, married sons and their families, all dependent relatives, and the family slaves.

The father, known as the **paterfamilias** (pat • uhr • fuh • MIL • ee • uhs), had absolute authority. He conducted religious ceremonies, made all important decisions, and supervised his sons' education. Roman women enjoyed a higher status than did Greek women. The mother managed the household, did the buying, and helped her husband entertain guests.

Religion

The early Romans believed that spirits inhabited everything. The spirits of the home were the most important. These included the *lares* (LAR • eez), who were ancestral spirits, and *penates* (puh • NAYT • eez), guardians of the storeroom. Family worship focused on Vesta, guardian of fire and hearth. Other spirits governed every aspect of farm life.

Contacts with other peoples, however, changed Roman beliefs. Jupiter, for example, was at first an Indo-European sky god. The Etruscans gave Jupiter

SECTION 1

Closure

The Roman Republic was designed for a small city-state in the Italian Peninsula. What advantages did Rome have that caused its growth? *(strategic location, trade, skilled legions, resettlement policy)* How did the Romans keep the loyalty of the people they conquered? *(granting citizenship and sharing political power)*

Review Answers

1. ***republic:*** a form of government in which those entitled to vote choose their government leaders; ***consul:*** chief executive who ran the government and served as military commander; ***veto:*** right of one consul to refuse to approve acts of the other; ***checks and balances:*** principle that prevented any one part of the government from becoming too powerful; ***praetor:*** judge who created most of the laws of Rome through decisions in court cases; ***censor:*** registered people according to their wealth to determine how much tax they should pay; ***tribune:*** elected official in the Assembly of Tribes who could veto Senate bills and acts of public officials; ***dictator:*** during emergency Senate gave this citizen absolute power for six months; ***patrician:*** member of powerful aristocratic class; ***plebeian:*** commoner; ***legion:*** most important military unit of Roman army consisting of 4,500 to

● The pope still bears the title Pontifex Maximus.

6,000 men; ***paterfamilias:*** father in the Roman family who had absolute authority
2. ***Romulus:*** legendary founder of Rome; ***Pontifex Maximus:*** high priest elected for life by a special assembly of 17 tribes
3. ***Po River:*** great river valley in northern Italy; ***Latium:*** west-central plains region where Latins settled; ***Tiber River:*** river along which Rome was built; ***Rome:*** heart of Roman civilization; city built on seven hills along Tiber River; ***Rubicon River:*** located on the northeast coast; northern boundary of Roman Republic's territory in 265 B.C.
4. Latin farmers learned from Etruscans to pave roads, drain marshes, and build sewers. The Latins absorbed much of the highly developed Etruscan culture.
5. Rome was located at the easiest Tiber River crossing for many miles and became a center of land trade routes.
6. (a) The three groups of citizens were: Senate, Assembly of Centuries, Assembly of Tribes. **(b)** The Senate was the most powerful. **(c)** Senators controlled public funds, political appointments, foreign policy, and sometimes acted as a court. **(d)** The nobles were rich and could afford to hold unpaid public office.

SECTION 2

Focus/Motivation
Have the students refer to the map on page 149. Ask:

a human form. Later, after the Romans conquered the Greeks, Jupiter took on the characteristics of the chief Greek god, Zeus. From the Etruscans the Romans also adopted the practice of trying to learn a god's will by observing the internal organs of animals or the flight of birds.

In time the old family religion became a state religion with temples, ceremonies, and processions. The high priest, elected for life by a special assembly of 17 tribes, was called the Pontifex Maximus.

SECTION 1 REVIEW

1. **Define** republic, consul, veto, checks and balances, praetor, censor, tribune, dictator, patrician, plebeian, legion, paterfamilias
2. **Identify** Romulus, Pontifex Maximus
3. **Locate** Po River, Latium, Tiber River, Rome, Rubicon River
4. **Understanding Ideas** What did the Latins learn from the Etruscans?
5. **Interpreting Ideas** How was Rome ideally located for trade?
6. **Analyzing Ideas** **(a)** Name the three groups of citizens that helped govern Rome during the Republic. **(b)** Which group was the most powerful? **(c)** Why? **(d)** How were the nobles able to control the government?

2 The Roman Republic Expanded into the Entire Mediterranean Region

By the middle 200s B.C., the Roman Republic had extended its power over all of the Italian Peninsula south of the Rubicon River. The addition of so much land and so many new people to the republic increased its power and strength, but the burden of defending the republic also increased.

Rome Versus Carthage

Rome soon came into contact with Carthage, a large and powerful city on the coast of North Africa (see map, page 149). Originally a Phoenician colony, Carthage became a great commercial power with an empire that spanned the western Mediterranean. The Carthaginians boasted that the Mediterranean was a "Carthaginian lake," in which people could not so much as wash their hands without Carthage's permission.

After the Romans occupied southern Italy, Carthage feared that they would also try to take Sicily, with its Carthaginian colonies and markets. The Romans feared that the Carthaginian navy would close the Adriatic Sea and the narrow Strait of Messina between Italy and Sicily. These fears sparked a series of devastating wars between the two cities.

Rome and Carthage fought three wars which, despite intervals of peace, lasted from 264 B.C. to 146 B.C. We call them the Punic Wars because the Latin adjective for "Phoenician" was *punicus.*

The opponents were well matched. Rome had the better army; Carthage had the better navy. Carthage had more wealth. Roman lands were more compact and more easily defended. At first Carthaginian military commanders had greater skill, but later Rome also acquired able generals.

The First Punic War. The First Punic War began in 264 B.C. Initially Rome had no navy, but soon built one using a captured Carthaginian vessel as a model. The Romans used land tactics at sea, equipping their ships with "boarding bridges." The Romans would ram their ship into a Carthaginian ship and then let down the bridge so that heavily armed soldiers could stampede across and take the enemy. This clever Roman tactic succeeded, and in 241 B.C. Carthage asked for peace. The Romans made Carthage pay a large **indemnity**—money for the damages it had caused—and forced Carthage to give up control of Sicily. Within a few years, the Romans conquered all of Italy and had major overseas holdings. But the Carthaginians thirsted for revenge.

The Second Punic War. The Second Punic War began in 218 B.C. In Spain Hannibal, one of the greatest generals of all time, assembled an army including an infantry, a cavalry, and 50 war elephants. They marched across what is now southern France and began the job of crossing the Alps into Italy in August. The crossing proved to be an incredible disaster, made doubly difficult by early snows and landslides. Almost half the army and most of the elephants perished. At the end of September, Hannibal led his remaining soldiers, half-starved and half-frozen, into the Po Valley (see map, page 149).

Despite the condition of Hannibal's army, the Roman armies were no match for him. He defeated several of the Roman armies, which then retreated to their fortified cities. Since Hannibal had no

1A, 1C, 3A, a4B, a4C, a4K, a4L

● Answers will vary. Students might suggest that if Hannibal had not lost his men or war elephants, he would have overwhelmed the Roman armies.

■ In the Senate Cato ended every speech — no matter what the subject — with "Carthage must be destroyed."

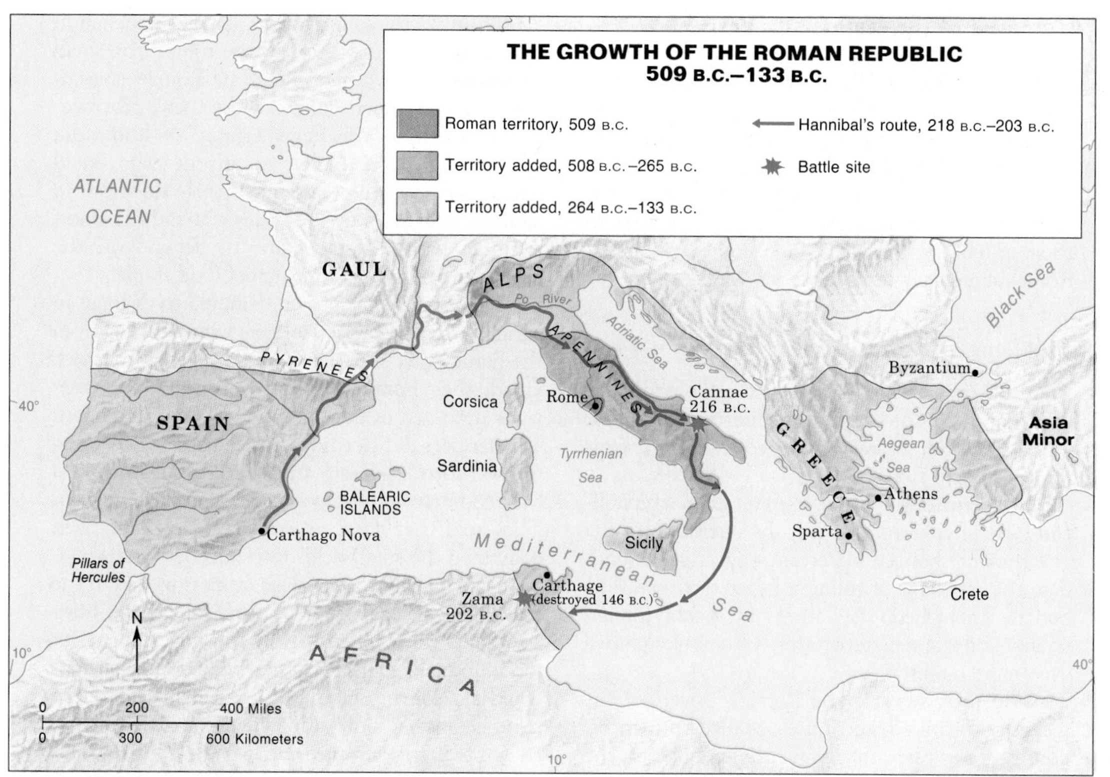

Learning from Maps *The destruction of Carthage made Rome the greatest power in the Mediterranean. What territories did Rome acquire after 265* B.C.? **Spain, Athens, Sparta, Crete, Carthage**

siege equipment, he could not attack the cities. Instead he spent 15 years ravaging the southern Italian countryside. He also tried to win away the Roman Republic's allies. The Roman policy of sharing citizenship and political power proved its value, however, and the majority of the republic's allies remained loyal.

Finally the Romans turned the tables by invading Africa and threatening Carthage. Hannibal's government ordered him home to defend the city. In Africa he finally met his match—the Roman general Scipio (SIP • ee • oh). In 202 B.C. at the battle of Zama, near Carthage, the brilliant Scipio defeated Hannibal and his army, ensuring the supremacy of Greco-Roman civilization in the Mediterranean (see map, this page).

Once more Carthage asked for peace and had to pay a huge indemnity. It also gave up its Spanish colonies. The city of Carthage remained independent, but it had lost all its power.

The Third Punic War. Although Carthage no longer threatened the power of Rome, some Roman war veterans passionately hated Carthage. Under pressure from these groups, the Senate ■ finally decided to crush Carthage. On a flimsy excuse, Rome declared war against Carthage in 149 B.C. After a bitter siege, the city fell in 146 B.C. The Romans razed Carthage and sold the surviving population into slavery.

What If?

Hannibal

Hannibal's army suffered devastating losses as they crossed the Alps. Even so, the Roman legions were no match for the remnants of the once-mighty Carthaginian forces. How do you think the course of world history would have been different if Hannibal had lost none of his men or war elephants when he ● crossed the Alps?

Why does it appear likely that Rome would come into conflict with Carthage? *(Student responses should include the idea that Rome's expansion threatened Carthaginian control of the western Mediterranean. The proximity of Roman territory to Carthaginian Sicily was also a threat.)* Ask students to examine the map and speculate why Rome became involved in the eastern Mediterranean. *(Answers might include the following: to protect and control the Adriatic; to gain control of trade in the East; to provide protection for territory already conquered.)*

Presentation
Relating Past To Present (Average/Group)
Have students read the subsection "Changes in agriculture" on page 150. Ask: How do the problems that Roman soldiers returning from the Punic Wars faced resemble problems of present-day veterans? *(Answers will vary. Students may mention that veterans in the United States received education under G.I. bills, VA loans for housing, and had organizations such as the American Legion and Veterans of Foreign Wars to speak for them. Vietnam War veterans faced less interest in their problems—such as drug abuse, physical rehabilitation, and psychological difficulties resulting from the war—until recently, perhaps because the war was so unpopular. The United*

149

1C, 1D, 3A

● King Pyrrhus of Epirus's victory over Rome was so costly that we use the term *pyrrhic victory* today to mean a "hollow victory."

■ The *equites* are sometimes called the equestrian order. The term originally applied to all citizens who served on horseback in the army.

States has never faced large-scale ravages from war in the 20th century, so the problems Romans faced on the land are not the same.)

SECTION 2

Closure

Victory in the Punic Wars over Carthage enabled Rome to dominate the Mediterranean region. Ask: How did the Romans organize the lands they conquered? *(politically as provinces; economically by leasing much public land into large estates called latifundia)*

Review Answers

1. ***indemnity:*** money paid by one country to another for the damages it caused during a war; ***latifundia:*** large Roman estates; ***equites:*** class of Roman business people who had great wealth but little political power; ***crucifixion:*** cruel execution by suffocation on a cross

2. ***publican:*** tax collector under Roman tax farming system; ***Spartacus:*** famous leader of a large Roman slave revolt

3. ***Carthage:*** a large and powerful commercial city on coast of North Africa; ***Sicily:*** island located southwest of Italy where Carthage had colonies and markets; ***Zama:*** battle near Carthage where Hannibal and his army were defeated in 202 B.C.

4. (a) Carthage was the world's greatest sea power, but it feared Rome

Conquest of the Hellenistic East

During the Second Punic War, Macedonia had been allied with Carthage. Out of revenge Rome started a war against Macedonia and defeated it in ● 197 B.C. The Greek cities now came under Roman "protection." The Romans soon defeated the Seleucid king and gave parts of his territory in Asia to their allies. By 146 B.C., after more conquests, Rome's supremacy in the east was total.

Problems of Roman Expansion

The Roman state had grown from a loose alliance of Italian cities into a great Mediterranean power. The expansion, however, created many problems for the Roman Republic.

Government. Rome itself retained a republican form of government. But the operation of the government changed in certain ways to accommodate the problems of ruling a larger territory. The Senate controlled the army, finances, foreign affairs, and the new territories. The nobles gained even more power.

The provinces. The Romans governed the recently organized territories, called provinces, poorly. They did not grant the people of the provinces citizenship, nor did they make them allies as they did with the people of conquered Italian cities. Instead the Romans taxed the people of the provinces without mercy.

Provincial cities became centers of local government, and new cities sprouted in rural regions throughout the republic's territories. The provinces became a collection of city-states, each one subject to Rome. Each province had a Roman governor called a *proconsul,* appointed by the Senate and backed by a Roman army of occupation. Because his term of office lasted for only one year and he received no salary, the proconsul often took bribes and neglected the needs of the people.

The proconsuls were not the only Romans who became wealthy by stealing from the provinces. In Rome the censors contracted with officials called *publicans,* who agreed to collect the taxes and pay a fixed amount to the Roman treasury. The publicans could then keep whatever they collected in excess of this fixed sum. This system of collecting taxes, called *tax farming,* provided another example of the widespread corruption that plagued the provinces.

Changes in agriculture. Rome's annexation of distant territories lessened the role of the small citizen-farmer in Roman life. The Roman government owned much land in the new provinces and leased it in very large estates, or ***latifundia*** (lat • uh • FUHN • dee • uh), to anyone who could pay the price. Only wealthy people could afford to rent the land and buy the slaves who did the work. As time passed Rome came to depend on the provinces for grain, Rome's chief food staple.

The Punic Wars also contributed to changes in agriculture. The farmer-soldiers who returned from the Punic Wars were sickened to find their livestock killed, their homes in ruins, olive groves or vineyards uprooted or burned, and the land untended. The farmers did not have enough money to bring the war-torn land back into cultivation, nor could they compete with the low price of imported grain. They sold their land to wealthy people who then combined the small fields into huge latifundia.

Many of the now landless farmers moved to the cities. Not all of them could find jobs there, however, and they depended on the government for food. To make matters worse, the displaced farmers could no longer serve in the army because the republic allowed only landowners to fight. All that these landless veterans could do was sell their votes to the highest bidder.

Growth of commerce. As farming declined in Italy, trade within Rome's vast empire increased. The businesspeople of Rome formed a class called **equites** (EK • wuh • teez). They had great wealth ■ but little political power. In addition to wealth from trade, they made money from contracts for public works, tax farming, and the loot of war.

Social change. The decline of the independent farmers and the growth of jobless masses in the cities weakened the ideals of discipline and devotion to the state. Romans now judged people by their wealth rather than their character.

Other changes had also taken place. As Rome expanded, victorious generals enslaved their enemies. Many of these slaves enjoyed relatively humane treatment. For example, owners often let skilled slaves keep part of what they earned to buy their freedom later. And by Roman law a freed slave became a citizen.

Other slaves led miserable lives. They often revolted. The most brutal revolt, led by a slave named Spartacus, began in 73 B.C. More than 70,000 slaves took part in this revolt. However, by

CONNECTIONS: THEN AND NOW

Baths

Ancient peoples were just as fond of taking a plunge into water as we are. The Romans were particularly fond of bathing and built many large public pools and baths. These pools and baths were often filled with water of different temperatures, heated either by natural hot springs or by furnaces. The Roman bather would go from one pool to the other, combining dips with exercises followed by massages with fine oils.

Some of the Roman bath houses also contained libraries, sports facilities, and shops. The public bath was a social gathering place where people could meet, gossip, and even do business. The largest public bath in Rome is credited as the main achievement of its builder, the Emperor Caracalla, who ruled in the A.D. 200s.

The Romans built baths wherever they settled. One such place in England, which had natural hot springs, became known as the city of Bath (top). People enjoyed its refreshing waters long after the Romans left England.

Today public baths are used as neighborhood gathering places and are extremely popular throughout Japan. There is also a very ornate public bath in Moscow, the capital of the Soviet Union, and in Budapest, Hungary (below). In the United States, outdoor and indoor public swimming pools provide the same enjoyment and recreation the ancient Romans knew.

71 B.C. the Roman army had crushed the uprising. The generals crucified Spartacus and 6,000 of his followers. **Crucifixion,** in which the accused was tied to a cross and left to die a slow and agonizing death from suffocation, was a common Roman method of execution.

SECTION 2 REVIEW

1. **Define** indemnity, latifundia, equites, crucifixion
2. **Identify** publican, Spartacus
3. **Locate** Carthage, Sicily, Zama
4. **Summarizing Ideas** **(a)** How were Rome and Carthage in competition with each other? **(b)** What were the final results of the Punic Wars?
5. **Determining Cause and Effect** **(a)** How did the government of Rome change as a result of the conquest of new territories? **(b)** What effect did the Punic Wars have on Roman agriculture?

3 The Roman Republic Was Transformed into an Empire

By 133 B.C. the Roman Republic faced many problems. Although courageous leaders attempted reform, the days of the republic were numbered.

The Gracchi

Two brothers, Tiberius and Gaius Gracchus (GRAK • uhs), were among the first to attempt reforms. Elected tribune in 133 B.C., Tiberius saw that some senators used public land for their own benefit. He therefore limited the amount of public land they could use. He also moved many landless citizens from the cities to work the land confiscated from

would try to take Sicily and Carthage's trading markets. The Romans feared Carthage would close the Adriatic Sea and the Strait of Messina. **(b)** After the First Punic War, Carthage had to pay an indemnity and give up control of Sicily. After the Second Punic War, Carthage had to pay an indemnity and give up its Spanish colonies. After the Third Punic War, Carthage was destroyed. Rome's victory ensured the supremacy of Greco-Roman civilization in the Mediterranean.
5. (a) Rome retained a republican form of government, but the nobles gained power through control of the Senate, which ruled the new territories. The new provinces became city-states under a Roman proconsul, but they were ruled poorly, taxes were heavy, and corruption was common. **(b)** Rome's annexation of distant territories after the Punic Wars lessened the role of the small citizen-farmer in Roman life. The farmer-soldiers did not have enough money to bring the war-torn land back into cultivation, nor could they compete with the price of cheap grain imported from the provinces. They sold their land to wealthy people who combined the small fields into latifundia.

SECTION 3

Focus/Motivation
Gaius Gracchus used public funds to purchase grain that was sold to the poor

below cost. A parallel can be drawn between this practice and the public welfare programs in the United States today. You might stimulate a discussion about these similarities by making the following statement: The government should use public funds to assist private citizens.

Presentation
Classifying Ideas (Average/Group)
Have the students make a chart with four columns and two rows. The columns should be labeled: *Triumvirate, Participants, Reasons for Forming,* and *Reasons for Breaking Up.* The rows should be labeled: *First Triumvirate* and *Second Triumvirate.* Students should fill in the chart with information found on pages 152-153. Next to *First Triumvirate* under *Participants* should be: Caesar, Pompey, and Crassus. Under *Reasons for Forming* should be: To unite against their enemies. Under *Reasons for Breaking Up* should be: Crassus killed, Pompey jealous of Caesar, war broke out between Pompey and Caesar. Next to *Second Triumvirate* under *Participants* should be: Octavian, Marc Antony, and Lepidus. Under *Reasons for Forming* should be: To unite against Caesar's assassins. Under *Reasons for Breaking Up* should be: Lepidus forced to retire, Antony and Octavian fought each other.

the senators. Although this policy made him popular with the masses, it angered and frightened many senators. A mob of senators and their sympathizers clubbed Tiberius and 300 of his followers to death.

His brother Gaius, elected tribune in 123 B.C., tried to increase the power of the Assembly of Tribes. Gaius used public funds to purchase grain to be sold to the poor at low prices. Other measures improved the political status of the equites. Again these policies outraged the senators. They soon gathered together 3,000 supporters of Gaius, killed them, and declared Gaius an enemy of the republic. To escape a public trial, Gaius committed suicide.

The violent deaths of the Gracchi marked a turning point in Roman history. From this point on, violence became the primary tool of Roman politics and replaced respect for the law.

Marius and Sulla

Gaius Marius (MER • ee • uhs), a military hero, also attempted reform. In 105 B.C. Marius defeated Germanic invaders and changed the course of Roman history. To fill his legions, he signed up any citizen, regardless of whether he had land or not. The soldiers served not only for pay but also for booty—whatever they could steal from the enemy and all the slaves they could bring home. When they were discharged, the soldiers expected their general to reward them with public land. In other words Marius had substituted a professional army for an army of draftees. As other generals followed these practices, armies became loyal to their leaders instead of to the Roman government.

The consul Lucius Cornelius Sulla showed what an ambitious general could do with a professional army. He led his legions from Asia Minor to Rome and drove out Marius, who had seized the city. A bloody civil war then broke out between the followers of Marius and Sulla. By 82 B.C. Sulla had triumphed. With terrible brutality and complete disregard for the law, Sulla executed thousands of Roman citizens.

Sulla ruled as a military dictator until 79 B.C. He placed all the powers of government in the hands of the Senate, which he enlarged by 300 members. Increasingly, however, army commanders who could count on the loyalty of their troops could force the Senate to do their bidding.

The First Triumvirate

Julius Caesar, a nephew of Marius, gained popularity during this period. An opponent of Sulla's, Caesar narrowly escaped assassination by bribing the guards Sulla sent to kill him. After Sulla's retirement, Caesar used spellbinding oratory and lavish gifts of grain to build a huge following among the poor citizens of Rome.

Realizing that his popularity with the people had made him many enemies in the Senate, Caesar joined forces with two popular generals, Pompey (PAHM • pee) and Crassus, in 60 B.C. The three formed a political alliance that became known as the First Triumvirate. (The word *triumvirate* means "rule of three.") With the support of the other triumvirs, Caesar became consul in 59 B.C.

Caesar in Power

Caesar realized that he could not win power without a loyal army, so he made himself proconsul of Gaul, a region in what is today France (see map, page 149). In his 10 years as proconsul, Caesar brought all Gaul under Roman rule and showed his superb abilities as a military leader and organizer. Caesar issued written reports about his campaigns and victories to keep the people of Rome informed. Students of Latin still read these clearly detailed reports known as *Commentaries on the Gallic Wars.*

Crassus died in battle in 53 B.C. Pompey, meanwhile, grew jealous of Caesar's rising fame. To head off his rival, Pompey had himself made sole consul. He then persuaded the Senate to order Caesar to return home without his army. Caesar refused to give up his military command and take second place to Pompey. Instead he led his army toward Rome in 49 B.C.

When Caesar reached the Rubicon River (the border between Cisalpine Gaul and Italy), a messenger from the Senate met him with the decree that he would be declared a rebel if he crossed the river with his army. Caesar hesitated a short time, and then made his decision. He ordered his army to march on to Rome. Today when people make an irreversible decision, we say they have "crossed the Rubicon."

Pompey and his followers fled to Greece, leaving the way open for Caesar to assume power. He first secured his power in Italy and Spain and

● **Friends of Caesar later murdered Pompey in Egypt.**
■ **This is the Julian calendar.**
▲ **From *caesar* came the Russian word *czar* and the German word *kaiser*, meaning "emperor."**

● defeated Pompey in Greece. He then went to Egypt, which had increasingly come under Roman domination. There Caesar put Cleopatra, a daughter of the ruling Ptolemy (TAHL • uh • mee) family, on the throne as an ally of Rome.

In 46 B.C. Caesar returned to Rome, where the Senate appointed him dictator for life. Caesar kept the republican form of government, but he was king in everything but name.

Caesar proved to be an able politician as well as general. He granted citizenship to many people in the provinces and gave public land to veterans and grain to the poor. Caesar reduced the Senate to the position of an advisory council and raised its membership to 900 senators. He also ordered the estab-
■ lishment of a calendar of 365 1/4 days, which was used in Europe until A.D. 1582.

The conservative families of Rome did not welcome Caesar's new status. Some 60 men who envied his great power formed a conspiracy against him. Two of these were men Caesar considered friends: Gaius Cassius and Marcus Brutus. On the stormy Ides of March (March 15), 44 B.C., the conspirators stabbed Caesar to death in the Senate.

Learning from Pictures *Augustus considered himself a citizen and tried to exemplify good citizenship, even using his own money to restore temples.*

The Second Triumvirate

Although Caesar had chosen his 18-year-old grandnephew Octavian as his heir, a scramble for power erupted after Caesar's death. While Octavian was in Greece, Marc Antony, a general and an ally of Caesar, and Lepidus (LEP • uh • duhs), Caesar's second-in-command, drove out the conspirators and took control in Rome. The three men—Octavian, Marc Antony, and Lepidus—then formed the Second Triumvirate in 43 B.C.

Antony led an army east and reconquered Syria and Asia Minor from the armies of Brutus and Cassius. Then, having fallen in love with Cleopatra, he joined her in Egypt. Meanwhile Octavian forced Lepidus to retire from political life and built up his own power in Italy.

Octavian: the First Augustus

Antony and Octavian divided the Roman world. Antony took the east and Octavian the west. In time, however, Octavian persuaded the Senate to declare war on Antony and Cleopatra. In 31 B.C., in a great naval battle at Actium in Greece, Octavian defeated their fleet. The following summer Octavian captured Alexandria. Seeing that they could not escape, both Antony and Cleopatra committed suicide. The wars had finally ended, but so had the republic.

Determined to avoid his granduncle's fate, Octavian proceeded cautiously. The Senate appointed Octavian sole ruler, but he carefully preserved the outward appearance of the republic.

The Senate gave Octavian the title *Augustus*, which means "set aside for religious purposes" or "sacred." He has been known ever since as Augustus Caesar, or simply Augustus. Many later Roman rulers used the name *Caesar* as part of their titles. ▲

Historians generally refer to Augustus as the first Roman emperor, although he did not actually use the title. Beginning with the reign of Augustus, the Roman state became the Roman Empire. Under his rule Rome's territory stretched from Spain in the west to Syria in the east and from the Rhine and Danube rivers in the north to Egypt and the Sahara in the south.

153

3A, a4A, a4D, a4F, a4G, a4H, a4M

SECTION 3

Closure

Ask students how the death of the Gracchi brothers marked a turning point in Roman history. *(Violence became an accepted tool of Roman politics and replaced respect for the law.)* How did the triumvirates exemplify this change? *(All triumvirs had a falling out with one another; one won out and became sole ruler.)*

Review Answers

1. ***Marius:*** leader who defeated the Germans and reorganized Roman army, substituting a professional army for one of draftees; ***Sulla:*** Roman general who defeated the followers of Marius and made himself military dictator; ***Pompey:*** Roman general and consul who tried and failed to limit Caesar's power; ***Cleopatra:*** queen of Egypt who joined forces with Marc Antony against Octavian; ***Marc Antony:*** member of the Second Triumvirate who was defeated by Octavian at the Battle of Actium; ***Nero:*** cruel and unpredictable Julian emperor who was widely hated and who committed suicide; ***Hadrian:*** Roman emperor, patron of arts, and able administrator; ***Marcus Aurelius:*** last of the Good Emperors
2. ***Actium:*** site of naval battle in Greece where Octavian defeated Antony and Cleopatra
3. **(a)** The First Triumvirate was a political alliance of Caesar, Pompey, and Crassus. **(b)** Each had

● **Statements will vary. They should include references to the end of the Republic.**

READ
● WRITE
INTERPRET
CONNECT
THINK

BUILDING HISTORY STUDY SKILLS

Writing About History: Formulating a Thesis Statement

The first step in writing an essay is to determine what you wish to describe, explain, or prove. The information or the data you have gathered helps you to complete this step. You can then use the information you have collected and your stated purpose to formulate a thesis statement. A thesis statement expresses the main idea of your essay. It serves the same function as the topic sentence of a paragraph, which expresses the main idea of the essay.

A thesis statement follows these criteria:

- It is a generalization.
- It uses significant data to express a point of view.
- It measures how the various parts of the data interact with or relate to each other.

How to Formulate a Thesis Statement

To formulate a thesis statement, follow these steps.

1. Choose a topic of interest. Begin to collect facts about the general topic and keep detailed notes.
2. Begin to refine the topic. Look for related facts. Make a generalization based on the related facts.
3. Organize the collected facts. Discard those facts that have no bearing on the general statement, or refine the statement even further to include the facts.
4. Write a thesis statement using the characteristics given above. Refine the generalization, turning it into a thesis statement that can be proven and that meets the criteria listed above.

Developing the Skill

Study the data below about significant events during the Roman Republic. As you read the data, think about what thesis statement you can formulate.

- The Senate, the Assembly of Centuries, and the Assembly of Tribes helped govern Rome.
- Over hundreds of years, the plebeians gained many rights.
- After the Punic Wars, slavery became widespread, and a new class of urban poor was created.
- The gap between the rich and the poor widened.
- Although the common people of Rome had many rights, the nobility dominated the government.
- The attempts by the Gracchi to bring about land and government reform failed because of resistance from wealthy landowners.
- After Marius promised his soldiers booty from their campaigns, soldiers began to be more loyal to their generals than to Rome.
- Julius Caesar became so powerful that the Senate named him dictator for life.
- Civil war followed Caesar's assassination, and the republic ended with the reign of Octavian.

The facts all relate to conditions during the Roman Republic. The first two statements show that the republic gave many rights to its citizens and that many groups shared in governing Rome. The next eight facts, however, detail events that led to the end of the republic. A generalization relating all these facts might be: The Roman Republic had a democratic government, but various events combined to end the republic. Another way of formulating this generalization, thus turning it into a thesis statement, is:

Although many people were allowed to take part in Roman government, the power of the landowning nobility and the growth of a professional army loyal to generals doomed the Roman Republic. ●

Practicing the skill. What other thesis statement can you formulate from this data?

To apply this skill, see Applying History Study Skills on page 175.

An upper-class banquet in Pompeii

The Julian Emperors

Augustus died in A.D. 14. For the next 54 years, relatives of Julius Caesar, called the Julian Emperors, ruled the empire (see chart, page 156). Tiberius, who reigned from A.D. 14 to A.D. 37, was the adopted son of Augustus. Tiberius proved to be an adequate ruler. His brutal and insane successor Caligula (kuh • LIHG • yuh • luh)—who even appointed his favorite horse as consul—was murdered.

Claudius, an intelligent and scholarly man who administered the empire wisely, followed Caligula. During his rule the Roman legions conquered Britain. But even Claudius could not escape the violence that almost always marked the imperial succession.* According to reports, his wife Agrippina poisoned him, perhaps with tainted mushrooms, in A.D. 54.

A disastrous fire swept Rome during the reign of Nero (A.D. 54–A.D. 68). Many people believed that the emperor started the fire. Whether or not the emperor was to blame, the Romans hated him because of his cruel and unpredictable policies. Facing certain assassination, Nero committed suicide in A.D. 68.

The Good Emperors

After the death of Nero, a number of emperors supported by the army ruled Rome. Then, in A.D. 96, Emperor Nerva came to the throne. He was the first of a group of five, known as the Good Emperors, who ruled Rome for almost 100 years. A Spanish general, Trajan, ruled from A.D. 98 to A.D. 117 and added new territories that brought the empire to its greatest size—about the size of the United States today (see map, page 159).

Hadrian, Trajan's successor, supported art and proved an able ruler. Born in Spain, he understood the provinces and spent much time organizing and Romanizing them. To help protect the boundaries of the empire, Hadrian built fortifications along the frontiers and encouraged frontier peoples to enter the army. He disapproved of conquering neighboring regions and gave up the areas that Trajan had acquired in Asia.

* The Romans never developed a formal policy of succession. Although many emperors named their successors, the Roman army often refused to accept the new emperors and assassinated them.

After the uneventful reign of Antoninus Pius, Marcus Aurelius, the last of the Good Emperors, began his reign in A.D. 161. A well-educated man who preferred studying Stoic philosophy to fighting wars, he nevertheless had to defend the empire against invaders from the north and east. These invaders would play a key role in the future of the empire.

SECTION 3 REVIEW

1. **Identify** Marius, Sulla, Pompey, Cleopatra, Marc Antony, Nero, Hadrian, Marcus Aurelius
2. **Locate** Actium
3. **Summarizing Ideas** **(a)** What was the First Triumvirate? **(b)** Why was it formed?
4. **Interpreting Ideas** **(a)** Why was Julius Caesar so popular with the common people of Rome? **(b)** Why was he killed?
5. **Analyzing Ideas** **(a)** Why was the Second Triumvirate formed? **(b)** What caused it to break apart?
6. **Understanding Ideas** What powers did Augustus hold as ruler of the Roman Empire?

4 The Romans Developed a Distinctive Society and Culture

Several essential characteristics helped the Romans build their empire and maintain it in peace. The Romans had a talent for ruling others and maintained their authority through an efficient government both at home and abroad. Law, military organization, and widespread trade and transportation held the empire together and brought peace for more than 200 years.

The period from the beginning of Augustus' reign until the death of Marcus Aurelius (27 B.C. to A.D. 180) is known as the time of the **Pax Romana,** or the "Roman Peace." The world has rarely known such continuing unity, peace, and stability.

Government

The Roman government provided the strongest unifying force in the empire and ruled a population of about 100 million people. The government maintained order, enforced the laws, defended the

many enemies in the Senate, so they decided to form the triumvirate.
4. (a) Julius Caesar was popular because he gave grain and public land to the poor and granted citizenship to many people in the provinces. He also reduced the Senate to the position of an advisory council.
(b) The conspirators did not like Caesar's status as dictator for life and envied his power.
5. (a) The Second Triumvirate was formed to drive out the conspirators who killed Caesar and to control Rome. **(b)** Octavian forced Lepidus to retire from political life. Marc Antony and Octavian divided the Roman world, but Octavian persuaded the Senate to declare war on Antony and Cleopatra.
6. Augustus was the sole ruler.

SECTION 4

Focus/Motivation
To introduce students to the daily life of Rome, have them turn to the picture on page 158. Ask students to study the picture but not to read the caption. What does the picture tell us about Roman amusements? Occupations? Social classes? After discussing the picture, have students read the caption.

1B, 3A, 4A

● Discussion topic: Cities throughout the Roman Empire were centers of culture. Ask students to name five major Roman cities.

Presentation
Comparing Ideas
(Average/Group)
Parallels are often drawn between the Roman Empire and the United States. Two areas where similarities are evident are in government and law. Ask the students to reread the subsection "Law" on this page. Drawing on what they already know of the United States Constitution, ask them to cite comparisons between the Twelve Tables and the United States Constitution. Also ask them to draw parallels between the Roman judicial system and the United States judicial system. *(Answers will vary. Students should include that the Twelve Tables could be modified and expanded just as the Constitution may be amended, judges interpreted the laws, and an accused person was considered innocent until proven guilty.)*

Emperors of the Pax Romana
27 B.C.—A.D. 180

27 B.C.–A.D. 14	Augustus
A.D. 14–A.D. 68	Julian Emperors Tiberius (14–37)* Caligula (37–41) Claudius (41–54) Nero (54–68)
A.D. 68–A.D. 69	Army Emperors Galba, Otho, Vitellus (Chosen by various legions during a succession crisis)
A.D. 69–A.D. 96	Flavian Emperors Vespasian (69–79) Titus (79–81) Domitian (81–96)
A.D. 96–A.D. 180	The Good Emperors Nerva (96–98) Trajan (98–117) Hadrian (117–138) Antoninus Pius (138–161) Marcus Aurelius (161–180)

*Indicates dates of reign

frontiers, and provided relief when fires or earthquakes damaged areas.

The position of emperor was a demanding one. He had to make all policy decisions. He appointed the officials who controlled the provinces and ran the entire government. The role of emperor entailed too many responsibilities for all but the ablest people, however. If a weak, incompetent, or selfish emperor reigned, effective government depended on the strength of the other government officials.

From the time of Augustus on, emperors appointed and promoted government officials on the basis of their ability alone. The positions were highly desired not only for the salary but also for the honor.

The Provinces

The provinces were governed more efficiently during the time of the Pax Romana than they had been under the republic, partly because the government in Rome kept a closer check on provincial governors. Any citizen in the provinces could appeal a governor's decision directly to the emperor.

The western provinces, especially Gaul and Spain, benefited greatly from their closeness to Roman civilization. The Romans constructed many ● new cities in the western provinces, each a small version of imperial Rome, complete with a senate building, theaters, and public baths. Most of the cities had **aqueducts**—bridgelike structures that carried water from the mountains. Most cities also had paved streets and sewer systems. Wealthy citizens of the provinces took great pride in their cities. They donated large sums of money for public buildings, streets, schools, and entertainment.

Law

Roman law also unified the empire. The code of the Twelve Tables had been created in a small agricultural society, and these laws had to be changed to address the many needs of a huge empire.

The Romans modified and expanded the Twelve Tables in two ways. First, the government passed new laws as needed. Second, judges interpreted the old laws to fit new circumstances. Both ways ensured that Roman law could adapt to fit the customs of all peoples throughout the provinces.

Roman judges helped develop the belief that certain basic legal principles apply to all humans. For example, Roman law established an idea we believe in today—that an accused person is considered innocent unless proven guilty.

In later years the Roman system of law became the foundation for the laws of all the European countries that had been part of the Roman Empire. Roman law also had a strong influence on the laws of the Christian Church.

The Army

Augustus had reorganized the Roman army. The Praetorian Guard—first organized by Augustus to guard the *praetorium*, or headquarters of the commander-in-chief—was a small, elite force stationed in Rome to protect the emperor. Citizens who served for 20 years made up the legions that were stationed in great fortified camps along the frontiers. People often settled around these camps, and

156

these settlements eventually grew into towns and cities.

Other forces from the provinces or the border tribes aided the Roman army. The soldiers enlisted for 25 years in return for the promise of Roman citizenship at the end of their enlistment. Thus a population of trained soldiers was established to help guard the frontiers. An estimated 250,000 to 300,000 soldiers guarded the empire at the time of Augustus' death. Although this number increased under later emperors, the total number of Roman soldiers probably never exceeded 500,000.

In some regions the Romans built great lines of fortifications for protection. In Britain, for example, Hadrian's Wall stretched entirely across the island in the north. A line of forts ran between the Rhine and Danube rivers. Between the great camps of the legions lay protective ditches, fortresses, and walls. Many portions of these walls still stand as reminders of Roman military glory.

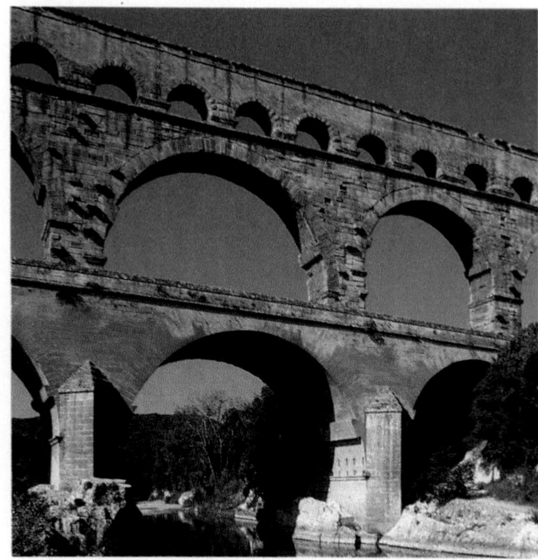

Learning from Pictures *A grooved channel, cut into the top of the aqueducts, carried fresh water from distant springs to large Roman cities.*

Trade and Transportation

Throughout the time of the Pax Romana, agriculture remained the primary occupation of people in the empire. In Italy itself most farmers worked on large estates devoted to vineyards or livestock. The provinces contained more small farms.

A new type of agricultural worker, a tenant farmer known as a **colonus,** began to replace slaves on the large estates. Each of these farmers received a small plot of land from the owner. The colonus had to remain on the land for a certain period and had to pay the owner of the land with crops. A colonus worked long, hard hours and had little to show for it.

The vast empire provided great opportunities for commerce, and the exchange of goods was easy. Taxes on trade remained low, and people everywhere used Roman currency. Rome and Alexandria became the empire's greatest commercial centers.

From the provinces Italy imported grain and raw materials such as meat, wool, and hides. From Asia came silks, linens, glassware, jewelry, and furniture to satisfy the tastes of the wealthy. India exported many products such as spices, cotton, and other luxury products that Romans had never known before.

Manufacturing also increased throughout the empire. Italy, Gaul, and Spain made inexpensive pottery and textiles. As in Greece most work was done by hand in small shops.

Transportation greatly improved during the early period of the empire. An estimated 180,000 miles (288,000 kilometers) of paved highways joined military outposts with cities in the interior, and highways linked all provincial cities to Rome—the origin of the saying, "All roads lead to Rome." Bridges spanned rivers, and an imperial post carried correspondence from the emperor and his officials to all parts of the empire. However, even with improved transportation and communications, it took a Roman messenger at least 10 weeks to cross the empire, traveling at top speed and using every known means of transportation.

Living Conditions

The Pax Romana provided prosperity to many people, but citizens did not share equally in this wealth. The rich citizen usually had both a city home and a country home. Each residence included many conveniences, such as running water and baths.

The lives of the wealthy included much time for leisure—rest, exercise, public baths, and banquets. Reclining on couches, many wealthy Romans ate and drank enormous quantities at banquets. These

157

1B, 3A, a1C

lavish banquets frequently offered exotic foods. For example:

Appetizers
Jellyfish and eggs
Patina of brains cooked with milk and eggs
Boiled tree fungi with peppered fish-fat sauce
Sea urchins with spices, honey, oil and egg sauce

Main Course
Fallow deer roasted with onion sauce, rue, Jericho dates, raisins, oil and honey
Boiled ostrich with sweet sauce
Turtle dove boiled in its feathers
Roast parrot
Dormice stuffed with pork and pine kernels
Ham boiled with figs and bay leaves, rubbed with honey, baked in pastry crust
Flamingo boiled with dates

Dessert
Fricassee of roses with pastry
Stoned dates stuffed with nuts and pine kernels, fried in honey
Hot African sweet-wine cakes with honey

Most Romans, however, ate three simple meals each day, including foods such as bread, cheese, and fruit. Many ate only cereal and vegetables.

Extreme differences separated the lives of the wealthy from those of the poor. The average Roman lived with very little furniture. The bed was the main piece of furniture, and chairs were chiefly camp stools or benches. Many of the 1 million residents of Rome lived in crowded three- or four-story concrete apartment houses, where fire posed a constant threat because of the candles and torches used for light. The massive wooden beams used in construction made the fires more intense. These fires, as well as the collapse of cheaply constructed buildings, often claimed hundreds of lives.

Most Romans were poor and hardworking. Some worked as artisans or farmers, but they had little security because of frequent unemployment and low wages. In Rome landlords charged high rents, but the government provided free grain to residents of the capital. This helped, but no one could survive on free grain alone.

The number of slaves in the empire declined greatly during the Pax Romana. With the end of

Learning from Pictures *Romans enjoyed music and games. This mosaic from Pompeii shows a group of musicians that includes a female flutist.*

● Britain, Gaul, Armenia, Syria, Judea, Egypt, and all of the Mediterranean coastline and the Black Sea

■ Many people attribute the origins of bullfighting to the events of the Roman arena, but bullfighting originated in the Iberian Peninsula during Carthaginian ownership, ca. 200s B.C.

1A, 1B, 3A, a4B, a4C, a4K

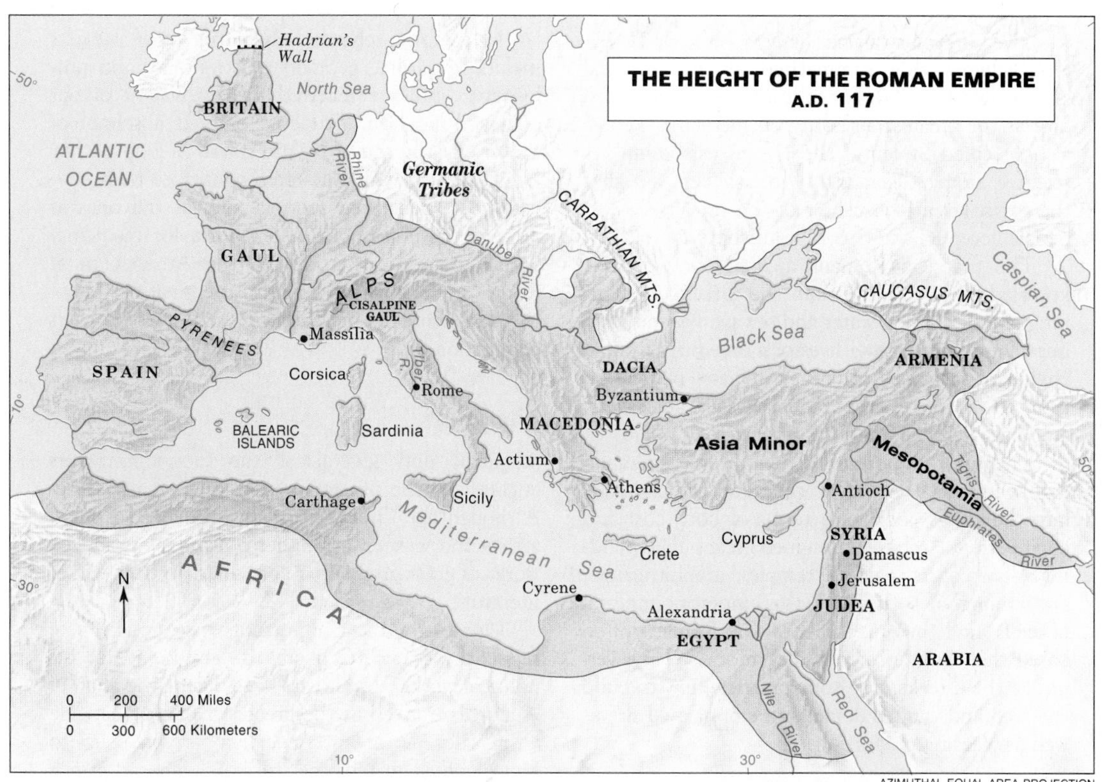

Learning from Maps *The Romans controlled the largest empire in the ancient world. What territories did the Romans acquire between 133* B.C. *and* A.D. *117?* ●

foreign conquests, the Romans no longer captured and enslaved prisoners of war. As a result, the price of slaves rose dramatically. In addition, most people could not afford to feed, clothe, and care for a slave. An owner of a large estate might find it more profitable to free a slave and make that slave a colonus.

Amusements

Romans enjoyed the theater, especially light comedies and satires. Performers such as mimes, jugglers, dancers, acrobats, and clowns became quite popular. Romans also enjoyed savage and brutal sports. They made Greek sports such as boxing bloodier by using brass knuckles. As many as 250,000 spectators watched chariot racing in the huge Circus Maximus of Rome, a kind of racetrack. Organized "fan clubs" for the popular chariot racers had many members.

Thousands of Romans also enjoyed spectacles in the Colosseum, the great amphitheater in Rome. Wild beasts, made more savage by hunger, fought one another in the arena. Sometimes humans fought against animals. Often condemned criminals or slaves were thrown into the arena to be killed by the beasts.

Combats between gladiators—trained fighters who were usually slaves—drew the largest crowds. The gladiators sometimes fought animals, but they often fought one another. The fights usually ended in death for one or both fighters. When a gladiator was wounded, he appealed for mercy to the crowd, ■ who signaled whether he should be killed or spared.

Science, Engineering, and Architecture

The Romans were less interested in scientific research to increase knowledge than in collecting and organizing information. Galen, a physician

159

who lived in Rome during the A.D. 100s, wrote several volumes that summarized all the medical knowledge of his day. For centuries people regarded him as the greatest authority on medicine. People also accepted Ptolemy's theories in astronomy. A scientist from Alexandria, Ptolemy believed that the earth lay at the center of the universe. Most people accepted this theory until the A.D. 1600s.

The practical Romans applied the scientific knowledge they gained from the Greeks in planning cities, building water and sewage systems, and improving farming and livestock breeding. Roman engineers surpassed all other ancient peoples in their ability to construct roads, bridges, aqueducts, amphitheaters, and public buildings.

The most important contribution of Roman architects was the use of concrete, which made large buildings possible in terms of both cost and engineering. Architects designed great public buildings—law courts, palaces, temples, amphitheaters, and triumphal arches—for the emperor, imperial officials, and the government. The Romans often based their buildings on Greek models. However, unlike the Greeks, the Romans knew how to build the arch and vaulted dome, and emphasized size as well as pleasing proportion.

Education

The Romans trained their children to be loyal citizens and to be obedient to their elders and superiors. They received their early education at home. The Roman father taught the sons farming and the duties of citizenship. The mother instructed the children in reading, writing, and arithmetic. Children also memorized the Twelve Tables.

The matron of the family taught her daughters to manage a household. In wealthy households girls also learned to sing, dance, paint, and play musical instruments. And although most Roman women did not receive a formal education, many upper-class women were well educated.

Every important town or city throughout the Roman Empire had elementary, secondary, and higher level schools. A boy or girl of the free classes entered elementary school at the age of seven and studied reading, writing, arithmetic, and music. At about the age of 13, boys entered a secondary school, where they studied grammar, Greek, literature, composition, and expressive speech. Former Greek slaves often taught the courses.

In rhetoric schools, where the chief subjects included oratory, geometry, astronomy, and philosophy, students received the equivalent of our college education. Students entered a school of rhetoric at the age of 16 and stayed as long as they liked. Wealthy students often continued their education at specialized schools such as the ones at Athens for philosophy, Alexandria for medicine, and Rhodes for rhetoric. In the Athenaeum at Rome, students could listen to the great orators of the day. Students in all schools paid fees for their educations.

Literature

Augustus and several of the Good Emperors encouraged the development of art and literature. Although the Greeks strongly influenced Roman artists and writers, a number of Romans produced works of great originality, particularly in the field of literature.

One of the most important writers of the late republic was Cicero, a great orator noted for his political works. Virgil, who lived during the reign of Augustus, ranked as the greatest Roman poet. He wrote the epic poem, *Aeneid,* a sort of sequel to Homer's *Iliad.* It tells the story of Aeneas, a prince of Troy and a supposed ancestor of the Latins. When the Greeks captured Troy, Aeneas fled and, after many adventures, came to Italy. His descendants Romulus and Remus founded Rome. Another Roman poet, Horace, wrote of human emotions in odes, satires, and epistles (letters). Yet another poet, Ovid, wrote love lyrics and the *Metamorphoses,* a collection of legends written in verse (see page 161).

Tacitus, one of the greatest Roman historians, wrote *Annals,* a history of Rome under the Julian Emperors, which shows his criticism of the government established by Augustus. He worried about the luxurious living of the wealthy and the lack of public virtue. Another of his works, *Germania,* provides the best account of the Germanic tribes along the borders. However, Tacitus may have exaggerated the virtues of the Germanic peoples because he wrote the book to shame the Romans for their low moral standards.

Plutarch, a Greek, wrote *Parallel Lives.* This work includes a series of biographical sketches, one of a famous Greek followed by one of a Roman whose life in some way resembled the Greek's life.

160

● **Students might enjoy reading more about mythology. *Bullfinch's Mythology* is an excellent source.**

LITERATURE

● **The *Metamorphoses***

Ovid, who lived from 43 B.C. to A.D. 17, was one of the best-known Roman poets. Although he wrote many works, his most famous was the *Metamorphoses,* 15 books of mostly Greek and some Roman mythology. With this work Ovid produced a masterpiece, or great work, for which he was hoping to become immortal. Using lively descriptions, he particularly demonstrates the richness of Greek mythology. Generations of poets and painters used his work for inspiration. The selection below recounts the story of Daedalus and Icarus, whom the legendary King Minos of Crete held prisoner.

DEDALE PERD SON FILS ICARE
Icare c'eſt en vain que ta foibleſſe aſpire
Au Sacre' cabinet des Merueilles des Dieux,
La ſeule foy te peut guinder iuſques aux Cieux,
Autrement tu fondras ton aiſleron de Cire.

“ Homesick for homeland, Daedalus hated Crete
And his long exile there, but the sea held him.
'Though Minos blocks escape by land or water,'
Daedalus said, 'surely the sky is open,
And that's the way we'll go. Minos' dominion
Does not include the air.' He turned his thinking
Toward unknown arts, changing the laws of nature.
He laid out feathers in order, first the smallest,
A little larger next it, and so continued,
The way that panpipes rise in gradual sequence.
He fastened them with twine and wax, at middle,
At bottom, so, and bent them, gently curving,
So that they looked like wings of birds, most surely.
And Icarus, his son, stood by and watched him,
Not knowing he was dealing with his downfall,
Stood by and watched and raised his shiny face
To let a feather, light as down, fall on it,
Or stuck his thumb into the yellow wax,
Fooling around, the way a boy will, always,
Whenever a father tries to get some work done.
Still, it was done at last, and the father hovered,
Poised, in the moving air, and taught his son:
'I warn you, Icarus, fly a middle course:
Don't go too low, or water will weigh the wings down;
Don't go too high, or the sun's fire will burn them.
Keep to the middle way. And one more thing,
No fancy steering by star or constellation,
Follow my lead!' That was the flying lesson,
And now to fit the wings to the boy's shoulders.
Between the work and warning the father found
His cheeks were wet with tears, and his hands trembled.
He kissed his son (*Good-by,* if he had known it),
Rose on his wings, flew on ahead, as fearful
As any bird launching the little nestlings
Out of high nest into thin air. *Keep on,*
Keep on, he signals, *follow me!* He guides him
In flight—O fatal art!—and the wings move
And the father looks back to see the son's wings moving.
Far off, far down, some fisherman is watching
As the rod dips and trembles over the water,
Some shepherd rests his weight upon his crook,
Some plowman on the handles of the plowshare,
And all look up, in absolute amazement,
At those airborne above. They must be gods!
They were over Samos, Juno's sacred island,
Delos and Paros toward the left, Lebinthus
Visible to the right, and another island,
Calymne, rich in honey. And the boy
Thought *This is wonderful!* and left his father,
Soared higher, higher, drawn to the vast heaven,
Nearer the sun, and the wax that held the wings
Melted in that fierce heat, and the bare arms
Beat up and down in air, and lacking oarage
Took hold of nothing. *Father!* he cried, and *Father!*
Until the blue sea hushed him, the dark water
Men call the Icarian now. And Daedalus,
Father no more, called 'Icarus, where are you!
Where are you, Icarus? Tell me where to find you!'
And saw the wings on the waves and cursed his talents,
Buried the body in a tomb, and the land
Was named for Icarus. ”

161

1B, 3A, 3B, a1A, a4A, a4F, a4G, a4H, a4M

● **Many upper-class Jews, like King Herod, were largely Hellenized in their culture. A gulf developed between the court and the mass of Jewish people.**

SECTION 4

Closure

Describe the social classes of the Roman Empire. How did each live? How did the Romans influence our world today? *(Julian calendar, Roman alphabet, Latin language)*

Review Answers

1. ***Pax Romana:*** "Roman Peace" that lasted from 27 B.C. to A.D. 180: from the beginning of Augustus's reign until the death of Marcus Aurelius; ***aqueduct:*** bridgelike structure that carried water from the mountains to the cities; ***colonus:*** a tenant farmer that began to replace slaves on the large estates **2.** ***Praetorian Guard:*** small, elite military force stationed in Rome to protect the emperor; ***Galen:*** Roman physician who summarized the medical knowledge of his day; ***Ptolemy:*** astronomer who theorized that earth was the center of the universe **3.** Roman legions were stationed in great fortified camps to protect the frontiers. People settled around these camps, and these settlements grew into towns and cities. **4.** A new type of agricultural worker, a tenant farmer known as a colonus, began to replace slaves on large estates. These workers were given small plots of land to farm. In return they had to remain on the land for a certain period and pay the owner of the land with crops.

Language

The Romans learned the Greek alphabet from the Etruscans and later changed some of the letters. The Roman, or Latin, alphabet of 23 letters, plus the *J*, *Y*, and *W*, which the English added after Roman times, is the alphabet we use today.

Long after the end of the Roman Empire, the Latin language continued to be used, with some changes, in most of Europe. Most medieval European universities used Latin in their classes, and the Roman Catholic church conducted services in Latin until the 1960s. For centuries all governments in western Europe wrote their laws and decrees in Latin. Latin is the parent of the modern Romance (a word derived from *Roman*) languages—Italian, French, Spanish, Portuguese, and Romanian.

Many scientific terms have either Latin or Greek origins. Although the English language developed mainly from the language of the early Germanic peoples, more than one-third of all English words have Latin origins.

SECTION 4 REVIEW

1. **Define** Pax Romana, aqueduct, colonus
2. **Identify** Praetorian Guard, Galen, Ptolemy
3. **Understanding Ideas** How did the army contribute to the protection and expansion of the Roman Empire?
4. **Interpreting Ideas** How did farming change during the period of the Roman Empire?
5. **Analyzing Ideas** **(a)** Why did trade expand so rapidly throughout the empire? **(b)** What products were traded and where did they come from?
6. **Summarizing Ideas** Name three important Roman writers and describe the writings of each.

5 Christianity Took Root in Judea

The Romans respected the various religions practiced in the provinces, if only to keep peace. However, as Roman power expanded, the Roman emperor became more widely regarded as a divine monarch. The Romans expected every resident of the empire to honor the gods of Rome and the "divine spirit" of the emperor. Such a ritual act, the Romans believed, would demonstrate the people's loyalty to the state.

Jews and the Roman Empire

In Roman times most Jews lived in Judea, which became a Roman province in A.D. 6. As monotheists believing in a single god, Jews could not honor the Roman gods or the "divine spirit" of the emperor, and the Romans excused them from doing so.

Many Jews in Judea hoped they could win their independence and have a king in the tradition of David. They yearned for a king like David—for a Messiah. (Each Jewish king was anointed, or smeared with oil, as part of his coronation. The word *Messiah* means "the Anointed One.")

As the years of Roman rule continued and independence became increasingly unlikely, the Jews began to think of the Messiah as a divinely appointed liberator. Various individuals claiming to be Messiahs appeared from time to time in Judea, but the Romans usually executed them as rebels. Occasionally the Jews would turn to radical measures and revolt against the Romans. After the great revolt of A.D. 66–A.D. 70, the Romans sacked Jerusalem, slaughtered thousands of Jews, and destroyed the Second Temple. Only the western wall of the Temple withstood the onslaught. Today Jews consider this wall, also known as the Wailing Wall, the most sacred site of Judaism. ●

The destruction of the Second Temple marked a major turning point in Jewish history. With the Temple gone, priests ceased to be the religious leaders of Judaism. **Rabbis**—scholars learned in the scriptures and in commentaries on religious law—filled their role.

Under the rule of the emperors Trajan and Hadrian,* more Jewish revolts erupted in Judea. In the last one, led by Simon bar Kokhba, the Jews struggled fiercely against Emperor Hadrian. After the Romans brutally suppressed the revolt in A.D. 135, they banned all Jews from Jerusalem. Jewish communities outside Jerusalem, however, carried on the Jewish faith and culture.

Christianity, the religion founded by the Jewish teacher known as Jesus of Nazareth, arose out of this setting. Christianity drew on the expectations

*Hadrian changed the name of the region from Judea to Palestine.

for a Messiah common in the region during these centuries.

The Life and Teachings of Jesus

Roman histories say very little about Jesus and the early Christians. Our knowledge of Jesus comes mainly from the Gospels of Matthew, Mark, Luke, and John—the first four books of the New Testament of the Bible.

According to the Gospels, Jesus was born in Bethlehem, near Jerusalem, and grew up in the town of Nazareth. He was said to have been a carpenter and a student of the writings of the Jewish prophets. In time he began preaching. As he traveled through the villages of Judea, he gathered a small group of disciples, or followers. From these he chose 12, the Apostles, to help him preach.

Jesus spoke of "my Father in heaven," and his followers believed that Jesus was the Messiah. He traveled with his disciples as a wandering rabbi, depending on the charity of the people for his needs. According to the Gospels, he created great excitement among the people, performing miracles of healing and defending the poor and the oppressed.

The teachings of Jesus have become one of the greatest influences on the Western world. He accepted the Ten Commandments as guides to right living but gave them further meaning. According to the Gospel of Matthew, Jesus said:

> "Don't misunderstand why I have come—it isn't to cancel the laws of Moses and the warnings of the prophets. No, I come to fulfill them, and to make them all come true."

He summarized the 10 rules in two great commandments: People must love God above all else, and they must love others as they love themselves. His many teachings include:

(1) God cares more for people than for their laws. He desires a new relationship between himself and humans based on his love, to which people respond in faith.

(2) Jesus saw himself as the link that would reestablish the loving relationship that God desires. Jesus called this new relationship the "Kingdom of God." The "Kingdom of God" would be both here on earth and in an eternal life beyond this world.

(3) God will forgive people their sins if they will admit the wrong and ask to be forgiven. People must also forgive one another in recognition of what God has already done for them and must not seek revenge.

Learning from Pictures *This Christian mosaic depicts Jesus on the road to Calvary to be crucified.*

5. (a) The vastness of the empire, low taxes on trade items, and a uniform currency helped trade expand. **(b)** From the provinces Italy imported grain and raw materials such as meat, wool, and hides. From Asia came silks, linens, glassware, jewelry, and furniture. India furnished spices, cotton, and other luxury products. Italy, Gaul, and Spain made cheap pottery and textiles.

6. The orator Cicero was noted for his political works. Virgil wrote the *Aeneid,* an epic about the legendary ancestor of the Latins. Horace composed odes, satires, and epistles. Ovid wrote love lyrics and the *Metamorphoses,* a collection of legends in verse. The historian Tacitus wrote *The Annals of Rome* and *Germania,* a description of the Germanic tribes. Plutarch wrote *Parallel Lives,* biographical sketches of Greeks and Romans.

SECTION 5

Focus/Motivation

Early Christians were often persecuted by the authorities in the Roman Empire. However, persecution only helped to strengthen rather than weaken the spread of Christianity. Ask students why they think this was so. *(Answers will vary. Students might suggest that martyrs inspire others and many people may have converted because of this.)*

Jews and Christians

3A, 3B, a1A

Critical thinking activity: Compare the beliefs of Hinduism, Buddhism, Judaism, and Christianity.

suffered for their religious beliefs during this period. Ask the class if they can think of any religious groups in the United States or the world who are suffering persecution. Is it similar to the situations of the Jews and Christians under the Romans? *(Answers will vary. Students might mention Soviet Jews, Hindus in Pakistan, Muslims and Sikhs in India. Religious prejudice dies hard, and it exists in the United States and other Western nations despite freedom of religion. Today's persecutions are not often so extreme as those of ancient Rome, although Nazi Germany carried out genocide agains the Jews in the 1930s and 1940s.)*

Presentation
Relating Cause and Effect (Average/Group)
Write the following list of statements on the chalkboard or an overhead projector. Have students determine one or more effects for each of these causes.
1. Jews became extremely dissatisfied with their Roman masters. *(The dream of a Messiah became more intense.)*
2. The Romans sacked Jerusalem and destroyed the Second Temple. *(Priests ceased to be the religious leaders of Judaism. Rabbis became religious leaders.)*

The Death of Jesus

Jesus claimed that he was the Son of God. When he traveled to Jerusalem in about A.D. 30, many Jews there hailed him as the Messiah and as "King of the Jews." Others, especially the conservative priestly class of Jews, denied that he was the Messiah and regarded him as a revolutionary.

The Romans feared that Jesus wanted to lead an uprising, and they considered him an enemy of the state. Jesus was tried before Pontius Pilate, the Roman governor. Pilate acted reluctantly, apparently because he feared the trial would ignite yet another revolt. Eventually, however, he agreed to Jesus' crucifixion.

The Spread of Christianity

According to the Gospels, Jesus arose from the dead, remained on earth for 40 more days, and then ascended into heaven. His followers believed that the resurrection and the ascension proved that Jesus was the Messiah, calling him Jesus Christ, after the Greek word for messiah—*Christos.* The resurrection became the central message of Christianity. Through the death of Jesus Christ, the Son of God, who had died for the sins of the human race, all people could achieve redemption. The disciples of Jesus set out to spread this message. At first the disciples worked mainly in the Jewish communities of the Middle East.

One of the people who did the most to spread Christianity was a Jew named Saul. Born in the town of Tarsus in Asia Minor, Saul converted to Christianity, took the name Paul, and became a great Christian missionary. Paul carried on his work not only among Jews but among all peoples. Between about A.D. 45 and A.D. 65, he journeyed throughout the eastern Mediterranean region, spreading the teachings of Jesus and founding Christian communities. Paul visited Rome, where, according to tradition, he was put to death.

Paul's Epistles, or letters, to Christian congregations in Greece and Asia Minor form an important part of the New Testament. Paul insisted that Jesus was not just the Jewish Messiah but a divine universal savior who would soon return to judge the entire human race. By following the teachings of Jesus, all people could be saved from the consequences of their sins. They could avoid damnation and instead enjoy the bliss of salvation in paradise after death.

Christianity and Its Rivals

Christianity spread slowly, but its appeal increased as life in the Roman Empire became more difficult. Emperor worship and many of the old religions of the empire no longer offered comfort to many people. The Persian cult of Mithras did promise happiness after death, but it excluded women. The cult of Cybele (SIB • uh • lee) in Asia Minor and the Egyptian cult of Isis worshiped goddesses, but it was expensive to belong to these cults.

Christianity, on the other hand, accepted everyone and charged nothing. It welcomed the poor and rich alike and promised salvation after death. In this world Christians were expected to be good citizens and to obey the laws. They were encouraged to practice charity and to care for the poor and outcast.

Persecution of the Christians

At first the Roman government viewed Christians as a Jewish sect and thus freed them from the obligation to worship the emperor. However, by the A.D. 100s it recognized the difference, and Christians had to make a difficult choice.

The early Christians were good citizens. Their religion taught them to respect government, but they refused to worship the emperor as a god.

To the emperors this refusal defied Roman religion and law, and they outlawed Christianity, seized Christian property, and executed many Christians. Sometimes the Romans used the Christians as scapegoats,* blaming them for natural or political disasters. As the Roman writer Tertullian (tuhr • TUHL • yuhn) reported: "If the Tiber floods or the Nile fails to, the cry goes up: the Christians to the lions!" Many Christians became **martyrs,** put to death because they refused to renounce their beliefs. The Roman efforts, however, failed to stop the spread of Christianity.

In the A.D. 200s, civil wars shook the Roman Empire, and many people turned to Christianity. City dwellers of the middle and upper classes suffered greatly, and many of them converted to this new religion, which gave them hope. By the end

*Many ancient religions sacrificed goats to their god or gods in order to obtain forgiveness. The term *scapegoat* came to mean a person or thing bearing blame for the actions of others.

1A, 3A, 3B, a1A, a4A, a4B, a4C

- Christianity gradually became the official religion of the Roman Empire in the A.D. 300s.

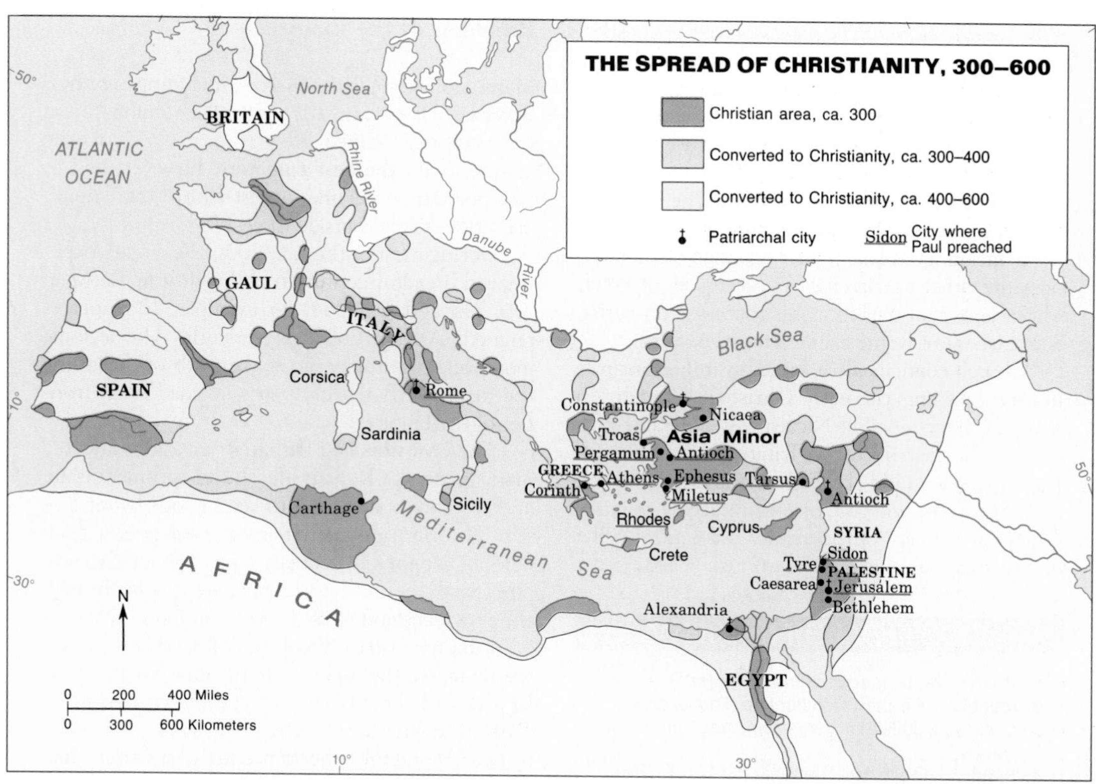

Learning from Maps *Christianity grew from a small sect to become the state religion of the Roman Empire. What patriarchal city lies due north of Jerusalem?* **Antioch**

of the A.D. 200s, the Christian Church had become too large for the government to punish all its members, and Roman law accepted Christianity as a religion.

The Success of Christianity

The position of the Christians vastly improved when Emperor Constantine became a supporter of Christianity. According to Constantine, in A.D. 312 he was leading his army into battle when he saw a blazing cross in the sky. Beneath it were the words *In Hoc Signo Vinces,* Latin words meaning "By this sign you will conquer." He placed himself and his army under the protection of the Christian God. After his victory he protected Christians and converted to Christianity on his deathbed in A.D. 337.

Constantine's successor, Theodosius (thee • uh • DOH • shuhs), banned pagan worship. Christian emperors persecuted the pagans, ordered the pagan temples destroyed, and abolished the Olympic Games because of their pagan rites. Within 400 years, Christianity had spread from its birthplace in Judea to all parts of the huge empire (see map, this page).

Organization of the Church

During the first few years after the crucifixion of Jesus, Christians saw little need for church organization. Christians lived together in groups, sharing their possessions and holding all property in common. They selected certain members to hold church services, preach, and help the sick and needy.

By the last years of the Roman Empire, a more definite church organization developed. The priests conducted services and performed baptisms and marriages. Above the priests were the bishops, who

165

1C, 1D, 3A, 3B, a4A, a4F, a4G, a4K

SECTION 5

Closure

Explain why Christianity took root in the Roman Empire. *(Its message had wide appeal during times of stress.)* You might mention that the Roman Empire itself, with its road system and political unity, facilitated Christianity's spread.

Review Answers

1. ***rabbi:*** scholar learned in the scriptures and commentaries about Judaic law; ***martyr:*** person who dies for his or her beliefs; ***patriarch:*** bishop of Rome, Constantinople, Alexandria, Antioch, or Jerusalem; ***pope:*** title given to patriarch of Rome, who claimed supremacy over other patriarchs
2. ***disciples:*** followers of Jesus; ***Constantine:*** Roman emperor who protected Christians; ***Theodosius:*** emperor who banned pagan worship and supported Christianity
3. ***Bethlehem:*** birthplace of Jesus; ***Jerusalem:*** center of Jewish religion; ***Nazareth:*** town where Jesus grew to maturity; ***Tarsus:*** Asia Minor town, birthplace of Paul the Christian missionary
4. (a) Jesus saw himself as the link reestablishing the loving relationship between God and humans. **(b)** Jesus taught people must love God above all else. They must love others as they love themselves. God will forgive people their sins, and people must forgive one another for wrongs.

were considered to be the successors of the apostles. A bishop headed the church in each city.

Five of the empire's cities—Rome, Constantinople, Alexandria, Antioch, and Jerusalem—gained special importance as administrative centers for the Christian Church. The bishops of these cities were called **patriarchs.** Over time the patriarch of Rome assumed the title of **pope** (from a Latin word meaning "father") and claimed supremacy over the other patriarchs. As successors of Peter, whom Jesus had named as his successor on earth, later bishops of Rome claimed broad powers.

Church councils also played an important role in strengthening the early Christian Church. In A.D. 325 the council at Nicaea (ny • SEE • uh) proclaimed the doctrine of the Trinity, the existence of three persons—God the Father, the Son, and the Holy Spirit—in one god, as a main article of faith. Today the concept of the Trinity is a central belief of Christians throughout the world.

SECTION 5 REVIEW

1. **Define** rabbi, martyr, patriarch, pope
2. **Identify** disciples, Constantine, Theodosius
3. **Locate** Bethlehem, Jerusalem, Nazareth, Tarsus
4. **Summarizing Ideas** **(a)** What did Jesus believe his mission to be? **(b)** State three teachings of Jesus.
5. **Analyzing Ideas** **(a)** What factors encouraged the spread of Christianity? **(b)** Why did the Romans persecute the Christians?
6. **Organizing Ideas** How was the early Christian Church organized?

6 A Weakened Roman Empire in the West Declined and Fell

The western part of the Roman Empire grew constantly weaker until it collapsed in the A.D. 400s. To understand this long period of decline, we must turn back to the time of the Good Emperors.

When Marcus Aurelius picked his successor in A.D. 180, he failed to show his usual wisdom. He appointed his weak, spoiled son Commodus (KAHM • uh • duhs). The end of the reign of Marcus Aurelius marked the beginning of the disintegration of the empire.

Problems of the Empire

Many capable soldier-emperors, including Septimus Severus, Diocletian (dy • uh • KLEE • shuhn), and Constantine, helped slow the decline of the empire. Even the best emperors, however, had to face population decline, unrest within the empire, and attacks from outside forces.

During most of the A.D. 200s, the empire experienced dreadful confusion and civil war. Between A.D. 235 and A.D. 284, for example, 20 emperors reigned. All but one died violently. The legions, moreover, did not perform their job of defending the frontiers. Barbarian tribes invaded every frontier of the empire.

The civil wars and barbarian invasions affected many aspects of Roman life. Travel became unsafe, and merchants hesitated to send goods by land or sea. The rural population grew even poorer than before. Population decreased throughout the empire, partly because a great plague spread through the provinces and caused several million deaths.

It became very difficult to collect taxes. Money was so scarce that people often paid taxes in grain. In A.D. 212 the government granted citizenship to all the peoples of the empire in order to collect from everyone the inheritance tax that citizens had to pay.

While taxes rose, money declined in value. The end of Roman expansion meant no new sources of gold. In addition, gold was being transported out of the empire because the rich continued to buy luxuries from abroad. To maintain the money supply, emperors minted new coins containing copper or lead as well as gold. When people realized that their coins had less gold in them, they refused to accept them at their face value.

In order to receive the same amount of gold as before, merchants raised their prices. We call the rise in prices caused by a decrease in the value of the exchange medium **inflation.** Inflation became so severe in some parts of the empire that people stopped using money and reverted to barter.

Only the major landowners remained relatively prosperous. As small farmers were forced to sell their land, large estates grew even larger. Many landowners left the cities and moved to their country estates. They organized and paid private armies and defied the government officials who came to collect taxes. With the decline in population, a danger that there might not be enough farmers

● Travel became unsafe so trade and population decreased.
■ Many emperors simply "adopted" their successors in order to ensure their succession.

Learning from Pictures
This relief sculpture shows a Roman legionary and an attacking barbarian. How did barbarian invasions affect Roman life? ●

arose. The emperor refused to permit farmers who inherited their land to leave it.

The people in the cities fared no better. Many artisans tried to leave their jobs in the cities to find work in the country. To prevent this the government made use of the workers' trade associations, called **collegia** (kuh • LEE • jee • uh). A law made workers' membership in the collegia compulsory. The government required members of the collegia to stay at their jobs and to perform certain public services. When some people tried to resign from the collegia, another law made membership not only compulsory but also hereditary.

Diocletian

The Roman Empire would probably have collapsed in the late A.D. 200s except for the efforts of two able emperors, Diocletian and Constantine. Their reforms and reorganizations postponed the collapse for nearly 200 years.

The son of a peasant, Diocletian had risen through the ranks of the army to become a general. The army made him emperor in A.D. 284, and he proved to be an able administrator.

Diocletian reorganized the administration of the empire. Realizing that the empire had grown too large for one person to manage, Diocletian appointed a co-emperor. Each co-emperor, known as an *augustus,* chose an assistant, called a *caesar,* ■ to help him rule and to be his successor.

Although the empire was not officially divided, each augustus administered approximately half of its territory. Diocletian ruled in the east, while Maximian ruled in the west.

Although Diocletian shared his power with others, he held supreme authority. He ended lawlessness within the empire and drove out the invading barbarian tribes. Diocletian also tried to improve commerce and manufacturing and to increase the wealth of the empire. However, his achievements did not endure. His policies proved impractical and difficult to enforce, and Rome drifted closer to economic ruin.

Constantine

The system of divided rule Diocletian established did not work well after he retired in A.D. 305. The rivalry between the co-emperors and their caesars

5. (a) Worship of the emperor and old religions offered no comfort. When the empire suffered civil wars in the A.D. 200s, many people turned to Christianity because it gave them hope. **(b)** Christians refused to worship the emperor as a god. The Romans saw this as defiance of Roman religion and law.
6. A priest served a parish. A bishop headed the church in a city. Patriarchs governed the five leading administrative centers at Rome, Constantinople, Alexandria, Antioch, and Jerusalem. The pope in Rome claimed supremacy.

SECTION 6

Focus/Motivation
Ask students what problems caused the fall of Rome. Write their responses on the chalkboard or an overhead projector. Next ask students if any of these problems or similar ones face the United States today. Write the responses in another column. Compare the two columns. Ask students how they think these issues might be handled in the United States. If you would like supplementary reading for this discussion, read Edmund Stillman's "Before the Fall" in *Horizon* (Autumn 1968). *(Answers will vary. Rome fell because of a combination of reasons: population decline; civil unrest; barbarian invasions; inflation and economic decline; inefficiency and corruption in government.*

1B, 1C, 3A

● Ostrogoths means "East Goths," Visigoths means "West Goths."

Presentation
Organizing Ideas
(Average/Group)
Have the students list in their notebooks the conditions brought about by Rome's decline. Call upon students to write their responses on the chalkboard or an overhead projector. The list should include the following: Anarchy—there was no effective government. Roads and bridges fell into disrepair. Trade and manufacturing almost disappeared. Travel was unsafe. Towns and cities were regularly attacked by barbarians. Most people left the cities. Crops were often destroyed and fields were overgrown with weeds. Learning declined. Libraries were destroyed. Ignorance and superstition replaced knowledge.

became intense, and civil war racked the empire. Constantine, who came to power as a caesar in A.D. 306, became sole emperor in A.D. 324. His reign is known for two great achievements: his protection of the Christian religion and his creation of a new capital on the site of the former Greek city of Byzantium. Named Constantinople, the new capital was dedicated in A.D. 330. Today it is the Turkish city of Istanbul.

After Constantine's death in A.D. 337, the empire enjoyed some 50 years of stability. However, inefficiency and corruption plagued the government, and the poor suffered greatly. The Spanish emperor Theodosius was the last ruler to control a unified empire. After his death in A.D. 395, his two weak sons shared the throne. By A.D. 400, two empires existed, one in the west and one in the east. The one in the west grew constantly weaker. Power had shifted to the east, the center of wealth. Although the empire in the west collapsed in the A.D. 400s, the empire in the east remained until 1453 (see Chapter 8).

The Germans

It might seem that the western Roman Empire would have fallen apart from inner weaknesses alone. However, pressures from the outside also mounted as enemies attacked every frontier of the empire. The most important of these outsiders were the Germans, who lived beyond the Rhine and north of the Danube rivers. One Germanic tribe, the Ostrogoths, eventually migrated southeast to settle north of the Black Sea. Another tribe, the ● Visigoths, occupied land north of the Danube River (see map, page 169).

Germans in the empire. The northern frontier of the Roman Empire along the Rhine and Danube rivers had strong fortifications designed to stop the Germans. As early as the reign of Augustus, however, many Germans began crossing the frontier peacefully.

About A.D. 375 the Huns, an Asiatic tribe, began moving into the region north of the Black Sea. The nomadic Huns lived by raiding and plundering, and their fierceness terrified the people of Europe.

Pressure by the Huns pushed many German tribes into the empire. Roman officials mistreated the new settlers, however, and in A.D. 378 the Visigoths revolted. In a battle at Adrianople, they destroyed a Roman army and killed its leader, the eastern emperor Valens.

An ambitious leader named Alaric now became king of the Visigoths. In A.D. 401 he led the Visigoths west into Italy (see map, page 169). Alaric captured Rome in A.D. 410 and savagely sacked the city. Amid the destruction, the Senate issued a momentous decree:

> "The devastations of Alaric the Barbarian have destroyed imperial Rome, burnt its records, and ransacked its treasuries. You can no longer rely on Rome for finance or direction. You are on your own."

Final invasions of the west. The two parts of the empire drifted further apart. The east revived and gained strength, while the west sank into ruin as barbarians poured in everywhere (see map, page 169). One tribe of barbarians, the Vandals, so savagely destroyed everything in their path that today we use the word *vandal* to mean one who causes senseless destruction.

In the mid-400s Attila, a fierce leader of the Huns, led an attack on Gaul. An army of Romans and Visigoths defeated the Huns in a great battle at Châlons in A.D. 451. Attila himself died two years later. His army quickly broke up, and the Huns no longer threatened the empire. But it was now too late to save the western Roman Empire, which was weakened and shattered beyond repair.

A barbarian commander overthrew Romulus Augustulus, the last Roman emperor in the west, in A.D. 476. Because of this event, people sometimes refer to the "fall" of the Roman Empire in A.D. 476. Actually, no such thing as a single "fall" occurred, but instead the empire had gradually disintegrated.

Results of Rome's Decline

European civilization suffered a grave setback when the western Roman Empire collapsed. The Germans who invaded the west established tribal kingdoms, but they proved incapable of ruling an empire. The result was **anarchy**—the absence of any government at all.

Wandering bands of barbarians regularly attacked towns and cities. Most people left the cities in search of both food and greater safety. In the country, however, soldiers often trampled crops during battles, and weeds choked the fields. Learning declined, for no government existed to set up

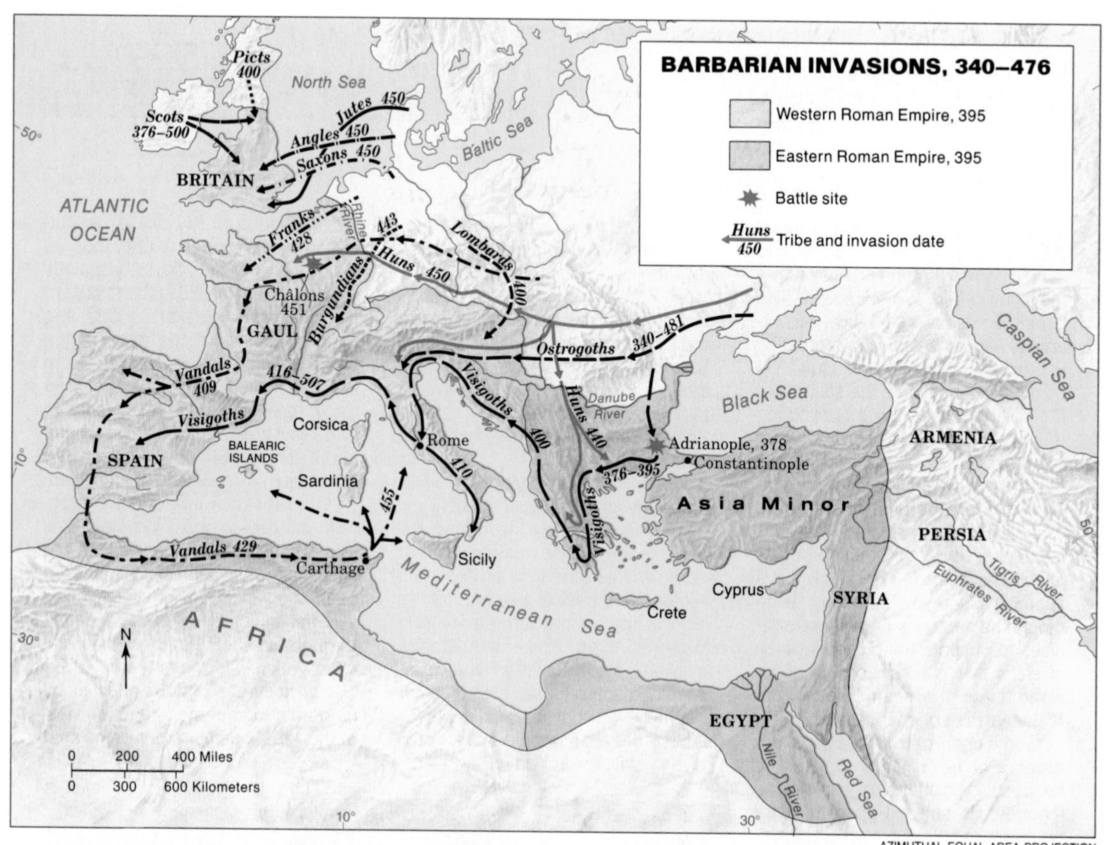

Learning from Maps *During the* A.D. *300s and* A.D. *400s, Germanic invaders threatened the frontiers of the Roman Empire. What Germanic group first invaded the empire?* **Ostrogoths**

stores of knowledge, were destroyed. The number of literate and learned people grew smaller and smaller. Knowledge of the world and the past declined and was replaced by ignorance and superstition. Without cities, trade, communication, and literacy of some kind, civilization could not survive.

Why Rome Declined

But *why* did Rome decline? How did this mighty empire that accomplished so much disappear? For centuries historians have debated these questions. Some historians have stressed the institution of slavery as the initial cause of Rome's decline. Slavery produced a class of people who were always discontented and often in revolt. It tended to make slave owners brutal, selfish, and lazy. However, the period of the empire.

The army also has been blamed as a weakening factor. After the time of the Good Emperors, poor leaders and lax discipline plagued the once mighty legions. Military interference in the choice of an emperor made the government unstable.

Barbarian invasions played an important role in Roman collapse. However, tribes of barbarians lived on the frontiers throughout the time of both the Roman Republic and the Roman Empire. Their numbers were small compared to the millions of people who lived within the empire. Not until the empire had declined were the mass of barbarians able to break through the frontiers.

The important point to remember is that no one factor caused Rome to decline. Like many other complex movements and events in history,

169

SECTION 6

Closure

Ask: If you had to describe how the Western Roman Empire looked in the A.D. 400s, how would you do so? *(anarchy, wandering barbarians, cities depopulated, trade declined, fields abandoned, learning declined, libraries destroyed)*

Review Answers

1. ***inflation:*** rise in prices caused by a decrease in the value of the exchange medium; ***collegia:*** workers' trade association; ***anarchy:*** absence of any form of government

2. ***Commodus:*** Roman Empire began to decline under this weak son of Marcus Aurelius; ***Ostrogoths:*** Germanic tribe that settled north of the Black Sea; ***Visigoths:*** Germanic tribe that moved westward occupying land north of the Danube River; ***Huns:*** Asiatic tribe whose raids terrified Europe; ***Alaric:*** Visigoth leader who captured and plundered Rome in A.D. 410; ***Attila:*** leader of Hun attack on Gaul; ***Romulus Augustulus:*** last Roman emperor in the West

3. ***Constantinople:*** new Roman capital created by Constantine, today called Istanbul; ***Black Sea:*** north of Constantinople where the Ostrogoths settled; ***Rhine River:*** frontier of Roman Empire, north of which the Germans lived; ***Danube River:*** Visigoths first occupied land north of this river; ***Adrianople:*** battle where Visigoths

LINKING GEOGRAPHY TO HISTORY

Aristotle's Views of World Geography

People have always been curious about the world, and since the beginnings of time they have tried to describe it. The Greek philosopher Aristotle, for example, was the first to use observation to prove that the earth was round. He pointed out that when the shadow of the earth crosses the moon during an eclipse, the edge of that shadow is circular. He also recognized that the height of some stars along the horizon increases as one travels north. Aristotle correctly stated that this could only occur if the observer was traveling over the curved surface of a sphere. Curiously enough, even though he surely had many opportunities to observe the disappearance of ships over the horizon, he never wrote about this most obvious proof of the earth's spherical shape.

Some people saw Aristotle as the essence of the armchair explorer, for he used logic alone to explain his theories. He saw no need to verify his premises through experimentation. For example, Aristotle believed that he could explain the habitability of the earth solely as a function of distance north or south of the equator. He based this theory on observations of people who lived around the shores of the Mediterranean Sea. He saw no reason to explore north or south of the Mediterranean to gather further ideas.

According to Aristotle, if the earth is a sphere and the sun is revolving around it, those parts of the earth where the sun is most directly overhead—around the equator—must be far hotter than elsewhere on earth. Aristotle knew of the excessively high temperatures recorded in North Africa along the southern shores of the Mediterranean. If it became so hot and unbearable some 30° north of the equator, Aristotle reasoned life must actually be impossible at the equator.

Aristotle called those uninhabitable parts of the earth close to the equator the *torrid zone.* Further, he suggested that areas of the earth far from the equator composed a *frigid zone.* This frigid zone, Aristotle surmised, would be perpetually frozen and therefore totally uninhabited. According to Aristotle, the *temperate zone,* a region lying between the uninhabitable torrid and frigid regions, composed the habitable portion of the earth.

Aristotle believed that a south temperate zone existed to balance the north temperate zone in which he lived. However, he assumed that travel between the temperate zones would be impossible because of the intense heat of the torrid zone that separated them. Some of Aristotle's followers also accepted the existence of a south temperate zone, but they believed that it would be uninhabited because people there would have to walk upside down.

Aristotle certainly would be surprised by the modern world. Indonesia, one of the most populous nations on earth, sits in the middle of the torrid zone. Alaska, Canada, and Finland, located in the heart of the frigid zone, enjoy pleasant, warm summers filled with sunshine. And the people of Argentina, Australia, and New Zealand, who live in the south temperate zone, walk on the ground just as people in the north do.

Like Aristotle, modern-day geographers use logic to develop new theories. However, their theories are also based on statistics gathered over long periods of time. They test the accuracy of these theories through experimentation and careful observation. Today, compared to the clear, accurate vision offered by modern geographers, Aristotle's view of the world seems rather fanciful.

Ptolemy, the celebrated mathematician, astronomer, and geographer, used the observations of Aristotle and other Greek philosophers to develop the Ptolemaic System. This represented a stationary earth in the center of the universe with the sun, moon, and stars revolving around it.

1B, 1D, 3A, a1D, a4A, a4D, a4F, a4H

the disintegration of the empire resulted from a combination of different forces. Between A.D. 200 and A.D. 400, no aspect of Roman life—political, economic, or social—escaped decay, each one acting upon the others.

Political weakness. Rome tried to control the entire Mediterranean world with a government designed for a small city-state. The miracle is that it worked for 600 years. In an age of slow transportation, the empire grew too fast and became too large for the kind of governmental organization the Romans had set up.

Another political weakness was the lack of civilian control of the military. Many emperors did win the loyalty of the army, but the emperor had to be strong to keep the legions loyal. Ambitious generals often seized control, assassinated the emperor, and assumed the throne. The common soldiers lost a sense of loyalty to Rome and instead served anyone who could pay them more.

Economic decline. The economic decline proved even more devastating than the political decline. Government expenses were heavy. Taxes had to finance the construction of public buildings, the maintenance of the army, and, later, the cost of two capitals—one in the west and one in the east. Heavy taxes could not support the government. For centuries the Roman government maintained itself on rich plunder from foreign wars. After Trajan, however, this source of revenue was exhausted.

Some emperors tried to fix prices and regulate business activity, but they failed. Decreased revenue for the government resulted in unrepaired roads and bridges and increased banditry. The greater danger in travel led in turn to a decrease in trade. When trade declined, manufacturing suffered and both eventually disappeared. Agriculture suffered the same fate as trade and commerce. Small farmers—once the strength of the empire—gradually lost their lands to a few very powerful landowners.

The Roman economy did not produce enough wealth to support a great civilization permanently. Wealth was concentrated in too few hands, and poverty steadily increased.

When the barbarians invaded the empire, Roman armies fought heroically, but when they lost, the empire lacked the leadership to recover. Moreover, morale collapsed because of the grinding oppression of the government. Taxes and public service crushed the urban middle class. The farmers were now *coloni* (plural of *colonus*) and paid heavy taxes, while the great landowners did not pay their share of taxes. The corrupt courts did not serve justice. Yet the government seemed to be locked into this system and unable to change it.

Social decay. A third force of great importance was social decay. Early Romans may have been rude and uncultured, but they were stern, virtuous, hardworking, and patriotic. They had a strong sense of duty and believed in serving their government. Romans of the later empire lost this patriotism, took little interest in government, and lacked political honesty. For example, at a time when barbarians threatened every frontier, thousands of soldiers deserted, and countless legions abandoned frontier posts.

The Roman Heritage and Christianity

In the ruins of the Roman world, two key ideas did survive in the west—the Roman heritage and the presence of Christianity. The barbarians whose kingdoms had once been part of the Roman Empire were influenced by its customs and civilizations. The leaders of the barbarian peoples remembered that unity under an emperor had once existed. Ambitious rulers in later centuries tried to regain this unity.

At the same time, Christianity became the official church, that is, the one religion recognized by the state. Its leaders would play key roles in the post-Roman world. In addition, the Christian Church became the main preserver of Roman ideas and civilization.

SECTION 6 REVIEW

1. **Define** inflation, collegia, anarchy
2. **Identify** Commodus, Ostrogoths, Visigoths, Huns, Alaric, Attila, Romulus Augustulus
3. **Locate** Constantinople, Black Sea, Rhine River, Danube River, Adrianople, Châlons
4. **Understanding Ideas** Describe the economic problems of the Roman Empire under the rule of Diocletian and Constantine.
5. **Interpreting Ideas** **(a)** What was the system of divided rule? **(b)** What were the problems caused by this organization?
6. **Synthesizing Ideas** **(a)** What was the major reason for the collapse of the Roman Empire in the west? **(b)** Give examples to support your answer.

destroyed Roman army and killed eastern emperor Valens; ***Chalons:*** battle where Roman and Visigothic armies defeated Huns in A.D. 451
4. Small farmers were forced to sell their land to latifundia owners, who often refused to pay taxes. Inflation occurred, money was scarce, and the coinage was debased so that people resorted to barter. The population declined, and the government worried that there would not be enough farmers to feed the population. Artisans left the cities to find work in the country.
5. (a) Diocletian appointed a co-emperor, called an *augustus,* and each administered half the empire. Each co-emperor chose an assistant, called a *caesar,* to help him rule and to be his successor. **(b)** rivalry between co-emperors and caesars
6. (a) and **(b)** Answers will vary. There was no single reason, but students should suggest the following: First, the economy declined because government expenses were heavy. Taxes rose. Even unbearably heavy taxes could not produce enough revenue. Second, political weakness saw Rome try to control the entire Mediterranean with a government originally designed for a small city-state. Third, social decay saw the Romans of the later empire take little interest in government, political honesty, and patriotism.

PERSPECTIVES: LEGACIES OF THE PAST

The Roman Empire collapsed more than 1,500 years ago. But in many ways it never died. Instead, it continues to influence people throughout the world even today.

Take language, for example. The Romans based their alphabet on that of the Greeks—who had borrowed theirs from the Phoenicians. But the modern letters that you see on this page are a direct gift from the Romans. So are Roman numerals. Even the planets of our solar system show the influence of imperial Rome because they bear the names of Roman gods—Mars, Mercury, and Venus, for example. Our calendar is based on the one developed by Julius Caesar in 46 B.C. July bears the name of Julius Caesar himself, August that of his successor, Augustus Caesar. The last day of the week, Saturday, honors the Roman god Saturn.

Latin, the language of the Romans, developed directly into the Romance languages of Italian, Romanian, French, Spanish, and Portuguese. The common origins of these languages becomes evident when you examine a few of their words. For example, the Latin word *luz,* meaning "light" is similar to the Italian word *luce,* and the French word *lumière.* And the Spanish word *luz* is exactly the same as the Latin word. Although the English language is a mixture of Old Norse, Old German, Latin, and Norman French, 60 percent of English words have Latin origins. For example, the word "republic" comes from *res publica,* Latin for "things belonging to the people." "Senate" came from the Roman council of elders, the *senatus.*

Rome's legacy remains highly visible throughout the countryside of southern Europe, North Africa, and the Middle East. Roman bridges still span French and Spanish rivers, and roads that once connected Rome with its provinces survive today. In each city they conquered, the Romans added their own urban plan—a grid system of roads, temples, a central forum, baths, and theaters. Many cities that flourished under the Romans, such as Alexandria, Antioch, and the rebuilt Carthage, owe their layout to Roman engineers.

The ruins of Roman buildings, themselves largely based on Greek models, inspired generations of architects. Michelangelo used Roman models to design St. Peter's Basilica in Rome in 1547. And Thomas Jefferson studied Roman architecture when he built his home, Monticello, in 1770. Roman law left its imprint on the world, too. Codified in the second and third centuries, Roman laws were adopted by many countries in Europe and the East after the empire fell. Through Spain, Roman law became the foundation

172

of the law of New Spain and remained in force when the territories became Texas and New Mexico. France's Napoleonic Code was based on Roman law. It was this law that the former French province of Louisiana used even after it became a state.

In hundreds of ways, Rome speaks to us all. But why? Why not the Persian or the Ottoman Empire? What made Rome so special? For one thing, the Roman Empire was huge. It once included what is today Italy, France, Spain, Portugal, Switzerland, Austria, Greece, Romania, Asia Minor, Libya, Syria, Morocco, and Tunisia, as well as parts of Great Britain and Germany. Across its far-reaching roads Rome sent not just legions but also commerce and culture.

Rome also lasted a long time. Founded, according to legend, in 753 B.C., it lived over 1,200 years, until the last Roman emperor, Romulus Augustulus, was deposed in A.D. 476. When Rome fell, the city of Constantinople laid claim to the entire Roman world. The Eastern Roman, or Byzantine, Empire carried on the heritage and organization of Rome for another 1,000 years, until it fell to the Turks in 1453.

The East was not the only place to keep the Roman tradition alive. The Germanic rulers who overran the empire saw themselves as successors to the Romans. The Frankish ruler Charlemagne, who spoke fluent Latin, was crowned "Emperor of the Romans" in A.D. 800, wearing a Roman toga and sandals.

In 962 Otto the Great founded the Holy Roman Empire, uniting the lands of Germany and Italy into a loose confederation of states. This empire lasted almost 1,000 years, until the reign of Napoleon.

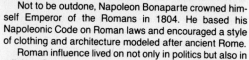

Not to be outdone, Napoleon Bonaparte crowned himself Emperor of the Romans in 1804. He based his Napoleonic Code on Roman laws and encouraged a style of clothing and architecture modeled after ancient Rome.

Roman influence lived on not only in politics but also in religion. Christianity, first scorned by Roman authorities, was made an official state religion in the fourth century and took on many Roman features. Church structure and organization were modeled after Roman government. Roman law became the model for canon, or church, law, and the pope became the center of Christianity. Christian churches were styled after Roman government centers or "basilicas."

Over the centuries, our Roman heritage has been idealized, romanticized, and often sanitized. While much about Rome was corrupt and unappealing, it was Rome's sense of grandeur, its power, and its organization that made everybody want to be a Roman, and that ultimately passed its legacy down to us.

Photos *Page 172: Charlemagne (top), Roman Senate (bottom left), United States Congress (bottom right); Page 173: Monticello (top left), St. Peter's Basilica (top right), Roman Colosseum (bottom left), Roman theatrical masks (bottom right)*

173

Reviewing Important Terms

1. e; **2.** f; **3.** g; **4.** h; **5.** c; **6.** d; **7.** a; **8.** b; **9.** i; **10.** j.

Developing Critical Thinking Skills

1. (a) The Third Punic War, First Triumvirate, Julian Emperors; **(b)** reign of Julius Caesar, life of Jesus, German invasions; **(c)** Estruscan invasions, Carthaginian invasions, Hun invasions; **(d)** Virgil's *Aeneid,* letters of Paul, Battle of Adrianople; **(e)** reforms under the Gracchi, founding of Constantinople, division of empire

2. The Roman Republic was democratic to a certain degree, although the aristocrats dominated the government. The empire was an absolute monarchy.

3. Written laws allowed everyone to be aware of their rights and obligations. Basic legal principles were applied to all people in the empire.

4. (a) and **(b)** Answers will vary. Students could state that the Roman system of law became the foundation of the laws of several European countries.

5. (a) Citizens of the Roman Empire could no longer look to Rome for protection. **(b)** Answers will vary.

6. Answers will vary. Similarities include: Only adult male citizens could vote and hold office; the commoners had a say in lawmaking; officials held office for short terms. In Athens citizens could participate in all branches of government, serve on juries, and hold office. In Rome citizens elected representatives to run the government. In Athens the Assembly was the most powerful body, in Rome the Senate.

1B, 1D, 3A, 3B, a4A, a4K

Reteaching

Have students review the Chapter Summary and the appropriate section and questions in the Unit Synthesis. Discuss the concepts until students demonstrate a clear understanding of the material.

CHAPTER 7 REVIEW

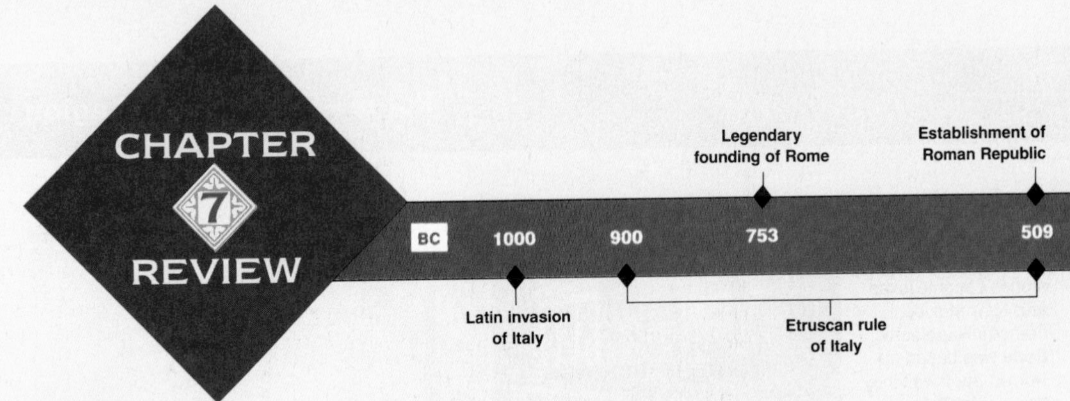

Chapter Summary

The following list contains the key concepts you have learned about Rome.

1. The early inhabitants of Italy included the Latins, the Etruscans, and the Greeks.
2. The Romans dominated the entire Mediterranean region by the 100s B.C.
3. Early Rome was a republic. The most important governing bodies were the Senate, the Assembly of Centuries, and the Assembly of Tribes.
4. After the struggle of the orders, the plebeians had many rights. The nobility, however, actually controlled the republic.
5. The growing importance of the army brought the Roman Republic to an end as military commanders repeatedly gained control of Rome's government. The last and most successful of these military leaders was Julius Caesar.
6. Caesar's grand-nephew Augustus, who succeeded him, became the first emperor. From the 20s B.C. onward, Rome was an empire, not a republic.
7. The abilities of the emperors varied greatly, but they all maintained internal stability and a continued expansion of Roman territory until the late A.D. 100s.
8. Education and literature flourished, as did engineering and architecture. However, corruption and political disorder gradually increased.
9. One of the world's great religions—Christianity—began in Judea. It was based on the teachings of Jesus.
10. Despite persecutions, Christianity spread.
11. About A.D. 300 two reforming emperors, Diocletian and Constantine, helped restore the empire.
12. Political, economic, and social factors all led to the collapse of the Roman Empire in the west.
13. The Christian Church helped preserve Roman civilization after the western half of the empire lost its strength and was overrun by invaders in the A.D. 400s. Only in the east did the descendants of the Romans preserve their independence in an empire centered on the city of Constantinople.

On a separate sheet of paper, complete the following review exercises.

Reviewing Important Terms

Match each of the following terms with the correct definition below.

a. latifundia
b. consul
c. veto
d. indemnity
e. inflation
f. Pax Romana
g. patriarch
h. republic
i. crucifixion
j. checks and balances

____ 1. The rise in prices that a decrease in the value of the exchange medium causes
____ 2. "Roman Peace"
____ 3. Bishop of one of the five most important early Christian cities
____ 4. Form of government in which voters elect their leaders
____ 5. Refuse to approve
____ 6. Money for the damages of war
____ 7. Large estate during the later Roman Republic and the Roman Empire
____ 8. One of the two chief executives who ran the government and who was also an army commander during the Roman Republic
____ 9. Method of execution in which the accused is tied to a cross and left to die a slow and agonizing death from suffocation
____ 10. Principle that prevents any one part of the government from becoming too powerful

Developing Critical Thinking Skills

1. **Understanding Chronology** Place the three items in each of the following lists in chronological order:
   - **(a)** The First Triumvirate, the Third Punic War, the Julian Emperors
   - **(b)** The German invasions, the life of Jesus, the reign of Julius Caesar
   - **(c)** The Hun invasions, the Carthaginian invasions, the Etruscan invasions
   - **(d)** The letters of Paul, Virgil's *Aeneid,* the battle of Adrianople
   - **(e)** Reforms under the Gracchi, founding of Constantinople, division of the empire

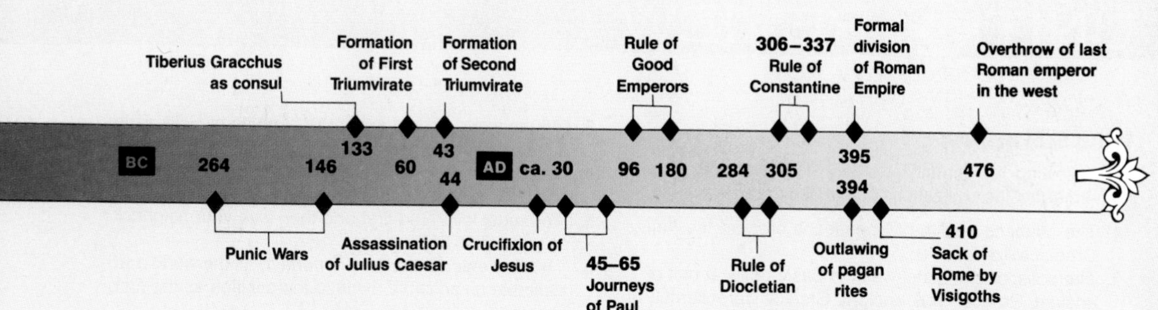

2. **Contrasting Ideas** How did the government of the Roman Republic differ from that of the Roman Empire?
3. **Interpreting Ideas** How did the use of written law help to strengthen the Roman government?
4. **Analyzing Ideas** **(a)** What do you consider to be the most important contribution that the Romans made to civilization today? **(b)** Give reasons to support your answer.
5. **Analyzing Primary Sources** Reread the decree of the Roman Senate on page 168. **(a)** Why did the Senate issue the decree? **(b)** If you had been a Roman citizen, how would you have reacted to the decree?
6. **Comparing Ideas** Compare the role of citizens in Athenian democracy with that of citizens in the Roman Republic. What are the similarities and differences? (You may wish to refer to Chapters 5 and 6 for information on Athenian democracy.)

Relating Geography to History

Compare the extent of Roman territory shown on the maps on pages 149, 159, and 169. **(a)** What was the farthest extent of Roman territory to the east? **(b)** When did these boundaries represent the farthest extent of Roman territory?

Relating Past to Present

1. The Roman Republic had a citizen army instead of a professional army. **(a)** What kind of army do we have in the United States today? **(b)** What are the advantages and disadvantages of each type of army?
2. **(a)** Discuss how the persecution of the Christians in Rome affected the spread of Christianity. **(b)** Choose a country where religious persecution exists today. What effect does this have on the members of the religious group being persecuted? **(c)** On the religion worldwide?
3. The Roman historian Tacitus used his treatise *Germania,* which is about the Germanic tribes, to criticize the corruption and immorality of Roman society. Choose a modern book, play, or movie that comments on contemporary events or people and describe the "message" that is being put forward.

Applying History Study Skills

Before completing this activity, review Building History Study Skills on page 154.

Study the following data on the policies and practices of Julius Caesar. Then formulate a thesis statement based on the data.

- Caesar resettled landless soldiers throughout Gaul.
- Caesar employed people on public works.
- Caesar tried to reduce the debt of farmers.
- Caesar expanded Roman citizenship to the peoples outside Italy.
- The Senate declared Caesar dictator for life.
- Senators who felt that Caesar was trying to destroy the republic assassinated him on the Ides of March, 44 B.C.

Investigating Further

1. **Determining Historical Accuracy** Read Shakespeare's play *Julius Caesar.* **(a)** How did Shakespeare depict Caesar? **(b)** How did Shakespeare depict Cassius? **(c)** Based on what you have read about Caesar in this chapter, is the character in the play historically accurate? **(d)** Was Caesar really trying to become a dictator? **(e)** According to the play, how did Brutus justify his role in the assassination of Caesar?
2. **Writing a Report** In A.D. 79 an eruption of Mount Vesuvius destroyed the city of Pompeii in southern Italy. The volcanic ash that buried Pompeii preserved the ruins, and from them we can learn much about daily life during the period. Prepare a written report on the destruction of Pompeii. Include information that clearly indicates that the citizens of Pompeii were caught by surprise when the volcano erupted. Two useful sources are the article "Last Moments of the Pompeians" (*National Geographic,* November 1961) and Ron and Nancy Goor's *Pompeii: Exploring a Roman Ghost Town* (Harper & Row Junior Books).
3. **Dramatizing History** Use resources in your school or public library to find more information on the plot to assassinate Julius Caesar. Then write a script of a scene in which the conspirators decide when they will kill Caesar.

Relating Geography to History
(a) *to the east:* Mesopotamia, Syria, and Armenia; *to the south:* the interior of Egypt; **(b)** between A.D. 98 and A.D. 117

Relating Past to Present
1. (a) professional; **(b)** Answers will vary. A citizen army provides a large supply of soldiers. However, a country may suffer defeat because it does not have a well-trained military force. A professional army is a well-trained force ready to resist attack, but it may become too powerful.
2. (a) Persecution made Christians stronger in their faith. Non-Christians began to feel there must be something to the new religion if people were willing to die for it. **(b)** Answers will vary. **(c)** Such persecution may strengthen members in their faith and resolve and gain sympathy worldwide.
3. Answers will vary.

Applying History Study Skills
People who initially admired Caesar's methods soon feared his power and plotted to kill him.

175

Reviewing Concepts

1. ***Demosthenes*** resisted Macedonian encroachment on to the Peloponnesus; 2. ***Xerxes*** attacked the Greeks and their fleet; 3. ***Alexander the Great*** desired a worldwide empire; 4. ***Pericles*** ruled during the Golden Age; 5. ***Jesus*** preached in the Judean countryside about the love of God; 6. ***Augustus*** was the emperor who established the Pax Romana to maintain control of the Mediterranean; 7. ***Homer*** wrote the *Iliad;* 8. ***Thucydides*** was the first real historian; 9. ***Hannibal*** led a Carthaginian invasion of Italy from the north; 10. ***Paul*** was a great missionary.

Applying Critical Thinking Skills

1. Answers will vary. Students should include definitions of democracy and republic, and a comparison of the Greek Assembly and the Roman Senate.

2. (a) Answers will vary. Students should include a specific analysis of how minority groups like the hoplites and plebeians received concessions from the upper classes.

(b) Roman law was much more specific and absorbed additional cultural values from neighboring lands.

3. Answers will vary. Students should include the Greek emphasis upon the individual and general daily life, while the Romans emphasized the corporate nature of their government, civilization, and religion. Both glorified their gods and constructed buildings and monuments to serve the community.

4. Answers will vary. Both were golden ages during which the people had economic prosperity, political

1A, 1B, 1D, 3A, 3B, a4A, a4F, a4G, a4H, a4J, a4L

Reteaching

Have students review the Chapter Summary and the appropriate section and questions in the Unit Synthesis. Discuss the concepts until students demonstrate a clear understanding of the material.

UNIT 2 REVIEW

Unit Summary

The following list contains the key concepts you have learned about the civilizations of the Mediterranean world.

1. The Minoans and the Mycenaeans created the first Greek civilizations.
2. The polis, or city-state, was the basic political unit of ancient Greece. The ancient Greeks were fiercely loyal to their own city-state, and they could seldom unite for very long.
3. The two most famous city-states were Sparta and Athens. Sparta was a militaristic state, while Athens gradually evolved into a democracy.
4. After stopping two Persian invasions, the city-states united under the leadership of Athens. This union was short-lived, however, and the city-states soon fought the devastating Peloponnesian War. Only when an outside invader, Philip of Macedon, conquered Greece was the region once again united.
5. Against the background of the Peloponnesian War, Athens underwent an unprecedented Golden Age. Athenian ideals of art, literature, and democracy were valuable contributions to Western civilization.
6. Alexander the Great created an empire that included Egypt, Asia Minor, and Persia. During this empire classical Greek culture merged with eastern cultures to form Hellenistic culture.
7. On the Italian Peninsula, the Latins, Etruscans, and Greeks influenced the culture of Rome. In time the Romans conquered the entire Mediterranean region and became a great empire.
8. The Romans made many contributions to Western civilization. Engineers constructed aqueducts; artists, sculptors, and writers created many original works; and architects first used concrete to build public buildings. Roman law formed the basis of our legal code, and from the Latin language emerged our present Romance languages.
9. Christianity developed in Judea and spread throughout the Roman Empire.
10. Although the Roman Empire in the west collapsed in A.D. 476, the empire in the east preserved the Roman heritage and traditions.

On a separate sheet of paper, complete the following review exercises.

Reviewing Concepts

Name the individuals who might have made the following statements. Explain why each statement is significant.

1. "King Philip of Macedon should not be allowed to rule over the Greeks."
2. "If I succeed at Salamis, I will have victory over all the Greeks."
3. "All the world should enjoy the benefits of Hellenistic culture under my rule."
4. "We must make Athens a center of culture, beauty, and good government."
5. "You must love God first and then love your neighbor as yourself."
6. "I wish to extend the *Pax Romana* to all the world and eliminate all possible rivals to my position as the first consul."
7. "I will write of the great legends of the ancient Greeks and how they conquered Troy."
8. "I believe that all information should be classified so that study will be rational and knowledge will advance."
9. "I will invade Italy from the north and conquer Rome with my elephants from North Africa."
10. "I will spread the teachings of Jesus throughout the world and write letters to answer people's questions about ethics."

Applying Critical Thinking Skills

1. **Comparing Ideas** In what way did the concept of Greek democracy differ from the Roman concept of a republic?
2. **Interpreting Ideas (a)** Trace the development of written law from Draco to Pericles to the Twelve Tables to Roman imperial law. Consider the individual rights of citizens, women, and slaves. **(b)** Why was Roman law considered superior to Greek law?
3. **Analyzing Ideas** How did sculpture, architecture, painting, mosaics, drama, and poetry reflect the religions and philosophies of Greece and Rome?
4. **Synthesizing Ideas** What do these two periods in history have in common: Athens under the rule of Pericles and Rome under the rule of Augustus?

Relating Geography to History

(a) How was the geography of ancient Greece different from that of ancient Italy? **(b)** How was the geography of these two countries similar? **(c)** How did the geography of each region influence the civilization that developed?

Writing About History

1. Assume that you are either a member of the Greek Council of 500 or a Roman noble during the reign of Caesar Augustus. Write a diary describing what you did during a typical week. Describe the major landmarks you passed, the people you met, and the government activities in which you took part. Include a description of your home and family and any family activities in which you participated. Also, describe your job and friends.

stability, and a higher standard of living.

Relating Geography to History

(a) and **(b)** Ancient Greece suffered from mountains separating each peninsular "finger" pointing into the Mediterranean, resulting in political fragmentation. Ancient Italy had a seaward location and a mild climate like Greece, but Italy did not suffer the consequences of physical division into city-states. **(c)** The Greeks developed highly-independent city-states, while the Romans expanded to control first the peninsula, and then the entire Mediterranean. Both developed colonies to support large populations.

2. Write an essay describing the Greek and Roman contributions to the development of government in the United States. Focus especially on the separation of powers, checks and balances, the role of citizens, and the powers of the legislature.

Further Readings

Bowra, C. M., ed. *Classical Greece.* New York: Time-Life Books. Shows the famous buildings, sculptures, and reliefs of ancient Greece.

Brion, Marcel. *Pompeii and Herculaneum: The Glory and the Grief.* New York: Crown Publishing. Describes these two ancient cities as they look today.

Bulfinch, Thomas. *Bulfinch's Mythology.* New York: Avenel Books. Describes various Greek myths, gods, and goddesses.

Hadas, Moses, ed. *Imperial Rome.* New York: Time-Life Books. Describes the history of the Roman Empire.

Lane Fox, Robin. *The Search for Alexander.* New York: Little, Brown and Company. Analyzes the life of Alexander the Great.

Unit Two Chronology

Date	Political and Social Developments	Technological and Scientific Advances	Visual Arts and Literature	Religious and Philosophical Thought
3000 B.C.–1500 B.C.	Minoan civilization **5*** Mycenaean invasion of Greece **5**		Minoan art **5**	Minoan bull worship **5**
1500 B.C.–500 B.C.	Latin invasion of Italy **7** Trojan War **5** Greek Age of Kings **5** Etruscans rule Italy **7** Draco's law codes **5**	Hippocrates and medicine **6** Pythagoras **6**	*Iliad* and *Odyssey* **5**	Greek polytheism **5**
500 B.C.–250 B.C.	Roman Republic begins **7** Cleisthenes **5** Golden Age of Greece **6** Persian Wars **5** Peloponnesian War **5** Alexander the Great **6**	*Elements* (Euclid) **6** Greek temples **6**	Sophocles **6** Parthenon **6** *Republic* **6** *Politics* **6** Euripides **6**	Roman lares and penates **7** Socrates **6** Cynicism, Stoicism, Epicureanism **6**
250 B.C.–0	Punic Wars **7** Rome invades Greece and Egypt **7**	Roman roads **7**	Virgil's *Aeneid* **7** Ovid's *Metamorphoses* **7**	
0–A.D. 250	Pax Romana **7** Caesar Augustus **7**	Galen and medicine **7** Ptolemy **7** Colosseum in Rome **7**	Tacitus' *Germania* **7** Plutarch's *Parallel Lives* **7** Paul's Epistles **7**	Roman emperor worship **7** Christianity and Paul's mission **7**
A.D. 250–A.D. 500	Roman civil wars **7** Constantine moves to Byzantium **7** Barbarian invasions of West **7** Rome falls **7**			Christianity official religion **7**

*Indicates chapter in which development is discussed

177

1B, 3A, a1C, a2G, a2J

Focus/Motivation
Ask students to study the map on page 102. Point out that the map shows the major geographic features of the Mediterranean Region. Ask for volunteers to locate the sites of Rome and Athens on the map. Then point out that the Unit Two Synthesis will deal with these two civilizations as well as others that developed in the Mediterranean Region.

Civilizations of the Mediterranean World

5 Greek City-states Developed in the Mediterranean Region

On the southern end of the mountainous Balkan Peninsula, as well as in Asia Minor and on the nearby islands, one of the greatest civilizations the world has ever known—Greek civilization—developed.

Early Greek City-states

A great civilization—Minoan civilization—flourished on the island of Crete in the Mediterranean Sea between about 2000 B.C. and 1400 B.C. Although the great civilizations of nearby Egypt and the Fertile Crescent influenced Minoan civilization, the Minoans added ideas of their own. Remains show that they equipped the royal palace and the homes of the nobles with running water. They were decorated with colorful frescoes—paintings made on wet plaster walls. Artisans made beautiful, delicately carved figures of ivory, stone, gold, silver, and bronze.

While Minoan civilization was developing, important changes were taking place on the Greek mainland. Beginning about 2000 B.C. a warlike people known as the Mycenaeans entered Greece from the north. The Mycenaeans conquered Crete and were in turn influenced by Minoan civilization. By 1200 B.C., however, the major Mycenaean cities had been destroyed and more primitive Greeks—the Dorians—moved into the peninsula.

Because of the geography of Greece and their own tribal organization, the early Greeks established city-states, such as Athens and Sparta, in the ninth and eighth centuries B.C. The Greek word for city-state—polis—originally meant a fort, a refuge in time of danger. As a village or city grew up around the fort, *polis* came to mean not only the fort, but also the city and its surrounding region.

Greek Government and Society

The early city-states were monarchies that constantly waged war among themselves. Despite this warfare, the Greeks gradually made significant advances. For example, they developed religious beliefs that sought to explain the mysteries of the physical world, the passions that could make people lose self-control, and how to gain such benefits as long life, good fortune, and abundant harvests. Because the gods were thought to be pleased by displays of strength and courage, the Greeks held athletic contests in their honor. Most famous were the games at Olympia, held every fourth year in honor of Zeus.

Over time, the Greeks developed new forms of government. First, nobles—the chief landowners—began to govern many city-states in a form of government known as aristocracy. As the Greek people chafed under the rule of aristocracies, many city-states adopted tyrannies in which a strong leader—a tyrant—seized power. Tyrants were not always harsh rulers. To the contrary, many of the tyrants were excellent rulers who encouraged trade and passed just laws.

As Greek government changed from monarchy to aristocracy to tyranny, the idea of popular government—that people could and should rule themselves and not be ruled by others—began to take root in many city-states. When cities ousted their tyrants, some restored the old monarchies or aristocracies. Others developed the form of government called democracy—a government in which all citizens took part.

Sparta and Athens

Similarities and differences existed among Greek city-states. The wide range of differences shows clearly in a comparison of the two city-states that became the most important, Sparta and Athens.

Sparta. The population of Sparta was divided into three groups. The citizens descended from the Dorian invaders controlled the government. The Spartans called the second group of people by the Greek word that meant "neighbors." They were free, but were not citizens. They lived in the towns, and most of them worked in commerce and industry. Some "neighbors" became rich, but they could never be citizens. The lowest group were the helots. Because the Spartans lived in constant fear of a helot revolt, they tried to prevent the helots from developing any leaders.

Sparta regulated the lives of its citizens from birth to death. All the rules had a single basic aim: to make every adult male citizen part of an efficient military machine designed to control the conquered people and extend Spartan power.

Athens. As in Sparta, the population of Athens was divided into three groups. First were the citizens. Next came the aliens—those who were not Athenians—who were called metics. Most metics were merchants or skilled workers. They were free but could not own land or take part in government. Metics, however, paid the same taxes as citizens and moved about freely. At the bottom were the slaves.

After the Age of Kings, Athens had an aristocratic government. However, four rulers—Draco, Solon, Pisistratus (pi • SIS • truht • uhs), and Cleisthenes (KLYS • thuh • neez)—helped change the political development of Athens. Each ruler helped Athens move closer to democracy until Cleisthenes established what we call direct democracy. That is, all citizens participated directly in making decisions.

Daily Life in Athens

The citizens of Athens and the other Greek city-states lived in much the same way. Their lives consisted of work, recreation, and the fulfillment of their responsibilities to the city-state.

Farming was the most honored occupation for an Athenian. More than half of all citizens were farmers. Foreign trade and manufacturing were also important to the Athenian economy.

Although the Athenians built magnificent temples and other public buildings, their private homes remained simple. Athenians believed that money should be spent on buildings to benefit the whole community, not on private homes.

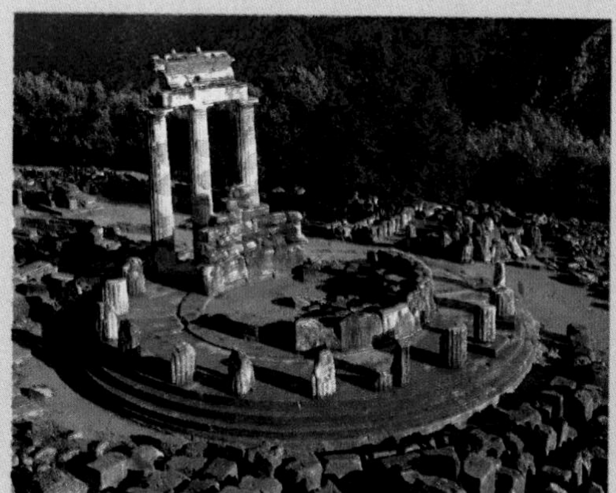

Temple of Athena at Delphi

Expansion of Greek Civilization

In 546 B.C. Cyrus of Persia conquered the Greek city-states on the western shores of Asia Minor. Then three Persian emperors—Cyrus, Darius, and Xerxes—sent huge armies to conquer the mainland Greeks. However, by 479 B.C. a combined Greek army had defeated the remnants of the Persian army at Plataea (pluh • TEE • uh).

After these destructive wars, the Greek city-states made several attempts to unify. The most notable was the Delian League under the leadership of Athens.

During this time Pericles (PER • uh • kleez) rose to power in Athens. Under his rule Athens became a complete democracy.

Even the firm control of Athens under Pericles could not unify the Greek city-states, however. Tensions between the city-states rose until a devastating war known as the Peloponnesian War broke out. After almost a generation of warfare, Athens finally surrendered to Sparta in 404 B.C.

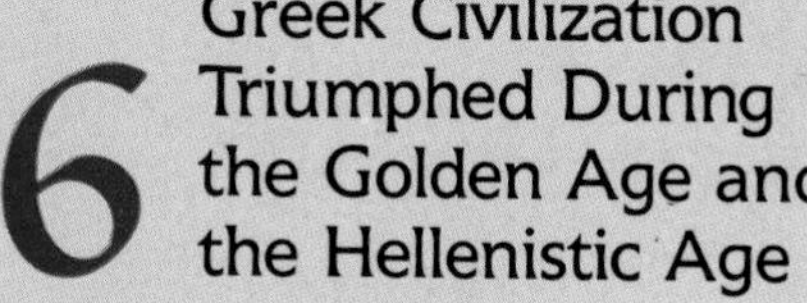

6 Greek Civilization Triumphed During the Golden Age and the Hellenistic Age

Greek culture reached new heights during the 400s B.C., a period so magnificent we call it the *Golden Age.*

179

1B, 3A, a1B, a1C

Presentation Understanding Relationships (Average/Group)
Point out to students that Western civilization owes much to the ancient civilizations of Greece and Rome. Then write the words *Greece* and *Rome* on the chalkboard or an overhead projector, and have students help to compile a list of the contributions of these ancient civilizations. *(The list under Greece should include democracy, architecture, painting, philosophy, and mathematics and science. Under Rome the list should include republic, language, law, and Christianity. You may wish to elaborate on each of these contributions in a class discussion.)*

Greek Art

After the Persian Wars, the wealth and power of Athens attracted artists and teachers from throughout Greece to the city.

Architecture. The Athenians made beauty a part of their daily life. They showed their love of Athens, and their pride in it, by erecting many impressive public buildings such as temples, gymnasiums, and theaters. They decorated these structures—such as the magnificent Parthenon that crowned the Acropolis—with their finest works of art, especially sculpture.

Painting. The best-preserved Greek paintings are those used to decorate vases. Vase painters illustrated everyday life as well as myths. They delighted in showing graceful and natural movements of their subjects.

Sculpture. Three great sculptors typify Greek sculpture. First was Myron, whose most famous figure is the Discus Thrower. The second was Phidias (FID • ee • uhs), who created the two wonderful statues of Athena in the Parthenon. The third was Praxiteles (prak • SIT • uh • leez), who crafted delicate, lifelike, and often life-sized figures.

The nature of Greek art. Greek art reflected how Greeks viewed themselves and the world. First, Greek art glorified humans as the most important creatures in the universe. Second, Greek art symbolized the pride of the people in their city-states. At the same time, it honored the gods, thanked them for life and fortune, and tried to win their favor. Third, all Greek art expressed Greek ideals of harmony, balance, order, and moderation—the qualities of simplicity and restraint. Finally, the Greeks believed in combining beauty and usefulness. To them, the useful, the beautiful, and the good were closely bound together.

Philosophers and Writers

The Greeks were eager to learn all they could and to think through everything that the human mind is capable of understanding. These characteristics are clearly shown in the record of the Greek thinkers and writers.

Socrates. One of the greatest thinkers and teachers of all time was Socrates (SAHK • ruh • teez), who lived in Athens from 469 B.C. to 399 B.C. Socrates wanted people to learn to think for themselves and not imitate their elders. Only then could they learn wisdom.

Battle of Issus

Socrates inspired great love among his followers, but he also made enemies. Even though Socrates honored the gods of the city, his enemies accused him of denying the existence of the many Greek gods. He was found guilty of teaching false religion and corrupting the minds of Athenian youth and was sentenced to death.

Plato. After Socrates' death, his student Plato began to teach in the grounds of the Academy, a public park and athletic field. One of Plato's major works is the *Republic,* in which he described his belief that the ideal government would be led by the most intelligent people of the polis.

Aristotle. Among Plato's students in the Academy was a young man named Aristotle, who founded his own school at Athens in 335 B.C. In order to describe the principles of government, Aristotle studied the political organization of 150 city-states and recorded his conclusions in a book called *Politics.* He concluded that the best government was one in which the middle class—those people who were neither wealthy nor poor—played an important role.

Mathematics and science. In the 500s B.C., before the Golden Age, Pythagoras (puh • THAG • uh • ruhs), a philosopher and mathematician, wrote that everything could be explained or expressed with numbers. He is probably best known for the Pythagorean theorem, the geometric theory which states that the square of the hypotenuse of a right triangle is equal to the sum of the squares of the other two sides.

History. The Greeks were the first people to take the writing of history seriously. Herodotus and Thucydides were the first great historians of the Western world.

Greek drama. The Greeks were the first people to write dramas—plays usually involving conflict and emotion through action and dialogue. It is in this form of literature that they excelled. Playwrights wrote both tragedies—showing the major character struggling unsuccessfully against fate—and comedies, in which the central characters succeeded in solving their problems.

Alexander the Great

In 359 B.C. a remarkable young man known as Philip of Macedon became king of Macedonia to the north of Greece and proceeded to conquer the quarrelsome Greek city-states. But it was Philip's son Alexander who had a lasting impact on history. By 331 B.C. Alexander had conquered Asia Minor, Syria, Egypt, Mesopotamia, and the Persian Empire and was attempting to conquer India. After a long campaign, however, he turned back and started the long journey home. On the journey, in 323 B.C., Alexander died in Babylon.

Although Alexander's empire broke up shortly after his death, his policies had long-lasting impact. Greek culture spread rapidly, and merged with other cultures to become what is known as Hellenistic culture.

Hellenistic Culture

Hellenistic society included a small class of very wealthy people and a large class of miserably poor people. However, the middle class grew because of the many opportunities for wealth.

Trade, the most profitable activity, radiated from the main trading centers in the cities of Alexandria, in Egypt; Rhodes, on the island of Rhodes off the coast of Asia Minor; and Antioch, in Syria. Trade routes now connected the whole Mediterranean world and even reached as far east as India.

The philosophers of the Hellenistic Age were more concerned with ethics than with fundamental questions of reality and human existence. There were three chief schools, or groups—the Cynics, the Stoics, and the Epicureans. The Cynics taught that people should seek virtue only. Stoics believed that divine reason directed the world. Epicureans taught that the aim of life was to seek pleasure and avoid pain.

Greeks of the Hellenistic Age were outstanding scientists. For example, Euclid developed geometry into a system by showing how geometric statements of truth, or theorems, develop logically from one another. And Archimedes (ahr • kuh • MEED • eez) used geometry to measure spheres, cones, and cylinders. He also calculated the value of π (pi)—the ratio of the circumference of a circle to its diameter—and used mathematics to explain the principle of the lever.

7 Rome Ruled the Western World for Centuries

The date 146 B.C. is often given as the end of the Hellenistic Age because by that year the Romans had extended their power over a large part of the eastern Mediterranean.

The Roman Republic

Although many peoples inhabited the Italian Peninsula in ancient times, the people who had the greatest impact on world history were the Romans. Early in their history, the Romans set up a republic, a form of government in which voters elect their leaders. Three groups of citizens helped govern Rome: the Assembly of Centuries, the Assembly of Tribes, and the Senate.

For more than 200 years after the founding of the Republic, the Romans fought many wars against neighboring peoples in Italy. By 265 B.C. the Romans controlled all of Italy south of the Rubicon River on the northeast coast. Both military organization and wise policies helped the Romans achieve their victories.

Roman Expansion in the Mediterranean

Rome soon came into contact with Carthage, a large and powerful city on the coast of North Africa. In a series of three wars, called the Punic Wars, the Romans completely destroyed their rival city. At the same time, Rome conquered the Hellenistic East.

Rome's annexation of distant territories lessened the role of the small citizen-farmer in Roman life. As land and slaves became more expensive, many citizen-farmers lost their lands and moved to the cities where they joined the unemployed masses.

181

1B, 1D, 3A, 3B, a1A, a1B, a1C

Closure
After rereading the paragraphs on Plato and Socrates on page 180, ask students whether they agree with Plato's or Aristotle's political beliefs. *(Students should give reasons for their choice.)*

From Republic to Empire

By 133 B.C. the Roman Republic faced many problems. Although leaders such as Tiberius, Gaius Gracchus (GRAK • uhs), Gaius Marius (MER • ee • uhs), and Lucius Cornelius Sulla attempted reforms, their programs met with little success.

Julius Caesar, who became dictator for life in 46 B.C., had the most impact. Although Caesar kept the republican form of government, he was king in everything but name. The conservative families of Rome did not welcome Caesar's new status, however, and he was assassinated in 44 B.C.

A scramble for power between Caesar's chosen heir Octavian and Marc Antony erupted soon after Caesar's death. But by 31 B.C. Octavian had defeated Marc Antony and taken the title *Augustus,* which means "set aside for religious purposes" or "sacred." He has been known ever since as Augustus Caesar, or simply Augustus, and is considered the first Roman emperor.

Roman Society and Culture

Law, military organization, and widespread trade and transportation held the empire together and brought peace for over 200 years—a period known as the Roman Peace, or Pax Romana.

Trade and transportation. Throughout the time of the Pax Romana, agriculture remained the primary occupation of people in the empire. In Italy itself most farmers worked on large estates devoted to vineyards or livestock. The provinces contained more small farms.

The vast empire provided great opportunities for commerce, and the exchange of goods was easy. Taxes on trade were low, and Roman currency was used everywhere. Rome and Alexandria in Egypt became the empire's greatest commercial centers.

Manufacturing also increased throughout the empire. Italy, Gaul, and Spain made inexpensive pottery and textiles. As in Greece, most work was done by hand in small shops.

Living conditions. The Pax Romana provided prosperity to many people, but wealth was not evenly distributed. The rich citizen usually had both a city home and a country home. Each residence included many conveniences, such as running water and baths. In contrast, the average Roman lived in a poorly constructed apartment building with very little furniture.

Science, engineering, and architecture. The Romans were less interested in scientific research to increase knowledge than in collecting and organizing information. Galen, a physician, wrote several volumes that summarized all the medical knowledge of his day. Ptolemy's theories in astronomy were also widely accepted. A scientist from Alexandria, Ptolemy believed that the earth was the center of the universe. Most people accepted this theory until the A.D. 1600s.

Education. Every important town or city throughout the Roman Empire had elementary, secondary, and higher level schools. A boy or girl of the free classes entered elementary school at the age of seven and studied reading, writing, arithmetic, and music. At about the age of 13, boys entered a secondary school, where they studied grammar, Greek, literature, good writing, and expressive speech. Greeks who had been slaves often taught the courses.

Literature. Although Greek influence was strong, a number of Romans produced literary works of distinction. For example, students still study the works of Cicero, Tacitus, Virgil, Ovid, and Plutarch to catch a glimpse of how the Romans thought and lived.

Christianity

One of the world's great religions—Christianity—began during the Roman Empire in the Roman-controlled territory of Judea. It was founded by a Jew known as Jesus of Nazareth.

Roman histories do not refer to Jesus at all. Our knowledge of Jesus comes mainly from the Gospels of Matthew, Mark, Luke, and John—the first four books of the New Testament of the Bible.

According to the Gospels, Jesus was born in Bethlehem, grew up in Nazareth, worked for a time as a carpenter, and began preaching as a young adult. Jesus spoke of "my Father in heaven," and his followers believed that Jesus was the Messiah, the Son of God.

The teachings of Jesus have become one of the greatest influences on the Western world. He accepted the Hebrew Ten Commandments as guides to right living but gave them further meaning. He summarized the 10 rules in two great commandments: People must love God above all else, and they must love others as they love themselves. His many teachings include:

1B, 3A, 3B, a1A, a1C, a4A, a4F, a4H, a4I

Question 1 of the Synthesis Review corresponds to Section 5; Question 2, to Section 6; Question 3, to Section 7; Question 4 asks students to synthesize information from Sections 5 and 7 of the synthesis.

The Colosseum in Rome

(1) God cares more for people than for laws.

(2) Jesus saw himself as the link that would reestablish the loving relationship that God desires. Jesus referred to this new relationship the "Kingdom of God."

(3) God will forgive people their sins if they will admit that they are wrong and ask to be forgiven.

The Romans feared that Jesus wanted to lead an uprising, and they considered him an enemy of the state. Consequently, Jesus was tried before Pontius Pilate, the Roman governor, who sentenced him to be crucified.

According to the Gospels, Jesus arose from the dead, remained on earth for 40 more days, and then ascended into heaven. His followers believed that the resurrection and the ascension proved that Jesus was the Messiah, calling him Jesus Christ, after the Greek word for messiah—*Christos*. The resurrection became the central message of Christianity. Through the death of Jesus Christ, the Son of God, who had died for the sins of the human race, all people could achieve redemption. The disciples of Jesus set out to spread this message, and within 400 years, Christianity had spread from its birthplace in Judea to all parts of the huge Roman Empire.

As Christianity spread, it developed a strict organization. Priests conducted services and performed baptisms and marriages. Above the priests were the bishops, who were considered the successors of the apostles. A bishop headed the church in each city. Over time, the bishop of Rome assumed the title of pope and claimed supremacy over the church.

The Collapse of the Empire in the West

During most of the A.D. 200s, the empire experienced dreadful confusion, civil war, and barbarian invasions. Travel became unsafe, and merchants hesitated to send goods by land or sea. People fled the cities. The rural population grew even poorer than before. Population decreased throughout the empire, partly because of a great plague that spread through the provinces and caused several million deaths.

The Roman Empire would probably have collapsed in the late 200s except for the efforts of two able emperors, Diocletian (dy • uh • KLEE • shuhn) and Constantine. Their reforms and reorganizations revived the empire. Nevertheless, their reforms could not postpone the collapse forever, and by A.D. 476 German barbarians had sacked imperial Rome—the empire was finished.

But *why* did Rome decline? How did this mighty empire that accomplished so much disappear? For centuries, historians have debated these questions. Some cite political weaknesses; the empire was too large to be governed efficiently. Others cite economic decline, including spiraling inflation. Still others cite social decay, the growth of the empire eroded the traditional values of the Romans. The important point to remember, however, is that no one cause was responsible for Roman decline. Like many other complex movements and events in history, it resulted from a combination of political, economic, and social forces.

In the ruins of the Roman world, however, two key ideas did survive in the West—the Roman heritage, including language and law, and the presence of Christianity. Both forces continue to influence life today—1,500 years after the collapse of the mighty Roman Empire.

SYNTHESIS REVIEW

1. **Summarizing Ideas** What were the three forms of government developed by the Greeks?
2. **Analyzing Ideas** How did Greek art reflect the ideals of Greek society?
3. **Interpreting Ideas** How did foreign conquests weaken the Roman Republic?
4. **Synthesizing Ideas** Why were the Romans able to establish a great empire, while the Greeks could never unify for very long?

Review Answers

1. The three forms of government developed by the Greeks were aristocracy, tyranny, and democracy.
2. Greek art reflected the ways in which the Greeks viewed themselves and the world. In art they glorified humans as the most important creatures; symbolized the pride of the people in the city-states; honored the gods; expressed Greek ideals of harmony, balance, order, moderation; and combined beauty with usefulness.
3. The role of the small citizen-farmers was lessened as land and slaves became more expensive, forcing many citizen-farmers to join the unemployed masses in the cities.
4. Greek geography and tribal organization caused them to establish rival city-states. Standard law, military organization, and widespread trade and transportation kept the Roman Empire united.

Introducing the Unit
Point out that while the Roman Empire in the West collapsed in the A.D. 400s, other brilliant civilizations flourished following this momentous event. In Unit Three students will examine these civilizations. Next ask students to read the titles of the chapters of this unit on page 185. Ask students to point out on a wall map the areas of the world they will be studying in each chapter. Point out that Chapters 8, 9, 12, and 13 examine the brilliant contributions of non-Western societies in the centuries following the collapse of Rome. In many ways, these civilizations were more advanced than those that developed in Europe at that time. Ask students to remember this point as they study Unit Three.

UNIT THREE

The World in Transition

◀ *Marco Polo leaving Venice*

Unit Goals
After studying Unit Three, students will be able to:

1. Describe how the Byzantine Empire influenced Kievan Rus.
2. Analyze the beliefs of Islam and compare the religion with Christianity, Hinduism, Buddhism, and Judaism.
3. Explain the spread of Islam and note Islamic contributions to civilization.
4. Outline the story of the rise of the Merovingians and Carolingians, including the role of the mayors of the palace.
5. Explain feudalism and the manorial system in medieval Europe.
6. Discuss how nations developed in Europe.
7. Describe the achievements of the Tang and Song dynasties in China.
8. Analyze the beginnings of Japanese and Korean civilization.
9. List the major civilizations of Africa and the Americas and describe the achievements of each.

CHAPTER (pages 186–203)

8 The Byzantine Empire Preserved the Heritage of Rome

(395 – 1589)

CHAPTER OVERVIEW

Although the Roman Empire in the West collapsed, the traditions and culture of Rome continued in the East in the Byzantine Empire. This empire lasted for centuries because of its political strength, good defenses, and prosperous economy.

The Byzantines passed on classical learning and created their own masterpieces, such as the church of Hagia Sophia. Justinian's Code, which preserved Roman law, was probably the greatest Byzantine contribution to civilization.

Byzantine influence extended to and strongly influenced Kievan Rus, which made up the territory that later became known as Russia. Missionaries from Constantinople converted many Eastern Slavs to Byzantine Christianity in the 900s. The Byzantine church grew rapidly in Kievan Rus.

The Mongols conquered Kiev in the 1200s and retained control there for almost 200 years. Mongol rule influenced Kievan society in several ways, but the most important cultural development of this period, the growth of the Orthodox church, took place despite the Mongol presence. Eventually Mongol rule was thrown off, and the princes of Moscow established an independent Russian state, centered in Moscow.

SUGGESTED LESSON PLAN			
Day	**Objectives**	**Suggested Activities**	**Materials**
1	U1,* C1-2	Introducing the Unit (page 184) Introducing the Chapter (page 186) Section 1 (pages 187-94), Focus/Motivation (page 187), Presentation (page 188), Closure (page 194), Suggested Teaching Strategies, Enrichment Activities, Daily Quiz, Suggested Assignments (page 185B)	ATE, Pupil's Edition, Teacher's Resource-Bank™
2	U1, C3-5	Section 2 (pages 196-99), Focus/Motivation (page 196), Presentation (page 196), Closure (page 198), Suggested Teaching Strategies, Enrichment Activities, Daily Quiz, Suggested Assignments (page 185C)	ATE, Pupil's Edition, Teacher's Resource-Bank™
3	U1, C5-7	Section 3 (pages 199-201), Focus/Motivation (page 199), Presentation (page 200), Closure (page 200), Suggested Teaching Strategies, Enrichment Activity, Daily Quiz, Suggested Assignments (page 185D)	ATE, Pupil's Edition, Teacher's Resource-Bank™
4	U1, C1-7	Chapter 8 Form A Test, Reteaching Worksheet, Chapter 8 Form B Test	Teacher's Resource-Bank™ or Workbook and Test Booklet

*C refers to applicable Chapter Objective, U refers to applicable Unit Goal.

BOOKS FOR THE TEACHER

Harcave, Sidney. *Russia: A History.* Lippincott. Provides a general history of Russia. The first chapters of the book are appropriate for this chapter.

Hussey, J. M. *The Byzantine World.* Harper & Row. Introduces the Byzantine Empire and analyzes how the Byzantines preserved the Roman heritage.

Rice, David T. *The Byzantines.* Praeger. Emphasizes social and cultural history.

Sherrard, Philip. *Byzantium.* Time-Life. Discusses the military, political, social, and cultural life of Byzantium, which later became Constantinople—the center of the Byzantine Empire.

Vernadsky, G. *The Mongols and the Russians.* Yale University Press. Gives one of the best accounts on the subject.

BOOKS FOR THE STUDENT

Almedinger, E. M. *Land of Muscovy: The History of Early Russia.* Farrar, Straus & Giroux. Describes life in Russia between 1400 and 1600.

Asimov, Isaac. *Constantinople.* Houghton Mifflin. Gives a general history of the Byzantine Empire.

Jacobs, David. *Constantinople and the Golden Horn.* American Heritage. Examines one of the most interesting cities in the world.

Moscow, Henry. *Russia Under the Tsars.* American Heritage. Analyzes Russian autocracy.

MULTIMEDIA MATERIALS

The Arab's World: Past and Future (mp, 52 min.), EBE. Evaluates the role of the Arab in world history.

Byzantine Empire (mp, 14 min.), Coronet. Outlines the empire and its important cultural contributions.

Our Heritage from the Byzantine Empire (fs), McGraw-Hill. Analyzes how the Byzantines preserved Western civilization.

Section (pages 187–194)

1 The Byzantine Empire Helped Preserve Western Civilization

The Byzantine Empire lasted for 1,000 years after the fall of the Western Roman Empire. The empire gained its strength from a highly centralized government with an efficient bureaucracy and a good army and navy. In addition, the empire was located at a crossroads of trade. Classical learning and Roman law were preserved by the Byzantines, who developed a distinct culture and religion.

SUGGESTED TEACHING STRATEGIES

1. **Preteaching Vocabulary (Basic)** You many wish to preteach the following important vocabulary terms: dowry (*page 188*); icon (*page 190*); iconoclast, iconoclastic controversy, heresy, excommunication (*page 191*); mosaic (*page 193*). Ask students to compare the terms *icon* and *mosaic*.
2. **Understanding Ideas (Average/Group)** Have interested students do research on the history of the Eastern Orthodox church. In their reports they should investigate the following: What is the background of the break between Roman and Orthodox Christianity? Where are most Orthodox worshipers found today? How does Orthodox doctrine differ from Roman Catholic doctrine? Which rites, ceremonies, and holidays are the same? Which are different? Sources include Huston Smith's *The Religions of Man* (Harper & Row) and Paul Johnson's *A History of Christianity* (Atheneum). Use the reports as the basis for a class discussion.

*3. **Thinking About History: Identifying Bias (Basic)** Have students reread "Building History Study Skills" on page 192. Then have them complete Critical Thinking Worksheet 19 in the TEACHER'S RESOURCEBANK™.

ENRICHMENT ACTIVITIES

1. **Making Connections (Basic)** The far-flung nature of the spice trade can be dramatized on a map of the world. Have students glue actual spices to the areas of the world from which they come. Students will need to consult encyclopedias to discover the origin of various spices: for example, cloves from Tanzania or paprika from the Balkans.
2. **Group Project (Average/Group)** A group of students might prepare a presentation on Constantinople. Some students should draw maps of the city and its favorable location. They might draw sketches of Hagia Sophia and a chronological chart of historical events in the city. Have students put their sketches and charts on the bulletin board. One member of the group could prepare an oral report to give to the class. Sources include "Constantine's City" in Philip Sherrard's *Byzantium* (Time-Life); David Jacobs's *Constantinople and the Golden Horn* (American Heritage); John Freely's *Blue Guide Istanbul*, 2d. ed. (W.W. Norton); and *The Birth of Western Civilization* (McGraw-Hill), edited by Michael Grant.
3. **Understanding Church Architecture (Challenging)** Have students research and write a report on the architecture of Christian churches. Tell them that during the period of Roman persecution, Christians met in small places of worship. After Christianity became the official religion, it needed special places of worship. The old temples were small and civic services or processions usually took place outside. The Christians needed room inside a building to hold the worshipers. The students' reports should answer the question of how Christians met this need. They might begin with the *basilicas*—rectangular assembly halls or courts—that developed in Byzantium. Students should explain terms like *apse, choir, nave,* and *basilica* that became permanent features of Christian architecture. Some students might wish to present slides or photographs showing early architecture. Others might wish to make a scale model of a church.

DAILY QUIZ

To assess understanding of Section 1, give the class the following quiz. (Each item is worth 10 points.)

1. (T or F) By the early 500s, the Roman Empire in the West had fallen to barbarian invasions, while the empire in the East had developed enough stability to start a great political, economic, intellectual, and artistic revival. *(T)*
2. The leader of the Eastern Roman Empire, who regained many territories of the old empire in the Mediterranean, was ________. *(Justinian)*
3. Which of these did *not* threaten the Byzantine Empire? Persians, Muslims, Russians, Turks *(Russians)*
4. This empress helped improve the status of women in the Byzantine Empire and encouraged her husband to stay in Constantinople and fight the Nika Rebellion. *(Theodora)*
5. (T or F) The Byzantine emperors relied on a skilled bureaucracy, an excellent navy, and control of the trade routes to keep their power. *(T)*
6. The dispute over the use of holy pictures of Jesus, the Virgin Mary, and the saints, which rocked the Byzantine church in the 700s and 800s, was called the ________ ________. *(iconoclastic controversy)*

7. Which Byzantine missionary developed an alphabet during the 800s because the Slavs had no written language? *(Cyril)*
8. Byzantine art glorified religion with pictures and designs formed by inlaid pieces of stone, glass, or enamel called ________. *(mosaics)*
9. What was very likely the greatest Byzantine contribution to civilization? *(preservation of Roman Law)*
10. In 1453 the city of Constantinople fell to what people? *(Ottoman Turks)*

SUGGESTED ASSIGNMENTS

1. **Skill Worksheet (Basic)** Have students complete Skill Worksheet 8 in the TEACHER'S RESOURCEBANK™.
2. **Geography Application Sheet (Basic)** Have students complete "Geography Application Sheet: Constantinople—Crossroads of Europe and Asia," in the TEACHER'S RESOURCEBANK™.
3. **Profile Worksheet(Average/Group)** Have students complete Profile Worksheet 8 in the TEACHER'S RESOURCEBANK™.
4. **Critical Thinking Worksheet (Average/Group)** Have students complete Critical Thinking Worksheet 18 in the TEACHER'S RESOURCEBANK™.
5. **Critical Thinking Worksheet (Basic)** Have students complete Critical Thinking Worksheet 19 in the TEACHER'S RESOURCEBANK™.

Section (pages 196–199)

2 Kievan Rus Developed Strong Ties with the Byzantine Empire

Eastern Europe was invaded by Vikings in the 800s. The Vikings dominated the trade routes and built several cities, the strongest of which was Kiev. Agriculture and trade were the basis of the Kievan economy. Vladimir I of Kiev and his people converted to Byzantine Christianity in the 900s, and the Kievan church became part of the Eastern Orthodox church when Christendom split in 1054.

SUGGESTED TEACHING STRATEGIES

1. **Preteaching Vocabulary (Basic)** You may wish to preteach the following important vocabulary terms: steppe, boyar (*page 196*); metropolitan, taiga (*page 198*). Ask students how the steppe differs from taiga.
2. **Word Scramble (Basic)** Reproduce the following scrambled words and their clues and distribute copies to the class.

a. tpespe	Vast grassy plain
b. lrua	Mountain range separating Europe and Asia
c. asureia	Name for the land mass that contains the continents of Europe and Asia
d. pniered	River on which Kiev is situated
e. atgai	Forest zone with abundant rainfall and cold temperatures
f. naeapsts	Largest social class in Kievan Rus
g. acusucsa	Mountain range in southern Europe

(Answers: a. steppe; b. Ural; c. Eurasia; d. Dnieper; e. taiga; f. peasants; g. Caucasus)

ENRICHMENT ACTIVITIES

1. **Art Project (Average/Group)** Interested students may show pictures or slides of religious art that illustrate Byzantine influence on later Russian art and architecture. Sources include Robert Wallace's *The Rise of Russia* (Time-Life) and Ian Grey's *History of Russia* (American Heritage).
2. **Writing a Report (Challenging)** Encourage students to do research on the Viking traders in eastern Europe and Kievan Rus. They should learn what products the Vikings bought and sold, where they came from and where they traded, what conditions they met on their voyages, and how some of them came to be permanent settlers in Kievan Rus. Students might wish to write their reports in a diary form. For example, they could briefly describe a Viking trader's daily experiences on a commercial trip down the Volga River. Have students read their reports to the class.

DAILY QUIZ

To assess understanding of Section 2, give the class the following quiz. (Each item is worth 10 points.)

1. (T or F) The steppe is an evergreen forest that stretches across eastern Europe and central Asia. *(F)*
2. The great plain of Eurasia is bordered by three large mountain ranges. Name two. *(Carpathians in west, Caucasus in south, Urals in east)*
3. (T or F) The city of Novgorod prospered because of its key location on the Dnieper River, providing access to the Black Sea and Constantinople. *(F)*
4. (T or F) The culture of Kievan Rus was dominated by religious themes in literature and art. *(T)*
5. List three goods the Kievan Rus sold to the Byzantines. *(agricultural goods, wood, iron, salt, slaves)*
6. List three goods the Kievan Rus received from the Byzantine Empire. *(wine, silk, religious art objects, spices, precious stones, steel blades, horses)*
7. Nobles in Kievan Rus were known as ________. *(boyars)*
8. Yaroslav the Wise issued the *Pravda Russkaia,* which was Rus's first ________ ________. *(law code)*
9. The veche was a ________ meeting of all heads of households with the local prince in the cities of Kievan Rus. *(town)*
10. What religion did Vladimir embrace in 988 as the official religion of Kievan Rus? *(Byzantine or Orthodox Christianity)*

SUGGESTED ASSIGNMENTS

1. **Understanding Geography (Basic)** Have students use an outline map of eastern Europe and central Asia to locate the following items: Ural Mountains, Carpathian Mountains, Caucasus

Mountains, Volga River, Don River, Vistula River, Dnieper River, Kiev, Novgorod, Moscow, Constantinople, Black Sea, Baltic Sea. On this map have them next locate by arrows the route of the Viking traders and Mongol invaders. Then discuss the importance of geography in the movement of peoples. Indicate to students that the lack of mountains and the presence of the steppe allowed invasions to take place easily down to the present day.

2. **Comparing Past and Present (Average/Group)** Have interested students study the history of Kiev at its height in the 1000s and read about its history since that time. Then have them write a report on how Kiev fares today — its population, economic activities, and cultural and political life as capital of the Ukrainian S.S.R. Use the students' reports as the basis for a class discussion comparing cities with a great past and a less glorious present (Constantinople, Berlin, Vienna, Calcutta, Venice).

Section 3 (pages 199–201)

The Mongols Established a Vast Empire in Eurasia

Kievan Rus declined and fell to the Mongols in the 1200s. Unfriendly neighbors and religious conflicts isolated Eastern Slavs from western Europe. The Mongols increased internal trade, built roads, and improved methods of taxation and communication. During this period the Russian Orthodox church became increasingly independent of Constantinople. In 1480 Ivan III refused to pay further tribute to the Mongols and became the first ruler of an independent state called Russia.

SUGGESTED TEACHING STRATEGIES

1. **Preteaching Vocabulary (Basic)** You may wish to preteach the following important vocabulary term: czar (*page 200*). Point out that *czar* is a translation of *caesar*.
2. **Debating the Issues (Average/Group)** Select a group of students to debate the following proposition: Mongol rule was good for the Kievan Rus. The debate should include questions and comments from the audience. Sources for further research include Sidney Harcave's *Russia: A History* (Lippincott); G. Vernadsky's *The Mongols and the Russians* (Yale University Press); Ian Grey's *History of Russia* (American Heritage); and John Chambers's *The Devil's Horsemen* (Atheneum).

ENRICHMENT ACTIVITY

Writing Assignment (Basic) Have students write a short description of the life of a Kievan peasant, member of the clergy, or a noble during the period of Mongol rule. Students may use the textbook and encyclopedias for background information. Call upon students to read their essays to the class.

DAILY QUIZ

To assess understanding of Section 3, give the class the following quiz. (Each item is worth 10 points.)

1. What Asiatic people conquered Kievan Rus in 1240? *(Mongols)*
2. How far west did the Mongols go? *(Hungary, Poland)*
3. (T or F) The Mongols tried to force Kievan Rus to adopt Mongol customs. *(F)*
4. (T or F) The Poles and Lithuanians were converted to Orthodox Christianity just like Kievan Rus. *(F)*
5. List the two obligations the peasants had to landlords. *(labor; payment of money or goods)*
6. Name three Mongol contributions to Kievan society. *(roads; improved methods of taxation and communication; Mongol words)*
7. During the period of Mongol rule, what institution expanded and became increasingly independent? *(Orthodox church)*
8. What people supported Moscow's rise to prominence because its rulers paid them taxes, or tribute? *(Mongols)*
9. What city became the "third Rome"? *(Moscow)*
10. (T or F) Ivan IV used secret police to control Russia. *(T)*

SUGGESTED ASSIGNMENTS

1. **Review Worksheet (Basic)** Have students complete Review Worksheet 8 in the TEACHER'S RESOURCEBANK™.
2. **Report (Challenging)** Have interested students do research on the life of Ivan IV, "the Terrible," and write a three-page essay on his life and reign. Ask students to read their essays to the class. Use the reports as the basis for a class discussion on the development of the autocracy in Russia. Ask students to discuss how Russia's past method of rule carried to the present century, for example dictatorships under Stalin and his successors. How do the reforms of Gorbachev fit into this tradition?

For suggested lesson plan, additional teaching strategies, enrichment activities, daily quizzes, and suggested assignments, see pages 185A–185D.

Introducing the Chapter
This chapter covers the changes in the East after the decline of the Roman Empire. To help students understand some of these changes and what influence they had, use the example of Russia. Have students make a chart with the following headings: *Vikings, Christian Missionaries,* and *Mongols.* Explain that these three groups greatly influenced the early development of the nation that later was called Russia. Before beginning the chart, have students look at the map on page 197 to locate the areas from which the three groups of people came. What routes of access were open to them? Was Russia easily accessible?

As students read the chapter, have them complete the chart by listing the influence of each of these groups on Russia's development.

Chapter Objectives
After studying Chapter 8, students will be able to:

1. Describe how the Byzantine Empire helped preserve Western civilization.
2. List Byzantine cultural developments.
3. Describe the geographical characteristics of eastern Europe and how they influenced the development of Kiev and Moscow.
4. Summarize the contributions of the Vikings and Slavs to Kievan Rus.

CHAPTER 8

The Byzantine Empire Preserved the Heritage of Rome

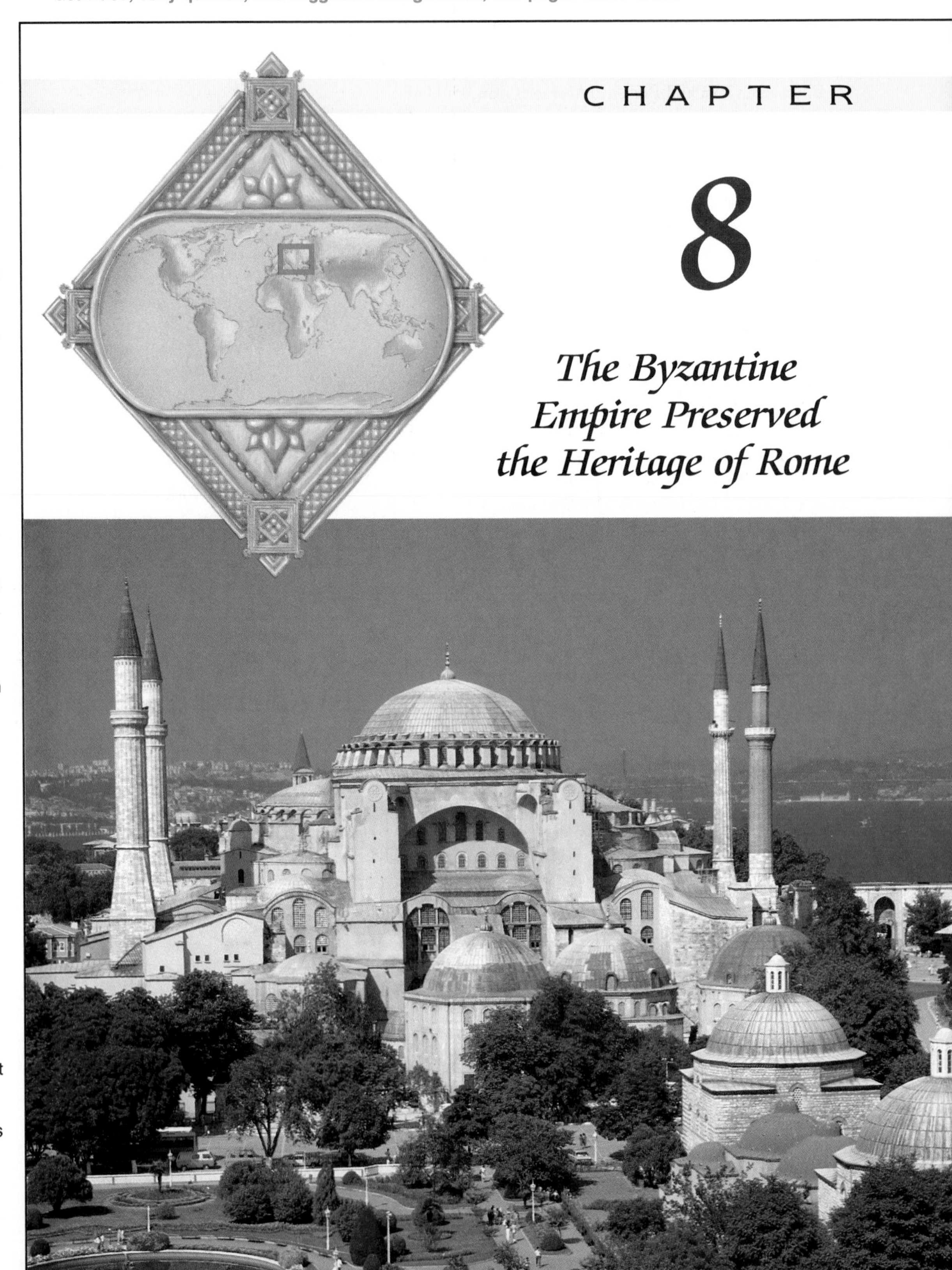

Constantinople's official name was New Rome, founded because emperors disliked Rome's Senate and republican traditions. Emperors also needed to be closer to the frontiers that needed their attention. The citizens of Constantinople were always called *Romaioi.*

1B, 3C, a1A, a4A, a4F

CHAPTER FOCUS

Place Eastern Europe, Asia Minor, and Russia

Time

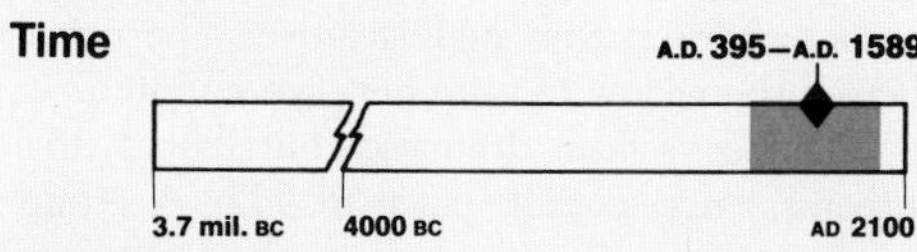

Significance

In the West the collapse of the Roman Empire resulted in fragmentation—the disappearance of strong governments and the division of land into isolated regions that were cut off from one another. However, the Roman Empire in the East maintained its traditions and kept out barbarian invaders. This new eastern empire took its name—the Byzantine Empire—from Byzantium, the ancient name for Constantinople. The empire lasted more than 1,000 years, from the formal split of the Roman Empire in 395 to the Turkish conquest of Constantinople in 1453. It created a distinct culture and a distinct branch of Christianity—the Byzantine church, later called the Eastern Orthodox church.

The Byzantines had the greatest influence upon Kievan Rus (KEE • ef • uhn ROOS), a land that eventually became known as Russia. As the Rus and other peoples of the territory struggled for political identity, they looked to the Byzantine Empire for religious and cultural inspiration. Although the Mongols plundered Kievan Rus in the 1200s, the Mongol influence was more political than cultural. As a result, the people of the area continued their Byzantine traditions.

Terms to Define

dowry	steppe
icon	boyar
iconoclast	metropolitan
heresy	taiga
mosaic	czar

People to Identify

Justinian	Methodius
Theodora	Vladimir I
Cyril	Ivan IV

Places to Locate

Constantinople	Kiev
Volga River	Lithuania

Questions to Guide Your Reading

1 How did the Byzantine Empire help preserve Western civilization?
2 How did the Byzantine Empire influence Kievan Rus?
3 How did Russia develop?

◀ *Hagia Sophia in Istanbul*

Amid the ruins of the Roman world, the magnificent city of Constantinople rose to become a great cultural and economic center. One historian noted the city's splendor.

> *"Around A.D. 1000 Christian Constantinople undoubtedly boasted over 500,000 inhabitants and may well have approximated 1,000,000. It was incomparably the largest city in Christendom, and, since the waning of the splendors of Baghdad, probably surpassed any other in the known world. . . .*
>
> *Strangers were lost in . . . eloquence when describing the magnificence of New Rome [Constantinople] and the impression which a visit to it produced upon them. Its denizens [residents] took this homage as a matter of course. To them their capital was not only 'The City guarded by God,' it was 'The City' —as if all other communities in the world were merely secondary towns."*

Constantinople, head of the Byzantine Empire, preserved the traditions of the Greco-Roman world for future generations.

1 The Byzantine Empire Helped Preserve Western Civilization

While barbarians plundered the Western Roman Empire in the 400s and 500s, the Byzantine Empire in the East thrived. Although surrounded by enemies, the Byzantine Empire maintained its independence for more than 1,000 years.

The Reign of Justinian

In the year 500, the Eastern Roman Empire included Greece and the northern Balkan Peninsula, Asia Minor, Syria, Palestine, Egypt, and Cyrenaica. Although Germanic tribes had attacked the eastern empire even before marching on the western empire, the East had withstood the attacks. By the early 500s, the Western Roman Empire had broken down into a group of Germanic tribal kingdoms (see map, page 188). The Eastern Roman Empire, on the other hand, had ousted the barbarians and was primed for a great political, economic, intellectual, and artistic revival.

5. Write a summary of the economy, social classes, government, and religion of Kievan Rus and Muscovy.
6. Describe the Mongol invasions of eastern Europe and how they affected social and political developments in Russia.
7. Outline the parallel rise of Moscow and the Russian Orthodox church.

SECTION 1

Focus/Motivation

Have students turn to the pictures of Hagia Sophia, built by Emperor Justinian, on pages 186 and 193. Then have them read the description of Hagia Sophia in the subsection "Architecture" on pages 193-94. Ask students what they can infer about the Byzantine Empire from this subsection. *(Answers will vary. Students might include: Religion was a major part of Byzantine life; the Byzantines were skilled architects; Byzantine art emphasized religion; the empire must have been wealthy to afford such an impressive structure.)* Then ask students why they think similar religious structures are infrequently built today. *(Answers might include the following: Governments do not usually provide funds for religious structures; church building is dependent upon less substantial private funding.)*

1A, 1B, 3C, a4A, a4B, a4C

- At the time of Justinian, the empire was Hellenistic. No Turks yet lived in Asia Minor and no Arabs lived in Egypt. The most dangerous enemies of the Byzantines were the Persians, who sacked Antioch in 540. Justinian's costly military campaigns to recover the West allowed the Persians to make encroachments in the East.

Presentation
Summarizing Ideas (Average/Group)
Have students develop in their notebooks a chart listing the political, military, and economic strengths of the Byzantine Empire. The following should be listed under *Political:* autocratic, highly centralized government; bureaucracy of trained officials; skillful diplomats. Under *Military:* good defenses; good intelligence system; good navy. Under *Economic:* wealth based on agriculture, manufacturing, and trade; Constantinople at crossroads of trade between Europe and Asia; government regulated manufacturing and trade to produce large tax revenues.

After the students complete this chart, encourage students to discuss how these strengths might be important in making a nation strong today.

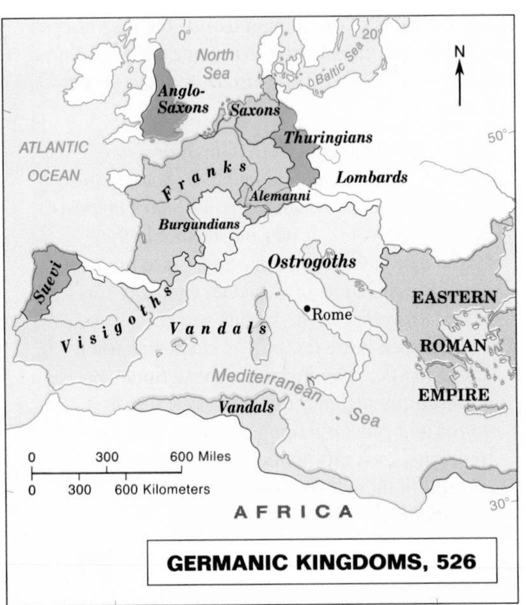

Learning from Maps *The Germanic invaders established kingdoms as far south as northern Africa. What group controlled northern Italy?* Ostrogoths

Emperor Justinian, who ruled from 527 to 565, led this revival and accomplished so much that the 37 years of his reign marked one of the most splendid periods in Byzantine history. Justinian's uncanny instinct for judging the abilities of others allowed him to choose exceptional people to help him rule the empire. Two wise choices were his wife, Theodora, and the commander-in-chief of his army, Belisarius (bel • uh • SAR • ee • uhs).

Theodora. The Byzantine Empire had several famous empresses, but the most extraordinary was Justinian's wife, Theodora. Theodora spent her early childhood with the circus, where her father trained bears. A pretty, witty, and intelligent girl, Theodora became an actress in her early teens. Soon she met and fell in love with Justinian. Although Byzantine law forbade marriage between high imperial officials and actresses, Justinian ignored the law and married Theodora in 523.

With Theodora's encouragement, Justinian changed Byzantine law to improve the status of women. Justinian decreed that a husband could not beat his wife and that a woman could sue for divorce if her husband mistreated her. Justinian changed the law prohibiting women from owning property. The new law allowed a woman to own property equal to the value of her **dowry,** the money or goods that she brought to her husband when the couple married. Furthermore, Justinian repealed an old law that forced a widow to surrender her children to a male relative. The new law allowed the widow to raise her own children.

Theodora's most dramatic contribution to her husband's success took place in 532. A group of senators, angry about high taxes, had organized a revolt known as the Nika Rebellion. As the leaders of the rebellion threatened to crown a new emperor, a cowering Justinian prepared to flee Constantinople. However, Theodora urged him to stay and fight. In a fierce battle, Justinian's troops hacked 30,000 rebels to death, ensuring that he would remain on the throne.

Belisarius. Justinian's appointment of Belisarius as commander-in-chief of the army proved as successful and unconventional as his choice of a wife. An officer of peasant stock who had little money, Belisarius had very little military experience. He was a friend of Theodora, however, and he had made a name for himself leading the troops that crushed the Nika Rebellion.

While the new Germanic kingdoms in the west quarreled among themselves, Justinian's armies, under the capable leadership of Belisarius, regained many territories in the Mediterranean region. As a result of these conquests, the Byzantine Empire reached its greatest territorial extent during Justinian's reign (see map, page 189). ●

The legacy of Justinian. After Justinian's death in 565, the empire suffered almost 50 years of civil wars, made worse by attacks from the outside. From the East came the Persians, whom Justinian's successors defeated in the late 500s. Meanwhile, an Asiatic group, the Avars, and a European people, the Slavs, invaded the Balkan Peninsula. The Lombards sacked Italy. By the early 600s, Germanic tribes had won back most of the territory that Justinian's armies had spent so much time conquering.

During the 600s the Byzantine Empire faced a new and highly energetic force—the armies of the Muslim Empire (see Chapter 9). The Muslims soon conquered Armenia, Syria, Palestine, and much of North Africa, including Egypt. After 650 the eastern empire consisted of little more than Asia Minor, the southern Balkan Peninsula, parts of Italy, and the nearby islands.

188

● Byzantine emperors began military reforms when barbarian cavalry proved superior in battle to the heavily armed legionaries. Byzantine power then stemmed from cavalry who wore steel caps and mail shirts, and carried swords, daggers, bows, and a lance. The emperors also hired mercenaries until the empire could no longer afford this luxury.

1A, 1B, 3C, a4B, a4C, a4H

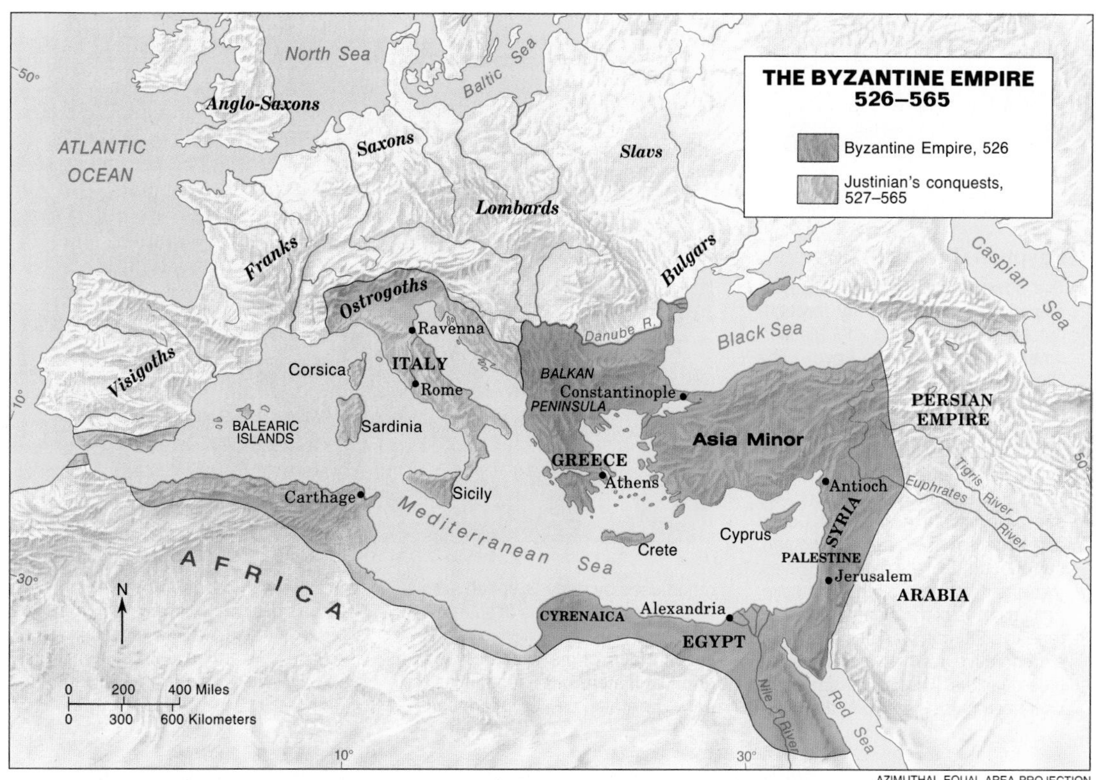

Learning from Maps *Justinian, perhaps the greatest of the Byzantine emperors, reunited most of the lands around the Mediterranean coast. What parts of the former Western Roman Empire did he reconquer?* **Italy, southern Spain, North Africa**

Strengths of the Empire

Several factors helped the Byzantine Empire survive for more than 1,000 years. It had political, military, and economic strength, and its people adapted skillfully to change.

Political strength. A highly centralized and autocratic government headed by an all-powerful emperor ruled the Byzantine Empire. Well-paid, efficient, skillful, and usually loyal officials carried out imperial commands and policies. Even during times of weak emperors or civil war, these officials made sure the empire ran smoothly.

The Byzantines practiced especially shrewd diplomacy. Their excellent intelligence service kept the emperor well informed of important foreign developments. They often bribed foreign officials to obtain information. To cement alliances Byzantine emperors often arranged marriages between Byzantine princesses and foreign princes. The Byzantines also routinely provoked one neighbor to attack another in order to prevent either one from attacking the empire. Today we use the term *byzantine* to describe tricky or devious policies.

Military strength. Byzantine rulers developed effective frontier, infantry, cavalry, and engineering corps to defend the empire. The government ● provided its soldiers with medical services and rewarded them with land grants. The military developed instruction manuals and established schools to teach leaders the latest strategies. It also replaced the bow and lance with the sword and javelin and designed a more protective armor.

During the 600s the Byzantines built a strong navy. Ships had battering rams, but the sailors' secret weapon was a flammable liquid called "Greek fire," which they hurled to set enemy ships ablaze. So carefully did the Byzantines guard their secret

189

1B, 1C, 1D, 3B, 3C, a1A

- The Byzantine gold coin, which Westerners called the *bezant,* was the standard coinage in much of the world far beyond Constantinople. Coins have been found in the Far East.
- Persians captured the silk trade, but silkworms were smuggled into Constantinople, where silk became a government monopoly.

History Through the Arts

WEAVING

Egyptian Christian Cloth

The power of the Byzantine Empire helped spread Christianity throughout the lands around the Mediterranean Sea, including Egypt. The Copts, as Egyptian Christians were called, combined aspects of Christian art that had developed in Italy and Byzantium with traditional Egyptian styles to form Coptic art.

In this ancient woven fabric, we see an excellent example of Coptic art. An elegant Byzantine woman, surrounded by a spiral of waves, gazes out from the cloth. This spiral design is one of the oldest in Mediterranean culture. It was being used as a decorative form long before the time of Jesus. The ducks that fill the circles on four sides typify the decoration used by early Egyptian artists, who portrayed all kinds of animal and plant life.

The face of the woman, stylized and two-dimensional, resembles the early portraits on Egyptian coffins and mummy cases. However, the woman's headdress, jewels, and robe look very much like the mosaic picture of a Byzantine empress in an early Christian church in Ravenna, Italy.

that even today no one knows its exact formula. The best guess is that Greek fire contained a combination of naphtha, sulphur, and saltpeter (potassium nitrate).

Economic strength. Because of its abundant agriculture, manufacturing, and trade, the East had always been the richest part of the Roman Empire. At the heart of the empire lay Constantinople, a city of grandeur with a population of 1 million inhabitants. Its advantage lay in its location. Situated on the border of Asia and Europe, the city overlooked the strategic Bosphorus, the narrow straits that linked the Black and Mediterranean seas (see map, page 191). Such a location allowed the Byzantines to control the vital trade routes linking Europe and Asia.

Merchandise from as far away as Scandinavia, China, and India poured into the markets of Constantinople. There and throughout the empire, the government regulated trade and manufacturing to produce large tax revenues. The emperor used the taxes to pay government officials and soldiers and to build great public buildings.

The Christian Church

Important figures in the early Christian Church included the patriarchs of Rome, Constantinople, Alexandria, Antioch, and Jerusalem. In time the pope and the church in Rome gained supreme authority in the West. However, the Byzantines did not recognize this authority. In the East the patriarch of Constantinople came to be the most important church leader.

The Byzantine faith provided a source of both weakness and strength for the Byzantine Empire. Because Christianity formed such a vital part of Byzantine life, the Byzantines argued bitterly and endlessly about minute details of ritual and doctrines concerning beliefs. Often, Byzantine leaders considered these arguments more important than broad matters of imperial policy, such as taxes or defense.

The most significant religious argument concerned holy pictures of Jesus, the Virgin Mary, and the saints, called **icons**, from *eikon,* the Greek word for "portrait." Many Byzantines revered icons,

190

1A, 1B, 3B, 3C, a1A, a4A, a4B, a4C, a4F

● The iconoclastic controversy led the popes to turn from the Byzantine emperors to the Franks, a rising power in the West.

which they kept in their homes and worshiped at church. Some Byzantines, however, were **iconoclasts,** who felt that the presence of icons constituted idol worship and should be suppressed.

The **iconoclastic controversy,** the argument between the supporters and the opponents of icons, rocked the empire for more than a century. In 730 Emperor Leo III outlawed the use of icons in an attempt to curb the power of the church and monasteries, which owned most of the icons. However, largely because people refused to give up their icons, the Byzantine emperors abandoned their ● efforts to suppress icon worship in 843. In the meantime the controversy had drastically affected the empire's relations with Europe.

Most people in western Europe, unlike those in the Byzantine Empire, could not read or write. Western clergy, therefore, considered visual images essential in teaching about Christianity. After

Learning from Pictures *This Byzantine wood carving depicts the Empress Irene, who ruled the Byzantine Empire between 780 and 802.*

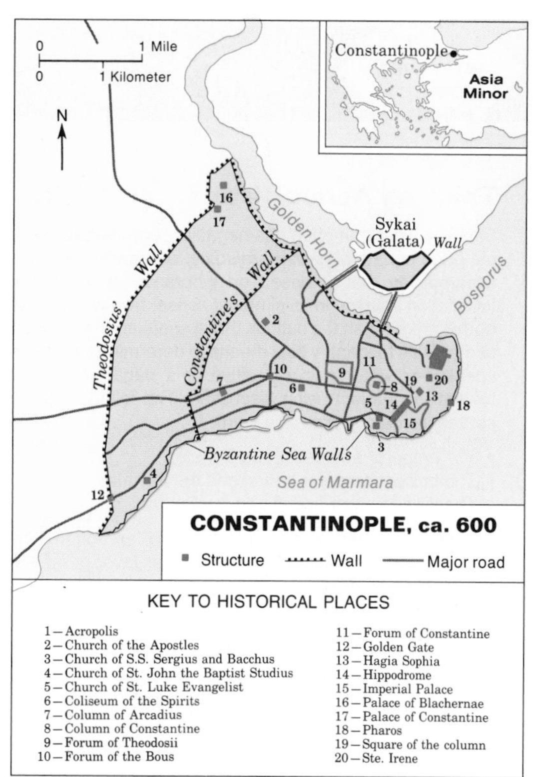

Learning from Maps *Constantinople's location on vital trade routes made it a great commercial center. What bodies of water protected the city?*
Bosporus, Sea of Marmara, Golden Horn

Emperor Leo III forbade the use of icons in the Byzantine Empire, the pope called a council of bishops. The council declared opposition to icons a **heresy,** or an opinion that conflicts with church doctrine, and excommunicated the iconoclasts. **Excommunication** entails barring a person from church membership and excluding the person from taking part in any church ceremonies, including baptism, marriage, and communion.

The declaration of iconoclasm as a heresy led to friction between the pope and the patriarch of Constantinople. The friction grew steadily worse over the years until finally the Christian Church split in 1054. In the West it became known as the Roman Catholic church, with the pope as its head. In the East it became known as the Eastern Orthodox church, with the patriarch of Constantinople as its head. This division between Roman Catholic and Eastern Orthodox Christendom still exists.

191

1B, 3C, a1A, a4A, a4E, a4G, a4I, a4J

READ
WRITE
INTERPRET
CONNECT
THINK

BUILDING HISTORY STUDY SKILLS

Thinking About History: Identifying Bias

Bias is a word that often has negative connotations. People often equate bias with *prejudice,* a negative (or positive) opinion that is based on ignorance or is without foundation in truth. In its simplest sense, however, bias is nothing more than the outlook that a speaker or writer presents. Thus to identify bias means to determine whether a speaker or writer has a positive or a negative attitude toward the subject being discussed. The following three sentences demonstrate the point.

- The emperor addressed the Senate.
- The brilliant emperor addressed the Senate.
- The silly emperor addressed the Senate.

The first statement is a simple report of an action. The statement is not biased; it shows neither favor nor disfavor. In the second statement, the word *brilliant* conveys a positive feeling toward the emperor. In the third statement, the word *silly* creates a negative feeling.

Being able to identify bias in writing and in speeches is an important skill to have, not only as you study history, but also as you read newspapers and magazines or watch newscasts on television. It helps you decide whether you are reading a factual report or one that shows the author's biased opinion.

How to Identify Bias

To identify bias, follow these steps.

1. Look for clues. Check for words or phrases that convey a positive or negative attitude.
2. Assess the evidence. Decide for yourself whether you agree or disagree with the bias on the basis of the evidence presented.

Developing the Skill

Procopius, an official in Constantinople, wrote *The Secret History* describing the rule of Justinian and Theodora. Read the excerpt below in order to identify bias.

> "They were a pair of blood-thirsty demons. . . . For they plotted together to find the easiest and the swiftest means of destroying all races of men and all their works, assumed human shape, became man-demons, and in this way convulsed the whole world. . . . He never even gave a hint of anger or irritation to show how he felt towards those who had offended him; but with a friendly expression on his face and without raising an eyebrow, in a gentle voice he would order tens of thousands of quite innocent persons to be put to death, cities to be razed to the ground, and all their possessions confiscated for the Treasury. . . . His ambition being to force everybody into one form of Christian belief he wantonly destroyed everyone who would not conform, and that while keeping up a pretense of piety. For he did not regard it as murder, so long as those who died did not happen to share his beliefs."

The excerpt includes many words that condemn Justinian and Theodora. For example, *bloodthirsty demons* and *man-demons* give the impression that they were truly evil people.

Practicing the skill. Read an article in your local newspaper and determine whether the article shows bias.

To apply this skill, see Applying History Study Skills on page 203.

Empress Theodora

Emperor Justinian I

192

Answers will vary. Students might speculate that if the Germanic tribes had destroyed both the Byzantine and Western Roman empire, the learning of classical times might have been lost forever.

Byzantine Culture

The Byzantine Empire performed a great service for civilization. Although its scholars produced little that was original, they did preserve and pass on the classical learning of Greece, Rome, and the Orient. For more than 1,000 years, while western Europe struggled to develop a new way of life, Constantinople served as the center of a brilliant civilization.

Not only did the Byzantines preserve the culture of the Mediterranean world, they also carried it beyond the borders of their empire. Cyril (SIR • uhl) and Methodius (muh • THOH • dee • uhs), two brothers who lived in the 800s, illustrate the role of the Byzantines in this cultural diffusion. As missionaries the brothers worked to convert the Slavs of central and eastern Europe to Christianity. Cyril wanted to teach the Slavs to read the Bible, but the Slavs had no written language. So Cyril created an alphabet that evolved into the Cyrillic (suh • RIL • ik) alphabet. Today many Slavic peoples of central and eastern Europe, including the Russians, still use the Cyrillic alphabet or one derived from it.

Cyril and Methodius converted many Slavs to Christianity. Descendants of these converts still follow the Eastern Orthodox faith.

Art. Byzantine art glorified religion. Murals covered the walls and ceilings of churches. Floors, walls, and arches glistened with colored **mosaics**—pictures or designs formed by inlaid pieces of stone, glass, or enamel. Artists used both painting and mosaics to create icons. The location of a particular person's image in the church indicated that person's importance to church doctrine. For example, an image of Jesus always occupied the dome of the church.

The subjects of Byzantine art, whether angels, saints, or martyrs, appeared stiff and artificial. The calm, meditative faces resembled Buddhist art in their purpose—to inspire reverence and to emphasize the importance of renouncing the pleasures of this life to prepare for the afterlife.

Architecture. Architecture, especially religious architecture, was the greatest form of Byzantine art. The finest Byzantine building ever built—indeed, one of the architectural masterpieces of the world—is the church of Hagia Sophia (meaning "holy wisdom") in Constantinople.

Justinian ordered the construction of Hagia Sophia in 532. A huge building in the form of a cross, the church measures 240 feet (73 meters) wide by 270 feet (82 meters) long. The interior once glittered with breathtaking decorations that reflected the sunlight streaming through lofty windows. Murals, mosaics, stone carvings, and metalwork covered every surface. Insets of ivory, silver, and jewels adorned the pulpit. The patriarch's throne was solid silver.

A huge dome, 165 feet (50 meters) high, dominates the cathedral. Resting on massive columns instead of walls, the dome illustrates the talent of Byzantine architects, who first solved the difficult problem of placing a round dome over a rectangular building.

What If?

The Byzantine Empire

The Byzantine Empire helped preserve the Greco-Roman heritage of the ancient world. How do you think the course of world history would have changed if the Germanic tribes had toppled the Byzantine Empire at the same time they plundered the imperial city of Rome?

Learning from Pictures *Today the Turkish government maintains the church of Hagia Sophia as a museum. What art covered the walls and ceilings of Byzantine churches?* **religious murals**

1B, 3C, a1A, a1B, a4A, a4F, a4G, a4H, a4L

Two major losses occurred in 1071: the Normans (descendants of Vikings) drove the Byzantines from southern Italy, and the Seljuk Turks defeated them at the Battle of Manzikert in Armenia. The Turks thereafter were a constant threat in Asia Minor.

SECTION 1

Closure

Ask students to list the accomplishments of the Byzantine Empire. Ask: How was it able to survive 1,000 years longer than its counterpart, the Western Roman Empire? *(political, military, and economic strengths)*

Review Answers

1. ***dowry:*** money or goods a wife brings to a marriage; ***icon:*** picture of religious figures; ***iconoclast:*** believed that presence of icons was heretical idol worship; ***iconoclastic controversy:*** argument between supporters and opponents of icons; ***heresy:*** opinion conflicting with church doctrine; ***excommunication:*** expelling a person from the church; ***mosaic:*** picture or design formed by inlaid pieces of glass, stone, or enamel
2. ***Justinian:*** Byzantine emperor during 500s who revived culture and reconquered much of the old Roman Empire; ***Greek fire:*** flammable liquid used by Byzantines to set enemy ships on fire; ***Slavs:*** Asiatic people who migrated north of the Black Sea; ***Hagia Sophia:*** beautiful Byzantine cathedral built by Justinian in Constantinople
3. ***Constantinople:*** capital of Byzantine Empire, located between Black and Aegean seas
4. (a) Justinian conquered most of the western rim of

When Hagia Sophia was completed in 537, one Byzantine writer called it a church "the like of which had never been since Adam, nor ever will be." And the great Byzantine historian Procopius (pruh • KOH • pee • uhs) described his feelings after first entering the church.

> "The church . . . is distinguished by indescribable beauty, for it excels both in its size and in the harmony of its proportion. . . . It is singularly full of light and sunshine; you would declare that the place is not lighted by the sun from without, but that the rays are produced within itself, such an abundance of light is poured into this church. . . .
>
> The entire ceiling is covered with pure gold, which adds glory to its beauty, though the rays of light reflected upon the gold from the marble surpass it in beauty. . . . Who could tell of the beauty of the columns and marbles with which the church is adorned? One would think that one had come upon a meadow full of flowers in bloom: who would not admire the purple tints of some and the green of others, the glowing red and glittering white . . . ? Whoever enters there to worship perceives at once that it is not by any human strength or skill, but by the favour of God that this work has been perfected; his mind rises sublime to commune with God, feeling that He cannot be far off, but must especially love to dwell in the place which He has chosen."

Justinian himself solemnly consecrated the church. As he first entered Hagia Sophia, he exclaimed, "O Solomon, I have outdone thee!" He was referring to King Solomon of Israel, who built a magnificent temple in Jerusalem. The splendor of Solomon's temple is described in the Bible.

The Preservation of Roman Law

Probably the greatest Byzantine contribution to civilization was the preservation of Roman law. Early in his reign, Justinian ordered his scholars to collect and organize all Roman law. The entire collection is known as the *Corpus Juris Civilis* (Latin for "Body of Civil Law"). It is also called Justinian's Code and includes four parts—the *Code*, the *Digest*, the *Institutes*, and the *Novels*.

The *Code* was a collection of Roman laws, omitting repetitions, inconsistencies, and statutes dealing with Roman religion. The *Digest* consisted of a summary of the writings of the great Roman legal experts, organized alphabetically by ideas. The *Institutes* was a textbook on the basic principles of Roman law. Justinian's own laws were included in both the *Institutes* and the *Novels*. In western Europe Roman law was studied chiefly from the *Digest* and *Institutes*. Justinian's Code forms the basis of many modern European legal systems.

Decline of the Empire

In the 1000s the Seljuk Turks, originally a nomadic people from central Asia, captured most of Asia Minor. This vital area included the Byzantine Empire's "breadbasket" and the source of soldiers for its army. When the Turks prepared to attack Constantinople, the Byzantine emperor appealed to the West for help. Western Europeans responded in 1096 and 1097 with the First Crusade, recapturing western Asia Minor for the Byzantines (see Chapter 11). During the Fourth Crusade in 1204, however, the crusaders attacked the Byzantine Empire and captured Constantinople.

After 50 years of Western rule, the Byzantines recaptured the city and reorganized the empire. Although the empire continued to exist for almost 200 years, it never regained its former strength. In the 1400s a new Asiatic people, the Ottoman Turks, rose to power in the region. When they captured Constantinople in 1453, the Byzantine Empire finally came to an end.

SECTION 1 REVIEW

1. **Define** dowry, icon, iconoclast, iconoclastic controversy, heresy, excommunication, mosaic
2. **Identify** Justinian, Greek fire, Slavs, Hagia Sophia
3. **Locate** Constantinople
4. **Analyzing Maps** **(a)** Using the map on page 189, describe the area of the Roman Empire in the west that Justinian had conquered by 565. **(b)** What peoples were affected by these conquests?
5. **Understanding Ideas** What factors enabled the Byzantine Empire to survive as long as it did?
6. **Evaluating Ideas** What did Cyril and Methodius contribute to the civilization of central and eastern Europe?

1B, 1D, a1B

CONNECTIONS: THEN AND NOW

Spices

Do you realize that when you have a bowl of chili you are eating food seasoned with the same kinds of spices that the Incas in Peru used 2,000 years ago? Whether you eat at home or in a restaurant (top right), at almost every meal, you are enjoying the taste of a spice—ginger in ginger ale or gingerbread, oregano in spaghetti sauce, anise in licorice, and mint in peppermints.

More than 800 years ago, the Aztecs in Mexico ground hot chili peppers and mixed them with other spices to make chili powder. Today hot peppers are used throughout the world. People in tropical countries believe that hot food stimulates the liver and promotes good health.

Black and white pepper can give us almost the same zing found in hot chilis. The black peppercorn is the whole berry, which is picked while it is green and set out to dry. White pepper is made from the core of the ripe berry. Pepper was originally grown on the western coast of India and was brought to Europe by traders who often passed through the markets of Constantinople on their journey.

When barbarians pillaged Rome in 410, the ransom they demanded included pepper as well as gold and silver. Pepper was later used as money, and dock workers had to have their pockets sewn shut so they would not steal it from the ships they were unloading.

In the 1400s spices from the East were in great demand in Europe. Explorers began to search for new and faster routes to bring pepper and other spices from India to Europe. Columbus hoped to find such a route to India when he sailed west and landed at Santo Domingo.

As trade has become international, so has the taste for foreign dishes and flavors. Today, spices are sold all over the world, as in these markets in the Middle East (center and bottom right).

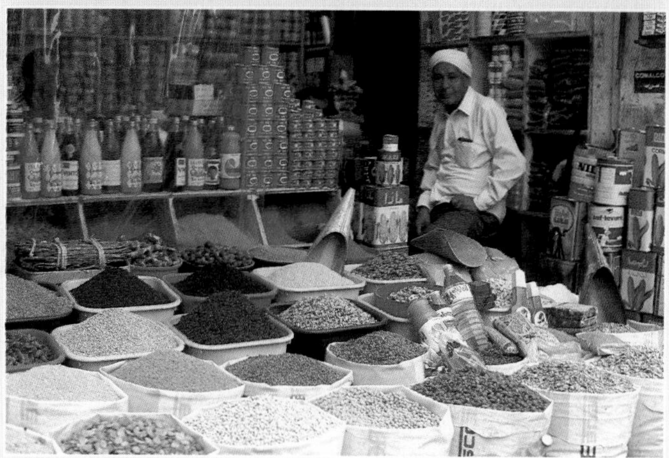

the Mediterranean, including North Africa, Spain, Italy, Corsica, Sardinia, and Sicily.
(b) Justinian penetrated Lombard, Avar, Frankish, and Visigoth territories.
5. A highly centralized government, skillful bureaucracy, and effective military enabled the Byzantine Empire to withstand foreign invasions.
6. Cyril and Methodius converted the Slavs to Christianity and developed the Cyrillic alphabet to give the Slavs a written language.

SECTION 2

Focus/Motivation
Have students turn to the map on page 197; then ask the following questions: What geographic features of eastern Europe and Central Asia are most outstanding? *(Students should note the general flatness of the terrain; the abundance of rivers; the higher mountain ranges on the east, west, and south; and the fact that the region of European Russia is almost landlocked.)* How might these features have influenced the development of Kievan Rus? *(Answers will vary. Students should include the following: Much of Kievan Rus is a flat plain that makes it easy to invade; the river system provides arteries for trade and transportation; most of the land outside the Arctic region is suitable for farming; European Russia is almost landlocked, encouraging the search for warm-water ports.)*

Presentation
Organizing Ideas (Average/Group)
Write the following list of events in the history of Kievan Rus on the chalkboard or an overhead projector. Then have students copy the list in their notebooks and write *1* before the event that took place first, *2* before the event that took place second, and so on.

(4) Rurik ruler of Novgorod

2 Kievan Rus Developed Strong Ties with the Byzantine Empire

During the early days of the Byzantine Empire, the Slavs who lived north of the Black Sea began to trade with Constantinople. The Byzantines greatly influenced the political and social lives of these Slavs.

The Physical Setting

A vast, grassy, almost treeless plain called the **steppe** stretches across eastern Europe and central Asia. It extends from the Arctic Ocean and the Baltic Sea south to the Black and Caspian seas, and from the Carpathian (kahr • PAY • thee • uhn) Mountains in Europe east to Manchuria in eastern Asia. Only the Ural (YOOR • uhl) Mountains, which run north and south and separate the continents of Europe and Asia, break the plain. Because the two continents form a single great landmass, they are sometimes called Eurasia.

The European part of the steppe is generally known as eastern Europe. Three mountain ranges —the Carpathians in the west, the Urals in the east, and the Caucasus (KAW • kuh • suhs) in the south—border the region (see map, page 197). Black, fertile soil makes the grassy steppe ideal for farming, especially in the area now known as the Ukraine.

A number of large rivers crisscross the steppe and provide a network of transportation within the region. The Dvina (duh • vee • NAH) and the Vistula (VISH • chuh • luh) rivers flow directly into the Baltic Sea. The Dniester (NEES • tuhr), the Dnieper (NEE • puhr), and the Don rivers empty into the Black Sea. The Volga and Ural rivers, because they flow into the landlocked Caspian Sea, are much less useful for trade than the other rivers of the steppe.

Slavic and Viking Influences

People have lived in the southern part of eastern Europe since Neolithic times. According to Herodotus, Greek merchants traded with the peoples north of the Black Sea. Later, Asian barbarians invaded the region. Beginning in the A.D. 200s, Slavs settled much of eastern Europe. Because the Slavs were peaceful and had only a very loose political organization, other invading peoples, including the Huns, Avars, and Magyars, often conquered them and made them pay tribute.

During the 800s Vikings from Scandinavia swept into eastern Europe. However, they came more as traders than as conquerors. Each fall they sailed up the rivers from the Baltic Sea and from Lake Ladoga (see map, page 197). When winter came, they loaded their ships on large sleds and hauled them across the snow to one of the rivers that flowed into the Black Sea. When the ice melted in the spring, they sailed south to trade in the Black Sea region. After trading their goods, they retraced their route to their Scandinavian homeland.

Kievan Rus

Several cities sprang up along the Viking trade routes. Two such cities were Novgorod (Russian for "new fort"), south of Lake Ladoga, and Kiev, on the Dnieper River. Kiev prospered because of its strategic location astride the rich trade route that extended from Constantinople to the Baltic Sea (see map, page 197).

According to legend, in the 860s the people of Novgorod asked Rurik, a Viking military leader, to help defend their city. Rurik and his successors became rulers of Novgorod and other principalities, including Kiev. The Slavs called both the Vikings and the area they controlled Rus. The word *Russia* is probably derived from this name.

Kiev grew to be the most important principality in Rus. The city of Kiev served as the capital of Rus from about 882 to 1169. Although the rulers of individual principalities paid tribute to the prince in Kiev in exchange for military protection, the degree of their loyalty varied, depending on the Kievan prince's power. Many of the smaller towns remained semi-independent.

Government

The prince of each of the cities of Kievan Rus at times ruled with the advice of a council of **boyars,** or nobles. Another important institution widely used in both Kiev and Novgorod was the *veche,* or town meeting. Here, at the request of the prince, the heads of all of the households met in the public

(2) Invasion by Huns, Avars, and Magyars
(3) Viking traders in Russia
(6) Kiev reached greatest power under Yaroslav the Wise
(5) Kievan Rus converted to Orthodox Christianity
(1) Slavs settled Eastern Europe

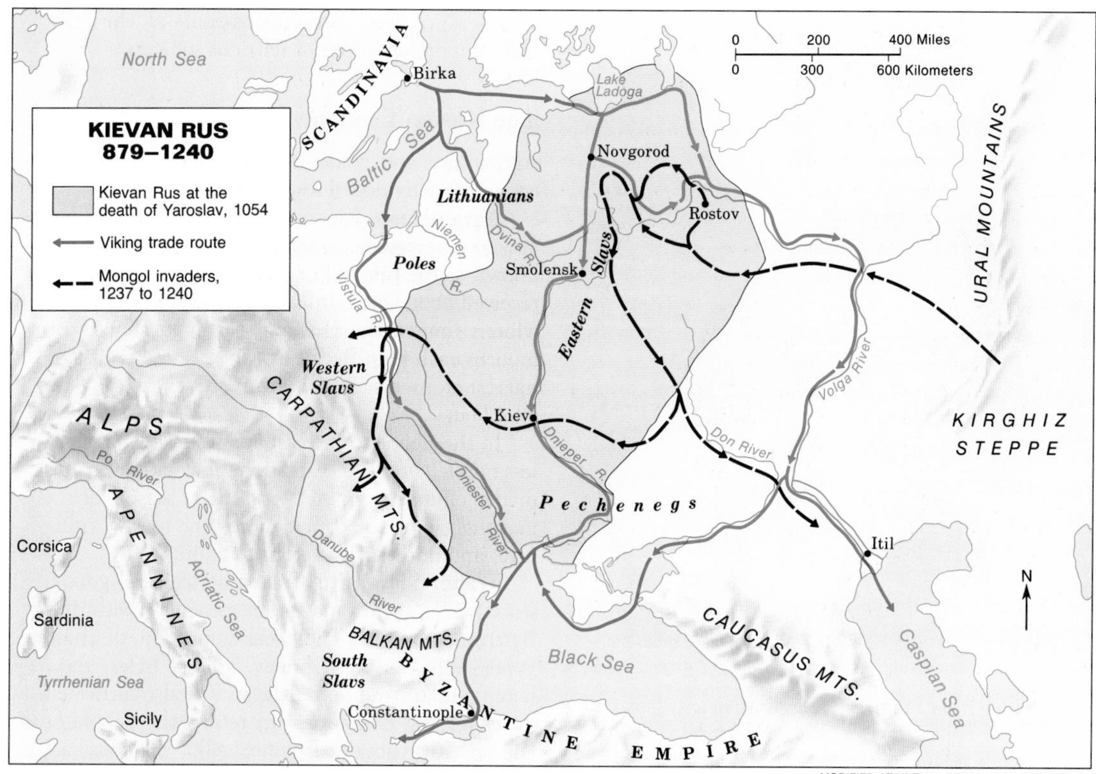

Learning from Maps *Kievan Rus controlled semi-independent principalities. What geographic feature lies south of the Ural Mountains?* Kirghiz steppe

marketplace. They considered such matters as calls to war, disputes between princes, and special emergency laws proposed by the prince.

Kievan Rus's greatest period came during the reign of Yaroslav I, called Yaroslav the Wise, who ruled from 1019 to 1054. Yaroslav's domain included about 7 million people. He issued Rus's first law code, the *Pravda Russkaia,* which remained in force in parts of the region until 1550.

Religion

In the 980s Vladimir I of Kiev invited missionaries from several faiths to address his boyar council and offer reasons why his people should convert to their religion. The prince rejected Islam because it prohibited the drinking of wine (see Chapter 9). He rejected Judaism because the Romans had expelled the Jews from Palestine in 135, leading Vladimir to believe that the Jews' god lacked political power.

Christian services in Germany failed to impress Vladimir's envoys, but those who went to Constantinople and attended services in Hagia Sophia reported the following:

> "We know not whether we were in heaven or on earth. For on earth there is no such splendor or such beauty, and we are at a loss how to describe it. We only know that God dwells there among men. . . . Every man, after tasting something sweet, is afterward unwilling to accept that which is bitter, and therefore we cannot any longer remain pagans."

Influenced by the reports of his envoys and by his desire to marry Anna, the Byzantine emperor's sister, Vladimir converted to Christianity in 988. He immediately ordered the baptism of Kievans and the destruction of pagan statues. Although many Kievans continued to worship the spirits of their

197

1B, 1D, 3C, a1A, a1B

SECTION 2

Closure

Ask students to explain why the Kievan ruler, Vladimir I, rejected Islam, Judaism, and Western Christianity. *(Islam prohibited the drinking of wine; the Jews' god lacked political clout, allowing the Romans to expel the Jews from Palestine; Western services did not impress Vladimir's envoys.)* Why did he accept Byzantine Christianity? *(He wanted to marry the Byzantine emperor's sister Anna, and Byzantine ceremonies impressed Kievan envoys.)*

Review Answers

1. ***steppe:*** vast, treeless plain in Eurasia; ***boyar:*** noble of Kievan Rus; ***metropolitan:*** a chief bishop of the Orthodox church; ***taiga:*** forest region of northern Russia
2. ***Vikings:*** Scandinavian traders and raiders who journeyed to Russia; some stayed to rule city-states; ***Rurik:*** Viking military leader and legendary first king of the Rus; ***Yaroslav the Wise:*** Kievan Rus ruler of 1000s who codified law; ***Pravda Russkaia:*** Russia's first law code
3. ***Arctic Ocean:*** body of water bordering Russia on north; ***Baltic Sea:*** western body of water separating Russia from Sweden; ***Black Sea:*** body of water bordering Asia Minor, eastern Europe, and Russia; ***Caspian Sea:*** landlocked body of water east of Black Sea; ***Ural Mountains:*** mountains

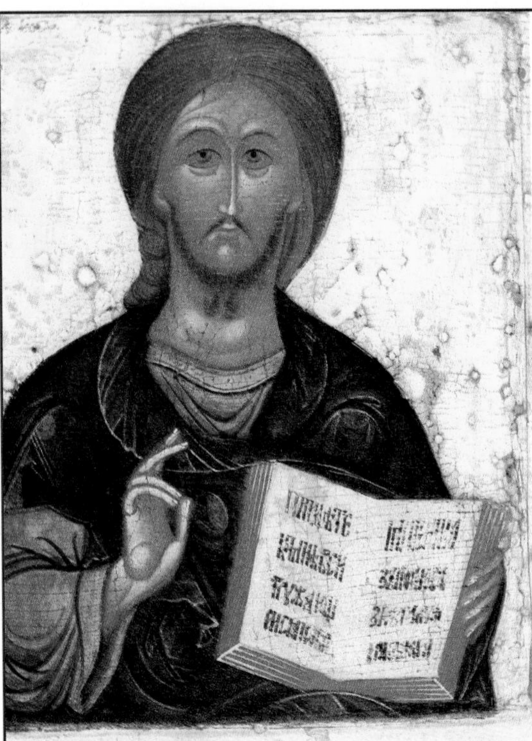

Learning from Pictures *This Russian icon shows Christ the Pantocrator, or almighty ruler, his right hand raised in a gesture of benediction.*

ancestors and ancient gods of nature, the Byzantine church became increasingly important as a spiritual force. When the Christian Church split in 1054, the Kievan church became a part of the Eastern Orthodox church; the patriarch of Constantinople chose the chief bishop, or **metropolitan,** of the Kievan church. New monasteries, which soon became great centers for social services, education, and artistic expression, further strengthened the church.

Religious feelings and subjects dominated Kievan culture in this period. Although authors wrote epic poems and historical chronicles about wars and the personal tragedies associated with war, religious hymns and sermons constituted the bulk of Kievan literature. Icon painting became the dominant Kievan art form. However, artists made no attempt to show figures as three-dimensional. The Kievans believed that the second of the Ten Commandments, "You shall not make a carved image for yourself," prohibited any art resembling sculpture. Thus they chose mosaics, frescoes, and icons—which were two-dimensional—as the only correct representations of religious subjects.

The Kievan Economy

Agriculture and trade were the most important economic activities in Kievan society.

Agriculture. Kievan Rus contained two major agricultural regions. In the north lay the forest zone known as the **taiga** (TY • guh). Although the taiga received abundant rainfall, the brutally cold, long winters limited the growing season to about four months each year. Because of the need to grow and harvest crops in such a short time, everyone worked long hours.

In the steppe to the east and south of the taiga, less rain fell and less vegetation grew. However, the milder climate permitted a growing season of six months, giving the people more time to sow, cultivate, and harvest their crops of grain.

Trade. Kievan Rus traded agricultural goods, wood, iron, salt, and other products with the Byzantine Empire. The most important of these goods were fur, wax, honey, animal hides, flax, hemp, burlap, and hops. Kievan Rus also furnished slaves for the Byzantines. In return the people of Kievan Rus obtained wine, silk, religious art objects, spices, precious stones, steel blades, and horses from the Byzantines. From western Europe the Rus received textiles, glassware, and metals. By the early 1000s, trade had helped make Kievan Rus as strong and wealthy as any western European power. Scholars estimate that Kiev's population was larger than that of Paris, which was the most populous city in western Europe.

Kievan Social Classes

In the varied economy of Kievan Rus, several social classes emerged. The highest class included the local princes and their families. Below the princes came the boyars. Next were the artisans and merchants, who lived in the towns and devoted themselves entirely to trade.

The clergy formed another important group in Kievan society. They not only performed religious ceremonies but also ran schools, hospitals, and other charities.

The largest social class, however, consisted of peasants. The peasants lived in small villages and produced the agricultural output of Kievan Rus.

1B, 1C, 3C, a1B, a4A, a4F, a4G, a4H, a4I, a4J, a4L

● Some historians believe that the Mongols retreated because Europe was too mountainous and lacked grazing land.

SECTION 2 REVIEW

1. **Define** steppe, boyar, metropolitan, taiga
2. **Identify** Vikings, Rurik, Yaroslav the Wise, *Pravda Russkaia*
3. **Locate** Arctic Ocean, Baltic Sea, Black Sea, Caspian Sea, Ural Mountains, Dvina River, Vistula River, Volga River, Novgorod, Kiev
4. **Analyzing Ideas** Why did Vladimir I choose Byzantine Christianity?
5. **Seeing Relationships** What ties did Kievan Rus have with the Byzantine Empire?
6. **Contrasting Ideas** What were the differences between the northern and southern agricultural regions in Kievan Rus?
7. **Classifying Ideas** Describe the social classes in Kievan Rus.

3 The Mongols Established a Vast Empire in Eurasia

After the rule of Yaroslav the Wise ended in 1054, Kiev declined in power and wealth. The Kievan rulers gave their younger sons outlying towns to rule as independent principalities. These princes and their descendants fought among themselves and with the ruler of Kiev to expand their own territories. Kiev's trade declined because of raids by the Polovtsy, Asiatic peoples who controlled the region south of Kiev after 1055. Also, the Italians developed new trade routes throughout the Mediterranean region that competed with the Kievan routes.

After a group of princes sacked Kiev in 1169 and again in 1203, the city's prosperity ended. As these princes continued to fight among themselves, new invaders took advantage of Kiev's weakness. These new invaders, the Mongols, came from the Asian steppe west of the Urals.

The Mongols in Eastern Europe

The Mongols first attacked eastern Europe in force in 1237. Kievan resistance proved too weak to halt the Mongols, and by 1240 they had conquered and burned almost every city in Kievan Rus.

The Mongols pushed on across the Carpathian Mountains into Hungary and across the plains into Poland. After defeating the Hungarian and Polish armies, however, the Mongol leader rushed back to the Mongolian capital in central Asia to help ● choose a new ruler. Thus Hungary and Poland, although terribly damaged by war and savage plundering, escaped continuing Mongol rule. The Kievan region, however, remained under Mongol control until the late 1400s.

Society Under the Rule of the Mongols

The Mongols did not try to impose their way of life on the people they conquered. They wanted only to collect taxes. Taxes were often harsh, but as long as they were paid, the Mongols allowed the people to retain their own government and customs. The local landlord collected taxes and administered justice. Peasants had two obligations to their landlords—labor at specified times and a payment either in money or in goods. The second obligation was considered more important. Most peasants in the north, the area between the Volga and Oka rivers, did not have landlords and paid taxes directly to the government.

The Mongols grazed their flocks on the steppe north of the Caspian Sea and the Sea of Azov, where they had little contact with the Slavs. Although they formed only a small ruling class, the Mongols did influence the society of the Eastern Slavs in several ways. They built important roads and improved methods of taxation and communication. Some of their words filtered into the language that came to be called Russian.

Learning from Pictures *Genghis Khan, a leader of the Mongols, was a skilled politician. He won a faithful following by rewarding those loyal to him.*

dividing Europe from Asia; ***Dvina River:*** river in northwestern Russia emptying into Baltic Sea; ***Vistula River:*** river in Poland emptying into Baltic Sea; ***Volga River:*** river in central Russia emptying into Caspian Sea; ***Novgorod:*** city south of Lake Ladoga; ***Kiev:*** leading city of Kievan Rus, on Dnieper River
4. Vladimir I was impressed with the rituals of Byzantine Christianity and wanted to marry the sister of the Byzantine emperor.
5. Kievan Rus traded with and shared common religious ties with Byzantium.
6. The cold northern agricultural regions in Kievan Rus had a shorter growing season but a greater average annual precipitation than the southern agricultural regions, which had less rainfall but a longer growing season.
7. The highest social class of Kievan Rus consisted of the local princes and their families. Next came the boyars, followed by artisans and merchants. The clergy also formed an important group. The largest social class consisted of peasants.

SECTION 3

Focus/Motivation
Ask students to hypothesize about the conditions under which a city as formidable as Kiev could be captured. Write

1B, 3B, 3C, a1A, a1B

● The Grand Prince brought many Mongols into his administration, assigning them Russian towns to govern and tax.

■ The Muscovite princes took over as their own the Mongol idea of empire and ability for military organization.

▲ The Slavs called Constantinople *Czargrad*, the city of the emperor.

their responses on the chalkboard or an overhead projector. *(Answers will vary. They might include the following: Authority was divided as Kievan rulers granted towns to younger sons to rule. Local leaders began fighting among themselves and could not unite against an attack.)*

Presentation
Relating Cause and Effect (Average/Group)
Write each of the following effects on the chalkboard or an overhead projector. Have students determine the cause or causes for each of the effects.

1. ***Effect:*** Trade declined in Kievan Rus
   Causes: **a.** Raids by Asiatic peoples to the south; **b.** Italians developed new trade routes in Mediterranean
2. ***Effect:*** Russia suspicious of western Europeans
   Causes: **a.** Territorial rivalry with Poland and Lithuania; **b.** Russians were Orthodox Christians; Poles and Lithuanians were Western Christians

SECTION 3

Closure
The rulers of Muscovy and the leaders of the Russian Orthodox Church spoke of Moscow as the "third Rome." Ask students what this meant to Russians of the time. *(Rome fell to heresy; Constantinople—the*

Learning from Pictures *The Byzantines influenced the religion and architecture of the Eastern Slavs. The Russians modified the dome style into an onion shape.*

During the time of Mongol rule, the Slavs of eastern Europe had little contact with central and western Europe. Lithuania and Poland took territory from the northern part of Kievan Rus in the late 1300s, forming a kingdom hostile to the Eastern Slavs. Religious conflicts also existed. The Poles had been converted to Western Christianity. The Eastern Slavs clung to their Orthodox faith, which set them apart from both the Poles and the Mongols. The Eastern Slavs grew suspicious of Europeans and their influence. This suspicion became a deep-seated one that has not disappeared to the present day.

The Rise of Moscow

In time Mongol rule grew weaker, and the princes of the region became more independent. During the early 1300s, Moscow, or Muscovy, became the strongest principality, partly because it cooperated with the Mongols. In return for this cooperation, the Mongols awarded Prince Ivan I, who ruled Moscow from 1325 to 1341, the title of Grand ● Prince. Ivan's power increased further when the chief metropolitan of the Orthodox church moved to Moscow in 1328.

By the time of Ivan III, who ruled as Grand Prince from 1462 to 1505, Moscow was so powerful that it refused to pay taxes to the Mongols. In 1480 ■ Ivan III overthrew Mongol rule. He united many principalities and emerged as the first ruler of an independent state called Russia.

In 1533, at the age of only 3, Ivan IV became ruler of Russia. Because of Ivan's youth, however, the boyars wielded power. The young boy watched powerlessly as the boyars fought each other, tortured captive opponents, and murdered political prisoners.

In an impressive ceremony in 1547, Ivan declared himself the heir of the Roman and Byzantine empires and took the title **czar,** the Russian word for "caesar." ▲ As czar, Ivan IV reformed Yaroslav's laws, reestablished trade with western Europe, and opened Siberia for Russian settlement.

When Ivan's wife died mysteriously, he blamed the boyars for her death. He immediately formed a secret police who dressed in black uniforms and rode black horses. These fearsome agents carried broomsticks to show how they would sweep the streets of trouble and execute all traitors.

Ivan used the secret police to control Russia. They arrested boyars and distributed the boyars' land to Ivan's supporters. Ivan later sent the secret police to execute the metropolitan of Moscow and routinely ordered the massacres of all the residents of villages. In a fit of rage, he even killed his own son. Such ferocious acts of cruelty earned Ivan IV the nickname "Ivan the Terrible," or "Ivan the Awesome." Nevertheless, Ivan IV established the nature of the new Russian state. The state would be huge, including old Kievan Rus and Siberia. And it would be autocratic, with one person ruling as czar.

The Growth of the Church

As in western Europe, the church in Russia continued to expand its landholdings, primarily through gifts from people who saw these donations to the church as a guarantee of spiritual salvation. By 1500 the Orthodox church owned as much as one-fourth of all cultivated land in Russia.

During the Mongol period, the Russian Orthodox church became increasingly independent of the patriarch of Constantinople. In 1448 the metropolitan of the Orthodox church in Moscow took office without the authority of Constantinople. The final break with Constantinople occurred in 1589, when Moscow's metropolitan was crowned patriarch and proclaimed equal with those of other Eastern Orthodox churches.

The Russians rewrote the history of how their country had been Christianized to give the Russian

1B, 3B, 3C, a1A, a1B, a4A, a4F, a4G, a4H, a4I, a4L, a4M

History Through the Arts

PAINTING

Sacred Icons

As Christianity spread into Kievan Rus in the 900s, the people were baptized and told to destroy their pagan idols. Holy pictures, or icons, were hung in lavish new churches. Gold- or silver-painted backgrounds made the icons easier to see in dimly lit interiors. Troops marching into battle also carried icons. In this icon from Kiev, we see three popular Byzantine saints: St. Vassilios; the eloquent St. John Chrysostom; and St. Grigorios Theologos, who was often shown shedding blood into the sacrificial chalice or cup.

Despite their flat, two-dimensional style, icons conveyed both individuality and a sense of godliness. Byzantine artists were expected to lead pure lives to demonstrate this feeling of holiness. Only then were they worthy enough to transfer God's goodness to men and women.

Orthodox church important theological support for its independence. The Russians now claimed that Andrew, one of the original 12 apostles of Jesus, brought Christianity to Russia directly from Jerusalem. They confidently proclaimed Moscow as the "third Rome." In 1510 a Russian abbot wrote that the first Rome had fallen because of heresy and the second Rome (Constantinople) had fallen because of infidels, or people who were not Christians. The third Rome (Moscow), he said, was destined to be the final one that would bring spiritual light to the whole world.

This new confidence affected Russian architecture and art. The Cathedral of the Assumption in Moscow exemplifies the artistry and religious fervor of the period. The church has the domed-roof style so popular in both the Byzantine and Russian cultures. Every inch of the church's interior walls exhibited some form of artwork. Sparkling chandeliers and candles illuminated every alcove. The face of Jesus adorned the highest central dome. The cathedral, full of grandeur and beauty, was designed to produce a strong mystical response from the people. Even today, people marvel at this early Russian masterpiece.

SECTION 3 REVIEW

1. **Define** czar
2. **Identify** Polovtsy, Mongols, third Rome, Ivan III, Ivan IV
3. **Locate** Sea of Azov, Lithuania, Poland, Moscow
4. **Determining Cause and Effect** What were some of the reasons for Kievan Rus's isolation from, and suspicion toward, western Europe?
5. **Summarizing Ideas** How did the Mongol rulers maintain control over the Kievan territories?
6. **Understanding Ideas** What two obligations did the peasants have to their landlords?
7. **Analyzing Ideas** How did Muscovy become independent from Mongol rule?

"second Rome"—fell to Islam; Moscow was the final center of the Christian world.)

Review Answers

1. ***czar:*** Russian "caesar," or emperor

2. ***Polovtsy:*** Asiatic people who raided Kiev and contributed to its decline; ***Mongols:*** invaders from Asiatic steppe; ***third Rome:*** Moscow; ***Ivan III:*** Grand Prince of Moscow who overthrew Mongol rule; ***Ivan IV:*** took title of "czar"

3. ***Sea of Azov:*** north of Black Sea; ***Lithuania:*** country in southeastern Baltic region; ***Poland:*** country bordering Russia on west; ***Moscow:*** capital of Russia whose early rulers overthrew Mongols

4. The Kievan Rus were suspicious of Western Europeans because of territorial rivalries and religious conflicts.

5. The Mongols allowed the local rulers to retain their government in return for paying taxes to the Mongols.

6. Peasants provided labor at specified times and a payment in either money or goods.

7. Moscow's princes cooperated with the Mongols, united many principalities, and became strong enough under Ivan III to refuse to pay tribute to the Mongols.

201

Reviewing Important Terms

1. dowry; **2.** icons; **3.** Iconoclasts; **4.** iconoclastic controversy; **5.** heresy; **6.** Excommunication; **7.** Mosaics; **8.** boyars; **9.** steppe; **10.** metropolitan; **11.** taiga; **12.** czar.

Developing Critical Thinking Skills

1. (a) Byzantine Empire; **(b)** Byzantine Empire; **(c)** Kievan Rus; **(d)** Kievan Rus; **(e)** Muscovite Russia; **(f)** Mongol Empire; **(g)** Kievan Rus; **(h)** Byzantine Empire
2. (a) People of the Byzantine Empire copied Roman and Greek traditions, but they developed the unique art of mosaics and spectacular religious architecture. The codification of Roman law was an equally great Byzantine contribution. **(b)** They adopted the Byzantine form of Christianity, the Cyrillic alphabet, and an autocratic form of government.
3. (a) Cities like Kiev became centers of trade because of their location on the Viking trade routes. **(b)** The Mongol invasion stopped cultural development and limited contacts with the West.
4. (a) The Russians developed the claim that Moscow was the Third Rome. The metropolitan of Moscow became a patriarch independent of Constantinople. **(b)** It gave religious backing to independence movements against the Mongols.
5. (a) 1200-1500; **(b)** 300-600; **(c)** 900-1200; **(d)** 900-1200

1B, 1D, 3B, 3C, a1A, a4A, a4F, a4I, a4M

Reteaching

Have students review the Chapter Summary and the appropriate section and questions in the Unit Synthesis. Discuss the concepts until students demonstrate a clear understanding of the material.

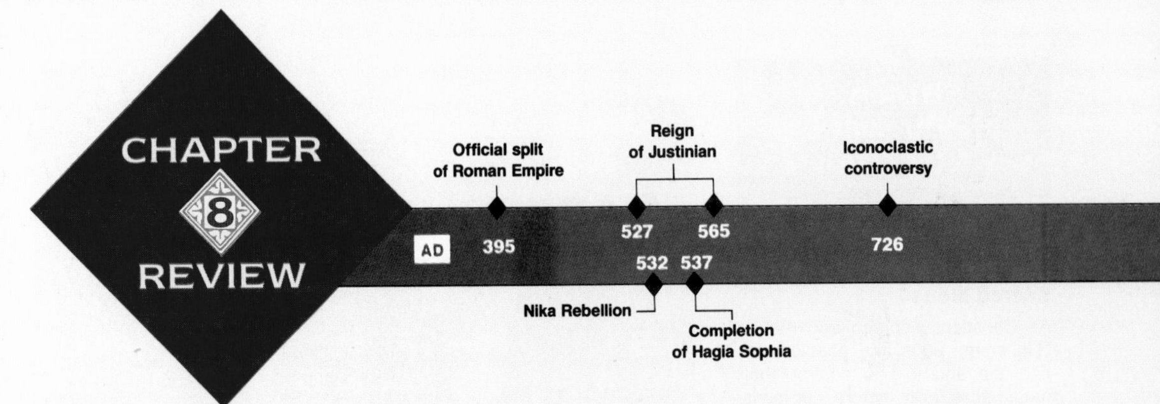

Chapter Summary

The following list contains the key concepts you have learned about the Byzantine Empire and its heritage.

1. A brilliant and sophisticated civilization, the Byzantine Empire helped preserve the heritage of Greco-Roman civilization.
2. Justinian, one of the most famous Byzantine emperors, survived the Nika Rebellion, extended the borders of the empire, and ordered the building of Hagia Sophia.
3. The Byzantine Empire survived for 1,000 years because of political, military, and economic strengths.
4. In 1054 the Christian Church split into two churches—the Roman Catholic church and the Eastern Orthodox church.
5. The main inheritor of Byzantine traditions was Kievan Rus, located on the vast, almost treeless steppe of eastern Europe.
6. Kievan Rus became a flourishing society based on agriculture and trade.
7. Although the Mongols conquered Kievan Rus, they had little long-lasting influence on local institutions and culture in the region around Kiev and Novgorod.
8. As Mongol control weakened, a strong state, centered in Moscow, started to emerge in the 1400s.
9. In the 1500s Ivan the Terrible took the title *czar* and firmly established the large Russian state.

On a separate sheet of paper, complete the following review exercises.

Reviewing Important Terms

Supply the term that correctly completes each sentence.

1. The money or goods that a bride brings to her husband when the couple is married is called a ________.
2. Holy pictures of Jesus, the Virgin Mary, and the saints, typically used in devotions, are called ________.
3. ________ felt that the presence of icons constituted idol worship and should be suppressed.
4. The argument between the supporters and the opponents of icons was called the ________ ________.
5. Church leaders label an opinion that conflicts with church doctrine ________.
6. ________ entails barring a person from church membership and excluding the person from taking part in any church ceremonies such as baptism, marriage, and communion.
7. ________ are pictures or designs formed by inlaid pieces of stone, glass, or enamel.
8. In Kievan Rus, the princes sometimes ruled with the advice of a council of ________, or nobles.
9. Much of eastern Europe consists of a grassy, almost treeless plain called the ________.
10. When the Christian Church split in 1054, the Kievan church became a part of the Eastern Orthodox church, with its chief bishop, the ________, chosen by the patriarch of Constantinople.
11. The forest zone in northern Kievan Rus was known as the ________.
12. Ivan IV declared himself the heir of the Roman and Byzantine empires and took the title ________, the Russian word for "caesar."

Developing Critical Thinking Skills

1. **Classifying Ideas** Classify each of the following statements as characteristic of the Byzantine Empire, Kievan Rus, the Mongol Empire, or Muscovite Russia.
   (a) Justinian established Law Code.
   (b) Princesses married foreign princes to help cement alliances.
   (c) The *veche* settled disputes.
   (d) First Russian law code compiled.
   (e) Ivan III united territories into Russia.
   (f) Semi-independent city-states developed.
   (g) Rulers gave younger sons outlying towns to rule independently.
   (h) Government regulated trade and manufacturing to produce large tax revenues.
2. **Summarizing Ideas** **(a)** Describe Byzantine art, architecture, and law. **(b)** What features of Byzantine culture did the people who eventually formed Russia adopt?
3. **Relating Cause and Effect** **(a)** In eastern Europe, how did the Viking trade routes affect the growth of

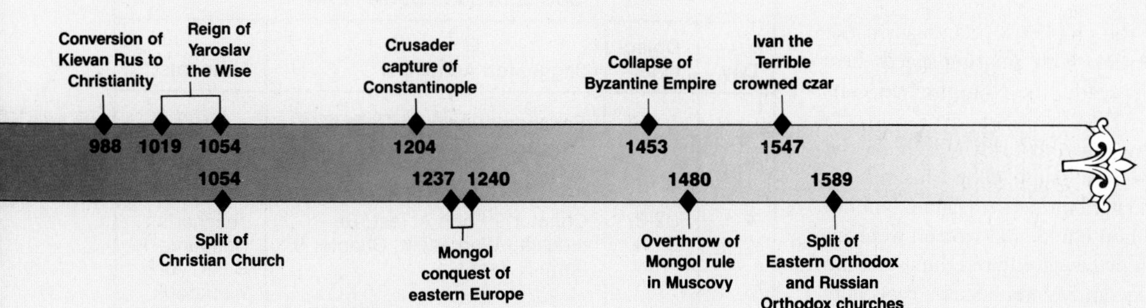

cities such as Kiev? **(b)** What effects did the Mongol invasion have on Kievan Rus?

4. **Analyzing Ideas** **(a)** How did the Russian Orthodox church branch out from the Eastern Orthodox church? **(b)** How was the Eastern Orthodox church in the region of Kievan Rus strengthened during Mongol rule?
5. **Understanding Chronology** Indicate whether each of the following events occurred between 300 and 600, 600 and 900, 900 and 1200, or 1200 and 1500.
   (a) Mongols capture Kiev.
   (b) Justinian rules the Byzantine Empire.
   (c) Yaroslav I rules.
   (d) Eastern church splits from the Roman Catholic church.

Relating Geography to History

(a) On an outline map of the present-day Soviet Union, trace the rivers mentioned in this chapter and label the body of water into which each river flows. **(b)** Using the maps on page 197 and Chapter 12, page 281, compare the territories of Kievan Rus with the Kipchak Empire (Golden Horde). What areas overlap? What territory of Kievan Rus is not included in the Kipchak Empire?

Relating Past to Present

1. Use either *The Statesman's Yearbook* or a world almanac from your library to obtain a list of products that the Soviet Union and Turkey import and export today. Compare this list with what was traded between the Byzantine Empire and Kievan Rus.
2. Visit a Greek or Russian Orthodox church and a Roman Catholic church. Write a report on the types of art, architecture, and decorative pieces you observe. Try to explain any similarities or differences you observe between these modern churches and the descriptions of the ancient churches in this chapter.

Applying History Study Skills

Before completing this activity, review Building History Study Skills on page 192.

Read the following excerpt from *Of the Buildings of Justinian* by Procopius. Then identify whether the author is neutral, biased in favor of Justinian, or biased against Justinian. Provide evidence, such as words or phrases that convey positive or negative attitudes, that supports your conclusions.

> "The Emperor Justinian . . . succeeding to the throne when the state was decayed, added greatly to its extent and glory by driving out from it the barbarians. . . . As for religion, which he found uncertain and torn by various heresies, he destroyed everything which could lead to error, and securely established the true faith upon one solid foundation. Moreover, finding the laws obscure through their unnecessary multitude, and confused by their conflict with one another, he firmly established them by reducing the number of those which were unnecessary, and in the case of those which were contradictory, by confirming better ones."

Investigating Further

1. **Writing a Report** Use encyclopedias or books about the Byzantine Empire to prepare a written report about the emperor Justinian. Include in your report a description of his life and his accomplishments.
2. **Interviewing People** Interview someone from Eastern Europe (Greece, Russia, Turkey, or the Ukraine) to gather information on the celebrations of special religious occasions, such as Christmas, Easter, weddings, baptisms, and funerals. Present your findings in an oral report to the class. Ask members of the class to compare this information with their own experiences on similar occasions.
3. **Drawing a Building Plan** Using pictures in encyclopedias and the photograph on page 186 of this chapter as models, draw a building plan of the church of Hagia Sophia. Display your plan on the bulletin board.
4. **Researching** Use resources in the school and public libraries to undertake a research project on Yaroslav the Wise's law code, the Pravda Russkaia. Make special note of its similarities to Justinian's Code. Be prepared to present an oral report on your findings to the class.

Relating Geography to History

(a) Students should list the Dvina and Vistula rivers that flow into the Baltic Sea; the Dniester, Dnieper, and Don rivers that flow into the Black Sea; and the Volga and Ural rivers that flow into the Caspian Sea. **(b)** Most of southern Kievan Rus is occupied by the Kipchak Empire. The northern reaches of Kievan Rus are not included.

Relating Past to Present

1. Answers will vary. Students should mention that Turkey exports cotton, hazelnuts, tobacco, raisins, and chromium ores. It imports crude oil, machinery, chemicals, motor vehicles, and iron and steel. The Byzantine Empire also traded agricultural products and exported manufactured goods, while Turkey imports manufactured goods. The Soviet Union exports clocks and watches, manganese ore, cotton, paper, and vegetable oil. It imports grain, manufactured consumer goods, and machinery and equipment. The Soviet Union still imports manufactured goods as did the Kievan Rus. However, the trading of furs and hides is no longer so important.
2. If students are unable to visit Orthodox or Roman Catholic churches, they may find information on church architecture in the school or public libraries.

Applying History Study Skills

Procopius admires Justinian, extolling his virtues as a great religious, political, and military leader, who also established a clear set of laws.

203

CHAPTER (pages 204–221)

9 Islam Became a Powerful Force from Spain to India

(570 – 1707)

CHAPTER OVERVIEW

The religion of Islam, founded by the prophet Muhammad in the A.D. 600s, spread outward from Arabia with amazing speed. Less than a century after Muhammad's death, the Muslims had conquered a vast empire.

Islamic government was tightly organized, with each of the three parts of the empire governed by a caliph. The Muslims encouraged trade, manufacturing, and agriculture. In Islamic families the father was absolute head of the household, and women were expected to be obedient. Because Islamic law prohibited the use of the human form to depict God, the decorative arts became especially important. The Muslims excelled in science, medicine, and mathematics. Muslim culture declined after 1000, and leadership of the empire passed from the Arabs to the Turks.

The Muslims entered India in the 700s but did not make significant conquests for about 300 years. By the early 1300s, however, the Muslims, under the Delhi sultans, controlled all of northern India and the Deccan. After the decline of the Delhi sultanate, Babur established the Mogul Empire, which lasted until the 1700s.

SUGGESTED LESSON PLAN

Day	Objectives	Suggested Activities	Materials
1	U2-3,* C1-4	Introducing the Chapter (pages 204-05) Section 1 (pages 205-10), Focus/Motivation (page 205), Presentation (page 206), Closure (page 209), Suggested Teaching Strategies, Enrichment Activities, Daily Quiz, Suggested Assignments (page 203B)	ATE, Pupil's Edition, Teacher's Resource-Bank™
2	U3, C5-7	Section 2 (pages 210-15), Focus/Motivation (page 211), Presentation (page 211), Closure (page 214), Suggested Teaching Strategies, Enrichment Activities, Daily Quiz, Suggested Assignments (page 203B)	ATE, Pupil's Edition, Teacher's Resource-Bank™
3	U2-3, C8-9	Section 3 (pages 215-19), Focus/Motivation (page 215), Presentation (page 216), Closure (page 218), Suggested Teaching Strategies, Enrichment Activity, Daily Quiz, Suggested Assignments (page 203C)	ATE, Pupil's Edition, Teacher's Resource-Bank™
4	U2-3, C1-9	Chapter 9 Form A Test, Reteaching Worksheet, Chapter 9 Form B Test	Teacher's Resource-Bank™ or Workbook and Test Booklet

*C refers to applicable Chapter Objective, U refers to applicable Unit Goal.

BOOKS FOR THE TEACHER

Encyclopaedia Britannica, eds. *The Arabs: People and Power.* Bantam. Describes the history and religion of the Muslims from Muhammad's time to the present.

Hitti, Philip K. *History of the Arabs.* Macmillan. Presents a thorough treatment of the subject.

Spear, Percival. *India.* University of Michigan Press. Reviews information pertinent to this chapter.

Watt, W. Montgomery. *What Is Islam?* Praeger. Discusses the teachings of Islam.

BOOKS FOR THE STUDENT

Clifford, Mary Louise. *The Land and People of the Arabian Peninsula.* Lippincott. Includes chapters on the early history of the Arabian Peninsula, Muslim customs, and the Islamic religion.

Edmonds, I. G. *Islam.* Franklin Watts. Presents information on Islamic beliefs, the life of Muhammad, and the influences of Jewish and Christian beliefs on Islam.

Powell, Anton. *The Rise of Islam.* Warwick Press. Includes a variety of topics and illustrations.

Shulberg, Lucille. *Historic India.* Time-Life. Features a chapter on the Mogul Empire.

Townson, Duncan. *Muslim Spain.* Lerner Publications. Discusses Islamic religion and culture in Spain.

MULTIMEDIA MATERIALS

The Arab's World: Past and Future (mp, 52 min.), EBE. Two lectures by Arnold Toynbee, evaluating the role of the Arab in world history.

India's History: Mogul Empire to European Colonization (mp, 11 min.), Coronet. Traces the growth and decline of the Mogul Empire on the Indian subcontinent and the eventual rise of European interest in India.

Iran: Landmarks in the Desert (mp, 27 min.), Chatsworth. Traces Persian history through the artistry of architects, painters, and artisans, with particular emphasis on the Muslim influence.

Moslem World: The Beginnings and Growth (mp, 11 min.), Coronet. Depicts the history of the Muslim world and its impact on Western culture.

Section 1 (pages 205–10)
Islam and the Muslim Empire Spread Outward from Arabia

SECTION OVERVIEW

The Islamic religion was founded by the prophet Muhammad in the A.D. 600s. This new religion included belief in one God, a code of ethics, a sacred book called the Koran, and five chief obligations for its followers. The empire begun by Muhammad spread outward and eventually included most of the Middle East, North Africa, and Spain. Early in their history, Muslims split into two rival groups, the Sunnis and the Shiites. This division has persisted into modern times.

SUGGESTED TEACHING STRATEGIES

1. **Preteaching Vocabulary (Basic)** You may wish to preteach the following important vocabulary terms: hegira (*page 206*); mullah, mosque (*page 207*); caliph (*page 208*); imam (*page 210*). Ask students to rank the Muslim clerics in order of importance. (*caliph, imam, mullah*)
2. **Understanding Ideas (Average/Group)** Organize the class into four groups for a discussion based on "Muhammad as a Man of His Time" in Edwin Fenton's *Thirty-two Problems in World History* (Scott, Foresman). Assign one of the four introductory questions from the reading to each group. Students are to read the selection, discuss the question within their group, and share their conclusions with the rest of the class. To prepare for the discussion, students might read a short account of Muhammad's life, such as the one in Will Durant's *Age of Faith* (Simon and Schuster).

ENRICHMENT ACTIVITIES

1. **Preparing an Oral Report. (Average/Group)** Interested students might present oral reports to the class on the following topics: (a) the history of Islam; (b) the moral teachings of Islam; (c) the religious obligations of Islam. Sources include Marcus Bach's *Major Religions of the World* (Abingdon); Joseph Gaer's *How the Great Religions Began* (New American Library); Huston Smith's *Religions of Man* (Harper & Row); and Desmond Stewart's *The Arab World* (Time-Life).
2. **Analyzing Ideas (Average/Group)** Have students reread the subsection "The Faith of Islam" on pages 206-207. Ask them how Muslims viewed slavery. (*The faith permitted slavery, but slaves had to be treated humanely.*) Then ask students how the Islamic ideas concerning slavery compared with those of the Greeks, Romans, and the Christians. Have interested students undertake additional research on slavery in Muslim countries up to the present century. They should prepare oral reports to give before the class. Use the information in these reports as the basis for further discussion on slavery and religion.

DAILY QUIZ

To assess student understanding of Section 1, give the class the following quiz. (Each item is worth 10 points.)

1. The nomadic Arabs who herded sheep and were organized into tribes were called ________. (*Bedouins*)
2. Muhammad called the Supreme Being, one God, or ________. (*Allah*)
3. At the age of 40, Muhammad had to flee for his life to Medina. This is called the ________, or "flight." (*hegira*)
4. The central belief of Islam is simple: "There is no God but Allah, and ________ is his prophet." (*Muhammad*)
5. The ________ is the Muslim holy book. (*Koran*)
6. List the five chief obligations of Islam. (*recite the words of witness; pray five times per day facing Mecca; make a pilgrimage to Mecca; give alms; fast during Ramadan*)
7. These Muslim men, or ________, are the "priests" of Islam and learned in Islamic faith and law. (*mullahs*)
8. Muslim governors of territory, "successors to the prophet," were called ________. (*caliphs*)
9. The Moors, or Muslims from Spain, threatened to control all of ________ until they lost to the Franks in the Battle of Tours. (*France or Europe*)
10. A people called ________ helped the Muslims win control of Spain in the 700s. (*Berbers*)

SUGGESTED ASSIGNMENTS

1. **Profile Worksheet (Basic)** Have students complete Profile Worksheet 9 in the TEACHER'S RESOURCEBANK™.
2. **Critical Thinking Worksheet (Average/Group)** Have students complete Critical Thinking Worksheet 20 in the TEACHER'S RESOURCEBANK™.

Section 2 (pages 210–15)
Muslims Created an Advanced Civilization

SECTION OVERVIEW

The Muslims created a stable society in which economic and cultural activity flourished. In Muslim society the basic social unit was the extended family, with the father as absolute head. The Muslims excelled in science, medicine, and mathematics. After the year 1000, Muslim culture declined, and leadership passed from the Arabs to the Turks.

SUGGESTED TEACHING STRATEGIES

1. **Preteaching Vocabulary (Basic)** You may wish to preteach the following important vocabulary terms: caliphate *(page 210)*; dower *(page 211)*; millet *(page 214)*; sultan *(page 215)*. Ask students how a dower differs from a dowry. *(A dowry is a settlement made by the bride's family to the groom.)*
2. **Performing a Drama (Average/Group)** Have members of the class perform skits from *The Arabian Nights*. Some suggestions are "Sinbad the Sailor," "Ali Baba and the Forty Thieves," or "Aladdin and His Lamp." After the skits have been presented, conduct a discussion on what aspects of Muslim life and values they reveal.

ENRICHMENT ACTIVITIES

1. **Comparing Past and Present (Average/Group)** Have students make bulletin board displays, write reports, or perform short dramatizations comparing the role of women in the Muslim Empire with the role of Muslim women today. They should consider the varying degrees of outside influences, especially Westernization, on Muslim women. They should indicate what has been accepted from the West and what has been rejected. For articles on the role of Muslim women today, students should consult the *Readers' Guide to Periodical Literature*.
2. **Writing Research Reports (Challenging)** Have interested students research and prepare written or oral reports on various aspects of Muslim culture. Have some students check encyclopedias for biographical studies of artists, scientists, mathematicians, and physicians. Other students could consult "Mohammedan Culture and Philosophy" in Bertrand Russell's *A History of Western Philosophy* (Simon and Schuster).

DAILY QUIZ

To assess student understanding of Section 2, give the class the following quiz. (Each item is worth 10 points.)

1. (T or F) Because they were originally desert nomads, the Arab leaders of the Muslim Empire had little interest in ocean-going trade. *(F)*
2. List two of the three caliphates in the Arab Muslim Empire. *(Baghdad; Cairo; Cordova)*
3. Which of these products from Damascus or Toledo became world famous? steel swords, pottery, glassware, leather goods *(steel swords)*
4. As in ancient Rome, the ______ was the absolute head of the household in Muslim society. *(father)*
5. What is the holy book used to educate all good Muslims? *(Koran)*
6. (T or F) The Muslims probably learned to make paper from the Chinese. *(T)*
7. (T or F) Rhazes, a Muslim physician, wrote about surgery, smallpox, and measles. *(T)*
8. (T or F) The Arabs made few contributions to the development of mathematics. *(F)*
9. (T or F) Slaves called millets provided bodyguards to the sultan and a highly disciplined infantry for the Ottoman Empire. *(F)*
10. The first Turkish people to seize much of Asia Minor and extend their rule within the Muslim Empire were the ______ ______. *(Seljuk Turks)*

SUGGESTED ASSIGNMENTS

1. **Geography Application Sheet (Basic)** Have students complete "Geography Application Sheet: Damascus, the Pearl of the Desert," in the TEACHER'S RESOURCEBANK™.
2. **Comparing Ideas (Basic)** In Islamic society, state governments, the family, and the mosque took responsibility for education. Have the students compare the role of Islamic society in education with the way responsibility for education is organized in the United States.

Section (pages 215–19)

3 Muslim and Mogul Rulers Brought Important Changes to India

SECTION OVERVIEW

After the collapse of Gupta rule in northern India, disorder prevailed until the reign of Harsha. After his death the region split into numerous small states controlled by the Rajputs. Between 712 and 1236, Muslims took control of northern India, and further Muslim conquests were made by the Delhi sultans. In the 1500s Babur set up the Mogul Empire. The Moguls fostered unity and orderly government in India.

SUGGESTED TEACHING STRATEGIES

1. **Relating Ideas (Basic)** Have students reread the subsection "Tamerlane" on page 216. Then ask them to describe how Tamerlane affected India and neighboring peoples. *(Answers will vary. Students should mention that Tamerlane weakened India under the Delhi sultans, disrupted other parts of the Muslim Empire by destroying Baghdad and Damascus, and postponed the Ottoman capture of Constantinople by defeating the sultan in battle at Angora.)* Then relate to students that Tamerlane's influence was short-lived. In this respect he resembled Mongol rulers in Kievan Rus: creating great fear and destruction but no lasting government or culture.

*2. **Reading About History: Understanding Sequence (Basic)** To clarify the events in this section, have the class make a descriptive time line. This can be done independently or in class on the chalkboard or an overhead projector. The completed time line should include the following events:

606	Harsha governed empire in northern India.
647	Harsha assassinated; northern India split into numerous small states, ruled by Rajputs.
712	Muslims conquered the Indus Valley.
1193	Muslims occupied Delhi.
1206	Beginning of Delhi sultanate
1398	Tamerlane captured Delhi, slaughtered inhabitants, and returned to Samarkand.
1526	Babur conquered Delhi and brought Rajput princes under control; set up Mogul Empire.
1556-1605	Reign of Akbar, the greatest Mogul ruler
1707	After death of Aurangzeb, Mogul Empire began to disintegrate.

ENRICHMENT ACTIVITY

Comparing Ideas (Basic) Have students prepare charts in their notebooks of the religious differences between Hindus and Muslims. Completed charts should be similar to the following chart.

MUSLIM	HINDU
Strict monotheism	Many gods
Prohibited representations of God	Idols allowed
Equality of all before God	Caste system
Purdah and harem	No purdah or harem
No taboo on beef	Cow sacred
Alcoholic beverages forbidden	Beverages fermented
No music in worship	Music in religious ceremonies

DAILY QUIZ

To assess student understanding of Section 3, give the class the following quiz. (Each item is worth 10 points.)

1. Who gained control of the Ganges Valley by using cavalry, elephants, and infantry, but later was assassinated by his army because of his oppressive rule? *(Harsha)*
2. (T or F) The Rajput rulers claimed divine origins, intermarried with Hindus, and adopted the caste system. *(T)*
3. The Muslim invasion of India began in the early 700s when Indian ________ began attacking Muslim ships in the Arabian Sea. *(pirates)*
4. (T or F) The Rajputs adopted advanced law codes. Their literature, however, did not reflect fair codes of conduct, respect for women, or mercy for defeated warriors. *(F)*
5. About the year 1000, Turkish Muslims began invading India from an area now called ________. *(Afghanistan)*
6. ________, who claimed to be descended from Genghis Khan, defeated the Golden Horde and conquered most of northern India. *(Tamerlane)*
7. (T or F) The tenets of the Muslim and Hindu religions are very similar. *(F)*
8. (T or F) The Muslims left no real lasting contributions in Indian life. *(F)*
9. The mystic prophet who attempted to bring about a union of Hinduism and Islam was ________. *(Nanak)*
10. After attempting a union of Hinduism and Islam, this mystic then founded the ________ religion. *(Sikh)*

SUGGESTED ASSIGNMENTS

1. **Understanding Geography (Average/Group)** Have interested students prepare maps comparing the Muslim Empire's various components: the Arab caliphates, the lands of the Seljuk Turks, Tamerlane's empire, the Ottoman Empire, and the Mogul Empire. Project the maps on an overhead projector to illustrate for the class the extent of each empire.
2. **Skill Worksheet (Basic)** Have students complete Skill Worksheet 9 in the TEACHER'S RESOURCEBANK™.
3. **Critical Thinking Worksheet (Basic)** Have students complete Critical Thinking Worksheet 21 in the TEACHER'S RESOURCEBANK™.
4. **Review Worksheet (Basic)** Have students complete Review Worksheet 9 in the TEACHER'S RESOURCEBANK™.

For suggested lesson plan, additional teaching strategies, enrichment activities, daily quizzes, and suggested assignments, see pages 203A–203D.

Introducing the Chapter
Have students turn to the map of the Muslim Empire on page 209. Ask them to speculate about the religious motives of the Muslims for spreading Islam. *(Answers should include the desire for religious converts and for spiritual reward for spreading the holy word.)* Next ask students to suggest more practical reasons for Muslim expansion. *(Answers will vary. Students might include the following: the need for more living space or more fertile land; desire for military conquest; desire for expansion of trade; diverting people's attention from problems at home.)* Help students to understand that people often act from a variety of motives.

Chapter Objectives
After studying Chapter 9, students will be able to:

1. Describe the Bedouin nomadic life.
2. Summarize Muhammad's life.
3. Outline Islam's five chief obligations and religious restrictions.
4. Compare the Sunni and Shiite groups.
5. Summarize the Muslim governmental organization and Muslim treatment of non-Muslims under their control.
6. Describe Islamic culture—families, society, art, and scientific developments.
7. Explain the Turkish

CHAPTER 9

Islam Became a Powerful Force from Spain to India

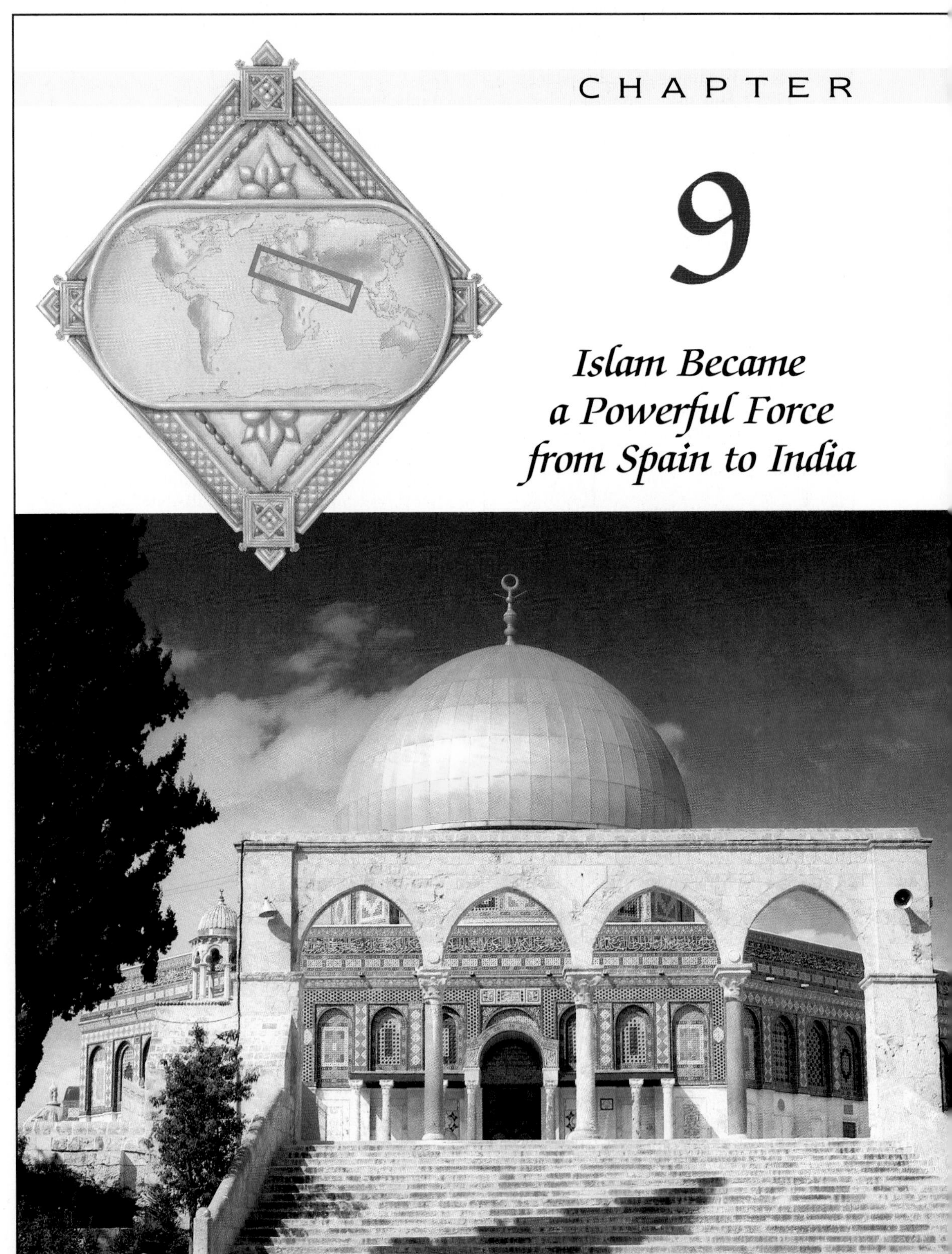

CHAPTER FOCUS

Place Arabia, North Africa, Southern Europe, and India

Time 570—1761

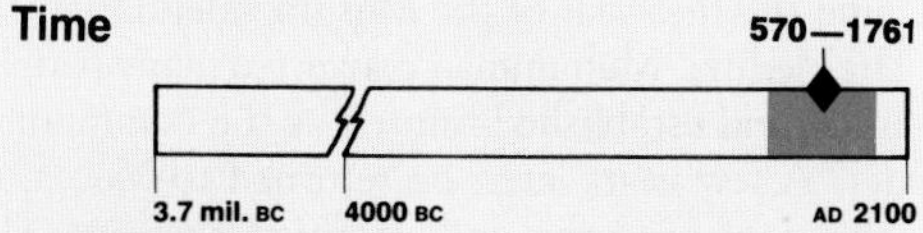

Significance

In the 600s the prophet Muhammad founded Islam, the youngest of the world's major religions. In only a few decades, this young religion captured the fervent support of millions of people and spread from Muhammad's homeland of Arabia west into the Mediterranean region and east into India.

Military conquest contributed greatly to the success of Islam. Indeed, Muhammad preached that the followers of Islam—known as Muslims—had to fight for their beliefs. "The sword is the key of heaven and hell," he said. However, Muhammad also offered spiritual teachings, encouraging people to lead humble, generous, and tolerant lives. Many who sought religious faith to guide their lives received and accepted this powerful messages.

As Islam spread, it encouraged the establishment of well-organized and vigorous states. Economic and cultural life flourished. Islamic philosophers, scientists, and artists created works that greatly influenced Western and Muslim cultures.

Terms to Define

hegira	imam
mullah	caliphate
mosque	dower
caliph	sultan

People to Identify

Muhammad	Babur
Abu Bakr	Akbar
Janissaries	Shah Jahan
Tamerlane	Aurangzeb

Places to Locate

Jiddah	Cairo
Mecca	Cordova
Medina	Delhi
Baghdad	Samarkand

Questions to Guide Your Reading

1 How did Islam and the Muslim Empire spread outward from Arabia?
2 What characteristics of their culture allowed the Muslims to create an advanced civilization?
3 What important changes did Muslim and Mogul rulers bring to India?

A story in Muslim literature tells of a sultan named Schariar (shahr • i • YAHR). Each night he married a new wife, and each morning he ordered her execution because he believed that no wife would remain loyal. However, one of these wives, Scheherezade (shuh • her • uh • ZAHD), told him an entertaining story which pleased him so much that he did not order her execution the following day. Night after night she continued to charm him with her stories. After a thousand and one nights of her storytelling, the sultan became convinced that this wife would remain forever faithful, and he abandoned all thoughts of executing her.

The collection of the "thousand and one" folk stories and fairy tales of Indian, Persian, or Arabic origin were translated from Persian into Arabic as early as 850 and have been enjoyed by people throughout the world for centuries. But it was not until the late 1700s that they were brought together in the collection we know today as the Thousand and One Nights, *or* Arabian Nights.

The collection includes the Sinbad stories, "Aladdin and His Magic Lamp" and "The History of Ali Baba" (source of the familiar phrase "Open Sesame"). These stories and others from the Thousand and One Nights *are among the most widely read in history.*

1 Islam and the Muslim Empire Spread Outward from Arabia

While the Byzantines ruled Asia Minor and the Balkan region, a new empire—the Muslim, or Arab, Empire—took shape to the south and east. The Muslims, like the Byzantines, developed a civilization that for centuries far surpassed that of Western Europe. It began in Arabia.

The Physical Setting

South of the Fertile Crescent lay the great peninsula of Arabia. Most of it consisted of a desert plateau with such sparse vegetation that it could only support herders and their flocks of sheep. These herders, called Arabs or Bedouins (BED • uh • wuhnz), lived as nomads, moving their flocks from one grazing area to another. They were organized into tribes, each

◀ *Dome of the Rock in Jerusalem*

influence on the Muslim world.
8. Outline the effects of the invasions of Muslims and Tamerlane on India.
9. Contrast Muslim and Hindu beliefs.

SECTION 1

Focus/Motivation
On the chalkboard or an overhead projector, write the following quotation from Abu Bakr on the death of Muhammad. Tell students that Abu Bakr was Muhammad's father-in-law and probably his first convert.

"Muslims! If you adored Muhammad, know that Muhammad is dead. If it is God whom you adore, know that he lives on; He never dies. Forget not this verse of the Koran: 'Muhammad is only a man charged with a mission; before him there have been men who received the divine message and died.' "

Lead a class discussion on this quotation, using the following questions as a guide: According to this speech, what was Muhammad's role in the Islamic religion? How would this speech encourage Muslims to continue their faith even after the death of Muhammad? *(Students should answer that Muhammad received a divine message. It became his mission to spread the word of God (Allah) and the Islamic religion. God, the true object of the Islamic*

1A, 1B, 1C, 3B, a1A
a1B

● The teachings of the Koran serve as the basis for all Muslim law, secular and religious.

faith, continued to exist, even though Muhammad had died.)

Presentation
Contrasting Ideas (Average/Group)
Organize the class into four or five groups. Have each group compare several world religions with Islam by making a wall chart headed by columns labeled with the religions they wish to compare: Islam, Christianity, Judaism, Hinduism, etc. In the left-hand column they should include titles such as *Founder, Major beliefs, Geographical locations or major centers, Unique features,* and *Schisms.* Have students post their charts on the bulletin board. Compare the information each group has selected. How are the charts similar? How are they different? Then use the information on the charts as the basis for a class discussion on the development of major religions. Ask students how the religions fare today. Are they aggressive in seeking converts? Are they split by doctrinal or other issues? Are they growing or declining?

ruled with an iron hand by a sheikh (SHEEK), or chief.

Some coastal regions of Arabia with greater rainfall could support more people. Here towns grew up. The Arabs who lived in these centers became traders. Goods from Asia and Africa entered the port of Jiddah (JID • uh) and then were taken overland to Mecca, the starting point of a caravan route running north to Syria. Consequently the Arabs who lived in towns met people of other cultures and were more influenced by the mainstream of civilization in the Fertile Crescent than the nomadic Bedouins.

The Life of Muhammad

Muhammad, the founder of Islam,* was born in Mecca about 570. Orphaned at an early age, Muhammad spent his youth in poverty. Having had little formal education, Muhammad probably never learned to write. As a young man, he became a camel driver and a caravan trader.

Because Muhammad lived in a major trading city that had contact with the outside world, he was exposed to Judaism and Christianity. As he met foreign traders and traveled to Christian and Jewish areas north of Mecca, Muhammad began to think seriously about religious and ethical questions. Although the Arabs worshiped many gods, meditation and prayer convinced Muhammad that there was only one god, whom he called Allah.

When he was about 40 years old, Muhammad had a great religious experience. He believed that Gabriel the archangel, or chief angel, approached him and ordered him to preach the word of Allah to the Arabs. Muhammad did not claim to have any supernatural powers. Like Moses, he considered himself a prophet and teacher.

Mecca's rulers bitterly opposed Muhammad's preaching. Mecca, an important center of trade, was also the site of a yearly pilgrimage that Arabs made to worship in the sacred Kaaba (KAHB • uh), a small stone building filled with the statues of many gods. The travelers brought income to many of Mecca's merchants. The rulers feared that Muhammad's preaching of a new religion would threaten the pilgrimage and cause the merchants to lose money.

*In Arabic the word *Islam* means "submission to the will of God."

Fearing for his life, Muhammad took his little band of followers to the nearby town of Medina. The event became known as the **hegira** (hi • JY • ruh), meaning "flight." It remained such an important event in Muhammad's life that the date, 622, became the first year of the Muslim calendar.

In Medina, Muhammad converted many people to Islam and established himself as the community leader. A few years later, he returned to Mecca at the head of an army and captured the city. He destroyed the idols in the Kaaba and made it Islam's holiest place. The only symbol he left in the temple was the Black Stone. Muhammad believed that Abraham had built the Kaaba and placed in it, as a sign of Allah's power, the stone sent from heaven.

The fall of Mecca convinced many Arabs that Muhammad was a prophet too strong to oppose. With a combination of wise policies, tolerance, and force, he converted many of the Bedouin tribes to his new religion. By 632, when Muhammad died, a large part of Arabia had accepted Islam (see map, page 209).

The Faith of Islam

The central belief of Islam is "There is no God but Allah, and Muhammad is his prophet." Like most religions, Islam has a holy book, definite rules for its believers, and emphasis on certain moral teachings.

The holy book of Islam is the Koran (meaning "recital"). The Koran presents Muhammad's most important teachings and includes many concepts and teachings also found in the Bible and the Torah. For example, the Koran recounts the creation of the world and the teachings of major prophets and of Jesus. Muhammad accepted the Bible and the Torah as part of Allah's revelations, and he taught respect for Christians and Jews. Muhammad also taught that the Koran was Allah's guide for all people and that it had existed in heaven, but he believed that no person before himself had been worthy of receiving it.

● All Muslims recognize the Koran as their sacred book. Because it was written in Arabic, and because Arabs discouraged its translation into other languages, Arabic became the common language of Muslims in matters of religion, law, and literature.

According to the Koran, a Muslim must meet five important obligations known as *The Pillars of Faith:* (1) Recite the words of witness, "There is no

Learning from Pictures *Islam's holiest shrine is the Kaaba located in Mecca, where Muslims go to fulfill the Third Pillar of Faith.*

God but Allah, and Muhammad is his prophet." (2) Pray five times a day facing Mecca, the holy city of Islam. (3) If possible, make a pilgrimage to Mecca at least once in a lifetime. (4) Give alms—money or food—to the needy. (5) Fast, or go without food and drink, from sunrise to sunset during the month of Ramadan—the ninth month of the Muslim year. The month is considered sacred because it was the month in which Muhammad had his vision of the archangel Gabriel and received Allah's instructions, later written in the Koran.

Muhammad required and emphasized the virtues of temperance, humility, justice, generosity, tolerance, obedience to authority, and courage. Islam allowed a Muslim man to have as many as four wives, but only if he treated them all with equal kindness. The faith also permitted slavery, but slaves had to be treated humanely. Muslims were forbidden to drink alcoholic beverages or to eat pork, believing, as the Jews did, that pigs were unclean.

In contrast to the teachings of Jesus, Muhammad praised what he called the jihad (ji • HAHD), or holy war—fighting to defend or spread the faith of Islam. According to Muhammad a fallen warrior's sins were forgiven and he received promised rewards in heaven.

Islam permits no religious images, such as statues, because Muhammad forbade his followers to make representations of human or animal forms. No elaborate ceremonies characterize the faith, and no formal priesthood exists. However, **mullahs,** men learned in Islamic faith and law, perform priestly duties. At a service in a Muslim temple, or **mosque,** the people pray together under the guidance of a leader. On Friday, the holy day in the week, all male worshipers must gather at noon for prayer and a sermon. The faith requires women to offer the same prayers at home or in a special section of the mosque set aside for them. A woman must also obey her husband, care for his children, and manage his household.

The Spread of Islam

When Muhammad died in 632, an assembly of Muslims chose Abu Bakr (UH • boo BAK • uhr), his father-in-law and probably his first convert, as his

207

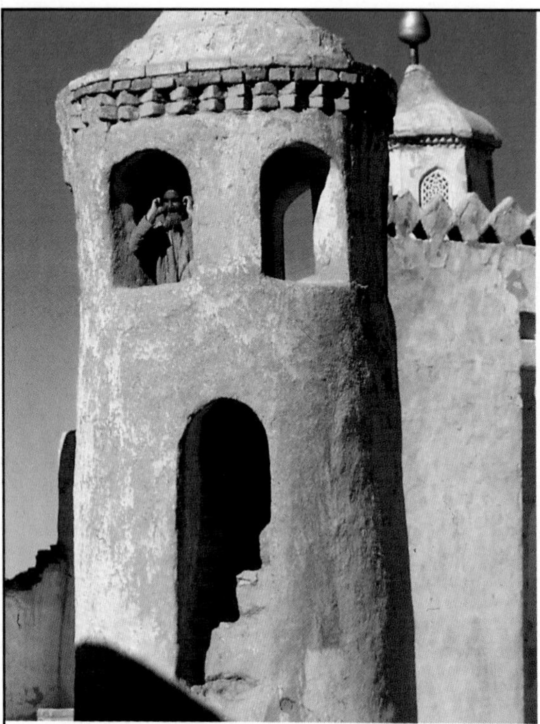

Learning from Pictures *A muezzin, or crier, calls the hour of daily prayers from the minaret of a mosque in Turkestan.*

successor. Abu Bakr used the title **caliph,** meaning "successor to the prophet." When Abu Bakr died, an assembly chose his friend and counselor, Umar, as caliph. To avoid civil wars over the succession, both Abu Bakr and Umar followed a policy aimed at conquering neighboring territories of non-Muslims. This policy diverted attention from the selection of the new caliph.

Fortunately for the caliphs, the Arabs had many opportunities for conquest in the 600s. Years of conflict had weakened both the Byzantine and Persian empires.

The Arab policy toward conquered peoples made their conquests easier. Fierce and fearless in battle, the Arabs were generous in victory. Non-Muslims who surrendered could choose either to accept Islam or to pay an annual tribute, or tax. However, some who refused to do either received the death penalty. Few of the conquered chose to die; they either paid the tribute or converted to Islam. Those who paid the tribute could keep their religion and customs but could not hold government office.

In less than 100 years after the death of Muhammad, the Islamic prophet's followers had swept through Arabia, Palestine, Syria, Armenia, Mesopotamia, Persia, part of India, and all of North Africa, including Egypt (see map, page 209). Then they took to the sea and eventually conquered the islands of the Mediterranean, from which they controlled the vital trade routes of the southern Mediterranean.

An attempt to take Constantinople failed. However, at the western end of the Mediterranean Sea, Muslims successfully entered Europe. A people of North Africa, called the Berbers, had recently converted to Islam and eagerly sought conquest. In 711 a Berber general named Tariq led an expedition

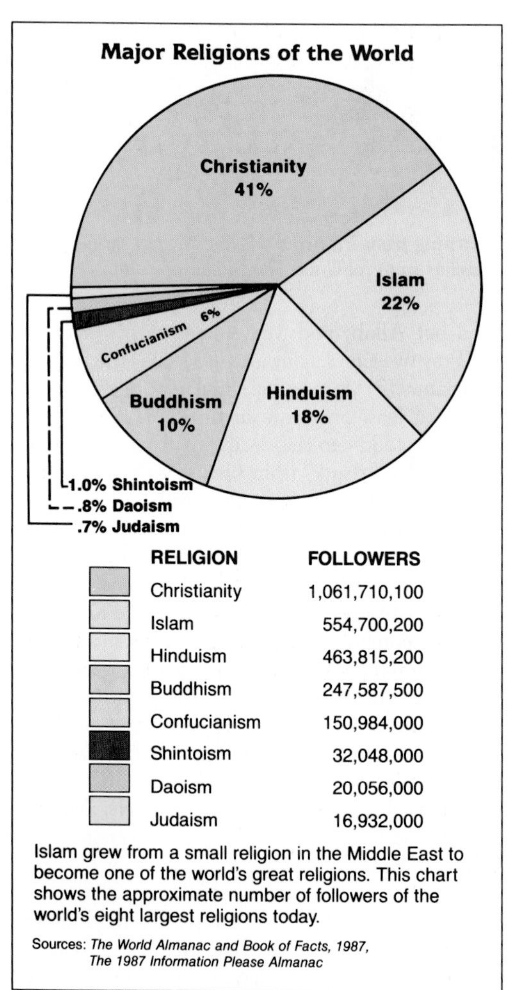

RELIGION	FOLLOWERS
Christianity	1,061,710,100
Islam	554,700,200
Hinduism	463,815,200
Buddhism	247,587,500
Confucianism	150,984,000
Shintoism	32,048,000
Daoism	20,056,000
Judaism	16,932,000

Islam grew from a small religion in the Middle East to become one of the world's great religions. This chart shows the approximate number of followers of the world's eight largest religions today.

Sources: *The World Almanac and Book of Facts, 1987, The 1987 Information Please Almanac*

208

1A, 1B, 3B, a4A, a4B, a4C, a4L

● **Answers will vary. However, students may suggest that if the Byzantine Empire had collapsed in 718, it could not have preserved the heritage of Rome.**

What If?

Constantinople

The Muslims attempted to conquer Constantinople in 718, but Byzantine armies successfully defended the city. How do you think the course of history would have been different if the Muslims had toppled the Byzantine Empire? ●

against the Visigoths in Spain, past the great rock that guards the strait between Africa and Europe. The rock became known as Jabal-al-Tariq, the "Mountain of Tariq." Europeans later altered the name to Gibraltar.

Spain was an easy conquest, and within seven years the Moors, Muslims of Spain, had passed beyond the Pyrenees to raid the plains of what is now central France. In 732 the Franks defeated them near the town of Tours (see map, this page). Driven back into Spain, the Moors continued to rule there for over 700 years.

In the 1800s the American author Washington Irving traveled throughout Spain. After visiting the Alhambra, the beautiful palace of the Moorish kings in Granada, a province of southern Spain, Irving wrote:

> "Their career of conquest, from the rock of Gibraltar to the cliffs of the Pyrenees, was as rapid and brilliant as the Moslem victories of Syria and Egypt. Nay, had they not been checked on the plains of Tours, all France, all Europe, might have been overrun with the same facility as the empires of the East. . . .
>
> Where are they? Ask the shores of Barbary and its desert places. . . . They have not even left a distinct name behind them, though for nearly eight centuries they were a distinct people. . . . A few broken monuments are all that remain to bear witness to their power and dominion, as solitary rocks, left far in the interior, bear testimony to the extent of some vast inundation. Such is the Alhambra; . . . an elegant memento of a brave, intelligent, and graceful people, who conquered, ruled, flourished, and passed away."

Learning from Maps *Two of the most important Islamic cities were Cordova and Baghdad. Where is Islam's holiest city?* **Mecca, Arabia**

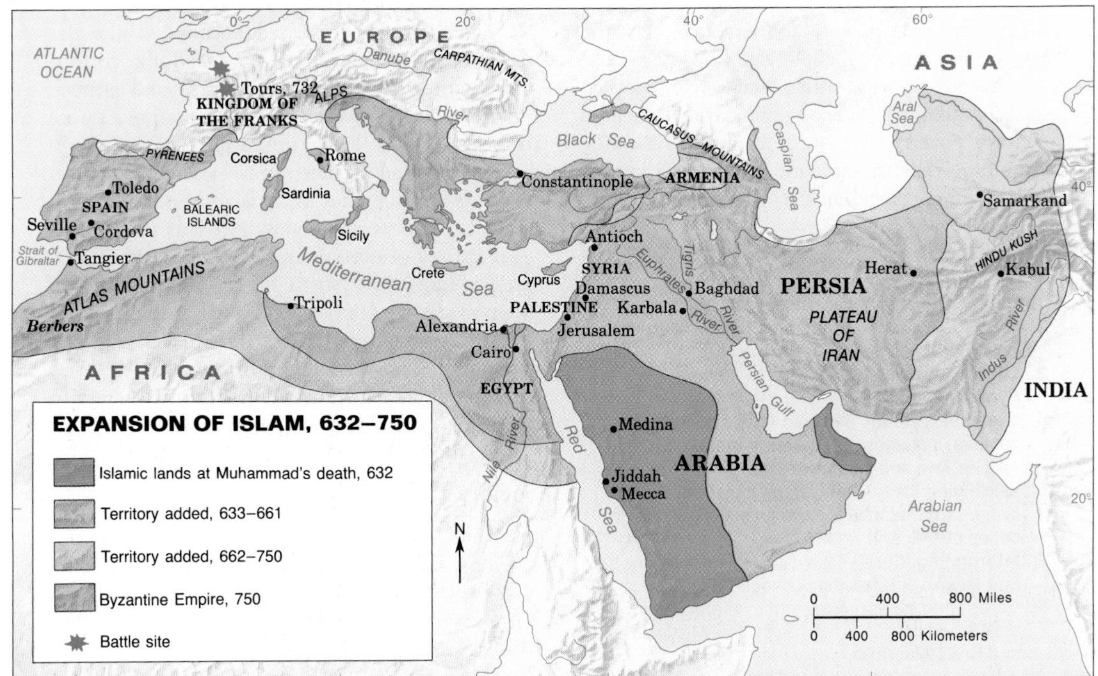

SECTION 1

Closure

Ask students to define the religious obligations of a Muslim. What similarities exist between Islam and other major religions? *(Answers will vary. Students should mention the one god—monotheism—of most world religions; virtues of humility, justice, and tolerance; charitable giving; fasting.)* Differences? *(pilgrimage to Mecca; forbidding of alcoholic beverages, although some branches of Christianity practice this.)*

Review Answers

1. ***hegira:*** flight in 622 of Muhammad from Mecca to Medina that marked first year of Muslim calendar; ***mullah:*** man learned in Islamic faith who performs priestly duties; ***mosque:*** Muslim temple; ***caliph:*** title meaning "successor to the prophet"; ***imam:*** Shiite leader having both spiritual and secular authority
2. ***Bedouin:*** Arab who lived as a nomad; ***Muhammad:*** founder of Islam; ***Allah:*** the one Islamic God; ***jihad:*** holy war to defend or spread Islam; ***Abu Bakr:*** successor to Muhammad and first caliph; ***Berbers:*** North African people who converted to Islam; ***Jabal-al-Tariq:*** Berber name for Gibraltar; ***Moors:*** Muslims of Spain
3. ***Arabia:*** peninsula between Persian Gulf and Red Sea, and home to Islam; ***Jiddah:*** Mecca's port on Red Sea; ***Mecca:***

1B, 1C, 3B, a1A, a1C, a4A, a4E, a4F, a4G, a4H, a4L

In 680 a civil war marked the beginning of the schism between Sunnites, who accepted the Umayyeds—a family from Mecca—and Shiites, who supported Ali, Muhammad's son-in-law. By the 900s the Shiites would have dominated the Muslim Empire but for the intervention of the devoutly Sunni Seljuk Turks.

holy city of Muhammad in Arabia; ***Medina:*** city in Arabia that was Muhammad's refuge and where he first established Islam; ***Pyrenees:*** mountain range between France and Spain; ***Tours:*** battle in France where Franks defeated Moors
4. Arabic became the common language of Muslims in religion, law, and literature because Arabs discouraged the translation of the Koran—written in Arabic—into other languages.
5. (a) The central belief of Islam is there is but one God, Allah, and Muhammad is his prophet. **(b)** The five chief obligations of a Muslim are: (1) Recite the words of witness: "There is no God but Allah, and Muhammad is his prophet." (2) Pray five times a day facing Mecca. (3) If possible, make a pilgrimage to Mecca. (4) Give alms. (5) Fast from sunrise to sunset during the month of Ramadan.
6. The Muslims were lenient toward the people they conquered. Non-Muslims who surrendered could choose either to accept Islam or pay an annual tribute. Some who refused both were killed. Those who paid the tribute could keep their religion and customs.
7. Sunnis claimed the Koran was the only mediator between believers and Allah. Shiites believed the imam, rather than the Koran, was the intermediary.

Islam Divides

Early in the history of Islam, rival groups began to emerge. Disputes arose over Muhammad's successors and over differing interpretations of the Koran. These divisions have persisted into modern times.

One group, the Sunnis (SOON • neez), claimed that the only intercessor between believers and Allah was the Koran. Another group, the Shiites (SHEE • yts), believed that a person, rather than the Koran itself, was the proper intermediary between Allah and believers. Shiites looked to this person, called the **imam,** as having both spiritual and secular authority. In countries where the Shiite sect dominated, the supreme religious authority also led the government.

The interpretation of the Koran by the faithful remained basic to both Islamic groups. According to Islamic belief, the Koran could not contain errors because Allah had dictated it directly to Muhammad. However, in order to establish the authority needed for the particular community, a decision had to be made concerning which verses or ideas took precedence over others.

As Islam spread beyond Arabia, numerous opportunities arose for direct contact with Christian and Jewish concepts and practices. By the 700s, Muslim mystics, people who said they could communicate directly with Allah, had adopted some Christian values. For example, they accepted voluntary poverty, a part of Christian doctrine maintaining that the amount of money a person has is less important than his or her faith in God.

SECTION 1 REVIEW

1. **Define** hegira, mullah, mosque, caliph, imam
2. **Identify** Bedouin, Muhammad, Allah, jihad, Abu Bakr, Berbers, Jabal-al-Tariq, Moors
3. **Locate** Arabia, Jiddah, Mecca, Medina, Pyrenees, Tours
4. **Evaluating Ideas** Why did Arabic become the common language of Muslims in matters of religion, law, and literature?
5. **Identifying Ideas** **(a)** List the major beliefs of Islam. **(b)** Describe the five chief obligations or duties of a Muslim.
6. **Interpreting Ideas** How did Muslims treat the non-Muslim peoples they conquered?
7. **Comparing Ideas** Explain the differences in beliefs and practices between Sunni Muslims and Shiite Muslims.

2 Muslims Created an Advanced Civilization

The tightly organized Islamic government gave its rulers great authority. Within the stable society that developed, both economic and cultural activity flourished.

Government and Economy

The caliph, the supreme civil, military, and religious leader of the vast Muslim Empire, headed the government. Although an elected office at first, the position of caliph later became hereditary. The territory of the empire, then organized into provinces, came under the leadership of Arabs.

Because the empire became more and more difficult to rule, it was later divided into three parts, or **caliphates,** ruled by caliphs in Baghdad, Cairo, and Cordova.

The Arabs had long been traders, and Muhammad had encouraged commerce. India and China sent goods across the Indian Ocean to the Persian Gulf and the Red Sea, then overland to the ports of Syria and to Cairo and Alexandria in Egypt.

Manufacturing increased because of the demands of trade. The empire produced silk, cotton, and linen textiles, as well as tapestries and carpets. Luxuries such as jewelry, perfumes, and spices were in great demand. Metal products included objects made of gold, silver, steel, brass, and copper. Steel swords from Damascus in Syria and from Toledo in Spain became world-famous. Artisans produced a great variety of pottery and glassware. Other artisans in Tangier in North Africa and Cordova in Spain made fine leather goods.

The Arabs also encouraged the development of agriculture. They introduced fruits, vegetables, and other products native to one part of the empire to other areas where they might grow.

Society and Art

In Islamic families, as in many other cultures and religions, the father was the absolute head of the household. The family provided the individual with both economic security and physical protection. Muslims respected the elderly and showed concern for the needs of all members of the extended

● Later Muslim civilizations such as those in Persia and India began to use figures in art that were unconnected to religion.

■ The Arabs absorbed a good deal of Byzantine culture when an early caliph moved the capital from Medina to Damascus in 660.

1B, 3B, a1A, a1B, a1C

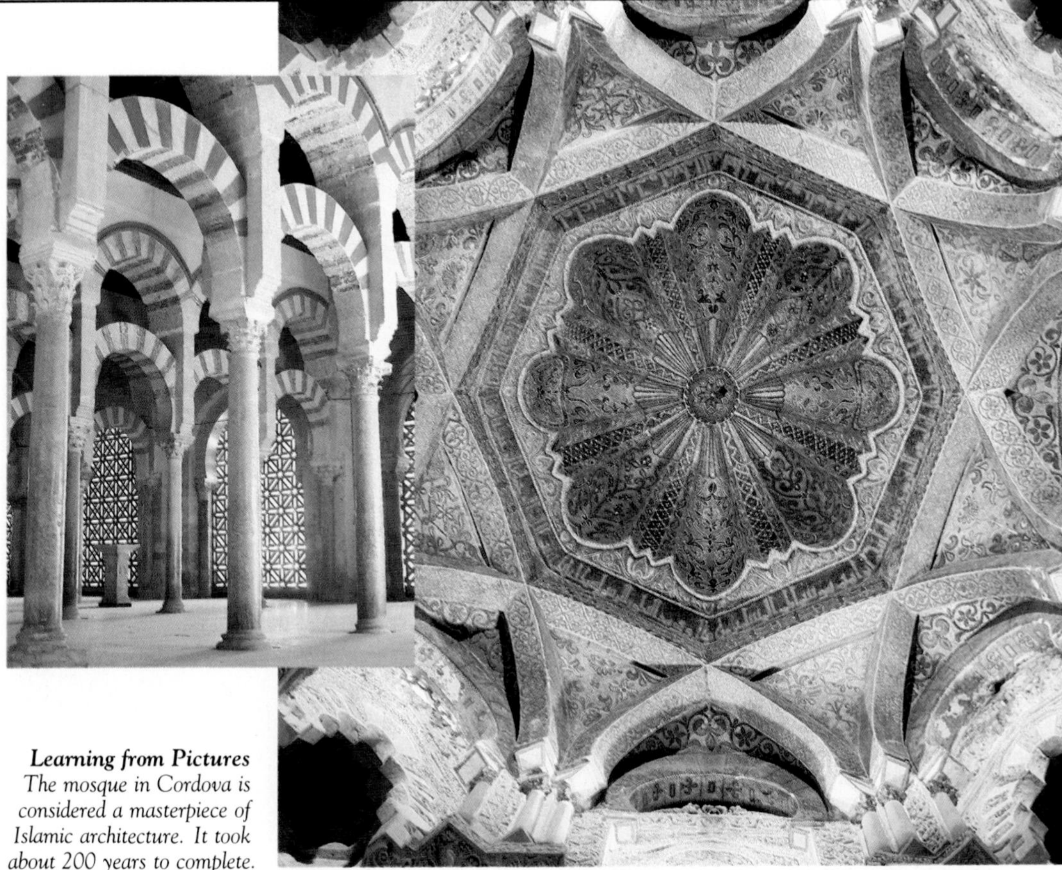

Learning from Pictures *The mosque in Cordova is considered a masterpiece of Islamic architecture. It took about 200 years to complete.*

family—parents, children, grandparents, aunts, uncles, and cousins.

Women had a clearly defined position in Islamic society. The Koran says, "Good women are obedient." A father or husband accepted responsibility for a woman's behavior. Parents arranged marriages for their children, and the groom gave his bride a special marriage gift called a *sadaq* or *mahr,* meaning **dower.** This gift did not represent a purchase price, but rather a gesture of love. In the event of a divorce, the bride kept this money.

The Koran extended more rights to women than they had received under traditional Arab law. For example, many Muslim women obtained an education and owned property. The Koran also forbade the killing of unwanted infant girls, a traditional Bedouin custom. And if a man divorced his wife, he had to continue to support her. She also was free to remarry. Although Muslim women later lost many of these rights, they still received the protection of either their husbands or brothers.

State governments had large educational systems, but the family and the mosque also took responsibility for education in Islamic society. The abilities to speak well and to write were considered the standards for an educated person. Subjects of required study were based on the Koran. A person with a superior intellect might be expected to memorize as many as 300,000 religious quotations.

Because Islamic law prohibited the use of the human form to depict Allah, the decorative arts and calligraphy assumed a special importance. Islamic art often used geometric and floral designs. Pictures of people showed only non-religious subjects, such as hunting or fighting battles. ●

Advances in Science and Mathematics

Though divided politically, the Muslim world remained united in one great civilization. The Arabs adopted the best ideas, customs, and institutions they found. For example, they combined the ■

SECTION 2

Focus/Motivation
Write the following words on the chalkboard or overhead projector, and explain to students that they are derived from Arabic.

algebra	damask
almanac	lemon
apricot	muslin
astrolabe	orange
chemistry	sherbet
cotton	sofa

Tell students the derivations of several of the words: *damask,* a fabric woven with a pattern, was originally made in Damascus. *Muslin,* a cotton cloth, originally came from the town of Mosul in Mesopotamia. For a more exhaustive list, see Duncan Townson's *Muslim Spain* (Lerner Publications). Interested students might research the derivations of the other words.

Ask the class what these words reveal about contact between Europe and the Arabic world. *(Answers will vary. Students should include the following: The words indicate that considerable trade was carried on between East and West. The words* algebra, astrolabe, *and* almanac *indicate a technical and intellectual influence.)*

Presentation
Organizing Ideas (Average/Group)
Have students make a chart in their notebooks

1B, 3B

listing Muslim accomplishments in science, medicine, and mathematics. The completed chart should include under *Science:* perfected the astrolabe, perfected map making, developed geography into a science. Under *Medicine:* Rhazes wrote about surgery, diseases of the eye, smallpox, and measles; compiled medical encyclopedia. Under *Mathematics:* perfected algebra as a science, introduced Arabic numerals to the West. When the students have completed the chart, have a class discussion on this material.

CONNECTIONS: THEN AND NOW

Medicine

Who was the first person in your life to set eyes on you? Most likely it was a doctor (below). Doctors and medicine have existed since ancient times. Early Egyptian books contain directions for setting fractures, and X-rays of mummies reveal healed bones.

We believe the Greeks were the first people to record their scientific research so that others could use it. They had medical centers where people could go, first to be cured, and then to offer sacrifices to the gods in thanks. The Romans established a medical school in Egypt. There Galen, a famous Greek physician, conducted studies whose results were used in Europe for the next 1,300 years.

In the Middle East, the Arabs developed their own interests in medicine. Legend says that in 765 the founder of Baghdad had incurable indigestion, so the doctors sought help from a Persian medical school. From then on, Persian doctors practiced in Baghdad and taught the Muslims about surgery performed with anesthesia. They established traveling clinics whose doctors went from place to place by camel, caring for the sick (above).

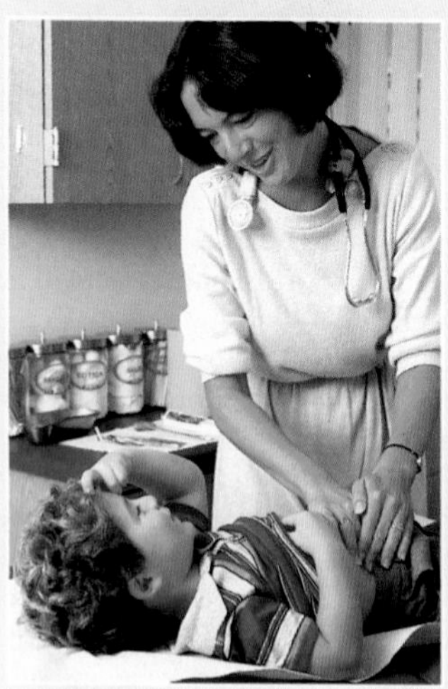

When the Muslims invaded Spain, they brought their medical knowledge to the Spanish universities. From there it soon spread to other European centers of learning. Monks in Italy had preserved the old medical knowledge, and now, combined with the new learning, medicine was taught at Italian universities. Farther north, young men studied medicine at the universities of Paris, Oxford, and Cambridge. These colleges are still well known for medical studies.

scientific and philosophical ideas of Greece, Rome, and Asia.

Muslim scientists wrote handbooks and encyclopedias on many subjects. Their geographers and navigators, known as the finest in the world, perfected the astrolabe, a small instrument used to determine latitude by calculating the positions of planets and stars. And from the Chinese, Muslims learned the art of papermaking.

Muslims added much medical knowledge to that developed by Hippocrates and Galen. At Baghdad in the early 900s, Rhazes (RAY • zeez), a

● The Arabs influenced Spanish music and rhythm. The words *fanfare, lute, guitar,* and *tambourine* have Arabic origins.

Muslim physician, wrote about surgery, diseases of the eye, smallpox, and measles. He compiled a huge medical encyclopedia which, translated into Latin, was used in Europe for centuries.

About the same time that Rhazes wrote, Avicenna (av • uh • SEN • uh), an Arabian philosopher and physician, used ancient Greek sources to write the *Canon of Medicine,* a medical textbook organized like an encyclopedia. Then in the 1100s, Averroës (uh • VER • uh • weez), a Spanish-Arabian physician and philosopher, wrote highly regarded commentaries based on Aristotle's works and on Plato's *Republic.* His interpretations of Aristotle influenced later Jewish and Christian writers.

Muslims excelled at mathematics and perfected algebra as a science. Our word *algebra* comes from the Arabic words *al-jabr,* meaning "the reunion of broken parts." Mathematicians of India developed the system of Arabic numerals, but the Arabs transmitted the system to the West. The Arabs also contributed the concept of zero to mathematics.

Arab scholars were particularly influential in the development of geography as a science. They used the observations of travelers as well as astronomical calculations to perfect mapmaking. Arab geographers adopted a Hindu idea that each hemisphere of the world had a center, or summit, equally distant from the four cardinal points of north, south, east, and west. Christopher Columbus based his conclusion that the earth was not flat on this theory.

The Spread of Muslim Culture

Europeans encountered Muslim culture in two ways. One was through contact with Spain, where the Muslim culture flourished. The cities of Cordova and Toledo became famous centers of learning, and Seville was known for art and luxury. ● Christian and Jewish scholars then carried Muslim learning from Spain into western Europe. Europe was also affected by Muslim culture through the Crusades—the attempts by Europeans to recapture the Holy Land from the Muslims from about 1100 to about 1300 (see Chapter 11). In Palestine and other Muslim regions, the crusaders learned of Muslim achievements and later returned home with ideas that greatly influenced European culture.

The great era of Muslim culture, however, lasted from about 700 to 1000. After that time those who believed in "following the letter of the Koran" rose to power in the Muslim world. These people opposed free thought and foreign ideas. At the same time, Turk and Mongol invaders disrupted trade and destroyed cities throughout the Muslim world. Only in Spain, which remained independent from the rest of the Muslim world, did Muslim culture continue to flourish.

The Turks

In the late 900s, the Seljuk Turks of central Asia migrated to Baghdad, where they adopted Islam.

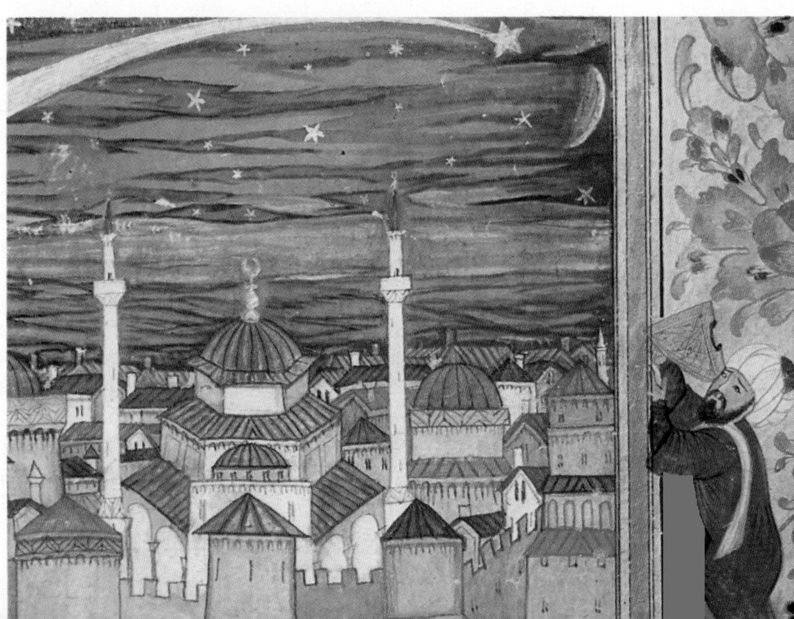

Learning from Pictures *This Muslim astronomer uses a quadrant to calculate the altitude of a meteor. What navigational instrument did Muslim scientists perfect?*
astrolabe

SECTION 2

Closure

Ask students to enumerate the many accomplishments of Muslim scientists, philosophers, and mathematicians during the height of the Muslim Empire. Why does the West owe so much to these individuals? *(Muslims preserved classical learning and passed on achievements of their own.)*

Review Answers

1. ***caliphate:*** one of three divisions of the Muslim Empire; ***dower:*** groom's marriage gift to bride; ***millet:*** community of religious minorities within Ottoman Empire; ***sultan:*** Turkish ruler
2. ***Rhazes:*** Muslim physician; ***Ottomans:*** Turks; ***Janissaries:*** powerful, disciplined slave bodyguards of sultans;
3. ***Baghdad:*** capital of one of caliphates of Muslim Empire; ***Cairo:*** capital of caliphate in Egypt; ***Cordova:*** capital of caliphate in Spain; ***Damascus:*** Syrian city noted for steel products; ***Toledo:*** center of learning in central Spain; ***Tangier:*** North African city; ***Seville:*** city in southwestern Spain;
4. The Muslim Empire produced silk, cotton and linen textiles, tapestries, carpets, jewelry, perfumes, spices, pottery, and glassware. It also produced metal products of gold, silver, steel, brass, and copper. Damascus in Syria and Toledo in Spain produced steel swords.

History Through the Arts

WEAVING

Oriental Carpets

People have been weaving rugs for at least 3,000 years. Used first as protection against cold, carpets soon had other purposes as well. They became symbols of wealth and popular items of trade. In Turkey, Persia, and central Asia, rug weaving became a great art. Many Oriental carpets remain unsurpassed for their texture, richness of color, and beauty of design.

Through the centuries, Muslims who could afford them have knelt and prayed on beautiful rugs. During prayer, the rug must be placed on the floor so that the arch in the design points toward Mecca, Muhammad's birthplace. The prayer rug shown here was woven in Turkey during the late 1600s or early 1700s. Typical of almost all Oriental carpets, it has a border of wide and narrow stripes and various geometric and stylized designs. The parts of the carpet have specific meanings. The color red, for example, stands for happiness and wealth. The trees above the arches are probably symbols of the tree of life.

During the 1000s they seized much of Asia Minor from the Byzantines and extended their rule into the Muslim territories of Syria and Mesopotamia. For the next 200 years, conflicts among Arabs, Turks, Byzantines, and Crusaders raged throughout the eastern Mediterranean area.

During the first half of the 1300s, a group of Turks called Ottomans (after their first ruler, Osman) surged through Asia Minor before invading Europe and establishing a capital at Adrianople, northwest of Constantinople. In the late 1300s they moved against Constantinople itself. Although the Mongols temporarily halted the Ottoman advance, the Turks eventually captured the city in 1453 and made it the capital of the Ottoman Empire.

The Ottoman rulers allowed conquered non-Muslims to practice their own religion. Religious minorities, grouped into communities called **millets,** exercised some self-government. They could establish their own schools, administer a civil government with its own courts, and collect taxes. However, any Muslim involved in a crime was not subject to the millet's authority.

A group of slaves called Janissaries* contributed to the Ottoman successes in battle and in government. The Janissaries, carefully instructed in

*Most of the Janissaries had been taken as prisoners of war. In later times, children taken from conquered Christians were often raised as Janissaries.

Islamic beliefs and laws, were organized into a standing army of disciplined, trained infantry. As bodyguards to the Turkish rulers, the **sultans,** they became influential in the government. Encouraged by promotions for merit and by a system of rewards and punishments, they represented a source of great strength. Later they gained much power and became a danger to the government, somewhat like the Praetorian Guard of the Roman Empire.

SECTION 2 REVIEW

1. **Define** caliphate, dower, millet, sultan
2. **Identify** Rhazes, Ottomans, Janissaries
3. **Locate** Baghdad, Cairo, Cordova, Damascus, Toledo, Tangier, Seville
4. **Summarizing Ideas** What items were manufactured in various locations throughout the Islamic Empire?
5. **Describing Ideas** Describe the organization of an Islamic family.
6. **Classifying Ideas** List what you consider to be the three most important scientific contributions of Islamic culture.
7. **Evaluating Ideas** How did the Ottoman Turks use the Janissaries in the organization of their government?

3 Muslim and Mogul Rulers Brought Important Changes to India

Islam also had profound effects far to the east of Arabia. Gupta rule in India came to an end in the 500s. At that time the Huns swept through the mountain passes and conquered all of northern India. Disorder and confusion disrupted the region until a ruler named Harsha brought peace.

Harsha's Rule

By the early 600s, the Huns had been overcome, and three warring states controlled the Ganges Valley. In 606 Harsha became the rajah in one of these kingdoms and built an effective army that included a cavalry and an infantry, as well as trained war elephants that wore enormous armor plates.

In six years Harsha conquered what had been the Gupta Empire. The Deccan, the rugged hill country south of the Narbada River, proved unconquerable, and Harsha never subdued it. Instead he settled down to govern his empire in northern India, which for a long time he did wisely and well. A Chinese Buddhist pilgrim to India wrote of the excellence of Harsha's early reign. He reported that the law-abiding people enjoyed low taxes, a high standard of living, and an excellent educational system.

Evil advisers victimized Harsha in the last years of his reign, and he became cruel and suspicious. By 647 his rule became so oppressive that the army had him assassinated.

The Rajputs

After Harsha's death northern India split into numerous small states, ruled over by the Rajputs (RAHJ • poots).* Descended from tribes that had migrated from central Asia into northern India during the 400s and 500s, the Rajputs claimed divine origins. They intermarried with Hindus, adopted the Hindu religion with its caste system, and took control of the small states.

Rajput rule was generally stable. Literature of the time included codes of conduct stressing respect for women, fair fighting in combat, and mercy for fallen warriors. Advanced codes of law also governed Rajput society. Courts used the testimony of sworn witnesses or written statements to decide civil cases. A man's children inherited his property, and his family supported his widow. The Rajputs also strictly enforced the caste system. Marriages could be arranged only between persons of similar caste.

Northern Indians under the Rajputs took great pride in their land. One visitor wrote that Indians "believe that there is no country but theirs, no nation like theirs, no kings like theirs, no religions like theirs, no science like theirs."

As it always had been and would long remain, agriculture in the small, self-sufficient villages served as the foundation for the economy of northern India. Villagers worked their own small plots of land, but policy required that they give free labor to the government once a month. Trade thrived, with people exchanging goods and services both within the village and between villages. And overseas trade flourished—with some trade monopolies, groups that controlled a good or a service, reaping large profits.

* *Rajput* means "son of a king."

Fine leather goods came from Tangier in North Africa and Cordova in Spain.
5. In Muslim families the father was the absolute head of the household. Muslim families cared for the extended family. The Koran defined the role of a Muslim woman as one of obedience, and a father or husband was responsible for her behavior. Parents arranged marriages in Muslim families.
6. Answers will vary. Students should include: perfecting the astrolabe, algebra, and mapmaking; introducing concept of zero to mathematics; introducing Arabic numerals to the West; medicine in the works of Rhazes and Avicenna.
7. The Ottomans used Janissaries—Christian slaves instructed in Islam—as a trained infantry and bodyguards to the sultan. At first a source of strength, the Janissaries later gained too much power and became dangerous to the government.

SECTION 3

Focus/Motivation
You might use the following statements and questions to stimulate class discussion: Early in his reign Harsha was a wise ruler; in later years he became a tyrant. Do you think that a person who holds power for a long time will inevitably become tyrannical? The Taj Mahal

215

was built at tremendous cost in money and labor. Do you think governments are justified in building elaborate monuments? *(Answers will vary. Students should be able to support their opinions.)*

Presentation
Interpreting Ideas (Average/Group)
Organize the class into two groups and hold an informal discussion with one group of students representing the Muslims' point of view and the other representing the Hindus' point of view. Have the two groups discuss their religious differences and the benefits that their respective religions brought to India. Students may want to do additional reading. Suggested sources include Huston Smith's *The Religions of Man* (Harper & Row); Lucille Shulberg's *Historic India* (Time-Life); and Desmond Stewart's *Early Islam* (Time-Life).

Muslim Invasions of India

In the early 700s, Indian pirates from the Indus Valley began attacking Muslim ships in the Arabian Sea. About 712 the Muslims struck back by conquering the Indus Valley. They governed the valley as a Muslim province but gave the Indians considerable freedom. Muslim criminal law applied to everyone, but courts cited Indian law in civil cases.

For about 300 years, the Muslims made no further conquests in India. Meanwhile, Turkish Muslims had occupied the area now called Afghanistan, northwest of the Indus River. About the year 1000, the Turks surged through the northwest mountain passes into India. One by one the small states of the Rajput princes fell to the conquerors. In battle the Indians always outnumbered the Turks and used their lumbering war elephants. However, the Muslims, adopting tactics originally developed by Alexander the Great, used their cavalry to stampede the elephants back upon the Indian troops. In 1193 the Muslims occupied Delhi, and by 1236 they controlled all of northern India.

The Delhi sultans. In 1206 one Muslim leader, a Turkish slave-general, founded the Mamluk dynasty. Because the Mamluk rulers used Delhi as their capital, they are called the Delhi sultans. Although the sultans were fanatical and cruel, they kept northern India unified for about 300 years. Early in the 1300s, one of the Delhi sultans conquered the Deccan. By 1320, resistance to the Muslims had collapsed throughout most of the Indian subcontinent.

Two Delhi sultans represent the worst and the best of Muslim rule in India. Probably the worst was Muhammad Tughluq (tuhg • LUHK), who ruled from 1325 to 1351. He murdered his father and fed the flesh of a rebel nephew to the rebel's wife and children. He once ordered the evacuation of Delhi and forced its inhabitants to march 600 miles south to a new capital.

Perhaps the best of the Delhi sultans was Firuz Shah, a social reformer and cultured man, who reigned from 1351 to 1388. He laid out more than 2,000 gardens and built five large canals. He also set up an employment agency for young men and a marriage bureau for young women. The bureau not only found husbands for the young women but also gave them marriage gifts.

Tamerlane. First civil wars and then the devastating onslaught of the Mongol leader Tamerlane interrupted the rule of the Delhi sultans. Tamerlane (Timur the Lame), born in Afghanistan in 1336, claimed to be descended from Genghis Khan, a great Mongol leader, and was as ferocious as his supposed ancestor. Following the usual pattern of Asiatic nomad warriors, he created an army and established his power in central Asia, with his capital at Samarkand. Then, about 1380, he began a career of conquest. After defeating the Golden Horde—Mongols who had invaded eastern Europe in the 1200s—north of the Caspian Sea, he led his army into India.

Tamerlane captured Delhi in 1398 and is said to have slaughtered about 100,000 of its inhabitants. When his campaign ended, he returned to Samarkand, taking with him all of Delhi's surviving artisans and leaving the city to die. Tamerlane reportedly said of the deserted capital, "For two whole months, not a bird moved in the city." After returning to Samarkand, Tamerlane moved westward again. He captured and looted Baghdad and Damascus and massacred their inhabitants. In 1402, his forces defeated the Ottoman Turks and captured the sultan in a great battle at Angora (modern Ankara) in Asia Minor. At the time the Turks were threatening what was left of the Byzantine Empire. Their defeat at the hands of the Mongols saved Constantinople for another 50 years.

In his late 60s, Tamerlane planned a campaign against China, wanting to conquer it as Genghis Khan had. However, Tamerlane died in 1405 before he could accomplish his goal.

Tamerlane's successors in India ruled until 1450. At that time the Delhi sultans regained power and maintained their rule until 1526.

Results of Muslim Rule

Despite the interruption of Tamerlane and his Mongol successors, the first period of Muslim rule in India had important and lasting consequences. Most northern Indians and nearly all southern Indians were Hindus. At first the Muslims ruthlessly slaughtered Hindus. Later they seemed content to confiscate land, leaving village life to go on as it had in the past. Even so, many Hindus converted to Islam, either to gain favor with the conquerors or to escape from the Hindu caste system.

Profound religious differences separated Muslims and Hindus. The Hindu worship of many gods

READ
WRITE
INTERPRET
CONNECT
THINK

BUILDING HISTORY STUDY SKILLS

Reading About History: Understanding Sequence

A sequence is the order in which things happen in time. Sequencing events, then, is arranging these events in the order in which they occurred. Sequencing helps you to organize information. From the pattern of the data, you can determine how events are related to each other. The relationship among these events can help you to identify other important ideas such as cause and effect and historical significance.

How to Sequence Information

To sequence information, follow these steps.

1. Identify what you hope to learn by sequencing the information being studied.
2. Look for calendar references, clue words, and time periods. Calendar references include centuries, years, and dates. Clue words include *first, second, after, before, meanwhile,* and *later.*
3. Determine whether there is an implied sequence or a cause-and-effect relationship. For example, could one event have happened without the other taking place?
4. List the events in sequence.
5. Make a statement about the relationship between the items, actions, or events included. What is the significance of the pattern of data?

Developing the Skill

You can better understand the expansion of Islam by organizing significant events sequentially. The following statements about the spread of Islam are not listed in the order they occurred. As you read the list, try to determine the proper sequence.

1. Muhammad's preaching was opposed, and in 622 he fled to Medina.
2. By 632, when Muhammad died, a large part of Arabia had accepted Islam.
3. Muhammad's successors pursued a policy aimed at conquering the territory of non-Muslims.
4. Muhammad considered himself a prophet and a teacher, and believed that there is only one god, Allah.
5. Muhammad became the leader of the community in Medina.
6. The Muslims were generous toward conquered peoples, who had to accept the religion of Islam or pay a tribute.
7. In 732, the Franks defeated the Moors and drove them back to Spain.
8. Less than a century after the death of Muhammad, his followers had conquered Palestine, Syria, Mesopotamia, part of India, Egypt, and the rest of North Africa.

The correct sequence of events would be: 4, 1, 5, 2, 3, 8, 6, and 7. The first statement (4) establishes Muhammad as the leader. Muhammad's beliefs are an implied part of the sequence. Muhammad has to be preaching something in order to be expelled from Mecca (1). Muhammad then became the leader of Medina (5). The date 632 completes Muhammad's achievements (2). His successors (3) would have to follow after his death. They conquered neighboring territories and then went to India, Egypt, and the rest of North Africa (8). Their conquering policy (6) is then explained as an implied part of the sequence. The Franks prevented the Muslim expansion into other parts of Europe in 732 (7).

Practicing the skill. Using the guidelines for sequencing information, make a list of important events at your school and arrange them in sequence. Include events such as special assemblies, school-sponsored club activities, and sports competitions.

To apply this skill, see Applying History Study Skills on page 221.

Muhammad's son-in-law, Imam Ali, in battle

217

1A, 1B, 1C, 3B, 2D, a1A, a1B, a1C, a4B, a4C, a4F

SECTION 3

Closure

Ask students to explain why many Hindus converted to Islam. *(to gain favor with Muslim conquerors and to escape the caste system)*

Review Answers

1. ***Harsha:*** rajah in northern India who conquered what had been the Gupta Empire; ***Rajputs:*** descendants of tribes from central Asia who ruled small states in northern India; ***Tamerlane:*** ferocious Mongol leader who captured Delhi, Baghdad, and Damascus before defeating and capturing the Ottoman sultan; ***Urdu:*** Muslims introduced this language combining Persian and Arabic words with Hindu grammar; ***Babur:*** descendant of Tamerlane who brought Rajputs under his control and established the Mogul Empire; ***Mogul:*** Muslim Empire that dominated India from 1526 to 1761; ***Akbar:*** Mogul ruler noted for religious toleration; ***Shah Jahan:*** Mogul emperor who built Taj Mahal; ***Nanak:*** in attempting to synthesize Islam and Hinduism, this prophet became the first guru of the new Sikh religion
2. ***Delhi:*** city in north central India that was long India's capital; ***Samarkand:*** Tamerlane's capital in central Asia; ***Angora:*** battle in 1402 in Asia Minor in which Tamerlane defeated Ottoman Turks; ***Agra:*** Indian city south of Delhi

and of idols repelled the Muslims. Hindus used music in their religious ceremonies; Muslims did not. The Hindu caste system contradicted Muslim belief in the equality of all people before Allah. Muslims introduced the seclusion of women—called *purdah*—into India. They also introduced the harem of several wives, which Hindus rejected. The Muslims ate the cows so sacred to the Hindus, while Hindus ate pork, which the Muslims thought unclean. In addition, Hindus drank fermented beverages that Muslims rejected.

However, the Muslims made several contributions to Indian life. They introduced a new and important language, Urdu. This language combined Persian and Arabic words with Hindu grammar and was used in addition to other official languages. Indian architects learned from the Muslims how to build the dome and the arch. Also, the Muslims borrowed paper, gunpowder, and the art of making porcelain from the Chinese and introduced it to India.

Learning from Maps *Babur defeated the Delhi sultans at the battle of Panipat. What two cities on the west coast of the subcontinent remained independent from Mogul rule?* **Goa, Calicut**

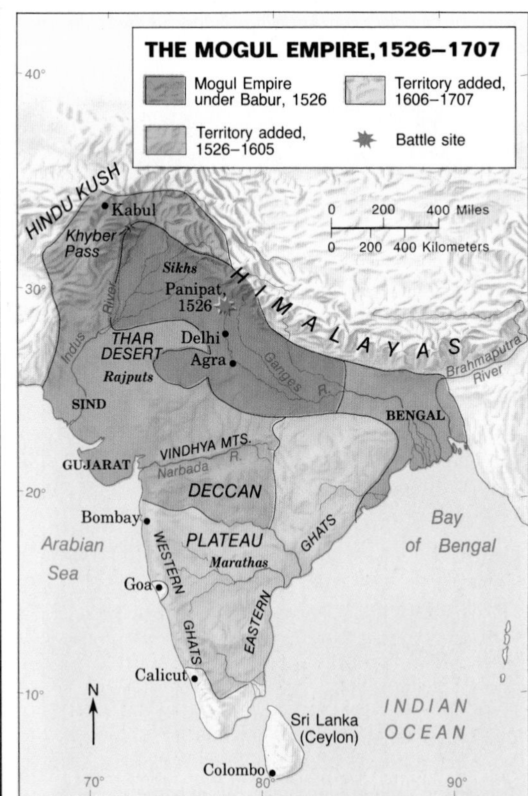

The Mogul Empire

As the Delhi sultanate grew weaker, Rajput princes again struggled for control of India. Thus, as in the time of Tamerlane, India lay open to Mongol attack. It came under the leadership of the youthful and talented "Babur the Tiger," a descendant of Tamerlane. He captured Delhi in 1526 and brought the Rajputs under his control. Then he set up the Mogul Empire (see map, this page), which lasted until 1761.*

Although Babur died in 1530, a series of energetic and talented rulers controlled the empire he had founded and united northern and southern India. While Tamerlane had made Indians fear Mongol rulers, the Moguls encouraged unity, orderly government, and the arts.

Babur's grandson, Akbar, considered the greatest of the Mogul emperors, reigned from 1556 to 1605. He fostered toleration for all religions, one of his greatest contributions to Indian civilization. Akbar repealed the special tax that non-Muslims had been forced to pay. He took a Hindu wife and encouraged Hindu as well as Muslim artists. These artists, supported by the royal household, created delicate and colorful miniature paintings based on the styles of Persia.

The rule of the Mogul emperor Shah Jahan, from 1628 to 1658, was outstanding. He is best known for ordering the construction of two famous buildings—the magnificent Taj Mahal at Agra and the Hall of Private Audience in the Red Fort at Delhi. The Taj Mahal, made of marble inlaid with semiprecious gems and built as a tomb for Shah Jahan's favorite wife, remains one of the architectural wonders of the world. In the cornices of the Hall of Private Audience are carved these famous lines: "If on earth be an Eden of Bliss, It is this, it is this, it is this."

These great buildings of marble were enormously expensive both in monetary and in human terms. Their cost became a grinding tax burden on

*In 1761 the Afghans pillaged Delhi. Although Mogul rulers continued to use the title of emperor until 1858, they had no power. Therefore, historians usually list the year 1761 as the end of the Mogul Empire.

218

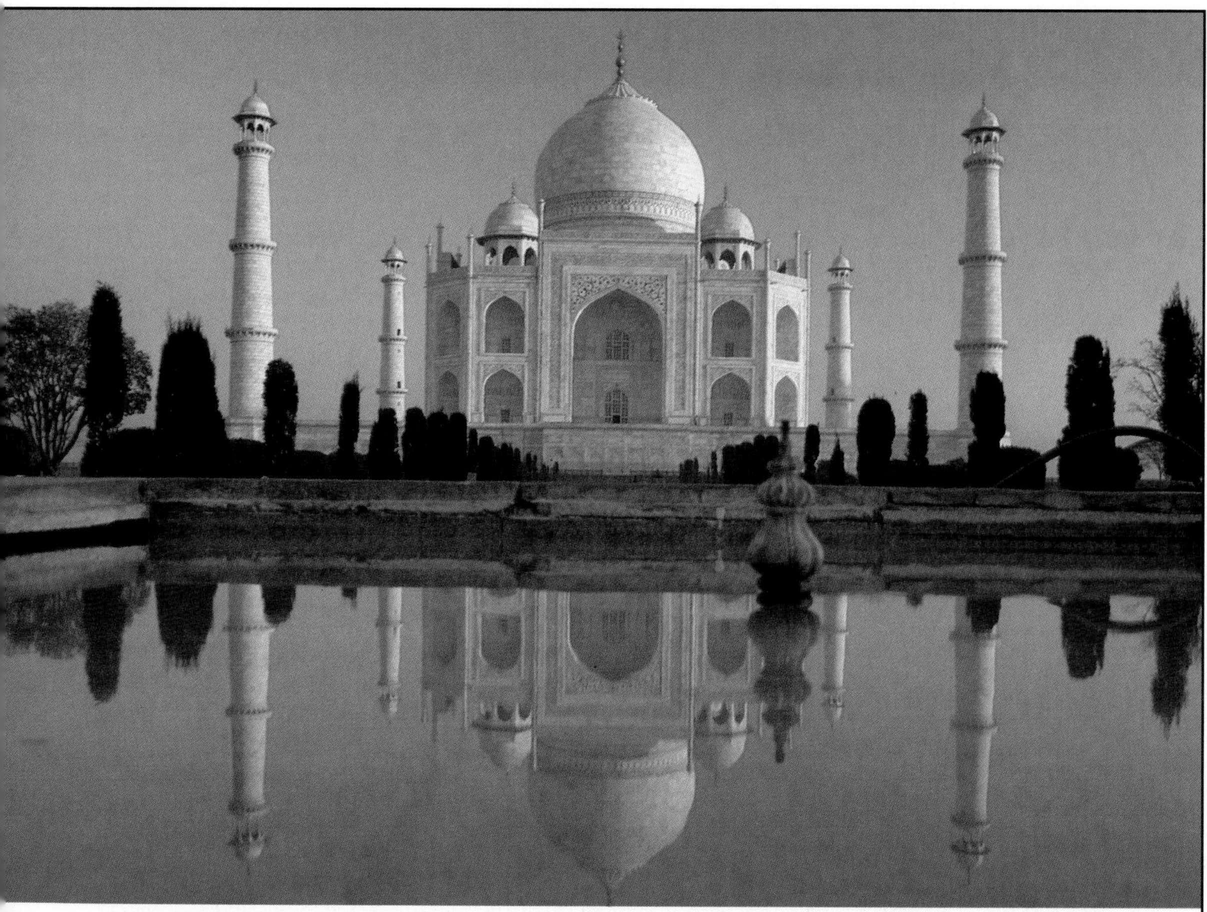

Learning from Pictures *The Taj Mahal's decorative details, gardens, and pools typify the blending of Muslim and Hindu cultures.*

Shah Jahan's subjects. It took 22,000 workers 22 years to finish the Taj Mahal.

The Moguls attempted a grand synthesis of Hindu and Muslim cultures. In the late 1400s, Nanak, a mystic prophet who was born a Hindu, attempted to bring about a total union of these two faiths. Out of his teachings grew a new religion—the Sikh (SEEK) faith. This faith stressed loving devotion to one god and the brotherhood of all, ideas that conflicted with Hindu beliefs. Nanak became the first guru (leader or teacher) of the Sikh faith. By the late 1600s, the Sikhs had become militant. As their military power developed, they became fierce enemies of the Mogul Empire and the Muslims.

In 1658, Aurangzeb (AWR • uhng • zeb), Shah Jahan's son, had his ailing father imprisoned and declared himself emperor. A fanatical Muslim, Aurangzeb began a campaign of persecution against people of other faiths, an act which led to revolts throughout his empire—by Sikhs and Rajputs in the north and among the peoples of the Deccan to the south.

Although the Mogul Empire reached its greatest territorial extent under Aurangzeb, his policies of persecution seriously weakened it. After his death in 1707, the empire began to disintegrate.

SECTION 3 REVIEW

1. **Identify** Harsha, Rajputs, Tamerlane, Urdu, Babur, Mogul, Akbar, Shah Jahan, Nanak
2. **Locate** Delhi, Samarkand, Angora, Agra
3. **Evaluating Ideas** Why were Turkish Muslims and the Mongols able to conquer northern India?
4. **Contrasting Ideas** What differences between Muslims and Hindus led to antagonisms?
5. **Identifying Ideas** Why was Akbar considered the greatest of the Mogul emperors?

and site of Taj Mahal
3. The Turkish Muslims and the Mongols conquered India because they faced no strong opposition. The Muslims attacked the Rajput states one by one. The Mongols under Tamerlane struck when the Delhi sultans faced civil wars. At the time of Babur's conquest, the Rajput princes were struggling to regain power.
4. The Muslims were repelled by the many Hindu gods and idols. Muslims believed in equality, which contradicted the Hindu caste system. The Muslims introduced purdah and the harem, which Hindus disliked. Muslims ate the meat of cows, animals that Hindus held sacred, while Hindus ate pork, which Muslims thought unclean. Hindus drank fermented beverages, which Muslims prohibited. Hindus used music in their ceremonies while Muslims did not.
5. Akbar is considered the greatest Mogul ruler because he fostered religious toleration and encouraged the arts.

219

Reviewing Important Terms
1. hegira; **2.** Mullahs; **3.** mosque; **4.** caliph; **5.** imams; **6.** caliphates; **7.** millets; **8.** Janissaries.

Developing Critical Thinking Skills
1. (a) The Muslims introduced the Urdu language, dome, and arch, and imported paper, gunpowder, and porcelain-making from China. **(b)** The aforementioned were positive. **(c)** Negative effects included religious persecution and long-lasting conflicts over religious differences.
2. He adopted monotheism.
3. The Koran included similar concepts, teachings, and prophecies.
4. The decorative art and calligraphy flourished. In architecture Muslims used the arch and dome. In mathematics they perfected algebra and introduced Arabic numerals. Muslim scientists wrote handbooks and encyclopedias. They perfected the astrolabe and were skilled mapmakers. The responsibility for education was shared by family, mosque, and state governments.
5. The Muslim caliphate in Spain became a flourishing center of culture that passed Arabic and classical learning into Europe.
6. Answers will vary. Students should mention that the Ottoman Turks allowed non-Muslim minorities to have some self-government. The Ottomans were probably more tolerant of religious minorities than the Moguls. Some Mogul emperors attempted to combine Hindu and Muslim culture.
7. (a) Hegira of Muhammad, Muslim conquest of Spain, Battle of Tours; **(b)** Harsha's conquest of the

1B, 1D, 3B, a1A, a1C, a4A, a4F, a4G, a4H, a4I, a4L

Reteaching
Have students review the Chapter Summary and the appropriate section and questions in the Unit Synthesis. Discuss the concepts until students demonstrate a clear understanding of the material.

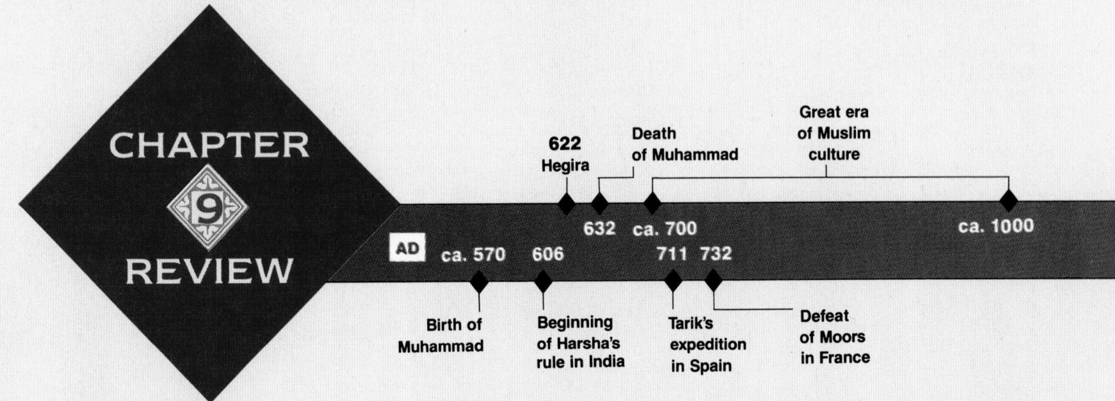

Chapter Summary

The following list contains the key concepts you have learned about Islam.

1. The rise of Islam transformed much of Asia and parts of Africa and Europe. Its early believers spread the Islamic faith aggressively, resulting in the most rapid spread of a new religion the world has ever seen.
2. Although the first wave of Muslim conquests died down in the 700s, the Muslims made further advances in India 400 years later.
3. A new Muslim expansionist force, the Ottoman Turks, rose to prominence in the 1300s and 1400s.
4. The faith of Islam emphasized humility and obedience. The result was the creation of stable states throughout the Muslim world.
5. The Muslims encouraged economic activity, and they became great traders, linking east and west.
6. The stable Islamic societies also promoted notable advances in science, philosophy, and art. Muslim contributions to medicine, mathematics, and geography had considerable influence on later scientific work.
7. In India the Muslim presence was felt at first in the 700s. It came to be of major significance only in the 1100s, when the Muslims conquered northern India.
8. Muslim rule brought new ideas and a new language, Urdu, to India. It also brought unrest and upheaval. The Muslims came as conquerors, and they persecuted the Hindus.
9. The Mogul Empire that conquered India in the 1500s was much more peaceful than earlier Muslim rulers. The Moguls encouraged the arts, most notably represented by the building of the Taj Mahal.

On a separate sheet of paper, complete the following review exercises.

Reviewing Important Terms

Supply the term that correctly completes the sentence.

1. Muhammad's flight to Medina is known as the ________.
2. ________ are learned in Islamic faith and law and perform priestly duties.
3. A ________ is a Muslim temple.
4. The successor to the prophet was called a ________.
5. Shiites believed that ________ were intermediaries between Allah and the people.
6. The Muslim Empire was divided into three parts called ________.
7. Communities of religious minorities were called ________.
8. ________ were bodyguards to Turkish rulers.

Developing Critical Thinking Skills

1. **Classifying Ideas** **(a)** Discuss the effects of the Muslim conquest on Indian culture. **(b)** Which effects do you think were positive? **(c)** Which were negative?
2. **Analyzing Ideas** How did trade in the ancient world influence Muhammad's ideas?
3. **Comparing Ideas** In what ways is the Koran similar to the Bible and the Torah?
4. **Synthesizing Ideas** Although the Muslim world was politically divided, it developed a high level of civilization. Using evidence from the textbook, explain how Muslims made advances in trade, art, math, science, and education.
5. **Interpreting Ideas** Why was Muslim Spain important to Europe's cultural development?
6. **Contrasting Ideas** Compare the treatment of non-Muslims in the Ottoman Empire and the Mogul Empire.
7. **Understanding Chronology** In each of the groups below, place the three events in chronological order.
   (a) Battle of Tours
   Hegira of Muhammad
   Muslim conquest of Spain
   (b) Taj Mahal built
   Delhi sultanate established
   Harsha's conquest of Gupta Empire
   (c) Delhi conquered by Tamerlane
   Hindus and Sikhs persecuted by Aurangzeb
   Mogul Empire established by Babur
   (d) Christian values adopted by Muslim mystics
   Abu Bakr named first caliph
   Constantinople captured by Ottoman Turks
8. **Evaluating Ideas** Why did the Mogul Empire begin to disintegrate?

220

1A, a4A, a4B, a4C, a4D, a4E, a4F, a4G, a4H, a4I, a4J, a4K, a4L, a4M

Gupta Empire, Delhi sultanate established, Taj Mahal built; **(c)** Delhi conquered by Tamerlane, Mogul Empire established by Babur, Hindus and Sikhs persecuted by Aurangzeb; **(d)** Abu Bakr named first caliph, Christian values adopted by Muslim mystics, Constantinople captured by Ottoman Turks **8.** Aurangzeb's persecution caused the Mogul Empire to disintegrate.

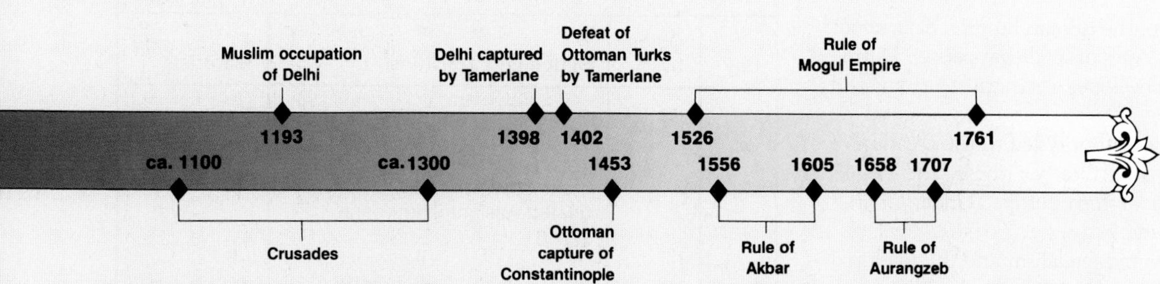

Relating Geography to History

Write a general description of the territorial changes that occurred in North Africa, southern and eastern Europe, and western Asia from about 550 to 1450. Use these maps for comparison: the Byzantine Empire in 565 (page 189) and Expansion of Islam (page 209).

Relating Past to Present

1. In early Islamic society, women were expected to be obedient and were kept in seclusion. Discuss the roles of women today in Muslim countries such as Egypt and Turkey. Compare these roles with the more traditional roles of women in such countries as Saudi Arabia and Iran. Use current sources to obtain information.
2. Many English words have been borrowed from other languages. For example, the coffee tree was introduced in Arabia in the 1400s. Coffee made from ground and roasted coffee beans became a favorite beverage of the Arabs. From Arabia, coffee spread to Egypt and Turkey and then to Europe and North America. Look up the word *coffee* in your dictionary. Where does it come from? Then research the origin and the use of tea. What can you conclude about the relationship between borrowed words and trade?

Applying History Study Skills

Before completing this activity, review Building History Study Skills on page 217.

All Muslims are expected to make at least one pilgrimage to Mecca during their lifetime. The following selection describes the events that occur during this pilgrimage. Read the selection. Then list the events in sequence.

> "Scarcely had the first smile of morning beamed . . . when we arose, bathed, and proceeded in our pilgrim garb to the sanctuary [the Kaaba]. We entered by the principal northern door, descended two long flights of steps, traversed the cloister, and stood in the sight of the Bait Allah [House of God]. . . . We proceeded to the open pavement . . . where we performed the usual two prostrations in honor of the mosque. This was followed by a cup of holy water and a present to the . . . carriers, who for the consideration distributed a large earthen vaseful in my name to poor pilgrims. We then advanced toward the eastern angle of the Kaabah, in which is inserted the Black Stone, and standing about ten yards from it, repeated with upraised hands, 'There is no God but Allah alone, Whose covenant is truth, and Whose servant is victorious. . . .' After which we approached as close as we could to the stone. . . . Then commenced the ceremony of Tawaf, or circumambulation, our route being the . . . low oval of polished granite immediately surrounding the Kaabah. . . . At the conclusion of the Tawaf, it was . . . advisable to kiss the stone. . . . In the evening, . . . I again . . . repaired to the . . . [Kaaba]."

Investigating Further

1. **Writing a Report** An important event in a Muslim's life is a pilgrimage to Mecca, the birthplace of Muhammad. In some years more than 400,000 Muslims visit the ancient city. Using encyclopedias, magazine articles, or other library reference materials, prepare a report on the holy places in Mecca and the religious ceremonies that take place during the pilgrimage. How do these ceremonies differ from religious ceremonies of other religions such as Christianity, Judaism, and Hinduism?
2. **Preparing an Oral Report** Oriental carpets made in Persia (Iran) have long been popular in the United States. Research and report to the class on the history and background of these rugs. Include the following information in your report:
   (a) How were the rugs made?
   (b) What were the importance and symbolic meaning of rugs in the Persian home?
   (c) How did the subject matter and design of the rugs reflect Islamic teaching?
   Among the books you might use are *Oriental Rugs: Antique and Modern* (Dover) by Walter Hawley and *Oriental Rugs: A Comprehensive Guide,* edited by Murray L. Eiland (N.Y. Graphic Society).

Relating Geography to History
Justinian recaptured most of the Mediterranean coastline of the old Roman Empire. The Muslim Empire took over North Africa, Spain, and almost all of the Byzantine Empire. By 1450 Christian rulers controlled the Italian city-states, most of Spain, and France. Muslim expansion took Persia and India.

Relating Past to Present
1. Answers will vary. In Egypt and Turkey, women are educated, mingle freely in society, vote, and wear Western dress. Women in Saudi Arabia and Iran are more restricted.
2. The word ***coffee*** comes from the Italian word *caffe*, a word in turn derived from Turkish and Arabic. Borrowed vocabulary indicates extensive trade and trade patterns. The word **tea** derives from the Chinese word *t'e* used for the plant.

Applying History Study Skills
Bathing; two prostrations; repeat Muslim words of witness; kiss the stone.

CHAPTER (pages 222–47)

10 Feudal Lords and the Church Dominated Medieval Europe

(432 – 1328)

CHAPTER OVERVIEW

The period following the collapse of the Roman Empire, from about 500 to 1500, is called the Middle Ages or medieval period. During this period the people of Europe developed distinctive customs and institutions.

The absence of a central ruling authority led to the creation of small, weak kingdoms by barbarian tribes. Of these, the Franks emerged as the dominant force in western Europe. Under Charlemagne they developed a vast empire.

Medieval life was organized around feudalism and the manorial system. Feudalism was the political system of the Middle Ages. Under feudalism lords granted land to vassals in return for military service and other aids. The relationship was based on mutual rights and obligations. The manorial system was the economic system of the Middle Ages. Manorialism was based on the self-sufficient manor worked by serfs.

The Christian church was active and influential in both spiritual and secular matters. It had great influence in secular affairs through its powers of excommunication, interdict, and taxation, and many popes claimed authority over monarchs. At the same time, however, many problems plagued the church.

Britain experienced a series of invasions by Angles, Saxons, Jutes, and Danes. The Normans under William the Conqueror made the last successful invasion of Britain. The monarch was made subject to law when nobles forced King John to accept the Magna Carta. During the 1200s the English Parliament and common law began to develop. In France the Capetian kings added to royal territory and developed a strong central government. In Germany and Italy, the Holy Roman Emperors began a struggle for power with the papacy.

SUGGESTED LESSON PLAN			
Day	**Objectives**	**Suggested Activities**	**Materials**
1	U4,* C1-3,	Introducing The Chapter (pages 222-23) Section 1 (pages 223-28), Focus/Motivation (page 223), Presentation (page 224), Closure (page 227), Suggested Teaching Strategies, Enrichment Activities, Daily Quiz, Suggested Assignments (page 221B)	ATE, Pupil's Edition, Teacher's Resource-Bank™
2	U5, C4-5,	Section 2 (pages 228-33), Focus/Motivation (page 229),	ATE, Pupil's Edition,
	C8	Presentation (page 229), Closure (page 231), Suggested Teaching Strategies, Enrichment Activities, Daily Quiz, Suggested Assignments (page 221C)	Teacher's Resource-Bank™
3	U5, C6-7	Section 3 (pages 233-37), Focus/Motivation (page 233), Presentation (page 235), Closure (page 236), Suggested Teaching Strategies, Enrichment Activities, Daily Quiz, Suggested Assignments (page 221D)	ATE, Pupil's Edition, Teacher's Resource-Bank™
4	U6, C9-10	Section 4 (pages 238-43), Focus/Motivation (page 238), Presentation (page 238), Closure (page 241), Suggested Teaching Strategies, Enrichment Activities, Daily Quiz, Suggested Assignments (page 221E)	ATE, Pupil's Edition, Teacher's Resource-Bank™
5	U6, C11-12	Section 5 (pages 243-45), Focus/Motivation (page 243), Presentation (page 243), Closure (page 244), Suggested Teaching Strategies, Enrichment Activity, Daily Quiz, Suggested Assignments (page 221F)	ATE, Pupil's Edition, Teacher's Resource-Bank™
6	U4-6 C1-12	Chapter 10 Form A Test, Reteaching Worksheet, Chapter 10 Form B Test	Teacher's Resource-Bank™ or Workbook and Test Booklet

*C refers to applicable Chapter Objective, U refers to applicable Unit Goal.

BOOKS FOR THE TEACHER

Chodorow, Stanley, ed. *The Other Side of Western Civilization.* Harcourt Brace Jovanovich. Includes a collection of articles on various aspects of medieval life.

Coulton, G. G. *Medieval Village, Manor and Monastery.* Harper & Row. Presents a detailed study of these institutions.

Durant, Will. *The Age of Faith.* Simon and Schuster. Features a thorough and popular account of this period.

Gahshof, F. L. *Feudalism.* Harper & Row. Discusses the feudal system in Europe.

Heer, Frederick. *The Medieval World.* New American Library. Describes social life of the Middle Ages.

BOOKS FOR THE STUDENT

Asimov, Isaac. *Dark Ages.* Houghton Mifflin. Discusses the period from the Germanic invasions to the end of the Carolingian Dynasty in Europe.

Rowling, Marjorie. *Life in Medieval Times.* Putnam. Concentrates on the social groups of the period; analyzes how people in the countryside and in the cities lived.

Unstead, R. J. *Living in a Medieval Village.* Addison-Wesley. Features account of village life.

Williams, Jay. *Life in the Middle Ages.* Random House. Focuses on daily life of the period; includes illustrations.

MULTIMEDIA MATERIALS

Charlemagne: Holy Barbarian (mp, 25 min.), Learning Corp. Contrasts the cultural contributions of Charlemagne with the ruthless means he used to accomplish his goals.

Civilization: The Great Thaw (mp, 52 min.), Time-Life. Describes the building of the great cathedrals and abbeys in twelfth-century Europe.

Medieval Times: Role of the Church (mp, 14 min.), Coronet. Explores the influence of the church on medieval society and its role in shaping European history.

Middle Ages: Rise of Feudalism (mp, 20 min.), EBE. Examines the origins and development of feudalism, from the barbarian invasions to the time of the Crusades.

The Middle Ages (fs), Educational Audio-Visual. Discusses the structure of society; the roles of agriculture, religion, and chivalry; and the world view of the average person during medieval times.

Section (pages 223–28)

1 Frankish Rulers Governed Much of Western Europe for Centuries

SECTION OVERVIEW

After the collapse of the Roman Empire, Germanic tribes overran Europe. One group, the Franks, created a strong kingdom in what is today France, Belgium, and the Netherlands. Charlemagne, the greatest Frankish king, governed an extensive empire that included most of western Europe. After his death the empire declined and fell victim to invasions from every direction.

SUGGESTED TEACHING STRATEGIES

1. **Preteaching Vocabulary (Basic)** You may wish to preteach the following important vocabulary terms: Middle Ages, medieval *(page 223)*. Have students look up the definitions to these important terms in the glossary.
2. **Understanding Chronology (Basic)** Write the following events on the chalkboard or an overhead projector. Have students copy them in their notebooks. Then have students arrange the events in chronological order by writing *1* before the event that took place first, *2* before the event that took place second, and so on.

    <u>(3)</u> Clovis conquered the Visigoths and southwestern Gaul.
    <u>(4)</u> Clovis's kingdom was divided among his heirs.
    <u>(2)</u> Clovis conquered the other Frankish tribes and controlled all northern Gaul.
    <u>(6)</u> Pepin II made the office of mayor of the palace hereditary.
    <u>(1)</u> Clovis became king of a Frankish tribe.
    <u>(5)</u> Mayors of the palace gained power.

ENRICHMENT ACTIVITIES

1. **Reading for Depth (Average/Group)** To help students obtain a more detailed picture of Frankish society and rulers, have them read excerpts from the works of Gregory of Tours and Einhard. Gregory, bishop of Tours in the 500s, wrote a 10-volume history of the Franks. Einhard, author of a biography of Charlemagne, studied at the palace school at Aix-la-Chapelle. Most anthologies of original sources in Western civilization contain excerpts from these two works. One source is Richard J. Burke's *The Ancient World* (McGraw-Hill).
2. **Contrasting Ideas (Average/Group)** Have interested students read encyclopedias or monographs on the Viking gods and goddesses. Ask them to list the major ones and be prepared to discuss the role of each in Viking lore. Then use the information on the Viking god-heroes as the basis for a class discussion comparing Viking gods with those of Greece and Rome.

DAILY QUIZ

To assess student understanding of Section 1, give the class the following quiz. (Each item is worth 10 points.)

1. Who became the first ruler of the Franks in 481? *(Clovis)*
2. Like Constantine 150 years before, Clovis won a battle and fulfilled a vow to his wife to make what religion the official religion in his kingdom? *(Christianity)*
3. What was the title of the chief of the royal household, whose position became hereditary in 700 under Pepin II? *(mayor of the palace)*
4. What man defeated the Muslims at the Battle of Tours in 732? *(Charles Martel)*
5. What religious leader crowned Pepin the Short as the king of the Franks—and whose successors later used this as an excuse to depose or install kings? *(pope)*
6. Why was Charlemagne crowned in 800 as "Emperor of the Romans"? *(Charlemagne was regarded as successor to the emperors in Rome and had unified much of Europe.)*
7. (T or F) Charlemagne created a palace school to encourage the education of nobles and the preservation of ancient Latin manuscripts. *(T)*

8. (T or F) After Charlemagne's death, the empire could best be characterized as a strong, united entity, with Charlemagne's grandchildren cooperating to protect the pope and successfully resist invasions by other tribes. *(F)*
9. The Vikings came from ________. *(Scandinavia)*
10. (T or F) The Vikings used their oared ships to plunder towns for treasure, search for food, and gain control of northern European towns. *(T)*

SUGGESTED ASSIGNMENTS

1. **Writing a report (Average/Group)** Have interested students read a biography of Charlemagne or a work on all the early Frankish rulers. Then ask them to write a three-page review of the book they read. Students should discuss in their reports not only the contents but also the author's point of view. Does the author view the subject with favor or disfavor? Ask the students to state whether the book enhanced their knowledge of this period of history.
2. **Creating a Model (Challenging)** Students with creative talent might like to build a scale model or draw or paint a picture of a Viking ship. Ask them to be prepared to explain to the class the features of the ship, its special seaworthiness, strengths and weaknesses, where the Vikings sailed, and what they used the ships for. Students might like to compare Viking ships with the Greek trireme and the later European ships used on the voyages of discovery.

Section (pages 228–33)

2 Medieval Life Was Based on Feudalism and the Manorial System

SECTION OVERVIEW

Within a century after Charlemagne's death, organized government had disappeared in Europe. Political power was divided among local lords who ruled their individual fiefs. Between lord and vassal, a number of rights and obligations existed. This political system was called feudalism. The manor was the economic center of life for both noble and serf.

SUGGESTED TEACHING STRATEGIES

1. **Preteaching Vocabulary (Basic)** You may wish to preteach the following important vocabulary terms: feudalism, vassal, fief, primogeniture *(page 228)*; manor *(page 229)*; domain, serf *(page 230)*; chivalry *(page 231)*. Ask students to explain feudalism and the manorial system.
2. **Understanding Ideas (Basic)** You might use the following diagram to help students understand feudal relationships. It illustrates that a person could be, and often was, both lord and vassal. For example, Ethelrod owes allegiance and obligation to Geoffrey, and is in turn owed dues by his vassals. The same is true of Archbishop Rufus, who could receive his fief from a layman and also grant fiefs to laymen. Point out that this is a highly simplified representation of a complicated system.

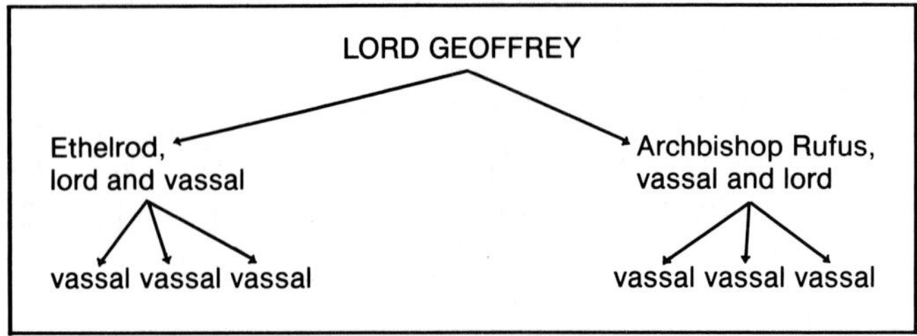

3. **Writing a Diary (Average/Group)** Have students write a diary entry for a typical day in the life of a noble, serf, page, squire, or knight. Call upon students to read their entries, and use them as a basis for discussing life on the medieval manor.

*4. **Thinking About History: Distinguishing a Fact from a Value Statement (Average/Group)** Ask students to read a discussion of the feudal system from a source other than this textbook. Then ask the students to list several facts and identify any value statements that may also appear in the source.

ENRICHMENT ACTIVITIES

1. **Researching Ideas (Average/Group)** Have students work in small groups to present oral or written reports on a particular aspect of feudalism. Sources include: Jay Williams's *Life in the Middle Ages* (Random House); Claire and Richard Winston's *Daily Life in the Middle Ages* (American Heritage); and *Horizon Book of the Middle Ages* (American Heritage), edited by Norman Kotker.
2. **Interpreting Ideas (Average/Group)** Have students read about coats of arms in the subsection "Chivalry" on pages 231 and 233. Then ask students to draw or sketch a coat of arms for themselves. Have them consider events, people, places, or animals—perhaps pets—that were or are significant in their lives. They may wish to incorporate these symbols into their coat of arms. Perhaps the family name will suggest a symbol. For example, the English writer C. P. Snow included snowflakes in his coat of arms when the queen of England made him a lord. Students may wish to consult works on heraldry or genealogy in their school or local libraries. Use the sketches as the basis of a class discussion on modern uses for personal or corporate emblems or logos: the Mercedes star, AT&T's stylized globe, and so on. Ask students to name several other uses of these devices.

DAILY QUIZ

To assess student understanding of Section 2, give the class the following quiz. (Each item is worth 10 points.)

1. (T or F) Feudalism developed to provide law and order at a local level when the Carolingian kings lost most of their power after the death of Charlemagne. *(T)*

2. The lord granted land to a ________, who held the land in return for services he gave the lord. *(vassal)*
3. The grant of land is called a ________. *(fief)*
4. Name one of three ways of carrying out feudal justice. *(trial by battle; compurgation, or oath taking; ordeal)*
5. The economic basis of medieval life was a large estate, including a village called a ________. *(manor)*
6. Peasants bound to the land were called ________. *(serfs)*
7. The lord's share of this estate was known as the ________. *(domain)*
8. (T or F) Because peasants lived on the land, they had plenty of meat to eat. *(F)*
9. The ________ was a strong tower that included storerooms, barracks, workshops, and the lord's living quarters. *(keep)*
10. The code of conduct for knights, from the French word *cheval,* was ________. *(chivalry)*

SUGGESTED ASSIGNMENTS

1. **Critical Thinking Worksheet (Basic)** Have students complete Critical Thinking Worksheet 22 in the TEACHER'S RESOURCEBANK™.
2. **Art Projects (Average/Group)** Have interested students make posters, dioramas, or other objects for display on the following: castles, the plan of a manor, armor, heraldry, chivalry, life on a manor. Sources include Charles Oman's *Castles* (Beekman House); Trevor Cairns's *The Middle Ages* (Lerner Publications); and R. J. Unstead's *Living in a Medieval Castle* (Addison-Wesley).
3. **Skill Worksheet (Basic)** Have students complete Skill Worksheet 10 in the TEACHER'S RESOURCEBANK™.

Section 3 (pages 233–37) The Church Had Many Roles in the Middle Ages

SECTION OVERVIEW

The church touched almost every aspect of medieval life. The members of the clergy were organized in a hierarchy with parish priests at the bottom and the pope at the top. The church had its own laws, courts, and the power of taxation. Both secular and regular clergy played an important role in education and social, political, and economic life. At the peak of its power, however, the church was troubled by internal problems.

SUGGESTED TEACHING STRATEGIES

1. **Preteaching Vocabulary (Basic)** You may wish to preteach the following important vocabulary terms: sacrament *(page 233)*; monasticism, abbot *(page 234)*; canon law, interdict, tithe, simony *(page 236)*; Inquisition *(page 237)*. Ask: What is the difference between canon law and secular law? *(canon law applies to the church)*
2. **Analyzing Ideas (Average/Group)** Ask students to read the subsection "Problems of The Church" on pages 236 and 237. Ask them how they think these problems began. *(Answers will vary. Students might suggest that the church's political interests and involvement in the feudal structure led it away from spiritual concerns.)* Ask students to keep these problems in mind, because they will be reading about the struggles of the popes and Holy Roman Emperors in Section 5 of this chapter. Explain also that despite early reform movements, the worldliness of the church would persist and that finally some members went into open revolt. This revolt was called the Reformation.
3. **Contrasting Ideas (Challenging)** Have students reread the subsection "Monasticism" on page 234. Then have them do research in encyclopedias to find information about monastic life in other religions—Buddhism, for example. Have students report this information to the class. Use their information as the basis of a class discussion on why monasticism became a part of Christianity and other religions. Ask: Did it appeal to the ancient Egyptians, the Greeks, the Romans, and the Indus and Ganges valley civilizations?

ENRICHMENT ACTIVITIES

1. **Understanding Music (Basic)** The church played an important role in the development of music in Europe. Obtain a recording of Gregorian chants and play it for the class.
2. **Understanding Art and Architecture (Average/Group)** The monastery at Lindisfarne, which produced the illuminated Bible shown on page 235, was the first establishment of Celtic Christianity in England. One or more students can prepare an oral report on Celtic art. One source is "The Celts," *National Geographic* (May 1977). You may also present the film, *Chartres Cathedral* (30 min., color, EBE). Have interested students pursue further the subject of art and church architecture. Some communities may have large cathedrals that would be well worth a visit by the entire class. See Nikolaus Pevsner's *An Outline of European Architecture* (Penguin) for background information.
3. **Preparing a Research Report (Average/Group)** Have students work in small groups to prepare oral or written reports on the spread of Christianity in Ireland and England. A source on the spread of Christianity in Ireland and England is Trevor Cairns's informative and readable *Barbarian, Christian, and Muslim* (Lerner Publications). Have students read their reports to the class. Use the information as the basis of a class discussion on the spread of Christianity throughout Europe. Ask students to speculate why Ireland—on the fringes of Europe—became a great Christian spiritual center in the early Middle Ages. *(Answers will vary.)* Tell students that the Romans never conquered Ireland, and after the Anglo-Saxon conquest of Britain, Ireland was cut off from the rest of Europe. It had an independent and well-educated clergy who established centers of learning. However, when the Irish clergy—mostly monks—quarreled with Roman clergy chiefly over the issue of how to calculate the date for Easter, they left Ireland. Many Irish monks settled in monasteries on the continent or became missionaries.

DAILY QUIZ

To assess student understanding of Section 3, give the class the following quiz. (Each item is worth 10 points.)

1. List three of the four levels of the church hierarchy. *(priest, bishop, archbishop, pope)*
2. Name three administrative divisions of the church. *(parish, diocese, province)*
3. What organization advised the leader of the Western church? *(curia)*
4. (T or F) Monks and nuns belong to the secular clergy. *(F)*
5. An individual who was cut off completely from the church and its sacraments, excluded from Christian society, and not allowed burial in church grounds was said to be ______. *(excommunicated)*
6. Who established an order of monks at Monte Cassino, Italy, and adopted a complex set of standards to guide their lives? *(St. Benedict)*
7. What country became the greatest center of Christian culture in Europe from 500 to 800? *(Ireland)*
8. The books produced by hand during the medieval period, which gave the monks an opportunity to beautify the text, are called ______ ______. *(illuminated manuscripts)*
9. (T or F) The "Peter's Pence" was a church tax of one penny a year on every household in England and Scandinavia. *(T)*
10. Name one of the two religious orders established to reform the church. *(Franciscans, Dominicans)*

SUGGESTED ASSIGNMENTS

1. **Art Project (Average/Group)** A group of interested students can make drawings, posters, or collages illustrating the daily schedule of monks or nuns during the Middle Ages. Students should research the topic. Sources include: Anne Boyd's *Life in a Fifteenth-Century Monastery* (Lerner Publications); Anne Fremantle's *Age of Faith* (Time-Life); and Eileen Power's *Medieval People* (Harper & Row).
2. **Critical Thinking Worksheet (Basic)** Have students complete Critical Thinking Worksheet 23 in the TEACHER'S RESOURCEBANK™.

Section (pages 238–43)

4 Kings and Nobles Struggled for Power in England and France

SECTION OVERVIEW

Angles, Saxons, and other Germanic peoples invaded Britain about 450. They established several small kingdoms that later were nearly overwhelmed by Viking invaders. The Anglo-Saxons finally drove out the Vikings, but they in turn were defeated by Normans from France. Kings in England and France increased their power over the nobles. In England the Exchequer was established, royal courts were strengthened, and the jury system developed. Parliament and common law developed in the 1200s. The Capetians in France gained territory, developed a strong central government, and increased tax revenues.

SUGGESTED TEACHING STRATEGIES

1. **Preteaching Vocabulary (Basic)** You may wish to preteach the following important vocabulary terms: shire *(page 238)*; Magna Carta *(page 240)*; common law *(page 242)*. Review with students the significance of the Magna Carta.
2. **Organizing Information (Basic)** On the chalkboard or an overhead projector, draw a time line showing the following dates: 1066-1087; 1100-1135; 1154-1189; 1215; 1265; 1272-1307. Have students identify the appropriate individual and his accomplishments next to each year. *(1066-1087: William the Conqueror brought feudalism to England; 1100-1135: Henry I set up the Exchequer to handle finances and sent out judges to hold court; 1154-1189: Henry II required every freeman to serve in the king's army, reorganized the Exchequer, appointed grand and petit juries, and gained land in France; 1215: King John accepted the Magna Carta; 1265: Simon de Montfort summoned the Great Council; 1272-1307: Edward I divided the king's court into three branches.)*
3. **Preparing an Oral Report (Average/Group)** Organize the class into groups to prepare oral reports on some of the early rulers of England and France. Suggested monarchs include: *England*—Alfred the Great, Edward the Confessor, William I, Henry I, Henry II, John, Richard the Lion-Hearted, and Edward I; *France*—Hugh Capet, Louis VII, Philip Augustus, Louis VIII, Louis IX (St. Louis), and Philip IV.
4. **Illustrating Ideas (Basic)** Write the following "equation" on the chalkboard or an overhead projector: CELTS + ANGLES + SAXONS + JUTES + DANES + NORMANS = ENGLISH Ask students what they think this "equation" means. *(Answers will vary. English people are descended from these various tribes. Over the course of years, these people assimilated through intermarriage.)* Ask students to suggest possible results of this assimilation. *(Answers will vary. Students should include the following: the creation of the English language and the development of common laws, traditions, customs, and ideas.)*

ENRICHMENT ACTIVITIES

1. **Comparing Past and Present (Average/Group)** Have interested students compare the life of Eleanor of Aquitaine to the life of the wife of a recent American president. They should discuss the influence each woman had on political developments during her lifetime. One source on Eleanor of Aquitaine is Desmond Seward's *Eleanor of Aquitaine* (Time Books). Students can use the *Readers' Guide to Periodical Literature* to find articles on presidential wives from Mrs. Woodrow Wilson to the present.
2. **Creating an Illuminated Manuscript (Average/Group)** Have interested students do research on the illuminated manuscripts

made by the monks during the Middle Ages. They may want to look at examples in art books or encyclopedias in the school or local libraries. Those students who have access to art museums with collections of illustrated manuscripts should visit them. Ask students to report on the pages they saw and describe what kinds of subject matter interested the monks who thus included it in their work. Those students with artistic talent may want to make an illuminated manuscript.

DAILY QUIZ

To assess student understanding of Section 4, give the class the following quiz. (Each item is worth 10 points.)

1. After which Germanic tribe did southeastern Britain get the name "England"? *(Angles)*
2. What Anglo-Saxon ruler first kept the Danes from conquering England? *(Alfred the Great)*
3. (T or F) William the Conqueror had little trouble ruling England because the Saxons readily adopted the language, customs, and ideas of the Normans. *(F)*
4. The ________ ________, compiled by William the Conqueror's commissioners, depicts an accurate portrayal of England in the 1000s. *(Domesday Book)*
5. (T or F) Henry II of England established the grand jury and circuit judge system to provide better local justice. *(T)*
6. Henry II's attempt to increase royal authority by reducing that of the church led to a dispute with the Archbishop of Canterbury. What was this archbishop's name? *(Thomas Becket)*
7. In 1215 what document did the English nobility force King John to sign? *(Magna Carta)*
8. Name the two houses of the English Parliament. *(House of Lords, House of Commons)*
9. (T or F) Hugh Capet ruled most of what is today France and was selected king when Charlemagne's last heir died. *(F)*
10. (T or F) The Capetian kings continually had to resist the English who controlled large sections of French territory, particularly in Aquitaine and Gascony. *(T)*

SUGGESTED ASSIGNMENTS

1. **Profile Worksheet (Basic)** Have students complete Profile Worksheet 10 in the TEACHER'S RESOURCEBANK™.
2. **Comparing Ideas (Average/Group)** Ask interested students to trace the development of representative government in England and France. How did the two countries go about creating representative bodies? *(Answers will vary. England's Parliament grew from an extension of membership in the Great Council to knights and burgesses. Eventually two houses—Lords and Commons—formed. Parliament had the important power of approving new taxes. In France the Capetian kings created a strong administration and sided with the townspeople against the feudal lords.)* Tell the students that a French parliamentary body, the Estates-General, did exist but the kings always managed to keep it in check, and its meetings grew more and more infrequent.

Section (pages 243–45)

5 Popes and Emperors Clashed over Germany and Italy

SECTION OVERVIEW

Conflicts arose over the temporal authority of the church, as the Holy Roman Emperors who controlled Germany and northern Italy struggled for power with the papacy. Pope Gregory VII made sweeping claims to power, and under Innocent III the papacy reached the height of its prestige and influence. Strong emperors, among them Frederick Barbarossa and Frederick II, tried unsuccessfully to unite Germany and Italy.

SUGGESTED TEACHING STRATEGIES

1. **Understanding Ideas (Basic)** Remind students that they read in Section 1 that in 800 the pope crowned Charlemagne as "Emperor of the Romans." In 962 another pope crowned Otto I of Germany with this same title. Tell the students that this new Roman empire is called the *Holy Roman Empire*. It lasted from Charlemagne's rule until the early 1800s—more than 1,000 years. Its power waxed and waned, largely depending on the emperor's strength of personality or military prowess. Next tell students that the earliest struggles of the Holy Roman Emperors were with the very popes who crowned them. Ask students how this new Holy Roman Empire differed from (1) the Roman Empire in the West and (2) the Byzantine Empire in the East. *(Answers will vary. Students should mention that the old Roman emperors took second billing to no one. There was no struggle with a religious authority in Rome. By the time Christianity was established in the Roman Empire, the emperors in the West had left Rome to defend the frontiers, and the popes could not yet fulfill the supremacy they later claimed. The Byzantine emperors differed from the Holy Roman emperors in that the Byzantines combined both the pope's and emperor's position in one—the emperor.)* Tell students that this is a concept known as caesaropapism.The Byzantine emperors were clearly dominant over the patriarchs at Constantinople. In addition, the pope first crowned the Frankish king as emperor, in part because the Byzantine emperors gave him little support against barbarian invasions of papal lands in Italy.
2. **Writing a Research Report (Challenging)** Have students prepare oral or written reports on significant people of this period, such as Frederick Barbarossa, Gregory VII, Innocent III, or Frederick II. Sources include Will Durant's *The Age of Faith* (Simon and Schuster); E. Kantorowicz's *Frederick the Second, 1194-1250* (Ungar); and Paul Johnson's *A History of Christianity* (Atheneum).

ENRICHMENT ACTIVITY

Performing a Drama (Average/Group) Interested students might stage a dramatization or present a television news report on Henry IV's pilgrimage to the pope's residence at Canossa. Students should assume the following roles: a newscaster, Henry IV, Pope Gregory

VII, a German noble, and two or three townspeople. The newscaster should give a background of events leading to the pilgrimage and then interview Henry and Gregory for their views of the controversy. Encourage the rest of the class to give their opinions on the incident. Sources for information include Anne Fremantle's *Age of Faith* (Time-Life) and Will Durant's *The Age of Faith* (Simon and Schuster).

DAILY QUIZ

To assess student understanding of Section 5, give the class the following quiz. (Each item is worth 10 points.)

1. Which of these was elected king of Germany by feudal lords in 936? Otto I, Frederick III, George I, Charlemagne. *(Otto I)*
2. Name the political unit covering Germany and Northern Italy. *(Holy Roman Empire)*
3. (T or F) Pope Gregory VII believed he had to solve the issue of lay investiture in order to guarantee the independence of the church. *(T)*
4. Excommunicated by Pope Gregory VII, ______ soon had to give in on the issue of lay investiture. *(Henry IV)*
5. The ______ ______ ______ stipulated that the emperor could grant lands and secular powers to church officials, but only the church could choose the bishops and grant them their spiritual powers. *(Concordat of Worms)*
6. Frederick I and Frederick II failed to unite Germany because they were interested in the wealthy city-states in what European country? *(Italy)*
7. What pope from 1198-1216 led the papacy to its height of power and prestige? *(Innocent III)*
8. (T or F) The pope used the interdict to intimidate King John of England into accepting his decisions. *(T)*
9. (T or F) By the 1200s the seeds of German unification had been planted, and it had become obvious that Germany would soon become a united country. *(F)*
10. (T or F) During the 1100s quarrels in Italy centered on the Lombard League, Frederick I, and Pope Innocent III. *(T)*

SUGGESTED ASSIGNMENTS

1. **Review Worksheet (Basic)** Have students complete Review Worksheet 10 in the TEACHER'S RESOURCEBANK™.
2. **Comparing Ideas (Challenging)** Have students review the subsection "Innocent III and Papal Power" on page 245. Then have them compare the powers of the medieval pope with those of Pope John Paul II today. Students might wish to consult the *Readers' Guide to Periodical Literature* on the present-day papacy. They might also wish to review the process of Italian unity, the Latern Treaties of 1929, and the extent of church activities today compared with those of the High Middle Ages. *(Answers will vary. Students should mention that Pope Innocent III had substantial territories as a temporal ruler while John Paul II has only the Vatican City. The spiritual powers of both popes are very great. Perhaps John Paul II carries greater weight with a worldwide Catholic membership, whereas Innocent's prestige did not extend beyond Europe. On the other hand, students might argue that secular interests are broader than in the religious Middle Ages.)*

Teacher's Notes

For suggested lesson plan, additional teaching strategies, enrichment activities, daily quizzes, and suggested assignments, see pages 221A–221H.

Introducing the Chapter
Explain to the students that the Middle Ages is a transition period between the Roman period and the modern period. Call upon students to suggest words or phrases that they associate with the medieval period. Write these on the chalkboard or an overhead projector. *(Accept answers such as the church, knights, castles, armor, kings and queens, monks, peasants, and the jury.)* Ask students if any items on the list can be found in modern society. *(Answers will vary; for example, the use of the jury has continued to the present time.)*

Chapter Objectives
After studying Chapter 10, students will be able to:

1. Outline the story of the rise of the Merovingians and Carolingians, including the role of the mayors of the palace.
2. Discuss the mutual benefits the Frankish kings and popes enjoyed as the Franks became the "official protectors" of Rome.
3. Summarize the collapse of the Frankish kingdom and the role the Vikings played in western European history.
4. Use these terms—*vassal, fief, lord*—to summarize the basic principles of feudalism.
5. Describe feudal justice, warfare, and chivalry.
6. List the hierarchical roles played by church leaders and the importance

CHAPTER 10

Feudal Lords and the Church Dominated Medieval Europe

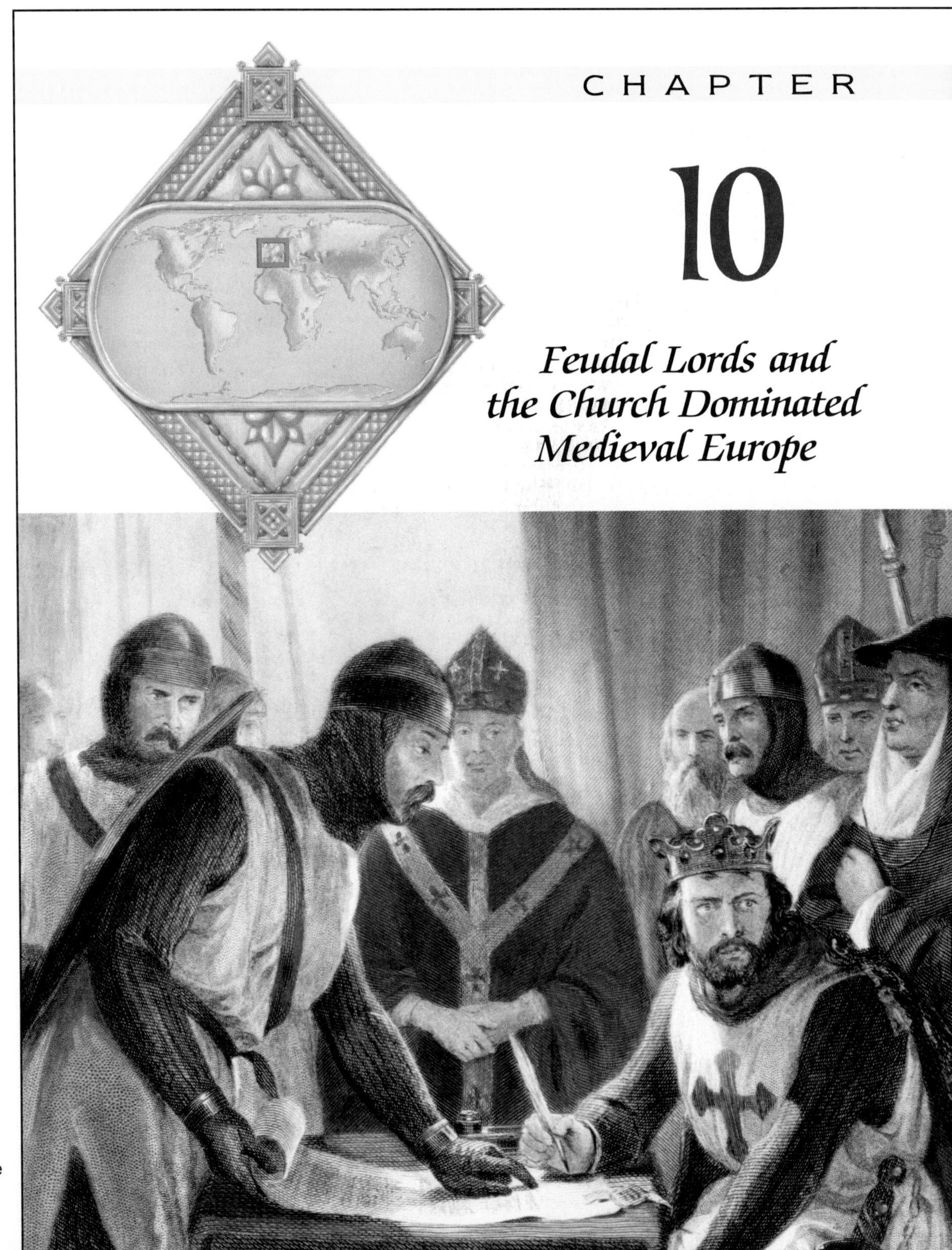

CHAPTER FOCUS

Place Western Europe

Time 432–1328

3.7 mil. BC — 4000 BC — AD 2100

Significance

While the Byzantine and Muslim empires flourished in the East, no strong empire emerged in what had been the western part of the Roman Empire. The Roman Empire did not end with a sudden crash, however. Rather, it slipped away a little at a time. A border fort would be abandoned. Mail would no longer come to a city. Slowly, what had been a magnificent empire became splintered ruins.

The period in western European history following the collapse of the Roman Empire, from about 500 to about 1500, is called the **Middle Ages,** or the **medieval** period. (The word *medieval* comes from the Latin words *medius,* meaning "middle," and *aevum,* meaning "age.")

The people of that time never thought of themselves as living in a "middle age." They thought of human history as a chain of events that had begun in the Biblical era and continued to their own time. Although these people had little understanding of the past, they developed new customs and institutions to suit the conditions under which they lived.

Terms to Define

Middle Ages	serf
feudalism	Inquisition
manor	Magna Carta

People to Identify

Charlemagne	William the Conqueror
Vikings	Hugh Capet

Places to Locate

Papal States	Hastings
Normandy	Worms

Questions to Guide Your Reading

1 How did Frankish rulers gain control of western Europe?
2 Why was medieval life organized around feudalism and the manorial system?
3 What was the role of the church during the Middle Ages?
4 What prompted conflict between kings and nobles in France and England?
5 Why did popes and emperors clash over Germany and Italy?

In the Middle Ages, most Europeans were peasants who eked out a meager living in the fields, often working from dawn to dusk. As one historian noted:

> *"The sun rose early, . . . but not much earlier than the peasants of the little village of Belcombe. . . . Within most of the houses men were stirring . . . taking a look at the sky before they ate a brief meal . . . of a lump of bread and a draught of ale. . . . Then they . . . fetched their scythes and rakes from the sheds, and started off. . . . On entering the field the peasants broke up in little groups, some going to one and some to another part of the meadow. . . .*
>
> *In one corner of the field John Wilde and his two sons, Richard and Roger, kept to their tasks for some time without pause. . . . All three continued until the sun was getting well up into the heavens, when they stopped their work and left the field together with many others. As they passed the church John glanced at the Mass clock on its wall near the door, and saw by the shadow . . . that they had good time before the service, as it was not yet eight."*

These hardworking peasants formed the backbone of a society attempting to restore order out of the chaos that followed the collapse of the Roman Empire in the West. In time a new social and political order emerged.

1 Frankish Rulers Governed Much of Western Europe for Centuries

After the Roman Empire in the west collapsed, many Germanic tribes, including Visigoths, Vandals, Burgundians, and Ostrogoths, plundered Europe and established several small kingdoms. Most tribes, however, did not create strong governments. Of all the Germanic tribes, the Franks played the greatest role in European history. The Franks first entered the Roman Empire near the mouth of the Rhine River in the A.D. 300s. They settled in the area of northern Gaul that corresponds roughly to the present-day nations of Belgium and the Netherlands.

◀ *King John signing the Magna Carta*

of monasticism in the medieval church.
7. Describe some of the problems facing the medieval church.
8. Describe the roles of the peasant and lord under the manorial system.
9. Outline the rise of Christianity in England and Ireland, Anglo-Saxon rule in England, and the effects of the Norman Conquest.
10. Compare the evolution of royal power in England and France, and explain the creation of Parliament in England.
11. Discuss the symbolic importance of the struggles between popes and Holy Roman Emperors, especially those between Gregory VII and Henry IV.
12. Explain the importance of Innocent III to the history of the church.

SECTION 1

Focus/Motivation
In the year 800 Pope Leo III crowned Charlemagne "Emperor of the Romans" in St. Peter's in Rome. Ask students why they think Charlemagne would want to emphasize the fact that he ruled "with God's blessing." *(Answers will vary. Students might suggest that religion was an integral part of people's lives, and that people would be more inclined to accept Charlemagne's rule if they thought it was graced by God.)*

Ask the class how this would ensure a ruler's continued reign and succession by his or her

1B, 4B, a4L

● Answers will vary. Students might suggest that had the Moors won the Battle of Tours in 732, they could not have been stopped. They would have destroyed the Germanic kingdoms and replaced Christianity with Islam. The Moors might also have joined with Arabs coming from the east.

descendants. *(Students might note that descendants of the ruler would be seen as inheriting divine grace, thus assuring their succession after the ruler's death.)*

Presentation Analyzing Ideas (Average/Group)
Organize the students into groups in order to discuss how each of the following contributed to the decline of the Frankish Empire.

1. Treaty of Verdun *(divided empire into three parts)*
2. Incompetent rulers *(fought among themselves instead of uniting against powerful local chiefs)*
3. Muslims *(conquered and occupied Sicily, Sardinia, and Corsica, and terrorized the entire Mediterranean coast)*
4. Magyars *(came from Asia, and after a century of terrifying raids settled in what is today Hungary)*
5. Vikings *(raided the Frankish Empire and settled in northwestern France, which they called Normandy)*

Clovis and the Merovingians

In 481 an able ruler named Clovis became king of one of the Frankish tribes. He and his successors were called Merovingians because Clovis traced his family back to an ancestor named Meroveg. Although brutal, cruel, and apparently without a conscience, Clovis excelled as a military leader. His troops conquered the other Frankish tribes and soon controlled all of northern Gaul.

A few years after Clovis became king, an important event took place. Influenced by his Christian wife, he vowed to accept her religion if he won a certain battle. When he won the battle, he not only kept his vow but also ordered 3,000 of his warriors to receive baptism. Clovis became a strong supporter of Christianity, and he and the Franks gained the support of the Church.

Later, Clovis seized southwestern Gaul from the Visigoths. Even though he ruled most of what is today France (which took its name from the Franks), Clovis failed to pass on to his successors either his strong leadership qualities or his united kingdom. In accordance with Frankish custom, Clovis's sons divided the kingdom among themselves.

The later Merovingian kings thought only of the pleasures and luxuries of palace life. One writer of the period tells of a Merovingian king who spent his time combing his long yellow curls with a jeweled comb. Because these "do-nothing kings" left the business of governing to palace officials, the chief of the royal household, called the mayor of the palace, became the real ruler. About 700, Pepin II, the mayor of the palace of one kingdom, succeeded in making the office of mayor hereditary. His successors were Frankish kings in everything but name.

Charles Martel and Pepin the Short

Pepin's able son, Charles Martel (meaning "Charles the Hammer"), succeeded Pepin as the mayor of the palace. In 732 Spanish Moors invaded France. Charles Martel's cavalry defeated the Moors near Tours, in central France, thus halting the Muslim advance in western Europe and removing an immediate danger and a constant menace.

When Charles Martel died in 741, he left a large and strong kingdom for his son Pepin III, or Pepin the Short. In 751 an assembly of Franks took the throne from the Merovingian king and elected Pepin king of the Franks. Three years later the pope traveled to France and personally crowned Pepin "king by the grace of God." Later popes claimed this action established a precedent, or an example to be followed in the future, which gave the popes the authority to install and depose kings.

What If?
Battle of Tours
The Frankish victory at Tours in 732 halted Muslim expansion in Europe. How do you think modern European culture would be different if the Moors had won the battle? ●

While the pope was in France, he asked Pepin for help against the Lombards, a Germanic tribe that was ravaging central Italy and threatening Rome. Pepin led an army of Franks into Italy and defeated the Lombards. He then took territory around Rome from the Lombard king and gave it to the pope. This gift of land, called the Donation of Pepin, created the Papal States, a region that would be ruled by popes for centuries.

History does not record whether the pope and Pepin made an agreement that Pepin would defend Rome in exchange for his coronation by the pope. Certainly, however, these events began an alliance between the Franks and the pope that greatly strengthened both sides. The way now opened for the greatest of all Frankish kings, Charlemagne (SHAHR • luh • mayn).*

Charlemagne's Empire

Pepin's son Charlemagne assumed the Frankish throne in 768 and ruled until 814. Although he had little formal education, this deeply religious and highly intelligent king became one of history's outstanding rulers.

Like many kings of his day, Charlemagne spent much of his life at war. He defeated the Lombards in Italy, the Saxons in northern Germany, and the Avars in central Europe. Although he failed in his attempt to conquer all of Muslim Spain, he drove the Moors back across the Pyrenees, thus gaining a

*Charlemagne's Latin name was *Carolus Magnus* (from which comes the name of his dynasty, *Carolingian*). The Germans called him *Karl de Grosse*. Translated into English, all these names mean "Charles the Great."

Learning from Pictures *Charlemagne was a patron of learning and encouraged the development of art, science, and literature.*

small strip of Spanish territory. By the end of his reign, Charlemagne controlled much of western Europe (see map, this page).

On Christmas Day in the year 800, Charlemagne knelt at worship in St. Peter's Church in Rome. Pope Leo III placed a crown on Charlemagne's head and declared him "Emperor of the Romans." The new title had little to do with the Frankish Empire, but it signified that Charlemagne, who had united much of Europe for the first time in 400 years, was regarded by many people as the successor to the emperors of Rome. Charlemagne's coronation by the pope also dramatized the close ties between the Frankish people and the Christian Church.

Government. Charlemagne's empire consisted of several hundred regions, each ruled by a representative called a count. Each count raised an army and administered the laws within his own lands. Charlemagne established his capital at Aix-la-Chapelle (AYK-SLAH-shuh • PEL), which today is Aachen (AHK • uhn), West Germany, but he traveled extensively throughout his empire. He also appointed officials called *missi dominici* (MI • see dohm • i • NEE • chee), Latin for "the lord's messengers." The missi dominici traveled throughout the empire to listen to complaints, to review the effectiveness of the laws, and to make certain the counts served the emperor rather than themselves.

The government levied no direct taxes on land or people because the emperor's vast estates produced enough revenue to cover most of the government's low expenses. Each person who lived in the

Learning from Maps *Charlemagne conquered much of Europe before his death in 814. Where did he establish his capital?* **Aix-la-Chapelle**

225

● Charles the Bald's kingdom

empire contributed to the army in some way. Wealthy lords provided the cavalry, and free peasants usually served as soldiers three months a year. Thus the emperor had an army at no expense to himself or the government.

Education and learning. Greatly interested in education, Charlemagne founded a school at the palace for his own children and the other young nobles. He invited learned scholars from throughout western Europe to teach in the school. The emperor also assembled scholars from all over Europe to produce a readable and authentic Bible. He ordered bishops to create libraries by copying ancient Latin manuscripts and to organize schools for the children of nobles and for intelligent children from the lower classes.

Although Charlemagne never learned to write, he could read. One of his favorite books, St. Augustine's *City of God,* urged all Christians to love God, and Charlemagne vigorously encouraged people throughout the empire to convert to Christianity. Sometimes he even forced people to convert, giving them a choice between baptism and execution.

Learning from Maps *Lothair's kingdom, with many important cities, was the first kingdom to break up. In* ● *what kingdom was Paris located?*

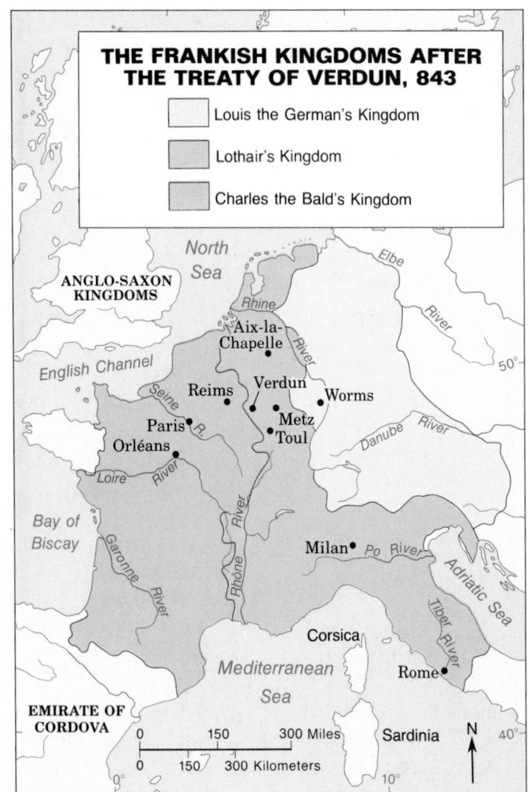

The Decline of the Frankish Empire

Charlemagne's energy, ability, and personality unified the empire during his lifetime. But the empire crumbled during the reign of Charlemagne's only surviving son, Louis the Pious. After Louis died, his three sons agreed to divide the empire into three parts: the eastern kingdom, the middle kingdom, and the western kingdom (see map, this page). Their agreement, signed in 843, was called the Treaty of Verdun.

Poor leaders, Charlemagne's descendants fought among themselves instead of uniting against powerful and ambitious local rulers. By 870 the middle kingdom broke up and was divided between the eastern and western kingdoms. But the great lords of these two kingdoms no longer obeyed the Carolingian monarchs. Instead they chose their own kings.

Charlemagne's empire splintered not only because of internal feuds but also because invaders swarmed into the empire from every direction. In the late 800s, Europe suffered from invasions more terrible than the invasions of the 400s (see map, page 227).

The Muslims came from North Africa and terrorized the Mediterranean coast, conquering Sicily, Sardinia, and Corsica. From the east came the Slavs, who pressed into central Europe. From Asia came a new group of nomads, the Magyars (MAG • yahrz). Magyar tactics so resembled those of the earlier Huns that Europeans called them Hungarians. After a century of terrifying raids, the Magyars settled down and established a kingdom in what is now the country of Hungary.

The Vikings

The most feared of all invaders, however, came from Scandinavia, in the north. The Germanic peoples of what are now the countries of Norway, Sweden, and Denmark called themselves Vikings. The English called them Danes, while other Europeans called them Northmen, or the Norse.

226

● The Vikings attacked in longboats powered by 16 pairs of oarsmen. The ships each held as many as 60 men.

■ The Vikings, or Normans, who conquered Sicily assimilated Muslim culture and made Palermo the greatest city in Europe outside Constantinople.

1A, 1B, 4B, a4B, a4C

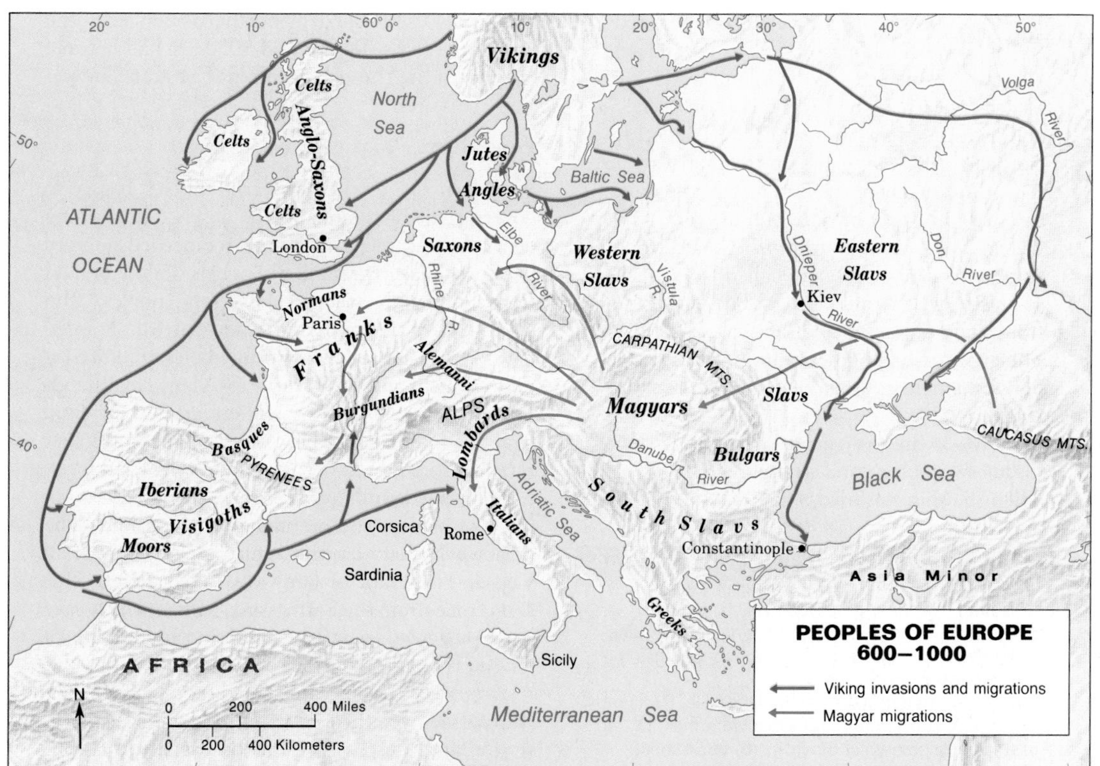

Learning from Maps *The Vikings migrated from the north to all parts of Europe. What body of water separated the Viking homeland from the Western Slavs?* **Baltic Sea**

Although the Vikings had kings and nobles, their government was surprisingly democratic for its time. The Vikings honored work, and all classes worked. Most people owned their own land, and few large estates existed. Assemblies of landowners made the laws.

During the 800s climate changes and a growing population apparently caused a serious food shortage in Scandinavia. Many Vikings sailed from their ● homeland in search of food and treasure. Sturdy Viking ships, propelled partly by sails but mostly by oars, skirted the coasts of Europe and plied the rivers of Germany, France, and the eastern Baltic area. They sailed across the Atlantic Ocean to Iceland, then on to Greenland and North America. In time the Vikings settled in England, Ireland, ■ France, eastern Europe, and later, elsewhere in Europe. A large settlement of Vikings in northwestern France gave the region its name, Normandy, from the French word *Normans,* for "Northmen."

As chaos engulfed medieval Europe, the Vikings continued their conquests, trading with the strong and pillaging the weak. Skilled in siege operations, they sometimes captured strongly fortified towns. Savage and cruel people, the Vikings seem to have enjoyed battle. They used their axes and swords to strike terror into people everywhere. A Viking once complained that "peace lasted so long that I was afraid I might come to die of old age, within doors, on a bed."

The Vikings' customs and myths centered on god-heroes, who led their people bravely in life and symbolically sailed away in death. Archaeologists have excavated Viking burial mounds in Europe that include boats and implements to be used in the afterlife. Sometimes the Vikings placed the dead person in a boat, set the boat adrift, and burned it. In 922 Ibn Fadlan, an Arab, attended the funeral of a Viking chieftain along the Volga. A historian wrote the following about Fadlan's experience:

SECTION 1

Closure
Ask students to trace the connection of Charlemagne's crowning as Holy Roman Emperor to the old Roman Empire in the West. What similarities existed between the new and old empires? What differences? Ask students how they think the Byzantine emperor would have reacted to the "re-creation" of the Roman Empire in the West.

Review Answers
1. ***Middle Ages:*** period between ancient times and modern period; ***medieval:*** from the Latin word *medius,* meaning "middle," and *aevum,* meaning "age"
2. ***Franks:*** Germanic tribe that settled in northern Gaul; ***Clovis:*** founder of Merovingian dynasty; ***Merovingians:*** dynasty of Frankish kings; ***Charles Martel:*** defeated the Moors at Tours; ***Pepin the Short:*** elected king of the Franks; ***Charlemagne:*** Emperor of the Romans; ***Louis the Pious:*** Charlemagne's son; ***Magyars:*** nomadic Asiatic people who established a kingdom in Hungary; ***Vikings:*** Scandinavians who were the most feared invaders in Europe
3. ***Papal States:*** region in central Italy that popes ruled; ***Aix-la-Chapelle:*** Charlemagne's capital city; ***Normandy:*** northwestern France

1B, 4B, a4A, a4F, a4G, a4H, a4K, a4M

● The word *vassal* is of Celtic origin.

4. (a) Clovis conquered other Frankish tribes, became a Christian and forced 3,000 of his men to be baptized, and later seized southwestern Gaul from the Visigoths. **(b)** Charles Martel was an able Frankish mayor of the palace who stopped the Muslim advance in western Europe at Tours.
5. (a) Pepin the Short, mayor of the palace under the Merovingians, became king of the Franks when an assembly of Franks elected him and the pope crowned him. **(b)** The pope's crowning of Pepin caused later popes to claim they had the authority to install and depose kings.
6. Charlemagne's empire was divided into several hundred regions ruled by counts. Charlemagne sent *missi dominici* to check on the counts, report on the effectiveness of the laws, and listen to complaints. The people paid no direct taxes. The army consisted of lords and peasants who donated their time and resources at no cost to the government. Charlemagne founded a school at the palace, invited scholars from western Europe to teach there, and ordered the church to copy ancient Latin manuscripts and establish schools.
7. Charlemagne's empire was torn apart by internal feuds among his descendants and by outside invaders.

"A girl slave volunteered to be burned with her master, Ibn Fadlan relates. His ship was hauled onto land and wood placed beneath. A tent was raised on deck and a brocaded mattress set on it. The richly clothed corpse was seated on the mattress. . . .

On the day of the burial, . . . the slave girl said, 'Lo, I see my lord and master . . . he calls to me. Let me go to him.' Aboard the ship waited the old woman called the Angel of Death, who would kill her. The girl drank from a cup of nabidh and sang a long song. She grew fearful and hesitant. At once the old woman grasped her head and led her into the tent.

Inside the tent the girl died beside her master by stabbing and strangling. Then the ship was fired."

SECTION 1 REVIEW

1. **Define** Middle Ages, medieval
2. **Identify** Franks, Clovis, Merovingians, Charles Martel, Pepin the Short, Charlemagne, Louis the Pious, Magyars, Vikings
3. **Locate** Papal States, Aix-la-Chapelle, Normandy
4. **Summarizing Ideas** **(a)** What were the accomplishments of Clovis? **(b)** of Charles Martel?
5. **Interpreting Ideas** **(a)** How did Pepin the Short become king of the Franks? **(b)** What precedent did the crowning of Pepin establish?
6. **Organizing Ideas** How did Charlemagne change government and education in his empire?
7. **Determining Cause and Effect** Give two reasons for the breakup of Charlemagne's empire.

2 Medieval Life Was Based on Feudalism and the Manorial System

On the continent of Europe, organized government again disappeared within a century after Charlemagne's death in 814. Europe became a continent of small, independent local governments. We call the political system that evolved in Europe feudalism. **Feudalism,** a political system in which kings and powerful nobles granted land to other nobles in return for loyalty, military assistance, and services, was firmly established in northern France by the end of the 900s. By the mid-1000s, it had become the way of life throughout most of western Europe.

Feudalism

Feudalism arose when powerful nobles began to govern their own lands in the absence of a strong central government. In return for needed military help, weak kings granted the nobles the use of land from the royal estates. The strong nobles, who often had more land than they needed, granted part of this land to less powerful nobles in return for military help and other services. Many small landholders who needed protection gave their land to more powerful nobles. The small landholder retained the right to occupy and work the lands but had to provide military service to the noble.

The person who granted land was a lord. The person who held land in return for services was a **vassal.** The grant of land was called a **fief.** This term comes from the Latin word *feudum,* which gave rise to the word *feudal.* The granting and holding of a fief was really a contract between lord and vassal. ●

In time the fief became hereditary. Legal ownership passed from the lord to his son, while legal possession and use passed from the vassal to his son. Since a fief could not be divided, the eldest son always inherited it—a system called **primogeniture** (pry • moh • JEN • uh • chuhr). However, many lords held more than one fief.

Women could influence society and politics, but their legal property rights were limited. A woman could include fiefs in her dowry. However, her husband would take over the dowry, and she controlled it only if he died.

Local lords held many of the powers of government, and the king became just another feudal lord. In theory every holder of land became a vassal to the king, but in practice the king had power only over those who lived on the king's feudal lands.

The church, too, became part of the feudal system. By the 900s the church owned vast amounts of land, some of which it granted as fiefs to nobles in return for military protection.

Feudal relationships. Keeping three things in mind will help you understand the relationship between lord and vassal:

(1) It was an honorable relationship between legal equals. Only nobles could be vassals. The greater lords were vassals and tenants of the king.

● In the late Middle Ages, military service could be substituted by a monetary payment called *scutage.* The church and towns that were part of fiefs often paid scutage.

■ In 1215 a church council condemned trial by ordeal. Trial by battle lasted longer.

Learning from Pictures *This stained glass window depicts the relationship between a lord and his vassal. In the feudal relationship, who had more obligations, the vassal or the lord?* vassal

The less powerful lords were vassals and tenants of the greater lords, and so on down.

(2) The same man might be both vassal and lord—vassal to a more powerful lord above him and lord to a less powerful vassal below him.

(3) It was a very personal relationship. Each man owed loyalties and obligations only to the lord immediately above him or to the vassal immediately below him.

Obligations of feudalism. Under the feudal contracts, the vassal had more obligations than the lord. The vassal promised to provide the lord a certain number of fully equipped cavalry riders and infantry soldiers, and he agreed to pay their expenses while at war. ●

The vassal had to make special payments to help cover the lord's extraordinary expenses such as ransom if the lord became captive in war. The vassal also had to house and feed the lord and his companions for a certain number of days a year, attend such ceremonies as the marriage of the lord's daughter, and serve on the lord's court to administer justice.

Feudal justice. Feudal justice differed from Roman justice. Decisions at trials were made in one of three ways:

(1) *Trial by battle.* The accused and the accuser, or men representing them, fought a duel. The outcome of the duel determined guilt or innocence.

(2) *Compurgation, or oath-taking.* The accused and the accuser each gathered a group of people who swore that "their" man was telling the truth. Compurgators, the oath-takers, were similar to the character witnesses in today's trials. ■

(3) *Ordeal.* The accused carried a piece of hot iron in his hand, or walked through fire, or plunged his arm into a pot of boiling water to pick up a hot stone. If his wounds healed rapidly, he was judged innocent; otherwise he was guilty.

Warfare. Frequent wars plagued the medieval period. Sometimes two kingdoms fought. Other times a king tried to subdue a powerful, rebellious vassal. Most wars, however, stemmed from private fights between feudal lords or between lords and vassals.

In the early Middle Ages, the knight, or fighting man, wore an iron helmet and a shirt of chain mail—small metal links hooked together to form flexible armor. The knight carried a sword, a large shield, and a lance. Armor became complicated in later medieval times, as metal plates replaced chain mail. Metal armor was so heavy that a knight often had to be hauled or boosted onto his horse.

For nobles, wars represented opportunities for glory and wealth, but to the rest of society, wars brought suffering and famine. The church tried to limit private wars. It issued decrees, known together as the Peace of God, which set aside certain places, such as churches, where fighting was not permitted. The church tried to get all lords to accept another decree, known as the Truce of God, which forbade fighting on weekends and holy days. Gradually more days were added to the Truce of God, until only 80 legal fighting days a year remained. Restrictions on fighting, however, could almost never be strictly enforced. Private wars continued until kings became strong enough to stop them.

The Manorial System

While feudalism was essentially a governmental and military system, the manorial system became the economic system. The **manor,** a large estate that included the manor house, pastures, fields, and a village, became the economic unit of the early Middle Ages, just as the fief had become the

SECTION 2

Focus/Motivation

Explain to students that chivalry (an unwritten code of behavior) required a knight to be brave, fight fairly, be loyal to his friends, keep his word, treat conquered foes gallantly, and be especially courteous to women. Ask students if they feel that chivalry is alive today. Why or why not? *(Answers will vary. Have students give examples from their personal experiences.)*

Presentation

Illustrating Ideas (Average/Group)

Draw a step diagram on the chalkboard or on an overhead projector to help students understand feudal society. Label the steps from top to bottom as follows: *king, lords, lesser lords, knights, townspeople and free people,* and *serfs.* Have students copy the labels into their notebooks. Then have students assign symbols to represent each of these groups and explain why they used that particular symbol. *(Answers will vary. For example, a crown for a king because he wears one.)*

1B, 4B, a1C, a4A

● Peasants were obliged to use the lord's mill to grind all grain. Control of windmills and watermills allowed the lords to keep a strong hold over the peasantry.

Learning from Pictures *Manorial banquets or feasts were often held at the end of the harvest season. What items did the manor import?* iron, salt, tar

governmental unit. While a small fief had only one manor, large fiefs had several.

Because no central authority or organized trade existed, each manor tried to be self-sufficient—or able to produce everything it needed. Most manors produced their own food, clothing, and leather goods. Only a few items, such as iron, salt, and tar, were imported.

The lord and several peasants shared the land of a manor. The lord kept about one-third of the manor land, called the **domain,** for himself. The domain was often divided into several plots, although it might form one large block near the lord's house. The peasants paid to use the remaining two-thirds of the land. In exchange they gave the lord part of their crops, worked on his land, performed other services on the manor, and paid many kinds of taxes.

A typical manor village, usually on a stream that furnished water power for its mill, had houses clustered together for safety a short distance away from the manor house or castle. The land of the manor extended out from the village and included vegetable plots, cultivated fields, pastures, and forests.

The cultivated land of the manor was often divided into three large fields for growing grain. Only two of the three fields were planted each year so that the third field could lie fallow, or unplanted, to regain its fertility. The three large fields in turn were divided into small strips. Peasants had their own strips in each field. If the lord's domain was divided, he too had strips in each field.

Peasant Life

Most of the peasants on a manor were **serfs,** or people bound to the land. Serfs could not leave the land without the lord's permission, and the price of his permission was usually more money than they could afford. Serfs were not slaves, for they could not be sold away from the land. If the land was granted to a new lord, the serfs became the new lord's tenants.

Manors had some free people who rented land from the lord. Free people included the skilled workers necessary to the village economy, such as millers, blacksmiths, and carpenters. Most villages also had a priest to provide for the spiritual needs of the villagers.

Long hours spent doing backbreaking work in the fields made daily life very hard. The laborers' meager diet consisted mainly of coarse black bread, cabbage and a few other vegetables, cheese, and eggs. Beer was plentiful in northern Europe, and wine in the grape-growing regions of the south. People rarely ate meat because they needed animals to help them work the fields and because they were not allowed to hunt on the lord's land.

We know little about the life of ordinary people in medieval times. However, historians tell us that because of diseases and starvation, the average life expectancy was probably less than 40 years. Because people in their forties were regarded as old, medieval society was a much younger society than ours. People could become prominent by their twenties, and a bright child would be encouraged at an early age. When a village priest found a particularly intelligent boy, he could arrange to have him

230

● The peasants were a conservative force in society. Their life and outlook changed little until the mid-1800s, when the Industrial Revolution affected rural areas.

■ In German the word for "castle" is *burg* (*bourg* in French). What the French call *faubourgs* (outside the burg), we would today call suburbs.

1B, 4B, a1C

educated for a career in the church, and thus a life in the wider world.

However, people rarely escaped the village. People usually died where they had been born. If a terrible disaster struck, such as a famine that lasted many years, villagers might flee. Usually, however, they stayed on, struggling to keep small families ● alive.

One of the few things we know about family life during these early years of the Middle Ages is that a child's status was sometimes determined by the mother rather than by the father. If a serf married a woman from a free family, for example, the couple's children might be considered free people rather than serfs.

The Life of the Nobility

When people today think of the Middle Ages, they sometimes picture luxurious castles and knights in ■ shining armor. However, the nobles did not necessarily lead luxurious or even easy lives.

A castle, or a fortified home for a lord, served as a base for protecting the surrounding countryside and enforcing the lord's authority. Most people today picture a castle as a great stone structure. Actually, stone castles were not constructed until much later in the Middle Ages. Throughout the early medieval period, castles were relatively simple structures built of earth and wood.

Located on hills or in other places that were easy to defend, castles were built for defense, not for pleasant living. If a castle had to be built in flat country, a ditch often filled with water, called a moat, surrounded the outer walls. A drawbridge across the moat enabled people to reach the gate to the courtyard inside the walls. In case of an attack, the drawbridge was raised.

The main part of the castle was the keep—a strong tower that contained storerooms, barracks, and workshops, as well as the lord's living quarters. In the great hall, the lord received visitors. Here the family also lived during the day. The lord and his family usually had a separate bedroom, but everyone else slept in the great hall. There was little furniture. The thick walls, with their small, usually glassless windows, made the rooms dark, damp, and chilly. Fowl, dogs, and other small animals ran across the filthy, straw-covered floors.

The lord spent most of his day looking after his land and dispensing justice to his vassals and serfs. He might have to spend some time each year fighting, either to help his own lord or to resolve a quarrel with another lord.

The lord and the head of a peasant family each depended a great deal on help from his wife and children. Medieval people viewed marriage as a way to advance one's fortunes, perhaps by inheriting new lands. Marriage also produced children, who had to be cared for. A lord had to provide a dowry for a daughter. For a son he had to provide either land or a position serving the church or the king.

When not fighting, the nobles and vassals amused themselves with mock battles called tournaments. In early medieval times, tournaments often led to loss of life, but later they became more like pageants.

Chivalry

During the 1100s **chivalry,** a code of conduct for knights, changed feudal society. The word *chivalry* comes from the French word *cheval,* meaning "horse." A knight usually rode a horse when he performed deeds demanded by the code of chivalry.

In the early days, becoming a knight was quite simple. Any noble, after proving himself in battle, could be knighted by any other knight. As time passed, chivalry became much more complex.

To become a knight, a boy had to go through two preliminary stages of training supervised by a knight. First, at the age of seven, a boy became a page, or knight's attendant, learning knightly manners and beginning his training in the use of weapons. Then, in his early teens, the boy became a squire, or knight's assistant. He continued his training in both manners and weapons. He took care of the knight's horses, armor, weapons, and clothing. When he was considered ready, the squire accompanied the knight into battle. After the squire proved himself worthy in battle, an elaborate religious ceremony initiated him into knighthood.

Chivalry required a knight to be brave—sometimes foolishly brave. He had to fight fairly. Tricks and strategy were considered cowardly. A knight had to be loyal to his friends, keep his word, and treat conquered foes gallantly. In addition, he had to be especially courteous to women.

Chivalry greatly improved the rough and crude manners of early feudal lords. Behavior, however, did not become perfect by any standards. The knight extended courtesy only to people of his own

SECTION 2

Closure

Ask students to summarize why the society of the Middle Ages was organized with such a rigid sense of rights and obligations—everyone had a place in that society. *(The dangers and unsettled conditions required that a lord provide protection to people on his fief. Vassals and peasants owed him military service or produce and work on the land in return.)*

Review Answers

1. ***feudalism:*** a political and military system based on the granting of land in return for loyalty, military assistance, and services; ***vassal:*** person granted land from a lord in return for services; ***fief:*** grant of land from a lord to a vassal; ***primogeniture:*** inheritance of a fief only by the eldest son; ***manor:*** economic unit of the Middle Ages, consisting of a large estate with manor house, fields, and a village; ***domain:*** portion of manor the lord kept for his own use; ***serf:*** worker on a manor who was bound to the land; ***chivalry:*** a code of conduct for knights
2. (a) Feudalism was a political system in which kings and nobles granted land to other nobles in return for loyalty, military assistance, and services. **(b)** Feudalism arose because of the breakdown of a central government after Charlemagne's death.

1B, 4B, a4A, a4E, a4F, a4G, a4H, a4J

Local lords governed their own lands. To get military help, kings granted lords the use of land from the royal estates. The strong lords in turn granted land they did not need to lesser lords in return for military assistance. Lesser landholders received protection in return for giving up their land to a lord.
3. The lord granted use of the land and guaranteed protection to the vassal. The vassal promised to provide the lord a certain number of cavalry riders and foot soldiers and agreed to pay their expenses while at war. Other obligations included housing and feeding the lord and his companions for a certain number of days, paying the lord's ransom should he be captured in war, attending ceremonies such as marriages in the lord's family, and serving on the lord's court.
4. Under feudal justice decisions were made by (1) *trial by battle,* in which the accused and accuser met in a duel, the outcome determining guilt or innocence; (2) *compurgation,* in which the accused and accuser each gathered people who swore their person told the truth; (3) *ordeal,* in which an accused person was inflicted with a wound, and the speed with which it healed determined guilt or innocence.
5. The lord kept about one-third of the manor land—the domain—while

READ
WRITE
INTERPRET
CONNECT
●THINK

BUILDING HISTORY STUDY SKILLS

Thinking About History: Distinguishing a Fact from a Value Statement

A fact can be verified or proved. A value statement is an opinion that represents a particular point of view. For example, a writer can state that Charlemagne was a successful ruler. That statement is a value statement because it is based upon the writer's definition of "successful."

Sometimes a fact and a value statement may be included in the same sentence. For example, in the book *Life of Charlemagne,* the author states that Charlemagne spoke Latin and Greek and was so eloquent that he could have taught both languages. Charlemagne's mastery of the two languages is a fact that can be verified. However, the degree of his mastery of the languages is a value statement. In your study of history, and later as you assume the responsibilities of citizenship, such as voting, it is important for you to be able to distinguish between facts and value statements.

How to Distinguish a Fact from a Value Statement

To distinguish a fact from a value statement, follow these steps.

1. Review the difference between a fact and a value statement.
2. Identify clue words that suggest values. For example, adjectives such as *great, wonderful,* and *horrible* are "feeling" words. "I" statements such as *I believe* or *In my opinion* indicate a point of view.
3. Ask questions about the sentence. Is it open to different interpretations? Does it contain "feeling" words or "I" statements?

Developing the Skill

The statement below tells how feudalism is best defined. Which sentences contain facts? Which sentences contain value statements?

> "The simplest way will be to begin by saying what feudal society was not. Although the obligations arising from blood-relationship played a very active part in it, it did not rely on kinship alone. . . . Feudal ties . . . developed when those of kinship proved inadequate. . . .
>
> European feudalism should therefore be seen as the outcome of the violent dissolution of older societies. It would in fact be unintelligible without the great upheaval of the great Germanic invasions which, by forcibly uniting two societies originally at very different stages of development, disrupted both of them and brought to the surface a great many . . . social practices of an extremely primitive character."

In the quotation, the author emphasizes the social and economic aspects of feudalism. He begins by stating a fact: it (feudalism) did not rely on kinship alone. You know from reading this chapter that this statement is a fact because lord-vassal relations often did not depend on kinship. The value statements are developed by the use of words such as *simplest, unintelligible,* and *primitive.* These statements are open to interpretation and depend on definitions and data the author provides.

Practicing the skill. Select a newspaper article about a person or a current event. Then identify the facts and the value statements.

To apply this skill, see Applying History Study Skills on page 247.

Farming on the manor

class. Toward all others his attitude and actions were likely to be coarse and arrogant.

In addition to codes of conduct, other traditions originated in feudal times. As early as the 1000s, knights carried personal symbols mounted on banners or shields into battle. In the 1100s it became customary for sons to inherit these banners and shields from their fathers. Later, three-dimensional crests, mostly of aggressive animals such as lions and hawks, were added to helmets. In time these crests became badges of nobility.

By the 1200s the crest, helmet, and shield had been incorporated into a family coat of arms. When a knight stayed at an inn, he hung his coat of arms outside. In later times coats of arms such as Richard II's white heart or the rose and crown of England were incorporated into signs that identified the inn where the person had stayed.

SECTION 2 REVIEW

1. **Define** feudalism, vassal, fief, primogeniture, manor, domain, serf, chivalry
2. **Summarizing Ideas** **(a)** What was feudalism? **(b)** Why did it develop?
3. **Classifying Ideas** What were the obligations of vassals and lords under the feudal relationship?
4. **Interpreting Ideas** Explain the three methods of trial under feudal justice.
5. **Evaluating Ideas** Describe the ways in which land on a manor was divided and used.
6. **Sequencing Ideas** Under the rules of chivalry, what were the steps leading to knighthood?

3 The Church Had Many Roles in the Middle Ages

Central governments in medieval Europe were weak or did not exist at all. Therefore, the church performed many of the responsibilities of modern governments. In one way or another, the church touched the lives of most medieval people.

The Church Hierarchy

Members of the clergy were organized in ranks according to their power and responsibilities. The levels of this hierarchy (HY • uh • rahr • kee), starting at the bottom, were as follows:

(1) *The parish priest.* The parish priest, usually of peasant origin, had little formal education. He served the people in his parish, the smallest division of the church. The poorest clergy member, the priest could hardly be distinguished from the peasants among whom he lived.

Though at the bottom of the hierarchy, the priest was in one sense the church's most important officer, for he administered five of the seven sacraments. The **sacraments** consisted of special ceremonies at which the participants received the direct favor, or grace, of God to help them ward off the consequences of sin. By the 1100s leaders of the church recognized seven ceremonies as sacraments—baptism, Holy Eucharist (communion), confirmation (admission to church membership), penance (acts showing repentance for sins), ordination (holy orders), matrimony, and extreme unction (the anointing of the dying). The parish priest conducted church services in his parish and administered all the sacraments except confirmation and ordination. He supervised the moral and religious instruction of his people and the moral life of the community. Often, however, the beliefs of villagers were as much pagan and superstitious as they were Christian. For example, the villagers sometimes relied on local "wise women" and "cunning men" for spiritual help.

(2) *The bishop.* A number of parishes made up a diocese (DY • uh • suhs), which the bishop managed. The cathedral church, or official church of the bishop, was located in the most important city of the diocese. (*Cathedra* is the Latin word for the bishop's throne, or chair.) The king or great nobles usually controlled the selection of a bishop. Bishops, frequently chosen for their family connections and political power, were often feudal lords or vassals who had vassals themselves.

(3) *The archbishop.* An archbishop managed a diocese and had all the powers of a bishop. In addition, he exercised some authority over the other dioceses and bishops in his province, which consisted of several dioceses. An archbishop could summon provincial councils of the clergy to decide questions of church belief and policy.

(4) *The pope and his curia.* The pope had a group of counselors, called the curia, to advise him. Cardinals, the most important members of the curia, advised the pope on legal and spiritual matters. Beginning in 1059 the cardinals elected the new pope.

the peasants paid for the use of the remaining land in crops, by working the lord's domain, and with other services and taxes. The manor land consisted of the lord's house or castle, the village, and vegetable plots, cultivated fields, pastures, and forests.

6. To become a knight, a boy became first, at age seven, a page, learning manners and the use of weapons. In his early teens, he became a squire or knight's assistant. As a squire, he took care of the knight's horses, armor, weapons, and clothing. When he was considered ready, he accompanied the knight into battle. After proving himself worthy of knighthood, the youth was initiated into knighthood in an elaborate religious ceremony.

SECTION 3

Focus/Motivation

Write the following statement on the chalkboard or an overhead projector:

"In the Middle Ages, Europe was the church, and the church was Europe."

Have students read the opening statement to Section 3 on this page and then ask if the statement supports or refutes the statement on the chalkboard. Ask them to give other evidence in support or refutation. *(Answers will vary.)*

1B, 3B, 4B, a1A

Students should include the following: The church ran schools and copied manuscripts. The pope claimed political as well as spiritual power. Church leaders held positions of power as feudal lords and as advisers to kings and nobles. Monks were innovators in agriculture, and monasteries carried on widespread trading activities. The church cared for widows and orphans, established hospitals, orphanages, and poorhouses, and buried the dead.)

Learning from Pictures *These Benedictine monks are reading in the relaxed atmosphere of a monastery's garden.*

Only in the church hierarchy could a commoner rise in the world. It did not happen often, but a man of great ability, regardless of birth, might rise to great heights in the church. For example, Callistus I was originally a slave of a Christian master in Rome. He was later freed, and in time he became a bishop. From about 217 to 222 he served as pope.

Monasticism

The medieval church was much like a present-day government. Everyone became a member, just as we become citizens. Priests, bishops, and the pope belonged to what was called the secular clergy. They lived *in saeculo,* a Latin phrase meaning "in the world," or "among ordinary people." They administered the sacraments and preached the gospel. A second group of church people, called regular clergy because they lived according to a strict rule, or *regula,* was the monastics—monks and nuns.

Monks and nuns believed that one of the best ways to live a perfect Christian life was to withdraw from the world and its temptations and serve God through prayer, fasting, and self-denial. At first each monk lived alone. Later, monks gathered in religious communities called monasteries and nuns lived in convents. The way of life in monasteries and convents was called **monasticism.**

Monasticism lacked organization and direction until the early 500s. About that time Benedict, a young Roman noble, became disgusted with worldly corruption and left Rome to become a hermit. In time his reputation for holiness attracted so many followers that he established a monastery at Monte Cassino in central Italy. Benedict drew up a set of standards to regulate the lives of the monks. Monasteries throughout Europe adopted this set of standards, called the Benedictine Rule.

According to the Benedictine Rule, a monk could own absolutely nothing. Everything he used or wore belonged to the community of monks. The **abbot,** the elected head of the community, controlled and distributed all property. The monks promised to obey the abbot in all things.

Monks spent several hours every day in prayer, but they were also expected to work. The abbot assigned each monk certain tasks in and around the monastery.

Monasteries fulfilled the intellectual and charitable needs of medieval society. Monks were often the most learned scholars of the time, and the monastery libraries were the main preservers of the literature of ancient civilizations and the early church. Several monasteries also ran schools to train the clergy.

Over the years monasteries became very rich. As an act of piety, a noble might leave his land to a monastery. Or a monastery might receive a large gift in return for accepting a young man as a monk. There were fewer convents than monasteries, and the convents were not as rich as monasteries. Like the monasteries, however, convents usually gave some of their wealth to the needy in nearby communities. Monks and nuns often cared for the sick, fed the hungry, and clothed the poor.

Some monks left the monasteries to become missionaries, a practice that existed long before the time of Benedict. St. Patrick in Ireland and St. Augustine in England were among those who did important missionary work.

Christianity in Ireland and England

Christian missionaries arrived in Ireland in the 400s. St. Patrick, the best known missionary,

234

PRINT DESIGN

Lindisfarne Gospels

During the early Middle Ages, monks were among the few people in Europe who could read and write. In monastery workshops they copied by hand almost all the books dating from this period. In this age of great faith, the work that was copied most often was the Bible. The monks were painstakingly careful, for a manuscript containing the word of God was considered a sacred object whose visual beauty should reflect the importance of its contents. To glorify God, the monks illuminated, or illustrated, the pages with gold leaf and intricate designs.

The Lindisfarne Gospels, among the most beautiful of the early illuminated books, were produced around 700 in the monastery of Lindisfarne. Now called Holy Island, Lindisfarne is a peninsula that becomes an island at high tide. One of England's early centers of learning, Lindisfarne lies off the northeastern coast of England.

The beginning of the Gospel According to St. John, part of the New Testament shown here, features a decorative border of interlaced ribbons, circles, and other designs. The Latin words mean, "In the beginning was the Word, and the Word was with God."

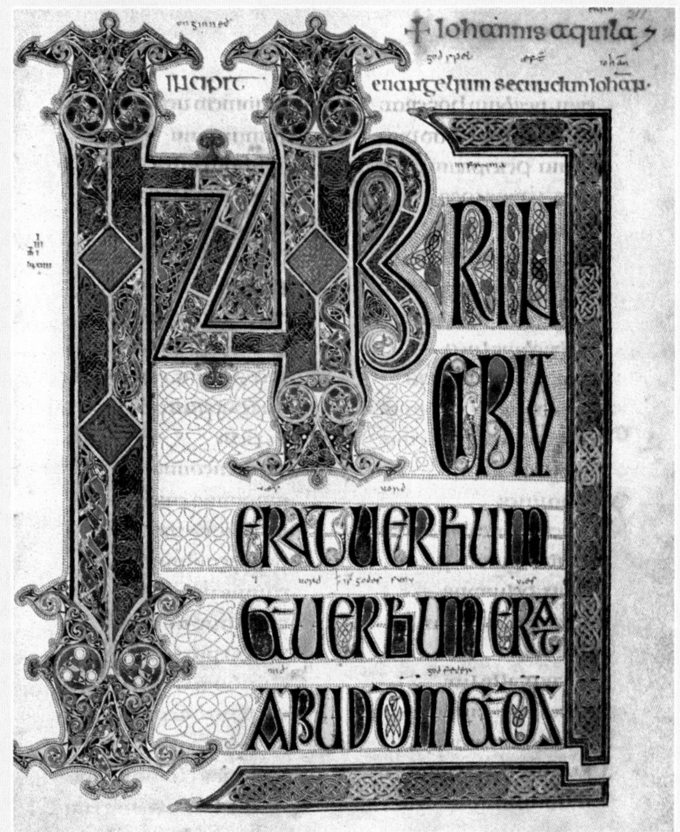

began his work there in 432. Several monastic schools provided the basis of an advanced culture that lasted from about 500 to about 800. Missionaries and teachers from Irish schools went to all parts of the British Isles and to the royal families on the continent of Europe. During this time Ireland became the greatest center and preserver of ancient and Christian culture in western Europe.

About 600 Pope Gregory I sent missionaries to England. Led by a monk named Augustine, the missionaries converted many people. Soon all England accepted Christianity. Augustine, made the first archbishop of Canterbury, eventually became known as St. Augustine of Canterbury. Canterbury became the center of the Christian Church in England.

The Church and Medieval Life

Both the secular and the regular clergy played a leading part in medieval institutions and in life. The church sought the most intelligent people among all classes to become members of the clergy. During the early Middle Ages, church leaders were almost the only educated people in Europe.

Since printing was unknown in the early Middle Ages, all books had to be copied by hand. Monks did most of this work. To relieve the tedious work of copying and to beautify the texts, the monks often added small paintings at the beginning of a page or in the margins. The gold leaf and brilliant colors they used brightened the pages so much that such works are called illuminated manuscripts.

Presentation
Organizing Information (Average/Group)
Place an outline of a chart titled **HIERARCHY OF THE MEDIEVAL CHURCH** on the chalkboard or an overhead projector. Label two columns *Rank* and *Duties.* Have students complete the chart in their notebooks. After the students have completed the assignment, have them compare their charts with the following: the lowest rank is that of parish priest—conducted church services; administered all the sacraments except confirmation and ordination; supervised moral and religious instruction and moral life of the community; bishop—managed a diocese; administered the sacraments of confirmation and ordination; appointed and removed parish priests; managed church property; archbishop—had all the powers of a bishop; had some authority over bishops and other dioceses in the province; at the top is the pope—leader of the Western church.

235

● The great church reformer, Pope Leo IX (1049-1054), forced married priests to give up either their wives or the priesthood.

SECTION 3

Closure

Ask students why they think monastic life had such an appeal in the Middle Ages. *(Answers will vary. In an unsettled world, a perfect Christian life might be found by withdrawing from it through prayer, fasting, and self-denial. The church dominated intellectual life—scholars would find the monastic libraries appealing. Monks and nuns also performed missionary and charitable duties.)*

Review Answers

1. ***sacrament:*** a special Christian ceremony in which participants received the grace of God; ***monasticism:*** system of monasteries and convents in which Christians withdrew from the world to lead a life of prayer, fasting, and self-denial; ***abbot:*** head of a monastery; ***canon law:*** church law; ***interdict:*** church's punishment of an entire region by withholding some sacraments; ***tithe:*** church tax representing one-tenth of a person's income collected from all Christians; ***simony:*** purchase of church office; ***Inquisition:*** church efforts to eliminate heresy **2.** ***curia:*** advisers to the pope; ***cardinals:*** most important members of the curia who elected popes beginning in 1059; ***St. Francis of Assisi:*** founder of a preaching order of monks; ***St. Dominic:***

These manuscripts were the finest artistic works produced during the early Middle Ages.

Political role. The church also became a political force during the Middle Ages. In the Papal States, the pope was both the political and spiritual ruler. Many popes claimed supreme political power for the church. They decreed that all monarchs in Europe had to obey the pope. Church leaders also held positions of power as feudal lords and as advisers to kings and nobles. The church preached that people should obey the laws of kings unless these laws conflicted with church laws.

The church had its own code of law, called **canon law,** and its own courts where members of the clergy were tried. The church enforced its laws by using excommunication and interdict.

Excommunication cut an individual off from the church. He or she could not receive the sacraments or be buried in sacred ground. All Christians had to avoid the excommunicated person, and the state treated him or her like a criminal. An excommunicated person was thought to be surely damned after death.

To punish an entire region, the church issued an **interdict.** No religious services could be held in the region, and only the sacraments of baptism and extreme unction could be administered. Everyone who lived in the region was in danger of eternal damnation.

As do present-day national governments, the church in the Middle Ages had the power of taxation. Through the parish priest, the church collected the **tithe,** or one-tenth of a person's income, from all Christians. In England and Scandinavia, the church collected "Peter's Pence," a tax of one penny a year on every household. The church also received fines collected by its courts and fees charged for the performance of ceremonies such as baptism and marriage. Finally, the church received vast income from church-owned lands. In the early 1200s, when the church reached the peak of its power, it had a larger income than all the kings of Europe combined.

Economic life. The moral ideas of the church affected all economic life. The church opposed people gaining wealth by exploiting others. It insisted that labor was in keeping with the dignity of free people.

Monks were leaders in agriculture. They developed new ways of raising crops, breeding cattle, and cultivating fruit. They cleared forests, drained swamps, and built dikes and roads to increase the amount of land that could be farmed.

Monasteries carried on widespread trading activities. They owned their own pack animals, ships, markets, and warehouses. Their trade routes were carefully mapped.

Social role. The church considered the family a sacred institution. It forbade divorce and took responsibility for all widows and orphans. It also took complete charge of all social work, such as relief for the poor.

To relieve the sick and distressed, the church established hospitals, orphanages, and poorhouses. Special religious orders provided hospital care, care of lepers, burial of the poor, and general charity.

Problems of the Church

At the peak of its power, the church faced several problems.

(1) *Lay investiture.* The tremendous wealth of the church created a problem, especially after church leaders became feudal lords and vassals. Nobles often rewarded their loyal friends or relatives by appointing them bishops and abbots, a procedure known as lay investiture. No one questioned a king's or a noble's right to grant a bishop or an abbot a fief and to have him become a vassal. The church, however, did object to kings and nobles naming bishops and abbots. Church leaders firmly believed that only a church member could grant spiritual authority to another member of the church. In the case of a bishop, a ring and crosier, or staff, symbolized this authority. A king or lord who granted a new bishop his fiefs often insisted on giving him his ring and crosier as well.

(2) *Worldly lives of the clergy.* Some members of the clergy lived in luxury. People criticized them because they seemed more interested in wealth than in holy living. ●

(3) *Simony.* In feudal times people often paid to get positions in the church, a practice called **simony** (SY • muh • nee). The purchaser expected to make money through his position, either from church income or by charging high fees for performing religious services.

(4) *Heresy.* The church did not permit anyone to question the basic principles, or doctrines, that served as the foundation of the Christian religion. People who denied the truth of these principles or preached unauthorized doctrines were considered

1B, 3B, 4B, a4A, a4F, a4G, a4H, a4K, a4L

History Through the Arts

METAL SCULPTURE

Reliquary of St. Faith

This golden image of St. Faith illustrates an important feature of medieval religion. It shows the devotion Christians had for the relics, or remains, of saints. During the last Roman persecution of Christians, in the early 300s, the Romans killed Faith, a French girl. Almost 500 years later, tales of miracles she had performed began circulating, and the church declared Faith a saint. Pilgrims soon flocked to the church in France where some of her remains had been taken. Many of these pilgrims made offerings of gold, jewels, and other valuables. In about 985, these precious metals and stones were used to make this reliquary, a container for relics. St. Faith's skull is in a cavity in the back, wrapped in a covering of silver.

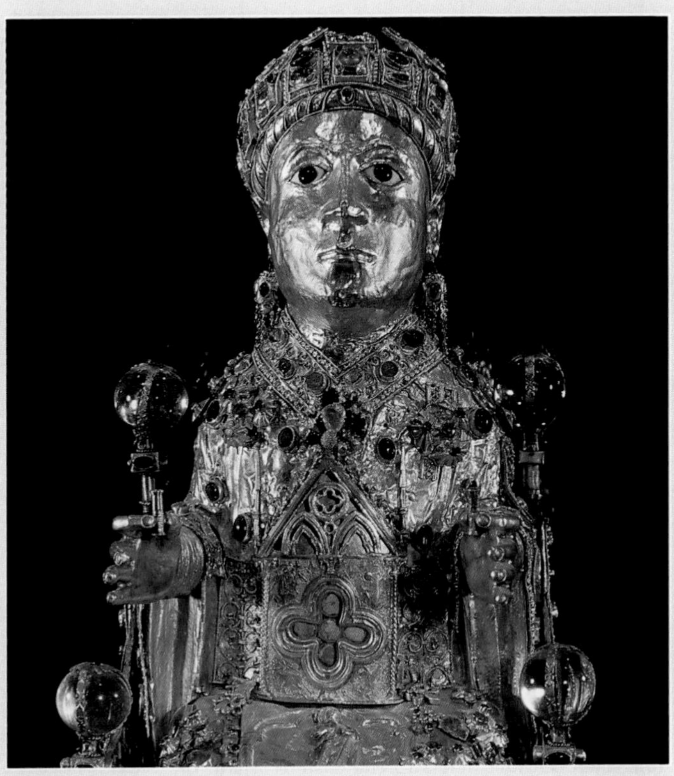

heretics, or unbelievers, guilty of the unpardonable sin of heresy, which brought eternal damnation. Heresy threatened the church itself, as treason does a modern government.

Attempts at church reform were made by many church leaders and lay rulers who tried to solve church problems through various measures. Two religious groups, or orders, established in the 1200s dedicated themselves to reform. They were the Franciscans, founded by St. Francis of Assisi in 1209, and the Dominicans, founded by St. Dominic in 1216. Members of both of these religious orders lived and preached among the people instead of secluding themselves in monasteries as members of most other religious orders did.

In the mid-1200s the pope ordered the Dominicans to seek out heretics and to eliminate heresy. During this search, known as the **Inquisition,** anyone suspected of heresy could be tried in secret and tortured in order to force a confession. Heretics who confessed they had been wrong were required to perform penance. The Inquisition condemned heretics who did not reform and turned them over to the civil government to be punished, usually by burning at the stake. The church thought these severe penalties were necessary to save the souls of heretics and to prevent the spread of heresy throughout Christendom.

SECTION 3 REVIEW

1. **Define** sacrament, monasticism, abbot, canon law, interdict, tithe, simony, Inquisition
2. **Identify** curia, cardinals, St. Francis of Assisi, St. Dominic
3. **Summarizing Ideas** Name the positions in the church hierarchy and briefly describe the duties of each position.
4. **Classifying Ideas** In what three ways did the medieval church resemble a state?
5. **Evaluating Ideas** How did the church contribute to medieval life?
6. **Interpreting Ideas** **(a)** What four major problems faced the church during the Middle Ages? **(b)** How do you think each problem hurt the power and status of the church?

founder of Dominicans
3. The *parish priest* was at the lowest level of the church hierarchy. He conducted services in the village church and supervised moral and religious instruction. From his cathedral city, the *bishop* managed a diocese consisting of several parishes. An *archbishop* exercised authority over other bishops in his province, which consisted of several dioceses. The *pope,* assisted by the curia and cardinals, sat at the top of the hierarchy and was the spiritual head of the church.
4. The church performed many of the responsibilities of a central government and resembled a state because (1) nearly everyone became a member, (2) it had its own laws and courts, (3) it had the power of taxation.
5. The church contributed to medieval life in the following ways: monks copied books by hand and created beautiful illuminated manuscripts. Monks were also leaders in agricultural development. The church took complete charge of all social work—hospitals, orphanages, poorhouses, and charity. It also exercised a great moral and religious influence.
6. (a) The problems of the medieval church included lay investiture, worldly lives of some clergy, simony, and heresy. **(b)** Answers

will vary. Students should include that these activities undermined people's confidence in the church, and that the church began to appear as a political authority interested in wealth and power rather than in its spiritual duties.

SECTION 4

Focus/Motivation
Write the following excerpts from the Magna Carta on the chalkboard or an overhead projector.

"Scutage [a tax paid instead of military service] or aid [grant to a king] shall be levied in our kingdom only by the common counsel of our kingdom . . . ."

"No freeman shall be captured or imprisoned . . . except by lawful judgment of his peers or by the law of the land."

"To no one will we sell, to no one will we deny or delay right of justice."

Ask students if these statements sound familiar. (Refer them to the American Bill of Rights.) Mention to students that the Magna Carta later became the basis for England's unwritten constitution and influenced the United States Constitution.

Presentation
Understanding Ideas (Average/Group)
Have students examine the map of the growth of

4 Kings and Nobles Struggled for Power in England and France

In Europe before the 1000s, kings and lords often struggled for power in a kind of feudal tug of war. Some great lords, as powerful as the kings themselves, served them only when it was convenient. However, a number of kings were able to impose their will on their subjects. From this struggle gradually emerged such kingdoms as England and France, where the king's authority grew stronger than that of the lords.

Anglo-Saxon England

About 450, not long after the last Roman legions left Britain, several Germanic tribes invaded the island. Although they first came as raiders, they soon began to settle. Two of these tribes, the Angles and the Saxons, became so powerful that we refer to their descendants as Anglo-Saxons even today. Even though the Saxons came to dominate the Angles and the other tribes, the Angles gave their name to the land. The word *England* comes from *Engla-land,* meaning "land of the Angles." The name *England* refers to the eastern island of the British Isles, except for Scotland in the north and Wales in the west.

The Anglo-Saxons in Britain formed several small independent kingdoms. Later these kingdoms combined into three important ones: (1) Northumbria, in what is now southern Scotland and northern England; (2) Mercia, in central England; and (3) Wessex, in southern England. In time the Anglo-Saxons divided these kingdoms into governmental districts called **shires.** Officials known as shire-reeves (which became the word *sheriffs*) governed these districts.

Alfred the Great. By the early 800s, the Wessex kings controlled practically all of England. However, their rule was soon challenged by the ferocious raiders from the north, the Vikings. At first the Danes—as the Anglo-Saxons called the Vikings—met little resistance, and they quickly conquered much of England. Then, in 871, Alfred the Great came to the throne of Wessex determined to drive the Danes from English soil. First, he persuaded them to leave Wessex by paying them a huge tribute, or sum of money. He spent the next five years reorganizing his army and building a fleet of

Learning from Pictures *Although tortured to death, St. Edmund, an Anglo-Saxon king, never renounced his faith. Here he gives alms to the poor.* †

ships. In 876, when he felt that his forces were strong enough, he attacked the Danes. The war raged for a decade, and in 886 the Danes sued for peace. The peace treaty limited Danish settlement to northeast Mercia and much of Northumbria. In this region, called the Danelaw, the Danes could live under their own laws and govern themselves.

Although best known as a warrior-king, Alfred the Great made many contributions to learning. An educated and scholarly man, he wanted his people to be educated also. To this end he established a number of schools and invited the best scholars from Ireland and Europe to teach in them. Alfred himself undertook the translation of a number of books from Latin to Anglo-Saxon. And at his command, scholars began a history of England from the earliest times. Work on this history,

†St. Edmund as alms giver, M736 F. 9r.: The Pierpont Morgan Library, New York

known as the *Anglo-Saxon Chronicle,* continued for some 250 years after Alfred's death in 899.

Danish rule. During the 900s Alfred's successors won back much of the remaining Danish-held land in England. At the same time, they unified the country, strengthened its government, and spread Christianity throughout the land. However, by the end of the century, England once again came under attack from the Danes. By 1013 they had conquered the whole of the country.

In 1019, under the rule of King Canute of Denmark, England became part of a large kingdom that included most of Scandinavia. Canute, who spent much of his time in England, ruled wisely. Canute's sons, however, had neither his intelligence nor his skill, and they proved to be weak rulers. By 1042 the Danes had been driven from England and the Anglo-Saxon nobles had chosen Edward the Confessor, as their new king.

The Norman Conquest

Edward the Confessor's background—part Anglo-Saxon and part Norman—created problems upon his death. When he died childless in 1066, Duke William of Normandy, a distant relative, claimed the English throne. The Anglo-Saxon nobles refused to recognize William's claim, selecting Edward's brother-in-law, Harold of Wessex, instead. So in 1066 William gathered a fleet of ships and an army of nobles and landed at Hastings, on the southeastern coast of England. In short order he defeated the Anglo-Saxon forces and declared himself King William I of England.

It took William, usually called William the Conqueror, several years to overcome Anglo-Saxon resistance. It took many more years for the Norman conquerors to overcome the hatred of the defeated Anglo-Saxons. The Anglo-Saxons did not adopt Norman ideas, customs, or language willingly. Anglo-Saxon, a Germanic language, remained the language of the people. Norman French, a Romance language based on Latin, became the language of the nobles. As time went on, however, the culture of England, including laws and customs, became as much Norman as Anglo-Saxon.

Feudalism in England

William the Conqueror, who ruled from 1066 to 1087, imported feudalism from France to England. However, he carefully altered feudalism in England so that the king, rather than the nobles, held the authority. To weaken the lords and prevent them from uniting, William gave his followers fiefs scattered throughout England.

William the Conqueror laid the foundation for a centralized government by requiring each feudal lord to swear allegiance directly to him. Thus all the feudal lords became vassals of the king.

To determine the population and wealth of England, William sent out commissioners to gather information on everyone in the country. This information helped to determine taxation. The survey became known as the *Domesday Book* (or *Doomsday Book)* because people said that it would be easier to escape doomsday, God's final judgment, than to avoid the royal commissioners.

Reforms Under William's Successors

One of William the Conqueror's sons, Henry I, ruled from 1100 to 1135. He made the central government more efficient by setting up a new department known as the Exchequer (eks • CHEK • uhr) to handle the kingdom's finances. Henry's other contribution was in the legal system. He wanted to weaken the feudal lords by having cases tried in the king's courts rather than in feudal courts. He sent traveling judges out to hold court sessions throughout the country.

Henry II, who reigned from 1154 to 1189, further increased royal authority. He allowed nobles to pay him instead of doing military service, then used the money to hire mercenaries. In this way he had an army loyal to him rather than to the nobles. He later raised a national army by requiring every freeman to obtain arms and serve. Henry reorganized the Exchequer to keep careful accounts of the government's finances.

Henry II made great use of the traveling judges. He established definite circuits, or routes, on which the judges were to travel. Thus they became known as circuit judges.

To let the judge know what cases should be tried, the king appointed groups of men called juries in each district. A grand jury consisted of 25 or more men who submitted the names of suspected criminals to the judge. In the 1200s the petit (PET • ee) jury of 12 developed. (*Grand* is the French word for "large," and *petit* the French word for "small.") At first petit juries decided only civil

France on page 242 or a wall map in the classroom showing this subject. Point out that Henry II of England inherited a number of French provinces from his mother and father: Anjou, Maine, Normandy, and Touraine. When Louis VII of France had his marriage to the heiress, Eleanor of Aquitaine, annulled by the church in 1152, Henry promptly married her. He thus got the additional provinces of Auvergne, Guienne, and Aquitaine. Although a vassal of the king of France, Henry was still a very powerful and dangerous vassal, owning lands or holding fiefs larger than France itself. Point out to students that the feudal system had long-term consequences for England and France. The English held some French territory for another 500 years (when Mary Tudor gave up Calais in the 1500s). Later, students will read about the Hundred Years' War and the very different cultures that emerged in two close neighbors. Use the information on Henry II's and Eleanor of Aquitaine's possessions as the basis for further discussion on how the feudal system worked.

1B, 4B, a1D

Learning from Pictures
King Henry II is shown doing penance at Thomas Becket's shrine.

cases, such as disputes over land. The feudal procedures of ordeal and combat still tried criminal cases. In time, however, petit juries decided criminal cases, too. In this way the king's law replaced feudal law.

In his efforts to increase royal authority, Henry II sought to transfer trials of certain members of the clergy from church courts to royal courts. The Archbishop of Canterbury, Thomas Becket, refused to allow this transfer, and the two men, once the best of friends, became bitter enemies. Four of the king's knights, thinking they were doing the king a great favor, murdered the archbishop in his cathedral.

Henry II denied any part in the assassination of Thomas Becket. Faced with papal excommunication, however, he was forced to abandon further attempts to reduce the power of the church. Thomas Becket became a saint, and his shrine in Canterbury became the most popular holy place in England for pilgrims to visit.

The last years of Henry II were troubled. His sons plotted against each other and united to plot against their father. His marriage to Eleanor of Aquitaine was stormy. Because he had received lands in France as part of Eleanor's dowry, England became further embroiled in wars in France. Nevertheless, Henry II helped consolidate the powers of the crown over the feudal lords. Later kings built upon his government and judicial institutions.

King John and the Magna Carta

One son of Henry II, King John, is famous for bringing on a revolt among the nobles of the realm by forcing them to pay taxes that they considered unjust. On June 15, 1215, the English nobles forced John to accept a document known as the **Magna Carta** (Latin for "great charter"), which protected the liberties of the nobles. Some provisions of the Magna Carta, however, dealt with the rights of England's ordinary people. These provisions have

240

come to be considered the most important ones in the document.

King John made several promises. He agreed not to collect any new or special tax without the consent of the Great Council, a body of important nobles and church leaders who advised the king. He promised not to take property without paying for it, and he agreed not to sell, refuse, or delay justice. The king also promised to grant any accused person a trial by a jury of peers, or equals. The Magna Carta meant that the king was not above the law—the king had to obey the law just as his subjects did, or they would be free to rebel against him.

Although the charter was not considered significant at the time, later political thinkers regarded many of its clauses as important precedents. Today the Magna Carta is considered one of the world's great documents, spelling out the rule of the law.

The Magna Carta forms part of the British Constitution, a series of great documents and acts of Parliament rather than one document such as the Constitution of the United States. Although the Magna Carta was a feudal document, it served as the basis for the establishment of parliamentary democracy in England and for the War of Independence that followed in the American colonies.

The original purpose of the Magna Carta was to protect the nobles, not to establish a constitutional government. Because the nobles were powerful, the rights they claimed were later extended to other classes of people. The document became the cornerstone of constitutional government and representative democracy.

Parliament and Common Law

In the century that followed the signing of the Magna Carta, the two most important developments in English history were the evolution of Parliament and the growth of common law.

Parliament. In the 1260s nobles revolted against King Henry III. The leader of the nobles, Simon de Montfort, ruled England for several months. He hoped to get greater support for the nobles' cause by broadening the representation in the Great Council.

In 1265 de Montfort summoned representatives of the middle class to meet with the higher nobles and clergy in the Great Council. There were two knights from each shire and two burgesses, or citizens, from each of several towns.

Learning from Pictures *The Magna Carta established the principle of limited government by restraining the power of the English monarch.*

De Montfort was killed in battle and the revolt was crushed, but the precedent of including knights and burgesses in the Great Council had been set. Later monarchs found it simpler to do business with a representative body of knights and burgesses than with crown officials. In time this representative body came to be called Parliament. It was eventually divided into two parts, or houses. The upper house consisted of nobles and clergy and was called the House of Lords. The lower house was made up of knights and burgesses and was called the House of Commons. Within a few years, this was the accepted form of representation.

The early Parliament did not have the power to pass laws, but it did have the important right of refusing to agree to new and special taxes. As the cost of running the central government increased, new taxes were necessary, and Parliament's approval became vital. Over the years Parliament used this power to its advantage.

Common law. One of England's greatest monarchs, Edward I, who ruled from 1272 to 1307,

SECTION 4

Closure
Ask students to trace the beginnings of the English Parliament. Why did Simon de Montfort wish to broaden the representation in the Great Council? *(to get greater support for the nobles who were rebelling against King Henry III)* Who did he include? *(knights from the shires and burgesses from the towns)* What important power did Parliament have from an early date? *(the right of refusing to approve new or special taxes)*

Review Answers
1. ***shire:*** district in kingdoms of Anglo-Saxon England; ***Magna Carta:*** Great Charter signed by King John protecting liberties of the English nobility; served as basis for liberties for all the people; ***common law:*** law codes based on judges' decisions
2. ***Anglo-Saxons:*** Germanic tribal invaders of England; ***Alfred the Great:*** greatest Anglo-Saxon king; ***Edward the Confessor:*** Anglo-Saxon king; ***Normans:*** successfully invaded England from France in 1066; ***William the Conqueror:*** Norman duke who claimed the English throne and defeated the Anglo-Saxons at Hastings; ***Thomas Becket:*** archbishop of Canterbury who quarreled with Henry II of England; ***Eleanor of Aquitaine:*** her dowry of lands in France on her marriage to Henry II embroiled England in wars with France; ***Simon de***

● southwestern coast, small area on coast south of Flanders

Montfort: leader of nobles' revolt in England against Henry III; ***Hugh Capet:*** founder of Capetian dynasty in France
3. ***Hastings:*** battle in southeastern England; ***Canterbury:*** town in southeastern England; ***Ile-de-France:*** region around Paris; ***Aquitaine:*** province in south-central France; ***Gascony:*** province in southwestern France
4. (a) The king could not collect any new tax without the consent of the Great Council; property could not be taken without payment; justice could not be refused, sold, or delayed; an accused person was entitled to a trial by a jury of peers. **(b)** The Magna Carta made the king subject to the law.
5. (a) Parliament developed from the Great Council. Later this representative body came to be called Parliament and was divided into a House of Lords and a House of Commons. **(b)** Common law developed through the verdicts of judges in the royal courts.
6. (a) The Capetians ruled only a small region around Paris. Feudal lords ruled the rest of France and resisted royal authority. **(b)** The Capetians had the advantage of not dividing the kingdom among sons.
7. by adding to royal lands, developing a strong centralized government, and increasing tax revenues

divided the king's court into three branches. The Court of the Exchequer kept financial accounts and tried tax cases. The Court of Common Pleas tried cases between private citizens. The Court of the King's Bench heard cases that concerned the king or the government.

Each of the three royal courts handed down many verdicts. Each year the courts collected the most important verdicts and wrote them down. These written decisions became the basis for future decisions made in the king's courts and in the circuit courts. This type of law, based on judges' decisions rather than on a code of statutes like Roman law, is known as **common law.** It received this name because it was common to all of the people of England. Common law forms the basis for the present-day legal systems in the United States and in England.

Rise of the Capetian Kings in France

When the last Carolingian king of France died without an heir in 987, an assembly of nobles chose Hugh Capet (kuh • PAY), a French noble, as king. Capet and his descendants, called the Capetians (kuh • PEE • shuhnz), ruled for more than 300 years.

As king, Hugh Capet ruled only a small region around Paris called the Ile-de-France (EEL-DUH-FRAHNS). *Ile* is the French word for "island," and this region was indeed an island of royal authority in the midst of feudal lands. Even in the Ile-de-France, the king's vassals resisted his authority.

The rest of what is today France was divided into provinces ruled by feudal lords (see map, this page). The Capetians set out to unite these provinces and to develop a strong central government.

The Capetian kings' method of succession allowed them to outlast many other noble families, including the Carolingian kings. Instead of dividing their kingdom among their sons, the Capetians allowed only the eldest son of a king to inherit. This method worked for more than 300 years.

The history of the Capetian kings demonstrates the feudal struggle for power. Strong kings increased royal lands and authority. Weak kings

Learning from Maps *The growth of France took place from the center, the Ile-de-France.*
● *What were the English possessions in France in 1328?*

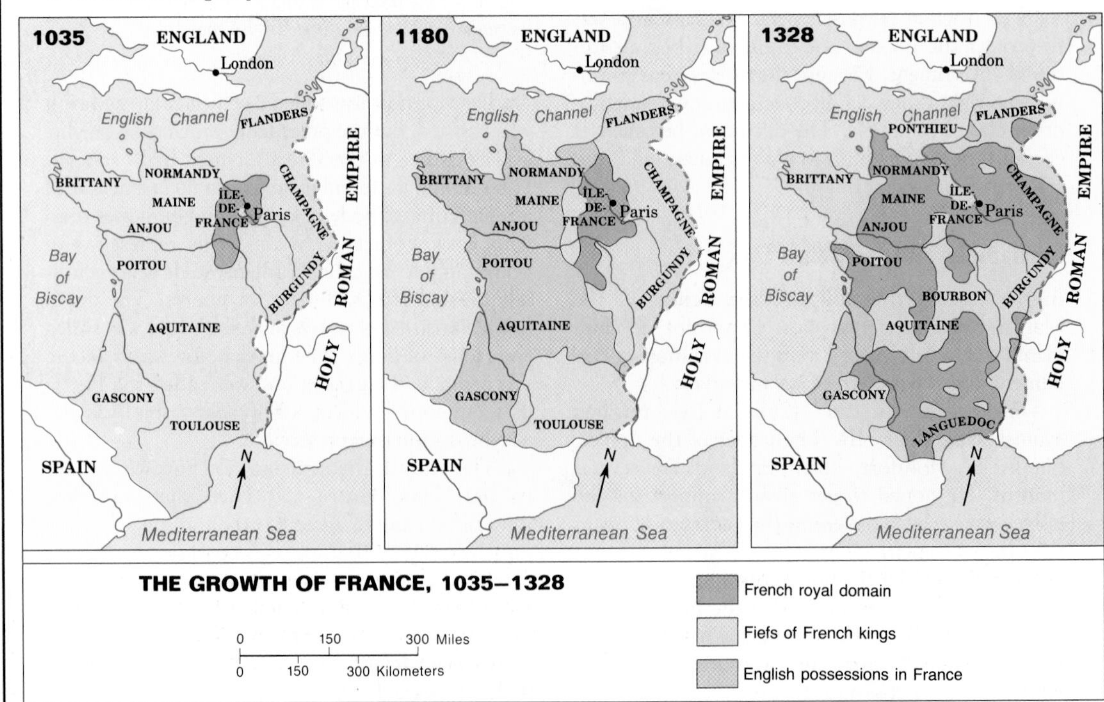

● In the rivalry for the imperial title the supporters of Lothair, the Duke of Saxony, were called *Guelphs;* supporters of the Hohenstauffen family were called *Ghibellines.* This struggle spread from Germany to Italy and went on for centuries. The Guelphs favored the popes and the Lombard League. The Ghibellines supported the Holy Roman Emperors.

1B, 4B, a4A, a4F, a4G, a4H, a4I, a4K, a4L

allowed nobles to regain power. Fortunately for the Capetians, enough strong kings ruled to outweigh the losses of the weaker kings.

The strong Capetian kings increased their power in three ways: by adding to the royal lands, by developing a strong central government, and by increasing the revenue from taxes.

The growth of royal territory. Kings sometimes married the daughters of great feudal lords to add to the royal lands. By doing so, they gained fiefs that were often included in the daughters' dowries. Kings also increased their royal territory by claiming the lands of those noble families that died out.

After 1066, when William of Normandy conquered England, the territorial problems of the Capetians became even more complicated. For centuries the English kings owned vast territories in France. Strong Capetians watched for a chance to regain these lands. The shrewd Philip Augustus, king of France from 1180 to 1223, seized much English-owned land in France. By 1328, when the last Capetian king died, the only major English landholdings in France included parts of the provinces of Aquitaine and Gascony (see map, page 242).

Central government. To maintain a strong government, the Capetians needed loyal, well-trained officials. They could not rely on feudal lords. Philip Augustus sent out loyal inspectors to investigate, hear complaints, report to the King's Council, and conduct government affairs.

The Capetians set up two new government departments. A Chamber of Accounts collected the taxes, and a supreme court, called the Parlement of Paris, heard appeals from all parts of the kingdom. Trained officials, like those in the King's Council, staffed and ran these departments.

Revenues. A strong central government needed money to pay the army, government officials, and other expenses. The expanding royal territory produced more wealth, as did fees and fines from royal courts. Because a wealthier country would produce more revenue from taxes, the Capetians encouraged the growth of towns, trade, and manufacturing. This policy caused townspeople to support the Capetians against the feudal lords. By the early 1300s, France was a strong, well-organized country, and the power of the king was greater than that of the nobles. However, the three sons of Philip IV died without a male heir, and in 1328 the long line of the Capetians ended.

SECTION 4 REVIEW

1. **Define** shire, Magna Carta, common law
2. **Identify** Anglo-Saxons, Alfred the Great, Edward the Confessor, Normans, William the Conqueror, Thomas Becket, Eleanor of Aquitaine, Simon de Montfort, Hugh Capet
3. **Locate** Hastings, Canterbury, Ile-de-France, Aquitaine, Gascony
4. **Interpreting Ideas** **(a)** Name four of the main provisions of the Magna Carta. **(b)** Why was the Magna Carta important?
5. **Evaluating Ideas** How did each of the following develop in England: **(a)** Parliament, **(b)** common law.
6. **Classifying Ideas** **(a)** What problems did the Capetian kings of France face? **(b)** What advantage did the kings have?
7. **Analyzing Ideas** Explain how the strong Capetian kings added to their power.

5 Popes and Emperors Clashed over Germany and Italy

Although people throughout Europe recognized the spiritual authority of the church, many conflicts arose over the church's temporal authority, or its role in worldly affairs. The greatest threat to the power of the medieval popes came from the German rulers of the revived Holy Roman Empire.

The Holy Roman Empire

Part of Italy had belonged to Charlemagne's empire. After Charlemagne's death in 814, Italy fell into a state of feudal anarchy. Several of Charlemagne's descendants held the title of "Emperor of the Romans" or "Holy Roman Emperor," without really ruling Italy. Later no one had even the title. ● The pope ruled the Papal States. The Byzantine Empire held some parts of Italy. Muslims held the island of Sicily and often invaded the Italian mainland.

In Germany the great feudal lords elected Otto I, known as Otto the Great, as king in 936. A powerful and forceful ruler, he might have developed a strong kingdom in Germany, like that of the Capetians in France, had he not been more interested in Italy.

SECTION 5

Focus/Motivation
Write on the chalkboard or an overhead projector the following decree of excommunication issued by Innocent III, or read it to the class:

"We excommunicate, anathematize [condemn], curse and damn him, as oathbreaker, blasphemer, incendiary, as faithless and as a criminal and usurper . . . . We order that henceforth anyone who gives him help or favor, or supplies him and his troops with food, clothing, ships, arms or anything else which he can benefit from shall be bound by the same sentence; any cleric, moreover, of whatever order of dignity, who shall presume to say the divine service for him, may know he has incurred the penalty due to one of his rank and order."

Ask students what effect they think excommunication would have on a ruler spiritually, personally, and politically. *(Answers will vary. Students should include the following: The excommunicated person is removed from the church and its sacramental life, running the risk of eternal damnation. Excommunication could damage the ruler's pride and reputation. Since the decree forbids Christians to give any form of support to the excommunicated person, vassals are released from allegiance to*

243

1B, 3B, 4B, a4A

● Shortly after Gregory VII's victory at Canossa, the pope and Henry fought again. Once again the pope excommunicated Henry. This time, however, Gregory had to flee from Rome to Salerno. His own allies, the Normans, sacked Rome, and Gregory died embittered and defeated in 1085.

their lord, leaving him without military protection.)

Presentation
Analyzing Ideas (Average/Group)
Ask students to identify the powers of the pope. Put their responses on the chalkboard or an overhead projector. *(Answers will vary. Students should include: interdict, excommunication, moral authority, ability to tax.)* Ask students to identify the ruler's powers. *(Answers should include: power to raise an army, collect taxes, bring people to justice in courts, and make laws.)* Hold a discussion on the following question: Which person seems to have had the most power? *(Answers will vary. Students should be encouraged to support their choice with logical arguments.)*

SECTION 5

Closure
Ask students why the German rulers of the Holy Roman Empire were so interested in Italy. *(wealth from trade)* Ask: Why do you think this distrubed the popes? *(Popes also were secular rulers of lands in central Italy; a powerful emperor was not in the papacy's best interest.)* What was the result of the papal-imperial struggle so far as Germany and Italy were concerned? *(Neither country was united until the 1800s.)*

Learning from Pictures *Emperor Otto had his son crowned as co-emperor by Pope John XIII. Who had Otto's title of Holy Roman Emperor 162 years before this coronation?* **Charlemagne**

Otto seized some territory in northern Italy. Then Pope John XII begged Otto's help in his struggle with the Roman nobles. Otto supported the pope, who crowned him "Emperor of the Romans" in 962. Otto later made his own secretary pope, and for the next 40 years, German kings chose the popes.

Although Otto's title was the same as that given Charlemagne 162 years earlier, he ruled a much smaller area—just Germany and northern Italy. This empire, called the Holy Roman Empire, was a shadowy sort of empire, but it lasted, in name at least, for centuries. It established a unique relationship between Germany and Italy that continued for more than 800 years, to the great harm of both regions.

The power of the Holy Roman Emperors reached a high point under Emperor Henry III, who reigned from 1039 to 1056. Like Charlemagne, Henry regarded the church as a branch of the royal government that should do what the emperor expected. During Henry's reign three different men claimed to be pope. Henry III deposed all three of these claimants and had a German "elected" to the papacy. He also chose the next three popes.

Struggle with the Papacy

Henry III's son, Emperor Henry IV, was only six years old when his father died. Powerful nobles in Germany took advantage of Henry's youth and reestablished their feudal powers. At the same time, the church increased its powers. After Henry IV became old enough to rule, Gregory VII, one of the great medieval church leaders, became pope.

The new pope sought to restore the papacy to power. He believed that as God's representative he had supreme power not only over the church but also over all temporal rulers and their subjects. As pope, Gregory used the most terrible punishments of the church—excommunication and interdict—in his conflicts with emperors, kings, and nobles. Gregory's greatest struggle was with Henry IV.

The struggle between Gregory VII and Henry IV concerned the issue of lay investiture. Henry IV insisted that he had the right to appoint bishops within the Holy Roman Empire. Gregory disagreed and excommunicated the emperor. He released all of Henry's subjects from their oaths of allegiance and urged them to elect another emperor.

Fearing rebellion, Henry decided to appeal to the pope for mercy. During the bitter winter of 1077, he set off to meet the pope at the castle of Canossa, high in the mountains of northern Italy.

At great risk Henry and his attendants reached the rugged Alpine summit. The most dangerous part of the journey, however, was the descent down the ice-covered jagged peaks. Cautiously the travelers slipped and slid a few feet at a time. The queen and her attendants sat on makeshift slides made of oxen skins, as guides directed their descent. Some horses were also placed on makeshift slides, and others were dragged across the ice and through crevices to the mountain base.

When Gregory learned that Henry had defied the cruel weather to make his treacherous journey, he ordered him to come to the castle at Canossa. ● When Henry arrived, he laid his royal regalia down and stood humbly, barefoot and dressed as a pilgrim, waiting for the pope's invitation to enter the castle. For three days Henry suffered the piercing chill of the freezing weather. On the fourth day, he was admitted to the castle. He agreed to several conditions of his forgiveness, and Gregory absolved his excommunication.

The struggle over lay investiture, however, continued during the reign of Henry's son. Finally, in

● Emperor Frederick II could read and speak Latin, Greek, French, German, Italian, and Arabic. The long struggle between popes and Hohenstauffens ended in a papal victory when, at age 16, Frederick II's grandson Conradin was defeated and beheaded in the public square at Naples. The Hohenstauffens were thus exterminated.

1B, 4B, a4A, a4F, a4G, a4H, a4K, a4L

1122 at the German city of Worms (VAWRMS), an assembly of church leaders, nobles, and representatives of the Holy Roman Emperor reached an agreement known as the Concordat of Worms. The emperor agreed to grant only lands and secular powers to church officials. The church officials should elect bishops and grant them their spiritual powers. The emperor promised not to try to influence the elections.

Even though the Concordat of Worms established the popes as spiritual leaders, the bitter struggle between popes and emperors did not end. The emperors still meddled in Italian politics and continued to threaten the popes' rule in the Papal States. The popes therefore opposed all attempts of the Holy Roman Emperors to rule any part of Italy.

Frederick Barbarossa

Frederick I, called Frederick Barbarossa (meaning "Frederick of the Red Beard"), ruled Germany from 1152 to 1190. Like the emperors who preceded him, Frederick could have made a determined effort to unite the empire, but he was more interested in Italy.

The rich city-states of Lombardy in northern Italy—Bologna, Parma, Padua, Verona, and Milan—had become increasingly independent trade centers. Each city-state had a wealthy merchant class. Frederick knew that if he could capture these rich city-states he would be a very rich ruler. So he sent representatives to take over the governments in the cities. When Milan refused to receive his representative, Frederick captured the city, destroyed it, and drove out its people.

The other Lombard city-states, aided by the pope, united to form the Lombard League. They raised an army and defeated Frederick in 1176. According to the peace settlement, the cities recognized Frederick as overlord in return for his agreement that they could govern themselves.

Innocent III and Papal Power

Innocent III, who was pope from 1198 to 1216, led the papacy to the height of its prestige and power. A learned and intelligent man, Innocent wrote books about law, theology, and Christian discipline. He was also a skillful diplomat and one of the greatest political leaders in all church history.

Innocent III made even more sweeping claims and enforced them more successfully on behalf of papal power than had Gregory VII. Innocent III believed himself supreme over the clergy and all temporal rulers. To Innocent, emperors and kings were merely servants of the church. Thus Innocent claimed the right to settle all political and religious problems. No person or group could do more than advise him.

Innocent intervened in disputes throughout Europe and made free use of his powers of excommunication and interdict. In a quarrel with King John, Innocent placed England under interdict. To have the interdict lifted, John had to become the pope's vassal and pay money every year to Rome. Innocent dominated all of Italy. In Germany he overthrew two kings and put his own choices on the throne.

Innocent III dominated almost all of Europe because of his seemingly superhuman ability and energy. Even so, he was successful partly because conditions in Europe were favorable to his claims and activities. Later popes were less skillful, and circumstances were less favorable. Thus they did not attain the power or influence that Innocent had possessed.

Nevertheless, Germany and Italy never united. The Holy Roman Emperor Frederick II attempted to unite the two areas in the early 1200s. Like earlier emperors, however, Frederick failed. ●

The attempts to unite Germany and Italy not only failed but also prevented either country from being united. Germany remained a jumble of independent cities and feudal states over which the emperor had little authority. Italy was fragmented too, with the Lombard cities in the north, the Papal States in the central region, and the Kingdom of Sicily in the south. Neither Germany nor Italy became a unified nation until the 1800s.

SECTION 5 REVIEW

1. **Identify** Otto I, Pope John XII, Henry III, Frederick Barbarossa, Frederick II
2. **Locate** Canossa, Worms
3. **Identifying Ideas** **(a)** What was the major issue in the conflict between Gregory VII and Henry IV? **(b)** How was the issue resolved?
4. **Classifying Ideas** What were the provisions of the Concordat of Worms?
5. **Analyzing Ideas** Why was the papacy of Innocent III so important?

Review Answers

1. ***Otto I:*** elected king of Germany in 936 by feudal lords; ***Pope John XII:*** crowned Otto I emperor of the Romans in return for help against Roman nobles; ***Henry III:*** Holy Roman Emperor during whose reign the power of the emperor reached a high point; ***Frederick Barbarossa:*** Holy Roman Emperor from 1152 to 1190; ***Frederick II:*** Holy Roman Emperor from 1215 to 1250

2. ***Canossa:*** town where Pope Gregory VII forgave Holy Roman Emperor Henry IV; ***Worms:*** town in southwestern Germany where concordat on lay investiture was reached

3. (a) lay investiture; **(b)** Henry entered the church after begging Gregory's forgiveness, but the issue of lay investiture was not resolved until the Concordat of Worms in 1122.

4. Church officials would elect bishops and grant them spiritual powers, while the emperor would not interfere in the elections and would grant only lands and secular powers to church officials.

5. Innocent III led the papacy to the height of its power, dominating almost all of Europe.

Reviewing Important Terms
1. Middle Ages, or medieval period;
2. Feudalism; **3.** vassal;
4. fief; **5.** primogeniture;
6. domain; **7.** serfs; **8.** chivalry; **9.** sacraments;
10. abbot; **11.** Interdict;
12. simony.

Developing Critical Thinking Skills
1. The Franks provided a strong government and gained church support. The mayors of the palace and Charlemagne revived education and preserved Latin learning.
2. It marked his recognition as successor to the Roman emperors and the close ties between Franks and popes.
3. (a) because it owned vast lands, some of which it granted as fiefs to laymen. Popes, bishops, and abbots served as feudal lords and vassals. **(b)** because popes claimed that they were politically supreme and that all monarchs had to obey them. The church had the power of taxation and its own laws and courts.
4. (a) Henry II of England tried to transfer trials of the clergy from church to royal courts. Becket refused to allow this.
(b) Henry IV insisted on the right to lay investiture, but Gregory VII disagreed.
5. (b) 481; **(d)** 732; **(e)** 800; **(f)** 987; **(c)** 1066; **(a)** 1122; **(g)** 1215
6. (a) William the Conqueror scattered fiefs and forced feudal lords to swear allegiance directly to him. Henry I established the Exchequer and used royal courts. Henry II created a professional army, established circuits for judges, and appointed juries. Capetian kings added to royal lands, established

1B, 3B, 4B, a1C, a4A, a4E, a4F, a4G, a4H, a4K, a4L

Reteaching
Have students review the Chapter Summary and the appropriate section and questions in the Unit Synthesis. Discuss the concepts until students demonstrate a clear understanding of the material.

CHAPTER 10 REVIEW

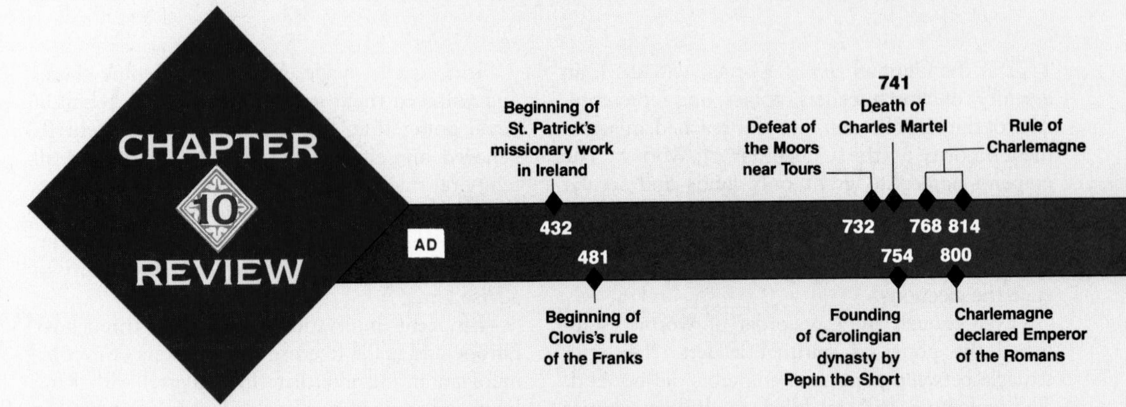

Chapter Summary

The following list contains the key concepts you have learned about feudal lords and the church in medieval Europe.

1. After the Roman Empire declined, Germanic tribes plundered Europe and established a series of short-lived kingdoms.
2. Clovis, king of a Frankish tribe, and the Merovingians who succeeded him created a large kingdom in France. The greatest Frankish king, Charlemagne, created an empire that included much of western Europe.
3. Two important medieval institutions were feudalism and the manorial system. Feudalism was a political system in which lords granted fiefs to vassals in return for military duty and other services. The manorial system was an economic system based on the self-sufficient manor, worked mainly by serfs.
4. During the Middle Ages, the church performed many functions. The church had its own laws and the power of taxation.
5. Monasticism attracted many people. Both secular and regular clergy played important roles in education, politics, economics, and social life.
6. Certain difficulties and problems, such as lay investiture, the worldly lives of the clergy, simony, and heresy, plagued the medieval church.
7. During the rule of the Anglo-Saxons in England, the people accepted Christianity and the Danes (Vikings) invaded. Although the Anglo-Saxons drove the Danes out of England, the Normans soon arrived.
8. The English ruler himself was made subject to the law when King John was forced to accept the Magna Carta. Parliament and common law developed in England during the 1200s.
9. French kings gradually extended their authority. The Capetians—Hugh Capet and his descendants—added territory, developed a strong central government, and increased tax revenues.
10. Holy Roman Emperors, who struggled for power with the papacy, controlled much of Germany and Italy.

On a separate sheet of paper, complete the following review exercises.

Reviewing Important Terms

Supply the term that correctly completes the sentence.

1. The period in western European history following the collapse of the Roman Empire, from about 500 to about 1500, is called the ________ ________.
2. ________ was the political system that flourished in Europe during the medieval period.
3. The person who held land in return for services was called the ________.
4. A ________ was a grant of land.
5. The custom of allowing only the eldest son to inherit land is called ________.
6. Under the manorial system, the lord kept about one-third of the manor land, called the ________.
7. In medieval Europe most peasants who lived on manors were ________, or people bound to the land.
8. The code of conduct for knights was known as ________.
9. Special rites or ceremonies at which participants receive the grace of God to help ward off the consequences of sins are called ________.
10. The elected head of a community of monks was called an ________.
11. ________ occurred when the church punished an entire region.
12. In feudal times people often paid to get positions in the church, a practice called ________.

Developing Critical Thinking Skills

1. **Identifying Ideas** Why were the Franks the most important Germanic tribe in western Europe?
2. **Interpreting Ideas** Why was Charlemagne's title as "Emperor of the Romans" significant?
3. **Evaluating Ideas (a)** How did the church become part of the feudal system in Europe? **(b)** In what ways was the church independent of the feudal system?
4. **Contrasting Ideas** Discuss the conflicts between church and state that arose in the disputes between **(a)** Henry II and Thomas Becket **(b)** Henry IV and Gregory VII.
5. **Sequencing Information** Give the correct date for each of the following events and arrange them in chronological order.

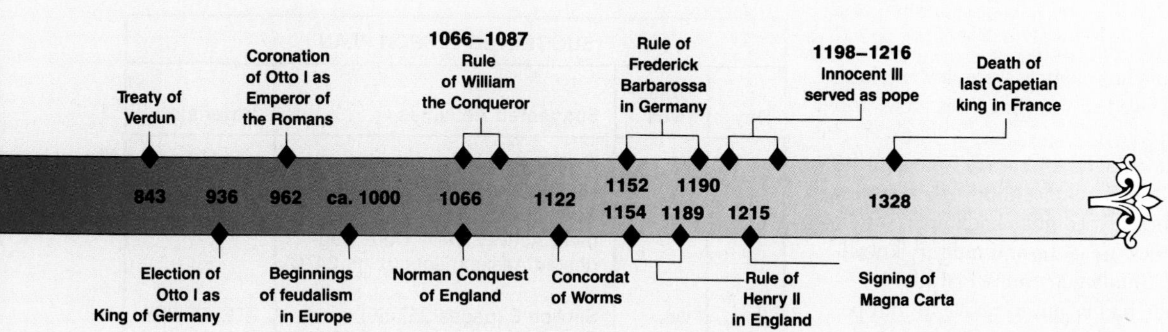

(a) Concordat of Worms signed
(b) Clovis became king of Frankish tribe
(c) Invasion of England by William the Conqueror
(d) Battle of Tours
(e) Charlemagne crowned Emperor of the Romans
(f) Capetian line of kings founded
(g) Signing of Magna Carta

6. **Analyzing Ideas** In both England and France, kings increased their power at the expense of the nobility. **(a)** List the ways in which William the Conqueror and his successors and the French Capetian kings added to their power and developed central governments. **(b)** Explain how these measures increased royal authority and decreased the nobles' power.

Relating Geography to History

Compare the map of Charlemagne's Empire on page 225 with the map of territorial changes resulting from the Treaty of Verdun on page 226. Then write a paragraph describing how Charlemagne's death affected the boundaries of his empire.

Relating Past to Present

1. Compare life on a medieval manor with life on a modern American farm. In which place would you find greater self-sufficiency? You may want to refer to books or magazines in your library for information about life on American farms.
2. Use a book on American civics or government to find the following information: **(a)** What kinds of cases go before a modern-day grand jury? **(b)** Why do some cases use a petit jury while others use only a judge? **(c)** What is the role of the judge? **(d)** What are the different types of courts in your state? Now compare your findings with the information in this chapter about the beginning of the court system in England.

Applying History Study Skills

Before completing this activity, review Building History Study Skills on page 232.

Read the following quotations about the role and status of women during the Middle Ages. Then identify one fact and one value statement in each quotation.

> "In addition to providing for their families' physical survival, peasant women also provided moral, emotional and spiritual sustenance. . . . There would be much in the harshness of life to justify and explain. As the daughter, as the female, the peasant woman's life would never be without responsibility. She would be the first child picked to work and the one always expected to assist in the maintenance of the family."

> "The women of the ninth century enjoyed an increased capacity to share in the inheritance of property. Women had always been eligible to receive certain movable goods from either their own relatives or from their husbands but now law and practice allowed women to inherit immovables. A reason for this trend may be discerned from a deed from the eighth century in which a doting father left equal shares of his property to his sons and daughters."

Investigating Further

1. **Analyzing Ideas** Read the medieval play *Everyman* (Dutton). **(a)** Describe five of the main characters. **(b)** What values does the church want people to cherish the most? **(c)** What is the importance of good deeds?
2. **Writing a Report** Obtain a copy of Eileen Power's *Medieval People* (Harper & Row), which tells the story of a peasant's life during the reign of Charlemagne. Read the selection "Madame Eglentyne," in which the author describes everyday life in a nunnery. Then prepare a written report that answers the following questions: **(a)** What religious duties were performed by the nuns? **(b)** What evidence of "worldliness" is given?
3. **Constructing a Model** Use resources in your school or public library to find more information about medieval manors. Then construct a scale model showing a typical manor.

a bureaucracy, and professional army, collected taxes, and had the Parlement of Paris hear appeals. They encouraged the growth of towns, trade, and manufacturing. **(b)** Answers will vary. Royal control of the courts weakened the nobles' hold on feudal justice. Paid armies made monarchs less dependent on nobles.

Relating Geography to History
The Frankish Empire was divided after the death of Louis the Pious. By the Treaty of Verdun, the western part, Charles the Bald's kingdom, served as the nucleus of France. The eastern kingdom, Louis the German's share, became Germany. These two kingdoms absorbed the middle kingdom, Lorraine.

Relating Past to Present
1. Medieval manors tried to be self-sufficient and had little contact with other manors. People today are more interdependent, agriculture is tied to a world market, and few farms are self-sufficient.
2. **(a)** Grand juries hear murder, rape, larceny, arson, burglary, and treason cases. **(b)** Citizens have the right to trial by jury when the penalty will be imprisonment for more than six months. **(c)** The judge maintains order in the courtroom, decides whether evidence is relevant, advises the jury on the law, and applies the law as the jury's verdict indicates. **(d)** Answers will vary according to state.

Applying History Study Skills
Answers will vary.

247

CHAPTER (pages 248–273)

11 Trade Revived and Nations Developed in Europe

(1000 — 1500)

CHAPTER OVERVIEW

During the late Middle Ages, significant changes were slowly taking place in Western Europe. Trade revived, towns and cities grew, and nation-states began to emerge.

In 1095 Pope Urban II called for the First Crusade to regain the Holy Land from the Muslims. Other Crusades followed, but they were military failures. However, these expeditions had important effects on Europe: they introduced new weapons and military knowledge, increased royal power, and stimulated commercial life.

Even before the Crusades, trade had begun to revive in Europe. The towns of northern Italy dominated the lucrative trade with the East. The towns in Flanders and the Hanseatic League also shared in the new commercial wealth. This revival of European trade led to the development of a manufacturing system, a banking system, and investment of capital.

As trade revived, towns grew in important trade locations. Townspeople gained important liberties, and merchants and skilled workers organized guilds. The middle class became prominent, and the number of serfs declined.

Medieval culture flourished in the cities. Vernacular languages developed, and universities were founded. Philosophers such as Peter Abelard and Thomas Aquinas tried to reconcile faith and reason. Architecture and the other arts still remained mostly in the service of the church.

Following the Hundred Years' War and the Wars of the Roses, governments grew stronger in England and France. Patriotism developed in England, France, and a unified Spain, but Germany and Italy remained politically disunited.

As monarchs became stronger, papal authority diminished with the Babylonian Captivity and the Great Schism.

SUGGESTED LESSON PLAN

Day	Objectives	Suggested Activities	Materials
1	U6,* C1	Introducing the Chapter (page 248) Section 1 (pages 249-53, Focus/Motivation (page 249), Presentation (page 250), Closure (page 252), Suggested Teaching Strategies, Enrichment Activities, Daily Quiz, Suggested Assignments (page 247B)	ATE, Pupil's Edition, Teacher's Resource-Bank™
2	U6, C2-3	Section 2 (pages 253-57), Focus/Motivation (page 253), Presentation (page 255), Closure (page 256), Suggested Teaching Strategies, Enrichment Activity, Daily Quiz, Suggested Assignments (page 247C)	ATE, Pupil's Edition, Teacher's Resource-Bank™
3	U6, C4-5	Section 3 (pages 257-59), Focus/Motivation (page 257), Presentation (page 258), Closure (page 258), Suggested Teaching Strategies, Enrichment Activity, Daily Quiz, Suggested Assignments (page 247D)	ATE, Pupil's Edition, Teacher's Resource-Bank™
4	U6, C6	Section 4 (pages 259-64), Focus/Motivation (page 259), Presentation (page 260), Closure (page 264), Suggested Teaching Strategies, Enrichment Activity, Daily Quiz, Suggested Assignments (page 247E)	ATE, Pupil's Edition, Teacher's Resource-Bank™
5	U6, C7-8	Section 5 (pages 265-69), Focus/Motivation (page 265), Presentation (page 266), Closure (page 268), Suggested Teaching Strategies, Enrichment Activity, Daily Quiz, Suggested Assignments (page 247E)	ATE, Pupil's Edition, Teacher's Resource-Bank™
6	U6, C9	Section 6 (pages 269-71), Focus/Motivation (page 269), Presentation (page 269), Closure (page 270), Suggested Teaching Strategies, Enrichment Activity, Daily Quiz, Suggested Assignments (page 247F)	ATE,Pupil's Edition, Teacher's Resource-Bank™
7	U6, C1-9	Chapter 11 Form A Test, Reteaching Worksheet, Chapter 11 Form B Test	Teacher's Resource-Bank™ or Workbook and Test Booklet

*C refers to applicable Chapter Objective, U refers to applicable Unit Goal

BOOKS FOR THE TEACHER

Barraclough, Geoffrey. *The Medieval Papacy.* Harcourt Brace Jovanovich. Gives history of the papacy; includes illustrations.

Copleston, Frederick. *Medieval Philosophy.* Torchbooks. Discusses the philosophy of the Middle Ages from traditional Catholic perspectives.

Oldenbourg, Zoe. *The Crusades.* Ballantine. Gives detailed account of 200 years of war.

Tuchman, Barbara. *A Distant Mirror.* Knopf. Provides colorful panorama of the close of the Middle Ages.

BOOKS FOR THE STUDENT

Evan, Rhodes. *An Army of Children.* Dial. Describes the Children's Crusade.

Fremantle, Anne. *Age of Belief.* Mentor. Provides good introduction to medieval philosophy.

Unstead, R. J. *Living in a Crusader Land.* Addison-Wesley. Describes everyday life in four crusader kingdoms.

MULTIMEDIA MATERIALS

The Crusades (fs), Educational Audio-Visual. Explores the causes of the Crusades.

The Crusades: Saints and Sinners (mp, 27 min.), Learning Corp. Describes the First Crusade.

Medieval England: The Peasants' Revolt (mp, 31 min.), Learning Corp. Reveals the weaknesses of the economic and social systems of medieval England.

Medieval Times: Guilds and Trades (mp, 14 min.), Coronet. Focuses on trade in the medieval world.

Medieval Times: The Crusades (mp, 14 min.), Coronet. Evaluates the effects of the Crusades.

Section (pages 249–253)

1 The Crusades Changed the Lives of the People of Europe

SECTION OVERVIEW

Pope Urban II's call for a Crusade in 1095 touched off a series of Crusades that continued until the late 1200s. The First Crusade regained the Holy Land for Christianity and established four small feudal states there. Succeeding Crusades had little success, and the Muslims recaptured the Holy Land. The Crusades, however, had other lasting effects. Military technology improved, royal power increased, and new goods and ideas entered Europe.

SUGGESTED TEACHING STRATEGIES

1. **Preteaching Vocabulary (Basic)** You may wish to preteach the following important vocabulary term: Crusade (page 250). Ask students what the word *crusade* means today.
2. **Interpreting Ideas (Average/Group)** Below is an excerpt from Pope Urban II's speech at Clermont, France. Distribute copies of this speech to the class.

"... Your brethren who live in the East are in urgent need of your help, and you must hasten to give them the aid which has often been promised them. For, as the most of you have heard, the Turks and Arabs have attacked them and have conquered the territory of Romania [the Byzantine Empire] as far west as the shore of the Mediterranean and the Hellespont. . . . They have killed and captured many, and have destroyed the churches and devastated the Empire. . . . On this account I . . . beseech you as Christ's heralds to publish this everywhere and to persuade all people of whatever rank . . . to carry aid promptly to those Christians. . . . I say this to those who are present; it is meant also for those who are absent. Moreover, Christ commands it.

All who die by the way, whether by land or by sea, or in battle against the pagans, shall have immediate remission of sins. . . . With what reproaches will the Lord overwhelm us if you do not aid those who, with us, profess the Christian religion! Let those who have been accustomed unjustly to wage private warfare against the faithful now go against the infidels and end with victory this war which should have been begun long ago. . . . Let those who have been fighting against their brothers and relatives now fight in a proper way against the barbarians."

Lead a class discussion on the pope's reasons for calling for a Crusade. *(Answers will vary. Students should include the following: aiding Eastern Orthodox church, retribution for atrocities committed by Seljuk Turks, fulfillment of God's will, forgiveness of sins, honor, and to end fighting among French nobles.)*

3. **Relating Ideas (Average/Group)** Have students write short essays describing the First, Second, and Third Crusades. Ask for volunteers to read their essays to the class.

ENRICHMENT ACTIVITIES

1. **Writing a Letter (Basic)** Have students write letters from a bishop, noble, noble's wife, or merchant to a friend describing how the Crusades have affected his or her life. A noble's wife might write that as a result of her husband's being away she has learned to manage a manor. The bishop can write about the prestige he has gained, and the merchant the expansion of his business. Have students share their letters with the class.
2. **Film (Average/Group)** The film *The Crusades: Saints and Sinners* (27 min., color, Learning Corporation) provides an excellent vehicle for a class discussion of the First Crusade. Discuss the following question: Were the Crusades an expression of Christian faith or just a series of cruel wars? During the discussion be sure that students become aware of the variety of reasons people had for going on a Crusade.

DAILY QUIZ

To assess student understanding of Section 1, give the class the following quiz. (Each item is worth 10 points.)

1. Which aggressive people gained control of the Holy Land from the Arabs, with the result that Christians wanted to drive them out? *(Seljuk Turks)*

2. In 1095 which pope asked the feudal nobles to drive the unbelievers out of the Holy Land? *(Urban II)*
3. What emblem did the crusaders wear stitched to their garments? *(cross)*
4. Name one state the crusaders established. *(Edessa, Antioch, Tripoli, Jerusalem)*
5. What did the crusaders introduce in their states in the Holy Land? *(feudalism—subdivided land into fiefs)*
6. (T or F) The Second Crusade led to additional conquests by the Christian knights. *(F)*
7. (T or F) The Fourth Crusade saved Constantinople from the inevitable attack by the Turks. *(F)*
8. (T or F) The Children's Crusade was a tragic failure. *(T)*
9. List two military weapons or tactics the crusaders learned from the Muslims or the Byzantines. *(crossbow, new siege tactics, gunpowder)*
10. List three European social or political changes brought about by the Crusades. *(improved status of women, prestige for church, rise of kings, decline of feudalism, cultural mixing, new products)*

SUGGESTED ASSIGNMENTS

1. **Critical Thinking Worksheet (Average/Group)** Have students complete Critical Thinking Worksheet 24 in the TEACHER'S RESOURCEBANK™.
2. **Research (Average/Group)** Have students read about the Crusades in encyclopedias and books in their school or public libraries. Then ask them to select one Crusade and make an in-depth report on it: Who led it? Where did the crusaders go? What did they accomplish or fail to accomplish? Then ask students to report their findings to the class. The reports may serve as the basis for a class discussion on the term *crusade* and how it is used in other contexts (politics, for example) and other eras.

Section (pages 253–256)

2 Trade Increased in Europe

SECTION OVERVIEW

Although trade had nearly died out in Europe after the 400s, it slowly revived. Italian traders were the first to make contact with the East. In time, northern Europe developed thriving trading towns, such as those in Flanders and the members of the Hanseatic League. As trade grew, fairs were held that provided central marketplaces for the exchange of goods. The domestic system of manufacturing and banking developed, marking the beginning of a market economy and the modern capitalist economic system.

SUGGESTED TEACHING STRATEGIES

1. **Preteaching Vocabulary (Basic)** You may wish to preteach the following vocabulary terms: usury (*page 253*); barter economy, domestic system (*page 255*); capital, market economy (*page 256*). Ask students to give an example of a product that might be produced by the domestic system today.
2. **Understanding Geography (Basic)** Produce a wall map of Europe or an outline map that can be shown on an overhead projector or reproduced on paper for each student. Have students trace the main medieval trade routes and note the lands, bodies of water, and cities along these routes. Lead a discussion using the following questions as a guide: What goods were traded and where did they come from? *(From Asia came spices, perfumes, dyes, silks, cotton, linen, and art products in gold, silver, and ivory. The Middle East supplied textiles, rugs, grain, and fruit. European goods included furs, timber, fish, and grain from the Baltic region; wine, oil, leather, arms, and armor from Spain; metal goods and glassware from Venice; fine woolen cloth from England and Flanders; wine from France.)* Ask the class what the Hanseatic League was and how it operated. Have them locate major Hanseatic ports on their maps. *(The Hanseatic League was an association of trading cities in northern Europe that promoted and protected trade among its members. Major Hansa ports include Lübeck, Cologne, Danzig, Hamburg, Bremen, and Rostock.)* Ask students to explain why fairs were important to trade. *(Fairs, particularly those of Champagne, provided a central marketplace for the exchange of goods.)*
3. **Writing a Diary (Average/Group)** Have students write a diary entry by a boy or girl who has just returned from the fair at Champagne. They are to describe their day at the fair, including the items of trade and the entertainments. Use the diaries as the basis for a class discussion comparing medieval fairs with present-day county or state fairs in the United States.

ENRICHMENT ACTIVITY

Performing at a Fair (Challenging) Medieval fairs were not only centers of trade, they were also centers of entertainment. Musicians, dancers, storytellers, actors, and jugglers were among the performers one could watch at a fair. Have students research medieval music and dance, musical instruments, and other forms of entertainment. You might have students use the information they have gathered to perform medieval entertainments for the class. Sources for this project include encyclopedias and recordings of medieval music. Archibald Davidson's and Willi Apel's *Historical Anthology of Music* (Harvard University Press) provides notated music for students who can play instruments.

DAILY QUIZ

To assess student understanding of Section 2, give the class the following quiz. (Each item is worth 10 points.)

1. Name one reason trade fell drastically after the 400s. *(thieves, shortage of money, poor roads, invasions, church laws against usury)*
2. What country became the first region to benefit from the new growth of trade? *(Italy)*
3. What factors favored the revival of trade in this country? *(Its*

towns had not declined as much as those elsewhere, and it was well positioned on trade routes between northern Europe and Asia.)

4. Flanders became important as a _______ center. *(textile or woolen trade)*
5. (T or F) The Hanseatic League existed primarily to establish colonies in Slavic lands. *(F)*
6. _______ in northeastern France was famous for its trade fairs. *(Champagne)*
7. Manufacturing that takes place in workers' homes is called the _______ _______. *(domestic system)*
8. We call the economy that exchanges goods for other goods without money _______ _______. *(barter economy)*
9. What economic system developed in Europe, in which private individuals invested wealth in businesses in order to produce profits? *(capitalism)*
10. What activity developed in Italy from the word meaning the "moneychanger's table"? *(banking)*

SUGGESTED ASSIGNMENTS

1. **Research Reports (Average/Group)** Have students write reports on one of the medieval trading cities, focusing on that city's role in reviving trade. Medieval cities that students might choose include Venice, Florence, Genoa, Bruges, Ghent, Hamburg, Lübeck, Danzig, and Bremen. Sources include Trevor Cairns's *The Middle Ages* (Lerner Publications) and Norman Kotker's *Horizon Book of the Middle Ages* (American Heritage).
2. **Contrasting Past and Present (Average/Group)** Have interested students do further study on the history of banking. They should examine economic histories in their school or local libraries. They may wish to select a particular banking family, such as the Fuggers of Augsburg or the Medici of Florence, and examine their origins, growth, and decline. Other students may wish to study some of the methods used by bankers then that are still in use or have been modified over the course of time. Have students present their findings in an oral report to the class.

Section (pages 257–259)

3 The Growth of Towns Brought Great Social and Political Change

SECTION OVERVIEW

With the revival of trade, towns and cities expanded. The growth of towns contributed to the breakdown of feudalism, as townspeople gained political liberties from the lords. A middle class, composed of merchants and craftspeople, developed, and guilds were formed to regulate trade and manufacturing.

SUGGESTED TEACHING STRATEGIES

1. **Preteaching Vocabulary (Basic)** You may wish to preteach the following important vocabulary terms: merchant guild, craft guild, apprentice (*page 257*); journeyman (*page 258*). Ask students to compare the guilds of medieval Europe with the labor unions of today.
2. **Understanding Ideas (Basic)** Have students write a paragraph describing a medieval city. They should include geographic location, sanitation, housing, and daily life. After students have completed the assignment, use their paragraphs as a basis for a class discussion. Ask students about geography's role in the development of medieval towns and in the development of their own city or a nearby city. Compare architecture, city planning, and sanitation in medieval towns with those in modern cities.
3. **Contrasting Past and Present (Average/Group)** A group of students might investigate the extent to which trade and cities are related today. Information for such a project may be obtained from the Chamber of Commerce or city hall. Some questions to be answered are: What means of transportation for goods (railroads, shipping, and so on) are available? What items produced in the city are consumed mostly outside the city? What goods made outside the city are consumed in the city? What products pass through the city destined for other places? Are there any commercial conventions or fairs in the city? Students should compare their findings with what they have learned about medieval trade.

ENRICHMENT ACTIVITY

Newspaper Reporting (Average/Group) Have interested students write newspaper stories on the Black Death. As background they can read Daniel Cohen's *The Black Death: 1347-1351* (Franklin Watts); Philip Ziegler's *The Black Death: A Study of the Plague in 14th-Century Europe* (Harper & Row); or Barbara Tuchman's *A Distant Mirror* (Knopf). Use the stories as the basis for a class discussion on public reaction to the current epidemic of AIDS. Ask students if they see similarities between the Black Death and AIDS. You might wish to point out that modern medicine has virtually eliminated many previously deadly diseases, such as smallpox, malaria, typhus, and polio.

DAILY QUIZ

To assess student understanding of Section 3, give the class the following quiz. (Each item is worth 10 points.)

1. List two reasons why towns survived or began to grow again in the 900s. *(As trade grew, towns became trade centers at harbors, mouths of rivers, or transfer points, all conditions for exchanging goods and services; also, a middle class emerged.)*
2. During the feudal period, who generally controlled the towns? *(nobles)*
3. (T or F) Serfs who escaped and lived in town for a year and a day became free. *(T)*
4. (T or F) Townspeople were not tried in town courts, but in king's and lord's courts specified by town charters. *(F)*
5. (T or F) Townspeople could not sell freely in the town market without paying tolls to the outside fair organizers. *(F)*
6. (T or F) Merchant guilds gained a monopoly in towns, fixed

prices and standards of quality, and also functioned as welfare organizations. *(T)*

7. The first step a man went through to become a guild member was serving as an ________ . *(apprentice)*
8. What is the second step called? *(journeyman)*
9. What were the middle class or merchants, masters, and skilled workers called? *(bourgeoisie, burghers, or burgesses)*
10. List two problems that existed in medieval cities. *(sewage, crowds, darkness, epidemics, no police)*

SUGGESTED ASSIGNMENTS

1. **Understanding Geography (Basic)** Have students complete "Geography Application Sheet: The Black Death Devastates Europe," in the TEACHER'S RESOURCEBANK™.
2. **Critical Thinking Worksheet (Average/Group)** Have students complete Critical Thinking Worksheet 25 in the TEACHER'S RESOURCEBANK™.

Section 4 (pages 259–264) The Culture of the Middle Ages Flourished in Towns and Cities

SECTION OVERVIEW

Medieval culture flourished with the revival of cities. Although Latin was still spoken by most educated people, writers began to use vernacular languages. At medieval universities scholastic philosophers, including Abelard and Aquinas, sought to reconcile faith and reason. Science made few significant advances during this period. The themes of painting and sculpture were generally religious.

SUGGESTED TEACHING STRATEGIES

1. **Preteaching Vocabulary (Basic)** You may wish to preteach the following important vocabulary terms: vernacular language, troubadours (*page* 259); miracle play (*page* 260); scholasticism (*page* 263). Ask students what kind of music today might compare to the songs of the troubadours.

*2. **Making Connections with History: Literature and History (Basic)** Have students reread "Building History Study Skills" on page 262. Then have them read a few passages from Chaucer's *Canterbury Tales* in class. Next have them make the connection between this literary work and history. One source is *Classics of Western Thought* (Harcourt Brace Jovanovich), edited by Karl F. Thompson. To reinforce the readings, you might show *From Every Shires Ende: The World of Chaucer's Pilgrims* (mp, 38 min., color, International).

ENRICHMENT ACTIVITY

Researching Ideas (Average/Group) Have students work together in small groups to prepare written or oral reports on the medieval university. Sources include: Marjorie Rowling's *Life in Medieval Times* (Putnam); Frederick Heer's *The Medieval World* (New American Library); and Anne Fremantle's *Age of Faith* (Time-Life).

DAILY QUIZ

To assess student understanding of Section 4, give the class the following quiz. (Each item is worth 10 points.)

1. Traveling singers called ________ helped popularize vernacular literature in the Middle Ages. *(troubadours)*
2. (T or F) The *fabliaux* were comic French short stories, usually told in verse, making fun of chivalry. *(T)*
3. The short dramas on religious or biblical subjects often performed at Easter and Christmas were called ________ ________ . *(miracle or mystery plays)*
4. Name the author of *The Divine Comedy* and the author of *Canterbury Tales. (Dante Alighieri, Geoffrey Chaucer)*
5. The attempt of medieval philosophers to reconcile faith and reason is called ________ . *(scholasticism)*
6. Name the authors of *Yes and No* and *Summa Theologica. (Peter Abelard, Thomas Aquinas)*
7. What did most large communities attempt to build and beautify during the late medieval period? *(church, cathedral)*
8. (T or F) Romanesque architecture had heavily domed roofs with very small windows, thick walls, and thick pillars. *(T)*
9. Gothic cathedrals utilized ________ ________ to support high walls. *(flying buttresses)*
10. (T or F) The new Gothic cathedral style got its name from artists who admired the buildings of the early Visigoths. *(F)*

SUGGESTED ASSIGNMENTS

1. **Critical Thinking Worksheet (Average/Group)** Have students complete Critical Thinking Worksheet 26 in the TEACHER'S RESOURCEBANK™.
2. **Art Projects (Average/Group)** Have students work together in groups to make diagrams, posters, collages, or dioramas illustrating some aspect of medieval art and architecture. Suggested topics include Romanesque and Gothic cathedrals, stained-glass windows, statuary, or illumination.
3. **Skill Worksheet (Basic)** Have students complete Skill Worksheet 11 in the TEACHER'S RESOURCEBANK™.

Section 5 (pages 265–269) Patriotic Feelings Spread Throughout Western Europe

SECTION OVERVIEW

Many of the nations of Western Europe developed out of the fiefs and states of feudal days. In England, after years of war and disorder,

Henry VII founded the Tudor dynasty and established a strong government. Louis XI unified France, ravaged by the Hundred Years' War, into a strong monarchy. Ferdinand and Isabella created an absolute monarchy in Spain. Only Germany and Italy remained disunited.

SUGGESTED TEACHING STRATEGIES

1. **Preteaching Vocabulary (Basic)** You may wish to preteach the following important vocabulary term: patriotism (page 265). Ask students how patriotism affects their lives today.
2. **Interpreting Ideas (Basic)** Have students reread the subsection "The Hundred Years' War" on pages 265-266. Empasize that in the late Middle Ages, the change in the nature of warfare greatly weakened feudalism. The use of the longbow and the cannon dealt it a mortal blow. Discuss with the class the use of these weapons and the advantages they provided over traditional combat.
3. **Writing an Essay (Challenging)** Have students write essays discussing which side of the Hundred Years' War had more justification for fighting. Call upon volunteers to read their papers to the class. Students should understand that it is difficult, if not impossible, to make such a judgment.

ENRICHMENT ACTIVITY

Biographical Sketches (Average/Group) Have interested students prepare biographical sketches of important people of this period: for example, Henry V, Henry VII, and Richard III of England; Joan of Arc, Charles VII, and Louis XI of France; or Ferdinand and Isabella of Spain. Students should share their reports with the rest of the class.

DAILY QUIZ

To assess student understanding of Section 5, give the class the following quiz. (Each item is worth 10 points.)

1. Name one cause of the Hundred Years' War. *(English claims to French provinces, English attempts to take the French throne, English-French rivalry over Flanders)*
2. (T or F) The use of the longbow and cannon strengthened the power of feudal lords in their conflicts with kings. *(F)*
3. Name one way Parliament gained control over the English king. *(Parliament had to approve any change in the law, only Parliament could impose taxes, the king could spend money only for the purpose for which Parliament had appropriated it.)*
4. The Wars of the Roses ended with King ________ ____ founding the ________ dynasty. *(Henry VII, Tudor)*
5. The French representative body resembling the English Parliament was called the ________ ________. *(Estates-General)*
6. This French king, nicknamed "The Spider," preferred diplomacy to war in making France strong. *(Louis XI)*
7. "The Spider's" most powerful adversary ruled the duchy of ________. *(Burgundy)*
8. Which two Spanish monarchs, whose marriage led to the unification of Spain, drove the Moors and Jews from their country? *(Ferdinand, Isabella)*
9. (T or F) The Holy Roman Emperor often sacrificed his power to the nobility and the electors to gain his title. *(T)*
10. After 1437 members of the ________ family almost always succeeded in being elected Holy Roman Emperor. *(Hapsburg)*

SUGGESTED ASSIGNMENTS

1. **Writing Reports (Average/Group)** Have interested students do research on the English Wars of the Roses. They should provide background material on the participants; show why the wars occurred and how they affected (1) the English monarchy, (2) the nobility, and (3) the rest of the population. Have them prepare oral reports to give to the class. Use their findings as the basis for a class discussion on the breakdown of feudalism in England and on the continent.
2. **Dramatiziation (Challenging)** Some students might wish to prepare a short dramatization of some event in the life of Joan of Arc, for example, her hearing of voices, her first meeting with the dauphin (Charles VII), or her trial. Numerous materials exist on the life of Joan of Arc, including the play by George Bernard Shaw, which will help students in this assignment.
3. **Profile Worksheet (Basic)** Have students complete Profile Worksheet 11 in the TEACHER'S RESOURCEBANK™.

Section (pages 269–271)

The Temporal Power of the Church Was Challenged

SECTION OVERVIEW

In the late Middle Ages, the church was plagued by a number of problems. People began to question the power and teachings of the church. This new attitude was reflected in the conflict between Pope Boniface VIII and King Philip IV of France, the Babylonian Captivity, the Great Schism, and the heretical teachings of John Wycliffe in England and John Huss in Bohemia.

SUGGESTED TEACHING STRATEGIES

1. **Understanding Ideas (Basic)** Ask students to reread the subsections "The Babylonian Captivity" and "The Great Schism" on pages 269 and 271. Then have them discuss how important the papal crisis must have been to the rest of Christian Europe. *(Answers will vary. Students might mention that political rivalries, such as those between England and France, would determine which pope the country would support. French kings would support the pope at Avignon and English kings the pope in Rome.)* Tell students that the confusion caused by the split in the church led to a *conciliar movement.* This movement means that church councils would settle the great theological questions and others arising in

the church. Ask students if they see any parallel movement with the nations of Europe. *(Answers will vary. Students might mention that parliaments developed in England and France which could offset the power of the monarchs. The church councils likewise would modify the powers of the pope.)* How did this conciliar movement work out? *(A church council at Constance did end the Great Schism, but it had difficulty reaching agreement on reforms. The result was that the popes remained powerful within the church.)*

2. **Performing a Drama (Challenging)** The conflict between Pope Boniface VIII and Philip IV of France can be used as the basis for a dramatic sketch to be acted out for the class. The reasons for the French king's taxation of the clergy, the calling of the Estates-General in 1302, the issuing of the papal bulls, and the capture and release of the pope might be included in this presentation. The following references may be used: Anne Fremantle's *Age of Faith* (Time-Life); Paul Johnson's *A History of Christianity* (Atheneum); and Geoffrey Barraclough's *The Medieval Papacy* (Harcourt Brace Jovanovich).

ENRICHMENT ACTIVITY

Understanding Art and Architecture (Average/Group) Have interested students research the city of Avignon in France, the seat of the popes during the Babylonian Captivity. Ask them to prepare a report to present to the class on (1) life in the city and papal court at the time and (2) the actual buildings used by the popes. Tell students that Avignon remained a papal possession long after the popes returned to Rome—until the French Revolution 200 years ago. The buildings are of interest architecturally and historically. Some students may be able to obtain slides or illustrations to show to the rest of the class.

DAILY QUIZ

To assess student understanding of Section 6, give the class the following quiz. (Each item is worth 10 points.)

1. (T or F) As kings developed control of their nation's territories, the church gained more temporal power. *(F)*
2. (T or F) When King Philip IV of France attempted to tax the church, Pope Boniface VIII's resistance resulted in the Babylonian Captivity. *(T)*
3. After the French gained control of the papacy, the religious headquarters for the Roman Catholic church moved to the city of ________. *(Avignon)*
4. (T or F) The French popes, according to some historians, were more interested in wealth and political power than the spiritual welfare of their people. *(T)*
5. (T or F) The Great Schism resulted in only one pope. *(F)*
6. (T or F) The Council of Constance fell apart during the Great Schism. *(F)*
7. (T or F) *The Defender of the Peace,* by Marsilius of Padua and John of Jandun, stated that the church had only spiritual authority. *(T)*
8. In England, ________ ________ attacked the wealth of the church, immorality among the clergy, and the pope's claim to absolute authority. *(John Wycliffe)*
9. In Bohemia, ________ ________ criticized the church's excesses and was burned at the stake. *(John Huss)*
10. (T or F) Many of the critics of the church were intellectuals and members of the clergy who had been educated by the church. *(T)*

SUGGESTED ASSIGNMENTS

1. **Review Worksheet (Basic)** Have students complete Review Worksheet 11 in the TEACHER'S RESOURCEBANK™.
2. **Outlining (Basic)** Have the students outline Section 6 for further understanding of the important points.

For suggested lesson plan, additional teaching strategies, enrichment activities, daily quizzes, and suggested assignments, see pages 247A–247G.

Introducing the Chapter
The Crusades, the growth of towns, a rising middle class, and the emergence of strong monarchies challenged the church's control of feudal society. The clash between traditional values and new or foreign influences is a recurring historical theme. Lead a class discussion on this theme, using the following questions as a guide: Can you recall other societies you have studied in which this process occurred? Can you think of any instances today in which modern, secular ideas are in conflict with traditional values? *(Answers will vary. Students may provide any number of reasonable examples of past societies in which this process occurred: for example, Egypt under Akhenaton; the Aryans and later the Muslims in India; Christianity in the Roman world. An example in today's world is the Muslim Middle East. The Muslim nations appear to want Western technology but not Western ways or values.)*

Chapter Objectives
After studying Chapter 11, students will be able to:

1. Outline the causes, events, and results of the Crusades and their impact on Europe, the Middle East, and the Byzantine Empire.
2. Summarize the reasons for the revival of European trade and list the major articles of trade.

CHAPTER 11

Trade Revived and Nations Developed in Europe

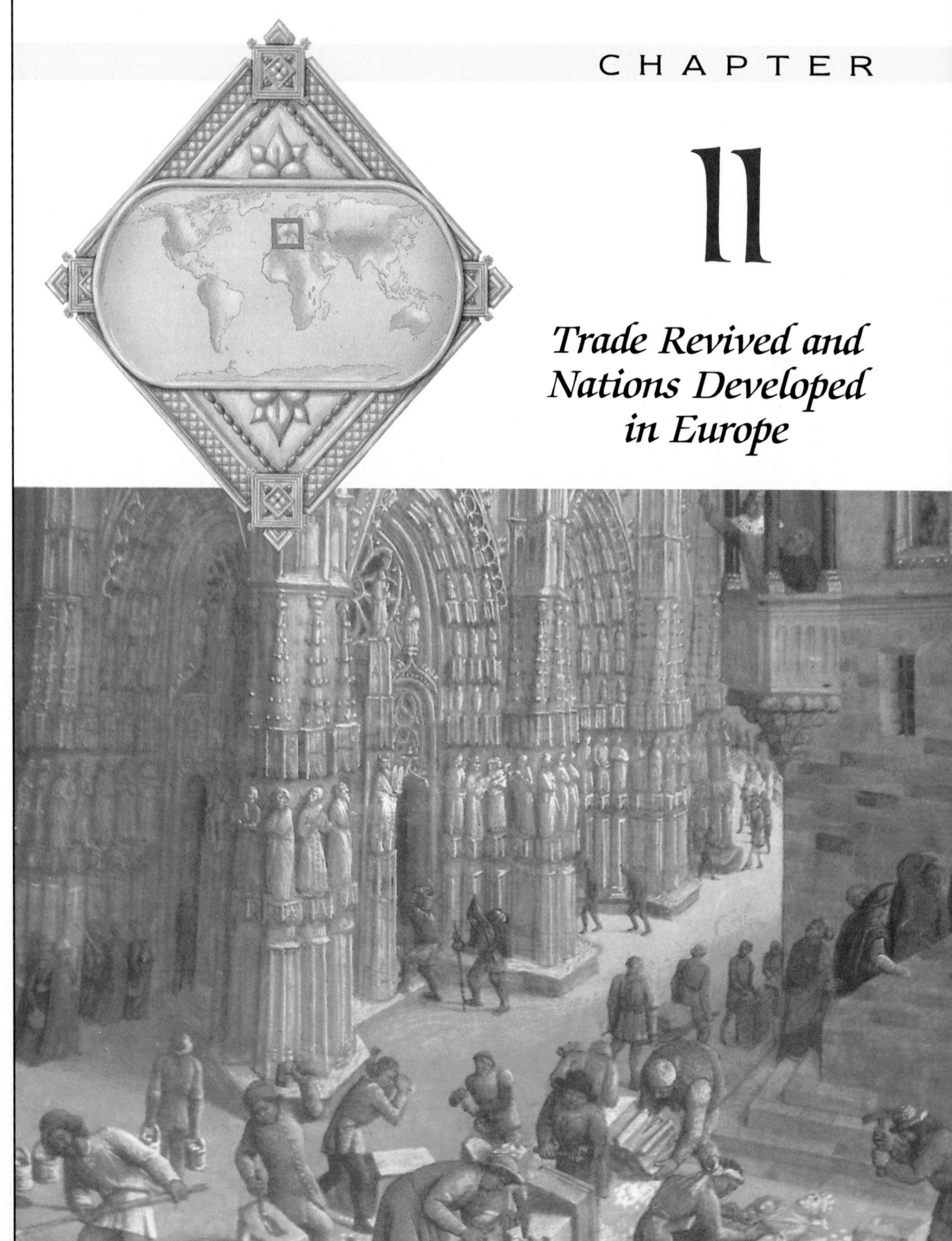

CHAPTER FOCUS

Place Western Europe

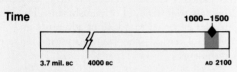

Time 1000–1500

3.7 mil. BC 4000 BC AD 2100

Significance

In a world where changes occur rapidly and mass media bombard us with a steady stream of information, it is difficult to imagine a time when change was slow and information scarce. During the Middle Ages, however, news traveled by word of mouth, few books existed, and most people could not read.

During the Middle Ages, Europe provided a world of striking contrasts. On the one hand were faith and chivalry; on the other hand, drudgery, violence, and ancient pagan and magical beliefs. Dark, filthy streets surrounded a majestic cathedral. Serfs lived in miserable huts below the noble's hilltop castle.

Great changes occurred during the Middle Ages, too. Cities became powerful centers of social and political change. Trade revived as people began to look outward, away from Europe.

Christians and Muslims came into conflict in the Middle East. Crusader armies fought the Muslims and returned to Europe, little realizing that they themselves had been conquered—by new and remarkable ideas that still influence the world today.

Terms to Define

capital	craft guild
market economy	apprentice

People to Identify

crusaders	Joan of Arc
Louis VII	Charles VII

Places to Locate

Venice	Avignon

Questions to Guide Your Reading

1 In what ways did the Crusades change the lives of the people of Europe?
2 What was the economic impact of the increase in trade in the late Middle Ages?
3 How did the growth of towns bring about great social and political change?
4 In what ways did the culture of the Middle Ages flourish in towns and cities?
5 What were the results of the spread of patriotism throughout western Europe?
6 How was the temporal power of the church challenged and weakened?

◀ *Building a medieval cathedral*

The Song of Roland is one of the earliest and best-known epic poems of medieval Europe. Written in the 1000s, the poem depicts the death of Roland, a courageous and loyal knight in Charlemagne's army. When the army fought the Moors in Spain, Roland was fatally wounded in an ambush of Charlemagne's rear guard. The following verse describes the last act of the dying hero:

> *"With deadly travail, in stress and pain,*
> *Count Roland sounded the mighty strain. Forth from his mouth the*
> *bright blood sprang,*
> *And his temples burst for the very pang.*
> *On and onward was borne the blast,*
> *Till Karl [Charlemagne] hath heard as*
> *the gorge he passed,*
> *And Naimes and all his men of war.*
> *'It is Roland's horn,' said the Emperor,*
> *'And, save in battle, he had not blown.'"*

By the later Middle Ages, knights from all over Europe, like Roland, were answering the call to battle in foreign lands.

1 The Crusades Changed the Lives of the People of Europe

During the Middle Ages, Christians regarded Palestine, where Jesus had lived and taught, as the Holy Land. The Arabs conquered Palestine in the 600s. Although most Arabs were Muslims, they usually tolerated other religions. If Christians or Jews paid their taxes and observed other regulations, they could live in Palestine and practice their religion openly. For centuries Christian pilgrims visiting Palestine met with little interference from the Arab rulers. European traders could generally do business there.

During the 1000s, however, the Seljuk Turks, a warlike people from central Asia who had adopted the Muslim faith, conquered Palestine and attacked Asia Minor, a part of the Byzantine Empire. When the Turks threatened the capital city of Constantinople, the Byzantine emperor appealed to the pope in Rome. Because Christian pilgrims to Palestine came home with reports of persecutions at the hands of the Turks, the Byzantine emperor's appeal for help found a warm reception in Europe.

3. Describe markets and fairs, the manufacturing system, and banking.
4. Explain why the rights of townspeople increased and serfdom declined during this era.
5. Describe the development and purpose of guilds, the rise in importance of the middle class, and life in medieval towns.
6. Discuss the culture that flourished in towns.
7. Analyze how the Hundred Years' War affected the establishment of strong central monarchies in France and England.
8. Discuss the steps leading toward the unification of Spain and how the Holy Roman Empire continued to be a loose union of states.
9. Describe the actions and events that eroded authority of the church.

SECTION 1

Focus/Motivation
Distribute copies of the following to the class.

"The Crusaders, less civilized in most respects than the peoples whose lands they were invading, had a more efficient military machine. When the heavy cavalry of the European knights first appeared in the East, they must have looked like creatures from another planet. It is hard today to see how they could have done what they did, marching and fighting under the blaze of the summer sun, broiling beneath the heavy metal

1A, 1B, 3B, 4B, a4B, a4C

● The Christian Church had split into two parts in 1054. One of Pope Urban II's goals was to reach an understanding with Byzantium and reunify the church.

armor that covered them, maddened by fleas and lice and mosquitoes they could not reach with their gauntleted hands. When they were well led by a commander like Richard (the Lion-Hearted), they were fairly impervious to attack from the lighter-armed foe.

With arrows sticking out of them all over, they looked like hedgehogs. Yet when on their huge armor-clad horses, they charged in a steady thundering line, nothing could resist them."

Lead a class discussion on motives that led people to go on the Crusades. *(Answers should include: The church forgave crusaders' sins, promised heaven for those who died fighting, and protected the crusader's property and family in his absence. Crusaders' debts were canceled and criminals were relieved of punishment. Love of adventure lured knights, who hoped to gain land or plunder; merchants saw new opportunities for trade.)*

Presentation
Classifying Ideas
(Average/Group)
Put the outline of a chart titled **THE CRUSADES** on the chalkboard or an overhead projector. Label two columns as follows: *Motives* and *Effects*. Subdivide the *Motives* column into *Religious* and *Worldly*. Have students complete

The Pope's Call for a Crusade

Pope Urban II was eager to regain the Holy Land ● from the Muslims. He called a great meeting of church leaders and French nobles at Clermont, France, in 1095. At the meeting he urged the powerful feudal nobles to stop fighting among themselves and to join in one great war against the "unbelievers."

Urban's plea fired his listeners with enthusiasm, and they joined in one mighty cry, "God wills it!" From Clermont people traveled throughout France preaching the cause. Those who joined the expeditions sewed a cross of cloth on their garments. They were called crusaders, from the Latin word *cruciata*, meaning "marked with a cross."

People joined the **Crusades,** the expeditions to regain the Holy Land, for many different reasons. The lure of lands and plunder in the rich Middle East dazzled the knights. Merchants saw a chance to make money. The pope promised both heavenly and earthly rewards. Those who died on a Crusade were said to go straight to heaven. The pope also guaranteed church protection of the crusader's property and family during his absence. Debtors who joined a Crusade had their debts canceled. Criminals were relieved of punishment. Thus the Crusades appealed to a love of adventure and the promise of reward—the desire to escape debts or punishment.

The First Crusade

French and Norman nobles led the First Crusade, which lasted from 1096 to 1099. In three organized armies, they marched across Europe to Constantinople (see map, this page).

Not surprisingly, the crusaders received a hostile reception in Constantinople. The Byzantine emperor had asked for some assistance, but now, seeing three armies approaching the city, he feared they might capture and plunder the capital. After

Learning from Maps *Most of the Crusades were launched from France. Which Crusade took the longest route to the Holy Land?* **Third Crusade**

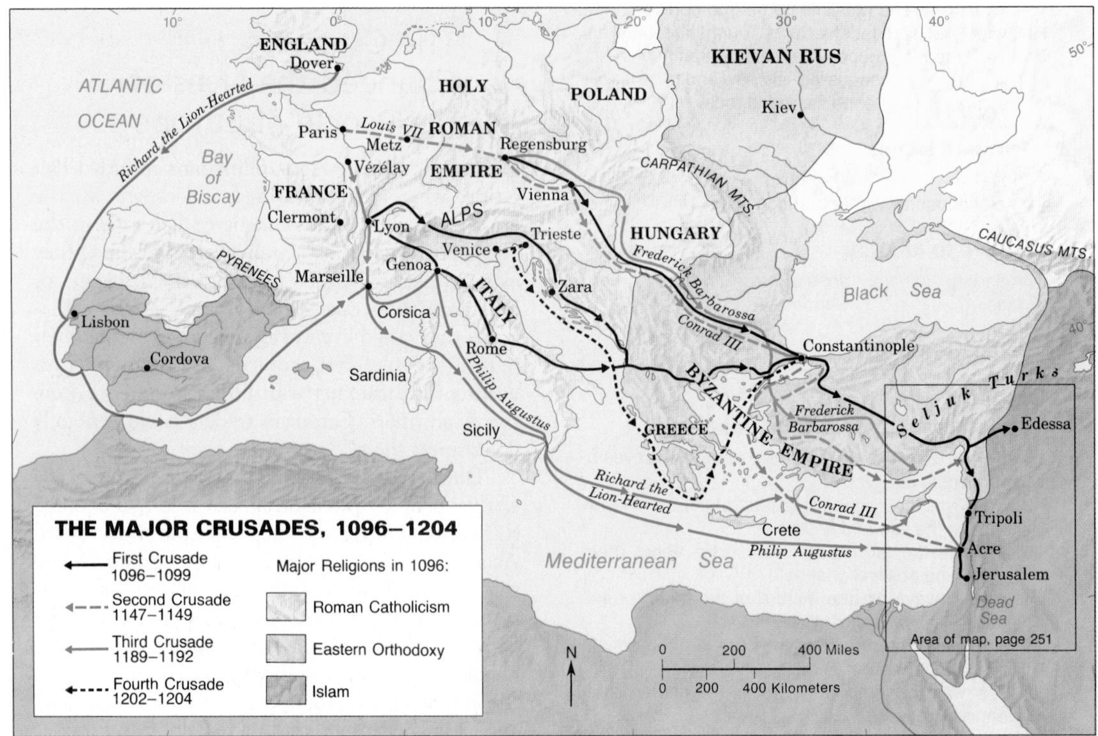

1A, 1B, 1C, 3B, 4B, a1C, a4B, a4C

● Pope Urban II died two weeks after the crusaders captured Jerusalem on July 15, 1099.

■ Kingdom of Jerusalem

much discussion the Byzantines allowed the crusaders to pass through Constantinople to begin their long, hot march across Asia Minor toward Palestine.

In their wool and leather garments and their heavy armor, the crusaders suffered severely from the heat. Because they had few pack animals, a shortage of food and water plagued them. Additional problems erupted when the leaders quarreled over fiefs in the lands they captured. Despite these difficulties, however, the crusaders forged on to capture the city of Antioch. Then they marched toward Jerusalem. If the Turks had not also been quarreling and disunited, the expedition would have failed.

Conditions improved as the crusaders marched down the seacoast toward Palestine. Fleets of ships from the Italian cities of Genoa and Pisa brought reinforcements and supplies. The crusaders captured Jerusalem after a short battle and slaughtered ● the Muslim inhabitants. One leader wrote to the pope that his horse's legs had been bloodstained to the knees from riding among the bodies of the dead Muslims.

In the Middle East the crusaders set up four small states: the County of Edessa, the Principality of Antioch, the County of Tripoli, and the Kingdom of Jerusalem (see map, this page). They introduced European feudalism and subdivided the land into fiefs controlled by vassals and lords. For almost a century, the Europeans occupied these lands. Brisk European trade, with goods carried mostly in Italian ships, sprang up. Christians and Muslims lived in close proximity and grew to respect each other. Many Christians adopted Eastern customs and came to prefer Eastern food and clothing.

The Second Crusade

The Second Crusade began in 1147, after the Turks had recaptured the important city of Edessa and threatened the Kingdom of Jerusalem. In this Crusade King Louis VII of France and the Holy Roman Emperor Conrad III led their armies across Europe to the Holy Land.

The armies of the two monarchs met many misfortunes on the march to the Holy Land. They fought separately and did not join forces until they reached Damascus, which the Turks held. Even then the large combined forces of Louis and Conrad failed to capture the city. After only two years, their armies returned to Europe in disgrace.

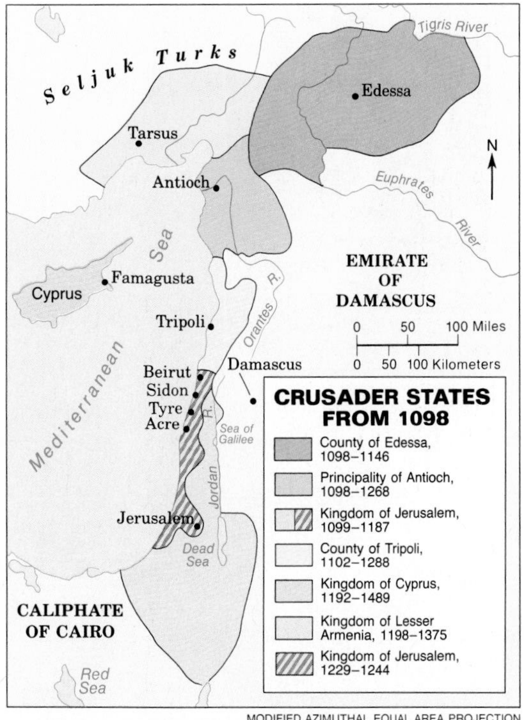

Learning from Maps *The Turks eventually conquered the crusader states. What crusader state did the Third Crusade attempt to reconquer?* ■

The Third Crusade

In 1187 the news reached Europe that the Muslim leader Saladin (SAL • uh • din) had recaptured Jerusalem. Europe responded with the Third Crusade, the "Crusade of the Three Kings," from 1189 to 1192. King Richard the Lion-Hearted of England, King Philip Augustus of France, and Emperor Frederick Barbarossa of the Holy Roman Empire each started out at the head of a great army to regain the Holy Land.

Once again the Europeans failed. Barbarossa drowned on the way to the Holy Land, and most of his army turned back. Philip and Richard quarreled, and Philip took his army home to seize English lands in France. Several times Richard might have gained the whole Kingdom of Jerusalem by diplomacy, but he preferred military attempts. In the end he made no significant gains. As a result of this Crusade, an estimated 300,000 Christians and Muslims lost their lives.

the chart in their notebooks. After students have completed the assignment, have them compare their charts. *(Charts should include the following information.* Motives: Religious—*Church forgave crusaders' sins, promised heaven for those who died fighting, and protected the crusader's property and family in his absence.* Worldly—*Debts were canceled and criminals were relieved of punishment; love of adventure lured knights, who hoped to gain land or plunder; merchants foresaw new opportunities for trade.* Effects: *The Crusades have been called successful failures because although they failed to regain the Holy Land, they succeeded in enriching and changing European life. Europeans learned new military technology such as the crossbow and gunpowder; political changes included the growth of royal and church power and the weakening of the power of feudal lords; women's status improved; exchange of ideas occurred; Italian cities benefited commercially; and new products were introduced into Europe.)*

1B, 3B, 4B

SECTION 1

Closure

Ask students why the popes called for Crusades. *(To regain the Holy Land for Christianity after pilgrims reported persecutions and the Byzantine emperors appealed for help against the Seljuk Turks.)* Then ask students if they believe any current animosities between the West and the Muslim Middle East have their roots in the Crusades. *(Answers will vary.)*

Review Answers

1. ***Crusade:*** expedition to regain the Holy Land for Christianity
2. ***Urban II:*** pope who called for the First Crusade; ***Louis VII:*** king of France who led an army in the Second Crusade; ***Conrad III:*** Holy Roman Emperor who led an army in the Second Crusade; ***Saladin:*** Muslim leader whose recapture of Jerusalem led to the Third Crusade
3. ***County of Edessa:*** Crusader state in southeastern Asia Minor; ***Principality of Antioch:*** Crusader state north of Palestine and west of Syria; ***County of Tripoli:*** Crusader state south of Antioch; ***Kingdom of Jerusalem:*** Crusader state in southern Palestine
4. People went on the Crusades for religious and worldly reasons. The church forgave crusaders' sins, promised heaven for those who died fighting, and protected the

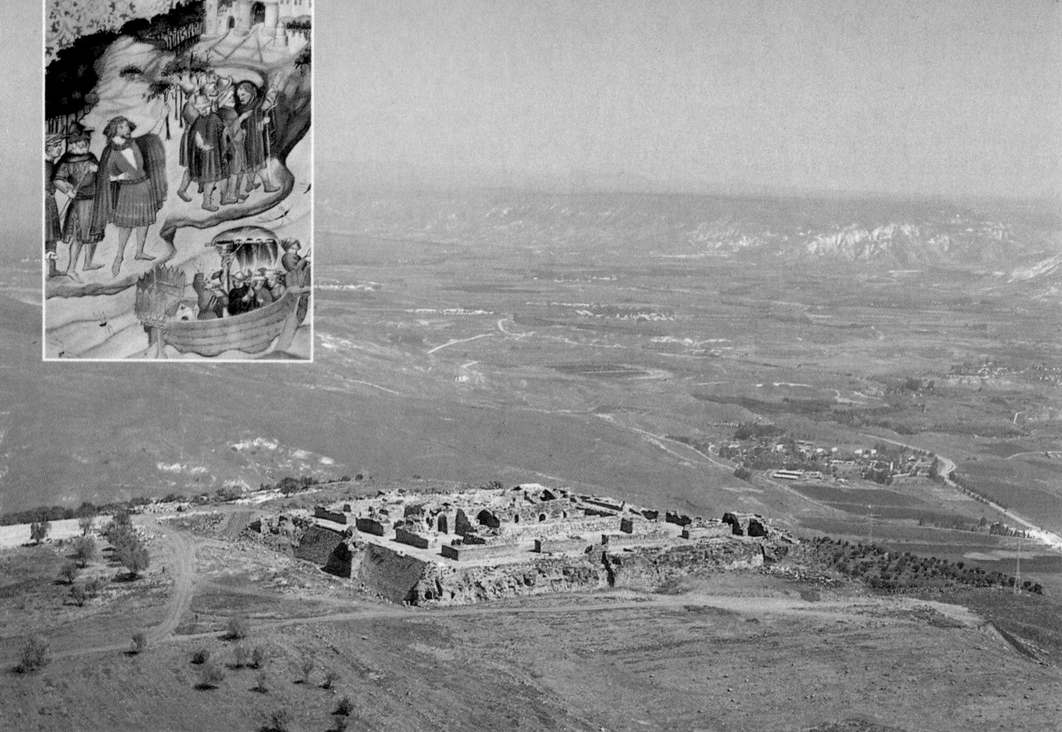

Learning from Pictures *Pilgrims arriving in the Holy Land (inset) built castles to protect themselves and to keep control of the land. Belvoir was built overlooking the Sea of Galilee.*

Later Crusades

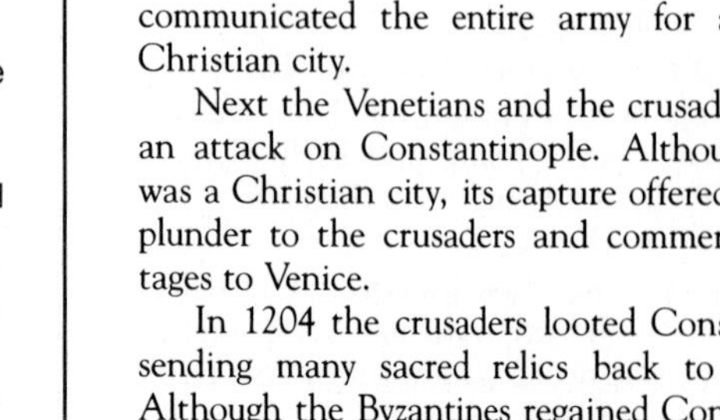

Pope Innocent III persuaded a group of French knights to embark on the Fourth Crusade in 1202. The city-state of Venice provided transportation, at the same time persuading the crusaders to attack Zara, a city on the Adriatic coast. Zara, a Christian city, was also a commercial rival of Venice. After the crusaders captured Zara, Pope Innocent excommunicated the entire army for attacking a Christian city.

Next the Venetians and the crusaders planned an attack on Constantinople. Although it, too, was a Christian city, its capture offered irresistible plunder to the crusaders and commercial advantages to Venice.

In 1204 the crusaders looted Constantinople, sending many sacred relics back to the West. Although the Byzantines regained Constantinople and a part of their lands after 50 years, they never regained their strength. The once-mighty empire finally collapsed when the Turks seized Constantinople in 1453.

A tragic episode in the story of the Crusades occurred in 1212, when a group of young children, believing they could triumph where their elders had failed, undertook their own march to the Holy Land. This Children's Crusade had untrained leaders and no equipment. The pope turned back some of the children. Others reached Marseilles in France, only to be tricked into boarding ships that carried them off to be sold to Muslim slave traders.

Additional Crusades were undertaken after 1204, although historians differ on how many took place. The Crusades continued until 1291, when the Muslims captured the last Christian stronghold, in Acre (AHK • ruh). For 200 years a constant flow of Europeans streamed into the Holy Land. Over that period, however, the religious zeal of the crusaders had steadily dwindled.

252

Results of the Crusades

From a military standpoint, all the Crusades except the first failed. The Muslims eventually recaptured Jerusalem and the rest of Palestine.

However, Europeans learned about many things of military importance, including the crossbow, a sophisticated bow and arrow held horizontally and fired by pulling a trigger. The crusaders also learned to use carrier pigeons as messengers. From the Byzantines the Europeans learned new siege tactics such as undermining walls and using catapults to hurl stones. In addition, they may have learned about gunpowder from the Muslims, who probably acquired their knowledge of this explosive from the Chinese.

In Europe the Crusades increased the power of kings and decreased the power of feudal lords. Kings imposed new taxes and led armies drawn from their entire countries. Many nobles died fighting, while others sold political liberties to towns in order to raise money to go on a Crusade. The church also assumed more political power because of its leadership role in initiating the Crusades.

The Crusades had other important results. For example, the status of women changed. With their husbands absent, many wives managed feudal estates. Europeans were influenced, too, by the ideas exchanged among the crusaders from different countries and between the crusaders and the other peoples they met.

Commercial changes also occurred. Italian cities benefited from their role in transporting crusading armies. Europeans discovered products from the Middle East—rice, sugar, lemons, apricots, and melons, among other things—which stimulated trade in such goods. Cotton cloth was also introduced into Europe in the form of muslin (cloth of Mosul, a city in Persia) and damask (cloth of Damascus).

SECTION 1 REVIEW

1. **Define** Crusade
2. **Identify** Urban II, Louis VII, Conrad III, Saladin
3. **Locate** County of Edessa, Principality of Antioch, County of Tripoli, Kingdom of Jerusalem
4. **Analyzing Ideas** Why did people join the Crusades?
5. **Interpreting Ideas** The Crusades are sometimes called "successful failures." **(a)** What is meant by this description? **(b)** Do you agree or disagree? Why?

2 Trade Increased in Europe

Trade nearly died out in western Europe after the 400s. Manors became increasingly self-sufficient, growing or making nearly everything they used. Towns and cities, which depended on trade and manufacturing, decreased in both population and size. Some towns disappeared completely.

Those who wanted to trade faced many obstacles—little money, poor roads, and few bridges. Each feudal lord charged tolls for the use of roads and bridges in his territory. Thieves on land and pirates at sea made travel dangerous.

Church laws also made trade difficult. The church insisted on a "just price" that did not permit the seller to make a large profit. The church prohibited the purchase of articles for resale at higher prices—in other words, retail selling. It also prohibited **usury** (YOOZH • uh • ree), which at that time meant the charging of interest on loans. Although people discovered various ways to overcome these prohibitions, restrictions still hampered the growth of trade.

Trade Routes

Trade first began to revive in Italy, largely because neither trade nor towns had declined as much there as elsewhere. Also, the geographic location of the Italian Peninsula favored trade. Italy lay between northern Europe, where people were becoming interested in goods from Asia, and the Middle East, where such goods could be bought. The Italians became the great European distributors, acting as go-betweens for traders from Asia, on the one hand, and traders from central and northern Europe, on the other.

During the late 900s and early 1000s, Italian traders began to make contacts with the Middle East. By a combination of force and negotiation, the Italian city-states of Venice, Genoa, and Pisa won trading rights in Constantinople, Syria, Palestine, and North Africa.

At the time of the Crusades, ships from Italian city-states carried crusaders to the Holy Land and brought back rich cargoes from the East. From Italian seaports these goods traveled by pack train through northern Italy and across the Alps into

crusaders' property and families in their absence. Debts were canceled and criminals were relieved of punishment. Love of adventure lured knights, and merchants saw new trade opportunities.

5. (a) The Crusades have been called successful failures because although they failed to regain the Holy Land from the Muslims, they succeeded in enriching and changing European life. Europeans learned new military technology, monarchs gained power over feudal lords, and the status of women improved. Europe was stimulated intellectually. Italian cities benefited commercially. Europeans discovered new foods and fabrics.

(b) Answers will vary. Students will probably agree because of the enrichment of Europe commercially and intellectually, and the stabilizing of Europe through weakening of the power of feudal lords.

SECTION 2

Focus/Motivation

The rise of towns and cities went hand in hand with the revival of trade. The Italian cities first benefited. Then as trade spread northward, new routes opened. In the far north a number of cities located on or near the Baltic and North seas formed a union of merchant guilds. This union was called the Hanseatic League (from

1B, 1D, 4B

● The cities of the Hanseatic League also fought among themselves. The league's power declined with the rise of Denmark, England, the Netherlands, Russia, and Poland.

Hansa, or "merchant guild" in German). The chief city of the league was Lübeck, followed by Cologne. The league began as an organization to protect merchants, and it soon turned into a profit-making organization with the goal of monopolizing trade. On a wall map, point out the leading cities of the Hanseatic League *(Lübeck, Cologne, Danzig, Bremen, Hamburg, Breslau, Kracow, Brunswick, Lüneberg, Rostock)* Ask students what products were traded in the cities of the league. *(fur, timber, fish, and grain)* Tell students that the Hanseatic League's monopoly of trade led many kings and merchants to seek alternate trade routes. The Hanseatic cities never gave any reciprocal privileges. The league began to decline even before the discovery of the New World and the establishment of newer trade routes. Ask students if any such trading leagues exist today. *(Answers will vary. Students might point out that the European Communities, OPEC, and the British Commonwealth are groups that extend trading privileges among members and set prices. The United States often grants "most-favored nation" status to trading partners in return for reciprocity on tariffs, etc. from that nation.)* Tell students that uneven trading arrangements such as those the Hanseatic League held with the areas with which it

CONNECTIONS: THEN AND NOW

Tolls

Toll roads are not modern inventions. If you had been part of a camel caravan in the Middle Eastern city of Petra more than 2,000 years ago, you would have paid a stiff toll before leaving the city.

About this time the Romans built a network of highways extending from the Wall of Hadrian in northern England to the Persian Gulf. Repairs were financed by the collection of tolls at the city gates. Many of the roads were still in use in the Middle Ages (right).

In medieval times some tolls were collected by barring the road with a pike, or pole, and then turning the pike to allow the traveler to pass. Early in the development of the North American colonies, private companies built "turnpikes" and charged travelers tolls to use them. Now the states build roads, either with money from the federal government or with tolls collected from users of those roads. And some states, such as Florida, charge tolls for driving on the beach (far right).

Rivers and canals have also provided natural opportunities for toll stations. By the year 1300, there were more than 35 places along the Rhine River, in Germany, where fees were collected. In England travelers were charged for passage both over and under London Bridge. Today ships pay tolls to go through Canada's Welland Canal and through the Suez and Panama canals.

central and northern Europe. This overland trade route led to the growth and increasing wealth of cities in Germany, Lombardy, and southern France.

Trade also revived in northern Europe. Before the year 1000, Viking traders from Kiev, in what is now the Soviet Union, traveled regularly to the Black Sea and on to Constantinople to collect goods from the East. They transported these items to the cities of northern Europe.

The region of Flanders, today part of Belgium and northern France, gained importance. It was the meeting point of trade routes that led across France, down the Rhine River from Germany, across the English Channel from England, and south from the coasts of the Baltic Sea. Moreover, people throughout Europe eagerly sought the fine woolen cloth that was the chief product of Flanders. During the 1200s Flanders became the textile headquarters of Europe. Cities such as Ghent and Bruges became thriving centers of population and wealth.

Hamburg, Lübeck, and Bremen became the most important commercial cities on the North and Baltic seas. Because Germany lacked a strong central government, these trading cities formed an alliance called the Hanseatic League. Eventually the league had more than 70 member cities. It became a powerful influence on the commerce of northwestern Europe during the 1300s and 1400s.

The Hanseatic cities set up permanent trading posts in Flanders, Scandinavia, England, and Russia. Any member that failed to abide by league agreements lost its trading privileges. If a ruler revoked the privileges of any Hanseatic traders, the league stopped all shipments of goods to that country. Sometimes league members waged small-scale wars in order to regain trading rights. ●

Learning from Pictures *Bruges, known as the "City of Bridges," was one of the chief Hanseatic cities and became the financial hub of northern Europe. Other cities in northern Europe also became trading centers.*

Articles of Trade

By far the most profitable trade for medieval merchants was in luxury goods from Asia and the Middle East. Because these highly valued articles were in short supply, merchants could charge exorbitant prices and make enormous profits. The Crusades caused a great increase in demand for spices, medicines, perfumes, dyes, and precious gems from Asia. Manufactured goods included silk, cotton, and linen fabrics, as well as gold, silver, and ivory art objects. The Middle East also supplied textiles, rugs, grain, and fruit.

Europe offered various products in exchange for Asian goods. The Baltic region supplied fur, timber, fish, and grain. From Spain came wine, oil, leather, and weapons and armor. Other European products included metal goods and glassware from Venice, fine woolen cloth from England and Flanders, and wine from France.

Markets and Fairs

As trade grew, merchants needed places where they could exchange goods. Many villages had weekly market days, but these local markets did not attract large crowds. Some merchants began to sell goods during religious festivals. Then some feudal lords established fairs for the sale of imported goods. They realized that they could become wealthy by charging fees, or taxes, on the merchandise sold. The feudal lords guaranteed special protection to merchants who held a fair.

Champagne, a region in northeastern France that lay directly along the trade route between Italy and northern Europe, held the most important and best-known fairs. In Champagne traders exchanged the textiles, wool, and wines of Europe for Asian luxury goods. Six fairs, each lasting four to seven weeks, were held annually at four towns in the region. Held at different times, the fairs provided a central marketplace for all of Europe.

A simple **barter economy**—that is, one in which goods and services are exchanged for other goods and services without the use of money—could not meet the needs of fairs as large and elaborate as those of Champagne. Even though little money might actually change hands at a fair, the value of goods had to be fixed in terms of a common medium of exchange. Since many different kinds of coins existed, a special class of money changers became important at the fairs. They estimated the value of the currency of one region in relation to the currency of another. In this way the money changers helped in the exchange of goods.

Fairs helped to create ties between regions and to broaden the narrow outlook of the people. Travelers came from great distances to attend large fairs, which offered entertainment in addition to the opportunity to buy and sell. Jugglers, clowns, and musicians entertained the crowds just as they do at county and state fairs today.

Manufacturing, Banking, and Investment

Three important developments resulted from the revival of European trade—a manufacturing system, a banking system, and the practice of investing capital.

Manufacturing grew out of trade. In a new method of production called the **domestic system,** manufacturing took place in workers' homes rather

traded provoke ill will and can encourage harsh treatment in return. Japan's superiority in exports to the United States at the same time it is reluctant to allow United States imports into Japan is an example.

Presentation
Analyzing Information (Average/Group)
On the chalkboard or an overhead projector, draw a chart with the headings *factors discouraging trade/ early middle ages* and *factors encouraging trade/ later middle ages.* Have students copy the headings into their notebooks and fill in the chart. *(Completed charts should contain the following information: (Discouraging: shortage of money, roads poor, few bridges, robbers and pirates, tolls, and church laws; Encouraging: interest in goods from Asia and the Middle East, Hanseatic League, formation of shipping companies, domestic system, and banking)*

1B, 1D, 4B, 4I, a1C, a3B, a3C, a3D, a3G, a3H, a3I

- ● Lombard Street in London, long the financial center of Europe, got its name from the Lombards (Italians) who operated banking branches there.
- ■ As first used in the 1100s and 1200s, the word *capital* did not apply exclusively to money; it could mean funds, a quantity of merchandise, or a sum of money. It did not take on its modern meaning until the 1770s.

SECTION 2

Closure

Tell students that the developments resulting from the revival of trade—manufacturing based on the domestic system, banking, and investing of capital—were extremely important to the economic dominance of European countries up to the present century (at least to the end of World War I).

Have students explain how each development contributed to the growth of capitalist economies.

Review Answers

1. ***usury:*** the charging of interest on loans of money in medieval times; ***barter economy:*** one in which goods or services are exchanged for other goods or services without the use of money; ***domestic system:*** method of production in which work was done in workers' homes rather than in a shop or factory; ***capital:*** wealth earned, saved, and invested to make profits; ***market economy:*** an economy in which land, labor, and capital are controlled by individuals; formed the basis of the modern capitalist system **2.** ***English Channel:*** important trade route between Normandy and England; ***Flanders:*** area of northern France and southern Belgium that produced woolen cloth; ***Ghent:*** city in Flanders; ***Bruges:*** city in Flanders north of Ghent; ***Hamburg:***

History Through the Arts

WEAVING

Medieval Tapestry

The large stone castles of the Middle Ages were cold, dark, and damp. To make their homes warmer and more cheerful, nobles often hung tapestries on the walls. These skillfully woven fabrics were both decorative and practical. They not only gave protection against the cold but also could easily be packed up and moved. The hangings were woven so that they could be cut into smaller pieces and resewn to fit rooms of various sizes.

The weavers of France and Flanders were especially skilled. They made tapestries with complicated pictures—usually with religious, historical, or mythological themes. The tapestry shown here, "A Walk on the Bank of the Loire," was woven in France around 1500. Flowers form the background for scenes illustrating the daily life of the nobles. Tapestries such as this one are highly valued for the skill with which even the smallest details are woven.

than in a shop or factory. A good example of the domestic system was the woolen industry. In this system an individual would buy wool and then distribute it to several workers. For an agreed price, each worker performed a particular job, such as spinning, weaving, or dyeing. The individual who owned the wool then collected the finished cloth and sold it for the highest price possible. The domestic system began in towns, but by the end of the Middle Ages, it had spread to the countryside.

Banking also developed in the later Middle Ages. In addition to evaluating and exchanging various currencies, money changers now began to provide other services. The word *bank* comes from ● the Italian word *banca,* meaning the "money changer's table."

Lending money was the most important service early bankers performed. Rulers, nobles, and merchants often needed to borrow funds to finance their activities. During the early Middle Ages, Jews had done much of the moneylending because the Christian Church forbade usury. By the mid-1200s, however, many Christians became involved in moneylending.

Officially these Christian moneylenders did not charge interest. Instead they paid themselves by collecting rents and fees for services and damages. They also eased the transfer of funds from one place to another by developing special notes, called letters of credit, to be used instead of money. A person could take a letter of credit issued by a banker in Ghent and cash it with another banker in Venice. This somewhat resembled our modern-day checking accounts.

With the growth of trade also came **capital,** ■ which is wealth earned, saved, and invested in order to produce profits. People with capital began investing it in businesses such as shipping companies. With the increase in trade, shipbuilding and the financing of voyages became good investments. Each investor contributed part of the cost and received a share of the profits.

These three factors laid the foundation for the emergence of a **market economy,** an economy in which land, labor, and capital are controlled by individuals. It was the market economy that formed the basis of the modern capitalist system (see Chapter 19).

1D, 4A, 4B, a1B, a4A, a4F, a4M

SECTION 2 REVIEW

1. **Define** usury, barter economy, domestic system, capital, market economy
2. **Locate** English Channel, Flanders, Ghent, Bruges, Hamburg, Lübeck, Bremen
3. **Determining Cause and Effect** **(a)** What caused trade to decline during the early Middle Ages? **(b)** What effect did this have on western Europe?
4. **Summarizing Ideas** Why were fairs important in medieval society?
5. **Understanding Ideas** **(a)** What is capital? **(b)** How was capital invested in medieval Europe?

3 The Growth of Towns Brought Great Social and Political Change

The growth of towns and cities accompanied the revival of trade in the Middle Ages. In fact, trade and cities always grow together. In a town or city, we find all the conditions needed for exchanging goods and services.

Beginning in the late 900s, existing towns began to grow larger. New towns grew at locations important for trade—natural harbors, the mouths of rivers, and transfer points, where cargo was shifted from oceangoing ships to river barges.

The Rights of Townspeople

As towns grew, it became clear that the town dweller did not fit into the manorial system. Townspeople made their living by manufacturing and trade. They played little part in the villages' agricultural economy.

Townspeople wanted to control their own governments. Under feudalism, however, lords controlled the town and would give up control only in exchange for something. Sometimes townspeople won rights of self-government by peaceful means. In some cases, however, they resorted to violence and even war.

Some lords granted political liberties to towns in order to encourage their development. Sometimes towns bought charters of liberties—written statements of their rights—from their lords.

Town and city charters differed widely from place to place. In time, though, everyone who lived in a town in Europe was assured of at least four basic rights:

(1) *Freedom.* No matter what their birth or origin, people who lived in a town had a chance to become free. If officials did not challenge them for a year and a day, they became free. This broke all ties to a manor or manor lord. A serf who escaped to a town could thus become free.

(2) *Exempt status.* Inhabitants of towns were exempt, or free, from having to perform any services on the manor.

(3) *Town justice.* Towns had their own courts, made up of prominent citizens familiar with local customs, which tried cases involving townspeople.

(4) *Commercial privileges.* Townspeople had the right to sell goods freely in the town market and to charge tolls to all outsiders trading there.

Guilds

As trade increased and towns grew larger and wealthier, medieval merchants began to unite in associations. Because of the dangers of travel, traders often assembled convoys—groups that travel together for safety. Arranging such convoys, however, took much planning and money. Gradually merchants founded associations called guilds.

In each town a **merchant guild** gained a monopoly—the sole right to trade there. Merchants from other towns or foreign nations could not trade in that town unless they paid a fee. The guilds also set standards of quality for manufactured goods. In addition, guilds acted as charitable organizations. They made loans to members and looked after those who were in any kind of trouble. For example, they supported the widows and children of deceased members.

In time the skilled workers who were engaged in manufacturing formed **craft guilds.** Each of these guilds included all of the people engaged in one particular craft, such as shoemaking or weaving. These guilds regulated wages and set hours and conditions of labor. They also set prices and conditions for selling the goods, disciplined workers, looked after ill or disabled members, and supervised the training of skilled workers. A master worker, or fully accepted member of the guild, had to be a male.

A candidate for membership in a craft guild went through two preliminary stages of training which took years to complete. In the first stage, he served as an **apprentice.** When he was still a boy,

Hanseatic river port in northern Germany; ***Lübeck:*** Hanseatic port on Baltic; ***Bremen:*** Western European Hanseatic port near North Sea
3. (a) Western European trade declined during the early Middle Ages because manors were self-sufficient; there were obstacles to trade such as a shortage of money, poor roads, few bridges, thieves, pirates, and numerous tolls; and church laws prohibited profit and usury. **(b)** These restrictions hampered trade; towns and cities decreased in population and size.
4. Fairs provided a central marketplace where merchants could exchange goods. Fairs were also festive occasions that helped break down the isolation of each region and the narrow perspective of the people.
5. (a) Capital is wealth earned or saved to be invested in a business opportunity to produce profits. **(b)** Medieval capitalists invested in shipbuilding and financing voyages, the domestic system, and banking, particularly money lending.

SECTION 3

Focus/Motivation
Explain to the class how new towns originated in the Middle Ages. Merchants on their routes would stop at castles or at a bishop's residence for lodging and protection. When space was no longer

1B, 1C, 1D, 4B, a1C

- Many wives of master craftsmen—particularly in weaving—worked with their husbands, and often took over the business when their husbands died.
- During the 1100s, for example, most English towns held from 1,000 to 6,000 people.

available, merchants settled outside the castle walls and built new walls to protect settlements. Gradually, this new section became more important than the old castle. The word for castle is *burg* in German and *bourg* in French. In English the terms *burg* and *borough* came to mean "town" or "city." Ask students to name cities in the United States that have *burg* or *borough* in their names. Examples are Pittsburgh, Harrisburg, Greensboro, Lynchburg, or St. Petersburg.

Presentation
Comparing Ideas (Average/Group)
Hold a class discussion on the advantages and disadvantages of urban living. Ask students whether they would prefer to live in the city or the country. If a great majority prefer one type of environment, you might supply arguments for living in the other. The discussion should be followed by a comparison of life in medieval towns with life in cities today.

SECTION 3

Closure
Ask students to explain the differences among an apprentice, a journeyman, and a master worker. *(An apprentice is a boy legally bound to a master worker in order to learn a trade. A journeyman is a skilled worker still employed by a*

Learning from Pictures *Guilds monitored the quality of products, such as cabinets. Guilds also decided whether a journeyman could become a master.*

his parents apprenticed him—bound him by legal agreement and often after paying a hefty fee—to a master worker to learn a trade. He lived at the home of the master. The master gave the apprentice food, clothing, training, and moral guidance. The apprentice promised to obey his master, to keep the secrets of his craft, and to behave properly. The period of apprenticeship varied from 3 to 12 years.

After completing his apprenticeship, a young man became a journeyman. A **journeyman** was a skilled artisan who worked for a master for daily wages. After working for wages for some time, he could become a master by submitting proof of his skill—a "masterpiece," or piece of work judged worthy of a master. If the guild masters approved his work, the journeyman could open a shop of his own.

Toward the end of the Middle Ages, the line between masters and journeymen became much more distinct and much harder to cross. The journeyman usually remained a wage earner all his life. Increased prosperity turned masters into an industrial aristocracy. Often the master's son inherited the business and position without performing the required apprenticeship.

The Rise of the Middle Class

A new class of merchants, master workers, and skilled workers emerged in medieval society. The members of this class were called *burgesses* in England, *bourgeoisie* (boorzh • wah • ZEE) in France, and *burgers* in Germany—all from the word *burg,* or *borough,* meaning "town."

The rise to prominence of this class during the later Middle Ages transformed European society. Townspeople tended to want stable and uniform governments that would protect trade and property, so they usually favored kings over nobles. To gain their support, kings began to consult them and to employ them in government positions.

Life in Medieval Towns

Medieval towns and cities, small by modern standards, had from 5,000 to 10,000 people. According to some estimates, in the 1300s Paris had a population of about 80,000. Ghent and Bruges, with about 50,000 inhabitants each, were considered huge. London, with about 35,000, was far above average size.

Physically compact, the medieval city often stood on top of a hill or at the bend of a river so that it could be defended easily. Because city land was scarce and valuable, houses were built five or six stories high. To increase the space inside a building, each story projected out a little farther than the one below. Thus at the top the houses almost met in the middle of the street. Each city had some particularly fine buildings such as a cathedral, a town hall, and the guild halls.

A medieval city would have offended the eyes and noses of people today. Sewage littered dark, filthy streets and was dumped into open gutters that were cleared only when it rained. Epidemics ran rampant. There was no street lighting. Servants accompanied law-abiding people who ventured out at night to protect them from robbers, for there were no police. Despite the uncomfortable conditions, however, life in a medieval city was not completely unpleasant. The medieval city was a busy and interesting place, alive with activity and an array of people—peddlers, lawyers, merchants, strolling actors, musicians, and jugglers.

● This *enclosure* took place from the 1500s to the 1700s.
■ The last major occurrences of the bubonic plague in Europe were in Marseilles in 1720, Moscow in 1770, Odessa in 1814, and the Balkans in 1841.

1B, 1C, 4B, a1B, a1C, a4A, a4F, a4G, a4H, a4L, a4M

The Decline of Serfdom

As the number of townspeople increased, the number of serfs declined. The growing towns offered serfs a chance to improve their hard lives. They might escape to the town and become free. Even if they did not, the town changed their way of living. Because the town needed food, serfs could sell their produce for money. Thus they could pay for the use of their lands in money rather than in labor.

Changes in agricultural methods also caused the number of serfs to decline. In England, for ● example, some landowners fenced off part of their land for sheep pastures, eliminating the need for shepherds. This action left some serfs without work and forced them into the cities. A devastating epidemic that began in the mid-1300s also contributed to the decline of serfdom.

The Black Death

In 1346 the bubonic plague, which Europeans called the Black Death, swept into Europe. It was brought to Genoa, Italy, by infected rats on board a merchant ship from a port on the Black Sea. The plague was transmitted to humans in two forms, the bubonic plague and the pneumonic plague. The bubonic plague erupted when rats infected with a bacterium became infested with fleas. The fleas bit people, and these people soon showed symptoms of the plague—infected lymph glands accompanied by painful swelling and high fever. Often, black spots broke out on the body, which might have been the reason for the name Black Death. The pneumonic plague, which attacks the lungs, was transmitted directly from one infected person to another. This horrible disease was almost always fatal to anyone contracting it.

It is difficult to estimate the total number of deaths throughout Europe. They happened so rapidly that often the survivors could not keep up with burying the dead. Bodies were loaded on carts and dumped in common graves outside the town. Entire villages and towns were emptied. Some estimates say that as many as one-third of Europe's population died and as many as 75 million people died worldwide. England lost one-third of its population. These devastating losses disrupted the continent's social, economic, and religious institutions. ■ Europe was left in a decline from which it did not recover for 100 years.

SECTION 3 REVIEW

1. **Define** merchant guild, craft guild, apprentice, journeyman
2. **Analyzing Ideas** Why are towns and cities essential to trade?
3. **Interpreting Ideas** **(a)** How did townspeople gain the rights of self-government? **(b)** What were the most important of these rights?
4. **Comparing Ideas** What were the differences between merchant guilds and craft guilds?
5. **Determining Cause and Effect** **(a)** What caused the growth of towns? **(b)** How did this growth contribute to the decline in the number of serfs? **(c)** How did the Black Death affect these towns?

4 The Culture of the Middle Ages Flourished in Towns and Cities

Civilization developed only after early humans settled in towns and cities. In a similar way, the culture of the Middle Ages did not flourish until city life revived.

Language and Literature

After the Roman Empire collapsed, Latin became the written language of western Europe. For centuries most educated people spoke a form called Medieval Latin. During the Middle Ages, however, the common people began to speak **vernacular languages,** or "everyday" speech that varied from place to place. These languages included English, Italian, French, German, and Spanish.

Vernacular literature. In time writers also began to use vernacular languages. The troubadours' songs were one of the first forms of vernacular literature. **Troubadours,** or traveling singers, wrote lyrical poems of love and chivalry, which they sang in the castles and courts of feudal lords. They also went from town to town singing, in this way helping to spread the vernacular language.

Another form of vernacular literature was the national epic. An English epic about King Arthur and his Knights of the Round Table became popular throughout Europe. France had its *Song of Roland.* Germans had the *Nibelungenlied,* a legend of how the hero Siegfried captured a magic treasure guarded by a dragon.

master worker who pays him wages. The master worker has passed the tests of the craft, joins the guild, and may open a shop.)

Review Answers

1. ***merchant guild:*** powerful association that monopolized trade; ***craft guild:*** included all of the people engaged in one particular craft; ***apprentice:*** a boy legally bound for several years to a master worker; ***journeyman:*** skilled worker who had completed his apprenticeship
2. Because they provide opportunities to exchange goods and services
3. (a) Some feudal lords granted towns political liberties, while others sold them charters of liberties. **(b)** freedom, exemption from manorial service, town justice, and commercial privileges
4. Merchant guilds were organizations of the traders in a town. Craft guilds were composed of workers in a particular craft.
5. (a) the revival of trade **(b)** The towns offered serfs a chance to gain their freedom. **(c)** The death toll caused towns to go into a decline.

SECTION 4

Focus/Motivation
Below is an excerpt from Dante Alighieri's *The Divine Comedy,* Canto XXVI, Ulysses. Read or distribute copies to the class.

"He answered me: 'Forever round this path Ulysses and Diomedes [in the war against Troy, Greek heroes who are being punished for their joint guilt] move in such dress, united in pain as once they were in wrath; there they lament the ambush of the Horse [wooden horse by which Troy was destroyed] which was the door through which the noble seed of the Romans issued from its holy source; there they mourn that for Achilles [coerced by Ulysses and Diomedes into going to Troy] slain Sweet Deidamia [Achilles' love, died of grief] weeps even in death; there they recall the Palladium [sacred statue of Pallas Athena on which the safety of Troy depended] in their pain.'"

Dante sought his material in the literature of ancient Greece and Rome. Name two epic poems that were his sources. *(Homer's* Iliad *and Virgil's* Aeneid*).*

Presentation
Comparing Architecture (Average/ Group)
Write the following list of characteristics on the chalkboard or an overhead projector, or give a printed copy to students. Students are to write the letter *R* next to the characteristics of Romanesque churches and the letter *G* next to the characteristics of Gothic churches. The answers are given in parentheses. frescos *(R);* flying buttresses *(G);* thick walls *(R);* domes

History Through the Arts

LITERATURE

The Canterbury Tales

The pilgrims in Geoffrey Chaucer's *The Canterbury Tales* represent almost every social class in English society. In the *Prologue* Chaucer parades a colorful cast of characters, each with an interesting story to tell, before the reader. The rhyming poetry and subtle satire of *The Canterbury Tales* make them fun to read even today. The following verses from the *Prologue* show Chaucer's mastery of description and satire:

"There was a *Knight,* a most distinguished man,
Who from the day on which he first began
To ride abroad had followed chivalry,
Truth, honour, generousness and courtesy. . .

There also was a *Nun,* a Prioress,
Her way of smiling very simple and coy.
Her greatest oath was only 'By St. Loy!'
And she was known as Madam Eglantyne.
And well she sang a service, with a fine
Intoning through her nose, as was most seemly,
And she spoke daintily in French extremely . . .

A *Monk* there was, one of the finest sort
Who rode the country; hunting was his sport.
A manly man, to be an Abbot able;
Many a dainty horse he had in stable. . . .

There was a *Merchant* with a forking beard
And motley dress; high on his horse he sat,
Upon his head a Flemish beaver hat
And on his feet daintily buckled boots.
He told of his opinions and pursuits . . .

They had a *Cook* with them who stood alone
For boiling chicken with a marrow-bone, . . .
But what a pity—so it seemed to me,
That he should have an ulcer on his knee. . . .

A *Doctor* too emerged as we proceeded;
No one alive could talk as well as he did
On points of medicine and of surgery, . . .

This *Pardoner* had hair as yellow as wax,
Hanging down smoothly like a hank of flax.
In driblets fell his locks behind his head
Down to his shoulders which they overspread;
Thinly they fell, like rat-tails, one by one.
He wore no hood upon his head, for fun . . .

Now I have told you shortly, in a clause,
The rank, the array, the number and the cause
Of our assembly in this company
In Southwark, at that high-class hostelry . . ."

The growth of towns created an audience for a new kind of literature that the French called *fabliaux* (FAB • lee • oh), which were short comic stories written in rhymed verse. The fabliaux mocked the lofty ideals of chivalry, ridiculed human foolishness, and criticized the clergy in particular. Animal stories or fables like that of Reynard the Fox grew increasingly popular among the more worldly and cynical people who lived in the towns and cities.

Another form of vernacular literature that developed during the Middle Ages was the mystery play, or **miracle play.** These short dramas on religious or biblical subjects were first written in Latin and enhanced the church services at Easter and Christmas. Later, as towns grew, miracle plays were written in vernacular languages, lengthened, and presented to large audiences in town marketplaces. One very popular miracle play was *Noye's Fludde (Noah's Flood).* It told the story of how Noah built his ark, col-

● It is not surprising that women were excluded. Religion was a cornerstone of medieval life, but a male-dominated clergy determined theology and wrote the rules of morality. Aquinas himself said that the role of a woman was to preserve the species or provide food and drink.

lected pairs of all creatures, and kept them and his family safe during the great flood.

Dante and Chaucer. Two great writers, Dante and Chaucer, represent the flowering of medieval vernacular literature. Dante Alighieri (DAHN • tay al • uhg • YER • ee) was born in Florence, Italy, in 1265. He wrote his scholarly works in Latin. When writing poetry, however, he preferred the Italian dialect of his native Tuscany. Because Dante used the Tuscan dialect in his most famous works, which were widely read throughout Italy, it became the written language of all Italy. Thus Dante is considered the father of modern Italian.

Dante's greatest work is *The Divine Comedy.* It tells of a pilgrimage on which Dante is guided by the Roman poet Virgil. Together the two pass through hell, purgatory, and heaven. They meet the souls of famous people, both good and evil. A work of this sort gave Dante the opportunity to criticize the society of his own time, and he used it fully. *The Divine Comedy* reflects the period in which Dante lived.

Geoffrey Chaucer was born in England in 1340. He wrote his *Canterbury Tales* in the form of a series of stories told by a group of pilgrims on their way to Thomas Becket's shrine in Canterbury. Chaucer used the Midland dialect of English to poke good-natured fun at the English and to satirize the clergy. Because of the popularity of his writings, this dialect became the forerunner of modern English.

Learning from Pictures *In* The Divine Comedy *Dante reflects on the fate of his soul. Here Dante and his beloved Beatrice are in Paradise.*

Education

During the early Middle Ages, only a few nobles and some clergy were educated, mainly at monasteries or by teachers in the church. Gradually, ● however, schools admitted any males who wanted to study. Located in prosperous towns, these schools had simple beginnings. A teacher could set up a place of instruction and try to attract students, who enrolled in the school by paying a fee. This educational system resembled that of Athens when Plato and Aristotle taught.

As teachers and students increased in number, they united to form guilds for both protection and privileges. Such a guild was called a *universitas,* a Latin word meaning "an association of people." Gradually the word *university* came to mean an association of people organized for the purpose of teaching and learning.

Four great universities developed between 1000 and 1200. Those at Paris and at Oxford, in England, specialized in theology, or the study of religious doctrine, and the liberal arts, which included Latin grammar, logic, rhetoric, arithmetic, geometry, astronomy, and music. The University of Bologna, in Italy, taught Roman law and canon, or church, law. The University at Salerno, also in Italy, specialized in medicine. By the 1300s towns throughout western Europe had universities.

In time medieval universities established standard courses of study, with uniform requirements for the various stages of progress. These stages were represented by academic degrees. The degree of bachelor of arts showed that a student had finished the apprenticeship. After further study and examination, the student qualified for the degree of master of arts and could then teach. The student was admitted to the guild of teachers at a ceremony that

(R); high, thin walls *(G);* stained-glass windows *(G);* dark interiors *(R);* tall spires *(G);* pointed arches *(G);* strong columns *(R);* low, flat towers *(R);* and sculpture in relief adorning the walls *(G).*

261

1B, 4B, a1A, a4A, a4F, a4G, a4L

READ
WRITE
INTERPRET
●CONNECT
THINK

BUILDING HISTORY STUDY SKILLS

Making Connections with History: Linking Literature to History

The literature of a society as found in novels, poems, and stories gives us information about the values and culture of a people. The content is fiction, but the ideas often indicate what the people of that society believed and what they felt was important. Literature helps us understand the intangible or underlying values and beliefs of a society.

How to Link Literature to History

To link literature to history, follow these steps.

1. Identify the source. Is the selection a novel, a poem, or a story? When was it written? Why was it written?
2. Explain the contents. What is the selection about? What is the main theme? Who are the characters?
3. Identify the values or beliefs being expressed.
4. Connect the literature to history. Does the literature represent an ideal, or does it describe a real event? Does it support or contradict the historical facts?

Developing the Skill

The troubadours' love songs focused on courtship. In the following poem, the troubadour Cercamon sings of his lady. Read the poem and attempt to explain the historical link.

> "Now that the air is fresher
> and the world turned green,
> I shall sing once more
> of the one I love and desire,
> but we are so far apart
> that I cannot go and witness
> how my words might please her.
>
> I sing of her, yet her beauty
> is greater than I can tell,
> with her fresh color, lovely eyes,
> and white skin, untanned
> and untainted by rouge.
> She is so pure and noble
> that no one can speak ill of her.
>
> But above all, one must praise,
> it seems to me, her truthfulness,
> her manners and her gracious speech,
> for she never would betray a friend;
> and I was mad to believe
> what I heard tell of her
> and thus cause her to be angry.
>
> I never intended to complain;
> and even now, if she so desires,
> she could bring me happiness
> by granting what I seek.
> I cannot go on like this much longer,
> for since she's been so far away
> I've scarcely slept or eaten."

Written in the 1100s, the poem is about romantic love. The young man has lost his love because he listened to lies about her. Now he is sorry about their separation.

The poem reflects the age in which it was written, with the woman represented as an ideal—pure, noble, gracious, and loyal, with "lovely eyes, white skin, untanned and untainted. . . ." It demonstrates the attitude of men toward women during the age of chivalry. Women were regarded as the weaker sex and, according to the code of chivalry, had to be protected and defended. The poem describes the woman in idealistic terms and places her on a pedestal.

Practicing the skill. Using the information on linking literature to history, choose a poem or novel written by a 20th-century author and find characteristics in the work that reflect modern times.

To apply this skill, see Applying History Study Skills on page 273.

An English knight

262

was called the commencement because it signified the beginning of work as a teacher. Only then could the student study one of the specialties offered at medieval universities—theology, law, or medicine.

Philosophy

During the Middle Ages, the classic works of the ancient Greek and Roman philosophers came to the attention of western Europe by way of the Moors in Spain. As a result, European scholars spent much time trying to reconcile Aristotle's ideas with those of the early church writers. Aristotle emphasized human reason. The early church writers, however, emphasized faith. The attempt of medieval philosophers to reconcile early church writers' faith and Aristotle's reason is often called **scholasticism.** The aim of the scholastic philosophers was to discover how people could improve themselves in this life by reason and also ensure salvation in the life to come.

Peter Abelard (AB • uh • lahrd), who taught in Paris in the 1100s, was an important scholastic philosopher. In his book *Sic et Non* (*Yes and No*), he raised many questions about church doctrine. After each question he placed his opinions of scripture from the Bible, decrees of the popes, and the writings of church philosophers. Many of these opinions conflicted with one another. Abelard made his students think and inquire. His motto was "By doubting we come to inquiry, and by inquiring we perceive the truth."

Probably the greatest of all medieval philosophers was Thomas Aquinas, a Dominican friar. His principal work, *Summa Theologica,* written in the late 1200s, summarizes Christian thought at that time. In it Aquinas examined each point of church doctrine and tried to show that it could be arrived at by logic or reason as well as by faith. Today the *Summa* forms one of the bases for the teaching of theology in Roman Catholic schools.

Science

Medieval thinking was deductive, leaving little room for scientific progress. In other words, an idea was taken from an authority, usually the Bible, accepted as true, and used as a basis for reasoning. Classical writings, like those of Galen and Ptolemy, formed the basis of much medieval science.

While the Arabs preserved the great accomplishments of Hellenistic science, only two subjects received serious attention in the West: mathematics and optics (the study of light). Europeans regarded mathematics as important because of its use in counting, calendars, trade, and measuring. They considered optics important because of their belief that God's influence was carried by light. In these subjects some important work was done, especially in the 1200s, 1300s, and 1400s. It was not until the 1550s, however, that major interest in science reappeared and led to vast changes in the understanding of the physical world.

Art and Architecture

During the Middle Ages, most artists dedicated themselves to glorifying God. Church architecture became the primary art form, and the other arts embellished or beautified it.

Between 1000 and 1150, most architects used the arches, domes, and low horizontal lines characteristic of Roman architecture. This style later came to be called *Romanesque* (meaning "similar to the Roman"). Because of the enormous weight of the domed stone roof, the walls of a Romanesque church could have only a few small windows. The style resulted in very dark, eerie interiors, but the simple style of the columns and arches gave the building dignity and serenity. Romanesque churches contained little sculpture, but frescoes adorned the walls.

During the mid-1100s, master builders in western Europe developed a radically different style of church architecture. Critics ridiculed this style because it did not conform to the standards of classical architecture. These critics called the new style *Gothic,* after the barbarian Goths. Despite the origin of the name, Gothic has come to be considered one of the most beautiful styles of architecture ever developed.

In contrast to the low, heavy Romanesque churches, the spires of Gothic churches soared delicately above the roofs of the surrounding town. Outside the walls, builders used rows of supporting ribs, called flying buttresses, which they connected to the church with arches. Because the buttress carried part of the weight of the roof, the walls could be high and thin, with large windows. Everything in Gothic churches—pointed arches, tall spires, and high walls—reached toward heaven.

263

1B, 4B, a4A, a4F, a4H, a4K, a4L

SECTION 4

Closure

Ask students to identify features of the medieval university that may still exist in modern universities. *(Answers will vary. Students should mention the setting of standards and curriculum requirements, the granting of academic degrees and the elaborate graduation ceremonies.)* How do they differ? *(No longer do males only attend the university. The emphasis has shifted away from theology to technical subjects.)*

Review Answers

1. ***vernacular language:*** the everyday speech of a particular locality; ***troubadours:*** traveling singers who wrote poems of love and chivalry; ***miracle play:*** short medieval drama with a religious or biblical subject; ***scholasticism:*** attempt by medieval philosophers to reconcile faith and reason
2. ***Dante:*** author of *The Divine Comedy;* ***Chaucer:*** writer whose *Canterbury Tales* satirized English society; ***Abelard:*** scholastic philosopher at University of Paris; ***Aquinas:*** philosopher whose principal work, *Summa Theologica,* summarizes Christian thought
3. The *fabliaux* were short comic stories in rhymed verse that made fun of chivalry and the foolishness of human beings. Medieval epics were long poems about

Learning from Pictures *The flying buttresses of Notre Dame support the high walls used in Gothic architecture. Reims Cathedral (inset) provides a beautiful example of lofty Gothic interiors.*

The inside of the Gothic church also differed from that of the Romanesque church. Statues of saints and rulers lined the interiors, sculpture in relief adorned the walls, and stained-glass windows let in shafts of sunlight.

In many ways Gothic churches exemplified the changing world of the late Middle Ages. The tall structures rose above the growing town. Marketplaces in the shadows of their walls teemed with traders. Religious pageants and miracle plays were performed both within the churches and outside their carved doors. All the skills of the medieval world went into building these monuments to God.

SECTION 4 REVIEW

1. **Define** vernacular language, troubadours, miracle play, scholasticism
2. **Identify** Dante, Chaucer, Abelard, Aquinas
3. **Comparing Ideas** How did the *fabliaux* differ from the epics?
4. **Summarizing Ideas** How did the church teach the Bible's stories to those who could not read?
5. **Organizing Ideas** What was the organizational structure of medieval universities?
6. **Comparing Ideas** What were some of the differences between the Romanesque and Gothic styles of architecture?

● Castillon

5 Patriotic Feelings Spread Throughout Western Europe

Under feudalism in the early Middle Ages, the people of a country did not look to a central government for defense or help, nor did they feel any loyalty toward the country as a whole. Instead, their loyalty lay with a local feudal lord, a manor village, or a town.

Gradually, however, nations began to form. The development of a nation usually started with the growth of patriotism among its people. **Patriotism** is a feeling of loyalty to the country as a whole. It gives the feeling of belonging to a large society rather than to only a small locality.

England

The authority of the English king, although partially restricted by Parliament, increased in various ways. These included the development of a single system of law and courts and an increase in revenue as the country grew more prosperous. Also, the military strength of a professional army and the support of the townspeople strengthened the king's position against the feudal lords.

Consequently, the power of feudal lords decreased. Manors began to disappear as the number of serfs declined. Increasingly, villages and farms of free peasants dotted the English countryside.

The Hundred Years' War. English prosperity and the development of a strong national government suffered a setback during a long war with France. The Hundred Years' War, which began in 1337, had three basic causes. First, the English king Edward III claimed the provinces of Aquitaine and Gascony in France. Second, he tried to seize the French throne when the last male Capetian died. Third, England and France competed for control of commercially rich Flanders. The war brought two important developments.

(1) The use of two new weapons—the longbow and the cannon—weakened feudalism. The English longbow was 5 or 6 feet (1.5 or 1.8 meters) long, with a range up to 400 yards (360 meters). English foot soldiers armed with longbows completely defeated a French feudal cavalry at Agincourt (AJ • uhn • kohrt) in 1415. Knights on horseback were no match for foot soldiers with longbows.

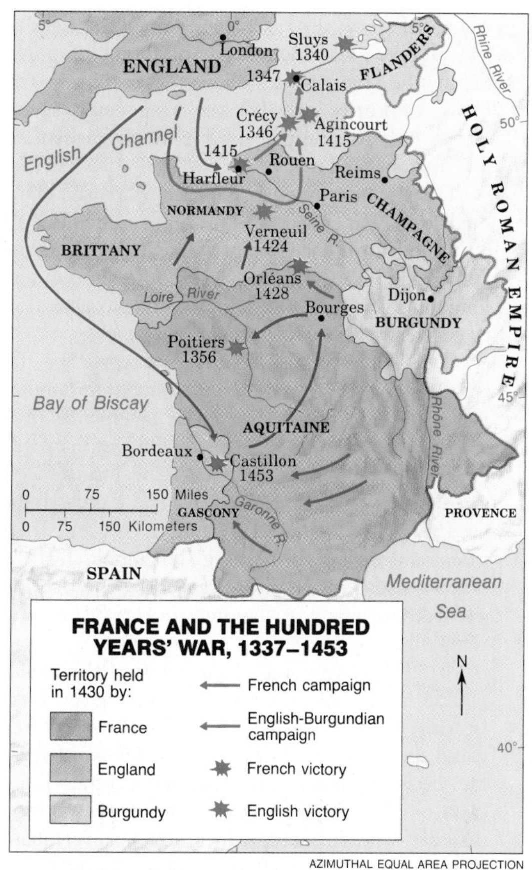

Learning from Maps *The English defeated the French for control of the English Channel in 1340, at the battle of Sluys. What battle did the French win in the south?* ●

Europeans may have learned the use of gunpowder from the Muslims during the Crusades. To this knowledge they added the use of the gun. At first the gun was only a crude tube of wood and metal out of which exploding gunpowder hurled stones or chunks of metal. Cannons developed from these rather simple weapons. Castles no longer provided strong protection for the feudal lord and his soldiers. One powerful blast from a cannon could break through a castle's thick walls.

(2) The English Parliament temporarily gained more power over the king. Through its right to grant or withhold tax revenues, Parliament forced some weak English kings during time of war to agree to a number of rights: (a) Parliament, as well as the king, had to approve any restatement or

national heroes and their great deeds.
4. The church taught the Bible through religious dramas called miracle plays. They were written in Latin and added to the church services at Easter and Christmas. Later these miracle plays were translated into vernacular languages, lengthened, and presented in marketplaces to large audiences.
5. Medieval universities contained standard courses of study, with uniform requirements for the various stages of progress. These stages were represented by academic degrees.
6. Romanesque churches are characterized by round arches, domes, low horizontal lines, thick walls, few windows, and dark interiors. There was little sculpture inside Romanesque churches, but many were adorned with frescoes. Gothic churches are characterized by high, thin walls with large windows, flying buttresses, pointed arches and tall spires. The interiors of Gothic churches were decorated with statues, reliefs, and large stained-glass windows.

SECTION 5

Focus/Motivation

During the Hundred Years' War, Joan of Arc, an uneducated peasant girl in her teens, heard "voices" telling her to leave her small village and help France defend the city of

265

Orléans. Charles, the uncrowned king of France, reluctantly agreed to give Joan command of his armies, and under her leadership the French forced the English to retreat. Eventually she was captured by enemy forces, turned over to English authorities, and tried and convicted of witchcraft. She was burned at the stake. Ask students why Charles would give command of his armies to a young girl. *(Answers will vary. The French had been suffering defeat after defeat. Joan persuaded them she was sincere about the "voices" from a heavenly source that told her to defend Orléans.)* The execution of Joan of Arc made her a martyr. Ask: How did her death help the French in the Hundred Years' War? ***(Her martyrdom strengthened French patriotism and the will to resist the English.)***

Presentation Relating Cause and Effect (Average/Group)
Put the following lists on the chalkboard or an overhead projector. List causes to the left and effects to the right.

Causes
1. Use of the longbow
2. Development of cannons
3. English kings needed money to fight wars
4. England lost the Hundred Years' War

Effects
a. Kings could devote

change of a law; (b) Parliament gained the right to levy all taxes, and any new tax had to be proposed first by the House of Commons rather than by the House of Lords; and (c) the king could spend money only for the purpose for which Parliament had appropriated it.

Despite many English victories, when the Hundred Years' War ended in 1453, England had lost all of its lands in France except Calais (see map, page 265). Actually, these losses helped England in the long run. Now the English king could pay attention to governing his own country.

The Wars of the Roses. A struggle for the throne between the York and Lancaster families began in 1455 and delayed the emergence of a strong centralized government in England. In this civil war—the Wars of the Roses—the Yorkists used a white rose as their badge, and the Lancastrians used a red rose. Small bands of nobles and their vassals did most of the fighting. The monarchy benefited because of the chaos caused by the fighting and because many of the great nobles of England were killed.

In 1485 Henry Tudor, a member of the House of Lancaster, ended the wars by defeating the Yorkist king, Richard III. He seized the throne of England and married a daughter of the House of York. He became Henry VII, founder of the Tudor dynasty. The English people, tired of war and disorder, willingly accepted the strong government that Henry VII established.

France

The history of France during the 1300s and 1400s resembled that of England. Capetian kings had developed a strong monarchy, although the Hundred Years' War with England caused French kings to lose some of their power. France suffered much more than England during that war because much of the fighting took place on French soil. Bands of robbers ravaged the already devastated French countryside. Even during the periods of relative peace, starvation plagued the citizens. The following excerpt describes the misery of the people in 1421:

> "And in truth when good weather came, in April, those who in the winter had made their beverages from apples and sloe plums emptied the residue of their apples and their plums into the street with the intention that the pigs of St. Antoine would eat them. But the pigs did not get to them in time, for as soon as they were thrown out, they were seized by poor folk, women and children, who ate them with great relish, which was a great pity, each for himself; for they ate what the pigs scorned to eat, they ate the cores of cabbages without bread or without cooking, grasses of the fields without bread or salt."

Joan of Arc. During the Hundred Years' War, rivalry broke out between two branches of the royal family—Burgundy and Orléans—making it difficult for the French to fight the English. Defeat followed defeat. However, French fortunes in the war were revived by an uneducated peasant girl in her teens, Joan of Arc. Joan said she had heard voices telling her to leave her small village and help defend the city of Orléans, which was under English attack. She persuaded the French authorities of her sincerity and made her way to the city. In 1429, inspired to greater efforts by Joan's presence, the weary French troops rallied and saved the city. That same year Joan helped the heir to the French throne take the crown as Charles VII.

Enemy forces captured Joan and turned her over to English authorities. A church council tried and convicted her of heresy and witchcraft. She was burned at the stake by the English in 1431. As the sentence was being carried out, an English leader cried, "We are lost! We have burned a saint!"

Joan's fate created a strong patriotic feeling among the French. Her example helped to bring about the successful conclusion of the war in 1453. The French finally drove the English out and reestablished a strong monarchy.

The Estates-General. In 1302 Philip IV established the Estates-General, a representative assembly resembling the English Parliament. It took its name from the groups that attended the meetings: members of the clergy (First Estate), nobles (Second Estate), and townspeople (Third Estate). During the Hundred Years' War, when France lacked a strong king, the Estates-General controlled finances and passed laws. For a time during the war, it looked as if the Estates-General might become the real ruler of France. When the war ended, however, Charles VII emerged strong enough to rule without the Estates-General, which

266

Students should note that despite the dominance of men in medieval society, a number of women rulers had a significant impact: Eleanor of Aquitaine, Empress Matilda, and Blanche of Castile—the mother of (Saint) Louis IX of France.

seldom met thereafter. It never gained the right to approve taxes, which was so important for the English Parliament. In France the king could levy taxes on his own authority.

Louis XI. Louis XI, one of the most remarkable French kings, further strengthened the French monarchy during his reign from 1461 to 1483. Louis avoided war except as a last resort, preferring to use diplomacy, at which he was a master. His opponents called him "The Spider." He used any methods to get what he wanted. His administration was harsh and taxes were heavy, but he used the money to strengthen the kingdom.

Louis XI used diplomacy to build an alliance against the powerful Duke of Burgundy, Charles the Bold. He did so by persuading the leaders of Switzerland, an independent nation, that a strong Burgundy would threaten Swiss freedom.

The Swiss did Louis's fighting for him. They armed themselves with pikes, long poles with metal spearheads. These Swiss pikes proved highly effective against cavalry charges, and, like the English longbows, they helped end the military supremacy of feudal knights. In 1477 the Duke of Burgundy was killed in battle. Since the duke had no son, Louis XI seized much of the territory of Burgundy.

The French king soon met with more good luck. French nobles now ruled various provinces that had once been part of the royal territory. Louis claimed their lands because several of these nobles died without heirs. In this way he obtained the provinces of Anjou, Maine, and Provence for the crown. He gained Brittany by marriage. Thus all of France was unified under the monarchy.

As the power of French kings increased, the power of French feudal lords declined. However, French nobles remained rich and influential until the middle of the 1700s. They had many privileges, including exemption from taxes.

As feudalism declined, French peasants did not gain as much personal freedom as the English did. Unlike the English, they still had to pay many dues and owed services to the manor and its lord.

Spain

By 1400 four principal Christian kingdoms—Portugal, Castile-León, Navarre, and Aragón—had emerged on the Iberian Peninsula (see map, this page). Granada, the last stronghold of the Moors in Spain, also shared the peninsula.

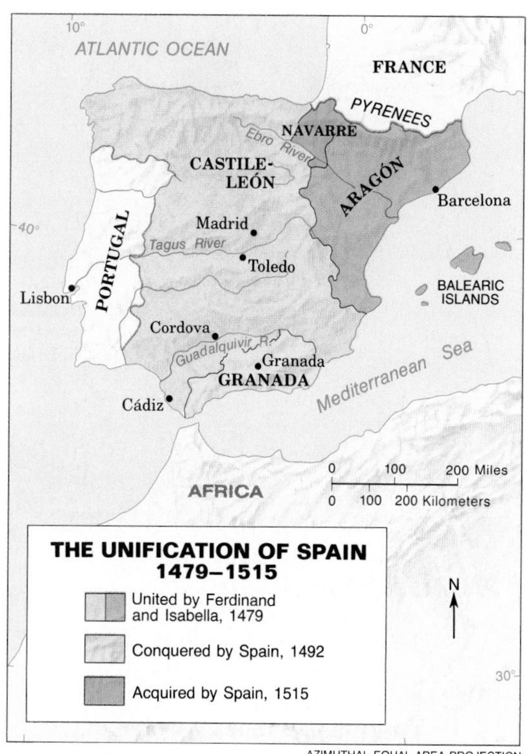

Learning from Maps *The fall of Granada completed the reconquest of Spain. In what year did Spain acquire Navarre?* 1515

The first real step toward unification of the peninsula came in 1469, when Isabella of Castile-León married Ferdinand of Aragón. The two kingdoms remained separate, but their rulers joined forces in a war against the Moors, capturing Granada in 1492. In the 1500s Ferdinand and Isabella united Castile-León and Aragón to form the new nation of Spain and added the kingdom of Navarre to its territories.

Ferdinand and Isabella made Spain a powerful monarchy. They took powers away from the church courts and the nobles. Ardent Catholics, they looked with displeasure at the many Moors and Jews in their kingdoms. Even after the fall of Granada, Moors had continued to live peacefully in Spain. Jews had been there from the time of the Roman Empire.

In 1492 Ferdinand and Isabella ordered all Jews within their two kingdoms to become Christians or leave. Several years later they offered the

more time to ruling England
b. The end of knights on horseback
c. Castles were no longer a strong defense
d. Parliament gained concessions from the kings.
Have students match each cause at the left with an effect at the right. (*Answers:* *1=b, 2=c, 3=d, 4=a*)

267

1A, 1B, 4B, 4D, a4B, a4C

• Anti-Semitism began in France. Edward I expelled the Jews from England in 1290, and German Jews were forced to live in their own communities, or ghettos. In Italy, by contrast, they lived under the protection of the pope in Rome and established a major center of learning at Padua.

SECTION 5

Closure
Have students identify events that encouraged patriotism in European countries during the Middle Ages. *(Answers will vary. Students might note Joan of Arc's rallying of the French against the English and their allies.)*

Review Answers
1. *patriotism:* feeling of loyalty to the country as a whole
2. *Joan of Arc:* French peasant girl who led French troops during the Hundred Years' War; ***Charles VII:*** French king whom Joan served; ***Estates-General:*** French representative assembly; ***Charles the Bold:*** duke of Burgundy; ***Ferdinand and Isabella:*** rulers of Aragón and Castile-León; ***Hapsburgs:*** family that gained control of vast amounts of territory in the Holy Roman Empire
3. *Burgundy:* powerful duchy in east central France; ***Orléans:*** city saved from English by Joan of Arc; ***Portugal:*** country on Iberian peninsula; ***Castile-León:*** kingdom in west central Spain; ***Navarre:*** kingdom in northern Spain; ***Aragón:*** kingdom in eastern Spain; ***Granada:*** last stronghold of Moors in southeastern Spain
4. (a) the weakening of feudalism and the temporary strengthening of the English Parliament; **(b)** Henry VII

Learning from Maps *In 1500 the Holy Roman Empire included lands in Italy as well as in Germany. However, local rulers held most of the power. What countries border the Holy Roman Empire?* **France, Papal States, Republic of Venice, Hungary, Poland**

Moors the same choice. Most people of both groups chose to leave rather than accept Christianity. In the long run, this policy weakened Spain because • the Moors and Jews had been leaders in industrial and commercial activity.

The Holy Roman Empire

England, France, and Spain each formed strong nations after 1100. However, Germany and Italy—the regions that made up the Holy Roman Empire—did not become unified nations until the 1800s. The Holy Roman Emperor lacked the power to exercise complete control.

In the early days, the rulers of many German states elected the Holy Roman Emperor. Gradually, the number who could vote for emperor decreased. Finally, by a decree in 1356, Emperor Charles IV ruled that only seven electors would choose the emperor.

The electors feared giving too much power to one of their own group or to any other powerful prince. As a result, for many years they elected only princes who had little land or power. The Holy Roman Emperor had no real authority, but he did have prestige. For this reason the election became an occasion for bribery and the trading of political favors.

Around 1300 a member of the Hapsburg family, which ruled a small state in what is now Switzerland, was elected emperor. The Hapsburgs, although only weak princes with little land, used the prestige of the title of Holy Roman Emperor to arrange marriages with powerful families. Through marriage the Hapsburg family gained control of the duchy of Austria and nearby lands. Many other

● Although Germany failed to unite, the German people remained dynamic and expansive. German knights, such as those in the Teutonic Order, missionaries, and colonists moved into eastern Europe. Many ethnic Germans today wish to leave the Soviet Union or Eastern Europe and return to Germany, particularly West Germany.

1B, 3B, 4B, 4D, a1A, a4A, a4F, a4H, a4L

well-planned marriages eventually gave them control of vast amounts of territory in the empire.

After 1437 the Hapsburgs maneuvered cleverly enough to ensure that the Holy Roman Emperor was always a member of their family. However, even the most powerful Hapsburg emperor did not rule all of Germany, but only the family lands. Germany, made up of more than 300 separate and independent governments, remained a nation in name only.

Italy, too, suffered from being a part of the Holy Roman Empire. Another problem that delayed Italian unification was that the country was divided, as by a belt across the middle, by the Papal States ruled by the pope.

SECTION 5 REVIEW

1. **Define** patriotism
2. **Identify** Joan of Arc, Charles VII, Estates-General, Charles the Bold, Ferdinand, Isabella, Hapsburgs
3. **Locate** Burgundy, Orléans, Portugal, Castile-León, Navarre, Aragón, Granada
4. **Summarizing Ideas** **(a)** What were two important results in England of the Hundred Years' War? **(b)** What ruler brought to an end the Wars of the Roses and established a strong monarchy in England?
5. **Analyzing Ideas** **(a)** Why was the reign of Louis XI important to France? **(b)** What territory did he gain?
6. **Interpreting Ideas** Explain why Italy and Germany failed to become unified nations during the later Middle Ages.

6 The Temporal Power of the Church Was Challenged

Innocent III, the most powerful of all the popes, made himself both the supreme ruler of the church and the judge of political questions throughout Europe. After his time, however, the temporal, or worldly, power of the church began to weaken. This occurred for two major reasons.

First, Europe was changing. Kings developed strong national governments with rich treasuries. The importance of townspeople grew, and they often felt that the restrictions of church laws hindered trade and industry.

Second, the wisdom of the Muslims and the pagan Greeks appeared in Europe as a "new learning." However, much of it conflicted with the teachings of the church. As a result a spirit of skepticism, or questioning, began to develop. People criticized the church because of its great wealth, its methods of raising money, and the worldly lives of some members of the clergy.

Boniface VIII Versus Philip IV

A serious clash between the church and secular authority erupted over the issue of whether the clergy had to obey national laws or pay taxes. In 1294 Philip IV of France (Philip the Fair) demanded that the clergy pay taxes to the national treasury. His demand angered Pope Boniface VIII. Although the pope was educated and cultured, he was proud, tactless, and eager for power. The pope argued that the clergy did not have to pay taxes. As the struggle wore on, Philip the Fair summoned the first meeting of the Estates-General in 1302. On this occasion Philip accused the pope of simony and heresy and protested Boniface's demands. He also demanded that a general council of the church bring Boniface to trial. The French king then had his envoy in Italy seize the pope and hold him prisoner. Although quickly released, Boniface died soon afterward. After his death the political power of the papacy lessened.

The Babylonian Captivity

Shortly after Boniface's death, Philip IV managed to have one of his French advisers elected pope. The new pope moved the headquarters, of the papacy from Rome to Avignon (a • veen • YOHN), in southern France. The next six popes were also French, and Avignon remained the papal capital for nearly 70 years.

This period of papal history—from 1309 to 1377—is known as the Babylonian Captivity, named after the Hebrew captivity in Babylonia. For 1,000 years, Rome had been the center of the church in the West. With the pope living in France, people in other countries became suspicious of the French monarch's control of the church. The French popes seemed more interested in their luxurious households than in the spiritual welfare of Christians. Rome fell into lawlessness in the pope's absence.

5. (a) Louis XI used diplomacy to extend French territory and create a unified absolute monarchy. **(b)** He gained Burgundy, Anjou, Maine, Provence, and Brittany.
6. Germany and most of Italy belonged to the Holy Roman Empire. Few of the emperors were powerful enough to establish strong central authority. Italy also suffered from being divided across the middle by the Papal States.

SECTION 6

Focus/Motivation
Write the following quotations on the chalkboard or an overhead projector.

"They who believe in the infallibility of the pope and openly say so are blasphemers."
—John Huss

"The Bible is for the government of the people, by the people, and for the people."
—John Wycliffe

Ask students to identify the criticism of the church and the heretical ideas contained in these lines. *(Students should mention that Huss attacked papal infallibility. Wycliffe placed the authority of the Bible above papal authority.)*

Presentation
Relating Cause and Effect (Average/Group)
Put the following sets of statements on the

chalkboard or an overhead projector. Ask students to identify each statement as "cause" or "effect."

1. Papal power declines. *(effect)* Boniface VIII is temporarily imprisoned. *(effect)* Boniface VIII and Philip IV clash over issues. *(cause)*
2. People are critical of the lifestyle of the popes. *(effect)* Rome becomes lawless. *(effect)* Popes reside in Avignon, France. *(cause)*

SECTION 6

Closure
Have students enumerate the difficulties facing the church in the late Middle Ages. *(Babylonian Captivity, Great Schism, criticism by Church reformers)*

Review Answers
1. ***Boniface VIII:*** pope who quarreled with Philip IV of France about the clergy paying taxes to the king; ***Babylonian Captivity:*** the removal of the papacy from Rome to Avignon; ***Great Schism:*** a division of the church into hostile groups over political matters; ***John Wycliffe:*** cleric and teacher at Oxford who attacked the church's wealth, immoral clergy, and papal authority; ***John Huss:*** Bohemian teacher who denounced church abuses
2. ***Avignon:*** southern French city; ***Constance:*** Swiss city and site of church council on reform; ***Prague:*** capital of Bohemia

LINKING GEOGRAPHY TO HISTORY

The World of Arab Geographers

Between 900 and 1400, people's knowledge of the world greatly increased. This expanded understanding, in large part, resulted from the travels of a number of Arab geographers. Ibn-Haukal, one of the earliest of these Arab geographers, explored some of the most remote parts of Africa and Asia between 943 and 973. On one of his voyages along the east coast of Africa, he reached a point just 20°N of the equator. He noted that thousands of people lived in those latitudes. This finding disproved Aristotle's theory that areas near the equator would be totally uninhabitable.

Other Arab geographers made important discoveries about the climates of the world. In fact, the Arabs published the world's first climatic atlas in the 900s. It included observations about temperature patterns from places south of the equator and proved emphatically that Aristotle's *torrid zone* did not exist. Then in 985 a geographer named Al-Maqdisi drew a map showing 14 world climatic regions in place of the three identified by Aristotle. Al-Maqdisi noted that climates varied not only with latitude, but also with location east and west. In addition, he suggested that much of the Southern Hemisphere consisted of oceans, while most of the Northern Hemisphere consisted of land.

During the mid-1100s, Edrisi, a Muslim who lived in Palermo, Sicily, began to compile the huge volume of data accumulated by Arab travelers. When Edrisi doubted the accuracy or precision of information about the location of a mountain, river, or coastline, he sent out trained geographers to make careful observations. With this fund of accurate information, Edrisi wrote what he called a *new geography.* Completed in 1154, it bore the interesting title of *Amusement for Him Who Desires to Travel Around the World.*

Edrisi's book corrected a number of mistaken notions. For example, he refuted the ideas that land completely encircled the Indian Ocean and that the Caspian Sea was a gulf of the world ocean. Unfortunately for the European explorers of the 1500s, Edrisi's book was not translated from Arabic into Latin until 1619.

Ibn-Batuta, born in Morocco in 1304, ranks among the greatest geographers and explorers of all time. At the age of 21, Ibn-Batuta set out on a pilgrimage to Mecca. During his journey he became increasingly intrigued with the people he met and the lands he saw. Before he reached Mecca, Ibn-Batuta committed himself to a life of travel, determining never to take the same route twice.

His journeys took him to practically every part of the known world. He sailed along the Red Sea, visited Ethiopia, and continued south along the shores of Africa's east coast. He went as far as Kilwa, 9°S of the equator. Ibn-Batuta then headed northward to explore the lands surrounding the Black Sea. From there he trekked across the vast grasslands of the Russian steppes, finally arriving in the fabled caravan city of Samarkand. Still impatient to see more, he climbed the snow-covered peaks of Afghanistan and crossed into India. He also visited a number of islands in the Indian Ocean and explored part of what today is Indonesia. Ultimately he reached China.

Not content with having seen more of Asia than any person of his time, Ibn-Batuta next visited Spain. He then returned to Africa and journeyed across the Sahara, traveling all the way to Tombouctou. During his nearly 30 years of traveling, he covered more than 75,000 miles (280,000 kilometers).

He finally settled in Morocco, not far from his native home, where he wrote his great work, *The Travels of Ibn-Batuta.* Thus, beginning with Ibn-Haukal and ending with Ibn-Batuta, the geographers of the Muslim world kept the light of geographic knowledge burning brightly for more than 400 years.

Arab geographers in Istanbul

1B, 3B, 4B, a1A, a4A, a4F, a4H, a4L

The Great Schism

The 1370s were an especially difficult time for the papacy. A French pope was persuaded to leave Avignon and return to Rome, where he died. The threats of a Roman mob forced the College of Cardinals to elect an Italian pope. But in 1378 the French cardinals elected a French pope, who remained at Avignon. The Italian pope excommunicated the French pope and cardinals; the French pope excommunicated the Italian pope and cardinals.

The period from 1378 to 1417 is known as the Great Schism (SIZ • uhm), meaning a division into hostile groups. For political reasons each of the two popes had the support of certain national rulers. Generally, the people and clergy of a country followed the choice of their ruler.

In 1414 a church council met at Constance in Germany to attempt to heal the schism and to consider reforms of all the weaknesses of the church. The council quickly dealt with the schism by deposing both the Italian and French popes. It agreed that a new pope should be elected, but not until a program of reforms had been adopted.

The Council of Constance had more difficulty agreeing on a program of reforms. Everyone agreed that corruption in the church and immorality among the clergy must end. However, when a definite plan was proposed to deal with a problem, the delegates disagreed so strongly that no conclusion could be reached.

After long and bitter debate, the council decided that church councils should be called regularly to deal with problems, including needed reforms. The council drew up a statement of reforms and the cardinals then elected a new pope.

Continued Criticism of the Church

The Babylonian Captivity and the Great Schism weakened the authority and prestige of the papacy and increased criticism of the church. Some of this criticism came from within the church itself.

In 1324 two members of the Franciscan order, Marsilius of Padua and John of Jandun, wrote an influential work called *Defender of the Peace.* According to the writers, the pope was only the elected head of the church and had no other power. The authors believed that all power belonged to the members of the church, who could delegate this power only to a general church council. A council had authority to make broad reforms in the entire church, including the papacy.

John Wycliffe. John Wycliffe, a member of the clergy and a teacher at Oxford University, adopted and spread these beliefs in England in the late 1300s. He attacked the wealth of the church, immorality among the clergy, and the pope's claim to absolute authority. He also said that Jesus Christ could save one's soul without the aid of a priest and that the means of salvation was in the Bible, not in the clergy. It is believed that in about 1382 Wycliffe encouraged the translation of the Bible from Latin into English. This enabled people to read scripture for themselves and learn what to believe and how to act.

John Huss. Wycliffe's books were widely read both in England and in Europe. His writings influenced John Huss of Bohemia, a teacher at the University of Prague. Huss became popular with the people of Bohemia by denouncing abuses in the church, but he angered the clergy and was excommunicated in 1410. Huss appeared before the Council of Constance to answer charges of heresy. In 1415 the council tried and condemned him as a heretic and ordered him burned at the stake.

By the end of the 1400s, the church seemed to have weathered the worst of its troubles. The demand for councils had died away, and the popes, wealthier than ever, held unchallenged authority over the church. The accusations of Wycliffe and Huss that the church ignored spiritual needs made little impact. Yet those spiritual needs later caused far greater problems for the popes than had the Babylonian Captivity and the Great Schism.

SECTION 6 REVIEW

1. **Identify** Boniface VIII, Babylonian Captivity, Great Schism, John Wycliffe, John Huss
2. **Locate** Avignon, Constance, Prague
3. **Analyzing Ideas** What caused the decline of the church's temporal power after the reign of Innocent III?
4. **Interpreting Ideas** Describe the dispute between Boniface VIII and Philip IV.
5. **Summarizing Ideas** **(a)** What were the Babylonian Captivity and the Great Schism? **(b)** Why did they weaken the church?
6. **Understanding Ideas** **(a)** Explain the importance of the ideas of *Defender of the Peace.* **(b)** How were these ideas further developed by both Wycliffe and Huss?

3. The church's temporal power declined because (1) national governments became stronger and richer; (2) townspeople believed church law restricted trade and industry; (3) new interest in the learning of the Muslims and ancient Greeks led to questioning of church doctrine; (4) people criticized the church for its great wealth, its methods of raising money, and the worldly lives of some clergy.
4. Philip demanded the clergy pay taxes to the French treasury. Boniface VIII argued that they did not have to pay.
5. (a) The Babylonian Captivity from 1309 to 1377 was a period when French popes ruled from Avignon. The Great Schism lasted from 1378 to 1418. Rival French and Italian popes were elected, shattering the church's unity. **(b)** Both events weakened papal authority and increased criticism of the church.
6. (a) *Defender of the Peace* stated that the pope was only the elected head of the church and had no other power. **(b)** Wycliffe also denied the absolute authority of the pope and the need for clergy in achieving salvation. The means of salvation was in the Bible. Huss was influenced by Wycliffe's writings and further denounced church abuses.

271

Reviewing Important Terms

1. vernacular language; **2.** Scholasticism; **3.** domestic system; **4.** Crusades; **5.** barter economy; **6.** journeyman; **7.** market economy; **8.** usury; **9.** merchant guild; **10.** craft guilds; **11.** Miracle plays; **12.** Patriotism; **13.** Apprenticeship; **14.** Troubadours.

Developing Critical Thinking Skills

1. Europeans learned new military technology and siege tactics. Royal powers increased while those of the nobility decreased. The church's political strength increased. Women's status changed because many wives managed estates for their absent husbands. The introduction of new ideas and new products influenced Europeans.

2. Abelard and Aquinas tried to reconcile the faith of the early church writers with Aristotle's reason.

3. (a) Romanesque: round arches, domes, low horizontal lines, thick walls, few windows, dark and simple interiors. Gothic: height and delicate appearance; flying buttresses; high, thin walls with large windows; pointed arches; tall spires; and elaborate interiors. **(b)** It did not conform to classical standards. Critics called it *Gothic,* after the barbarian Goths, to ridicule it.

4. (a) The Crusades and the products of Asia revived trade and caused cities to grow. Town fairs helped break down regional isolation. Medieval capitalists invested in shipbuilding, voyages, manufacturing, and banking. **(b)** It encouraged the development of merchant and craft guilds, town self-government, and led to the decline of serfdom.

1B, 1D, 4A, 3B, 4B, 4D, a4A, a4F, a4H

Reteaching

Have students review the Chapter Summary and the appropriate section and questions in the Unit Synthesis. Discuss the concepts until students demonstrate a clear understanding of the material.

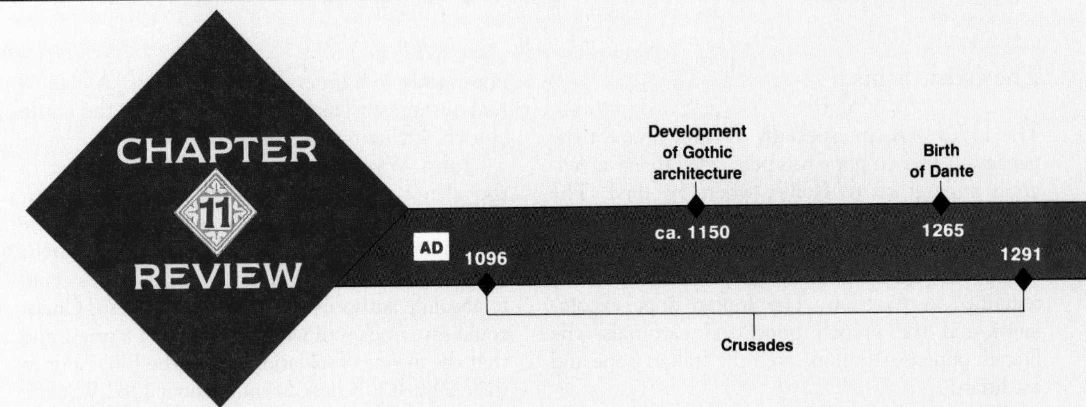

Chapter Summary

The following list contains the key concepts you have learned about the revival of trade and the rise of nations in medieval Europe.

1. The Crusades were organized by Christians chiefly to regain the Holy Land from the Muslims. They had several important effects on Europe: the introduction of new weapons, increased royal power, the weakening of feudal lords, and intellectual and commercial stimulation.
2. Even before the Crusades, trade had begun to revive in Europe. Italians acted as distributors for traders from Asia and from central and northern Europe. Flanders had great commercial importance, as did the Hanseatic League. Trade was enhanced by fairs and led to the development of a monetary and banking system.
3. Towns grew as trade revived. Townspeople gained important rights including freedom, town justice, and commercial privileges. Merchants and artisans organized guilds.
4. Medieval culture flourished with the revival of towns. Vernacular languages developed and were used by such writers as Dante and Chaucer. At great universities scholastic philosophers, including Abelard and Aquinas, sought to reconcile faith and reason. Examples of outstanding medieval architecture are the Romanesque and Gothic churches.
5. National governments continued to grow stronger. After the Hundred Years' War and the Wars of the Roses, England's government became centralized under Henry VII, founder of the Tudor dynasty.
6. In France, Joan of Arc and the French victory over the English in the Hundred Years' War spurred patriotism. Louis XI added much land to the royal territory and helped unify France.
7. In Spain Ferdinand and Isabella created a strong monarchy but weakened the country by driving out the Moors and Jews. Germany and Italy remained disunited until the 1800s.
8. A quarrel between Philip IV of France and Pope Boniface VIII weakened papal authority. The reformers Wycliffe and Huss criticized the church.

On a separate sheet of paper, complete the following review exercises.

Reviewing Important Terms

Supply the term that correctly completes each sentence.

1. Everyday speech is called ________ ________.
2. ________ was the attempt of medieval philosophers to reconcile faith and reason.
3. A method of production in which the workers performed their jobs in their homes was called the ________ ________.
4. ________ were expeditions by Christians to regain the Holy Land from the Muslims.
5. In a ________ ________, goods are exchanged for other goods without the use of money.
6. A skilled artisan who worked for a master for daily wages was a ________.
7. In a ________ ________, land, labor, and capital are controlled by individuals.
8. In the Middle Ages, the church prohibited ________, or the charging of interest on loans.
9. In medieval towns, the organization that gained a monopoly, the sole right to trade there, was called a ________ ________.
10. In the late Middle Ages, the skilled workers who were engaged in manufacturing formed ________ ________.
11. ________ ________ were short dramas on religious or biblical subjects first written in Latin to enhance the church services at Easter and Christmas.
12. ________ is a feeling of loyalty to the country as a whole.
13. ________ was the first stage of training in a craft.
14. ________ were traveling singers who wrote love poems.

Developing Critical Thinking Skills

1. **Summarizing Ideas** What were the effects of the Crusades on Europe?
2. **Analyzing Ideas** How did the teachings of Peter Abelard and Thomas Aquinas build upon those of Plato and Aristotle?
3. **Comparing Ideas** **(a)** Describe the Romanesque and

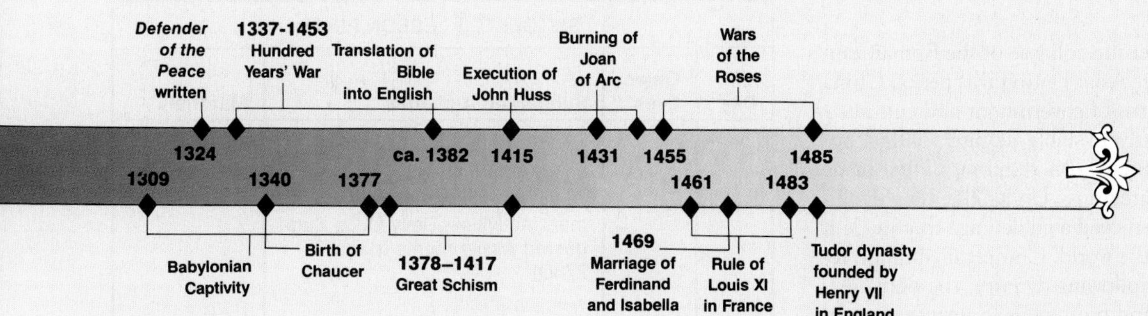

Gothic styles of church architecture. **(b)** Why was the name *Gothic* used for the newer style?

4. **Understanding Cause and Effect** **(a)** What caused trade to increase in Europe in the late Middle Ages? **(b)** In what ways did the increase in trade affect the economy of Europe?
5. **Interpreting Ideas** **(a)** Why was the Black Death so devastating to Europe? **(b)** Why did European recovery take such a long time?

Relating Geography to History

Use the map of the Crusades on page 250 and the map of Europe today on page R12 in order to do the following exercises.

1. List the bodies of water, cities, and islands that Richard's fleet passed through or visited.
2. List the cities and bodies of water crusaders passed through in the First and Fourth Crusades.

Relating Past to Present

1. In the late Middle Ages, the longbow, the cannon, and the pike changed the nature of warfare and contributed to the decline of feudalism. Read Chapter 3 in James Burke's *Connections* (Little, Brown) to find out more about medieval weapons. **(a)** Then name some of the weapons developed in the 1900s. **(b)** What effects have these weapons had on the modern world?
2. Consult your village, town, or city planning agency to obtain the following information:
   (a) What are some of the major building code regulations for housing?
   (b) How are sewage, clean water, and garbage removal provided for or regulated?
   (c) Compare your information with what you have learned about towns and cities in the Middle Ages.

Applying History Study Skills

Before completing this activity, review Building History Study Skills on page 262.

Read the following poem written by a French noble in the 1100s. Then answer the questions that follow.

> "I love the springtide of the year
> When leaves and blossoms do abound,
> And well it pleases me to hear
> The birds that make the woods resound
> With their exulting voices.
> And very well it pleases me
> Tents and pavilions pitched to see,
> And oh, my heart rejoices
> To see armed knights in panoply [full armor]
> Of war on meadow and on lea [pasture]. . . .
>
> And well I like a noble lord
> When boldly the attack he leads,
> For he, whene'er he wields his sword,
> Inspires his men by his brave deeds,
> Their hearts with courage filling.
> When tide of battle's at the flood,
> Each soldier then, in fighting mood,
> To follow should be willing,
> For no man is accounted good
> Till blows he's given and withstood."

1. Why does the poet long for the springtime?
2. How does he feel about the fighting lord?
3. What is the theme of the poem, and which sentences help you to identify the theme?
4. **(a)** How is the poem similar to the troubadour's love song on page 262? **(b)** How is it different?

Investigating Further

1. **Writing a Report** Using encyclopedias or books on the Middle Ages, collect additional information about one of the Crusades. You might find "Triumph of the First Crusade to the Holy Land," *National Geographic* (December 1963), helpful in your research. Then pretend you are a crusader and write an imaginary diary of your experiences on your journey to the Holy Land.
2. **Presenting an Oral Report** Read *Song of Roland* in Gerald Simons's *Barbarian Europe* (Time-Life), which depicts the values of chivalry and the love of battle. Present an oral report on your findings to the class.

5. (a) The losses of population disrupted the continent's social, economic, and religious institutions. **(b)** because of the loss in population.

Relating Geography to History

1. English Channel, Atlantic Ocean, Strait of Gibraltar, Mediterranean Sea, Marseilles, Genoa, Sicily, Crete, Cyprus, Acre.
2. First Crusade: Adriatic Sea, Fourth Crusade: Adriatic Sea, Aegean Sea, Mediterranean Sea.

Relating Past to Present

1. (a) tanks, airplanes, atomic bombs, missiles **(b)** These weapons also threatened the civilian population. Nuclear weapons threaten world existence.
2. (a), (b), (c) Answers will vary.

Applying History Study Skills

1. for chivalry and combat
2. The lord inspires men with his bravery.
3. combat and pageantry; "To see armed knights in panoply"; "When boldly the attack he leads"; "For no man is accounted good Till blows he's given and withstood."
4. (a) begins with the beauties of nature **(b)** emphasizes combat

273

CHAPTER (pages 274–291)

12 Civilization in East Asia Reached New Heights

(100–1644)

CHAPTER OVERVIEW

While the West was struggling after the collapse of the Roman Empire, civilizations flourished in East Asia. During this period China and Japan established stable patterns of government and culture.

Chinese society remained relatively stable despite political upheavals, invasion, and war. Because of this stability, China made notable achievements in art and literature. Under the Tang dynasty, poetry flourished, and China enjoyed a golden age that made it the most sophisticated country in the world. Chinese civilization remained at a high level under the following dynasty, the Song. Although the country was wealthy and prosperous, a new tax system reduced many peasants from landowners to tenant farmers.

In the 1200s the nomadic Mongols invaded China and established the Yuan dynasty. They brought economic growth, governmental reorganization, and more contact with Europeans.

In Japan, Shintoism and deep reverence for the emperor profoundly influenced Japanese society. Other strong influences came from Chinese culture. The Japanese developed a feudal political system and their own distinctive forms of literature and art.

Peoples on the margins of Chinese civilization in Korea and Indochina felt its effect in culture and religion while still maintaining a degree of independence.

SUGGESTED LESSON PLAN

Day	Objectives	Suggested Activities	Materials
1	U7-8,* C1-2	Introducing the Chapter (page 274) Section 1 (pages 275-80, Focus/Motivation (page 275), Presentation (page 276), Closure (page 279), Suggested Teaching Strategies, Enrichment Activities, Daily Quiz, Suggested Assignments (page 273B)	ATE, Pupil's Edition, Teacher's Resource-Bank™
2	U7, C3-5	Section 2 (pages 281-83), Focus/Motivation (page 281), Presentation (page 281), Closure (page 282), Suggested Teaching Strategies, Enrichment Activity, Daily Quiz, Suggested Assignments (page 273C)	ATE, Pupil's Edition, Teacher's Resource-Bank™
3	U8, C6-9	Section 3 (pages 284-89), Focus/Motivation (page 284), Presentation (page 285), Closure (page 287), Suggested Teaching Strategies, Enrichment Activities, Daily Quiz, Suggested Assignments (page 273D)	ATE, Pupil's Edition, Teacher's Resource-Bank™
4	U7-8 C1-9	Chapter 12 Form A Test, Reteaching Worksheet, Chapter 12 Form B Test	Teacher's Resource-Bank™ or Workbook and Test Booklet

*C refers to applicable Chapter Objective, U refers to applicable Unit Goal

BOOKS FOR THE TEACHER

Goodrich, L. Carrington. *A Short History of the Chinese.* Harper & Row. Emphasizes the early periods of Chinese history.

Hall, John Whitney. *Japan: From Prehistory to Modern Times.* Delta Books. Profiles Japanese history.

Morton, W. Scott. *China: Its History and Culture.* Lippincott. Presents a general history of China, with chapters on the Tang and Song dynasties.

Samsom, G. B. *Japan: A Short Cultural History.* Appleton-Century-Crofts. Surveys cultural life of Japan from early history to the Tokugawa shogunate.

BOOKS FOR THE STUDENT

Bloodworth, Dennis. *The Chinese Looking Glass.* Farrar, Straus & Giroux. Presents easy-to-read, entertaining account of traditional Chinese society.

Rugoff, Milton. *Marco Polo's Adventures in China.* American Heritage. Gives colorful account of Polo's journey.

Statler, Oliver. *Japanese Inn.* Random House. Portrays life in ancient Japan.

Turnbull, S. R. *The Samurai.* Macmillan. Gives detailed account of the samurai, with pictures and battle maps.

MULTIMEDIA MATERIALS

Ancient Chinese (mp, 24 min.), Independent Film. Shows how China's history and deeply rooted traditions have continued longer than those of any other civilization.

Ancient Orient (mp, 14 min.), Coronet. Portrays the religions, philosophies, and arts of ancient India, China, and Japan.

Japan: Miracle of Asia (mp, 30 min.), EBE. Describes Japan's rise from a feudal society to a leading industrial nation.

Men Who Made History: Genghis Khan (fs), EBE. Examines the conquests of Genghis Khan and his influence on history.

Past and Present China (fs), Visual. Describes Chinese life during several dynasties. Titles appropriate for Chapter 12: "The Han and Tang Dynasties," "The Song and Yuan Dynasties," "The Home in Imperial China."

People in History: Marco Polo (fs), Educational Audio-Visual. Examines Marco Polo's influence on world history and the social conditions of his time.

Section 1 (pages 275–280)

China Flourished Under a Restored Empire

SECTION OVERVIEW

After the reunification of China under the short-lived Sui dynasty, the Tang dynasty promoted artistic creativity and economic expansion. Buddhism spread rapidly but was suppressed. The Tang dynasty was eventually overthrown and, after years of disunity and civil war, replaced by the Song dynasty. Foreign trade expanded, the arts flourished, the civil service system was perfected, and gunpowder and printing were invented. Agricultural productivity increased greatly during the Tang and Song dynasties, but a change in the tax system left many peasants struggling for survival. Under the Song, more Chinese lived in cities and towns, where they dominated China's social and cultural life.

SUGGESTED TEACHING STRATEGIES

1. **Writing a Diary (Basic)** Have students write diary entries describing a typical day of a peasant and of a city-dweller during the Song dynasty. Read some of the entries aloud. Then lead a discussion comparing the two life styles.
2. **Preparing an Oral Report (Average/Group)** Tea, porcelain, printing, and gunpowder constitute a partial list of Chinese contributions to the world. Have students work in small groups to research and give oral reports on these contributions and their influence on the world. Students may use the following sources: Joesph Needham's *Science and Civilization in China* (Cambridge University Press); and Derk Bodde's *China's Gift to the West* (American Council on Education).

ENRICHMENT ACTIVITIES

1. **Printing Demonstration (Average/Group)** An interested student can demonstrate the art of printing. Edward H. Schafer's *Ancient China* (Time-Life) has a clear and easy-to-follow presentation that will help the student prepare.
2. **Comparing Ideas (Average/ Group)** Have students reread the material on peasant life in Europe during the Middle Ages (see Chapter 10, pages 229-231). Then ask them to write an essay comparing peasant life in Europe with that in China under the Tang. How did the tax system the Tang instituted compare with the labor and dues under the manorial system?

DAILY QUIZ

To assess student understanding of Section 1, give the class the following quiz. (Each item is worth 10 points.)

1. Under what dynasty did the Chinese defeat the Turks, make contact with India, and lead Chinese civilization to its "golden age"? *(Tang)*
2. What type of literature — history, prose, epic, poetry — characterized by the success of Li Bai and Du Fu, became the most popular literary form during the 700s? *(poetry)*
3. What Indian religion greatly influenced Chinese religious life until the 800s? *(Buddhism)*
4. (T or F) Politically the period of the Song Empire could best be characterized as being filled with unrest because of civil war and foreign invasion. *(T)*
5. (T or F) The Song eliminated the system of civil service exams because too much cheating and favoritism had made them unworkable. *(F)*
6. (T or F) During the Tang dynasty, the Chinese invented gunpowder but did not use it immediately for warfare. *(T)*
7. What new crop did the Chinese begin producing during the Song dynasty? *(tea)*
8. The new tax on land begun by the emperors during the Tang dynasty forced many peasants to become ________ ________. *(tenant farmers)*
9. (T or F) During the Song dynasty, many people moved into the cities, even though the great majority of the Chinese people still lived in the country. *(T)*
10. For centuries the Chinese have used the "five flavors" in seasoning their food. Name the five. *(bitter, salty, sour, hot, sweet)*

SUGGESTED ASSIGNMENTS

1. **Critical Thinking Worksheet (Average/Group)** Have students complete Critical Thinking Worksheet 27 in the TEACHER'S RESOURCEBANK™.
2. **Chinese Cooking (Challenging)** Have interested students study recipes for simple meals in Chinese cookbooks. Then have them prepare dishes that can be savored by the entire class, asking each student to determine which of the "five flavors" — bitter, salty, sour, hot, and sweet — or combination thereof each dish contains. If your school is situated near a Chinese restaurant, you may wish to have the entire class use the lunch hour for experiencing Chinese cooking. This suggestion need not apply solely to Chinese cooking but may be used for learning about Thai, Vietnamese, or Japanese foods as well.

Section (pages 281–283)

2 Central Asian Nomads Invaded China and the West

SECTION OVERVIEW

Kublai Khan, a grandson of Genghis Khan, established the Yuan dynasty in North China in 1271. Under Mongol rule China made notable economic progress, contact with Europeans increased, transportation and communications were improved, and local governments were made responsible to the central government. The countries of Indochina adopted features of both Indian and Chinese civilizations, but they also developed national literatures and individual styles of art.

SUGGESTED TEACHING STRATEGIES

1. **Understanding Ideas (Basic)** Ask students to reread the subsection "The Mongol Empire" on pages 281-282. Then have them write an essay describing the means by which the Mongols achieved their conquests in Asia and Europe. They should include in their essays the features of Mongol military technology and tactics *(specially designed saddles and stirrups that enabled Mongol warriors to fire arrows accurately; their speed, mobility, and use of columns of riders)*.
2. **Writing a Diary (Average/Group)** Have students take the role of European people who have just gotten word that the Mongols of the Golden Horde have invaded their territory. They should include in their diaries their fears, the excitement, and then the actual attack and its aftermath. Students may wish to do additional research on the Mongols in encyclopedias or books in their school or local library. Use their diary entries as the basis for a class discussion on the effects of war on the civilian population. During the discussion point out that, in general, modern wars have a much greater impact on civilians than did earlier wars.
3. **Comparing Past and Present (Challenging)** Have students reread the subsection "Civilization Developed in Indochina" on page 283. Then have them do additional research in their school or local library on one of the countries of Indochina — Cambodia (Kampuchea), Laos, Vietnam, Burma, Malaysia, and Thailand. Ask students to write a three-page report on the history — past and present — of the country they have selected. Read one report on each country to the class. Then use the information provided as the basis of a class discussion on outside influences — Chinese or Indian religions and culture, Westernization, Communism — on each country.

ENRICHMENT ACTIVITY

Poetry Reading (Basic) Have interested students read and report on Samuel Taylor Coleridge's poem "Kubla Khan," quoted in the text on page 282. You might have one or two students read this poem to the class.

DAILY QUIZ

To assess student understanding of Section 2, give the class the following quiz. (Each item is worth 10 points.)

1. (T or F) The Mongols were a nomadic people who depended upon the horse for rapid mobility. *(T)*
2. (T or F) The Mongols did not enjoy combat but became excellent warriors because they needed to defend their homeland from constant attack. *(F)*
3. Which of these areas did the Mongols *not* conquer — South China, North China, Korea, Japan? *(Japan)*
4. Which ruler was recognized as head — Great Khan — of the whole Mongol Empire? *(Kublai Khan)*
5. What Venetian merchant traveled to China and stayed there for 20 years during the 1200s? *(Marco Polo)*
6. (T or F) In contrast to the Chinese, the Mongols valued accomplishment in literature and the arts. *(F)*
7. (T or F) After Kublai Khan died, China experienced a long period of prosperity and plenty. *(F)*
8. (T or F) Later Chinese historians denounced the Mongols as savages. *(T)*
9. (T or F) For the most part, the countries of Indochina adopted the political structure of India. *(F)*
10. (T or F) Most people in Indochina practiced Buddhism. *(T)*

SUGGESTED ASSIGNMENTS

1. **Research Reports (Average/Group)** Some students might prepare written or oral reports on the travels of Marco Polo. Sources include Milton Rugoff's *Marco Polo's Adventures in China* (American Heritage), and Marion Koenig's *The Travels of Marco Polo* (Golden Press).
2. **Contrasting Ideas (Average/Group)** Have interested students do research on the culture of three countries of Indochina: Cambodia (Kampuchea), Laos, and Vietnam. Have them prepare an oral or written report on the differing peoples, languages, religions, and artistic and literary achievements of Indochina.
3. **Profile Worksheet (Basic)** Have students complete Profile 12 in the TEACHER'S RESOURCEBANK ™.

Section (pages 284–289)

3 Japan Developed Its Own Government, Society, and Culture

SECTION OVERVIEW

Japan has had two enduring characteristics — the Shinto religion and a deep reverence for its emperor. Early emperors were strong, but later emperors lost power to the leading families, who fought for the position of shogun. At the local level, a feudal system developed. Although frequent warfare occurred, the feudal period was a time of economic and cultural growth. Buddhism spread and inspired landscape architecture, the tea ceremony, and *No* plays.

SUGGESTED TEACHING STRATEGIES

1. **Preteaching Vocabulary (Basic)** You may wish to preteach the following important vocabulary terms: shogun, samurai, Bushido, seppuku, daimyo (*page 286*). Ask students to compare the feudal system of Japan with that of medieval Europe.

*2. **Reading About History: Reading a Chart (Basic)** Have students reread "Building History Study Skills" on page 288. Then on the chalkboard or an overhead projector, draw a time line showing the dates listed below. Have students read the time line and then volunteer to put the appropriate event next to each year.

405	Chinese writing introduced into Japan
550	Buddhism brought to Japan
702	Law code modeled on the Chinese
794	New capital of Heian-kyo built
early 800s-mid-1100s	Fujiwara family controlled central government
1192	The Minamoto introduced the role of shogun
1291	Mongol invasion fleet dispersed by *Kamikaze*
1338	Ashikaga family took over the shogunate

3. **Organizing a Report (Average/Group)** Organize the class into groups to work on reports on the samurai. Suggested topics include: samurai armor and weapons; the life and code of the samurai; battle tactics; and a description of Japanese feudalism. Groups should present their findings to the rest of the class. Sources include S. R. Turnbull's *The Samurai: A Military History* (Macmillan) and Jonathan N. Leonard's *Early Japan* (Time-Life).

ENRICHMENT ACTIVITIES

1. **Understanding Customs (Average/Group)** Have interested students research the Japanese tea ceremony. Then ask them to dramatize it before the class — first without explanation and then again explaining the steps and their significance.
2. **Interpreting Literature (Challenging)** Assign advanced readers to read *The Tale of Genji.* After their reading, have students write a brief report describing court life and explaining the customs of Japanese society that influence Genji's behavior.

DAILY QUIZ

To assess student understanding of Section 3, give the class the following quiz. (Each item is worth 10 points.)

1. List the four main Japanese islands. *(Honshu, Kyushu, Shikoku, Hokkaido)*
2. (T or F) The *Kamikaze* protected the Japanese from Kublai Khan's Mongol fleet. *(T)*
3. What is the foremost religion in Japan, whose name means the "way of the gods"? *(Shinto)*
4. What religion did Chinese missionaries bring to Japan in 550? *(Buddhism)*
5. Just as the Romans borrowed cultural ideas from the Greeks, the Japanese borrowed many of their cultural traditions from the ______ . *(Chinese)*
6. The Fujiwara family best exemplifies the control some families exercised over what national political leader? *(emperor)*
7. Important families controlled the government by developing the new position of ______ . *(shogun)*
8. Warrior landlords, or ______, led military units. *(samurai)*
9. These warlords followed a code called ______ that stressed bravery, loyalty, and honor. *(Bushido)*
10. ______ controlled Korea through much of its history, influencing politics and culture. *(China)*

SUGGESTED ASSIGNMENTS

1. **Critical Thinking Worksheet (Average/Group)** Have students complete Critical Thinking Worksheet 28 in the TEACHER'S RESOURCEBANK™.
2. **Review Worksheet (Basic)** Have students complete Review Worksheet 12 in the TEACHER'S RESOURCEBANK™.
3. **Skill Worksheet (Basic)** Have students complete Skill Worksheet 12 in the TEACHER'S RESOURCEBANK™.
4. **Geography Application Sheet (Basic)** Have students complete Geography Application Sheet 6 in the TEACHER'S RESOURCEBANK™.

For suggested lesson plan, additional teaching strategies, enrichment activities, daily quizzes, and suggested assignments, see pages 273A–273D.

Introducing the Chapter
Refer students to a world map or the map of Asia on page 276. Ask them to speculate about how Japan could borrow so extensively from Chinese culture and yet resist a complete cultural and political takeover by the Chinese. *(Answers will vary. Students should include the following: The proximity of Japan to China would make it possible for a traveler to visit Japan. However, as the Mongols discovered, invasion of the islands was difficult. This relative isolation made it possible for the Japanese to choose which cultural influences they would accept and which they would reject.)*

CHAPTER

12

Civilization in East Asia Reached New Heights

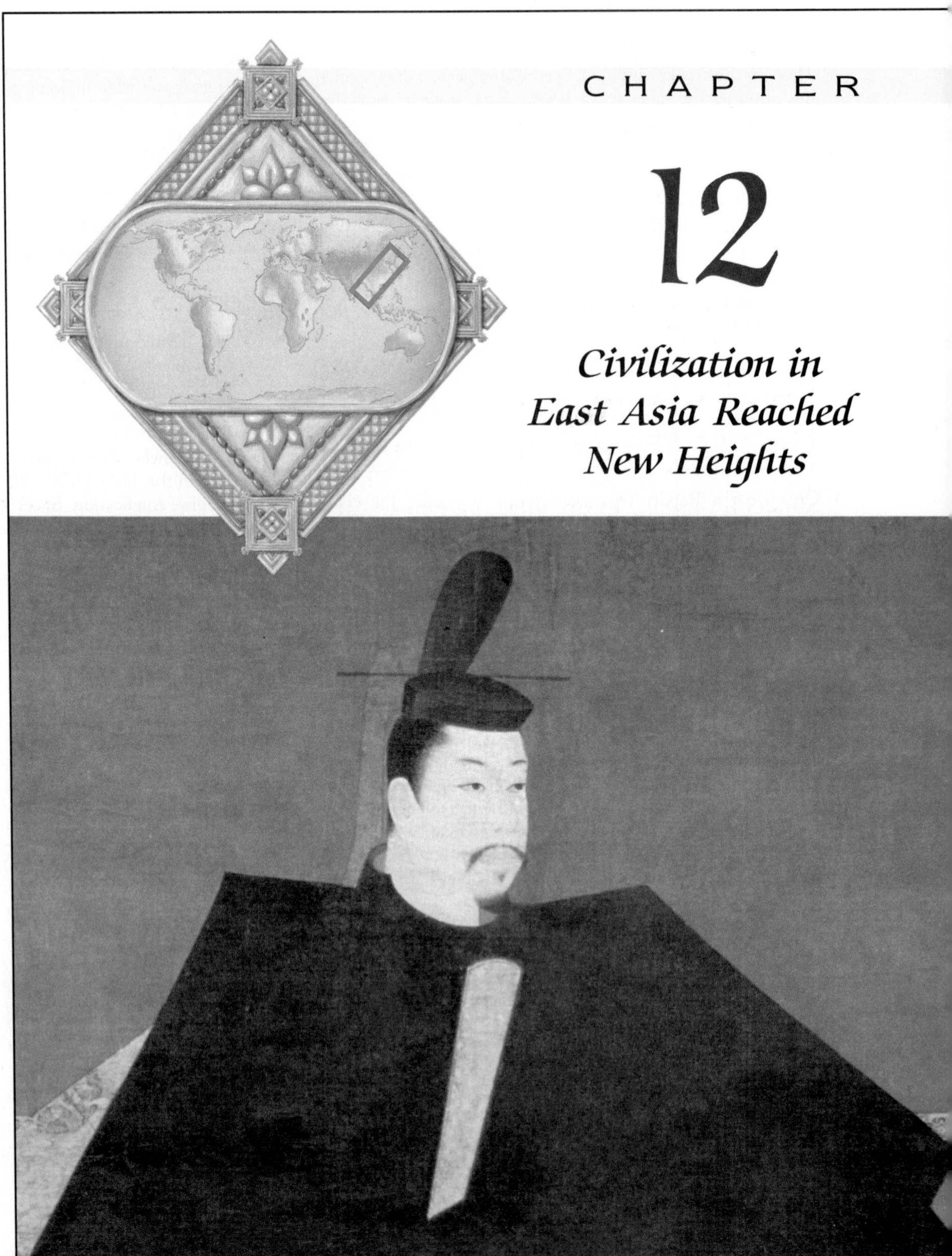

CHAPTER FOCUS

Place China, Indochina, Japan, and Korea

Time 100–1644

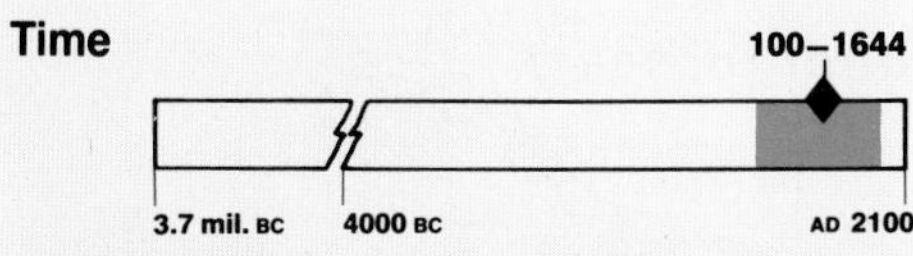

Significance

From about 500 to 1644, great civilizations flourished in East Asia. The Chinese and Japanese established complex patterns of government, society, and culture. The attitudes and institutions they developed influenced Korea and Indochina as well as other neighboring countries and have lasted into modern times.

The Chinese developed a remarkably inventive civilization, even though the region experienced a considerable amount of political unrest during this period. Chinese culture extended far beyond the country's borders. Korea and Indochina felt China's strong influence, although they managed to maintain their own political and cultural identities.

A different civilization emerged on the islands of Japan. Although enormously influenced by Chinese culture, the Japanese developed their own distinct culture and created traditions as long-lasting as those of China.

Through their literature, art, religion, and political structure, these two countries, over more than a thousand years, advanced to a level of social and intellectual achievement that the West could well envy.

Terms to Define

shogun	Bushido
samurai	daimyo

People to Identify

Li Bai	Kublai Khan
Du Fu	Rabban Bar Sauma
Genghis Khan	Ashikaga

Places to Locate

Grand Canal	Karakorum
Chang'an	Kyoto
Beijing	Kamakura
Hangzhou	Korea

Questions to Guide Your Reading

1 In what ways did China flourish under a restored empire?
2 Who were the central Asian nomads who invaded China and the West?
3 In what ways did the Japanese develop their own politics, society, and culture?

◀ ***Shogun Yoritomo Minamoto***

Written in the late 1500s or early 1600s, a strict code of chivalry and conduct called Bushido *acted as a guide for the Japanese samurai, or warriors. Reminiscent of the standards expected of the knights during the medieval period in Europe, one part of the code stated:*

> *"One who is a samurai must before all things keep constantly in mind, by day and by night, from the morning when he takes up his chopsticks to eat his New Year's breakfast to Old Year's night when he pays his yearly bills, the fact that he has to die. That is his chief business. If he is always mindful of this, he will be able to live in accordance with the paths of Loyalty and Filial Duty, will avoid myriads of evils and adversities, keep himself free from disease and calamity and moreover enjoy a long life. He will also be a fine personality with many admirable qualities."*

1 China Flourished Under a Restored Empire

In the West the Roman Empire never recovered after its collapse in the late 400s. In the East, however, the Chinese defeated the Huns and other invaders from Tibet and Mongolia and established a unified empire. By the 600s this empire emerged stronger, wealthier, and grander than the Han dynasty.

The Sui and Tang Dynasties

The short-lived Sui (SWEE) dynasty succeeded in reuniting China in 589. In their brief period of power, Sui rulers oversaw the building of one of the engineering marvels of the ancient world—the Grand Canal. By skillfully using existing waterways between the Huang He and Chang Jiang, and also by digging new ones, the Chinese successfully linked North and South China for the first time in history. This efficiency in engineering did not extend to governing, however, for the Sui rulers proved overambitious and unskilled in administration. They tried unsuccessfully to conquer southern Manchuria and northern Korea and were defeated by invading Turks in 615. An uprising in

Chapter Objectives
After studying Chapter 12, students will be able to:

1. Describe the Tang dynasty and how the Buddhist religion influenced its political life.
2. Summarize the social, cultural, and economic changes that the Song brought to China.
3. Outline the Mongol conquest of China and Asia and the cultural changes imposed upon the Chinese by the victors.
4. Summarize early contacts between Europeans and the Chinese under the Mongols.
5. Describe the influences of Chinese and Indian culture upon the peoples of Indochina.
6. Describe Japan's physical setting, climate, and geographical advantages.
7. Summarize Shintoism and Buddhism within the Japanese context.
8. Outline Japanese feudalism, its relation to political development, and the concept of *Bushido.*
9. Describe the Chinese cultural impact upon Japan and Korea.

SECTION 1

Focus/Motivation
The Tang land tax turned many Chinese peasants into tenant farmers. Ask students why the income of a farmer is unpredictable. Of what advantage is a single tax based on land? What are

the disadvantages? Ask students to suggest alternatives to this system. *(Answers will vary. Students might include the following: Farmers' incomes are unpredictable because they are at the mercy of the elements. A tax on land provides the government with a guaranteed income. In good years farmers can make a profit because they have more crops to sell and their tax remains fixed. In bad years farmers have to pay the fixed rate although their income drops. As alternatives, students might suggest a tax based on the amount of crops grown, a reduction in the tax rate during bad years, or delayed tax payments.)*

Presentation Summarizing Ideas (Average/Group)

Have students make a chart with three columns in their notebooks. Each column should be labeled with one of the following headings: *Sui dynasty, Tang dynasty,* and *Song dynasty.* Ask students to reread the subsections "The Sui and Tang Dynasties" and "China Under the Song Dynasty," on pages 275-280. Then ask students to list under the appropriate dynasty the major accomplishments of each. *(The list under the Sui dynasty should include: reunited China, Grand Canal built to link North and South China. The list under the Tang dynasty should include: defeated*

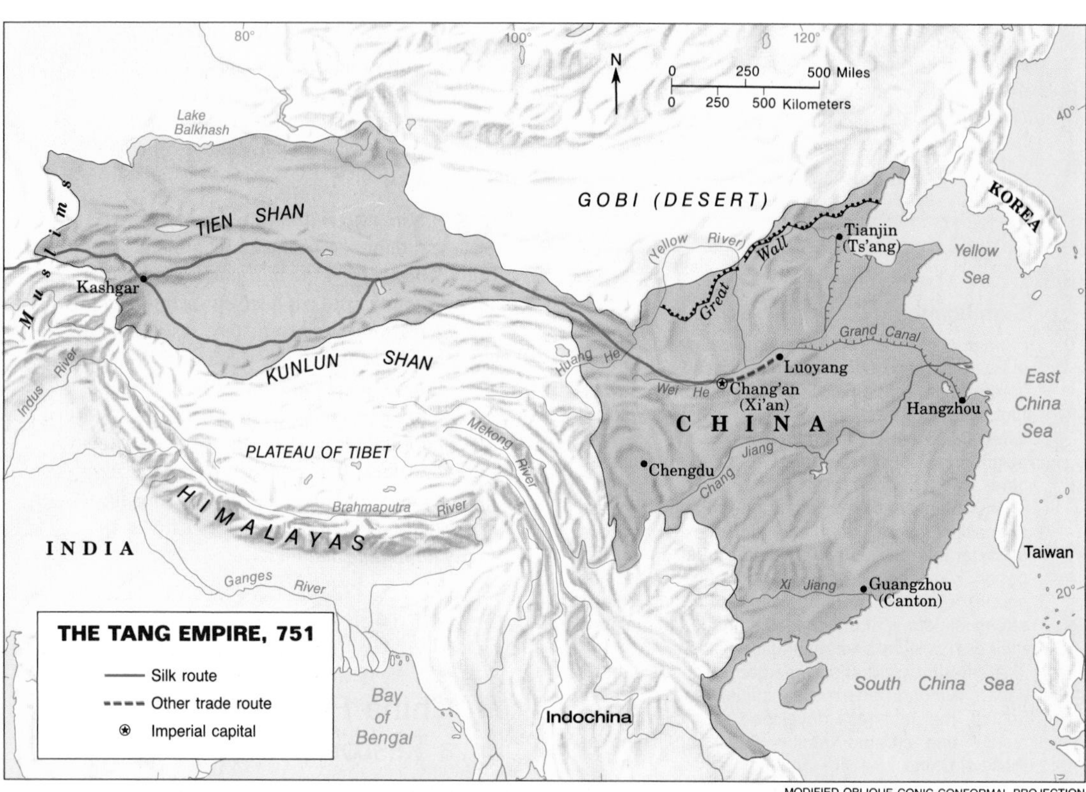

Learning from Maps *In 751 the Muslims defeated the Chinese on China's western frontier at the Battle of Talas. Which city on the Silk Route is located in the Tien Shan?* **Kashgar**

618 ended the Sui dynasty and ushered in a new dynasty—the Tang.

Expansion under the Tang. The early Tang rulers defeated the invading Turks to the north and west and extended China's frontiers farther west than ever before (see map, this page). Tang rulers made contact with India and the Muslim Empire, and Chinese ideas greatly influenced China's eastern neighbors, Korea and Japan. This contact with other peoples also influenced and enhanced the culture of China.

The Tang established their capital at Chang'an (CHAHNG • AHN). During the 700s and 800s, about 2 million people lived in and around Chang'an, making it the largest city in the world at that time. The city served not only as the center of government but also as a center of culture. People from many parts of the world made Chang'an their home. In its marketplaces Arabs, Persians, Jews, Greeks, and native Chinese shopped side by side.

Like the Han dynasty centuries earlier, the Tang gave China a golden age. Although the Tang dynasty itself lasted only until 906, it began a 1,000-year period during which China could be described as the most powerful, the most sophisticated, and the wealthiest country in the world.

Literature under the Tang. During the Tang dynasty, numerous Chinese poets created an abundance of beautiful literature. Later Chinese anthologies, or literary collections, include more than 48,900 poems by more than 2,300 Tang poets. Although exact opposites in terms of personality, two writers of the 700s represent the best of these poets.

Li Bai (LEE BY), a Daoist, spent a great deal of his life seeking pleasure. His writings—happy, light, and elegant—described the delights of life. According to Chinese legend, Li Bai became tipsy and drowned while reaching from a boat for his reflection in the moonlit water.

● Some Chinese considered Buddhism a foreign religion and disliked it for that reason.

History Through the Arts

SCULPTURE

Tang Camel

This lively ceramic figure of a two-humped camel, approximately 2.5 feet (.75 meters) tall, was used as a tomb figure during the Tang dynasty (618–906). The practice of burying pottery replicas of servants and favorite animals was widespread in ancient times. It replaced the older, more primitive custom of killing slaves and cattle in order to provide the dead person with company and food in the afterworld.

In addition to servants and animals, the Chinese also buried figures of musicians, dancers, bodyguards, and grooms. Although tomb figures were made long before the Han dynasty (202 B.C.–A.D. 220), the realistic horses and camels of the Tang period are regarded as the finest.

The brilliant colors, the sense of drama, and the joyous pose of this camel are typical of the rebirth in art that took place under Tai Zong (TY ZOOHNG), the second Tang emperor. During his reign China experienced great prosperity and expanded its borders. Ceramists began to borrow colors and motifs from Persia, India, and Syria, becoming more international in style.

invading Turks and extended frontiers, poetry flourished, gunpowder invented, first book printed [Diamond Sutra], and a new system of taxation. The list under the Song dynasty should include: expanded foreign trade, perfected porcelain making and landscape painting, perfected civil service system.) Call upon a student to put his or her chart on the chalkboard or an overhead projector. Use this information to conduct a class discussion on the Tang and the Song rulers.

Du Fu (DOO FOO), on the other hand, possessed a serious, even solemn, nature and devoutly followed the teachings of Confucius. His carefully written lyrics showed his deep concern about the suffering and tragedy of human life.

Religion in Tang China. Missionaries from India introduced Buddhism into China during the Han dynasty. Under the Tang dynasty, Buddhism reached its peak there. Wealthy believers donated land for monasteries. Many different sects developed, the most famous of which is known by its later Japanese name, Zen. Zen Buddhism stressed meditation as a means to enlightenment and showed a marked similarity to Daoism. Many Chinese peasants found Buddhism and Daoism closely related. Inspired by the example of Buddhism, the people organized Daoist sects and parishes so that Daoism became a religion. In later centuries the religion of the common people in China contained a complicated blend of Buddhist and Daoist teachings.

In time the growing wealth of Buddhist monasteries began to alarm government officials. They tried to tax the monastery lands and sometimes seized the monasteries' precious art objects for the emperor's treasury. In the middle of the 800s, an insane, fanatically anti-Buddhist emperor began to ● persecute Buddhists. He destroyed 40,000 shrines and 4,600 monasteries and forced 260,000 monks and nuns to give up their religious duties and return to ordinary life. Buddhism continued to exist as a religion in China, but it never again became as important a force in Chinese life.

A revival of Confucianism occurred during the Tang dynasty. The government further developed civil service examinations so that once again Chinese scholars stressed the Confucian classics. The construction of temples for worshiping Confucius reinforced this emphasis on Confucian philosophy, and it continued as the main religion of China's governing classes until the early 1900s.

The decline of the Tang dynasty. The Tang dynasty reached its height about 750 and then gradually declined under weak emperors. By 900, tax revenues had diminished, nomadic peoples had invaded, and governors in the provinces had challenged the emperors' power. The Tang dynasty was overthrown in 906 when the last emperor, a child, was murdered.

China Under the Song Dynasty

In 960 Zhao Kuangyin (JOW KWAHNG • YIN) established the Song (SOOHNG) dynasty. Like the Tang, the Song faced foreign invasions and civil wars.

By the mid-900s the principal foreign pressure came from Mongols called the Khitan, in the north. They had occupied Chinese territory in southern Manchuria and in time invaded as far south as the Huang He. When the Khitan threatened the Song capital at Kaifeng (KY • FUHNG), the Song emperors kept the peace only by paying a

277

1A, 1B, a1A, a1C, a4B, a4C

● Hangzhou

■ During the Tang dynasty, civil service examinations were open to aristocrats only. Under the Song this changed, and it became possible for boys of lowly origins to rise to high government positions. In practice only sons of wealthy landlords became scholar-officials.

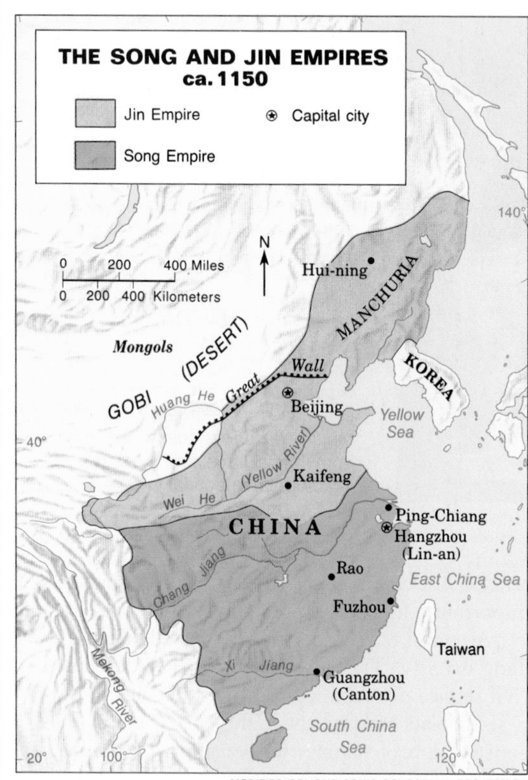

Learning from Maps *Foreigners established the Jin dynasty in the north, dividing China and forcing the Song south. What city became the capital of the Song?* ●

huge tribute. By 1042 these tributes cost the Song more than 200,000 ounces of silver annually, a tremendous burden.

Another central Asian people, the Jurchen, moved into Manchuria and took over northern China. This again divided China. The Jurchen established the Jin dynasty in the north, with its capital at Beijing (BAY • JING), while Hangzhou (HAHNG • JOH) became the capital of the Song dynasty in the south (see map, this page).

Culture. Despite the problems of the Song emperors, Chinese civilization remained at a high level under their rule. Foreign trade expanded, boosting the hard-pressed treasury. Overseas commerce centered on Hangzhou and Guangzhou (GWAHNG • JOH). A thriving caravan trade also brought goods in from central Asia and India.

A Chinese customs list of the year 999 shows exports of gold, silver, and copper "cash" (a small coin). It also lists porcelain—a fine, translucent pottery—which from this period on was one of China's most valuable exports. Song artisans perfected the art of making porcelain, creating delicate vases as thin as eggshell.

Song artists also produced beautiful landscape paintings. Inspired partly by the Daoist love of nature, they painted scenes of natural grandeur, with jagged mountain peaks rising above misty hills and rushing water. Many of these landscapes were painted on silk.

The civil service system. The Chinese further improved their civil service system during the Song dynasty. Examinations took place in the capital every three years. To qualify for these, an individual first had to pass an examination at the local level. Fewer than 10 percent of those who tried this succeeded, and fewer than 10 percent of that group passed the national examination.

Because of the intense competition for civil service employment, steps had to be taken to prevent ■ cheating and corrupt practices by government officials, who might accept bribes or be swayed by friends. Candidates were identified by numbers, not names, and guards watched them take the examination. Clerks then copied the candidates' papers so that no one's handwriting would be recognized. Finally, three judges read each paper.

Great inventions. The Chinese invented gunpowder during the Tang dynasty but used it at that time only in firecrackers. They first used it for warfare as an explosive around the year 1100.

Printing was an even greater invention of the Chinese. They had learned very early how to make ink and paper. The first step toward printing probably came in A.D. 175, during the Han dynasty, when the Chinese classics were carved in stone. Artisans could copy these writings by carefully fitting damp paper over the stone inscription and patting the flat surface with soot. This resulted in a white-on-black image of the original.

The next step in printing probably came with seals of metal or wood on which an inscription was carved in reverse. By the 600s such seals had become quite large, and the images they created resembled today's block prints.

The oldest printed book is the *Diamond Sutra,* a Buddhist religious text printed in China in 868, during the Tang dynasty. It was made in the form of a roll of six sheets of paper pasted together. Carved blocks were used to print the words on the roll.

278

Movable type, by which separate characters can be arranged freely to form words and sentences, apparently came into China from Korea about 1030. The characters were made of wood, porcelain, or copper. This technique did not become common in China, however. Since the Chinese language consists of so many characters, printers would have had to make about 40,000 separate movable blocks to represent them all. For this reason the Chinese preferred blocks carved with an entire page of text.

Peasant life. By about 1050 China's population may have exceeded 100 million. The population consisted mostly of peasants, who lived and worked in the countryside. Two important changes took place in peasant life during the Tang and Song dynasties.

One change stemmed from technological improvements in agriculture. Many extensive water-control projects had been built in South China. As a result, the number of irrigated fields where rice could be grown increased. In addition, a new kind of quick-ripening rice from Southeast Asia made it possible to grow two crops of rice each year instead of only one. Also from Southeast Asia came an entirely new crop, tea, which soon became a popular drink throughout China.

Thus agricultural productivity greatly increased, especially in South China. Peasants had more work to do than ever before, but they also had a greater chance to produce surplus food. That surplus could be sold in the many small market towns found in rural areas.

The second important change in the life of the peasants resulted from a change in the agricultural tax system during the Tang dynasty. In the past, individuals had been taxed. Every peasant owed the government a certain amount of agricultural produce and labor each year. However, peasants living on the tax-free estates of high officials did not have to pay taxes. After the 700s the land itself was taxed, and tax-free estates no longer existed. Taxes had to be paid in produce according to the amount of land a person owned.

The government benefited from this change, but the peasants did not. They could not escape to

SECTION 1

Closure

Ask students to explain how Buddhism came into China and what effect it had upon Chinese religion. *(Indian missionaries introduced Buddhism. Many different sects developed; Zen Buddhism was the most famous. Its similarity to Daoism inspired a blend of Buddhism and Daoism that appealed to the common people.)*

Learning from Pictures *The Chinese emperor had important administrative and ceremonial obligations (right). The Song emperors relaxed at the Lotus Pavilion (above).*

279

1B, 1C, a1A, a1C, a4A, a4H, a4K, a4L

Review Answers

1. ***Li Bai:*** Daoist poet of the Tang dynasty; ***Du Fu:*** Confucian poet of the Tang dynasty; ***Zen:*** Japanese name for the most famous form of Chinese Buddhism; ***Diamond Sutra:*** a Buddhist text that is the world's oldest printed book
2. ***Grand Canal:*** linked North and South China between Huang He and Chang Jiang; ***Chang'an:*** Tang capital city; ***Kaifeng:*** Song capital city; ***Beijing:*** Jin capital city; ***Hangzhou:*** capital city of Song dynasty
3. Sui, Tang, Song, Jin
4. (a) To qualify, an individual had to pass an exam at the local level. **(b)** Guards watched during testing. Examinations were numbered and recopied by clerks to prevent bribery of corrupt officials. Three judges read each paper.
5. During the Han dynasty, printers fitted damp paper onto a carved stone and patted the flat surface with soot, making a likeness of the original. The next step came with seals on which an inscription was carved in reverse. Eventually, blocks were carved with an entire page of text.
6. Water-control projects and quick-ripening rice greatly increased agricultural productivity. Lords placed new taxes on the land instead of on individual peasants. Many peasants were forced to sell their land and become tenant farmers.

tax-free estates when they produced too little to pay taxes. Instead they had to sell their land and become tenant farmers. As tenant farmers they paid the landlords high rents, sometimes half the crops they raised. From Song times on, the power of landlords became a serious problem in China. It was not solved until the 1900s.

For many Chinese peasants, the new tax system made life a struggle for survival. To avoid losing their land, they had to stay out of debt. If they lost their land and became tenant farmers, they worried about not having enough food to eat after paying their rent. During the growing season, they worked in the fields from early morning until sundown. During the winter they repaired their simple tools and wove cloth. Young children were kept busy collecting firewood, bringing in water, and watching the family's chickens or pigs. Only for a short time each winter could they go to school—if their village had one—to learn a little writing and arithmetic.

Two or three times a year, peasant families had a chance to relax at festivals held in the villages. Everyone would gather to watch jugglers or acrobats and to enjoy feasting and music. Then the daily routine of hard work would begin again.

City life. During the Song period, a larger share of China's population than ever before came to live in cities and towns. Hangzhou, the capital of the dynasty after 1127, had a population of almost 1 million. Marco Polo, a merchant and explorer from Venice, visited the city in the 1200s and recorded his amazement at its size and beauty. In addition to Hangzhou, several smaller cities and many towns were scattered throughout the empire. Although outnumbered by rural peasants, the city dwellers dominated Chinese society and culture.

The cities of Song China bustled with activity. Huge shipments of rice, fish, and vegetables arrived daily in the marketplaces. Streets were jammed with traffic—carts for transporting goods, sedan chairs in which wealthy people were carried along by servants, peddlers with their goods on bamboo poles, and large numbers of pedestrians. Boats and barges jammed the canals that crisscrossed many cities in South China. Shops specializing in luxury goods—embroidered silks, pearl necklaces, chess sets, and printed books—lined the main streets. Shops selling noodles, candles, and other articles of everyday use lined the narrow side streets and alleyways. Amusement quarters provided puppet shows, plays, and performances by dancers and acrobats.

Officials and wealthy merchants lived in fine homes surrounded by gardens and artificial lakes. Ordinary people lived in crowded apartments, with only one or two rooms for an entire family. Some people had no homes at all. They begged for food and slept wherever they could find shelter. The government set up hospitals and orphanages to help the poor. It also gave food and money to the needy after disasters. However, poverty remained a serious problem in China's cities. In times of great floods or famines, peasants would crowd into the cities and increase the numbers of poor.

Chinese food. Many of the foods found in Chinese homes and restaurants today were also served during the Song dynasty. The development of agriculture in South China made rice the basic food of the Chinese diet. Ordinary people ate rice three times a day, with small portions of dried fish or pork on the side. Wealthy people enjoyed a healthier diet. They could afford fresh fruits and vegetables and greater quantities of fish and meat.

Whether rich or poor, the Chinese prepared their food in the same way. Because of a scarcity of firewood, food had to be cooked as quickly as possible. Meat and vegetables were cut into small pieces first and then stir-fried for only a few minutes. The Chinese used chopsticks instead of forks and knives, probably because they served the food already cut into bite-sized pieces. Various spices and seasonings added flavor. For centuries the Chinese had believed in the concept of "the five flavors"—bitter, salty, sour, hot, and sweet. They tried to achieve a mixture of these flavors in the meals they cooked, which made even simple peasant food varied and interesting in taste.

SECTION 1 REVIEW

1. **Identify** Li Bai, Du Fu, Zen, *Diamond Sutra*
2. **Locate** Grand Canal, Chang'an, Kaifeng, Beijing, Hangzhou
3. **Organizing Ideas** List the names of the four dynasties established in China from 589 to the 1200s.
4. **Interpreting Ideas** **(a)** How did a person qualify for the civil service exams? **(b)** How were the exams administered?
5. **Expressing Ideas** Describe the invention and development of printing in China.
6. **Summarizing Ideas** What were two important changes in the lives of Chinese peasants that took place during the Tang and Song dynasties?

1A, 1B, a1B, a1C, a4B, a4C

2 Central Asian Nomads Invaded China and the West

The nomadic peoples who lived in central Asia, to the north and northwest of China proper, inhabited lands not well suited to farming. As a result, they raised horses and sheep and spent their lives moving their herds from one pasture to another. Often they covered vast distances in a year. The hardships of outdoor life made these nomads sturdy and self-reliant. They were also fierce warriors. A strong leader could organize these rival clans of nomads into a disciplined fighting force ready to conquer vast lands.

Such leaders emerged among the Huns and other central Asian nomadic tribes. Many invaded China over the centuries, but the greatest nomadic leader of all times was Genghis Khan (JENG • guh SKAHN). With his fighting force of Mongols, he created the largest empire the world has ever known (see map, this page).

The Mongol Empire

The Mongols inhabited the area to the northwest of China, a region now called Mongolia. At most, they numbered 2 million people. At its height the Mongol army consisted of about 130,000 cavalry troops. Usually no more than 30,000 of these troops engaged in any one campaign. With their superior military technology and battle tactics, however, they were able to conquer vast and heavily populated territories.

Before the invention of firearms, warriors on horseback had a great advantage over soldiers on foot. Mongol troops, who took extra horses with

Learning from Maps *Mongol cavalries captured much of Asia. The Mongol's armada, however, was not very successful. What country did the Mongols try to invade across the East China Sea?* **Japan**

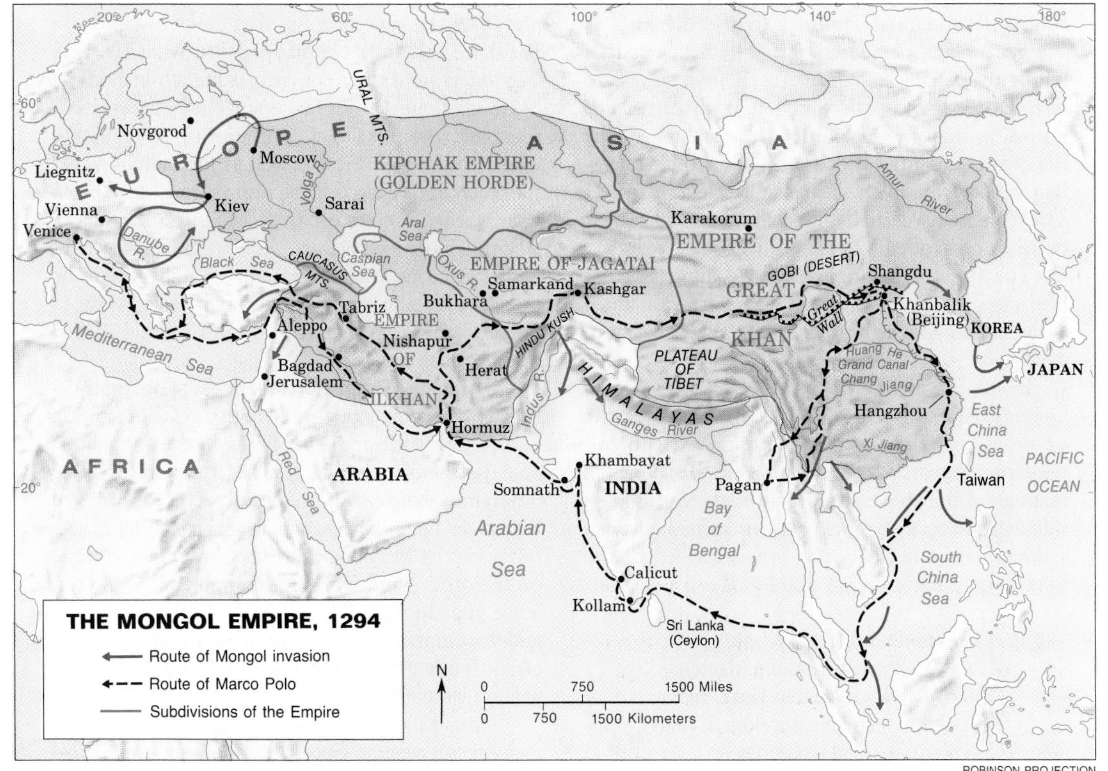

SECTION 2

Focus/Motivation
Use the map of the Mongol Empire on this page as the basis for a class discussion. Ask students to name the areas included in the empire. *(China, Korea, central Asia, Persia, Mesopotamia, and eastern Europe.)* Ask students why they think the empire was divided into four parts. *(Answers will vary. Students might suggest that the empire was so large it had to be divided for administrative purposes.)* Have students speculate on why the Mongols succeeded in conquering so large an area. *(Answers might include the following: superior military technology and tactics, and a well-trained, highly organized army.)* As students read the section, have them check their hypotheses against the text.

Presentation
Relating Past and Present (Average/Group)
Have students reread the subsection "Civilization Developed in Indochina" on page 283. Ask them to name the countries of Indochina. *(Cambodia, Laos, and Vietnam. Geographers often include Burma, Malaysia, and Thailand as well.)* Then ask students to describe the effects that Indian and Chinese civilization had on

● **Kublai Khan used the government institutions developed by the Chinese to rule his Chinese territories. The Mongols recognized the superiority of Chinese culture over their own.**

the peoples of Indochina. *(Students should point out that Chinese Buddhism, Daoism, and Confucianism were transplanted from China, and Buddhism became the main religion of most people in Indochina. Indian influence is evident in Cambodia, especially in temple architecture. Hinduism was also strong.)* Ask students what they believe to be the relationship between China and Indochina today. *(Answers will vary. Students might point out that though both China and the three countries of Indochina—Cambodia, Laos, and Vietnam—are Communist nations, the Chinese have fought a border war with Vietnam and those two nations support rival groups in war-torn Cambodia.)*

SECTION 2

Closure

Have students explain why and how the Mongols established large empires and what contribution they made in China. *(Answers will vary. Students should point out that the nomadic Mongols were self-reliant and hardy, and under a capable leader like Genghis Khan they became a superb military force, conquering vast territories with their superior military technology and tactics. In China the Mongols improved communications and made local governments directly responsible to the government in Beijing. The emperors under later*

them on campaigns, could cover up to 90 miles (145 kilometers) in one day. Specially designed saddles and iron stirrups enabled them to fire arrows with deadly accuracy while moving at full speed. On the open plains of central Asia, they learned to make good use of their speed and mobility on horseback. In battle seemingly endless columns of Mongol riders surrounded the enemy in the same way that they surrounded wild game. Equally important, the Mongolian soldiers enjoyed combat. It provided a test of their abilities and a way to acquire riches, honor, and personal power.

In the early 1200s, Mongols under Genghis Khan swept down from Karakorum (kar • uh • KOHR • uhm), their headquarters. They captured Beijing and renamed it Khanbalik (kahn • buh • LEEK). They then turned westward, conquering central Asia and most of Persia. Under Kublai Khan (KOO • bluh KAHN), a grandson of Genghis Khan, the Mongols completed their conquest of China. The Mongols also conquered Korea and tried unsuccessfully to conquer Japan.

Another grandson of Genghis Khan, Batu, invaded Europe, sweeping with his troops across Russia, Poland, and Hungary to the outskirts of Vienna. They plundered city after city, either killing the inhabitants or taking them as slaves. To terrified Europeans, the Mongolian forces became known as the Golden Horde—"golden" for all the riches they acquired and "horde" after the Mongolian word *ordo,* which means "elite cavalry force." The Mongols eventually left Poland and Hungary, but they controlled Russia for almost 200 years.

The Mongol Empire was divided into four parts (see map, page 281). These four parts remained united for about a century and then slowly began to drift apart.

In 1260 Kublai Khan was given the title of Great Khan and recognized as the head of the whole Mongol Empire. He incorporated the cultural refinements of the Chinese in his personal manners and at his court. In addition to the magnificent palace in Beijing, he also owned a lavish summer palace north of the city, described by the English poet Samuel Taylor Coleridge:

> "In Xanadu did Kubla Khan
> A stately pleasure-dome decree,
> Where Alph, the sacred river, ran
> Through caverns measureless to man
> Down to a sunless sea."

Life under Mongol rule. In 1271 Kublai Khan established the Yuan (YOO • AHN) dynasty in North China with Beijing as his capital. Yuan forces defeated the Song dynasty in South China in 1279 and ruled all of China until 1368. ●

Under Mongol rule China made notable economic progress. During more than a century of invasion and warfare, its population had declined from 100 million to only 59 million. With the restoration of peace, however, the population began to increase.

Kublai extended the Grand Canal from the Huang He to Beijing in order to ship rice from South China to his new and expanding capital city. Next to the canal he built a stone-surfaced highway that stretched for 1,100 miles (1,770 kilometers) between Hangzhou and Beijing. A messenger could cover this distance in 40 days. Kublai also linked China to India and Persia by post roads or mail routes, which greatly improved trade.

Contacts with Europeans. During Mongol rule Europeans and Chinese became better acquainted with one another. Among the Europeans living in China at this time were Russian artisans and soldiers captured by the Golden Horde, a Parisian goldsmith kidnapped in what is now Yugoslavia, and the nephew of a French bishop.

King Louis IX of France and the pope in Rome sent ambassadors to China during the 1200s. Christian missionaries, as well as the famous Venetian merchant Marco Polo, also traveled to China. Polo's Chinese counterpart, Rabban Bar Sauma of Beijing, journeyed across Asia to Persia, then to Constantinople, and eventually to Italy, where he talked with the pope. Bar Sauma also went to France, where he met King Philip IV and visited the University of Paris.

Chinese-Mongol differences. The Yuan dynasty had brought certain benefits to China. But a natural antagonism existed between the conquerors and the conquered that resulted from the striking differences between Mongol and Chinese ways of living. To begin with, their languages differed. As warriors, the Mongols valued action. The Chinese, on the other hand, valued accomplishment in literature and the arts. The Chinese disliked the smell and appearance of the invaders, who did not wash often. They also objected to the freedom Mongol women were allowed.

When Kublai Khan died in 1294, he left China to weak successors. Seven Mongol emperors ruled

● The civilizations of Southeast Asia were never dominated by either Chinese or Indian culture. The region had cultural and political diversity. Confucianism, for example, did not have a missionary zeal as did Buddhism and Hinduism. In this way the adoption of Chinese culture became a matter of choice for the non-Chinese people of the region.

1B, 2D, a1A, a1C, a4A, a4F, a4H, a4K

Learning from Pictures *This tranquil scroll painting from the Yuan dynasty illustrates the Mongol's admiration of horses.*

China over the following 26 years. During this period the country experienced many problems. The Huang He flooded, destroying crops and causing famine throughout the land. Many secret organizations calling for revolution sprang up. Finally, in 1368, the Yuan dynasty came to an end with the overthrow of the last Mongol emperor.

Later Chinese historians denounced the Mongols as savages. They claimed that the Yuan dynasty had no lasting effect on China. The Mongols did, however, influence China in important ways. Among other things, they improved communications and made local governments directly responsible to the central government in Beijing. Later Chinese dynasties built upon the Mongols' political reforms by concentrating greater power in the hands of the emperor.

Civilization Developed in Indochina

Historically Indochina consists of the countries of Cambodia, Laos, and Vietnam. However, geographers include the countries of Burma, Malaysia, and Thailand as well. Indochina is located on a peninsula that borders China on the north and India on the northwest. As a result, the region shows the influences of both of these cultures. During much of their history, the countries of Indochina were part of the Chinese Empire. At times, however, they were able to maintain their independence because of their location far from the center of Chinese rule.

Buddhism, which was adopted from the Chinese, helped shape the culture of Indochina. Daoism and Confucianism also were transplanted from China. And, for the most part, the countries of Indochina adopted the Chinese political structure. However, they retained their own languages.

Early in the history of Indochina, people from India settled in the region, bringing their language, art, and religion. Evidence of their cultural impact can still be found in the southern part of the peninsula. Religious art, temples, and sculpture show this influence. In present-day Cambodia (Kampuchea), ruins of the city of Angkor Thom (ANG • kawr TAHM), particularly at the huge temple of Angkor Wat, offer reminders of Indian influence. Reliefs with scenes from the Hindu epics adorn this structure, one of the architectural wonders of the Far East. Although Hinduism was strong in this area due to the Indian influence, Buddhism remained the main religion of most of the people.

During the late 1300s, a form of writing easier than Chinese developed in Indochina. Also at this time, a national literature and a native style of art ● arose in parts of the region.

SECTION 2 REVIEW

1. **Identify** Genghis Khan, Kublai Khan, Batu, Golden Horde, Rabban Bar Sauma
2. **Locate** Karakorum, Indochina
3. **Understanding Ideas** How were the Mongols able to conquer so much land in Asia so quickly?
4. **Analyzing Ideas** **(a)** Why did the Chinese despise the Mongols? **(b)** What were some of the good features of Mongol rule?
5. **Organizing Ideas** How did Kublai Khan improve communications in China?
6. **Summarizing Ideas** How were the countries of Indochina able to maintain their own identities?

dynasties thus became more powerful.)

Review Answers

1. ***Genghis Khan:*** Mongol leader who captured Beijing, central Asia, and most of Persia; ***Kublai Khan:*** grandson of Genghis Khan who completed the conquest of China; ***Batu:*** grandson of Genghis Khan who invaded Europe; ***Golden Horde:*** name given to Mongols by Europeans; ***Rabban Bar Sauma:*** Chinese traveler who visited Europe
2. ***Karakorum:*** city in Mongolia that served as Mongol headquarters; ***Indochina:*** historically consists of countries of Cambodia, Laos, and Vietnam; geographically also includes Burma, Malaysia, and Thailand
3. The Mongols used superior military technology and tactics to conquer territory. Numerous columns of Mongol riders surrounded enemies. Specially designed saddles and stirrups enabled them to fire arrows accurately while moving at full speed.
4. **(a)** The Chinese despised the Mongols because of different languages, the Mongol emphasis on action in contrast with Chinese appreciation for the arts, and the terrible smell and appearance of the invaders. They also objected to the freedom allowed Mongol women. **(b)** The Mongols brought peace to China,

1B, 2D, a1B

● The warm ocean currents allowed double cropping of rice in the south. The seafaring tradition is also strong in Japan.

■ Discussion topic: A comparison of the Japanese islands with the British Isles *(Both are protected from invasion by the surrounding waters.)*

improved communications, increased contacts with Europeans, and made local governments responsible to the central government. **5.** Kublai Khan extended the Grand Canal and built a stone-surfaced highway next to it between Hangzhou and Beijing. He also built post roads linking China with India and Persia, which facilitated trade. **6.** The peoples of Indochina spoke separate languages, developed a form of writing easier to master than Chinese, a national literature, and a native style of art. These, in addition to a location far from the center of Chinese rule, helped each country develop and maintain its own identify.

SECTION 3

Focus/Motivation

Write Article 1 of the 1947 constitution of Japan on the chalkboard or an overhead projector.

"The Emperor shall be the symbol of the State and of the unity of the people, deriving his position from the will of the people with whom resides sovereign power."

Lead a discussion on the role of the emperor in Japan, using the following questions as a guide. According to the 1947 constitution, on what basis does the emperor of Japan rule? *(In modern Japan the emperor derives his power from the will of the people.)* Tell students that in traditional Japan the

3 Japan Developed Its Own Government, Society, and Culture

Japan consists of a chain of islands in the Pacific Ocean off the northeast coast of Asia. Most of the country's large population lives on the four main islands—Honshu (HAHN • shoo), Kyushu (kee • OO • shoo), Shikoku (shi • KOH • koo), and Hokkaido (hah • KYD • oh).

The Physical Setting

Because it is so mountainous, only about one-sixth of the area of Japan can be used for farming. However, this farmland produces more food than do most other places in the world, thanks to abundant rainfall, plentiful sunlight, long growing seasons, and the diligence of Japanese farmers. The plentiful water supply provides easy irrigation and, in modern times, is also a source of electric power. The rains ● also support heavy timber growth. Nature is not entirely kind to Japan, however. Earthquakes, tidal waves, and typhoons often strike the islands, causing extensive damage.

Until modern times the seas surrounding Japan ■ shielded the islands from foreign influences. This protection allowed the Japanese to choose whether they wanted to have contact with other peoples. At times in their history, they have been very interested in the outside world, especially China. At other times they have preferred to live in isolation.

The Mongols under Kublai Khan tried several times to conquer Japan, but they failed. In 1281, for example, a Mongol fleet of 3,500 ships carrying more than 100,000 soldiers assembled to invade Japan. However, an extraordinarily powerful typhoon, or "Divine Wind," which the Japanese call the *Kamikaze,* dispersed the fleet.

Japan's Beginnings

Long ago the people of Japan migrated to the islands from the Asian mainland. The two oldest and most basic characteristics of their society have been the ancient Shinto religion and a deep reverence for their emperor.

Shinto means "the way of the gods." It teaches that spirits live in such objects as sand, waterfalls, and great trees. Shintoism lacks established scripture, specific doctrine, and priests. It contains, however, numerous gods called *Kami,* meaning "superior." The Kami help especially in promoting fertility in families and crops. From one viewpoint Shinto is not so much a religion as a set of prayers and rituals to satisfy the Kami.

Reverence or respect for the emperor is also a foundation of Japanese life. According to tradition, Jimmu, the first emperor, was crowned in 660 B.C. The Japanese chose this date in A.D. 601 by counting back 1,260 years, a period of time borrowed from the Chinese as representing a major historical cycle.

Jimmu probably was a mythical figure. The first real, or historic, emperor, Sujin, reigned in the 300s. He, and his successors, claimed divine descent from the sun goddess. Official denial of this belief was not announced until 1945, after the Japanese defeat in World War II. In the entire history of Japan, only one imperial family has ruled, making it the longest unbroken dynasty in the history of the world.

Early History of Japan

Only sketchy records of early Japanese history exist. The Chinese, however, knew about Japan before A.D. 100. Chinese writing was introduced and adopted in Japan about 405. Another Chinese influence filtered in about 550, when a monk brought Buddhism to Japan. At first the emperor's conservative advisers opposed the new religion. One of them even threw a statue of Buddha into a canal. But soon after, when an epidemic broke out, the advisers interpreted the illness as a sign of the new religion's power, and the emperor allowed several Buddhist monasteries to be built. Buddhism then won many converts among nobles at the emperor's court.

In later centuries Buddhism spread among the common people and became an important part of Japanese life. It did not replace Shinto, however. For most of Japanese history, the two religions coexisted peacefully, and people believed in both religions at the same time. They celebrated important events, such as births and marriages, according to Shinto rituals. They held funerals according to Buddhist rituals.

Japanese adoption of Chinese writing and Buddhism led to the introduction of other Chinese

CONNECTIONS: THEN AND NOW

Parks and Gardens

There are times when you just want to "get away from it all." When this happens to people in Japan, many seek a garden such as this one (bottom left) to refresh their spirits. Gardens in Asia are designed to imitate nature. They are miniature representations of the world, where rocks stand for mountains, ponds represent oceans, and sand and gravel are rivers. Frequently the gardens are open and in harmony with the hills around them.

In contrast, some gardens, particularly in China, are completely walled. Inside, visitors enjoy special views that change with the time of day or the seasons. Sometimes there are platforms where one can sit and look at the moon.

Some private homes and many public parks in Japan have tea gardens with paths leading to small houses. There tea is served with great ceremony. The public parks are lined with rows of cherry trees, and in springtime families have picnics under the blossoms. The Japanese sent similar cherry trees, now planted around the Tidal Basin in Washington, D.C., so that Americans could enjoy them, too.

You may have camped out in one of the many national or state parks in the United States. People who live in or near cities visit Central Park in New York, the Public Gardens in Boston, Grant Park in Chicago, or Golden Gate Park in San Francisco. The people of Victoria, British Columbia, enjoy walking and sitting in the Butchart Gardens (below right). The Tivoli Gardens (above) in Copenhagen, Denmark, and the Prater in Vienna, Austria, have giant Ferris wheels and other entertainments. A number of parks in the United States have special themes. Sometimes they contain animals and are game preserves.

emperors claimed divine descent from the sun goddess. What advantage would an emperor of early Japan have over a modern emperor? *(An emperor who claimed divine descent would be more secure. Few people would dare to overthrow a divinely appointed ruler.)*

Presentation
Interpreting Ideas (Average/Group)
Have the students turn to the map on page 289. In a classroom discussion, ask them to describe the geography of Japan. *(mountainous islands)* Ask them to explain how the geography of Japan influenced Japanese history and culture. *(The seas surrounding Japan shielded the islands from unwanted foreign influences, making it possible for the Japanese to choose whether or not to have contact with the outside world.)*

285

ideas and ways of life. The Japanese also adopted Chinese artistic designs, road engineering, medical knowledge, a system of weights and measures, and styles of clothing.

The Japanese sent their first ambassadors to China in 607. Japanese students returning from China in the 640s believed Japan inferior in various ways and worked to have other aspects of Chinese culture adopted in their country.

In 702 Japan's emperor issued a law code modeled on one from China's Tang dynasty. The code regulated all aspects of life in Japan and established a highly centralized government under the emperor. In 794 the Japanese built a capital named Heian-kyo (HAY • ahn-KYOH), which became the modern city of Kyoto. In Heian-kyo members of the ruling class began to modify some of the practices that had been adopted from China, creating their own distinctive culture. For example, earlier poetry had been written in Chinese. Japanese poets now began writing in their own language.

Women enjoyed a high position in upper-class society in Heian-kyo. They could own property, and they played an important role in the literary life of the capital. Several women wrote diaries. Around the year 1000, Lady Murasaki Shikibu (moohr • uh • SAHK • ee SHEE • kee • boo) wrote *The Tale of Genji,* the world's first novel. It tells the story of Prince Genji, the perfect courtier. Written in a quiet, sensitive style and filled with poems about the beauties of nature, it became one of the masterpieces of Japanese literature.

Feudal Japan

Although emperors continued to reign in Heian-kyo, after the early 800s the centralized political system adopted from China gradually fell into decline. In its place Japan developed a system of local power that in many ways resembled feudalism, the system that governed Europe at this time.

In Japan the feudal system contained two conflicting sources of power. One was an indirect form of central government under which an important family held power in the name of the emperor. The other source of power existed outside the control of the central government. It consisted of military units that had authority in the territories they occupied.

Central government. The first family to gain control over the emperor and to use his power to their advantage were the Fujiwara (foo • jee • WAH • rah). By holding important government offices and by marrying into the emperor's family, the Fujiwara controlled the central government from the early 800s to the mid-1100s.

After a long power struggle, the Minamoto (mi • nah • MOH • TOH) family took control of the government in 1185. They held power until 1338. In 1192 the Minamoto introduced a new kind of official called the **shogun.** On paper the shogun was the chief officer of the emperor and was expected to be dutiful to him. In practice he was the agent of the Minamoto and of the powerful families that succeeded them. From this time on, gaining control of the shogunate, or office of shogun, became the major aim of any ambitious family.

The shogun also was the chief military officer of the central government. In addition, he controlled finance, law, the courts, and appointments to office. He often governed from his military headquarters at Kamakura. In 1338 the Ashikaga (ah • shee • KAH • gah) family took over the shogunate from the Minamoto. They controlled the office for more than 200 years.

Local military rule. The leading families and their shoguns had power, but they were not strong enough to extend this power to local levels. There, warrior-landlords called **samurai** (SAM • uh • ry) led the military units. The power of a samurai rested on his control of land, on his descent from earlier local leaders, and on his ability with the sword. The samurai followed a code called **Bushido** (BOOH • shee • doh) that stressed bravery, loyalty, and honor. Samurai had to endure great physical hardship without complaint and could have no fear of death. They regarded **seppuku** (se • POO • koo), a form of ceremonial suicide also known as hara-kiri, or "belly slitting," as the honorable way to avoid torture, execution, or defeat in battle.

In time, the samurai developed an order of ranking among themselves. At the top were the **daimyos** (DY • mee • ohz), who gained the loyalty of the lesser samurai. As the power of the daimyos increased and they became like petty kings, the samurai lost both power and prestige.

Life in Feudal Japan

Rival military units competed for power at the local level, and leading families competed for the shogunate, making warfare a frequent occurrence in

286

● a ritual to produce a sense of spiritual calm

Learning from Pictures *Japanese people often prepare food at the dinner table as they eat. What was the purpose of the tea ceremony?*

SECTION 3

Closure

Ask students why invoking the Mandate of Heaven did not occur in Japan. *(In Japan's entire history, only one dynasty has ruled.)* Japan's emperors were officially regarded as descendants of the sun goddess as late as the end of World War II. How is the emperor regarded today by the Japanese people? *(Answers will vary. The emperor is a constitutional monarch and is only a figurehead in the Japanese democracy.)*

feudal Japan. Nevertheless, considerable economic and cultural growth took place during the feudal period.

Instead of weakening the country, warfare seems to have enriched it. The daimyos encouraged peasants to grow larger crops, since larger crops meant more taxes for the daimyos. They also promoted and taxed trade, financing their military campaigns with the money they received.

For ordinary people, the frequent warfare offered a chance to rise in the world. Any man who could use a sword or a lance could join a daimyo's army. If he proved himself a good fighter and leader, he might be promoted to a higher rank. Or he might even lead a revolt against his daimyo and become a daimyo himself.

The spread of Buddhism. A religious awakening occurred during the feudal period in Japan. Buddhists established new sects, including several that taught that salvation could come through faith alone. According to the older Buddhist sects, a person had to make contributions to monasteries and study Buddhist scriptures to achieve salvation. Only wealthy people could afford that. The new sects appealed to ordinary people.

Zen Buddhism, a sect introduced from China in the late 1100s, particularly interested warriors. Zen stressed salvation through enlightenment, not faith. To achieve enlightenment, a person had to engage in long hours of meditation and rigorous self-discipline. Warriors found that practicing Zen gave them the courage they needed to fight.

Zen and Japanese culture. The Ashikaga shoguns strongly supported Zen Buddhism. They built Zen monasteries throughout the country and encouraged the artistic efforts of Zen monks. Several new art forms inspired by Zen developed during the late 1300s and early 1400s, at the height of Ashikaga power. One was landscape architecture, the art of designing gardens. By the careful arrangement of rocks, trees, and water, Zen believers tried to represent the essential beauty of nature.

Another new art form was the tea ceremony, a ritual designed to produce spiritual calm. A few people gathered in a small, simply furnished room that overlooked a garden. They sat quietly while one of them slowly and deliberately made tea. Then they drank the tea, admired the pottery bowls in which it was served, and enjoyed the beauties of nature in the garden outside.

287

1B, a1B, a4B, a4F, a4I

Review Answers

1. ***shogun:*** powerful official who controlled the Japanese emperor; ***samurai:*** warrior landlords who ruled local areas; ***Bushido:*** samurai code of honor; ***seppuku:*** ceremonial suicide; ***daimyo:*** samurai with the highest status
2. ***Shinto:*** ancient religion of Japan; ***The Tale of Genji:*** world's first novel, written by Lady Murasaki Shikibu; ***Ashikaga:*** family that controlled the shogunate after 1338; ***Sejong:*** Yi ruler of Korea in the mid-1400s who directed the development of the Korean alphabet
3. ***Kyoto:*** early Japanese capital on island of Honshu; ***Kamakura:*** military headquarters city of shoguns in east-central Honshu; ***Korea:*** peninsula south of Manchuria
4. Favorable features of Japanese geography include large amounts of rainfall, producing much water for irrigation and a large supply of timber. Until modern times the surrounding seas have shielded the islands from invasion. Unfavorable geographic features include the large percentage of mountainous land unsuitable for farming and frequent damaging earthquakes, tidal waves, and typhoons.
5. Two major Chinese contributions to Japan were writing and Buddhism. Other influences include artistic design, road engineering, medical knowledge,

READ
WRITE
• INTERPRET
CONNECT
THINK

BUILDING HISTORY STUDY SKILLS

Interpreting Visuals: Reading a Chart

Charts are visual ways of organizing information in order to show relationships. For example, a time line is a chart for recording the order of events. A classification chart groups information so that it can be compared easily. An organization chart shows relationships within a system or group. Lines are connected to show who has authority over whom. A flow chart illustrates the steps in a process, and a family tree diagrams the structure of a family.

How to Read a Chart

To read a chart, follow these steps.

1. Identify the type of chart and its purpose.
2. Identify the details.
3. Relate the details to each other.

Developing the Skill

The following chart is an organization chart. It records the structure of Japanese society under the feudal system. The emperor is at the top of the feudal structure. Under him is the shogun. The daimyos are under the shogun, the samurai under the daimyos, and the merchants, peasants, farmers, and craft workers are on the bottom of the chart.

The dotted lines show weak or formal rule. The solid lines show real power. The relationship of the samurai to the daimyo can be seen, as can the relationship of the daimyo to the shogun and that of the shogun to the emperor. By reading the chart, you can see clearly that the daimyos possessed the real power in feudal Japan.

A samurai warrior on horseback

Practicing the skill. Using the above information on charts, draw an organization chart that shows the structure of the United States government. You may need to use an American history textbook to find the information necessary to practice this skill.

To apply this skill, see Applying History Study Skills on page 291.

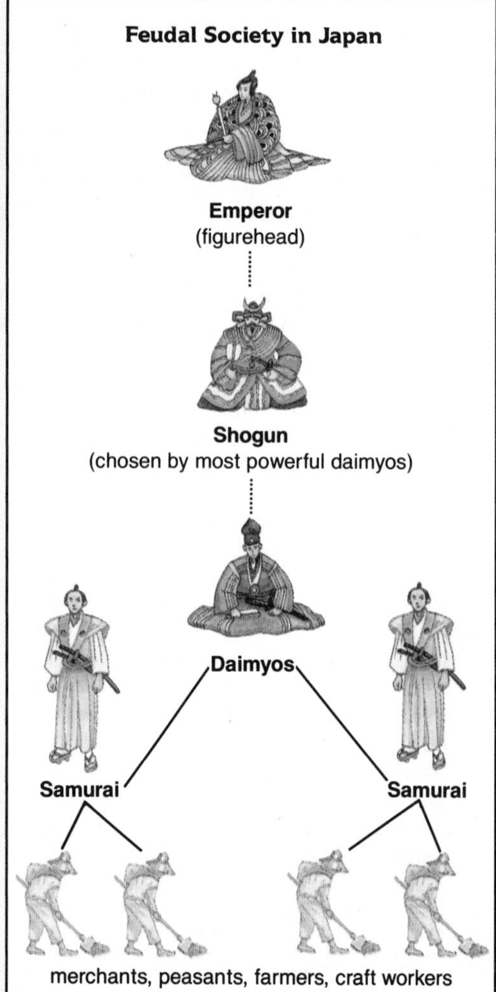

1A, 1B, 2D, a1A, a4A, a4B, a4C, a4F, a4H, a4L, a4M

● Much of China's culture that influenced Japan was introduced by way of Korea.

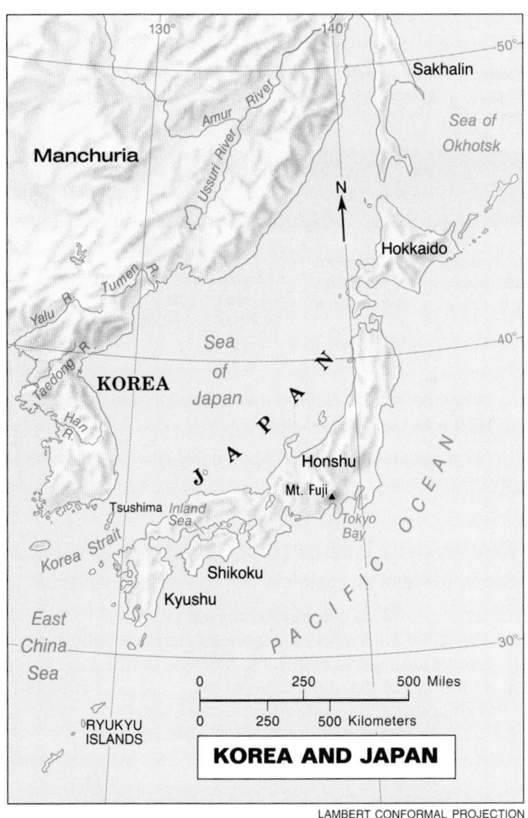

Learning from Maps *The Koreans built a great wall on the northern frontier to protect themselves from invasion. What body of water separates Japan and Korea?* **Sea of Japan**

Another artistic expression of Zen was the *No* play. First performed in the 1300s, *No* plays were highly stylized dance dramas, usually on religious subjects. Like Greek plays, *No* plays were performed on a bare stage by male actors wearing masks, while a chorus chanted the story.

The Ashikaga retained control of the shogunate until 1573 but had no political influence after about 1460. Real power rested with the many daimyos, who now began to fight among themselves for supremacy. For about a century, Japan had no central government.

Civilization Developed in Korea

Korea occupies a peninsula on the eastern border of the Chinese mainland (see map, this page). China controlled the peninsula for much of Korea's history and, as a result, greatly influenced Korea's political and cultural development. China first invaded Korea in 200 B.C., during the Han dynasty. ● At this time the Chinese began to transmit their culture to Korea.

After the fall of the Han dynasty, three independent kingdoms, with shifting boundaries, took control of the peninsula. The kingdom of Silla (SI • luh) eventually emerged as the strongest and unified the country in 668. During the Tang dynasty, Korea once again became a colony of China but kept its own ruling dynasty. Buddhism was introduced to Korea during this period. Then Korea became part of the Mongol Empire, and when the Mongols were expelled, a new dynasty, the Yi (YEE), was founded in 1392. This dynasty survived until 1910, when Japan annexed Korea.

Buddhism had the most important religious influence on Korea. Its teachings can be seen in the country's culture, philosophy, and morality. In 845 Buddhism was made the state religion. Scholars studied the Confucian classics, and the government adopted the Chinese civil service system, based on the teachings of Confucius. The Koreans did not, however, completely copy the Chinese. They retained both their native dress and their own language. Sejong (SA • ZHONG), a Yi emperor who ruled in the mid-1400s, directed the development of a Korean alphabet. The Koreans also invented a method of printing using movable metal type that the Chinese later adopted.

SECTION 3 REVIEW

1. **Define** shogun, samurai, Bushido, seppuku, daimyo
2. **Identify** Shinto, *The Tale of Genji,* Ashikaga, Sejong
3. **Locate** Kyoto, Kamakura, Korea
4. **Comparing Ideas** Compare the favorable and unfavorable features of Japanese geography.
5. **Interpreting Ideas** What were China's major contributions to and influences on Japan?
6. **Organizing Ideas** **(a)** Name the two centers of power in Japanese feudalism. **(b)** How did they complement each other? **(c)** How did they conflict with each other?
7. **Analyzing Ideas** How did Zen Buddhism influence Japanese culture?
8. **Identifying Cause and Effect** What effect did years of Chinese domination have on Korean culture?

weights and measures, and clothing styles. The Japanese modeled their law code after one from the Tang in China.

6. **(a)** Feudal Japan had two conflicting powers: an indirect form of central government under which an important family held power in the emperor's name, and military units with authority over local territories. **(b)** Because the central government was not strong enough to extend its power to local levels, the samurai took control. **(c)** Conflict arose when rival military units competed for power at the local level and leading families competed for the shogunate.

7. Zen Buddhism inspired new Japanese art forms such as landscape architecture, the tea ceremony, and *No* plays.

8. Chinese Buddhism influenced Korean culture, philosophy, and morality. The Koreans adopted Buddhism as the state religion, studied Confucian classics, and instituted the Chinese civil service system.

289

Reviewing Important Terms

1. Seppuku; **2.** shogun; **3.** daimyos; **4.** Samurai

Developing Critical Thinking Skills

1. (a) Chinese classics were carved in stone, then copied on paper over stone inscriptions. Next seals were carved with an inscription in reverse. Movable type was the last step. **(b)** Answers will vary. Printing was a cumbersome technique in the Chinese language. Printing exposed many more people to literature and contributed to worldwide cultural diffusion.

2. (a) Water-control projects were built that increased the number of irrigated fields where rice could be grown. Quick-ripening rice made possible two crops a year. **(b)** South China; **(c)** More people moved to the cities.

3. (a) The Tang eliminated tax-free estates, and peasants paid taxes in produce according to the amount of land owed. **(b)** The government received a tax on all land, but peasants could no longer avoid taxes by escaping to tax-free estates.

4. to be the chief officer of the emperor

5. The emperor of Japan claimed divine descent. The emperor of China did not. The emperor of Japan exercised little power, while the Chinese emperor was powerful.

6. The Koreans adopted Buddhism, studied Confucian classics, and instituted the civil service.

Relating Geography to History

Qin Ling Range, the Gobi, arid land in Xinjiang, Tien Shan, Kunlun Shan.

1A, 1B, a1A, a1C, a4A, a4F, a4G, a4H, a4I, a4L, a4M

Reteaching

Have students review the Chapter Summary and the appropriate section and questions in the Unit Synthesis. Discuss the concepts until students demonstrate a clear understanding of the material.

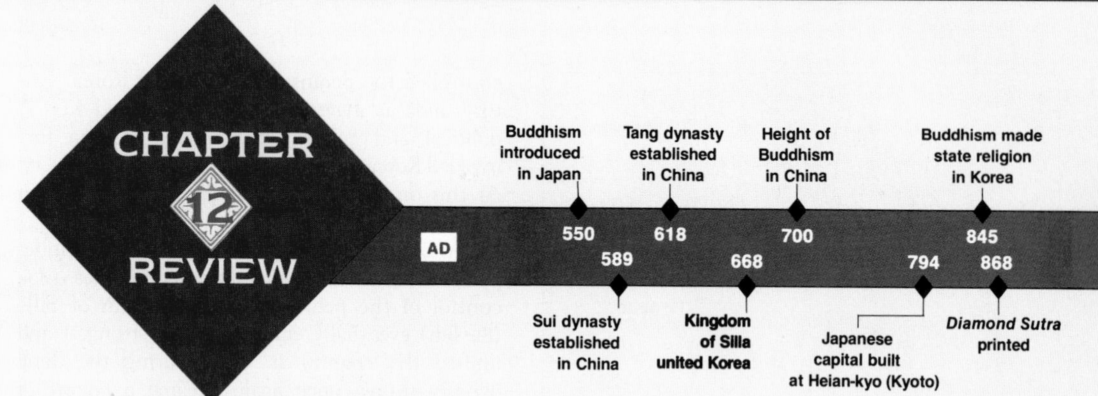

Chapter Summary

The following list contains the key concepts you have learned about the civilizations of China, Indochina, Japan, and Korea.

1. A unified empire was reestablished in China in 589 by the Sui dynasty. Soon China was stronger and wealthier than ever before.
2. During the Tang and Song dynasties, the Chinese civil service system was perfected. Important inventions, such as gunpowder and printing, were made.
3. In the 1200s the nomadic Mongols of central Asia were united into a powerful fighting force under Genghis Khan and, later, his grandson Kublai Khan. They conquered China, Persia, and much of eastern Europe.
4. Mongol rule brought economic growth to China. Also under the Mongols, population increased, roads and canals were built, and trade developed with other peoples. The Chinese resented the Mongols. However, later Chinese dynasties used the Mongol's political method of concentrating greater power in the hands of the emperor.
5. The countries of Indochina were controlled by China during much of their histories. As a result, Chinese culture greatly influenced these countries.
6. Japan was influenced by China but created its own distinct culture. Its island location made it safe from foreign invasion. The difficult terrain encouraged a political system in which there was both central and local power.
7. Two of the most basic characteristics of Japanese society are the Shinto religion and a deep reverence for the emperor. The Shinto religion lacks established scripture, doctrine, and priests. It contains numerous gods called Kami. Japanese emperors claimed divine descent from the sun goddess. In all of its history, Japan has been ruled by only one imperial family.
8. Japan developed a feudal political system. The central government was controlled by the shogun, who held power in the name of the emperor. At the local level, power was in the hands of the samurai, warrior-landlords. The most powerful samurai were the daimyo.
9. Korea, although dominated by China for most of its history, managed to develop its own culture. The Koreans had their own native dress as well as their own language and developed their own alphabet. Movable type was invented in Korea.

On a separate sheet of paper, complete the following review exercises.

Reviewing Important Terms

Supply the term that correctly completes each sentence.

1. ________ was a ceremonial suicide in Japan.
2. The chief officer of a Japanese emperor who was always careful to be dutiful to him was the ________.
3. At the top of the samurai were the ________, who, as their power increased, became petty kings.
4. ________ were warrior-landlords in Japan.

Developing Critical Thinking Skills

1. **Understanding Cause and Effect** **(a)** What were the steps in the development of printing? **(b)** What effect did the invention have on China and eventually the rest of the world?
2. **Analyzing Ideas** **(a)** What agricultural improvements took place in China during the Tang and Song dynasties? **(b)** What part of China was most affected by these changes? **(c)** How did these changes influence city life in China?
3. **Interpreting Ideas** **(a)** Explain the tax reforms introduced during the Tang dynasty. **(b)** Why was this change good for the government and bad for the peasants?
4. **Summarizing Ideas** Why was the position of shogun established in Japan?
5. **Comparing Ideas** How was the role of emperor in Japan different from the role of emperor in China?
6. **Analyzing Ideas** In what ways did the Chinese influence the culture of Korea?

Relating Geography to History

Using the map of China on page 70 and the map of the Tang Empire on page 276, list the physical obstacles a merchant would have to overcome while traveling along the Silk Route.

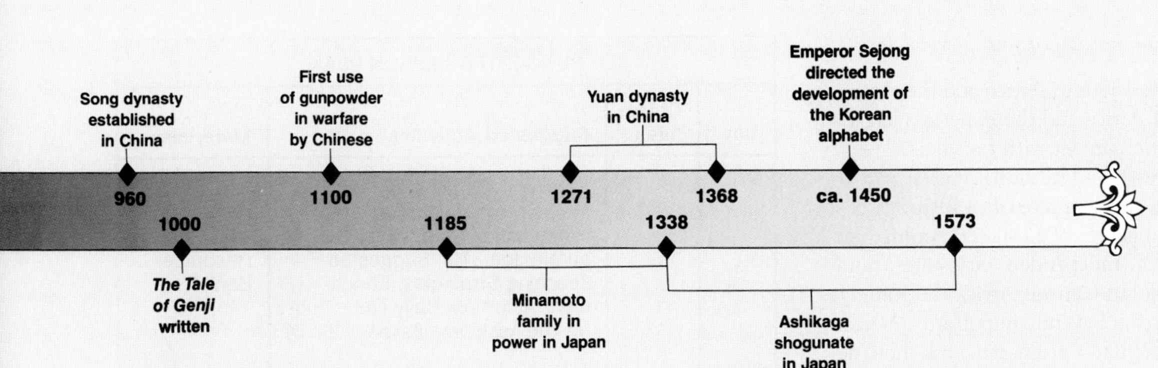

Relating Past to Present

1. Consult an American history textbook to learn how and why the United States government introduced civil service examinations in the late 1800s. Compare the beginnings of the American civil service exam to the beginnings of the civil service exam in China.
2. Describe the development of printing in early China. How are today's copy machines similar to the block prints of early China? What impact have mass-produced paperback books had on our society today?

Applying History Study Skills

Before completing this activity, review Building History Study Skills on page 288.

Look again at the steps for reading a chart. Then complete the following exercise.

Study the chart in column 2 of this page. It shows the Confucian Five Relationships and how they operate. Then answer the following questions.

1. What type of chart is it?
2. **(a)** According to the chart, what does a son owe to a father? **(b)** A father to a son? **(c)** What is the obligation of a younger brother to an older brother? **(d)** What is the obligation of a wife to a husband? **(e)** What is the obligation of a husband to a wife?
3. Would you characterize the relationships as unequal or as complementary? Why?
4. Which of the five relationships relate to the family? Why?
5. What is the purpose of the five relationships?

Investigating Further

1. **Writing a Report** Read poems by the Chinese poets Li Bai and Du Fu. One possible source is Cyril Birch's *Anthology of Chinese Literature* (Grove Press). What do these poems tell you about life in China?
2. **Presenting an Oral Report** Find out more about Marco Polo's impressions of the Chinese people. You might want to read Ronald Latham's *The Travels of Marco Polo* (Penguin) to learn about Chinese life and social customs. Report your findings to the class.

Confucian Five Relationships

The Five Relationships and the attitudes they involve can be set out as follows:

Father Is kind Gives protection Provides education	**Son** Shows respect Accepts father's guidance Cares for him in old age and performs the customary burial ceremonies
Elder Brother Sets an example of refinement and good behavior	**Younger Brother** Respects the character and experience of the elder
Husband Carries out his family duties Is honorable and faithful Provides for his wife and family	**Wife** Looks after the home Is obedient Diligently meets the needs of her husband and children
Elder Gives encouragement Shows consideration toward younger people Sets a good example	**Junior** Shows respect Defers to the advice of those with more experience Is eager to learn
Ruler Acts justly Strives to improve the welfare of his people Is worthy of loyalty	**Subjects** Are loyal Serve their ruler Honor their ruler because of his position and character

Relating Past to Present

1. The Pendleton Act of 1883 created a Civil Service Commission authorized to hire workers on the basis of open examinations. This law was passed to eliminate corruption in government. The Chinese civil service examinations were begun to bring society into harmony with the Confucian teaching.
2. *See* **1 (a)** under Developing Critical Thinking Skills. Mass-produced paperbacks have exposed more people to a variety of reading materials.

Applying History Study Skills

1. classification chart
2. (a) The son owes the father respect, accepts his guidance, takes care of him in his old age, and sees that he is buried. **(b)** kindness, protection, and an education; **(c)** respect his character and experience; **(d)** A wife must be obedient to her husband, look after the house, and meet the needs of her husband and children. **(e)** A husband must be honorable and faithful to his wife, provide for her and the family, and carry out family duties.
3. Answers will vary.
4. the first three; the family was the most important unit in Chinese society (*See* Chapter 4, pages 84-86.)
5. The purpose of the five relationships is to illustrate the importance in Confucianism of the family and the family's ancestors. The emperor is the head of the country just as the father is the head of the family.

291

CHAPTER (pages 292–313)

13 Africa and the Americas Produced Complex Civilizations

(1800 B.C.–A.D. 1500)

CHAPTER OVERVIEW

Our knowledge of events before the 1500s in Africa and the Americas is fragmentary. The peoples of Africa and the Americas left few written records, and there was little contact with outsiders.

Through the study of languages, oral traditions, music, and archeological finds, historians have reconstructed the histories of a variety of African cultures. The kingdoms of Cush and Axum dominated the interior of eastern Africa. Independent city-states, notable for trade, grew up on the coast. In Central Africa the Karanga kingdom controlled a large area. Several important African societies—Ghana, Mali, and Songhai—prospered and then declined in West Africa.

People who migrated from Asia settled the Americas over many centuries. The most advanced culture of the Americas was that of the Maya of southern Mexico and Central America. The decline of the Maya was followed by the rise of other civilizations such as the Toltecs and Aztecs of central Mexico and the Incas of Peru. In North America many different cultures existed.

SUGGESTED LESSON PLAN

Day	Objectives	Suggested Activities	Materials
1	U9,* C1-4	Introducing the Chapter (page 292) Section 1 (pages 293-97), Focus/Motivation (page 293), Presentation (page 294), Closure (page 296), Suggested Teaching Strategies, Enrichment Activity, Daily Quiz, Suggested Assignments (page 291B)	ATE, Pupil's Edition, Teacher's Resource-Bank™
2	U9, C5	Section 2 (pages 297-303), Focus/Motivation (page 297), Presentation (page 298), Closure (page 301), Suggested Teaching Strategies, Enrichment Activity, Daily Quiz, Suggested Assignments (page 291B)	ATE, Pupil's Edition, Teacher's Resource-Bank™
3	U9, C6-7	Section 3 (pages 303-06), Focus/Motivation (page 303), Presentation (page 304), Closure (page 305), Suggested Teaching Strategies, Enrichment Activity, Daily Quiz, Suggested Assignments (page 291C)	ATE, Pupil's Edition, Teacher's Resource-Bank™
4	U9, C8-9	Section 4 (pages 306-11), Focus/Motivation (page 306), Presentation (page 308), Closure (page 310), Suggested Teaching Strategies, Enrichment Activities, Daily Quiz, Suggested Assignments (page 291D)	ATE, Pupil's Edition, Teacher's Resource-Bank™
5	U9, C1-9	Chapter 13 Form A Test, Reteaching Worksheet, Chapter 13 Form B Test	Teacher's Resource-Bank™ or Workbook and Test Booklet
6	U1-9	Unit Three Review Worksheet, Unit Three Test	Teacher's Resource-Bank™ or Test Booklet

*C refers to applicable Chapter Objective, U refers to applicable Unit Goal.

BOOKS FOR THE TEACHER

Bailey, Helen, and Abraham Nasatir. *Latin America: The Development of Its Civilization.* Prentice-Hall. Surveys Latin American history, with several chapters on the earliest cultures.

Davidson, Basil. *Africa in History.* Macmillan. Surveys much of African history.

Oliver, Roland, and J. D. Fage. *A Short History of Africa.* Penguin. Introduces the history of Africa.

Soustelle, Jacques. *Daily Life of Aztecs.* Stanford University Press. Covers all aspects of Aztec life.

BOOKS FOR THE STUDENT

Chu, Daniel, and Elliott Skinner. *A Glorious Age in Africa.* Tells the story of three African kingdoms: Ghana, Mali, and Songhai.

Cox, Harold. *Man Comes to America.* Little, Brown. Details early life in America.

Fichter, George S. *How the Plains Indians Lived.* Details the life styles of the Plains people.

Whitlock, Ralph. *Everyday Life of the Maya.* Putnam. Examines social life, government, and religion of the Mayas.

MULTIMEDIA MATERIALS

Ancient Africa (mp, 27 min.), International. Studies the development and cultural heritage of African civilizations before the advent of the Europeans.

Ancient New World (mp, 16 min.), Churchill. Portrays the rise of early civilizations in Central America. Includes Olmecs, Toltecs, Maya, and Aztecs.

The Ancient Peruvian (mp, 28 min.), Independent Film. Explores art, architecture, religion, and society of pre-Columbian Peru.

The Search for Black Identity: Proud Heritage from West Africa (fs), Guidance Associates. Examines the cultural, political, and economic life of the African empires and kingdoms and examines their many achievements.

The Story of the Aztecs (mp, 19 min.), Films. Studies Aztec culture and its influence on modern Mexico.

Section (pages 293–297)

1 Many Methods Uncovered Africa's Early History

SECTION OVERVIEW

In spite of a harsh environment, the people of SubSaharan Africa made important cultural and political advances in the 2,000 or so years before A.D. 1500. Scholars have learned much about Africa's early history through the study of languages, oral traditions, music, and archaeological finds. The village was the basic unit of African society and economy. Chiefs or elders exercised political authority, and women played a crucial role in African societies because the societies were matrilineal.

SUGGESTED TEACHING STRATEGIES

1. **Preteaching Vocabulary (Basic)** You may wish to preteach the following important vocabulary terms: tropical rain forest, jungle (*page 294*); savanna, linguist, oral tradition, matrilineal (*page 295*). Ask students to differentiate between a tropical rain forest and a jungle.
2. **Understanding Methods (Average/Group)** Have students write paragraphs describing the various methods used to interpret Africa's past, such as the study of oral traditions, music, plants, and language. Ask volunteers to read their essays to the class.

ENRICHMENT ACTIVITY

Making Connections (Challenging) The feature on page 296 explains that the trumpet has been used in music since earliest times. Some students might want to investigate the history of other instruments that were first used in ancient civilizations and are still found in different cultures throughout the world. The drum and the harp are among the instruments that might be investigated. Have students share their findings with the class.

DAILY QUIZ

To assess student understanding of Section 1, give the class the following quiz. (Each item is worth 10 points.)

1. List the four major African Rivers. *(Nile, Zaire, Zambezi, Niger)*
2. Name the two major African deserts. *(Kalahari, Sahara)*
3. What is the relatively dry grassland in SubSaharan Africa called? *(Savanna)*
4. List geographical, climatic, or topographical barriers that discouraged inland exploration by those outside Africa. *(absence of harbors, few navigable rivers and harbors, wet climate allows the breeding of disease-carrying insects)*
5. What is the name of the basic family of closely-related languages in Africa? *(Bantu)*
6. What do linguists do? *(study languages)*
7. (T or F) The spread through Africa of a common language took little time as the conquering Nigerians quickly dominated central and then southern Africa, imposing their culture on their conquered neighbors. *(F)*
8. (T or F) Oral tradition in Africa, as in other ancient cultures, passed poems, songs, and stories from one generation to another. *(T)*
9. (T or F) Scholars of music theorize that Indonesians migrated to Africa centuries ago. *(T)*
10. (T or F) Life in the African villages was closely bound to the agricultural cycles of planting and harvesting. *(T)*

SUGGESTED ASSIGNMENTS

1. **Bulletin Board Display (Average/Group)** Assign groups of students to prepare a bulletin board display of maps and pictures of Africa.
2. **Research Project (Challenging)** Thor Heyerdahl constructed a raft and sailed from Africa to the Americas to prove his theory that there may have been such an ancient migration of people. Have students read about Heyerdahl's theory in *National Geographic* (January 1971). After their reading, have students prepare a report analyzing the possibility of such a migration, based on the evidence presented.

Section (pages 297–303)

2 City-states and Kingdoms Arose Throughout Africa

SECTION OVERVIEW

A variety of kingdoms, empires, and small city-states arose in Africa before 1500. South of Egypt the kingdoms of Cush and Axum flourished. City-states along the East African coast dominated coastal trade. In Central Africa the Karanga built a kingdom based on the mining of gold. Three major kingdoms—Ghana, Mali, and Songhai—developed in West Africa.

SUGGESTED TEACHING STRATEGIES

1. **Writing a Letter (Average/Group)** Have students write a letter to a friend about daily life in an African village or in a city such as Napata, Great Zimbabwe, or Tombouctou. Call upon students to read their letters to the class.
2. **Researching Ideas (Average/Group)** Have students work in small groups to prepare reports on the kingdoms and societies mentioned in this section, or biographical sketches of Ibn Battuta, Mansa Musa, or Sunni Ali. Suggested sources include: Robert Coughlin's *Tropical Africa* (Time-Life); Basil Davidson's *African Kingdoms* (Time-Life); Leon E. Clark's *Through African Eyes*, vol. III (Praeger); and Daniel Chu's *A Glorious Age in Africa* (Doubleday). Each group should present its findings to the class.

*3. **Writing About History: Paraphrasing Information (Basic)** Have students reread "Building History Study Skills" on page 299. Then have them reread the subsection "East Africa and Trade" on page 300 and paraphrase the subsection.

ENRICHMENT ACTIVITIES

1. **Illustrating Ideas (Average/Group)** One of the outstanding cultural achievements of Africa has been its art. Interested students might prepare a bulletin board display or present an oral report, supplemented with slides or pictures shown on an opaque projector, on some aspect of African art.
2. **Relating Past and Present (Challenging)** Have interested students research the Coptic church in Egypt. The Copts were descendants of ancient Egyptians. Their language was the language of Egypt before Arabic superseded it when the Muslims conquered the country. The name *Copt* has come to mean "Christian Egyptians." Coptic Christians adhered to the Monophysite heresy, meaning the single nature of Christ. Coptic Christians belong to neither Latin or Greek Christianity (Roman Catholic or Greek Orthodox), and after the Arab conquest in the 600s they also ceased to speak Greek. Students might wish to comment on the role and future of Copts living in today's Egypt, faced as it is by Islamic fundamentalism. With the departure of many Europeans, particularly in cities like Alexandria, the Coptic way of life and position in society (so well described in Lawrence Durrell's *Alexandria Quartet*) may be regarded as precarious. Ask students to find out how many Egyptians belong to the Coptic church today. They may present their findings in an oral or written report.

DAILY QUIZ

To assess student understanding of Section 2, give the class the following quiz. (Each item is worth 10 points.)

1. (T or F) The kingdom of Cush exported gold, granite, and timber from its trade center at Kerma. *(T)*
2. The people of Cush, particularly those in Meroë, developed the technological skills to work with what metal? *(iron)*
3. Which country led by King Ezana conquered Cush in A.D. 325? *(Axum)*
4. The spread of this religion to East Africa created the favorable conditions for trade along the coast. *(Islam)*
5. (T or F) The most famous of the East African city-states was Napata. *(F)*
6. The control of what natural resource by the Karanga led to the great trade expansion along the Indian Ocean? *(gold)*
7. The West African kingdom of Ghana began its decline after being attacked by ________. *(Berbers)*
8. (T or F) Ghana, the earliest of the West African kingdoms, served as a trade center for salt and gold. *(T)*
9. Which Mali city became the center of art, literature, education and culture? *(Tombouctou)*
10. Under Sunni Ali, the West African kingdom of Songhai kept a fleet of warships to protect commerce along the ________ River. *(Niger)*

SUGGESTED ASSIGNMENTS

1. **Skill Worksheet (Basic)** Have students complete Skill Worksheet 13 in the TEACHER'S RESOURCEBANK™.
2. **Critical Thinking Worksheet (Average/Group)** Have students complete Critical Thinking Worksheet 29 in the TEACHER'S RESOURCEBANK™.
3. **Critical Thinking Worksheet (Average/Group)** Have students complete Critical Thinking Worksheet 30 in the TEACHER'S RESOURCEBANK™.
4. **Understanding Geography (Basic)** Have students complete "Geography Application Worksheet: Gold and Salt—Resources That Built Kingdoms" in the TEACHER'S RESOURCEBANK™.
5. **Profile Worksheet (Basic)** Have students complete Profile Worksheet 13 in the TEACHER'S RESOURCEBANK™.

Section (pages 303–306)

3 People Migrated from Asia to the Americas

SECTION OVERVIEW

Over many centuries waves of different peoples migrated from Asia to the Americas across what is now the Bering Strait. By about 1500 B.C. people had begun to live in villages, and farming provided most of the food supply. The cultures of the peoples of North America varied according to the geography of the region.

SUGGESTED TEACHING STRATEGIES

1. **Preteaching Vocabulary (Basic)** You may wish to preteach the following important vocabulary terms: adobe (*page 305*); tepee (*page 306*). Point out that adobe is still a popular building material in the southwestern United States.

2. **Researching Ideas (Average/Group)** Organize the class into several small groups. Assign each group one of the cultures studied in this section. Have them write a report on its culture.
3. **Demonstrating Music (Challenging)** The peoples of the Americas produced a great variety of musical instruments, songs and dances. Students might like to perform some of them for the class. Sources include: John Bierhorst's *Music of the North American Indians* (Four Winds).

ENRICHMENT ACTIVITIES

1. **Writing a Report (Average/Group)** Have interested students examine the concept of the land bridge as it applies to Asia and North America. Have them write a brief report that covers the peoples who crossed the land bridge, where they went after the crossing, and what cultural characteristics they have lost or retained from their previous Asian homeland.
2. **Illustrating Ideas (Challenging)** Have interested students prepare a report or illustrated lecture (using slides or pictures that may be posted on the bulletin board) on the social history of the peoples of North America. They should compare their dress, food, life style, religion, and social customs. Some students may have access to recordings of music or articles of clothing, weapons of war, or farming implements that they can bring to class.

DAILY QUIZ

To assess student understanding of Section 3, give the class the following quiz. (Each item is worth 10 points.)

1. (T or F) Europeans aggressively followed up the Viking discovery of North America in 1000. *(F)*
2. The Americas include these two great river systems. *(Mississippi, Amazon)*
3. Which of the following crops is not native only to the Western Hemisphere? —corn, rice, beans, squash, potatoes *(rice)*
4. (T or F) Early Western Hemisphere peoples developed highly complex cultures, applied the wheel and plow to agriculture, and learned how to manufacture crude iron tools. *(F)*
5. The land bridge between Asia and North America is now covered by a body of water known as the ________. *(Bering Strait)*
6. (T or F) By the time of Columbus' voyage in 1492, people depended on farming for much of their food supply only as far north as Mexico and as far south as northern Peru. *(F)*

Matching

7. *(b)* Lived with an economy based on fishing; became expert carvers, woodworkers and weavers
8. *(d)* Tribal peoples who lived in tepees and hunted buffalo
9. *(c)* Had a sophisticated culture in the Eastern Woodlands
10. *(a)* Lived in permanent settlements in the southwestern United States.

a. Pueblo
b. Northwest
c. Mound Builders
d. Great Plains

SUGGESTED ASSIGNMENTS

1. **Studying Maps (Average/Group)** Have students do research on the various peoples of North America. Then ask them to prepare a map showing where these peoples — often called Native Americans or Indians — lived. Students may wish to consult atlases in their school or local libraries. Post the best maps on the classroom bulletin board. Use the information from the maps as the basis for a class discussion on words that appear today in the names of states (e.g., Iowa, Kansas, Illinois) and other geographical names (e.g., Cheyenne, Sioux, Yuma, Yakima, Seminole, Miami).
2. **Report (Average/Group)** Have interested students research the role of women in the early societies of North America and prepare a written or oral report. They may select either one tribe or do a comparative study of several tribes in a selected region of the continent. They should include in their reports what tasks women had in the economy and household, and their role and place in the family. Ask the students to deliver or read their reports to the class.

Section (pages 306–311)

Empires Rose and Flourished in Mexico and Peru

SECTION OVERVIEW

In Mexico, Central America, and South America, more advanced civilizations developed as early as 1500 B.C. The earliest cultures were the Olmecs in Mexico and the Chavin in Peru. Later the Maya developed a great civilization in Central America and Yucatán, which suddenly declined about A.D. 900. Other elaborate civilizations followed. Central Mexico was invaded from the north by the Toltecs. After about 1325 the Aztecs became the dominant people in central Mexico. At about the same time, the Incas created an empire in the Andes of South America.

SUGGESTED TEACHING STRATEGIES

1. **Preteaching Vocabulary (Basic)** You may wish to preteach the following important vocabulary terms: chinampa (*page 310*); quipu (*page 311*). Ask students to contrast quipus with hieroglyphics and cuneiform.
2. **Writing an Essay (Challenging)** Have students write a short essay on the development of agriculture among the Mayan, Aztec, and Inca peoples. These essays should discuss crops grown, farming techniques used, and extent of agricultural production. Read selected essays to the class, and use the information provided as the basis for a class discussion comparing farming in the Americas with farming in the ancient Middle East, Africa, and Asia.
3. **Making a Chart (Average/Group)** Write the headings of the following chart on the chalkboard or an overhead projector. Have students copy the headings and complete the chart in their notebooks.

CHARACTERISTICS OF MAYAN CIVILIZATION		
Architecture	**Intellectual Achievements**	**Religion**
Constructed steep pyramids Used the most advanced techniques of the time	Created accurate calendar Developed a counting system based on 20 Invented writing system	Involved astrology Gods were varied and changed form Worshiped peaceful gods Practiced human sacrifice in times of crisis

ENRICHMENT ACTIVITIES

1. **Relating Past and Present (Average/Group)** Have students work in groups to prepare oral reports comparing Aztec and Inca culture with modern Mexican and Peruvian culture. Possible topics are government, religion, and art. Sources include: Hammond Innes's *The Conquistadors* (Knopf) and Jonathan N. Leonard's *Ancient America* (Time-Life). Students should check encyclopedias and the *Reader's Guide to Periodical Literature* for information on Mexico and Peru.
2. **Researching Ideas (Challenging)** Have interested students examine Mayan society and prepare a short paper on it. They should investigate Mayan social classes, religion, government, and customs.

DAILY QUIZ

To assess student understanding of Section 4, give the class the following quiz. (Each item is worth 10 points.)

1. (T or F) Several early cultural groups in Central and South America included pyramids in their religious rites. *(T)*
2. (T or F) The Mayans never studied astronomy and were unable to develop an accurate calendar. *(F)*
3. (T or F) The Mayans frequently engaged in sacrifices and cannibalistic rituals to please their bloodthirsty gods. *(F)*
4. (T or F) The Toltecs, ruled by the military, built pyramids, practiced human sacrifice, and worshiped Quetzalcoatl. *(T)*
5. Which of these was the Aztec capital? Chichen Itza, Cuzco, Tenochtitlán, Teotihuacan *(Tenochtitlán)*
6. (T or F) The Aztecs were great "borrowers," who learned to use metals, to weave, and to make pottery. *(T)*
7. (T or F) The Aztec chinampas allowed for a very productive form of agriculture. *(T)*
8. The Aztecs believed that the sun god and the war god demanded ________ ________ in return for favors. *(human sacrifices)*
9. What does the word "Incas" mean? *(children of the sun)*
10. (T or F) The Incas established irrigation systems, roads, and a public school system, and "wrote" quipus to send messages. *(T)*

SUGGESTED ASSIGNMENTS

1. **Review Worksheet (Basic)** Have students complete Review Worksheet 13 in the TEACHER'S RESOURCEBANK™.
2. **Report (Average/Group)** Have interested students research Aztec methods of warfare in their school or public local libraries. They should indicate the types of weapons the Aztecs used, the kind of clothing or armor they wore, and what kinds of fighting units they formed. *(Aztecs fought with a number of weapons, the most deadly of which was a two-handed sword. This sword was made of hardwood and had razor-sharp blades made of obsidian. This blade was so sharp it could cut off the head of a horse. The Aztecs also used a bow, a sling that threw egg-sized stones, and a javelin, or lightweight spear, some of which had cords so they could be pulled back during a skirmish.)*

Teacher's Notes

For suggested lesson plan, additional teaching strategies, enrichment activities, daily quizzes, and suggested assignments, see pages 291A-291E.

Introducing the Chapter
Have students turn to the maps on pages 294, 298, 304, and 307, or display a physical map of the continents of Africa, North America, and South America in the classroom. Ask students to suggest possible reasons for the isolation of the Americas and SubSaharan Africa. *(Answers should include the following: The vast distances created by the Atlantic and Pacific oceans isolated SubSaharan Africa and the Americas; Europeans were reluctant to pursue uncharted courses to the south; the Sahara separated much of the African continent from the busy North African coast.)*

Ask students to explain how geography and climate contributed to the diversity of cultures in these two areas. *(Answers should include the following: Mountain ranges, deserts, and rain forests tended to isolate societies in Africa and the Americas; Africa lacked good harbors and had few navigable rivers; the variations in Africa's climate—deserts, savannas, and rain forests—made it difficult for people to migrate to unsettled lands and survive. Geography also produced different types of livelihood in different societies. For example, occupations such as farming or raising cattle depended upon geographic location.)*

CHAPTER

13

Africa and the Americas Produced Complex Civilizations

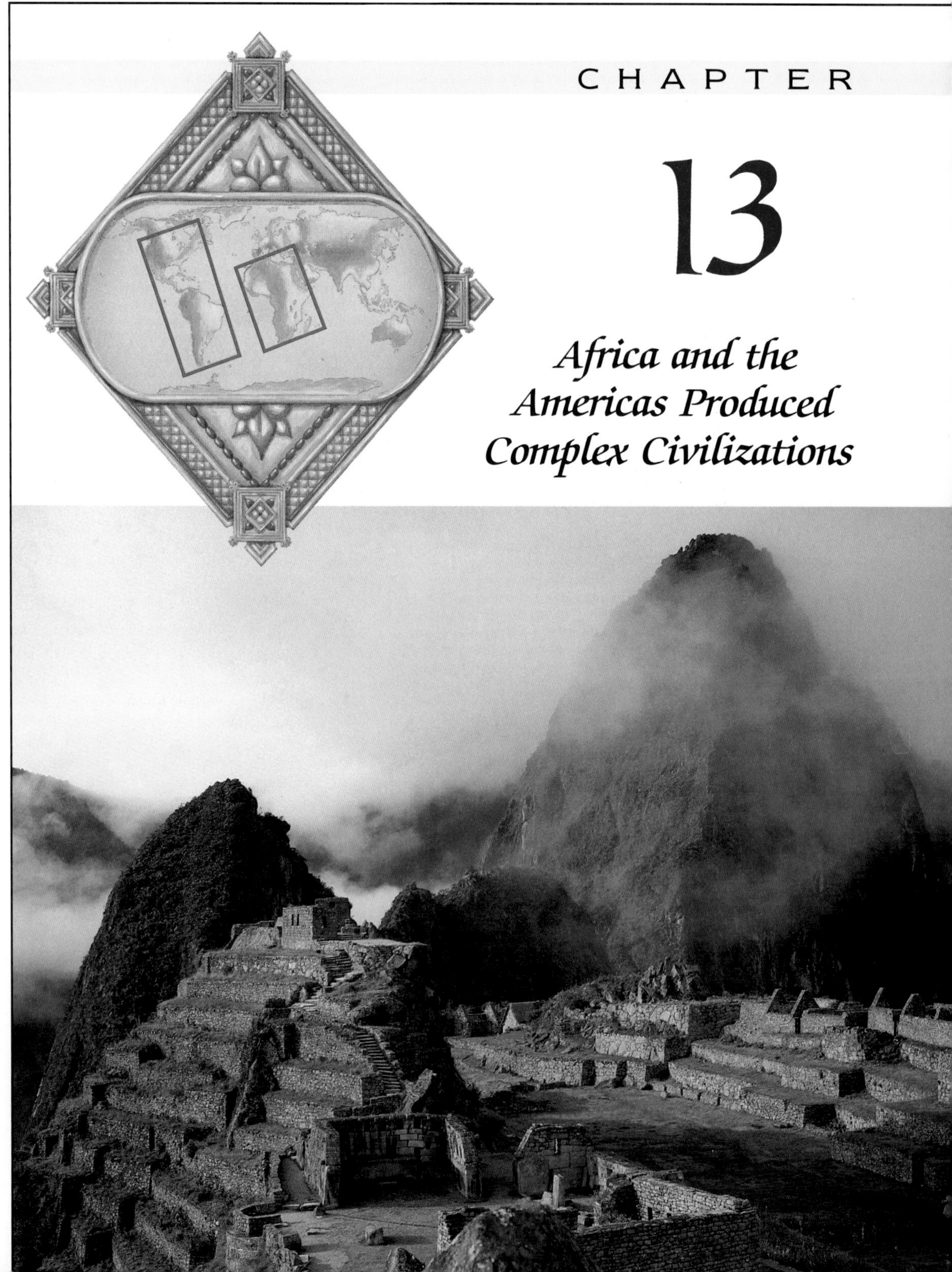

CHAPTER FOCUS

Place Africa and the Americas

Time

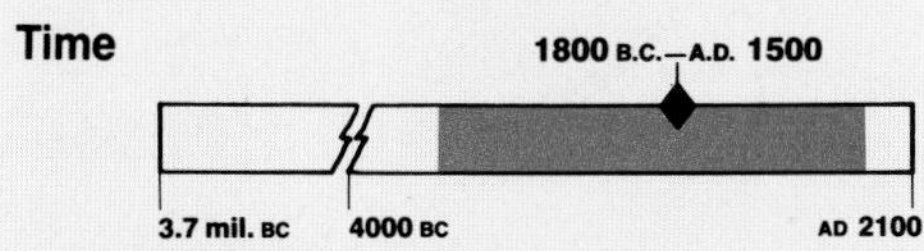

Significance

Because we have few written records of peoples who lived in Africa south of the Sahara and in the Americas, we know much less about events before 1500 in those regions than we do about events in Europe and Asia. Often we must reconstruct early African and American history from artifacts and ancient folk traditions. As a result, our historical knowledge of Africa and the Americas remains fragmentary.

Despite the lack of written records, we know that complex, highly sophisticated societies, remarkable for their political forms and their cultural achievements, developed in both Africa and the Americas. On these continents archaeologists are only beginning to uncover the walls of elaborate cities and fortresses and the foundations of huge temples.

Although the early peoples of Africa and the Americas had little influence on or contact with other parts of the world, understanding these vigorous and varied societies will help you to understand human history. These societies exhibit both contrasts and similarities between European and Asian societies of the same period.

Terms to Define

jungle	adobe
savanna	chinampa
linguist	quipu

People to Identify

Karanga	Olmecs
Mansa Musa	Maya
Sunni Ali	Aztecs

Places to Locate

Niger River	Ghana
Sahara	Andes Mountains
Axum	Yucatán Peninsula

Questions to Guide Your Reading

1 How did historians uncover Africa's early history?
2 What major city-states and kingdoms arose throughout Africa?
3 How did people migrate from Europe and Asia to the Americas?
4 What were the major accomplishments of the empires in Mexico and Peru?

◀ *Machu Picchu, Peru*

On July 24, 1911, in the Peruvian Andes, the American archaeologist Hiram Bingham uncovered the fabled lost city of the Incas—one of the greatest civilizations of the Americas. Bingham marveled at what he saw:

> *"Suddenly I found myself confronted with the walls of ruined houses built of the finest quality of Inca stone work. It was hard to see them for they were partly covered with trees and moss, the growth of centuries, but in the dense shadow, hiding in bamboo thickets and tangled vines, here and there walls of white granite . . . carefully cut and exquisitely fitted together. . . .*
>
> *Surprise followed surprise in bewildering succession. . . . Suddenly we found ourselves standing in front of the ruins of two of the finest and most interesting structures in ancient America. Made of beautiful white granite, the walls contained blocks of Cyclopean size, higher than a man. The sight held me spellbound. . . .*
>
> *I could scarcely believe my senses as I examined the larger blocks . . . and estimated that they must weigh from ten to fifteen tons each. Would anyone believe what I had found?"*

Bingham's discovery, called Machu Picchu, was only one of many glorious cities built by the peoples of the Americas. At the same time, African peoples were creating equally spectacular civilizations.

1 Many Methods Uncovered Africa's Early History

Written records, surviving monuments, and ruins provide evidence of the great civilizations that thrived in North Africa before 1500. Equally important developments were taking place in the rest of Africa—the vast portion of the continent south of the Sahara known as SubSaharan Africa.

The Physical Setting

Most of the vast expanse of SubSaharan Africa rests on a high plateau. Here and there, however, basins and deep valleys dent this plateau.

Chapter Objectives
After studying Chapter 13, students will be able to:

1. Draw a rough outline map of Africa and label the four major rivers, two deserts, rain forest, and savanna.
2. State how African geography, topography, and climate provided an almost impenetrable barrier to outsiders.
3. Summarize how oral tradition helped preserve African culture.
4. Describe the role of women in African society.
5. Outline cultural development in Cush, the coastal city-states, and in Central and West Africa.
6. Describe the characteristics of the people who migrated across the Bering Strait.
7. Write a paragraph summarizing North American Indian cultural developments.
8. Summarize the evolution of early cultures that culminated in the Mayan civilization.
9. Compare the culture of early Central and South American kingdoms with that of the Aztecs and Incas.

SECTION 1

Focus/Motivation
Have students study the map on page 294. Ask them to identify the natural regions of Africa. Lead a class discussion, using the following questions as a guide: What are the two largest natural regions in Africa? *(desert and*

293

1A, 1B, 2B, a4B, a4C

grassland) What do the natural regions tell us about the amount of farmland in Africa? *(The savannas and part of the rain forest are suitable for farming, but the larger portion of Africa is unsuitable for farming.)* What other activities might be conducted in these regions? *(The lumber and rubber industries could prosper in the rain forest. Few activities, except possibly mining and herding, could be carried on in the desert.)*

Presentation
Analyzing Ideas (Average/Group)
Much of the local history of Africa has been recorded in poetry and song and in this way was passed down from generation to generation. Over a period of many years, these histories often became folklore and may contain as much fiction as fact. Conduct a class discussion by asking the students to name some folk songs or stories with which they are familiar. Also ask what the themes of some of these stories are, and why they think that these songs and stories eventually took on the characteristics of fables rather than factual histories.
(Answers will vary. Students might include excerpts from the following: Greek mythology, the Arabian Nights Entertainments, Aesop's Fables. Themes will cover

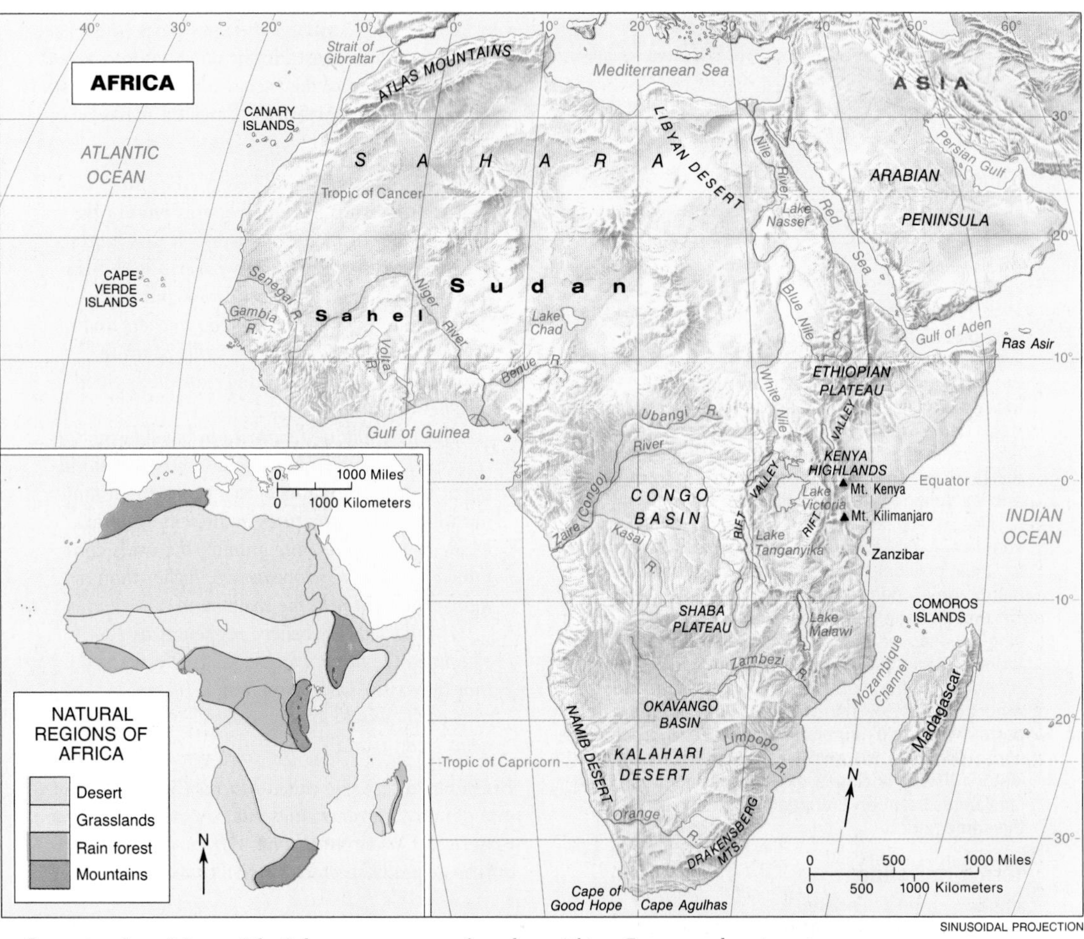

Learning from Maps *The Sahara covers most of northern Africa. Between what rivers is the Kalahari Desert located?* **Orange and Zambezi rivers**

The plateau. The great plateau of SubSaharan Africa straddles the equator like a giant inverted bowl, uplifted in the center and then dropping sharply to the shoreline. Only in Liberia, Ghana (GAHN • uh), and the Ivory Coast—on Africa's western bulge—and in Mozambique (moh • zuhm • BEEK)—in the east—does the slope rise more gently.

The steep shoreline contains few harbors. Most major rivers, including the Niger (NY • juhr), Zaïre (zah • EER), or Congo, and the Zambezi (zam • BEE • zee), are navigable only for relatively short distances into the interior because of numerous rapids. Although these rivers limited trade, they also protected many parts of Africa from invasion. The absence of good natural harbors and navigable rivers has also hindered communication and contact among the African peoples.

Rain falls irregularly throughout much of Africa. In the north lies the enormous Sahara, and in the south, the Kalahari (kal • uh • HAHR • ee) Desert (see map, this page). In contrast, some areas of western and central Africa receive more than 100 inches (254 centimeters) of rain each year. There, vast forests called **tropical rain forests** thrive. People often mistakenly call these forests jungles. However, a **jungle** is a thick growth of plants found in a tropical rain forest wherever sunlight penetrates the dense umbrella of tall trees and reaches the forest floor.

The wet climate of the rain forests provides fertile breeding grounds for insects that carry deadly diseases. For example, mosquitoes transmit malaria and yellow fever, and the tsetse (SET • see) fly carries sleeping sickness. Although modern medicine can treat these diseases, many Africans perished from them in earlier centuries.

Although no mountain ranges break the plateau, isolated mountain peaks dot its eastern part. Some, such as Mount Kenya and Mount Kilimanjaro (kil • uh • muhn • JAHR • oh), jut thousands of feet above the plateau.

The basins. Five deep basins dent the plateau. Each more than 600 miles (965 kilometers) wide, these basins sink more than 5,000 feet (1,525 meters) below the top of the plateau.

The Rift Valley. Perhaps the most remarkable geographic feature of SubSaharan Africa is the Great Rift Valley. Formed thousands of years ago when a part of the plateau sank, this steep-sided structural crack runs north and south near the plateau's eastern edge. Today many long, narrow lakes lie in the rift valley.

The Sahel. A vast area of relatively dry grasslands called **savannas,** dotted with a few trees and thorny bushes, stretches across Africa immediately south of the Sahara. In this region, known as the Sahel (suh • HAYL), sparse, unpredictable rainfall often results in severe droughts.

Rediscovering the African Past

Scholars rely on a variety of methods to understand the African past during the time before the people there developed writing. For example, **linguists**—scholars who study languages—have used computers and mathematics to compare the roots of words and common vocabulary. This technique—lexicostatistics—has helped solve the mystery of how Bantu, a family of closely related languages spoken in many parts of Africa, spread. The study suggests that for centuries wave upon wave of peoples have migrated throughout SubSaharan Africa.

An original "cradle land" of the Bantu language was in the southeastern region of what is today Nigeria. From there, beginning perhaps 2,000 years ago, Bantu-speaking people began to migrate southward into what are today the countries of Cameroon and Gabon. By the A.D. 700s, Bantu was spoken in central Africa as well as on the island of Zanzibar, in the Indian Ocean off the coast of Africa (see map, page 298).

The study of **oral traditions**—poems, songs, or stories passed by word of mouth from one generation to another—has been another source of information about specific African clans, villages, and dynasties. Africans have always had a strong sense of their own history. Individual families or villages preserved the memory of important events by incorporating them into poetry or song. People then passed these stories on from one generation to the next, with each generation adding to the tradition. In a similar way, the royal households of African kingdoms paid professional reciters to record in song the important events of a dynasty. Anthropologists and historians have now written down much of this oral tradition.

Other fields of scholarship have also helped unlock the secrets of Africa's past. For example, scholars who study music have discovered similarities in the design and tuning of xylophones found in East Africa and Indonesia, in Southeast Asia. These similarities suggest that at some early date, people migrated from Asia to Africa. Similarly, scientists have studied the spread to Africa of the banana, a plant that grows in Southeast Asia. And linguists have studied the Malagasy language, spoken on the island of Madagascar in the Indian Ocean off the east coast of Africa. Malagasy has many words in common with languages spoken on the islands of Indonesia. From these fields of study—the study of music, plants, and language—scholars have determined that people from Indonesia migrated to East Africa about A.D. 300.

Scholars have also discovered that the people of SubSaharan Africa were particularly adept at coping with their often harsh environment. Although wheat and barley could not be cultivated south of the Sahara near sea level, the people there were able to domesticate a variety of crops. For example, the people of the Sahel domesticated millet, sorghum, pennisetum, and eleusine. In later centuries these grains became the staple crops of the people of SubSaharan Africa. In addition, farmers cultivated sesame, which through the process of cultural diffusion was introduced in Sumer about 2350 B.C.

Although the people of SubSaharan Africa domesticated various crops, changes in the climate of the Sahel soon altered patterns of agriculture. Between about 2500 B.C. and 2300 B.C. the region became much drier. As a result the people of the region relied increasingly on herding.

almost every human condition. A reason for events being recorded in this manner is that most of the people in the early societies were unable to read or write, so the only way for them to communicate events of the past was through word of mouth. As time went on, these stories or songs became embellished as generations were removed from the actual event and more fiction than fact was incorporated.)

SECTION 1

Closure

Ask students to list the major geographical features of SubSaharan Africa. *(plateau, basins, the Rift Valley, and the Sahel)*

Review Answers

1. ***tropical rain forest:*** vast forested regions in western and central Africa receiving more than 100 inches of annual rainfall; ***jungle:*** thick growth of plants found on forest floor in tropical rain forests; ***savanna:*** dry grasslands; ***linguist:*** scholar who studies languages; ***oral tradition:*** poems, songs, or stories passed by word of mouth from one generation to another; ***matrilineal:*** societies in which people trace their ancestors through mothers rather than their fathers

2. ***Niger River:*** long river in West Africa; ***Zaïre (Congo) River:*** major world river with mouth on south central Atlantic coast; ***Zambezi River:*** flows into Indian Ocean on southeastern coast; ***Sahara:*** great North African desert; ***Kalahari Desert:*** desert along southwestern coast

3. (a) The small number of natural harbors, lack of navigable rivers, the Sahara and Kalahari deserts, and dense rain forests made contact difficult among peoples in the interior. **(b)** People settled in small, independent villages as farmers or herders.

4. Oral traditions in the

CONNECTIONS: THEN AND NOW

Trumpets

The sound of trumpets has been echoing around the world for thousands of years. The first trumpets were made from hollow branches or reeds. They were used to frighten away evil spirits, to make mournful sounds at funerals, and in the evening to appeal to the sun to return the next day. In some parts of Switzerland, the alpenhorn still sounds the evening prayer. In Romania and Tibet, men play long wooden trumpets at funerals.

Early Africans used horns to send messages over long distances (far right). In present-day Nigeria, horns are still sounded at celebrations (above). The Aztecs used trumpets to call the rain gods, and horns of silver, copper, and wood were used by the Incas in Peru. Incas also had clay trumpets with bells shaped like jaguar heads.

Both the Egyptians and the Hebrews used metal trumpets to attract the attention of the gods. The Bible says that when Joshua fought the battle of Jericho, the blast of seven trumpets made the walls fall down. Today, at the ceremony to celebrate the Jewish New Year, the *shofar* is sounded. Carved from a ram's horn as in ancient times, the sounding of the horn reminds Jewish worshipers of their ancient origins.

Trumpets as we know them are shaped like those used in Europe since 1500. Many musicians feel that the peak of trumpet performance has come only recently from the contributions of America's great jazz musicians, such as Wynton Marsalis (below left) and Chuck Mangione (below right).

● The later Christian kingdom of Nubia was strong enough to prevent the Muslim invaders from crossing the First Cataract of the Nile River until the 1200s. Arab traders settled in Red Sea ports by the 800s and gradually penetrated Nubia. After a Nubian prince converted to Islam in the 1300s, Islam eventually predominated.

1B, 2A, 2B, a1C, a4A, a4F, a4G, a4H, a4L

Archaeology has also added much to our understanding of African history. Excavation sites throughout the continent have revealed details of daily life in early Africa. Much of this work has helped to either support or disprove what has been learned from oral traditions and other sources.

Patterns of Life

Based upon the scholarly studies of the African past, experts have drawn several conclusions about patterns of life in early Africa. They believe that most Africans lived in small, independent villages and were farmers or herders. Relationships of kinship, age, and sex provided the ties that bound the different societies together. Within this system women played a crucial role. As laborers they performed much of the agricultural work. In Great Zimbabwe women worked in the mines. Scholars believe that societies in many parts of SubSaharan Africa were matrilineal. In **matrilineal** (ma • truh • LIN • ee • uhl) societies, people trace their ancestors through their mothers rather than their fathers. In such societies, a boy inherited from his mother's brother rather than from his father.

Chiefs or elders usually exercised authority over the village. However, since land was plentiful and migration became a real choice for those who were unhappy, a chief's rule had to be fair. Life in the African villages was closely bound to the agricultural cycles of planting and harvesting. Through the rise and fall of numerous kingdoms, the village survived as the basic unit of society and the economy. Its persistence makes it a vital part of the African heritage.

SECTION 1 REVIEW

1. **Define** tropical rain forest, jungle, savanna, linguist, oral tradition, matrilineal
2. **Locate** Niger River, Zaïre (Congo) River, Zambezi River, Sahara, Kalahari Desert
3. **Linking Geography and History** **(a)** What geographic factors made contact difficult among peoples in Africa's interior? **(b)** How did the geography of Africa influence patterns of settlement?
4. **Summarizing Ideas** What nonwritten evidence identifies early African developments?
5. **Understanding Ideas** What conclusions have scholars reached about patterns of life in early Africa?

2 City-states and Kingdoms Arose Throughout Africa

A remarkable variety of kingdoms, empires, and small city-states arose in the different areas of Africa before 1500. These kingdoms were as diverse as the African geography.

Cush

Along the Nile River, south of the major centers of ancient Egypt, lies an area known as Nubia. A ● source of gold, granite, and timber, it also thrived as an important trade center. Here, caravans hauled goods from the Red Sea to barges on the Nile. And here arose a powerful kingdom known as Cush (see map, page 298).

Cush traces its roots to the city of Kerma, a trading center of southern Nubia that the Egyptians founded about 1800 B.C. The Egyptians greatly influenced this region. Nevertheless, the pottery, jewelry, and other ornaments uncovered in this area show that a distinctly local Nubian culture emerged.

Learning from Pictures *These ruins of the kingdom of Cush are located in the Sudan.*

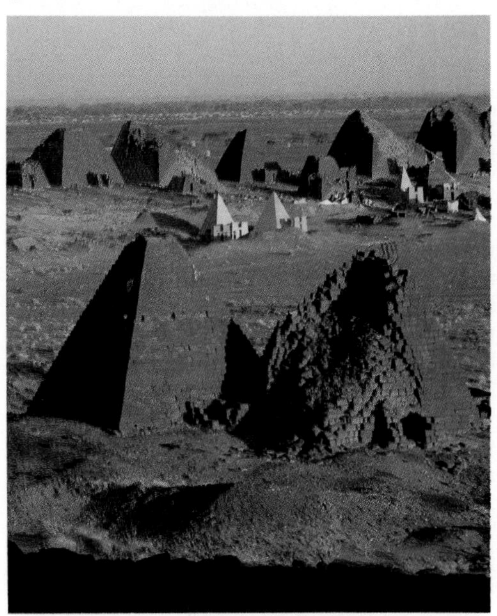

form of poems, songs, and stories provide information on African clans, villages, and dynasties.
5. The spread of certain languages, music, and plants can be studied to identify migrations of people. Most Africans lived in small independent villages as farmers or herders. Relationships of kinship, age and sex provided the ties that bound the different societies together.

SECTION 2

Focus/Motivation
Have students read the subsection on Axum on page 300. Then tell them that many Ethiopians believe that the biblical Queen of Sheba had her capital at Axum and that her son Menelik by King Solomon was the first king of Ethiopia. Many historians, however, believe that the Queen of Sheba came from Saba (Sheba), a country situated across the Red Sea in what is today Yemen and Aden.

Tell students that the Ethiopian legend is an example of oral traditions in the study of African history. Another example they will read about is Prester John, a legendary king, who intrigued the Portuguese in the 1400s. They believed Prester John was king of a wealthy Christian country — perhaps Ethiopia — that the Muslims threatened to conquer. In the Age of Exploration, the

1A, 1B, 1D, 2A, 2B, a4B, a4C

● **Cushite temple and pyramid ruins are in desert lands today. In 500 B.C., however, large herds of cattle lived off the land. This indicates only that the rainfall was much greater.**

Portuguese would search for Prester John and wage war against the Muslims. At the same time, they could take control of the lucrative trade routes.

Ask students how Christianity penetrated to the kingdom of Axum. *(King Ezana converted to Christianity in A.D. 325, and the region has remained Christian since then.)*

Presentation
Relating Ideas (Average/Group)
Ask students to name the major items that SubSaharan Africans traded. *(Gold, slaves, and salt were the chief items of trade, but they also traded iron, war elephants, rhinoceros horn, incense, spices, and ivory.)*
Ask: What were the principal trading kingdoms or empires? *(Cush, Axum, the city-states along the East African coast, the Karanga people of Zimbabwe, and Ghana, Mali, and Songhai in West Africa)* Next ask students how geography influenced this trade. *(Answers will vary. Students should point out that control of sea routes across the Red Sea and the Indian Ocean enabled Cush, Axum, and city-states like Kilwa to thrive in the east, while control of caravan routes across the Sahara and the major rivers such as the Niger enabled great empires like Ghana, Mali, and Songhai to become major powers in West Africa.)*
Tell students that the Arabs

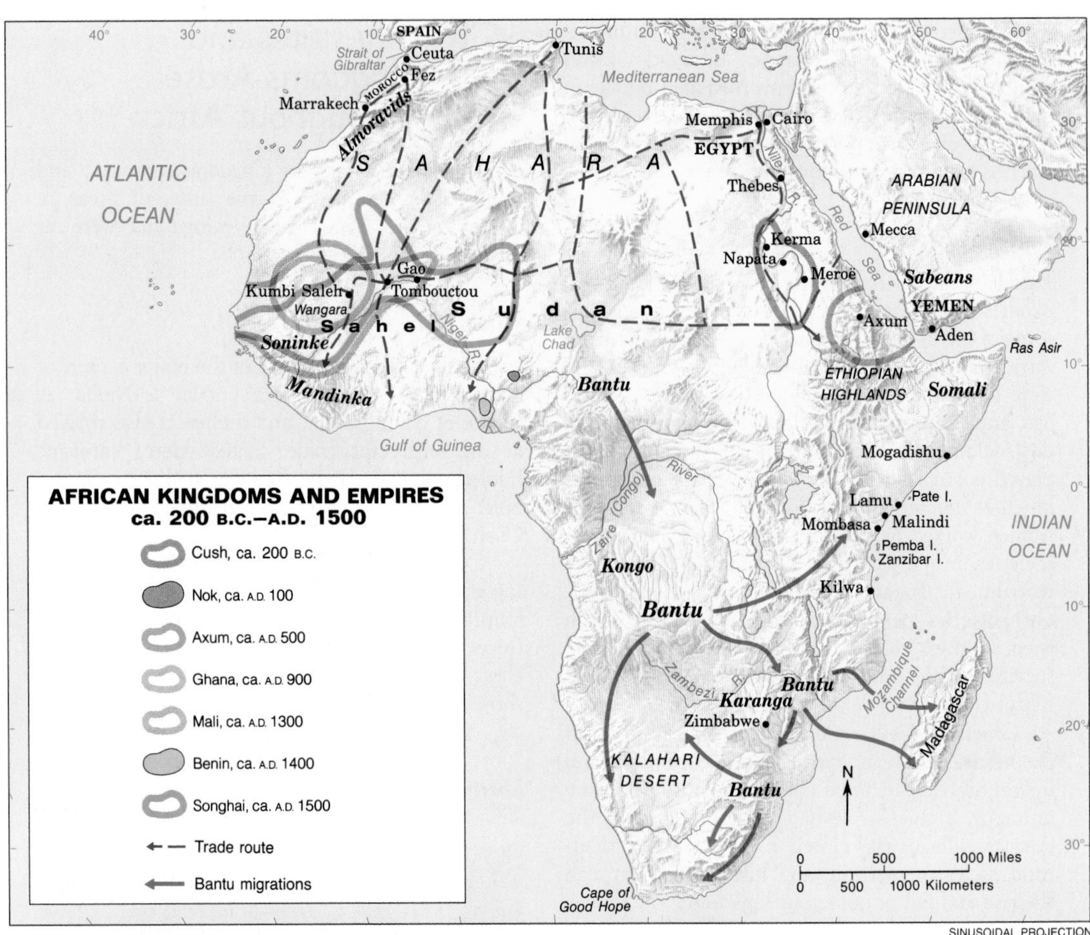

Learning from Maps *African civilizations were thriving during the height of the Roman Empire. How many years does the map cover?* **1,700 years**

Over the next centuries, Cush became a distinct kingdom. It had its own dynasty and a capital at Napata (NAP • uht • uh), a city upstream from Kerma. But it maintained close cultural and economic ties with Egypt. By the 1100s B.C., Cush had become virtually independent of Egypt, and about 750 B.C. it conquered Upper Egypt. For about 100 years—until the Assyrians, armed with iron weapons, invaded in 671 B.C.—a Cush dynasty ruled a unified Egypt.

With the Assyrian invasion, the Cush kingdom weakened. Following the Assyrian plunder of Napata in 591 B.C., the kingdom reorganized itself around a new capital at Meroë (MER • uh • wee) and began a new period of growth and cultural achievement. Meroë was one of the earliest centers of iron working in Africa. Today, the remains of huge heaps of slag, the waste from smelting, rise out of the desert, indicating the importance of this ancient activity.

The Cush kingdom also controlled trade routes from the Red Sea to the Nile. Caravans brought Hellenistic, Persian, and Indian influences that the people of Meroë adapted to their own culture.

The brilliant Cush civilization reached its height from 250 B.C. to A.D. 150. The people erected impressive pyramids and temples and crafted exquisite pottery and ornaments. Then the ●

1B, 1C, 2B, a4D, a4F, a4G

READ
● WRITE
INTERPRET
CONNECT
THINK

BUILDING HISTORY STUDY SKILLS

Writing About History: Paraphrasing Information

As you study world history and perfect your writing skills, you will use many primary and secondary sources. You might either quote or paraphrase these sources. *Quoting* is repeating exactly the words of the author or speaker. *Paraphrasing* is translating something into your own words. Putting something into your own words often helps you think about what you have read and makes it easier to understand and remember, especially for tests. If you are writing a report, paraphrasing will help you to avoid plagiarizing, or copying the words and ideas of others without acknowledging the source.

How to Paraphrase Information

To paraphrase information, follow these steps:

1. Define the main idea of the selection.
2. Indicate the details—bits and pieces of information related to the main idea.
3. Put the main idea and details in your own words.
4. Compare your statement with the original selection by asking questions:
   - Have you written a complete thought?
   - Does it make sense?
   - Does it have new information that focuses on meaning?

Developing the Skill

The following document describes the founding of the East African city of Kilwa. Read the document. Then define the main idea and paraphrase the document in a few sentences.

Arab dhows sailing

"The story goes that there was a Sultan of Shiraz named Hasan bin Ali. . . . One day he saw a vision of a rat with an iron snout nibbling and gnawing at the walls. From this he foreboded the ruin of the country, and so, . . . the whole family, seven in number, sailed away from the doomed country in as many ships. Of these it was the sixth that came to Kilwa. At the time of the immigration Kilwa was an island only at high tide. . . . The new-comers found a Muslim already settled there with his family, and a mosque. From him they learned that the country belonged to the chief of the neighboring district, who was then absent on a hunting expedition. After a few days, he returned to Kilwa, and the stranger, being pleased with the island, offered, through the mediation of the friendly Muslim, to buy it. The chief named his terms, which were that the stranger should surround the whole island with colored cloth. This was soon done, and the chief took the cloth and surrendered the island. All the while, however, he cherished the secret intention of returning with an armed force to destroy the immigrants and carry off their goods. This was guessed by the Muslim, who had acted as interpreter, so he warned the strangers to provide for their safety in time. Accordingly, as soon as the chief's back was turned, they set to work and dug a trench in the neck of the land joining Kilwa to the continent. . . . The chief . . . waited for the tide to go down and leave a dry passage to Kilwa; but the water never subsided, so he returned to his own country defeated and disappointed."

The topic of the selection is the founding of the East African city of Kilwa. The details focus on why the sultan fled his home, how he took possession of Kilwa, and how he secured the island. A paraphrased statement of the selection might be:

According to legend, the Sultan of Shiraz had a vision telling of impending ruin for his country. He gathered his family, and they fled in seven ships. One of the ships landed at Kilwa, where a sympathetic Muslim helped the sultan buy the area from the local chief. Warned that the chief was going to invade, the sultan and his family dug a deep trench to protect Kilwa. Since Kilwa was now an island, the chief abandoned it. And that is how Kilwa became an island.

Practicing the skill. Reread the selection by Hiram Bingham on page 293 and put it into your own words.

To apply this skill, see Applying History Study Skills on page 313.

became important traders in this region. They also made great inroads into traditional and Christian countries by converting the people to Islam. Islam still predominates throughout North Africa and large sections of East Africa. The slave trade also occupied an important part of the economy of these civilizations, but it did not affect the world until the advent of European traders and the establishment of European empires with plantation economies.

1B, 1D, 2A, 2B, a1B, a1C

● Ethiopia adopted Coptic Christianity, which had absorbed many practices from Judaism and pagan religions. In the 1520s Arabs from Somalia began a *jihad*, or holy war, against the Ethiopians. The Ethiopians appealed to the Portuguese, who sent 400 musketeers from their possessions in India and defeated the Arabs.

Cush civilization mysteriously declined. Although scholars do not know why, many believe that it involved the rise of a rival state—Axum.

Axum

Situated in the Ethiopian Highlands south of Cush, Axum straddled the trade routes from the Red Sea into Egypt and the interior of Africa (see map, page 298). As Cush declined, Axum became a major competitor for control of this trade and sent war elephants, rhinoceros horns, tortoise shells, incense, and spices to the Mediterranean world by way of Egypt.

Finally, in A.D. 325, King Ezana (AH • zah • nah) of Axum inflicted a crushing defeat on Cush and established a thriving kingdom. During his reign Ezana converted to Christianity, and the religion, which incorporated many elements of the people's traditional beliefs, has remained an important influence in the region.

For the next 400 years, Axum controlled the African side of the Red Sea trade. Its influence beyond this region, however, ended with the rise of Islam. By the early 700s, Muslim forces controlled both the Arabian and the African sides of the Red Sea.

East Africa and Trade

No large kingdoms like Cush and Axum emerged on the coast of East Africa. Instead, a series of city-states that dominated coastal trade in the Indian Ocean arose. The seasonal monsoon winds provided a reliable means of travel. Sailors explored the seas and developed trade routes linking all shores of the Indian Ocean. Africans exported gold, slaves, ivory, hides, and tortoise shells and imported porcelain and weapons.

The spread of Islam to northeastern Africa also created favorable conditions for trade. Along the East African coast, a golden age began in the 700s and lasted through the 1300s. The opportunity to make money in Africa attracted merchant families, adventurers, and refugees fleeing the Shiite-Sunnite conflicts in Arabia and Persia. They settled on islands and easily defensible spits of land, where they soon established several thriving trading centers.

Over several generations a unique African culture—Swahili (swah • HEE • lee)—developed on the East African coast. The people of this culture spoke Swahili, a Bantu language with Arabic and Persian influences. Although the Swahili were not a unified ethnic group, their common pursuits—especially trade—and language bound the people together.

Learning from Pictures *This ritual charm discovered in the present-day nation of Zaire belonged to Bantu-speaking people.*

The earliest of the city-states—Mogadishu (mahg • uh • DISH • oo), Lamu, Pate (PAH • tay), and Malindi—lay in the north. Gradually, commercial activity shifted southward. By the 1100s Kilwa, the most famous city-state, was the leading port along the African coast.

Under Kilwa's leadership, coastal civilization flourished. Ibn Battuta (IB • uhn bah • TOO • tah), a famous Muslim traveler of the 1300s, described Kilwa as one of the most beautiful and well-constructed towns in the world. Recent archaeological excavations have uncovered a massive trade center and a large mosque that reveal the city's wealth and achievements. ●

Central Africa and Great Zimbabwe

Kilwa grew as a port for the shipment of gold mined along the Zambezi River in central Africa. For centuries gold and other goods had reached the coast from there, passing eastward through small-scale

300

1B, 1C, 1D, 2A, 2B, a1B, a1C

The trans-Saharan trade was based mainly on three very profitable items: salt, gold, and slaves.

SCULPTURE

Royal Figure from West Africa

The people of Ife, in what is now southwestern Nigeria, began making life-sized bronze heads more than 600 years ago. Historians believe that the original inhabitants of the region—the Yoruba (YAWR • uh • buh) people—had crafted terra cotta sculpture for centuries.

About 700 years ago, however, immigrants from the northeast swept into the area and founded the city of Ife. It was these immigrants who taught the Yoruba the intricate art of making bronze sculptures and introduced the concept of divine kingship.

The magnificent example of bronze casting shown here depicts one of these kings. The beaded crown tells us that the head is that of a very important king. The vertical lines represent ritual scarring—a practice still followed by people in some parts of Africa. A beard and a mustache were attached to the holes around the mouth.

After a king died, the bronze head was attached to a wooden body and carried throughout the city. The ceremony indicated that although the king was dead, the power of the office lived on in his successors.

SECTION 2

Closure

Ask students to describe the relationship of ancient Egypt with African kingdoms on the upper Nile. *(In ancient times the region of Nubia contained the kingdom of Cush, which had a highly developed civilization and carried on trade with Egypt. Cush was weakened by the Assyrian conquest and by the rise of Axum in Ethiopia.)*

trade networks based on the exchange of essential items such as salt, tools, or cloth.

The growth of Indian Ocean trade after the 900s dramatically increased the demand for gold. With this increased demand came a consolidation of control over the mining of gold and its shipment to the coast. In about 800 the Karanga, a people who immigrated onto the plateau land of what is today Zimbabwe (zim • BAHB • wee), achieved this control. Gradually, the Karanga asserted control over local peoples and mining activities. Archaeologists have located more than 7,000 mine shafts, indicating the importance of mining to the local economy.

Although we have little definite information about the Karanga people, scholars believe they built fortified enclosures and probably attained great wealth and power. Great Zimbabwe, the largest and most famous of these fortresses, became the administrative and religious center of the Karanga state. Its 32-foot- (10-meter-) high and 17-foot- (5-meter-) thick walls consist of some 900,000 large granite blocks and show the advanced construction methods this society used.

Excavation of the site revealed a rapid and seemingly mysterious decline in the 1400s. Scientists now believe that the area may have experienced an ecological disaster. One theory is that the population grew so quickly that it outpaced dwindling water and food resources. Without enough food and water, people starved, and the brilliant civilization declined.

Kingdoms and Cultures of West Africa

In West Africa, between Lake Chad and the Atlantic Ocean, important African kingdoms flourished. They included Ghana, Mali (MAHL • ee), and Songhai (SAWNG • hy). Knowledge of these kingdoms comes largely from oral tradition and from the writings of African scholars and Muslim traders.

The wealth and strength of these kingdoms depended on control of the trade routes across the Sahara. At the desert's edge, traders exchanged gold, extracted from the forest zone south of the Sahel, for salt, mined in the Sahara. The people of the Sahel needed the salt to flavor and preserve their food. The traders from the north wanted the gold for coins and for buying goods from Europe. At the site where this gold-for-salt exchange took place, important commercial cities grew and flourished. Indeed, West Africa produced most of the world's gold until 1500. In time traders in these cities also exchanged ivory and slaves for horses, textiles, linen, books, paper, and weapons.

In these civilizations monarchs ruled, assisted by officials. Often adorned with gold, these monarchs presided over elaborate ceremonies and administered justice. According to the Muslim historian Al-Bakri, trial by wood was common:

301

1B, 2B, a1A, a1C

- In 1076 Berber Almoravids, a puritanical Islamic sect, captured Ghana's capital.
- The modern nation of Ghana is not located in the same lands as was the earlier kingdom. It is on the Gulf of Guinea to the southeast.

Review Answers

1. ***Mansa Musa:*** ruler under whom Mali reached the peak of its power; ***Sunni Ali:*** ruler whose policies made Songhai a powerful and efficient kingdom
2. ***Kerma:*** Egyptian-founded city from which Kingdom of Cush grew; ***Napata:*** capital of independent Cushite kingdom; ***Meroë:*** capital of Cush after Assyrians plundered Napata; ***Kilwa:*** the most famous city-state on the East African coast; ***Lake Chad:*** large lake in West Africa that was eastern border of important African kingdoms; ***Ghana:*** earliest of large West African kingdoms, reached peak in 900s; ***Mali:*** successor kingdom to Ghana, on upper Niger River, reached peak in 1300s; ***Tombouctou:*** capital of Mali and important center of Muslim learning; ***Songhai:*** third kingdom in West Africa, important in 1400s and 1500s; ***Gao:*** trading city and center of Songhai kingdom
3. Gold and iron ore were mined in Africa.
4. A series of city-states that dominated coastal trade along the Indian Ocean arose in East Africa. Seasonal monsoon winds provided reliable means of travel, while sailors explored the seas and developed trade routes linking all shores of the Indian Ocean. The spread of Islam to northeastern Africa also created favorable conditions for

Learning from Pictures *This bronze plaque depicting soldiers wearing helmets and decorative robes is from the kingdom of Benin in West Africa.*

> "When a man is accused of denying a debt or having shed blood or some other crime, a headman takes a thin piece of wood, which is sour and bitter to taste, and pours upon it some water which he then gives to the defendant to drink. If the man vomits, his innocence is recognized and he is congratulated. If he does not vomit and the drink remains in his stomach, the accusation is accepted as justified."

Below the royal family and government officials on the social scale came merchants, farmers, fishers, and cattle breeders. Slaves, whose numbers remained small, ranked at the bottom of the social scale.

Ghana. Ghana, the earliest of these kingdoms, traced its origin to Kumbi Saleh, a trading village founded in the 200s and situated in the southeastern part of modern Mauritania (mawr • uh • TAY • nee • uh). Ghana was at its peak in the 900s, but its period of prosperity was short-lived. In the 1000s a Muslim religious revival and the preaching of a Holy War stirred up Berber tribes, who had once controlled trade in the Sahara. They invaded Ghana. The kingdom never recovered from this attack and in 1235 ceased to exist.

Mali. The rise of a successor kingdom—Mali—followed the fall of Ghana. This new kingdom came to power in the region that had been Ghana, as well as in vast areas to the north and west and along the upper Niger River. Under Mansa Musa, who ruled from 1307 to 1332, Mali's power reached its peak. When Mansa Musa made his pilgrimage to Mecca, 60,000 other pilgrims, including 500 slaves each carrying a 4-pound (1.8 kilogram) bar of gold, accompanied him. Upon his return, Musa supported education, the arts, and building. His capital, Tombouctou (tohn • book • TOO), became an important center of Muslim learning, with a large university that attracted scholars from Egypt and Arabia.

When Ibn Battuta visited Mali shortly after Mansa Musa's death, the wealth and peace of the kingdom astounded him. He wrote:

> "They [the people of Mali] are seldom unjust and have a greater abhorrence of injustice than any other people. Their Sultan shows no mercy to any one guilty of the least act of it. There is complete security in their country. Neither traveler nor inhabitant in it has any thing to fear from robbers or men of violence. They do not confiscate the property of any white man who dies in their country, even if it be uncounted wealth. On the contrary, they give it into the charge of some trust-worthy person among the whites, until the rightful heir takes possession of it."

Although disputes over dynastic succession weakened Mali, it managed to maintain control over the desert trade routes until the 1400s. Then in 1468 Sunni Ali, leader of a region that had broken away from Mali's authority, captured Tombouctou, beginning the age of the third kingdom—Songhai.

Songhai. The kingdom of Songhai was centered on the important trading city of Gao (GOH). From there it controlled a kingdom about the size of all western Europe. Sunni Ali, its most important ruler, hoped to avoid a succession crisis after

Answers will vary. Students might comment that invaders from China, Mongolia, and Russia would have had continuous overland access to North America from Asia, opening North America to the conquests and settlement by many peoples.

1A, 1B, 1C, 1D, 2B, 2C, a4A, a4F, a4G, a4H, a4L

his death. Therefore, he established a government designed to ensure tighter control over his subjects. He divided the kingdom into provinces, each with a governor and officials who reported directly to the king in his capital at Gao. He also built a fleet of warships to enforce peace along the Niger River, which had become a major route of African commerce. His policies made Songhai a powerful and efficient kingdom that continued to thrive until the Moroccans invaded in 1591.

SECTION 2 REVIEW

1. **Identify** Mansa Musa, Sunni Ali
2. **Locate** Kerma, Napata, Meroë, Kilwa, Lake Chad, Ghana, Mali, Tombouctou, Songhai, Gao
3. **Summarizing Ideas** What metals were mined in the ancient kingdoms of Africa?
4. **Understanding Ideas** What factors helped make East Africa a center for trade?
5. **Analyzing Ideas** (a) Give evidence to support the idea that Ghana, Mali, and Songhai were powerful, wealthy kingdoms. **(b)** What role did trade play in their development?

3 People Migrated from Asia to the Americas

From the beginning of history until about 500 years ago, the peoples of the Eastern and Western hemispheres had virtually no contact with each other. Although daring Viking explorers landed at several places on the coast of North America around the year 1000, accounts of their voyages were not well known, and other explorers did not follow up their journeys. Old European maps show a vast blank space or fanciful islands where what we now call the Western Hemisphere lies. Europeans seemed unaware that millions of people already inhabited that vast region of the world.

The Physical Setting

The Americas stretch more than 9,000 miles (14,500 kilometers) from Greenland in the north to Cape Horn at the southern tip of South America. Not surprisingly, geographic contrasts typify this enormous expanse of land.

Almost every type of climate and terrain can be found somewhere in the Americas. Jagged mountains curve like a rugged backbone near the western coast of the Americas. Known as the Rocky Mountains in North America, they extend through Mexico and into South America, where they are called the Andes Mountains. To the east of the mountains on both continents are flatter lands dotted here and there by mountains.

The Americas also include two of the world's great river systems. In North America the Mississippi River drains much of the continent and provides a major transportation route. In South America the Amazon River, second only to the Nile in length, flows almost 3,900 miles (6,275 kilometers) from the Andes through dense rain forests before emptying into the Atlantic Ocean.

The Great Migrations

While the Ice Age still gripped the earth, people migrated from Asia to the Americas across what is now the Bering Strait, off the coast of Alaska. This strait marks the narrowest point between the continents of Asia and North America. During several periods in the past, a "bridge" of land stood there. Even when water covered the land, the strait spanned only a few miles, and people in boats could have crossed it easily.

Neither a single large migration nor a continuous flow of people from Asia populated the Americas. Rather, over the centuries a series of waves of different peoples crossed to the Americas. Changes in Asia's climate may from time to time have forced people northeastward and across the strait. From there they drifted toward warmer climates. Finding some areas already inhabited by earlier immigrants, they would move on, looking for a favorable place to settle.

Some people moved into the eastern and central areas of North America. Others drifted farther south, through Mexico and Central America and

What If?

The Bering Strait

Prehistoric peoples migrated across a land bridge linking Asia and North America. How do you think the course of world history would have been different if this land bridge still existed?

trade, while the opportunity to make money in Africa attracted merchant families, adventurers, and refugees fleeing Islamic religious conflicts. The Swahili language bound the people together.
5. (a) The three kingdoms controlled profitable trade routes across the Sahara. Mali also controlled the territory to the north and west of Ghana and along the Upper Niger. Tombouctou, the capital of Mali, became an important center of learning under Mansa Musa. Songhai controlled an even larger area. Under Sunni Ali, Songhai warships enforced peace along the Niger River, a major trade route. **(b)** Answers will vary. Students might state that trade helped in the spread of culture through the exchange of ideas and created the wealth to support education and the arts. Wise rulers encouraged trade that brought this wealth and political power.

SECTION 3

Focus/Motivation

Whether people in the Americas developed their own civilizations or had contact with other people and learned from them is frequently debated. Ask students to comment on theories about groups that might have influenced people in the Americas. *(Answers will vary. Students might include the Chinese, Scandinavians, or*

303

1A, 1B, 2C, a1C, a4B, a4C

● **Throughout the world maize is second only to rice as a staple crop. The word *corn* is used for maize in America, but corn is a generic word for grain of any kind, such as the "wheat" referred to in the English Corn Laws.**

Polynesians.) Ask students what evidence there is for these theories. *(Students may point out the discovery of the Vinland map, similarities in architectural styles between the pyramids of Egypt and those of Mexico, the similarity of Asian and South American art objects, and the voyages of Thor Heyerdahl.)*

Explain to students that although evidence exists for some of these theories, the evidence is not conclusive. Interested students may use the following sources to pursue the topic: Samuel Eliot Morison discusses Irish and Viking influences in *The European Discovery of America* (Oxford University Press). George E. Stuart's *Discovering Man's Past in the Americas* (National Geographic Society) touches on the topic in Chapters 2 and 7. Jonathan N. Leonard's *Ancient America* (Time-Life) has an illustration on the subject.

Presentation
Summarizing Ideas (Average/Group)
Write the following items on the chalkboard or an overhead projector:

1. Built communal houses of adobe
2. Lived by hunting wild buffalo
3. Expert woodworkers and weavers
4. Built earthen mounds as burial sites
5. Placed high value on deeds of bravery

Learning from Maps *Many cities in North America are named after Indian tribes. What Indian people settled along the Bering Strait?* **Eskimos**

across the narrow Isthmus of Panama. From there all South America spread out before them.

The Development of Agriculture

The first people to reach the Americas were nomads who lived by hunting and gathering. Their descendants, however, discovered a new way of life—farming. The earliest traces of farming in the Western Hemisphere have been found in parts of south-central and northeastern Mexico, along the coast of Peru, and in the southwestern United States. Scholars believe that the first farmers planted sunflowers (for seeds), corn, beans, squash, ● and a variety of other crops. In South America and on the islands of the Caribbean, farmers raised various root crops, mainly manioc and other crops similar to sweet potatoes. In the highlands of Peru, the potato was the most important food. As archaeologist Hiram Bingham stated:

The word *pueblo* is Spanish and means "people," "settlement," or "town." In the Southwest it applies to the Indian settlements made of adobe.

"Few Americans realize how much we owe to the ancient Peruvians. Very few people appreciate that they gave us the white potato, many varieties of Indian corn, and such useful [medicines] as quinine. . . ."

Farming began at about the same time in both hemispheres but developed more gradually in the Americas. The plow was not invented in the Americas partly because animals large enough to pull it, such as horses, were not available there. For the same reason, the ancient people of the region did not use wheeled implements in agriculture, although ancient toys unearthed in Mexico show that the people did know of the wheel. In the highlands farmers used digging sticks to plant rows of seeds. They also used dead fish as fertilizer.

Agriculture produced enough to support village life and the beginnings of towns. By the time of Columbus's voyage in 1492, people as far north as the northeastern United States and Canada and as far south as Argentina depended on farming for much of their food supply. In Mexico and in the Andes Mountains, agriculture and food storage formed the basis of civilizations as advanced as those of Egypt and Sumer.

The North Americans

In what is today the United States and Canada, many different cultures and some highly organized societies thrived (see map, page 304). The cultures of these peoples often depended on the geography of the region they inhabited.

Southwest. The Pueblo (poo • EB • loh) people created a well-developed culture in what is now the southwestern United States. These farmers lived in permanent settlements and used **adobe**, a sun-dried brick, to build communal houses—ancient versions of our apartment houses. They erected many multistoried houses, some with as many as 800 rooms, and clustered others together beneath overhanging cliffs so they could be better defended.

Northwest. Several tribes with economies based largely on fishing lived on the northwest coast of North America. Expert woodworkers and weavers, these people crafted majestic totem poles—great wooden carvings of people and beasts that symbolized tribal history.

Great Plains. An entirely different culture flourished in the Great Plains, which stretch between the Rocky Mountains and the Mississippi River. Here, tribal peoples lived by hunting the

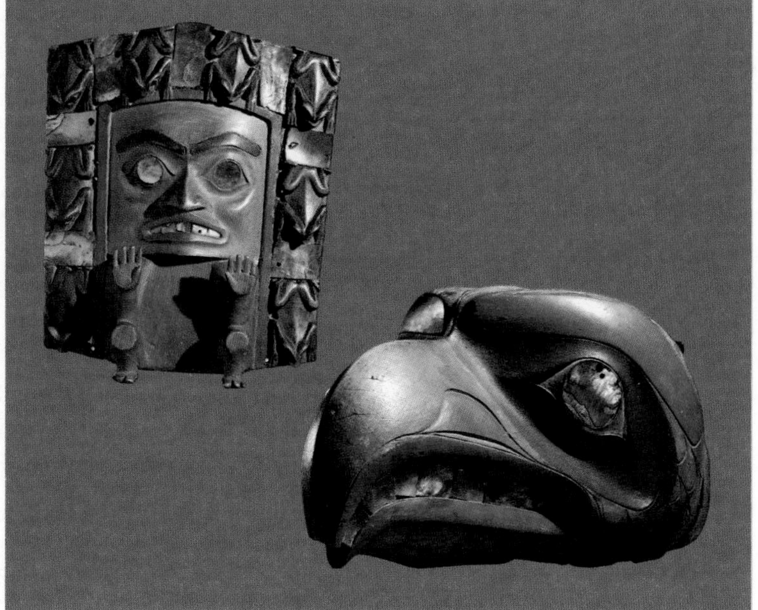

Learning from Pictures *The Tsimshian Indians of the Northwest, known for their expert woodwork, carved these two ceremonial masks.*

Next list the following four tribes on the board or overhead projector:

a. Pueblos
b. Mound Builders
c. Plains tribes
d. Northwest coast tribes

After students have reread the subsection "The North Americans" on pages 305-306, ask them to match the name of the tribe with the characteristic that best describes it. *(Answers: 1-a, 2-c, 3-d, 4-b, 5-c)*

SECTION 3

Closure

Ask students to name some of the plants farmers in the Americas grew in settled agriculture. *(sunflowers, corn, beans, squash, sweet potatoes)* How did farming differ in the Americas from farming elsewhere? *(no plows, no wheeled implements, no horses or other large farm animals)*

Review Answers

1. ***adobe:*** sun-dried brick used by farmers in southwestern United States to build communal houses; ***tepee:*** cone-shaped tent made of hides by the Plains people
2. ***Pueblo people:*** farming peoples in southwestern United States who lived in adobe communal houses; ***Plains people:*** tribal peoples of Great Plains who hunted huge herds of buffalo and lived in tepees
3. ***Rocky Mountains:*** mountain range in western North America;

305

1B, 1D, 2C, a1A, a1C, a4A, a4G, a4H, a4L

Andes Mountains: mountain range in western South America
4. Changes in Asia's climate may have motivated early peoples to migrate to the Americas.
5. (a) Important crops grown in the Americas include sunflowers, corn, beans, squash, sweet potatoes, and manioc. **(b)** Productivity was limited because the plow had not been invented in the Americas, the wheel was apparently not used in agriculture, and animals such as the horse were unavailable for farm work.
6. Pueblo people lived in permanent settlements and used adobe to build communal houses. Northwestern tribes fished and became expert woodworkers and weavers. Tribal peoples of the Great Plains followed the buffalo herds and lived in tepees. In the Eastern Woodlands, people developed a high level of culture and artistic ability. They constructed large earthen mounds that required communal cooperation.

SECTION 4

Focus/Motivation
Write the following quotations on the chalkboard or an overhead projector.

"The revolting nature of their religious rites should not blind us to the fact that the Aztecs were the culmination of a remarkable cultural development. . . . In manners, dress, design,

Learning from Pictures *This cliff dwelling in Mesa Verde National Park, Colorado, is sheltered by a spruce forest and is named the Spruce Tree House Ruin.*

huge herds of wild buffalo that roamed the land. The Plains peoples ate the meat of the buffalo and used its hide to make clothing and to build their cone-shaped tents, called **tepees.** Skilled fighters, they placed a high value on deeds of bravery.

Eastern Woodlands. The Eastern Woodlands stretch from what is now Canada to the Gulf of Mexico and from the Atlantic Ocean to the Mississippi River. There one of North America's most sophisticated cultures flourished. The peoples of the region are sometimes called the Mound Builders because of the many earthen mounds they constructed throughout the area.

The tools, jewelry, and weapons found in mounds built as burial places reveal that these peoples had highly developed artistic skills. Some of the mounds are in the shapes of animals. One such mound in Ohio, the Great Serpent Mound, extends more than 1,300 feet (400 meters) in length. Although archaeologists recognize that building the mounds obviously required cooperative effort, they do not know what happened to the builders.

SECTION 3 REVIEW

1. **Define** adobe, tepee
2. **Identify** Pueblo people, Plains people
3. **Locate** Rocky Mountains, Andes Mountains
4. **Understanding Ideas** What may have motivated early peoples to migrate to the Americas?
5. **Summarizing Ideas** **(a)** List the important crops grown in the Americas. **(b)** What factors limited farmers' productivity?
6. **Contrasting Ideas** How did the various cultures of North America differ?

4 Empires Rose and Flourished in Mexico and Peru

By about 1500 B.C., the peoples along the coast of Peru and in central Mexico lived in villages. In another 500 years, ceremonial and trading centers, made possible by the food surplus of many villages,

About 1,300 years ago, a people known as the Moche lived along the northern coast of Peru. They built irrigation systems and knew how to make elaborate jewelry, but they had no written language or calendar. Recent discoveries at Sipán in Peru contain artifacts in a warrior's tomb that may provide clues to the history of the Moche.

1A, 1C, 2C, a1A, a1C, a4B, a4C

began to appear. Unlike cities in other regions of the world, the central areas of these cities were reserved for priests and high officials. The common people lived in nearby farming villages. The societies of these cities remain mysterious because scholars have not deciphered their hieroglyphic writings.

The Olmecs

The earliest of these cultures in Mexico, the Olmecs (OHL • meks), left giant stone heads and many objects made of jade. Carved from basalt that had to be transported from quarries 80 miles (129 kilometers) away, each stone head weighs 16 to 18 tons. Although scholars remain mystified about how the Olmecs moved the giant stones, they believe that only a highly sophisticated society could have developed the technology to do so. Scholars also believe that the Olmecs developed a priestly class and worshiped a god represented by the image of a jaguar. In the highlands of Peru and along its coast, a culture called Chavin (shuh • VEEN) developed about the same time. The Chavin also worshiped the jaguar. Both the Olmec and Chavin cultures mysteriously disappeared about A.D. 200.

The Maya

One of the most advanced cultures of the Americas was that of the Maya, who occupied the tropical lowlands of Central America considerably before 1000 B.C. (see map, this page). Skilled architects and engineers, the Maya built many steep pyramids. For example, recent excavations of the Mayan city of El Mirador in Guatemala show that one pyramid soared 18 stories and had a base about the size of three football fields.

The Maya also studied astronomy. They learned to predict solar eclipses and devised a calendar more accurate than the one used in Europe at the time. The Maya developed a counting system that was based on the number 20 and that included the zero. They also used a writing system based on pictograms, ideograms, and phonograms. Much of the Mayan script, however, remains undeciphered, and the Spaniards destroyed nearly all Mayan manuscripts. Nevertheless, the ruins of magnificent cities lead scholars to believe that the Maya used their writing and mathematical knowledge to record the dates of kings' reigns, their ritual ceremonies, and their knowledge of astronomy.

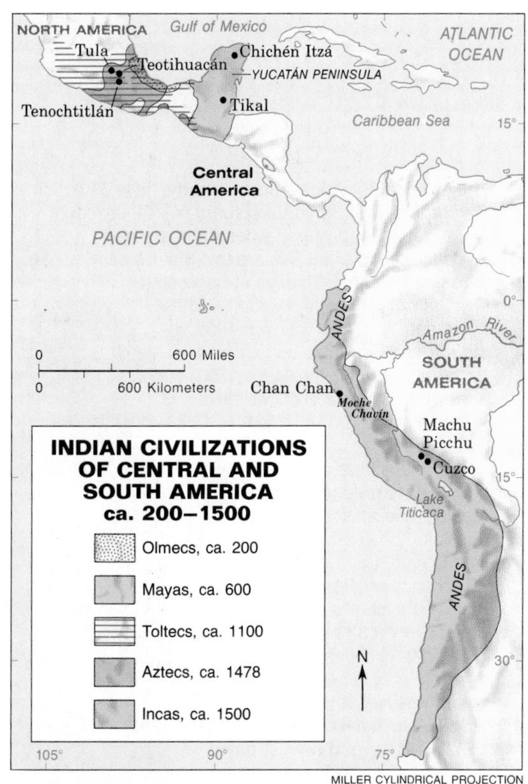

Learning from Maps *The Toltecs controlled the largest Indian empire of North America. What Indian people controlled the west coast of South America?* Incas

The Maya produced a great deal of food, perhaps more efficiently than European farmers of the time. This food helped support noble and priestly classes, whose members did not perform any manual labor. The complex religion of the Maya involved astronomy and the worship of many gods who were thought to change their forms at will. Sometimes in periods of crisis, such as droughts, Mayan priests offered human sacrifices to the gods, hoping for rain.

About A.D. 900 a mysterious catastrophe struck the Mayan civilization. The population declined sharply and people fled the ceremonial centers. Although scholars can only speculate, any number of disasters could have caused this decline. The agricultural methods used by the Maya may have worn out the soil. A foreign invasion may have overwhelmed them, or possibly a peasant revolt may have overthrown the nobles and priests.

Text continues on page 310.

and architecture, they rivaled medieval Europe; the largest of their temples were almost as grand as the pyramids of Egypt; their gardens as beautiful as Babylon; their stonework matched the structures of ancient Greece; their plastered and lime-washed palaces were as fine as those of Moorish Spain."

"Peru was probably the world's best-governed country in the turbulent 1550s. Well-built roads threaded its great mountains, crossing precipitous gorges on suspension bridges. A message service of trained relay runners kept Cuzco in touch with all parts of the empire. Irrigation canals and other skilled engineering works such as agricultural terraces ensured plenty of food, and a nationwide social security system took care of the basic wants of individuals."

Lead a class discussion of Aztec and Inca society, using the following questions as a guide: What do the authors consider special features of these societies? *(Both had strong central governments to organize building projects and, in the case of the Incas, a social security system.)* What can you infer about Aztec society? *(The quotation suggests that Aztec artisans were highly skilled and that nature was important as represented in their gardens.)* Ask: What can you infer about Inca life? *(In the Inca Empire great importance was placed on communication, so the Incas built irrigation systems and terraces; suitable farmland was scarce; and the government played a large role in people's lives with its social security system.)*

Presentation Organizing Ideas (Average/Group) Write the following headings on the chalkboard or an overhead projector: *Architecture, Intellectual Achievements,* and *Religion.* Have students make a chart in their notebooks showing the characteristics of Mayan civilization under the three headings. *(The characteristics under Architecture should include: constructed step pyramids, used the most advanced techniques of the time. Under Intellectual Achievement: created accurate calendar, developed a counting system based on 20, invented writing system. Under Religion: involved astrology, gods were varied and constantly changing, worshiped peaceful gods, practiced human sacrifice in times of crisis.)*

PERSPECTIVES: LEGACIES OF THE PAST

The calendar is a mess. Some months have 31 days, some have 30, and February has 28—except, of course, in "leap years," when February has 29 days instead of 28. We are told that it's easy to remember that leap days always occur in years divisible by four—such as 1984, 1988, and 1992. But the year 1900, although it was divisible by four, was not a leap year. Neither were 1700 and 1800. The year 2000 will be a leap year, but 2100 (4 × 525 = 2100) will not be.

For thousands of years people have tried to make the calendar as accurate as possible. Yet we still don't have it quite right. Each year is still 26 seconds off. Fortunately, that's not a lot—it's off by one day out of every 3,323 years.

As imprecise as this is, our calendar is better than what our ancestors put up with. The year 46 B.C. had 445 days. In A.D. 1582, October had only 21 days. And in 1752, Americans went to bed the night of September 2nd and awoke the morning of September 14th.

People have kept track of time for their own survival. To know when to plant or when to prepare for floods and storms, people learned to watch the movements of the sun, moon, and stars. Many early cultures worshiped these heavenly bodies and devised calendars to know when to hold religious festivals. A lunar month—from one full moon to the next—was one good measure of time everyone could *see.* But, because each solar year contains about 12.37 lunar months, the sun cycle and the moon cycle didn't fit together. People had to choose between the two or try to harmonize them.

The Babylonians may have been the first to use a formal calendar. Following the moon cycle, they alternated between 29- and 30-day months, which only added up to 364 days—not a full year. The ancient Chinese and, later, the Hebrews and Muslims also used the lunar cycle.

The Egyptians counted 365 days between the *annual* risings of the Nile and divided the year into 12 30-day months with 5 extra days. This was closer than the Babylonian calendar, and it compensated for the extra ¼ day each year has.

The Calendar—Will We Ever Get It Straight?

The ancestor of the calendar we use today was invented in Rome—although the early Romans were quite nonchalant about calendrical accuracy and made do with a 10-month, 304-day year. About 700 B.C., two new months were added—Januarius and Februarius—making the year 355 days long. By the time Julius Caesar came to power in 59 B.C., the Roman calendar was more than two months behind—and the spring festival was ridiculously being celebrated in July. With the help of the Greek astronomer Sosigenes, Caesar changed the calendar to 365 days, adding one extra day every fourth February. Caesar rewarded himself by changing the name of the month Quintilis to his own, Julius (July). His successor Augustus, not to be outdone, changed the next month, Sextilis, to Augustus.

Things went along pretty smoothly for the next 1,500 years until a pope in Rome noticed that the annual date for Easter—the first full moon after the spring equinox—was getting later and later in the year. He discovered that the Julian (Julius Caesar's) calendar was about 11 minutes too long. Over 1,500 years this had put an extra 10 days on the year. So in 1582 Pope Gregory XIII declared that the day after October 4 would be October 15. To prevent this problem from recurring, he had to find a way of eliminating three days about every 400 years. He did this by abolishing leap day in all turn-of-the-century years except those divisible by 400. Therefore, 1600 remained a leap year, but 1700, 1800, and 1900 each lost the leap day. This made the calendar correct to within 26 seconds a year, or one day every 3,323 years.

Roman Catholic countries adopted the Gregorian calendar immediately. Protestant countries were reluctant. When England and its colonies, including America, finally adopted the calendar in 1752, they were 11 days behind. After Parliament announced that the day after September 2, 1752, would be September 14, angry people shouting "Give us back our 11 days!" mobbed the House of Commons. Landlords protested losing two weeks' rents, and everyone protested changing dates for holidays and birthdays. But in America, Ben Franklin advised people not to regret the lost time but to rejoice that one could "lie down in peace on the second of the month and not . . . awake till the morning of the 14th."

In Orthodox Christian countries—Greece, Russia, Romania, Serbia, Bulgaria, and others—the Julian calendar continued. The Russian Orthodox church still follows the Julian calendar and celebrates Christmas 13 days later than western Christians. Russia kept the Julian calendar until the 1917 Communist Revolution. The ensuing loss of 13 days led to the oddity that the Communist "October Revolution" had to be celebrated in November.

Some people argue for a "world calendar." Each 52-week year would begin with Sunday, and leap days would be tacked on at the end of the year whenever necessary. Such a change is hard to make, and many people would protest, but it has been done before. "Time stops for no man," but time has frequently been rearranged—on paper.

Photos *Page 308: Jewish omer calendar (top); Pope Gregory XII presenting calendar (bottom); Page 309: Stonehenge (top); Egyptian calendar (middle); Aztec calendar (bottom)*

309

1B, 1C, 2C, a1A, a1C, a4A

• The Aztecs adopted the legend of Quetzalcoatl. Tradition says that Quetzalcoatl was white and bearded, and had committed a sin or been overthrown by a rival god. Quetzalcoatl promised to return. The Spanish took advantage of the Indian belief in this legend when, as white, bearded conquistadors, they came to Mexico.

SECTION 4

Closure

Ask: What disasters occurred to the advanced civilizations of Central America, Mexico, and Peru? *(Olmec and Chavin mysteriously disappeared about A.D. 200, the Mayan population declined and people fled the ceremonial centers about A.D. 900, subject peoples revolted and Spanish explorers helped destroy the Aztec Empire, and the Spanish conquered the Incas.)*

Review Answers

1. *chinampa:* floating artificial island on which the Aztecs farmed; ***quipu:*** knotted string used by the Incas to keep records
2. *Olmecs:* early culture in Mexico; left giant stone heads and many jade objects; ***Chavin:*** culture developed in highland and coastal Peru about the same time as Olmecs; ***Maya:*** most advanced culture of the Americas, occupied southern Mexico and nearby Central America; ***Toltecs:*** people who invaded central Mexico from the north; ***Quetzalcoatl:*** Toltec god; ***Aztecs:*** warlike people of central Mexico; ***Incas:*** people who built an empire in the Andes
3. *Tula:* Toltec capital; ***Yucatán Peninsula:*** peninsula in Central America that was part of Mayan civilization; ***Chichén Itzá:*** chief Mayan city in the Yucatán; ***Tenochtitlán:*** Aztec capital; ***Cuzco:*** Inca capital

Learning from Pictures *This Mayan observatory is located in Chichén Itzá. What Toltec influences do the ruins of Chichén Itzá reflect?* religion and design

The Toltecs

About A.D. 650 a people called the Toltecs (TOHL • tecks) invaded central Mexico from the north. Ruled by a military class, the Toltecs built a capital city at Tula (TOO • luh) and by 1100 had spread their influence as far south as the Yucatán Peninsula (see map, page 307). There they encountered the Maya, who were rebuilding their civilization. The influence of Toltec religion and designs is noticeable in the ruins of Chichén Itzá (chuh • CHEN uht • SAH), the chief Mayan city.

Like the Maya, the Toltecs built pyramids. However, they never produced art as advanced as that of the Maya. The Toltecs extended trade much farther than had the Maya and introduced the working of gold and silver. The Toltecs also spread • the worship of their god, Quetzalcoatl (ket • SAHL • kwaht • uhl), represented by a feathered serpent, and practiced human sacrifice.

The Aztecs

Around A.D. 1200 peoples from the north launched further invasions of central Mexico. Unlike the Toltecs, these peoples probably lived as hunters and gatherers at the time of their arrival. A number of these groups fought one another in central Mexico. Out of these struggles emerged the strongest group—the Aztecs.

The Aztecs had been wandering warriors. According to legend their priests had instructed them to settle where they saw a sign—an eagle sitting on a cactus and devouring a serpent. They finally saw the sign on one of a pair of islands in Lake Texcoco (tes • KOH • koh) in Mexico. There they built their city of Tenochtitlán (tay • nawch • tee • TLAHN).

From about 1325 on, the Aztecs increased their power until they dominated central Mexico. Conquered tribes paid them tribute in gold, turquoise, corn, animals, and slaves.

By building causeways and stone foundations, the Aztecs expanded Tenochtitlán to make room for great pyramid-temples, marketplaces, and palaces for the nobles and wealthy families. The city may have had more than 100,000 inhabitants at its period of greatest power and prestige in the 1400s.

The Aztecs incorporated into their culture the inventions of peoples they conquered or with whom they traded. They soon learned metalwork, weaving, pottery-making, the calendar, and mathematics. Their artisans produced finely finished pieces of art.

The Aztecs perfected farming on **chinampas**—artificial islands in the region's many lakes. The use of chinampas was perhaps the most productive form of agriculture in the world.

The military dominated Aztec society. Warfare carried great prestige and led to wealth and power. The Aztecs believed that the sun god and the god of war demanded human sacrifices in return for favors. Hundreds of captives from defeated tribes might be put to death each year. In 1487, at the height of their power, the Aztecs sacrificed 20,000 captives on their pyramid altars.

Just as the great Aztec civilization had grown rapidly, so it was to fall in a very short time. By the end of the 1400s, surrounding peoples who had been paying tribute to the Aztecs revolted. But the final blow to the Aztec Empire came from foreign conquerors—the Spanish explorers of the 1500s.

The Incas

At about the same period that the Aztecs built their civilization in Mexico, another group created a civilization in the Andes Mountains of South America. These people based their religion on sun worship. Their name—Incas—means "children of the sun."

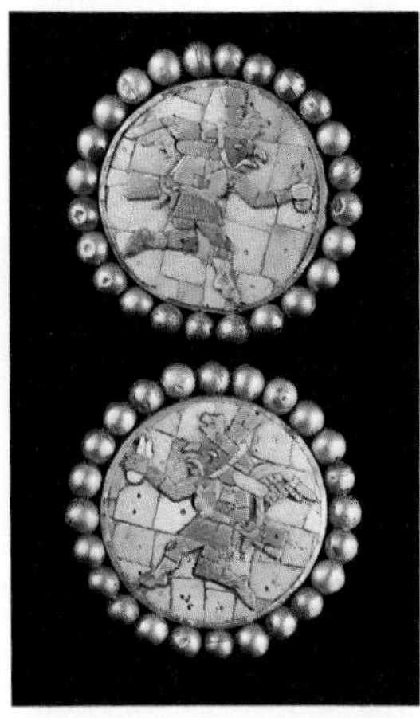

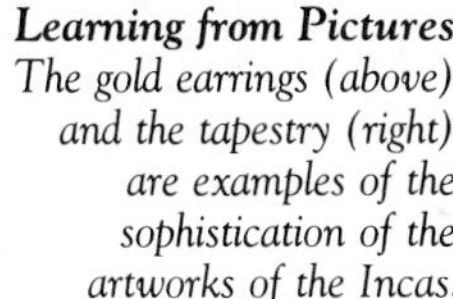

Learning from Pictures *The gold earrings (above) and the tapestry (right) are examples of the sophistication of the artworks of the Incas.*

The Inca Empire expanded steadily. By about 1470, it extended along most of the west coast of South America and far into the Andes, covering much of the present-day nations of Peru, Ecuador, Bolivia, and Chile. As in ancient Egypt, everything belonged to the ruler, and everyone owed absolute obedience to him. Although an autocrat, the emperor used his power to improve the empire.

The Inca capital was Cuzco (KOO • skoh), known as the "City of the Sun." The Incas built fortresses and irrigation systems and laid paved roads from one end of their realm to the other. Pack animals called *llamas* carried goods, and swift runners brought news to the Inca capital. The rulers of the empire prevented local famines by maintaining storehouses and by moving food supplies to villages when crops failed.

After conquering their neighbors, the Inca rulers sought to eliminate tribal diversity in their empire. In order to pacify and colonize newly conquered lands, they moved entire villages to the new lands. They established an educational system, particularly for the children of the nobility, that taught the Inca religion and history. Even today millions of native people in the five South American countries of Peru, Ecuador, Bolivia, Chile, and Argentina speak the Inca language—Quechua (KECH • wuh).

Although the Incas did not have a system of writing, they did keep records by means of the **quipu** (KEE • poo)—a kind of knotted string used to assist the memory. They were quite advanced in the practice of medicine, using anesthetics and even performing a primitive kind of brain surgery.

Just as they did with the Aztecs, the Spaniards conquered the Incas in the 1500s. Yet many aspects of this fabulous civilization lived on in the isolated highland valleys of the Andes.

SECTION 4 REVIEW

1. **Define** chinampa, quipu
2. **Identify** Olmecs, Chavin, Maya, Toltecs, Quetzalcoatl, Aztecs, Incas
3. **Locate** Tula, Yucatán Peninsula, Chichén Itzá, Tenochtitlán, Cuzco
4. **Determining Cause and Effect** What factors contributed to the growth of large populations in Mexico and Peru?
5. **Summarizing Ideas** How did the Incas prevent famines?
6. **Comparing Ideas** **(a)** How were the civilizations of the Maya, Aztecs, and Incas similar? **(b)** How were they different?

4. Civilizations in Mexico and Peru developed effective irrigation systems that allowed greater productivity. The Aztecs perfected the chinampas, or floating gardens, that had perhaps the greatest productivity of any form of agriculture in the world.
5. The Incas prevented famines by maintaining storehouses and by moving food supplies to villages when crops failed.
6. (a) Maya, Aztec, and Inca civilizations were similar in their skillful engineering projects, understanding of astronomy and mathematics, use of a calendar, and building of great cities. All three achieved great levels of agricultural productivity.
(b) The Mayan civilization lasted a long time, from 1000 B.C. to A.D. 900 and beyond, but both Aztecs and Incas lasted only about 300 years, from the 1200s to the 1500s. **Aztecs and Maya practiced human sacrifice. The Incas had no system of writing, but the Maya did. The Incas sought to eliminate tribal diversity by pacifying and colonizing conquered lands, but the Aztecs made the subject peoples pay tribute, thus paving the way for revolt.**

Reviewing Important Terms
1. b; **2.** e; **3.** a; **4.** d; **5.** c; **6.** g; **7.** f; **8.** j; **9.** h; **10.** i.

Developing Critical Thinking Skills
1. (a) Maya; **(b)** Meroë; **(c)** Ghana; **(d)** Mali; **(e)** Kilwa; **(f)** Aztecs
2. (a) The Maya used the most advanced techniques to build pyramids. Their knowledge of astronomy was extensive. They devised a calendar. They developed a counting system based on the number 20, and they invented a writing system. **(b)** Answers will vary. Maya and Europeans shared abilities in architecture, astronomy, and mathematics.
3. (a) The melting and molding of ores requires special knowledge. The construction of public buildings requires engineering skill, creative ability, and governmental organization. **(b)** The Karanga mined gold and used it as a trade item. They used their wealth to build the large fortress of Great Zimbabwe. The Aztecs used metals and produced fine pieces of art. By building causeways and stone foundations, they made room in Tenochtitlán for great pyramids, temples, marketplaces, and palaces.
4. (a) East African exports included hides, tortoiseshells, ivory, slaves, and gold. Imports included porcelain and weapons. The West Africans traded salt, gold, slaves, and ivory. They imported horses, textiles, books, paper, and weapons. **(b) (c)** The tributaries of the large agricultural empires traded corn, gold, turquoise, animals,

1B, 1D, 2A, 2B, 2C, a1A, a1C, a4A, a4H, a4I

Reteaching
Have students review the Chapter Summary and the appropriate section and questions in the Unit Synthesis. Discuss the concepts until students demonstrate a clear understanding of the material.

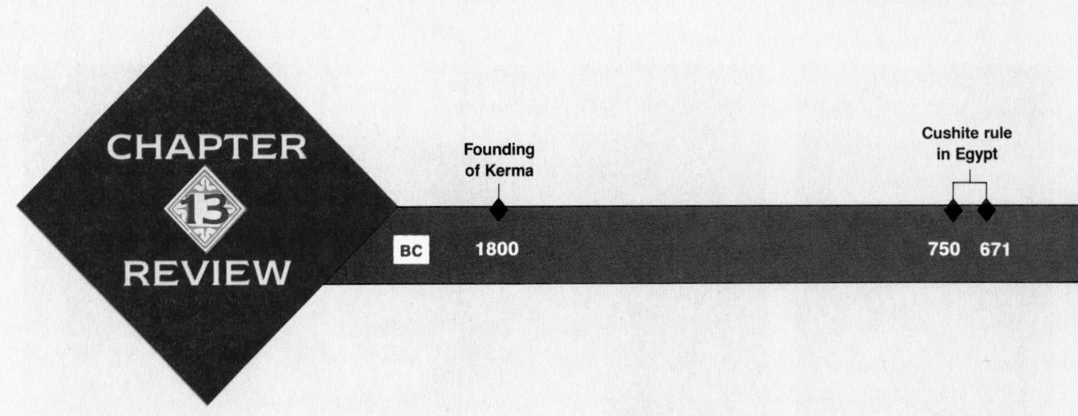

Chapter Summary

The following list contains the key concepts you have learned about civilizations in Africa and the Americas.

1. SubSaharan Africa lies on a great plateau, broken here and there by basins and the Great Rift Valley.
2. Scholars have used linguistics, oral traditions, music, and archaeology to unlock the African past.
3. Africans lived primarily in small villages where families were very important.
4. The great kingdoms of Cush and Axum dominated the interior of eastern Africa.
5. Independent city-states, noted for their trading activity, were established on Africa's eastern coast. The region experienced a golden age that lasted from the 700s through the 1300s.
6. In central Africa, Zimbabwe controlled a large area.
7. To the west, large kingdoms such as Mali, Ghana, and Songhai developed. These kingdoms controlled the vital gold-for-salt trade of the western Sudan.
8. Successive waves of immigrants from Asia settled the Americas. Many crossed the land bridge that linked Asia and the Americas.
9. North American tribes included the fishers of the Northwest, the hunters of the Plains region, the Pueblo farmers of the Southwest, and the Mound Builders of the Eastern Woodlands.
10. As agriculture and small towns developed, several great cultures arose—the Olmecs, Maya, Toltecs, and Aztecs of Mexico and Central America, and the Incas of Peru.

On a separate sheet of paper, complete the following review exercises.

Reviewing Important Terms

Match each of the following terms with the correct definition in column two.

a. savanna	**f.** adobe
b. linguist	**g.** tepee
c. oral traditions	**h.** tropical rain forest
d. chinampa	**i.** jungle
e. quipu	**j.** matrilineal

__ **1.** Scholar who studies languages
__ **2.** Kind of knotted string developed by the Incas to keep records and assist the memory
__ **3.** A vast area of relatively dry grasslands
__ **4.** Artificial island that the Aztecs created for agriculture
__ **5.** Poems, songs, or stories passed by word of mouth from one generation to another
__ **6.** Cone-shaped tent made of buffalo hide
__ **7.** Sun-dried brick
__ **8.** Society in which people trace their ancestors through their mothers rather than their fathers
__ **9.** Forest where annual rainfall exceeds 100 inches (254 centimeters)
__ **10.** A thick growth of plants found in a tropical rain forest wherever sunlight penetrates the dense umbrella of tall trees and reaches the forest floor

Developing Critical Thinking Skills

1. **Classifying Ideas** Supply the name of the area or culture that completes each statement.
   (a) The ______ developed a counting system based on 20.
   (b) ______ was an early East African center of ironworking.
   (c) The first West African kingdom to build up gold-for-salt trade was ______ .
   (d) Tombouctou, the capital of ______, was a center of Muslim learning.
   (e) ______ became the most famous city-state for East African trade.
   (f) The ______ of Mexico farmed on floating artificial islands.
2. **Interpreting Ideas** **(a)** What evidence supports the claim that the Maya were one of the most advanced cultures of the Americas? **(b)** In what ways were the Maya as advanced as the Europeans of the same period?
3. **Evaluating Ideas** **(a)** How do the use of metals and the type of buildings that are constructed reflect the accomplishments of a civilization? **(b)** Give an example from one African and one American civilization to support your answer.

and slaves. The North American peoples were largely nomadic people who traded among themselves. **(d)** Answers will vary.
5. The Maya, Toltecs, and Aztecs used pyramids as religious centers and altars. The American pyramids indicate the importance of religion, a high degree of social organization, and advanced techniques of engineering and building in those civilizations.

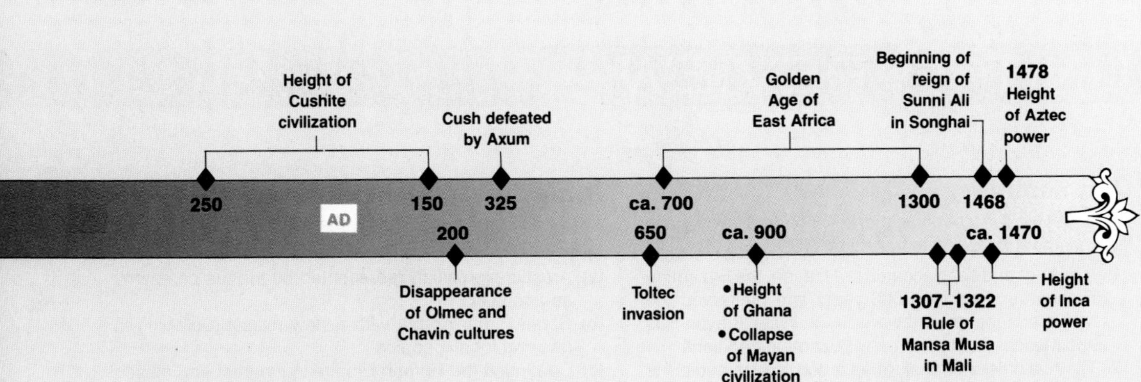

4. **Summarizing Ideas** **(a)** What types of trade developed across the Sahara and along the eastern coast of Africa? **(b)** What items were traded in the American civilizations? **(c)** Who traded with whom? **(d)** What similarities or differences in trade do you notice in all of these civilizations?
5. **Analyzing Ideas** Review the functions of the pyramid structures of the Maya, Toltecs, and Aztecs. What do these structures tell us about the cultures they represent?

Relating Geography to History

(a) Using information in this chapter, trace on maps of Africa and the Americas the migration routes of the peoples who later established the great civilizations. **(b)** What climatic and geographical obstacles did they have to overcome? **(c)** What approximate dates are given for these migrations?

Relating Past to Present

1. The Bush people of the Kalahari Desert and the Bantu-speaking peoples of East and South Africa live much the same way as their ancestors did hundreds of years ago. Use encyclopedias, history books, or other reference books on Africa to find out more about the culture of one of these groups.
2. Many English words have roots in Latin American cultures. Use your dictionary to find the origin of these words: *chocolate, hammock, potato, quinine, tapioca, tobacco, tomato, avocado.*

Applying History Study Skills

Before completing this activity, review Building History Study Skills on page 299.

Read the following excerpt in which Olauda Equiano describes his Nigerian home.

> “In our buildings we study convenience rather than ornament. Each master of a family has a large square piece of ground, surrounded with a moat or a fence. . . . Within this, are his houses to accommodate his family and slaves, which if numerous, frequently present the appearance of a village. In the middle, stands the principal building, appropriated to the sole use of the master and consisting of two apartments; in one of which he sits in the day with his family, the other is left for the reception of his friends. . . . On each side are the apartments of his wives, who also have their separate day and night houses. The habitations of the slaves and their families are distributed throughout the rest of the enclosure. These houses never exceed one story in height; they are always built of wood . . . crossed with wattles and neatly plastered within and without. . . .”

1. What is the main idea of Equino's description?
2. In two complete sentences, paraphrase the main idea of the excerpt.

Investigating Further

1. **Writing a Report** In 1911 Hiram Bingham discovered the Inca city of Machu Picchu in the wilderness of the Andes Mountains. Read his account in *Lost City of the Incas* (Atheneum). Check other sources to determine if additional research has discovered new information about the purpose of this city, the organization of its society, the uniqueness of its buildings, or its methods of farming. Write a report discussing your findings. Conclude your report by discussing why this fabulous city remained undiscovered for so many centuries.
2. **Preparing an Oral Report** Form study groups to prepare oral reports on the Indians of North America. Each group can choose one Indian culture to research. Assign each member of the group a particular area of study, such as clothing, shelter, transportation, or religious beliefs. One source for your research is Alvin Josephy's *The Indian Heritage of America* (Knopf). Another source may be scholars at a local college or university.
3. **Constructing a Chart** Use resources in your school or public library to locate more information on the decline of the kingdoms of Africa and the Americas discussed in this chapter. Then prepare a chart that lists the reasons for the decline of these kingdoms in three categories: political, economic, and social.

Relating Geography to History

(a), (b) and (c) Answers will vary.

Relating Past to Present

1. Answers will vary.
2. ***chocolate:*** from Nahuatl *xocoatl;* ***hammock:*** from Taino; ***potato:*** from Taino; ***quinine:*** from Quechua; ***tapioca:*** from Tupi; ***tobacco:*** from Taino; ***tomato:*** from Nahuatl; ***avocado:*** from Nahuatl.

Applying History Study Skills

1. Equiano's purpose is to show that Nigeria's homes are built for the convenience of the master, yet they remain simple and without ornamentation.
2. These utilitarian Nigerian houses are really a collection of buildings centered on the principal building for use of the master. Surrounding his residence is a compound that includes additional residences, constructed of wood, for his wives and slaves.

313

Reviewing Concepts
1. Dante; 2. Charlemagne; 3. Marco Polo; 4. Muhammad; 5. William the Conqueror; 6. John; 7. Akbar

Applying Critical Thinking Skills
1. **(a)** Japanese; **(b)** Islamic; **(c)** Byzantine; **(d)** Kievan Rus; **(e)** Maya; **(f)** Chinese
2. **(a)** The Christian Church split into two branches because of doctrinal and political reasons. The split became final in 1054, when the pope and the patriarch at Constantinople excommunicated each other. **(b)** The Western church became known as the Roman Catholic church, while the Byzantine church is known as the Eastern Orthodox church. **(c)** Disputes in Islam arose over Muhammad's successor and interpretations of the Koran. **(d)** Sunnites claimed the only mediator between believers and Allah was the Koran. The Shiites believed the imam was the proper intermediary between Allah and believers.
3. Answers will vary. Students should see that trade and cities were important to civilizations in western Europe, China, Russia, and West Africa as centers for the exchange of materials, valuables, crafts, and learning.
4. Islamic science was advanced. Muslim doctors used anesthesia, started traveling clinics, and set bones. Little scientific progress was made in Europe, but some technological advances were made in mathematics and optics. Arabic became a common language among Muslims. In India the Muslims introduced Urdu, a combination of Persian and Arabic words with Hindu grammar. In Europe, Latin

1A, 1B, 1D, 2C, 3B, 4B, 4D, a1A, a1C, a4A, a4D, a4E, a4H, a4K, a4L

Reteaching
Have students review the Chapter Summary and the appropriate section and questions in the Unit Synthesis. Discuss the concepts until students demonstrate a clear understanding of the material.

UNIT 3 REVIEW

Unit Summary

The following list contains the key concepts you have learned about the world in transition.

1. A brilliant and sophisticated civilization, the Byzantine Empire survived for 1,000 years and preserved the heritage of the ancient world in the West. Kievan Rus and Muscovy adopted many Byzantine traditions.
2. The rise of Islam transformed much of Asia and parts of Africa and Europe. Its early believers spread the Islamic faith aggressively.
3. The great Frankish king Charlemagne created an empire that included much of western Europe.
4. Two important medieval institutions were feudalism and the manorial system.
5. During the Middle Ages, the church in western Europe performed many functions.
6. Kings in France and England gradually extended their authority in the late Middle Ages.
7. The Crusades were organized chiefly to regain the Holy Land from the Muslims.
8. Towns grew and medieval culture flourished as trade revived. Townspeople gained freedom from services on the manor, town justice, and commercial rights.
9. Under the rule of the Sui, Tang, and Song dynasties, the Chinese made notable achievements.
10. In the 1200s the nomadic Mongols of central Asia were united into a powerful fighting force under Genghis Khan.
11. Japan was influenced by China but created its own distinct culture.
12. From ancient times through the 1500s, a remarkable variety of societies arose on the African continent. The great kingdoms included Cush, Axum, Zimbabwe, Ghana, Mali, and Songhai.
13. Immigrants from Asia settled the Americas. Civilizations developed, particularly in Mexico and Peru.

Reviewing Concepts

Identify the person who might have made each of the following statements:

1. "I used my native Italian language to describe a spiritual pilgrimage through hell, purgatory, and heaven."
2. "I was crowned Emperor of the Romans in 800."
3. "I traveled extensively over the Mongol Empire as a trader, keeping a record of my experiences."
4. "I asked my followers to believe in one god, Allah, and accept me as his prophet."
5. "I conquered England in 1066 but also retained control over large territories of France."
6. "I was forced by my nobles to sign a charter protecting their rights and limiting my power."
7. "I showed religious tolerance by marrying a Hindu princess and repealing the special tax on non-Muslims."

Applying Critical Thinking Skills

1. **Classifying Ideas** Name the culture that each of the following statements describes.
   (a) Artistic expression represented by the tea ceremony and *no* plays
   (b) Spread from Arabia with a new religion believing in one god for all peoples
   (c) Continued the Roman Empire in the east and helped Christianity spread into Russia
   (d) Decided issues of peace or war at the *veche,* or town meeting
   (e) Built steep pyramids as ceremonial centers; had a counting system based on 20 and a calendar that could predict solar eclipses
   (f) Perfected civil service examinations
2. **Summarizing Ideas** **(a)** Explain why the Christian Church divided. **(b)** Identify its two branches. **(c)** What factors contributed to the split in Islam? **(d)** What two sects emerged?
3. **Synthesizing Ideas** Trade and city life are considered essential to the strength of a civilization. Defend or oppose this idea as it would apply to any three of the following: western Europe, China, Russia, western Africa.
4. **Comparing Ideas** Compare the western European culture of the Middle Ages to the Islamic culture of the same period with regard to scientific accomplishments, language and literature, and concepts of law and justice.

Relating Geography to History

Study the maps of Africa and the Americas on pages 294 and 304 and the map of the world on pages R2–R3. **(a)** What geographic factors isolated the peoples of SubSaharan Africa from people in the rest of the world? **(b)** What geographic factors isolated the peoples of North and South America from people in the rest of the world?

Writing About History

1. Work with other members of your class to write a scene from a play in which a representative from Mali, one of Charlemagne's lords, a Muslim mullah, a Song emperor, a Tokugawa shogun, and an Inca prince debate the merits of their civilizations.
2. Use encyclopedias and recent issues of periodicals such as *National Geographic* to write a report on archaeological excavations in the Americas and Africa.

Further Readings

Bengtsson, Frans G. *The Long Ships.* New York: New American Library. Discusses Viking life.

Holmes, George, ed. *The Oxford Illustrated History of Medieval Europe.* New York: Oxford University Press. Shows territorial changes in Europe, 400–1500.
Parker, Henry. *A History of Mexico.* Boston: Houghton Mifflin. Recounts events in history of Mexico.
Ritchie, Rita. *The Year of the Horse.* New York: Dutton. Details life in Genghis Khan's empire.
Stewart, Desmond. *Early Islam.* New York: Time, Inc. Recounts the history of the beginnings of Islam.
Tuchman, Barbara. *A Distant Mirror: The Calamitous 14th Century.* New York: Ballantine Books. Analyzes life in Europe during the 1300s.

Unit Three Chronology

Date	Political and Social Developments	Technological and Scientific Advances	Visual Arts and Literature	Religious and Philosophical Thought
0–A.D. 500	Angles, Jutes, and Saxons in England **10*** Mayan civilization **13** Height of Cush kingdom **13** Cush defeated by Axum **13**	Maya develop calendar and zero **13** Paper in China **12** Axum dry-stone construction **13** Mexican pyramids **13**	Byzantine mosaics **8**	St. Patrick in Ireland **10** Ezana converted to Christianity **13**
500–750	Sui and Tang dynasties in China **12** Justinian's empire **8** Muslim invasion of Spain and Indus Valley **9** Battle of Tours **10** Feudalism begins **10**	Beginning of Golden Age in East Africa **13**	Hagia Sophia **8** Illuminated manuscript **10** Tang porcelain **12**	Buddhism in Japan **12** Muhammad **9** Islam in East Africa **13**
750–1000	Karanga state; Ghana civilization **13** Height of Mayan civilization **13** Charlemagne **10** Viking invasions **8** Alfred the Great **10** Song Dynasty **12**	Norse navigational techniques **10** Three-field system **10** Stirrup **10** Arabs invent zero **9** Construction of Great Zimbabwe **13**	Cyrillic alphabet **8** *Diamond Sutra* **12** *The Tale of Genji* **12** *Anglo-Saxon Chronicles* **10**	Origins of scholasticism **11**
1000–1250	Norman Conquest **10** Toltecs **13** Yaroslav I **8** Barbarossa **10** Innocent III **10** Magna Carta **10**	Chinese gunpowder **12** Optics **11** Textile "home" industry **11** Flying Buttress **11**	Gothic cathedrals **11** Nigerian bronze sculpture **13** Universities–Paris and Bologna **11** *Domesday Book* **10**	Concordat of Worms **10** Division of Roman and Eastern churches **8** Crusades begin **11** Constantinople falls to crusaders **8**
1250–1500	Mongols in Russia **8** 100 Years' War **11** Tamerlane in Delhi **9** Yuan dynasty **12** Marco Polo **12** Fall of Constantinople **8** Bubonic plague **11** Mali and Songhai **13** Height of Aztec and Inca civilizations **13**	Inca irrigation and roads **13** Incan quipus **13**	*Defender of the Peace* **11** Wycliffe's English Bible **11** *The Divine Comedy* **11** *Canterbury Tales* **11**	Babylonian Captivity **11** Great Schism **11** John Huss executed **11**

*Indicates chapter in which development is discussed

served as the language of the church and educated people. Common people spoke vernacular languages. The Koran served as the basis of Islamic law and justice. In Europe decisions at feudal trials were made by trial by battle, compurgation, and ordeal. As kings increased their power, cases began to be tried in royal courts rather than feudal courts.

Relating Geography to History

(a) The absence of navigable rivers, the Sahara and Kalahari deserts, impenetrable tropical rain forests, and the high plateau with few good harbors along the coastline formed intimidating barriers to exploration or trade. **(b)** The tremendous distances across the Atlantic and Pacific oceans isolated the Western Hemisphere from the rest of the world.

1B, 3B, a1A, a1B, a1C

Focus/Motivation
Remind students that the Roman Empire in the West collapsed in A.D. *476* and was replaced by a series of weak kingdoms. At the same time, however, civilizations in other parts of the world — the Middle East, Asia, Africa, and the Americas — were thriving. Discuss with students some of the ways in which these civilizations influenced Europe in later centuries. *(Students might point out that Arabic numerals, printing, and gunpowder were developed in these civilizations and that African art had a great impact on artists of the 1900s, such as Pablo Picasso.)*

UNIT THREE SYNTHESIS

The World in Transition

8 The Byzantine Empire Preserved the Heritage of Rome

In the West the collapse of the Roman Empire resulted in the disappearance of strong governments. However, the Roman Empire in the East—the Byzantine Empire—maintained its traditions and kept out barbarian invaders.

The Byzantine Empire

By the early 500s the empire in the West had broken down into a group of Germanic tribal kingdoms. The Eastern Roman Empire, on the other hand, had ousted the barbarians and had begun a great political, economic, intellectual, and artistic revival under the leadership of Emperor Justinian. Although many problems plagued the Byzantine Empire after Justinian's death, its political, military, and economic strengths helped it survive for more than 1,000 years.

The Church. In religion, the Byzantines recognized the patriarch in Constantinople rather than the pope in Rome as head of the Christian Church. Then after years of arguments over the role of icons, or holy pictures, in services, the Christian Church officially split in 1054. In the West, it became known as the Roman Catholic church. In the East, it became known as the Eastern Orthodox church.

Byzantine culture. Of all the Byzantine contributions to world civilization, the greatest was probably the preservation of Roman law. Early in his reign, Emperor Justinian ordered his scholars to collect and organize all Roman law. The entire collection is known as the *Corpus Juris Civilis* (Latin for "Body of Civil Law"). It is also called Justinian's Code. It remained in force until the Ottoman Turks toppled the empire and captured Constantinople in 1453.

Kievan Rus

A vast, grassy, almost treeless plain called the steppe stretches across eastern Europe and central Asia. On the western portions of the steppe, another civilization—Kievan Rus—arose.

Kiev, one of many city-states in the region, prospered because of its strategic location astride rich trade routes. In time, Kiev became the most powerful city in a region that included many semi-independent principalities.

Religion dominated Kievan culture. Although authors wrote epic poems and historical chronicles about wars and the personal tragedies associated with war, religious hymns and sermons constituted the bulk of Kievan literature. Icon painting became the most distinctive Kievan art form.

The Mongols

After the rule of Yaroslav the Wise ended in 1054, Kiev declined in power and wealth. By 1240 fierce Mongol invaders from Central Asia had conquered and burned almost every city in Kievan Rus. The Mongols retained control of the Kievan region until the 1400s.

In time, Mongol rule grew weaker and the princes of the region became more independent. During the 1300s Moscow, or Muscovy, became the strongest principality. By the late 1400s, Muscovy had overthrown Mongol rule and become the capital of an independent state called Russia.

9 Islam Became a Powerful Force from Spain to India

In the 600s the prophet Muhammad founded Islam, the youngest of the world's major religions.

Islam and the Muslim Empire

The central belief of Islam is: "There is no God but Allah, and Muhammad is his prophet." The holy book of Islam is the Koran (meaning "recital"). The Koran presents Muhammad's most important teachings and includes many concepts and teachings also found in the Bible and the Torah.

According to the Koran, a Muslim must meet five chief obligations known as *The Pillars of Faith:* (1) Recite the words of witness: "There is no God but Allah, and Muhammad is his prophet." (2) Pray five times a day facing Mecca. (3) If possible, make a pilgrimage, or a journey to a holy place, to Mecca at least once in a lifetime. (4) Give assistance to the needy. (5) Fast from sunrise to sunset during the month of Ramadan.

In contrast to the teachings of Jesus, Muhammad praised what he called the jihad (ji • HAHD), or holy war—fighting to defend or spread the faith of Islam. Following this principle, Muhammad's successors spread Islam throughout the Middle East and along the shores of the Mediterranean.

Muslim Civilization

The tightly organized Islamic government gave its rulers great authority. Within the stable society that developed, both economic and cultural activity flourished. Though the Muslim Empire later divided, the Muslim world remained united in one great civilization. The Arabs adopted the best ideas, customs, and institutions they found. For example, they combined the scientific and philosophical ideas of Greece, Rome, and Asia.

Muslim and Mogul Rulers in India

About the year 1000, the Turks surged through the northwest mountain passes and into India. One by one the small states of the local Rajput princes fell to the conquerors. In 1193 the Muslims occupied Delhi, and by 1236 they controlled all of northern India in what is called the Delhi sultanate.

First civil wars and then the devastating onslaught of the Mongol leader Tamerlane interrupted Muslim rule. Despite these interruptions, the first period of Muslim rule in India had important and lasting consequences. Many Indians converted to Islam, and the Muslims introduced a new and important language, Urdu.

Dome of the Rock in Jerusalem

As the Delhi sultanate grew weaker, Rajput princes again struggled for control of India. Thus, as in the time of Tamerlane, India lay open to Mongol attack. It came under the leadership of the youthful and talented "Babur the Tiger," a descendant of Tamerlane who set up the Mogul Empire, which lasted until 1761.

10 Feudal Lords and the Church Dominated Medieval Europe

The period in western European history following the collapse of the Roman Empire, between ancient times and the modern period (from about 500 to about 1500), is called the Middle Ages.

Frankish Rulers

After the Roman Empire collapsed, many Germanic tribes, including Visigoths, Vandals, Burgundians, and Ostrogoths, plundered Europe and established kingdoms. Of all the Germanic tribes, the Franks played the greatest role in history. The greatest Frankish ruler was Charlemagne, who assumed the throne in 768 and ruled until 814. By the end of his reign, he controlled much of western Europe.

Although Charlemagne was a powerful ruler who organized an efficient government, his empire soon crumbled not only because of internal feuds, but also because invaders—Muslims, Slavs, Vikings, and Magyars—swarmed into the empire from every direction.

317

1B, 1D, 3B, 4B, a1A, a1C, a2G, a2I, a2J

Presentation
Seeing Relationships (Average/Group)
Point out that England developed a constitutional form of government even though it remained a monarchy. At the same time, France developed into an absolute monarchy. Ask: Why do you think this happened? *(Students might suggest that England had a tradition of royal restraint that began with the Magna Carta, while France lacked these traditions.)*

Feudalism and the Manorial System

We call the political system that evolved in Europe after the death of Charlemagne feudalism. Feudalism, a political system in which kings and powerful nobles granted land to other nobles in return for loyalty, military assistance, and services, was firmly established throughout most of western Europe by the 1000s.

While feudalism was essentially a governmental and military system, the manorial system became the economic system. The manor, a large estate including a village, became the economic unit of the early Middle Ages.

The lord and several peasants shared the land of a manor. Most of the peasants on a manor were serfs, or people bound to the land. But serfs were not slaves, for they could not be sold away from the land.

The Church in the Middle Ages

Central governments in medieval Europe were weak or did not exist at all. Therefore, the church performed many of the responsibilities of modern governments.

Members of the clergy were organized in ranks according to their power and responsibilities. The levels of this hierarchy (HY • uh • rahr • kee), starting at the bottom, were the parish priest, the bishop, the archbishop, and the pope and his curia. In addition, monks and nuns provided valuable services for the church.

England and France

Kings and lords often struggled for power. From this struggle gradually emerged such kingdoms as England and France, where the king's authority grew stronger than that of the lords.

England. In 1066 Duke William of Normandy invaded and conquered England. One of William's successors, John, brought on a revolt among the nobles by forcing them to pay taxes that they considered unjust. In 1215 the nobles forced John to accept a document known as the Magna Carta (Latin for "great charter") in which he accorded them many rights. Although the charter was not considered significant at the time, later political thinkers regarded many of its clauses as important precedents.

King John signing the Magna Carta

In the century that followed the signing of the Magna Carta, the two most important developments in English history were the evolution of Parliament—the legislative body of England—and the growth of common law—the type of law based on judges' decisions.

France. In 987 an assembly of nobles chose Hugh Capet (kuh • PAY), a French noble, as king. Capet and his descendants, called the Capetians, ruled France for over 300 years and steadily increased royal power by adding to the royal lands, by developing a strong central government, and by increasing the revenue from taxes.

Germany and Italy

During the 1000s the Holy Roman Emperors who ruled what is today Germany and northern Italy often clashed with the papacy because the emperors claimed the right to appoint bishops. After years of conflict, the issue was finally settled in 1122 when an assembly of church leaders, nobles, and representatives of the Holy Roman Emperor reached an agreement known as the Concordat of Worms. The Concordat provided that only the church could select bishops.

11 Trade Revived and Nations Developed in Europe

During the Middle Ages people gradually began to look outward, away from Europe, seeking new products and new ways of making money.

318

The Crusades

During the 1000s the Seljuk Turks conquered Palestine and interfered with Christian pilgrims who were trying to visit the sites of the life of Jesus. In response, Pope Urban II called for a war to regain the Holy Land from the Muslims. The series of wars that followed is called the Crusades.

From a military standpoint, all the Crusades except the first failed. However, Europeans learned about many things of military importance, including the crossbow, a sophisticated bow and arrow held horizontally and set off by a trigger, and perhaps the use of gunpowder.

Trade

Trade nearly died out in western Europe after the 400s. Slowly, however, it began to revive—first in Italy where neither trade nor towns had declined as much as elsewhere. Later, trade revived in northern Europe as well.

Four important results of the revival of European trade were: a monetary system, a manufacturing system, a banking system, and the practice of investing capital.

The Growth of Towns

The growth of trade spurred the growth of towns. As the number of towns increased and their populations grew, a new class of merchants, master workers, and skilled workers emerged in medieval society. The rise of this class, in turn, encouraged the growth of nations. Townspeople tended to want stable and uniform governments that would protect trade and property, so they usually favored kings over nobles.

The Culture of the Middle Ages

Two great writers, Dante and Chaucer, represent the flowering of medieval literature. Dante Alighieri (DAHN • tay al • uhg • YER • ee) was born in Florence, Italy, in 1265. Dante's greatest work is *The Divine Comedy.* Geoffrey Chaucer of England wrote his *Canterbury Tales* in the form of a series of stories told by a group of religious pilgrims.

The later Middle Ages also witnessed the growth of universities. By the 1300s universities could be found in towns throughout western Europe. And in architecture, the soaring Gothic style replaced the earlier Romanesque style that had been based on Roman architecture.

Nations

In the late Middle Ages, European monarchs continued the process of national consolidation.

In England, the authority of the monarch, although partially restricted by Parliament, increased in various ways. These included the development of a single system of law and courts and an increase in revenue as the country grew more prosperous.

The history of France during the 1300s and 1400s resembled that of England. Philip IV, for example, established the Estates-General, a representative assembly resembling the English Parliament. But strong French kings curtailed its powers and seldom called it into session.

Spain had been divided into four kingdoms during the early Middle Ages. In the 1500s, however, Ferdinand and Isabella united Castile-León and Aragón to form the new nation of Spain, added the kingdom of Navarre to its territories, and made Spain a powerful monarchy.

Unlike England, France, and Spain, Germany and Italy—the regions that made up the Holy Roman Empire—did not become unified nations until the 1800s.

The Temporal Power of the Church

The late Middle Ages also witnessed changes in the status of the church. By the early 1300s, French kings named the popes, who ruled the church from

Building a cathedral

319

1B, 3B, 4B, a1C

Closure
Ask: Why do we know less about the early civilizations of SubSaharan Africa and the Americas than we do about other civilizations that developed about the same time? *(SubSaharan Africa and the Americas had less contact with the outside world.)*

Avignon in southern France rather than from Rome. This period of papal history—from 1309 to 1377—is known as the Babylonian Captivity.

The situation for the church worsened after 1378 when two popes, one French and one Italian, claimed power during a period called the Great Schism. Although the conflict was resolved, both the Babylonian Captivity and the Great Schism weakened the authority and prestige of the papacy and increased criticism of the church.

12 Civilization in East Asia Reached New Heights

From the 100s to 1644 great civilizations flourished in East Asia.

China

The Sui dynasty succeeded in reuniting China in 589. In their brief period of power, Sui rulers oversaw the building of one of the engineering marvels of the ancient world—the Grand Canal. However, an uprising in 618 ended the Sui dynasty, which was replaced by the Tang dynasty.

Although the Tang dynasty itself lasted only until 906, it began a 1,000-year period during which China could be described as the most powerful, the most sophisticated, and the wealthiest country in the world. It was also during the Tang dynasty that the Chinese invented printing.

The next dynasty, the Song, faced both foreign invasion and civil wars. Nevertheless, Song rulers maintained Chinese civilization and expanded trade.

Shogun Yoritomo Minamoto

Nomadic Invasions

In the 1200s the Mongols under the leadership of Genghis Khan captured Beijing and renamed it Khanbalik (kahn • buh • LEEK). They then turned westward, conquering central Asia, most of Persia, and Korea.

Japan

Only sketchy records of early Japanese history exist. We do know that Chinese influences were very strong and that the centralized political system adopted from China gradually fell into decline after the early 800s. In its place Japan developed a system of local power that in many ways resembled feudalism, the system that governed Europe at this time.

In Japan the feudal system contained two conflicting sources of power. One was an indirect form of central government under which an important family held power in the name of the emperor. The other source consisted of military units that had authority in the territories they occupied.

In 1192 the Minamoto family introduced a new kind of official called the shogun. Officially he was the chief officer of the emperor and was always careful to be dutiful to him. In fact, however, he was the agent of the powerful families.

The leading families and their shoguns had power, but they did not control enough to extend this power to local levels. There, warrior-landlords called samurai (SAM • uh • ry) led the military units.

Japan's neighbor to the east, Korea, also developed civilization. There both Japanese and Chinese influences were evident.

13 Africa and the Americas Produced Complex Civilizations

Because we have few written records of peoples who lived in Africa south of the Sahara and in the Americas, we know much less about events before 1500 in those regions than we do about events in Europe and Asia. We do know that complex, highly sophisticated societies developed.

320

Question 1 of the Synthesis Review corresponds to Section 8, Question 2, to Section 9; Question 3, to Section 10; Question 4, to Section 11; Question 5, to Section 12; Question 6, to Section 13. Question 7 asks students to synthesize information from various sections of the synthesis.

1B, 2A, 2B, 2C, a1C, a4A, a4F, a4G, a4H, a4I, a4K, a4L, a4M

Machu Picchu, Peru

Africa's Early History

Experts have drawn several conclusions about life in early Africa. They believe that most Africans lived in small, independent agricultural villages ruled by chiefs. Relationships of kinship, age, and sex bound the different societies together. Within this system women played a crucial role.

African City-states and Kingdoms

Along the Nile River, south of the major centers of ancient Egypt, lies an area known as Nubia, which was the site of Cush. Cush maintained close cultural and economic ties with Egypt, and about 750 B.C. it conquered Upper Egypt. Later the kingdom of Axum arose in the Ethiopian highlands.

No large kingdoms like Cush and Axum emerged on the coast of East Africa. Instead, a series of city-states that dominated coastal trade in the Indian Ocean arose.

The growth of Indian Ocean trade after the 900s dramatically increased the demand for gold. The Karanga, a people who first immigrated onto the plateau land of what is today Zimbabwe (zim • BAHB • wee) about 800, achieved control of this trade.

In West Africa, between Lake Chad and the Atlantic Ocean, several important African societies developed. The most powerful included Ghana, Mali, and Songhai.

The Americas

While the Ice Age still gripped the earth, people migrated from Asia to the Americas across a land bridge that then linked the two continents near what is today the Bering Strait. These early immigrants lived by hunting and gathering. Their descendants, however, learned to farm.

In what is today the United States and Canada, many different cultures and some highly organized societies thrived. The cultures of these peoples often depended on the geography of the region they inhabited.

Empires in Mexico and Peru

Several cultures developed in Mexico. Early cultures included the Olmecs, the Maya, and the Toltecs. Then about A.D. 1200 peoples from the north launched further invasions of central Mexico. One of these groups, the Aztecs, soon dominated central Mexico. The Aztecs incorporated into their culture the inventions of peoples they conquered or with whom they traded. They soon learned the use of metals, weaving, pottery-making, the calendar, and mathematics.

At about the same period that the Aztecs built their civilization in Mexico, another group created a civilization in the Andes Mountains of South America. These people based their religion on sun worship. Their name—Incas—meant "children of the sun."

The Inca Empire expanded steadily. By the late 1400s it extended along most of the west coast of South America and far into the Andes, covering much of the present-day nations of Peru, Ecuador, Bolivia, and Chile.

SYNTHESIS REVIEW

1. **Understanding Ideas** What was the greatest Byzantine contribution to civilization?
2. **Interpreting Ideas** Why did Muslims attempt to spread their faith?
3. **Summarizing Ideas** What were the basic principles of feudalism and the manorial system?
4. **Analyzing Ideas** How did the growth of towns in the Middle Ages affect the growth of national states?
5. **Comparing Ideas** How did the governmental system of Japan resemble feudalism in Europe?
6. **Relating Cause and Effect** How did geography affect migrations into the Americas?
7. **Synthesizing Ideas** Why do you think the Byzantines and the Muslims were able to control large empires when Europe was fragmented?

Review Answers

1. preservation of Roman law
2. Muhammad praised what he called the jihad, or holy war — fighting to defend or spread the faith of Islam.
3. Feudalism was a political system in which kings and powerful nobles granted land to other nobles in return for loyalty, military assistance, and services. The manorial system was an economic system based on the manor, or large estate. The lord and several peasants shared the land of a manor. Most of the peasants on a manor were serfs, or people bound to the land.
4. Townspeople tended to want stable and uniform governments that would protect trade and property, so they usually favored kings over nobles.
5. It was based on local power consisting of an important family holding power in the name of the emperor and military units that had authority in the territories they occupied.
6. The Americas were isolated except in the distant past when a land bridge connected North America and Asia.
7. Answers will vary. Students might suggest that the Byzantines and the Muslims had efficient governments at a time when various waves of invaders had overwhelmed the West and set up a series of rival kingdoms.

Introducing the Unit

Have students study the map on pages R12-R13. Point out that the map shows nations in Europe today. Then tell students that the emergence of nations is a relatively recent phenomenon that has occurred since the 1500s. To illustrate this point, have students compare the map on pages R12-R13 with the political map of Europe on page 378. Ask: How does the territory of France differ in the two maps? *(France is much larger today.)* Then point out that students will be studying the growth of nations in Unit Four.

UNIT FOUR

The Emergence of Modern Nations

◀ *A European Renaissance seaport*

Unit Goals

After studying Unit Four, students will be able to:

1. Analyze the impact that the Renaissance, the Reformation, and the Scientific Revolution had on history.
2. Describe the reasons for and the results of European explorations in the Americas, Africa, and Asia.
3. Trace the steps in the development of France, Prussia, Russia, and Austria.
4. Discuss the development of constitutional government in England and the United States.
5. Analyze how the Enlightenment influenced the French Revolution.
6. Describe the French Revolution and the rise of Napoleon.
7. Summarize the accomplishments of the Ming and Qing dynasties.
8. Describe the Tokugawa shogunate.
9. State why Europeans became interested in Africa and then compare the three different types of slavery—African slavery, Portuguese slavery, and the slavery systems of other nations.

UNIT FOUR THE EMERGENCE OF MODERN NATIONS

CHAPTER (pages 324–353)

14 The Renaissance, Reformation, and Scientific Revolution Changed Europe

(1350 – 1700)

CHAPTER OVERVIEW

The Renaissance began in Italy and grew out of humanism. Important Italian humanists included Petrarch and Machiavelli. In northern Europe, humanism was reflected in the works of Erasmus and More. The Renaissance in art was one of the greatest creative outbursts the world has known.

During this period a movement known as the Reformation split the Christian Church in western Europe. In Germany Martin Luther taught that salvation would be granted by faith alone. In England Henry VIII broke from the Church of Rome and created the Anglican church. Another challenge came from John Calvin, who emphasized predestination and the community of believers.

The Catholic church initiated a Counter-Reformation and set out to redefine church doctrine and to reform abuses. It published an *Index of Prohibited Books,* revived the Inquisition, and founded new religious orders.

Due to the religious changes of the Reformation and the development of the printing press, the close-knit community of the village began to break down. Gradually, new information challenged popular beliefs.

In the 1500s a new way of pursuing knowledge gave rise to the Scientific Revolution. Important advances were made in astronomy, physics, and anatomy. By the 1700s the scientific point of view dominated European thought.

SUGGESTED LESSON PLAN

Day	Objectives	Suggested Activities	Materials
1	U1,* C1-9 C1-2	Introducing the Unit (pages 322-23) Introducing the Chapter (pages 324-25) Section 1 (pages 325-32), Focus/Motivation (page 325), Presentation (page 326), Closure (page 332), Suggested Teaching Strategies, Enrichment Activities, Daily Quiz, Suggested Assignments (page 323B)	ATE, Pupil's Edition, Teacher's Resource-Bank™
2	U1, C3-4	Section 2 (pages 332-36), Focus/Motivation (page 333), Presentation (page 334), Closure (page 336), Suggested Teaching Strategies, Enrichment Activity, Daily Quiz, Suggested Assignments (page 323C)	ATE, Pupil's Edition, Teacher's Resource-Bank™
3	U1, C4	Section 3 (pages 336-41), Focus/Motivation (page 337), Presentation (page 338), Closure (page 340), Suggested Teaching Strategies, Enrichment Activity, Daily Quiz, Suggested Assignments (page 323D)	ATE, Pupil's Edition, Teacher's Resource-Bank™
4	U1, C5-7	Section 4 (pages 341-47), Focus/Motivation (page 341), Presentation (page 343), Closure (page 346), Suggested Teaching Strategies, Enrichment Activity, Daily Quiz, Suggested Assignments (page 323E)	ATE, Pupil's Edition, Teacher's Resource-Bank™
5	U1, C8-9	Section 5 (pages 347-51), Focus/Motivation (page 347), Presentation (page 347), Closure (page 350), Suggested Teaching Strategies, Enrichment Activity, Daily Quiz, Suggested Assignments (page 323F)	ATE, Pupil's Edition, Teacher's Resource-Bank™
6	U1, C1-9	Chapter 14 Form A Test, Reteaching Worksheet, Chapter 14 Form B Test	Teacher's Resource-Bank™ or Workbook and Test Booklet

*C refers to applicable Chapter Objective, U refers to applicable Unit Goal.

BOOKS FOR THE TEACHER

Becker, Carl L. *The Heavenly City of the Eighteenth-Century Philosophers.* Yale University Press. Provides a philosophical basis for the Enlightenment.

Durant, Will. *The Reformation* and *The Renaissance.* Simon and Schuster. Gives a thorough and enjoyable account of these two periods.

Lucas, Henry S. *The Renaissance and Reformation.* Harper & Row. Surveys this period of history.

BOOKS FOR THE STUDENTS

Cowie, Leonard W. *The Reformation.* John Day. Provides short, informative overview of the Reformation.

Hale, John R. *The Renaissance.* Time-Life. Presents a variety of illustrations and charts.

Marzieh, Gail. *Life in the Renaissance.* Random House. Gives colorful account of the period; many illustrations.

Simon, Edith. *The Reformation.* Time-Life. Describes the social and religious aspects of the times.

MULTIMEDIA MATERIALS

Galileo: Challenge of Reason (mp, 27 min.), Learning Corp. Describes Galileo's conflict with the church.

A Matter of Conscience: Henry VIII and Thomas More (mp, 25 min.), Learning Corp. Provides edited version of *A Man for All Seasons.*

The Saga of Western Man: I, Leonardo da Vinci (mp, 54 min.), McGraw-Hill. Portrays the life of da Vinci and the enormous influence of his ideas on the intellectual history of the Western world.

Section (pages 325–332)

1 Renaissance Writers and Artists Created Outstanding Works

SECTION OVERVIEW

The Renaissance was a period of great intellectual and artistic activity that began in Italy and eventually spread to northern Europe. The basis of the Renaissance was humanism. Italian humanists studied ancient Greek and Roman culture; northern European humanists were also interested in the early Christian period. Renaissance artists realistically portrayed natural life and forms and used perspective. In art and in literature, human beings became the center of concern.

SUGGESTED TEACHING STRATEGIES

1. **Preteaching Vocabulary (Basic)** You may wish to preteach the following important vocabulary terms: Renaissance *(page 325)*; humanist *(page 326)*; perspective *(page 329)*; utopia *(page 331)*. Ask students what they think a utopian society might be like.
2. **Writing an Essay (Average/Group)** Have students write essays explaining the basis of Renaissance thought and how it influenced education, politics, and individualism. Some students may want to make an outline before writing the essay. *(Students should mention that Renaissance thought was based on humanism, a study of classical literature. Renaissance scholars emphasized education in order to learn how things worked. They believed people should take an active interest in practical affairs such as politics. Humanists emphasized individual dignity and achievement.)*
3. **Contrasting Art (Basic)** Have students review the art of early Egypt (pages 24, 25) and then contrast this flat, two-dimensional rendering with the Renaissance paintings in this chapter (pages 329, 330, 332). Some students might want to give illustrated oral reports contrasting the two types of art. They can find additional examples in art books in the library.

ENRICHMENT ACTIVITIES

1. **Discussing a Film (Average/Group)** The film *Saga of Western Man: I, Leonardo da Vinci* (54 min., color, McGraw-Hill) is an excellent vehicle for a discussion of Leonardo da Vinci and the Renaissance concept of the universal person. Ask students if they think it is possible to be a universal person today. If so, ask them to give examples from today's world. (Answers will vary.)
2. **Learning History Through Art (Average/Group)** As the feature on page 330 explains, the unicorn symbol has appeared in various cultures throughout history. Some students might wish to learn more about the legends surrounding the unicorn. One source is Nancy Hathaway's *The Unicorn Book* (Viking). After researching the topic, students can make a bulletin board display comparing unicorn legends from various cultures.

DAILY QUIZ

To assess student understanding of Section 1, give the class the following quiz. (Each item is worth 10 points.)

1. *Renaissance* is a French word that means ________. *(rebirth)*
2. In what country do historians believe the Renaissance began? *(Italy)*
3. (T or F) The humanists of the 1300s initially studied the Greek and Roman classics and stressed the study of grammar, rhetoric, history, and poetry. *(T)*
4. (T or F) Humanists such as Petrarch emphasized science to the exclusion of religion, music, and art. *(F)*
5. What was the title of Niccolò Machiavelli's famous book that described government as it should work? *(The Prince)*
6. This Dutch humanist was interested not only in Greek and Roman culture but also in early Christian philosophers. *(Desiderius Erasmus)*
7. (T or F) Thomas More's *Utopia* described a society in which the church and state cooperated. *(F)*
8. The artist who painted the frescoes on the ceiling of the Sistine Chapel in Rome was ________. *(Michelangelo)*
9. The playwright who produced characters such as Hamlet, Macbeth, and Romeo and Juliet was ________ ________. *(William Shakespeare)*
10. (T or F) Hans Holbein the Younger is noted for his scenes of the countryside and peasant life in his native Flanders. *(F)*

SUGGESTED ASSIGNMENTS

1. **Critical Thinking Worksheet (Basic)** Have students complete Critical Thinking Worksheet 31 in the TEACHER'S RESOURCEBANK™.
2. **Critical Thinking Worksheet (Basic)** Have students complete Critical Thinking Worksheet 32 in the TEACHER'S RESOURCEBANK™.
3. **Analyzing Ideas (Average/Group)** Have interested students research Lorenzo Valla's criticism of ancient texts. Then have them identify the Donation of Constantine and explain how Valla discovered that this document was a forgery.

Section (pages 332–335)

2 The Protestant Reformation Changed Religious Attitudes

SECTION OVERVIEW

Increasing criticism of the church developed into a religious revolution that split the church in western Europe. The first break occurred in Germany, where the use of indulgences to raise money produced an outcry. Martin Luther protested the sale of indulgences and taught that salvation was attained by faith alone. Luther's opposition to church doctrines led to his break from the Church of Rome. Other Protestant movements gained strength. In England, Henry VIII broke with the pope and created the Anglican church.

SUGGESTED TEACHING STRATEGIES

1. **Preteaching Vocabulary (Basic)** You may wish to preteach the following important vocabulary terms: Reformation, indulgence *(page 333)*; 95 theses *(page 334)*; sect *(page 335)*. Ask students to name sects of the various religions of the world with which they are familiar.
2. **Understanding Ideas (Basic)** Have students read the subsections, "The Origins of the Reformation" on page 333, "Luther's Break With the Medieval Church" on pages 334-335, and "The Spread of Protestantism" on page 335. Ask them to speculate on why Germany was sensitive to church abuses and why the main thrust of the "Reformation" occurred in that country. *(Answers will vary. Students should point out that Germany had no strong central government to prevent the pope from making monetary demands on the people. Humanism was strong in Germany, encouraging church reformers such as Luther. The political divisions of Germany also encouraged the princes to make gains at the expense of both the Holy Roman Emperor and the church.)*
3. **Staging a Debate (Challenging)** Johann Eck, defender of the church, staged a famous debate with Luther. Have two students debate the issues that divided Luther and the church. "Luther Versus the Church: Conflicts in Doctrine" in Louis Synder et al., *Panorama of the Past* (Houghton Mifflin) contains points that can be used by both sides. Henry S. Lucas's *Renaissance and Reformation* (Harper & Row) also has a detailed account of the controversy.

ENRICHMENT ACTIVITY

Interpreting Ideas (Challenging) Have interested students research the life of Martin Luther. They may want to examine biographies or encyclopedias in their school or local libraries. Have them pay particular attention to the evolution of Luther's thoughts — from simple reform to a major revolution — and thus a break with the Church of Rome. Ask them to speculate on how serious a course it was for a monk to confront the hierarchy of the church. Why was Luther compelled to do what he did? *(Answers will vary. Students might mention Luther's concern as a youth for his salvation, his failure to get comfort from the existing church, and his belief that indulgences would not provide the salvation that only simple faith could provide. Therefore the church had to change. When it denounced Luther and then excommunicated him, Luther broke completely with it and formed his own church.)*

DAILY QUIZ

To assess student understanding of Section 2, give the class the following quiz. (Each item is worth 10 points.)

1. (T or F) At the time of the Reformation, Germany had a strong central government headed by the Holy Roman Emperor, a weak church, and a large number of imperial cities that followed the emperor's commands. *(F)*
2. The church sold ________, or pardons from punishment for sin, in order to help pay for the rebuilding of St. Peter's in Rome. *(indulgences)*
3. (T or F) The northern humanists had no interest in church reform. *(F)*
4. The Holy Roman Emperor summoned Martin Luther to the Imperial Diet in this German city in order to put the papal excommunication into effect. *(Worms)*
5. What was the name of the Holy Roman Emperor? *(Charles V)*
6. While under the protection of the Elector of Saxony, Martin Luther translated the ________ into German so that literate Christians could read it for themselves. *(Bible)*
7. Members of the Lutheran clergy are called ________. *(ministers)*
8. One of the early sects, the ancestors of the modern-day Baptists, were called ________. *(Anabaptists)*
9. The religious truce which allowed the princes of Germany to determine the religion in their states was known as the ________. *(Peace of Augsburg)*
10. Which English king broke away from the Church of Rome and formed the Anglican church because the pope would not grant him a divorce? *(Henry VIII)*

SUGGESTED ASSIGNMENTS

1. **Autobiographical Report (Average/Group)** An autobiography provides rich information for historians about the life of a person

and about society and the customs of that person's time. Have students prepare oral or written reports on an autobiography of their choice. They should discuss the information the autobiography gives about family relationships, education, cultural life, and ways of earning a living during the period in which the person lived.

2. **Synthesizing Ideas (Average/Group)** Have interested students research the reasons for the creation of the Anglican Church in England during the Reformation. They should examine encyclopedias, biographies, and histories of England in their school or local libraries. In their study they should compare the personal reasons for Henry VIII's decision with the growth of Protestant ideas in England, to determine how the resulting church is different from Luther's church, the sects, and Calvinism (about which they will read in Section 3). Have students prepare either an oral or written report, both of which can be presented to the class.

Section (pages 336–341)

3 The Roman Catholic Church Met New Challenges

SECTION OVERVIEW

The religion founded by John Calvin became a powerful, widely supported movement that challenged the Catholic church even in areas where the church was strong. The Catholic church realized that some reforms were needed and began in the 1530s a revival within known as the Counter-Reformation. The Council of Trent defined church doctrine, and the church founded new religious orders to combat Protestantism and bring members back to the fold.

SUGGESTED TEACHING STRATEGIES

1. **Preteaching Vocabulary (Basic)** You may wish to preteach the following important vocabulary terms: predestination, theocracy *(page 336)*; Counter-Reformation *(page 337)*. Ask students to name any theocracies that are in existence today.
2. **Comparing Ideas (Basic)** Ask students to present a discussion between John Calvin and Ignatius of Loyola. A moderator should ask them to explain their beliefs, to describe the methods they used to create self-disciplined followers, and whether they see any similarities in their approaches.
3. **Understanding Ideas (Average/Group)** Divide the class into small groups. Have each group discuss the following questions and then have the groups share their conclusions. How did Calvin's teachings on predestination differ from Catholic teaching? How might Calvin have felt about the persecution of the Huguenots in France? Why did Genevan laws prohibit dancing and other popular entertainment? Students will need to do additional reading. Sources include Sydney Eisen and Maurice Filler, eds., *The Human Adventure* (Harcourt Brace Jovanovich), and Will Durant's *The Reformation* (Simon and Schuster).

*4. **Making Connections with History: Using Art to Understand Values (Average/Group)** Have students examine the painting of the Council of Trent by Titian on page 337. Ask them to determine when the artwork was produced, explain what major theme the artwork represents, identify the subject of the work, and use the theme and subject to help explain the values of the historical period in which the work was created.

ENRICHMENT ACTIVITY

Mapping Religion (Average/Group) Have interested students prepare two maps of European religions. The first map should show the religious divisions made in 1555 at the Peace of Augsburg. The second map should show Europe at the end of the Counter-Reformation, about 1600. Post the maps on the bulletin board. Use the divisions thus shown as the basis for a class discussion on the geographical spread of Protestantism and the successes made by the Catholic church in recovering some lands for the church.

DAILY QUIZ

To assess student understanding of Section 3, give the class the following quiz. (Each item is worth 10 points.)

1. What French religious leader moved to Geneva, Switzerland, and developed a complete and clear set of beliefs that had a powerful influence in Europe? *(John Calvin)*
2. Those who followed his beliefs in France were called ________. *(Huguenots)*
3. In 1598 the king of France issued a decree giving Protestants freedom of worship and some political rights. What was the name of this decree? *(Edict of Nantes)*
4. Protestants called ________ played a vital role in England and in the English colonies of North America. *(Puritans)*
5. The ________ was a court that tried heretics. *(Inquisition)*
6. The ________ ________ ________ ________ prohibited Catholics from reading certain works. *(Index of Prohibited Books)*
7. The Council of ________ reaffirmed church doctrines, banned the sale of indulgences, and tightened discipline for the clergy. *(Trent)*
8. What religious order founded some of the best colleges in Europe, where they combined humanist values with theology? *(Society of Jesus, or Jesuits)*
9. Who founded this religious order? *(Ignatius of Loyola)*
10. (T or F) The Catholic Counter-Reformation had little success slowing the spread of Protestantism in Poland, Germany, and France. *(F)*

SUGGESTED ASSIGNMENTS

1. **Profile Worksheet (Basic)** Have students complete Profile Worksheet 14 in the TEACHER'S RESOURCEBANK ™.
2. **Skill Worksheet (Basic)** Have students complete Skill Worksheet 14 in the TEACHER'S RESOURCEBANK™.

3. **Biographical Report (Average/Group)** Have students study the lives of one of the following individuals of the Reformation period. They may wish to use resources in their school or local libraries. Have them write a three-page report on the accomplishments of this individual. They should present their reports to the class.

Huldrych Zwingli	John Calvin
Pope Paul III	Ignatius of Loyola
Henry IV of France	John Knox
Michael Servetus	Catherine de' Medici

4. **Report (Challenging)** Have interested students study the wars of religion in France during the 1500s. They may wish to use histories of France or encyclopedias to help them in their research. They should prepare an oral or written report to give to the class. In their reports they should discuss the growth of Protestantism, the numbers and classes of people involved, the fighting between forces of the Catholic party and those of the Huguenots, and the War of the Three Henrys (Henry of Guise, Henry III of Valois, and Henry IV of Navarre.)

Section (pages 341–347)

4 Popular Culture Took New Forms and Influenced Daily Life

SECTION OVERVIEW

Before the 1500s the lives of most Europeans consisted of work from sunrise to sunset, with some recreations. They depended upon magic and witchcraft to account for the unexplained or unusual events of daily life. The invention of printing, the Reformation, and the Counter-Reformation brought new ideas into the village and drastically changed village culture. The standard of living increased in Europe until the wars of religion during the Reformation.

SUGGESTED TEACHING STRATEGIES

1. **Preteaching Vocabulary (Basic)** You may wish to preteach the following important vocabulary terms: broadside, almanac (*page 344*); standard of living, inflation (*page 345*). Ask students what almanacs are still published.
2. **Writing a Diary (Basic)** Have each student write a diary entry by a child in the 1400s describing a holiday in his or her village. Call upon volunteers to read their entries to the class.
3. **Understanding Technology (Average/Group)** Have interested students research the development of the printing press through time. Have them use resources in their school or local libraries. They should then prepare an oral or written report on improvements made in the press, the volume of works that could be printed, and the packaging and selling of the products. Those students who live in areas with printing or publishing companies might be able to visit them, obtain literature, and enhance their reports with material on the latest achievements in printing technology. Have them present their reports to the class.

ENRICHMENT ACTIVITY

Writing a Research Report (Average/Group) Interested students might prepare reports on witchcraft during this period. Sources include Edith Simon's *The Reformation* (Time-Life); Will Durant's *The Reformation* (Simon and Schuster); and Will and Ariel Durant's *The Age of Reason Begins* (Simon and Schuster).

DAILY QUIZ

To assess student understanding of Section 4, give the class the following quiz. (Each item is worth 10 points.)

1. (T or F) Most parish priests shared their parishioners' beliefs in good and evil spirits. *(T)*
2. (T or F) Peasants often consulted "wise men" or "wise women" to obtain remedies for their problems. *(T)*
3. (T or F) Although uncommon in Europe in the 1500s and 1600s, witch hunts indicated that the normal harmony of the village had broken down. *(F)*
4. (T or F) "Rough music" was a popular ceremony which poked fun at the familiar sights and scenes of village life. *(T)*
5. Who brought broadsides and pamphlets into the village? prince, peddler, gypsy, troubadour *(peddler)*
6. The most common of early books or pamphlets, besides the Bible, was the ________. *(almanac)*
7. (T or F) Sometimes villagers turned angrily on their neighbors or outsiders who upset their traditions or sense of proper behavior. *(T)*
8. (T or F) As a result of economic changes, by the 1500s the standard of living had risen in Europe. *(T)*
9. (T or F) After the Black Death cut Europe's population by perhaps one-third, the peasants prospered because their goods and labor were in demand. *(T)*
10. What two sources of protein were an important part of the diet of Europeans everywhere? *(cheese, eggs)*

SUGGESTED ASSIGNMENTS

1. **Oral Report (Average/Group)** Have interested students report on housing during the 1500s and 1600s. They should describe how peasants and townspeople lived, how their life styles differed, and what types of housing construction they used. Students should take into consideration variations between religious groups, between town and country, and between social classes. Students will want to examine literature on rural and city life in their school or local libraries. Have them present their material in an oral report to the class. Use their findings as the basis for a class discussion on housing and life styles then and now.
2. **Making a Chart (Challenging)** Have students select one European country and prepare a chart showing what the people of that country ate during the 1500s and 1600s, and what they eat today. They should research this topic in encyclopedias in their school or local libraries. They may wish to obtain literature from the government information offices of their selected country or from the World Health Organization and other United Nations

agencies. On this chart they should list popular items of diet and indicate their use or disuse now. Use their findings as the basis for a class discussion on the diet of the country shown on the chart and the foods that Americans eat today.

Section (pages 347–351)

5 The Scientific Revolution Swept Europe

SECTION OVERVIEW

In the 1500s and 1600s Europeans began to question traditional opinions about the world and to experiment for themselves. This new system of investigation gave rise to a transformation in thinking known as the Scientific Revolution. New discoveries were made in astronomy, physics, anatomy, and other areas. By the 1700s, the scientific point of view dominated European thought.

SUGGESTED TEACHING STRATEGIES

1. **Preteaching Vocabulary (Basic)** You may wish to preteach the following important vocabulary terms: Scientific Revolution *(page 347)*; scientific method, geocentric theory, heliocentric theory *(page 348)*. Ask students to enumerate recent scientific inventions that have revolutionized the world of science.
2. **Comparing Ideas (Average/Group)** Divide the class into two groups. Have one group serve as supporters of the geocentric theory of the universe. The other group should support the heliocentric theory espoused by Copernicus. Have each group select one member of the group to be its spokesperson. Ask each spokesperson to present the argument for his or her respective position. Members of the opposing group should ask questions from the floor. The spokesperson and supporters may answer them. After the class has exhausted the arguments for and against both theories, ask them to name the steps adopted by the new scientists which form the best of the scientific method. *(performing experiments, using mathematics)*
3. **Explaining Ideas (Average/Group)** Explain to the class that since the Scientific Revolution, researchers conduct experiments to arrive at knowledge and truth. This is known as the *inductive method.* This was a radical departure from the *deductive method* used in the Middle Ages, where "truth" was arrived at by following the maxims of established authority. Ask students to describe the steps of inductive reasoning and contrast these with the deductive method. *(In the deductive method, conclusions are drawn from general principles assumed to be true. The inductive method accumulates specific facts or individual cases to arrive at general conclusions. Both of these methods are used in research today.)*

ENRICHMENT ACTIVITY

Writing Biographical Sketches (Basic) Have students write short biographical sketches about scientists of the period and their accomplishments. Students may refer to encyclopedias or biographies for information. Additional sources are Will and Ariel Durant's *The Age of Reason Begins* and *Age of Louis XIV* (Simon and Schuster).

DAILY QUIZ

To assess student understanding of Section 5, give the class the following quiz. (Each item is worth 10 points.)

1. Who believed that the position of the stars affected human life? alchemists, astronomers, astrologers, physicians *(astrologers)*
2. Name two instruments that helped scientists observe and measure their scientific experiments. *(barometer, microscope, thermometer, telescope)*
3. Ptolemy's theory is called the _______ _______ of the universe. *(geocentric theory)*
4. Copernicus helped develop the _______ _______ of the universe. *(heliocentric theory)*
5. _______ _______, using mathematics to test Copernican theory, determined that the orbits the earth moved in were ellipses, not circles. *(Johannes Kepler)*
6. (T or F) Galileo helped develop the first telescope. *(T)*
7. _______ wrote *On the Fabric of the Human Body,* using illustrations to depict human anatomy. *(Vesalius)*
8. Who was the French philosopher and scientist who argued that all thought had to follow the clear, orderly progression of scientific reasoning? *(Descartes)*
9. This English scientist explained why the planets moved as they did by his laws of motion and universal gravitation. *(Isaac Newton)*
10. The Englishman Joseph Priestley and the Frenchman Antoine Lavoisier conducted experiments with the element _______. *(oxygen)*

SUGGESTED ASSIGNMENTS

1. **Review Worksheet (Basic)** Have students complete Review Worksheet 14 of the TEACHER'S RESOURCEBANK™.
2. **Scientific Experiment (Challenging)** Have interested students devise a scientific instrument of their choice, such as a telescope, and bring it to the class. Other students might wish to set up a computer program using data that explains the heliocentric theory of the universe, scientific formulas, etc. These projects should be brought to class. Ask the project or program designers to explain their work to the rest of the class, using the scientific method introduced during the Scientific Revolution. Use the experiments as the basis for a class discussion on the progress made in science since the 1600s.

For suggested lesson plan, additional teaching strategies, enrichment activities, daily quizzes, and suggested assignments, see pages 323A-323D.

Introducing the Chapter Put the following two quotations on the chalkboard or an overhead projector.

"It is therefore vanity to seek after perishing riches.
It is also vanity to seek honors. . . .
It is vanity to mind this present life, and not those things which are to come."
—Thomas à Kempis

"It is true that men who have labored with some show of excellence have already given knowledge of themselves to the world; and this alone ought to suffice them; I mean the fact that they have proved their manhood and achieved renown. Yet one must needs live like others; and so in a work like this there will always be found occasion for natural bragging, which is of diverse kinds."
—Benvenuto Cellini

Lead a discussion comparing medieval thought to Renaissance thought, using the following questions: In which passage is heaven considered more important than this world? *(Thomas à Kempis)* In which passage are honors and fame considered more important? *(Cellini)* In which passage does human achievement seem to be more praised? *(Cellini)* Which do you think was written during the medieval period? *(Thomas à Kempis)* During the Renaissance? *(Cellini)*.

CHAPTER 14

The Renaissance, Reformation, and Scientific Revolution Changed Europe

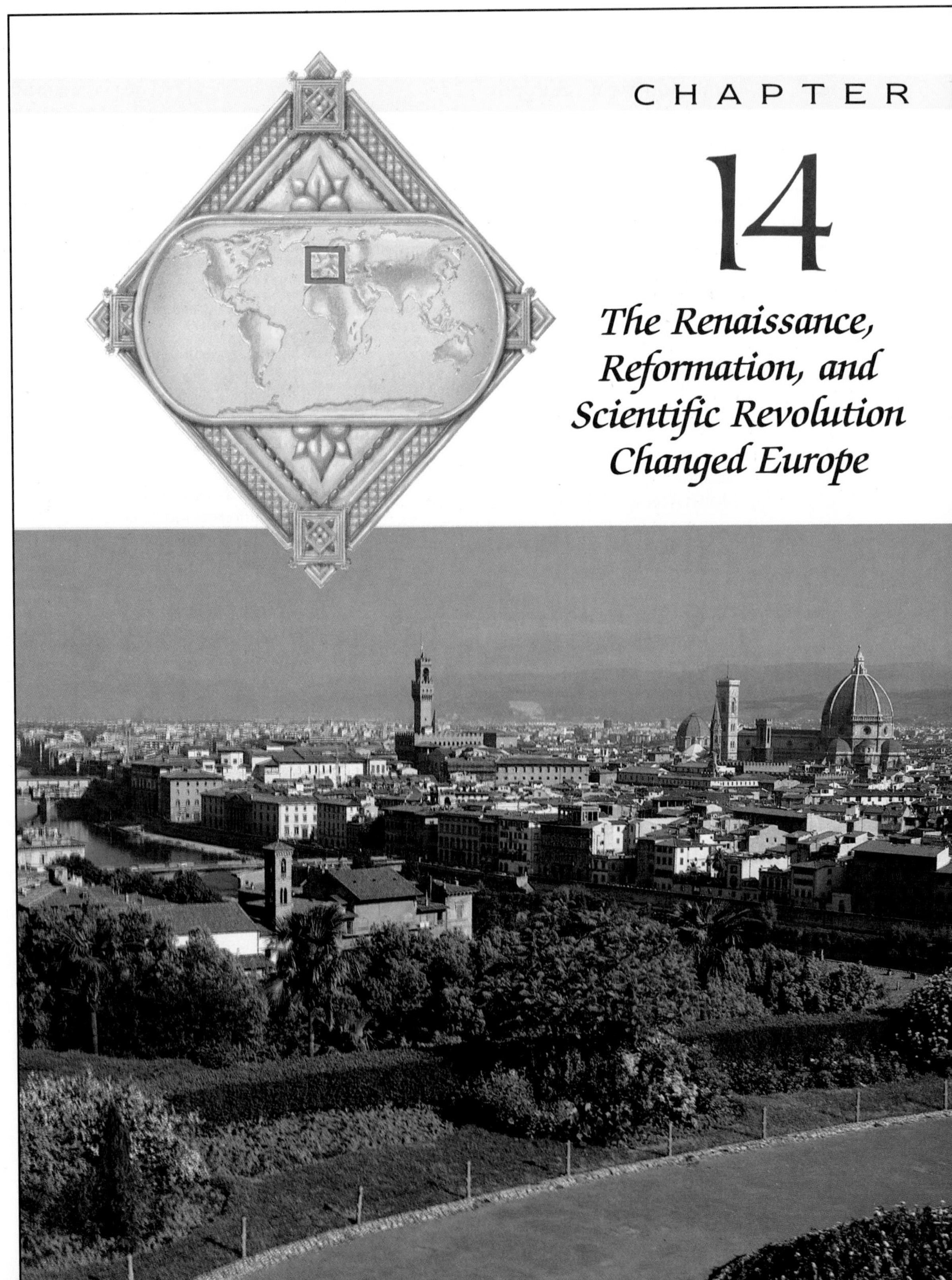

CHAPTER FOCUS

Place Europe

Time

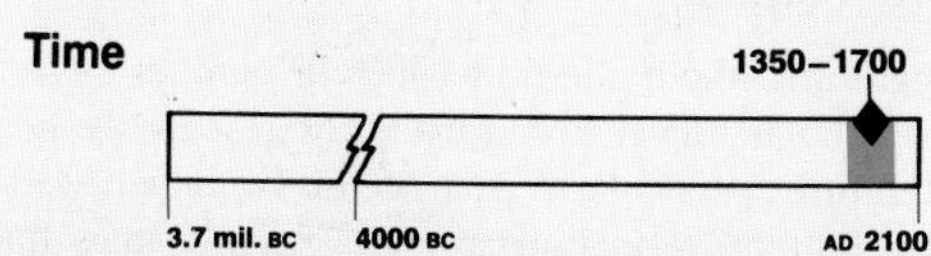

Significance

If you were to think about the differences between medieval and modern times, you would probably think first of the great difference in the material goods available. Today we have compact disc players, VCRs, and other luxuries and conveniences that medieval people never dreamed of. However, another and perhaps even greater difference exists—a difference in attitudes. Beginning in the 1300s, people gradually began to look for new ways to explain what happened in the world in which they lived.

The changes in attitude that altered how people viewed themselves as well as their world did not occur overnight. Many historians believe that the changes grew out of a philosophical and artistic movement that began in Italy about 1350. Because it centered on a revival of interest in the classical learning of Greece and Rome, we call this movement the **Renaissance** (REN • uh • sahnts), a French word meaning "rebirth." Some scholars think of the Renaissance as merely a continuation and development of the Middle Ages. Others think of the Renaissance as a break with medieval life and medieval thought—as the beginning of modern times.

Terms to Define

Renaissance	indulgences
perspective	Scientific Revolution
Reformation	heliocentric theory

People to Identify

Leonardo da Vinci	John Calvin
Johann Gutenberg	Nicolaus Copernicus
Martin Luther	Galileo

Places to Locate

Florence	Worms

Questions to Guide Your Reading

1 What major works did Renaissance writers and artists create?
2 Why did the Reformation take place?
3 How did Calvinism and the Counter-Reformation affect religion in Europe?
4 How did popular culture change during the Renaissance and the Reformation?
5 Why was the Scientific Revolution important?

◀ *Florence, Italy*

On November 4, 1966, newscasts across the world carried reports of a staggering natural disaster. In northern Italy the Arno River had burst over its banks, sending torrents of swirling floodwaters cascading through the museums, cathedrals, and libraries of Florence. When the waters receded, they left layer upon layer of sewage and muck. Within days, hundreds of people—mostly students—converged on the water-logged city to help with the massive cleanup.

Why would news of a flood in northern Italy electrify people across the world? Quite simply because that city of only 150,000 people contained the world's greatest store of Renaissance art and literature. As one reporter noted:

> *"It is fair to say that much of what we know today of painting and sculpture, of architecture and political science, of scientific method and economic theory, we owe to the artists, politicians, statesmen, bankers, and merchants of the Renaissance—that explosion of intellectual and artistic energy in Italy between 1300 and 1600. And Florentines stood at the turbulent center of the Renaissance."*

Throughout Europe the outpouring of creativity that was the Renaissance changed the course of Western civilization.

1 Renaissance Writers and Artists Created Outstanding Works

Scholars use the term *Renaissance* to refer not only to a philosophical and artistic movement but also to the period during which it flourished. The period of the Renaissance saw many developments, including the invention of the printing press, advances in science, and a new emphasis on reason.

The Origins of the Italian Renaissance

A renewed interest in Roman literature and life characterized the Renaissance. In many ways it was natural that this interest would reawaken in Italy. Ruins of the mighty Roman Empire dotted the Italian countryside and served as constant reminders of Roman glory. The tradition of Rome as the capital city of a vast empire lived on in the popes, who made Rome the seat of the Roman

Chapter Objectives

After studying Chapter 14, students will be able to:

1. Define humanism and its influence on art and literature.
2. Identify and compare the major Italian and Northern Renaissance artists and writers.
3. Explain the causes of the Reformation, paying particular attention to Martin Luther's grievances against the church.
4. Describe the fragmentation of the Roman Catholic church, the spread of Protestantism by the sects, the Anglican church, and Calvinism; and the steps the Catholic church took during the Counter-Reformation to reform the church.
5. Describe how superstition and violence affected the lives of ordinary people.
6. Discuss how printing revolutionized education and society.
7. Describe the changes in daily life of people from 1350 to 1700.
8. Discuss the causes of the Scientific Revolution and the advances scientists made in the studies of astronomy, physics, and anatomy.
9. State how the theories of Descartes and Newton influenced the scientific world.

SECTION 1

Focus/Motivation

To highlight the differences between medieval and

1A, 1B, 4C, a1A, a1C, a4B, a4C

● Venice

■ The Medici family ruled Florence from the 1400s to 1737. They were very rich and furnished three popes (Leo X, Clement VII, and Leo XI) and two queens of France, Catherine de' Medici and Marie de' Medici.

Renaissance art, show examples from these two periods to the class. Have students study the illustrations in the textbook. Then let them look through books with color reprints of medieval and Renaissance art from your school or public library. You might be able to obtain slides from your school's art department. Call upon students to make general observations about medieval paintings. *(For example, medieval art lacks depth or perspective, the figures are stiff and elongated, facial expressions lack emotions, the background is frequently a solid color.)* Ask students about the characteristics of Renaissance painting. *(Students' responses should include: use of perspective, realistic figures, facial expressions that convey emotions, natural landscapes as background.)*

Presentation Matching (Average/Group)

Write the following lists on the chalkboard or an overhead projector. You may wish to reproduce them for distribution to the class. Have students match each artist in one list with his work in the other list.

1. Giotto
2. Leonardo da Vinci
3. Michelangelo
4. Raphael
5. Titian
6. Brueghel

Catholic church. The Crusades and trade with the Middle East brought Italians into contact with Byzantine civilization, whose scholars had preserved much learning from classical Greece and Rome. Even before the fall of Constantinople in 1453, many Byzantine scholars had fled to Italy to escape the troubled political climate of their native land. These scholars brought with them a great appreciation and knowledge of the Greek and Roman classics.

Florence, Rome, Venice, Milan, and Naples were the most important cities of the Renaissance. These cities had grown rich through trade. Their citizens included many educated, wealthy merchants who saw themselves and their city as a reflection of the ancient polis. In Florence, for example, the Medici (MED • uh • chee) family grew wealthy first as bankers and then as rulers of the city-state. Lorenzo Medici, who was known as "the Magnificent," became a great patron of the arts and ■ wanted to make Florence the most glorious city in Europe.

Learning from Maps *Many Italian cities became centers of Renaissance learning. Which major* ● *Renaissance city is on the northern Adriatic coast?*

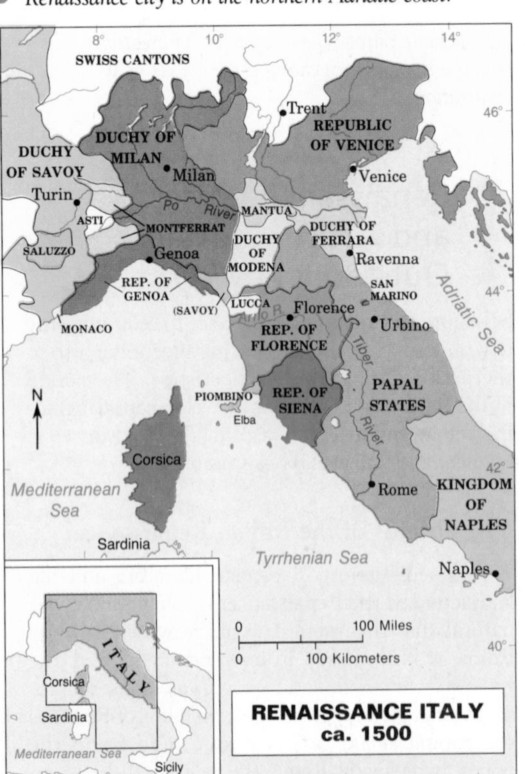

The Humanities

Beginning about the mid-1300s, a number of Italian scholars developed a lively interest in classical literature, particularly that of the Romans. Medieval scholars who had studied ancient times had tried to make everything they learned harmonize with Christian doctrine. The Italian scholars of the 1300s, on the other hand, studied the ancient world in an attempt to imitate its great achievements.

These Italian scholars stressed the study of grammar, rhetoric, history, and poetry, using classical texts. We call these studies the *humanities;* people who specialized in the humanities were called **humanists.** Humanists searched out Greek and Latin language manuscripts. Often they would find more than one copy of a work. If the copies differed, humanists compared the different versions to determine which was correct. In doing so they developed a critical attitude that had been lacking in much medieval scholarship.

As humanists studied classical manuscripts, they began to acquire a new outlook on life. They came to believe that it was important to know how things worked. This belief led them to emphasize education. However, they also wondered whether a life that consisted only of contemplation gave a person enough opportunities to lead a meaningful life. Humanists became more and more convinced that a person had to become actively involved in practical affairs such as politics or patronage of the arts.

Humanists viewed existence not only as a preparation for life after death but also as a joy in itself. They thought that men and women, despite all their faults, were intelligent beings who could make their own decisions. Along with a belief in individual dignity came an admiration for individual achievement. Many remarkable individuals of this period displayed a variety of talents. A person might be not only a poet and musician but also a scientist and painter.

Writers of the Italian Renaissance

One of the first humanists, the Florentine Francesco Petrarch (PEE • trahrk), lived from 1304 to 1374. Like many of the humanists, Petrarch became famous as a scholar and as a teacher. He

History Through the Arts

LITERATURE

The Book of the Courtier

In 1528 the Italian diplomat and writer Baldassare Castiglione (kahs • teel • YOH • nay) published what was probably the most famous book of the Renaissance, *The Book of the Courtier.* Castiglione's work is both a book on courtesy and an explanation of the role of the refined courtier as a successor to the coarse knight of the Middle Ages. The setting for the book is the court of the dukes of Urbino, an Italian city-state where the author lived many happy years. Castiglione's characters are real people who reflect in fictional conversations on how gentlemen and gentlewomen ought to act in polite society. Castiglione wrote:

"I would have him speak not always of serious subjects but also of amusing things, such as games and jests and jokes, according to the occasion. He should always, of course, speak out fully and frankly, and avoid talking nonsense. . . .

He should have a knowledge of Greek as well as Latin [and] he should be very well acquainted with the poets, and no less with the orators and historians, and also skilled at writing both verse and prose, especially in our own language. . . .

Gentleness is most impressive in a man who is a capable and courageous warrior. . . . He should . . . above all avoid affectation. Next let him consider well whatever he does or says, the place where he does it, in whose presence, its timing, why he is doing it, his own age, his profession, the end he is aiming at, and the means that are suitable. . . .

He will not speak evil. . . . Our courtier will avoid foolish arrogance; he will not be the bearer of bad news; he will not be careless in sometimes saying things that may give offence, instead of striving to please; he will not be obstinate. . . . He will not be an idle or lying babbler, nor a stupid flatterer or boaster, but will be modest and reserved. . . .

The courtier should . . . take great care to give a good impression of himself. . . . [There are men who are] convinced they are being terribly witty and amusing, [when] they use filthy and indecent language in the presence of noble ladies, and often to their face. And the more they make the ladies blush, the more they are convinced that they are being good courtiers. . . . The only reason they behave in such a beastly fashion is because they believe it makes them the life . . . of the party. . . . To acquire this reputation they indulge in the most shameful and shocking discourtesies. . . . Sometimes they push one another downstairs, belabor each other with sticks and bricks, throw handfuls of dust in each other's eyes, cause their horses to collapse on one another . . . then at table they hurl the soup, or the sauce or jelly, in one another's face, and they burst out laughing. . . .

[The lady must have] those virtues of the mind . . . in common with the courtier, such as prudence, magnanimity . . . and many others besides, and also the qualities that are common to all kinds of women, such as goodness and discretion, the ability to take good care . . . of her husband's belongings and house and children, and the virtues belonging to a good mother. . . . And her serene and modest behaviour . . . should be accompanied by a quick and vivacious spirit. . . .

She should know how to choose topics suitable for the kind of person she is addressing. . . . She should not introduce . . . jests and jokes into a discussion about serious things. She should not . . . [pretend] to know what she does not know, but should seek modestly to win credit for knowing what she does. . . . In this way she will be adorned with good manners. . . . Thus she will be not only loved but also revered by all."

7. Dürer
8. Holbein

a. Paintings and sculpture have massive dignity
b. Pioneered an emphasis on realism
c. Works noted for rich colors
d. Noted for copper engravings and woodcuts
e. Made use of scientific experiments in paintings
f. Painted lively scenes of village life
g. Painted portraits of Erasmus and Sir Thomas More
h. Noted for madonnas
(Answers: 1-b, 2-e, 3-a, 4-h, 5-c, 6-f, 7-d, 8-g)

1B, 4C, a1B, a1C, a1D

Petrarch's great friend, Giovanni Boccaccio (1313-1375), wrote the *Decameron,* a series of stories set against the Black Death.

also wrote poetry, and his sonnets to Laura, the imaginary ideal woman, are considered some of the greatest love poems in literature.

Petrarch's main influence, however, stemmed from his ideas about virtue and about the Romans. He thought the Romans had set the best examples of ethical behavior and believed they could best be imitated if one studied their writings. This study of the writings of the ancients, particularly the Romans, came to be called *classical education.* A command of the Latin language, as written by ancient writers, became the mark of an educated person.

Although the humanists remained deeply committed to Christian teachings, they sometimes felt a tension between their commitment to the study of the Romans and their commitment to Christianity. Petrarch, for instance, agonized over his lust for fame (a well-known Roman ambition), which he feared would hurt his chances for salvation. Like most Italian humanists, Petrarch thought it important to lead a full and active life here on Earth, even if that meant devoting less time to purely spiritual concerns.

Niccolò Machiavelli (mahk • yah • VEL • lee) of Florence, a diplomat and historian who lived from 1469 to 1527, probably ranks as the most illustrious of the many Renaissance writers. In 1513 he wrote a famous essay, *The Prince,* which described government not in terms of lofty ideals but as Machiavelli felt government actually worked. He believed that in the real world, power counts much more than noble ideals. "It is safer to be feared than loved," he said.

The Prince advised rulers to maintain the safety of their states by whatever means they thought necessary and not to let considerations of honesty, justice, or honor hamper them. Today we use the word *Machiavellian* to describe people who use deceit and who have little regard for morality in their effort to get what they want.

Machiavelli can be considered a humanist because he looked to the ancient Romans for models and because such matters as the workings of politics interested him. However, his lack of concern for morality in *The Prince* set him apart from the other humanists, who considered virtue their main aim.

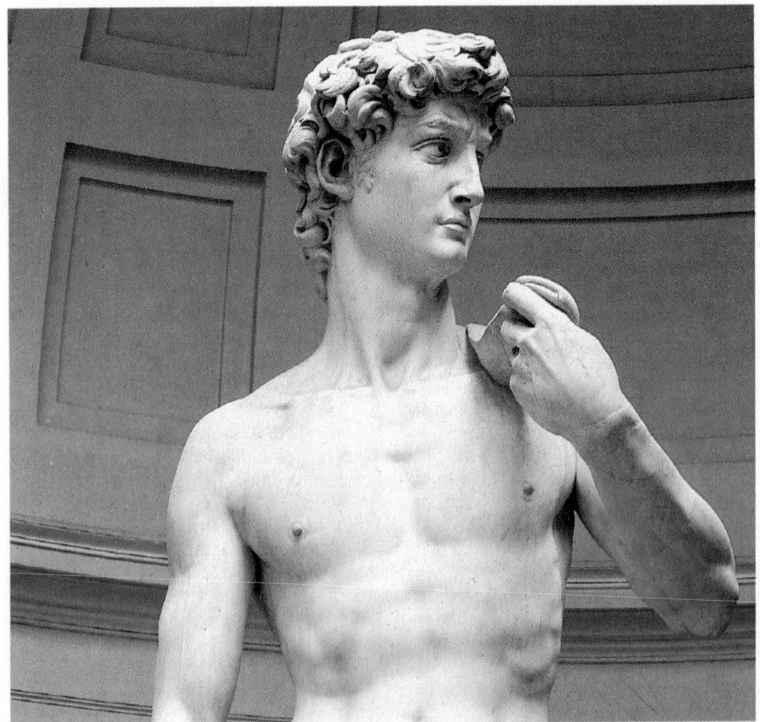

Learning from Pictures *Michelangelo, the famous Renaissance artist, sculpted this marble statue of David, king of ancient Israel. Michelangelo has been noted as one of history's greatest sculptors.*

328

History Through the Arts

PAINTING

Realism and Perspective

The changes in painting from medieval to modern times can be seen in the work of the great early Renaissance artist Giotto. In this painting the angel of God tells St. Anne that she will have a child, Mary, who will be the mother of Jesus. Giotto makes us feel the scene is an actual event rather than a symbolic one by giving a three-dimensional quality to the lighted room, to the rooftops that recede into the dark, and to the faces of the women and the angel.

Giotto was an architect as well as an artist. His attention to architectural detail and perspective heightens the realism of his work. Note, for example, how he realistically portrayed the staircase leading to the balcony above the entrance. Like other Renaissance artists, Giotto was interested in showing a building or a landscape as it appeared through a person's own eyes. Later Renaissance painters developed perspective mathematically and portrayed distances with great accuracy.

Italian Renaissance Artists

Art as well as literature flourished during the Renaissance. In an outburst of creativity, Italian artists produced some of the world's most exquisite masterpieces.

Medieval paintings stressed the world beyond everyday life—a world associated with religious subjects—and depicted formal and stylized figures. The most noticeable characteristic of Renaissance painting, on the other hand, is its realism. Renaissance painters admired the intensely realistic art of the Romans, and they depicted realistic and lifelike human figures in Renaissance paintings. Even the backgrounds of these paintings differed from those of medieval paintings. Earlier artists had portrayed the Holy Land. Renaissance painters showed the rugged countryside that they knew.

Renaissance painters could make their works lifelike because they had learned a very important technique of painting called **perspective.** By making distant objects smaller than those in the foreground, and by arranging the objects in certain ways, an artist could create the illusion of depth on a flat canvas.

Giotto (JAW • toh), who lived from 1276 to 1337, and Masaccio (mah • ZAHT • choh), who lived from 1401 to 1428, pioneered the emphasis on realism. According to legend, a fly in one of Giotto's paintings looked so lifelike that an observer tried to brush it off the picture. Masaccio painted light and shadows to give the effect of depth to objects.

Italian painters of the late 1400s and early 1500s displayed such genius that historians often call this period the High Renaissance. Among the many great painters of this period, four made particularly outstanding contributions.

Leonardo da Vinci (duh • VIN • chee)—artist, musician, architect, mathematician, and scientist—lived from 1452 to 1519. He used his experiments

329

1B, 4C, a1B, a1C

History Through the Arts

PAINTING

Lady with a Unicorn

The work of the great Italian artist Raphael reflected the intellectual and artistic ideals of the Renaissance. His paintings combined spirituality and artistry with the search for realism and truth that characterized his age. Raphael studied and worked in Florence, in the schools of Michelangelo and Leonardo da Vinci. He became so accomplished that he was called to Rome to help decorate the Vatican. Each year millions of visitors to Rome marvel at some of his most famous works.

In his paintings Raphael conveyed a feeling of balanced space, giving the viewer a sensation of tranquillity and joy. In this painting we see a Renaissance lady holding a baby unicorn. The unicorn is snugly enclosed in the lady's arms, yet relaxed in the spaciousness of her lap. The main figure takes up almost the entire canvas and the landscape stretches back into the distance; yet there is no sense of crowding. The glowing fabric of the lady's dress and the beauty of her pendant reveal the splendor of Renaissance taste.

Raphael's respect for antiquity are demonstrated in the little unicorn, a fabled animal that appeared in the art of ancient civilizations. During the Middle Ages, the unicorn was often used in Christian art as a symbol for the purity of Christ and the Virgin Mary.

in science to enhance his painting. Studies of anatomy helped him draw the human figure, and mathematics helped him organize the space in his paintings. People throughout the world still marvel at his mural, *The Last Supper.* Probably his most famous painting is the portrait called *Mona Lisa.*

Another master of Renaissance art, Michelangelo Buonarroti (my • kuh • LAN • juh • loh bwaw • nah • RAW • tee), lived from 1475 to 1564. Millions of people have visited the Sistine Chapel of the Vatican, the residence of the pope in Rome, and looked with wonder at the frescoes Michelangelo painted on the ceiling.

Although a brilliant painter, Michelangelo preferred sculpture. Both his paintings and his stone carvings of such biblical figures as David and Moses suggest a massive dignity. Almost as versatile as Leonardo, Michelangelo also wrote poetry and worked as an architect, helping design St. Peter's Basilica in Rome.

Raphael (raf • ee • EL), who lived from 1483 to 1520, became so popular in Florence that the pope hired him to help beautify the Vatican. His frescoes in the papal chambers include *The School of Athens,* which depicts the great philosophers of classical Greece. Raphael also painted exquisite madonnas, representations of the Virgin Mary.

Titian (TISH • uhn), who lived from about 1488 to 1576, spent most of his life in his native Venice. His works, such as *The Assumption of the Virgin,*

330

● Sir Thomas More held important government positions for many years under King Henry VIII of England. His refusal to accept the Act of Supremacy making the king head of the Church of England brought him imprisonment in the Tower and execution for treason in 1535.

1B, 1D, 4C, a1B, a1C

portray a vivid sense of drama and are noted for their rich colors. The Holy Roman Emperor and the king of France sponsored many of Titian's works, and he became one of the first painters to become rich through his work.

Dozens of other artists prospered in Italy in the 1400s and 1500s. Princes supported many of these artists. The princes thought they would achieve lasting fame if they became patrons of the arts. One way a prince could be remembered was to have a great artist paint his portrait. Thus the patrons helped foster the enormous creativity of the period.

The Northern Renaissance

Humanist thought spread beyond Italy. Numerous mountain passes, such as the Brenner and the Great Saint Bernard, pierce the rugged Alps and allow people—and ideas—to pass from Italy to northern Europe. The Danube, Rhône, and Rhine rivers provide even easier routes. New ideas, often carried by northern European students who had studied in Italy, soon traveled to Germany, the Netherlands, France, and England.

Printing. A remarkable new process—printing—also helped ideas spread. Hundreds of years earlier, the Chinese had learned how to create a wooden block into which writing or pictures could be etched. Printers smeared ink on the block and pressed the block onto paper, which absorbed the ink. Then the block was reinked. In this way the writing or pictures could be reproduced many times. The Chinese had also learned how to assemble the block from separate pieces, or type, that could be used again and again.

The Arabs captured some Chinese people who knew how to make paper and perfected the production of paper. The Moors of Spain later introduced paper to Europe. In the 1400s printing began to appear in Europe, where it had its first great impact on intellectual life.

Scholars believe that in about 1450, Johann Gutenberg of Mainz, Germany, was the first European to use movable type to print books. Gutenberg developed a printing press on which he printed a copy of the Bible between 1453 and 1456. Many publishers adopted the printing press, and books soon helped spread new ideas to a large audience.

The Dutch scholar Desiderius Erasmus (i • RAZ • muhs) was the greatest humanist of northern Europe. He learned about the ideas of the Italian humanists from printed books. Erasmus, who lived from 1466 to 1536, entered a monastery as a young man but soon decided to spend his life studying the ancient Greeks and Romans.

Unlike the Italian humanists, Erasmus and other northern humanists were interested in the early Christian period as well as in early Roman and Greek culture. Erasmus believed that in its early years, Christianity had existed in harmony with classical civilization. He applied to his study of the Bible the critical method that the Italian humanists had developed, arguing for a return to the original, simple message of Jesus. Erasmus was saddened that the medieval scholars had made Christian faith less spiritual and more complicated and ceremonial. He published stinging criticisms of the church's lack of spirituality, a popular subject among the northern humanists.

Erasmus's most famous book, *In Praise of Folly,* ridiculed ignorance, superstition, and vice among the clergy and ordinary Christians. Erasmus criticized fasting, pilgrimages to religious shrines, and even the church's interpretation of some parts of the Bible.

Erasmus's friend Thomas More, the English humanist, took a similar view. In 1516 More published *Utopia,* a book in which he criticized the society of his day by describing an imaginary ideal society. According to More, the ideal society would consist entirely of free citizens who would elect their own governing officials. Conscientious citizens, not police, would enforce laws. Money and greed would vanish, and everyone would practice a simple, ethical religion. More's *Utopia* became so popular that today **utopia** means "an ideal place or society."

English literature. Renaissance literature in England reached its peak in the late 1500s and early 1600s in the plays of William Shakespeare. Like many other playwrights, Shakespeare often used familiar plots, but he built masterpieces of poetic drama around them.

Shakespeare's characters grapple with the questions that humanists asked about virtue and morality. Few writers have been able to portray personality and human emotions with Shakespeare's skill. The jovial Falstaff, the moody Hamlet, the young lovers Romeo and Juliet, and the tragic Macbeth seem as real today as when Shakespeare first created them.

331

1B, 4C, a1A, a1C, a4A, a4F, a4H

SECTION 1

Closure

Ask students to enumerate the chief characteristics of humanism. *(revival of interest in the classical world, and the study of its grammar, rhetoric, history, and poetry; emphasis on education; active participation in practical affairs; belief in individual dignity)*

Review Answers

1. ***Renaissance:*** philosophical and artistic movement based on a revival of interest in classical learning; ***humanist:*** scholar who studied grammar, rhetoric, history, and poetry, using classical texts; ***perspective:*** making distant objects smaller than those in the foreground and creating the illusion of depth; ***utopia:*** ideal place or society, a term originating with Thomas More's book of that name.
2. ***Francesco Petrarch:*** Italian humanist poet concerned with Roman virtue: ***Niccolò Machiavelli:*** author of *The Prince,* an essay describing government, not in terms of lofty ideals but as it actually worked; ***Leonardo da Vinci:*** Italian artist, musician, architect, mathematician, and scientist; ***Michelangelo:*** Italian sculptor, painter, poet, and architect famous for his statues of Moses and David and paintings in the Sistine Chapel; ***Johann Gutenberg:*** first European to use movable type to print

● **printed illustrations**

Learning from Pictures *This painting by Dürer depicts the deposition of Christ. What possibilities did* ● *Dürer see for art in the mass production of books?*

Northern Renaissance Artists

The dynamic new painting techniques of Italian artists inspired artists outside of Italy. Northern European merchants carried Italian paintings home, and painters from northern Europe studied with Italian masters, thus spreading the arts of Italy to northern Europe.

Perhaps the most creative artists lived in Flanders; these artists perfected the technique of painting in oils on canvas. The brothers Hubert and Jan van Eyck, who lived in Flanders in the 1400s, paid great attention to detail in works such as *The Adoration of the Lamb,* the altarpiece of the cathedral at Ghent.

One of the greatest Flemish artists, Pieter Brueghel (BROO • guhl) the Elder, painted in the mid-1500s. Brueghel loved the countryside and the peasants of his native Flanders and painted lively scenes of village festivals and dances. He also used his paintings as a means to criticize the intolerance and cruelty he saw around him.

The German artist Albrecht Dürer (DYUR • uhr), who lived from 1471 to 1528, was famous for his copper engravings and woodcuts. During Dürer's lifetime the printing press made mass production of books possible. Dürer became one of the first to see the possibilities of printed illustrations in books.

Although a German, Hans Holbein the Younger (1497–1543) did most of his work in other countries. Holbein traveled throughout Europe to paint portraits of famous people, such as Erasmus, Thomas More, and King Henry VIII of England. This emphasis on portrait painting reflects the Renaissance interest in the individual and in fame among the political leaders of the time.

SECTION 1 REVIEW

1. **Define** Renaissance, humanist, perspective, utopia
2. **Identify** Francesco Petrarch, Niccolò Machiavelli, Leonardo da Vinci, Michelangelo, Johann Gutenberg, Desiderius Erasmus, Thomas More, William Shakespeare, Pieter Brueghel the Elder, Hans Holbein the Younger
3. **Locate** Florence, Venice, Milan, Flanders
4. **Interpreting Ideas** Why did the Renaissance begin in Italy?
5. **Analyzing Ideas** Why did humanism spread northward?
6. **Summarizing Ideas** **(a)** What was the most notable characteristic of Renaissance painting? **(b)** How was it achieved?

2 The Protestant Reformation Changed Religious Attitudes

About 1500 several northern humanists suggested that the Roman Catholic church had lost sight of the spiritual mission proclaimed by Jesus. Instead of setting an example of moral leadership, they said, popes acted as political leaders and warriors. Instead of encouraging inner piety, priests concerned themselves with the details of ceremonies. The church as a whole, the humanists claimed, seemed more interested in its income than in saving souls. The northern humanists sought a new emphasis on personal faith and spirituality. When the Catholic church ignored their concerns, a new generation of reformers urged believers who were unhappy with traditional religion to form a new church. This religious revolution, which split the church in western Europe and created several new churches, is called the **Reformation.**

The Origins of the Reformation

The first break with the Roman Catholic church occurred in Germany, where the political situation of the time helped lay the foundation for the Reformation. Unlike some countries during the early 1500s, Germany lacked a strong central government. Although Germany formed the core of the Holy Roman Empire, the empire included about 365 independent states. A number of imperial cities with a great deal of freedom existed side by side with principalities. The weak emperor could not control independent ideas about religion within the German states or keep the pope from demanding money.

Pope Leo X continued the rebuilding of St. Peter's Basilica in Rome. The pope charged an enthusiastic monk named Johann Tetzel with raising funds in northern Germany. Using a technique that had become accepted in the church, Tetzel asked people to buy **indulgences,** or pardons from punishment for sin.

Indulgences, part of the sacrament of penance, had originally been a reward for exceptionally pious deeds, such as helping a poor person go on a Crusade. Renaissance popes, however, sold indulgences simply to raise money.

This misuse of indulgences appalled the northern humanists, who wanted the church to become more spiritual. The concern grew especially strong in Germany, where political leaders gave sellers of indulgences great freedom of movement. One unhappy observer, Martin Luther, protested Tetzel's behavior in 1517.

Martin Luther's Protest

Martin Luther was born in 1483 to a moderately prosperous peasant family in the small mining community of Eisenleben in Saxony. Luther's family made sure he received a good education. Although he planned to become a lawyer, as a young man Luther considered himself a terrible sinner, and he desperately worried about the salvation of his soul. One summer day as he walked home, a sudden storm overtook him. A blinding bolt of lightning struck close by. Luther cried out, "Help, dear Saint Anne, I will become a monk!" He gave up studying law in order to enter a monastery and spend his life in search of salvation.

Luther found that the church's methods for overcoming sin gave him no comfort. He did all the things required of him, including making a trip to holy places in Rome. Nothing, however, relieved his feeling of damnation.

One evening while Luther studied the Bible, a revelation, or new understanding, came to him. Suddenly Luther realized that all the ceremonies and good deeds made no difference in saving a sinner. The only thing that counted, Luther believed, was an inner faith in God. As long as people did

Learning from Pictures *This religious statue in a Renaissance village is being restored and blessed after it was mutilated during Reformation violence.*

books; ***Desiderius Erasmus:*** greatest humanist of northern Europe; ***Thomas More:*** English humanist who published *Utopia* to criticize the society of his day; ***William Shakespeare:*** English playwright who wrote masterpieces of poetic drama; ***Pieter Brueghel the Elder:*** Flemish painter of village life; ***Hans Holbein the Younger:*** German painter noted for portraits of famous people

3. ***Florence:*** important center of Renaissance culture in north-central Italy; ***Venice:*** commercial and cultural city at head of the Adriatic; ***Milan:*** city in north-central Italy just south of the Alps; ***Flanders:*** coastal region north of France

4. The Renaissance began in Italy because of Italy's numerous reminders from Roman times. Trade brought Italians into contact with Byzantines, who had preserved the classics.

5. through travels by northern European students who studied in Italy and through the invention of printing

6. (a) The most notable characteristic of Renaissance painting was the realism it gave to natural life and forms. **(b)** This was achieved through the use of perspective.

SECTION 2

Focus/Motivation
Briefly discuss with the class the definition of the

333

● **Luther wrote the 95 theses in Latin, a clear sign that he did not want to break at that point with the church.**

term *reformation* (the process of improving or correcting). Ask students if they think change is occurring in the Catholic church today. Ask students to suggest specific practices that have been adopted or are under debate that might indicate a reform movement. *(Answers will vary. Students might respond with the following: more modern translations of the Bible, replacing Latin with vernacular languages in church services, the marriage of priests, admission of women to the clergy.)* Ask also if there are some efforts to maintain traditional forms of ritual and belief.

Ask students if they see any parallels between recent controversies and the conflicts of the 1500s. *(Answers will vary. Students might say that both are attempts to make religion more personal and spiritually rewarding, or that both are concerned with religion's place in society.)*

Presentation Understanding Chronology (Average/Group)
The following is a list of events in Martin Luther's life. Write these items on the chalkboard or an overhead projector. Ask students to copy the list in their notebooks. Then have them arrange the events in chronological order by writing *1* before the event that took place first, *2*

Learning from Pictures *Even though Martin Luther had humble beginnings, he earned a degree from the University of Erfurt.*

not rely on their own actions, but believed God would save them, they could receive salvation by God's grace. Luther later described this revelation as the opening of the "doors into paradise."

On the basis of this new insight, he developed beliefs which later became known as Lutheranism. Luther believed that a simple faith could lead everyone to salvation. Thus he believed Tetzel committed a criminal act by asking poor people to give up their precious money for false promises of forgiveness.

In 1517 Luther challenged Tetzel by posting on the church door at Wittenberg **95 theses,** or statements, about indulgences. Sales of indulgences began to decline. The news quickly spread across Europe that a monk had publicly challenged the selling of indulgences.

Luther clearly considered himself a reformer within the main tradition of the church. Surprised at the widespread impact of his ideas, Luther had no wish to break with the church. But because his ideas challenged church practices, church leaders denounced him.

Luther's Break with the Medieval Church

By 1520 Luther openly disagreed with many church doctrines. The sole religious authority, he said, was the Bible. Popes and bishops should not tell a person what to believe. Luther believed that ceremonies did not counteract sins and that priests had no special role in helping people to salvation. God viewed all people with faith equally. Luther considered his church a "priesthood of all believers."

Taking advantage of the power of the printed word to spread ideas, in 1520 Luther wrote three publications that outlined his doctrines, attacked the pope, and called on all Germans to support his views. Pope Leo X declared Luther a heretic and excommunicated him.

To put the excommunication into effect, the new Holy Roman Emperor Charles V summoned Luther in 1521 to the Imperial Diet, a special meeting of the rulers of the empire, at the city of Worms (VOHRMZ). The emperor commanded Luther to renounce his ideas. When Luther refused, the Diet of Worms banished him from the empire and prohibited the sale or printing of his works. Luther was now considered an outlaw. Because Germany lacked a strong government, however, the powerless emperor could not enforce the Diet's ruling. The Elector of Saxony, Frederick the Wise, protected Luther and provided a place for him to hide while the uproar caused by the confrontation at the Diet of Worms died down.

In 1522, while under the protection of Frederick the Wise, Luther translated the New Testament of the Bible into German. By 1534 he had translated the entire Bible from Hebrew and Greek. Now all literate Christians in Germany could read the Bible for themselves.

Emperor Charles V continued to oppose Luther's doctrines and did what he could to keep Lutheranism from spreading. The princes who supported Luther protested the emperor's treatment of Lutheranism. Because of the protest, the followers of Luther and all later reformers came to be called "Protestants."

● Luther closed the monasteries and convents, married the former nun Katharina von Bora, and had six children.

■ During Henry VIII's reign, England made little headway in becoming Protestant. The move toward Protestantism occurred under the leader appointed to rule England during the minority of Edward VI.

1B, 4C, a1A, a1C

Luther's works continued to circulate, and his ideas continued to spread. In time he established a ● new church called the Lutheran church. Luther kept the organization of the new church as simple as possible. Lutheran clergy, called ministers, had no special powers; they served merely to guide their congregations to the true faith. Ministers also had less importance than Catholic priests had, because Luther permitted only the two sacraments mentioned in the Bible—baptism and communion—rather than the seven sacraments practiced in the Roman Catholic church.

The Spread of Protestantism

Luther had touched a very deep desire among the people of Europe for a simpler, more direct faith. Within a short time after he took his stand, many rulers in the German states established the Lutheran church within their domains. In addition, dozens of other reformers appeared who were dissatisfied with both the Roman Catholic church and the Lutheran church.

Charles V attempted to stop the spread of Protestantism, but for about 10 years he was too busy fighting the Ottoman Turks and the French. Then in 1544 he sent his armies against the Protestant princes in Germany for both religious and political reasons. The emperor won most of his battles with the princes, but in the end he could not defeat them or the Lutheran church. Charles V finally reached a compromise with the princes with the signing of the Peace of Augsburg in 1555.

One of the provisions of the Peace of Augsburg stated that each German ruler had the right to choose the religion for his state. His subjects had to accept the ruler's decision or move away. Almost all the princes of northern Germany accepted Luther's faith.

The sects. Hundreds of new religious groups emerged in much of Germany and Switzerland in the 1520s and 1530s. These groups, known as **sects,** did not form organized churches with clear-cut rules, authority, discipline, and membership. The sects were societies of a few people gathered together, usually with a preacher as their leader.

Most of the sects later died out. One that survived was known as the Anabaptists. The ancestors of the modern-day Baptist denomination, the Anabaptists believed that infants should not receive baptism because they could not understand the significance of the ceremony. Instead, they believed baptism should be offered only to adults who accepted the Anabaptist faith.

The Anglican church. In England the Protestant Reformation came about by entirely different means than in Germany. True, some Protestant ideas had filtered into England by the 1520s. The English also had a tradition of resistance to the popes that went back to John Wycliffe in the 1300s. However, King Henry VIII caused the break between England and the Roman Catholic church between 1529 and 1536. The break was a political move that had little to do with religious doctrine. In fact, before 1529 Henry VIII had defended the church so well against Martin Luther's ideas that the pope had granted Henry the title of "Defender of the Faith"—a title that the present monarch of England still bears.

England's break with Rome took place because Henry VIII wanted to divorce his wife, Catherine of Aragon, for not producing a male heir to the throne. The king believed that a continuing strong monarchy depended on having a son to succeed him. The royal couple had a daughter, Mary, but England had no tradition of a ruling queen. Furthermore, Henry had fallen in love with Anne Boleyn, a lady-in-waiting at the court, and wanted to be rid of Catherine.

Although the Catholic church forbade divorce, the pope could make exceptions. Pope Clement VII, however, refused to dissolve Henry's marriage. Clement made his decision in part because the troops of Catherine of Aragon's nephew, the Holy Roman Emperor Charles V, had captured and sacked Rome in 1527.

Pope Clement's refusal to grant the divorce infuriated Henry, who withdrew England from the Catholic church and created a new church. In a series of laws, Parliament created the Church of England with the king as its head. Although the Church of England, or Anglican church, slowly acquired some Protestant doctrines, it kept the ■ organization and many of the ceremonial features of the Catholic church.

Of course, Henry VIII's church granted his divorce. The king married not only once again but five times. He finally fathered a son, the future Edward VI, although not by Anne Boleyn. More important, by creating the Anglican church and making England Protestant, he created a refuge for people who held the new religious ideas.

before the event that took place second, and so on.

(3) Posted 95 theses on church door
(1) Entered a monastery
(5) Refused to withdraw his ideas at the Diet of Worms
(4) Published three books outlining his ideas
(2) Had a religious experience convincing him salvation was possible through faith alone
(6) Translated the Bible from Latin into German

1B, 4C, a1A, a1C, a4A, a4F, a4H, a4L

- Calvin introduced many principles of democracy into church organization. The congregation elected the minister and chose laymen called presbyters to control church policy.
- The St. Bartholomew's Day Massacre (August 24, 1572) of Huguenots renewed the fighting between Catholics and Protestants in France.

SECTION 2

Closure

Ask: Why did the northern humanists criticize the Roman Catholic church? *(Popes acted not as spiritual leaders but as warriors and politicians. Priests were concerned with ceremonies, not piety. The church was interested in income instead of saving souls.)*

Review Answers

1. ***Reformation:*** religious revolution that split the Christian Church in western Europe; ***indulgence:*** pardon given in return for repentance; ***95 theses:*** Luther's protests against indulgences that he posted on the church door at Wittenberg; ***sect:*** religious group of a few people with a preacher as leader
2. ***Johann Tetzel:*** monk who sold indulgences in northern Germany to raise money to rebuild St. Peter's in Rome; ***Martin Luther:*** leader of Protestant Reformation who believed that salvation could be achieved by faith alone; ***Charles V:*** Holy Roman Emperor who summoned Luther to the Diet of Worms; ***Henry VIII:*** English king who broke with Roman Catholic church and formed Anglican church
3. ***Wittenberg:*** city in Germany where Luther posted his 95 theses
4. The Reformation began in Germany over the abuse in issuing indulgences.

SECTION 2 REVIEW

1. **Define** Reformation, indulgence, 95 theses, sect
2. **Identify** Johann Tetzel, Martin Luther, Charles V, Henry VIII
3. **Locate** Wittenberg
4. **Understanding Ideas** What specific issue started the Reformation?
5. **Interpreting Ideas** What was the religious compromise of the Peace of Augsburg?
6. **Contrasting Ideas** What were the main differences between Luther's ideas and those of the Roman Catholic church?
7. **Analyzing Ideas** Why did Henry VIII break away from the Roman Catholic church?

3 The Roman Catholic Church Met New Challenges

Lutheranism, the sects, and Anglicanism did not pose a major problem for the Catholic church except in a few areas of northern Europe. However, another reformer, the French-born John Calvin, and his followers challenged the Catholic church even in countries such as France, where the Catholic faith remained strong. After 1550 the followers of Calvin and a remarkable Catholic revival known as the Counter-Reformation dominated the religious conflict in Europe.

Calvin and Calvinism

Huldrych Zwingli (TSVING • lee), the vicar at the cathedral in Zurich in the early 1500s, was greatly influenced by the humanist writings of Erasmus, whom he met in 1516. Zwingli was leading the forces of religious reform in Switzerland when he heard about Luther's 95 theses. Zwingli and Luther met and discovered that they basically agreed on doctrine but disagreed about forms of worship and the use of images. Zwingli's supporters, for example, whitewashed wall decorations in churches.

In 1531 Zwingli died in a battle between Catholics and Protestants, but the French Protestant John Calvin carried on the work of the Reformation in Switzerland. Calvin founded a Protestant church that had a powerful and popular following. Calvin formulated a complete and clear set of beliefs, the *Institutes of the Christian Religion,* published in 1536. This work laid down exactly what the faithful ought to believe on every major question of religion. Calvin thus provided his followers, known as Calvinists, with a code that united them and gave them strength in the face of opposition and persecution.

In 1536 Calvin settled in the free city of Geneva, where Calvinism became the official religion. Calvin retained Luther's reliance on faith and on the Bible, but he placed a new emphasis on the community of believers. He believed that God had decided, at the beginning of time, who would be saved and who would be damned—a belief known as **predestination.** Those predestined (or chosen beforehand) for salvation were called "the elect." They formed a special community of people who were expected to live up to their position by following the highest moral standards. These standards included devoutness, dislike of frivolity, self-discipline, attendance at sermons for the purpose of denouncing one's sins, and complete dedication to God's wishes.

Calvin became almost all-powerful in Geneva. He made the city a **theocracy,** or a government ruled by a clergy claiming God's authority. By attaching such great importance to righteous living, Calvin regulated the conduct of the citizens down to the smallest detail. Laws prohibited dancing, card playing, showy dress, and profane language. Violation of these laws brought extremely severe punishment.

Calvinism soon spread to France, where its converts became known as Huguenots (HYOO • guh • nahts). Although France remained primarily Roman Catholic, by the mid-1550s Huguenots composed about one-fifteenth of the French population. Many high-ranking nobles and prosperous townspeople adopted the Calvinist doctrines. The Catholic French monarchs, who wanted a strongly united kingdom, considered the Huguenots a threat to national unity. To the kings of France, as to most European rulers of the time, a subject who differed with his or her king in matters of religion committed treason.

Beginning in 1562 the Huguenots defended themselves in a series of bloody civil wars with the Catholics. In 1598 King Henry IV issued a decree called the Edict of Nantes (NANTS), which gave the Huguenots freedom of worship and some political rights.

● Paul III, a member of the Farnese family, was a Renaissance pope who supported the arts and artists, especially Michelangelo, who completed the *Last Judgment* in the Sistine Chapel for the pope. At the same time, Paul supported church reforms and it was under his reign (1534-1549) that the Council of Trent began its deliberations.

1B, 4C, a1A, a1C

Calvinist minorities also existed in Poland and Hungary in eastern Europe. The Calvinists met with the most success, however, in Scotland, in the northern Netherlands, and in some parts of Germany. In these countries the strength of the Calvinists among ordinary people persuaded rulers to change their views. In a form called *Puritanism,* Calvinism would also play a vital role in England and in the English colonies of North America. By 1600 the Calvinist churches were the strongest of the many Protestant churches that had been established in Europe.

The Counter-Reformation

The Catholic church took a long time to realize that Protestantism posed a serious threat. The pope at first dismissed Luther's criticisms as "a monk's quarrel." However, a number of people within the Catholic church, including Erasmus, had called for internal reforms even before Luther appeared. As the breakup of the church continued, these reformers eventually convinced the pope of the drastic need for change.

In the 1530s a major reform effort known as the **Counter-Reformation,** or the Catholic Reformation, began in the Catholic church. Initially created to foster a more spiritual outlook in the Catholic church, the Counter-Reformation also clarified the doctrines of the church and pursued an aggressive campaign against Protestants.

Counter-Reformation tactics. Pope Paul III, who reigned as pope from 1534 to 1549, began the deliberate policy of reviving a more spiritual outlook in the Catholic church. He appointed devout and learned men as bishops and cardinals and required bishops to live and work in their home dioceses.

Pope Paul III brought the medieval Inquisition to Rome from Spain, where authorities had been trying and punishing so-called heretics since 1478. The Inquisition borrowed many of its cruel punishments, including burning at the stake, from governments, which had long used such methods against the worst criminals and traitors. The Inquisition viewed its chief purpose not as punishing Protestants but as keeping Catholics within the church.

In 1557 Pope Paul IV introduced another method of combating heresy. He established the *Index of Prohibited Books,* which forbade Catholics to read certain books. The Index was a recognition of the important part printing had played in spreading the Reformation. Before the printing press, the church could easily find and burn manuscript copies of heretical work. After printing was developed, it became far easier to prohibit what people could read than to try to burn all the books. The Catholic church maintained the Index as late as 1966, when the Second Vatican Council finally abandoned it.

The Council of Trent. Pope Paul III knew ● that no counterattack against Protestantism would be possible unless Catholic doctrines were well defined. Because church authorities often disagreed about complicated doctrines, such as the role of priests, heresy was difficult to oppose. In 1545 Paul summoned a council of church leaders to the Italian city of Trent. The Council of Trent, which met in three sessions from 1545 to 1563, defined official church doctrine with the same precision Calvin had used to define his faith.

Learning from Pictures *Pope Paul III commissioned the Venetian painter Titian to record the Council of Trent in session.*

Luther protested with his 95 theses.

5. The Peace of Augsburg of 1555 allowed each prince in Germany to choose the religion for his state.

6. The Roman Catholic church taught that salvation was possible through good works and through the sacraments. Luther taught that salvation was possible through faith alone. Luther rejected all the sacraments of the church except baptism and communion.

7. Henry VIII broke away from the Roman Catholic church so he could dissolve his marriage, remarry, and produce a male heir. Divorce was forbidden by the church, and the pope refused to grant an exception.

SECTION 3

Focus/Motivation

Put the following statement by John Calvin on the chalkboard or an overhead projector, or distribute copies to the class.

"We assert, that . . . God has once for all determined, both whom he would admit to salvation, and whom he would condemn to destruction. We affirm that this counsel [position], as far as concerns the elect, is founded on his gratuitous [freely given] mercy, totally irrespective of human merit; but that to those whom he devotes to condemnation, the gate of life is closed by a just and

1B, 4C, a1A, a1C, a4A, a4B, a4C, a4I

irreprehensible [unblamable], but incomprehensible judgment."

Lead a discussion about Calvin's statement, using the following questions as a guide: How is election for salvation determined? *(God determines who will be saved.)* Can one work to gain salvation? Explain. *(There is nothing one can do to change one's destiny.)* Why do you think members of the elect would work to be devout, self-disciplined, and dedicated to God's wishes, when they were already assured of salvation? *(Answers will vary. Students might mention to set a good example for others, or to prove oneself a worthy recipient of God's choice.)*

Presentation
Making Generalizations (Average/Group)
Put the following groups of statements about the Reformation and Counter-Reformation on the chalkboard or an overhead projector. Have students make one generalization based on each group of statements.

1. Southern and eastern Europe and Ireland remained firmly Catholic. France and the Netherlands were split religiously. Switzerland, northern Germany, England, Scotland, and the Scandinavian countries were Protestant. ***(Generalization:** As a result*

READ
WRITE
INTERPRET
●CONNECT
THINK

BUILDING HISTORY STUDY SKILLS

Making Connections with History: Using Art to Understand Values

In 1508 Pope Julius II commissioned Michelangelo to paint the ceiling of the Sistine Chapel in Rome. Perched atop a new type of scaffolding that he had designed for the project, Michelangelo worked until 1512 to complete the commission. The result of his work has often been called the best example of Renaissance art in the world.

By studying the works of art produced during a specific period in history, we can learn much about the values of the people who lived during that period. Much of the art of the Middle Ages in western Europe, for example, reflects the religious nature of the society. The backgrounds of paintings focus not on real scenery but on heavenly backdrops, symbols, or gold reflections. People's faces reflect piety rather than individuality, and the figures themselves do not appear three-dimensional. Renaissance art retains religious themes while reflecting the humanistic and secular values of the time.

How to Use Art to Understand Values

To use art to understand values, follow these steps.

1. Identify when the artwork was produced. What historical period does the artwork represent?
2. Explain what major theme the artist is attempting to illustrate. Does the artwork depict a religious theme? Does it show daily life?
3. Identify the subject of the work of art and note the details.
4. Use the theme and the subject to help explain the values of the historical period in which the work was created.

Developing the Skill

The illustration at the bottom of this page shows details from Michelangelo's *The Creation of Adam* on the ceiling of the Sistine Chapel in Rome. The painting reflects the values of the southern Renaissance.

The painting has a religious theme, similar to paintings of the Middle Ages. The subject is God's creation of Adam; however, the details focus on the humanity and individuality of Adam. Michelangelo captures Adam at the very moment that God holds out his hand to give life to Adam, whom God has created in his own image. Michelangelo portrays Adam as weak—barely able to lift his arm to receive the gift of life from God. God, on the other hand, appears supremely powerful.

Based on the painting, what conclusions can you draw about values during the cultural explosion of the Renaissance? The painting shows the concern with religious themes, as does medieval art. Michelangelo, however, depicts figures as intensely human and realistic. The painting captures the beauty of Adam's face, his reflection of God's power and glory, and the heroic individualism at the beginning of life. The painting shows that during the Renaissance people were intensely religious. At the same time, they believed in the dignity of human beings.

Practicing the skill. Find an illustration of a modern work of art. How does this artwork reflect the values of modern society?

To apply this skill, see Applying History Study Skills on page 353.

● The Jesuits took a special vow of obedience to the pope. They were not under local church jurisdiction, and this made them particularly effective during the Counter-Reformation. Because of their close connections to the papacy, however, the Jesuits came under attack in the Catholic monarchies during the 1700s.

1B, 4C, a1A, a1C

The Council of Trent banned the sale of indulgences and tightened discipline for the clergy. In most cases, however, the council reaffirmed the importance of those doctrines that Protestants rejected. It emphasized the need for ceremonies, arguing that God ought to be worshiped with pomp and splendor. It noted that people must depend on priests because God granted forgiveness only through the church, not on personal merit. The council stressed that although everyone enjoyed free will, a person's fate after death depended not only on his or her faith, as Luther claimed, but on ceremonial church actions as well.

The decisions made at the Council of Trent worked effectively for the Catholic church. Many people found Protestantism's simplicity and austerity appealing, but many others took comfort from ancient ceremonies, beautifully decorated churches, the authority of priests, and the idea that one could perform good works to gain salvation. The Counter-Reformation thus had its effect. By the 1600s the Reformation had slowed down.

Soldiers of the Counter-Reformation

A new aggressiveness on the part of the Catholic church became a major reason for the success of the Counter-Reformation. This aggressiveness took many forms. Better-educated priests worked more forcefully for the church. The old religious orders reformed their rules, while new religious orders such as the Society of Jesus, known as Jesuits, formed.

Ignatius of Loyola founded the Jesuits in 1534. Loyola was a Spanish soldier who walked with a limp because his leg had been shattered fighting for Charles V against the French. Loyola's long period of recovery from his injury gave him time to read about the lives of Jesus and the saints. Like Martin Luther, Loyola wondered how he could attain salvation despite his sins. The answer came to him in a vision that he recorded in 1548 in his book *Spiritual Exercises.* According to Loyola, salvation could be achieved by self-discipline and a tremendous effort of will to do good deeds—in other words, by one's own actions. Loyola soon convinced six fellow students at the University of Paris—but not his fellow student John Calvin—to take religious vows and to follow him. In 1540 Pope Paul III recognized Loyola's group as an official order of the Catholic church.

Learning from Pictures *Loyola believed that educating and disciplining children were the best ways to prepare them for adult life.*

Loyola organized the Jesuits like a military body, with military discipline and the strictest obedience. He was the order's general; the members were his soldiers. The Jesuits quickly became the most disciplined and effective agents in spreading Catholicism. Within 16 years the Jesuits had 1,500 members. Their missions took them as far away as China and Japan. In Europe their preaching and their hearing of confessions slowed the spread of Protestantism in Poland, Germany, and France. ●

The Jesuits stressed education. They founded some of the best colleges in Europe, combining humanist values with theology to turn out learned, fervent supporters of the church.

The Jesuits opposed killing heretics because they believed that, given a chance to discuss religion with a Protestant, they could convert the person and thus gain a soul. Unfortunately, few other religious groups took such a nonviolent view in

of the Reformation, religion divided Europe.)
2. Many new universities appeared in Europe in the 1400s and 1500s. Protestant belief in studying the Bible stressed the importance of reading. The Jesuits and other religious orders set up schools to strengthen the faith of Catholics. ***(Generalization:*** *As a result of Catholic and Protestant attempts to strengthen their followers' faith, education became more important.)*
3. Protestant governments took responsibility for the leadership of the established church. Catholic rulers often obtained considerable control over their churches. The pope made concessions to retain the loyalty of rulers. ***(Generalization:*** *The power of national governments increased, while the power of the pope declined.)*

339

1A, 1B, 4B, 4C, a1A, a1C

● Italians took an intense interest in church reform, but their concerns were more a carryover from humanism than an expression of outright revolt. The court of Renée, the duchess of Ferrara, was a center of reform. Students might like to research this topic.

SECTION 3

Closure

Ask students to recall earlier societies that were strongly organized around religion, as was John Calvin's theocracy in Geneva. *(Answers will vary. Students might point out that in many societies—especially in Mexico and Central America—the clergy had extremely powerful roles, yet a secular ruler was always in place in most societies. But the pharaohs of Egypt, the Byzantine emperors, and the caliphs of Islam—who assumed the role of religious leaders in their realms—came close to creating theocracies. Calvin's Geneva was one of the first where the clergy totally dominated the government.)*

Review Answers

1. ***predestination:*** a belief that God had decided who would be saved and who would be damned; ***theocracy:*** a government ruled by a clergy; ***Counter-Reformation:*** Catholic reform to counteract the spread of Protestantism
2. ***Huldrych Zwingli:*** Zurich churchman who established Protestant reform in Switzerland; ***John Calvin:*** French Protestant who carried on Zwingli's work in Switzerland and wrote the *Institutes of the Christian Religion;* ***Pope Paul III:*** led movement for spiritual revival in the Catholic church; ***Ignatius of Loyola:***

Learning from Maps *The Reformation did not gain many converts in southern Europe. What religions were dominant in England? Sweden? Italy?* **Anglican, Lutheran, Roman Catholic**

the 1500s. The period from the 1530s through the mid-1600s was a time of devastating religious wars—sometimes interrupted by long truces—in Germany, Switzerland, France, and the Netherlands. Not until the mid-1600s, when the wars ended, could the results of the Reformation and the Counter-Reformation be fully seen.

Results of the Religious Upheaval

The most striking result of the great religious struggle of the 1500s was the emergence of many different churches in western Europe. In Italy, although Protestantism never made much headway as a broad movement, interest in church reform ● remained strong. Most of the people of southern and eastern Europe and the native population of Ireland remained firmly Catholic. France and the Netherlands had large numbers of Protestants. In Switzerland, northern Germany, England, Scotland, Norway, Denmark, and Sweden, various Protestant faiths became the established churches, backed by the central government (see map, this page).

1B, 4C, a1A, a1C, a4A, a4F, a4I

Another far-reaching result of the Reformation and Counter-Reformation was a new interest in education. Many new universities had appeared in the 1400s and 1500s because of the humanists' concern for learning. After the mid-1500s enrollments increased dramatically, and the religious reformers supported this trend.

Protestants believed that people could find their way to Christian faith by studying the Bible. As a result, reading became increasingly important. In their schools the Jesuits and other new religious orders worked to strengthen the faith of the Catholics. Education did not mean tolerance of new ideas, however. Luther, Calvin, and their followers felt obliged to set up standards of faith and religious practice. Neither the Protestant nor the Catholic authorities permitted views that differed from their own.

The Reformation led to an increase in the power of national governments and to a decrease in the power of the pope. In Protestant regions each government took responsibility for the leadership of the official church. In Catholic areas rulers often obtained considerable control over their churches in return for remaining loyal to the pope.

SECTION 3 REVIEW

1. **Define** predestination, theocracy, Counter-Reformation
2. **Identify** Huldrych Zwingli, John Calvin, Pope Paul II, Ignatius of Loyola
3. **Locate** Zurich, Geneva
4. **Understanding Ideas** **(a)** What were the main ideas of John Calvin? **(b)** Why did Calvinism spread so rapidly throughout Europe?
5. **Evaluating Ideas** **(a)** Why was the Council of Trent summoned? **(b)** What actions did it take? **(c)** Do you think it was successful?
6. **Summarizing Ideas** What role did the Jesuits play in the Counter-Reformation?

4 Popular Culture Took New Forms and Influenced Daily Life

The ideas that shaped the Renaissance, the Reformation, and the Counter-Reformation involved relatively few people. Ordinary people had their own views about themselves and the world around them.

Magic and Witchcraft

Most Europeans lived in small villages and spent their entire lives raising food and combating nature to survive. People close to the land could never predict what life would bring. They never knew when a cow might suddenly fall ill, when lightning might burn down a cottage, or when milk would fail to turn into butter.

The world of spirits. Since people considered God to be a distant, unknowable force, they thought spirits populated the world. Although good spirits abounded, demons, or devils, made life difficult. Because people believed in spirits, nothing was considered an accident. If lightning struck a house, a demon had caused it. If the butter would not form, a demon had prevented it. If a pitcher of milk spilled or a woman could not have a baby, the cause stemmed from the evil work of a demon. Many "superstitions," such as the belief that walking under a ladder might bring bad luck, began during this period.

Village priests usually tolerated these beliefs or at least pretended to ignore them. To the ordinary villager, the priest could offer no better explanations of how the world worked. The priest was likely to say that misfortune was God's will or God's punishment for sin. However, villagers often found certain of the priest's actions helpful. For example, every spring in a special ceremony, the priest would go out to the fields to bless the earth and pray for good crops. His blessing of a husband and wife at a wedding supposedly gave the couple a good start in life, and baptism was thought to safeguard a newborn child.

The priest, however, was not the only person to whom the villagers turned in times of trouble. They also looked to a so-called "wise" or "cunning" man or woman. This person, usually fairly old, was thought to have a special understanding of the way the world operated. Ordinary people would explain their problem—a lost ring, a cruel husband, a sick pig, or even an ominous sign—to these "wise" folk. Since people believed nothing happened by accident, anything unusual, such as a frog jumping into a fishing boat, was taken as a warning. The wise man or woman would explain what the warning meant and would sometimes recommend a remedy to ward off evil. The remedy might include a good-luck charm to wear, a strange spell to chant, or a potion to drink.

founder of the Jesuits
3. ***Geneva:*** city in western Switzerland where Calvin established theocracy; ***Zurich:*** Swiss city where Zwingli led Reformation
4. (a) Calvin preached reliance on faith and the Bible, but he also gave new importance to the community of believers. His most important teaching was the doctrine of predestination.
(b) The Calvinists' energy and determination in winning converts spread the religion rapidly.
5. (a) to define church doctrines and make reforms in church customs and practices **(b)** The council banned the sale of indulgences, tightened discipline for the clergy, emphasized free will, and endorsed the role of ritual, ceremonies, and good deeds in attaining salvation. **(c)** The Council of Trent was successful because the Roman Catholic church managed to define official church doctrine with the same precision Calvin had used to define his faith.
6. The Jesuits became effective agents in spreading Catholicism and turning back Protestantism in some areas. They founded colleges that were among the best in Europe and turned out fervent supporters of the church.

SECTION 4

Focus/Motivation
During the episodes of witch hunting, many innocent people were

341

1B, 4B, 4C, a1A, a1C

killed. Read the following excerpts to the class, or distribute copies for students to read.

"She rubbed with her salve and brought about the death of Lienhart . . . Geilen's three cows, of Brucabauer's horse, two years ago of Max Petzel's cow. . . . In short, she confesses that she destroyed a large number of cattle over and above this. A year ago she found bleached linen on the common and rubbed it with her salve, so that the pigs and geese ran over it and perished shortly thereafter."

"Innocent have I come into prison, innocent I must die. For whoever comes into the witch prison must become a witch or be tortured until he invents something out of his head. . . . The executioner put the thumbscrews on me . . . so that the blood ran out of the nails and everywhere. . . . Thereafter they first stripped me, bound my hands behind me, and drew me up in torture. . . . Eight times did they draw me up and let me fall again. . . . I confessed in order to escape the great anguish and bitter torture."

Discuss these excerpts with the class, using the following questions as a guide: Of what crimes is the woman in the first excerpt accused? *(killing farm animals)* Might these occurrences have had natural causes? *(Accept all reasonable explanations.)*

342

● The great witch hunts of the 1500s and 1600s carried over to the English colonies in North America, where persecution was particularly intense in Salem, Massachusetts, in the 1690s.

Learning from Pictures *Although peasants led difficult lives, they celebrated many holidays, including wedding feasts. This Brueghel painting shows one such wedding feast.*

The belief in witchcraft. Wise people were often called "good witches." However, if their relationships with their neighbors turned sour, wise people might be accused of being "bad witches." In many cases the person accused of witchcraft would be an elderly widow. Perhaps too weak to work, with no husband or family to support her, she would be the most defenseless person in the community and an easy target for attack.

Stories about witches became more sensational as they spread throughout the countryside. Outrageous accusations were made; a person might be accused of flying on a broomstick, sticking pins into dolls, or dancing with the devil in the woods at night. When the majority of people believed an accusation, a wise person would be unable to convince a mob that the accusation was untrue. In some cases the priest might be asked to hold a ceremony to exorcise, or drive out, a demon that was thought to have taken over the witch's body. In other cases, the accused person might be dragged to a bonfire, tied to a stake, and burned, perhaps with the approval of the local lord.

"Witch hunting" signaled that the normal harmony and cooperation of village life had broken down. Witch hunting showed a dark side of the ordinary person's view of how the world worked.

An enormous outburst of witch hunting occurred in Europe in the mid-1500s and lasted for more than 100 years. Religious leaders were ready to attack witches, whom they regarded as rivals for their own position as advisers in times of trouble. Political authorities were eager to use law courts to prosecute witches. But as witch hunting began to lead to hysteria, religious and political authorities made a deliberate effort to slow down the prosecution of witches. After 1700 only a handful of cases came to trial, and very few of these trials resulted in the execution of the accused person. ●

Forms of Recreation

For most people, daylight meant work and night meant sleep. Because they had only crude farming methods, people needed all their daylight hours for raising food. Villagers limited evening activities because they were exhausted from working all day and because they could not afford the candles needed for light. Still, they did find time for relaxation.

Every village had a gathering place, such as the village green, where people came together to drink, sew, do simple chores, and tell stories. Some people played games such as skittles (a form of bowling) and dice. Occasionally traveling companies of actors passed through a village and put on a simple show. Holidays occurred frequently. The church decreed some holidays. Others honored a local saint or a local tradition. During the holidays, the

CONNECTIONS: THEN AND NOW

Games

People throughout the ages have played games for amusement and diversion. In some cultures, games gave children an opportunity to learn skills that would be useful to them in later life. In addition, games provided relief and relaxation from the routine of hard work in the home or the fields.

In ancient Greece a favorite game of children used knucklebones of sheep similar to the way that we use dice today.

More than 400 years ago, the Flemish artist Pieter Brueghel painted the large picture shown here (above). The picture is almost an encyclopedia of the games played by children of Brueghel's time. Brueghel loved to show the activities of peasants and working people. This painting depicts at least 80 games, including everything from marbles to hockey to ring-around-the-rosy and hoop rolling.

Many games are played by adults as well as by children. Baseball, for example, can be a pickup game in a neighborhood park or a schoolyard, or a competition among professional athletes. In recent years people of all ages have been fascinated by the new games and twists on old games that electronics and the computer have made possible.

The wide appeal of games to people of all ages may account for a feature of Brueghel's painting that has never been explained. Some people think that all the people playing games in his paintings look like adults. Perhaps Brueghel wanted to suggest that adult activities are no different from the games that children play. However, we cannot know for sure. What we do know is that many of these games and activities are still amusements today (left), for children as well as for grownups throughout the world.

What problems do you see in trying to accurately determine a person's guilt or innocence by the procedure described in the second excerpt? *(A person might admit to a crime he or she did not commit just to end the torture.)* Why do you think people might accuse others of witchcraft? *(In times of anxiety, people may try to find scapegoats on whom to lay blame.)* Ask students if they can think of other peoples in history who have become scapegoats during times of troubles? *(Answers will vary. Students might mention the Christians in the early Roman Empire.)*

Presentation Comparing Ideas (Average/Group)

In "rough music" ceremonies, villagers poked fun at village life. Ask students to name present-day means of criticizing or poking fun at the government or important people. *(Answers will vary. Responses might include movies, plays, protest marches, political cartoons, newspaper editorials, and books.)* Ask students to bring in examples of cartoons, articles in periodicals, or editorials that satirize public figures or contemporary themes. Have them explain to the class how they do so.

343

● Research topic: The new techniques that have revolutionized printing in recent years

villagers sometimes dressed up and would often put on their own ceremonies.

A favorite ceremony poked fun at the familiar sights and scenes of village life. In different parts of Europe, this ceremony had different names— "rough music," "charivari," "abbeys of misrule." The basic ceremony was always much the same. The young men of the village formed a procession and marched along, ridiculing the accepted customs or the foolish people of the village. For example, two young men would impersonate a couple known to everyone because the wife beat the husband. The impersonators would be pulled along in a cart and, as they passed by, the other villagers would jeer and hoot at them. The same sort of ridicule might be directed at an old man who had a young wife.

Sometimes the marchers had more serious targets; often they wanted to show how things would look if the poor or the weak had power. They would dress a fool like a bishop, or they would put the poorest man on a throne. At this point, the jokes lost their lightheartedness and symbolized the resentment the villagers felt about the hard lives they led and about the privileges of those who ruled them.

Violence and Protest in the Village

Villagers lived in close-knit communities. They could turn angrily on neighbors or on outsiders who seemed to upset their traditions or their sense of proper behavior. At times of hardship or famine, these neighbors or outsiders became the targets of more than jokes.

Sometimes people would burn an official's house and beat or kill the official. The women of the village often led these attacks. Since women were responsible for feeding their families, they felt strongly the impact of taxes or food shortages. Women dealt firsthand with bakers and other suppliers of food. If the women suspected that a baker hoarded bread or sent it elsewhere for higher profits, they might ransack the baker's shop.

The authorities sometimes tried to break up public gatherings because they feared the gatherings would result in violence. If the king sent troops to quiet a disturbance, the women would stand in the front line, because people knew that soldiers would be more reluctant to shoot at women than at men.

Printing and the Spread of Knowledge

In the 1500s the world beyond the village began to affect village life. Printed works and, in some areas, traveling preachers, inspired the changes. ●

Few ordinary villagers could read. Often even the village priest could not read. Nevertheless, soon after the invention of printing, publishers started selling popular works. Single printed sheets known as **broadsides** began to appear. A broadside usually had a picture and some verses that made fun of a favorite object of humor, such as monks. Books and broadsides arrived in the village in the packs of peddlers who brought goods from the outside world. When the villagers gathered around a fire in the evening, they enjoyed listening to someone read the latest book or a new broadside.

While romances and epics of the classical age appealed to the nobility, publishers quickly found subjects that appealed to country folk and produced cheap books for this new market. The most common books were **almanacs,** the ancestors of *The Farmer's Almanac* of today. Arranged like a calendar, an almanac made predictions about the weather and the prospects for growing crops. Almanacs also contained traditional superstitious advice about daily living, such as the warning that if you put on your left shoe before your right shoe in the morning, you would have bad luck all week. Almanacs became best-sellers because they reflected the beliefs about nature and life that made up the ordinary person's view of the world.

Soon after Luther's break with the church, new religious ideas reached the villages. Sometimes preachers came to visit. More often, different kinds of books came out of the peddlers' packs. Some of Erasmus's writings took the form of simple stories that attacked the church. Perhaps people heard the stories read in the evening at village get-togethers. Certainly the messages of Luther and Calvin traveled in this way, as did translations of the Bible.

As Protestants and Catholics battled for the loyalties of ordinary people, leaders of both sides encouraged the founding of primary schools in the villages and towns. Both Protestant and Catholic leaders believed that knowledge would lead a person to support the faith; but the leaders did not hesitate to encourage their followers to use force against their enemies, including religious opponents. It was better, many said, to kill a heretic than to allow a soul that was damned to live. In the

344

Learning from Pictures *By the end of the 1400s, Germany had become the center of printing in Europe. More than 60 German towns had printing presses.*

long run, however, education assisted by the printing press helped people to understand that those of differing faiths could live together in peace and worship as they chose.

Changes in Daily Life

In addition to religious and political changes, economic changes resulted in a higher standard of living. The measure of the quality of life of a people or a country is called the **standard of living.** The standard of living is not strictly limited to income or economic output; it also includes working conditions, home life, the environment, health, and leisure.

Population and inflation. After the Black Death of the 1300s cut Europe's population by perhaps one-third, to about 50 million, the peasants prospered. Their goods and labor were in demand, and they enjoyed a relatively high standard of living.

By 1550, when the wars of religion had begun to ravage Europe, conditions changed. The population had grown tremendously, surpassing its pre-Black Death high of about 74 million in 1300 to reach about 78 million by 1550.

With the growth of the population came **inflation,** a rise in prices for goods. After 1550 wages could not keep up with the rise in prices, especially of farm products.

Diet. By 1700 half the population ate cereals rather than bread. White bread made from wheat was a rarity. Meat was scarce and expensive, but fish was not. Salt, needed to preserve fish and meats, had long been an important item of trade in Europe. Cheese and eggs, cheap sources of protein, were an important part of the diet everywhere. Western Europeans drank a lot of milk, but they complained that merchants sold watered-down milk. Butter, limited to northern Europe, was not widely used until the 1700s.

The spices that had earlier come to Europe from the East had been largely luxury items. By the 1500s the spice trade increased; Luther said Germany had more spices than grain. However, the spice trade declined by the late 1600s as traders introduced Europeans not only to new vegetables—asparagus, spinach, lettuce, green beans, tomatoes, and melons—but also to the new luxuries of coffee, tea, and chocolate.

Not everyone enjoyed the new and varied diets. Wealthy people in the cities could live better than

345

1B, 4C, a1B, a1C

● Research topic: The effect of diet on health and life expectancy

SECTION 4

Closure

Ask students to explain how printing influenced the lives of ordinary people. *(Students should respond that although few people could read, broadsides, almanacs, and the vernacular Bible helped spread new ideas and helped in the understanding of old ones. With the establishment of primary schools, people eventually gained a better appreciation of the world beyond the village.)*

Review Answers

1. ***broadside:*** single printed sheets often making fun of a favorite object of humor; ***almanac:*** book containing predictions about the weather, crops, and traditional superstitious advice about daily living; ***standard of living:*** the measure of the quality of life of a people or a country; ***inflation:*** a rise in prices for goods
2. ***"rough music":*** form of ridicule of people or existing society
3. Almanacs were popular because they reflected the beliefs about nature and life that made up the ordinary person's view of the world.
4. The standard of living declined after the 1550s because the population had grown, prices rose, wages declined, and the wars of religion ravaged Europe.
5. Traditional culture declined because people

Learning from Pictures *This Brueghel painting captures a moment from a country dance—one of the few diversions for the common people.*

most of the peasants and the urban poor, who ate largely the same simple meals they had eaten for ● centuries.

The table settings and customs that we know today were not common in the 1300s and 1400s. People ate mostly with their fingers, picking what they wanted from one large dish which everyone shared. In some areas people ate from wooden plates. Guests brought their own knives; individual forks and spoons did not come into use until the 1500s. People drank beverages from a common cup passed around the table.

Housing. The growing cities of Europe began to use brick and stone in construction after the 1500s. In the countryside, however, peasants continued to live in thatched-roof cottages as they had in the Middle Ages.

Most rural houses were small. Because glass was expensive and sometimes not available even for the wealthy, most houses had shutters rather than glass windows.

Most peasants endured harsh living conditions. Their houses reflected the overwhelming poverty of rural life and contained few possessions—a large cooking pot, a table, a bench, and a few tools. Those who were fortunate had a bed; others slept on sacks filled with straw. Enmeshed in poverty, with little hope of escaping their fate, many peasants sought refuge in the cities.

The Decline of Traditional Culture

The migration from countryside to city further altered traditional popular culture. In the city, food came from a shop rather than from the fields. Local governments often helped out when disaster loomed. If famine struck, local government authorities distributed bread. If plagues broke out, the government set up hospitals and quarantines.

Gradually, more sophisticated attitudes began to take hold among the residents of towns and cities. In particular, people's understanding of how things happened in the world began to change. Demons and spirits no longer dominated views of daily life. People sought rational explanations for day-to-day events, and there now seemed less need for magic and "wise" folk. This development has been called the "disenchantment" of the world—the removal of "enchantment," or magic, from nature. One of the most important influences on the growth of this new attitude was the creation of modern science.

SECTION 4 REVIEW

1. **Define** broadside, almanac, standard of living, inflation
2. **Identify** "rough music"
3. **Understanding Ideas** Why were almanacs such popular books for country people?
4. **Analyzing Ideas** Why did the standard of living for many peasants decline after 1550?
5. **Interpreting Ideas** Why did traditional culture decline?

5 The Scientific Revolution Swept Europe

Unlikely though it may seem, belief in magic helped create the revolution in thinking that led to modern science. In the 1500s it was not only ordinary people who thought hidden forces controlled the world; the early scientists also hoped to discover what they called the secrets of nature. Alchemists were early scientists who used spells and magic formulas to try to change one substance into another—for example, lead into gold. Astrologers believed that the position of the stars in the sky affected human life.

What made the early scientists more than just alchemists or astrologers was that they had very general interests. They wanted to find out why stones fall, why the stars seem to move, or what function the heart serves. They attempted to uncover the invisible structure of the universe by performing experiments and using mathematics—two methods that proved more effective than chants or spells.

The success of these early investigators in solving ancient problems in astronomy, physics, and anatomy created a new way of thinking that no longer relied on magic. This new way of pursuing knowledge is today called science. Before the 1600s the word *science* meant "knowledge." After the 1600s the meaning of the word evolved into the narrower, specialized meaning it has today.

Experiments and Mathematics

The Europeans' ideas about the universe had come to them from the ancient Greeks and Romans. People considered Aristotle and Galen to be absolute authorities who knew the truth. However, as the humanists unearthed more classical manuscripts, they found that even the respected writers of the ancient period did not all agree with each other. As people began to examine the world around them—for example, the movement of stars in the sky—they made observations that did not correspond to ancient beliefs.

As a result, people in the 1500s began to question traditional opinions. They began to observe and experiment for themselves. Most importantly, they described nature without any reference to previous beliefs. The foundation of this approach was the principle of doubt; nothing was to be believed unless it could be proved by experiment or mathematics. This approach became the new way of studying the world. The transformation in thinking that occurred during the 1500s and 1600s as a result of this new system of investigation is known as the **Scientific Revolution.**

The new approach relied heavily on the scientists' ability to conduct scientific experiments. Scientists did not have great research laboratories like those of today, where they could test and measure their experiments in a controlled environment. However, they did have newly invented instruments, such as the barometer, the microscope, and the thermometer, which improved their ability to observe and measure. At the same time, improved mathematical calculations became essential to investigations of nature. The method of inquiry that includes carefully conducted experiments and

moved from the countryside to the cities, where more sophisticated attitudes took hold and people sought more rational explanations for the events around them.

SECTION 5

Focus/Motivation
In his *Dialogue on the Two Great Systems of the World,* Galileo seemed to say that the heliocentric theory of the universe as explained by Copernicus was true. Galileo was called before the Inquisition and questioned closely. He was ordered by the church to recant (to make an open confession of error), which he did. Legend says, however, that after his public denial that the earth moves, Galileo whispered: "But it does move!" Ask students why the church disapproved of the Copernican system. *(It seemed to contradict the Bible.)*

Presentation
Analyzing Ideas (Average/Group)
Lead a classroom discussion about Renaissance science and technology, using the following questions as a guide: What were the results of the following discoveries, inventions, and new ideas? barometer, microscope, and thermometer *(improved ability to observe and measure);* Harvey's explanation of blood

1B, 4C, a1A, a1C

● Ask: How do you use the scientific method in your science classes?

circulation, Vesalius's description of the anatomy of the human body, and Leeuwenhoek's use of the microscope to discover bacteria *(medical knowledge grew)*. Ask students how our world would be different if the following discoveries or inventions had not been made; printing press *(books would be rare and expensive)*; Newton's law of universal gravitation *(scientists could not have sent astronauts to the moon)*; the discoveries of Harvey, Vesalius, and Leeuwenhoek *(people would probably live shorter and less healthy lives because medicine would be less advanced)*.

mathematical calculations—to verify the results of the experiments—is called the **scientific method.**

Most Europeans in the 1500s and 1600s continued to believe in astrology, magic, and witchcraft. Educated people, however, began to adopt the scientific approach to evidence.

Astronomy, Physics, and Anatomy

New frontiers in science attracted people with interests in different fields of study. Five Europeans in particular—Copernicus, Kepler, Galileo, Vesalius, and Harvey—became pioneers of modern astronomy, physics, and anatomy.

Copernicus. For centuries astronomers had believed in the theory Ptolemy stated about A.D. 100: that the earth was the center of the universe and that the other planets and the sun moved around it. Ptolemy's theory is called the **geocentric** ("Earth-centered") **theory,** from the Greek words *geo,* meaning "Earth," and *kentron,* meaning "center."

In the early 1500s, a Polish scientist named Nicolaus Copernicus discovered ancient writings arguing that the sun was the center of the universe. This theory became known as the **heliocentric theory,** from the Greek word *helios,* meaning "sun." After a long period of study and observation, Copernicus became convinced that the heliocentric theory best explained all the known facts of astronomy of his time. In 1543 Copernicus published his conclusions in a book titled *On the Revolutions of the Heavenly Spheres.*

The book caused little excitement at the time. Few people believed in the heliocentric theory because it seemed to contradict the evidence of the senses. Anyone could "see" that the sun and planets moved around the earth. Anyone could "feel" that the solid earth did not move.

Learning from Pictures *Along with his many other discoveries, the astronomer Galileo found that the sun's reflected light creates the moon's glow.*

Copernicus could not test and prove the heliocentric theory with the instruments or the mathematics available to him. Proof had to wait for the work of two later scientists, a German named Kepler and an Italian named Galileo.

Kepler and Galileo. Johannes Kepler, a brilliant mathematician who lived in the early 1600s, used mathematics to test the heliocentric theory of Copernicus. At first Kepler could not make the theory fit the observed facts. It is said that he calculated the problem 70 times before he discovered the error. Copernicus had written that the earth and other planets went around the sun in orbits, or paths in space, that were exact circles. Kepler discovered that the orbits were not exact circles but ovals called ellipses. Now other facts made sense. The heliocentric theory of the universe *could* be proved mathematically.

Because Kepler's proof could not be seen or observed, only mathematicians understood it. An Italian professor of mathematics, Galileo Galilei, provided proof that non-mathematicians could understand.

Galileo had read of a Dutch eyeglass-maker who put two glass lenses together in a tube to make a telescope. By looking through the telescope, a person could see distant objects more clearly. Galileo made a telescope for himself. By modern standards Galileo's telescope was only a small one, but it allowed him to see more of the heavens than anyone had ever seen. He could see the mountains and valleys of the moon and the rings around the planet Saturn. He observed sunspots. He proved that the earth rotated on its axis. His discovery that the moons of Jupiter revolve around the planet helped disprove the geocentric theory of Ptolemy by showing that not every heavenly body revolves around the earth.

Galileo published his findings in 1632 in a work called *Dialogue on the Two Great Systems of the World.* His work caused much more of an uproar than had the work of Copernicus. Many people now wanted telescopes. Many others believed telescopes to be the devil's work and refused to have anything to do with them. Scholars who accepted the authority of Ptolemy refused to believe the heliocentric theory. The church disapproved because the theory seemed to contradict the Bible. The church further insisted upon its right to condemn any scientific explanations that differed from Scripture. The Inquisition summoned Galileo to Rome, where it ordered him to renounce his belief that the earth moves around the sun. Galileo did so, but legend tells us that as he left the Inquisition room he said, "Yet it *does* move." The new ideas continued to advance.

Galileo was interested in physics as well as astronomy. Perhaps the most remarkable of his discoveries disproved the popular belief that heavier bodies fall faster than lighter ones. Galileo proved mathematically that, in the absence of air friction, all objects fall at the same speed regardless of their weight. This discovery laid the foundation for the modern science of mechanics, the study of matter in motion. Galileo further showed that the laws of physics operate in the heavens just as they do on Earth.

Vesalius and Harvey. Andreas Vesalius, a Flemish scientist, pioneered the study of anatomy. Vesalius refused to accept the descriptions of human muscles and tissues that Galen had written 1,400 years earlier. Vesalius conducted his own investigations to see how the human body was constructed. In 1543, the same year that Copernicus published his book, Vesalius published a landmark work in the history of medicine called *On the Fabric of the Human Body.*

Equally important was the work of William Harvey, an English physician. Using laboratory experiments, Harvey described the circulation of the blood through veins and arteries, the working of the body's most important muscle—the heart—and the function of the blood vessels.

The Triumph of Science

The effects of these discoveries were felt throughout Europe. So much had been accomplished. Knowledge had advanced so far that the scientists' methods became examples for everyone.

Just as new religious orders of the Counter-Reformation spread the revived faith in the church, scientific "orders" helped spread developments of the Scientific Revolution. Galileo belonged to the Accademia dei Lincei, founded in Rome in 1601. King Charles II granted a charter to the Royal Society in London in 1662, and Louis XIV established the French Academy of Sciences in 1666. The printing press helped the scientists just as it had the religious reformers. Most societies published journals so that scientists everywhere could read of work being done throughout Europe.

349

1B, 4C, a1A, a1C

SECTION 5

Closure

Ask students how the belief in magic helped bring about the Scientific Revolution. *(Answers will vary, but students should point out that the alchemists and astrologists who sought the secrets of the universe pointed the way for scientists with more general interests. These scientists used mathematics and performed experiments that did not rely on magic.)*

Review Answers

1. *Scientific Revolution:* a new way of thinking about the world that relied on questioning and experimentation; ***scientific method:*** method of inquiry including experimentation and mathematical calculations; ***geocentric theory:*** earth-centered theory of the universe; ***heliocentric theory:*** sun-centered theory of the universe

2. *Nicolaus Copernicus:* Polish astronomer who became convinced that the known facts of astronomy were best explained by the heliocentric theory; ***Johannes Kepler:*** mathematician who proved Copernicus's heliocentric theory correct by showing that the orbits of the planets are elliptical, not circular; ***Galileo:*** mathematician who helped prove heliocentric theory; also made discoveries in physics; ***Andreas Vesalius:*** pioneer in the study of anatomy; ***William Harvey:*** physician

Learning from Pictures *Descartes wrote a book agreeing with Copernican theory, but he stopped its publication when Galileo was summoned by the Inquisition.*

Descartes. One of the most influential advocates of science was René Descartes (day • KAHRT), a French philosopher and scientist who lived from 1596 to 1650. Educated at a Jesuit college, Descartes decided to become a soldier in order to learn more about the world around him. He saw little fighting as a soldier and thus had ample time to think.

Descartes rejected everything based on anyone else's authority. He decided to start fresh with a new philosophy based on his own reason. In his *Discourse on Method* (1637), he argued that everything had to be proved. Descartes believed that the fact that he could think proved that he existed: "I think, therefore I am," he said. This was his first truth. From this basic truth, Descartes established a method of inquiry in which all thoughts would follow the clear, orderly progression of scientific reasoning.

Bacon and Pascal. Descartes's contemporary, the English philosopher Francis Bacon, put the case even more strongly. Science, Bacon thought, would help humanity conquer nature and would end all the suffering in the world. Blaise Pascal, a French philosopher and scientist, opposed such ideas because they ignored the power of faith and the need to rely on God. Few people took notice of Pascal. Instead they made a hero of Isaac Newton, an English mathematician and philosopher who was considered the supreme example of the new reasoning powers of science.

Newton. In 1687 Newton, one of the greatest scientists of all time, published his *Mathematical Principles of Natural Philosophy.* It combined and related the contributions of Copernicus, Kepler, and Galileo. These early scientists had shown that the planets, including the earth, revolve around the sun. But they had not been able to explain *why* the planets moved as they did.

Newton's book contained his laws of motion and universal gravitation, which explained the movements of the planets. His law of universal gravitation states that all bodies attract each other with a force that can be measured. This force holds the whole system of sun and planets together by keeping them in their orbits.

Newton's work had a tremendous influence on the thinking of his own era and on all later scientific thought. The English poet Alexander Pope described Newton's great impact: "Nature and nature's laws lay hid in night; God said, 'Let Newton be,' and all was light."

Other scientific discoveries. New discoveries were made elsewhere in Europe. Working independently of each other, both Newton and Gottfried Wilhelm Leibniz (LYP • nits), a German philosopher and mathematician, developed calculus, a branch of mathematics that studies continuously changing quantities. A Dutch scientist, Anton van Leeuwenhoek (LAY • vuhn • hook), used the microscope, an invention of the late 1500s, to discover bacteria. The microscope enabled him to study a whole new world of life that could not normally be seen by the human eye.

Robert Hooke of England, who lived from 1635 to 1703, also worked with the microscope. The first person to identify cells in living matter, Hooke examined a thin slice of cork and noticed that it consisted of small rectangular "rooms." He called these "rooms" *cells* because they looked like the cells in which bees store honey.

The English scientist Robert Boyle is known as the founder of modern chemistry, the study of the

1B, 4C, a1A, a1C, a4A, a4H, a4I

Learning from Pictures *This painting, which hangs in the palace at Versailles, shows the establishment of the Academy of Science in 1666. It symbolizes the emphasis that people during the Enlightenment placed on science.*

composition of materials and the changes they undergo. Another English chemist, Joseph Priestley, discovered the element later called oxygen. (Elements are the fundamental substances that make up matter.)

A French scientist, Antoine Lavoisier (luhv • WAHZ • ee • ay), named oxygen. Lavoisier showed that fire was not an element, as many had believed. He proved that fire was the result of the rapid combination of oxygen with another substance. Lavoisier also demonstrated that matter is indestructible; it can be changed from one form into another, but it cannot be created or destroyed. For example, when water boils, it does not disappear. It forms steam, which combines with the air. The water's form has changed, but the water has not disappeared. Lavoisier's discovery is known as the law of conservation of matter.

By the time Priestley and Lavoisier made their discoveries, the scientific point of view dominated European thought. Many Europeans of the 1700s spoke of their changing times as an "Age of Enlightenment."

SECTION 5 REVIEW

1. **Define** Scientific Revolution, scientific method, geocentric theory, heliocentric theory
2. **Identify** Nicolaus Copernicus, Johannes Kepler, Galileo, Andreas Vesalius, William Harvey, Isaac Newton, Joseph Priestley, Antoine Lavoisier
3. **Interpreting Ideas** How did Descartes and Bacon adapt the ideas of science to their writings?
4. **Summarizing Ideas** What were Newton's scientific contributions?

who first understood and described the circulation of the blood and the functions of the heart and blood vessels: ***Isaac Newton:*** English scientist who wrote about the universal laws of motion and gravitation that explained the movements of the planets; ***Joseph Priestley:*** English chemist who discovered oxygen; ***Antoine Lavoisier:*** French scientist who named oxygen and demonstrated that matter is indestructible

3. Descartes argued that all thoughts had to follow the clear, orderly progression of scientific reasoning. Bacon wrote that science would help humanity conquer nature and would end all suffering in the world.

4. Newton combined and related the scientific contributions of Copernicus, Kepler, and Galileo. His laws of motion and universal gravitation explained the movements of the planets.

Reviewing Important Terms

1. Renaissance; **2.** humanists; **3.** perspective; **4.** Reformation; **5.** indulgences; **6.** theocracy; **7.** Scientific Revolution; **8.** heliocentric theory

Developing Critical Thinking Skills

1. (a) Descartes; **(b)** Newton; **(c)** Luther; **(d)** Lavoisier; **(e)** Loyola
2. (a) Petrarch fostered the study of Roman classics to imitate their ethical behavior. **(b)** his ideas on government and politics **(c)** Erasmus applied humanist analyses to the Bible and criticized ignorance, superstition, and vice among Christians. **(d)** Shakespeare's characters faced the questions of virtue and morality that humanists addressed. Answers will vary. Students should be able to justify their opinions.
3. (a) Salvation was possible through faith alone. **(b)** He permitted only the two sacraments mentioned in the Bible—baptism and communion. **(c)** Ministers were allowed no special powers.
4. (a) a major reform movement within the Catholic church; **(b)** Its aims were to create a more spiritual outlook within the church, define church doctrines, and pursue an aggressive campaign against Protestants. **(c)** It was successful in that many needed reforms were made within the Catholic church.
5. Villagers thought the world was populated by spirits. Good spirits helped people, but more often demons or devils made life difficult.

1B, 4C, a1A, a1C, a4A, a4F, a4H, a4L

Reteaching

Have students review the Chapter Summary and the appropriate section and questions in the Unit Synthesis. Discuss the concepts until students demonstrate a clear understanding of the material.

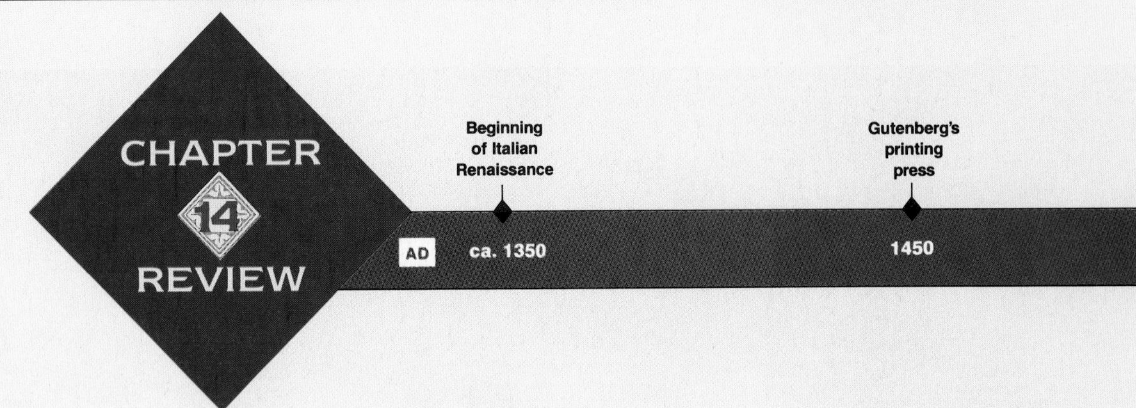

Chapter Summary

The following list contains the key concepts you have learned about the Renaissance and the Reformation.

1. In the late 1300s, a literary and artistic movement known as the Renaissance swept Italy and then the rest of western Europe.
2. The humanists, such as Petrarch, Erasmus, and More, emphasized a renewed interest in classical learning, a critical spirit, and an enthusiasm for life in this world.
3. The Renaissance also inspired masterpieces in painting and sculpture.
4. In Germany, Martin Luther broke away from the Roman Catholic church and began the Protestant Reformation. The doctrines he developed, known today as Lutheranism, spread throughout northern Europe.
5. In England the Anglican church was founded under Henry VIII.
6. John Calvin's teachings spread from Switzerland to much of Europe.
7. In the 1530s the Roman Catholic church began a major revival effort known as the Counter-Reformation. At the Council of Trent, church leaders defined official doctrines. The church used the Inquisition and the Index to combat heresy. New religious orders, such as the Jesuits, tried to halt the spread of Protestantism.
8. The development of the printing press and the religious changes of the Reformation brought new ideas to the lives of ordinary people. New attitudes toward nature and toward the community took hold.
9. The Scientific Revolution transformed the methods and understanding of astronomy, physics, and anatomy. Europeans made important technological and scientific achievements. The new scientific attitude would dominate future European thought.

On a separate sheet of paper, complete the following review exercises.

Reviewing Important Terms

Supply the term that correctly completes each statement.

1. The creative movement that began in Italy in the mid-1300s and included a revival of interest in the classical learning of ancient Greece and Rome was called the ________ .
2. People who used classical texts to study grammar, rhetoric, history, and poetry were called ________ .
3. The painting technique in which painters make distant objects smaller than those in the foreground and arrange the objects in certain ways to make them appear more realistic is called ________ .
4. The religious revolution, which split the church in western Europe and created several new churches, is called the ________ .
5. The sale of ________ by the church in Germany sparked the Reformation.
6. Calvin made Geneva a ________ in which the government was ruled by a clergy claiming God's authority.
7. The ________ ________ marked the development of a new way of thinking about the world.
8. Nicolaus Copernicus caused controversy with the ________ ________ , which contradicted what most people believed about the relationship between the earth and the sun.

Developing Critical Thinking Skills

1. **Identifying Ideas** Identify the historical figure who could have made each of the following statements.
   (a) "I think, therefore I am."
   (b) "The law of gravitation is a universal law."
   (c) "Salvation is possible through faith alone."
   (d) "All matter is indestructable."
   (e) "Individual actions can bring salvation."
2. **Evaluating Ideas** Identify what each of the following people contributed to the humanist movement. Which person do you think made the greatest contribution? Why? **(a)** Petrarch; **(b)** Machiavelli; **(c)** Erasmus; **(d)** Shakespeare
3. **Summarizing Ideas** Identify what Martin Luther's ideas were on each of the following: **(a)** salvation; **(b)** the sacraments; **(c)** the clergy.
4. **Interpreting Ideas (a)** What was the Counter-Reformation? **(b)** What did it try to accomplish? **(c)** How successful was it?
5. **Understanding Ideas** During the time of the Reformation, most people in Europe lived in small villages.

1A, a4A, a4B, a4C, a4D, a4E, a4F, a4G, a4H, a4I, a4J, a4K, a4L, a4M

6. People began to question traditional opinions.

Relating Geography to History

(a) Italy's location in the middle of the Mediterranean Sea was ideal for transshipping products from the Middle East and Northern Europe. **(b)** Students and the printing press carried ideas north.

Relating Past to Present

1. (a) Answers will vary. **(b)** One advantage is that a Renaissance person would have a broad outlook on life. A disadvantage might be that a person would not be an expert in any one field.
2. (a) Printing made books cheaper and more readily available. Knowledge and new religious ideas spread through the villages.
(b) Radio and television have made the people of today more aware of world problems.

Applying History Study Skills

1. Since these two works of art depict deities, they demonstrate that both Greek and Renaissance societies were concerned with religion.
2. The difference between the values of the two societies as shown in these works of art is in the way they viewed dieties. Michelangelo depicts God as powerful and awe-inspiring, particularly next to Adam. On the other hand, Praxiteles' Hermes does not inspire awe or reverence, but is on a more human level.

1513 Machiavelli's *The Prince*
1516 More's *Utopia;* Erasmus's *In Praise of Folly*
1517 Luther's 95 theses
1521 Diet of Worms
ca. 1530 Beginning of the Counter-Reformation
1534 Founding of Jesuits
1536 Calvin's *Institutes of the Christian Religion*
1543 Copernicus's *On the Revolutions of the Heavenly Spheres*
1545 Council of Trent
1555 Peace of Augsburg
1563 Council of Trent
1632 Galileo's *Dialogue*
1637 Descartes's *Discourse on Method*
1687 Newton's *Mathematical Principles of Natural Philosophy*

Describe how villagers explained the natural events that occurred in their lives.

6. **Analyzing Ideas** How did the Scientific Revolution change the way people viewed themselves and their world?

Relating Geography to History

Study the map of Europe on pages R12–R13 in the Atlas. **(a)** Why was Italy ideally suited to establish trade with the Middle East? **(b)** How did the ideas of the Italian Renaissance spread to northern Europe?

Relating Past to Present

1. A Renaissance person is defined as one who is knowledgeable in both science and art. **(a)** Give an example of someone in today's world who might be called a Renaissance person. **(b)** What are the advantages and disadvantages of this combination of knowledge for an educated person?
2. **(a)** How did the invention of printing revolutionize the spread of knowledge and ideas in Europe during the time of the Reformation? **(b)** Describe how radio and television have changed our understanding of the world.

Applying History Study Skills

Before completing this activity, review Building History Study Skills on page 338.

Look again at Michelangelo's *The Creation of Adam* on page 338. Then look at the statue of Hermes by Praxiteles in column 2.

1. How do these works of art show similarities between the values of Greek and Renaissance societies?
2. How do they show differences?

Investigating Further

1. **Writing a Report** Leonardo da Vinci was one of the greatest geniuses of the Renaissance. Prepare a written report on Leonardo's talents and achievements.

You may use the following sources: "The Scope of Genius" in John Hale's *The Renaissance* (Time-Life Books) and "Leonardo da Vinci" in *Horizon Book of the Renaissance* (American Heritage).

2. **Preparing an Oral Presentation** The invention of the printing press caused a revolution in communication. Find out more about Gutenberg's invention and its development. Sources include: Douglas McMurtie's *The Book: The Story of Printing and Bookmaking* (Oxford University Press) and "The Birth of Printing" in Edith Simon's *The Reformation* (Time-Life Books). Present your findings to the class.
3. **Writing a Biography** In encyclopedias or biographies, read more about one of the Renaissance artists or writers that you read about in this chapter. Prepare a short biography of that person. Be certain that your biography discusses the person's major achievements.

353

CHAPTER (pages 354–393)

15 *Strong Monarchies Helped European States Expand*

(1400–1800)

CHAPTER OVERVIEW

For centuries Italians had dominated trade with the East. In the late 1400s, however, other European countries began to search for new trade routes to Asia. Improved maps, navigational instruments, ships, and cannons all aided this search. In addition, strong monarchs who had great wealth played an important role by subsidizing voyages of exploration.

Fueled by the economic theory of mercantilism, which stressed the importance of colonies as sources of raw materials and markets for manufactured goods, European exploration soon turned to colonization. Portugal and Spain led the way in exploration and were the first to gain vast colonial empires. However, their empires soon went into decline. Spain, in large part, lost power because of a long and costly war with one of its territories, the Dutch Netherlands. The Netherlands went on to become a major trading nation during the 1600s.

France became a dominant power in Europe during the 1600s. Cardinal Richelieu, Louis XIII's chief minister, strengthened the monarchy at the expense of the French nobles. He also strengthened France's international position through clever diplomatic and military policies during the Thirty Years' War. Louis XIV continued Richelieu's domestic and foreign policies, and during Louis's long reign France enjoyed great power and prestige. In this period, the French planted colonies in North America and competed with the English in India.

In Russia, Peter the Great built a strong central government and moved to Westernize his country. Catherine the Great continued Peter's policies and greatly expanded Russia's territory southward around the Black Sea and eastward across the lands of Siberia.

After losing power in Germany during the Thirty Years' War, Austria consolidated its power in the east and south. However, the state of Prussia under Frederick the Great began to challenge Austrian rule.

SUGGESTED LESSON PLAN

Day	Objectives	Suggested Activities	Materials
1	U1-2* C1-2	Introducing the Chapter (pages 354-55) Section 1 (pages 355-59), Focus/Motivation (page 355), Presentation (page 356), Closure (page 358), Suggested Teaching Strategies, Enrichment Activities, Daily Quiz, Suggested Assignments (page 353B)	ATE, Pupil's Edition, Teacher's Resource-Bank™
2	U2, C3	Section 2 (pages 362-66), Focus/Motivation (page 362), Presentation (page 363), Closure (page 365), Suggested Teaching Strategies, Enrichment Activity, Daily Quiz, Suggested Assignments (page 353C)	ATE, Pupil's Edition, Teacher's Resource-Bank™
3	U2, C4-5	Section 3 (pages 366-76), Focus/Motivation (page 367), Presentation (page 368), Closure (page 376), Suggested Teaching Strategies, Enrichment Activities, Daily Quiz, Suggested Assignments (page 353D)	ATE, Pupil's Edition, Teacher's Resource-Bank™
4	U3, C6-7	Section 4 (pages 376-83), Focus/Motivation (page 377), Presentation (page 378), Closure (page 382), Suggested Teaching Strategies, Enrichment Activity, Daily Quiz, Suggested Assignments (page 353E)	ATE, Pupil's Edition, Teacher's Resource-Bank™
5	U3, C8-9	Section 5 (pages 383-91), Focus/Motivation (page 383), Presentation (page 384), Closure (page 389), Suggested Teaching Strategies, Enrichment Activity, Daily Quiz, Suggested Assignments (page 353F)	ATE, Pupil's Edition, Teacher's Resource-Bank™
6	U2-3 C1-9	Chapter 15 Form A Test, Reteaching Worksheet, Chapter 15 Form B Test	Teacher's Resource-Bank™ or Workbook and Test Booklet

*C refers to applicable Chapter Objective, U refers to applicable Unit Goal.

BOOKS FOR THE TEACHER

Alexander, John T. *Catherine the Great: Life and Legend.* Oxford University Press. Details the life of Catherine the Great.

Elliott, John H. *Imperial Spain 1469-1716.* St. Martin's. Gives an account of the development of the Spanish Empire.

Massie, Robert K. *Peter the Great.* Knopf. Offers a complete picture of the life of this Russian ruler.

Mitford, Nancy. *The Sun King: Louis XIV at Versailles.* Harper & Row. Features court life at Versailles to illustrate absolutism.

Morison, Samuel. *The European Discovery of America.* Oxford University Press. Offers a detailed account of the northern voyages of discovery from 500 to 1600.

Parry, J. H. *The Spanish Seaborne Empire.* Knopf. Describes the conquests of Cortes and Pizarro and discusses Spanish and Indian life in the empire.

Prescott, W. H., *The Conquest of Peru.* New American Library. Discusses the Spanish victory over the Incas. A classic on the subject.

BOOKS FOR THE STUDENT

Berger, Josef. *Discoverers of the New World.* American Heritage. Covers the major explorers of the western hemisphere. Recommended for high school students.

Blitzer, Charles. *The Age of Kings.* Time-Life. Discusses the rise of absolutism with emphasis on the Thirty Years' War and Louis XIV.

Humble, Richard. *The Explorers.* Time-Life. Uses a large number of excellent illustrations to describe the great voyages of discovery and exploration.

Marrin, Albert. *Aztecs and Spaniards: Cortes and the Conquest of Mexico.* Atheneum. Details the rise of the Aztec empire and describes the clash between the Spanish and the Aztecs.

Sanderlin, George. *Eastward to India.* Harper & Row. Concentrates on Vasco da Gama's voyage, with chapters on Prince Henry and Cabral. Original sources are woven into the text in a lively narrative style.

Stearns, Monroe. *Louis XIV of France.* Franklin Watts. Provides a very readable account of the life of the Sun King.

MULTIMEDIA MATERIALS

The Age of Exploration (2 fs), Educational Audio-Visual. Features the Portuguese and Spanish explorers and conquistadors.

Europe and the Age of Discovery (fs), Educational Audio- Visual. Examines the causes and effects of European exploration in the 1500s and 1600s.

European Expansion (mp, 25 min.), McGraw-Hill. Discusses how exploration and discovery affected the world.

The Rise of National Monarchies (2 fs), Multi-Media Productions. Traces the emergence of absolutism as it occurred in France, Spain, and England.

Saga of Western Man: Fourteen Ninety-Two (mp, 60 mins.), McGraw-Hill. Re-creates the voyage of Columbus and lists the significant events of the year in which he sailed.

The Sun King (mp, 30 mins.), NET. Examines the personal life of Louis XIV of France.

The Thirty Years' War (2 fs), Educational Audio-Visual. Shows how the Thirty Years' War helped to reshape European affairs and to lay the foundations for nationalism and capitalism.

Section 1 (pages 355–359)

Europeans Had New Reasons for Exploring Overseas

SECTION OVERVIEW

A great era of European exploration and discovery began in the late 1400s, aided by changes in technology, politics, economics, and society. Europe experienced a Commercial Revolution, and a new economic theory called mercantilism developed. A variety of social changes led people to participate in exploration and colonization.

SUGGESTED TEACHING STRATEGIES

1. **Preteaching Vocabulary (Basic)** You may wish to preteach the following important vocabulary terms: compass, astrolabe, latitude, galley *(page 356)*; Commercial Revolution *(page 357)*; joint-stock company, mercantilism *(page 358)*; favorable balance of trade, tariff, subsidy *(page 359)*. Ask students how important the theory of mercantilism was to colonial empire-building.
2. **Writing a Letter (Average/Group)** Ask students to imagine they are sixteenth-century sailors about to sail from Europe on a voyage of exploration. Then ask them to write letters to a friend discussing what dangers they expect to encounter and what they hope to achieve by this voyage. Have the students share their letters with the rest of the class.

ENRICHMENT ACTIVITIES

1. **Illustrating Ideas (Basic)** The most common type of ship used for exploration was the carrack. Interested students might like to use encyclopedias and other books to find information on the carrack and its improvement over other sailing ships. Then have them prepare sketches and diagrams of carracks for display on the bulletin board.
2. **Conducting an Interview (Average/Group)** Have students study the *History Through the Arts* feature on page 357. Then ask them to interview a sailor, airline pilot, or navigator to discover the kinds of navigational instruments used today. Suggest that the students use the following questions in their interviews: Do you use an astrolabe? Why or why not? What other instruments do you use? How do these instruments help you in your work?

DAILY QUIZ

To assess student understanding of Section 1, give the class the following quiz. (Each item is worth 10 points.)

1. When did European navigators create a true compass by fixing a magnetized needle to a card marked with directions? *(during the 1300s)*

2. What two disciplines did the astrolabe apply to navigation? *(astronomy and geometry)*
3. What kind of ships conducted most European coastal trade before and during the 1400s? *(galleys)*
4. How did shipbuilders of the late 1400s change the location of a ship's rudder? *(they moved it from the side to the stern)*
5. Who financed the voyages of exploration of the 1400s and 1500s? *(the stronger and more ambitious central governments that emerged during this period)*
6. Who led the way in the minting of coins that had a fixed value? *(the Italian cities)*
7. Which economic theory maintained that the world contained only a fixed amount of wealth? *(mercantilism)*
8. How do tariffs on foreign goods influence buying habits? *(they discourage people from buying foreign goods.)*
9. How did home countries keep strict economic control of their colonies? *(governments passed laws preventing colonists from buying foreign-manufactured goods and from selling raw materials to any country but the home country)*
10. Why did French Huguenots and English Puritans decide to resettle in the New World? *(to escape religious and political persecution in their homelands)*

SUGGESTED ASSIGNMENTS

1. **Geography Supplement (Basic)** Have students complete the Map Skills Worksheet, titled *Identifying Direction, Scale, and Legend,* in the Geography Supplement of the TEACHER'S RESOURCEBANK™.
2. **Researching a Topic (Average/Group)** Have interested students use resources in the school and public libraries to research one of the joint-stock companies of the 1500s and 1600s, such as the Dutch East India Company, the British East India Company, or the Hudson's Bay Company. The results of their research may be presented in different ways: an essay, an oral report, or a collection of captioned illustrations suitable for posting on the bulletin board.

Section (pages 362–366)

2 Portugal and Spain Took the Lead in Exploration

SECTION OVERVIEW

Portugal and Spain led Europe in exploration and in the acquisition of overseas territory. Under the leadership of Prince Henry the Navigator, Portuguese sea captains explored the coast of Africa, sailed around its southern tip, and landed in India. Columbus, sailing in the other direction, made landfall on the islands later known as the West Indies. Other enterprising explorers such as Vespucci, Balboa, and Magellan soon followed Columbus's westward route, providing Europe with a fund of knowledge about this "New World" in the Western Hemisphere.

SUGGESTED TEACHING STRATEGIES

1. **Preteaching Vocabulary (Basic)** You may wish to preteach the following important vocabulary terms: triangular trade, Middle Passage *(page 365)*. Ask the students to discuss the impact of the Middle Passage on slaves and slave traders.
2. **Illustrating Ideas (Average/Group)** Provide students with outline maps of Africa. Ask the students to use these outlines to develop a map titled *Major Sources and Destinations of African Slaves, Early 1500s to Mid-1800s.* Suggest that they use historical atlases and encyclopedias to find the information needed for this map. Select a number of students to display their maps on the bulletin board.

ENRICHMENT ACTIVITY

Presenting a Report (Average/Group) Have students present to the rest of the class oral or written reports on one of the European explorers. Sources for information on these explorers include George Sanderlin's *First Around the World* (Harper & Row) and *Eastward to India* (Harper & Row); Josef Berger's *Discoverers of the New World* (American Heritage); and Richard Humble's *The Explorers* (Time Life).

DAILY QUIZ

To assess student understanding of Section 2, give the class the following quiz. (Each item is worth 10 points.)

1. Who founded a school for navigators in Portugal? *(Prince Henry the Navigator)*
2. The Portuguese traded ______ and ______ with the people of West Africa for slaves. *(cotton goods, weapons, liquor)*
3. (T or F) In 1488 Bartholomeu Dias sailed around the Cape of Good Hope eastward across the Indian Ocean to India. *(F)*
4. Which Portuguese explorer accidentally reached the east coast of South America in 1500? *(Pedro Alvares Cabral)*
5. For which explorer is America named? *(Amerigo Vespucci)*
6. Why did Ferdinand Magellan name the great ocean to the west of South America the *Pacific*? *(because it appeared so calm)*
7. (T or F) The Portuguese divided their Asian colonies into large agricultural estates on which they grew sugar for export. *(F)*
8. Why did Europeans become involved in the African slave trade? *(because their new overseas empires began to require slave labor)*
9. (T or F) After the Spanish annexed Portugal in 1580, they limited Portuguese trade and neglected the colonies the Portuguese had established. *(T)*
10. Who took advantage of Portuguese weakness and seized control of much of the Asian trade in the 1600s? *(the Dutch and English)*

SUGGESTED ASSIGNMENTS

1. **Critical Thinking Worksheet (Average/Basic)** Have students complete Critical Thinking Worksheet 33, in the TEACHER'S RESOURCEBANK™.

2. **Geography Supplement (Average/Group)** Have students complete Geography Application Sheet 8, titled *Westward, Ho! Using Winds and Currents,* in the Geography Supplement of the TEACHER'S RESOURCEBANK™.

Section (pages 366–376)

3 Spain Created a Vast Empire in Europe and Overseas

SECTION OVERVIEW

In the late 1500s, Spain replaced Portugal as Europe's leading colonial power. The Spaniards established settlements in the Caribbean and Central and South America and developed a centralized form of government for their colonies. Gradually, however, the Spanish Empire declined. This decline in power, in part, resulted from a long and costly war that Spain conducted with one of its European territories, the Dutch Netherlands.

SUGGESTED TEACHING STRATEGIES

1. **Preteaching Vocabulary (Basic)** You may wish to preteach the following important vocabulary terms: viceroy *(page 367)*, guerrilla warfare *(page 374)*. Ask students to name recent wars in which guerrilla tactics have been used effectively.
2. **Writing an Essay (Challenging)** Have students write an essay on one of the two most prominent Spanish conquistadors of the 1500s, Cortes and Pizarro. Sources for information on these two adventurers include Bernal Diaz del Castillo's *The Conquest of New Spain* (Penguin); Cecil Howard's *Pizarro and the Conquest of Peru* (American Heritage); and Irwin Blacher's *Cortex and the Aztec Conquest* (American Heritage).

ENRICHMENT ACTIVITIES

1. **Analyzing Ideas (Average/Group)** On the chalkboard or an overhead projector, draw the following chart listing the troubles that Charles V faced as ruler of Spain and the Holy Roman Empire. Once they have identified the problems, lead students in a discussion on how Charles met some of these challenges. A similar discussion could be held on the reign of Philip II.

CHALLENGES FOR CHARLES V	
Spain	**Holy Roman Empire**
Considered "foreigner" by Spanish	Defending empire against the Turks
Inefficient government	Religious wars
Lack of industrial growth	Widely scattered territories
Food shortages	

2. **Relating Past and Present (Challenging)** In the 1600s Spain was troubled by inflation and dwindling gold and silver reserves. The United States has also had to contend with inflation problems several times in its history. Interested students might like to compare the impact of inflation on Spanish and American societies. Suggest that students consult the *Readers' Guide to Periodical Literature* for magazine articles on inflation in the United States in recent years. For information on the Spanish economy in the 1600s the students may refer to J. H. Elliott's *Imperial Spain 1469-1716* (St. Martin's). Have the students present their findings in an oral report to the rest of the class.

DAILY QUIZ

To assess student understanding of section 3, give the class the following quiz. (Each item is worth 10 points.)

1. What area in Asia remained of interest to Spain as a colony? *(the Philippine Islands)*
2. Which agency in Spain carefully planned and directed the development of the Spanish Empire? *(the Council of the Indies)*
3. What was the major asset of the Spanish Empire? *(mineral resources)*
4. Who succeeded to Charles V's territories when he split them in 1556? *(Charles's son, Philip, received Spain and its possessions; Charles's brother, Ferdinand, received the territories of the Holy Roman Empire)*
5. Why was Philip II known by his subjects as "The Prudent King?" *(because he insisted on personally approving every important decision of state)*
6. Who led the revolt of the northern Netherlands against the Spanish? *(William the Silent, Prince of Orange)*
7. The colonial empire the Dutch established differed significantly from that of Spain because the Dutch were interested in ________, not settlement. *(trade)*
8. (T or F) The importation of gold and silver from the colonies drove up prices in Spain. *(T)*
9. (T or F) During the 1500s Spain had a thriving and enterprising middle class. *(F)*
10. (T or F) Spain's government was highly centralized but very inefficient. *(T)*

SUGGESTED ASSIGNMENTS

1. **Researching a Topic (Average/Group)** Have interested students use resources in the school and public libraries to research the life of a Dutch painter of the 1600s, such as Rembrandt or Vermeer. During the next lesson, have the students present their findings in an oral report to the rest of the class. Suggest that they accompany their report with examples of the painter's work.
2. **Constructing a Genealogical Table (Challenging)** Remind students that the Hapsburg family came to the throne of Spain through a number of arranged marriages. Then, to demonstrate how the Hapsburgs extended their territories through marriage, ask students to research and prepare a genealogical table of the

Hapsburg family in the 1500s. In the next lesson, ask the students to display their tables on the bulletin board.

3. **Profile Worksheet (Basic)** Have students complete Profile Worksheet 15 in the TEACHER'S RESOURCEBANK™.

*3. **Reading About History: Making Inferences (Average/Group)** To reinforce the skill lesson presented on page 380, have students discuss why great care should be taken when using primary sources to make inferences about important historical events.

Section 4 (pages 376–383)

France Emerged as a Great Power

SECTION OVERVIEW

In the 1600s the leadership of Europe passed from Spain to France. Cardinal Richelieu, Louis XIII's chief minister, strengthened the French monarchy and worked to make France dominant in Europe. Following Richelieu's policies, Louis XIV built France into a world power. However, territorial ambitions led Louis to fight in wars that gained little and hurt France economically.

SUGGESTED TEACHING STRATEGIES

1. **Preteaching Vocabulary (Basic)** You may wish to preteach the following important vocabulary terms: tax farming (*page 377*); intendant (*page 378*); divine right of kings (*page 381*); balance of power (*page 382*). Ask the students to discuss what problems might arise from the system of tax farming.
2. **Illustrating Ideas (Basic)** To underscore the way in which the balance of power operates, on the chalkboard draw the diagrams shown below. Refer the students to diagram (1) and point out that France, as the most powerful country in Europe, probably could defeat any of the other European countries. Next, refer the students to diagram (2) and point out that when enough European countries allied against France, they balanced French power. Mention that this happened during the War of Spanish Succession, when England, the Dutch Netherlands, the Austrian Hapsburgs, and others joined the Grand Alliance to fight France.

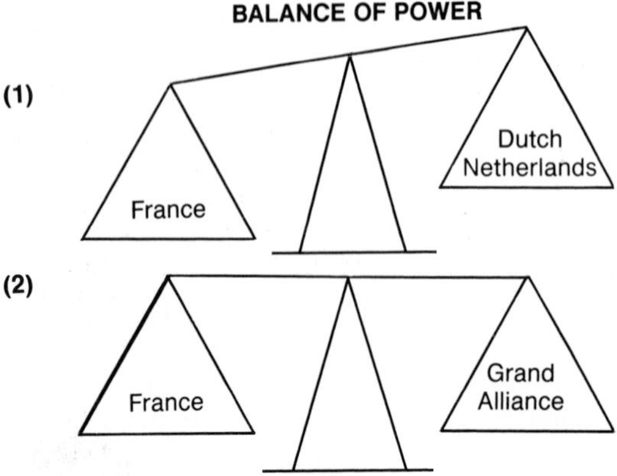

ENRICHMENT ACTIVITY

Writing a Paragraph (Average/Basic) Ask students to study both the picture of Louis XIV on page 379 and the picture of Versailles on page 380. Then ask them to use these pictures to write two paragraphs, one on a foreigner's impression of France after visiting Versailles, the other on a foreigner's impression of Louis XIV. Select a number of students to read their paragraphs to the rest of the class.

DAILY QUIZ

To assess student understanding of Section 4, give the class the following quiz. (Each item is worth 10 points.)

1. What French king reportedly remarked, "Paris is worth a Mass"? *(Henry IV)*
2. What special order guaranteed religious freedom and political rights to the Huguenots? *(Edict of Nantes)*
3. What were the results of the Duke of Sully's financial policies? *(a sizable surplus in the royal treasury)*
4. Which Huguenot seaport was attacked in 1627 by royal forces commanded by Cardinal Richelieu? *(La Rochelle)*
5. What treaty ended the Thirty Years' War and greatly strengthened France? *(Treaty of Westphalia)*
6. What series of rebellions erupted in France between 1648 and 1652? *(Fronde)*
7. Which French king proclaimed, "L'état, c'est moi"? *(Louis XIV)*
8. Two advisers chosen by Louis XIV were ________ ________ ________, an expert in finance, and ________ ________ ________, a military genius who reorganized the French army. *(Jean Baptiste Colbert, Marquis de Louvois)*
9. What treaty ended the War of Spanish Succession, by which France lost many colonial possessions to Great Britain? *(Treaty of Utrecht)*
10. Which explorer sailed down the Mississippi to the Gulf of Mexico and claimed the entire inland region of North America for France? *(Robert de La Salle)*

SUGGESTED ASSIGNMENTS

1. **Constructing a Map (Average/Group)** Provide students with outline maps of North America. Have students use these outlines to construct a map titled *French Exploration of North America.* Suggest that they use historical atlases and encyclopedias to find information on the travels of such French explorers as Jacques Cartier, Samuel de Champlain, and Robert de La Salle. Have students transfer this information to their maps. Encourage the students to display their maps on the bulletin board.

2. **Writing a Biographical Sketch (Challenging)** More than any other person, Cardinal Richelieu was responsible for the strengthening of the French monarchy during the 1600s. Ask interested students to use resources in the school and public libraries to write a biographical sketch of this French priest-politician.
3. **Skill Worksheet (Basic)** Have students complete Skill Worksheet 15 in the TEACHER'S RESOURCEBANK™.

Section 5 (pages 383–391)

Monarchs in Eastern and Central Europe Expanded Their Power

SECTION OVERVIEW

After gaining independence from the Mongols, the princes of Moscow—the most powerful rulers in Russia—sought to add new lands to their realm and centralize their power. By the mid-1600s, the power of the Central Russian government had been firmly established. Peter the Great began to Westernize Russia and tried to extend its territories southward to the warm-water ports of the Black Sea. Catherine the Great continued Peter's foreign policies and greatly increased the lands under Russian rule.

In the mid-1700s, the Austrian Hapsburgs dominated political life in Central Europe. However, the German state of Prussia, guided by the strong Hohenzollern rulers Frederick William I and Frederick the Great, soon began to challenge Hapsburg authority.

SUGGESTED TEACHING STRATEGIES

1. **Identifying Ideas (Basic)** Write the following statements on the chalkboard or reproduce them for the class. Have the students put a *P* for Peter the Great or a C for Catherine the Great before each statement to identify which ruler it describes.

   a. _______ had a temper and suffered from epilepsy. *(P)*
   b. _______ supported the arts, science, and literature. *(C)*
   c. _______ defeated Sweden and won Swedish territory. *(P)*
   d. _______ forced nobles to wear European-style clothing. *(P)*
   e. _______ made the Church a branch of government under the control of the ruler. *(P)*
   f. _______ visited Europe to learn about the West. *(P)*
   g. _______ participated in the partitioning of Poland. *(C)*
   h. _______ gained control of the Sea of Azov. *(C)*

2. **Organizing a Class Discussion (Average/Group)** Have students carefully study the map on page 390. Then lead them in a discussion of the following questions: How was the Austrian Hapsburg empire divided? What difficulties would this division present for Hapsburg rulers? How were Prussia and the Austrian Hapsburg empire similar?

ENRICHMENT ACTIVITY

Interpreting Ideas (Average/Group) Have students carefully study the pictures of Peter the Great, Catherine the Great, Maria Theresa, and Frederick the Great in this section. Then ask the students to suggest adjectives that describe the way each ruler appears. Have them indicate evidence in each picture that supports their choice of adjectives.

DAILY QUIZ

To assess student understanding of Section 5, give the class the following quiz. (Each item is worth 10 points.)

1. The most important factor that isolated Russia from the rest of Europe was the country's _______. *(geography)*
2. Which dynasty ruled Russia for 300 years, beginning in 1613? *(Romanov)*
3. One of Peter the Great's major goals was to acquire _______ _______ _______ on the Sea of Azov and the Black Sea. *(warm-water ports)*
4. What city was known as Russia's "window to Europe"? *(St. Petersburg)*
5. Catherine the Great not only wrested control of the Black Sea from the Turks, but she also took the largest share in the _______ of _______. *(partition, Poland)*
6. What was the agreement by which the rulers of Europe promised to allow Maria Theresa to inherit Austrian Hapsburg lands intact? *(Pragmatic Sanction)*
7. What family ruled Brandenburg-Prussia? *(Hohenzollern)*
8. Which ruler doubled the size of the Prussian army and made it the best and most efficient fighting force in Europe? *(Frederick William I)*
9. Frederick the Great invaded _______, Maria Theresa's richest province, in 1740. *(Silesia)*
10. Through the _______ _______, Maria Theresa gave up the alliance with Great Britain and allied with Hapsburg Austria's traditional enemy, France. *(Diplomatic Revolution)*

SUGGESTED ASSIGNMENTS

1. **Review Worksheet (Basic)** Have students complete Review Worksheet 15 in the TEACHER'S RESOURCEBANK™.
2. **Writing a Biographical Sketch (Challenging)** Organize the class into two groups. Have one group prepare a biographical sketch of Catherine the Great and the other group prepare a biographical sketch of Maria Theresa. The *Great Lives Observed* series (Prentice-Hall) has volumes on both subjects. Other sources that might be useful include Miriam Kochan's *Catherine the Great* (St. Martin's) and Edward Crankshaw's *Maria Theresa* (Viking). During the next lesson, select students from both groups to share their sketches with the rest of the class. Then lead the class in a discussion comparing these rulers.
3. **Critical Thinking Worksheet (Basic)** Have students complete Critical Thinking Worksheet 34 in the TEACHER'S RESOURCEBANK™

For suggested lesson plan, additional teaching strategies, enrichment activities, daily quizzes, and suggested assignments, see pages 353A-353F.

Introducing the Chapter
European exploration from the 1400s to the 1600s used to be referred to as the "discovery" of Asia, Africa, and the Americas. Ask students why they think the word "discovery" is now rarely used to describe the activities of Columbus, Magellan, and others. *(The word "discovery" reflects a cultural bias, suggesting that Asia, Africa, and the Americas were uninhabited or without cultures or civilizations before the coming of the Europeans.)* Then ask students to speculate on how the native populations of these areas reacted to the arrival of the Europeans. *(Answers will vary. Students may suggest such things as awe, fear, anger, or friendliness.)* Finally, ask students to suggest how these native populations and the Europeans differed. Before students discuss this final point, you may want to refer them to Chapters 12 and 13 for information on the background of non-Western peoples. *(Answers will vary. Students may suggest such things as physical appearance, dress, religion, or attitudes toward nature. Students' answers should be reviewed and revised as study of this chapter progresses.)*

CHAPTER 15

Strong Monarchies Helped European States Expand

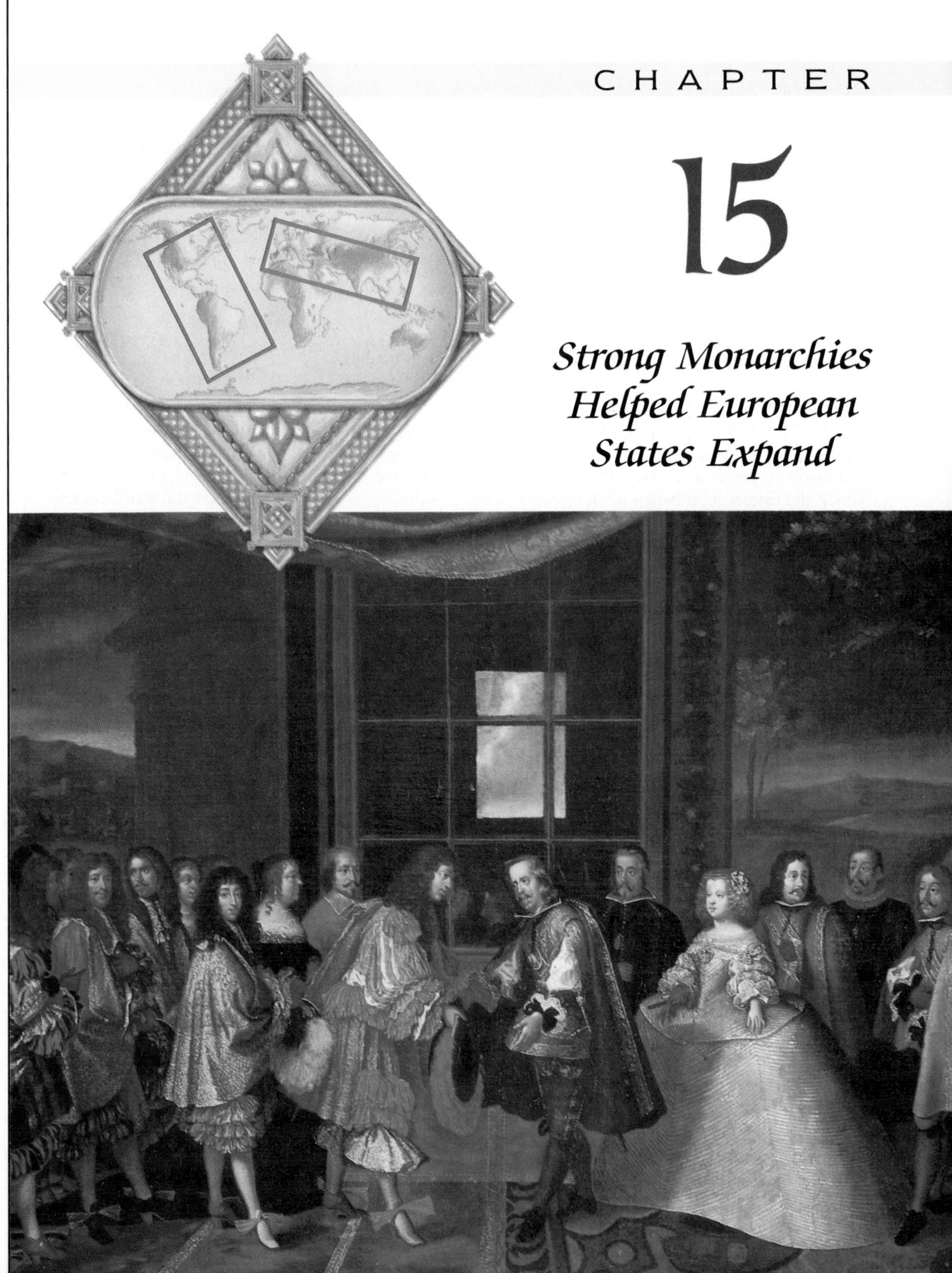

CHAPTER FOCUS

Place Europe, Asia, North and South America

Time

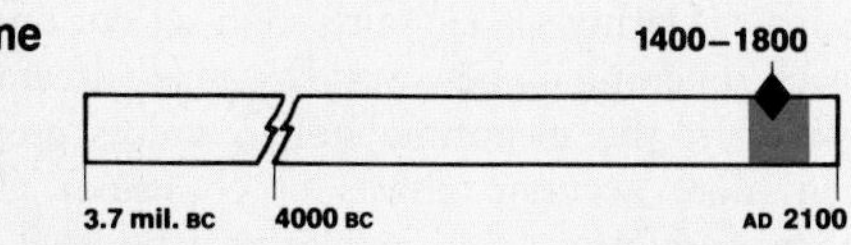

Significance

In 1400 Europe's monarchs lacked the wealth and power of the rulers of China, India, Africa, the Americas, and even Europe's neighbor, the Ottoman Empire. Less than 400 years later, however, Europe had become the dominant civilization on earth. This remarkable transformation of relationships among the world's peoples is one of the most significant developments in history.

European expansion occurred only after technological, economic, and political changes had taken place in Europe. Central governments grew larger and more powerful, while local governments became weaker. By the 1600s a system of government called **absolute monarchy** had become more popular in Europe than those systems that favored representative government or local self-rule. In an absolute monarchy, the ruler determines policy without consulting either the people or their representatives.

Terms to Define

absolute monarchy
mercantilism
favorable balance of trade
tariff
subsidy
triangular trade
Middle Passage
balance of power

People to Identify

Vasco Núñez de Balboa
Ferdinand Magellan
Ferdinand I
Peter the Great
Catherine the Great
Maria Theresa

Places to Locate

Isthmus of Panama
Versailles
St. Lawrence River
Moscow

Questions to Guide Your Reading

1 What technological, political, and economic forces allowed European countries to embark upon overseas expansion?
2 Why did the Portuguese fail to maintain their large empire?
3 How did Spain's huge empire in the New World affect economic and political developments in Spain itself?
4 How did the kings of France go about establishing an absolute monarchy?
5 How were the reigns of Catherine the Great, Maria Theresa, and Frederick the Great similar?

Archaeologists believe the recently discovered ruins on Haiti's north shore may be those of the first Spanish settlement in North America—Christopher Columbus's lost colony, La Navidad. Kathleen A. Deagan, confident that her search for the colony has ended, writes:

> *"Just before midnight on Christmas Eve, 1492, a sleepy helmsman gave the tiller of Christopher Columbus's flagship,* Santa Maria, *to the ship's boy. . . . The hapless lad promptly ran the ship onto a coral reef off the north coast of Haiti. . . . Attempts to free the vessel failed, the planking opened, and the Admiral abandoned her for* Niña. . . .
>
> *Columbus appealed for help to Guacanagari, the Indian . . . chief, whose village was about four miles from the wreck. The Indians helped unload supplies, . . . dismantle the ship's timbers and boards, and carry them . . . to the village. . . . Thus the tiny settlement—named for the infant child of Christmas, La Navidad—was established. . . . We can only speculate upon what happened next. When Columbus returned 11 months later, he found the settlement burned and all his men dead. . . . The site was forgotten for nearly 500 years. Now, . . . our team . . . believes we have found it again."*

Christopher Columbus was only one of many Europeans who spread Western civilization throughout the world.

1 Europeans Had New Reasons for Exploring Overseas

Before the 1400s Europeans had not been totally isolated. Marco Polo traveled to China, the crusaders tried to wrest the Holy Land from the Arabs, and other Europeans engaged in the spice trade. But most Europeans had neither the interest nor the ability to explore foreign lands. By the late 1400s, however, technology, politics, economics, and society had changed significantly. These changes sparked European interest in foreign lands and provided the opportunity to explore them. Soon adventurous Europeans discovered new routes to these lands. These discoveries opened up an era of exploration that lasted for the next 400 years.

◀ *A royal summit, Louis XIV and Philip IV*

Chapter Objectives

After studying Chapter 15, students will be able to:

1. List the technological advances that made European exploration possible.
2. Define the term *mercantilism* and explain the role that colonies played in mercantilism.
3. Compare Portuguese and Spanish colonial policies.
4. Trace the major events in the revolt of the Spanish Netherlands.
5. Identify the factors that contributed to the decline of the Spanish Empire.
6. Describe Cardinal Richelieu's program for strengthening the central government of France.
7. Identify the causes of the Thirty Years' War and list the principal consequences of the Treaty of Westphalia.
8. Explain how Peter the Great attempted to Westernize Russia.
9. Describe how Frederick William I and Frederick the Great strengthened Prussia's government.

SECTION 1

Focus/Motivation

Have students compare European exploration between 1400 and 1600 with present-day space exploration. Ask students what factors enabled the United States and the Soviet Union to undertake space-exploration programs. ***(Answers will vary. Students may suggest such factors as technology, financing, government support,***

1B, 4E, a4A

● that it was round

■ The Europeans probably learned the principle of the compass from the Arabs, who, in turn, had learned it from the Chinese.

an atmosphere of inquiry, national rivalries, and people willing to risk their lives.) Then have students suggest which of these factors were important during the Age of Exploration. *(Answers will vary. Students' answers should include the following: technological developments such as the compass, astrolabe, and new ships; government financing; curiosity about the world; rivalry among European nations; and ambitious and daring people.)*

Presentation
Constructing a Chart (Average/Group)
Have students construct charts showing the technological advances discussed in this section and how each of these advances aided exploration. Select a number of students to display their finished charts on the bulletin board.

Technological Advances

The first European explorers wanted to reach Asia to acquire spices, silks, and jewels—very valuable trading items, even in small amounts. A ship filled with spices had a cargo worth more than 100 times that of a ship filled with timber or grain.

Spices, silks, and jewels came mainly from India, China, and the islands of Southeast Asia. To compete successfully with powerful Arab and local traders, the Europeans needed better maps, navigation instruments, ships, and guns—in short, a more advanced technology.

Mapmaking. Mapmaking improved during the Renaissance because of the growing interest in the writings of ancient geographers and the desire for pictorial accuracy. Most scholars knew—as Ptolemy's maps had shown—that the world was round. Renaissance mapmakers added information about Africa and Asia. Their early globes showed Madagascar, Java, and Japan, but not, of course, North and South America. Observers could see that the distance from Europe to Asia was shorter to the west—across the Atlantic Ocean—than to the east. Daring sea captains soon set out on their travels, opening up new worlds scarcely dreamed of before. In the meantime Italian sailors prepared even more accurate charts of coastlines. These charts were essential for explorers, who used them to record their routes so that others could follow.

Learning from Pictures *The Dutch painter Vermeer painted this mapmaker at work. In the 1400s what did most scholars believe about the shape of the earth?* ●

Navigation instruments. Just as important, navigation instruments helped make it possible for ships to sail out of the sight of land without losing their bearings. One such instrument was the **compass.** As early as the 1100s, European navigators had learned that an iron needle rubbed against a piece of lodestone—a kind of magnetic rock—would become magnetized and turn toward the north. At first they floated the magnetized needle on a piece of cork in water. In the 1300s, by fixing the needle to a card marked with directions, they created a true compass. ■

Another important navigation instrument, the **astrolabe,** applied astronomy and geometry to navigation and allowed sailors to determine the relative height of stars and planets. Using this information they could calculate a ship's **latitude,** its distance north or south of the equator.

New ships. Long-distance exploration also required improvements in ships. In 1400 the Arabs, the Indians, and the Chinese were making better ships than the Europeans, but by 1600 European ships were the best in the world.

Before and even during the 1400s, long ships called **galleys** conducted most European coastal trade. Slaves or prisoners of war strained at the 50 or 60 oars that propelled the galley. In deeper ocean waters, traders used sailing ships. Before the late 1400s, however, these small and clumsy ships could sail only in the direction in which the wind blew.

In the late 1400s, ship designers in Portugal and Spain made important improvements. They reduced the width of ships in proportion to their length, made smaller and different-shaped sails, and moved the location of the rudder—a device used for steering—from the side to the rear, or stern, of the ship. These improvements allowed ships to sail against the wind, to travel quickly, and to be steered with reasonable accuracy.

TECHNOLOGY

A Mariner's Astrolabe

The process of determining a vehicle's position and directing its movement is called navigation. The word *navigation* comes from two Latin words—"navis," meaning "ship," and "agere," meaning "to drive."

The explorers of the 1500s sailed the oceans with only a few simple instruments such as the compass and the astrolabe to guide them. But with these, along with the stars and the sun, they navigated the world. They could plot and hold a course, measure their progress, and estimate their position in relation to land.

The bronze astrolabe shown here was an instrument used to measure latitude. It has an outer edge divided into degrees, and a movable center bar with pointers on each end. Grasping the astrolabe by the ring at the top, the viewer sighted along the bar, rotating it until one of the pointers aimed at the sun. The figure at the other end of the instrument indicated the correct latitude. This is the origin of the expression "shooting the sun."

The astrolabe became obsolete with the invention of the sextant, an instrument navigators use to measure the angular distance between two points such as the horizon and the sun.

The cannon. Europeans first used the cannon in war during the 1400s. Until this time naval warfare had consisted of ramming and boarding an enemy vessel. Shipboard cannons and the handguns sailors carried now helped Europeans defeat the vastly larger navies of their enemies.

Political Change

Technological advances alone could not have made successful explorations possible. Money provided by the stronger and more ambitious central governments that emerged in Europe in the 1400s and 1500s financed these expeditions.

By the 1400s and 1500s, dynastic ambitions and rivalries between countries often made the central governments enthusiastic supporters of new exploration and colonization. And governments appealed to the patriotism of their citizens to help build empires.

Economic Change

The development of new economic policies and methods also played an important part in carrying out exploration. In some cases developments that had already begun, such as the use of money and the services provided by banks, simply changed to accommodate the needs of exploration. In other cases the old methods of doing business became inadequate, and Europeans worked out new ones. The changes in the European economy were so extensive that some historians have referred to the period from 1400 to 1750 as the **Commercial Revolution.**

Standardized money. Money, essential to growth, had been in short supply. Also, its value had not yet been standardized—that is, the value of certain coins might change depending on the amount of precious metal used to make them. Until the 1400s the scarcity of precious metals from which coins were made, the great variety of coins in use, and the lack of a fixed value for money handicapped Europeans.

During the 1400s, however, Europeans developed standard systems of money. The Italian cities led the way in minting coins that had a fixed value. The gold florin of Florence and the ducat (DUHK • uht) of Venice became very dependable. Later, the Spanish kings used silver and gold shipped from the New World to pay debts owed their bankers. These payments helped relieve the shortage of precious metals in Europe.

The standardization of money made economic transactions much more reliable. Anyone who accepted a florin in payment for goods or services knew that the money was worth a certain amount and could be used to buy other goods or services.

357

1B, 1D, 4E, 4I, a3B, a3C, a3D, a3E, a3G, a3H, a3I

● Because of their ability to make loans to governments, some European banking families—such as the Medici in Florence and the Fuggers in Augsburg—became very powerful.

■ Both the British East India Company and the Dutch East India Company, which controlled trade with Asia, were joint-stock companies.

SECTION 1

Closure

Ask students to imagine that they live in sixteenth-century Europe. Then ask them to discuss which factors they would consider most important in making a decision to become an explorer or a settler in the New World. *(Students might mention religious freedom or wealth.)*

Review Answers

1. ***absolute monarchy:*** system of government in which the ruler determines policy without consulting either the people or their representatives; ***compass:*** instrument used for navigational purposes consisting of a magnetized needle attached to a card marked with directions; ***astrolabe:*** instrument used to calculate latitude; ***latitude:*** distance north or south of the equator; ***galley:*** long ship propelled by oars; ***Commercial Revolution:*** changes in the European economy that took place between 1400 and 1750; ***joint-stock company:*** a business organization that raised money by selling stock, or shares, in the company to investors; ***mercantilism:*** theory that suggested the world contained only a fixed amount of wealth; to increase its share, a country had to take some wealth away from other countries; ***favorable balance of trade:*** situation in which a country sells more goods than it buys in a foreign country;

CONNECTIONS: THEN AND NOW

Money

In early times any object that everyone accepted as valuable could serve as money. The Romans, for example, paid their soldiers with what was then a prized commodity, salt. From this custom we get the phrase "worth one's salt." Other items that have been used as money include shells, tobacco, feathers, and whale teeth.

Probably the first money made specifically as a medium of exchange appeared in China during the Shang dynasty. Because farmers often had traded spades and knives for other goods, this ancient money was shaped like spades.

Increasingly, rare metals, especially gold and silver, came to be used as money. They were fashioned into coins, which could be carried easily.

Governments jealously guarded the right to make coins and to establish their value. Often, however, government officials would clip pieces off coins. Then they would melt these pieces down to make more coins so that they could buy more. During the 1500s this process brought on inflation and was stopped only when milled, or grooved, edges were put on coins (above). These edges enabled people to see at once if the coins had been clipped.

About this time, too, paper money became more common. The Chinese, the first to use both paper and movable type, were also the first to use paper money, about the year A.D. 1060. Paper money was even more convenient than coins and became especially useful as long-distance trade grew increasingly important.

This in turn encouraged the growth of international trade and banking. The large sums that banks now accumulated made it possible for them to loan money to governments and major trading ● companies who financed large overseas expeditions.

Joint-stock companies. Individual merchants often combined their resources in a new type of business organization called a **joint-stock company.** Such a company raised money by selling stock, or shares, in the company to investors. These shareholders became co-owners. Shareholders divided profits according to the numbers of shares of stock they owned. Joint-stock companies raised large amounts of money from people willing ■ to invest in their activities.

Despite their contributions to the Commercial Revolution and the growth of capitalism, no Italian city-states such as Florence or Venice financed explorations or established overseas colonies. As the age of exploration began, economic leadership in Europe shifted. Trade that previously had been concentrated in the Mediterranean area and southern Germany now moved to the Atlantic nations. So in Portugal, Spain, and France, monarchs and their advisers not only financed voyages but also controlled exploration and the building of overseas empires. These monarchs understood what the great merchant families of Venice, Genoa, Florence, and Augsburg had not—that overseas possessions could bring power to their dynasties and great riches to their countries.

Mercantilism

The political and economic changes associated with overseas expansion also contributed to a new economic theory called **mercantilism.** According to this theory, the world contained only a fixed amount of wealth. To increase its share, a country had to take some wealth away from another country. More wealth meant more power. Therefore, a country's government had to do all it could to increase the country's wealth. For this reason many countries sought overseas possessions.

Balance of trade. A nation could gain wealth by mining gold and silver either at home or in its colonies. It could also get these precious metals by selling more goods than it bought in foreign countries, thus creating a **favorable balance of trade.** By bringing money into a country, a favorable balance of trade strengthened the country itself and weakened its foreign rivals, who paid for the goods they bought and thus depleted their supplies of gold and silver.

To gain a favorable balance of trade, a nation could take several measures:

(1) It could reduce the amount of goods imported into the country by imposing **tariffs,** or import taxes, on foreign goods. The importer paid the tax and added that amount to the selling price of the goods. The higher price discouraged people from buying foreign goods.

(2) It could try to increase the value of its exports. Manufactured goods were the most valuable kind of exports because they sold for more money than raw materials; woolen cloth, for instance, brought more than raw wool. Therefore, mercantilist nations encouraged manufacturers, exporters of manufactured goods, and shipbuilders. In many cases governments made grants of money called **subsidies** to help establish new industries and build ships.

(3) It could try to make itself self-sufficient by producing everything it needed, plus a surplus of goods for export. The self-sufficient nation did not have to depend on foreign countries, which were always rivals and might at any time become active enemies. The desire for self-sufficiency helped to stimulate the race for colonies.

The role of colonies. Colonies played an important part in mercantilism. Those that produced gold and silver were the most desirable. Next best were those which produced raw materials that could not be produced at home. By buying these materials in its colonies, a nation could avoid buying from a foreign rival. Thus money did not go out of the nation or empire, and it maintained complete control of its wealth.

Finally, mercantilist theory put a high value on colonies as markets for the manufactured goods of the home country. Governments passed strict laws to prevent colonists from buying foreign manufactured goods or selling their raw materials anywhere except the home country. In this way the home country kept strict economic control of its colonies.

Social Change

Government policies alone could not create a willingness to explore and settle overseas. Because of the changes in society, however, exploration and resettlement abroad became attractive to some people.

The great increase in the population during the 1400s and 1500s caused overcrowding on the land. As a result, many people sought better opportunities. One such prospect was a life at sea. Sailors were paid, fed, and given a place to stay. Other adventurous people hoped that, despite harsh living conditions in the colonies, settling overseas would give them a fresh start and a better life.

Many more people went to the colonies hoping to reap quick profits. Tales of gold and jewels and of fabulous cities like the legendary El Dorado in South America persuaded thousands that easy wealth lay overseas.

Others—like the French Huguenots and the English Puritans—went overseas to escape religious or political persecution at home. Those who went for other reasons, such as to spread Christianity or to expand Europe's trade, comprised a small minority. On the whole, hardships caused by social change prompted people to participate in Europe's expansion.

Sometimes a combination of reasons caused people to seek refuge in new lands. However, regardless of the reasons, thousands resettled during this period.

SECTION 1 REVIEW

1. **Define** absolute monarchy, compass, astrolabe, latitude, galley, Commercial Revolution, joint-stock company, mercantilism, favorable balance of trade, tariff, subsidy
2. **Summarizing Ideas** Describe the improvements in navigational instruments and ship construction that made long-range exploration possible.
3. **Analyzing Ideas** Why was the standardization of money important?
4. **Interpreting Ideas** What role did colonies play in mercantilism?
5. **Synthesizing Ideas** What were some of the reasons people left Europe to settle in the colonies?

tariff: import tax imposed on foreign goods; ***subsidy:*** grant of money made by governments to encourage businesses to establish new industries

2. Long-range explorations were made possible by new and better maps; new navigation instruments, such as the compass and the astrolabe; and improvements in the rudder and the shape of sails.

3. Standardization of money gave coins a fixed value, making economic transactions much more reliable. This, in turn, encouraged the growth of international commerce and the rise of banks.

4. Colonies that produced gold or silver or raw materials that were not available in the home country were important because the home country did not have to buy these items from a foreign country. In this way the home country was able to maintain complete control of its wealth. Colonies also served as markets for the manufactured goods of the home country.

5. Hardships caused by social change prompted many people to settle in the colonies. Many went to the colonies with the hope of making quick profits. Others went overseas to escape religious persecution or political problems. Still others went to convert the native populations to Christianity or to expand Europe's foreign trade.

359

1A

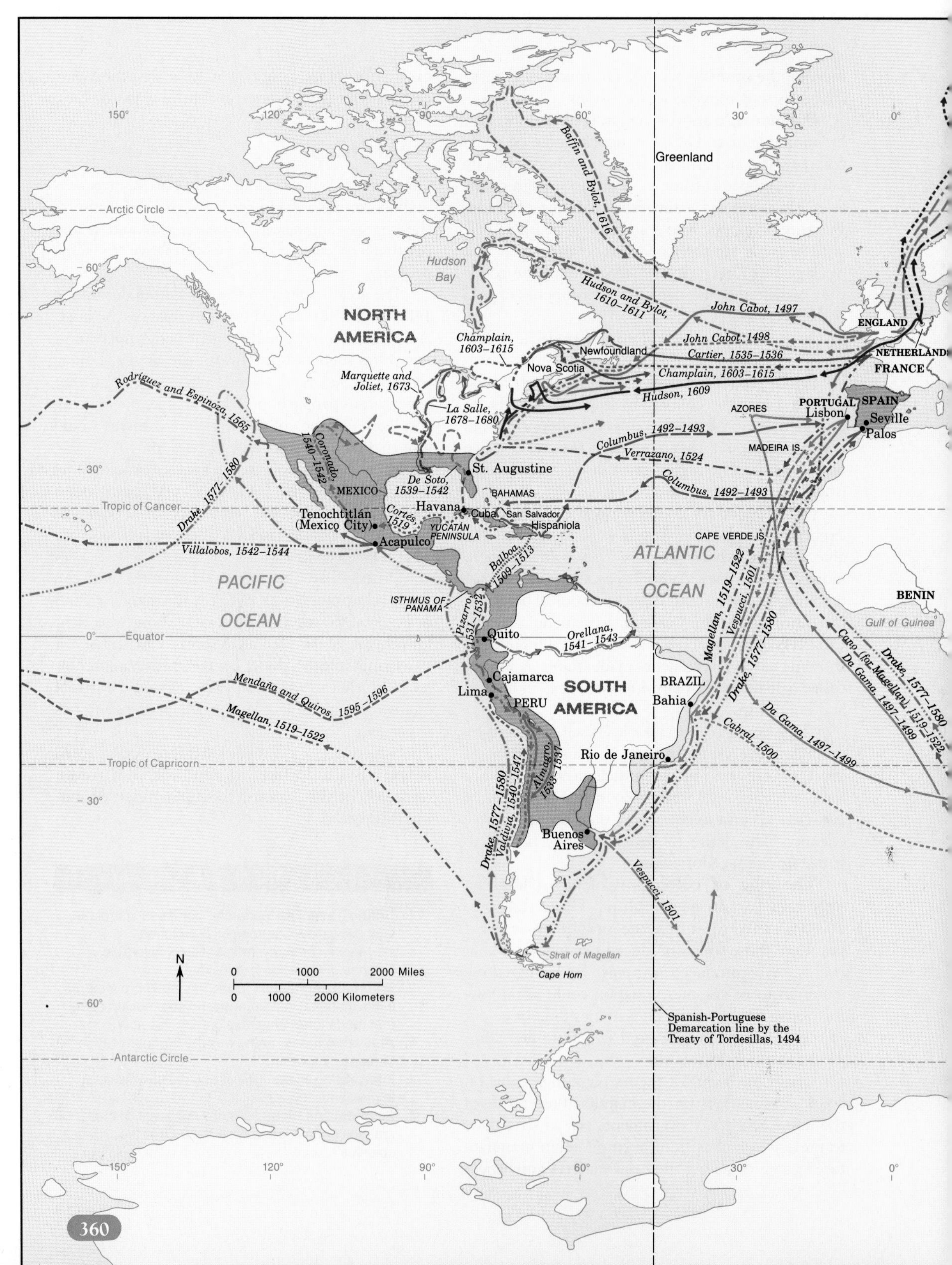

Greenland
Baffin and Bylot, 1616
Arctic Circle
Hudson Bay
Hudson and Bylot, 1610–1611
NORTH AMERICA
John Cabot, 1497
John Cabot, 1498
Cartier, 1535–1536
Champlain, 1603–1615
Hudson, 1609
ENGLAND
NETHERLANDS
FRANCE
PORTUGAL
SPAIN
Lisbon
Seville
Palos
AZORES
MADEIRA IS.
Champlain, 1603–1615
Newfoundland
Nova Scotia
Marquette and Joliet, 1673
La Salle, 1678–1680
Rodríguez and Espinoza, 1565
Coronado, 1540–1542
De Soto, 1539–1542
St. Augustine
Columbus, 1492–1493
Verrazano, 1524
Columbus, 1492–1493
MEXICO
Havana
BAHAMAS
Cuba
San Salvador
Hispaniola
Tropic of Cancer
Drake, 1577–1580
Tenochtitlán (Mexico City)
Cortés, 1519
YUCATÁN PENINSULA
Acapulco
Villalobos, 1542–1544
CAPE VERDE IS.
ATLANTIC OCEAN
PACIFIC OCEAN
Balboa, 1509–1513
ISTHMUS OF PANAMA
Pizarro, 1531–1532
BENIN
Gulf of Guinea
Equator
Quito
Orellana, 1541–1543
Magellan, 1519–1522
Vespucci, 1501
Drake, 1577–1580
Cano (for Magellan), 1519–1522
Da Gama, 1497–1499
Drake, 1577–1580
Cajamarca
Lima
PERU
SOUTH AMERICA
BRAZIL
Bahia
Mendaña and Quiros, 1595–1596
Magellan, 1519–1522
Da Gama, 1497–1499
Cabral, 1500
Rio de Janeiro
Tropic of Capricorn
Almagro, 1535–1537
Valdivia, 1540–1547
Drake, 1577–1580
Buenos Aires
Vespucci, 1501
Strait of Magellan
Cape Horn
N
0 1000 2000 Miles
0 1000 2000 Kilometers
Spanish-Portuguese Demarcation line by the Treaty of Tordesillas, 1494
Antarctic Circle
150° 120° 90° 60° 30° 0°
30° 60° 0° 30° 60°

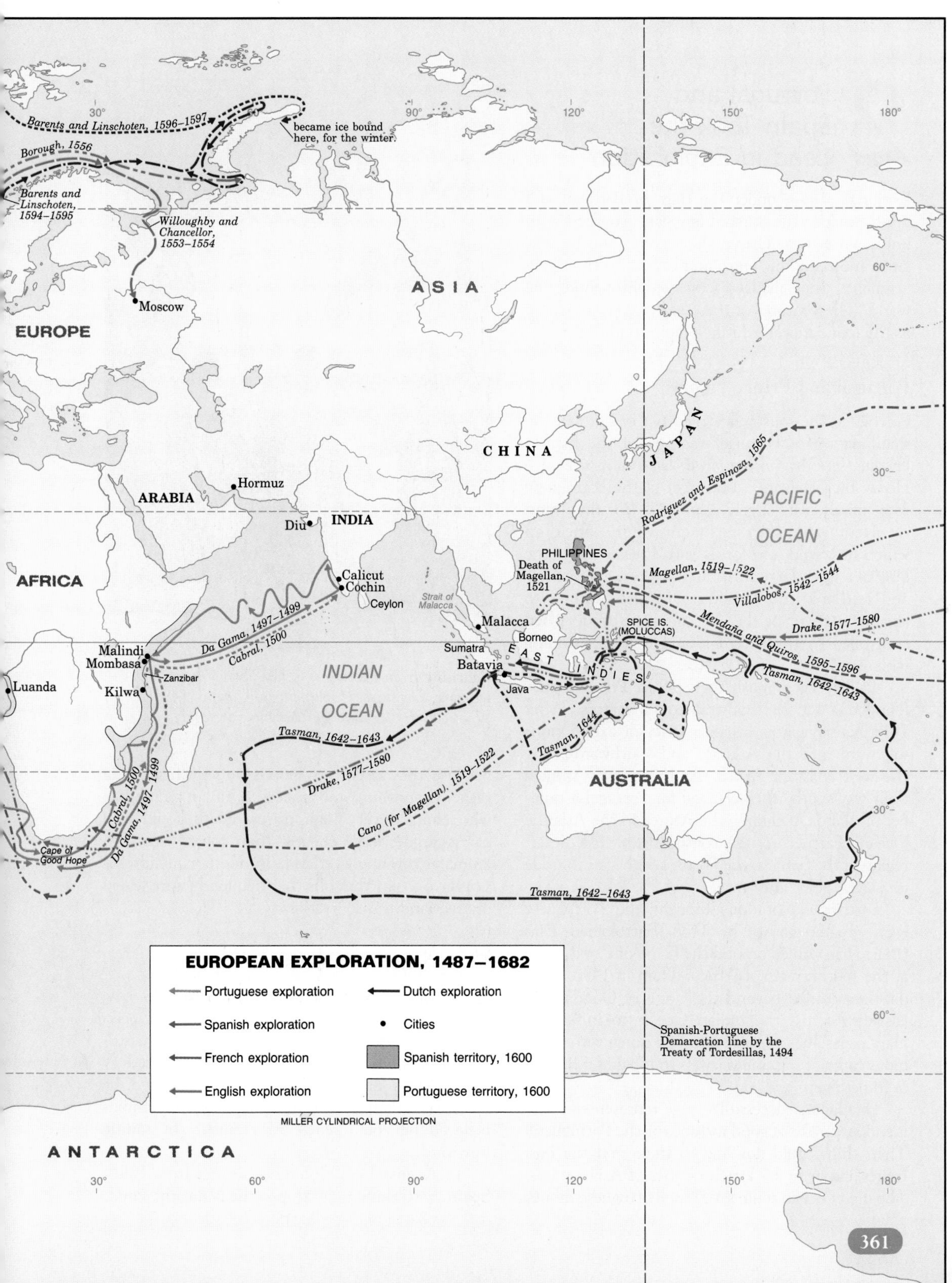
EUROPEAN EXPLORATION, 1487–1682
Portuguese exploration
Dutch exploration
Spanish exploration
Cities
French exploration
Spanish territory, 1600
English exploration
Portuguese territory, 1600
MILLER CYLINDRICAL PROJECTION
Barents and Linschoten, 1596–1597
became ice bound here, for the winter.
Borough, 1556
Barents and Linschoten, 1594–1595
Willoughby and Chancellor, 1553–1554
Moscow
EUROPE
ASIA
CHINA
JAPAN
ARABIA
Hormuz
INDIA
Diu
AFRICA
Calicut
Cochin
Ceylon
Strait of Malacca
Malacca
PHILIPPINES
Death of Magellan, 1521
Borneo
Sumatra
EAST INDIES
Batavia
Java
SPICE IS. (MOLUCCAS)
Malindi
Mombasa
Zanzibar
Kilwa
Luanda
Da Gama, 1497–1499
Cabral, 1500
INDIAN OCEAN
PACIFIC OCEAN
Rodriguez and Espinoza, 1565
Magellan, 1519–1522
Villalobos, 1542–1544
Mendaña and Quiros, 1595–1596
Drake, 1577–1580
Tasman, 1642–1643
Tasman, 1644
Cano (for Magellan), 1519–1522
AUSTRALIA
Cape of Good Hope
Spanish-Portuguese Demarcation line by the Treaty of Tordesillas, 1494
ANTARCTICA
30°
60°
90°
120°
150°
180°
0°

1B, 1D, 4E, a4A

● Henry's school was located at Sagres, near Cape St. Vincent, at the southwestern tip of Portugal.

■ Spain

▲ On his voyage, Columbus carried with him a copy of Marco Polo's book, *Descriptions of the World.*

SECTION 2

Focus/Motivation

Point out that one reason for the voyages of exploration was the European desire for a new trade route to Asia. To help students understand this desire, lead a discussion using the following questions as a guide: What were the existing trade routes between Europe and Asia? *(Refer students to pages 253-254 for help in answering this question. Arab traders brought Asian goods to the eastern Mediterranean region by overland caravans. From there Italian traders dominated the distribution of goods to northern Europe.)* Did goods go directly from their source to consumers? *(No, products from Asia went through many lands and many hands before reaching consumers.)* What happened to the price of goods as they were transported from Asia to Europe? Why? *(As goods passed from trader to trader the price increased, not only because the traders wanted to make a profit, but also because they passed on the cost of doing business, such as paying tolls.)* How do you think the discovery of water routes to Asia might change this situation? *(An all-water route to Asia would bypass costly overland caravans and eliminate the cost of paying intermediaries.)*

2 Portugal and Spain Took the Lead in Exploration

Explorers sailing under the flags of Portugal and Spain made the first European voyages into unknown waters. Driven by curiosity and by religious and economic aims, and backed by their governments, they made discoveries throughout the world. The ventures of these early pioneers served as the foundation for future empire-building.

Portugal and Prince Henry

Perched at the southwestern corner of Europe, the small nation of Portugal was one of the first to become seriously interested in exploration. Prince Henry the Navigator, a member of the Portuguese royal family, was largely responsible for this interest. Henry wanted to start a crusade in Africa—in which he would join forces with Prester John, the king of a legendary Christian kingdom—to encircle and outflank the Muslims. He also wanted to acquire a share of the African slave trade, then controlled by the Muslims, and to begin trading with Asia.

To help accomplish these goals, Prince Henry ● founded a school that trained navigators. After 1418 his navigators began a series of explorations westward into the Atlantic and southward along the west coast of Africa. As they slowly worked their way south, they claimed for Portugal a number of islands, including the Azores in the Atlantic Ocean. Farther to the south, below the desert region of the Sahara, the Portuguese began to trade for slaves, gold, and ivory.

Further explorations brought the Portuguese even greater gains. In 1488 Bartolomeu Dias (DEE • ahsh) sailed around the Cape of Good Hope at the southern tip of Africa. Then in 1498 Vasco da Gama sailed beyond the Cape of Good Hope eastward across the Indian Ocean to India (see map, pages 360–61). He returned home with a fabulous cargo of spices and jewels that paid for his trip 60 times over.

Da Gama's successful voyage represented a tremendous stroke of good fortune for the Portuguese. Their ships could now sail to India and the East Indies and bring back rich cargoes of Asian goods. The direct ocean route saved the Portuguese money because they could buy goods directly from Asia rather than from Arab traders or Italian merchants who charged very high prices. Ships could also carry cargoes more cheaply than could wagons or animals traveling overland. In addition, ships did not have to pay the tolls that frequently were levied on overland transportation.

Learning from Pictures *The Ciboney Indians welcome Christopher Columbus to Cuba in 1492. What country sponsored Columbus's voyage?* ■

Christopher Columbus

Spain, too, became interested in the search for new trade routes. Its rulers, King Ferdinand and Queen Isabella, decided to finance a voyage by Christopher Columbus, an Italian navigator. Inspired by ▲ the writings of Marco Polo and influenced by Ptolemy's description of the round earth, Columbus believed he could reach Asia quickly by sailing westward.

In August 1492 Columbus set sail from Palos, Spain, with three small ships—the *Niña,* the *Pinta,*

● Answers will vary. Students might suggest that Latin America would reflect British rather than Spanish traditions.
■ that it was not a part of Asia, but was a "New World"

and the *Santa Maria*—and crossed the Atlantic. In October his small fleet landed on a tiny island that Columbus named San Salvador (see map, pages 360–61). After visiting several other islands in the area, Columbus returned triumphantly to Spain in the spring of 1493 to report his discoveries. Because he believed the islands lay off the east coast of India, Columbus called them the "Indies" and their inhabitants "Indians." He had discovered the islands that were later to be known as the West Indies. Although Columbus made three more voyages to the "Indies" between 1493 and 1504, he believed until his death that he had landed off the coast of Asia.

Dividing the New Lands

In the early days of exploration, Spain and Portugal often claimed the same newly discovered lands. Finally, they agreed to let Pope Alexander VI settle their disputes. In 1493 he drew on a world map a line of demarcation down the middle of the Atlantic Ocean, from the North Pole to the South Pole. He granted Spain the rights to all newly discovered lands west of the line. Portugal could claim all those to the east of the line. A year later, the Treaty of Tordesillas (tawrd • uh • SEE • yuhs) between Spain and Portugal moved the line farther west (see map, pages 360–61).

Obviously, because the earth is round, if either Spain or Portugal had continued to explore and claim lands in the direction allowed, their claims would have eventually overlapped on the other side of the world. For practical purposes, however, the pope's line of demarcation worked well. For example, a Portuguese captain, Pedro Álvares Cabral (kuh • BRAHL), reached the east coast of South America by accident in 1500. He had sailed for India along da Gama's route, but strong winds had blown him far off course, forcing him westward. When he claimed what is now Brazil for Portugal, Spain honored his claim because he had landed east of the line fixed by the Treaty of Tordesillas.

In 1529 Spain and Portugal agreed to extend the line completely around the globe. Thus Spain took control of most of Central and South America, while Portugal exploited Asia.

What If?

Christopher Columbus

Christopher Columbus reached the Americas and claimed the lands he discovered for Spain. How might the history of the world have been different if Columbus had sailed as a representative of the English monarch rather than the Spanish monarch? ●

Vespucci, Balboa, and Magellan

Other explorers followed Columbus westward. Between 1497 and 1503, another Italian, Amerigo Vespucci (veh • SPOO • chee), took part in several Portuguese expeditions across the Atlantic. Vespucci became convinced that the land he saw was not part of Asia but was instead what he called a "New World." After reading Vespucci's writings, a German geographer named the new land America after Vespucci (whose first name, in Latin, is *Americus*).

In 1513 a Spaniard named Vasco Núñez de Balboa crossed the Isthmus of Panama and looked out on a vast ocean, which he called the South Sea and claimed for Spain. It now seemed clear that the

Learning from Pictures *Amerigo Vespucci uses an astrolabe as he works on maps. What did Vespucci conclude about the land he saw across the Atlantic?* ■

Presentation
Writing an Article
(Average/Group)
Have students write a news story for an imaginary Portuguese or Spanish newspaper of the 1500s. The article should be entitled "A New Land Has Been Found" and should explain why this event is important for the country involved.

363

1B, 1D, 4E

Learning from Pictures
Vasco Núñez de Balboa, the discoverer of the Pacific Ocean, later lost the favor of the Royal Governor of Panama, who had him executed for treason.

New World really was a distinct landmass, separate from Asia. Ferdinand Magellan, a Portuguese navigator sailing for Spain, proved it.

In 1519, with five ships, Magellan set out from Spain, crossed the Atlantic to South America, and sailed along its eastern shore until he reached the southernmost tip. After passing through the strait now named for him, Magellan found himself in a great ocean. Because it appeared to be very calm, he named it the Pacific Ocean, from the Latin word *pacificus,* meaning "peaceful." This was the same ocean Balboa had named the South Sea.

Magellan sailed westward across the Pacific and reached the Philippine Islands, claiming them for Spain. There, in 1521, he died in a fight with the islanders. The crew sailed on. Only one ship and 18 crew members survived to finish the historic voyage, returning to Spain in 1522. For the first time, people had sailed completely around the earth.

Portuguese Expansion

After the voyages of Dias and da Gama, the Portuguese pursued Henry the Navigator's dream of dominating trade with Asia.

The Portuguese in the East. About 1510 the Portuguese conquered part of the southwest coast of India, making the port of Goa (GO • uh) their administrative center. From India they attacked and conquered Malacca (muh • LAHK • uh), a city on the southwest coast of Malaya. From there they moved east to take the fabled Moluccas (muh • LUHK • uhz), a group of islands that Europeans called the Spice Islands because cloves, nutmeg, and other spices grew there in abundance.

The Portuguese next gained footholds in China and Japan. They then turned their attention to the island of Ceylon (now Sri Lanka), off the southeast coast of India, adding it to their chain of trading bases. With its key location between Goa and Malacca and its tea and spices, Ceylon helped the Portuguese dominate European trade with the East Indies.

The Portuguese in the New World. Portugal's colonies in Asia, though important, were small trading bases. In the New World, however, the Portuguese founded a much larger colony in Brazil. They divided this huge country into enormous agricultural estates on which they grew sugar for export.

364

The Slave Trade

As they did in Asia, the Portuguese went to Africa to trade. At first the Portuguese, largely at the request of Christian missionaries who wanted to convert the continent's inhabitants, maintained friendly relations with the Africans. The Portuguese treated the monarch of the Kongo kingdom as a legitimate and "brother" king to the Portuguese ruler. In turn, the king of the Kongo welcomed the newcomers and accepted baptism. His advisers adopted European dress and manners. Envoys from the Kongo traveled to Europe, and the king corresponded with the pope. The cordial relations, however, soon collapsed when the economic interests of Portuguese traders became evident.

Portuguese economic interests in Africa centered largely on slavery, holding people in servitude. Slavery had been practiced since the earliest times. Europeans themselves had been used as slaves in the Byzantine Empire and in the Arab and Turkish empires. During the 1500s, however, the new overseas empires of the Europeans began to require slave labor.

The trade grew very gradually, beginning in earnest when the Portuguese set up sugar plantations on the islands of Príncipe and São Tomé off the coast of West Africa. To operate efficiently and profitably, these plantations required large numbers of slaves. Plantation owners acquired their slaves from the African mainland. As plantation agriculture spread to Brazil and the Caribbean islands, the demand for slaves increased. By the early 1600s, the slave trade served as the chief purpose of European relations with Africa.

The growth of the slave trade. The Portuguese began to lose their grip on international commerce when Spain annexed Portugal in 1580. The Dutch emerged as the leading naval power and took over some of Portugal's colonies, most notably the East Indies. In addition, the slave trade came under their control. Later, the English and the French also became involved in the slave trade.

Triangular trade. The transatlantic slave trade was just one aspect of a system known as the **triangular trade.** In the first stage of this system, merchants shipped cotton goods, weapons, and liquor to Africa, in exchange for slaves or gold. The second stage—called the **Middle Passage**—was the shipment of slaves across the Atlantic to the Americas. There the traders sold the slaves for produce from the plantations. To complete the triangle, merchants used the plantations' products, such as molasses and sugar, to make rum. The triangular trade began anew when they used the rum as well as cloth metal, and guns to buy more African slaves.

Middle Passage. The Middle Passage had a brutal and dehumanizing effect on all involved. The traders chained the slaves in the overcrowded hold of the ship to prevent them from jumping overboard or organizing a rebellion aboard ship. The slaves had little food or water and no provision for sanitation. Many died before they ever reached their destination.

In the 1500s slave traders transported about 2,000 slaves a year from Africa. At the height of the trade in the 1780s, they seized as many as 80,000 slaves a year. Historians estimate that a total of 11 million to 14 million Africans lived through the horrible journey of the Middle Passage to become slaves in the Americas. Possibly as many died during the process of enslavement by fellow Africans and on the hard trip from the interior of Africa to the coast, where still other Africans sold the slaves to Europeans for shipment overseas. This tragic loss meant that Africa's population did not increase between 1650 and 1800, when Europe's population grew rapidly. Despite the tragedy of the slave trade, strong states arose that helped to protect their own people from slave raiders. In time these states conquered large areas of West Africa where most of the slave trade was centered.

In the late 1600s, for example, the Ashanti state developed on the Gold Coast bordering the Gulf of Guinea in West Africa. At about this time the economy of the Gold Coast experienced rapid change. The Europeans who had arrived in the late 1400s had been interested primarily in gold. But by the 1700s the traders actively engaged in the slave trade. Ashanti rulers responded to this trade by limiting the slaves traded to prisoners of war, and Ashanti flourished throughout the 1700s and 1800s.

To the east of Ashanti two other kingdoms—Benin and Dahomey—arose. These kingdoms pursued completely different policies toward the slave trade. Benin took little part in the trade after the early 1500s when the ruler outlawed the export of male slaves.

Since the Europeans were almost exclusively interested in male slaves to do manual work on colonial plantations, the ban effectively meant that Benin had nothing to do with the slave trade.

SECTION 2

Closure

At first the Portuguese and other European traders were interested in a number of African trade goods. In time, however, these traders focused on the trading of slaves. Ask: Why did the slave trade become so important for Europeans? *(to supply laborers for the colonies)*

Review Answers

1. ***triangular trade:*** system through which European merchants shipped weapons and liquor to Africa, exchanging them for slaves; the slaves were then transported to the Americas and sold to plantation owners for produce from the plantations; these American products were then shipped to European markets; ***Middle Passage:*** the second stage of the triangular trade, involving the shipment of slaves from Africa across the Atlantic to the Americas

2. ***Prince Henry the Navigator:*** member of the Portuguese royal family who founded a school for navigators; ***Prester John:*** legendary Christian king in Africa with whom Henry the Navigator wanted to join forces; ***Bartholomeu Dias:*** Portuguese explorer who sailed around the Cape of Good Hope; ***Vasco de Gama:*** Portuguese explorer who sailed around Africa and across the Indian Ocean to India; ***Treaty of Tordesillas:*** treaty between Spain and Portugal that moved the papal line of demarcation farther west;

1B, 1C, 1D, 4E, a4A, a4H, a4L

● Critical thinking activity: Ask the students to compare African attitudes toward slavery with those held by the people of early Athens and Rome.

Pedro Álvares Cabral: Portuguese captain who claimed Brazil for Portugal; ***Amerigo Vespucci:*** explorer for Portugal who became convinced that the land across the Atlantic was not a part of Asia, but was a "New World"; ***Vasco Núñez de Balboa:*** Spanish explorer who crossed the Isthmus of Panama and claimed the Pacific Ocean for Spain; ***Ferdinand Magellan:*** Portuguese navigator sailing for Spain who undertook the first circumnavigation of the world and proved that the New World was a distinct landmass
3. *Azores:* islands in the Atlantic Ocean west of Portugal; ***Cape of Good Hope:*** southern tip of Africa; ***San Salvador:*** small island north of Cuba; ***Brazil:*** country on the east coast of South America; ***Isthmus of Panama:*** narrow strip of land joining North and South America; ***Strait of Magellan:*** narrow channel through the southernmost tip of South America; ***Philippine Islands:*** group of islands on the western edge of the Pacific Ocean; ***Malacca:*** city on the southwest coast of Malaya; ***Moluccas:*** group of islands in the East Indies also known as the Spice Islands; ***Ceylon:*** island located in the Indian Ocean off the southeast coast of India
4. (a) He believed he could reach Asia quickly by sailing across the Atlantic. **(b)** He discovered several islands in the Caribbean that later became known as the West Indies.

Although the ban was eased in the 1700s, the slave trade never became an important part of Benin's economy. In contrast, Dahomey based its economy in large part on the slave trade.

African slavery. Not all Africans participated in the slave trade with Europeans, but many Africans had practiced slavery well before the arrival of the Europeans. African slavery was very ● different from that of the Americas, however.

African slavery included a wide range of relationships, from voluntary service to enforced captivity of prisoners of war. While the slavers sold children captured in raids, Africans usually considered the children born to enslaved women as free because their fathers were often free men. Most slaves sold in the international slave trade were adult males, whose labor would be productive on plantations. African societies generally allowed slaves to buy back their freedom, and they treated slaves as people with a role in society. Europeans, on the other hand, considered slaves as property to be bought or sold for profit.

Because Europeans rarely ventured beyond Africa's coast, they needed the help of Africans in gathering and transporting slaves. Some African societies and individuals willingly joined in the slave trade to obtain arms and other goods from Europe. In turn, neighboring groups either had to participate in the trade or become its victims. The demand for slaves led to increased slave raiding that accelerated the cycle of violence in African life and had a disastrous effect on the future of the continent.

Weakness of the Portuguese Empire

Portugal rapidly acquired wealth and a vast empire, but the empire declined almost as swiftly as it rose. Three main factors hastened this decline. First, the Portuguese government, neither strong nor well organized, had difficulty controlling its officials at home and found it impossible to control them in its colonies.

Second, transporting products home from the colonies drastically reduced Portugal's population. Portuguese ships made enormous profits in trade, but they carried so much cargo that they were top-heavy and thus dangerous to sail. The voyage from Portugal to India took six to eight months. The ships, often manned by inexperienced sailors and usually in bad repair, might be beset by storms and the crew lost to accident or disease. Each year Portugal sent out its strongest, most daring young men as sailors or traders. Sometimes only half of those who set out returned. Because Portugal had a small population to begin with, the losses could not easily be replaced.

Third, Spain annexed Portugal in 1580, and Portugal did not regain its independence until 1640. In the meantime Spain limited Portuguese trade and neglected the colonies that the Portuguese had established.

Taking advantage of these weaknesses, the Dutch and English captured much of the Asian trade from the Portuguese in the 1600s. Small Portuguese colonies survived in Africa, India, and China, but they no longer served as sources of great wealth. Only Brazil and Angola remained major Portuguese colonies.

SECTION 2 REVIEW

1. **Define** triangular trade, Middle Passage
2. **Identify** Prince Henry the Navigator, Prester John, Bartholomeu Dias, Vasco da Gama, Treaty of Tordesillas, Pedro Álvares Cabral, Amerigo Vespucci, Vasco Núñez de Balboa, Ferdinand Magellan
3. **Locate** Azores, Cape of Good Hope, San Salvador, Brazil, Isthmus of Panama, Strait of Magellan, Philippine Islands, Malacca, Moluccas, Ceylon
4. **Interpreting Ideas (a)** Why did Christopher Columbus set sail across the Atlantic Ocean? **(b)** What was the result of his exploration?
5. **Summarizing Ideas (a)** What route did Magellan follow? **(b)** What did Magellan and his crew accomplish?
6. **Synthesizing Ideas** What weaknesses made it difficult for Portugal to maintain its colonial empire?

3 Spain Created a Vast Empire in Europe and Overseas

Throughout the 1500s Spain, the most powerful nation in Europe, had the largest overseas empire. However, within just 150 years, Spain's power declined. The reasons for the rise and rapid decline of the Spanish Empire are woven through an intricate network of historical events.

Learning from Pictures *Hernando de Soto discovered the Mississippi River and searched for gold in what is today Tennessee and Arkansas.*

Spain's Colonial Empire

Portugal's main interests, with the exception of Brazil, lay in Africa and Asia. Spain, on the other hand, turned most of its energies to the Americas. In Asia only the Philippine Islands remained of any great interest to Spain as a colony.

Beginning with the voyages of Columbus and Balboa, Spaniards explored the West Indies, Central America, and parts of the mainland of North and South America (see map, pages 360–61). They failed to find the spices they sought and quickly learned that America was not Asia and that the lands they explored were not the East Indies. However, America's good climate, the fertile soil, and rich mineral resources provided other opportunities.

Spanish colonization of the New World began in the West Indies. From Santo Domingo, in what is today the Dominican Republic, Spanish explorers went forward to conquer Puerto Rico, Cuba, and parts of the South American coast. From Puerto Rico, Juan Ponce de León (PAHN • suh DAY lee • OHN) sailed northward in 1513 and explored what is today the state of Florida.

Other explorers went to Yucatán in Mexico and learned of the great Mayan civilization that had flourished there. In 1519, with 10 ships and 600 men, Hernando Cortés invaded Mexico. After defeating the Aztec ruler Montezuma (mahnt • uh • ZOO • muh), Cortés captured and destroyed the wealthy ancient city of Tenochtitlán—on the ruins of which the Spanish built Mexico City—and eventually conquered the entire Aztec Empire. Horses and guns, unknown in the Americas, helped the small Spanish force overcome the much larger Aztec armies.

The Spaniards had also heard of a great and rich civilization in South America. In 1530 Francisco Pizarro led an expedition of 180 men and 27 horses from the Isthmus of Panama to the Inca Empire in what is now Peru and seized it for Spain.

In time Spain controlled a vast empire in the West Indies, Central America, southern North America, and a large part of South America. The Spaniards became colonizers in the true sense of the word. Unlike the Europeans in Africa and Asia, who became mainly traders, the Spaniards in the Americas established settlements.

Spain also developed a centralized form of government for its colonies. **Viceroys**, representatives of the monarch, reported to the Council of the Indies in Spain. The council carefully planned and directed the development of Spain's empire.

Spain grew enormously rich from its colonies and their valuable silver mines in the regions that are now Bolivia and northern Mexico. Although agriculture and trade retained their importance, mineral resources became the Spanish Empire's main asset.

The Europeans passed on diseases new to the Americas. The native inhabitants had no resistance

Text continues on page 370.

5. (a) He sailed around South America, and across the Pacific Ocean. Although Magellan was killed in the Philippines, his crew continued on to Spain. **(b)** Magellan proved that the New World was separate from Asia.
6. The Portuguese government was neither strong nor well organized; the empire was a drain on the country's small population; and, after the Spanish annexation of Portugal in 1580, Portugal's trade was limited and its colonies were neglected.

SECTION 3

Focus/Motivation
On the chalkboard or an overhead projector, write this statement by Francisco Pizarro, the conqueror of the Incas: "The New World is a cow for our milking." Lead a class discussion on Spanish attitudes toward the Americas, using the following questions as a guide: How must Pizarro have regarded the native populations of the Americas? *(Answers will vary, but most students will recognize that Pizarro viewed the native populations as inferior and their lands ripe for exploitation.)* In what ways did he think to use the native populations and their lands? *(Answers will vary, but most students will suggest that he thought he would get the most gold, silver, and other resources out of the land at the lowest possible cost.)* When the students

have completed this section, ask them to discuss if the Spaniards acted in the manner suggested by Pizarro. *(Students should note that the Spaniards forced native Americans to work for them and drained the colonies of gold and silver.)*

Presentation
Writing an Essay (Average/Group)
Organize the class into two groups. Have members of one group imagine they are native Americans during the 1500s. Then ask them to write an essay detailing their first encounters with the Spanish. Have members of the other group imagine they are Spanish conquistadors. Ask them to write an essay describing their first encounters with the native Americans. Select members of each group to share their essays with the rest of the class.

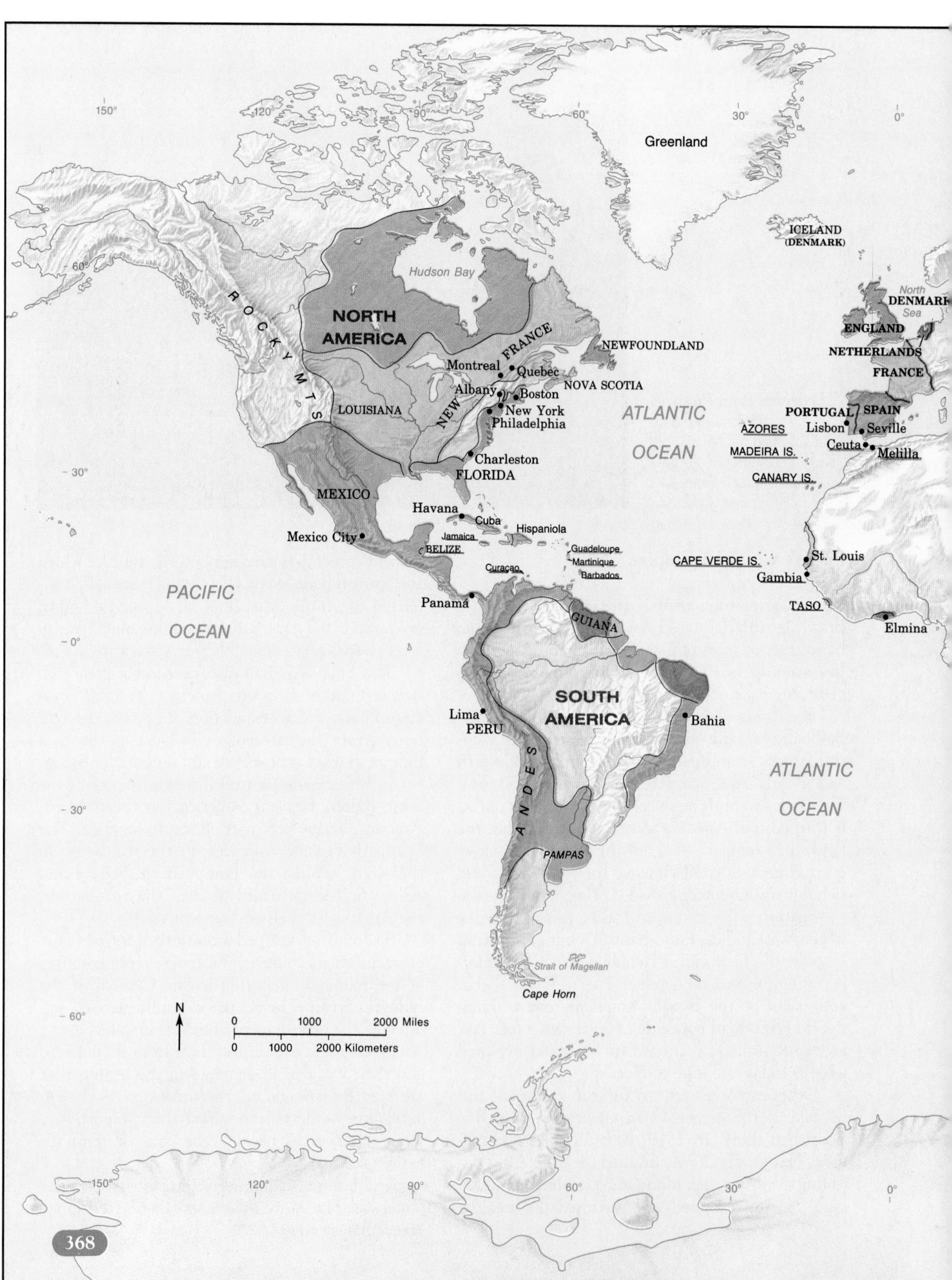

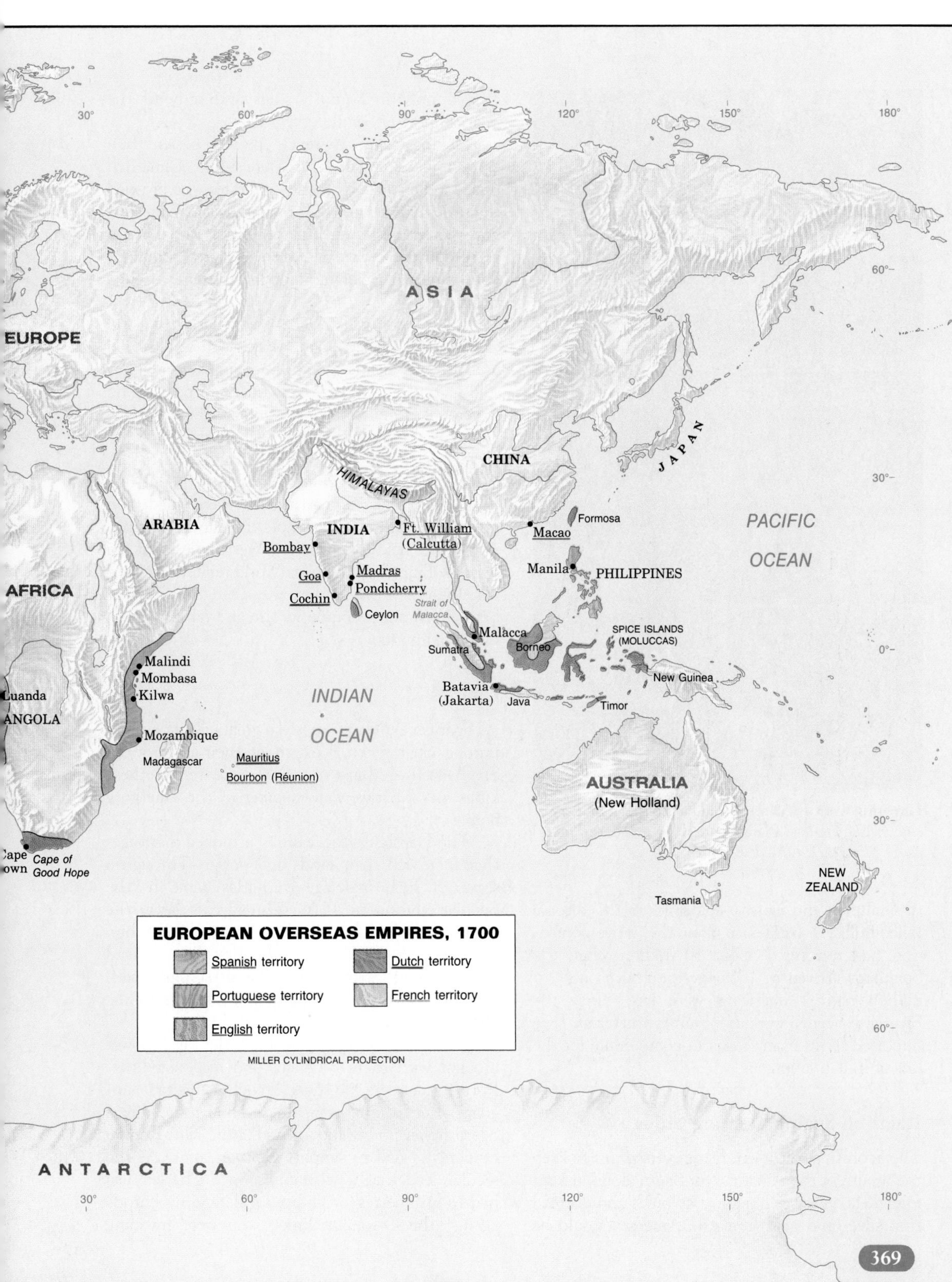

EUROPEAN OVERSEAS EMPIRES, 1700
Spanish territory
Dutch territory
Portuguese territory
French territory
English territory
MILLER CYLINDRICAL PROJECTION
ASIA
EUROPE
AFRICA
ARABIA
INDIA
CHINA
JAPAN
HIMALAYAS
Ft. William (Calcutta)
Bombay
Goa
Madras
Pondicherry
Cochin
Ceylon
Strait of Malacca
Malacca
Sumatra
Borneo
Batavia (Jakarta)
Java
Timor
Macao
Formosa
Manila
PHILIPPINES
SPICE ISLANDS (MOLUCCAS)
New Guinea
PACIFIC OCEAN
INDIAN OCEAN
Malindi
Mombasa
Kilwa
Luanda
ANGOLA
Mozambique
Madagascar
Mauritius
Bourbon (Réunion)
Cape Town
Cape of Good Hope
AUSTRALIA (New Holland)
Tasmania
NEW ZEALAND
ANTARCTICA
30°
60°
90°
120°
150°
180°
0°

369

1B, 4E, a1D

Smallpox epidemics played a major part in Cortes's victory over the Aztecs.

Learning from Pictures *The Hapsburgs were very enthusiastic hunters. Here Charles V observes the ladies as they take their turn at the hunt.*

to smallpox, and massive epidemics of this disease killed millions. In Mexico alone the native population had numbered about 10 million when the Spaniards arrived in 1519; by the 1600s only 1.5 million native Americans were left. Since the Spaniards needed workers for mines and farms, they imported slaves from Africa to compensate for the loss of Indian labor.

Raids on Spain's Treasure Ships

The Spanish government made every effort to keep the wealth of the Americas for Spain alone. It kept foreigners out of the Spanish colonies and decreed that silver and gold from the Americas could be carried only in Spanish ships and only to the Spanish port of Seville.

Making rules, however, proved easier than enforcing them. Spanish treasure ships became rich prizes and attractive targets for pirates who prowled the seas. Late in the 1500s, Spain developed a convoy system, with warships to escort the treasure vessels on the voyage across the Atlantic to Spain. For a time, at least, most of the treasure reached Spain safely.

Spain's colonial rivals—particularly England and France—envied Spain's American wealth and used various means to capture a share of it. They sold manufactured goods in American ports. And instead of trying to suppress piracy, these nations encouraged pirates to attack Spanish ships.

Spain's rivals also established colonies in the New World, paying no attention to the pope's line of demarcation. Some inroads were made on Spanish territory; for example, England, Holland, and France held islands in the West Indies. But the Spanish Empire in the New World remained otherwise intact until the early 1800s. Let us now turn to Spain itself and examine its rise and fall as a great European nation.

Charles V

As Spanish explorers created a great empire outside Europe, Spanish kings expanded their authority in Spain itself. Perhaps one of the greatest of these kings was Charles V, a member of the Hapsburg family.

The Hapsburgs successfully arranged marriages that increased their lands and power. Through a series of such marriages, Charles came to the Spanish throne in 1516. Three years later, the electors of the Holy Roman Empire chose him emperor. Though he was the first king named Charles to rule Spain, he was the fifth Charles with the title Holy Roman Emperor and is known in history as Charles V.

Charles V found that his titles and power brought with them problems and responsibilities. Born in Flanders, he spoke French as his first language. But as king of Spain, he had to acquire a Spanish viewpoint, and as head of the Holy Roman Empire, he had to support German aims. As the secular leader of Christian Europe, Charles also had to assume responsibility for defending Europe against the Ottoman Turks, who were invading

370

central Europe and attacking European ships in the Mediterranean.

Charles V halted the Turkish penetration of central Europe by driving the Turks away from Vienna in 1529. Then in 1555, the Peace of Augsburg temporarily settled the religious wars between Lutherans and Roman Catholics in Germany. Nonetheless, the nearly continuous wars drained Spain's human and financial resources.

In addition, Spain lacked industries and the government did little to encourage them. It also had difficulty feeding its people, because so much land was devoted to raising sheep for wool. Food prices quintupled between 1500 and the mid-1600s. The Spanish government, though tightly controlled by the king, could not operate efficiently over a territory that included land scattered throughout Europe as well as colonies in the New World.

Charles V realized that this scattered empire had become too large for any one monarch to rule alone. In 1556 he gave up his throne and divided his vast territory between members of his family. Charles's son, Philip II, received Spain and its possessions, and his branch of the family became known as the Spanish Hapsburgs. Charles's brother, Ferdinand I, king of Hungary and Bohemia, became Holy Roman Emperor and founded the Austrian Hapsburgs.

Charles V retired to a monastery, where he continued to take an interest in political affairs. However, largely because of his rich and unhealthy diet, which consisted of sardine omelettes, eel pies, and pickled partridges, he did not live long.

Philip II

Unlike his father Charles V, Philip II was born and educated in Spain and proudly considered himself a Spaniard. Philip II had such a dedicated sense of responsibility to his country that he had almost no private life. No matter escaped his attention, and he worked long hours at the business of being king. He wanted to make Spain stronger at home so that it might continue as Europe's leading power. Philip II made the central government responsible only to the king, and he moved the capital to Madrid.

Philip II also saw himself as the leader of the Counter-Reformation. A very devout Catholic, Philip ordered the Spanish Inquisition to redouble its efforts to find and stamp out heresy at home. Abroad, Philip became involved in wars to defend Catholicism and advance Spain's glory. These wars drained the Spanish treasury. Taxes never kept up with expenses, and the bankers charged more and more interest on loans they made to Spain. The government's financial problems grew worse, and Philip declared bankruptcy four times. Near the end of his reign, the national debt stood at 100 million ducats, and the interest payments alone on this sum took two-thirds of all government revenues.

Undeterred by these financial problems, Philip built a new royal residence, El Escorial, 30 miles from Madrid. From there Philip, surrounded by mountains of government papers, drew the reins of the government so tightly that he almost paralyzed the administration. Because he insisted upon approving every important decision personally, Philip's subjects called him "The Prudent King." In fact, Philip II's communication with his enormous empire became so slow that one of his governors wrote, "If Death had to come from Spain, I would live forever."

Philip found it impossible to subdue all the enemies of Spanish power and of Catholicism. His war with the Ottoman Empire in the Mediterranean ended in a draw. An attempted Spanish invasion of England in 1588 with an Armada, or huge fleet of ships, ended in disaster. And an attempt to invade France to prevent a Protestant from becoming king proved an expensive failure. The most costly disaster, however, resulted from Philip's policy toward the Netherlands.

The Rise of the Dutch

The 17 provinces of the Netherlands that Philip II inherited had been a great trading center and one of Europe's richest areas since the Middle Ages. Their people had a proud tradition of independence. By the 1550s Calvinism was already making headway in the area. Philip II's harsh treatment of his subjects in the Netherlands led to catastrophe for Spain.

The people of the Netherlands strongly distrusted Philip. Unlike his father Charles V, who had been born in the Netherlands, Philip was a Spaniard. Philip turned this distrust into outright rebellion by making three fundamental errors. First, he ignored the long tradition of self-rule of the Netherlands and insisted that he, not the local nobles, held all authority. Second, he taxed the

Text continues on page 374.

371

1B, a1A, a1C, a2A

372

PERSPECTIVES: LEGACIES OF THE PAST

In the last decades of the 1700s, revolutions shook both sides of the Atlantic. In 1776 the 13 British colonies of North America declared their independence. In 1789 the French people overturned the absolute power of King Louis XVI and established a limited monarchy.

In both cases, important documents marked political change: the Declaration of Independence in the United States in 1776 and the Declaration of the Rights of Man in France in 1789. The two share many features and ideas.

Undoubtedly, the French were inspired by the American example. But the common elements are not just due to imitation. The documents resemble each other because both drew on similar ideas.

It was the time of the Enlightenment, also called the Age of Reason. People were beginning to question old institutions. They no longer accepted, for example, that monarchies were the natural order of things. In this climate of critical evaluation, the two declarations were born. Both claimed the sanction of God. The Americans wrote in 1776 that men "are endowed by their Creator with certain unalienable rights." The French in 1789 proclaimed the rights of man "under the auspices of the Supreme Being."

Both documents drew on the political ideas of John Locke, who had brilliantly defended the English Revolution of 1688. Locke had maintained that men are "by nature, all free, equal, and independent." Governments, he said, were established by people and could be changed by people—if necessary, by force.

There are two other striking parallels between the two declarations. First, each presented ideas in general terms; *all* mankind, in *all* societies, had the same rights the Americans and

Two Declarations of Freedom

the French now claimed. Second, each carefully avoided a clear statement on the issue of slavery. Neither, however, explained how slavery could be reconciled with universal freedom.

There were also major differences between the two documents; they came out of different societies. The Declaration of Independence was the product of a country at war. The government in London refused to negotiate with the colonies. King George III declared the colonies in a state of rebellion. Bloody battles at Bunker Hill and Quebec resolved little except to strengthen the determination of the American freedom fighters. State assemblies were setting up governments to replace British officials who had fled or been thrown out. Many nations, including France, sympathized with the colonies.

Thus special features of the Declaration can be placed in perspective. Written largely by Thomas Jefferson, the document was carefully composed and elegantly written. It took pains to explain American actions to the outside world. It went from general principles to a lengthy set of charges against George III. The king, it said, had proved himself a tyrant "unfit to be the ruler of a free people." The Declaration vividly invited other oppressed peoples to follow the American lead. When governments become despotic, peoples must respond: "It is their right, it is their duty, to throw off such government."

In contrast, the Declaration of the Rights of Man came out of a country at relative—though uneasy—peace. The French had just overcome an unjust division into three estates: the clergy, the nobles, and the commoners. The commoners (the Third Estate) had chafed under the injustice of this division. They were the most numerous and the most heavily taxed. Why should they have little voice in government? They had rebelled and formed a national assembly. Now they prepared to write a constitution. The Declaration of the Rights of Man was composed to guide the constitution makers.

The Declaration of the Rights of Man lacked the organization and the brilliant force of its American counterpart, but its purpose was clear: to remind France's citizens of "the natural, inalienable, and sacred rights of man."

Starting with a statement of general principles, the Declaration followed with 17 specific claims. There was no direct attack on the king; no direct call for other peoples to follow the French in overturning an unjust government.

Instead, the Declaration took aim at specific abuses of the Old Regime. No one, it said, should be persecuted for religious beliefs. Taxation should depend on income. Public offices should be open to all.

While the American Declaration was a war cry for a society under attack, the French Declaration was intended to stabilize the new order. Yet it failed! The king balked at his diminished role. Some revolutionaries wanted to spread the new order beyond France's border, plunging the nation into war with its neighbors. Quarrels over the role of the Roman Catholic church led to civil war. France then fell under a dictatorship that ignored the very rights the Declaration of the Rights of Man so eloquently guaranteed.

Thus, the Declaration of the Rights of Man was overwhelmed by events, whereas the Declaration of Independence led Americans to victory and freedom.

Photos Page 372: Thomas Jefferson (top), signing the Declaration of Independence (bottom); Page 373: revolution in Paris (top), John Locke (middle), Declaration of the Rights of Man (bottom)

373

1B, 4A, 4E, a1A, a1C

History Through the Arts

PAINTING

Young Woman with a Water Jug

What does this young lady see as she gazes through the window? The map on the wall behind her is of the far-flung Dutch provinces, and perhaps it has led her thoughts to faraway places.

The window lets light in on her starched linen headdress, and the sun sparkles on the metal pitcher and tray, defining the pattern on the Oriental rug. The rug is an example of the varied goods that overseas trade brought to the Dutch people after they had won their independence from Spain.

In the 1600s Dutch merchants grew rich enough to buy handsome silks and linens for their wives and to commission artists to paint for them. Artists flourished in the prosperous economy of the Netherlands, and Jan Vermeer, who painted this picture, was one of the finest. His painting gives us an accurate look at daily Dutch life.

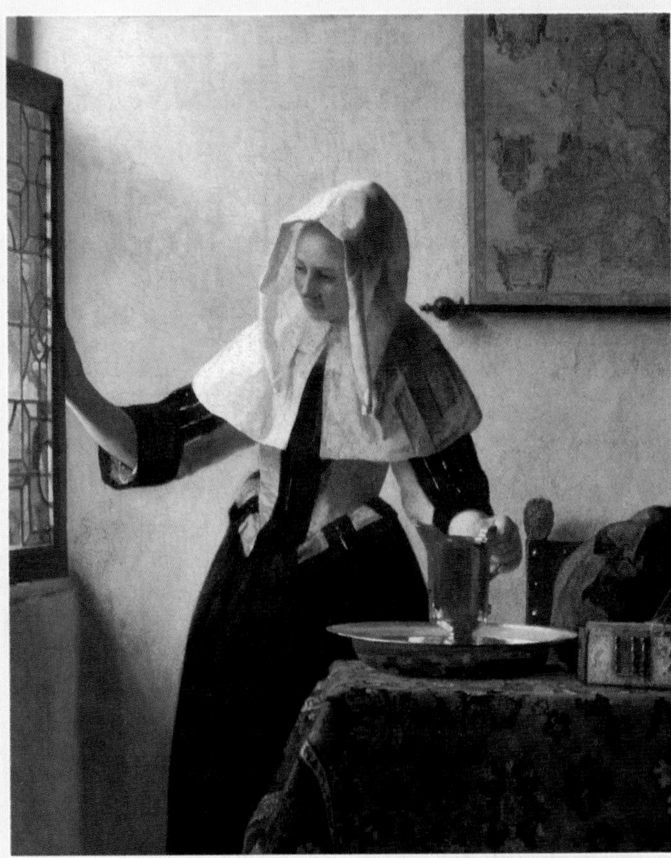

The Metropolitan Museum of Art, Gift of Henry G. Marquand, 1889. Marquand Collection, (89.15.21)

Netherlands' trade heavily to finance Spanish wars. Third, he persecuted the Calvinists.

Philip could not stop the revolt that erupted in 1568. The people of the Calvinist northern provinces lived on land that was below sea level, protected by large dikes. They simply opened the dikes, flooded the country, and left Philip's army helpless. William the Silent, prince of Orange, led the revolt of the northern provinces. He relied on quick strikes, raids by bands of his soldiers to keep the Spanish army off balance. Today we call this military technique **guerrilla warfare.**

In 1581, under William the Silent's leadership, the northern provinces declared their independence from Spain and became the Republic of the United Provinces. Today they are called simply the Netherlands.

William was assassinated in 1584, but his sons continued the struggle against Spain. Eventually, in 1609 the Spaniards agreed to a truce. By this time the Spaniards had won back the loyalty of the southern provinces of the Netherlands, partly because Philip promised the heavily Catholic southern provinces greater self-rule. The region remained under the rule of Spain and was known as the Spanish Netherlands (see map, page 378). In 1713 when the Austrian Hapsburgs took possession, it was called the Austrian Netherlands. Since 1830 it has been the independent kingdom of Belgium.

Dutch society. The people of the northern provinces of the Netherlands—the Dutch—created one of Europe's most remarkable societies. Primarily traders, they dominated European commerce

374

● Even Marranos—Jews who had converted to Christianity—were expelled from Spain.

throughout the 1600s. Their ships carried most of the world's trade. The city of Amsterdam became a world financial center. Dutch banks, trading companies, manufacturing enterprises—especially shipbuilding—and overseas colonies became models of efficiency.

The Dutch had an extraordinarily open society. Although only Calvinists could hold political offices, the government allowed all inhabitants freedom of religion. Victims of religious persecution elsewhere found tolerance in the Netherlands.

Amsterdam also became the liveliest cultural center in Europe. The philosopher René Descartes, Hugo Grotius (GROH • shee • uhs), the scholar of international law and freedom of the seas, and the painter Rembrandt thrived in this comfortable and inspiring setting.

The Dutch colonial empire. The Netherlands lay on the North Sea, and the Dutch, a seafaring people, built very efficient ships and became excellent sailors. In the age of exploration, Dutch merchants set up a number of companies to trade in various parts of the world. In 1602 the Dutch combined several of their trading companies into one powerful organization, the Dutch East India Company. The Dutch government gave this company the sole right to carry on trade between the Netherlands and Africa and the East Indies.

The Dutch established their first colony in Asia in 1619 at Batavia (now Jakarta) on the island of Java. From Java the Dutch expanded westward to take the island of Sumatra and eastward to seize the valuable Spice Islands from the Portuguese. Next came Malacca and the island of Ceylon, as well as Cochin on the southwest coast of India. In 1652 the Dutch founded a colony at the Cape of Good Hope, which helped them supply and protect their trade routes to Asia and along the African coast (see map, pages 368–69).

The Portuguese had held only strategic points along the coasts in order to control the sea lanes. The Dutch, however, realized that a successful empire required much more extensive control over both the land and the people. They did not stop with establishing a trading post at Batavia, for example, but took over the entire island of Java, with its large population and its sugar, tea, coffee, and spices.

The Dutch gained some commercial influence even in Japan. Since they had not come as missionaries, the shogun—the Japanese military ruler—allowed the Dutch to trade in Japan and to operate a trading post at Nagasaki.

In the New World, the Dutch founded colonies in the West Indies, South America, and North America. In 1626 they purchased Manhattan Island from the Indians. There they founded New Amsterdam, which later was called New York City.

The colonial empire that the Dutch established differed significantly from that of Spain. At no time did the Dutch try to convert the people they conquered to Christianity, nor did they force them to speak Dutch or to live under the laws of the Netherlands. The Dutch came as traders, to make money. In this sense the overseas empire of the Netherlands reflected the businesslike society of the home country.

Decline of the Spanish Empire

Spain's loss of the Netherlands in 1581 marked the beginning of the decline of the mighty Spanish Empire. The chief reason for this decline stemmed from the gold and silver that flowed into Spain from the colonies. Spanish rulers used the gold and silver to finance wars. Even with this wealth, they still needed to borrow money for their military campaigns. The government also minted new coins, driving up prices in Spain. And because it cost more to produce goods in Spain than in other countries, Spanish industries never developed.

An enterprising middle class might have helped Spanish industries develop despite these obstacles. Spanish nobles preferred military careers. In addition, by the early 1500s Ferdinand and Isabella had ● expelled first the Jews and the Moriscos—Moorish converts to Christianity who were suspected of secretly practicing Islam. Both the Jews and the Moriscos had once formed a vital part of Spain's middle class.

Spain thus developed an imbalance of trade. Much Spanish wealth simply passed through Spain on its way to buy goods from other nations. It was said that the treasure from the Americas was like rain on the roof—it poured down but drained away. With the gold and silver received for goods they sold to Spain, Spain's enemies—France, England, and the Netherlands—developed their own industries and grew strong at Spain's expense.

The Spanish government also adopted other unwise policies: building large warships instead of smaller commercial ships, selling monopolies that

375

SECTION 3

Closure
Have students compare the decline of the Spanish Empire to the decline of the Portuguese Empire. Ask: How were the causes of the decline of these two empires similar? How were they different? *(Students might note economic factors.)*

Review Answers
1. ***viceroy:*** representative of monarch in the Spanish colonies; ***guerrilla warfare:*** quick strikes and raids by small bands of soldiers designed to keep the opposing army off balance
2. ***Charles V:*** member of the Hapsburg family of Austria who became King of Spain and Holy Roman Emperor; ***Philip II:*** son of Charles V who succeeded to the Spanish throne after Charles divided his territory in 1556; ***Ferdinand I:*** brother of Charles V who succeeded Charles as Holy Roman Emperor
3. ***Vienna:*** city on the Danube River in Austria; ***Madrid:*** city in central Spain
4. (a) Philip II's religious views led him to order the Spanish Inquisition to redouble its efforts to wipe out heresy in Spain. **(b)** In Europe, Philip II's religious views led to a number of costly wars.
5. At no time did the Dutch attempt to convert the native populations of their colonies to Christianity, nor did they force these native populations to adopt Dutch laws and ways of life. Rather, the Dutch were

History Through the Arts

PAINTING

Rembrandt Self-portrait

The successful Dutch revolt against the Spanish monarch created a new society, one that was dominated by Protestants rather than Catholics. In this new society, the middle class rose to power and made way for a new art, concerned more with daily life than with religion.

Dutch artists, no longer dependent upon the church or the aristocracy for patrons, could paint what they liked. Their new subjects consisted of wealthy merchants who, proud of their success, clamored to have their portraits painted.

In the mid-1600s, the Netherlands probably had more painters than any other country. About this time, in 1633, the 27-year-old Rembrandt van Rijn settled in Amsterdam. He was brilliant in his ability to capture a person's spirit and personality on canvas, as is evident in this deeply moving self-portrait. It is one of 60 self-portraits that Rembrandt did during his lifetime. Here the artist, an aging and financially troubled man, lets us see inside his soul.

restricted trade, taxing wool exports, and setting up customs barriers that drove prices up. Economic discontent caused people to leave Spain.

Spain's inefficient government also contributed to the empire's decline. And in the colonies, shutting out all foreign trade encouraged attacks by England, France, and the Netherlands. Although the Spanish monarchy survived with its absolute powers intact, the country never regained its prominence in international affairs.

SECTION 3 REVIEW

1. **Define** viceroy, guerrilla warfare
2. **Identify** Charles V, Philip II, Ferdinand I
3. **Locate** Vienna, Madrid
4. **Analyzing Ideas** **(a)** How did Philip II's religious views affect government policy within Spain? **(b)** How did they affect Spain's relations with the rest of Europe?
5. **Contrasting Ideas** How did the Dutch colonial empire differ from the Spanish colonial empire?
6. **Interpreting Ideas** Why did Spanish power decline in the late 1500s?

4 France Emerged as a Great Power

Following Spain's slow decline, France emerged as the leading European power. It had recovered rapidly from the religious wars of the 1500s, thanks to the policies of King Henry IV, the first monarch of a new royal house in France, the Bourbons. Assisted by two cardinals of the Roman Catholic church, the Bourbons would make the monarchy absolute in France. Under Louis XIV, France became the dominant power in Europe.

Henry IV

Henry IV, who had lived in Navarre—a tiny kingdom that straddled the Pyrenees between France and Spain—was the first of the Bourbon family to be king of France. He had been a Huguenot, but he realized he could not rule France successfully as a member of a religious minority. He wanted a strong,

● Henry IV also hoped to better the lives of the peasants, promising them "a chicken in every pot."

● united, and peaceful kingdom; therefore, he converted to Catholicism, reportedly remarking, "Paris is well worth a Mass." However, to protect his Huguenot friends, he issued a special order, the Edict of Nantes, guaranteeing freedom of worship and political rights. This edict defused the religious conflict and ended the civil wars.

Henry also attempted to resolve other major problems. Powerful nobles had undermined royal authority in the 1500s. Henry either persuaded them to join the central government or quieted them with large bribes, thus regaining real control over the whole country.

France's financial difficulties, however, defied easy solutions. The French system of taxation was inefficient, corrupt, and unjust. As in the Roman Empire, **tax farming,** selling the right to collect taxes to private individuals called tax farmers, was common. These tax farmers paid the government a fixed sum, collected all they could, and kept any surplus. Some estimates show that less than half of the taxes collected reached the French treasury. Only the tax farmers got rich. Also, since the nobles and clergy paid no taxes, the tax burden fell most heavily on the peasants.

Henry showed wisdom in choosing the Duke of Sully as minister in charge of finances. However, even he could not make the system fair. Nobles and clergy continued to be free from taxation. Nevertheless, Sully limited the expenditures of the royal household, fired dishonest tax collectors, and supervised the tax farmers more closely. The result was a sizable surplus in the treasury, which provided funds to build up trade and industry.

Cardinal Richelieu's Program for France

Henry's son and successor, Louis XIII, was only eight years old when a fanatic monk stabbed his father to death in 1610. The boy's scheming mother, Marie de Medici, became regent—the ruler of France until Louis came of age.

At the age of 16, Louis XIII took control of the government. He was not a strong ruler, but he quickly learned to select good advisers and to support them against all opposition. Louis XIII chose as his chief minister Cardinal Richelieu (RISH • uhl • oo), who ran the government of France from 1624 until 1642. It was Richelieu who created the system by which France was governed until the French Revolution nearly 150 years later.

Learning from Pictures *Cardinal Richelieu founded the French Academy to support literature. Today the Academy still awards literary prizes.*

A political genius, Richelieu had a keen understanding of the possibilities of politics and diplomacy. He wanted to make the king supreme in France, and France supreme in Europe. To accomplish the first aim, he set out to destroy the power of the nobles and the remaining political independence of the Huguenots that had been granted by the Edict of Nantes. In addition he wanted to strengthen France economically by continuing Sully's policy of encouraging trade and industry. To make France supreme in Europe, Richelieu planned to reduce the power of the Spanish and Austrian Hapsburgs.

Huguenots. Richelieu believed that the provisions of the Edict of Nantes that allowed the Huguenots to control fortified cities were politically dangerous. The Huguenot cities, which were like states within a state, made strong centralized government impossible. In 1627 Richelieu himself, temporarily trading his cardinal's hat for a military helmet, directed the attack on the Huguenot seaport of La Rochelle and other fortified towns.

interested solely in trade.
6. Spanish power declined in the late 1500s chiefly because the importation of gold and silver from the Americas drove up prices in Spain. These high prices prevented the growth of Spanish industry. Spain's failure to develop an enterprising middle class added to such economic problems. Finally, government inefficiency and unwise policies prevented Spain from becoming a truly great power.

SECTION 4

Focus/Motivation

Point out to the class that Louis XIV of France was a firm believer in the divine right of kings. In a book entitled *Political Ideas Derived from the Very Words of Holy Scripture,* Bishop Bossuet offered a definition of the divine-right theory. On the chalkboard or an overhead projector, write the following quotation from Bishop Bossuet:

"The royal authority is sacred. God established kings as his ministers and reigns through them over his people. For such a reason the royal throne is not the throne of a man, but the throne of God himself. . . . The person of kings is sacred and . . . any attack on them is sacrilege. . . . One should obey the prince on grounds of religion and of conscience. Royal authority is absolute. The prince owes an explanation to no one for what he orders."

377

1A, 1B, 4D, 4E, a1A, a1C, a4B, a4C

● the Spanish Hapsburgs

Lead a class discussion on the divine-right theory, using the following questions as a guide: What are the characteristics of royal power? *(It is sacred and absolute.)* What is the relationship between rulers and God? *(Rulers are established by God and receive their power from God.)* What is the responsibility of subjects to their ruler? *(Subjects must obey the ruler unquestioningly.)* What limitations, if any, do you think there should be on a ruler? *(Answers will vary. Many students will suggest that the ruler should not be above the law.)*

Presentation Illustrating Ideas (Average/Group)
Have students listen to records of some of the music performed at the court of Louis XIV. Most public libraries have recordings of music by such period composers as Jean Baptiste Lully, Robert Cambert, and François Couperin. After they have listened to the recordings, ask students to discuss the ways in which the music is appropriate for Louis' ideas about royalty.

● ***Learning from Maps*** *France gained the territory of Alsace from the Holy Roman Empire after the Treaty of Westphalia. Who controlled land northwest of Alsace?*

After stubborn but futile resistance, the Huguenots asked for peace. Richelieu took away their special rights in fortified cities, but he allowed the Huguenots to continue to worship freely, hold public office, and attend schools and colleges.

Nobles. The cardinal next turned to the problem of the nobles, to finish the work that Henry IV had begun. It was a difficult and dangerous task. Moving first to crush the nobles' military power, he ordered that all fortified castles not necessary for the defense of France be leveled. The nobles complained in vain.

After Richelieu reduced the nobles' military power, he reduced their political power. With the king's consent, the cardinal appointed as governors of provinces only those who favored a strong monarchy. He also strengthened the power of the local administrators known as **intendants.** For these positions he chose middle-class people, who had no interest in advancing the power of the nobles. Richelieu gave the intendants strong administrative powers and made them directly responsible to the king, who appointed them and could remove them.

The Bohemian rebellion—and the Thirty Years' War—began in May 1618 with an incident known as the *Defenestration of Prague.* In this, Bohemian Protestants threw two Catholic officials appointed by the Holy Roman Emperor from a window of the palace of Prague.

1B, 4D, 4E, a1A, a1C

The Thirty Years' War

Richelieu's foreign policy was as determined and coldly calculating as his policy at home. He did not allow his position as a Catholic cardinal to interfere with his primary goal of strengthening France at the expense of the Hapsburgs. The Thirty Years' War offered a golden opportunity to achieve this purpose.

The Thirty Years' War actually consisted of a series of wars interrupted by intervals of peace. It began because the religious conflicts between Protestants and Catholics in Germany had never completely died down following the Peace of Augsburg in 1555. Constant rivalry continued among the more than 300 German princes, who also wanted to be independent of the Holy Roman Emperor. In addition, France, Denmark, and Sweden were all looking for opportunities to diminish the power of the Hapsburgs and the Holy Roman Empire.

When the Holy Roman Emperor suppressed a Protestant rebellion in Bohemia in 1620, Protestant German princes and Protestant Danes went to war against him. The emperor defeated the king of Denmark, who had to promise not to interfere in German affairs. Sweden then took up arms.

Cardinal Richelieu favored the Swedes over the Catholic Hapsburgs, but he believed that it was in France's interest to prolong the war without involving France directly. The other nations would become weak from fighting, while France remained strong. Most of the battles of the Thirty Years' War took place in Germany, which lost about one-third of its population to casualties, famine, and disease. In 1635, however, France actively joined the war against the Hapsburgs. By 1648 the French and their allies had claimed victory.

The participants in the Thirty Years' War signed the Treaty of Westphalia in 1648. This agreement was a landmark because it made changes that affected western Europe for centuries. Territorial changes outlined in the treaty greatly strengthened France, which received Alsace, a valuable territory along the Rhine River.

The Treaty of Westphalia also recognized the Netherlands and Switzerland as independent nations, which weakened the Hapsburgs. The Hapsburgs suffered further blows because the peace made the princes in Germany virtually independent of the Holy Roman Emperor.

Because the Austrian Hapsburgs no longer exercised any real authority in Germany, they began to look eastward rather than westward. They became more interested in their own possessions—Austria, Bohemia, and Hungary—and eventually created a new empire centered along the Danube River instead of in Germany.

The Sun King

Although France emerged powerful from the Peace of Westphalia, a series of rebellions erupted between 1648 and 1652. These rebellions are known as the Fronde, from the French word for "sling." The rebels—Frondeurs—were compared to mischievous schoolboys using slingshots when the teacher looked away. Nobles led the rebellions, but many peasants and the citizens of Paris also supported them. The Fronde threatened the centralized royal power that Richelieu and his successor Cardinal Mazarin had built up. The Frondeurs

Learning from Pictures *Louis XIV was such a patron of the arts that the 1600s in French art is sometimes called the "Century of Louis XIV."*

379

1B, 4D, 4E, a4A, a4G, a4J, a4L

READ
WRITE
INTERPRET
CONNECT
THINK

BUILDING HISTORY STUDY SKILLS

Reading About History: Making Inferences

As you study history, you often read a source in order to understand the facts of the event or events the author is explaining. For example, read the following description of Versailles:

> "The palace of Versailles cost 5 million livres out of a total state budget of 120 million livres. . . . In 1682, 22,000 workers were laboring on it; the next year, there were 36,000. In 230 acres of gardens, 1,400 fountains were installed, and 25,000 full-grown trees were transplanted in one year so that Louis XIV would not have to wait for saplings to grow."

The facts of the quotation are obvious. Thousands of people worked on the palace at Versailles (below) and the construction cost a great deal of money. By "reading between the lines," however, you can find information that is only implied—that Louis XIV possessed great power.

When you read between the lines, you are developing your reasoning ability to discover new meanings. In this way you can identify something that the writer does not actually state. Your identifications are called inferences.

How to Make Inferences

To make inferences, follow these steps.

1. Select the main idea or literal interpretation.
2. Look for clues that suggest additional meaning, such as key phrases or emotional words.
3. Add the clues to the original interpretation.
4. Create a revised meaning based on the connection between the stated idea and the implied ideas.

Developing the Skill

In the following selection from *A Description of the East India Company,* Peter Van Dam, an officer of the company, describes how the Dutch government stimulated and promoted trade by establishing the East India Company. What inferences can you make about the key to the company's success?

> "The Company's charter authorized it to make alliances with princes and potentates east of the Cape of Good Hope and beyond the Straits of Magellan, to make contracts, build fortresses and strongholds, name governors, raise troops, appoint officers of justice, and perform other necessary services for the advancement of trade. . . . The Company after the date of this charter has made great progress in the Indies. It has captured a number of fortresses from the Spaniards and the Portuguese . . . and has established trading posts at several places. It was decided as a consequence that it was desirable to establish a formal government in the Indies."

The selection states that the company could make treaties and set up governments. The key phrases "made great progress" and "as a consequence" are clues that can help you "read between the lines." These phrases indicate that although the company was set up for trade, it had many political successes. One inference that you can make is that the company owed its economic success to the political powers that it enjoyed. Control of certain political rights were linked to the development of trade. The Dutch East India Company was a political as well as an economic organization.

Practicing the skill. Read a political article in the daily paper or listen to a televised news program that focuses on a political issue. Then list 10 facts and any inferences you can make.

To apply this skill, see Applying History Study Skills on page 393.

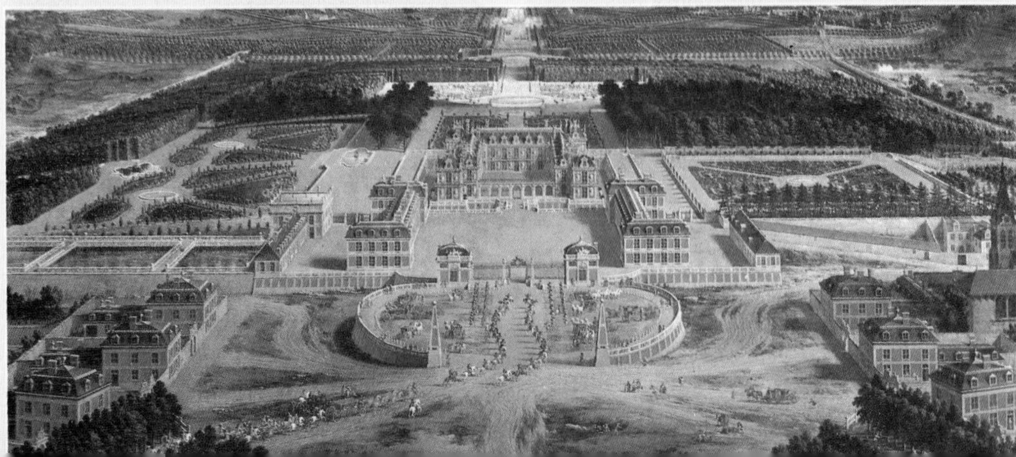

● Although extravagant, Louis XIV's court was regimented and often very dull. "Always the same pleasures, always at the same time and always with the same people," was one courtier's comment on life at Versailles.

wanted to revive the independence of local regions and the power of the nobility. Mazarin crushed the Fronde, but with some difficulty. No major attempts to restrict the royal power were made for more than 135 years.

Louis XIV—whose 72-year reign from 1643 to 1715 was the longest in French history—benefited from this strengthening of central authority. As a small boy, Louis had witnessed the rebellious nobles of the Fronde in Paris. He decided to remove himself from the dangers and humiliation he had faced, make his power absolute, and allow no opposition. To accomplish his goals, he built an enormous palace at Versailles (vur • SY), a few miles outside of Paris, where he established his court and moved the French government. The elaborate palace cost the equivalent of about 1 billion dollars in today's currency—an immense sum that strained the French economy.

The palace emphasized the grandeur and power of Louis XIV and France. Louis believed in the **divine right of kings**, meaning that God had ordained him to govern France. "L'état, c'est moi," ("I am the state,") Louis proclaimed.

To increase royal authority over the nobility, Louis insisted that the most important nobles of France live at Versailles. There they had to serve him at all times, helping him dress in the morning, joining him in the hunt—a passion with the Bourbons—performing the ceremonies of the court, and handing him his nightshirt when he went to bed. In this way Louis kept his eye on the nobles. Instead of trying to gain power by fighting the monarchy, the ● nobility now could advance only by getting royal favors and offices.

Versailles and its absolute king became the ideal of European royalty. Other monarchs built smaller copies of the palace. European nobility adopted French clothing, manners, cooking, and language. Louis XIV adopted as his personal emblem the sun, whose rays symbolized the extent of his power and influence. He looked like a king, lived like a king, and behaved like a king. He also took the business of being a king seriously.

Louis chose competent advisers, although he alone made the decisions. One of his most outstanding advisers was Jean Baptiste Colbert (kawl • BAIR), an expert in finance. Colbert, a member of the middle class, followed Sully's ideas in promoting economic development. He tried to build up French industry at home and French trade abroad. He granted government subsidies to private companies to build new industries or strengthen existing ones. He placed high tariffs on foreign imports, improved transportation, and replanted forests.

Like Sully, Colbert also tried to eliminate corruption and waste in the tax-farming system. His efforts resulted in the accumulation of enough money to finance all the economic improvements in France, maintain a large army, and support exploration abroad. Colbert encouraged French companies to establish colonies and carry on trade with Canada, the West Indies, and East Asia.

Louis XIV was concerned that the French were still not unified in their religious beliefs. The Huguenots, he believed, disturbed the unity of the country and weakened the central authority. Consequently, in 1685 he revoked the Edict of Nantes, ending the policy of toleration for Protestants. More than 100,000 productive citizens fled France rather than become Catholics. This action hurt the French economy, but Louis considered national unity and obedience to the crown more important.

The Wars of Louis XIV

Louis chose as his minister of war the Marquis de Louvois (loov • WAH), a military genius who completely reorganized the army. Soldiers were promoted on the basis of merit rather than commissions purchased for them. Louvois also created a quartermaster's department to furnish supplies to his troops so that they did not always have to live off the land. Officers and soldiers received extensive training and followed strict discipline. The officer responsible for this training, General Jean Martinet, furnished a word to the language: anyone who is a strict disciplinarian is called a *martinet*. By the early 1700s, the French had a force of 400,000 well-trained soldiers—an army larger and more powerful than Europe had ever seen.

Why did Louis XIV need such a large army? He had territorial ambitions and was convinced that French security depended on achieving France's natural frontiers. The Alps, the Mediterranean Sea, the Pyrenees, the Atlantic Ocean, and the English Channel already protected France on the southeast, south, west, and northwest. Like Richelieu, Louis wanted to make France even safer by reaching the Rhine River, its natural frontier to the northeast and east. To gain his ends, Louis XIV fought four wars between 1667 and 1713.

381

1A, 1B, 4D, 4E, a1D, a4B, a4C

SECTION 4

Closure

On the chalkboard or an overhead projector, write the following quotation by Lord Acton: "Power tends to corrupt and absolute power corrupts absolutely." Then select members of the class to debate the following: "Lord Acton's observation is perfectly illustrated by the reign of Louis XIV."

Review Answers

1. ***tax farming:*** selling the right to collect taxes to private individuals called tax farmers; ***intendant:*** local administrator in the French governmental system; ***divine right of kings:*** theory that stated God had ordained rulers to govern; ***balance of power:*** maintaining an equilibrium in international politics
2. ***Duke of Sully:*** Henry IV's minister in charge of finances; ***Marie de Medici:*** mother of Louis XIII who served as regent of France until Louis came of age; ***Cardinal Richelieu:*** Louis XIII's chief minister; ***Cardinal Mazarin:*** Richelieu's successor, chief minister for Louis XIII and Louis XIV; ***Jean Baptiste Colbert:*** expert in finance and adviser to Louis XIV; ***Marquis de Louvois:*** Louis XIV's minister of war, who completely reorganized the French army; ***Jacques Cartier:*** French explorer who sailed up the St. Lawrence River to the site of present-day Montreal
3. ***Navarre:*** tiny kingdom straddling the Pyrenees

Learning from Maps *Louis XIV extended French territory to the north, south, and east. What territory did he add to the south of France?* **Roussillon**

Louis XIV's goals alarmed the other European countries, which united to counteract the great power of France. At various times the Netherlands, England, Sweden, Spain, and Denmark, as well as Austria, Brandenburg, and other German states, formed alliances to amass enough power to equal or surpass that of France. Maintaining an equilibrium in international politics is known as the **balance of power.**

The wars took a tremendous toll on France's resources. By the end of Louis XIV's third war in 1697, the treasury was empty. Louis even melted down the royal silver to help pay for his wars.

War of the Spanish Succession. The War of the Spanish Succession was Louis XIV's last war. It was fought over the question of who should succeed to the throne of Spain. The last Spanish Hapsburg king had died in 1700, leaving the throne to a French prince, the grandson of Louis XIV.

The other European nations feared the prospect of Bourbon rulers in both Spain and France, particularly if the two thrones would ever merge under one monarch. Louis refused to promise that the two thrones would never be merged, so the nations of Europe declared war on France. Battles raged throughout Europe, on the high seas, and in America. French armies and fleets met defeat everywhere, and Louis finally submitted to a peace agreement in 1713.

The European settlement in 1713. The Treaty of Utrecht, which ended the War of the Spanish Succession, became important in the history of both Europe and America. It recognized Louis XIV's grandson as King Philip V of Spain, but provided that the French and Spanish crowns were never to be united. Great Britain had become France's chief enemy, since the treaty gave it lands in the New World at the expense of France.

The French Colonial Empire

The empire that France began to lose after the War of the Spanish Succession had begun in the early 1500s when French explorers such as Jacques Cartier (kahr•TYAY) made several voyages to North America. Cartier's voyage up the St. Lawrence River as far as Montreal gave the French a claim to much of eastern Canada. Not until 1608, however, did they make any permanent settlement. In that year Samuel de Champlain founded Quebec.

France then established several other settlements in the St. Lawrence Valley and in the Great Lakes region. The French developed a profitable fur trade with the Indians and engaged in fishing off Newfoundland and Nova Scotia.

Between 1679 and 1683, Robert de La Salle sailed down the Mississippi River to the Gulf of Mexico and claimed the entire inland region of North America for France. He named the region Louisiana in honor of King Louis XIV. French settlement in North America grew very slowly, however. Elsewhere in the New World, the French occupied Haiti and the sugar-producing islands of Guadeloupe and Martinique in the West Indies.

The French also expanded to the east. On the southeast coast of India, the French East India

Company, formed in 1664, established a trading post at Pondicherry and controlled part of India through the 1700s.

The Legacy of Louis XIV

Louis XIV died in 1715. The French people had tired of his endless wars in which so many lives were lost and so much money wasted. The long reign itself had exhausted the French. Nevertheless, despite his defeats, the Sun King had made France the most powerful nation in Europe. While Great Britain became the strongest colonial power within Europe, France remained the largest, the richest, and the most influential nation. Moreover, for more than 50 years after the king's death, the French government was remarkably stable. Louis XIV's great-grandson and successor, Louis XV, who reigned from 1715 to 1774, held unquestioned authority, though in fact a succession of ministers ran the country.

SECTION 4 REVIEW

1. **Define** tax farming, intendant, divine right of kings, balance of power
2. **Identify** Duke of Sully, Marie de Medici, Cardinal Richelieu, Cardinal Mazarin, Jean Baptiste Colbert, Marquis de Louvois, Jacques Cartier
3. **Locate** Navarre, La Rochelle, Alsace, Versailles, Alps, English Channel, Rhine River
4. **Understanding Ideas** What were the causes of the Thirty Years' War?
5. **Synthesizing Ideas** What goals did Cardinal Richelieu have for French domestic and foreign affairs?
6. **Summarizing Ideas** List some of the provisions of the Treaty of Westphalia.
7. **Interpreting Ideas** **(a)** How did the construction of Versailles contribute to the absolute power of Louis XIV? **(b)** Why did Louis XIV revoke the Edict of Nantes?

5 Monarchs in Eastern and Central Europe Expanded Their Power

While the countries of western Europe strengthened their national governments at the expense of local governments or class interests such as the nobility, the new empires of Russia, Prussia, and Austria grew up in eastern and central Europe.

Russian Isolation

After more than 200 years of Mongol rule, Russia became independent in 1480. By this time the rulers of Moscow had become the most important in Russia, and they continued to expand their power and their territory by conquests, marriages, and alliances. Moscow's rulers differed widely in their abilities, but a few had the qualities needed to build a large and powerful state.

Several factors—both physical and cultural—tended to separate Russia from western Europe. One was the Asian influence resulting from Mongol domination. Second, Western civilization had reached Russia from Constantinople and the Byzantine Empire, not from the West. Russia's religion was Eastern Orthodox rather than Roman Catholic or Protestant. Russia's use of the Cyrillic alphabet posed a barrier to communication with the rest of Europe, which used the Roman alphabet.

Most important, Russia's geography isolated the country from the rest of Europe. The country was almost entirely landlocked. The stronger kingdoms of Sweden and Poland blocked Russia from the Baltic Sea. To the south the Ottoman Turks held the Black Sea coast. To the west the vast plains of Poland and eastern Europe hindered commercial contacts. Russia's many navigable rivers did not flow into the great oceans and seas of commerce.

After the death of Ivan the Terrible in 1584, Russia underwent a long period of unrest. Nobles fought for power, false pretenders claimed the throne, and Russia's neighbors invaded. Finally, in 1613 a national assembly elected as czar Michael Romanov, the first of the Romanov dynasty that would rule Russia for 300 years.

In the mid-1600s, the Romanov monarchy faced a number of crises. It quieted rebellious townspeople by granting monopolies on trade and handicraft. It tried but failed to repress religious dissenters called "Old Believers," who broke away from the official church. The government succeeded, however, in crushing rebellious Cossacks, runaway peasants who had settled on Russia's southeastern frontier. Also, the Romanovs established serfdom more firmly during this time.

between France and Spain; ***La Rochelle:*** seaport on France's west coast; ***Alsace:*** territory along the Rhine River; ***Versailles:*** enormous palace outside Paris built by Louis XIV; ***Alps:*** mountain range on France's southeast border; ***English Channel:*** narrow body of water marking France's northwest border; ***Rhine River:*** river marking parts of France's north and northeast borders
4. The chief causes were: conflicts between Protestants and Catholics; rivalry among German rulers; and desire of France, Denmark, and Sweden to weaken the Hapsburgs and the Holy Roman Empire.
5. to make the king supreme in France, and France supreme in Europe
6. The chief provisions included: France received Alsace; Sweden received lands along the Baltic and North seas; Brandenburg received lands along the Baltic Sea and several areas in Germany; the Dutch Netherlands and Switzerland were recognized as independent; and German princes were made virtually independent of the Holy Roman Empire.
7. (a) Louis XIV moved the government and important nobles to Versailles.
(b) The Huguenots, by disturbing the religious unity of the country, threatened Louis' authority.

SECTION 5

Focus/Motivation
Have students turn to the map on page 385 and

locate the city of Archangel, Russia's principal port until the founding of St. Petersburg in 1703. Ask: What might Archangel's location on the Arctic Ocean indicate about its usefulness as a port? *(The port probably would be icebound for a good part of the year.)* Ask: What conclusions can you draw from this about the policies of Peter the Great and Catherine the Great? *(Answers will vary. Most students will note that this would explain the drive to attain warm-water ports—an integral part of the policies of both Peter and Catherine.)*

Presentation
Writing a Report (Average/Group)
Organize the class into two groups. Have members of one group research and write brief reports on the cultural changes Peter the Great made in his efforts to Westernize Russia. Ask members of the other group to research and write similar reports on the political changes made by Peter. Select members of each group to read their reports to the rest of the class.

Learning from Pictures *Peter the Great launched Russia on the path toward modernization and brutally crushed any who opposed his policies.*

By dealing with these problems firmly, the czars thus created a Russian form of absolutism. In 1682 Peter I, a czar with remarkable vision, came to the throne. He would use this power to influence both Russia and Europe.

Peter the Great

Czar Peter I ruled Russia from 1682 to 1725. An energetic giant of a man—6 foot 9 inches tall—he had dark hair and eyes, a swarthy complexion, and a prominent nose, and he suffered from epilepsy. Peter also had a violent temper and was capable of great cruelty. It has been said that he murdered his son Alexis. This intemperate and ruthless czar decided that Russia's future lay toward Europe.

One of Peter's major goals was to break through Russia's landlocked position and acquire warm-water ports on the Sea of Azov and the Black Sea. However, the Ottoman Empire blocked those ambitions. It controlled all the land between the Black Sea and the Mediterranean Sea. Peter realized that to defeat the Turks he would need two things—help from western Europe and a stronger, more efficient Russia.

Peter's foreign mission. In 1697 Peter, who often disguised himself as a private citizen, went with a Russian delegation to several countries in western Europe to negotiate an alliance against the Turks. The mission failed in this purpose, but it was of great importance because the czar learned about the West. He met scientists and artisans and trained officers to return to Russia. He even worked as a carpenter in a Dutch East India Company shipyard to learn ship construction.

Learning from Pictures *Peter the Great wore this gold crown shortly after he became czar of Russia in 1682.*

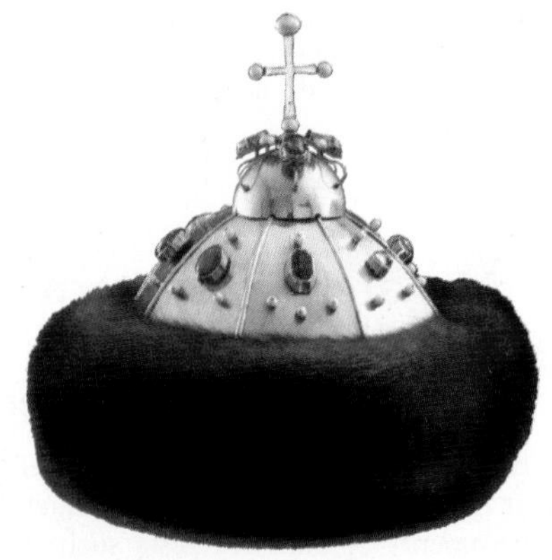

● Peter built St. Petersburg near the site of a great battle victory of the thirteenth-century Russian hero, Alexander Nevsky.
■ the Sea of Azov, the Black Sea, and the Caspian Sea

Westernization. Peter decided to remodel Russia along Western lines. He reorganized his army along French lines and equipped it with the best European weapons. He then tested this army in a long war (1700–1721) with Sweden, which resulted in Russia's gaining territory with access to the Baltic Sea. Peter also ended Sweden's short-lived role as a great power in Europe.

In this new territory at the eastern end of the Gulf of Finland (see map, this page), Peter built a completely new city, St. Petersburg (now Leningrad). In 1703 he moved the capital from Moscow to St. Petersburg, bringing the center of Russian government closer to the nations of western Europe. ● As Russia's "window to Europe," St. Petersburg symbolized the new Russian policy of Westernization.

Westernization meant that women abandon their isolation and take part in community life. The czar forced the nobles to give up their long robes—suitable for Russia's long, bitterly cold winters—and wear European-style short coats. Peter also ordered the men to shave off their long beards.

Much more important, however, were Peter's changes in Russian trade, finance, industry, and government. Armies and navies cost money, and to get it, Peter taxed nearly everything—from long beards to the birth of babies. He also encouraged the development of foreign trade and manufacturing.

In government Peter followed the absolutist ideas of Louis XIV of France. The czar had complete control of a highly centralized administration, and the nobles were merely his agents. The Orthodox church, too, fell under Peter's control. And, as in France, the monarchy also controlled local governments.

The nobility. Peter created a new service nobility, whose rank and privileges depended on the amount of government service performed rather than on family status. In return for government service, Peter granted the nobles large estates with thousands of serfs—many of them formerly free peasants. Peter's changes not only increased the number of serfs but also worsened their condition. At a time when serfdom was declining rapidly throughout western Europe, the czar began a policy of binding the Russian serfs to their lords as well as to the land. The serf's owners could buy and sell them much like slaves. Frequent uprisings occurred as the peasants lashed out at their superiors who had inflicted this unhappy lot upon them. The government brutally crushed all such rebellions.

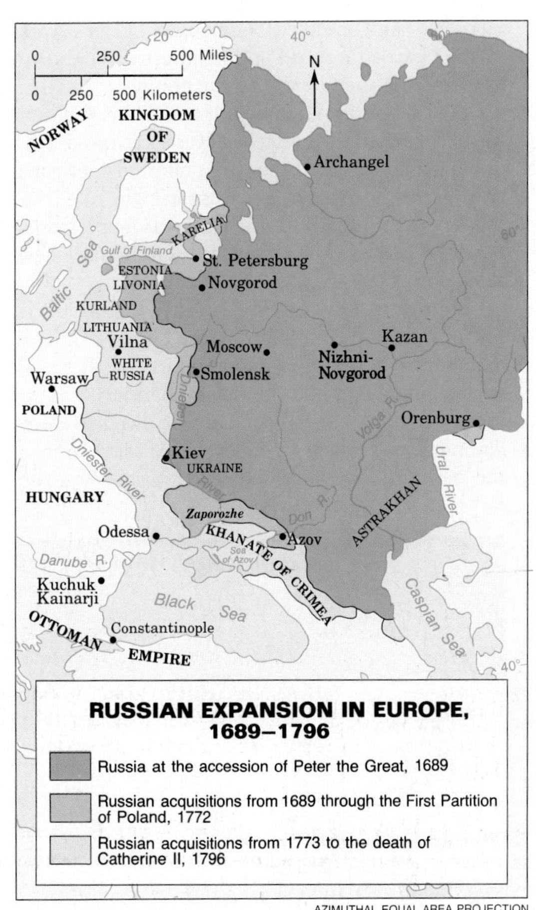

Learning from Maps *Russia eventually won the ports it needed to increase trade. On which bodies of water are these ports located?* ■

Although Peter the Great failed to westernize Russian society completely, under his leadership the nation rose to great power. He is called Peter the Great because he achieved astounding success in modernizing and centralizing the czarist monarchy and extending the nation's frontiers.

Catherine the Great

The male Romanovs who followed Peter the Great during the 1700s did not survive long. Three were

385

1B, 4D, 4E, a1D

● By the end of Catherine's reign, more than 90 percent of the Russian people were serfs.

murdered and one died of smallpox. Peter's work was not carried forward until Catherine II, known as Catherine the Great, became empress.

A princess from a small German state, Catherine had married the heir to the Russian throne. Her unpopular husband, Peter III, preferred Germans and Germany to anything Russian. He ruled for only six months in 1762 and then was murdered by powerful nobles who supported Catherine. She ruled until 1796.

Domestic and foreign policy. Catherine II certainly did not earn her title "the Great" from her domestic policy. Catherine's support for the arts, science, literature, and the theater had little meaning or value to most Russians, who lived in deep ignorance and poverty. She extended serfdom into the new lands she acquired, and the masses—the common people—lived much as they had before. Under Catherine II the nobility, however, became more westernized. They spoke French and lost touch with most of the Russian people. The vast differences between rulers and ruled help explain the undercurrent of discontent that finally exploded in revolution in the 1900s.

It was Catherine's foreign policy—a continuation of the expansionist policies of Peter the Great—that brought her fame. Russia still sought warm-water ports through the control of the Sea of Azov and the Black Sea. In a successful war against the Turks, Catherine won control of the Sea of Azov, most of the northern shore of the Black Sea, and a protectorate over the Crimea.

The Polish question. Catherine also made great territorial gains in the west. There the large

Learning from Pictures
Catherine the Great supported liberal ideas. She had schools and hospitals built, promoted education for women, and extended religious tolerance.

386

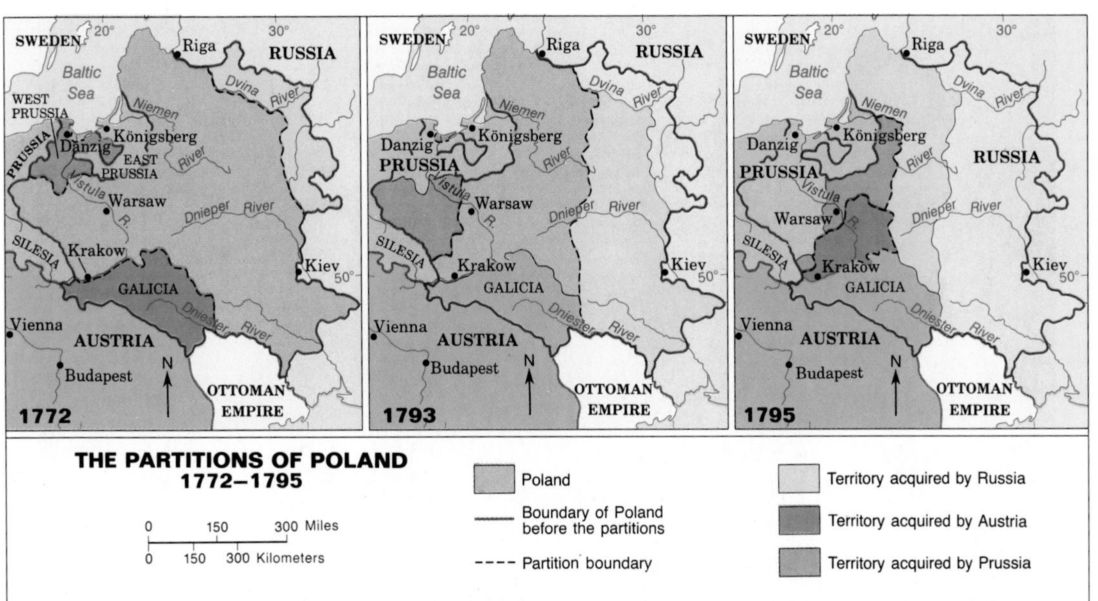

Learning from Maps *In less than 25 years Poland shrank to less than half its original size. Which country took most of Poland's land?* **Russia**

kingdom of Poland had many weaknesses. The nobles elected its kings. The election campaigns to determine who would be king invited domestic and international troubles. Prussia, Austria, France, and Russia each repeatedly plotted to put its favorite on the Polish throne.

Only nobles were represented in Poland's legislature, the Diet. The Diet rarely accomplished anything because any one member could veto any legislation being considered.

Poland contained large minority groups of various nationalities and religions. The Roman Catholic Poles and their leaders often discriminated against and oppressed the minorities, and sometimes they appealed to Prussia, Austria, or Russia for help.

In 1772 these three powers decided to take advantage of Poland's weak condition and seize a slice of Polish territory. This action is known as the First Partition of Poland (see map, this page).

Unable to resist the partition, the Poles tried in 1791 to reform and strengthen their nation by adopting a new constitution. This new constitution would have established a hereditary monarchy and abolished the veto privileges in the Diet. However, in 1793 Russia and Prussia took a second helping of Polish lands. The rebellion that broke out over this Second Partition was crushed, but it brought about the Third Partition in 1795 by Austria, Prussia, and Russia. With that, Poland disappeared from the map of Europe until 1919.

Catherine the Great had not only wrested control of the Black Sea from the Turks but also had acquired the largest share of Poland. She had added 200,000 square miles (520,000 square kilometers) of territory to her empire. Russia's borders now extended well into central Europe, and Russia became a force to consider in the European balance of power.

Russian Expansion

Russia's expansion differed from that of the western European countries. Instead of expanding overseas, Russia expanded overland. In addition to the political expansion south and west, Russian settlers, spearheaded by the freedom-loving Cossacks, moved eastward. In 1581 the Cossacks conquered the remnants of the Mongol Golden Horde and captured their capital city of Sibir. With that, the way lay open to the vast, sparsely populated region east of the Urals known as Siberia.

387

1B, 4D, 4E, a1A, a1C, a4L

● Answers will vary. Students might note that it would have increased tensions between the Soviet Union and the United States.

Learning from Pictures *Maria Theresa was one of Austria's most popular rulers. Among her 16 children was Marie Antoinette, future queen of France.*

This region's rich fur trade drew many people. Much like the pioneers of the American West, the early Russian settlers built small posts for trade and defense that grew into the towns and cities of Siberia. By the 1640s the Russians had reached the Pacific Ocean. At the Amur River they came in contact with the Chinese, who resisted Russian expansion into their country. In 1689 the Russians and Chinese signed a treaty that fixed the boundary between them north of the Amur River and provided for Chinese-Russian trade. Russia traded furs and raw materials with the Chinese in exchange for silk and tea. Also, by 1741 the Russians had crossed the Bering Strait to establish a colony in Alaska in North America.

Hapsburg Austria

The Austrian Hapsburgs lost much territory in the Thirty Years' War. In the 100 years after the war, however, Austria won new lands. These gains came in the form of lands won from the Turks in central Europe and the Balkans and territories received as a result of the Treaty of Utrecht, which ended the War of the Spanish Succession. The Hapsburgs now had an empire that extended to Hungary and the Italian Peninsula.

In 1740 Emperor Charles VI died, leaving no sons and only his 23-year-old daughter, Maria Theresa, to inherit Austria and the other Hapsburg lands. Charles had spent most of his reign trying to persuade other European rulers to sign an agreement called the Pragmatic Sanction. By this agreement the rulers of Europe promised to allow Maria Theresa to inherit the Hapsburg lands intact.

Although the laws of the Holy Roman Empire prevented Maria Theresa from being elected

What If?

Russian Expansion

Instead of expanding westward, Russia expanded overland to the east and colonized Alaska. If the Russians had colonized all of what is now Canada as well as Alaska, how might the history of the United States have been different? ●

388

empress, in 1745 she became Holy Roman Empress by making certain that her husband was elected emperor.

Maria Theresa inherited a patchwork of territories and peoples: Germans, Hungarians, Italians, Belgians, Romanians, Poles, Bohemians, Serbs, Croatians, and Slovenes. This great variety led to many conflicts of language, religion, and nationality within the empire.

Several German states envied Hapsburg power. Bavaria, in southern Germany, jealously guarded its lands and independence, sometimes by forming alliances with France against the Hapsburgs. In the north, Saxony and Hanover—whose rulers had been kings of England since 1714—also preferred to act independently of the Holy Roman Empire. Austria's chief rival, however, was Brandenburg-Prussia, a small north German state which in 1740 did not even have a common boundary with Austria.

The Rise of the Hohenzollerns

During the Middle Ages, the Hohenzollerns (HOH • uhn • zahl • uhrns) had ruled only a small territory in southern Germany. However, the ambitious family wanted to increase its power, influence, and landholdings. Near the end of the Middle Ages, one branch of the family settled in Brandenburg, in northern Germany. The ruler of Brandenburg eventually became an elector of the Holy Roman Empire.

During the Reformation the Calvinist Hohenzollerns seized lands belonging to the Catholic church in their territories. By the end of the Thirty Years' War in 1648, they ruled several widely scattered territories in Germany, including Prussia, which bordered the Baltic Sea.

One of the greatest of the Hohenzollerns, Frederick William, called the Great Elector, guided his state through the difficult last years of the Thirty Years' War. He then turned to the rebuilding and further strengthening of Brandenburg-Prussia. The Great Elector reorganized the armies of all his lands into one strong force. He also improved the tax collection system and encouraged agriculture, industry, and transportation.

The Hohenzollerns

1640–1688	Frederick William, the Great Elector
1688–1713	Frederick I
1713–1740	Frederick William I
1740–1786	Frederick II (the Great)

Learning from Pictures *Frederick the Great encouraged industry and agriculture. The German people considered him a strong king and a great military hero.*

Beginning with the reign of Frederick I, the Great Elector's successor and the first king of Prussia,* all the Hohenzollern possessions in northern Germany were called Prussia. The original duchy of Prussia became known as East Prussia.

Frederick William I. Frederick I, one of the many European rulers who tried to imitate Louis XIV of France, built a lavish palace in the style of Versailles. His son and successor, Frederick William I, disliked French ways intensely. He got rid of much of this luxury when he became king in 1713.

Frederick William I used the money he saved to strengthen Prussia. He doubled the size of the Prussian army and made it the best and most efficient

*As a reward for supporting the Hapsburgs in the War of the Spanish Succession, the Holy Roman Emperor granted Frederick I the title "King of Prussia" in 1701.

SECTION 5

Closure

Point out to students that Catherine the Great and Frederick the Great have been characterized as "enlightened despots." Such leaders justified their absolute rule by claiming to govern in the interests of their subjects. Ask students to note the differences and similarities between Catherine and Frederick and other monarchs such as Louis XIV and Peter the Great. Then ask students if they feel that Catherine and Frederick were truly enlightened.

Review Answers

1. ***Peter the Great:*** Russian czar who ruled from 1682 to 1725; ***Catherine the Great:*** princess of a small German state who, through marriage, became empress of Russia in 1762; ***Maria Theresa:*** ruler of Austria and other Hapsburg lands who came to the throne in 1740; ***Frederick William I:*** member of the Hohenzollern family who became ruler of Prussia in 1713; ***Frederick the Great:*** son of Frederick William I who built Prussia into a major European power

2. ***Moscow:*** city in central Russia; ***Black Sea:*** inland sea that formed part of the southern border of Russia; ***Sea of Azov:*** small inland sea joined to, and to the north of, the Black Sea; ***Gulf of Finland:*** northeastern extension of the Baltic Sea; ***St. Petersburg:*** city, now known as Leningrad,

at the eastern end of the Gulf of Finland; ***Crimea:*** peninsula on the northern shore of the Black Sea; ***Siberia:*** vast area to the east of the Ural Mountains; ***Amur River:*** river flowing into the Pacific Ocean that marked part of the Russian-Chinese border; ***Bavaria:*** state in southern Germany; ***Silesia:*** rich province in the north of Austrian Hapsburg lands; ***Berlin:*** capital city of Prussia
3. The following factors separated Russia from Western Europe: Russia had experienced years of Asian influence under Mongol rule; Western civilization had reached Russia through the Byzantine Empire, not through the West; Russia was almost entirely landlocked; the vast plains of Poland and eastern Europe hindered commercial contacts; and Russia's major rivers did not flow into the oceans and seas used for trade routes.
4. (a) Peter the Great tried to Westernize Russia culturally by insisting that women abandon their isolation and take part in community life. He also forced nobles to wear European-style clothing and to cut off their long beards. Politically, he followed the example of Louis XIV of France by creating a highly centralized government that completely controlled the nobles, the church, and local governments. **(b)** Catherine the Great gained the Sea of Azov, most of the northern shore of the Black Sea, and a

Learning from Maps *Great Britain gained no new territories in Europe, according to the Peace of 1763. Who controlled Silesia?* **The Hohenzollerns**

fighting force in Europe. A strict disciplinarian, Frederick William ran Prussia like a military barracks. At his palace, he treated his 14 children harshly. One of his few extravagances was recruiting, drafting, or even kidnapping tall soldiers to form his regiment of giants, the Potsdam Guards. Other European rulers knew the king of Prussia would owe them a great debt if they could furnish a soldier over six foot seven (2 meters) for this regiment.

In addition to strengthening the army, Frederick William I reorganized the civil service and encouraged trade and the development of new industries. Tax collecting and government spending were carefully planned to provide the Prussian treasury with a surplus for emergencies. And, convinced that all children should have a primary education, Frederick William I issued a decree requiring all parents to send their children to school.

Frederick the Great. Toward the end of his life, Frederick William I worried that his son Frederick had shown little interest in either military life or government service. Instead, the youth wrote poetry, played the flute, and read philosophy. The king used the harshest methods, even imprisonment, to force his heir to become the kind of son he desired. Frederick and a companion tried to escape

390

1B, 4D, 4E, a4A, a4F, a4G, a4H, a4I

● However, Frederick made little effort to end discrimination against Jews.

the country, but they were caught. The king forced the son to watch as his friend was beheaded.

After this ordeal, the son seemed to have submitted to his father's wishes. Frederick William I need not have worried. Frederick II—or Frederick the Great—proved to be an even stronger ruler than his father. He became king in 1740, the same year that Maria Theresa became ruler of Austria.

Conflict Between Prussia and Austria

Though Frederick William I had signed the Pragmatic Sanction guaranteeing Maria Theresa her Hapsburg possessions, Frederick II argued that it did not apply to him. Almost immediately after becoming king, Frederick marched the strong army his father had created into Maria Theresa's richest province, Silesia. Prussia had no legal claim to Silesia. But it was a valuable region, populated largely by Germans, with rich farmlands and iron deposits, and its possession would greatly add to Frederick's own lands. Frederick did not declare war on Austria, and he took the Austrians by surprise. He said later that in seizing Silesia he lost only 20 men and 2 officers.

European and world war. The conquest of Silesia marked the beginning of two major European wars—the War of the Austrian Succession, which lasted from 1740 to 1748, and the Seven Years' War, from 1756 to 1763. Almost all of Europe became involved at one time or another. And, because European countries had colonies overseas, the fighting was not limited to Europe. Battles were also fought, notably between Great Britain and France, in India and North America. In America the Seven Years' War is known as the French and Indian War.

At one point Prussia, surrounded by enemies in Europe, was getting financial help only from Great Britain. Three times, enemy armies invaded the Prussian capital of Berlin. Fighting against great odds, Frederick dashed from one front to another to direct his troops in holding off the invaders. For all his great skill, he was spared only because Czar Peter III of Russia, who admired Frederick, made peace with Prussia. From then on the fighting decided nothing. Both sides agreed to the Treaty of Hubertusburg in 1763. Under its terms Prussia kept Silesia.

The years of peace. Frederick the Great spent the first 23 years of his reign at war. He spent the last 23 showing that he also had a genius for organization and administration. He expanded and further improved public education and the already excellent Prussian civil service system. He continued the Hohenzollern policy of religious freedom. ● For example, when the pope dissolved the Jesuit order in 1773, Frederick II invited its members to Protestant Prussia. He made legal and court reforms and encouraged trade and manufacturing. Through Frederick's hard work and wise direction, the expanded state of Prussia recovered the prosperity it had lost during the long years of war.

Prussia continued to make territorial gains. Frederick the Great helped to bring about the First Partition of Poland in 1772. By taking Polish territory along the Baltic coast, he linked Prussia and East Prussia. When he died in 1786, Frederick left a greatly enlarged and prosperous nation. Prussia had become a formidable rival of Austria for control of the German states and a first-class power in Europe.

The Diplomatic Revolution. Maria Theresa recognized that she could never recover Silesia, but she was determined not to lose any more of her possessions. To accomplish this, she gave up the old alliance with Great Britain—first formed in the long series of wars against Louis XIV—and made instead an alliance of Hapsburg Austria with its ancient enemy, Bourbon France. This was the Diplomatic Revolution, or reversal of alliances, made during the Seven Years' War. For many years afterward, France and Austria steadfastly opposed Great Britain and Prussia.

SECTION 5 REVIEW

1. **Identify** Peter the Great, Catherine the Great, Maria Theresa, Frederick William I, Frederick the Great
2. **Locate** Moscow, Black Sea, Sea of Azov, Gulf of Finland, St. Petersburg, Crimea, Siberia, Amur River, Bavaria, Silesia, Berlin
3. **Understanding Ideas** What factors separated Russia from western Europe?
4. **Interpreting Ideas** **(a)** Describe how Peter the Great tried to Westernize Russia both culturally and politically. **(b)** How did Catherine the Great continue Peter's foreign policy?
5. **Summarizing Ideas** What conditions in Poland made it easy for foreign powers to divide the country?
6. **Analyzing Ideas** **(a)** What were the reasons for the War of the Austrian Succession? **(b)** What were its results?

protectorate over the Crimea. She also extended Russian territory westward by taking large areas of Poland.

5. Poland had several weaknesses. Nobles elected the Polish kings, and the election campaigns invited interference from foreign nations, who plotted to put their favorites on the Polish throne. Also, the Polish Diet represented only the nobles, and this body could get little done because any one member could veto legislation. Finally, the Polish Roman Catholic majority often discriminated against the country's many ethnic and religious minorities, and these minorities sometimes sought help from foreign nations.

6. (a) The War of the Austrian Succession was caused by the Prussian invasion of the Austrian Hapsburg province of Silesia in 1740. **(b)** By the terms of the Treaty of Hubertusburg, which finally ended the conflict in 1763, Prussia was allowed to keep Silesia.

391

Reviewing Important Terms

1. absolute monarchy; **2.** astrolabe; **3.** Commercial Revolution; **4.** joint-stock company; **5.** mercantilism; **6.** favorable balance of trade; **7.** tariff; **8.** subsidies; **9.** Tax farming; **10.** intendants; **11.** Middle Passage; **12.** balance of power.

Developing Critical Thinking Skills

1. mapmaking, new navigational instruments, improvements in shipbuilding, the cannon
2. The increase in population caused overcrowding, and the religious and political persecution that developed after the Reformation forced many people to leave Europe.
3. The Dutch dominated world trade, and the city of Amsterdam was one of the world's leading financial centers. Perhaps the most remarkable feature of Dutch society was its openness.
4. (a) Portuguese colonies were small, consisting of little more than trading bases. The Spanish, on the other hand, conquered large areas, established permanent settlements, and developed a centralized form of government for their colonies. **(b)** introduced the slave trade
5. (a) They lost territories, and the German princes became virtually independent of the Holy Roman Empire. **(b)** The Austrian Hapsburgs turned their attention eastward and gained new lands. **(c)** France
6. (a) Peter the Great tried to Westernize Russia culturally, while Catherine the Great primarily attempted to expand Russia's borders. **(b)** Both waged wars around the Black Sea

1B, 1D, 4D, 4E, a1A, a1C, a1D, a4A, a4F, a4H, a4L

Reteaching

Have students review the Chapter Summary and the appropriate section and questions in the Unit Synthesis. Discuss the concepts until students demonstrate a clear understanding of the material.

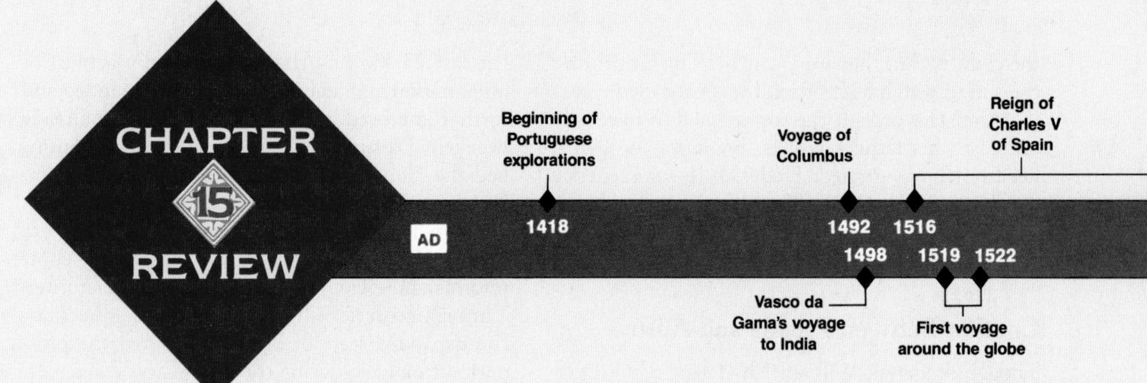

Chapter Summary

The following list contains the key concepts you have learned about European expansion and the formation of strong, centralized monarchies in Europe from about 1400 to about 1800.

1. Europeans were able to expand overseas because they developed or improved techniques in mapmaking, navigation, ship design, and weaponry.
2. The Commercial Revolution enabled Europeans to begin large-scale overseas expansion.
3. The development of new economic policies and methods also played an important part in carrying out exploration.
4. The political and economic changes associated with overseas expansion also contributed to a new economic theory called mercantilism.
5. Portuguese and Spanish explorers took the lead in discovering new lands and trade routes that paved the way for Europe's domination of the world.
6. The Portuguese developed the slave trade in Africa.
7. Spain established a vast colonial empire and became the greatest power on the European continent until the mid-1600s. It lost this superiority because it developed an imbalance of trade, squandered its resources in continuous wars, and neglected the national economy.
8. After the Dutch declared their independence from Spain, they created a large overseas empire. They dominated European commerce throughout the 1600s.
9. Cardinal Richelieu and Louis XIV humbled both the Spanish and Austrian Hapsburgs and made France an absolute monarchy. Their ambitions to achieve France's natural frontiers brought France into a series of wars.
10. During the 1700s Peter the Great and Catherine the Great extended both the powers of the central government and the boundaries of Russia.
11. War between the rising power of Hohenzollern Prussia and the Hapsburgs of Austria over the province of Silesia brought most of Europe into wars fought in Europe, North America, and India.

On a separate sheet of paper, complete the following review exercises.

Reviewing Important Terms

Supply the term that correctly completes each statement.

1. In an _______ _______ the ruler determines policy without consulting the people or their representatives and has complete power.
2. The captain of a ship at sea can determine latitude by means of an instrument called the _______.
3. The changes in the European economy were so considerable that some historians have referred to the period from 1400 to 1750 as the _______ _______.
4. A _______ _______ _______ raised money by selling shares in the company to investors.
5. An economic theory called _______ maintained that the world contained only a fixed amount of wealth and that to obtain a larger share, one country had to take some wealth away from another country.
6. By selling more goods in foreign countries than it buys, a country creates a _______ _______ _______ _______.
7. A _______ is an import tax on foreign goods.
8. Government grants of money called _______ helped establish new industries and build ships.
9. _______ _______ was a term for selling the right to collect taxes to private individuals.
10. In France, Cardinal Richelieu strengthened the power of the local administrators known as _______.
11. The _______ _______ was the shipment of slaves across the Atlantic Ocean to the West Indies or the southern colonies of British North America.
12. The principle of maintaining an equilibrium in international politics is known as the _______ _______ _______.

Developing Critical Thinking Skills

1. **Interpreting Ideas** What changes in technology made it possible for Europeans to explore foreign lands?
2. **Summarizing Ideas** What social changes in Europe created a willingness to explore and settle overseas?
3. **Evaluating Ideas** Why was Dutch society considered one of Europe's most remarkable societies?
4. **Comparing Ideas** **(a)** How was Spanish colonization different from Portuguese colonization? **(b)** How

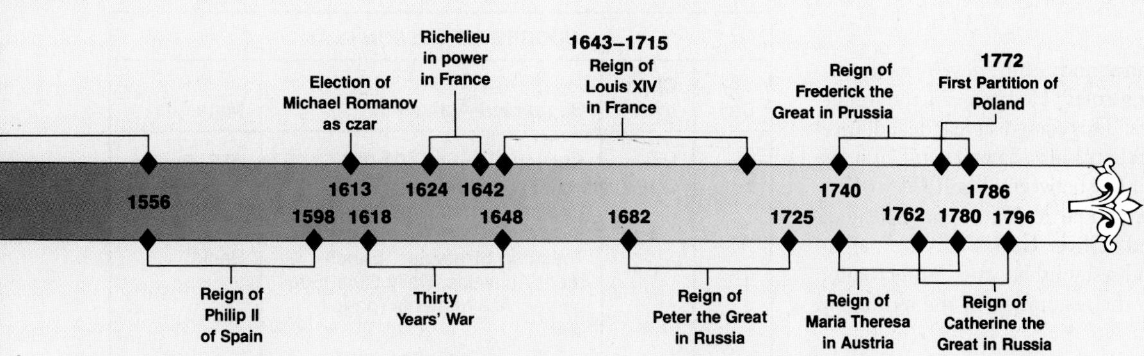

did Portuguese expansion affect the history of Africa?

5. **Understanding Ideas** **(a)** How did the Thirty Years' War weaken the Austrian Hapsburgs? **(b)** How did Austria benefit in the 100 years after the war? **(c)** Which country benefited most from this?
6. **Contrasting Ideas** **(a)** Compare the reigns of Peter the Great and Catherine the Great. **(b)** How were they similar? **(c)** What were the important accomplishments of each?
7. **Synthesizing Ideas** Explain how Cardinal Richelieu and Louis XIV strengthened the central government in France over local, religious, and class interests.
8. **Analyzing Ideas.** What factors enabled Prussia under the Hohenzollern family to create a strong, centralized government and become a great European power by the mid-1700s?

Relating Geography to History

During the Age of Exploration, certain geographical areas were important to navigation, exploration, and trade routes. Using the map on pages 360–61 and information in your textbook, explain the geographical importance of the following: **(a)** Cape of Good Hope, **(b)** Strait of Magellan, **(c)** African coast.

Relating Past to Present

1. It has been said that Louis XIV's control of a large and fine army gave him the desire to use it. Does the existence of great armies today lead to the same result? Explain your answer.
2. The 1600s are often called the "French century." What nation do you think the 1900s will be named after? Give reasons for your answer.

Applying History Study Skills

Before completing this activity, review Building History Study Skills on page 380.

Queen Elizabeth I addressed her troops on August 9, 1588, as they prepared to fight the Spanish Armada sent by Philip II. Read the selection. What inferences can you make about Queen Elizabeth?

> "Let tyrants fear! I have always so behaved myself that, under God, I have placed my chiefest strength and safeguard in the loyal hearts and good will of my subjects; and therefore I am come amongst you, as you see, at this time, not for my recreation and disport, but being resolved, in the midst and heat of the battle, to live or die amongst you all, and to lay down for my God, for my kingdom, and for my people, my honour and my blood. . . .
>
> I know I have the body of a weak and feeble woman, but I have the heart and stomach of a king, and of a king of England too, and think foul scorn that Parma or Spain, or any prince of Europe, should dare to invade the borders of my realm; to which, rather than my dishonour shall grow by me, I myself will take up arms. . . ."

1. Why is Elizabeth making the speech?
2. What does the speech tell you about Elizabeth's relationship to her people?
3. What does Elizabeth mean by "I have the body of a weak and feeble woman, but I have the heart and stomach of a king?"
4. What inferences can you make about Elizabeth's role as a ruler?
5. What inferences can be made about Elizabeth as a person?

Investigating Further

1. **Relating Literature to History** The novels of Alexander Dumas deal with France during the reign of Louis XIV. Read one of these novels to discover more about life in France during this period. *The Three Musketeers* would be especially appropriate.
2. **Conducting Research** St. Petersburg (now Leningrad), founded by Peter the Great, became a symbol of the new Russian policy of Westernization. Using books in your library, prepare a short report on St. Petersburg, concentrating mainly on its founding.
3. **Constructing a Chart** Use resources in your school or public library to find information on the Romanov czars. Then construct a family tree showing the imperial succession between Peter the Great and Catherine the Great.

and also consolidated their power by eliminating competition from the nobility. **(c)** Peter created a highly centralized government that controlled the nobles, the church, and the local governments. Catherine greatly expanded the boundaries of Russia.
7. They centralized authority by eliminating the Huguenots privileges and weakening the political power of the nobles.
8. a series of strong leaders

Relating Geography to History
(a) stopping-off point for Dutch ships on their way to the East Indies; **(b)** a passageway from the Atlantic to the Pacific; **(c)** stopping-off points for European traders and a source of slaves, gold, and ivory

Relating Past to Present
1. Answers will vary. However, students may point out that world conflicts create concern about a possible confrontation between the United States and the Soviet Union.
2. Answers will vary. However, students may suggest the United States.

Applying History Study Skills
1. She is preparing England for battle with Spain.
2. Elizabeth respects the English people, and they respect her.
3. She means that even though she may look weak she has great inner strength.
4. She was a strong leader.
5. She was a courageous woman.

CHAPTER (pages 394–419)

16 The English-speaking World Took a New Political Course

(1485–1800)

CHAPTER OVERVIEW

During the 1500s England, like France and Spain, developed a central government headed by a strong ruler. However, in the 1600s Parliament began to assert its powers. This caused a great deal of friction between Parliament and two Stuart kings, James I and Charles I. In time, this friction led to a civil war between Charles I's royalist forces and supporters of Parliament. The royalists were defeated, and in 1649 Charles was executed. Oliver Cromwell, the parliamentary leader, took control and established the Protectorate. Cromwell's death, however, led to the restoration of the monarchy in 1660.

Differences between the monarch and Parliament continued, and in the Glorious Revolution of 1688, Parliament deposed James II and declared William and Mary joint rulers. The new monarchs accepted the Bill of Rights, which limited royal authority. By the 1700s Britain was a limited constitutional monarchy.

For much of the 1500s, England had been preoccupied with home affairs and lagged behind Portugal and Spain in the race for overseas empires. The defeat of the Spanish Armada, however, encouraged England to establish colonies in India and North America. These North American colonies exercised considerable self-government, and the only area where the home country intervened was the economy. However, this intervention led to conflict when the British tried to enforce trade laws and impose new taxes. The Revolutionary War broke out between Great Britain and the American colonists in 1775, and the following year the colonists declared independence. The war ended with the American victory at Yorktown.

The new American nation was first loosely organized under the Articles of Confederation. A new constitution provided a federal system with both central authority and state governments. The central power was divided among three branches of government.

SUGGESTED LESSON PLAN

Day	Objectives	Suggested Activities	Materials
1	U4,* C1-2	Introducing the Chapter (pages 394-95) Section 1 (pages 395-400), Focus/Motivation (page 395), Presentation (page 396), Closure (page 398), Suggested Teaching Strategies, Enrichment Activity, Daily Quiz, Suggested Assignments (page 393B)	ATE, Pupil's Edition, Teacher's Resource-Bank™
2	U4, C2	Section 2 (pages 400-02), Focus/Motivation (page 400), Presentation (page 401), Closure (page 402), Suggested Teaching Strategies, Enrichment Activities, Daily Quiz, Suggested Assignments (page 393C)	ATE, Pupil's Edition, Teacher's Resource-Bank™
3	U4, C3, C4-5	Section 3 (pages 403-08), Focus/Motivation (page 403), Presentation (page 404), Closure (page 407), Suggested Teaching Strategies, Enrichment Activities, Daily Quiz, Suggested Assignments (page 393D)	ATE, Pupil's Edition, Teacher's Resource-Bank™
4	U4, C6	Section 4 (pages 410-12), Focus/Motivation (page 410), Presentation (page 410), Closure (page 412), Suggested Teaching Strategies, Enrichment Activities, Daily Quiz, Suggested Assignments (page 393E)	ATE, Pupil's Edition, Teacher's Resource-Bank™
5	U4, C7, C8-9	Section 5 (pages 412-17), Focus/Motivation (page 413), Presentation (page 413), Closure (page 416), Suggested Teaching Strategies, Enrichment Activities, Daily Quiz, Suggested Assignments (page 393E)	ATE, Pupil's Edition, Teacher's Resource-Bank™
6	U4, C1-9	Chapter 16 Form A Test, Reteaching Worksheet, Chapter 16 Form B Test	Teacher's Resource-Bank™ or Workbook and Test Booklet

*C refers to applicable Chapter Objective, U refers to applicable Unit Goal.

BOOKS FOR THE TEACHER

Ashley, Maurice. *England in the Seventeenth Century.* Penguin. Discusses the social and artistic history of England.

Boorstin, Daniel J. *The Americans: The Colonial Experience.* Random House. Examines the colonial character.

Middlekauff, Robert. *The Glorious Cause.* Oxford University Press. Describes the vital events and personalities of the American Revolution.

Wedgewood, C.V. *The Trial of Charles I.* Penguin. Covers the trial and execution of the second Stuart king.

BOOKS FOR THE STUDENT

Forbes, Esther. *Johnny Tremain.* Tells the story of the American Revolution through the eyes of a young man.

Fraser, Antonia. *Mary, Queen of Scots.* Delacorte Press. Illustrates the life of one of the more colorful figures of the 1500s.

Kurtz, Henry Ira. *John and Sebastian Cabot.* Franklin Watts. Discusses the lives of this father and son who undertook voyages of exploration for England.

Ross, Josephine. *The Tudors.* Putnam. Describes England's rise to greatness under the monarchs of this dynasty.

Williams, Jay. *The Spanish Armada.* American Heritage. Covers the events leading up to the sailing of the Armada, the battles, and the outcome.

MULTIMEDIA MATERIALS

Age of Absolute Monarchs in Europe (mp, 14 min.), Coronet. Focuses on James I of England and Louis XIV of France.

America: Making a Revolution (mp, 52 min.), Time-Life. Explains how and why the American Revolution was won.

The Elizabethan Age (fs), Educational Audio-Visual. Surveys social life in England during the reign of Elizabeth I.

The English Revolution (2 fs), New York Times. Details the tensions between Crown and Parliament that plunged England into decades of civil and political strife.

Section (pages 395–400)

1 The Tudors and the Stuarts Clashed with Parliament

SECTION OVERVIEW

Although frequently at odds with Parliament, Elizabeth I managed it well and was able to get most of what she wanted from its members. This was not the case with James I and Charles I. They violently disagreed with Parliament over several issues.

SUGGESTED TEACHING STRATEGIES

1. **Preteaching Vocabulary (Basic)** You may wish to preteach the following important vocabulary terms: revolution *(page 395)*; gentry, burgesses *(page 397)*; covenant *(page 400)*. Ask the students to list the political revolutions that have taken place in the 1900s.
2. **Organizing Ideas (Average/Group)** Have the students list in their notebooks the problems that Elizabeth I, James I, and Charles I faced in their dealings with Parliament. Then ask the students to organize this information into chart or table form. Encourage students to retain their charts and tables for revision purposes.

ENRICHMENT ACTIVITY

Writing a Biographical Sketch (Average/Group) Have the students work in small groups to prepare biographical sketches of the English rulers mentioned in this section. Sources the students might find useful include Joseph Ross's *The Tudors* (Putnam) and Antonia Fraser's *Mary, Queen of Scots* (Delacorte). In addition, the series *Kings and Queens* (St. Martin's) includes biographies of Mary Queen of Scots, Elizabeth I, James I, and Charles I. Have the groups select representatives to read their sketches to the rest of the class.

DAILY QUIZ

To assess student understanding of Section 1, give the class the following quiz. (Each item is worth 10 points.)

1. Mary I was nicknamed _______ _______ because, in her efforts to rid England of clergy who would not conform to Catholic laws, she had almost 300 people burned at the stake. *("Bloody Mary")*
2. Why did the prospect of Mary Queen of Scots' succeeding to the throne of England horrify English Protestants? *(because she was a Catholic)*
3. Philip II of Spain sent a fleet of 130 ships, which he called the _______ _______, to invade England. *(Invincible Armada)*
4. People who wanted to purify the Anglican church of all its Catholic trappings were called _______. *(Puritans)*
5. (T or F) The gentry was made up of merchants and professional people from the towns and cities. *(F)*
6. According to Henry IV of France, this king was "the wisest fool in Christendom." *(James I)*
7. James I ordered an English translation of the Bible. This Bible is known as the _______ _______, or the King James Version. *(Authorized Version)*
8. What did Charles I agree to do when he signed the Petition of Right? *(not to levy taxes without the consent of Parliament, not to declare martial law nor to quarter soldiers in private homes during peacetime, and not to imprison people without a specific charge)*
9. Charles I used the Court of _______ _______ to prosecute critics of government policy. The Parliament of 1640 later disbanded this court. *(Star Chamber)*
10. (T or F) For the Scottish Presbyterians, loyalty to their church — the Kirk — came before loyalty and obedience to King Charles I. *(T)*

SUGGESTED ASSIGNMENTS

1. **Profile Worksheet (Basic)** Have students complete Profile Worksheet 16 in the TEACHER'S RESOURCEBANK ™.

2. **Researching (Challenging)** Inform students that people in Great Britain commemorate the Gunpowder Plot each November 5 by burning Guy Fawkes in effigy and setting off fireworks. Interested students might like to use resources in the school and public libraries to find out more about either the plot that gave rise to this celebration or the celebration itself. Have the students share their findings with the rest of the class.

Section 2 (pages 400–402) The King and Commons Went to War

SECTION OVERVIEW

To raise money to crush the Scottish and Irish rebellions, Charles I had to call Parliament into session. However, Parliament continued to work at reducing his authority. When radical members attempted to pass a bill reorganizing the Anglican church, Charles forcibly entered the House of Commons to arrest them. As a result of this unwise act, a civil war erupted. The parliamentary forces were victorious, and Charles I was executed. Oliver Cromwell assumed leadership of the country as Lord Protector. In 1660, however, the monarchy was restored when Parliament invited Charles II to take the throne.

SUGGESTED TEACHING STRATEGIES

1. **Preteaching Vocabulary (Basic)** You may wish to preteach the following important vocabulary term: constitution *(page 402)*. Ask: What is the importance of a constitution to the smooth operation of government?
2. **Defending a Point of View (Average/Group)** Select members of the class to make short presentations defending one of the following statements:
   (a) Charles I was within his rights when he entered the House of Commons to arrest the radical leaders.
   (b) Parliament's cause in the civil war was just.
   (c) Charles I was guilty of arrogance, not treason, and he should not have been executed.

   After students have completed their presentations, encourage all members of the class to debate the points of view made in the three statements.

ENRICHMENT ACTIVITY

Debating a Topic (Challenging) Point out to the students that at the beginning of the civil war, Parliament banned the playing of sports and the performance of plays since they were "spectacles of pleasure, too commonly expressing . . . mirth and levity" and not in keeping with the solemn times at hand. Interested students might like to hold a debate on the appropriateness of allowing entertainments to continue during times of national danger or periods of national mourning. The debate topic might be "All sports events and entertainments should be canceled during times of war." After the debate, ask the rest of the class for their opinions on the topic.

DAILY QUIZ

To assess student understanding of Section 2, give the class the following quiz. (Each item is worth 10 points.)

1. The religious group whose members controlled the House of Commons during the Long Parliament was the ______. *(Puritans)*
2. (T or F) Religious tensions in Ireland, Scotland, and England contributed to the outbreak of civil war in 1642. *(T)*
3. The royalists, or ______, supported Charles I in the civil war. *(Cavaliers)*
4. Oliver Cromwell, the parliamentary leader, organized his forces into the ______ ______ ______. *(New Model Army)*
5. Why did Charles I's execution strengthen the cause of the monarchy? *(because many people considered Charles a martyr)*
6. How did Cromwell try to control England's social life? *(by closing theaters and limiting popular entertainment)*
7. From 1653 to 1658, Cromwell held the title of Lord ______. *(Protector)*
8. (T or F) The Navigation Act of 1651 permitted English goods to be carried on Dutch ships to reduce English transportation costs. *(F)*
9. (T or F) Cromwell ended up dismissing Parliament and ruling alone, just as Charles I had done. *(T)*
10. The new Parliament of 1660 invited ______ to return to England from exile and take the throne. *(Charles II)*

SUGGESTED ASSIGNMENTS

1. **Writing a Diary (Average/Group)** Have students prepare diary entries for a day in the life of either a royalist soldier or a member of the New Model Army. In their diary entries, students might like to explore the reasons why these soldiers decided to join the king's cause or Parliament's. Ask for volunteers to read their entries to the class. Use these diary entries as the basis for a class discussion on the civil war.
2. **Researching a Topic (Challenging)** Have interested students do further research on the battles of the civil war. Suggest that students use resources in the school and public libraries to complete their research. Have students present their findings in a written, illustrated report.

Section 3 (pages 403–409) England Established a Constitutional Monarchy

SECTION OVERVIEW

During the reign of Charles II, the English political scene began to change with the emergence of the first political parties. In addition, individual rights were strengthened with the passage of the Habeas Corpus Act. Then, with the Glorious Revolution, James II was forced to abdicate and Parliament invited William and Mary to become joint rulers. Parliament asserted its authority over the monarchy with the Bill of Rights, and the cabinet became increasingly important. By the 1700s Great Britain had become a limited constitutional monarchy.

SUGGESTED TEACHING STRATEGIES

1. **Preteaching Vocabulary (Basic)** You may wish to preteach the following important vocabulary terms: natural rights, habeas corpus *(page 405)*; cabinet *(page 407)*; prime minister, limited constitutional monarchy *(page 408)*. Ask students why Great Britain's system of government is called a limited constitutional monarchy. *(There are limits on the monarch's powers.)* Ask them to name the governmental system of the United States. *(federal republic)*
2. **Writing a Letter (Average/Group)** Ask the students to imagine they have lived through the Commonwealth and Restoration periods in England. Have them write a letter to a friend in another country describing life during these times. The letter should contain a comparison of life in the two periods. Students may want to check encyclopedias and other books in the library for more information on the topic. Encourage the students to read their letters to the rest of the class.

*3. **READING ABOUT HISTORY: Identifying a Point of View (Basic)** To reinforce the skill lesson presented on page 409, have students explain how a point of view is different from a fact.

ENRICHMENT ACTIVITIES

1. **Role-playing (Average/Group)** Organize interested students into two groups, one representing the Whigs, the other representing the Tories. Have the students consult this textbook or other history books to discover the issues that divided these two political parties. The two groups should then meet separately and develop logical arguments on the issues. Then bring the two groups together in a mock session of Parliament. You may wish to serve as the Speaker to ensure that members are recognized when they want to speak.
2. **Comparing Ideas (Challenging)** Interested students may like to take part in a panel discussion comparing the views of Thomas Hobbes and John Locke. Suggest that they use the following sources to research the works of these two philosophers: Stuart Hampshire, ed., *Age of Reason* (Mentor); Isaiah Berlin, ed., *Age of Enlightenment* (Mentor); and W. T. Jones's *Hobbes to Hume* (Harcourt Brace Jovanovich).
3. **Writing a Report (Challenging)** Interested students might like to write a report on the theater in England during the Restoration period. Suggest that they include in their reports such subjects as famous actors of the period, the types of theaters used, and the plays performed. A useful source of information on this topic is Emmett L. Avery and Arthur H. Scouten's *The London Stage, 1660-1700* (Southern Illinois University Press).

DAILY QUIZ

To assess student understanding of Section 3, give the class the following quiz. (Each item is worth 10 points.)

1. (T or F) The beginning of the Restoration was marked by the return of a Stuart king to the English throne. *(T)*
2. (T or F) Charles II continued the commercial policies established by Lord Protector Oliver Cromwell during the Commonwealth. *(T)*
3. The political party that supported a strong hereditary monarchy was called the ______ Party. *(Tory)*
4. The ______ favored a weak monarch and a strong Parliament. *(Whigs)*
5. What event caused the Glorious Revolution? *(James II's Catholic wife gave birth to a son — the heir to the throne — who would be raised as a Catholic.)*
6. The philosopher who set down his political ideas in a book titled *Leviathan* was ______ ______. (Thomas Hobbes)
7. ______ ______ believed that rulers who failed to protect the people's natural rights had broken the social contract between ruler and ruled and could be replaced. *(John Locke)*
8. The ______ ______ ______ declared that Parliament would choose the ruler, who would merely be an official subject to parliamentary laws. *(Bill of Rights)*
9. How did the make up of the cabinet change during the reign of William and Mary? *(Before that time the cabinet had been made up of Whigs and Tories. During William and Mary's reign, it became clear that government ran more smoothly when the cabinet consisted of members of the majority party in the House of Commons of Parliament.)*
10. Why is Great Britain a limited constitutional monarchy? *(There are limits on the monarch's powers.)*

SUGGESTED ASSIGNMENTS

1. **Critical Thinking Worksheet (Basic)** Have students complete Critical Thinking Worksheet 35 in the TEACHER'S RESOURCEBANK™.
2. **Critical Thinking Worksheet (Basic)** Have students complete Critical Thinking Worksheet 36 in the TEACHER'S RESOURCEBANK™.
3. **Skill Worksheet (Basic)** Have students complete Skill Worksheet 16 in the TEACHER'S RESOURCEBANK™.

Section 4 (pages 410–412)

English Sea Power Helped Establish a Large Empire

SECTION OVERVIEW

The English were latecomers in the race for colonial empires. The defeat of the Spanish Armada, however, encouraged the English to found colonies in the Americas and Asia. Merchants established companies to trade in these new lands, and by the 1700s England had become a leader in world commerce and a major colonial power.

SUGGESTED TEACHING STRATEGIES

1. **Preteaching Vocabulary (Basic)** You may wish to preteach the following important vocabulary term: sea dogs *(page 410)*. Ask students what part the sea dogs played in England's colonial expansion. *(They attacked Spanish treasure ships.)*
2. **Organizing Ideas (Average/Group)** Have students construct a chart showing the information on the English colonial empire presented in this section. Suggest that they use such column-headings as *Location, Government,* and *Economic Practices* in their charts. Use these charts as a starting point for a discussion comparing the colonial empires of Portugal, Spain, the Dutch Netherlands, France, and England.

ENRICHMENT ACTIVITY

Interpreting Illustrations (Average/Group) Have students study the picture of Sir Francis Drake's ship *Golden Hind* on page 410. Then ask the students the following questions. What would life have been like on the *Golden Hind?* What are some of the problems that might have arisen for Drake and his sailors on their circumnavigation of the world? *(Life would have been hard. Sailors faced the threats of storms and homesickness.)*

DAILY QUIZ

To assess student understanding of Section 4, give the class the following quiz. (Each item is worth 10 points.)

1. ________ ________, an Italian sea captain, explored the coasts of Newfoundland, Nova Scotia, and New England in 1497 to give England a claim in the New World. *(John Cabot)*
2. (T or F) English sea dogs like Francis Drake and John Hawkins were both traders and pirates. *(T)*
3. The attacks by the English sea dogs greatly angered ________ of Spain. *(Philip II)*
4. The English East India Company set up trading posts at Bombay, ________, and ________ in India. *(Calcutta, Madras)*
5. While searching for the ________ ________, Henry Hudson explored the river in eastern North America and the bay in northern Canada that now bear his name. *(Northwest Passage)*
6. (T or F) The English founded settlements in North America primarily for commercial purposes. *(T)*
7. (T or F) Unlike other colonial empires, the English did not use slavery in their colonies. *(F)*
8. (T or F) Self-government set England's empire apart from other European colonial empires. *(T)*
9. The first mercantilist regulation passed by the English government that affected the North American colonies was the ________ ________ of 1651. *(Navigation Act)*
10. ________ became a respectable occupation as the American colonists sought ways to evade mercantilist trade regulations. *(Smuggling)*

SUGGESTED ASSIGNMENTS

1. **Writing an Essay (Average/Group)** Have the students prepare an essay on the English sea dogs and other pirates of the period covered in Section 4. Suggest that the students use the following sources in preparing their essays: George Sanderlin's *The Sea-Dragon* (Harper & Row); Hugh F. Rankin's *Golden Age of Piracy* (Holt, Rinehart and Winston); and Franklin R. Stockton's *Buccaneers and Pirates of Our Coast* (Macmillan). During the next lesson, ask for volunteers to read their essays to the rest of the class.
2. **Relating Past and Present (Average/Group)** Ask the students to write a report on the various reasons why people came to the Americas to settle. To gather information for their reports, the students might read "Why English Settlers Came to America" in Edwin Fenton's *Thirty-two Problems in World History* (Scott, Foresman). Ask the students to include in the final paragraph of their reports speculation on why people emigrate to North America today. Use the students' reports as a starting point for a discussion on how motives for emigration have or have not changed since colonial times.

Section 5 (pages 412–417)
The American Revolution Created a New Nation

SECTION OVERVIEW

After the French and Indian War, Great Britain tried to enforce trade laws and impose new taxes on the colonies. Colonial resistance to these British policies led to open conflict in 1775. Fighting continued until 1783 when, after a devastating defeat at Yorktown, the British recognized American independence. The new American nation was first governed by the Articles of Confederation. A new constitution, ratified in 1788, established a federal system of government.

SUGGESTED TEACHING STRATEGIES

1. **Preteaching Vocabulary (Basic)** You may wish to preteach the following important vocabulary terms: federal system of government *(page 416)*, executive branch, legislative branch, judicial branch *(page 417)*. Ask the students why the framers of the Constitution divided the federal government into three branches. *(so that no one branch would be too powerful)*
2. **Analyzing Ideas (Average/Group)** Read the Declaration of Independence aloud to the class. Have the students list the arguments for independence enumerated in the document. Then ask them to point out the ways in which the ideas of Thomas

Hobbes and John Locke are reflected in the Declaration. Frederick Gentiles and Melvin Steinfield's *Hang-ups from Way Back*, vol. 2 (Harper & Row), which discusses the influence of various philosophers on the Declaration, might help the students in their analysis of the document.

ENRICHMENT ACTIVITIES

1. **Preparing an Oral Report (Average/Group)** Have interested students research and prepare oral reports on American art and crafts of the colonial period, such as metalworking, furniture making , architecture, and painting. Useful sources for information on this topic include encyclopedias, illustrated art books in the library, and issues of *American Heritage* magazine. Encourage the students to read their reports to the rest of the class.
2. **Holding a Panel Discussion (Challenging)** Have three students assume the roles of the following colonists: radical Samuel Adams, moderate John Dickinson, and conservative Thomas Hutchinson. These three should discuss what actions the colonies should pursue in response to Great Britain's policies. The students may refer to Larry Cuban and Philip Roden's *Promise of America: The Starting Line* (Scott, Foresman) for a model of this discussion. Students might also consult American history textbooks and encyclopedias for further information.

DAILY QUIZ

To assess student understanding of Section 5, give the class the following quiz. (Each item is worth 10 points.)

1. The _______ _______ _______ War, known as the Seven Years' War in Europe, settled British-French rivalry in North America. *(French and Indian)*
2. In response to the Stamp Act of 1765, the colonists began a trade _______ against British products. *(boycott)*
3. The colonists' rallying cry soon became "no taxation without _______." *(representation)*
4. What did the colonists call the laws the British government passed in response to the Boston Tea Party? *(Intolerable Acts)*
5. Among the "unalienable rights" mentioned in the Declaration of Independence were life, _______, and the _______ _______ _______. *(liberty, pursuit of happiness)*
6. (T or F) Many British people were against the Revolutionary War, and some even sympathized with the American efforts to win independence. *(T)*
7. (T or F) The American colonists' strength in the Revolutionary War lay in the organization of their army and navy. *(F)*
8. The aid of what European country was a major factor in the American victory at Yorktown? *(France)*
9. The United States Constitution divided governmental power between the central, or _______, government and the individual _______ governments. *(federal, state)*
10. The first _______ amendments to the Constitution, known collectively as the _______ _______ _______, guaranteed the basic rights of all citizens of the United States. *(10; Bill of Rights)*

SUGGESTED ASSIGNMENTS

1. **Constructing a Chart (Basic)** Have the students construct charts showing the causes of the American Revolution. Suggest that they use such column-headings as *Political, Economic,* and *Social* in their charts. Encourage the students to retain their charts for revision purposes.
2. **Review Worksheet (Basic)** Have students complete Review Worksheet 16 in the TEACHER'S RESOURCEBANK™.

For suggested lesson plan, additional teaching strategies, enrichment activities, daily quizzes, and suggested assignments, see pages 393A-393F.

Introducing the Chapter
On the chalkboard or an overhead projector, write the following excerpt from a speech Elizabeth I made to Parliament in 1601.

"There will never a queen sit in my seat with more zeal to my country, care for my subjects, and that sooner with willingness will venture her life for your good and safety, than myself. For it is not my desire to live nor reign longer than my life and reign shall be for your good. And though you have had, and may have many princes, more mighty and wise, sitting in this state; yet you never had, or shall have any that will be more careful and loving."

Lead the class in a discussion, using the following questions as a guide: What seems to be Elizabeth I's view of the purpose of a monarch? *(Answers will vary. Most students will suggest that Elizabeth believes a monarch should serve his or her subjects.)* What impact do you think this speech might have had on members of Parliament? *(Answers will vary. Some students will suggest that the members of Parliament would be ready to cooperate with Elizabeth because of the caring attitude.)* How does Elizabeth I's view of monarchy compare to that of Louis XIV of France? *(Answers will vary. Most students will note that Louis XIV thought that he was ordained to rule by God, and he owed no one an*

CHAPTER 16

The English-speaking World Took a New Political Course

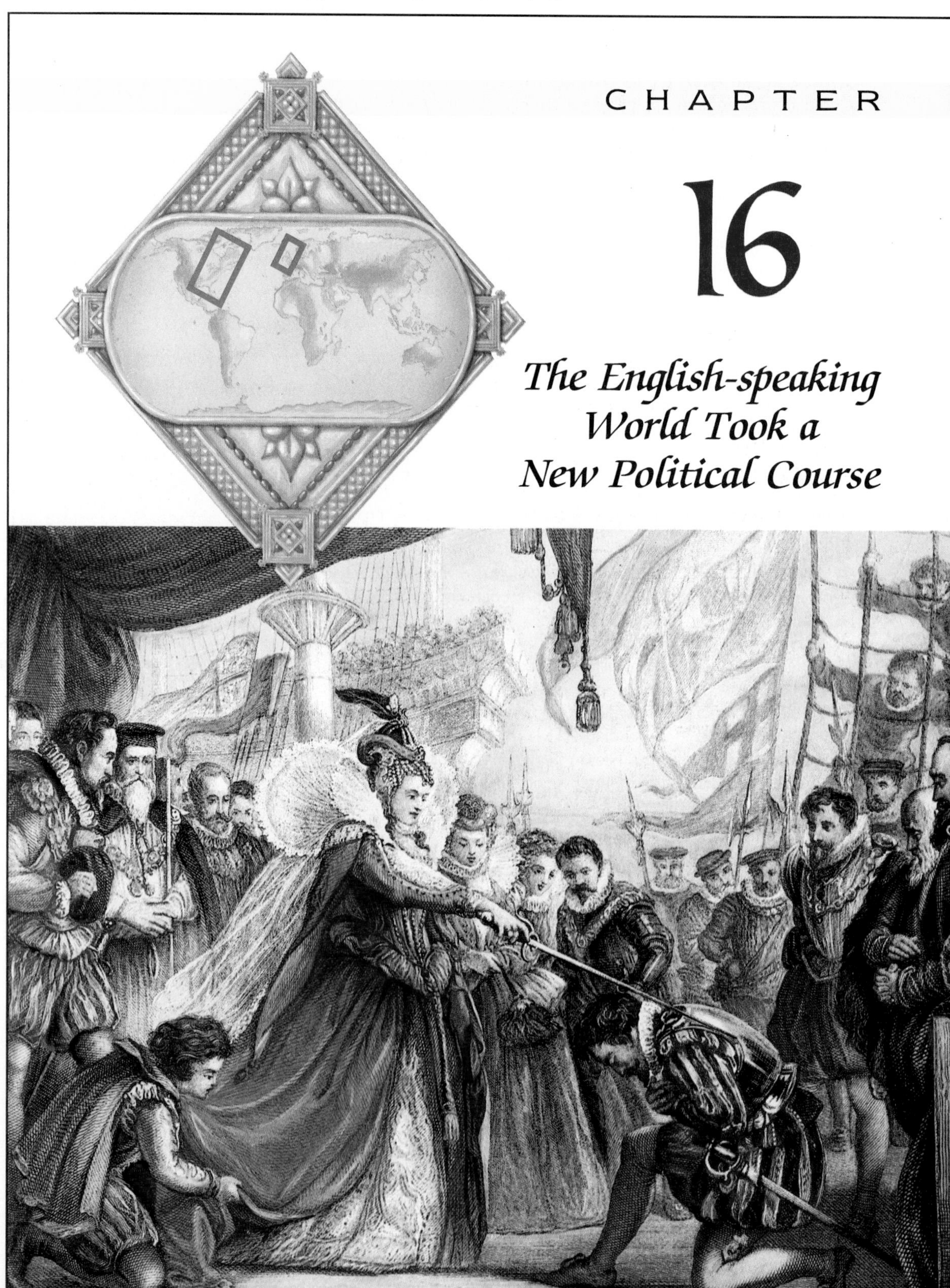

CHAPTER FOCUS

Place The British Isles, North America, India

Time 1485–1800

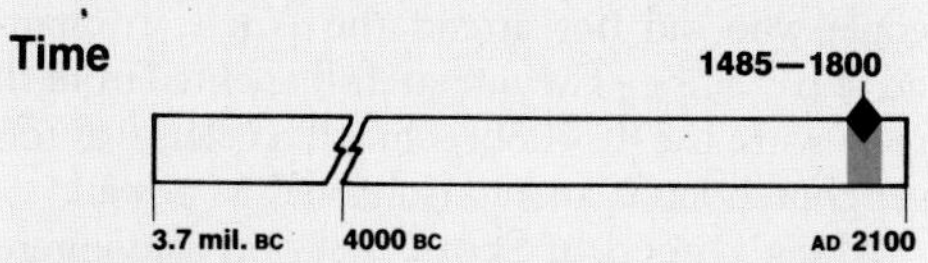

Significance

England experienced much turmoil from the end of the 1400s to the beginning of the 1800s. The Tudor monarchs, who ruled from 1485 to 1603, had established Protestantism in England by naming the Anglican church the official church of England. However, other reformers called *Puritans* wanted to go further in reforming the church.

Continual clashes occurred between those who favored the Puritans and Parliament and those who favored the Anglican church and the monarchy. The struggle between these two factions erupted into a violent civil war.

In addition to the problems at home, rebellions in Ireland, Scotland, and later the North American colonies also troubled English rulers. Through all of this upheaval, however, England moved toward a parliamentary government and emerged as one of the strongest empires in the world.

Terms to Define

revolution	covenant	habeas corpus
gentry	constitution	cabinet
burgesses	natural rights	sea dogs

People to Identify

Elizabeth I	James II	Thomas Jefferson
Charles I	Sir Francis Drake	
Oliver Cromwell	Henry Hudson	Paul Revere

Places to Locate

English Channel	Jamestown
Ulster	Mississippi River
Bombay	Yorktown

Questions to Guide Your Reading

1 How did the Tudor monarchs and the Stuart monarchs differ in their relationship with Parliament?
2 What issues divided the English monarchy and Parliament?
3 Why did the King and the commons go to war in England?
4 How did England's colonial empire differ from those of other European powers?
5 What political arguments did the supporters of the Glorious Revolution and the American Revolution use to justify their actions?

Elizabeth I, the forceful queen who ruled England from 1558 to 1603, had a strong, sometimes contradictory personality. In the following passage, the author Lytton Strachey gives us a glimpse of this fascinating and vibrant queen.

> *"While the Spanish ambassador declared that ten thousand devils possessed her, the ordinary Englishman saw in King Hal's full-blooded daughter a Queen after his own heart. She swore; she spat; she struck with her fist when she was angry; she roared with laughter when she was amused. And she was often amused. A radiant atmosphere of humour coloured and softened the harsh lines of her destiny, and buoyed her up along the zigzags of her dreadful path. Her response to every stimulus was immediate and rich: to the folly of the moment, to the clash and horror of great events, her soul leapt out with a vivacity, an abandonment, a complete awareness of the situation, which made her, which makes her still, a fascinating spectacle."*

Elizabeth I, one of England's strongest monarchs, led her country successfully through a very turbulent time in its history.

1 The Tudors and the Stuarts Clashed with Parliament

Chapter 15 described the struggle between central governments and local authorities for control in European countries. In these countries the central governments usually won, and the most extreme form of central government—absolute monarchy—became common. Of all the revolts in the mid-1600s, the most severe took place in England. The clash there led in the 1640s and 1650s to civil war and **revolution**—a radical attempt to change the very structure of a country's government. Although the English Revolution did not succeed, it influenced both English history and political ideas throughout Europe.

The Reign of Mary Tudor

In the late 1400s, a new royal family, the Tudors, became England's rulers. Following the turbulence

◀ ***Elizabeth I knighting Francis Drake***

explanation for his behavior. Elizabeth viewed the monarch as the servant of his or her subjects.)

Point out that Elizabeth I respected the power of Parliament and worked to avoid confrontations with that body. As they read Chapter 16, have students note the attitudes toward Parliament of Elizabeth's successors and the problems these attitudes caused.

Chapter Objectives

After studying Chapter 16, students will be able to:

1. Identify the problems that faced Elizabeth I.
2. Describe the causes of the English civil war.
3. Compare the political philosophies of Hobbes and Locke.
4. Identify the safeguards against absolute monarchy established in England.
5. Explain why the British government is described as a limited constitutional monarchy.
6. List the characteristics of England's North American colonies.
7. Trace the events of the American Revolution.
8. Describe the federal system of government established by the United States Constitution.
9. Explain the worldwide effect of United States independence.

SECTION 1

Focus/Motivation

Have the students study the chart on page 398.

1B, 4A, 4D, a1D

● Many people believe the plot was instigated by agents of Elizabeth's secretary of state, Sir Francis Walsingham.

Then lead the class in a discussion, using the following questions as a guide: What was the relationship between Elizabeth I and Mary Queen of Scots? *(Most students will note that they were cousins.)* What was the relationship between Mary Queen of Scots and James I of England? *(They were mother and son.)* On what was James I's claim to the English throne based? *(He was the great-great-grandson of Henry VII.)* What evidence does the chart provide that Henry VII used marriage as a political and diplomatic tool? *(He attempted to build alliances with leading rulers of Europe by having his children marry into their families.)* Why do you think Parliament continually urged Elizabeth I to marry and have children? *(If Elizabeth married and had children, the Protestant succession would be assured. However, if Elizabeth died childless, the throne might pass to one of Elizabeth's Catholic relatives.)*

Presentation
Identifying Ideas
(Average/Group)

Write the following lists on the chalkboard or an overhead projector. Then ask students to match the rulers with the policies. Point out that rulers may have more than one policy.

1. Mary I
2. Elizabeth I
3. James I
4. Charles I

Learning from Pictures *This coin (both sides pictured) commemorates the wedding of Philip II of Spain to Mary I of England.*

of the Wars of the Roses, the first Tudor king, Henry VII, brought stability and prosperity to England. The Tudors made the same efforts to strengthen their powers as did the rulers of France and Spain. Of the five Tudor monarchs, Henry VIII, who reigned from 1509 to 1547, and his daughter Elizabeth I, who reigned from 1558 to 1603, had the greatest success. Henry VIII established a new official church in England, the Anglican church.

After the short reign of sickly Edward VI, Mary I, the oldest daughter of Henry VIII, ascended the throne at the age of 37 and became the first reigning queen of England. Her unhappiness and her devotion to Catholicism shaped her attitude. Though she did not lack courage or kindliness, she had a fierce determination to make England a Catholic nation again. Her unpopular marriage to Philip II of Spain, the leader of the Counter-Reformation, worried her Protestant subjects. Their worries proved to be well-founded. Mary, determined to rid England of those clergy who would not conform to the laws of the Catholic church, burned close to 300 people at the stake, including Thomas Cranmer, the archbishop of Canterbury. For this reason she was given the nickname "Bloody Mary." The queen's persecutions shocked the English, and Mary totally failed to destroy Protestantism.

The Reign of Elizabeth I

When Mary I died in 1558, her half-sister Elizabeth became queen. Elizabeth I used parliamentary acts to help make England Protestant. For example, people who did not attend the Anglican church had to pay a fine. The monarchy benefited from the break with the Catholic church because it took over church lands and consolidated its powers.

Mary Queen of Scots. Religion also entered into the question of who should succeed Elizabeth. In a monarchy the oldest child usually inherits the throne. But Elizabeth did not marry and had no children. Her closest relative and heir—Mary Stuart, queen of Scotland, or Mary Queen of Scots as she is more commonly known—was Catholic.

The prospect of Mary Queen of Scots becoming queen of England horrified English Protestants. However, it also delayed the plans of Philip II of Spain to invade England and force a Catholic ruler on the English people.

In 1568, to escape problems in Scotland, the headstrong Mary fled to England, only to be imprisoned by Elizabeth. Later, Mary foolishly plotted with Philip II's ambassadors in England to kill Elizabeth and seize the English throne. Reluctantly, Elizabeth signed the Scottish queen's death warrant, and in 1587 Mary was beheaded. With Mary dead, Philip II no longer had any reason to postpone his plans to invade England. ●

The Spanish Armada. In 1588 Philip sent a fleet of 130 ships, which he called the "Invincible Armada," north toward the English Channel. The English summoned all their ships to intercept the Spanish Armada. The swift, maneuverable English ships had the advantage. They also had guns that fired faster and had a longer range than the guns on the Spanish ships. The English managed to damage and sink a number of the lumbering Spanish vessels. The Spaniards ran low on ammunition and attempted to escape to the North Sea. A terrible storm—the "Protestant Wind"—began to blow, further battering the Spanish vessels. Some of the Spanish ships reached the open sea and attempted to limp home around Scotland and Ireland. Many of them foundered on the rocky, desolate coasts of these two countries. Only about 50 ships managed to return to Spain. The combination of bad weather and skilled English seafaring had proved deadly for Philip II's enormous Armada. With Spain no longer a threat and Elizabeth's throne and

However, Elizabeth did not force her subjects to accept her religious beliefs, for she did not want "to pry windows into men's souls."

Protestantism secure, England turned to exploring overseas. However, Elizabeth's government still faced two major problems.

The religious problem. The religious issue in England was unsettled. The monarchy had led the break with the pope and the establishment of Protestantism in England, but many people believed that the change had not gone far enough. They wanted to "purify" the English church even further. These people, called *Puritans,* objected to the continuation of many Catholic practices. Although the Anglican church had abolished the Mass, it still had bishops. Priests still dressed in elaborate robes for religious services, and the congregation still knelt during services. The Puritans thought these customs too Catholic and wanted to abolish them.

Like many monarchs of the time, the Protestant Tudors thought religious disunity threatened England's stability. They wanted all their subjects to be united in the Anglican faith. Therefore, they persecuted both the remaining Catholics and the Puritans. Not only did they fail to stamp out either group, they created a dangerous enemy in the Puritans.

The Puritans set very strict moral standards and became increasingly unhappy about the Anglican church and the quality of the clergy. Eventually, that unhappiness made the Puritans willing to revolt against their ruler. Queen Elizabeth, however, refused to allow any changes in the Anglican church. The Anglican church became a permanent institution largely through the force of her personality.

Elizabeth I and Parliament. In England, Parliament, the body of representatives from the whole country, had the right to approve all taxes and pass laws. Parliament gained power and prestige in the 1530s, when Henry VIII used it to pass the laws that made England a Protestant nation. Moreover, people looked to Parliament as a restraint on the monarchy because it represented the wishes of people outside the central government.

Parliament had two houses. The House of Lords consisted of nobles and higher clergy. The House of Commons represented two classes: gentry and burgesses. The **gentry** owned land and had social position. The younger sons of nobles, who could not inherit their fathers' titles or positions, sometimes moved into the gentry. Merchants and professional people from the towns and cities made up the **burgesses.**

Learning from Pictures *The English built the tower of London as a fortress but later used it as a prison. Mary I briefly imprisoned Elizabeth I in the tower.*

The gentry and burgesses mingled to a surprising extent in England. Class lines were blurred compared with those in continental Europe. Rich merchants who owned land might be considered gentry. Younger sons of nobles might enter professions and come to be regarded as burgesses. Together the two groups had considerable power that the monarch had to respect.

Elizabeth I summoned 10 Parliaments during her reign, and they met for a total of 140 weeks. She managed Parliament very cleverly, obtaining all the taxes she needed without letting the members influence her policy too directly. Although angered at their petitions urging her to marry, Elizabeth nevertheless always respected the members' freedom of speech in their meeting hall. Despite her skill at managing Parliament, Elizabeth found it increasingly difficult to prevent its members, particularly the Puritans, from questioning government policies. Under the reigns of her less clever successors, Parliament's questions became increasingly numerous and more challenging. Eventually, members of Parliament began a revolution when the monarchy refused to listen to their views.

a. Ordered a new translation of the Bible
b. Managed Parliament cleverly
c. Agreed to the Petition of Right
d. Attempted to rid England of clergy who refused to conform to Catholic law
e. Fined people who did not attend the Anglican church
f. Prosecuted government critics in the Court of Star Chamber
g. Raised money by selling titles of nobility
h. Tried to impose a prayer book on the Scots
(Answers: 1-d; 2-b, e; 3-a, g; 4-c, f, h.)

397

1B, 4A, 4D, 4G, a1D

However, persecution of Catholics continued. In response to this persecution, a group of Catholics led by Guy Fawkes planned to blow up the Houses of Parliament while James was in attendance. But this Gunpowder Plot was discovered on November 5, 1605, and Fawkes and his fellow conspirators were executed.

SECTION 1

Closure

Some historians have suggested that Charles I's personality made his clash with Parliament inevitable. Ask: What aspects of Charles I's character and behavior contributed to his problems with Parliament? *(Student answers might include: Charles was arrogant, tactless, and aloof—even from his own advisers; he took arbitrary measures when people would not comply with his wishes, such as imprisoning those who would not loan him money; he had an extravagant life style and a love of religious ritual.)*

Review Answers

1. ***revolution:*** a radical attempt to change the structure of a country's government; ***gentry:*** people who owned land and had social position; ***burgesses:*** merchants and professional people from the towns and cities; ***covenant:*** solemn agreement **2.** ***Mary I:*** oldest daughter of Henry VIII who was fiercely determined to return England to the Catholic faith; ***Philip II:*** king of Spain, leader of Counter-Reformation, and husband of Mary I; ***Elizabeth I:*** half-sister of Mary I who became queen in 1558 and made England a Protestant country through a series of parliamentary acts; ***Mary Queen of Scots:*** Catholic heir to the throne during Elizabeth I's reign; ***James I:*** King of Scotland and son of Mary Queen of Scots

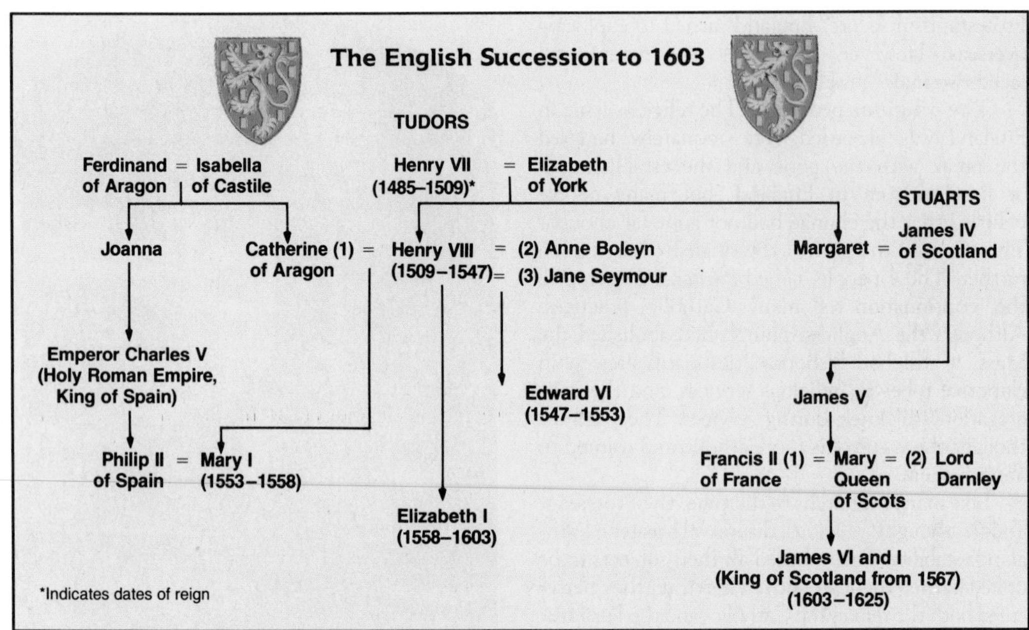

The Roots of the English Revolution

Between 1603, when Elizabeth died, and 1640, relations between the monarchy and its subjects deteriorated. The main stages in that deterioration suggest how and why it happened.

James I. The first problem arose almost immediately. King James VI of Scotland, a member of the Stuart family and the son of Mary Queen of Scots, succeeded Elizabeth to the English throne as James I of England.* He was tall and had blue eyes. At age 39, he had thin brown hair, a straggly beard, and spindly legs. The gangly king was also coarse in his habits. The French ambassador said that "where he wishes to assume the language of a king his tone is that of a tyrant, and where he condescends he is vulgar." But James had a taste for learning and was a man of considerable intelligence. Even so, he lacked common sense. According to Henry IV of France, he was "the wisest fool in Christendom."

James managed to rule in Scotland by pitting one faction against another and keeping the powerful church of Scotland under control. His English subjects suspected that, as a foreigner, he did not really understand how their parliamentary system worked. At his first Parliament, some of its members drew up an Apology of the House of Commons, a document that arrogantly explained the way its authors thought England ought to be ruled. James, who strongly believed in the divine right of kings, openly ignored their advice.

Finance and foreign policy occupied the attention of James I during much of his reign. He left the Puritans alone and even pleased them by ordering a new translation of the Bible into English. This Bible, known as the Authorized Version, or King James Version, is still one of the most widely used English translations.

James I's troubles came not from the Puritans but from Parliament. The 1600s was a time of inflation and growing government activity. James could never collect enough money in taxes to finance his policies. When the taxes passed by Parliament proved insufficient, he raised money by selling titles of nobility, granting monopoly rights to private companies, and increasing customs duties. Parliament objected to these methods. It also objected to James's attempt to create an alliance with England's old enemy, Spain.

*From this time on, England and Scotland were ruled by the same monarch.

Charles I. At the time of his death in 1625, James I and his subjects had an uneasy relationship. The tension between the monarchy and the people increased during the reign of his son Charles I, who ruled from 1625 to 1649. Brave, arrogant, and tactless, Charles believed in the divine right of kings just as firmly as his father had. His high opinion of the role of the monarch kept him aloof even from his own advisers. Charles had few friends and had none of the common touch of his father. An unhappy marriage to the Catholic French princess Henrietta Maria completed his isolation.

When Charles I could not persuade Parliament to give him funds, he tried to force people to loan him the money he needed and imprisoned many who refused. The king's policies led to a terrible confrontation with Parliament during 1628 and 1629. The members presented Charles with a document known as the Petition of Right. Desperate for money, Charles signed the petition, promising not to levy taxes without the consent of Parliament, not to declare martial law or to quarter soldiers in private homes in peacetime, and not to imprison people without a specific charge. Although Charles had signed the petition, he continued to levy taxes. When members of the House of Commons protested, he dissolved Parliament.

For the next 11 years, Charles refused to call Parliament into session, hoping never to have to do so again. During this time he used drastic methods to collect taxes and revived long-ignored dues and royal fees.

Charles I took his job as head of the Anglican church seriously. He favored a very formal and ritualistic Protestantism, which irritated the Puritans. They also despised the extravagant life of the royal family. Charles in turn increased the restrictions on Puritans. For example, he limited sermons to those that concerned the Ten Commandments and required government approval for the printing of any religious books. As a result of these restrictions, thousands of Puritans left the country for a new life in America during the 1630s. Those who stayed behind became determined opponents of the king's policies.

These Puritans were joined by some members of Parliament and many lawyers who thought the king's rule was tyrannical. Charles avoided the system of common law by offering cheap and rapid justice in the royal courts. In these courts decisions were made in secret by judges, not by juries.

Learning from Pictures *This patent of nobility, issued by Charles I in 1627, is considered a work of art. It shows Charles seated on the throne and the royal lion of England.*

who assumed the English throne after Elizabeth's death in 1603; ***Charles I:*** son of James I whose arrogance, lack of tact, and belief in the divine right of kings brought him into conflict with Parliament

3. ***English Channel:*** narrow stretch of water separating southern England from France

4. Elizabeth did not marry and had no children, and during the first part of her reign her closest heir was Mary Queen of Scots, a Catholic.

5. She called frequent parliaments and always respected the members' rights of free speech, even when she considered their questions, suggestions, and criticism too personal in nature.

6. James I's troubles with Parliament concerned finance. When taxes imposed by Parliament proved insufficient for his needs, James raised money by selling titles of nobility, granting monopoly rights to private companies, and raising customs duties. This greatly aggravated members of Parliament, who also disliked James's attempts to forge an alliance with Spain.

Charles I's problems with Parliament also concerned financial matters. When he could not persuade Parliament to give him funds, Charles tried to force people to loan him money, imprisoning those who refused.

7. (a) Although Protestantism had been established as the state religion of

399

1B, 4A, 4D, 4G, a1C, a2J, a4A, a4F, a4H, a4L

● Since that time, no reigning British monarch has entered the House of Commons.

England, many people felt that the changes in the church had not gone far enough. These people, the Puritans, wanted to purify the church further.
(b) In time, the Puritans became increasingly unhappy with the established church in England, and they led a revolution against the monarch.

SECTION 2

Focus/Motivation

Point out that when the English civil war began in the late summer of 1642, Charles I had barely 1,000 troops under his command. Continue by mentioning that even those most loyal to Charles seemed to have joined his cause with little enthusiasm. For example, Sir Edmund Verney — who was killed in the first year of fighting — noted that he "did not like the quarrel." However, Verney said he could not do "so base a thing as to forsake" Charles in his "hour of need." Then lead a class discussion on the beginning of the civil war, using the following questions as a guide: Why do you think people were slow to join Charles I's cause? *(Student answers might include: people hoped that Charles and Parliament might yet reach a compromise; people were reluctant to join what might be a losing cause; the gentry—who largely were supporters of Charles—would have been involved in harvesting on their estates.)* Why do you

Common-law lawyers resented these rivals to the circuit court system, especially because they believed the king controlled the judges. One royal court, the Court of Star Chamber—named for the wall and ceiling designs in the room where it met—was particularly efficient at prosecuting Puritans and critics of government policy. People bitterly hated the Star Chamber.

It seemed to many English people that Charles I was increasingly imposing his own absolute rule. Those who opposed the growing power of the central government waited for an opportunity to reverse this trend.

The Scots. When Charles tried to impose a standard prayer book on his Scottish subjects, the opportunity came. The Scots had accepted a branch of Puritanism known as Presbyterianism. Elders known as *presbyters,* rather than bishops, ruled the Presbyterian church. The Presbyterians had their own prayer book. In 1638 they responded to Charles's attempt to Anglicanize the Presbyterian service by signing a National Covenant. In this **covenant,** or solemn agreement, the Scots swore to the death that changes in the church in Scotland violated both their religion (modeled after Calvinism) and acts of the Scottish Parliament. Moreover, the king seemed to be reestablishing Catholic practices in Scotland. Though the Scottish Presbyterians did not question their loyalty to King Charles, loyalty to their church—the Kirk—came before loyalty to the king. Charles I insisted on being obeyed, so the Scots assembled an army to fight for their religious freedom. In desperate need of money to fight the Scots, Charles called Parliament into session in 1640.

SECTION 1 REVIEW

1. **Define** revolution, gentry, burgesses, covenant
2. **Identify** Mary I, Philip II, Elizabeth I, Mary Queen of Scots, James I, Charles I
3. **Locate** English Channel
4. **Summarizing Ideas** What religious problems plagued the royal succession when Elizabeth I came to the throne?
5. **Synthesizing Ideas** How did Elizabeth I control Parliament?
6. **Understanding Ideas** What difficulties arose between Parliament and each of the first two Stuart kings?
7. **Analyzing Ideas** **(a)** What issues divided Protestants in England? **(b)** How did those issues influence English politics?

2 The King and Commons Went to War

The Parliament of 1640—known as the *Long Parliament*—reconvened periodically for 20 years. The Puritans who controlled the House of Commons took a number of actions that limited absolute monarchy in England. For example, they abolished the king's power to dissolve Parliament and passed a law requiring that Parliament meet at least once every three years. They ended all forms of illegal taxation, abolished the Court of Star Chamber, and executed two of the most hated advisers of the king.

The Irish Problem

While the Long Parliament worked at reducing the king's authority, Charles also faced trouble in Ireland. England had ruled Ireland since the late 1100s, but it had never brought the Irish completely under control. The English conquerors seized land belonging to Irish owners and gave it to English settlers, who were mostly Anglicans. In time these landowning Anglo-Irish settlers became the upper class and controlled most of the wealth of Ireland. Later, Scottish Presbyterians settled in the northern region called Ulster. Mostly farmers and merchants, they became the middle class. The majority of the native Irish remained Roman Catholic, were tenant farmers, and formed the lower social and economic classes. In 1641, led primarily by the Irish Catholics, the Irish rebelled against England.

The rebellion in Ireland and the Scottish invasion of England forced Charles I at first to concede to Parliament and then to accept the changes that resulted. Later, however, the most radical Puritan group tried to pass an act that would abolish the appointment of bishops in the Anglican church. This group also issued a complete list of grievances against Charles I. As a staunch defender of the Anglican church, whose motto might have been "No bishop, no king," Charles I at that point led troops into the House of Commons and tried to ● arrest the leaders of the opposition. This hostile act led to the outbreak of a civil war in 1642 between supporters of the king and supporters of Parliament.

1B, 4A, 4D, 4G, a1A, a1C, a2J

● The soldiers of the New Model Army were called *Ironsides* because their helmets had metal extensions that covered the sides of their faces.

English Civil War

It was difficult to determine whether a citizen favored the king or Parliament. Generally, the king's supporters, called *royalists* or Cavaliers, after the king's cavalry, included Anglicans, Roman Catholics, nobles, and anyone who disagreed with the Puritans on political or religious issues. The Puritans supported Parliament. They were sometimes called Roundheads, after the Puritan soldiers who tucked their hair under their helmets. Anyone who believed that the powers of the king ought to be severely curbed joined the Puritan opposition.

Oliver Cromwell, leader of the Puritans, organized his forces into a New Model Army that the Cavaliers could not match. The New Model Army ● had well-drilled, disciplined, and zealous soldiers who charged into battle singing hymns. They easily outfought the royalists. After two defeats in battle, Charles I surrendered in 1646.

This surrender initiated a great maneuvering among various political and religious groups for control of the government. Chief among these groups were the Presbyterians, who held a majority in Parliament, and the Independents, led by Cromwell, who made up a majority of the army. Cromwell's Independents won the struggle. They used troops to keep all Anglican and Presbyterian members from entering the House of Commons, leaving only 60 members, all Independents. This remnant of the Long Parliament became known as the Rump Parliament, since it was the only part of the parliamentary body left sitting.

Death of the king. The Rump Parliament abolished both the monarchy and the House of Lords. It proclaimed England a *commonwealth,* a

Learning from Pictures
Oliver Cromwell was very modest. He is said to have told the artist not to make him look handsome, but to paint him "warts and all."

think people like Sir Edmund Verney were with Charles from the beginning? *(Student answers might include: they thought it was the correct thing to do; they would support the king, right or wrong.)* Finish the discussion by mentioning that Parliament proved to be Charles I's most effective recruiter. In September, 1642, its members declared that all people who refused to give complete support to the parliamentary cause would have their property confiscated. The gentry and nobility could no longer remain neutral, and many of them saw Charles I as their natural ally.

Presentation
Writing a Script
(Average/Group)
Interested students might like to prepare a script for a "You Are There" radio program. The date for the program would be January 30, 1649, the day that Charles I was executed. Suggest that the students explore in their script the events that led to the execution—Charles's belief in the divine right of kings, his violation of the Petition of Right, his efforts to establish the Anglican church in Scotland, and so on. Mention that interviews with Charles I, Oliver Cromwell, and other major figures involved in the events leading up to the execution might also be included. Have the students "broadcast" their program for the rest of the class.

1B, 4A, 4D, 4G, a1D, a2J, a4A, a4H, a4J

● Some political opponents within Cromwell's camp held revolutionary ideas. One group, the Levelers, called for universal manhood suffrage, while the more radical Diggers demanded an end to the ownership of all private property.

SECTION 2

Closure

Ask: Was the execution of Charles I justified? *(Answers will vary.)*

Review Answers

1. ***constitution:*** document outlining the fundamental laws and principles that govern a nation
2. ***Long Parliament:*** the Parliament of 1640 that reconvened periodically for the next 20 years; ***Cavalier:*** supporter of the king, also known as a Royalist; ***Roundhead:*** Puritan soldier who sided with Parliament; ***Oliver Cromwell:*** leader of the Puritans; ***New Model Army:*** well-drilled, disciplined Puritan soldiers, organized by Oliver Cromwell; ***Rump Parliament:*** remnant of Parliament—consisting of 60 Independent members—left after Cromwell's forces had barred entry to all Anglican and Presbyterian members
3. The costs of suppressing the rebellions in Scotland and Ireland forced Charles I to concede to Parliament and then accept the changes it enacted. However, when radicals in Parliament tried to pass an act abolishing the appointment of bishops in the Anglican church, Charles led troops into the House of Commons to arrest radical leaders. Charles I's hostile act led to the outbreak of the civil war.

word used at that time to mean a republic, and appointed a special court to try Charles I for treason. The court condemned Charles and beheaded him in front of the palace at Whitehall in 1649. Charles I faced death courageously. This advanced the cause of the monarchy as many people now considered Charles a martyr. His courage enabled the English to overlook his faults and made it easier for Charles's son, who fled to France after his father's death, to return later as king. Meanwhile, Oliver Cromwell took control of England and became essentially a military dictator.

Cromwell's Commonwealth

Oliver Cromwell was a devout, honest, and upright Puritan who possessed the qualities of a powerful orator and skilled leader. However, he believed that only he could govern correctly. He suppressed all political and religious opposition with great severity. He even tried to control the country's social life by closing all theaters and limiting many other forms of popular entertainment.

Although Cromwell held considerable power, he was a reluctant dictator. He preferred a parliamentary, republican government and made several attempts to create one. He tried twice to establish a **constitution**—a document outlining the fundamental laws and principles that govern a nation. One such document, known as the Instrument of Government, was the first written constitution of a major European nation. It gave Cromwell the title of Lord Protector and provided that landowners would elect Parliament. Cromwell held the title of Lord Protector from 1653 until 1658, a period often called the *Protectorate.*

Cromwell's government might have been overthrown except for three factors: (1) It had enough money from taxes and the sale of confiscated royalist lands to support itself and its army. (2) Its enemies, the Irish and the royalists, had no organized army. Cromwell suppressed the Irish so mercilessly that his name inspires hate even today, and the royalists never posed a serious threat. (3) Its own army was disciplined and powerful.

Cromwell's domestic policy of developing manufacturing and trade related directly to his foreign policy. During the troubled times of the civil war in England, Dutch merchants and shipowners had built up a profitable trade. Cromwell challenged the Dutch by having Parliament pass the Navigation Act of 1651. This act required that all imports into England be shipped in English ships or the ships of the country producing the goods.

Cromwell's policies led to a commercial war with the Dutch from 1652 to 1654. Because the Dutch carried so much of the world's trade, they realized that the freedom of the seas was at stake. England seized the lucrative Portuguese slave trade away from the Dutch in 1654, but the war ended indecisively. During the war, however, the English navy gained prestige, and Cromwell demonstrated that the English government would use its might to strengthen English commerce.

The End of the Revolution

Cromwell's experiment with republican government failed. He quarreled almost as much with Parliament as had the Stuart kings, and parliamentary ● resentment of central power resurfaced. Shortly before his death in 1658, Cromwell dissolved Parliament and ruled alone. His son Richard, who succeeded him as Lord Protector, was a weak leader who could not win the necessary support of the army.

By 1660 the English people, too, had undergone a change in feelings. Though some had favored the execution of Charles I, Cromwell's rule had brought only confusion and resentment. After some hesitation, the new Parliament of 1660 invited Charles II, the son of Charles I, to return to England from exile. The English Revolution ended, and although the country seemed to have weathered its troubles, another 30 years would pass before anyone could be certain that any lessons—especially the need to give Parliament an important role in government—had been learned.

SECTION 2 REVIEW

1. **Define** constitution
2. **Identify** Long Parliament, Cavalier, Roundhead, Oliver Cromwell, New Model Army, Rump Parliament
3. **Interpreting Ideas** How did rebellions in Scotland and Ireland influence the civil war in England?
4. **Summarizing Ideas** **(a)** In what ways did the Long Parliament limit absolute monarchy in England? **(b)** How did the civil war begin?
5. **Synthesizing Ideas** Why was Oliver Cromwell unable to establish a permanent republic in England?

1B, 4A, 4D, 4G, a1A, a1C, a2G, a2J

● Charles replied to this lampoon: "This is very true: for my words are my own, and my actions are my ministers."

Learning from Pictures *In 1660 Charles II returned to England where the people gave him an enthusiastic welcome.*

4. **(a)** The Long Parliament limited absolute monarchy in England by abolishing the king's power to dissolve Parliament, passing a law requiring that it meet at least once every three years, and ending all forms of illegal taxation. It also abolished the Court of Star Chamber. **(b)** The civil war began after Charles I led troops into the House of Commons to arrest radical leaders.
5. Cromwell found that he was almost continuously at odds with Parliament. In 1658, Cromwell's experiment with republicanism ended when he dismissed Parliament and ruled alone. His son was a weak leader, and by 1660 the English people favored a return to monarchy.

3 England Established a Constitutional Monarchy

The struggles between king and Parliament did not end in 1660. An echo of the crisis occurred in the 1680s. After that uncertainty passed, however, the English created a stable government that linked monarch and Parliament in a close, workable partnership.

Charles II and the Restoration

The revolution ended in 1660, when Charles II regained the throne. The period of his rule is called the Restoration, because monarchy had been restored in England.

Charles II was well over six feet tall. He had dark brown hair and eyes, and he resembled his Medici and Bourbon ancestors. Charles was quite dignified, but because he also loved entertainment and good times, people called him the "Merry Monarch." Charles removed the restrictions on the theater and other forms of entertainment that the stern Puritans of the Commonwealth had legislated. A lampoon of the time said of Charles II:

> "We have a pretty witty king
> Whose word no man relies on:
> He never said a foolish thing,
> And never did a wise one."

Despite this lampoon, Charles II had learned ● much from his years in exile. He said he had no desire "to go on his travels again." When his policies met opposition, he gave in, although he often used roundabout methods to gain his ends. Charles continued Cromwell's commercial policy, which eventually led to wars with the Dutch. During

SECTION 3

Focus/Motivation

On the chalkboard or an overhead projector, write the following passages from the English Bill of Rights:

"That it is the right of the subjects to petition the king, and all . . . prosecutions for such petitioning are illegal.

That excessive bail ought not to be required, nor excessive fines imposed, nor cruel and unusual punishments inflicted."

Lead the class in a discussion, using the following questions as a guide: What rights are being protected? *(The right to speak freely against a ruler's policies*

403

1B, 4A, 4D, 4G, a1A, a1D, a2A, a2B, a2C, a2D, a2G, a2J, a2K, a4A

● a number of leading English nobles

and to be free from excessive punishment.) How did these alter existing policies? *(Under existing policies, people could be prosecuted for petitioning the king. Also, fines and punishments were set at the whim of the court.)* Why do you think people considered these rights important enough to put them into law? *(Answers will vary. Students might suggest that since absolute rulers had violated these rights so often in the past, people felt that the only way to ensure their protection was to put them into law.)* Do similar laws exist in the United States? *(Most students will mention the Bill of Rights.)*

Presentation
Determining Cause and Effect (Average/Group)
Make copies of the three statements below and distribute them to members of the class. Tell students that each statement is a cause for which they must determine an effect.

1. James, a Roman Catholic, would succeed his brother Charles II as king of England. *(England's first political parties, the Whigs and the Tories, developed.)*
2. England and Scotland were united into one kingdom. *(Trade barriers between the countries were removed.)*
3. Neither George I nor George II understood the larger issues of British government. *(The cabinet became more and more important.)*

these wars England seized the Dutch settlement of New Amsterdam in North America and renamed it New York. Charles wanted an alliance with France, but English protests forced him to oppose France. This shift marked the beginning of 150 years of rivalry between England and France for mastery of the sea and for colonial power.

Charles II tolerated Roman Catholics and hoped to lift some of the legal restrictions on them in England. However, his attempt to do so met with such strong parliamentary opposition that he abandoned the effort.

Political Parties Develop

Because Charles II and his Portuguese queen, Catherine of Braganza, had no children, it seemed clear that Charles's younger brother James, a Roman Catholic, would succeed him. The issue of royal succession led to the development of England's first political parties.

Two groups of almost equal strength—*Tories* and *Whigs*—evolved in Parliament. Like Cavaliers and Roundheads, the terms Tories and Whigs were nicknames. The original Tories had been Irish Catholic guerrillas. The Whigs had been Presbyterian guerrillas in southwestern Scotland. The Tories wanted a strong hereditary monarch, but not an absolute one. They strongly supported the Anglican church but would willingly accept a Roman Catholic ruler provided that the heirs were Protestant. The Whigs favored a weak monarch and a strong Parliament. They vigorously opposed the idea of a Roman Catholic ruler.

James II and the Glorious Revolution

Charles II died in 1685 and his brother the Duke of York came to the throne as James II. The fair-haired, humorless, and stubborn James had learned less in exile than had Charles. As a Roman Catholic and an ardent believer in royal absolutism, like that of Louis XIV in France, he antagonized both Whigs and Tories.

Like Charles, one of James's main problems involved the succession to the throne. James's daughters, Mary and Anne, were both raised as Protestants, and both married Protestant princes.

Learning from Pictures *William III and Mary II were the only monarchs in English* ● *history who ruled with equal power. Who invited them to become England's monarchs?*

● In this state of nature, Hobbes said, life was "solitary, poor, nasty, brutish, and short."

■ Locke's ideas on natural rights were greatly influenced by the writings of the first century B.C. Roman philosopher, Cicero.

1B, 4A, 4D, 4F, 4G, a1A, a1D, a2A, a2B, a2C, a2D, a2G, a2J, a2K

However, James's first wife died, and he was married again, this time to a Roman Catholic princess, Mary of Modena. In 1688 Mary gave birth to a son, who would by law succeed his father before his older half-sisters. Since the boy was a Catholic like his father and mother, English Protestants feared a whole line of Catholic rulers on the throne of mostly Protestant England.

Now all the groups who opposed James combined to bring about the event known as the Glorious Revolution. Whigs and Tories agreed that James must abdicate. A number of leading nobles invited James's daughter Mary and her Dutch husband William of Orange to take the throne of England. Although William landed in England with an army in 1688, armed force was hardly necessary. Unable to rally anyone to his support and fearful of assassination, James fled to France. Parliament gave the crown to William III and Mary II as joint rulers.

New Ideas About Government

The English civil war and the events that followed led not only to changes in government but also to new ideas about government. The English philosopher Thomas Hobbes lived through the civil war and was disturbed by the chaos it created. He set forth his political philosophy in a book called *Leviathan,* published in 1651.

Hobbes explained that groups of people first lived in anarchy, what he called a "state of nature." ● Life was violent and dangerous under these circumstances, so people chose a leader to rule them. In order to maintain a stable society, people made an unwritten "social contract." Hobbes argued that under this contract they had to give the monarch absolute power, or anarchy would again result. The people retained only the right to protect their own lives.

John Locke, another English philosopher, adopted many of Hobbes's ideas but interpreted them differently. Locke supported Parliament in the struggle that led to the overthrow of James II. Earlier, he established the principles on which the supporters of the Glorious Revolution acted in 1688, and in 1690 he published these principles in his *Two Treatises on Civil Government.*

Like Hobbes, Locke believed that people had first lived in a state of anarchy and then made a social contract. However, he believed that people had given up only some of their individual rights and had kept others. The rights they kept, called **natural rights,** included the right to live, the right ■ to enjoy liberty, and especially the right to own property.

According to Locke, a ruler who violated these rights violated natural law and broke the unwritten social contract. The people had the right to overthrow such a ruler and replace him with another ruler who pledged to observe and protect their rights. Locke thus provided grounds for the people to force James II to leave the throne and for Parliament to offer the crown to William and Mary. Locke's ideas would influence later revolutions in America and France.

Safeguards Against Absolute Rule

Parliament passed safeguards against arbitrary rule as early as the reign of Charles II. In 1679 it passed an important measure, the *Habeas Corpus Act.* This act provided that anyone who was arrested could obtain a writ, or order, demanding to be brought before a judge within a specified period of time. The judge would decide whether the prisoner should be released or charged and tried for a crime. The writ itself was called **habeas corpus,** Latin for "you shall have the body." The Habeas Corpus Act protected individuals against illegal arrest and unlawful imprisonment.

Before granting the throne to William and Mary in 1689, Parliament required them to accept in advance certain fixed conditions named in a document known as the *Bill of Rights.* The Bill of Rights declared that Parliament would choose the ruler, who would be merely an official, subject to parliamentary laws. The ruler could not proclaim or suspend any law, impose any tax, or maintain an army in peacetime without Parliament's consent. Parliament had to meet frequently, and the monarch could not interfere in the elections of its members. The Bill of Rights guaranteed the right of the members of Parliament to express themselves freely.

The Bill of Rights also protected private citizens. All citizens had the right to petition the government for relief of any injustice. In addition, no one could be required to pay excessive bail or be subjected to cruel and unusual punishment.

In 1689 Parliament also passed the *Act of Toleration.* This act granted freedom of conscience and the right of public worship to those Protestants (now called Dissenters) who were not members of

1B, a1C

CONNECTIONS: THEN AND NOW

Theaters

People have enjoyed going to see plays and entertainment since the earliest times. In ancient Greece and Rome, performances were given in great open-air arenas (right). In ancient Japan the *No* plays were popular entertainment.

During the Middle Ages, sacred stories and plays with Christian themes, called *morality plays,* were performed in or near churches. By the time of the Renaissance, special buildings were built for the performances. These buildings came to be known as *theaters.*

Perhaps the most famous theater in history was the Globe (below). This octagon-shaped theater was built in the late 1500s on the south bank of the Thames River, across from London. Most of William Shakespeare's plays had their earliest performances in the Globe.

Londoners flocked to see the latest comedies and tragedies of writers like Shakespeare, Christopher Marlowe, and Ben Jonson. These writers did not write morality plays. Imitating the models of classical Greece and Rome, they created dramas that were full of romance, humor, violence, and despair.

Plays had to be performed in the daytime, when there was enough natural light to illuminate the stage. The center of the theater was open to the sky. Ordinary tradespeople sat or stood in this open area, ready to be rained upon if the weather turned bad. Nobles and rich merchants sat in boxes around the sides of the theater. The stage itself was covered by an overhanging roof.

The human emotions explored by the plays of the Elizabethan and Restoration periods are so universal that many of the plays continue to be performed. Love, ambition, madness, and revenge were the themes of ancient Greek dramas. The same themes are still used by modern playwrights. Our enjoyment of the theater is one way in which we are linked with our ancestors.

406

the Anglican church. It did not, however, bring about complete religious freedom. For example, Roman Catholics still lived under heavy restrictions, and no Dissenters could hold public office.

In 1701 Parliament passed the Act of Settlement, designed to keep Roman Catholics off the English throne. The act provided that if William III should die with no children to succeed him, Mary's sister, Anne, would inherit the throne. If Anne had no children, the throne would go to another Protestant granddaughter of James I, the German Electress Sophia of Hanover.

Parliament Rules England

The Bill of Rights and the Act of Settlement marked the end of the long struggle between monarch and Parliament to determine who would rule the country. By 1700, although England remained a monarchy, Parliament held the power. However, Parliament did not represent all the people. Hereditary nobles and higher clergy made up the House of Lords. Even the House of Commons, which was gradually becoming the more powerful of the two houses, was not particularly representative. Only about 15 percent of the male population—the gentry who were landowners and the powerful commercial people—had the right to vote for members of the House of Commons.

In the 50 years following 1689, Parliament continued to gain importance as the real power in the government of England. During this time the organization and institutions characteristic of today's English government gradually emerged.

For centuries, English monarchs had met with advisers to discuss government problems. Beginning in the time of Charles II, a smaller group of advisers began to meet separately. Most of them were *ministers,* or heads of government departments. They made policy and dealt with issues effectively because they were leaders in Parliament. This group became known as the **cabinet.**

At first the cabinet included both Whigs and Tories. However, during the reign of William III, it became clear that the government ran more smoothly when most of the ministers of the cabinet belonged to the majority party in the House of Commons. Thus the monarch chose his or her ministers accordingly.

Several additional changes increased parliamentary control of the English government during and following the reign of William III. Parliament gained the right to declare war, and the monarch stopped vetoing acts of Parliament. Queen Anne, who reigned from 1702 to 1714, was the last monarch to veto an act of Parliament.

Act of Union

Before he died, William III urged the union of England and Scotland. He perhaps feared that Scottish resentment of rich England might lead the Scots to take sides with France again. In 1707 the Parliaments of England and Scotland passed the Act of Union. This act merged the two countries into one kingdom, known as Great Britain. The act abolished the Scottish Parliament and gave the Scots seats in the English House of Lords and House of Commons.

Learning from Maps *In 1707, Parliament united Scotland and England into the kingdom of Great Britain. What cities are outside the kingdom of Great Britain?* **Dublin; Londonderry**

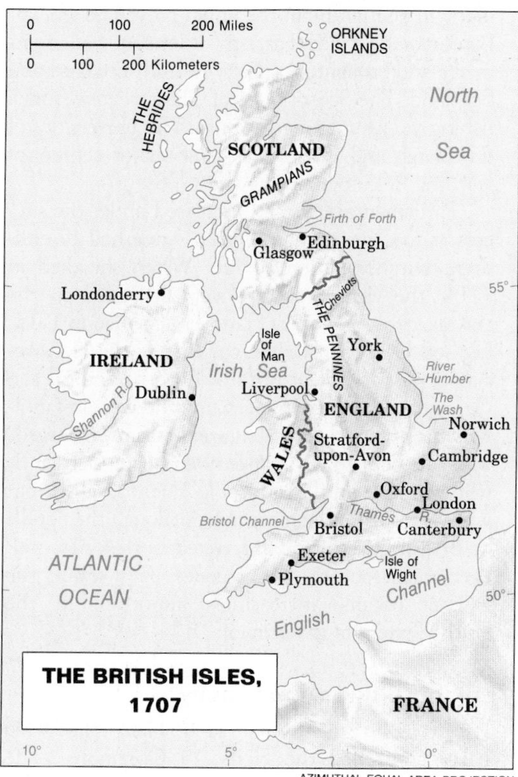

SECTION 3

Closure

Have students compare the British constitution with the United States Constitution. Ask: How is the British constitution different from the Constitution of the United States? *(The British constitution is not a single written document like that of the United States. Rather, it consists of a number of great documents—like the Magna Carta and the Bill of Rights—acts of Parliament, and a number of unwritten traditions.)*

Review Answers

1. ***natural rights:*** rights to life, liberty, and property; ***habeas corpus:*** Latin phrase meaning "you shall have the body"; ***cabinet:*** ministers, or heads of government departments, who act as advisers to the monarch; ***prime minister:*** chief minister of the cabinet, the real leader of the government; ***limited constitutional monarchy:*** monarchy in which a king or queen occupies the throne, but whose powers are limited by a constitution
2. ***Charles II:*** son of Charles I who came to the throne in 1660, beginning the period called the Restoration; ***Tories:*** members of a political party in Parliament who wanted a strong hereditary monarchy; ***Whigs:*** members of a parliamentary political party who favored a weak monarch and a strong Parliament; ***James II:*** brother of Charles II who came to

1B, 1C, 4A, 4D, 4G, a1A, a1C, a2A, a2C, a2D, a2E, a2F, a2G, a2H, a2J, a2K, a2L, a4A, a4F, a4G, a4L

● Since George I spoke no English and Sir Robert Walpole, his chief minister, spoke no German, they communicated in Latin.

■ The title of "prime minister" was not given official recognition in Great Britain until 1937.

the throne in 1685. A strong believer in absolutism, he antagonized both the Whigs and the Tories; ***William III:*** son-in-law of James II, invited to take the throne after James' abdication; ***Thomas Hobbes:*** English philosopher, author of *Leviathan;* ***"social contract":*** according to Hobbes, unwritten agreement giving a monarch absolute power; ***John Locke:*** English philosopher who outlined his political ideas in *Two Treatises on Civil Government;* ***Act of Toleration:*** act of Parliament granting freedom of conscience and right of public worship to non-Anglican Protestants; ***Robert Walpole:*** leader of the Whigs and first prime minister of Great Britain

3. Parliament tolerated James II, a Catholic, as long as his Protestant daughters seemed destined to succeed him. However, James and his second wife had a son, who automatically became heir apparent. Since both James and his second wife were Catholics, it was assumed that their son would be raised Catholic. Therefore, Parliament undertook the Glorious Revolution, forcing James to abdicate and offering the crown to his daughter Mary and her husband, William.

4. Hobbes believed that in the past people had lived in a state of anarchy. To develop and maintain a stable society, the people made an unwritten "social contract" giving absolute power to their chosen

Learning from Pictures *George I founded the Knights of the Bath, shown here in a procession at Westminster. What language did George I speak?* German

Some people opposed the union at first, particularly in Scotland, but the union proved beneficial. By removing trade barriers, it encouraged commerce and brought prosperity to both England and Scotland. The Scottish city of Glasgow grew from a fishing village into a great port. The universities of Edinburgh and Glasgow became major centers of learning in Europe during the 1700s.

Parliamentary control increased under the successors to Queen Anne. Queen Anne had 17 children, but none survived her. When she died in 1714, the elector of Hanover succeeded to the throne. Since Sophia of Hanover also died in 1714, her son George I became the first of the Hanoverian dynasty of Great Britain. Both he and his son George II were born in Germany and were unfamiliar with British government and customs. George I, ● who ruled until 1727, spoke no English. George II, who was king until 1760, spoke fluent English, but with a strong German accent. Although the details of British government interested both kings, neither understood the larger issues. As a result, the cabinet became increasingly important in the British system of government.

A Constitutional Monarchy

For over 20 years—from 1721 to 1742—the Whig party controlled the House of Commons. The recognized leader of the Whigs, Sir Robert Walpole, always became a minister. Walpole had strong leadership capabilities and came to be recognized as the **prime minister,** first minister, although the early prime ministers usually carried the title of "First Lord of the Treasury." Under ■ the rule of the Hanoverians, the prime minister became the real head of the government and Great Britain became a **limited constitutional monarchy.** It was a monarchy in that a king or queen sat on the throne. It was limited and constitutional in that a constitution limited the monarch's powers, and the monarch had to consult Parliament.

The British constitution is not a single written document like that of the United States. It consists partly of great documents that include among others the Magna Carta, the Petition of Right, and the Bill of Rights. It also includes acts of Parliament, which any succeeding Parliament may change. Several features of the British governmental system have never been written down; for example, the powers of the prime minister and the functions of the cabinet are based largely on tradition. The prime minister rather than the monarch selects the other members of the cabinet. Together the prime minister and the cabinet plan and carry out government policy.

Great Britain is one of the oldest constitutional governments in the world today. Its limited monarchy became a model for governments of many other nations, and the British experience became a guide to those who wanted to abolish absolute monarchy elsewhere.

SECTION 3 REVIEW

1. **Define** natural rights, habeas corpus, cabinet, prime minister, limited constitutional monarchy
2. **Identify** Charles II, Tories, Whigs, James II, William III, Thomas Hobbes, "social contract," John Locke, Act of Toleration, Robert Walpole
3. **Understanding Ideas** What role did the issue of Roman Catholicism play in the Glorious Revolution?
4. **Comparing Ideas** Compare and contrast the political philosophies of Thomas Hobbes and John Locke.
5. **Interpreting Ideas** **(a)** How did the English Bill of Rights limit the powers of the monarch? **(b)** How did it protect private citizens?
6. **Analyzing Ideas** Why did the cabinet gain importance during the reigns of William and Mary, Anne, George I, and George II?

READ
WRITE
INTERPRET
CONNECT
THINK

BUILDING HISTORY STUDY SKILLS

Reading About History: Identifying a Point of View

A point of view presents a person's outlook on a subject or an event. It is important to know the author's point of view in order to determine the accuracy of the information presented. By understanding the author's viewpoint, you can tell which data has been ignored or which data has been exaggerated. You can also evaluate how reliable the information is.

How to Identify a Point of View

Follow these guidelines to identify a point of view.

1. State the author's topic.
2. Identify the main idea.
3. Determine how and why emphasis has been placed on the main idea.
4. Select words and phrases that signal an opinion, emotion, or exaggeration.
5. Indicate ideas or facts about the subject that the author did not include.
6. State the author's point of view.

Developing the Skill

The issue of how and why government is organized was an integral part of the English Civil War and the Glorious Revolution. Thomas Hobbes in *Leviathan* and John Locke in *Two Treatises on Government* contributed their thoughts to the discussion. Read the selections from their works. What are their points of view? How are their ideas similar? How are they different?

" In the first place, I put for a general inclination of all mankind, a perpetual and restless desire of power after power, that ceaseth only in death. . . . during the time men live without a common power to keep them in all awe, they are in that condition which is called war; . . . as is of every man, against every man. . . . In such condition, there is no place for industry . . . and consequently no culture of the earth; no navigation . . . no commodious building; . . . no arts; no letters; no society; and which is worst of all, continual fear, and danger of violent death; and the life of man, solitary, poor, nasty, brutish, and short. . . .

The only way . . . they may nourish themselves and live contentedly; is, to confer all their power and strength upon one man, or upon one assembly of men, that may reduce all their wills, . . . unto one will. . . . This is more than consent, or concord; it is a real unity of them all, in one and the same person, made by covenant of every man with every man . . . This done, the multitude so united in one person, is called a COMMONWEALTH. "

(Thomas Hobbes, *Leviathan*)

" . . . *Political power* is that power, which every man having in the state of nature, has given up into the hands of the society . . . And this *power has its original only from compact,* . . . and the mutual consent of those who make up the community. . . .

The reason why men enter into society, is the preservation of their property; and the end why they chuse and authorize a legislative, is, that there may be laws made, and rules set, as guards and fences to the properties of all the members of the society, . . . whenever the *legislators endeavor to take away, and destroy the property of the people,* or to reduce them to slavery under arbitrary power, they put themselves into a state of war with the people, who are thereupon absolved from any farther obedience. "

(John Locke, *Second Treatise*)

Both men discussed how governments are formed. Hobbes claimed that man in a state of nature was in constant disorder. He formed a government to insure protection, prosperity, and order for himself. Man gave up his individual will to a ruler. Revolution was never justified because the ruler protected the common good. The signal words are *fear, danger, brutish, concord, unity,* and *consent.*

Locke believed that man in a state of nature had political power and formed a society to protect property. Government was a contract between the ruler and the governed. The government's purpose was to protect individual rights. Locke said that the contract can be broken if the ruler does not protect property. The signal words are *arbitrary* and *slavery.*

Practicing the skill. Choose a current political article from a periodical and identify the point of view.

To apply this skill, see Applying History Study Skills on page 419.

The natural right of assembly

leader. The people retained only the right to protect their own lives. Locke also believed that people, to avoid anarchy, had made a social contract with their chosen leader. However, he thought that the people had retained most of their rights, and no one could take these rights from them.

5. (a) The Bill of Rights limited the monarch's power by declaring him or her subject to Parliament's laws. According to the Bill of Rights, the monarch could not proclaim or suspend laws, levy taxes, or maintain a peacetime army without Parliament's consent. Also, the Bill of Rights required that Parliament meet frequently, that its members be elected without interference from the monarch, and that its members be guaranteed freedom of speech. **(b)** The Bill of Rights granted private citizens the right to petition the government for relief of injustice and prohibited the imposition of excessive bail and cruel and unusual punishment.

6. The Bill of Rights and the Act of Settlement gave Parliament the real power of government in England. Since cabinet members were also members of Parliament, the importance of the cabinet grew during the reigns of William and Mary and Anne. The cabinet began to play an even more important role during the reigns of George I and George II, since neither monarch understood British government.

409

1D, 4E

● Hawkins, as treasurer of the navy, was responsible for building the fleet that defeated the Spanish Armada. Raleigh, as well as being an explorer, historian, and poet, was also responsible for introducing potatoes and tobacco to England and Ireland.

SECTION 4

Focus/Motivation
When England gained overseas possessions, its leaders had to decide how to administer these distant territories. To stimulate discussion on colonial administration, ask students the following questions: How would you have run overseas territories in the 1600s? Who would you choose to direct the colonies? Would the colonies be for trade or for settlement? If the colonies were to be for settlement, who would settle in them? How much control would you exercise over the "interior" of a colony? How would trade between the home country and the colonies operate? *(Refer the students to the discussion of Portuguese, Spanish, Dutch, and French colonies in Chapter 15.)*

Presentation
Making Connections (Average/Group)
Point out that in 1626 the Dutch purchased Manhattan Island from American Indians and founded the colony of New Amsterdam. Later the English ousted the Dutch and renamed the colony New York. The use of the term *New* implies that there was an "old" place of the same name in Europe. Ask students to identify "New" places along the eastern coast of North America that were named for "old" places in England. *(Student answers might include: New Bedford, MA; New Britain, CT;*

4 English Sea Power Helped Establish a Large Empire

Spain and Portugal established vast overseas empires during the 1500s, while England remained preoccupied with problems at home. Even though these problems persisted during the 1600s, English mariners began explorations that allowed England to claim lands in the Americas and Asia. English merchants founded companies to trade in these new lands, in addition to English companies that traded in the Baltic and Russia. By the mid-1600s English naval power had become a major force. By the 1700s Europe began to recognize British naval supremacy on the high seas. At the same time, the British merchant fleet began to overtake the Dutch fleet in the amount of goods carried. By the 1760s England's colonial empire had no serious competition in North America or India.

Explorers and Sea Dogs

Shortly after Columbus landed in the Western Hemisphere in 1492, King Henry VII commissioned an Italian captain named John Cabot to sail to North America. In 1497 and 1498 he explored the coasts of Newfoundland, Nova Scotia, and New England. Although Cabot's voyages gave the English a claim in the New World, almost a century passed before the English took steps to develop this territory.

During the reign of Queen Elizabeth I, in the second half of the 1500s, a hardy breed of sea captains appeared in England. The English called this group of traders and pirates **sea dogs.** These men—John Hawkins, Francis Drake, and Walter ● Raleigh, among others—challenged Portuguese and Spanish monopolies of overseas trade. They also made important voyages of exploration. Sir Francis Drake, for example, sailed westward from North America across the Pacific Ocean, around the southern tip of Africa, and north to England. In 1580 he became the first English sea captain to sail around the globe.

However, the English sea dogs were better known for plundering foreign shipping. They stole from Spanish ships not protected by convoys, and they seized slaves being shipped from Africa and sold them in Spanish colonies. The attacks by

Learning from Pictures *Francis Drake's ship, the* Golden Hind, *captured many Spanish treasure ships. Here it is seizing a load of gold from Peru.*

English sea dogs greatly angered King Philip II of Spain. He protested to Queen Elizabeth, but she claimed that she was helpless to control them. Secretly she supported the sea dogs and shared what they had stolen. Despite their involvement in piracy, the sea dogs played a part in England's defeat of the Spanish Armada in 1588, and they strengthened the seafaring tradition of the island nation.

The English in India

The defeat of the Spanish Armada encouraged the English to establish colonies overseas. In 1600 Queen Elizabeth I granted a charter to a trading company called the English East India Company.

This company set up trading posts at Bombay, Calcutta, and Madras in India. The company dealt mainly with local rulers because the Mogul Empire had declined in power. To gain the support of these rulers, the company helped those who were weak, used force without hesitation against those who opposed the company, and extended generous "gifts" to those who might be swayed by bribery.

The English East India Company eventually set up a few trading posts in Malaya and the East Indies, but India remained the company's headquarters and chief source of trade and wealth. The English East India Company rapidly became extremely wealthy and powerful, with a vast fleet of merchant ships and warships to protect its interests.

The English in the Americas

Because of its great interest in Asia, England was slow to establish colonies in North America. Initially, the English explored North America in hopes of finding a northwest passage to India—a water route around the Americas to the north and west. The Spanish dominated the southern route around Cape Horn in South America.

Henry Hudson searched unsuccessfully for the northwest passage, but in 1609, on a voyage for the Dutch, he charted much of the coast of eastern North America and explored the river which now carries his name. On a voyage for the English one year later, he explored Hudson Bay in northern Canada.

As the search for a northwest passage to India continued, the English began to establish colonies along North America's east coast. The first of these colonies were founded by private companies or individuals. The English established the first permanent settlement at Jamestown, Virginia, in 1607. In 1620 they founded the second settlement, Plymouth, in what is now the state of Massachusetts.

The English founded the settlements primarily for commercial purposes since they no longer wanted to be dependent on imports from Asia. Investors hoped that the settlers would raise products that would make the home country more self-sufficient. However, the North American colonies proved to be a disappointment. Few of the original investors made a profit or even got their money back. Many colonists had reasons other than profit for settling in the New World. These people hoped to find greater political and religious freedom and to make better lives for their families.

As in other colonial empires, the British used slavery in their colonies, especially those in southern North America and the West Indies. Settlements on the Caribbean islands, such as Barbados, were commercially successful largely because of slave labor.

Self-government set Britain's empire apart from other European colonial empires. Most English colonies had some form of representative assembly, or governing body, although official control remained firmly in the hands of the home country.

New Cumberland, NJ; New Durham, NH; New Gloucester, ME; New Hyde Park, NY; New London, CT; New Windsor, MD; New Hampshire; and New Jersey.)

Learning from Pictures *Henry Hudson signs the contract with the Amsterdam Chamber of the Dutch East India Company to search for a northwest passage to China.*

411

1D, 4E, 4G, a4A, a4G, a4H, a4L

● This policy of loose enforcement was referred to as *salutary neglect.*

SECTION 4

Closure

Remind students of the old saying, "The sun never sets on the British Empire." Have them suggest what this old saying meant. *(Since it covered such a vast area, it was always daytime somewhere in the empire.)*

Review Answers

1. ***sea dogs:*** English sea captains who were both traders and pirates
2. ***John Cabot:*** Italian sailor, commissioned by England, who explored the North American coast; ***Sir Francis Drake:*** first Englishman to sail around the world
3. ***Bombay:*** city on western coast of India where English East India Company set up a trading post; ***Calcutta:*** city in northeastern India where English East India Company set up a trading post; ***Madras:*** city on eastern coast of India where English East India Company set up a trading post; ***Hudson Bay:*** bay in northern Canada explored by Henry Hudson; ***Jamestown:*** first permanent English settlement in America, located on central eastern coast of North America; ***Plymouth:*** second permanent English settlement in America, located on northeastern coast of North America; ***Barbados:*** island in the southern West Indies that was commercially successful due to slave labor
4. During the 1500s England was preoccupied

Mercantilism and the British Colonies

The British government, however, did intervene in colonial economies by following mercantilist principles. Mercantilism maintained that colonies existed for the benefit of the home country. Colonies supplied needed raw materials and furnished a market for Britain's manufactured products.

The British government passed a number of mercantilist regulations that affected its North American colonies, beginning with the Navigation Act of 1651. One regulation required that certain colonial products could be sold only in the home country, even though the colonists might have received higher prices for the products in another country. Other regulations discouraged colonists from manufacturing. For example, the British government forbade colonists to ship woolen cloth that they had manufactured to places outside their colony.

These trade regulations aroused resentment, and colonists found many ways to evade them. Colonists avoided paying taxes whenever and however they could. Smuggling became a respectable occupation, difficult to prevent because the long American coastline had many harbors and inlets. Until the mid-1700s, however, the English government only loosely enforced its trade restrictions. ●

SECTION 4 REVIEW

1. **Define** sea dogs
2. **Identify** John Cabot, Sir Francis Drake
3. **Locate** Bombay, Calcutta, Madras, Hudson Bay, Jamestown, Plymouth, Barbados
4. **Understanding Ideas** Why did England fail to develop a large colonial empire at the same time as Spain and Portugal?
5. **Explaining Ideas** What methods did the East India Company use to extend its influence throughout India?

5 The American Revolution Created a New Nation

Although the North American colonists of the 1700s resented British trade regulations, they disliked the French along their borders even more. After the defeat of the French, however, the North American colonists struggled with the British over many issues and finally declared their independence.

British-French Rivalry

While the British established colonies along the Atlantic coast of North America, the French developed settlements to the north and west in what was called New France. In the 1700s, American settlers moved westward across the Appalachian Mountains in search of new land. Conflict with the French was inevitable if this westward movement continued.

When Louis XIV threatened the balance of power in Europe during the reign of Charles II, the English opposed him. The wars in Europe had their counterparts in North America, mostly in frontier skirmishes. The colonies counted on British assistance for defense against the French and their Indian allies.

The decisive conflict that settled British-French rivalry in North America was the French and Indian War (1754–1763), known as the Seven Years' War in Europe. The Treaty of Paris in 1763 confirmed the sweeping British victories not only in North America but all over the world. The British now dominated the region from the Atlantic Ocean to the Mississippi River and from the Gulf of Mexico almost to the Arctic Ocean.

Increased Control over the Colonies

The worldwide conflicts between 1754 and 1763 had left the British with a large debt. The British fought in North America to protect the colonists. The British government, therefore, felt justified in asking the colonists to help pay the cost of this protection and relieve British taxpayers of some of their heavy burden.

However, British governments during the 1760s lacked a consistent policy toward their greatly expanded North American empire. The colonists nevertheless came to believe that the British intended to curb their liberties. In 1763, following an Indian uprising, the British forbade any colonists to settle in the land west of the Appalachian Mountains. Great Britain also attempted to bring its colonies under closer economic control by enforcing mercantilist trade regulations. The Sugar Act of 1764 imposed new taxes on sugar and many

History Through the Arts

METALWORKING

Sons of Liberty Bowl. Paul Revere II U.S., 1735–1818 Silver H.: 5½ in. D.: 5 13/16 in. Gift by Subscription and Francis Bartlett Fund. The Museum of Fine Arts, Boston

Engraved Sons of Liberty Bowl

Paul Revere is best known for the midnight ride he made to warn the Minutemen that the British were coming, before the battles at Lexington and Concord. Revere, however, was also a fine silversmith.

In the early American colonies, there were no banks to keep silver coins. Consequently, silver coins were often melted down and crafted into household objects. Teapots and serving trays were marked with the name or family crest of the owner and the initials of the silversmith.

In addition to being a silversmith, who crafted many lovely silver pieces before and after the American Revolution, Paul Revere was also a patriot. Among his work was this exquisite bowl made in honor of the patriotic society called the Sons of Liberty. This organization was founded in 1765 to establish a communications network among the colonial leaders and to involve other colonists in violent protests against the British and British sympathizers. The Sons of Liberty claimed that they were fighting for their rights as British subjects.

The engraved symbols of freedom—signatures, liberty bell, and flags representing the Magna Carta and the Bill of Rights—symbolize the colonists' fight, first for their rights as British subjects, then for their right to independence.

other items imported into North America from non-British colonies. The British were determined to collect these taxes.

In 1765 Parliament passed the Stamp Act. This law required that the colonists pay a tax—in the form of special stamps—on wills, mortgages, contracts, newspapers, pamphlets, calendars, playing cards, and almanacs. The colonists unified in opposition to the Stamp Act. They found a common ground in their opposition and began to think as a single people, not as people from 13 separate colonies. They began a trade boycott of British products. Their refusal to buy British goods brought economic pressure on British merchants, who complained to Parliament. As a result, the British repealed the Stamp Act in 1766.

Each time the British repealed one law, they devised another. And with each new law, the colonists increased their resistance. The colonists argued that they had no representatives in the British Parliament, and "taxation without representation" constituted tyranny. Between 1763 and 1775, relations between the British government and the American colonies grew steadily worse.

Intensified Conflict

King George III, who reigned from 1760 to 1820, was the first "thoroughly British" monarch of the House of Hanover. This meant that he was born in England and placed England's interests over those of his German possession of Hanover.

George also believed that Parliament had too much power in the constitutional system governing Great Britain. He determined to select his own ministers from the "King's Friends" in Parliament. Politics became extremely unsettled in Great Britain. Six prime ministers came to power during an eight-year period. Against this background of parliamentary confusion, the crises leading to the final break with the American colonies unfolded. As the colonists hardened their resistance to British policy, George III became equally determined to coerce them. By 1770 he found a prime minister who was willing to carry out this objective—Lord North.

The colonists were by no means united in wanting independence. However, as tensions increased, many colonists believed that their rights could be

with problems at home.
5. To extend its influence among local rulers, the East India Company helped weak rulers, used force against those who opposed the company, and gave generous "gifts" to those who could be swayed by bribery.

SECTION 5

Focus/Motivation
On the chalkboard or an overhead projector, write the following quotations. Tell students that the final quotation refers to Great Britain's restrictions on American trade with the West Indies.

"Give me liberty or give me death."

"No taxation without representation."

"There ought to be no more New England men, New Yorkers . . . but all of us Americans."

"I know not why we should blush to confess that molasses was an essential ingredient in American independence."

Ask students what causes for revolution they can infer from these quotations. *(desire for political liberty, political representation, national unity, and economic freedom)*

Presentation Understanding Chronology (Average/Group)
Write the following events on the chalkboard or an

4A, 4G, a1A, a1C, a1D, a2A, a2J, a4A

● to seize guns and gunpowder the colonists had stored nearby

■ Other people involved in writing the Declaration of Independence included Benjamin Franklin and John Adams.

overhead projector, and have students copy the list. Then ask students to arrange the events in their correct chronological order by writing *1* before the event that took place first, *2* before the event that took place second, and so on.

(5) Battle of Yorktown
(1) Intolerable Acts
(6) Treaty of Paris
(4) Declaration of Independence
(3) Battle of Lexington and Concord
(2) First Continental Congress

Learning from Pictures *This engraving shows the British breaking ranks at the battle of Concord. Why did British troops march into Concord?* ●

guaranteed only if the colonies became completely independent.

About one-third of the colonists, called *loyalists* (also known as *Tories*), strongly opposed independence. Another one-third, called *patriots* actively favored independence. The remainder of the colonists did not take sides. In 1773 Lord North's British government allowed the English East India Company to ship tea directly to the colonies, in effect giving the company a monopoly on tea sales. Angry colonists, upset at the prospect of a monopoly, threw the tea into Boston harbor. The British responded to the "Boston Tea Party" by closing the port of Boston to all shipping. Colonists called this act and a series of other laws passed in 1774 the Intolerable Acts.

The patriots resented the Intolerable Acts and decided to take action. In the fall of 1774, delegates from 12 of the 13 colonies—Georgia did not attend—met in Philadelphia in the First Continental Congress. The delegates demanded that the colonists be granted the full rights of British people. The delegates also pledged to support each other in the future and agreed to meet the following year if Great Britain did not repeal the Intolerable Acts.

In April 1775 British troops marched from Boston to seize guns and gunpowder that the colonists had stored nearby. At the towns of Lexington and Concord, the British met with armed resistance and retreated to Boston. The American Revolution had begun.

The Declaration of Independence

When delegates to a Second Continental Congress met in Philadelphia, the spirit of independence was stronger. The delegates voted to declare their freedom from Great Britain. On July 4, 1776, they adopted the Declaration of Independence, which established the United States of America as an independent nation. Thomas Jefferson, the declaration's principal author, expressed American sentiments with nobility and grandeur. The Americans wanted the whole world to read their declaration. ■

The Declaration of Independence shows the influence of political philosophers such as John Locke. It states that all people are created equal and are given by their Creator certain "unalienable rights" that cannot be taken from them. Among these rights are "life, liberty, and the pursuit of happiness." This idea—that every human being has the right to equal opportunity and must be treated with equal justice—is the foundation of the democratic ideal. Although the ideal was not stated to include women or slaves, the demand for equality created a new aim in politics.

The declaration also stated that all powers of government belong to the people. No government can exist without the consent of its citizens, because citizens create governments to protect individual rights. If a government fails to protect or attempts to destroy the people's rights, the people have the right "to alter or to abolish" the government and to set up a new government that will safeguard their rights.

These were extreme ideas, even for those who had rejected the unlimited authority of monarchs. Such ideas were especially bold when stated by a group of small, weak colonies against powerful Great Britain.

The War for Independence

Each side had advantages and weaknesses as the war began. The Americans were fighting to defend

1A, 4A, 4G, a1B, a1C, a2J, a4B, a4C

their own homes in territory they knew well. The British had to fight more than 3,000 miles (4,800 kilometers) from home, bringing with them most of their military supplies and equipment.

The American Revolutionary War was not popular in Great Britain. Many people did not support it, and some even sympathized with the Americans. The British had not favored large armies since the struggles of the 1600s between crown and Parliament. Therefore, King George III had to hire mercenaries, many of them foreign.

Nevertheless, Great Britain's strength lay in the organization of its army and navy. British troops were well trained, and the British fleet was the strongest in the world.

The lack of unity among the American states also helped the British. The states voluntarily sent representatives to the Continental Congress, but all of the Congress's proposals for action had to be sent back to the states for approval. In addition to the time required for the states to approve proposals, the colonial government faced other problems. To meet the immediate need of financing the war, the Continental Congress borrowed money and printed its own paper money. However, since it had no way of paying its debts, its credit was poor.

The weaknesses of the American government made it difficult to build a strong army. At first, American forces consisted mostly of poorly trained and undisciplined volunteers. The American troops

Learning from Maps *The American victory at Saratoga helped the revolutionary forces secure French aid. What city outside the colonies did the Americans capture?* **Montreal**

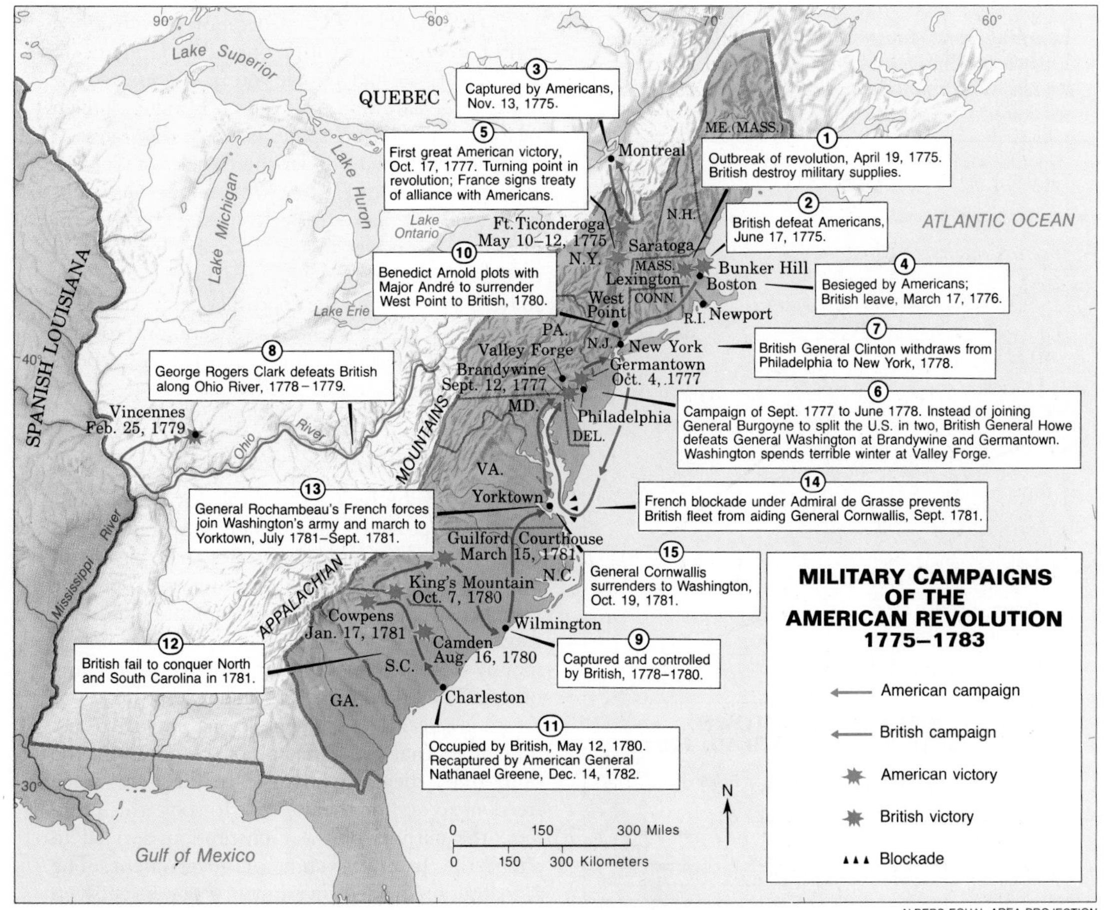
MILITARY CAMPAIGNS OF THE AMERICAN REVOLUTION 1775–1783
American campaign
British campaign
American victory
British victory
Blockade
1 Outbreak of revolution, April 19, 1775. British destroy military supplies.
2 British defeat Americans, June 17, 1775.
3 Captured by Americans, Nov. 13, 1775.
4 Besieged by Americans; British leave, March 17, 1776.
5 First great American victory, Oct. 17, 1777. Turning point in revolution; France signs treaty of alliance with Americans.
6 Campaign of Sept. 1777 to June 1778. Instead of joining General Burgoyne to split the U.S. in two, British General Howe defeats General Washington at Brandywine and Germantown. Washington spends terrible winter at Valley Forge.
7 British General Clinton withdraws from Philadelphia to New York, 1778.
8 George Rogers Clark defeats British along Ohio River, 1778–1779.
9 Captured and controlled by British, 1778–1780.
10 Benedict Arnold plots with Major André to surrender West Point to British, 1780.
11 Occupied by British, May 12, 1780. Recaptured by American General Nathanael Greene, Dec. 14, 1782.
12 British fail to conquer North and South Carolina in 1781.
13 General Rochambeau's French forces join Washington's army and march to Yorktown, July 1781–Sept. 1781.
14 French blockade under Admiral de Grasse prevents British fleet from aiding General Cornwallis, Sept. 1781.
15 General Cornwallis surrenders to Washington, Oct. 19, 1781.
QUEBEC
Montreal
Ft. Ticonderoga May 10–12, 1775
Saratoga
Lexington
Bunker Hill
Boston
Newport
West Point
New York
Germantown Oct. 4, 1777
Valley Forge
Brandywine Sept. 12, 1777
Philadelphia
Vincennes Feb. 25, 1779
Yorktown
Guilford Courthouse March 15, 1781
King's Mountain Oct. 7, 1780
Cowpens Jan. 17, 1781
Camden Aug. 16, 1780
Wilmington
Charleston
ME. (MASS.)
N.H.
MASS.
N.Y.
CONN.
R.I.
PA.
N.J.
MD.
DEL.
VA.
N.C.
S.C.
GA.
SPANISH LOUISIANA
APPALACHIAN MOUNTAINS
Lake Superior
Lake Michigan
Lake Huron
Lake Ontario
Lake Erie
Ohio River
Mississippi River
ATLANTIC OCEAN
Gulf of Mexico
90°
80°
70°
60°
40°
30°
N
0 150 300 Miles
0 150 300 Kilometers
ALBERS EQUAL AREA PROJECTION

415

1A, 4A, 4G, a1A, a1C, a2A, a2G, a2J, a4B, a4C

SECTION 5

Closure

Ralph Waldo Emerson referred to the exchange of gunfire at Concord in 1775 as "the shots that rang round the world." Ask: What do you think Emerson meant by this? ***(Answers will vary. Most students will suggest that the colonists' challenge to Great Britain, the most powerful nation in the world, would have far-reaching repercussions.)***

Review Answers

1. ***federal system of government:*** system in which power is divided between the central, or federal, government and the governments of the individual states; ***executive branch:*** branch of government that enforces the laws; ***legislative branch:*** branch of government that makes the laws; ***judicial branch:*** branch of government that interprets and applies the laws
2. ***Lord North:*** British prime minister who took office in 1770 determined to force the Americans into accepting British colonial policies; ***loyalist:*** colonist who strongly opposed independence; ***patriot:*** colonist who actively supported the drive for independence; ***Bill of Rights:*** first 10 amendments to the Constitution
3. ***Concord:*** one of the small towns outside Boston where the British first met armed resistance from colonists; ***Yorktown:*** scene of decisive American and

could seldom successfully oppose the well-trained British forces in a large-scale battle. But the Americans had good leaders, particularly General George Washington, who commanded the Continental Army. In addition, military officers from other nations came to help the Americans.

The fighting. Most of the fighting took place between 1776 and 1781, with neither side winning a clear victory (see map, page 415). After the Americans surrounded and defeated a British army under General John Burgoyne at Saratoga in October 1777, Lord North offered peace to the Americans. By the time the terms reached America, however, the colonies had signed an alliance with France. Spain and the Netherlands also joined the war against the British. In 1781 the Americans and their French allies won a decisive battle at Yorktown, Virginia (see map, this page).

Learning from Maps *During the siege of Yorktown, Virginia, the British were trapped with their backs to the sea. What country provided the Americans with sea power?* **France**

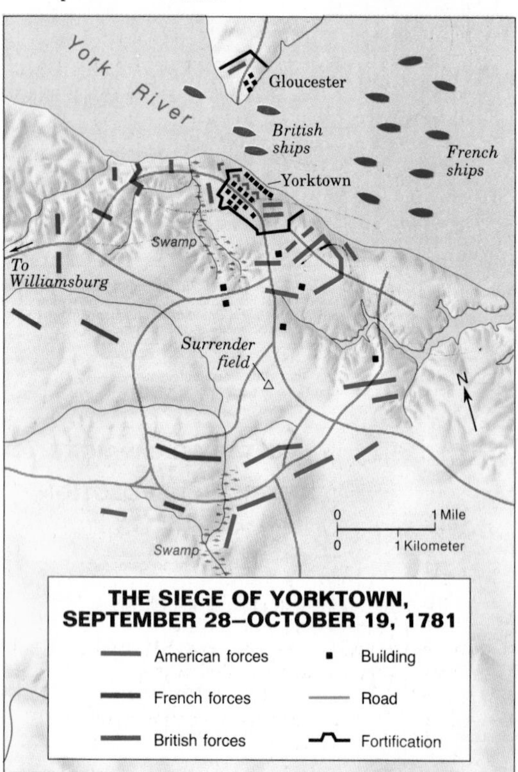

Ending the war. The British still had more troops in America than George Washington had in the Continental Army, and the British navy, after losing command of the sea at Yorktown, soon regained it. But the British people were tired of the costly American war.

In 1783 after two years of negotiation, with Benjamin Franklin as the shrewd and persuasive chief American negotiator, the British and the Americans and their allies signed the Treaty of Paris. The Americans won not only independence but also a territory much larger than the original 13 colonies (see map, page 417).

The Articles of Confederation

In 1781 the American states ratified, or accepted, the Articles of Confederation, a plan of government the Second Continental Congress had adopted in 1777. The Articles of Confederation provided for a central government, with a one-house Congress in which each state had a single vote. Congress had the power to declare war, make peace, conduct foreign relations, and settle disputes between the states.

The government under the Articles of Confederation lasted from 1781 to 1789, but because of its weaknesses, it lacked effectiveness. The government had no power to tax, to coin money, or to regulate trade with foreign countries or among the states. Laws required the approval of at least nine of the states. The Articles of Confederation provided for no chief executive officer, and the only courts were state courts, which tried all cases.

The Constitution

Americans soon realized that the Articles of Confederation provided inadequate government. In 1787 delegates from the states met again in Philadelphia to draw up a constitution to provide the framework for a new government. The delegates of the Constitutional Convention unanimously elected George Washington as its presiding officer. They then turned to the issue at hand—to create a central government strong enough to act on matters that concerned all of the states. At the same time, they wanted to leave the states some freedom to act for themselves. To solve this problem, the authors of the Constitution decided to adopt the **federal system of government.** The Constitution divided governmental powers between

416

● the Mississippi River
■ Some representatives felt that their state legislatures would not ratify the Constitution unless these amendments were added.

1A, 4A, 4G, a1A, a1C, a2A, a2G, a2J, a4A, a4E, a4F, a4L

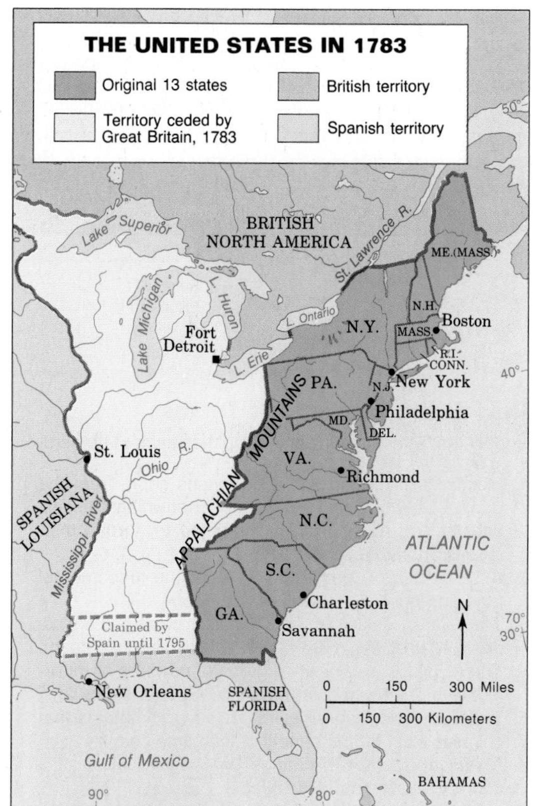

Learning from Maps The Treaty of Paris gave the United States territory west of the Thirteen Colonies.
● What was the western border of the new nation?

the central, or federal, government and the individual states. It gave the federal government the power to declare war, make treaties, coin money, raise armies, and regulate trade with foreign countries. All other powers belonged to or were shared by the states and the people.

The framers of the Constitution created three branches of the federal government. The **executive branch** (the president) enforced the laws, the **legislative branch** (Congress) made the laws, and the **judicial branch** (the federal courts) interpreted and applied the laws. The framers gave each branch certain powers and specified in the Constitution how each branch of government acted as a check on the others.

The first 10 amendments of the Constitution, added in 1791, are known collectively as the Bill of Rights. They specifically guarantee the basic rights of every United States citizen. Among others, these rights include freedom of religion, speech, press, assembly, and petition. In addition, rights regarding search, seizure, and a public trial by a jury are listed. Many representatives to the Constitutional ■ Convention insisted on spelling out these rights so that no question could arise as to what rights citizens did or did not have.

Effects of American Independence

The American Revolution put into practice the ideas of John Locke and other political philosophers. These ideas had previously existed only on paper. The Declaration of Independence contains two basic founding principles of democracy: that all people have certain unalienable rights and that all the powers of government belong to the people and are exercised only with the consent of the governed. The American experience gave encouragement to people everywhere who opposed domination by absolute monarchy and privileged classes.

The democracy that the Americans achieved in 1789, however, was very different from democracy today. The states restricted voting to adult, free males, who usually owned property. Women could not vote, and the large black slave population had no political rights at all.

Clearly, many liberties still had to be won. But from the American Revolution emerged a new kind of government and a new relationship among citizens. This may not have been what most Americans who opposed Great Britain intended when the Revolution began. However, their common beliefs and the economic and political needs of the new nation created a country that inspired loyalty.

SECTION 5 REVIEW

1. **Define** federal system of government, executive branch, legislative branch, judicial branch
2. **Identify** Lord North, loyalist, patriot, Bill of Rights
3. **Locate** Concord, Yorktown
4. **Interpreting Ideas** How did mercantilism affect the British colonies in North America?
5. **Evaluating Ideas** How did the Declaration of Independence show the influence of John Locke?
6. **Analyzing Ideas** Why were the Articles of Confederation ineffective?

French victory over the British, located on the Chesapeake Bay in Virginia
4. Mercantilism restricted American colonial trade by specifying that certain American goods could be sold only in Great Britain. Also, mercantilism placed restrictions on American manufacturing.
5. Locke's ideas on natural rights are reflected in the Declaration's recognition of "unalienable rights." Locke had justified the Glorious Revolution in England by claiming the ruler had violated natural law. Americans justified their revolution on similar grounds.
6. The Articles of Confederation were ineffective because they were weak. The main weaknesses were that Congress lacked the power to tax and the power to regulate trade, there was no president, so enforcement of the laws was left to the states, and the only courts were state courts.

417

Reviewing Important Terms
1. gentry, burgesses; **2.** constitution; **3.** Habeas Corpus Act; **4.** cabinet; **5.** mercantilism; **6.** revolution.

Developing Critical Thinking Skills
1. (a) Taxes imposed by Parliament did not provide enough money to finance James I's policies. Parliament objected to his alternative methods of raising money. Charles I's problems with Parliament also concerned financial matters. When he could not persuade Parliament to give him funds, Charles tried to force people to loan him money and imprisoned those who refused. Charles also clashed with Parliament over other measures he used to get the English people to comply with his wishes. **(b)** issues of church and state separation, the authority of the king
2. (a) Mary I's efforts to return England to the Catholic faith, which involved the burning at the stake of close to 300 heretics, made many English people fearful of Catholicism.
(b) passed the Act of Settlement
3. Elizabeth I obtained all the taxes she needed without letting members of Parliament influence her policy too directly. James I, however, had to sell titles of nobility, grant monopoly rights, and increase customs duties to raise money to finance his policies. Charles I tried to force people to loan him money and imprisoned many who refused, causing a terrible confrontation with Parliament. William and Mary agreed to Parliament's demands for control of finan-

1A, 1B, 1D, 4A, 4G, a1A, a1C, a1D, a2A, a2G, a2J, a4A, a4F, a4G, a4H, a4L

Reteaching
Have students review the Chapter Summary and the appropriate section and questions in the Unit Synthesis. Discuss the concepts until students demonstrate a clear understanding of the material.

CHAPTER 16 REVIEW

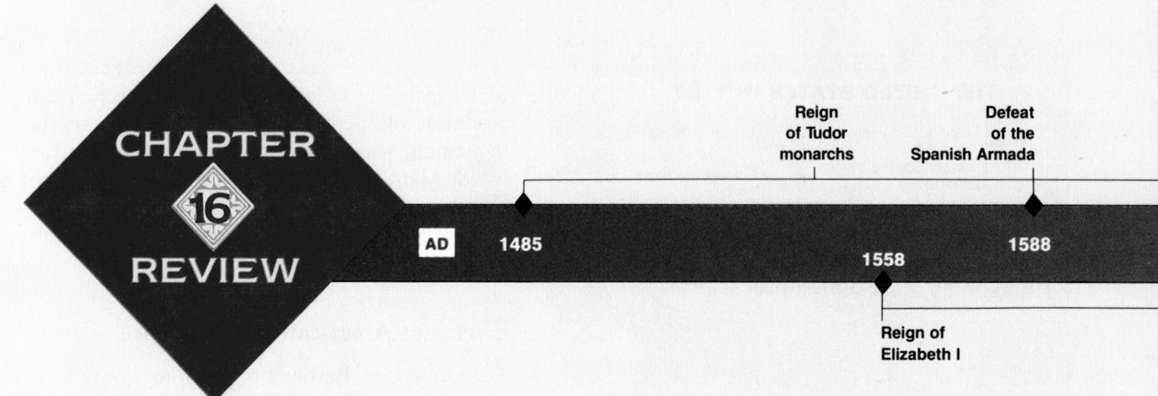

Chapter Summary

The following list contains the key concepts you have learned about political developments and the revolutions in the English-speaking world.

1. Elizabeth I faced threats from Spain abroad, and from Catholics and Puritans at home. She established a strong central government while respecting the rights of members of Parliament.
2. The Stuarts believed in the divine right of kings. They got into endless quarrels with Parliament over taxation and a wide variety of other issues.
3. Oliver Cromwell and the Puritans defeated King Charles I and established a republic called the Commonwealth. Cromwell made England strong, but his experiment in republican government failed. After his death the English restored the monarchy under Charles II.
4. Under the later Stuarts, England always faced the issue of a Catholic succession to the throne. This issue led to the formation of political parties called Whigs and Tories. They finally created the permanent Protestant succession. In time Parliament passed the Settlement Act, which was designed to keep Catholics off the English throne.
5. Thomas Hobbes and John Locke each formed a theory of government based on a social contract between rulers and ruled. Locke's ideas that the people had the right to overthrow a ruler who violated the contract gave the English and the Americans justification for revolution.
6. By the 1760s Great Britain had an overseas empire in North America and India which was largely unchallenged.
7. Great Britain had been involved in worldwide conflicts from 1754 to 1763. This left the British heavily in debt, making it necessary for them to raise taxes. However, when they attempted to tax their North American colonies, they ran into opposition.
8. The American colonists disagreed with the way the British governed them. Unable to change British policy, the 13 colonies chose independence.

On a separate sheet of paper, complete the following review exercises.

Reviewing Important Terms

Supply the term that correctly completes each statement.

1. Members of the House of Commons came from the ________, who represented the landowning classes, and the ________, who represented the urban merchants and professional people.
2. A ________ is a document outlining the fundamental laws and principles that govern a nation.
3. The ________ ________ ________ protected individuals against illegal arrest and unlawful imprisonment.
4. The ________ was a small group of advisers or ministers who dealt with government policy and issues.
5. The economic theory called ________ maintains that colonies exist for the benefit of the home country.
6. A radical attempt to change the very structure of a country's government is called a ________.

Developing Critical Thinking Skills

1. **Understanding Ideas** **(a)** Why did James I and Charles I quarrel with Parliament? **(b)** What issues precipitated the civil war in the 1640s?
2. **Evaluating Ideas** **(a)** Why did Catholicism cause fear among the majority of English people during the 1500s and 1600s? **(b)** What did the English Parliament do in 1701 to prevent Catholics from becoming kings and queens of England?
3. **Comparing Ideas** Compare the strengths and weaknesses of Parliament and monarchs during the reigns of Elizabeth I, Charles I, and William and Mary.
4. **Applying Ideas** **(a)** How did the English and French colonies in North America differ from one another? **(b)** In what other ways did the English and French differ as they struggled for leadership of the European world?
5. **Explaining Ideas** What works of English political philosophers helped the American authors of both the Declaration of Independence and the Constitution?

Relating Geography to History

Use the maps of the North American colonies on pages 415 and 416 to answer the following questions. **(a)** What advantages did the English

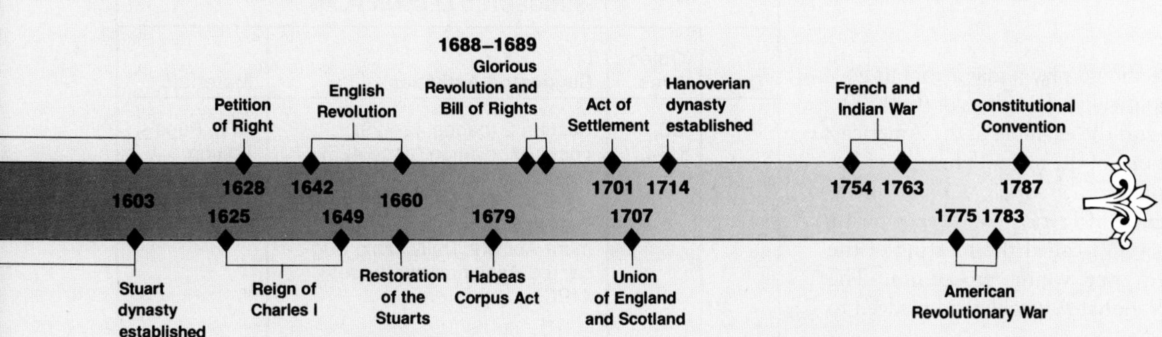

colonies along the Atlantic seaboard have over the French colonies in Canada and the west? **(b)** What geographical disadvantages did Great Britain have in fighting a war with the American colonies? What geographical advantages?

Relating Past to Present

1. The Petition of Right, the Habeas Corpus Act, the English Bill of Rights, and the Act of Toleration covered many important rights of individual citizens. List the rights protected by these measures. Use American civics or government books to find out how many of these rights are protected today by the United States Constitution.
2. The British monarchy today has little power, yet the monarchy as an institution is widely respected and supported in Great Britain. The monarch still serves certain functions in Great Britain and the nations of the Commonwealth. Examine textbooks that discuss comparative government or articles about British life today and list some important functions that the monarch still performs. You might want to compare the political role of Queen Elizabeth II with that of Elizabeth I, listing the powers that belonged to the earlier queen which do not belong to the current queen.

Applying History Study Skills

Before completing this activity, review Building History Study Skills on page 409.

Look again at the steps for identifying a point of view on page 409. Then complete the following exercise.

During the English Civil War, the victorious Parliamentarians and their generals sought to devise a new government for England. A small party of radicals, called the *Levelers,* demanded a radical change for the government of England. Their point of view is represented in the Putney Debates, from which the following selection is taken. Read the excerpt below and try to identify the point of view presented.

> “I do hear nothing at all that can convince me why any man that is born in England ought not to have his voice in election of burgesses. It is said that if a man have not a permanent interest, he can have no claim; and we must be no freer than the laws will let us to be . . . and I do think that the main cause why Almighty God gave men reason, it was that they should make use of that reason, and that they should improve it for that end and purpose that God gave it [to] them . . . I do not find anything in the law of God, that a lord shall choose twenty burgesses, and a gentleman but two, or a poor man shall choose none: I find no such thing in the law of nature, nor in the law of nations . . . and am still of the same opinion, that every man born in England cannot, ought not, neither by the law of God nor the law of nature, to be exempted from the choice of those who are to make laws and for him to live under, and for him (for aught I know) to lose his life under.”

1. **(a)** What is the main idea? **(b)** How is the main idea repeated and emphasized?
2. What are the signal words?
3. Which ideas has the speaker neglected to mention?
4. Why are the speaker's ideas considered radical?
5. What is the speaker's point of view about men and their relationship to his government?

Investigating Further

1. **Writing a Report** Prepare a report about the Spanish Armada. Discuss the following in your report: What was the background of the Spanish-English conflict? Why did Philip II want to conquer England? How was religion a factor? How was Elizabeth I regarded by other European monarchs? How was the Spanish fleet defeated? What was the significance of the English victory? You can use encyclopedias or Garrett Mattingly's *Armada* (Houghton Mifflin) as sources for your research.
2. **Presenting an Oral Report** Rulers such as Queen Isabella of Spain and Queen Elizabeth I of England supported voyages of exploration. Using books in your library, find out more about these rulers and why they supported these adventures. Include examples of voyages of exploration in your research. Present an oral report about your findings to the class.

cial matters before they took the throne.
4. (a) The English developed colonies along the Atlantic coast of North America, while the French established colonies in the interior, north and west of the English. **(b)** Their differences of opinion over who would lead Europe spilled over into their American colonies and culminated in the French and Indian War.
5. *Leviathan* by Thomas Hobbes and *Two Treatises on Civil Government* by John Locke.

Relating Geography to History

(a) superior communications, short defensive and supply lines, protection by the British fleet, and a mountain barrier; **(b)** The British had to travel a great distance to the field of battle, and they lacked the knowledge of the land on which they were fighting. However, because of their superior sea power, the British could attack wherever they desired along the American coast.

Relating Past to Present

1. Answers will vary.
2. Answers will vary.

Applying History Study Skills

1. (a) the equality of all men; **(b)** The speaker uses reason, the law of God, and the law of nature.
2. I do think; I do not find; I find no such thing.
3. Answers will vary.
4. Answers will vary.
5. Men have a right to choose those who make the rules by which they must live.

419

CHAPTER (pages 420–451)

17 The French Revolution Changed the Course of World History

(1715–1829)

CHAPTER OVERVIEW

The English ideal that the people should play a major role in government influenced the French political philosophers of the 1700s. The writings of these *philosophes,* and the example of the American Revolution, helped to bring about one of the major upheavals of European history—the French Revolution.

Discontent with the Old Regime in France had been growing since the mid-1700s. When Louis XVI called the meeting of the Estates-General, conflict erupted over voting procedures. The Third Estate proclaimed itself a National Assembly and pledged to write a new constitution.

The Constitution of 1791, adopted by the National Assembly, created a limited monarchy. Invasion by Prussian and Austrian troops touched off riots that ended this government. The National Convention, which succeeded the National Assembly, proclaimed a republic and executed the king. Threatened with new invasions and civil war, the National Convention conscripted an army and suppressed domestic opposition through the Reign of Terror. The Directory, the next government of France, was corrupt and inefficient. It was overthrown by Napoleon Bonaparte in a coup d'état.

Napoleon ruled France as a military dictator, but he also initiated many reforms. By 1808 Napoleon dominated Europe. However, after several military defeats, he was forced to abdicate. He soon returned but was decisively defeated at Waterloo. Napoleon's wars cost France and Europe greatly, but his conquests spread revolutionary ideas and feelings of nationalism throughout Europe.

After 1815 governments in Europe sought to restore and maintain political order. At the Congress of Vienna, the leaders of the European powers adopted the principles of legitimacy and territorial compensation and began to forge new alliances. And under Prince Klemens von Metternich's leadership, most European governments suppressed liberal ideas and nationalist aspirations.

SUGGESTED LESSON PLAN

Day	Objectives	Suggested Activities	Materials
1	U3*, U5, C1	Introducing The Chapter (pages 420-21) Section 1 (pages 421-24), Focus/Motivation (page 421), Presentation (page 421), Closure (page 424), Suggested Teaching Strategies, Enrichment Activity, Daily Quiz, Suggested Assignments (page 419B)	ATE, Pupil's Edition, Teacher's Resource-Bank™
2	U3, U5-6, C2	Section 2 (pages 424-29), Focus/Motivation (page 425), Presentation (page 426), Closure (page 428), Suggested Teaching Strategies, Enrichment Activity, Daily Quiz, Suggested Assignments (page 419C)	ATE, Pupil's Edition, Teacher's Resource-Bank™
3	U6, C3-4	Section 3 (pages 429-34), Focus/Motivation (page 429), Presentation (page 430), Closure (page 433), Suggested Teaching Strategies, Enrichment Activities, Daily Quiz, Suggested Assignments (page 419D)	ATE, Pupil's Edition, Teacher's Resource-Bank™
4	U6, C5-6	Section 4 (pages 434-39), Focus/Motivation (page 435), Presentation (page 436), Closure (page 438), Suggested Teaching Strategies, Enrichment Activities, Daily Quiz, Suggested Assignments (page 419E)	ATE, Pupil's Edition, Teacher's Resource-Bank™
5	U6, C7-8	Section 5 (pages 439-44), Focus/Motivation (page 439), Presentation (page 440), Closure (page 443), Suggested Teaching Strategies, Enrichment Activities, Daily Quiz, Suggested Assignments (page 419F)	ATE, Pupil's Edition, Teacher's Resource-Bank™
6	U3, C9	Section 6 (pages 444-49), Focus/Motivation (page 445), Presentation (page 446), Closure (page 448), Suggested Teaching Strategies, Enrichment Activities, Daily Quiz, Suggested Assignments (page 419G)	ATE, Pupil's Edition, Teacher's Resource-Bank™
7	U3, U5-6, C1-9	Chapter 17 Form A Test, Reteaching Worksheet, Chapter 17 Form B Test	Teacher's Resource-Bank™ or Workbook and Test Booklet

*C refers to applicable Chapter Objective, U refers to applicable Unit Goal.

BOOKS FOR THE TEACHER

Brinton, Crane. *The Anatomy of Revolution.* Vintage. Offers a comparative analysis of the French, English, American, and Russian revolutions.

Cobb, Richard, and Colin Jones, eds. *Voices of the French Revolution.* Salem House. Provides a vivid picture of the Revolution through the words of those who lived it.

Herold, J. Christopher. *The Horizon Book of the Age of Napoleon.* Harper & Row. Explains Napoleon's impact on Europe. Includes illustrations.

Hibbert, Christopher. *The Days of the French Revolution.* William Morrow. Features an engrossing account of the Revolution from the Tennis Court Oath to Napoleon's seizure of power.

Manceron, Claude. *Twilight of the Old Order.* Knopf. Provides a picture of France on the brink of revolution through depictions of scores of incidents and images.

BOOKS FOR THE STUDENT

Cairns, Trevor. *The Old Regime and the Revolution.* Lerner Publications. Describes the end of the Old Regime and the onset of the Revolution. Includes illustrations.

Dowd, David L. *The French Revolution.* American Heritage. Offers a well-illustrated description of the Revolution.

Dupuy, Trevor N. *The Military Life of Napoleon.* Franklin Watts. Details the life of Napoleon from military school to the Battle of Waterloo.

Harris, Nathaniel. *The Fall of the Bastille: A Day That Made History.* Dryad. Details the events of July 14, 1789 and attempts to explain why France suffered a revolution.

World Leaders: Past and Present Series. Chelsea House. Includes biographies of Danton, Robespierre, Napoleon, and Metternich.

MULTIMEDIA MATERIALS

The French Revolution: The Bastille (2 fs), Learning Corp. Details the events leading up to the storming of the Bastille.

The French Revolution: The Terror (2 fs), Learning Corp. Demonstrates how political intrigues and problems that grew out of the Revolution led to the Reign of Terror.

Napoleon: The End of a Dictator (mp. 26 min.), Learning Corp. Examines the events that led to Napoleon's downfall.

The Napoleonic Era (2 fs), EAV. Traces Napoleon's rise and his impact upon both France and the rest of Eruope.

Section (pages 421–424)

1 The Enlightenment Applied Scientific Ideas to Politics

SECTION OVERVIEW

During the mid-1700s a number of French philosophers, or *philosophes,* applied the scientific principles of the Enlightenment to the study of human behavior. As a result, such philosophes as Diderot, Montesquieu, Voltaire, and Rousseau began to write reasoned critiques of French society. The writings of these Enlightenment thinkers had a great influence on future political developments in France.

SUGGESTED TEACHING STRATEGIES

1. **Preteaching Vocabulary (Basic)** You may wish to preteach the following important vocabulary terms: Enlightenment, rationalism *(page 421)*; philosophes *(page 422)*; salon, popular sovereignty *(page 423)*; enlightened despotism *(page 424)*. Ask: Why do you think the people of the 1700s referred to their times as *The Age of Enlightenment?*
2. **Understanding Chronology (Average/Group)** Write the following events on the chalkboard or an overhead projector and have students copy the list. Then, to help students understand the development of the Enlightenment, ask them to arrange the events in chronological order. Suggest that they write *1* before the first event, *2* before the second event, and so on.

   __ First volume of the *Encyclopedia* published *(4)*
   __ Rousseau wrote his prize-winning essay for the Academy of Dijon *(3)*
   __ *The Social Contract* published *(5)*
   __ Voltaire's *Letters on England* published *(1)*
   __ United States Constitution written *(6)*
   __ Montesquieu published *The Spirit of the Laws (2)*

ENRICHMENT ACTIVITY

Analyzing Ideas (Average/Group) Show the class the two filmstrips titled *The Enlightenment.* These filmstrips may be obtained from Social Studies School Service, 10200 Jefferson Boulevard, Room 1, P.O. Box 802, Culver City, CA 90232. After they have viewed these filmstrips, lead students in a discussion on the impact of Enlightenment thinking. Ask: How did the ideas of such Enlightenment philosophers as Voltaire and Rousseau influence social and political life in eighteenth-century Europe?

DAILY QUIZ

To assess student understanding of Section 1, give the class the following quiz. (Each item is worth 10 points.)

1. (T or F) The Enlightenment philosophers believed they could apply the scientific method and use reason to explain human nature logically. *(T)*
2. One characteristic of the Enlightenment was ______, or the belief that truth can be arrived at solely by reason or logical thinking. *(rationalism)*
3. Which philosophe published 35 volumes of the *Encyclopedia* between 1751 and 1780? *(Denis Diderot)*
4. ______, or gatherings of the social, political, and cultural elite, gave philosophes the opportunity to meet and discuss the major issues of the day. *(Salons)*

5. In Montesquieu's perfect government, power was divided among three parts: the legislative, the ______, and the ______. *(executive, judicial)*
6. Montesquieu's idea of ______ and ______ influenced the framers of the United States Constitution. *(checks, balances)*
7. (T or F) Voltaire did not like freedom of speech because it disrupted the rule of law. *(F)*
8. On what basic foundation, according to Jean-Jacques Rousseau, should just laws and wise governments be based? *(popular sovereignty)*
9. Why might it be argued that Rousseau should not be included among the philosophers of the Enlightenment? *(Because he distrusted the use of reason, one of the major principles of Enlightenment thinking.)*
10. What system of government did most philosophes favor? *(enlightened despotism)*

SUGGESTED ASSIGNMENTS

1. **Critical Thinking Worksheet (Average/Group)** Have students complete Critical Thinking Worksheet 37 in the TEACHER'S RESOURCEBANK™.
2. **Presenting an Oral Report (Average/Group)** Have interested students research and present oral reports on one of the philosophes of the Age of Enlightenment. Useful sources for information on Enlightenment thinkers include Carl L. Becker's *The Heavenly City of the Eighteenth-Century Philosophers* (Yale University Press); Peter Gay's *Age of Enlightenment* (Time-Life); and Harold Nicolson's *The Age of Reason* (Doubleday).

Section (pages 424–429)

2 Revolution Swept Across France

SECTION OVERVIEW

Under the Old Regime in France, great inequalities existed among the three Estates. The Third Estate was the largest, yet it possessed the least wealth, power, and privilege. When the need for increased revenue led Louis XVI to call a meeting of the Estates-General, the Third Estate saw its chance to increase its political power. However, its demand for a new voting procedure in the Estates-General was denied. In response the Third Estate proclaimed itself a National Assembly and pledged to write a new constitution. Louis XVI's attempt to disperse the National Assembly by force led to the storming of the Bastille, and revolutionary violence quickly swept the country.

SUGGESTED TEACHING STRATEGIES

1. **Preteaching Vocabulary (Basic)** You may wish to preteach the following important vocabulary terms: primogeniture, bourgeoisie, tithe *(page 425)*. Ask: Why do you think the bourgeoisie wanted political power?
2. **Organizing Ideas (Average/Group)** Make copies of the following chart and distribute them to students.

THE OLD REGIME		
Estate	**Membership**	**Conditions**
First		
Second		
Third		

Have students organize the information on pages 424-425 of Section 2 by completing the chart. Suggest that students retain these charts for revisions purposes.

ENRICHMENT ACTIVITY

Preparing a Newscast (Average/Group) Interested students might like to prepare an imaginary newscast from Paris on July 14, 1789. The program, involving several reporters, might be recorded on tape complete with background noises of mob scenes. For help in preparing the newscast, students may consult "The Storming of the Bastille" in Sydney Eisen's and Maurice Filler's *The Human Adventure,* vol. 1 (Harcourt Brace Jovanovich); and Douglas Liversidge's *The Day the Bastille Fell* (Franklin Watts). Have students play their taped newscast to the rest of the class.

DAILY QUIZ

To assess student understanding of Section 2, give the class the following quiz. (Each item is worth 10 points.)

1. Who were members of the First Estate? *(Clergy of the Roman Catholic Church)*
2. Which estate constituted about 97 percent of the French population? *(Third Estate)*
3. (T or F) The Second Estate consisted of the bourgeoisie. *(F)*
4. The bourgeoisie wanted ______ ______ equal to their economic strength. *(political power)*
5. What did the terms *liberty* and *equality* mean to peasants and artisans? *(The right to eat and to receive some reward for their labor.)*
6. To deal with the financial crisis, Louis XVI called a meeting of what group in 1789? *(Estates-General)*
7. (T or F) According to tradition, nobles could not represent the Third Estate. *(F)*
8. (T or F) By the Tennis Court Oath, Louis XVI swore to meet all the demands of the Third Estate. *(F)*
9. Why did the people of Paris storm the Bastille on July 14, 1789? *(To find weapons with which to protect the National Assembly against troops of Louis XVI.)*
10. (T or F) The violent events of July 1789 in Paris were repeated throughout France. *(T)*

SUGGESTED ASSIGNMENTS

1. **Critical Thinking Worksheet (Basic)** Have students complete Critical Thinking Worksheet 38 in the TEACHER'S RESOURCEBANK™.
2. **Researching (Average/Group)** Interested students might like to find out more about how the French celebrate their national holiday, July 14—Bastille Day. Suggest that students use resources in the school and public libraries to find out what ceremonies take place every Bastille Day. The *Readers' Guide to Periodical Literature* may provide them with sources of information on the special celebrations in July 1989 that marked the bicentennial of the storming of the Bastille.

Section (pages 429–434)

3 After a Period of Turmoil, the French Overthrew the Monarchy

SECTION OVERVIEW

The National Assembly assumed power in the disorder following the storming of the Bastille. The assembly abolished the last remnants of feudalism, issued the Declaration of the Rights of Man, and passed a series of reforms. It also drafted the Constitution of 1791, which created a limited monarchy. However, invasion by Prussian and Austrian troops—instigated, in part, by Louis XVI—touched off riots that brought down the monarchy.

SUGGESTED TEACHING STRATEGIES

1. **Preteaching Vocabulary (Basic)** You may wish to preteach the following important vocabulary terms: émigrés, departments *(page 430)*; conservatives, radicals, moderates *(page 433)*. Ask: In the political context, do the terms *conservative, radical,* and *moderate* mean the same today as they did during the French Revolution?
2. **Analyzing Ideas (Average/Group)** With students, review the ideals of the French Revolution—liberty, equality, fraternity—and their meaning for the French people. Then put the following statement on the chalkboard or on an overhead projector: The Constitution of 1791 was not true to the ideals of the Revolution. Ask students to provide evidence to support the statement. *(Students' answers will include such points as: voting was restricted to males who paid taxes, and neither people who owned no land nor women could hold office.)* Then lead a class discussion using the following questions as a guide: Whose interests did the Constitution of 1791 protect? *(the bourgeoisie)* Why might the writers of the Constitution have been reluctant to give people without property the right to vote? *(Answers will vary. Many students will suggest that the writers of the Constitution may have thought that such people did not have a sufficient stake in the country to be entrusted with that responsibility.)*
3. ***Thinking About History: Examining How Perspective Influences Viewpoints (Average/Group)** To reinforce the skill lesson presented on page 432, ask students to suggest how Olympe de Gouges might have viewed the Constitution of 1791 if she had been a member of the Second Estate.

ENRICHMENT ACTIVITIES

1. **Illustrating Ideas (Average/Group)** The national anthem of France, the "Marseillaise," is a stirring recollection of the spirit of the French Revolution. Have several students give a presentation of the "Marseillaise." They should read a translation of the lyrics, and sing or play a record of the French version.

   Other students might like to research the origins of the song. Ask them to provide answers to the following questions: When was the "Marseillaise" composed? *(in April 1792)* What is the origin of its name? *(It was adopted as a marching song by revolutionary troops from the city of Marseille.)* When was it adopted as the national anthem of France? *(The National Convention adopted the song on July 14, 1795.)*
2. **Analyzing Primary Sources (Average/Group)** Official documents are an important source of information for historians. To underscore this point, assign selected students to read portions of the Declaration of the Rights of Man. Excerpts may be found in Sydney Eisen and Maurice Filler's *The Human Adventure,* vol. 1 (Harcourt Brace Jovanovich). Ask these students to identify the Enlightenment ideas contained in this document. Then have other members of the class compare the Declaration of the Rights of Man with the English Bill of Rights and the American Declaration of Independence.

DAILY QUIZ

To assess student understanding of Section 3, give the class the following quiz. (Each item is worth 10 points.)

1. (T or F) The National Assembly abolished the special privileges of the First and Second Estates. *(T)*
2. What document, adopted by the National Assembly in August, 1789, was strongly influenced by the English Bill of Rights, the writings of Rousseau, and the Declaration of Independence? *(Declaration of the Rights of Man)*
3. What three words became the slogan of the French Revolution? *(liberty, equality, fraternity)*
4. (T or F) The émigrés helped organize support for the revolution in foreign countries. *(F)*
5. (T or F) The National Assembly seized church lands and sold them to raise money to pay off the public debt. *(T)*
6. Which group held the most political power under the Constitution of 1791? *(wealthy men)*
7. Louis XVI and his family attempted to flee France, but they were apprehended at the small town of ________. *(Varennes)*
8. Which political faction sat on the left in the Legislative Assembly and helped create the political continuum of left-center-right? *(Radicals)*
9. The Declaration of ________ invited European rulers to help Louis XVI restore the French monarchy to its full power. *(Pillnitz)*

10. Why did the Commune want to abolish the monarchy? *(Because its members believed Louis XVI was guilty of plotting with foreign rulers to overthrow the Constitution of 1791.)*

SUGGESTED ASSIGNMENTS

1. **Illustrating Ideas (Basic)** Remind students that the French Revolution was not confined to the streets of Paris. Rather, revolutionary activities took place throughout the country. To illustrate this point, first provide students with outline maps of France. Then, have them place on their maps the following revolutionary centers in 1789: Nantes, Le Havre, Rouen, Paris, Lille, Nancy, Strasbourg, Besancon, Grenoble, Valence, Marseille, Montpellier. Then ask students to note in which departments these centers are located. *(Nantes—Loire-Atlantique; Le Havre, Rouen—Seine-Maritime; Paris—Paris; Lille—Nord; Nancy—Meurthe-et-Moselle; Strasbourg—Bas-Rhin; Besancon—Doubs; Grenoble—Isere; Valence—Drome; Marseille—Bouches-du-Rhone; Montpellier—Herault)*
2. **Researching (Average/Group)** Interested students might like to find out more about the supporters of the Paris Commune, the *sans-culottes.* Suggest that students use resources in the public library. Inform students that the Dewey classification number for the French Revolution is 944.04. Have the students present their findings in a brief oral report titled "The *Sans-culottes:* Their Role in the Early Days of the French Revolution."
3. **Skill Worksheet (Basic)** Have students complete Skill Worksheet 17 in the TEACHER'S RESOURCEBANK™.

Section (pages 434–439)

4 The French Republic Faced Disorder at Home and War Abroad

SECTION OVERVIEW

The National Convention proclaimed France a republic, fought against the First Coalition, and suppressed domestic opposition with the Reign of Terror. The Convention brought about many reforms in France, but the ruthlessness of the Reign of Terror resulted in chaos. In 1795 the Directory replaced the National Convention as the governing body of the country, but it was corrupt and inefficient. With conditions in the country worsening, Napoleon Bonaparte seized control of the government in a coup d'état.

SUGGESTED TEACHING STRATEGIES

1. **Preteaching Vocabulary (Basic)** You may wish to preteach the following important vocabulary terms: universal manhood suffrage *(page 434)*; conscription, counterrevolution *(page 435)*; coup d'état *(page 439)*. Ask: Why was universal manhood suffrage so important to the members of the Third Estate?
2. **Class Discussion (Average/Group)** To generate discussion among the students, show films on topics covered in Section 4. Films that might be useful include *Man and State: Burke and Paine on Revolution* (27 min., color, BFA Educational Media), in which Edmund Burke, an articulate conservative, and Thomas Paine, a leading revolutionary, debate their conflicting views regarding people, political change, and liberty while elements of the French Revolution are acted out before them; and *Napoleon: The Making of a Dictator* (28 min., color, Learning Corp.), which portrays the motives and events leading to Napoleon's coup d'état.

ENRICHMENT ACTIVITIES

1. **Illustrating Ideas (Average/Group)** Play a recording of "Marat/Sade," sung by Judy Collins (*In My Life*, Elektra Records), for the class. Then lead the class in a discussion, using the following questions as a guide: From which Estate do you think this song emerged? From which group in the Estate? What changes did they want to see? *(This song would have emerged from the peasants of the Third Estate, who were seeking the reduction of privilege and power for the ruling class, economic improvement, and political rights.)* What was their attitude toward their leaders? *(Answers will vary. Many students will note that the song appeals to the leaders for help, but indicates great contempt for what leaders such as Marat had become.)* Did the people feel the revolution had turned out the way they had intended? *(The revolution had not turned out the way they intended because they had not gained what they wanted.)*
2. **Debating Ideas (Challenging)** On the chalkboard or on an overhead projector, write the following quotation from Louis Blanc, a nineteenth-century politician and journalist: "It is a falsehood to say that the Terror saved France, but it may be affirmed that it crippled the Revolution." Then ask interested students to debate the impact of the Reign of Terror on the French Revolution, using Blanc's statement as a starting point for class discussion.

DAILY QUIZ

To assess student understanding of Section 4, give the class the following quiz. (Each item is worth 10 points.)

1. The two major groups in the National Convention were the ______ and the ______. *(Girondists, Jacobins)*
2. Who was the leader of the extreme radicals in the National Convention? *(Jean-Paul Marat)*
3. What was the first action taken by the National Convention when it assumed power? *(It proclaimed the end of the monarchy and the establishment of a republic.)*
4. (T or F) The National Convention established the Committee of Public Safety to direct the army in crushing foreign invaders. *(T)*
5. The leaders of the Reign of Terror included the powerful Jacobins ______ and ______. *(Danton, Robespierre)*
6. What was the "national razor" used to execute people convicted of treason during the Reign of Terror called? *(guillotine)*
7. What important reform did the National Convention institute in the French colonial empire? *(It abolished slavery.)*

8. What government was created by the Constitution of 1795? *(Directory)*
9. Which two countries joined Great Britain in the Second Coalition? *(Austria and Russia)*
10. How did Napoleon Bonaparte come to power in France? *(through a coup d'état)*

SUGGESTED ASSIGNMENTS

1. **Critical Thinking Worksheet (Basic)** Have students complete Critical Thinking Worksheet 39 in the TEACHER'S RESOURCEBANK™.
2. **Writing Biographical Sketches (Average/Group)** Have students prepare biographical sketches on individuals of the French Revolution such as Danton, Marat, Robespierre, Charlotte Corday, and Marie Antoinette. Useful sources of information on these people include Stanley Loomis's *Paris in the Terror* (Lippincott) and Robert R. Palmer's *Twelve Who Ruled* (Atheneum). Students may present their findings to the class.

Section (pages 439–444)

5 Napoleon Built an Empire That Spread Across Europe

SECTION OVERVIEW

Napoleon ruled France as a military dictator. However, he also instituted important domestic reforms, such as the Napoleonic Code, the Bank of France, and a system of public education. Through a number of military victories, Napoleon completely dominated Europe by 1808. But Napoleon's attempts to enforce the Continental System involved him in a costly war with Spain and Portugal and prompted his disastrous invasion of Russia. The nations of Western Europe united to defeat Napoleon, and he was forced to abdicate and retire to the island of Elba. He returned to France and raised an army, but was finally defeated at Waterloo. The Bourbon monarchy was then restored to France, but Napoleon's conquests had spread revolutionary ideas and spurred feelings of nationalism throughout the European continent.

SUGGESTED TEACHING STRATEGIES

1. **Preteaching Vocabulary (Basic)** You may wish to preteach the following important vocabulary terms: plebiscite *(page 439)*; nationalism *(page 441)*; scorched-earth policy *(page 443)*. Ask: How did the spread of nationalism change the political map of Europe?
2. **Identifying Ideas (Average/Group)** Have students study the map of Napoleon's empire in 1810 on page 442. Ask students to make lists in their notebooks of the following: areas that were part of the French Empire, states controlled by Napoleon, states allied with Napoleon, and independent European states. Then, ask students why they think Napoleon was unable to conquer the Russian Empire. *(Answers will vary. Most students will suggest that the territory was so vast that it would have been difficult to conquer and control.)*
3. **Writing a Letter (Average/Group)** Have students write letters from a French soldier to a family member, describing the French retreat from Moscow. Suggest that they refer to pages 442-443 of the textbook for information on Napoleon's invasion of Russia. Call upon students to read their letters to the class.

ENRICHMENT ACTIVITIES

1. **Analyzing Ideas (Average/Group)** Francisco Goya painted scenes of the horror of the Peninsular War. With help from the art department or the library, prepare a slide presentation or use art books to show his paintings to the class. Ask students to discuss what the artist's intentions might have been and what impact his paintings might have had on people who saw them.
2. **Presenting Oral Reports (Average/Group)** Much of Napoleon's fame rested on his military exploits. Interested students might like to present a detailed report on some of Napoleon's military engagements. Useful sources of information on this subject include Fletcher Pratt's *The Battles That Changed History* (Doubleday); Trevor N. Dupuy's *The Military Life of Napoleon* (Franklin Watts); and Claude Manceron's *Austerlitz* (W. W. Norton).
3. **Writing a Script (Challenging)** Interested students might like to prepare a "You Are There" program from Waterloo, starting shortly before the battle began. Interviews with prominent military leaders should be included, along with descriptions of the fighting. Students participating in this exercise should refer to Edward S. Creasy's *The Fifteen Decisive Battles of the World* (Dutton); Manual Komroff's *The Battle of Waterloo* (Macmillan); and Trevor N. Dupuy's *The Military Life of Napoleon* (Franklin Watts) for useful background information.

DAILY QUIZ

To assess student understanding of Section 5, give the class the following quiz. (Each item is worth 10 points.)

1. The period of European history from 1799 to 1814 is known as the ________ Era. *(Napoleonic)*
2. What was the name of the first five years of Napoleon's rule? *(Consulate)*
3. What was the agreement, reached in 1801, between Napoleon and the pope that acknowledged Catholicism as the religion of most French citizens? *(Concordat)*
4. What sea battle almost destroyed the French and Spanish fleet in 1805? *(Trafalgar)*
5. What is the name for Napoleon's blockade of Great Britain? *(Continental System)*
6. Napoleon's armies helped to awaken a spirit of ________ among the peoples they conquered. *(nationalism)*
7. What action led to Napoleon's occupation of Portugal? *(In 1807 Portugal refused to observe the Continental System.)*
8. What policy used by the Russian army caused great problems for Napoleon in Russia? *(scorched-earth policy)*

9. After escaping from Elba, Napoleon triumphantly marched into Paris on March 20, 1815, beginning the period known as the _______ _______. *(Hundred Days)*
10. What is the name of the island in the South Atlantic to which Napoleon was exiled after his defeat at Waterloo? *(St. Helena)*

SUGGESTED ASSIGNMENTS

1. **Geography Supplement (Average/Group)** Have students complete Geography Application Sheet 9 in the TEACHER'S RESOURCEBANK™.
2. **Writing an Editorial (Average/Group)** Organize the class into two groups. Assign one group to write editorials for a British newspaper, and the other for a French newspaper. The subjects of the editorials will be the Battle of Trafalgar and the Continental System. Have each student exchange his or her completed editorial with a student from the other group. Then have students write a letter to the editor responding to the editorial they have received.
3. **Profile Worksheet (Basic)** Have students do Profile Worksheet 17 in the TEACHER'S RESOURCEBANK™.

Section (pages 444–449)

6 Peace Was Restored to Europe

SECTION OVERVIEW

Nationalism and liberalism, two great forces in the post-Napoleonic world, played only a small role at the Congress of Vienna. Diplomats met there to restore legitimate rulers to power and reshuffle territories to maintain a balance of power. Metternich, whose ideas dominated European politics for years, worked to suppress liberal and nationalistic movements that threatened absolutism.

SUGGESTED TEACHING STRATEGIES

1. **Preteaching Vocabulary (Basic)** You may wish to preteach the following important vocabulary terms: legitimacy *(page 445)*; indemnity, reaction, reactionaries *(page 447)*; liberalism *(page 448)*. Ask: How do conservatism and liberalism differ?
2. **Identifying Ideas (Average/Group)** Have students compare the map of Napoleon's empire in 1810 on page 442 with the map of Europe after the Congress of Vienna on page 446. Select a number of students to make a brief presentation to the class describing compensations and the balance of power.

ENRICHMENT ACTIVITIES

1. **Writing a Newspaper Article (Average/Group)** Have students write an article based on an imaginary interview with one of the following European leaders: **(a)** Metternich, explaining why he favors measures such as the Carlsbad Decrees; **(b)** Czar Alexander, explaining why he promotes the Holy Alliance; **(c)** George Canning, explaining why England is withdrawing from the Quintuple Alliance; **(d)** Talleyrand, explaining why he feels France should be accepted into the European community.
2. **Analyzing Ideas (Average/Group)** Lord Byron took a keen interest in Greece's war for national independence and emphasized the achievements of classical Greece in his poetry. A group of students might like to read and analyze some of Lord Byron's poetry, noting the influences of classical Greece.
3. **Presenting a Play (Challenging)** An excellent short play entitled *The Plot to Turn Back the Clock* can be found in Henry Abraham's and Irwin Pfeffer's *Enjoying World History* (Amsco). Ask four volunteers to give a presentation of the play to the class. The questions that accompany the play should be reproduced and passed out for students to discuss and answer.

DAILY QUIZ

To assess student understanding of Section 6, give the class the following quiz. (Each item is worth 10 points.)

1. (T or F) The Congress of Vienna of 1815 undertook to settle the political and territorial questions arising from the Napoleonic Wars. *(T)*
2. Who represented Austria at the Congress of Vienna? *(Prince Klemens von Metternich)*
3. Which European country did the participants of the Congress of Vienna wish to weaken? *(France)*
4. What do we call extremists who not only oppose change but generally desire to turn back the clock to the time before certain changes occurred? *(Reactionaries)*
5. Which four countries constituted the Quadruple Alliance? *(Russia, Prussia, Great Britain, and Austria)*
6. Which European monarch urged that all rulers pledge themselves to rule as Christian princes by signing the Holy Alliance? *(Czar Alexander I)*
7. What was the aim of the Concert of Europe? *(To maintain peace and the status quo)*
8. (T or F) The Carlsbad Decrees ended German government censorship of university students' newspapers. *(F)*
9. (T or F) French troops representing the Quintuple Alliance suppressed a revolt against the king of Spain in 1823. *(T)*
10. Which European nation won independence from the Ottoman Empire in 1829 despite receiving little assistance from the rest of Europe? *(Greece)*

SUGGESTED ASSIGNMENTS

1. **Review Worksheet (Basic)** Have students complete Review Worksheet 17 in the TEACHER'S RESOURCEBANK™.
2. **Researching Ideas (Average/Group)** Interested students might like to do further research on the life of the leader of the Congress of Vienna, Prince Klemens von Metternich. Have the students present their findings to the class.

Teacher's Notes

For suggested lesson plan, additional teaching strategies, enrichment activities, daily quizzes, and suggested assignments, see pages 419A–419G.

Introducing the Chapter
On the chalkboard or on an overhead projector, write the following definition of the term *revolution:* an overthrow of a government or social system, with another taking its place. Explain to students that many factors contribute to a political revolution. Then, write the following factors on the chalkboard or on an overhead projector:

1. Political, economic, and social conditions prior to the Revolution
2. Aims of the Revolution
3. Revolutionary leaders
4. Education and social background of revolutionary leaders
5. Supporters of the Revolution
6. Opposition to the Revolution

Ask students to copy these factors into their notebooks. As students read Chapter 17, have them point out how these various factors contributed to the French Revolution.

Chapter Objectives
After studying Chapter 17, students will be able to:

1. Discuss the philosophy of the Enlightenment writers in France.
2. Enumerate the reasons for discontent among the French people in the 1700s.
3. Discuss the principles contained in the Declaration of the Rights of Man.
4. List the reforms made by the National Assembly.
5. Outline the most significant events of the Reign of Terror.

CHAPTER 17

The French Revolution Changed the Course of World History

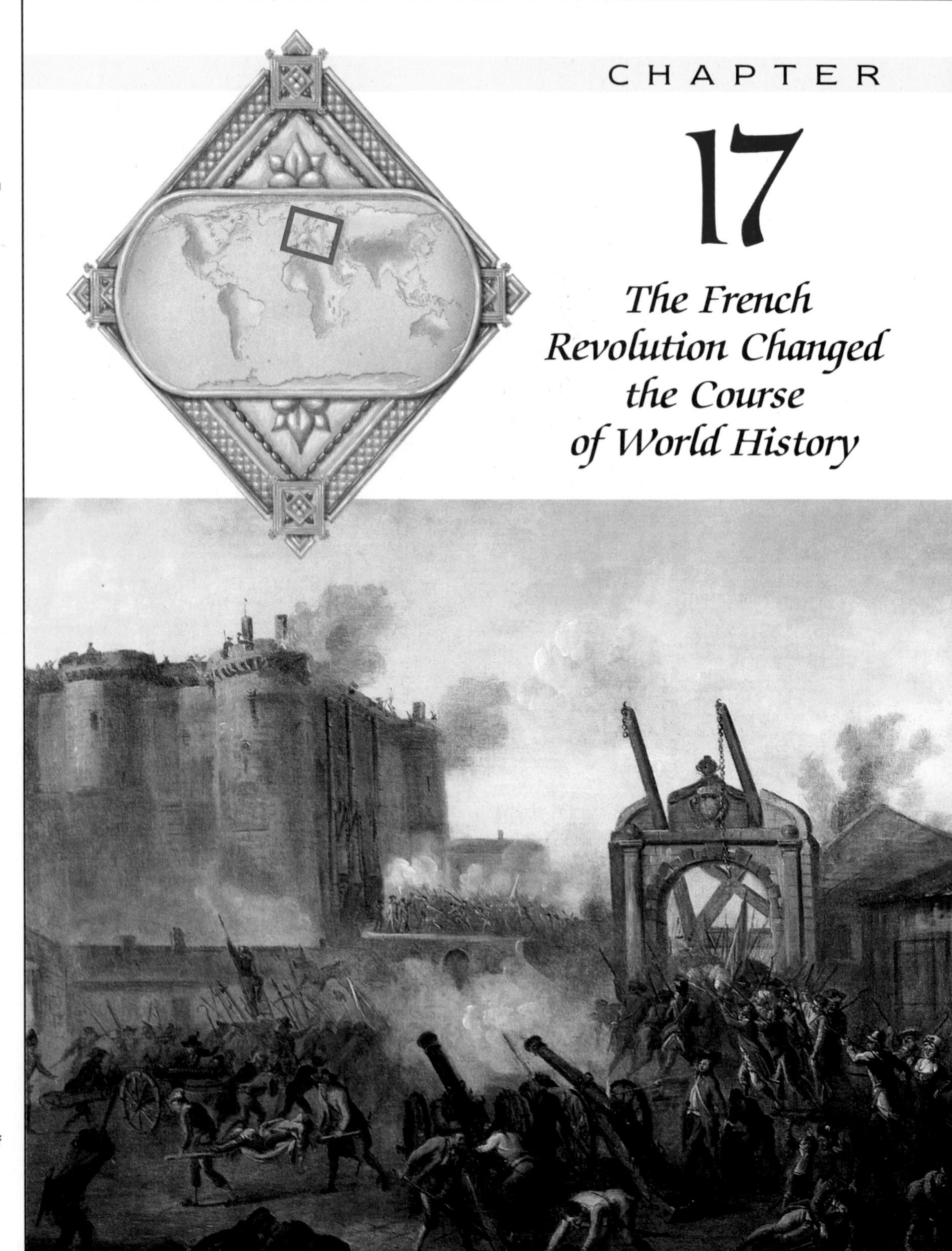

CHAPTER FOCUS

Place France and the rest of Europe

Time

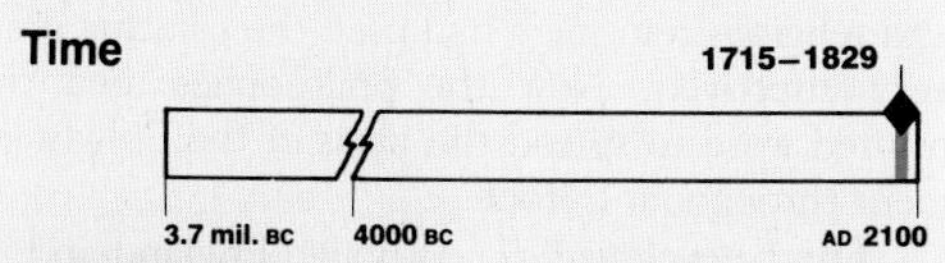

Significance

The English ideal that people should have a voice in government greatly influenced French political writers of the 1700s. These writers spread this idea, paving the way for one of the greatest revolutions in history—the French Revolution. The American Revolution, with its central theme of the freedom and dignity of human beings, helped inspire the French people to overthrow the existing government and establish a government based on these ideals.

The beginning of this revolutionary tradition represents an important step in the development of the modern world. Our ancestors in the 1700s regarded change as dangerous and as something to be avoided. Our times differ markedly; now many people in the West regard change as useful. This totally new attitude about change permits us to accept the period of the French Revolution as a positive turning point in modern history.

Terms to Define

Enlightenment	conscription
philosophe	coup d'état
bourgeoisie	legitimacy

People to Identify

Denis Diderot	Maximilien Robespierre
Rousseau	Napoleon
Louis XVI	Metternich

Places to Locate

Paris	Austerlitz
Corsica	St. Helena

Questions to Guide Your Reading

1 How did the philosophy of the Enlightenment influence people's views on government in the 1700s?
2 How did the makeup of the three estates in France affect the outlook of each on the eve of the meeting of the Estates-General?
3 How did the National Assembly reorganize the French political system between 1789 and 1791?
4 Why did the French Revolution take a more extreme course in 1792?
5 How did Napoleon create an empire?
6 How did the Congress of Vienna try to restore absolutism?

◀ *The taking of the Bastille*

Although Baroness Emmuska Orczy wrote the novel The Scarlet Pimpernel *years after the French Revolution, in it she captured the spirit of an age that transformed the social order. She wrote:*

> *"During the greater part of the day the guillotine had been kept busy at its ghastly work: all that France had boasted of in the past centuries, of ancient names, and blue blood, had paid toll to her desire for liberty and for fraternity. . . . But this was as it should be: were not the people now the rulers of France? Every aristocrat was a traitor . . . for two hundred years now the people had sweated, and toiled, and starved, to keep a lustful court in lavish extravagance; now the descendants of those who had helped to make those courts brilliant had to hide for their lives—to fly, if they wished to avoid the tardy vengeance of the people."*

Like many revolutions, the French Revolution traced its roots to early political writers.

1 The Enlightenment Applied Scientific Ideas to Politics

The European people of the 1700s referred to their century as an "Age of Enlightenment." They believed themselves the first to have discovered the "light" of logical thinking revealed by science. Spurred by Descartes's methodology for understanding the truth and by Newton's explanation of the working of the universe, researchers had made great advances in the physical sciences. During the **Enlightenment** philosophers believed they could apply the scientific method and use reason to logically explain human nature.

Characteristics of the Enlightenment

During the 1700s an increasing number of people began to believe that every natural phenomenon had both a cause and an effect. The thinkers of the Enlightenment attempted to test everything by observation and to determine the cause-and-effect relationships between natural events.

Another characteristic of the Enlightenment was **rationalism,** the belief that truth can be

6. Explain how Napoleon came to power.
7. Describe the Continental System and evaluate Napoleon's effectiveness in reorganizing Europe.
8. Outline Napoleon's policies and show how they contributed to the collapse of his empire.
9. List the terms of the Congress of Vienna and discuss the alliances that grew out of this conference.

SECTION 1

Focus/Motivation
Point out to students that the free exchange of ideas was the life-blood of the Age of Enlightenment. Then ask them to carefully study the picture on page 422. Ask the students how this picture illustrates the exchange of ideas. *(Answers may vary. Most students will suggest that the picture shows a number of philosophes meeting to hear the readings of the works of other philosophes and to discuss the important issues of the day.)*

Presentation
Identifying Ideas (Average/Group)
On the chalkboard or on an overhead projector, write the following list of names:

a. Jean d'Alembert
b. Denis Diderot
c. Marie-Therese Geoffrin
d. Baron de Montesquieu
e. Jean-Jacques Rousseau
f. Voltaire

1B, 4A, 4F, a1A, a1C

● Catherine the Great of Russia provided financial assistance for Diderot while he worked on the *Encyclopedia.*

Then, write the following statements on the chalkboard or on an overhead projector:

1. Wrote *The Spirit of the Laws,* in which he tried to describe the perfect government
2. Edited the *Encyclopedia*
3. Thought that people were born good but that environment, education, and laws corrupted them
4. Exemplified the spirit of the Enlightenment
5. Famous salon organizer
6. Assisted in the editing of the *Encyclopedia*
Ask students to match the statements with the person they best describe.

(Answers: 1. d 2. b 3. e 4. f 5. c 6. a)

arrived at solely by reason, or rational, logical thinking. Because of this central belief, historians often refer to the Age of Enlightenment as the Age of Reason.

Thinkers during the Enlightenment also believed in natural law. The discoveries of Newton and other scientists seemed to support the idea of an orderly universe. Many individuals came to feel that natural law governed the universe and all of its creatures.

God, they believed, had created the world and made rules for all living things. Just as the law of gravity governed the physical movement of planets, so other laws governed human behavior. In order to live in harmony, people had to use reason to discover natural law. If they lived according to this natural law and made their government and other institutions conform to it, the world would become a perfect place. Thus the thinkers of the Enlightenment became convinced that progress would always take place.

Crusaders of the Enlightenment

Their contemporaries called the thinkers of the Enlightenment **philosophes** (fee • luh • ZAWFS); *philosophe* is the French word for "philosopher." The philosophes were not only philosophers, however, but also critics of society. They wrote to one another, and they published their ideas in books, plays, pamphlets, newspapers, and "encyclopedias." Before and during the Reformation, the humanists and religious reformers had used the printing press very effectively. Now the philosophes used the printed word to spread the ideas of the Enlightenment throughout Europe.

The *Encyclopedia.* Although England and its allies curbed Louis XIV's expansion of French rule and maintained the balance of power, France remained both the strongest political power and the dominant cultural influence in Europe. Educated people throughout Europe spoke and wrote French. They read the *Encyclopedia,* a handbook or reference book on the Enlightenment, which became the most famous publication of this period.

The philosophe Denis Diderot (dee • DROH) ● edited the *Encyclopedia.* Working 14 hours a day in a tiny attic, he and his assistant, Jean d'Alembert (dal • uhm • BAR), published the first edition of the *Encyclopedia* in 35 volumes between 1751 and 1780.

The leading philosophes all contributed articles to the *Encyclopedia.* Their writings criticized the church, the government, the slave trade, torture,

Learning from Pictures *Marie-Thérèse Geoffrin's salon provided the opportunity for authors to hear readings from other writers' works, like those of Voltaire.*

- For a time during the 1750s, Frederick the Great of Prussia was a patron of Voltaire.

taxes, and war. They covered nearly every subject—many of them technical in nature—in the rational, questioning style of the Enlightenment.

The French authorities frowned on critical writings, however, and they imprisoned Diderot and several other philosophes. Nevertheless, people throughout Europe bought illegal editions of the *Encyclopedia,* read it, and adopted its ideas enthusiastically.

Salons. Philosophes gravitated to France, particularly to Paris. There famous hostesses set up **salons,** or gatherings of the social, political, and cultural elite, in their homes. One such hostess, Marie-Thérèse Geoffrin (zhaw • FRAN), had a chef who cooked superb meals for her gatherings. Amid lavish entertainment and witty and intelligent conversation, the philosophes could meet one another and discuss the important issues of the day.

Political Criticism

The philosophes critically examined the political and social institutions of their day. They tried to learn how these institutions had developed. They analyzed the power of kings, the special position of the church, and the privileges of clergy and nobles. Several philosophes attacked the idea of privileged classes. They thought that political and social institutions should be changed to benefit everyone instead of just certain groups.

Montesquieu. In the early 1700s, English political ideas and institutions became popular in France. A number of French philosophes adopted the ideas of John Locke, about whom you read in Chapter 16. In 1748 Baron de Montesquieu (mahn • tuhs • KYOO) published *The Spirit of the Laws,* in which he tried to describe what he considered a perfect government. After studying all existing governments, Montesquieu concluded that the English had the most nearly perfect form. He wrote that its greatest strength lay in the fact that power was divided equally among the three branches of government: the legislative, which made the laws; the executive, which administered them; and the judicial, which interpreted and applied them. Each branch balanced and checked the power of the others.

Montesquieu's high opinion of the English form of government was based on a misunderstanding of it. As you know from reading Chapter 16, the legislative and executive powers were largely combined in the House of Commons rather than separated into the two branches of government. Nevertheless, Montesquieu's ideas carried great weight in the formation of limited monarchies in Europe. In the United States, his concept of checks and balances influenced the framers of the Constitution in 1787.

Voltaire. The French writer François-Marie Arouet, known as Voltaire, exemplified the spirit of the Enlightenment. After serving two sentences in the Paris prison called the Bastille (ba • STEEL), Voltaire fled for a time to England. He commented on the British political system and English customs in *Letters on England* (1734), which helped popularize English ideas in France.

When he returned to France, Voltaire savagely attacked everything he considered sham or superstition. He fought against intolerance and injustice, and he managed to reverse several legal decisions—unfortunately not always before the defendants had been unjustly punished. He did so by rallying public opinion and rousing people to oppose barbaric tortures and religious intolerance. Voltaire is credited with a famous statement on freedom of speech: "I do not agree with a word you say, but I will defend to the death your right to say it."

Rousseau. Jean-Jacques Rousseau (roo • SOH) first gained attention in 1749 by writing a prize-winning essay for the Academy of Dijon. The academy asked, "Has the reestablishment of the sciences and the arts tended to purify or corrupt social morality?" Rousseau responded that civilization had corrupted people. He said that history repeats itself in cycles of decay, and that we had only to look at Egypt, Greece, Rome, and Byzantium for examples.

In his most famous book, *The Social Contract,* published in 1762, Rousseau wrote that people are born good but that environment, education, and laws corrupt them. The free and good state into which people are born can be preserved only if they live under a government that they have chosen and can control. In other words, just laws and wise governments must be based upon **popular sovereignty**—that is, created by and subject to the will of the people. This idea of Rousseau's had enormous influence.

In some ways, Rousseau belongs outside the Enlightenment. In an age of reason, he distrusted reason, believing that it brought on corruption and misery, not progress. Rousseau preferred a kind of pastoral state, free of complicated institutions. By the 1780s many people who had tired of rationalism

423

1B, 4A, 4F, 4G, a1A, a1C, a4A, a4F, a4H

SECTION 1

Closure

On the chalkboard or on an overhead projector, write Voltaire's famous statement on free speech:

"I do not agree with a word you say, but I will defend to the death your right to say it."

Ask students to discuss how Voltaire may have viewed Louis XIV of France and Charles I of England.

Review Answers

1. *Enlightenment:* period during which philosophers believed they could apply the scientific method and use reason to logically explain human nature; ***rationalism:*** belief that truth can be arrived at solely by reason; ***philosophes:*** French word for "philosopher"; ***salons:*** gatherings of social, political, and cultural elite in France; ***popular sovereignty:*** belief that government is created by and subject to the will of the people; ***enlightened despotism:*** system of government in which absolute monarchs ruled according to the principles of the Enlightenment

2. *Marie-Thérèse Geoffrin:* wealthy salon hostess; ***Voltaire:*** French writer who fought against intolerance and injustice, exemplified the Enlightenment; ***Jean-Jacques Rousseau:*** author of *The Social Contract,* who believed people were born good but were corrupted by education and laws

accepted Rousseau's philosophy of the "natural man." He had great influence in the later years of the Enlightenment.

Enlightened Despotism

The philosophes argued and worked to make a better world based on reason. They did not criticize religion and people's faith so much as they fought superstition, the institution of the church, and the ignorance of some of the clergy. They did not dislike monarchy itself so much as they disliked absolute monarchy. Most philosophes favored **enlightened despotism**—a system of government in which absolute monarchs ruled according to the principles of the Enlightenment.

In countries with absolute monarchies and strong censorship, the rulers and clergy fought the ideas of the philosophes. They prohibited the publishing of books by philosophes, or they severely censored the books, removing any material unflattering to public officials or the church. The public hangman symbolically burned many books. The clergy thundered from their pulpits against the philosophes, whom they accused of undermining the church.

Faced with this unfavorable attention, the philosophes became cautious. They wrote "Persians" when they meant "Parisians," as Montesquieu did with his *Persian Letters.* Voltaire, who did not wish to repeat his earlier imprisonment in France, moved to a residence near Geneva, Switzerland, out of reach of the French authorities.

Later, other people, not content to merely discuss such ideas, preferred instead to act upon them. By the late 1780s, France, the home of the Enlightenment, became the setting for a major political and social revolution.

SECTION 1 REVIEW

1. **Define** Enlightenment, rationalism, philosophes, salons, popular sovereignty, enlightened despotism
2. **Identify** Marie-Thérèse Geoffrin, Voltaire, Jean-Jacques Rousseau
3. **Relating Ideas** How did the *Encyclopedia* influence Europeans during the 1700s?
4. **Contrasting Ideas** How did Montesquieu's ideas of government differ from those of Rousseau?
5. **Analyzing Ideas** How did England and English ideas influence the French philosophes?

2 Revolution Swept Across France

When the French Revolution began in 1789, the rest of Europe watched in horrified astonishment. For more than 100 years, France had been the largest and most powerful European nation. Within a few months, however, the king lost his power to make laws, and eventually the people's elected representatives voted for his execution. These new rulers wrote a constitution and reformed many laws. The radical change made people feel that they were living in a new era. They began to refer to the period before 1789 as the Old Regime.

The Old Regime

How did the French Revolution happen? To answer that question, we must look first at the Old Regime. You will recall from earlier chapters that the French kings constructed an absolute monarchy in which the king's will was law. You will remember, too, that the French organized their society into three estates. Great inequality existed among these estates. The First and Second Estates had the fewest people, but they also had the most wealth, power, and privilege.

First Estate. The First Estate consisted of the clergy of the Roman Catholic church and totaled less than 1 percent of the population. The church retained many of the privileges it had held since the Middle Ages. Only church courts could try priests and bishops. The clergy did not have to pay taxes, but they agreed to make a "free gift" of money to the French king. The church owned about one-tenth of all French land and received enormous amounts of money from rents, taxes, and fees. The higher clergy—archbishops, bishops, and abbots—held most of this wealth. As a result, some of these people had become lazy, worldly, and neglectful of their spiritual duties.

In contrast, the lower clergy, made up of the parish priests, performed most of the work and received very low pay. In addition to giving religious guidance, they fed the poor and provided all education.

Second Estate. The nobility, the Second Estate, represented less than 2 percent of the population. They still had special privileges and customs

The average artisan earned 20 *sous* a day, while peasants were lucky to make a daily wage of 8 *sous.* Some average prices: bread—1 *sou* per pound; beef—3 *sous* per pound; wine—3 *sous* per pint; eggs—10 *sous* per dozen; a good pair of shoes—60 *sous;* a shirt—30 *sous.*

that had originated in feudal times—the right to wear a sword; **primogeniture,** or the right of the eldest son to inherit titles and lands; and the right to function as "lord of the manor." The nobles paid few taxes, if any, and they still collected feudal dues from the peasants. Only nobles held the highest positions in the army and government. Although some cared about the welfare of France, as a class the nobility were thoughtless, irresponsible, and extravagant.

Third Estate. The rest of the people of France—approximately 97 percent—belonged to the Third Estate. This estate was itself subdivided into three groups.

At the top stood the **bourgeoisie** (boorzh • wah • ZEE)—the city-dwelling middle class—made up of merchants, manufacturers, and professional people such as doctors and lawyers. Many of them possessed wealth and education. Below the bourgeoisie came the laborers and artisans of the cities. The peasants ranked at the bottom of the Third Estate and often led miserable lives, mired in inescapable poverty. By the 1700s few peasants remained serfs, but most still owed feudal dues and services such as working on the roads. They paid rent for the land they worked, the heaviest taxes, and one-tenth of their income—the **tithe**—to the church. They worked long and hard, but they had no voice in making or changing the laws that kept them under the absolute and crushing control of their landlords and the king.

Growing Discontent

In the mid-1700s discontent in France began to grow. Several factors explain this discontent. The first resulted from the growth of the French population. Families had more children to support, and they needed more food and money.

Changing economic conditions in France also spurred discontent. In order to get more money, the nobles, clergy, and some of the bourgeoisie who owned land raised the rents they charged peasants. They hired lawyers to find old feudal dues that had fallen into disuse. Then they forced the peasants to pay these dues in addition to their already heavy taxes and other obligations. The nobles and clergy also tried to sell things they had once given away. For example, instead of letting peasants pick up twigs and branches in the woods for use as fuel, the landlords sold them firewood.

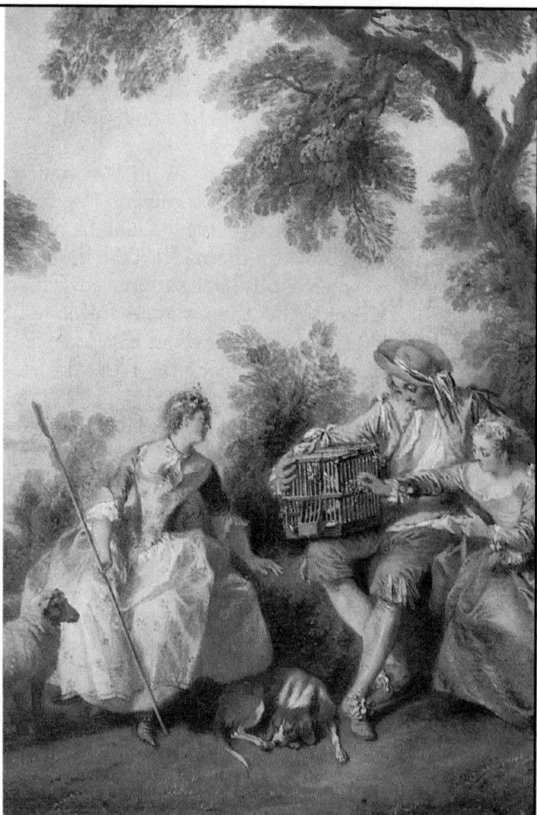

Learning from Pictures *Nobles dressed up as peasants to idealize peasant life. Peasant life though, was harsh, oppressive, and anything but idyllic.*

In the cities, laborers found food prices rising higher and higher, but wages were not going up as quickly. The artisans and peasants resented the rich, who collected their rents, lived in big houses, and had plenty to eat. The poor blamed the king for allowing prices to get so high. They loathed having to pay taxes when the nobles and clergy did not. Sometimes the poor took to the streets and rioted against these higher prices and taxes. Travelers' diaries of the period tell of the robbery and violent crime this widespread misery sparked. The poor economic conditions also reinforced the determination of the first two estates to protect their most important privilege: freedom from taxation.

Although the bourgeoisie prospered during the 1700s, they too became discontented. They wanted political power equal to their economic strength. Merchants and manufacturers resented paying taxes when the nobles and clergy did not. The bourgeoisie also wanted their sons to have

3. The leading philosophers contributed articles to the *Encyclopedia.* Their writing criticized the church, government, the slave trade, taxes, and war. People throughout Europe adopted these ideas enthusiastically.
4. Montesquieu praised the English form of government for its division of power among legislative, executive, and judicial branches. His ideas were later embodied in the United States Constitution. Rousseau wrote that government ought to be based on the free choice of the people.
5. Montesquieu's *Spirit of the Laws,* which described his ideas on the perfect government, was strongly influenced by England's political system. Voltaire's *Letters on England,* which discussed the English political system and English customs, helped to popularize English ideas among the philosophes.

SECTION 2

Focus/Motivation
"It was the best of times, it was the worst of times." So began Charles Dickens's *A Tale of Two Cities,* a novel about the French Revolution. Remind students that French society was organized into three classes called estates—the first consisted of the clergy; the second consisted of the French nobility; and the third, and by far the largest, consisted of the bourgeoisie, laborers and artisans, and peasants.

1B, 4A, 4G, a1A, a1C

Louis XV's disdain for others is illustrated by the following incident. He ordered Paris jewelers to make a necklace of close to 650 diamonds at a cost of nearly 1.6 million livres—about $2.5 million in present-day money. When the jewelers delivered the completed necklace, Louis claimed to have no knowledge of the transaction, and refused to pay.

Ask students to interpret the quote from *A Tale of Two Cities* in terms of how it might apply to the organization of French society. *(Answers may vary. Most students will point out that for the First and Second Estates it was the best of times, since they enjoyed great wealth and special privileges. For the Third Estate, however, it was the worst of times. Although some bourgeoisie had wealth, they also had to pay high taxes. Laborers, artisans, and peasants lived lives of great poverty, and they had no say in the making of the laws.)*

Presentation Relating Cause and Effect (Average/Group) On the chalkboard or on an overhead projector, write the following three groups of statements. For each numbered statement, have students determine whether each of the two following statements can best be described as a cause or as an effect.

1. French nobles felt the economic pinch of the mid-1700s.
a. _____ Nobles raised the rents they charged peasants. *(E)*
b. _____ Prices began to rise in France. *(C)*
2. The bourgeoisie were discontented.
a. _____ Their sons could not hold important positions in the church, army, and government. *(C)*
b. _____ Mercantilist regulations governed wages and prices. *(C)*

important positions in the church, army, and government. However, only nobles could hold such positions.

The bourgeoisie wanted a say in government policy mainly because the government interfered with business. The bourgeoisie had at first welcomed mercantilism. By the mid-1700s, however, they disliked mercantilist regulations governing wages and prices. And they wanted freedom to trade with foreign countries without interference.

Discontent simmered among the First and Second Estates, too. Since the reign of Henry IV, the nobility and upper clergy had disliked the increasing concentration of power in the hands of French kings. France became larger and its kings more powerful, with larger armies at their disposal. The nobles did not profit from this trend; instead, they lost much of their influence.

Different Grievances, Similar Ideas

The various groups in French society had different kinds of grievances, but they shared the same ideas and used the same words to express them. They all talked of "liberty" and "equality" as their natural rights. For peasants and artisans, liberty and equality meant the right to eat and to have some reward for their labor. For the bourgeoisie, liberty and equality meant the freedom to trade without restrictions. It also meant the right to advance to the highest levels of society on merit alone. They called this "equality of opportunity." For the nobility, liberty and equality meant the liberty to enjoy their ancient privileges and to limit the authority of the king. Even though they meant different things to different people, these ideas of liberty and equality unified France's various groups in a major challenge to the king's power in 1789.

The Financial Crisis

The crisis that now paralyzed France stemmed from many years of conflict. The wars of Louis XIV had left France saddled with a huge debt. In 1715 a new king began his reign, and for 25 years France enjoyed peace. But the national debt continued to grow. Wise rulers might have averted this financial crisis, which ultimately toppled the monarchy, but the Bourbons lacked that wisdom.

Louis XV. King Louis XV's reign, the second longest in French history, lasted 59 years—from 1715 to 1774. Only five years old when he came to the throne, Louis XV began his reign backed by the goodwill of the French people, who called him "Louis the Well-Beloved." The intelligent Louis XV might have become a great king, but in later years his laziness, personal vices, intrigues, and uncaring attitude toward the French people exhausted their initial goodwill.

When taxes did not produce enough money to meet expenses, Louis XV borrowed more and more from the bankers. He turned his back on those people who summoned up enough courage to urge him to economize. Warned that his actions endangered France, Louis XV remarked, "It will survive for my time. After me, the deluge."

Louis XVI. In 1774 Louis XVI succeeded Louis XV as the ruler of France. Marie Antoinette, the daughter of the Austrian empress Maria Theresa and the wife of Louis XVI, seemed destined for tragedy. She served as the target for all people determined to undermine the monarchy. To begin with, her marriage to Louis XVI was part of an unpopular alliance between Austria and France. She had beauty, grace, and charm, but she chose her friends unwisely and meddled in politics. In time the French people came to hate her.

King at the age of 19, Louis XVI cared more for hunting than governing. But France's worsening debt, which had grown rapidly because of French assistance to the United States during the American Revolution, forced him to tackle his governmental tasks.

Louis XVI sought help from financial experts. They all gave him the same advice: tax the first two estates. Each time new taxes were proposed, however, the nobles protested and refused to cooperate. Sometimes they led riots that the king had difficulty putting down. By 1787 the country had exhausted its credit, and bankers refused to lend the government more money. France faced financial disaster.

Reluctantly Louis XVI decided to convene the Estates-General at Versailles in May 1789. He hoped that by calling together the representatives of all three estates, not just of the nobility, he could get approval for his plan to tax the wealthy.

The Meeting of the Estates-General

At the time the king called the meeting of the Estates-General, France was suffering from high

● When a deputy of the king ordered the representatives to disperse, the Count de Mirabeau replied, "You should seek permission to use force; for only the power of bayonets will dislodge us."

unemployment and serious inflation in addition to the government's financial crisis. Moreover, the harvest of 1788 had been poor, and food prices had soared. Peasants and urban laborers were finding that they had to spend more than 60 percent of their income just for bread.

The planned meeting of the Estates-General created feelings of excitement and expectation among the people. The Abbé Sieyès (see • ay • YES), who became a leading revolutionary, published "What Is the Third Estate?"—a pamphlet that everyone in France talked about. In it Sieyès wrote:

> "What is the Third Estate?
> Everything. What has it been,
> till the present, in the political order?
> Nothing. What does it ask?
> To become something."

The French people hoped the meeting of the Estates-General would solve their problems.

No one knew exactly what powers and rules the Estates-General had, because it had not met for 175 years. Many people felt that if it had power only to advise the king, and not to make and carry out laws, the meeting would be useless. They also argued about the rules. In the past the three estates had met separately, and each estate had cast one vote. This procedure had always allowed the clergy and nobles of the First and Second Estates to outvote the Third Estate.

Many representatives of the Third Estate were young lawyers acquainted with the ideas of Montesquieu and Voltaire. A few nobles, like the Count de Mirabeau, also consented to represent the Third Estate. As the representatives of the majority of the people, they insisted on having a real voice in decisions without being automatically outvoted by the other two estates. The Third Estate had as many representatives as the First Estate and Second Estate combined. Therefore, it wanted the three estates to meet together, with their representatives voting as individuals.

The Estates-General assembled first in a combined meeting on May 5, 1789. Louis XVI instructed the delegates to follow the old custom of each estate meeting separately and voting as one body. The representatives of the Third Estate refused. They claimed that the Estates-General represented the French people, not the three classes. Therefore, all the representatives should meet together and vote as individuals.

Always hesitant, Louis XVI failed to take action. As a result, on June 17, 1789, the Third Estate proclaimed itself the National Assembly. The rebellious representatives then invited the delegates of the other two estates to join them in working for the welfare of France. When the king had the representatives of the Third Estate locked out of their meeting place, they met at a nearby indoor tennis court. There, on June 20, they made a pledge called the Tennis Court Oath. The representatives declared that they would not adjourn ● until they had written a constitution for France and had seen it adopted. Finally the king gave in and ordered the three estates to meet together.

Learning from Pictures *The Tennis Court Oath was the decisive challenge to the absolute monarchy in France, established by Louis XIV.*

3. The French government became bankrupt.
a. ______ France fought many wars and supported the American Revolution. *(C)*
b. ______ The king called the Estates-General. *(E)*

427

SECTION 2

Closure

Refer the students to the statement by Abbé Sieyès on page 427. Ask students what evidence they can provide to support Abbé Sieyès's statement about the Third Estate.

Review Answers

1. ***primogeniture:*** the right of the oldest son to inherit titles and lands; ***bourgeoisie:*** city-dwelling middle class; ***tithe:*** one-tenth of a person's income that is paid to the church
2. ***Louis XVI:*** came to the French throne at the age of 19 in 1774, cared more for hunting than governing; ***Abbé Sieyès:*** wrote a pamphlet called "What Is the Third Estate?" and became a leading revolutionary
3. The social structure of France during the Old Regime was based on three classes, or estates: the First Estate (clergy), the Second Estate (nobles), and the Third Estate (approximately 97 percent of the population, including the bourgeoisie, artisans and peasants).
4. Discontent began to grow because poor economic conditions placed heavy burdens on peasants and artisans, the bourgeoisie wanted political power equal to their economic strength and freedom from mercantilist restrictions, and the nobles and upper clergy resented the growing power of the king.
5. (a) To the peasants "liberty" and "equality" meant

CONNECTIONS: THEN AND NOW

Independence Days

Most modern nations celebrate a day in honor of their nation each year. For many this takes the form of an independence day, marking the date when the nation became a distinct political unit.

The oldest such independence day is August 1 in Switzerland. It commemorates the day in 1291 when three Swiss cantons, or states, agreed to form a union. Switzerland has now grown to 21 cantons, and they all celebrate their independence on August 1.

After World War II, many colonies of European nations gained independence. Each year some hold festivals celebrating their freedom, such as the ones in India (below left) and in Mexico (below right).

Even nations so ancient that they cannot record an independence date have established a national festive day. For example, in England there are fireworks on Guy Fawkes Day, November 5, to commemorate the day in 1605 when the government uncovered and foiled a plot to blow up Parliament.

A number of nations consider themselves to be creations of revolutions. The French observe Bastille Day every July 14. It marks the day in 1789 on which a Paris mob stormed the dreaded royal prison, the Bastille. The French people regard this event as the beginning of their freedom in modern times.

In the United States, Americans observe a holiday on July 4, the day in 1776 on which the Declaration of Independence was adopted. Americans celebrate the day with parades, speeches, and fireworks (above).

About the time of the American Revolution, Europeans first applied the techniques for making fireworks to the making of rockets for warfare. One of the earliest military uses of rockets occurred in the War of 1812 between the United States and Great Britain. After the British bombarded Fort McHenry, in Baltimore, Maryland, the American poet Francis Scott Key wrote a poem describing the battle, which he had watched. Later his poem, set to music, became the American national anthem. Today, as Americans watch "the rockets' red glare" during Independence Day fireworks displays, they are reminded of the link between the beauty of the celebration and the seriousness of battle.

1B, 4A, 4G, a1A, a1C, a4A, a4F, a4G

● The storming of the Bastille, which cost the lives of about 100 people, won the release of just seven prisoners.

The Spread of the Revolution

Now Louis XVI tried to do secretly what he dared not do openly. He began to bring troops to Paris and to Versailles, where the representatives were meeting. Fearing that he planned to drive out the National Assembly by force, the people of Paris took action. On July 14, 1789, they stormed and captured the Bastille, the hated prison-fortress, in search of weapons. They planned to use the weapons to defend the National Assembly against the royal troops.

This outbreak of violence in Paris led to the formation of a new government for the city. Under the leadership of General Lafayette, the French hero who had fought for American independence in the Revolutionary War, a people's army—the National Guard—was formed. The tricolor—a flag bearing vertical red, white, and blue stripes, which has remained the flag of France—replaced the white flag of the Bourbons with its *fleur de lis* (lily) symbols.

The events in Paris were repeated throughout France. In July and August, a "Great Fear" swept across the land. The peasants believed rumors that the nobles planned to send bandits into the countryside to crush them and the Revolution. They feared that the nobles would hoard grain and starve the peasants into submission. Eager to take revenge for old wrongs, the peasants attacked and often destroyed monasteries and manor houses. They burned the hated documents that recorded rents, feudal dues, and other obligations. They killed some of the nobles and their agents, as well as some government officials, especially tax farmers. These actions showed how widespread people's hatred of the social system of the Old Regime had become.

SECTION 2 REVIEW

1. **Define** primogeniture, bourgeoisie, tithe
2. **Identify** Louis XVI, Abbé Sieyès
3. **Explaining Ideas** Describe the social structure of France during the Old Regime.
4. **Interpreting Ideas** Why did discontent grow in France during the mid-1700s?
5. **Analyzing Ideas** **(a)** How were the terms "liberty" and "equality" interpreted by the peasants? **(b)** by the bourgeoisie?
6. **Understanding Ideas** **(a)** Why did Louis XVI call a meeting of the Estates-General? **(b)** Why did representatives of the Third Estate insist that all three groups of the Estates-General meet and vote together?

3 After a Period of Turmoil, the French Overthrew the Monarchy

Chaos engulfed France after the storming of the Bastille and the outbreaks of violence throughout the country. With the support of the people, the National Assembly assumed power.

The End of the Old Regime

Many members of the National Assembly felt that they could deal with revolutionary violence only by removing the oppression and injustice that produced it. In a little more than a month, they took several important steps in this direction.

As of August 4, 1789, the National Assembly abolished the last remnants of feudalism in France. Delegates repealed the tithe and canceled all feudal dues and services owed by the peasants. They also did away with the special privileges of the First and Second Estates.

Following these reforms, on August 27, 1789, the assembly adopted the Declaration of the Rights of Man. The English Bill of Rights, the writings of Rousseau and other philosophers, and the American Declaration of Independence strongly influenced this document.

The Declaration of the Rights of Man stated that men are born equal and remain equal before the law. It proclaimed freedom of speech, of the press, and of religion. It guaranteed men the right to take part in their government and to resist oppression and declared that all citizens had an equal right to hold public office. The Declaration of the Rights of Man also assured the right to personal liberty, which men could lose only after a fair trial and conviction. The Declaration stated and defined the principles that became the slogan of the French Revolution: "liberty, equality, fraternity."

These rights, however, were not extended to women. During the Revolution a group of women led by a Parisian housewife, Olympe de Gouges (duh • GOOZH), wrote a declaration of rights for women, but the National Assembly rejected it. The leaders of the Revolution were not ready to grant women legal rights or to share political participation with them. They believed in equality for men, but they did not believe that women were the equals of men.

that all people had the right to eat and have some reward for their labor. **(b)** To the bourgeoisie the terms meant the liberty to trade without restrictions and the right to advance to the highest levels of society on merit alone.
6. (a) Louis XVI called a meeting of the Estates-General to help pull France back from the verge of bankruptcy. **(b)** In the past each estate had met separately and cast one vote as a body. Therefore, the clergy and the nobles together could always outvote the Third Estate.

SECTION 3

Focus/Motivation
Write the following terms on the chalkboard or on an overhead projector: *conservative, radical, moderate.* Ask students to find the definitions of these terms on page 433. Then, have students determine which category each of the following might have belonged to and why: monarch, clergy, nobility, bourgeoisie, artisans, laborers, peasants. *(Answers may vary. Most students will suggest that the monarch, clergy, and nobility probably would be conservative because they might lose their privileged position in society through change. Some members of the bourgeoisie would be moderate because they might be afraid of losing what financial gains they had made. Others would be radical since they might believe that gaining political power*

1B, 4A, 4G, a1A, a1C, a4A

● Attempting to squelch the Revolution, and for food shortages and the high price of bread

was more important than financial well-being. Artisans, laborers, and peasants probably would be radical since they had nothing to lose and everything to gain through change.)

Presentation
Writing an Editorial (Average/Group)
Have interested students write editorials reacting to Louis XVI's flight and his capture at Varennes. Mention to students that after the king's attempted escape, public opinion on what to do with him was divided. Suggest that they reflect this division of opinion in their editorials. Have students read their editorials to the rest of the class.

Learning from Pictures *This engraving depicts Parisian women marching to Versailles on* ● *October 5, 1789. For what did these women blame the king?*

Although the National Assembly swept away the remains of feudalism in France, the Old Regime died hard. Many nobles fled to Great Britain, to Italy, and across the Rhine to Germany. There they plotted continuously to overturn the Revolution and set the clock back. These **émigrés** (EM • ee • gray)—French for "emigrants"—became a constant source of trouble for France for the next few years.

Some nobles remained at Versailles with the king. Their opposition to some of his policies had helped start the Revolution. Now, however, most nobles sided with the king against the National Assembly and others who insisted on change. The nobles urged the king to use force to restore the Old Regime. Taking their advice, Louis XVI again called troops to Versailles.

When news of this reached the people, a crowd led by women marched from Paris to Versailles. They believed that the king was trying to squelch the Revolution. They also blamed the king for food shortages and the high price of bread. The crowd stormed into the palace and forced Louis XVI, Marie Antoinette, and their family to return to Paris with them, away from the plotting and scheming royal advisers.

The National Assembly accompanied the royal family to Paris. There the Assembly held meetings in a public hall, where spectators often interrupted the debates with shouts or rose to give their own opinions from the gallery. This kind of open, democratic participation in government would have been unthinkable before 1789.

Reforms in Government

The abolition of feudalism and the issuing of the Declaration of the Rights of Man established the guiding principles of the French Revolution. The National Assembly then began to work out the details. Between 1789 and 1791, the Assembly passed more than 2,000 laws aimed at correcting abuses and setting up a new government.

The Assembly reformed France's administrative structure. It abolished the provinces and divided France into 83 districts called **departments.** It also called for the election of all local officials.

Because it had assumed responsibilities along with its new powers, the National Assembly also assumed the burden of the debt. In November 1789 the National Assembly seized land that belonged to the Catholic church and offered it for sale to the public. The proceeds from the sale could then be used to pay off the public debt. The wealthier peasants, who had been renting this land, bought a good portion of it.

430

● Jean-Baptiste Drouet, the man responsible for apprehending the royal coach at Varennes, said that he was struck by the resemblance of one of the passengers "to the effigy on the fifty-livre *assignat* (bank note)."
■ southwest

1A, 1B, 4A, 4G, a1A, a1C, a4B, a4C

In 1790 the Assembly issued the Civil Constitution of the Clergy. This law stated that people in the parishes and dioceses would elect their clergy. The government—as a compensation for seizing church lands—assumed church expenses and paid the salaries of priests and bishops. The pope refused to allow the clergy to accept this arrangement, and most obeyed him. Some clergy became émigrés, while others helped the remaining nobles stir up opposition to the Revolution.

The Constitution of 1791

In 1791 the National Assembly finally finished writing a constitution for France. This constitution limited the authority of the king and set up a government divided into three branches—executive, legislative, and judicial.

The constitution greatly reduced the powers of the king. He could not proclaim laws, nor could he block laws passed by the legislature. Taxpaying male voters elected the members of the one-house legislature—the Legislative Assembly. The National Assembly was dissolved, and no one who had been a member could run for election to the Legislative Assembly. Only men who owned considerable property could hold office. The Constitution of 1791 did not permit women to vote or run for office. Despite the guarantees of equal rights and powers by the Declaration of the Rights of Man, under France's new constitution wealthy men held most of the political power.

Louis XVI reluctantly consented to the limitations that the new constitution imposed on him. At the same time, he encouraged the émigrés to plot with foreign governments. The king hoped that such plots would lead to the overthrow of the new government and a return to the Old Regime.

Some of the king's advisers urged him to flee and seek help directly from nations friendly to the monarchy. On the night of June 21, 1791, Louis XVI, Marie Antoinette, their young son and daughter, and the king's sister slipped out of Paris and tried to escape to the Austrian Netherlands. Louis disguised himself as a coachman, but the military escort for his coach, as well as the enormous coach itself, aroused suspicion. Louis's profile was on every coin in the kingdom, and he was recognized and stopped at Varennes, a town near the ● border. The revolutionaries arrested Louis and his family and sent them back to Paris.

Despite Louis XVI's unsuccessful flight, the National Assembly decided to allow him to remain king. Louis pledged that he would abide by the new constitution. People hoped that under the new constitutional monarchy, France could recover without further revolutionary disturbances. Instead, the attempted escape marked a revolutionary turning point. People no longer trusted the king, and they publicly discussed creating a republic.

The Legislative Assembly and War

The new government provided for by the Constitution of 1791 went into effect in September 1791, but it lasted less than a year. The revolutionaries had been more skillful in overthrowing the Old Regime than in creating a sound government to replace it. They had set up a weak executive and a powerful but inexperienced legislature elected by a minority of the population.

Three factions, or groups of people with differing attitudes, sat in the Legislative Assembly. One group believed that the Revolution had gone far enough. They considered the ideal form of

Learning from Maps *Revolutionaries forced Louis XVI and his family to move to the Tuileries palace. What direction is Versailles from Paris?* ■

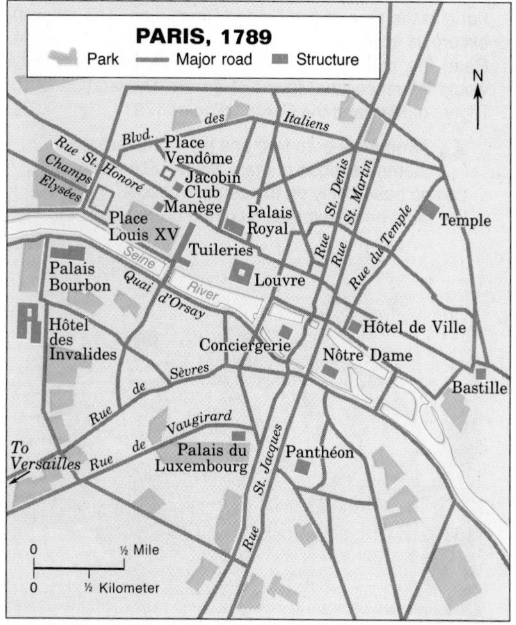

1B, 4A, 4G, a1A, a1B, a1C, a1D, a4A, a4B, a4E, a4G, a4L

READ
WRITE
INTERPRET
CONNECT
●THINK

BUILDING HISTORY STUDY SKILLS

Thinking About History: Examining How Perspective Influences Viewpoints

A person's perspective often influences how he or she views events. Many factors, including education, social class, religion, age, sex, ethnic group, and personality, shape a person's perspective and influence his or her viewpoint. For example, a wealthy man might feel that only people who own property should be allowed to vote, because they have a stake in the society. In this case, the man's social class influences his viewpoint on voting rights. You can understand events in history more clearly if you can determine the way different groups of people interpret the meanings of these events.

How to Examine How Perspective Influences Viewpoints

To examine how perspective influences viewpoints, follow these steps.

1. Identify the goal or purpose of your analysis.
2. Determine what factors shape the person's perspective.
3. Identify how the person views specific events in history.
4. Determine how the person's perspective influences his or her viewpoint.

Developing the Skill

Olympe de Gouges was from the lower middle class in Paris at the time of the French Revolution. The following excerpt is from her "Declaration of the Rights of Women." Read the excerpt and determine how her perspective would influence her viewpoint on the Declaration of the Rights of Man and the Constitution of 1791.

> " Woman is born free and her rights are the same as those of man. Social distinctions can be based only on the common good. . . . The law must be an expression of the general will; all citizens, men and women alike, must be equally eligible for all public offices, positions, and jobs, according to their capacity and without any other criteria than those of their virtues and talents. [Women] . . . have the right to go to the scaffold; they must also have the right to go to parliament. . . . Women, wake up . . . recognize your rights. Man, the slave, has multiplied his strengths. . . . What advantages have you got from the Revolution? "

The goal is to determine if Olympe de Gouges would view the events of the Revolution as steps toward liberty. Her words show her concern for political justice and rights for women. She believes that if women can fight and die for the Revolution, they are entitled to its benefits. Her perspective as a woman influences her viewpoint.

The Declaration of the Rights of Man made no mention of women. Olympe de Gouges wrote her declaration in response to this omission, asking, shouldn't the people who "go to the scaffold" also have the right "to go to parliament"?

Olympe de Gouges would condemn the Constitution of 1791 as a denial of liberty. It reinforced property rights for upper-class men. People had to own property before they could have the right to vote. Women could not own property, so they could not vote. Olympe de Gouges's perspective would influence a point of view that the Revolution was not over because it had not gone far enough in guaranteeing liberty for all people.

Practicing the skill. How might the perspective of a wealthy factory owner and that of an unemployed laborer influence their viewpoints on a new law lowering taxes and canceling unemployment insurance?

To apply this skill, see Applying History Study Skills on page 451.

A patriotic women's club at the time of the French Revolution

432

Learning from Pictures *During the Revolution, the food shortage was so severe that women in Paris stormed the Hôtel de Ville searching for food.*

government to be one in which the king had limited authority. They were the **conservatives**—that is, they did not want to change existing conditions. Another group called the **radicals** wanted to get rid of the king, set up a republic, and institute far-reaching changes. A third group, the **moderates,** had no extreme views. They sided with either conservatives or radicals depending on the issues.

In the hall where the Legislative Assembly met, conservatives sat on the right, moderates in the center, and radicals on the left. Since the French Revolution, the terms *right* (conservative), *center* (moderate), and *left* (radical) have meant different slants of political opinion.

The Legislative Assembly frequently deadlocked on domestic issues, but it united in facing a foreign threat. Before the Legislative Assembly first met, Marie Antoinette's brother, Emperor Leopold II of Austria, and King Frederick William II of Prussia had issued the Declaration of Pillnitz. This declaration invited European rulers to help Louis XVI restore the monarchy to its full power.

The fear of foreign invasion electrified the Legislative Assembly. Each group in the Assembly hoped that a successful foreign war would increase its own influence. Louis XVI favored war because he hoped that foreign armies would defeat the French army and restore his authority. Only a few farsighted people feared that war would lead to dictatorship. With only seven members opposed, in April 1792 the Legislative Assembly voted to declare war on Austria. It hoped to keep Prussia and the other German states out of the war, but it failed in that objective. Soon afterward an army of Austrian and Prussian troops invaded France and headed toward Paris.

The End of the Monarchy

The invasion of France by Austrian and Prussian armies touched off mass uprisings in Paris. A group of radicals seized control of the city government and set up an organization called the Commune.*

When the Prussian commander, the Duke of Brunswick, vowed to destroy Paris and punish the revolutionaries if any harm came to the royal family, members of the Commune threatened the Legislative Assembly with violence unless it abolished the monarchy. The Commune accurately accused Louis XVI of plotting with foreign monarchs to overthrow the Constitution of 1791. Revolutionary troops arrived from Marseilles to help defend Paris, singing their marching song—the *Marseillaise*—which became France's national anthem.

On August 10, 1792, the Legislative Assembly, coerced by the Commune, voted to suspend the office of king. Troops marched on the Tuileries palace, massacred many of the king's guards, and imprisoned Louis XVI and his family in the Temple (see map, page 431). The Commune now ruled Paris, and the Legislative Assembly tried to govern France.

With the monarchy suspended, France needed a new constitution. The Legislative Assembly voted itself out of existence and set a date for the election of delegates to a National Convention to draw up a new constitution for France. In late 1792, in the

*People called *sans-culottes* (san-skyoo • LAHT) offered the greatest support to the Commune. The term *sans-culottes* means "without knee breeches"—the craftsworkers, artisans, apprentices, and small shopkeepers of Paris who belonged to the *sans-culottes* wore long pants, while the nobility and rich bourgeoisie wore knee breeches. It became unfashionable to dress like the nobles and the wealthy, so in this way, revolution and social class influenced fashion. In the 1800s and 1900s, all men in the West began wearing long pants.

SECTION 3

Closure

Suggest to students that it sometimes is easier to state a goal than to achieve it. Ask: How do the Declaration of the Rights of Man and the Constitution of 1791 illustrate the truth of this suggestion?

1B, 4A, 4G, a1A, a1C, a4A, a4F, a4G, a4K

● Danton, Robespierre, and Marat all voted for the death sentence. Most of the Girondists voted for a sentence of life imprisonment or exile.

■ The monarchy may have been preserved for a longer period of time and the French government would not have changed to include the civil liberties outlined in the Declaration of the Rights of Man.

Review Answers

1. ***émigré:*** noble who fled France during the Revolution; ***department:*** administrative district of France established by the National Assembly; ***conservative:*** person who did not want to change existing conditions; ***radical:*** person who wanted to get rid of the king, set up a republic, and institute far-reaching changes; ***moderate:*** person with no extreme views on the issues at hand

2. ***Olympe de Gouges:*** leader of a group of women who wrote a declaration of rights for women that was rejected by the National Assembly; ***Duke of Brunswick:*** Prussian military commander who vowed to destroy Paris and punish the revolutionaries if any harm came to Louis XVI and his family

3. ***Varennes:*** French town near the border of the Austrian Netherlands—present-day Belgium

4. The National Assembly seized church lands and offered them for sale, using the proceeds to pay off the public debt.

5. The Constitution of 1791 limited the authority of the king and set up a government divided into three separate branches—the executive, legislative, and judicial. The Legislative Assembly was to consist of one house, elected by male voters. To hold office a man had to own considerable property. Women were not permitted to vote or to run for office.

midst of great danger, with a foreign war and political turmoil at home, France faced both a national election and a complete change of government.

SECTION 3 REVIEW

1. **Define** émigré, department, conservative, radical, moderate
2. **Identify** Olympe de Gouges, Duke of Brunswick
3. **Locate** Varennes
4. **Understanding Ideas** How did the National Assembly try to pay off the French government's enormous debt?
5. **Explaining Ideas** Describe the organization of the French government under the Constitution of 1791.
6. **Analyzing Ideas** **(a)** What three political groups made up the Legislative Assembly? **(b)** What were their political views?

4 The French Republic Faced Disorder at Home and War Abroad

The delegates to the National Convention were elected by **universal manhood suffrage**—every man could vote, regardless of whether he owned property. Although some 7 million qualified voters lived in France, only 10 percent cast their ballots.

The National Convention

The National Convention held its first meeting in September 1792. The delegates, like those in the Legislative Assembly, were divided into three main groups. This time, however, no one supported the king. On the right sat the Girondists (juh • RAHN • duhsts), so called because many of them came from the department of the Gironde in southwestern France. The Jacobins (JAK • uh • buhns), members of a radical political club of that name, sat on the left. Among the most powerful Jacobins were Georges-Jacques Danton and Maximilien Robespierre. The third group consisted of delegates that had no definite views. Later most of these delegates came to favor the Jacobins. The Convention also included some Jacobins who were extreme radicals and wanted reforms that would benefit all classes in society, including the *sans-culottes.* Jean-Paul Marat (muh • RAH), a doctor from Paris, led these radicals.

The National Convention governed France for three years. As soon as it met, it proclaimed the end of the monarchy and the beginning of a republic. Besides drawing up a new constitution, it had to assume many of the responsibilities of government. It had to suppress disorder and revolt at home and fight a war against foreign invaders.

The National Convention tried Louis XVI on charges of plotting against the security of the nation. Putting a king on trial was serious business. The Convention studied carefully the records of the Long Parliament, which had tried and executed Charles I in England 143 years earlier. The Convention declared Louis XVI guilty and by a margin of one vote sentenced him to death. On January 21, 1793, Louis was beheaded by the guillotine (GIL • uh • teen), a new device believed by its inventor to allow for quick and more humane executions. ●

Exporting the Revolution

Even before Louis's execution, the National Convention heard encouraging news. The French army had defeated the Austrian and Prussian forces and stopped the invasion. The French followed up their military victories by invading the Austrian Netherlands and capturing Brussels. Joyful over these victories, the National Convention declared that the French armies would liberate all the peoples of Europe from oppression.

The French decision to export the ideas of the Revolution by force of arms alarmed the monarchs of Europe. Great Britain, the Netherlands, Spain, and the kingdom of Sardinia joined Austria and Prussia to form an alliance against France called the First Coalition. For a time, the enemies of France succeeded in driving French troops out of the Austrian Netherlands, and they invaded France again.

In 1793 the National Convention took steps to meet these dangers. It set up the Committee

What If?

Louis XVI

Louis XVI was a weak monarch who was more interested in hunting than in governing France. How do you think world history would have been different if Louis XVI had been a strong king like Louis XIV? ■

● Supporting the establishment of the Revolutionary Tribunal, Danton declared, "Let us embody terror, so as to prevent the people from doing so."

Learning from Pictures *The beheading of Louis XVI shocked most of Europe. Even the United States, which a few years earlier had succeeded in its own revolution, condemned the execution.*

of Public Safety to direct the army in crushing all foreign invaders. It also established a court called ● the Revolutionary Tribunal to try "enemies of the Revolution."

To meet the danger of invasion, the Committee of Public Safety adopted **conscription**—the draft. All men between 18 and 45 were liable for military service. As a force of loyal, patriotic young men, the French army took on a new spirit. Many of the nobles who had been professional officers had fled as émigrés, so now men of all classes who proved their ability and daring could serve as officers. For the first time, a country called upon the talents and abilities of its entire population to fight a war.

Despite the army's optimism, the war created many problems for France. In the cities, working people demanded that the government do something about food shortages and rising prices. In the countryside the clergy refused to take the oath of loyalty to the Revolution. Instead they organized small armies of peasants to fight against it. Some nobles joined them. In western France, particularly in the department of the Vendée (vahn • DAY), the "Royal and Catholic army" fought against the French revolutionary army. The term that describes their activities is **counterrevolution,** because it was aimed counter to, or against, the Revolution. In short, counterrevolutionaries supported the Old Regime.

Jacobins, including Danton and Robespierre, controlled the Convention. They arrested many Girondist delegates who opposed their policies. Charlotte Corday, a woman from Normandy influenced by Girondist propaganda, journeyed to Paris and assassinated Marat. The Revolutionary Tribunal sent her to the guillotine for her crime.

The Reign of Terror

To meet the danger of opposition and revolt within France, the Convention started a systematic program to suppress all opposition. The Reign of Terror, as it became known, lasted from September 1793 to July 1794. According to one delegate, "What constitutes the Republic is the complete destruction of everything that is opposed to it."

The Revolutionary Tribunal conducted swift trials and handed down harsh sentences. It arrested, tried, and executed many people on mere suspicion. Marie Antoinette became an early victim of the Reign of Terror. The Jacobins directed the Reign of Terror not only against the nobility, however. The guillotine—the "national razor"—chopped off the heads of people of all classes suspected of disloyalty to the Revolution. The revolutionaries executed twice as many people from the bourgeoisie as nobles and clergy, and nearly three times as many peasants and laborers as people from all other classes. Danton and Robespierre sent their Girondist opponents and Olympe de Gouges to the scaffold. They also arrested the extreme radical followers of Marat. The Revolutionary Tribunal condemned Antoine Lavoisier, the famous chemist, because he had been involved

6. (a) Conservatives, radicals, and moderates made up the Legislative Assembly. **(b)** The conservatives did not want to change the existing political situation; the radicals, on the other hand, wanted to get rid of the king and set up a republic; moderates held no extreme views on political change.

SECTION 4

Focus/Motivation

Mention that in order to protect the Revolution against domestic enemies, the Committee of Public Safety instituted the Reign of Terror. All persons suspected of counterrevolution were arrested. The evidence against most of these people was meager at best, but thousands were sentenced to die on the guillotine. It has been estimated that more than 10,000 people were killed during the Reign of Terror. Next, on the chalkboard or on an overhead projector, write the following quotation:

"O Liberty, O Liberty, what crimes are committed in thy name!"

Point out to the students that Madame Roland, the wife of the Girondist leader, uttered this just before her death on the guillotine in 1793. Discuss the quotation with the class, using the following question as a guide: How could the same people who had adopted the Declaration of the Rights of Man also take part in the Reign of Terror?

435

1B, 4A, 4G, a1A, a1C, a1D, a2G

● Danton met his death courageously, admonishing the executioner not to forget "to show my head to the people. It's well worth a look."

■ Just before his execution on April 5, Danton predicted that Robespierre would follow him to the guillotine within three months. Robespierre was executed on July 28, just three weeks later than Danton had anticipated.

Presentation
Understanding Chronology (Average/Group)
Put the following events on the chalkboard or on an overhead projector, and have students copy the list into their notebooks. Then have them arrange the events in chronological order by writing *1* before the event that took place first, *2* before the event that took place second, and so on.

(3) Reign of Terror
(5) Napoleon's coup d'état
(1) First Meeting of Natinal Convention
(2) Louis XVI beheaded
(4) Directory created

in tax farming under the Old Regime. It sent him to death with the words, "The Republic has no need of genius."

In the spring of 1794, Danton felt that the Reign of Terror had accomplished its purpose and should be relaxed. But Robespierre became even more fanatical and accused Danton of disloyalty to the Revolution. He had Danton and his followers ● put to death.

For 100 days Robespierre carried out a policy of suppression that aroused fear even among his supporters. He was convinced that only he could protect the Revolution from its enemies. Finally, a few brave members of the National Convention called a halt. In July 1794 they arrested Robespierre and ■ guillotined him. The Reign of Terror was over.

Work of the National Convention

Despite the dangers and difficulties of the time, the National Convention made many reforms in France. It began codifying French laws. It provided for a national system of public education, and it abolished slavery in the French colonies.

In addition, the Convention adopted the metric system of weights and measures. Today most parts of the world use the metric system. The Convention also adopted a new calendar with colorful names that reflected the seasons, such as *Thermidor* for the time of heat (roughly July) and *Ventôse* for the time of wind (roughly March). This calendar did not survive, however, perhaps because it also increased the number of days in a week from 7 to 10—an arrangement that met with little support among working people!

Meanwhile, the citizen army swept to victory. By 1795 the French had driven invaders from French soil and conquered territory as far as the Rhine River in Germany. Even more important, the First Coalition began to break up. However, the French paid a heavy price for victory. At home the spirit of militarism allowed the National Convention to use the army to quell any opposition. It crushed an uprising in Paris in October 1795, indicating that the new government did not welcome any opposition. In other countries, the French army behaved so harshly and with such arrogance that the people it supposedly "liberated" hated it.

Learning from Pictures *The Reign of Terror ended with the execution of Robespierre and the closing of the Jacobin club.*

History Through the Arts

PAINTING

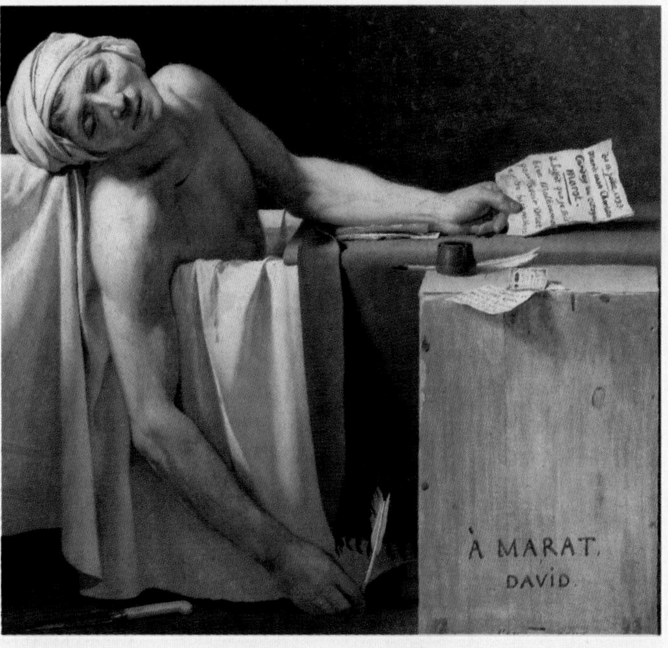

The Death of Marat

It is hardly surprising that the art of France reflected the shattering changes brought about by the Revolution. In subject, in mood, and in technique, these changes are evident in this work by Jacques-Louis David. The Jacobin leader Jean-Paul Marat was stabbed to death by Charlotte Corday as he was bathing. She had been convinced by the Girondists that he was a cruel tyrant. (Marat suffered from a painful skin disease caught while he was hiding in the sewers, and he could find relief only by sitting in a warm bath.)

Because of its bizarre circumstances, Marat's assassination was not a conventional subject for a painting. But David—himself a revolutionary who at one time presided over the Convention—was a great artist and succeeded in creating a moving and forceful painting. In Marat's hand is a letter from his assassin. The knife that she plunged into his chest lies on the floor. The painting's stark drama is highlighted by David's simple inscription, "To Marat."

The Directory

In 1795 the National Convention drafted another constitution. Universal manhood suffrage disappeared and only property owners could vote. The wealthy controlled the government, as they had under the rule of the National Assembly. The new constitution established an executive branch of five men called *directors.* The directors gave their name to the government created by the Constitution of 1795: the Directory.

Although the Directory governed France for four years, it pleased neither the radicals nor the conservatives. Weak, corrupt, and selfish, the five directors constantly quarreled among themselves and could not agree on how to solve any of France's problems. Prices skyrocketed out of control, and the peasants, *sans-culottes,* and all the poor people in France suffered. But the directors made no effort to improve the desperate situation. They did not interfere with the activities of corrupt business leaders and speculators. As a result, the economic situation got worse. When crowds protested the government's inability to act, the directors called in the army to put down the unrest. A worker in Paris summed up his feelings this way:

> "Under Robespierre blood was spilled and we had bread. Now blood is no longer spilled and we have no bread. Perhaps we must spill some blood in order to have bread."

The Directory soon became as unpopular as the Old Regime. It repeated history by going bankrupt, and it prepared the way for military dictatorship.

Napoleon Bonaparte

The Directory did encourage good leadership in the French army. The continuing war with Great Britain, Austria, and Sardinia provided opportunities for able military leaders. During this period, from 1795 to 1799, a relatively unknown general named Napoleon Bonaparte caught the public's

437

1B, 4A, 4G, a1A

● Napoleon said that he dispersed the mob by giving them "a whiff of grapeshot."

■ Napoleon's unconventional approach to war gained him a reputation as a gambler and risk-taker. Napoleon replied to such charges by saying he preferred glorious defeats to ordinary victories.

SECTION 4

Closure

Refer students to the statement by the Parisian worker on page 437. Ask: Are violent periods like the Reign of Terror justified if they produce benefits for the majority of the people?

Review Answers

1. ***universal manhood suffrage:*** the right of every man to vote, regardless of whether he owns property; ***conscription:*** the draft for military service, used by the Committee of Public Safety to create a national French army; ***counterrevolution:*** actions aimed counter to, or against, the Revolution; ***coup d'état:*** seizure of power by force
2. ***Georges-Jacques Danton:*** Jacobin leader in the National Convention; ***Maximilien Robespierre:*** Jacobin leader in the National Convention; ***Jean-Paul Marat:*** leader of the extreme radicals in the National Convention
3. ***Brussels:*** central Belgium; ***Vendée:*** western France; ***Corsica:*** island in the Mediterranean south of Genoa, Italy
4. The three main groups in the National Convention were the Girondists on the right, the Jacobins on the left, and a large group in the middle that at first supported neither, but later came to favor the Jacobins.
5. **(a)** The Reign of Terror was a program instituted by the Convention to suppress all opposition to the Revolution. It lasted from

Learning from Pictures *Although Napoleon was not the eldest son, at the age of 16 he became the head of his family after his father's death.*

attention. As a general at age 26, he had suppressed ● the uprising in Paris that attempted to prevent the establishment of the Directory.

Born in 1769 on the French island of Corsica, Napoleon Bonaparte attended military school in France and graduated as an artillery officer. He might have remained there had the Revolution not given him the opportunity to rise to the rank of general.

Bonaparte bundled extraordinary energy into a five-foot-two-inch (1.6-meter) frame. Requiring only two to three hours of sleep a night, he combined overwhelming ambition with a vain and domineering personality. Either despite or because of these traits, the general proved to be a superb organizer and administrator in both political and military affairs. Above all, he had military genius.

Napoleon Bonaparte ranks among the great generals of all time. Because of the dominant role Napoleon played beginning in 1796, the wars that the French fought from then until 1815 are generally known as the Napoleonic Wars.

Napoleon's genius lay in his ability to rapidly move troops and to mass forces at critical points on the battlefield. These techniques gave him an advantage over his opponents' older, slower tactics. ■

In Italy Napoleon quickly showed his ability. He took a small, weak, and poorly equipped French army and, within weeks, so organized and inspired it that he forced the Sardinians to make peace. Napoleon defeated the Austrians twice, and in 1797 he forced them to sign a humiliating peace treaty that gave France control of all of northern Italy.

Napoleon's successes made him so popular in France that the Directory worried that he might seize power. Napoleon, on the other hand, continually sought new conquests to keep his name before the French people. He proposed to weaken the British in a military campaign that would cut off their trade with the Middle East and India. The Directory quickly agreed, since such a campaign would keep him out of Paris.

Napoleon's campaign met with disaster. The British destroyed the French fleet near Alexandria in Egypt, thus cutting off the French army's supply lines. Napoleon left his army to its fate and secretly returned to France. He concealed the true situation in Egypt and made exaggerated claims of victories.

Napoleon became the popular hero of the time. However, his popularity could not change the facts. France faced a truly dangerous situation. The British had organized a Second Coalition against France that included Austria and Russia. Coalition forces drove French armies out of Italy, and French control over the other conquered states slipped.

Napoleon's Seizure of Power

As conditions worsened, many people believed that only Napoleon could win victory abroad and restore order at home. People afraid that royalists might seize control organized a plot to overthrow the government and place Napoleon in power. The plotters wanted stability in France to insure that they could keep the nationalized property they had bought and the power they had acquired. Abbé Sieyès, one of the chief conspirators, said, "We had reached the point when it was a question of thinking of saving, not the principles of the Revolution, but the men who had made it." In 1799 three directors resigned and two were arrested, leaving the way open for change. Troops with bayonets surrounded the legislature and forced most of its members to leave. Those that remained turned the government over to Napoleon and his fellow plotters.

A seizure of power by force is called a **coup d'état** (kood • ay • TAH), meaning literally a "stroke of state." Napoleon himself said later, "I found the crown of France lying on the ground, and I picked it up with a sword."

SECTION 4 REVIEW

1. **Define** universal manhood suffrage, conscription, counterrevolution, coup d'état
2. **Identify** Georges-Jacques Danton, Maximilien Robespierre, Jean-Paul Marat
3. **Locate** Brussels, Vendée, Corsica
4. **Summarizing Ideas** Describe the three main groups that made up the National Convention.
5. **Analyzing Ideas** **(a)** What was the Reign of Terror? **(b)** What kinds of people were among its victims?
6. **Explaining Ideas** Explain the circumstances that made Napoleon's coup d'état possible.

5 Napoleon Built an Empire That Spread Across Europe

Although Napoleon's government kept the form of a republic, the coup d'état of 1799 had made him dictator of France. From 1799 until 1814, Napoleon influenced events in France and the rest of Europe to such a great extent that this period is known as the Napoleonic Era, or the Age of Napoleon.

The people of France accepted Napoleon's dictatorship. Some, weary of the long period of chaos, wanted stability. Others were afraid to protest because they feared arrest. Instead of trying to abolish the changes brought on by the Revolution, Napoleon supported them. He respected the ideals of the Declaration of the Rights of Man and did not restore serfdom and feudal privileges. He reassured the peasants that the land they owned would remain theirs.

However, liberty under Napoleon meant only freedom of opportunity. It was not liberty from control, because Napoleon believed that the people should obey orders given by a leader.

Napoleon and the Consulate

Napoleon reorganized and centralized the administration of France to give himself unlimited power. The executive branch, made up of three consuls, gave its name to the first five years of Napoleon's rule—the Consulate. In an attempt to appeal to popular admiration for the strength and virtues of ancient Rome, Napoleon took the title of First Consul—the title used in the Roman Republic.

As First Consul, Napoleon commanded the army and navy. He also had the right to appoint and dismiss all officials and to propose all new laws. None of the Consulate's legislative bodies had any real power; they merely rubber-stamped Napoleon's decrees.

Napoleon submitted the constitution of his new government to the people for a vote, a procedure known as a **plebiscite** (PLEB • uh • syt). People could vote only yes or no and could not make any changes. Nevertheless, a vast majority of French voters approved the new constitution.

People usually remember Napoleon for his military leadership. However, his work in government had more importance and a longer-lasting effect. Under Napoleon's direction, scholars completed the revision and organization of all French law begun by the National Convention. Many governments in Europe and elsewhere copied this system, called the Napoleonic Code.

Napoleon established the Bank of France because he wanted a central financial institution. Although the bank was privately owned, the government closely supervised it.

The government also established the public education system planned by the National Convention. This system included elementary schools, high schools, universities, and technical schools. A central agency called the University of France supervised and directed these schools.

The Civil Constitution of the Clergy of 1790 had ruptured relations between the Roman Catholic church and the French government. Napoleon ended the conflict by reaching an agreement called the *Concordat* with the pope in 1801. The Concordat acknowledged Catholicism as the religion of most French citizens, but it did not abolish the religious toleration guaranteed by the Declaration of the Rights of Man. Most important, the church gave up claims to the property the government had seized and sold during the Revolution.

September 1793 to July 1794. **(b)** People from all classes suspected of disloyalty to the Revolution were beheaded. In fact, more laborers and peasants went to the guillotine during the Reign of Terror than members of any other class.
6. Napoleon's coup d'état was made possible because the Second Coalition was threatening France from without, while the weaknesses of the Directory had led to disorders at home. Many people in France believed that Napoleon, a popular hero, was the only one who could win victory abroad and restore order at home. Therefore, a plot was organized to overthrow the government and place Napoleon in power.

SECTION 5

Focus/Motivation
Write the following quotations on the chalkboard or on an overhead projector.

"I shall respect public opinion when its judgments are legitimate, but it has whims that must be scorned. It is the duty of the government to enlighten public opinion, not to follow it in its errors."

"One can lead a people only by promising it a future; a chief of state is a seller of hopes."

"Constitutions should be short and obscure . . . . A constitution should be drafted in such a way that it will not hinder the

1B, 4A, a1A, a1D

• **In extravagance, Napoleon's coronation matched any formal event of Louis XIV's reign. For example, on its journey from the Tuileries palace to Notre Dame, Napoleon's golden coronation coach was preceded by six cavalry regiments and 24 ornamented carriages. The whole procession was accompanied by close to 80,000 foot soldiers.**

actions of a government and not force the government to violate it . . . If there are problems with a government that is too strong, there are many more with a government that is too weak. Things won't work unless you break the law every day."

"My system is very simple. I believe that in the circumstances, it is necessary to centralize power and increase the authority of the government in order to build a nation. I am the constitution-making power."

Use these quotations as a starting point for a class discussion on Napoleon's views of public opinion and government. At the end of the discussion, ask students if they think Napoleon's government was the kind of government the revolutionaries had wanted. *(Most students will note that the Revolution had replaced one form of absolute rule with another.)*

Presentation
Word Scramble
(Average/Group)
Put the following scrambled words and definitions on the chalkboard or on an overhead projector. Have students unscramble the letters to spell out the words.

1. *traoplug* — Country on the Iberian Peninsula that refused to observe the Continental System
2. *psohej* — Brother of Napoleon who was made king of Spain

In a display of shrewd and skillful diplomacy, Napoleon destroyed the Second Coalition against France. In 1799 he convinced Russia to desert the coalition. By 1801 Austria asked France for peace, and in 1802 Great Britain and France signed a peace treaty. For a time it looked as though Napoleon would keep his promises to the French people—peace won by military victory, firm and steady government, and economic prosperity.

Napoleon as Emperor

In France Napoleon moved to increase his power by making it permanent and hereditary. In another plebiscite in 1804, the French people voted to declare France an empire. First Consul Napoleon Bonaparte became Emperor Napoleon I.

The coronation of Napoleon in the Cathedral of Notre Dame in Paris inaugurated the empire, later known as the First Empire. One part of the elaborate ceremony was especially significant. The pope had come to Paris to crown the new emperor. However, when the time came for him to place the crown on Napoleon's head, Napoleon seized the crown and placed it on his head himself. Thus he demonstrated that the power and authority that he held were not given to him by anyone but himself.

The First Empire expanded far beyond France's old boundaries. But throughout Europe people wanted to destroy Napoleon's empire. The British became his most determined adversaries once they realized that his ambition threatened their commerce, their empire, and their control of the seas. Great Britain renewed the war against France and in 1805 organized the Third Coalition. Austria, Russia, and Sweden allied themselves with Great Britain; Spain was allied with France. Napoleon planned to defeat the British navy and then invade Great Britain.

However, in 1805 a British fleet led by Admiral Horatio Nelson defeated a combined French and Spanish fleet near Trafalgar off the southern coast of Spain. Nelson was killed in the battle, but not before he had almost destroyed the French and Spanish fleet. Napoleon succeeded spectacularly, however, in land battles against Austria and Russia.

The Continental System

Because they inflicted defeat upon him, Napoleon had nothing but contempt for the British, calling them "a nation of shopkeepers." He believed that if the British lost their foreign trade and its profits, they would be willing to make peace on his terms. Therefore, he ordered a blockade of the British Isles and forbade anyone in the French Empire or its allied states to trade with the British. This blockade was called the Continental System, because Napoleon controlled so much of the continent of Europe.

The British responded with a blockade of their own against the French. They ordered ships of neutral countries to stop at British ports to get a license before trading with France or its allies. Napoleon, in turn, ordered the French navy to seize any neutral ship that obeyed the British order.

This conflict placed neutral nations in an awkward position. If they disregarded the British order, the British might capture their ships. If they obeyed the British, the French might seize their ships. The Continental System and the British blockade hit especially hard at the United States, for it depended heavily on trade with both Great Britain and the continent of Europe. Both France and Great Britain stopped American ships, but British ships did the most damage to American trade. This conflict, in part, brought about the War of 1812 between Great Britain and the United States.

Although the British blockade hurt France, Napoleon continued to win battles against the powers in the Third Coalition. He struck his enemies before they could unite effectively. In December 1805 Napoleon smashed the combined forces of Russia and Austria at Austerlitz, a town north of Vienna. Shortly thereafter, the Third Coalition collapsed.

The Reorganization of Europe

By 1808 Napoleon completely dominated Europe (see map, page 442). He forced Austria and Prussia to sign humiliating peace treaties. Czar Alexander I allied Russia with France. Napoleon ruled the Austrian and Dutch Netherlands and Spain, and forced Denmark and the Papal States into alliances. To stop the possibility of any Russian gains, Napoleon formed the territory that Prussia had taken from Poland into the Grand Duchy of Warsaw, which he gave to his ally, the king of Saxony.

Since 1795 various treaties had given France the right to intervene in the affairs of the many small German states. Napoleon organized the most

Learning from Pictures *As emperor, Napoleon brought back a number of institutions similar to those of the old monarchy. For example, he gave princely titles to members of his family.*

3. *leendraax* — Czar of Russia who withdrew from the Continental System
4. *asiurs* — Country in which Napoleon's Grand Army suffered a disastrous defeat
5. *blea* — Island to which Napoleon was sent after his abdication
6. *dhruedn adsy* — Period of Napoleon's rule after his return from exile
7. *traolowe* — Battle that marked Napoleon's final defeat
8. *ts. neelha* — Island in the South Atlantic where Napoleon died
9. *linanoamtsi* — Powerful movement in Europe spurred by Napoleon's conquests
(Answers: 1-Portugal, 2-Joseph, 3-Alexander, 4-Russia, 5-Elba, 6-Hundred Days, 7-Waterloo, 8-St. Helena, 9-nationalism)

important of these states into the Confederation of the Rhine, with himself as protector. He abolished the Holy Roman Empire in 1806 and forced its emperor to take the lesser title of emperor of Austria. He unified all the small northern Italian states into the Kingdom of Italy and made them dependencies of France. He also placed members of his large family on the thrones of the countries he had conquered.

Napoleon did not limit the changes he made in Europe to enlarging his empire and reorganizing the conquered territories. On the contrary, he instituted far-reaching changes. Wherever the French army went, it put the Napoleonic Code into effect, abolished feudalism and serfdom, and introduced the modern methods of the French army.

Without intending to, the French also helped awaken in the people they conquered a spirit of **nationalism,** or love of one's country rather than of one's native region. In France the events of the Revolution and the stirring words of the Declaration of the Rights of Man had produced feelings of patriotism for the country as a whole, rather than just for local regions. People thought of themselves as French, with a country and ideals worth fighting for. Now these same feelings of loyalty and patriotism for their homelands appeared among the conquered peoples, and they wanted to rid themselves of French rule.

In 1808 Napoleon ruled Europe, but time worked on the side of his enemies. The coalitions reformed and his opponents' armies grew stronger. The generals who opposed Napoleon in the field copied his methods of moving and massing troops rapidly. Other nations, especially Great Britain and Prussia, had learned how to train large bodies of troops. And, as you have read, nationalism strengthened Napoleon's opponents.

The Peninsular Campaign

To the south of France, on the Iberian Peninsula, lay Spain and Portugal. In 1807 Portugal refused to observe the Continental System because the nation's prosperity depended on trade with Great Britain. In retaliation the French army occupied Portugal and drove its king into exile.

Napoleon then decided to conquer Spain. After forcing the Spanish king to abdicate, Napoleon made his brother Joseph king of Spain. Resenting a foreign king, the Spanish people revolted in 1808. The British sent an army under Arthur Wellesley,

441

1A, 1B, 4A, a1A, a1D, a4B, a4C

the future Duke of Wellington, to help the Spanish and Portuguese drive out the French. In spite of everything Napoleon did, he failed to suppress the Spanish uprising and defeat the British.

The Peninsular Campaign, as this war was called, lasted from 1808 to 1814. Napoleon continued to control Spain's government, but the campaign drained French military resources when the emperor needed them elsewhere.

In 1814 the Spanish, with British help, captured Madrid and drove out Joseph Bonaparte. They then drew up a new constitution that provided for a limited monarchy. The Spanish revolt and the new constitution illustrated the tremendous influence of the ideals of the French Revolution. It also showed the rising spirit of nationalism and opposition to Napoleon.

Catastrophe in Russia

Czar Alexander I of Russia, who reigned from 1801 to 1825, viewed Napoleon's domination of Europe with alarm and distrust. The French Continental System had disrupted a long-established exchange of Russian grain and raw materials for British manufactured goods. Gradually, the czar relaxed his

Learning from Maps *Napoleon controlled the European coastline from the Mediterranean to the North Sea. On which other seas did he control some coastline?* **Baltic Sea and Adriatic Sea**

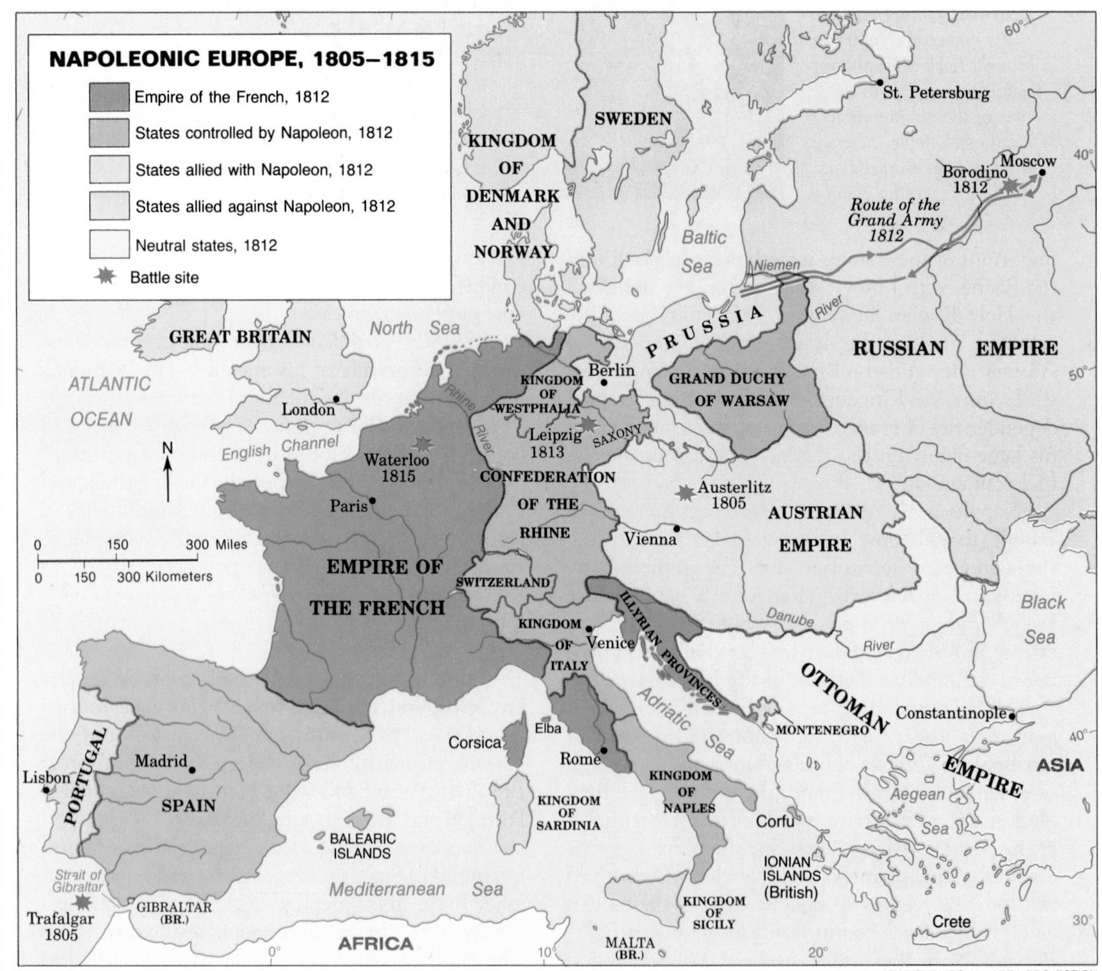

442

enforcement of the Continental System in Russia, and in 1812 he announced the resumption of trade with Great Britain.

Inefficient as it was, the blockade remained Napoleon's only way of striking at the British. He found it intolerable for Russia, a French ally, to openly ignore it. Napoleon decided to invade Russia, and he exerted pressure on all parts of his empire to supply soldiers.

When finally assembled, Napoleon's Grand Army totaled 600,000 soldiers. However, this huge force differed greatly from the enthusiastic, loyal, and patriotic armies of the early French Empire. Fewer than half of the soldiers were French. The majority of the Grand Army consisted of soldiers from Napoleon's conquered states or from countries he forced to be his allies. The soldiers had little heart for this war.

In May 1812 Napoleon's army began its march eastward toward Russia (see map, page 442). Instead of battling the French on the vast plains of western Russia, the Russian army retreated slowly, drawing Napoleon's army deeper into the country. As they retreated, the Russians practiced a **scorched-earth policy,** burning or destroying crops and everything else that might be of value to the invaders.

In mid-September 1812 the French captured Moscow and Napoleon entered the Kremlin. But it was a hollow victory. As soon as the French entered the city, the Russians set it afire so that nothing would be left for their enemies. The fire destroyed so many buildings that the French troops had no housing. To make matters worse, the harsh Russian winter lay ahead, and Russian troops lurked in the countryside, endangering the Grand Army's long supply line from France. Napoleon had not expected the Russians to destroy the food supply that his troops and horses needed. Many soldiers in the Grand Army fell ill or starved. Faced with these horrible hardships, Napoleon decided to retreat to France.

Napoleon's retreat from Moscow ranks as one of the greatest military disasters of all time. The Russian winter struck with exceptional force. In addition to the snow and bitter cold, the French troops had to pass back through the devastated countryside, where the Russians attacked the bedraggled soldiers without mercy. Cossacks and peasants captured or killed stragglers. Discipline broke down, and many troops deserted. Napoleon abandoned his army to fend for itself and hurried to France to raise new forces to defend his empire. When the Grand Army reached Prussia in December, it had lost four-fifths of its troops. The Russian army followed the retreating French and invaded Napoleon's empire.

Final Defeat

Everywhere in western Europe, monarchs broke their alliances with Napoleon and joined the invading Russians. Napoleon faced overwhelming odds. Prussia, Austria, Great Britain, and Sweden joined Russia in a new and final alliance to crush France.

Napoleon tried his old strategy of striking before his enemies could unite, but this time he was too late. In October 1813 Napoleon's forces and the army of the new alliance met at Leipzig, in Saxony. The allies beat the French decisively, and Napoleon retreated into France. A series of brilliant military maneuvers by Napoleon did not prevent the allies from capturing Paris in March 1814.

Napoleon tried to abdicate in favor of his son, but failing to get any support, he gave up all claims to the throne for himself and his family. The allies granted him a pension and allowed him to retire to the small island of Elba off the west coast of Italy.

The victorious allies now had to make peace with France. They wanted to make sure the country could never again disrupt European affairs. They agreed that France could keep the boundaries of 1792. They also restored the Bourbon monarchy to the throne in the person of Louis XVIII, brother of the executed Louis XVI.*

The Hundred Days

During 1814 and early 1815, the restored Bourbons made many enemies among the French people. Learning of the discontent in France, Napoleon plotted his return. He escaped from Elba and landed in France on March 1, 1815.

When Louis XVIII sent troops to capture Napoleon, the emperor faced them, saying, "If there is one among you who wishes to kill his emperor, he can do so: here I am!" Resistance quickly crumbled, and Napoleon led a triumphant

*Royalists referred to the young son of Louis XVI and Marie Antoinette as King Louis XVII. He is believed to have died in prison in 1795.

SECTION 5

Closure

On the chalkboard or on an overhead projector, write French writer Madame de Stael's description of Napoleon:

"He was an able chess player, and the human race was the opponent to whom he proposed to give checkmate."

Then ask students if Madame de Stael's statement is an apt description of Napoleon's "Grand Design" for Europe.

Review Answers

1. ***plebescite:*** procedure in which a government measure is submitted to the people for a vote; ***nationalism:*** love of one's nation; ***scorched-earth policy:*** burning and destroying crops and everything else that might be of value to an invading army
2. ***Horatio Nelson:*** British admiral whose fleet defeated the combined French and Spanish fleets at Trafalgar; ***Duke of Wellington:*** British military leader who commanded the army that defeated Napoleon at Waterloo; ***Czar Alexander I:*** Russian ruler who withdrew from the Continental System; ***Louis XVIII:*** brother of Louis XVI, restored to the throne by the allies after Napoleon abdicated
3. ***Trafalgar:*** cape on the Atlantic coast of southwestern Spain, near Gibraltar; ***Austerlitz:*** Austrian town, north of Vienna;

1B, 4A, a1A, a4A, a4F,
a4G, a4H, a4L

● On St. Helena Napoleon remarked to one of his guards, "If I had succeeded I should have been the greatest man known to history."

Leipzig: located in Saxony; ***Elba:*** island in the Mediterranean between Corsica and Italy; ***Waterloo:*** near Brussels; ***St. Helena:*** island in the South Atlantic, off the West African coast
4. The French people accepted Napoleon's dictatorship because some wanted security after a long period of instability. Others feared arrest if they protested. In addition, people were willing to accept Napoleon's dictatorship because he kept the reforms made during the Revolution.
5. (a) Napoleon declared war on Russia because Alexander I defied Napoleon's Continental System. **(b)** After the capture of the burned and ruined capital of Moscow, the campaign ended with the disastrous retreat to France. Then, Russia and Prussia allied and invaded Napoleon's empire.
6. (a) In the Battle of Waterloo, the combined armies of Prussia, Great Britain, and the Dutch Netherlands defeated the army Napoleon had assembled after his escape from Elba. **(b)** Napoleon surrendered to the British, who exiled him to the South Atlantic island of St. Helena, where he lived under constant guard until his death in 1821.
7. Wherever the French army went, the Napoleonic Code was put into effect, feudalism and serfdom were abolished, and the modernized methods of the French army were introduced. Indirectly, the

army into Paris on March 20, beginning a period called the Hundred Days. Since a frightened Louis XVIII had scurried across the frontier to Brussels, Napoleon once again ruled France. Acting immediately to avoid war, Napoleon renounced all claims to territories that had belonged to his empire.

The emperor hoped that disputes among his opponents over the division of territory in Europe would keep them from opposing his return, but he was mistaken. Under the command of the Duke of Wellington, the combined armies of Prussia, Great Britain, and the Netherlands moved toward France. Napoleon once more assembled a French army to battle them.

On June 18, 1815, the allied and the French armies met in battle at Waterloo, near Brussels, where the allies dealt Napoleon a humiliating defeat. Napoleon abdicated again, and the Bourbons again returned "in the baggage," it was said, of the allies.

Napoleon surrendered to the British, asking at first to be allowed to go to the United States. When denied that, he asked to take refuge in England. The British refused this request also. Instead they sent the defeated emperor to live under constant guard on the lonely, dismal island of St. Helena in ● the South Atlantic. There Napoleon died in 1821.

Government of France 1774–1814

1774	Louis XVI became king
1789	Third Estate, as National Assembly, assumed power
1791	Legislative Assembly, with Louis XVI as constitutional monarch, began rule
1792	Monarchy suspended and National Convention began governing
1795	Directory took control
1799	Consulate established, with Napoleon as First Consul
1804	Napoleon crowned emperor
1814	Napoleon overthrown and Bourbon monarchy restored

As the years passed, Napoleon's legend grew. People forgot the wars and Napoleon's failures and remembered only his glories and achievements. In people's minds, Napoleon was transformed from a vain and ambitious dictator into the "Little Corporal," the "Good Emperor," and the "true patriot of the Revolution." In 1840 the British allowed the French to take his body back to Paris, where it lies to this day under the dome of the Invalides, the magnificent home for old soldiers that Louis XIV had built.

SECTION 5 REVIEW

1. **Define** plebiscite, nationalism, scorched-earth policy
2. **Identify** Horatio Nelson, Duke of Wellington, Czar Alexander I, Louis XVIII
3. **Locate** Trafalgar, Austerlitz, Leipzig, Elba, Waterloo, St. Helena
4. **Interpreting Ideas** Why were the people of France willing to accept Napoleon's dictatorship?
5. **Analyzing Ideas** **(a)** Why did Napoleon declare war on Russia? **(b)** How did his Russian campaign end?
6. **Summarizing Ideas** **(a)** What nations were involved in the battle of Waterloo? **(b)** What happened to Napoleon afterward?
7. **Synthesizing Ideas** How did the conquests of the French under Napoleon influence other European peoples?

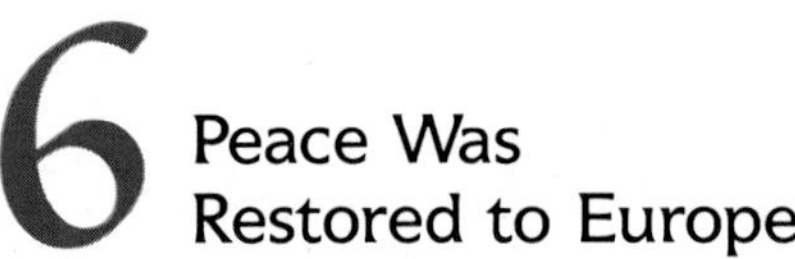

6 Peace Was Restored to Europe

With the final defeat of Napoleon in 1815, Europe reached an important turning point. For more than 25 years, the most powerful political influence on the continent had been the French Revolution. Even though Napoleon did not always uphold the ideals of the Revolution—liberty, equality, and fraternity—he did carry its influence throughout Europe.

As long as Napoleon ruled France, the governments of other nations feared that France would export political unrest or rebellion and challenge their authority. Once they defeated Napoleon, the major European powers were determined to restore order, keep peace, and squelch the ideas of the Revolution. After 1815 they followed policies designed

● Talleyrand was the member of the National Assembly who suggested confiscating church lands to help raise funds to cover government debts. He also was one of Napoleon's chief advisers until he openly criticized the emperor's policies on Spain and Russia.

Learning from Pictures *Two of the most influential diplomats at the Congress of Vienna were Talleyrand (seated second from right) and Metternich (standing far left).*

to maintain stability and to suppress any danger of political upheaval.

The Congress of Vienna

Stability could be achieved only by settling political and territorial questions arising from the Napoleonic Wars. The Congress of Vienna, a conference held in the Austrian capital, undertook the settling of these questions. The congress began in September 1814, while Napoleon was in exile on Elba. About 700 diplomats attended at one time or another. Napoleon's return from exile interrupted the congress in 1815, but after his final defeat at Waterloo, the congress resumed its work.

Despite the presence of many notable figures, only a few people made the real decisions at the Congress of Vienna. Great Britain, Austria, Russia, and Prussia had done the most to defeat Napoleon. Their four representatives were Lord Castlereagh (KAS • uhl • ray), foreign secretary of Great Britain; Prince Klemens von Metternich, chief minister of Austria and chairman of the conference; Czar Alexander I of Russia; and King Frederick William III of Prussia. Metternich, however, was the chief architect of the policies drawn up by the congress.

Surprisingly, the representative of defeated ● France, Charles Maurice de Talleyrand, played an important part at the Congress of Vienna. A shrewd negotiator, Talleyrand wielded great influence as the representative of Louis XVIII.

The Principles of the Congress of Vienna

Four principles guided the decisions of the Congress of Vienna. (1) **Legitimacy,** which meant that all former ruling families should be restored to their thrones, had to be upheld. (2) The balance of power had to be restored in Europe. This meant that the nations of Europe had to keep any one nation from becoming too powerful. (3) France had to be weakened. (4) The countries that suffered most at the hands of Napoleon, especially the four great powers—Great Britain, Austria, Russia, and Prussia—had to be compensated for their losses.

Legitimacy. At Talleyrand's urging, the Congress of Vienna made settlements based on the principle of legitimacy. The Bourbon monarchy, already restored in France, also returned to power in Spain and in the Kingdom of the Two Sicilies. Monarchies were also restored in Portugal and in the Kingdom of Sardinia.

Compensation and the balance of power. The winning powers soon quarreled over the division of spoils. The two most difficult problems concerned Poland and the German state of Saxony. From Prussia's Polish territory, Napoleon had created the Grand Duchy of Warsaw, which he had

French army also helped awaken a spirit of nationalism in the areas that it conquered.

SECTION 6

Focus/Motivation
Reproduce the following quotation from Prince Klemens von Metternich for the class.

"There is a rule of behavior common to individuals and to states which has been proven correct because it has been practiced over the centuries and in everyday life. This rule declares that 'man should not dream of changing things while emotionally excited about the matter; wisdom directs that at such moments we should limit ourselves to maintaining the status quo.'

If all kings will only accept this rule and prove by word and action their determination not to change things without careful thought, they will find people everywhere who support them. If the governments establish the principle of stability, this will not exclude future improvement of conditions . . . . There should be respect for change and new development along slow, peaceful paths."

Have students study the quotation, and then lead them in a discussion, using the following questions as a guide:

1. What principles seemed to guide Metternich's

1A, 1B, 4A, a1A, a1C, a2G, a4B, a14C

thinking? *(stability, maintaining the status quo, and change only after careful thought)*

2. Based on this quotation, was Metternich a conservative or a reactionary? *(If necessary, refer the students to the definition of the term* reactionary *on page 447. Accept any answers that can be supported by evidence from the quotation.)*

Complete the discussion by mentioning that students will learn more about the views of Metternich in Section 6.

Presentation
Organizing Ideas (Average/Group)

Make copies of a chart divided into three columns with the headings *Alliance, Participants,* and *Goals* and distribute them to the class.

Have students complete the chart by entering information on the alliances discussed in Section 6. Encourage students to retain their charts for revision purposes.

given to his faithful ally, the king of Saxony. Russia now demanded this territory. Prussia agreed to this, provided that the king of Saxony be deposed and Saxony be given to Prussia.

Both Great Britain and Austria opposed this arrangement. Great Britain did not want to see Russia become too strong. Austria feared that the addition of Saxony might make Prussia too powerful in German affairs. For a time the threat of war loomed. Then Talleyrand suggested a compromise that settled the argument. Most of what had been the Grand Duchy of Warsaw went to Russia. Prussia got the rest of it, along with part of Saxony (see map, this page).

The Netherlands, one of Napoleon's early conquests, received the Austrian Netherlands and became the single Kingdom of the Netherlands. As compensation for this loss, the Austrians gained the northern Italian states of Venetia and Lombardy. Austrian Hapsburgs also became rulers of the northern Italian states of Parma, Modena, and Tuscany.

In addition to gaining the largest share of the Grand Duchy of Warsaw, Russia had acquired Finland as a result of war with Sweden. Since Sweden had fought against Napoleon, it received Norway, formerly a Danish possession. This territorial adjustment punished Denmark for cooperating with Napoleon. Prussia, in addition to its share of

Learning from Maps *France was allowed to keep its pre-Napoleonic boundaries at the Congress of Vienna. What kingdoms gained territories to the north of France?*

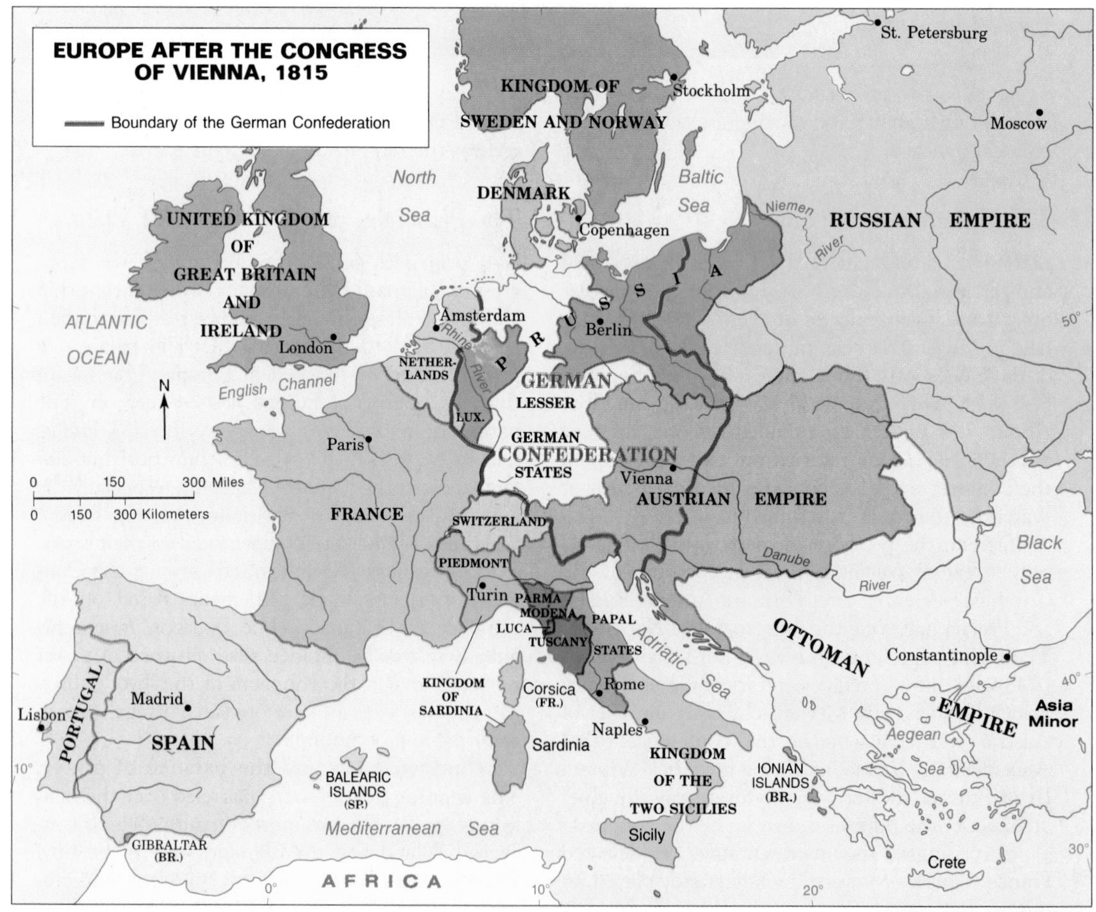

446

Saxony and Poland, received an area along the lower Rhine River.

Although Great Britain did not receive any territory in continental Europe, it did gain possessions overseas. They included several islands in the French West Indies and the Mediterranean island of Malta. From the Danish the British gained Helgoland, an island in the North Sea. From the Dutch they took Cape Colony in Africa and what became British Guiana in South America.

France held in check. All of this territorial reshuffling set up a ring of strong states around France so that it could not again threaten the peace of Europe. The diplomats, however, did not consider the feelings of the people who lived in these regions that changed hands. They parceled out territories as if these lands were uninhabited deserts.

France was stripped of its conquests, and its boundaries were returned to what they had been in 1792. In addition, it had to pay a large **indemnity**—a compensation to other nations for damages it had inflicted on them. France also had to pay for forts that the victorious nations now maintained on the French borders.

Reaction, Absolutism, and Nationalism

A time of **reaction** followed the first few years after the Napoleonic Era. This means that those in authority wanted to return to the conditions of an earlier period. **Reactionaries** are extremists who not only oppose change, but generally would like to turn the clock back to the time before certain changes occurred. After 1815 the victors in Europe attempted to restore conditions to what they had been before the French Revolution.

In Spain, the Two Sicilies, and the states of northern Italy, the reinstated rulers abolished the constitutions that had been adopted during Napoleon's rule. They returned to absolutism as if nothing had ever happened. Switzerland alone retained its constitutional government but had to promise to remain neutral in European wars. The European powers guaranteed this neutrality.

Napoleon's conquests resulted in the spread of new political ideas and the rise of nationalism, which the reactionary powers considered dangerous and tried to stamp out. National feelings began to have such wide influence that they became accepted as a basic political ideal. Writers, artists, and politicians promoted nationalism by stressing the people's shared history, common language, or cultural achievements.

The desire for national unity caused concern among the major powers of the time, and they tried to hold it back. For a while they succeeded, and the Congress of Vienna left nationalist groups disappointed. Some Italians, for example, had hoped for a united Italy. Their hope went unfulfilled. To make matters worse, many Italian states were placed under a hated foreign rule. The major powers also blocked the desire of the Polish people for national independence. Nor was self-government granted to national groups living within the Austrian Empire.

The German desire for national unity came closer to fulfillment. Napoleon had consolidated many of the German states into the 16-member Confederation of the Rhine. Now more states, including Prussia, formed the German Confederation, which had 39 members. Austria dominated this confederation, since an Austrian delegate always presided over the confederation's assembly.

Alliances Among the Great Powers

The idea of revolution still haunted the governments of Europe. As a result, they believed that a special watch had to be kept for the lurking dangers that might upset the peace they had so painstakingly created.

The Quadruple Alliance. The four allies that had finally defeated Napoleon—Great Britain, Austria, Russia, and Prussia—agreed in 1815 to continue their alliance. This became known as the Quadruple Alliance. The chief purpose of the alliance was "to guarantee Europe from dangers by which she may still be menaced"—that is, revolutionary movements. Members of the alliance agreed to make sure that France carried out the terms of the peace treaty. They planned to hold periodic conferences to keep the major powers in agreement on matters that concerned them all.

The Holy Alliance. Czar Alexander I of Russia doubted that alliances alone could maintain peace and prevent revolutions. He firmly believed in absolute monarchy. However, he believed just as firmly that Christian moral principles and a strong sense of duty should guide monarchs. Shortly before joining the Quadruple Alliance, he urged that all rulers pledge themselves to rule as Christian princes by signing an agreement called the Holy

447

SECTION 6

Closure

European history from about 1815 to the 1840s is sometimes referred to as the Age of Metternich. Ask: What impact did Metternich have on European politics in the first half of the nineteenth century?

Review Answers

1. ***legitimacy:*** principle holding that all former ruling families should be restored to their thrones; ***indemnity:*** compensation a vanquished nation has to pay to other nations for damages it inflicted on them during a war; ***reaction:*** desire to return to the conditions of an earlier period; ***reactionary:*** extremist who not only opposes change but wishes to turn the clock back to the time before certain changes occurred; ***liberalism:*** political movement that extolled the American and French revolutions with their ideals of individual rights and the rule of law
2. ***Castlereagh:*** foreign secretary of Great Britain; ***Talleyrand:*** representative of France at the Congress of Vienna; ***Metternich:*** chief minister of Austria and chair of the Congress of Vienna
3. ***Saxony:*** southeast of Denmark; ***Kingdom of the Netherlands:*** the Netherlands and the northern part of Belgium; ***Venetia:*** territory around Venice; ***Lombardy:*** northern Italy; ***Malta:*** island in the Mediterranean south of Sicily

Alliance. All the rulers of Europe signed it except the British king; the Turkish sultan, who was not a Christian; and the pope, who refused to be instructed in Christian principles by the Orthodox czar.

Those rulers who signed the Holy Alliance did so only to humor the czar and had little intention of following its principles. Castlereagh scoffingly called it "a piece of sublime mysticism and nonsense."

The Concert of Europe. Out of the more practical Quadruple Alliance grew what was called the Concert of Europe—a form of international government by concert, or agreement. It was aimed at maintaining peace and the *status quo* (a Latin phrase meaning roughly "the condition in which things exist"). In this case the status quo meant maintaining the balance of power established by the Congress of Vienna.

The first of the periodic conferences provided for by the Quadruple Alliance met in 1818. France, having fulfilled the terms of the peace settlements, returned to the European family of nations and was admitted to the Quadruple Alliance, making it a Quintuple Alliance. The Concert of Europe lasted until 1848.

The Age of Metternich

For 30 years after the Congress of Vienna, Prince Metternich influenced Europe so strongly that the period is sometimes known as the Age of Metternich. A reactionary, Metternich believed strongly in absolute monarchy. He looked with fear and horror at constitutions and liberalism. The movement known as **liberalism** extended the principles of the American and French revolutions with their ideals of individual rights and the rule of law. Metternich believed in suppressing completely such ideas as freedom of speech, religion, and the press.

Metternich aimed to prevent war or revolution and to preserve absolutism. He had little difficulty achieving these goals in Austria. He set up an efficient secret police system to spy on revolutionary organizations and individuals. Liberals were imprisoned, fined, or exiled.

Because Austria controlled the German Confederation, Metternich persuaded the rulers of most German states to adopt the same methods. Hapsburg rulers in northern Italy made sure that no revolutionary movements would succeed there. In France, King Louis XVIII moved cautiously in domestic affairs. However, he quite willingly joined in suppressing revolutions elsewhere.

Political Liberalism

The ideas of liberals greatly influenced politics during the 1800s. These ideas could be seen in the internal political conflicts of Great Britain, France, Italy, Germany, and the United States. Liberalism

Learning from Pictures *Political liberalism in Russia culminated with the Decemberist uprising. After the death of Alexander I, troops rebelled against the new czar in December 1825. The uprising failed to establish either a democratic republic or a constitutional monarchy.*

1B, 4A, 4G, 4J, a1A, a1C, a2G, a4A, a4H, a4K

● The Carlsbad Decrees also banned student clubs, which were the hotbed of the debate on nationalism.

took many different forms in these countries, but certain key ideas remained identical. These included a belief in the importance of individual liberty—freedom of thought, religion, and economic opportunity. Above all, liberals hated the tyranny of absolute rule. Thus they worked to secure constitutions and other legal safeguards to limit governmental authority and protect civil liberties. Most liberals did not believe that all people should have the right to vote. Instead, most believed that voting should be limited to men with property and education.

Reaction to Metternich

Liberals reacted strongly to the decisions of the Congress of Vienna and to Metternich's actions to check liberalism. A number of uprisings occurred in Europe, and Metternich turned the Concert of Europe into an instrument of suppression. Whenever a threat to the status quo appeared, representatives of the five powers gathered to discuss ways of handling it. Austria, Russia, and Prussia went further. They agreed to act in concert to put down any attempt at revolution anywhere.

Great Britain could not agree to this last step. It opposed interfering in the attempts of liberal popular movements to overthrow absolute rulers. Great Britain itself had a representative government. The British people as a whole sympathized with other peoples in their struggles to institute similar governments. More important, Great Britain depended on trade. Meddling in the internal affairs of other countries might hurt British commerce. Under the influence of George Canning, who became foreign secretary in 1822, Great Britain withdrew from the Quintuple Alliance.

The Metternich System in Operation

For a time the Metternich system operated successfully. When discontent flared up among German university students in 1819, Metternich called together the leaders of the larger states of the German Confederation at Carlsbad in Bohemia. At his insistence they adopted measures known as the Carlsbad Decrees. The decrees placed students and faculty members of the universities under strict ● watch. They censored newspapers and periodicals and formed an organization to search for secret revolutionary activities. These measures prohibited political reforms that conflicted with absolute monarchy.

Because of repression, several underground movements began that opposed the status quo. In 1820 a revolt in Spain forced King Ferdinand VII to restore the constitution he had abolished. This alarmed the four continental members of the Quintuple Alliance. Despite British protests they sent a French army to Spain. In 1823 they restored Ferdinand to full power, brutally crushing the revolt and its leaders.

The Spanish revolt inspired other uprisings in 1820. In the Kingdom of the Two Sicilies, revolutionaries forced the ruler to grant a constitution. An Austrian army put down this revolt. In Portugal, too, the people forced the ruler to accept a constitution. A few years later, however, he abolished it and assumed absolute power.

In 1821 nationalism upset the international order when the Greeks revolted against the Ottoman Turks. Influenced by Metternich, European rulers refused Greek pleas for aid. However, many individuals came to the support of the Greeks, either as volunteers or by sending arms. One of these volunteers was Lord Byron, the British poet, who died of a fever in Greece in 1824.

Finally Russia, Great Britain, and France brought pressure on the Ottoman sultan. By the Treaty of Adrianople in 1829, Greece became an independent state. The Serbs and Romanians, to the north on the Balkan Peninsula, received some rights of self-government within the Ottoman Empire.

Greek independence demonstrated the first real failure of the Metternich system in Europe. It showed that the sense of nationalism encouraged by the French Revolution could not be suppressed forever.

SECTION 6 REVIEW

1. **Define** legitimacy, indemnity, reaction, reactionary, liberalism
2. **Identify** Castlereagh, Talleyrand, Metternich
3. **Locate** Saxony, Kingdom of the Netherlands, Venetia, Lombardy, Malta
4. **Synthesizing Ideas** Give an example of the principle of legitimacy as it operated at the Congress of Vienna.
5. **Organizing Ideas** **(a)** What was the Quadruple Alliance? **(b)** the Holy Alliance? **(c)** the Concert of Europe?

4. The Congress of Vienna restored the Bourbons to the thrones of France, Spain, and the Kingdom of the Two Sicilies. Monarchies were also restored in Portugal and the Kingdom of Sardinia.
5. (a) An alliance of four countries—Great Britain, Austria, Russia, and Prussia—that had defeated Napoleon **(b)** An agreement, instituted by Czar Alexander I, that called upon all European monarchs to use Christian moral principles and a strong sense of duty to guide their decisions as rulers **(c)** The nations of the Quadruple Alliance and France

Reviewing Important Terms

1. a; **2.** i; **3.** e; **4.** h; **5.** c; **6.** f; **7.** b; **8.** g; **9.** d; **10.** j; **11.** k; **12.** l; **13.** m.

Developing Critical Thinking Skills

1. (a) every natural phenomenon had a cause and an effect; truth could be arrived at solely by rational thinking; natural laws governed science and human behavior; and if people lived by these laws, the world would become a perfect place; **(b)** by compiling the *Encyclopedia*
2. (a) The consequences of his policies would fall on future generations. **(b)** He had a cynical attitude.
3. (a) calling of the Estates-General; Tennis Court Oath; capture of the Bastille; **(b)** Declaration of the Rights of Man; Constitution of 1791; Reign of Terror; **(c)** Louis XVI becomes king; flight to Varennes; Napoleon crowned emperor; **(d)** First Coalition formed; Continental System; Napoleon invades Russia; **(e)** Peninsular Campaign; Hundred Days; Waterloo. **(f)** Congress of Vienna; signing of Holy Alliance; Greek independence
4. (a) a one-house legislature; only men who owned considerable property could vote or hold office; the executive was weak; **(b)** delegates elected by universal manhood suffrage; established France as a republic, and set up the Committee of Public Safety; **(c)** The wealthy controlled the government and an executive of five directors. Only property owners could vote. **(d)** executive branch composed of three Consuls; real power in the hands of Napoleon; legislature composed of several

1B, 4A, 4F, 4G, 4J, a1A, a1C, a2G, a4A, a4J

Reteaching

Have students review the Chapter Summary and the appropriate section and questions in the Unit Synthesis. Discuss the concepts until students demonstrate a clear understanding of the material.

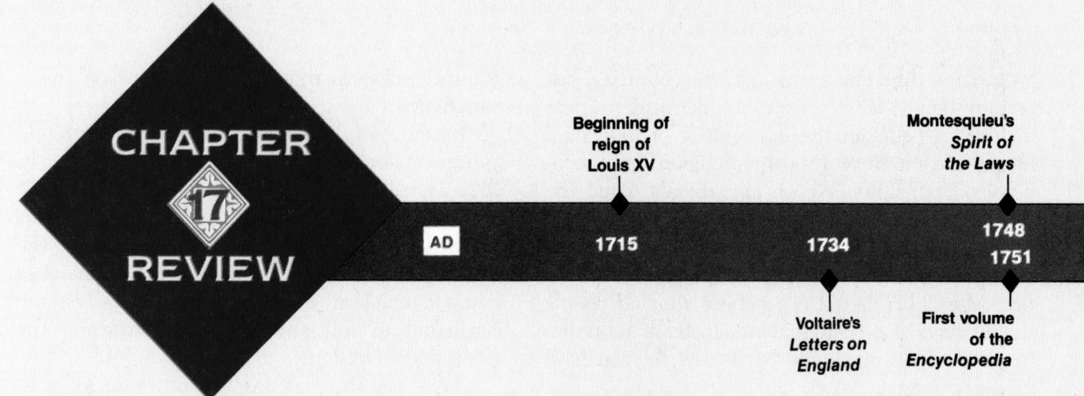

Chapter Summary

The following list contains the key concepts you have learned about the French Revolution and the Napoleonic Era.

1. During the Enlightenment thinkers began to criticize the established political institutions.
2. The philosophes included Diderot, Montesquieu, Voltaire, and Rousseau.
3. Discontent in France and Louis XVI's failure to solve the government's continuing financial crisis were the direct causes of the French Revolution.
4. In 1789 Louis XVI summoned a meeting of the Estates-General in an attempt to solve the financial crisis of the monarchy. When Louis XVI insisted on following the old voting procedures, the Third Estate met separately and proclaimed itself the National Assembly.
5. The National Assembly issued the Declaration of the Rights of Man and wrote the Constitution of 1791, creating a limited constitutional monarchy. Invasion by Austrian and Prussian troops to restore absolute power to the king touched off riots that led to the end of the monarchy in 1792.
6. The National Convention proclaimed a republic and executed the king. With France threatened by new invasions, it drafted an army to defend the nation and suppressed opposition at home with the Reign of Terror.
7. The inefficient and corrupt Directory followed the National Convention.
8. In 1799 Napoleon Bonaparte took over the government in a coup d'état. Napoleon ruled France as a military dictator and extended French control over much of Europe.
9. Napoleon became emperor and ruled Europe. French troops of the empire carried the ideals of the Revolution to other European nations. In response to French invasion, feelings of nationalism were ignited throughout Europe.
10. After several military defeats, Napoleon abdicated and went into exile on Elba in 1814. Napoleon soon escaped, only to be defeated again at Waterloo.
11. The Congress of Vienna and later alliances attempted to restore the status quo in Europe.
12. Despite the efforts of the reactionaries, the ideals of liberalism and nationalism could not be suppressed. In the 1820s several rebellions against reactionary policies broke out.

On a separate sheet of paper, complete the following review exercises.

Reviewing Important Terms

Match each of the following terms with the correct definition below.

a. Enlightenment
b. scorched-earth policy
c. moderate
d. popular sovereignty
e. department
f. conscription
g. coup d'état
h. conservative
i. bourgeoisie
j. enlightened despotism
k. reactionary
l. liberalism
m. émigré

___ **1.** Movement stressing the use of reason to logically explain human nature
___ **2.** City-dwelling middle class in France
___ **3.** One of 83 administrative districts in France
___ **4.** Person who does not want to change existing conditions
___ **5.** Person with no extreme views
___ **6.** Government policy requiring people to serve in the army
___ **7.** Burning or destroying crops and everything else that might be of value to the enemy
___ **8.** Seizure of power by force
___ **9.** Government by free choice of the people
___ **10.** System of government in which absolute monarchs ruled according to the principles of the Enlightenment
___ **11.** A person who not only opposes change but generally would like to go back to the time before changes occurred
___ **12.** Movement that extended the principles of the American and French revolutions with their ideals of individual rights and the rule of law
___ **13.** French for "emigrant," person who fled France during the Revolution and plotted continuously to overturn the Revolution and set the clock back

450

1A, 4F, 4G, a4A, a4B, a4C, a4D, a4E, a4F, a4G, a4H, a4I, a4J, a4K, a4L, a4M

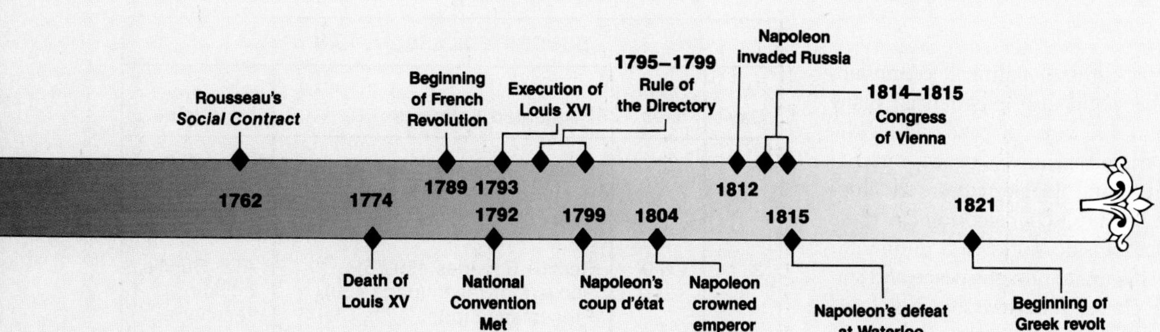

Developing Critical Thinking Skills

1. **Understanding Ideas** **(a)** What were the major ideas of the Enlightenment? **(b)** How did Diderot help spread these ideas?
2. **Analyzing Ideas** **(a)** What did Louis XV mean when he said: "After me, the deluge"? **(b)** What do you think this statement shows about his attitude toward France?
3. **Understanding Chronology** In each of the following groups, place the items in the correct chronological order: **(a)** capture of the Bastille, calling of the Estates-General, Tennis Court Oath; **(b)** Constitution of 1791, Declaration of the Rights of Man, Reign of Terror; **(c)** flight to Varennes, Napoleon crowned emperor, Louis XVI becomes king; **(d)** First Coalition formed, Continental System, Napoleon invades Russia; **(e)** battle of Waterloo, Hundred Days, Peninsular Campaign; **(f)** Congress of Vienna, Greek independence, signing of Holy Alliance
4. **Summarizing Ideas** How was the French government organized under each of the following: **(a)** the Legislative Assembly; **(b)** the National Convention; **(c)** the Directory; **(d)** the Consulate.
5. **Synthesizing Ideas** **(a)** What were the lasting effects of the French Revolution? **(b)** In what ways did Napoleon both fulfill and destroy its ideals? **(c)** Did the Congress of Vienna fail to restore absolutism?

Relating Geography to History

Compare the map of Napoleonic Europe on page 442 with the map of Europe after the Congress of Vienna on page 446. Then write a paragraph describing the resulting boundary changes.

Relating Past to Present

1. The French Revolution completely altered the political structure of Europe. **(a)** What effects are revolutions having on life in today's world? **(b)** Where are revolutions currently taking place?
2. Spain used guerrilla warfare against Napoleon's forces. **(a)** How is guerrilla fighting conducted? **(b)** Describe how guerrilla fighting was used in a modern war. **(c)** Why is this type of warfare often effective against modern armies?

Applying History Study Skills

Before completing this activity, review Building History Study Skills on page 432.

Edmund Burke was a British gentleman and a member of Parliament during the French Revolution. He published his *Reflections on the Revolution in France* in 1790. Read the excerpt below and explain how his perspective influences the way in which he views the events of the French Revolution.

> "The fresh ruins of France, which shock our feelings wherever we turn our eyes, are not the devastation of civil war; they are the sad but instructive monuments of rash and ignorant counsel in time of profound peace. . . . Whilst they are possessed of these notions, it is vain to talk to them of the practice of their ancestors, the fundamental laws of their country, the fixed form of a constitution, whose merits are confirmed by the solid test of long experience. . . . They have the 'rights of men.' . . . But to form a free government; that is, to temper together these opposite elements of liberty and restraint in one consistent work, requires much thought, deep reflection, . . . a powerful and combining mind. This I do not find in those who take the lead in the National Assembly."

Investigating Further

1. **Determining Cause and Effect** Read *A Tale of Two Cities* by Charles Dickens. Describe how the French Revolution affected the lives of the main characters.
2. **Applying Ideas** The ideas of Montesquieu and Rousseau influenced political and social thought in the 1700s. Describe how their ideas were reflected in the Declaration of the Rights of Man and the constitutional monarchy set up by the National Assembly in 1791. A suggested resource for your research is J. Bronowski's and B. Mazlish's *Western Intellectual Tradition: From Leonardo to Hegel* (Harper & Row).

assemblies without real authority
5. (a) Class divisions and privileged positions ended. **(b)** Everyone had equal opportunity to rise in society, and public office was open to everyone. France was far from a democracy. The legislature was powerless and the French had no say in their government. **(c)** Although several monarchies were restored, absolutism was regained only in Spain and the two Sicilies.

Relating Geography to History

Most of what had been the Grand Duchy of Warsaw went to Russia. Prussia got the rest of it and part of Saxony. The Netherlands received the Austrian Netherlands and became the single kingdom of the Netherlands. The Austrians gained Venetia and Lombardy. Austrian Hapsburgs ruled Parma, Modena, and Tuscany. Sweden received Norway. Prussia received an area along the lower Rhine River.

Relating Past to Present

1. (a) Answers will vary. **(b)** Central America
2. (a) By small bands **(b)** Guerrillas destroyed railroads, bridges, and factories. **(c)** Modern equipment is ineffective in jungles and mountainous areas. Guerrilla armies are spread out, camouflaged, and depend on surprise and secrecy.

Applying History Study Skills

Answers will vary. Most students will suggest that Burke's social position would influence his view.

451

CHAPTER (pages 452–477)

18 The Countries of Asia Experienced a Transition

(1368-1868)

CHAPTER OVERVIEW

While Europe was undergoing great cultural, political, economic, and social change, the rest of the world also experienced many changes. China enjoyed more than 400 years of peace under the Ming and Qing dynasties. During these centuries of peace, internal trade increased, the population grew, and popular culture developed. However, Ming and Qing emperors discouraged foreign trade and tried to keep contact with the outside world to a minimum. Similarly, in Japan the Tokugawa shogunate brought peace and stability after a long period of political chaos. Tokugawa shoguns closed the country to most foreigners, and Japan developed in isolation.

European influence began to be felt increasingly in Asia in the 1700s. The Portuguese were the first to reach China and Japan. Jesuit missionaries won many converts but were eventually expelled from both countries. The British developed a lucrative trade with China, but disagreements between the two countries brought about the Opium War. Japan, isolated until the 1800s, came under Western influence when the United States and European powers negotiated the opening of several Japanese ports.

Elsewhere in Asia three Islamic empires — the Ottoman, the Persian, and the Mogul — began to decline. The downfall of the Mogul Empire opened the way for the British to dominate in India. After the British victory over the French in the Seven Years' War, most of India came under the control of the British East India Company. After the Indian Mutiny of 1857 the East India Company was dissolved, and India came under the British government.

SUGGESTED LESSON PLAN

Day	Objectives	Suggested Activities	Materials
1	U7* C1-3,	Introducing the Chapter (pages 452-53) Section 1 (pages 453-63), Focus/Motivation (page 453), Presentation (page 454), Closure (page 461), Suggested Teaching Strategies, Enrichment Activity, Daily Quiz, Suggested Assignments (page 451B)	ATE, Pupil's Edition, Teacher's Resource-Bank™
2	U8, C4-5	Section 2 (pages 463-69), Focus/Motivation (page 463), Presentation (page 464), Closure (page 468), Suggested Teaching Strategies, Enrichment Activity, Daily Quiz, Suggested Assignments (page 451C)	ATE, Pupil's Edition, Teacher's Resource-Bank™
3	C6-9	Section 3 (pages 469-75), Focus/Motivation (page 469), Presentation (page 470), Closure (page 474), Suggested Teaching Strategies, Enrichment Activities, Daily Quiz, Suggested Assignments (page 451D)	ATE, Pupil's Edition, Teacher's Resource-Bank™
4	U7-8, C1-9	Chapter 18 Form A Test, Reteaching Worksheet, Chapter 18 Form B Test	Teacher's Resource-Bank™ or Workbook and Test Booklet
5	U1-8	Unit Four Test	Teacher's Resource-Bank™ or Workbook and Test Booklet
6		Mid-Book Test	Teacher's Resource-Bank™ or Workbook and Test Booklet

*C refers to applicable Chapter Objective, U refers to applicable Unit Goal.

BOOKS FOR THE TEACHER

Hibbert, Christopher. *The Great Mutiny, India 1857.* Viking. Offers an exciting account of the mutiny.

Moorhouse, Geoffrey. *India Britannica.* Harper & Row. Tells the story of three centuries of British rule in India.

Spear, Percival. A *History of India, Volume 2.* Penguin. Covers Indian history from the coming of the Moguls to independence.

BOOKS FOR THE STUDENT

Clavell, James. *Shogun.* Atheneum. Offers an exciting, panoramic view of traditional Japan.

Reynolds, Robert L. *Commodore Perry in Japan.* American Heritage. Provides a full account of Perry's expedition; many colorful illustrations.

Sears, Stephen W., ed. *The Horizon History of the British Empire.* American Heritage. Details the history of the British Empire.

MULTIMEDIA MATERIALS

Forbidden City (mp, 43 min.), Films. Shows the splendor of the Ming and Qing dynasties through artifacts and paintings in Beijing.

India's History: British Colony to Independence (mp, 11 min.), Coronet. Covers British colonization of India, the Indian Mutiny of 1857, and the growth of the nationalist movement.

Iran: Landmarks in the Desert (mp, 27 min.), Chatsworth. Portrays Persian history through the artistry of architects, painters, and artisans.

Past and Present China (fs), McGraw-Hill. Studies relations between China and the West from earliest times to the present.

Section (pages 453–463)

1 China Changed Gradually Under the Ming and Qing Dynasties

SECTION OVERVIEW

During the Ming dynasty, China's interest in foreign trade and sea power declined. Despite Ming efforts to protect the northern frontier, the Manchus conquered China in the 1600s and established the Qing dynasty. During both the Ming and Qing dynasties, new patterns of commerce and trade began to appear. A weakened army, the breakdown of government services, and increasing uprisings and rebellions contributed to the decline of the Qing dynasty and the opening up of the country to Europeans. Chinese isolation was finally ended by the Opium War and a series of humiliating treaties with Europeans.

SUGGESTED TEACHING STRATEGIES

1. **Preteaching Vocabulary (Basic)** You may wish to preteach the following important vocabulary terms: junk *(page 454)*; queue *(page 455)*; philology *(page 457)*; free trade *(page 460)*; extraterritoriality *(page 461)*. Ask students why the Chinese were opposed to free trade.
2. **Relating Cause and Effect (Average/Group)** Put the following groups of statements on the chalkboard or on an overhead projector. For each numbered statement, have students determine whether each of the two following statements can best be described as a cause or as an effect.

   a. Ming emperors stopped financing naval expeditions.
   (C) Confucianism was the philosophy of the government.
   (C) Defending the northern frontier became costly.

   b. Peasants became discontented.
   (E) The number of uprisings and rebellions increased.
   (C) Taxes increased while services decreased.

*3. **Thinking About History: Analyzing Consequences (Average/Group)** To reinforce the skill lesson presented on page 462, ask students to discuss why it is important to consider both the immediate and the long-term consequences when a decision is made.

ENRICHMENT ACTIVITY

Analyzing Ideas (Average/Group) Lead the class in a discussion about the role of women in China, using the following questions as a guide: How did the growth of cities contribute to the decline of the status of women? *(In the cities women no longer had an important economic role.)* How did this contrast with the status of women in the country? *(In rural China women were part of an economic unit in which everyone had to work to survive.)* Why did foot-binding develop in China? *(It was a sign of social and economic status, for foot-binding indicated that a woman's husband or father was rich enough that she did not need to work.)* What connection do you see between the economic role of a woman and her status in society? *(Answers will vary.)*

DAILY QUIZ

To assess student understanding of Section 1, give the class the following quiz. (Each item is worth 10 points.)

1. (T or F) The Chinese probably invented the compass. *(T)*
2. (T or F) As followers of Confucius, the Ming emperors viewed merchants as very important members of society. *(F)*
3. To protect China's northern frontier, the Ming emperors strengthened the ________ ________ and built new observation towers. *(Great Wall)*
4. The Qing, to distinguish the Chinese from the Manchus, forced Chinese men to wear their hair in a ________. *(queue)*
5. New crops from the Americas, such as peanuts, tobacco, and ________ ________ — the "poor man's food" — were introduced into China during the Qing dynasty. *(sweet potatoes)*
6. Why was foot-binding a sign that a woman was of high social standing? *(It indicated that her father or husband was wealthy enough not to need her to work to help support the family.)*
7. (T or F) Portugal's commercial impact on China was far more important than its religious impact. *(F)*
8. What product did the British desire when they first began to trade with China in the early eighteenth century? *(tea)*
9. What two actions by the British gave rise to the conflict between China and Great Britain known as the Opium War? *(The British attempted to establish free trade with China and they began to pay for Chinese tea with opium.)*
10. What rebellion of the mid-1800s seriously weakened the Qing dynasty? *(Taiping Rebellion)*

SUGGESTED ASSIGNMENTS

1. **Explaining Relationships (Average/Group)** Have students write brief paragraphs explaining how each of the following contributed to the decline of the Qing dynasty. Students may need to refer to pages 458-463 to complete this assignment.
   - **a.** Soldiers of the Manchu army had lost much of their skill as warriors.
   - **b.** The population increased.
   - **c.** Officials become corrupt.
   - **d.** Discontent over increased taxes and decreased services spread widely.
2. **Presenting an Oral Report (Challenging)** Interested students might like to undertake further reading on the Taiping Rebellion in China and present their findings to the class in an oral report. Two selections on the subject may be found in Sydney Eisen's and Maurice Filler's *The Human Adventure* (Harcourt Brace Jovanovich), vol. 2. "The Taiping Rebellion."
3. **Profile Worksheet (Basic)** Have students complete Profile Worksheet 18 in the TEACHER'S RESOURCEBANK™.
4. **Skill Worksheet (Basic)** Have students complete Skill Worksheet 18 in the TEACHER'S RESOURCEBANK™.

Section (pages 463–469)

2 Japan Prospered Under the Rule of the Tokugawa Shoguns

SECTION OVERVIEW

After years of warfare in Japan, the Tokugawa shogunate was established in 1603. This shogunate brought Japan a long period of relative tranquility, known as the Great Peace of the Tokugawa. During the Tokugawa period, cities grew in both size and importance, and improvements were made in agriculture and industry. These developments, in part, led to the rise of a popular culture in Japan. A major reason for this progress was the Tokugawa policy of isolation, which eliminated almost all foreign contacts. With the arrival of Commodore Matthew Perry in the 1850s, however, Japanese isolation came to an end.

SUGGESTED TEACHING STRATEGIES

1. **Preteaching Vocabulary (Basic)** You may wish to preteach the following important vocabulary term: consulate (*page 468*). Ask students what the difference is between a consulate and an embassy?
2. **Making Generalizations (Average/Group)** For each of the following generalizations, have students provide three supporting statements from this section.

   Generalization: The shogun placed restrictions on the daimyos to discourage revolts.
   - *a. The shogun would not allow lesser daimyos to build new castles within their domains.*
   - *b. The daimyos had to spend every other year in Yedo, the shogun's capital.*
   - *c. The daimyos had to leave their families in Yedo when they returned to their domains.*

   Generalization: The shoguns created a stable society.
   - *a. Sons were required to follow the occupations of fathers.*
   - *b. Membership in social classes became hereditary.*
   - *c. All warriors were required to live in the castle town of their daimyo.*

   Generalization: Changes occurred in Tokugawa Japan.
   - *a. Internal trade expanded.*
   - *b. Cities grew.*
   - *c. Merchants and artisans gained wealth.*

ENRICHMENT ACTIVITY

Analyzing Ideas (Challenging) Point out to students that over time the samurai developed a code of ideal behavior. At the core of this code — which was called *bushido,* or "the way of the warrior" — was the belief that the samurai owed absolute loyalty to their masters. Suggest that the best example of *bushido* in action was the act of revenge committed by a group of 47 *ronin,* or masterless samurai, that took place during the Tokugawa shogunate. These 47 warriors patiently waited more than a year for the right moment to kill Kira, the shogunate official who was responsible for their master's death. After, they committed *seppuku* — ritual suicide — en masse.

The following excerpt describes the reaction of the Japanese people to this incident, both at the time and at later periods. Make copies of the excerpt and pass them out to the students. Have students read the excerpt, and then lead them in a discussion on how this excerpt helps to explain the historical developments during the Tokugawa shogunate.

"The public outburst of sympathy and admiration for the forty-seven ronin was immediate and virtually unanimous. Even among a number of the shogunate officialdom there was a widespread desire to [forgive] them. Yet the ronin had broken fundamental Tokugawa laws . . . and after a period of a few months of hesitation, they were directed to [commit suicide]. It is significant to note, as an indication of the attitudes of the times, however, that the estates of Kira's grandson . . . were at the same time confiscated on the grounds that . . . he had failed to fight to the death in defense of his grandfather.

In their martyrdom . . . the band of forty-seven ronin achieved a folk immortality that can be matched by few others in Japan's history. Their story, which has been rendered . . . in every imaginable medium of the performing arts . . . is simply without challenge the most popular of all among Japanese audiences. By their noble conduct they bequeathed to all later generations an example of the spirit of pre-modern samurai at its best."

DAILY QUIZ

To assess student understanding of Section 2, give the class the following quiz. (Each item is worth 10 points.)

1. (T or F) Until the late 1500s, feudal Japan followed a course of political development more like that of Europe than that of China. *(T)*
2. (T or F) Before the establishment of the Tokugawa shogunate, Japan's capital city had been Yedo. *(F)*
3. How long did the Tokugawa shogunate rule Japan? *(about 250 years)*
4. (T or F) The Tokugawas kept the daimyos' families "hostage" in the capital city, greatly reducing the possibility of a daimyo revolt. *(T)*
5. What is the period from 1600 to 1868 in Japan sometimes called? *(The Great Peace of the Tokugawa)*
6. Give two reasons why the Tokugawa were able to keep peace in Japan. *(The restrictions they placed on the daimyos and the disarming of the peasants helped the Tokugawa keep the peace. The Tokugawa's policy of isolation also helped them keep the peace.)*
7. (T or F) The Tokugawa were anxious to trade with the Portuguese for fire arms. *(F)*
8. (T or F) The Japanese view of social classes placed warriors first, followed, in descending order, by peasants, artisans, and merchants. *(T)*
9. (T or F) The changes that took place in Tokugawa Japan were similar to those that took place in China during the Ming and Qing dynasties. *(T)*
10. How did Japan reach a decision on whether or not to accept Western influence and modernize? *(A civil war broke out between traditional and progressive forces. The progressive forces were victorious and, under the Emperor Meiji, Japan began to modernize.*

SUGGESTED ASSIGNMENTS

1. **Critical Thinking Worksheet (Basic)** Have students complete Critical Thinking Worksheet 40 in the TEACHER'S RESOURCEBANK™.
2. **Researching (Challenging)** A group of students might like to research and prepare an oral report on the opening of Japan by Commodore Matthew Perry. The report should explain the reasons for Japan's isolation, Perry's motives for his journey, and the reception Perry's party received upon its arrival in Japan. Suggest that the students use such sources as "The Closing of Japan" and "The Opening of Japan" in Sydney Eisen's and Maurice Filler's *The Human Adventure,* vol. 2 (Harcourt Brace Jovanovich).

Section 3 (pages 469–475)

The Islamic Empires of Asia Declined

SECTION OVERVIEW

Beginning with the Ottoman Empire in the late 1600s, the three Islamic empires of Asia went into decline. The failure of the Mogul Empire left India open to British influence. After the British victory over the French in the Seven Years' War, the British East India Company essentially ruled India. The company's control was not challenged until the 1850s, when the Indian Mutiny led to its dissolution. The British government then took over rule of India.

SUGGESTED TEACHING STRATEGIES

1. **Preteaching Vocabulary (Basic)** You may wish to preteach the following important vocabulary term: sepoy *(page 474)*. Ask students to explain how the British East India Company used sepoys to extend its power over India.
2. **Writing an Editorial (Average/Group)** Ask students to read either the short description "The Black Hole of Calcutta" in Ralph O. West's *The Human Side of World History* (Ginn) or the longer, more detailed account in Noel Barder's *Black Hole of Calcutta* (Houghton Mifflin). Have them use these readings as the basis for a short newspaper editorial calling for prompt action by the British against the Indians and French. Have the students read their editorials to the rest of the class.

ENRICHMENT ACTIVITIES

1. **Analyzing Ideas (Average/Group)** Show students the filmstrip on Süleyman the Magnificent from the *Villains, Heroes, and History Series* (Opportunities for Learning). After they have viewed the filmstrip, lead them in a discussion on the following questions: How was Süleyman able to come so close to conquering Europe? Why did he fail?
2. **Preparing a Newscast (Average/Group)** The entire class might like to help in developing a newscast on the Indian Mutiny. The program should include the immediate background of the rebellion, interviews with Indians who resent British domination, and interviews with officials of the British East India Company. Suggest that the students refer to pages 474-475 for information. Additional sources of information include "India: The Great Sepoy Mutiny, 1857" in Louis Snyder's *Panorama of the Past,* vol. 2 (Houghton Mifflin) and Christopher Hibbert's *The Great Mutiny, India 1857* (Viking). Have the class put on a mock broadcast of the program.

DAILY QUIZ

To assess student understanding of Section 3, give the class the following quiz. (Each item is worth 10 points.)

1. Which European city did Süleyman the Magnificent nearly capture? *(Vienna)*
2. What was the title of the chief ministers of the sultans of the Ottoman Empire? *(grand viziers)*
3. What was the capital of the Safavid Persian Empire? *(Isfahan)*
4. ________ ________ extended Persia's boundaries to their furthest extent since the times of Darius and Xerxes. *(Nader Shah)*

5. Which was the weakest of the three Muslim empires by the 1700s? *(Mogul Empire)*
6. Who controlled Great Britain's trade with India? *(British East India Company)*
7. Which British military leader defeated the French and their Indian allies in a series of decisive battles? *(Robert Clive)*
8. When did the British start imposing their way of life on the Indian people? *(during the 1830s)*
9. What action by the British East India Company precipitated the Indian Mutiny? *(The issue of a new rifle that used cartridges that were rumored to be greased with cow and pig fat offended both the Hindu and Muslim sepoys.)*
10. How did the Indian Mutiny affect the British East India Company? *(After the mutiny, the British government dissolved the company and took over direct rule of India.)*

SUGGESTED ASSIGNMENTS

1. **Review Worksheet (Basic)** Have students complete Review Worksheet 18 in the TEACHER'S RESOURCEBANK™.
2. **Critical Thinking Worksheet (Basic)** Have students complete Critical Thinking Worksheet 41 in the TEACHER'S RESOURCEBANK™.
3. **Identifying Ideas (Average/Group)** Point out to the students that the colonial experience in India left an indelible mark on Great Britain, especially on the English language. Have students use dictionaries and encyclopedias to find words in the English language that have Indian origins. Ask students to compile the words into a "dictionary." Have students compare the entries in their dictionaries during the next lesson.

Teacher's Notes

For suggested lesson plan, additional teaching strategies, enrichment activities, daily quizzes, and suggested assignments, see pages 451A–451E.

Introducing the Chapter Before students begin the chapter, have them review what they have already learned about the early cultures of Asia. Refer students to Chapter 3 (India), Chapter 4 (China), Chapter 9 (Islamic Asia), and Chapter 12 (China and Japan). Assign individuals to present brief reviews of the major cultures and civilizations of each region.

As students read the chapter, have them note the political, economic, social, and cultural changes in these areas of the world. After completing their reading, have students update their reports and describe the changes that occurred in each area during the period covered in the chapter.

CHAPTER 18

The Countries of Asia Experienced a Transition

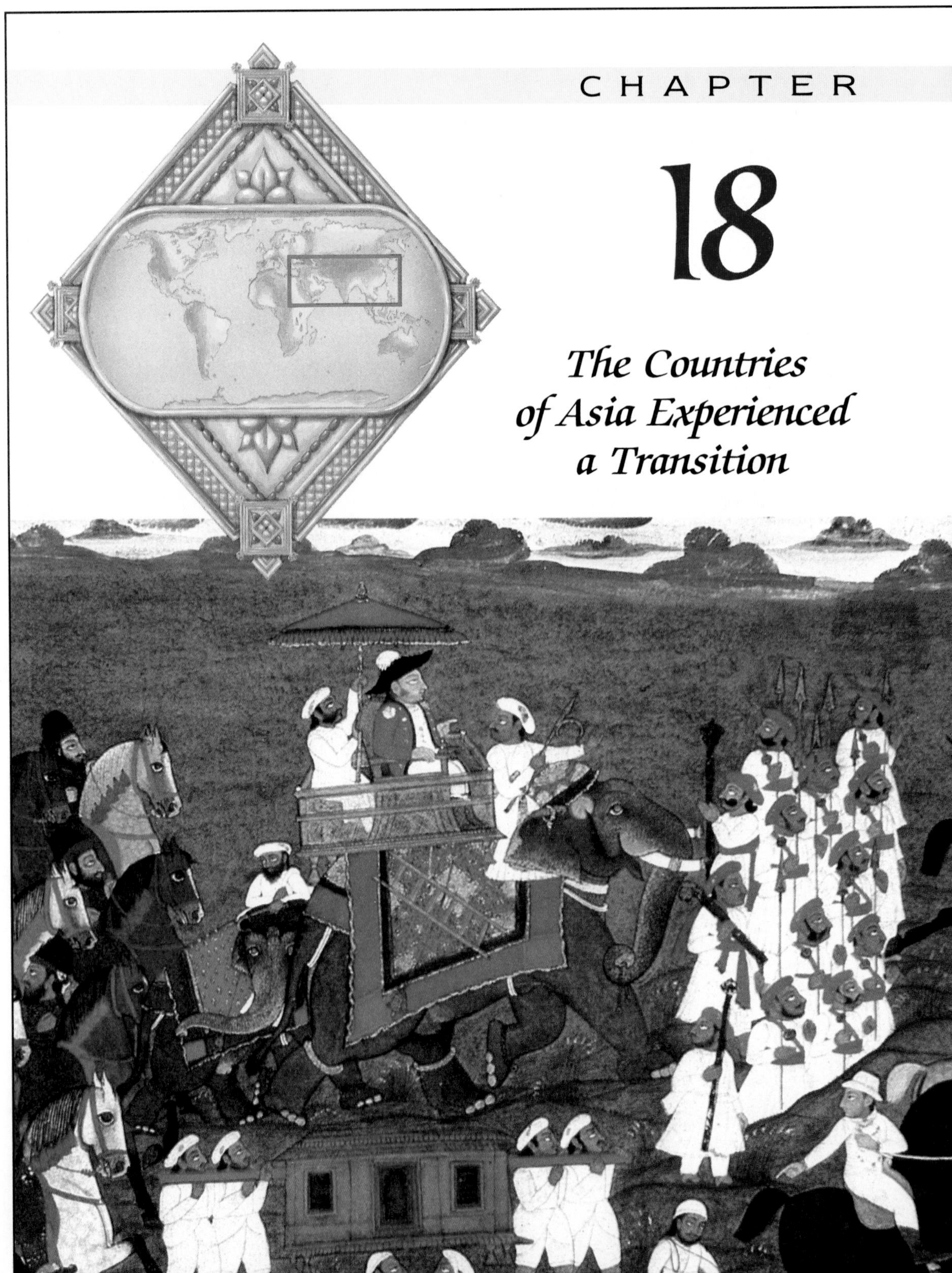

CHAPTER FOCUS

Place China, Japan, the Middle East, and India

Time

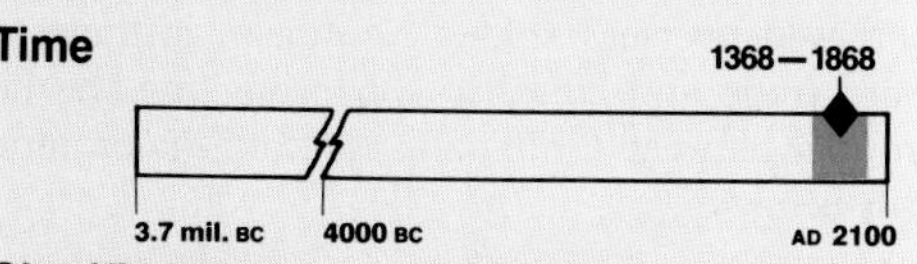

Significance

Between 1400 and the mid-1800s, many of the dominant countries in Asia reached a political and cultural peak and then began to decline. In China and Japan, following centuries of remarkable political and technological achievement, rulers attempted to keep their countries stable by opposing change and contact with the outside world. This stability, however, had a price. These civilizations stagnated. Although in 1500 China and Japan had civilizations at least as advanced as those in Europe, after 1500 these civilizations gradually fell behind.

The Ottoman, Persian, and Mogul empires reached the zenith of their political and cultural power in the 1500s and 1600s. However, decline also overtook these three empires.

As a result all these once splendid civilizations proved weak and ineffective when challenge came from the outside world. In some cases these empires were vulnerable not only to outside influence but also to colonization.

Terms to Define

junk
queue
philology
free trade
consulate
sepoy

People to Identify

Kangxi
Tokugawa Ieyasu
Matthew Perry
John Sobieski
Mahmud II
Nader Shah
Robert Clive
Lord Cornwallis

Places to Locate

Manchuria
Shanghai
Hong Kong
Nagasaki
Tehran
Delhi

Questions to Guide Your Reading

1 How did the Ming and Qing dynasties deal with the Europeans, and how did the Europeans finally gain a foothold in China?
2 By what means did the Tokugawa shoguns create a centralized, powerful government, and how were they able to keep Japan isolated?
3 How did Europeans gain control of trade in Asian nations and control of government in India?

◀ *A British parade in India*

One of the greatest contributions of the Japanese to the literary world is a form of poetry called haiku, *which when translated means "comic," or "lighthearted." Known as the poetry of the common people, haiku consists of very short verses—17 syllables at most—that subtly convey ideas and achieve a desired effect. The following are some of these charming verses by the Japanese poet Matsuo Basho, who wrote in the 1600s.*

"There goes my best hat
as down comes rain on my bald
pate, plop! plop! Oh well. . ."

"Low clouds are shattered
into small distant fragments
of moonlit mountains."

"Swallows, spare those bees
humming westward at evening
laden with honey."

"Scattered on the sand
like jewels, seashells tangled
in kelp and rubbish. . ."

"The best I have to
offer you is the small size
of the mosquitoes."

"On a journey, ill,
and over fields all withered, dreams
go wandering still."

From ancient times Asian civilizations had fascinated Europeans. However, Asian rulers did not always consider contact with Europeans desirable.

1 China Changed Gradually Under the Ming and Qing Dynasties

In 1368 Zhu Yuanzhang (JOO YOO • EN • JAHNG), a former Buddhist monk, overthrew the Yuan dynasty of the Mongols in China. At that time he established the Ming, or "brilliant," dynasty, which remained in power until 1644, when the Qing (CHING), or "untarnished," dynasty replaced it. Very little rebellion or warfare occurred in China during these two dynasties. This lengthy period of peace greatly contributed to China's stability and allowed it to maintain its culture.

Chapter Objectives
After studying Chapter 18, students will be able to:

1. Show how Confucian thought influenced Ming policy towards the outside world.
2. Summarize the accomplishments of the Qing dynasty and list the reasons for its collapse.
3. Identify the sources of the conflict between the British and the Chinese during the early 1800s.
4. Discuss the accomplishments of the Tokugawa shogunate.
5. Describe the changes that took place in Tokugawa Japan.
6. Discuss the causes of the decline of the Ottoman Empire.
7. Outline the history of Persia from 1500 to 1800.
8. Explain how the British expanded their authority over India.
9. List the causes of the Indian Mutiny.

SECTION 1

Focus/Motivation
Point out to students that while China is one of the world's major powers, people in the West really know little about the history of that country's people and culture. Ask students what they know about the Chinese people and how they live. List responses on the chalkboard or an overhead projector. Have students copy the list, and then ask them if any of the items on the list reveal anything about the political, economic, or so-

1A, 1B, 2D, a1A, a1C, a4B, a4C

● The capital of the Ming Empire was first at Nanjing, then at Beijing. Neither are seaports.

cial history of the Chinese people. Next, ask students why we know so little. *(Most students will mention China's geographic isolation and the Chinese people's belief that all other people were barbarians.)* As students read this section, have them add more specific information on China's religion, trade, education, and government to their lists.

Presentation Relating Cause and Effect (Average/Group)
Write the following groups of statements on the chalkboard or an overhead projector. For each numbered statement, have students determine whether each of the two following statements can best be described as a cause or as an effect.

1. Ming emperors stopped financing naval expeditions.
_C_ Confucianism was the philosophy of the Ming government.
_C_ Defending the northern frontier became costly.

2. Ming emperors promoted the tribute system.
_C_ Emperors wanted to increase security.
_E_ The emperor entertained and gave lavish gifts.

3. Chinese internal trade expanded.
_E_ Certain regions began specializing in particular goods.
_C_ Cities continued to grow.

Ming Policy Toward the Outside World

During the early Ming period, the Chinese were probably the most skillful sailors in the world. They built large, solid ships known as **junks,** some of which were over 400 feet (125 meters) long. Since the early 1100s, the Chinese had used the compass, which they probably invented, in navigation. They also drew detailed charts of Asian sea routes. In 1407 the emperor financed a Chinese fleet that sailed all the way around Southeast Asia to India. Another Chinese fleet crossed the Indian Ocean and reached Aden, at the southern tip of the Red Sea, in 1415.

These and other voyages occurred almost 100 years before Vasco da Gama sailed from Portugal to India by going around the tip of Africa. The Chinese clearly had the ability to become a great seafaring power, as both Portugal and England later did. However, the naval expeditions of the early Ming period ended suddenly in the mid-1400s. The later Ming emperors—unlike Henry the Navigator in Portugal or Queen Elizabeth in England—had little interest in seapower or in overseas trade. They stopped financing naval expeditions and for a time outlawed overseas trade. Confucian attitudes toward trade and concern over protecting the land frontier between China and central Asia prompted this behavior.

Learning from Maps *After the beginnings of the Age of Exploration in the 1400s, many European traders visited Guangzhou (Canton). What is the name of the* ● *capital of the Ming Empire? Is it a seaport?*

Confucian Attitudes Toward Trade

After defeating the Mongol conquerors in 1368, the Ming emperors tried to rid China of all Mongol influences. They looked to the great ages of China's past for inspiration and tried to re-create the grandeur of the Han, Tang, and Sung dynasties. As part of that effort, the Ming emperors restored Confucianism—to which the Mongols had paid only lip service—as the official philosophy of the government.

Confucian philosophy divided society into four classes. First in order of importance were the scholar-officials, who governed the country for the emperor. Next came the peasants, who produced food and paid the taxes that supported the empire. Artisans, who made useful objects, came third. At the bottom of the social order were the merchants. The Chinese regarded them as "parasites" who made profits from selling things that the peasants and artisans had produced. The Chinese, then, regarded trade as a necessary evil, not as something desirable.

As followers of Confucius, the Ming emperors tried to keep trade with other countries to a minimum. Unlike European monarchs influenced by mercantilism, the emperors of China did not believe that foreign trade benefited the country. Instead, they received tribute from governments in Korea, Japan, and Tibet. In return the emperors gave the rulers of these nations lavish gifts. However, the emperors did not intend for these exchanges to increase China's wealth. Instead, they designed the tribute system to enhance China's prestige and security.

The Northern Frontier

After their victory over the Mongols, the Ming emperors wanted to make sure that no central Asian people ever again would conquer China. They therefore concentrated their efforts on securing the long northern land frontier rather than on venturing into overseas trade.

To protect that frontier, they strengthened the Great Wall and built new observation towers. They encouraged Chinese soldiers to move with their families into the frontier zone, offering the soldiers free land there in exchange for defending the strategic mountain passes.

In 1421 the Ming moved the imperial capital from Nanjing, in central China, to Beijing, in the north (see map, page 454). From there, only 40 miles (64 kilometers) south of the Great Wall, the emperors tried to prevent the nomadic tribes of the north from uniting into a powerful fighting force. Individual tribes that submitted to the Ming sent yearly tribute missions to Beijing and exchanged gifts. In return for their loyalty, the Ming emperors gave the chiefs of the nomadic tribes titles, money, and honors.

Defending the frontier required constant attention and cost a great deal of money. In addition, the emperors had to entertain and present lavish gifts to the hundreds of nomads who came to Beijing on the yearly tribute missions. The Ming emperors did not have the financial resources to encourage overseas expeditions as well. Therefore, primarily to save money for frontier defense, the Ming emperors ended the overseas expeditions of the early 1400s.

The Founding of the Qing Dynasty

Throughout most of the Ming period, the northern frontier remained secure. Occasionally, small bands of nomads seeking greater riches than they could obtain through the tribute system surged across the frontier, but the Chinese always succeeded in driving them away.

In the early 1600s, however, a new and very serious threat emerged in Manchuria, to the northeast of China. There a chieftain named Nurhachi (NOOHR • HAHCH • EE) unified the many tribes into a single people—the Manchus. After conquering Korea and Inner Mongolia in the 1630s, the Manchus captured Beijing in 1644 with the help of a Chinese general. The Manchus then established the Qing dynasty, which survived until 1911. Once again, despite all the efforts of the Ming, "barbarians" had conquered China and had established their own dynasty.

Even though the Qing dynasty was non-Chinese, it actually became one of the most "Chinese" in outlook. The Qing emperors adopted Chinese culture and used traditional Chinese techniques of government in their rule.

The adoption of the Chinese tradition was exemplified by the Emperor Kangxi (KAHNG • SHEE), who ruled from 1661 to 1722. Kangxi knew the Chinese classics well and sponsored many important literary projects. He presided over the examination system and appointed successful candidates to civil service positions. He supervised efforts to control flooding on China's major rivers and to establish storehouses throughout the land to hold grain for use in case of famine. The emperor urged both officials and the common people to behave virtuously. In short, Kangxi ruled in accordance with the teachings of Confucius, just as the Ming emperors had done.

At the same time, Kangxi and the other Qing emperors tried to preserve distinctions between the Manchus—who were a minority in the empire—and the Chinese people. All Manchus had to study the Manchu language and Manchu cultural traditions. The Qing forbade the Chinese people to marry Manchus or to settle in northern Manchuria. The dynasty maintained this region as a tribal homeland for the Manchus. Finally, the Qing required all Chinese men to wear their hair in a single braid, called a **queue** (KYOO). The queue distinguished the Chinese from the Manchus and signified Chinese submission to Manchu rule.

The Ming and Qing Economies

The Qing emperors, like those of the Ming dynasty, believed that agriculture was the basis of China's wealth. They maintained traditional political institutions, and they supported traditional Chinese ideas and values. Neither the Ming nor the Qing emperors showed any interest in change. Nevertheless, change occurred. For example, new patterns of commerce and trade began to appear.

The trend toward the growth of cities begun during the Song dynasty continued under the rule of the Ming and Qing emperors. Urban growth contributed to the expansion of trade within China. In theory the Chinese looked down on the merchants. In practice they needed them to supply the urban population with food, textiles for clothing, and other essential goods.

4. The status of women declined.

_C_ In the city women did not have an economic role.

_E_ The practice of footbinding was introduced.

5. Peasants became discontented.

_E_ The number of uprisings and rebellions increased.

_C_ Taxes increased while services decreased.

1A, 1B, 1C, 1D, a1A, a1C, a4B, a4C

● Ricci gained acceptance at the Qing court by presenting clocks and a huge map of the world to the emperor.

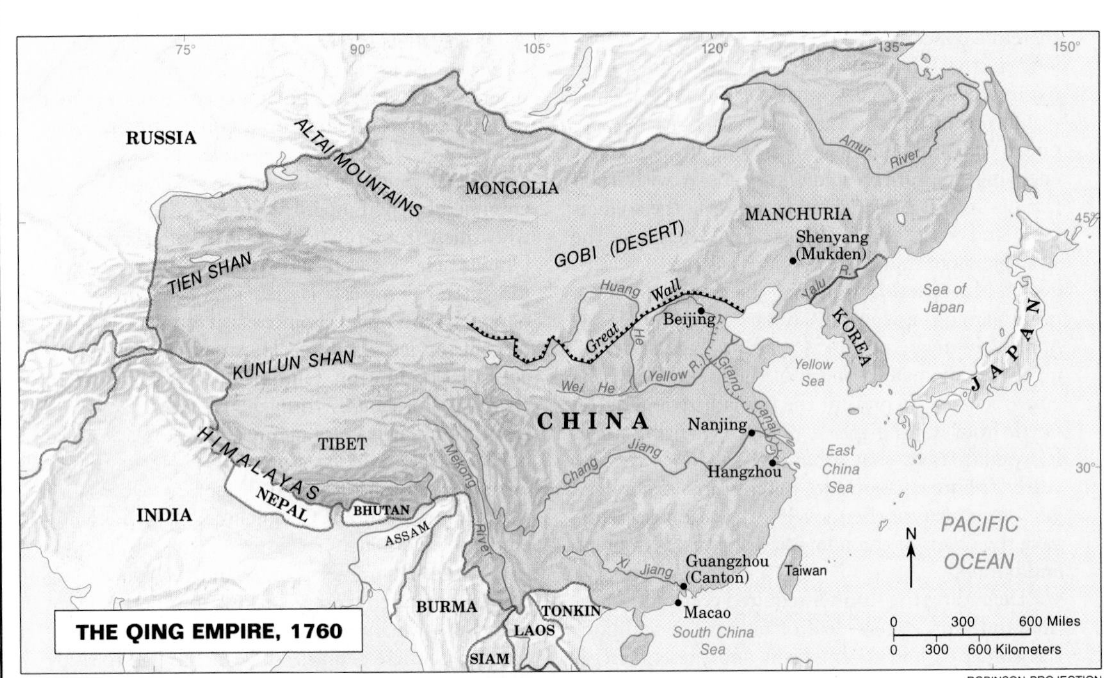

Learning from Maps *The Qing dynasty's northern border extended beyond the Great Wall to the Amur River. In what region of China is the Amur River located?* Manchuria

Certain regions of the country began specializing in the production of certain goods. For example, Guangzhou (GWAHNG • JOH), in the south, became a center for the manufacture of woks—the shallow iron cooking pans that the Chinese still use for cooking today. And the region near Shanghai in central China became a center for the weaving of cotton cloth.

Traders transported goods from these manufacturing centers by barges and junks along the rivers, canals, and coastal waters to Beijing, the new and rapidly growing capital city, and to other large urban centers such as Guangzhou and Shanghai.

● An Italian missionary, Father Matteo Ricci, who traveled through China in 1583, gives a fascinating description of the Grand Canal and the hazards of traveling on it.

> "So great is the number of boats that frequently many days are lost in transit by crowding each other, particularly when water is low in the canals. To prevent this, the water is held back at stated places by wooden locks, which also serve as bridges. . . . At times it happens that the rush of water is so high and strong, at the exit from one lock or at the entrance to another, that the boats are capsized and the whole crew is drowned. The boats of the Magistrates and of other government dignitaries are drawn up the stream, against the current, by wooden devices on the shore, and the expense for such hauling is paid by the Government. . . ."

The Chinese shipped goods such as tea and silk by caravan to central Asia and as far away as Russia. In addition, Chinese ships continued to sail to Southeast Asia and India to trade, despite the government's disapproval of such voyages.

Despite the growth of cities, the vast majority of China's people continued to live in the countryside, where they increased the amount of land under cultivation. New crops such as sweet potatoes, peanuts, and tobacco were introduced from the Americas. The sweet potato became known as "the poor man's food" in south China because it thrived in soils unsuited to the growing of rice. It also provided more basic nutritional value than most other crops.

456

● The practice of acupuncture developed during the Ming and Qing dynasties.

■ artisans

The Growth of Popular Culture

As in Europe the growth of cities and the increasing wealth of urban merchants and artisans in China encouraged the rise of popular culture. As early as the Yuan dynasty in the 1300s, city people read novels and watched plays written in the common, everyday language rather than in the literary language. During the Ming and Qing periods, these popular novels and plays increased in number. Old tales about bandits, corrupt officials, and beautiful women, which had once been recited by storytellers in the streets, now appeared in inexpensive books written by professional authors. The writings of this period realistically portrayed Chinese society and family life.

Scholarship also flourished under the rule of the Ming and Qing emperors. During the Ming dynasty, Chinese scholars wrote both long and detailed histories of earlier dynasties as well as essays on Confucian ethics. During the Qing dynasty, scholars studied the history of words, or **philology.** As the humanists had done in Europe during the Renaissance, Chinese scholars applied intensive study to ancient writings to determine their exact meaning.

A few scholars, mostly Daoists, compiled encyclopedias of plants and animals. In 1579 a scholar completed a huge book describing almost 2,000 animal, vegetable, and mineral drugs used in Chinese medicine. The book included information, for ● example, on how to inoculate people against smallpox. In contrast to Europe, however, pure science and the scientific method did not take hold in China.

City life contributed to the development of popular culture and scholarship, but it also contributed to a decline in the status of Chinese women. In rural China everyone, including women, had to work on the land so that families could survive. In the cities, however, women did not have such an important economic role. Officials and wealthy merchants grew very accustomed

Learning from Pictures *These Chinese silk weavers are working on a manual loom during the Qing dynasty. To what social class did textile workers belong?* ■

1B, a1A, a1C, a4A

● the binding of women's feet

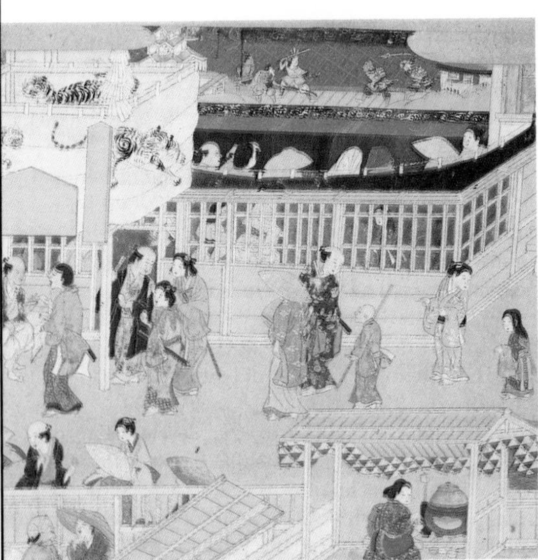

Learning from Pictures *This picture scroll shows a street scene during the Ming dynasty. What Ming* ● *practice did the Qing rulers try to ban?*

to thinking of women as useless playthings. The practice of foot-binding illustrated this changing attitude toward women.

When a girl reached the age of five, her parents bound her feet tightly with strips of cloth, forcing each foot to bend into an upside-down U-shape. Gradually, over the course of several years, the arch of each foot would break. This created what the Chinese called a "golden lotus," a tiny foot half the normal size and curved under instead of straight. Foot-binding was extremely painful and made it very difficult for women to walk. It indicated that a woman's father or husband was rich enough that the woman did not need to work to help support the family. For this reason few peasant women had bound feet. This practice, which began among the upper classes in the Song period, spread throughout Chinese society and reached a peak under the Ming dynasty. The Qing rulers did not approve of foot-binding and tried unsuccessfully to ban it. The Chinese did not entirely give up the practice until the mid-1900s.

The Decline of the Qing Dynasty

By about 1800 the Qing dynasty had entered the stage of decline in the pattern of dynastic cycles. After more than a century of peace, the soldiers of the Manchu army had lost much of their skill as warriors. They had grown used to peacetime life. Despite government policies to keep them separate from the Chinese people, the soldiers had developed closer ties to the Chinese and had become more and more like them in their behavior and values. Sensing that the Manchu army was weak, central Asian tribes began to threaten China's northern frontier.

Under the rule of the Qing, government services for the people also collapsed. China's population had doubled—from approximately 150 million in the late Ming period to 300 million by 1800. Peace and increases in agricultural output contributed significantly to this population growth. Chinese peasants raised more crops, making it possible to feed more people. However, increases in population were not matched by increases in either the number or the efficiency of government officials. During the late Ming period, the government had about 20,000 officials, or one for every 7,500 people. In 1800 the Qing government still consisted of only 20,000 officials—now only one for every 15,000 people.

As in the past, local officials relied on powerful local rural families, the gentry, to make the political system work. These local officials collected taxes from the peasants, sending the revenue to the government. They also supported local schools and supervised road repairs and other public works projects. In return the emperor permitted them to keep a small portion of the taxes they collected.

In normal times this system functioned very smoothly. A small number of government officials could administer the affairs of a large country. However, during the late Qing period, corruption among government officials caused serious problems. High-ranking bureaucrats began to use their positions in the emperor's service to acquire great personal fortunes. They pressured local officials throughout China to give them money and expensive gifts.

Those local officials, forced to pay bribes or lose their jobs, pressured the gentry for more tax revenues. The gentry in turn demanded more taxes from the peasants. Less and less of the money collected went to provide necessary services such as flood control and road repairs. Instead, the money ended up in the hands of high-ranking government officials.

458

At first the Portuguese were warmly received by the Chinese. But because of the piratical activities of many Portuguese sea captains, they were expelled in 1522.

Discontent and Rebellion

In 1796 discontent over increased taxes and decreased services erupted into a great peasant rebellion. Members of the White Lotus Society, a secret society that had risen up against the Mongols centuries earlier, led this revolt, called the White Lotus Rebellion. The government finally succeeded in restoring peace in 1804 after a long and expensive struggle. The emperor then tried to eliminate official corruption, but he lacked the financial resources to increase the number of officials and to create reforms in government at the local level. Thus the basic cause of discontent remained, and uprisings and rebellions occurred frequently.

The Qing dynasty seemed to be following in the footsteps of all previous Chinese dynasties. It had gained the Mandate of Heaven in battle and had achieved great heights. Now, however, a discontented people challenged the dynasty. If the pattern of past Chinese history had repeated itself, eventually a powerful rival to the Qing emperor would have emerged, defeated the Qing army in battle, and claimed the Mandate of Heaven for himself. The new emperor would then have established a new and more vigorous dynasty.

Chinese history did not follow that traditional pattern, however. Just as the Qing dynasty started its decline, new peoples appeared in China—Europeans.

The Portuguese in China

The first Portuguese ships reached the southeastern coast of China about 1514. After many years of negotiation, the Chinese allowed the Portuguese to establish a trading station at Macao (muh • KOW) in 1557. Portugal's impact, however, was not limited to trade.

The Jesuit missionaries who arrived on Portuguese ships enjoyed considerable success in China. They used their knowledge of advanced Western astronomy to gain admission to the emperor's circle. By helping to revise the Chinese calendar, they proved themselves useful to the emperor, whose duties still included predicting eclipses and the timing of the seasons. The emperor appointed the Jesuit missionaries to official positions in his palace, which gave them the opportunity to convert numerous high-ranking Chinese officials to Christianity.

In the 1700s, however, the Qing emperors turned against the Jesuits, claiming they had become too involved in politics. The emperors denounced Christianity as a subversive anti-Confucian sect. The number of converts to Christianity dwindled following this denouncement.

By this time troubles at home and competition from the Dutch had weakened Portugal's position in Asia. Portugal and the Roman Catholic church had to retreat from China. Thus Christianity never became an important religion in China.

Learning from Pictures *In the 1500s the Chinese allowed Europeans to establish trading stations. The opening of these stations boosted Chinese commerce.*

459

The British in China

In the early 1700s, British ships began arriving frequently at Guangzhou, where the British had established a trading post in 1699. The British came to China to buy tea, which the Dutch had introduced to Europe in the 1600s. Great Britain was rapidly becoming "a nation of tea drinkers," and the British regarded Chinese teas as the best in the world.

The British East India Company monopolized the new trade in Chinese teas. The company agreed to accept Chinese restrictions on its activities in order to get adequate supplies of tea. The Chinese allowed company ships to dock only at Guangzhou and to trade only with a small number of officially licensed Chinese merchants. These merchants in turn paid large fees to the Chinese government. The government allowed only a few representatives of the British East India Company to stay in Guangzhou, where they lived in a special "foreign settlement" outside the city walls. They could not bring their families with them, and they had to abide by Chinese laws.

For a time the Chinese government succeeded in controlling the British with trading and housing restrictions. They kept contact between the British and the Chinese to a minimum. In the late 1700s, however, two new developments led to a deterioration in British-Chinese relations and eventually led to war between these two countries.

Free trade ideas. The first development that led to the crisis between China and Great Britain was the spread of **free trade** ideas from the West. Free trade, which developed as a reaction to mercantilism, illustrated the belief that government should not restrict or interfere in international trade. Not all British traders worked for the British East India Company. Those who tried to operate independently in Asia resented the monopolies enjoyed by the British company. Resentment also grew among American traders, who began sailing from New England to China in the 1780s.

The British government also expressed increasing concern about securing additional overseas markets for the products of British industry. It sent official missions to Beijing in 1793 and again in 1816 to request that the Chinese open several more ports to British ships. Both ended in dismal failure.

In 1834 the British government went a step further in initiating a free trade policy. It decided that the British East India Company had not been aggressive enough in encouraging British exports. It therefore abolished the company's monopoly on trade with China. The British government sent an official to Guangzhou for trade talks, but the Chinese rebuffed this official's efforts.

Learning from Pictures *One of the Chinese products highly prized by Europeans for European markets was porcelain, like this finely crafted decorative plate.* †

The opium trade. The other development that resulted in war between China and Great Britain involved the steady expansion of the tea trade. The British East India Company had paid for its purchases of Chinese tea with cotton from India. Eventually, Chinese demand for this cotton, used to supply the many weavers in central China, reached its limit. The British demand for tea, however, continued to increase. The company had to find some new product to exchange for tea. The product they chose was opium, a habit-forming narcotic.

British India produced opium and exported it to China in increasing quantities from the late 1700s onward. Opium addiction spread among the Chinese people, and the Chinese government grew alarmed. It also expressed concern that so much of China's silver supply helped to pay for the growing volume of opium imports. Chinese authorities demanded that opium sales be stopped and that all opium cargoes be turned over to them.

†The Metropolitan Museum of Art, Purchase, The Lucille and Robert H. Gries Charity Fund, 1970.

460

● because its ships were better armed and its sailors were better trained
■ The Opium War broke out when a representative of the emperor seized an opium consignment at Guangzhou and burned it.

Learning from Pictures *The British were victorious in this battle near Guangzhou. Why was the British navy so successful against the Chinese?* ●

The Opium War in China. When the Chinese tried to suppress the opium traffic in South China and insisted on maintaining the traditional ■ tribute system, a war broke out between China and Great Britain. This conflict—known as the Opium War or the First Anglo-Chinese War—lasted from 1839 to 1842.

During the Opium War, the Chinese army and naval forces proved no match against the better-armed and better-trained British. A small British naval force, which included iron-hulled steamships, moved up the coast from Guangzhou, defeating Chinese resistance with relative ease. In 1842 the British secured control of an important region near Nanjing (nahn • JING). At that point the Qing officials agreed to negotiate on British terms.

The treaty of 1842, which ended the Opium War, compelled China to give the island of Hong Kong to the British and to open the cities of Xiamen (Amoy) and Shanghai to foreign trade. These ports, together with Guangzhou, became the first Chinese treaty ports. No tariff of more than 5 percent could be charged on British goods entering these ports. A further provision stated that British subjects in these ports would be governed by British, not Chinese, laws and would be tried in British courts. This exemption of foreigners from the laws of the nation in which they live or do business is called **extraterritoriality.**

Great Britain could not hold its privileged trade monopoly in China for long. France and other Western powers, including the United States, soon demanded and received similar trade treaties with provisions for extraterritoriality. China did not negotiate these trade treaties but was forced to sign them. The Chinese called them "unequal treaties."

The Taiping Rebellion

An event that occurred in China itself made the intrusion of the Western powers easier. In the mid-1800s southern and central China were torn by a rebellion that threatened to overthrow the Qing. The leader of this revolt was a southern Chinese influenced by Christian teachings. He claimed to be the younger brother of Jesus, charged with the mission of establishing a new dynasty—the Taiping (ty • PING), or "Great Peace." His ideas attracted many followers among the Chinese.

When the government tried to suppress the Taiping movement, it turned into a political rebellion. The Taiping Rebellion lasted from 1850 to 1864 and caused great destruction in southern China and the Chang Jiang valley. The rebels were never able to establish the Mandate of Heaven. With the aid of some regional armies and foreign adventurers, the Qing finally suppressed the rebels.

SECTION 1

Closure

Lead the class in a discussion of the following question: Can the Ming and Qing periods be considered a time of cultural development for China? Why or why not? *(Answer: Cultural development did occur under the Ming and Qing. However, Confucian policy of keeping trade to a minimum did not allow the culture to expand as it might have.)*

1B, a1A, a1D, a4A, a4F, a4G, a4K

Review Answers

1. ***junk:*** large ship first built during the Ming period; ***queue:*** single braid required of all Chinese men; ***philology:*** study of the history of words; ***free trade:*** trade free of government restrictions; ***extraterritoriality:*** exemption of foreigners from the laws where they live or do business
2. ***Nurhachi:*** chieftain who unified the nomadic tribes of Manchuria; ***Kangxi:*** emperor of the early Qing period who adopted Chinese culture and government
3. ***Beijing:*** city in east central China; ***Manchuria:*** province in northeastern China; ***Guangzhou:*** port on Xi River; ***Shanghai:*** port at the mouth of the Chang Jiang; ***Macao:*** port on South China Sea; ***Hong Kong:*** port on South China Sea
4. The Ming emperors devoted much attention and money to defending the northern frontier, leaving them without financial resources for overseas trade and expeditions.
5. (a) Society's four classes were scholar-officials, peasants, artisans, and merchants.
(b) in Confucian philosophy, merchants were considered parasites. The Ming looked on trade as a necessary evil, and therefore, tried to keep trade with other countries to a minimum.
6. The reasons for the Qing decline were: Central Asian tribes threatened the frontier; a decrease in government efficiency; official corruption; discontent over

READ
WRITE
INTERPRET
CONNECT
●THINK

BUILDING HISTORY STUDY SKILLS

Thinking About History: Analyzing Consequences

Every human action and decision produces a consequence or result. For example, if you stayed up until about 2:00 A.M. last night and had to get up at 6:00 A.M. this morning, the consequence would probably be that you are exhausted today. Or if you decided to study very hard for a test, the consequence would probably be that you received a good grade on the test. Since history deals with human actions, analyzing the consequences of these actions will help you gain new insights into historical events. Knowing the consequences helps you analyze the impact of change. Consequences can be immediate or long-range, positive or negative.

How to Analyze Consequences

To analyze consequences, follow these steps.

1. Identify the purpose or goal of the action or decision that you are studying. Ask: What did the person or persons hope to achieve?
2. State the positive and/or negative consequences of the decision or action.
3. Identify the immediate and the long-range consequences of the action or decision.
4. Form a conclusion by asking whether the action or decision helped to achieve the purpose or goal.

Developing the Skill

The statement below by H. G. Creel describes the civil service examinations in China. As you read the statement, consider what consequences the examinations had for the government of China.

> "The civil service examination system . . . was competitive, objective, and open to practically everyone of ability. It broke down class distinctions, feudalism, and artificial barriers of race, tribe, religion and color. . . . It brought many of the ablest men of the country into government service. In so far as it was effective, it assured that officials were men of culture, not mere wasters who had inherited their position."

The purpose of your study is to analyze the consequences that the civil service system had on Chinese government and society. Creel mentions the positive outcomes of the system. The examinations contributed to social mobility in that anyone could take them; the examinations had a performance requirement rather than a class requirement. People from different classes could be chosen for positions by scoring well. Therefore, the system provided for intelligent leadership by the ablest people. Other positive consequences included a common philosophy of rule, a commitment to ethical and moral beliefs as the foundation of leadership, and the stability of the system. The Chinese emperor might have changed, but the bureaucratic system remained intact, orderly, and continuous.

In the short term, the system promoted education. Long-term consequences of the system included stability and order.

What were the overall consequences of the civil service system on Chinese government and society? The civil service system promoted unity and the learning of new ideas.

Practicing the skill. In your local newspaper, read an article dealing with a government decision or policy. Then analyze the consequences that this decision or policy might have.

To apply this skill, see Applying History Study Skills on page 477.

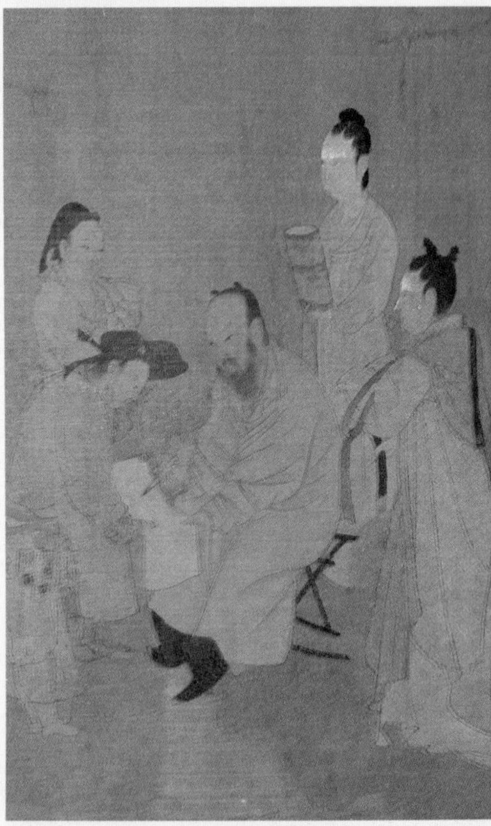

Chinese scholars with scrolls

1B, a1A, a1C, a4A, a4F, a4I, a4K, a4L, a4M

● **Point out that at the same time English nobles were fighting a war of succession—the Wars of the Roses.**

The Taiping Rebellion, however, weakened both the Qing dynasty and the country. To raise money, the government established a system of internal tariffs. These tariffs hurt trade without providing much help to the central treasury because tariff collectors stole most of the money. Then foreigners took over the collection of customs duties in Chinese ports, further weakening China's control over its revenues.

During the Taiping Rebellion, the Qing could not protect foreign citizens as Western governments had demanded. In 1856, war with Great Britain again broke out, and British forces, with French aid, again defeated the Chinese.

This forced the Chinese to sign another "unequal treaty," which opened additional treaty ports on the coast and along the Chang Jiang. The Chinese had to allow the British to open an embassy in Beijing, the Qing capital. Other foreign powers soon followed Great Britain's example by opening their own embassies in Beijing. In addition, Great Britain took possession of a small section of the Chinese mainland opposite Hong Kong. And the Chinese government pledged to protect Christian missionaries and their converts.

In separate treaties, Russia gained even more than trade privileges and extraterritoriality. It received territory north of the Amur River and east of the Ussuri River, bordering on the Sea of Japan. In the southern part of this newly gained territory, the Russians founded the port of Vladivostok.

SECTION 1 REVIEW

1. **Define** junk, queue, philology, free trade, extraterritoriality
2. **Identify** Nurhachi, Kangxi
3. **Locate** Beijing, Manchuria, Guangzhou, Shanghai, Macao, Hong Kong
4. **Interpreting Ideas** Why did foreign trade and overseas explorations experience a decline during the Ming dynasty?
5. **Summarizing Ideas** **(a)** What were the four classes of society, according to Confucianism? **(b)** How did the Ming emperors reinforce this philosophy?
6. **Evaluating Ideas** Why did the Qing dynasty decline?
7. **Understanding Ideas** **(a)** Why were the Jesuits successful at first in converting people in China to Christianity? **(b)** Why did they later lose favor with the Chinese emperor?
8. **Understanding Cause and Effect** **(a)** What were the causes of the Taiping Rebellion? **(b)** What was the result of this rebellion in China?

2 Japan Prospered Under the Rule of the Tokugawa Shoguns

China's culture influenced that of early Japan. However, until the late 1500s, feudal Japan followed a course of political development more like that of Europe than of China.

In the late 1400s, the Japanese daimyos began ● fighting among themselves for survival and supremacy. The struggle among the daimyos resulted in the creation of a political system that was a cross between feudalism and centralized monarchy. The Japanese established this hybrid system, known as the Tokugawa (TOH • KOOG • AH • WAH) shogunate, in 1603. It survived until 1868.

Founding of the Tokugawa Shogunate

In 1467 rival branches of the Ashikaga (AH • SHEE • KAH • GAH) family in Japan became involved in a dispute over the naming of the next shogun. This conflict marked the beginning of 100 years of almost constant warfare in Japan. Local daimyos, sensing the weakness of the Ashikaga, fought for control of the country. Three daimyos in turn emerged in the late 1500s as victors in this long struggle. They succeeded in establishing themselves as overlords to the other daimyos but not as absolute rulers of all Japan.

Oda Nobunaga. The first of these overlords, Oda Nobunaga (NOH • BOO • NAH • GAH), began his career as a minor daimyo. He succeeded, by means of conquest and alliances, in capturing the city of Kyoto in 1568. Nobunaga ended the Ashikaga shogunate in 1573 and then started to consolidate his power in central Japan. Before he could defeat his remaining rivals, however, one of his own vassals killed him.

Toyotomi Hideyoshi. Another vassal, Toyotomi Hideyoshi (TOH • YOH • TOH • MEE HEE • DAY • OH • SHEE), assumed Nobunaga's position as overlord. Born in 1537 to a humble peasant family, Hideyoshi had risen to a high position in Nobunaga's army, from warrior to general. In the 1580s Hideyoshi defeated several powerful daimyos in battle, and by threats and diplomacy, he forced the others to pledge their loyalty to him.

Hideyoshi thus did not destroy the powers of the defeated daimyos but weakened them by reduc-

increased taxes and decreased services caused uprisings and rebellions. **7. (a)** The Jesuit missionaries used their knowledge of advanced Western astronomy to gain admission to the emperor's circle. By helping to revise the Chinese calendar, they proved themselves useful to the emperor, whose duties still included predicting eclipses and the timing of the seasons. **(b)** In the 1700s the Qing emperors turned against the Jesuits, claiming they had become too involved in politics.
8. (a) The leader claimed to be the younger brother of Jesus, charged with the mission of establishing a new dynasty—the Taiping. His ideas attracted a wide following among the Chinese. **(b)** To raise money to cover the cost of putting down the rebellion, the government established a system of internal tariffs which hurt trade. Foreigners took over the collection of foreign customs duties in Chinese ports.

SECTION 2

Focus/Motivation
Set up a situation in the classroom to illustrate the split in Japanese authority between the shogun and the daimyos before the rise of the Tokugawa. Name a responsible pupil as student teacher to review the answers to the day's homework questions while you sit in the back of the room. Two groups of two or three students each should be told before class

to contradict any of the answers given by the class and accepted by the student teacher. After a while the result of such a lesson will be confusion. At this point ask the students what the classroom situation has to do with feudalism in Japan. *(Some students will see similarities between the role of the teacher and the Japanese emperor, the student teacher and the shogun, and the dissenting students and the daimyos.)* Point out to the students that, similar to the situation in the classroom, the power structure under Japanese feudalism was cause for turmoil and confusion.

Presentation Comparing Ideas (Average/Group)

In teaching about feudalism in Tokugawa Japan, it might be useful to build on students' knowledge of feudalism in Europe. Ask students in what ways feudalism in Japan was similar to feudalism in Europe and in what ways it was different. *(Students will note parallels between samurai and knights, bushido and the code of chivalry, the daimyos and great nobles. Students may also point out that nothing like the shogunate existed in Europe. However, students should conclude that the basic European characteristics of feudalism, such as power based on landholding, no strong central government, and local loyalties among people, were all present in Japan.)*

Learning from Pictures *Japanese warriors regularly exercised and meditated to keep fit for battle. What country did Japan invade in 1592?* Korea

ing the size of their territories so they could not threaten him again. He also carried out a "sword hunt" to disarm the peasants. Thereafter, peasants could no longer rise to become warriors. Only men born into warrior families could become warriors.

In 1592 the ambitious Hideyoshi sent an army to invade Korea. Hideyoshi took this action for two reasons. He wanted to build an extensive empire, and he also wanted to keep Japanese warriors busy with battles overseas while he increased his power at home. At first the Japanese invasion force succeeded. As the battles continued, however, the Korean navy began sinking Japanese ships carrying troop reinforcements, and a Chinese army aiding the Koreans pushed the invaders back to the coast. When Hideyoshi died in 1598, the Japanese withdrew to their homeland.

Tokugawa Ieyasu. Hideyoshi's most powerful vassal, Tokugawa Ieyasu (EE • AY • YAH • SOO), succeeded him as overlord. Ieyasu established his capital at Yedo (Tokyo). Other daimyos resisted Ieyasu, but he defeated them in 1600. Then in 1603 he forced the emperor to name him shogun. The Tokugawa family retained the title of shogun for the next 250 years—a period known as the Tokugawa shogunate.

Like Toyotomi Hideyoshi, Tokugawa Ieyasu did not destroy his defeated rivals. Instead Hideyoshi made them swear oaths of loyalty to him and his family. He allowed the daimyos, who then numbered about 250, to retain possession of their private domains. However, he reserved for himself the right to expand or reduce the size of their territories in the future.

Within his own domain, each daimyo governed almost as an absolute ruler. The local peasants paid taxes that the daimyo used to support both himself and those in his service, particularly the samurai. The Tokugawa family had its own very large domain, which included about one-fourth of the land area of Japan. Thus the Tokugawa did not rule the entire country directly, nor did they personally tax the entire population. In this way Japan maintained a degree of political and economic decentralization.

Tokugawa Power

As overlords the Tokugawa did have considerable influence over the behavior of the lesser daimyos. Behind this influence lay Tokugawa wealth and military power. The Tokugawa shoguns prohibited the less powerful daimyos from building new castles within their domains and from entering into alliances with other daimyos. The daimyos had to spend every other year in Yedo, the shogun's capital, and they left their families there as hostages when they returned to their own domains. In this manner the Tokugawa shoguns maintained control over the daimyos.

The expense of maintaining two grand residences—one in Yedo and one in the provinces—and of traveling to and from Yedo in elaborate processions drained the financial resources of most daimyos. The daimyos could no longer afford to engage in revolt. The threat that the Tokugawa shoguns might execute their sons and heirs if they did revolt provided another powerful restraint on the daimyos.

1A, 1B, a1A, a1B, a1C, a4B, a4C, a4G

The Great Peace of the Tokugawa

The Tokugawa shoguns came to power in 1600 because of war, but they brought Japan a long era of peace. For more than 250 years, Japan did not experience rebellion or other violent upheavals. The period from 1600 to 1868—the end of the shogunate—is sometimes called the Great Peace of the Tokugawa.

The hostage system and other controls over the daimyos served to keep the peace. So did the disarming of the peasants, a policy that Hideyoshi began and the later Tokugawa shoguns continued. Japan also enjoyed peace because the Tokugawa adopted a policy of isolation. They had permitted overseas trade for only a brief period.

Foreign contacts. Even before the invasion of Korea under Hideyoshi, Japanese sailors and traders had traveled overseas. In the early 1400s, during the Ashikaga shogunate, Japanese ships had sailed to Korea and China seeking profitable trade. If refused, as often happened, the Japanese resorted to piracy, seizing whatever they could from the local inhabitants.

These Japanese traders sailed mostly from those ports in western Japan closest to the Asian mainland. The goods they brought back—whether paid for or stolen—contributed to the wealth of local daimyos in that part of the country.

The Portuguese in Japan. In the mid-1500s the daimyos found another source of wealth: trade with the Portuguese, whose ships began appearing in Japanese waters. Portuguese traders introduced two things to Japan that later Tokugawa shoguns considered undesirable: the musket and Christianity. The musket, a forerunner of the modern rifle, gave its possessor an enormous advantage over an opponent armed with only a sword. Christianity was undesirable because it taught loyalty to a power greater than the Tokugawa shogun.

Christian missionaries. In the wake of Portuguese traders came Christian missionaries, chief among them the Jesuits, who had achieved notable success during the Counter-Reformation in Europe. The Jesuits concentrated their efforts on converting the daimyos to Christianity. They had discovered that it was easier to first convert a daimyo and then build churches and seek converts throughout the domain that he controlled. By the early 1600s, the missionaries had converted almost 500,000 Japanese to Christianity.

Closing the country. The success of the Jesuits alarmed the Tokugawa shoguns. Fearing that Japanese Christians might revolt against their rulers, the shoguns outlawed Christianity. Then, in the early 1600s, the shoguns forced Portuguese traders and Christian missionaries to leave Japan.

By this time the Portuguese faced stiff competition from the Dutch in the spice trade in the islands off the coast of Southeast Asia as well as in Japan. The Dutch had accepted a strictly controlled trading relationship with the Tokugawa shogunate. The shoguns allowed only a few Dutch merchants to live in Nagasaki, a port city on the island of Kyushu. In addition, the shoguns themselves controlled the small amount of trade Japan conducted with the Dutch.

Even that limited trading was curtailed when the Tokugawa "closed the country" in the late 1630s. They prohibited the building of oceangoing ships and also banned travel abroad by Japanese.

Learning from Maps *Yedo was the capital of the Tokugawa shogunate. On what island is the city Yedo located?* Honshu

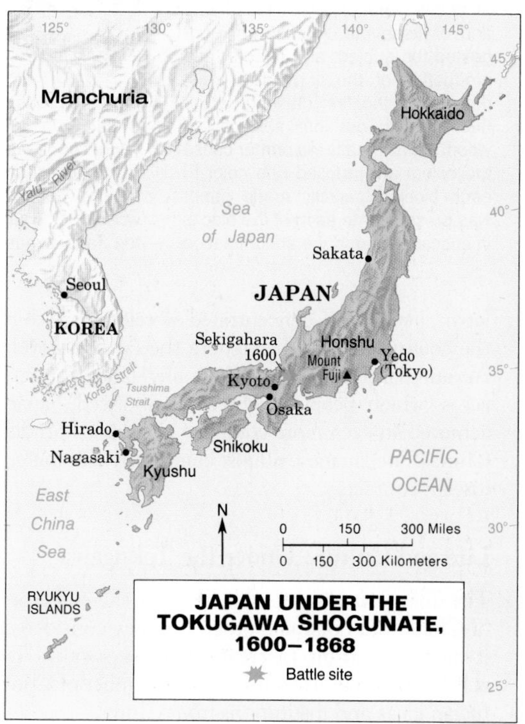

LAMBERT CONFORMAL CONIC PROJECTION

465

PAINTING

Evening Squall at Ohashi

The emergence of popular culture in Tokugawa Japan was reflected in the subjects of woodblock prints. Recreational and theatrical scenes as well as scenes of such commonplace activities as fishing and farming were captured by the gifted artists and printmakers of the 1700s and 1800s.

In this woodblock print by Ando Hiroshige, working people are opening umbrellas over their heads to protect themselves from the rain as they hurry over a wooden bridge. The artist shows a single moment caught in time. As we look at the picture, we can almost sense the suddenness of the storm and feel the sensation of the rain on our skin.

Prints such as this were the result of a collaboration of skilled artists and craftspeople. A publisher suggested the subject and directed the production of the print. The artist then made the first drawing, which the engraver cut into a series of woodblocks. Finally the printer chose the colors and applied one color to each block. Specially made paper was pressed onto each of the blocks in succession, and the accumulation of color produced the total picture. Usually an edition of about 200 impressions was printed, to be sold in the publisher's shop.

The technique of printing by woodblock was first developed while the Tang dynasty held the Mandate of Heaven in China and was brought into Japan in the 700s. In the late 1700s and early 1800s, as the technique became more popular, it began to reflect the tastes of a people emerging from a feudal society into the modern world.

Japan, like China, concentrated on relations within the country and tried to ignore the outside world. As an island country without any land frontiers across which people might slip unnoticed, Japan achieved an even more complete isolation than did China. The Japanese almost completely eliminated foreign contacts.

Life and Culture Under the Tokugawa

The Tokugawa shoguns, like most of the emperors of China, did not value progress. They considered it more important to create a stable society. To achieve this goal, they borrowed a number of Confucian ideas and institutions from China.

First they adopted—with some modification—the Confucian structure of social classes. They ranked warriors, who performed roughly the same role as scholar-officials in China, first. Peasants, artisans, and merchants followed in descending order of importance.

In Japan people belonged to these classes by birth. Sons followed the occupations of their fathers, and the authorities allowed no one, male or female, to move freely about the country. For example, a person born into an artisan family in the city of Osaka remained a member of the artisan class in Osaka for life.

Second, the Tokugawa shoguns encouraged education in the Confucian classics for members of

466

the warrior class. The shoguns established schools in every domain to prepare young warriors for their new peacetime role as government officials. However, the shoguns did not adopt the Chinese civil service examination system. In Japan warriors became officials by heredity alone. Males born into low-ranking warrior families worked as low-ranking officials in their domains. Those born into high-ranking families served as high-ranking officials.

As a further means of maintaining control, the shoguns required all warriors to live in the castle town of their daimyo. Instead of living off the income of their own estates in the countryside, they now received yearly payments from their daimyo. A warrior's rank determined the amount. This policy deprived warriors of the opportunity to develop independent sources of wealth or power. It also eliminated their opportunities to revolt against their lords.

Change in Tokugawa Japan

As in China, the rulers of Japan could not prevent social, economic, and political change. Much of the change that occurred resembled the change that occurred in China. Cities grew in both size and importance. Internal trade expanded, and various regions began to specialize in different crops and handicrafts. The growth of cities and the increasing wealth of merchants and artisans led to the rise of a popular culture. By the early 1700s, new forms of literature, theater, and art had taken root. All these new forms catered to the tastes and life styles of ordinary city residents.

The End of Japanese Isolation

As part of the Tokugawa plan for keeping Japan isolated, the Japanese government refused to give shelter to ships of other nations during storms. They treated shipwrecked sailors harshly. Such treatment of American whaling and merchant ships finally brought Japanese isolation to an end.

In 1853 United States President Millard Fillmore sent a naval force to Japan under Commodore Matthew Perry. Perry had orders to negotiate a commercial treaty that would open Japanese ports to American trade as well as guarantee the safety of American sailors. He presented a letter from President Fillmore that urged the Japanese to accept the

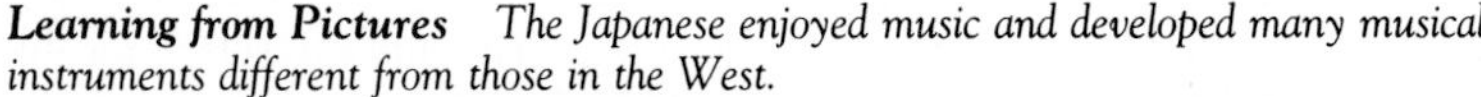

Learning from Pictures *The Japanese enjoyed music and developed many musical instruments different from those in the West.*

1B, a1A, a1C

Eager to learn about the West, a young samurai named Yoshida Shoin attempted to stow away on the *Missouri,* one of Commodore Perry's ships. He carried only a pen and paper with which to record his experiences in foreign lands. However, American sailors turned him over to the shogunate authorities, who threw him into prison.

SECTION 2

Closure

Mention to the students that many of the people who wanted to modernize Japan were followers of a patriot-scholar named Sakuma Shozan. He believed that Japan would be able to withstand Western influence only if it employed a combination of "Western science and Eastern morals." Ask students if this has happened in Japan. *(To a great extent it has.)*

Review Answers

1. *consulate:* diplomatic office headed by consul
2. *Oda Nobunaga:* daimyo overlord who ended the Ashikaga shogunate in 1573; ***Toyotomi Hideyoshi:*** vassal to Oda Nobunaga who succeeded him as overlord; ***Tokugawa Ieyasu:*** overlord who established a shogunate that lasted more than 250 years; ***Matthew Perry:*** commander of a naval force to Japan who had orders to negotiate a treaty to open Japanese ports to U.S. trade and guarantee the safety of U.S. sailors
3. *Kyoto:* city in south-central Honshu; ***Yedo:*** city on Tokyo Bay in east-central Honshu; ***Nagasaki:*** city on western coast of Kyushu
4. The less powerful daimyos were not allowed to build new castles within their domains or enter into alliances with other daimyos. They had to spend every other year in Yedo, the shogun's capital, and

treaty, and he promised he would return for an answer the following year.

In Japan the American visit sparked controversy. Some powerful leaders favored military resistance and continued isolation. Others believed that Japan could not hold out, and their views prevailed. The shogun reluctantly agreed to negotiate when Perry returned in 1854.

Colorful ceremonies accompanied the negotiations, symbolic of the two contrasting cultures. The Japanese gave the Americans beautiful silk, lacquer ware, and other articles exquisitely made by hand. The Americans presented the Japanese with guns, a telegraph set, and a model railroad train on which dignified Japanese officials took rides.

The negotiations led to the Treaty of Kanagawa (kuh • NAHG • uh • wuh) in 1854, a turning point in Japanese history. The Japanese opened two ports to Americans for shelter and trade. Within two years Japan signed treaties with Great Britain, Russia, France, and the Netherlands. Several Japanese seaports were opened where representatives of foreign nations had the right to live, trade, purchase naval supplies, and establish **consulates**—diplomatic offices headed by consuls.

At first, conservative Japanese isolationists ignored foreign consuls and kept contacts with foreigners to a minimum. Nevertheless, in 1858 the Japanese and the United States governments agreed to exchange diplomatic representatives. The Japanese now admitted more American consuls and opened more treaty ports to the United States. Similar treaties with other nations soon followed.

The Decision to Modernize

The end of isolation brought Japan face to face with a great question. Should Japan resist Western influence, by force if necessary? Or should the nation try to become strong in the only way the imperial powers would respect—by Westernizing and industrializing?

The decision did not come about without a struggle. In the 1860s a civil war broke out between rival factions of the samurai warrior class. On one side were those who wanted to maintain the existing political system. On the other were progressive samurai who saw the need to modernize Japan, if only to keep Japan strong and independent. They pushed for the ouster of the shogun and the restoration of the emperor's powers. The pro-emperor forces won out in 1868. The last Tokugawa shogun resigned and turned his extensive domain over to the emperor. The daimyo soon followed suit. The emperor, a boy of 15, took the name Meiji (MAY • JEE), meaning "enlightened rule," for his reign.

Learning from Pictures *Encouraged by the Tokugawa shogunate, artists carved these miniature Japanese sculptures, called netsukes, in a variety of images. Many netsukes depict Westerners (left) as comical. Other netsukes relate to Japanese history, like this traditional dancer (right).*

a1A, a1C, a4A,
a4F, a4G, a4H, a4L

● Vienna

Learning from Pictures This painting depicts Sultan Süleyman at the Battle of Mohács. What European capital did ● Süleyman almost capture?

SECTION 2 REVIEW

1. **Define** consulate
2. **Identify** Oda Nobunaga, Toyotomi Hideyoshi, Tokugawa Ieyasu, Matthew Perry
3. **Locate** Kyoto, Yedo, Nagasaki
4. **Interpreting Ideas** How were the Tokugawa shoguns able to control the daimyos?
5. **Understanding Ideas** Why did the Tokugawa shoguns decide to "close the country"?
6. **Summarizing Ideas** What Chinese ideas and institutions did the Tokugawa shoguns adopt?
7. **Contrasting Ideas** How did the way in which Japan ended its isolation differ from the way in which China did?

3 The Islamic Empires of Asia Declined

Followers of the Muslim faith spread the word of Allah from the Iberian Peninsula to the East Indies. By the 1500s three large Islamic empires existed in the central part of that vast stretch of land from Bengal in India to the Balkan Peninsula: the Ottoman Empire, Persia, and the Mogul Empire.

The rulers of these Muslim states set up strong central governments. They also faced deep religious divisions with lasting quarrels between Shiites and Sunnis.

The Ottoman Empire

After the Ottoman Turks conquered Constantinople in 1453, they continued to expand overland while Europe expanded overseas. Led by Süleyman (SOO • lay • mahn) the Magnificent, the Turks conquered Hungary and nearly captured the Hapsburg capital at Vienna in 1529. They may have failed in their capture of Vienna only because heavy rains prevented the sultan from bringing forward his heavy siege cannon.

Nearly a half century later, in 1571, Philip II of Spain inflicted a great naval defeat on the Turks at Lepanto. Later, the Turks surrendered control of Hungary, but in 1683 they again nearly captured Vienna. Troops led by the Polish king John Sobieski halted their attack.

Despite these defeats and great territorial losses, the Ottoman Empire still had considerable vitality in the late 1600s. Turks lived in the heart of the empire in Asia Minor. Christians inhabited the Balkans, and Muslim Arabs lived in the old Fertile Crescent and along the Mediterranean shore of North Africa. From the capital at Constantinople, the sultans and their grand viziers (vuh • ZIRZ)—who had duties similar to a prime minister's—ruled this diverse mass of people.

leave their families there when they went back to their own domains. The expense of maintaining two residences and traveling between them, as well as the threat of violence to their families, kept the daimyos from revolting.
5. The Tokugawa shoguns closed the country because they saw unrestricted foreign trade and Christianity as possible sources of revolt against them.
6. The Tokugawa shoguns adopted — with some modifications — the Confucian view of social classes. The Tokugawa shoguns also encouraged education in the Confucian classics.
7. Conservative Japanese isolationists held out successfully against any real contacts with outsiders. Even after 1858, the opening of Japan was a slow, deliberate process. China, on the other hand, had its isolation broken by being forced to sign "unequal treaties" that opened treaty ports on the coast and along the Chang Jiang to Western countries.

SECTION 3

Focus/Motivation
Have students study the map of the Ottoman Empire on page 470. Then ask students the following questions: **(a)** What was the farthest extent of the empire. *(much of Eastern Europe — almost to Vienna, the shores of the Black Sea, parts of North Africa)* **(b)** Who drove the

● the lands around the Sea of Azov and the Black Sea

Ottomans from North Africa? *(the armies of Napoleon)* **(c)** Which country won independence from the Ottoman Empire in the 1820s? *(Greece)* **(d)** In what region were a number of independent states formed in the 1870s? *(Balkans)*

Mention to students that in this section they will learn some of the reasons for the decline of the Ottoman Empire.

Presentation Classifying Information. (Average/Group) Write the following events on the chalkboard or on an overhead projector. Have students place the events in their correct chronological order by writing *1* before the event that took place first, *2* before the event that took place second, and so on.

- *(3)* Lord Cornwallis named governor general
- *(1)* Nader Shah sacked Delhi
- *(4)* English became the language of instruction in Indian schools
- *(7)* Queen Victoria proclaimed Empress of India
- *(2)* Black Hole of Calcutta
- *(6)* British East India Company dissolved
- *(5)* Sepoy Rebellion.

Decline begins. After Süleyman the Magnificent died in 1566, the empire began its slow decline. Food production could not keep pace with the growing population and the economy suffered because the empire lost control of both the silk and spice trades. The Turks also lost lands around the Black Sea and the Sea of Azov to the Russians. Corruption, rebellious Janissaries, and problems concerning the succession also weakened the empire.

Attempts at reform. Napoleon's army, which invaded the Ottoman possession of Egypt in 1798, spread the ideas of the French Revolution to the Ottoman Empire. These ideas greatly influenced Selim III, who ruled the empire from 1789 to 1807. He enacted enlightened reforms in administration, in taxation, and in the military. However, conservatives and Janissaries opposed to change overthrew him.

Selim's successor, Mahmud II, had more success with reform. Although Great Britain, France, and Russia forced him to recognize Greek independence in 1829, Mahmud destroyed the Janissaries—using their poor performance against the Greek rebels as an excuse—and introduced autocratic reforms. The Ottoman Empire continued under this reformed system of rule until the early 1900s. Although reduced in prestige and power, the Ottoman Empire continued to influence international affairs.

Persia

The peoples of Persia, the land lying between the Ottoman Empire and the Mogul Empire of India, had become part of the early Islamic empire. In 1501 a Turkic dynasty called the *Safavids* (say • FAH • vuhdz) established a very strong central

Learning from Maps *At its zenith, the Ottoman Empire controlled eastern Europe and north Africa. What lands did the Turks lose to the Russians?*

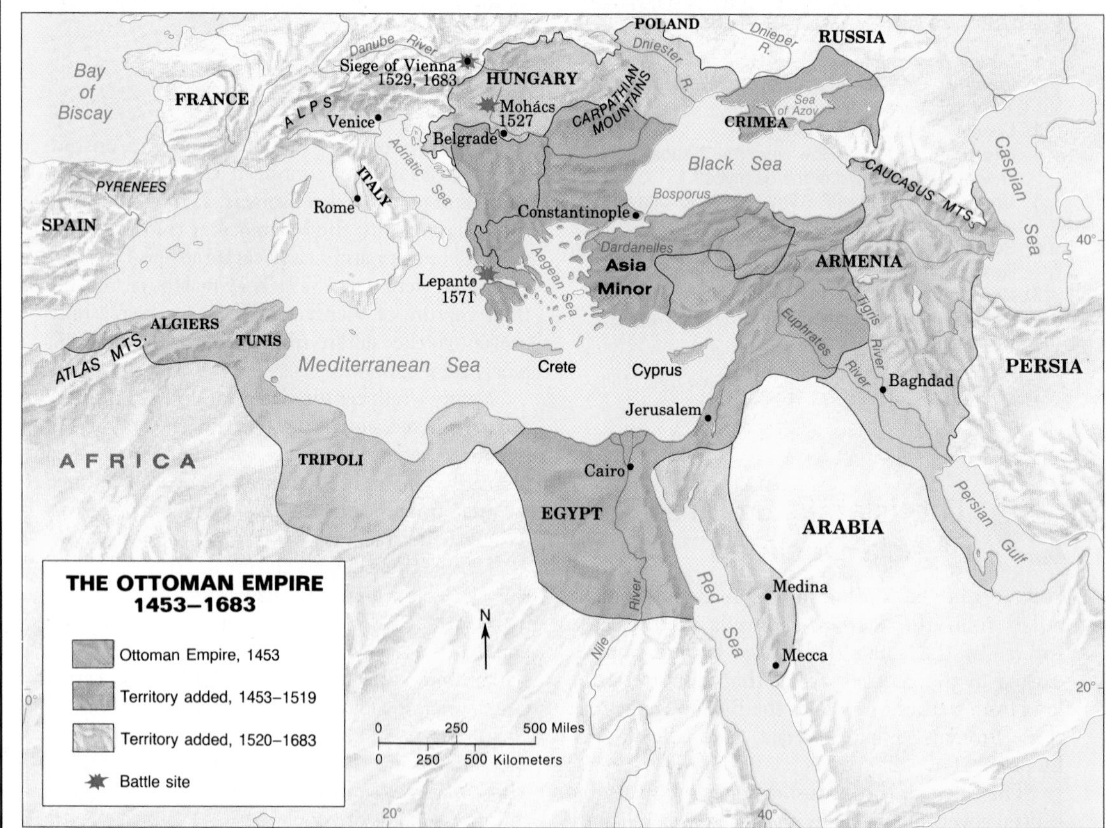

● because of its protest movement and the strength it gave to the central government of the Persian Empire

government with its capital at Isfahan. The Safavids, under the rule of Shah Abbas I, brought Persian society to new heights in the late 1500s and early 1600s. Isfahan, with its brilliant royal court, was considered one of the great cities of the Muslim world. Shah Abbas's reign saw a flowering of literature—especially poetry—and of the arts—particularly calligraphy and textile and carpet design. During this same period, Persian was adopted as the language of diplomacy in much of the Islamic world.

In one respect Persia resembled the northern Europe of the 1500s. The Safavids followed the Shiite element of Islam, and they ruthlessly forced Shiism as the state religion upon the Persian population. Some historians have compared Shiite Islam to Protestantism because of its protest movement and the strength it gave to the central government. Most important to later history is the contribution the Shiite Muslims made to modern Iranian nationalism. Shiism gave the Persians—today's Iranians—a separate identity from the greater number of Sunnis—Turks and Arabs—who lived around them. This nationalism would have a strong effect on Iran in the 1900s.

The close ties between religion and government had both positive and negative aspects. The Shiite Safavids encouraged religious education, and many of the best students became members of the clergy or went into the law—professions that were closely related in strict Islamic societies. In time religious and legal leaders came to wield great power in the government. However, many of them opposed the government's efforts at change and modernization. Others became corrupt and supported only those government policies that would increase their power and wealth.

The rulers who succeeded Abbas proved increasingly inept, and in 1736 the Safavid dynasty fell. The Persian nobles then elected a brilliant military leader, Nader Shah, as their new ruler. Through numerous conquests Nader Shah extended Persia's boundaries to their greatest extent since the time of Darius and Xerxes. But after one of his own tribesmen assassinated Nader Shah in 1747, Persia lost these conquered lands. Persia then divided into a number of small states. At the end of the 1700s, the Qajar (kah • JAHR) dynasty—another Turkic people—established a Persian monarchy with its capital at Tehran.

Learning from Pictures *Shah Abbas I, leader of the Safavids, leads a battalion against the* ● *Uzbeks. Why do historians compare the Shiite branch of Islam to Protestantism?*

471

LINKING GEOGRAPHY TO HISTORY

The Mercator Projection: A Map for Navigators

When people look at a map, they usually have no idea of which projection cartographers used to construct that map. However, almost everyone has heard of or seen the most frequently used projection—the Mercator—developed by Gerhard Mercator in 1569.

On his projection Mercator drew the lines of latitude and longitude as straight lines that crossed each other at right angles so that navigators could draw straight lines to plot courses. This meant that the distance between parallels, or lines of latitude, increased as latitude increased. If, however, Mercator had drawn the parallels with even spacing, as they are on a globe, straight lines plotted on them would not be true compass bearings.

The actual mathematical computations that Mercator used to develop his projection were complex, but the idea behind his projection was quite simple. Picture a spherical balloon inside a hollow cylinder. Next, imagine that the balloon has lines of latitude and longitude marked on it and that the line marking the equator just touches the wall of the cylinder. Now imagine blowing up the balloon. As the balloon stretches, the lines of longitude lie as straight lines along the walls of the cylinder and the lines of latitude are stretched apart in proportion. As a result, the farther poleward you look the greater the distortion in scale. And although land shapes appear correct, their areas are greatly distorted. Nevertheless, for every point on the map, the angles shown are correct in every direction. This allows a navigator to plot a straight line course, because a line connecting any two points follows an exact compass direction.

While the Mercator projection is a valuable navigational tool, it has been used far too frequently to depict the world on a flat surface. It seems convenient because the shapes of the continents are correct and are easily recognized. However, as a result of regularly seeing the Mercator projection, many people have no idea of the sizes of the continents in relation to one another.

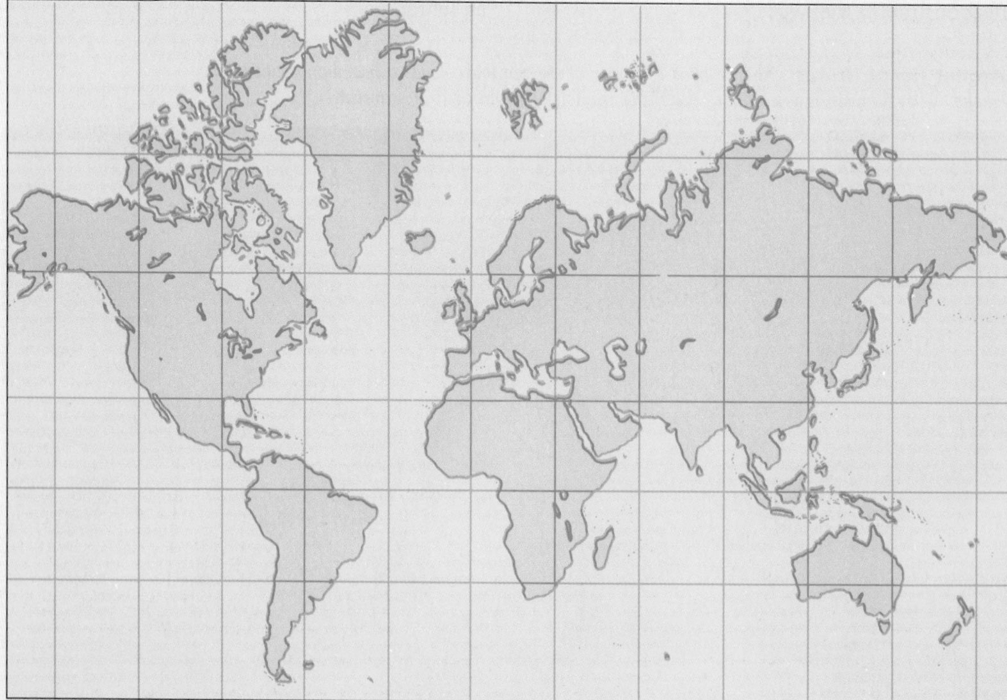

On the Mercator projection, landmasses retain their true shape.

472

1B, 4E, a1A, a1C, a4A

● the French and their Indian allies

The Mogul Empire in India

The Mogul Empire had become the weakest of the three Muslim empires by the 1700s. Still, the wealth of India attracted traders. People believed the country had impressive supplies of jewels and gold. European travelers could see that India's rulers enjoyed luxurious life styles unmatched by those of any European monarchs. India's great cities, such as Agra and Delhi, seemed much larger than any city in Europe. Agriculture flourished on the subcontinent, where the monsoon season allowed more than one harvest a year.

Nevertheless, by the mid-1600s Mogul rulers faced financial difficulties that weakened the central government. The Moguls maintained huge and expensive armies supplied with enormous cannons. They believed they needed these forces to hold their empire together. In addition, the court became more luxurious and more expensive to support. To pay these costs, the Mogul emperors increased taxes. Sometimes as much as one-third of the peasants' income from the land went to pay these taxes. As a result, the peasants' levels of production and prosperity declined, further reducing the revenue base. Nevertheless, the Moguls expanded the size of the bureaucracy so that it could collect taxes more efficiently.

In 1739 Nader Shah, the powerful new Persian ruler, sacked Delhi and confiscated the jewel-encrusted Peacock Throne of the Moguls. The Moguls lost their wealth, their prestige, their army, and much of their territory. Nader Shah effectively destroyed Mogul power in India, although a shadow emperor remained on the throne in Delhi until the 1850s. During the remainder of the 1700s, the Marathas, Sikhs from the Punjab, and Afghan Muslim invaders fought for control of the country. With India torn by dissension, Europeans could more easily conquer it.

The British in India

The Mogul Empire had the least success of the major Muslim empires in confronting European power. To the east of India the Chinese and Japanese managed to keep Europeans out altogether for a long time. In India, however, the Mogul emperors could neither dislodge the Portuguese in the 1500s nor could they resist the English. By the 1600s the English began to replace the Portuguese as the major European presence in India. Over the years this presence grew.

Learning from Pictures *Robert Clive laid the foundation for the expansion of Britain's Indian empire. Who did Clive defeat for control of India?* ●

The British East India Company, founded in 1600, controlled England's trade with India. By the 1700s the company's chief rival was the French East India Company. Both the English and the French trading companies desired commercial profits, not Indian colonies. Very few English or French citizens lived in India.

Competition between the governments of Britain and France ultimately resulted in the Seven Years' War, which began in 1756. This occurred as the Mogul Empire was dissolving into hundreds of small states. Taking advantage of the chaos, the British and the French made alliances with rival Indian rulers.

The British trading post at Calcutta lay within the important Indian state of Bengal, whose ruler was allied with the French. In 1756 Bengali troops captured Calcutta and imprisoned 146 British citizens, locking them up overnight in a small jail cell that became known as the "Black Hole of Calcutta." By the next morning, 123 of the prisoners had died of suffocation.

The British East India Company, under its military leader Robert Clive, fought back with fury. In a series of decisive victories, Clive crushed the

473

1A, 1B, 2D, 4E, a1A, a1C, a4B, a4C

SECTION 3

Closure

Point out to students that some British people characterized India as "the jewel in the crown of the empire." Ask students why they think the British valued their Indian colonial possessions so highly. *(India was a valuable source of natural resources and trade for the British.)*

Review Answers

1. ***sepoy:*** British-trained local soldier in India
2. ***John Sobieski:*** Polish king who halted the Turks' attack at Vienna; ***Mahmud II:*** Selim III's successor who destroyed Janissaries and introduced autocratic reforms in the Ottoman Empire; ***Nader Shah:*** Persian military leader who extended Persia's boundaries to their greatest extent since the times of Darius and Xerxes; ***Robert Clive:*** military leader for British East India Company; ***Lord Cornwallis:*** governor general of India in the late 1780s
3. ***Lepanto:*** scene of naval battle in Mediterranean where Spanish inflicted great defeat on Turks; ***Black Sea:*** inland sea north of Constantinople; ***Sea of Azov:*** inland sea north of Black Sea; ***Isfahan:*** Safavid capital in Central Persia; ***Tehran:*** Iranian capital city in north-central Persia (Iran), south of Caspian Sea; ***Delhi:*** Indian capital city located in north-central India; ***Bengal:*** province at the mouth of the Ganges

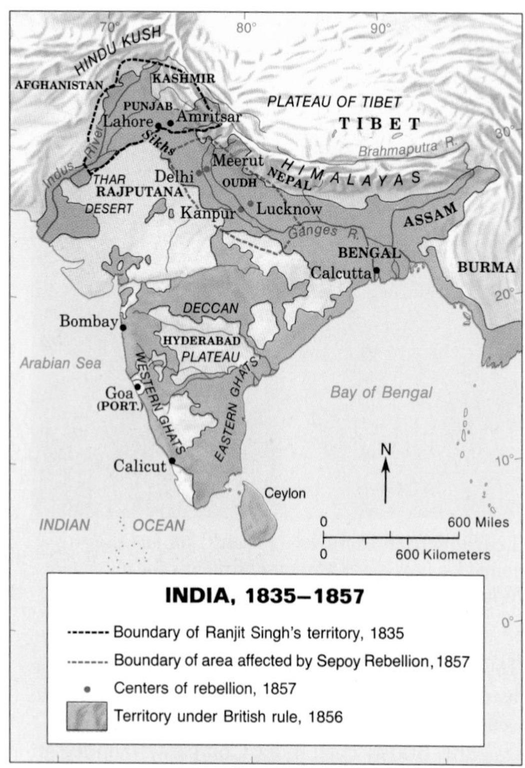

Learning from Maps *The British eventually acquired control of the two largest river deltas in India. Which river delta did the British acquire first?* Ganges

French and their Indian allies. The Treaty of Paris in 1763 left the French with a few tiny footholds along the coast and gave the British a free hand in India.

Expansion of British Authority

After the Seven Years' War, the British government became uneasy at the thought of a commercial company controlling the lives of millions of Indian people. In the 1770s the government assumed the right to appoint the company's highest official, the governor general. However, the company remained free to earn profits and to use its officials and troops as it chose.

In the late 1780s, the British government named Lord Cornwallis—the same man who surrendered at Yorktown—to be governor general of India, an appointment that would have long-lasting effects. One of Cornwallis's first actions was to clean up widespread corruption among company employees. For this purpose he created a civil service of company officials who were forbidden to have any part in the company's commercial activities. Blaming some of the corruption on Indian employees, Cornwallis ordered them excluded from all important company positions. Indian resentment over this discrimination lasted for years.

As time went on, the British were drawn deeper into the quicksands of Indian political rivalries. Several strong Indian states engaged in constant jealous rivalries and even warfare. The British took advantage of these rivalries and wars to win control of these regions. Religious hatred between Hindus and Muslims, and the caste system, which prevented Indians from uniting against the foreigners, helped the British. The British usually did not need to employ any of their own troops. Instead, when actual fighting was necessary, they made use of local troops called **sepoys** (SEE • poys), who were trained and led by British officers. In this way the British East India Company extended its power over the Indian subcontinent. By 1857 the British East India Company ruled about three-fifths of the subcontinent directly. It ruled most of the rest indirectly through its control over local princes. Great Britain also controlled the island of Ceylon, which it had seized from the Dutch during the time of the Napoleonic Wars.

Until about 1830 the British made no attempt to impose their way of life on India. In the 1830s, however, English became the language of instruction in Indian schools, and Indian pupils studied Western literature, history, and science.

The British also enforced several social reforms. They prohibited slavery and the killing of infant girls. They declared the ritual suicide known as suttee illegal. And the British suppressed Thuggee, a religious cult that required its members to commit ritual murder and robbery. It is from this cult that we get our word *thug*.

The Indian Revolt

India in the mid-1800s presented the strange spectacle of a huge land, with millions of people and an ancient civilization, controlled by a foreign commercial corporation. The British population in India had grown rapidly and by this time included British wives and families.

Indians resented the British and their increasing tendency to impose Western ways of life upon India. The sepoys were particularly dissatisfied because they had been forced to fight for the British in numerous campaigns in Afghanistan and Burma. In 1857 they revolted.

The immediate cause of the Indian Revolt, or Sepoy Rebellion, involved a new kind of rifle that the British East India Company issued in 1857. The cartridges for this rifle had been greased to make the bullets slide more easily through the barrel. In order to load his rifle, the sepoy had to bite off part of the cartridge. According to rumors, the cartridges were greased with the fat of cows and pigs. The Hindus regarded the cow as sacred. Muslims were forbidden to eat pork. India's forces included both Hindus and Muslims. Thus, biting the cartridge would violate the religious customs of both groups.

Agitators whipped up existing resentments by claiming that the company had purposely tried to insult the two religions. With help from the Indian people, the sepoy troops staged a widespread and violent mutiny against their British masters.

The Indian Revolt almost drove the British out of India, but troops sent from Great Britain finally suppressed the rebellion. To discourage future rebellions, the British executed leading sepoys by shooting them out of cannons. In 1858 the British Parliament dissolved the British East India Company and transferred the rule of India to the British government. In 1877 Queen Victoria was proclaimed Empress of India, and Great Britain filled the void left by the passing of the Moguls.

SECTION 3 REVIEW

1. **Define** sepoy
2. **Identify** John Sobieski, Mahmud II, Nader Shah, Robert Clive, Lord Cornwallis
3. **Locate** Lepanto, Black Sea, Sea of Azov, Isfahan, Tehran, Delhi, Bengal
4. **Contrasting Ideas** **(a)** In what ways were the three Islamic empires similar? **(b)** In what ways were they different?
5. **Synthesizing Ideas** How do you explain the rise of the European powers and the relative decline of the Islamic empires during the period from 1400 to 1800?
6. **Summarizing Ideas** What were the results of the Seven Years' War in India?
7. **Analyzing Ideas** **(a)** What led to the Indian Revolt? **(b)** How did this change the government in India?

Learning from Pictures
The massacre at Cawnpore during the Sepoy Rebellion left many women and children dead. This atrocity would affect Indian and British relations for a long time.

4. (a) The rulers set up strong central governments. They also faced religious divisions with lasting quarrels between Shiites and Sunnis. **(b)** Shortages of gold and food existed in the Ottoman Empire. The empire's economy also suffered because it lost control of both the silk and spice trades. The Persians devoutly followed Shiism as a state religion, and that gave them an identity separate from the other Muslims. The Indians faced European colonization.
5. Religious fanaticism, conservative absolute monarchs, the fear of involvement in war, and European empire-building all helped to stunt development in the Muslim empires. These empires also did not share in the technological and industrial revolutions of Europe.
6. After the Seven Years' War, most of India was left under the control or influence of Great Britain.
7. (a) The immediate cause of the Indian Revolt involved a new kind of rifle issued in 1857. In order to load the rifle, the sepoy had to bite off part of the cartridge. According to rumors the cartridges were greased with the fat of cows (sacred to Hindus) and pigs (forbidden to Muslims). Biting the cartridges would violate the religious customs. **(b)** In 1858 the British Parliament dissolved the British East India Company and transferred the rule of India to the British government.

Reviewing Important Terms
1. junks; 2. queue; 3. philology; 4. free trade; 5. consulates; 6. Sepoys

Developing Critical Thinking Skills
1. The Ming dynasty strengthened the Great Wall, built new observation towers, and encouraged soldiers to move their families into the frontier. The Ming capital was moved to Beijing while emperors bribed nomadic chieftains with titles, honors, and money in return for loyalty.
2. The ways that the Tokugawa maintained peace were: the hostage system; the disarming of peasants; and the policy of isolation which eliminated almost all foreign contacts, allowing Japan to create a stable society.
3. Foreign pressures, governmental ineptitude, questions of succession, and corrupt officials frequently opposed to modernization helped cause the decline of these empires.
4. In the 1700s the British began to trade opium from India for Chinese tea. Opium addiction spread among the Chinese. After the Opium War, the British developed treaty ports in China. The British defeated the French in the Seven Years' War which gave control of India to the British East India Company.
5. (a) The Japanese faced the possible loss of their culture, social class system, and even independence as in China.
(b) Japan became a modern industrial nation.
6. (a) In China, Jesuit missionaries became involved in palace politics and were forced to leave the country. The British traded opium from India for Chinese

1B, 3B, 4E, a1A, a1C, a4A, a4F, a4G, a4H, a4L

Reteaching
Have students review the Chapter Summary and the appropriate section and questions in the Unit Synthesis. Discuss the concepts until students demonstrate a clear understanding of the material.

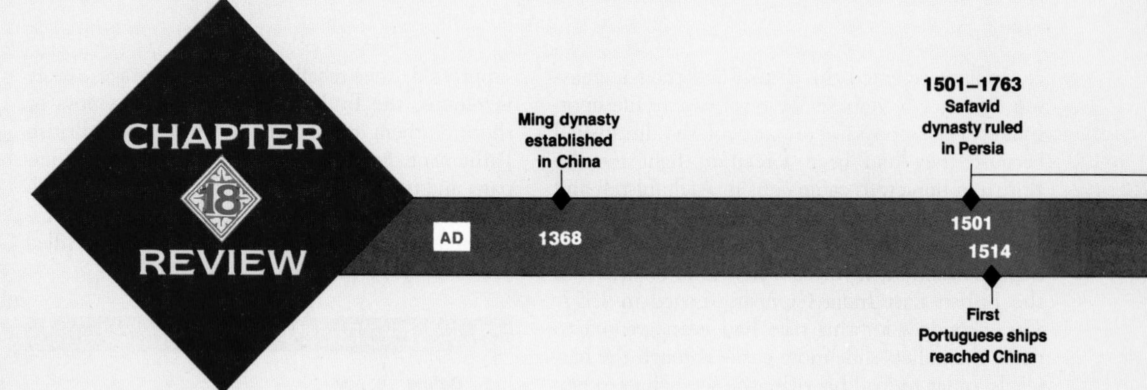

Chapter Summary

The following list contains the key concepts you have learned about the non-European world in the era of European expansion.

1. The rulers of the Ming and Qing dynasties tried to isolate China by prohibiting Chinese merchants from trading overseas and by restricting foreign merchants to special settlements inside China.
2. The Ming and Qing emperors brought peace to China, but by the late 1700s, corruption among officials increased taxes, and decreased services led to discontent and rebellion. This made it difficult for the Chinese emperors to keep out the British. China's defeat in the Opium War with Great Britain forced China to deal with the outside world. Other rebellions in China allowed foreigners to make further inroads into China.
3. As the nations of Europe did in the 1500s and 1600s, the Japanese struggled over who was to be supreme—the central government run by the shoguns or the local lords called daimyos.
4. The Tokugawa shoguns established internal peace and in the 1630s closed Japan to foreign missionaries and merchants, except for a few Dutch traders. In 1853 the United States sent a naval force to Japan to negotiate a treaty for trading privileges and to guarantee the safety of American sailors. These negotiations led to the Treaty of Kanagawa in 1854. This opened up Japan to other foreign nations.
5. The Ottoman Empire remained a threat to central and eastern Europe until 1683, after which it began a gradual decline. Under Selim III some reforms, inspired by the French Revolution, were attempted. His successor, Mahmud II, introduced autocratic reforms, and the Ottoman Empire was ruled under this system until the early 1900s.
6. The Safavid dynasty brought Persia to great cultural and political heights, and it forced the Persian people to adopt the Shiite form of Islam as the official religion. After the Safavid dynasty fell, Nader Shah assumed power. He extended Persia's boundaries to their greatest extent since the time of Darius and Xerxes. After his assassination Persia lost these lands and divided into smaller states.
7. Unlike their counterparts in China and Japan, the Mogul emperors could not keep European traders out of India. The Seven Years' War between Great Britain and France resulted in British domination in India.
8. India was governed by the British East India Company, which managed to create resentment among the Indian troops trained by the British. In 1857 the Indians rebelled in what is known as the Indian Revolt, or Sepoy Rebellion. The British put down the rebellion and dissolved the British East India Company. They transferred the rule of India to the British government. Some years later Queen Victoria was proclaimed Empress of India.

On a separate sheet of paper, complete the following review exercises.

Reviewing Important Terms

Supply the term that correctly completes each statement.

1. Early Chinese ships were called ________.
2. The Manchu emperors forced Chinese men to wear their hair in a long braid called a ________ to indicate their submission to them.
3. Like the humanists in Europe, Chinese scholars became interested in ________, the history of words.
4. Under ________ ________ the government does not restrict or interfere in international trade.
5. Diplomatic offices headed by consuls are called ________.
6. ________ were native Indian troops trained by British officers.

Developing Critical Thinking Skills

1. **Summarizing Ideas** List the steps taken by the Ming dynasty to protect China's northern frontier.
2. **Explaining Ideas** How was the Great Peace of the Tokugawa maintained?
3. **Interpreting Ideas** In what ways were the decline of the Ottoman Empire and of the Persian Empire the same?
4. **Comparing Ideas** Compare the way the British established trade in China with the way in which they established it in India.

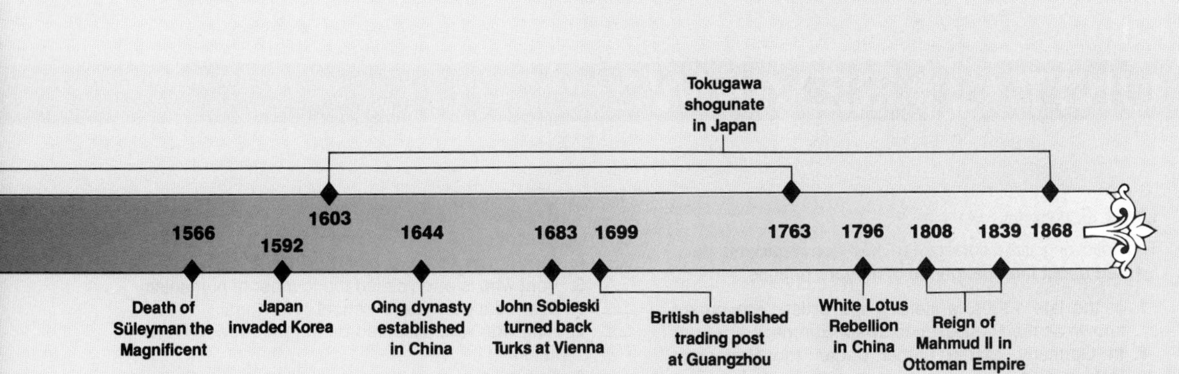

5. **Analyzing Ideas** **(a)** What issues concerned the Japanese in deciding whether to modernize their country? **(b)** What was the result of this decision?
6. **Understanding Relationships** Describe the results of European contact with each of the following: **(a)** China; **(b)** Japan; **(c)** India.

Relating Geography to History

Turn to the map on page 474 and answer the following questions: **(a)** Why did British control begin along the coast and move gradually inland? **(b)** Looking at British acquisitions from 1835 to 1857, what geographic pattern did they follow? **(c)** Why did the British have more difficulty controlling the interior than the areas along waterways?

Relating Past to Present

1. Review the military problems of the Ming and Qing dynasties along their land borders with central and northern Asia. Then use the *Readers' Guide to Periodical Literature* to find magazine articles that deal with the tensions between China and the Soviet Union in recent years. What are the reasons for the tensions between these two countries?
2. Europeans transmitted their culture to the areas of the world that came under their domination. Choose an area of the world today that is experiencing the influence of Western ideas and culture. Describe some of these influences. What impact might they have on the traditional way of life in the area?
3. The British excluded the Indians from any official positions in the British East India Company. Naturally the Indians developed a deep resentment over this policy of exclusion. How do you think this superior attitude that colonial rulers had over their subjected people has affected the relationship between the former colonial power and its former colony?

Applying History Study Skills

Before completing this activity, review Building History Study Skills on page 462.

Read the following selection from a 1636 Tokugawa edict banning contact with foreigners. Then answer the questions that follow.

> "No Japanese ships may leave for foreign countries. . . . No Japanese may go abroad secretly. If anyone tries to do this, he will be killed, and the ship and owner(s) will be placed under arrest while higher authority is informed. . . . No offspring of Southern Barbarians [Europeans] will be allowed to remain. Anyone violating this order will be killed and all his relatives punished according to the gravity of the offense."

1. What consequences did people who ignored the decree face?
2. What do you think were the positive and negative long-term consequences of the decree?

Investigating Further

1. **Writing a Report** As you read on page 466, the art form of woodblock prints became popular in Japan during the Tokugawa period. Use books in your library to write a report answering the following questions: Why was this art form so popular? What was its subject matter? How did Japanese woodblock prints change in the 1800s? One source for your research might be Seiichiro Takahashi's *Traditional Woodblock Prints of Japan* (Weatherhill).
2. **Presenting an Oral Report** Prepare an oral report describing how Indians reacted to British rule. The following selections are possible sources: "The Sepoy Rebellion" and "The Growth of National Feeling in India" in Sydney Eisen and Maurice Filler's *The Human Adventure,* Volume 2 (Harcourt Brace Jovanovich).
3. **Writing an Essay** The opium trade became a major problem between Great Britain and China. Write an essay describing the dilemma of the Chinese officials in attempting to stop the opium traffic. Also describe how the British used the Opium War to make demands on the Chinese. One possible source is "The Opening of China" in Sydney Eisen and Maurice Filler's *The Human Adventure,* Volume 2 (Harcourt Brace Jovanovich).

tea. Opium addiction spread among the Chinese, and they lost much of their silver supply paying for the opium. **(b)** Japan permitted foreign trade for a brief period, later closed the country to foreigners, and then reopened it after Perry's journey. Westernization and industrialization strengthened Japan. **(c)** The British made English the national language, Indian pupils studied western subjects, and the British instituted social reforms.

Relating Geography to History

(a) The British needed supply ships and the protection of the navy to develop coastal posts and make contacts with the interior. **(b)** Beginning with two footholds on the coast, the British moved along waterways into the interior. **(c)** Transportation and troop and naval support became more difficult as the British moved farther inland.

Relating Past to Present

1. Answers will vary.
2. Answers will vary.
3. Answers will vary.

Applying History Study Skills

1. They faced death, and their relatives would be punished according to the gravity of the offense committed.
2. The Japanese maintained a purity of culture, untainted by European traditions. However, they lost considerable trade income and did not share the technological and industrial innovations that traders and merchants might have brought with them.

Reviewing Concepts

1. b; **2.** a; **3.** g; **4.** e; **5.** i; **6.** c; **7.** d; **8.** f; **9.** h; **10.** j

Applying Critical Thinking Skills

1. The Renaissance emphasized individual dignity, stressed human values, and expressed a concern with life in this world. Renaissance artists painted portraits in a realistic style, showing human emotions.
2. Humanism led many people to develop a new enthusiasm for life in this world. The Scientific Revolution represented a new approach to studying the world. People explained things experimenting for themselves.
3. (a) European nations hoped to get from their colonies gold and silver or raw materials that could not be produced at home. **(b)** Colonists were expected to buy the manufactured products of the home country. In some colonies the natives were forced to work for the Europeans, and some native cultures were destroyed.
4. Parliament gained the following powers at the expense of the monarch: The Petition of Right demanded no taxes be imposed without Parliament's consent; the Habeas Corpus Act protected the rights of those arrested and imprisoned; the Bill of Rights limited the monarch's powers and protected private citizens; the Act of Settlement provided for orderly succession; Parliament gained the right to declare war, and monarchs ceased to veto acts of Parliament.
5. (a) During the Ming and Qing dynasties, cities developed, trade expanded, regions began to specialize in particular goods, agriculture expanded, new crops were introduced, and

1B, 3B, 4A, 4C, 4E, 4F, 4G, 4J, a1A, a4A, a4B, a4C, a4D, a4E, a4F, a4G, a4H, a4I, a4J, a4K, a4L, a4M

Reteaching

Have students review the Chapter Summary and the appropriate section and questions in the Unit Synthesis. Discuss the concepts until students demonstrate a clear understanding of the material.

UNIT 4 REVIEW

Unit Summary

The following list contains the key concepts you have learned about the emergence of modern nations.

1. In the late 1300s, a literary and artistic movement known as the Renaissance swept Europe.
2. In Germany, Martin Luther began the Protestant Reformation.
3. The Scientific Revolution of the 1500s and 1600s transformed the methods and understanding of astronomy, physics, and anatomy.
4. In the 1400s and 1500s, Europeans expanded overseas. Portuguese and Spanish explorers took the lead in discovering new lands and trade routes.
5. The rulers of Europe centralized government in their hands and established absolute monarchies in France, Russia, Prussia, and Austria.
6. In England monarchs and Parliament clashed throughout the 1600s.
7. In the 1700s the British colonists in what is today the United States revolted and set up their own government.
8. During the Enlightenment thinkers began to criticize the established political institutions.
9. Growing discontent in France and Louis XVI's failure to solve the government's continuing financial crisis led to the French Revolution in 1789.
10. Through a series of steps, France became first a republic and then an empire under Napoleon Bonaparte. When Napoleon was defeated in 1815, the European powers attempted to restore the Old Regime.
11. China and Japan tried to protect their cultures from outside influences.
12. The Ottoman, Persian, and Mogul empires declined in the 1700s. India then became a target for European colonialism as Great Britain began taking control in the late 1700s.

On a separate sheet of paper, complete the following review exercises.

Reviewing Concepts

Match each of the following people with the appropriate description from the list below:

a. Leonardo da Vinci	**f.** Michelangelo
b. Peter the Great	**g.** Maria Theresa
c. Prince Henry	**h.** Machiavelli
d. Louis XVI	**i.** Petrarch
e. Bartholomeu Dias	**j.** Charles V

___ **1.** Built a new capital in Russia that would be a "window to Europe"
___ **2.** Painted the *Mona Lisa*
___ **3.** Hapsburg ruler protected by the Pragmatic Sanction
___ **4.** Sailed around the southern tip of Africa
___ **5.** Poet who is often called the founder of humanism
___ **6.** Started a navigators' school in Portugal
___ **7.** King who was executed during the French Revolution
___ **8.** Painted the murals on the ceiling of the Sistine Chapel
___ **9.** Italian Renaissance thinker who wrote about politics and government
___ **10.** Hapsburg who was both king of Spain and Holy Roman Emperor

Applying Critical Thinking Skills

1. **Interpreting Ideas** In what ways did European art of the 1500s and 1600s reflect the new ideas and attitudes of the Renaissance?
2. **Analyzing Ideas** How did the ideas of humanism and the Scientific Revolution change Europe?
3. **Understanding Ideas (a)** According to the theory of mercantilism, what benefits did European nations hope to gain from colonial empires? **(b)** How did the building of empires affect the people of the colonial areas?
4. **Classifying Ideas** List the powers that Parliament gained at the expense of the English monarch between 1603 and 1714.
5. **Describing Ideas (a)** Describe the changes that occurred in China during the rule of the Ming and Qing dynasties. **(b)** How were they similar to the changes that took place under the Tokugawa shogunate in Japan?
6. **Comparing Ideas** Compare the goals and achievements of the French Revolution to those of the American Revolution.

Relating Geography to History

How did the relative locations of China and Japan make it easier for the governments in those countries to shun contact with foreigners, while the relative location of the Ottoman Empire made such isolation more difficult?

Writing About History

1. Find information on Japanese and Chinese painting in the 1700s and the 1800s. Then find sources that explain how Japanese and Chinese artists influenced European and American artists. Present your findings in a written report.
2. Develop a comparative essay explaining the unique features of Japanese, Chinese, European, Indian, and Ottoman cultures in the 1700s and the 1800s.

the population increased.
(b) In Tokugawa Japan cities grew in size and importance, internal trade expanded, and various regions began to specialize in different crops and handicrafts.
6. The goals of the French Revolution were liberty and equality. The French Revolution ended class divisions and abolished the privileged position of the nobles and clergy. Independence was the main goal of the American Revolution. Independence was achieved and the restrictions imposed by mercantilism were ended.

Relating Geography to History

China, protected by almost impenetrable mountains in the west and a cold plateau region to the north, could almost seal its borders and ports to anyone. Japan, isolated by seas, surrounded by rocky coasts, and protected by the vast Pacific to the east, could also isolate itself. The Ottoman Empire rested astride major trade routes between Europe and the Middle East and was much nearer large centers of population.

Writing About History

1. Answers will vary.
2. Answers will vary.

Further Readings

Bainton, Roland H. *Here I Stand: A Life of Martin Luther.* Nashville: Abingdon Press. Recounts major events of Luther's life.

Dickens, Charles. *A Tale of Two Cities.* New York: New English Library. A novel set in London and Paris at the time of the French Revolution.

Ferguson, Wallace K. *The Renaissance.* New York: Holt, Rinehart & Winston. Analyzes the causes of the Renaissance and compares the Italian Renaissance to the Northern Renaissance.

Turnbull, Stephen. *Samurai Warriors.* New York: Blandford Press. Provides an illustrated history of Japanese warriors.

Unit Four Chronology

Date	Political and Social Developments	Technological and Scientific Advances	Visual Arts and Literature	Religious and Philosophical Thought
1300–1450	Growth of Italian city-states **14*** Ming dynasty **18**	Prince Henry the Navigator **15** Printing press **14**	Italian Renaissance **14**	Humanism **14**
1450–1550	Treaty of Tordesillas **15** Columbus **15** Da Gama **15** Henry VIII **14** Cortés **15** Magellan **15** Beginnings of Safavid dynasty **18**	Copernicus **14** Vesalius **14**	Northern Renaissance begins **14** *The Prince* **14** *Utopia* **14** *Institutes* **14** Da Vinci **14** Michelangelo **14** Fresco art **14** Dürer **14**	Luther **14** Diet of Worms **14** Anglican church **15** Counter-Reformation **14** Council of Trent **14** *Institutes of the Christian Religion* **14**
1550–1650	Peace of Augsburg **14** Edict of Nantes **14** Michael Romanov **15** Spanish Armada **15** Thirty Years' War **15** Tokugawa shogunate **18** Qing dynasty **18** Richelieu **15** Süleyman the Magnificent **18**	Kepler **14** Galileo **14** Microscope **14** European shipbuilding **15**	Rembrandt **15** Shakespeare **14**	King James Version of the Bible **16**
1650–1750	Louis XIV **15** Glorious Revolution **16** Peter the Great **15** Maria Theresa **15** Frederick the Great **15** Act of Union **16**	Newton **14** Versailles **15**	*Leviathan* **16** *Two Treatises on Civil Government* **16**	Enlightenment **17** Voltaire **17** Rousseau **17** Jesuits banned from China **18**
1750–1850	Catherine the Great **15** Partitioning of Poland **15** American Revolution **16** French Revolution **17** Napoleon **17** Congress of Vienna **17** Selim III **18**		*Encyclopedia* **17** Japanese woodblock printing **18** Silverwork by Paul Revere **16** *The Social Contract* **17**	French Commune **17** Declaration of the Rights of Man **17** U.S. Constitution **16**

*Indicates chapter in which development is discussed

1B, 3B, 4C, a1C

Focus/Motivation
Have students study the map on pages R12-R13. Point out that the map shows nations in Europe today. Then tell students that the emergence of nations is a relatively recent phenomenon that has occurred since the 1500s. To illustrate this point, have students compare the map on pages R12-R13 with the political map of Europe on page 378. Ask: How does the territory of France differ in the two maps? *(France is much larger today.)* Then point out that they will be studying the growth of nations in the Unit Four Synthesis.

UNIT FOUR SYNTHESIS

The Emergence of Modern Nations

14 The Renaissance, Reformation, and Scientific Revolution Changed Europe

A great burst of creativity began in Italy in the 1300s. Because this movement centered on a revival of interest in the classical learning of Greece and Rome, we call it the Renaissance (REN • uh • sahnts), a French word meaning "rebirth."

Renaissance Writers and Artists

Beginning about the mid-1300s, a number of Italian scholars, such as Francesco Petrarch (PEE • trahrk), developed a lively interest in classical literature, particularly that of the Romans. These Italian scholars stressed the study of grammar, rhetoric, history, and poetry, using classical texts. We call these studies the *humanities;* people who specialized in the humanities are called humanists.

Art as well as literature flourished during the Renaissance. The most noticeable characteristic of Renaissance painting, however, is its realism as shown in the works of artists such as Giotto (JAW•toh), Masaccio (mah•ZAH •choh), Leonardo da Vinci (duh VIN • chee), Michelangelo Buonarroti (my • kuh • LAN • juh • loh bwaw • nah • RAW • tee), Raphael, and Titian (TISH • uhn).

Over time the Renaissance spread beyond Italy. Trade, transportation, and the invention of printing helped this spread.

The Reformation

About 1500 several northern humanists suggested that the Roman Catholic church had lost sight of the spiritual mission proclaimed by Jesus. When the Catholic church ignored their concerns, reformers urged believers to form a new church. This religious revolution, which split the church in western Europe and created several new churches, is called the Reformation.

The first break with the Roman Catholic church occurred in Germany, where some people opposed the church's policy of selling indulgences, or pardons from punishment for sin. The most vocal of these critics was Martin Luther, a German monk, who founded Lutheranism.

Calvin and the Counter-Reformation

In Switzerland, many rural areas remained Catholic, while the free cities developed a form of Protestantism significantly different from Luther's. The most prominent form of Protestantism was Calvinism, founded in Switzerland by John Calvin.

In response to the Reformation, the Catholic church launched a major reform movement known as the Counter-Reformation, or the Catholic Reformation, in the 1530s. Initially created to foster a more spiritual outlook in the Catholic church, the Counter-Reformation also clarified the doctrines of the church and pursued an aggressive campaign against Protestants.

The most striking result of the great religious struggle of the 1500s was the emergence of many different churches in western Europe. Another far-reaching result was a new interest in education. The Reformation also led to an increase in the power of national governments and a decrease in the power of the pope.

Popular Culture

At the time of the Renaissance and the Reformation, most Europeans lived in small villages and spent their entire lives raising food and combating nature to survive. Over time, however, changes did occur. Many people sought their fortunes in the growing towns and cities. Gradually, more

Florence, Italy

sophisticated attitudes began to take hold among the residents of towns and cities. In particular, people's understanding of how things happened in the world began to change. Demons and spirits no longer dominated views of daily life. People sought rational explanations for day-to-day events.

The Scientific Revolution

Science also changed as scientists worked to uncover the secrets of nature. These early investigators began to question traditional opinions and to observe and experiment for themselves. Most importantly, they described nature without any reference to previous beliefs. The foundation of this approach was the principle of doubt: nothing was to be believed unless it could be proved by experiment or mathematics. This approach became the new way of studying the world. The transformation in thinking that occurred during the 1500s and 1600s as a result of this new system of investigation is known as the Scientific Revolution.

15 Strong Monarchies Helped European States Expand

In 1400 Europe's monarchs lacked the wealth and power of the rulers of China, India, Africa, the Americas, and even Europe's close neighbor, the Ottoman Empire. Less than 400 years later, however, Europe had become the dominant civilization on earth.

Reasons for Exploration

Several factors encouraged the Europeans to explore the world. First, technological advances such as improved mapmaking, better navigation instruments, sturdier ships, and new weapons made long voyages possible. Second, newly powerful central governments encouraged exploration and colonization to enhance their prestige. Third, the development of new economic policies and methods played an important part in carrying out exploration. And finally, social changes such as overcrowding in Europe and the desire to seek religious freedom stimulated exploration.

Portugal and Spain

Explorers sailing for Portugal and Spain made the first European voyages into unknown waters. The Portuguese, encouraged by Prince Henry the Navigator, explored the coast of Africa and found a water route to India. The Spanish sent expeditions to the Americas to stake out an empire there.

One tragic aspect of this empire building was the slave trade. As Spain and Portugal established colonies, they imported African slaves to work the lands. This inhumane trade in human beings lasted until the 1800s.

Portugal rapidly acquired wealth and a vast empire, but its decline was almost as swift as its rise. Three main factors hastened this decline. First, the Portuguese government, neither strong nor well organized, had difficulty controlling its colonial officials. Second, many ships sank transporting products home from the colonies. The resulting loss of life drastically reduced Portugal's population. Third, Spain annexed Portugal in 1580, and Portugal did not regain its independence until 1640.

Taking advantage of these weaknesses, the Dutch and English captured much of the Asian trade from the Portuguese in the 1600s. Small Portuguese colonies survived in Africa, India, and China, but they no longer served as sources of great wealth. Only Brazil remained a major Portuguese colony.

The Spanish Empire

Spain turned most of its colonial energies to the Americas. By the 1530s it controlled almost all of Central and South America.

1B, 4A, 4E, 4G, a1D, a2F, a2I

Presentation
Comparing Ideas
(Average/Group)
Explain to students that great governmental changes occurred in Europe in the 1600s and 1700s which had repercussions as far as the North American continent. Ask students to compare the changes that occurred in the governments of England, the United States, and France during this period. *(Students should mention that each of these countries experienced a revolution during this period. England developed a constitutional monarchy. A document known as the Bill of Rights essentially gave Parliament all of the power. The United States was established and a government was set up which adopted a constitution guaranteeing the rights of all of its citizens. France set up a republic which also drafted a constitution guaranteeing the rights of its citizens. However, the French Republic was unstable and this eventually led to the rise of Napoleon.)*

Spain also developed a centralized form of government for its colonies. Representatives of the monarch, called viceroys, reported to the Council of the Indies in Spain.

As Spanish explorers created a great empire outside Europe, Spanish kings expanded their authority in Spain itself. Perhaps one of the greatest of these kings was Charles V, who was Holy Roman Emperor as well as king of Spain. However, Charles's nearly continuous wars drained Spain's human and financial resources. In addition, Spain itself lacked industries and the government did little to encourage them. It also had difficulty feeding its people because so much land was devoted to raising sheep for wool. Finally, though tightly controlled by the king, the government could not operate efficiently over a territory that was scattered throughout Europe and the Americas.

Charles V realized that this scattered empire had become too large for any one monarch to rule alone. In 1556 he gave up his throne and divided his vast territory between his son, who became Philip II of Spain, and his brother, who became Holy Roman Emperor Ferdinand I.

France

In the mid-1600s, France emerged as a European power. It had recovered rapidly from the religious wars of the 1500s, thanks to the policies of King Henry IV, the first monarch of a new royal house in France, the Bourbons. Assisted by two able cardinals of the Roman Catholic church, the Bourbons would make the monarchy absolute in France. Under Louis XIV, France became the dominant power on the European continent.

Eastern and Central Europe

While the countries of western Europe strengthened their governments, new empires grew up farther east. In the 1600s the czars of Russia successfully dealt with many problems and created a Russian form of absolutism. Perhaps the greatest czar of this period was Peter the Great, who took power in 1682. Under his able rule, Russia claimed new territories and established closer ties with the West. Other rulers such as Catherine the Great further strengthened the monarchy. At the same time, the Hapsburgs of Austria and the Hohenzollerns of Prussia expanded their powers.

16 The English-speaking World Took a New Political Course

While nations on the continent of Europe were establishing absolute monarchies, England was developing a constitutional form of government.

The Tudors and the Stuarts

In the late 1400s, a new royal family, the Tudors, became England's rulers. The Tudor rulers brought stability and prosperity to England. When the throne passed to the Stuarts, however, relations between Parliament and the monarchs steadily deteriorated. Charles I even tried to rule without calling Parliament. Desperate for money, Charles finally assembled the legislative body in 1640.

Civil War

The Parliament of 1640, controlled by the Puritans, attempted to curb the powers of the monarch. Because of rebellions in both Ireland and Scotland, Charles I agreed to these limits. In 1642, however, the feisty monarch tried to arrest the leaders of Parliament. This action provoked a violent civil war that resulted in the king's execution and the establishment of a republican form of government under the Puritan Oliver Cromwell.

By 1660 the English people had undergone a change in feelings. Some had favored the execution of Charles I, but Cromwell's rule had brought only confusion and resentment. After some hesitation,

Queen Elizabeth I and Sir Francis Drake

the new Parliament of 1660 invited Charles II, the son of Charles I, to return to England from exile.

Constitutional Monarchy

Charles II had learned much from his years in exile and cooperated with Parliament. His brother, James II, however, clashed with the legislative body. Finally, when his Catholic wife gave birth to a son, the political parties of Whigs and Tories agreed that James must abdicate. A number of leading nobles invited James's daughter, Mary, and her husband William of Orange to take the throne of England. In 1689 William and Mary ascended the throne in what is known as the Glorious Revolution.

The English Revolution brought about safeguards against absolute monarchy in England. For example, in 1679 Parliament passed an important measure, the Habeas Corpus Act. This act provided that anyone who was arrested could obtain a writ, or order, demanding to be brought before a judge within a specified period of time. And before granting the throne to William and Mary, Parliament required them to accept certain fixed conditions named in a document known as the Bill of Rights. The Bill of Rights declared that Parliament would choose the ruler, who would be merely an official subject to parliamentary laws. The ruler could not proclaim or suspend any law, impose any tax, or maintain an army in peacetime without Parliament's consent. Parliament had to meet frequently, and the monarch could not interfere in the elections of its members. The Bill of Rights guaranteed the right of the members of Parliament to express themselves freely. By 1700, although England remained a monarchy, Parliament held the power. In the 50 years following 1689, Parliament continued to gain importance as the real power in the government of England. The organization and institutions characteristic of today's English government gradually emerged.

The English Empire

Spain and Portugal established vast overseas empires during the 1500s while England remained preoccupied with problems at home. Even though these problems persisted during the 1600s, English mariners began explorations that allowed England to claim lands in the Americas and Asia. Most notable were the Thirteen Colonies in North America and the commercial empire of the British East India Company in Asia.

The American Revolution

Although the North American colonists of the 1700s resented British trade regulations, they disliked the French along their borders even more. After the defeat of the French in 1763, however, relations between the colonists and the British steadily worsened. Finally, in 1776 the colonists declared their independence. After years of struggle, the British officially recognized the young nation—the United States of America—in 1783.

The new nation first attempted a loose union of states under the Articles of Confederation. When it became evident that the Articles did not give the central government enough power, the nation adopted the Constitution, which provided for a much stronger federal government. To guarantee the rights of the American people, the Constitution included the Bill of Rights—10 amendments specifying the basic rights of every United States citizen.

17 The French Revolution Changed the Course of World History

The English ideal that people should have a voice in government greatly influenced French political writers of the 1700s. These writers spread this idea, paving the way for one of the greatest revolutions in history—the French Revolution.

The Enlightenment

The people of the 1700s referred to their century as an "Age of Enlightenment." They believed themselves the first to have discovered the "light" of logical thinking revealed by science. During the Enlightenment philosophers believed they could apply the scientific method and use reason to logically explain human nature.

Their contemporaries called the thinkers of the Enlightenment philosophes (fee • luh • ZAWFS); *philosophe* is the French word for "philosopher." The philosophes were not only philosophers, however, but also critics who examined the political and social institutions of their day.

483

1B, 4A, 4E, 4G, a1C, a2A, a2F, a2G, a2J, a2K

Closure

Ask students to suggest reasons why China and Japan shut out the outside world. *(Students might suggest that the Chinese and Japanese leaders feared that exposure to the outside world would erode their influence and control over their people and their institutions.*

Storming the Bastille

The French Revolution

The French kings constructed an absolute monarchy based upon the division of society into three groups or estates. The First and Second Estates that included the clergy and the nobility had the fewest people, but they also had the most wealth, power, and privilege. The Third Estate, which included more than 90 percent of the people, had almost no power.

In the mid-1700s discontent in France began to grow. Several factors explain this discontent. The first resulted from the growth of the French population. Families had more children to support, and they needed more food and money. Second, the Third Estate chafed under a growing burden of taxation and spiraling prices, and the bourgeoisie clamored for a greater voice in government. Even the First and Second Estates were dissatisfied because they resented the absolute power of the monarch.

When a beleaguered Louis XVI called a meeting of the Estates-General in 1789, discontented groups throughout France hoped that the assembly would make necessary reforms. When the assembly finally met, the king proclaimed that each estate would meet separately and have equal power. In response, the delegates of the Third Estate boldly proclaimed themselves the National Assembly and proceeded to enact reforms.

Fearing that the king planned to close the National Assembly, the people of Paris took action. On July 14, 1789, they stormed and captured the Bastille, the hated prison-fortress, in search of weapons. They planned to use the weapons to defend the National Assembly against the royal troops. The French Revolution had begun.

The End of the Monarchy

Quite rapidly, the National Assembly became the real government of France and enacted reforms. As of August 4, 1789, the National Assembly abolished the last remnants of feudalism in France. Following these reforms, on August 27, 1789, the Assembly adopted the Declaration of the Rights of Man, guaranteeing basic human rights. Between 1789 and 1791, the Assembly passed more than 2,000 laws aimed at correcting abuses and setting up a new government. And in 1791 it finished writing a new constitution for France that established a constitutional monarchy.

When Austria and Prussia invaded France, a group of radicals seized control of the Paris government and established what they called the Commune. The Commune accurately accused Louis XVI of plotting with foreign monarchs to restore absolutism in France. On August 10, 1792, the Legislative Assembly, coerced by the Commune, voted to suspend the office of king.

The French Republic

A new legislative body, the National Convention, met in 1792. As soon as it met, it proclaimed the end of the monarchy and the beginning of a republic. The Convention also tried Louis XVI on charges of plotting against the security of the nation and ordered his execution. Fearful of counter-revolutionaries and foreign invasions, the Convention then instituted the Reign of Terror, during which thousands were executed.

In spite of the dangers and difficulties of the time, the National Convention brought about many reforms in France. It began organizing French laws into a single system, or code. It provided for a national system of public education, and it abolished slavery in the French colonies.

In 1795 the National Convention drafted another constitution under which the Directory controlled France. Although the Directory governed for four years, it pleased neither the radicals nor the conservatives. Finally, in 1799 Napoleon Bonaparte took over the government.

Napoleon

Though the government he set up kept the form of a republic, Napoleon became first dictator and then

Question 1 of the Synthesis Review corresponds to Section 14 of the synthesis, Question 2, to Section 15; Question 3 to Section 16; Question 4, to Section 17; Question 5, to Section 18. Question 6 asks students to synthesize information from Sections 16 and 17 of the synthesis.

1B, 3B, 4J, a1C, a4A, a4H, a4I, a4K, a4L, a4M

emperor of France. Under his rule, the French armies conquered most of Europe. In 1812, however, Great Britain, Austria, Sweden, and Russia united against the French. In March 1814 Paris fell to the allied armies, and Napoleon was exiled to the island of Elba. Although Napoleon returned to France in 1815, he was decisively defeated at the Battle of Waterloo in 1815.

Peace

After the final defeat of Napoleon in 1815, European leaders met at the Congress of Vienna to redraw the map of Europe. Four principles guided the decisions of the Congress of Vienna: (1) Legitimacy, which meant that all former ruling families should be restored to their thrones, had to be upheld. (2) The balance of power had to be restored in Europe. This meant that the nations of Europe had to keep any one nation from becoming too powerful. (3) France had to be weakened. (4) The four powers—Great Britain, Austria, Russia, and Prussia—had to be compensated for the losses they had suffered at the hands of Napoleon.

Although the delegates to the Congress of Vienna attempted to restore the old order, they ultimately failed. The national feelings that Napoleon had aroused throughout Europe became powerful forces in the years following the Congress of Vienna.

18 The Countries of Asia Experienced a Transition

Between 1400 and the mid-1800s, many of the countries in Asia reached a political and cultural peak and then began to decline.

China

Under the reign of the Ming and Qing dynasties, China enjoyed more than 400 years of peace. Except for the fighting that occurred when the Qing dynasty overthrew the Ming dynasty, very little rebellion or warfare occurred. This period of peace greatly contributed to China's stability.

Just as the Qing dynasty started its decline in the late 1700s, new peoples appeared in China—Europeans. First the Portuguese, and then the British and the Russians claimed trading privileges in China—often with disastrous effects for the Chinese people.

Japan

In the late 1400s, the Japanese daimyos began fighting among themselves for survival and supremacy. The struggle among the daimyos resulted in the creation of a political system roughly halfway between feudalism and centralized monarchy. The Japanese established this hybrid system, known as the Tokugawa (TOH • KOOG • AH • WAH) shogunate, in 1603. It survived until 1868. Unlike in China, the Tokugawa shoguns successfully kept out the Europeans. Nevertheless, in 1858 the Japanese and the United States governments agreed to exchange diplomatic representatives. The Japanese now admitted more American consuls and opened more treaty ports to the United States. Similar treaties with other nations soon followed. With the establishment of contacts with the West came a decision to modernize Japan.

Islamic Empires

By the 1500s three large Islamic empires existed: the Ottoman Empire, Persia, and the Mogul Empire. The rulers of these three empires met with varying degrees of success in combatting European influences. Perhaps the least successful, however, were the Mogul leaders of India. There, the British steadily increased their powers until India became an official part of the British Empire in 1877.

SYNTHESIS REVIEW

1. **Understanding Ideas** Why did Martin Luther split with the Roman Catholic church?
2. **Classifying Ideas** What factors encouraged European explorations?
3. **Determining Cause and Effect** How did the English Revolution encourage the growth of constitutional government?
4. **Seeing Relationships** How did the discontent of the French people lead to the French Revolution?
5. **Summarizing Ideas** Which Islamic empire had the least success in combating the influence of the Europeans?
6. **Synthesizing Ideas** How did the English Revolution influence the French Revolution?

Review Answers

1. Luther disagreed with the church over the selling of indulgences, or the buying of pardons from punishment for sins.
2. Reasons for exploration were technological advances; powerful central governments which encouraged exploration; the development of new economic policies; social changes.
3. Following the revolution, Parliament, in order to curtail the power of the monarch, forced the new monarchs to accept the Bill of Rights which made them subject to parliamentary law.
4. The French king gave the Third Estate, to which 90% of the French people belonged, equal power with the First and Second Estates. The Third Estate responded by taking control of the government.
5. India had the least success combating the influence of the Europeans.
6. The English established a constitutional monarchy following their revolution. The French followed the English example by setting up a constitutional monarchy after their revolution. However, it failed in France.

Introducing the Unit
Ask students to look around the classroom to name items that are machine-made in factories. *(Students should mention almost everything in the classroom.)* Point out that although almost all the items we use in our daily lives are machine-made in factories, only 200 years ago most items were handmade in people's homes. Tell students that the great change from handmade to machine-made products is the result of the Industrial Revolution that they will be studying in this unit. Ask: How has this change in the way goods are produced changed people's lives? *(Students might suggest that it has made a greater variety of products available to more people and therefore raised the standard of living.)* Conclude by asking students to keep their answers in mind as they study the unit.

UNIT FIVE

The Development of Industrial Society

◀ Construction *by Thomas Hart Benton*

Unit Goals

After studying Unit Five, students will be able to:

1. Explain the factors that made the Industrial Revolution possible and evaluate the effects of the Industrial Revolution.
2. Explain the economic theories of Adam Smith, Thomas Malthus, David Ricardo, and Karl Marx.
3. List the major developments in the physical, biological, and social sciences during the 1800s and the 1900s.
4. Compare the major artistic and literary movements of the late 1800s.
5. Compare the political developments that took place in Great Britain, the United States, Latin America, Italy, Germany, Russia, and Austria-Hunary during the late 1800s and the early 1900s.
6. Analyze European imperialism in the late 1800s.

487

CHAPTER (pages 488–513)

19 The Industrial Revolution Transformed the Modern World

(1600-1900)

CHAPTER OVERVIEW

The Industrial Revolution began in Great Britain and transformed the world. It was preceded by an agricultural revolution that increased production and decreased the demand for human labor.

The Industrial Revolution was the result of a series of remarkable inventions and technological innovations. Each invention or innovation introduced seemed to stimulate the development of others. The replacement of waterpower by steam power was basic to the Industrial Revolution. Almost as important was the development of improved steelmaking methods. Industrial developments led to improvements in transportation and communication.

The Industrial Revolution made large-scale production possible. The factory system brought together large numbers of people who performed simple, repetitive tasks for wages. Men, women, and children worked long hours for little pay. Workers lived in crowded tenements, while members of the middle class—many of whom were factory owners—lived a more comfortable life.

Business practices were vastly altered by the Industrial Revolution. Mass production and the assembly line fostered the growth of large corporations.

During this period new economic and political theories were advanced. Adam Smith and David Ricardo said that governments should not interfere with the operation of business. Humanitarian reformers such as John Stuart Mill believed that government should intervene to improve social conditions. Socialists called for public ownership of all means of production. Karl Marx predicted the overthrow of capitalism and advocated proletarian revolution.

Workers, meanwhile, began to protest unemployment, low wages, and poor working conditions. Governments responded to some of these demands by passing laws to reform working conditions.

SUGGESTED LESSON PLAN

Day	Objectives	Suggested Activities	Materials
1	U1* C1-2	Introducing the Unit (pages 486-87) Introducing the Chapter (pages 488-89) Section 1 (pages 489-95), Focus/Motivation (page 489), Presentation (page 490), Closure (page 493), Suggested Teaching Strategies, Enrichment Activity, Daily Quiz, Suggested Assignments (page 487B)	ATE, Pupil's Edition, Teacher's Resource-Bank™
2	U1, C3-4	Section 2 (pages 495-99), Focus/Motivation (page 495), Presentation (page 496), Closure (page 498), Suggested Teaching Strategies, Enrichment Activity, Daily Quiz, Suggested Assignments (page 487C)	ATE, Pupil's Edition, Teacher's Resource-Bank™
3	U1, C5-6	Section 3 (pages 499-501), Focus/Motivation (page 499), Presentation (page 499), Closure (page 500), Suggested Teaching Strategies, Enrichment Activity, Daily Quiz, Suggested Assignments (page 487D)	ATE, Pupil's Edition, Teacher's Resource-Bank™
4	U2, C7-8	Section 4 (pages 502-07), Focus/Motivation (page 502), Presentation (page 503), Closure (page 505), Suggested Teaching Strategies, Enrichment Activity, Daily Quiz, Suggested Assignments (page 487E)	ATE, Pupil's Edition, Teacher's Resource-Bank™
5	U2, C9	Section 5 (pages 507-11), Focus/Motivation (page 507), Presentation (page 508), Closure (page 510), Suggested Teaching Strategies, Enrichment Activity, Daily Quiz, Suggested Assignments (page 487F)	ATE, Pupil's Edition, Teacher's Resource-Bank™
6	U1-2 C1-9	Chapter 19 Form A Test, Reteaching Worksheet, Chapter 19 Form B Test	Teacher's Resource-Bank™ or Workbook and Test Booklet

*C refers to applicable Chapter Objective, U refers to applicable Unit Goal.

BOOKS FOR THE TEACHER

Berlin, Isaiah. *Karl Marx: His Life and Environment.* Time-Life. Offers a balanced portrait of this controversial figure.

Heilbroner, Robert L. *The Worldly Philosophers.* Simon and Schuster. Details the lives of the great economic thinkers.

Henderson, W. O. *The Industrialization of Europe 1780-1914.* Harcourt Brace Jovanovich. Approaches the topic by looking at the individuals, inventions, and groups involved.

Mumford, Lewis. *The City in History.* Harcourt Brace Jovanovich. Evaluates the importance of the city during the early Industrial Revolution.

Stearns, Peter N. *The Other Side of Western Civilization,* Vol. II. Harcourt Brace Jovanovich. Includes numerous articles on the effects of industrialization on society.

BOOKS FOR THE STUDENT

Buchell, S. C. *Age of Progress.* Time-Life. Includes many illustrations of inventions.

Fessenden, Nicholas B. *The Impact of the Industrial Revolution.* Harcourt Brace Jovanovich. Offers an excellent analysis of the impact of industrialization on society.

Forman, James D. *Capitalism.* Franklin Watts. Provides a concise introduction to the subject.

Holland, Ruth. *Mill Child.* Crowell-Collier Press. Portrays child labor in America in a novelistic style.

Rius, L.C. *Marx for Beginners.* Pantheon. Explains the basic ideas of Marxism in an equal mixture of illustration and narrative.

Weisberger, Bernard A. *Captains of Industry.* American Heritage. Provides an interesting portrait of the leaders of the American industrial revolution. Includes many illustrations.

MULTIMEDIA MATERIALS

Early Victorian England and Charles Dickens (mp. 30 min.), EBE. Portrays the startling contrasts of morality and hypocrisy, splendor and squalor, prosperity and poverty in Victorian England.

The Industrial Revolution (2 fs), Educational Audio-Visual. Covers the causes of the revolution and the social changes it brought about.

The Industrial Revolution in England (mp. 26 min.), EBE. Explains the changes that took place in England during the 1800s.

Man and the Industrial Revolution (mp. 20 min.), McGraw-Hill. Explores the development of industrialization in England and its effects on daily life.

Meaning of the Industrial Revolution (mp. 11 min.), Coronet. Examines the industrial achievements that revolutionized Western civilization.

Section 1 (pages 489–495) The Industrial Revolution Began in Great Britain

SECTION OVERVIEW

The Industrial Revolution began in Great Britain because of that country's favorable balance of factors of production. The revolution in industry was preceded and made possible by a revolution in agriculture. The replacement of waterpower by steam power and new methods of making steel were essential to the Industrial Revolution. The changes brought forth by the Industrial Revolution made better transportation both necessary and possible. And rapid communications developed with the invention of the telegraph and of the cable.

SUGGESTED TEACHING STRATEGIES

1. **Preteaching Vocabulary (Basic)** You may wish to preteach the following important vocabulary terms: enclosure movement, factors of production *(page 490)*; mechanization, domestic system, factory system *(page 491)*. Ask: How important to the Industrial Revolution was the introduction of the factory system? *(It helped make the mass production of goods possible.)*
2. **Constructing a Chart (Average/Group)** Have students construct a chart of the inventors listed below and their inventions. Suggest that students use the following three column headings for their charts: *Inventor, Invention, Function of Invention.*

   Jethro Tull | Richard Arkwright
   Charles Townshend | Samuel Crompton
   John Kay | Edmund Cartwright
   James Hargreaves | Eli Whitney

   Encourage students to keep their charts for revision purposes.
3. **Analyzing Ideas (Average/Group)** A striking feature of the Industrial Revolution was the rate of change in transportation and communications. To help students understand the bewildering rate of change, have them list five areas of modern technology that are undergoing rapid change. *(Most students will note such areas as computers, robots, electronic communications, automobiles, airplanes, and space travel.)* Discuss with the class the level of technology in these areas 10 years ago, at the present, and ten years in the future. For example, 10 years ago people required considerable technical training to use a computer. Today "user-friendly" personal computers almost work themselves. Computers will almost certainly become more and more accessible over the next 10 years. Then ask: What does the next 10 years hold for other technologies?

ENRICHMENT ACTIVITY

Illustrating Ideas (Average/Group) Have students work in small groups to make collages or posters depicting the development of one of the following: roads, canals, railroads, steamboats. Sources for ideas for illustrations include: Ralph Andrist's *Erie Canal* (American Heritage) and *The Pictorial Story of Railways* (Hamlyn), edited by E. L. Cornwell.

DAILY QUIZ

To assess student understanding of Section 1, give the class the following quiz. (Each item is worth 10 points.)

1. What are the three factors of production? *(land, labor, and capital)*

2. What is the term for the movement to fence off common lands into individual holdings, begun in England in the seventeenth century? *(enclosure)*
3. What two inventions did Jethro Tull develop? *(seed drill and horse-drawn cultivator)*
4. (T or F) Viscount Charles Townshend developed the practice of crop rotation. *(T)*
5. (T or F) The Englishman Edmund Cartwright invented a faster weaving process with the power loom, the shuttle operated by waterpower. *(T)*
6. What process made the development of the modern steel industry possible? *(Bessemer process)*
7. Who invented vulcanization, the basis of the modern rubber industry? *(Charles Goodyear)*
8. Who perfected a steam-propelled moving engine in 1814? *(George Stephenson)*
9. Who invented the telegraph? *(Samuel Morse)*
10. Where did the American steel industry grow? *(around Pittsburgh and the Great Lakes region)*

SUGGESTED ASSIGNMENTS

1. **Understanding Chronology (Basic)** Put the following lists of events on the chalkboard or an overhead projector, and have students copy them in their notebooks. Then have them arrange the events in each group in chronological order by writing *1* before the event that took place first, *2* before the event that took place second, and so on. Review students' lists during the next lesson.

   (4) The steamboat *Great Western* crossed the Atlantic Ocean.
   (2) Fulton's *Clermont* began service on the Hudson River.
   (3) The *Rocket* began locomotive service between Liverpool and Manchester.
   (1) Construction of canals began.

   (1) Volta built the first battery.
   (3) Morse invented the telegraph.
   (2) Ampère worked out the principles of the magnetic effect of an electric current.
   (4) Field laid a cable across the Atlantic Ocean.
2. **Presenting a Report (Challenging)** Have students research, prepare, and present oral or written reports on one of the inventors or inventions mentioned in this section. Useful sources of information on this subject include: Ruby L. Radford's *Inventors in Industry* (Julian Messner); *Men of Science and Invention* (American Heritage), edited by the editors of *American Heritage;* Anthony Feldman and Peter Ford's *Scientists and Inventors* (Facts on File); Donald Clarke's *Great Inventors and Discoveries* (Marshall Cavendish); Mitchell Wilson's *American Science and Invention* (Simon and Schuster), and Irmingarde Eberly's *Famous Inventors for Young People* (Dodd, Mead).
3. **Profile Worksheet (Basic)** Have students complete Profile Worksheet 19 in the TEACHER'S RESOURCEBANK™.
4. **Outlining (Basic)** To reinforce student understanding of the key concepts presented in Section 1, have them outline the section. Remind students to use the correct form for their outline.

Section 2 (pages 495–499)

The Factory System Changed Working and Living Conditions

SECTION OVERVIEW

The introduction of steam-powered machines brought about the introduction of the factory system. Workers, now dependent on wages, were subject to many rules and regulations as well as to discomfort and danger on the job. Even very young children worked in the factories and mines. Living conditions for the working class were bad, while the middle class lived comfortably and gained importance and power in society.

SUGGESTED TEACHING STRATEGIES

1. **Determining Cause and Effect (Average/Group)** On the chalkboard or an overhead projector, write the following list of pairs of statements and have students copy the list into their notebooks. Then ask students to identify which statement in the pair is a cause (C) and which is an effect (E).

   a. *E* The introduction of steam-powered machinery made work easier.
   C People could learn to work a machine in a few days.
   b. *C* Women and young workers did not have set working methods and did not expect high wages.
   E Employers preferred to hire women and young people.
   c. *E* Early textile factories employed mainly children and young adults under 30.
   C Children and young adults would work for lower wages than would men.
   d. *C* Machines became more and more available.
   E Older skilled workers found themselves unemployed.
   e. *C* Older skilled workers found themselves unemployed.
   E Many unemployed people sent their children to work in factories to make up for their loss of income.
2. **Interpreting Ideas (Average/Group)** Copy the following table onto the chalkboard or an overhead projector, or make reproductions of the table and distribute them to the class.

AVERAGE AGE AT DEATH FOR DIFFERENT SOCIAL GROUPS			
	Gentry	Tradespeople	Laborers
Rutland	52	41	38
Truro	40	33	28
Derby	49	38	21
Manchester	38	20	17
Bethnal Green	45	26	16
Liverpool	35	22	15

Point out that Rutland was an agricultural area in central England, Truro was a tin-mining center, and the other locations listed in the table were major industrial centers. Have students carefully study the table. Then lead them in a discussion, using the following questions as a guide: Which social group generally lived the longest? The shortest? Why? Why do you think all social groups lived longer in Rutland? Based on what you have read in this section, what do you think life was like for laborers in Derby, Manchester, Bethnal Green, and Liverpool? Does this explain their short life expectancy? Why or why not?

ENRICHMENT ACTIVITY

Writing an Editorial (Average/Group) One of the most deplorable aspects of the early Industrial Revolution was the use of child labor. Organize the class into two groups. Have members of one group write editorials attacking the employment of children in factories. Have the other group write letters to the editor from factory owners explaining the need for child labor. As background reading, students might like to consult "Child Labor in Factories" in Sydney Eisen's and Maurice Filler's *The Human Adventure,* vol. 2 (Harcourt Brace Jovanovich) and Ruth Holland's *Mill Child* (Crowell-Collier Press). Select members of each group to read their editorials or letters to the rest of the class.

DAILY QUIZ

To assess student understanding of Section 2, give the class the following quiz. (Each item is worth 10 points.)

1. (T or F) Under the new factory system, employers needed more skilled and experienced workers. *(F)*
2. (T or F) Many workers who had lost their jobs because of the introduction of machines sent their children to work in the factories to make up for the loss of income. *(T)*
3. (T or F) Since factory owners wanted to produce goods as cheaply as possible, when the cost of raw materials went up they lowered workers' wages. *(T)*
4. (T or F) Men and women were given equal pay if they did the same work. *(F)*
5. Among the worst features of early industrialization was the employment of ________. *(children)*
6. (T or F) Most laborers earned enough to afford a daily diet of fresh meat, milk, and vegetables. *(F)*
7. (T or F) As a result of the Industrial Revolution, the middle class grew in power and prestige. *(T)*
8. While some working-class women took jobs in factories, many others continued to work in a traditional field for women ________ ________. *(domestic service)*
9. (T or F) According to some writers of the day, a woman's nature equipped her only for raising children and caring for the home. *(T)*
10. What field had become almost entirely a female profession? *(elementary school teaching)*

SUGGESTED ASSIGNMENTS

1. **Critical Thinking Worksheet (Basic)** Have students complete Critical Thinking Worksheet 42 in the TEACHER'S RESOURCEBANK™.
2. **Comparing Ideas (Average/Group)** Have students write a paragraph comparing and contrasting the life style of workers with the life style of the middle class during the Industrial Revolution. Some students may want to make an outline before writing the paragraph. Points they should cover are living conditions, clothing, food, and education.

Section 3 (pages 499–501) New Methods and Giant Businesses Produced an Industrial Economy

Mass production, based on division of labor, interchangeable parts, and the assembly line, transformed several industries. This transformation was accompanied by a change in the way business was organized. The corporation, whose system of limited liability attracted shareholders, became the dominant form of business organization. As these corporations grew, they often formed monopolies and cartels. Despite efforts to stabilize economies, the Industrial Revolution brought alternating periods of prosperity and decline, a pattern known as the business cycle.

SUGGESTED TEACHING STRATEGIES

1. **Preteaching Vocabulary (Basic)** You may wish to preteach the following important vocabulary terms: capitalism, commercial capitalism, industrial capitalism, division of labor *(page 499)*; mass production, sole proprietorship, partnership *(page 500)*; corporation, monopoly, cartel, business cycle, depression *(page 501)*. Ask students to describe the economic conditions during a depression. *(widespread unemployment, low output)*
2. **Constructing a Chart (Average/Group)** Have students construct a chart showing the advantages and disadvantages of the three major forms of business organization—sole proprietorships, partnerships, and corporations. Select certain students to display their charts on the bulletin board.

ENRICHMENT ACTIVITY

Analyzing Ideas (Challenging) Some people believe we are entering a new age—a post-industrial age. Ask students to suggest what is meant by the phrase *post-industrial age.* Then have them discuss whether the era of industrialization is over for Western nations. Ask them to provide evidence for their views.

DAILY QUIZ

To assess student understanding of Section 3, give the class the following quiz. (Each item is worth 10 points.)

1. (T or F) In industrial capitalism merchants bought, sold, and exchanged goods. *(F)*
2. (T or F) Eli Whitney used division of labor to make muskets in the early nineteenth century. *(T)*
3. The division of labor and the system of interchangeable parts

constituted two essential elements of _______ _______. *(mass production)*

4. What is the arrangement whereby each worker performs a special task on unfinished products as they pass by on a conveyor belt? *(assembly line)*
5. Who was the American auto manufacturer who used the mass production system to lower the cost of cars? *(Henry Ford)*
6. (T or F) Corporations are similar to partnerships in that stockholders are responsible for all debts incurred. *(F)*
7. (T or F) J. P. Morgan and a number of associates formed the first billion-dollar corporation in the United States. *(T)*
8. A _______ is a group of corporations that have combined to gain control of all parts of an industry. *(cartel)*
9. A country's economy usually goes through alternating periods of prosperity and decline, a pattern known as the _______ _______. *(business cycle)*
10. During the American Civil War, the United States could not ship cotton to Great Britain. The resulting shortage of cotton caused a _______ in the British textile industry. *(depression)*

SUGGESTED ASSIGNMENTS

1. **Critical Thinking Worksheet (Basic)** Have students complete Critical Thinking Worksheet 43 in the TEACHER'S RESOURCEBANK™.
2. **Writing an Essay (Average/Group)** American financiers and industrialists of the late 1800s and early 1900s included Ford, Morgan, Carnegie, and Rockefeller. Have students choose two of these industrialists and use encyclopedias and biographies to find information on their careers. Then have students write a short essay comparing and contrasting the two in the following areas: education, age at which they began their own business, innovations they developed that advanced industrialism, ways in which they used their wealth to help others, and public sentiment toward them. In the course of their research, students may find other areas in which to make comparisons. Have students read their essays to the rest of the class.

Section 4 (pages 502–507)

Living and Working Conditions Gradually Improved

SECTION OVERVIEW

During the Industrial Revolution, economists argued about what role government should play in the economy. Adam Smith and David Ricardo advocated laissez-faire. Others, such as social reformer John Stuart Mill, argued that government should intervene to protect working people. In time the British government did enact a number of reforms that improved working conditions. However, the interests of employers and workers continued to conflict. To strengthen their position, workers began to organize unions. Only later, however, did these unions become legal.

SUGGESTED TEACHING STRATEGIES

1. **Preteaching Vocabulary (Basic)** You may wish to preteach the following important vocabulary terms: free enterprise *(page 502)*; laissez-faire, utilitarianism *(page 504)*; strike *(page 506)*; unions, collective bargaining *(page 507)*. Ask: What are the major arguments for and against laissez-faire? *(for: encourages productivity and initiative; against: allows many businesses to engage in unethical practices)*
2. **Analyzing Ideas (Average/Group)** Write the following quotation by Thomas Malthus on the chalkboard or an overhead projector.

   "The power of population is indefinitely greater than the power in earth to produce subsistence [food] for man. Population, when unchecked, increases in a geometrical ratio. Subsistence only increases in an arithmetical ratio."

   Call upon a volunteer to explain the difference between a geometric and an arithmetic progression. *(In a geometric progression, each number after the first is formed by multiplying the preceding number by a constant factor. For example. 1-3-9-27 is a geometric progression in which the common factor is 3. An arithmetic progression is a series in which a constant quantity is added to each number to form the next. An example of an arithmetic progression is 1-4-7-10, in which the constant is 3.)* Ask students why Malthus was concerned about the difference between these two ratios. *(Because a geometric progression increases faster than an arithmetic progression, Malthus was concerned that population would outpace food supply.)* What factors did Malthus fail to take into account? *(inventions that would greatly increase crop production and limit the growth of population)*
3. **3.* **Interpreting Visuals: Determining Cause and Effect (Average/Group)** To reinforce the skill lesson presented on page 503, have students trace the social, political, and intellectual changes that led to the Industrial Revolution.

ENRICHMENT ACTIVITY

Relating Past to Present (Average/Group) Write the following sentence on the chalkboard or an overhead projector: Unions may have served a need, but now they have outlived their usefulness.

Ask students to discuss whether or not they agree with this statement. Use the following questions as a guide for discussion: What do you remember about the forerunners of unions in another time you have studied? *(Some students will mention the guilds that developed during the Middle Ages to protect artisans from competition and help them in time of need.)* What conditions prompted workers to form unions? *(Student answers will include such points as poor working conditions, low pay, and long hours.)* Were workers able to gain rights without organizing? *(Many students will suggest that organizing unions was the most effective way of balancing the power of the industrialists.)* Were workers justified in creating unions? Why or why not? *(Students should support their answers with evidence.)* What do today's workers hope to gain by belonging to a union? *(Student answers will include such points as health care and retirement benefits.)*

DAILY QUIZ

To assess student understanding of Section 4, give the class the following quiz. (Each item is worth 10 points.)

1. Which two natural laws did Adam Smith believe regulated all business and economic activity? *(supply and demand and competition)*
2. Adam Smith's perfect economic system was one of complete ________ ________. *(free enterprise)*
3. Who was the economist who expounded the idea known as the "iron law of wages"? *(David Ricardo)*
4. What theory stated that for a law to be useful it had to lead to "the greatest good for the greatest number"? *(utilitarianism)*
5. What act passed by the British Parliament in 1819 prohibited the employment of children under nine years of age in the textile industry? *(Factory Act)*
6. What is the term for the situation in which a whole group of workers refuses to work? *(strike)*
7. What are associations organized to negotiate settlements of workers' grievances called? *(unions)*
8. What legislation passed by the British Parliament in 1799 forbade workers to unite in order to demand higher wages and better working conditions? *(Combination Acts)*
9. (T or F) The French and German governments legalized unions some years after the British government had taken this step. *(T)*
10. What is the process by which union and management representatives meet to negotiate wages, hours, and working conditions and, on reaching an agreement, write a binding contract that lasts for a set period of time? *(collective bargaining)*

SUGGESTED ASSIGNMENTS

1. **Skill Worksheet (Basic)** Have students complete Skill Worksheet 19 in the TEACHER'S RESOURCEBANK™.
2. **Writing a Handbill (Average/Group)** Have students write a handbill composed by a worker in the 1800s protesting working conditions in his or her factory. Point out to students that a handbill is often passed out on street corners and, therefore, should be written in a style that gains a reader's attention. Have students read their handbills to the class, or select a few students to display their handbills on the bulletin board. Use the handbills as the basis for a class discussion focusing on how working conditions have improved since the early Industrial Revolution.
3. **Researching Ideas (Challenging)** Point out to students that before the organization of unions, some workers took violent action to protest low wages and working conditions. Interested students might like to conduct further research into groups of British workers who took violent action, such as the Luddites or the Swing movement. Useful sources of information on these groups include Christopher Hibbert's *The English: A Social History, 1066-1945* (W.W. Norton); E.P. Thompson's *The Making of the English Working Class* (Penguin); E.J. Hobsbawm's and George Rude's *Captain Swing* (Penguin); and Douglas Liversidge's *The Luddites* (Franklin Watts).

Section (pages 507–511)

5 Socialists Proposed Radical Changes

SECTION OVERVIEW

As the Industrial Revolution progressed, some people became alarmed at the growing gap between the rich and the poor. These people came to feel that laissez-faire capitalism exploited the poor, and the only way to remedy this was to introduce another form of economic system—socialism. Some utopian socialists wanted to create ideal cooperative communities. Karl Marx, on the other hand, advocated a workers' revolution that would eventually lead to the pure communism of a classless society.

SUGGESTED TEACHING STRATEGIES

1. **Preteaching Vocabulary (Basic)** You may wish to preteach the following important vocabulary terms: socialism *(page 507)*; utopian socialists, bourgeoisie, proletariat *(page 510)*; authoritarian socialism, communism, democratic socialism *(page 511)*. Organize the class into two groups. Ask one group to compile a list of countries that presently have Communist economic systems. Have the other group compile a similar list of socialist countries today.
2. **Identifying Ideas (Average/Group)** On the chalkboard or an overhead projector, write the following two lists and ask students to copy the lists into their notebooks. Then ask students to match each statement in the first list with the most suitable term or name in the second list.

   1. System of government in which the government owns the means of production and operates them for the welfare of all the people
   2. English humanist during the Renaissance and writer of a book titled *Utopia*
   3. Utopian socialist who established cooperative communities in both Britain and the United States
   4. Author of the *Communist Manifesto* and *Das Kapital* and founder of communism
   5. Another name for the owners of property
   6. The working class
   7. People who believe that socialism can be achieved through education and the ballot box
   8. The International Workingmen's Association

   a. bourgeoisie
   b. democratic socialists
   c. First International
   d. Karl Marx
   e. proletariat
   f. Robert Owen
   g. socialism
   h. Thomas More

(Answers: 1. g; 2. h; 3. f; 4. d; 5. a; 6. e; 7. b; 8. c)

ENRICHMENT ACTIVITY

Analyzing Ideas (Average/Group) Parts of the *Communist Manifesto* might be discussed and criticized in class. Excerpts may be found in Sydney Eisen's and Maurice Filler's *The Human Adventure,* vol. 2 (Harcourt Brace Jovanovich). Begin the discussion with the following question: In the 1840s Marx and Engels felt that a worldwide workers' revolution was close at hand. Why do you think this revolution never materialized? *(Students might point out improvements in working conditions.)*

DAILY QUIZ

To assess student understanding of Section 5, give the class the following quiz. (Each item is worth 10 points.)

1. (T or F) Socialists wanted to establish an economic system that would abolish the profit motive and competition. *(T)*
2. (T or F) Utopian socialists adopted Thomas More's book, *Utopia,* as their bible. *(F)*
3. Who was the owner of a large mill in New Lanark, Scotland, who believed that people were naturally good? *(Robert Owen)*
4. What was the name of the pamphlet in which Karl Marx and Friedrich Engels outlined their ideas on society? *(Communist Manifesto)*
5. What was the name that Marx gave to profits? *(surplus value)*
6. Marx believed that in time capitalist society would divide into two classes, the owners—or ________—and the workers—or ________. *(bourgeoisie, proletariat/proletarians)*
7. Since many people would not readily accept socialism, Marx thought that the workers initially would have to control the government in a "________ of the ________." *(dictatorship, proletariat)*
8. Why did Marx refer to his ideas as scientific socialism? *(because he thought he was describing objective laws of historical development—laws that would work inevitably)*
9. (T or F) Today we call a political system in which the government owns most of the means of production, controls economic planning, and ignores basic human and civil rights a dictatorship of the proletariat. *(F)*
10. (T or F) Democratic socialists believe that socialism can only be achieved through violent revolution. *(F)*

SUGGESTED ASSIGNMENTS

1. **Review Worksheet (Basic)** Have students complete Review Worksheet 19 in the TEACHER'S RESOURCEBANK™.
2. **Writing a Report (Average/Group)** Assign certain students to write reports on utopian socialists such as Robert Owen and Charles Fourier. Suggest that students give special consideration to why the programs of these utopians failed. For information on the utopians, have students refer to Edmund Wilson's *To the Finland Station* (Doubleday) and Frank E. Manuel's *The Prophets of Paris* (Harper Torchbooks). Ask students to present their reports to the rest of the class.

Teacher's Notes

For suggested lesson plan, additional teaching strategies, enrichment activities, daily quizzes, and suggested assignments, see pages 487A–487H.

Introducing the Chapter Have students choose three tasks that can be done either by machine or by their own labor—for example, washing dishes, copying information on a piece of paper, and traveling a particular distance. Then have students perform each task, following these steps: (1) Measure the time required for the completion of the task—first by machine, then by individual labor. (2) Evaluate the quality of the product or service by each method.

Ask students to draw some conclusions from the experiments concerning the impact of technology on their daily lives. *(Student answers should make reference to the speed or quality of goods produced.)* Explain that this technology has its roots in the change in methods of production brought about by the Industrial Revolution.

CHAPTER 19

The Industrial Revolution Transformed the Modern World

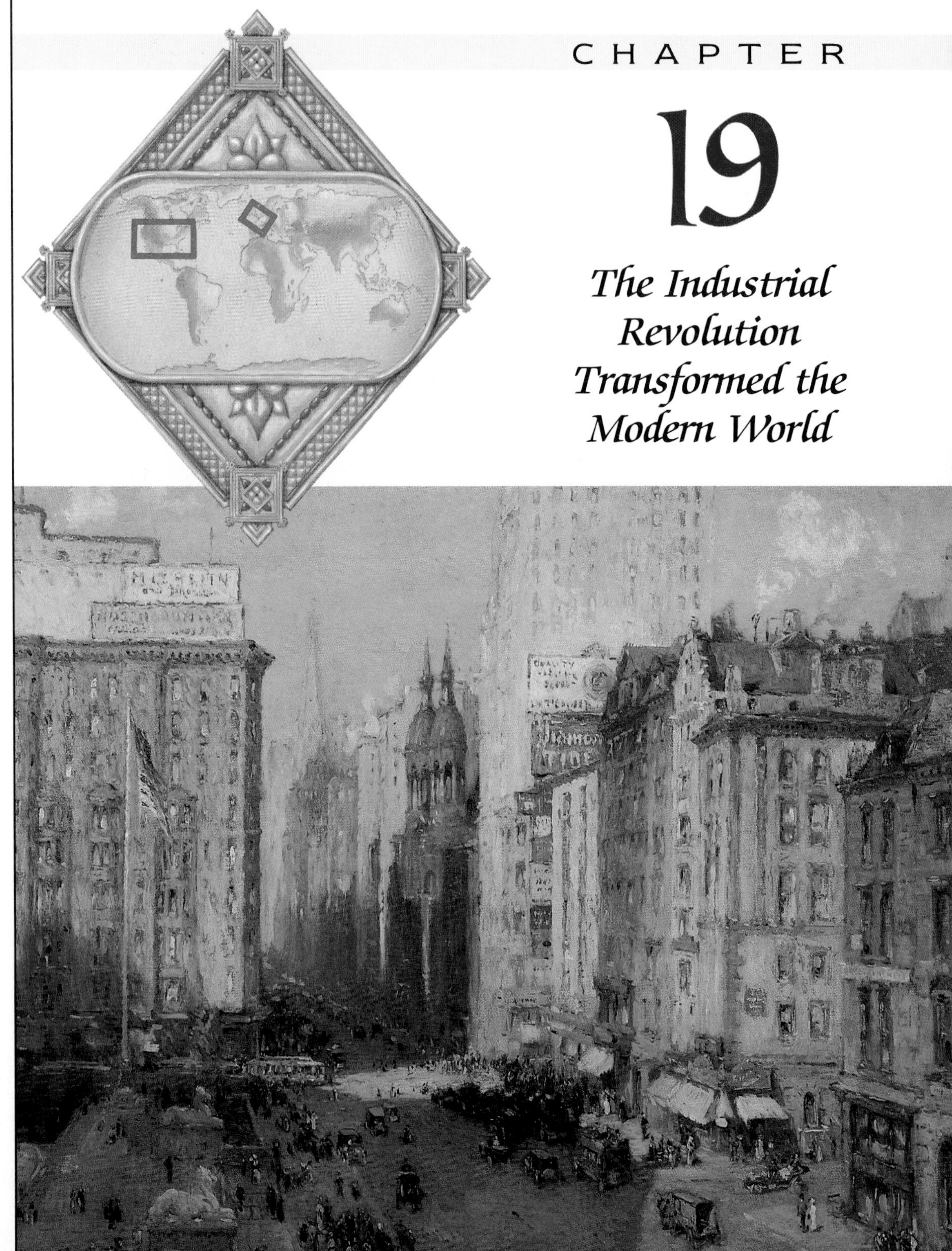

CHAPTER FOCUS

Place Great Britain, the United States, France, and Germany

Time 1600–1900

3.7 mil. BC 4000 BC AD 2100

Significance

The Scientific Revolution of the 1500s and 1600s expanded human understanding of the world through the work of scientists such as Isaac Newton. The struggles of people who fought for the right to be considered as individuals, to be equal before the law, and to have a voice in their own governments spawned great political revolutions. During the 1600s, 1700s, and 1800s, these revolutions changed Great Britain, North America, and France.

Now we will focus on a third kind of revolution, one that is neither scientific nor political. This revolution began in the 1700s, when power-driven machines began to perform much of the work that people had done before. The changes this industrial technology brought about affected manufacturing, or industry, so deeply that they are referred to as the **Industrial Revolution.** The Industrial Revolution led to such significant changes in the way goods were produced and in the way people lived that it completely transformed the world.

Terms to Define

factors of production	corporation
mechanization	business cycle
mass production	free enterprise

People to Identify

Eli Whitney	Charles Goodyear
James Watt	Samuel Morse
Henry Bessemer	Adam Smith

Places to Locate

London	Manchester
Liverpool	Silesia

Questions to Guide Your Reading

1 Why did the Industrial Revolution begin in Great Britain?
2 How did the factory system change working and living conditions?
3 What new methods and types of businesses produced an industrial economy?
4 What problems led workers to protest the effects of industrialization?
5 What political and economic changes did socialists seek?

◀ *New York's Fifth Avenue 1913*

The rhythmic grating of the rocking chair against the wooden planks of the front porch punctuated the still summer evening. An American farmer of English and German heritage peacefully scanned the land he and his ancestors had tilled for three generations. The farmer's granddaughter saw the pride in the old man's eyes and asked him to tell her about his life.

The old man thought for a moment and then began:

> *"I think back to all the stories I heard the old folks tell when I was a boy in the 1890s—stories about how our ancestors had left the old country and migrated to America. They farmed and ranched, eking out a living from the land. They did not have tractors, planters, and harvesters. They could not drive a car on paved roads to buy frozen foods at supermarkets or frilly things at fancy stores. I think about how hard they worked, and about how different our lives are because of them."*

The old man's face crinkled with a smile as he continued:

> *"I look back over my life and I realize that I have lived in one of the most exciting times in American history. As a boy I knew the old pioneers. As a young man at the turn of the century I saw more changes within a few years than generations of old folks had seen in a lifetime. And now, I look out onto this land and I see the promise of modern technology fulfilled, a better life for the generations to come, and new frontiers to explore."*

The conversation between the grandfather and his granddaughter took place during the early 1970s in Texas, but the rapid changes the old man witnessed were the product of the Industrial Revolution, which changed the way goods were produced and the way people lived.

1 The Industrial Revolution Began in Great Britain

A revolution in agriculture preceded and made possible the Industrial Revolution. Both the agricultural revolution and the Industrial Revolution began in Great Britain.

Chapter Objectives

After studying Chapter 19, students will be able to:

1. List the factors of production and explain their importance to the process of industrialization.
2. Trace the development of the inventions and technological innovations that were essential to the Industrial Revolution.
3. Describe how the factory system changed working and living conditions during the Industrial Revolution.
4. Discuss the changing roles of women in a newly industrialized society.
5. Identify the elements that made mass production possible.
6. Describe the pattern known as the business cycle.
7. Explain the economic theories of Adam Smith, Thomas Malthus, and David Ricardo.
8. Describe the development of the reform movement and the beginnings of labor unions.
9. Discuss the theory of scientific socialism formulated by Karl Marx.

SECTION 1

Focus/Motivation

Before students read the section, pose the following situation: You are the ruler of a less developed, agricultural country. What conditions must exist in your country in order for it to become industrialized? *(Student answers should include: efficient central government; rich natural*

1B, 1C, 1D, 4H, 4I, a1B, a1C

• Some farm laborers, their jobs threatened by these technological innovations, destroyed farm machines and burned down barns and hayricks. Factory workers, too, took to machine-breaking. They were known as Luddites, because their supposed leader was a young apprentice named Ned Ludd.

resources; increasing population; inventive genius; and a willingness to adopt, adapt, and take chances.) Write student responses on the chalkboard or an overhead projector. Have students read the section and make a list of the factors of production. *(land, capital, and labor)* Then, ask students to classify the answers they gave under the appropriate factor of production.

Presentation Understanding Relationships (Average/Group)
Write the following list on the chalkboard or an overhead projector. In each pair, one invention or discovery depended on the other. Have students identify which invention or discovery of each pair came first.

1. *(1)* loom
   (2) flying shuttle
2. *(2)* spinning jenny
   (1) flying shuttle
3. *(1)* spinning mule
   (2) power loom
4. *(2)* street lamps
   (1) gas from coal
5. *(1)* rubber
   (2) vulcanizing
6. *(1)* oil
   (2) kerosene

The Agricultural Revolution

Before the 1600s English villagers used common lands jointly for pastures and other agricultural endeavors. Then in the 1600s, English farmers began to fence off, or enclose, these common lands into individual holdings. The farmers combined scattered lands to form larger holdings that were efficient for large-scale farming. This **enclosure movement** continued into the 1700s. Finally, in the early 1800s, the increased demand for agricultural products in growing cities and the need for Great Britain to feed its own people during the Napoleonic Wars made large-scale farming a necessity.

The enclosure movement had two significant results. First, as large landowners added to their holdings, they forced owners of small plots to either become tenant farmers or give up farming and move to the cities. Second, since land did not have to be farmed in common, farmers could experiment with their new methods of farming without having to seek the consent of the other villagers.

Among the first who experimented in the early 1700s were the so-called "gentlemen farmers" such as Jethro Tull. Concerned about the wasteful practice of scattering seeds by hand over a wide area, Tull invented a seed drill, which made it possible to plant seeds in regular rows.

Experiments showed Tull that crops grew better if he periodically removed the weeds and broke up the soil between the rows of plants. Tull invented a horse-drawn cultivator to do this work.

Another English gentleman farmer, Viscount Charles "Turnip" Townshend, found a way to avoid another wasteful practice. Traditionally, farmers left some of their fields unplanted, or fallow, each year to allow nutrients to replenish the soil. By repeated experiments Townshend learned that alternating different kinds of crops would preserve soil fertility. For example, he would plant grain crops such as wheat and barley one year and root crops such as turnips the next. This system, called **crop rotation,** has become a basic principle of modern farming.

Additional improvements in machinery made farm labor easier and increased production. For example, iron plows replaced wooden ones. An American blacksmith, Robert Ransome, invented an iron plow in three parts so that a farmer could replace a broken part at low cost, rather than having to buy a whole new plow every time one part broke.

Some of the new agricultural techniques and machines were expensive. Farmers who could afford them made large profits, but many farmers with small holdings could not afford additional equipment.

By the 1800s improvements in agriculture had decreased the demand for farm laborers. Many unemployed farm workers moved to the cities, • where they created a large labor force.

Factors of Production

The Industrial Revolution that followed the agricultural revolution began in Great Britain because a certain combination of conditions existed there. Great Britain had what economists call the **factors of production,** or the basic resources necessary for industrialization: land, capital, and labor.

When economists speak of *land,* they are referring to all natural resources, of which Great Britain had an abundant supply—particularly of coal and iron ore. Furthermore, Britain's excellent harbors facilitated trade, and its many rivers provided waterpower and inland transportation.

Great Britain also had access to capital. *Capital* includes money and goods such as tools, machinery, equipment, and inventory, which are used in the production process. Since the Commercial Revolution, many British people had grown wealthy from trade and could use this wealth to invest in new businesses.

In addition to land and capital, Great Britain had an abundant supply of industrial workers, primarily because the agricultural revolution had forced many farm laborers to seek jobs in cities. Furthermore, Great Britain could supply management to direct the development of industry. Traditionally, the British considered it honorable for young people from the upper and middle classes to go into business. Many became managers, and a few people of the lower class now had some opportunity to succeed in business.

Several other conditions help explain why the Industrial Revolution began in Great Britain. The British Isles and overseas colonies represented huge markets that created a large demand for British goods. Additional trade opportunities also existed in many other parts of the world, which could be reached by the British navy and merchant fleet, the best in the world. Equally important was the British government's concern for commercial interests. Parliament passed laws that protected businesses and helped them expand.

The Textile Industry

The cotton textile industry was the first industry in Great Britain to undergo **mechanization,** the use of automatic machinery to increase production. Although England had imported cotton cloth since the late Middle Ages, in the 1600s English businesses began importing raw cotton and employing spinners and weavers to make it into cloth. This industry was an example of the **domestic system,** a system in which men and women work in their homes. Although production increased, all the work was still done by hand, and England could not produce enough cotton cloth to meet the demand for it.

New inventions. The first step toward mechanization came with the improvement of the loom for weaving cloth. A loom is set up with a series of threads, called the warp, strung from top to bottom. The loom operator pushes a shuttle containing the woof, or the thread running crosswise to the warp, back and forth across the loom in a very time-consuming process. In 1733 a clockmaker named John Kay invented the flying shuttle, a cord mechanism that moved the woof thread more rapidly across the loom. Now the weavers could weave faster than the spinners could produce thread on their simple spinning wheels. The demand for thread rose so dramatically that some people offered a prize for a better spinning machine.

James Hargreaves, a poor English worker, won the prize in 1764 with a machine that he named the spinning "jenny" in honor of his wife. This machine could produce eight times as much thread as a single spinning wheel. Five years later Richard Arkwright made further improvements with a machine called the water frame, a spinning machine driven by waterpower.

Workers could use the jenny and the small, hand-operated, and relatively inexpensive flying shuttle in their homes. However, most people who worked at home could not afford the expensive water frame, which required waterpower and more space. For this reason Arkwright opened a spinning mill, bringing workers and machines together in one place to make goods. Employees worked a set number of hours for a certain amount of money. By 1784 Arkwright employed several hundred workers. This mill marked the beginning of the modern **factory system.**

In 1784 Samuel Crompton combined the best features of the spinning jenny and the water frame in another machine, the spinning mule. Now weavers could get plenty of fine-quality thread. However, even with the flying shuttle, the weavers failed to meet the demand for cloth.

In 1785 an English minister, Edmund Cartwright, met the need for a faster weaving process

Learning from Pictures *Calico cotton cloth, once imported from India, is shown here being manufactured in a Lancashire, England, cotton mill.*

491

1B, 1C, 1D, 4H, 4I, a1C

● In the 20 years between 1750 and 1770, British cotton exports increased tenfold.

with his invention of a loom powered by water. Using this power loom, one person could weave as much cloth as 200 hand-loom operators. About the same time, one of Kay's sons invented a way to print colored patterns on cotton cloth.

Effects of mechanization. With all these improvements, cotton cloth became cheaper to produce and sell. As the price went down, the demand increased, and so did the need for more raw cotton. In 1701 England imported 1 million pounds (450,000 kilograms) of cotton. In 1802 it imported 60 million pounds (27 million kilograms).

Most of the imported raw cotton came from the southern United States. At first, cotton cultivation had not been profitable there because it was difficult to remove the seeds to prepare the cotton for market. By hand, one person could clean only one pound (.45 kilogram) of cotton a day. In 1793 Eli Whitney invented the cotton gin, a machine that could do the work of 50 people. Equipped with Whitney's invention, the southern United States met the demands of the British textile manufacturers and became the cotton-producing center of the world.

Learning from Pictures *The Bessemer process shown here serves as part of the manufacturing process of railroad tracks.*

Steam Engines

Waterpower drove the early machines of the Industrial Revolution. Although waterpower represented a great improvement over human, animal, and wind power, it did have drawbacks. A factory had to be located beside a stream or river, preferably near a natural waterfall or a place where a dam could be built. Often this location was not near transportation, raw materials, a labor supply, or markets. A second drawback was that the water flow could vary greatly with the seasons. People began to look for a continuous, dependable, and portable power source; they found it in steam.

People had observed the power contained in steam since ancient times. It was not until 1712, however, that Thomas Newcomen, an English engineer, produced the first successful steam engine. Initially, workers used Newcomen engines to pump water from mines. These crude machines were more powerful and dependable than water wheels, but they were slow and expensive to operate.

In the 1760s James Watt, a Scottish instrument maker and engineer, studied the Newcomen engine. He invented several improvements and in 1769 produced the modern steam engine. Industry quickly adapted the Watt engine to drive the new spinning and weaving machines. As a result of Watt's invention, steam replaced water as industry's major power source.

Iron and Steel

The invention and availability of more and more machines produced a great demand for iron to make them. From early times people in the British Isles had produced iron, using wood or charcoal to fuel the forges needed to separate the element from its ore. Then someone discovered that coal worked even better than wood or charcoal. As the Industrial Revolution continued, iron and coal became the two major raw materials of modern industry. Great Britain had an enormous advantage over other countries, because it had large amounts of these two resources.

Many early steam engines exploded because the iron used to build them could not withstand the high pressure of steam. Industry needed a stronger, harder metal. Suppliers met this need with steel, which is iron with certain impurities removed. The early process for making steel was

492

● The first steam locomotive was built in 1803 by Richard Trevithick, an engineer from Cornwall, England.

slow and expensive, however, and the metal remained rare until the 1850s. During that decade an American, William Kelly, and an Englishman, Henry Bessemer, discovered a new way of making steel. The **Bessemer process** involved forcing air through the molten iron to burn out carbon and other impurities. The process reduced the cost so much that steel became what it is today—the basic material of industrial civilization.

Industrialization in Other Fields

Using steam engines and iron and steel, British manufacturers quickly introduced power-driven machinery in many industries. The production of shoes, clothing, ammunition, and furniture became mechanized, as did printing and papermaking. People used machines to cut and finish lumber, to process foods, and to make other machines.

Some new inventions and innovative processes had important by-products. These by-products often developed into separate industries. For example, iron smelteries used coke, a by-product of coal, to improve the smelting process. Then someone discovered that the gases that coal released during the coke-making process could be burned to give light. During the 1830s London became one of the first cities to pipe in gas to burn in street lamps. By the 1850s hundreds of cities throughout the Western world used gas to light streets and homes.

The production of rubber created another new industry during the 1800s. Rubber was first used to make waterproof shoes and coats, but they became sticky in warm weather. In 1839, after years of experimenting, Charles Goodyear of the United States discovered a process of "curing" rubber to make it more elastic and usable. He mixed the raw rubber with sulfur and then heated the mixture. Goodyear's method, called *vulcanizing,* became the basis of the modern rubber industry.

The oil industry developed after 1850, when people discovered how to use crude oil, or petroleum, to produce paraffin for candles, lubricating oil for machinery, and kerosene for lighting and heating.

Transportation

The Industrial Revolution also transformed transportation. When the revolution first began, land transportation was almost the same as it had been during the Middle Ages. Roads, little more than trails blurred with thick dust in dry weather and buried in deep, slippery mud when it rained, made travel difficult.

A passenger in a stagecoach could travel 50 miles (80 kilometers) in one day, barring unforeseen delays. Packhorses and clumsy wagons carrying heavy goods made even less progress in a day's journey.

Roads and canals. Industrialization made improved transportation necessary. Factories required delivery of raw materials, and finished products had to be transported to markets as quickly as possible. A Scottish engineer, John McAdam, worked out a new way of building roads that improved travel conditions. Layers of carefully selected small stones topped a roadbed of large stones. These roads, called macadam roads, served as models for engineers in later times. Today road builders use asphalt to bind the smaller stones together.

Great Britain and other countries of western Europe also had extensive networks of rivers that served as water highways. Some canals connected them, but workers constructed many more canals after engineers began using locks—gates that regulate the level and flow of water. Many canals were built between 1760 and 1850. However, although canals provided a cheaper and slightly faster form of transportation than roads, new forms of transportation soon competed with them.

Railroads and steamboats. Watt's steam engine offered many possibilities for new means of transportation. In 1814 George Stephenson, an ● English engineer, perfected a steam-propelled moving engine, or locomotive, that ran on rails. In 1829 Stephenson's famous locomotive, the *Rocket,* pulled a line of cars from Liverpool to Manchester at an amazing speed for that time—29 miles (46 kilometers) per hour. Networks of railroads soon connected much of the Western world. Continuous improvements—steel rails, air brakes, more comfortable coaches, and special cars for different kinds of freight—made railroad transportation fast, safe, and affordable.

Many people tried adapting the steam engine to ships. Robert Fulton, an American who established the first regular inland steamboat service, received credit for accomplishing this task. His boat, the *Clermont,* was launched on the Hudson River in 1807, and immediately began regular trips between

SECTION 1

Closure

Point out to students that the Industrial Revolution was made possible by a series of interconnected inventions and technological developments. Ask: Which invention or technological development do you think was the most important for the Industrial Revolution? *(Students might suggest the steam engine because it provided a new source of power.)*

Review Answers

1. ***Industrial Revolution:*** introduction of industrial technology that changed the way goods were produced; ***enclosure movement:*** fencing off common land into individual holdings suitable for large-scale farming; ***crop rotation:*** alternating different types of crops to preserve soil fertility; ***factors of production:*** basic resources necessary for industry—land, capital and labor; ***mechanization:*** the use of automatic machinery to increase production; ***domestic system:*** system under which work is done in workers' homes; ***factory system:*** system which brings people and machines together in one place to produce goods **2.** ***agricultural revolution:*** improvements in agriculture including crop rotation and enclosure; ***James Hargreaves:*** invented the spinning jenny; ***Richard Arkwright:*** invented the water frame; ***Eli Whitney:*** invented the cotton gin; ***James***

1B, 1D, 4H, 4I, a1C, a3A, a3B, a3G, a3I

Watt: developed the steam engine; ***Henry Bessemer:*** developed cheaper process of producing steel by forcing air through molten iron to burn off impurities; ***John McAdam:*** developed a method of building better roads by layering stones on each other; ***Robert Fulton:*** American who established first regular steamboat service: ***Samuel Morse:*** invented telegraph and Morse Code; ***Cyrus Field:*** laid transatlantic telegraph cable
3. ***London:*** city in southeast England; ***Liverpool:*** port on northwestern coast of England
4. (a) As large landowners added to their holdings, small farmers were forced either to become tenant farmers or to give up farming and move to cities. Also, it was easier for individual owners of large farms to experiment with new agricultural methods than it had been when numerous farmers had to agree. **(b)** It made farm work easier, increased production, and eventually led to a fall in the demand for farm labor, causing many farm workers to move to the cities in search of jobs.
5. The Industrial Revolution began in Great Britain because that country had an abundant supply of the factors of production—land, labor, and capital. Also, the British colonies provided a huge market for British manufactured goods, and Parliament passed laws that protected industries and helped them

Learning from Pictures *This scene of the Mississippi River is by Currier and Ives, publishers of hand-colored prints depicting United States social history.*

New York City and Albany. Steamboats soon appeared on many of the rivers and lakes of the world.

In 1838 the *Great Western,* a ship operated only by steam, crossed the Atlantic Ocean in 15 days, less than half the time it took a sailing ship. Samuel Cunard of Great Britain, who founded the Cunard Line shipping company, provided regular steamboat service across the Atlantic. Soon ships built of iron and steel instead of wood moved goods all over the world in less time and for less money than ever before.

The Communications Revolution

Science played only a small role in the invention of textile machinery, the steam engine, the locomotive, and the steamship. These inventions represented the work of amateur inventors and engineers and did not come from the scientist's laboratory. In communications, however, science played a significant role in the development of technology.

From early times people had observed electricity and its connection with magnetism, but they had put their knowledge to little practical use. For one thing, no one had found a way to provide a steady flow of electric current. About 1800 an Italian, Alessandro Volta, built the first battery, a device that provided a steady current of electricity. Soon afterward André Ampère of France worked out principles governing the magnetic effect of an electric current.

Samuel Morse of the United States put the work of Volta and Ampère to practical use. Morse sent an electrical current over a wire to a machine at the other end of the wire. Each time the electricity passed along the wire, the machine clicked. Morse worked out a system of dots and dashes—the Morse code—by which these clicks could be translated into letters of the alphabet. By 1844 Morse's invention, the telegraph, had become a practical communication instrument. Soon telegraph wires, stretched across continents, transmitted ideas at the speed of electricity.

People also found a way to carry electricity under the sea by using cables—heavily insulated telegraph wires. Early in the 1850s, a cable across the English Channel connected Great Britain with the European continent. However, spanning the great distance of the Atlantic Ocean presented enormous difficulties. Not until 1866 did Cyrus Field and a group of Americans finally lay a cable across the Atlantic Ocean. Soon afterward cables connected all continents of the world.

The Spread of Industry

For various reasons the rapid changes in agriculture, industry, transportation, and communications had little effect on the European continent for several years. Many continental European countries did not have raw materials or large, accessible markets in which to sell their products. Great Britain, in order to keep its monopoly on new methods, prohibited the export of machines. It also refused to allow skilled workers to leave the country. In addition, the wars of the French Revolution and the Napoleonic Era slowed Europe's industrial development.

France, however, did develop some industry, especially textiles, iron, and mining. The French government helped this development in two ways. First, it imposed high tariffs to keep out foreign manufactured goods. Second, it encouraged the construction of railroads. However, in the 1800s France remained largely an agricultural country.

Industry grew slowly in the German states because Germany had no efficient central government to aid industrial growth. Although some factories were established in the middle 1800s, real industrialization had to await the unification of Germany in the 1870s.

The United States eagerly adopted British inventions and methods. The United States had everything that it needed for industrial development—national unity and a vast country with rich natural resources. It also had a rapidly increasing population, inventive genius, and a willingness to adopt, to adapt, and to take business risks.

A network of canals and railroads crept across the United States during the 1800s, and industry moved west as transportation developed. The steel industry grew in Pittsburgh and the Great Lakes region, and farm machinery was manufactured in Chicago. By 1869 a railroad connected the east and west coasts of the United States. By 1870 the United States was second only to Great Britain as a manufacturing nation.

Along with the growth of American industry came significant changes in farming. Eli Whitney's cotton gin enabled the southern states to supply cotton to the British textile industry. Another invention was a machine for harvesting grain, patented by Cyrus McCormick in 1834. The McCormick reaper, drawn by horses, freed many farmers from the slow, backbreaking work of cutting grain with a sickle or a scythe. Other inventions, such as the mechanical thresher for separating the grains of wheat from their stalks and hulls, followed.

SECTION 1 REVIEW

1. **Define** Industrial Revolution, enclosure movement, crop rotation, factors of production, mechanization, domestic system, factory system, Bessemer process
2. **Identify** agricultural revolution, James Hargreaves, Richard Arkwright, Eli Whitney, James Watt, Henry Bessemer, John McAdam, Robert Fulton, Samuel Morse, Cyrus Field
3. **Locate** London, Liverpool
4. **Determining Cause and Effect** **(a)** How did the enclosure movement lead to changes in agriculture? **(b)** What were the principal effects of the agricultural revolution?
5. **Analyzing Ideas** Why did the Industrial Revolution begin in Great Britain?
6. **Summarizing Ideas** Why was the Bessemer process so important to industry?
7. **Identifying Ideas** What were four important developments in transportation during the Industrial Revolution?

2 The Factory System Changed Working and Living Conditions

For centuries skilled artisans produced goods of all kinds in their homes or in small shops. The artisan controlled the training of apprentices, the quality and price of goods, and the pace of each workday. During the 1700s the opportunity for a higher standard of living lured thousands of English farm workers to the city to work in the factories spawned by the Industrial Revolution. The emergence of these factories was only one of the many changes the Industrial Revolution created.

The Effect of Machines on Work

The introduction of steam-powered machinery made work easier to do. Instead of spending several years as an apprentice learning a trade, a person could learn to work a machine in a few days.

Employers looked for people who could learn a few simple tasks and soon discovered that women and children could operate machines as efficiently as men. Employers preferred to hire young men and women rather than older, skilled people. Young people did not have set working methods and did not expect high wages. Women and children would work for lower wages than men. Consequently, the

expand.

6. The Bessemer process, which was a method for removing impurities from iron, reduced the cost of steel production so much that steel became the basic material of industrial civilization.

7. Four important transportation developments were canals, railroads, steamboats, and better roads.

SECTION 2

Focus/Motivation

Pose the following situation for students: You are the ruler of the less developed country discussed in the *Focus/Motivation* exercise for Section 1. You have determined the conditions that your country will need to industrialize. What changes do you think industrialization will make on your culture and way of life? Would people continue to perform the same jobs or would ways of earning a living change? *(Students might suggest that people who previously farmed might become factory workers.)* Would people continue to live in the same locations? *(Students might suggest that places of residence might change as workers moved closer to the factories.)* Might the time parents spend with their children change? *(Students might suggest that parents might work in a factory rather than at home and be less available to their children. Some students might also point out that children might be*

working too.)
Have students compare their responses with the information they obtain from this section.

Presentation
Analyzing Information (Average/Group)
Lead a discussion about the role of women in industrial society, using the following questions as a guide: How did the lives of working-class women in the 1800s compare with the lives of middle-class women? What jobs were open to women in the late 1800s? What jobs are available to women today from which they were barred as recently as 20 years ago? *(construction worker, police officer, fire fighter)* Why do you think changes have occurred? Does discrimination against women in the labor force still exist in terms of wages, types of jobs, or opportunity for advancement? Suggest that students refer to pages 498-499 for information on these topics.

early textile factories employed mainly children and young adults under the age of 30.

As machines became more and more available, older skilled workers often found themselves unemployed. Factories no longer needed their abilities as weavers or spinners but would not hire them for simpler work. To make up for their loss of income, many of these people sent their children to work in textile factories while they looked for odd jobs in the cities or on nearby farms.

The Wage System

The factory system differed from the domestic system. Factories brought together large numbers of people. Instead of working on a product from beginning to end, each worker performed only a small part of the entire job. Instead of working in a shop with a few others, dozens of people worked in the same room, under the direction of a shop supervisor.

Under the domestic system a master served as both worker and employer. Under the factory system, a few masters became factory owners, but most became workers. Instead of owning a shop or some tools, artisans now worked for the people who owned the machines and the factories. Factory owners paid their workers wages based on the number of hours worked or the amount of goods produced.

Several factors determined factory workers' wages. First, employers wanted to produce goods as cheaply as possible. Thus, factory owners set wages in relation to other costs of production. For example, if the cost of land or capital increased, the owners lowered wages.

Second, competition for jobs lowered wages. But wages rose when there were not enough workers to do a particular job.

Third, wages often depended on what people could earn at other kinds of work. For example, early employers in textile factories wanted to attract young women as workers. So the employers paid young women more than they would have earned as household servants.

Fourth, wages took into account the needs of a worker and his or her family. Adult men earned higher wages than adult women because people thought men should support the family. Women were thought to be adding "a little something" to a man's wage, even if in reality a woman was the only one earning money for her family.

Workers who earned wages depended entirely on their earnings. Under the domestic system, artisans had owned their tools and the shops they worked in, and apprentices had eventually become masters. Now, someone else employed most workers throughout their lives.

Factory Rules and Regulations

Factory work changed people's work habits. Workers had many rules to follow. They had to arrive at work promptly. They could eat meals and take breaks only at set times, and they could leave only with permission. They worked whether it was hot or cold, winter or summer, day or night. Breaking the rules or missing work for any reason could result in heavy fines, pay cuts, or losing a job.

In the early factories, workers spent 14 hours a day, 6 days a week, on the job. Instead of the work being adjusted to the seasons, as it was under the domestic system or on farms, factory workers had to adjust their lives to the demands of machines, and the machines never needed to rest. Some workers even complained that people in authority expected them to become machines themselves.

Factories were uncomfortable places; they were noisy, dirty, and poorly ventilated. The air was hot and steamy in summer and cold and damp in winter. Sanitary facilities were primitive. Early machines had no safety devices, and serious injuries occurred frequently. Employers provided no accident insurance or other form of compensation for injury.

One of the worst features of early industrialization concerned child labor. Five-year-old children were commonly employed in cotton mills and mines. Conditions were particularly bad in coal mines, where women and children pulled carts through tunnels that were too low to allow a donkey or a grown man to pass through.

Abusive situations in factories soon scandalized Great Britain. In 1832 a parliamentary committee investigated working conditions of children in textile mills. The following exchange between the committee and 23-year-old Elizabeth Bently illustrates the committee's findings:

> "What time did you begin work at the factory?—When I was six years old. . . .
>
> What were your hours of labor in that mill?—From five in the morning till nine at night. . . .

● In Manchester, England, in the 1840s, life expectancy for working-class people was about 35 years.

FURNITURE

Thonet Rocker

In the 1840s Michael Thonet, an Austrian cabinetmaker, invented a process that revolutionized furniture making. In 1860 he used this process to craft the bentwood rocker shown here. The chair may look familiar because similar chairs are still sold in stores today. Thonet's patent consisted of bending solid wood by steaming it and then clamping a thin strip of steel along one side. This process eliminated complex jointing and carving. It meant that Thonet could hire local people, rather than expensive artisans, for his European factories. Men did the cutting and bending; women and children did the sanding, polishing, and packing.

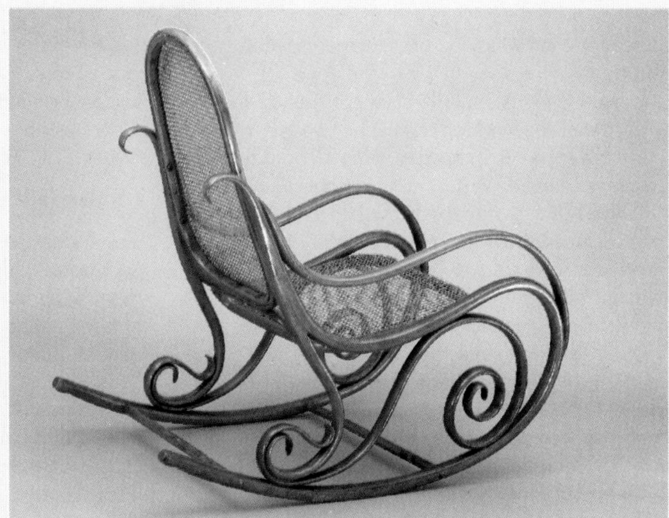

Rocking chair by Gebrüder Thonet. 1860. Bent beechwood; cane, 37 1/2" h. Collection, The Museum of Modern Art, New York. Gift of Cafe Nicholson.

Well before the Industrial Revolution affected the rest of the furniture industry, Thonet's chairs, hat stands, and other pieces were being produced in a factory and marketed to the new middle class. By the end of the 1800s, Thonet's company was making 4,000 pieces of furniture a day— more than 1 million a year—a triumph in mass production.

Were the children [beaten] . . . ?—Yes. . . . What was the reason for that?—[The overlooker] was angry.

Had the children committed any fault?—They were too slow. . . .

You are considerably deformed in your person in consequence of this labor?—Yes, I am.

At what time did it come on?—I was about thirteen years old when it began coming, and it has got worse since. ”

Living Conditions of Workers

Life in the mines and factories was hard and monotonous, and life in the workers' homes was not much better. Working people lived in cramped and poorly maintained apartment houses called tenements. As many as a dozen people shared a room. As late as 1840, one out of every eight working-class families in Manchester, England, lived in cellars. Many children shared one bed in a sparsely furnished room. The illness, death, or unemployment of a working father or mother could drive a family to the brink of starvation.

Although the working classes suffered during the Industrial Revolution, their living standard improved considerably when cheap goods produced in the factories became available to them. During the 1800s real wages (wages measured in terms of what they will buy) increased rapidly.

Conditions in industrial cities during the Industrial Revolution were shocking compared to living ● and working conditions today. Compared to conditions in rural areas or nonindustrial cities at the same time, however, they were not so bad. The lower economic classes, whether peasants or artisans, had always worked long and hard. They had always suffered from periodic famines and epidemics. And women and children had always worked hard, especially in rural areas.

The Development of the Middle Class

During the Industrial Revolution, the balance of economic and political power shifted from agriculture to industry. As more jobs became available in cities, the middle class grew. This group consisted of many kinds of people—bankers, manufacturers,

497

1B, 1C, 1D, 4H, 4I, a1A, a1C, a4A

● **Many women who had worked at home went to work in factories.**

SECTION 2

Closure

Ask students how the Industrial Revolution affected the middle class. *(As more jobs became available in cities, the middle class grew.)*

Review Answers

1. *Manchester:* city in central England

2. Machines changed the way work was done by cutting down the training period for a job. People began to work in factories on a small part of a job rather than at home on the entire project.

3. Wages of factory workers were determined in several ways: they were lower when many people were competing for jobs and higher when there were fewer workers; they were set in relation to other costs of production; they often depended on what people could earn at other kinds of work; they took into account the needs of a worker and his or her family.

4. Factories were uncomfortable places—noisy, dirty and poorly ventilated.

5. (a) In the late 1800s women worked in textile mills or as domestic servants. They also became nurses, social workers, and teachers. **(b)** Women moved from rural areas to the cities, earned wages for their labor, and entered new professions.

merchants, lawyers, doctors, engineers, professors, and their families.

The life of the middle class contrasted sharply with that of the working class. The two groups lived apart—workers in crowded slums, middle-class people in larger houses in more spacious neighborhoods. The two groups dressed differently. Workers wore work shirts and trousers, while lawyers and merchants wore suits. Working-class women dressed in plain skirts and blouses, but the women of the middle class wore lace and frills.

Middle-class people benefited more than workers from the early Industrial Revolution. The laboring poor who worked on farms or in factories continued to suffer economically as had their parents and grandparents. But for the middle class, it was a time of increasing prestige and political recognition. Members of the middle class owned property and could afford to hire servants, to eat well, and to enjoy some comfort.

The members of the middle class were able to send their children to school to receive training for good jobs. Often the younger generation inherited money and social position from their parents.

Learning from Pictures *These young girls are working in a garment shop. How did industrialization affect the working-class women?* ●

Aristocratic government leaders sought the advice of middle-class economists. Soon government leaders became as concerned about the future of industry as they were about the future of agriculture.

Industrialization Affected Women's Lives

The Industrial Revolution affected women of different classes in different ways. In the past, in addition to working in the fields, women had made clothing at home, spun yarn, woven cloth, and prepared all meals. They manufactured goods for sale and assisted their husbands in craft shops or small family businesses. However, the Industrial Revolution moved most manufacturing into factories. Now all classes of people purchased food and clothing at large markets instead of making these products at home. As a result, important work that women previously had to do at home could now be done by others elsewhere.

Working-class women. The early textile mills hired women to tend machines that spun cotton into thread, a job that required little skill. Many women who had spun thread at home took jobs in the new factories. People referred to these jobs as "women's jobs," although a few men also performed them. Industrialization changed the location of work for working-class women, but it did not raise the status of their jobs.

While some working-class women took factory jobs, many others continued to work at a traditional job for women—domestic service. For centuries young, single women had been hired as maids, cooks, and nannies in other people's houses or businesses. And many men had worked as grooms, gardeners, footmen, coachmen, valets, and butlers. After industrialization more middle-class families could afford to hire servants. As a result, more jobs for servants became available.

As the number of farms declined during the Industrial Revolution, rural areas offered fewer jobs. Daughters of farm families now took jobs as servants in the city. For many country women, domestic service represented a first step into city life. Becoming a servant did not require special skills. In addition, servants lived with the families for whom they worked. Thus an employer guaranteed a young woman moving from the country a place to live and food to eat. After living for a while in the city as a servant, a young woman often took a job in a shop or factory.

As early as 1875, more than one-third of France's primary school teachers were women.

Middle-class women. The Industrial Revolution brought new wealth and greater luxury to middle-class women, who could hire servants to cook, clean, and take care of their children. While their husbands left home to go to work each day, middle-class wives stayed home. Middle-class people placed increasing emphasis on the idea that women belonged at home and men belonged in the working world. According to some writers of the day, a woman's nature equipped her only for raising children and caring for the home. More and more people considered earning money, even by doing chores in the house, as a corruption of "true womanhood." Some women accepted and enjoyed this role, but others began to express a very different attitude.

This new attitude arose in Great Britain, where in the mid-1800s many middle-class women did not marry. Many came from families who could not support them throughout their lives. Therefore, they had to support themselves by going to work. Some women whose families could support them believed that women should have the opportunity to work if they wanted to. This idea gradually gained acceptance.

During the late 1800s, more jobs became available for women. The demand for public health care created a need for nurses and social workers, greatly increasing opportunities for women.

Demands also arose for improvements in education. College courses were opened to women, and special women's colleges were established. As public education spread in the 1870s and 1880s in France and Great Britain, the need for teachers increased. Women began to enter the teaching field in large numbers. By the end of the 1800s, elementary school teaching had become almost entirely a female profession.

SECTION 2 REVIEW

1. **Locate** Manchester
2. **Evaluating Ideas** How did machines change the way work was done?
3. **Interpreting Ideas** How were the wages of factory workers determined?
4. **Summarizing Ideas** Describe working conditions in factories and mines.
5. **Classifying Ideas** **(a)** What jobs were open to women in the late 1800s? **(b)** How did these jobs affect their lives?

3 New Methods and Giant Businesses Produced an Industrial Economy

Throughout the 1800s inventions, new sales methods, and new methods of production and distribution of goods transformed industry. The rapid growth caused by these developments brought many changes to the factory system and to the organization of businesses. Some of these changes date back to the early Industrial Revolution. Others came about after 1870 as a result of scientific contributions.

The factory system also introduced a new phase in the development of **capitalism**—the economic system in which individuals rather than the government control the factors of production. Before the Industrial Revolution, most capitalists were merchants who bought, sold, and exchanged goods. We call this type of capitalism **commercial capitalism.** However, because the capitalists of the Industrial Revolution became more involved in producing and manufacturing goods themselves, the capitalism of this period is often referred to as **industrial capitalism.**

Division of Labor

As we have seen, industrialization changed the methods of production. Instead of relying on a master and his apprentices, factory owners hired large numbers of unskilled laborers, divided the manufacturing process into a series of simple steps, and then assigned a step to each worker. This process was a form of **division of labor.** Because a large number of items could be produced in a given length of time, the cost of the items diminished. The use of machinery helped the division of labor, since machines performed many of the steps.

Interchangeable Parts

The American inventor Eli Whitney used division of labor to make muskets in the early 1800s. In Whitney's factory some people worked on musket barrels, others on trigger mechanisms, and still others on the wooden stocks or handles.

The use of interchangeable parts for his firearms became an essential part of Whitney's system. He designed machinery that unskilled workers

SECTION 3

Focus/Motivation
Have students study the picture on page 500. Then lead them in a discussion, using the following questions as a guide: What benefits might the assembly line have for industry? for workers? *(Students might suggest that since workers need to learn only one task, time is saved in training, and production costs are lowered. Also, students might suggest that workers who lack skills and would otherwise have difficulty finding a job could work on an assembly line.)* What disadvantages does the assembly line have for workers? *(Student answers should include: boredom, loss of pride in work, and danger of injury.)*

Presentation
Explaining Relationships (Average/Group)
Have students write paragraphs explaining the role of each of following in mass production: division of labor, interchangeable parts, and assembly line. (Students may need to reread pages 499-500.) Have students compare their paragraphs with those of other members of the class.

1B, 1D, 4H, 4I, aC, a1C, a3A, a3B, a3G, a3I, a4A

● Frederick Taylor did time-motion studies of assembly-line procedures to see how long it took workers to do particular tasks. Taylor analyzed his findings and made suggestions as to how the workers might cut down movement and, therefore, do their tasks in less time.

SECTION 3

Closure
Point out to the students that in the late 1800s some people in Europe and the United States became alarmed by the growth of big corporations. Ask: What advantages and disadvantages do monopolies and cartels pose for a country's economy? *(Students might suggest that they allow more goods to be produced but that they limit competition.)*

Review Answers
1. ***capitalism:*** economic system in which individuals rather than the government control the factors of production; ***commercial capitalism:*** early phase of capitalism in which capitalists bought, sold, and exchanged goods; ***industrial capitalism:*** period of capitalism in which capitalists were involved in producing and manufacturing goods themselves; ***division of labor:*** dividing the manufacturing process into a series of steps, each step then being assigned to a worker; ***mass production:*** system of manufacturing large numbers of identical items; ***sole proprietorship:*** business owned and controlled by one person; ***partnership:*** business owned and controlled by two or more people; ***corporation:*** business organization in which individuals buy shares of stock, elect directors to decide policies, hire managers, and receive dividends according to the number of shares they

Learning from Pictures *In 1913, Henry Ford's main plant was located in the Detroit suburb of Highland Park.*

could operate. This machinery turned out identical, interchangeable parts. This development made division of labor possible in a product composed of several parts that had to fit together. Whitney's system resulted in the speedy production of a large number of inexpensive muskets that could be easily repaired. If part of a musket broke, repair involved inserting an identical replacement part. Other manufacturers, realizing the usefulness of interchangeable parts, quickly adopted Whitney's principle.

The Assembly Line

Division of labor and the system of interchangeable parts constituted two essential elements of **mass production.** Mass production is the system of manufacturing large numbers of identical items.

A third element of mass production is the assembly line. Until the late 1800s, separate parts were brought together and assembled into a final product at a central point—a slow and inefficient process. Then manufacturers devised the assembly line. A conveyor belt carried the unfinished products past each worker in turn. As each item passed, each worker performed a special task. The assembly line saved time and energy and increased the number of times per hour a worker could perform the assigned task.

Henry Ford saw great potential in the mass-production system. By applying it to the manufacture of automobiles, he founded one of the largest industries in the United States. A conveyor belt carried the frame of the automobile from one worker to the next. Each worker made a small contribution to the finished product by adding one or more of the 5,000 interchangeable parts that composed the Model T Ford. Mass production lowered the price of automobiles and made them available ● to most American families.

American and European industrialists began to mass-produce clothing, furniture, and machinery. Because mass production usually lowered the cost of an item, more people could buy more things and enjoy a higher standard of living.

Rise of the Corporation

Before the Industrial Revolution, most businesses were either sole proprietorships or partnerships. A business owned and controlled by one person is a **sole proprietorship,** while a **partnership** is a business owned and controlled by two or more people. Although both types of business organizations give their owners considerable freedom to make economic decisions, both types have disadvantages. For example, both sole proprietors and partners are responsible for all debts even if the debts exceed the original amount of investment. In addition, sole proprietorships and partnerships usually remain small. Small companies with few workers cannot use mass-production methods or afford to buy the machinery necessary for large-scale production.

As the scale of business grew during the 1800s, so too did the corporation. A **corporation** is a business organization in which individuals buy shares of stock, elect directors to decide policies and hire managers, and receive dividends according to the number of shares they own. In contrast to sole proprietors and partners, the shareholder's financial responsibility is limited to the amount that he or she invests. For this reason corporations attract greater numbers of investors.

In the late 1800s, corporations increased greatly both in the amount of capital invested and in the size of the manufacturing establishment or group of enterprises. In 1901 American financier J. P. Morgan and his associates formed the United States Steel Company, the first of many billion-dollar corporations. Banks and other financial institutions played an increasingly important role in forming and operating these large corporations.

Increasing the size of a corporation, however, did not solve all the corporation's problems. A large manufacturing enterprise could produce goods at a lower cost than a small one. To get lower costs, however, the factory had to operate at full capacity, turning out as many goods as possible. Sometimes the factory produced so many goods that selling them all became a problem.

If a number of corporations were producing the same products, competition became very keen. The smaller and less efficient businesses suffered if they tried to sell their products by cutting prices. Often these smaller firms had to sell out to larger firms.

As a result, although the size of individual corporations increased steadily, the number of corporations in some industries decreased. Sometimes a corporation would buy so many smaller companies that it would create a monopoly. A **monopoly** is the control of the total production or sale of a good or service by a single firm. In the United States, corporations such as Standard Oil and United States Steel created monopolies.

By 1900 many corporations in Germany had combined to control entire industries. These combinations of corporations were known as **cartels.** For example, a cartel might own coal and iron mines, steel mills, and factories that used steel to build machines, thus controlling all parts of an industry.

Business Cycles

As industrial production became more and more important, it influenced a country's entire economy. The Industrial Revolution brought alternating periods of prosperity and decline—a pattern known as the **business cycle.**

When one industry did well, other industries also prospered. If, for example, there was a great demand for machines, there would also be a demand for the coal and iron needed to make them. If, on the other hand, a large firm reduced its orders of iron and laid off workers, other companies would also be affected. The iron suppliers might have to cut down production and lay off workers. The workers then would have to find other jobs, because without wages they could not pay their rent or buy food. When the number of available workers exceeded the number of jobs available, employers could reduce wages. The effects would go on spreading to other industries, until the entire economy was in a **depression**—the lowest point of a business cycle.

These economic fluctuations affected the lives of all the people in an industrialized country, even those people who did not work in factories. In addition, events in one country could affect the economy of another country. During the American Civil War, for example, the United States could not ship cotton to Great Britain. The shortage of cotton set off a depression in the British textile industry.

SECTION 3 REVIEW

1. **Define** capitalism, commercial capitalism, industrial capitalism, division of labor, mass production, sole proprietorship, partnership, corporation, monopoly, cartel, business cycle, depression
2. **Identify** interchangeable parts, assembly line
3. **Evaluating Ideas** **(a)** What is the chief advantage of mass production? **(b)** What three elements are needed to make mass production possible?
4. **Comparing Ideas** What advantages did corporations have over sole proprietorships and partnerships?
5. **Analyzing Ideas** Why did corporations grow larger as the Industrial Revolution progressed?

hold. Also, shareholders' financial responsibility is limited to the amount invested; ***monopoly:*** control of the total production or sale of a good or service by a single company; ***cartel:*** combination of corporations that controls an entire industry; ***business cycle:*** economic pattern of alternating periods of prosperity and decline; ***depression:*** lowest point of a business cycle

2. ***interchangeable parts:*** identical parts for use in mass production; ***assembly line:*** arrangement whereby each worker performs a special task in assembling a product as it passes by on a conveyor belt

3. **(a)** The chief advantage of mass production is that it usually lowers the cost of an item. **(b)** Three elements that make mass production possible are division of labor, interchangeable parts, and the assembly line.

4. In sole proprietorships and partnerships, the owners are responsible for all business debts, regardless of their investment. In a corporation, the shareholder's financial responsibility is limited to the amount invested. Corporations, therefore, could attract greater numbers of investors because individual risk was lessened.

5. Competition forced smaller and less efficient companies out of business. Many of these smaller companies were swallowed up by larger corporations. In some

501

1B, 4H, 4I, a1C

● **Smith said that in pursuing their own selfish ends, individuals would be led, as if by an "invisible hand," to achieve the greatest good for all.**

cases a large corporation became a monopoly.

SECTION 4

Focus/Motivation Reproduce the following quotations for students.

"It is not from the benevolence [kindliness] of the butcher, the brewer, or the baker that we expect our dinner, but from their regard to their self-interest. We address ourselves not to their humanity, but their self-love and never talk to them of our necessities, but of their advantages."
—Adam Smith

"I confess that I am not charmed with the ideal of life held out by those who think that the normal state of human beings is that of struggling to get on; that the trampling, crushing, elbowing, and treading on each other's heels, which form the existing type of social life, are the most desirable lot of human beings."
— John Stuart Mill

Have students carefully read the quotations. Then lead them in a discussion on the views expressed by the two economists, using the following questions as a guide: According to Smith, what motive drives people? *(self-interest)* How do you think Mill views Smith's idea? *(He is "not charmed" with it.)* Which of the two economists do you think would be involved in a movement to reform industry? Why? *(Mill; supporting answers will vary.*

4 Living and Working Conditions Gradually Improved

As the Industrial Revolution progressed, the interests of employers often conflicted with the interests of workers. Employers needed workers who would come to work on time, do their jobs quickly and well, follow the rules of the factory, and accept relatively low wages.

Workers, on the other hand, needed wages high enough to support their families even in time of illness or high prices. They wanted some control over their work hours, the conditions in the factories, and the conditions in the towns where they lived. Nevertheless, governments, influenced by certain economic theories that had become widespread as the Industrial Revolution progressed, at first refused to yield to workers' demands.

Adam Smith

During the Enlightenment of the 1700s, a group of economists attacked the ideas of mercantilism, the economic theory based on the belief that the world contained only a fixed amount of wealth and that in order to increase its wealth, a country had to take some wealth from another country. These economists believed that natural laws governed economic life. Any attempt to interfere with these natural economic laws was certain to bring disaster. Adam Smith, a Scot, best stated the views of these economists in his book *The Wealth of Nations,* published in 1776.

Smith reasoned that two natural laws—the law of supply and demand and the law of competition—regulate all business and economic activity. In any business, Smith believed, prices—and therefore profits—will be fixed by the relationship of supply to demand. If an article is scarce and in great demand, people will pay a high price for it. Thus profits from its sales will rise. People will then invest their money to produce more of the scarce article. Soon the supply of the article will exceed the demand for it.

Now each manufacturer will face competition. In order to get people to buy a product, the manufacturer will have to reduce the price or improve the quality, or both. If too many manufacturers produce the same article, the price of the item will go down so far that some manufacturers will not make enough money to cover their costs. The least efficient businesses—those that are so poorly organized and managed that their production costs are high—may be forced out of business. When such manufacturers quit producing the article, the supply of the article will decrease and the price will go up. Then the capable, efficient, and well-organized producers will make a reasonable profit.

Adam Smith wrote that every person should be free to go into any business and to operate it for the greatest advantage. The result, Smith said, would benefit everyone. Laborers would have jobs, investors and owners would make profits, and buyers would receive better goods at lower prices. Smith's system was one of complete **free enterprise.** ●

Smith's ideas appealed to industrialists because the forces he outlined supposedly worked automatically. Smith argued that if anything interfered with the absolutely free working of supply and demand and competition, the system could not work well. Laws and regulations, such as those imposed under mercantilism, were thought of as interfering with the workings of natural law.

Learning from Pictures *Adam Smith asserted that if business or government undermined the laws of a free competitive market, economic life would break down.*

READ
WRITE
● INTERPRET
CONNECT
THINK

BUILDING HISTORY STUDY SKILLS

Interpreting Visuals: Determining Cause and Effect

Understanding history requires that you identify the causes of historical events and determine their effect on history. A *cause* is the reason that something happened. An *effect* is the result or consequence of an action or a situation. Usually an event, an idea, or a situation results from several causes. Causes can be divided into two types. Underlying causes are long-term. Immediate causes lead directly to an event. For example, practicing a sport may lead to a championship. The immediate cause of that victory, however, is the winning game.

How to Determine Cause and Effect

To determine cause and effect, follow these steps.

1. Identify the focal point of your study.
2. Determine the underlying causes. For example, did new ideas cause people to act in a certain way?
3. Identify the immediate cause. For example, did a political candidate win or lose an election because bad weather resulted in a low voter turnout?
4. Formulate a conclusion about the significance of the causes and effects of a historical event.

Developing the Skill

Economists often wonder why industrialization suddenly "takes off" at a certain time in a particular place. Walter Rostow, a twentieth-century economic historian, has advanced the theory that every society develops according to a dynamic production pattern that consists of five stages. The chart below explains the five stages of Rostow's theory.

The chart shows that in stage one, the economy is based on agriculture. Traditional values prevail. The underlying causes for the Industrial Revolution are economic, political, social, and intellectual. Economically, there needs to be an agricultural surplus that generates capital. The traditional social structure declines with the rise of a commercial class. A centralized national government encourages economic modernization. Ideas about the benefits of profit are praised rather than degraded. The immediate cause of the production pattern originates from a surge of production and the rapid expansion in one industry, which serves as the basis for modernization. The significance of the process is that in order for the Industrial Revolution to occur, a social, political, and intellectual change must take place. The economic system is intertwined with the culture and the value system.

Practicing the skill. Use the characteristics of society on the chart as the basis for constructing your own chart on the development of the space industry.

To apply this skill, see Applying History Study Skills on page 513.

Rostow's Theory of Industrial Development

Characteristics	Stage One: *Traditional Society*	Stage Two: *Pre-Conditions for Take-Off*	Stage Three: *Take-Off*	Stage Four: *Drive to Maturity*	Stage Five: *Age of Mass Consumption*
Economy	• agricultural • limited production	• agricultural surplus • surplus capital • expansion of trade	• surge of technology • rapid expansion of industry	• technology extended to all sectors	• increased production and use of durable goods
Society	• hierarchical social structure	• beginning of a commercial class	• Entrepreneurial class more dominant	• urbanization • skilled and professional workers increase	• rise of a new middle class • shift to suburbs
Political Power	• regionally based power in the hands of landowners	• centralized national government	• groups in power encourage economic modernization	• industrial leaders highly influential	• social welfare • more resources for military
Values	• belief that change will not occur	• spirit of progress	• investment of capital for profit becomes important	• emphasis on technology • expectation of progress	• acquisition of consumer goods important

*"Rostow's Theory of Industrial Development" (chart) is based on information from *The Stages of Economic Growth* by W. W. Rostow. Published by Cambridge University Press (England), 1971.

Students may suggest that Mill believed that government should intervene to protect working children and improve housing and factory conditions.) End the discussion by informing students that they will learn more about the economic theories of Adam Smith and John Stuart Mill in Section 4.

Presentation
Understanding Chronology (Average/Group)
Write the following list of events in the history of the British labor movement on the chalkboard or an overhead projector, and have students arrange the events in chronological order.

(5) Parliament passed laws allowing strikes.
(3) Parliament passed a law permitting laborers to meet in order to agree on wages and hours.
(4) Ten Hours Act passed.
(6) Collective bargaining became accepted practice.
(1) According to British law, persons who combined with others to demand better working conditions could be imprisoned.
(2) Large protest movements occurred in northern England.

1B, 1C, 4H, 4I, a1C

Thomas Malthus and David Ricardo

Smith's ideas received strong support from Thomas Malthus and David Ricardo. Malthus was an Anglican clergyman who became a professor of economics. In his book *An Essay on the Principle of Population,* published in 1798, he wrote that population increases present the greatest obstacle to human progress. People, he said, multiply more rapidly than the food supply increases, despite such checks as famines, epidemics, and wars. He believed that human misery and poverty are inevitable.

David Ricardo was an English businessman who built up a large fortune early in life and then was elected to the House of Commons. He, too, wrote that working-class poverty was inevitable. In his book *Principles of Political Economy and Taxation,* published in 1817, Ricardo stated that supply and demand determined wages. When labor was plentiful, wages remained low. When it was scarce, wages soared. As population grew, Ricardo wrote, more and more workers would become available and wages would inevitably drop. Ricardo's idea became known as the "iron law of wages."

Malthus and Ricardo painted a grim picture of the worker, condemned to inevitable poverty and suffering by unchangeable laws. Understandably, the new social science of economics became known as the "dismal science."

Laissez-faire

The writings of economists supported early industrialists who wanted to buy labor, like any other commodity, as cheaply as possible. Economic theories also indicated that governments should not interfere with the operations of business. This attitude was summed up in the French phrase **laissez-faire** (le • say-FAYR), meaning "let do" or leave things alone.

The British put the theory of laissez-faire into practice during the 1800s. Formerly either the government or the guilds had regulated the quantity and quality of goods produced, the hours and wages of workers, and the qualifications of apprentices and masters. In the middle 1800s, most regulations were discontinued. Tariffs, which had been used to regulate foreign trade, were abolished. Free trade became the rule. Other European countries and the United States adopted many features of laissez-faire economics, although not as completely as Britain.

Growing Interest in Reform

As time went on, more and more people realized that things could not be left entirely alone. Humanitarians—people who work to improve the conditions of others—urged reforms. Ministers preached against what they considered the unchristian selfishness of businesspeople.

Influential writers made people aware of the terrible conditions in mines and factories. The great English writer Charles Dickens used his novels *Dombey and Son* and *Hard Times* to attack selfish business leaders. In *David Copperfield* Dickens described his own wretched boyhood experiences as a worker in a warehouse. Essayists and critics such as Thomas Carlyle and John Ruskin denounced the materialism—the obsession with money and the neglect of spiritual values—of their times.

Many people began to feel that government needed to regulate work hours and set minimal standards for wages and working conditions. These people argued that such laws would not interfere with the natural workings of the economy.

In Great Britain some reformers adopted Jeremy Bentham's ideas. Bentham strongly believed that every act of a society should be judged in terms of its utility, or usefulness. His theory was thus known as **utilitarianism.** A law was useful, and therefore good, said Bentham, if it led to "the greatest good for the greatest number" of people. The "greatest good" meant whatever brought happiness to the most people. Bentham believed that people needed education so they could determine what things were good for them.

Bentham and his followers advocated reform of the prison system and education as well as legal reform. They thought government should create conditions to enable as many people as possible to find happiness.

John Stuart Mill

Philosopher John Stuart Mill, although a believer in laissez-faire, criticized the economic injustices and inequalities of British society. Mill worked to correct the problems associated with industrialization. He thought government should intervene to protect working children and improve housing and factory conditions. Mill's father had been associated with Bentham and had taught his son the principles of utilitarianism.

504

History Through the Arts

LITERATURE

Hard Times

English novelist Charles Dickens (1812–1870) achieved lasting fame for his portrayal of British society during the early Industrial Revolution. The following excerpt describes Coketown, a town spawned by the Industrial Revolution.*

"It was a town of red brick, or of brick that would have been red if the smoke and ashes had allowed it; but as matters stood it was a town of unnatural red and black like the painted face of a savage. It was a town of machinery and tall chimneys, out of which interminable serpents of smoke trailed themselves for ever and ever, and never got uncoiled. It had a black canal in it, and a river that ran purple with ill-smelling dye, and vast piles of buildings full of windows where there was a rattling and a trembling all day long, and where the piston of the steam-engine worked monotonously up and down like the head of an elephant in a state of melancholy madness. It contained several large streets all very like one another, and many small streets still more like one another, inhabited by people equally like one another, who all went in and out at the same hours, with the same sound upon the same pavements, to do the same work, and to whom every day was the same as yesterday and tomorrow, and every year the counterpart of the last and the next. . . .

Seen from a distance . . . Coketown lay shrouded in a haze of its own, which appeared impervious to the sun's rays. You only knew the town was there, because you knew there could have been no such sulky blotch upon the prospect without a town. A blur of soot and smoke, now confusedly tending this way, now that way, now aspiring to the vault of Heaven, now murkily creeping along the earth, as the wind rose and fell, or changed its quarter: a dense formless jumble, with sheets of cross light in it, that showed nothing but masses of darkness:—Coketown in the distance was suggestive of itself, though not a brick of it could be seen. . . .

The streets were hot and dusty on the summer day. . . . Stokers emerged from low underground doorways into factory yards, and sat on steps, and posts, and palings, wiping their swarthy visages, and contemplating coals. The whole town seemed to be frying in oil. There was a stifling smell of hot oil everywhere. The steam-engines shone with it, the dresses of the Hands were soiled with it, the mills throughout their many stories oozed and trickled it."

*Coke is the residue left after distillation of coal or other materials such as petroleum. Coke was often used as fuel.

Mill believed government should work for the well-being of all its citizens. Governments would pass good laws, he said, only if the laws met the interests of all individuals and groups. People would obey laws if they felt they had a part in making the laws. Mills wrote that because governments must represent all citizens, everyone of a certain age, including women, should be allowed to vote. "All human beings have the same interest in good government," he wrote in 1861. "The welfare of all is alike affected by it, and they have equal need of a voice in it to secure their share of its benefits."

In Mill's view individual liberty, which included the liberty to think as one pleased and to express one's views, was a basic human right. Mill believed governments should guarantee that liberty.

Early Reform Laws

Great Britain made the first attempts to improve working conditions through legislation. The earliest laws dealt with the employment of women and children. Working conditions for these two groups, in particular, scandalized many people.

SECTION 4

Closure

Ask: What reforms helped improve the lot of workers? *(Factory Act of 1819, Ten Hours Act, legalization of unions)*

Review Answers

1. *free enterprise:* economic system in which every person is free to go into any business and operate it to the greatest advantage; ***laissez-faire:*** French phrase meaning "leave things alone," applied to a situation where government does not interfere with the operations of business; ***utilitarianism:*** Jeremy Bentham's idea that every act of a society should be judged in terms of its utility; ***strike:*** protest in which an entire group of workers refuses to work; ***union;*** association of workers; ***collective bargaining:*** process of negotiation between union and management over wages, hours, and working conditions, with agreements being written into a contract that would last for a fixed time period

2. *Adam Smith:* author of *The Wealth of Nations* who argued that two natural laws—supply and demand, and competition—regulated the economy; ***Thomas Malthus:*** professor of economics and author who believed that population increase posed the greatest challenge to human progress; ***David Ricardo:*** English business leader and politician who believed supply and

demand determined wages; ***Charles Dickens:*** great English author who used novels to attack selfish business leaders; ***Jeremy Bentham:*** propounded the theory of utilitarianism; ***John Stuart Mill:*** believed in laissez-faire, but believed government should work for the well-being of all
3. ***Lyons:*** southeastern France; ***Silesia:*** Czech-Polish border
4. (a) Smith believed these laws regulated all business and economic activity. In any business, prices and profits would be fixed by the relationship of supply to demand. If an article was scarce and in great demand, people would pay a high price for it. Profits from its sale would rise and people would invest their money to produce more of the scarce article. Soon the supply of the article would exceed the demand for it. Then each manufacturer would face competition. The least efficient businesses would be forced out of business. When such manufacturers stopped producing the article, the supply would decrease and the price would go up again. **(b)** that the free enterprise system was the best for everyone
5. Bentham believed every act of a society should be judged in terms of its utility, or usefulness. A law was useful and good if it led to the "greatest good for the greatest number" of people. He believed people needed education so they could determine

The Factory Act of 1819 illustrates how bad working conditions had become. The act prohibited the employment of children under nine years of age in cotton mills. Children between the ages of 9 and 18 could work no more than 12 hours a day. In 1833 this law was applied to all textile factories. Children between the ages of 9 and 13 could work no more than 9 hours daily, and those between ages 13 and 18 could work no more than 12 hours a day.

Nine years later another law prohibited the employment in mines of all women and girls and of boys under 10. A great advance came in 1847 with the passage of the Ten Hours Act. This law established a 10-hour working day for women and for children under the age of 18 in textile factories. Since it was not profitable to keep the factories running when the women and children were gone, textile factories adopted the 10-hour workday for all workers.

Despite these reform laws, the conditions under which many workers labored remained harsh. Laws often were not strictly enforced, and they did not solve all of the workers' problems. For example, the factory reform laws did not deal with wages. Eventually, workers would achieve improved working conditions through more organization and government legislation.

Worker Strikes

One way that workers could protest poor working conditions and low wages was for a group of them to refuse to work. A group of miners, for example, who believed they were being paid too little for their work would refuse to enter the mines. When an entire group of workers refused to work, they were said to be on **strike.** Workers often made a list of their demands and told the employer they would not work until these demands were met. Employers sometimes agreed to give the strikers what they wanted. At other times the employers either fired all the strikers and hired new workers, or waited until the workers returned to work.

Hundreds of strikes took place in industrial countries during the first half of the 1800s. The strikers usually made two kinds of demands—higher wages for workers and more control over working conditions.

Strikes were usually local events. But in some cases, the strikes spread from one town to another. In the 1830s, for example, shoemakers in one French town after another went out on strike demanding higher wages. Tailors and carpenters went on similar waves of strikes.

Learning from Pictures *These young textile workers in Philadelphia are on strike. In the early 1900s, 1.7 million children under 16 were employed.*

1B, 4H, 4I, a1C, a3A, a3I, a4A, a4G, a4H, a4L

● However, in 1834 six farm laborers from the village of Tolpuddle in Dorset were transported to Australia for seven years for forming a workers' association.

Sometimes strikes began as demands for higher wages but became protests against general working and living conditions of the working class. Strike leaders demanded a reorganization of society to end the differences between rich and poor, employers and workers.

Large protest movements occurred in northern England in 1811 and 1812; in the silk-weaving city of Lyons, France, in 1831 and 1834; and in Silesia, in eastern Europe, in 1844. The protests ended when the governments sent troops to arrest protesting workers.

The Union Movement

In order to strengthen their position, workers sought ways to organize permanently. They felt their efforts would be more successful if they belonged to associations of workers. These associations would collect dues and use the money to pay workers while they were on strike. The associations could plan actions and coordinate the demands of different types of workers in the same factory. These associations came to be called **unions.**

Organizing unions was not easy. English, French, and German law, for instance, regarded workers' associations as illegal. When English workers tried to unite anyway, employers persuaded Parliament to pass laws against them. The Combination Acts of 1799 stated that persons who united with others to demand higher wages, shorter hours, or better working conditions could be imprisoned.

Eventually, however, the workers began to make some progress. In 1825 Parliament passed a law that permitted laborers to meet in order to agree on wages and hours. Finally, in the 1870s Parliament passed laws legalizing strikes. The French government legalized unions in 1884, and the German government followed suit in 1890.

Now that workers had gained the legal rights to form unions and to strike, they had more power to deal with employers. Gradually, factory owners granted unions recognition; they agreed that union representatives could speak and bargain for all the members. Union and management representatives met to negotiate wages, hours, and working conditions. If the bargainers could agree, they wrote their agreements into a contract that would last for a fixed period of time. This process of negotiation, called **collective bargaining,** became accepted only during the 1900s.

SECTION 4 REVIEW

1. **Define** free enterprise, laissez-faire, utilitarianism, strike, union, collective bargaining
2. **Identify** Adam Smith, Thomas Malthus, David Ricardo, Charles Dickens, Jeremy Bentham, John Stuart Mill
3. **Locate** Lyons, Silesia
4. **Evaluating Ideas** **(a)** According to Adam Smith, how did the law of supply and demand and the law of competition work? **(b)** What conclusion did Smith draw from these laws?
5. **Interpreting Ideas** How was the theory of utilitarianism applied to social reform?
6. **Summarizing Ideas** What were the two kinds of demands usually made by strikers?
7. **Analyzing Ideas** Why were unions created?

5 Socialists Proposed Radical Changes

In the economy that resulted from the Industrial Revolution, a few people became enormously rich, but most remained poor. The uneven distribution of wealth disturbed many people. Some reformers became convinced that laissez-faire capitalism was not the best economic system. They argued that laws could not do enough to remedy inequalities. The only way to distribute wealth more evenly, they thought, was to change the ownership and operation of the means of production. The means of production include the capital and equipment used to produce and exchange goods—for example, land, mines, railroads, factories, stores, banks, and machines.

Socialism

Some reformers of the 1800s advocated a political and economic system called **socialism.** In this system the government owns the means of production and operates them for the welfare of all the people.

Socialists wanted to establish an economic system that would abolish the profit motive and competition. They believed that everyone, not just capitalists and owners, had a right to share in the profits of industry.

The early socialists believed that people could live at peace with each other if they lived in small cooperative settlements, owning all the means of

Text continues on page 510.

what things were good for them. Therefore, Bentham and his followers advocated reform of the education system. They also called for reforms in the prison and legal systems. By and large. Bentham and his followers thought government should create conditions to enable as many people as possible to find happiness.

6. Strikers usually demanded higher wages and more control over their working conditions.

7. Workers felt their efforts would be more successful if they formed associations that could plan actions and coordinate the demands of different types of workers in the same factory. These associations came to be called unions.

SECTION 5

Focus/Motivation

On the chalkboard or an overhead projector, draw the following diagram that shows Kark Marx's theory of the stages of the class struggle in history.

TRIBES
Shared Property
Shared Work

↓

SLAVERY
Slaveowners; Slaves

↓

FEUDALISM
Landowners; Serfs

↓

CAPITALISM
Capitalists; Proletariat

↓

COMMUNISM
Classless Society

1B, 1C, 1D, 1E, 4E, 4H, 4I, 5H, a1B, a1C, a1B, a3C, a3G, a3I

Lead the class in a discussion on the diagram, using the following questions as a guide: What similarities do you see between the slavery, feudalism, and capitalism stages? Which previous stage did Marx think communism would resemble? *(tribes)* End the discussion by pointing out that Marx's theories are outlined in Section 5.

Presentation
Interpreting Ideas
(Average/Group)
Have students study the picture of New Harmony on page 510. Then ask students to suggest reasons for the short life of this cooperative community. *(Student answers will include: arguments over sharing of work and profits, people did not like other members of the community, desire to have a choice in goods to buy.)*

PERSPECTIVES: LEGACIES OF THE PAST

Historians consider the Industrial Revolution one of the two most important changes that have taken place in the history of the world. Just as the start of agriculture did 10,000 years ago, the Industrial Revolution marks a turning point in history.

The Industrial Revolution is, of course, a more recent change. Just 200 years ago, people could produce goods only by using their own muscles, the muscles of animals, or unreliable sources of power such as wind (in windmills) or water (in watermills). As a result, production was limited.

The Industrial Revolution made it possible to produce goods in abundance. Now people could use machines driven by fuels such as coal and oil. And the supply of these fuels seemed unlimited.

This remarkable change began at a particular time, the late 1700s, and in a particular country, Great Britain. Why then and why there?

For one thing, after the mid-1700s, the demand for manufactured goods such as cloth grew rapidly and outran the capacity of small, rural clothmakers, who often worked in their own homes. The population grew faster than the supply of goods. Moreover, European countries had established empires in other parts of the world: North and South America, Asia, and Africa. A European country that could produce goods quickly and cheaply had existing markets—both at home and overseas. The demand was there. The problem was how to satisfy it. Here, Britain had an advantage over its European neighbors. Because of advances in agriculture, Britain had better farm machinery and more scientific methods of cultivation than the rest of Europe. This paved the way for industry because fewer farm workers were needed, and more workers were available for other jobs.

The Story Behind the Industrial Revolution

In contrast, Britain was a country with limited government, enthusiasm for change, and a stimulating contact with the outside world. By the 1780s the Industrial Revolution had begun to transform the textile industry, and in 1785 Richard Arkwright applied the technology of the steam engine to textile production.

More than any other invention, the steam engine drove the Industrial Revolution forward by providing a source of power that did not depend upon human muscle or the power of the wind or moving water. The growth in power now available to produce goods was remarkable. An average worker using only muscle can provide one-tenth of one horsepower. Most 18th-century watermills reached five horsepower. But the steam engines of 1800 could produce between 6 and 20 horsepower.

Industrial change spread in two important ways. First, new industries sprang up as people applied the steam engine to new uses. Second, the Industrial Revolution crossed from Britain to other countries. Between 1815 and the 1850s, steam engines, factories, and railroads began to appear in parts of France, Belgium, Holland, Germany, and northern Italy.

After 1870 the Industrial Revolution entered still another phase. It is the period that extends to the present, and some historians call it the "Second Industrial Revolution." Electric power and the internal combustion engine now joined the steam engine. Many of the latest products of industry—the telephone, the automobile, radio, and television—became available to almost all citizens of industrialized countries.

The great industrial transformation that had begun in the special conditions of Great Britain soon encircled the globe.

Already wealthy because of trade with the outside world, Britain could afford to invest in new ventures. In addition, the British government safeguarded property against seizure by the government. Both these facts provided a perfect climate for individual and industrial innovation. Thus, a talented inventor like James Watt, who devised an efficient steam engine, found himself richly rewarded for his work—in a country where such wealth was secure.

Even the other wealthy countries of western Europe could not match Britain's advantages. By 1763 France had lost much of its empire to Britain, and in 1789 a revolution toppled the Bourbon monarchy. The Netherlands, another rich nation, had a small population and lacked Britain's manufacturing experience.

Industrial change was even less probable in non-Western nations such as China. There, society valued stability and continuity over change. The Chinese saw themselves as members of an advanced and self-contained society, one that did not need contact with the outside world. Chinese were even prevented from settling overseas.

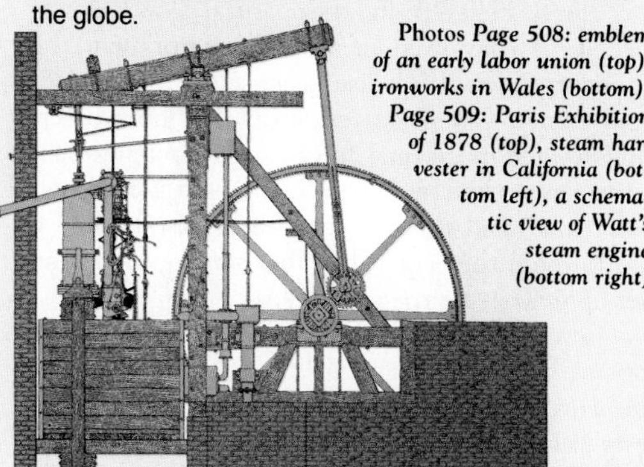

Photos Page 508: emblem of an early labor union (top), ironworks in Wales (bottom); Page 509: Paris Exhibition of 1878 (top), steam harvester in California (bottom left), a schematic view of Watt's steam engine (bottom right)

509

1B, 4H, 4I, a1A, a1C

● **Marx was able to devote all his time to writing because Engels, a wealthy factory owner, provided financial support for him and his family.**

SECTION 5

Closure
Refer students to Karl Marx's statement on society under pure communism — "From each according to his abilities, to each according to his needs." Ask: Do you think any of the present-day Communist societies have achieved this level? Why or why not? *(None have achieved pure communism.)*

Review Answers
1. *socialism:* system in which the government owns the means of production and operates them for the welfare of all people; ***utopian socialist:*** person who attempted to establish model communities; ***bourgeoisie:*** owners of property; ***proletariat:*** working class; ***authoritarian socialism:*** system, established through violent revolution, in which the government owns the means of production and controls economic planning; ***communism:*** another name for authoritarian socialism; ***democratic socialism:*** system, established through peaceful, democratic means, in which the government owns the means of production but individuals retain partial control over economic planning through the election of public officials
2. *Thomas More:* English humanist who described a model community in the book *Utopia;* ***Robert Owen:*** utopian socialist who believed in the natural goodness of people and

Learning from Pictures *Robert Owen's cooperative community of New Harmony, located in southern Indiana, lasted only two years.*

production in common and sharing the products. The socialists tried to work out detailed schemes for model communities and then tried to persuade people to set up the communities. Thomas More, an English humanist, described such a model community in 1516 in his *Utopia.* Thus these early socialists were sometimes called **utopian socialists.**

In Great Britain the most influential utopian socialist was Robert Owen, who lived from 1771 to 1858. As a boy Owen quit school and went to work. By the age of 19 he managed a large cotton mill. Eventually, he became both owner and manager of a large mill in New Lanark, Scotland.

Owen believed in the natural goodness of people. If they lived in a good environment, he thought, they would cease to act selfishly. As a factory owner, Owen felt responsible for his workers and devoted much time and money to making their lives happier and more secure. He built nice homes for them, paid them decent wages, established a store where they could buy inexpensive food, and set up schools for their children.

Owen believed, however, that workers should not be completely dependent on their employers. He encouraged workers to form unions. He also established cooperative communities in both Great Britain and the United States.

The Theories of Karl Marx

Some thinkers grew impatient with early socialism, which they regarded as impractical. Their primary objections, however, concerned capitalism and the Industrial Revolution. Karl Marx, a journalist and the most important of these critics, was born in Prussia in 1818. Marx's radical political views made him unpopular in his own country. Forced to leave, he eventually settled in London, where he lived until his death in 1883.

Marx believed that all the great changes in history came from changes in economic conditions. In 1848, with a fellow German, Friedrich Engels, Marx published the *Communist Manifesto,* a pamphlet outlining his ideas. ●

Marx wrote that human history had moved through several stages. First, people had shared property and worked together in small communities or tribes. Then slavery arose. Some people owned all the property as well as people who were forced to work for them. Feudalism followed slavery, according to Marx. Under feudalism, landowners controlled the lives of serfs, who depended on them for land and food. Capitalism emerged from feudalism and brought with it industrial development. Capitalists owned machinery and tools and employed workers in their factories.

Marx stated that each stage of history involved inequality, and therefore struggle, between those who owned property and those who did not. In the capitalist stage, for example, the struggle existed between the owners, or **bourgeoisie** (boorzh • wah • ZEE), and the working class, or **proletariat** (proh • luh • TAYR • ee • uht).

Marx argued that all wealth is created by labor. Under capitalism, he said, labor receives only a small fraction of the wealth it creates. Most of the wealth goes to the owners in the form of profits, which Marx called surplus value. As a result of this unequal distribution of wealth, the capitalist system necessarily suffered from increasingly severe depressions because working people lacked money to buy the products manufactured in the factories. He thought the time would soon come when capitalist society would divide into two classes—a few capitalists and a vast mass of workers, or proletarians. The proletarians, concentrated in cities, would suffer poverty and unemployment.

In these circumstances the proletarians in the most advanced and industrialized nations would

1B, 4H, 4I, a1A, a1C, a4A, a4J, a4K, a4L

● Marx was somewhat bemused by the way his ideas were adopted by other socialists. A few months before his death he told Engels, "All I know is that I am not a Marxist!"

unite, seize power by force in a revolution, and establish socialism. Since many people would not readily accept socialism, initially the workers would have to control the government. Marx referred to this phase as the "dictatorship of the proletariat." After a period of education, people would become experienced in working together cooperatively. Force would no longer be needed, and the state would "wither away." This last stage, characterized by a truly classless society, Marx called *pure communism*.

Marx believed that pure communism was the inevitable outcome of human history. Each person would contribute what he or she could and would receive what he or she needed. Marx said, "From each according to his abilities, to each according to his needs."

In Marx's time the terms *communism* and *socialism* were used in many different ways. To Marx and Engels, a communist was one who believed that people could live cooperatively without being forced to do so.

Marx called his variety of socialism "scientific socialism" because he thought he was describing objective laws of historical development—laws that would work inevitably. Marx published many of his ideas in *Das Kapital* (German for "capital"), a book that analyzed capitalism in detail.

Variations of Marxist Socialism

In the mid-1800s socialists began forming political parties to put their ideas into practice. The ideas of Marx and Engels influenced many of these parties. ● Marxist, or radical, socialists generally believed in the necessity of revolution to overthrow the capitalist system. They wanted to establish a system in which the government owns almost all the means of production and controls economic planning. Today we call this economic and political system—which ignores basic human rights—**authoritarian socialism,** or **communism.**

Another group of socialists, though influenced by Marx, believed that socialism could develop gradually through education and democratic forms of government. These moderate socialists believed that when enough people became educated about socialism, they would elect socialist representatives to their government. Then the government would take over the means of production peacefully. The owners would be paid for their property, and the

Learning from Pictures *Karl Marx did not foresee how collective bargaining would better working conditions, avoiding the dictatorship of the proletariat.*

government would operate the means of production in the interest of all the people. Today we call this type of socialism **democratic socialism.** Under democratic socialism, unlike under authoritarian socialism, the people retain basic human rights and partial control over economic planning through the election of government officials. Individuals may own private property, but the government controls at least some of the means of production.

Marx believed that workers had to unite in order to fight capitalism successfully. In 1864 he helped found the International Workingmen's Association, called the First International. This organization disbanded in 1876. A Second International was formed in 1889, after Marx's death. Torn by disagreements between moderate and radical socialists, it survived only into the early 1900s. Elsewhere, particularly in Russia, Marx's ideas would have profound effects.

SECTION 5 REVIEW

1. **Define** socialism, utopian socialist, bourgeoisie, proletariat, authoritarian socialism, communism, democratic socialism
2. **Identify** Thomas More, Robert Owen, Karl Marx
3. **Sequencing Ideas** Describe the stages of history, according to Marx, that would lead to pure communism.
4. **Contrasting Ideas** How do authoritarian socialism and democratic socialism differ?

established a number of cooperative communities in Great Britain and the United States; ***Karl Marx:*** journalist, co-author of the *Communist Manifesto,* and founder of communism
3. First there had been small communities in which people shared property and work. Then came a number of stages that involved class struggles. Slavery arose first, followed by feudalism. Capitalism then emerged from feudalism. Marx thought the time would come when the working class would revolt and establish a dictatorship of the proletariat. After a period of education, people would be able to work together cooperatively and the state would "wither away." This last stage, characterized by a truly classless society, would constitute pure communism.
4. Authoritarian socialism, or communism, is supported by radical socialists. They want to establish through violent revolution a system in which the government owns almost all of the means of production and controls economic planning. Moderate socialists support democratic socialism. Under this system, which is attained through democratic means, the people retain basic human rights and partial control over economic planning through the election of government officials.

Reviewing Important Terms
1. Industrial Revolution; **2.** factors of production; **3.** crop rotation; **4.** Automation; **5.** Bessemer process; **6.** depression; **7.** strike; **8.** laissez-faire; **9.** Capitalism; **10.** monopoly; **11.** corporation

Developing Critical Thinking Skills
1. For centuries workers had labored in small shops and controlled the pace of their work. With the Industrial Revolution, workers labored in factories for wages.
2. (a) She viewed them as terrible. **(b)** Browning describes how the children have to drag their burdens through the coal-dark mines, or how they drive machines all day long in factories. **(c)** Laws were passed regulating the age at which children could start work and the hours that they could work.
3. (a) Mass-production methods could not be used by small companies nor could small companies afford to buy the machinery necessary for large-scale production; corporations could. **(b)** Workers protested long hours, low wages, and poor working conditions in the factories brought about by technology. They sought to strengthen their position by organizing unions.
4. Many working-class women who had previously worked at home began to work in factories. However, they were given jobs that required little skill and were paid low wages. Married middle-class women were expected to stay home, rear children, and enjoy the luxuries industrialization produced. Single middle-class women had greater job opportunity than in the

1B, 1D, 4H, 4I, a1A, a1C, a4A, a4F, a4M

Reteaching
Have students review the Chapter Summary and the appropriate section and questions in the Unit Synthesis. Discuss the concepts until students demonstrate a clear understanding of the material.

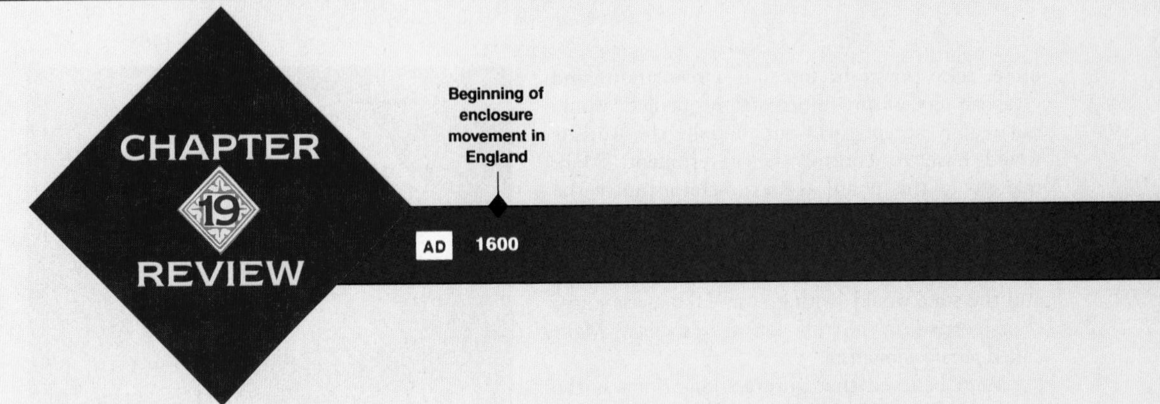

Chapter Summary

The following list contains the key concepts you have learned about the Industrial Revolution and the resulting changes in political and economic thought.

1. The Industrial Revolution–changes brought about by the introduction of power-driven machinery–began in Great Britain. In time the Industrial Revolution transformed the world.
2. The Industrial Revolution was preceded by an agricultural revolution.
3. The replacement of waterpower by steam power was basic to the Industrial Revolution. Almost as important was the development of the Bessemer process, a new method of making steel, that made steel readily available to the newly founded industries.
4. Transportation improved with better roads, networks of canals and railroads, and the use of steam power in ships. The wireless telegraph made rapid communication possible.
5. By gathering workers together in factories, the Industrial Revolution brought an end to the traditional practices of artisans who had worked in their homes or in small shops.
6. Factory workers became dependent on wages and no longer controlled the pace of their work because they had to do what they were told.
7. Living and working conditions were often poor during the early Industrial Revolution.
8. A series of innovations in business practices accompanied the Industrial Revolution. Mass production–based on the division of labor, interchangeable parts, and the assembly line–transformed several industries and permitted the growth of enormous corporations.
9. Workers began to protest harsh working conditions and low wages. The first labor unions were organized to seek improvements in working conditions and to obtain higher wages.
10. Socialists like Karl Marx believed that a more fundamental transformation of politics and society was necessary.

On a separate sheet of paper, complete the following review exercises.

Reviewing Important Terms

Supply the term that correctly completes each sentence.

1. The changes industrial technology brought about affected manufacturing so deeply that they are referred to as the ______ ______.
2. The basic resources necessary for industrialization (land, labor, and capital) are called the ______ ______ ______.
3. Alternating crops to replenish nutrients in the soil is called ______ ______.
4. ______ is the use of automatic machinery to increase production.
5. The ______ ______ involved burning impurities such as carbon out of iron with a blast of air forced through molten metal.
6. A ______ occurs at the lowest point in the business cycle.
7. A ______ occurs when a group of workers refuses to work.
8. The idea that government should not interfere with the operations of business is called ______.
9. ______ is an economic system in which individuals control the factors of production.
10. A ______ is the control of the total production or sale of a good or service by a single firm.
11. A ______ is a business organization in which individuals buy shares of stock, elect directors to decide policies and hire managers, and receive dividends according to the number of shares they own.

Developing Critical Thinking Skills

1. **Determining Cause and Effect** How did the Industrial Revolution change the relationship between workers and employers that had existed during the Middle Ages?
2. **Using Primary Sources** Laws regulating child labor did not exist in the 1700s. For example, during the early years of the Industrial Revolution, it was common for five-year-old children to work in damp, dark coal mines or poorly ventilated textile mills for as long as 14 hours a day. The lines below, from a poem by Elizabeth Barrett Browning, describe the life of working-class children.

512

1A, a4A, a4B, a4C, a4D, a4E, a4F, a4G, a4H, a4I, a4J, a4K, a4L, a4M

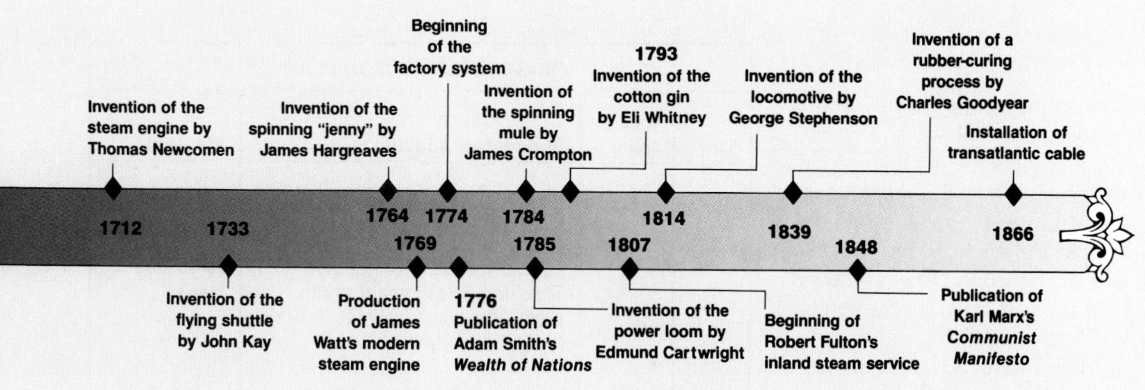

> 'For oh,' say the children, 'We are weary,
> and we cannot run or leap;
> For all day, we drag our burden tiring
> Through the coal-dark underground;
> Or all day, we drive the wheels of iron
> In the factories, round and round.'

(a) How did Browning view working conditions in Great Britain? **(b)** What evidence in the poem supports your answer? **(c)** Based on information in this chapter, how were working conditions gradually improved?

3. **Relating Ideas** Why might each of the following be considered a result of advances in technology? **(a)** corporations **(b)** unions
4. **Analyzing Ideas** How did industrialization affect the lives of women?
5. **Summarizing Ideas** **(a)** What problems did workers face during the Industrial Revolution? **(b)** What problems did employers encounter?
6. **Understanding Ideas** **(a)** Why did Adam Smith's ideas appeal to industrialists? **(b)** Why did industrialists oppose the ideas of Karl Marx?

Relating Geography to History

Using information in this chapter, write a short essay on the relationship between geography and the Industrial Revolution. For example, how might working conditions have been different if the geography of Great Britain and the United States had not been suited to growing cotton or producing coal?

Relating Past to Present

1. During the Industrial Revolution, many countries held exhibitions to showcase the latest technological developments. Investigate some of the important technological achievements of the 1980s. Use this information to design a poster for a similar exposition in the near future.
2. Use resources in your school or public library to construct a chart showing how long it took to travel from New York to California in 1850, 1900, 1930, and today. Your chart should include what form of transportation people used in each of the years listed.

Applying History Study Skills

Before completing this activity, review Building History Study Skills on page 503.

In the following excerpt from *The Stages of Economic Growth,* W. W. Rostow suggests why the Industrial Revolution began in England. Read the excerpt. Then answer the questions that follow.

> Now why Britain? Why not France? . . .
> The French . . . were too rough with their Protestants. They were politically and socially too inflexible, caught up . . . in . . . a caste society. The best minds and spirits of eighteenth-century France . . . had to think about political, social and religious revolution rather than economic revolution. Moreover the French were committed heavily to ground warfare in Europe; and they cheated on shipping and naval strength . . . when ships mattered greatly. . . .
> Britain alone was in a position to weave together cotton manufacture, coal and iron technology, the steam-engine, and ample foreign trade to pull it off.

1. What question is Rostow posing?
2. What are the underlying causes for France's inability to industrialize?
3. What are the underlying causes for Britain's industrializing first?

Investigating Further

1. **Practicing Map Skills** By the 1850s iron and coal had become the two major raw materials of modern industry. Using an atlas, draw an outline map of the world showing the global distribution of these resources today.
2. **Relating Literature to History** Read the chapter entitled "No Way Out" in *Hard Times* by Charles Dickens. As you read, consider the differences between the worker (or "hand") and the owner of the factory. **(a)** How did Dickens portray industrial society in the 1800s? **(b)** What aspects of that society did he seem to be criticizing? **(c)** Why would Dickens be accurate in his description?

the past, especially in such fields as public health care and teaching.
5. (a) Workers faced long hours, low wages, and poor working conditions in the factories. **(b)** Employers faced machine breaking, strikes, and large-scale protest movements. They also faced fierce competition, possible loss of capital investment, and government regulation.
6. (a) Adam Smith believed in free enterprise, which allowed industrialists to operate their businesses free of government regulations. **(b)** They had no choice but to oppose Marx because his ideas meant the end of their ownership of the means of production.

Relating Geography to History
Answers will vary. However, students should mention the relationship between natural resources and industry.

Relating Past to Present
1. Posters might include pictures of computers, satellites, sports cars, or jets.
2. Answers will vary. Charts should illustrate the reduction in travel time in the modern age.

Applying History Study Skills
1. Rostow posed the question why the Industrial Revolution began in Great Britain.
2. According to Rostow, the French were too rough with their religious minorities and too inflexible politically and socially. They also neglected their navy.
3. Britain alone was in the situation of having all the necessary factors of production in the correct balance.

513

CHAPTER (pages 514–541)

20 The Industrial Age Revolutionized Science and Culture

(1800–1928)

CHAPTER OVERVIEW

In the 1800s technological innovation continued, especially in the areas of communications and transportation. Science and art reflected the impact of this technology and the sense of progress that it engendered. Developments in the physical sciences centered on the atomic theory, and the theories of Einstein revolutionized the study of matter and energy. In the biological sciences, research expanded and increased knowledge of the cell theory. Darwin's theory of evolution had great impact, as did the new science of genetics, founded by Mendel.

The advances in science were accompanied by advances in medicine that improved health and extended human life. New drugs were developed, and researchers discovered the importance of a balanced diet.

The social sciences — political science, economics, and history — became more scientific. New fields of study included anthropology and sociology. In psychology two approaches were developed to study the human mind. Behaviorism, based on Pavlov's work, stressed observable, measurable responses; Freud explored the unconscious and developed psychoanalysis.

The arts reflected the changes in society. Artists of the romantic movement emphasized emotion and love of nature. In the mid-1800s writers and artists began to portray life realistically. Later, impressionist painters sought to capture the impressions of a fleeting moment. By the close of the 1800s, painters and sculptors were experimenting with intensely individualistic art forms.

Among the many social changes that occurred during this period were the rapid growth of urban populations and the gradual acceptance of universal public education. Education for women, however, was limited to the secondary and college levels. The spread of education increased interest in public issues and expanded the demand for newspapers, magazines, and books.

SUGGESTED LESSON PLAN

Day	Objectives	Suggested Activities	Materials
1	U3–4,* C1–2	Introducing the Chapter (pages 514–15) Section 1 (pages 515–18), Focus/Motivation (page 515), Presentation (page 515), Closure (page 518), Suggested Teaching Strategies, Enrichment Activity, Daily Quiz, Suggested Assignments (page 513B)	ATE, Pupil's Edition, Teacher's Resource-Bank™
2	U3, C3–4	Section 2 (pages 518–24), Focus/Motivation (page 519), Presentation (page 520), Closure (page 523), Suggested Teaching Strategies, Enrichment Activities, Daily Quiz, Suggested Assignments (page 513C)	ATE, Pupil's Edition, Teacher's Resource-Bank™
3	U3, C5–6	Section 3 (pages 524–29), Focus/Motivation (page 525), Presentation (page 525), Closure (page 528), Suggested Teaching Strategies, Enrichment Activities, Daily Quiz, Suggested Assignments (page 513D)	ATE, Pupil's Edition, Teacher's Resource-Bank™
4	U3, C7–8	Section 4 (pages 529–34), Focus/Motivation (page 529), Presentation (page 530), Closure (page 534), Suggested Teaching Strategies, Enrichment Activities, Daily Quiz, Suggested Assignments (page 513E)	ATE, Pupil's Edition, Teacher's Resource-Bank™
5	U4, C9	Section 5 (pages 534–39), Focus/Motivation (page 535), Presentation (page 536), Closure (page 538), Suggested Teaching Strategies, Enrichment Activities, Daily Quiz, Suggested Assignments (page 513D)	ATE, Pupil's Edition, Teacher's Resource-Bank™
6	U3–4 C1–9	Chapter 20 Form A Test, Reteaching Worksheet, Chapter 20 Form B Test	Teacher's Resource-Bank™ or Workbook and Test Booklet

*C refers to applicable Chapter Objective, U refers to applicable Unit Goal.

BOOKS FOR THE TEACHER

Eissler, K. R. *Sigmund Freud: His Life in Pictures and Words.* Harcourt Brace Jovanovich. Offers a comprehensive study of the life of Freud.

Ralling, Christopher. *The Voyage of Charles Darwin.* Mayflower

Books. Condenses Darwin's autobiographical writings on his voyage to the Galapagos Islands.

Talmon, J. L. *Romanticism and Revolt: Europe 1815–1848.* Harcourt Brace Jovanovich. Studies the romantic movement and its relationship with the revolutions of the period.

Troyat, Henri. *Tolstoy.* Doubleday. Provides an engrossing portrait of the great novelist.

BOOKS FOR THE STUDENT

Berger, Melvin. *Famous Men of Modern Biology.* T. Y. Crowell. Contains chapters on Pasteur, Darwin, and Mendel.

Chester, Michael. *Relativity.* W. W. Norton. Explains relativity clearly and concisely for young readers; includes graphs and charts.

Karp, Walter. *Charles Darwin and Origin of Species.* American Heritage. Offers an explanation of Darwin's theories suitable for high school students; includes illustrations.

Neimark, Anne E. *Sigmund Freud: The World Within.* Harcourt Brace Jovanovich. Offers a biography of Freud written in the form of a novel.

MULTIMEDIA MATERIALS

Fight Against Microbes (mp. 29 min.), International. Presents the contributions of Jenner, Pasteur, Koch, Lister, Fleming, and others.

Freud: The Hidden Nature of Man (mp. 29 min.), Learning Corp. Dramatizes Freud's concept of the human personality.

Impressionism in Art and Music (2 fs), Educational Audio-Visual. Explores parallels between impressionist art and music.

Romanticism in Art and Music (mp. 26 min.), McGraw-Hill. Portrays European cultural life in the first half of the 1800s.

Section (pages 515–518)

1 Advances Continued in Technology and Communication

SECTION OVERVIEW

Developments in communications begun during the Industrial Revolution continued in the late 1800s. Most notable among these were the telephone and the wireless telegraph. Discoveries by Michael Faraday and technological applications developed by Thomas Edison made electricity a viable source of power. Also, the development of the internal-combustion engine soon revolutionized transportation.

SUGGESTED TEACHING STRATEGIES

1. **Understanding Relationships (Basic)** On the chalkboard or an overhead projector, write the following two lists. Then have students arrange the developments or inventions in each group in the order that they became important.

Communications

(3) Marconi invented instruments for sending and receiving radio waves.
(2) Heinrich Hertz proved that electromagnetic waves existed.
(4) Marconi sent the first wireless message across the Atlantic Ocean.
(1) James Clerk Maxwell asserted the existence of invisible waves that travel through space at the speed of light.

Electricity

(2) Faraday generated electricity through the use of magnets.
(1) Ampère showed how electricity produced magnetism.
(4) Edison developed a central powerhouse and invented a transmission system.
(3) The dynamo, or electric generator, was developed.

2. **Presenting a Report (Average/Group)** Have students research, prepare, and present oral or written reports on one of the inventors or inventions mentioned in this section. Useful sources of information on this subject include: Ruby L. Radford's *Inventors in Industry* (Julian Messner); American Heritage, eds., *Men of Science and Invention* (American Heritage); Anthony Feldman and Peter Ford's *Scientists and Inventors* (Facts on File); Donald Clarke's *Great Inventors and Discoveries* (Marshall Cavendish); Mitchell Wilson's *American Science and Invention* (Simon and Schuster); and Irmingarde Eberly's *Famous Inventors for Young People* (Dodd, Mead).

ENRICHMENT ACTIVITY

Illustrating Ideas (Average/Group) Have students work in small groups to make collages depicting the development of one of the following: telephone, telegraph, electricity, automobile, airplane. Sources for ideas for illustrations include: Valerie Moolman's *The Road to Kitty Hawk* (Time-Life); Phil Drackett, ed., *The Encyclopedia of the Motorcar* (Crown); and Ralph Stein's *The Treasury of the Automobile* (Golden Press). Have students display their collages on the bulletin board.

DAILY QUIZ

To assess student understanding of Section 1, give the class the following quiz. (Each item is worth 10 points.)

1. (T or F) By the 1900s most people thought of technology and progress as the same thing. *(T)*
2. Who patented the telephone in 1876? *(Alexander Graham Bell)*
3. (T or F) James Clerk Maxwell proved the existence of electromagnetic waves by transmitting and receiving them. *(F)*
4. Who developed the wireless telegraph? *(Guglielmo Marconi)*
5. (T or F) Michael Faraday disproved the work of Andre Ampère when he generated an electric current through the use of magnets. *(F)*
6. (T or F) Waterfalls, such as Niagara Falls, were used to generate electricity. *(T)*
7. Why was the electric motor not a very useful means of moving vehicles? *(because it had to be connected to its power supply)*

8. In this engine the burning of fuel takes place in a closed cylinder. *(internal-combustion engine)*
9. Who built the first successful gasoline-driven automobile in the United States? *(Charles and Frank Duryea)*
10. Who first successfully flew an airplane in powered, sustained, and controlled flight? *(Orville and Wilbur Wright)*

SUGGESTED ASSIGNMENTS

1. **Identifying Ideas (Basic)** Point out that during his life, Thomas Edison received close to 1,300 patents for various inventions and technological developments — almost one patent for every three weeks of his life. Have students use encyclopedias to identify some of Edison's technological innovations. Then ask them to make a list of those innovations that have had an impact on their lives. *(Student answers probably will include: phonograph, movie projector, light bulb, electric power station.)*
2. **Writing a Report (Challenging)** Interested students might like to do further research for a written report on the great expositions where scientific and technological developments are displayed for the public. Useful sources of information on this subject include: John Allwood's *The Great Expositions* (Macmillan) and Robert W. Rydell's *All the World's a Fair* (University of Chicago Press). Have students present their reports to the rest of the class.

Section (pages 518–524)

2 Advances in Science and Medicine Helped Improve Human Life

SECTION OVERVIEW

The physical and biological sciences developed rapidly during the 1800s and early 1900s. Such scientists as Roentgen, the Curies, Planck, and Einstein contributed to an understanding of the atom, matter, and energy. In the biological sciences, research in cell theory was carried on by several scientists. And the new science of genetics answered many questions about inheritance.

Advances in medicine and surgery lengthened life and contributed to an increase in population. The isolation of germs and improved sanitation reduced the spread of disease. Improvements in diet and food storage also contributed to a longer life span.

SUGGESTED TEACHING STRATEGIES

1. **Preteaching Vocabulary (Basic)** You may wish to preteach the following important vocabulary terms: physical sciences *(page 518)*; radioactivity, quantum theory, special theory of relativity *(page 520)*; biological sciences, evolution *(page 521)*; genetics *(page 522)*; pasteurization *(page 523)*. Ask: What is the difference between the physical and the biological sciences? *(Physical sciences deal with inanimate objects; biological sciences deal with animate creatures.)*
2. **Writing Biographical Sketches (Average/Group)** Organize the class into pairs. Each pair is to select a scientist mentioned in the section and prepare a biographical sketch. One of the two students should concentrate on the life and background of the scientist, the other on the scientist's work and its influence. Useful sources of information include: Louis Untermeyer's *Makers of the Modern Mind* (Simon and Schuster) and Isaac Asimov's *Asimov's Biographical Encyclopedia of Science and Technology* (Doubleday). Have the pairs of students present their biographical sketches, in oral or written form, to the rest of the class.

ENRICHMENT ACTIVITIES

1. **Analyzing Ideas (Challenging)** In recent years magazines and newspapers have had numerous articles on topics related to genetics. Have students do further reading on DNA, gene splicing, or other topics in genetics research. They should consult the *Readers' Guide to Periodical Literature* for sources. When students have completed their reading, hold a discussion on the benefits and dangers of recent experiments in the area of genetics.
2. **Illustrating Ideas (Average/Group)** Organize the class into groups to make posters on nutrition and diet for display on the bulletin board. Some students might make posters of today's ideas about a balanced meal or about foods to avoid, such as junk food. Students might consult a nutritionist, the local hospital, and/or the home economics department. Other students might make posters illustrating nineteenth-century knowledge of the value of proper nutrition.

DAILY QUIZ

To assess student understanding of Section 2, give the class the following quiz. (Each item is worth 10 points.)

1. (T or F) The physical sciences deal with the inanimate, or nonliving, aspects of nature. *(T)*
2. Russian chemist Dimitri Mendeleyev developed the first workable classification of the elements, called the ________ ________. *(Periodic Table)*
3. ________ ________ developed the equation $E=mc^2$ and formulated the special theory of relativity. *(Albert Einstein)*
4. ________ ________ developed the theory of natural selection and wrote *The Origin of Species*. *(Charles Darwin)*
5. (T or F) Darwin's theories were not particularly controversial because the work of Lamarck, which had covered similar ground, had been readily accepted by the general public. *(F)*
6. (T or F) Pasteur developed the germ theory of disease, showing that harmful bacteria called germs cause illness. *(T)*
7. What two anesthetics were first used in the 1840s? *(ether and chloroform)*
8. Which German physician isolated the germ that causes tuberculosis and identified the germ responsible for Asiatic cholera? *(Robert Koch)*
9. This drug, made available in the 1890s, reduced pain and fever. *(aspirin)*
10. ________ ________ discovered penicillin in 1928. *(Alexander Fleming)*

SUGGESTED ASSIGNMENTS

1. **Making Comparisons (Challenging)** Have students research the death rate, birth rate and average life span of Americans. They should compare these figures with statistics from a country in Asia, Africa, or South America. Useful sources for such information include: *Statistical Abstract of the United States* (Department of Commerce), *Facts on File,* and the *Readers' Guide to Periodical Literature.* Students also may contact an insurance company for information. Students should report their findings to the class.
2. **Understanding Relationships (Average/Group)** Some of the science fiction plots of writers such as Jules Verne and H.G. Wells have since become reality. Several students might like to review books by these authors and prepare oral reports on the devices described, such as submarines, rockets, and balloons. Another group of students might like to review works of modern science fiction writers and report on the predictions about space travel.
3. **Profile Worksheet (Basic)** Have students complete Profile Worksheet 20 in the TEACHER'S RESOURCEBANK ™

Section (pages 524–529)

3 The Population Grew and Became More Mobile

SECTION OVERVIEW

During the 1800s Western society underwent many changes. There was a huge population increase and cities grew rapidly, creating sanitation and public order problems. As sports and cultural activities developed, people of all classes began to find new ways to spend their leisure time.

SUGGESTED TEACHING STRATEGIES

1. **Preteaching Vocabulary (Basic)** You may wish to preteach the following important vocabulary term: emigration *(page 525).* Ask students why people choose to emigrate.
2. **Organizing Information (Basic)** Have students list in their notebooks the improvements in diet and food storage that contributed to the increase in life expectancy during the late 1800s and early 1900s. Ask students to compare their lists with those of other members of the class.

ENRICHMENT ACTIVITIES

1. **Creating a Bulletin Board Display (Average/Group)** You might have students work in small groups to make bulletin board displays of leisure activities of the 1800s and of today. Then use the displays as a starting point for a discussion on the similarities and differences between activities in the two periods. Students should refer to textbook pages 526–529 for information on leisure activities of the 1800s. Other useful sources of information include: S. C. Burchell's *Age of Progress* (Time-Life) and Christopher Hibbert's *Daily Life in Victorian England* (American Heritage).
2. **Writing a Letter (Average/Group)** Have students imagine they are nineteenth century city-dwellers. Ask them to write a letter to a friend in the country. The letters should describe life in the city, and should include such topics as opportunities for work and leisure activities. Call upon students to read their letters to the rest of the class. Use the lists as the basis for a class discussion of city life at that time.

DAILY QUIZ

To assess student understanding of Section 3, give the class the following quiz. (Each item is worth 10 points.)

1. Life expectancy increased after 1850 because more food became available and more was known about the relationship between diet and ________. *(health)*
2. Many people emigrated to the United States to escape economic hardship or to avoid ________ and ________. *(oppression, discrimination)*
3. What was the greatest spur to the growth of cities? *(the factory system)*
4. (T or F) Technological developments, such as iron pipes, toilets, and water systems, led to improvements in sanitation in urban areas in the late 1800s. *(T)*
5. (T or F) In 1829 Sir Robert Peel organized a permanent police force for London. *(T)*
6. (T or F) Suburbs developed in the late 1800s despite poor public transportation systems. *(F)*
7. What was one of the first games to change from an informal community activity to a professional spectator sport in Great Britain? *(football, or soccer)*
8. (T or F) At the end of the nineteenth century, the church still was the primary source of cultural activities in most of the large cities. *(F)*
9. The ________ ________ in London contained a large book collection and was open for public use. *(British Museum* or *British Library)*
10. This amusement park opened in Brooklyn, New York, in 1895. *(Coney Island)*

SUGGESTED ASSIGNMENTS

1. **Critical Thinking Worksheet (Basic)** Have students complete Critical Thinking Worksheet 44, in the TEACHER'S RESOURCEBANK™.
2. **Geography Supplement (Basic)** Have students complete the Geography Fact Sheet titled *Urbanization Around the World* in the Geography Supplement of the TEACHER'S RESOURCEBANK™.
3. **Geography Supplement (Basic)** Have students complete the Geography Application Sheet titled *Manchester: The Growth of an Industrial Giant* in the Geography Supplement of the TEACHER'S RESOURCEBANK™.

Section (pages 529–534)

4 Interest in the Social Sciences and Education Increased

SECTION OVERVIEW

During the 1800s, the scientific method of inquiry was applied to the study of people and society. Historians established stricter methods for their work, emphasized original sources, and used their writings to encourage nationalism. Two new social sciences — anthropology and sociology — emerged. In psychology, Pavlov discovered the conditioned reflex while Freud introduced the idea of the unconscious and the process of psychoanalysis.

After 1870, governments in western Europe and the United States began to pass laws making some form of education universal and compulsory. However, education for girls and women was still limited. The spread of education contributed to increasing literacy. Newspapers became especially important, and people became better informed about the issues and events that affected their lives.

SUGGESTED TEACHING STRATEGIES

1. **Preteaching Vocabulary (Basic)** You may wish to preteach the following important vocabulary terms: social sciences *(page 529)*; social Darwinism *(page 531)*; psychoanalysis *(page 532)*. Ask the students what approaches applied to the natural sciences were also applied to the social sciences in the 1800s.
2. **Relating Past to Present (Challenging)** Have students find statistics on educational levels achieved by women in the United States. Useful sources of information include: *Statistical Abstract of the United States* (Department of Commerce); *World Almanac and Book of Facts* (Newspaper Enterprise Associates); and *Facts on File*. Select certain students to report their findings to the rest of the class.

ENRICHMENT ACTIVITIES

1. **Interviewing (Challenging)** Select two students, one to play Ivan Pavlov, the other to play Sigmund Freud. Have the rest of the class stage an interview with Pavlov and Freud, asking some of the following questions: What have you learned about human behavior? What information led you to these conclusions? How do you think your ideas can help people? For background information, have students consult encyclopedias and Richard Attignaneis's *Freud for Beginners* (Pantheon).
2. **Holding a Panel Discussion (Challenging)** Have four students assume the roles of an industrialist, a government official, an army officer, and a worker of the 1800s. Each person is to give reasons for supporting free public education. Have other members of the class participate by questioning the speakers.

DAILY QUIZ

To assess student understanding of Section 4, give the class the following quiz. (Each item is worth 10 points.)

1. (T or F) During the 1800s history became based more and more on the study of original documents and the careful organization of facts. *(T)*
2. (T or F) James George Frazer first used the term *Kultur* to describe the set of beliefs and behaviors that all people in a society share. *(F)*
3. (T or F) Sociologist Herbert Spencer applied Darwin's theories to the study of human communities. *(T)*
4. _______ _______ discovered the conditioned reflex. *(Ivan Pavlov)*
5. Who developed the process of psychoanalysis? *(Sigmund Freud)*
6. (T or F) By 1800, most western European countries had established some form of universal public schooling. *(F)*
7. (T or F) For the most part, children of the lower classes attended school only as long as the law required. *(T)*
8. (T or F) In most schools of the late 1800s, boys and girls studied the same subjects. *(F)*
9. As more and more people were able to read, daily _______ became especially popular in the late 1800s. *(newspapers)*
10. New technology, such as the _______, which set type by machine rather than by hand, and the electric-powered _______ _______, improved the printing process. *(linotype, rotary press)*

SUGGESTED ASSIGNMENTS

1. **Critical Thinking Worksheet (Basic)** Have students complete Critical Thinking Worksheet 45, in the TEACHER'S RESOURCEBANK™.
2. **Writing an Editorial (Average/Group)** Have students write an editorial for a newspaper in the 1800s advocating the higher education of women or free compulsory education. Have students read their editorials to the rest of the class. Then select members of the class to present nineteenth-century arguments against these two positions.

Section (pages 534–539)

5 Literature, Music, and Art Reflected the Spirit of the Times

SECTION OVERVIEW

Literature, art, and music reflected the social and economic developments of the industrial age. The romantic movement stressed emotion, love of nature, and interest in the past. In the mid-1800s writers and artists turned to realism, providing a more accurate picture of life. By the end of the 1800s, musicians and artists were experimenting freely with many different approaches.

SUGGESTED TEACHING STRATEGIES

1. **Preteaching Vocabulary (Basic)** You may wish to preteach the following important vocabulary terms: romantic movement,

romanticism *(page 534)*; realism *(page 536)*; regionalism, naturalist, impressionist *(page 538)*. Ask students to describe the difference between romanticism and realism.

*2. **Interpreting Visuals: Using Art as a Historical Document (Basic)** To reinforce the skill lesson presented on page 537, have the students apply the steps taught in the lesson to the illustrations on pages 535, 538, and 539.

ENRICHMENT ACTIVITIES

1. **Preparing Oral Reports (Average/Group)** Have students work in small groups to prepare oral reports on literary, musical, and artistic movements of the 1800s. Each group is to select a theme—romantic painters, for example—and prepare short biographies and lists of accomplishments for about five artists. Illustrations, slides, posters, or records should be included in the presentations. Students might consult the *Library of Art* series (Time-Life) and the art series by Crown Publishers. Other useful sources of information include: David Jacobs's *Beethoven* (American Heritage); Pierre Courthion's *Manet* (Abrams); Meyer Schapiro's *Van Gogh* (Abrams); Douglas Cooper's *Toulouse-Lautrec* (Abrams); and Eric Blom, ed., *Grove's Dictionary of Music and Musicians* (St. Martin's).
2. **Analyzing Ideas (Average/Group)** Play for the class a representative orchestral piece from the classical period, such as Mozart's *Eine Kleine Nachtmusik,* and a piece from the romantic period, such as Tchaikovsky's *Piano Concerto in B-Flat Minor.* Ask students to identify which piece is classical and which is romantic. Have students describe the differences between the two compositions. Help them by asking the following questions: How do the pieces differ in terms of dynamics (loud and soft)? In regularity of tempo? In apparent size of orchestra? In emotions expressed? End the discussion by asking the students the following question: What effects were romantic composers trying to achieve?

DAILY QUIZ

To assess student understanding of Section 5, give the class the following quiz. (Each item is worth 10 points.)

1. (T or F) Romantic writers emphasized reason and showed things as they really were. *(F)*
2. (T or F) Some romantic authors, such as Sir Walter Scott, Victor Hugo, and Alexander Dumas, told stories set in the medieval period. *(T)*
3. (T or F) James Fenimore Cooper and Washington Irving were American romantic authors. *(T)*
4. What German romantic composer's *Pastoral Symphony* captured the atmosphere of the countryside? *(Beethoven)*
5. Romantic composers Schubert and Schumann are especially remembered for their great songs, or ______. *(lieder)*
6. (T or F) Romanticism in architecture expressed itself in the Romanesque revival of the mid-1800s. *(F)*
7. (T or F) In the United States, realism took the form of regionalism, or the portrayal of everyday life in different parts of the country. *(T)*
8. Toward the end of the 1800s, a group of writers called ______ carried realism further, describing ugly and sordid aspects of everyday life. *(naturalists)*
9. What did the impressionists attempt to do with their paintings? *(to give a vivid impression of people and places as they might appear in a brief glance)*
10. What French sculptor gave some of his work a deliberately unfinished quality? *(Auguste Rodin)*

SUGGESTED ASSIGNMENTS

1. **Critical Thinking Worksheet (Challenging)** Have students complete Critical Thinking Worksheet 46, in the TEACHER'S RESOURCEBANK™.
2. **Skill Worksheet (Basic)** Have students complete Skill Worksheet 20 in the TEACHER'S RESOURCEBANK™.
3. **Review Worksheet (Basic)** Have students complete Review Worksheet 20 in the TEACHER'S RESOURCEBANK™.

For suggested lesson plan, additional teaching strategies, enrichment activities, daily quizzes, and suggested assignments, see pages 513A–513F.

Introducing the Chapter
Explain to the class that something as important as the Industrial Revolution affected not just business, but all of human activity. Science and art in the 1800s were changed greatly by the Industrial Revolution, as students will learn in this chapter. Ask students to speculate on how industrialization would affect scientists, artists, and writers. *(Students should mention the new subjects that artists and writers had to deal with and think about, the advanced technology that scientists could use for their experiments, and the general atmosphere of progress in Western society.)*

Chapter Objectives
After studying Chapter 20, students will be able to:

1. Describe the developments that made electricity a practical source of power.
2. Identify the importance of the internal-combustion engine.
3. List the major developments in the physical sciences during the 1800s and 1900s and identify the scientists responsible for these developments.
4. Summarize the contributions of Jenner, Pasteur, Lister, and Koch to the improvement of public health standards.
5. Discuss the reasons for population growth after the Industrial Revolution.
6. Describe the changes in life styles that took place

CHAPTER 20

The Industrial Age Revolutionized Science and Culture

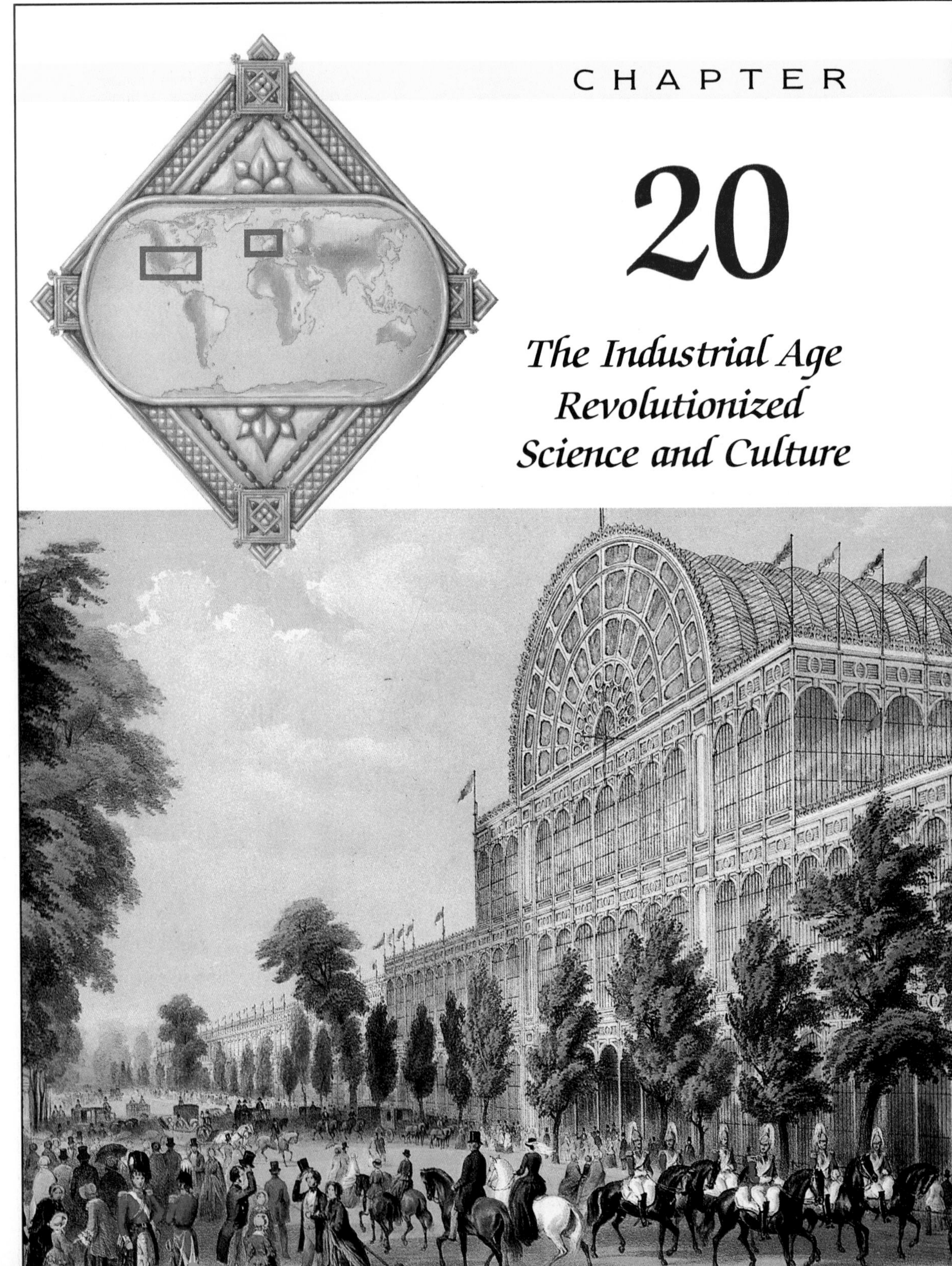

CHAPTER FOCUS

Place The United States and Europe

Time 1800–1928

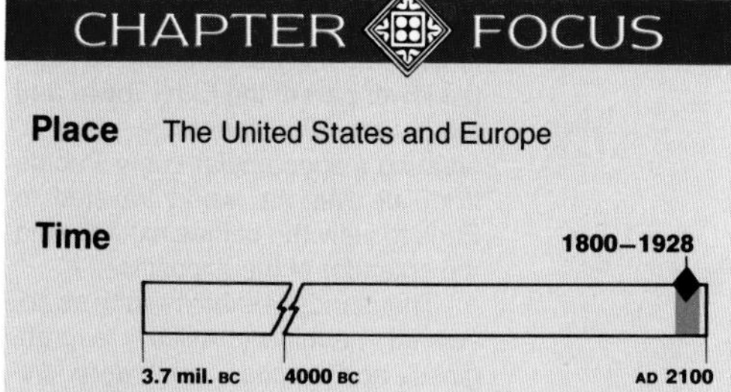

Significance

In addition to changing the economy and society, the Industrial Revolution had a profound effect on science, art, music, and literature. Improved technology brought about sweeping changes in transportation and communication. Scientists developed new theories to explain the physical world. Advances in medicine greatly improved people's lives. Some people began to apply scientific methods to the study of people, both as individuals and as members of social groups.

In the 1800s compulsory education laws in many countries led to the creation of public schools. As more and more people were educated, a larger audience for intellectual and cultural activities developed.

Some writers and artists glorified progress, science, and change. Others, however, disagreed with this view. They looked to the past and insisted that no scientific theory could ever describe the true spiritual nature of human beings. In music, sculpture, and painting, styles changed frequently and rapidly, responding to the impact of industrialization on people's lives.

Terms to Define

physical science	pasteurization
radioactivity	social science
genetics	romantic movement

People to Identify

Alexander Graham Bell	Charles Darwin
Thomas Edison	Sigmund Freud
Pierre and Marie Curie	Emily Davies

Places to Locate

Kitty Hawk	Paris

Questions to Guide Your Reading

1 What advances were made in technology and communication?
2 What advances were made in science and medicine?
3 What factors helped spur population growth?
4 When did interest in the social sciences and educational institutions develop?
5 How did literature, music, and art reflect the spirit of the times?

Stories of "the good old days" transcend both time and generations. In the following excerpt from Sparks from the Anvil, *Carl Schmidgall, an American inventor and a pioneer in mechanical engineering, recounts boyhood memories of conversations among visitors to his father's blacksmith shop in the early 1900s.*

"During the winter months, I have seen and heard many a good political discussion while they sat and stood around our cannon stove. [The upright portion of the stove was shaped like the barrel of a cannon.] There were some hot arguments sometimes over subjects ranging from religion and politics to the welfare of the country. It was here where such men from the crossroads of life met, and during these periods of my entering the shop as a small boy, until I grew to manhood, the information I gained from their talks and arguments gave me much to think about. I learned the philosophy of a better life.

There was at times much humor connected with their talks, but there was also present many times the reverence of religion and the ways of mankind. To me all of these things meant that there was room for study—to venture out into the world and to help make it a better place to live in. All through my later years away from the old blacksmith shop, little recollections of it have kindled a spark within my heart which has inspired me."

Vivid memories of the blacksmith shop and the people he met there inspired Schmidgall as he grew up. By 1916 he was president of his own manufacturing company. Several of his inventions—all of them based on the technology of the Industrial Revolution—are still used today.

1 Advances Continued in Technology and Communication

Beginning about 1870, manufacturers increasingly applied the findings of pure science to their businesses, generating a new wave of industrial growth. The application of scientific solutions to industrial problems resulted in: (1) inventions that provided rapid communication over long distances; (2) the

◀ *The Great Exhibition of London, 1851*

in Europe during the 1800s.
7. Summarize the contributions made to the social sciences during the 1800s.
8. Discuss the growth of public education and its impact on Western society.
9. Compare romanticism with realism and describe new experiments in art.

SECTION 1

Focus/Motivation
To introduce the section, you might hold a discussion on the influence of science, technology, and invention in today's world. Use the following questions as a guide: In the past, inventors found it hard to make a living, while today they seem to be in a more favored position. How might you account for this? *(Answers will vary. Some students may suggest that as scientists improved the quality of life, their prestige increased. People began to look to scientists for solutions to some of life's problems.)* What does this indicate about the role of science and technology in the contemporary world? *(Some students will suggest that the industrialized nations of the world depend upon science and technology and therefore give special status to their scientists.)*

Presentation
Identifying Ideas (Average/Group)
On the chalkboard or an overhead projector, write the following two lists and

515

1B, 1D, 4H, 4I, a1C, a3A, a3B, a3G, a3H, a3I

● In his experiments, done 10 years before Faraday's, Ampère produced similar findings, but he rejected them as being of little importance.

have the students copy them into their notebooks. Have students match the invention or scientific development in the first list with the inventor or scientist in the second list.

1. Sent the human voice over a long distance by means of an electrical circuit
2. Invented instruments for sending and receiving radio waves
3. Found that by moving a magnet through a coil of wire an electrical current could be generated in that wire
4. Developed an electric light bulb that glowed for two days
5. Pioneered the development of the internal-combustion engine
6. Undertook the first powered, sustained controlled flight

a. Alexander Graham Bell
b. Gottlieb Daimler and Karl Benz
c. Thomas Edison
d. Michael Faraday
e. Guglielmo Marconi
f. Orville and Wilbur Wright

(Answers: 1. a; 2. e; 3. d; 4. c; 5. b; 6. f)

POSTER ART

Paris Exposition Poster

In 1889 the French held a spectacular exposition in Paris to celebrate the one hundredth anniversary of the French Revolution. In its many buildings, the exposition featured examples of the tremendous industrial progress that had been made during the nineteenth century. To celebrate the exposition, the French newspaper *Le Figaro* published a special supplement using this poster as its cover. In the foreground is the Seine River; the famous Eiffel Tower soars in the background. At the time the tower was the tallest structure in the world. It stands as a monument to the engineering skills and achievements of the 1800s.

The 1889 exposition was the first to use electricity extensively. At night the lower part of the Eiffel Tower and the surrounding fountains were lit, creating a spectacular show. People from all over the world traveled to Paris to view the unique exhibits and the splendor of the exposition.

Thousands of exhibits such as advanced machinery, military aircraft, glass, and applied arts were displayed. From a high-moving platform in the Gallery of Machines, under the arch of the Eiffel tower, visitors viewed the inventions developed during the Industrial Revolution. The exposition demonstrated to the world that the 1800s had indeed been technically dynamic. It also provided a preview of technology that would characterize everyday life in the 1900s.

Today, people flock to World's Fairs, which, like the 1889 exposition, showcase technological advances.

development and use of new sources of power; and (3) the creation of new products and materials and the improvement of old ones.

By 1900 most people thought of technology and progress as the same thing. Many individuals viewed science as an endless source of new ideas and inventions. Machines seemed capable of constantly improving the quality of life. There appeared to be no end to the progress made possible by industrialization. People thought that science and technology could solve any problems that the Industrial Revolution might create.

Communications

An important development in the communications field occurred in the 1870s when Alexander Graham Bell sent the human voice over a long distance by means of an electrical circuit. Bell, an American, patented his telephone in 1876. Then in 1895 an Italian inventor, Guglielmo Marconi, developed a way to send messages through space without wires.

Marconi's invention was based on the work of two earlier scientists, James Clerk Maxwell of Great Britain and Heinrich Hertz of Germany. Maxwell had made a mathematical study of electricity and magnetism. In 1864 he asserted the existence of invisible electromagnetic waves that travel through space at the speed of light. In the 1880s Hertz not only proved that such waves did exist, by transmitting and receiving them, but also measured their length and speed.

Marconi invented instruments for sending and receiving these radio waves, as they came to be called. His wireless telegraph soon proved itself valuable for ship-to-ship and ship-to-shore communication. In 1901 he sent the first wireless message across the Atlantic Ocean.

Electricity

As industry grew during the 1800s, manufacturers continued to search for new and better power sources. In the 1870s a tremendous new power source—electricity—was developed.

An English scientist, Michael Faraday, discovered the scientific key to the problem in 1831. From the work of Ampère and other scientists, Faraday knew that electricity could produce magnetism. He ● wanted to find out whether magnetism could produce electricity. He found that by moving a magnet through a coil of wire he could generate an electric current in the wire.

Faraday concentrated primarily on exploring the nature of electricity. Others used his discovery to develop the dynamo, or electric generator. Driven either by a steam engine or by waterpower,

516

● Edison received only three months of formal education, and that when he was eight years old.

■ Kitty Hawk, North Carolina

the dynamo transformed mechanical power into electrical energy. This energy in turn could generate power to run machinery in factories.

English and American inventors kept trying to make practical use of another scientific discovery about electricity—that a current passing through certain kinds of wire caused the wire to glow. Here was a possible source of light for city streets, homes, and factories. Electric light bulbs were first produced in 1845, but they burned out in a matter of minutes. In 1879 Thomas Edison, an American, made a bulb that glowed for two days before burning out. In a few years, after further improvements, electric lighting replaced gas lighting.

To make electricity practical, it had to be transmitted from the place it was generated to the place it would be used. After much work on the problem, Edison developed a successful central powerhouse and transmission system that began operating in 1882 in New York City, London, and Milan.

The electrical industry grew rapidly. Waterfalls, such as Niagara Falls, were tapped to run huge dynamos, whose hydroelectric power was sent long distances through wires. Tremendous dams were built in many countries to provide artificial sources of waterpower.

As large-scale production and transmission of electricity became available in the late 1800s, electric motors replaced steam engines in factories. Where hydroelectric power was either unavailable or too expensive, steam engines turned the generators at central powerhouses.

The Internal-combustion Engine

The electric motor had one significant limitation—it had to be connected to its power supply. Therefore, it was not very useful as a means of moving vehicles.

Automobiles. In the late 1800s, several European inventors worked on engines that would use a portable fuel supply of oil or gasoline to propel individual vehicles. The device was called the internal-combustion engine because the combustion, or burning, of fuel took place inside a closed cylinder. (In the steam engine, combustion takes place outside the cylinder.) Pioneers in this field included Gottlieb Daimler and Karl Benz of Germany and Louis Renault of France. In 1893 Charles and Frank Duryea (duhr • ee • AY) built the first successful gasoline-driven automobile in the United States. Three years later the American inventor Henry Ford produced his first automobile.

Airplanes. Since the 1700s people had used balloons filled with gases lighter than air to float above the ground. Beginning in the 1800s, inventors tried to devise a heavier-than-air machine that would actually fly. Many early airplanes were not designed to carry people. The first people to succeed in flying an airplane in powered, sustained, controlled flight were Wilbur and Orville Wright of the United States. They achieved this feat at Kitty Hawk, North Carolina, in 1903. The flight lasted 12 seconds and covered 120 feet (37 meters).

The Wright brothers' achievement was another example of the combination of science and technology. The Wrights succeeded where others had failed because they had studied aerodynamics—the principles governing the movement of air around objects—and had used the internal-combustion engine to propel their plane through the air. From this modest beginning, today's multi-billion dollar airplane industry developed.

Learning from Pictures *In 1909 Louis Bleriot was the first pilot to fly across the English Channel. Where did the first successful airplane flight take place?* ■

517

1B, 4H, 4I, a1C, a4A, a4H, a4L

SECTION 1

Closure

Point out that the scientific developments and inventions discussed in Section 1 all had an impact on nineteenth-century life. Ask the students which of these developments or inventions has had the most influence on daily life today. *(Answers will vary.)*

Review Answers

1. ***Alexander Graham Bell:*** developed the telephone, which he patented in 1876; ***Guglielmo Marconi:*** invented the wireless telegraph; ***Thomas Edison:*** invented electric light bulb and central powerhouse to transmit electricity; ***Wilbur and Orville Wright:*** first to fly an airplane in powered, sustained, controlled flight; ***internal-combustion engine:*** engine in which fuel was burned inside a closed cylinder; ***aerodynamics:*** principles governing the movement of air around objects
2. The three developments resulting from applying scientific solutions to industrial problems are: inventions that provided rapid communication over long distances; the development and use of new sources of power; the creation of new products and materials and the improvement of old ones.
3. Marconi's scientific developments employed the work of two earlier scientists, James Maxwell of Great Britain and Heinrich Hertz of Germany. Maxwell asserted the existence of

SECTION 1 REVIEW

1. **Identify** Alexander Graham Bell, Guglielmo Marconi, Thomas Edison, Wilbur and Orville Wright, internal-combustion engine, aerodynamics
2. **Classifying Ideas** What three developments resulted from applying scientific solutions to industrial problems?
3. **Evaluating Ideas** What ideas of earlier scientists did Marconi use?
4. **Summarizing Ideas** What developments made electricity a new source of power?
5. **Interpreting Ideas** How was the internal-combustion engine first used?

2 Advances in Science and Medicine Helped Improve Human Life

The **physical sciences** are those sciences that deal with the inanimate, or nonliving, aspects of nature. They include astronomy, geology, physics, and chemistry. The most significant developments in the physical sciences during the 1800s and early 1900s centered on the atomic theory.

The Atomic Theory

According to modern atomic theory, all matter in the universe consists of very small particles called atoms. The arrangement and structure of these atoms and their chemical combinations with each other account for the different characteristics of the materials that make up our world.

We can trace the beginnings of the atomic theory, as we can many other scientific ideas, back to the Greek philosophers, such as Democritus. For many centuries, however, atomism was only one of several philosophical theories about physical reality. During the Scientific Revolution of the 1500s and 1600s, people began to accept the atomic theory as part of science, although neither experimental proof nor mathematical demonstration yet supported it.

John Dalton, an English chemist and schoolteacher, became the first scientist to obtain convincing experimental data about the atom. In 1803 he outlined a method for "weighing" atoms. After studying the ratios of elements in various gases, Dalton assigned an arbitrary weight of one to the lightest element, hydrogen. Dalton then expressed the weights of all of the other known elements in relation to it.

During the 1800s many scientists explored the paths opened up by Dalton, learning much about the atom. In 1869 a Russian chemist, Dmitri Mendeleyev (men • duh • LAY • uhf), produced the first workable classification of the elements. Although somewhat modified, Mendeleyev's *Periodic Table* is a familiar feature of modern chemistry textbooks.

Modern atomic theory originated in the study of chemistry. However, it soon became part of physics—the science of matter and energy. This began to occur when scientists studying heat and gases explained their findings with a new theory of atoms in motion.

In the 1800s some scientists began to think of heat as the result of the motion of a body's atomic particles. In a cold substance—ice, for example—the atoms move relatively slowly. In a hot substance—such as scalding water—the atoms move much more vigorously, even colliding with one another. When water boils, the atoms move extremely fast and the water turns into a gas—water vapor. These discoveries established the atomic theory as a part of physics.

The Structure of the Atom

In 1895 a German physicist, Wilhelm K. Roentgen (RENT • guhn), was sending electricity through a vacuum inside a glass tube. He noticed that a fluorescent substance on a table nearby glowed brightly when the electric current was switched on in the tube. Roentgen immediately concluded that the tube was sending out a new form of ray. Soon he discovered that the rays penetrated many substances, including human skin and tissue, and would leave an image on a photographic plate. Because he did not know what caused this powerful penetrating radiation, Roentgen named the rays *X rays*. X rays became an important diagnostic tool in medicine, and their existence raised new questions about the physical world.

An English physicist, J. J. Thomson, probed further into the nature of matter. In 1897 he discovered the electron, a tiny particle that had a negative electrical charge. Thomson announced that an electron was more than 1,000 times lighter than

CONNECTIONS: THEN AND NOW

Science Fiction

Storytellers since the time of the ancient Greeks have enjoyed imagining that people are capable of breaking the laws of nature and gaining fantastic strength or powers. They have also invented amazing machines (right) and mythical figures with magical abilities.

Since the time of the Scientific Revolution, these fantasies have often taken a special form, inspired by the achievements of science. They are usually referred to as science fiction.

A favorite subject of science fiction has been travel in space. In fact, one of the earliest works of science fiction was written by Johannes Kepler, who played a major part in the revolution in astronomy during the 1600s. Kepler wrote a book called *The Dream,* in which he imagined his mother flying to the moon on a broomstick. This book created problems for his mother, for it was used as evidence that she was a witch. However, it is one of the most imaginative descriptions of life in space ever written.

Science fiction was particularly popular in the 1700s and 1800s. The French philosopher Voltaire imagined a visit to earth by an enormous native of the star Sirius. An English novelist, Mary Wollstonecraft Shelley, invented a medical student called Victor Frankenstein, who created a monster out of a corpse. In the late 1800s, a French writer, Jules Verne, wrote a series of stories about incredible journeys—in a balloon, on a rocket, and even on a submarine. The English novelist H.G. Wells imagined a machine that could stop time and Martians who invaded Earth (bottom right).

In more recent times, much of science fiction—in films as well as books—has dealt with outer space (bottom left). But the basic theme has remained the same: fantastic people or creatures who can do things that normally are impossible. By showing us the impossible, science fiction tries to teach us something about the limits under which we live.

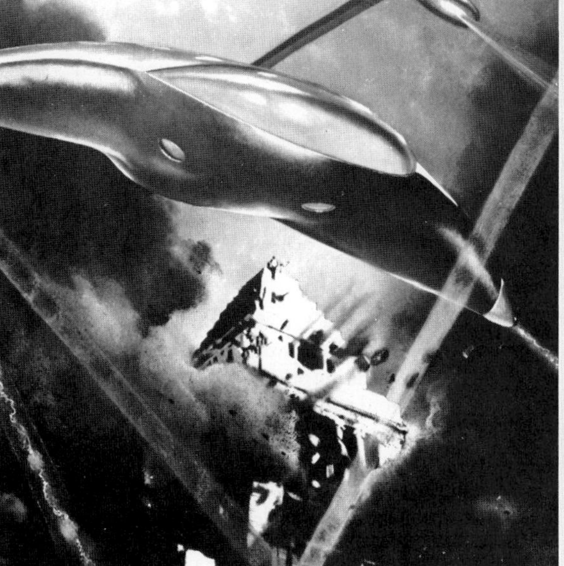

invisible electromagnetic waves that travel through space at the speed of light. Hertz proved the existence of such waves by transmitting and receiving them, and he also measured their length and speed.

4. Electricity became a new source of power as a result of Faraday's discovery that electric current could be produced by magnetism and Edison's development of a central powerhouse and transmission system.

5. The internal-combustion engine was first put to use in powering automobiles and airplanes.

SECTION 2

Focus/Motivation

To compare medical practices of the 1800s with those of the present, read to the class the following quotation, which describes conditions during the Civil War. Have students discuss how medical knowledge of the causes of infection and disease has advanced since then.

"Few medical men then knew why wounds become infected or what causes disease; the treatment of wounds and disease, consequently, ranged from the inadequate through the useless to the downright harmful. . . . The idea that a surgical dressing ought to be sterilized never entered anyone's head. . . . If a surgeon's instruments were so much as rinsed off between operations at a field hospital, the case was

● Marie Curie died of leukemia caused by radiation from the elements she was studying.

an exception. In camp, diseases like typhoid, dysentery, and pneumonia were dreaded killers. . . . It has been estimated that two and one-half Union deaths resulted from disease for every single combat loss, while the ratio on the Confederate side was three to one."

Presentation Understanding Chronology (Average/Group)
Write the list below on the chalkboard or an overhead projector. Have students number the statements in the order in which they became important.

- (4) Thomson discovered the electron.
- (3) Roentgen discovered the X ray.
- (1) Dalton outlined a method for "weighing" atoms.
- (7) Einstein developed the special theory of relativity.
- (5) Rutherford described the atom.
- (8) Bohr discovered that the behavior of atoms revealed atomic structure.
- (2) Mendeleyev developed the *Periodic Table.*
- (6) Planck put forward the quantum theory.

Learning from Pictures *The German-born Albert Einstein emigrated to the United States before Hitler came to power.*

the smallest known atom, and he theorized that all atoms contained electrons. Therefore, he said, subatomic particles (that is, particles inside atoms), rather than the atoms themselves, must be the true building blocks of all matter in the universe.

While most physicists reluctantly accepted the electron's existence, a French husband-and-wife team of chemists, Pierre and Marie Curie, provided new evidence that atoms were not the simple, indivisible particles pictured by earlier scientists. The Curies experimented with uranium and radium. They found that the atoms of these elements constantly disintegrated and released energy on their own. This process is called **radioactivity.** Elements that disintegrate and release this energy are called radioactive elements.

Ernest Rutherford of Great Britain combined Thomson's ideas about electrons and the Curies' discovery of disintegrating atoms in a new theory of the atom. Rutherford maintained that at the center of the atom lay an extremely small and heavy core, or nucleus. Electrons whirled in circular orbits around the nucleus. When Rutherford bombarded the nucleus with heavy particles from radioactive elements, he found that it held even smaller particles, which he called protons. With this discovery scientists no longer thought of the atom as a solid piece of matter.

Later scientists modified Rutherford's description of the atom. He had thought in terms of two subatomic particles—electrons and protons. However, his successors discovered another, the neutron, and eventually more than 30 elementary atomic particles.

Planck and Einstein

In 1900, the German physicist Max Planck disproved the then-common belief that energy was continuous and that it could be divided into any number of smaller units. Planck proved that energy could be released only in definite "packages," which he called *quanta* (the plural of *quantum,* the Latin word for "how much"). Planck's **quantum theory** formed the basis for a completely new approach to the study of matter and energy.

In 1905 an extraordinary young German scientist, Albert Einstein, wrote four papers that revolutionized physics. In his first paper, Einstein examined some of the basic concepts of mechanics and tried to prove the existence of atoms. Einstein realized that if large grains of pollen were put into a gas or liquid, movement of the grains could be observed under a microscope. An earlier scientist had also made this observation but could not explain why the grains of pollen moved. In his paper Einstein maintained that the movement of pollen resulted from atoms hitting the grains.

In his second paper, Einstein extended Planck's quantum theory to describe the nature of light. Planck believed that light was a continuous wavelike phenomenon. Einstein used mathematics to show that light can also consist of a cascade of minute particles of energy. Einstein's theories were not confirmed by other scientists until the mid-1920s, but in time they led to the development of improvements such as the electric eye that triggers automatic door openers.

In his third paper, Einstein developed the **special theory of relativity.** He concluded the following: (1) No particles of matter can move faster than the speed of light. (2) Motion can be measured only relative to some particular observer. Thus it does not make sense to speak of absolute motion, space, or time.

A brief fourth paper developed Einstein's equation $E = mc^2$. According to this equation,

● In 1805 a German naturalist, Lorenz Oken, first suggested that all living organisms consisted of small living particles, or cells.

E (energy) equals *m* (mass) multiplied by c^2 (the speed of light squared). This formula states that a small amount of mass can be transformed into a tremendous amount of energy.

Einstein's theories overturned long-held ideas. Isaac Newton and the scientists who followed him had thought of the universe in terms of three dimensions: length, breadth, and depth. They claimed that gravity forces all particles of matter to move toward one another. Einstein declared that all events occur not only in the three dimensions of space but also in a fourth dimension—time. This four-dimensional system he called the *space-time continuum*. Gravity, he said, is not a property of matter, but rather a property of the space-time continuum.

By 1912 the theories of Max Planck and Albert Einstein paved the way for more advanced scientific discoveries. Niels Bohr, a student of J. J. Thomson, became intensely interested in atomic structure. Dispensing with traditional scientific approaches, Bohr applied the quantum theory to the challenging problem. He discovered that the behavior of atoms reveals atomic structure.

Cell Theory in Biology

Scientists of the 1800s were as interested in explaining the nature of life as they were in exploring the nature of nonliving matter. However, matter is extremely complex in the **biological sciences**—those sciences dealing with living organisms.

Biologists had long been familiar with the idea of cells, the tiny units of living matter. Various scientists of the 1600s examined living matter under their microscopes, seeing what we now know to be plant and animal cells. The cells of different species were of different shapes and sizes, but these early observers did not draw any general conclusions about them.

In 1858 the work of the German scientist ● Rudolf Virchow expanded the cell theory. Virchow showed that the destruction or change of cells by some outside force or agent caused disease in living organisms. From his study of cells, Virchow also concluded that every new cell must come from some older cell and that only living matter can produce new living matter. Thus by the late 1800s, scientists generally accepted the cell as the basic unit of living matter.

Lamarck's Theory of Inheritance

The cell theory, however, could not account for the rich variety of plants and animals on the earth. Until the mid-1800s most people explained the variety of living things by the concept of "special creation." They believed that all the different kinds of plants and animals had been created at one time.

One group of scientists, however, offered a different theory. They argued that the thousands of kinds of modern plants and animals had evolved, or developed, from common ancestors of long ago. This kind of development through change is called **evolution.**

In science new theories often raise new questions. Those who believed in evolution now had to explain how plants and animals had evolved. In the early 1800s, a French biologist, Jean Baptiste Lamarck, suggested that living beings changed their form in response to their environment. A giraffe, for example, acquired a long neck because it always had to stretch to eat leaves high up in trees. Such changes were then passed on by inheritance to its descendants. Conversely, other characteristics might gradually disappear if they were not used at all. Lamarck maintained that changes of this sort, continuing from generation to generation for millions of years, could have produced present-day plants and animals out of the first bits of living matter.

Lamarck's theory did not become a part of modern biology because it was later disproved. However, it influenced other scientists, among them a British biologist named Charles Darwin.

Darwin's Theory of Evolution

Charles Darwin had spent 25 years studying plant and animal life. In 1859 he published his theory of evolution in a book called *On the Origin of Species by Means of Natural Selection.*

Darwin began with a well-known biological fact—no two creatures are exactly alike, and offspring are not exactly like their parents. He combined this fact with the ideas of Thomas Malthus. Malthus believed that there were always more creatures born than could survive, because of natural dangers and restrictions, including the limited food supply. Therefore, Darwin said, in any generation some creatures would survive and some would perish. Those who survived would, in general, be

521

1B, 4H, a1C

those whose characteristics were best adapted to the existing environment. This idea is often called the "survival of the fittest." The strongest survivors would live to produce offspring, who would then repeat the process. Thus, Darwin claimed, one could explain the evolution of all forms of life.

According to Darwin's theory, the ancestors of the giraffe may not have had long necks, but they gave birth to offspring that were not exactly like their parents. Some had necks slightly longer than their parents had. Others had shorter necks. In an environment where leaves were found on tall trees, the offspring with the longer necks had an advantage. They could eat the leaves on the higher branches. Therefore, Darwin believed that nature "selected" the longer-necked offspring. These offspring lived and gave birth to another generation. The short-necked giraffes starved. Once again natural selection was repeated, and the longer-necked individuals survived.

Darwin's theory had a great impact on other scientists. It inspired them to gather evidence that would either prove or disprove it—evidence they looked for in the records of fossils as well as in the study of living organisms. However, the theory of natural selection stirred up controversy because (1) it placed human beings in the animal kingdom, an idea many believed incorrect, and (2) many people believed that it contradicted the story of Creation in the Bible.

Learning from Pictures *Darwin gathered most of the material for his theory of evolution during a surveying expedition off the coast of South America.*

Genetics

Darwin left an important question unanswered: why were the offspring not exactly like their parents? Unknown to Darwin, a monk in Austria, Gregor Mendel, had been gathering evidence that would answer this question. Mendel founded **genetics**—the study of the ways in which inborn characteristics of plants and animals are inherited by their descendants. He did much of his research in the 1860s and 1870s, although other scientists did not know about it until later.

Mendel worked in a quiet monastery garden, where he bred pea plants. He mated tall plants with short plants, which produced not medium-sized pea plants, but all tall plants. Then Mendel fertilized these tall offspring with their own pollen and was surprised to find that they produced a mixed generation of both short and tall plants. In some way the characteristic of shortness had been hidden in the tall plants.

From these experiments Mendel concluded that inborn characteristics were not necessarily blended or mixed together. Instead, he believed, they were all inherited as if they were separate particles. For example, tall plants could carry and pass on to the next generation the particles that would cause shortness.

The Fight Against Disease

Remarkable breakthroughs in medicine accompanied the advances in science and helped prolong human life. Until the late 1800s, two out of every three children died while very young. Epidemics killed more people than did wars, famines, or natural disasters. Little was known about the causes of diseases. Scientists had seen bacteria under the microscope as early as the 1600s but had not suspected their connection with disease.

Smallpox, one dreaded disease common among children, swept through cities in periodic epidemics. A well-known saying of the time was that mothers did not count their children until they had had smallpox and lived through it.

522

● Initially, the scientific community rejected much of Pasteur's work. Some leading scientists ridiculed Pasteur, calling him an idiot and an amateur.

Edward Jenner. An English physician of the late 1700s, Edward Jenner, made a thorough investigation of smallpox in the hope of finding a way to prevent it. He learned that milkmaids who had once had cowpox (a mild disease similar to smallpox) did not get the dreaded disease even during an epidemic. After years of experimenting, Jenner developed the principle of *inoculation,* which had been known in India 1,300 years earlier. In 1796 Jenner made a *vaccine* from the fluid in cowpox sores and scratched it into the skin of a boy's arm. The boy had a mild case of cowpox but quickly recovered. When the boy was later exposed to smallpox, he did not contract it.

Louis Pasteur. Jenner had developed a method of preventing smallpox through inoculation, but he did not know the scientific principle that made it work. This principle came to light in the late 1800s through the work of the French chemist Louis Pasteur. ● Until Pasteur's time scientists believed that certain living things, including bacteria, sprang to life out of nonliving matter. This process was called *spontaneous generation.* Pasteur's experiments showed that bacteria reproduced like other living things and traveled from place to place in the air, on people's hands, and in other ways.

Pasteur learned that bacteria are responsible for many phenomena. For example, some cause fermentation, turning grape juice into wine or making milk sour. In the 1860s Pasteur developed a process of heating liquids to kill bacteria and prevent fermentation—a process that was named **pasteurization** in his honor. He also determined that some bacteria cause diseases in animals and humans. These harmful bacteria are called *germs* or *microbes.*

During the 1870s Pasteur experimented with the germ that caused anthrax, a disease often fatal to both animals and humans. He produced a vaccine containing weakened anthrax germs, which he injected into animals. This prevented them from catching the disease. He determined that when weakened germs enter the body, the system builds up substances called antibodies to fight them. These antibodies remain in the body and are strong enough to kill the more deadly germs if exposure occurs. Thus Pasteur showed why Jenner's smallpox inoculations had been effective.

Pasteur used this same technique in fighting rabies, a fatal disease communicated to humans by dogs or other animals infected with a certain virus (a minute organism smaller than bacteria). In the 1880s Pasteur found a way to weaken the rabies virus. He injected the vaccine he produced into a boy who had been bitten by a rabid dog, and the boy survived.

Learning from Pictures *Louis Pasteur never profited monetarily from his discoveries, but humankind benefited immeasurably from his experiments with bacteria.*

The Development of Surgery

Through the centuries surgery had been a desperate measure, always painful and often fatal. Surgeons dared to attempt only those operations that could be completed in a few minutes, such as tooth extractions and limb amputations. Patients had to be forcibly held down, or their senses dulled with liquor or opium.

In the 1840s it was discovered that ether and chloroform would cause unconsciousness or deaden sensation and thus eliminate pain. Such anesthetics not only relieved the patients' suffering but also made longer operations possible.

Even after anesthetics came into use, however, many patients survived the surgeon's knife only to die from infection soon afterward. Pasteur's discoveries about germs helped to resolve this dilemma.

SECTION 2

Closure

Point out to students that many of the scientific and medical developments discussed in Section 2 met with opposition and disbelief when they were first introduced. Ask the students why they think scientific innovations are not always readily accepted by the scientific community and society at large.

Review Answers

1. ***physical science:*** science that deals with the inanimate, or nonliving, aspects of nature; ***radioactivity:*** process of disintegration in which certain elements release energy; ***quantum theory:*** theory that energy can be released only in definite amounts; ***special theory of relativity:*** theory that stated that no particles of matter can move faster than the speed of light, and that motion can be measured only relative to some particular observer; ***biological science:*** science dealing with living organisms; ***evolution:*** theory that plants and animals developed from common ancestors; ***genetics:*** study of the ways in which inborn characteristics of plants and animals developed by inheritance; ***pasteurization:*** process of heating liquids to kill bacteria and prevent fermentation

2. ***John Dalton:*** devised a method for "weighing" atoms; ***Dmitri Mendeleyev:*** Russian chemist who produced the first workable

1B, 4H, a1C, a4A, a4H, a4L

● Anesthetics caused unconsciousness or deadened sensation, whereas opium or liquor merely dulled the senses.

classification of the elements; ***Wilhelm Roentgen:*** German physicist who discovered X rays; ***Pierre and Marie Curie:*** French chemists who investigated radioactivity; ***Max Planck:*** German physicist who developed the quantum theory; ***Albert Einstein:*** German scientist who revolutionized physics, stating that all events occur in four dimensions—the three dimensions of space and the fourth dimension of time; ***Gregor Mendel:*** founder of genetics; ***Edward Jenner:*** English physician who developed the principle of inoculation **3. (a)** Dalton devised a method for "weighing" atoms; **(b)** Thomson discovered the electron; **(c)** Rutherford described the atom in terms of subatomic particles—electrons and protons. **4.** Einstein's chief contributions were extending Planck's quantum theory to light; developing the equation $E=mc^2$, which meant that a small amount of mass could be transformed into a tremendous amount of energy; developing a theory of relativity. **5. (a)** Lamarck believed living things changed their form in response to their environment. These changes would be passed on to descendants, and characteristics not needed would gradually disappear. According to Darwin, those creatures best suited to the existing environment would survive and pass on their characteristics to offspring, while the less fit would die off. **(b)** Many

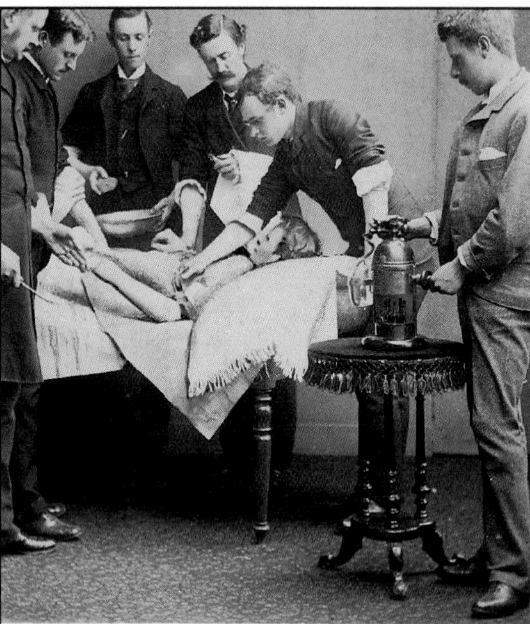

Learning from Pictures *The discovery of anesthetics led to new surgical techniques. Why were anesthetics* ● *better than liquor and opium for deadening pain?*

An English surgeon, Joseph Lister, studied Pasteur's work and developed antisepsis—the process of killing disease-causing germs. Lister used carbolic acid as an antiseptic; milder chemicals later came into use for this purpose. The use of antiseptics helped reduce bacterial infection not only in surgery but also in childbirth and in the treatment of battle wounds. Hospitals, once houses of death, became houses of healing.

Other Medical Advances

A German physician, Robert Koch, made discoveries that reinforced those of Pasteur. In 1882 he isolated the germ that causes tuberculosis. He also identified the germ responsible for Asiatic cholera and developed sanitary measures, such as water filtration, to prevent disease.

The discoveries of Pasteur, Lister, and Koch were the starting point of an international fight against disease. Knowing the nature and role of germs and viruses, scientists could now isolate the causes of many diseases and develop vaccines for inoculation.

Scientists traced some epidemic diseases, including malaria and yellow fever, to germs carried in the bodies of mosquitoes and transmitted by their bite. Thus the battle against disease was extended to the mosquitoes that carried it. Bubonic plague, found to be carried by fleas on rats, was brought under control in Western countries through rat-extermination campaigns.

Scientists developed and tested many new medicines. Aspirin, which became available in the 1890s, reduced pain and fever. Insulin, developed in the 1920s, saved diabetics from certain death and enabled them to lead normal lives. Other medicines were used to treat bacterial infections. For example, Alexander Fleming of Great Britain discovered penicillin in 1928. The sulfonamides, or sulfa drugs, were developed in Germany in the 1930s. However, neither penicillin nor the sulfas came into wide use until the 1940s.

SECTION 2 REVIEW

1. **Define** physical science, radioactivity, quantum theory, special theory of relativity, biological science, evolution, genetics, pasteurization
2. **Identify** John Dalton, Dmitri Mendeleyev, Wilhelm Roentgen, Pierre and Marie Curie, Max Planck, Albert Einstein, Gregor Mendel, Edward Jenner
3. **Classifying Ideas** **(a)** What contributions to atomic theory were made by Dalton? **(b)** Thomson? **(c)** Rutherford?
4. **Summarizing Ideas** What were Albert Einstein's major contributions to physics?
5. **Contrasting Ideas** **(a)** Explain how Lamarck's theory of evolution differed from that proposed by Darwin. **(b)** What differences of opinion did Darwin's theory cause?
6. **Evaluating Ideas** In what ways did Gregor Mendel's ideas build upon Darwin's theory?
7. **Identifying Ideas** What were four great contributions made by Louis Pasteur?

3 The Population Grew and Became More Mobile

From about 1600 to 1750, the population of Europe grew very little. When the Industrial Revolution began, 140 million people lived in Europe. By 1850, only 100 years later, the population had increased to 266 million. The rate of population growth during most of the period was highest in Europe and the United States, the areas in which industrialization advanced most rapidly. The progress made possible by science and technology helped produce this rapid population growth.

Improvements in Diet and Food Storage

Another reason that life expectancy increased after 1850 was that more food became available, and more was known about the relationship of food to health. In the early 1900s, biologists discovered the importance of vitamins and minerals in the diet. Diseases resulting from vitamin deficiencies, such as beriberi and rickets, were wiped out in advanced regions of the world.

Science and technology combined to produce better methods of preserving and transporting food. Pasteurization was one important step. So was refrigeration, which also retards the growth of bacteria. Refrigerators appeared in the late 1800s. They later became an indispensable household feature in many industrialized countries. Refrigerated railroad cars were first used around 1850 to transport meats, fruits, and vegetables. All these developments made a balanced diet available year-round.

Emigration

As the population grew in industrialized countries, it also became more mobile. Large numbers of people moved across national boundaries and oceans to foreign lands. The great movement shifted away from Europe to North and South America, Africa, Australia, and New Zealand.

Like so many other changes, this movement to other lands, or **emigration,** intensified after 1870. Between 1870 and 1900, more than 10 million people left Europe for the United States alone. This mass movement of people has no equal in human history.

Many people fled from countries with poor economic conditions, such as Ireland and Italy. Other people, such as Jews, Armenians, and Slavs, fled oppression and discrimination. The general trend of movement was toward the more sparsely populated nations in northern and western Europe, where rapid industrialization had created a great demand for factory labor. Higher wages in these countries attracted people, and steamships and trains made travel faster, safer, and affordable.

Learning from Pictures *Tiny Ellis Island in New York Harbor symbolized hope for immigrants, who traveled from Europe on overcrowded ships. More than 16 million people passed through the island on their way into the United States between 1892 and 1943.*

people disagreed with Darwin's theory because it placed human beings in the animal kingdom, and it contradicted the biblical story of creation.

6. Darwin failed to explain why offspring were not like the parents. Mendel theorized that inborn characteristics were not necessarily blended or mixed but were inherited as if they were separate particles.

7. Pasteur's four great contributions were showing that microscopic organisms are not spontaneously created; proving bacteria can be killed by heat; introducing the germ theory of disease; and explaining the principle of inoculation.

SECTION 3

Focus/Motivation

Ask students to study the picture of Ellis Island on this page. Then ask them to discuss what reasons might cause people to leave their homelands and travel thousands of miles in cramped, unpleasant conditions to a new, unknown land, such as the United States or Australia. *(Student answers should include: to escape religious or political persecution, to seek better economic and social opportunities, and to find uninhabited lands.)*

Presentation
Constructing a Graph (Average/Group)

Have students draw bar graphs showing the increase in urban population

525

1B, 1C, 4H, a1C

● The police were also known as "Peelers," after their founder.

and the decrease in rural population in the United States since 1790. Ask them to draw graphs for the following years:

	Rural	Urban
1790	95%	5%
1850	85%	15%
1900	60%	40%
1980	37%	63%

Have students determine during which years urban population made the greatest increase. Then ask them to explain this, based on what they have read in Section 3.

The Shift to the Cities

As the population increased, changes in agriculture, industry, and transportation produced another striking result—the rapid growth of cities. As employment opportunities on farms declined, the developing industries located in or near cities offered new jobs. The factory system became the greatest spur to city growth.

Many early factories were located in already established cities, which then grew tremendously. The population of Manchester, England, for example, expanded from 25,000 in 1772 to 455,000 in 1851. When factories were built in rural areas, cities grew up around them. City living became the way of life for more and more people.

Before the Industrial Revolution, the vast majority of people lived in rural areas or in small villages. By 1900, however, in many nations more people lived in or near cities than in the countryside. In Great Britain about 10 percent of the population lived in cities in 1800. By 1921 that figure had grown to 80 percent. Similar changes took place in other countries. In 1800 not a single city in the Western world had a population of 1 million. Yet only 100 years later, cities such as New York, London, Paris, and Berlin each had more than 1 million inhabitants.

Sanitation and Public Order

Until very late in the century, cities did not have sewers. European and American cities of the 1800s differed significantly from cities today. People got their daily water supply from public fountains because houses did not have running water inside. The water in fountains came from polluted rivers, and no one knew how to purify it.

Neither public nor private garbage collection companies existed, so people dumped garbage on the streets. In cities smoke from the factories added to the smells from sewage and garbage. Thus people thought of cities as foul-smelling places.

After the 1870s the situation began to change. Technological advances made possible many improvements such as iron pipes, toilets, and water systems. Cities installed closed public sewers and piped water into houses. City governments passed laws requiring better heating systems and better construction of buildings. Governments also installed street lights and paved roads.

The governments of the growing cities also found they needed a new kind of police force. Law enforcement officers had to patrol streets to prevent robberies, direct crowds safely, and protect the lives and property of city dwellers.

In 1829 Sir Robert Peel, a leader of the House of Commons, organized a permanent police force for the city of London. This force was responsible for maintaining order and making sure that people obeyed the law. The London police were nicknamed "bobbies" after Peel's first name, Robert, and ● are still called that today. Other major cities soon followed London's lead and established police forces.

The Development of Suburbs

As cities grew and became more crowded, their boundaries expanded to include surrounding areas. In addition, people moved outside cities to new areas called suburbs—residential areas on the outskirts of cities. Suburbs first began to develop in the late 1800s. Families lived in the suburbs, where there was less crowding, noise, and dirt, but their working members journeyed each day to jobs in the city.

Railroad and bus lines made this daily travel possible. During the late 1800s, more and more cities established public transportation systems so that people could travel between home and work. At first ordinary working people could not afford the fares of trains and horse-drawn buses. Only employers, managers, merchants, and professionals enjoyed these transportation luxuries. They could afford to live fairly long distances from work, in the new suburbs, while factory workers had to live within walking distance of their jobs. By the end of the 1800s, however, lower fares made it possible for most city dwellers to ride trolleys or horse-drawn buses to work.

Leisure and Cultural Activities

Many currently popular forms of entertainment first developed during the 1800s. Before that time, of course, people enjoyed concerts, plays, games, and sports. As the populations of cities grew during the industrial age, the numbers and variety of these activities increased. Large audiences now paid to hear professional musicians perform or to watch professional athletes compete.

1B, 4H, a1C, a4A

Teams usually consisted of whole villages, and the playing field could cover more than a dozen square miles. The game was very violent, with deaths a common occurrence. During the 1500s football deaths reached such a level that Elizabeth I banned the game.

Learning from Pictures *This football match, played around 1900, was sponsored by a British ladies' football club. Who is known as the "Father of Football"?* Walter Camp

Sports. People had participated in athletic events for many centuries. The rich hunted and played a form of tennis. The poor organized informal games on the village common. In fact, we can trace the origins of soccer, rugby, and football to a game played by villagers using an inflated pig's bladder as a ball.

During the 1800s, however, many games became more organized. In Great Britain, "football" (known as soccer in the United States) was among the first games to change from an informal community activity to a professional spectator sport. Rugby and the American game of football then evolved from this early kicking game.

According to legend, in 1823 a young student at Rugby School in England caught a kicked ball during a "football" game. Instead of dropping it on the ground to kick toward the opponents' goal, he held it and ran toward the goal. Although the boy's teammates and the spectators admonished him for violating the rules of the game, the idea of running with the ball eventually won favor and in time led to the organization of a game called *rugby*.

"Football" clubs for working-class people were created in the 1850s. By that time laws granted factory workers Saturday afternoon and Sunday as rest days. Groups of players gathered each week to compete, and the rest of the community came to watch.

Soon certain clubs had reputations for their skill, and they attracted large crowds. Many people who did not play football themselves knew the rules of the game and enjoyed watching it. In the 1860s the London Football Association drew up official rules for games called *soccer* and *rugby*, and in 1871 the association established a national competition among football clubs.

Americans played soccer before rugby was introduced in England. Then in 1880 an American named Walter Camp, known as the "Father of Football," adapted rugby, and the game we know as football evolved. Although professional football leagues were not established in the United States until 1920, by the mid-1880s many soccer and rugby players were full-time athletes. "Football" had evolved into three sports played by amateurs and professionals and watched by paying spectators.

527

SECTION 3

Closure

Point out to students that population changes had an impact on the way people lived in the late 1800s. Ask students how the growth and change in the makeup of the population influenced people's leisure and cultural activities. *(Students might suggest that the growing cities provided more opportunities for leisure activities.)*

Review Answers

1. ***emigration:*** movement to other lands
2. ***Sir Robert Peel:*** British politician who organized a permanent police force in London; ***"bobbies":*** nickname for London police, derived from Peel's first name; ***Walter Camp:*** "father" of American football
3. ***New York:*** second largest city in the United States, located on the northeastern coast; ***Paris:*** French capital city located in central northern France; ***Berlin:*** East German capital city located in central East Germany
4. Pasteurization was one important improvement in the preservation of food in the 1800s. Refrigeration, which retards the growth of bacteria, was another. Refrigerators became an indispensable feature in the home in most industrialized countries, and refrigerator cars on railroads preserved foods during transport.
5. New technology such as iron pipes, toilets, and water systems made possible

Concert halls, museums, and libraries. Before the 1800s individuals and private groups sponsored most cultural activities. Musicians performed concerts in the homes of the rich or as part of religious services. Wealthy individuals who wanted to commemorate a family or personal event commissioned paintings. Individual families and religious or civic groups also commissioned paintings and sculpture for display in homes, churches, or clubs.

During the 1800s art and music became available to many people. City governments built concert halls and opera houses, and theaters presenting a wide variety of plays opened in both large and small towns. Music halls offered popular entertainment and vaudeville*, generally to working-class audiences, while middle-class people usually preferred classical drama.

Cities began to support symphony orchestras, bands, and choral groups. Performances took place in large concert halls. Bands played on Sunday afternoons in parks, where people picnicked, fished, or strolled.

During the 1800s art collections originally displayed in private homes and churches were moved to public museums. The Louvre (LOOV) museum in Paris had contained the art collections of the kings of France. Now it became a public museum. Paintings were organized and displayed by historical period and by the country of the artist. The museum received money from the French government, which wanted to educate its citizens in matters of art.

Great libraries were opened, among them the Bibliothèque Nationale in Paris and the British Museum (now called the British Library) in London. These libraries contained large book collections and were open to public use in the 1840s. In some cities, too, lending libraries with small collections offered books to subscribers for a small fee.

*Vaudeville, named after a town in France where popular songs were composed, consisted of light, often comical theatrical performances that frequently combined dialogue, dancing, pantomime, and singing.

Learning from Pictures *La Scala opera house was opened in Milan, Italy, in 1778. Early operas centered around scenery, song, and pastoral themes.*

Learning from Pictures This painting of a croquet game in the park was done by Winslow Homer in 1866. This great American painter began his career as a magazine illustrator.

Public parks and urban planning. Crowded cities had few places for outdoor recreation. When railroads were built, people often rode trains to the countryside. They could spend the day there, away from the congestion, noise, and dirt of city streets. Some people demanded, in addition, that city governments provide parks within cities for recreation.

By the end of the 1800s, many cities had playgrounds for children. Private lands were donated or purchased by city governments and given to the people as public parks. Large areas inside city limits—for example, the Bois de Boulogne (BWA duh boo • LOHN) in Paris and Central Park in New York City—were set aside as public parks.

During the late 1800s, amusement parks appeared in some cities. To entertain the crowds who visited them, the amusement parks offered games and rides, circuslike shows, and food. One famous amusement park, Coney Island, opened in 1895 in Brooklyn, New York, and is still in operation today.

SECTION 3 REVIEW

1. **Define** emigration
2. **Identify** Sir Robert Peel, "bobbies," Walter Camp
3. **Locate** New York, Paris, Berlin
4. **Interpreting Ideas** Describe how the preservation of food was improved after 1850.
5. **Summarizing Ideas** What improvements in the cities were made possible by new technology?
6. **Classifying Ideas** What new forms of leisure activities developed in the 1800s?

4 Interest in the Social Sciences and Education Increased

In 1800 illiteracy was widespread, even in those countries of the world that were becoming industrialized. In European countries schools were private. Religious groups ran the majority of these schools. Only wealthy or middle-class people could afford to educate their children. Most children either did not go to school at all or went for only a few years.

During the 1800s interest in education and in a new field of study, the **social sciences,** grew rapidly. The social sciences consist of those branches of knowledge that study people as members of society. This group of studies deals with many subjects—economic development, political institutions, history, and relations among people. The idea of making the study of these subjects objective and factual—of treating them like sciences—was new in the 1800s.

Political Science and Economics

The study of politics dates back to the Greek philosophers Plato and Aristotle. Later it was the subject of such thinkers as Machiavelli, Locke, and Rousseau. In the 1800s the study of politics became known as *political science,* and writers tried to study law and government in the scientific manner of physicists and biologists.

closed public sewers and indoor plumbing. Other improvements included better heating and better construction of buildings, street lights, and paved roads.

6. New forms of leisure activities included professional spectator sports, performances in concert halls and opera houses, plays performed in theaters, and popular entertainment in music halls. In addition, cities supported museums, libraries, symphony orchestras, bands, and choral groups.

SECTION 4

Focus/Motivation

Put the following quotations on the chalkboard or an overhead projector.

"[The job of history] is to show what actually happened. . . . The strict presentation of the facts . . . is undoubtedly the supreme law."
Leopold von Ranke

"History is nothing more than a tableau [scene] of crimes and misfortunes."
Voltaire

"The history of the world is but the biography of great men."
Thomas Carlyle

Ask students to choose the statement that best reflects their view of history and to explain the reasons for their choice. If they do not agree with any of the statements, have them write their own definition of history.

1B, 4H, a1C

● Research topic: Trace the development of one of the social sciences founded in the 1800s

Presentation Organizing Ideas (Average/Group)
Write the following lists on the chalkboard or an overhead projector. Ask students to match each individual in the first list with his work or theory in the second.

1. Voltaire
2. James George Frazer
3. Auguste Comte
4. Herbert Spencer
5. Ivan Pavlov
6. Sigmund Freud

a. French philosopher who influenced the development of sociology.
b. Compared the customs of different societies
c. Discovered the conditioned reflex
d. Influenced historians to concentrate on the study of ordinary people
e. Discussed his theories in a book titled *A General Introduction to Psychoanalysis*
f. Applied Darwin's theory to society

(Answers: 1. d; 2. b; 3. a; 4. f; 5. c; 6. e)

● Another social science, *economics,* was already well developed in the work of Adam Smith. However, not until the later 1800s did economists begin to imitate scientists by collecting and arranging statistics in order to test their theories.

History

Like political science, the study of history dates back to the Greeks. History, too, underwent change in the 1800s. Influenced by nationalism, many scholars wrote histories detailing the accomplishments and glories of their native countries. In addition, historical writing became based more and more on the systematic study of original materials and the careful organization of facts. Historians began a massive search for evidence of the past in documents, diaries, letters, and other sources. New interpretations of history began to emerge.

Another way historians encouraged nationalism was by observing and including in their studies all the people in a society. Here a writer of the 1700s proved influential—the French philosopher Voltaire, who was noted for his attention to social and intellectual history. His works inspired many historians to concentrate less on wars and great leaders and more on the study of ordinary people and how they lived. Later historians, influenced by Darwin, also tried to interpret historical events in terms of evolution.

Anthropology

It was in the 1800s that scientists realized how old the earth was and how long humans had lived on it. They found prehistoric cave paintings, discovered Egyptian, Sumerian, and Assyrian remains, and excavated such ancient cities as Troy and Mycenae.

Anthropologists also began to explore the continuity in the attitudes of human societies and in the way people relate to one another. An English anthropologist, E. B. Tylor, adopted the German term *kultur* to describe the set of beliefs and behaviors that a society shares. He discussed this concept in his book *Primitive Culture* (1871). In it he looked at one particular subject, religion, as it evolved in all human cultures.

Another English anthropologist, James George Frazer, took this approach further in his book *The Golden Bough* (1890). Frazer compared the customs of different societies and tried to show links between those societies through magical beliefs, religion, and attitudes toward authority. The study of similarities and differences among various societies has remained a major interest of anthropologists.

Learning from Pictures *In 1923 Howard Carter (left) and A. R. Callender crated artifacts from the tomb of Tutankhamen for shipment to England.*

Sociology

Sociology—the study of human relationships in society—also first appeared in the 1800s. The writings of the French philosopher Auguste Comte greatly influenced this branch of the social sciences. He argued that the study of society should follow scientific methods by using objective facts and avoiding personal interpretations.

In the late 1800s, sociologists became particularly interested in adopting the theories of the biological sciences. Herbert Spencer, for example, used Darwin's theory of evolution as the basis for studying human communities. As you have read, Darwin claimed that nature "selected" certain individuals—those most fit to survive—and allowed others to die. In his *Principles of Sociology,* published between 1877 and 1896, Spencer applied this theory of natural selection to society. A society, he said, includes superior people who are well adapted to it. In exercising their "natural rights," these people also contribute to the progress of civilization. At the same time, a society will contain inferior types—

the poor, the lazy, the ignorant, the criminal—who contribute nothing.

Spencer wrote that human society, like the plant and animal worlds, had evolved from lower to higher forms through natural selection. If so-called inferior types were permitted to die out, then society would ultimately consist exclusively of superior people. This application of Darwin's theory came to be known as **social Darwinism.** However, as social problems grew more severe and society became more complex during the 1800s, sociologists rejected social Darwinism.

Psychology

Psychology, another new science of the 1800s, studied the human mind—how it works and how it affects behavior. Psychology's origins trace back to the works of Greek thinkers, and since it did not involve experimentation, most people considered it a branch of philosophy. However, in the mid-1800s a number of scientists decided to make psychology an experimental science like biology.

Pavlov. Darwin's theory of evolution had a strong impact on the new science of psychology. Among other things, it influenced psychologists to study animal behavior and to apply their findings to humans. The most famous of these early experimenters was a Russian biologist, Ivan Pavlov.

In the 1890s Pavlov discovered the conditioned reflex. Psychologists had long known that certain behavior was automatic. A child does not have to be taught to pull his or her hand away from fire, but removes it automatically. In the same way, a dog does not have to be taught to salivate, or water at the mouth, when eating food. Psychologists call this kind of involuntary response a *reflex action.*

By experimenting with dogs, Pavlov proved that an animal could be conditioned, or taught, to have certain reflex actions. First, he offered food to a dog. The dog salivated. Second, he rang a bell each time the food was presented to the dog. The animal salivated and also began associating the sound of the bell with food. Finally, Pavlov offered no food to the dog but rang the bell. The dog salivated. It had been conditioned to salivate when it heard the bell. As a result of his research, Pavlov believed that all habits, even mental activity, constitute a series of connected conditioned reflexes.

Freud. In the early 1900s, the Austrian physician Sigmund Freud (FROID) developed another explanation of human behavior. Freud introduced the revolutionary concept of the unconscious—the mental processes of which a person is unaware—as a determining factor in behavior.

Freud had hypnotized certain mentally disturbed patients. He had found that under hypnosis they could remember past experiences that they could not otherwise recall. Freud believed that these early experiences had led to their illness. He treated his patients by gradually bringing the disturbing memories, fears, and conflicts back to the level of consciousness. To do this he studied their dreams and encouraged them to talk about whatever came into their minds. Then he interpreted these dreams and thoughts to show what lay beneath them in the unconscious mind.

Freud believed that troubled patients had unknowingly forced unpleasant experiences into the unconscious. To cure such people, it was necessary to make them aware of these experiences again.

Learning from Pictures *Sigmund Freud's pioneering work in psychoanalysis had a great influence on art, literature, and education.*

531

1B, 1D, 4H, a1C

● Discussion topic: How public education has changed since the 1800s

LITERATURE

Alice's Adventures in Wonderland

The modern era witnessed a new attitude toward children—that of treating them as children and not as small adults. One reflection of this change was the publication of books for young people that would amuse rather than instruct them. A landmark children's story was Lewis Carroll's *Alice's Adventures in Wonderland*, a fantasy both humorous and menacing. The drawings that accompanied it, by John Tenniel, were a high point in the art of illustration, perfectly capturing the story's whimsy and lack of logic. Here Alice is shown with the ill-tempered Duchess. Alice in Wonderland continues to entertain children of all ages in many countries of the world.

Freud called this process of revealing and analyzing the unconscious **psychoanalysis.** He discussed his theory fully in a book titled *A General Introduction to Psychoanalysis,* published in 1920.

Later, some psychologists challenged details of Freud's theories. However, much of his basic theory and method forms the foundation of psychiatry—the study and treatment of mental illness.

● Growth of Public Education

The American and French revolutions, with their ideas of liberty, equality, and representative government, made it seem important to provide education for all citizens. In the years following the revolutions, both France and the United States took steps to establish public school systems. Many people opposed the idea, however. They feared that education would encourage revolutionary ideas and make people less willing to do farm and factory work. They also believed that the cost of education would result in increased taxes.

As the years went by, many other factors encouraged the development of free public education—schooling free of charge for all, regardless of social class. Schools were easier to establish in larger towns and cities than in rural areas. Industrialists wanted literate workers as well as more engineers, scientists, and skilled technicians. Other people believed that schools other than government-established schools would not develop patriotic citizens. Military leaders wanted educated soldiers for their armies. As more people gained the right to vote, they voted for more education. They believed that education would improve their children's chances for a better life.

After 1870 governments in western Europe and the United States began to pass laws making some form of education both universal and compulsory. In a number of countries, the government provided only elementary education. In others the government also funded secondary, or high school, public education. In the United States, many public school systems were expanded to include kindergarten for young children and state universities for advanced study. Many new subjects, especially the sciences, were added to the curricula, and vocational and technical training were introduced.

Teachers had to take special courses that prepared them to teach new subjects.

In European nations the central governments established and controlled schools. In the United States, where local governments were stronger, the individual states established schools and set standards. Local school districts administered schools and levied taxes to support them.

For the most part, children of the lower classes attended school only as long as the law required. Then they went to work to earn money to help support their families. Middle-class children, however, went on to secondary school and often to college.

Education for Women

During the 1800s a great deal of debate focused on education for women. Some people argued that most educational courses were either unsuitable or unnecessary for women. Other people insisted that education was important because it made women better wives and mothers. Still others said that women should have equal opportunity in every aspect of society, including education and the opportunity to have careers outside the home.

Toward the end of the 1800s, when many countries passed laws guaranteeing education for all, elementary education for girls was included. However, opportunities for secondary education remained limited. In the United States, as in Great Britain and France, high schools for girls offered different courses than did schools for boys. Girls' schools emphasized foreign languages, literature, history, and home economics. Boys, on the other hand, studied sciences, mathematics, and philosophy, as well as classics, history, and literature.

Many people objected to the practice of having different courses for boys and girls. For example, Emily Davies, an Englishwoman, urged her government to improve women's education sufficiently to allow women to attend the universities. In 1865 she said:

> "We are not encumbered [burdened] by theories about equality and inequality of mental power in the sexes. All we claim is that the intelligence of women, be it great or small, shall have full and free development. And we claim it not especially in the interests of women, but as essential to the growth of the human race."

Learning from Pictures *These women are studying subjects traditionally studied only by males. What are these subjects?* **sciences, mathematics, and philosophy**

533

1B, 1D, 4H, a1C, a4A, a4F, a4G, a4H, a4I, a4M

SECTION 4

Closure

After they have read the section, ask students the following questions: What do you think should be the purpose of education? Who should be taught? What subjects should be taught? How do your responses compare to attitudes held by people in the 1800s? *(Students should note that in the 1800s far fewer people received educations.)*

Review Answers

1. ***social science:*** a branch of knowledge that studies people as members of society; ***social Darwinism:*** application of Darwin's theory of evolution to human society; ***psychoanalysis:*** a process of revealing and analyzing the unconscious
2. ***sociology:*** the study of human relationships in society; ***Herbert Spencer:*** wrote *Principles of Sociology,* in which he developed the theory of social Darwinism; ***psychology:*** study of the human mind; ***Ivan Pavlov:*** psychologist who discovered the conditioned reflex; ***Sigmund Freud:*** considered the "father" of modern psychology
3. An objective, scientific approach to the study of politics, economics, and history was adopted in the 1800s.
4. (a) By experimenting with dogs, Pavlov proved an animal could be conditioned to have certain reflex actions. **(b)** Pavlov found that all habits, even

Few colleges admitted women as students during the 1800s. Therefore, those people who believed that women should have the opportunity to receive university educations opened colleges for women. In the United States, Mary Lyon founded the Mount Holyoke Female Seminary in 1837. This school later became Mount Holyoke College. In Great Britain, Girton College opened in 1874 and Newnham College opened in 1875. Today these colleges are part of Cambridge University.

The Effects of Education

The spread of education had many positive results. People became better informed about current issues and took an active interest in a variety of government activities. Since more people could read, massive quantities of newspapers, magazines, and books were published and distributed to people of all ages.

Newspapers, which were not widely read before 1800, became especially popular and important. During the 1800s newspapers expanded their coverage to include politics, foreign affairs, and art and science. To attract readers the editors also included weekly stories by famous authors such as Zola and Dickens.

Newspapers often advocated a particular political position. They either supported or criticized the policies of one government figure or another and often featured humorous political cartoons. France, for example, had republican newspapers and monarchist newspapers as well as Catholic newspapers.

As more and more people bought newspapers, the prices decreased. Publishers also used advertising as a way of increasing income, attracting readers, and keeping prices low. In addition, new technology, such as the linotype, which set type by machine instead of by hand, and the electric-powered rotary press, improved printing processes. The invention of the telegraph made it possible for reporters to transmit the news quickly. Reporters could now extend their coverage to distant places and transmit news to their hometown newpapers.

As newspapers grew, so did the number of job opportunities for journalists and editors. In the past, writing had been something that people did in addition to their other work. It was not a full-time profession. In the 1800s, however, journalism became an accepted and respected occupation. Consequently, more people viewed journalism as an exciting career.

SECTION 4 REVIEW

1. **Define** social science, social Darwinism, psychoanalysis
2. **Identify** sociology, Herbert Spencer, psychology, Ivan Pavlov, Sigmund Freud
3. **Analyzing Ideas** How did the study of politics, economics, and history change in the 1800s?
4. **Interpreting Ideas** **(a)** Describe Pavlov's experiments in conditioning. **(b)** What were his findings?
5. **Classifying Ideas** List some of the reasons for the growth of public education.
6. **Comparing Ideas** What were some of the arguments for and against the education of women in the 1800s?
7. **Determining Cause and Effect** Describe the effects of the spread of education.

5 Literature, Music, and Art Reflected the Spirit of the Times

Literature, music, and art reflected the dramatic social and economic developments of the industrial age. Even in their most personal statements, artists portrayed in their works a sense of the rapidly changing times and of the influences of revolutionary scientific ideas.

Romanticism

Many writers of the early 1800s belonged to what is known as the **romantic movement,** or **romanticism.** Their work appealed to sentiment and imagination and dealt with the "romance" of life—life as it used to be, or as they thought it ought to be, rather than as it actually was. The romantic movement was partly a reaction to the Enlightenment, the movement in the 1700s that had emphasized reason and progress. Romantics glorified feeling, emotion, and instinct. They idealized nature and the golden past.

The romantic movement was also a product of the revolutions of the 1700s and 1800s. Political revolution in France had overturned the old order of society and released the spirit of liberty and equality. So, too, romanticism overturned the formal structures that literature and art had possessed in the 1700s and released a spirit of creativity, enthusiasm, and individuality.

Learning from Pictures *Edgar Degas sculpted this small bronze statue entitled* Little Fourteen-Year-Old Dancer. *His ballet paintings have long had worldwide popularity.* †

In Great Britain the most famous romantics were a group of young, intense poets whose works were filled with emotion and a strong love for beauty and nature. The works of romantic poets such as William Wordsworth, Percy Bysshe Shelley, John Keats, Lord Byron, and Samuel Taylor Coleridge are among the classics of literature.

Many romantic writers glorified the past, especially the Middle Ages with its chivalrous knights, ladies, and castles. For example, in *Ivanhoe,* the Scottish novelist Sir Walter Scott wrote about the days of knighthood. *The Hunchback of Notre Dame,* by the French author Victor Hugo, was also set in medieval times. Alexandre Dumas told the tale of *The Three Musketeers,* who roamed France in the days of Cardinal Richelieu.

Interest in the past was related to the growing nationalism of the times. Many writers turned to folklore, songs, and the history of their own countries for their subject matter. Germany was not yet a unified nation in the early 1800s, but a national literature arose there. The Grimm brothers collected the famous fairy tales that bear their name. This collection remains a favorite of children even today. Friedrich von Schiller wrote of liberty in *William Tell,* a drama about a Swiss hero. Johann Wolfgang von Goethe (GUHR • tuh), a master of poetry, drama, and the novel, also wrote during this period of rising national feeling. The drama *Faust,* the story of a man's bargain with the devil, is the most famous of Goethe's works.

Romanticism also influenced American writers of the early 1800s. James Fenimore Cooper wrote adventure stories that idealized the Indian and the frontier. Washington Irving produced romantic stories set in New York's Hudson River valley.

Romantic Music

In music, as in literature, the 1800s began with a shift to romanticism. One of the leaders of this transition was the German composer Ludwig van Beethoven (BAY • toh • vuhn). Beethoven brought to music the same interests and aims that the British poets of his time brought to literature. He expressed his love of nature in a symphony (known as the *Pastoral Symphony*) devoted entirely to evoking the atmosphere of the countryside. His call for liberty and freedom dominated the one opera he wrote, *Fidelio,* as well as the final movement of his last symphony. Beethoven wrote his music to arouse powerful and passionate emotion. Like all the other romantics, he praised human heroism and achievement and thought that people should express their feelings strongly.

The romantic movement led to a great outpouring of music, especially in Austria and Germany. Johannes Brahms composed powerful symphonies and concertos. Although they were classical in form, they surged with rich, intensely emotional music. Franz Schubert, Robert Schumann, and Felix Mendelssohn brought to their music the lyric quality of romantic poetry. Schubert and Schumann are especially remembered for their great songs, or *lieder.*

†The Metropolitan Museum of Art, Bequest of Mrs. H. O. Havemeyer, 1929. The H. O. Havemeyer Collection.

mental activity, are a series of connected conditioned reflexes.

5. Industrialists wanted literate workers as well as more engineers, scientists, and skilled technicians. Other people wanted government schools in order to develop patriotic citizens. Military leaders wanted educated soldiers for their armies. In addition, many parents believed education would improve their children's chances for a better life.

6. Some people argued most education was unsuitable or unnecessary for women. Others insisted education was important because it made women better wives and mothers. Still others said women should have equal opportunity in every area, including education.

7. With the spread of education, people became more informed about issues and took greater interest in government activities. Since more people could read, newspapers, magazines, and books began to be published in massive quantities. As people became more educated and informed, they began to have more say in the events that affected their lives.

SECTION 5

Focus/Motivation

Use slides, posters, or pictures from art books to display samples of the following art styles: romantic (works by such artists as Delacroix, Turner, and

535

Constable); realistic (works by such artists as Monet and Renoir); post-impressionist (works by such artists as Cezanne, Gauguin, and Rodin). Without identifying the art styles, have students point out the characteristics of each style of painting. *(Students will probably observe the following: Some paintings burst with action and drama and display deep emotions, color, and vitality — romantic. Some attempt to portray people and everyday life as accurately as possible — realism. Some use color and light to capture fleeting moments; they do not present reality but rather suggest it — impressionist. Some are more abstract with emphasis on color, forms, and shapes — post-impressionist.)*

After completing the section, show students the pictures again and have them identify the style to which each belongs.

Presentation
Analyzing Ideas (Average/Group)
Read to the class a selection of poems by Wordsworth, Shelley, Keats, and Byron. Then ask students to discuss what elements of romanticism are illustrated by the poetry selection. *(Answers will depend on poems chosen, but students should recognize such elements as a love of nature and beauty, the use of emotional language, the glorification of times past, and nationalist sentiments.)*

Learning from Pictures *Frédéric Chopin was a self-taught pianist, whose musical genius began to show early in his childhood.*

Frédéric Chopin (SHOH • pan), a Polish-born composer who lived in France, wrote graceful yet dynamic piano pieces. Franz Liszt of Hungary used native folk songs and dances in some of his compositions. He also developed the tone poem, a symphonic piece based on a literary or philosophical theme, often taken from romantic literature.

In Russia, Peter Ilich Tchaikovsky (chy • KAHF • skee) wrote highly emotional and melodic symphonies, operas, ballet music, and orchestral works. Often his compositions were built around stories, such as the fairy tale of *The Nutcracker,* the romance of *Romeo and Juliet,* and Napoleon's defeat at Moscow in the *1812 Overture.* He and other Russian composers, especially Modest Mussorgsky—known for his opera *Boris Godunov*—developed nationalistic music that emphasized Russian folk themes. As in literature, strong national feeling was an essential part of the romantic movement in music.

The greatest Italian operatic composer of the 1800s was Giuseppe Verdi. His best-known works, such as *Otello* and *Aïda,* contain some of the most beautiful and dramatic music ever written for the human voice. In keeping with the spirit of his times, the stories and themes of many of his early operas were highly nationalistic. Verdi's operas inspired a generation of Italians who were not yet politically united.

In Germany the greatest operatic composer of the 1800s was Richard Wagner (VAHG • nuhr). He called his operas "music dramas," and in them he combined singing, music, dancing, costumes, and scenery to create a spectacular theatrical effect. Like his contemporaries, Wagner was an intense nationalist. He based many of his operatic plots on German myths.

Several composers of the late 1800s followed in the general tradition of romantic music. They are sometimes called *post-romantics.* Gustav Mahler of Austria, for example, used huge orchestras and choruses to perform his lengthy symphonies. Another trend, however, was to break away from older styles. Claude Debussy (deb • yoo • SEE) of France developed unusual harmonies and rhythms in trying to create delicate musical impressions of clouds, sea, or moonlight.

Romantic Painting and Architecture

Although Germans, Austrians, Russians, and Italians dominated the music world in the 1800s, the outstanding painters and sculptors were French.

In the 1820s and 1830s, romantic painters, like romantic writers, chose subjects from the past and depicted scenes bursting with action and drama. Such a painter was Eugène Delacroix (del • uh • KRWAH) of France. Landscape painters John Constable and J. M. W. Turner of Great Britain reflected the romantic interest in nature. Their work had intense color and vitality, partly because they often painted outdoors instead of working in their studios.

Romanticism in architecture expressed itself first in the so-called Gothic revival of the mid-1800s. This was an attempt to re-create a great period of the past. The British Houses of Parliament as well as many American churches, college buildings, and other public structures of the time were designed in the Gothic style.

The Rise of Realism

The rich imagination as well as the ornate style of the romantics produced a type of literature and art of little relevance to the lives of most people. In the mid-1800s writers and artists began to abandon this approach and turn to **realism,** the realities of everyday life. One of the most important realists was Gustave Flaubert (floh • BAIR) of France. His novel *Madame Bovary* described with extraordinary attention to detail the life of an ordinary woman. In Great Britain, Mary Ann Evans wrote realistic novels under the name George Eliot. In one of

READ
WRITE
● INTERPRET
CONNECT
THINK

BUILDING HISTORY STUDY SKILLS

Interpreting Visuals: Using Art as a Historical Document

Works of art are not isolated from society but are created as part of human activity. Works of art often reflect the values of the artist as well as those of his or her society. The artist may be criticizing social conventions or political practices or reflecting the values of the historical period. By paying attention to the details and themes that the artist depicts, you can gain a better understanding of the historical period. Asking questions, such as the ones below, is an important part of viewing a work of art and helps you to understand its significance.

- What is the painting telling you about politics, society, or the people of the historical period?
- To what extent is the artist reflecting or criticizing the society?
- To what extent is the painting a document?

How to Use Art as a Historical Document

To use art as a historical document, follow these steps.

1. Identify the historical period of the work of art.
2. Explain the theme of the painting.
3. Connect the theme to the historical period.
4. Indicate whether the artwork reflects or criticizes the society and explain how it does so.

Developing the Skill

Study Honoré Daumier's painting *The Washerwoman* (right). What is it saying about working class people? How is it connected to the life style of the working class?

Daumier rebelled against the romantic tradition in art and sympathized with the working class. Instead of aristocracy and nature, Daumier's art reflects social realities. The Industrial Revolution created an urban working class with laboring chores. The theme of *The Washerwoman* focuses on the dignity and humanity of the working people. The artwork sensitively portrays poor, working people as having strength and dignity; harsh working or living conditions do not prevent the humanity of the individual from being revealed.

Is there a message in this particular painting? Daumier is realistically portraying the hardship and struggles by showing the heavy bundle the woman carries and the posture of both figures. These are not people to pity, however. Instead, the artist portrays the humanity of his subjects.

Daumier's painting is telling us about the social effects of the Industrial Revolution. Although members of the working class led difficult lives, they retained both their humanity and their individuality.

Practicing the skill. Visit a local art museum or look in an art history book to find a modern painting. Study the painting carefully so that you may interpret what the artist is saying. Using the steps above, try to determine how this work of art could be used as a historical document.

To apply this skill, see Applying History Study Skills on page 541.

537

SECTION 5

Closure
Point out to students that the development of realism was a reaction to romanticism. Ask students what social and economic conditions of the mid-1800s might have turned artists and writers away from romanticism toward realism. *(Students might note the labor conditions in factories or the rapid rate of change.)*

Review Answers
1. ***romantic movement:*** body of literary and musical works that appealed to sentiment and imagination; ***romanticism:*** another term for romantic movement; ***realism:*** expression of realities of everyday life in art; ***regionalism:*** artistic portrayal of everyday life in local sections of a huge country; ***naturalist:*** artist who described the ugly and sordid aspects of life while carefully screening emotion from his or her work: ***impressionist:*** artist who tried to give a vivid impression of people and places as they might appear at a brief glance
2. ***William Wordsworth:*** British romantic poet; ***Ludwig van Beethoven:*** German composer; ***Peter Ilich Tchaikovsky:*** developed nationalistic Russian music that emphasized folk themes; ***War and Peace:*** Tolstoy's novel that portrayed war as a vast confusion of misery and death; ***Claude Monet:*** French impressionist painter; ***Paul Cézanne:*** painter whose landscapes and still lifes

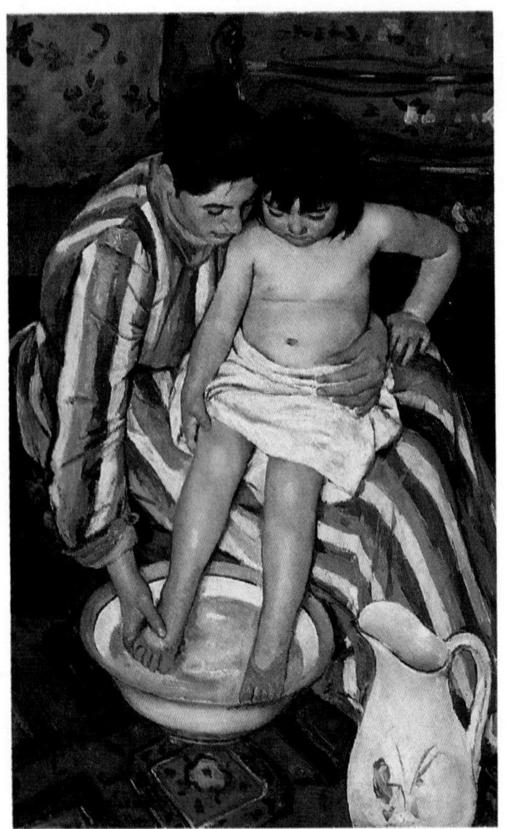

Learning from Pictures *The American impressionist Mary Cassatt lived in France. Her favorite theme was motherhood as shown in this painting titled* The Bath.

her novels, *Middlemarch,* she focused on country life of the Victorian period.

Often the realists made social and economic conditions their theme. The Russian Leo Tolstoy, in his monumental novel *War and Peace* (published in 1868–69), portrayed war not as a romantic adventure but as a vast confusion of misery and death. The Norwegian dramatist Henrik Ibsen brought human problems onto the theater stage. His play *A Doll's House* (1879) advocated the equality of husband and wife in marriage.

In the United States, realism took the form of **regionalism**—the portrayal of everyday life in different parts of the huge country. Examples are Mark Twain's novels *Tom Sawyer* (1876) and *Huckleberry Finn* (1884), with their earthy and humorous depiction of life along the Mississippi River.

Toward the end of the 1800s, a number of writers called **naturalists** carried realism even further. They described the ugly and sordid aspects of everyday life, carefully screening emotion and opinion from their writings. The French novelist Émile Zola was a leader of this approach. He wrote as if he were a scientist objectively studying and carefully recording all human activities. Though people objected to his frankness, his exposure of shocking conditions in industries helped bring reform. Another realist was the English novelist Charles Dickens, who often wrote about the poor people of London.

In painting, the kind of realism that portrayed people and everyday life in the industrial age characterized the works of the French artists Gustave Courbet (koor • BAY) and Honoré Daumier (doh • MYAY). Another kind of realism was attempted by a group of French painters who are known as **impressionists.**

Impressionist painting flourished during the 1860s and 1870s. Impressionist painters tried to give vivid impressions of people and places as they might appear in a brief glance. To do this, the impressionists studied light and color. They experimented with small patches of different colors placed side by side to create shimmering effects. Claude Monet (moh • NAY) and Pierre-Auguste Renoir (REN • wahr) were leading impressionist painters.

Experiments in Art Forms

In painting and sculpture, romanticism and realism were brief movements, followed quickly by intensely individualistic experimentation. There was less nationalism in art than in literature or music, and more "art for art's sake." Like writers and musicians, painters and sculptors often rebelled against the materialism and mechanization of an industrial world.

In the late 1800s, painters abandoned tradition in favor of experimentation. Form, color, and emotion became more important than subject matter. Realism was left to the newly invented camera, and painting styles became highly individualistic.

Paul Cézanne's landscapes and still lifes emphasized the forms and shapes of his subjects. He began to move beyond surface appearances to explore the abstract qualities of color and design. This shift away from showing recognizable, real scenes influenced other artists.

Learning from Pictures *The French impressionist Pierre-Auguste Renoir's painting,* Le Moulin de la Galette, *depicts a cafe in Paris.*

Also influential was Paul Gauguin (goh • GAN). Gauguin, who left Europe to live in Tahiti, stressed color and simple, flat shapes in his paintings. Henri Matisse painted many decorative scenes of southern France. He, too, emphasized design at the expense of realism. The Dutch painter Vincent van Gogh (van GOH) expressed intense emotions in his work. He used thick blobs of pure color, swirling brush strokes, and distorted perspectives and made no pretense at realism. Edgar Degas, Henri de Toulouse-Lautrec (too • LOOZ • luh • TREK), and Édouard Manet (ma • NAY) all painted scenes of Parisian life in their own personal style.

The French sculptor Auguste Rodin (roh • DAN) also broke with tradition. Some of his statues included unworked portions of the marble from which they were carved, giving his work a deliberately unfinished quality. Rodin rejected the traditional demands that art should show people, objects, and scenes as they appeared in real life. The growing interest in abstract forms marked the end of the emotional strivings of romanticism and pointed the way toward the new artistic interests of the 1900s.

SECTION 5 REVIEW

1. **Define** romantic movement, romanticism, realism, regionalism, naturalist, impressionist
2. **Identify** William Wordsworth, Ludwig van Beethoven, Peter Ilich Tchaikovsky, *War and Peace,* Claude Monet, Paul Cézanne, Vincent van Gogh
3. **Summarizing Ideas** **(a)** Briefly explain the romantic movement of the early 1800s. **(b)** Give three examples of romanticism in each of the following: literature, music, art, and architecture.
4. **Evaluating Ideas** How did Tolstoy and Ibsen use the ideas of realism in their literature?
5. **Understanding Ideas** **(a)** What was the aim of the impressionist painters? **(b)** How did they accomplish it?

emphasized forms and shapes of subjects, also explored the abstract qualities of color and design; ***Vincent van Gogh:*** Dutch painter who expressed intense emotions

3. (a) Romantics glorified freedom, emotion, and instinct and looked to nature and the past. **(b)** *Literature:* Sir Walter Scott glorified the past in *Ivanhoe;* the Grimm brothers' fairy tales encouraged nationalism; Schiller wrote about liberty in *William Tell; Music:* Chopin wrote graceful yet dynamic piano pieces; Tchaikovsky's works were highly emotional and melodic, Mussorgsky wrote nationalistic music; *Art:* Delacroix depicted scenes bursting with action; Turner and Constable illustrated nature; *Architecture:* the Gothic revival expressed romanticism; the British Houses of Parliament and American churches and college buildings were built in the Gothic style.

4. Tolstoy, in his novel *War and Peace,* showed war not as a romantic adventure but as a vast confusion of misery and death. Ibsen, in his play *A Doll's House,* advocated the equality of husband and wife in marriage.

5. (a) to give vivid impressions of people and places; **(b)** Impressionists studied light and color and experimented with small patches of different colors placed side by side to create shimmering effects.

Reviewing Important Terms

1. h; **2.** i; **3.** g; **4.** f; **5.** c; **6.** d; **7.** b; **8.** a; **9.** e

Developing Critical Thinking Skills

1. After 1870 new inventions such as the telephone and wireless telegraph made rapid communication possible. The use of electricity became widespread, and the development of the internal-combustion engine improved transportation.
2. The work of Pasteur, Lister, and Koch provided doctors with an understanding of what caused disease. As a result doctors were able to control malaria and yellow fever by the extermination of mosquitoes that carried these diseases. Similarly, they were able to control bubonic plague by the extermination of rats. In addition, there was a general reduction of infectious diseases through sanitary measures such as garbage disposal, water purification, cleanliness in food preparation, and development of new drugs.
3. **(a)** Flaubert; **(b)** Eliot; **(c)** Ibsen; **(d)** Twain; **(e)** Beethoven; **(f)** Tchaikovsky; **(g)** Tolstoy; **(h)** Verdi
4. Advances in science were accompanied by breakthroughs in medicine in such areas as prevention and cure of diseases, antiseptics, and the development of new drugs. In addition, through the physical and biological sciences more was known about the relation of diet to health and better methods of preserving and transporting food were developed.
5. **(a)** Romanticism was a reaction to the drabness of life resulting from industrialization. Romanticism

1B, 1D, 4H, a1C, a4A, a4E, a4J, a4K, a4M

Reteaching

Have students review the Chapter Summary and the appropriate section and questions in the Unit Synthesis. Discuss the concepts until students demonstrate a clear understanding of the material.

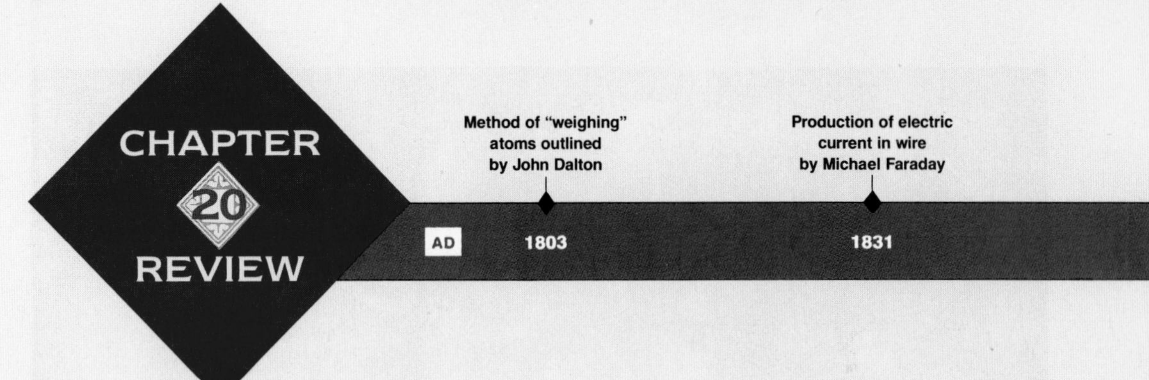

Chapter Summary

The following list contains the key concepts you have learned about advances in technology, science, education, and the arts between 1800 and 1928.

1. After 1870 new inventions such as the telephone and wireless telegraph made rapid communication possible. The use of electricity became widespread, and the development of the internal-combustion engine improved transportation.
2. Science developed rapidly during this period. In the physical sciences, the atomic theory became the basis for understanding matter. The brilliant work of Einstein revolutionized the study of energy and matter.
3. Significant progress also was made in the biological sciences. Knowledge about the cell, the basic unit of living matter, increased. The theory of evolution proposed by Darwin had an enormous impact. And the new science of genetics, founded by Mendel, answered many questions about biological inheritance.
4. Jenner, Pasteur, Lister, and Koch made advances in medicine. New drugs and medical techniques, such as surgery with anesthesia, were developed.
5. Improvements in diet and food storage changed people's lives, while immigration to the cities changed population patterns.
6. Those who studied the behavior of people as members of societies began to use scientific methods. Their fields of study came to be known as the social sciences and included new techniques for understanding history, politics, and economics. These new social sciences also included anthropology, sociology, and psychology.
7. Compulsory education won gradual acceptance in western Europe and the United States in the late 1800s. More and more people learned to read and write. This educated audience made possible the publication of books, magazines, and newspapers that presented a wide range of opinions and ideas.
8. The arts reflected the social and economic changes of the industrial age. In the early 1800s, many writers, musicians, and artists were caught up in the romantic movement, which emphasized emotion, nature, and nationalism.
9. In the late 1800s, romanticism gradually gave way to realism. In painting and sculpture, romanticism and realism were followed by an intensely individualistic period.

On a separate sheet of paper, complete the following review exercises.

Reviewing Important Terms

Match each of the following terms with the correct definition below.

a. physical science
b. special theory of relativity
c. social science
d. romantic movement
e. genetics
f. biological science
g. realism
h. regionalism
i. impressionists

____ **1.** the portrayal of everyday life in different parts of the country
____ **2.** artists who painted people and places as they might appear in a brief glance
____ **3.** deals with the realities of everyday life
____ **4.** deals with living organisms
____ **5.** studies people as members of society
____ **6.** deals with the "romance" of life
____ **7.** $E=mc^2$
____ **8.** deals with nonliving aspects of nature
____ **9.** studies the ways in which inborn characteristics of plants and animals are inherited by their descendants

Developing Critical Thinking Skills

1. **Summarizing Ideas** What were four of the technological advances during the period from 1870 to 1900 that made life easier?
2. **Understanding Ideas** What medical advances saved lives in the late 1800s and early 1900s?
3. **Classifying Ideas** Identify the name of the author or composer of each of the following literary or musical works: **(a)** *Madame Bovary,* **(b)** *Middlemarch,* **(c)** *A Doll's House,* **(d)** *Tom Sawyer,* **(e)** *Fidelio,* **(f)** *The Nutcracker,* **(g)** *War and Peace,* **(h)** *Aïda.*
4. **Determining Cause and Effect** How did advances in

1A, a4A, a4B, a4C, a4D, a4E, a4F, a4G, a4H, a4I, a4J, a4K, a4L, a4M

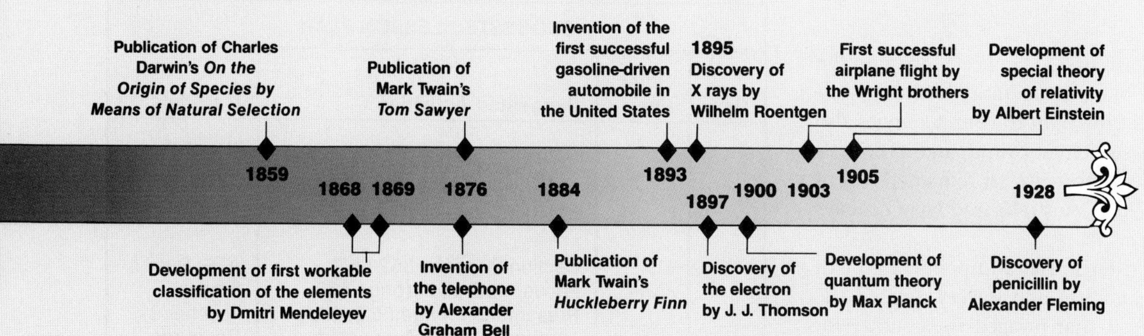

the physical and biological sciences affect the development of other branches of knowledge?

5. **Analyzing Ideas** Why might each of the following be considered a response to industrialization: **(a)** romanticism; **(b)** realism; **(c)** compulsory education.

Relating Geography to History

Select a particular author, composer, or artist discussed in this chapter. Use encyclopedias or other references to find out if he or she traveled extensively. Then write a short summary explaining how that person's environment and the extent of his or her travel may have affected his or her contributions to literature, music, or art.

Relating Past to Present

1. To investigate medical progress during the 1900s, interview a physician, nurse, pharmacist, or public health official in your community. You may wish to include the following questions: **(a)** How have medical advances made during the 1800s been improved upon? **(b)** What has been the most significant medical breakthrough in recent years? Record the responses to such questions for use in a general discussion of current medical technology.
2. Newspapers and news magazines became very popular during the late 1800s. What newspapers and news magazines can you find on the newsstands in your town or city? Select two or three of these and find out the year in which they were first published. Did any of the publications originate in the 1800s or early 1900s? If so, ask your librarian about the availability of early issues. Notice the kinds of articles and advertisements that ran when the magazine or newspaper first appeared. How do they compare with those printed today? What do the advertisements suggest about changes in society over a period of time?

Applying History Study Skills

Before completing this activity, review Building History Study Skills on page 537.

Several historical themes of the first half of the 1800s are combined in *Le Moulin de la Galette* by French painter Pierre-Auguste Renoir, shown on page 539. The painting is part of the impressionist school and shows people in a common meeting place in a French city. Study the painting and answer the following questions.

1. **(a)** How would you define *impressionism*? **(b)** How is it portrayed in *Le Moulin de la Galette*?
2. How does the setting of the painting show the middle class?
3. **(a)** What is the theme of the painting? **(b)** How do you know?
4. **(a)** Are the people portrayed in the painting different from the traditional ideal of men and women? **(b)** If so, in what ways?
5. Compare *Le Moulin de la Galette* to Daumier's *The Washerwoman*. What similarities or differences can you identify?

Investigating Further

1. **Writing a Report** Using books on the history of art, research Honoré Daumier's paintings on political themes. You might use Helen Gardner's *Art Through the Ages* (Harcourt Brace Jovanovich) or H. W. Janson's *History of Art* (Prentice-Hall) as sources. What is the subject of each painting? What techniques did Daumier use to influence public opinion? Why might a painting or other work of art sometimes have a greater impact than a written commentary?
2. **Preparing a Book Report** Writers of the early 1800s sought to appeal to the emotions and sentiments of their readers. They turned to nature and the past for inspiration, and their stories were often filled with adventure, romance, and personal heroics. Read one of the following novels and explain how it reflected the ideas of the romantic movement: Sir Walter Scott's *Ivanhoe* (Pocket Books); Rafael Sabatini's *Scaramouche* (Houghton Mifflin); Baroness Emmuska Orczy's *The Scarlet Pimpernel* (Macmillan).
3. **Preparing a collage** Using posterboard and a variety of magazines that may be discarded, make a collage of products that might be displayed in a 1980s exposition.

glorified life as it used to be, or ought to be, rather than as it actually was. **(b)** Realism accepted industrialization. Social and economic conditions were frequent realist themes. **(c)** Compulsory education was demanded by the industrialists who wanted literate workers as well as more engineers, scientists and skilled technicians.

Relating Geography to History
Answers will vary.

Relating Past to Present
1. (a) and **(b)** Answers will vary depending upon the individuals students choose to interview.
2. Answers will vary depending upon what newspapers and magazines are available at the local newsstands.

Applying History Study Skills
1. (a) Vivid impressions of people and places as they might appear at a glance; **(b)** The painting expresses the feelings of warmth, friendliness, and good cheer of a visit with friends.
2. The people in the painting appear to be well-dressed.
3. (a) The theme appears to be one of people enjoying life. **(b)** The smiles of the people at the tables, the gentle movement of the dancers, and the warmth of the conversations can clearly be seen.
4. (a) Yes. **(b)** The men and women are mixing quite freely together. The women do not appear to be subordinate to the men, as they would be in the traditional style.
5. Answers will vary.

CHAPTER (pages 542–571)

21 Reforms Swept Through Many Areas of the World in the 1800s

(1794-1911)

CHAPTER OVERVIEW

In Great Britain a series of reform laws passed between 1832 and the early 1900s made the government more democratic. The most important change was the expansion of the right to vote. Changes also took place in the relationship between Great Britain and its colonial possessions. Canada gained self-government but remained part of the British Empire. By the early 1900s, Australia and New Zealand too had joined the British Empire.

The United States experienced territorial and political growth during the 1800s. However, sectionalism and slavery divided the country. This resulted in a civil war that ravaged the country for several years. The postwar period in the United States was marked by industrialization, increased immigration, and reforms in women's rights.

In France, the first half of the 1800s was a time of turmoil. In 1830 Charles X was forced to abdicate; his successor, Louis Philippe, was overthrown in 1848. The Second Republic was set up, but Louis Napoleon soon created the Second French Empire. As Emperor Napoleon III, he involved France in many unsuccessful foreign ventures. Defeat in the Franco-Prussian War marked the end of the Second Empire. The Third Republic of France, established after the fall of Napoleon III, was beset by many internal political problems.

In Latin America, unrest became widespread as news of the American and French revolutions spread. The French colony of Haiti was the first to wage a successful revolt, followed by Spanish and Portuguese possessions in Central and South America. By 1825 nearly all of Latin America had become independent. Hoping to gain economically from the vast new market of independent Latin America, Great Britain and the United States opposed European intervention in the Western Hemisphere. Then, in 1823 the United States issued the Monroe Doctrine, warning European countries to respect the independence of the newly created governments.

SUGGESTED LESSON PLAN

Day	Objectives	Suggested Activities	Materials
1	U5* C1-2,	Introducing the Chapter (pages 542-543) Section 1 (pages 543-552), Focus/Motivation (page 543), Presentation (page 544), Closure (page 550), Suggested Teaching Strategies, Enrichment Activity, Daily Quiz, Suggested Assignments (page 541B)	ATE, Pupil's Edition, Teacher's Resource-Bank™
2	U5, C3-4	Section 2 (pages 552-557), Focus/Motivation (page 552), Presentation (page 553), Closure (page 555), Suggested Teaching Strategies, Enrichment Activity, Daily Quiz, Suggested Assignments (page 541C)	ATE, Pupil's Edition, Teacher's Resource-Bank™
3	U6, C5-7	Section 3 (pages 557-562), Focus/Motivation (page 557), Presentation (page 558), Closure (page 562), Suggested Teaching Strategies, Enrichment Activity, Daily Quiz, Suggested Assignments (page 541D)	ATE, Pupil's Edition, Teacher's Resource-Bank™
4	U5, C8-9	Section 4 (pages 562-569), Focus/Motivation (page 563), Presentation (page 564), Closure (page 567), Suggested Teaching Strategies, Enrichment Activities, Daily Quiz, Suggested Assignments (page 541E)	ATE, Pupil's Edition, Teacher's Resource-Bank™
5	U5-6 C1-9	Chapter 21 Form A Test, Reteaching Worksheet, Chapter 21 Form B Test	Teacher's Resource-Bank™ or Workbook and Test Booklet

*C refers to applicable Chapter Objective, U refers to applicable Unit Goal.

*C refers to applicable Chapter Objective, U refers to applicable Unit Goal.

BOOKS FOR THE TEACHER

Bailey, Helen, and Abraham Nasatir. *Latin America: The Development of Its Civilization.* Prentice-Hall. Surveys Latin American history; contains several sections pertinent to this chapter.

Horne, Alistair. *The Fall of Paris.* St. Martin's. Details the siege of Paris in 1870–71.

Mackenzie, Midge. *Shoulder to Shoulder.* Knopf. Documents the history of the suffragette movement in Great Britain. Includes many illustrations.

McPherson, James M. *Battle Cry of Freedom: The Civil War Era.* Oxford University Press. Explains the causes of the Civil War and details military events from Fort Sumter to Appomattox.

Parry, J.H. *The Spanish Seaborne Empire.* Knopf. Offers a scholarly study of the Spanish Empire and its collapse.

Strachey, Lytton. *Queen Victoria.* Harcourt Brace Jovanovich. Provides a very readable biography of the queen.

Talmon, J. L. *Romanticism and Revolt: Europe 1815–1848.* Harcourt Brace Jovanovich. Discusses the influence of romanticism on the political revolts of this period.

BOOKS FOR THE STUDENT

Cairns, Trevor. *Power for the People.* Lerner Publications. Provides a short, easily readable account of this era.

Noble, Iris. *Emmeline and Her Daughters.* Julian Messner. Features a readable biography of Emmeline Pankhurst.

Perry, George, and Nicholas Mason. *The Victorians: A World Built to Last.* Viking. Sheds light on this fascinating age through a collection of short pieces by many experts on the period. Includes many illustrations.

Prago, Albert. *The Revolutions in Spanish America.* Macmillan. Offers a concise and interesting account of the drive for freedom in Latin America.

Western, Irving. *I Accuse.* Julian Messner. Provides an account of the Dreyfus case in novel form.

Young, Bob and Jan. *Liberators of Latin America.* Lothrop, Lee & Shephard. Portrays some of the leading personalities of the Latin American independence movement.

MULTIMEDIA MATERIALS

The 1848 Revolutions (2 fs), Educational Audio-Visual. Examines and analyzes the revolutions in France, Austria, Hungary, Italy, and Germany.

The Latin Americas: Wars for Independence in Spanish South America (mp, 29 min.), NET. Assesses the influence of Bolívar and San Martín in the establishment of new nations in South America.

Nineteenth-Century Nationalism (2 fs), Educational Audio-Visual. Traces the origins of nationalism and its development up to World War I.

Revolts and Reforms in Europe 1815–1848 (mp, 16 min.), Coronet. Analyzes the struggles between the conservative nobility and political and social reformers.

Section (pages 543–522)

1 Liberal Theories Affected Great Britain and Its Empire

SECTION OVERVIEW

Although Great Britain had become a limited constitutional monarchy, the right to vote was severely restricted. A number of reforms during the 1800s made the government of Great Britain more democratic. The most important change was the expansion of the franchise to virtually all the people in the country. Changes also took place within the British Empire, where Canada, Australia, and New Zealand became self-governing dominions, maintaining close ties with Great Britain.

SUGGESTED TEACHING STRATEGIES

1. **Preteaching Vocabulary (Basic)** You may wish to preteach the following important vocabulary terms: liberalism *(page 543)*; suffrage *(page 544)*; home rule, suffragette *(page 547)*. Ask students to compare the eighteenth-century meaning of the word *liberal* with the way it is viewed today.
2. **Illustrating Ideas (Average/Group)** Have students study the picture at the bottom of page 550. Provide students with outline maps of North America. Then ask students to use historical atlases and encyclopedias to find the routes followed by the American and Canadian transcontinental railroads. Have students trace these routes on their outline maps. Finally, use these outline maps as a starting point for a class discussion on the geographical problems that faced the construction companies that built the transcontinental railroads.

*3. **Reading About History: Understanding Ideology (Average/Group)** To reinforce the skill lesson presented on page 548, ask students to suggest how ideology might influence the way historians interpret historical events.

ENRICHMENT ACTIVITY

Analyzing Ideas (Challenging) Point out that the illustration on textbook page 546 is from Sir Thomas Malory's *Morte d'Arthur.* These legends of King Arthur were also immortalized by the most famous poet of the Victorian Age — Alfred, Lord Tennyson. Have students read various parts of Tennyson's *Idylls of the King* and prepare oral or written reports suggesting why these stories had such appeal for the Victorians. To illustrate their reports, some students may wish to dramatize one of the Arthurian legends.

DAILY QUIZ

To assess student understanding of Section 1, give the class the following quiz. (Each item is worth 10 points.)

1. (T or F) Before 1832 the rights to vote and to hold public office in Great Britain were severely restricted. *(T)*
2. What names did the two major political parties in Great Britain adopt during the 1830s? *(Liberals, Conservatives)*
3. Which group petitioned Parliament to adopt such reforms as universal manhood suffrage and the secret ballot? *(Chartists)*
4. Which four-time prime minister enacted many political reforms during the 1800s? *(William Gladstone)*
5. Which socialist organization helped to found the British Labour Party? *(Fabian Society)*
6. (T or F) Herbert Asquith, prime minister from 1908 to 1916, adopted extensive social welfare legislation, including laws that

provided for better housing, child care, old-age pensions, and health and unemployment insurance. *(T)*

7. What was the name given to women who fought for the right to vote? *(suffragettes)*
8. (T or F) Lord Durham, governor general of Canada, wrote a report advocating that all British colonies be given their independence immediately. *(F)*
9. What opened western Canada to immigration? *(Western Canada was opened to immigration by the completion of the Canadian Pacific Railway.)*
10. (T or F) Australia originally had been settled by utopian socialists led by the Fabian Society. *(F)*

SUGGESTED ASSIGNMENTS

1. **Skill Worksheet (Basic)** Have students complete Skill Worksheet 21 in the TEACHER'S RESOURCEBANK™.
2. **Writing an Editorial (Average/Group)** Ask students to write an editorial supporting one of three issues: the Chartist program, the Parliament Bill of 1911, or women's suffrage. Have students share their editorials with the class.
3. **Preparing Biographical Sketches (Average/Group)** Have students work in small groups to prepare written or oral biographical sketches on influential figures of the Victorian Era, such as Queen Victoria, Benjamin Disraeli, William Gladstone, Charles S. Parnell, George Bernard Shaw, Herbert Asquith, Emmeline Pankhurst, or Christabel Pankhurst. Students should focus on these figures' accomplishments and the influence they had on the events of their time. Useful sources of information on these personalities include: Giovanni Costigan's *Makers of Modern England* (Macmillan); Neil Grant's *Benjamin Disraeli* (Franklin Watts); and Iris Noble's *Emmeline and Her Daughters* (Julian Messner).

Section (pages 552–557)

2 The United States Expanded and Changed

SECTION OVERVIEW

In 1788 the United States consisted of 13 states along the Atlantic coast and territory that extended west to the Mississippi River. During the 1800s the United States expanded rapidly. Sectionalism and slavery, however, divided the country and led to a civil war that ravaged the country for four years. Although the war left deep scars, it paved the way for a number of reforms, including voting rights for women. After the Civil War the United States experienced phenomenal growth, due in large part to immigration.

SUGGESTED TEACHING STRATEGIES

1. **Preteaching Vocabulary (Basic)** You may wish to preteach the following important vocabulary terms: sectionalism, secede *(page 554)*. Ask: Can such large countries as the United States and Canada ever be free of sectionalism? Why or why not?
2. **Researching (Average/Group)** The entire class might be involved in a project studying immigration to the United States from Europe in the 1800s. *Historical Statistics of the United States* (Department of Commerce) contains figures on the numbers of immigrants to this country broken down by year and country or region of origin. Groups of students should determine the total number of immigrants from each country and region of Europe for the periods 1820–1859 and 1860–1899. Another group should calculate the total number of immigrants from all countries and regions worldwide during each period. Using these figures, another group should determine what percentage of total immigration each country contributed. These percentages can be used to create two pie charts, which can be displayed on the bulletin board. Have students use these pie charts as a reference point in a discussion of the following questions: From what part of Europe did most immigrants in the earlier period come? in the later period? Were the immigrants' reasons for coming to the United States the same in both periods? Explain your answer.

ENRICHMENT ACTIVITY

Preparing a Bulletin Board Display (Average/Group) Have students make a bulletin board display depicting aspects of the westward movement. Students might include illustrations of covered wagons, gold mining and mining towns, trading with native Americans, and clothing of the period. Ask students to write brief captions for the illustrations included in the display.

DAILY QUIZ

To assess student understanding of Section 2, give the class the following quiz. (Each item is worth 10 points.)

1. In the late 1700s, the land bounded by the Appalachians, the Ohio and Mississippi rivers, and the Great Lakes was known as the ________ ________. *(Northwest Territory)*
2. (T or F) The Northwest Ordinance of 1787 guaranteed that people living in the territories would have rights equal to those who lived in the original 13 states. *(T)*
3. What territory did the United States purchase from Napoleon in 1803 for $15 million? *(Louisiana)*
4. Which Mexican territory, declared an independent republic in 1836, was annexed by the United States in 1845? *(Texas)*
5. (T or F) The Gadsden Purchase of 1853 extended the northwestern border of the United States to the Pacific Ocean. *(F)*
6. During the presidency of ________ ________ the United States underwent a "great democratic revolution." *(Andrew Jackson)*
7. During the first half of the nineteenth century, a rivalry developed between the three sections of the country—the Northeast, a region of growing cities and industry; the ________, an area of many large farms; and the ________, a frontier region. *(South, West)*
8. What was the greatest issue dividing the United States in the mid-1800s? *(slavery)*
9. The Thirteenth Amendment to the Constitution abolished slavery, the Fourteenth Amendment gave former slaves

_______ and equal protection under the law, and the Fifteenth Amendment gave them the right to _______. *(citizenship, vote)*

10. Who organized the 1848 women's rights conference in Seneca Falls, New York? *(Elizabeth Cady Stanton and Lucretia Mott)*

SUGGESTED ASSIGNMENTS

1. **Critical Thinking Worksheet (Basic)** Have students complete Critical Thinking Worksheet 47 in the TEACHER'S RESOURCEBANK™.
2. **Critical Thinking Worksheet (Basic)** Have students complete Critical Thinking Worksheet 48 in the TEACHER'S RESOURCEBANK™.
3. **Geography Supplement (Basic)** Have students complete "Geography Application Sheet 12: European Migration to the Americas" in the Geography Supplement of the TEACHER'S RESOURCEBANK™.
4. **Geography Supplement (Basic)** Have students complete "Geography Application Sheet 11: The Price of Making Cotton King" in the Geography Supplement of the TEACHER'S RESOURCEBANK™.

Section (pages 557–562)

3 France Underwent Revolutions and Changes of Government

SECTION OVERVIEW

In France Charles X tried to restore the Old Regime and was forced to abdicate. His successor, Louis Philippe, was overthrown during the revolution of 1848. Parisians proclaimed the Second Republic, and Louis Napoleon was elected president. However, by cleverly winning the support of many different factions, he created the Second French Empire. French defeat in the Franco-Prussian War marked the end of his rule and of the Second Empire. The Third Republic was established but faced internal political problems.

SUGGESTED TEACHING STRATEGIES

1. **Preteaching Vocabulary (Basic)** You may wish to preteach the following important vocabulary terms: anarchist, coalition *(page 562)*. Have students discuss why coalition governments might lead to political instability.
2. **Comparing Ideas (Average/Group)** Interested students might like to work together to construct a chart that shows the similarities and differences between the reigns of Charles X and Louis Philippe. Suggest that students cover such topics as ascension to the throne, economic policies, foreign policies, domestic policies, and end of reign.

ENRICHMENT ACTIVITY

Preparing a Script (Average/Group) The entire class might become involved in the preparation of a script for a "You Are There" program about the Paris Commune of 1871. Descriptions of conditions under the Commune and interviews with the Communards, members of the National Assembly, and National Assembly troops should be included in the script. Sources for the preparation of such a program include: S.C. Burchell's *Age of Progress* (Time-Life) and Alistair Horne's *The Fall of Paris* (St. Martin's). Select certain students to perform the script for the rest of the class.

DAILY QUIZ

To assess student understanding of Section 3, give the class the following quiz. (Each item is worth 10 points.)

1. (T or F) Charles X, an ardent believer in equality and liberty, enacted liberal reforms on coming to the throne. *(F)*
2. (T or F) Louis Philippe's support for legislation favorable to French workers won him the title of "Citizen King." *(F)*
3. (T or F) The establishment of the "national workshops" in 1848 marked the first appearance in modern times of the idea that a government has a responsibility to do something about unemployment. *(T)*
4. (T or F) Louis Napoleon, while posing as a champion of democratic rights, sought to stifle free speech by imposing strict censorship and driving all his critics from France. *(T)*
5. By cleverly manipulating the votes of a plebiscite, Louis Napoleon won consent to take the title _______ _______ _______. *(Emperor Napoleon III)*
6. (T or F) In order to quiet discontent at home, Napoleon attempted to win glory in two ill-fated ventures in the Crimea and Mexico. *(T)*
7. In a desperate attempt to regain support of the French people, Napoleon went to war against neighboring _______ in 1870. *(Prussia)*
8. Following the 1870 war, many Parisians, incensed at the terms of the Treaty of Frankfort, set up an independent council, called the _______, to rule the city. *(Commune)*
9. What radical group, which believed in the abolition of all governments through violence, set off bombs and attempted to assassinate government officials? *(anarchists)*
10. Who was at the center of an espionage case that led to deep divisions in the Third Republic? *(Captain Alfred Dreyfus)*

SUGGESTED ASSIGNMENTS

1. **Writing a Newspaper Article (Average/Group)** Have interested students write a newspaper report of the espionage trial of Captain Alfred Dreyfus. Suggest that they include in their reports the impact the trial had on French society. A useful source of information on the Dreyfus Affair is Irving Western's *I Accuse* (Julian Messner). Have students read their newspaper reports to the rest of the class.
2. **Researching Ideas (Average/Group)** Some students might like to do further research on Ferdinand de Lesseps and the construction of the Suez Canal. Suggest that they focus their research on the physical problems de Lesseps and his engineers had to face in digging the canal. Have students present their findings in oral

reports to the rest of the class. Students might illustrate their reports with maps and diagrams of the canal.

3. **Profile Worksheet (Basic)** Have students do Profile Worksheet 21 in the TEACHER'S RESOURCEBANK™.

Section 4 (pages 562–569)

The Nations of Latin America Gained Independence

SECTION OVERVIEW

By the late 1700s there was increasing discontent in Latin America, fueled by news of the revolutions in America and France. A successful revolt took place in the French colony of Haiti in 1794, and revolutions soon followed in Mexico, Central America, and South America. Spain and Portugal, weakened by internal problems, offered little resistance. By 1825 much of Latin America had achieved independence.

SUGGESTED TEACHING STRATEGIES

1. **Preteaching Vocabulary (Basic)** You may wish to preteach the following important vocabulary terms: hacienda, peninsular, creole, mestizo, mulatto *(page 563)*. Ask: How was the social hierarchy organized in colonial Latin America?
2. **Quick Quiz (Average/Group)** Write the following lists on the chalkboard or an overhead projector. Have students match each item at the left with a description at the right.

1. creoles	a. leader of a peasant revolt in Mexico in 1810
2. mestizos	b. militia general who proclaimed himself emperor of Mexico
3. mulattoes	c. native-born whites
4. Toussaint L'Ouverture	d. leader who was made president of Great Colombia
5. Miguel Hidalgo	e. people who were part Indian and part white
6. Agustín Iturbíde	f. leader of the revolt in Haiti
7. Simón Bolívar	g. Argentine general who freed Chile
8. José de San Martín	h. people of black and white ancestry.

(Answers: 1-c, 2-e, 3-h, 4-f, 5-a, 6-b, 7-d, 8-g)

ENRICHMENT ACTIVITIES

1. **Preparing Biographical Sketches (Average/Group)** Have students prepare oral or written reports on the leaders who fought for Latin American independence. Useful sources of information on these leaders include: Bernardine Bailey's *Famous Latin American Liberators* (Dodd, Mead); Irene Nicholson's *The Liberators* (Praeger); Paul Rink's *Quest for Freedom: Bolivar and the South American Revolution* (Julian Messner); and Ronald Syme's *Toussaint: The Black Liberator* (William Morrow). Ask students to present their reports to the rest of the class.
2. **Making a Dramatic Presentation (Average/Group)** Interested students might like to present a talk show featuring people from colonial Latin America. The group should include individuals from various classes and racial backgrounds. Each person should describe his or her way of life, and the good and the bad aspects of that life. One student should act as host or moderator of the show.

DAILY QUIZ

To assess student understanding of Section 4, give the class the following quiz. (Each item is worth 10 points.)

1. Why did the Brazilian city of Rio de Janeiro grow during the 1700s? *(because of its location near gold mines)*
2. What were the white, European-born rulers of Latin American colonial society called? *(peninsulars)*
3. (T or F) By the 1700s people of mixed race—mestizos and mulattoes—constituted the majority of the population in Latin America. *(T)*
4. (T or F) The revolutionary events in North America and France had little impact on people in Latin America. *(F)*
5. Who led the slave and mulatto revolt against the French in Haiti? *(Toussaint L'Ouverture)*
6. (T or F) The Mexican republic was established when a group of generals overthrew the dictatorial Emperor Agustín I in 1824. *(T)*
7. The three great leaders of South American liberation were Bolivar, ________ ________, and ________. *(San Martín, O'Higgins)*
8. In what declaration did the United States government warn European nations not to interfere in the Western Hemisphere? *(Monroe Doctrine)*
9. (T or F) During the 1820s, Latin Americans showed interest in creating a "United States of Latin America," and actually formed a union in the 1840s. *(F)*
10. Which social class derived great benefits from Latin American independence? *(creole upper classes)*

SUGGESTED ASSIGNMENTS

1. **Critical Thinking Worksheet (Basic)** Have students complete Critical Thinking Worksheet 49 in the TEACHER'S RESOURCEBANK™.
2. **Review Worksheet (Basic)** Have students complete Review Worksheet 21 in the TEACHER'S RESOURCEBANK™.

Teacher's Notes

For suggested lesson plan, additional teaching strategies, enrichment activities, daily quizzes, and suggested assignments, see pages 541A–541E.

Introducing the Chapter
This chapter contains several terms that are important for students to understand. Some of these have been introduced in previous chapters. Before beginning the chapter, discuss the meaning of the following terms: liberalism, suffrage, home rule, sectionalism, secede, anarchist, and coalition. *(liberalism: philosophy advocating freedom of the individual, civil rights, and peaceful change in society through the law; suffrage: voting rights; home rule: self-government; sectionalism: rivalry among various sections of a country; secede: to formally withdraw from a larger body, such as a political union; anarchist: person who believes in the abolition of all governments through force; coalition: temporary alliance of nations, political parties, or other such groups for some specific purpose)* At the end of the chapter, have students refer to the context in which these terms were used.

CHAPTER 21

Reforms Swept Through Many Areas of the World in the 1800s

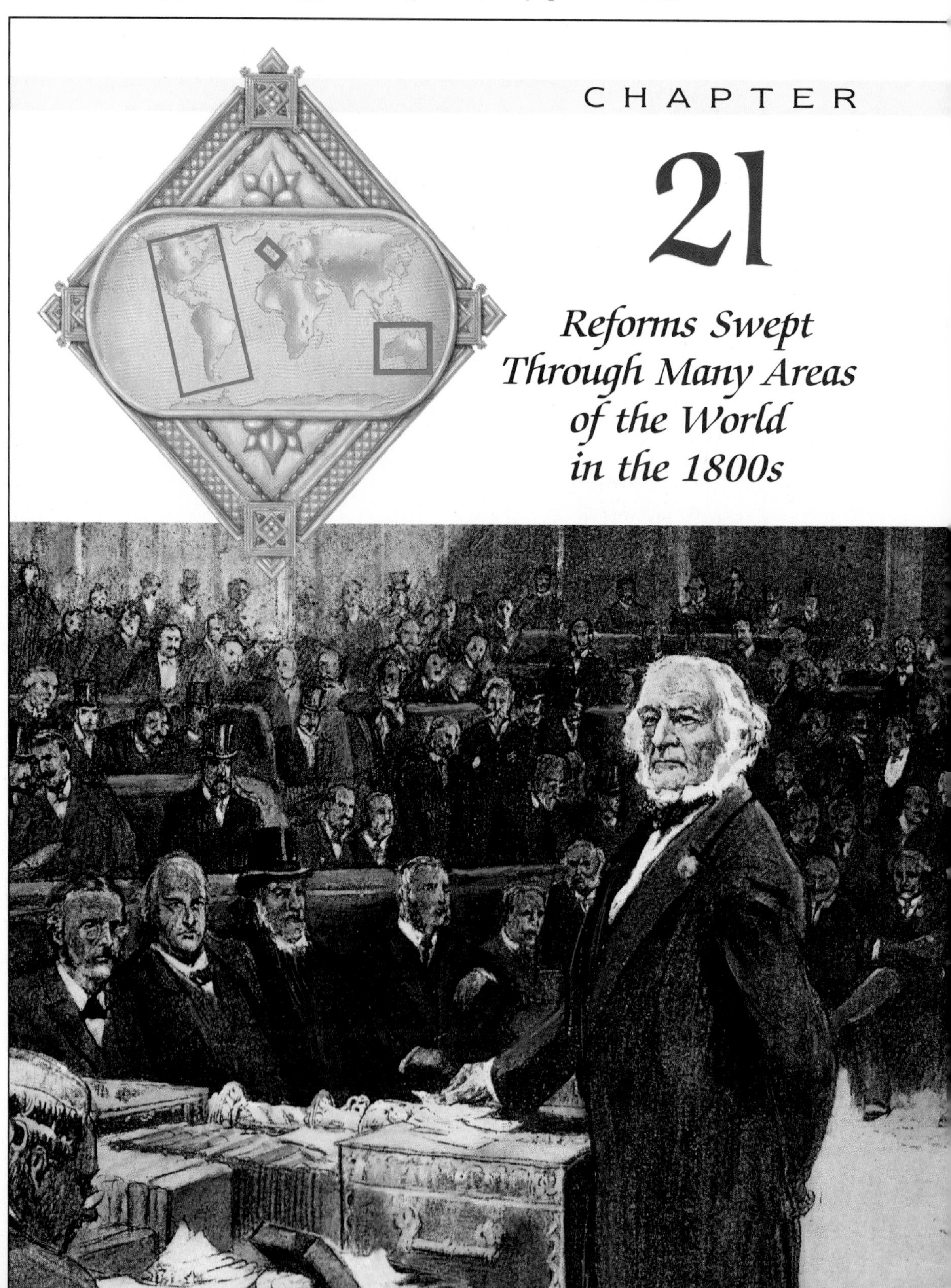

CHAPTER FOCUS

Place The British Empire, the United States, France, and Latin America

Time 1794–1911

3.7 mil. BC 4000 BC AD 2100

Significance

As the Industrial Revolution swept through Europe and the United States, people clamored for social and political reforms. An upper-middle class who profited from the Industrial Revolution emerged. Many members of this class believed in the political philosophy of **liberalism,** which advocated representative government, the protection of individual rights by law, and the ability of people to think and work as they please.* In many countries these reforms came through new laws. In others, however, it took revolutions and wars to win more rights.

The British Parliament passed laws extending rights to many citizens and granting its colonies self-government. In the United States, sectional tensions erupted in a bloody civil war before constitutional amendments extended citizens' rights. In France people endured riots, revolution, unstable governments, and wars before securing a democratic government. And leaders of revolutions set up republics throughout Latin America.

Terms to Define

liberalism	anarchist
sectionalism	mestizo

People to Identify

Benjamin Disraeli	Alfred Dreyfus
Louis Napoleon	Simón Bolívar

Places to Locate

Quebec	Florida
New South Wales	Texas
New Zealand	Mexico

Questions to Guide Your Reading

1 In what ways did liberal theories affect Great Britain and its empire?
2 How did social change affect the United States?
3 What effect did revolutions and changes of government have in France?
4 How did the Latin American nations gain independence from European powers?

*Liberalism in the 1800s differed greatly from liberalism today. For example, the liberals of the 1800s wanted to restrict voting to educated male property owners.

Florence Nightingale was a heroic Englishwoman who fought long-standing prejudices to make nursing a respectable profession. During the Crimean War, under terrible circumstances, she reorganized the inept military hospitals into efficient, sanitary places for saving lives. The following excerpt from Cecil Woodham Smith's biography, Florence Nightingale, *describes the admiration and respect she earned from the doctors and fighting men who observed her during the war.*

> *"In January, 1855 there were 12,000 men in hospital and only 11,000 in the camp before Sebastopol; and still the shiploads came pouring down. It was, Miss Nightingale wrote, 'calamity unparalleled in the history of calamity.'*
>
> *In this emergency she became supreme. She was the rock to which everyone clung.*
>
> *Her calmness, her resource, her power to take action raised her to the position of a goddess. The men adored her. . . . The doctors came to be absolutely dependent on her."*

The voices of women struggling for recognition of their rights through political reform were beginning to be heard in the 1800s.

1 Liberal Theories Affected Great Britain and Its Empire

Those who believed in liberalism were often active in politics during the 1800s. In Great Britain and in parts of the British Empire, for example, liberals helped enact a number of reforms aimed at protecting political and civil liberties. Some reforms extended the right to vote to working men and to women. Another abolished slavery, which had denied human and civil rights to black people.

British Reforms of the 1800s

Great Britain was one of the first European nations to abolish divine-right monarchy. The Glorious Revolution of 1688 (see Chapter 16) made Parliament the real ruler of the country. Great Britain became a limited constitutional monarchy with executive power vested in a cabinet headed by the prime minister.

◀ *William Gladstone in the House of Commons*

Chapter Objectives
After studying Chapter 21, students will be able to:

1. Identify the important reforms made in Great Britain between 1832 and 1867.
2. Describe the political changes that took place in Canada, Australia, and New Zealand during the 1800s.
3. Discuss the territorial growth of the United States from 1787 to 1853.
4. Explain the causes and results of the Civil War.
5. Identify the reasons for the French revolutions of 1848.
6. Discuss the effects of the Franco-Prussian War on France.
7. Describe the internal political problems faced by France in the late 1800s and early 1900s.
8. Explain the causes, goals, and results of the Latin American revolutions.
9. Identify the internal problems that faced Latin American nations after independence.

SECTION 1

Focus/Motivation
You might introduce this chapter with a discussion of the meaning of democracy as we know it today. Ask the class what elements are necessary for a society to be considered democratic. *(Student responses will probably include characteristics such as: voting rights, freedom of speech and the press, freedom of religion, absence of discrimination,*

1B, 4A, 4G, a1A, a1C, a2D, a2E, a2G, a2J, a2K, a2L

● In some districts, called "rotten boroughs," the population had greatly decreased or completely disappeared.

■ These were called "pocket boroughs" because the lord had the representative "in his pocket."

and equality of opportunity.) Have students read the subsection "Voting restrictions" on page 544. Then ask them: What conditions in Great Britain were undemocratic? *(A large portion of the population could not vote or hold office, the country was run for and by the upper classes, and there was discrimination against Catholics, Jews, and Dissenters.)* Upon completion of the section, have students indicate the reforms made to change each of these conditions.

Presentation Illustrating Ideas (Average/Group)

Have students work together to make a bulletin board display on life during the Victorian Age. They should include such topics as clothes, furniture, architecture, morals, and literature. Students may use encyclopedias and books in the library as sources for information and illustration ideas.

Voting restrictions. Theoretically the House of Commons represented all the British people. The voters of each district elected the members of Commons. The government, however, was not a complete democracy because not all the people had a chance to participate in it. The rights to vote and to hold public office were severely restricted in several ways: (1) Only property owners and a few other privileged people could vote. (2) Catholics, Jews, and Dissenters (non-Anglican Protestants) could not hold political office. (3) People voted in the open rather than in private. Unscrupulous people could ensure "cooperation" of bribed or intimidated voters. (4) The boundaries of election ● districts, or boroughs, had not been changed since 1664, even though the distribution of population had changed dramatically. (5) In some boroughs nobles who were members of the House of ■ Lords controlled the choosing of a representative. (6) Only men who owned considerable property could be elected to the House of Commons.

The Reform Bill of 1832. As time went on, the middle class and the workers began to demand reforms. At first the upper classes resisted reforms because they feared a political change might bring about a reign of terror just as it had in the French Revolution. Then, from 1793 to 1815, British involvement in wars with France provided a convenient excuse for delaying action.

After Napoleon's defeat, Britain, like continental Europe, experienced a period of reaction that threatened even long-established civil liberties such as the right of *habeas corpus.* Reformers who once might have tried to gain the king's support could find no help because of George III's insanity and George IV's incompetency. However, in 1829, near the end of George IV's reign, one piece of reform legislation passed. The Catholic Emancipation Act permitted the election of Roman Catholics to Parliament if they recognized the Protestant monarch as the legitimate ruler of Great Britain.

As time went on, the middle class and the laboring class demanded more extensive reforms. Several times the House of Commons passed bills that gave more people the right to vote and reapportioned election districts more fairly. Each time, the House of Lords refused to pass the bill. When the Whigs came to power in 1830, the cabinet forced the new king, William IV, to announce that he would create as many new lords as necessary to give the bill a majority in the House of Lords. To avoid this move, the lords grudgingly gave in and passed the bill in 1832.

The Reform Bill of 1832 took seats in the House of Commons away from the less populated boroughs and gave the seats to the new industrial cities. It also lowered property qualifications for voting. Now about 1 out of every 30 Englishmen could vote. As a result, people made wealthy by the Industrial Revolution gained parliamentary power, and this new class now had a voice in government.

The Whig Party, which had forced the passage of the Reform Bill of 1832, had the support of the new voters. Since many voters favored even more liberal reforms, the party changed its name and became the Liberal Party. The Tory Party of the large landowners, who had opposed the reforms and hesitated to go any further, became known as the Conservative Party.

Social and economic change. Vital social and economic developments took place after 1832. In 1833 Parliament passed an act that provided for the gradual abolition of slavery throughout the British colonies. The act gave freedom to all children under the age of six; all children six and older were to be free within seven years.

The Liberal Party soon forced the adoption of other reforms. The government took a timid first step toward free public education by giving financial support to private and church schools. Another reform abolished imprisonment for debt.

The Liberal Party also helped repeal the unpopular Corn Laws. For many years Britain's Corn Laws had set high tariffs on imported grain. By raising prices on imports, the Corn Laws protected expensive British grain against competition from cheaper foreign crops. British landowners benefited because they could sell their grain at high prices; however, the high prices created a hardship for workers who had to buy grain products or starve. In 1846, after a bitter fight, Parliament repealed the Corn Laws. Grain could now be imported into Britain free of tax. The repeal of the Corn Laws represented Britain's first step toward free trade.

Chartism. Beginning in the 1830s, a group known as the Workingman's Association petitioned Parliament to adopt reforms such as universal manhood **suffrage,** or voting rights, and the secret ballot. These proposals were made in a document called *A People's Charter,* and those who advocated them became known as *Chartists.* They proposed complete democracy for Great Britain.

● Through Disraeli's foreign policy, Great Britain gained control of the Suez Canal, and Queen Victoria became empress of India.

■ Not all people were impressed by Disraeli's success. John Bright, Liberal MP and founder of the Anti-Corn Law League, remarked of him, "He is a self-made man and he worships his creator."

1B, 4A, 4G, a1A, a1C, a2D, a2E, a2G, a2J, a2K, a2L, a4A

The Chartists held conventions in 1839, 1842, and 1848. Although the Chartists made relatively mild proposals, many people believed they threatened the very foundations of society. In 1848 the British authorities worried that revolution might occur in Great Britain. But the Chartists were not unified in their aims, and the movement died out.

Despite the failure of the Chartist movement, Parliament eventually adopted most of the reforms its members advocated. Workers continued to demand voting rights, and many others who favored more democratic government joined them. Leaders of both the Conservative and Liberal parties came to realize that reforms might gain the gratitude and the votes of the new voters.

In 1867 Parliament passed a second Reform Bill with more sweeping reforms than the first. It almost doubled the number of those who could vote. By lowering property qualifications, the second Reform Bill extended the vote to most city industrial workers. However, household servants, members of the armed forces, agricultural workers, and women did not gain voting rights.

Learning from Pictures *Thomas Sully portrayed Queen Victoria shortly after she became queen. Her reign was the longest in British history.*

Disraeli and Gladstone

William IV died in 1837. Since he had no male heirs, the throne went to his 18-year-old niece, Victoria. She interfered very little in the government and allowed her prime ministers a free hand. Victoria reigned from 1837 until 1901, a 64-year period so outstanding in British history that it became known as the *Victorian Era.*

Learning from Pictures *Disraeli was Queen Victoria's favorite prime minister. What did he achieve* ● *in foreign policy between 1874 and 1880?*

Two outstanding prime ministers—Benjamin Disraeli and William Gladstone—dominated the political arena between 1866 and 1894. Benjamin Disraeli led the Conservative Party and served twice as prime minister. In addition to his wit and shrewdness, Disraeli had an intense interest in foreign affairs and the expansion of the British Empire. ■

Disraeli's first term as prime minister lasted only a few months. He first became prime minister when Lord Derby resigned in February of 1868, but he was defeated by Gladstone and the Liberals in the general election held later that year. During his second ministry, from 1874 to 1880, Britain gained control of the Suez Canal and Queen Victoria became Empress of India.

William Gladstone led the Liberal Party and served four terms as prime minister. He was devout, cautious, and formal. His formality even bothered

1B, 4A, 4G, 4H, a1A, a1C

● Victoria much preferred the charming, flamboyant Disraeli. And Disraeli knew how to win over the queen. He noted to a friend, "Everyone likes flattery; and when it comes to Royalty you should lay it on with a trowel."

History Through the Arts

DRAWING

The Victorians and King Arthur

Waving farewell to the magical sword Excalibur, Sir Bedivere watches as the mysterious Lady of the Lake takes back the weapon that had served his beloved King Arthur for so many years.

This ancient legend of Arthur, the ideal king, and his Knights of the Round Table dates back to the 600s. Stories about the good and powerful leader were spread by word of mouth throughout England, Wales, and France for centuries. Then, in the 1400s, the English writer Sir Thomas Malory adapted these tales, and William Caxton, one of England's first printers, published them. Children and adults have loved reading them ever since.

King Arthur was a special favorite during the Victorian Era. This scene was drawn in 1893 by Aubrey Beardsley, who was only 21 when he was commissioned to illustrate the King Arthur stories. Beardsley established a personal form of art, blending the ornate curves of art nouveau (new art) with the feeling and pattern of Japanese prints. He quickly became the leading illustrator of his day. But Beardsley did not live to enjoy his fame. He died of tuberculosis when he was only 25. Although often imitated, his exquisite, flat black-and-white style has remained unique.

●Queen Victoria, who complained, "Mr. Gladstone addresses me as if I were a public meeting." Gladstone concerned himself with British domestic and financial matters. Under his leadership, Parliament attempted additional reforms, many of which went into effect.

Gladstone first became prime minister in 1868. One of his finest achievements as prime minister was the passage of the Education Act of 1870, which created a national elementary education system. The passing of this act meant that the children of the working classes could now receive an elementary education for a small fee. Elementary education became free in England in 1891.

In 1872, under Gladstone's leadership, Britain adopted the secret ballot. Now a man could vote as he chose, without fearing that he might suffer because someone disapproved of his politics. The secret ballot also reduced bribery, which had been common, and protected the workers in the cities from intimidation by their bosses.

In 1884 Gladstone and the Liberals pushed through Parliament the third Reform Bill, which gave the vote to most agricultural workers. In the following year, 1885, the Redistribution Bill divided Britain into electoral districts approximately equal in population. Although this bill did not achieve complete equality in representation, it was an important step in this direction.

546

The Irish Question

One area in which the Liberals proved unsuccessful was the "Irish Question." In 1801 the Act of Union had joined Ireland and Great Britain to form the United Kingdom of Great Britain and Ireland. The Act of Union disbanded Ireland's Parliament, leaving the Irish with little representation in the British Parliament. In addition to resenting the poor parliamentary representation, the Irish people—mostly Roman Catholics—resented having to pay taxes to help support the Anglican church.

The Irish hated British rule, especially the absentee landlords who owned much of the land. Several times in the mid-1800s, the potato crop failed, and famine swept Ireland. The worst famine came in 1848, causing many Irish people to abandon their homes and flee to the United States. Those who remained wanted new land laws and **home rule,** or self-government. Gladstone tried unsuccessfully to get home-rule bills passed. Finally, the Conservatives made concessions to the Irish during the 1890s, and the "Irish Question" ceased to be troublesome for the next few decades.

British Reforms of the Early 1900s

Social reform accompanied political reform. During the late 1800s and early 1900s, the labor union movement grew stronger in Great Britain. Socialism, too, attracted many followers.

Social reforms. In 1884 a group of intellectuals founded the Fabian Society, a socialist organization aimed at "reconstructing society in accordance with the highest moral possibilities." At first the Fabians worked through the established political parties. In 1906 they helped workers, frustrated over the policies of the Liberal and Conservative parties, to found a new organization, the British Labour Party.

In 1905 the Liberal Party came to power. Under Herbert Asquith, prime minister from 1908 to 1916, the Liberals adopted extensive social welfare legislation. Laws provided for child care, old-age pensions, better housing, and health and unemployment insurance. In order to pay for all of these welfare benefits, Parliament raised taxes.

Changes within Parliament. The budget of 1909 increased taxes for the wealthy. Because the House of Lords opposed the budget, the Liberals took steps to decrease the power of the lords. The Parliament Bill of 1911 took away the lords' powers to veto tax and appropriation bills and allowed them only to delay passage of other bills. The lords bitterly opposed the act and passed it only after George V, who had become king in 1910, threatened to create enough new Liberal lords to pass it.

Within a month after the passage of the Parliament Bill, Liberals and workers achieved another vital goal. Parliament passed a law giving members of the House of Commons a salary of 400 pounds ($2,000) a year. Although by today's standards the amount seems small, it was a good salary for that time. It meant that a person without an independent income could afford to serve in Parliament.

Women's voting rights. Since the late 1880s, many women in Great Britain had demanded the right to vote. Led by energetic and outspoken women like Christabel Pankhurst and her mother, Emmeline, they were known as **suffragettes** because they wanted suffrage for all women. Suffragettes petitioned Parliament and marched. Many expected that women would receive the right to vote in 1910, but this did not happen.*

Reforming the Parliamentary System

1829	Catholic Emancipation Act permitted Roman Catholics to be elected to Parliament
1832	First Reform Bill redistributed seats in Parliament and lowered property qualifications for voting
1867	Second Reform Bill further lowered property qualifications, almost doubling electorate
1872	Secret ballot adopted
1884	Third Reform Bill gave vote to most farm workers
1885	Redistribution Bill divided Britain into approximately equal electoral districts
1911	Parliament Bill took away power of lords except to delay passage of bills
1928	All British women over the age of 21 were granted voting rights

*In 1919, a bill gave the right to vote to women over the age of 30 if they or their husbands owned property. In 1928 another bill granted all British women over the age of 21 the right to vote.

547

1B, 4I, a1A, a1B, a4A, a4E, a4G, a4H, a4J, a4K, a4L

READ
WRITE
INTERPRET
CONNECT
THINK

BUILDING HISTORY STUDY SKILLS

Reading About History: Understanding Ideology

An ideology is a body of ideas on which a particular system is based. In the 1800s in Europe, the two conflicting ideologies were liberalism and conservatism. Liberalism was based on the political philosophy of the French Revolution and the Enlightenment. Those who followed the ideology of political liberalism believed in a constitution that protected individual rights. The role of the government was to protect these rights. An economic liberal believed in the freedom of the individual to pursue economic gain without government interference.

On the other hand, conservatism was the ideology of the old order that was hostile to the French Revolution and the Enlightenment. Those who followed the ideology of political conservatism believed in a traditional government system that upheld the privileges of the upper classes. Economic conservatives believed in the government's role to manage the economy so that the state would prosper.

Understanding an ideology helps you determine the extent to which a person's position is based on his or her belief in an ideology rather than the facts. For example, to what extent is a newspaper's support for a presidential candidate determined by ideology?

How to Understand Ideology

To understand an ideology, follow these steps.

1. Define the ideology. Find out what a person's ideology is by determining how he or she views change and the role of government.
2. Make connections. How does the ideology affect the author's viewpoint or the development of the author's argument?
3. Categorize the ideology. Is it economic or political?

Developing the Skill

The cartoons on the right were printed during the debate over the extension of suffrage to the workingman in 1867 in Great Britain. The argument sharply divided the liberals and the conservatives. Study the cartoons to determine the ideology of each of the cartoonists.

The political cartoon on the top expressed the liberal ideology. The cartoonist depicted the workingman as an angel carrying his tools, while drinking holy water from a font in a church. The cartoonist must have favored change and supported the government's extension of the right to vote, because he drew the worker in such a positive way.

The political cartoon on the bottom expressed the conservative ideology. In this cartoon the workingman is portrayed as a slovenly drunkard. This cartoonist's sympathy with the conservative ideology was apparent by the negative way in which he depicted the workingman. The cartoonist opposed change because he would not want the government to extend voting rights to the undeserving worker.

Practicing the skill. Find a political cartoon in your local newspaper. By using the skills listed above, attempt to determine the political ideology of the cartoonist.

To apply this skill, see Applying History Study Skills on page 571.

1A, 1B, 4E, a1B, a1C, a4B, a4C

Changes Within the British Empire

As Great Britain instituted social and political reforms, other changes occurred within the British Empire. Settlers in the British colonies of Canada, Australia, and New Zealand benefited from the liberal policies being enacted in Great Britain.

Canada

The French Canadians in Lower Canada (part of what is now Quebec) and British settlers in Upper Canada (part of what is now Ontario) had long been discontented with British rule. The problem arose primarily because the British Canadians wanted even more self-government, and the French-Canadians resented British rule.

During the 1830s a business depression, unemployment, and crop failures led to uprisings in both Lower and Upper Canada. The French Canadians tried to establish an independent French republic, while the British Canadians sought greater freedom from British officials. Neither revolt met with success.

The Durham Report. In 1838 the British government sent a new governor general, Lord Durham, to Canada to try to settle disagreements between the English- and French-speaking Canadians. A leader of the Liberal Party, Durham had helped write the Reform Bill of 1832. He was given broad powers to reform Canada's government.

In 1839 Lord Durham submitted a report to Parliament with a basic recommendation that became a guide for all later British colonial policy.

Learning from Maps *In Canada the British avoided the mistakes they had made in the 13 American colonies. What is Canada's smallest province?* **Prince Edward Island**

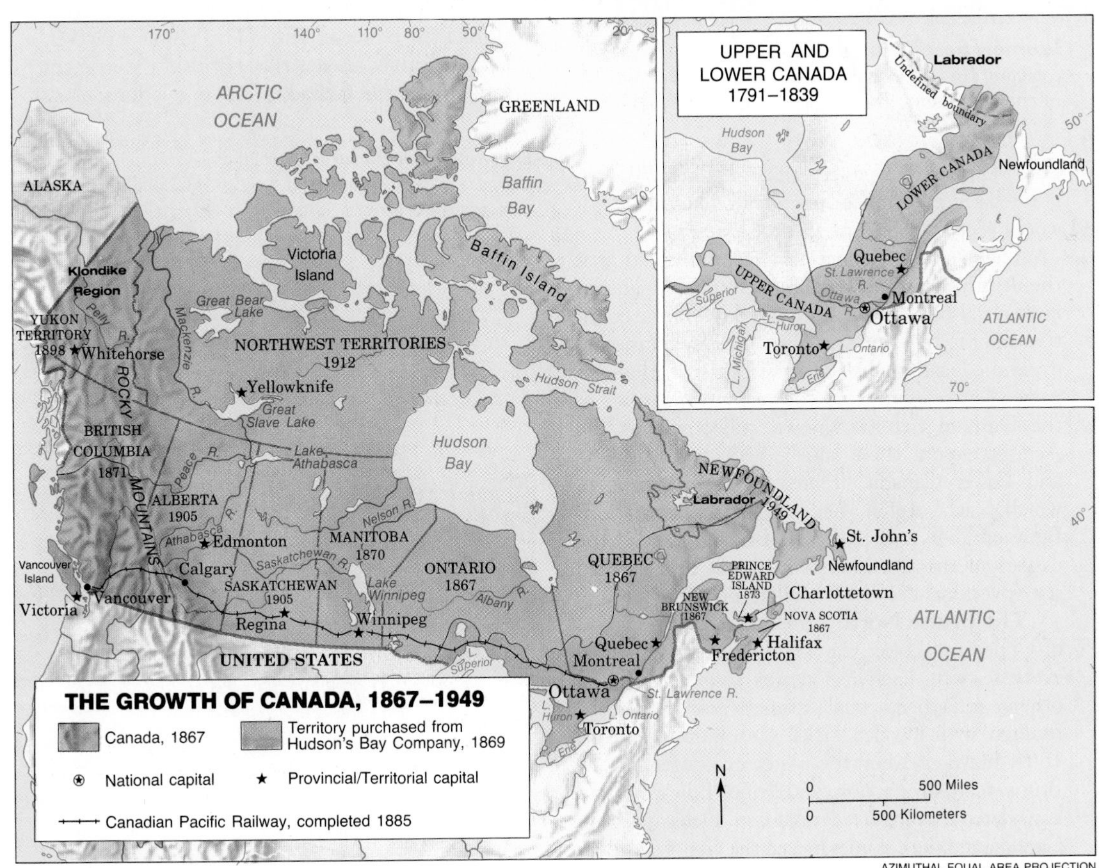

549

SECTION 1

Closure
Mention that in a speech in 1844, Benjamin Disraeli noted that the British government should implement policies on Ireland that would "effect . . . all those changes which a revolution would affect by force." Ask: Why do you think a solution to the Irish Question required such drastic changes?

Review Answers
1. ***liberalism:*** political philosophy that advocated representative government, the protection of individual rights by law, and the ability of people to think and work as they please; ***suffrage:*** voting rights; ***home rule:*** self-government; ***suffragette:*** woman who wanted voting rights for all women
2. ***Chartists:*** advocates of reforms, such as universal manhood suffrage and the secret ballot; active in the 1830s and 1840s; ***Queen Victoria:*** ruled from 1837-1901; interfered very little in government and allowed prime ministers a free hand; ***Benjamin Disraeli:*** Conservative Party leader and twice prime minister in the late 1800s; particularly interested in foreign affairs and enlarging the British Empire; ***William Gladstone:*** Liberal Party leader who served four terms as prime minister in the late 1800s; ***Fabian Society:*** organization of socialist intellectual reformers who helped found the British Labour Party; ***Christabel***

Learning from Pictures *This picture of Victoria, the capital of British Columbia, was taken in 1890. Victoria is among the most "British" of Canada's cities.*

Lord Durham suggested that if Great Britain granted self-government to colonies like Canada, it would keep these colonies in the empire.

The Durham Report also recommended that the British government aid immigration to Canada, build a railroad to help unite and develop the country, reform the tax and the court systems, and expand education. In 1840 the British Parliament passed laws to carry out the recommendations of the Durham Report. Known collectively as the Acts of Union, these laws joined Upper Canada and Lower Canada. It created a Parliament in which each region had equal representation. Between 1846 and 1848, the British enlarged the powers of the Canadian Parliament and granted self-government to the Canadian people.

The British North America Act. The union of Upper and Lower Canada did not work well in every respect. Each region was suspicious of the other, and their equal strength in Parliament resulted in many deadlocks. A solution came in 1864, however, when the eastern colonies of New Brunswick, Nova Scotia, and Prince Edward Island considered forming a federal union. Delegates from Canada and the colonies met in the city of Quebec. They recommended a plan of federation, which the British Parliament approved as the British North America Act of 1867. The act created the Dominion of Canada with the provinces of Ontario, Quebec, Nova Scotia, and New Brunswick.

By the terms of the British North America Act, each province kept its own legislature to deal with local affairs. The federal Parliament, which dealt with national problems, met in Ontario at the Dominion capital, Ottawa. Dominion government was a parliamentary democracy with a cabinet based on the British model. The Liberal and Conservative political parties in Canada resembled those in Great Britain. The party in power appointed the premier, who had much the same influence as the British prime minister.

The Canadian provinces did not become completely independent through the British North America Act. Instead, Canada remained part of the British Empire and recognized the British king or queen, whose representative, the governor general, had the power of veto. (This power, however, would be rarely used.) The British government greatly influenced Canada's foreign relations.

Learning from Pictures *Great transcontinental railroads traversed the vast distances of Canada just as they did in the United States.*

● More than 162,000 British convicts were transported to Australia between 1788 and 1868, when the practice officially ended. Most of them were petty criminals and the sentences they received ranged from seven years to life.

1A, 1B, 1C, 4E, a1C, a4B, a4C

Territorial growth. In 1869 Canada purchased a huge area, including the present Northwest Territories, from the Hudson's Bay Company, a private trading company in Canada. Because the Canadians feared that the United States would try to annex all or part of this vast area, they quickly created the province of Manitoba in the southeast portion of the area. British Columbia and Prince Edward Island became provinces during the 1870s, bringing the number of provinces in the Dominion to seven.

The completion in 1885 of the Canadian Pacific Railway (see map, page 549) opened western Canada to immigration. As a result, two more provinces—Alberta and Saskatchewan—joined the Dominion of Canada in 1905.*

The discovery of gold in the Klondike region led to the development of northwestern Canada. During the late 1890s, thousands of prospectors rushed to the area searching for gold. The Klondike gold rush brought so many people that the area was organized as the Yukon Territory in 1898.

Australia

Australia is a huge island, a continent in itself. Yet for centuries it remained unknown to the rest of the world. The European explorers who sailed into the Pacific Ocean in the 1500s missed it entirely. The Dutch sighted the continent in the early 1600s and named it New Holland, but considered it too poor to colonize. Captain James Cook, an English sailor on a scientific expedition for the navy, sailed along Australia's eastern shore in 1770. He named the region New South Wales, because of its resemblance to southern Wales, and claimed it for Great Britain.

Before the American Revolution, Great Britain sent many convicted prisoners to North America. After the British lost their 13 American colonies, they decided to send convicts to Australia. The first shiploads arrived in New South Wales in 1788, ● and soon the convicts founded the town of Sydney on the southeast coast. Free settlers arrived shortly afterward with land grants. Convicts who served their time and gained their freedom were allowed to remain in Australia and own land. However, these two groups did not always get along.

*In 1949 Newfoundland and its dependency, Labrador, became the tenth province of the Dominion of Canada.

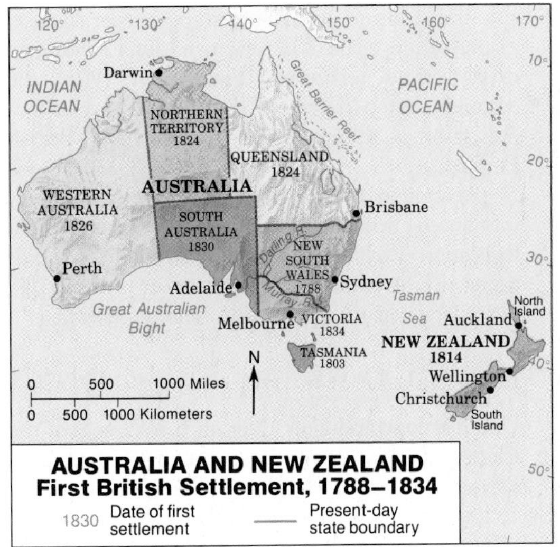

Learning from Maps *Australia is the world's only nation that occupies an entire continent. What city is the westernmost state capital?* **Perth**

Australia experienced a lawless period in the early 1800s. Clashes among immigrants, exconvicts, and gangs of escaped convicts called bushrangers occurred frequently. Uncaring people hunted down and almost exterminated many of the aborigines (ab • uh • RIJ • uh • neez), the original inhabitants of Australia, as if they were animals.

In 1829 the British claimed the entire continent of Australia. By 1836 the colonies of Tasmania, Western Australia, and South Australia had been organized. The colony of Victoria was formed in 1851, and Queensland in 1859 (see map, this page).

The discovery of gold in 1851 in the new colony of Victoria brought a flood of immigrants to Australia. Soon the colonial legislatures began to pass acts that allowed only white people to immigrate. This "White Australia" policy antagonized many nations, particularly in the Orient. The Australian government strictly enforced the policy, however, and admitted only a few immigrants from countries other than Great Britain.

The Australian colonies developed independently for many years. They modeled their legislatures after the British Parliament, except that both upper and lower houses were elected. (In New South Wales, the members of the upper house were appointed for life.) In the 1890s the Australian

Pankhurst: suffragette leader in the late 1800s and early 1900s; ***Lord Durham:*** Liberal Party leader and governor general of Canada who submitted a report to Parliament recommending self-government for Canada and other colonies; ***Maori:*** native of New Zealand
3. ***Ontario:*** Canadian province to the north of lakes Ontario and Superior; ***Quebec:*** mostly French-speaking province in northeast Canada; ***Ottawa:*** city at the southern end of the border between Quebec and Ontario; ***Australia:*** island continent located where the Pacific and Indian oceans meet; ***New Zealand:*** island nation in the Pacific
4. (a) In Great Britain in the early 1800s, only property owners and a few other privileged persons could vote. Catholics, Jews, and Dissenters could not hold political office. Voting was done openly instead of by secret ballot. Because election district boundaries had not been changed for many years, the membership of the House of Commons did not adequately represent the voters and in some districts the choice of representatives was controlled by members of the House of Lords. Only men with considerable property could be elected to the House of Commons. **(b)** The Reform Bill of 1832 reapportioned voting districts so the new industrial cities were better represented

1B, 4E, a1C, a4A, a4F, a4H, a4J, a4K

and it lowered property qualifications for voting so more factory owners, bankers, and merchants could vote.
5. Seats in the House of Commons were taken away from the less populated boroughs and given to the new industrial cities; property qualifications for voting were lowered; and voting rights were extended to most city industrial workers.
6. According to the terms of the British North America Act, each province kept its own legislature to deal with local affairs; the federal Parliament, which dealt with national problems, met in Ontario at the Dominion capital; the Dominion government was a parliamentary democracy with a cabinet based on the British model; the party in power appointed the premier.
7. Students answers will vary. However, they should include: the gradual abolition of slavery throughout the empire, the provision of financial support to private and church schools —a first step toward public education, and the abolition of imprisonment for debt.

SECTION 2

Focus/Motivation
During the 1800s many Americans felt that it was the destiny of the United States to expand to the Pacific Ocean. Americans thought this was so obvious, they called it the nation's "manifest destiny."

colonies began to consider forming a federal union as protection against European nations seeking to expand their territories. Finally, in 1901, the colonies united to create the Commonwealth of Australia—a self-governing part of the British Empire.

Australian trade unions and the Labor Party influenced Parliament to adopt a great deal of social legislation. Parliament passed bills establishing old-age pensions, compulsory arbitration of labor disputes, and wage-fixing boards, among others.

New Zealand

Dutch sailors, and later Captain Cook, sighted the islands of New Zealand, southeast of Australia. Private companies developed the islands in the 1820s and 1830s. A treaty with the Maori (MOW • uhr • ee) chieftains, the native rulers of the islands, established British control in 1840. A few years later, the British Parliament gave New Zealand a constitution, and the islands became a self-governing colony.

Disputes over land brought the British settlers into conflict with the native inhabitants, and several Maori wars took place in the 1840s and 1860s. In other respects the development of New Zealand resembled that of Australia. The discovery of gold and the establishment of restricted immigration occurred in 1861. In 1893 New Zealand became the first country in the world to adopt voting rights for women. In 1907 New Zealand joined the British Empire as a dominion.

SECTION 1 REVIEW

1. **Define** liberalism, suffrage, home rule, suffragette
2. **Identify** Chartists, Queen Victoria, Benjamin Disraeli, William Gladstone, Fabian Society, Christabel Pankhurst, Lord Durham, Maori
3. **Locate** Ontario, Quebec, Ottawa, Australia, New Zealand
4. **Understanding Cause and Effect** **(a)** Why was the Reform Bill of 1832 necessary in Great Britain? **(b)** How did the bill affect the British government?
5. **Summarizing Ideas** What important political reforms were made in Great Britain between 1832 and 1867?
6. **Analyzing Ideas** Explain the terms of the British North America Act of 1867.
7. **Organizing Ideas** Name two social reforms passed by the British Parliament in the 1800s.

2 The United States Expanded and Changed

When the United States ratified its Constitution in 1788, the new nation consisted of 13 states along the Atlantic coast and additional territories that stretched westward to the Mississippi River. The country's population totaled about 4 million people, most of whom lived in farming communities in the eastern states.

The young nation was born during a time of European turmoil, and most Americans wanted to stay out of European affairs and develop their nation in peace. They did this so successfully that, during the next 100 years, the territory of the United States grew to almost 4 times its original size and its population increased to 60 million. By 1900 the United States took its place among the great nations of the world.

Territorial Growth

Many European powers expanded overseas and set up colonies. The United States, in contrast, expanded overland, within the continent of North America. Unlike European countries, the new nation expanded without acquiring any colonies.

The Northwest Territory. The land bounded by the Appalachian Mountains, the Ohio and Mississippi rivers, and the Great Lakes was known as the Northwest Territory. States that had originally claimed this area turned the land over to the United States when they ratified the Articles of Confederation. Once the country had gained independence, hundreds of settlers pushed across the mountains into the Northwest Territory. In 1787 Congress passed the Northwest Ordinance to provide some form of government for the settlers.

The Northwest Ordinance of 1787 guaranteed that people who lived in territories would have rights equal to those who lived in the original 13 states. It provided that the Northwest Territory would be divided into states and admitted into the Union on an equal basis with existing states. When a territory had 5,000 adult males, it could form a legislature to govern the territory. Then, when a territory had 60,000 inhabitants, it could adopt a constitution and apply for statehood. The ordinance, therefore, ensured orderly expansion.

1A, 1B, a4B, a4C

Many people left their homes on the Atlantic seaboard to settle the Northwest Territory. These settlers knew that their territories would be admitted to the Union as equal states. As a result, 10 new states joined the United States between 1791 and 1820.

Completing the expansion. Most of the principles of the Northwest Ordinance were applied to all new lands as the country continued to expand. In 1803 Napoleon sold the vast territory of Louisiana (which Spain had ceded to France) to the United States for $15 million. Extending westward from the Mississippi River roughly to the Rocky Mountains, the so-called Louisiana Purchase almost doubled the size of the United States. The United States also purchased Florida from Spain in 1819 (see map, this page).

In 1836 American settlers in Mexican territory south of the Louisiana Purchase declared themselves independent and established the Republic of Texas. The United States annexed Texas by treaty in 1845, and war with Mexico resulted. The United States won the Mexican War and gained the Mexican Cession, a huge region that became the states of Utah, Nevada, California, and parts of Arizona, Colorado, New Mexico, and Wyoming.

In 1846 a treaty with Great Britain gave the United States the Oregon Country. The states of

Learning from Maps *In its westward expansion, the United States encountered little opposition. How long did it take the nation to stretch from coast to coast?* **72 years (1776-1848)**

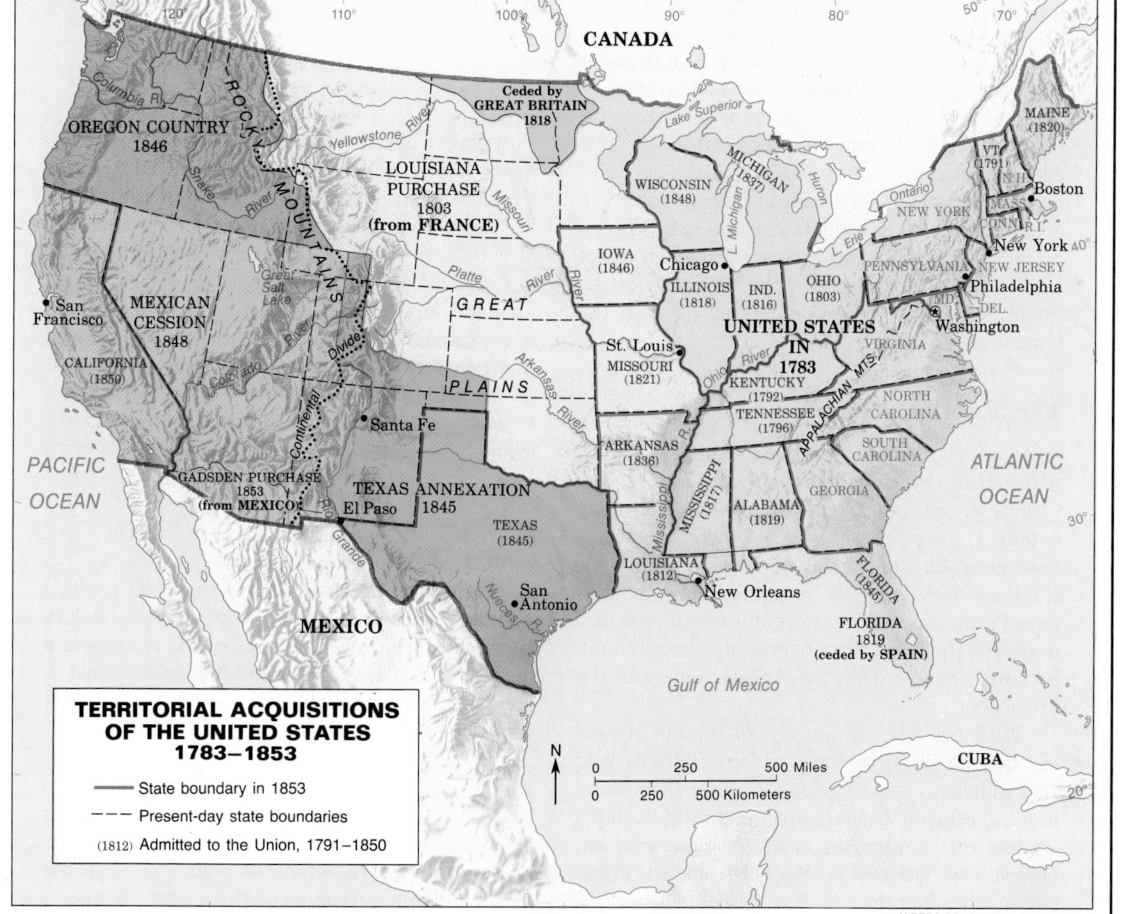

ALBERS EQUAL AREA PROJECTION

On the chalkboard write the following statement made in 1845 by newspaper editor John L. O'Sullivan.

"[It is] our manifest destiny to overspread the continent allotted by Providence for the free development of our yearly multiplying millions."

Ask students what O'Sullivan meant by this statement. What practical reason for expansion is hinted at in this statement? *(population increase)* Then ask students to speculate about other reasons for expansion. *(Answers will include: desire for new farmland, the need for resources, the fur trade, and adventure.)*

Presentation
Analyzing Ideas (Average/Group)

A panel discussion might be held on the issue of slavery in the South, covering such topics as slaves' living conditions, the slave family, religion, economic value of slavery, and effects of slavery on slave and master. Useful sources of information on this issue include: Eugene D. Genovese's *Roll, Jordan, Roll* (Vintage); Kenneth Stampp's *The Peculiar Institution* (Random House); and Lerone Bennett Jr.'s *Before the Mayflower* (Johnson Publishing Company).

1C, a1A, a1B, a1C, a2A, a2B, a2C, a2D, a2E, a2F, a2G, a2H, a2K, a2L

Oregon, Washington, Idaho, and parts of Montana and Wyoming were created from this land.

Finally, in 1853 the United States bought a small strip of land known as the Gadsden Purchase, in what is now southern New Mexico and Arizona, from Mexico for $10 million.

Thus, by the 1850s, the relatively new nation stretched from coast to coast and from Mexico to Canada. During the next 50 years, settlement caught up with territorial acquisitions. The discovery of gold in California in 1848 led to the California gold rush. Cattle ranchers, farmers, and miners settled in the plains and mountains of the western United States.

Political Growth

In the early days of the United States, some states had allowed only white male property owners to vote. The new states farther west imposed no such property qualifications. In time eastern states dropped property qualifications for male voters.

During the presidency of Andrew Jackson in the early 1830s, many changes occurred. Public education became widespread. An increasing number of political offices became elective instead of appointive. Political candidates came to be chosen by party conventions rather than by small groups of legislators. Foreign visitors spoke frequently of the "great democratic revolution" taking place in the United States.

The Slavery Question

Although the United States had a unified federal government, **sectionalism**—a rivalry among the various sections of the country—plagued the young nation. During the early 1800s, three major sections emerged: the Northeast, a region of growing cities and industry; the South, an area of many large farms, especially cotton and tobacco plantations; and the West, a frontier region of small, independent farms between the Appalachians and the Mississippi.

With such different ways of life, it is not surprising that people from each of these sections held very different views on such issues as internal improvements at federal expense, tariffs, banking and currency, and public lands. As time went on, however, the question of slavery became the greatest issue dividing the country.

Black slavery existed in the American colonies almost from the beginning. The Constitution accepted slavery but left its regulation up to the states. In states where slavery existed, only the state government could abolish it.

People in the southern states believed they needed slaves to harvest their crops of cotton and tobacco. Therefore, slavery increased in the South, especially after the invention of the cotton gin made cotton a profitable crop.

Both cotton and tobacco crops exhausted the soil. Southerners needed new lands and moved to the unsettled lands of the territories, bringing with them the institution of slavery. The question soon arose: Should slavery be permitted in the new territories? Southerners argued that Congress did not have the power to prohibit slavery in the territories; Northerners and Westerners argued that it did. A growing number of people came to advocate the abolition of slavery.

Secession and Civil War

The slavery question, as well as the issue of states' rights versus the federal government, led to bitter sectional quarrels throughout much of the 1800s. Southern states threatened many times to **secede,** or withdraw from the Union. Each time, compromises staved off secession. Then in 1860 Abraham Lincoln was elected president. Lincoln headed the newly formed Republican Party, which had pledged to prevent the spread of slavery into the territories.

Shortly after the election, South Carolina seceded and other southern states followed. They formed the Confederate States of America, with Jefferson Davis as president. Eventually 11 southern states joined the Confederacy.

President Lincoln and Congress said the Constitution did not give a state the right to secede. They declared that the Southerners had rebelled and that the United States government had a duty to suppress the rebellion. Efforts to compromise proved useless. By 1861 the Union and Confederate States of America were engaged in a bloody civil war that would last four years.

The Civil War was the most costly conflict in which the United States had been involved up to that time. It has been called the first modern war because it introduced new and lethal devices such as explosive shells, ironclad warships, and the Gatling gun, a forerunner of the machine gun.

554

● **By 1863, however, Great Britain had found other sources of cotton, such as Egypt.**

Learning from Maps *President Lincoln led the North in the fight to save the Union. What major battle was fought in the North?* **The Battle of Gettysburg**

Many European nations favored the Confederacy. Industrial and commercial interests hoped the war would weaken their business competitors in the Northeast. ● The British needed Southern cotton and frequently aided Confederate ships by letting them use British ports. Napoleon III of France took advantage of the conflict to intervene in Mexico.

As time went on, it became clear that the agricultural South lacked the industries and railroads necessary to supply its armies. The end finally came in April 1865, when the Confederacy surrendered. The Union was preserved.

In January 1863 President Lincoln had issued the Emancipation Proclamation, freeing slaves in

SECTION 2

Closure

On the chalkboard write the following statement: The Civil War ensured that sectionalism would continue to plague the United States. Then ask: Do you agree or disagree with this statement? Why? *(Students should mention that southerners held deep resentment following the Civil War and still do in some areas of the south.)*

Review Answers

1. ***sectionalism:*** rivalry among the various sections of the United States; ***secede:*** to withdraw from the Union

2. ***Northwest Ordinance:*** provided form of government for American territories west of the Appalachians; ***Grimké sisters:*** abolitionists who also spoke out for equality for women; ***Elizabeth Cady Stanton, Lucretia Mott:*** coorganizers of 1848 women's rights conference in Seneca Falls, New York

3. ***Louisiana Purchase:*** region extending westward from the Mississippi River roughly to the Rocky Mountains; ***Mexican Cession:*** region consisting of what are today Utah, Nevada, and California, and parts of Arizona, Colorado, New Mexico, and Wyoming; ***Oregon Country:*** territory that included present-day states of Oregon, Washington, and Idaho, and parts of Montana and Wyoming;

555

1B, 1C, 4A, 4H, a1A, a1C, a2B, a2C, a2G, a2K, a2L

Gadsden Purchase: region that is today southern Arizona and New Mexico
4. United States territory expanded as follows: the Northwest Ordinance divided the Northwest Territory into states and provided for their admission into the Union; the Louisiana Territory was purchased from France in 1803; Florida was obtained from Spain in 1819; Texas was annexed in 1845; war with Mexico gained the Mexican Cession; a treaty with Great Britain in 1846 gained the Oregon Country; the Gadsden Purchase of 1853 added territory in the Southwest.
5. The new western states imposed no property qualification on voting rights. In the eastern states, property qualifications for male voters were gradually dropped. Public education became more widespread, political offices became elective instead of appointive, and political candidates came to be chosen by party convention.
6. Southern planters needed new lands to which they could move when they exhausted the soil on their old lands. As they moved onto the new lands, they wanted to take their slaves with them. Many Americans did not want slavery in the territories, and in 1856 the new Republican Party took a stand against it. When Abraham Lincoln was elected president as a Republican in 1860, South Carolina immediately seceded and was soon followed by other Southern states. Civil war resulted.

those parts of the country "still in rebellion against the United States." However, many plantation owners in the South did not honor the proclamation, and many slaves did not know about it. Following the Civil War, Congress passed three amendments to the Constitution: The Thirteenth Amendment abolished slavery, the Fourteenth Amendment gave former slaves citizenship and equal protection under the law, and the Fifteenth Amendment granted them the right to vote. Although in some areas of the country these laws were not strictly enforced, the amendments strengthened the principle of equality before the law.

The cost of preserving the Union had a tragically high price. The North and South together had lost nearly 600,000 people. Families had been torn apart as brother fought against brother. Freedom did not solve all the problems of the former slaves. The war left deep scars on the nation that remained well into the 1900s.

A Changing Nation

The United States experienced phenomenal growth from 1865 to 1900 primarily as a result of industrialization. Cities doubled and tripled in size, and a network of railroads crisscrossed the nation to link the cities together.

Immigration. Another important factor in this growth was immigration. For many decades people had come to the United States from England and Scotland. In the mid-1800s, a heavy wave of immigration came from two other regions—Ireland, which suffered severe potato famines, and Germany, where many people fled from revolutions in 1848.

In the late 1800s, immigration increased from southern and eastern Europe, especially Italy, Russia, and Austria-Hungary. The United States absorbed more immigrants than any other country in the world and soon became known as a "melting pot."

Woman suffrage. Many women had campaigned for the abolition of slavery. Some of these abolitionists, such as the sisters Sarah Moore Grimké and Angelina Emily Grimké, had begun publicly to address the status of women. They insisted that equality be extended to women as well as men.

In 1848 a women's rights conference, organized by Elizabeth Cady Stanton and Lucretia Mott, was

Learning from Pictures *Wyoming was the first state in the United States to grant woman suffrage. And some other states soon followed. Here Boston women vote in a municipal election.*

held in Seneca Falls, New York. The delegates drew up a list of demands, including suffrage for women.

In the 1890s and early 1900s, many women continued the campaign for the right to vote. Finally in 1920, with the ratification of the Nineteenth Amendment to the Constitution, women won the right to vote.

SECTION 2 REVIEW

1. **Define** sectionalism, secede
2. **Identify** Northwest Ordinance, Grimké sisters, Elizabeth Cady Stanton, Lucretia Mott
3. **Locate** Louisiana Purchase, Mexican Cession, Oregon Country, Gadsden Purchase
4. **Organizing Ideas** List the steps in the territorial expansion of the United States from 1787 to 1853.
5. **Analyzing Ideas** In what ways did the United States become more democratic during the 1800s?
6. **Interpreting Ideas** How did the issue of slavery lead to the Civil War in the United States?

3 France Underwent Revolutions and Changes of Government

The Congress of Vienna restored the Bourbon monarch, King Louis XVIII, to the throne of France following Napoleon's exile in 1814. Louis, glad to be king and unwilling to upset the situation, carried on many of the reforms established between 1789 and 1815. He retained the Bank of France, the state-supported schools, and the Napoleonic Code. He accepted a constitution that limited his power and established a legislature to assist in governing the country. The constitution gave only the wealthy people the right to vote.

Charles X

When Louis XVIII died in 1824, his brother, Charles X—an ardent believer in absolute monarchy—succeeded him. As soon as he became king, Charles antagonized his subjects. First, he pledged that the government would reimburse the *émigrés* whose estates had been seized and sold to the peasants. This unpopular policy meant taxing all the people for the benefit of the emigrant nobles, who had opposed any progress or democracy in France. Second, Charles abolished most of the liberal provisions of the weak constitution his brother had accepted and tried to restore many features of the Old Regime.

Charles's actions caused trouble in France. Since 1789 the nation had learned too much about throwing off autocratic rule to accept these changes peacefully. In July 1830 a revolt spread throughout the country. Faced with growing hostility, Charles X abdicated.

The successful revolt in France inspired revolutions elsewhere. Two months after Charles's abdication in 1830, for example, the Belgians declared independence from their Dutch rulers.

Louis Philippe, the "Citizen King"

The leaders of the French revolt of 1830 wanted to be rid of Charles X, but they could not agree on the kind of government they wanted after his departure. Those favoring a republic lacked the strength to win. Finally, they reached a compromise and all groups agreed on the choice of another king. They selected Louis Philippe, Duke of Orléans, who belonged to a branch of the Bourbon family but had a record of liberal beliefs.

Louis Philippe was in a delicate position. He was a king, but an elected king. From the experience of Charles X, Louis Philippe knew that he could be deposed if he did not have the support of the majority of the French people. Therefore, he tried hard to please the people and called himself the "Citizen King."

The upper-middle class benefited more than any other class during the reign of Louis Philippe. After the revolt of 1830, the right to vote was extended to 200,000 of the wealthiest citizens, which included many newly rich manufacturers. Under Louis Philippe workers could not organize, and the government outlawed labor unions. High tariffs placed on imported goods benefited the owners of industries because they kept foreign-made goods out of France. However, the tariffs resulted in higher prices for domestic goods.

While the middle class generally favored Louis Philippe, he faced opposition from both monarchists and republicans. One group of monarchists wanted a direct descendant of Charles X to be king, while another group, the Bonapartists, wanted to revive Napoleon's empire.

SECTION 3

Focus/Motivation

Reproduce the following quotation by Alexis de Tocqueville for the class. It describes the French revolutions of 1848.

"I spent the whole afternoon in walking about Paris. Two things in particular struck me: the first was . . . the uniquely and exclusively popular character of the revolution that had just taken place; the omnipotence it had given to . . . the classes who work with their hands . . . . Although the working classes had often played the leading part in the events of the First Revolution, they had never been the sole leaders and masters of the State. . . . The Revolution of July (1830) was effected by the people, but the middle class had stirred it up and led it, and secured the principal fruits of it. The Revolution of February (1848), on the contrary, seemed to be made entirely outside the bourgeoisie and against it."

Lead a discussion on the quotation, using the following questions as a guide: What classes of people were responsible for the revolution of 1848, according to de Tocqueville? *(the working classes)* When the author refers to the "First Revolution," which revolution does he mean? *(the revolution that began in 1789)* What does the author see as the difference between the July Revolution of 1830 and the February Revolution of 1848?

1B, 4A, 4G, a1A, a1B, a1C

(The July 1830 revolution was led by the middle class, whereas the February 1848 revolution was led by the lower classes against the middle class.)

Presentation
Writing a Paragraph (Average/Group)
Have students write a paragraph comparing and contrasting the empires of Napoleon I and Napoleon III. Suggest that students pay close attention to styles and systems of government under the two emperors. Select a number of students to read their paragraphs to the rest of the class.

The republicans stood at the other extreme from the monarchists. They believed that France should become a republic and should grant political rights and social changes to benefit all the people. Most French workers agreed. They disliked Louis Philippe's anti-labor measures and the high prices that resulted from his tariff policy. Food shortages and widespread unemployment increased discontent between 1846 and 1848.

The Roman Catholics, especially the higher clergy, also disliked Louis Philippe. They opposed the separation of church and state, a policy begun during the French Revolution and continued by Napoleon and Louis Philippe.

The Revolutions of 1848

In 1848 opposition to the regime of Louis Philippe erupted into violence. Trouble began over the principle of free speech. In February opponents of the government organized meetings where they criticized official policy. Louis Philippe issued a decree prohibiting the final meeting.

The publication of the decree sparked riots in Paris. The disorders did not seem serious until the National Guard, summoned to restore order, joined the rioters. The disturbances forced Louis Philippe to abdicate and flee to England.

The people of Paris established a temporary government and proclaimed the Second French Republic in 1848. (The First Republic had lasted from 1792 until 1804, when Napoleon became emperor.) The most active group in the new government consisted of the urban working classes, whose leaders believed in socialism. Because economic depression and widespread unemployment had paralyzed France, the socialist members of the government established "national workshops" to give people work. This action marked the first appearance in modern times of the idea that the government has a responsibility to remedy chronic unemployment.

Adopting universal manhood suffrage, the Second Republic held elections in April to choose a National Assembly to write a constitution for a permanent government. When the new National Assembly met in June, conservative members in the majority voted to stop the program of national workshops.

This action led to violent rioting in Paris. Fearing a widespread revolution, the Assembly allowed army officers to assume power. For three days Paris became a battlefield. Finally, the army crushed the rebellion and imprisoned, exiled, or executed its socialist leaders. Karl Marx, the founder of modern socialism, was expelled from France.

Louis Napoleon

The new constitution written by the National Assembly provided for a republican form of government, with an elected president. The president would serve a four-year term and would not be eligible for a second term. The National Assembly would be a single legislative body, consisting of representatives elected by universal manhood suffrage.

In December 1848 the Republic held its first elections. Instead of electing as president someone who had helped to create the Second Republic, however, the voters overwhelmingly chose Louis Napoleon Bonaparte, the nephew of Napoleon.

Louis Napoleon wanted to be more than a president. He began to work for the support of various influential groups in France. Like his uncle, he did everything he could to gain the backing of the army. To win support from French Catholics, he helped the pope suppress an attempt by Italian patriots to set up a republic in Rome. He also repealed certain laws so that the Catholic church could have more control over French education.

Economically, Louis Napoleon favored the middle class by encouraging the development of manufacturing and railroads. At the same time, however, he tried to keep the favor of the workers through actions such as setting up a program of public works that gave jobs to many. To the peasants, who owned their land, the newly elected president spoke of his devotion to the principle of private property. He reminded the peasants of the prosperity he had brought them through better transportation and larger markets. He also established a new bank that provided funds for agricultural improvements.

In addition, Louis Napoleon posed as a champion of democratic rights. Meanwhile, however, he limited criticism of his actions through strict censorship and by driving his critics out of France.

Louis Napoleon now employed the plebiscite, a device his uncle had used so successfully. He asked the French people to permit him to draft a new constitution for the Second French Republic. Most people believed that he was defending law and order. They voted almost 12 to 1 in his favor.

558

History Through the Arts

PAINTING

The Gleaners

"This art offends me and disgusts me," said the French director of fine arts about the work of Jean-François Millet. Millet not only rejected the popular romanticized style of his day—the 1850s and 1860s—but also used peasants and workers as his subjects.

Millet, a peasant himself, worked on the land until the age of 19 when he begain studying with another artist. Understandably, then, he identified heavily with the peasant class.

Gleaners are the poorest peasants, who gather the leavings from a field after reaping. In this painting Millet makes them appear noble and dignified. That The *Gleaners* seems sentimental and idealized today is evidence of constantly changing tastes and values in art.

The Second French Empire

The new constitution extended Louis Napoleon's term as president to 10 years. Although it gave him greater power, he remained dissatisfied. He wanted to follow in the footsteps of his uncle, Napoleon I—and Napoleon I had been an emperor.

In 1852 Louis Napoleon held another plebiscite for another constitution. By cleverly manipulating the votes, Louis Napoleon won consent to take the title Emperor Napoleon III. (He called himself the "third" Napoleon because Napoleon I had had a son. "Napoleon II" had never reigned and died in 1832.)

On the surface the Second French Empire looked like a democracy. It allowed for a constitution and a legislature elected by universal manhood suffrage. In reality, however, France came under a new style of absolutism. The legislature could pass only those laws proposed by the emperor. The legislature had no power over spending and could not question the emperor's ministers.

People suspected of opposing the government could be imprisoned or exiled without trial. Newspapers were strictly censored. The government warned that any paper criticizing the emperor or his government would be warned twice, then shut down. Freedom of speech did not exist. Liberal professors in the universities lost their jobs. With all these restrictions, it became impossible to organize opposition to the government of Louis Napoleon.

Problems in the Crimea and Mexico

In order to quiet discontent at home, Napoleon III tried to win glory abroad. The weakening Ottoman Empire gave him his chance.

Because of earlier agreements, Russia claimed the right to protect all Orthodox Christians living under the rule of the Ottoman Turks. Similarly, France protected the Roman Catholics. In the 1850s both Russia and France claimed jurisdiction over certain holy places in Palestine, which was part of the Ottoman Empire. The Ottomans granted privileges to the Roman Catholics but did not do the same for the Orthodox Christians. The czar demanded these same privileges for the Orthodox Christians. Napoleon III took a firm stand against these Russian demands and formed an alliance with Great Britain, which feared Russian expansion toward the eastern Mediterranean.

The Ottoman Turks, backed by France and Great Britain, resisted Russian claims in the Palestine dispute. The three allies declared

559

1B, 4E, a1A, a1C

● Have students compare the Charge of the Light Brigade with Pickett's Charge at the Battle of Gettysburg.

Learning from Pictures *Known as the Lady with the Lamp, Florence Nightingale tended to the wounded with her nursing corps during the Crimean War.*

war in March 1854, and full-scale fighting began six months later. The fighting took place mostly in the Crimea, in southern Russia.

The Crimean War has been called "the most unnecessary war in history." The hostilities were conducted with inefficiency and wastefulness. The famous poem "The Charge of the Light Brigade," by Alfred, Lord Tennyson, described one tragic event ● of the war. A brigade of 600 horsemen charged across a valley and were cut to pieces by enemy fire. The following are two verses from the poem.

> "Half a league, half a league,
> Half a league onward,
> All in the valley of Death
> Rode the six hundred.
> 'Forward the Light Brigade!
> Charge for the guns!' he said.
> Into the valley of Death
> Rode the six hundred. . . .
>
> Cannon to right of them,
> Cannon to left of them,
> Cannon in front of them
> Volley'd and thunder'd;
> Storm'd at with shot and shell,
> Boldly they rode and well,
> Into the jaws of Death,
> Into the mouth of hell,
> Rode the six hundred."

Despite the carnage of the war, the conflict did have two constructive results. First, modern field hospitals to care for the wounded came into use. Second, Florence Nightingale established professional nursing of the wounded.

It took two years of fighting, with huge losses on both sides from battle and disease, for the allies to defeat Russia. France won glory but little else.

Napoleon III now turned to building the French colonial empire. In North Africa he took advantage of a native revolt to strengthen French rule over Algeria, which had begun in 1830. In 1859 French engineers began constructing the Suez Canal in Egypt. In Asia, Napoleon established French control over Cambodia, thus beginning a move into Indochina. He also tried, although unsuccessfully, to intervene in Mexico. From 1863 until 1867, French troops protected the Archduke Maximilian, the brother of the emperor of Austria, who had become ruler of Mexico with Napoleon's help. The Mexicans hated Maximilian and finally overthrew and executed him in 1867.

Napoleon now faced mounting pressures in France. The elections held in 1869 showed strong opposition by both liberals and conservatives.

The Franco-Prussian War

Napoleon III decided to try another bold and risky venture, hoping to regain the support of all groups in France. At this time Prussia was working to unite all the German states under its leadership (see Chapter 22). By opposing this unification, Napoleon could gain the support of almost all French people because they distrusted Prussia.

Napoleon really hoped that Prussia would back down and that war would not be necessary. However, Otto von Bismarck, the head of the Prussian government, had decided that war with France would help to achieve German unification. Bismarck made a series of clever maneuvers that angered the French, and in July 1870 the French legislature declared war on Prussia.

French defeat. From the start of the Franco-Prussian War, the French suffered disastrous defeats. Napoleon III went to the front to take command of the army, and at the battle of Sedan, he fell into the enemy's hands.

Immediately after the capture of Napoleon III, the Legislative Assembly proclaimed the fall of the Second French Empire and the establishment of a Third Republic. The new government tried to defend the nation, but Paris fell to the Prussians in January 1871, signifying the end of the war.

560

In seven days of fighting, known as "the bloody week," more than 30,000 Parisians were killed. On May 27, the last 150 Communards were captured and summarily executed in Père Lachaise cemetery. Every May the working people of Paris honor the Communards by laying wreaths at the spot where the last 150 met their deaths.

1B, a1A, a1C

France Under German Domination

Bismarck drew up the Treaty of Frankfort, which dictated harsh terms to France. France had to give up the territories of Alsace and the eastern part of Lorraine on the French-German border. It also had to pay a huge indemnity to Germany within three years. German troops were to occupy northern France until they paid the indemnity.

In February 1871 Bismarck permitted the election of a National Assembly to decide whether France wanted to sign the peace treaty or to resume the war. The republicans urged renewal of the war. The monarchists took the position that France had already suffered defeat and should negotiate with the conquerors. About 70 percent of the elected delegates were monarchists—not because the French people favored monarchy, but because they wanted peace.

As in the revolutions of 1848, the people of Paris were strongly republican. They had fought almost alone to defend the city against the Prussians and were angered by the peace terms.

In March the socialists and radical republicans of Paris, supported by the National Guard, set up a municipal council to govern the city. It was called the Commune, like the Paris government established in 1792 during the French Revolution. The Communards, members of the Commune, proposed a program to reform France. Their program included decentralization—the redistribution of power from the central government to regional and local governments—separation of church and state, and replacement of the army by a national guard.

Disagreement between the Communards and the National Assembly resulted in a violent revolutionary uprising in Paris. Troops sent by the National Assembly entered Paris and fought several bitter and bloody battles against the Communards, defeating them in May 1871. The National Assembly immediately approved the Treaty of Frankfort.

The government borrowed money to pay the Germans the indemnity, and German soldiers left France in September 1873.

The Third Republic

After the fall of Napoleon III, quarreling factions in the National Assembly were unable to agree on a constitution until 1875. Finally, the assembly passed a group of laws known as the Constitution of 1875, which officially made France a republic.

The Third Republic included a president, elected by the legislature for a term of seven years. The cabinet of ministers had to approve the president's actions and was responsible for government policy. Although the constitution did not specifically provide for a premier, or prime minister, the position soon became established.

Learning from Pictures *Many famous buildings such as the Tuileries, the old royal palace, were burned during the fighting of 1871 in Paris.*

561

1B, 4G, a1A, a1C, a2H, a2L, a4A, a4F, a4H, a4L

SECTION 3

Closure

Point out that the existence of a myriad of political parties led to political instability in France in the early 1900s. Ask: Which other countries have been plagued by a similar situation in recent years? *(Answers will vary. Most students will mention Italy or Israel.)*

Review Answers

1. ***anarchist:*** person who believes in the abolition of all government through force; ***coalition:*** political groups temporarily united in support of a common cause
2. ***Louis XVIII:*** Bourbon monarch restored to the throne of France following Napoleon's exile; ***Charles X:*** king of France forced to abdicate in 1830; ***the "Citizen King":*** Louis Philippe, a member of the Bourbon family chosen king following the revolt of 1830; ***Florence Nightingale:*** established professional nursing of the wounded; ***Archduke Maximilian:*** brother of the Austrian emperor; became ruler of Mexico with Napoleon III's help in 1863; ***Alfred Dreyfus:*** Jewish officer in the French army falsely accused of treason
3. (a) The class that benefited most from the rule of Louis Philippe was the upper middle class. **(b)** Both monarchists and republicans opposed Louis Philippe.
4. By cleverly manipulating the votes in a plebiscite,

During the late 1800s, France faced many problems, created mostly by groups represented in the legislature. One group wanted to make war on Germany in revenge for the Franco-Prussian War. Another group was hostile to the Catholics. Still another backed French expansion overseas, along the lines begun by Napoleon III. The conservative republicans managed to steer a course that avoided extremes; their legislation encouraged education and legalized trade unions. But the nation lacked financial stability, and unemployment soared.

In the 1890s a financial scandal rocked France. The crisis stemmed from the failure of the Panama Company, which had been formed to build a canal across the Isthmus of Panama. Ferdinand de Lesseps, the man responsible for building the Suez Canal, had been president of the company, and thousands of French people had invested in it. It failed because of dishonesty, mismanagement, and malaria, which killed many of the French working on the canal in the jungles of Panama. Accusations of bribery against a number of legislators endangered the government.

Another threat to the republic came from extremists of the labor movement; clashes occurred between workers and troops. **Anarchists,** who believed in the abolition of all governments by force, set off bombs and attempted to assassinate public figures, including the president.

The Dreyfus case. The most serious danger to the Third Republic arose in 1894. An attempt to betray French military secrets to Germany was uncovered. A court accused and convicted Captain Alfred Dreyfus, a Jewish officer, and sentenced him to life imprisonment. However, evidence soon came to light indicating that Dreyfus had been falsely convicted. Even so, the French army command would permit no criticism of its actions. Monarchists, many Catholics, and anti-Semites—people who dislike Jews—supported the army.

The real traitor was discovered, but the army cleared him. Émile Zola, a famous French novelist, wrote an open letter, *"J'Accuse"* ("I Accuse"), in which he placed blame on the army command and its supporters for this scandal. Although many responsible for the false charges against Dreyfus confessed, his name was not cleared until 1906.

The Dreyfus case led to a clash between the two major groups in France—those who had condemned Dreyfus and supported the army, and those who supported his cause.

Reform and political instability. After the Dreyfus case, French republicans planned several reforms. They took steps to end the favored position that Napoleon I had given the Roman Catholic church in France in 1801. The church and the state were officially separated in 1905, and France had complete religious freedom.

The existence of many different political parties caused political instability in France in the early 1900s. The parties ranged from the monarchists on the far right to radical socialists on the far left. Major parties contained a number of "splinter groups," or smaller divisions. No one party ever completely controlled the French government. In order to get anything done, parties temporarily united to form **coalitions,** or political groups organized in support of a common cause.

SECTION 3 REVIEW

1. **Define** anarchist, coalition
2. **Identify** Louis XVIII, Charles X, the "Citizen King," Florence Nightingale, Archduke Maximilian, Alfred Dreyfus
3. **Interpreting Ideas** **(a)** Which class benefited most during the rule of Louis Philippe? **(b)** What groups opposed Louis Philippe?
4. **Analyzing Ideas** How did Louis Napoleon become emperor?
5. **Evaluating Ideas** How did the results of the Franco-Prussian War affect France?
6. **Explaining Ideas** Describe France's internal political problems in the late 1800s and early 1900s.

4 The Nations of Latin America Gained Independence

By the early 1800s, the ideologies behind the French Revolution and Napoleonic Wars had strongly affected the political and social thinking of many Europeans. The people in Spain and Portugal's Latin American colonies also felt some of the effects. In time strong independence movements swept the region extending from the northern border of Mexico southward to the tip of South America. These independence movements traced their roots to the structure of colonial economies and societies, and once started, they spread rapidly.

Colonial Economy

Both the Spanish and Portuguese followed mercantilist principles in organizing their colonies. They wanted to provide as much income as possible for the rulers of the home country, for merchants engaged in overseas trade, and for the white colonists. In the Latin American colonial system, silver, gold, and plantation crops such as sugar provided the profits.

Large, self-sufficient farming estates called **haciendas** (hahs • ee • EN • duhz) and smaller farms of various sizes became the major economic units of colonial Latin America. Monarchs granted some enormous estates to conquistadors, or conquerors, and to court favorites. Huge land grants dotted California during the Spanish period, for example, and many of the grants survived under United States rule.

Many people who received these grants eventually sold them to rich merchants and mining entrepreneurs who wanted to diversify their investments. Landowners who did not live on their haciendas hired overseers to manage them.

In parts of Latin America, such as the Caribbean, much of the Indian population died as a result of disease and forced labor on the land or in the mines. Although the Indians later became free subjects under Portuguese and Spanish law, many worked for wages and became bound to their occupations because of debt. The demand for labor, however, became so great that the Spanish and Portuguese then imported black African slaves to relieve the labor shortage.

In the 1690s the Portuguese discovered gold in the Minas Gerais (MEE • nuhs zhuh • RYS) region of Brazil. The city of Rio de Janeiro, which became the colonial capital in 1763, grew because of its location near the mines. The gold discovery also brought on a labor shortage in other regions of Brazil. The Portuguese answered the shortage by importing more black slaves.

The wealth of the Spanish and Portuguese colonies impressed visiting Europeans. Mexico City, Lima, and other cities had large populations and imposing cathedrals and government palaces. The colonial governments built immense fortresses, like the one guarding the port of San Juan in Puerto Rico, to protect the water approaches to the cities from pirates and sea dogs.

Learning from Pictures *Many West Indian economies depended on slave labor. The slaves shown here are working on an indigo plantation in the 1700s.*

Colonial Society

Social classes based on privilege divided colonial society. The highest ranks of society consisted of the royal bureaucrats, the owners of large estates, and the great merchants. An enormous social gap opened between these classes and the town workers, peasants, and slaves.

Racial discrimination made the situation in Latin America worse than in Europe. White people, called **peninsulars** because they were born in Spain or Portugal, ruled colonial society. Whites born in the colonies—called **creoles**—suffered social snobbery and job discrimination at the hands of the peninsulars.

Indians and blacks shared the bottom of the social pyramid. Many of them did not speak the language of the ruling class. Furthermore, laws upheld racial distinctions.

By the 1700s people of mixed race became the majority in Latin American society: **Mestizos** were of Indian and white background, and **mulattoes** were of black and white ancestry. Distribution of mestizos and mulattoes varied considerably. For example, mestizos became prominent in Mexico, but in Brazil mulattoes became the largest group. Mestizos and mulattoes usually faced social and racial barriers constructed by the peninsulars and creoles. In the Andes, southern Mexico, and parts of Central America, Indians remained the largest group.

Louis Napoleon won the right to take the title Emperor Napoleon III.

5. By the Treaty of Frankfort, France lost Alsace and eastern Lorraine; in addition, France had to pay a huge indemnity; German troops occupied northern France until the amount was paid.

6. In the late 1800s and early 1900s, factions in the French legislature disagreed bitterly. The Dreyfus case led to a clash between two major groups in France. Strikes and labor troubles caused difficulty and there was political instability due to the large number of political parties and factions.

SECTION 4

Focus/Motivation

The cost and inconvenience brought about by Spain's mercantilist policies in Latin America is illustrated in this tale of the production of a handkerchief. Read and discuss this passage with the class, focusing on the economic problems of this system and why some people might object *(consumers)* or approve *(merchants)*. You might want to have a map available to point out the cities mentioned in this long journey taken by the cotton.

"A Spanish broker bought a pinch of good cotton at the fair in Portobello; a Spanish ship carried it to Seville; a broker sold it to the agent of a mill in Flemish Ghent; after another ocean voyage

1B, 4E, 4G, a1A, a1B, a1C, a2H, a2L

the cotton was carded, the thread spun, the fabric woven, the handkerchief fashioned; the delicate confection journeyed again, first to Seville, then to Portobello, then overland to Panama, then by sea to Callao and Lima; in due course it was sold to a fine lady in the Viceregal court of Peru, or even in Tucumin or faraway Buenos Aires. The pennyworth of cotton had become a two dollar handkerchief. . . ."

Presentation
Analyzing Ideas (Average/Group)
Have students study and compare the maps of Latin America on pages 565 and 568. Then ask them to discuss why they think the Spanish and Portuguese colonial empires were dismantled in a little more than 30 years. *(Answers will vary. Most students will point to the inefficiency of colonial government, the inequality of colonial society, and the examples of revolution in the United States and France.)*

Learning from Pictures *Toussaint-Louverture was the leader of Haitian independence. He struggled to free slaves and resisted Napoleonic rule.*

Catholic church. The Roman Catholic church wielded great power and an enormous influence in the Spanish and Portuguese colonies. Missionaries who accompanied the explorers and conquistadors immediately began converting the Indians to Catholicism. The missionaries not only took an interest in Indian culture, but in many cases they also tried to prevent the government and colonists from abusing the Indians.

By the 1700s the Jesuits had become extremely powerful and rich, through the ownership of haciendas, town property, mines, and thousands of slaves. During the mid-1700s Spanish and Portuguese kings dissolved the Jesuit order in their kingdoms and seized all their colonial property.

Social life. Spain and Portugal greatly influenced social customs in the colonies. The male-dominated society of the Iberian Peninsula carried over into Latin America. For example, men had a rigid conception of family honor, and they believed in restricting the younger women of the household. A man could kill an unfaithful wife and go unpunished.

At lower levels of society, women, by necessity, participated more actively in economic life. Often they headed the households and their families lived on their earnings. Many women in the towns ran small businesses.

Growing Discontent

By the late 1700s, the Spanish and Portuguese colonies underwent administrative reform and economic growth, inspired in part by the Enlightenment (see Chapter 17). Nevertheless, the revolutionary events in British North America and France in the late 1700s aroused interest, particularly among discontented creoles. Although the creoles had begun to fill many upper-level positions in the colonial government, King Charles III of Spain sent peninsulars to take over the top jobs.

Not only did the creoles suffer discrimination in the colonial bureaucracy, but Spain's economic policy also angered them. Charles III began to relax some of the stiff mercantilist restrictions, and creole merchants feared they might lose their monopolies.

The Spanish and Portuguese colonists fared even worse than the British colonists. Spain and Portugal had little industry, so their merchants supplied the colonies with goods from Great Britain and France, after taking a substantial profit for themselves. Widespread smuggling resulted. The Spanish colonists also resented having to pay taxes to finance Spain's wars.

The colonists in Latin America believed they had good reason to rebel. In 1815 the creole revolutionary Simón Bolívar (see • MOHN boh • LEE • vahr) stated, "The hatred that the Peninsular has inspired in us is greater than the ocean which separates us."

Haiti's Slave Revolution

By the early 1800s, Spain's American colonies were ripe for revolution. The first successful revolt, however, took place in the French colony of Haiti, on the island of Hispaniola in the West Indies.

In Haiti a small number of French planters grew sugarcane and coffee trees on plantations tended by African slaves. When the French Revolution broke out, the free mulattoes demanded the same rights as French settlers. In 1794 the black slave population rebelled. Mulattoes and blacks united under the leadership of François-Dominique Toussaint-Louverture (too • SAN loo • ver • TOOR), a freed slave, and won control of the island.

Napoleon sent an army to try to reestablish French authority. The French captured Louverture, and he died a prisoner in France in 1803. Later, a

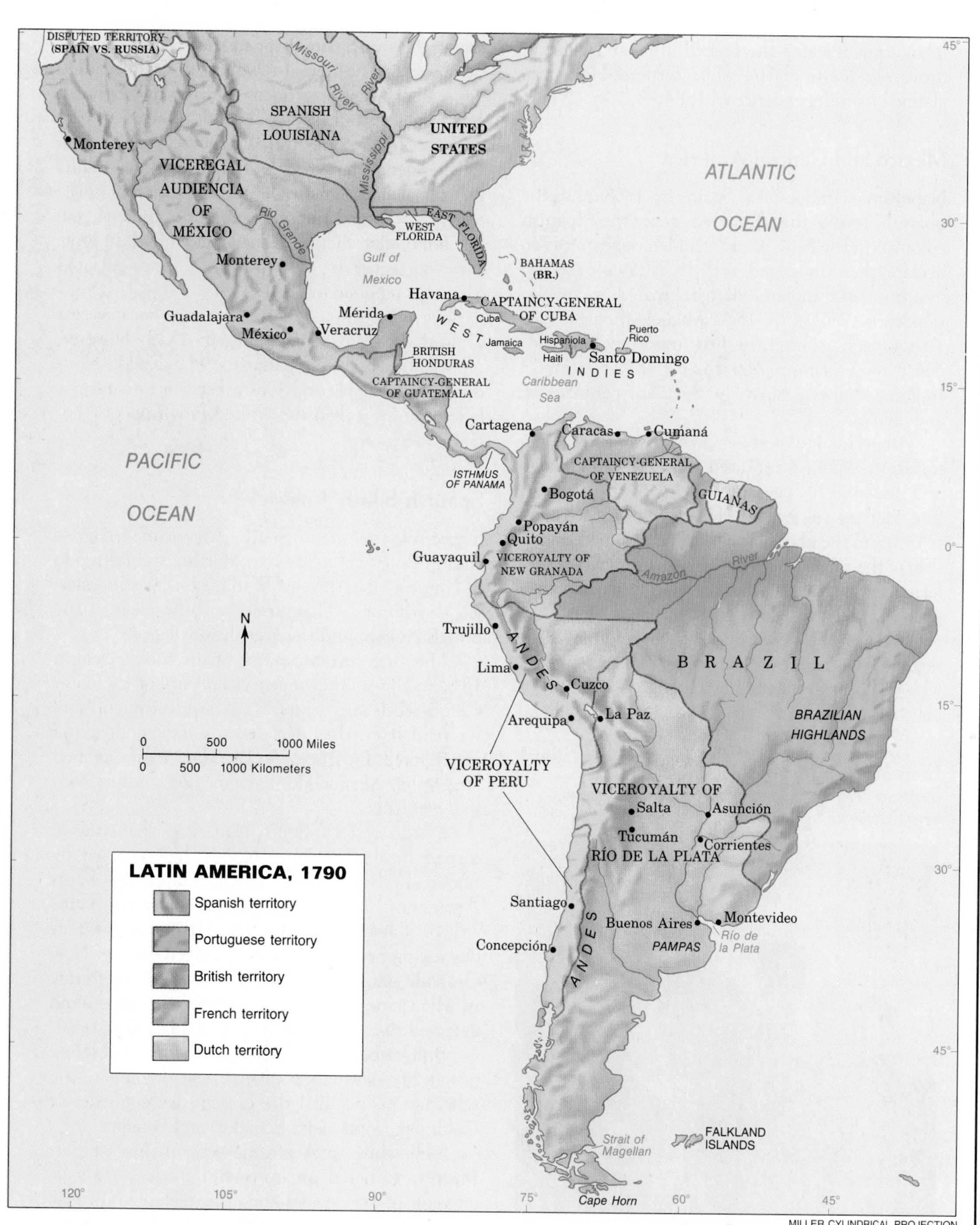

Learning from Maps *Spain allowed little colonial participation in governing its New World colonies. What six cities are located in the Viceroyalty of Peru?* **Lima, Trujillo, Arequipa, Santiago, Concepción, and Cuzco**

565

1B, 4E, 4G, a1A, a1C, a2H, a2L

● **Bernardo O'Higgins was chosen as the first president of independent Chile. He attempted to introduce the principles of the French Revolution — liberty, fraternity, and equality — to his country, but he was bitterly opposed by conservative Chileans. Rather than plunge the country into civil war, O'Higgins resigned and went into exile in 1823.**

rebel army defeated the French army and killed or drove out many of the white settlers. Haiti proclaimed its independence in 1804.

Mexico and Central America

Napoleon's conquest of Spain in 1808 and the Spanish revolt that followed gave the Spanish colonists in the New World a golden opportunity to declare their independence. In Mexico, creoles, mestizos, and Indians all participated in revolutionary activities. In 1810 Miguel Hidalgo (ee • THAHL • goh) started the first important independence movement in Mexico. He led an army of Indian peasants against the Spanish, peninsulars, and creoles.

After Hidalgo's forces achieved some early victories, the Spanish captured and executed Hidalgo and dispersed his peasant army in 1811. A priest, José Morelos (moh • RAY • lohs), who wanted land reform and the abolition of slavery, assumed leadership of the rebels. Upper-class Mexican creoles preferred things the way they were, and in 1815 they captured and shot Morelos.

In 1814 the very conservative Ferdinand VII regained the throne of Spain. The Mexican creoles, who had been frightened by Hidalgo, looked favorably upon Ferdinand. However, in 1820 liberal army rebels in Spain stripped the king of some of his powers. The liberal rebellion in Spain caused upper-class Mexicans to fear that the new Spanish government would apply liberal reforms in the colonies. Therefore, in 1821 they carried out an independence movement of their own. A militia general named Agustín de Iturbide (ee • toor • BEE • thay) proclaimed himself Emperor Agustín I, but his unpopular dictatorial rule did not last long. Mexican generals overthrew him and declared Mexico a republic in 1824.

For a brief time, Central America became part of Iturbide's Mexican empire. In 1823, however, representatives from Guatemala, El Salvador, Honduras, Nicaragua, and Costa Rica met to form a federal union called the United Provinces of Central America.

Learning from Pictures *José de San Martín, the great hero of Argentine independence, is shown here (left) with his military staff.*

Spanish South America

Three of the great South American leaders—Simón Bolívar, José de San Martín, and Bernardo O'Higgins—had traveled or studied in North America and Europe. They knew well the ideas of the Enlightenment and the French Revolution.

The first revolt against Spain took place in 1810 in the southernmost viceroyalty of La Plata. Creole rebels seized control of the government, and six years later, they declared the independence of the United Provinces of La Plata, later named Argentina. Meanwhile, Paraguay declared its own independence.

In the rest of South America, the struggle turned into a long and bloody civil war led by Simón Bolívar, called "the Liberator" by Latin Americans. Bolívar started the revolt in his native city of Caracas in 1810. He did not succeed in destroying Spain's power in the viceroyalty of New Granada until 1819. Then he raised another army in what is now Venezuela, crossed the Andes, and defeated the Spanish at Boyacá (bah • yuh • CHAY).

Bolívar became president, with almost absolute power, of a new nation called Great Colombia. The new nation included the present-day countries of Colombia, Venezuela, Ecuador, and Panama.

Meanwhile an Argentine general, José de San Martín, gathered an army and made a difficult crossing of the Andes into the region known as Chile. He joined forces with the Chileans, led by Bernardo O'Higgins, and overcame Spanish resistance there in 1818. ●

From Chile, San Martín's forces sailed north to capture the city of Lima in Peru. The Spanish viceroy fled, and San Martín declared the independence of Peru in 1821. Royalist forces, however, remained in parts of Peru. Internal squabbling among the independence leaders led some Peruvians to invite Bolívar to help them defeat the Spanish. San Martín then withdrew, turning leadership over to the ambitious Bolívar.

In August 1824 Bolívar won a major victory over the forces led by the Spanish viceroy at Junín (hoo • NEEN) in Peru. By December of that year, the revolutionaries achieved total victory over the forces loyal to Spain at Ayacucho (eye • uh • KOO • choh). Peru was free. In 1825 the northern territory of Upper Peru became a separate republic, named Bolivia in honor of Bolívar.

Brazil

When Napoleon's army invaded Portugal in 1808, King John VI and his family fled to Brazil. Once there, John elevated Brazil to a realm equal to Portugal and opened its ports to foreign trade. Even after the overthrow of Napoleon, King John stayed in Brazil. In 1820, however, a revolt broke out in Portugal, and the Portuguese persuaded King John to return home.

The Portuguese then tried to return Brazil to the status of a colony. Angered Brazilian creoles persuaded Pedro, King John's son who had stayed in Brazil, to become ruler of an independent Brazil. Brazil declared its independence as a constitutional monarchy in 1822, and Pedro I ruled as its emperor until 1831.

The new nations of Brazil and Argentina struggled over territory that lay between them. Patriots in this disputed territory gained independence in 1825, calling their new country Uruguay.

Almost all of Latin America had thus become independent by 1825. Portugal lost its entire New World empire. The Spanish lost all their colonies except Cuba and Puerto Rico. Elsewhere in Latin America, only Jamaica, the Guianas, British Honduras, and a few smaller islands in the Caribbean remained under colonial rule.

Foreign Reactions to Independence

The British hoped to benefit from Latin American independence. They were eager to increase their trade with the region, which they imagined to be richer than it really was. Also, the British viewed the Latin Americans as potential allies against continental Europe, which was growing more conservative. For this reason, the British had provided the rebels with small amounts of arms, primarily in South America.

Learning from Pictures *Influenced by the Enlightenment, the creole Simón Bolívar led the independence movement in northern South America.*

The War of 1812 with Great Britain had distracted the United States. In addition, the United States did little to help the Latin American revolutionaries, because it did not wish to anger Spain while trying to get that country to give up Florida. Even after Spain ceded Florida in 1819, the United States had no Latin American policy until late in the administration of President James Monroe. Like the British, however, Americans saw the region as a vast new market and became alarmed when the Spanish tried to regain their colonies in the 1820s.

In 1823 President James Monroe sent a message to Congress that came to be known as the Monroe Doctrine. It declared that the United States would not intervene in Europe's affairs or interfere in any of Europe's remaining colonies in the Western Hemisphere. At the same time, the United States would oppose any attempt by European nations to reestablish lost colonies, to form new colonies, or to interfere with any of the American governments in the Western Hemisphere.

SECTION 4

Closure

Point out that since independence most Latin American countries have been ruled by a succession of *caudillos* — military dictators. Ask: Do you think that the way most Latin American countries achieved independence led to their history of military dictatorship? Why or why not? *(Answers will vary. Should students answer yes, they should explain that most Latin American nations achieved independence by military uprisings which led to a history of military dictatorship. However, should students answer no, then they should mention that the U.S. gained independence by a military uprising and this did not lead to a history of military dictatorship.)*

567

Review Answers
1. ***hacienda:*** large, self-sufficient farming estate; ***peninsular:*** white person living in Latin America who was born in Spain or Portugal; ***creole:*** native-born white person in Latin America; ***mestizo:*** person of part Indian and part white background; ***mulatto:*** person of part black and part white ancestry
2. ***Simón Bolívar:*** creole revolutionary, known as "the Liberator" by Latin Americans; country of Bolivia named for him; ***Toussaint L'Ouverture:*** freed slave who led the slave and mulatto revolt against the French in Hispaniola; ***Miguel Hidalgo:*** started the first important independence movement in Mexico when he led a rebellion of Indian peasants in 1810; ***Agustín Iturbíde:*** upper-class militia general who declared himself emperor of Mexico in 1821; ***José de San Martín:*** Argentine general who liberated Chile from Spain; ***Bernardo O'Higgins:*** Chilean army leader who fought with San Martín; ***Monroe Doctrine:*** statement issued by President Monroe opposing European intervention in American affairs
3. ***Rio de Janeiro:*** city on southeastern coast of Brazil; ***Lima:*** city in west-central Peru; ***Haiti:*** western part of the island of Hispaniola; ***Caracas:*** city on northern coast of Venezuela; ***Boyací:*** battle site in central Great Colombia; ***Great Colombia:*** region in northwestern South America, included the

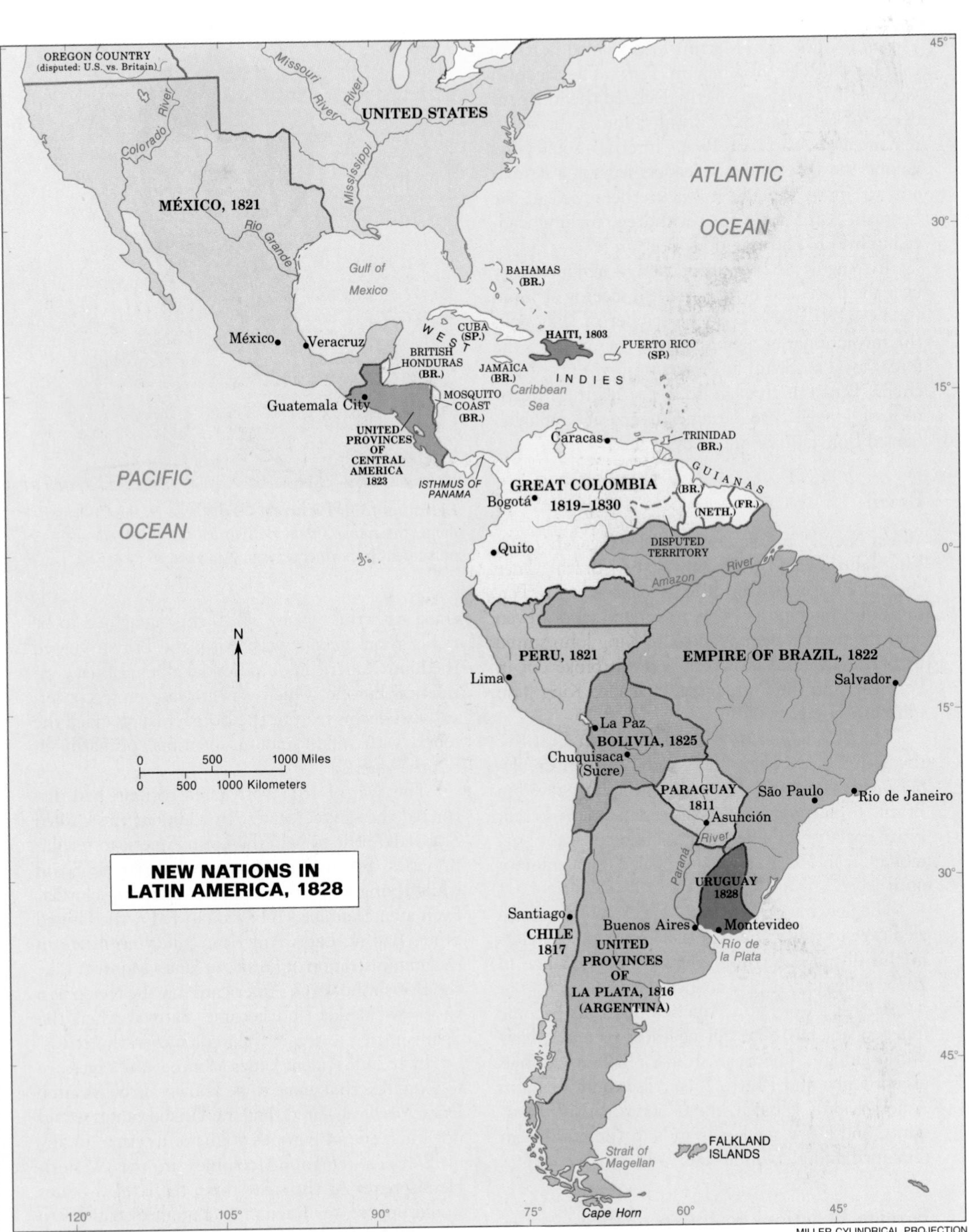

Learning from Maps *Within a short span of years, the huge Spanish and Portuguese empires became independent nations. What regions remained Spanish colonies?* **Cuba and Puerto Rico**

Although European leaders denounced the Monroe Doctrine, no nation of Europe tried to defy it or test it. The combination of British and United States power discouraged other European countries from meddling in Latin American affairs.

Latin American Unity

Enormous distances, geographical barriers, and regional rivalries prevented unity among the new Latin American countries. Of the former Spanish and Portuguese territories, only Brazil managed to maintain national unity. Ecuador and Venezuela broke away from Great Colombia. The United Provinces of Central America crumbled into five separate countries, and Argentina was threatened with internal divisions. By 1840 Latin America contained 17 independent nations.

In 1826 Bolívar called a congress of the Latin American nations to meet at Panama to promote unification. Only Colombia, Peru, Central America, and Mexico attended. Although the Panama Congress failed, many Latin Americans cherished the ideal of unity.

Internal Problems

Independence gave the creole upper classes in Latin America the benefits they had hoped for. They sold more goods abroad at higher prices than ever before, and they could buy manufactured goods more cheaply. However, the creoles rarely built lasting political institutions. Latin American governments came to power as often by rebellion as by elections.

Political instability stemmed in part from the failure to establish strong central governments. The conflict between liberals and conservatives also kept some countries in a state of turmoil. Conservatism thrived in part because the colonial governments never prepared local people for political leadership. During colonial times, the figure of the king bonded together different interests within colonial society. After gaining independence, Brazil had an emperor, but nations with republican institutions had no substitute for a king. In some countries, dictators filled this gap. Dictatorial government provided political stability but no freedom. Conservatism worked against social change and for the preservation of the status quo.

The new governments of Latin America did little to promote social justice. The creole upper classes had little interest in eliminating the inequalities inherited from colonial society. Conservatives believed that reforms had gone too far. In addition, the new Latin American nations lacked the economic resources to finance welfare.

The creoles abolished slavery in every country—though in some not until the 1850s, and in Brazil not until 1888. For the most part, creoles sought to take over the positions of privilege. They also battled to take over communal lands that belonged to the Indian population, claiming that such lands slowed economic progress. The haciendas continued to grow during the next 100 years.

The position of the Roman Catholic church also became a tremendous issue in the new nations. Liberals proposed changes in the powers of the church. They wanted the government to take over functions that the church had performed in colonial times. For example, they thought the government, rather than the church, had the exclusive right to run schools. In some countries, liberals proposed that the government take over the church's extensive landholdings. Conservatives, on the other hand, opposed the loss of church rights.

With all these conflicts, the first 50 or 60 years of independence proved difficult in many Latin American countries. However, in the latter part of the 1800s, trade and government tax revenues increased, and many controversies were concluded successfully. Latin American countries began to achieve some stability and economic growth.

SECTION 4 REVIEW

1. **Define** hacienda, peninsular, creole, mestizo, mulatto
2. **Identify** Simón Bolívar, Toussaint-Louverture, Miguel Hidalgo, Agustín de Iturbide, José de San Martín, Bernardo O'Higgins, Monroe Doctrine
3. **Locate** Rio de Janeiro, Lima, Haiti, Caracas, Boyacá, Great Colombia, Junín
4. **Explaining Ideas** What was the outcome of the revolution in Haiti?
5. **Summarizing Ideas** **(a)** What were the goals of the revolutions that took place in Mexico and Central America? **(b)** What were the results?
6. **Synthesizing Ideas** Why did unification of large regions in South America ultimately fail?
7. **Relating Ideas** **(a)** What were the economic and social problems facing the creoles in Latin America on the eve of independence? **(b)** What problems were evident after independence?

present-day countries of Venezuela, Colombia, Bolivia, and Ecuador; ***Junín:*** city in Andes Mountains northeast of Lima, Peru.

4. Although Toussaint-Louverture died in a French prison, Haiti proclaimed its independence in 1804.

5. (a) The goals were to become free of Spanish authority and establish independent nations. **(b)** Mexico became a republic in 1824. For a brief time, Central America was part of the Mexican empire. By 1823, however, the nations of Honduras, Guatemala, El Salvador, Nicaragua, and Costa Rica formed a federal union known as the United Provinces of Central America.

6. The unification of large regions of South America failed partly because of enormous distances, geographical barriers, and regional rivalries.

7. (a) The creoles suffered social snobbery and job discrimination. In addition, Spain's economic policies threatened creole merchants' monopoly of trade. **(b)** The major problem facing these countries was political instability.

569

Reviewing Important Terms

1. Liberalism; 2. Home rule; 3. Suffragettes; 4. Sectionalism; 5. anarchist; 6. coalition; 7. creoles; 8. Mestizos

Developing Critical Thinking Skills

1. (a) Chartists wanted universal manhood suffrage, the secret ballot, and complete democracy for Great Britain. (b) Parliament eventually adopted most of the Chartists' suggested reforms, such as extending voting rights, the secret ballot, and setting up equal electoral districts.
2. (a) Louis Napoleon tried to gain the support of the army and every section of French society. He had himself named Napoleon III and tried to win glory abroad by fighting the Crimean War, building the Suez Canal, intervening in Mexico, strengthening control of Algeria and establishing French rule in Cambodia. (b) Answers will vary. (c) Explanations will vary. Students' explanations should support their answers.
3. The revolutionary events in British North America and in France aroused the interest of Latin Americans. The creoles suffered discrimination, their monopoly on trade was threatened by Spanish economic policies, and they resented paying taxes to finance Spanish wars.
4. (a) The Monroe Doctrine stated that the United States would oppose any attempt by European nations to interfere in the Western Hemisphere. (b) The American government saw Latin America as a vast new economic market and became alarmed when the Spanish attempted to regain their colonies.

1B, 4A, 4G, 4I, a1A, a1B, a1C, a4A, a4F, a4L

Reteaching

Have students review the Chapter Summary and the appropriate section and questions in the Unit Synthesis. Discuss the concepts until students demonstrate a clear understanding of the material.

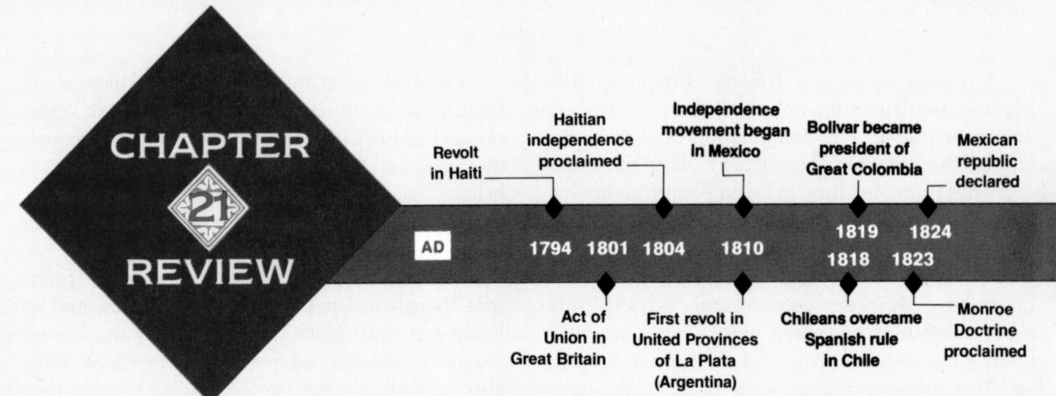

Chapter Summary

The following list contains the key concepts you have learned about political changes in the British Empire, the United States, France, and Latin America during the 1800s and early 1900s.

1. Many reforms occurred in Great Britain in the 1800s and early 1900s. With the Reform Bill of 1832 and agitation from people such as the Chartists, voting rights were greatly broadened in England. In the early 1900s, women finally gained the right to vote.
2. Queen Victoria gave her prime ministers a great deal of power. Two dominant prime ministers of the Victorian Era were Benjamin Disraeli, leader of the Conservative Party, and William Gladstone, leader of the Liberal Party. Under these two prime ministers, many political changes occurred in Great Britain.
3. The labor union movement and socialism grew in Great Britain in the late 1800s and early 1900s. This movement led to the rise of the Labour Party. When the Liberal Party came to power in 1905, Great Britain adopted extensive welfare legislation.
4. Britain's social and political reforms extended to colonies within the British Empire. Canada, Australia, and New Zealand were allowed self-government while remaining within the British Empire.
5. Territorial growth and sectionalism in the United States led to conflict over the issue of slavery. Eventually, the North and South fought a bitter civil war.
6. Following the Civil War, Congress passed the Thirteenth, Fourteenth, and Fifteenth Amendments to the Constitution. These Amendments abolished slavery, made former slaves citizens, and gave black men the right to vote. Women in the United States were given the right to vote in 1920, when the Nineteenth Amendment was ratified.
7. France experienced a series of upheavals in 1830, 1848, and 1871 that rekindled the revolutionary spirit of the 1790s. Each time, politics soon returned to more stable forms. The monarchy was eventually abolished, as was the position of emperor that Napoleon III created for himself. By the early 1900s, France was a republic, governed by coalitions of parties that represented monarchist, liberal, and socialist beliefs.
8. In the early part of the 1800s, revolutions took place throughout Latin America. Following their independence from Spain, most Latin American countries set up democratic governments.
9. The peoples of Latin America had many regional, economic, racial, and social differences. For these reasons, they did not unite but split into many nations after their wars for independence in the early 1800s. Only Brazil managed to maintain national unity.

On a separate sheet of paper, complete the following review exercises.

Reviewing Important Terms

Supply the term that correctly completes each statement.

1. ________ was a movement whose followers believed that people ought to be free to think and work as they please.
2. ________ ________ is a term for self-government.
3. ________ were women who wanted voting rights for all women.
4. ________ is a rivalry among the various sections of a country.
5. An ________ believes in the abolition of all government.
6. A ________ is formed by political groups organized in support of a common cause.
7. People called ________, who were whites born in the Latin American colonies, led the revolutions in South America.
8. ________ are people of mixed Indian and white ancestry.

Developing Critical Thinking Skills

1. **Analyzing Ideas** **(a)** What were the aims of the Chartists? **(b)** How did they contribute to the growth of democracy in Great Britain?
2. **Interpreting Ideas** Louis Napoleon Bonaparte once said, "I believe that from time to time men are created . . . in whose hands the destinies of their countries are placed. I believe myself to be one of those men." **(a)** How did Louis Napoleon attempt to fulfill this

1A, 4G, a4A, a4B, a4C, a4D, a4E, a4F, a4G, a4H, a4I, a4J, a4K, a4L, a4M

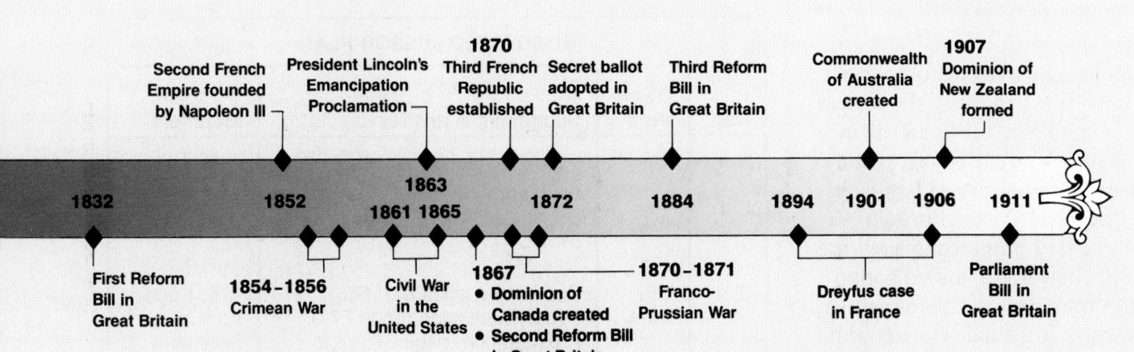

prophecy? **(b)** Would you describe his actions as liberal or reactionary? **(c)** Explain.

3. **Understanding Ideas** What conditions favored revolutions in Latin America during the 1800s?
4. **Summarizing Ideas** **(a)** What was the Monroe Doctrine? **(b)** Why was it issued?
5. **Explaining Ideas** How did the geography of Latin America prevent unity among these countries?

Relating Geography to History

Turn to the map on page 553 and answer the following questions. **(a)** After 1783, how did the United States acquire most of its territory? **(b)** Was the land in your state part of the United States before the 1800s? **(c)** If not, when was it acquired? **(d)** How long did it take for the United States to expand its borders from the Mississippi River to the Pacific Ocean? **(e)** Why might such rapid growth encourage the development of liberalism and nationalism?

Relating Past to Present

1. Before taking office, William Gladstone pledged, "My mission is to pacify Ireland." Review the events that prompted Gladstone to make this remark. Then investigate the situation in Ireland today. Which of the problems faced in the 1880s have lingered into the present? How has the British government dealt with the problems in the 1980s?
2. How did the spread of liberalism inspire the start of the women's suffrage movement in Great Britain and the United States? Even though women now have the vote, some people are still working to extend the rights of women. What are some of the reforms that women have called for during the last decade?

Applying History Study Skills

Before completing this activity, review Building History Study Skills on page 548.

Read the following selection from William Gladstone's speech to Parliament on April 8, 1886, supporting home rule for Ireland.

"... Our intention is, Sir, to propose to the House of Commons that which, as we think ... will liberate Parliament from the restraints under which of late years it has ineffectually struggled to perform the Business of the country; ... obtain an answer ... to the question whether it is or is not possible to establish good and harmonious relations between Great Britain and Ireland on the footing of those free institutions to which Englishmen, Scotchmen, and Irishmen are alike unalterably attached. ... In point of fact, law is discredited ... in Ireland upon this ground especially–that it comes to the people of that country with a foreign aspect, and in a foreign garb. These Coercion Bills of ours ... are stiffly resisted by the Members who represent Ireland in Parliament. The English mind ... is estranged from the Irish people and the Irish mind is estranged from the people of England and Scotland."

1. How does Gladstone defend his view of home rule for Ireland?
2. Does Gladstone's position represent a liberal or conservative ideology? How do you know?
3. Is Gladstone's ideology economic or political? Write a response to Gladstone from another ideology. How did you determine what would be included in your response?

Investigating Further

1. **Presenting an Oral Report** Use encyclopedias to learn more about the ministries of Benjamin Disraeli and William Gladstone. Give an oral report on the types of programs each supported and how they influenced the direction of Great Britain's domestic and foreign policy.
2. **Writing a Report** During the revolutions of 1848, the people of Paris set up a provisional government and proclaimed the Second French Republic. Prepare a report explaining the form that this republic was to take. One source you may use is the "Proclamations of the French Provisional Government, February-March, 1848" in Louis Snyder's *Fifty Major Documents of the Nineteenth Century* (Van Nostrand Reinhold).

5. The size of the region and geographical barriers, such as the Andes Mountains and the Amazon River, prevented unity.

Relating Geography to History

(a) The U.S. acquired most of its territory by treaties with foreign powers.
(b) Answers will vary.
(c) Answers will vary.
(d) It took the U.S. about 45 years to expand from the Mississippi River to the Pacific. **(e)** Answers will vary. Most students will note that individualism bred by frontier conditions might have encouraged the development of liberalism, while the rapid growth of the country helped the development of nationalist feelings.

Relating Past to Present

1. Answers will vary.
2. The idea that all people are equal and should participate in government inspired the movement for women's rights. Answers will vary, but might include equal job opportunities and elimination of sexual harassment.

Applying History Study Skills

1. Gladstone defends his view by suggesting that British law is foreign to the Irish, and that many of the bills passed by Parliament were opposed by Irish members.
2. Gladstone's position represented liberal ideology, because most liberals were for home rule. Gladstone supports home rule.
3. It is political. Answers will vary.

571

CHAPTER (pages 572–597)

22 *Unification of New Nations Added to Rising Tensions in Europe*

(1806-1913)

CHAPTER OVERVIEW

During the 1800s Italian nationalism became a strong force. However, revolts in 1830, 1848, and 1849 failed to unify the Italian kingdoms. Cavour, chief minister of Sardinia, made an alliance with France's Napoleon III to challenge Austrian power in Italy. Although France broke the agreement, Sardinia gained Lombardy; after further revolts, four northern Italian states voted to join Sardinia. Then Garibaldi with his army of Red Shirts conquered the Kingdom of the Two Sicilies. By 1870, Italy was a unified nation.

In Germany the first major step toward unification came in 1818, when Prussia set up the Zollverein. To exclude Austria while uniting the other German states, Prussia fought three wars: the Danish War, the Seven Weeks' War, and the Franco-Prussian War. Prussian victory in the Franco-Prussian War resulted in the unification of the German states into the German Empire.

With Bismarck as chancellor, the newly formed nation made great strides in industrialization. However, Bismarck came into conflict with two groups — Catholics and socialists. Then, in 1890, Bismarck clashed with the new emperor, William II, and resigned.

Russia in the 1800s had a repressive, autocratic government. Although Alexander II abolished serfdom in 1861, the peasants gained little. Alexander's assassination put an end to liberal reforms. After the Revolution of 1905, the czar promised an elected Duma and individual liberties. Soon after the revolution, however, reactionaries came back into control, and autocratic government returned.

In response to the nationalistic revolts of 1848 and the defeat by Prussia in 1866, Austrian leaders created the Dual Monarchy of Austria-Hungary. Government power was shared by Hungary and Austria, but this arrangement did not solve the problem of nationalities in the empire. In the Balkans, the rise of nationalism led to several wars and interference by the European powers. A number of Balkan states gained their independence, and the territory of the Ottoman Empire shrank dramatically.

SUGGESTED LESSON PLAN

Day	Objectives	Suggested Activities	Materials
1	U5* C1-2	Introducing the Chapter (page 572–573) Section 1 (pages 573–577), Focus/Motivation (page 573), Presentation (page 574), Closure (page 575), Suggested Teaching Strategies, Enrichment Activity, Daily Quiz, Suggested Assignments (page 571B)	ATE, Pupil's Edition, Teacher's Resource-Bank™
2	U5, C3-4	Section 2 (pages 577–583), Focus/Motivation (page 577), Presentation (page 578), Closure (page 582), Suggested Teaching Strategies, Enrichment Activity, Daily Quiz, Suggested Assignments (page 571C)	ATE, Pupil's Edition, Teacher's Resource-Bank™
3	U5, C5-6	Section 3 (pages 583–587), Focus/Motivation (page 583), Presentation (page 584), Closure (page 586), Suggested Teaching Strategies, Enrichment Activity, Daily Quiz, Suggested Assignments (page 571C)	ATE, Pupil's Edition, Teacher's Resource-Bank™
4	U5, C7-8	Section 4 (pages 587–591), Focus/Motivation (page 587), Presentation (page 588), Closure (page 590), Suggested Teaching Strategies, Enrichment Activity, Daily Quiz, Suggested Assignments (page 571D)	ATE, Pupil's Edition, Teacher's Resource-Bank™
5	U5, C9	Section 5 (pages 591–595), Focus/Motivation (page 591), Presentation (page 592), Closure (page 594), Suggested Teaching Strategies, Enrichment Activity, Daily Quiz, Suggested Assignments (page 571E)	ATE, Pupil's Edition, Teacher's Resource-Bank™
6	U5 C1-9	Chapter 22 Form A Test, Reteaching Worksheet, Chapter 22 Form B Test	Teacher's Resource-Bank™ or Workbook and Test Booklet

*C refers to applicable Chapter Objective, U refers to applicable Unit Goal.

BOOKS FOR THE TEACHER

Hibbert, Christopher. *Garibaldi and His Enemies.* Little, Brown. Covers the main events in Italian unification.

Kinross, Lord. *The Ottoman Centuries.* William Morrow. Details the rise and fall of the Turkish empire.

Macartney, C. A. *The Hapsburg Empire: 1790–1918.* Macmillan. Discusses the major personalities and problems of the Hapsburg family.

BOOKS FOR THE STUDENT

Apsler, Alfred. *Iron Chancellor.* Julian Messner. Offers an interesting portrait of Bismarck. Specially written for high school students.

Crankshaw, Edward. *The Shadow of the Winter Palace.* Viking. Details life in Russia in the century before the revolution.

Leeds, Christopher. *The Unification of Italy.* Putnam. Provides a highly readable, thorough account of Italian unification.

Smith, Denis M., ed. *Garibaldi.* Prentice-Hall. Evaluates the career of Garibaldi through an examination of original sources.

MULTIMEDIA MATERIALS

Bismarck: Germany from Blood and Iron (mp, 30 min.), Learning Corp. Traces the development of modern Germany from 1815 through the late 1800s.

Continental Europe in Revolution: 1789–1890 (7fs), EBE. Offers a comprehensive picture of the subject. Titles appropriate for Chapter 22 include: "The Unification of Italy (1848–1870)" and "The Rise of Germany (1860–1890)."

Germany: Feudal States to Unification (mp, 14 min.), Coronet. Follows the growth of Prussian power and the extension of Prussian control over other German states.

The Making of the German Nation (4 fs), Educational Audio-Visual. Traces the growth of German power. Title appropriate for Chapter 22: "The Creation of the German Empire from Bismarck Through World War I."

Unification of Italy (mp, 14 min.), Coronet. Follows the struggle for Italian unification from Napoleon's invasion of Italy in 1805 to the plebiscite of Rome in 1870.

Section (pages 573–577)

1 After Years of Struggle, Italy Became a Unified Nation

SECTION OVERVIEW

In the 1830s and 1840s, Giuseppe Mazzini led an unsuccessful Italian unification movement. Leadership in the unification movement ultimately came from the kingdom of Sardinia. Through Sardinia's cooperation with France and finally with Prussia, Austria was forced to abandon its Italian possessions. Garibaldi added the Kingdom of the Two Sicilies, and by 1870 Italy was a unified nation.

SUGGESTED TEACHING STRATEGIES

1. **Preteaching Vocabulary (Basic)** You may wish to preteach the following important vocabulary term: Risorgimento *(page 574)*. Ask: Why do you think the movement toward Italian independence and unification was called a resurgence or reawakening? *(Most students will note that the drive for independence was a resurgence of a movement first started after Napoleon's invasion of Italy in 1805.)*
2. **Researching (Challenging)** Giuseppe Verdi's early operas often had nationalistic themes. Refer students to Chapter 20 for information on this point. Students might investigate Verdi's early works, such as *Nabucodonosor,* and explain why they inspired nationalistic feelings in many Italians. If possible, portions of some of his operas might be played for the class.

ENRICHMENT ACTIVITY

Holding a Panel Discussion (Average/Group) Have three interested students assume the roles of Cavour, Mazzini, and Pius IX. They are to discuss their plans for Italian unification. Mazzini should argue for a republic, Pius IX for a federation with himself as head, and Cavour for a constitutional monarchy under the king of Sardinia. Hold a "plebiscite" of members of the class to see which form of government they would prefer.

DAILY QUIZ

To assess student understanding of Section 1, give the class the following quiz. (Each item is worth 10 points.)

1. Napoleon's conquests gave the Italian peninsula something resembling unity for a few years, but the Congress of ______ divided Italy once again. *(Vienna)*
2. The Italian nationalist movement, with its goals of liberation and unification, became know as the ______, the Italian word for "resurgence." *(Risorgimento)*
3. Who founded the Italian patriotic society known as "Young Italy" in 1831? *(Giuseppe Mazzini)*
4. Which group of Italians wanted to establish a republic in Italy? *(liberals)*
5. Count ______, a leader of Italian nationalism and unity, served as premier of Sardinia. *(Cavour)*
6. In an attempt to unite Italy in 1858, representatives of the kingdom of Sardinia signed a secret treaty of alliance with ______ against Austria. *(Napoleon III)*
7. Who led the Red Shirts against the Kingdom of the Two Sicilies in 1860? *(Giuseppe Garibaldi)*
8. (T or F) In the fall of 1860, the leaders of the nationalist movement agreed to establish an Italian republic. *(F)*
9. What marked the completion of the unification of Italy? *(the plebiscite of Rome in 1870)*
10. What secret society was formed by the leaders of Sicily after unification? *(the Mafia)*

SUGGESTED ASSIGNMENTS

1. **Understanding Chronology (Basic)** Have students construct a time line showing the major events in the drive for Italian unification, and display their time lines on the bulletin board.

2. **Writing a Biographical Sketch (Average/Group)** Assign students oral or written reports on one of the following individuals and his role in the Italian unification: Cavour, Garibaldi, Mazzini, Pius IX, Victor Emmanuel II. Useful sources of information on these individuals include: Christopher Leeds's *The Unification of Italy* (Putnam) and R.A. McLeod's *Cavour and Italian Unity* (Exposition).
3. **Profile Worksheet (Basic)** Have students complete Profile Worksheet 22 in the TEACHER'S RESOURCEBANK™.

Section (pages 577–583)

2 Prussia Created a Unified and Powerful German Empire

SECTION OVERVIEW

The Zollverein, a customs union, was the first step toward cooperation among the German states. Otto von Bismarck, chief minister of Prussia, built a strong army and brought about German unification through a series of wars. The German Empire was proclaimed in 1871 when King William I of Prussia became emperor.

SUGGESTED TEACHING STRATEGIES

1. **Preteaching Vocabulary (Basic)** You may wish to preteach the following important vocabulary term: kaiser *(page 582)*. Ask: Which other European leader used a similar title to kaiser? *(the Russian czar)*
2. **Understanding Chronology (Average/Group)** Write the following groups of events on the chalkboard or on an overhead projector. Have students arrange the events in each group in the correct chronological order.

<u>*(2)*</u> Denmark attempted to annex Schleswig.
<u>*(1)*</u> Christian IX came to the Danish throne.
<u>*(4)*</u> Prussia and Austria received joint ownership of Schleswig and Holstein.
<u>*(3)*</u> Prussia and Austria declared war on Denmark.

<u>*(4)*</u> Austria surrendered its rule of Holstein to Prussia.
<u>*(3)*</u> Bismarck provoked Austria into declaring war on Prussia.
<u>*(1)*</u> Bismarck persuaded Napoleon III to remain neutral if war developed between Austria and Prussia.
<u>*(2)*</u> Bismarck formed an alliance with Italy.

<u>*(2)*</u> France declared war on Prussia.
<u>*(4)*</u> The German Empire was proclaimed at Versailles.
<u>*(3)*</u> The southern German states became allies of Prussia.
<u>*(1)*</u> The North German Confederation was formed.

ENRICHMENT ACTIVITY

Preparing a Newscast (Average/Group) A group of students might prepare a short newscast from the Hall of Mirrors at Versailles on the day William I was proclaimed emperor of Germany. Reporters should interview William I, Bismarck, and a German soldier about how the empire was formed and what the empire means to them. Also, reporters should interview French citizens for their feelings on what took place at Versailles. Have students "broadcast" their newscast to the rest of the class.

DAILY QUIZ

To assess student understanding of Section 2, give the class the following quiz. (Each item is worth 10 points.)

1. Who were the Junkers? *(the aristocratic landowners of Prussia)*
2. Beginning in 1819, Prussia and other German states signed a number of treaties that set up a customs union called the ________. *(Zollverein)*
3. What touched off demands for liberal reforms throughout Germany in the mid-1800s? *(the 1848 uprisings in France)*
4. Who said that German policy would be carried out "by iron and blood"? *(Otto von Bismarck)*
5. Over which two small states did Prussia and Austria go to war with Denmark? *(Schleswig and Holstein)*
6. The Treaty of ________ ended the Seven Weeks' War between Prussia and Austria in 1866. *(Prague)*
7. How did Bismarck persuade the southern German states to unite with the rest of Germany? *(by provoking a war with France)*
8. What were the terms of the treaty that ended the Franco-Prussian War? *(France was occupied by German troops, it forfeited Alsace and part of Lorraine to Prussia, and it had to pay a huge indemnity.)*
9. In the new German Empire, what title did the head of government hold? *(kaiser)*
10. What were the names of the two houses of the legislative branch of the German government? *(Bundesrat, Reichstag)*

SUGGESTED ASSIGNMENTS

1. **Critical Thinking Worksheet (Basic)** Have students complete Critical Thinking Worksheet 50 in the TEACHER'S RESOURCEBANK™.
2. **Researching (Challenging)** Interested students may wish to undertake further research into the wars that Bismarck waged to unify Germany. Useful sources of information on Bismarck include: Alfred Apsler's *Iron Chancellor* (Julian Messner) and Edward Crankshaw's *Bismarck* (Viking). Have students share their findings with the rest of the class.

Section (pages 583–587)

3 Industrialization and Socialism Created Opposition to Bismarck

SECTION OVERVIEW

Despite his successful leadership as chancellor of the German Empire, Bismarck encountered opposition. He attempted to reduce the power of the Catholic Church in the *Kulturkampf.* Industrialization — aided by political unification, gains from the Franco-Prussian War, and government policies — bolstered socialist strength. Bismarck tried to control the socialists, first through repressive measures and then through a broad program of social reform.

SUGGESTED TEACHING STRATEGIES

1. **Understanding Words (Basic)** Reproduce the following list of scrambled words and their clues and distribute to the class.

a. ampkurtlukf	German word meaning "war of civilization"
b. hurr	River valley in Germany where a huge steel industry developed
c. aoclis cremdsoat	A new German political party formed in 1869
d. chiegrats	Legislative assembly used by socialists to air their grievances
e. noir nelchoracl	Nickname of Otto von Bismarck
f. limwail	Kaiser who forced Bismarck to resign

(Answers: a-kulturkampf, b-Ruhr, c-Social Democrats, d-Reichstag, e-Iron Chancellor, f-William)

*2. **Writing About History: Writing a Comparison Essay (Basic)** To reinforce the skill lesson presented on page 586, have students write a brief paragraph comparing industrial development in Germany with industrial development in Great Britain.

ENRICHMENT ACTIVITY

Analyzing Ideas (Average/Group) Organize the class into groups of four or five students to discuss the following statement: Bismarck was one of the greatest political leaders of the nineteenth century. Appoint group leaders to direct and record the results of the group discussions. Have the groups decide whether they agree or disagree with the proposition by listing both the good and bad aspects of Bismarck's career. After the task has been completed, reassemble the class and have each group present its findings.

DAILY QUIZ

To assess student understanding of Section 3, give the class the following quiz. (Each item is worth 10 points.)

1. (T or F) All Germans supported Bismarck's quest for a powerful, centralized government during the 1870s. *(F)*
2. Why did Bismarck oppose the pope's long-standing claim to the right to administer church property in Germany? *(because he felt that it amounted to foreign interference in German domestic affairs)*
3. Bismarck's *Kulturkampf* was aimed at Germany's ______. *(Catholics)*
4. (T or F) The fact that industrialization came later in Germany than in Great Britain and France proved to be a benefit for Germany. *(T)*
5. (T or F) Under Bismarck's leadership, the German government worked to stifle industrial development. *(F)*
6. Which new political party, founded on the idea that the government should own all major industry, began to gain strength in the Reichstag during the 1870s? *(Social Democrats)*
7. How did Bismarck attempt to control the socialists in 1878? *(He pushed through laws prohibiting newspapers, books, and pamphlets that spread socialist ideas and banned public meetings held by socialists.)*
8. How did Bismarck "steal the socialists' thunder?" *(He passed a number of social and economic reforms proposed by the socialists.)*
9. Why did William II force Bismarck to resign as chancellor? *(because he thought Bismarck was too powerful)*
10. What move by William II brought Germany into competition with Great Britain? *(his strengthening of the German navy)*

SUGGESTED ASSIGNMENTS

1. **Writing a Paragraph (Basic)** Have students write a paragraph on whether they agree or disagree with the following statement: "It was a wise decision on the part of William II to force Bismarck to resign." Students should defend their position.
2. **Researching (Average/Group)** Industries such as steel production and arms manufacture grew rapidly during Bismarck's years in power. Have students research and report to the class, using charts they have prepared, on the development of these industries in Germany in the late 1800s.
3. **Skill Worksheet (Basic)** Have students complete Skill Worksheet 22 in the TEACHER'S RESOURCEBANK™.

Section (pages 587–591)

Despite Reforms, Russia Remained a Rigid Autocracy

SECTION OVERVIEW

Although Alexander II abolished serfdom in Russia and attempted other reforms, radical groups wanted more drastic measures. After Alexander's assassination, his successors used all means to stamp out liberalism. Russia's defeat in the Russo-Japanese War ignited the bloody Revolution of 1905. Nicholas II was forced to promise individual liberties and an elected Duma, but the government gradually returned to oppressive autocracy.

SUGGESTED TEACHING STRATEGIES

1. **Preteaching Vocabulary (Basic)** You may wish to preteach the following important vocabulary terms: autocrat *(page 587)*; terrorism *(page 588)*; pogrom *(589)*. Ask students to suggest terms

for the word *autocrat.* *(Student suggestions should include: absolute ruler, despot, dictator, totalitarian, tyrant.)*

2. **Illustrating Ideas (Average/Group)** The art of Fabergé has been reproduced in many illustrated books. An interested student might bring one of these books from the public library and show the class other examples of the extraordinary eggs that were produced for the Russian royal family. Another student might want to research the enameling process in more detail and report to the class.

ENRICHMENT ACTIVITY

Analyzing Ideas (Average/Group) Students could present readings to the class from various works of Russian literature. The dialogue between Bazarov the Nihilist and an elderly man in *Fathers and Sons* by Ivan Turgenev will serve as the basis for a discussion of the philosophy of nihilism. Another appropriate reading is "The Grand Inquisitor" from *The Brothers Karamazov* by Feodor Dostoyevsky.

DAILY QUIZ

To assess student understanding of Section 4, give the class the following quiz. (Each item is worth 10 points.)

1. The three groups that comprised the population of European Russia were the Great Russians, the White Russians, and the ________. *(Ukrainians)*
2. The czar ruled the huge Russian Empire as an ________, or one who holds absolute power. *(autocrat)*
3. What program forced non-Russians in the empire to speak Russian, accept the Orthodox faith, and adopt Russian customs? *(Russification)*
4. In the Balkans the czars backed ________ the union of all Slavic peoples under Russian leadership. *(Pan-Slavism)*
5. In 1861 Alexander II issued the ________ ________ that freed all serfs. *(Emancipation Edict)*
6. Which radical group wanted to abolish the whole political and social structure and build a new Russia? *(Nihilists)*
7. Which political group urged its members to live among the Russian peasants as teachers or doctors? *(Populists)*
8. The radical movement known as the ________ ________ favored the use of terrorism. *(People's Will)*
9. "________ ________," when the czar's troops shot at a group of unarmed strikers, marked the beginning of the Revolution of 1905. *(Bloody Sunday)*
10. The October Manifesto provided for the election of a parliament called the ________. *(Duma)*

SUGGESTED ASSIGNMENTS

1. **Critical Thinking Worksheet (Basic)** Have students complete Critical Thinking Worksheet 51 in the TEACHER'S RESOURCEBANK™.
2. **Writing a Report (Challenging)** The nineteenth century was an outstanding artistic period in Russian history. To acquaint students with this period, ask them to prepare written reports on the life and work of one of the following: Aleksandr Pushkin (writer), Nikolai Gogol (writer), Ivan Turgenev (writer), Feodor Dostoyevsky (writer), Leo Tolstoy (writer), Anton Chekhov (playwright), Mikhail Glinka (composer), Aleksandr Borodin (composer), Modest Mussorgsky (composer), Nicolai Rimsky-Korsakov (composer), Peter Tchaikovsky (composer). Select students to read their reports to the rest of the class.

Section 5 (pages 591–595)

Austria-Hungary's Interest Focused on the Balkans

SECTION OVERVIEW

The formation of the Dual Monarchy of Austria-Hungary left minority groups dissatisfied. To compensate for a loss of influence in Germany and Italy, the Dual Monarchy tried to gain influence and territory in the Balkans, where Ottoman influence was beginning to decline. Taking advantage of the rise of nationalism in the Balkans, Austria-Hungary and other foreign countries began to intervene in the region for their own ends.

SUGGESTED TEACHING STRATEGIES

1. **Constructing a Chart (Basic)** To help students trace the development of the independence movement in the Balkans, have them construct a chart showing, in the correct chronological order, the Balkan states that gained independence in the 1800s and early 1900s.
2. **Illustrating Ideas (Average/Group)** Draw the following diagram on the chalkboard and use it as a starting point for a discussion on the organization and problems of Austria-Hungary. The following questions will help the discussion: Why did Austria create the Dual Monarchy? What powers were left with the central government? Why do you think the central government insisted on those particular powers? What advantages did Hungary gain by this arrangement?

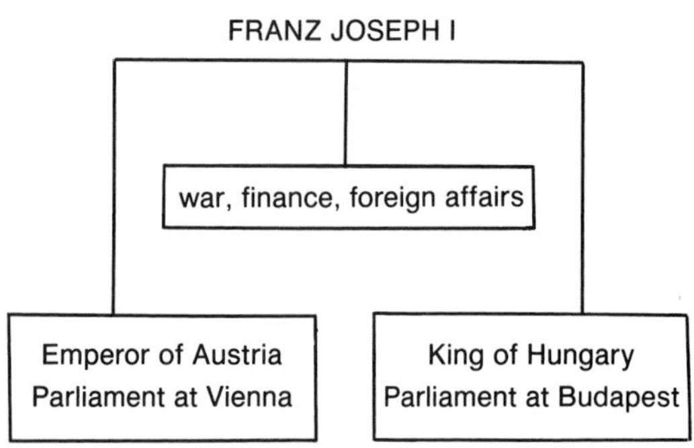

ENRICHMENT ACTIVITY

Comparing Ideas (Challenging) Have interested students hold a discussion on the similarities and differences between the decline of the Ottoman Empire and another great empire, such as the Roman Empire. Ask students to try to answer the following question in their discussion: Do all great empires follow the same pattern — rise, peak, stagnation, decline, and disintegration?

DAILY QUIZ

To assess student understanding of Section 5, give the class the following quiz. (Each item is worth 10 points.)

1. To what ethnic group did many people who lived in Hungary belong? *(Magyars)*
2. Who led the Hungarian revolt against Austrian domination in 1848? *(Louis Kossuth)*
3. How did Austria solve the problem of increasing Hungarian demands for freedom? *(by forming the Dual Monarchy, in which the Hungarians shared power with the Austrians)*
4. What were the two government centers of Austria-Hungary? *(Vienna and Budapest)*
5. What economic issue caused friction between Austria and Hungary? *(the issue of tariffs)*
6. (T or F) The Ottoman Empire was weakened by pervasive favoritism, bribery, and corruption. *(T)*
7. Which European power followed a policy of Pan-Slavism and encouraged Balkan nationalist groups like the Serbs and Bulgarians? *(Russia)*
8. Which liberal democratic western nation intervened on the side of the autocratic Turks against Balkan nationalist groups? *(Great Britain)*
9. The Treaty of San Stefano granted independence to Romania, ________, and ________. *(Montenegro, Serbia)*
10. In 1912 Bulgaria, Serbia, Greece, and Montenegro formed an alliance known as the ________ ________ to fight the Ottoman Empire. *(Balkan League)*

SUGGESTED ASSIGNMENTS

1. **Review Worksheet (Basic)** Have students complete Review Worksheet 22 in the TEACHER'S RESOURCEBANK™.
2. **Writing an Editorial (Average/Group)** Have students write an editorial for a newspaper on one of the Balkan territories demanding independence, such as Serbia or Bulgaria. The paper's position should be nationalistic, arguing for the independence of the particular group.

For suggested lesson plan, additional teaching strategies, enrichment activities, daily quizzes, and suggested assignments, see pages 571A–571F.

Introducing the Chapter
Have students study the following maps: "Unification of Italy" (page 577) and "Unification of Germany" (page 582). Ask students to identify the dominant or leading state in the unification of each nation. *(Sardinia and Prussia)* Ask students to speculate on what problems might have hindered Italian and German unification. *(Student answers should include: rivalries among different states, unwillingness of rulers to give up their power, and fear of the smaller states that they would be absorbed by bigger states.)* Then ask students what factors they think would tend to promote unity. *(Students answers should include: common language, common cultural heritage, and geographic unity.)*

You might contrast the situation in Italy and Germany with the problems of the Austrian and Ottoman empires. Point out that Germany and Italy tried to bring together peoples that had much in common; Austria-Hungary and the Ottoman Empire struggled to keep together many distinct nationalities with diverse interests.

CHAPTER 22

Unification of New Nations Added to Rising Tensions in Europe

CHAPTER FOCUS

Place Europe

Time 1806–1913

3.7 mil. BC | 4000 BC | AD 2100

Significance

For about 100 years, from the mid-1700s to the mid-1800s, relations among the major nations of Europe had remained the same. However, a new force—nationalism—would disrupt and permanently alter those relationships.

Nationalism, which linked people through ties of history, language, culture, and territory, caused much upheaval in Europe in the mid-1800s. In divided Italy and Germany, nationalistic feelings fueled successful efforts to unify these two nations. Feelings of nationalism also resulted in the emergence on the European continent of two strong economic and political powers—the kingdom of Italy and the German Empire.

During the second half of the 1800s, therefore, political life in Europe changed significantly. In eastern Europe, for example, nationalism became an increasingly important political influence as various nationalist groups began to agitate continually for self-government. After more than a century of relative stability, the European situation was becoming more and more unsettled as well as more complex.

Terms to Define

Risorgimento, terrorism, kaiser, pogrom, autocrat

People to Identify

Cavour, Alexander II, Iron Chancellor, Francis Joseph I

Places to Locate

Venetia, Bavaria, Papal States, Bulgaria, Saxony, Cyprus

Questions to Guide Your Reading

1 How, after years of struggle, did Italy finally become a unified nation?
2 How did Prussia create a unified and powerful German Empire?
3 In what ways did socialism create opposition to Bismarck?
4 Why did Russia remain a rigid autocracy?
5 Why did Austria-Hungary's interest focus on the Balkans?

Giuseppe Mazzini, who lived from 1805 to 1872, was one of the three rulers of the republic set up in Rome during the ill-fated revolution of 1848–1849. He expresses his anger and sadness at losing the struggle in the following excerpt from a letter he wrote to the French woman novelist George Sand on June 28, 1849, as French forces overwhelmed Rome.

> *"I am looking on at the agony of a great city, and my soul is sharing her agony. Since the 20th (in consequence of the treachery of an officer), the soldiers of General Oudinot are in the breach. Rome is not a fortress; it is a town eighteen miles in circumference. . . . (The French) proceed, an inch a day, with the help of covered passages. They killed our brave officers singly. They try to crush our batteries with large cannon. . . . They cut off our water-supplies. They seize our provisions and our cattle, which come from the country. They throw bombs night and day. They do not even respect the hospitals. . . . The war which they make upon us is base and cowardly. Oudinot will not face our barricades; but by tiring the population out, harassing our soldiers, killing people with his bombs, and cutting off our provisions, he will end by exciting those elements of fear and local egoism which always exist in a town, however heroic it may be."*

The upheaval in Rome was only one of many that erupted in Europe in the mid-1800s.

1 After Years of Struggle, Italy Became a Unified Nation

The conquests of Napoleon I had given the Italian Peninsula something resembling unity for a few years. The Italians, inspired by the liberal and nationalistic ideals of the French Revolution, had overthrown several rulers of the Italian states. However, after the Congress of Vienna in 1815, Italy was again divided. Austria annexed Lombardy and Venetia. The rest of Italy was fragmented into several large and small states. These states were either dominated by Austria or ruled by reactionary monarchs who tried to wipe out any advances made during Napoleon's time (see map, page 577).

◀ *Celebrating Italian unification*

Chapter Objectives
After studying Chapter 22, students will be able to:

1. Identify the leaders of the Italian unification movement.
2. Trace the events leading to Italian unification and describe the problems facing Italy after unification.
3. Identify the major events in Germany's unification.
4. Describe the government of the German Empire.
5. List the factors that made Germany's rapid industrialization possible.
6. Summarize the social reforms adopted under Bismarck.
7. Explain the aims of Russian foreign policy.
8. Discuss why the Revolution of 1905 failed.
9. Describe the strengths and weaknesses of the Dual Monarchy, and explain the decline of the Ottoman Empire.

SECTION 1

Focus/Motivation
The following lines are part of the "Garibaldi Hymn," generally considered the national anthem of Italy.

"Two seas and the Alps shall our Italy bound; The oppressor no more in our land shall be found!"

Ask students what these lines indicate about the goals of Italian nationalists during the mid-1800s. Who is the "oppressor"? Assign a group of students to locate a translation of the complete song. Ask them

● The paper was named *Il Risorgimento,* from which the nationalist movement took its name.

to identify the additional ideals described in the lyrics. How do these compare with the ideals in our own national anthem, "The Star-Spangled Banner"?

Presentation
Making a Poster
(Average/Group)
Divide the class into small groups to make bulletin board posters advocating Italian unification. Posters should show the republican, monarchist, and papal points of view toward unification.

Early Movements Toward Unification

Italian nationalism became a strong force in the early 1800s when many thinkers and writers tried to revive interest in Italy's traditions. This nationalistic movement, with its goals of liberation and unification, became known as the **Risorgimento** (ree • sor • jee • MEN • toh)—the Italian word for "resurgence." Because nationalists could not support their cause openly, they formed secret societies. An early group of this sort was the Carbonari (kahr • buh • NAH • ree). One of its most famous members, Giuseppe Mazzini, greatly influenced later Italian history.

Mazzini, born in 1805, envisioned a united Italy, and he devoted his entire life to this goal. Mazzini spent time both imprisoned and exiled for his part in an unsuccessful uprising against Sardinia in 1830. In 1831 he called for all Italian patriots to join a new movement, known as Young Italy, to spread the ideals of the Risorgimento. Mazzini described Young Italy as "a brotherhood of Italians who believe in Progress and Duty."

In 1848 liberals and nationalists led rebellions in several of the Italian states. These rebellions forced the rulers of Sardinia, the Kingdom of the Two Sicilies, and Tuscany to grant constitutions to their subjects, and overthrew Austrian rule in Lombardy and Venetia. Revolutionaries seized Rome in 1849 and set up a republic that Mazzini and two other leaders governed. All but one of these revolutionary movements soon failed. The Austrian army succeeded in recapturing some of its former possessions in northern Italy during the summer of 1849. Former rulers returned to power, revoking the constitutions. The revolt succeeded only in Sardinia, which remained independent.

Despite the failure of the revolts of 1848 and 1849, Italian patriots continued their efforts. They now agreed on their principal aim—a united Italy. However, they could not agree on how to achieve unity or what the ideal form of government would be after unification had succeeded.

Many Italians, especially the Catholic clergy, wanted a federation of Italian states headed by the pope. Liberals, however, wanted an Italian republic. They opposed federation, partly because the papacy had turned against liberalism after 1849. Still others wanted a constitutional monarchy under King Victor Emmanuel II of Sardinia, who sympathized with liberal aims.

Learning from Pictures *Count Cavour sought an alliance with Napoleon III to evict the Austrians and unify Italy under Sardinia's leadership.*

Cavour in Sardinia

The chief minister or premier, Count Camillo Benso di Cavour (kahv • OOHR), and not the king of Sardinia, actually governed the nation. Born in 1810, Cavour was a well-educated and widely traveled aristocrat. He edited a nationalist newspaper ● in 1847, took part in the revolutions of 1848, and in 1852 became premier of Sardinia.

Cavour disliked absolutism and admired the British system of parliamentary government. He wanted Italy to be both united and industrialized under Sardinia's leadership.

Cavour reorganized and strengthened the Sardinian army. He helped to establish banks, factories, and railroads, encouraged shipbuilding, and negotiated treaties with other countries to increase trade. Under the slogan "A free church in a free state," he tried to reduce the political influence of the Roman Catholic church. He expelled the politically powerful Jesuit order from the country. He

● They adopted the uniform in imitation of Garibaldi, who always wore a bright red shirt in battle.

also brought Sardinia to prominence through its participation on the side of France and Great Britain in the Crimean War and in the peace conference at Paris in 1856 that ended that war.

Napoleon III and War with Austria

Since Austrian control of part of northern Italy presented the greatest obstacle to Italian unity, Cavour searched for allies against that nation. He proposed an alliance of France and Sardinia against Austria. Although Napoleon III always sought ways to increase French prestige, he hesitated at first to take this step because he feared antagonizing the pope and French Catholics. However, he hoped that with Austria driven out of Italy, France could dominate a weak confederation of Italian states. Cavour, on the other hand, believed that with Austria out of Italy, the other Italian states would join Sardinia to form a strong alliance against both France and Austria.

In 1858 Cavour and Napoleon met secretly to plan a war against Austria. Napoleon agreed that if Austria could be provoked into declaring war on Sardinia, France would send troops to help drive the Austrians out of Lombardy and Venetia. In return for this help, Cavour promised to give the French-speaking regions of Nice and Savoy that then belonged to Sardinia to France. In 1859 Cavour began his preparations for war. Austria played right into Cavour's hands by demanding that the military buildup in Sardinia be stopped in three days. When Cavour rejected Austria's "attempt to interfere in the affairs of Sardinia," Austria, as Cavour had hoped, declared war.

At first the war went according to Cavour's plans. The combined Sardinian-French forces quickly drove the Austrians out of Lombardy and marched on into Venetia. Italian patriots in Tuscany, Modena, and Parma overthrew their Austrian rulers and asked to be annexed to Sardinia.

Napoleon III had not planned on this happening, however. He did not want a strong, united Italy any more than he wanted a united Germany. He feared that if the war lasted a long time, Prussia, for its own ends, might help Austria. Napoleon had no desire to get involved in a war against both Austria and Prussia. In July 1859, only three months after the war began, Napoleon signed a secret armistice with Austria. According to its terms, Sardinia received Lombardy, but Austria kept Venetia. The agreement also returned Austrian rulers to Tuscany, Modena, and Parma.

This armistice marked a severe setback for Cavour and the Italian nationalists. Napoleon III had delivered only half of his side of the bargain—control of Lombardy to Sardinia. However, he insisted on collecting his full price—Nice and Savoy. Afraid of losing even the partial victory, King Victor Emmanuel II agreed to the French terms.

The Italian people, however, refused to give up their goals. Popular feeling ran far ahead of governmental caution. Rebellions in Parma, Modena, and Tuscany again expelled the Austrian rulers and set up popular temporary governments. The people of Romagna, a province in the Papal States, also revolted. When all of these areas held elections, the voters overwhelmingly favored joining Sardinia.

Garibaldi's Red Shirts

The southern half of the Italian Peninsula, together with the large island of Sicily, made up the Kingdom of the Two Sicilies. A harsh Bourbon king ruled this kingdom. Earlier revolts there had failed, but it now became the target of the Italian nationalists. Giuseppe Garibaldi, a man devoted to Italian freedom, led the way.

Garibaldi was born in Nice in 1807. As a youth, he joined Mazzini's Young Italy movement. In 1834, after being involved in a revolutionary plot in Piedmont, Garibaldi had to flee for his life to Latin America. Returning to Italy, he fought in the revolutions of 1848. Forced to flee again, he lived in the United States for a few years, returning once more to Italy in 1854.

With financial assistance secretly furnished by Cavour, Garibaldi recruited an army of 1,100 soldiers. They called themselves Red Shirts because of ● the uniform they wore into battle. In the spring of 1860, Garibaldi and his Red Shirts invaded Sicily, where the people welcomed them. Crossing to the Italian mainland, Garibaldi and his forces seized Naples, the capital city, and drove Francis II and his forces north to the border of the Papal States.

Garibaldi planned to continue his march north to capture Rome and then Venetia. But Cavour, afraid that Garibaldi might try to set up a republic, sent an army south to stop Garibaldi's advance. In the process Sardinia annexed most of the territory of the Papal States.

SECTION 1

Closure

Mention that Giuseppe Mazzini referred to Count Cavour as a "pale ghost of Machiavelli." Ask: What do you think Mazzini meant by this comment? *(Most students will suggest that Mazzini thought the methods used by Cavour were similar to the cunning, duplicitous approach advocated by Machiavelli.)*

Review Answers

1. ***Risorgimento:*** Italian word meaning "resurgence"; name given to the Italian nationalist movement in the 1800s
2. ***Carbonari:*** secret society of Italian nationalists; ***Young Italy:*** movement founded by Giuseppe Mazzini to spread the ideals of the Risorgimento among Italians; ***Victor Emmanuel II:*** king of Sardinia who became ruler of the kingdom of Italy; ***Cavour:*** chief minister of Sardinia who became the engineer of Italian unification; ***Garibaldi:*** leader who freed the Kingdom of the Two Sicilies from Bourbon rule; ***Red Shirts:*** soldiers of Garibaldi's army, so called because of the uniform they wore into battle; ***Francis II:*** harsh Bourbon ruler of the Kingdom of Two Sicilies
3. ***Lombardy:*** northern Italy, bordering on Switzerland; ***Venetia:*** northeastern Italy; ***Sardinia:*** island in the Mediterranean south of Corsica; ***Kingdom of the Two Sicilies:*** southern Italy and Sicily; ***Tuscany:*** region

around the city of Florence; ***Modena:*** northern Italy, bordering on Venetia; ***Parma:*** northwest of Modena; ***Romagna:*** south of Venetia; ***Papal States:*** east of Tuscany from Rome to Romagna; ***Turin:*** city of central Piedmont
4. Mazzini was an idealistic Italian patriot and revolutionary leader who devoted his life to Italian unity. In 1849, with two others, he briefly headed a republican government in Rome. His influence in Italy was tremendous.
5. In 1848-49 rebellions took place in Sardinia,the Kingdom of the Two Sicilies and Tuscany; Austrian rule was overthrown in Lombardy and Venetia; and a republic was established in Rome. However, in all of the states but Sardinia the revolts were eventually put down. In 1852 Cavour became chief minister of Sardinia. In 1858 Cavour and Napoleon III made a secret agreement to fight Austria. In 1859 war between Sardinia and Austria led to Sardinia gaining Lombardy. In 1860 Sardinia annexed Parma, Modena, Tuscany and Romagna. Garibaldi seized Sicily and Naples; he and Cavour agreed to the establishment of a kingdom of Italy. Elections in all states except Venetia and Rome made unification official. In 1866 Italy gained Venetia in the Seven Weeks' War. In 1870 the Franco-Prussian War forced Napoleon III to withdraw his troops from Rome, and its citizens voted for union with Italy.

In the fall of 1860, Garibaldi and Cavour met in Naples where Garibaldi reluctantly agreed to abandon his plan to conquer the entire Italian Peninsula. For the sake of Italian unification, Cavour persuaded Garibaldi to support the establishment of the kingdom of Italy, with Victor Emmanuel II of Sardinia as its ruler.

Final Unification

In 1860 elections were held everywhere in Italy except in Venetia and Rome. The people voted overwhelmingly for national unity under the king of Sardinia. Representatives of the various states met at a parliament in the Sardinian capital of Turin in February 1861, where they confirmed Victor Emmanuel II as king of Italy "by grace of God and the will of the nation."

The new kingdom included all of Italy except Venetia, which still belonged to Austria, and the western part of the Papal States around the city of Rome, which the pope ruled (see map, page 577). European governments were left primarily with two choices—either to recognize the new state or to fight it. The embarrassed Napoleon III stopped short of making war on the new country but did send French troops to Rome to prevent the Italian nationalists from seizing it.

Unification was completed when Italy gained Venetia in the Seven Weeks' War of 1866. When the Franco-Prussian War broke out in 1870, Napoleon III had to recall his troops from Rome. The Italians entered the city, and the citizens of Rome voted overwhelmingly for union with Italy. Later that year Rome was proclaimed the capital of the kingdom of Italy.

Problems of a United Italy

Although now politically united, Italy still had many problems. Few Italians had experience with self-government, and scandals frequently rocked the young nation. The various regions of the country remained divided by their own traditions and independence. Tensions arose between the industrialized north and the agricultural south. In Sicily

Learning from Pictures
The aspirations of Italian nationalism were strengthened by Garibaldi's liberation of Sicily, where the Red Shirts defeated an army 20 times its size.

● One result of this instability was massive emigration. In the 50 years after unification, more than 5 million people left Italy for the Americas.

Learning from Maps *By agreeing to help Sardinia against the Austrians, France received Nice and Savoy. What year did France receive these territories?* **1860**

local leaders organized a secret society known as the Mafia. The society formed a kind of state within the state, which the central government was powerless to control.

Italy's leaders admired the military strength of Germany and hoped to follow a similar course in their own country. Within a few years, Italy had the world's third largest navy and the third largest merchant marine.

Italy paid for this military buildup by taxing its people heavily, a policy that sparked strikes, riots, and peasant uprisings, particularly in Sicily, in the 1890s. Looking for victories that would build the country's prestige, Italy engaged in expensive colonial ventures in Africa. A brief war against the Ottoman Empire in 1911 cost a great deal of money and brought Italy little in return. Although unified, Italy had not achieved stability. ●

SECTION 1 REVIEW

1. **Define** Risorgimento
2. **Identify** Carbonari, Young Italy, Victor Emmanuel II, Cavour, Garibaldi, Red Shirts, Francis II
3. **Locate** Lombardy, Venetia, Sardinia, Kingdom of the Two Sicilies, Tuscany, Modena, Parma, Romagna, Papal States, Turin
4. **Analyzing Ideas** Who was Mazzini and what was his place in Italian history?
5. **Organizing Ideas** Trace the steps toward Italian unification as they occurred in the following years: 1848–49, 1852, 1858, 1859, 1860, 1866, and 1870.
6. **Explaining Ideas** Describe the problems that Italy faced following its unification in 1870.
7. **Understanding Ideas** Why did France and Sardinia form an alliance against Austria?

2 Prussia Created a Unified and Powerful German Empire

The inability of the German people to form an enduring union before the late 1800s appears as a great historical mystery. The Germans shared a common language and history. Several times, vigorous, intelligent rulers came close to achieving a strong central government, but all of them failed. In the mid-1800s Germany remained what it had been for centuries—a patchwork of independent states. Each has its own laws, currency, and rulers. By the late 1800s, Prussia took the lead in uniting these states.

Prussia as Leader

The Prussians built a strong and prosperous state in the 1700s during the reigns of Frederick William I and his son Frederick the Great. A new situation arose when Napoleon I dominated Prussia from 1806 until 1812. He seized Prussian lands, formed new states from them, and gave them to his relatives and allies. To prevent Prussia from becoming a military threat, he limited the size of the Prussian army and levied a large indemnity. He also forced Prussia to support an occupation army within its territory and contribute soldiers to the French armies.

Rome was then proclaimed the capital of the kingdom of Italy.
6. Many problems remained after Italian unification. Few Italians were experienced in self-government, and scandals were common. The various regions of the country remained divided from one another by their own traditions and independence. Tension grew between the industrialized north and the agricultural south. In Sicily the secret society of the Mafia became a state within a state. Italy's attempt to be a military and imperialist power led to heavy taxes. This and governmental inefficiency led to peasant uprisings in the countryside and strikes and riots in the cities.
7. Since Austrian control of part of northern Italy presented the greatest obstacle to Italian unity, Cavour searched for allies against that nation. He proposed an alliance of France and Sardinia against Austria. Napoleon III agreed to the alliance to increase French prestige.

SECTION 2

Focus/Motivation
Put the following statement by Bismarck on the chalkboard, or reproduce it for the class.

"Prussia must collect her forces and hold them in reserve for a favorable moment, which has already come and gone several times. Since the treaties of Vienna, our frontiers have been ill designed for a healthy body politic. The great question of our time will be decided not by speeches and resolutions of majorities . . . but by blood and iron."

Lead the class in a discussion about Bismarck, using the following questions as a guide: What are the "treaties of Vienna" to which Bismarck refers? *(the Congress of Vienna in 1815, which ended the Napoleonic Era)* Why might Bismarck think Prussia's frontiers were "ill designed"? *(The Congress of Vienna gave Prussia much important territory, but Prussian lands were broken up by many smaller German states.)* What policies does the statement recommend? *(maintaining a reserve army and becoming strong by war)*

Presentation
Constructing a Chart (Basic)
Have students work together to develop a two-column chart showing the government of the German Empire. In one column have students list the positions and branches of the government—kaiser, chancellor, bundesrat, and reichstag. In the other column, have them enter the powers of the listed positions and branches. Then use the chart for a discussion comparing the German system of government with the federal system of the United States.

The Prussians found ways around Napoleon's restrictions, however. For example, the strength of Prussia had long rested on its army, which the French had now restricted in size. But the Prussians craftily drafted all able-bodied men and required them to serve short army terms, during which time they received intensive military training. They then went into the reserves, and a new group of men was drafted into the regular army. Thus trained men, not really part of the regular army, could be called into active service when needed. Technically Prussia observed the limits placed on its standing army by the French and at the same time kept available a large force of trained soldiers.

Napoleon's territorial changes in Germany also worked in Prussia's favor. Austria had been Prussia's strongest rival for leadership of the German states. An Austrian Hapsburg had held the position of Holy Roman Emperor since the 1400s, thus giving Austria a vague claim over the German states. Napoleon abolished the Holy Roman Empire and reorganized and consolidated many German states into the Confederation of the Rhine.

In addition, Napoleon's rule stimulated nationalism in the German states as it had throughout Europe. Some of Germany's greatest thinkers and writers were active during the period of the French Revolution and Napoleon. Frederick the Great himself had despised the German language and usually wrote and spoke French. Now Germans began to appreciate their language, their past, and their traditions.

German nationalism favored Prussia more than Austria. The population of Prussia was mostly German. In Austria, although the Germans ruled, many other nationalities, including Hungarians, Romanians, Italians, and Slavs, held the majority. Most of them wanted independence from Austria so that they could establish their own national governments.

The revived Prussian state played a major part in the final struggle against Napoleon. Prussian armies fought at Waterloo, and Prussia earned the right to be one of the four great powers represented at the Congress of Vienna. It also joined the Quadruple Alliance.

In 1815 the Congress of Vienna turned Napoleon's Confederation of the Rhine into the German Confederation with additional members that included Prussia. The Congress gave Prussia much important territory, including two-thirds of Saxony and an area along the lower Rhine River. Prussian lands now stretched almost unbroken from Russia to the Rhine and beyond. Prussia had a well-organized and efficient government and a strong economy.

The Zollverein

The first major step toward German unity after the Congress of Vienna concerned the economy. The tariffs that each state levied made movement of goods from one German state to another extremely difficult. The Prussians even placed tariffs on items shipped from one Prussian possession to another. The tariffs increased the prices of goods while reducing the amount sold.

The drive for freer movement of goods was begun by the Junkers (YOOHN • kuhrz)—the aristocratic landowners of Prussia—who wanted to sell their farm products. In 1818 they persuaded the king of Prussia to abolish all tariffs within his territories. Beginning the next year, Prussia and other German states made a number of treaties that set up a customs union called the Zollverein (TSAWL • fer • yn). By 1844 it included almost all of the German states except Austria.

The Zollverein benefited its members by making prices both lower and more uniform. It also led to the spread of industrialization in the German states by providing a wide, free market for German goods and by offering tariff protection against foreign competition. The German states adopted uniform systems of weights, measures, and currency. Manufacturers produced and sold more goods, and business leaders became strong supporters of German unification.

The establishment of the Zollverein had no immediate political effects, and each of the various states in the German Confederation continued to act independently. However, by making its members economically dependent on one another the Zollverein paved the way for later political unification.

In the years after the Congress of Vienna, strong nationalistic and democratic movements emerged within the states of the German Confederation. In 1848 uprisings in France touched off demands for liberal reforms throughout Germany. Agitation was intense for a while, and elections were held for representatives to a National Assembly in Frankfurt to try to unify Germany. Eventually, however, the demands of liberals for representative government were defeated. German unification was to be accomplished by the policies of a king and his powerful chancellor.

Bismarck and Prussian Strength

William I became king of Prussia in 1861. In 1862 he appointed Otto von Bismarck, a conservative Junker politician, to head the Prussian cabinet.

Bismarck opposed democracy and the idea of a parliament. He also believed in Prussian destiny to lead the German people to unification. He was willing to use trickery, bribery, or military force to help Prussia fulfill this destiny. Bismarck had great contempt for idealists, regarding them as mere talkers, not people of action. He once said of German policy that it could not be carried out by "speeches and majorities . . . but by iron and blood."

For years Bismarck really ruled Prussia. He had the full cooperation of the king and the generals in charge of the army. They agreed with Bismarck on the necessity of reorganizing and further strengthening the Prussian army. First, however, the government had to increase taxes.

When the Prussian parliament refused to approve the money for a military expansion program, Bismarck simply dismissed it and collected the taxes without parliamentary authorization. In so doing, he ignored the protests of the liberals. He planned to quiet critics with military victories.

Bismarck and his generals proceeded to build the Prussian army into a great war machine. Prussian military strategists tried to plan for every possible situation that their army might encounter in the field.

Learning from Pictures *Bismarck's diplomatic abilities led to his appointment as head of the Prussian cabinet. His military policy brought about German unification under the leadership of Prussia.*

579

1B, 4J, a1C

Bismarck equated progress with acquiring territory and broadening the Prussian sphere of influence. As Benjamin Disraeli noted, "his idea of progress was evidently seizing something."

Unification Through War

To increase the power and size of Prussia, Bismarck had to overcome two major obstacles: First, he had to drive Austria out of its position of leadership in the German Confederation. Second, he had to overcome Austria's influence over the southern German states, which he considered the major opponents to Prussian leadership. He accomplished these objectives in three wars—the Danish War, the Seven Weeks' War, and the Franco-Prussian War.

The Danish War. On the border between Denmark and Germany lay two small states—the duchies of Schleswig and Holstein (see map, page 582). The population of Holstein, which had been part of the German Confederation since 1815, was entirely German. Schleswig's population included a mixture of Germans and Danes. The Danish king ruled the two duchies under a constitution that provided separation from Denmark. In 1863 King Christian IX came to the Danish throne. At the insistence of many Danes, he proclaimed a new constitution under which he tried to annex Schleswig to Denmark.

Both Prussia and Austria protested the new Danish constitution. Together they demanded that it be revoked. When Denmark refused, Prussia and Austria declared war on Denmark. Denmark had hoped for help from France and Great Britain, but neither acted. In 1864, after three months of fighting, Denmark surrendered.

The peace treaty gave the two duchies to Prussia and Austria jointly. That arrangement caused problems, however. Austria demanded that the two duchies form a single state within the German Confederation. Prussia opposed this settlement. After bitter quarreling, Prussian and Austrian leaders agreed that Prussia would administer Schleswig, and Austria would administer Holstein.

The Seven Weeks' War. As Prussian influence expanded, Bismarck moved to drive Austria out of the German Confederation. He prepared the way with a series of skillful diplomatic actions ensuring that no one would aid Austria. First, he persuaded Napoleon III of France to remain neutral if war broke out between Prussia and Austria. In return for its neutrality, France demanded certain territory then held by the southern German states. Bismarck persuaded Napoleon III to put these demands in writing, but the clever Prussian never did the same with his vague promises to Napoleon.

Bismarck next formed an alliance with the new nation of Italy. In return for fighting against Austria, Italy would receive the Austrian territory of Venetia. Then, by various complicated moves, Bismarck provoked Austria into declaring war on Prussia in 1866.

Austria had not counted on the superb training and preparation of the Prussian army. In fact, Prussia's conduct of the war came as a surprise to the whole world. Prussian forces took advantage of modern technology, moving by train and communicating via the telegraph. Prussia defeated the Austrians in only seven weeks.

The Treaty of Prague ended the so-called Seven Weeks' War in the summer of 1866. Under its lenient terms Austria approved the dissolution of the German Confederation and surrendered Holstein to Prussia. The Italians gained Venetia.

In 1867 several northern German states united with Prussia to form the North German Confederation. Each state had self-government, but the king of Prussia was hereditary president of the Confederation. As the largest state, with the most powerful industry and army, and with the greatest number of representatives, Prussia dominated the legislature of the new confederation.

Only the three southern states of Bavaria, Baden, and Württemberg and the southern part of Hesse-Darmstadt remained outside Prussia's influence. If they could be persuaded to join Prussia, German unity would be complete.

The Franco-Prussian War. Bismarck decided that the way to unite the southern states with the rest of Germany was to provoke a war with France. His opportunity came in 1870 when Spain was looking for a new ruler. The Spaniards offered the throne to Prince Leopold, a cousin of the king of Prussia. Napoleon III took a strong stand against this development because it meant that both Prussia and Spain would be ruled by the Hohenzollern family. He dispatched notes to Prussia and Spain asking that Leopold turn down the offer.

Leopold did withdraw, but the French ambassador gambled further. He insisted that King William I of Prussia pledge publicly that no member of the Hohenzollern family would ever be a candidate for the Spanish throne.

The French ambassador delivered the French demand to King William at a resort known as Ems. The king's vague reply made the ambassador request another meeting to discuss the subject. The

580

● in the Hall of Mirrors of the palace of Versailles

■ In 1871 Georges Clemenceau seethed at the way the Germans had insulted France at Versailles, and he vowed revenge. In 1919, as leader of the French delegation to the Paris Peace Conference at Versailles, Clemenceau demanded that the Germans be severely punished.

1B, 4J, a4A

king told the ambassador that he would not be able to meet with him again at Ems.

Bismarck received a dispatch from the king at Ems summarizing his meeting with the French ambassador. Bismarck decided to use it to trick Napoleon III into declaring war on Prussia. He altered the dispatch slightly and made it sound as though the king had dismissed the ambassador offensively and contemptuously. Then Bismarck released the so-called Ems dispatch to the newspapers.

Outraged at the humiliation of the Ems dispatch, France declared war on Prussia. Bismarck then showed the leaders of the southern German states the 1865 document in which Napoleon III had demanded their territory for France. He persuaded them that France posed a greater danger than Prussia. Bismarck thus converted the states from rivals into allies against France and secured their help in winning a Prussian victory.

The Franco-Prussian War was short but decisive. No outside nation made any move to help France. Superbly trained, well equipped, and ably led, the Prussian army totally defeated the French within only a few months.

Bismarck had been lenient with Austria following its defeat because he did not want as enemies its large German population. He had no such feeling about France, however. France was occupied by German troops, lost Alsace and part of Lorraine, and had to pay a huge indemnity.

Formation of the German Empire

For Germany the peace was not as important as an event that took place before the signing of the treaty. On January 18, 1871, representatives of the allied German states met in the Hall of Mirrors of ■ the palace of Versailles near Paris. There they

Learning from Pictures *This painting depicts the ceremony proclaiming the German* ● *Empire. Where did the ceremony take place?*

1A, 1B, 4J, a4B, a4C

● Bavaria, Baden, Württemberg, and the southern part of Hesse-Darmstadt

■ Point out that *kaiser* is the German form of the word *caesar*.

SECTION 2

Closure

Many people characterized Bismarck as a master of *realpolitik.* Point out that this German term, meaning "politics of reality," is used to describe an artful, shrewd approach to politics that completely disregards ideology. Ask students to suggest what actions taken by Bismarck to unify Germany illustrate *realpolitik.*

Review Answers

1. ***kaiser:*** title of the German emperor
2. ***Junkers:*** aristocratic Prussian landowners; ***William I:*** king of Prussia after 1861; ***Treaty of Prague:*** ended the Seven Weeks' War; ***Iron Chancellor:*** nickname of Bismarck; ***Bundesrat:*** appointive federal council, the upper house in the German Empire's legislature; ***Reichstag:*** German lower house, an elective legislative assembly
3. ***Saxony:*** province south of Prussia and north of Czechoslovakia; ***Schleswig:*** duchy south of Denmark; ***Holstein:*** duchy south of Schleswig; ***Bavaria:*** province in southeastern Germany; ***Württemberg:*** province west of Bavaria
4. (a) The Zollverein was a customs union, including almost all the German states except Austria, that set uniform prices for goods. It also helped the spread of industrialization in the German states.
(b) By building economic

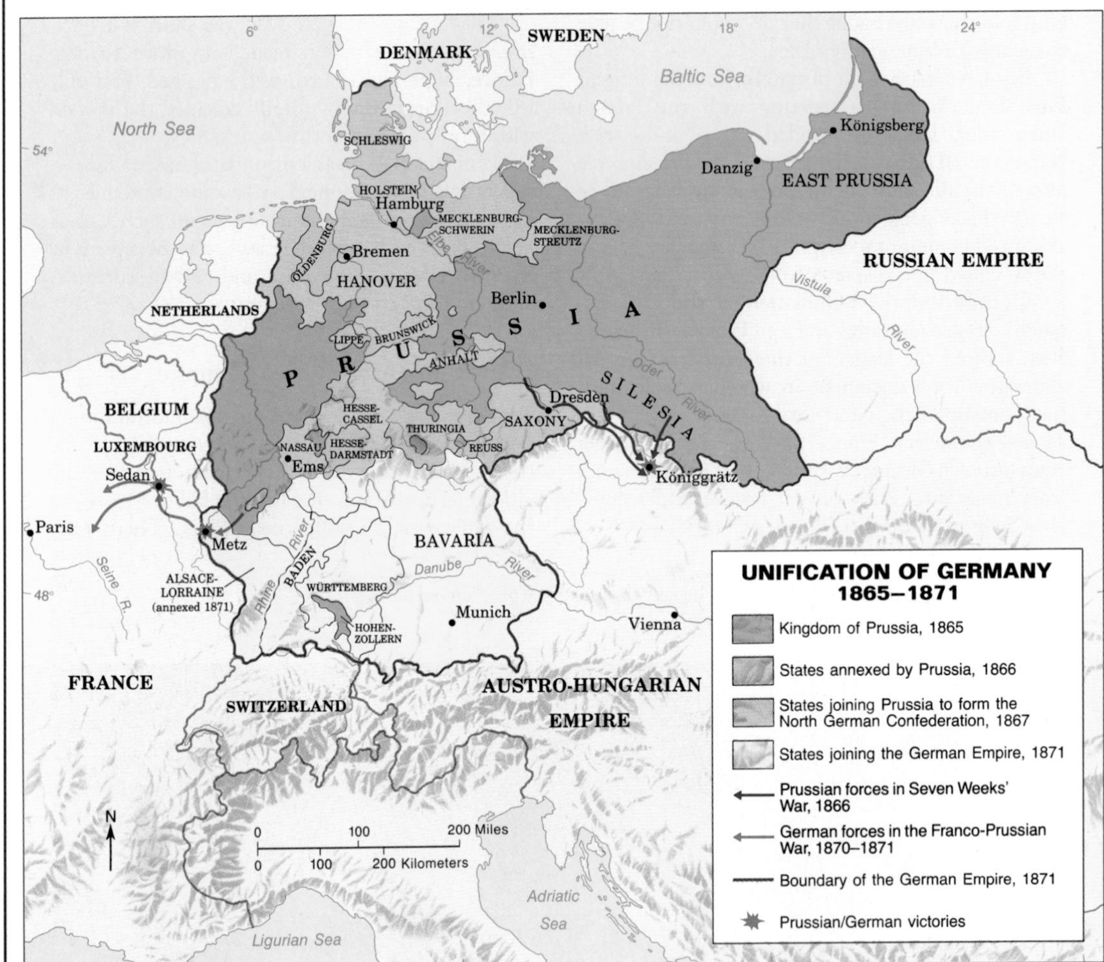

Learning from Maps *The liberal southern German states hesitated to join conservative* ● *Prussia. What were the names of these states?*

issued an official proclamation declaring the formation of the German Empire, which included all of the German states except Austria (see map, this page). Berlin, the Prussian capital, also became the capital of the new empire.

King William I of Prussia was proclaimed German emperor. Bismarck became the chancellor—or chief minister—of the German Empire, with the nickname of the "Iron Chancellor" because of his policy of "iron and blood."

Much as he disliked constitutions, Bismarck accepted one that united the 25 German states in a federal form of government. Each state had its own ruler as well as the right to handle its own domestic matters, including public health, education, law enforcement, and local taxation.

The federal government controlled all common matters, such as national defense, foreign affairs, and commerce. The emperor, called the **kaiser** ■ (KY • zuhr), headed the German government. He was not an absolute monarch, but he did have tremendous power. He could appoint the chancellor, and he commanded the army and navy. The kaiser could declare a defensive war on his own, and he could order an offensive war with the agreement of the upper house of the legislature.

The legislative branch of the government contained two houses. The Bundesrat (BOON • duhs • raht), or upper house, was a federal council, with 58 appointed members.

The Reichstag (RYKS • tahg), or legislative assembly, made up the legislature's lower house. Its nearly 400 members were elected by universal manhood suffrage. The Bundesrat drew up all the bills for consideration by the Reichstag and could veto its actions. The Bundesrat and the kaiser acting together could dismiss the Reichstag. This combination thus made it almost impossible for the Reichstag to pass any liberal democratic laws that the Bundesrat or kaiser might oppose.

The German constitution strongly favored Prussian interests. The king of Prussia had become kaiser of Germany. Prussia had the greatest number of delegates in the Bundesrat. As the most populous state, it also had the largest number of delegates in the Reichstag.

SECTION 2 REVIEW

1. **Define** kaiser
2. **Identify** Junkers, William I, Treaty of Prague, Iron Chancellor, Bundesrat, Reichstag
3. **Locate** Saxony, Schleswig, Holstein, Bavaria, Württemberg
4. **Analyzing Ideas** **(a)** What was the Zollverein? **(b)** Did it serve the purpose for which it was founded?
5. **Organizing Ideas** Prussia fought three wars to unite Germany. **(a)** Name each war. **(b)** List what territory was acquired as a result of each.
6. **Explaining Ideas** How did Bismarck persuade the southern German states to accept Prussian leadership of Germany?
7. **Summarizing Ideas** Name the powers held by the kaiser.

3 Industrialization and Socialism Created Opposition to Bismarck

Because the constitution did not give Bismarck the absolute monarchy he wanted, he tried to achieve it in other ways. However, in the years after the formation of the German Empire, he had to accept many compromises to make the political system work. Even though the constitution did not give the people much voice in their own affairs, the government had to take their demands into account.

Opposition to Bismarck

In spite of rigid control by the aristocratic Prussians, the new German federal government soon ran into difficult problems. Dissatisfied groups formed political parties that opposed Bismarck's policies. Some wanted the government to be more liberal and democratic and to enact social reforms. Others feared Bismarck's military policy and the ever-growing army and navy.

Representatives in the legislative assembly from the southern German states, especially those from Bavaria, resented the interference of the federal government in what they considered to be their local affairs. They thought their own state governments should deal with such matters.

Relations with the Roman Catholic church presented special problems for Bismarck. The pope's long-standing claim of the right to administer church property seemed to Bismarck like foreign interference in German domestic affairs. He came to see the Catholic church as a threat to the German Empire. The fact that the southern German states were mostly Catholic strengthened this feeling.

In 1872 Germany and the papacy broke diplomatic relations. Bismarck then initiated the anti-Catholic *Kulturkampf*—German for "war of civilization"—in which Germany passed strict laws to control the Catholic clergy and Catholic schools. The laws expelled the Jesuits and stated that all the Catholic clergy had to be Germans who had been educated in German schools.

This religious policy stirred up opposition among the German people. The Catholics formed a political party to oppose the *Kulturkampf* and to work for other changes. Many non-Catholic liberals also joined the opposition. By 1880 Bismarck began to modify the *Kulturkampf* because he needed the support of the Catholic Party. Bismarck reestablished diplomatic relations with the papacy and repealed the laws against Catholics. By 1887 the *Kulturkampf* had ended.

Industrial Development Under Bismarck

Bismarck wanted to transform Prussia into an industrial giant. Germany contained a rich store

interdependence among the German states, it helped pave the way for later political union.
5. (a) and **(b)** The Danish War brought the duchy of Schleswig under Prussian administration. The Seven Weeks' War gained Holstein, Hanover, Hesse-Cassel, Nassau, and the free city of Frankfort. The Franco-Prussian War gained Alsace and part of Lorraine.
6. Bismarck showed the leaders of the southern German states the 1865 document in which Napoleon III had demanded their territory for France. He persuaded them their greatest danger was from France, not Prussia. In doing so he converted the states from rivals into allies.
7. The kaiser appointed the chancellor, commanded the army and navy, controlled foreign policy, could declare a defensive war, and could order offensive war with agreement of the Bundesrat. In addition, he controlled enough votes in the Bundesrat to block any constitutional amendment; together with the upper house, he could dismiss the lower house.

SECTION 3

Focus/Motivation
Write the following two statements by Bismarck on the chalkboard: **1.** Politics is the doctrine of the possible, the attainable. **2.** Politics is the art of the

583

next best.

Have students hypothesize about the beliefs of a political leader who would make these statements. (Student responses might include: the politician recognizes that the public should be promised only what the politician can deliver; or that the politician sees a need for compromise in politics. At the completion of the section, ask students how well Bismarck's actions in domestic affairs corresponded with his ideas stated above.

Presentation Comparing Ideas (Average/Group)
Interested students might like to compare the social legislation enacted in Germany with that enacted in the United States. They should review the social reforms passed under Bismarck (page 585). Then have them consult American history textbooks to find out when similar reforms were passed in the United States. Have students share their findings with the class.

History Through the Arts

PAINTING

Two Men Looking at the Moon

Many artists were inspired by the nationalistic spirit that flooded Europe during and after the Napoleonic Era. Art, literature, and music were all affected by this movement. Caspar David Friedrich, a German landscape artist, painted the work at the right. He was a patriotic German, who admired German art of the Middle Ages. He deliberately included in his paintings some of its common motifs. Among these were gnarled and twisted trees, like the one shown in this painting entitled *Two Men Looking at the Moon.* This brooding nighttime scene, with its air of melancholy, is typical of the romantic movement. Romanticism emphasized the past and thus was especially appealing to Germans, who, in the early 1800s, were taking a new interest in their national traditions and customs.

Staatliche Kunstsammlungen Desden, DDR

Romanticism inspired nationalism which, by the mid-1800s, had become a major movement in Germany.

of natural resources, including the great coal and iron deposits in the Ruhr valley, where a huge steel industry developed. The German government owned the railroads, and it managed them in order to promote industrial development. In addition, a system of canals provided cheaper, though slower, transportation.

The fact that industrialization came later in Germany than in Great Britain and France proved to be an advantage for Germany. German industries could use the best methods and most advanced machinery that had been developed elsewhere. German scientists then worked out further changes and improvements.

Under Bismarck's leadership, the government helped industry in many ways. It standardized money and banking laws throughout the empire. Postal and telegraph services—the means of communication by which so much business was conducted—were centralized. The government encouraged German industrialists to form cartels. In addition, Germany adopted a high-tariff policy to protect its industries from foreign competition. Germany rapidly became an industrial nation, and soon rivaled Great Britain and France.

Socialism in Germany

With the growth of German industry, cities grew rapidly, and a class of factory workers appeared. German laborers, like those in other nations, wanted decent working conditions. Some people believed that the action of the cartels led to lower wages for workers and higher prices for consumers. Many thought that these various problems needed government action. They wanted the government to pass laws that would benefit workers and regulate industry.

Just as in other European nations, socialist reformers in Germany went even further, advocating government ownership of all major industries. German socialists banded together in 1869 to form the Social Democratic Party. The party grew quickly, with most of its members coming from the ranks of the city workers. In 1871 it elected two members to the Reichstag. By 1877 that representation had increased to 12.

Even if the Social Democrats had had a much greater representation, they could have done very little. The Reichstag could not pass any laws that

● Have students compare Bismarck's efforts to control dissent with those made by Emperor Napoleon III in France.

the Bundesrat opposed. Since the Bundesrat represented the hereditary rulers, there was little chance that it would propose or pass the laws that the socialists wanted. The Reichstag, however, served as a good public forum in which socialist members could express their grievances and make promises of what they would do if given the power.

Bismarck's Antisocialist Campaign

Every gain in socialist voting strength—and every new demand for reform—alarmed Bismarck. When the Social Democrats won 500,000 votes in the election of 1877, the chancellor decided to use all of his power to fight them. His opportunity came in 1878, when two attempts to assassinate the emperor occurred. Neither of the would-be assassins had any connection with socialism, and Bismarck knew this. However, he took advantage of the public concern to accuse the Social Democrats of plotting the attempts. The emperor and the Bundesrat dissolved the Reichstag and called for new elections. A widespread campaign against socialists and their ideas followed.

The election did not change the strength of the Social Democrats in the Reichstag. Bismarck, ● however, pushed through laws aimed at repressing the socialists. The new laws prohibited newspapers, books, or pamphlets from spreading socialist ideas and banned public meetings of socialists.

Despite such restrictive laws, the socialists continued their efforts, and by 1884 Social Democratic representation in the Reichstag had increased to 24. As he did in the *Kulturkampf,* Bismarck had to re-examine his tactics in order to see how to achieve his aims against a growing opposition.

Since repression had failed, the Iron Chancellor was forced to try another tactic. He decided to grant many of the reforms the socialists had proposed. If the government granted reforms, Bismarck believed, people would have less reason to join the socialists, and their support would collapse.

Bismarck's new policy was called "stealing the socialists' thunder." He said that he wanted to pass laws to help workers so that the Social Democrats would "sound their bird call in vain." Beginning in 1883, he put through several far-reaching reforms. First came insurance against sickness, then insurance against accidents—both paid for by employers. Other laws limited working hours, provided for certain holidays from work, and guaranteed pensions for disabled and retired workers.

Germany thus adopted a pioneering program of government-directed social reforms. The reforms did not wipe out socialism in Germany, but they did eliminate many of the workers' grievances. Many other industrial nations later copied this program of social legislation.

Learning from Pictures *As capital of the German Empire, Berlin became a thriving cultural and political center. This picture shows the center of Berlin and the Spree River in 1890.*

585

1B, 4J, a1C, a4A, a4D, a4F, a4G, a4H, a4L

SECTION 3

Closure

Mention that a French diplomat said of Bismarck that all the noble sentiments were unknown to him save one: "devotion to his country's ambition." Ask: Based on what you have learned about Bismarck, do you think this description of him is accurate?

Review Answers

1. ***Kulturkampf:*** program, initiated by Bismarck in 1872, to restrict the power of the Roman Catholic Church in Germany; ***Social Democratic Party:*** Germany's socialist party, formed in 1869; ***William II:*** grandson of William I who became emperor in 1888 and forced Bismarck to resign

2. Three problems faced by the German Empire were: political demands by parties that opposed Bismarck's policies, resentment by south German states of government interference in local affairs, and strained relations between Germany and the Roman Catholic Church.

3. Major factors in Germany's rapid industrialization were political unification; French gold and iron mines gained after the Franco-Prussian War; good transportation; plentiful natural resources; the availability of advanced methods and machinery already pioneered by Great Britain and France; government aid in providing uniform and centralized ser-

READ
● WRITE
INTERPRET
CONNECT
THINK

BUILDING HISTORY STUDY SKILLS

Writing About History: Writing a Comparison Essay

To make comparisons is to identify both similarities and differences. Writing a comparison essay helps us to see relationships, make connections between conflicting ideas, and analyze the similarities and differences between these ideas.

How to Write a Comparison Essay

To write a comparison essay, follow these steps.

1. State the topic for comparison.
2. On a separate sheet of paper, write the categories for comparison. The categories should be broad points under which similarities and differences on the topic can be listed.
3. List the similarities and differences under each category, then begin writing the essay, further explaining these similarities and differences.
4. In the last paragraph, form a conclusion that synthesizes the information in your essay. The conclusion should be more than a summary. It should be an analytical statement of comparison, using the categories that you developed.

Developing the Skill

If you were to write an essay comparing Italian and German unification, you could establish the categories of comparison as leadership, methods, and results. Study the following essay and identify the categories.

> "A renewed spirit of nationalism marked the late 1800s in Europe. Nationalism triumphed in both Italy and Germany. The unification of these nations was accomplished because of the leadership of Cavour and Garibaldi in Italy, and of Bismarck in Germany.
>
> Cavour's skill lay in his ability to direct political events to his own grand scheme. After he started a war with Austria in 1859, France entered on the side of Italy. Cavour also succeeded in getting Lombardy and some of the central states annexed to Italy.
>
> Garibaldi led his republican army in rebellion in the Kingdom of the Two Sicilies and, in a compromise with Cavour, made them part of the kingdom of Italy.
>
> German unification did not have the multiple leadership and republican elements that existed in Italian unification. However, the manipulation of Austria and the provoking of war were similar characteristics. Bismarck manipulated events and took advantage of opportunities. He united the southern part of Germany with the rest of the country when he stirred up nationalistic and emotional feelings against France after provoking a war with that nation. Republicanism and liberalism were not part of German unification.
>
> Italian unification, although it did involve war, incorporated the ideals of republicanism and nationalism and had two leaders, Cavour and Garibaldi. The unification of Germany included nationalism but came about through Bismarck's policies of "iron and blood.""

Notice that the first paragraph identified the topic and stated the categories. The second, third, and fourth paragraphs developed the categories of leadership, methods, and results. The concluding paragraph synthesized the categories by showing the different methods of unification.

Practicing the skill. After reading current newspaper or magazine articles, write a comparison essay on the views of any two political candidates.

To apply this skill, see Applying History Study Skills on page 597.

A caricature of Bismarck

The Resignation of Bismarck

Emperor William I died in 1888. His son, Frederick III, reigned for only a few months before he, too, died and was succeeded by his son, William II. The young monarch and the old chancellor soon disagreed violently. William II felt that Bismarck was too powerful. Bismarck resented the way that the young emperor took away the powers the chancellor had used wisely for years. He also feared that William was too rash and undisciplined to use his considerable authority wisely.

For a long time, Bismarck had thought himself indispensable to Germany. However, in 1890 William forced him to resign, which he did with a great deal of bitterness. Although he and William II later reconciled, Bismarck never again served Germany in an official role.

With Bismarck gone, William II set out to expand Germany's colonial empire. He increased the size and strength of the German army and began to build up the German navy. This move brought Germany into competition with Great Britain, which was at that time the world's strongest naval power. William signed new agreements with neighboring nations, and by the early 1900s, Germany emerged stronger than ever before.

SECTION 3 REVIEW

1. **Identify** *Kulturkampf,* Social Democratic Party, William II
2. **Organizing Ideas** What were three problems faced by the German Empire in the 1870s and 1880s?
3. **Analyzing Ideas** What were the major factors responsible for Germany's rapid industrial development?
4. **Explaining Ideas** **(a)** Describe the most important social reforms adopted under Bismarck. **(b)** Why did he favor these reforms?
5. **Interpreting Ideas** How did Bismarck attempt to destroy socialism?

4 Despite Reforms, Russia Remained a Rigid Autocracy

By the mid-1800s Russia had the largest territory and population of any European nation. Yet it remained weak. Industrial development, which so strengthened the West, lagged in Russia. Most of the country's extensive natural resources lay undeveloped. Ports blocked by ice for much of the year, or exits from the seas controlled by other countries, made Russia almost entirely landlocked. This situation led to continuous Russian attempts to win access to the Mediterranean, past Constantinople and the Dardanelles. These efforts led to conflicts with the Ottoman Empire, which controlled the Dardanelles.

Russia had another problem. Unlike Great Britain or France, it lacked unity. The huge Russian Empire included a great variety of peoples and national groups. Most people in the European part of Russia belonged to one of three related groups: (1) the Great Russians, in central and northern Russia, (2) the Ukrainians, in the south, and (3) the White Russians, in the west. Most of them belonged to the Orthodox church. Scattered throughout the empire were smaller racial, national, and religious groups speaking a variety of languages. Many of these groups, such as the Poles and Finns, had been conquered by the Russians and disliked Russian rule.

Russian Domestic and Foreign Policies

The liberal movement that influenced other European nations so strongly in the 1800s made little headway in Russia. The czar ruled the huge Russian Empire as an **autocrat**—meaning, one who holds absolute power. Although the czars tried to maintain autocracy, liberal political developments in western Europe affected the country.

Russia had felt the influence of the West from before the time of Peter the Great. Improved transportation and communication made this influence stronger still. Nationalistic ideas appealed to the Russian minorities, especially to the strongly patriotic Poles and Finns. By the early 1800s, liberalism began to attract some of the educated members of the Russian aristocracy.

Faced with problems caused by liberal ideas and restless nationalities, the czars took harsh measures. To counteract liberalism the government strictly censored speech and the press and rejected all demands for a constitution. To lessen the nationalities' tensions, in the 1830s Czar Nicholas I began a program of "Russification." This program forced non-Russian peoples in the empire to use the

vices and high tariffs; and government encouragement of cartels.
4. (a) Social reforms adopted under Bismarck included sickness and accident insurance, both paid by employers; limits on working hours and provision for holidays; and payments to old or disabled workers. **(b)** He thought that if these reforms were granted, people would have less reason to join the socialists.
5. Bismarck attempted to destroy socialism by "stealing the socialists' thunder" and passing laws to help workers.

SECTION 4

Focus/Motivation

Write the following quotation by a nineteenth-century Russian on the chalkboard, or reproduce it for the class.

"In Europe the principle of personality is supreme; with us it is the communal principle. Europe is pagan; Russia — holy Christian. In the West reigns apparent liberty, a liberty like that of a wild animal in the desert. The true liberty is found among us, in the East."

Discuss with students the writer's attitude toward the West. For example, the author believes that the Russian life style is better than that of the West; that

1B, 4J, a1C

● To all intents and purposes, freed serfs remained tied to their masters. Leo Tolstoy summed up this relationship between noble and peasant thus: "I sit on a man's back, choking him and making him carry me, and yet assure myself and others that I am very sorry for him and wish to ease his lot by all possible means—except by getting off his back."

Russia is religious, and the West is not; that what appears to be liberty in the West is actually lack of control, unlike true Russian freedom.

Point out to students that in the 1800s a conflict between Russian and Western ideas resurfaced in Russia. Westernizers wanted to adopt certain aspects of Western life, while Slavophiles stressed Russia's uniqueness and wanted to retain Russian religion, culture, and values. Ask students to recall when this issue had been debated earlier. *(Students should remember the policy of Westernization begun by Peter the Great.)*

Presentation
Writing a Diary (Average/Group)
Have interested students write a diary entry for a typical day in the life of a Russian noble, serf, writer, Jew, or Populist. You might want to discuss with the class the status of serfs before and after emancipation, the position of artists, or the condition of Jews in Russia. For an account of the life of nobles and serfs, students might read "Nobles and Serfs in Tsarist Russia," in L. S. Stavrianos's *Readings in World History* (Allyn and Bacon). Call upon students to read their entries to the rest of the class.

Russian language, accept the Orthodox religion, and adopt Russian customs.

The Russian rulers had two goals for their foreign policy: (1) In the Balkans they backed Pan-Slavism—the union of all Slavic peoples under Russian leadership. (2) Elsewhere the Russian rulers followed the program of expansion, begun under the first czars, east into Asia and south toward the Ottoman Empire. Russian expansion, however, suffered a setback with the empire's defeat in the Crimean War when it lost territory.

Alexander II and Reforms

Alexander II became czar in 1855. Although he was basically conservative and autocratic, public opinion strongly influenced him, and he heeded the liberals' demand for freedom for all serfs.

Serfdom had taken a different form in Russia than it had in the rest of Europe. After the time of Peter the Great, serfs were bound to persons and not to the land. They could not leave their villages or masters' homes unless so ordered by government officials or permitted to do so by their owners. Although unable to move freely from the land, and largely under the control of their masters, serfs still retained a few civil rights such as the right to sue in court.

Toward the middle of the 1800s, nobles who, under pressure from radical intellectuals, felt guilty about owning serfs began to support the campaign against serfdom. Also, factory owners began to urge that the serfs be freed. The industrialists did not believe in liberal ideas, however; they simply needed workers for their factories. Another group, the "enlightened state bureaucrats," or government employees, also urged freedom for the serfs and convinced Alexander II to consider abolishing this institution.

In response to these urgings, Alexander II appointed committees to study the problem of the serfs. In 1861 he issued the Emancipation Edict that freed all the serfs. The terms of the edict also provided that the government would give the nobles bonds for their land and that peasants or former serfs could buy small tracts of land from the government.

● Emancipation did not really improve conditions for the former serfs. Some of the land they had previously farmed was sold to them in small plots and at high prices. Most freed serfs could not afford to buy enough land to earn the payments for the land, pay the taxes, and still make a living. Therefore, they had to rent additional land from their former owners—and rents were high. Some former serfs, unable to either buy or rent land, moved to the growing towns and cities, where they became a source of cheap labor for the factories.

Alexander II attempted other liberal reforms. Beginning in 1864 he allowed each province of European Russia to have an assembly of nobles and of delegates elected by townspeople and peasants. These assemblies decided local taxes and controlled public health, schools, assistance for the poor, and some public works programs.

Alexander also reformed the courts. Civil and criminal cases, formerly tried in secret by administrative officials, were now tried by juries in open courts. However, trials for political offenders accused of plotting against the government were held in secret.

Alexander's policies did not please everyone. People with extremely conservative views opposed them and tried to convince the czar that such actions endangered the position and privileges of the ruler and the nobles. Liberals considered Alexander's reforms as only modest first steps and pointed out the need for further changes. Radicals criticized Alexander even more strongly.

Radicals and Government Reaction

Several groups carried on radical political activity in Russia. The Nihilists (NY • uh • luhsts)—whose name comes from the Latin word *nihil,* meaning "nothing"—were active in the 1860s. They wanted to abolish the whole political and social structure and build a completely new Russia. They rebelled against the traditions of family, school, and society. They believed in keeping nothing of the old values and standards.

In the 1870s another group, the Populists, urged its followers to live among peasants as teachers and doctors. Some believed that all the large estates of the nobles should be seized and the land divided among the peasants. After the government arrested many Populists, some Russian radicals turned to violent action, joining a movement known as the People's Will. These radicals favored the use of **terrorism**—bombings and assassinations of high officials by political groups—to force the government to grant their demands.

1B, 4J, a1C

History Through the Arts

JEWELRY DESIGN

Fabergé Egg

This unusual piece of art is an enameled gold egg containing a completely accurate model of the Gatchina Palace near St. Petersburg. Only five inches (13 centimeters) high, it even includes a tiny flag flying from the palace tower. It is decorated with pearls and diamonds. Historians think this egg was given to the mother of Czar Nicholas II on Easter morning, 1902. It was customary for the Russian royal family to exchange eggs like this one every Easter. An egg symbolized the resurrection of Jesus as well as the ancient concepts of fertility and the earth's rebirth in spring.

The Gatchina egg, as it is called, was created in the jewelry firm of Carl Fabergé, in St. Petersburg. Founded in 1842, this company employed the finest jewelers and goldsmiths in all of Europe. These artisans also designed magnificent boxes, clocks, tableware, and jewelry. It was the series of eggs, however, that made Fabergé's reputation. Most of the eggs were signed by Michael Perchin, who was one of the few native Russians employed by Fabergé.

The famed House of Fabergé was closed in 1918 by officials of the new government. In order to raise money, the government sold all but 10 of the eggs. Today, many of these priceless eggs are housed in private collections and museums.

Radical activity frightened Alexander II, and in the late 1860s, he turned to repressive measures. Gradually, however, he became convinced that additional reforms were necessary. Ironically, a terrorist assassinated him in 1881.

The assassination of Alexander II ended liberal reforms and led to another intensive campaign of repression. Alexander III and his successor, Nicholas II, used every available means to stamp out liberalism—censorship, control of the church and of education, spies and informers, even imprisonment and exile. They intensified "Russification." They severely persecuted Jews in massacres called **pogroms** (POH • gruhmz). Under the slogan "One Czar, One Church, One Language," other minorities felt the heavy hand of oppression.

The attempt to preserve the old order met with much opposition both open and underground. The development of industry in Russia had produced a class of city workers who wanted the right to form unions and to strike. Middle-class industrialists wanted a voice in the government. Liberals and radicals became more determined than ever to gain reforms.

The attempts of the Russian government to suppress all of these varied aims produced an explosive situation. Terrorism increased. Socialists, who in 1898 had founded the Social Democratic Labor Party in imitation of the German Social Democratic Party, grew increasingly radical in their demands. Clearly the government's reaction had backfired.

589

1B, 4J, a1C

Even members of the armed forces demonstrated against the czar's autocratic rule. In June of 1905 the crew of the battleship *Potemkin,* the flagship of the Black Sea fleet, mutinied and took to the streets of Odessa. Within 24 hours the whole city was in a revolutionary fervor.

SECTION 4

Closure

On the chalkboard or on an overhead projector write the following statement: The history of Russia might have been different if Nicholas II had taken note of the warning issued by the Revolution of 1905. Ask: Do you agree or disagree with this statement? Why or why not?

Review Answers

1. ***autocrat:*** one who holds absolute power; ***terrorism:*** assassinations and bombings committed by political groups; ***pogrom:*** persecution and murder of Jews
2. ***"Russification":*** program begun by Nicholas I to force non-Russian peoples to use the Russian language and customs and adopt the Orthodox religion; ***Pan-Slavism:*** the union of all Slavic peoples under Russian leadership; ***Emancipation Edict:*** 1861 document issued by Alexander II that freed all serfs; ***Nihilists:*** radical reform group that wanted to abolish the political and social structure and build Russia anew; ***People's Will:*** radical group that favored the use of terrorism; ***Social Democratic Labor Party:*** Russian socialist party founded in 1898; ***Duma:*** parliament established by the October Manifesto
3. The most important aims were Pan-Slavism and expansion of the empire eastward and southward.

The Revolution of 1905

In 1904 and 1905, Russia fought a war with Japan in East Asia. To the surprise of the world, the Japanese dealt the Russians a humiliating defeat. Russia's defeat exposed a government that was corrupt and inefficient, as well as autocratic, reactionary, and oppressive. The defeat in turn spurred almost all of the discontented groups in the country to action.

On January 22, 1905, "Bloody Sunday," the czar's troops shot at a group of unarmed strikers on their way to deliver a petition to the czar. The incident triggered the Revolution of 1905. Workers struck and held demonstrations. Merchants closed their stores, and industrialists shut down their factories. Lawyers refused to plead cases, and servants deserted their employers. Czar Nicholas II faced a crisis. Russian autocracy had to yield or perish. He reluctantly decided to yield.

The czar issued a decree called the October Manifesto, which guaranteed individual liberties and provided for the election of a parliament called the Duma. These measures ended the strikes and the revolution.

After the end of the Russo-Japanese War in 1905, the czar's government could better deal with its critics at home. The czar dismissed two sessions of the Duma because its members insisted that the czar's ministers be responsible to the Duma. Then in 1907 the czar changed the qualifications for voting so that only large landowners could vote. This resulted in a more conservative Duma, and one more cooperative with the czar.

The revolutionary movement of 1905 failed to achieve more widespread results for three main reasons: (1) The army remained loyal to the czar and thus would not overthrow the regime. (2) The French, bound to Russia by a military alliance, lent money to support the government. (3) The various

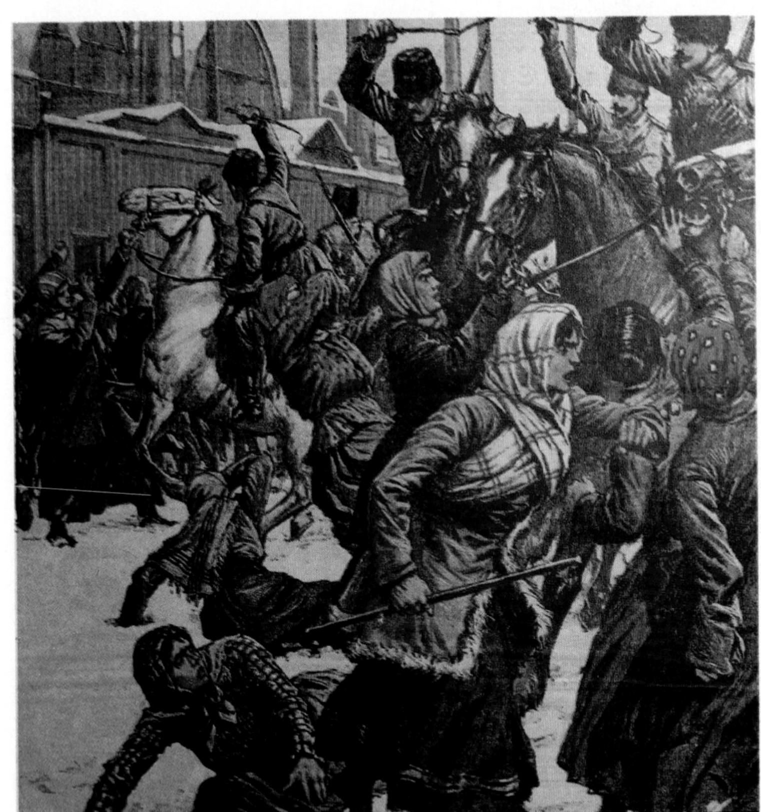

Learning from Pictures *After shooting into the crowd of protestors on Bloody Sunday, Russian Cossacks dispersed the crowd with whips.*

Learning from Pictures *In 1906 the first national assembly in Russian history was elected.*

revolutionary groups remained divided in their goals. Moderates feared radical demands. Radicals disagreed among themselves. Workers lost heart and deserted their leaders.

The reactionaries learned nothing from the Revolution of 1905. The government hunted down, imprisoned, exiled, or executed revolutionary leaders. Using all the repressive measures just as before, the government tried to remain as it had been—an autocracy.

SECTION 4 REVIEW

1. **Define** autocrat, terrorism, pogrom
2. **Identify** "Russification," Pan-Slavism, Emancipation Edict, Nihilists, People's Will, Social Democratic Labor Party, Duma
3. **Interpreting Ideas** What were the most important aims of Russian foreign policy?
4. **Summarizing Ideas** **(a)** What groups favored the abolition of serfdom in Russia? **(b)** Did emancipation improve the condition of the serfs? **(c)** Why or why not?
5. **Organizing Ideas** **(a)** List the liberal reforms that Alexander II accomplished in Russia. **(b)** What did he do with regard to the serfs?
6. **Analyzing Ideas** **(a)** Why did the Revolution of 1905 fail to achieve its goals? **(b)** How did Nicholas II respond to the Revolution of 1905?

5 Austria-Hungary's Interest Focused on the Balkans

"When France sneezes, all Europe catches cold," the Austrian leader Metternich said in 1848. He was referring to the fact that uprisings in France had set off revolts in almost every other European nation. The Austrian Empire proved no exception.

In Vienna demonstrators and the army clashed. A frightened Emperor Ferdinand ordered Metternich, his chief minister, to resign. After having dominated European affairs for well over 30 years, Metternich now fled the country. In 1848 Ferdinand himself abdicated, and the throne went to the 18-year-old Francis Joseph I.

Uprisings occurred in Hungary, too. The people of this region—one of the largest parts of the Austrian Empire—chafed under Austrian rule. Most of them were Magyars—descendants of the nomadic warrior group that had migrated to Hungary from Russia and Romania in the 900s. The Magyars spoke a language unlike other European languages and maintained a distinctive culture. A strong nationalist movement centered on making

4. (a) Groups favoring abolition of serfdom included liberal reformers, nobles, government officials, and middle-class industrialists. **(b)** Emancipation did not improve the living conditions of the serfs. **(c)** Peasants could not afford enough land to allow them to earn the payments for the land, pay taxes, and still make a living. Therefore they had to rent additional land from landlords at high rents.
5. (a) Alexander created elected provincial assemblies of nobles and delegates that decided local issues. He also reformed the courts. **(b)** Alexander II freed the serfs.
6. (a) The Revolution of 1905 failed to achieve its goals because the army remained loyal to the czar; the French supported the government with money; and revolutionary groups were not united. **(b)** Nicholas II issued the October Manifesto and created the Duma. However, after the Russo-Japanese War ended, Nicholas II dismissed two sessions of the Duma and changed the voting qualifications so only large landowners could vote.

SECTION 5

Focus/Motivation

Write the following statement on the chalkboard: The problem of nationalities was the Achilles' heel of the Dual Monarchy and the Ottoman Empire. Make sure students understand that "Achilles' heel" means

591

1A, 1B, 4J, a1C, a4B, a4C, a4F

● Romanians and Italians

a weak or vulnerable point. Next, write on the chalkboard a list of the nationalities in each kingdom. Under the Dual Monarchy list Germans, Magyars, Czechs, Serbs, Croats, Rumanians, Poles, and Italians. The list under the Ottoman Empire should include Serbs, Greeks, Rumanians, Bulgarians, Albanians, Montenegrins, Russians, Jews, Egyptians, and other North Africans.

Ask students why they think so many nationalities might cause difficulties in governing an empire. *(Most students will suggest such things as differences of religion, customs, and languages.)* Have students hypothesize about solutions to the problem. *(Student responses might include the imposition of a national language or religion.)*

Presentation
Class Discussion (Average/Group)

The Ottoman Empire during this period was called "the sick man of Europe." Discuss why the major powers gave this nickname to the Ottoman Empire. Focus on governmental, economic, and social weaknesses of the empire. Before the discussion, you might have the students reread the subsection "The Ottoman Empire" on page 593. As an alternative, read to the class "Decline of the Ottoman Empire" and "On the Eve of Partition" from L. S. Stavrianos's *Readings in World History* (Allyn and Bacon).

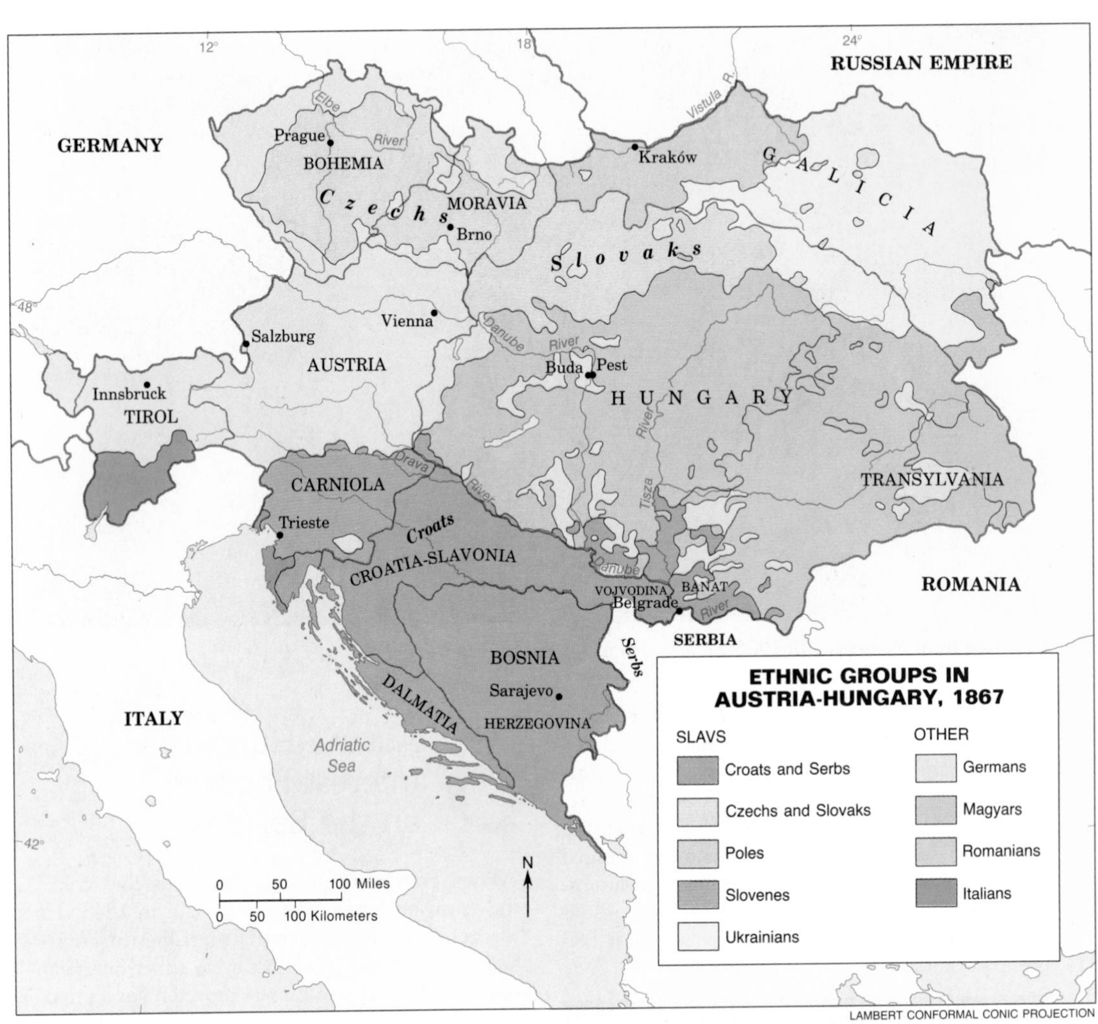

Learning from Maps *The Germans of Austria and the Magyars of Hungary were equals under the Dual Monarchy. What other non-Slavic peoples lived in Austria-Hungary?*

the Magyars dominant in Hungary and freeing the region from Austrian domination.

The Hungarian patriot Louis Kossuth led the revolt in 1848. For a time it looked as though Hungary would gain its independence, and in 1849 Kossuth was elected "responsible governor president" by the Hungarian Diet. However, Austria, with Russia's assistance, soon defeated the revolutionaries. Czar Nicholas I offered his help because he feared that the revolt might spread to Russian Poland. Kossuth fled the country. This ended, for a time, any further Hungarian attempts at independence.

Formation of the Dual Monarchy

For almost 20 years after the Revolution of 1848, Austria managed to keep liberalism and nationalism from becoming major issues. However, after Austria's defeat by Prussia in 1866, Hungarians demanded more freedom. Austria solved this problem in 1867 by forming the Dual Monarchy—also called Austria-Hungary—in which the Hungarians shared power with the Austrians.

The Dual Monarchy had a common ruler, Francis Joseph I, whose title was Emperor of

Austria and King of Hungary. Although three ministries—war, finance, and foreign affairs—conducted government business for the whole empire, Austria and Hungary each had its own parliament. The Austrian parliament met in Vienna; the Hungarian met in Budapest.

From an economic standpoint, the Dual Monarchy proved a practical arrangement. The various parts of the empire fitted together into one economic unit. Hungary, chiefly agricultural, furnished raw materials and food. Austria, strongly industrial, produced manufactured goods. Each provided a market for the other.

Many problems existed, however. Because of its manufacturing interests, Austria wanted high protective tariffs. As a farming region, Hungary favored low tariffs and freer trade.

Nor did the formation of the Dual Monarchy solve the problem of nationalities. The Austrian Germans and the Hungarian Magyars dominated the population in each of their separate national states. National minorities—the Czechs, Serbs, Croats, Romanians, Poles, and Italians—existed in both Austria and Hungary. These people benefited very little from the Dual Monarchy and continued to agitate for self-government.

Other problems arose over command and language in the common army. The Austrians spoke German. The Hungarians spoke Magyar, or Hungarian, which had been declared the official language of Hungary. Some soldiers also spoke the various Slavic languages.

Bismarck, to strengthen Prussia and form a united Germany, declared war on Austria in 1866. Its defeat in the Seven Weeks' War forced Austria out of positions of power in Germany and Italy. To compensate for this setback, and hoping to gain influence and territory, the Dual Monarchy turned toward the Balkans, a region to the southeast controlled chiefly by the Ottoman Empire.

The Ottoman Empire

By the 1800s the Ottoman Empire had declined dramatically. The completely autocratic government had a sultan, or commander-in-chief, who controlled both governmental and religious affairs. Early sultans had been responsible rulers, but later sultans turned to the pleasures of palace life and left government business to lesser officials. These government officials acted as both administrators and military commanders, since the army and the government were one and the same. Favoritism, bribery, and corruption existed everywhere.

Economic and social weaknesses. The Ottoman rulers did little to improve agriculture, maintain irrigation systems, or build public works projects such as roads, hospitals, and schools. The tax system discouraged both agriculture and industry, and production declined. Most peasants planted only enough land to produce a crop that they could harvest quickly and hide from the tax collector. The subject peoples of the Ottoman Turks did not regard their rulers favorably. Many of the people living in the empire were Christians or Jews. In strictly religious matters, the Turks granted toleration to non-Muslims under their own religious leaders. However, when Jews or Christians planned rebellions or plotted with enemy powers, the Turks slaughtered them mercilessly.

Discontent in the Balkans

In the early 1800s, the rise of nationalism increased discontent in the Balkan area of the Ottoman Empire. The Balkan region contained several different peoples—Serbs, Bulgarians, Romanians, and Slavs, for example—all of whom wanted to govern themselves.

The Turks tried to suppress nationalistic movements. During the 1820s the Greeks and Serbs revolted. Aided by outside powers, Greece gained independence in 1829, and Serbia achieved a degree of self-rule. Encouraged by these successes and by the evident weakness of the Turks, Serbia and Greece tried to gain more territory.

Foreign countries intervened for their own ends in the struggles between the Turks and these nationalist groups. Russia supported Balkan nationalists for several reasons. The Russians were Slavs like the Bulgarians and Serbs. In addition, like many of the discontented Balkan groups, the Russians were Orthodox Christians. More importantly, if the Ottoman Empire collapsed, Russia hoped it might be able to gain control of the water route from the Black Sea to the Mediterranean.

The Russian drive toward the eastern Mediterranean caused the British to support the crumbling Ottoman Empire. Great Britain did not want the Russians in the Mediterranean, where they might challenge British sea power.

593

1A, 1B, 4J, a1C, a4B, a4C

SECTION 5

Closure

Have the students compare the Congress of Vienna of 1815 with the Congress of Berlin in 1878. Ask: How were the aims and outcomes of the Congress of Vienna and Congress of Berlin the same? How were they different?

Review Answers

1. ***Magyars:*** descendants of the nomadic warrior group that migrated to Hungary in the 900s; ***Louis Kossuth:*** Hungarian patriot who led an unsuccessful revolt against Austrian authority in 1848; ***Francis Joseph I:*** first ruler of the Dual Monarchy; ***Treaty of San Stefano:*** treaty of 1878 that gave a number of Balkan states their independence; ***Balkan League:*** alliance of Greece, Bulgaria, Serbia, and Montenegro that defeated the Turks in 1912

2. ***Romania:*** state on the western coast of the Black Sea; ***Budapest:*** city in north-central Hungary; ***Serbia:*** state in the Balkans south of Hungary; ***Montenegro:*** state north of Albania on the Adriatic Sea; ***Bulgaria:*** state south of Romania; ***Bosnia:*** state west of Serbia; ***Herzegovina:*** state between Bosnia and Montenegro; ***Cyprus:*** island in the northeastern Mediterranean Sea; ***Rhodes:*** island in the Mediterranean off southwestern Turkey

3. **(a)** The Dual Monarchy was formed in 1867. **(b)** It

● Serbia, Montenegro, Romania, Bulgaria, Albania

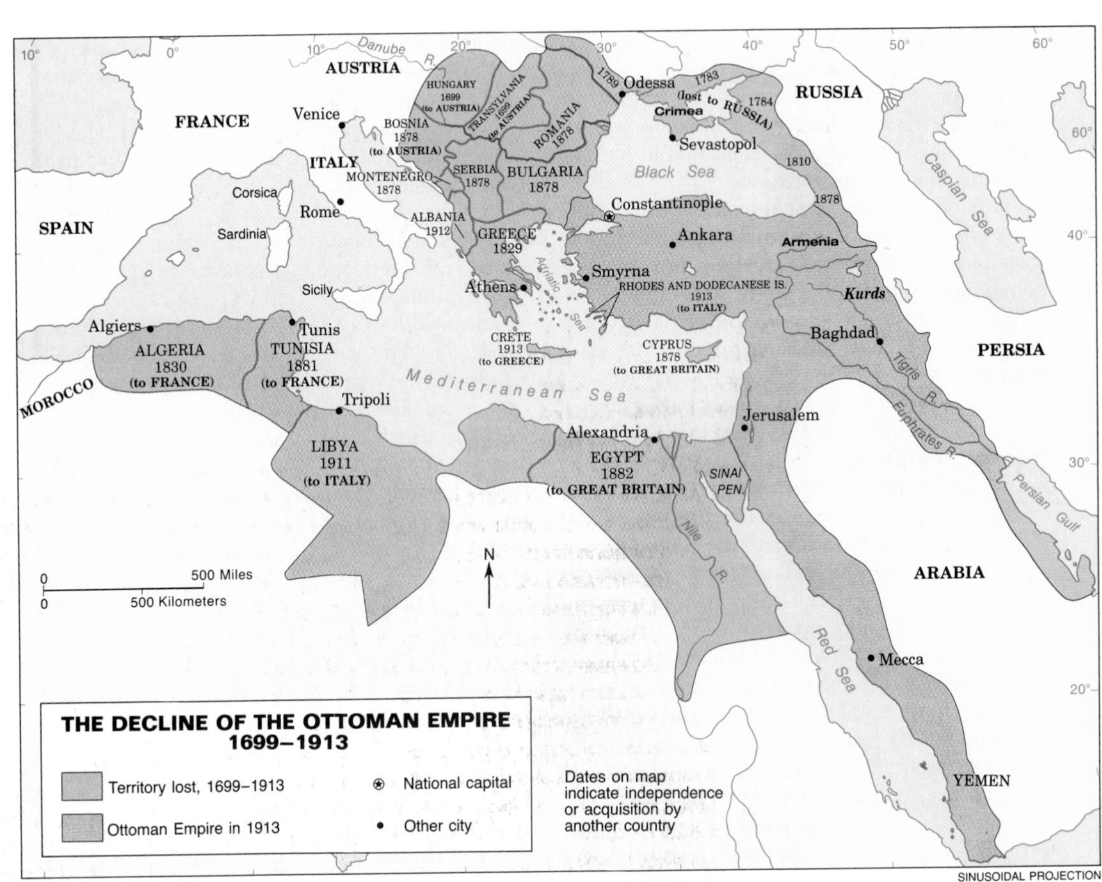

Learning from Maps *Greek independence sparked nationalism in the Balkans. What other countries in the Balkans became independent?*

It was a curious alignment of nations. The autocratic Russian government promoted the freedom and independence of the Balkan peoples. Democratic Great Britain supported the autocratic Turks in suppressing freedom.

The Congress of Berlin and the Balkans

In 1875 revolts broke out in several Turkish provinces in the Balkans. Two years later Russia decided to support the rebels and declared war on the Ottoman Empire. The Turks were defeated and forced to sign the Treaty of San Stefano in 1878. The treaty granted independence to Romania, Montenegro, and Serbia. It also created an enlarged Bulgaria, which Russian troops then occupied for some years. The new boundaries of Bulgaria extended to the Aegean Sea in the eastern Mediterranean.

The sudden increase of Russian influence in the Balkans alarmed other European powers. Before the Treaty of San Stefano could go into effect, a group of nations led by Great Britain and Austria forced the Russians to consent to an international conference at Berlin.

All the major European powers met at the Congress of Berlin in 1878. The Congress approved several terms. Serbia, Montenegro, and Romania retained their independence. Bulgaria was granted self-government, but its area was reduced in size, and it was kept within the Ottoman Empire—thus removing Russia's access to the Aegean Sea. Austria continued to govern Bosnia and Herzegovina but was not permitted to annex them.

594

The British were given the right to occupy and administer the island of Cyprus, long held by the Turks. The Turkish sultan still officially ruled the island, but Great Britain actually took it over. The use of Cyprus as a naval base increased Great Britain's power in the eastern Mediterranean and kept Russia out of this region.

Other nations continued to reduce both the size and the power of the Ottoman Empire. France, Great Britain, and Italy each seized parts of its African territory. In 1908 Bulgaria became completely independent. In the same year, Austria broke the agreement of the Congress of Berlin by annexing Bosnia and Herzegovina outright. In 1912 Italy seized several islands in the southeastern Aegean Sea, including Rhodes. The island of Crete revolted in 1896 and 1905, which resulted in a degree of self-government and, finally, annexation by Greece in 1913.

In 1912 and 1913, two wars between independent Balkan nations and the Ottomans further altered national boundaries and increased international tensions. Bulgaria, Serbia, Greece, and Montenegro, known as the Balkan League, declared war on the Ottoman Empire and quickly defeated it. The Balkan League wanted to take and divide among themselves the Balkan territories of the Ottoman Empire. However, they could not agree on the partition of the Turkish territories and hostilities broke out again in 1913. This time, Serbia, Greece, Montenegro, Romania, and the Ottoman Empire fought against and defeated Bulgaria.

As a result of the first war, Serbia gained a seaport on the Adriatic, and Albania became independent. Bulgaria claimed considerable territory in the central Balkans and along the Aegean Sea. As a result of the second war, however, Bulgaria suffered humiliating territorial losses to Serbia and Greece and was left with only a small outlet on the Aegean.

By the end of 1913, the territory of the Ottoman Empire in Europe had shrunk dramatically. It included only the city of Constantinople and a small region that gave it control of the vital water route from the Black Sea to the Mediterranean (see map, page 594). The stage was set for a showdown of the major European powers.

Everywhere in Europe, therefore, aggression and expansion marked the behavior of nations both new and old in the early 1900s. Tension and hostility began to rise to dangerous levels. Overseas rivalries, the result of a new force—imperialism—only made matters worse.

Learning from Pictures *This cartoon shows the European powers as vultures waiting for the independence of the Balkans and the fall of the Ottoman Empire.*

SECTION 5 REVIEW

1. **Identify** Magyars, Louis Kossuth, Francis Joseph I, Treaty of San Stefano, Balkan League
2. **Locate** Romania, Budapest, Serbia, Montenegro, Bulgaria, Bosnia, Herzegovina, Cyprus, Rhodes
3. **Summarizing Ideas** **(a)** When was the Dual Monarchy formed? **(b)** What were its strengths and weaknesses?
4. **Organizing Ideas** How was the Ottoman Empire reduced in size between 1878 and 1913?
5. **Interpreting Ideas** **(a)** Why did the Western nations fear Russian influence in the Balkans? **(b)** What prompted the Congress of Berlin?

was strong economically, with agricultural Hungary balancing industrial Austria. Its chief weaknesses were disagreement over tariffs, friction among national minorities, and confusion in the army over language differences.
4. The Ottoman Empire was reduced in size in 1878 when Serbia, Montenegro, and Romania became independent, Bosnia and Herzegovina were transferred to Austria, and Cyprus went to Great Britain; when several African territories were seized by France, Great Britain, and Italy; in 1908 when Bulgaria became independent; in 1912 when Italy seized islands in the Aegean Sea and when Albania became independent; and in 1913, when Crete was annexed by Greece.
5. (a) Great Britain did not want the Russians in the Mediterranean, where they might challenge British sea power. Russian support of Pan-Slavism promoted independence movements in the western sections of the Ottoman Empire and threatened the traditional balance of power in western Europe. **(b)** The actions of Russia alarmed the European powers. Before the Treaty of San Stefano could go into effect, a group of nations led by Great Britain and Austria forced the Russians to consent to an international conference at Berlin that would rewrite the treaty.

595

Reviewing Important Terms

1. Risorgimento; **2.** kaiser; **3.** autocrat; **4.** terrorism; **5.** pogroms

Reviewing Critical Thinking Skills

1. (a) Similarities include the following: One state led the drive for unification, and wars were fought for unification. Differences: Sardinia lost territory but Prussia only gained territory, and the Italian unification movement had more than one leader. **(b)** Answers will vary. Most students will note that unification was a gradual process.
2. Bismarck took whatever steps were open to him to build the empire. For example, he saw that he would be more successful in the war against Denmark with Austria as an ally, and later, he went to war with Austria. After defeating Austria, Bismarck was lenient with them.
3. (a) The liberal movement made little progress because the czar held absolute power. **(b)** Some spoke about abolishing the entire political and social structure. Some advocated that the large estates of the nobles be seized and the land divided among the peasants, and some advocated the use of terrorism.
4. (a) In Italy and Germany, nationalism helped unify people of the same racial and cultural background. **(b)** Nationalism caused the czar to force non-Russians to adopt Russian culture. **(c)** The Dual Monarchy allowed the Hungarians to share power with the Austrians. **(d)** As Ottoman power decreased, nationalist groups within its Empire began to call for independence.

1A, 1B, 4J, a1C, a4A, a4F, a4H, a4I, a4J, a4L

Reteaching

Have students review the Chapter Summary and the appropriate section and questions in the Unit Synthesis. Discuss the concepts until students demonstrate a clear understanding of the material.

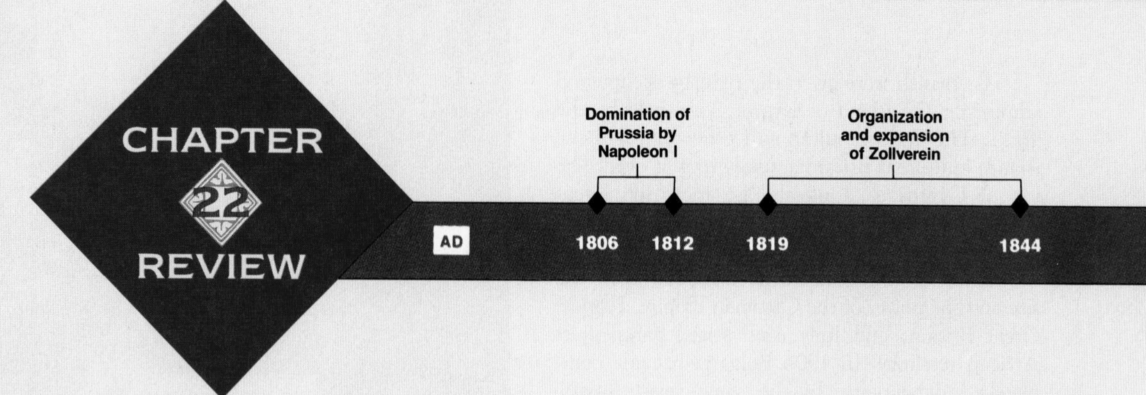

Chapter Summary

The following list contains the key concepts you have learned about the unification of Italy and Germany as well as about problems that arose in other European nations in the late 1800s and early 1900s.

1. Major new forces entered the European scene with the formation of a united Italy and a united Germany.
2. Italy was unified in 1870 due to the efforts of Mazzini, Garibaldi, and Cavour. A kingdom was established with Rome as its capital.
3. The kingdom of Prussia led the German unification under the leadership of Otto von Bismarck.
4. In both cases, but especially that of Germany, aggressive behavior accompanied the new unity. The Italians militarized rapidly, until their navy was the third largest in the world. The Germans went further, using three victorious wars to crush rivals and strengthen German national feeling.
5. Bismarck clashed with the new emperor, William II, and was forced to resign in 1890. However, Germany remained both prosperous and aggressive.
6. In Russia the czar maintained autocratic control over the country, despite such reforms as the freeing of the serfs.
7. Discontent and rebellion continued in the Austrian Empire even after Austria-Hungary, the Dual Monarchy, was created. Holding its various nationalities together was a major problem of the Dual Monarchy.
8. As the Ottoman Empire declined, discontent in its Balkan territories led to two Balkan wars in 1912 and 1913, with the result that international tensions increased. This would eventually lead to a greater show of hostility.

On a separate sheet of paper, complete the following review exercises.

Reviewing Important Terms

Supply the term that correctly completes each statement.

1. The nationalistic movement in Italy, with its goals of liberation and unification, was called ______ .
2. The emperor or king of Prussia was called the ______ .
3. An ______ is someone who holds absolute power.
4. Bombings and assassinations of high officials by political groups are called ______ .
5. The massacres of the Jews in czarist Russia were called ______ .

Developing Critical Thinking Skills

1. **Comparing Ideas** **(a)** What were the similarities and differences between the processes of unification in Italy and Germany? **(b)** What generalizations can you make about how these two nations came into existence?
2. **Analyzing Ideas** Otto von Bismarck once remarked, "Politics is the art of the possible, the art of the attainable." How did Bismarck's actions in forming the German Empire demonstrate his belief in this statement?
3. **Interpreting Ideas** **(a)** Why did the liberal movement make little progress in Russia during the 1800s? **(b)** How did Russian radicals attempt to bring about change?
4. **Understanding Relationships** Why might each of the following events be considered a response to the rise of nationalism? **(a)** Unification of Italy and Germany; **(b)** Start of the "Russification" program **(c)** Establishment of the Dual Monarchy; **(d)** Further decline of the Ottoman Empire.

Relating Geography to History

You read in Chapter 15 about the rivalry between Prussia and Austria to dominate central Europe. To study the outcome of this struggle, compare the two maps on pages 390 and 582. How did the balance of power change during the period from 1763 to 1871? Using the information in this chapter and in Chapter 15, briefly explain how Prussia came to rule the German Empire.

Relating Past to Present

1. The Zollverein was a major step toward German unity. **(a)** Who belonged to this customs union? **(b)** How did the various member states benefit from economic

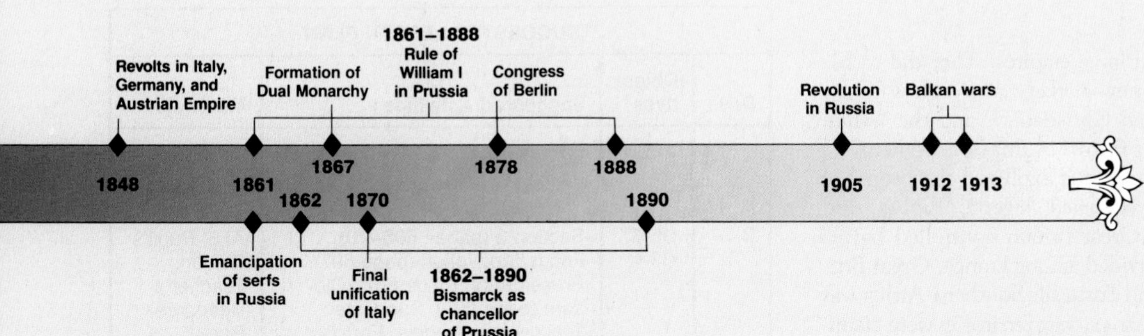

cooperation? **(c)** Using American history or civics books, find out about the laws regulating trade among the states in this nation. Can the states impose or collect tariffs? **(d)** Can the federal government grant special trade concessions to any one state or region? **(e)** What evidence of trade among the states can you find in your home?

2. Review the objectives of Russia's foreign policy during the 1800s. Then clip newspaper and magazine articles that illustrate foreign-policy objectives of the Soviet Union today. Compare the objectives of the 1800s with those of the present day. What seem to be the similarities and differences?

Applying History Study Skills

Before completing this activity, review Building History Study Skills on page 586.

Read the following statements. The first is from a speech by Otto von Bismarck on his view of the unification of Germany. The other is from a letter by Giuseppe Garibaldi on his conquest of Naples. How are their views of unification different? How are they similar?

> "Germany does not look to Prussia's liberalism, but to her power. The south German states . . . would like to indulge in liberalism, and because of that no one will assign Prussia's role to them! Prussia must collect her forces and hold them in reserve for an opportune moment, which has already come and gone several times. . . . Not by speeches and majorities will the great questions of the day be decided—that was the mistake of 1848 and 1849—but by iron and blood."

(Otto von Bismarck. Speech to the Reichstag on September 30, 1862)

> "Having reached the strait, it became necessary to cross it. To have reinstated Sicily in the great Italian family was certainly a glorious achievement. But what then? Were we, in compliance with diplomacy, to leave our country incomplete and maimed? What of the two Calabrias, and Naples, awaiting us with open arms? And the rest of Italy still enslaved by the foreigner and the priest?. . .
>
> I entered Naples with the whole of the southern army as yet a long way off in the direction of the Straits of Messina, the King of Naples having, on the previous day, quitted his palace to retire to Capua.
>
> At Naples, as in all places we had passed through since crossing the strait, the populace were sublime in their enthusiastic patriotism, and the resolute tone assumed by them certainly had no small share in the brilliant results obtained."

(Garibaldi's Report on the Conquest of Naples)

1. How did Bismarck feel about liberalism?
2. **(a)** How did Garibaldi feel about the role of the people in uniting Italy? **(b)** How did his opinion differ from Bismarck's?
3. What does Bismarck mean by the expression "iron and blood"?
4. **(a)** How was Garibaldi greeted in Naples? **(b)** What might Bismarck have said about this greeting?
5. What was the primary difference between Garibaldi's and Bismarck's approaches to unification?

Investigating Further

1. **Presenting an Oral Report** Read Garibaldi's entire "Proclamation to the Italians," and Bismarck's entire "iron and blood" speech in a source such as Louis Snyder's *Fifty Major Documents of the Nineteenth Century* (Van Nostrand Reinhold). Give an oral report explaining why each of these documents might be considered an expression of nationalism. Discuss which one is more idealistic and why.
2. **Writing a Report** Garibaldi and his comparatively small army succeeded in conquering the Kingdom of the Two Sicilies, which later became part of a united Italy. Prepare a written report on Garibaldi's exploits in Sicily. One source for your report is "Garibaldi and His Thousand Redshirts Win Palermo" in Louis Snyder and Richard Morris's *A Treasury of Great Reporting* (Pocket Books).

Relating Geography to History

In 1763 Austria was the dominant power in central Europe. In 1871 the newly formed German Empire was dominant. Frederick the Great challenged Austria in a series of wars. Bismarck, through a series of wars, drove Austria from its position of leadership.

Relating Past to Present

1. (a) The Zollverein included almost all the German states except Austria. **(b)** Members benefited from lower and more uniform prices. **(c)** In the United States the states cannot impose tariffs. **(d)** The federal government cannot grant trade concessions to any one state. **(e)** Answers will vary.

2. The main aims of Russian foreign policy in the 1800s were Pan-Slavism and expansion of the empire eastward and southward. The Soviet Union today dominates the Eastern European countries.

Applying History Study Skills

1. Bismarck had little regard for liberalism.

2. (a) Garibaldi believed the people brought about the revolution. **(b)** Garibaldi liked to have popular support, while Bismarck liked to maintain control over all of society.

3. Most students will suggest that Bismarck means strength and war.

4. (a) The people enthusiastically greeted Garibaldi as a great leader. **(b)** Most students will suggest that Bismarck would probably have felt it was wasting precious energy.

5. Garibaldi depended upon popular support, while Bismarck desired complete control.

CHAPTER (pages 598–627)

23 Imperialist Powers Competed in Many Areas of the World

(1798–1914)

CHAPTER OVERVIEW

In the 1800s many nations formed large empires. They did so because of a need for raw materials, new markets, and outlets for excess population. A desire to spread Christianity, and the "white man's burden" were also important factors in this development.

Imperialism divided the continent and exploited the people of Africa. In North Africa, France occupied Algeria, Tunisia, and Morocco; Italy seized Libya; and Great Britain controlled Egypt. Western and central Africa were divided among France, Great Britain, Belgium, Germany, Spain, and Portugal. Southern Africa was dominated by the British. In East Africa, vast territories were claimed by Portugal, Great Britain, Germany, Italy, and France.

During the Meiji Era, Japan underwent rapid industrialization and developed a strong army. Japanese fear of imperialism in Asia led them into the Sino-Japanese War. Japan's victory gave Westerners an excuse to intervene and gain additional territory in Asia.

Southeast Asia was also subjected to imperialism. Only Siam remained independent. Islands in the Pacific became valuable as coaling stations and naval bases.

In Latin America, the United States intervened to aid Venezuela against Great Britain. The United States also became directly involved in Cuban affairs by going to war with Spain. The Spanish-American War resulted in an American victory but revealed the need for a United States canal across the Isthmus of Panama. As the Caribbean area became more important, President Theodore Roosevelt issued the Roosevelt Corollary to the Monroe Doctrine.

SUGGESTED LESSON PLAN

Day	Objectives	Suggested Activities	Materials
1	U6,* C1	Introducing the Chapter (pages 598–99) Section 1 (pages 599–602), Focus/Motivation (page 599), Presentation (page 600), Closure (page 602), Suggested Teaching Strategies, Enrichment Activity, Daily Quiz, Suggested Assignments (page 597B)	ATE, Pupil's Edition, Teacher's Resource-Bank™
2	U5-6, C2-3	Section 2 (pages 602–06), Focus/Motivation (page 603), Presentation (page 604), Closure (page 605), Suggested Teaching Strategies, Enrichment Activity, Daily Quiz, Suggested Assignments (page 597C)	ATE, Pupil's Edition, Teacher's Resource-Bank™
3	U5-6, C3-4	Section 3 (pages 606–10), Focus/Motivation (page 607), Presentation (page 607), Closure (page 609), Suggested Teaching Strategies, Enrichment Activity, Daily Quiz, Suggested Assignments (page 597C)	ATE, Pupil's Edition, Teacher's Resource-Bank™
4	U6, C5-7	Section 4 (pages 610–16), Focus/Motivation (page 611), Presentation (page 611), Closure (page 615), Suggested Teaching Strategies, Enrichment Activity, Daily Quiz, Suggested Assignments (page 597D)	ATE, Pupil's Edition, Teacher's Resource-Bank™
5	U6, C8-10	Section 5 (pages 616–19), Focus/Motivation (page 617), Presentation (page 618), Closure (page 618), Suggested Teaching Strategies, Enrichment Activity, Daily Quiz, Suggested Assignments (page 597E)	ATE, Pupil's Edition, Teacher's Resource-Bank™
6	U5-6, C11-14	Section 6 (pages 619–25), Focus/Motivation (page 619), Presentation (page 621), Closure (page 624), Suggested Teaching Strategies, Enrichment Activity, Daily Quiz, Suggested Assignments (page 597F)	ATE, Pupil's Edition, Teacher's Resource-Bank™
7	U5-6, C1-14	Chapter 23 Form A Test, Reteaching Worksheet, Chapter 23 Form B Test	Teacher's Resource-Bank™ or Workbook and Test Booklet
8	U1-6	Unit Five Review Worksheet, Unit Five Test	Teacher's Resource-Bank™ or Workbook and Test Booklet

*C refers to applicable Chapter Objective, U refers to applicable Unit Goal.

BOOKS FOR THE TEACHER

Morris, Edmund. *The Rise of Theodore Roosevelt.* Coward, McCann. Describes Roosevelt's earlier career, with chapters on his role in the Spanish-American War.

Pakenham, Thomas. *The Boer War.* Random House. Presents comprehensive coverage of this war.

Pakenham, Valerie. *Out in the Noonday Sun.* Random House. Offers an entertaining description of British colonialism during the Edwardian Era.

BOOKS FOR THE STUDENT

Achebe, Chinua. *Things Fall Apart.* Fawcett. Describes the impact of British imperialism and missionary activity on the people of Nigeria.

Freidel, Frank. *The Splendid Little War.* Dell. Offers a highly readable account of the Spanish-American War.

Sears, Stephen W. *The Horizon History of the British Empire.* American Heritage. Provides a thorough account of the rise and fall of the British Empire.

Werstein, Irving. *Land and Liberty: The Mexican Revolution.* Contemporary Books. Brings to life this turbulent period of Mexico's history.

MULTIMEDIA MATERIALS

Colonization: Ogre or Angel? (mp. 30 min.), McGraw-Hill. Depicts the growth of British colonies and examines the impact of industrialization and consequent awakening to self-determination of non-European populations.

Imperialism (3 fs), Educational Audio-Visual. Defines and analyzes European imperialism and then examines it more closely through three case studies.

India's History: British Colony to Independence (mp. 11 min.), Coronet. Covers the exploitation of India's resources, the Indian Mutiny of 1857, and the growth of the nationalist movement.

The Unfinished Revolution (mp. 53 min.), NET. Depicts the 1910 revolution in Mexico.

Section 1 (pages 599–602)

Several Forces Stimulated Imperialism

SECTION OVERVIEW

In the late 1800s, imperialism became a dynamic force in world affairs. Many nations had political, economic, and social motives for establishing overseas colonies. Industrialization had created a need for economic self-sufficiency, new markets, places to invest surplus capital, and outlets for population. Nationalism, missionary motives, and the "white man's burden" were also important factors that stimulated imperialism.

SUGGESTED TEACHING STRATEGIES

1. **Preteaching Vocabulary (Basic)** You may wish to preteach the following important vocabulary terms: imperialism *(page 599)*; colony, protectorate, condominium, concession, sphere of influence *(page 602)*. Ask: How do spheres of influence operate?
2. **Analyzing Ideas (Average/Group)** Obtain a collection of Rudyard Kipling's poems. Read to the class the complete version of "The White Man's Burden" and other poems, such as "Gunga Din" and "Fuzzy-Wuzzy." Then lead students in a discussion of Kipling's work, using the following questions as a guide: Were your ideas about "The White Man's Burden" changed by hearing the full version of the poem? Why or why not?

ENRICHMENT ACTIVITY

Making a Bulletin Board Display (Average/Group) Organize the class into groups to prepare cartoons or other illustrations on the theme of the "white man's burden" or some other motive for imperialism. Completed projects can be displayed on the bulletin board.

DAILY QUIZ

To assess student understanding of Section 1, give the class the following quiz. (Each item is worth 10 points.)

1. (T or F) Nineteenth-century imperialism developed out of the mercantilistic policies of the major European powers. *(F)*
2. Increased industrial production spurred demand for such traditional raw materials as iron and ________ . *(coal)*
3. European nations wanted to become ________ in raw materials because they did not want to depend on other countries for such items during times of war. *(self-sufficient)*
4. (T or F) Some imperialists argued that the customs of the native peoples of the colonies could be remolded to create new markets for manufactured goods. *(T)*
5. (T or F) Some European countries used native peoples from the colonies to bolster their military forces. *(T)*
6. Some nationalists believed the excess population of their countries could be settled in ________ to produce raw materials and purchase goods manufactured in the homeland. *(colonies)*
7. (T or F) Missionary work in the colonies was carried out only by the Roman Catholic church. *(F)*
8. Trained medical missionaries spread knowledge of medicine, ________ , and ________ as well as Christianity. *(hygiene, sanitation)*
9. Who was the British poet and author who wrote about the "white man's burden?" *(Rudyard Kipling)*
10. In a ________ ________ ________, one nation has special, sometimes exclusive, economic and political privileges that are recognized by other nations. *(sphere of influence)*

SUGGESTED ASSIGNMENTS

1. **Identifying Ideas (Basic)** Write the following terms on the chalkboard or an overhead projector: protectorate, concession,

sphere of influence. Ask students to copy the terms in their notebooks. Then ask students to provide an example of each from the late nineteenth century. Suggest that students present their answers in the following fashion: Protectorate — Egypt, of Great Britain. Have students compare their answers with those of other members of the class.
2. **Researching (Average/Group)** It has been argued that several of the motives that promoted imperialism were never fulfilled. Organize the class into seven groups, and have each group research one of the seven forces for imperialism given in this section. Each group should discuss its findings and then choose one member to report to the class on whether or not the aim was fulfilled. Two sources are D. K. Fieldhouse's *The Colonial Empires* (Dial) and *Western Civilization,* vol. 2, edited by W. L. Langer (Harper & Row).

Section (pages 602–606)

2 Europeans Made Claims in North Africa and the Sudan

SECTION OVERVIEW

Throughout history many different peoples had conquered North Africa. During the 1800s, for example, the region was part of the Ottoman Empire. By the end of the century, however, France, Great Britain, and Italy had laid claim to most of the territory of North Africa.

SUGGESTED TEACHING STRATEGIES

1. **Illustrating Ideas (Basic)** Have students study the map on page 607. Ask students to speculate why the Fashoda Incident, involving Anglo-French competition for control of the Sudan, developed. *(Answers will vary. Most students will point out that control of the Sudan would give France possession of territory in an unbroken line from the Atlantic to the Red Sea. Similarly, British control of the Sudan would provide a link between Egypt and their East African colonies.)*

*2. **Thinking About History: Determining Relevancy (Basic)** To reinforce the skill lesson on page 604, have students suggest why information on British merchant shipping might be relevant to a study of the Suez Canal.

ENRICHMENT ACTIVITY

Producing a Newscast (Average/Group) Rivalry between France and Germany over Morocco brought Europe close to war. Interested students might research the Agadir Incident of 1911, when Kaiser William II sent a gunboat to the Moroccan port of Agadir. Students could then prepare a newscast, designed for a German audience, on this incident. The tension between Germany and France should be conveyed by explaining William's position and by giving a hostile review of past French imperialism in North Africa.

DAILY QUIZ

To assess student understanding of Section 2, give the class the following quiz. (Each item is worth 10 points.)

1. Four Muslim states — Morocco, Algiers, Tunis, and Tripoli — together were known as the ________ ________. *(Barbary States)*
2. (T or F) The Algerians welcomed the French troops as liberators in 1830. *(F)*
3. Which two countries became embroiled in a bitter dispute over possession of Morocco? *(France and Germany)*
4. What was the title of the Turkish viceroy in Egypt? *(khedive)*
5. Why did Great Britain want to gain control of the Suez Canal? *(It was a vital trade route between Great Britain and such colonies as India, Australia, and New Zealand.)*
6. Why did the British occupy the whole of Egypt after 1882? *(to protect the Suez Canal)*
7. What kind of vegetation is found in the geographic region known as the Sudan? *(savanna)*
8. In which battle did British troops under General Herbert Kitchener defeat a Sudanese army? *(Omdurman)*
9. What was the event that nearly brought France and Great Britain to war in the Sudan? *(Fashoda Incident)*
10. Why did Italy seize control of Tripoli? *(It wanted to join the other European powers in establishing an empire.)*

SUGGESTED ASSIGNMENTS

1. **Critical Thinking Worksheet (Basic)** Have students complete Critical Thinking Worksheet 52 in the TEACHER'S RESOURCEBANK™.
2. **Illustrating Ideas (Average/Group)** Have students work together to construct a large-scale map of the Suez Canal. Suggest that they use atlases to locate the necessary information.
3. **Researching Ideas (Challenging)** Interested students might like to do further research on the Fashoda Incident. Have them look in the school and public libraries to locate information.
4. **Skill Worksheet (Basic)** Have students complete Skill Worksheet 23 in the TEACHER'S RESOURCEBANK™.

Section (pages 606–610)

3 Several European Nations Carved Up SubSaharan Africa

SECTION OVERVIEW

By the end of the 1800s, the forces of imperialism had overwhelmed practically the whole of the African continent. Western and Central Africa were divided by several European nations, and by 1900 Liberia was the only independent nation in these regions. Portugal, Great Britain, and Germany all claimed territories in East Africa. And in southern Africa, the Union of South Africa was formed as a British dominion after the Boer War.

SUGGESTED TEACHING STRATEGIES

1. **Preteaching Vocabulary (Basic)** You may wish to preteach the following important vocabulary terms: direct rule, paternalism, assimilation, indirect rule *(page 609)*. Ask students to discuss what impact the various kinds of colonial rule might have on local populations.
2. **Presenting a Report (Average/Group)** Students might research and prepare an oral or written report on the Boer War. An excellent source of information on this topic is Thomas Pakenham's *The Boer War* (Random House). Students should present their reports to the rest of the class.

ENRICHMENT ACTIVITY

Illustrating Ideas (Average/Group) Provide students with examples of African art for them to view. The school or public library probably contains several books, or the art department may be able to provide slides. Ask the class to suggest reasons why nineteenth-century Europeans judged African art as "barbaric." *(Student answers might include that it was unlike what Europeans were accustomed to, or that it was associated with aspects of African life that Europeans also considered "barbaric.")*

DAILY QUIZ

To assess student understanding of Section 3, give the class the following quiz. (Each item is worth 10 points.)

1. What first attracted Europeans to West Africa? *(the slave trade)*
2. What ancient West African city did the French claim? *(Tombouctou)*
3. Which West African kingdom tried to stop British expansion in the region? *(Ashanti)*
4. Why was Liberia able to remain independent? *(American diplomatic pressure discouraged European takeover attempts.)*
5. What European monarch carved out a huge personal empire in Central Africa? *(Leopold II of Belgium)*
6. The descendants of the original Dutch settlers in southern Africa were called ________. *(Boers)*
7. What Zulu leader created a thriving empire with a strong army in southern Africa? *(Shaka)*
8. What British speculator took control of South African diamond production? *(Cecil Rhodes)*
9. Since they believed that Africans were unfit to rule themselves, many Europeans practiced ________, a system of governing colonies in much the same way that parents guide their children. *(paternalism)*
10. (T or F) Economically, Africans benefited more than Europeans from imperialism. *(F)*

SUGGESTED ASSIGNMENTS

1. **Preparing an Oral Report (Average/Group)** In 1871 Henry Stanley began a famous search for Dr. David Livingstone, a Scottish missionary and explorer. Students might like to do further research on Stanley's two-year search and present their findings in oral reports to the rest of the class. One useful source of information is "Stanley Finds Livingstone" in Sydney Eisen's and Maurice Filler's *The Human Adventure,* vol. 2 (Harcourt Brace Jovanovich).
2. **Writing an Essay (Challenging)** In the late 1800s and early 1900s, big game hunting became a major sport in Africa. Even President Theodore Roosevelt undertook a hunting safari there after leaving office in 1909. Some students might like to research and write a brief essay on big game safaris in Africa. Useful sources of information include: Peter Capstick's *Safari: The Last Adventure* (St. Martin's); Brian Gardner's *The African Dream* (Putnam); and Valerie Pakenham's *Out in the Noonday Sun* (Random House). Ask for volunteers to read their essays to the rest of the class.

Section 4 (pages 610–616)

Europeans Expanded Their Influence in South and East Asia

SECTION OVERVIEW

After the Indian Mutiny of 1858, India was directly controlled by the British government. British rule brought some improvements along with many injustices. However, one improvement — better education for the Indians — eventually fostered Indian nationalism, and in the late 1800s, several groups began to agitate for Indian independence.

The Meiji Era in Japan was noted for rapid modernization and industrialization and the establishment of a new system of government. Japanese fear of the growing strength of imperialism led the country into the Sino-Japanese War. The Japanese victory, rather than halt Western interference in Asia, provided the Western powers with a pretext for seizing more territory.

SUGGESTED TEACHING STRATEGIES

1. **Identifying Ideas (Basic)** Have students study the map on page 615. Then have them enter in their notebooks the various possessions of the following nations: Great Britain, France, Germany, the Netherlands, Russia, Japan, and the United States. Then ask them to discuss the power struggle in Asia, using the following questions as a guide: Which nation seems to have the strongest foothold in Asia? What steps did the various European nations take to prevent others from gaining too much power in the region?
2. **Writing a Letter (Average/Group)** Organize the class into two groups. Have one group write letters from British civil servants in India to Parliament giving reasons why the British should remain in India. The other group should write letters from Indian nationalists to Parliament requesting independence. Have students share their letters with the class.

ENRICHMENT ACTIVITY

Holding a Panel Discussion (Challenging) A small group of students might present a panel discussion on the beneficial and harmful effects of British imperialism in India. Refer students to the discussion of the effects of imperialism in India on page 610. Encourage students to compare and contrast these effects with the effects of imperialism on Africa, discussed in the previous two sections of the chapter.

DAILY QUIZ

To assess student understanding of Section 4, give the class the following quiz. (Each item is worth 10 points.)

1. What method did the British authorities use to control both British India and local India? *(divide and rule)*
2. What impact did the importation of cheap British cotton goods have on the Indian handicraft industry? *(It practically destroyed the local handicraft industry.)*
3. (T or F) The British imposed themselves above Indian society as a sort of super-caste. *(T)*
4. (T or F) For the most part, British education had little impact on Indian society. *(F)*
5. The ________ ________ ________, a political party founded in 1885, favored a gradual advance toward independence through democratic methods. *(Indian National Congress)*
6. What was the accepted name given to the change from the Tokugawa shogunate to imperial government in Japan? *(the Meiji Restoration)*
7. (T or F) The Japanese constitution of 1889 had two purposes—to impress Western governments with Japan's progress and to give the Japanese people a somewhat limited voice in national affairs. *(T)*
8. The new Japanese constitution established a two-house national assembly called the ________, one house of which was elected. *(Diet)*
9. (T or F) The mostly agricultural Japanese economy could not support the ambitious industrialization programs of the late 1800s. *(F)*
10. The Treaty of ________, which ended the Sino-Japanese War, displeased Russia and the other European nations that had colonial interests in Asia. *(Shimonoseki)*

SUGGESTED ASSIGNMENTS

1. **Critical Thinking Worksheet (Basic)** Have students complete Critical Thinking Worksheet 53 in the TEACHER'S RESOURCEBANK™.
2. **Writing an Essay (Average/Group)** Ask students to write brief essays describing the social, political, and economic changes of the Meiji Restoration. Suggest that students refer to pages 612-614 for background information on these subjects. Have students read their essays to the class.
3. **Profile Worksheet (Basic)** Have students complete Profile Worksheet 23 in the TEACHER'S RESOURCEBANK™.

Section (pages 616–619)

5 Foreign Influence in Southeast Asia and the Pacific Increased

SECTION OVERVIEW

Expanding their empires in the East, Great Britain, France, and the Netherlands claimed territories in Southeast Asia. As the European powers set up colonies around the world, the Pacific islands became valuable as coaling stations and naval bases. France, Great Britain, and Germany established claims in the area. The United States gained Hawaii, the Philippines, Guam, and Wake Island, and shared the Samoa Islands with Germany.

SUGGESTED TEACHING STRATEGIES

1. **Preteaching Vocabulary (Basic)** You may wish to preteach the following important vocabulary term: buffer state *(page 617)*. Ask: Can you think of examples of buffer states in present times?
2. **Presenting an Oral Report (Average/Group)** Students may be interested in preparing and presenting oral reports based on the following articles from *American Heritage:* "Funston Captures Aguinaldo" (February 1956); "The Sham Battle of Manila" (December 1960); "The Great White Fleet" (February 1964).

ENRICHMENT ACTIVITY

Researching Ideas (Average/Group) Have a group of students use books in the library to find information about Captain Alfred T. Mahan, a naval scholar whose ideas greatly influenced the imperialists of the 1890s. *(Mahan's main point was that nations that control the seas control the world.)* Have students prepare reports focusing on the following questions: What were Mahan's ideas? How did the United States government respond to Mahan's arguments? Ask students if they think Mahan's theories still hold true today.

DAILY QUIZ

To assess student understanding of Section 5, give the class the following quiz. (Each item is worth 10 points.)

1. What was the importance of the island of Singapore, on the tip of the Malay Peninsula? *(It guarded the Strait of Malacca, one of the most vital trade routes in the world.)*
2. Which country acted as a buffer state between French Indochina and British-controlled Burma? *(Siam)*
3. (T or F) A series of revolts in the Dutch East Indies during the late 1800s convinced the Dutch government to give the colonies their independence. *(F)*
4. What was the primary motive for the imperialist powers to take control of Pacific islands? *(to use them as coaling stations and naval bases)*
5. In the late 1800s, the most serious rivalry over territory in the Pacific involved the ________ ________. *(Samoa Islands)*

6. What crops did American businesses and other foreign investors develop on the Hawaiian Islands? *(sugarcane, pineapples)*
7. In what year did the United States officially annex the Hawaiian Islands? *(1898)*
8. After which war did the United States win control of the Philippines and Guam? *(The Spanish-American War)*
9. (T or F) Some Filipinos welcomed the American invasion and even fought with American troops against the Spanish. *(T)*
10. _______ _______ led a Filipino uprising to win independence from the United States. *(Emilio Aguinaldo)*

SUGGESTED ASSIGNMENTS

1. **Writing a Paragraph (Average/Group)** Point out that many Americans referred to the Spanish-American War as the "splendid little war." Ask students to write a paragraph explaining the reasons why this war was so named. Have students read their paragraphs to the rest of the class.
2. **Writing an Editorial (Average/Group)** Organize the class into two groups. Have one group write a newspaper editorial supporting American involvement in imperialism. Ask the other group to write a newspaper editorial opposing American imperial ambitions. Have students from both groups read their editorials to the rest of the class. Use these editorials as a starting point for a discussion on American imperialism.

Section 6 (pages 619–625)
Latin America Became Involved with Imperialist Powers

SECTION OVERVIEW

The Spanish-American War of 1898 and the building of the Panama Canal marked an escalation of United States involvement in Latin America. The rationale for this increased involvement was explained in the Roosevelt Corollary to the Monroe Doctrine. American involvement in Latin American affairs sometimes caused problems. For example, the Mexican revolution of 1910 and American response to it led to tensions between Mexico and the United States that did not ease until 1917.

SUGGESTED TEACHING STRATEGIES

1. **Preteaching Vocabulary (Basic)** You may wish to preteach the following important vocabulary term: arbitration *(page 620)*. Ask: In what fields other than diplomacy might arbitration be used? *(Answers will vary. Most students will suggest the settlement of labor disputes.)*
2. **Interpreting Cartoons (Average/Group)** There are a number of cartoons on United States imperialism in Latin America. Have each student bring a cartoon to class or draw a cartoon. Students should be called upon to interpret each other's cartoons. Useful sources for such cartoons include: Thomas Bailey's *American Pageant* (D. C. Heath) and *A Diplomatic History of the American People* (Appleton-Century-Crofts).

ENRICHMENT ACTIVITY

Preparing a Panel Report (Challenging) Three students might work together to present a panel report on the Spanish-American War. Each member should research one aspect of the war. Topics to be covered include the causes, fighting, and outcome of the war. Sources include Frank Freidel's *The Splendid Little War* (Dell) and Thomas Bailey's *A Diplomatic History of the American People* (Appleton-Century-Crofts). Students should also check the index of *American Heritage* for appropriate articles.

DAILY QUIZ

To assess student understanding of Section 6, give the class the following quiz. (Each item is worth 10 points.)

1. The Americans acquired a taste for _______, which they bought in Central America, and for _______, which came mostly from Brazil. *(bananas, coffee)*
2. Foreign investors often were granted special favors by Latin American governments — for example, monopoly privileges, free land, and exemption from _______. *(taxes)*
3. On what did most Latin American governments spend the loans they obtained from foreign banks? *(on strengthening their armies and navies)*
4. (T or F) When Latin American countries could not or would not repay foreign loans, the loaning countries often occupied the ports and took control of customs collection. *(T)*
5. Between which two countries was the dispute that the United States insisted should be settled by arbitration? *(Venezuela, Great Britain)*
6. The sinking of which American ship was the spark that set off the Spanish-American War? *(the Maine)*
7. Where did most of the fighting in the Spanish-American War take place? *(Cuba)*
8. From which country did the United States "take" the Panama Canal Zone by guaranteeing Panama's freedom? *(Colombia)*
9. What was the name given to President Theodore Roosevelt's statement that the United States would act as an "international police force" to protect the independence of any country in the Western Hemisphere? *(the Roosevelt Corollary to the Monroe Doctrine)*
10. In which Latin American country was there the greatest political upheaval during the age of imperialism? *(Mexico)*

SUGGESTED ASSIGNMENTS

1. **Review Worksheet (Basic)** Have students complete Review Worksheet 23 in the TEACHER'S RESOURCEBANK™.
2. **Unit Review Worksheet (Basic)** Have students complete Unit 5 Review Worksheet in the TEACHER'S RESOURCEBANK™.

For suggested lesson plan, additional teaching strategies, enrichment activities, daily quizzes, and suggested assignments, see page 597A–597F.

Introducing the Chapter
Have students read the Chapter Focus for Chapter 23 on page 599. Ask the class to determine from the Focus why imperialism did not emerge until the late 1800s. The class discussion should focus on the effects of the American and French revolutions, the Napoleonic Wars, nationalism, and the rise of democracy. Guide the discussion with the following questions: How was colonial expansion discouraged by these events and historical trends? Why do you think the situation began to change around 1870? At the end of the chapter, have students compare their answers with what they have read.

Chapter Objectives
After studying Chapter 23, students will be able to:

1. Identify the political, economic, and social motives for imperialism.
2. Outline the steps in the colonization of Africa.
3. Describe European competition for control of Africa.
4. Compare the costs and benefits of imperialism for Africans.
5. Trace the rise of Indian nationalism.
6. Describe the results of the Meiji Restoration.
7. List the causes and results concerning the Sino-Japanese War.
8. Identify and locate the Southeast Asian possessions of the various world powers.
9. Describe the reasons

CHAPTER 23

Imperialist Powers Competed in Many Areas of the World

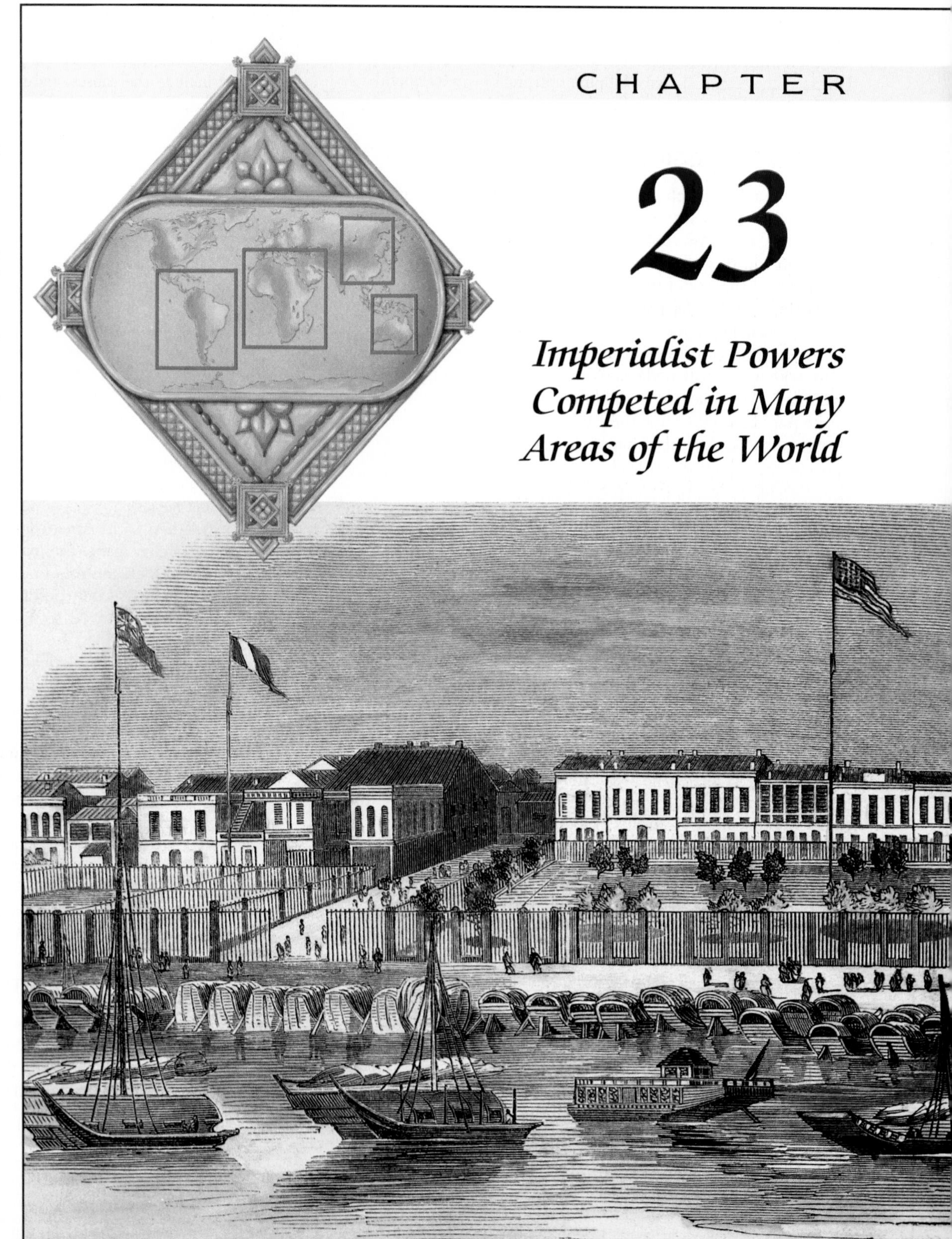

CHAPTER FOCUS

Place Africa, Asia, the Pacific, and Latin America

Time 1798–1914

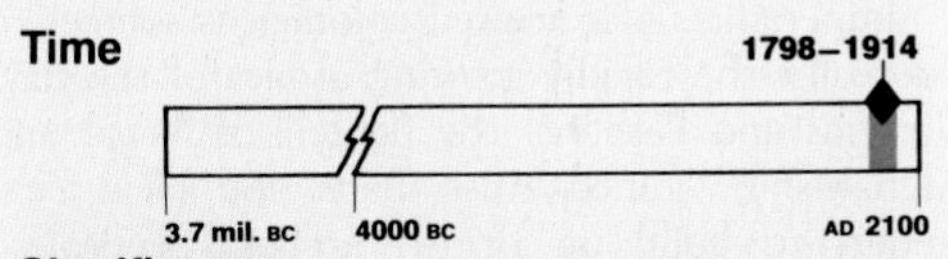

Significance

Beginning in the late 1400s and continuing into the 1700s, European nations extended their power to Asia and the Americas. By the late 1700s, however, this interest declined. Great Britain and France had lost colonies in North America. Also, the French Revolution and Napoleonic Wars had prompted Europeans to focus more attention on European affairs.

Beginning about 1870 several factors rekindled interest in establishing colonies. During the next 40 years, many nations became involved in a new kind of empire building called **imperialism**—the domination by a powerful nation over the political, economic, and cultural affairs of another nation or region. Imperialism differed from the colonization of the 1500s and 1600s. Colonies established after 1870 were both more heavily populated and more thoroughly dominated. By the early 1900s, European nations, the United States, and Japan had brought most of the world under their control.

Terms to Define

imperialism, colony, protectorate, concession, direct rule, paternalism, assimilation, indirect rule

People to Identify

Rudyard Kipling, Ashanti, Boers, Cecil Rhodes

Places to Locate

Suez Canal, Brazzaville, Singapore, Panama Canal

Questions to Guide Your Reading

1 What forces stimulated imperialism?
2 How did Europeans win control of North Africa?
3 What colonies did Europeans carve out of Sub-Saharan Africa?
4 How did imperialism in South and East Asia differ from imperialism in Africa?
5 Why did imperialist powers claim colonies in the Pacific?
6 How did the United States become an imperialist power?

◀ *European trading centers in Guangzhou, China*

In 1869 the New York Herald *hired journalist Henry Stanley to locate Dr. David Livingstone, who had disappeared in Africa. In 1871 Stanley finally located Livingstone and wrote of their meeting.*

> *"So I did that which I thought was most dignified. I pushed back the crowds, and, passing from the rear, walked down a living avenue of people until I came in front of the semicircle of Arabs, in front of which stood the white man with the gray beard. As I advanced slowly toward him I noticed he was pale, looked wearied. . . . I would have run to him, only I was a coward in the presence of such a mob. . . . So I did what cowardice and false pride suggested was the best thing—walked deliberately to him, took off my hat, and said, 'Dr. Livingstone, I presume?'*
>
> *'Yes,' said he, with a kind smile, lifting his cap slightly."*

Stanley's highly publicized trip did much to spark European interest in Africa.

1 Several Forces Stimulated Imperialism

Imperialism arose out of a complex mixture of political, economic, and social forces, although historians do not agree on which influences were most dominant.

Desire for Self-sufficiency

After 1850 the Industrial Revolution accelerated as new sources of power, new machinery, and new industries were developed. Increased industrial production spurred the demand for traditional raw materials such as iron and coal. In addition, the new factories needed other raw materials such as manganese and tungsten for making steel alloys, copper for the electrical industry, and rubber for a variety of uses. Industrialization also brought rising standards of living in Europe and the United States and increased demands for products such as coffee, tea, and spices.

Although none of the industrialized nations produced all of these products, none of the leaders of these nations wanted to depend on other

for imperialist interest in the Pacific islands.
10. Explain how the United States acquired possessions in the Pacific.
11. Give examples of economic imperialism in Latin America.
12. Discuss the causes and results of the Spanish-American War.
13. Explain the Roosevelt Corollary.
14. Trace the development of tensions between Mexico and the United States after the Mexican Revolution of 1911.

SECTION 1

Focus/Motivation

Ask the class for a definition of imperialism *(Answers will vary. One suggestion might be: the practice of establishing colonies in order to control raw materials and markets.)* Then remind students that after 1870 Europe and the United States experienced new industrial growth. Have students speculate about the relationship between industrialism and imperialism by asking the following questions: What effect would industrialization have on a nation's resources after several decades? *(Raw materials might be depleted; excess manufactured goods might begin to accumulate.)* What steps might a nation take to solve these problems? *(It would acquire new lands rich with raw materials, and search for new markets for its goods.)* How might population growth during the Industrial Revolution have been related to the establishment of colonies? *(Nations might seek to export excess population.)* Ask students if they can think of other economic motives for imperialism. Have them record these motives in their notebooks and compare them with what they read in this section.

Presentation
Constructing a Chart (Average/Group)
Have the students draw a chart in their notebooks categorizing the motives for imperialism. Suggest that they use the following headings: *Political, Economic,* and *Social. (Students should enter the following under these headings: Economic — the need for self-sufficiency and new markets to invest surplus capital. Political — outlets for increased population, and the rise of nationalism. Social — religious motives and the "white man's burden.")*

nations for raw materials. Government leaders feared that in the event of war their countries would be at the mercy of an enemy. Thus the leaders of the industrial nations concluded that the best solution was to become self-sufficient by gaining control of the sources of the raw materials they needed.

Need for New Markets

After 1870 new technology made it possible to produce goods in enormous quantities. Indeed, manufacturers had to produce large quantities of goods in order to realize a profit. Only when the new and expensive machinery was used to full capacity could it pay for itself and generate profits for its owners.

Even with their rising standards of living, people in Europe and the United States could not buy all the goods on the market. In order to sell all of the goods they produced, industrialists began to look for new markets in nonindustrialized regions, especially in Asia, Africa, and Latin America.

Imperialists believed that if people in nonindustrialized areas were aware of manufactured goods and if the goods were available, they would buy them. Imperialists even argued that the customs of these people might be remolded to create new markets. Advocates of imperialism wrote articles describing how busy European and American factories would be, and how much profit they would earn, if only the people of central Africa could be persuaded to wear shirts and ties.

Many people argued that industrialized nations should control their new markets abroad, just as they controlled the colonial sources of their raw materials. Industrialists wanted their governments to guarantee them exclusive rights to sell in these markets. At the same time, they demanded protective tariffs to assure their exclusive markets at home.

Nationalism

Nationalism, a strong force throughout the 1800s, became particularly powerful between 1870 and 1914. Many nationalists now argued that having colonies added to their nations' strength and prestige. The recently unified nations of Germany and Italy felt that they had to build up colonial empires in order to compete with longtime colonial powers such as Great Britain, France, and the Netherlands. However, it is notable that the British, who already had a large empire, entered the imperialistic race for colonies as enthusiastically as did the Germans or Italians. National "honor" would not allow the British to watch territorial prizes go to rival nations.

Imperialists also viewed colonies as sources of troops for the rapidly growing armies of the day. Gurkhas and Pathans, the fighters of Nepal and Afghanistan, joined Australians and New Zealanders to build up British armies. Senegalese troops from West Africa fought for the French.

A large navy was even more important than a large army to protect widely scattered colonies and far-ranging merchant ships. For many years steam-powered ships burned coal, and the range of a steamship was "from coal to coal." Thus the coaling station, a place where warships and merchant ships could refuel, became strategically important for military and commercial purposes. Tiny islands with nothing to offer except their strategic location became coaling stations or naval bases. Often these stations became objects of fierce competition among naval powers.

Outlets for Population

Rapid population growth accompanied industrialization. Industrial development created many jobs, but in Europe there was not enough work to employ all the new job seekers. As a result, people left Europe in great numbers and immigrated to the United States, Latin America, and Australia.

Nationalists regretted seeing these people leave because the emigrants often became naturalized citizens of the countries in which they settled, breaking all ties with their former homelands. How much better, the nationalists thought, if emigrants would instead settle in one of the colonies. There they would remain loyal subjects under the political control of their home country. Although many new colonies were already heavily populated or were so remote that they attracted few European settlers, these drawbacks did not trouble the nationalists.

Missionary Motives

The urge to spread the Christian religion influenced colonial expansion during the 1500s and 1600s. Although Roman Catholic missionaries had continued their work since that time, they increased their activities during the period of

Learning from Pictures *This missionary classroom was in the Philippines. What types of knowledge did missionaries spread?* **medicine, hygiene, and sanitation, as well as Christianity**

imperialism. Growing numbers of Protestant missionaries also attempted to convert people in the colonies to Christianity.

Missionaries did other important work as well. Education became a regular missionary activity. Trained medical missionaries went out from Europe and the United States. Consequently, knowledge of medicine, hygiene, and sanitation spread with Christianity.

The "White Man's Burden"

Closely related to the missionary motive was the idea that the people of advanced Western nations had a duty to transmit Western ideas and techniques to more "backward" people. People were considered backward if their religion or their culture differed from those of the West.

The British poet Rudyard Kipling wrote a poem that urged members of his race to "take up the white man's burden."

> "Take up the white man's burden—
> Send forth the best ye breed—
> Go bind your sons to exile
> To serve your captives' need;
> To wait in heavy harness,
> On fluttered folk and wild—
> Your new-caught, sullen peoples,
> Half-devil and half-child."

Kipling was referring to the obligation to carry Western civilization to those he considered less fortunate. The French spoke of their "civilizing mission." The people of each industrial nation considered its civilization and culture to be the highest and, therefore, the one most suited for enlightening the "backward" peoples of the earth.

Opponents of imperialism claimed that the only burden the white man wanted to take up was the burden of colonial wealth, which he wanted to carry back home as fast as possible. Such opponents, however, formed a minority with little influence in their countries.

The Nature of Imperialism

Imperialism created bitter rivalries among the imperial powers and hatred among the colonized peoples. Rivalries led to the building of larger armies and navies and eventually to world conflict.

In the beginning, European governments did not actively plan imperialism. Usually it began with the work of individuals such as merchants, explorers, scientists, or missionaries. Sometimes the Europeans met with resistance and violence from the local inhabitants. Then European soldiers appeared, followed by government officials to protect the interests of their citizens. Builders, engineers, and technicians who opened mines and built roads,

601

1B, 1C, 1D, 4K, a4A, a4I, a4M

SECTION 1

Closure

On the chalkboard or an overhead projector, write the following quotations:

"What enterprise is more noble and more profitable than the reclamation from barbarism of fertile regions and large populations?" Winston Churchill

"Because a man has a black face and a different religion from our own, there is no reason why he should be treated like a brute." King Edward VII

Ask: Which quotation best sums up imperialist attitudes of the late 1800s?

Review Answers

1. ***imperialism:*** the domination by a powerful nation over the political, economic, and cultural affairs of another nation or region; ***colony:*** area in which a foreign nation gained control over a region and its local population; ***protectorate:*** region in which, although a native ruler kept his title, a foreign power actually ruled; ***condominium:*** region ruled by two nations as partners; ***concession;*** grant of economic rights and privileges in a given area; ***sphere of influence:*** region in which one nation has special economic and political privileges that are recognized by other nations

2. ***"white man's burden":*** idea that Western nations had a duty to transmit their ideas and techniques to

railroads, bridges, and dams usually followed the soldiers and officials. Then the region would be developed for the benefit of the developers. The local population had very little, if any, say in this process.

Loans to local rulers often provided the initial wedges of imperialism. If the local rulers spent the money recklessly, they found themselves heavily in debt and were forced to grant economic privileges. Economic privileges often led to political control. Europeans often used this means of gaining control of an area or region.

Several terms used in connection with imperialism need explanation. Originally a colony was a settlement established in another region by citizens of a country. Early examples of colonies include the ancient Greek colonies throughout the Mediterranean and the British colonies in North America. During the imperialistic era, however, a **colony** was an area in which a foreign nation gained total control over a given region and its local population. A colony was first gained by settlement or conquest and then annexed, becoming a part of the empire.

In a **protectorate,** the local ruler kept his title, but officials of the foreign power actually controlled the region. The "protecting" power kept out other foreign nations. In a **condominium,** two nations ruled a region as partners. A **concession** was the grant of economic rights and privileges in a given area. Concessions were given to foreign merchants or capitalists who wanted to trade, to build railroads, or to develop mineral deposits and other natural resources. Concessions held exclusively by one foreign power were called monopoly concessions. A **sphere of influence** was a region in which one nation had special, sometimes exclusive, economic and political privileges that were recognized by other nations.

SECTION 1 REVIEW

1. **Define** imperialism, colony, protectorate, condominium, concession, sphere of influence
2. **Identify** "white man's burden"
3. **Determining Cause and Effect** **(a)** Why did European interest in colonies decline between the late 1700s and the late 1800s? **(b)** Why was interest in colonies rekindled in the late 1800s?
4. **Summarizing Ideas** Describe four motives behind imperialism that were related to the Industrial Revolution.

2 Europeans Made Claims in North Africa and the Sudan

Throughout history many conquerors, including the Romans, the Byzantines, and the Arabs, imposed their rule on North Africa. In the 1800s most of the region belonged to the Ottoman Empire, although Turkish control was weak.

The French in North Africa

For a long time, expert Muslim seafarers known as the Barbary pirates operated off the coast of North Africa, taking a heavy toll on Mediterranean shipping. The term *Barbary* means "of the Berbers"—a people of North Africa who had converted to Islam during the 600s. Four Muslim states—Morocco, Algiers, Tunis, and Tripoli—made up the so-called Barbary States. (These countries are now called Morocco, Algeria, Tunisia, and Libya.)

The operations of the Barbary pirates gave the French, who wanted to compensate for the loss of French prestige after the defeat of Napoleon in 1815, an excuse to intervene in North Africa. The French complained about the Barbary pirates to the Algerian ruler and received what they considered an insulting reply. In 1830 a French force occupied Algeria, arrested the ruler, and settled down to stay. For more than 40 years, the French had to fight against almost continuous local rebellions and violence.

Economically, however, the struggle for Algeria proved worth the price. Many French people and other Europeans moved to Algeria, taking over the best land and running the nation's businesses. Algeria soon became an exporter of farm products, wine, and meat, playing an important role in French economic life.

Seizure of Tunisia. East of Algeria lies Tunisia, a small country with a long history. Its capital, Tunis, grew up near once-formidable Carthage, the rival of ancient Rome. A poor and underdeveloped country, Tunisia belonged to the Ottoman Empire. Its Turkish ruler, the bey of Tunis, spent money lavishly and cared little about financial management. He borrowed heavily from European bankers until they refused him further loans. The French government, seeing a chance to gain influence, lent him more money.

When the French loan was due, the bey raised the already high taxes, inciting rebellion. In 1869 a commission of the bey's creditors was established to restore order and reorganize Tunisia's finances. The commission included representatives of the British, French, and Italian governments.

All three of these nations wanted Tunisia. Italy, in the process of becoming united and eager to gain colonies, had encouraged many Italians to emigrate to Tunisia. In a complicated series of negotiations, France and Great Britain reached an agreement, which was announced in 1878 at the Congress of Berlin. The French were to have a free hand in Tunisia, and the British could occupy the island of Cyprus. Italy—new, poor, and inexperienced at the diplomatic game—was ignored.

In 1881 the French declared Tunisia a protectorate. The bey remained ruler in name, but the senior French official in Tunis wielded the power. French rule brought certain improvements to Tunisia—public order, roads, schools, industries, and sound finances. However, religious differences, local pride, and a rising spirit of nationalism inspired many Tunisians to work for independence.

Rivalry over Morocco. After acquiring Algeria and Tunisia, France felt it needed Morocco in order to protect its interests in North Africa. Morocco's strategic location along the narrow Strait of Gibraltar made it a tempting prize for imperialist nations. However, so many European countries wanted Morocco that each one was afraid to take it because doing so might trigger a war.

By the early 1900s, France was willing to take the necessary risks to acquire Morocco. As a result, France and Germany became entangled in a bitter dispute over Morocco. A compromise was eventually reached in 1911. France was given a free hand in Morocco, while Germany received territory in West Africa. Spain acquired the small northern strip of Spanish Morocco, and the city of Tangier came under international control. The rest of rich Morocco became a French protectorate.

The British in Egypt

Egypt had been part of the Ottoman Empire for centuries. However, by the mid-1800s, the empire was crumbling. The Turkish viceroy in Egypt, called the khedive (kuh • DEEV), had become almost entirely independent. The khedive still paid some tribute to the Ottoman sultan but ruled Egypt with absolute authority.

Learning from Pictures *French cavalry crushed resistance in Tunisia in order to forestall Italian ambitions in North Africa.*

the more "backward" peoples of Africa and Asia
3. (a) European interest in colonies declined because Great Britain and France had lost colonies in North America; the French Revolution and Napoleonic Wars kept attention focused on European affairs; capital formerly invested abroad was being used to finance industrialization at home; and democratic, nationalistic, and reform movements kept attention focused on internal affairs. **(b)** Interest in colonies was rekindled by the nationalistic desire to increase prestige and military strength, Christian missionary zeal, and the idea that the advanced Western nations had a duty to transmit their culture to "backward" people.
4. Motives for imperialism related to the Industrial Revolution included the desire for national self-sufficiency in raw materials, the need for new markets for manufactured goods, the search for new areas in which to invest capital profitably, and the need for areas where surplus populations could live.

SECTION 2

Focus/Motivation
Have students locate the Suez Canal on a map of the world. Then have them speculate on why control of the canal became such an important aspect of British imperial policy. *(Most students will note that the majority of British colonies lay to the east of*

1B, 4K, a1A, a1C, a4A, a4E, a4F, a4H, a4I, a4J

Africa. Ships traveling between Great Britain and these colonies had to sail around Africa. The Suez Canal offered a quicker route from Great Britain to the colonies in Asia, India, Australia, and New Zealand.)

Presentation Summarizing Ideas (Average/Group)
Have students summarize European imperialism in North Africa by asking them to construct a table. This table should show the countries of North Africa, the European nations that controlled these countries, and the reasons why the European nations took control. Encourage students to retain their tables for revision purposes.

READ
WRITE
INTERPRET
CONNECT
●THINK

BUILDING HISTORY STUDY SKILLS

Thinking About History: Determining Relevancy

As you do research in history, you often must sift through mountains of information to find what you need. As you do so, you need to be able to distinguish between relevant and irrelevant information. Relevant information includes the data that applies to your topic or purpose. For example, if you are researching the topic of how the Japanese resisted European imperialism, the shogun's response to Commodore Perry's ultimatum would be relevant information. A description of the beauty of Kyoto, the emperor's residence, would not be relevant because it would not help you explain the resistance to imperialism.

How to Determine Relevancy

To determine relevancy, follow these steps.

1. State the topic that you are researching.
2. Identify categories that will help you to organize the topic.
3. Look for definitions, descriptions, details, and evidence on your topic.
4. Examine each piece of information and relate it to the topic. Use the categories that you have devised and discard all the information that has no bearing on them.

Developing the Skill

If you were researching the impact that imperialism had on European economies, you might use two categories—*costs* and *benefits*. Read the following two selections and determine whether either would be relevant in your research. The first excerpt is from a speech by the British imperialist Joseph Chamberlain. The second is from the writings of Marco Polo.

> “We have suffered much in this country from depression of trade. We know how many of our fellow-subjects are at this moment unemployed. Is there any man in his senses who believes that the crowded populations of these islands [the British Isles] could exist for a single day if we were to cut adrift from us the great dependencies which now look to us for protection and assistance, and which are the natural markets for our trade? . . . If tomorrow it were possible, as some people apparently desire, to reduce by a stroke of the pen the British Empire to the dimensions of the United Kingdom, half at least of our population would be starved.”

> “On the interior side of the palace are large buildings with halls and chambers, where the Emperor's private property is placed, such as his treasures of gold, silver, gems, pearls and gold plate, and in which reside the ladies and secondary wives. These rooms are only for him and no one else has access to them.”

In the first excerpt, Chamberlain discusses one of the major benefits of imperialism. It provides trade outlets and also helps to feed the many people of Great Britain. It would be relevant in your research of the costs and benefits of imperialism.

The second excerpt, however, would not be relevant to your topic. It merely discusses Marco Polo's impression of the emperor's palace. In addition, Marco Polo lived centuries before the imperialism of the 1800s that you are researching.

Practicing the skill. Read the excerpt from Rudyard Kipling on page 601. Then determine whether it would provide relevant information about the costs and benefits of imperialism.

To apply this skill, see Applying History Study Skills on page 627.

Morocco's reception of the French ambassador

● **British Prime Minister Benjamin Disraeli bought the stock without waiting for Parliament's approval. If Parliament had not ratified the deal, Disraeli would have been personally liable for the huge loan he had taken out to make the purchase.**

In 1854 a French company headed by Ferdinand de Lesseps gained a concession to build a canal through the Isthmus of Suez. The Egyptian government bought almost half of the stock in the company. Individual French citizens bought most of the remaining shares.

Ismail Pasha, the khedive when the canal was completed in 1869, had very expensive habits and little concern with financial management. Between 1869 and 1879, he increased the foreign debt of his government by more than 20 times. Finally, foreign banks refused to lend him more money.

Ismail's solution to his financial problem was to sell Egypt's stock in the Suez Canal. This action provided an opportunity for the British, who wanted to control the canal because it was a vital link in the trade route between Great Britain and India, Australia, and New Zealand. In 1875 the ● British government bought the Egyptian stock and became the largest single stockholder. Because the British owned so much of the stock and because the rest was so widely scattered among private investors, the British gained virtual control of the canal.

After an Egyptian rebellion in 1882, a British fleet bombarded Alexandria, landed troops, and soon occupied the entire country. There they remained, claiming that they had to safeguard the Suez Canal, their main route to India. The Egyptian government remained outwardly independent, but the British actually ruled.

Anglo-Egyptian Sudan

The Sudan, a vast geographic region of savannas south of the Sahara, stretches from the Atlantic Ocean to the Nile River valley and beyond. In the imperialistic era, the term *Sudan* also referred to a specific eastern part of this region south of Egypt. Arabs and various local tribes inhabited this region, which Egypt claimed.

After Great Britain established control over Egypt in 1882, the Sudan became important to the British. Since the upper Nile River flows through the Sudan, control of the region would afford a chance to build dams to store water for irrigation and to control the flow of water in the lower Nile. France also wanted the Sudan, both because of its possessions farther west and because it already had a toehold on the Red Sea (French Somaliland) and wanted to extend its territory inland.

In 1881 Muhammad Ahmad, taking the title Mahdi, or Islamic savior, organized a revolt in the Sudan. Mahdi's troops captured Khartoum and established a government that ruled until 1898. In that year, Great Britain ordered a military force to move into the Sudan. Under General Herbert Kitchener, these troops defeated a Sudanese army at Omdurman and then moved farther south.

Meanwhile the French sent an expedition from the French Congo, under Major J. B. Marchand. Marchand and his small force of Senegalese soldiers made a daring two-year journey through some 3,000 miles (5,000 kilometers) of tropical rain forest. In July 1898 Marchand reached Fashoda, on the upper Nile River, and raised the French flag.

The British force reached Fashoda in September, and Kitchener insisted that the French flag be lowered and the British and Egyptian flags be raised. Tension was relieved only when both officers decided to ask their governments for further instructions.

Since neither government really wanted war, they negotiated a settlement of what became known as the Fashoda Incident. The French recognized the British as masters of the Sudan, in return for recognition of all their possessions in French West Africa. Great Britain and Egypt established a condominium in the Sudan, known as the Anglo-Egyptian Sudan. In this way Great Britain established political dominance of this area.

The Italians in Libya

Desert covered most of Tripoli, a region lying to the west of Egypt. Like Tunisia, it belonged to the Ottoman Empire, but Turkish control was weak. Italy was interested in joining the other European powers by establishing an empire. The region had almost no economic value, but, as one diplomat put it, when Italy came to the table, only the crumbs were left. So Italy decided to eat the crumbs.

First, Italy secured guarantees of neutrality from several European powers. Then in 1911 Italy declared war on the Ottoman Empire. Although the Turks showed surprisingly strong resistance, the Italians finally defeated them.

Italy took Tripoli as a colony and renamed it Libya. It was a profitless victory. Except for a narrow strip along the coast, the land was barren. The small population violently opposed Italian rule. As a result, the expense of maintaining troops in Libya drained the Italian economy.

SECTION 2

Closure

Ask: How would you characterize the motives of the European imperial powers in North Africa—political, economic, or social? *(Students should point out that all three factors played a role and should provide examples.)*

Review Answers

1. ***Barbary pirates:*** Muslim seafarers who operated off the Mediterranean coast of North Africa, taking a huge toll on European shipping; ***Fashoda Incident:*** 1898 crisis in the Sudan brought on by conflicting British and French interests there
2. ***Algeria:*** northwestern Africa; ***Tunisia:*** east of Algeria; ***Suez Canal:*** link between Red and Mediterranean seas; ***Anglo-Egyptian Sudan:*** south of Egypt, west of Ethiopia
3. (a) The operations of the Barbary pirates gave the French, who wanted to compensate for the loss of French prestige after the defeat of Napoleon in 1815, an excuse to intervene in North Africa. The French complained about the Barbary pirates to the Algerian ruler and received what they considered an insulting reply. In 1830 a French force occupied Algeria. **(b)** The French loaned the bey of Tunis money. When the French loan was due, the bey raised the already high taxes, inciting rebellion. A commission of the bey's creditors was established to restore order and also to

605

1C, 1D, 4K, a4A, a4H, a4L

● Point out that the capital of Liberia, Monrovia, is named after President James Monroe of the United States.

reorganize Tunisia's finances. An international commission negotiated a settlement between the several European powers that wanted to control Tunisia. By this settlement, the French were given a free hand in Tunisia. A few years later, the French declared Tunisia a protectorate. **(c)** After acquiring Algeria and Tunisia, France felt it needed Morocco to protect its interests in North Africa. After 1900, France and Germany attempted to occupy the territory until a compromise settled the bitter dispute. Germany received territory in West Africa while the French received a free hand in Morocco.
4. (a) The financially-strapped khedive, Ismail Pasha, sold Egypt's stock in the Suez Canal to finance his expensive habits. The British purchased the Egyptian stock and became the largest single stockholder, gaining virtual control of the canal.
b) After an Egyptian rebellion in 1882, a British fleet bombarded Alexandria, landed troops, and occupied the country. They remained there, claiming they had to safeguard the Suez Canal, their main route to India.
5. After Great Britain established control over Egypt, the Sudan became important to the British. Since the upper Nile River flows through the Sudan, control of the region would afford a chance to build dams for irrigation and control the flow of water.

SECTION 2 REVIEW

1. **Identify** Barbary pirates, Fashoda Incident
2. **Locate** Algeria, Tunisia, Suez Canal, Anglo-Egyptian Sudan
3. **Summarizing Ideas** **(a)** How did the French gain Algeria? **(b)** Tunisia? **(c)** Morocco?
4. **Understanding Ideas** **(a)** How did the British gain control of the Suez Canal? **(b)** How did they become virtual rulers of Egypt?
5. **Interpreting Ideas** Why did the British want to control the Sudan?

3 Several European Nations Carved up SubSaharan Africa

In the 1500s and the 1600s, the first great period of European colonization, several nations established trading posts on the east and west coasts of Sub-Saharan Africa. The imperialism of the late 1800s increased interest in this vast portion of Africa.

Competition for West Africa

West Africa had been a major center of the slave trade. First the Portuguese and the Dutch, and later the British and the French, had established trading posts along the coast. When most European countries abolished the slave trade in the early 1800s, these former slaving centers turned increasingly to other types of commerce. They traded in palm oil, hides and feathers, ivory, rubber, and other natural products from the interior. Eager to control this trade, the Europeans began to push inland.

By pushing into the interior, European countries sought to link their coastal possessions. In the "bulge" of western Africa, the French pushed inland and claimed the ancient city of Tombouctou. They also increased the number of commercial settlements in the coastal areas of French Guinea, the Ivory Coast, and Dahomey. By 1900 France had claimed a vast area called French West Africa (see map, page 607).

In many cases the French as well as other Europeans met with fierce resistance in their drive to colonize Africa. In what is today Senegal, for example, the ruler Samari Touré signed an agreement with the French in the late 1800s. When the French broke their part of the bargain Touré led his people in revolt. For seven years the French were unable to subdue the fiesty Touré and his forces. Finally in 1898, the superior fire power of the French troops paid off, and Touré was captured. In another instance of heroic resistance, the king of Dahomey resisted the French until 1894.

The British competed with the French throughout West Africa. They too sought to connect their coastal settlements and expand into the interior. The Gold Coast (modern Ghana) particularly interested them. From their coastal bases there, the British thrust inland, coming up against the powerful African kingdom of Ashanti. By 1901, however, Great Britain had annexed all the territory of Ashanti and made the Gold Coast a colony.

The British also expanded into Nigeria, a territory to the east of the Gold Coast that took its name from the Niger, one of the great rivers of ● Africa. Control of the Niger River assured control of a huge region rich in resources. In 1861 the British annexed the port city of Lagos and then pushed steadily inland. African merchants and Muslim states resisted the British. But British military forces crushed all African resistance and made Nigeria a protectorate.

By the early 1900s, France, Britain, Germany Spain, and Portugal had claimed all of West Africa except Liberia (see map, page 607). Settled by freed slaves from the United States, Liberia had become an independent republic in 1847.

Although economically and militarily weak, Liberia maintained its independence. It no doubt would have become the protectorate of an ambitious European power if not for its special relationship to the United States. American diplomatic pressure discouraged European attempts to take over the small republic.

Competition for Central Africa

Henry Stanley's successful search for Dr. David Livingstone did much to publicize the possibilities for imperialistic development in Africa. Stanley tried but failed to interest the British government in the vast area he had explored. He then turned to King Leopold II of Belgium, who did want the region. After much national and international maneuvering, Leopold, acting as a private citizen, carved out a personal empire of 900,000 square miles (2.3 million square kilometers).

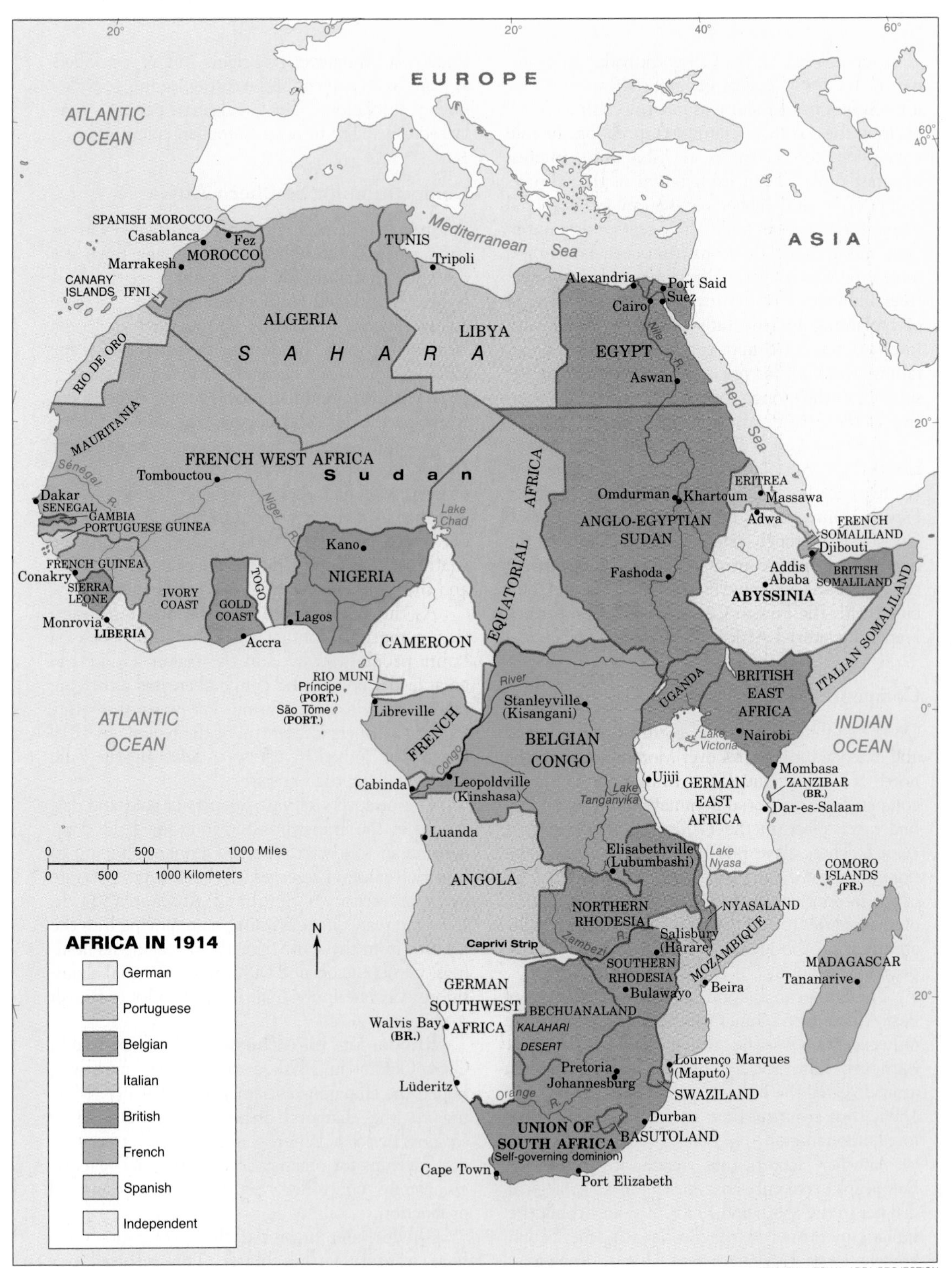

SECTION 3

Focus/Motivation

Read the following poem by the African poet David Diop. Ask students to comment on the poem by asking the following questions: What is the poet's point of view on the effect of imperialism on the Africans? How does it compare with the point of view of the poem by Rudyard Kipling quoted on page 601?

"The White Man killed my father,
My father was proud. . . .
The White man burnt my brother beneath the noonday sun.
My brother was strong.
His hands ran with black blood.
The White Man turned to me;
And in the Conqueror's voice said,
"Boy! a chair, a napkin, a drink."

Presentation
Illustrating Ideas (Average/Group)

Have students refer to the map of Africa on this page. Then ask them to suggest why there was friction between France, Germany, and Great Britain over their African possessions. *(Most students will point out that possessions held by one European power prevented another European power from holding huge tracts of Africa. For example, German East Africa broke*

607

1D, 4K

● *Boer* is the Afrikaans word for "farmer."

up a line of British possessions stretching from Egypt to South Africa.)

608

Leopold's rule of the Congo provides an example of the worst aspects of imperialism. His only interest was in extracting as much wealth as possible from the colony. Forming a corporation, he sold concessions to speculators who shared his interest in a fast profit. Their exploitation of the Congo's supply of natural rubber became an international scandal. Leopold set aside whole regions as monopolies and uprooted Africans from their homes and forced them to collect rubber. Large areas of rubber trees and vines were destroyed without any thought of replanting for the future. Finally, faced with international criticism of conditions in the Congo, falling world rubber prices, and dwindling rubber supplies in the Congo, Leopold transferred ownership to the Belgian government in 1908.

North of Leopold's Congo, Pierre de Brazza founded the city of Brazzaville on the lower Zaire (Congo) River in 1880, thus laying the basis for French claims to an area known as the French Congo. The French extended their claims to the northeast, gaining control of a large region north of the Congo and adjoining French West Africa. Combined with the French Congo, this region formed French Equatorial Africa (see map, page 607).

Competition for East Africa

On the east coast of Africa, Portugal strengthened and extended its control over Mozambique. To the north of Mozambique, Great Britain and Germany competed for territorial domination. Slave raiding had taken place in the 1700s and 1800s in East Africa. These slave raids disrupted political relations among African peoples and made penetration of the interior easier. At the same time, the efforts of missionaries to end the slave trade focused public attention on the area and helped to justify European intervention.

The European nations rapidly carved the rest of East Africa into colonies (see map, page 607). The only exception was the ancient empire of Ethiopia. Although Italy invaded Ethiopia, the Ethiopian army defeated the Italians at Adwa (AHD • wuh) in 1896, thus ensuring their country's freedom from foreign domination.

Another factor that made it easier for ● Europeans to colonize East Africa was an ecological disaster in the 1880s and 1890s. Scholars think the Italians in Eritrea or the Russians in the Sudan brought cattle carrying a fatal disease known as rinderpest. Whatever its origins, rinderpest killed as many as 80 percent of the cattle, leading to widespread starvation. The weakened people often lacked the ability to resist European colonization.

Competition for Southern Africa

European settlement in South Africa began in 1652, when Dutch settlers founded Cape Town as a resupplying station for ships sailing to the East Indies. The Dutch settlement grew into a large colony called Cape Colony. During the Napoleonic Wars of the early 1800s, the British seized Cape Colony, which then became a British possession.

As British administration became established, many people left the colony and moved to the north and east. These people were Boers (BOHRZ)—descendants of the original Dutch settlers, who had their own language, known as Afrikaans. In the new territories the Boers carved out three colonies—Natal (nuh • TAL), on the southeast coast, the Orange Free State to the west, and the Transvaal (trans • VAHL) to the north.

As the Boers moved into the new territories, they came into contact with the Zulu people, a Bantu people who lived in the region. Under the great leader Shaka, the Zulu had created a thriving empire with a strong army. For years this army fought the Boers for control of the region. In 1879 the British joined in the war, defeating the Zulu and destroying their empire.

The discovery of vast reserves of gold and diamonds in the Transvaal soon intensified the competition in southern Africa. Germany, hoping to find rich mineral reserves, declared a protectorate over the territory of Southwest Africa in 1884. In the same year, Great Britain began moving into the interior from the south, greatly increasing its holdings. Closely associated with these territorial acquisitions was one individual, Cecil Rhodes, a British speculator.

Rhodes and his influence. Rhodes arrived in Cape Colony in 1870, a sickly young man who hoped the climate would improve his health. Moving to the diamond fields in northern Cape Colony, he soon demonstrated a talent for business and a genius for organization. Within 20 years he completely controlled South African diamond production.

Rhodes later organized the colonization of a huge territory farther north. This territory was named Rhodesia after him. In 1890 Rhodes sent several hundred adventurers into Rhodesia in search of gold. He staked his reputation and much of his fortune on this hope. When little gold was found, it became essential for Rhodes to make up his losses by increasing production and profits in the Transvaal mines.

In 1895 a colleague of Rhodes tried to topple the Transvaal government, which had restricted mining operations. The attempt failed, but Great Britain's apparent support of the attempt made relations between the Boers and the British openly hostile. In 1899 war broke out. After three years of costly fighting, the British defeated the Boers and imposed a settlement that favored mining interests.

To ensure Boer support of the peace, the British allowed the Boers to continue using the Afrikaans language in their schools and courts. The British also provided funds for Boers—though not for Africans—to rebuild their destroyed farms. In 1910 a federal constitution united the Cape Colony, Natal, the Transvaal, and the Orange Free State into the Union of South Africa, a British dominion. The constitution made it virtually impossible for nonwhites to be given voting rights. The settlement of the South African War, or the Boer War, thus laid the basis for the later development of a system of complete racial segregation.

European Government in Africa

The European powers that established empires in Africa generally used one of two forms of government in their territories. France, Germany, Belgium, and Portugal practiced direct rule. Great Britain practiced indirect rule.

Direct rule. In colonies with **direct rule,** the imperialist power controlled all levels of government and appointed its own officials to govern. The Europeans based this type of government on their belief that the Africans could not rule themselves. As a result of this belief, the Europeans practiced **paternalism,** the system of governing colonies in much the way that parents guide their children.

The European nations practiced various forms of direct rule. For example, the French encouraged **assimilation,** in which the people of the colonies abandoned their local cultures and adopted all aspects of French culture. When the French judged that most of the people of a colony had been assimilated, the territory would be made a department of France.

Indirect rule. Under the British system of **indirect rule,** a British governor and a council of advisers made colonial laws, but local rulers exerted some authority. The British chose indirect rule largely because they lacked enough workers to staff all the governments of their vast empire, which by then covered almost one-fourth of the earth's land surface.

Costs and Benefits of Imperialism

Imperialism was a harsh experience for all of Africa. However, the costs and the benefits resulting from European expansion were unevenly distributed across the continent.

The Europeans constructed roads and railroads. These means of transportation were used mostly to connect areas of European settlement with the coast. They also served to make African products available for the world market. The Europeans built cities, but crowded and unsanitary slums grew up around them. Europeans introduced medicines to help people live longer and healthier lives. However, development reduced the amount of land available for crop cultivation, contributing to malnutrition among the African people. One of

Learning from Pictures *This battle during the Boer War took place in the Transvaal. What other regions were united into the Union of South Africa?* ●

SECTION 3

Closure

Ask: Why did it take so long for Europeans to penetrate into the African interior? *(Students should point out that at first the Europeans wanted only trading posts. Later they wanted colonies.)*

Review Answers

1. *direct rule:* colonial situation in which an imperialist power controls all levels of government and appoints its own officials to govern; ***paternalism:*** system of governing colonies in much the way parents guide their children; ***assimilation:*** situation in which people abandon their own culture and adopt another; ***indirect rule:*** situation in which representatives of an imperialist power make colonial laws, but local rulers continue to exert some authority

2. *Ashanti:* powerful West African kingdom whose territory was annexed by the British to form the Gold Coast colony; ***Henry Stanley:*** journalist and explorer who located Dr. David Livingstone; ***Leopold II:*** Belgian king who created a personal empire in the Congo region; ***Pierre de Brazza:*** French explorer who founded Brazzaville in the French Congo in 1880; ***Boers;*** descendants of original Dutch settlers in South Africa; ***Afrikaans:*** language used by the Boers; ***Cecil Rhodes:*** speculator instrumental in establishing British control over the whole of South Africa

1B, 1C, 1D, 2D, 4K, a4A, a4E, a4G, a4I, a4M

● Discussion topic: How imperialism in Asia differed from imperialism in Africa

3. By pushing into the interior, European countries sought to link their coastal possessions. The interior regions had resources European countries wanted to control.
4. (a) The Boer War had its roots in the Transvaal government's restrictions on the development of gold fields. Apparent British support of an attempt to topple the Transvaal government led to openly hostile relations between the Boers and the British.
(b) After the war the British imposed a settlement that favored mining interests, but the Boers were allowed to continue using the Afrikaans language in their schools and courts. The British also provided funds for Boers to rebuild their destroyed farms. Later, a federal constitution united Cape Colony, Natal, Transvaal, and the Orange Free State into the British dominion of the Union of South Africa. This constitution made it almost impossible for nonwhites to be given voting rights, thus setting the stage for the development of a system of complete racial segregation.
5. The imperialist powers built roads and railroads, making African produce available for the world market. They built cities, but crowded and unsanitary slums appeared. New medicines prolonged life, but Europeans contributed to malnutrition by reducing the land available for crop cultivation. In some areas economic prosperity and a

the great tragedies of imperialism was the economic effect it had on the people. Europeans paid Africans the lowest possible wages, thus forcing them to become migrant workers. As such, imperialism changed the very fabric of African society—the family—because migrant workers would move to cities and leave their families at home to eke out meager existences.

Despite the hardships, some individuals and groups in African society did benefit. In West Africa, profits that Africans earned from the rubber trade helped to finance the cultivation of cocoa plants. The spread of cocoa farming, in turn, brought prosperity and raised living standards. In Uganda, British support of cotton cultivation gave rise to a large class of wealthy peasant producers. Even in South Africa, the gold discoveries brought prosperity for African farmers for a brief period, who sold more food to the growing population.

The introduction of Western laws and courts often benefited the unprotected members of society, especially women. Africans adapted to foreign cultures that missionary and government schools introduced. From the experience came a new group of African leaders in the 1900s.

SECTION 3 REVIEW

1. **Define** direct rule, paternalism, assimilation, indirect rule
2. **Identify** Ashanti, Henry Stanley, Leopold II, Pierre de Brazza, Boers, Afrikaans, Cecil Rhodes
3. **Interpreting Ideas** Why did the Europeans want territorial possessions in the interior of Africa?
4. **Determining Cause and Effect** **(a)** What were the reasons for British and Boer competition? **(b)** What were the results of the Boer War?
5. **Evaluating Ideas** What were some of the costs and benefits of imperialism in Africa?

4 Europeans Expanded Their Influence in South and East Asia

The strong forces of imperialism that swept Africa in the 1800s brought important and fateful changes to South and East Asia. In these regions, however, the changes were not as abrupt as they were in so ● many parts of Africa.

British Imperialism in India

As you read in Chapter 18, the British government ruled India directly after the Sepoy Rebellion in 1858. But British control of the subcontinent remained essentially the same as it had been under the British East India Company. British India still made up about three-fifths of the subcontinent. The rest consisted of over 550 states, headed by local princes. The British government, through its viceroy, controlled the local princes' right to make treaties and declare war, either with foreign countries or with one another. Great Britain also regulated Indian internal affairs when it seemed necessary.

To control both British India and Indian states, the British government used the old Roman method of "divide and rule." It granted favors to those princes who cooperated with British rule and dealt harshly with those who did not. It treated Hindus and Muslims equally but did little to ease religious hatred between them.

The British were interested chiefly in profitable trade in India. To achieve it, they maintained public order by ending the many local wars and massacres. They set up an efficient governmental administration that built roads, bridges, railroads, factories, hospitals, and schools. They tried to improve agricultural methods, public health, and sanitation.

Many of these improvements helped the Indians, but other effects of British rule were harmful. The Indian handicraft industry almost disappeared. British cotton mills made cloth so cheaply that it could be transported to India and sold for less than handwoven Indian products. Local artisans had to search for work in the cities or eke out a meager living from farming small plots of land.

During the late 1800s and early 1900s, British rule in India had created a situation in which the peoples of two very different cultures lived side by side with almost no contact. The British had imposed themselves above Indian society as a superior race, a sort of super-caste. The British formed exclusive social circles, open to any European but closed to any Indian, no matter how distinguished. Posted everywhere—in railway carriages and waiting rooms and even on park benches—were signs reading "for Europeans only." For generations all Indians were subjected to contemptuous treatment by the British.

Critical thinking activity: Discuss with students how imperialism often created a clash between traditional values and progress. Ask students to think of parts of the world where this clash is still going on today.

The Rise of Indian Nationalism

Although the British did not mingle socially with the Indians, Western civilization had a powerful impact on India. For one thing, it led to a serious conflict of values.

Both Hinduism and Islam stressed age-old customs and respect for tradition. Western culture, on the other hand, emphasized material progress and political change. Indians, especially educated Indians, regarded Europeans as materialists who cared little for the higher values of mind, soul, and spirit.

British education had a profound effect on India. Before British rule, only Brahmans were educated. Indian merchants might be schooled only in reading, writing, and mathematics. Men of other castes and all women went uneducated. During the 1800s the British East India Company, the British government, missionaries, and private individuals started schools and colleges in India. They educated only a small percentage of the people, but among other things, they taught them about nationalism and the ideals of democracy. Indian scholars could, and did, use quotations from British writers to condemn British imperialism. Many Indians also came to learn about and believe in the ideas of socialism.

A movement for Indian self-rule began in the late 1800s. Not all Indian nationalists supported the same approach. Some, especially those who had been educated in British schools and universities, wanted to advance toward independence gradually and by democratic methods. They also wanted to keep certain aspects of Western culture and industry that they thought could benefit India. The Indian National Congress, a political party founded in 1885, advocated this moderate approach.

Other people wanted to break all ties with Great Britain in an effort to sweep away all Western influence. The Hindus, particularly, wished to revolt not only against Western culture but also against Islam. The views of this second group alarmed Indian Muslims. They were a minority in the land, and British rule protected them from discrimination and violence. They feared that if British rule were removed, their future might be in danger. The Muslims were therefore much less enthusiastic about driving out the British than were the Hindus. In 1906 Muslims formed the Muslim League to protect their interests. The independence movement in India gathered strength very slowly, and the British kept the country under a tight rein.

Learning from Pictures *In 1875 the Prince of Wales, later to become Emperor of India, took a tour of India. Here the city of Bombay welcomes him.*

rise in the standard of living occurred. Other results included the introduction of Western laws and courts and the building of schools.

SECTION 4

Focus/Motivation

Have students study the picture on this page. Ask the following questions: What does the picture show about the life of the British in India? What does it show about the relationship between the British and the Indians? *(Most students will suggest the picture shows that the British led lives of luxury, pomp, and ceremony, and that the Indians were forced to serve the British.)*

Presentation

Analyzing Ideas (Average/Group)

Lead the class in a discussion of the role that Western thought and ideas played in the modernization of Japan during the Meiji Restoration. A good source for information on this topic is "The Modernization of Japan" in Sydney Eisen's and Maurice Filler's *The Human Adventure,* vol. 2 (Harcourt Brace Jovanovich).

The Meiji Restoration in Japan

While imperialism remained firmly entrenched in India, it took a different course in Japan. Although European influence in Japan became strong after the overthrow of the Tokugawa shogunate in 1868, Europeans did not dominate Japan as they did India. Rather, the Japanese under the rule of the Meiji emperors controlled their own affairs and began to industrialize.

Real power in the Meiji government was exercised not by the emperor but by samurai from several domains in western Japan. These samurai had grown impatient under the strict, hereditary system of the Tokugawa period, in which birth, not ability, counted. They persuaded the emperor that Japan must take the road toward modernization. Even though the samurai were members of Japan's traditional ruling class, they advocated and carried out radical changes in Japan.

The Meiji Restoration, as the change from the Tokugawa shogunate to imperial government is called, was really a social, political, and economic revolution. It corresponded in its scope to the revolutions in the Western nations during the 1700s.

The old system of social classes was abolished, and all Japanese became free to choose the occupations they wished. The government established universal compulsory education and almost wiped out illiteracy. For nearly 300 years Japanese commoners had been denied the right even to own swords. Only samurai, as members of the warrior class, had been allowed to bear arms. Now this restriction was removed, and a new, highly centralized and modernized military, in which all Japanese men had to serve, was created.

A centralized government replaced the political system of the Tokugawa period. The city of Yedo, renamed Tokyo, became the new imperial capital, and the domains fell under the control of government officials. The central government imposed taxes on the Japanese people as a whole, and it established laws that applied to the entire population.

During the 1880s an appointed commission wrote a constitution, which the emperor accepted

Learning from Pictures
The Meiji empress inspects the rice fields of the Imperial Palace. Notice the Western-style military uniforms worn by her escorts.

612

Point out that the West continues to be fascinated by Oriental styles. For example, Oriental styles in furniture are very popular in the United States.

PAINTING

The Influence of Japanese Art

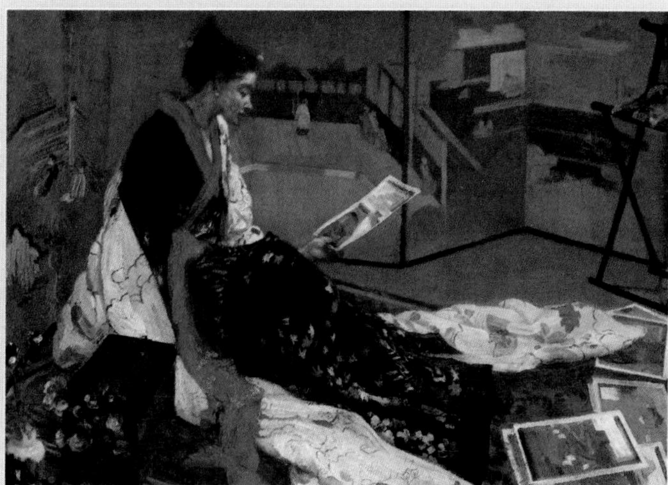

Courtesy of the Freer Gallery of Art, Smithsonian Institution, Washington, D. C. # 04.75

Although she wears a kimono and is studying Japanese woodblock prints, the woman in this painting is not Oriental. Rather she is a model used by the American painter James McNeill Whistler (1834–1903). Many years later Whistler would paint a picture of his mother in a similar pose but with more restrained colors.

Like many artists of his time, Whistler studied in Paris. There he discovered the enchantments of Oriental art, particularly Japanese prints, which became increasingly popular in Europe during the period. Though his paintings reflected the influence of Europe, Whistler eventually adapted the use of both Oriental subjects and techniques.

Whistler was a leader of the new attitude of "art for art's sake." A flamboyant figure for his time, Whistler sued an art critic in 1878 who criticized him for "flinging a pot of paint in the public's face." Although Whistler won the libel suit, the horrendous court costs eventually forced him into bankruptcy.

and proclaimed in 1889. The constitution had two major purposes—to impress Western governments with Japan's progress and to provide the Japanese people a limited voice in national affairs.

The leaders of the Meiji government were monarchists who did not believe in democracy. However, they knew from their study of Western history that political absolutism led to popular discontent. Although the new constitution gave the emperor supreme power, it established a two-house national assembly, called the Diet, one house of which was elected. Initially, only those Japanese who owned a substantial amount of property had the right to vote, and the elected house of the Diet had very limited powers.

The new constitution and the Diet satisfied most Japanese. The government did not have to deal with the problems of political instability that afflicted so many other nations that were struggling to modernize. It could concentrate its energies and its resources on promoting industrialization and economic development. Japanese leaders believed that their nation had to either catch up with the Western nations in technology and wealth or face the humiliation of foreign domination.

Industrialization

Fortunately, Japan was in a position to make rapid economic and industrial progress. Its traditional agricultural economy had created surpluses that could be used to finance industrialization. The government invited foreign experts to Japan to help modernize transportation and communications. The government also used factory machinery purchased from several Western countries and enacted a new commercial code to encourage private investment in industrial enterprises.

By 1900 Japan had acquired the foundations of an industrial economy. Railroads, the telegraph, and telephones linked Japanese cities. Banks existed throughout the country. Light manufacturing, especially of textiles, was well developed, and Japan had begun exporting machine-made cotton cloth and silk to other countries. The money that these exports earned helped to pay for imports of industrial raw materials such as iron and petroleum, which Japan lacked. The Japanese then used these raw materials in steel production and shipbuilding. Although Japan's economy remained smaller and weaker than the economies

613

1B, 4K, 5A

of the Western nations, the gap gradually narrowed. In fact, Japan was the first country in Asia to industrialize.

Nevertheless, Japan's leaders continued to feel threatened by imperialist expansion in Asia. This fear motivated the Japanese to embark on a course of imperialist expansion themselves.

The Sino-Japanese War

The territory that most interested Japan was the nearby Korean Peninsula, long a dependency of China. Korean authorities had to refer all matters involving foreign relations to the Chinese emperor. No foreigners were allowed into the country. However, Russia, France, and the United States were all interested in gaining trade privileges there. Fearing that a Western-controlled Korea might threaten its safety, Japan began to demand privileges in the Korean Peninsula.

Japan maintained that Korea was independent, while China still claimed Korea as a dependency. In 1876, out of this confusion, Japan secured a treaty that opened three Korean ports to Japanese trade. China then allowed the Koreans to make similar treaties with six Western nations.

Learning from Pictures *This was the scene at Yokohama in 1871, as Prince Iwakura left for the United States on Japan's first foreign mission.*

In 1894 a rebellion broke out in Korea. Both Japan and China sent armed forces to end it. It was a turbulent situation that exploded into the brief Sino-Japanese War, in which Japan defeated China. (*Sino* means "Chinese.")

In addition to trade privileges, the Japanese wanted territory. The Treaty of Shimonoseki (shim • uh • noh • SEK • ee) in 1895 forced China to recognize the complete independence of Korea. China also had to give to Japan the island of Formosa and the nearby islands, the Pescadores. In another provision of the treaty, China gave Japan the strategic Liaodong (LEE • AYOOH • DOOHNG) Peninsula on the southern coast of Manchuria. At the tip of the Liaodong Peninsula, which juts into the Yellow Sea, lay the excellent harbor of Port Arthur (see map, page 615). Finally, China also had to pay Japan an indemnity equivalent to $150 million.

Russia and the East Asian Mainland

The Treaty of Shimonoseki displeased the Russians, who did not want a strong power in Korea close to their naval base at Vladivostok. In addition, Russia wanted to build a railroad across Manchuria and the Liaodong Peninsula to Port Arthur.

With these plans afoot, Russia was more than willing to help China keep Japan away from the Asian mainland. France, which had recently signed an alliance with Russia, was also willing to help. Germany, eager to be on better terms with Russia and perhaps to weaken the alliance between France and Russia, also offered its services. In a joint note, Russia, France, and Germany advised the Japanese government to withdraw from the Liaodong Peninsula.

The Japanese were furious, but they were not able to resist such powerful forces. They gave the Liaodong Peninsula back to China in return for a larger indemnity. France and Russia gave China loans to help pay the indemnity to Japan.

The Price of European Assistance

China had to pay a price for this financial help, however. China had to pledge that no foreign power would receive any special rights in Chinese

614

1A, 4K, 5A, a4B, a4C

● **Discussion topic: Why Japan was able to maintain its independence, while China fell increasingly under foreign domination**

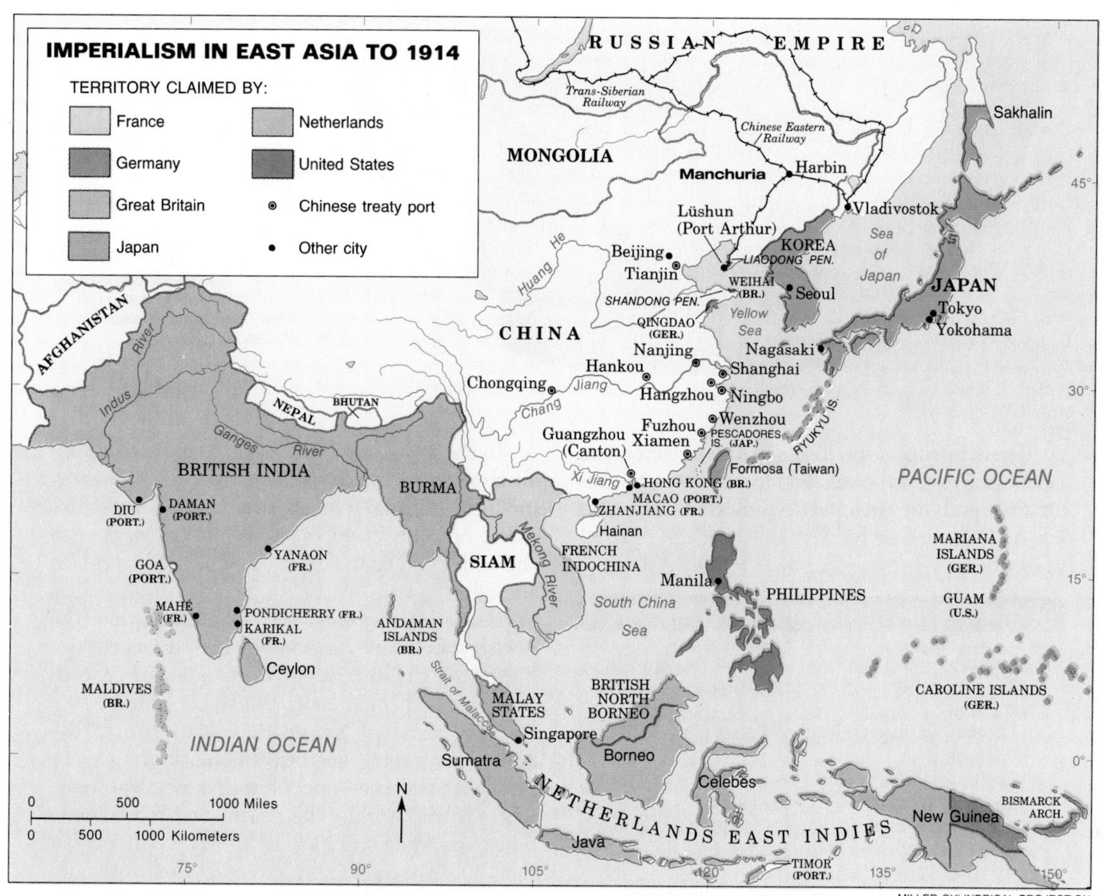

Learning from Maps *The Portuguese empire in East Asia had dwindled by 1914. What two trading centers did Portugal still control?* **Macao and Goa**

financial affairs unless France and Russia received them too. Great Britain and Germany quickly made similar loans with similar provisions.

Beginning in 1896, the Europeans placed still more demands on China. France demanded and received special trading privileges and the right to develop mineral resources in southern China. It also received a 99-year lease to the territory of Zhanjiang and the right to build a railroad linking southern China with the French protectorate in ● Indochina.

Germany received a 99-year lease to the port of Qingdao (CHING•DOW) and surrounding territory on the south shore of the Shandong Peninsula. Germany also received mining rights and permission to build a railway in Shandong.

Great Britain would not be left out. It negotiated for more trading privileges in the Chang Jiang valley and the right to build a naval base at Weihai on the north shore of the Shandong Peninsula to balance the German base at Qingdao.

Russia demanded and received the right to lease a tax-free right-of-way for its railroad across Manchuria—to be called the Chinese Eastern Railway. It also received permission to police the Manchurian route as well as certain other extraterritorial privileges. In effect, northern Manchuria would be under Russian economic and military domination. In a further and secret treaty, Russia and China formed an alliance pledging mutual assistance in case either should become involved in war with Japan.

SECTION 4

Closure

On the chalkboard or an overhead projector, write the following quotation by Lord Curzon, viceroy of India from 1899 to 1905: "As long as we rule India we are the greatest power in the world. If we lose it we shall drop straight away to a third-rate power."

Ask: Does this quotation help to explain the way the British behaved in India? Why or why not? *(Students might mention that the British acted the way they did because they believed India was vital to their prestige.)*

Review Answers

1. ***Indian National Congress:*** Indian political party, founded in 1885, that advocated advance to independence through democratic means and the adoption of certain aspects of Western culture; ***Muslim League:*** organization formed in 1906 by Indian Muslims to protect their interests; ***Treaty of Shimonoseki;*** ended Sino-Japanese War in 1895; ***Chinese Eastern Railway:*** Russian railroad across Manchuria
2. ***Formosa:*** island off east coast of central China; ***Liaodong Peninsula:*** located in Yellow Sea area between Korea and Manchuria; ***Vladivostok:*** Russian port on Sea of Japan located near Korea and eastern Manchuria
3. Among the beneficial effects of British rule were the maintenance of public order; the improvement of

615

government; protection against foreign invasion; and better transportation, education, and health facilities. However, competition from cheap British imports caused the Indian handicraft industry to disappear and many artisans to lose their means of livelihood. Another harmful effect of British rule was the creation of a wide social gulf between the British and Indians.

4. (a) The Meiji Restoration was revolutionary because it changed the social, political, and economic structure of Japan.
(b) The system of social classes was abolished, and universal compulsory education and the draft were established. A highly centralized and modernized military was created, and a centralized government was established. This government concentrated its energies on industrialization and economic development.

5. Chinese-Japanese competition for control of Korea led to the Sino-Japanese War. After its defeat, China was forced to recognize the independence of Korea; to cede Formosa, the Pescadores, and the Liaodong Peninsula to Japan; and to pay an indemnity. Russia, France, and Germany forced Japan to restore the Liaodong Peninsula to China in return for money. The foreign powers also loaned China money to help pay for the return of the peninsula.

Learning from Pictures *This Chinese porcelain punch bowl was imported for European markets. The bowl depicts the European trading centers at Canton.*

These territorial privileges greatly angered the Japanese. Western powers had forced them to give up the spoils of their victory. Both China and Japan recalled these humiliations over the next 50 years when they strove for power in East Asia.

SECTION 4 REVIEW

1. **Identify** Indian National Congress, Muslim League, Treaty of Shimonoseki, Chinese Eastern Railway
2. **Locate** Formosa, Liaodong Peninsula, Vladivostok
3. **Evaluating Ideas** What were the beneficial and harmful effects of British rule in India?
4. **Analyzing Ideas** **(a)** In what sense can the Meiji Restoration be considered a revolution? **(b)** What were its results?
5. **Determining Cause and Effect** Describe the causes and results of the Sino-Japanese War.

5 Foreign Influence in Southeast Asia and the Pacific Increased

The tide of imperialism did not stop in South Asia and East Asia. It also affected Southeast Asia and the islands of the Pacific.

Imperialism in Southeast Asia

In the late 1400s and early 1500s, European traders explored the East Indies. In the seaports of these islands and on the nearby mainland, Portuguese and Dutch merchants enjoyed a rich and active trade until the early 1800s.

In the 1800s and early 1900s, European imperialism came to Southeast Asia as it did to nearby India and China. The area became an important source not only of spices but also of the world's tea and coffee and later of such valuable products as tin and oil.

British successes. It was natural that the British should take an interest in the kingdom of Burma, on the eastern border of India. By 1886 all of Burma had come under British control.

The island of Singapore, on the tip of the Malay Peninsula, guarded the entrance to the Strait of Malacca—one of the most vital trade routes in the world. The British first moved onto Singapore, then uninhabited, in 1819. Throughout the 1800s they gradually extended their influence northward to include large parts of the peninsula up to the southern border of Siam (today known as Thailand). They created a city at Singapore, which became an important naval base in the empire.

French gains. The eastern part of the mainland of Southeast Asia contained several small, weak nations that were under Chinese influence. Beginning in the late 1700s, French merchants gained trading rights at seaports on the South China Sea. In the late 1800s, French imperialists forced China to give up its claim to the area, and the French became the dominant power in what became known as French Indochina.

Siam. The kingdom of Siam was better organized than were other parts of Southeast Asia. The British on the Malay Peninsula and the French in Indochina nibbled at the borders of Siam. To maintain their independence, Siamese rulers skillfully maneuvered British interests against French interests. The British and French finally agreed that an

● Point out that many Americans saw their country's imperial policy as an extension of Manifest Destiny.

■ Students might suggest that Asia, Africa, and the Pacific would have retained more of their traditional societies and that tensions caused by colonial rivalries would not have occurred.

1B, 1D, 4K, a4L

independent Siam was a useful buffer state between their possessions. A **buffer state,** located between two hostile powers, is a small country that often lessens the possibility of conflict between them.

The Dutch East Indies. The Dutch East India Company, formed in 1602 to exploit the island possessions of the Netherlands, succeeded in doing so for many years. By the late 1700s, however, it had become corrupt and inefficient. In 1798 the government of the Netherlands revoked the company's charter and took over the administration of the Netherlands East Indies.

The Dutch East India Company had used a system of forced labor in the East Indies. The Dutch government somewhat improved working conditions for the locals. By the late 1800s, however, several local revolts convinced the government of the Netherlands to make basic reforms in the administration of its richest imperial possession.

Interest in the Pacific Islands

Only a few of the islands and island groups in the Pacific were economically attractive to the imperialist powers. These few areas had large local populations that, it was hoped, could be persuaded to want and buy manufactured goods. Some of the areas had fertile soil that could support rich plantations. Other islands had minerals to be mined. Imperialism in most of the Pacific islands, however, was based on another motive—the need for coaling stations and naval bases. Since the imperialist powers competed in the Pacific, as elsewhere, none was willing to trust the others for its coal supplies and naval repairs. Each of the powers, therefore, sought out its own Pacific islands. By 1900 imperialist nations controlled almost all the islands (see map, page 618).

The Samoan Islands. In the late 1800s, the most serious rivalry over territory in the Pacific involved the Samoan Islands. Here the United ● States played a major role. American interests in Samoa had been developing for a number of years. In 1878 Americans gained the right to use the harbor city of Pago Pago (PAHNG • oh PAHNG • oh), on the island of Tutuila (toot • uh • WEE • luh), as a trading post, coaling station, and naval base. Great Britain and Germany secured similar rights in other parts of the Samoan Islands.

For a number of years, rivalry among the three foreign nations for control of the Samoan Islands simmered until they teetered on the brink of war. To prevent further trouble, the three nations set up a system of joint control in 1889, but it soon failed.

In 1899 the rivals signed a treaty ending the dispute. Great Britain, preoccupied with the South African War, withdrew its interests. The United States established firm control over Tutuila and six other small islands whose combined area was only about 75 square miles (195 square kilometers). Together, these possessions became known as American Samoa. Germany gained control of all the other islands in the Samoan group, which eventually became known as Western Samoa.

The Hawaiian Islands. Far more important to the United States than its Samoan possessions were the Hawaiian Islands (see map, page 618). This group of islands had fertile soil, plentiful rainfall, and a mild climate. Foreign traders and missionaries, including Americans, had begun settling there in the 1820s but interfered little with the government and economy of the locals. After 1865, however, businesses from the United States and other foreign nations began to develop sugarcane and pineapple plantations on the islands.

The local rulers of the Hawaiian Islands resented foreign influence and announced that they intended to bring it to an end. American planters then asked the United States representative in the islands to call for a force of American marines. Hawaiian troops, ill-prepared to match this show of force, refused to fight. By 1893 foreign business leaders, supported by American marines, were in control of the islands, and in 1898 the United States annexed the islands.

The Philippines, Guam, and Wake Island. Since the 1500s and 1600s, the Philippine Islands and Guam in the western Pacific Ocean had been parts of Spain's far-flung empire. In 1898 the United States declared war on Spain. Most of the fighting occurred in Cuba and Puerto Rico, but the

What If?

Imperialism

In the late 1800s and early 1900s, European countries carved out empires in Africa, Asia, and the Pacific. How do you think world history would have been different if the Europeans had not established these empires? ■

SECTION 5

Focus/Motivation

The following passage is President McKinley's explanation of how he arrived at his decision to annex the Philippines. Read the passage aloud or reproduce it for the class.

"I walked the floor of the White House night after night until midnight; and I am not ashamed to tell you, gentlemen, that I went down on my knees and prayed to Almighty God for light and guidance more than one night. And one night late it came to me this way — I don't know how it was, but it came (1) that we could not give them back to Spain — it would be cowardly and dishonorable; (2) that we could not turn them over to France or Germany — our commercial rivals in the Orient — that would be bad business and discreditable; (3) that we could not leave them to themselves — they were unfit for self-government . . . ; and (4) that there was nothing left for us to do but to take them all, and to educate the Filipinos, and uplift and Christianize them, and by God's grace do the very best we could by them."

Lead a discussion using the following questions as a guide: What reasons did McKinley give for annexing the Philippines? *(He claimed to have no alternative; he gave both practical and idealistic reasons.)* What was his attitude toward the Filipinos? *(He felt*

● **the Philippines**

they were unfit for self-government, uneducated, and pagan.) Do you think he was more concerned about the United States or the Philippines? *(Students might note that his main concern seemed to be for the prestige, power, and economic interests of the United States. As evidence, students might point to his condescending attitude toward the Filipinos.)*

Presentation
Quick Quiz
(Average/Group)
Read the following statements. Have students write in their notebooks the country or area each statement describes.
1. This kingdom on the eastern border of India came under British control in the late 1800s. *(Burma)*
2. France replaced China as the dominant power in this region. *(French Indochina)*
3. Rivalry existed between the United States, Great Britain, and Germany in these islands. *(Samoan Islands)*

SECTION 5

Closure
Point out that the United States had fought a war to free itself of domination by the imperial power, Great Britain. Ask students to discuss how they think Americans reconciled this fact with American imperial ambitions of the late 1800s and early 1900s.

first United States military action against Spain took place in the Pacific.

When war erupted, United States naval forces were in peak condition. Under orders from Assistant Secretary of the Navy Theodore Roosevelt, four cruisers and two gunboats under the command of Commodore George Dewey steamed from the British port of Hong Kong and moved quickly into the harbor of Manila, the capital of the Philippine Islands. Early on the morning of May 1, Dewey's forces attacked the decrepit Spanish fleet. By noon the Spanish ships were sunk or in flames and the city of Manila was at Dewey's mercy. Within a few months, American land forces, supported by local revolutionaries, defeated the Spanish forces in Manila. With the collapse of Spanish power at Manila, the entire Philippine Islands came under the control of the United States. At about this time, American forces also occupied Guam, a small, Spanish-held island east of the Philippines (see map, this page).

Some Filipinos welcomed the Americans and even fought with them against the Spaniards. Most of the local population, however, had suffered under Spanish rule for centuries and saw little advantage in changing one foreign master for another. Led by Emilio Aguinaldo (ahg • ee • NAHL • doh), Filipino locals fought for independence for three years against thousands of American troops. The Filipinos used guerrilla warfare against the better-equipped United States army, but were finally defeated in 1902.

Besides acquiring the Philippine Islands and Guam, the United States also took possession of Wake Island in the central Pacific. Thus the United States acquired yet another link in a strategic chain of island possessions running from its west coast across the vast distances of the Pacific Ocean all the way to East Asia.

● ***Learning from Maps*** *Spain's empire in the Pacific Ocean crumbled after the Spanish-American War. What islands does the United States possess under the terms of the peace treaty?*

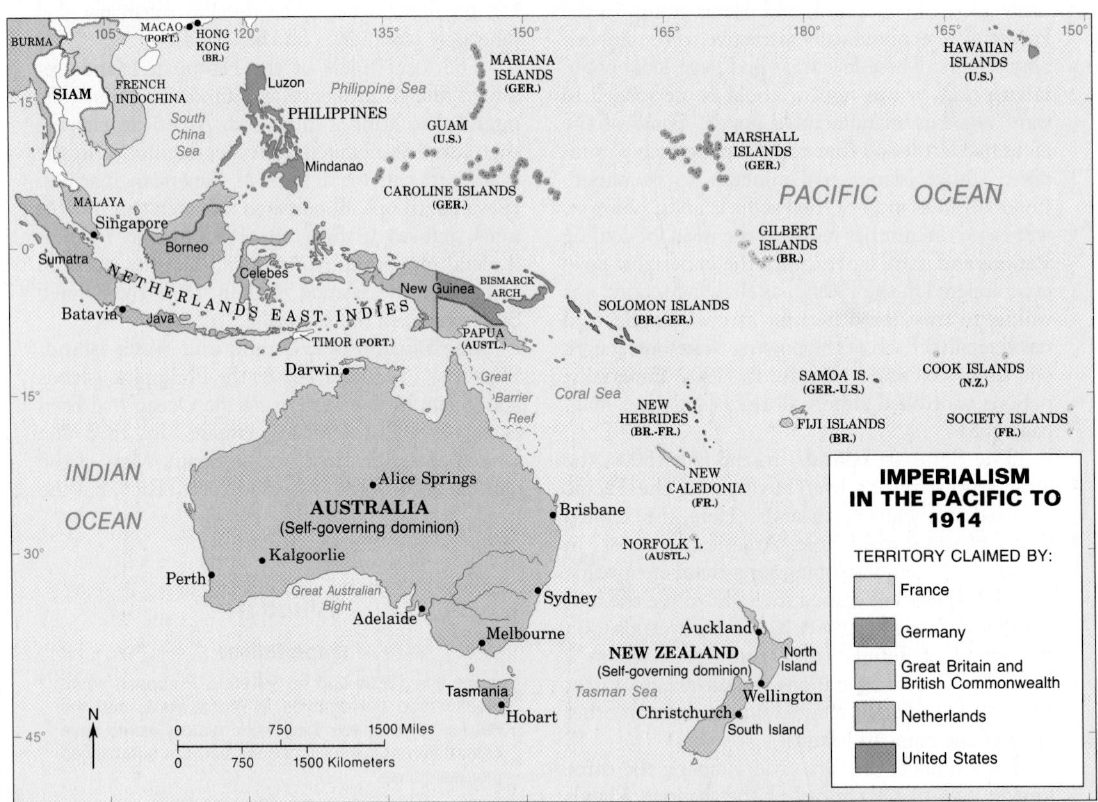

618

SECTION 5 REVIEW

1. **Define** buffer state
2. **Identify** Emilio Aguinaldo
3. **Locate** Singapore, Samoa, Philippines
4. **Analyzing Maps** Using the map on page 618, list the Southeast Asian possessions world powers had acquired by 1914.
5. **Interpreting Ideas** Why was Siam a useful buffer state?
6. **Analyzing Ideas** Why were the Pacific islands important possessions?

6 Latin America Became Involved with Imperialist Powers

Imperialism in Latin America differed from that in the Pacific. Although the Latin American countries were weak, the Monroe Doctrine of the United States, along with Great Britain's navy and its commercial policy, prevented them from being turned into colonies again. Nevertheless, the countries of Latin America experienced economic interference as they increasingly attracted European and American investment.

New Opportunities for Trade

As the pace of the Industrial Revolution increased in Europe and the United States, more agricultural products and raw materials were purchased from Latin American countries. Americans, for example, acquired a taste for bananas, which they imported from Central America, and for coffee, which came mostly from Brazil. They bought sugar made from sugarcane grown in Cuba, and they smoked cigars made from Cuban tobacco.

The British purchased large quantities of wool, which their factories needed, as well as wheat, beef, and mutton from Argentina and Uruguay. Chile mined nitrates from natural deposits in its northern deserts and sold them to the industrial countries to make fertilizers and explosives. Brazil exported natural rubber from its vast Amazon forests.

Railroads were built to bring these goods to Latin American port cities. The ports were also improved to ease the loading of the newly perfected steamships. All these developments brought prosperity to those countries of Latin America that had the opportunity to engage in trade. Argentina especially benefited from these developments. However, other Latin American countries such as Bolivia and Paraguay hardly participated in trade at all. In these countries, nearly all trade benefits were concentrated in the capital cities and the ports.

As had occurred in the United States, a few of the Latin American countries—most notably Argentina, Brazil, Uruguay, and later Cuba—attracted a large number of immigrants from Europe. In those Latin American countries with the greatest export trade, industries also began to develop. Imperialists built factories such as sugar mills to process export goods. Other new factories—textile mills, flour mills, and metalworking shops—produced consumer goods for local markets.

Economic Imperialism

Foreign investors owned many of the new railroads, ranches, plantations, and mines in Latin America. Central governments granted these investors many special favors—for example, monopoly privileges, free land, and exemption from taxes—in the hope that the foreigners would develop the economy by establishing new businesses there. However, the investors usually sent the profits from these businesses and the interest payments from loans back to their own countries.

The central governments in Latin America now had more tax revenues. As a result, foreign banks willingly lent them funds for public improvements. Central governments spent some of this money on strengthening their armies and navies, which made it easier to suppress internal rebellions. However, a revolution often toppled the government that had borrowed the money, and the new government would refuse to pay the old debts. In addition, although Latin Americans spent some money to install electricity and streetcars in the capital cities, much money was wasted on payments to powerful politicians.

Unpaid loans frequently led to intervention by the foreign powers. European banking and business leaders would persuade their governments to pressure the Latin American governments for payment. Sometimes warships and troops were sent to compel payment. A typical method involved taking over the collection of the customs—the principal tax—and holding back enough money to pay the debts.

Review Answers

1. ***buffer state:*** small state located between two hostile powers that often lessens the possibility of conflict between those two powers
2. ***Emilio Aguinaldo:*** leader of the revolt in the Philippines against American control
3. ***Singapore:*** tip of Malay Peninsula; ***Samoa:*** island in the Pacific Ocean located east of Australia and northeast of Fiji; ***Philippines:*** group of islands in the Pacific south of Formosa and east of French Indochina
4. *Great Britain:* Burma, Singapore, Malay Peninsula, northern Borneo, southeast New Guinea, Pacific islands; *France:* French Indochina, Pacific islands; *Netherlands:* Dutch East Indies; *Germany:* northeastern New Guinea, Pacific islands; *United States:* Philippines, Hawaiian Islands, other islands; *Japan:* Korea, number of islands
5. Siam was independent and lessened the possibility of conflict between France and Great Britain.
6. A few of the Pacific islands were valuable for their rich soil or mineral wealth. Most, however, were important as coaling stations or naval bases.

SECTION 6

Focus/Motivation

Exaggerated and sensational stories of Spanish atrocities in Cuba had ap-

4K, a2G

● Point out that possession of the Falklands — known as the Malvinas by the Argentines — has continued to cause friction between Great Britain and Argentina. In 1982, after Argentine troops occupied the islands, this friction became open warfare.

peared in many American newspapers in 1898 and played an important role in bringing about the Spanish-American War. If possible, read or show to the class examples of the "yellow journalism" of this period. Then ask students if they think yellow journalism is still practiced today. You might have students bring in samples of one story as it is covered by various newspapers and magazines and have the class judge the objectivity of each presentation. Or you might have students write two short articles on an actual news event. They should first write an objective presentation of the facts. Then have them write the same story in a sensational, but credible, style. Have volunteers read their stories in class and ask other students to identify the different versions.

Learning from Pictures *This railroad funded by the United States runs through a banana plantation in Costa Rica.*

American Intervention

As the United States became an industrial power, it began to challenge Great Britain, its main rival for dominance of the Western Hemisphere. In the early 1800s, the Americans had not enforced the Monroe Doctrine in any region farther away than Central America when the offender was Great Britain. For example, the British had occupied the Falkland Islands, near the tip of South America, in ● 1837. Although Argentina protested, the United States did not support the Argentinians.

In 1895, however, the United States did intervene in a dispute between Great Britain and Venezuela. Early in the 1800s, Great Britain had acquired British Guiana (gy • AN • uh), on the northern coast of South America. On a number of occasions, Great Britain had tried to extend the boundary of British Guiana westward into territory claimed by Venezuela.

Venezuela had asked the United States for support in its demand that the border dispute be submitted to **arbitration**—negotiation for a settlement of the dispute by a party agreed upon by all sides. When Great Britain refused to arbitrate, President Grover Cleveland insisted that they do so. Finally, Great Britain, preoccupied with the South African War, submitted, and the dispute with Venezuela was settled. The United States had championed the cause of a weak Latin American nation against powerful European interests. Beyond this, however, the United States had its own motives for helping Venezuela. The gold thought to be in the region was now more accessible to American investors.

The Spanish-American War

In 1898 the United States became even more deeply involved in Latin American affairs. Its involvement grew out of disputes with Spain.

The main cause of tension between Spain and the United States was Cuba (see map, page 624), a Spanish colony in the West Indies. For many years the Cubans had been unhappy under Spanish rule. Several rebellions flared, which the Spanish government suppressed with great difficulty. These rebellions alarmed United States citizens and corporations that had invested money in Cuba, especially in its railroads and its sugar plantations and mills.

Concern for American-owned property was only one reason for the tense relations between the United States and Spain. Many Americans felt sympathetic toward Cuba's desire for independence and indignant over Spanish treatment of the Cuban rebels. Anti-Spanish speeches and writings by Cubans who had settled in the United States and sensational stories in American newspapers telling of Spanish atrocities in Cuba stirred these sentiments.

More anger arose in 1898 when an American battleship, the *Maine,* exploded in Havana harbor, and 260 Americans perished. The *Maine* had been sent to Cuba to protect American citizens and their property. No one knew the cause of the explosion, but many in the United States assumed that the Spaniards were to blame. American newspapers played on this assumption, encouraging a rising popular demand in the United States for war with Spain.

Spain showed some willingness to come to terms with the United States regarding the difficulties in Cuba. President McKinley and his cabinet did not want war. However, American leaders felt unable to resist the popular demand for aggressive measures and declared war in April 1898. To pacify its members who opposed rising

American imperialism, Congress declared that the United States was fighting only on behalf of Cuban independence and had no intention of taking the island for itself.

Cuban leaders had not wanted United States intervention, which they feared as much as Spanish rule. Judging themselves capable of winning the war on their own, Cubans regarded American intervention as interference.

The war lasted only a few months, and after being defeated both on land and on the sea, Spain asked for peace. The Treaty of Paris was signed in December 1898.

The United States government did not invite the Cubans to the peace conference. Instead it dealt only with Spain. By the terms of the peace treaty, Spain surrendered its claim to Cuba. It also ceded Puerto Rico, in the Caribbean, and the Pacific island of Guam to the United States. In addition, Spain sold the Philippines to the United States for $20 million.

Following the war, United States troops occupied Cuba. Americans established schools, built roads, provided sanitation, and eradicated yellow fever. The United States government also recognized Cuba's independence. However, Cuba was not turned over to its own leaders but to a provisional military government. Although the United States government permitted a Cuban assembly to draw up a constitution, it insisted that the Cuban constitution include the so-called Platt Amendment. This amendment gave the United States the right to intervene in Cuba whenever it thought orderly government was endangered. The United States also insisted on having four naval bases in Cuba but later agreed to only one—Guantánamo Bay.

The Panama Canal

In addition to governing its new and far-flung possessions, the United States now had to defend them. The major problem of defense came to light during the Spanish-American War.

Before the war the American battleship *Oregon* had been stationed on the Pacific coast of the United States. When war became likely, this battleship was summoned to strengthen American forces in the Caribbean Sea. It had to race around the entire South American continent, a distance of over 11,000 miles (17,600 kilometers), to reach the Caribbean. The United States realized at this point that it would either have to build two complete navies to protect its empire or find an easier and quicker way to route warships between the Atlantic and Pacific oceans.

A canal across the Isthmus of Panama had long been considered. The same French company that built the Suez Canal tried unsuccessfully to build a canal across Panama. In the late 1800s, the United States government began negotiating for

Learning from Pictures *On July 1, 1898, Theodore Roosevelt, along with Cuban troops called* Mambis, *led American troops in the Battle of Santiago. They captured this high ground overlooking the city of Santiago and the fort* El Viso.

Presentation Identifying Words (Average/Group)

Write the following lists on the chalkboard or an overhead projector. Have students unscramble each word in the list and then match it to a description in the second list.

1. oelrovste *(Roosevelt)*
2. molbocia *(Colombia)*
3. ziad *(Diaz)*
4. nwislo *(Wilson)*
5. ilalv *(Villa)*

a. Dictotor of Mexico for 34 years
b. President who obtained the treaty to build the Panama Canal
c. President who refused to recognize Huerta's government
d. Mexican revolutionary who raided a New Mexican border town
e. Before independence Panama was a province of this nation

(Answers: 1-b, 2-e, 3-a, 4-c, 5-d)

permission and a right-of-way to build a canal. It asked Colombia for a lease to a strip of land across the isthmus in Panama, at that time a province of Colombia (see map, page 624).

After a treaty had been negotiated, the Colombian senate adjourned without ratifying it, a move that angered people in the United States and in the province of Panama. The people of the province wanted the canal because it would create great benefits for them. When negotiations seemed to break down, certain Panamanian business leaders and some American residents of Panama began a revolution to gain independence from Colombia.

American warships stationed at Panama prevented Colombian troops from moving in to suppress the revolt, and the revolution succeeded. The United States then quickly recognized the independence of Panama. In 1903 the new government of Panama gave the United States all the rights necessary to build a canal across Panama.

The Panama Canal, one of the world's greatest achievements in engineering, opened in 1914. It would probably have been impossible to build without recently invented power shovels and other new machines. Medical science, too, played a vital part. Cuban and American scientists had discovered that mosquitoes carry yellow fever, a disease that contributed to France's inability to build a canal across Panama. By destroying the mosquitoes, scientists controlled the spread of the disease, thus enabling the construction crews to work in the jungles of Panama.

The new canal shortened the sea route from New York to San Francisco by over 5,000 miles (8,000 kilometers) and the sea route from New York to the new territory of Hawaii by 4,400 miles (7,100 kilometers). Fleets in the Atlantic and Pacific oceans could now be quickly shifted when necessary. Merchant ships of all nations paid a toll to use the canal. The toll was well worth the price because the shortened route lowered the operating cost of a ship, far outweighing the amount of the toll itself.

The Panama Canal also had an important effect on the countries of Central and South America that bordered the Caribbean Sea. Formerly this region had been a sleepy backwater of the world, a dead end of commerce. The canal made it a thriving worldwide trading center.

Learning from Pictures *The two doors being installed at the Gatun Locks are actually floatable metal structures 65 feet wide (about 20 meters) and 7 feet thick (about 2 meters).*

The Roosevelt Corollary

Long before the completion of the Panama Canal, the United States recognized that any strong European power with a foothold in the Caribbean region could threaten the canal or the sea lanes leading to it. Therefore the United States adopted a new policy regarding foreign influence in Latin America.

In 1904 President Theodore Roosevelt's State of the Union address included a section on Latin America. Roosevelt said that if any situation threatened the independence of any country in the Western Hemisphere, the United States would act as an "international police power" to prevent a foreign country from stepping in. This statement became known as the Roosevelt Corollary to the Monroe Doctrine. It was regarded as a natural consequence of the earlier policy, and it would be called into use several times in the coming years.

Although European and American investors supported the Roosevelt Corollary, Latin Americans were enraged at the implication that they could not manage their own affairs. Thus Latin American nations supported a statement made by Luis Drago, foreign minister of Argentina. He had vehemently denied the European or American right to collect foreign debts—a declaration known as the Drago Doctrine.

LINKING GEOGRAPHY TO HISTORY

The Berlin Conference: Making a New Map of Africa

The continent of Africa has a distinctive location. It sits directly on the equator and reaches almost as far north as it does south of the earth's midline. In addition, Africa occupies an amazingly central position in relation to the other landmasses of the world. The Americas lie to the west, Eurasia to the north and east, Australia to the southeast, and Antarctica to the south. Africa's central location, along with its huge size and vast stores of mineral wealth, made it a prime target for colonization by European nations during the 1800s. As you have read in this chapter, each of the European colonial powers created spheres of influence in Africa. Among the most significant of these powers was Germany. Otto von Bismarck, the German imperial chancellor, planned not only to expand Germany's control in Africa but also to play his country's European rivals one against the other, thereby weakening their influence. By the 1880s Germany had begun to carry out these plans by establishing colonies in locations designed to obstruct the imperial designs of other European powers. For example, the Germans had taken Cameroon which lay between French colonies, and German East Africa separated two huge British colonies. Then in 1884 Bismarck called for a meeting in Berlin to complete the division of Africa among all interested parties.

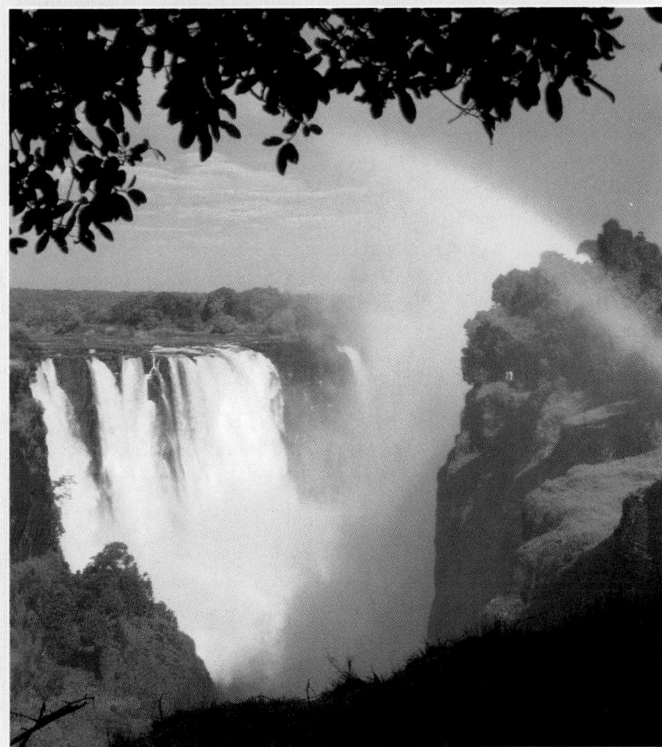

Victoria Falls, on the Zambia-Zimbabwe border

At the time of the Berlin Conference many Africans still lived under their own government. With absolutely no regard for local boundaries, the representatives carved up the continent among themselves. These representatives argued over, drew, erased, and redrew the boundary lines of their new colonies. Huge parcels of land changed hands, sometimes simply at the whim of one representative. Often, people from the same ethnic group found themselves separated and ruled by different colonial powers. Conversely, the new boundaries frequently threw together ethnic groups hostile to one another. Also, in drawing boundary lines the representatives ignored such natural boundaries as rivers and mountain ranges. Ignorant of the continent's geography, the representatives had no idea of the location of such natural dividing lines.

Probably no meeting in history has had the lasting impact on a continent that the Berlin Conference had on Africa. In many ways the decisions made at the Berlin Conference still plague Africa today. Much of Africa secured independence after 1950, but the colonial boundaries established by the Berlin Conference had acquired the legitimacy of time. Even though many of these boundaries were arbitrary and a possible cause for future trouble, the leaders of the new African nations feared that drawing new boundaries might result in complete chaos. Yet at the same time these leaders found they could not make the old boundary lines function. For many Africans, loyalty to their ethnic group still had far greater meaning than national identity. Conflicting loyalties had disastrous consequences in many countries.

623

1A, 1B, 4K, a1C, a4B, a4C

SECTION 6

Closure

Have students compare American control of the Panama Canal with British control of the Suez Canal. Ask: Why was control of these waterways important to the United States and Great Britain? *(because of their strategic locations)*

Review Answers

1. *arbitration:* negotiation for settlement of a dispute by a party agreed upon by all sides involved
2. *Maine:* American battleship blown up in Havana harbor; ***Platt Amendment:*** part of the Cuban constitution giving the United States the right to intervene whenever it thought orderly government was endangered; ***Roosevelt Corollary:*** President Theodore Roosevelt's extension of the Monroe Doctrine claiming for the United States "international police power" to protect the independence of any Latin American country; ***Porfirio Díaz:*** dictator of Mexico for 34 years whose regime collapsed in 1910; ***Victoriano Huerta:*** general who seized control of the Mexican government in 1913; ***Emiliano Zapata:*** peasant leader who voiced the Mexican people's demands for rights to the land; ***Venustiano Carranza:*** a constitutionalist who led a rebellion against the Huerta government; ***Pancho Villa:*** Mexican revolutionary leader

Further United States Expansion

Because of political disturbances and defaults on loans, the United States continued to expand its influence in the Caribbean. It created military governments in Nicaragua from 1912 to 1933, in Haiti from 1915 to 1934, and in the Dominican Republic from 1916 to 1924. Cuba was again subjected to an occupation government from 1906 to 1909, and United States marines were stationed there from 1917 to 1922.

The United States intervened in these countries for several reasons. During the early 1900s, world tensions increased and the economies of the Caribbean nations almost collapsed. The United States feared that governments might fall into anarchy or into the hands of leaders who would refuse to pay the debts owed to foreign banks. European nations might have used this refusal to pay debts as an excuse to intervene in the Caribbean region.

In 1917 the United States purchased from Denmark three of the Virgin Islands east of Puerto Rico. With this purchase the United States added another base to assure its control over the Caribbean. At the same time, Puerto Ricans became United States citizens and received a few more rights of self-government in order to guarantee their loyalty in dangerous times.

Mexico's Revolution

The greatest upheaval in Latin America during the age of imperialism was the Mexican Revolution. For 34 years one dictator, Porfirio Díaz (DEE • ahs), had dominated Mexico. He had permitted foreign companies to develop many of Mexico's natural resources and had allowed the major landowners to buy up much of the country's land from poor peasants. In 1910, although Mexico appeared outwardly stable, Díaz's regime suddenly collapsed.

Learning from Maps *Imperialism in the Caribbean Sea was checked by the Roosevelt Corollary. Which island is part of the United States?* Puerto Rico

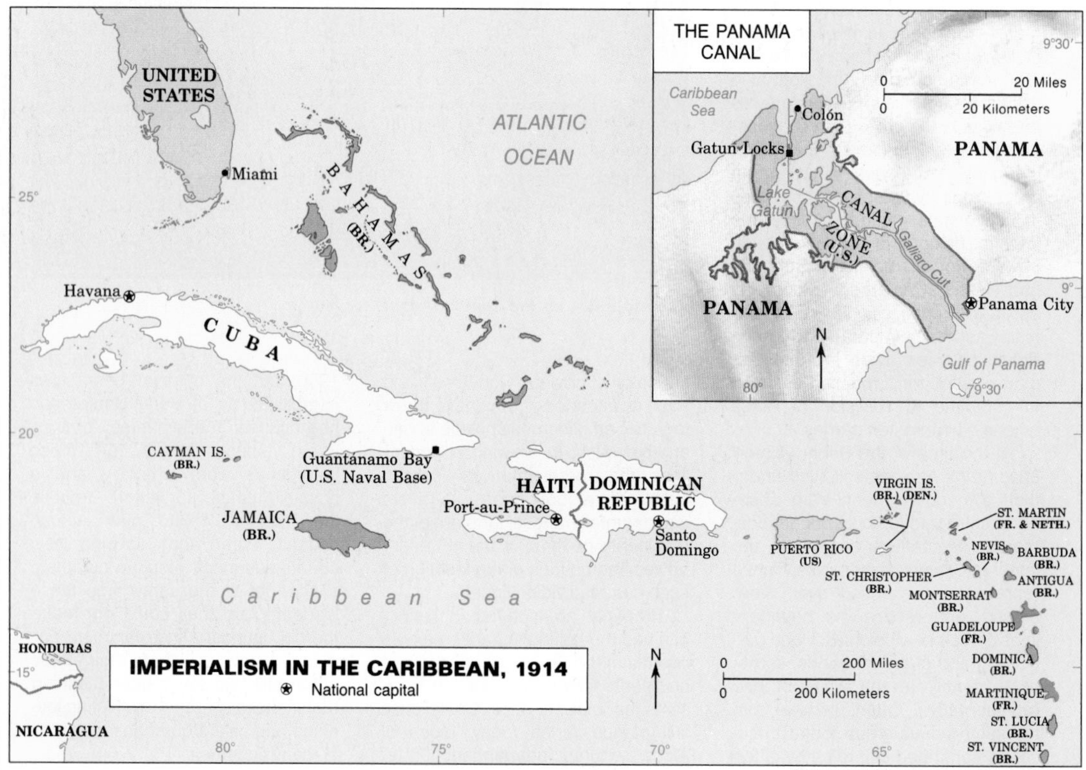

1B, 4K, a1C, a4A, a4E, a4G, a4H, a4L

● He had raided a New Mexico border town, killing a number of American citizens.

Learning from Pictures *The Mexican revolutionary Pancho Villa is shown here sitting in the Presidential Chair. Why was the United States pursuing Villa?*

A rebellion against the aging dictator put Francisco Madero in power in 1911. He was assassinated in 1913, and Victoriano Huerta (WERT • uh), one of Díaz's former generals, seized control of the government. A rebellion led by constitutionalist Venustiano Carranza against Huerta then began and later deepened into intensive civil warfare among various factions. The war dragged on for 10 years and cost perhaps 1 million lives. Underlying these struggles were widespread demands for rights to the land. The peasant leader Emiliano Zapata (sah • PAH • tah) voiced these demands.

The violence and unrest in Mexico frightened American investors who had billions of dollars invested there. President Woodrow Wilson refused to recognize Huerta's government and tried to force Huerta's overthrow. President Wilson opposed the Huerta regime because it was imposed upon the Mexican people without their consent. Wilson also ignored requests to send troops into Mexico to protect American lives and property, instead choosing a policy known as "watchful waiting." However, in 1914, after the arrest of some American soldiers, United States marines were sent to occupy Veracruz. President Wilson also allowed shipment of arms to Carranza and persuaded England to withdraw its support of the Huerta regime. Two years later, United States troops were sent into Mexico to capture Pancho Villa (VEE • yuh), a revolutionary leader who had raided a border town in New Mexico, killing several Americans. Tensions between the two countries mounted, and for a time there was a threat of war. Tensions eased in 1917, when the United States withdrew troops from Mexico and focused its attentions on the world war in Europe.

SECTION 6 REVIEW

1. **Define** arbitration
2. **Identify** *Maine,* Platt Amendment, Roosevelt Corollary, Porfirio Díaz, Victoriano Huerta, Venustiano Carranza, Emiliano Zapata, Pancho Villa
3. **Locate** Cuba, British Guiana, Puerto Rico, Panama Canal, Nicaragua, Virgin Islands
4. **Summarizing Ideas** Give examples of economic imperialism in Latin America.
5. **Understanding Ideas** Explain how the United States exerted its influence **(a)** in Venezuela's dispute with Great Britain, and **(b)** in Cuba.
6. **Understanding Ideas** What were the results of the Spanish-American War?
7. **Interpreting Ideas** **(a)** Why was the United States interested in building the Panama Canal? **(b)** What were the results?

3. ***Cuba:*** island in the Caribbean south of Florida; ***British Guiana:*** northeastern South America east of Venezuela; ***Puerto Rico:*** island in Caribbean east of Dominican Republic; ***Panama Canal:*** artificial waterway in Central America connecting Caribbean Sea and Pacific Ocean; ***Nicaragua:*** between Costa Rica and Honduras; ***Virgin Islands:*** group of islands in the Caribbean east of Puerto Rico
4. Many of the new railroads, plantations, and mines in Latin America were foreign-owned. Foreign investors received monopoly privileges and exemption from taxes.
5. (a) President Cleveland supported Venezuela in its border dispute with Great Britain and insisted the matter be submitted to arbitration. **(b)** The United States intervened in the fight for Cuban independence and declared war on Spain. After the American victory, Cuba became a protectorate of the United States.
6. The Spanish-American War resulted in Cuban independence and acquisition of Puerto Rico, Guam, and the Philippines by the United States.
7. (a) The United States wanted a canal for military reasons, since it would enable fleets in the Atlantic and Pacific to be quickly combined when necessary. **(b)** Completion of the canal shortened travel distances and lowered the operating costs of shipping companies.

Reviewing Important Terms
1. f; **2.** b; **3.** d; **4.** c; **5.** h; **6.** e; **7.** g; **8.** a; **9.** k; **10.** j; **11.** l; **12.** i

Developing Critical Thinking Skills
1. (a) Italy; **(b)** Germany; **(c)** France; **(d)** Britain; **(e)** Spain; **(f)** Britain
2. (a) Economic imperialism involves the indirect control of one country over another by owning certain industries or other economic rights and privileges. Political imperialism usually involves outright control of a country by settlement or conquest. **(b)** Economic imperialism often led to political imperialism. Foreign-owned mines, plantations, and factories were sometimes attacked and damaged by locals. Foreigners who had invested money demanded their governments protect their investments. In response governments put pressure on local rulers or sent troops to restore order.
3. Economic exploitation, social discrimination, and disregard for native cultures created native resentment in the local population. The educational systems introduced by the Western nations taught the students about Western ideas such as nationalism and liberalism, and showed the conflict between what Western governments did and what they said.
4. (a) American diplomatic pressures discouraged European attempts to take over Liberia. **(b)** An attempt by Italy to invade Ethiopia was stopped at Adwa in 1896. **(c)** Under the Meiji government, the Japanese began a program of industrialization and modernization to catch up with the Western

1B, 1D, 4H, 4J, 4K, 5A, a1C, a4A

Reteaching
Have students review the Chapter Summary and the appropriate section and questions in the Unit Synthesis. Discuss the concepts until students demonstrate a clear understanding of the material.

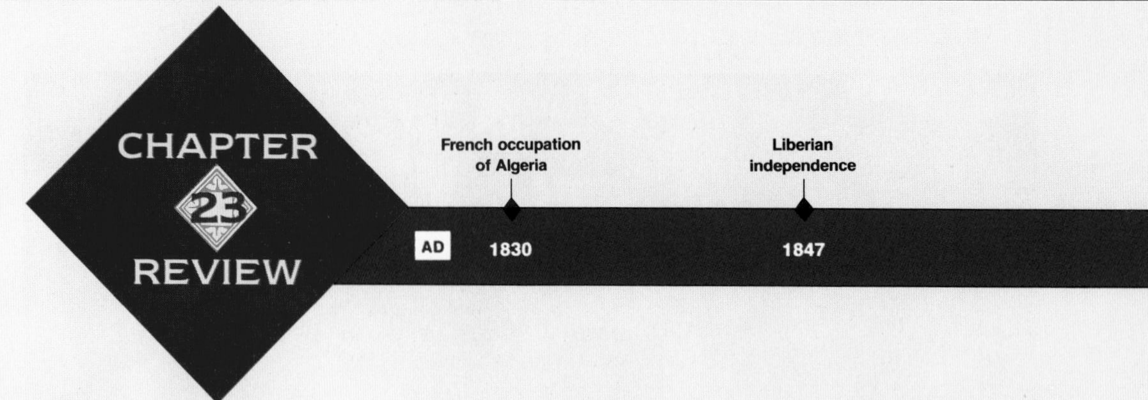

Chapter Summary

The following list contains the key concepts you have learned about imperialism in the late 1800s and early 1900s.

1. In the late 1800s, European nations became involved in a new kind of empire building—imperialism—that arose from the need for self-sufficiency, new markets, and places in which an ever-growing population could settle.
2. European nations divided up almost all of Africa in the late 1800s. Communication and transportation improved, slavery was abolished, and some Africans profited from the many economic investments foreigners made. For the most part, however, Africa was mercilessly exploited, and tensions developed that would lead to further struggles later in the 1900s.
3. In India the British government assumed direct control. However, the British set themselves up as a caste superior to the local population.
4. After a civil war in Japan, the emperor was restored to power in 1868. The Japanese then began a remarkably quick and successful process of industrialization.
5. Although foreign powers helped China resist the Japanese, the Chinese had to make concessions for receiving this assistance.
6. Imperialism was also a strong force in Southeast Asia and in the Pacific. By the late 1800s, the kingdom of Siam was the only area of Southeast Asia that remained free.
7. The Pacific islands became valuable as coaling stations and naval bases.
8. The countries of Latin America were weak and vulnerable to economic imperialism. The United States sought to extend its influence and to protect Latin America from powerful European interests.
9. The relatively easy American victory in the Spanish-American War dramatized the growing strength of the United States. In the early 1900s, the United States became increasingly involved in Latin American affairs, often invoking the Roosevelt Corollary to the Monroe Doctrine.

On a separate sheet of paper, complete the following review exercises.

Reviewing Important Terms

Match each of the following terms with the correct definition below.

a. paternalism
b. assimilation
c. imperialism
d. arbitration
e. direct rule
f. protectorate
g. sphere of influence
h. buffer state
i. colony
j. concession
k. indirect rule
l. condominium

___ **1.** System of government in which the local ruler kept his title but officials of the foreign power actually controlled the region
___ **2.** System in which the people of the colonies abandoned their local cultures and adopted all aspects of the colonial power's culture
___ **3.** Settlement of a dispute by a party agreed upon by all sides
___ **4.** The domination by a powerful nation over the political, economic, and cultural affairs of another nation or region
___ **5.** A small country that is located between two hostile powers and that often lessens the possibility of conflict between them
___ **6.** System of colonial government in which the imperialist power controlled all levels of government and appointed its own officials to govern the colony
___ **7.** A region in which one nation had special, sometimes exclusive, economic and political privileges that were recognized by other nations
___ **8.** System of governing the colonies just as parents guide their children
___ **9.** System of government under which the governor and a council of advisers made colonial laws, but local rulers exerted some authority
___ **10.** A grant of economic rights and privileges in a given area usually given to foreign merchants or capitalists
___ **11.** System whereby two nations ruled a region as partners
___ **12.** An area in which a foreign nation gained total control over a given region and its local population

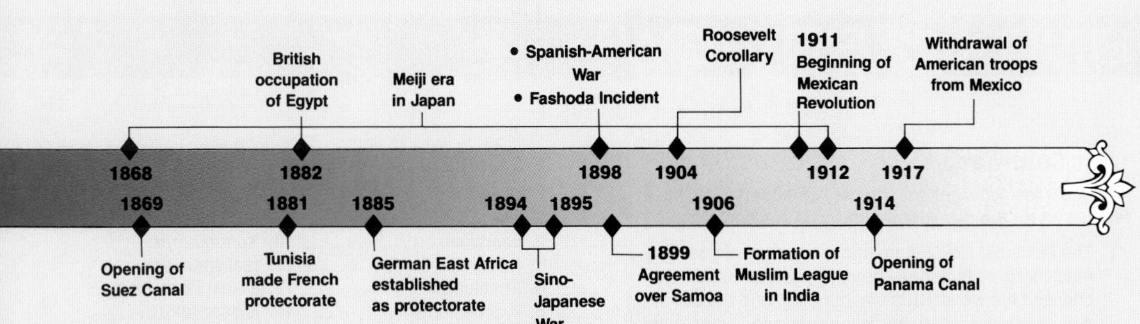

Developing Critical Thinking Skills

1. **Classifying Ideas** Name the imperialist nation that claimed each of the following territories: **(a)** Libya, **(b)** Togo, **(c)** Algeria, **(d)** Gold Coast, **(e)** Río de Oro, **(f)** Sudan.
2. **Contrasting Ideas** **(a)** How does economic imperialism differ from political imperialism? **(b)** Why did one often lead to the other during the late 1800s?
3. **Seeing Relationships** How did European imperialism encourage the growth of nationalism in other parts of the world?
4. **Summarizing Ideas** How were each of the following nations able to preserve their independence: **(a)** Liberia, **(b)** Ethiopia, **(c)** Japan, **(d)** Siam.
5. **Contrasting Ideas** In what ways did the colonial policy of the United States differ from that of other nations?
6. **Evaluating Ideas** What were the positive and negative effects of imperialism in Africa and in India?
7. **Analyzing Primary Sources** Reread the lines from the Rudyard Kipling poem "The White Man's Burden" on page 601. **(a)** What does Kipling mean by the phrase "white man's burden"? **(b)** How does he characterize the people who must be "served"? **(c)** Based on what you have learned about early African, Asian, and Indian civilizations, what arguments might you use to prove Kipling wrong?

Relating Geography to History

Use the world map on pages R4–R5 of the Atlas section to answer the following questions: **(a)** If the Suez Canal did not exist, what would be the shortest water route between London and Bombay? **(b)** If the Panama Canal did not exist, what would be the shortest water route between New York and Hawaii?

Relating Past to Present

1. Using a world atlas, prepare a map showing the distribution of natural resources in Africa. Compare this map with the map on page 607. **(a)** What resources did each imperialist nation stand to gain through its possession of African colonies? **(b)** Which of these resources are most important to industrial nations today?
2. Review the reasons for the United States government's decision to build a canal across the Isthmus of Panama. Then investigate the debate surrounding the 1978 decision to turn ownership of the canal over to Panama by the year 2000.

Applying History Study Skills

Before completing this activity, review Building History Study Skills on page 604.

Your topic is: "How did the Meiji Restoration speed the industrialization of Japan?" Which of the following items would be relevant to your topic?

1. Yedo was renamed Tokyo when it became the new imperial capital.
2. A system of universal education was set up in Japan.
3. Compulsory military service was established.
4. European nations began to set up trading barriers such as tariffs on Japanese goods.
5. The divinity of the emperor was stressed during the Meiji Restoration.
6. The special stipend for samurai was abolished during the Meiji Restoration.
7. Government policy was mainly decided by a group of able samurai from the daimyo domains of Satsuma and Choshu.
8. Political parties formed protest movements.

Investigating Further

1. **Conducting a Debate** Work with several of your classmates to find information on European imperialism in Africa. Prepare a debate on the following topic: *Resolved:* The Europeans exploited Africa and severely damaged the local cultures.
2. **Writing a Report** Imperialism arose out of a complex mixture of political, economic, and social forces. One of these was the missionary motive. Using books in your library, prepare a report on missionary activities in colonial areas.

nations in technology and wealth. **(d)** The British and French decided an independent Siam would be a useful buffer state between their possessions.
5. The United States did not occupy large areas of land in Asia, Africa, or Latin America. The Philippines and Puerto Rico each had an elected legislative assembly.
6. In Africa, the imperialist powers built roads and railroads and introduced medicine to prolong life. They reduced the land available to Africans for crop cultivation, contributing to malnutrition. In some areas economic prosperity and a rise in the standard of living occurred, and Western laws, courts, and schools were introduced. The British in India helped modernize the country but discriminated against the Indians.
7. (a) the "burden" of civilizing non-Western peoples; **(b)** ill-humored and childlike; **(c)** Accept all reasonable answers.

Relating Geography to History
(a) around Africa;
(b) around South America

Relating Past to Present
1. (a) Great Britain stood to gain diamonds, gold, coal, manganese, iron ore, uranium, tin, and copper. France stood to gain phosphates and iron ore. Belgium stood to gain uranium, coal, cobalt, copper, tin, and gold. **(b)** Answers will vary.
2. Answers will vary.

Applying History Study Skills
2. and **4.**

627

1A, 1B, 1D, 4G, 4H, 4I, 4J, 4K, 5A, a1C, a4A, a4E, a4F, a4G, a4H, a4I, a4L, a4M

Reteaching

Have students review the Chapter Summary and the appropriate section and questions in the Unit Synthesis. Discuss the concepts until students demonstrate a clear understanding of the material.

Reviewing Concepts

1. g; **2.** n; **3.** i; **4.** k; **5.** l; **6.** j; **7.** a; **8.** m; **9.** e; **10.** b; **11.** f; **12.** c; **13.** d; **14.** h

Applying Critical Thinking Skills

1. (a) The enclosure movement forced small landowners to become tenant farmers or move to cities. The invention of new agricultural techniques and machinery required fewer farm laborers, and many farm laborers moved to cities in search of work. **(b)** Factory owners needed a large pool of workers.

2. (a) Working people lived in cramped and crowded tenements. The middle class lived in larger houses in more spacious neighborhoods. **(b)** With industrialization, working-class women worked in factories or as domestic servants. Middle-class married women were expected to raise children and care for the home. **(c)** After the Industrial Revolution, people began having children earlier. **(d)** The Industrial Revolution provided people with more leisure time.

3. (a) a belief in the importance of individual rights; **(b)** Great Britain and the United States; **(c)** Russia and Austria

4. (a) Metternich was referring to the political and cultural influence France exerted in European affairs. **(b)** Accept all reasonable answers.

5. (a) weight of atoms; **(b)** radioactivity of uranium and radium; **(c)** theory of relativity; **(d)** theory of evolution; **(e)** smallpox inoculation; **(f)** germ theory of diseases; **(g)** antisepsis; **(h)** idea of the unconscious and psychoanalysis

UNIT 5 REVIEW

Unit Summary

The following list contains the key concepts you have learned about the development of industrial society.

1. The Industrial Revolution—the production of goods by machinery in factories—began in Great Britain and changed the world. Both steam power and the Bessemer process were extremely important to the early Industrial Revolution.
2. Workers began to protest harsh working conditions and low wages. The first labor unions were organized to seek improvements in working conditions.
3. Socialists like Karl Marx believed that a more fundamental transformation of politics and society was necessary and would resolve human problems.
4. After 1870 new inventions, scientific discoveries, compulsory public education, and a lively interest in the arts helped improve the quality of life.
5. Many social and political reforms occurred in Great Britain and the British Empire in the 1800s and early 1900s.
6. Territorial growth and sectionalism in the United States led to conflict over the issue of slavery. Eventually the North and South fought a bitter civil war.
7. France experienced political instability in the 1800s. By the early 1900s, France was a republic governed by coalitions of parties that represented monarchist, liberal, and socialist beliefs.
8. The peoples of Latin America gained their independence in the 1800s but did not unite.
9. Due to the efforts of Mazzini, Garibaldi, and Cavour, Italy was unified by 1870. In Germany, Prussia led the movement toward unification.
10. In Russia the czar maintained autocratic control over the country, while rebellion in the Austrian Empire led to the formation of the Dual Monarchy.
11. In the late 1800s, European nations became involved in a new kind of empire building—imperialism. Europeans established colonies in Africa, Asia, and the Pacific. In most of Latin America, imperialism was economic rather than political.

On a separate sheet of paper, complete the following review exercises.

Reviewing Concepts

Match each of the following individuals with the correct concept in column two.

a. Mazzini	**h.** Pankhurst
b. Bismarck	**i.** Mill
c. Spencer	**j.** Monet
d. Smith	**k.** Einstein
e. Marx	**l.** Metternich
f. Daumier	**m.** Kipling
g. Beethoven	**n.** Freud

____ **1.** romanticism in music	____ **8.** "white man's burden"
____ **2.** psychoanalysis	____ **9.** pure communism
____ **3.** liberalism	____ **10.** *Kulturkampf*
____ **4.** relativity	____ **11.** realism in art
____ **5.** absolutism	____ **12.** Social Darwinism
____ **6.** impressionism	____ **13.** laissez faire
____ **7.** Risorgimento	____ **14.** woman suffrage

Applying Critical Thinking Skills

1. **Interpreting Ideas** **(a)** How did the agricultural revolution help to create a large labor force in the cities? **(b)** Why was this necessary for the development of an industrial economy?
2. **Determining Cause and Effect** What effect did the Industrial Revolution have on each of the following: **(a)** living conditions, **(b)** women's lives, **(c)** family size, **(d)** use of leisure time.
3. **Understanding Ideas** During the 1800s liberalism emerged as a vital force in Europe. **(a)** What were some of the political ideas associated with liberalism? **(b)** In what nations did liberalism make the greatest progress? **(c)** the least progress?
4. **Analyzing Primary Sources** Metternich once commented, "When France sneezes, all Europe catches cold." **(a)** What do you think he meant by this remark? **(b)** In light of the actions taken by Napoleon III, would you agree or disagree with Metternich? Why or why not?
5. **Classifying Ideas** Identify the major accomplishments of each of the following scientists: **(a)** John Dalton, **(b)** Marie Curie, **(c)** Albert Einstein, **(d)** Charles Darwin, **(e)** Edward Jenner, **(f)** Louis Pasteur, **(g)** Joseph Lister, **(h)** Sigmund Freud
6. **Evaluating Ideas** **(a)** What conditions encouraged the growth of nationalism in Europe? **(b)** How did the spirit of nationalism affect the development of Italy? **(c)** of Germany? **(d)** of Austria-Hungary? **(e)** of Russia?
7. **Synthesizing Ideas** **(a)** How did the Industrial Revolution and the rise of nationalism rekindle the desire for colonies? **(b)** What other factors promoted the renewed interest in empire building? **(c)** How did the imperialism of the late 1800s differ from the colonization of the 1500s and 1600s?

Relating Geography to History

Turn to the map of Africa on page R16. **(a)** How many independent nations exist in present-day Africa? **(b)** How does this number compare with the number of nations shown on the map on page 607? **(c)** Which imperialist power gave up the most territory? **(d)** the least territory?

Writing About History

1. Choose one of the scientists discussed in Chapter 20. Then use resources in your school or public library to find what recent discoveries have advanced the work of this scientist. Write a report detailing your findings.
2. Write a newspaper article dated October 25, 1876, that tries to convince your readers that European countries should establish colonies.

Further Readings

Fieldhouse, D. K. *The Colonial Empires.* New York: Dell. Compares European and North American empire building from the 1500s to the 1900s.

Hibbert, Christopher. *Africa Explored: Europeans in the Dark Continent, 1769–1889.* New York: Penguin Books. Description of European exploration of Africa and the growing competition to carve spheres of influence throughout the world.

Mosse, Werner. *Alexander II and the Modernization of Russia.* New York: Collier. Comprehensive biography of Alexander II of Russia that analyzes his impact on Russian society, particularly the peasant classes.

Sinclair, Upton. *The Jungle.* New York: Signet Classics. Social critique of the Industrial Revolution in the United States. Graphic descriptions of abuses of workers.

Twain, Mark. *The Adventures of Huckleberry Finn.* New York: Signet Classics. One of many reprintings of the most famous (and probably the first) American novel about life on the Mississippi during the early nineteenth century.

Unit Five Chronology

Date	Political and Social Developments	Technological and Scientific Advances	Visual Arts and Literature	Religious and Philosophical Thought
1750–1800	Enclosure continues **19*** French and British anti-union activity **21**	Watt's steam engine **19** Cartwright's power loom **19** Cotton **19** Jenner and smallpox **20** Factory system **19**	*Wealth of Nations* **19** Beethoven **20** Shift to romanticism **20** Malthus's *Essay . . . Population* **19**	Commercial capitalism **19** Adam Smith **19** Robert Owen **19**
1800–1850	British industrial reform **19** Decline of Ottoman Empire **22** Zollverein **22** Revolutions of 1848 **21, 22** Latin American independence **21** Imperialism in China **23**	Fulton's *Clermont* **19** Stephenson's locomotive **19** McCormick's reaper **19** Goodyear's vulcanized rubber **19** Morse's telegraph **19** Mendeleyev's periodic table of elements **20**	Tchaikovsky, Wagner, and Verdi **20** Brothers Grimm **20** Goethe **20** *Communist Manifesto* **19** Victorian Age **21** Cooper and Irving **20**	Chartism **21** Utopians **19** David Ricardo **19** John Stuart Mill **19**
1850–1920	2nd and 3rd French Republics **21** European imperialism **23** Meiji Restoration **23** Spanish-American War **23** U.S. Civil War **21** Franco-Prussian War **21** Woman suffrage **21** Russo-Japanese War **22** Boer War **23** Establishment of Germany, Italy, Dual Monarchy **22** Reform Bills in Great Britain **21**	Darwin **20** Bessemer steel process **19** Transatlantic cable **19** Bell's telephone **20** Edison's light bulb **20** Suez Canal **21, 23** Pasteur **20** Wireless **20** Wright brothers **20** Panama Canal **23** Planck and Einstein **20**	*Das Kapital* **19** Dickens **19** *Principles of Sociology* **20** Realism **20** Impressionists **20**	*Kulturkampf* **22** Socialism **19** Nationalism **22** Social Darwinism **20** Liberalism **21** Universal education **21** Nihilism **22** Freud **20** "White Man's Burden" **23**

*Indicates chapter in which development is discussed

6. (a) Napoleon had spread the ideal of nationalism throughout Europe. **(b)** In Italy nationalism served as a force for liberation and unification. **(c)** It did the same in Germany. **(d)** The Dual Monarchy was created as a concession to allow Hungarians to share power with Austrians. **(e)** Under the program of "Russification," non-Russians in the empire were forced to adopt the Russian language, religion, and customs.

7. (a) The Industrial Revolution spurred the demand for raw materials, new markets, places to invest surplus capital, and outlets for excess population. Nationalists argued that colonies added to a nation's strength and prestige. **(b)** Other factors included the desire to spread Christianity and to take up the "white man's burden" of "civilizing the peoples" of Africa and Asia. **(c)** Imperialism was undertaken on a much larger scale than the earlier colonization.

Relating Geography to History

(a) Virtually the entire continent is free. **(b)** In 1914 only Ethiopia and Liberia were free. **(c)** Britain; **(d)** Spain

629

1B, 1C, 1D, 4H, 4I, a1B, a1C

Focus/Motivation
Ask students to imagine that they are living in the pre-industrial age. Point out that all labor is done by hand and that machine-made products are virtually nonexistent. Then have them suggest how their daily lives would be different. *(Students should mention that virtually every aspect of their lives would be different. There would be no factories to mass produce many of the products that they use daily.)* Conclude the activity by pointing out the Industrial Revolution that began in Great Britain transformed the ways that goods were produced and therefore changed the ways in which people lived.

UNIT FIVE SYNTHESIS

The Development of Industrial Society

19 The Industrial Revolution Transformed the Modern World

A revolution quite different from the Scientific Revolution of the 1500s or the political revolutions of the 1600s and the 1700s began in Great Britain in the 1700s. This revolution—the Industrial Revolution—transformed the ways goods were produced and profoundly affected the world.

The Early Industrial Revolution

The Industrial Revolution began in Great Britain because of a certain combination of conditions. Great Britain had what economists call the factors of production, or the basic resources necessary for industrialization: land, capital, and labor.

But even before the Industrial Revolution had begun, Great Britain experienced a revolution in agriculture. This revolution had started when British farmers began to fence off, or enclose, common lands into individual holdings efficient for large-scale farming.

By the 1800s, because of improvements in agriculture, farmers needed fewer farm laborers. Many unemployed farm workers moved to the cities, where they created a large labor force. Many of these workers found jobs in the cotton textile industry, which was the first industry in Great Britain to undergo mechanization—the use of automatic machinery to increase production.

The Factory System

Soon, inventors perfected the steam engine, which could be used to power machinery. This introduction of steam-powered machinery made work easier to do and made it possible to produce a wide array of products in a relatively short time. Most of these goods were manufactured in factories rather than in people's homes.

Life in the mines and factories of the early Industrial Revolution was hard and monotonous, and life in the workers' homes was not much better. Working people lived in cramped and poorly maintained apartment houses called tenements. At the same time, the middle class grew and enjoyed many luxuries unknown before the Industrial Age.

New Business Methods

The factory system introduced a new phase in the development of capitalism—the economic system in which individuals rather than the government control the factors of production. Before the Industrial Revolution, most capitalists were merchants who bought, sold, and exchanged goods. We call this type of capitalism commercial capitalism. However, because the capitalists of the Industrial Revolution became more involved in producing and manufacturing goods themselves, the capitalism of this period is often referred to as industrial capitalism.

Industrialization changed the methods of production and depended on division of labor, interchangeable parts, and the assembly line. It also gave rise to a new form of business organization—the corporation.

Improving Living Conditions

During the Enlightenment of the 1700s, a group of economists attacked the ideas of mercantilism. These economists believed that natural laws governed economic life, and that any attempt to interfere with these natural economic laws was certain to bring disaster. Adam Smith, a Scot, best stated the views of these economists. Smith wrote that every person should be free to go into any business and to operate it for the greatest advantage. The result, Smith said, would benefit everyone. We call this system of complete free enterprise *laissez-faire.*

As time went on, more people realized that things could not be left entirely alone. Many people, such as John Stuart Mill, felt that government needed to regulate work hours and set minimum standards for wages and working conditions. These people argued that such laws would not interfere with the natural workings of the economy. Over time, governments began to agree with these reformers.

Many workers, however, felt that governments were not moving fast enough. Sometimes these workers took matters into their own hands and refused to work until demands were met. We call such a work stoppage a strike.

In order to strengthen their position, workers sought ways to organize permanently into associations called labor unions. Although these organizations were at first outlawed, they later became legal.

Socialism

Some reformers of the 1800s advocated a political and economic system called socialism. In this system the government owns the means of production and operates them for the welfare of all the people.

Some thinkers grew impatient with early socialism, which advocated peaceful methods to attain goals. Karl Marx, the most important of these critics, believed that all the great changes in history came from changes in economic conditions. Under capitalism, he said, labor receives only a small fraction of the wealth it creates. Most of the wealth goes to the owners in the form of profits. As a result of this unequal distribution of wealth, the capitalist system necessarily suffered from increasingly severe depressions that would ultimately lead to a revolution led by the workers, or proletarians.

Marxist, or radical, socialists generally believed in the necessity of revolution to overthrow the capitalist system. They wanted to establish a system in which the government owns almost all the means of production and controls economic planning. Today we call this economic and political system authoritarian socialism, or communism.

Another group of socialists, though influenced by Marx, believed that socialism could develop gradually through education and democratic forms of government. Today we call this type of socialism democratic socialism. Under democratic socialism, the people retain basic human rights and partial control over economic planning through the election of government officials.

The Great Exhibition of London, 1851

20 The Industrial Age Revolutionized Science and Culture

In addition to changing the economy and society, the Industrial Revolution had a profound effect on science, art, music, and literature.

Technology and Communication

Beginning about 1870 manufacturers increasingly applied the findings of pure science to their businesses, generating a new wave of industrial growth. The application of scientific solutions to industrial problems resulted in: (1) inventions that provided rapid communications over long distances; (2) the development and use of new sources of power; and (3) the creation of new products and materials and the improvement of old ones.

Advances in Science and Medicine

The most significant developments in the physical sciences—those that deal with the inanimate, or nonliving, aspects of nature—during the 1800s and early 1900s centered on the atomic theory. This theory states that all matter in the universe consists of very small particles called atoms. The arrangement and structure of these atoms and their chemical combinations with each other account for the different characteristics of the materials that make up our world.

Scientists also investigated the biological sciences—those dealing with living organisms. Many

631

Presentation
Interpreting Ideas
(Average/Group)
Have students reread the subsection "Literature, Music, and Art" on this page. Ask: Why do you think artists moved away from romanticism and toward realism? *(Students might suggest that artists became more concerned with the problems of life in the Industrial Age.)* Then ask how the Industrial Revolution might have influenced this shift. *(Students might point out that society was changing from agricultural to industrial, and that the shift was a reaction against the poor working conditions of the early Industrial Revolution.)*

explored the structure of cells, the tiny units of living matter, in an attempt to better understand organic matter and thereby improve human life.

Population

The progress made possible by science and technology helped produce rapid population growth in industrialized countries. As the population grew, it also became more mobile. Large numbers of people moved across national boundaries and oceans to foreign lands. Others moved to cities to find jobs in the new factories.

Social Sciences and Education

During the 1800s interest in education and in the social sciences grew rapidly. The social sciences are disciplines that study people as members of society. These subjects include political science, economics, history, anthropology, sociology, and psychology.

Literature, Music, and Art

Literature, music, and art reflected the social and economic developments of the Industrial Age. Even in their most personal statements, the artists portrayed in their works a sense of the times and of the influences of scientific ideas and rapid change.

Many writers of the early 1800s belonged to what is known as the romantic movement. Their work appealed to sentiment and imagination and dealt with the "romance" of life—life as it used to be, or as they thought it ought to be, rather than as it actually was. In the mid-1800s writers and artists began to abandon romanticism and turn to realism, which emphasized the realities of everyday life.

21 Reforms Swept Through Many Areas of the World in the 1800s

During the late 1800s, people throughout the world clamored for reform. Their appeals met with varying degrees of success.

British Reforms

Although Great Britain was a limited constitutional monarchy with executive power vested in a cabinet headed by the prime minister, not everyone had a voice in government. In the 1800s, however, a series of reforms extended rights to the entire population. At the same time, vital social and economic reforms took place. Two outstanding prime ministers—Benjamin Disraeli and William Gladstone—helped push through many of these reforms.

As Great Britain instituted social and political reforms, other changes occurred within the British Empire. The British colonies of Canada, Australia, and New Zealand won self-government. Nevertheless, each maintained close ties with Great Britain.

The United States

Unlike European governments, the United States expanded without acquiring any colonies. Instead, it expanded across North America and gave new territories the opportunity to become states on an equal basis with the original 13 states.

Despite phenomenal growth, the United States had one significant problem—the unresolved issue of slavery. This issue, along with the issue of states' rights, led to a brutal civil war that raged between 1861 and 1865 and left much of the nation—particularly the South—in ruins. Nevertheless, the Union was preserved.

After the Civil War, the United States experienced phenomenal growth primarily as a result of industrialization and immigration.

France

For many years after the Congress of Vienna, the Bourbons continued to rule France. Then in 1830 a revolt forced King Charles X to abdicate. The leaders of the French revolt then chose Louis Philippe, Duke of Orléans, who belonged to a branch of the Bourbon family but who had a record of liberal beliefs, as king.

But in 1848 opposition to the regime of Louis Philippe erupted in violence. A new government—a republic—under the leadership of Louis Napoleon was soon proclaimed. Napoleon, however, had imperial ambitions similar to those of his illustrious uncle and soon proclaimed the Second Empire.

The Second Empire lasted until a humiliating defeat by Prussia toppled it in 1871. France once again proclaimed a republic.

Latin America

By the late 1700s, the Spanish and Portuguese colonies underwent administrative reform and economic growth, inspired in part by the Enlightenment. Nevertheless, the revolutionary events in British North America and France in the late 1700s aroused interest, particularly among discontented creoles, as upper-class Latin Americans were known. By the mid-1800s this discontent had become full-scale revolution, and the nations of Latin America had won their independence.

22 Unification of New Nations Added to Rising Tensions in Europe

In the late 1800s, the political situation in Europe changed significantly. Italy and Germany each became unified nations. Russia remained a rigid autocracy, and Austria and Hungary formed the Dual Monarchy.

Italy

Italian nationalism became a strong force in the early 1800s. Under the leadership of fiery patriots such as Giuseppe Mazzini, people in many parts of Italy clamored for national unity. Although the nationalists made some gains, they could not agree on what type of government the united Italy should have.

One group favored union under the leadership of Sardinia. There, the chief minister or premier, Count Camillo Benso di Cavour (kahv • OOHR), provided the major impetus for Italian unification. Throughout the 1850s and the 1860s, Cavour used diplomacy, war, and persuasion to achieve unity. Finally, in 1870 unification was completed when the Italians claimed Rome.

Prussia

Like Italy, Germany remained fragmented in the early 1800s. But during the 1860s and 1870s, the long-delayed process of centralization and consolidation under the leadership of Prussia began to pick up great speed.

Celebrating Italian Unification

Perhaps the person most responsible for German unification was the Prussian chancellor Otto von Bismarck, who used clever diplomacy and war against Denmark, Austria, and France to achieve unification in 1871.

The new German Empire was a federal union under the leadership of the Prussian kaiser, or emperor. The federal government controlled all common matters, such as national defense, foreign affairs, and commerce.

Opposition to Bismarck

In spite of rigid control by the aristocratic Prussians, the new German federal government soon ran into difficult problems. Dissatisfied groups formed political parties that opposed Bismarck's policies. Relations with the Roman Catholic church proved troublesome, and socialists clamored for government ownership of businesses. Through delicate diplomacy, however, Bismarck was able to deal with these problems and transform Germany into an industrial power.

In foreign policy Bismarck worked to build up Germany's military strength and develop a system of alliances to prevent Russia and France from becoming allies.

Russia

Ruled by an autocratic czar, Russia steadfastly opposed reform. Nevertheless, liberal ideals became popular among discontented Russians—particularly

633

1B, 4J, 4K, a1C

Closure

Ask students how imperialism increased world tensions in the late 1800s and the early 1900s. *(Students might suggest that as nations competed for colonies, conflicts arose over territory and trade.)* Point out that these tensions proved to have disastrous consequences for the world in the 1900s.

among intellectuals. Faced with problems caused by liberal ideas and restless nationalities, the czars took harsh measures.

Although the late 1800s witnessed reforms such as the freeing of the serfs during the reign of Alexander II, most reform efforts failed. And the czars continued to use repression to combat any erosion of their powers. Then in 1904 and 1905 the Russians fought a disastrous war with Japan. Defeat at the hands of the Japanese spurred all the discontented groups in the country to action and led to revolution. Although the beleaguered Czar Nicholas II granted a few reforms, he later reneged on his promises and resumed his policies of repression. This repression would have disastrous consequences for the Romanovs.

Austria-Hungary

The Hapsburgs in Austria also had to deal with the rising tide of liberalism in the late 1800s. And to combat nationalist demands in the empire, the Austrians formed the Dual Monarchy in which both Hungarians and Austrians played a vital role in government.

The formation of the Dual Monarchy failed to solve the problem of nationalities. The Austrian Germans and the Hungarian Magyars dominated the population in each of their separate national states. National minorities—the Czechs, Serbs, Croats, Romanians, Poles, and Italians—existed in both Austria and Hungary. These people benefited very little from the Dual Monarchy and continued to agitate for self-government.

The Dual Monarchy also faced problems abroad. In the late 1800s, the Hapsburgs clashed with the autocratic government of the Ottoman Empire over the Balkans. Although the Ottomans had ruled the Balkans for centuries, their influence steadily weakened as their empire declined.

23 Imperialist Powers Competed in Many Areas of the World

Beginning about 1870 several factors rekindled interest in establishing colonies. During the next 40 years, many nations became involved in imperialism—the domination by a powerful nation over the political, economic, and cultural affairs of another nation or region.

Background of Imperialism

Imperialism arose out of a complex mixture of political, economic, and social forces. These forces included a desire for self-sufficiency, the need for new markets, the search for national pride and prestige, the need for places where people could settle and still remain loyal to the home country, and the desire to convert people to Christianity.

Imperialism created bitter rivalries among the imperial powers and hatred among the colonized peoples. As European powers took over more and more of the world, these rivalries and hatreds intensified.

North Africa and the Sudan

In the 1800s most of North Africa and the Sudan belonged to the Ottoman Empire. Because Turkish control in many areas was weak, the Europeans scrambled to claim new colonies. The French claimed Algeria, Tunisia, and Morocco. The British established dominance in Egypt and the Sudan, and the Italians took Libya.

SubSaharan Africa

The Europeans repeated their colonial ambitions in SubSaharan Africa. During the empire building of the 1500s and the 1600s, the Europeans had established settlements on the coasts. In the late 1800s, however, the Europeans moved inland. By 1900 Europeans claimed all land in SubSaharan Africa except Liberia and Ethiopia.

Imperialism was a harsh experience for all of Africa. However, the costs and the benefits resulting from European expansion were unevenly distributed across the continent.

South and East Asia

The strong forces of imperialism that swept Africa in the 1800s brought important and fateful changes to South and East Asia although the changes were not as abrupt as they were in so many parts of Africa. In India, for example, the British had long played an important role. In the mid-1800s, they increased this role and made India a part of their vast empire.

Question 1 of the Synthesis Review corresponds to Section 19 of the synthesis, Question 2, to Section 20; Question 3, to Section 21; Question 4, to Section 22; Question 5, to Section 23. Question 6 asks students to synthesize information from various sections of the synthesis.

1B, 1D, 4K, a1C, a4A, a4F, a4H, a4I, a4L

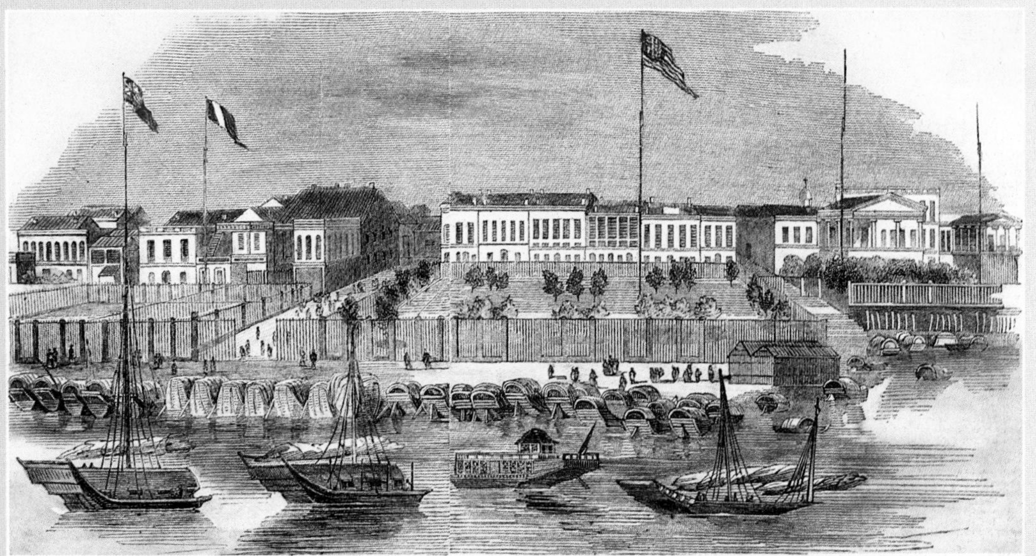

European trading centers in Canton, China

Although European influence in Japan became strong after the overthrow of the Tokugawa shogunate in 1868, Europeans did not dominate Japan as they did India. Rather, the Japanese under the rule of the Meiji emperors controlled their own affairs and industrialized. At the same time, China came increasingly under European domination even though it remained nominally independent.

Southeast Asia and the Pacific

The tide of imperialism did not stop in South and East Asia. It affected Southeast Asia and the islands of the Pacific as well. The British, the French, and the Dutch claimed parts of Southeast Asia and several islands in the Pacific. The United States claimed the Philippines, Hawaii, Guam, and Wake Island.

Latin America

Imperialism in Latin America differed from that in the Pacific. Although the Latin American countries were weak, the Monroe Doctrine of the United States, along with Great Britain's navy and its commercial policy, prevented them from being turned into colonies again. Nevertheless, the countries of Latin America experienced economic interference as they increasingly became a field for investment from Europe and the United States. We call this type of imperialism, economic imperialism because the colonial power controls the subject area's economy rather than its government.

In two areas, Cuba and Puerto Rico, however, a foreign government did take political control. These islands had been a part of the Spanish Empire for centuries. But in 1898 the United States defeated Spain in the Spanish-American War and claimed the islands. Cuba later became independent, while Puerto Rico became a commonwealth of the United States. And in Panama, the United States built a canal and ruled the territory known as the Canal Zone.

SYNTHESIS REVIEW

1. **Interpreting Ideas** Why did the Industrial Revolution begin in Great Britain?
2. **Determining Cause and Effect** How did the Industrial Revolution alter population patterns?
3. **Comparing Ideas** How did political developments in France and Great Britain differ in the late 1800s?
4. **Understanding Ideas** How did Bismarck deal with the socialists?
5. **Analyzing Ideas** What factors led Europeans to found colonies in the late 1800s?
6. **Synthesizing Ideas** Why do you think democracy triumphed in Great Britain and the United States but failed in Russia?

Review Answers

1. Great Britain had what economists call the factors of production, or the basic resources necessary for industrialization: land, capital, and labor. Also, the political system allowed free economic competition.
2. The increased availability of food and the recognition of the relationship between diet and health also improved life expectancy. Large numbers of people moved across national boundaries and oceans to foreign lands. Cities also grew.
3. France underwent revolutions in 1848 and 1871. In Great Britain a series of peaceful reforms extended rights to the entire population.
4. Bismarck implemented his own socialist reforms to reduce the socialists' political support.
5. a desire for self-sufficiency, the need for new markets, the search for national pride and prestige, the need for places where people could settle and still remain loyal to the home country, and the desire to convert people throughout the world to Christianity
6. Answers will vary. Students might point out that the United States and Great Britain had long histories of constitutional government that valued human rights, while Russia had a long history of rigid autocracy and an absolute monarch.

Introducing the Unit
Ask students to study the map on page 644. Point out that the map shows Europe in 1914 and that in Unit Six they will be studying the events that sparked World War I and the rise of totalitarian dictatorships that led to World War II. Ask for volunteers to locate the sites of Berlin and Vienna on the map. Then point out that Unit Six will explain the historical significance of these two cities during World War I and World War II.

UNIT SIX

World War in the Twentieth Century

◀ *The British Rescue at Dunkirk*

Unit Goals

After studying Unit Six, students will be able to:

1. Identify the causes of World War I.
2. Identify the social, political, and economic results of World War I.
3. Explain the United States's role in World War I.
4. Describe how the peace terms of World War I changed Europe.
5. Explain why the prosperity that followed World War I crumbled into a worldwide depression during the 1930s.
6. Analyze the rise of Fascist dictatorships in Italy and Germany during the 1930s.
7. Summarize the rise of communism in the Soviet Union.
8. Identify the political systems that developed in Turkey, Persia, and Africa after World War I.
9. Assess the effects of the worldwide depression on Latin America.
10. Identify the causes of World War II.
11. Identify the social, political, and economic results of World War II.
12. Describe and assess the role of the United States in World War II.
13. Summarize the political changes in Europe that followed World War II.

UNIT SIX WORLD WAR IN THE TWENTIETH CENTURY

CHAPTER (pages 638–663)

24 World War I and the Russian Revolution Altered the Course of History

(1882–1920)

CHAPTER OVERVIEW

In the early 1900s nationalism, imperialism, militarism, and a system of alliances led to extreme international tension and an intense armaments race. The spark that set off World War I occurred in the Balkans when Archduke Francis Ferdinand of Austria-Hungary was assassinated by a Serbian nationalist. This touched off war between Austria and Serbia, and because of the system of alliances, most of the major European nations as well as Japan and China were soon at war. After initial advances by the Central Powers and counterattacks by the Allies, the war reached a deadly, costly stalemate.

By 1917 economic backwardness, poverty, and the devastation of World War I resulted in the Russian Revolution. The czar was overthrown and a provisional government was formed. However, the Bolsheviks under Lenin overturned this moderate government, and later a civil war ended in a Communist victory.

The United States had remained neutral for nearly three years. It sent munitions and other supplies to the belligerents, principally to the Allies. The sinking of American ships by German U-boats, the Zimmermann telegram, and other factors caused the United States to enter the war on the side of the Allies in 1917.

President Wilson defined the American war aims in his Fourteen Points. American troops helped turn the tide of battle and bring about the collapse of the Central Powers.

The Versailles Treaty ended the war with Germany. It declared Germany guilty of starting the war and dictated large reparation payments to the Allies. In other treaties Austria-Hungary was broken up, and new nations were established in eastern Europe.

Included in the Versailles Treaty was the creation of the League of Nations. President Wilson hoped that the League could maintain world peace; the United States, however, did not join the League.

SUGGESTED LESSON PLAN

Day	Objectives	Suggested Activities	Materials
1	U1* C1-2	Introducing the Unit (pages 636–37) Introducing the Chapter (pages 638–39) Section 1 (pages 639–45), Focus/Motivation (page 639), Presentation (page 640), Closure (page 643), Suggested Teaching Strategies, Enrichment Activity, Daily Quiz, Suggested Assignments (page 637B)	ATE, Pupil's Edition, Teacher's Resource-Bank™
2	U3, C3-6	Section 2 (pages 645–51), Focus/Motivation (page 645), Presentation (page 645), Closure (page 650), Suggested Teaching Strategies, Enrichment Activities, Daily Quiz, Suggested Assignments (page 637C)	ATE, Pupil's Edition, Teacher's Resource-Bank™
3	U7, C7-9	Section 3 (pages 651–54), Focus/Motivation (page 651), Presentation (page 652), Closure (page 653), Suggested Teaching Strategies, Enrichment Activity, Daily Quiz, Suggested Assignments (page 637D)	ATE, Pupil's Edition, Teacher's Resource-Bank™
4	U4, C10-11	Section 4 (pages 654–58), Focus/Motivation (page 654), Presentation (page 655), Closure (page 656), Suggested Teaching Strategies, Enrichment Activity, Daily Quiz, Suggested Assignments (page 637E)	ATE, Pupil's Edition, Teacher's Resource-Bank™
5	U2, U4 C12-13	Section 5 (pages 658–61), Focus/Motivation (page 658), Presentation (page 658), Closure (page 659), Suggested Teaching Strategies, Enrichment Activity, Daily Quiz, Suggested Assignments (page 637F)	ATE, Pupil's Edition, Teacher's Resource-Bank™
6	U1-4, U7 C1-13	Chapter 24 Form A Test, Reteaching Worksheet, Chapter 24 Form B Test	Teacher's Resource-Bank™ or Workbook and Test Booklet

*C refers to applicable Chapter Objective, U refers to applicable Unit Goal.

BOOKS FOR THE TEACHER

Fischer, Louis. *The Life of Lenin.* Harper Colophon Books. Presents the life, philosophy, and personality of Lenin.

Massie, Robert K. *Nicholas and Alexandra.* Atheneum. Portrays the end of the Romanov dynasty.

Mee, C. L., Jr. *The End of Order.* Dutton. Describes the writing of the Versailles Treaty. Includes character sketches of the main participants.

Smith, Gene. *When the Cheering Stopped.* William Morrow. Features narrative of Wilson's fight for the ratification of the Versailles Treaty and his debilitating illness.

Stokesbury, James L. *A Short History of World War I.* William Morrow. Focuses on informative and concise coverage of World War I.

Toland, John. *No Man's Land.* Doubleday. Gives detailed description of the campaigns and prominent personalities of the last year of the war.

Tuchman, Barbara W. *The Guns of August.* Macmillan. Analyzes the beginning of World War I.

BOOKS FOR THE STUDENT

American Heritage eds. *The American Heritage History of World War I.* American Heritage. Includes interesting narrative and excellent photographs and other illustrations.

Bowen, Ezra. *Knights of the Air.* Time-Life. Features a combination of narrative, photographs, and diagrams.

Everett, Suzanne. *World War I.* Rand McNally. Illustrates the history of the war.

Feuerlicht, Roberta. *Desperate Act: The Assassination of Franz Ferdinand at Sarajevo.* McGraw-Hill. Portrays the assassination in a style suitable for high school students.

Reeder, Red. *Bold Leaders of World War I.* Little, Brown. Features portraits of 12 men and women who played important roles in World War I.

MULTIMEDIA MATERIALS

Causes of World War I (2 fs), Educational Audio-Visual. Examines the political, economic, and social causes of World War I.

Russia: Czar to Lenin (mp, 30 min.), McGraw-Hill. Documents the causes and outbreak of the Russian Revolution.

The Great War (7 fs), Multi-Media. Examines the world situation that led to the war, the war itself, and the efforts to make a lasting peace.

World War I: The Background (mp, 13 min.), Coronet. Describes the militaristic and nationalistic rivalry, entangling alliances, and international tension of the prewar years, reaching back to 1870.

World War I: Building the Peace (mp 11 min.), Coronet. Dramatizes the writing of the treaty at the conference at Versailles, its provisions, and its effect on the map and peoples of Europe.

World War I: The War Years (mp 13 min.), Coronet. Reviews the relative advantages of the Allies and the Central Powers. Discusses German strategy and its failure, the major campaigns of the middle war years, and the final phases of the war.

Section (pages 639–645)

1 Conflicting National Interests Set the Stage for War

SECTION OVERVIEW

Four factors—nationalism, imperialism, militarism and the system of alliances—helped bring on World War I. The Balkans were the center of intense nationalist rivalries and competition among the major powers. Archduke Francis Ferdinand's assassination was the spark that ignited this "powder keg of Europe." Austria issued an ultimatum to Serbia. When Serbia did not accept all the terms, Austria declared war. This declaration created a chain reaction in Europe involving all the major powers.

SUGGESTED TEACHING STRATEGIES

1. **Understanding Chronology (Basic)** Put the following list of events on the chalkboard, and have students arrange the events in chronological order.

(3) Austria-Hungary declared war on Serbia.
(7) Germans marched into Belgium.
(10) Italy entered the war against its former allies.
(1) Archduke Francis Ferdinand was assassinated.
(5) Germany declared war on Russia.
(9) Japan entered the war against Germany.
(2) Austria-Hungary issued an ultimatum to Serbia.
(4) Russia mobilized troops.
(6) Germany declared war on France.
(8) Great Britain declared war on Germany.

2. **Using a Map (Average/Group)** Use the map on page 644 as the basis for a discussion of the basic strategic position of the two alliances in World War I. Ask these questions: What were the geographical advantages and disadvantages of the Triple Entente? Of the Triple Alliance? How might the close grouping of the Triple Alliance nations help them to combine and coordinate forces? To what extent might this advantage be reduced by having to fight a two-front war? How might the distance between the Triple Entente nations be both an advantage and a disadvantage? What effect might control of the seas have on the war?

ENRICHMENT ACTIVITY

Presenting a Newscast (Average/Group) Have students divide into groups to research events surrounding the assassination of Francis Ferdinand. Two good sources are Sydney Eisen's and Maurice

Filler's "The Assassination of Archduke Franz Ferdinand" in *The Human Adventure,* vol. 2 (Harcourt Brace Jovanovich); and *The American Heritage History of World War I,* edited by the editors of American Heritage. Groups should prepare reports for a class newscast. One group can report from Sarajevo and provide a summary of the assassination itself; other groups can report on government reactions in Paris, London, Vienna, St. Petersburg, Berlin, and Washington. One or more groups can prepare editorials to be read during the newscast.

DAILY QUIZ

To assess student understanding of Section 1, give the class the following quiz. (Each item is worth 10 points.)

1. List three "causes for peace" in the world prior to World War I. *(Red Cross, communications improved, Olympic Games, philanthropy, Nobel and his awards, Palace of Peace, The Hague, and limitation of armaments)*
2. Name two areas where imperialistic goals helped heighten prewar international tensions. *(Africa, China, Middle East, and the Pacific Islands)*
3. The glorification of armed strength is sometimes called ________ . *(militarism)*
4. What military branch of each country conducted a particularly major buildup as the countries competed for colonial power? *(navy)*
5. Name one of the two major alliance networks—and its members—in Europe prior to World War I. *(Triple Alliance—Germany, Austria-Hungary, Italy; Triple Entente—France, Russia, Great Britain)*
6. What mountainous region in southeastern Europe could be called a "powder keg" because of the Pan-Slavic and nationalist movements? *(Balkans)*
7. Which country in the Balkan region wanted to add Bosnia and Herzegovina, and developed close ties with Russia to make these gains? *(Serbia)*
8. The assassination of Archduke ________ ________ resulted in Austria-Hungary declaring war on Serbia. *(Francis Ferdinand)*
9. The invasion of what neutral country forced Britain to enter World War I? *(Belgium)*
10. (T or F) The Ottoman Empire and Bulgaria ended neutrality by the end of 1915 and joined the war on Germany's side. *(T)*

SUGGESTED ASSIGNMENTS

1. **Critical Thinking Worksheet (Basic)** Have students complete Critical Thinking Worksheet 54 in the TEACHER'S RESOURCEBANK™.
2. **Researching Ideas (Challenging)** Have students research the relationship between the rise of nationalism and militarism prior to World War I and develop an argument that illustrates how these factors gave rise to dictatorships during the 1930s and set the stage for World War II. Students should find information on this subject in their school or local library.

Section (pages 645–651)

2 The Nations of the World Fought a New Kind of War

SECTION OVERVIEW

The French halted the early German advance near Paris, and eventually the western front became a stalemated war of attrition, fought mainly in trenches. When the Allies blockaded the North Sea, Germany countered with submarine warfare. British propaganda, the Zimmermann telegram, and Germany's resumption of unrestricted submarine warfare influenced the United States to enter the war on the Allied side in 1917.

SUGGESTED TEACHING STRATEGIES

1. **Preteaching Vocabulary (Basic)** You may wish to preteach the following important vocabulary terms: propaganda *(page 648)*; war of attrition *(page 650)*; contraband, atrocity *(page 651)*. Ask: How did trade with the belligerents affect the United States?
2. **Map Work (Average/Group)** Divide the class into groups to make maps of the principal battles of World War I. Maps can be done as posters or as overlays for overhead projectors. Students should sketch the topographical or defensive features that figured in the battle and choose symbols to represent the opposing armies and show their movements.

ENRICHMENT ACTIVITIES

1. **Presenting Oral Reports (Average/Group)** Students might prepare oral reports on some of the weapons and military techniques used during World War I. Sources include *Tanks and Weapons of World War I,* edited by Bernard Fitzsimmons (Beekman House); Ezra Bowen's *Knights of the Air* (Time-Life); Edwin P. Hoyt's *The Zeppelins* (Lothrop, Lee & Shepard); and Dorothy and Thomas Hobbler's *Trenches* (Putnam).
2. **Researching Ideas (Challenging)** Divide the class into three groups representing the United States, Great Britain, and Germany. Each group is to research the issues that could be exploited by its country for propaganda. Some examples are the sinking of the *Lusitania,* American loans and shipments of contraband to the Allies early in the war, the British blockade, war heroes and air aces, and the violation of Belgian neutrality. Have each group prepare propaganda in the form of cartoons, posters, editorials, speeches, or songs. Sources include Suzanne Everett's *World War I* (Rand McNally); and Frank Freidel's *Over There* (Little, Brown). Have each group present their findings to the class in an oral presentation.

DAILY QUIZ

To assess student understanding of Section 2, give the class the following quiz. (Each item is worth 10 points.)

1. List three members of the Central Powers or three members of the Allied Powers. *(Central Powers: Germany, Austria-Hungary, Bulgaria, Ottoman Empire; Allied Powers: France, Britain, Russia, Italy, Belgium, Portugal, Ireland, Montenegro, Albania, Greece, Serbia, Romania, Poland)*
2. List three developments in military tactics and weaponry that affected the fighting in World War I. *(machine gun, tank, airplane, U-boat or submarine, poison gas, and trenches)*
3. What segment of society produced the war materials on the home front as most of the men went to war? *(women)*
4. (T or F) Most governments involved in World War I made use of propaganda in the newspapers and magazines, portraying the enemy as brutal and subhuman. *(T)*
5. Who were the two primary foes on the eastern front? *(Russia and Germany)*
6. Where did the British and French attack in an attempt to send supplies to Russia? *(Gallipoli)*
7. What did Germany send to destroy British ships and starve the British people into submission? *(U-boat or submarine)*
8. At ________ Germany tried to "bleed" the French army to death. *(Verdun)*
9. War material supplied by neutral nations to belligerents is called ________. *(contraband)*
10. Unrestricted submarine warfare and the Zimmermann telegram incident resulted in which powerful country entering the war on the Allied side? *(the United States)*

SUGGESTED ASSIGNMENTS

1. **Critical Thinking Worksheet (Basic)** Have students complete Critical Thinking Worksheet 55 in the TEACHER'S RESOURCEBANK™.
2. **Profile Worksheet (Basic)** Have students complete Profile Worksheet 24 in the TEACHER'S RESOURCEBANK™.

Section 3 (pages 651–654)

The Russian Revolution Ended the Czarist Regime

Economic backwardness, in addition to continuing poverty, and the devastation of World War I helped bring revolution to Russia. In March 1917 the czar was overthrown and a provisional government was formed. In November the Bolsheviks under Lenin overturned this moderate government, and a civil war ended in a Communist victory.

SUGGESTED TEACHING STRATEGIES

1. **Forming Hypotheses (Challenging)** Have students use their knowledge of Russia in the late 1800s and early 1900s to make hypotheses about the causes of the Bolshevik Revolution. Ask students to name two principal means societies use to bring about change. *(reform and revolution)* If students fail to respond, ask how the people of France in the late 1700s and Great Britain in the 1800s brought power to the middle class. What reform measures did czars Alexander II and Nicholas II institute? *(freeing of the serfs, provincial assemblies, legal reforms, increased liberties, and creation of the Duma)* Why were these reforms ineffective? *(The reforms made only minor changes in the society, whereas major changes were required.)* What reforms would have been more effective? *(Students' answers may vary.)*
2. **Interpreting Ideas (Average/Group)** How did World War I expose Russia's weaknesses? *(The demands of the war revealed the country's lack of railroads, roads, and industry needed to equip and supply Russia's army.)*

ENRICHMENT ACTIVITY

Preparing Biographical Sketches. (Average/Group) Have students prepare oral or written reports on one of the following leading persons of the Russian Revolution: Nicholas II, Rasputin, Alexander Kerensky, Trotsky, Lenin, and Stalin. Sources include: Kay M. Teall's *From Tsars to Commissars* (Julian Messner).

DAILY QUIZ

To assess student understanding of Section 3, give the class the following quiz. (Each item is worth 10 points.)

1. (T or F) The Russian Revolution of 1905 brought about no real changes. *(T)*
2. Why did Nicholas II remain almost an absolute ruler? *(He did not trust the Duma.)*
3. What three weaknesses exposed during World War I affected Russia's ability to equip and supply its army? *(lack of railroads, roads, and industry)*
4. Most members of the Petrograd Soviet were moderate socialists called ________. *(Mensheviks)*
5. Radical socialists were called ________. *(Bolsheviks)*
6. ________ ________ was the revolutionary Bolshevik leader. *(Nikolai Lenin)*
7. Opposition forces tried to overthrow the ________ in a civil war. *(Communists)*
8. The ________ adopted the color red because it was the symbolic color of European revolutionary socialism. *(Communists)*
9. Why did the Allies aid White forces with arms and money? *(They were angry because Russia had signed separate peace treaties with the Central Powers and they feared that if the Communists gained control of Russia, the revolution would spread.)*
10. (T or F) The Allies made no attempt to prolong the Russian civil war. *(F)*

SUGGESTED ASSIGNMENTS

1. **Constructing a Time Line (Average/Group)** Have students make a time line for the period 1905-1936 that includes each major event dated in Section 3. Then have students identify the

cause-and-effect-relationship that developed among specific events.

2. **Drawing Conclusions (Average/Group)** In 1917 Kaiser William II, although he was anticommunist, allowed Lenin to pass safely through Germany on the way to Russia. Have students write a paragraph that addresses the following questions: On what basis can the kaiser's action be justified? *(He wanted to get Russia out of the war by stirring up a revolution.)* In what ways did it prove to be foolish? *(In the long term, Russia became a threat to Germany in the East.)* From this example, what conclusions can you reach about conflicts between short-term and long-term goals? Can you think of other examples in history of enemies cooperating to oppose a common enemy? What results did such action have? *(Answers will vary. However, students should cite specific events and support their opinions with facts.)*

Section (pages 654–658)

4 After Achieving Victory, the Allies Drafted Peace Terms

SECTION OVERVIEW

The Communist Party seized control of the Russian government in November 1917 and soon signed a peace agreement with Germany. The Russians published the Allies' secret territorial aims; in response President Wilson expressed more idealistic aims in his Fourteen Points. The German offensive in the spring and summer of 1918 failed, and the Central Powers collapsed in the Balkans and the Middle East. When the Allies met in Paris to draft peace treaties, their representatives faced the problems of territorial demands, reparations, and establishing an organization to maintain world peace.

SUGGESTED TEACHING STRATEGIES

1. **Comparing Past and Present (Average/Group)** Have students look in current magazines and newspapers for events that relate to the six general proposals of Wilson's Fourteen Points. Stories on economic barriers and limits on armaments are apt to be readily available. Discuss whether Wilson's ideals are desirable and realistic. What advantages and disadvantages does each one entail? Are Wilson's proposals being put into practice today? Why or why not?

*2. **Interpreting Visuals: Using a Map as a Historical Document** Have students conduct research on the spread of communism from 1960 to the present by looking at maps. Then have them identify nations that might be vulnerable to the spread of communism.

ENRICHMENT ACTIVITY

Debating Ideas (Challenging) Two students, representing Wilson and Clemenceau, might hold a debate on the subject of a peace of justice versus a peace of vengeance. Other students can act as reporters, questioning the debaters. Before presenting the program, students might consult L. S. Stavrianos's "Wilson's Fourteen Points" in *Readings in World History* (Allyn and Bacon); T. A. Bailey's *A Diplomatic History of the American People* (Appleton-Century-Crofts); and C. L. Mee, Jr.'s "Negotiating the Treaty of Versailles" in *The End of Order* (Dutton). Students might also read more about other peace conferences discussed in the textbook, such as the Congress of Vienna, and other wars, such as the American Civil War, to see how the victors treated the defeated peoples.

DAILY QUIZ

To assess student understanding of Section 4, give the class the following quiz. (Each item is worth 10 points.)

1. Woodrow Wilson said the United States entered World War I to "make the world safe for ______." *(democracy)*
2. What Allied Power, divided by revolution, left the war in 1918 and signed the Treaty of Brest-Litovsk, badly damaging the Allied war effort? *(Russia)*
3. (T or F) The six general proposals of the Fourteen Points included freedom of the seas for all nations and removal of all economic barriers or tariffs. *(T)*
4. (T or F) Wilson's fourteenth point suggested the establishment of a "general association of nations." *(T)*
5. What was the last Central Power still fighting, despite the loss of Kaiser William II, who had abdicated? *(Germany)*
6. The Allies agreed that a ______ treaty should be written for each of the defeated Central Powers. *(separate)*
7. Which countries comprised the Big Four? *(Italy, Great Britain, France, and the United States)*
8. Which country was the only Allied Power not invited to the peace conference? *(Russia)*
9. Payments for war damages are called ______. *(reparations)*
10. Many of the victors believed that only ______ ______ would teach Germany and Austria the consequences of war. *(harsh treatment)*

SUGGESTED ASSIGNMENTS

1. **Skill Worksheet (Basic)** Have students complete Skill Worksheet 24 in the TEACHER'S RESOURCEBANK™.
2. **Writing an Editorial (Average/Group)** Divide the class into six groups. Have each group work together to write an editorial for a French, British, Italian, American, Russian, or German newspaper, respectively. They are to express their country's position on issues at the peace conference—the independence of nationalist groups, territorial claims, and reparations. Before writing, students may want to reread "Problems Facing the Peacemakers" on pages 656 and 658.
3. **Comparing Ideas (Challenging)** Have students research American foreign policy during the 1980s and write a comparison of President Wilson's role in American foreign policy with that of President Bush. Students should be able to find sources of information in their school or local library. They may also con-

sult the *Readers' Guide to Periodical Literature* for more recent information on this subject.

Section 5 (pages 658–661)
The Peace Treaties Created a "New Europe"

SECTION OVERVIEW

The Versailles Treaty forced Germany to acknowledge guilt for starting the war, to pay reparations, to cede territory, to surrender its colonies, and to limit its military force. The peace treaty also changed the political map of Europe. All of the Central Powers and Russia lost territory, and several new nations were created in Europe and the Middle East. The League of Nations was established, but the United States did not join.

SUGGESTED TEACHING STRATEGIES

1. **Conducting Interviews (Average/Group)** Organize the class into groups of three. In each group have one student assume the role of a newspaper reporter and the others of a German and a French citizen. The time is after the signing of the Treaty of Versailles. Ask the reporter in each group to compile a list of questions regarding the treaty's provisions for France and Germany. The interviewees should answer the questions as they think their person would respond in historical context. The responses should be based on material on pages 658–659. For additional information, students might read Edwin Fenton's "The Treaty of Versailles and the German Position" in *Thirty-two Problems in World History* (Scott, Foresman).
2. **Using Maps (Average/Group)** To help the class understand the territorial changes made after World War I, pass out two copies of the outline map of Europe in the Geography Supplement of the TEACHER'S RESOURCEBANK™ to each student. On one, students should show Europe before World War I; on the other, Europe after World War I. Have them note the territorial changes resulting from World War I.

ENRICHMENT ACTIVITY

Researching Ideas (Average/Group) Divide the class into groups to study the creation of the League of Nations and the failure of the United States to join. Each group should select a specific topic, such as Wilson's role in the founding of the League, reactions of representatives at Versailles to the League, or reception of the League in the United States. Sources include Sherrill E. Aberg's *Woodrow Wilson and the League of Nations* (Scholastic); C. L. Mee, Jr.'s *The End of Order* (Dutton); and T. A. Bailey's *A Diplomatic History of the American People* (Appleton-Century-Crofts). Students should also check the index of *American Heritage* magazine to find appropriate articles.

DAILY QUIZ

To assess student understanding of Section 5, give the class the following quiz. (Each item is worth 10 points.)

1. What was the name of the treaty that ended World War I in 1919? *(Treaty of Versailles)*
2. Name one of the German objections to the treaty. *(war guilt, reparations, "blank check" for reparations, loss of territory)*
3. (T or F) Germany did not lose Berlin as a result of the peace treaty. *(T)*
4. (T or F) The treaty provisions attempted to destroy Germany's ability to wage war, maintain a navy, or compete economically with France. *(T)*
5. Which Central European country became several nations as a result of the war? *(Austria-Hungary)*
6. Unlike Finland, Latvia, Lithuania, and ________, Greece was not created as a buffer state against Soviet Russia after World War I. *(Estonia)*
7. Name one of the League of Nation's aims. *(promote international cooperation, reduce armies or armaments, and maintain peace)*
8. Name two of the League's main or satellite agencies. *(Assembly, Council, Secretariat, World Court)*
9. Name three of the five intended permanent members of the Council. *(Great Britain, France, Italy, Japan, and the United States)*
10. Name two nations that did not, or were not permitted to, join the League right away. *(Germany, Russia, and the United States)*

SUGGESTED ASSIGNMENTS

1. **Preparing a Book Report (Average/Group)** Have students write short book reports on books dealing with World War I. They may choose either fiction or nonfiction works. Suggested books include the following: John Dos Passos's *Three Soldiers* (Houghton Mifflin); Barbara Tuchman's *The Guns of August* (Macmillan); and Robert Graves's *Goodbye to All That* (Doubleday).
2. **Review Worksheet (Basic)** Have students complete Review Worksheet 24 in the TEACHER'S RESOURCEBANK™.

For suggested lesson plan, additional teaching strategies, enrichment activities, daily quizzes, and suggested assignments, see pages 637A–637F.

Introducing the Chapter
Discuss the concept of a world war with the students, using the following questions: What does the term *world war* mean? *(a conflict that spreads to all major inhabited regions of the world)* Had any previous military conflicts qualified as world wars according to this definition? *(Answers will vary. However, students should suggest that several wars during the 1700s involved most of the European nations. One of these, the Seven Years' War, was fought throughout Europe, in the Americas, and in India.)* What circumstances do you think would cause a world war? *(threat of world conquest by one power, an alliance system, or rival imperialist claims)* As students read the chapter, have them refine their concept of whether World War I was actually a world war. Point out that although fighting reached many distant areas of the world, it did not reach all areas of the world. For example, no battles were fought in North or South America, Southeast Asia, or much of Africa.

CHAPTER 24

World War I and the Russian Revolution Altered the Course of History

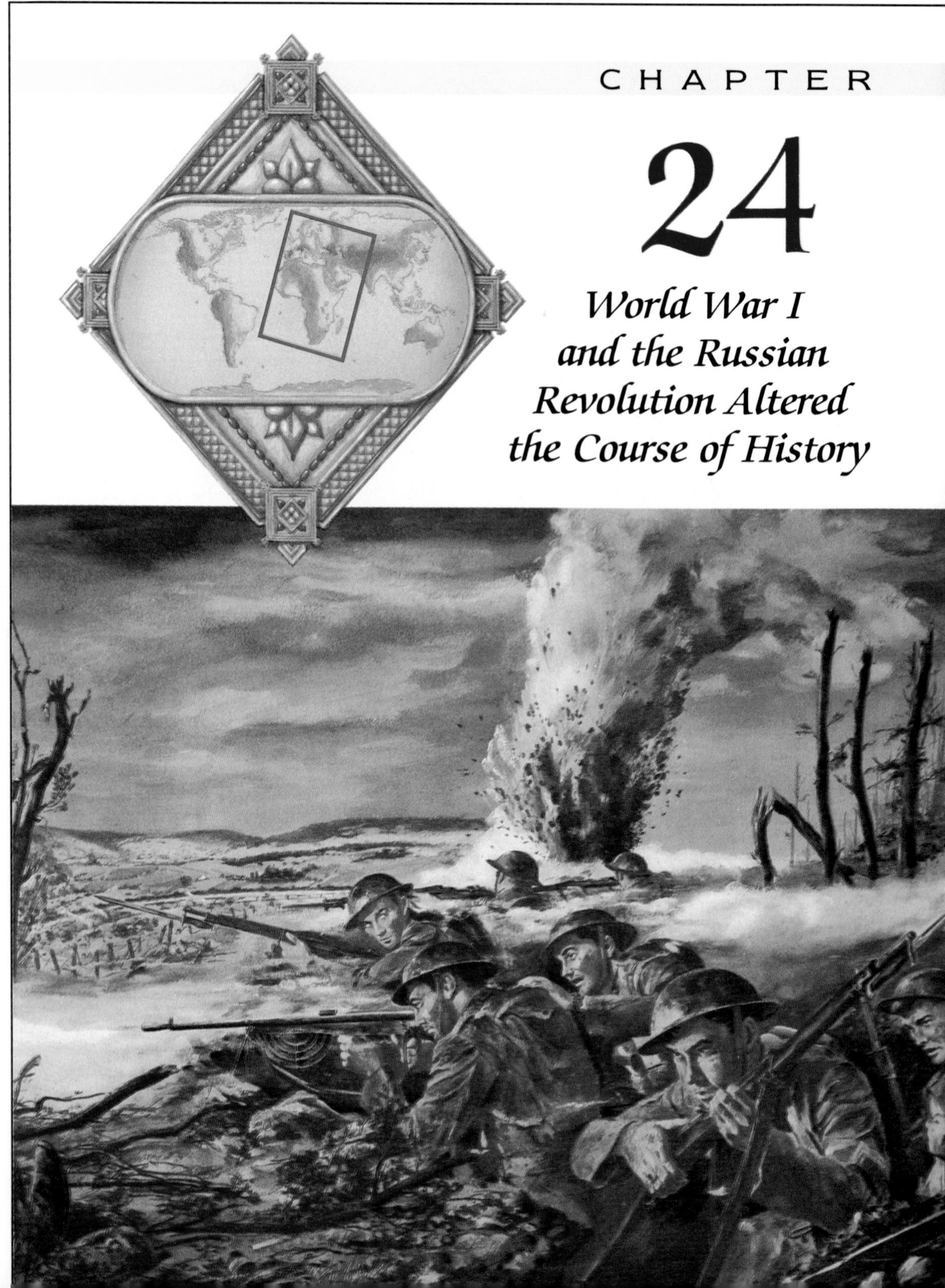

CHAPTER FOCUS

Place Europe, Africa, and the Middle East

Time 1882–1920

Significance

During the late 1800s, world leaders had striven to promote cooperation among nations. Philanthropists—people interested in the welfare of the human race—gave time and money to encourage cooperation between nations. For example, Andrew Carnegie, an American financier, built the Palace of Peace at The Hague, in the Netherlands, where diplomats could hold international conferences designed to reduce world tensions.

Representatives of several nations met at The Hague in 1899 and again in 1907 in an effort to limit armaments. Even as nations met to discuss peace, however, they prepared for war. The war that began in the summer of 1914 resembled no previous war. For the first time in history, industrial technology played a major role.

Because of the devastation that the war caused, the people of the time rightly called it the Great War. We know the Great War as World War I.

Terms to Define

militarism
mobilize
entente
ultimatum
belligerent
propaganda
contraband
Fourteen Points

People to Identify

Andrew Carnegie
Archduke Francis Ferdinand
Woodrow Wilson
Alfred Zimmermann
Ferdinand Foch
Big Four

Places to Locate

Sarajevo
western front
Polish Corridor
Czechoslovakia

Questions to Guide Your Reading

1 What conflicting national interests set the stage for war?
2 In what ways did the nations of the world fight a new kind of war?
3 How did the war bring about the Russian Revolution and the end of the czarist regime?
4 After defeating the Central Powers, what peace terms did the Allies draft?
5 How did the peace treaties create a "new Europe" after World War I?

As in all other wars, the soldiers of World War I came to realize that terror and death stalk both sides. The following excerpt from All Quiet on the Western Front *describes a German soldier's feelings upon the death of an enemy.*

> *"The rattle of machine-guns becomes an unbroken chain. Just as I am about to turn around a little, something heavy stumbles, and with a crash a body falls over me into the shell-hole, slips down, and lies across me— . . .*
>
> *The silence spreads. I talk and must talk. So I speak to him and say to him: 'Comrade, I did not want to kill you. . . . You were only an idea to me before. . . . But now, for the first time, I see you are a man like me. . . . Forgive me, comrade. We always see too late. . . . Why do they never tell us that you are . . . like us, that your mothers are just as anxious as ours, and that we have the same fear of death, and the same dying and the same agony—Forgive me, comrade; how could you be my enemy? If we threw away these rifles and this uniform you could be my brother.'"*

The events that culminated in the horror soldiers experienced on battlefields during World War I began with conflicting national interests among European nations during the late 1800s and the early 1900s.

1 Conflicting National Interests Set the Stage for War

Some historians have referred to the decades before 1914 as a period of "international anarchy." Each nation in Europe pursued policies without regard for the wishes or interests of its neighbors. These conflicting interests set the stage for war.

Since the Congress of Vienna in 1815, relations among European powers had been more or less harmonious. Beginning in the late 1800s, however, cooperation among nations broke down as intense rivalries increased. These rivalries grew both within Europe as new nations were formed, and overseas as a result of imperialism.

In *The Guns of August,* Barbara Tuchman describes an event in England that temporarily brought the European nations together and marked the transition between the old and the new.

◀ *American soldiers in trenches east of Paris, 1918*

Chapter Objectives
After studying Chapter 24, students will be able to:

1. Identify the conflicting national interests that set the stage for World War I.
2. Briefly trace the expansion of World War I.
3. List the Allied Powers and the Central Powers.
4. Describe the innovations in warfare during World War I.
5. Explain why the war reached a stalemate by 1916.
6. Summarize the reasons why the United States entered World War I.
7. List Russia's reasons for entering World War I.
8. Compare the government of Russia under Czar Nicholas II with government under Lenin and the Bolsheviks.
9. Summarize the causes and effects of the civil war in Russia.
10. State the importance of the Fourteen Points.
11. Summarize the problems facing the peacemakers at the end of World War I.
12. List the major provisions of the Versailles Treaty.
13. Summarize the purpose and the organization of the League of Nations.

SECTION 1

Focus/Motivation
Bismarck had predicted that "some foolish thing in the Balkans" would ignite the next war. Ask: What conditions in the Balkans might have led Bismarck to this conclusion? Have stu-

4J, 4K, 5B, 5F

● Discussion topic: The advantages and disadvantages of nationalism

dents review what they learned in Chapter 22 about growing nationalism and outside involvement in the Balkans. Then ask the following questions: How did Balkan nationalists fare in their fight for independence in the 1800s? What interests did Russia, Great Britain, Austria-Hungary, and Germany have in the region? How did these interests conflict? What would happen if nationalistic conflicts and major-power tensions came together? Conclude by pointing out that some historians believe that if Germany had not allied with Austria-Hungary, and Russia with Serbia, the war would have been just another Balkan war.

Presentation Analyzing Ideas (Average/Group)

Ask students to discuss how communication has changed since the early 1900s. Then ask them to speculate on what effect improved communication may have on the incidence or outcome of international conflicts today. *(Some students might suggest that the development of satellites and other monitoring devices contribute to a nation's security. Students may also point out that "hot lines" available to national leaders allow immediate communication during emergency situations.)*

"So gorgeous was the spectacle on the May morning of 1910 when nine kings rode in the funeral of Edward VII of England that the crowd, waiting in hushed and black-clad awe, could not keep back gasps of admiration. In scarlet and blue and green and purple, three by three the sovereigns rode through the palace gates, with plumed helmets, gold braid, crimson sashes, and jeweled orders [military decorations] flashing in the sun. After them came . . . heirs, . . . queens . . . and a scattering of special ambassadors from uncrowned countries. Together they represented seventy nations in the greatest assemblage of royalty and rank ever gathered in one place and, of its kind, the last. The muffled tongue of Big Ben tolled nine by the clock as the cortege left the palace, but on history's clock it was sunset, and the sun of the old world was setting in a dying blaze of splendor never to be seen again."

As rivalries intensified in the early 1900s, the great powers plunged toward war, pressed forward by four factors: nationalism, imperialism, militarism, and the system of alliances.

Nationalism and Imperialism

Spurred by the nationalism that developed after the French Revolution and the Napoleonic Wars, national groups throughout the 1800s tried to unite under governments controlled by their own people. This desire to unite all the people of a nation under ● a single government, however, had explosive possibilities in a Europe where a single government often ruled many nationalities.

In the early 1900s, the imperialist nations came to the brink of war several times as they scrambled to partition Africa among themselves. Germany and France, for example, narrowly avoided war over their rival claims to Morocco on two occasions between 1905 and 1911. They managed to settle each incident with makeshift compromises that usually left one of the participants dissatisfied.

Militarism

The glorification of armed strength, or **militarism,** dominated the thinking of many European leaders before World War I. These leaders believed that only the use of force could solve problems among nations. According to these leaders, a militarily strong nation usually got what it wanted, as Prussia had proved in its wars with Denmark, Austria, and France. Weaker nations lost out, as Italy had learned from its imperialistic ventures in Africa.

In the late 1800s, European nations built reserve armies of soldiers who were drafted, given military training, and then returned to civilian life. These soldiers could be called into service at any time. If one nation **mobilized,** or organized its resources for combat, other nations would mobilize for their own protection. It was a cyclical process that was difficult to stop once it had begun.

As international rivalries intensified, each European nation believed it necessary to keep its armed forces stronger than those of any potential enemy. Armies grew larger as spending for new weapons and for the fortification of national boundaries multiplied. In the 1890s Germany began to build a large and modern navy to rival that of Great Britain. France, the United States, Japan, and Italy followed Germany's example. Great Britain responded by expanding its navy even more.

The System of Alliances

During the late 1800s, the unification of Germany and of Italy shifted the balance of power in Europe. Germany, more than Italy, created an entirely new situation. In place of a group of relatively weak states, a powerful German Empire, under the leadership of Prussia, emerged. Otto von Bismarck, the skillful and ruthless German chancellor, shaped its ambitious foreign policy.

The Triple Alliance. Bismarck feared that France would seek revenge for its 1871 defeat in the Franco-Prussian War by trying to regain Alsace-Lorraine, which it had lost to Germany. He therefore dedicated his foreign policy to keeping France isolated and without allies. Bismarck particularly wanted to prevent a Franco-Russian alliance because it would serve to isolate Germany diplomatically and—at worst—mean that Germany would have to fight on both its eastern and western borders in the event of war.

In 1879 Bismarck formed the Dual Alliance, a mutual defense pact between Germany and Austria-Hungary. Then in 1881 the chancellor set up the Three Emperors' League, a secret agreement among the emperors of Germany, Russia, and Austria-Hungary.

Learning from Pictures *In 1906 the British Navy launched a new type of battleship called the dreadnought that featured heavy armor plating and batteries of big guns.*

In 1882 Bismarck agreed to Italy's request for the Triple Alliance, a pact among Germany, Austria-Hungary, and Italy. Bismarck considered Italy a weak link in the Triple Alliance; however, the forging of the alliance isolated France and therefore enabled Bismarck to accomplish his primary foreign policy goal.

The formation of the Triple Alliance completely upset the balance of power in Europe. For a while, Bismarck's skillful diplomacy kept France isolated. France, however, became uneasy and began to seek allies.

The Reinsurance Treaty. In 1885 a Balkan crisis, sparked by Bulgarian nationalism in Eastern Rumelia (a Turkish province in the Balkan region), resulted in the dissolution of the Three Emperors' League. Russian nationalists, who resented Germany's support of Austria-Hungary in the Balkans, demanded that the Russian government make an alliance with France. However, the Russian government hesitated to sever diplomatic relations with Germany and suggested instead that Germany enter into a new treaty that would exclude Austria-Hungary. The Reinsurance Treaty of 1887 provided for neutrality in case either Russia or Germany became involved in a defensive war.

In 1888 William II became kaiser and soon dismissed Bismarck. Bismarck's careful plans collapsed as William II abandoned Bismarck's policies.

The Triple Entente. France, meanwhile, had been trying to gain allies. The opportunity arose after William II allowed the Reinsurance Treaty to collapse. An economic crisis shook Russia, and the czar sought a loan. The French hurried to lend the money and took other steps to win Russia's friendship. In 1894 France and Russia formed an alliance, making Bismarck's fear of facing potential enemies on two sides a reality.

After 1888 Germany entered the race for colonies with full force, demanding its "place in the sun." William II also began a great naval buildup. The rapid growth of the German navy troubled the British. Germany also began to interfere with some of Great Britain's imperial schemes, as goods from German industries competed with British goods in world markets.

Great Britain, too, began to look for allies. In 1904 the British and the French reached an agreement over the control of Morocco and Egypt. The agreement was an **entente** (ahn • TAHNT)—a friendly understanding or agreement between nations—rather than an alliance. Still, in order to

641

5B, a1C

● Gavrilo Princip was sent to prison, where he died of tuberculosis in 1918.

counterbalance the Triple Alliance, Great Britain and Russia had to come to an agreement as well. Reaching such an agreement proved difficult, however, because of the two nations' rivalry in the Middle East. But with French help they finally arrived at an understanding in 1907. The resulting alignment of France, Russia, and Great Britain was called the Triple Entente. Both France and Russia also had secret understandings with Italy, which meant that the Italians had a foot in both camps.

Dangers of the alliance system. By 1907 the alliance system threatened world peace because it divided Europe into two armed camps. Should hostilities develop between any two rival powers, all six nations would become involved in the fighting, whether or not the original dispute concerned all of them. A minor quarrel could lead to serious consequences, as events in 1914 would prove.

The Balkan Powder Keg

The many conflicts that plagued the Balkans gave rise to the region's nickname—"powder keg of Europe." Amid the growing system of alliances, the powder keg threatened to explode.

Nationalists in Serbia, which had become independent in 1878, hoped to make their country the center of a large Slavic state. They wanted Slavic territories still under Ottoman and Austro-Hungarian rule to become part of this state. The Serbian nationalists especially wanted the provinces of Bosnia and Herzegovina (hert • suh • goh • VEE • nuh) because Serbia was landlocked and these two provinces would provide an outlet on the Adriatic Sea.

The decision of the Congress of Berlin in 1878 to make the two provinces protectorates of Austria-Hungary (see Chapter 22) severely disappointed the Serbs. After Austria-Hungary annexed Bosnia and Herzegovina in 1908, infuriated Serbian nationalists distributed propaganda against Austria-Hungary to win sympathy for their cause. The rivalry between the two groups intensified.

Hoping to assume leadership of a Slavic league, Russia supported Serbia's nationalistic goals. Great Britain, however, opposed Pan-Slavism, the nationalist movement that pressed for the political and cultural unity of all Slavs under Russian leadership. The British distrusted Russian influence in the Balkans. They also feared for the safety of the Suez Canal, their main route to India and Britain's most important colonial possession.

These rivalries heightened tensions in the Balkans. Another factor made the situation even more explosive. To strengthen the Triple Alliance and make up for the weakness of Italy, the young, arrogant William II of Germany sought new allies. He began negotiating to bring the Ottoman Empire into the Triple Alliance and thereby extend German influence into the Balkans.

Germany also planned to build a railroad from Berlin through the Balkans to Constantinople and on to Baghdad, near the Persian Gulf. This plan aroused many fears. The British regarded the proposed railroad as a threat to the sea route through the Suez Canal, their Mediterranean-Red Sea "lifeline" to India. They feared that such a railroad would provide a better route to India. The Russians feared that Germany would become a strong protector of the Ottoman Empire. This would diminish Russia's age-old hope of gaining Constantinople, the Dardanelles, and the Bosporus.

Germany's actions in the Balkans complicated an already confused situation and resulted in what Bismarck had carefully avoided—the strengthening of ties between Great Britain and Russia. Both countries wanted to resist German expansion in the Balkans. Austria-Hungary, on the other hand, feared Pan-Slavism and won Germany's support in its opposition to Slavic nationalism.

Assassination at Sarajevo

The spark that touched off the explosion of the Balkan "powder keg" and led to war came on June 28, 1914. The heir to the Austro-Hungarian throne, Archduke Francis Ferdinand, and his wife were visiting Sarajevo (sahr • uh • YE • voh), the capital of Bosnia and Herzegovina, on a mission of goodwill. As they rode in an open automobile, a young man fired a revolver, killing both the archduke and his wife.

The assassin, Gavrilo Princip, belonged to the Black Hand, one of the many secret societies of Serbian nationalists opposed to Austro-Hungarian ● rule. Although Princip had acted without the authority of the Serbian government, certain Serbian leaders were aware of his plans and had furnished arms and ammunition.

The assassination brought to a head the long struggle between Serbia and Austria-Hungary. The Austro-Hungarian government was determined to punish the Serbs. But before Austria-Hungary

642

● He was on a mission of goodwill.

Learning from Pictures *Gavrilo Princip fires the fatal shots at Archduke Francis Ferdinand and his wife. Why was the Archduke in Sarajevo?*

acted, it wanted to make sure of German support in case the Russians tried to help Serbia. Germany promised to back Austria-Hungary in anything Austria-Hungary did. Encouraged by this so-called blank check, the Austro-Hungarians presented an **ultimatum** to the Serbian government. An ultimatum puts forth the final terms offered for a settlement. It states that if the ultimatum is rejected, negotiations will end and the country that issued the ultimatum will use force.

War Between Austria-Hungary and Serbia

In its ultimatum Austria-Hungary made the following demands: (1) The Serbian government would condemn all propaganda against Austria-Hungary and suppress publications and societies that opposed Austria-Hungary. (2) Serbia would ban from its schools books and teachers who did not favor Austria-Hungary. (3) Serbia would dismiss any officials who had promoted propaganda against Austria-Hungary. (4) Austro-Hungarian judges would conduct the trial of those accused of the crime at Sarajevo. (5) Serbia had to accept all of these terms within 48 hours or Austria-Hungary would declare war.

The Serbian government returned a mild and conciliatory reply. Serbia accepted all the terms except the last two, but offered to submit the entire dispute to the international court at The Hague. However, assuming that Austria-Hungary would not accept this offer, the Serbian government ordered mobilization.

In spite of the Serbian reply, Austria-Hungary declared war on Serbia on July 28, after the time limit on the ultimatum had elapsed.

Mobilization of Europe

All attempts to persuade Austria-Hungary to continue negotiations proved futile, especially since Germany continued to support Austria-Hungary. Russia prepared to defend Serbia by mobilizing troops along the Russian–Austro-Hungarian border. Expecting Germany to join Austria-Hungary, Russia also sent troops to the German border.

Germany immediately demanded that Russia cancel mobilization within 12 hours or face war. Russia ignored this ultimatum, and on August 1, 1914, Germany declared war on Russia. Convinced that France was prepared to side with Russia and hoping to gain a military advantage by swift action, Germany declared war on France two days later.

Great Britain Enters the War

The great powers had guaranteed Belgian neutrality in 1839, shortly after Belgium gained its independence. Under the terms of this guarantee, Belgium agreed to stay out of any European war and not to help any **belligerents,** or warring nations. In turn, the other powers agreed not to attack Belgium. However, Belgium's location was of great importance to Germany's military plans. The German General Staff counted on the German army to mobilize, strike, and knock France out of the war before the Russians could attack from the east. Because the Franco-German border was hilly and heavily fortified with the Maginot Line, the Germans planned to attack through Belgium on the coastal plain between France and Germany (see map, page 644).

After the German government declared war on France, it sent an ultimatum to Belgium, demanding that German troops be allowed to cross Belgian territory. The British protested, insisting that Germany observe Belgian neutrality. The German foreign minister replied that surely Great Britain would not fight over "a scrap of paper."

SECTION 1

Closure

Ask students how they think the chain of events that sparked World War I might be compared to recent events in the Middle East. Then ask students to consider the danger of the alliance system among nations today. Tell students as they read the chapter that they should look for reasons why foreign policy decisions must always be made as carefully as possible.

Review Answers

1. ***militarism:*** glorification of armed strength; ***mobilize:*** to organize a nation's resources for combat; ***entente:*** friendly understanding or agreement between nations; ***ultimatum:*** the final terms offered for a settlement; if rejected, negotiations are ended; ***belligerent:*** warring nation **2.** ***Triple Alliance:*** pact among Germany, Austria-Hungary, and Italy created by Bismarck to isolate France; ***Triple Entente:*** agreement among France, Great Britain, and Russia formed to balance the power of the Triple Alliance; ***"powder keg of Europe":*** phrase describing the Balkans because conflict there spread to the rest of the continent; ***Pan-Slavism:*** nationalist movement that pressed for the political and cultural unity of all Slavs under Russian leadership; ***Archduke Francis Ferdinand:*** heir to the Austro-Hungarian throne **3.** ***Serbia:*** independent

1A, 5B, a4B, a4C

Balkan state; ***Bosnia:*** province under Austro-Hungarian rule; ***Adriatic Sea:*** arm of the Mediterranean Sea between Italy and the Balkan Peninsula; ***Sarajevo:*** capital of Bosnia and Herzegovina and site of assassination of Archduke Francis Ferdinand
4. (a) Serbia wanted to acquire territories from the Ottoman Empire and Austria and to become the nucleus of a large Slavic state. Russia supported Serbia's goals, hoping to become the leader of a Slavic league. Great Britain opposed Russian and German expansion, fearing for the safety of the Suez Canal, its most important possession in that region. Germany wanted to expand its influence in the Balkans by bringing the Ottoman Empire into the Triple Alliance and by building a Berlin-to-Baghdad railroad. **(b)** It divided Europe into two armed camps.
5. The event that "lit the fuse" in 1914 was the assassination at Sarajevo of Archduke Francis Ferdinand.
6. Belgium's neutrality had been guaranteed by the major European powers in 1839. Germany, however, wanted to attack France and demanded the right to cross Belgian territory. Great Britain protested that the neutrality guarantee should be observed. When Germany marched into Belgium, Great Britain declared war on Germany.

Learning from Maps *Defensive alliances polarized Europe into two armed camps. What great powers belonged to the Triple Entente?* **France, Russia, and Great Britain**

German soldiers marched into Belgium on August 4, 1914, secure in the kaiser's message—"You will be home before the leaves have fallen from the trees." Great Britain declared war on Germany later that day.

Expansion of the War

Within six weeks after Gavrilo Princip had assassinated Archduke Francis Ferdinand and his wife at Sarajevo, the rapidly modernizing nation of Japan had entered the war on the side of Great Britain and France. In addition, all the nations of the Triple Alliance and the Triple Entente except Italy were at war. The Italian government took the position that the Austro-Hungarians and Germans had acted as aggressors when they marched through neutral Belgium. Thus the Triple Alliance, a defensive treaty, did not require Italy to help them.

● the Battle of Jutland

Italy remained neutral for nine months, while each side pleaded desperately for its help. Finally, Italy signed secret treaties with Great Britain, France, and Russia that guaranteed Italy a share of the spoils of war in case of victory over Germany and Austria-Hungary. In May 1915 Italy entered the war against Germany and Austria-Hungary, its former allies.

In the meantime, Germany had been negotiating to win other allies. In November 1914 the Ottoman Empire had plunged into the war on the side of Germany and Austria-Hungary. The Turks, although not a strong military power, occupied a strategic position. Their control of Constantinople and the Dardanelles bottled up Russia's Black Sea fleet. It also prevented Russia's allies from sending supplies through the Mediterranean and Black seas. Germany also persuaded Bulgaria to enter the war in October 1915.

SECTION 1 REVIEW

1. **Define** militarism, mobilize, entente, ultimatum, belligerent
2. **Identify** Triple Alliance, Triple Entente, "powder keg of Europe," Pan-Slavism, Archduke Francis Ferdinand
3. **Locate** Serbia, Bosnia, Adriatic Sea, Sarajevo
4. **Identifying Ideas** **(a)** Describe the chief aims in the Balkans of the following nations: Serbia, Russia, Great Britain, and Germany. **(b)** Why was the alliance system dangerous?
5. **Summarizing Ideas** What event can be said to have "lit the fuse" in 1914?
6. **Evaluating Ideas** How did Belgium play a strategic role in the outbreak of World War I?

2 The Nations of the World Fought a New Kind of War

The soldiers who marched enthusiastically off to war in the summer of 1914 thought they would win a quick and decisive victory and come home as heroes in time to celebrate the New Year. They were wrong—tragically wrong.

The Belligerents

Germany, Austria-Hungary, Bulgaria, and the Ottoman Empire became known as the Central Powers. Notice on the map on this page that they formed an almost solid block of territory from the North Sea to the Persian Gulf. This geographical proximity gave them an advantage for easy communication and rapid troop movements. Another advantage was Germany's well-organized, well-trained, and well-equipped army.

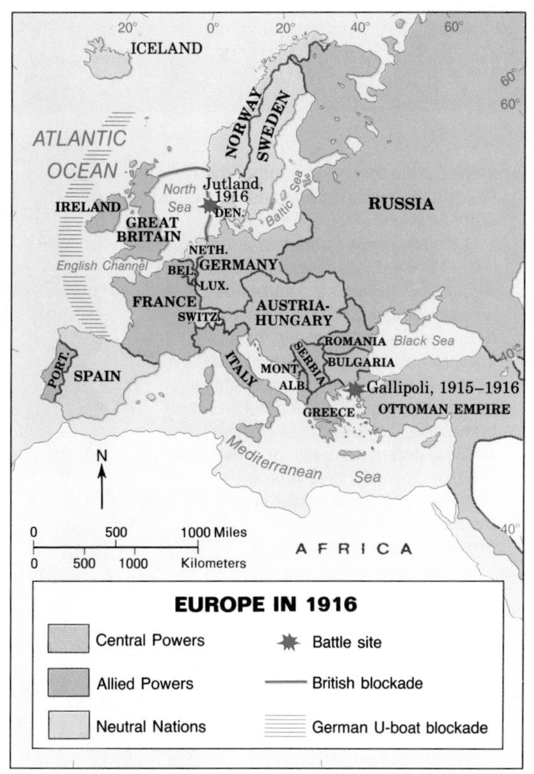

Learning from Maps *The British set up a naval blockade in the North Sea to cut off Germany's sea routes. What battle was fought to break the blockade?* ●

Great Britain, France, Russia, and their partners in the war became known as the Allied Powers, or the Allies. Although they did not have the geographic advantages of the Central Powers, they had more soldiers and a greater industrial potential. They also controlled the seas. Therefore, they could obtain food and raw materials more easily and could blockade and attempt to starve the Central Powers.

As a result of diplomatic maneuvers, Greece and Romania joined the Allies in 1916. Eventually 32 countries made up the Allied side. Many of

Text continues on page 648.

SECTION 2

Focus/Motivation
Ask students to scan the information under "Innovations in Warfare" on page 648. Then have them identify elements in the text that indicate how World War I differed from previous wars. Ask the following questions: How were battlefield conditions unique? *(Trench warfare was used almost exclusively.)* How did the field of battle expand? *(War spread from land and the ocean surface to include the air and ocean depths.)* What impact would this expansion have? *(It required more complicated strategic planning and caused greater casualties.)* What attempts were made to rally public opinion? *(Propaganda was used.)*

Presentation
Comparing Ideas (Average/Group)
Draw on the chalkboard or an overhead projector a chart with two vertical columns. Title one column "Reasons the United States Should Not Enter the War" and the other column "Reasons the United States Should Enter the War." Have students fill in the columns by reviewing pages 645–651. After listing these characteristics on the board, conduct a class discussion on the similarities and differences between World War I and other foreign wars the United States entered.

PERSPECTIVES: LEGACIES OF THE PAST

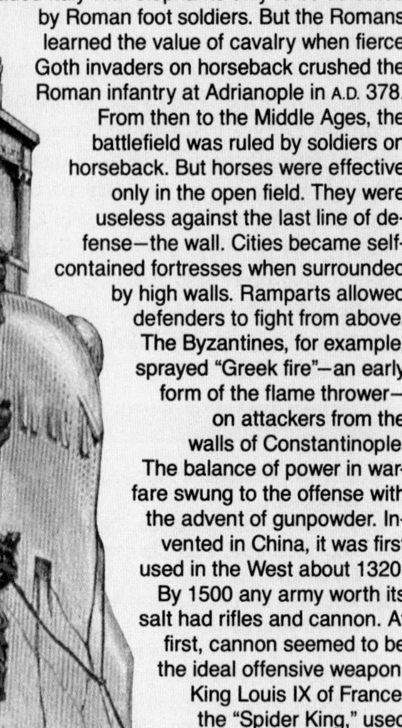

Armies have fought each other throughout history. What has determined the outcome of these wars?

One answer is the bravery—or cowardice—of the individual soldier. Another answer is the skill of the commander.

Most battles and wars, however, have been decided by weapons. In some eras, armed forces have used offensive weapons against which the enemy could find no successful defense. More commonly, the advantage has rested with the defensive side. Today we have the ultimate defensive weapon—nuclear arms. Their power is so awesome that their mere presence discourages attack.

In the early eras of warfare, most weapons were muscle-powered: swords in the hands of Roman legionnaires, lances and longbows in the hands of medieval knights and archers. Innovative generals added mechanical devices. The ancient Assyrians and Egyptians put sharp blades on the wheels of their chariots, and Alexander the Great used huge catapults.

Animal power augmented human power. In 217 B.C. Hannibal invaded Italy with elephants only to be defeated by Roman foot soldiers. But the Romans learned the value of cavalry when fierce Goth invaders on horseback crushed the Roman infantry at Adrianople in A.D. 378.

From then to the Middle Ages, the battlefield was ruled by soldiers on horseback. But horses were effective only in the open field. They were useless against the last line of defense—the wall. Cities became self-contained fortresses when surrounded by high walls. Ramparts allowed defenders to fight from above. The Byzantines, for example, sprayed "Greek fire"—an early form of the flame thrower—on attackers from the walls of Constantinople.

The balance of power in warfare swung to the offense with the advent of gunpowder. Invented in China, it was first used in the West about 1320. By 1500 any army worth its salt had rifles and cannon. At first, cannon seemed to be the ideal offensive weapon. King Louis IX of France, the "Spider King," used cannon to destroy the castles of upstart nobles—and to create a powerful and

646

centralized French monarchy. But it was not long before the cannon was put to defensive use—it could destroy attacking armies as easily as it destroyed fortifications.

At the start of the 1800s, Napoleon Bonaparte used combinations of attacking artillery, infantry, and cavalry with dazzling success. He battered the enemy lines with heavy guns, sent his infantry charging in to break the foe, then crushed the retreating troops with his cavalry. This type of offense seemed unstoppable. It was, but only for a while. Defense caught up in the form of transportation. In the American Civil War, railroads made it possible for reinforcements to reach retreating armies quickly. The Battle of Bull Run (July 1861) provided a clear example of this strategy.

The Civil War was one of the first great conflicts fought with firearms. It was won only when one side had been worn down after years of fighting—not destroyed quickly in Napoleonic fashion.

World War I was directed by generals who tried to imitate Napoleon. There were long artillery barrages to soften the enemy, followed by mass infantry charges. But now a new weapon had come to the fore—the machine gun. In the hands of determined defenders in trenches or behind fortifications, machine guns made a quick Napoleonic victory impossible. World War I ended, as had the American Civil War, with one side collapsing from exhaustion.

World War II brought a shift to the offense, based on fast-striking weapons such as the tank and the airplane. Hitler's war machine quickly crushed Poland (September 1939) and France (May–June 1940).

The tide of the war against Germany turned not because of new defenses against the tank and the plane. It turned when the Allies were able to produce more offensive firepower than the Germans. Against such force, Hitler's last stand in "Fortress Berlin" was doomed.

World War II in the Pacific was ended by the most fearsome offensive weapon ever developed—the atomic bomb. But it was an offensive weapon only as long as it was possessed by one side alone. As other nations learned to build it, it became the final defense. In a war between nuclear powers there can be no winners.

You have heard of homicide (the killing of a person) and genocide (the killing of a race). "Nuclear war," an opponent of nuclear weapons said, "is omnicide (the destruction of all)."

Photos *Page 646: Trojan horse (top), medieval catapult (bottom left), English knights fighting invaders (bottom right); Page 647: tank in World War I (top), atomic explosion (middle), American aircraft carrier (bottom left), F–16 fighters (bottom right)*

647

1A, 5B, 5E, a4A, a4B, a4C

them, however, joined late in the war and made only token contributions to the war effort.

Innovations in Warfare

World War I was an industrialized war. Industry produced weapons with the same efficient mass production methods that it had applied to other items.

One of the most important weapons of World War I was the machine gun. Its sweeping, rapid-fire spray of bullets made it so deadly that armies often found any advance difficult and costly. To protect themselves from the machine gun's raking fire and from artillery bombardments, soldiers dug elaborate systems of trenches.

Both sides used weapons that had never been tried before. In 1916 the British introduced the tank, an armored vehicle on which guns were mounted. Tanks enabled troops to tear through barbed wire and break through enemy lines.

Another untried weapon was the recently invented airplane. Although these first airplanes were not very maneuverable or fast, they sometimes engaged in air battles called dogfights. However, the airplanes were primarily used for observing troop movements and for dropping explosives.

Germany became the first nation to make extensive use of submarines. Its U-boats (from the German word *unterwasser,* meaning "underwater") damaged Allied shipping. The Germans also introduced poison gas, which the Allies later employed.

Except for the wars of the French Revolution, most previous European wars had been fought by professional soldiers whose only source of income was their military pay and rations. In contrast, armies of drafted civilians fought the battles of World War I. Those who could not fight worked at home to help the war effort. Many women participated by working in factories. This type of war became known as total war. To stir the patriotism of the people, governments made wide use of **propaganda**—ideas, facts, or rumors spread deliberately to further one's cause or to damage an opposing cause. Newspapers and popular magazines portrayed the enemy as brutal and subhuman, while praising national aims and achievements.

The War from 1914 to 1916

Germany's attack on France, launched through neutral Belgium, nearly succeeded. By September, German troops had reached the Marne River near Paris. But the French army stood fast and Paris was saved.

The Battle of the Marne changed the entire nature of the war. Germany's hope of swift victory ended. Both armies dug trenches on the western front, which stretched from the Swiss border to the shores of the North Sea.

On the eastern front, the Russians completed mobilization much more quickly than the Germans had expected. One Russian army moved westward toward Budapest, the capital of Hungary. A second army moved through East Prussia, threatening the important Baltic seaport of Danzig.

In late August this second Russian army met a German force in a fierce battle at Tannenberg, in East Prussia (see map, this page). The Russians

Learning from Maps *The Central Powers controlled most of Russia's land around the Baltic Sea. What port city did the Russians control?* **St. Petersburg/Petrograd**

648

CONNECTIONS: THEN AND NOW

Codes and Ciphers

Codes have been used as secret ways of communicating for thousands of years. The ancient Egyptians flew code flags on their ships, and in medieval Europe the Beggars' Association marked houses with signs meaning "food" or "vicious dog." Anyone who knows the key to a code, whether the code consists of flags, signs, or smoke signals, can understand the message.

Most often we think of codes as involving secret messages, danger, and spying activities in wartime (above). The most common way to devise codes for secret messages is by the use of ciphers. A cipher is a letter, number, or symbol that replaces the normal alphabet in a coded message. Since the Japanese and the Chinese languages do not use alphabets, they cannot be used to create ciphers. But all other languages have found this the best method of sending secret, coded messages.

By the time of World War I, coded communication had become so important that the British decided to create a special department of cryptanalysts or cryptographers. These were people who studied ways of solving codes and ciphers. The department operated in the Office of Naval Intelligence and helped the war effort significantly. For example, the British captured the keys to two German codes: the book of naval codes and the official diplomatic cipher system. These keys enabled the British to read a number of vital secret messages and helped them figure out how other German codes worked.

Today computers (above) and satellite dishes (top) have become the main tools for cryptographers. Although they are now much more complicated, codes and ciphers remain an essential form of communication.

649

1A, 1C, 5B, 5E, a4A, a4B, a4C

SECTION 2

Closure

Ask: How did the Russian Revolution of 1917 affect public opinion regarding American entry into the war? *(Americans would more readily accept a war in which the lines were drawn between democratic and nondemocratic countries.)*

Review Answers

1. ***propaganda:*** ideas, facts, or rumors spread deliberately to further one's cause or to damage an opposing cause; ***war of attrition:*** slow wearing-down process in which each side tries to outlast the other; ***contraband:*** war materials supplied by a neutral to a belligerent nation; ***atrocity:*** brutal crime of war
2. ***Central Powers:*** Germany, Austria-Hungary, Bulgaria, and the Ottoman Empire; ***Allied Powers:*** Great Britain, France, Russia, and their partners; ***U-boats:*** German submarines; ***Lusitania:*** British passenger liner sunk by a German submarine off the coast of Ireland; ***Woodrow Wilson:*** president of the United States during World War I; ***Alfred Zimmermann:*** German foreign minister who sent a secret telegram to the German ambassador in Mexico with instructions to draw Mexico into the war on Germany's side
3. ***Marne River:*** site of the Battle of the Marne, near Paris; ***western front:*** stretched from the Swiss border to the shores of the

retreated after suffering a humiliating defeat. Soon afterward the Germans launched an offensive in the east and drove the Russians completely out of Germany and eastward into Russian Poland.

The Gallipoli campaign. Russia had a large army, but it lacked enough guns and ammunition to properly equip its soldiers. In 1915 Great Britain and France decided on a daring venture to try to help Russia. They would attempt to force their way through the Dardanelles and capture Constantinople on the Bosporus and Sea of Marmara.

At first the British and French thought that bombardment from their heavily armed battleships would force the Ottomans to surrender Constantinople. After five days of Allied bombardment, troops landed on the Gallipoli (guh • LIP • uh • lee) Peninsula in an effort to establish a foothold on the beach. The Turks, supervised by German officers, resisted stubbornly. After eight months of fighting and the loss of 145,000 men killed or wounded, the Allies abandoned the attempt.

Naval warfare. Since the British had not achieved quick victory on land, they decided to blockade the North Sea to keep merchant ships from reaching Germany. Originally the British set up the blockade to prevent the Germans from getting raw materials to manufacture war equipment. Gradually, however, the blockade became an attempt to starve the German people and ruin their economy.

Germany also set up a naval blockade. Employing its fleet of U-boats, Germany attempted to force Great Britain to surrender by sinking ships carrying food and munitions to the British.

In May 1915, without warning, a German submarine sank the British passenger liner *Lusitania* off the coast of Ireland. The sinking of the *Lusitania,* which carried a cargo of war materials to England, killed 1,200 people, including 128 Americans. Woodrow Wilson, the American president, warned Germany that the United States would not tolerate another such incident. For the next two years, Germany used submarine warfare only sparingly. It did not wish to provoke the neutral Americans into entering the war on the side of the Allies.

In May 1916 the only large naval battle of the war was fought by Germany and Britain off the coast of Jutland in the North Sea. Neither side could claim total victory, but the German navy retired into the Baltic Sea, where it remained until the end of the war.

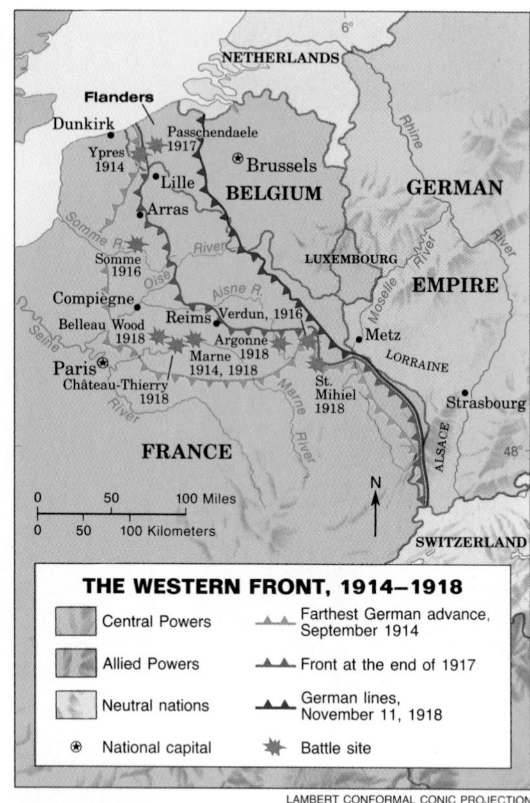

Learning from Maps *The Germans never captured the city of Paris. What French cities fell to the Germans?* **Lille, Arras, Compiègne, and Reims**

The War of Stalemate

By 1916 the war had reached a stalemate on land as well as at sea. Each side realized that it could not break through the other's line of trenches. A small area of land on the western front changed hands again and again, costing each side thousands of lives. The conflict had become a **war of attrition**—a slow wearing-down process in which each side tries to outlast the other.

The most famous example of such warfare occurred at Verdun, in northeastern France (see map, this page). The Germans attacked Verdun in February 1916, hoping to use the Verdun offensive to bleed the French army to death. However, after six months of fighting, the Germans gave up. At Verdun, Germany lost 330,000 soldiers; French losses were 350,000.

650

1D, 5B, 5I, a1C, a1D, a2A, a2B, a2K, a4A, a4F, a4H, a4J, a4L

The Role of the United States

When World War I began in 1914, the United States declared its neutrality. Most Americans viewed the war as a European affair in which the United States should not become involved.

Trade with the belligerents. Nevertheless, the war soon affected the United States. As the strongest industrialized neutral nation, the United States became a supplier of food, raw materials, and munitions. The government insisted on the right of American citizens and business firms to trade freely with either side. However, if an American ship carried **contraband**—war materials supplied by a neutral to a belligerent nation—the goods could be seized. The United States also insisted on the right of its citizens to travel in safety on ships of any nation, neutral or belligerent.

Because of the United States' neutrality, its government could not lend money to either side. Yet the government made no effort to stop banks, corporations, or private citizens from buying bonds of foreign governments or selling goods on credit.

At the beginning of the war, American investors and businesspeople dealt with both sides. However, as the British blockade of Germany tightened, American trade became more and more one-sided. Soon the United States traded only with the Allies, who paid for most of the goods with money borrowed from American interests.

American entry into the war. Britain's propaganda impressed Americans far more than did Germany's. Graphic stories of German **atrocities**—brutal crimes of war, often committed against defenseless civilians—angered Americans. Many of these stories were untrue, but many Americans believed them because the United States got most of its war news from British sources.

In 1917 the issue of American involvement was settled. In January the German foreign minister, Alfred Zimmermann, sent a secret telegram to the German ambassador in Mexico. It instructed him to draw Mexico into the war on Germany's side. In exchange, Germany promised Mexico the return of parts of the southwestern United States that Mexico had lost in 1848. The British intercepted the telegram, decoded it, and sent it to Washington. Publication of the Zimmermann telegram in American newspapers enraged the public.

At the same time, Germany, faced with extreme food and munitions shortages, decided that the war must end before all hope of victory vanished. Germany decided to resume unrestricted submarine warfare, taking the chance that the United States would not enter the war or, if it did, that Germany could defeat Britain before the United States had time to mobilize. German submarines attacked any naval vessel, enemy or neutral, found in what Germany determined to be a "war zone."

Meanwhile, in March 1917, revolutionaries overthrew the autocratic czarist government of Russia. The leaders of the revolution promised to establish a constitutional government. After the czar's government fell, all the major Allied powers had democratic governments. Americans would more readily accept a war in which the lines were drawn between democratic and nondemocratic countries.

On April 2, 1917, President Woodrow Wilson appeared before Congress. Announcing that "the world must be made safe for democracy," he asked for a declaration of war. On April 6 Congress voted to declare war on Germany and to enter the war on the side of the Allies.

SECTION 2 REVIEW

1. **Define** propaganda, war of attrition, contraband, atrocity
2. **Identify** Central Powers, Allied Powers, U-boats, *Lusitania,* Woodrow Wilson, Alfred Zimmermann
3. **Locate** Marne River, western front, Danzig, Tannenberg, Gallipoli Peninsula, Jutland, Verdun
4. **Summarizing Ideas** **(a)** As the war began, what advantages did the Central Powers have? **(b)** the Allied Powers?
5. **Classifying Ideas** Name some important new weapons and military techniques introduced in World War I.
6. **Analyzing Ideas** **(a)** How was the United States as a neutral power affected by World War I? **(b)** What factors led to its entry into the war?

3 The Russian Revolution Ended the Czarist Regime

Russia, torn by revolutionary disturbances throughout the 1800s, faced continuing problems in the early 1900s. The Revolution of 1905 brought about

North Sea; ***Danzig:*** Baltic seaport; ***Tannenberg:*** site of a battle in East Prussia; ***Gallipoli Peninsula:*** land extending from the coast of Turkey; ***Jutland:*** peninsula extending from Germany into the North Sea; ***Verdun:*** city in northeastern France, site of a German attack
4. (a) The Central Powers formed an almost solid block of territory from the North Sea to the Persian Gulf, providing easy communication and opportunity for rapid troop movements. The Central Powers also had well organized, well equipped, and well trained armies. **(b)** The Allied Powers had more soldiers, greater industrial potential, and control of the seas.
5. The machine gun, trench warfare, the tank, armed aircraft, and submarines were introduced in World War I.
6. (a) The United States declared neutrality in 1914, but soon became a supplier of food, raw materials, and munitions. **(b)** The United States entered the war primarily because of German atrocities against civilians, public outrage concerning the Zimmermann telegram, and German attacks on Allied navy vessels.

SECTION 3

Focus/Motivation
Ask students to list some of the problems that might lead to a revolution. *(Answers will vary but should include poverty and economic backwardness.)*

Lead the class in a discussion of whether or not these problems, which Russia was experiencing prior to revolution, were immediately solved by the revolution. *(No, because Russia was plunged into a civil war following the overthrow of the czar, and most of the government's efforts went into solving this problem rather than dealing with economic problems.)* Ask students whether they think people's lives improve immediately following a revolution. *(Most students will point out that in most cases their situation worsens and only improves after a considerable period of time.)*

Presentation Summarizing Ideas (Average/Group)
Write the following items on the chalkboard or an overhead projector:

1. elected legislative body in Russia
2. masses of soldiers in the Russian army
3. Socialist members of the Petrograd Society
4. radical Socialists
5. Bolshevik leader
6. group organized to train Russian workers to become a revolutionary force
7. formed the basis of Russian communism
8. "Land, Peace, and Bread"

Ask students to match each statement above with the correct item from the following list:

Learning from Pictures *Czar Nicholas II and his family were the last absolute monarchs of Europe. What was the last order the czar gave the Duma? What was the Duma's response?* **Disband: refused to dissolve**

no real changes. The elected legislative body, the Duma, had little power. The czar, Nicholas II, did not trust the Duma and remained an almost absolute ruler. Many of the Russian people, long denied the democratic rights and civil liberties that they had been promised, joined secret societies that often committed violent acts to express their members' frustration.

Grave economic problems also confronted Russia, which lagged far behind western European countries in its industrial development and agricultural methods. For example, in 1914 industrial workers made up only 1.5 percent of Russia's population, compared with 40 percent of Great Britain's population. Debts, taxes, and rents kept most Russian peasants in poverty despite their 1861 emancipation.

Russia in World War I

World War I exposed Russia's weaknesses. The country lacked enough railroads and good roads, and its industry could not adequately equip or supply its army. The Ottoman Empire's entrance into the war on the side of the Central Powers cut Russia off from outside supplies.

The Allies had counted heavily on the Russian "steamroller"—the great masses of soldiers in the Russian army. When war came, however, Russian troops proved to be poorly equipped and badly led. The courage of the Russian soldiers could not hide an inefficient and corrupt government, which was completely unfit to deal with the problems of modern warfare. Nevertheless, for more than three years, Russian troops held back more than half the troops of the Central Powers. During this period more than 2 million Russians were killed, approximately 5 million were wounded or crippled, and more than 2 million were taken prisoner. If the Russians had not fought so well, the Allies might have lost the war.

The spring of 1917 found the Russian people weary of hardships and disheartened by the appalling casualties they had suffered in the war. The people had lost all faith in their government and in Czar Nicholas II. Strikes and street demonstrations broke out in Petrograd, as St. Petersburg had been called since 1914. The czar ordered his troops to crush the demonstrations. When the Duma demanded reforms in the government, Nicholas dissolved the legislative body.

In the past the government had always been able to use the army against disturbances such as those in Petrograd. Now, however, the soldiers joined the rioters. The Duma, encouraged by the army's disobedience, refused the czar's order to disband.

On March 15, 1917, unable to control either his subjects or his army, Nicholas II abdicated. He and his family were executed the following year. The Romanov dynasty that had maintained Russian autocracy for 300 years was finished.

Lenin and the Bolsheviks

A liberal provisional government was set up to rule Russia until a constitutional assembly could be elected to choose a permanent system of government. While the provisional government tried to restore order, a rival force worked for change in Russia.

Known as the Petrograd Soviet of Workers' and Soldiers' Deputies (*soviet* is the Russian word for council), the rival force had been quickly organized when disorders began in Russia. The leaders modeled the Petrograd Soviet on similar organizations that had participated in the Revolution of 1905. Most members of the Petrograd Soviet were moderate socialists called Mensheviks. The organization also included a small number of radical socialists, known as Bolsheviks.

Other soviets similar to the one in Petrograd sprang up. Many people throughout Russia supported their program, which was more attractive than that of the provisional government. The program called for immediate peace, land reform, and the turning over of factories to the workers.

The leader of the Bolsheviks, Nikolai Lenin, was born Vladimir Ilyich Ulyanov, but he assumed the name Nikolai Lenin as a young man. An intelligent and forceful person, Lenin came from the middle class and had studied law. After his older brother was executed by the czarist police as a revolutionary, Lenin became a revolutionary himself.

On April 16, 1917, Lenin returned to Russia from exile in Switzerland. His first act was to insist that all governing power be turned over to the soviets.

Lenin was a radical socialist, but he favored a modified Marxism, partly because of the conditions that existed in Russia. Lenin believed that because Russia had comparatively little industry and only a small working class, the forces of history there might not move in the direction Marx had predicted. Therefore, he advocated the establishment of a small group of dedicated Marxists. This group would train the workers to become a revolutionary force. Lenin's adaptation of Marxism formed the basis of what we now know as Russian communism. His slogan, "Land, Peace, and Bread," reached the hearts of the masses.

On November 7, 1917, the Bolsheviks overthrew the provisional government and seized control of Russia. This revolution is often called the Second Russian Revolution (the first having been in March), or the Bolshevik Revolution. In the spring of 1918, the Bolsheviks renamed themselves the Communist Party.

Civil War

The Communists signed peace treaties with each of the Central Powers early in 1918 at Brest-Litovsk. Russia anxiously made peace on any terms, since its army was exhausted from three years of bitter fighting. The harsh treaties forced Russia to give up a sizable amount of territory.

The new regime then turned its attention to internal problems. The Communists faced much opposition within Russia, not only from former aristocrats and other reactionaries, but also from middle-class liberals and the Mensheviks. In scattered groups, opposition forces tried to overthrow the Communists in a civil war.

Learning from Pictures *Germany allowed Lenin to pass through its territory on his way back to Russia from Switzerland. German leaders hoped that the fiery Bolshevik would take Russia out of the war.*

The Communists had adopted red, the symbolic color of European revolutionary socialism, as their color. For this reason they became known as the Reds. Those who opposed the Communists were called the Whites. The civil war, which began in early 1918, lasted almost three years, adding to the devastation begun by World War I. The Red Army—as the forces of the new government were called—fought many battles with the White armies, leaving an appalling trail of destruction.

The Allies had been angered by the new Russian government's signing of separate peace treaties with the Central Powers. They also feared that if the Communists gained control of Russia, the revolution would spread. Therefore, the Allies aided the White forces with arms and money. Several nations, including the United States, even sent small forces of troops to help overthrow the Communist government. The Allies helped prolong the civil war, but they could not change the result. By 1921 the Communists had completely defeated the White forces.

a. Bolsheviks
b. Marxists
c. Lenin's Marxism
d. Duma
e. Mensheviks
f. Lenin's slogan
g. Nikolai Lenin
h. "Steamroller"

(Answers: 1. d; 2. h; 3. e; 4. a; 5. g; 6. b; 7. c; 8. f)

SECTION 3

Closure

Ask: Why did the Communists become known as "Reds"? *(The Communists adopted red as their color because it symbolized European revolutionary socialism.)*

Review Answers

1. ***Petrograd Soviet:*** rival force of the liberal provisional government set up in Russia after the revolution; ***Mensheviks:*** moderate socialists; ***Bolsheviks:*** radical socialists; ***Nikolai Lenin:*** Bolshevik leader; ***Reds:*** Communists
2. ***Brest-Litovsk:*** Soviet city where the treaty between Germany and Russia was signed at the end of World War I
3. **(a)** The Russian people were weary of hardships and disheartened by the casualties of the war. **(b)** Nicholas II abdicated the throne and a provisional government was set up. **(c)** The far-reaching effects of the revolution included the formation of a Communist government in Russia.

5B, a1C, a4A, a4F, a4G, a4H, a4K, a4M

4. The Petrograd Soviet program wanted immediate peace, land reform, and the turning over of factories to the workers.
5. Lenin advocated a modified Marxism and the creation of a Marxist group to train the workers.
6. The signing of the peace treaty in 1918 allowed the new regime to turn its attention to internal problems.

SECTION 4

Focus/Motivation
Ask students to estimate the level of morale among the Allied and Central Powers before and after America's entry into the war. Ask these questions: How important to a nation's war effort is its morale? In what specific ways can morale affect the war effort of a democratic country, such as Great Britain? *(Low morale might lead to unrest that could bring down the government.)* In what specific ways can morale affect the war effort of an autocratic country, such as czarist Russia or the German Empire? *(An autocratic government might be less concerned with morale, believing that it can still retain control despite an unpopular war.)*

SECTION 3 REVIEW

1. **Identify** Petrograd Soviet, Mensheviks, Bolsheviks, Nikolai Lenin, Reds
2. **Locate** Brest-Litovsk
3. **Understanding Cause and Effect** **(a)** What were the causes of the Russian Revolution in March 1917? **(b)** What were the immediate effects of the Revolution? **(c)** What were the far-reaching effects?
4. **Organizing Ideas** What kind of program did the Petrograd Soviet propose for Russia?
5. **Explaining Ideas** Explain the type of Marxism that Lenin advocated for Russia.
6. **Analyzing Ideas** How did the signing of the peace treaty by the Communists in 1918 help the new regime establish power?

4 After Achieving Victory, the Allies Drafted Peace Terms

President Wilson's statement of America's aim in entering the war—to make the world "safe for democracy"—held a lofty and idealistic theme. However, the November 1917 Russian Revolution and Russia's signing of a separate peace treaty with Germany at Brest-Litovsk dampened Allied morale. Meanwhile, the Russians published the terms of the secret treaties signed by the Allies when Italy entered the war.

The Fourteen Points

The revelation that their governments were fighting for bits of land made the war seem shoddy to many people on the Allied side. British Prime Minister David Lloyd George tried to undo the bad impression these revelations left. He stated more idealistic aims in a speech to Parliament. However, it was President Wilson who best expressed what many people thought the Allied aims should be. In a speech to Congress in January 1918, Wilson announced his **Fourteen Points.** Six of the points contained plans of a general nature (points 1–5 and 14). The eight remaining points dealt with specific countries and regions, such as Russia, Belgium, Alsace-Lorraine, and the Balkans.

The six general proposals may be summarized as follows: (1) No secret treaties. (2) Freedom of the seas for all nations. (3) Removal of all economic barriers or tariffs. (4) Reduction of national armaments. (5) Fair adjustment of all colonial claims, with equal consideration given to the people of a region and the nation. (14) Establishment of "a general association of nations," which would guarantee political independence and protection to large and small states alike.

The Fourteen Points caught the imagination of people everywhere and raised the morale of Allied troops. Copies dropped behind the German lines made the German people willing to surrender. Some historians believe, however, that Wilson made one serious mistake. During the war, when his influence was the greatest, he did not make the Allies promise to accept the Fourteen Points.

Defeat of the Central Powers

The Treaty of Brest-Litovsk with Russia allowed the Germans to withdraw troops from the eastern front and concentrate their efforts on a huge offensive in the west during the spring and summer of 1918. This offensive represented a last desperate gamble to break through the Allied lines, capture Paris, and end the war before the Americans could arrive in strength and turn the tide.

The German offensive lasted until mid-July. It almost succeeded. In May the Germans reached the Marne River, only 37 miles (59 kilometers) from Paris. By this time, however, more than 250,000 Americans were landing in France every month.

Under a newly organized joint command, headed by the French general Ferdinand Foch (FAWSH), the Allied forces stopped the Germans in June at Château-Thierry (shah • toh-tye • REE). In July the Allies began to counterattack. A final Allied push in September at St. Mihiel (san mee • YEL) and in the Argonne Forest forced the German armies back to the borders of Germany (see map, page 650).

At the same time, conditions worsened for the Central Powers in the Middle East and the Balkans. Bulgaria, seeing little hope for victory or for help from its allies, surrendered first, in September 1918. The Turks soon asked for peace also. By November a revolution in Austria-Hungary had brought the old Hapsburg Empire to an end. Austria and Hungary then formed separate governments.

In Germany the government of Kaiser William II soon collapsed. Woodrow Wilson had said he

● Students may suggest that if the United States had gone to war with Mexico, Americans would have been defending their own soil and would have been unable to help the Allies defend Europe.

■ Economic dislocations helped bring on the Great Depression and the rise of dictatorships.

5B, a1C, a4L

Learning from Pictures *These victorious American soldiers march through the Arch of Triumph, France's equivalent of our Tomb of the Unknown Soldier.*

would deal only with a government that truly represented the German people. Many Germans, wishing to end the war, looked upon the kaiser as an obstacle to peace. On November 9 the kaiser abdicated and the German Republic was proclaimed.

On November 11, 1918, the chancellor of the new German Republic signed an **armistice,** an agreement to stop fighting until a treaty can be drawn up. The armistice provided that at the eleventh hour on the eleventh day of the eleventh month of 1918, all fighting would cease. The Germans grimly signed the armistice in a railroad car in the forest of Compiègne (kohmp • YAYN) in France.

According to the severe terms of the armistice, Germany had to cancel the Treaty of Brest-Litovsk that it had forced the Russians to sign. Germany also had to surrender all its submarines and a large part of its surface fleet. In addition, it had to release all war prisoners and turn over munitions that might make additional fighting possible. The Allies reserved the right to occupy all German territory west of the Rhine River and a narrow strip of land along the east bank of the Rhine.

What If?

Nations at War

How do you think world history would have been different if the United States had gone to war with Mexico in 1917? Do you think the results of World War I would have been different? Why or why not? ●

Costs of the War

The costs of World War I stagger the imagination. Each of the belligerent nations suffered enormous and lasting consequences. Reliable estimates indicate that the war left more than 10 million soldiers dead and over 20 million more wounded—many of them crippled for life.

Militarily, Russia suffered the most severely, losing more than 2 million people. Germany lost almost that many, and France and its colonies lost nearly 1.5 million. Austria and Hungary counted 1.25 million dead after the war, Great Britain almost 1 million. American lives lost numbered 115,000.

For the first time in history, civilian casualties numbered almost as many as those among the armed forces. Naval blockades, artillery and aerial bombardments, famine, disease, and political violence all took their toll. The destruction of property was appalling. One historian has estimated that the total cost was $400 billion. ■

The Peace Conference at Paris

After the armistice in November 1918, the Allies faced the task of arranging peace terms. President Wilson had written and spoken of a peace conference in which both sides would write a treaty that was fair to all. However, the war had caused so much bitterness and had cost so much in terms of human lives and property that the Allies were determined to dictate the terms of peace.

Delegates of the victorious nations met in Paris in January 1919. Almost all the Allied Powers sent representatives. Russia, in the midst of a civil war, was the only Allied power not invited.

The Allies agreed to call in representatives of the defeated powers only to accept the terms of the treaties. They decided that a separate treaty should be written for each of the defeated Central Powers. Since Austria and Hungary now had separate governments, five treaties had to be drawn up. In

Presentation
Evaluating Ideas (Average/Group)
Have students discuss Wilson's statement of America's aim in entering the war—"to make the world safe for democracy." Then ask the students to evaluate whether the United States achieved its goal. *(Students should point out that the Russian Revolution and Russia's signing of a separate peace treaty with Germany dampened Allied morale and, ultimately, the effectiveness of Wilson's ideals.)*

SECTION 4

Closure

Have students review the problems facing the peacemakers as explained on pages 656 and 658. Then ask them to explain why territorial claims were difficult to reconcile.

Review Answers

1. ***Fourteen Points:*** Woodrow Wilson's plan for the Allied aims to end the war; ***armistice:*** agreement to stop fighting until a treaty can be drawn up; ***reparation:*** payment for war damages
2. ***Ferdinand Foch:*** French general in command of the joint Allied forces in 1918; ***Paris Peace Conference:*** delegates of the victorious nations in World War I who met at Versailles in 1919; ***Big Four:*** most powerful Allies at the peace conference—Great Britain, France, U.S. and Italy; ***Big Three:*** the major allied powers after Orlando left the conference—Britain, France, and the U.S.; ***League of Nations:*** a general association of nations suggested by Wilson to guarantee political independence and protection to large and small states alike
3. ***Château-Thierry:*** near Luxembourg on the western front; ***St. Mihiel:*** south of Chateau-Thierry; ***Rhineland:*** western province of Germany; ***Saar River valley:*** eastern border of Lorraine; ***Tirol:*** northern Italy; ***Trieste:*** eastern Italy; ***Fiume:*** northwestern Yugoslavia

History Through the Arts

PAINTED GLASS

Duchamp and the Dadaists

World War I raged violently for four years. When it ended, more than 20 million soldiers and civilians had lost their lives. Such devastation did not go unnoticed in the art world. Artists expressed their anger and bitterness over the war by producing anti-art, works that mocked the values of a society that could have supported the war. This school of art was called *Dada.** Some critics refer to Dadaistic works as non-art.

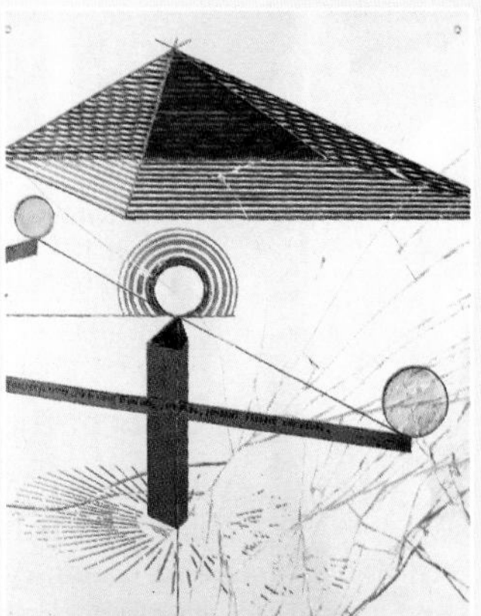

Buenos Aires, 1918. Oil paint, silver leaf, lead wire, and magnifying lens on glass (cracked), 19½ × 15⅝" (49.5 × 39.7 cm), mounted between two panes of glass in a standing metal frame, 20⅛ × 16¼ × 1½" (51 × 41.2 × 3.7 cm), on painted wood base 1⅞ × 17⅞ × 4½" (4.8 × 45.3 × 11.4 cm); overall height 22′ (55.8 cm). Collection, The Museum of Modern Art, New York. Katherine S. Dreier Bequest.

Marcel Duchamp's painted glass (1918) is an example of Dada art. Its seemingly meaningless design served to criticize the war-mad world. Even its title is Dadaistic, or nonsensical: "To be looked at (from the other side of the glass) with one eye close to, for almost an hour." When this piece and others by Duchamp were accidentally cracked, the artist seemed not to care. He said the fracture lines enhanced his initial design. Perhaps Duchamp, like other Dadaists, believed the war had cracked the world beyond repair.

**Dada* is a French word for wooden horse. A sculptor and a German writer accidently discovered the word in a dictionary. They liked the sound and brevity of the word and because a wooden horse is useless, as they believed the violence of World War I was, they applied it to the art form.

theory, the representatives of all the victorious nations had a hand in writing the treaties. In fact, the work had been done in advance, behind the scenes, by the leaders of the four most powerful Allies—Great Britain, France, the United States, and Italy. Known as the Big Four, the leaders were Prime Minister David Lloyd George of Great Britain, Premier Georges Clemenceau (klem • uhn • SOH) of France, President Woodrow Wilson of the United States, and Premier Vittorio Orlando of Italy.

Problems Facing the Peacemakers

By 1919 Europe faced a confusing political situation. Republics replaced hereditary monarchies in the three great empires of Germany, Austria-Hungary, and Russia. A fourth empire, that of the Ottoman Turks, tottered on the brink of collapse. Nationalist groups pressed their claims in Russia and the defeated empires. Each group wanted independence, self-government, and unity within the borders of a single nation. Nationalism took hold in colonial possessions as well.

Territorial claims. The victorious nations had many conflicting territorial demands that they found difficult to reconcile. France wanted, above all, security from another German attack. It insisted on the return of the former provinces of Alsace and Lorraine, which had been guaranteed in the Fourteen Points. In addition, it demanded that the French boundary be extended to the Rhine River so that France would possess the Rhineland, a territory located on the west bank of the Rhine in Germany. France also demanded the Saar River valley, with its valuable deposits of coal.

Italy claimed the Tirol region and the city of Trieste in accordance with the secret treaties it had made in 1915. It also claimed Fiume (FYOO • may), although this port city had not been promised in the secret treaties. Lloyd George, Wilson, and Clemenceau gave in willingly on the Tirol region. However, Wilson steadfastly opposed giving Fiume to Italy. The controversy became so bitter that Orlando left the conference and went home in disgust. The Big Four then became the Big Three.

Belgium, which had suffered under wartime German occupation, requested two small portions of German territory along the border. Great Britain wanted Germany's African colonies. It also insisted that the German navy be destroyed and that Germany be prohibited from building warships.

During the war Japan had occupied the previously German-held Marshall, Caroline, and Mariana islands, as well as Qingdao and most of the Shandong Peninsula. Japan now demanded permanent ownership of all these regions. It also asked that the powers recognize its "special position" in China. This meant, in effect, that in any further

READ
WRITE
● INTERPRET
CONNECT
THINK

BUILDING HISTORY STUDY SKILLS

Interpreting Visuals: Using a Map as a Historical Document

The Congress of Vienna in 1815 resulted in border changes in Europe (see maps entitled "Napoleonic Europe, 1805–1815," Chapter 17, page 442 and "Europe After the Congress of Vienna, 1815," Chapter 17, page 446). Studying changes in the map of Europe before and after the Congress of Vienna helps you to understand the political and historical development of Europe before World War I.

A major goal of the participants at the Congress of Vienna was keeping France in check to prevent the aggression that Napoleon had engaged in. Consequently, the Austrian Netherlands (Belgium) united with Holland (Dutch Netherlands) to act as a buffer state. The Rhineland became the border of Prussia. Savoy and Genoa were added to Sardinia to make Sardinia a larger state along the border of France. Lombardy and Venetia in northern Italy were given to Austria to lessen the temptation to invade France. The changes at the Congress of Vienna did not allow for self-determination; the overall principle focused on the balance of power. Do you notice any other balance-of-power provisions based on the changes in the two maps? What consequences did this have for the historical development of Europe?

How to Use a Map as a Historical Document

To use a map as a historical document, follow these steps.

1. Identify the topic of the map.
2. Identify the historical context of the map.
3. Explain what information about the topic is included on the map.
4. Connect the information on the map to the historical context of the topic.
5. Make comparisons with other maps.

Developing the Skill

World War I created new borders on the map of Europe. The Treaty of Versailles changed the nature of Europe's geography, economy, and politics. Studying a map of Europe before and after the Treaty of Versailles, just as you have studied a map of Europe before and after the Congress of Vienna, also helps you to understand the political and historical development of Europe. Now look at the maps entitled "Europe on the Eve of World War I, 1914" on page 644 and "Europe After the Paris Peace Settlements, 1919–1920" on page 659. How did Europe change? How did these changes affect European history?

The historical context involves the impact of World War I on Europe. The maps illustrate many ways in which Europe changed after World War I. Germany lost Alsace-Lorraine to France; Serbia became part of Yugoslavia; Austria-Hungary was divided into Austria, Hungary, Czechoslovakia, and Yugoslavia. Poland reappeared, and the Soviet Union became the Union of Soviet Socialist Republics. The Polish Corridor was created out of part of Germany, and Germany lost part of its access to the Baltic Sea. The maps give clues as to the impact on European history. The large empires could no longer serve as a balancing force, and Europe was divided into many small countries. An attempt was made to prevent German aggression (as at the Congress of Vienna there was an attempt to prevent French aggression). Alsace-Lorraine and the Polish Corridor, for example, were two limits on Germany. However, the changes also contained the seeds of a future war because of the political aspects of German antagonism and national security interests.

Practicing the skill. Look at a map of Europe showing non-Communist nations at the end of World War II. Then look at a recent map showing the Soviet Union and that country's satellite nations. What can you conclude about the spread of communism since 1945?

To apply this skill, see Applying History Study Skills on page 663.

The Big Four at Versailles

4. (a) Wilson's six general proposals were: no secret treaties; freedom of the seas; removal of all tariffs; reduction of national armaments to the minimum necessary for defense; fair adjustment of colonial claims; formation of a general association of nations. **(b)** The Fourteen Points raised the morale of the Allied troops and made the German people more willing to consider surrender.
5. (a) France demanded Germany return Alsace and Lorraine and cede the Rhineland and the valley of the Saar River. **(b)** Italy demanded the Tirol region and the cities of Trieste and Fiume. **(c)** Great Britain demanded all of Germany's African possessions. **(d)** Belgium demanded two small portions of German territory along its border. **(e)** Japan demanded ownership of the Marshall, Caroline, and Mariana islands as well as Qingdao and the Shandong Peninsula in China. It also asked the powers to recognize its "special position" in China.
6. (a) Wilson believed in a "peace of justice" because he thought it was the only kind of settlement that would not create new hatred and desire for revenge, which might lead to another war. **(b)** Other leaders opposed this belief because they felt the defeated should be taught a lesson. France and Belgium argued that Germany should be divided up and disarmed completely.

5B, a1C, a4A, a4H, a4I, a4L

Wilson was compassionate toward the defeated peoples. He had grown up in the Reconstruction South, where Southerners received a "peace of vengeance."

SECTION 5

Focus/Motivation
Write on the chalkboard or on an overhead projector the following quotation from one of the British delegates to the Paris Peace Conference:

"We arrived determined that a peace of justice and wisdom should be negotiated: we left it conscious that the Treaties imposed upon our enemies were neither just nor wise."

Have students hypothesize about the type of treaty that would cause a delegate to the peace conference to make such a statement. *(For example, the victors did not include the defeated in the negotiations; the defeated were forced to give up large amounts of territory; the defeated were forced to pay large indemnities; the defeated were forced to disarm beyond a reasonable point; the Allies received unequal benefits from the treaty.)* As students read the section, have them note the characteristics of the treaty that were "neither just nor wise."

Presentation
Identifying Ideas (Average/Group)
Have students review the map on page 659 and identify the nine new countries that were added to Europe as a result of World War I.

seizure of Chinese territory, Japan was to have the first choice and the largest share. A bitter fight and Japan's threat to leave the conference caused Wilson to give in on the Shandong Peninsula.

Reparations and peacekeeping. The destruction caused by the war brought up the problem of **reparations**—payment for war damages. Who should pay for restoring the land? Did war damages include damage to property only? Or should reparations also include pensions to wounded veterans and to widows and orphans?

Finally, the conference had to consider the issue of a world organization to maintain peace. The formation of a League of Nations had widespread appeal, but many European leaders doubted its chances for success.

The Peace: Justice or Vengeance?

Early in the conference, two conflicting viewpoints surfaced. The British, French, and Italian governments had appeared to support the Fourteen Points. Yet they had never really given up the aims stated in the secret treaties—to divide the territories taken from the Central Powers among themselves after the war. The Fourteen Points represented a "peace of justice," whereas the terms of the secret treaties represented a "peace of vengeance."

Wilson believed that the conference must write a "peace of justice." Many people disagreed. The war had left bitterness, hatred, and a longing for revenge. Many of the victors believed that the defeated must be taught a lesson. Only harsh treatment could teach Germany and Austria the consequences of starting a war.

SECTION 4 REVIEW

1. **Define** Fourteen Points, armistice, reparations
2. **Identify** Ferdinand Foch, Paris Peace Conference, Big Four, Big Three, League of Nations
3. **Locate** Château-Thierry, St. Mihiel, Rhineland, Saar River valley, Tirol, Trieste, Fiume
4. **Summarizing Ideas** **(a)** What were the six general proposals of Wilson's Fourteen Points? **(b)** What effect did the Fourteen Points have?
5. **Interpreting Ideas** Describe the territorial demands the following nations made after World War I: **(a)** France; **(b)** Italy; **(c)** Great Britain; **(d)** Belgium; **(e)** Japan.
6. **Evaluating Ideas** **(a)** Why did Wilson believe in a "peace of justice"? **(b)** Why did others oppose this belief?

5 The Peace Treaties Created a "New Europe"

The victors made separate treaties with each of the five Central Powers. The most famous was the Versailles Treaty with Germany.

The Versailles Treaty

In May 1919 leaders of the new German Republic were called in, presented with a peace treaty, and told to sign it. The Germans complained bitterly that the treaty did not follow the Fourteen Points. They objected especially to two features. First, the treaty made Germany admit that it alone was guilty of starting the war and therefore must pay reparations. Second, the treaty did not specify the amount of reparations. In spite of their protest, the Germans had no choice but to sign.

Under the Versailles Treaty, Germany agreed to pay $5 billion in reparations within two years and an unspecified sum later. In 1921 the Allies set the total amount at $33 billion. The treaty also provided for the formation of the League of Nations and for numerous territorial adjustments.

Germany lost considerable territory along its northern, western, and eastern borders (see map, page 659) as well as its overseas colonies. Germany agreed not to fortify the Rhineland, which Allied troops would occupy for an unspecified period of time. The Saar Valley would fall under the administration of the League of Nations for 15 years. During that time all of the coal mined in the area would go to France in partial payment of reparations. At the end of 15 years, the people of the region were to vote on whether to continue under the League, to become part of France, or to rejoin Germany.

The restored nation of Poland received a large area of German land. This region included the Polish Corridor, which cut off East Prussia from the rest of Germany and gave Poland an outlet to the Baltic Sea. Danzig became a free city administered by the League of Nations.

Germany had to abolish conscription and could not maintain a reserve army. It was not allowed to manufacture heavy artillery, tanks, military airplanes, or poison gas. In addition, Germany could have no submarines and no battleships larger

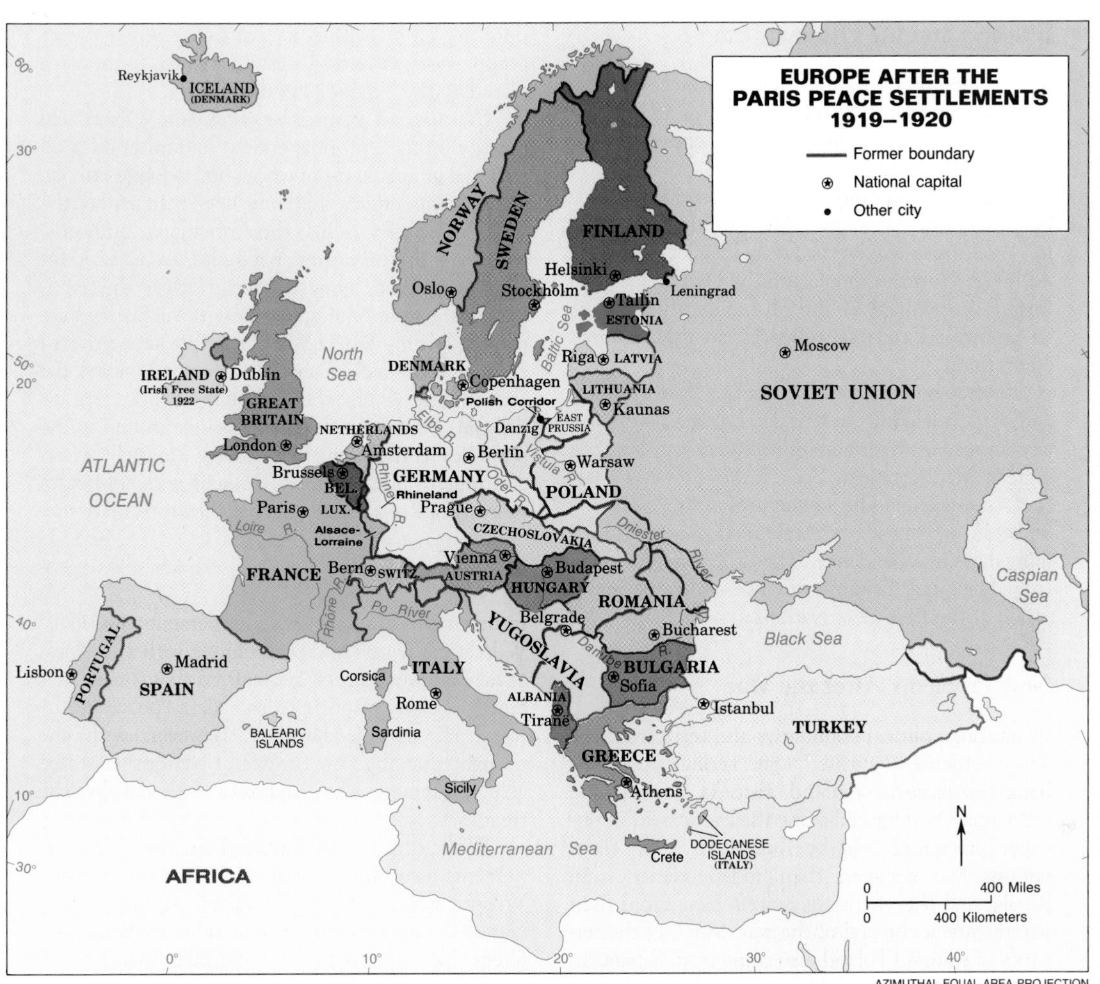

Learning from Maps *After World War I nine new countries were added to the continent of Europe. Which of these countries now had a coastline on the Mediterranean Sea?* **Yugoslavia**

than 10,000 tons. The authors of the treaties imposed these measures to ensure that Germany would be a peacekeeping nation. However, although the Allies made strict rules for Germany, they had weak means of enforcing them.

Austria-Hungary

The Dual Monarchy split in two as the war ended. Therefore, the victors arranged one treaty with Austria in September 1919 and a separate treaty with Hungary in June 1920. Austria, now recognized as an independent republic, lost the southern Tirol and the city of Trieste to Italy. The new republic could not grow enough food for its people or supply its industries with adequate raw materials. Austria rapidly sank into financial crisis and poverty.

Hungary lost a great deal of the territory it had governed under the Dual Monarchy to the new nation of Czechoslovakia that included Czechs, Slovaks, and Ruthenians. In the western Balkans, the new nation of Yugoslavia united the former independent kingdoms of Serbia and Montenegro, the former Hapsburg provinces of Bosnia and Herzegovina, and a section of the Adriatic coast.

SECTION 5

Closure

Ask students to review pages 660–661 and describe the organization of the League of Nations.

Review Answers

1. ***mandate:*** area to be administered by the government of an advanced nation; ***economic sanction:*** refusal to trade with an offending member nation of the League of Nations
2. ***Treaty of Versailles:*** peace treaty signed with Germany to officially end World War I; ***World Court:*** the Permanent Court of International Justice that worked closely with the League of Nations and was located at The Hague
3. ***Polish Corridor:*** strip of land in the northern part of Poland; ***Czechoslovakia:*** formed in 1918 from territories formerly part of the Austro-Hungarian Empire—bordered by east Germany, Poland, the Soviet Union, Austria, and Hungary; ***Yugoslavia:*** bordered by Austria, Hungary, Romania, Bulgaria, Greece, Albania, Italy, and the Adriatic Sea; ***Finland:*** part of Russia until 1918—bordered by Norway, Russia, the Gulf of Finland, the Gulf of Bothnia, and Sweden; ***Estonia:*** formerly part of Russia—bordered by Russia, Latvia, and the Baltic Sea; ***Latvia:*** formerly part of Russia—bordered by Russia, Estonia, Lithuania, and the Baltic Sea; ***Lithuania:*** formerly part of Russia—bordered by Russia, Poland, Latvia, and

5B, a1C, a2A, a2B, a2K, a2L

the Baltic Sea
4. (a) Germany was required to pay $5 billion in reparations within two years and an unnamed sum later. **(b)** Germany was to lose all of its colonies. They were divided among Japan, Great Britain, Australia, and New Zealand, who were to supervise them on behalf of the League of Nations.
(c) Conscription and a reserve army were abolished in Germany, and the manufacture of heavy artillery, tanks, military airplanes, poison gas, battleships over 10,000 tons, and submarines was forbidden.
5. (a) Nations that lost territory were Germany, Austria, Hungary, Bulgaria, the Ottoman Empire, and Russia. Nations that gained territory were France, Belgium, Great Britain, Japan, Italy, and Greece. **(b)** Nations created in Europe were Poland, Czechoslovakia, Yugoslavia, Finland, Estonia, Latvia, and Lithuania.
6. Two problems created by the peace settlement were: the isolation of Russia from western Europe by buffer states along its western borders, and the guaranteeing of the rights of remaining national minorities.
7. (a) The aims of the League of Nations were to promote international cooperation and to maintain peace. **(b)** The League's main agencies were an Assembly (a lower house composed of representatives of all member nations), a Council (an upper house composed of 15

Bulgaria and the Ottoman Empire

The victors also penalized Bulgaria. According to the terms of its peace treaty, signed in 1919, Bulgaria lost territory, including its outlet to the Aegean Sea, which went to Greece.

The Ottoman Empire paid an even higher price for being on the losing side. Its treaty, signed in 1920, resulted in a great loss of territory. Although Constantinople and the Dardanelles and Bosporus remained in Turkish hands, they had to be unfortified and controlled by an international commission.

Several new nations—Palestine, Trans-Jordan, and Syria (including present-day Lebanon)—eventually emerged from former Turkish territory along the eastern Mediterranean Sea. Turkish territory farther east became the country of Iraq. Only the kingdom of Hejaz in Arabia, however, gained immediate independence. The others were administered by Great Britain or France under the supervision of the League of Nations.

New Problems After the War

By altering political boundaries and territories, the peace settlements created some serious problems. Four new nations—Finland, Estonia, Latvia, and Lithuania—had formed along the Baltic Sea, in territory previously held by Russia. In 1918 these nations had declared their independence from Russia, and the victorious powers recognized their sovereignty at the end of the war. Much of the territory of restored Poland also came from Russia. In addition, Russia lost the province of Bessarabia, in the southwest, to a greatly enlarged Romania.

Another problem grew out of the attempt to solve the problem of national self-determination by uniting people of each nationality under their own government. This did not always succeed. For example, there were 250,000 German-speaking Austrians in the Tirol, which came partly under Italian rule. Germans lived in Danzig and the Polish Corridor. Almost 3 million former Austrian subjects—a German-speaking group called Sudeten Germans—lived in Czechoslovakia.

These national minorities, people of one nationality living under a government controlled by another nationality, presented a problem. Therefore, all five treaties contained clauses in which each government pledged to treat fairly any minority group within its borders. Each minority group was guaranteed certain rights, to be protected by the League of Nations.

Dissatisfied minorities. President Wilson held out the promise of independent nationhood for all national groups, most of whom had belonged to one of the great empires that vanished at the end of the war. But peoples such as the Armenians and Kurds, who lived in the Ottoman Empire, never saw this promise fulfilled. They suffered greatly at the hands of the larger national groups under which they were placed. During World War I, the Ottoman government had carried out terrible atrocities against the Armenians, whom the Ottomans believed to be disloyal. Today some Armenians live in one of the republics constituting the Soviet Union. Others continue to live in Turkey. Today Kurds hold out a forlorn hope of a Kurdistan that they can call home.

The League of Nations

In helping to draft the peace settlements, President Wilson made several compromises with the ideals of his Fourteen Points. He realized that the treaties failed in many respects to provide a "peace of justice." He consoled himself, however, with the thought that the new League of Nations would be able to remedy the injustices inflicted by the treaties.

While diplomats hammered out the treaty settlements, a special commission, which included Wilson, wrote the covenant of the League of Nations. This covenant, adopted by the Paris conference, became part of the Versailles Treaty.

Organization. According to the covenant, the League of Nations had two main aims: (1) to promote international cooperation, and (2) to maintain peace by settling disputes peacefully and by reducing armaments. The League was to include all independent sovereign nations. Three main agencies—an assembly, a council, and a secretariat—would conduct League business. The League was to work closely with a related but independent body, the Permanent Court of International Justice, or World Court, located at The Hague.

The Assembly was to be a sort of lower house composed of representatives of all member nations. Regardless of size, each nation was to have one vote. The Council, an upper house, was to be composed of 9 member nations (later increased to 15). It was to consist of 5 permanent members—Great

1D, 4K, 5B, a4A, a4B, a4C, a4H, a4L

● Those who opposed the League of Nations claimed that in order to keep the peace, the organization must have exclusive control of armed forces and an enforceable world law.

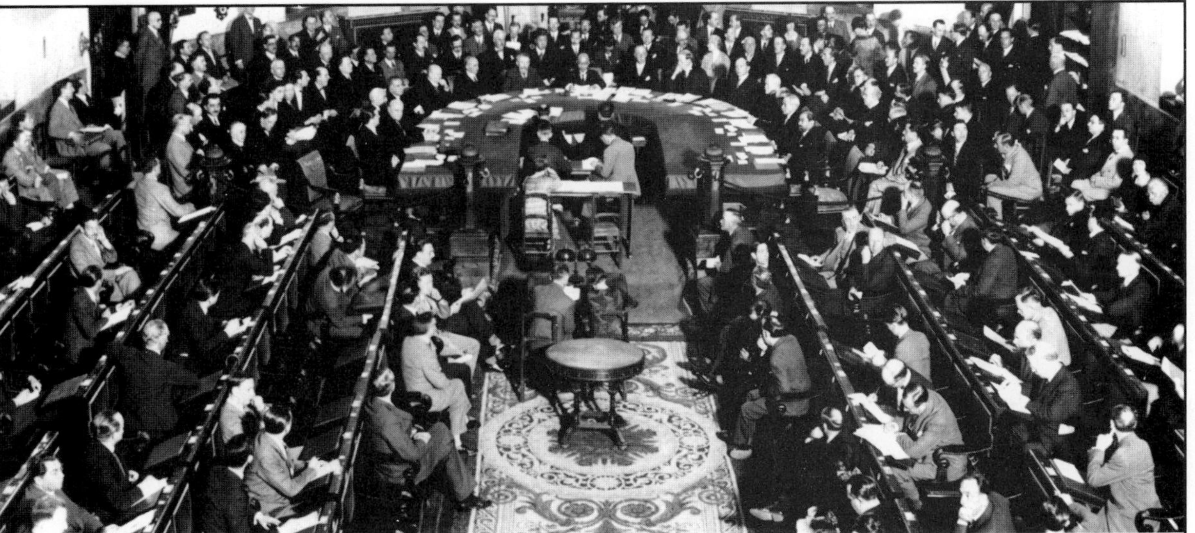

Learning from Pictures The lack of support by the United States did not discourage the League of Nations. It held its first public meeting in Madrid, Spain, in 1920.

Britain, France, Italy, Japan, and the United States—the victorious powers of the war. The remaining seats on the Council were to be filled by rotation from among the other nations.

Peacekeeping measures. The League of Nations provided a way to deal with the many problems created by imperialism in so-called "backward" regions of the world. Until the people of an area were considered ready for independence, the League took the area in trust and assumed responsibility for it. The League assigned the area as a **mandate** to be administered by the government of an advanced nation. The administering nation had to pledge that it would prepare the people of the area for self-government and would make annual reports to the League about the area's progress.

The members of the League of Nations agreed not to resort to war, promising to submit any disputes to the World Court or specially convened commissions for arbitration. The League of Nations covenant provided that if a member nation broke this agreement, the League could impose penalties. Possible penalties included breaking diplomatic relations, imposing **economic sanctions**—the refusal to trade with the offending member nation—or blockades. Military force would be considered only as a last resort.

Although the League of Nations had been Wilson's idea, the United States never became a ● member of the organization. Some senators disapproved of the League itself, while others wanted changes in the Versailles Treaty, which included the League covenant, and refused to ratify the treaty. President Wilson prophetically stated that if the United States did not join, another war would be fought.

Despite the absence of the United States, the 42 member nations represented at the League's first meeting at Geneva in November 1920 held an optimistic view of the future. Germany could not join the League until 1926, and Russia did not become a member until 1934. By 1935 membership in the League included 62 nations.

SECTION 5 REVIEW

1. **Define** mandate, economic sanction
2. **Identify** Treaty of Versailles, World Court
3. **Locate** Polish Corridor, Czechoslovakia, Yugoslavia, Finland, Estonia, Latvia, Lithuania
4. **Summarizing Ideas** Summarize the provisions of the Versailles Treaty concerning: **(a)** reparations; **(b)** Germany's colonies; **(c)** German military power.
5. **Using Maps** **(a)** Name six nations that lost territory and six nations that gained territory as a result of the peace treaties. **(b)** What new nations were created in Europe?
6. **Evaluating Ideas** How did the peace settlements create problems with regard to Russia and national minorities?
7. **Interpreting Ideas** **(a)** What were the aims of the League of Nations? **(b)** What were its main agencies? **(c)** What provisions did it make for peacekeeping?

members), and a Secretariat (a staff to manage the routine business). An independent but related body was the Permanent Court of International Justice, or World Court. **(c)** Peacekeeping provisions included having its member nations promise not to resort to war and pledge to submit disputes to arbitration by the World Court or by special commissions. Further, if a member broke its pledge to submit to arbitration or went to war, the League could impose penalties, such as economic sanctions. The use of military force was considered a last resort.

Reviewing Important Terms
1. e; **2.** f; **3.** a; **4.** h; **5.** g; **6.** b; **7.** c; **8.** d

Developing Critical Thinking Skills
1. (a) The immediate cause of World War I was the assassination of Archduke Francis Ferdinand. **(b)** Underlying causes were nationalism, imperialism, militarism, and alliances.
2. (a) Some of the ideals in the Fourteen Points were (1) no secret treaties, (2) freedom of the seas, (3) restriction of armaments. **(b)** Obstacles to Wilson's efforts included the demand for reparations from Germany, and skepticism over the League of Nations.
3. The Allies were not in favor of the new Russian government. The Allies helped prolong the civil war by aiding the enemies of the new Russian government.
4. (a) As a result of the peace negotiations, the Central Powers lost territory and power. The victors gained power and territory. **(b)** Although these changes did not ignore the causes, they did not correct them. **(c)** The reshuffling of boundaries and creation of new states did not satisfy all the nationalist desires.
5. (a) Austria-Hungary lost the most; **(b)** Bulgaria lost the least. **(c)** Russia lost territory. **(d)** Russia was isolated and new national minorities were formed.
6. (a) Answers will vary. **(b)** The students might answer militarism or idealism.
7. (a) Answers may vary. **(b)** Students may cite the alliance system and the assassination.

1B, 5B, a4A, a4B, a4C, a4H, a4L

Reteaching
Have students review the Chapter Summary and the appropriate section and questions in the Unit Synthesis. Discuss the concepts until students demonstrate a clear understanding of the material.

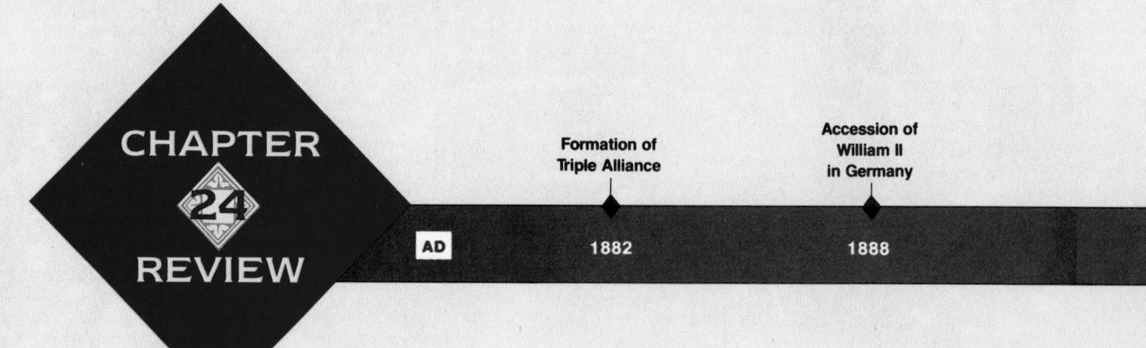

Chapter Summary

The following list contains the key concepts you have learned about World War I and the Russian Revolution.

1. Suspicions among European nations intensified in the early 1900s. These suspicions were caused by strong national feelings, the spread of imperialism, growing militaristic buildups, and a system of rival alliances.
2. The 1914 assassination of Archduke Francis Ferdinand in Sarajevo sparked World War I.
3. Within a few months, almost all the nations of Europe, plus Japan, were at war.
4. Everyone expected the conflict to be over quickly and decisively. Instead, the struggle dragged on for four long years of trench warfare.
5. In Russia a revolution toppled the 300-year-long rule of the Romanov dynasty and abolished the monarchy.
6. Germany tried and failed in a final drive to break the military deadlock. In early 1918 Russia and Germany signed a peace treaty that put Russia out of the war. The Americans provided the fresh troops and new resources that helped defeat the Central Powers.
7. Although the war ended in 1918, the problems it caused continued to plague governments for years. Many lives had been lost, much property had been destroyed, and many problems remained unresolved.
8. After the war national groups demanded recognition, especially in eastern Europe. The victors wanted to punish the losers. Violence erupted in Germany, Russia, and the former Austro-Hungarian and Ottoman territories.
9. Woodrow Wilson's Fourteen Points offered idealistic goals that might have created a peaceful and lasting framework among nations after the war. At the Paris Peace Conference, however, many of these goals were forgotten as the Allies sought to collect reparations for their wartime losses and to gain additional territory.
10. Many hoped the League of Nations would help keep the peace and settle disputes among countries. However, the United States did not join, and the League's efforts were thus crippled from the start.

On a separate sheet of paper, complete the following review exercises.

Reviewing Important Terms

Match each of the following terms with the correct definition below.

a. entente	**e.** mandate
b. contraband	**f.** reparations
c. militarism	**g.** armistice
d. belligerent	**h.** ultimatum

____ **1.** Territory being prepared for independence
____ **2.** Payment for war damages
____ **3.** Friendly agreement between nations
____ **4.** Final terms offered for a settlement
____ **5.** Agreement to stop a war
____ **6.** War materials supplied by a neutral to a belligerent nation
____ **7.** Glorification of armed strength
____ **8.** Warring nation

Developing Critical Thinking Skills

1. **Classifying Ideas** **(a)** What was the immediate cause of World War I? **(b)** What were four underlying causes?
2. **Contrasting Ideas** President Wilson believed World War I would be the "war to end all wars." **(a)** What ideals in the Fourteen Points worked toward this goal? **(b)** What obstacles blocked Wilson's efforts to carry out his plan?
3. **Interpreting Ideas** How did the Allies view the Russian Revolution and civil war?
4. **Evaluating Ideas** **(a)** How did peace negotiations readjust the balance of power in the world? **(b)** Did these changes correct the causes of World War I or ignore them? **(c)** Explain.
5. **Using Maps** Study the map on page 659. **(a)** Which of the Central Powers lost the most territory as a result of World War I? **(b)** Which of the Central Powers lost the least? **(c)** Which Allied Power lost territory? **(d)** Based on evidence in this map, what new problems might have been created by changing the political boundaries of Europe?
6. **Using Pictures** As you learned in this chapter, governments used propaganda to encourage citizens to support the war effort. Locate a copy of a propaganda poster from the era. **(a)** What techniques or symbols used in the

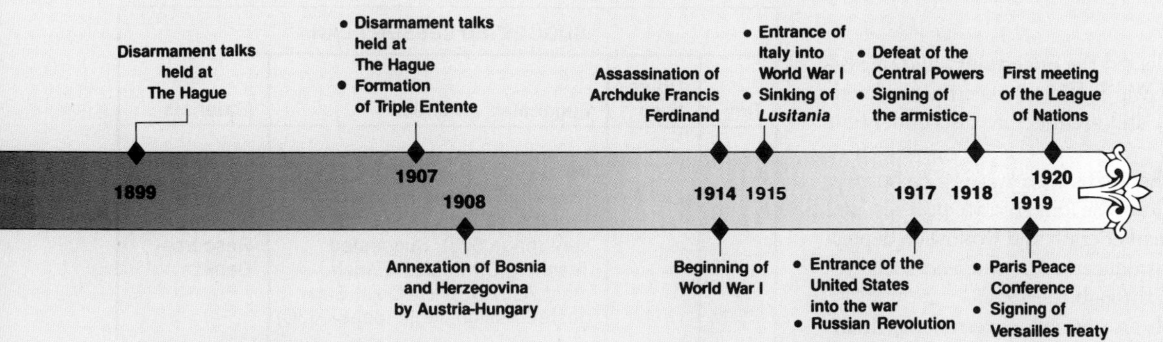

poster might arouse a sense of patriotism? **(b)** To what other emotions does this poster seem to appeal?

7. **Analyzing Information** In assessing World War I, Prime Minister Lloyd George once commented that "no one at the head of affairs quite meant war. It was something into which they glided, or rather staggered and stumbled." **(a)** Do you agree with this interpretation of the war? **(b)** What evidence in the chapter supports your answer?

Relating Geography to History

Using information from this chapter, draw a map showing the reorganization of European nations after World War I. Then use encyclopedias or other library references to show the reorganization of European nations immediately following World War II and the later realignment of Communist nations.

Relating Past to Present

1. Review the following causes of World War I: nationalism, militarism, imperialism, and international alliances. Which of these forces are still present in the world? Clip newspaper or magazine articles that support your answer.
2. Before World War I, the Balkan region was known as the "powder keg of Europe." **(a)** Why was it given this name? **(b)** Are there any similar trouble spots in the world today? **(c)** If so, what actions might be taken to keep them defused? **(d)** What can be done to prevent another Balkan situation from occurring?
3. In 1899 and again in 1907, several nations participated in disarmament conferences held at The Hague. Using the *Readers' Guide to Periodical Literature,* locate articles about recent disarmament talks between the United States and the Soviet Union. Are any of the obstacles to disarmament the same as those faced in the late 1800s and early 1900s? Are any unique to the present? Explain.

Applying History Study Skills

Before completing this activity, review Building History Study Skills on page 657.

Study the maps entitled "Europe in 1916" on page 645 and "The Eastern Front 1914–1918" on page 648. Then answer the following questions to help you use the maps as historical documents.

1. Why would the Central Powers be more successful in the east than in the west?
2. Why was the Brest-Litovsk line important to the Central Powers?
3. Which side do you think had the greater strategic advantage? Why?
4. Why do you think Switzerland was neutral?
5. What military strategy enabled the Allied Powers to win? Why?
6. What strategy could the Central Powers have followed that might have enabled them to succeed? Why?
7. Why can these maps be described as historical documents?

Investigating Further

1. **Writing a Report** While troops bogged down in the muddy trenches of Europe, other battles were taking place in the skies. Write a short report on developments in air warfare during World War I. Also investigate the pilots who flew these missions, such as Baron von Richthofen (the "Red Baron"), Eddie Rickenbacker, or members of the Lafayette Escadrille. One source for your report is Quentin Reynolds's *They Fought for the Sky: The Dramatic Story of the First War in the Air* (Holt, Rinehart and Winston).
2. **Preparing a Book Report** Read one of the following novels and present a book report to the class: Ernest Hemingway's *A Farewell to Arms* (Scribner); Erich Maria Remarque's *All Quiet on the Western Front* (Fawcett); Willa Cather's *One of Ours* (Random House). Note the author's point of view on war. How does it compare with the idealism expressed by President Wilson at the start of World War I?
3. **Conducting Research** Using a variety of references from your library, conduct research on one of the following World War I topics: **(a)** the role of blacks, **(b)** the role of women, **(c)** music and literature of the period, **(d)** military technology. Report your findings to the class.

Relating Geography to History

Maps should show that realignment of European nations and the spread of communism.

Relating Past to Present

1. All of these forces seem to be present today.
2. (a) Because of the many conflicts between Balkan countries and the major powers. **(b)** Students might mention the Middle East and Central America. **(c)** Students may suggest international peace conferences. **(d)** Communication among world leaders and careful consideration of foreign policy may help.
3. Fear and distrust on each side continues to be a problem. The sophistication of nuclear weapons makes inspection and detection more difficult today.

Applying History Study Skills

1. Because Russia had most of its army in Europe and the Central Powers could trap or push back Russian troops
2. It enabled the Central Powers to control eastern Europe.
3. The Allies had greater access to the sea, and surrounded the Central Powers on three sides.
4. Probably because it bordered both Allied nations and Central Powers
5. Allies were able to attack on several fronts, maintain their line of defense in western Europe, and force Central Powers back.
6. The Central Powers may have been more successful if they could have prevented Allied access to the Atlantic.
7. Because they connect geographical information to a time in history

663

CHAPTER (pages 664–689)

25 The Great Depression Helped the Rise of Totalitarian Dictatorships

(1919–1936)

CHAPTER OVERVIEW

Attitudes, ideas, and the arts reflected the uncertainty and uneasiness of the times following World War I. Writers experimented with new forms, and music, painting, and architecture also underwent many changes in style.

The United States entered the 1920s on a wave of prosperity. However, overproduction of food, unwise foreign trade policies, and stock speculation led to a stock market crash and worldwide depression. Although the New Deal introduced economic and social reforms, the Depression continued through the 1930s.

Postwar France struggled with an unstable government, financial difficulties, and labor unrest. Great Britain was also badly hurt by the war and by the economic nationalism that followed. Ireland continued to pose problems for the British. In 1921 southern Ireland became a self-governing dominion. Finland, the Baltic states, and Czechoslovakia remained democracies, but conditions elsewhere in eastern Europe were less favorable for democracy.

Postwar Italy experienced economic problems and labor unrest. Mussolini, leader of the Fascist Party, offered a program of relief, and, capitalizing on the fear of communism, slowly turned Italy into a police state. The Weimar Republic in Germany was unpopular. Hitler, leader of the Nazi Party, won many followers by appealing to their nationalistic spirit and fear of communism. Once in office, he began to turn Germany into a police state. Political opposition was eliminated, and particularly harsh treatment was reserved for "inferior races," especially Jews.

After the Communist takeover in Russia, or what became known as the Soviet Union, Lenin became head of the government. He brought a measure of central control to the economy. Stalin increased this control with the Five-Year plans, designed to industrialize the Soviet Union and collectivize its agriculture. In the process he created a police state.

SUGGESTED LESSON PLAN

Day	Objectives	Suggested Activities	Materials
1	U4,* C1–3	Introducing the Chapter (pages 664–65) Section 1 (pages 665–70), Focus/Motivation (page 665), Presentation (page 666), Closure (page 669), Suggested Teaching Strategies, Enrichment Activities, Daily Quiz, Suggested Assignments (page 663B)	ATE, Pupil's Edition, Teacher's Resource-Bank™
2	U5, C4–6	Section 2 (pages 671–74), Focus/Motivation (page 671), Presentation (page 671), Closure (page 673), Suggested Teaching Strategies, Enrichment Activity, Daily Quiz, Suggested Assignments (page 663C)	ATE, Pupil's Edition, Teacher's Resource-Bank™
3	U5, C7	Section 3 (pages 674–78), Focus/Motivation (page 674), Presentation (page 675), Closure (page 677), Suggested Teaching Strategies, Enrichment Activity, Daily Quiz, Suggested Assignments (page 663D)	ATE, Pupil's Edition, Teacher's Resource-Bank™
4	U6, C8–9	Section 4 (pages 679–85), Focus/Motivation (page 679), Presentation (page 679), Closure (page 683), Suggested Teaching Strategies, Enrichment Activity, Daily Quiz, Suggested Assignments (page 663E)	ATE, Pupil's Edition, Teacher's Resource-Bank™
5	U7, C10	Section 5 (pages 685–87), Focus/Motivation (page 685), Presentation (page 685), Closure (page 686), Suggested Teaching Strategies, Enrichment Activity, Daily Quiz, Suggested Assignments (page 663F)	ATE, Pupil's Edition, Teacher's Resource-Bank™
6	U4–7 C1–10	Chapter 25 Form A Test, Reteaching Worksheet, Chapter 25 Form B Test	Teacher's Resource-Bank™ or Workbook and Test Booklet

*C refers to applicable Chapter Objective, U refers to applicable Unit Goal

BOOKS FOR THE TEACHER

Kirkpatrick, Ivone. *Mussolini: A Study in Power.* Hawthorn. Presents a thorough and engrossing account of the man, his personality, and his career.

Shirer, William L. *The Collapse of the Third Republic.* Simon and Schuster. Contains information on the Third Republic.

Toland, John. *Adolf Hitler.* Doubleday. Presents new information about Hitler's early years.

BOOKS FOR THE STUDENT

Archer, Jules. *Twentieth Century Caesar: Benito Mussolini.* Julian Messner. Provides a highly readable biographical sketch of Mussolini.

Conkin, Paul K. *The New Deal.* T. Y. Crowell. Gives concise account of the New Deal.

Gibson, Michael. *Russia Under Stalin.* Putnam. Portrays life under Stalin in text and photographs.

Switzer, Ellen. *How Democracy Failed.* Atheneum. Provides interviews with Germans who were teenagers in the 1930s.

Unstead, R. J. *The Twenties and The Thirties.* MacDonald Educational. Consists of a two-volume history with an excellent visual presentation of the decades.

MULTIMEDIA MATERIALS

Biography Series: Mussolini (mp, 26 min.), McGraw-Hill. Covers Mussolini's life from the end of World War I to his death in 1945.

Fascist Dictatorships (4fs), Educational Audio-Visual. Examines the historical and philosophical roots of fascism and the rise to power and subsequent fall of Mussolini and Hitler.

Golden Twenties (mp, 68 min.), McGraw-Hill. Presents a classic film on the events of the 1920s in the United States.

Minister of Hate (mp, 27 min.), McGraw-Hill. Explores the techniques of mass thought control evolved by the Nazi propagandist Joseph Goebbels.

Section (pages 665–670)

1 An Uneasy Postwar Era Affected the Arts and Ideas

SECTION OVERVIEW

In the two decades after World War I, Europe and the United States experienced profound uneasiness and uncertainty. The war itself had caused many artists to reject the past and to experiment with their art. Writers criticized the times and explored new themes and techniques. Musicians, painters, and architects also rejected earlier forms and experimented with new styles. Even popular culture felt the changes, as new styles of music and films, some of them conveying a pessimistic outlook, flourished.

SUGGESTED TEACHING STRATEGIES

1. **Preteaching Vocabulary (Basic)** You may wish to preteach the following important vocabulary terms: totalitarian regime *(page 665)*; surrealism *(page 666)*; cubism *(page 668)*; functionalism, international style *(page 670)*. Ask students to name any totaltitarian regimes in existence today. *(Answers will vary.)*
2. **Understanding Ideas (Average/Group)** Discuss with the class the impact of films on American society. Ask the following questions as a guide: Have films impacted American society morally? If yes, how? If no, why not? Have the people involved in the film industry generally made good role models? Are filmmakers responsible for what they show on the screen? Do most film producers use discretion when creating a film? *(Accept all reasonable answers.)*

ENRICHMENT ACTIVITIES

1. **Group Project (Average/Group)** Divide the class into four groups. Each group should be assigned one of the following architects: Le Corbusier, Mies van der Rohe, Gropius, and Wright. Students should answer these basic questions: What did these architects attempt to do? Did they accomplish their goals? Students should use an opaque projector to display photographs of the architects' most important buildings and point out their main characteristics. Sources include: Edwin and Joy Hoag's *Masters of Modern Architecture* (Bobbs-Merrill); Tom Wolfe's *From Bauhaus to Our House* (Farrar, Straus & Giroux).
2. **Preparing a Slide Presentation (Challenging)** Have students make slide presentations on one of the art movements of the period — cubism, surrealism, art deco, or abstract painting. If slides are unavailable, students can show reproductions under an opaque projector. Have students identify and contrast the philosophies behind the various movements. Sources include: William Rubin, ed., *Pablo Picasso: A Retrospective* (Museum of Modern Art); Victor Arwas's *Art Deco* (Abrams); and Malcolm Haslam's *The Real World of the Surrealists* (Rizzoli).

DAILY QUIZ

To assess student understanding of Section 1, give the class the following quiz. (Each item is worth 10 points.)

1. (T or F) After studying the arts and literature of the post–World War I era, it can be said that this was an era of uncertainty, discontent, and disillusionment. *(T)*
2. (T or F) Freud's psychology helped explain why people could act destructively and irrationally, while Einsteinian physics intensified the uncertainty and doubts that people had about traditional attitudes. *(T)*
3. Which of these novelists does NOT "fit" in the Twenties? Marcel Proust — Washington Irving — Thomas Mann — Franz Kafka *(Washington Irving)*
4. (T or F) Ernest Hemingway expressed frustration and disillusionment over human behavior. *(T)*
5. (T or F) French poet T.S. Eliot followed very formal, traditional rules of composition and rhyme. *(F)*
6. (T or F) Musicians like Arnold Schoenberg, Igor Stravinsky, and Anton Webern experimented with traditional musical forms, sometimes even developing new scales or instrument combinations. *(T)*
7. (T or F) Pablo Picasso was trying, through his art, to express his concept of what nature is. *(F)*
8. Name one popular leisure-time activity many Americans took part in during the 1920s. *(listening to radio, dancing to jazz, attending films, watching musicals, going to the theater)*

9. Name one American musical composer or uniquely American popular music form. *(Cole Porter, Irving Berlin, jazz, blues)*
10. Which of these men was the architect noted for blending a building with its environment as in the prairie style? Marcel Proust — Frank Lloyd Wright — James Joyce — Georges Braque *(Frank Lloyd Wright)*

SUGGESTED ASSIGNMENTS

1. **Presenting a Report (Average/Group)** Have students present reports on the music mentioned in this section, discussing its distinctive features and what it indicates about the musicians and the period in which it was written. Students might want to bring records to class to play excerpts. Records can usually be obtained from public libraries. You may wish to ask a music teacher to visit the class to lend some expertise to the discussion. Sources include Leonard Feather's *The New Edition of the Encyclopedia of Jazz* (Horizon); Eric Blom, ed., *Grove's Dictionary of Music and Musicians* (St. Martin's); and David Ewen's *All the Years of American Popular Music* (Prentice-Hall).
2. **Critical Thinking Worksheet (Basic)** Have students complete Critical Thinking Worksheet 56 in the TEACHER'S RESOURCEBANK ™

Section (pages 671–674)

2 Postwar Prosperity Crumbled into a Worldwide Depression

SECTION OVERVIEW

The United States entered a period of economic prosperity and isolation after World War I. However, overproduction of food and other goods, low wages paid to workers, economic nationalism, and speculation in investments led in 1929 to a stock market crash and a worldwide depression. In 1933 President Roosevelt introduced the New Deal to revive the American economy.

SUGGESTED TEACHING STRATEGIES

1. **Preteaching Vocabulary (Basic)** You may wish to preteach the following important vocabulary terms: economic boom, Prohibition, economic nationalism *(page 671)*; market speculation, Great Depression *(page 672)*. Ask students why Prohibition was unsuccessful.
2. **Classifying Information (Average/Group)** Have students define *relief* and *reform*. *(Relief is short-term aid; reform is change to bring about long-term benefit.)* During the Great Depression Congress passed New Deal legislation to help bring an end to the economic crisis. Some of this legislation fell under the category of relief, while others fell under the category of reform. Ask students to make a chart listing New Deal relief and reform policies. The completed chart should be similar to the following one:

NEW DEAL PROGRAMS

Relief	Reform
Granting money to the states for relief — food, shelter, and clothing for the needy	Strictly supervising banks and stock exchanges
Creating a public-works program for jobs	Providing for unemployment and old-age benefits under Social Security Act
Paying farmers to take land out of production and to plant crops that would revitalize soil	Establishing a 40-hour work-week and a minimum wage
Buying and storing surplus crops	Guaranteeing workers the right to establish unions
	Creating the Tennessee Valley Authority

Have students think of ways that the relief measures might also be reforms, and vice versa. For example, paying farmers to take land out of production is also a reform aimed at bringing supply in line with demand.

ENRICHMENT ACTIVITY

Panel Discussion (Average/Group) A panel of students might discuss the pros and cons of the New Deal. Questions to investigate include: How do relief programs like those of the New Deal affect people's incentive to work? How would too much government regulation of business affect the economy? How would too little regulation affect it?

DAILY QUIZ

To assess student understanding of Section 2, give the class the following quiz. (Each item is worth 10 points.)

1. (T or F) Immediately after World War I, the U.S. emerged a world leader and actively led the world in pursuing new avenues of peace and prosperity. *(F)*
2. What was one thing from the "Roaring Twenties" that made it such a socially revolutionary time? *(automobile, airmail delivery, telephone, movies, jazz, prohibition, women's suffrage, women working in the general workforce)*
3. (T or F) Wages for industrial workers did not keep pace with productivity, and farmers overproduced food resulting in surplus products that drove consumer prices down. *(T)*
4. (T or F) The world trade economy suffered because of protective tariffs designed to preserve each country's industries and agricultural production. *(T)*
5. What was the event that triggered the Great Depression? *(the crash of the stock market)*
6. (T or F) Great Britain devised a system of "imperial preferences" that lowered tariffs on products coming in from other European countries. *(F)*

7. What was FDR's program of relief and reform called? New Deal — New Freedom — New Nationalism — Square Deal *(New Deal)*
8. (T or F) FDR initiated legislation that regulated the banks and stock exchanges. *(T)*
9. (T or F) FDR managed to successfully oppose the Social Security Act that provided minimum wages for workers, and benefits for retirees. *(F)*
10. (T or F) Under the New Deal programs the government became less involved with the economic and social welfare of the individual citizen. *(F)*

SUGGESTED ASSIGNMENTS

1. **Critical Thinking Worksheet (Basic)** Have students complete Critical Thinking Worksheet 58 in the TEACHER'S RESOURCEBANK™.
2. **Biographical Reports (Average/Group)** Have each student make a short oral presentation of a figure of the "Roaring Twenties," such as Babe Ruth, Rudolph Valentino, Mary Pickford, Lillian Gish, Clarence Darrow, Al Capone, Sinclair Lewis, F. Scott Fitzgerald, Red Grange, Knute Rockne, Helen Wills, Gertrude Ederle, Gene Tunney, and Charles Lindbergh. Students should consult Frederick Lewis Allen's *Only Yesterday* (Harper & Row) and Time-Life eds., *This Fabulous Century,* vol. III (Time-Life).

Section (pages 674–678)

3 Europe Experienced Political Tensions After World War I

SECTION OVERVIEW

After World War I, France was plagued by heavy debts, unstable government, and a lack of security. The coalition Popular Front government improved conditions for workers but brought on high inflation. Great Britain faced severe economic problems and labor unrest. British difficulties with Ireland subsided somewhat when southern Ireland was given its independence. Eastern Europeans tried to solve their economic problems by land redistribution, industrialization, and economic nationalism.

SUGGESTED TEACHING STRATEGIES

1. **Preteaching Vocabulary (Basic)** You may wish to preteach the following important vocabulary terms: planned economy *(page 674)*; general strike *(page 675)*; nationalize *(page 676)*. Ask students why a general strike might cause an economic crisis.
2. **Making Generalizations (Average/Group)** Put the following groups of three statements on the chalkboard. Have students make a generalization based on each group.
   a. France owed money that it had borrowed during and after the war.
   b. Inflation was growing in France.
   c. Expenses of the French government continued to be high.
   Generalization: *France had serious economic problems.*

   a. By 1921 about 2 million workers were out of work in Great Britain.
   b. In 1926 British coal miners went on strike.
   c. Later in 1926, the British government had to use troops to put down a general strike.
   Generalization: *In the 1920s Great Britain faced unemployment and labor unrest.*

ENRICHMENT ACTIVITY

Illustrating Ideas (Challenging) Have each student bring in a photograph, preferably one that shows a particular event or action. Put the collection of photographs on the bulletin board. Have each student select five of the photographs and for each write a brief paragraph describing the scene, the photographer's purpose, and what details a historian 100 years from now might think reflect our times.

DAILY QUIZ

To assess student understanding of Section 3, give the class the following quiz. (Each item is worth 10 points.)

1. Name one economic problem western European powers faced at the end of World War I. *(unemployment, overproduction)*
2. France built what line to protect itself from the Germans after World War I? *(Maginot Line)*
3. The French signed a series of bilateral treaties with other European powers to isolate: Italy — Germany — Soviet Russia — Spain. *(Germany)*
4. The members of the French trade unions and British laborers used this tactic to resist military dictatorship and low wages, respectively. *(general strike)*
5. This socialist leader, elected French premier in 1936, united the French political parties into a workable coalition government and developed a social welfare program for workers: Leon Blum — Ramsay MacDonald — Béla Kun — Eamon De Valera. *(Leon Blum)*
6. (T or F) Political struggles in the French National Assembly and British Parliament centered upon labor's rights to strike, minimum wages, maximum hours and social security-type legislation. *(T)*
7. Great Britain granted independence to the southern Catholic section of what island? *(Ireland)*
8. (T or F) Eastern European nations faced the same industrial problems as France and Britain during the Twenties. *(F)*
9. Which of these was NOT a Baltic Republic that managed to maintain a democratic government? Estonia — Latvia — Hungary — Lithuania *(Hungary)*
10. Which of these was NOT an eastern European dictator during the interwar period? Admiral Nicholas Horthy — Béla Kun — Marshal Józef Pilsudski — Ramsay MacDonald *(Ramsay MacDonald)*

SUGGESTED ASSIGNMENTS

1. **Writing a Report (Average/Group)** Have students write a report on the Maginot Line, using visual aids such as charts and pictures to enhance the report. Sources include: Thomas Parrish, ed., *Encyclopedia of World War II* (Simon and Schuster) and Robert Weinick's *Blitzkrieg* (Time-Life).
2. **Explaining Relationships (Average/Group)** Have students write a brief paragraph explaining in detail how each of the following contributed to the postwar problems in France and Great Britain:
   - **a.** demobilization of armed forces
   - **b.** huge war debt
   - **c.** labor unrest
   - **d.** war-damaged areas in France
   - **e.** policy of economic nationalism in Great Britain

Select certain students to read their paragraphs to the rest of the class.

Section (pages 679–685)

4 Fascist Dictatorships Were Established in Italy and Germany

SECTION OVERVIEW

Italy and Germany suffered heavily from World War I. In Italy the government seemed powerless to remedy the problems of high debt, unemployment, and inflation. Mussolini was able to gain control of the government and set up a fascist dictatorship. In Germany the Weimar Republic was unpopular and faced many of the same economic problems. The Nazis, led by Hitler, transformed Germany into a police state and crushed all opposition. Like Mussolini, Hitler promised to restore the glories of his country's past.

SUGGESTED TEACHING STRATEGIES

1. **Preteaching Vocabulary (Basic)** You may wish to preteach the following important vocabulary terms: fascism *(page 679)*; corporate state *(page 680)*. Ask students to compare a fascist state to a democracy.
2. **Analyzing Ideas (Average/Group)** On the chalkboard or an overhead projector list the following terms: Nationalism, Militarism, Particularism, Authoritarianism, Anti-Semitism, Anti-Communism. Have students define each of these terms. Then discuss the unique characteristics of German history as they would apply in each category. *(Nationalism: Germans knew they had been the last country to unite in Europe. Their unity was indeed fragile and after World War I was threatened by the Allied occupation of German territory. Militarism: Prussia had existed because its military, which consumed 60% of its budget, was disciplined and trained enough to preserve the country from threats by Poland, Russia, Austria, etc. With no army after WW I, Germany lost its identity with Prussia. Particularism: Prior to the Napoleonic Wars, each authoritarian prince ruled his tiny principality from a castle. In each region the prince had the final authority to approve or disapprove the actions of a citizen. People began to look at these princes almost as "father" figures, benevolent dictators. In contrast to England, there was no historic resistance to authority in Prussia, so people looked for an "all-knowing" father-like leader to provide guidance during the rough times after World War I. Anti-Semitism had, for centuries, been an oft-times bitter public emotion, frequently expressing itself in pogroms, riots in the Jewish quarter, or, as in Nazi Germany, the forced wearing of the Star of David. During economic hard times, people could blame a scapegoat. Anti-Communism: Communism threatened the middle and lower-middle class with loss of status and possessions, and loss of identity in a rapidly industrializing world. Hitler took these strands and wove them together to organize his Nazi party in Germany.)*

*3. **Thinking About History: Analyzing Documents (Average/Group)** Using the information students have learned about analyzing documents in this chapter, have them read and analyze other political documents from this era.

ENRICHMENT ACTIVITY

Researching Ideas (Average/Group) Historians have long disagreed as to what degree history is influenced by individuals. Some historians think that the decisions of individual leaders are crucial factors in the major events of their day. Another group argues that leaders are subtly controlled by social forces and have very little freedom of action. The conditions in Germany and Italy, these historians claim, were ripe for nazism and fascism, and similar movements would have arisen without Hitler and Mussolini. Have students take a tentative position on this question and do research to find evidence supporting their position. Ask for volunteers from each side to share their findings with the class. Then take a vote to see which position has more support among class members.

DAILY QUIZ

To assess student understanding of Section 4, give the class the following quiz. (Each item is worth 10 points.)

1. (T or F) Fascism and communism are both totalitarian governments that maintain rigid control of the state by using force and censorship. *(T)*
2. (T or F) Fascism and communism have similar motives, encouraging the workers to revolt in order to establish a classless society and to share the profits of an industrialized society. *(F)*
3. What Italian Fascist gained control of Italy in the 1920s? *(Mussolini)*
4. The Italian Fascists violently opposed and destroyed what opposing political groups? *(Communists, Socialists)*
5. What color shirts did the Italian Fascists wear? white — brown — blue — black *(black)*
6. Name one problem the Weimar Republic faced during the Twenties. *(inflation, unemployment, signed Versailles Treaty)*

7. What party, led by Hitler, rose to power during the early 1930s? *(Nazi Party)*
8. Hitler's *Mein Kampf* — *Das Kapital* — *The Communist Manifesto* — *Der Fuhrer* described his goals and the spirit of the racist Nazi movement. *(Mein Kampf)*
9. Name one way the Nazis persecuted the Jews before they developed the Final Solution. *(deprived them of civil rights; humiliated them; murdered them; forced them to wear a yellow star; segregated them; confiscated their property or businesses; boycotted their businesses; vandalized their synagogues, homes or businesses)*
10. (T or F) After gaining power, Hitler rearmed Germany, militarized the Rhineland and signed an alliance with Mussolini, measures that effectively destroyed the Versailles Treaty. *(T)*

SUGGESTED ASSIGNMENTS

1. **Biographical Sketches (Average/Group)** Have students research and then write a biographical sketch of either Hitler or Mussolini.
2. **Profile Worksheet (Basic)** Have students complete Profile Worksheet 25 in the TEACHER'S RESOURCEBANK™.
3. **Critical Thinking Worksheet (Average/Group)** Have students complete Critical Thinking Worksheet 57 in the TEACHER'S RESOURCEBANK™.
4. **Skill Worksheet (Basic)** Have students complete Skill Worksheet 25 in the TEACHER'S RESOURCEBANK™.

Section (pages 685–687)

5 A Dictatorship Is Established in the Soviet Union

SECTION OVERVIEW

After the death of Lenin in the Soviet Union, a bitter and merciless struggle between two opposing factions occurred. Joseph Stalin emerged the leader. Stalin initiated the first Five-Year Plan in 1928 with the purpose of turning the Soviet Union into a modern, industrialized society. A second Five-Year Plan was begun in 1933. Both had varying degrees of success. In order to maintain a totalitarian dictatorship, Stalin set up a police state with rigid controls.

SUGGESTED TEACHING STRATEGIES

1. **Preteaching Vocabulary (Basic)** You may wish to preteach the following important vocabulary terms: collective farm, command economy *(page 685)*; purge *(Page 686)*. Ask students if the Soviet Union has had purges in recent decades.
2. **Constructing a Time Line (Basic)** To help students better understand the economic and political development of the Soviet Union under communism in the 1920s and 1930s, have them make a time line chronologically listing the important events relating to this period.

ENRICHMENT ACTIVITY

Biographical Sketches (Challenging) Have interested students prepare a biographical sketch on Lenin, Trotsky, or Stalin. Sources include Wyatt Blassingame's *Joseph Stalin and Communist Russia* (Garrard) and the CBS News Staff's *Lenin and Trotsky* (Franklin Watts).

DAILY QUIZ

To assess student understanding of Section 5, give the class the following quiz. (Each item is worth 10 points.)

1. What economic policy did Lenin devise which permitted some local capitalism in order to help develop the economy for later socialist control? New Deal — NEP — USSR — FDIC *(NEP)*
2. Who removed Leon Trotsky and gained control of the government after Lenin died in 1924? *(Stalin)*
3. The ______ ______ ______ was initiated to monitor and increase industrial, agricultural, and educational growth, and to produce more heavy industry and collectivize the farms. *(Five-Year Plan)*
4. (T or F) Wealthier peasants were permitted to keep their land under Stalin's economic plan. *(F)*
5. (T or F) Under the second economic plan begun in 1933, consumer goods production increased as less emphasis was placed on the expansion of heavy industry. *(F)*
6. (T or F) Stalin used the secret police, party purges, and terror to rule Russia, but hesitated to try and spread revolution to the world before consolidating Russian socialism. *(T)*
7. Most power in the Soviet government lay in the hands of the ______. *(Politburo)*
8. The organization founded by Lenin to help spread the Communist revolution throughout the world is called the ______. *(Comintern)*
9. (T or F) During the 1920s and 1930s the outside world viewed the Soviet Union with fear, suspicion, and hostility. *(T)*
10. Many people deported by Stalin were sent to ______, in northern Russia. *(Siberia)*

SUGGESTED ASSIGNMENTS

1. **Comparison Essay (Challenging)** Under Lenin's New Economic Policy a certain measure of free enterprise existed. Small, individually owned businesses and home industries were permitted to operate for a profit, and individuals could buy, sell, and trade farm products. This was to stimulate the Soviet economy. Recently, the Soviet government has allowed capitalistic enterprises to reappear in order to stimulate their economy. Have interested students research and then write an essay comparing the Soviet economy under the NEP and under the new policy of *perestroika*. For recent information students may consult the *Readers' Guide to Periodical Literature*.
2. **Review Worksheet (Basic)** Have students complete Review Worksheet 25 in the TEACHER'S RESOURCEBANK™.

For suggested lesson plan, additional teaching strategies, enrichment activities, daily quizzes, and suggested assignments, see pages 663A–663F.

Introducing the Chapter
Subtle changes in attitudes toward science, art, progress, and industrialization resulted from World War I. Lead a discussion using the following questions: What were some of the advances in physics, biology, medicine, and the social sciences that we read about in Chapter 20? *(Answers should include the following: the development of the atomic theory, special theory of relativity, genetics, pasteurization, anesthetics, and antiseptics; the systematic study of political science, economics, history, anthropology, sociology, and psychology.)* How were systems of education changing? *(Public education was spreading.)* How do you think these things affected people's hopes for improving society? *(There was optimism that science and education could improve society.)* How do you think people felt about science after World War I since scientific knowledge produced the armaments for war? *(Most people no longer believed that science necessarily improved society.)* What were most people's views in general following World War I? *(People in general became more pessimistic about the future after World War I.)*

Chapter Objectives
After studying Chapter 25, students will be able to:

1. Summarize the general attitude of the times as they were expressed in the

CHAPTER 25

The Great Depression Helped the Rise of Totalitarian Dictators

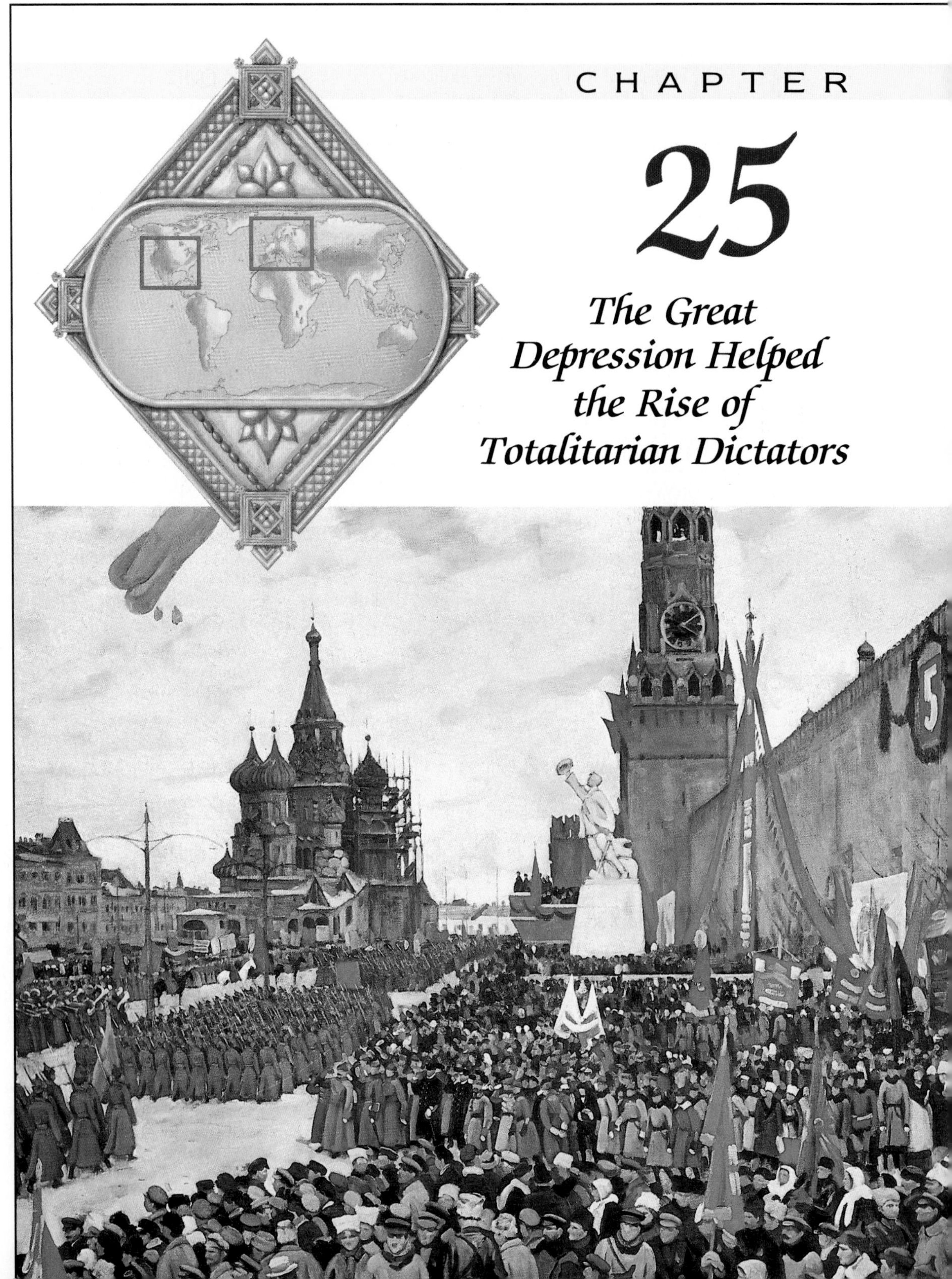

CHAPTER FOCUS

Place Europe and the United States

Time

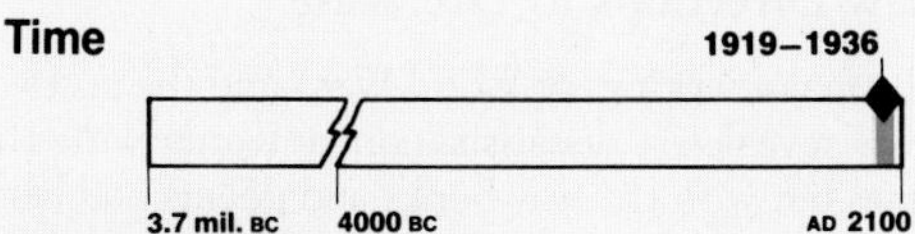

Significance

World War I, according to Woodrow Wilson, was fought to make the world "safe for democracy." For a time immediately following the war, it seemed as if this aim had been achieved.

However, the war dramatically changed how people viewed the world. Disgusted by the death and destruction of World War I, writers and painters began reacting against traditional forms of literature and art.

The tremendous economic prosperity that appeared immediately after the war soon crumbled into a terrible economic depression. This caused a cynical view of life to prevail.

Postwar tensions extended into politics as many democratic nations struggled to survive, particularly in Europe. **Totalitarian regimes**—highly centralized governments that allowed no opposition and held total control—seemed to offer Europeans security amid the instability and uncertainty of the period. Tragically, this era served only as a prelude to an even more devastating war.

Terms to Define

cubism	fascism
functionalism	corporate state
market speculation	collective farm
nationalize	purge

People to Identify

Pablo Picasso	Adolf Hitler
Benito Mussolini	Joseph Stalin

Places to Locate

Ural Mountains	Vladivostok

Questions to Guide Your Reading

1 How did the uneasiness of the postwar era affect the arts and the development of new ideas?
2 How did postwar prosperity eventually crumble into a worldwide depression?
3 What political tensions developed in postwar Europe?
4 How were totalitarian dictatorships established in postwar Italy and Germany?
5 How did Stalin firmly establish communism in the Soviet Union?

◀ *A Red Army parade in Moscow*

During the 1930s a natural disaster overtook the American farmer as an 18-month drought destroyed farmland from Texas to the Dakotas. As the drought continued, wind blew the dry topsoil into swirling dustclouds, turning the region into what became known as the Dust Bowl. These conditions forced many farm families to leave their homes. In his novel, The Grapes of Wrath, *John Steinbeck describes the hardships of Dust Bowl families as they prepare to leave Oklahoma for the fields of California.*

> *"In the little houses the tenant people sifted their belongings and the belongings of their fathers and of their grandfathers. Picked over their possessions for the journey to the west. The men were ruthless because the past had been spoiled, but the women knew how the past would cry to them in the coming days. . . . How can we live without our lives? How will we know it's us without our past? No. Leave it. Burn it. . . . And they piled up the goods in the yards and set fire to them. They stood and watched them burning, and then frantically they loaded up the cars and drove away, drove in the dust. The dust hung in the air for a long time after the loaded cars had passed."*

Just as these families experienced hardships, so, too, did many millions struggle during the years between the two world wars.

1 An Uneasy Postwar Era Affected the Arts and Ideas

World War I disrupted people's lives. Everything seemed unsettled, and all traditional values seemed under attack. A journalist writing in 1938 offered an impression of these times:

> "Spiritually and morally, civilization collapsed on August 1, 1914—the civilization . . . which with all its shortcomings did give more satisfaction to more people than any other yet evolved. Young people cannot realize how the world has been coarsened and barbarized since 1914. They may feel the loss of security . . . but they cannot appreciate how much else has been lost."

arts and literature of the post–World War I era.
2. List the new developments in science.
3. Outline the changes in people's tastes as revealed in popular culture and architecture.
4. List reasons why Americans sometimes refer to the 1920s as the "Roaring Twenties."
5. Outline the origins of the Great Depression, focusing particularly on the interrelationships of the United States' and world economies.
6. Identify the major programs initiated in the New Deal and understand how each helped to alleviate some of the economic hardships caused by the Great Depression.
7. Compare the problems European nations faced during the two decades after World War I.
8. Compare the motivations, methods and class support of fascism and communism, particularly in Italy and Germany during the interwar period.
9. Describe Mussolini's and Hitler's rise to power, methods of control, and the reasons for their overwhelming support by the general public.
10. Trace Lenin's and Stalin's adaptation of Communist principles to Russian problems.

SECTION 1

Focus/Motivation
Begin the section by displaying a painting from the Renaissance period, one from the baroque or from

the rococo period, and one from the Romantic period. Ask students to describe what they see. Next show the students paintings by Picasso, Braque, Dali, and Kandinsky. Ask students to describe these paintings. Show them the main difference between modern art and earlier art by explaining that modern art does not portray objective reality; its enjoyment or understanding depends upon a person's subjective interpretation. Point out to students that this subjective interpretation characterizes much of this period's art. (This exercise can also be done with literary selections from Dickens and Joyce.) Ask students why they think art became subjective in this period. Ask them what this increased subjectivity indicates about standards, including standards of beauty or justice, during the post–World War I era.

Presentation
Identifying Ideas (Average/Group)
On the chalkboard or on an overhead projector write the following two lists and have students copy them into their notebooks. Have students match the description in the first list with the artist, writer, musician, architect, or film director in the second list.

1. French novelist who believed that the only reality is sensation, or what is felt through the senses.

The work of the leading thinkers, writers, and artists of the time heightened this sense of disquiet and uncertainty.

The Effects of New Scientific Ideas

Following World War I, many people rejected the beliefs of reason and progress first expressed during the Enlightenment. Instead they felt a sense of helplessness and cynicism. Scientists, who since the 1600s had been proving that human beings could solve almost any problem, had begun to suggest something else in the early 1900s. During this period some people interpreted the ideas of psychologist Sigmund Freud, for example, to mean that people could no longer be quite so confident about the powers of rational thought.

Freudian psychology. Sigmund Freud had developed theories of the unconscious (see Chapter 20). He believed that the unconscious mind governed human behavior. In Freud's opinion people were generally unaware of the mental processes of the unconscious. Freud had begun writing in the early 1900s, but his ideas about the unconscious mind and irrationality did not gain popularity until after World War I. If people believed that they could not rationally control their actions, then much that seemed bewildering could be explained. These ideas seemed to help people understand why the dreadful devastation of World War I had taken place, why things had not turned out as they had hoped, and why the uneasiness was continuing.

Einstein's physics. The theory of relativity made Albert Einstein famous (see Chapter 20). In this theory he had argued that even such seemingly absolute and definite concepts as space, motion, and time had to be seen as relative, or dependent on one another. This concept gave comfort to those who denied that any standard, whether of morality or of artistic taste, was absolute. Believers in this concept argued that attitudes depended on the individual—that they were relative to each person. They claimed that Einstein's physics supported their view.

Certainty in basic scientific measurements no longer seemed possible. As a result, people believed that science no longer provided indisputable knowledge. This change in attitude destroyed the assumption that constant progress would unlock the secrets of nature. It also added to a sense of unease and a lack of confidence in the future. The scientists intensified, rather than relieved, the uncertainty and the doubts about traditional attitudes that marked the postwar world.

New Directions in Literature

The major writings of World War I and the postwar years revealed a dissatisfaction not only with the times but with the way books and poems had been written in the past. Writers experimented with form and, influenced by Freud, began to probe unconscious motivations. The German historian and philosopher, Oswald Spengler, set the mood for the era with *The Decline of the West.* Spengler believed that all civilizations pass from youth to maturity, and from maturity to old age and eventually death. In his book Spengler predicted that European civilization would disintegrate. World War I had been only the first step in the process.

Novels. The French novelist Marcel Proust suggested that people could not make realistic or proper judgments by reasoning and thinking. Proust believed that the only reality is sensation, or what is felt through the senses. In exhaustive detail, Proust vividly brought to life the sensations of taste, touch, and smell. His main work, *Remembrance of Things Past,* is a multivolume novel. The first part appeared in 1913, but most of it was published after World War I. In the 1920s his work became famous and was widely read.

Thomas Mann, Proust's German contemporary, used as his themes the constant presence of death amid life and the alienation of the writer from society. A constant atmosphere of decadence and sadness prevails in his novels—reflecting the moods of the 1920s and 1930s. The somber atmosphere is most notable in *The Magic Mountain* (1927). This book, set in a tuberculosis sanitarium, deals symbolically with the moral sickness of Europe.

After the war the works of Franz Kafka, the Czech writer, were particularly influential in Germany—even though Kafka spent all but the last year of his life in Prague. In his works, most of which became popular after his death, Kafka used a technique known as **surrealism**—an attempt to portray and interpret life as if it took place in a dream. In *The Trial* (1925), the main character is being tried in a hostile atmosphere for a crime he knows nothing about. In *The Castle* (1926), a man is looking for someone, but despite searching through endless

● The musical *Cats,* by Andrew Lloyd Weber, is based on T.S. Eliot's book of poetry entitled *Old Possum's Book of Practical Cats.*

PAINTING

The City by Fernand Léger

During World War I many soldiers suffered from the effects of poison gas. One of these was the French artist Fernand Léger. Before he entered the army, Léger painted glorified machines and technology. While recovering in a hospital, he realized that individuals were more important than things. When he began painting again, Léger included people in his canvases. In this painting of city life, human figures descend the staircases, walk on the streets, and appear in the posters.

Léger's interest was not only in painting but in set design as well. He conceived, directed, and produced sets for ballets and motion pictures.

Philadelphia Museum of Art: A. E. Gallatin Collection

Léger was part of the cubist movement in art that started in Paris about 1907. Cubists portrayed objects broken down into their basic geometric forms. In theory a cubist painter stepped into the picture and then walked around the subject, trying to show all the sides at once. Thus the artist could expand what the human eye could see.

corridors and seeing many other people in the castle, he can never accomplish his goal. Kafka's writings later influenced the work of many writers.

The Irish writer James Joyce caused a great stir during this period. In his sometimes bewildering masterpiece, *Ulysses* (1922), Joyce tried to convey everything that happened to a man and everything the man thought, both consciously and unconsciously, in a single day. Joyce used a technique called stream of consciousness. Influenced by psychoanalysis, the technique demands that everything that comes into a character's mind be recorded or noted on paper. *Ulysses* is difficult to understand because it lacks normal punctuation and skips about at random. *Ulysses* was a revolutionary work that broke away from many of the traditions of the novel. It revealed both the dissatisfaction with the past and the restlessness of the people of the postwar era.

The American writer Ernest Hemingway wrote in clear, simple prose. His aim, especially in *A Farewell to Arms* (1929), was to express the disillusionment over human behavior that was so common in the years after World War I.

Poetry. The American-born poet T. S. Eliot, ● who spent most of his life in England, best expressed through his poetry the break with traditional forms and the deep pessimism of the postwar years. In his most famous poem *The Waste Land* (1922), Eliot gave a despairing description of a world without faith, incapable of restoring its spiritual and moral values. Many other poets of this period also abandoned traditional rhyme and meter. Instead they wrote poetry without rhyme that had lines of varying lengths. They also experimented with punctuation and even with the physical appearance of their poems.

New Directions in Music and Painting

Musicians and painters rejected traditional forms and styles with the same determination as did the writers of this period. Some of the new ideas of musicians and painters began before World War I, but they did not take hold until the unsettled postwar years.

Music. One of the pioneers of the new direction in music was Igor Stravinsky. Born in Russia,

2. Spanish surrealist painter who attempted to symbolize the unconscious
3. Czech writer who used surrealism in an attempt to interpret life as if it took place in a dream
4. French artist who was one of the first to introduce the style of art called cubism
5. American architect who helped develop the skyscraper, as well as a style of architecture called functionalism
6. Austrian musician who wrote atonal music
7. American film director who made films about human intolerance and cruelty
8. American composer who wrote music with catchy melodies for the "Big Bands"

a. Louis Sullivan
b. D.W. Griffith
c. Walter Schoenberg
d. Irving Berlin
e. Marcel Proust
f. Georges Braque
g. Salvador Dali
h. Franz Kafka

(Answers: 1. e; 2. g; 3. h; 4. f; 5. a; 6. c; 7. b; 8. d)

1B, 5B, 5F, a1B, a1C

History Through the Arts

FILMS

Charlie Chaplin in *Modern Times*

Mechanization created feelings of uneasiness in many people. One of these people was the brilliant comedian Charlie Chaplin. Characterizing the human spirit in its loneliness and humor, he used the new invention, the movie, as the vehicle for his satire. One of his most famous films was *Modern Times,* which was released in 1936. The movie depicts him, in his usual role as a gentle tramp, at work in a huge factory. Here he is shown tightening bolts on an endless assembly line. In pursuit of one neglected bolt, he knocks other workers over, upsets the entire factory routine, and ends as a captive of the machinery.

he lived most of his life in western Europe and the United States. Stravinsky's *The Rite of Spring* (1913) caused a disturbance at its first performance because it broke so completely with traditional music composition. Stravinsky directed different instruments to be played in different keys at the same time, creating a sound that many people found disturbing.

Three Austrians, Arnold Schoenberg and his students Alban Berg and Anton von Webern, were even more revolutionary. They wrote what is called atonal music. In Schoenberg's atonal compositions, he completely abandoned the conventional eight-tone musical scale and used instead a twelve-tone scale. Schoenberg and his followers avoided such traditional forms as the sonata, the symphony, and the concerto. They wrote pieces for unusual collaborations of instruments, such as Webern's *Quartet for Violin, Clarinet, Saxophone, and Piano.* Their melodies were not developed in the traditional way, and their music often sounded strange and unfamiliar. This discordant music is controversial even today.

Painting. The same rejection of traditional forms and styles occurred in the field of painting. Artists of the early 1900s overturned the standards of beauty and the recognizable portrayal of nature taken for granted since the Renaissance.

The first pioneers of this new style of art were the Spaniard Pablo Picasso and the French artist Georges Braque, who worked in Paris. They created a new art style called **cubism,** which emphasized geometric forms, shapes, and designs. Using shapes such as cones, cylinders, spheres, flat planes, and especially cubes, they showed the abstract structures of the objects they painted, not their surface appearance. In fact, Picasso and Braque often depicted the objects from several different perspectives at the same time. Thus, for example, one would see half a face in profile and the other half from the front.

Picasso justified the severe distortions of reality in his artwork by saying that "nature and art, being two different things, cannot be the same thing. Through art we express our concept of what nature is not." Like the composers of the time, Picasso

668

● A cultural renaissance, or rebirth, took place among black artists, writers, and musicians, during the 1920s, centering around New York City's black community of Harlem.

knew that his work disturbed many people, but that was part of his purpose. He was protesting the easy acceptance of old forms.

Other painters turned away from traditional art in various ways. Surrealistic painters attempted to symbolize the unconscious. Their works featured perfectly painted objects that did not seem to relate to one another. The Spanish surrealist Salvador Dali painted *The Persistence of Memory* (1931), which depicts a dreamlike landscape with what looks like liquid clocks draped over a tree branch and the edge of a shelf. Other artists, notably the Russian, Wassily Kandinsky, and the Dutchman, Piet Mondrian, painted purely abstract designs.

Like the writers of the period, the musicians and the painters of the post-World War I era broke dramatically with the attitudes and styles of the past. They created works that reflected the pessimism and doubts of the people in the late 1920s and the 1930s.

Popular Culture

Novelists such as Franz Kafka and musicians such as Arnold Schoenberg appealed only to a small audience. Most people found escape from the disillusionment of troubled times in other new forms of entertainment.

Popular music. One favorite diversion was listening to music on phonograph records or on the radio. More and more households had radios in the 1920s and 1930s, and music aimed at a mass audience filled the air waves. This was the start of the era of the "Big Bands." These bands played dance music with catchy melodies written by composers such as Irving Berlin and Cole Porter. In addition, the musical, a type of play featuring song and dance, became a major attraction in the theater.

The most innovative popular musicians played a distinctive form of music known as jazz. Jazz began in the southern United States in the late 1800s. Performed primarily by black musicians, its style ● developed particularly in New Orleans. Using African as well as American music as inspiration, jazz emphasized individual experimentation. One of its major forms, the blues, concentrated on sad, pessimistic themes. The work of jazz musicians did not differ from the experimental and untraditional writing and painting of the day.

Film. The chief entertainment for popular audiences of the 1920s and 1930s came from another new art form, the film, or motion picture. Invented around the year 1900, motion pictures swept through Europe and the United States. Thousands of movie houses, or theaters, opened in the 1920s and 1930s. The first public showings occurred around 1910, and by the 1920s millions of moviegoers routinely waited in long lines to see their favorite films.

Film, too, reflected the pessimism of the postwar era. Although early movies were often simple dramas or hilarious comedies, they also carried disturbing messages. The greatest film directors—D. W. Griffith in the United States and Sergei Eisenstein in the Soviet Union—made powerful films about human intolerance and cruelty. Most movies, however, offered viewers an escape from the problems of a difficult world.

Learning from Pictures *The internationally known American jazz trumpet player Louis Armstrong (fourth from left), played with the King Oliver band during the early 1920s in Chicago.*

SECTION 1

Closure

Ask students to explain the impact that World War I had on the postwar attitudes. *(Answers will vary.)*

Review Answers

1. ***totalitarian regime:*** highly centralized government that allowed no opposition and held total control; ***surrealism:*** an attempt to portray and interpret life as if it took place in a dream; ***cubism:*** art style that emphasized forms, shapes and design; ***functionalism:*** form of architecture based on the principle that a building should be designed for its specific use; ***international style:*** form of functional architecture that was plain and severe and used uninterrupted expanses of steel and glass

2. ***Thomas Mann:*** German novelist who developed themes of death amidst life and the alienation of the writer from society; ***James Joyce:*** Irish writer who developed stream of consciousness technique; ***Ernest Hemingway:*** American writer who expressed disillusionment about human behavior; ***The Waste Land:*** poem by T.S. Eliot in which he gave a despairing description of a world without faith, incapable of restoring its spiritual and moral values; ***Igor Stravinsky:*** Russian composer who broke with most traditional methods of musical

1B, 5B, 5F, a1B, a1C, a4A, a4F, a4H, a4L

composition; ***Pablo Picasso:*** Spanish painter who introduced cubism; ***Frank Lloyd Wright:*** American architect who believed a building should be related to its environment
3. Popular culture was often escapist during the 1930s because people wanted to escape from the economic hardships of the Depression and the troubled political and international conditions.
4. (a) Experimentation in literature included Joyce's introduction of "stream of consciousness," and poets' abandonment of rhyme and experimentation with line length, stress and punctuation. **(b)** In music, Igor Stravinsky composed music in which instruments played in different keys at the same time; and jazz emphasized individual experimentation. **(c)** Among painters, Picasso and Braque created cubism; Dali attempted to symbolize the unconscious; and Kandinsky and Mondrian reduced painting to pure abstract design. **(d)** Griffith and Einstein made films about human intolerance and cruelty. **(e)** In architecture, Sullivan introduced functionalism; Wright stressed the relation of a building to its environment; and European architects developed the international style.

Learning from Pictures *This house named "Fallingwater" was designed by Frank Lloyd Wright in the 1930s. The house is built over a waterfall near Uniontown, Pennsylvania.*

Architecture

Architecture also underwent great change during the postwar years. New technical advances, such as the use of structural steel, made a remarkable transformation possible.

The American Louis Sullivan pioneered the new architecture. Not only did he help to develop the skyscraper, but he also developed a style called **functionalism.** The fundamental principle of functionalism is that a building should be designed for its specific use rather than according to popular style.

Louis Sullivan's pupil Frank Lloyd Wright adopted Sullivan's ideas and added his own. One of Wright's major theories stressed that buildings should be appropriate to their environment. For example, Wright's prairie houses in the Middle West were low buildings with long horizontal lines. In the 1920s Wright built the Imperial Hotel in Tokyo. Adapting the hotel to its location, he floated it on a cushion of mud instead of anchoring it rigidly to rock. Because of this adaptive construction, it was the only large structure in Tokyo to survive the severe earthquake of 1923.

European architects developed a new style of architecture. Influenced by Sullivan and Wright, a group including the Frenchman Le Corbusier and the German Walter Gropius developed a functional architecture called the **international style.** This style used uninterrupted expanses of steel and glass.

The new art forms all showed a radical change —a break as dramatic as the one between medieval and Renaissance styles. It was as if nothing—neither music, books, paintings, nor architecture—could be the same again after World War I.

SECTION 1 REVIEW

1. **Define** totalitarian regime, surrealism, cubism, functionalism, international style
2. **Identify** Thomas Mann, James Joyce, Ernest Hemingway, *The Waste Land,* Igor Stravinsky, Pablo Picasso, Frank Lloyd Wright
3. **Analyzing Ideas** What was the main function of popular culture during the 1930s?
4. **Interpreting Ideas** The 1920s and 1930s witnessed much experimentation in art forms. Give an example of this experimentation in each of the following categories: **(a)** literature, **(b)** music, **(c)** painting, **(d)** film, and **(e)** architecture.

● Young women, called flappers, showed their defiance of conventional conduct by wearing their dresses above the knee, bobbing their hair, wearing lipstick, smoking cigarettes, drinking alcohol illegally, and discussing sex openly.

1B, 4I, 5B, a1C, a3A, a3B, a3C, a3D, a3E, a3G, a3H, a3I

2 Postwar Prosperity Crumbled into a Worldwide Depression

Like France and Great Britain, the United States had fought on the victorious Allied side in World War I. Unlike the Europeans, however, the Americans had fought in the war for less than a year. The Atlantic Ocean had separated the United States from the battlefields, and therefore no American land had been devastated. The United States emerged much stronger economically at the end of the war. By 1918 both industry and agriculture had expanded tremendously, resulting in an **economic boom,** or sudden increase in prosperity.

Postwar Prosperity

The United States emerged from the war as the apparent successor to Great Britain in world leadership. The American involvement in the war had contributed greatly to the Allied victory, and the United States had also taken a strong role in drawing up the peace settlement.

The United States' new financial status most dramatically indicated its leadership role in the world. In 1914 the United States had owed about $4 billion to foreign governments and businesses. By 1919 these conditions had reversed, with foreign governments owing the United States government about $10 billion. Much more was owed to United States citizens who had bought foreign bonds.

However, the refusal of the United States to join the League of Nations indicated that the United States did not want the responsibility of world leadership. Americans seemed to want to sit back and enjoy their newfound prosperity and avoid any further entanglement in European affairs.

The Roaring Twenties

Historians have dubbed the 1920s the Roaring Twenties because of the fast pace of life and sometimes frantic pursuit of pleasure that marked the era. Some have attributed that atmosphere to the American exposure to European attitudes during World War I. However, other factors also contributed to this social change.

During the 1920s many changes affected people's lives. Automobiles became a popular means of transportation. Commercial airlines began carrying mail (passenger service did not begin until the 1930s). Telephones linked millions of homes, and movies became a favorite form of entertainment. During this era jazz became popular, new fast dances like the Charleston gained acceptance, and movie stars became public idols. Charles Lindbergh gained fame overnight for his solo flight across the Atlantic Ocean, a feat that had never before been accomplished.

This era of enormous confidence also prompted a revolt against traditional morality and standards. Changes brought more freedom for women as they won the right to vote and joined the work force in greater numbers than ever before. Another sign of ● changing morality came with the widespread evasion of **Prohibition**—the law forbidding the manufacture, sale, and transportation of alcoholic beverages. Smuggling and bootlegging—the illegal manufacture and sale of liquor—made Prohibition ineffective.

The Economy

Although the United States was prosperous, some flaws did exist. For example, wages paid to laborers did not keep pace with increased productivity. In other words, not enough money ended up in the hands of consumers to buy the goods being produced. Instead, profits went either to wealthy stockholders or toward reinvestment in new machinery and additional factories. Increased use of labor-saving machinery not only stimulated production but also increased unemployment.

Agriculture suffered as well. Farmers had greatly increased production during the war to help feed the Allies. But now that market had dried up. The use of modern machinery and methods led to a serious overproduction of food, and prices fell. In the wheat market especially, production far outweighed consumption in the 1920s.

Another flaw in the system occurred through **economic nationalism.** This is the policy a nation uses to improve its economic well-being by establishing protective tariffs and similar restrictions on the import and export of goods. A healthy world market depends on a free flow of goods from one country to another. In the 1920s, however, many countries set up tariffs to protect their own expanding industries from foreign competition. Each country's home market could not consume all that

SECTION 2

Focus/Motivation
Have students study the picture on textbook page 673, then read them the following lyrics from "Brother, Can you Spare a Dime?" a song popular during the Depression. A record may be available in a local library.

"They used to tell me I
was building a dream —
And so I followed the mob.
When there was earth to
plough and guns to
bear —
I was always there —
right on the job.
They used to tell me I was
building a dream —
With peace and glory
ahead —
Why should I be standing
in line just waiting for
bread?"

Ask students the following questions: What does the picture tell you about how people felt during the Depression? *(The picture conveys sadness, despair, and disillusionment.)* What does the song tell you about public attitudes during the Depression? *(People felt that they had worked hard but had somehow been let down.)* What steps might government take to restore people's faith? *(Accept all reasonable answers.)*

Presentation
Analyzing Ideas (Average/Group)
Conduct a panel discussion in which students might discuss the pros and cons of the New Deal. Questions to investigate

4I, 5B, a3F

● Discussion topic: Had the countries represented at the International Monetary and Economic Conference been able to come to an agreement to end economic nationalism, and had they been successful in promoting international cooperation, how might the course of history have been changed?

should include: How do relief programs like those of the New Deal affect people's incentive to work? How would too much government regulation of business affect the economy? How would too little regulation affect it? *(Answers will vary.)*

was being produced, and high tariffs made it difficult for foreign buyers to absorb the surplus.

During the 1920s the United States raised its tariffs to the highest level in its history. The United States insisted upon American dollars in exchange for goods sold abroad. High tariffs now made it hard for European countries to sell their goods in the United States. If they could not sell goods *to* the United States, then they could not acquire dollars to purchase goods *from* the United States. As a result, banks and businesspeople in the United States willingly lent money to Europeans so that they could buy American goods. But this practice merely created more indebtedness, and European nations already had heavy war debts.

Speculation, Panic, and Crash

Throughout the 1920s millions of Americans made **market speculations,** or risky investments, in the stock market in the hope of quick, high profits. The stock market is the organization through which a company's stock certificates are bought and sold. A company issues shares of stock to raise money for expansion. Investors buy these shares to make a profit or earn an income from the company's earnings known as dividends. During the 1920s prices of stocks sold on the New York Stock Exchange soared, and many investors did make large profits. Trouble rose, however, because much of the money invested in the stock market had been borrowed. Frequently, the only security the borrower had to offer to the lender was the hope of future profits from stock investments. Everyone had expected the prices of stocks to rise indefinitely.

However, on October 29, 1929, a wave of panic swept investors in the New York Stock Exchange. On this day prices sank to an all-time low when more than 16 million shares of stock were suddenly dumped on the market. No one would buy stocks while prices declined. As a result, many of the stocks on the exchange became virtually worthless. Vast fortunes vanished. Hundreds of banks, factories, mining companies, and business firms in the United States declared bankruptcy.

The Great Depression

The collapse of the New York Stock Exchange marked the beginning of a worldwide depression called the **Great Depression.** Some of the reasons for this economic crisis included the slowdown of business activity, the high rate of unemployment, and falling wages and prices. Many of the most reliable European banks closed their doors. By 1932 more than 30 million workers in countries throughout the world could not find jobs. Germany stopped paying reparations, and the Allied nations ceased the payments of war debts to the United States.

The strange thing about poverty during the Depression was that it occurred in the midst of abundant productivity. The prices of goods fell very low, but the goods could not be sold because people simply did not have the money to buy them. Manufactured products piled up in warehouses, and crops rotted. Some countries tried to force prices to rise by destroying surpluses. Canada burned part of its wheat crop. Brazil dumped coffee into the sea. European exports and imports declined more than 60 percent in three years, and United States trade abroad decreased by 68 percent.

Responses to the Great Depression

The United States responded to the Great Depression by continuing its policy of economic nationalism. It raised tariffs even higher and cut off American loans to Europe. Germany and Austria had wanted to establish a customs union to aid their economies. However, several European nations opposed the project, and the World Court banned it. In every case, it appeared, the immediate response to the Great Depression made recovery more difficult.

In 1933 an International Monetary and Economic Conference met in London, but it failed to promote greater financial cooperation among the industrial nations. Most of these countries had already decided upon economic nationalism as the proper answer to the Great Depression. ●

Great Britain tried to induce full employment and stimulate production by granting low-interest loans to its industries. In addition to raising its tariffs against foreign goods, in 1931 Great Britain formed a system for economic cooperation within its empire. In 1932 at a conference in Ottawa, Canada, Great Britain devised a system of "imperial preferences." Through this system the dominions and possessions within the British Empire agreed to levy low tariffs on one another's products. In a period of international economic uncertainty, they were attempting to become economically self-sufficient.

France, less industrialized than Great Britain, did not suffer as much during the Great Depression. However, French trade declined, unemployment increased, and industrial production dropped sharply. The uncertainty of the Depression years caused even greater political instability in France than the troubles following the war had created. In 1933 alone there were four changes of government.

Elsewhere in the world, the Great Depression caused unrest and violence. In Germany it helped destroy the Weimar Republic established at the end of the war. The representative governments that did survive the severe shock of the Great Depression had strong democratic traditions.

The New Deal

The United States had fallen behind most other industrial nations in creating social legislation. Unemployment insurance and government relief programs did not exist. As a result, when the Great Depression occurred, American workers had to rely on their savings, if any, and on charity provided by private organizations. People stood in breadlines to receive a bowl of soup or a plate of stew. Some earned money by selling apples in the streets.

Under President Herbert Hoover, the federal government tried to remedy these severe conditions, but the measures adopted were not extensive. Hoover believed that prosperity was "just around the corner."

Elections brought a new President, Franklin D. Roosevelt, to office in 1933. He immediately embarked upon a program of relief and reform called the New Deal. Under the provisions of the New Deal, the government granted money to each state for food, shelter, and clothing for the needy. The government also began a program of public works to provide employment.

Following Roosevelt's emergency relief program, Congress enacted a sweeping reform of America's economic system. Banks and stock exchanges were placed under strict regulation. The Social Security Act of 1935 provided for unemployment and old-age benefits. A 40-hour work week and minimum wage levels were established. The federal government had previously remained neutral or sided with the industrialists in labor disputes. Now it guaranteed workers the right to establish unions.

The federal government also tried to relieve the desperate situation of farmers by paying them to take land out of production and to plant crops that would revitalize the soil. Later the government adopted a program of buying and storing surplus

Learning from Pictures *In this scene from the Great Depression, women and children receive food from the New Hope Mission in New York City.*

SECTION 2

Closure

Ask students to list the economic conditions that caused the stock market crash of 1929. When they finish, ask them if any of these economic conditions exist today and if so, to discuss them.

Review Answers

1. ***economic boom:*** sudden increase in prosperity; ***Prohibition:*** law forbidding the manufacture, sale and transportation of alcoholic beverages; ***economic nationalism:*** policy of imposing protective tariffs and restrictions on import and export of goods; ***market speculation;*** risky stock investments in the hope of quick, high profits; ***Great Depression:*** worldwide depression beginning in 1929
2. ***"Roaring Twenties":*** term often used for the 1920s; ***Herbert Hoover:*** president at the beginning of the Depression; ***Social Security Act:*** provided for unemployment and old-age benefits; ***Tennessee Valley Authority:*** program to build a series of dams in the Tennessee River valley; ***Trade Agreements Act:*** allowed the president to make agreements with foreign countries for reciprocal tariff reductions
3. The U. S. was economically strong and had undamaged, expanded industry and agriculture. It had tipped the balance militarily in favor of the Allies and had taken a leading role in the peace settlement. Financially, the U.S. had now

1C, 1E, 4I, 5B, 5H, a1C, a4A, a4F, a4H, a4I, a4L, a4K

become a major creditor nation.
4. The U. S. raised its tariffs and insisted upon American dollars in exchange for goods. American banks and businesspeople lent money to European nations, making them dependent upon the U. S.
5. Buying power did not keep pace with productivity; increased used of labor-saving machinery reduced employment and created overabundance; economic nationalism hampered trade; uncontrolled speculation led to the stock market's collapse.
6. Great Britain tried to induce full employment and stimulate production through low-interest loans to its industries. Besides raising tariffs, Great Britain formed within its empire a system for economic cooperation.
7. (a) The New Deal was Franklin D. Roosevelt's program of direct relief and sweeping reform of the economy. **(b)** New Deal measures included granting of money to states for direct relief, providing employment through a public-works program, regulating banks and stock exchanges, and providing for unemployment and old-age benefits.

SECTION 3

Focus/Motivation
Lead a discussion on the problems facing Europe after World War I, using the following questions as a guide: What problems usually occur at the end of any

Learning from Pictures *President Roosevelt dedicated many public works. Here he is at the opening of a bridge that crosses the Choptank River in Maryland.*

farm crops. This program helped prevent the prices of farm goods from plunging.

Another federal program of far-reaching economic and social significance involved the establishment of the Tennessee Valley Authority, or TVA. Having established the TVA in the valley of the Tennessee River and its tributaries, the government built a series of multipurpose dams there, intending to generate cheap electricity, to help prevent floods and soil erosion, and to improve navigation.

The Roosevelt administration also tried to revive world trade. The Trade Agreements Act of 1934 allowed the president to make special agreements with foreign countries. If a foreign nation lowered its tariff rates on some American products, the president was empowered to lower American tariff rates on some of that foreign country's products. As a result of this and other measures, United States foreign trade began to recover.

Under the New Deal, the United States government became more deeply involved than ever before in the welfare of the individual citizen. It attempted in many ways to restore prosperity. However, the causes of the Great Depression remained too deeply rooted to be cured completely even by a program as ambitious as the New Deal. Only when the United States mobilized for war did the hardships caused by the Great Depression finally end.

SECTION 2 REVIEW

1. **Define** economic boom, Prohibition, economic nationalism, market speculation, Great Depression
2. **Identify** Roaring Twenties, Herbert Hoover, Social Security Act, Tennessee Valley Authority, Trade Agreements Act
3. **Summarizing Ideas** Why was the United States considered a world leader in the years following World War I?
4. **Analyzing Ideas** How did American economic policies during the 1920s and 1930s affect economic conditions in Europe?
5. **Organizing Ideas** What conditions helped to bring about the Great Depression?
6. **Understanding Ideas** What measures did Great Britain take to cope with the effects of the Great Depression?
7. **Explaining Ideas** **(a)** What was the New Deal? **(b)** Give some specific examples of its provisions.

3 Europe Experienced Political Tensions After World War I

The events of the postwar years put a strain on the older and more experienced European democracies, such as France and Great Britain. Demobilization of the armed forces led to widespread unemployment and intense competition for jobs. Many people could not find jobs because production by farms and factories had expanded to fill wartime needs, and now an overabundance existed.

Many Europeans believed that governments needed to take a more active role in economic matters to solve the unemployment problem. Before World War I, many people had believed that governments should not interfere in business matters. However, wartime needs had led several nations to adopt a **planned economy**—an economy in which governmental regulation and direction of national

● Construction of the Maginot Line seriously weakened the French system of alliances as France's allies became concerned about this defensive position.

resources was established to achieve economic stability. Since the system had worked well in wartime, why not use it to solve peacetime economic problems?

In the new European nations, such as Poland, different problems arose. Many of these new countries set up their governments more in imitation of Western systems than because of any deep devotion to democratic principles. Most of the people who administered them had no experience in democratic government. As a result, social and economic troubles increased, and serious signs of weakness began to appear.

France's Postwar Difficulties

During the four years of World War I, northern France had been a major battleground. At war's end, farmhouses and even entire cities lay in ruins, and trenches and shell holes scarred the land. Wharves needed replacing. Railroads and roads needed restoration. Most tragic of all, a high percentage of the young men of France had been killed.

Thus France emerged from World War I victorious but unstable. It still owed money that it had borrowed from its citizens and from the United States during and after the war. Inflation also took its toll. The burden of higher prices fell mostly on industrial workers and the lower middle class—those least able to pay.

The expenses of the French government soared for several reasons. The number of civil servants increased during and after the war. The government had to repair war-damaged areas and to pay interest on its heavy debt. But most important, perhaps, it had to pay for military security.

The Maginot Line. Twice in less than 50 years, the Germans had invaded France. To prevent this from happening again, the French rebuilt their army. They also constructed a series of steel and concrete fortifications that stretched nearly 200 miles (320 kilometers) along the borders of Germany and Luxembourg. This extensive line of fortifications was named the Maginot (MAZH • uh • noh) Line, after the minister of war who planned it.

Construction of the Maginot Line cost enormous sums of money. Since trench warfare had been a major feature of World War I, the French planned to make their defenses so strong that the country could never again be invaded overland from the east.

International affairs. In July 1922 Germany had informed the Allies that it could not continue to pay reparations on schedule. Despite British objections, France and Belgium therefore marched troops into Germany's coal- and iron-rich Ruhr Valley in January 1923. France intended to occupy the area and operate the steel mills there until it collected the money Germany owed. The German workers refused to cooperate, and the attempt ended in failure. The French then withdrew their troops.

By 1925 the political situation in Europe seemed to be improving. In that year, representatives from Great Britain, France, Germany, Belgium, Italy, Czechoslovakia, and Poland met at Locarno, Switzerland. There they signed a number of treaties known together as the Locarno Pact. The delegates to the conference pledged that their countries would settle peacefully all future disputes, guaranteed the existing Franco-German boundaries, and invited Germany to join the League of Nations. In addition, France signed mutual assistance treaties with both Poland and Czechoslovakia.

However, France's protective alliances began to show serious weaknesses. By the mid-1930s Belgium canceled its defensive alliance with France and declared itself neutral in any future war. France formed a shaky alliance with its prewar ally Russia, now under a Communist government. France's wartime ally Italy, now under the rule of a dictatorship, resumed its old opposition to France. In keeping with its aim of encircling Germany, France developed postwar alliances with Yugoslavia and Romania as well as with Poland and Czechoslovakia. However, these relatively weak nations, although they shared France's mistrust of Germany, were undependable allies. ●

Political unrest. In early 1934 a scandal in the French government touched off riots in Paris. Rioters demanded an end to the republican form of government. They called for a military dictatorship to "discipline" the country and to reunite the opposing parties.

The trade unions responded to the threat from the right-wing conservatives by calling a **general strike**—a refusal by workers in various industries to continue working until their demands are met. Shortly thereafter the parties of the left-wing organized a coalition government called the Popular Front. Its leader, Léon Blum, a socialist, became

war? *(Countries need to rebuild, reconcile grievances with other countries, pay war debts, return soldiers to civilian life, and change from a wartime to a peacetime economy.)* How do you think the nations of Europe should have gone about solving these problems? *(Accept all reasonable answers. Solutions should aim at a sharing of burdens by all classes of society, encouragement of democratic institutions, and international cooperation.)* As students read the section, have them note the specific problems each country faced and how successful each was in solving them.

Presentation
Analyzing Ideas (Average/Group)
After World War I many nations adopted economic nationalism. Have students compare the situation then with trade conditions today by asking the following question: Does the United States follow economic nationalism? *(The United States has sought to eliminate some, but not all, tariff barriers between itself and other nations.)* Can you name American industries in which economic nationalism is advocated? *(Students might refer to the automobile and electronics industries, which are threatened by competition from Japan.)* How might economic nationalism in these industries help America's economy? How might economic nationalism hurt the

1E, 5B, 5H, a1C

American economy? *(It might help by protecting American industry. It might hurt as other nations would retaliate by placing a tariff on goods that they import from the United States, causing U.S. exports to drop.)*

premier of France in 1936. United for the moment against the threat of a coup d'état, Blum's government carried out many reforms.

The Popular Front first persuaded the leaders of industry to grant an immediate pay raise to all workers. The government then established a 40-hour work week and granted every worker the right to a paid vacation. It also promised to protect labor union organizers, and it set up a system for the arbitration of labor disputes. The Bank of France came under public control and the armaments industry was partially **nationalized**—put under government control or ownership.

Prices, however, continued to rise to such levels that the increased wages did little to help. In addition, industrialists proved uncooperative. Blum's ministry lasted only one year. Through his leadership in this brief period, however, France's government developed great power and determination and enacted many important reforms.

After the fall of the Popular Front, the French working classes suffered severe setbacks. The 40-hour work week was abolished in 1938. Workers protested by organizing general sit-down strikes during which they stayed at their jobs but refused to work. Severe antilabor legislation followed.

France remained a democracy, but bitter divisions existed among the French people. They also feared German military power, which began regaining strength at an alarming rate.

Great Britain After World War I

Like France, Great Britain faced grave economic difficulties after World War I. A huge war debt owed both to people at home and to the United States made taxes extremely high.

British industry and trade suffered. The coal mines, on which industry depended, were beginning to give out. During the war the United States and Japan had taken over many of Great Britain's world markets. After the war Britain's run-down factories and worn-out machinery made competition with newer American or Japanese machines impossible.

In addition, the high tariffs of economic nationalism damaged British trade because Great Britain needed to sell abroad in order to pay for needed imports of food and raw materials.

Labor troubles. By 1921 the British government had to support about 2 million unemployed

Learning from Pictures *World War I left psychological as well as physical scars on people throughout Europe. Here a cafe in postwar Paris bustles, as the French people try to regain a sense of normalcy in their everyday lives.*

● Germany had plotted with the Irish rebels, the Sinn Fein, throughout the war, but did not come through with the promised help during the Easter Rebellion, causing the rebellion to collapse.

Learning from Pictures *The British attacked Liberty Hall, the headquarters of the Irish nationalists during the Easter Rebellion.*

workers. This high unemployment rate meant labor unrest. Labor unions fought hard to maintain the high wages and full employment rate of the war years. Industrialists fought just as hard to resist the unions' demands.

In 1926 the coal miners called a strike, and their action led to a general strike. Soon almost half of Great Britain's 6 million unionized workers had left their jobs. The British government declared a state of emergency and ordered soldiers and sailors to replace the striking workers. The general strike failed, and the miners returned to work. Later the government passed the Trades Disputes and Trade Unions Act of 1927, which controlled unions and made general strikes illegal.

Discontented workers found a spokesman in Ramsay MacDonald, leader of the Labour Party. Although the Labour Party grew stronger, it did not have a majority in the House of Commons. Therefore, MacDonald formed a coalition with the Liberal Party, which had declined in strength because it could not attract working-class members. MacDonald was elected prime minister in 1924 and again in 1929. His government brought about moderate reforms, such as the extension of unemployment benefits and old-age insurance. Thus Great Britain avoided the social unrest that toppled democratic institutions elsewhere in Europe during the postwar years.

Ireland. In the 1920s Great Britain faced a major problem in a country it had ruled for centuries. During the 1800s the British government and Irish nationalists struggled over the issue of home rule for Ireland. The matter of limited self-government was unresolved by 1914, and most Irish people continued to yearn for complete independence for their country.

During World War I, with Great Britain's attention focused elsewhere, Irish nationalists revolted in the Easter Rebellion of 1916. The British suppressed the rebellion, but fighting broke out again in 1918. For years the Irish Republican Army fought British troops in a series of violent and bitter struggles. ●

In 1921 the British submitted to Ireland's demands and signed a treaty dividing Ireland into two parts. The following year the southern part of Ireland became the Irish Free State, a self-governing dominion with loose ties to Great Britain. Six counties in the northern region of Ireland chose to remain in the United Kingdom, with representatives in the British Parliament. This region became known as Northern Ireland.

In 1937 the Irish Free State adopted a new constitution and the name Eire (AR • uh). Eamon De Valera (dev • uh • LER • uh) was elected its first prime minister. (In 1949 Eire became completely independent, calling itself the Republic of Ireland.)

SECTION 3

Closure
Ask students to review the major economic and political problems confronting Europe after World War I, and discuss how these situations were dealt with by each of the countries in this section.

Review Answers
1. ***planned economy:*** governmental regulation and direction of national resources; ***general strike:*** refusal by workers in various industries to continue working until their demands are met; ***nationalize:*** place under general governmental control or ownership
2. ***Maginot Line:*** series of defensive fortifications built by France along the frontiers of Germany and Luxembourg; ***Locarno Pact:*** group of treaties signed in 1925; ***Popular Front:*** French leftist coalition government; ***Ramsay MacDonald:*** British Labour Party leader who was twice elected prime minister; ***Easter Rebellion:*** 1916 uprising of Irish nationalists against British rule; ***Eamon De Valera:*** first prime minister of Eire; ***Józef Pilsudski:*** military dictator of Poland beginning in 1926
3. France's internal problems after World War I included the following: a great deal of its land, buildings and industrial machinery had been damaged or destroyed; many of its young men had been killed; the government

1E, 5B, 5H, a4A, a4F, a4G, a4I, a4K, a4L

owed large war debts; inflation was rampant; and building the Maginot Line and reconstruction projects led to high government expenses.
4. Great Britain faced a large war debt, heavy taxes, declining industry and trade, labor unrest due to the slumping economy, and unrest in Ireland.
5. Discontented workers found a spokesman in Ramsay MacDonald, leader of the Labour Party. MacDonald formed a coalition with the Liberals and brought about moderate reforms such as the extension of unemployment benefits and old-age insurance.
6. *Anschluss* meant the union of Austria with Germany. The peace treaties ending World War I prevented this.
7. Eastern European countries tried to improve their economies by breaking up large estates and distributing the land to peasants, promoting industrialization, and practicing economic nationalism.

Both religion and politics divided the island. Most people in the Republic of Ireland were Roman Catholic, while the majority in Northern Ireland were Protestant. These same problems continue to trouble relations between Great Britain and Ireland today.

Eastern Europe

While the countries of western Europe attempted to recover economically, the new nations of eastern Europe began to create their own economies. However, the eastern European nations lagged far behind the western democracies in industrial development. For centuries the economy of eastern Europe had focused on the manor, and serfdom existed in some areas until the mid-1800s. As late as World War I, the economy was still mainly agricultural, with a few wealthy aristocrats owning most of the land.

Immediately after the war, the governments of Czechoslovakia, Romania, Bulgaria, and the Baltic countries (Estonia, Latvia, and Lithuania) divided the large estates and gave the land to the peasants. Yet most peasants lacked the funds to buy the farm equipment, fertilizers, and seeds necessary to make their farms productive.

The breakup of the Russian and Austro-Hungarian empires disrupted old patterns of trade. Most of the new eastern European countries tried to industrialize and turned to economic nationalism to protect their industries. As a result, trade among the countries proved difficult. Goods produced by the new industries could not be sold to neighboring countries at a reasonable profit.

The push toward economic development created a period of instability in the new nations of eastern Europe. Finland, Czechoslovakia, and the Baltic countries managed to sustain democratic regimes, but few other nations in eastern Europe succeeded in doing so. Three examples help illustrate what happened.

Austria. The Austria created after the war was a small country. Many Austrians wanted *Anschluss* (union) with Germany, but the peace treaties forbade it. Austria's economic weakness—one-third of the country's people lived in Vienna, the former capital of a large empire—and a continuing struggle between socialists and conservatives weakened the democratic system. Each faction set up private armies in the streets. The country became less democratic, and the Catholic church played an important role in the battle for control of the Austrian government.

Hungary. Hungary was declared a republic in November 1918. In March 1919, Béla Kun, a Hungarian Communist who had participated in the Russian Revolution, overthrew the republic and tried to establish a Communist system modeled on Russia's new government. He planned to break up the large estates and distribute the land to the peasants. However, the aristocrats who owned the land bitterly opposed Kun and with outside help overthrew his government in August of the same year.

By 1920 Hungarian Admiral Nicholas Horthy, a reactionary representative of the military class, ruled Hungary. Under Admiral Horthy's rule, landlocked Hungary was called "a kingdom without a king, ruled by an admiral without a fleet." In 1921 the emperor Charles I tried to restore the Hapsburg monarchy. However, the Allies would not permit the Hapsburgs to return to power, and for the next 10 years, Hungary was ruled by the nobility.

Poland. Soon after the war, a constitutional assembly met in Poland. It adopted a democratic constitution closely modeled on that of France's Third Republic (see Chapter 21). However, bitter opposition from both the conservatives and liberals prevented the new government from operating effectively. In 1926 Poland followed the example of Hungary and turned to military dictatorship. Dictator Marshal Józef Pilsudski (peel • SOOT • skee) represented the aristocracy and the military.

SECTION 3 REVIEW

1. **Define** planned economy, general strike, nationalize
2. **Identify** Maginot Line, Locarno Pact, Popular Front, Ramsay MacDonald, Easter Rebellion, Eamon De Valera, Józef Pilsudski.
3. **Organizing Ideas** What internal problems did France experience after World War I?
4. **Summarizing Ideas** What were the causes of the economic problems faced by the British after World War I?
5. **Analyzing Ideas** Why was Great Britain able to avoid the social unrest that troubled other nations after World War I?
6. **Understanding Ideas** What prevented Austria from achieving *Anschluss*?
7. **Explaining Ideas** How did eastern European countries try to improve their economies after World War I?

678

4 Fascist Dictatorships Were Established in Italy and Germany

As it did elsewhere, the war and its aftermath took their toll in Italy and Germany. Heavy losses of life, a crushing burden of debt, unemployment, and inflation plagued these countries. In Italy labor troubles resulted in many violent strikes. The Italian government, a constitutional monarchy, seemed helpless to meet the pressing needs of this situation.

The Rise of Fascism in Italy

One person who did offer a positive plan was Benito Mussolini. The son of a blacksmith, he had been a socialist as a young man and had edited a socialist newspaper. His writings had brought him a term in jail and a period in exile. During World War I his views changed. Mussolini became an extreme nationalist, and the Italian Socialist Party expelled him. After Italy joined the Allies, he enlisted in the army and was wounded in battle.

When Mussolini returned from the war, he began to organize his own political party. He called it the Fascist Party and called its doctrine **fascism** (FASH • iz • uhm). The words *fascist* and *fascism* come from the Latin word *fasces*. In ancient Rome a *fasces* was a bundle of rods bound tightly around an ax. It symbolized governmental authority. The various groups of the nation, Mussolini said, should be bound together like the rods of the fasces. He defined fascism as "the dictatorship of the state over many classes cooperating."

In his book *Delivered from Evil*, Robert Leckie described Benito Mussolini's physical features and the imposing personality that brought him and the Fascist Party to power in Italy in the 1920s:

> "At . . . his full height. . . [he was] . . . remarkable for his commanding head and his broad low brow, piercing black eyes, wide mouth and jutting square jaw. Because of his great head, he gave the impression of physical strength. Yet, if he were to remove his outer garments, it would be seen that his shoulders were thin, his arching chest a pouting pigeon's breast and his arms and legs spindly. However, like Napoleon, he could strike fear into men twice his size with a direct glance from those astonishing eyes."

Fascism, like communism, relies on dictatorial rule and a totalitarian regime, in which the state

Learning from Pictures *Mussolini ordered military training for all males ages 6 to 83. These young soldiers, called "sons of the wolf," parade in Rome.*

SECTION 4

Focus/Motivation
Put the following quotation from Mussolini on the chalkboard or on an overhead projector.

"Democracy is talking itself to death. The people do not know what they want; they do not know what is the best for them. There is too much foolishness, too much lost motion. I have stopped the talk and the nonsense. I am a man of action. Democracy is beautiful in theory; in practice it is a fallacy. You in America will see that some day."

Lead a discussion using the following questions: What are the basic differences between a democratic and a dictatorial government? *(A democratic government is responsible to its citizens and guards their rights. A dictatorship controls citizens through force, and can take away their rights.)* What general weakness did Mussolini attribute to democracy? *(Mussolini believed democracy promoted talk, but no action.)* Do you think that there might be other reasons besides social conditions in Italy for his views? *(his personal character traits)* How would you respond to Mussolini's statement? *(Answers will vary.)*

Presentation
Analyzing Ideas (Average/Group)
Mussolini's march on Rome is a good subject for a newscast that can involve the entire class. In

5B, 5G, a1C

● Fascism, unlike communism, did not contain a political philosophy but was more of a reaction to the times.

the newscast the following questions should be considered: What was the role of the Black Shirts? How important was Mussolini's leadership? How did King Victor Emmanuel III react to the Fascist advance? What did Italian politicians expect would happen to the government that Mussolini formed? Students should consult Jerre Mangione's *Mussolini's March on Rome* (Franklin Watts); Ivone Kirkpatrick's *Mussolini: A Study in Power* (Hawthorn); and Laura Fermi's *Mussolini* (University of Chicago Press).

● maintains rigid control of the people through force and censorship. All authority belongs to the state, with individuals completely subordinate to it. However, important differences exist between communism and fascism. Communism, which is based on a socialist economy, seeks international revolution. It appeals to workers and promises a classless society. Fascism, on the other hand, is extremely nationalistic, appeals to the middle class, while promising to preserve all existing social classes, and defends the ownership of private property. Both systems violently oppose the other.

Mussolini Gained Power

Mussolini found his first followers among demobilized soldiers and discontented nationalists. Gradually, the Fascists attracted professionals, wealthy landowners, and businesspeople, especially large manufacturers interested in the anticommunist program. These new supporters gave the Fascists much financial assistance. Fascists also found strong support among the lower middle classes, who had been severely hurt by inflation, and among the unemployed.

Recognizing that strong anticommunism appealed to the people, Mussolini emphasized this in his program. Fascism began to stand for the protection of private property and of the middle class. Mussolini promised to prevent a proletarian revolution. At the same time, he offered the industrial working class full employment and social security. He also stressed national prestige, pledging that Italy would gain all its war aims and return to the glories of the Roman Empire.

The Fascist Party began a violent campaign against its opponents, especially socialists and communists. Rowdy groups broke up strikes and political meetings and drove properly elected socialist officials from office. The Fascists adopted the black shirt as their uniform and became known as the Black Shirts.

In October 1922 Black Shirt groups from all over Italy converged on Rome, claiming they were coming to defend Italy against a communist revolution. Liberal members of the Italian parliament insisted that the king declare martial law. When he refused, the cabinet resigned. Conservative advisers then persuaded the king to appoint Mussolini as the premier and to ask him to head a coalition government.

Mussolini had often criticized democracy as a weak and ineffective form of government. Once in office, he began to destroy democracy in Italy and set up a dictatorship. He appointed Fascists to all official positions both in the central government and in the provinces. He pushed through parliament a new election law providing that the party receiving the most votes would automatically gain two-thirds of the seats in the Chamber of Deputies, the lower house of parliament. After the Fascists won the election in 1924, the Chamber of Deputies voted to give Mussolini "decree powers"—which meant that his decrees would have the force of law. He took the title *il Duce* (DOO • chay), Italian for "the leader."

Italy as a Police State

Now all of the outward signs of a dictatorship began to appear. Opposition parties ceased to exist. The government suspended freedom of speech, freedom of the press, and freedom of assembly, as well as trial by jury. Labor unions came under government control, and strikes were outlawed. Uniformed police, as well as secret police, spied on everyone.

Mussolini became commander-in-chief of the army, navy, and air force and head of the police. Although he allowed the king to reign as a figurehead, real power lay in the hands of the Grand Council of the Fascist Party. Mussolini headed the Council.

The Corporate State

Mussolini argued that in a modern industrial society, representation according to geographic location was outmoded. Instead, he introduced a new and complicated system of government in which representation was according to profession or occupation. The country's major economic activities, such as agriculture, transportation, manufacturing, and commerce, were formed into syndicates that resembled corporations. Thus Italy became known as a **corporate state.**

By the 1930s, Italy had 22 of these syndicates. In each syndicate representatives of government, management, and labor met to establish wages and prices and to agree upon working conditions. Labor unions and capitalists alike had to submit to the will of Mussolini's government. Private property remained in the hands of its owners, and profits

680

were allowed. All parts of the society had to cooperate with one another for the welfare of the nation.

The Fascist dictator, Mussolini, sat at the top of the entire system. In addition to the changes in the government, he strengthened the army and navy and increased armaments. These two additional changes in Italy had a double purpose: unemployment was reduced, and military strength increased. Mussolini promoted war as a glorious, patriotic adventure.

The Weimar Republic

As with Italy, difficulties in postwar Germany gave rise to political change following World War I. In November 1918 Germany was declared a republic. The following year, an assembly met in the city of Weimar (VY • mahr) and drafted a constitution that made Germany a federal republic, known as the Weimar Republic.

Germany's new government had a president and a two-house parliament elected by universal suffrage. The parliament included the Reichsrat (RYKS • raht) and the Reichstag. The president appointed the chancellor, Germany's prime minister.

The Weimar Republic was not popular with the German people. The republic had been created in response to Woodrow Wilson's announcement that he would deal only with a government elected by the German people. Many Germans opposed a republican government, and because Weimar representatives had signed the humiliating Versailles Treaty, the German people viewed the republic as a traitorous government.

Many of the difficulties of the Weimar Republic reflected the economic, social, and political problems that faced all of Europe after the war. Unemployment was high, and inflation soared. For example, in 1913 a German mark was worth about 25 cents. In 1923 it took 1 trillion marks to equal 25 cents.

Within its first year, two attempted revolutions threatened the Weimar Republic. A Communist government took over Munich, the capital of the state of Bavaria, and attempted to withdraw the state from the federal union. Later in Berlin, a right-wing group tried to overthrow the republic and to elevate to power men of its own choosing. The republic was powerless to defend itself and in

Learning from Pictures *The value of the German mark fell so low that people baled it and sold it for fuel.*

both cases had to rely on temporary alliances with anti-republican groups.

The Bavarian Communist revolt was crushed by the "free corps"—private right-wing armies made up of demobilized soldiers loyal only to their generals. The attempted overthrow in Berlin was defeated when members of the legal government, fleeing the city, called for a general strike. The workers of Berlin left their jobs, paralyzing the city and making it impossible for the right-wing rebels to set up their own government.

The Nazis and Hitler

One of the many political parties that formed in Germany after World War I was the German Workers' Party. In 1920 the party, attempting to broaden its appeal, changed its name to the National Socialist German Workers' Party, or Nazi Party. The party did not represent the working class, as its name might indicate, but was extremely nationalistic and violently anticommunist. Promising to protect Germany from communism, the party in time attracted the support of wealthy business leaders and landowners.

One of the first Nazi recruits, an ex-soldier named Adolf Hitler, was born in Austria in 1889, the son of a minor government official. As a young

681

5B, 5G

● Hitler was an Austrian citizen, but he enlisted in the German army during the war, and emerged with the rank of corporal.

Learning from Pictures *Hitler (left) and Mussolini (right) review German troops in Berlin on one of Mussolini's many state visits.*

man, he had gone to Vienna, where he failed as an artist and worked at various odd jobs. In Vienna, where Jews contributed to the city's rich cultural life and had risen to respected positions, Hitler became resentful and violently anti-Semitic.

● Hitler served in the German army in World War I and later moved to the city of Munich, where he joined the Nazi Party. In 1923 Hitler took part in a Nazi uprising in Munich in the state of Bavaria. The uprising failed, and Hitler was sentenced to prison. While there, he wrote *Mein Kampf* (My Struggle), a rambling book that expressed the spirit of the Nazi movement. In this writing, Hitler left no room for doubt about his goals for the German nation. He wrote:

> "If the National Socialist [Nazi] movement really wants to be consecrated [honored] by history with a great mission for our nation . . it must find the courage to gather our people and their strength for an advance along the road that will lead this people from its present restricted living space to new land and soil."

After his release from prison, Hitler became the leader of the Nazis and wanted to implement his ideas. He possessed a hypnotic talent as an orator. In the confusion of the postwar years, his emotional speeches attracted enthusiastic listeners. The frustration, self-pity, and hatred Hitler expressed reflected the feelings of many Germans who believed that they had suffered a great humiliation in the Versailles Treaty. The war reparations and loss of territory made them eager to follow a leader they hoped would restore Germany's lost glory.

Hitler's program found appeal with almost every element in the German population. To farmers he promised land reforms. To the workers he offered better working conditions, social legislation, nationalization of big business, and the abolition of unearned profits. To nationalists Hitler promised to repeal the Versailles Treaty, especially the "war-guilt" clause. He said that he would restore Germany to equality in armaments and also regain all its lost territory and colonies to build a "Greater Germany." Like Mussolini, he promised protection against communism.

To these promises Hitler added his garbled racial doctrine. According to this doctrine, the Germans, as "Aryans" (a misapplied use of the word), were the "master race." All other races were inferior. As Hitler's power increased, his personal traits of intolerance, hatred, and contempt for non-Germanic people became the policies of the government.

Hitler's Rise to Power

The Nazis had few followers* until the Great Depression. In the election of 1930, however, many middle-class voters turned to the Nazi Party. These voters had experienced economic hardships and had lost their savings. In addition, many of them feared a Communist revolution. Two years later the Nazi Party won 230 seats in the Reichstag. Although the largest single party there, the Nazis did not have enough votes to form a government.

In January 1933, when it appeared that no other party could successfully form a government, the president of the republic, Paul von Hindenburg, appointed Hitler as chancellor.

Since the Nazis still lacked a majority, Hitler used the Nazis' private army—the storm troopers, or Brown Shirts—to intimidate the Reichstag.

*In 1921 the Nazi Party had 6,000 members; by 1932 it had 50,000 members.

5B, 5G, a4A, a4E, a4F, a4G, a4L, a4M

READ
WRITE
INTERPRET
CONNECT
●THINK

BUILDING HISTORY STUDY SKILLS

Thinking About History: Analyzing Documents

Documents are basic sources for historians. They are used to answer a question, to develop a theory, or to support a view of a historical event. Documents can be any information written on a particular subject and may consist of essays, books, charts, and graphs, to name a few. Reading and analyzing documents helps you to formulate your own view of events based on the evidence and your analysis. Using documents helps you to integrate information and form conclusions.

How to Analyze Documents

To analyze documents, follow these steps.

1. Explain the question, theory, or point of view being researched in the documents.
2. Classify the documents. Determine whether they deal with political, economic, or social issues.
3. Identify the source of the documents.
4. Determine the validity and bias of the documents.
5. Connect the documents to each other.
6. Formulate a thesis statement based on the connection found in the documents.

Developing the Skill

The following documents deal with Hitler's rise to power in Germany. The question the documents focus on is, "How did Hitler destroy parliamentary democracy in Germany?"

The Election Results

	November 1932	March 1933
National Socialists	196	233
Nationalists	51	53
People's Party & Bavarian People's Party	31	21
Catholic Center	70	73
Socialists	121	120
Communists	100	81

"On February 27, a week before the election, the Parliament building was set on fire. The event was described by the Nazis as the first move in a vast Communist conspiracy, and on the following day the President issued an Emergency Decree 'for the protection of the People and the State' and as 'a defensive measure against the Communist acts of violence': 'Articles 114, 117, 118, 123, 124 and 153 of the constitution . . . are suspended until further notice. Consequently, restrictions on personal liberty, on the right of free expression of opinion, including freedom of the Press, on the right of assembly and association . . . and warrants for house searches . . . are permissable beyond the legal limits normally laid down.'"

The documents should be classified as political since the subject of both is government. The source of the documents is Tony Edward's *History Broadsheets, Hitler & Germany 1919–1939*. The documents are unbiased since they merely state facts.

The chart of the election results tells us that there was a multiparty system in Germany's Weimar Republic after World War I. The parties are listed from extreme right-wing National Socialists (Nazis) to extreme left-wing Communists. In order to rule, a party had to have most of the seats, or a majority, in the Reichstag. No party was ever strong enough to have a majority without combining their votes with those of at least one other party. As the chart indicates, the Nazis won the most seats in the Reichstag in the election of November 1932 but did not have a majority. Their major competitors were the Communists and the Socialists at the other end of the political spectrum. However, following the election of 1933 the Nationalists formed a coalition with the Nazis giving them a majority in the Reichstag.

The second document helps explain how the Nazis were able to consolidate their power by destroying the opposition. The Emergency Decree was based on the burning of the Reichstag, which the Nazis unjustly blamed on the Communists. This played on the fear of disorder and revolution that people believed was caused by the Communists. The Emergency Decree also put restrictions on the Communists who were the Nazis' biggest rivals and to whom they lost seats in the Reichstag in the election of 1933.

Practicing the skill. Read the excerpt from *Mein Kampf* on page 682. What bias does the document show? What can you learn about Hitler's plans for Germany by studying the document?

To apply this skill, see Applying History Study Skills on page 689.

SECTION 4

Closure
Conduct a class discussion in which the students compare and contrast fascism and nazism.

Review Answers
1. ***fascism:*** doctrine proposed by Mussolini stating the state is supreme; ***corporate state:*** system of government in which representation is according to profession or occupation
2. ***Black Shirts:*** Fascist Party members so called because of the black shirts they wore; ***il Duce:*** "the leader," title assumed by Mussolini; ***Mein Kampf:*** book by Hitler that expressed the spirit of nazism; ***storm troopers:*** Nazis' private army; ***der Führer:*** "the leader," title taken by Hitler; ***Gestapo:*** Nazi secret police force; ***Third Reich:*** Hitler's regime, the "Third Empire" of Germany; ***Rome-Berlin Axis:*** alliance between Hitler and Mussolini
3. (a) Mussolini defined fascism as "the dictatorship of the state over many cooperating classes." He believed the state is supreme and individuals are completely subordinate to it and rigid control should be maintained by the government through force and censorship. **(b)** Mussolini's program appealed to the middle classes and promised to preserve the capitalist system and existing social classes. He also found many followers among demobilized sol-

5G, a1C

● Rather than a formal alliance, the Rome-Berlin Axis was at first an association. Ostensibly, its purpose was to defend civilization. However, as history was to prove, Hitler and Mussolini's real intentions were to form a partnership for the purpose of wresting European power from France and Great Britain, using any means possible.

diers and discontented nationalists. Gradually, the fascists attracted wealthy landowners, businesspeople, professionals, the lower-middle class and the unemployed.
4. The Weimar Republic was unpopular with the German people because they felt it had been created to satisfy Wilson's demand for a new German government elected by the people. Moreover, the Weimar government had signed the humiliating Versailles Treaty. It was also plagued by many of the social, political and economic problems that affected all of Europe.
5. Hitler's program included disbanding opposition parties and labor unions; giving the Gestapo increased power; suppressing opposition newspapers; placing all radio stations under government control; sending liberals, socialists and Communists to concentration camps; and subjecting members of "inferior races" to increasingly severe persecutions.
6. Economic hardships, unemployment and high prices contributed to political unrest and the rise of fascism and nazism.

Learning from Pictures *The Nazis used a variety of techniques to stamp out opposition to their regime. On the evening of May 20, 1933, for example, huge bonfires were lit at Berlin University and in other cities, and hysterical students burned books unacceptable to Nazism.*

Granted emergency powers to deal with an alleged Communist revolt, Hitler expertly used these powers to make himself a dictator.

The Nazi Program in Action

Once in power, Hitler, who often modeled his policies after Mussolini's totalitarian state, took the title *der Führer* (FYOOR • ur), German for "the leader." Quickly turning Germany into a police state, Hitler banned opposition parties, labor unions, and opposition newspapers, and placed radio stations under strict government control. To enforce these policies, Hitler gave the Gestapo, a secret-police force, wide-ranging powers.

Liberals, socialists, and Communists often ended up in large prisons called concentration camps. Members of the so-called inferior races increasingly suffered severe persecutions. Jews became particular targets of Nazi attacks. They were deprived of their civil rights, publicly humiliated, and even murdered by storm troopers. In some places the Nazis forced the Jews to live in segregated areas called ghettos and to wear yellow stars of David, the six-pointed star that is a symbol of Judaism, on their clothing. Hitler later carried this policy to monstrous extremes (see Chapter 27).

Like Mussolini, Hitler promised to restore the glories of his country's past as well as to bring Germany to full economic recovery. He called his regime the Third Reich. *Reich* is the German word for "empire." (The first empire in Germany had been the Holy Roman Empire, and the second was the German Empire of the Hohenzollerns.) Hitler promised the Germans that the Third Reich would last 1,000 years.

Hitler claimed that Germany's racial superiority justified taking land from the Slavs of eastern Europe in order to expand Germany's borders and provide living space for Germany's expanding population. Such expansion would necessitate a large, well-equipped army. Germany had been secretly rearming since the 1920s, and now it openly defied the terms of the Versailles Treaty.

According to the Versailles Treaty, the Rhineland was to be left unfortified. In the spring of 1936, Hitler's army marched into the Rhineland. France sent a note of protest; the other European powers did nothing.

Encouraged by his unexpected success in the Rhineland, Hitler sought an alliance with Mussolini in order to have support for future aggressive moves. In the fall of 1936, the two dictators formed an alliance and called it the Rome-Berlin Axis. ●

● Lenin suffered a paralytic stroke in May 1922, but was able to continue as head of the Soviet government until an incapacitating stroke a year before his death made this impossible.

■ As a young man, Stalin studied for the religious life at a seminary of the Georgian Orthodox Church.

1E, 4I, 5B, 5G, 5H, a1C, a4A, a4F, a4G, a4H, a4L

SECTION 4 REVIEW

1. **Define** fascism, corporate state
2. **Identify** Black Shirts, *il Duce, Mein Kampf,* storm troopers, *der Führer,* Gestapo, Third Reich, Rome-Berlin Axis
3. **Explaining Ideas** **(a)** Explain Mussolini's ideas about fascism. **(b)** List the various groups of people in Italy who supported him.
4. **Analyzing Ideas** Why was the Weimar Republic unpopular with the German people?
5. **Summarizing Ideas** Describe the main features of Hitler's program.
6. **Interpreting Ideas** What economic problems in Italy and Germany contributed to the rise of fascism and nazism?

5 A Dictatorship Is Established in the Soviet Union

As soon as the Communists seized power in 1917, they reorganized Russia's government. They moved the capital from Petrograd to Moscow. Lenin became the head of the cabinet, the Council of People's Commissars. The Communists also established a National Congress, a legislative body made up of more than 1,000 representatives. Officially, the National Congress had supreme authority. Real power rested with the People's Commissars.

Russia Under Lenin

In 1922 the Communist leaders gave Russia a new name, the Union of Soviet Socialist Republics (U.S.S.R.). This change indicated that power had been transferred to the soviets. After 1922 the Russian people became known as the Soviet people.

Politically the country was divided into separate republics joined in a federal union. Eventually 16 of these republics comprised the U.S.S.R.

Between 1918 and 1921, Soviet leaders had followed a policy known as War Communism. They nationalized the Russian industries. However, social and economic measures were not based on a long-range plan. The Communist leaders had to develop a program to build their "new society" in Russia.

Faced with economic collapse in 1921, Lenin announced the New Economic Policy (NEP) that allowed some free enterprise. The NEP permitted individuals to buy, sell, and trade farm products. The major industries—oil, mining, steel, and the railroads—remained under government ownership and management. Smaller businesses and home industries could be privately owned and operated for profit. Foreign capital was welcomed for the development of government-controlled industries, and investors were promised high rates of return.

Soviet agriculture remained a problem. During the revolution farmlands had been seized from the wealthy landlords and divided among the peasants. The government tried to persuade the peasants to form **collective farms**—land pooled into large farms on which people could work together as a group. On a collective farm, peasants could share the scarce modern machinery. However, the great majority of peasants held on to their small strips of land and to the old ways of farming.

A Power Struggle

When Lenin died in 1924, a power struggle erupted ● in the Communist Party. The main contenders were Leon Trotsky and Joseph Stalin. Trotsky, a talented party organizer, had almost single-handedly created the Red Army that defended the Bolshevik Revolution. Stalin was secretary general, or leader, of the Communist Party.

One issue in the power struggle concerned the future of the revolution. Trotsky followed the strict Marxist belief that the revolution should take place all over the world. Stalin, however, broke with accepted doctrine and advocated "socialism in one country"—the U.S.S.R. only. Stalin believed that after socialism succeeded there, the revolution would spread to the rest of the world.

A bitter, savage, and merciless struggle between the two factions began. By 1928, however, Stalin ■ emerged securely as leader. Trotsky went into exile and was later murdered in Mexico, reportedly on Stalin's orders.

The Five-Year Plan

In 1928 Stalin ended the NEP and returned to a completely controlled **command economy,** in which government planners make all economic decisions. The economic controls from 1918 to 1921 had been emergency measures. Now Stalin's goal was to make the planned economy a permanent feature in the Soviet Union.

SECTION 5

Focus/Motivation
Begin a class discussion by stating that in 1928 Stalin initiated the first Five-Year Plan, that returned the Soviet economy to a completely controlled, or command economy. Mention that in a command economy, the government takes over all of the means of production and controls both industry and agriculture. Ask students to explain what this statement means. *(Students should answer that the government determines what to produce and how much to produce.)* Ask students if the U.S. economy ever becomes a command economy. *(Students should answer that during a war the government makes more of the economic decisions but individual ownership continues.)*

Presentation
Summarizing Ideas (Average/Group)
Have students draw a time line for the Soviet Union from 1919 to 1936. Have students make inferences based on the time line. Ask the following questions: Were any of the events on the time line causes or results of other events? How? Which events on the time line do you think brought the greatest change? Why? What change did each bring? What effect might these events have had on subsequent history? *(Answers will vary.)*

1E, 4I, 5G, 5H, a1C

SECTION 5

Closure

Have students summarize the Five-Year Plans of 1928 and 1933 and discuss in what ways they were successful and in what ways they were failures.

Review Answers

1. ***collective farm:*** the pooling of a small farm into a large farm where peasants worked together; ***command economy:*** economy in which government planners make all economic decisions; ***purge:*** used by Stalin to rid the Communist Party of any members not loyal to him
2. ***U.S.S.R.:*** country in which the power was transferred to the Soviets; ***Trotsky:*** organizer of the Red Army and rival of Stalin after Lenin's death; ***Presidium:*** small committee elected by the Supreme Soviet to run the government when the Supreme Soviet was not in session; ***Politburo:*** Politicial Bureau of the Communist Party that exercised most of the power in the Soviet Union; ***Comintern:*** Third, or Communist, International founded by Lenin to spread the revolution
3. The NEP, formulated by Lenin, relaxed Marxist principles and allowed some free enterprise in order to stimulate the Soviet economy. Individuals were allowed to buy, sell and trade farm products. Major industries remained under government ownership and management, while smaller businesses and all home

Learning from Pictures *Stalin won the power struggle after Lenin's death even though Lenin had opposed him.*

A plan for economic growth, the first Five-Year Plan, was published in 1928. It set industrial, agricultural, and social goals for the next five years. It also laid plans for expanding the educational system and for building more hospitals and housing.

The Five-Year Plan stretched the resources of the Soviet Union to the breaking point in an attempt to turn the country into a modern, industrialized society. The expansion of heavy industries occurred at the expense of industries producing consumer goods.

The planners hoped that collective farming would produce enough food for the Soviet people as well as a surplus for export. Money received from farm exports would help pay for modern machinery, which would in turn advance the drive toward industrialization. Therefore, the future of the Soviet Union as an industrial nation depended on a rapid increase in farm production. All farms were to be merged into collectives. Peasants had to join or suffer severe consequences. The wealthier peasants who attempted to retain their lands faced execution, imprisonment, or exile.

The first Five-Year Plan succeeded in most industries. The government turned about 70 percent of the productive farmland into collective farms. A second Five-Year Plan, even more comprehensive than the first, began in 1933. This second program called for production increases in heavy industries. As a reward for the hard work and sacrifices, people could expect an increase in the production of consumer goods such as food and clothing. However, what actually happened was a decrease in consumer goods as the Soviet government placed all of its efforts on the expansion of heavy industry. Rather than receiving any reward for their hard work, the Soviet people faced higher prices as consumer goods became more scarce.

Stalin's Dictatorship

As the years passed, Soviet leaders admitted that it would take time for a classless society of pure communism to develop. In the meantime the Communist Party would rule.

A police state. The czars had used secret police and spies to maintain their absolute rule. Now Stalin used similar tactics. Under Stalin the Soviet people still experienced rule by fear. People had to conform to the "party line," the policy of the Communist Party, or face repression.

The Soviets had disestablished the Orthodox church and seized its property. They ridiculed religious worship and taught children atheism. Artists, writers, and musicians were ordered to produce "socialist realism" in the service of the state, with works subject to rigid control and censorship.

Government under Stalin. In 1936 Stalin proclaimed a new constitution for the Soviet Union. The Stalin Constitution, as it was called, preserved the essential framework that had existed under Lenin. The parliamentary body, called the Supreme Soviet, met twice a year. While in recess, its authority was assumed by the Presidium, a small committee elected by the Supreme Soviet. The Council of People's Commissars, later renamed the Council of Ministers, held executive and administrative authority.

On paper the Soviet government appeared to be democratic. In reality, however, most power lay in the hands of the Politburo (Political Bureau) of the Communist Party. As head of the party, Stalin controlled the Politburo. In other words, he held dictatorial powers, with virtually complete authority over the people.

The Soviet Union's totalitarian dictatorship under Stalin gradually grew harsher. In 1934, following the assassination of a high party official, Stalin began a **purge** of party members supposedly disloyal to him. Through intimidation, brutality,

1A, 4I, 5C, 5G, a4A, a4B, a4C, a4F, a4H, a4I

Learning from Maps *People Stalin deported were sent to labor camps in Siberia via the Trans-Siberian Railroad. What city is located at the eastern end of the railroad line?* **Vladivostok**

and public trials staged only for show, Stalin began to rid the party of all members who would not submit to his will. Scholars estimate that by 1939 nearly 8 million people had been arrested. Following arrest usually came deportation, imprisonment in forced labor camps, or execution.

The Comintern

Soviet foreign policy during the 1920s and 1930s contained contradictions. On the one hand, the new Communist government wanted to be accepted by the established nations of the world. On the other hand, its support of the Third International, also called the Communist International or the Comintern, alienated many countries. Lenin founded this organization in 1919 to help spread the revolution throughout the world. The Comintern continued to agitate for the overthrow of the governments of the capitalist democracies.

Communist parties existed in many countries outside Russia. The Comintern worked through these parties to incite workers and urge rebellion. Such open calls for revolution caused fear, suspicion, and hostility in the outside world.

SECTION 5 REVIEW

1. **Define** collective farm, command economy, purge
2. **Identify** Union of Soviet Socialist Republics, Trotsky, Presidium, Politburo, Comintern
3. **Explaining Ideas** Describe the New Economic Policy of Russia.
4. **Comparing Ideas** What was the main political difference between Trotsky and Stalin?
5. **Analyzing Ideas** **(a)** What economic policies did Stalin initiate? **(b)** What were the consequences for those who resisted Stalin's policies?

industries could be privately owned and operated for profit.

4. Trotsky believed the revolution had to take place all over the world. Stalin advocated "socialism in one country" — the Soviet Union. After socialism had succeeded there, the revolution would spread throughout the world.

5. (a) Stalin ended the NEP and tried to create a completely controlled economy. Heavy industry was vastly expanded at the expense of consumer goods. All farms were to be merged into collectives. It was hoped a surplus of farm goods could be produced for export to help pay for the industrial expansion. **(b)** Those who resisted Stalin's policies were deported, imprisoned in forced labor camps, or executed.

687

Reviewing Important Terms

1. Collective farms; 2. planned economy; 3. general strike; 4. economic nationalism; 5. Fascism; 6. economic boom; 7. market speculations; 8. surrealism; 9. cubism; 10. international style

Developing Critical Thinking Skills

1. (a) War Communism was a policy by which Soviet leaders nationalized Russian industries. (b) The NEP was an economic policy that permitted individuals to buy, sell, and trade farm products. The state still controlled major industries. (c) War Communism brought all aspects of economic life under government control. The NEP allowed a certain amount of free enterprise to exist.
2. (a) Demobilization created widespread unemployment and intense competition for jobs. (b) France and Great Britain had better-developed economic and political institutions.
3. Both rely on dictatorial rule. Communism is based on a socialist economy and seeks a classless society. Facism is a capitalist system and promises to preserve existing classes.
4. (a) The Weimar Republic was not popular with the German people because the Weimar representatives had signed the humiliating Versailles Treaty. (b) The Versailles Treaty was considered humiliating, and Hitler gained popularity by attacking it. (c) Hitler promised solutions to these problems.
5. (a) American industry and agriculture expanded tremendously. European countries had war debts,

1B, 1E, 4I, 5B, 5G, 5H, a1C, a4A, a4F, a4H, a4K, a4L

Reteaching

Have students review the Chapter Summary and the appropriate section and questions in the Unit Synthesis. Discuss the concepts until students demonstrate a clear understanding of the material.

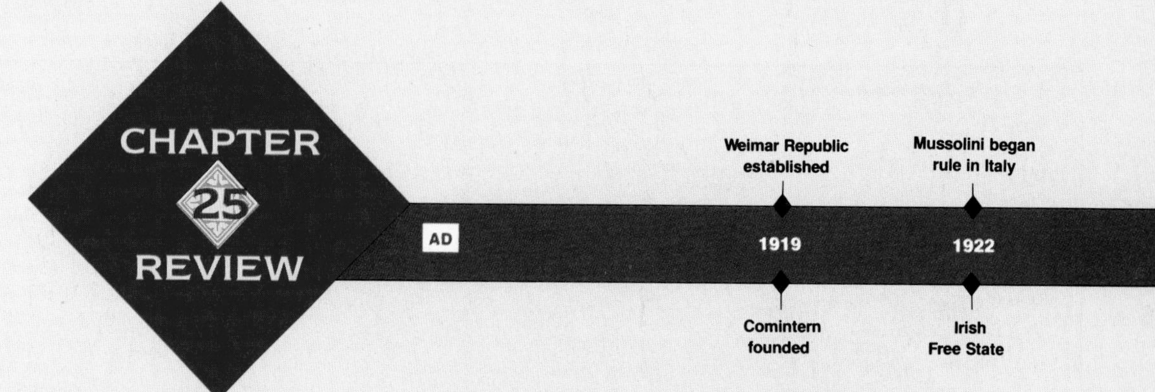

Chapter Summary

The following list contains the key concepts you have learned about political, social, and economic conditions in the United States and Europe following World War I.

1. The period following World War I was a time of major stresses and uncertainties.
2. The literature, music, art, and science of the time reflected the new outlook and the uncertainties of the period. James Joyce and Pablo Picasso abandoned traditional forms and created works that had disturbing implications. Even new popular art forms, film and jazz, had pessimistic overtones. The Western world had entered an unsettled and less optimistic era.
3. Following the victory in World War I, people in the United States realized that their country was the richest nation in the world. A sense of optimism and the influence of European contact brought about rapid change. The pace of life quickened during the decade appropriately called the Roaring Twenties.
4. The economic bubble burst with the stock market crash and the beginning of the Great Depression in 1929. President Franklin Roosevelt enacted policies for recovery known as the New Deal.
5. In Europe instability was widespread. The British and the French maintained their democratic traditions despite labor unrest and the problems of unemployment caused by the Great Depression. In eastern Europe, a number of the new nations abandoned democracy for rule by dictators.
6. In Italy and Germany, dissatisfaction with the weakness and hesitations of democratic governments led to an extreme form of dictatorship, fascism. Mussolini in Italy and Hitler in Germany established totalitarian regimes, and both had expansionist foreign ambitions that further undermined Europe's stability.
7. Following the civil war, Russia became the Soviet Union, with a government based on the principles of Marx and communism. However, when its first leader Lenin died, his successor Stalin maintained control only by brutally crushing his opponents and setting up a totalitarian dictatorship.

On a separate sheet of paper, complete the following review exercises.

Reviewing Important Terms

Supply the term that correctly completes each statement.

1. _______ _______ are formed when land is pooled into large farms on which people can work together.
2. Governmental regulation and direction of national resources to achieve economic stability occurs in a _______ _______.
3. A _______ _______ occurs when workers refuse to continue working until their demands are met.
4. When a country tries to improve its own economic well-being through protective tariffs and similar restrictions, it is adopting the policy of _______.
5. _______ was the doctrine of Mussolini.
6. A sudden increase in prosperity is called an _______ _______.
7. When people make _______ _______, they are investing in stocks in the hope of attaining quick, huge profits.
8. A technique used by artists to interpret or portray life as if it took place in a dream is called _______.
9. The painting style created by Pablo Picasso and Georges Braque, which emphasizes form, shape, and design, is called _______.
10. The plain and severe style of architecture that uses uninterrupted expanses of steel and glass is called _______.

Developing Critical Thinking Skills

1. **Summarizing Ideas** **(a)** What was War Communism? **(b)** What was the New Economic Policy? **(c)** How did each program attempt to stimulate the Soviet economy?
2. **Analyzing Ideas** **(a)** Why did the demobilization of troops put economic pressures on the nations of Europe? **(b)** Why were Great Britain and France better able to deal with these problems than the new nations of eastern Europe?
3. **Explaining Ideas** Explain the similarities and differences between fascism and communism.
4. **Organizing Ideas** How did each of the following contribute to the rise of nazism in Germany? **(a)** creation of the Weimar Republic, **(b)** signing of the Versailles Treaty, **(c)** high unemployment and soaring inflation

1A, a4A, a4B, a4C, a4D, a4E, a4F, a4G, a4H, a4I, a4J, a4K, a4L, a4M

5. **Comparing Ideas** **(a)** How did the economic situation in the United States compare with the economic situation in Europe during the postwar years? **(b)** What brought the boom years to an end?
6. **Interpreting Ideas** **(a)** How did the arts reflect the disillusionment of the postwar era? **(b)** How did popular culture reflect this disillusionment?

Relating Geography to History

Turn to the map titled "The Soviet Union in 1936" in this chapter, page 687, and to the one titled "Europe After the Congress of Vienna, 1815" Chapter 17, page 446. Then complete the following. **(a)** List the republics in the Soviet Union. **(b)** List the countries bordering the Soviet Union that were part of Russia in 1815. **(c)** Why had the Soviet Union lost a sizable amount of its territory after pulling out of World War I?

Relating Past to Present

1. **(a)** What did the leaders of the 1917 Russian Revolution hope to accomplish? **(b)** Based on what you know about conditions in the Soviet Union today, which of these goals have been achieved? **(c)** Which of these goals have not?
2. **(a)** List the programs that President Roosevelt instituted during the New Deal. **(b)** Which of these programs are still in existence? **(c)** Choose one of these and find out why this program has continued. **(d)** What is its main purpose? **(e)** Do any groups of people think the program should be discontinued? If so, why?

Applying History Study Skills

Before completing this activity, review Building History Study Skills on page 683.

Study the following documents. The first document is Stalin's justification of his methods in industrializing the Soviet Union. The second document is a chart summarizing the results of the Five-Year Plans. Decide how each document helps to answer the question "How was Stalin able to industrialize the Soviet Union?"

"It is sometimes asked whether it is not possible to slow down the tempo a bit, to put a check on the movement. No, comrades, it is not possible! The tempo must not be reduced! On the contrary, we must increase it as much as is within our powers and possibilities. . . .

To slacken the tempo would mean falling behind. And those who fall behind get beaten. . . . No, we refuse to be beaten! One feature of the history of old Russia was the continual beatings she suffered for falling behind, for her backwardness. She was beaten by the Mongol Khans. She was beaten by the Turkish beys. She was beaten by the Swedish feudal lords. She was beaten by the Polish and Lithuanian gentry. She was beaten by the British and French capitalists. . . . All beat her—for her backwardness: . . ."

The Five-Year Plans

	First 5-Year Plan		Second 5-Year Plan
	1928	1932	1937
Industrial production (million rubles)	18.3	43.3	95.5
Electricity (million kilowatts)	5.05	13.4	36.2
Steel (million tons)	4.0	5.9	17.7
Grain harvest (million tons)	73.3	69.6	75.0
Cattle (million head)	70.5	40.7	63.2

Investigating Further

1. **Writing a Report** Using encyclopedias and books, prepare a brief biographical sketch of Benito Mussolini.
2. **Presenting an Oral Report** Prepare a report on the response of the United States and European nations to the Great Depression, explaining why the policy of economic nationalism created more problems than it solved.

lagging industrial production, and labor unrest. **(b)** The stock market crash ushered in the Depression. **6. (a)** The writings revealed a dissatisfaction with the way past books and poems had been written. Musicians and painters also rejected earlier forms and styles. **(b)** Popular music and films generally offered escape.

Relating Geography to History

(a) Russian Soviet Federated Socialist Republic, Byelorussia Soviet Socialist Republic, Ukraininan S.S.R., Georgian S.S.R., Armenian S.S.R., Azerbaijan S.S.R., Turkmen S.S.R., Uzbek S.S.R., Kazakh S.S.R., Kirghiz S.S.R., Tadzhik S.S.R., Moldavian S.S.R. **(b)** Finland, Estonia, Latvia, Lithuania, Poland **(c)** The new Communist government made peace with the Central Powers on their terms and lost a sizable amount of its territory.

Relating Past to Present

1. (a) Soviet leaders hoped to set up a "new society" in Russia. **(b) and (c)** Students' opinions may vary. **2. (a)** Answers will vary. Students may list some of the following: Social Security Act, Works Progress Administration **(b)** Students may include Social Security and farm subsidies. **(c), (d), and (3)** Answers will vary.

Applying History Study Skills

By studying the two documents, students should be able to see how Stalin enabled the Soviet Union to industrialize over a short period of time.

CHAPTER (pages 690–709)

26 New Political Forces Emerged in Africa, Asia, and Latin America

(1900–1938)

CHAPTER OVERVIEW

Throughout the British Empire demands for political change became more vocal. Egypt, Trans-Jordan, and Iraq were granted independence, although Great Britain maintained influence in these countries. Palestine's future remained in doubt. The Indian independence movement gained momentum under the direction of Mohandas Gandhi. As a concession to demands for self-government, Great Britain issued the Statute of Westminster. Some former colonies were granted independence and treated as equals within the Commonwealth.

Demand for political change increased in other areas. Turkey broke with Islamic tradition and adopted Western customs and practices. Western industries and customs were introduced into Persia. Africans became more vocal in protesting colonial rule and demanding independence.

China suffered greatly in the process of modernizing. After the country was divided into spheres of influence among Western powers, anti-imperialist sentiments erupted in the Boxer Rebellion. The Kuomintang overthrew the Qing dynasty and tried to reform the country. An open break occurred between the Kuomintang and the Communist Party. By appealing to the peasants, Mao Zedong established a successful Communist government in a northern province of China.

After defeating China and Russia, Japan emerged as the dominant power in Manchuria and Korea. Japan's industry and population grew, and emigration met increasing foreign restrictions. In addition, many nations levied high tariffs against Japanese goods. Japanese society experienced changes in traditional customs and values. The inability of the government to satisfy political and economic demands led to the rise of military influence.

The 1920s brought economic prosperity and social change to Latin America. The Great Depression brought economic collapse and a drift toward authoritarian military regimes. To improve United States relations with Latin America, Roosevelt carried on the Good Neighbor policy.

SUGGESTED LESSON PLAN

Day	Objectives	Suggested Activities	Materials
1	U8,* C1–2	Introducing the Chapter (pages 690–91) Section 1 (pages 691–94), Focus/Motivation (page 691), Presentation (page 693), Closure (page 693), Suggested Teaching Strategies, Enrichment Activity, Daily Quiz, Suggested Assignments (page 689B)	ATE, Pupil's Edition, Teacher's Resource-Bank™
2	U8, C3,	Section 2 (pages 695–96), Focus/Motivation (page 695), Presentation (page 695), Closure (page 696), Suggested Teaching Strategies, Enrichment Activities, Daily Quiz, Suggested Assignments (page 689C)	ATE, Pupil's Edition, Teacher's Resource-Bank™
3	C4–5	Section 3 (pages 697–701), Focus/Motivation (page 697), Presentation (page 698), Closure (page 700), Suggested Teaching Strategies, Enrichment Activities, Daily Quiz, Suggested Assignments (page 689D)	ATE, Pupil's Edition, Teacher's Resource-Bank™
4	C6–7	Section 4 (pages 701–04), Focus/Motivation (page 701), Presentation (page 701), Closure (page 704), Suggested Teaching Strategies, Enrichment Activities, Daily Quiz, Suggested Assignments (page 689D)	ATE, Pupil's Edition, Teacher's Resource-Bank™
5	U9, C8–10	Section 5 (pages 704–07), Focus/Motivation (page 705), Presentation (page 705), Closure (page 707), Suggested Teaching Strategies, Enrichment Activities, Daily Quiz, Suggested Assignments (page 689E)	ATE, Pupil's Edition, Teacher's Resource-Bank™
6	U8–9, C1–10	Chapter 26 Form A Test, Reteaching Worksheet, Chapter 26 Form B Test	Teacher's Resource-Bank™ or Workbook and Test Booklet

*C refers to applicable Chapter Objective, U refers to applicable Unit Goal

BOOKS FOR THE TEACHER

Chesneaux, Jean, et al. *China: From the Opium Wars to the 1911 Revolution* and *China: From the 1911 Revolution to Liberation.* Pantheon. Examines the history of China from the Opium War during the 1800s to World War II.

Davidson, Basil. *Let Freedom Come: African Modern History.* Explores the independence movement in Africa. Several sections of the book discuss issues raised in this chapter.

Kinross, Lord. *Atatürk.* William Morrow. Discusses Mustafa Kemal and what he hoped to accomplish for Turkey.

Shirer, William L. *Gandhi: A Memoir.* Simon and Schuster. Provides a simply written journalistic account of Gandhi's career and personality.

BOOKS FOR THE STUDENT

Archer, Jules. *African Firebrand: Kenyatta of Kenya.* Julina Messner. Examines the story of Kenya's struggle for independence, told through the life of Kenyatta.

Rawding, F. W. *Gandhi and the Struggle for India's Independence.* Lerner. Introduces Gandhi's life.

Robertson, John R. *China: From Manchu to Mao.* Atheneum. Examines the history of the period.

Werstein, Irving. *The Boxer Rebellion.* Franklin Watts. Explores the rebellion in concise and informative terms.

MULTIMEDIA MATERIALS

Atatürk: The Father of Modern Turkey (mp, 26 min.), McGraw-Hill. Portrays the life of the man who modernized Turkey.

China in the Modern World (4 fs), Educational Audio-Visual. Focuses on political history from the fall of the Qing dynasty to the People's Republic. Titles appropriate for Chapter 26: "The End of Imperial China," "The Struggle for Power."

Fascist Dictatorships (2 fs), Educational Audio-Visual. "The Rise of Fascism" traces the rise of Mussolini; "Fascism in Action" traces the rise of Nazism, the spread of fascism, and fascism's defeat in World War II.

The Irish Question: 1800–1922 (2 fs), Multi-Media. Analyzes the relationship between Great Britain and Ireland from the Union of 1800 to the achievement of dominion status in 1922.

Mahatma Gandhi (mp, 26 min.), McGraw-Hill. Gives the life story of Gandhi, who led India to independence.

Section 1 (pages 691–694)

The British Empire Adjusted to the Postwar Era

SECTION OVERVIEW

After World War I, British colonies demanded self-government or independence. Egypt, Trans-Jordan, and Iraq were granted independence. In Palestine, Zionism and Arab nationalism increasingly conflicted, and the British sought support from both Jews and Arabs. Mohandas Gandhi led an independence movement for India based on passive resistance. Canada, Australia, New Zealand, and South Africa gained independence and joined Great Britain in the Commonwealth of Nations.

SUGGESTED TEACHING STRATEGIES

1. **Preteaching Vocabulary (Basic)** You may wish to preteach the following important vocabulary terms: Zionism *(page 692)*, passive resistance *(page 694)*. Ask students to list the main idea behind passive resistance. *(It aims to change public policy by having citizens refuse to cooperate with the government.)*
2. **Relating Past to Present (Average/Group)** Gandhi's program of passive resistance was eventually successful in achieving greater self-government for India. Ask students to speculate about how the outcome might have been different if the resistance had not been directed against a democratic country such as Great Britain. What might the reaction of an autocratic government such as Germany or the Soviet Union have been? *(The resistance movement might have been brutally crushed.)* Ask students if they can think of any present-day examples of repression of resistance movements. *(Students might point to the events in Poland in the 1980s.)*

*3. **Writing About History: Writing a Problem-Solution Essay (Basic)** Have students reread "Building History Study Skills" on page 693. Then have them reread "The Palestine Issue" on page 692. Ask them to write a problem-solution essay detailing how the British should deal with the issue of an independent Palestine in 1930.

ENRICHMENT ACTIVITY

Dramatizing History (Challenging) Two students might conduct an interview between Mohandas Gandhi and a reporter. The interviewer should ask questions concerning Gandhi's goals and methods, his philosophy of passive resistance, and the major events in his life. Sources for this activity include: William L. Shirer's *Gandhi: A Memoir* (Simon and Schuster) and Robert Payne's *The Life and Death of Mahatma Gandhi* (Dutton).

DAILY QUIZ

To assess student understanding of Section 1, give the class the following quiz. (Each item is worth 10 points.)

1. (T or F) After World War I, British colonies demanded more self-government or complete independence. *(T)*
2. The ______ invasion of Ethiopia forced Great Britain to maintain a presence in Egypt to protect the canal. *(Italian)*
3. The peace settlements after World War I gave ______ ______ the mandates of Trans-Jordan, Palestine, and Iraq. *(Great Britain)*
4. (T or F) The Balfour Declaration favored the creation of a Jewish state in Palestine. *(T)*
5. ______ ______ is considered the founder of Zionism. *(Theodor Herzl)*
6. (T or F) Most Arab states favored the creation of a Jewish homeland in Palestine. *(F)*
7. ______ ______ was the chief advocate of Indian nationalism, led the Indian National Congress, and promoted civil disobedience against the British. *(Mahatma Gandhi)*

8. (T or F) Indian leaders opposed the new constitution that Great Britain granted in 1935 because it did not provide for complete independence. *(T)*
9. Canada, Australia, New Zealand, and South Africa joined with Great Britain as equal partners in the ________ ________ ________. *(Commonwealth of Nations)*
10. (T or F) Unlike most other nations, Great Britain was not affected by the Great Depression. *(F)*

SUGGESTED ASSIGNMENTS

1. **Critical Thinking Worksheet (Average/Group)** Have students complete Critical Thinking Worksheet 60 in the TEACHER'S RESOURCEBANK™.
2. **Skill Worksheet (Basic)** Have students complete Skill Worksheet 26 in the TEACHER'S RESOURCEBANK™.

Section (pages 695–696)

2 Varied Political Forms Developed in Turkey, Persia, and Africa

SECTION OVERVIEW

Turkey, Persia, and Africa underwent political changes after World War I. Kemal Atatürk won for Turkey a more generous peace treaty and introduced Western customs. Reza Khan guided Persia (renamed Iran) away from Russian influence toward the West. In parts of Africa, the experiences of World War I, increasing education, and growing political organizations brought pressure for self-rule that would not be granted until after World War II.

SUGGESTED TEACHING STRATEGIES

1. **Classifying Ideas (Basic)** Put the following lists on the chalkboard or an overhead projector. Have students match each individual at the left with a statement on the right. More than one statement may apply to an individual.

1. Kemal Atatürk	a. Separated the Muslim religion from political affairs
2. Reza Shah Pahlavi	b. Introduced Western industries and customs into Persia
3. Jomo Kenyatta	c. Ordered his subjects to adopt Western clothing
4. Nnamdi Azikiwe	d. Suppressed political parties and strictly controlled the press and education
	e. Gave women the right to vote
	f. Became leader of a group in Kenya opposed to colonialism
	g. Became leader of group in Nigeria opposed to colonialism

(Answers: 1-a, c, e; 2-b, d; 3-f; 4-g)

2. **Dramatizing History (Average/Group)** Have two students assume the roles of a European missionary and an African. The missionary should try to persuade the African to attend the church school. Before presenting the skit, students should reread textbook page 696 and "Ibrahimo Becomes a Christian" and "A Missionary Meets His Match" in *The Colonial Experience: An Inside View* (Praeger), edited by Leon E. Clark. After the skit, use the following questions as the basis for a class discussion: Was the missionary successful? Why or why not? What benefits of the church school did he mention to the African? Will these things meet the African's needs? What similarities can you see between this skit and the relations between Africa and Europe in the 1920s?

ENRICHMENT ACTIVITY

Conducting Research (Challenging) Have interested students use resources in the school or public library to research the independence movements in Africa between World War I and World War II. Have students present their findings to the class.

DAILY QUIZ

To assess student understanding of Section 2, give the class the following quiz. (Each item is worth 10 points.)

1. The new influence throughout the developing countries of the world during the interwar period was **a.** nationalism, **b.** imperialism, **c.** isolationism, **d.** subservience. *(a)*
2. What Turkish nationalist led the Young Turks in the successful 1922 revolution? *(Mustafa Kemal)*
3. (T or F) Kemal Atatürk ordered his subjects to adopt Western clothing and to develop in the industrial traditions of Western powers. *(T)*
4. The new constitution of Turkey severed the long-lived relationship between the ________ religion and the Turkish government. *(Muslim)*
5. Reza Shah Pahlavi gained dictatorial control of what Middle Eastern country? *(Persia)*
6. In 1935 Persia became officially known as ________. *(Iran)*
7. Why were many Africans who had fought on the side of Great Britain and France disappointed after the war? *(They had hoped to be rewarded with greater political freedom.)*
8. (T or F) The Western education provided by colonial powers probably promoted African independence movements. *(T)*
9. ________ ________ of Senegal was one of the first leaders to agitate for independence. *(Léopold Senghor)*
10. Place the following items in chronological order: **a.** overthrow of the sultan in Turkey, **b.** World War I, **c.** change of name for Persia. *(b, a, c)*

SUGGESTED ASSIGNMENTS

1. **Making a Chart (Basic)** Have students make a chart comparing modernization in Turkey and in Iran during the period between World War I and World War II.

2. **Researching (Average/Group)** Have interested students write a brief biography of one of the people discussed in the section.

Section 3 (pages 697–701)

China Struggled to Become a Modern Nation

SECTION OVERVIEW

Despite the Open Door policy, foreign powers received special trading privileges throughout China. The Qing dynasty incited anti-foreign sentiment, which resulted in the unsuccessful Boxer Rebellion. Sun Yat-sen, leader of the Kuomintang, led a revolution and declared China a republic. His successor, Chiang Kai-shek, instituted some reform but did little for Chinese peasants. The Communists, led by Mao Zedong, fought with the Kuomintang. After the Long March, Mao established a successful regime in Shaanxi with the support of the local peasants.

SUGGESTED TEACHING STRATEGIES

1. **Writing a Diary (Average/Group)** Have students review events in China between the end of the Boxer Rebellion and the overthrow of the Qing dynasty. Then have students write a fictional diary entry for a day in the life of a peasant, student, city worker, or scholar-official during those years. Entries should reflect how the lives of ordinary people were affected by political changes in China.
2. **Dramatizing History (Average/Group)** Organize the class into four groups. Have each group work on an interview with either Sun Yat-sen, the dowager empress, Chiang Kai-shek, or Mao Zedong. The interviews should contain accounts of the people's early lives, their goals for China, and the problems they faced. Then bring the four individuals together for discussion and mutual criticism of their respective visions of China. Sources for this project include L. S. Stavrianos's "Sun Yat-sen Turns to the Soviet Union," "The Three People's Principles," and "Chiang Kai-shek Turns Against the Communists" in *Readings in World History* (Allyn and Bacon); and P. H. Clyde's and B. F. Beers's *The Far East* (Prentice-Hall).

ENRICHMENT ACTIVITY

Conducting Research (Challenging) Have interested students give an oral report on the Boxer Rebellion. Sources include: Irving Werstein's *The Boxer Rebellion* (Franklin Watts), and Peter Fleming's *The Siege of Peking* (Harper & Row).

DAILY QUIZ

To assess student understanding of Section 3, give the class the following quiz. (Each item is worth 10 points.)

1. As the European powers divided China into spheres of influence, the ______ ______ attempted to maintain an Open Door policy to protect its commercial interests. *(United States)*
2. In 1900 the ______ Rebellion erupted in China. *(Boxer)*
3. After the rebellion was crushed in 1901, the imperialist powers did not divide China because they realized that the nations of ______ and ______ would benefit the most from such a division. *(Russia and Japan)*
4. The political party led by Sun Yat-sen was called the ______. *(Kuomintang)*
5. Name the Three Principles of the People. *(people's rights, people's government, and people's livelihood)*
6. (T or F) Leaders known as warlords had acquired power during the last years of the Qing dynasty and controlled most of China when Sun Yat-sen attempted to overturn tradition. *(T)*
7. When Sun Yat-sen died, ______ ______ ______ took control of the Nationalists. *(Chiang Kai-shek)*
8. The Nationalists established their capital at ______. *(Nanjing)*
9. What Communist led the Long March away from the Nationalists to establish a northern base of support? *(Mao Zedong)*
10. The Communist army was also known as the ______ Army. *(Red)*

SUGGESTED ASSIGNMENTS

1. **Profile Worksheet (Basic)** Have students complete Profile Worksheet 26 in the TEACHER'S RESOURCEBANK™.
2. **Writing a Summary (Basic)** Have students write a paragraph summarizing developments in China between 1900 and 1933.

Section 4 (pages 701–704)

Japan Underwent Change and Increased its Military Strength

SECTION OVERVIEW

Japan's military power in Asia increased when it defeated China and then Russia in the early 1900s. Rapid industrialization and population growth in Japan brought pressure to increase exports and emigration. Social tensions appeared as various groups demanded change. Many younger Japanese began to question traditional values and to copy Western styles in their personal lives. During the 1920s the military led a more active role in the government and argued for a more independent course in foreign policy.

SUGGESTED TEACHING STRATEGIES

1. **Understanding Points of View (Average/Group)** Have the class reread the section "Social Tensions in the 1920s" on page 703 and list examples of the traditional values being questioned. Then organize the class into groups of two. One student in each group is to assume the role of an older Japanese person, the other a young student. The younger person wishes to abandon the tra-

ditional values and customs. The older person argues for the old customs. Have each person write his or her arguments on a sheet of paper. Afterward, bring the class together, read the arguments out loud, and discuss their validity.

2. **Writing an Editorial (Challenging)** Have students write an editorial either defending the attitudes of the Japanese military toward a "Monroe Doctrine for Asia" or attacking the power and values of the military.

ENRICHMENT ACTIVITY

Conducting Research (Challenging) One of the most controversial figures in the 1900s was Emperor Hirohito of Japan. Interested students might enjoy researching Hirohito's role in the military buildup that began in Japan in the 1920s and culminated in World War II. Have students research the topic and present their findings to the class during the study of Chapter 27. Students should evaluate whether the emperor was guilty of any crimes during the war.

DAILY QUIZ

To assess student understanding of Section 4, give the class the following quiz. (Each item is worth 10 points.)

1. (T or F) Japan was the first of all the Asian countries to industrialize. *(T)*
2. In 1902 Japan signed an alliance with _______ _______. *(Great Britain)*
3. Who mediated the settlement of the Russo-Japanese War in 1905? *(Theodore Roosevelt)*
4. Japan annexed Korea and renamed it _______. *(Chosen)*
5. Why did Japan have to sell its own goods abroad? *(to buy raw materials that it lacked)*
6. (T or F) During the 1920s the Japanese experienced amazing political unity among all groups of society. *(F)*
7. (T or F) After World War I, many young Japanese began to question the traditional values of their society, protest Japanese imperialism, and attempt to organize unions. *(T)*
8. Even though Japan had a constitution, the head of state was the _______. *(emperor)*
9. (T or F) During the 1920s in Japan, civilian authorities began to regain control of the military. *(F)*
10. Place the following in the correct chronological order: **a.** granting of universal manhood suffrage, **b.** Russo-Japanese War, **c.** annexation of Korea. *(b, c, a)*

SUGGESTED ASSIGNMENTS

1. **Comparing Ideas (Basic)** Have students write a paragraph explaining how the development of Japan after World War I differed from the development of China during the same period.
2. **Relating Past to Present (Average/Group)** Have students bring in newspaper or magazine articles about current developments in Japan. Ask for volunteers to read their articles to the class.

Section (pages 704–707)

5 The World Economic Crisis Shook Latin America

SECTION OVERVIEW

In the 1920s Latin American nations increased their industrial production and experienced changes in society. During the Depression, economic crisis led to military dictatorships. Relations with the United States improved when the Roosevelt administration fostered the Good Neighbor policy. However, economic nationalism soon strained the relationship.

SUGGESTED TEACHING STRATEGIES

1. **Supporting Generalizations (Average/Group)** For each of the following generalizations, have students provide supporting statements from this section.
   Generalization: Several factors ensured the military's success in gaining control of governments. *(The military appealed to the fears and hatred of lower classes against foreigners and the upper class. The military gained popularity by responding to some of the needs of the masses. The military used violence and repression.)*
   Generalization: Under the Good Neighbor policy, relations between the United States and Latin America improved. *(The United States joined with other American nations in an agreement called the Montevideo Pact. The United States withdrew American troops from Haiti. The United States surrendered its right to interfere in Panama. The United States canceled the Platt Amendment regarding Cuba.)*
2. **Panel Discussion (Challenging)** An interested group of students might discuss the following questions: Is it in the best interest of the United States to support dictators? What advantages and disadvantages does this policy bring? Is a foreign policy based on human rights practical? Why or why not? What examples can students give of successful and unsuccessful relationships with dictators? of successful and unsuccessful uses of a human rights approach? *(Accept all reasonable answers. Relationships with South Korea might be seen as successful, with Iran and Cuba as unsuccessful. President Carter's policies toward Brazil and South Africa can also be examined and evaluated.)* Students should consult the *Readers' Guide to Periodical Literature.*

ENRICHMENT ACTIVITY

Preparing a Chart (Basic) Have students use the textbook and encyclopedias to find information on Latin American governments in the 1930s. Then have them construct a chart showing each country and the form of government it had during the period.

DAILY QUIZ

To assess student understanding of Section 5, give the class the following quiz. (Each item is worth 10 points.)

1. (T or F) In the early 1900s, industrial products dominated the economy of Latin America. *(F)*
2. In the early 1900s, Mexico became a leading exporter of ______ . *(oil)*
3. The ______ class grew rapidly in Latin America as new jobs opened up in government service, commerce and industry. *(middle)*
4. (T or F) In most Latin American countries, the economic success of industry resulted in reform governments anxious to change the inequities of society. *(F)*
5. (T or F) During the Great Depression, the traditional export price of sugar, coffee, and nitrates remained stable. *(F)*
6. In the 1930s many cities throughout Latin America steadily lost population. *(F)*
7. (T or F) During the 1930s most Latin American governments were known for their stability and their liberal political and social programs. *(F)*
8. In 1936 General ______ ______ seized power in Nicaragua. *(Anastasio Somoza)*
9. Place the following events in the correct chronological order: **a.** Montevideo Pact, **b.** beginning of Trujillo dictatorship in the Dominican Republic, **c.** beginning of the Great Depression. *(c, b, a)*
10. (T or F) During the Great Depression most Latin American governments followed a policy of economic nationalism. *(T)*

SUGGESTED ASSIGNMENTS

1. **Critical Thinking Worksheet (Average/Group)** Have students complete Critical Thinking Worksheet 59 in the TEACHER'S RESOURCEBANK™.
2. **Review Worksheet (Basic)** Have students complete Review Worksheet 26 in the TEACHER'S RESOURCEBANK™.

For suggested lesson plan, additional teaching strategies, enrichment activities, daily quizzes, and suggested assignments, see pages 689A–689F.

Introducing the Chapter
During the 1920s and 1930s, many nations in Africa, Asia, and Latin America strove for independence from imperialist nations. Ask students to suggest why a country would prefer to strike out on its own rather than remain under the protection of another country. *(nationalism; desire for political, economic, or social self-determination)* List students' suggestions on the chalkboard or an overhead projector.

Then have students list the problems that are likely to occur when any nation gains independence. *(lack of strong political institutions, scarcity of qualified leaders, political infighting, and economic decline because of revolutionary activity)* At the end of the chapter, have students compare their lists with the information found in the textbook.

CHAPTER 26

New Political Forces Emerged in Africa, Asia, and Latin America

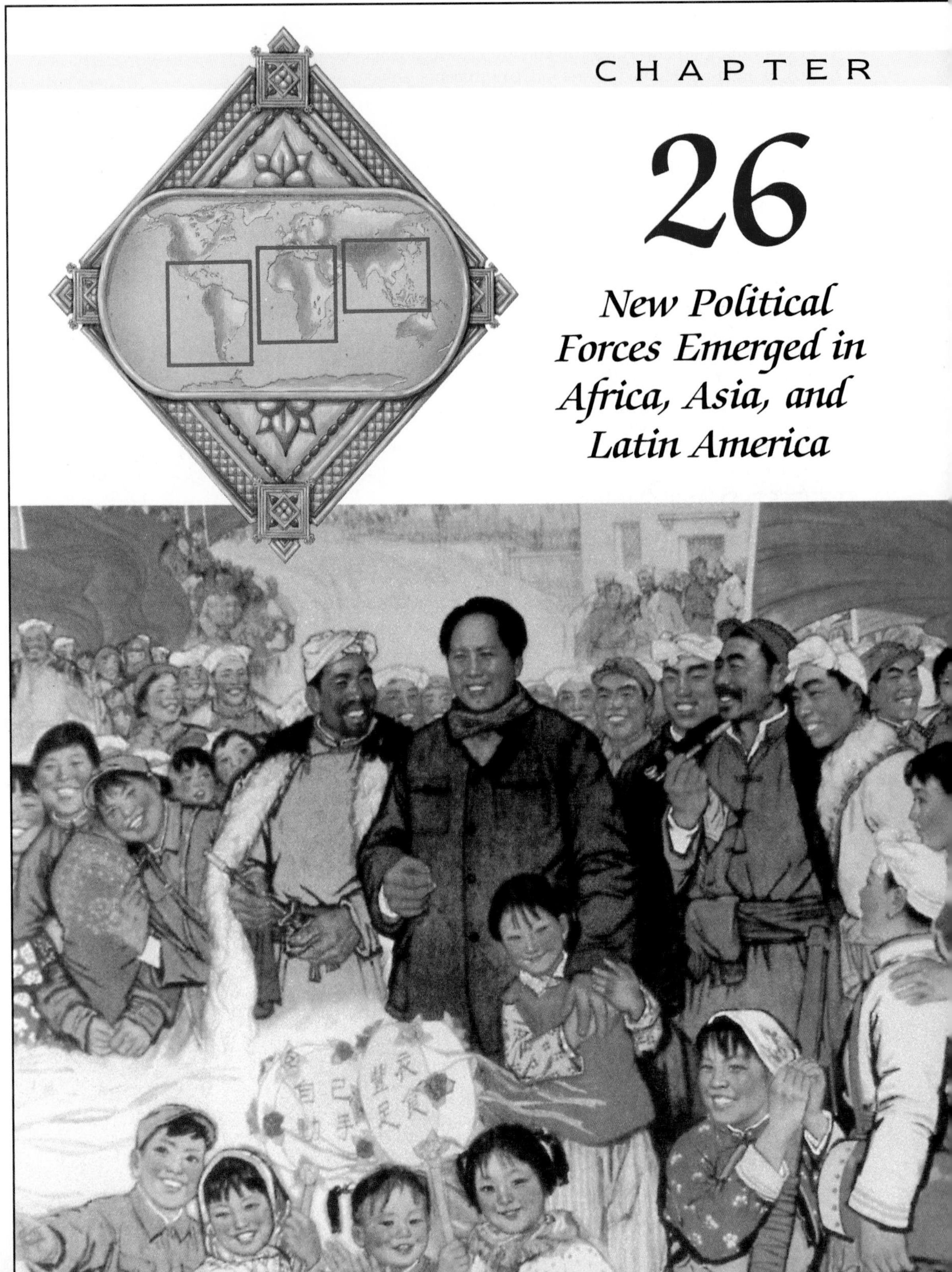

CHAPTER FOCUS

Place Africa, Asia, and Latin America

Time 1900–1938

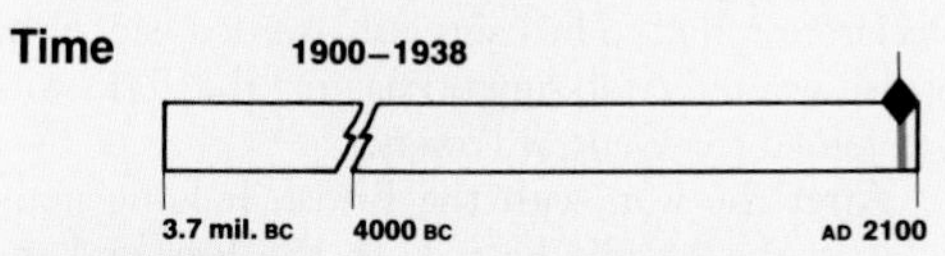

Significance

As you have read, Europe and the United States faced many social, political, and economic challenges during the early decades of the 1900s. In other parts of the world, however, people's main concern was with political change. Among the countries of the British Empire, India started on the path toward independence and others developed new relationships with Great Britain. The major independent countries of the Middle East—Turkey and Persia—also began rapid political transformation, and new political forces stirred throughout Africa.

At the same time, profound changes transformed the great civilizations of China and Japan. In China the dynastic cycle was finally broken, and the long and difficult process of creating new political structures began. Neighboring Japan set its course for economic growth and foreign expansion.

The countries of Latin America faced economic and social change as well as an uncertain relationship with the United States. Many Latin American governments, like others in the 1920s and 1930s, decided that strong centralized power provided the best answer to their problems.

Terms to Define

Zionism — passive resistance

People to Identify

Mahatma Gandhi — Chiang Kai-shek
Jomo Kenyatta — Fulgencio Batista

Places to Locate

Trans-Jordan — Haifa
Palestine — Shaanxi

Questions to Guide Your Reading

1 How did the British Empire adjust to the changes that World War I brought?
2 What forms of government developed in Turkey, Persia, and Africa?
3 On what principles was the Chinese republic based?
4 How did the military come to play a major role in the Japanese government?
5 Why did authoritarian governments come to power in many Latin American countries?

◀ *Chinese poster art honoring Mao Zedong*

In 1930 thousands of Indians peacefully demonstrated against the British salt tax. As the reporter Webb Miller wrote in the New Freeman, *however, the demonstration met with a violent and tragic end.*

> *“Suddenly, at a word of command, scores of native police rushed upon the advancing marchers and rained blows on their heads. . . . Not one of the marchers even raised an arm to fend off the blows. They went down like tenpins. From where I stood I heard the sickening whacks of the clubs on unprotected skulls. . . .*
>
> *Those struck down fell sprawling, unconscious or writhing in pain with fractured skulls or broken shoulders. In two or three minutes the ground was quilted with bodies. Great patches of blood widened on their white clothes. The survivors without breaking ranks silently and doggedly marched on until struck down.”*

India was only one area of the world convulsed in change after World War I.

1 The British Empire Adjusted to the Postwar Era

Although the British Empire had grown larger as a result of the Paris Peace Conference, its continued existence was threatened from within. People in all parts of this vast empire voiced demands for more freedom, for self-government, and even for complete independence.

Independence for Egypt

Technically, the Turks ruled Egypt, but since 1882 the British had been in control. In 1914, when the Ottoman Empire joined the Central Powers, Great Britain declared Egypt a protectorate. This protectorate formally ended in 1922. Great Britain continued to influence the Egyptian government, however, because of British interests in the Suez Canal.

During the 1920s and early 1930s, a strong independence movement grew in Egypt. In 1936 the British and Egyptian governments reached an agreement on the independence issue. In the previous year, Italy had invaded Egypt's neighbor,

Chapter Objectives
After studying Chapter 26, students will be able to:
1. Compare the Egyptian, Palestinian, and Indian movements for independence.
2. Summarize the terms of Statute of Westminster.
3. Describe the varied political forms that evolved in Turkey, Persia, and Africa.
4. Outline events in China's struggle to become a modern nation.
5. Discuss the importance of the Kuomintang, Sun Yat-Sen, Chiang Kai-shek and Mao Zedong and compare their respective solutions to China's problems.
6. Describe Japan's territorial designs and methods of modernization.
7. Summarize the military influence exerted on the Japanese government between the wars.
8. Trace the changes in the economy, society, and politics of Latin America.
9. Outline the growth of authoritarian regimes and the development of economic nationalism in Latin America.
10. Write a paragraph summarizing the relations between Latin America and the United States between the wars.

SECTION 1

Focus/Motivation
Begin class with a discussion about parents and children. Ask students to think of an experience in which the parents had already completed a task or found a solution to a problem. Then discuss how the

1B, 2D, 4E, 4K, 5A, a1C

● **Point out that Trans-Jordan later became known as Jordan. The wife of the current king of Jordan — King Hussein — was born in the United States as Elizabeth Halaby. When she married Hussein, she took the name Queen Noor al-Hussein.**

student, when faced with a similar challenge, refused to listen to a paternalistic comment prefaced with,

"When I tried that, I did . . ."

Now discuss how Western nations might exhibit a paternalistic attitude toward colonies by introducing the topic with the following quotation:

"The West, having sown its own national wild oats in the past, is now sometimes inclined to look with a combination of dismay and superior wisdom on the upstart countries which assert an allegedly anachronistic (outdated) desire to follow the same course."

Lead a discussion, using the following questions as a guide: Why would European countries, having fought for their own independence, "look with dismay" on colonial nations' desires for independence? *(Idealistically, European nations understood the ill effects of independence on the stability of the new nation's economy, political structure, and society. They also recognized the benefits of being a colony, such as military protection and regular trade. Selfishly, Europe had much to lose from the independence of its colonies.)* What did colonial powers stand to lose if their colonies became independent? *(supplies of raw materials; markets for manufactured goods; and geographical advantages, such as the transportation benefits of the Suez Canal).*

Ethiopia. The British needed Egyptian support to prevent further Italian aggression. Thus they agreed to help Egypt become a member of the League of Nations. The two nations also pledged mutual assistance in time of war. In addition, Egypt gave Great Britain military control of the Suez Canal for 20 years. With this agreement Egypt became completely independent, and it joined the League in 1937.

The Palestine Issue

The peace settlements after World War I gave Great Britain the mandates for Trans-Jordan, Iraq, and Palestine. These lands were all formerly part of the Ottoman Empire.

The spirit of nationalism had arisen among Arabs during the final years of the Ottoman Empire. It grew stronger after the British assumed control in the Middle East. Unable to extinguish this spirit, the British recognized the independence ● of Trans-Jordan in 1923. However, they maintained some control in the area through the presence of military advisers. By 1930 the British had also recognized the kingdom of Iraq as an independent nation. Again Great Britain retained some control, especially in military and financial matters.

Of the three Middle Eastern mandates, only Palestine now remained completely under British control. Palestine was important to the British because of its strategic location and because a vital oil pipeline from Iraq ended at the Palestinian port of Haifa. The British found themselves in a difficult position in Palestine, however.

Since the late 1800s, Jews from Europe had been establishing small colonies in Palestine. These colonists supported a nationalist movement called **Zionism,** which aimed to build a Palestinian homeland for the Jews.* In 1917 the British foreign secretary, Arthur Balfour, eager to secure Jewish support for the Allied war effort, told Zionist leaders that the British would "view with favor" the creation of a Jewish "national home" in Palestine. This Balfour Declaration, as it came to be called, also stated that the establishment of such a homeland should not threaten the civil and religious rights of non-Jews, who made up 98 percent of Palestine's population.

The British also had promised to aid the formation of an independent Arab state that might include parts of Palestine. Therefore, the Balfour Declaration had to be cautiously worded, since the British wanted Arab support against the Turks who had joined the Central Powers.

After the war, with the British holding mandates in the Middle East, both the Jews and the Arabs wanted Great Britain to fulfill its promises. While Britain sought an equitable solution to the problem, tensions between Arabs and Jews intensified. The Arabs viewed the number of Jews settling in Palestine as especially alarming.

During the 1930s many Jews fled Europe to avoid Nazi persecution. Hoping to calm the fears of the Arabs, the British placed strict limitations on the number of Jews allowed to immigrate to Palestine. Jewish settlers bitterly resented this policy, especially when Nazi persecution of European Jews increased. Thus, by trying to please everyone, the British had succeeded only in making the situation worse. The Palestine question continued to plague the British throughout the 1940s.

Independence Movements in India

As the largest of the British colonies, India posed even greater difficulties than did the Middle Eastern mandates. India had taken part in World War I on the side of the Allies, contributing both troops and money. In return, Great Britain had promised India a greater degree of self-government.

Any settlement for India had to recognize the tensions and hostilities present in Indian society. For example, an uneasy truce marked the relationship between Hindus and Muslims, and wide gulfs existed between upper-caste and lower-caste Hindus. Such a settlement also had to satisfy many conflicting demands. British conservatives completely opposed giving up this important part of the British Empire. Indian princes, many of whom were almost absolute rulers in their domains, also favored the existing state of affairs. Indian nationalists, on the other hand, wanted to rid India of British rule.

The chief advocate of Indian nationalism was Mohandas K. Gandhi, who in 1920 became leader of the Indian National Congress—India's most important political party. Many Indians looked

*Theodor Herzl, an Austrian Jew, is considered the founder of this Zionist movement. *Zion* is another name for Israel, the Jewish homeland.

692

4E, 4K, a1A, a4A, a4G, a4I, a4J

READ
● WRITE
INTERPRET
CONNECT
THINK

BUILDING HISTORY STUDY SKILLS

Writing About History: Writing a Problem-solution Essay

Writing a problem-solution essay includes analyzing a problem in order to provide a solution to the problem. For example, assume that a city's crime rates are increasing. Consequently, a problem can be identified—it is not safe to walk alone on city streets at night. The problem also has a logical solution—the mayor of the city and the city council could approve more funds so that the police could patrol the high crime areas more frequently at night.

How to Write a Problem-solution Essay

To write a problem-solution essay, follow these steps.

1. Identify the problem.
2. Describe the problem.
3. State a solution and relate it to the problem.

Developing the Skill

Mohandas Gandhi lived for a time in South Africa where he formulated many of his theories about nonviolence. Gandhi believed that practicing "satyagraha" would help end the injustice he witnessed in South Africa. *Satya* means truth and is the equivalent of love. Gandhi believed truth and love to be characteristics of the soul. *Agraha* means firmness or force. Satyagraha is therefore translated as "soul force." If you were to write an essay on the problem of injustice that Gandhi first faced in South Africa and the solution that he formulated, it might appear as follows.

> "On August 22, 1906, the *Transvaal Government Gazette* of South Africa published the draft of the Asiatic Registration Act, a law requiring all Indian people above the age of eight to submit to official registration and fingerprinting. People who did not have a certificate of registration would be fined and imprisoned. Gandhi, speaking to a large crowd in Johannesburg, told the people to pledge defiance of the ordinance and go to jail if necessary. Gandhi believed the people should protest rather than forfeit their right to free movement.
>
> Gandhi's solution to the problem was to develop the idea of satyagraha, which he said is 'the vindication of truth not by infliction of suffering on the opponent, but on one's self.' According to Gandhi, 'the opponent must be weaned from error by patience and sympathy.' Satyagraha reverses the 'eye for an eye' policy, which ends in making everyone blind. It returns good for evil until the evildoer tires of evil. This was Gandhi's plan for dealing with South African injustice."

The first paragraph identifies and defines the problem—the injustice of the South African government which requires the Indian people to carry registration certificates that monitor their movement and create racial distinctions. The solution that Gandhi develops is "satyagraha," or soul force. If you resist the law nonviolently and are willing to suffer the consequences, ultimately you will change the opposition. Gandhi's method, not to allow the protestor to adopt the methods of the oppressor, was designed to appeal to the conscience of the opposition.

Practicing the skill. Research the effects of Gandhi's solution and explain how they might be incorporated into the model problem-solution essay.

To apply this skill, see Applying History Study Skills on page 709.

Mohandas Gandhi with followers

Presentation
Analyzing Maps (Average/Group)
Distribute to each student two copies of an outline map of the world. Have students make maps of the British Empire in 1918 and in 1939. They should develop appropriate categories to be keyed by color. After students have completed their maps, have them draw three conclusions from the maps *(for example, how many colonies gained independence, how many remained under British control, where most of the colonies gaining independence were located).* Afterward, examine and evaluate students' choice of categories and conclusions in a class discussion.

SECTION 1

Closure
Ask students to summarize how the British Empire adjusted to the postwar world. *(The British gave many areas their independence but retained many colonies.)*

Review Answers
1. ***Zionism:*** movement to resettle Jews in Palestine; ***passive resistance:*** technique whereby citizens peacefully refuse to cooperate with their government in order to win concessions from it
2. ***Theodor Herzl:*** Austrian Jew and founder of Zionist movement; ***Arthur Balfour:*** British foreign secretary who, in 1917, pledged British support for a Jewish

1B, 4E, 4K, 5A, a1A, a4A, a4F, a4H, a4L

● Research topic: How Gandhi's policy of passive resistance influenced the civil rights movement in the United States

homeland; ***Mahatma Gandhi:*** leader of Indian National Congress; ***Statute of Westminster:*** an act of the British Parliament recognizing Canada, Australia, New Zealand and South Africa as independent and as partners with Great Britain in the Commonwealth of Nations

3. ***Trans-Jordan:*** British mandate south of Syria and east of Palestine; ***Palestine:*** south of Syria and northeast of Egypt; ***Haifa:*** port in Palestine

4. It promised that Great Britain would "view with favor" the establishment of a Jewish "national home" in Palestine, provided the civil and religious rights of non-Jews were protected. It was issued to secure additional Jewish support for the allied war effort.

5. He used passive resistance and urged Indians to give up their Western ways and strengthen their ancient culture.

6. The nations enjoyed mutual trade benefits.

on Gandhi as more than a political leader. They also revered him as a spiritual force, calling him *Mahatma* (muh • HAHT • muh), or "Great Soul." Gandhi wanted nothing short of complete self-government for India. He also urged Indians to give up Western ways and return to their ancient culture and religions.

Gandhi opposed all use of force and violence. As early as 1909, he expounded his reasons for favoring nonviolence over violence as a means of achieving Indian independence.

> "It is perfectly true that [the English] used brute force and that it is possible for us to do likewise, but by using similar means we can get only the same thing that they got. . . . [It is like] saying we can get a rose through planting a noxious weed. . . . We reap exactly as we sow. . . . [F]air means alone can produce fair results. . . . "

Drawing on ideas in Hindu scriptures and in the New Testament, Gandhi developed a political approach known as *nonviolent noncooperation.* This technique, a form of **passive resistance,** or civil disobedience, called for citizens to peacefully refuse to cooperate with their government in order to win concessions from it.

Among other things Gandhi's program of nonviolent noncooperation included refusing to buy British goods or to pay taxes. Such actions often resulted in imprisonment for Gandhi and many of his followers. In an attempt to control the nationalist movement, the British authorities issued orders restricting the civil liberties of many of its leaders. In addition, British soldiers often used force to break up nationalist political gatherings.

In 1935, after many committee reports and conferences, Great Britain granted India a new constitution that provided for home rule. However, the British viceroy still controlled India's national defense and foreign affairs. Committed to total self-government, the nationalists rejected the new constitution. During the next few years, discontent continued to simmer in India.

The Statute of Westminster

Even in those parts of the British Empire that already had a degree of self-government, people demanded greater independence. In Canada, New Zealand, Australia, and the Union of South Africa, Great Britain still appointed a governor-general. This official had a veto power over laws, although it was rarely used. Great Britain also controlled the foreign policy of these areas.

After World War I these dominions demanded complete self-government. Showing a remarkable readiness to accommodate, adjust, and accept the political realities, the British gave in without a struggle.

In 1931, by an act of Parliament called the Statute of Westminster, Britain recognized Canada, Australia, New Zealand, and South Africa as completely independent. The four nations joined with Great Britain as equal partners in a very loose organization called the British Commonwealth of Nations. The British Parliament had no power either to make laws for Great Britain's Commonwealth partners or to interfere in their affairs. However, each member agreed to declare its loyalty to the British monarch and to recognize its cultural ties with Great Britain.

Over the years several other British colonies became independent and joined the Commonwealth. Favorable trade arrangements with Great Britain made membership especially attractive. Like other major nations, Britain faced an economic depression after World War I and needed increased trade to stimulate its economy. As you have read, British trade abroad had been hurt by economic nationalism. Thus the Commonwealth's economic arrangement worked remarkably well for both Great Britain and the regions that had formerly been British colonies.

Politically, however, Great Britain's vast empire proved burdensome. In the Middle East and India especially, the empire became more a source of problems than one of support.

SECTION 1 REVIEW

1. **Define** Zionism, passive resistance
2. **Identify** Theodor Herzl, Arthur Balfour, Mahatma Gandhi, Statute of Westminster
3. **Locate** Trans-Jordan, Palestine, Haifa
4. **Understanding Ideas** What was the Balfour Declaration, and why was it issued?
5. **Analyzing Ideas** What methods did Mahatma Gandhi use in his efforts to gain independence for India?
6. **Evaluating Ideas** How did the British Commonwealth's arrangement benefit both Great Britain and its former colonies?

2 Varied Political Forms Developed in Turkey, Persia, and Africa

The nationalist feelings that swept the Middle East after World War I also affected the southwest Asian countries of Turkey and Persia and the whole of Africa. As a result new political forces began to stir.

Turkey Under Mustafa Kemal

The Treaty of Sèvres stripped the Ottoman Empire of all its territories except Turkey. Then in 1919 the Greeks invaded and seized part of Turkey. Inept and weak, the sultan could not even organize resistance to the invasion.

For some time a group of nationalists, called the Young Turks, had been trying to reform the corrupt Ottoman government. Discontent over the terms of the Treaty of Sèvres and shock at the sultan's inability to resist the Greeks finally forced the Young Turks into action. Under their able and energetic leader, Mustafa Kemal (kay • MAHL), they drove the Greeks out of Turkey and in 1922 overthrew the sultan.

With their revolution the Young Turks put an end to the Ottoman Empire and established the Republic of Turkey. They moved the capital from Constantinople to Ankara. For the republic's system of government, they selected a Western-style parliamentary democracy with a strong executive. In 1922 Mustafa Kemal became the republic's first president.

Kemal wanted Turkey to become a modern, progressive nation like the industrialized powers of the West. He therefore ordered the Turkish people to adopt Western ways. He prohibited the wearing of traditional clothing such as the fez, the traditional Turkish hat. In addition, he insisted that all Turks adopt family surnames, as Europeans had. He himself took the Muslim name *Atatürk*, meaning "father of the Turks." He also passed laws that gave women the right to vote and hold office, and he abolished polygamy—the practice of having more than one wife.

Atatürk drew up a new constitution that severed the long-lived relationship between the Muslim religion and the Turkish government. He abolished the position of caliph and tried to lessen Islam's influence over the Turkish people.

In a further effort to modernize, Atatürk introduced the Western calendar, the metric system of weights and measures, and the Roman alphabet. He also adopted a westernized program of economic development, paying subsidies to farmers and providing aid for new industries.

Modernizing Persia

Turkey's neighbor, Persia, had never come under Ottoman control. Rather, since the late 1700s, it had been ruled by shahs of the Qajar dynasty. In the early 1900s, however, both Great Britain and Russia established spheres of influence in Persia. Until the 1920s these two countries practically ran the Persian government.

In 1921 Reza Khan, a Persian army officer with strong nationalist sentiments, seized control of the government in a coup d'état. Some four years later, he deposed the ruling shah and assumed the throne, taking the title Reza Shah Pahlavi. Like Kemal Atatürk, Reza Shah wanted to modernize his country and free it from foreign domination. Therefore, he embarked on a massive reform program. He stripped the Muslim religious leaders of much of their power, reorganized and strengthened the army, built schools and hospitals, and gave

Learning from Pictures *The Shah of Persia (right) and Kemal Atatürk (left) met in 1934 in the city of Ankara, Turkey.*

SECTION 2

Focus/Motivation
Have students imagine that a young Turk, Persian, and African are visiting western Europe and the United States in the early 1920s. What impressions would they be apt to receive? *(wonder at the productive capacity of Western economies as shown in military equipment, buildings, and consumer goods; admiration of Western educational systems; perhaps approval of democracy and political freedom; and appreciation of a comfortable life for the average worker)* What changes might the three make in their own countries if given a chance? What difficulties would they encounter in making these changes? *(Accept all reasonable answers. Encourage students to develop their answers as they read the section.)*

Presentation
Panel Discussion (Average/Group)
Select a group of interested students to conduct a panel discussion on two distinct goals of nationalism — modernization and a return to traditional culture. Ask the class to explain why a nation would decide to modernize *(to improve standards of living, to build up military strength)* or to reverse modernization *(to improve the quality of life as opposed to material well-being).* Then have two students defend the modernizations made by Kemal

1B, 1C, 4E, 4K, 5A, 5B, a1C, a4A, a4E, a4F

European settlers consistently opposed reforms that gave Africans more self-government. On September 10, 1935, for example, a meeting of white settlers in Kenya denounced British policies.

Atatürk and Reza Shah Pahlavi, and have two students criticize them. Encourage other students to ask questions. Sources for this project include Desmond Stewart's *Turkey* (Time-Life), and Lord Kinross's *Atatürk* (William Morrow).

SECTION 2

Closure

Ask: Were Kemal Atatürk's and Reza Shah's efforts to modernize their countries successful? *(Answers will vary. Many students will point out that they both instituted new technology.)*

Review Answers

1. ***Young Turks:*** Turkish nationalists who wanted to reform their government; ***Reza Shah Pahlavi:*** Persian army officer who seized power in 1925; ***Nnamdi Azikiwe:*** leader of colonial opposition in Nigeria; ***Jomo Kenyatta:*** leader of colonial opposition in Kenya; ***Léopold Senghor:*** one of the young, Western-educated leaders of the Senegalese independence movement
2. ***Ankara:*** capital of Turkey; ***Iran:*** country located east of Iraq and west of Afghanistan
3. (a) They both wanted to modernize their countries. **(b)** Reza Shah began to use his power in an authoritarian manner.
4. African protest against colonialism increased because World War I had broadened Africans' experiences of the world, and education received from

women more rights. Reza Shah also introduced an ambitious economic development plan that improved the nation's transportation system and established many new industries. And in 1935 he announced that the country would be officially called by the name its own people called it—Iran.

Although Iran's constitution specified a limited monarchy, most of the power remained in Reza Shah's hands. The new leader soon began to use this power in an authoritarian manner, strictly controlling the press and suppressing political parties. His private police force ruthlessly put down any opposition to his government. Later in his reign, Reza Shah came to believe that he was divinely ordained, and he took the title "Shadow of God."

Africa After World War I

The many Africans who fought on the side of Great Britain and France during World War I expected to be rewarded with greater political freedom after the war. Like the Indians, they were disappointed.

Increased political activity. The years after World War I saw an increase in political activity among Africans. The war itself had served as a broadening experience for many. Military service took them away from their homes. For the first time, they became aware of the world beyond their immediate family and village. When these ex-soldiers returned home, they brought with them new ideas about freedom and nationalism. In time they put these ideas to work organizing anticolonial protest movements.

Colonial education also influenced many Africans to become politically involved. Missionary and government schools taught their African students the Western ideals of equality and self-improvement. Yet colonial governments denied these same Africans the opportunity for self-determination and economic advancement. As more and more Africans personally experienced this contradiction between Western teaching and the reality of colonialism, they realized that change had to come. Racism and political repression awakened in many Africans a desire to work for reform and even independence.

New political associations. Alarmed at the growing spirit of dissent among Africans, many colonial governments moved to close off all avenues of protest. However, Africans still found ways to organize. In Tanganyika, a former German colony whose mandate had been assigned to Great Britain, Africans from the lower ranks of the civil service formed a civil servants' association. Since the association was open to all Africans, it overcame traditional ethnic barriers. It soon became a center of anticolonial protest in Tanganyika. Similarly, railroad and dockworkers in both Nigeria and South Africa organized trade unions. These also became important forums for the expression of African grievances.

In response to the formation of these new political associations, colonial governments strengthened the authority of tribal chiefs who favored colonial rule. They rewarded these chiefs with pensions or positions of local power—judgeships, for example. At the same time, the colonial authorities agreed to institute some reforms. For instance, colonial governments placed restrictions on forced labor, the method by which most mining and construction companies obtained their workers. But a few cooperative chiefs and piecemeal reform could not stem the rising tide of African opposition to colonialism.

New leaders. By the 1930s Africans increasingly were calling for independence rather than reform. The loudest of these calls came from the group of young, Western-educated men—among them Nnamdi Azikiwe (ah • ZEEK • way) of Nigeria, Jomo Kenyatta (ken • YAHT • uh) of Kenya, and Léopold Senghor of Senegal—who had assumed the leadership of the anticolonial movement. Following Gandhi's example they organized demonstrations, strikes, and boycotts against their colonial rulers. They also employed Western methods of political organization to attract more people to their cause. By the end of the decade, these men led a growing movement dedicated to ending colonial rule.

SECTION 2 REVIEW

1. **Identify** Young Turks, Reza Shah Pahlavi, Nnamdi Azikiwe, Jomo Kenyatta, Léopold Senghor
2. **Locate** Ankara, Iran
3. **Comparing Ideas** (a) How were the reform programs of Kemal Atatürk and Reza Shah alike? (b) How were they different?
4. **Understanding Ideas** Why did many Africans become more involved in politics after World War I?
5. **Analyzing Ideas** How did colonial governments respond to the formation of African political associations?

● The Boxers were enraged that the Europeans were constructing railroads throughout China. Often the tracks ran through cemeteries where the remains of sacred ancestors were buried.

3 China Struggled to Become a Modern Nation

Many historians believe that in order to understand the changes that occurred in China during the 1920s, it is necessary to go back to events that took place around 1900. Until that time the imperialist powers of France, Germany, Great Britain, Japan, and Russia had maintained their spheres of influence mainly along the Chinese coast and up the Chang Jiang. At the turn of the century, however, they began to move into China's interior, carving out spheres of influence there as well.

The United States watched this new development with some concern. It did not want American merchants excluded from Chinese trade. In 1899, therefore, the American government appealed to the nations with interests in China to recognize what it called the Open Door policy. Under this policy all nations would have equal rights to trade anywhere in China. The nations contacted by the United States agreed to the policy, but in practice, they continued as before. None of these nations wanted to openly refuse to support the policy. Yet none truly intended to observe it.

Learning from Pictures *Sun Yat-sen, pictured with his wife, plotted the overthrow of the Qing dynasty from Japan during the Boxer Rebellion.*

The Boxer Rebellion

By the end of the 1800s, China's fate as a subservient nation seemed sealed. Foreign powers had won numerous grants of special privileges from the Chinese. Traders and missionaries traveled about the country's interior at will. And foreign governments all but ran China's largest cities.

In 1898, hoping to stem foreign interference by revitalizing his government, the young Qing emperor instituted a series of reforms to change the examination and governmental administration and to promote industry. The drastic nature of these reforms shocked China's conservative leaders. They called on the emperor's aunt, the aging empress dowager (widow of an earlier ruler) Cuxi (TSOO·SHEE), to take action. She quickly had the emperor imprisoned, and for the next 10 years she ruled China in his place.

The empress dowager chose to fight outside interference by doing everything she could to stir up hatred for foreigners, especially the missionaries. Her efforts strongly influenced the members of a patriotic movement called the Society of Righteous and Harmonious Fists. In English they became known simply as "Boxers." In what became known as the Boxer Rebellion, the Boxers roamed throughout China, attacking foreigners at every opportunity. Seeking protection, many foreigners fled to their embassies in Beijing. There they came under siege by an army of angry Boxers. ●

Despite their rivalries the imperialist nations were determined to protect their common interests in China. They decided to act jointly against the Boxers, sending to Beijing an army comprised of soldiers from Great Britain, France, Germany, Russia, Japan, and the United States. This army relieved the besieged embassies and put down the rebellion in 1901. The foreign powers then imposed heavy penalties on the Chinese, including a demand for payment of a large indemnity. In addition, the foreign powers claimed the right to maintain troops at Beijing and along the Chinese Eastern Railway to the coast.

foreigners revealed contradictions between Western teachings and colonial practice.

5. Colonial governments in Africa rewarded cooperative chiefs with pensions and positions of power. At the same time these governments instituted some reforms.

SECTION 3

Focus/Motivation

Have students recall what they have already learned about the Qing dynasty and European imperialism to try to predict the main forces and events in Chinese history in the early 1900s. Ask the following questions: How did the Qing dynasty benefit China? *(It provided security that brought peace and prosperity.)* What were its principal weaknesses? *(It reduced government services, its officials were corrupt, and the army was weak.)* Judging from their behavior elsewhere in the world, what would be the principal interest of Europe and the United States in China at this time? *(to expand trade and acquire colonies)* Based on these answers, what kinds of practices would you expect to occur in China? *(Special trading privileges would be granted by corrupt officials, foreign influence would be unchecked by a weakened military, and Chinese peace and prosperity would be endangered.)*

1B, 4E, 5A, a1C

● The 1987 film, *The Last Emperor,* traces the life of the boy emperor.

Presentation
Understanding
Chronology
(Average/Group)

Put the following list of events on the chalkboard or an overhead projector and have students arrange the events in chronological order.

(4) Republic was proclaimed by Sun Yat-sen.
(1) Dowager empress took over the throne.
(8) Long March began.
(2) Boxer Rebellion ended.
(3) Rebellion against Qing dynasty began.
(7) Kuomintang expelled all Communists from the Nationalist People's Party.
(6) Chiang Kai-shek assumed leadership of Kuomintang after death of Sun Yat-sen.
(5) Chinese Communist Party founded in Shanghai.

PAINTING

Chinese Painting

For many centuries Chinese painters saw only works of art that had been created within their own country. With the formation of the Chinese republic in 1912, however, painters began to study in Japan and Europe, bringing back new ideas and art forms.

Qi Huang (1863–1957), one of China's most famous poets and painters, lived through both of these periods. As a young man, he worked in the fields by day and learned to paint by night. By the age of 30, he had achieved recognition as a professional artist, had acquired a classical education, and had founded a poetry society.

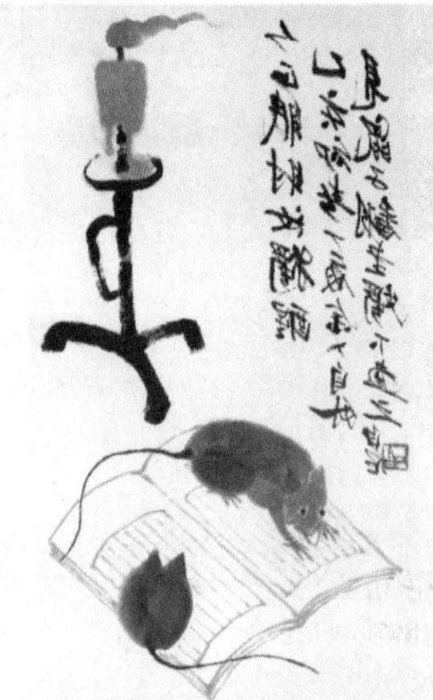

Chinese painters as well as calligraphers considered the mastery of brushstrokes very important. The artists wanted to be quick enough to paint or to write their impressions while they were still fresh in their minds. The blending of calligraphy and art, of poetry and painting, was accomplished most elegantly by Qi Huang. This painting, done in 1935, was strongly influenced by Japanese art. It illustrates the artist's respect for learning and shows how he pursued knowledge by candlelight at night. The inscription reads: "Returning home one night, I find mice perusing the pages of a book. Why are you awake when everyone else is sleeping?"

1980.98 *Browsing by Candlelight* Ch'i Huang. Ink and light color on paper. Gift of Madame fan Tchum-pi Courtesy Museum of Fine Arts, Boston

The crushing of the Boxer Rebellion brought China completely under foreign domination. Had it not been for China's neighbors, Russia and Japan, the other imperialist powers might have divided China into colonies. However, these other powers realized that, because of location, Russia and Japan would benefit most from any division of China. As it was, Russia had used the Boxer Rebellion as an excuse to move 100,000 troops to the northern Chinese province of Manchuria.

Overthrow of the Qing Dynasty

The Boxer Rebellion failed to fulfill its major aim—to drive all foreigners from Chinese soil. But it did foster a nationalistic sentiment among the Chinese people, especially the young and well-educated. Instead of attacking foreigners as the Boxers had done, these young nationalists advocated the reform of China itself. A new political party, the Kuomintang (KWOH • MIN • TANG), or Nationalist People's Party, grew out of this reform movement. Many members of the Kuomintang had studied in Europe or the United States. For example, the party's founder and leader, Sun Yat-sen, had spent most of his life in the United States, attended school in Hawaii, and studied medicine at a British college in Hong Kong.

Influenced by Western democratic ideas, these young nationalists wanted a constitutional government, with civil liberties guaranteed by a bill of rights. They also wanted China to industrialize, so that it could defend itself economically against the imperialist powers. In the nationalists' view, China would be able to protect itself against foreign domination only if it became a modern nation.

The Qing rulers, under pressure from nationalists, tried to carry out reforms. But for many Chinese, their efforts came too late. These people called for a complete break with the "Old China" and an end to the corrupt Qing dynasty.

In 1911 a series of revolts, led mostly by young army officers who supported Sun Yat-sen, spread throughout southern China. In a last, desperate gesture to preserve their dynasty, the Qing proclaimed a constitutional monarchy. The rebels, however, would accept nothing but a republic.

Forming the Chinese Republic

In February 1912 the Kuomintang forced the last Qing emperor, a young child, to abdicate. The ● Kuomintang then proclaimed China a republic. Sun Yat-sen described the republic's ruling philosophy as "The Three Principles of the People," or people's government, people's rights, and people's

698

● **Resentment of foreigners in China continued under the Chinese Republic. In 1927, for example, several Europeans were killed in riots in Nanjing.**

livelihood. These principles called for: (1) political unification and the ending of foreign influence; (2) a gradual change to democratic government, with full personal liberties and rights for all Chinese people; and (3) economic improvements, including industrializing and providing for a more equitable distribution of land.

Problems with the warlords. Proclaiming revolutionary change proved to be easier than accomplishing it. At first the Republic of China existed mainly on paper. The Kuomintang controlled only a small region around Guangzhou (GWAHNJ • JOH), in southern China. Warlords, who had acquired power during the last years of the Qing dynasty, ruled the rest of the country. These warlords refused to surrender their power to the Kuomintang without a fight. Some even hoped to defeat their rival warlords and start a new imperial dynasty.

The Nationalists—as members of the Kuomintang called themselves—hoped to defeat the warlords and establish the Republic of China as a strong central government. To fulfill this aim, they asked for help from foreign powers. Only the Soviet Union responded. In the early 1920s, the Soviets sent technical, political, and military advisers to help reorganize the Kuomintang and build up a modern Chinese army.

A split in the Kuomintang. When Sun Yatsen died in 1925, Chiang Kai-shek (CHANG KY • SHEK), a military commander who had trained with the Red Army in the Soviet Union, assumed leadership of the Nationalists. Under Chiang's command the Nationalist army grew stronger. In 1926 Chiang began a military campaign—called the Northern Expedition—against the warlords of the north. Warlord resistance collapsed when confronted by the efficient, highly motivated Nationalist troops. In quick succession the Nationalists seized Wuhan and Nanjing on the Chang Jiang. Two years later they occupied Beijing.

At the same time that the Kuomintang was expanding the area under its control, disagreements began to divide its membership. The left wing of the party, composed of socialists and Communists, wanted to put more power into the hands of peasants and workers. The conservative right wing opposed such radical change, especially any reforms designed to redistribute land and give it to the peasants. Chiang Kai-shek became the leader of this right wing.

In 1927, before the Kuomintang completed the Northern Expedition, Chiang expelled all Soviet advisers from the country and moved against the party's left-wing members. Troops loyal to Chiang attacked the Communist stronghold of Shanghai, arresting thousands of Communists and executing them on the spot. Those few who survived this onslaught went into hiding. Secure in the knowledge that the left-wingers no longer posed a threat to his leadership, Chiang established a Nationalist government in Nanjing. ●

The Nanjing Government

Chiang and his followers wanted a strong, efficient government, but not a democratic one. Eventually, they set up a one-party system with Chiang as virtual dictator.

Chiang tried to promote economic development, but lack of capital hindered his efforts to industrialize. Defense expenditures took much government revenue that could have been used for industrialization. Foreign control of many of China's natural resources also held back economic development.

Even so, by 1937 the area of China under Nationalist control had made notable progress. The Nationalists had begun a massive road construction program and had started to repair, rebuild, and extend the railroad system. In addition, they strengthened the financial system by establishing a national bank. They also improved all levels of the educational system.

However, the Nationalists failed to deal with two crucial problems. Because they needed the support of landowners and merchants, they made no changes in the oppressive, age-old system of land ownership or in the method of collecting taxes in the countryside. In short, they did nothing to eliminate the causes of suffering and discontent among Chinese peasants.

The Growth of Chinese Communism

In July 1921 a small group of Chinese intellectuals met in Shanghai and founded the Chinese Communist Party. Inspired by the example of the Russian Revolution and by the ideologies of Marx and Lenin, the founders of Chinese communism hoped to free their country from foreign domination and economic backwardness. They first set about

699

1A, 1B, 4E, 4I, 5A, 5G, a1C, a4B, a4C, a4G

SECTION 3

Closure

Ask students how the Boxer Rebellion hurt China. *(The Western powers put down the rebellion and then levied a large indemnity.)*

Review Answers

1. ***Open Door policy:*** policy that all nations would have equal rights to trade anywhere in China; ***Kuomintang:*** Nationalist People's Party founded by Sun Yat-sen; ***Sun Yat-sen:*** leader of Kuomintang; ***warlords:*** leaders of regional armies who acquired power during the last years of the Qing dynasty; ***Chiang Kai-shek:*** leader of Nationalists after 1925; ***Long March:*** two-year, 6,000-mile trek by the Chinese Communists; ***Mao Zedong:*** leader of the Chinese Communists
2. ***Nanjing:*** Nationalist Chinese capital on the Chang Jiang; ***Shanghai:*** city in coastal China; ***Jiangxi:*** province in southeastern China; ***Shaanxi:*** province in northwestern China.
3. **(a)** a Chinese uprising in 1901 against foreigners; **(b)** An international military force suppressed the rebellion and demanded payment for damages from China.
4. political unification and an end to foreign influence; a gradual change to democratic government with full personal liberties and rights for all Chinese; and economic improvements, including land reform and industrialization
5. The Nationalists constructed roads, extended

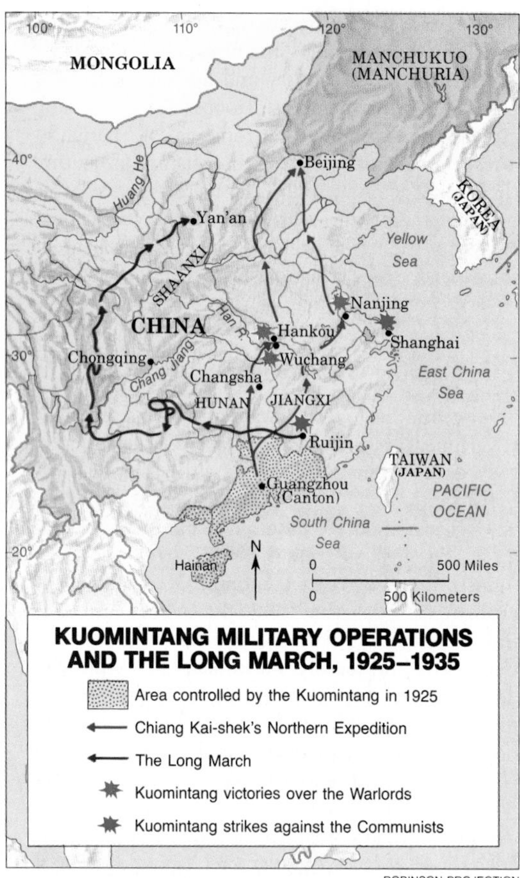

Learning from Maps *The Communists' Long March ended in military defeat. What city is at the end of the Long March?* **Yan'an**

building strong party organizations and labor unions in the cities. They also cooperated with the Kuomintang in efforts to defeat the regional warlords.

At first, when the Kuomintang was weak and in need of all the help it could get, the Nationalists welcomed Communist support. As the Communist Party grew stronger, however, conservative Nationalists became alarmed. Chiang Kai-shek purged the Communists from the Kuomintang in 1927, and executed many of them. In the early 1930s, when he realized that he had failed to destroy the Communist Party, Chiang undertook several large-scale military campaigns to "annihilate" communism once and for all.

The Long March. Those Communists who escaped the purge of 1927 fled first to Jiangxi province, in southeastern China. There they set up their own government—modeled after the Russian Communist regime—called the Chinese Soviet Republic. In late 1933, after repeatedly attacking the soviet, the Nationalist forces besieged it. Some months later the Communists broke through the Nationalist siege lines and evacuated Jiangxi.

In the famous Long March, lasting for more than a year, about 100,000 Communists made their way on foot to Shaanxi province in northwestern China. Under incredibly arduous conditions, they crossed 18 mountain ranges and 24 rivers, a distance of about 6,000 miles (10,000 kilometers). A few deserted on the march, but many more perished on the difficult journey. The 10,000 who did complete the march, along with 10,000 Communists already in Shaanxi, established their headquarters in the isolated mountain town of Yan'an. They chose a charismatic young man named Mao Zedong (MAOH ZEE • DAWNG) as their leader.

Mao Zedong. Born in the countryside of southeastern Hunan province, Mao had long argued that Chinese peasants, not the urban proletariat, could provide the best basis for a Communist revolution in China. Now, in a rural province far from the major cities of China, he had a chance to prove his arguments.

Mao and his followers introduced a program of land and tax reforms in Shaanxi province. To ensure the program's success, they met with the peasants and listened to their problems. The Communists also explained China's problems to the peasants and urged them to support the revolution.

Since the peasants of Shaanxi were suspicious of outsiders, at first they did not trust the Communists. However, when they found that the Communists were trying to understand and help them solve their problems, the peasants rallied to the Communist cause. Many volunteered to serve in the Communist army, called the Red Army. Others provided the Communists with useful information about the location and movement of Nationalist troops.

With the support of the local peasant population, the Communists managed to rebuild their strength and resist the efforts of the Nationalists to destroy them. In time they would take the offensive against the Nationalists.

1B, 4E, 5A, a1C, a4A, a4F, a4G, a4H, a4L

Remind students that Russia's humiliating defeat in the Russo-Japanese War sparked the Revolution of 1905.

Learning from Pictures On the Long March, Mao Zedong (on horseback) waged battle against Chiang Kai-shek's pursuing army and against regional warlords.

SECTION 3 REVIEW

1. **Identify** Open Door policy, Kuomintang, Sun Yat-sen, warlords, Chiang Kai-shek, Long March, Mao Zedong
2. **Locate** Nanjing, Shanghai, Jiangxi, Shaanxi
3. **Analyzing Ideas** **(a)** What was the Boxer Rebellion? **(b)** What were its results?
4. **Classifying Ideas** Describe Sun Yat-sen's three goals for the Chinese republic.
5. **Understanding Ideas** What successes did the Nationalists have in modernizing China?
6. **Evaluating Ideas** Why was Mao Zedong able to involve the peasants of Shaanxi in the Communist revolution?

4 Japan Underwent Change and Increased Its Military Strength

Japan had begun to modernize in the late 1800s. However, the economic, social, and political reforms achieved during that time had created problems. Japan's desire to expand on the Asian continent only exaggerated these problems.

Japanese Expansion

The reforms introduced by the leaders of the Meiji Restoration transformed Japan into a modern industrial and military power. This newly acquired status enabled Japan to embark on a policy of expansionism in the late 1800s. Gaining overseas possessions would serve two purposes. First, it would provide both new sources of raw materials for their country's growing industries and new markets for the products of those industries. Second, it would show the nations of the West just how far Japan had progressed. Other parts of Asia, especially China, seemed to provide the best opportunities for expansion.

Korea. Korea had long interested Japan. The Treaty of Shimonoseki that ended the Sino-Japanese War provided for Korean independence and forced China to cede Taiwan and the Pescadores to Japan. Very soon, however, Japan dominated the Korean government.

China indirectly caused another Japanese conflict, this one with Russia. After the Boxer Rebellion, most foreign powers withdrew their troops from China. However, a force of 100,000 Russian soldiers lingered on in Manchuria. Despite several protests by the Japanese government, Russia continued to drag its feet. Finally, the Japanese, who looked on Manchuria as a future sphere of influence, prepared to force out the Russians.

In 1902 Japan signed an alliance with Great Britain. Each nation agreed that the other had the right to defend its special interests in China, Manchuria, and Korea against any third power. The two powers agreed that if either one became involved in a war with a single power, the other would remain neutral. They would aid each other, however, if a third power joined the conflict. Although neither country openly admitted it, the alliance targeted Russia as a potential enemy.

The Anglo-Japanese alliance meant great prestige for Japan. The nation no longer stood alone but now had the support of the most powerful country in the world. The alliance also increased pressure on Russia to withdraw its troops from Manchuria. The Russians agreed to negotiate the issue with Japan, but they made little effort to actually begin talks.

The Russo-Japanese War. Early in 1904, without any declaration of war, the Japanese attacked and badly damaged the Russian fleet at Port Arthur

railroads, and started a national bank.
6. By carrying out land and tax reforms Mao won peasant support.

SECTION 4

Focus/Motivation
Have students compare the forces and trends in Japanese and Chinese society by asking the following questions: What major problems facing China were discussed in Section 3? *(Answers should include foreign influence, a weak military, backward economy, and disunity.)* Based on what you have already read, did Japan have the same problems? *(No. Japan was a united, industrializing nation with a relatively strong military and little foreign domination.)* What challenges did Japan face? *(Japan faced the dangers of militarism and problems accompanying rapid industrialization, such as the need to find markets for industrial goods, and changing values due to an economic shift from agriculture to industry.)*

Presentation
Using Maps (Average/Group)
Ask students to locate Japan on a wall map of the world. Point out that Japan's first efforts at expansion were into Korea and China. Ask students to locate both of these countries on the map. Then ask why these two areas would be logical choices for Japanese

1B, 1C, 4E, 5A, a1B, a1C, a4A

● Treaty of Portsmouth

expansionists. *(They are relatively close to Japan.)* Then ask students to locate the Soviet Union on the map. Point out that in the early 1900s the Soviet Union was known as Russia. Then ask: Why would Japanese expansion into Korea and China alarm the Russians? *(The Russians had a border with China and probably wanted spheres of influence there.)*

Learning from Pictures *After a five-month bombing siege, Port Arthur surrendered to Japanese forces. What treaty ended the Russo-Japanese War?*

in Manchuria. In retaliation the Russians sent part of their Baltic fleet to Asia. The Japanese navy, however, annihilated this Russian force of 32 ships at the Battle of Tsushima in 1905. Earlier, during the summer of 1904, Japanese troops had marched northward through Korea into Manchuria and defeated the Russians in a series of battles. Another Japanese force landed on the Liaodong Peninsula in Manchuria and, with the help of the navy, placed Port Arthur under siege.

Shorter supply lines, a better-prepared military, and greater support from its people helped Japan in the war against Russia. However, the Japanese army suffered heavy casualties, and the cost of the war strained the Japanese economy. As a result, the Japanese asked Theodore Roosevelt, president of the United States, to mediate the conflict. Roosevelt reluctantly agreed, and in 1905 he invited representatives from Japan and Russia to take part in negotiations at Portsmouth, New Hampshire. Later that year these representatives signed an agreement ending the Russo-Japanese War.

The Treaty of Portsmouth. Under this agreement, called the Treaty of Portsmouth, Russia ceded to Japan its lease on the Liaodong Peninsula, including Port Arthur, and control of the southern branch of the Chinese Eastern Railway. In addition, Russia agreed to withdraw all its troops, except for railway guards, from Manchuria. Also, instead of paying an indemnity, Russia turned over to Japan the southern half of the Russian island of Sakhalin, north of Japan. Finally, Russia gave the Japanese special fishing rights along its Siberian coast.

The Treaty of Portsmouth essentially gave Japan complete control of Manchuria. More importantly, it signaled that other countries recognized and respected Japan's position as a great power. A further indication of this recognition and respect came in 1910. When Japan proclaimed the annexation of Korea—renaming it Chosen (choh • SEN)—none of the other imperialist powers protested.

Problems of Modernization

In less than 50 years, Japan had advanced from a feudal agrarian nation to one of the world's leading industrial powers. Its victories over China and Russia had established it as a military power. However, these considerable achievements also created new problems for the island nation.

Industrialization and scientific development brought higher standards of living and improved medical care to Japan, spurring population growth. Cities grew rapidly, and every inch of suitable land was placed under cultivation. Even so, the increase in the food supply could not match the rapid population growth. And although the economy grew rapidly, it could not provide jobs for all those who wanted them. As a result Japanese people began to emigrate to Korea and Taiwan, as well as to Hawaii and other islands of the Pacific. Thousands more left for the United States.

In time the United States prohibited the immigration of Asians, while still permitting the immigration of Europeans. As proud people, the Japanese deeply resented such discrimination.

Japanese industrialization created yet another problem. Japan had to import raw materials, since it lacked almost all those needed in modern industry. To pay for these raw materials, it had to sell its own goods abroad. Since Japan also needed to import food, it had to export or face economic collapse.

In exporting goods, Japan met with restrictions, just as it did in its "export" of people. Many countries passed tariff laws to protect their home markets against Japanese competition. These countries argued that Japanese manufactured goods had an unfair advantage, since cheap Japanese labor enabled Japanese companies to charge lower prices for their goods.

1B, 5A, 5F, a1C

● **Discussion topic: How modernization of formerly traditional societies often results in social problems**

Social Tensions in the 1920s

Social and political stability marked the Meiji era. During this time the Japanese people were content with the rights their leaders were willing to give them. By the 1920s, however, the situation had changed. Economic development, universal education, and new ideas from the West had all contributed to a change in attitude among the Japanese people. The time had come, many Japanese said, for the people to benefit from the nation's economic advances.

Industrial workers organized labor unions and went out on strike for higher wages and better working conditions. Tenant farmers organized unions, too, and demanded lower agricultural rents. Urban intellectuals and university students, inspired by the victory of the Western democracies over Germany in World War I, argued that democracy was the wave of the future. They organized a movement for universal manhood suffrage, which they saw as an essential first step toward promoting democracy in Japan. Other Japanese became interested in socialism and communism. These people protested the government's expansionist policies and tried to organize a revolutionary political movement in Japan.

Also, some young Japanese began to question the traditional values of their society. These values required that young people obey and respect their parents, especially their fathers. When making decisions—taking a job or choosing a husband or wife, for example—young people had to accept their parents' choice. And military training taught young soldiers and sailors to follow orders without question or hesitation, even if following those orders might lead to their deaths. Japanese military leaders considered it an honor to die in battle for the emperor.

Few young Japanese rejected these values openly. In their private lives, however, they tried to escape, at least temporarily, and experience greater freedom. They listened to jazz and played baseball. Young women in the cities cut their hair short like "flappers" in the United States and refused to wear the traditional female attire of a long kimono. Eager to learn about other societies, young people cleared the bookstores of every Western novel. Japanese novels that dealt with the loneliness and frustration of individuals in Japanese society also enjoyed great popularity among the young. ●

Growing Influence of the Military

Japanese political leaders of the 1920s had difficulty finding answers to all the demands of the Japanese people. They granted universal manhood suffrage in 1925, yet they could not agree on what to do

Learning from Pictures *Japanese melodramatic theater, featuring colorful costumes and makeup and portraying historical or domestic events, is called Kabuki.*

1B, 1D, 5A, a1C, a4A, a4F, a4K, a4M

SECTION 4

Closure

Discuss with students how the humiliation of high tariffs against their products led many Japanese people to resent foreigners and helped set the stage for World War II.

Review Answers

1. ***Treaty of Portsmouth:*** treaty that ended the Russo-Japanese War in 1905

2. ***Port Arthur:*** Russian port on the Pacific; ***Sakhalin:*** island controlled partly by Japan in north Pacific

3. The Anglo-Japanese alliance meant that Japan now had the support of the most powerful country in the world.

4. Shorter supply lines, a better-prepared military and greater support from its people helped Japan in the war against Russia.

5. In Japan modernization brought overpopulation, scarcity of food and industrial raw materials, and increased tariff restrictions from trading partners.

6. The Japanese constitution provided that top-ranking officers recommend to the emperor who should serve as minister of war and minister of the navy. If the ministers of war and of the navy disapproved of a government policy, they could resign and force all the other ministers to resign. Since only members of the military could hold these two posts, the civilian authorities had almost no control over military affairs.

about other demands. In addition, they seemed to have no solutions to the country's growing economic problems. In this atmosphere of discord and dissatisfaction, the influence of the Japanese military grew steadily stronger.

The constitution of 1889 had granted special powers to the military. Top-ranking officers recommended to the emperor who should serve as the government's minister of war and minister of the navy. If the ministers of war and of the navy disapproved of a government policy, they could resign and force all the other ministers to resign as well. And since only members of the military could hold these two posts, the civilian authorities had almost no control over military affairs.

Until the late 1920s, military ministers generally cooperated with civilian members of the government. Then, however, the military ministers began to assert their special powers in order to influence government policy. In many ways their knowledge of World War I helped them expand their role in government. They saw the recent conflict as a new kind of war in which victory depended on total mobilization, not only of troops but also of the entire spiritual and material resources of the nation. Believing that victory in any future war would require the same kind of mobilization, they saw the discontent in Japan as a serious problem. It indicated weakness in Japanese society and constituted a threat to the nation's security in the event of war. To preserve the nation, the military ministers felt they must do everything in their power to eliminate this discontent.

The economic problems that Japan faced in the late 1920s also influenced military leaders to take a more active role in government. Officers in the army and navy believed that Western nations would never treat Japan as an equal. As proof of this, they pointed to the restrictions many Western nations had imposed on Japanese immigration and exports. They concluded, therefore, that the government's policy of cooperation with the Western powers was unproductive. In the future, they argued, Japan should pursue a more independent course, especially in Asia.

In time the military leaders began to insist that the Japanese people pay greater attention to traditional values. These leaders also called for a larger army and a stronger navy. In addition, they advocated a Japanese "Monroe Doctrine" that would give Japan special powers in East Asia similar to those exercised by the United States in the Western Hemisphere. In particular, the military leaders saw Manchuria as a target for future expansion. The growing influence of the military ultimately would have far-reaching consequences for all of Japanese society and for the rest of the world as well.

SECTION 4 REVIEW

1. **Identify** Treaty of Portsmouth
2. **Locate** Port Arthur, Sakhalin
3. **Understanding Ideas** Why was the Anglo-Japanese alliance so important for Japan?
4. **Determining Cause and Effect** Why were the Japanese able to defeat Russia in the Russo-Japanese War?
5. **Summarizing Ideas** What new problems were created by Japanese modernization?
6. **Analyzing Ideas** Why did the Japanese military begin to exert more influence over government policy in the late 1920s?

5 The World Economic Crisis Shook Latin America

As the 1920s began, Latin America appeared to be headed for prosperity. However, the region soon would suffer the effects of the worldwide economic crisis of the 1930s.

Economic Developments

Agricultural products, such as beef, wheat, sugar, coffee, and fruits continued to dominate the economy of Latin America. However, during the early 1900s, Mexico became a leading exporter of oil. Oil was also discovered in Venezuela, Peru, Bolivia, and Colombia. The mining of other resources, such as copper in Chile and Peru, tin in Bolivia, and bauxite in Guiana, also developed rapidly during this period. For the most part, British and American companies owned these oil and mining operations.

In addition, the 1920s saw a great expansion in the generation of electric and hydroelectric power, financed mainly by foreign investors. The energy that was produced enabled many Latin American countries to industrialize during the 1920s. For example, the larger countries in the region began

- **Critical thinking activity: How the social problems of Latin America resembled those in Japan at the same time**

FRESCOES

Rivera's *Fruits of Labor*

After World War I, life in Mexico changed dramatically. Diego Rivera, one of Mexico's greatest artists, recorded these changes. As a youth Rivera studied in Spain and France. After World War I, he joined the Cubist school in Paris and later traveled extensively throughout Europe. In Italy Rivera studied fresco painting.

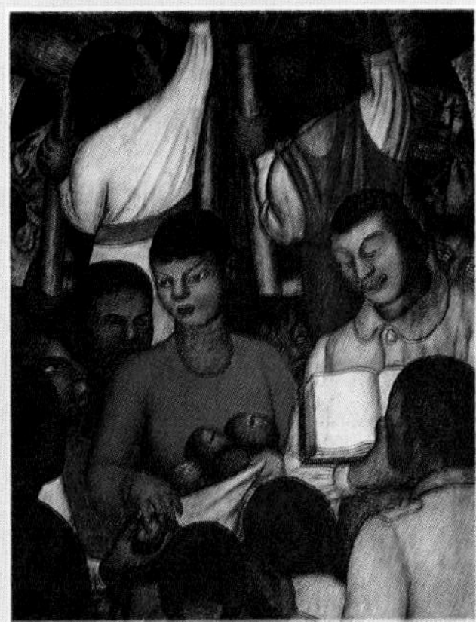

He returned to Mexico in 1921, where the clamor for social reform changed the direction of his work.

As a member of the art movement known as Social Realism, Rivera produced many paintings that dealt with current problems. Of particular interest are his works that show the plight of the peasants of Mexico. Another frequent subject in his paintings are children. The Mexican government liked Rivera's art and commissioned him to paint murals for many schools and government buildings. On the left is a detail from his mural *Fruits of Labor*—commissioned by the Ministry of Education in Mexico City—in which he honors working people and their children. This impressive fresco took Rivera and a crew of assistants from 1923 to 1929 to complete.

to produce textiles, construction materials, machinery, and automobiles. Oil refining and food processing became important industries at this time also.

Changes in Society

Industrialization contributed to the growth of cities. By 1935 Mexico City, Rio de Janeiro, São Paulo, and Buenos Aires all had 1 million or more inhabitants. These and other major cities in the region extended their transportation, sewer, and utilities systems to accommodate the influx of people and industries.

Industrialization also contributed to a change in Latin America's social structure. To provide labor for their growing industries, many countries—particularly Argentina, Brazil, and Chile—encouraged immigration from Europe. The new arrivals from across the Atlantic swelled the ranks of Latin America's working classes.

This growth, in turn, led to an increase in labor union activity. Although Latin American workers had first begun to organize in the late 1800s, the 1920s saw a surge in labor union membership. The Latin American unions, which were largely anarchist or socialist in outlook, employed the strike as the primary way to achieve their ends. As a result, by the late 1920s, practically every major city in Latin America had been hit by general strikes. Many governments mobilized police and troops to put down these strikes violently. Some governments went so far as to outlaw strikes and labor unions.

The middle class also began to grow as new jobs opened up in the professions, government service, and commerce. The increasing numbers of merchants, shopkeepers, and small-business owners added to this growth. Soon the sons of middle-class people took most of the places in the military academies. And changes in university programs created opportunities for middle-class youth in engineering, business, and public administration. Such developments gave the middle class potential access to greater power.

Political Changes

Political life in Latin America underwent sweeping change in the early 1900s. In Chile, Argentina, Peru, and Brazil, for example, political parties backed by the middle class emerged. Mexico, wracked by regional factionalism, opted for a single-party political system. Mexico's leaders hoped such a system would encourage a feeling of nationalism among the people and unify them behind the revolution that shook the country in the early 1900s. And in Uruguay reformers led by President José Batlle y Ordóñez (BAHT • yay ee or • THOWN • yas) enacted a broad reform program that included free elections, a social security system, and nationalization of the railroads and public utilities.

Even with these changes, democracy eluded most Latin American governments. Although many

SECTION 5

Focus/Motivation
Ask students the following questions: What conditions helped lead to dictatorship in Germany and Italy? *(economic hardship, the humiliation of defeat, a sense of military weakness, and lack of experience in democracy)* Which of these conditions might have existed in Latin America in the 1930s? *(economic hardship, not from war but from worldwide depression; no humiliation of defeat but resentment of imperialism; perhaps a sense of military weakness and a lack of democratic experience)*

At the end of the section, students might compare the dictatorships in Europe with those in Latin America. *(**Similarities:** military government, no democratic institutions, restriction of personal freedom; **Differences:** Latin American dictatorships did not pose an international threat; some maintained good relations with the United States and Western countries.)*

Presentation
Relating Past to Present (Average/Group)
Point out that in 1933 the United States agreed in the Montevideo Pact not to intervene in the internal or external affairs of another country. Ask: How closely has the United States followed this policy? How closely should it? Is it possible for the United States to be completely detached from Latin American affairs? *(Answers will vary.)*

Discuss with students the present-day situation in Central America. Ask: Is it in our national interest to become involved in this area? Why or why not? Have each student bring appropriate newspaper or magazine articles to class.

countries had passed laws granting universal manhood suffrage, throughout the region voting was largely restricted to literate males. In most countries this group accounted for less than 25 percent of the population. Furthermore, dishonesty and corruption marked many elections. In rural areas, for example, large landowners manipulated elections, controlling the way their tenants voted. And in some countries, forcible overthrow remained the typical way of changing governments.

The Effects of the Great Depression

As the 1920s drew to a close, prices for Latin America's major agricultural exports, such as sugar and coffee, began to fall. Chile's export economy suffered a particularly crippling blow. German scientists had perfected a process for making synthetic nitrates, used in fertilizers and explosives. As a result the bottom dropped out of the market for Chile's major export, nitrates.

The worldwide economic depression caused the prices of Latin America's exports to fall even further. Since they got such a small return on their exports, many Latin American nations found it impossible to import any but the most essential goods. Some countries stopped making payments on their foreign debt. As the region's economies continued to falter, unemployment became widespread, causing worker unrest.

Authoritarian Regimes

Economic crisis soon led to political crisis. Coups d'état overthrew most Latin American governments in the 1930s. In many cases these coups toppled constitutional systems that had worked for 30 to 40 years. Only Uruguay, which experienced a minor crisis between 1933 and 1935, and Mexico, which had undergone a revolution from 1911 to 1917, avoided major political upheaval.

The planters and exporters, whose fortunes had been wiped out during the Depression, no longer held power. Instead the military strongly influenced or controlled these new governments. In some countries American-trained military leaders came to power. The result was that the military became the best equipped to take power. In Nicaragua, for example, General Anastasio Somoza seized power in 1936, two years after assassinating his chief rival, nationalist guerrilla leader Augusto César Sandino. And in the Dominican Republic, General Rafael Trujillo (troo • HEE • yoh) began a 31-year dictatorship in 1930.

The new military officers considered the upper-class landowners and exporters corrupt, accusing them of having conducted dishonest elections and of allowing foreigners to take control of national resources. Consequently, the military leaders limited the landowners' political influence. At the same time, the new military governments broke the power of labor unions and other worker and peasant organizations. Many governments simply abolished these groups and jailed their leaders. Sometimes the military governments reacted more violently. In El Salvador, for example, the army massacred more than 10,000 peasants in an effort to destroy a popular movement led by Agustín Faribundo Martí, a one-time follower of Sandino in Nicaragua. And in Brazil, President Getúlio Vargas used arrests, mock trials, and torture in his crackdown on the National Liberation Alliance, a left-wing popular movement.

Some military leaders, however, saw that they could curb popular movements through persuasion rather than terror. A number of governments controlled the labor movements by recognizing and giving favors only to those unions loyal to the military. At the same time, many military governments tried to limit the appeal of left-wing movements by

Learning from Pictures *In 1933 police opened fire on Cubans in Havana who were celebrating the rumor that President Machado had resigned.*

1B, 1D, a1C, a4A, a4F, a4H, a4L

- Research topic: The current status of relations between the United States and Latin America

responding to some of the needs of ordinary people. These governments enacted some land reforms and passed laws giving workers benefits such as paid vacations and accident compensation.

Relations with the United States

In its relations with Latin America, President Franklin D. Roosevelt's administration tried to undo the ill will and suspicion created by the earlier United States policy of intervention. Roosevelt fostered a program, begun in the 1920s, called the Good Neighbor policy. This policy stressed mutual cooperation among the American nations and noninterference by the United States in Latin American affairs.

Then in 1933 the United States joined with other American nations in an agreement called the Montevideo (mahnt • uh • vuh • DAY • oh) Pact. This pact declared that "No state has the right to intervene in the internal or external affairs of another state." As proof of its intentions, the United States recalled the army units that had occupied Haiti since 1915. It also surrendered its right to interfere in the affairs of Panama.

A situation in Cuba, however, sorely tested the Roosevelt administration's commitment to the Montevideo Pact. In 1933 a group of radical reformers overthrew the Cuban dictator, Gerardo Machado. The new government immediately declared a socialist revolution and nationalized a number of companies owned by investors from the United States. In response the Roosevelt administration refused to grant diplomatic recognition to the new government. Once again it appeared that the United States would intervene, as was its right under the Platt Amendment (see page 621).

The United States did not directly interfere, but when a Cuban army sergeant, Fulgencio Batista, decided to overthrow the reformers, Roosevelt's envoy to Cuba encouraged him. Once in power, Batista received economic and military assistance from the United States. In order to strengthen Batista's regime, the United States signed a treaty with Cuba in 1934, canceling the Platt Amendment.

Economic Nationalism

Most Latin American governments during the 1930s followed a policy of economic nationalism. They reacted to the decline in markets for their exports by encouraging industry. In this way they hoped to become more self-sufficient. The Vargas regime in Brazil achieved the most success in this effort. By the time the army ousted Vargas in 1945, Brazil was producing many of its own consumer goods.

Foreign nations responded in a number of ways to this new Latin American initiative. On the whole the United States and Great Britain tried to discourage the Latin American effort to industrialize, since it constituted a threat to their investments and export markets in the region. The German government under Hitler, however, cleverly promoted exports of its own machinery to equip Latin American factories. In this way it hoped to undermine the financial and political influence of the United States and Great Britain.

The most significant act of economic nationalism occurred in Mexico in 1938. American- and British-owned oil companies operating in Mexico became involved in a wage dispute with their workers. When the Mexican Supreme Court ruled in favor of the workers, the foreign-owned oil companies refused to accept its decision. As a result, President Lázaro Cárdenas intervened and nationalized the oil industry.

At first the Roosevelt administration made angry threats and demands. However, supporters of the Good Neighbor policy soon prevailed, insisting on a more subtle approach. The administration then applied various indirect pressures, trying to force the Mexican government to pay the oil companies what they claimed their holdings were worth. Finally the two governments reached a compromise. With the threat of war in Europe growing, the United States thought it necessary to maintain good relations with Mexico.

SECTION 5 REVIEW

1. **Identify** Good Neighbor policy
2. **Locate** Mexico City, Buenos Aires
3. **Understanding Ideas** How did Latin American society change during the 1920s and 1930s?
4. **Analyzing Ideas** **(a)** What economic problems did Latin America experience in the late 1920s and the 1930s? **(b)** What impact did these problems have on political life in Latin America?
5. **Evaluating Ideas** How did the Good Neighbor policy affect relations between the United States and Latin America?

SECTION 5

Closure

Ask: How did the Great Depression affect Latin America? *(Unemployment rose, and worker discontent spread.)*

Review Answers

1. ***Good Neighbor policy:*** program fostered by President Franklin Roosevelt to improve relations with Latin America

2. ***Mexico City:*** city in central Mexico; ***Buenos Aires:*** city in eastern Argentina

3. Because of increased industrialization, cities grew. Transportation, sanitation, and electric services expanded. Many more people worked for wages, and trade unions became important. A middle class began to grow as universities provided training for new careers.

4. (a) Europe's demand for Latin American products and its supply of capital faltered. Prices for major agricultural products fell. **(b)** Unemployment became widespread, causing political unrest and the overthrow of most Latin American governments in the 1930s.

5. The United States signed the Montevideo Pact; withdrew American troops from Haiti; surrendered its right to interfere in Panama; canceled the Platt Amendment; and reached a compromise with Mexico over the seizure of American oil companies.

Reviewing Important Terms
1. Zionism; **2.** passive resistance.

Developing Critical Thinking Skills
1. (a) Nicaragua; **(b)** Turkey; **(c)** China; **(d)** India; **(e)** Cuba; **(f)** Iran
2. In 1935 Great Britain granted India a new constitution providing more self-government but not dominion status. Great Britain gave in to the demands of Canada, Australia, New Zealand, and the Union of South Africa without a struggle in 1931.
3. (a) by gradually creating democratic institutions and granting full personal liberties and rights to all Chinese people; **(b)** hostility from powerful warlords, little help from any foreign powers except the Soviet Union, and a split between the left and right wings in the Kuomintang
4. (a) The Nationalists began building roads and repairing, rebuilding, and extending railroads. They also improved finances and reformed the educational system. **(b)** They made no changes in the oppressive system of land ownership or in the method of collecting taxes in the countryside.
5. As a result of rapid modernization and industrialization, Japan's population increased dramatically. This problem was compounded when other countries restricted Japanese immigration. Industrial workers and tenant farmers organized unions and made demands. Urban intellectuals and university students organized social protest movements. Many young Japanese began to question traditional values

1B, 5A, a1B, a1C, a4A, a4E, a4F, a4G, a4H, a4J, a4K, a4L, a4M

Reteaching
Have students review the Chapter Summary and the appropriate section and questions in the Unit Synthesis. Discuss the concepts until students demonstrate a clear understanding of the material.

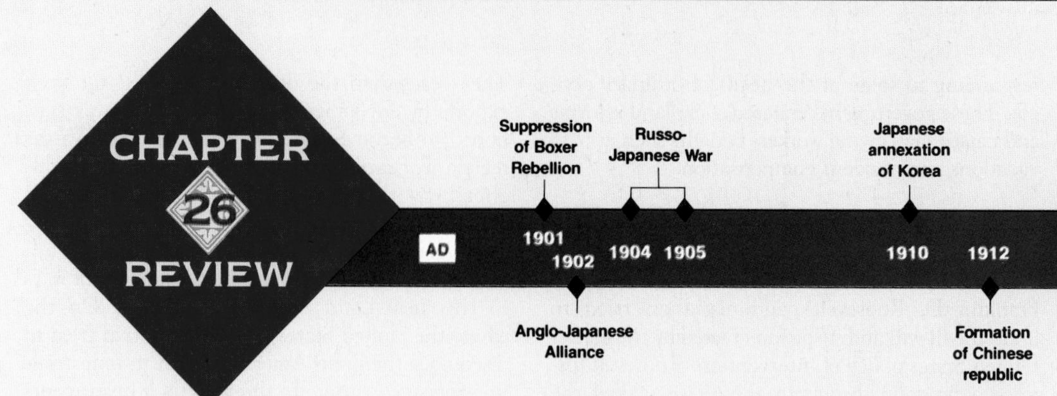

Chapter Summary

The following list contains the key concepts you have learned about the political forces that emerged in Africa, Asia, and Latin America in the early 1900s.

1. During the 1920s and 1930s, Egypt became completely independent, and Trans-Jordan and Iraq gained limited self-government. At the same time, Palestine's future remained in doubt, and India took its first steps toward independence.
2. Great Britain and its former colonies organized the Commonwealth of Nations.
3. Political and social reforms were attempted in Turkey and in Persia. Africa witnessed the stirrings of political activity that were to lead to major transformations in the years ahead.
4. The Chinese began the long and difficult process of adjusting to the modern world. Revolution brought imperial rule to an end, but the Kuomintang had trouble establishing its power in the new republic.
5. Dramatic change took place in Japan, which defeated first China and then Russia at the turn of the century. The Japanese also faced economic and social pressures after World War I.
6. Developments in Latin America reflected the worldwide economic crisis. The 1920s and 1930s were also a time of rapid social change, and in a number of countries, governments became more authoritarian.
7. Latin American relations with the United States improved as a result of the Good Neighbor policy, but economic nationalism led to a certain degree of tension.

On a separate sheet of paper, complete the following review exercises.

Reviewing Important Terms

Supply the term that correctly completes each sentence.

1. Many Jews supported ________, which aimed to build a Palestinian homeland for the Jews.
2. Gandhi's technique of ________ ________ called for citizens to peacefully refuse to cooperate with their government in order to win concessions from it.

Developing Critical Thinking Skills

1. **Classifying Ideas** Name the country in which each of the following people played vital leadership roles: **(a)** Anastasio Somoza, **(b)** Kemal Atatürk, **(c)** Chiang Kai-shek, **(d)** Mohandas Gandhi, **(e)** Fulgencio Batista, **(f)** Reza Shah Pahlavi.
2. **Comparing Ideas** After World War I, many colonies wanted independence. Compare the British reaction to demands for Indian independence with the reaction to similar demands from Canada, Australia, New Zealand, and the Union of South Africa.
3. **Interpreting Ideas** **(a)** How did Sun Yat-sen hope to bring democracy to China? **(b)** What obstacles prevented him from succeeding?
4. **Summarizing Ideas** **(a)** What changes did the Nationalists begin in China? **(b)** What problems did they fail to solve?
5. **Determining Cause and Effect** What economic and social problems did Japan face as a result of its rapid modernization and industrialization?
6. **Analyzing Ideas** Why did President Roosevelt support a continuation of the Good Neighbor policy during his administration?
7. **Analyzing a Primary Source** The lines below are from a poem entitled "Reproach" by Muhammad Iqbal, an Indian poet and a fervent nationalist who wanted independence for India. Read these lines, and answer the questions that follow.

> "Your fate, poor hapless India, there's no telling–
> Always the brightest jewel in someone's crown;
> Mortgaged to the alien, soul and body too,
> Alas–the dweller vanished with the dwelling–,
> Enslaved to Britain you have kissed the rod:
> It is not Britain I reproach, but you."

(a) What does Iqbal think India's fate will be? **(b)** Whom does he blame for this situation? **(c)** Why? **(d)** What actions do you think Iqbal might want the Indian people to take?

1A, 5A, a4A, a4B, a4C, a4D, a4E, a4F, a4G, a4H, a4I, a4J, a4K, a4L, a4M

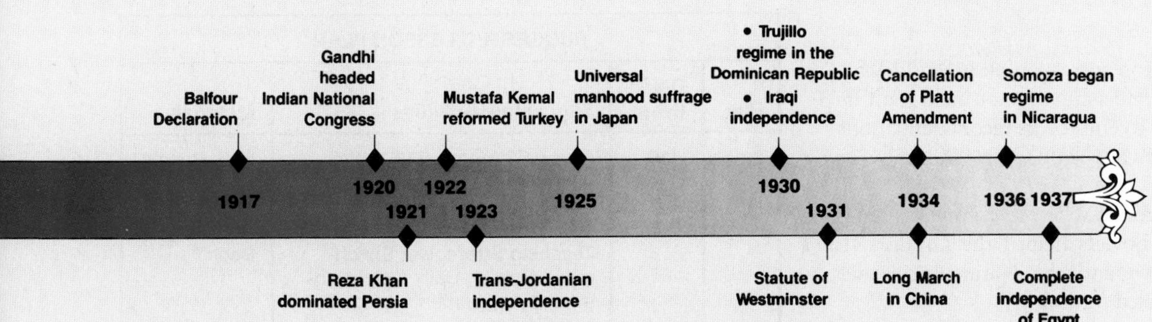

Relating Geography to History

Study the map of the Kuomintang military operations on page 700. **(a)** Where did Kuomintang victories over the warlords take place? **(b)** Where did Kuomintang strikes against the Communists take place?

Relating Past to Present

1. Examine a historical atlas containing a map of the Middle East in the 1930s. **(a)** What nations existed as mandates or protectorates? **(b)** What nations were independent? **(c)** How does this map compare with a map of the Middle East today? **(d)** What nations hold the land that once made up Palestine?
2. **(a)** What issue strained relations between the United States and Mexico in the 1930s? **(b)** Does this issue still cause difficulties between these two nations? Explain.
3. Review the information in this chapter on the importance of the military in Japan, Persia (Iran), and Latin America. Choose one of these areas. Use newspapers and magazines to determine what role the military plays in these areas today. Is the military stronger or weaker than it was in the 1920s and 1930s?

Applying History Study Skills

Before completing this activity, review Building History Study Skills on page 693.

Mohandas Gandhi organized the "Salt March" in India in 1930 to protest the British tax on salt. Read the following excerpt on the "Salt March" from *Gandhi* by Daniel R. Birch, D. Ian Allen, John U. Michaelis, and Robin J. McKeown. Then answer the questions that follow.

> "The salt deposits were surrounded by ditches filled with water and guarded by four hundred native Surat police. . . . Half a dozen British officials commanded them. The police carried *lathis*—five-foot clubs tipped with steel. Inside the stockade twenty-five native riflemen were drawn up.
>
> In complete silence the Gandhi men drew up and halted a hundred yards from the stockade. A picked column advanced from the crowd, waded the ditches, and approached the barbed wire stockade, which the Surat police surrounded, holding their clubs at the ready. Police officials ordered the marchers to disperse under a recently imposed regulation which prohibited gatherings of more than five persons in any one place. The column silently ignored the warning and slowly walked forward. . . .
>
> Suddenly, at a word of command, scores of native police rushed upon the advancing marchers and rained blows on their heads with their steel-shod *lathis*. Not one of the marchers even raised an arm to fend off the blows. They went down like tenpins. . . .
>
> Then another column formed while the leaders pleaded with them to retain their self-control."

1. What problem does the excerpt describe?
2. What is the solution to the problem?
3. How is the solution related to satyagraha?
4. **(a)** How would you evaluate the method? **(b)** Can nonviolence triumph over violence? **(c)** Why or why not?
5. Write a conclusion analyzing the method of nonviolence in response to the Salt Tax. Use your answers for question 4 to support your conclusion.

Investigating Further

1. **Writing a Report** Prepare a report on the rise of nationalism in Turkey. Your report should focus on the efforts of the Young Turks and the role of Mustafa Kemal. One possible source for your report is Desmond Stewart's *Turkey* (Time-Life Books).
2. **Preparing an Oral Presentation** Empress Cuxi—the empress dowager—held power in China from 1861 until her death in 1908. Using encyclopedias and books in your library, prepare a brief report on the life of the empress. In your report note reasons why her policies might have helped to bring about the end of the Qing dynasty.
3. **Constructing a Chart** Make a list of the major changes that took place in Latin America during the 1920s and 1930s. Then prepare a chart in which you classify each of the items on your list under one of the following headings: economic, social, or political.

and to adopt Western styles and values.
6. to help undo the ill will created by earlier American policies
7. (a) India will always be under another's control. **(b)** Iqbal blames the Indian people. **(c)** They accept British rule. **(d)** He might want them to rise up and throw out the British.

Relating Geography to History
(a) southern China; **(b)** northern China

Relating Past to Present
1. (a) Iraq, Palestine, Trans-Jordan, Lebanon, Syria, Kuwait, Bahrain, Qatar, Trucial Oman, Muscat and Oman, Aden; **(b)** Turkey, Iran, Iraq, Saudi Arabia, Yemen; **(c)** Today the former protectorates are independent. **(d)** Israel and Jordan
2. (a) the nationalization of the oil industry; **(b)** Economic relations still cause difficulties today.
3. Students should give reasons for their answers.

Applying History Study Skills
1. the tax on salt
2. a march of protest
3. The marchers did not respond with violence.
4. (a) Answers will vary. Some students might suggest that the method did not seem successful in this case. **(b)** Answers will vary. **(c)** Answers will vary. Many students might suggest that nonviolence can provide an example.
5. Answers will vary. Students might conclude that the nonviolent method resulted in no arrests.

CHAPTER (pages 710–739)

27 Local Aggressions Brought About World War II

(1921–1945)

CHAPTER OVERVIEW

The League of Nations failed to stop aggression after World War I because of basic weaknesses: its membership did not include all the major powers, and it lacked power to enforce its recommendations. The League failed to prevent Japan's attack on China and Italy's invasion of Ethiopia.

Civil war in Spain served as a prelude to war in Europe. Germany and Italy aided the Nationalists; Soviets helped the Loyalists. In 1939 the republic was overthrown and the Nationalist leader, Franco, set up a Fascist state modeled on Italy.

Germany became increasingly aggressive. Hitler sent troops into the Rhineland and later engulfed Austria, Czechoslovakia, and Memel, Lithuania. When German troops invaded Poland in September 1939, France and Great Britain declared war.

In the first two years of World War II, the German blitzkrieg overran Poland, Denmark, Norway, the Low Countries, and France. The Soviet Union, having signed a nonaggression pact with Germany, seized the Baltic States and defeated Finland. Dunkirk was a military disaster. The British saw their darkest days during the Battle of Britain. Germany made significant gains in the Balkans and North Africa and made a surprise attack deep into the Soviet Union. Japan continued its aggression in China and the Pacific. Its surprise bombing of Pearl Harbor brought the United States into the war on the Allied side.

Late in 1942 the tide of battle turned, with Allied counterattacks in the Soviet Union and North Africa and naval victories in the Pacific. Next came the invasion and surrender of Italy and the American strategy of "island hopping" in the Pacific. On June 6, 1944, Allied forces landed in Normandy, France. Germany was attacked from both east and west and was forced to surrender unconditionally. Japan surrendered only after the United States dropped atomic bombs on Hiroshima and Nagasaki.

SUGGESTED LESSON PLAN

Day	Objectives	Suggested Activities	Materials
1	U10,* C1–2	Introducing the Chapter (pages 710-11) Section 1 (pages 711-16), Focus/Motivation (page 711), Presentation (page 712), Closure (page 715), Suggested Teaching Strategies, Enrichment Activity, Daily Quiz, Suggested Assignments (page 709B)	ATE, Pupil's Edition, Teacher's Resource-Bank™
2	U10, C3–5	Section 2 (pages 716–20), Focus/Motivation (page 716), Presentation (page 717), Closure (page 719), Suggested Teaching Strategies, Enrichment Activity, Daily Quiz, Suggested Assignments (page 709C)	ATE, Pupil's Edition, Teacher's Resource-Bank™
3	U12, C6–7	Section 3 (pages 720–26), Focus/Motivation (page 721), Presentation (page 722), Closure (page 726), Suggested Teaching Strategies, Enrichment Activity, Daily Quiz, Suggested Assignments (page 709C)	ATE, Pupil's Edition, Teacher's Resource-Bank™
4	U12, C6–10	Section 4 (pages 726–31), Focus/Motivation (page 727), Presentation (page 728), Closure (page 730), Suggested Teaching Strategies, Enrichment Activity, Daily Quiz, Suggested Assignments (page 709D)	ATE, Pupil's Edition, Teacher's Resource-Bank™
5	U11–13, C11–12	Section 5 (pages 731–37), Focus/Motivation (page 731), Presentation (page 732), Closure (page 736), Suggested Teaching Strategies, Enrichment Activities, Daily Quiz, Suggested Assignments (page 709E)	ATE, Pupil's Edition, Teacher's Resource-Bank™
6	U10–13, C1–12	Chapter 27 Form A Test, Reteaching Worksheet, Chapter 27 Form B Test	Teacher's Resource-Bank™ or Workbook and Test Booklet
7	U1–13	Unit Six Review Worksheet, Unit Six Test	Teacher's Resource-Bank™ or Test Booklet

*C refers to applicable Chapter Objective, U refers to applicable Unit Goal

BOOKS FOR THE TEACHER

Davidowicz, Lucy S. *The War Against the Jews, 1933–1945.* Holt, Rinehart and Winston. Analyzes the Holocaust.

Toland, John. *The Rising Sun.* Random House. Details Japanese-American relations from 1911 to 1945.

Tuchman, Barbara W. *Stilwell and the American Experience in China.* Bantam. Traces relations between the United States and China from 1911 to 1945.

BOOKS FOR THE STUDENT

Churchill, Winston. *The Second World War.* Golden Press. Contains abridged version of Churchill's war memoirs. Includes numerous illustrations.

Lidz, Richard. *Many Kinds of Courage: An Oral History of World War II.* Putnam. Presents accounts of ordinary people who displayed a quiet courage in wartime crises.

Meltzer, Milton. *Never to Forget: The Jews of the Holocaust.* Portrays account of the persecution of Jews, with a section on the Jewish resistance.

Taylor, A. J. P. *The War Lords.* Atheneum. Includes short, personal biographies of Mussolini, Hitler, Churchill, Stalin, and Roosevelt, with numerous photographs.

AUDIO-VISUAL MATERIALS

The Causes of World War II (2 fs), Educational Audio-Visual. "1918–1933" studies the Treaty of Versailles and its treatment of Germany, post-World War I problems, the rise of fascism, the Locarno Pact, and the Kellogg-Briand Pact. "1933– 1941" covers the policies of the Nazis, the Spanish civil war, the Far East situation, the policy of appeasement, the outbreak of war, the fall of France, Germany's attack on Russia, and American and Japanese involvement.

Franco (mp, 26 min.), McGraw-Hill. Portrays the dictator's life, with particular emphasis on his early career.

Man of the Century: Churchill (mp, 54 min.), McGraw-Hill. Follows Winston Churchill from his role in the Boer War to World War II.

Second World War (3 mp), EBE. "Prelude to Conflict" (29 min.) portrays key events that led to war. "Triumph of the Axis" (25 min.) analyzes the triumphs of the Axis Powers during the first phase of the war. "Allied Victory" (28 min.) documents key events of the war from 1944 to Japan's surrender in 1945.

Twisted Cross (mp, 55 min.), McGraw-Hill. Traces the rise and fall of Hitler. Many of the scenes were excerpted from captured German films.

Section 1 (pages 711–716)
Local Conflicts Threatened World Peace

SECTION OVERVIEW

In the 1930s events in China, Ethiopia, and Spain threatened world peace. In 1931 Japan attacked Manchuria and established a puppet state. Japan withdrew from the League of Nations and invaded China Proper in 1937. Italy invaded Ethiopia, but the League made only mild efforts to arbitrate and apply sanctions. The Spanish civil war was won by Franco's Nationalist forces over the Loyalists. Germany and Italy aided Franco; the Soviet Union and foreign volunteers helped the Loyalists.

SUGGESTED TEACHING STRATEGIES

1. **Using a Map (Basic)** Have students study the map on page 713 and discuss the relationship between Japanese militarism and Japanese expansion.
2. **Interpreting Ideas (Average/Group)** Ask students to consider why economic and political instability led to civil war in Spain.

ENRICHMENT ACTIVITY

Presenting a Group Discussion (Average/Group) Organize the class into groups representing the delegations to the League of Nations from such countries as Great Britain, France, the Soviet Union, the Netherlands, and Switzerland. Japan has just invaded Manchuria. Have students try to avoid the mistakes of the League of Nations by adopting a plan of action to deal with such acts of aggression. Have students write out the resolutions they would recommend. Bring the groups together for a discussion of their proposals. Return to these ideas when discussing the United Nations in Chapter 28.

DAILY QUIZ

To assess student understanding of Section 1, give the class the following quiz. (Each item is worth 10 points.)

1. What was one weakness of the League of Nations? *(The United States, Germany and Russia were not included; no real external forces could be exerted.)*
2. What area did Japan invade first? *(Manchuria)*
3. Mussolini hoped to reclaim the past glories of ancient Rome by taking the African nation of ________. *(Ethiopia)*
4. (T or F) The League of Nations effectively stopped agression, applying successful sanctions against Italy and forcing Italy to withdraw from Ethiopia. *(F)*
5. (T or F) Before the civil war, Spain was a poor country, the Catholic church controlled the educational system, and the agricultural economy lagged behind European industry. *(T)*
6. (T or F) Franco and the Falange received aid from the Fascists in Italy. *(T)*
7. (T or F) The Loyalists, or Republicans, were groups of left-wing working-class parties. *(T)*
8. To which group did Russia send aid? *(Loyalists, Republicans)*
9. Germany and Italy saw a facist Spain as a part of their plan to surround ________ with unfriendly powers and threaten Great Britain. *(France)*
10. (T or F) Franco became the facist dictator of Spain and copied Italian policies for promoting economic growth. *(T)*

SUGGESTED ASSIGNMENTS

1. **Researching Ideas (Average/Group)** Students might prepare oral or written reports on the following topics: Japanese occupation of Manchuria, war in China, political background of the Spanish civil war, foreign involvement in the Spanish civil war, the war in Ethiopia, and the actions of the League of Nations. Sources include: John Toland's *The Rising Sun* (Random House); Hugh Thomas's *The Spanish Civil War* (Harper & Row); and Ivone Kirkpatrick's *Mussolini* (Hawthorn Books).
2. **Comparing Ideas (Challenging)** Organize the class into two groups. Have one group use a variety of references to compare Japanese aggression in Asia prior to World War II with Communist aggression in Asia prior to the Korean War. Have the second group use reference materials to compare Japanese aggression in Asia before World War II with Communist aggression in Asia before the Vietnam War. Then have the students present their findings to the class and discuss how aggression leads to war.

Section 2 (pages 716–720)

Hitler's Aggressions in Europe Sparked World War II

SECTION OVERVIEW

In 1938 Hitler annexed Austria to the Third Reich. In the same year, he demanded that Czechoslovakia give up the Sudetenland. Great Britain and France appeased Hitler by agreeing to this demand, but he soon occupied the remainder of Czechoslovakia. Under German pressure Lithuania ceded Memel, while Italy conquered Albania. On September 1, 1939, Germany invaded Poland, and Great Britain and France declared war on Germany.

SUGGESTED TEACHING STRATEGIES

1. **Preteaching Vocabulary (Basic)** You may wish to preteach the following important vocabulary term: appeasement *(page 718)*. Ask students why appeasement seemed to be an alternative to war in 1938.
2. **Identifying Ideas (Average/Group)** Ask students to scan page 716 and explain why Hitler was able to annex Austria. *(Students should suggest that the democratic nations had done little to halt the spread of fascism in Ethiopia and Spain. Students should also mention that the Austrian government did little to halt the expansion of the Nazi Party.)*

ENRICHMENT ACTIVITY

Preparing Dramatic Presentations (Challenging) Four students could assume the roles of Hitler, Mussolini, Chamberlain, and Daladier and present a skit based on the Munich Conference. Henry Abraham's and Irwin Pfeiffer's *Enjoying World History* (Amsco) contains a brief skit, "Meeting in Munich," which can serve as a guide. Other sources include: William L. Shirer's *The Rise and Fall of the Third Reich* (Simon and Schuster) and John Toland's *Adolf Hitler* (Doubleday). Another group of students could dramatize the historic meeting between Hitler and the Austrian chancellor in February 1938. An account of the meeting is in Sydney Eisen's and Maurice Filler's *The Human Adventure* (Harcourt Brace Jovanovich).

DAILY QUIZ

To assess student understanding of Section 2, give the class the following quiz. (Each item is worth 10 points.)

1. In 1938 Hitler annexed ________ to complete his *Anschluss*. *(Austria)*
2. (T or F) The French and British leaders continued to follow the policy of appeasement, hoping Hitler would be satisfied with his territorial acquisitions. *(T)*
3. What region of Czechoslovakia became the center of a dispute between Czechoslovakia and Germany? *(Sudetenland)*
4. As the tensions mounted in Europe, Hitler demanded a conference, to be held in ________. *(Munich)*
5. (T or F) Greece annexed parts of Czechoslovakia after Hitler's conference. *(F)*
6. (T or F) Franco and the Falange received aid from the Fascists in Italy. *(T)*
7. (T or F) The Loyalists, or Republicans, were groups of left-wing working-class parties. *(T)*
8. To which group did Russia send aid? *(Loyalists, Republicans)*
9. Germany and Italy saw a facist Spain as a part of their plan to surround ________ with unfriendly powers and threaten Great Britain. *(France)*
10. (T or F) Franco became the facist dictator of Spain and copied Italian policies for promoting economic growth. *(T)*

SUGGESTED ASSIGNMENTS

1. **Critical Thinking Worksheet (Basic)** Have students complete Critical Thinking Worksheet 61 in the TEACHER'S RESOURCEBANK™.
2. **Critical Thinking Worksheet (Basic)** Have students complete Critical Thinking Worksheet 62 in the TEACHER'S RESOURCEBANK™.

Section 3 (pages 720–726)

The Axis Made Significant Gains

SECTION OVERVIEW

On the western front a period of inactivity called the "phony" war existed, while on the eastern front Russia conquered eastern Poland, the Baltic States, and Finland. In the spring of 1940, Hitler's armies overran Denmark, Norway, the Netherlands, Belgium, Luxembourg, and France. Under Churchill's leadership, the British survived the Battle of Britain. Although neutral, the United States began to commit its resources to aid Great Britain. Churchill and Roosevelt outlined their war aims in the Atlantic Charter in the fall of 1941.

SUGGESTED TEACHING STRATEGIES

1. **Preteaching Vocabulary (Basic)** You may wish to preteach the following important vocabulary terms: blitzkrieg *(page 720)*; collaborator *(page 721)*; isolationist *(page 725)*. Ask: Why did isolationists oppose American intervention in World War II? *(They believed it was Europe's war.)*
2. **Understanding Chronology (Basic)** Put the following events tracing United States involvement in World War II on the chalkboard or an overhead projector. Have students arrange the events in chronological order.

   (1) A revised Neutrality Act allowed the sale of munitions to belligerent nations on a cash-and-carry basis.
   (5) Congress abolished restrictions prohibiting American merchant ships from being armed or entering war zones.
   (2) President Roosevelt transferred 50 old American naval destroyers to Great Britain.
   (4) Roosevelt and Churchill issued the Atlantic Charter.
   (3) Congress passed the Lend-Lease Act.
*3. **Reading About History: Understanding a Biographical Account (Average/Group)** Organize the class into groups. Have each group research the life of a different World War II leader. Students should present their findings to the class and discuss how many of the events in the lives of these leaders became historically significant.

ENRICHMENT ACTIVITY

Preparing a Panel Discussion (Challenging) Have students conduct a panel discussion on Roosevelt's actions in 1940 and 1941, based on the following question: Was Roosevelt justified in pursuing the course that he took in American relations with Great Britain? Sources include: James MacGregor Burns's *Roosevelt: The Soldier of Fortune* (Harcourt Brace Jovanovich); Thomas Bailey's *Probing America's Past: A Critical Examination of Major Myths and Misconceptions*, vol. 2 (D. C. Heath) and *A Diplomatic History of the American People* (Appleton-Century-Crofts).

DAILY QUIZ

To assess student understanding of Section 3, give the class the following quiz. (Each item is worth 10 points.)

1. What is the translation for the German term "blitzkrieg"? *(lightning war)*
2. (T or F) During the "phony" war Germany rolled over France and Spain with almost no opposition. *(F)*
3. The Germans took control of the Scandinavian Atlantic coastline to establish control of all European ______ and ______ ______. *(submarine and air bases)*
4. What great statesman took over the British government when Neville Chamberlain resigned? *(Winston Churchill)*
5. The successful British evacuation of continental troops occurred at ______. *(Dunkirk)*
6. (T or F) The French soon surrendered after Germany attacked in June 1940, and the Germans divided France into Occupied France and Vichy France. *(T)*
7. Who, as the leader of the Free French government, encouraged the French partisans to continue resisting the German occupation? *(Charles de Gaulle)*
8. (T or F) The Battle of Britain was a German air assault against the city of London, where radar helped turn the tide in favor of the British. *(T)*
9. (T or F) The isolationists in the United States supported the neutrality acts. *(T)*
10. President Roosevelt and Prime Minister Churchill announced their war aims and met on a British battleship to draw up a plan later called the ______ ______. *(Atlantic Charter)*

SUGGESTED ASSIGNMENTS

1. **Identifying Leadership Qualities (Average/Group)** Have students read selected excerpts from Winston Churchill's address to the British people following the evacuation of Dunkirk. Then ask them to write a paragraph describing the leadership qualities the British people attributed to Winston Churchill.
2. **Analyzing Ideas (Challenging)** Have students research the fall of France and the Battle of Britain. Then have them analyze why France fell to the Axis Powers early in the war and Britain overcame assaults by the Axis Powers.
3. **Skill Worksheet (Basic)** Have students complete Skill Worksheet 27 in the TEACHER'S RESOURCEBANK™.

Section 4 (pages 726–731)

The Soviet Union and the United States Entered the War

SECTION OVERVIEW

In June 1941 German armies invaded the Soviet Union as part of Hitler's master plan for a "New Order"—a Europe dominated by "Aryans." The invasion stalled in the winter of 1941–42. Hitler's "Final Solution" of the "Jewish Problem" resulted in the murder of about 6 million Jews. In December 1941 Japan attacked Pearl Harbor, in Hawaii, which brought the United States into the war.

SUGGESTED TEACHING STRATEGIES

1. **Preteaching Vocabulary (Basic)** You may wish to preteach the following important vocabulary term: Holocaust *(page 730)*.

Point out that the extermination of an entire race is referred to as genocide.

2. **Class Discussion (Average/Group)** An important film to show to the class is *Genocide* (Anti-Defamation League of B'nai B'rith, New York). It shows dramatic film footage of the Holocaust and traces the history of Hitler's "Final Solution" from the 1920s to 1945. Before showing the film, have students define the term *genocide (a purposeful, organized attempt to exterminate an entire people)*. After students have viewed the film have them explain what motives or appeals might influence people actively or passively to support policies of genocide.
3. **Relating Geography to History (Basic)** Have students discuss how the weather affected the Soviet defense in 1941.

ENRICHMENT ACTIVITY

Researching Ideas (Challenging) Have students do further reading about the siege of Leningrad. Harrison Salisbury's *Nine Hundred Days* (Avon) is an excellent source. Students should explore the following questions: What was life like for the average citizen in Leningrad before the siege? What were the most important effects of the siege on day-to-day life? Have students use the answers to these questions to write a first-person fictional account of a citizen's typical day in besieged Leningrad.

DAILY QUIZ

To assess student understanding of Section 4, give the class the following quiz. (Each item is worth 10 points.)

1. (T or F) During the fall of 1940, Germany held almost all of western Europe. *(T)*
2. (T or F) Italy's initial attack on North Africa failed as the British counterattacked. *(T)*
3. What important German general was known as the "Desert Fox?" *(Erwin Rommel)*
4. What country did Hitler attack in June 1941, after growing tensions about the occupation of the Balkans? *(Russia)*
5. (T or F) The Allies sent aid to the Soviet Union through Siberian ports and Iran. *(T)*
6. What were two of the three Soviet cities that the Nazis hoped to capture? *(Leningrad, Stalingrad, and Moscow)*
7. The Nazis planned to eliminate all ________ when they established their program for the "Final Solution." *(Jews)*
8. What is the systematic destruction of the European Jews by the Nazis called? *(Holocaust)*
9. (T or F) As soon as the Nazis conquered most of western Europe, the Japanese quickly planned an attack on the Western powers. *(T)*
10. Where did the Japanese launch an attack on December 7, 1941? *(Pearl Harbor)*

SUGGESTED ASSIGNMENTS

1. **Preparing an Oral Report (Average/Group)** A group of students might present an oral report on the Japanese attack on Pearl Harbor. The report should include a description of the American navy in the Pacific before the attack, including numbers of ships and their functions; American military damage suffered at Pearl Harbor; and military tactics used by the Japanese in the attack. Students should use the card catalogue in the library to locate appropriate books and could also check the index to *American Heritage* magazine for articles.
2. **Writing an Essay (Challenging)** Have students write an essay that focuses on the American belief in individualism and free enterprise, and the government controls imposed upon the American people during World War II. Students should present arguments for or against such controls and suggest hypothetical circumstances under which Americans might accept such controls today.

Section (pages 731–737)

5 Allied Victories over Germany and Japan Ended the War

SECTION OVERVIEW

In 1942 and 1943 the Allies made significant gains. Russia won a decisive victory at Stalingrad, and Allied invasions in North Africa and Italy were successful. The Allies gained control of the Atlantic, and in the Pacific started "island hopping" to reach Japan. After the invasion of Normandy, the Allies closed in on Germany from both east and west. The Germans surrendered after the fall of Berlin. Japan held out until atomic bombs were dropped on Hiroshima and Nagasaki. Japan's surrender in 1945 ended the costliest war in world history.

SUGGESTED TEACHING STRATEGIES

1. **Comparing Historical Documents (Basic)** You might show one of the following movies based on newsreels: *The Second World War: The Allied Victory* (mp, 28 min., EBE) or *You Are There: D-Day* (mp, 26 min., McGraw-Hill). After the films, ask the following questions: How did what you saw in the films differ from what you had imagined about conditions during the war? How did it differ from movies and television shows dealing with the war? *(Answers will vary.)* What is the danger of relying mainly on our imaginations or works of fiction in understanding the past? *(Imagination and art can change the past to suit its purposes or distort the truth accidentally.)* How can our imaginations and works of fiction help us understand the past? *(Imagination and art help us make reasonable inferences and fill in gaps in our knowledge, although risks of inaccuracy are present.)*
2. **Constructing a Chart (Average/Group)** Have students construct a chart that illustrates important German offensives.

ENRICHMENT ACTIVITIES

1. **Writing a Diary (Average/Group)** Have students imagine they served in the armed forces during World War II. Then have them

write a diary entry about their experiences during one day of the war. Remind the class that women also served in the various branches of the armed forces. Students might want to refer to the Time-Life series on World War II or to Trevor N. Dupuy's *The Military History of World War II* (Franklin Watts).

2. **Conducting Research (Challenging)** Have students prepare written or oral reports on World War II strategy or battles or on a topic such as the resistance movement or the home front. Students should consult the Time-Life series on World War II; *Picture History of World War II* by the editors of *Life* (Simon and Schuster); Cyril Falls's *Great Military Battles* (Macmillan); Oliver Warner's *Great Sea Battles* (Macmillan); Don Lawson's *An Album of World War II Home Fronts* (Franklin Watts); Stephen A. Sears's *The Battle of The Bulge* or *Air War Against Hitler's Germany* (American Heritage). Students should also check the index of *American Heritage* magazine for appropriate articles.

DAILY QUIZ

To assess student understanding of Section 5, give the class the following quiz. (Each item is worth 10 points.)

1. What were the three major Allies that finally defeated the Axis? *(Soviet Union, Great Britain, and the United States)*
2. Where did the turning point in the Russian theater of the war occur? *(Stalingrad)*
3. What southern European country did the Western Allies attack in 1943? *(Italy)*
4. What invention saved the Allied convoys from submarines? *(sonar)*
5. (T or F) New Guinea was the site of an American naval victory in the Pacific. *(F)*
6. What was the Allied strategy that bypassed certain Japanese island strongholds? *(island hopping)*
7. What was the day called when the Allies attacked at Normandy? *(D-Day)*
8. What was the name of the last German offensive on the western front, in December 1944? *(Battle of the Bulge)*
9. What was the name of the Japanese suicide dive-bombers that attacked the Allied fleet? *(Divine Wind or Kamikaze)*
10. What were the names of the two wartime conferences designed to establish a peaceful postwar world? *(Potsdam, Yalta)*

SUGGESTED ASSIGNMENTS

1. **Profile Worksheet (Basic)** Have students complete Profile Worksheet 27 in the TEACHER'S RESOURCEBANK™.
2. **Review Worksheet (Basic)** Have students complete Review Worksheet 27 in the TEACHER'S RESOURCEBANK™.

For suggested lesson plan, additional teaching strategies, enrichment activities, daily quizzes, and suggested assignments, see pages 709A–709F.

Introducing the Chapter
During the 1930s local conflicts threatened world peace and Hitler's aggressions in Europe brought about World War II. Students will understand this concept more clearly if they refer to the map on page 717. Ask students to explain why annexing Austria was important to Hitler. *(Students should suggest that the annexation of Austria meant that Germany shared a common border with its ally—Italy.)*

Chapter Objectives
After studying Chapter 27, students will be able to:

1. Trace the conflicts in Asia and Africa that led the world down the path to war.
2. Outline the problem in Spain that led to revolution, including an analysis of the foreign interests involved in the conflict.
3. Summarize Hitler's actions that led to the Munich Conference.
4. Describe Mussolini's attack on Albania.
5. State how the Nazi-Soviet nonaggression pact laid the groundwork for European hostilities.
6. Outline the successes of the Axis Powers early in World War II.
7. Describe the United States's gradual entry into the war on the side of the Allies.
8. Discuss how Hitler's invasion of Russia and campaign in North Africa over-extended his military.
9. Evaluate the causes and effects of Hitler's "New

CHAPTER 27

Local Aggressions Brought About World War II

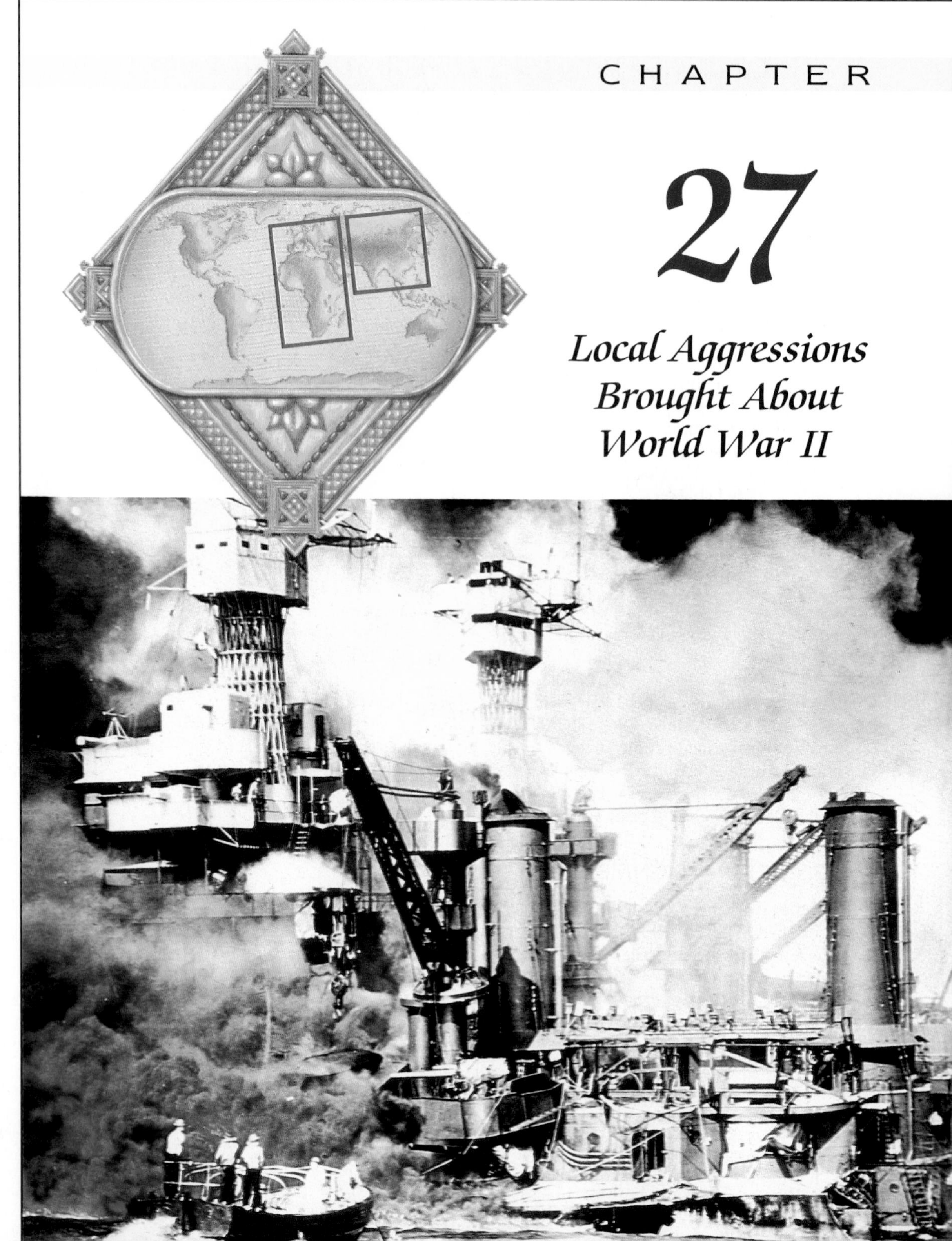

CHAPTER FOCUS

Place Asia, Africa, and Europe

Time

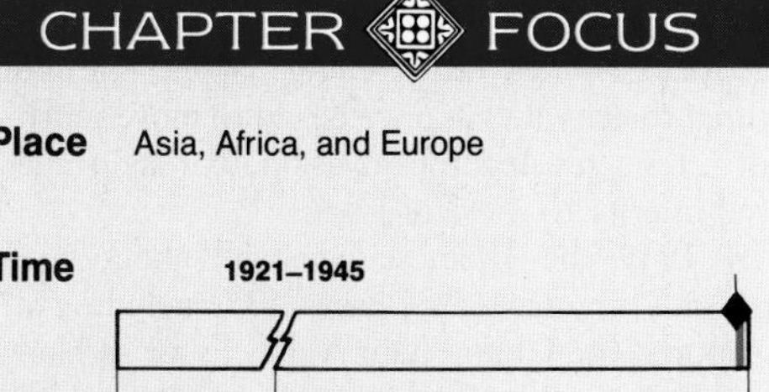

Significance

By the 1930s most European nations once more claimed loyalty to one of two opposing camps. One group included those nations generally satisfied with the World War I peace settlement. The other group consisted of dissatisfied nations. With each passing year, international relations between the two groups grew more strained.

Despite its serious weaknesses, the League of Nations tried valiantly to preserve the peace. Since the United States had never joined, however, and the Soviet Union was not admitted until 1934, the League's membership was incomplete. In addition, the League could not make laws for its members, but could only make recommendations that it had no means of enforcing. Peace became increasingly difficult to preserve, and in 1939 Japanese aggression in Asia and German aggression in Europe erupted in World War II.

Terms to Define

appeasement
blitzkrieg
collaborator
Holocaust

People to Identify

Benito Mussolini
Francisco Franco
Adolf Hitler
Neville Chamberlain
Joseph Stalin
Winston Churchill
Franklin Roosevelt
Hideki Tojo
Bernard Montgomery
Dwight Eisenhower

Places to Locate

Manchuria
Sudetenland
Maginot Line
Munich
Polish Corridor
Danzig
Dunkirk
El Alamein
Leningrad
Pearl Harbor
Philippine Islands
Yalta

Questions to Guide Your Reading

1 How did local conflicts threaten world peace?
2 How did Hitler's aggressions in Europe bring about World War II?
3 What significant gains did the Axis achieve in the early years of the war?
4 Why did the Soviet Union and the United States enter the war?
5 What Allied victories over Germany and Japan ended the war?

◀ *Pearl Harbor after Japan's surprise attack*

In the early morning hours of August 6, 1945, an American army sergeant sat resolutely at the wheel of a battered, mud-encrusted jeep. Propping a small pad of paper awkwardly against his knee, he wrote a loving note to his fiancée in the United States. A portion of the letter read:

> *"I've never doubted that we would win the war. After four years much of Europe is in ruins. During these last few weeks of occupation the guns have remained silent. Today men in my unit are preparing to board troopships for Japan. We're tired of war, but we're ready to do whatever it takes to win it."*

The young sergeant had no way of knowing that as he wrote, a B-29 bomber named Enola Gay *was en route to Japan, carrying the world's first atomic bomb. Before the soldier's fiancée received the letter, Japan had surrendered unconditionally, and World War II was over. The Allied victory came nearly six years after the beginning of World War II, but concern about world peace actually arose in the 1920s.*

1 Local Conflicts Threatened World Peace

Because of the political weakness of the League of Nations, the major powers held diplomatic conferences outside the organization. The first of these conferences was held in 1921 and 1922 in Washington, D.C. Nine of the powers having interests in East Asia (excluding the Soviet Union, which was not invited to the meeting) attended this Washington Conference.

Several treaties resulted from the conference. The Five-Power Treaty provided for a 10-year "naval holiday," during which no warships would be built. The participating nations also signed the Nine-Power Treaty, agreeing to take no additional territory from China and to maintain the existing Open Door policy. As a result of the Washington Naval Conference and other diplomatic settlements, peace was preserved throughout the 1920s.

The most optimistic of the international conferences took place in 1928 in Paris. The American secretary of state, Frank B. Kellogg, and the French foreign minister, Aristide Briand, drafted a treaty

Order" and "Final Solution."
10. Describe Japanese aggressions in the Pacific and the initial U.S. involvement in World War II.
11. Outline the Allied offensives against the Axis, comparing the methods used in Europe with those used in Asia.
12. Evaluate the individual Allied goals at Yalta and Potsdam, and the costs of the war to the world.

SECTION 1

Focus/Motivation
Read aloud the following quotation from Mussolini.

"A solemn hour is about to strike in the history of the Fatherland. . . . Not only is an army marching towards its objective, but forty million Italians are marching in unison with the army, all united because there is an attempt to commit against them the blackest of all injustices, to rob them of a place in the sun. . . . With Ethiopia, we have been patient for forty years."

Ask students the following questions: What is the purpose of the speech? *(Mussolini wanted to rally Italians to support the Ethiopian invasion.)* How does Mussolini justify the invasion? *(He creates a fictitious injustice—as if having Ethiopia as a colony is a right that is being stolen from Italy; also by inspiring revenge for Italy's defeat in 1896 at Adwa.)* What phrases does Mussolini use to appeal to Italian patriotism? *("solemn hour,"*

1B, 4K, 5B, 5G, a1B, a1C

● Discussion topic: The reasons that world peace was threatened despite the Kellogg-Briand Pact

"Fatherland," "forty million Italians. . . . marching in unison")

Presentation
Writing a Newspaper Article (Average/Group)
Have students write a newspaper article describing the Japanese occupation of Manchuria or the political background of the Spanish civil war. Stress that these articles, like all good journalism, should first establish the key facts and then provide background for perspective. The point of view can be objective, or slanted if the writer desires to gain sympathy for the democratic institutions threatened by the local conflicts leading towards war. Use the articles as the basis for a class discussion on events that threatened world peace.

condemning war. Eventually, more than 60 nations signed the Kellogg-Briand Pact, which made war "illegal," but no one had yet found a way to prevent ● war. In the 1930s, it became clear that such makeshift arrangements would no longer be effective.

Japanese Aggression in Asia

Beginning in the late 1920s, the military gained increasing power in Japan. In 1930 Japan's liberal prime minister, Yuko Hamaguchi (HAH • MAH • GOO • CHEE), was fatally shot. Political disorder followed, and within two years militarists controlled the Japanese government.

Attack on Manchuria. In September 1931 a mysterious explosion near the city of Mukden, Manchuria, damaged a Japanese-controlled railroad. Without warning and without the consent of China, Japanese troops occupied Mukden. The Republic of China appealed to the League of Nations for help. The Japanese delegate to the League stated that the occupation of Mukden was purely a local matter and warned the League not to interfere. This incident sparked a conflict between Japan and China that was to continue, intermittently, until 1945.

The League of Nations sent an investigating commission, headed by Lord Lytton of Great Britain, to Manchuria. At the same time, Japan continued its conquest. In 1932 Japan declared Manchuria to be an independent nation, under the name Manchukuo (MAN • CHOO • KWOH).

The Lytton Commission advised the League not to recognize Manchukuo's independence and recommended that the region be restored to China. When the League voted on this recommendation, only Japan opposed it. As a result of its diplomatic defeat, Japan withdrew from the League of Nations. Some historians regard Japan's successful aggression against China as the actual beginning of World War II.

The League's inability to restrain Japan's territorial ambitions showed that although the major nations joined in condemning aggression, they were unwilling to take drastic measures to stop it. Japanese aggression started a chain reaction that led to the collapse of peace in the West as well as in the East.

War in China. Confidently Japan pressed further demands on China. It announced its intention to extend its influence to all of China, not merely to outlying regions. In July 1937 Japanese and Chinese troops clashed near Beijing. Japanese armies captured the city and at once began to move southward. China resisted the invasion, but its armies proved inferior to those of Japan.

By 1939 the Japanese occupied about one-fourth of China (see map, page 713), including all its seaports, the Chang Jiang Valley as far as Hankou, and many cities in the interior. Still the Chinese stubbornly resisted. This resistance proved an enormous strain, not only on their own resources, but also on those of Japan. By 1939 Japan had lost nearly 500,000 troops in China and had spent $10 billion. Chinese losses were uncountable.

Italy's Conquest of Ethiopia

The Fascist Party in Italy, like the Communist Party in Russia, considered itself a ruling elite. Premier Benito Mussolini, the party's leader, focused his policy on improving the nation's economy through increased taxation, reduced government spending, and suppression of strikes.

Mussolini also sought to solve his country's economic problems by overseas expansion. Ethiopia, one of the few independent nations in Africa, became the object of his ambitions.

A border incident provided the pretext for aggression. In December 1934 an Italian border patrol in Italian Somaliland (so • MAHL • ee • land) clashed with an Ethiopian border patrol. Mussolini at once sent Italian forces from Eritrea (er • uh • TREE • uh) and Italian Somaliland to invade Ethiopia and "restore order."

Ethiopia, poorly prepared to resist such an invasion, asked the League of Nations for protection. The League maintained no armed forces and made only a minimal effort to bring the dispute to arbitration. In October 1935 Mussolini waged an all-out campaign to conquer and colonize the independent nation of Ethiopia.

The League then declared Italy an aggressor and applied economic sanctions—the stoppage of trade and other economic relations with an offending nation. The sanctions, although sweeping enough, generated only half-hearted observance. In a long war, the effects of the sanctions might have weakened Italy and forced it to give in to the League's demands. However, the poorly equipped Ethiopian army was not prepared to engage in a long war. The Italians triumphantly entered the

● Philippines, Guam, Wake, Hawaii

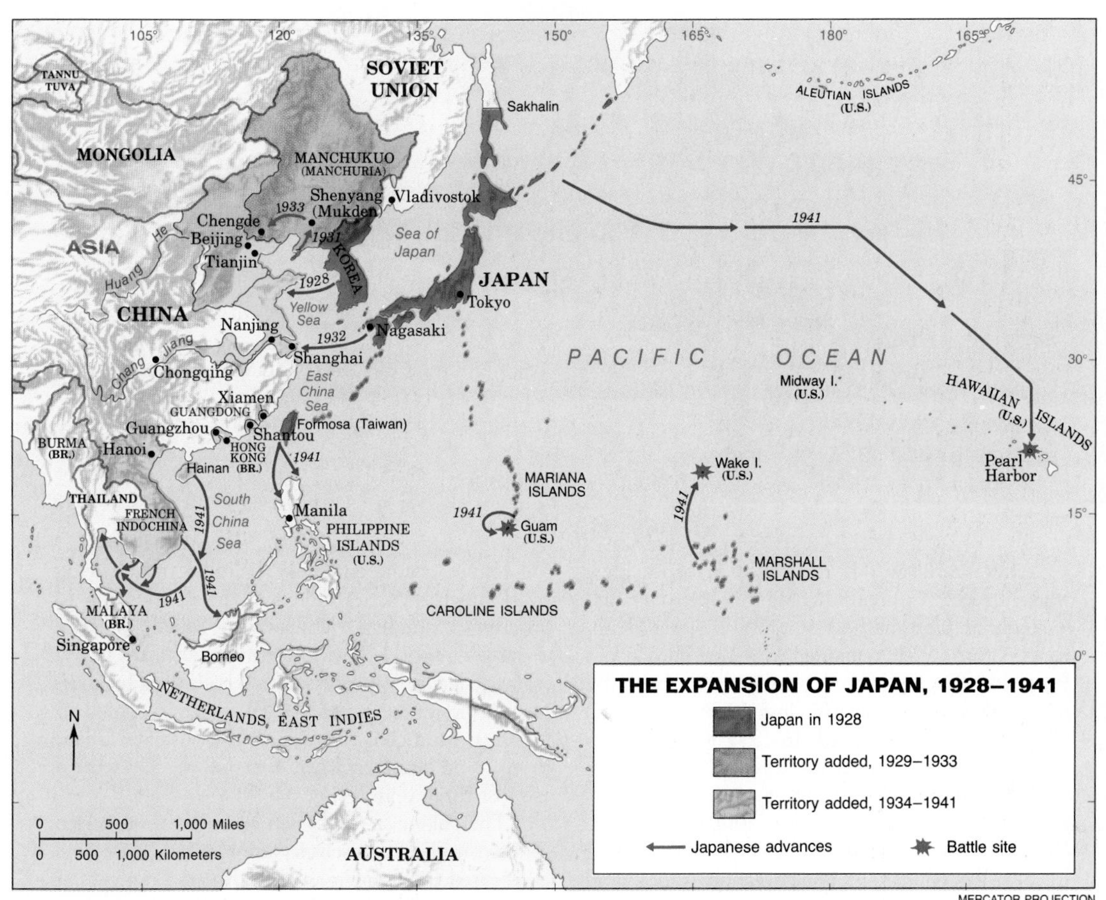

● ***Learning from Maps*** *Militarism was the driving force behind Japanese expansion. What groups of islands did the Japanese attack in 1941?*

Ethiopian capital, Addis Ababa (ad • uh SAB • uh • buh), in the spring of 1936. Mussolini declared Ethiopia a part of the Italian Empire and proclaimed the Italian king, Victor Emmanuel III, emperor of Ethiopia.

By this time the League of Nations' ineffectiveness had become apparent. During the summer of 1936, the League called off its sanctions on Italy. However, in 1937 Italy withdrew from the organization anyway. Thereafter, the League failed to command international respect. Its inability to prevent aggression, despite almost universal disapproval of Italy's actions, caused deep concern throughout the world. Meanwhile, Japan and Italy had learned that the democracies were apparently unwilling to go to war to prevent aggression.

Civil War in Spain

Economically Spain lagged far behind the rest of western Europe during the 1800s. Although some industry existed, the economy remained primarily agricultural. The nobility owned large estates that included much of the nation's land. The wealthy and powerful Catholic church controlled the educational system.

By the early 1900s, the Spanish government had become a constitutional monarchy. An elected parliament called the *Cortes* limited the king's power. Politically the country was unstable. Throughout the early 1900s, violent strikes, political assassinations, military plots, and separatist movements in the provinces plagued the nation.

713

1B, 5B, a1C, a4A

● Students might enjoy reading Ernest Hemingway's *A Farewell to Arms,* which deals with the civil war.

Learning from Pictures *This Spanish woman is assembling a fuselage in an airplane factory during the civil war. What country sent airplanes to help the Loyalists?* Soviet Union

After World War I, the chaos in Spain grew worse. In 1923 General Miguel Primo de Rivera led a revolt and established a military dictatorship. King Alfonso XIII remained as a figurehead, but Primo de Rivera, backed by the army, held the power. However, after Rivera lost the support of the army in 1930, he resigned. In 1931 King Alfonso abdicated, and Spain became a republic.

The Spanish Republic. Spain's new leaders planned to establish freedom of religion, separate church and state issues, and place the government in control of education. The government took land from the Catholic church and the nobility and gave it to landless peasants. The government barred members of the clergy from teaching in schools, and the Catholic church now had to pay its clergy. Workers received many benefits—shorter hours, better wages, the right to organize, and a voice in the management of business.

These sweeping reforms antagonized Spanish conservatives, who quickly organized a fascist party called the Falange (FAY • lanj)*. The Falange was determined to preserve the power of the army, the landowners, and the church, regardless of whom the voters might elect to office.

Nationalists versus Loyalists. In February 1936 a Popular Front government that included Socialists and Communists won a major election. The Spanish Popular Front, like the Popular Front in France, represented a coalition of left-wing working-class parties united in their opposition to fascism. Prominent rightists were jailed, and the Falange responded with terrorist acts. In July a Falange leader was assassinated. Following his murder, army uprisings, led by Falangists, erupted in Spanish Morocco, the Canary Islands, and Spain itself. The bitter civil war that followed lasted for almost three years.

The Falangist rebels, led by General Francisco Franco, called themselves Nationalists. Those who supported the republic were known as Loyalists, or Republicans. By the end of 1936, the Nationalists held most of northern and western Spain. The Loyalists controlled the east and southeast, most of the northern coastline, and the capital city of Madrid. ●

Foreign Assistance to Spain

The Spanish civil war soon became a small European war. Germany and Italy saw a fascist Spain as a part of their plan to surround France with unfriendly powers and threaten Great Britain. They sent fully equipped military units to bolster the Nationalist forces.

Sympathetic to the republican government, the Soviet Union sent planes, technicians, and military advisers. Soviet help to the Loyalists, however, was not nearly as extensive as that which Franco received from his fascist allies.

Volunteers from France, Great Britain, the United States, and other nations also clamored to

**Falange* is the Spanish word for "phalanx."

History Through the Arts

PAINTING

Guernica by Pablo Picasso

Although he lived in France, Pablo Picasso had been born in Spain and was keenly sympathetic to the Loyalist cause during the Spanish civil war. This painting expressed his outrage over the bombing of the town of Guernica, which had no strategic value. Using only blacks, grays, and whites, Picasso evoked anguish and horror with his distorted figures writhing in agony under a stark electric light. The painting was on tour in New York City in 1939 when World War II began. Picasso suggested that it stay in the United States until "the reestablishment of public liberties" in Spain. *Guernica* was returned to Spain in 1981 and was placed in the Prado museum in Madrid.

help the Spanish Republic. These antifascist volunteers became known as the International Brigade. The International Brigade, however, numbered only about 40,000, while Italy alone sent more than 50,000 trained troops to assist the Fascists.

The Spanish civil war brought into the open the seething struggle between fascism and socialism in Europe during the 1930s. It also became a testing ground for new weapons and tactics such as improved aircraft and strategic bombing missions.

The French and the British feared that the Spanish civil war might spread to the rest of Europe and involve them. In September 1936, at the suggestion of the French government, a nonintervention committee representing 27 nations was established. These nations unanimously agreed to a policy of nonintervention in Spain that included a blockade intended to halt the flow of volunteers and supplies to both sides. The blockade cut off most help to the Loyalists, but not German and Italian assistance to Franco. To Hitler and Mussolini, this constituted one more proof that Great Britain and France would do nothing to stop aggression unless it involved their own territory.

Spain Under Franco

By the spring of 1938, the Nationalist forces in Spain had grown strong enough for a large-scale offensive. They defeated the weakened Loyalist troops in March 1939, with the capture of Barcelona and Madrid. During the campaign to seize Madrid, one of Franco's generals announced that he had four columns—long narrow lines of troops—marching on the city and a fifth column within Madrid that would rise against the defenders at the appropriate time. The expression *fifth column* has come to mean traitors within a country who assist its enemies.

Franco then set up a fascist government modeled on Mussolini's dictatorship in Italy and became head of the state with unlimited power. He assumed the title *el Caudillo* (cow • DEE • yoh)—Spanish for "the leader." He was responsible, as one decree said, "only to God and history." Franco's political party, the Falange, was the only one permitted. Its national council, chosen by Franco, "advised" him on legislation.

The economic organization of Spain resembled that of fascist Italy, with syndicates, or corporations, organized according to occupations and economic activities. The government abolished free elections and most civil rights. Under Franco's regime, the old ruling groups—the army, the landowners, and the Roman Catholic church—continued to hold positions of power.

Although Spain had become a fascist dictatorship, Franco did not join the Rome-Berlin Axis

SECTION 1

Closure

Ask students to explain the ineffectiveness of the League of Nations in dealing with Japanese aggression in Asia and Italian aggression in Ethiopia. *(It had no power.)*

Review Answers

1. *Kellogg-Briand Pact:* treaty condemning war drafted by American secretary of state Frank B. Kellogg and French foreign minister Aristide Briand; ***Yuko Hamaguchi:*** Liberal prime minister of Japan fatally shot in 1930; ***Lytton Commission:*** group sent by the League of Nations to investigate the Japanese invasion of Manchuria; ***Falange:*** Spanish Fascist Party organized in the 1930s; ***Francisco Franco:*** leader of Falangist rebels, or Nationalists, in the Spanish civil war; ***Nationalist:*** Spaniard who favored the interests of the army, landowners, and the church; ***Loyalist:*** supported the republic and favored freedom of religion, free elections, separation of church and state, and secular education; ***International Brigade:*** antifascist volunteers from several foreign nations who fought on the Loyalist side

2. *Mukden:* south-central Manchuria; ***Manchukuo:*** Japanese-controlled Manchuria; ***Beijing:*** northern China proper; ***Chang Jiang Valley:*** eastern China; ***Somaliland:*** horn of Africa; ***Ethiopia:*** south of Egypt

5B, 5G, a1C, a4A, a4G,
a4H, a4L

3. The League of Nations sent the Lytton Commission to investigate. It voted to adopt the commission's suggestion to restore Manchuria to China. Japan defied the League, withdrew its membership and continued its aggression. When Italy invaded Ethiopia, the League's effort to arbitrate had no effect. It then applied economic sanctions, which were largely ignored and soon called off. Mussolini withdrew from the League. In both cases, the League proved helpless to stop the aggressors.
4. The Nationalists favored the army, landowners, and the church. The Loyalists supported the republic and favored freedom of religion, free elections, separation of church and state, and secular education. They distributed land and granted workers benefits.
5. **(a)** Great Britain and France established a nonintervention committee representing 27 nations. They set up a blockade that stopped most aid to the Loyalists but not German and Italian aid to Franco. **(b)** Germany and Italy felt this was proof that Great Britain and France would not stop aggression unless it involved their own territory.

SECTION 2

Focus/Motivation
Have students anticipate the acts of aggression to be discussed in this section by asking the following questions: Look at the map on page 717.

(see below). The civil war had devastated the country, and many years were to pass before economic recovery took place and hatred among Spaniards waned.

SECTION 1 REVIEW

1. **Identify** Kellogg-Briand Pact, Yuko Hamaguchi, Lytton Commission, Falange, Francisco Franco, Nationalist, Loyalist, International Brigade
2. **Locate** Mukden, Manchukuo, Beijing, Chang Jiang Valley, Somaliland, Ethiopia
3. **Evaluating Ideas** How did the League of Nations respond to the Japanese takeover of Manchuria and to Italy's invasion of Ethiopia?
4. **Contrasting Ideas** How did the political views of the Spanish Nationalists differ from those of the Loyalists?
5. **Summarizing Ideas** **(a)** What policy did Great Britain and France adopt regarding the Spanish civil war? **(b)** How did Germany and Italy view this policy?

2 Hitler's Aggressions in Europe Sparked World War II

As Germany grew stronger, Hitler's foreign policy became more aggressive. In 1933 he had taken Germany out of the League of Nations and announced his intention to rearm the country. In March 1936 German troops marched into the Rhineland, violating the Treaty of Versailles. In October 1936, following the outbreak of the Spanish civil war, Hitler and Mussolini formed a military alliance called the Rome-Berlin Axis and began referring to themselves as the Axis Powers.*

Shortly afterward, Japan and Germany pledged to work together to prevent the spread of Russian communism. The two countries signed an agreement called the Anti-Comintern Treaty, which Italy soon endorsed. Thus by the end of 1936, the nations that would eventually enter World War II as the Axis Powers—Germany, Italy, and Japan—had camouflaged their aggressive intentions under the pretense of resisting communism. Hitler became convinced that he could do as he pleased, and for a time he seemed right. The democratic nations had done very little to halt the spread of fascism in Ethiopia and Spain.

Annexing Austria

A Nazi party had been formed in Austria in the late 1920s. By the early 1930s, the extremely conservative Austrian government was doing little to resist Nazi inroads. By 1938 threats from both Hitler and Mussolini forced the Austrian government to include Nazi members in its cabinet.

When the Austrian chancellor offered to take a vote of the Austrian people on the question of *Anschluss* (union) with Germany, Hitler refused to permit it. The chancellor resigned, and a German army marched into Austria unopposed. In March 1938 Hitler proclaimed Austria a part of the Third Reich. The League of Nations took no action. Great Britain and France sent protests to Hitler, which he ignored. Once again, no stronger steps were taken. The democracies seemed to prefer inaction to the danger of war.

The addition of Austria enlarged Germany's population, territory, and resources. It also increased Hitler's influence in Europe. Strategically, Germany had now penetrated the heart of central Europe and reached a common border with its ally, Italy. A glance at the map on page 717 will show what the annexation of Austria did to Czechoslovakia, which Hitler had designated as the next objective in his expansion program. Germany now almost completely encircled the Czech republic. Nazi propaganda, however, claimed that Czechoslovakia had become "a dagger aimed at the heart of Germany."

Czechoslovakia and the Sudeten Crisis

Around the western rim of Czechoslovakia, in a region known as the Sudetenland (soo • DAYT • uhn • land), lived more than 3 million Germans. This territory, once part of the huge Hapsburg Empire, had been included in Czechoslovakia after World War I. A chain of mountains, which gave the new state a natural and defensible frontier, separated the Sudetenland from Germany and Austria. Czechoslovakia had fortified these mountains heavily. Now they had become a defensive line—second in importance in Europe only to France's Maginot Line.

*Mussolini originated the term *Axis Powers.* He claimed that an imaginary line drawn from Rome to Berlin formed the "axis" on which the world would turn from that time forward.

● ***Martial law*** **is military law applied in an occupied territory. It can also be invoked by a government during an emergency when civilian law enforcement agencies are unable to maintain public safety.**

Learning from Maps *Axis aggression was directed at poorly defended eastern Europe and Africa. What country in Africa did the Axis Powers invade?* **Ethiopia**

The Czech government tried to protect the rights of the Sudeten Germans. It allowed them to use the German language in their schools and to be represented fairly, according to population, in the parliament, the civil service, and the army. Still, many Sudeten Germans wanted union with Germany, and with the Nazi victory in Germany, a strong Nazi party grew in the Sudetenland.

After Germany's annexation of Austria, Sudeten Nazis demanded a completely self-governing Sudetenland. Hitler took up their cause, ranting against the Czech "oppression" of Germans. Nazi propagandists spread many fictitious stories of Czech discrimination and atrocities against the Sudetens. Riots broke out, and in September 1938 the situation became so critical that the Czech government placed the country under martial law. ●

Hitler said that the German army would invade the Sudetenland to "protect" Germany's "Sudetenland brothers." He also decreed that Germany

What nation do you think Hitler would attempt to take over first? Why? *(Answers will vary. Lead students to understand that traditional links to Austria would make it a logical choice.)* How would he go about the takeover? *(Students should see that political pressure would be preferable to armed attack.)* What sort of political pressure would be most effective? *(claims of Germany's supposed right to take over the country)* What other countries would you expect Hitler to seek? *(places with German-speaking populations, such as the Sudetenland and Danzig, then weak non-German lands)*

Presentation
Constructing a Time Line (Average/Group)
Develop with the class a time line of events preceding World War II. Completed time lines should include the following events: Germany occupies the Rhineland, March 1936; Spanish civil war begins, July 1936; Berlin Olympics, July 1936; *Anschluss* with Austria, March 1938; Germany annexes the Sudetenland, September 1938; Germany annexes Czechoslovakia and Memel, March 1939; Mussolini invades Albania, April 1939; Nazi-Soviet nonaggression pact signed, August 1939; Hitler attacks Poland, September 1939.

1B, 5B, 5G, a1B, a1C, a1D

● Discussion topic: The role of appeasement as it pertains to preventing war

would annex the Sudetenland. This was a disaster for Czechoslovakia. The loss of its heavily fortified mountain region would leave the country defenseless against Germany. When Germany sent troops to the frontier, the world waited tensely to see what action Czechoslovakia's allies would take.

The Czechs had defensive alliances with both France and the Soviet Union. The Soviet alliance provided that the Soviet Union would assist the Czechs only on the condition that France did likewise. France turned to Great Britain for support. Great Britain, however, urged France to be patient and advised the Czechs to make every possible concession to avoid war. The Czech government then granted increased independence for the Sudetens.

Still dissatisfied, Hitler began to increase Germany's military preparations. On September 22, 1938, he demanded that the Sudetenland be turned over to Germany. If it were not, he said, he would invade it and take it by force.

Learning from Pictures *German soldiers enter Prague as residents of the city stand somberly on the sidewalks.*

Appeasement at Munich

As tensions mounted in Europe, Hitler unexpectedly suggested a conference. It would be attended by Hitler, Mussolini, British Prime Minister Neville Chamberlain, and Edouard Daladier (duh • LAHD • ee • aye), the premier of France. The conference would begin on September 29 in Munich, and the participants would attempt to settle the Czech problem peaceably. Conspicuously absent from the meeting were the Soviet Union, which, along with France, had pledged to defend Czechoslovakia, and a representative of Czechoslovakia itself. The Soviet Union was not invited because Hitler wanted to isolate it from the West.

At Munich, Chamberlain and Daladier tried to avoid war at any cost. They accepted Hitler's demand that the Sudetenland be annexed to Germany. The policy they followed—attempting to preserve peace by yielding to the demands of the aggressor—is known as **appeasement.** Upon his return to London, Chamberlain triumphantly addressed a cheering crowd and announced, "I believe it is peace for our time."

Soon after the Munich Conference, France announced that it would neither honor its alliance with Czechoslovakia nor provide any assistance. Germany began to occupy the Sudetenland. The small country of Czechoslovakia, deserted by its allies, was now rendered defenseless. Yet another step had been taken toward the rule of force and chaos in international affairs. ●

In speaking of the Sudetenland, Hitler said, "This is the last territorial claim I shall make in Europe." In March 1939, however, Hitler sent his troops throughout the Czech area of Czechoslovakia and made it a German protectorate. He then declared the remainder of the country an independent state called Slovakia, which he soon seized.

Czechoslovakia had been the last democracy in Central Europe as well as the most prosperous of the nations formed after World War I. Yet within six months, this independent republic was erased completely from the map of Europe. As a result the League of Nations was compelled to cross still another name off its list of members. Now the League's helplessness could no longer be remedied. In the meantime the political situation in Europe headed rapidly toward chaos.

Unchecked Fascist Aggression

Not satisfied with Czechoslovakia, Hitler next moved toward Lithuania. Hitler's quarrel with that nation involved the former East Prussian port city of Memel (see map, page 717). Germany had

718

● time and a piece of Poland

surrendered Memel to the Allies under the Versailles Treaty. In 1923 Lithuania took the city.

After Hitler came to power, a Nazi party made up of the Germans in Memel demanded that Germany annex the city. Hitler echoed these demands. By March 1939 Lithuania could no longer withstand the pressure and ceded Memel and adjacent territory to Germany.

Still another nation lost its independence in the spring of 1939. Mussolini, once a model for other dictators, had by now become Hitler's imitator. In April 1939 Mussolini invaded Albania, on the east coast of the Adriatic Sea (see map, page 717). The Italians took the country in only a few days. King Zog and Queen Geraldine fled the country, and the king of Italy, who had recently become emperor of Ethiopia, gained an additional title—king of Albania.

Preparations for War

After Hitler took Czechoslovakia, British and French leaders could no longer maintain their illusions about the peaceful intentions of the fascist dictators. Britain and France therefore began to prepare for war. In France the premier was given special powers to speed wartime preparations. In Great Britain, Neville Chamberlain rushed a huge armaments program and a draft law through Parliament. France already had a defensive alliance with Poland. Great Britain announced that it, too, would help Poland if Germany attacked.

France also had a nonaggression treaty with the Soviet Union. Now Great Britain and France approached the Soviet leader, Joseph Stalin, suggesting a mutual alliance against Germany. Even though the Soviet Union had joined the League of Nations, while Japan, Germany, and Italy had dropped out, Soviet leaders remained suspicious of the Western democracies. Until this time, the Western nations—fearful of communism—had excluded the Soviet Union from all major decisions affecting Europe and the rest of the world. The Soviet leaders in turn feared that the Western powers would welcome a chance to turn Hitler loose on them.

The Soviets insisted that any mutual assistance pact they might sign with Great Britain and France guarantee the independence of Poland, Finland, and the Baltic countries of Estonia, Latvia, and Lithuania. The Soviets also wanted a military alliance with all of these countries to ensure immediate response in the event of a German attack. This suggestion brought instant protests from the nations involved. All but Lithuania had common borders with the Soviet Union. A military agreement would mean that, in case of a German attack, Soviet armies would have the right to move into their countries to meet the Germans. The negotiations dragged on, resulting in a stalemate.

The Nazi-Soviet Pact

At the same time Stalin was negotiating with Great Britain and France, he was carrying on secret negotiations with Germany. In August 1939 the Western democracies received a tremendous shock. Hitler proudly announced a German-Soviet nonaggression treaty. Soviet leaders in Moscow soon confirmed the announcement.

The reasons for such an agreement between openly declared enemies were not immediately apparent. However, many historians believe that neither the Germans nor the Soviets expected the treaty to be a lasting one. Both Hitler and Stalin may simply have been playing for time. Hitler wanted to assure himself of Soviet neutrality to prevent the outbreak of a two-front war while he dealt

Learning from Pictures *This cartoon satirizes Stalin's pact with Hitler. What did Stalin gain from the pact?* ●

SECTION 2

Closure
Have students discuss the problem unchecked Fascist aggression caused in Europe and compare it to current concern regarding the spread of communism.

Review Answers
1. ***appeasement:*** yielding to the demands of an aggressor in the hope of preserving peace
2. ***Axis Powers:*** Germany, Italy, and Japan; ***Anti-Comintern Treaty:*** pact signed by Japan, Germany and Italy by which they agreed to work together to prevent the spread of Soviet communism; ***Neville Chamberlain:*** British prime minister who attended the Munich Conference; ***Edouard Daladier:*** premier of France who attended the Munich Conference; ***Munich Conference:*** conference in Munich among Hitler, Mussolini, Chamberlain and Daladier that resulted in Chamberlain's policy of appeasement; ***Nazi-Soviet Pact:*** nonaggression treaty between Germany and the Soviet Union
3. ***Sudetenland:*** western rim of Czechoslovakia; ***Munich:*** city in southern Germany; ***Memel:*** port in Lithuania; ***Albania:*** eastern coast of Adriatic; ***Polish Corridor:*** linked Danzig to Poland; ***Danzig:*** between East Prussia and Germany
4. Hitler's annexation of Austria enlarged German population, territory, and resources; increased Hitler's

719

influence in Europe; extended German territory as far as the border of its ally, Italy; and almost completely surrounded the nation of Czechoslovakia.
5. In Czechoslovakia a Nazi Party was formed among the Sudeten German minority. Eventually this minority demanded complete self-government, which Hitler supported with claims of Czech "oppression" and atrocities. When riots broke out and the Sudeten Nazi leader fled to Germany, Hitler sent troops to the frontier. At the Munich Conference, Great Britain and France appeased Hitler by allowing Germany to annex the Sudetenland. Hitler later sent his troops into the Czech area of Czechoslovakia and made it a protectorate. He then declared the remainder of the country an independent state called Slovakia, which he soon seized.
6. In the summer of 1939 the French premier was given special powers to speed wartime preparations. Great Britain's Parliament rushed through an armaments program and a draft law. France already had a defensive alliance with Poland, and Great Britain announced that it too would aid Poland if it was attacked. Great Britain and France tried but failed to form a mutual defensive alliance with Russia.
7. (a) The pact was a nonaggression treaty between Germany and the Soviet Union.
(b) Many historians believe

with France and Great Britain. Stalin apparently hoped that Hitler would find himself bogged down in the West. This would give the Soviet Union adequate time to prepare for its eventual, inevitable encounter with Germany.

Publicly the Nazi-Soviet Pact pledged that Germany and the Soviet Union would never attack each other. Each would remain neutral if the other became involved in war. Secretly, however, the two dictators agreed to divide eastern Europe into spheres of influence. Germany was to take western Poland. The Soviet Union was to have a free hand in the Baltic countries, in eastern Poland, and in the province of Bessarabia, which it had lost to Romania in 1918.

Little doubt existed as to the meaning of the pact. The Western nations had lost a possible ally in the East, and Germany had secured a pledge of the Soviet Union's neutrality. It was a tremendous military advantage, which Hitler was quick to use.

Danzig and the Polish Corridor

The crisis that finally touched off World War II began in Poland. Hitler's dispute with that country involved the Polish Corridor, the strip of territory cut through Germany to allow Poland access to the seaport of Danzig (see map, page 717). Danzig, a free city protected by the League of Nations, was a port for both Germany and Poland.

Because Danzig had a large German population, Hitler claimed that the city had been "torn from the fatherland." He attacked the commissioner appointed by the League as a "foreigner."

A strong Nazi party, encouraged by propaganda and financial help from Berlin, developed in Danzig. By 1937 it controlled the city government. It took actions and issued demands that made relations with Poland increasingly difficult. The League commissioner was powerless to do anything.

After securing Austria and Czechoslovakia, Hitler intensified his campaign against Poland. The Nazis demanded the return of Danzig to the fatherland. A propaganda campaign claimed Polish mistreatment of the Germans in the Polish Corridor. Within a week after signing the nonaggression pact with the Soviet Union, Hitler demanded a "German Solution" to the "Polish Question": Danzig must be returned to Germany, and the Germans must be allowed to occupy a strip running through the Corridor.

On the morning of September 1, 1939, Hitler declared the annexation of Danzig to the Reich. At the same time, without warning, his air force made a massive attack on Poland. Nazi troops, led by tank columns, penetrated the border. Two days later Great Britain and France decided that they would not tolerate any further Nazi aggression. They kept their promises to Poland and declared war on Germany. Within 48 hours the unannounced attack on Poland had become the beginning of World War II.

SECTION 2 REVIEW

1. **Define** appeasement
2. **Identify** Axis Powers, Anti-Comintern Treaty, Neville Chamberlain, Edouard Daladier, Munich Conference, Nazi-Soviet Pact
3. **Locate** Sudetenland, Munich, Memel, Albania, Polish Corridor, Danzig
4. **Evaluating Ideas** How did Hitler's annexation of Austria benefit Germany?
5. **Sequencing Ideas** Describe the steps by which Hitler took over Czechoslovakia.
6. **Understanding Ideas** How did France and Great Britain prepare for war in 1939?
7. **Summarizing Ideas** **(a)** What was the significance of the Nazi-Soviet Pact? **(b)** What may have been Hitler's and Stalin's reasons for signing it?

3 The Axis Made Significant Gains

Hitler's invasion of Poland introduced the world to a new kind of warfare. The German attack was called a **blitzkrieg**—German for a "lightning war" conducted with great speed and force. Dive bombers screamed down from the skies, dropping explosives on cities below. Panzer* units—tanks and armored trucks—advanced swiftly. On September 27, 1939, after a brief but devastating war, the Poles surrendered to Hitler.

The "Phony" War

While Germany launched its attack on Poland, France moved its army up to the Maginot Line, the

*Panzer is from the German word for armor.

● The British air force gained momentary control of the sky over Dunkirk.

chain of fortifications guarding France's eastern frontier. British forces crossed the English Channel and landed on the northern coast of France. The British navy blockaded Germany's ports. The Germans massed troops behind the Siegfried Line, the system of fortifications they had built in the Rhineland. Although German submarines had begun to sink merchant ships—both enemy and neutral—there was little action on the western front. Despite the escalation of mobilization and arms production, newspapers began to speak of the "phony" war in western Europe. Many people referred to the "phony" war as a "sitzkrieg," or sitting war, instead of a blitzkrieg. However, they still hoped that an all-out war could be avoided.

As the Germans marched into Poland, the Soviet army massed on the Soviet-Polish border. Then, in accordance with the secret provisions of the Nazi-Soviet Pact, the Soviets moved into eastern Poland. Once again, Poland disappeared from the map of Europe. The Soviets also seized control of Estonia, Latvia, and Lithuania.

On November 30, 1939, the Soviet Union attacked Finland. The Finns appealed to the League of Nations, which expelled the Soviet Union for its aggression against a fellow member nation. Although the Finns fought bravely for three months, their resistance crumbled in March 1940.

Scandinavia and the Low Countries

On April 9, 1940, the "phony" war ended with a sudden German invasion of Denmark and Norway. Hitler had prepared the way in these Scandinavian countries by sending Germans there as workers. These Germans were to secure the services of native **collaborators,** people who were willing to assist their country's enemies. In a single day, German troops seized several of Norway's strategic North Sea ports. Both Denmark and Norway fell under German control.

The reasons for Hitler's invasion of these countries soon became clear. By seizing them, Germany had secured an outlet to the Atlantic. Thus Hitler made certain that his country's navy would not be bottled up in the Baltic Sea as it had in World War I. The long, irregular Scandinavian coastline gave Germany excellent submarine bases. The terrain also provided many good sites for airfields. Thus sea lanes to France and Great Britain were put in grave danger.

The British soon realized that Hitler posed an immediate threat to their safety. Neville Chamberlain, who symbolized the policy of appeasement, was forced to resign as prime minister in May 1940. He was succeeded by Winston Churchill, one of the few prominent politicians in the 1930s to attack appeasement and to warn against the Nazi menace.

Hitler, meanwhile, continued to attack. He intended to take as much territory as possible before his opponents could mount an offensive against him. On May 10, 1940, German armored units invaded the Low Countries—the Netherlands, Belgium, and Luxembourg. Luxembourg fell in one day, the Netherlands in five. When the Dutch city of Rotterdam resisted the German army, Hitler ordered his air force to attack it. Even while a surrender was being negotiated, Nazi bombers leveled the heart of the city. At the end of May, Belgium also surrendered.

Hitler's forces were now in a position to outflank France's Maginot Line. The German panzers drove westward toward the English Channel. At Dunkirk, a seaport in northern France, they cut off the British, Belgian, and French troops from the major French force to the south. Outnumbered and with no room to maneuver, the encircled Allied troops withdrew.

Evacuation of Dunkirk. At this point, the British air force was able to gain momentary

Learning from Pictures *The defeated Allies evacuate the beach at Dunkirk. What allowed the evacuation to succeed?* ●

both leaders were playing for time. Hitler wanted time to deal with Great Britain and France while the Soviets remained neutral. Stalin wanted time to prepare for a war with Germany, which he regarded as inevitable.

SECTION 3

Focus/Motivation

Have students read the excerpts from Winston Churchill's speeches on pages 722, 723, and 724. Ask: What makes these quotations inspirational? *(They appeal to national pride.)* How did FDR, Hitler and Mussolini use speeches and the radio to appeal to their particular audiences? Why was the radio such an important medium during the war? How could the individual leader use the radio to generate nationalism and resistance to the enemy or to promote propaganda against the ideas promoted by the enemy? *(The radio allowed leaders to reach a wide audience and was much more personal than enemy propaganda.)*

Now discuss how the excerpts met the British need for encouragement and patriotism during the period between the fall of France and the entry of the United States into World War II.

721

5B, 5G, a1C

Presentation Writing a Letter (Average/Group)
Have students write letters from a British student to an American student describing his or her reactions to Dunkirk and the Battle of Britain. Use these letters as the basis of a class discussion on British resistance against the Nazis.

control of the air to defend the trapped forces at Dunkirk from bombing attacks. Every available ship and boat in England, including fishing craft and rowboats, was ordered to Dunkirk. Between May 27 and June 4, some 340,000 men were safely transported across the channel to England.

For unknown reasons, Hitler decided not to attack the retreating allies. For three days he held back his tanks—a decision that later would be considered a costly Axis mistake because it allowed Britain to rally. Hitler's panzer leaders bombarded their superior officers with protests but received only a message that holding the tanks back was "the Führer's personal order."

Although the evacuation of Dunkirk was a military defeat for the Allies, the success of the astounding rescue operation helped raise British morale considerably. On June 4 Prime Minister Churchill addressed the British people in one of his most stirring speeches. His forceful and engaging voice boomed over the airwaves:

> "We shall go on to the end. We shall fight in France, we shall fight in the seas and oceans, we shall fight with growing confidence and growing strength in the air, we shall defend our Island, whatever the cost may be. We shall fight on the beaches, we shall fight on the landing-grounds, we shall fight in the fields and in the streets, we shall fight in the hills; we shall never surrender; and even if, which I do not for a moment believe, this island or a large part of it were subjugated and starving, then our Empire beyond the seas, armed and guarded by the British Fleet, would carry on the struggle, until, in God's time, the New World, with all its power and might, steps forth to the rescue and the liberation of the Old."

The Fall of France

After the evacuation of Dunkirk, the French were left to fight alone on the European continent. The Maginot Line was useless. Having taken Belgium, the Germans were in a position to attack France from the north, where few fortifications existed.

Germany began its offensive against France early in June 1940. The French fought a desperate, losing battle. Their army was neither trained nor equipped for this new kind of war. Northern France was a scene of utter confusion. Civilians, carrying whatever possessions they could save, blocked roads in their attempts to flee southward. German planes bombed and machine-gunned the helpless refugees, causing panic and disorder.

Mussolini, taking advantage of France's weakness, declared war on France and Great Britain on June 10, and Italian forces invaded southern France. On June 14 the Germans entered Paris, and French armed resistance collapsed. Rather than surrender, the French cabinet resigned.

Some of the French leaders, however, were willing to surrender. The aged Marshal Philippe Pétain (pay • TAN), a hero of World War I, formed a government and assumed dictatorial powers. Late in June Hitler forced the Pétain government to sign an armistice with Germany and Italy. Ironically, it was signed in the same railroad car where the Germans had signed the armistice to end World War I in November 1918.

The terms of the armistice were severe. German troops were to occupy northern France, including Paris, and a strip of territory along the Atlantic coast southward to Spain. France had to pay the costs of this occupation. The French navy was to be disarmed and confined to French ports. Pétain's government moved to the city of Vichy (VISH • shee), in the south. Thus France was divided into Occupied France, administered by the Germans, and Vichy France, which collaborated with the Germans. The Vichy government also controlled most French possessions in North Africa and the Middle East. This government became another symbol of appeasement and surrender to fascism.

The French resistance. Some of the French who wanted to continue to fight against Germany escaped to Africa or to England. Under the leadership of General Charles de Gaulle (duh GOHL), they formed the Free French government, with its headquarters in London.

Within France itself an underground movement, the resistance, flourished. Its members worked secretly to oppose the German occupation forces. Similar resistance movements developed in most of the other countries occupied by Germany. Members of some of these resistance groups were called *maquis* (mah • KEE)—a French term for scrubby undergrowth, common in the areas where resistance fighters hid. To cripple the Germans, the

● Students might enjoy viewing the film *Hope and Glory,* which describes the life of a London family during the war.

Learning from Pictures *Members of the French resistance, shown here after the liberation of Paris, helped Allied forces undermine German authority in occupied France.*

maquis engaged in sabotage. They blew up bridges, wrecked trains, and cut telephone and telegraph lines.

● The Battle of Britain

After France fell, French generals predicted that Great Britain, which they considered a weaker country, would "have her neck wrung like a chicken's in three weeks." (Churchill later commented: "Some chicken! Some neck!")

Hitler began scattered bombing raids on Great Britain, gradually increasing them in intensity. He then offered to negotiate a peace settlement, but the feisty British leaders rebuffed him.

At the end of June 1940, Churchill braced the British people for the treacherous battle that he was certain would soon come:

> "Hitler knows that he will have to break us in this island or lose the war. If we can stand up to him, all Europe may be free and the life of the world may move forward into broad, sunlit uplands. But if we fail, then the whole world, including the United States, including all that we have known and cared for, will sink into the abyss of a new Dark Age. . . . Let us therefore brace ourselves of our duties, and so bear ourselves that, if the British Empire and its Commonwealth last for a thousand years, men will say, 'This was their finest hour.'"

Hitler ordered his air force, the *Luftwaffe* (LOOFT • wahf • uh), to soften Great Britain for invasion. He shifted the Luftwaffe squadrons to airfields in occupied France and Belgium near England. Germany stepped up its devastating air attacks on Great Britain, striking civilian population centers, railroads, and industrial targets. The period of the heaviest attacks, from August through November 1940, is known as the Battle of Britain.

German bombers blasted British cities with explosives and firebombs. The Luftwaffe bombed London continually during September and October. In November the city of Coventry burned almost to the ground. The Germans wanted to lower morale and destroy the people's will to fight, but the undaunted British resolutely dug out of the ruins and fought on. Essential to their resistance was the highly successful defense by fighter planes of the Royal Air Force—the R.A.F.

British planes, though fewer in number, were of better quality than the German planes. Daring and superbly trained British pilots courageously flew combat missions day after day, night after night.

723

1C, 5B, a1B, a1C, a4A, a4D, a4E, a4F, a4G, a4I, a4K

READ
WRITE
INTERPRET
CONNECT
THINK

BUILDING HISTORY STUDY SKILLS

Reading About History: Understanding a Biographical Account

History is more than the factual study of events and the analysis of important issues. People, and the decisions they make, have a significant impact on history. One way to understand the role of people from a historical perspective is to study biographical accounts—secondary sources that are based on primary sources. Biographical accounts help to establish a person's place and significance in regard to a historical event.

How to Understand a Biographical Account

To understand a biographical account, follow these steps.

1. Explain the historical context of the account. For example, what events led up to the events of the person's life?
2. List the major events of the person's life.
3. Identify the person's beliefs.
4. Explain the person's responses to historical events.
5. Identify how other people have viewed the person.
6. Assess the historical significance of the individual. For example, what role did he or she play in the causes or the effects of the event?

Developing the Skill

Prime Minister Winston Churchill's leadership abilities in government and his influence as the author of books such as *The Second World War* and *A History of the English-speaking Peoples* affected not only British history, but world history as well.

The following excerpt from the prime minister's speech to the House of Commons in May 1940 and the wartime conferences listed below illustrate Churchill's place in world history. What information do the excerpt and the list suggest about Churchill's ideas and actions? How did other people view him?

> "I have nothing to offer . . . but blood, toil, tears, and sweat. You ask, what is our policy? I will say: it is to wage war by sea, land and air, with all our might and with all the strength that God can give us; to wage war against a monstrous tyranny, never surpassed in the dark, lamentable catalogue of human crime. That is our policy.
>
> You ask, what is our aim? I answer in one word. It is *victory:* victory at all costs, victory in spite of all terror, victory however long and hard the road may be, for without victory there is no survival."

The following list contains several of the wartime conferences Churchill attended during World War II.

- August 1941: Churchill and Roosevelt meet on a battleship off the coast of Newfoundland to issue the Atlantic Charter on postwar aims.
- December 1941: Churchill and Roosevelt meet in Washington, D.C., to confirm that the defeat of Germany will take precedence over the defeat of Japan.
- August 1942: Churchill confers with Stalin in Moscow and informs the Soviet leader that there can be no second front in Europe in 1942.
- August 1943: Churchill and Roosevelt meet in Quebec to confirm the Allied landings at Normandy and agree to landings in southern France.
- September 1944: Churchill and Roosevelt meet in Quebec to discuss victory plans.
- October 1944: Churchill and Stalin meet in Moscow to discuss eastern Europe's future.
- July-August 1945: Churchill, Truman, and Stalin meet at Potsdam to hammer out peace treaties.

Churchill became prime minister at a moment of disaster. The German armies occupied Holland, the Belgian king surrendered, and the French army was driven back to Paris. Although the outlook for Europe appeared dim, the inspiring words of Churchill's "blood, sweat, and tears" speech rallied the British people and encouraged them to persevere. His unwavering leadership at the wartime conferences contributed to the Allied victory, thus impacting world history.

Practicing the skill. Find excerpts from two of Roosevelt's speeches to Americans during World War II. How do these excerpts help you to determine Roosevelt's significance in world history?

To apply this skill, see Applying History Study Skills on page 739.

Winston Churchill amidst bombing damage

724

● One of the most vocal isolationists was Charles Lindbergh—the first person to make a solo flight across the Atlantic Ocean.

British planes also had the advantage of radar, a new electronic tracking device that could detect the number, speed, and direction of enemy aircraft or ships, even in darkness, fog, or clouds.

The R.A.F. challenged German control of the air and prevented German invasion across the channel. Of these British fighter pilots, Churchill said, "Never in the field of human conflict was so much owed by so many to so few."

The Germans continued their night bombing raids for almost two years. At the same time, British bombers made increasingly heavy raids on German cities. By the middle of 1941, air warfare had reached a stalemate. However, because of Germany's effective blockade of British shipping from European ports, there was a chance that Great Britain could be starved into surrendering. This might have happened had it not been for the United States.

United States Involvement

In the Neutrality Act of 1937, the United States expressed its determination to remain neutral in future wars. This legislation forbade Americans to sell war equipment to belligerent nations, prohibited loans to belligerents, prohibited Americans from sailing on ships of belligerents, and restricted the entry of American ships into war zones.

When war in Europe broke out in 1939, public opinion in the United States was divided. Many people believed that Nazi Germany threatened not only Europe but civilization itself. Other people believed that Europe's wars were of no concern to the United States. These **isolationists,** as they were called, had risen to power at the end of World War I, when they had succeeded in keeping the United States out of the League of Nations. Now, however, their power faded as the fear of a Nazi ● conquest of the world increased.

As the war progressed, the United States gradually became more involved. In 1939 a revised Neutrality Act allowed American firms to sell munitions to belligerent nations, but only on a cash-and-carry basis. In spite of German submarine attacks, the British still controlled the sea routes between the United States and Great Britain. Thus, in effect, this law permitted the sale of arms only to Great Britain.

After the disaster at Dunkirk and the fall of France, Americans' sympathies for the British increased. In September 1940 President Franklin D. Roosevelt, by executive agreement, transferred 50 old American naval destroyers to Great Britain. In exchange, Great Britain gave the United States long-term leases on British naval and air bases in Newfoundland, the British West Indies, and British Guiana. In that same month, Congress passed the first national draft law ever adopted by the United States during peacetime.

Early in 1941 Churchill appealed to the United States: "Give us the tools, and we will finish the job." In March, Congress passed the Lend-Lease Act, authorizing the president to supply war materials to Great Britain on credit. Now the direction of America's involvement became clear.

The Atlantic Charter

Because they wanted to avoid the criticism that the secret treaties of World War I had raised, President Roosevelt and Prime Minister Churchill announced the war aims of the two democracies. In August 1941 they met on board a British battleship off the coast of Newfoundland and drew up a statement that became known as the Atlantic Charter.

Among its provisions and in the spirit of Wilson's Fourteen Points, the charter stated that Britain and the United States: (1) sought no territorial gain, (2) would allow no territorial changes without the consent of the people concerned, (3) respected the right of all people to choose their own form of government, (4) believed that all nations should have equal rights to trade and to raw materials, (5) wanted nations to cooperate on economic matters to ensure everyone a decent standard of living, (6) believed people everywhere should have the right to security and "freedom from want and fear," (7) believed freedom of the seas should be guaranteed, and (8) believed that nations must abolish the use of force and establish a "system of general security," implying the formation of an international organization.

By the fall of 1941, the United States Navy was waging an undeclared war on German submarines. The nation had moved far away from its neutrality of 1937. The only remaining restrictions prohibited American merchant ships from being armed or entering war zones. In November 1941 Congress abolished even these restrictions. The United States, as a nonbelligerent ally, now gave the British "all aid short of war."

725

5B, a1C, a4A, a4G, a4H, a4K, a4L

● Research topic: The role that Rommel played in the plot to assassinate Hitler

SECTION 3

Closure

Have students explain why Danzig and the Polish Corridor sparked World War II. *(Hitler used them as an excuse to invade Poland.)*

Review Answers

1. ***blitzkrieg:*** German "lightning war" involving air attacks, artillery bombardment and armored raids; ***collaborator:*** person who aided his or her country's enemies; ***isolationist:*** American who believed the U.S. should not become involved in Europe's wars
2. ***"phony" war:*** period after Hitler's invasion of Poland when there was practically no action on the Western front; ***Winston Churchill:*** British prime minister who succeeded Neville Chamberlain; ***Philippe Pétain:*** French World War I hero who formed the government that signed an armistice with Hitler and Mussolini; ***Charles de Gaulle:*** French general who formed Free French government in London; ***maquis:*** nickname for the French resistance; ***Battle of Britain:*** peak period of Hitler's air attacks on England, from August through November 1940; ***Luftwaffe:*** Nazi air force; ***Neutrality Act of 1937:*** U.S. expressed determination to remain neutral in future wars; ***Lend-Lease Act:*** act authorizing the U.S. president to supply war materials to Great Britain on credit; ***Franklin D. Roosevelt:*** president of U.S. in

SECTION 3 REVIEW

1. **Define** blitzkrieg, collaborator, isolationist
2. **Identify** "phony" war, Winston Churchill, Philippe Pétain, Charles de Gaulle, maquis, Battle of Britain, Luftwaffe, Neutrality Act of 1937, Franklin D. Roosevelt, Lend-Lease Act, Atlantic Charter
3. **Locate** Maginot Line, Siegfried Line, Rotterdam, Dunkirk, Occupied France, Vichy France, Coventry
4. **Summarizing Ideas** What advantages did Germany gain by seizing Norway and Denmark?
5. **Evaluating Ideas** Why was the Maginot Line useless in June 1940?
6. **Sequencing Ideas.** Describe the progression of United States involvement in World War II, from the Neutrality Act of 1937 to giving Great Britain "all assistance short of war."

4 The Soviet Union and the United States Entered the War

In the fall of 1940, Germany held almost all of western Europe. It controlled the Atlantic coastline from the tip of Norway to Spain, and its submarines were allowed to use Spanish ports. Spain did not join in the fighting, but neither was it neutral. Franco called his country a "nonneutral nonbelligerent." Germany and Italy also controlled much of the western Mediterranean coastline, an important advantage for their side.

Great Britain still held Gibraltar, on the southern coast of Spain; the islands of Malta and Cyprus, in the Mediterranean; and Alexandria, in Egypt. British troops were stationed in Palestine and in Egypt, protecting the Suez Canal. In September the Japanese government joined the Rome-Berlin Axis as an ally of Hitler and Mussolini.

Eastern Europe and the Mediterranean

Mussolini, hoping to build a Mediterranean empire for Italy, sent his troops into Egypt and Greece in the fall of 1940. The decision proved to be unwise. The Greeks routed the invading Italian army, and the British stopped the advance into Egypt. In their counterattack the British took Tobruk, a port city of Libya (see map, page 727). The Italian invasion of British Somaliland at the same time also failed, and a counterattack by the British drove the Italians out of Ethiopia as well.

When Hitler turned his attention to the Balkans, Axis fortunes in eastern Europe improved. Germany seized Romania, which it needed for the rich oil fields there. In March 1941 pressure on Bulgaria resulted in the German occupation of that country. By November, Romania, Bulgaria, and Hungary had allied themselves with Germany.

In April 1941 Hitler invaded Yugoslavia, having failed to persuade its government to allow German troops to march through the country to Greece. In less than two weeks, the Germans had crushed Yugoslav resistance.

Next came Greece. Despite stubborn resistance by the Greeks, the German panzers prevailed. The British withdrew to the island of Crete, where the Germans used a new tactic. German troops parachuted onto Crete, and by the end of May the British had abandoned the island and fled to Egypt. Thus Germany controlled the entire Balkan Peninsula except for European Turkey, the city of Istanbul, the Dardanelles, and the Bosporus (see map, page 727). In June, Germany and Turkey signed a treaty assuring Turkish neutrality.

The German victories in Greece and Crete enabled Hitler to launch the next move in his giant strategy—a huge pincers movement aimed at the Suez Canal. One part of the Axis force was to come by way of North Africa, the other through Syria, Iraq, Trans-Jordan, and Palestine.

The rich oil fields of the Middle East would give Hitler a considerable advantage in the war because vital war equipment such as airplanes, tanks, and trucks needed fuel to operate. But Hitler failed to conquer the region. He had hoped that neutral Turkey would allow German troops to pass through its territory to British and French possessions in the Middle East. However, Turkey refused. Consequently, the British and Free French held Iraq and, in July 1941, drove the Vichy French out of Syria. One month later, Allied forces also occupied Iran.

Meanwhile, German forces had moved across the Mediterranean to North Africa. Throughout 1941 Italian and German troops led by General Erwin Rommel—known as the "Desert Fox"— ● fought the British in Libya. In the summer of 1942, Rommel's forces drove the British out of Libya and back into Egypt. At El Alamein, only 70 miles (112 kilometers) from Alexandria (see map, page 727), the German offensive began to falter for lack of

1A, 5B, a1C, a4A, a4B, a4C

Learning from Maps *World War II transformed Europe and North Africa into one huge battlefield. In which country did the Battle of the Bulge take place?* **Belgium**

supplies. The British made a stand, and Rommel remained stalled at El Alamein.

Germany's Attack on the Soviet Union

The Soviet Union regarded the German victories in the Balkans with alarm and anger. It considered the Balkans, especially Romania and Bulgaria, to be within its own sphere of influence.

At a Soviet-German conference in Berlin in November 1940, the Soviets demanded that Bulgaria, Istanbul, the Dardanelles, and the Bosporus be included in their sphere of influence. Hitler suggested instead that Germany should have Europe, and that the Soviet Union should establish a sphere in Asia. The Soviets rejected these suggestions.

On June 22, 1941, the war entered a new phase. Without a declaration of war, German

World War II; ***Atlantic Charter:*** statement of the democracies' war aims, drawn up by Churchill and Roosevelt in 1941

3. ***Maginot Line:*** French fortification on French-German border; ***Siegfried Line:*** German fortification on French-German border; ***Rotterdam:*** city in the Netherlands; ***Dunkirk:*** town in northern France; ***Occupied France:*** northern and western France; ***Vichy France:*** southern France; ***Coventry:*** northwest of London

4. a shipping outlet to the Atlantic, a long coastline useful for submarine bases, and good sites for airfields

5. Germany could outflank it through Belgium.

6. The United States took several steps to modify the strict neutrality it declared in the Neutrality Act of 1937. These included: the Neutrality Act of 1939; an executive agreement in 1940 transferring 50 old American destroyers to Great Britain; the Lend-Lease Act of 1941; and a congressional act in November 1941 removing restrictions on American merchant ships from being armed and entering war zones.

SECTION 4

Focus/Motivation

Put the following quotation by Adolf Hitler on the chalkboard or an overhead projector, or read it to the class.

"Human culture and civilization on this continent are

inseparably bound up with the presence of the *Aryan.* If he dies out or declines, the dark veils of an age without culture will again descend on this globe. . . .

We all sense that in the distant future humanity must be faced by problems which only a highest race, become master people and supported by the means and possibilities of an entire globe, will be equipped to overcome."

Ask the following questions: Why do you think a person would come to the conclusion that his race was superior? *(Answers will vary. They might include fear of unfamiliar peoples, insecurity about one's own worth, and revenge for a supposed injustice.)* How might Hitler's racism affect his policies within Germany? *(He might advance people that fit his category of "Aryan" and persecute all others.)* How might it affect Hitler's foreign policy? *(It might lead him to support racially similar nations and to oppose racially different nations. If this proved impossible, it might result in alliances of convenience, such as the alliance with the "yellow Aryan" Japanese.)*

Presentation
Conducting an Interview (Average/Group)
Have students interview relatives, friends or acquaintances who lived in the United States during the war years. Have the students ask them what they remember about the

LINKING GEOGRAPHY TO HISTORY

The World Ocean: Earth's Largest Region

The historical events discussed in this book all took place in specific areas, or regions, of the world. In fact, many of the chapters of the book are organized around the various regions of the world. However, largely because no humans live there, the greatest region on earth—the world ocean—receives little mention. Yet a sense of the geography of the world ocean is necessary for a full understanding of historical processes. The world ocean's size alone staggers the imagination. While geographers give names to four major oceans—the Arctic, Atlantic, Indian, and Pacific—in reality a series of narrow waterways and other sea passages connect all four to form just one great world ocean. Further, around the margins of this world ocean lie the seas, gulfs, and bays that extend its waters.

To gain a sense of the size of the world ocean, look at a globe. With your finger, trace a line on the globe through the four oceans, noting the waterways that connect them. As you can see, the name *Earth* is actually a misnomer. For the early Greek geographers, however, the world consisted of just one comparatively small body of water, the Mediterranean Sea, surrounded by large amounts of land. Hence, calling this planet Earth seemed appropriate to them. Had they known that more than 70 percent of the planet's surface was covered by water, they might have named it *Ocean.*

Actually, some Greek geographers did suggest that a world ocean existed. However, they located it incorrectly. To them the ocean consisted of an endless, boundless stream that flowed around the margins of the world. They believed that if people ventured far out upon this ocean, they would pass through a region of dense fog and ultimately arrive in an even more dreaded region where water and sky met. There they would find themselves cast into a world of darkness from which they would never return.

The voyages of exploration and discovery during the 1500s provided people with an understanding of the vastness of the world ocean. However, 400 years passed before people developed a similar understanding of the ocean floor. During these years most people assumed the floor of the ocean consisted of a vast level plain. However, exploration conducted in the second half of the 1900s showed clearly that the ocean bottom is as varied and broken as the earth's surface. In fact, some of the world's most spectacular scenery lies beneath the ocean's waters. The ocean floor's towering mountain ranges, enormous canyons, and expansive plains make their counterparts on land appear miniscule by comparison.

For example, one huge mountain range—the Mid-Atlantic Ridge—runs down the middle of the Atlantic Ocean for more than 10,000 miles (16,000 kilometers). Also, many long, narrow valleys cut into the floor of the Pacific Ocean. One of these valleys, the Mariana Trench, is so deep that if the world's highest mountain, Mount Everest, were dropped into it, more than one mile (1.6 kilometers) of ocean water would lie above the mountain's summit. While the ridges and trenches represent the most dramatic landforms of the ocean floor, in terms of area, plains dominate the ocean world. Like plains on land, these undersea plains are mostly smooth and flat.

Research also has shown that the ocean contains many minerals. In addition, some scientists have suggested that the abundant marine life of the world ocean may offer a solution to the problem of food shortages. In the years to come the world ocean may play a much greater role in history than it has in the past.

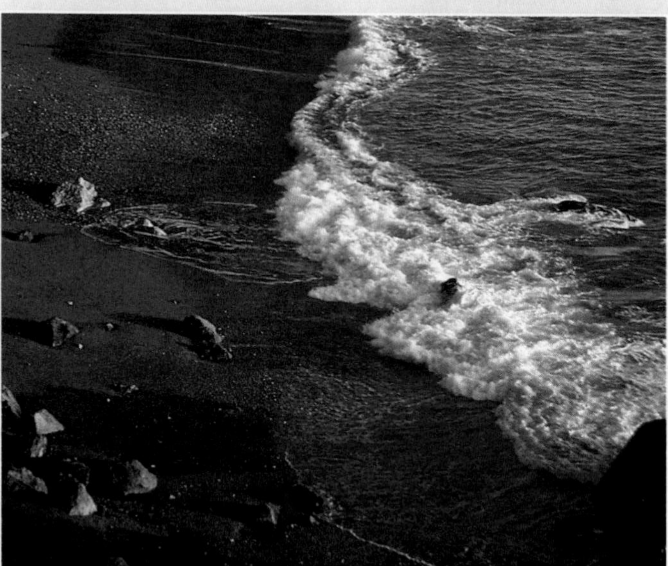

Big Sur, on the Pacific Coast of California

● Critical thinking activity: Ask students to describe the similarities and differences between Napoleon's attack on Russia and Hitler's attack on the Soviet Union. Point out that Stalin encouraged resistance by asking the people to defend "Mother Russia" rather than the Communist state.

armies invaded the Soviet Union. Hitler had opened a new front in the east, 2,000 miles (3,200 kilometers) long. Churchill declared that, although he did not admire communism, any nation that fought the Nazis was an ally and should receive help. The United States also declared its willingness to assist the Soviet Union.

As in World War I, sending aid to the Soviet Union became extremely difficult. Ships sailing the route across the Mediterranean and through the Dardanelles, the Bosporus, and the Black Sea risked submarine and air attacks from bases in Italy and the Balkans. The route through the Baltic Sea was impossible. Convoys to two Soviet ports, Murmansk and Archangel in the Arctic, had to pass the long, German-held coast of Norway. To avoid these dangers, the Allies developed a new route from the Persian Gulf across Iran by train and truck to the southern part of the Soviet Union.

The Soviet Defense

The initial thrust of the Nazi armies into the Soviet Union was tremendous. Everywhere the Soviet armies were driven back. Within a very short time, Moscow and Leningrad were under siege. There, however, the attack bogged down.

The Soviet defenders used the same scorched-earth tactics against Hitler that their ancestors had used against Napoleon. The retreating armies and civilians carried away what they could and destroyed everything else. Thus the territory the Germans gained was more a hindrance than a help. In addition, many Soviet soldiers remained, hiding out in swamps and forests and making daring guerrilla attacks on railroads, bridges and trains. ●

Hitler had expected the Soviet Union to surrender quickly. But the Soviet stand at Leningrad and Moscow disrupted his timetable. When the short Russian autumn came, Hitler faced the same decision Napoleon had had to make: Should he retreat or should he stand? Hitler chose to stand.

Soon the Germans had to face a new enemy—the bitterly cold Russian winter. The Soviets chose the winter for a counterattack, which was intended primarily to relieve pressure on Moscow. For the first time in World War II, the Germans retreated.

The year 1941 ended with the Germans deep inside the Soviet Union. In the spring of 1942, they struck southward, aiming to cut the Soviet supply line from Iran. One German spearhead drove toward the city of Stalingrad (see map, page 727). The southern part of the German army drove deep into the Caucasus. Fighting fiercely, the Soviets stopped the Germans before they reached their goal, the port of Baku on the Caspian Sea. North of the Caucasus, however, the Germans forced the Soviets all the way back to Stalingrad.

"New Order" and "Final Solution"

The invasion of the Soviet Union was part of Hitler's master plan for the creation of a "New Order" for Europe. Hitler wanted to organize the continent into a single political and economic system ruled from Berlin and dominated by the "Aryan race." According to this plan, the Soviet Union would supply Germany with food and raw materials. An official economic plan issued by the German government stated: "There is no doubt that . . . many millions of people will be starved to death if we take out of the country the things we need." Causing the Russians to starve did not concern Hitler. According to Nazi ideology, all Slavs were "racially inferior."

Another aspect of Hitler's "New Order" went into effect as the Germans continued their offensives. In 1941 Hitler ordered the annihilation of the entire Jewish population of Europe. The Nazis referred to this program as the "Final Solution" of the "Jewish Problem." This unbelievably barbaric goal was possible in Hitler's Germany because so many people had accepted as fact the Nazi theories about the racial superiority of the Aryans.

Jews by the hundreds of thousands were transported to eastern Germany and Poland. There they were held in "protective custody" in concentration camps. Among the most infamous were Dachau and Buchenwald in Germany, and Treblinka and Auschwitz in Poland. The captors used some inmates as slave laborers. Most, however, were murdered by poison gas or were shot.

In his book *Never to Forget,* Milton Meltzer quotes an SS* officer sent to a Polish death camp to deliver poison gas. There he witnessed the mass extermination of Polish Jews. The following excerpt is from the officer's handwritten account:

*Hitler's SS *(Schutzstaffel)* was an elite corps of officers sworn to absolute obedience. They served as Hitler's bodyguards and later took charge of intelligence, central security, and extermination of people in concentration camps.

day Pearl Harbor was bombed and President Roosevelt's radio address to the American people. Then have students write the interviews in a report as an eyewitness account, or present an oral report to the class. Use the reports as the basis for a class discussion on American entry into the war.

3B, 5B, 5G, a1C

● Critical thinking activity: Ask students to consider how history may have been different if Japan had not bombed Pearl Harbor in December 1941. Would the United States have entered the war? Why or why not?

SECTION 4

Closure

Ask: Why did the Japanese attack Pearl Harbor? *(They wanted to destroy the American fleet so that the United States would not rival the Japanese in the Pacific.)*

Review Answers

1. ***Holocaust:*** the systematic murder of European Jews by the Nazis
2. ***Erwin Rommel:*** German general who drove the British out of Libya but was finally defeated at El Alamein; ***"New Order":*** Hitler's plan for organizing Europe into a single political and economic system, ruled from Berlin; ***"Final Solution":*** an attempt to annihilate the entire Jewish population of Europe; ***Auschwitz:*** one of a number of concentration camps in which Jews were used as slaves or exterminated; ***Hideki Tojo:*** militaristic Japanese premier who came to power in 1941
3. ***El Alamein;*** village in northeastern Africa; ***Murmansk:*** city in northwestern Russia; ***Stalingrad:*** city in southern Russia; ***Pearl Harbor:*** inlet on coast of Hawaii and site of Japanese attack on United States navy in 1941; ***Gilbert Islands:*** islands in the South Pacific; ***Solomon Islands:*** Pacific islands southwest of the United States
4. In 1941 the Germans occupied Romania, Bulgaria, Yugoslavia, Greece, and Crete and signed a treaty

"They walked along the path, . . . and entered the death chambers. A sturdy SS man stood in the corner and told the wretched people in a clerical tone of voice: 'Nothing at all is going to happen to you! You must take a deep breath in the chambers. That expands the lungs. This inhalation is necessary because of illness and infection.' . . .

This gave some of these poor people a glimmer of hope that lasted long enough for them to take the few steps into the chambers without resisting. The majority realized—the smell told them—what their fate was to be. So they climbed the steps and then they saw everything. . . . They hesitated, but they went into the gas chambers, pushed on by those behind them, or driven by the leather whips of the SS. . . . Many people were praying. . . .

The SS forced as many in together as was physically possible. The doors closed. . . . After 28 minutes only a few were still alive. At last, after 32 minutes everyone was dead.

Men of the work squad opened the wooden doors from the other side. . . . The dead were standing upright . . . pressed together in the chambers. . . . One could see the families even in death. They were still holding hands. . . . Two dozen dentists opened the mouths with hooks and looked for gold. . . . The . . . corpses were carried in wooden barrows just a few meters away to the pits."

During the war, people in some western European countries, especially Denmark, tried to protect Jewish citizens. In eastern Europe, however, a long tradition of anti-Semitism made the Nazi program easier to carry out and its results more devastating.

By the time the Nazi government fell, its leaders and its followers had murdered an estimated 6 million European Jews. This systematic Nazi destruction of almost an entire race is referred to as the **Holocaust.** The Nazis also murdered nearly as many non-Jews—mainly Slavs, Gypsies, and members of the resistance.

Japanese Aggressions in the Pacific

The struggle against the Axis Powers received a major boost in December 1941, when expanding conflict and events in the Pacific area drew the United States into the war. Japanese militarism and aggression had increased throughout the 1930s. Early in 1939, with the situation in Europe growing increasingly tense, Japan saw a long-awaited chance to extend its control over East Asia. Japan's first move was to capture the island of Hainan (HI • nahn) and several small islands off the coast of French Indochina (see map, page 713). Thus Japan severed the British sea route from Hong Kong to Singapore. Neither France nor Great Britain could prevent this move.

After both the Netherlands and France fell, Japan made further aggressive moves in East Asia. The Japanese government declared the Netherlands East Indies to be under Japanese "protective custody." Japanese pressure forced the Vichy government to allow French Indochina to become a Japanese protectorate.

In September 1940 Japan formed an alliance with Germany and Italy. The United States responded to this action in three ways: by protesting violations of the Nine-Power Treaty, providing assistance to Chiang Kai-shek, and placing an embargo on the sale of oil and scrap iron to Japan. Japan thus became even more intent on removing any rivals that might jeopardize its oil reserves in the Netherlands East Indies. Now only the American-held Philippines and the Hawaiian Islands threatened Japanese supremacy in the Pacific. The United States, meanwhile, had already moved a large part of its Pacific Fleet to Hawaii.

During 1941 relations between the United States and Japan steadily deteriorated. Japan and the Soviet Union signed a five-year nonaggression treaty. An even more militaristic government came to power in Japan under Premier Hideki Tojo. By the middle of 1941, the Japanese government had begun to plan an attack upon the United States. However, in November the Japanese government also sent special "peace" mission representatives to Washington, D.C.

American Entry into the War

On December 7, 1941, while Tojo's representatives were still in Washington, the Japanese launched a surprise attack on the American naval base at Pearl Harbor, Hawaii. They intended to strike such a severe blow that the United States would not rival the Japanese in the Pacific. Several American ships

5B, 5F, 5G, a1C, a4A, a4E, a4I, a4J

• Three United States aircraft carriers—the *Enterprise,* the *Lexington,* and the *Saratoga*—were at sea and escaped the destruction at Pearl Harbor.

"THE GIRL HE LEFT BEHIND" IS STILL BEHIND HIM
She's a WOW
WOMAN ORDNANCE WORKER

Learning from Pictures *In the United States, posters like this one encouraged civilians to take part in the war effort.*

• were sunk; others were badly damaged. American dead totaled more than 2,300.

In an excerpt from his book *At Dawn We Slept,* historian Gordon Prange relates an eyewitness account of the attack on Pearl Harbor:

> "When the attack began, . . . the explosion of bombs, the whine of bullets, the roar of planes, the belching guns of aroused defenders, the acrid smell of fire and smoke—all blended into a nerve-racking [sound] of chaos. . . . Bombardiers still dropped their torpedoes, while dive bombers pounced like hawks. . . . Far above, high-level bombers rained their deadly missiles as fighters shuttled in and out, weaving together the fearful tapestry of destruction."

On December 8, 1941, Congress declared war on Japan, as did the British Parliament. Three days later, Germany and Italy declared war on the United States, and Congress replied with its own declaration of war. The United States became a full-fledged belligerent in World War II.

The Japanese quickly took advantage of American unreadiness. On the same day as the attack on Pearl Harbor, Japan began aerial attacks on the Philippines. Soon afterward the Japanese landed on Luzon. Within a month they captured the American island outposts of Guam and Wake. In less than three months, mainland areas of Burma, Thailand, and Malaya, including the British fortress of Singapore, fell to Japan (see map, page 733).

Japan went on to conquer a vast island empire: most of the Netherlands East Indies (Indonesia), the Philippines, and the Gilbert Islands. Australia remained the last stronghold of resistance in the southwest Pacific. It could be supplied only over a long route from Hawaii. Japanese landings on New Guinea and the Solomon Islands threatened this critically important supply line.

SECTION 4 REVIEW

1. **Define** Holocaust
2. **Identify** Erwin Rommel, "New Order," "Final Solution," Auschwitz, Hideki Tojo
3. **Locate** El Alamein, Murmansk, Stalingrad, Pearl Harbor, Gilbert Islands, Solomon Islands
4. **Summarizing Ideas** What gains did the Germans make in southeastern Europe in 1941?
5. **Interpreting Ideas** **(a)** What was Hitler's strategy concerning the Middle East? **(b)** How well did it succeed?
6. **Understanding Ideas** What event sparked the entry of the United States into World War II?

5 Allied Victories over Germany and Japan Ended the War

Representatives of 26 nations met in Washington, D.C., in January 1942 to unite in the common purpose of defeating the Axis. Chief among these Allies were Great Britain, the Soviet Union, and the United States. Other nations in Europe, Asia, and the Americas contributed what they could. Each nation pledged to use all its resources to defeat the Axis, not to sign a separate peace treaty, and to abide by the provisions of the Atlantic Charter.

assuring Turkish neutrality.
5. (a) Hitler's strategy was to attack the Suez Canal in a pincer movement, closing in from North Africa and from Turkey through western Asia. **(b)** However, Turkey refused to permit the Germans to cross its territory, the Vichy French were driven out of Syria, and the Allies held Iraq and Iran. The other pincer was stopped at El Alamein and thus failed to reach the Suez Canal.
6. The Japanese launched a surprise attack on the American naval base at Pearl Harbor.

SECTION 5

Focus/Motivation
Lead a class discussion in which students play the role of military advisers. The class must develop a strategy for counterattacking the Japanese after the Pearl Harbor disaster, sending troops an supplies to Great Britain, and delivering "Lend-Lease" trucks to the Soviets. Outline basic strategy, i.e. landing troops first in Africa; "island hopping" in the Pacific theater; attacking Sicily and Italy from Africa; running convoys to Britain and the Soviet Union; organizing convoys to send troops to Australia; etc. Have a student record the suggestions so a delegate can meet with FDR, Churchill, and Stalin to make specific recommendations about strategy to be coordinated with the Soviets and British.

5B, 5E

● The Allied air raids damaged German industry and communication.

Presentation
Conducting an Interview (Average/Group)
Have students interview relatives, friends or acquaintances who served in the armed forces during the war. Have students ask them what military life was like and obtain their comments on the following topics: basic training; life aboard ship (or at an airfield); barracks life; life at the front; C- and K-rations; KP duty; *Stars and Stripes* (newspaper); Armed Forces radio; entertainment; USO; V-mail; dog tags; weaponry; meeting civilians after liberation; POW camps (as guard or prisoner). Then have the students write the interviews in a report as an eyewitness account, or present an oral report to the class. Use the reports as the basis for a class discussion on the military during the war.

Important Offensives

The German offensive in the summer of 1942 pushed the Soviets back to Stalingrad (see map, page 727). There a tremendous battle, the most spectacular of the war, was fought for six months. The Germans penetrated the city, suffering terrible losses in the process. Instead of retreating, the determined Soviets defended their city—street by street and house by house.

In November 1942 the Soviets began a counterattack, encircling the German troops in Stalingrad. Although Hitler ordered his trapped forces to fight to the death, what was left of his army in the city surrendered in January 1943. The heroic and successful defense of Stalingrad was a crucial turning point in the war. The Germans never completely recovered from this defeat.

North Africa. The Allies also made progress in North Africa during 1942. Late in the summer, Allied reinforcements were rushed to El Alamein, where British troops were under German attack. In a decisive battle in October, troops under General Bernard Montgomery of Great Britain routed Rommel's force. They pushed the Germans westward across Libya into Tunisia.

In November 1942 American and British forces under General Dwight Eisenhower of the United States landed in Morocco and Algeria. They pushed eastward into Tunisia as Montgomery's army moved westward. Rommel's army was thus trapped between the two Allied forces. By the middle of May 1943, the Axis Powers in North Africa were forced to surrender.

As a result of Rommel's defeat, the Allies gained a stronghold in North Africa. Italy's African empire disappeared, and control of the French colonies in Africa passed to the Free French. The Allies had maintained control of the Suez Canal and had made the Mediterranean more secure for Allied naval operations.

The Invasion of Italy

Throughout 1942 Stalin demanded that the British and Americans open a second front in Europe to relieve the German pressure on the Soviet Union. The Allies argued that an attack before they were fully prepared would be too risky. Stalin suspected the Allies of hoping that Germany and the Soviet Union would destroy each other.

When the Allies secured North Africa, Stalin renewed his demands for a landing in Europe. Churchill insisted upon an attack on what he called the "soft underbelly of the Axis"—through Italy and the Balkans. In July 1943 Allied armies that had been fighting in North Africa landed on the strategic island of Sicily. Resistance was strong, but the Allies took the island in little more than a month. Then they bombed the Italian mainland in preparation for a landing.

In Italy, Mussolini was forced to resign, and Marshal Pietro Badoglio (buh • DOHL • yo) became premier. His first act was to dissolve the Fascist Party. When the Allied army landed on the southwestern Italian mainland in September 1943, the Italians surrendered unconditionally. They then declared war on Germany. German troops in Italy quickly filled the void left by the Italian Fascists. They skillfully resisted the Allied advance.

The War at Sea and in the Air

Meanwhile, the Allies were winning the Battle of the Atlantic. This conflict between German and Allied ships had begun in the spring of 1940. Although German submarines sank an enormous number of Allied ships, by the fall of 1943, destroyers and other armed ships escorted convoys of troop and supply ships sailing from the United States. Planes based both on land and on aircraft carriers also protected the convoys. New technological devices, such as sonar, located submarines.

Allied air attacks against Germany and the occupied countries intensified. At first the Allies, operating from bases in the British Isles, concentrated on strategic military sites. Later they attacked civilian areas as well. The Allies bombed almost every German city, severely damaging some. ●

The War in the Pacific

The Japanese advance in the Pacific suffered its first setback in May 1942. In the Battle of the Coral Sea, American and Australian air and naval forces defeated a Japanese fleet steaming toward Australia. Soon afterward an American fleet met a larger Japanese fleet pushing eastward to try to capture the Midway Islands, northwest of Hawaii (see map, page 733). The Americans defeated the Japanese in the crucial Battle of Midway, fought in June by ships and carrier-based planes. With these

Learning from Maps *The dropping of atomic bombs on two Japanese cities ended the war in the Pacific. Which Japanese cities were hit by atomic bombs?* **Nagasaki and Hiroshima**

two victories, the United States Navy began to turn the tide in the war against Japan.

Early in August 1942, to protect the Australian supply line, American marines landed on the Solomon Islands, seizing the airfield on Guadalcanal. This was the first invasion of Japanese-held territory and an important morale-booster for the United States. Four times in the next three months the Japanese launched savage attacks on the American forces. All were repulsed, with horrendous losses on both sides.

In 1943 the Allied nations took the offensive in the Pacific. Forces from Australia and New Zealand assisted sea, air, and land forces of the United States. Together, they waged a long series of battles aimed at driving the Japanese entirely out of the Solomon Islands. The Allies then adopted a strategy called "island hopping." Certain Japanese-held

733

5B, 5E

● Research activity: The innovations that contributed to the Allied effort: transportation, radar, dehydrated food, and antibiotics

Learning from Pictures *After suffering heavy casualties in fierce fighting to capture the island, American marines unload supplies on Iwo Jima.*

islands were captured, while others were bypassed and left helpless for lack of supplies.

During 1944 the Americans cleared the Japanese from the Marshall Islands, New Guinea, and the Marianas. Saipan and Tinian, in the Marianas, became bases for long-range bombing attacks on Japan. In October 1944 an American army under General Douglas MacArthur landed at Leyte (LAYT • ee) in the central Philippines. Shortly after the landing, the Japanese fleet suffered a crushing defeat in a great air and sea fight, the Battle of Leyte Gulf. After six months of heavy fighting, the Allies recovered the Philippine Islands.

Victory in Europe

As the Allies fought their way through Italy in late 1943, plans were being made for another, larger invasion of Europe—Operation Overlord—aimed at the heart of Germany. The landing was to be made on the beaches of the narrow, heavily wooded French peninsula of Normandy (see map, page 727).

The long-awaited landing came on June 6, 1944—D-Day as the military called it. Soldiers and supplies were transported across the English Channel in one of the most daring invasion operations in military history. Within a month, more than 1 million troops had landed in France. The Germans had expected a landing in France but were unable to discover the exact location of the assault. When they did find out, German forces rushed to meet the Allied invasion but were outnumbered.

After heavy fighting, Allied troops broke out of Normandy and into northern France. At the same time, Allied forces landed on the Mediterranean coast of France and fought their way northward. On August 25, 1944, Allied troops entered Paris. By September they faced the strongly fortified Siegfried Line along Germany's western frontier. ●

The drive from the east. In June 1944 the Soviets began a major drive against Germany from the east. By the end of 1944, the Red Army had taken Finland, Estonia, Lithuania, Latvia, Romania, and Bulgaria. The British assisted in driving the Germans out of Greece. Yugoslavia had been liberated earlier with the help of resistance fighters under Marshal Tito. By far the heaviest Soviet fighting, however, was in Poland. By July 1944 Soviet troops were approaching the eastern outskirts of Warsaw.

The drive from the west. The Americans pierced the "unconquerable" Siegfried Line in October after five weeks of fighting. The Allies captured port cities in France and Belgium, easing supply problems. The Allies also cleared Alsace and Lorraine of German troops.

734

The Germans still had enough strength for one desperate counterattack. Just before Christmas in 1944, they drove a 50-mile (80-kilometer) wedge into Allied lines in Belgium. After a costly 10-day battle—the Battle of the Bulge—the Allies turned back the German drive. Finally, in early spring 1945, German defenses collapsed. At the end of April, the German army in Italy surrendered unconditionally. Italian guerrillas pursued and captured Mussolini. He was shot, and his body was hung upside down and displayed to jeering crowds.

The Soviet and American armies made their first contact at Torgau, in eastern Germany, on April 25, 1945. It was agreed that the Soviets would take Berlin. On April 30, as the Soviets neared their objective, Hitler committed suicide.

Learning from Pictures *This Japanese war poster features a giant samurai fighting for the Axis Powers. Which countries belonged to the Axis Powers?*

Two days later the Soviets captured the battered and devastated city. Within a week the German high command surrendered unconditionally. May 8, 1945, was V-E Day—the day of victory in Europe.

Attacks on Japan

Though the war had ended in Europe, it continued in the Pacific. Long-range bombers from Saipan could now reach the main islands of Japan. Raids on Japanese industrial cities began early in 1945. However, the Allies needed still closer islands to use as fighter bases and emergency landing fields.

The first move was into a group of islands about 750 miles (1,200 kilometers) directly south of Tokyo. American marines landed on the volcanic island of Iwo Jima (see map, page 733) and captured it after a month of the most bitter fighting of the war. The Japanese resisted even more strongly as their home islands were approached. Okinawa, the largest of the Ryukyu Islands, was taken after more desperate fighting. At Okinawa, nearly 250 Allied ships were damaged by suicide attacks of Japanese pilots who crashed their planes into the ships. These suicide missions were called kamikaze attacks, meaning "Divine Wind." The Japanese believed that pilots who pledged to die for the emperor would save the empire, just as the Divine Wind had saved Japan from Chinese-Mongol attack in 1281. The kamikaze pilots were usually very young, most of them in their teens or early twenties. According to some historians, these pilots often had only about 12 hours of flight training. Their only mission was to select an appropriate target and die for the emperor while destroying it. An excerpt from a diary kept by a sailor includes a kamikaze pilot's last letter to his girlfriend:

> "Do not weep because I am about to die. If I were to live and one of my dear ones to die, I would do all in my power to cheer those who remain behind. I would try to be brave. . . .
>
> I pray for the happiness of you all, and I beg your forgiveness for my lack of piety.
>
> I leave for the attack with a smile on my face. The moon will be full tonight. As I fly over the open sea off Okinawa I will choose the enemy ship that is to be my target.
>
> I will show you that I know how to die bravely."

735

5B, 5E, a4L

Students may suggest that if the bombs had not detonated, the war with Japan would have continued and countless Allied lives would have been lost. If the Japanese had known that there were only two bombs, they might not have surrendered. If Germany had used the bomb first, the Allies might have lost the war.

SECTION 5

Closure

Ask students to explain why World War II was the most destructive war in history. *(New technology made deadlier weapons possible.)*

Review Answers

1. *Dwight Eisenhower:* American general in command of an Anglo-American army in North Africa; ***"soft underbelly of the Axis":*** southeastern Europe; ***"Island hopping":*** Allied strategy by which some Japanese islands were captured while others were bypassed and left helpless for lack of supplies; ***Douglas MacArthur:*** American general in command of the American army that landed at Leyte in the Philippines; ***Operation Overlord:*** Allied invasion of western Europe; ***V-E Day:*** May 8, 1945, when the German high command surrendered; ***V-J Day:*** September 2, 1945, when the Japanese surrendered
2. *Stalingrad:* city in southern Russia; ***Guadalcanal:*** one of the Solomon Islands, located in the Pacific, southwest of the United States; ***Saipan:*** island near Guam in the Pacific; ***Tinian:*** island near Guam in the Pacific; ***Normandy:*** western French coast; ***Iwo Jima:*** island between Saipan and Japan; ***Okinawa:*** island between Japan and the Philippines; ***Hiroshima:*** city in southern Japan;
3. (a) Stalin wanted a second front to relieve some of the German pressure on

Despite such determined resistance, the Allies continued their intensive bombing of Japan. Japanese ports were effectively blockaded, and the Japanese navy was immobilized. Nevertheless, the Japanese government still refused to surrender.

Yalta and Potsdam

Roosevelt and Churchill had long hoped to persuade Stalin to enter the war in the Pacific. Before the defeat of Germany, however, the Soviet Union had been completely occupied in defending itself. Moreover, it considered the war against Japan the business of the United States.

In February 1945 Roosevelt and Churchill met with Stalin at Yalta, in the Soviet Union. The Big Three, as these Allied leaders were called, agreed that Germany should be temporarily divided and occupied by Allied troops including those of France. The liberated areas of Europe were to have democratically elected governments. The Soviet Union was to enter the war against Japan. As compensation it was to receive several Japanese territories.

Another conference began on July 17, 1945, at Potsdam, near Berlin. Roosevelt had died in April, and Harry Truman was now president of the United States. He scheduled a meeting with the other members of the Big Three—Churchill and Stalin. However, before the conference ended on August 2, Clement Attlee of the Labour Party had become Britain's prime minister and replaced Churchill at the conference. The three leaders planned for the control and occupation of Germany and issued an ultimatum to Japan, demanding its unconditional surrender. Japan rejected the ultimatum.

However, the Allies now had a secret weapon—a workable atomic bomb. Scientists from many nations, including refugees from fascist-controlled countries, had worked to harness the enormous energy released by splitting atoms. They had succeeded in creating the most destructive weapon yet known. By using this weapon, the Allies would not need to invade Japan.

Learning from Pictures *On the grounds of Livadio Palace located in Yalta in the Soviet Union, the Big Three decide the fate of postwar Europe.*

Japanese Surrender

When the Japanese government refused to surrender, President Truman made an important decision—to use the atomic bomb against Japan. Accordingly, on August 6, 1945, an American B-29 bomber dropped the deadly weapon on Hiroshima.

Exploding with a force equal to 20,000 tons (18,144 metric tons) of TNT, the bomb killed some 80,000 of the 320,000 people in the city and leveled more than half of the buildings. Two days later the Soviet Union declared war on Japan. Soviet armies swept into Manchuria, where they met little resistance. On August 9 an American plane dropped a second and even more powerful atomic bomb on the city of Nagasaki.

What If?
The Atomic Bomb

The atomic bomb had been tested earlier in the war, but in August 1945 only two atomic bombs existed. One bomb was dropped on Hiroshima, and a few days later the second bomb was dropped on Nagasaki. How do you think world history might have been different if the bombs had not detonated, or if the Japanese had known that the Allies had no more atomic bombs? Since Germany was also developing atomic weapons near the end of the war, how might history have been different if Germany had actually produced the atomic bomb first?

Learning from Pictures *These sailors, veterans of the Iwo Jima and Okinawa landings, celebrate V–J Day on board their ship.*

On August 14 the Japanese surrendered unconditionally, asking only that the emperor be allowed to retain his title and authority as emperor. The Allies agreed, on the condition that he accept the orders of the supreme allied commander in the Pacific, General Douglas MacArthur. On September 2, 1945 (known as V-J Day), representatives of both sides signed the official Japanese surrender documents in a ceremony aboard the American battleship *U.S.S. Missouri* anchored in Tokyo Bay.

Costs of the War

World War II, to a much greater extent than World War I, was a war of movement and of machines. Military casualties were enormous. The war was the most destructive in history. More than 22 million people died, and more than 34 million were wounded. Battle losses of the Soviet Union alone have been estimated at 7 million lives, although an accurate count has never been made. Germany lost more than 2 million people in battle. Japan's total loss—civilian and military—was nearly 2 million. Great Britain, France, and the United States each lost hundreds of thousands in battle. Six million Jews died in German concentration camps and gas chambers. Millions of civilians were uprooted by the war or killed or injured by bombs.

As the war progressed, weapons and tactics became more devastating. More shocking, people grew accustomed to this increased destructiveness. By 1943 Allied air attacks on Axis civilian centers were accepted simply as part of modern warfare. The destruction of Hamburg and the atomic bombings of Japan did not immediately bring any great public protest. By 1945 the killing of civilians was accepted as a normal practice of war.

SECTION 5 REVIEW

1. **Identify** Dwight Eisenhower, "soft underbelly of the Axis," "island hopping," Douglas MacArthur, Operation Overlord, V-E Day, V-J Day
2. **Locate** Stalingrad, Guadalcanal, Saipan, Tinian, Normandy, Iwo Jima, Okinawa, Hiroshima
3. **Analyzing Ideas** **(a)** Why did Stalin want a second front? **(b)** How was it launched?
4. **Summarizing Ideas** What were the fates of Mussolini and Hitler?
5. **Classifying Ideas** List the chief decisions made at Yalta and Potsdam.
6. **Understanding Ideas** What action did the United States finally take against Japan to end the war?

the Soviet Union. **(b)** At Churchill's insistence, the attack was made via Sicily and Italy. Allied armies already in North Africa took Sicily in July 1943, then attacked Italy.
4. Mussolini was captured by Italian guerrillas and shot, and his body was displayed in public. Hitler committed suicide as the Soviets entered Berlin.
5. At Yalta the Allies agreed that Germany was to be temporarily divided and occupied by troops of the victorious powers, including France; the liberated areas of Europe were to have democratically elected governments; and the Soviet Union was to enter the war against Japan in return for various Japanese territories. At Potsdam, Truman, Attlee, and Stalin decided to issue an ultimatum to Japan demanding surrender and made various decisions regarding peace settlements in Europe.
6. To end the war, the U.S. dropped an atomic bomb on Hiroshima on August 6, 1945. Three days later, a second bomb was dropped on Nagasaki.

Reviewing Important Terms
1. d; **2.** e; **3.** b
4. f; **5.** c; **6.** a

Developing Critical Thinking Skills
1. (a) The Japanese conquest of Manchuria was the first major act of aggression after World War I. **(b)** Accept all reasonable answers regarding the point of no return.
2. (a) The supporters of the two sides became the respective belligerents in World War II. **(b)** Spain remained technically neutral during the war.
3. (a) France, Great Britain, Germany, and Italy; **(b)** France and Great Britain were eager to avoid war; Germany wanted to take over the Sudetenland; Italy supported Germany's demand. **(c)** The decisions doomed Czechoslovakia.
4. (a) Rommel was stopped at El Alamein; the Soviets defeated the Germans in the Battle of Stalingrad. American forces dealt Japan its first major defeats. **(b)** The succession of Axis victories came to an end.
5. The principal new weapon was the atomic bomb. Old weapons, such as tanks, planes, submarines, and artillery, were improved and used more extensively. Important new technology included radar and sonar. New tactics included the blitzkrieg, use of carrier-based airplanes, bombing of cities, island hopping, kamikaze attacks, and parachute troops.

1B, 5B, 5G, a1B, a1C, a4A, a4F, a4H, a4K, a4L

Reteaching
Have students review the Chapter Summary and the appropriate section and questions in the Unit Synthesis. Discuss the concepts until students demonstrate a clear understanding of the material.

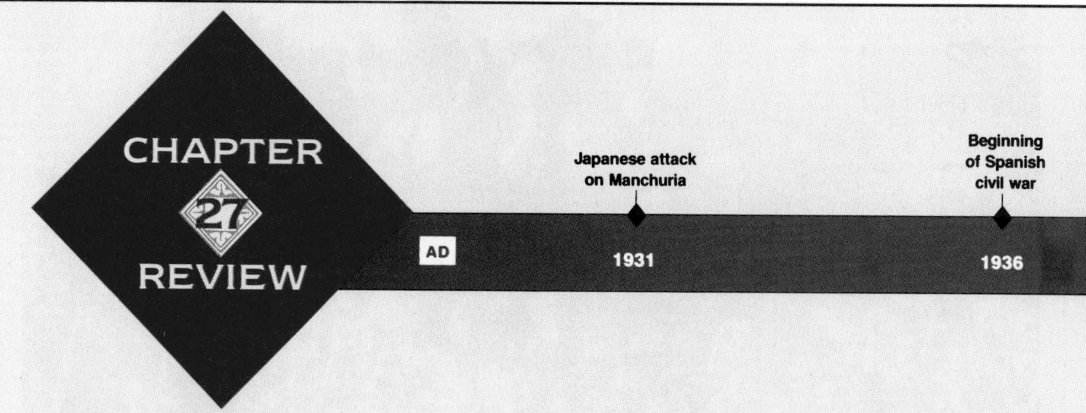

Chapter Summary

The following list contains the key concepts you have learned about World War II.

1. In the 1930s a series of aggressions by the Japanese and the Fascists brought about World War II. At first the democracies were reluctant to resist these aggressions, preferring a policy of appeasement.
2. The Japanese made gains in Manchuria and China. Italy captured Ethiopia, Fascists took over Spain following the country's civil war, and the Germans seized Austria and Czechoslovakia. The League of Nations proved incapable of halting these advances.
3. Only when Hitler invaded Poland in September 1939 did his principal opponents, Great Britain and France, decide at last to stand firm. They were at a severe disadvantage, because their obvious ally, the Soviet Union, had signed a nonaggression pact with Germany. Nevertheless, Great Britain and France declared war on Germany in 1939.
4. By the fall of 1940, the Axis Powers had conquered most of Scandinavia, defeated France, and forced British troops off the continent of Europe. They also had formed an alliance with Japan. During the next year, their success in battle reached its highest level and then began to decline.
5. Despite some isolationist opposition, the United States began to send supplies to Great Britain in 1940. During this same year, Great Britain's air force turned back German air attacks and prevented an invasion of England.
6. In 1941, after considerable successes in the Balkans, Germany suddenly attacked the Soviet Union. In that same year, the Japanese attacked the American fleet at Pearl Harbor, in Hawaii. This assault brought the United States into the war.
7. Within Germany, a vicious and barbaric policy of exterminating all the Jews of Europe was put into effect. The Holocaust diverted essential German efforts away from the front line. The Soviets counterattacked, and the German army was forced to engage in heavy fighting on the eastern front.
8. In 1943 the Allies invaded Sicily from North Africa. At the same time, they began an offensive to drive the Japanese out of the Pacific islands.
9. In 1944 the Allies invaded France. Finally, in 1945, they conquered Germany.
10. The atomic bombing of Hiroshima and Nagasaki forced Japan to surrender.
11. The cost of the war, in suffering and death, was worse by far than that of any other war in history.
12. The end of the war brought hope that the aims proclaimed in the Atlantic Charter of 1941—including an end to wars and self-determination and decent living conditions for all people—might now be realized.

On a separate sheet of paper, complete the following review exercises.

Reviewing Important Terms

Match each of the following terms with the correct definition below.

a. appeasement
b. Holocaust
c. blitzkrieg
d. maquis
e. isolationists
f. collaborators

____ 1. Members of resistance movements
____ 2. Those who oppose involvement in the affairs of other nations
____ 3. Systematic destruction of Jews by the Nazis
____ 4. People who cooperate with their country's enemies
____ 5. Lightning war
____ 6. Attempt to preserve peace by giving in to aggressor's demands

Developing Critical Thinking Skills

1. **Analyzing Ideas** **(a)** Many historians regard the Japanese conquest of Manchuria as the start of World War II. Why? **(b)** At what point do you think world war became inevitable? Explain.
2. **Evaluating Ideas** **(a)** In certain respects, the Spanish civil war was a preview of the global war to come. Why? **(b)** What role did Spain play once World War II started?
3. **Classifying Ideas** **(a)** Which nations participated in the conference at Munich? **(b)** What did each of these nations hope to achieve? **(c)** How did the decisions reached at Munich affect the future of Czechoslovakia?

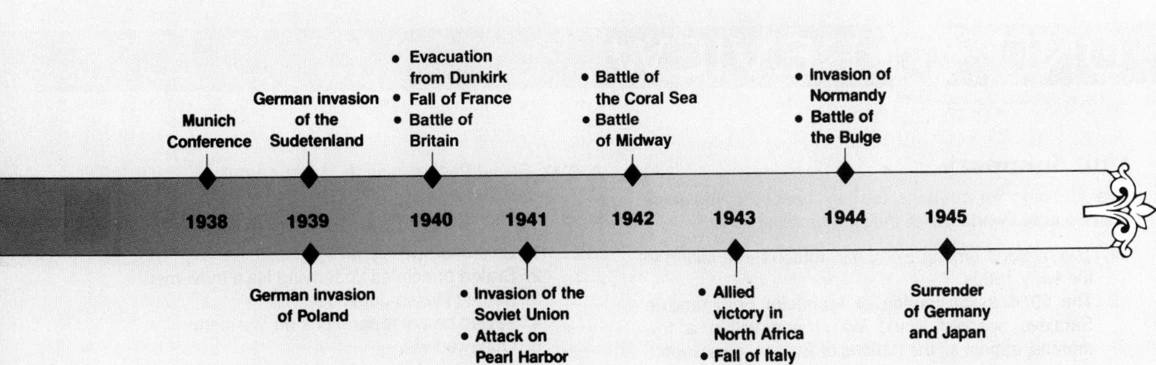

4. **Sequencing Ideas** **(a)** List the major events that occurred in the war during 1942. **(b)** Why might this year be considered a turning point in the war?
5. **Summarizing Ideas** What new weapons and military tactics were employed during World War II?

Relating Geography to History

Turn to the map on page 727. **(a)** What nations did the Axis Powers hold at the height of their power? **(b)** What nations remained neutral or nonaligned? **(c)** Based on information in this map, why might Churchill have considered Italy the "soft underbelly of the Axis"?

Relating Past to Present

1. "The next war," declared Albert Einstein after the bombing of Japan, "will be fought with stones." **(a)** What might he have meant by this comment? **(b)** What efforts are being made today to limit the production and sale of nuclear weapons?
2. Prior to American entry into the war, President Roosevelt called the United States the "arsenal of democracy." **(a)** What did he mean by this statement? **(b)** Does the United States still play this role in world affairs? **(c)** Why or why not? If possible, clip current articles that illustrate your answer.
3. Review the failure of the League of Nations to end Italian aggression in Ethiopia during the 1930s. Then find information on Soviet intervention in Afghanistan and Poland during the 1980s. **(a)** What actions did the United Nations take? **(b)** Were any of the problems faced by the United Nations similar to those experienced by the League? Explain.

Applying History Study Skills

Before completing this activity, review Building History Study Skills on page 724.

Read Mussolini's description of the nature of fascism. Then answer the questions below.

> "The foundation of Fascism is the idea of the state—its character, its duty, and its aims. The state guarantees the people's security, both within the nation and abroad. It represents the spirit of the nation. It is the state which educates its citizens. It makes them aware of their purpose in life and unites them. It leads men from primitive tribal life to the highest expression of human power, which is empire.
>
> But building an empire demands discipline . . . This fact explains the severe measures we must take against those who oppose this movement in Italy in the twentieth century. Never before has the nation stood more in need of authority, direction, and justice."

1. How did Mussolini define fascism?
2. What do you think Mussolini meant by the phrase "authority, direction, and justice"?
3. Use information in the chapter to determine if Mussolini's ideas coincided with his actions.
4. **(a)** What was Mussolini's place in Italian history? **(b)** In world history?

Investigating Further

1. **Researching Ideas** Review the information on codes in the Connections feature on page 649. Then use books in your library to investigate the use of codes during World War II.
2. **Writing a Report** Prepare a report on one of the following books about the Holocaust: Anne Frank's *Diary of a Young Girl* (Doubleday); John Hersey's *The Wall* (Pocket Books); Ilse Koehn's *Mischling, Second Degree* (Greenwillow); Arnost Lustig's *Night and Hope* (Avon); Elie Wiesel's *Night* (Avon). In your report, note whether the story is fiction or nonfiction. Also briefly discuss the background of the author. Then describe the way in which each of the central characters responded to Nazi persecution.
3. **Conducting an Interview** Interview a friend or relative who remembers the war years. Ask this person to explain the meaning of the following words or phrases: *victory garden, ration books, blackouts, dog tags, Rosie the Riveter, war bonds, C-rations, black market.* Try to discover other World War II terms that might be added to the list.

Relating Geography to History
(a) Norway, Finland, Estonia, Latvia, Lithuania, Poland, part of the Soviet Union, Austria, Czechoslovakia, Hungary, Romania, Yugoslavia, Bulgaria, Albania, Greece, Denmark, Netherlands, Belgium, France, and part of Libya, Tunisia, and Egypt; **(b)** Sweden, Switzerland, Spain, Portugal, Eire, Turkey, and Saudi Arabia; **(c)** Italy is a peninsula that can be attacked anywhere along its coastline.

Relating Past to Present
1. (a) Atomic bombs would so destroy civilization that people would be reduced to a primitive level. **(b)** Answers will vary.
2. (a) The United States would give war materials to countries resisting Axis aggression. **(b)** The United States plays this role today to a limited extent. **(c)** Answers will vary.
3. Refer to pages 712–13. Have students consult the *Readers' Guide to Periodical Literature* to find articles on recent actions of the United Nations.

Applying History Study Skills
1. the ideas of the state, which guarantees the people's security
2. The goals of the state would be achieved regardless of the measures necessary to achieve them.
3. Answers will vary.
4. (a) Students may suggest that Mussolini achieved short-lived success in Italian history as a Fascist leader. **(b)** Students may suggest that Mussolini was a threat to world peace.

Reviewing Concepts

1. f; **2.** h; **3.** i; **4.** j; **5.** a; **6.** d; **7.** c; **8.** g; **9.** b; **10.** e

Applying Critical Thinking Skills

1. (a) World War I forced industry and agriculture to expand. **(b)** Wages did not keep pace with the increase in productivity, and agriculture suffered from overproduction and falling prices.
2. (a), (b), (c), (d), and **(e)** Answers will vary. Students should support their choices with specific examples.
3. (a) Sun Yat-sen believed that the participation of the people in government should be increased gradually. Chiang Kai-shek gave the people little say in government. Mao Zedong believed that the people should participate in their support of the Communist Party. **(b)** All three were opposed. **(c)** Sun Yat-sen believed in land reform and industrialization. Chiang Kai-shek failed to reform landownership or the tax system. Mao Zedong promoted industrialization and land and tax reform. **(d)** Sun Yat-sen wanted a democratic society. Chiang Kai-shek introduced a one-party dictatorship. Mao Zedong created a Communist regime. **(e)** All three agreed on the need for modernization.
4. (a) expansion; **(b)** aggression
5. (a) The causes of World War I were nationalism, imperialism, militarism, and the system of alliances. Nationalism, imperialism, and militarism were also underlying causes of World War II. **(b)** Germany resented the treaty and sought revenge.
6. (a) The Atlantic Charter and the Fourteen Points

1B, 4I, 5A, 5B, 5G, a1B, a1C, a4A, a4E, a4F, a4G, a4H, a4I, a4J, a4K, a4L, a4M

Reteaching

Have students review the Chapter Summary and the appropriate section and questions in the Unit Synthesis. Discuss the concepts until students demonstrate a clear understanding of the material.

UNIT 6 REVIEW

Unit Summary

The following list contains the key concepts you have learned about world war in the twentieth century.

1. The rivalries among European nations intensified in the early 1900s.
2. The 1914 assassination of Archduke Ferdinand in Sarajevo sparked World War I and within a few months, almost all the nations of Europe, plus Japan, were at war.
3. A dramatic upheaval took place in Russia, where in 1917 a revolution abolished the monarchy. Following the civil war in Russia, a government based on the principles of Marx and communism was created.
4. Although World War I ended in 1918, the problems it caused continued to plague governments.
5. Woodrow Wilson's Fourteen Points offered idealistic goals, but as the Allies sought to collect reparations for their wartime losses and to gain additional territory, many of Wilson's goals were forgotten.
6. In 1920, 42 nations founded the League of Nations. However, the United States did not join, and the League's efforts were thus crippled from the start.
7. The new outlook and the uncertainties of the stressful period following World War I were reflected by the science, literature, music, and art of the time.
8. In the United States, a sense of optimism and the influence of European contact brought about rapid change during the decade called the Roaring Twenties.
9. The stock market crash marked the beginning of the Great Depression in 1929, and in Europe instability due to the depression was widespread.
10. In Italy and Germany, dissatisfaction with the weakness and hesitations of democratic governments led to an extreme form of dictatorship, fascism.
11. In territories controlled by Great Britain, major political changes took place during the 1920s and 1930s. Political and social reforms were also attempted in Turkey, Persia, China, Japan, and Africa.
12. Developments in Latin America reflected the worldwide economic crisis.
13. In the 1930s the League of Nations failed to halt aggressions by the imperial government of Japan and the Fascists, which brought about World War II. In 1945 the Allies conquered Germany and Japan.

On a separate sheet of paper, complete the following review exercises.

Reviewing Concepts

Match each of the following items with the correct description in column 2.

a. Kellogg-Briand Pact
b. Balfour Declaration
c. Nazi-Soviet Pact
d. Atlantic Charter
e. Zimmerman telegram
f. Fourteen Points
g. Yalta Conference
h. *Mein Kampf*
i. Treaty of Portsmouth
j. Versailles Treaty

____ **1.** Called for "peace with justice"
____ **2.** Stated principles underlying Nazi movement
____ **3.** Settled Russo-Japanese War
____ **4.** Levied heavy reparations on Germany
____ **5.** Outlawed war
____ **6.** Announced war aims of the democracies
____ **7.** Pledged Soviet Union's neutrality
____ **8.** Temporarily divided Germany
____ **9.** Favored creation of Jewish "national home"
____ **10.** Invited Mexico to join the Central Powers

Applying Critical Thinking Skills

1. **Summarizing Ideas** **(a)** How did World War I help bring about a boom period in the United States? **(b)** What conditions brought this period to an end?
2. **Classifying Ideas** Choose two of the following and discuss how they reflected the uncertainties of the period following World War I: **(a)** literature, **(b)** music, **(c)** painting, **(d)** architecture, **(e)** film.
3. **Contrasting Ideas** How did Sun Yat-sen, Chiang Kai-shek, and Mao Zedong differ in their plans for China's future? Include the following topics in your answer: **(a)** the role of the people; **(b)** foreign interference in China; **(c)** economic reforms; **(d)** constitutional government; **(e)** the need for modernization.
4. **Evaluating Ideas** **(a)** What were the foreign policy objectives of Italy, Germany, and Japan in the 1930s? **(b)** How did these nations achieve their objectives?
5. **Determining Cause and Effect** **(a)** Compare the causes of World War I with the causes of World War II. **(b)** Why might the Versailles Treaty be considered a cause of World War II?
6. **Comparing Ideas** **(a)** Compare the principles expressed in the Atlantic Charter with those listed in the Fourteen Points. **(b)** How did each of these documents seek to establish "peace with justice"?
7. **Analyzing Ideas** **(a)** How did the United States assist the Allies before December 1941? **(b)** Why did the United States move away from its neutral status?
8. **Determining Cause and Effect** **(a)** How did the bombings of Hiroshima and Nagasaki change the nature of warfare? **(b)** What other technological developments grew out of World War II?

Relating Geography to History

Refer to maps in Chapter 24 and Chapter 27. How did the map of Europe change after the Versailles Peace Conference? How did it change after the end of World War II?

took similar positions on such issues as freedom of the seas, equal trade opportunities, self-determination, arms reduction, and prohibiting the use of force. **(b)** The Atlantic Charter called for economic cooperation to ensure a decent standard of living for everyone. The Fourteen Points provided for a general association of nations to guarantee political independence and protection to all states.

7. (a) with economic assistance; **(b)** It feared a Nazi victory.

8. (a) The atomic bomb made war more impersonal and more horrible. **(b)** Other technological developments of the war included radar and sonar. Students may offer more items.

Relating Geography to History

Students should emphasize the differences in the creation of countries and the shift of boundaries in eastern Europe, in particular.

Writing About History

President Truman once declared, "Men make history and not the other way around." Use three of the following leaders as examples to explain Truman's statement: **(a)** Woodrow Wilson, **(b)** Sun Yat-sen, **(c)** Mustafa Kemal, **(d)** Mohandas Gandhi, **(e)** Winston Churchill.

Further Reading

Archer, Jules. *African Firebrand: Kenyatta of Kenya.* Julian Messner, New York. Tells the story of Kenya's struggle for independence during the turbulent 1950s and 1960s.

Feuerlicht, Roberta. *Desperate Act: The Assassination of Franz Ferdinand at Sarajevo.* McGraw-Hill, New York. Describes the events leading to war and the assassination of the archduke.

Marshall, S. L. A. *World War I.* McGraw-Hill, New York. Summarizes the war and its effects.

Richter, Hans Peter. *I Was There.* Dell, New York. Gives an eyewitness account of a boy who participated in German Youth.

Robertson, John R. *China: From Manchu to Mao.* Atheneum, New York. Chronicles twentieth-century China.

Sulzberger, C. L. *World War II.* McGraw-Hill, New York. Covers campaigns of World War II.

Unit Six Chronology

Date	Political and Social Developments	Technological and Scientific Advances	Visual Arts and Literature	Religious and Philosophical Thought
1880–1910	Triple Alliance and Triple Entente **24*** Boxer Rebellion **26** Russo-Japanese War **26**	Industrial Revolution continues **24** Einsteinian physics **25** Louis Sullivan **25**	Picasso, cubism **25** Motion pictures **25**	Freudian psychology **25** Zionism **26**
1910–1920	Chinese Republic **26** Assassination of Francis Ferdinand **24** World War I **24** *Lusitania* sunk **24** Russian Revolution **24** Treaties of Brest-Litovsk and Versailles **24**	U-boats **24** Machine guns **24** Poison gas **24** Tanks **24**	Proust **25** Stravinsky, Schoenberg, Berg, Webern **25**	Gandhi **26**
1920–1930	Weimar Republic **25** Chiang Kai-shek **26**, Mussolini **25**, Stalin **25**, Atatürk **26** Lenin's NEP **25** African and Asian nationalism **26** Fascism **25**	Frank Lloyd Wright **25** Auto, phone, radio **25** Industrialization **24–26**	Mann **25** Kafka and surrealism **25** Joyce's *Ulysses* **25** T. S. Eliot **25** Jazz **25**	Gandhi **26** Spengler's *The Decline of the West* **25**
1930–1939	Rise of Hitler **25** Great Depression **25** FDR's New Deal **25** Soviet purges **25** Kenyatta, Azikiwe **26** Long March **26**	TVA **25**	*The Grapes of Wrath* **25** Dali **25** Big Band Era **25**	
1939–1945	Germany invades Poland **27** Pearl Harbor **27** Yalta and Potsdam **27** Hiroshima **27**	Blitzkrieg **27** Nuclear power **27** Panzer units **27** Radar **27**		Meltzer's *Never to Forget* **27**

*Indicates chapter in which development is discussed.

741

1B, 1C, 4K, 5B, 5D, 5E,
a1C, a3A, a3G, a3H

Focus/Motivation
Point out to students that World War I and World War II involved more of the world than any previous wars in history. On a wall map of the world, illustrate this idea by pointing out the areas involved in the fighting. Ask: Why was so much of the world pulled into these wars? *(Students might suggest that technological advances made rapid communication and transportation possible. In addition, Europeans had established colonies throughout the world. When the Europeans went to war, so did their colonies.)*

UNIT SIX SYNTHESIS

World War in the Twentieth Century

24 World War I and the Russian Revolution Altered the Course of History

The war that began in the summer of 1914 resembled no previous war. For the first time in history, industrial technology, especially the mass production of armaments, played a major role. This horrifying war dragged on for more than four years, taking a terrible toll in lives and property.

Conflicting National Interests

Beginning in the late 1800s, cooperation among European nations broke down as intense rivalries increased. As rivalries intensified in the early 1900s, the great powers built up their military strength and formed secret alliances to protect themselves. Soon they were plunging toward war, pressed forward by four factors: nationalism, imperialism, militarism, and the system of alliances. In 1914 Europe was divided into two armed camps, and even a minor disagreement would threaten global devastation.

The minor incident that plunged Europe into war came in the Balkans on June 28, 1914, when the heir to the Austro-Hungarian throne, Archduke Francis Ferdinand, and his wife were assassinated. The assassin belonged to a secret society of Serbian nationalists who opposed Austria-Hungary.

The assassination brought to a head the long struggle between Serbia and Austria-Hungary. When Serbia did not accept all of the terms of an ultimatum issued by Austria-Hungary, Austria-Hungary declared war. Then on August 1, 1914, Germany declared war on Russia. Convinced that France was prepared to side with Russia and hoping to gain a military advantage by swift action, Germany declared war on France two days later. When German troops passed through neutral Belgium on their way to France, Great Britain declared war on Germany. Many other nations soon entered the war.

A New Kind of War

Germany, Austria-Hungary, Bulgaria, and the Ottoman Empire became known as the Central Powers. They fought the Allied Powers that included Great Britain, France, Russia, and their partners in the war. Eventually 32 countries made up the Allied side. Many of them, however, joined late in the war and made only symbolic contributions to the war effort.

Except for the wars of the French Revolution, most previous European wars had been fought by professional soldiers whose only source of income was their military pay and rations. In contrast, armies of drafted civilians fought the battles of World War I. Those who could not fight worked at home to help the war effort. Many women participated in the war effort by working in factories. This type of war became known as *total war.*

The war soon became a stalemate. Both sides dug long lines of trenches on the western front, which stretched from the Swiss border through Germany, France, and Belgium to the shores of the North Sea. On the eastern front, the Germans forced the Russians back into Poland. Only a few sea battles took place.

As the strongest industrialized neutral nation, the United States became a supplier of food, raw materials, and munitions. Then in 1917, when the Germans began attacking merchant ships, the United States entered the war on the side of the Allies.

The Russian Revolution

The spring of 1917 found the Russians weary of hardships and disheartened by the appalling casualties they had suffered. They had lost all faith in their government and Czar Nicholas II. Strikes and

American soldiers in trenches east of Paris, 1918

street demonstrations broke out in Petrograd, as St. Petersburg had been called since 1914. On March 15, 1917, unable to control his subjects or his army, Nicholas II abdicated. He and his family were executed the following year.

A liberal provisional government was set up to rule Russia until a constitutional assembly could be elected to choose a permanent system of government. While the provisional government tried to restore order, a rival force—the Marxist Bolsheviks—worked for change in Russia. By November the Bolsheviks, or Communists, under the leadership of Nikolai Lenin, had taken over the Russian government.

The Communists signed separate peace treaties with each of the Central Powers in the spring of 1918. The new regime then turned its attention to quelling a civil war that had erupted. By 1921 the Communists had completely defeated their opponents.

Peace Terms

President Wilson of the United States wanted the Allies to work out a just peace. But when the Central Powers finally surrendered in November 1918, the victorious Allies sought revenge. In a series of peace treaties, the Allies redrew the boundaries of Europe. They also humiliated Germany and declared the end of the Dual Monarchy.

The League of Nations

In helping to draft the peace settlements, President Wilson made several compromises with his ideals. He realized that the treaties failed in many respects to provide a "peace of justice." He consoled himself, however, with the thought that the new League of Nations would be able to remedy the injustices inflicted by the treaties.

However, the League of Nations had no real powers to help it maintain peace. In addition, the United States never joined the League.

25 The Great Depression Helped the Rise of Totalitarian Dictators

For a time after World War I, it appeared that the world had indeed been made "safe for democracy." Within a few short decades, however, events proved this assumption false.

Uneasiness in the Postwar Era

Following World War I, many people rejected the beliefs of reason and progress expressed during the Enlightenment. Instead, scientists, writers, and artists expressed a sense of helplessness and cynicism.

These intellectuals, however, appealed only to a small audience. Most people found escape from the disillusionment of troubled times in other new forms of entertainment that "Big Bands," jazz, and films provided.

Architecture also underwent great change during the postwar years. New technical advances, such as the use of structural steel, made skyscrapers and bold new architectural designs possible.

Worldwide Depression

The United States emerged from the war as the apparent successor to Great Britain in world leadership. But the refusal of the United States to join the League of Nations indicated that the United States did not want the responsibility of world leadership. Americans seemed to want to sit back and enjoy their newfound prosperity during what historians have named the Roaring Twenties.

Prosperity, however, was short-lived. The collapse of the American stock market plunged the United States and the rest of the industrial world into a severe economic depression known simply as the Great Depression.

743

1B, 4I, 5B, 5C, 5D, 5G, a1C

Presentation
Interpreting Ideas
(Average/Group)
Point out to students that many people called World War I "the war to end all wars;" yet, less than 30 years after the end of World War I, the world plunged into an even more devastating war. Ask students why they think this happened. *(Students might mention the harsh peace terms that Germany resented.)* Then discuss with students the current prospects for world peace.

A Red Army parade in Moscow

In response to the hardships of the Great Depression, voters in the United States elected Franklin D. Roosevelt president. Roosevelt quickly set up a series of measures, known as the New Deal, to combat the Depression. Only when the United States mobilized for war once more in the late 1930s, however, did the hardships caused by the Great Depression finally end.

Political Tensions

The events of the postwar years put a strain on the older and more experienced European democracies, such as France and Great Britain. France still owed money that it had borrowed from its citizens and from the United States during and after the war. And inflation soared.

Although conditions improved in the 1920s, the Great Depression brought havoc to France. Riots in 1934 almost toppled the government. In 1936 a socialist government took power, but it lasted only a year. Although France remained a democracy, bitter divisions still existed.

Like France, Great Britain faced grave economic difficulties after World War I. While Great Britain retained its democratic government, military dictatorships took power in the nations of eastern Europe.

Fascist Dictatorships

As it did elsewhere, the war and its aftermath took their toll in Italy and Germany. Heavy loss of life, a crushing burden of debt, unemployment, and inflation plagued these countries. In Italy the problems led to the rise of Benito Mussolini, whose Fascist Party set up a military dictatorship. In Germany Adolf Hitler and the Nazi Party came to power in the 1930s. In both countries the new leaders established totalitarian regimes that stripped the citizens of all human rights.

The Soviet Union

Similar developments occurred in the Soviet Union. Although Lenin had allowed some freedoms

1B, 4K, 5A, 5C, 5G, a2J, a2K

as well as free enterprise to exist under his New Economic Policy, his successor, Joesph Stalin, announced the end of the NEP and the return to a completely controlled economy. Through a series of bold Five-Year Plans, the Soviets tried to industrialize. This industrialization, however, concentrated on heavy industry and defense at the expense of consumer goods, creating shortages of the basic necessities of life. Just like the Fascists in Italy and the Nazis in Germany, Stalin created a totalitarian regime that deprived the people of basic human rights. In addition, the Soviets began to export communism to other parts of the world.

New Political Forces Emerged in Africa, Asia, and Latin America

The postwar years also witnessed profound changes outside Europe.

The British Empire

Although the British Empire had grown larger as a result of the Versailles peace agreements, its existence was threatened from within. People in all parts of the empire voiced demands for more self-government, and even for complete independence.

In the Middle East in 1923, the British recognized the independence of Trans-Jordan. By 1930 the British had also recognized the kingdom of Iraq as an independent nation. Then in 1936 the British and Egyptian governments agreed that Egypt would be independent but that Great Britain would control the Suez Canal for 20 years. Only Palestine remained under British control.

As the largest British colony, India posed even greater difficulties than did the Middle Eastern mandates. Indian nationalists clamored for complete independence. Finally, in 1935, after many committee reports and conferences, Great Britain granted India a new constitution that provided for home rule. However, the British viceroy still controlled India's national defense and foreign affairs. Committed to total self-government, the nationalists rejected the new constitution. During the next few years, discontent continued to simmer in India.

Even in those parts of the British Empire that already had a degree of self-government, people

Chinese poster art honoring Mao Zedong

demanded greater independence. After World War I these dominions demanded complete self-government. Showing a remarkable readiness to accommodate, adjust, and accept the political realities, the British gave in without a struggle.

Turkey, Persia, and Africa

The nationalist feelings that swept the Middle East after World War I also affected the Southwest Asian countries of Turkey and Persia and the whole of Africa. In Turkey an able and energetic leader, Mustafa Kemal (kay • MAHL), emerged as the republic's first president and worked to modernize the nation. In 1921 in Persia an army officer with strong nationalist sentiments seized control of the government in a coup d'état. Some four years later, he deposed the ruling shah and assumed the throne, taking the title Reza Shah Pahlavi. Like Kemal, Reza Shah wanted to modernize his country and free it from foreign domination. In Africa many leaders worked for independence; however, their success was limited.

China

In the 1800s the Western powers carved out spheres of influence in China. When the Chinese attempted to oust the foreigners during the Boxer Rebellion, the Westerners crushed the revolt and imposed heavy penalties on the Chinese. The humiliation of this defeat brought on a revolution against the Qing dynasty. In 1911 a series of

745

1B, 4I, 5A, 5B, 5G, a1C

Closure
Ask: How did World War II differ from all previous wars? *(It was more devastating and affected the civilian population to a greater extent.)*

revolts, led mostly by young army officers who supported Sun Yat-sen, spread throughout southern China. In a last desperate gesture to preserve their dynasty, the Qing proclaimed a constitutional monarchy. The rebels, however, would accept nothing but a republic. In 1912 the emperor abdicated and the republic was proclaimed.

But China's problems were far from over. The ruling political party, the Kuomintang, soon split into rival factions. On one side were the Nationalists, led by Chiang Kai-shek. Opposing them were the Communists, led by Mao Zedong. The two sides never resolved their differences, and until the late 1940s, continued to wage war.

Japan

By 1920 Japan had advanced from a feudal agrarian nation to one of the world's leading industrial and military powers. However, this rapid change brought a deterioration of traditional values. Although the economy grew rapidly, it could not provide jobs for all those who wanted them. As a result, Japanese people began to emigrate to Korea, Taiwan, and Hawaii, as well as other islands of the Pacific. Thousands more left for the United States.

In addition, Japan had to export goods in order to buy needed raw materials from other countries. Many countries, however, levied high tariffs on Japanese goods. The Japanese resented these tariffs. This resentment led many Japanese to accept the arguments of military leaders that Japan needed to become an imperialist power in order to survive.

Latin America

The 1920s brought prosperity to Latin America as it did to much of the world, and for a time the region seemed destined for stability. But the Great Depression dashed these prospects. Demand for the region's products shrank, and the United States and Europe halted investment in Latin America.

Economic crisis soon led to political crisis. Coups d'état overthrew most Latin American governments in the 1930s. In many cases these coups toppled constitutional systems that had worked for 30 to 40 years. Only Uruguay, which experienced a minor crisis between 1933 and 1935, and Mexico, which had undergone a revolution from 1911 to 1917, avoided major political upheaval.

27 Local Aggressions Brought About World War II

By the 1930s most European nations once more claimed loyalty to one of two opposing camps. One group included those nations generally satisfied with the World War I peace settlement. The other group consisted of dissatisfied nations that wanted change.

Threats to World Peace

Although many international conferences in the 1920s worked to maintain peace, several local conflicts erupted. In Asia, Japan, under the influence of its militaristic leaders, invaded Manchuria, set up the puppet state of Manchukuo, and invaded China itself. In Africa, Mussolini invaded and conquered Ethiopia. And in Spain a bitter civil war resulted in the establishment of a fascist government under the leadership of Francisco Franco.

Nazi Aggressions

Germany also embarked on a program of conquest in the 1930s. In March 1936 German troops marched into the Rhineland, violating the Treaty of Versailles. Then in October 1936, following the outbreak of the Spanish civil war, Hitler and Mussolini formed a military alliance called the Rome-Berlin Axis and began referring to themselves as the Axis Powers. Shortly afterward, Japan and Germany pledged to work together to prevent the spread of Russian communism.

Perhaps emboldened by the inability of the League of Nations to act, Hitler continued his conquests. In March 1938 his troops marched unopposed into Austria, and later that year he occupied the Sudetenland in Czechoslovakia. The next year he occupied all of Czechoslovakia. Even though the Czechs had alliances with Great Britain and France, the Western democracies were unwilling to defend their ally.

Wanting still more territory, Hitler took part of Lithuania in early 1939. About the same time, Mussolini conquered Albania.

Faced with all of this Fascist aggression, Great Britain and France prepared for war. Although the two countries tried to forge an alliance with Joseph Stalin of the Soviet Union, their negotiations

Question 1 of the Synthesis Review corresponds to Section 24 of the synthesis; Question 2, to Section 25; Question 3, to Section 26; Question 4, to Section 27. Question 5 asks students to synthesize information from various sections of the synthesis.

1B, 5B, 5E, 5G, 5I, a1C, a2K, a4A, a4G, a4H, a4I, a4L

failed. Instead, Stalin shocked the world by announcing that he had concluded a nonaggression pact with Germany. Publicly the Nazi-Soviet Pact pledged that Germany and the Soviet Union would never attack each other. Each would remain neutral if the other became involved in war. Secretly, the two dictators agreed to divide eastern Europe into spheres of influence.

Emboldened by the pact with Stalin, Hitler launched his next act of aggression with an attack on Poland on September 1, 1939. This time Great Britain and France stood by their ally and declared war. World War II had begun.

Axis Gains

On September 27, 1939, after a brief but devastating war, the Poles surrendered to Hitler. Then after several months of inaction, Hitler invaded Scandinavia, the Netherlands, Belgium, and France. By June 14, 1940, the Nazis were marching through Paris. Hitler tried to conquer Great Britain as well, but the British held their own, assisted by the United States. Although the United States remained officially neutral, it gave assistance to Great Britain in the form of war supplies.

Soviet and American Involvement

By late 1941 it appeared that the Axis Powers were winning the war, conquering much of eastern Europe and pushing into North Africa. Hitler failed, however, in his attempt to conquer the Middle East and its rich oil fields. By 1942 the British had stalled Nazi advances in North Africa.

On June 22, 1941, the war entered a new phase. Without a declaration of war, German armies invaded the Soviet Union. British Prime Minister Churchill declared that, although he did not admire communism, any nation that fought the Nazis was an ally and should receive help. The United States also declared its willingness to assist the Soviet Union. This assistance helped the Soviets stall the Nazi offensive.

The invasion of the Soviet Union was part of Hitler's master plan for the creation of a "New Order" for Europe. To build this New Order, the Nazis mercilessly slaughtered millions of Jews, Gypsies, and other groups whom they considered inferior races.

Pearl Harbor after Japan's surprise attack

The struggle against the Axis Powers received a major boost in December 1941, when Japan attacked the United States naval base at Pearl Harbor, Hawaii, and the United States declared war on the Axis Powers.

Allied Victory

Throughout 1942 the Axis Powers faced defeats on every front. Then with the Allied invasion of France in 1944, the war reached its final phase. By 1945 Germany surrendered. Japan soon followed suit after the United States unleashed the power of the first atomic bombs on Hiroshima and Nagasaki.

Even before the end of the war, Allied leaders Franklin Roosevelt of the United States, Winston Churchill of Great Britain, and Joseph Stalin of the Soviet Union had met at Yalta in the Soviet Union. The Big Three, as these Allied leaders were called, agreed that Germany should be temporarily divided and occupied by troops of the victorious powers, including France. Another conference began on July 17, 1945, at Potsdam, near Berlin. At this conference the leaders planned for the control and occupation of Germany.

SYNTHESIS REVIEW

1. **Comparing Ideas** How did World War I differ from earlier wars?
2. **Interpreting Ideas** Why did the Great Depression lead to political instability in Europe?
3. **Evaluating Ideas** What factors led many Japanese to favor the militarists?
4. **Understanding Ideas** What event precipitated Japan's surrender?
5. **Synthesizing Ideas** How did disillusionment with the World War I peace settlements lead to World War II?

Review Answers

1. For the first time in history, industrial technology, especially the mass production of armaments, played a major role.
2. Grave economic difficulties led to widespread discontent and resulted in political instability.
3. Many countries levied high tariffs on Japanese goods. The Japanese resented these tariffs. This resentment led many Japanese to accept the arguments of military leaders that Japan needed to conquer more territories to survive.
4. the dropping of the atomic bombs
5. The Germans believed that the peace agreements were unjust and thirsted for revenge. As a result, they were willing to follow Hitler who pledged a restoration of national honor and prestige.

747

Introducing the Unit
Have students look at the picture of Singapore on this page. Ask them to note the elements of both the traditional and modern worlds in the picture. *(old-style houses and boats in the foreground, modern skyscrapers in the background)* As students work through this unit, ask them to consider why this mixture of traditional and modern might serve as an excellent metaphor for the Asian experience in the twentieth century.

Unit Objectives
After studying Unit Seven, students will be able to:

1. Explain how postwar problems were settled in Europe.
2. Discuss how the cold war influenced Europe.
3. Explain why the Communist bloc developed in Europe.
4. Identify the major problems in the postwar world.
5. Outline the spread of communism after 1945.
6. Explain why Japan became a leading economic power after World War II.
7. Analyze how nations in Africa, the Middle East, and Southeast Asia achieved independence after World War II.
8. Summarize the impact of the Vietnam War.
9. Describe the conflicts in Latin America, Mexico, and the Caribbean Islands since 1945.
10. Outline the leadership role of the United States in world affairs from 1968 to the present.

UNIT SEVEN

The World Since 1945

◀ *Singapore, an example of modern Asia*

11. List signs of economic and political stability in Western Europe in the 1970s and 1980s.
12. Identify the political and economic challenges the Soviet Union and Eastern Europe faced in the 1980s.
13. Describe how technological changes affected ideas and behavior after World War II.
14. Identify changes in the arts and literature after 1945.
15. Summarize changes in the patterns of living in the postwar era.

749

CHAPTER (pages 750–773)

28 Challenges Faced Europe and North America in the Postwar Years

(1945–1968)

CHAPTER OVERVIEW

The United Nations, planned during World War II, was established in 1945 to help maintain worldwide peace. However, postwar hostilities hindered agreement on peace terms. Treaties were quickly completed with Italy and four other German allies, but the Austrian treaty required 10 years of negotiation. No final agreement was reached on Germany.

Eastern European nations became satellites of the Soviet Union. In an effort to contain communism, President Truman announced the Truman Doctrine and gave economic aid to Europe through the Marshall Plan. When the Soviet Union blockaded Berlin, a Western airlift supplied the city. Soon afterward, Germany was divided.

Cold-war rivalries led to the formation of the North Atlantic Treaty Organization (NATO), a mutual defense pact among the Western nations. The Soviet Union and its satellites responded by forming the Warsaw Pact.

Despite the tensions of the cold war, Europe experienced a very impressive economic recovery. Germany remained divided, but West Germany prospered economically. Great Britain became a welfare state but continued to face severe economic problems. France's president, Charles de Gaulle, steered the country on an independent course in international affairs. And European economic unity was advanced by the establishment of the Common Market.

The United States emerged as one of the world's superpowers, but the nation faced a number of problems in the postwar years. The consistent aim in foreign policy was to resist the ambitions of communist nations. At home, the presidents introduced social programs and domestic reforms that sought to maintain a flourishing economy.

Canada experienced considerable economic development after World War II. Close economic and military ties developed between Canada and the United States, but Canadians feared becoming too dependent on their neighbor to the south.

SUGGESTED LESSON PLAN

Day	Objectives	Suggested Activities	Materials
1	U1* C1–4	Introducing the Unit (pages 748–49) Introducing the Chapter (pages 750–51) Section 1 (pages 751–57), Focus/Motivation (page 751), Presentation (page 752), Closure (page 755), Suggested Teaching Strategies, Enrichment Activities, Daily Quiz, Suggested Assignments (page 749B)	ATE, Pupil's Edition, Teacher's Resource-Bank™
2	U2–5, C5–8	Section 2 (pages 758–62), Focus/Motivation (page 758), Presentation (page 758), Closure (page 761), Suggested Teaching Strategies, Enrichment Activity, Daily Quiz, Suggested Assignments (page 749C)	ATE, Pupil's Edition, Teacher's Resource-Bank™
3	U4, C 9–10	Section 3 (pages 762–67), Focus/Motivation (page 762), Presentation (page 763), Closure (page 766), Suggested Teaching Strategies, Enrichment Activity, Daily Quiz, Suggested Assignments (page 749D)	ATE, Pupil's Edition, Teacher's Resource-Bank™
4	U4–5, C10–11	Section 4 (pages 767–69), Focus/Motivation (page 767), Presentation (page 767), Closure (page 767), Suggested Teaching Strategies, Enrichment Activity, Daily Quiz, Suggested Assignments (page 749E)	ATE, Pupil's Edition, Teacher's Resource-Bank™
5	U4, C12–13	Section 5 (pages 769–71), Focus/Motivation (page 769), Presentation (page 769), Closure (page 770), Suggested Teaching Strategies, Enrichment Activity, Daily Quiz, Suggested Assignments (page 749E)	ATE, Pupil's Edition, Teacher's Resource-Bank™
6	U1–5 C1–13	Chapter 28 Form A Test, Reteaching Worksheet, Chapter 28 Form B Test	Teacher's Resource-Bank™ or Workbook and Test Booklet

*C refers to applicable Chapter Objective, U refers to applicable Unit Goal

BOOKS FOR THE TEACHER

Acheson, Dean. *Present at the Creation.* W. W. Norton. Provides an interesting and detailed eyewitness account of Truman's postwar foreign policy.

Halle, L. J. *The Cold War as History.* Harper & Row. Details the development of the cold war.

McClellan, Grant S., ed. *Canada in Transition.* H.W. Wilson. Provides a picture of Canada in a collection of articles.

Mee, C. L., Jr. *Meeting at Potsdam.* M. Evans. Discusses the participants and issues at the Potsdam Conference.

O'Neill, W.L. *Coming Apart: An Informal History of the United States in the 1960s.* Quadrangle. Surveys the social history of this turbulent decade.

Smith, Hedrick. *The Russians.* Ballantine. Offers a fascinating portrait of present-day Soviet society.

BOOKS FOR THE STUDENT

Downberg, John. *Eastern Europe: A Communist Kaleidoscope.* Dial. Presents an interesting account of life behind the iron curtain.

Harris, Nathaniel. *The Forties and Fifties.* MacDonald. Offers an illustrated history of the period from 1946 to 1959.

Haskins, James. *The Life and Death of Martin Luther King, Jr.* Lothrop, Lee & Shephard. Presents a highly readable portrait of the great civil rights leader.

Hoepli, Nancy L., ed. *The Common Market.* H. W. Wilson. Offers a series of articles about the European Economic Community.

Maclean, Fitzroy. *Tito.* McGraw-Hill. Summarizes the life of Yugoslavia's leader. Includes many illustrations.

Marshall, Charles B. *The Cold War: A Concise History.* Franklin Watts. Provides a brief account of the cold war.

Sterling, Dorothy. *Tear Down the Walls.* Doubleday. Details the history of the civil rights movement in the United States.

MULTIMEDIA MATERIALS

Apostle of Power: Dr. Martin Luther King, Jr. (mp, 14 min.), Screen News. Spans the years from the Montgomery bus boycott to the civil-rights leader's burial in Atlanta.

Canada: Our Great Northern Neighbor (2 fs), Prentice-Hall. Examines U. S.-Canadian ties and the problems of separatism.

The Cold War: The Early Period (1947–1953) (mp, 18 min.), McGraw-Hill. Identifies the events that led to the cold war.

The Common Market (2 fs), Educational Audio-Visual. Details the planning and organization of the Common Market.

Germany: The Road of Return (mp, 30 min.), Filmfare. Traces the development of divided Germany from the end of World War II to the present.

Section 1 (pages 751–757) Europe Attempted to Regain Stability

SECTION OVERVIEW

Although diplomats soon completed peace treaties with Italy and four other German allies, the Austrian treaty required 10 years of negotiations. Germany and Berlin were divided into four zones, and a temporary border was fixed. A flood of East German refugees to West Germany created problems, as did the question of rebuilding Germany's industry. At the Nuremberg trials, top Nazi leaders were convicted. Also, a program of denazification was undertaken.

In response to a worldwide desire for peace, the United Nations was established in 1945. Its aims were to maintain peace and security, to encourage respect for human rights, and to develop international cooperation.

SUGGESTED TEACHING STRATEGIES

1. **Preteaching Vocabulary (Basic)** You may wish to preteach the following important vocabulary terms: cold war *(page 751)*; veto power *(page 755)*; developing nation, developed nation *(page 757)*. Ask students to make a generalization about the locations of developing nations and developed nations. *(Most developing nations are in the Third World — Africa, Asia, and Latin America. Most developed nations are in the West — North America and Western Europe.)*
2. **Comparing Ideas (Average/Group)** Have students list the Allies' policies toward Germany after World War I. *(These included disarmament, territorial losses, enormous reparations, little economic aid.)* Review how this treatment affected Germany. *(It helped cause inflation, resentment toward the Allies and disenchantment with the Weimar government, and ultimately led to the rise of the Nazi government.)* Next have students list the Allies' treatment of Germany after World War II. *(It included disarmament, territorial losses, moderate reparations, substantial economic aid, and division and occupation of the country.)* Ask students how this treatment compares with that following World War I. *(Most student answers will point out the following: In both cases the policies reflect punishment and restriction of Germany's ability to renew war. The moderate repearations and substantial aid after World War II incidate that the Allies had learned from the failures of the Treaty of Versailles. These policies aimed at limiting the motivation for renewing war — economic hardship and revenge.)*

ENRICHMENT ACTIVITIES

1. **Using Primary Sources (Average/Group)** The purpose, function, and structure of the United Nations can be studied directly from its charter. You might go over the charter with students by reading and discussing sections of it. The document can be found in Sydney Eisen's and Maurice Filler's *The Human Adventure,* vol. 2 (Harcourt Brace Jovanovich).
2. **Preparing a Newscast (Average/Group)** Interested students might like to prepare an imaginary newscast from the Potsdam Conference. A reporter should interview students representing Truman, Stalin, and Churchill. Questions should focus on such topics as the Polish boundary, the division of Germany, German reparations, and the ultimatum to Japan. Sources for research on the conference include: C. L. Mee, Jr.'s *Meeting at Potsdam* (M. Evans) and T. A. Bailey's *A Diplomatic History of the American People* (Appleton-Century-Crofts).

DAILY QUIZ

To assess student understanding of Section 1, give the class the following quiz. (Each item is worth 10 points.)

1. In 1945 the Allies held conferences at _______ and _______ to try to plan postwar policy. *(Yalta, Potsdam)*
2. Which organization wrote the peace treaties that ended World War II? *(The Council of Foreign Ministers)*
3. Who led the provisional government that ran France until the proclamation of the Fourth Republic in 1946? *(Charles de Gaulle)*
4. Where did a special international court meet to try Nazi leaders for war crimes? *(Nuremberg)*
5. The Allies pursued a policy of _______, which included the removal of all former Nazis from positions of authority in Germany. *(denazification)*
6. Which world leader first used the term "united nations" to refer to the countries allied against the Axis powers? *(President Franklin D. Roosevelt)*
7. Where was the first meeting of the United Nations General Assembly held? *(San Francisco)*
8. What constitutes the General Assembly of the United Nations? *(representatives of all the member nations)*
9. Which nations are the five permanent members of the Security Council? *(the United States, Great Britain, the Soviet Union, France, and China)*
10. What is the goal of the World Health Organization? *(for all the peoples of the world to enjoy good health)*

SUGGESTED ASSIGNMENTS

1. **Critical Thinking Worksheet (Average/Group)** Have students complete Critical Thinking Worksheet 65 in the TEACHER'S RESOURCEBANK™.
2. **Identifying Ideas (Average/Group)** Ask students to write on a sheet of paper one recent accomplishment they associate with the UN. This accomplishment can be of a military, political, or humanitarian nature. *(Students may mention the work of UNICEF, UNDP, WHO, FAO, the World Bank, and other agencies.)* Then ask students to list any failures of the UN. *(Students may mention the inability of the UN to stop wars — the Arab-Israeli conflict, for example—or its failure to slow the nuclear arms race.)* Use students' lists as a starting point for a discussion.

Section 2 (pages 758–762) The Cold War Divided Europe

SECTION OVERVIEW

The United States announced the Truman Doctrine and the Marshall Plan in response to Soviet expansion in Eastern Europe. Fear of Soviet expansion also caused the formation of the North Atlantic Treaty Organization (NATO). The Soviet Union responded by establishing the Warsaw Pact. Despite rising cold-war tensions, internal dissent caused these two alliances to weaken.

SUGGESTED TEACHING STRATEGIES

1. **Preteaching Vocabulary (Basic)** You may wish to preteach the following important vocabulary terms: satellite, iron-curtain country, containment *(page 758)*; summit conference *(page 761)*. Ask students to identify the satellite nations of the Soviet Union during the 1940s and 1950s. *(Poland, East Germany, Czechoslovakia, Hungary, Bulgaria, and Romania. Point out to students that although Albania and Yugoslavia are sometimes considered satellites, during the 1950s they followed a course somewhat independent of the Soviet Union.)*
2. **Writing a Paragraph (Average/Group)** Have students write a paragraph on each of the following: the Truman Doctrine, the Marshall Plan, the Berlin airlift, NATO, and the Warsaw Pact. Have them explain each topic's origins in the postwar period, its contribution to Europe, and its effect on the tension between the two superpowers. Encourage students to share their paragraphs with other members of the class.

*3. **Reading About History: Identifying an Argument (Basic)** To reinforce the skill lesson presented on page 760, have students identify the argument the authors make on page 761 about summit conferences. *(that summit conferences rarely produced substantive results)*

ENRICHMENT ACTIVITY

Drawing a Political Cartoon (Average/Group) Have each student draw a political cartoon concerning an event discussed in this section. Remind students that political cartoons should express a point of view about an event and may make use of pointed captions, caricature, and satire. The cartoons might be displayed on the bulletin board.

DAILY QUIZ

To assess student understanding of Section 2, give the class the following quiz. (Each item is worth 10 points.)

1. In 1946, Winston Churchill stated that an _______ _______ had descended across Europe from the Baltic to Trieste. *(iron curtain)*
2. The Truman Doctrine, which called for the restriction of the spread of communism, is sometimes referred to as _______. *(containment)*
3. What was the more-frequently used name for the European Recovery Program? *(Marshall Plan)*
4. Which Yugoslav leader objected to Soviet domination of the internal affairs of his country? *(Marshal Tito)*
5. How did the Soviet Union respond to plans by the Western occupying powers to unite their zones of Germany? *(it blockaded Berlin)*

6. In what year was Germany officially divided into two countries? *(1949)*
7. In April 1949 twelve nations signed a mutual defense pact that established the _______ _______ _______ _______. *(North Atlantic Treaty Organization)*
8. What was the name of the mutual defense agreement signed by European Communist bloc countries? *(Warsaw Pact)*
9. What incident led to the cancellation of a summit conference between Premier Khrushchev and President Eisenhower in 1960? *(the shooting down of an American spy plane over the Soviet Union)*
10. Which European leader wanted to loosen his country's ties with NATO during the 1960s? *(Charles de Gaulle of France)*

SUGGESTED ASSIGNMENTS

1. **Critical Thinking Worksheet (Average/Group)** Have students complete Critical Thinking Worksheet 63 in the TEACHER'S RESOURCEBANK™.
2. **Writing a Report (Average/Group)** Interested students might like to prepare and write reports on the history of summit conferences. One useful source of information on this subject is Robert Wernick's "Summits of Yore: Promises, Promises and a Deal or Two" (*Smithsonian*, September 1986).
3. **Profile Worksheet (Basic)** Have students complete Profile Worksheet 28 in the TEACHER'S RESOURCEBANK™.
4. **Skill Worksheet (Basic)** Have students complete Skill Worksheet 28 in the TEACHER'S RESOURCEBANK™.

Section 3 (pages 762–767)

Western Europe Experienced Progress and Setbacks

SECTION OVERVIEW

One of the outstanding characteristics of postwar Europe was its economic recovery, particularly in West Germany. Great Britain adopted a moderate form of socialism, and the Fifth French Republic was established in France. Perhaps the most significant postwar development in Europe was the establishment of the Common Market, a major step toward European economic union.

SUGGESTED TEACHING STRATEGIES

1. **Preteaching Vocabulary (Basic)** You may wish to preteach the following important vocabulary terms: market economy, command economy *(page 762)*; welfare state *(page 764)*. Ask: What are the advantages and disadvantages of a welfare state? *(Answers will vary. Accept all reasonable answers.)*
2. **Illustrating Ideas (Average/Group)** To aid students' understanding of the history and purpose of the Common Market, you might show the two-part filmstrip *The Common Market* (Educational Audio-Visual). Then ask students why the organization came into existence and what it has accomplished so far.

ENRICHMENT ACTIVITY

Analyzing Ideas (Average/Group) Have students study the picture of the Berlin Wall on page 750. Then organize the class into two groups. Have one group of students imagine they are West Berliners and the other imagine they are East Berliners. Lead the two groups in a discussion of how they feel about the wall that divides their city. After the discussion, ask students to write a paragraph summarizing the feelings of Berliners about the wall. Students might like to read Peter Schneider's *The Wall Jumper* (Pantheon), which covers this subject in novel form.

DAILY QUIZ

To assess student understanding of Section 3, give the class the following quiz. (Each item is worth 10 points.)

1. Which European nation's economic recovery was referred to as a "miracle"? *(West Germany)*
2. Which West German chancellor established strong alliances with Western nations and worked for his country's acceptance by NATO? *(Konrad Adenauer)*
3. How did the East German government stem the flow of refugees fleeing to the West? *(by building walls and fences along the border between East and West)*
4. (T or F) In the postwar years, Great Britain became a welfare state, with the government providing for the social welfare of its citizens. *(T)*
5. Under the constitution of the Fifth French Republic, much power was concentrated in the hands of the _______. *(president)*
6. What caused President Charles de Gaulle to dissolve the French National Assembly and call a general election in 1968? *(violent student demonstrations and widespread strikes)*
7. In 1952 France, West Germany, Italy, and the _______ countries formed the European Coal and Steel Community. *(Benélux)*
8. The European Economic Community (EEC), also known as the _______ _______, planned to abolish tariffs and import quotas among member nations. *(Common Market)*
9. (T or F) Great Britain, Denmark, and Spain all were original members of the EEC. *(F)*
10. (T or F) The founding members of the EEC hoped for political as well as economic unity for Europe. *(T)*

SUGGESTED ASSIGNMENTS

1. **Writing a Report (Average/Group)** Interested students might like to write brief reports on the events of May 1968 that nearly brought down the government of Charles de Gaulle. A useful source of information on this topic is David Caute's *The Year of the Barricades* (Harper & Row). Have students read their reports to the rest of the class.
2. **Writing an Editorial (Challenging)** Have interested students write an editorial supporting or opposing a political union of the nations of Western Europe. Suggest that the students write their

editorials from an American viewpoint. Use these editorials as a starting point for a discussion on the impact of such a union on American economic and foreign policies.

Section (pages 767–769)

4 The Communist Bloc Faced Challenges in the Postwar Period

SECTION OVERVIEW

After the death of Stalin in 1953, Nikita Khrushchev became the leader of the Soviet Union. Khrushchev denounced Stalin's abuses and introduced a number of economic, social, and political reforms. His failure to revitalize the Soviet economy, however, led to his downfall.

During the 1950s and 1960s, a number of satellite nations rebelled against Soviet domination. However, efforts at democratization in East Germany, Hungary, and Czechoslovakia were put down by Soviet troops.

Like their Western counterparts, the nations of Eastern Europe attempted economic union. In 1949 the Council for Mutual Economic Assistance (COMECON) was established to coordinate industrial development and trade within the Soviet bloc.

SUGGESTED TEACHING STRATEGIES

1. **Understanding Chronology (Basic)** Write the following list of events on the chalkboard or an overhead projector and have students copy it in their notebooks. Then have students number the events in the correct chronological order.

    4 U–2 spy airplane shot down
    6 Khrushchev forced to resign
    3 Uprising in Hungary
    5 Berlin Wall built
    2 Khrushchev became Soviet premier
    1 Stalin died

2. **Researching (Average/Group)** Select students to work together to find out more about the Prague Spring and the Soviet invasion of Czechoslovakia in 1968. Useful sources of information on these topics include: Tad Szulc's *Czechoslovakia Since World War II* (Viking) and Z. A. B. Zeman's *Prague Spring* (Hill & Wang). Ask students to present their findings in an oral report to the rest of the class.

ENRICHMENT ACTIVITY

Writing a Script (Challenging) Interested students might like to develop a script for a "You Are There" program on one of the following topics: the Hungarian uprising; the building of the Berlin Wall; or the trial of Gary Powers, the U-2 pilot shot down over the Soviet Union. Stress that the bulk of the script should deal with the reactions of ordinary people. Have students perform the script for the rest of the class.

DAILY QUIZ

To assess student understanding of Section 4, give the class the following quiz. (Each item is worth 10 points.)

1. Nikita Khrushchev initiated a program of ________ in which he lifted restrictions on intellectuals, freed some political prisoners, and ended some of the terrorism of the secret police. *(de-Stalinization)*
2. List two ways in which Khrushchev loosened the central government's tight control on the economy. *(Incentives were given to increase agricultural production, and factory and farm managers were given much more control in order to meet production quotas.)*
3. What name was given to the foreign policy adopted by Khrushchev? *(peaceful coexistence)*
4. Who succeeded Khrushchev as leaders of the Soviet Union? *(Leonid Brezhnev and Aleksei Kosygin)*
5. Yugoslavia's growing independence from the Soviet Union after 1948 was known as ________. *(Titoism)*
6. Which country revolted against Soviet domination in 1956? *(Hungary)*
7. Which Czech leader instituted a series of reforms known as the "Prague Spring?" *(Alexander Dubcek)*
8. In which year did the Soviet-bloc nations establish the Council for Mutual Economic Assistance (COMECON)? *(1949)*
9. What was the main purpose of COMECON? *(to coordinate industrial development and trade within the Soviet bloc)*
10. What was the major weakness of COMECON? *(lacked trade flexibility)*

SUGGESTED ASSIGNMENTS

1. **Critical Thinking Worksheet (Average/Group)** Have students complete Critical Thinking Worksheet 64 in the TEACHER'S RESOURCEBANK™.
2. **Constructing a Chart (Average/Group)** Have students construct charts comparing the Common Market and COMECON. Suggest that students include such headings as "Members," "Purpose," "Strengths," and "Weaknesses" in their charts. Select students to display their charts on the bulletin board.

Section (pages 769–771)

5 The United States and Canada Entered a New Era After 1945

SECTION OVERVIEW

In the area of foreign policy after 1945, the consistent aim of the United States was to resist the spread of communism throughout the world. Domestically, the economy reached new heights of production, but it was hit by a number of recessions. Such serious problems as McCarthyism and civil rights and antiwar protests troubled the United States during this period.

After World War II, Canada experienced economic growth and it forged closer ties with the United States. However, many Canadians feared that American industries might eventually gain control of the Canadian economy.

SUGGESTED TEACHING STRATEGIES

1. **Preteaching Vocabulary (Basic)** You may wish to preteach the following important vocabulary terms: recession *(page 769)*; lobbying *(page 770)*. Ask: What is the difference between a recession and a depression? *(Essentially, a depression is deeper and more prolonged than a recession.)*
2. **Preparing an Oral Report (Average/Group)** Interested students might like to work together to prepare and present an oral report on the construction of the St. Lawrence Seaway. One source of information on this subject is the *National Geographic* article, "New St. Lawrence Seaway Opens the Great Lakes to the World" (March 1959).

ENRICHMENT ACTIVITY

Analyzing Ideas (Average/Group) Ask a student to obtain a copy of Martin Luther King, Jr.'s "I Have a Dream" speech. Then ask for a volunteer to read the speech to the class. In a class discussion, have students speculate on the impact the speech had on the American people in 1963. End the discussion by asking the following question: Has Dr. King's dream been fulfilled? Why or why not?

DAILY QUIZ

To assess student understanding of Section 5, give the class the following quiz. (Each item is worth 10 points.)

1. Which organization did President Eisenhower help to found in an attempt to halt Communist advances in Asia? *(Southeast Asia Treaty Organization or SEATO)*
2. What did the Eisenhower Doctrine entail? *(the provision of economic and military assistance to non-Communist countries in the Middle East)*
3. What was the major focus of American foreign policy during the presidency of Lyndon B. Johnson? *(Vietnam War)*
4. President Johnson's package of domestic reforms was known as the ________ ________. *(Great Society)*
5. Who was the major spokesman of the "conspiracy theory" during the 1950s? *(Senator Joseph McCarthy)*
6. Which landmark Supreme Court decision called for the end of segregation in American schools? *(Brown* v. *Board of Education of Topeka)*
7. Which civil rights leader, who insisted on the use of nonviolence in attaining his goals, won the Nobel Peace Prize in 1964? *(Martin Luther King, Jr.)*
8. Which country provided most of the capital for Canada's postwar industrial development? *(United States)*
9. What is the DEW Line? *(the Distant Early Warning Line, a line of radar installations across the Arctic to furnish early warnings of air attacks from the Soviet Union)*
10. How did the construction of the St. Lawrence Seaway help American and Canadian trade? *(It enabled oceangoing ships to reach all the ports on the Great Lakes.)*

SUGGESTED ASSIGNMENTS

1. **Constructing a Chart (Basic)** Have students make charts in their notebooks listing the postwar foreign policy actions of Presidents Truman, Eisenhower, Kennedy, and Johnson. Encourage students to compare their charts with those of other members of the class.
2. **Review Worksheet (Basic)** Have students complete Review Worksheet 28 in the TEACHER'S RESOURCEBANK™.

For suggested lesson plan, additional teaching strategies, enrichment activities, daily quizzes, and suggested assignments, see pages 749A–749F.

Introducing the Chapter
Ask students to suggest what the term *cold war* means *(conflict between Communist and Western nations waged by political and economic, rather than military, means).* Then ask the class why neither East nor West wanted a "hot" war. *(Many nations were still recovering from the devastation of World War II; the development of the atomic bomb increased the dangers of war.)*

Make certain students understand that the distrust and tension between Western and Communist nations were several decades old. Ask students what earlier events may have contributed to the distrust. *(Students should mention the following: Western intervention in the Russian civil war, loss of Soviet land through the Treaty of Versailles, temporary exclusion of the Soviet Union from the League of Nations, the Hitler-Stalin Pact, and the Allies' delay in starting a second front during World War II.)*

Chapter Objectives
After studying Chapter 28, students will be able to:

1. Discuss the various treaties and settlements that brought World War II to an end.
2. Describe the Nuremberg trials and the denazification program.
3. List the four major purposes of the United Nations.
4. Outline the organization of the United Nations.

CHAPTER 28

Challenges Faced Europe and North America in the Postwar Years

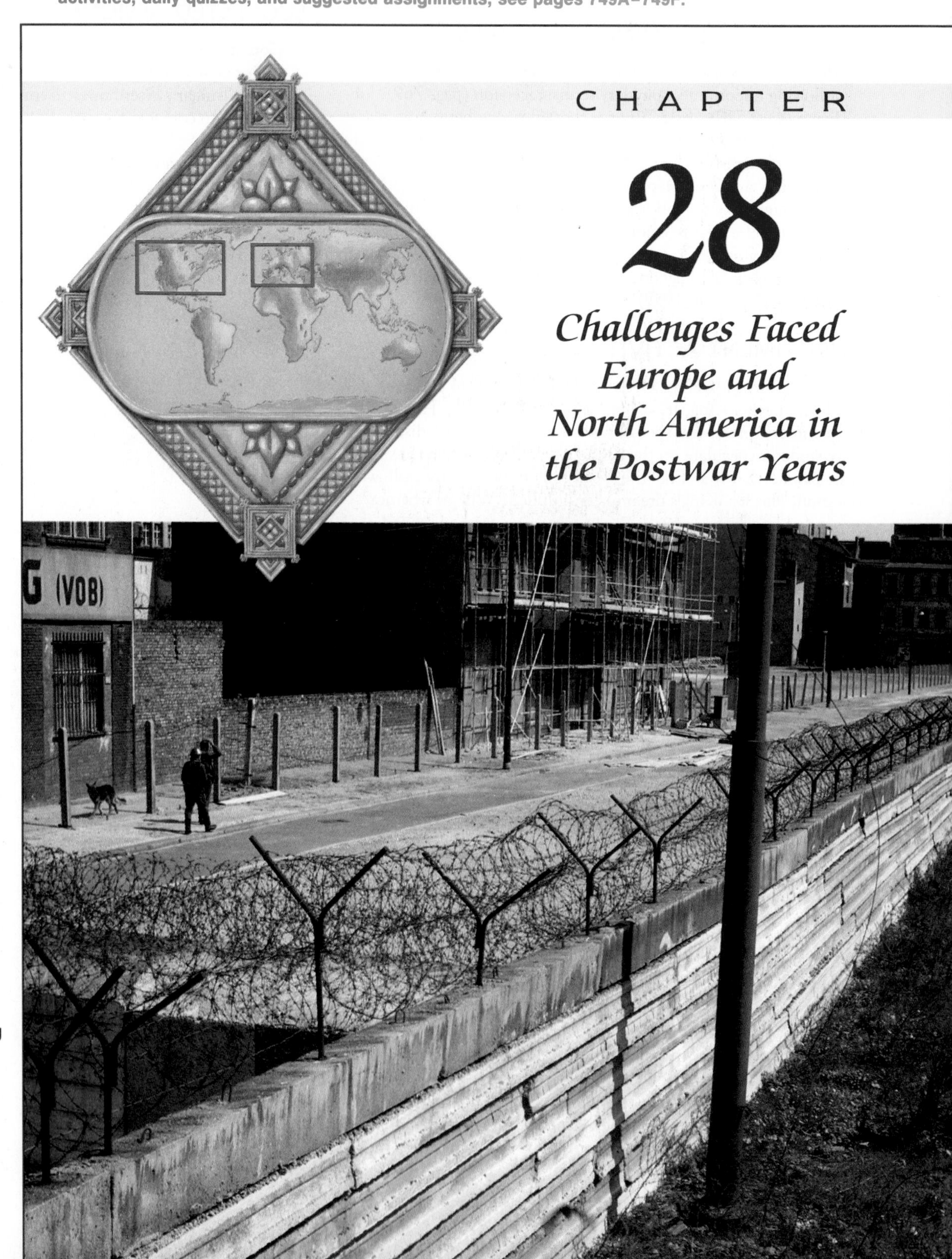

● The term *cold war* was coined by American journalist Herbert Bayard Swope. However, its usage was popularized by journalist and political commentator Walter Lippman.

CHAPTER FOCUS

Place Europe, the United States, and Canada

Time 1945–1968

3.7 mil. BC 4000 BC AD 2100

Significance

The Allies met several times before the end of World War II and mutually agreed to terms for the restructuring of postwar Europe. However, with the need to maintain an alliance against a common enemy removed, old antagonisms between the United States and the Soviet Union soon revived. The split that developed among the former Allies placed the democratic nations and other non-Communist countries, led by the United States, Great Britain, and France, on one side and the Communist nations, led by the Soviet Union, on the other side.

Suspicion and hostility between the Communist and Western nations led to the so-called **cold war**—waged by political and economic means rather than with weapons. The cold war shaped the foreign policies of the East and West, established the United States and the Soviet Union as "superpowers," and had a profound effect on world events after the end of World War II.

Terms to Define

veto power	containment
satellite	recession
iron curtain	lobbying

People to Identify

George C. Marshall	Ludwig Erhard
Marshal Tito	Alexander Dubcek
Nikita Khrushchev	Joseph McCarthy
Konrad Adenauer	Martin Luther King, Jr.

Places to Locate

Stettin	Oder-Neisse line
Trieste	East Prussia
Berlin	Nuremberg

Questions to Guide Your Reading

1 How did the victors attempt to settle Europe's postwar problems?
2 How did the cold war influence events in Europe?
3 What cooperative ventures contributed to the economic recovery of Western Europe?
4 How did the Communist bloc develop during the postwar era?
5 What challenges faced the United States and Canada in the postwar world?

In 1946 Sir Winston Churchill, the former prime minister of Great Britain, visited Westminster College in Fulton, Missouri. His address to an audience of students, faculty, and their distinguished guest, President Harry Truman, became one of the most memorable speeches of his career.

The recent takeovers by Soviet-backed Communist regimes in Eastern Europe had deeply disturbed the Western nations. The following excerpt from Churchill's speech describes the shadow of uncertainty that darkened postwar Europe—and the world.

> *"A shadow has fallen upon the scene so lately lighted by the Allied victory. . . . From Stettin in the Baltic to Trieste in the Adriatic, an iron curtain has descended across the Continent. Behind that line lie all the capitals of the ancient states of central and eastern Europe. . . . All these famous cities and the populations around them lie in what I must call the Soviet sphere, and all are subject in one form or another, not only to Soviet influence, but to a very high and, in many cases, increasing measure of control from Moscow. . . . I have felt bound to portray the shadow which, alike in the west and in the east, falls upon the world."*

This standoff between East and West colored world events during the postwar era.

1 Europe Attempted to Regain Stability

Throughout the war Allied leaders met to plan strategy and postwar policy. Many of their discussions centered on the proposed fate of postwar Germany. At the Yalta Conference in 1945, Churchill, Roosevelt, and Stalin agreed to divide both Germany and Austria into four zones. The United States, the Soviet Union, Great Britain, and France would each be responsible for administering one zone in each country. The four Allies would also divide Berlin and Vienna into four zones. The Allied Control Council, composed of military leaders of the occupying armies, would supervise the occupied regions. Decisions of this council had to be unanimous.

At the Potsdam Conference, later in 1945, Joseph Stalin, Clement Attlee (the new British

◀ *The Berlin Wall*

5. Discuss the development of the cold war.
6. Explain the purpose of the Truman Doctrine.
7. Outline the basic features of the Marshall Plan.
8. Explain why NATO and the Warsaw Pact were formed.
9. Describe the economic and political recovery of Western European nations after World War II.
10. Explain the purposes of the Common Market and COMECON.
11. Describe the efforts of Communist satellites to resist Soviet domination.
12. Identify the challenges facing the United States in the postwar years.
13. Discuss the relationship between the United States and its northern neighbor, Canada.

SECTION 1

Focus/Motivation

Put the following quotations on the chalkboard or an overhead projector, or reproduce them. Adolf Eichmann, one of the leaders of the Nazi extermination of the Jews, was captured in Argentina in 1960 and taken to Israel, where he was tried and hanged for crimes against the Jews and against humanity. Gideon Hausner was the attorney general for Israel at Eichmann's trial.

"If someone had said to me, 'Your father is a traitor' — I mean my own father is a traitor — and I had to kill him, I would have done it. But what was done was not of my doing.

I had the feeling of a Pontius Pilate. I felt that it was not with me that the guilt lay."

— Adolf Eichmann

"He is responsible because of the conspiracy and the plots for all that happened to the Jewish people — from the shores of the Arctic Ocean to the Aegean Sea, from the Pyrenees to the Urals. But his criminal responsibility for oppression, for torment, for starvation, for despoliation [looting], and for murder, derives from a legal principle which is very close to the principle of conspiracy. And that is the principle of the complicity in crime."

— Gideon Hausner

Lead students in a discussion of these two views, using the following questions as a guide: How does Eichmann discuss guilt? By what argument does Hausner find Eichmann guilty? Should soldiers be excused their wartime actions if they were under orders to carry them out? Why or why not?

Presentation
Making a Bulletin Board (Average/Group)
Have students make a bulletin board display focusing on the activities of WHO, UNICEF, UNESCO and other UN agencies. Students might write to the UN agencies in New York City or check the *Readers' Guide to Periodical Literature* for articles on these agencies.

prime minister), and Harry Truman agreed that a Council of Foreign Ministers, representing the Soviet Union, Great Britain, the United States, France, and China, should write the peace treaties. Decisions of this council also had to be unanimous.

Peacemaking Problems

At the end of World War II in Europe, the occupation zones which had been agreed upon at Yalta were set up, and the Allied Control Council and Council of Foreign Ministers began their work. However, such practical arrangements lasted only as long as the Allies remained on friendly terms. As postwar hostility grew, unanimous decisions by the councils became more and more difficult to reach.

The governments of the United States, the Soviet Union, and Great Britain had survived the test of war. Elsewhere, however, changes had to be made. For example, in 1946 a plebiscite, or a direct vote by the people on a national issue, abolished the monarchy and established a republican form of government in Italy. In France, a provisional government headed by General Charles de Gaulle ran the country until 1946, when the Fourth French Republic was proclaimed.

Much of the rest of Europe also faced major changes. Poland and Czechoslovakia had no national governments, Greece had a tottering monarchy, and the futures of both Germany and Austria seemed uncertain.

Postwar Treaties

Early in 1947, after months of heated debate, the Council of Foreign Ministers reached agreement on a treaty with Italy. The defeated nation renounced all claims to countries that it had invaded during the war. Italy also lost some territory to France, Yugoslavia, and Greece; and its colonies were placed under a trusteeship of the United Nations. In addition, Italy had to pay reparations.

The Council of Foreign Ministers also drew up treaties with the defeated countries of Romania, Hungary, Bulgaria, and Finland. These countries had to return territory they had taken and accept changes to their prewar boundaries. They also had to reduce the size of their armed forces and pay reparations to the nations that their armies had invaded.

The four-way occupation of Austria continued for years without any agreements as to peace terms. Finally, in 1955, a treaty with Austria was negotiated and signed.

First the Germans and then the Allies had occupied Austria for a total of 17 years. The treaty of 1955 made Austria a "sovereign, independent, and democratic state" with the same boundaries that had existed in 1938. The treaty also forbade political or economic union between Austria and Germany in "any form whatsoever."

German Settlements and Problems

It had taken the Council of Foreign Ministers 10 years to reach an agreement over Austria. But no final agreement was reached on what was to become of Germany.

The war devastated Germany and greatly reduced its territory. At the Potsdam Conference in 1945, the Allies had agreed to temporarily set Poland's western boundary at the Oder and Neisse rivers. Thus Poland now included part of prewar Germany within its borders. This transfer of territory to Poland stripped Germany of a large farming area that had formerly produced one-fourth of its food supply. Poland also took part of East Prussia, and the Soviet Union took the rest.

Germany's postwar population constantly increased as Germans who had formerly lived outside the boundaries of prewar Germany streamed into the country. Czechoslovakia, for example, insisted that Sudeten Germans who had supported Hitler's invasion of Czechoslovakia must leave the country. The Soviets adopted the same policy toward Germans in East Prussia and in the Soviet-controlled Baltic countries. Poland followed suit, expelling Germans from the area of prewar Poland as well as from the territory that they had taken from Germany following the war.

These moves, though not surprising in view of prewar troubles with German minorities, created a serious problem. The burden of housing, feeding, and employing these refugees fell on a shrunken and divided postwar Germany.

German Industry

The Allied Control Council solved the immediate problem of keeping Germany peaceful by swiftly disbanding all German land, air, and sea forces.

Learning from Pictures *The fierce fighting of World War II forced many people to flee from their homes. After the war Allies set up refugee centers, such as this one in Austria, to help people return to their homes.*

The council abolished the German General Staff, with all its military schools and institutions. To insure that German industry did not rearm, the Allies forbade the manufacture of big guns, tanks, and airplanes—even private or commercial planes.

The Allies also demanded the dismantlement of all industrial plants and equipment used in the war industry. This plan proved difficult to enforce, however, since the Allies first needed to answer the complex question of what constituted a war industry. A factory that manufactures tractors, for example, may easily be converted to produce tanks. In general, the Soviets and the French favored strict limits on German industry, while the Americans and the British were more lenient. The Allied Control Council, therefore, found it increasingly difficult to reach unanimous decisions regarding German industry. Meetings of the Council of Foreign Ministers proved unproductive. These complications and other complex problems you will read about later in this chapter led to the indefinite adjournment of the Council of Foreign Ministers in 1948.

Nuremberg Trials and Denazification

The military occupation of Germany revealed to the world the full extent of the horrors of German concentration camps. The Nazi policy of extermination led to the deaths of millions of people. More than 6 million of the estimated 10 million Jews living in Europe had been killed by the Nazis during the Holocaust. Many had died of disease and starvation in concentration camps. Others had been shot, hanged, or suffocated in gas chambers. Some, subjected to horrible tortures, served as subjects for so-called "scientific" experimentation on the human body. The Nazi victims also included almost 6 million non-Jewish Europeans—Poles, Czechs, Russians, Yugoslavs, Dutch, French, and Gypsies.

In 1945 and 1946 a special international court met at Nuremberg, Germany, to try the captured Nazi leaders responsible for these murders. Although Hitler was dead and some of his highest-ranking officers had escaped to Spain and Latin America, many Nazi leaders had been captured.

753

1B, 5B, 5G, a1D, a2I

● **Have students compare the Nuremberg trials with the trials of Argentine army officers involved in the "dirty war" in the 1970s.**

● The Nuremberg court charged 22 of the principal Nazi leaders with "conspiracy to wage aggressive war," "crimes against the peace," and "crimes against humanity" in the extermination camps, the slave-labor camps, and the conquered countries. In a series of trials, 12 of the defendants were sentenced to death, 7 were given life imprisonment, and 3 were acquitted. At the same time, the court declared the Nazi Party a criminal organization.

Trials of other war criminals continued for many years in postwar Germany. Hundreds of ex-Nazis were prosecuted, including high-ranking officers, camp guards, minor officials, and doctors who had taken part in "medical experiments." The convictions included murder, use of slave labor, and violation of the laws of war concerning the treatment of war prisoners and civilians.

In addition to trying Nazi leaders, the Allies also pursued a policy of denazification, which included removing former Nazis from positions of authority in government, industry, and education. Suspected Nazis had to appear before denazification courts and try to clear themselves. However, difficulties soon developed. The German economy had broken down almost completely. Its rebuilding required technically skilled leaders, many of whom had been Nazis. In addition, each of the four occupation zones had different criteria as to what degree of connection with the Nazi Party justified purging. By 1948 the denazification courts had almost ceased to function in Germany.

The United Nations

The wartime agreements that redrew the map of Europe also made plans for maintaining peace. In August 1944 representatives of Great Britain, the Soviet Union, China, and the United States met to draft a provisional charter for an organization to be known as the "United Nations." President Roosevelt had first used the term "united nations" in referring to the countries allied against the Axis Powers.

The leaders of the three major powers met at Yalta in February 1945. There Roosevelt, Churchill, and Stalin discussed the proposed charter and agreed on voting procedures to be followed in the United Nations. They set the time and place for the

Learning from Pictures *The Nuremberg trials determined that even though Nazi soldiers were following orders from their superiors when they committed war crimes, they were still responsible for their actions.*

754

● **Essay assignment: Compare the purposes and organization of the United Nations with the purposes and organization of the League of Nations.**

meeting of the first General Assembly, at which the final charter would be drawn up.

In April 1945 representatives from 51 nations met in San Francisco. After two months the General Assembly agreed to a final version of the Charter, which was then submitted to the government of each representative for ratification. By October 1945 the required number of nations had ratified the Charter, and the United Nations was established.

In the Charter, member nations agreed to the following purposes of the United Nations: (1) to maintain peace and security; (2) to promote equal rights and the self-determination of peoples; (3) to develop international cooperation; and (4) to encourage respect for human rights and fundamental freedoms without regard to race, sex, language, or religion.

The United Nations consists of six main bodies—the General Assembly, the Security Council, the Secretariat, the International Court of Justice, the Trusteeship Council, and the Economic and Social Council (see chart, page 756). The General Assembly, the Security Council, and the Secretariat make up the most important bodies of the organization.

The General Assembly. The General Assembly consists of representatives of all the member nations. The Assembly draws up the UN budget and assesses each member nation's share of the cost. Acting with the advice of Security Council, the General Assembly elects the Secretary-General and the judges of the International Court of Justice. In addition, it receives and considers the reports of the various agencies of the United Nations and recommends actions.

When a matter is brought to a vote in the General Assembly, each member nation has one vote. On procedural matters, those involving comparatively routine details, a simple majority vote is enough. Substantive, or important, matters require a two-thirds vote. Nations may also abstain—choose not to vote.

The Security Council. The Security Council maintains peace, settles disputes among nations, and prevents or resists aggression. It consists of representatives of 15 member nations who each have one vote. Five of these nations—the United States, Great Britain, the Soviet Union, France, and China—are called the Big Five and are permanent members. China was first represented by the government on Taiwan, or Nationalist China. However, since 1971 China has been represented in the UN by the People's Republic of China. Any one of the Big Five can prevent the Council from taking an important action by using its **veto power**—the power to defeat a measure with a single vote. The remaining 10 members of the Security Council are temporary. They are elected for two-year terms by the General Assembly and cannot be reelected immediately.

When the Security Council considers a dispute, it may ask questions of the parties involved, or, with their consent, send UN representatives to investigate. After the dispute has been discussed, the Council usually urges the nations involved to meet and work out their own solution. Sometimes it appoints mediators to aid the negotiations. The Council may suggest some kind of compromise, or it may send the case to the International Court of Justice in The Hague for a decision.

The Secretariat. The Secretary-General and a staff of several thousand clerical and administrative workers, technical experts, and advisers comprise the Secretariat. The Security Council nominates the Secretary-General, and the General Assembly elects him or her for a term of five years. The Secretary-General acts as mediator in international disputes, attends all Security Council and General Assembly meetings, and carries out tasks assigned by UN agencies. The Secretary-General also reports annually to the General Assembly on the progress of the United Nations' various programs.

Specialized agencies. In addition to the six main bodies of the United Nations, many specialized agencies serve a wide variety of functions. Each of these specialized agencies handles a single problem or a related set of problems. Every agency has its own charter, organization, membership, and budget.

The Technical Assistance Board supervises and coordinates the work of the specialized agencies, whose main aim is to help nations help themselves. It gives assistance only when requested by a government.

The United Nations International Children's Fund (UNICEF) was created to provide emergency supplies of food, clothing, and medicine to the children in postwar Europe. It became a permanent agency in 1953 and has set up long-range programs

SECTION 1

Closure

On the chalkboard or an overhead projector write the following statement about the UN.

The United Nations is a noble concept, but the organization itself is almost powerless to fulfill any of its purposes.

Have students discuss whether they agree or disagree with this statement. Ask them to support their points of view.

Review Answers

1. ***cold war:*** hostility between the Communist and Western nations; ***veto power:*** the power to defeat a measure with a single vote; ***developing nation:*** nation with limited resources, a rapidly growing population, an agricultural economy, and traditional life styles; ***developed nation:*** nation possessing a very high degree of economic sophistication

2. ***Allied Control Council:*** military leaders of the occupying armies who were to supervise the postwar occupation of Germany and Austria; ***Council of Foreign Ministers:*** ministers of the Soviet Union, Great Britain, the United States, France, and China responsible for writing peace treaties; ***Charles de Gaulle:*** general who headed the provisional government in France after Allied liberation; ***Nuremberg trials:*** trials of major Nazi leaders by a special international court that met at

Nuremberg, Germany; ***denazification:*** Allied policy that included the removal of Nazis from positions of authority in government, industry, and education; ***General Assembly:*** United Nations body that consists of representatives of all member nations; ***Security Council:*** United Nations body that maintains peace, settles disputes among nations, and also prevents or resists aggression. Consists of 15 representatives —10 revolving members and five permanent members; ***Big Five:*** permanent members of the Security Council: the United States, Great Britain, the Soviet Union, France, and China; ***Secretariat:*** the United Nations Secretary-General and clerical, technical, and administrative staffs
3. ***Trieste:*** city on the northern coast of the Adriatic Sea; ***Berlin:*** capital of East Germany located in northeastern Germany; ***Oder-Neisse line:*** Poland's western boundary, marked by the Oder and Neisse rivers; ***East Prussia:*** currently in northeastern Poland
4. The Austrian peace treaty restored sovereignty, independence, and democracy to Austria. It forbade political or economic union between Austria and Germany and restored prewar Austrian boundaries.
5. The Allies' order to dismantle German war industries was difficult to enforce because it was hard to determine what constituted a war industry. A more basic problem was

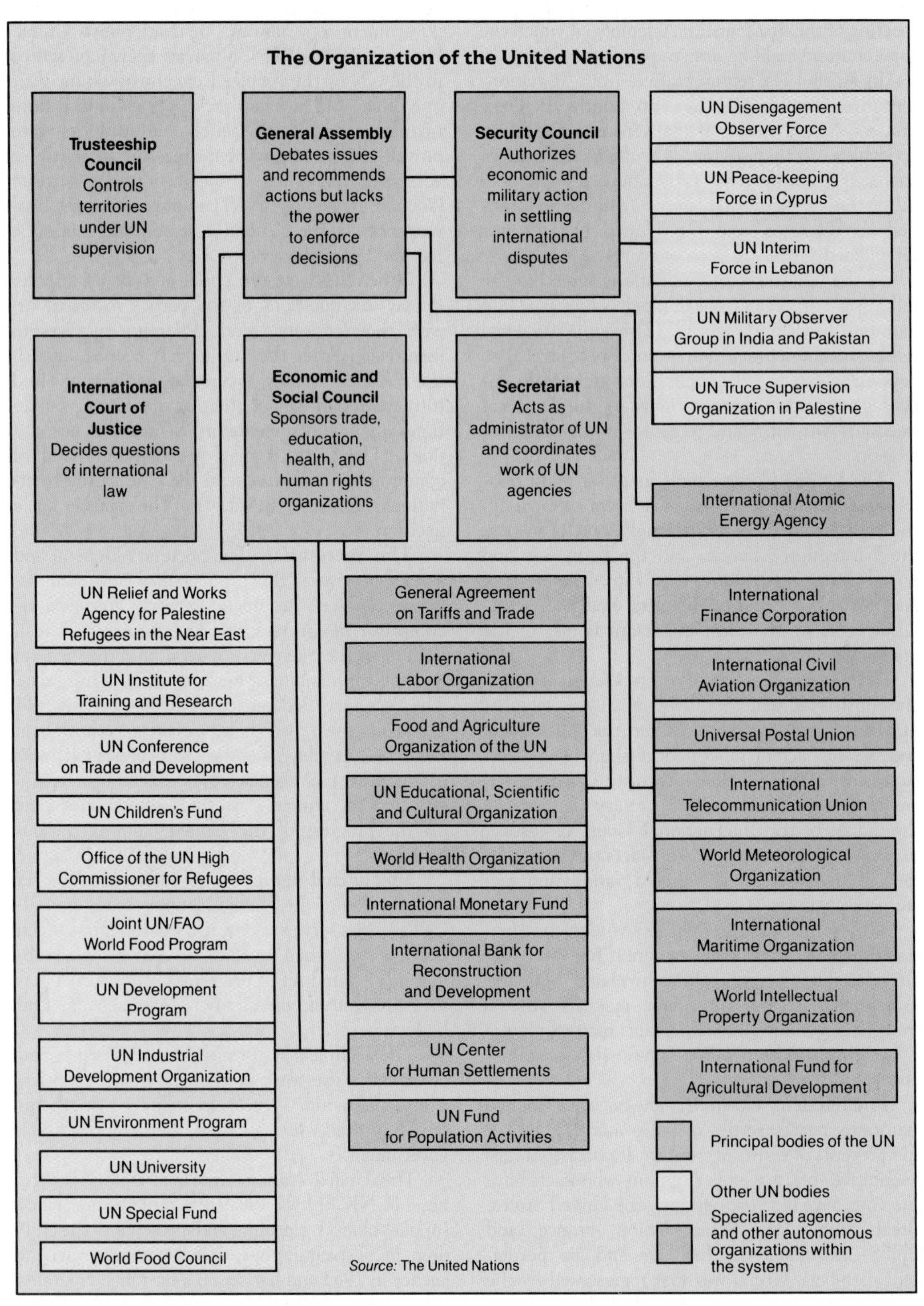

Source: The United Nations

5B, 5D, 5E, a4A, a4F, a4G, a4H, a4I, a4L

• Students may suggest that the Korean War, the Vietnam War, and other conflicts may have been prevented or resolved in a shorter time.

to combat disease, illiteracy, and malnutrition among the children of the world. UNICEF works primarily in developing nations,* helping establish community-based services in the areas of applied nutrition, child and maternal health, education, social-welfare services, and sanitation. UNICEF also directs emergency relief operations when natural disasters strike.

The World Health Organization (WHO) directs and coordinates international health programs. Its goal is for all peoples to enjoy good health. WHO provides governments with advice and assistance on expanding health services; trains doctors and health workers; controls and attempts to eradicate major diseases such as leprosy, malaria, tuberculosis, and smallpox; protects the health of mothers and children; improves sanitation and water supplies; and promotes mental health.

The United Nations Educational, Scientific, and Cultural Organization (UNESCO) was established to promote international collaboration in the fields of science, education, culture, and communication. Its major aims are to promote universal respect for justice, the rule of law, human rights, and fundamental freedoms for all. The major emphasis of this agency has been on stamping out illiteracy and on improving basic skills by establishing teacher-education programs, designing inexpensive school facilities, advising governments on curriculum reform and educational planning, and overseeing the production of textbooks and other educational materials.

The International Bank for Reconstruction and Development, or World Bank, helps to finance the rebuilding of devastated areas and developing regions. The World Bank encourages economic progress through such projects as railroads and power plants.

Another agency, the International Atomic Energy Agency (IAEA), works directly with the General Assembly and the Security Council to promote peaceful uses of atomic energy. The IAEA holds scientific meetings and establishes safety regulations.

*Economists often classify the nations of the world as developing or developed. **Developing nations** are characterized by limited resources, a rapid population growth rate, and agricultural economies with traditional life styles. In contrast, the **developed nations** have a high degree of economic sophistication. Of the more than 160 nations in the world today, only about 30 of them are considered developed.

Learning from Pictures *During the 1960s UNICEF provided needed medical services and supplies to children in Egypt.*

What If?
The United Nations

One of the main purposes of the United Nations is to maintain world peace. How might peace have been maintained in the postwar world if the UN General Assembly had the power to enforce decisions and the Big Five did not have veto power? •

SECTION 1 REVIEW

1. **Define** cold war, veto power, developing nation, developed nation
2. **Identify** Allied Control Council, Council of Foreign Ministers, Charles de Gaulle, Nuremberg trials, denazification, General Assembly, Security Council, Big Five, Secretariat
3. **Locate** Trieste, Berlin, Oder-Neisse line, East Prussia
4. **Explaining Ideas** Describe the principal terms of the Austrian peace treaty.
5. **Analyzing Ideas** What problems arose after the Allied Control Council limited German industry?
6. **Classifying Ideas** How have the specialized agencies of the UN helped people of the world?

the economic situation. The Soviets dismantled some industrial plants and shipped them east to replace Soviet factories, but stopped when they realized that serious unemployment resulted. In the Western zones, the British and Americans gradually became more lenient with the Germans. This was violently opposed by the French, who feared German industrial power.
6. UNICEF was created to provide emergency supplies of food, clothing, and medicine to children in postwar Europe. The WHO is a specialized agency with the purpose of directing and coordinating international health programs. UNESCO is an autonomous agency established to promote international collaboration in the fields of science, education, culture, and communication. The World Bank helps to finance the rebuilding of devastated areas. The IAEA works directly with the General Assembly and the Security Council to promote peaceful uses of atomic energy.

1B, 4I, 5B, 5C, 5G, a1C

Ethel Snowden first used the term *iron curtain* to describe the Soviet sphere of influence in her 1920 publication, *Through Bolshevik Russia.*

SECTION 2

Focus/Motivation
Tell the class that toward the end of World War II, the Soviet Union gained considerable influence in Eastern Europe. It promoted the establishment of Communist-controlled governments in a number of countries. Then have students reread Winston Churchill's "Iron Curtain" statement on page 751. Ask students what they think Churchill meant by this statement. Why is "iron curtain" an apt phrase for the Communist takeover of Eastern Europe? *("Curtain" connotes closing off these countries from the world's view. "Iron" implies that attempts to part the curtain would be extremely difficult.)*

Presentation
Constructing a Chart (Average/Group)
Have students construct charts contrasting NATO with the Warsaw Pact. Suggest that they include such information as members and the numbers of troops and weapons involved. Select students to display their charts on the bulletin board.

2 The Cold War Divided Europe

Difficulties over the writing of the treaties and over the governing of occupied Germany grew increasingly severe during the early postwar years. Many people in the West feared that Communist nations, led by the Soviet Union, planned to take over all of Europe.

Soviet Advances

The Soviets fought their way toward Germany at the end of World War II, liberating and occupying Poland and Germany's eastern allies—Romania, Bulgaria, and Hungary. The Soviets then set up Communist-controlled governments in these countries. In Albania and Yugoslavia, local Communists who had led resistance groups during the war established governments.

These nations came to be known as Soviet **satellites** because, like planets circling the sun, they depended upon the Soviet Union. The Soviet Union justified this ring of Communist countries surrounding its western borders as a badly needed buffer zone against the possibility of future German expansion.

In matters of both domestic and foreign policy, the satellite countries were subordinate to the Soviet Union. Following Winston Churchill's speech in 1946, in which he referred to the Communist takeover in Eastern Europe as the "iron curtain," the Soviet Union and its satellites were often referred to as **iron-curtain countries.**

The Soviet Union soon made known its intentions to foster communism throughout Europe. In 1947 a Soviet-sponsored agency, the Communist Information Bureau (Cominform),* began to publish propaganda about the supposed unity of European Communist parties. This campaign continued until the dissolution of Cominform in 1956.

The Truman Doctrine

Early in 1947 the United States emerged as the Western leader against Soviet expansion. In March 1947 President Truman, speaking before Congress, announced what came to be called the Truman Doctrine. The United States, Truman said, considered the continued spread of communism to be a threat to democracy. The United States would not try to stamp out communism in countries where it already existed, or in any country that freely chose communism. The United States would, however, use its money, materials, technical knowledge, and influence to help countries threatened by communism if they asked for help. This policy, referred to as **containment,** aimed at "containing," or restricting the spread of communism; it constitutes the Truman Doctrine.

Truman further declared that the United States would "support free peoples who are resisting attempted subjugation by armed minorities or by outside pressures." He asked Congress to appropriate $400 million to help defend Greece and Turkey from Communist aggression. His request was granted after a United Nations investigating committee reported that neighboring Communist

*Cominform was the successor to Comintern, which was dissolved in 1943.

● **Marshall served as chief of staff of the United States Army throughout World War II.**

countries were helping the Greek rebels try to overthrow the Greek government. With American financial and technical assistance, the Greek government put down the rebellion. Thus the United States demonstrated to the Communists its determination to enforce the policy of containment as outlined in the Truman Doctrine.

The Marshall Plan

The United Nations Relief and Rehabilitation Administration (UNRRA), formed in November 1943, provided emergency assistance for war-torn countries. Nations that had escaped invasion were asked to contribute one percent of their 1943 national income to the relief project. The United States, Great Britain, and Canada made the largest contributions. However, by 1947 Europe's most pressing need was for more economic assistance. For this help to be effective, distributing the funds would require a coordinated effort.

In 1947 United States Secretary of State ● George C. Marshall suggested a new policy that formed the basis for legislation adopted by Congress the following year. The European Recovery Program, often called the Marshall Plan, stipulated that the United States was prepared to assist Europe on certain terms. The European countries were to: (1) confer and determine their needs on a continental basis; (2) show what resources they could put into a common pool for economic rebuilding; (3) stabilize their currencies; and (4) try to remove trade barriers so that goods could flow freely throughout the continent. In this way prosperity was to be restored.

Eventually, 17 European nations participated in the European Recovery Program. Congress appropriated about $13 billion for the first four years of the program. Thus the United States economy shared its benefits with war-ravaged Europe. The United States also offered assistance to the Soviet Union and its satellites, but they rejected it.

The Cold War in Central Europe

Prewar Czechoslovakia had been the most democratic of all the Central European countries. The democratic postwar government, however, included many Communist officials.

In February 1948 national elections in Czechoslovakia showed a decline in the Communist vote. A few weeks later, shortly after the death (some thought murder) of the Czech foreign minister, the Communists held a new election. They presented a single list of party-approved candidates and wrote a new constitution, which the president of Czechoslovakia refused to sign. In June the president resigned and a Communist, who approved the constitution, succeeded him. Thus Czechoslovakia became a member of the Soviet-dominated Communist bloc* of Eastern Europe.

Only one break appeared in the iron curtain that divided East and West. During the spring of 1948, a disagreement arose between Joseph Stalin and Marshal Tito of Yugoslavia. Tito objected to Soviet domination and announced that Yugoslavia would follow an independent course. By June 1948 the split had become definite, and Yugoslavia was expelled from the Cominform.

The Division of Germany

By 1948 joint government in Germany by the four former Allies had become impossible. As a result, the country experienced great economic difficulty. The three Western occupying powers began discussions aimed at uniting their zones. In response, in June 1948 the Soviets blockaded all land and water traffic into Berlin from the West. They refused to allow trucks, barges, and trains to pass the checkpoints at the borders, thus threatening the people of West Berlin with starvation.

The Western nations acted swiftly during the Berlin blockade. The United States and Great Britain organized an airlift to supply West Berlin. They flew daily supplies of food and coal to the 2 million inhabitants of the Western sectors of the city. The airlift operated so efficiently that raw materials were supplied to West Berlin factories. In May 1949 the Soviet Union lifted its blockade of the city.

Meanwhile, the three Western occupying powers announced that if no peace treaty with Germany were written, they would unite their zones and allow the Germans to write a constitution and set up a democratic government. A constitutional assembly held on May 23, 1949, proclaimed the Federal Republic of Germany, known as West Germany.

*The Communist bloc consists of all satellite nations of the Soviet Union.

759

4I, 5B, 5C, 5G, a1C, a4A, a4E, a4F, a4H. a4I, a4J, a4K, a4L, a4M

READ
WRITE
INTERPRET
CONNECT
THINK

BUILDING HISTORY STUDY SKILLS

Reading About History: Identifying an Argument

When we hear the word *argument,* we often think of a disagreement or a dispute. However, when historians use the word argument, they are speaking of a thesis or main point supported by reasons and examples. Identifying the argument is the first step in determining its validity.

How to Identify an Argument

To identify an argument, follow these steps.

1. Explain the author's thesis or main point. Ask what the author is attempting to prove. You can look for key words and phrases such as *therefore, in conclusion, consequently,* or *I support.*
2. Identify the reasons supporting the main thesis. How does each reason elaborate on the main point?
3. Determine the examples that support the reasons.
4. Connect the thesis of the argument to the reasons and examples.

Developing the Skill

Read the following selection from Thomas G. Paterson's *On Every Front: The Making of the Cold War.*

> "The Cold War derived from three closely intertwined sources: the conflict ridden *international system,* the divergent *fundamental needs* and *ideas* of the major antagonists, America and Russia, and the diplomatic conduct or *tactics* of American and Soviet leaders. . . . Officials in Washington and Moscow abandoned any quest for a community of nations and instead built competing spheres of influence. They thereby expanded and protected what they respectfully [sic] perceived to be their interests, divided the world, and stimulated more conflict. . . . Two nations emerged from the rubble of World War II to claim first rank. The competitive interaction between the United States and the Soviet Union . . . contributed to the bipolarism of the immediate postwar years. . . . The major powers, in short, intervened abroad to exploit the political opportunities created by the destructive scythe of World War II. The stakes seemed high. A change in a nation's political orientation might presage [predict] a change in its international alignment. The great powers tended to ignore local conditions which might mitigate against alignment with an outside power. Americans feared that a . . . Communist Greece would look to the East and permit menacing Soviet bases on Greek territory or open the door to a Soviet naval presence in the Mediterranean. The Russians dreaded a conservative anti-Soviet Polish government . . . for it might prove so weak and so hostile to Moscow as to permit a revived Germany to send stormtroopers once again through the Polish corridor into the heart of Russia. A Communist China . . . might align with Russia; a Nationalist China would remain in the American camp. All in all, the rearranging of political structures *within* nations drew the major powers into competition, accentuating the conflict inherent in the postwar international system."

President Truman

The author's main point or thesis is that the origin of the cold war lies in the goals of the United States and the Soviet Union. Both nations, in their efforts to protect their big-power status and their national security, engaged in tactics that reinforced mutual suspicion. The competing ideologies were a basis for mutual mistrust.

The writer supports his thesis with details about the political situation at the end of World War II. He contends that the Soviet Union and the United States interfered in local conflicts because they saw their own power interests at stake. The examples that Paterson cites are in Greece, Poland, and China.

The author's argument is based upon his thesis that both powers, the United States and the Soviet Union, share responsibility for the development of the cold war.

Practicing the skill. Read a recent newspaper or magazine article that states a thesis or argument on a political point. Identify the argument using the skill you have just learned.

To apply this skill, see Applying History Study Skills on page 773.

760

In October 1949 a provisional Communist government, the German Democratic Republic, was established in the Soviet zone of Germany. This region became known as East Germany (see map, this page).

Political Alliances

With the Soviet takeover of satellite nations in Eastern Europe, many people feared a Soviet push to the West. Indeed, Churchill later said that only the fear of American atomic bombs had prevented the Soviet Union from overrunning Western Europe. Increasingly the Western nations felt a need to deter any Soviet drive.

The North Atlantic Treaty Organization. In April 1949 a mutual defense pact provided for creation of the North Atlantic Treaty Organization (NATO). Twelve nations originally signed the North Atlantic Treaty: the United States, Great Britain, France, Italy, Portugal, Norway, Denmark, Iceland, Canada, Belgium, the Netherlands, and Luxembourg. Greece and Turkey joined NATO in 1952, and West Germany followed in 1955 (see map, page 763). The signers agreed that if one member nation was attacked, all members would take united action against the aggressor.

In 1954 the NATO members drew up a detailed defense plan, calling for each nation to contribute to a standing NATO force of about 750,000 troops. The plan also asked for extensive commitments of ships and aircraft.

Not all the goals set in 1954 were reached. Consequently, NATO members came to rely more and more on American nuclear weapons rather than on the proposed force of ground troops.

The Warsaw Pact. The Soviet Union responded immediately to the strengthening of the North Atlantic Treaty Organization. In May 1955, in Warsaw, Poland, the Soviet government held a meeting of representatives of the European Communist bloc—the Soviet Union, Poland, East Germany, Czechoslovakia, Hungary, Romania, Bulgaria, and Albania (see map, page 763). Yugoslavia did not participate.

These nations adopted a 20-year agreement called the Warsaw Pact. The nations pledged, in the event of war, to furnish about 1.5 million troops. Adding these figures to the number of Soviet troops, the Warsaw Pact provided the Communist bloc with a potentially formidable force.

Learning from Maps *Today West Berlin is still divided into occupied sectors. In which sector is the Free University located?* **American**

Summit Conferences

After Stalin's death in 1953, many people in the West hoped that the world's leaders could meet to discuss problems and reach general agreements on various issues. Begun in the 1950s, these meetings, or **summit conferences,** involved the highest officials of the participating countries.

Summit conferences, which have occurred at irregular intervals during the last 30 years, have rarely produced substantive results. The May 1960

SECTION 2

Closure
Have students discuss the role that summit meetings play in international relations. Ask: How important are summit meetings to maintain good relations among nations? *(Accept all reasonable answers.)*

Review Answers
1. ***satellite:*** Communist country of Eastern Europe that is subordinate to the Soviet Union; ***iron-curtain country:*** an Eastern European country that is a satellite of the Soviet Union; ***containment:*** policy aimed at restricting the spread of communism; ***summit conference:*** meeting where the world's leaders attempt to reach general agreements on various issues
2. ***Cominform:*** Communist Information Bureau, used to foster communism
3. The purpose of the Truman Doctrine was to provide help to countries threatened by communism, and to support free peoples resisting attempted subjugation by armed minorities or outside forces.
4. The Marshall Plan provided aid to European countries on certain terms. The European countries had to determine their needs on a continental basis, show what resources they could put into a common pool, stabilize their currencies, and try to remove trade barriers.
5. Early in 1948 the Soviets stopped all traffic into Berlin from the West. The United States and

761

1E, 4I, 5B, 5C, 5D, 5E, 5H, 5I, a4A, a4F, a4H, a4I, a4L

Great Britain organized an airlift to supply West Berlin. The Soviet Union finally lifted its blockade in 1949. **6. (a)** The basic function of both organizations was to provide protection for member nations in case of attack. NATO signers agreed that an attack on one member nation was considered an attack on all. Warsaw Pact members pledged that in the event of war, each member would furnish troops in proportion to its population. **(b)** NATO was formed to deter any Soviet drive to extend its influence; the Warsaw Pact was signed in response to NATO.

SECTION 3

Focus/Motivation
Review with students the economic policies that were adopted after World War I. What were the results of these policies? *(Economic nationalism was a failure, hurting nearly every country practicing it.)* Then have students pretend that they are the chief economic ministers of Western European countries in the late 1940s. What would be their goals? *(Goals should include peace, stability, and rebuilding their nations' economies.)* What policies would they suggest to bring about economic recovery? What lessons could be learned from the failure of economic nationalism? *(Lead students to the conclusion that instead of protective tariffs and restrictions without a certain*

Learning from Pictures *President Eisenhower welcomes Nikita Khrushchev to the United States in 1959. The two leaders discussed many of the problems of the cold war.*

summit meeting between Premier Nikita Khrushchev (kroosh • CHAHWF) of the Soviet Union and President Dwight Eisenhower of the United States, for example, was canceled when news that an American spy plane had been shot down over the Soviet Union came to light. The plane had been photographing Soviet military operations. Still, most Americans agreed that it was important to keep lines of communication open with the Soviets.

Weakening Alliances

During the late 1950s, many NATO members became discontented with the organization for several reasons. First, the alliance had grown increasingly dependent for its defense on nuclear weapons, which could be used only when the president of the United States gave permission. This meant, in effect, that the United States controlled the defense of Europe. Second, because of the growing strength of Western Europe, and problems of the Soviet Union in its own sphere, Western leaders felt that the Soviets would not risk a military push in Europe. Third, with the development of long-range missiles Europeans feared that the Soviet Union could conquer Europe and threaten to destroy cities in the United States. In this case, they thought, the United States might not risk its own destruction in order to defend Western Europe from Soviet domination.

The chief challenge to NATO, however, came from the president of France, Charles de Gaulle. Wishing to take a more independent course, he withdrew some of the French troops from NATO in 1966 and asked the United States to give up its NATO bases in France. De Gaulle's successors supported the Western alliance. Nevertheless, they acted independently from NATO in dealing with the Communist bloc.

SECTION 2 REVIEW

1. **Define** satellite, iron-curtain countries, containment, summit conference
2. **Identify** Cominform
3. **Understanding Ideas** What was the purpose of the Truman Doctrine?
4. **Summarizing Ideas** What were the basic features of the Marshall Plan?
5. **Explaining Ideas** Briefly describe the East-West struggle over the city of Berlin.
6. **Analyzing Ideas** **(a)** What were the functions of NATO and the Warsaw Pact? **(b)** Why were these alliances formed?

3 Western Europe Experienced Progress and Setbacks

Thanks to the Marshall Plan and the resolve of the European people, postwar Western Europe experienced a remarkable economic and political recovery. Most of the nations of Western Europe were **market economies** in which private businesses and individuals answer three economic questions: (1) what goods and services should be produced; (2) how these goods and services should be produced; and (3) for whom these goods and services should be produced. In contrast, the Communist bloc nations had **command economies** in which the government made the economic decisions. The market economies of Western Europe helped those nations achieve a higher standard of living than that in Eastern Europe. In a relatively short time, Western Europeans cleared away the rubble of bombed cities and rebuilt roads, rail lines and bridges. Industries rapidly returned to full production.

1A, 1C, 1E, 5B, 5H, 5I,
a1C, a4B, a4C, a4G

Learning from Maps *Not all Western European nations belong to NATO. Which NATO nations border Warsaw Pact nations?* **West Germany, Greece, and Turkey**

The West German "Miracle"

The reconstruction and industrial development of West Germany progressed at such a remarkable rate that many people referred to it as the "German miracle." West Germany developed a capitalist economy, and by the 1950s its industrial production had more than doubled, making it the leading industrial nation in Western Europe.

During the postwar years, the West German government managed to provide housing and jobs for the many refugees from East Germany and other Eastern European nations. The labor of these refugees contributed to West Germany's rapidly

amount of consideration for other countries, some plan for economic cooperation similar to the Common Market might be attempted.)

Presentation
Summarizing Ideas (Average/Group)
Ask students to write a paragraph summarizing the similarities and differences among the postwar economic recoveries of the three major Western European countries — West Germany, France, and Great Britain. Have students compare their paragraphs with those of other members of the class.

1B, 1C, 1E, 5B, 5D, 5E, 5H, a1C

● The East German authorities referred to the Berlin Wall as an "antifascist rampart." The people of West Germany simply called it the "wall of shame."

growing economy. German industry flourished, thanks to technological innovation, a commitment to quality, and the absence of strikes and other labor troubles. The German automobile industry, for example, made impressive advances and became a strong competitor of its American counterpart. The West German currency, the mark, became one of the most stable in the world.

In his book, *Germany and the East-West Crisis,* William S. Schlamm describes how one West German built a successful business after the war.

> " . . . a young friend of mine, a former Sudeten-German, in 1948—when he was thirty-two—crossed the border of the German Soviet Zone and started to manufacture nylon stockings in West Germany. At the end of 1957, nine years later . . . his plant would be the pride of any United States chamber of commerce. Beautifully remodeled in 1957, it is an authentic example of shrewd rationalization techniques, of mechanical perfection, of tidiness and profitability. "

Two political parties, the Christian Democrats and the Social Democrats, dominated politics in the Federal Republic of Germany in the 1950s and 1960s. The first West German chancellor, Konrad Adenauer, was a Christian Democrat. Under Adenauer, West Germany established a strong alliance with the Western nations, and it joined NATO in 1955.

In 1963 Adenauer retired without having realized his dream of German reunification. Ludwig Erhard, a Christian Democrat, became chancellor, but by the late 1960s the Christian Democrats were losing ground to the Social Democrats.

Throughout the postwar period, Berlin remained a major trouble spot in the East-West struggle. With American assistance, West Berlin made an astonishing recovery from the devastation of war. In East Berlin, however, recovery stagnated. More and more people in East Berlin, discontented with the totalitarian Communist rule there, fled to West Berlin. Political refugees also streamed into West Berlin from East Germany and other satellite countries.

In 1961 the East German government tried to stop the flow of refugees to the West by building walls and fences along the boundary between the Allied and Soviet sectors of Berlin. They guarded crossing points at all times. East and West Berliners could move through these points only with authorization. This restriction stemmed the flow of refugees. East German guards shot at anyone trying to escape to West Berlin. The concrete portion of the Berlin Wall, topped by barbed wire, became a symbol of world tensions. ●

Great Britain After the War

In 1945 Clement Attlee, head of the Labour Party, defeated Winston Churchill and the Conservative Party and became prime minister of Great Britain. The Labour Party, a moderate socialist party, made many changes in the British economic and social systems. The government nationalized railroads, utilities, coal mines, and the Bank of England. Many welfare measures were passed, including free medical care for everyone. Great Britain became a **welfare state**—or one in which the government undertakes primary responsibility for the social welfare of its citizens.

Great Britain also faced many severe economic problems after the war. Its industrial equipment was outdated and inefficient. Many workers had been killed in the war. In addition, the country had lost, and continued to lose, scientists and managers. Many emigrated to Canada, Australia, and the United States.

Great Britain lost valuable colonies and possessions, and the cost of the nation's remaining overseas commitments created a heavy burden. British problems in Northern Ireland also flared.

Despite its many problems, Great Britain began to experience favorable economic development in the 1950s. The government reduced unemployment, stabilized its currency, improved housing conditions, and raised the general standard of living.

However, limited economic freedom and incentives resulted in a decline in these favorable trends. Great Britain's industrial productivity fell to one of the lowest levels in the industrialized world in the 1960s. Some of its principal industries, such as auto manufacturing, experienced hard times.

The Fifth French Republic

Postwar France also faced severe problems. In spite of assistance provided through the Marshall Plan, economic recovery came slowly. The French Empire crumbled in Southeast Asia and in North Africa, where bitter and costly struggles drained

764

● **Student agitation began in March 1968 at the University of Nanterre, just outside Paris. By May the troubles had spread to the University of Paris's Sorbonne campus in the Latin Quarter. Like the revolutionaries of 1789, 1848, and 1871, the students used the cobblestones from the Latin Quarter's streets for building barricades and for weapons.**

1E, 4I, 5B, 5D, 5H, 5I, a1C

Learning from Pictures *An example of West German technological innovation in the automobile industry was the Volkswagen plant in Wolfsburg, Germany. In the United States, this popular car, created by Dr. Ferdinand Porsche, was referred to as a "beetle."*

the nation's treasury. France's political parties bickered among themselves so much that they could not form a coalition long enough to run a stable government.

Finally, in 1958, the French legislature, under pressure from army leaders, authorized General Charles de Gaulle to write a new constitution and to rule by decree until its ratification. Thus, the Fourth French Republic ended without a struggle.

The new constitution, approved by French voters in October 1958, created the Fifth French Republic. The constitution concentrated much power in the hands of the president. The president appointed the prime minister and could dissolve the legislature and assume dictatorial powers in a national emergency. Through the prime minister, the president could enact laws unless a majority of the National Assembly opposed them.

General de Gaulle became the first president of the Fifth Republic. He ended France's colonial warfare and established stability at home. This stability was attained, however, at a high cost to the French taxpayer.

In foreign policy, de Gaulle was a nationalist, believing that Europe could prosper only under a system of national states. De Gaulle opposed British and American influence in Europe and wanted to keep Germany weak. He hoped to maintain close relations with the Soviet Union and Poland as a check on possible German aggression.

In the late 1960s political conditions within France became unstable. Violent riots shook the nation in 1968. Militant students demanded reforms in the educational system, and strikes for higher wages and better working conditions spread rapidly throughout industrial areas. To meet the crisis, de Gaulle dissolved the National Assembly and called for a general election. ●

To win a favorable vote, de Gaulle acknowledged the need for social improvements in France. When reelected, he approved a 15 percent increase in workers' wages. This concession strained the finances of the nation without increasing industrial production and led to spiraling inflation. De Gaulle's popularity declined. In April 1969, in a direct vote, the French people rejected his proposals for reform. The 79-year-old president resigned.

Other Western European Nations

Recovery in the other nations of Western Europe took many different paths. Denmark, Norway, and Sweden, for example, adopted democratic socialistic systems and established welfare states. Although these systems provided many social benefits, they resulted in very high taxes.

In Italy the Christian Democrat Party dominated the political arena during the 1950s and 1960s. Under Alcide de Gasperi, the prime

765

1B, 1D, 1E, 5B, 5D, 5F, 5H, 5I, a1C, a3G

SECTION 3

Closure

Have students discuss the following statement:

Efforts at economic cooperation, such as the Common Market, were the most important developments in postwar Europe.

Review Answers

1. ***market economy:*** economy in which private businesses and individuals make the economic decisions; ***command economy:*** economy in which the government makes the economic decisions; ***welfare state:*** state in which the government undertakes primary responsibility for the social welfare of its citizens
2. ***Konrad Adenauer:*** chancellor of West Germany; ***Ludwig Erhard:*** succeeded Adenauer as West German chancellor; ***EEC:*** European Economic Community
3. (a) Technological innovation, a commitment to quality, and the absence of strikes and other labor troubles helped German industry to flourish.
(b) Thanks to this industrial growth, West Germans enjoyed a stable economy and government and had a very high standard of living in the 1950s and 1960s.
4. (a) The Labour Party nationalized railroads, utilities, and coal mines and provided welfare programs for everyone.
(b) In the 1960s Great Britain's industrial productivity fell, as limited economic freedom led to a

ARCHITECTURE

Chapel by Le Corbusier

World War II, so devastating for people in Europe and elsewhere, also had among its casualties many great works of art. Numerous old and beautiful churches were damaged or destroyed. It was with great joy, then, that Europeans hailed the construction of this new place of worship. Built between 1951 and 1955 by the great architect Le Corbusier, the chapel stands proudly in the green fields of Ronchamp, in France.

Called Notre Dame du Haut, this was one of Le Corbusier's most famous works. The idea for its dramatic roof line came to the architect when he saw a large crab shell on a beach in Long Island, New York. The chapel, which almost resembles sculpture, was one of the first buildings completed by the architect after the war. It is unique both in design and overall effect.

Le Corbusier also developed the modular, or unit, system of design. In it all the architectural elements are similar, though not identical. They can be individually arranged, yet are well suited to mass production.

minister from 1948 to 1953, Italy established a capitalist economy and the country experienced industrial and agricultural growth.

By the 1960s the Socialist and Communist parties had gained considerable strength as labor unrest increased. At the end of the decade Italy's economic growth declined sharply. This decline contributed to the undermining of political stability.

Economic programs in Greece, Spain, and Portugal met with varying degrees of success. All three nations, however, were able to develop free-enterprise systems.

European Economic Cooperation

In the 1950s the French proposed that the nations that produced most of Western Europe's steel and coal unite their facilities and production. In 1952 France, West Germany, Italy, and the Benelux countries (Belgium, the Netherlands, and Luxembourg) formed the European Coal and Steel Community (ECSC). A central authority regulated production and prices, and members did not charge each other tariffs on coal or steel. A remarkable feature of the ECSC was its freedom from national control.

The Common Market

In 1957 the same six nations took another important step toward economic union by establishing the European Economic Community (EEC)—usually called the Common Market. The treaty provided for the gradual abolition of tariffs and import quotas among the six member nations. A common tariff would be placed on goods coming into the Common Market from nonmember nations. The member nations established the European Investment Bank with capital contributed by member governments. The bank's purposes included financing projects beyond the means of individual nations and investing in developing industries in poor areas of member nations.

The Common Market made steady progress toward European economic unity in the 1960s. In 1967 it adopted a five-year plan to provide greater price and wage stability and more uniform tax levels among member countries. Also in 1967 the EEC merged with the European Coal and Steel Community and the Atomic Energy Community, which the six nations had created to share information on the peaceful uses of atomic energy, to form

1E, 4I, 5B, 5C, 5G, 5H, a1C, a4A, a4F, a4G, a4H, a4K, a4L, a4M

the European Community, or EC. The European Community set up a single European commission with headquarters in Belgium.

The founding members of the Common Market had dreamed of political as well as economic unity for Europe. Although many unresolved issues stood in the way, the nations did seek ways to achieve political unification.

SECTION 3 REVIEW

1. **Define** market economy, command economy, welfare state
2. **Identify** Konrad Adenauer, Ludwig Erhard, EEC
3. **Understanding Cause and Effect** **(a)** Why did the West German economy experience tremendous growth after the war? **(b)** What effect did this have on the nation's economic and political stability?
4. **Summarizing Ideas** **(a)** What changes did the Labour Party bring about in Great Britain? **(b)** What problems did Great Britain begin to experience in the 1960s?
5. **Organizing Ideas** What were the provisions of the constitution that created the Fifth French Republic?

4 The Communist Bloc Faced Challenges in the Postwar Period

The death of Joseph Stalin, the Soviet dictator, in 1953 created a power struggle within the Soviet government. Eventually, Nikita Khrushchev emerged as Communist Party leader and in 1955 became Soviet premier.

The Soviet Union Under Khrushchev

Soon after he came to power, Khrushchev gave a speech in which he ridiculed Stalin for the political purges during the 1930s. By condemning Stalin for the imprisonment and death of many Communist Party members, Khrushchev hoped to win favor with the discontented Soviet people.

Khrushchev initiated a program called de-Stalinization in which he lifted restrictions on intellectuals and artists, freed many political prisoners, and ended some of the terrorism of the secret police. Stalin was publicly denounced. The city of Stalingrad became Volgograd. However, in spite of this public change in attitude, the government still tightly controlled Soviet society.

Khrushchev loosened the central government's tight grip on the economy. Incentives were given to increase agricultural production. Factory and farm managers were given more control in order to meet production quotas.

One major problem that continued under Khrushchev involved heavy investment in the defense industry rather than in agriculture or industries that produced consumer goods. Khrushchev's inability to deal with this problem eventually led to his forced resignation in 1964.

Soviet foreign policy under Khrushchev seemed less threatening than it had under Stalin as Khrushchev adopted a policy known as "peaceful coexistence." However, this temporary thaw in East-West relations lasted only until 1960, when an American U-2 spy airplane was shot down, leading to the cancellation of the planned summit talks. Diplomatic relations further deteriorated with the building of the Berlin Wall in 1961. Khrushchev's successors, Communist Party Secretary Leonid Brezhnev and Prime Minister Aleksei Kosygin, reversed many of Khrushchev's domestic and foreign policies.

East Germany

The history of East Germany differed greatly from that of West Germany after 1948. The German Democratic Republic faced harsh political and economic measures at the hands of the Soviet Union. As war reparations the Soviets seized $8 billion worth of industrial plants and transported the machines and equipment to the Soviet Union. The Soviets also forced 200 large industrial enterprises to produce goods for the Soviet Union. Until the mid-1950s the output of these industries amounted to about one-fourth of East Germany's total production. In addition, the division of Germany cut off East Germany from most of its natural resources, making economic recovery a slow and painful process.

Even though the East German standard of living remained low compared to that of West Germany, by the 1960s the East Germans had begun to make impressive economic progress. Within a decade East Germany had become highly industrialized and was one of the most technologically advanced members of the Communist bloc.

lack of incentives to reverse this trend.
5. Under the Fifth French Republic, the president appointed the prime minister. Through the prime minister, the president could enact laws unless the National Assembly opposed them.

SECTION 4

Focus/Motivation
Point out to students that Khrushchev described his policy of peaceful coexistence as "a policy of consolidating peace, easing international tension and doing away with the cold war." As they work through this section, ask students to consider whether Khrushchev's other policies supported peaceful coexistence. Ask students to discuss the following question: Do you think Khrushchev's support for peaceful coexistence was real? *(Answers will vary.)*

Presentation
Constructing a Time Line (Average/Group)
Have students construct time lines showing the major upheavals in the Soviet Union's satellite nations in the 20 years between 1948 and 1968. Encourage students to display their time lines on the bulletin board.

SECTION 4

Closure
Have students discuss postwar recovery in the

1E, 4I, 5B, 5C, 5G, 5H, 5J, a1C

● Dubcek referred to his program of reforms as "socialism with a human face."

Soviet Union and Eastern Europe. Ask students to compare the economic recovery in the Soviet bloc with that of Western Europe.

Review Answers

1. ***Nikita Khrushchev:*** the Soviet premier shortly after Stalin's death; ***Alexander Dubcek:*** Czech leader who introduced a number of reforms including greater political, economic, and social freedom; ***COMECON:*** the Council for Mutual Economic Assistance
2. Khrushchev's inability to reduce investment in defense and to increase investment in agriculture and the consumer goods industry led to his downfall.
3. (a) Yugoslavia resented the Soviet Union's attempts to dictate domestic and foreign policy. Hungarians wanted to adopt a democratic form of government and to withdraw from the Warsaw Pact. Czechoslovakia wanted to abandon communism in favor of "socialist democracy." Poland wanted greater control over its internal affairs. **(b)** The Soviet Union made little effort to interfere in Yugoslavia. Hungary and Czechoslovakia, however, were unsuccessful in their attempts to throw off Soviet control. The Soviet Union invaded both countries, putting down the rebellions.
4. (a) COMECON would coordinate industrial development and trade within the Soviet bloc. **(b)** COMECON lacked trading flexibility.

Upheavals in Eastern Europe

During the early postwar years, the Communist bloc seemed a solid, firmly knit group of nations united by common beliefs, policies, and goals. However, the satellite countries had once been independent nations, some with long-standing antagonisms toward the Soviet Union.

Yugoslavia's growing independence from the Soviet Union after 1948 aroused envy among the satellites. This independence, called "Titoism" after the leader of Yugoslavia, became a kind of goal for some people in the satellite countries. In 1953 Soviet tanks and troops put down a revolt by East German workers. In 1956 Poland threatened to revolt and, as a result, gained a small amount of independence in domestic policy-making.

In 1956 Hungary revolted against Soviet domination. At first Soviet troops withdrew, but they later returned and bloodily suppressed the revolt.

In 1968 Czechoslovakia, under Alexander Dubcek (DOOB • chek), began a program of reforms. ● Dubcek promised civil liberties, democratic political reforms, and a more independent political system. This short-lived period of freedom became known as the "Prague Spring." Within six months, Warsaw Pact troops, chiefly from the Soviet Union, invaded Czechoslovakia. They seized the reform leaders and replaced them with pro-Soviet people.

These upheavals pointed to several changes that seemed to be taking place between the Soviet Union and its satellites. First, many people in the satellites seemed less willing to accept continued Soviet domination. Second, the troops from satellite countries, promised in the Warsaw Pact, might prove of little help to the Soviet Union in the event of war.

Learning from Pictures *When the people of Czechoslovakia tried to institute reforms in 1968, the Soviet Union invaded the country.*

COMECON

In 1949 several Communist nations joined to form their own common market, the Council for Mutual Economic Assistance (COMECON). Its members included the Soviet Union, Poland, East Germany, Czechoslovakia, Hungary, Romania, Bulgaria, Albania,* and Mongolia. Over the years, China, North Vietnam, North Korea, and Yugoslavia have sometimes attended COMECON meetings.

The main purpose of COMECON was to coordinate industrial development and trade within the Soviet bloc. The organization tried to integrate the economies of its members and to expand trade with the capitalist countries.

COMECON was far less successful than its counterpart, the EEC, chiefly because COMECON lacked trading flexibility. Members conducted trade on a balanced nation-to-nation basis. Bulgaria, for example, would sign an agreement with Poland, providing for an exchange of a certain amount of Bulgarian products for products of about the same value received from Poland. No money would change hands in the trade. Deliveries from one country would be checked off against deliveries from the other.

COMECON members found this system cumbersome and unsatisfactory. Some members also objected to plans under which they supplied raw materials while other members—especially the Soviet Union—did the manufacturing.

For the first decade after the establishment of COMECON, the Soviet Union profited from its trading relationships with the Communist bloc countries. However, since the 1960s the Soviet Union has had to subsidize these bloc nations.

*Albania was expelled in 1961.

1E, 5B, 5D, 5H, 5I, a1B, a1C, a2C, a2J, a2K, a3B, a3C, a3F, a3J, a4A, a4F, a4H, a4K, a4M

SECTION 4 REVIEW

1. **Identify** Nikita Khrushchev, Alexander Dubcek, COMECON
2. **Interpreting Ideas** How did Khrushchev's economic policies lead to his eventual fall from power?
3. **Understanding Cause and Effect** **(a)** What caused political upheaval in some of the Eastern European countries in the 1950s and 1960s? **(b)** How did the Soviets handle these disturbances?
4. **Analyzing Ideas** **(a)** What was the purpose of COMECON? **(b)** Why was COMECON less successful than the Common Market?

5 The United States and Canada Entered a New Era After 1945

Despite flourishing economies and powerful roles in world affairs, the United States and Canada faced a number of problems in the postwar years. These difficulties included internal conflicts, political problems, and a gradual realization that economic growth has limits. Both nations, however, remained committed to maintaining positions of great influence.

Challenges Facing the United States

Between 1945 and 1968, three Democratic presidential administrations and two Republican presidential administrations represented the American people. Although these five presidents often had similar goals, they just as often differed on policies for carrying out their goals. Some of the problems that arose during this period proved extremely trying for the men who held the highest office in the land. Their decisions set precedents and shaped the way the American people viewed both the world and themselves during a critical period in their country's history.

Foreign policy. For the most part, United States foreign policy during the postwar period revolved around the containment of communism. As discussed earlier in this chapter, President Harry Truman successfully blocked a Communist attempt to take over the government of Greece. He also implemented the Marshall Plan, which helped European nations recover from World War II. During his administration the United States took part in the Berlin airlift and helped establish NATO. Both the Berlin airlift and the establishment of NATO were bold attempts to contain Soviet aggression in Europe. In Asia, the United States sent troops to South Korea in a police action to stop the Soviets and the Chinese from taking over the country (see Chapter 29).

Truman's successor, Dwight D. Eisenhower, brought the Korean War to an end and created the Southeast Asia Treaty Organization (SEATO) in an attempt to halt further Communist advances in that region. He also announced the Eisenhower Doctrine, which provided economic and military assistance to anti-Communist countries in the Middle East. During the administrations of John F. Kennedy and Lyndon B. Johnson, the war in Vietnam was the major focus of American foreign policy.

All of these undertakings were part of the cold war between Western and Communist nations. The United States, however, also had other concerns during this period. It provided economic assistance to developing nations in Latin America, Asia, and Africa. It also made major efforts to reduce tensions in troubled regions.

Domestic policy. At home, the United States presidents consistently aimed to resolve social and political problems and maintain a flourishing economy. Following the example of the New Deal, later presidents created new programs to address social problems. Social programs were launched during the Kennedy and Johnson administrations. President John F. Kennedy introduced a broad program of domestic reforms, highlighted by legislation to reduce social inequalities. His tragic assassination in November 1963 occurred before Congress had passed much of his proposed legislation.

Vice President Lyndon B. Johnson succeeded Kennedy and attempted to create what he called the Great Society. His program included much of Kennedy's domestic reform legislation, along with important new civil rights programs.

The economy. After World War II the American economy reached new peaks of productivity, with huge new industries and rapid growth of new construction. Nevertheless, during the 1940s and 1950s, several **recessions**—periods of temporary business slowdown and increased unemployment—occurred. The 1960s had no recession, but toward the end of the decade inflation soared.

SECTION 5

Focus/Motivation
Write on the chalkboard the following quotation from President Lyndon B. Johnson:

"The problem we face is to make the quality of American life — and I mean life for all Americans — match the quantity of our wealth. . . ."

Have students discuss what measures Johnson and other presidents took in the postwar years to solve this problem. *(Most students will suggest such measures as President Kennedy's New Frontier policies, Johnson's Great Society, and the civil rights legislation of the 1960s.)*

Presentation
Presenting an Oral Report (Average/Group)
In December 1955 Rosa Parks was arrested for riding in the "whites only" section of a bus in Montgomery, Alabama. Her action led to a nationwide protest movement. A group of students might prepare and present an oral report on the action taken by Rosa Parks, describing racial segregation in the South, the Montgomery bus boycott, and the eventual Supreme Court ruling on the case. Suggest that students use resources in the school or public library.

5C, 5G, a1B, a1C, a2B, a2C, a2D, a2E, a2F, a2G, a2H, a2I, a2J, a2K, a2L, a3J

● Point out that Dr. King was greatly influenced by the ideas of Mahatma Gandhi.

SECTION 5

Closure

In general, the relationship between the United States and Canada has been close. Ask students to summarize the reasons for this close relationship. *(Student answers might include: similar economic and political development, a long shared border, cultural similarities, and the two countries were allies in two world wars.)*

Review Answers

1. ***recession:*** period of temporary business slowdown; ***lobbying:*** pressuring members of the legislature to vote for or against a particular measure
2. ***SEATO:*** Southeast Asian Treaty Organization; ***Great Society:*** Johnson's plans for domestic reform; ***Joseph McCarthy:*** senator who publicized the "conspiracy theory" of communism; ***NAACP:'*** National Association for the Advancement of Colored People; ***Martin Luther King:*** civil rights leader; ***DEW Line:*** Distant Early Warning Line across the Arctic which warns against missile attack; ***St. Lawrence Seaway:*** waterway linking Great Lakes and Atlantic Ocean; ***Columbia River basin:*** joint development program by the U.S. and Canada that doubled water storage capacity of the Pacific Northwest
3. The major foreign-policy concern of United States presidents from 1945 to 1968 was the containment

Learning from Pictures *In an unusual occurrence, captured in this 1961 photograph, four American presidents appear together. From left to right they are: John F. Kennedy, Lyndon B. Johnson, Dwight D. Eisenhower, and Harry S Truman.*

Political unrest. Many of the American successes of the postwar world lasted for a relatively long period of time. However, the discouraging results of many of the defeats and setbacks surfaced almost immediately. For example, some Americans did not understand why the United States had allowed the Soviet Union to spread its sphere of influence throughout Eastern Europe and other parts of the world. A number of people tried to explain these setbacks by a "conspiracy theory." They believed that Soviet gains had occurred because certain people in the United States government were "soft on communism."

Senator Joseph McCarthy of Wisconsin became the most dramatic spokesman for the "conspiracy theory." Between 1950 and 1954 he questioned the loyalty of many government officials and built up a large following. In the process he damaged the reputations of many Americans.

In 1954 a Senate committee investigated McCarthy's conduct and found his charges groundless. The Senate then censured, or reprimanded, him for "conduct unbecoming to a Senator," and his influence collapsed.

Civil rights. Black Americans had been freed from slavery during the Civil War and had officially been granted their rights as citizens but, in fact, still lived under many social, political, and economic restrictions. In many regions, in both the North and the South, black people were prevented from voting and from obtaining decent educations, jobs, and housing. Dissatisfaction grew, especially after World War II. Organizations such as the Urban League and the National Association for the Advancement of Colored People (NAACP) worked to find employment and to secure civil rights for black Americans. These organizations achieved gains through legal action and **lobbying**—trying to persuade legislators to vote for or against a measure.

A turning point in the black civil rights movement came in 1954. In the landmark case of *Brown v. Board of Education of Topeka,* the United States Supreme Court unanimously declared that state laws requiring black children to attend separate schools were unconstitutional. States having such laws were ordered to integrate their schools "with all deliberate speed."

This important decision encouraged the growing civil rights movement of the late 1950s and 1960s. The most prominent civil rights leader was Dr. Martin Luther King, Jr., a Baptist minister. He ● advocated the use of nonviolent methods such as boycotts, marches, and sit-ins to bring about change. Blacks attempted to hold peaceful demonstrations and mass protests against discrimination. For his efforts in furthering the cause of civil rights through nonviolent means, Dr. King was awarded the Nobel Peace Prize in 1964. However, in spite of Dr. King's efforts, many of these protests resulted in violence. From 1964 to 1967, more than 100 people died in 329 riots across the nation.

Ironically, Dr. King died violently at the hands of an assassin. His murder in 1968 dealt a severe blow to the civil rights movement and sparked another wave of violence in cities across the country.

In the 1960s Congress passed several civil-rights and voting-rights acts that guaranteed political equality for blacks and other minorities.

Antiwar protest. A military issue that developed into a major social issue by the late 1960s was the continued involvement of American troops in Vietnam. Many antiwar protesters, particularly college students and civil rights supporters, expressed their discontent by staging demonstrations on university campuses. The protesters argued that United States involvement in Vietnam caused needless loss of life.

Antiwar protests sometimes ended in violence. At the 1968 Democratic National Convention in Chicago, a confrontation between antiwar protesters and the police interrupted the proceedings.

Antiwar protests later reached an all-time high and did not all end until the withdrawal of all American troops from Vietnam was completed in 1975.

Canadian Challenges

Active participation in two world wars ended the isolation policy Canada had maintained for many years. After World War II, Canada became a vigorous supporter of the United Nations and an important member of NATO, loaned almost $4 billion to other countries, and welcomed thousands of refugees from Europe.

Economic growth. Canada experienced considerable economic development after World War II. Much of the country remained basically agricultural. Production of crops such as wheat, barley, flax, and feed grains provided a surplus for export. During the 1960s, world food shortages forced China and the Soviet Union to purchase large quantities of Canadian grain. Most of the surplus disappeared.

Canada's industries also grew after World War II. The large Canadian forest areas provided many wood products. The wood pulp and paper industries expanded, with most of the paper sold to the United States. Development of electric power and improvement of transportation stimulated the mining of iron, coal, and uranium, and greater production of oil and gas. Aircraft, electrical, textile, and automobile industries developed in the provinces of Quebec and Ontario. The United States furnished much of the capital for this industrial development.

Relations with the United States. For more than a century Canada has had a close relationship with the United States. During and after World War II this relationship strengthened, especially with regard to military and economic affairs.

Canadian national defense relied heavily on the United States. Together the two nations built a line of radar installations, called the Distant Early Warning (DEW) Line, across the Arctic, to furnish early warnings of air attacks. They also established the North American Air Defense Command.

In 1959 close economic cooperation between Canada and the United States produced the St. Lawrence Seaway, a 2,400-mile (3,840-kilometer) waterway linking the Great Lakes and the Atlantic Ocean. The Seaway enables oceangoing ships to reach every port on the Great Lakes. Another important cooperative venture was the development of the Columbia River basin. This project doubled the water-storage capacity of the Pacific Northwest.

SECTION 5 REVIEW

1. **Define** recession, lobbying
2. **Identify** SEATO, Great Society, Joseph McCarthy, NAACP, Martin Luther King, DEW Line, St. Lawrence Seaway, Columbia River basin
3. **Explaining Ideas** Describe the foreign policy concerns of United States presidents from 1945 to 1968.
4. **Analyzing Ideas** **(a)** What was the "conspiracy theory"? **(b)** How did this theory develop?
5. **Interpreting Ideas** Why did political issues cause social dissent during the 1960s?
6. **Understanding Cause and Effect** **(a)** What effect did world shortages of food have on the Canadian economy? **(b)** Why?

of communism. Other concerns included providing economic assistance to developing nations and attempting to reduce tensions in troubled regions.
4. (a) Some Americans believed Soviet gains had occurred because certain government officials were "soft on communism."
(b) Senator Joseph McCarthy of Wisconsin developed this idea and publicized it.
5. Leaders of the civil rights and antiwar movements felt that they could not achieve their goals by working through political channels. Rather, they felt that social dissent was the only way to find solutions to such political issues as civil rights for minorities and the Vietnam War.
6. (a) During the 1960s world food shortages resulted in large purchases of Canadian grain by China and the Soviet Union, greatly helping the Canadian economy. **(b)** Canadian agriculture and industry expanded to meet these needs.

771

Reviewing Important Terms
1. cold war; **2.** iron-curtain countries; **3.** containment; **4.** welfare state; **5.** recession; **6.** lobbying

Developing Critical Thinking Skills
1. (a) In the General Assembly each member nation has one vote. **(b)** Nine votes will pass a resolution in the Security Council.
2. Communist-controlled governments were set up in Eastern Europe. When the Western powers moved to unite their occupation zones in Germany, the Soviets blockaded Berlin.
3. (a) After World War II, many Western nations feared that communism would spread. **(b)** The foreign policies of both the U.S. and the Soviet Union were designed to block the other.
4. The Marshall Plan and the Truman Doctrine stipulated that the U.S. was prepared to give needed aid to war-torn European countries on certain terms. It was hoped that these plans would minimize the influence of communism.
5. The Western nations designed NATO. The Soviet response to NATO was the Warsaw Pact. The purpose of both was to offer assistance to member nations in the event of an attack.
6. (a) The members wanted to establish an economic union to abolish tariffs and import quotas. **(b)** COMECON was created to coordinate industrial development and trade within the Soviet block.
7. In the 1960s Congress passed several civil-rights and voting-rights acts as a result of the work of civil rights leaders.

1B, 1D, 1E, 5B, 5C, 5G, 5H, a1C, a2D, a2F, a4A, a4E, a4F, a4H, a4I, a4J, a4K, a4L, a4M

Reteaching
Have students review the Chapter Summary and the appropriate section and questions in the Unit Synthesis. Discuss the concepts until students demonstrate a clear understanding of the material.

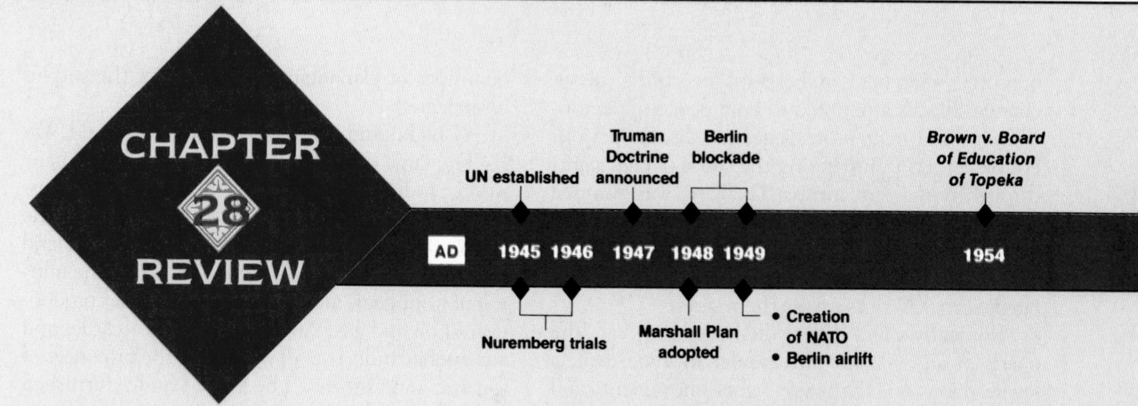

Chapter Summary

The following list contains the key concepts you have learned about Europe, the United States, and Canada.

1. After World War II, disagreements between the Soviet Union and the United States resulted in the cold war. Germany was divided into four zones and occupied by France, Great Britain, the United States, and the Soviet Union. Many Nazi leaders were brought to trial.
2. Following World War II, the United Nations was established to help maintain world peace. The UN also assumed an important humanitarian role in the promotion of human rights and world health.
3. The creation of satellite nations and establishment of the Cominform revealed Soviet plans to spread communism throughout the world. The Truman Doctrine and the Marshall Plan were attempts by the United States to contain communism.
4. The Soviet threat in Europe resulted in the formation of the North American Treaty Organization, which most Western European nations joined. The Soviet Union responded with the Warsaw Pact.
5. West Germany recovered quickly after the war. Great Britain faced difficult economic conditions while maintaining political stability. France experienced economic prosperity, despite the political uncertainties of the postwar period.
6. A major source of the growing wealth of Western Europe was the European Economic Community, which was founded in 1957. The organization attempted to eliminate trade barriers between nations.
7. The Communist bloc nations experienced economic and political discontent throughout the 1950s and 1960s. In 1956 the Hungarians revolted, and in 1968 Czechoslovakia attempted reforms. In 1961 they formed their own economic community, the Council for Mutual Economic Assistance (COMECON).
8. Demands for civil rights and opposition to the war in Vietnam confronted the United States during the Johnson administration.
9. Canada enjoyed a manufacturing and mining boom after 1945.

On a separate sheet of paper, complete the following review exercises.

Reviewing Important Terms

Supply the term that correctly completes each statement.

1. The ________ ________ was waged by political and economic means rather than with weapons.
2. ________ ________ is a name given to the Eastern European nations that depend directly on the Soviet Union.
3. The United States policy that attempted to restrict the spread of communism during the postwar era was called ________.
4. A state in which the government undertakes the primary responsibility for the social welfare of its citizens is called a ________ ________.
5. A period of temporary slowdown and increased unemployment is called a ________.
6. Trying to persuade legislators to vote either for or against a measure is called ________.

Developing Critical Thinking Skills

1. **Analyzing Ideas** **(a)** How are decisions made in the UN General Assembly? **(b)** How are decisions made in the Security Council?
2. **Summarizing Ideas** What developments in the occupation of Eastern Europe and Germany increased tensions between the Soviet Union and the Western nations?
3. **Explaining Ideas** **(a)** Why did the cold war develop? **(b)** How did it affect the postwar foreign policies of the major world powers?
4. **Interpreting Ideas** How were the Marshall Plan and the Truman Doctrine designed to carry out the containment policy?
5. **Organizing Ideas** What was the purpose of the alliance systems set up by the Western nations and by the Communist bloc after 1945?
6. **Understanding Ideas** **(a)** Why did the countries of Western Europe establish the Common Market? **(b)** Why did the countries of the Communist bloc establish COMECON?
7. **Synthesizing Ideas** How did the work of civil rights leaders such as Dr. Martin Luther King lead to changes in the United States' policy toward equal rights for all of its citizens?

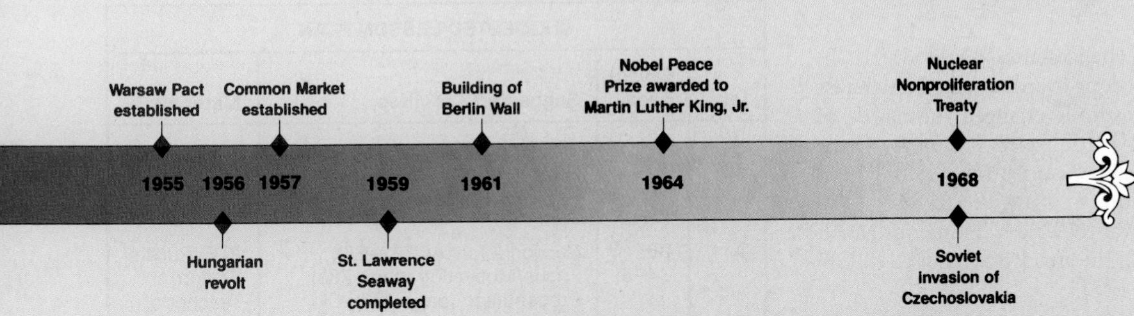

Relating Geography to History

Turn to the map on page 763. **(a)** Which European nations belong to NATO? **(b)** Which nations belong to the Warsaw Pact? **(c)** Which nations have remained neutral? **(d)** How has the system of alliances changed since World War II? **(e)** What factors account for this realignment?

Relating Past to Present

1. The policies of containment and economic aid were used after World War II to stem the spread of communism. **(a)** Does the United States still try to prevent the spread of communism? **(b)** Has the United States been successful in containing communism? **(c)** What method does it use today?
2. In the 1950s several satellite nations tried to free themselves from Soviet control. **(a)** Are there any instances today of satellite nations in Eastern Europe trying to lessen Soviet control? **(b)** To what extent have these nations been successful?
3. Cooperation between the United States and Canada has continued since 1945. Using information in the textbook and recent articles in the news, identify some of the ways in which Canada and the United States work together today. What actions might be taken to strengthen our ties with Canada?

Applying History Study Skills

Before completing this activity, review Building History Study Skills on page 760.

On March 12, 1947, President Truman addressed the Congress of the United States with a justification for containment as a basis for American foreign policy. Read the following excerpt from his speech and then answer the questions to help you identify his argument.

> "At the present moment in world history nearly every nation must choose between alternative ways of life. The choice is too often not a free one. . . . One way of life is based upon the will of the majority, and is distinguished by free institutions, representative government, free elections . . . and freedom from political oppression. . . . The second way of life is based upon the will of a minority forcibly imposed upon the majority. It relies upon terror and oppression, a controlled press . . . and the suppression of personal freedoms. . . . I believe that it must be the policy of the United States to support free peoples who are resisting attempted subjugation . . . I believe that our help should be primarily through economic and financial aid which is essential to economic stability and orderly political processes."

1. How is containment illustrated in President Truman's speech?
2. What reasons does President Truman use to support his main point?
3. How does the president feel about the Soviet Union? Are there examples to support his position? Explain your answer.
4. How would you define the Truman Doctrine?

Investigating Further

1. **Presenting an Oral Report** After Franklin Roosevelt's death, his widow, Eleanor Roosevelt, became the United States ambassador to the United Nations in New York City. Using the *Dictionary of American Biography* or the most recent edition of *Notable American Women*, research Eleanor Roosevelt's public life beginning with the years as first lady and ending with her career as a diplomat of the United States. Present your findings to the class.
2. **Writing a Report** The position of secretary-general of the United Nations is a demanding and sometimes controversial job. Prepare a written report by using the encyclopedias and books in your library to find out more about each of the following secretaries-general: Trygve Lie, Dag Hammarskjöld, U Thant, and Javier Pérez de Cuéllar.
3. Use resource materials in your library to research the satellite upheavals discussed in the chapter (Yugoslavia, 1945–48; Hungary, 1956; Czechoslovakia, 1968). Why did each nation try to free itself from Soviet control? Evaluate to what extent each of these nations was successful in its objectives.

Relating Geography to History

(a) Canada, Norway, Great Britain, Denmark, the Netherlands, Belgium, West Germany, France, Italy, Greece, Turkey, Luxembourg, Portugal, Iceland, and the United States; **(b)** the Soviet Union, Poland, East Germany, Czechoslovakia, Hungary, Romania, Bulgaria, and Albania; **(c)** Sweden, Finland, Ireland, Switzerland, Austria, and Yugoslavia; **(d)** NATO and Warsaw Pact members have acted independently of the U.S. and the Soviet Union. **(e)** the growing dependence on nuclear weapons for defense

Relating Past to Present

1. (a) Yes. **(b)** Answers will vary. **(c)** The U.S. uses economic aid and diplomatic pressure.
2. (a) and **(b)** Answers will vary.
3. Answers will vary.

Applying History Study Skills

1. President Truman illustrated containment as a struggle between representative government and a government in which the views of the minority are forced upon the majority.
2. Truman believed that the U.S. must aid those resisting terror and oppression by providing aid to promote stability.
3. Truman hated the motives of the Soviet Union. The statement, "The choice is too often not a free one . . ." indicates his knowledge of coercive Communist techniques to subjugate peoples.
4. Most students will define the Truman Doctrine as a policy of aid to developing countries to combat communism.

CHAPTER (pages 774–805)

29 *Asian Nations Struggled to Gain Stability*

(1945 to the present)

CHAPTER OVERVIEW

Asian countries experienced great changes after World War II. In China, Communists led by Mao Zedong overthrew the Nationalist government. The Communists drastically changed the nature of China's economy. Disputes among party leaders led to the Great Cultural Revolution in 1966. China broke with the Soviet Union and later resumed diplomatic relations with the United States.

Korea was divided after World War II. When Communist North Korea invaded South Korea in 1950, the attack was repulsed by UN forces. An armistice was signed in 1953.

After World War II, Japan lost its territorial gains but underwent remarkable agricultural and industrial recovery. In the late 1980s Japan was Asia's leading industrial power.

After independence, the Indian subcontinent was divided into India and Pakistan. India, under Nehru, adopted a mixed economy. Foreign relations were marred by conflicts with Pakistan and China. After a civil war, East Pakistan became the nation of Bangladesh.

The Philippines gained independence in 1946 but retained close ties with the United States. After a number of years under the authoritarian rule of Ferdinand Marcos, the Philippines returned to democracy in the mid-1980s. Indonesia under Sukarno and Suharto suffered from economic mismanagement. The new Federation of Malaysia was endangered by cultural and economic differences. After gaining independence, Burma tried to remain neutral in the ongoing East-West conflict.

In Indochina, France fought a long war and was defeated by the Communist-led Viet Minh. In the 1960s the United States became increasingly involved in Vietnam but withdrew in 1973. North Vietnam defeated South Vietnam in 1975. Other countries in Southeast Asia were also affected. Border disputes and refugee problems contributed to tensions in the region.

Asian countries encouraged industrialization with varied approaches, from authoritarian measures to international cooperation. Some countries enjoyed success, but throughout the region economic development proceeded at a slow pace.

SUGGESTED LESSON PLAN

Day	Objectives	Suggested Activities	Materials
1,2	U5,7* C1–3	Introducing the Chapter (pages 774–75) Section 1 (pages 775–83), Focus/Motivation (page 775), Presentation (page 776), Closure (page 781), Suggested Teaching Strategies, Enrichment Activity, Daily Quiz, Suggested Assignments (page 773B)	ATE, Pupil's Edition, Teacher's Resource-Bank™
3	U6, C4–6	Section 2 (pages 783–86), Focus/Motivation (page 783), Presentation (page 783), Closure (page 785), Suggested Teaching Strategies, Enrichment Activity, Daily Quiz, Suggested Assignments (page 773C)	ATE, Pupil's Edition, Teacher's Resource-Bank™
4	U7, C7–8	Section 3 (pages 786–91), Focus/Motivation (page 786), Presentation (page 786), Closure (page 790), Suggested Teaching Strategies, Enrichment Activity, Daily Quiz, Suggested Assignments (page 773D)	ATE, Pupil's Edition, Teacher's Resource-Bank™
5	U7, C9–10	Section 4 (pages 791–94), Focus/Motivation (page 791), Presentation (page 792), Closure (page 793), Suggested Teaching Strategies, Enrichment Activity, Daily Quiz, Suggested Assignments (page 773E)	ATE, Pupil's Edition, Teacher's Resource-Bank™
6,7	U7–8, 10 C9–13	Section 5 (pages 794–800), Focus/Motivation (page 794), Presentation (page 795), Closure (page 799), Suggested Teaching Strategies, Enrichment Activity, Daily Quiz, Suggested Assignments (page 773F)	ATE, Pupil's Edition, Teacher's Resource-Bank™
8	U7, C14–15	Section 6 (pages 801–03), Focus/Motivation (page 801), Presentation (page 802), Closure (page 802), Suggested Teaching Strategies, Enrichment Activity, Daily Quiz, Suggested Assignments (page 773G)	ATE, Pupil's Edition, Teacher's Resource-Bank™
9	U5–8, 10 C1–15	Chapter 29 Form A Test, Reteaching Worksheet, Chapter 29 Form B Test	Teacher's Resource-Bank™ or Workbook and Test Booklet

*C refers to applicable Chapter Objective, U refers to applicable Unit Goal.

BOOKS FOR THE TEACHER

Bonavia, David. *The Chinese.* Lippincott. Provides a first hand account of life in present-day China.

Collins, L., and D. Lapierre. *Freedom at Midnight.* Simon and Schuster. Offers an engrossing account of the movement for Indian independence.

Dawson, Alan. *55 Days: The Fall of South Vietnam.* Prentice-Hall. Details the last days of the South Vietnamese government.

Goulden, Joseph C. *Korea: The Untold Story of the War.* Time Books. Provides an up-to-date and highly informative account.

Halberstam, David. *The Best and the Brightest.* Random House. Portrays the people and decisions that involved the United States in Vietnam.

BOOKS FOR THE STUDENT

Archer, Jules. *Chou En-lai.* Hawthorn Books. Offers interesting insights into the life of this Chinese leader.

Edmonds, I. G. *Pakistan.* Holt, Rinehart and Winston. Traces the history of Pakistan to the present.

Herr, Michael. *Dispatches.* Knopf. Provides an episodic history of the Vietnam War.

Reischauer, E. O. *The Japanese.* Belknap Press. Portrays Japanese society and culture.

Terrill, Ross. *800,000,000: The Real China.* Delta. Offers a personal impression of life in China.

MULTIMEDIA MATERIALS

China: An End to Isolation (mp. 23 min.), ACI. The effect of Mao's central doctrine is examined in this look at China today.

Friendship First, Competition Second (mp. 25 min.), Time-Life. Shows how the Chinese, although enthusiastically adopting many Western sports, have retained many of their traditional entertainments.

The Japanese (mp. 52 min.), Carousel. Discusses the postwar recovery, growth, and Westernization of Japan. Narrated by Edwin O. Reischauer, former American ambassador to Japan.

One Nation: Many Peoples (mp. 25 min.), Time-Life. Stresses the ethnic diversity of the Chinese people.

Rise of Nationalism in Southeast Asia (mp. 16 min.), McGraw-Hill. Surveys the general conditions that gave rise to nationalism and examines the problems confronting the nations of Southeast Asia today.

Section (pages 775–783)

1 Communists Took Control in China and Created a New Society

SECTION OVERVIEW

In 1949 Mao Zedong established a Communist government on the Chinese mainland, forcing the Nationalists to withdraw to the island of Taiwan. Mao initiated a series of five-year plans to raise industrial and agricultural production. In the late 1970s, after Mao's death, Chinese leaders included some aspects of free enterprise in the economic planning. In the area of foreign affairs, China broke with the Soviet Union and reestablished relations with the United States. In the early 1950s North and South Korea fought an inconclusive war. Many of the issues that helped bring about the war still trouble the two Koreas today.

SUGGESTED TEACHING STRATEGIES

1. **Analyzing Ideas (Average/Group)** *Fall of China* (27 min., b & w, McGraw-Hill) presents differing opinions on why China became a Communist country. You might show this film and then lead a class discussion, using these questions as a guide: According to the film, why did the Communists gain control in China? Were all points of view represented in the film? What role should the United States have played in the Chinese civil war?
2. **Preparing an Oral Report (Average/Group)** Have students give oral reports on some aspect of Chinese history or society. Students might consider one of the following topics: the Great Cultural Revolution, education, family life, communes, the Four Modernizations, and the arts. Useful sources of information include: Loren Fessler's *China* (Time-Life) and Frederick K. Poole's *An Album of Modern China* (Franklin Watts). Students should also consult the *Readers' Guide to Periodical Literature* for appropriate articles.

ENRICHMENT ACTIVITY

Defending a Point of View (Average/Group) Write the following statement on the chalkboard:

The Korean War settled none of the issues for which it was fought.

Organize the class into two groups. Have one group develop an argument defending this statement and the other develop an argument refuting the statement. Then have each group select one or two representatives to present their arguments to the rest of the class. You may wish to use these arguments as the basis of a discussion on the causes and results of the Korean War.

DAILY QUIZ

To assess student understanding of Section 1, give the class the following quiz. (Each item is worth 10 points.)

1. Who led the Communist takeover of China in 1949? *(Mao Zedong)*
2. (T or F) The Great Leap Forward, China's second five-year plan, was so successful that its goals were fulfilled in only four years. *(F)*
3. (T or F) The Four Modernizations program encouraged industrial development to the point that in the mid-1980s China was the world's leading producer of coal, second-leading producer

of cement, and third-leading producer of steel. *(T)*

4. (T or F) The Great Proletarian Cultural Revolution was Mao Zedong's attempt to put Liu Shaoqi's ideas on the economy into practice. *(F)*
5. (T or F) Since the 1950s Sino-Soviet relations have been very cordial, reflecting the two nations' common interests, political philosophy, and goals. *(F)*
6. Which United States president opened diplomatic channels to China by visiting that country in 1972? *(Richard Nixon)*
7. (T or F) Taiwan occupies China's permanent seat on the United Nations Security Council. *(F)*
8. Taiwan's volume of ______ ______ equals that of all of mainland China. *(international trade)*
9. Who first commanded the United Nations troops who fought off the Communist invasion of South Korea? *(General Douglas MacArthur)*
10. (T or F) Since the signing of the armistice in 1953, South Koreans have lived under a democratic government. *(F)*

SUGGESTED ASSIGNMENTS

1. **Critical Thinking Worksheet (Basic)** Have students complete Critical Thinking Worksheet 67 in the TEACHER'S RESOURCEBANK™.
2. **Writing a Book Report (Average/Group)** Several perceptive and descriptive eyewitness accounts of China have been written in recent years. Students might select one of the following and present a book report to the class: Ross Terrill's *800,000,000: The Real China* (Delta); Orville Schell's *In the People's Republic* (Random House); John Fraser's *The Chinese: Portrait of a People* (Summit); Andrew Watson's *Living in China* (Rowan & Littlefield); and Lois Fisher's *A Peking Diary* (St. Martin's).
3. **Profile Worksheet (Basic)** Have students do Profile Worksheet 29 in the TEACHER'S RESOURCEBANK™.

Section 2 (pages 783–786)

Japan Became an Economic Giant in the Postwar World

SECTION OVERVIEW

After its defeat in World War II, Japan was occupied by American troops commanded by General Douglas MacArthur. The two aims of occupation were demilitarization and the creation of a democratic government. Japan's postwar recovery was so successful that Japan entered the 1980s as one of the world's leading industrial powers. This industrialization began to alter traditional Japanese society and political life.

SUGGESTED TEACHING STRATEGIES

1. **Illustrating Ideas (Average/Group)** Japan's economy has been growing at a remarkable rate since the 1960s. Have students use resources in the school and public libraries to find statistics on the Japanese economy — gross national product, personal income, productivity, balance of trade, unemployment, inflation rates, and so on — from the 1960s to the present day. Then have students work together to construct a number of graphs showing Japan's economic growth over the last 25 years. Have students display their graphs on the bulletin board.
2. **Writing an Editorial (Average/Group)** Have students write an editorial for a Japanese or an American newspaper. The editorial should take a position concerning the suggestion that the United States place a protective tariff on Japanese products.

ENRICHMENT ACTIVITY

Preparing a Book Report (Average/Group) After World War II, Elizabeth Vining, an American woman, became the teacher of the crown prince of Japan. An interested student might read about her experience in *Window for the Crown Prince* (Lippincott) and present a book report to the class. Suggest that the student pay close attention to the cultural misunderstandings that took place between teacher and pupil.

DAILY QUIZ

To assess student understanding of Section 2, give the class the following quiz. (Each item is worth 10 points.)

1. What were the two aims of the Allied occupation of Japan after World War II? *(to demilitarize the country and to create a democratic government)*
2. The "MacArthur constitution" called for the direct election of the ______, or parliament, with all adults having the right to vote. *(Diet)*
3. (T or F) The "MacArthur constitution" called for the abolition of the title of emperor. *(F)*
4. (T or F) Japan entered the 1980s as Asia's leading economic power and the world's third-ranking industrial nation. *(T)*
5. How did industrialization negatively affect life in Japan? *(It caused the price of land and housing to soar. It also created environmental pollution.)*
6. How did postwar economic development change the role of the family in Japanese life? *(It caused a decline in the emphasis on the family, which was traditionally the center of all Japanese life.)*
7. (T or F) Even today, Japan's military expenditures remain at about 1 percent of the GNP. *(T)*
8. (T or F) In response to continued pressure from the United States, the Japanese discontinued development of a self-defense force. *(F)*
9. Why did the reestablishment of diplomatic contacts between the United States and the People's Republic of China dismay the Japanese? *(The United States did not inform them of this step beforehand.)*
10. (T or F) By the mid-1980s disagreements over trade and defense policies had caused friction between the United States and Japan. *(T)*

SUGGESTED ASSIGNMENTS

1. **Summarizing Ideas (Average/Group)** The death of Emperor Hirohito in early 1989 rekindled the debate about the role of the emperor in Japan. Have students use the *Readers' Guide to Periodical Literature* to find articles about this debate. Then ask students to write a paragraph summarizing the Japanese people's feeling about the role of the emperor. Have students share their summaries with the rest of the class.
2. **Writing an Essay (Challenging)** Some people have suggested that Japanese management techniques were among the most important factors in Japan's economic recovery. Interested students might like to write an essay comparing Japanese and American approaches to business management. Useful sources of information on this topic include: *How the United States and Japan See Each Other's Economy,* edited by Isaiah Frank and Ryokichi Hirono (Committee for Economic Development); Frank Gibney's *Miracle By Design* (Times Books); William G. Ouchi's *Theory Z* (Avon); and *The Management Challenge: Japanese Views,* edited by Lester C. Thurow (MIT). Ask students to read their essays to the rest of the class.

Section (pages 786–791)

3 India, Pakistan, and Bangladesh Became Independent Nations

SECTION OVERVIEW

In 1947 the British colony of India received its independence and was divided into the states of India and Pakistan. India faced social and economic problems and conflicts with Pakistan and China. Pakistan, separated into two parts, also experienced domestic and foreign problems. After a civil war, the province of East Pakistan became the new nation of Bangladesh.

SUGGESTED TEACHING STRATEGIES

1. **Preteaching Vocabulary (Basic)** You may wish to preteach the following important vocabulary terms: non-alignment *(page 786)*; mixed economy *(page 788)*. Ask: How might a country benefit from following a policy of non-alignment? What costs might that country incur by following such a policy?
2. **Relating Past to Present (Average/Group)** The following passage comes from the Code of Manu, a Hindu book of sacred law:

   "A woman should never be independent. Her father has authority over her in childhood, her husband has authority over her in youth, and in old age her son has authority over her."

   Read the passage to the class and have students summarize what it indicates about the role of women in traditional Indian society. Then have students find newspaper or magazine articles about the opportunities open to Indian women today. Ask: What changes have taken place?

ENRICHMENT ACTIVITY

Presenting a Panel Discussion (Average/Group) A panel of four to six students might be organized to discuss India's economic problems and to suggest realistic ways to deal with these problems. Students should consult the *Readers' Guide to Periodical Literature* for contemporary information on India's economy.

DAILY QUIZ

To assess student understanding of Section 3, give the class the following quiz. (Each item is worth 10 points.)

1. The _______ _______ felt that its people would be secure only if they had their own state. *(Muslim League)*
2. Which state joined neither India nor Pakistan after independence? *(Kashmir)*
3. (T or F) Jawaharlal Nehru agreed with Mahatma Gandhi that after independence, India should return to its traditional way of life. *(F)*
4. In foreign affairs Nehru wanted to follow a policy of _______. *(non-alignment)*
5. (T or F) Indira Gandhi's years as prime minister were marked by the eradication of government corruption and the strengthening of democratic institutions. *(F)*
6. What was the goal of the Sikh extremists at Amritsar? *(independence for the province of Punjab)*
7. What is India's major economic problem? *(that its economy has failed to grow as fast as its population)*
8. Which political party called for greater autonomy for East Pakistan? *(Awami League)*
9. (T or F) Since it attained independence in 1971, Bangladesh has become the most economically developed nation in South Asia. *(F)*
10. Who was elected leader of Pakistan in 1988, becoming the first woman to serve as head of state of a Muslim nation? *(Benazir Bhutto)*

SUGGESTED ASSIGNMENTS

1. **Preparing an Oral Report (Average/Group)** Students might like to research and prepare oral reports on the causes of the war between West and East Pakistan, the war itself, the founding of Bangladesh, and the final settlement between Pakistan and India. Sources for such reports can be located by consulting the *Readers' Guide to Periodical Literature.* Have students present their reports to the rest of the class.
2. **Writing an Essay (Challenging)** One of the most pressing problems for Indian leaders in recent years has been the call for independence by the Sikhs. Interested students might like to research and write essays on this religious minority. Their essays should include information on the Sikhs' beliefs and on the history of the Sikhs' struggle for freedom. Suggest that students use resources in the school and public libraries to complete their research. Ask students to volunteer to read their essays to the rest of the class.

Section (pages 791–794)

4 The Countries of Southeast Asia Achieved Independence

SECTION OVERVIEW

After independence, the countries of Southeast Asia began the difficult process of political and economic development. The authoritarian rule of President Marcos in the Philippines was ended in the mid-1980s when the country returned to democracy. In Indonesia, authoritarian rule continued after General Suharto ousted President Sukarno in a coup. Conflicts between Malays and Chinese led to the forced secession of Singapore from the Federation of Malaysia. And Burma passed from a republic to a military dictatorship to a socialist democratic republic.

SUGGESTED TEACHING STRATEGIES

1. **Identifying Ideas (Basic)** Write the following lists on the chalkboard. Have students unscramble each word at the left and then match it with its description at the right.

1. racmso *(Marcos)*	a. Ethnic group forming a majority of the population in the Federation of Malaysia
2. armalit wla *(martial law)*	b. President of the Philippines who declared martial law in the 1970s
3. uksanor *(Sukarno)*	c. First premier of an independent Burma
4. hasruot *(Suharto)*	d. Launched a coup and became president of Indonesia in 1966
5. symaal *(Malays)*	e. Rule by the military
6. gaspnoier *(Singapore)*	f. Led Indonesia to independence and governed the country for 15 years
7. un u *(U Nu)*	g. Forced to secede from the Federation of Malaysia

(Answers: 1. b, 2. e, 3. f, 4. d, 5. a, 6. g, 7. c)

2. **Interpreting Ideas (Average/Group)** Point out that Singapore is one of the world's leading trade centers. Have students study the map on page 795. Then ask them to suggest what aspects of Singapore's geographic location would make it an important trading center. *(It lies directly on the Straits of Malacca, one of the world's busiest sea transportation routes.)*

ENRICHMENT ACTIVITY

Conducting an Interview (Average/Group) The entire class can become involved in producing a talk show about the governments of Southeast Asia. Have one student be the interviewer and five others portray the leaders of the Philippines, Indonesia, the Federation of Malaysia, the Republic of Singapore, and Burma. The interviewer should prepare a list of questions before the show. Suggested questions include: Why did your government move toward military rule or democracy? What are your country's major economic problems? How do you plan to solve them? The other students can be members of the studio audience. Allow time for the audience to ask questions after the formal interview has been completed.

DAILY QUIZ

To assess student understanding of Section 4, give the class the following quiz. (Each item is worth 10 points.)

1. How did President Ferdinand Marcos of the Philippines describe his government? *(constitutional authoritarianism)*
2. The assassination of which political figure sparked widespread rioting in the Philippines in 1983? *(Benigno Aquino)*
3. What action by a number of army officers caused President Marcos to flee the Philippines? *(These officers shifted their support from Marcos to Corazon Aquino.)*
4. (T or F) Presidents Sukarno and Suharto both ruled as virtual dictators in Indonesia. *(T)*
5. In 1963 the newly-independent countries of Malaya, Singapore, Sarawak, and Sabah united to form the ________ of ________. *(Federation, Malaysia)*
6. Which is the largest ethnic group in Singapore? *(Chinese)*
7. Who has dominated Singapore's political scene since the country's founding in 1965? *(Lee Kwan Yew)*
8. (T or F) Singapore's per capita income is the highest in Southeast Asia. *(T)*
9. Which military leader seized power in Burma in 1962? *(General Ne Win)*
10. (T or F) In foreign affairs Burma tried to remain neutral, not taking sides in the East-West conflict. *(T)*

SUGGESTED ASSIGNMENTS

1. **Comparing Ideas (Average/Group)** Have students study the *History Through the Arts* feature on page 792. Ask them to write in their notebooks a list of symbols of wealth in American society. *(Students might list an expensive home, fine jewelry, and a luxury car.)* Then have students compare these symbols of wealth with the Ikat cloth by writing a paragraph that answers the following question: Why do the respective societies value these items? *(Answers will vary. Most students will point out that in each case the item is rare and thus valuable. The American symbols might be seen as products of industrial technology, while the Ikat cloth is treasured for its age-old handcrafted technique.)* Have students compare their paragraphs with those of other members of the class.
2. **Writing a Report (Average/Group)** Some students might like to write reports on an eyewitness account of the events that brought about the fall of President Marcos of the Philippines. One such account is James Fenton's "The Snap Revolution" (*Granta 18*, 1986). A shorter version of this article may be found in *Eyewitness to History*, edited by John Carey (Harvard). Ask students to volunteer to read their reports to the rest of the class.

Section 5 (pages 794–800)
Conflict in Vietnam Affected Other Countries in Southeast Asia

SECTION OVERVIEW

French attempts to restore control over Indochina after World War II led to conflict. The Geneva Agreements of 1954 divided Vietnam into north and south sections, with Communists taking control in the north. Opposition groups soon began a guerrilla campaign to overthrow the government of South Vietnam. In time this developed into a full-scale war. During the 1960s the United States became more and more involved in this conflict. However, American troops were withdrawn in 1973. After the surrender of South Vietnam in 1975, North and South Vietnam were united. Vietnam then attempted to spread its revolutionary ideas throughout Southeast Asia.

SUGGESTED TEACHING STRATEGIES

1. **Preteaching Vocabulary (Basic)** You may wish to preteach the following important vocabulary term: domino theory *(page 796)*. Ask: In which area of the world other than Southeast Asia has the domino theory been cited to support American foreign-policy actions? *(Latin America)*

*2. **Reading About History: Identifying Fallacies in Reasoning (Basic)** To reinforce the skill lesson presented on page 799, ask students to suggest how the paragraph on the domino theory might be rewritten to avoid fallacies in reasoning.

ENRICHMENT ACTIVITY

Presenting an Oral History (Average/Group) Have interested students ask a Vietnam veteran from your community to speak to the class. The teacher should talk with the guest speaker prior to the classroom visit and screen student questions. Tell students that talking about the war can be difficult for many veterans.

DAILY QUIZ

To assess student understanding of Section 5, give the class the following quiz. (Each item is worth 10 points.)

1. Which European country controlled much of Indochina before World War II? *(France)*
2. Who led the largely Communist group known as the Viet Minh? *(Ho Chi Minh)*
3. Which major defeat caused the French to negotiate an end to the war with the Viet Minh? *(Dien Bien Phu)*
4. The ________ ________, signed in 1954, divided Vietnam into two zones at the 17th parallel. *(Geneva Accords)*
5. Who led the government of South Vietnam from the country's founding until 1963? *(Ngo Dinh Diem)*
6. By what name did the National Liberation Front become known in South Vietnam? *(Viet Cong)*
7. (T or F) United States involvement in the Vietnam conflict reached its height during the Kennedy administration. *(F)*
8. President Nixon introduced a policy of ________, which aimed at preparing the South Vietnamese to take over fighting the war. *(Vietnamization)*
9. Which group of insurgents established a Communist regime in Cambodia in 1975? *(Khmer Rouge)*
10. (T or F) Communist victories in Vietnam, Cambodia, and Laos during the mid-1970s forced Thailand to reconsider its close relationship with the United States. *(T)*

SUGGESTED ASSIGNMENTS

1. **Skill Worksheet (Basic)** Have students complete skill worksheet 29 in the TEACHER'S RESOURCEBANK™
2. **Constructing a Time Line (Basic)** Have students construct a time line tracing American involvement in Vietnam. Students' time lines should include the following events:

1957	War broke out in South Vietnam.
1959–62	President Eisenhower sent military and economic aid; President Kennedy continued the policy.
1963	Ngo Dinh Diem assassinated
1965	President Johnson ordered air attacks on North Vietnam.
1968	President Johnson announced a limited halt to bombing of North Vietnam. Peace conference held in Paris.
1970	President Nixon announced an invasion of Cambodia.
1973	The United States withdrew its remaining troops from South Vietnam.
1975	The South Vietnamese government surrendered.

3. **Analyzing Ideas (Average/Group)** Television brought the Vietnam War into the living rooms of the American people. Have students write a brief report analyzing the impact of television and radio on Americans' attitudes on the war. Sources of information on this topic include Phillip Knightley's *The First Casualty* (Harcourt Brace Jovanovich); Michael McClear's *The Ten Thousand Day War: Vietnam 1945–1975* (Avon); and Myra MacPherson's *Long Time Passing: Vietnam and the Haunted Generation* (Doubleday). Have students share their reports with the rest of the class.

Section (pages 801–803)

Asian Nations Sought Security and Economic Growth

SECTION OVERVIEW

During the postwar period, authoritarian regimes came to power in many Asian nations. They were able to do so because most Asian nations were plagued by such major problems as ethnic and cultural differences, threats from neighboring countries, and poor economic conditions. Asian governments used various approaches to encourage industrialization, but economic development proceeded slowly. To deal with this and other problems, the countries formed cooperative associations. In spite of the difficulties it faced, Asia continued to influence the West culturally and economically.

SUGGESTED TEACHING STRATEGIES

1. **Writing an Essay (Average/Group)** Have each student assume the position of the leader of one of the Asian countries mentioned in this chapter. After selecting the country, the student should decide which approach to industrialization his or her country ought to follow. Have students write short essays explaining the reasons for their choice. Call on students to present and defend their positions.
2. **Analyzing Ideas (Average/Group)** On the chalkboard write the following statement:

   The Pacific Rim is the area of the future.

   Have students discuss this statement, using the following questions as a guide: What do you think this statement means? Do you agree or disagree with this statement? Why or why not?

ENRICHMENT ACTIVITY

Conducting a Poll (Average/Group) Ask the students to conduct a poll among their friends and members of their families to discover the kinds of goods produced in Asia that they own or use. The students should ask such questions as:

1. What goods produced in Asia do you own or use?
2. Why did you purchase these goods? quality? price? special features?
3. Did you consider buying a similar American product if it was available? If not, why not?

Have the students write a report on the findings of their poll.

DAILY QUIZ

To assess student understanding of Section 6, give the class the following quiz. (Each item is worth 10 points.)

1. (T or F) Most of the countries of Asia were once colonies of the Western powers. *(T)*
2. (T or F) With the passage of time, democracy has grown in strength throughout Asia. *(F)*
3. (T or F) Ethnic and cultural diversity in Southeast Asia has encouraged tolerance of minorities and political pluralism. *(F)*
4. (T or F) In both Communist and non-Communist countries, fear of neighboring nations' intentions led to a desire for strong central government. *(T)*
5. (T or F) The desire for rapid economic development often encouraged rulers in Southeast Asia to employ authoritarian methods. *(T)*
6. (T or F) One of the primary reasons economic development in Southeast Asia has been slow is a shortage of available investment capital. *(T)*
7. What was the original purpose of ASEAN? *(to combat communism in Asia)*
8. Asian-made radios, cameras, video equipment, and automobiles, by and large, have dominated ________ ________ over the last decade. *(world markets)*
9. ________ ________ ideas on nonviolent resistance had a powerful impact on the civil rights movement in the United States. *(Mahatma Gandhi's)*
10. Hong Kong, Japan, South Korea, Singapore, and Taiwan are sometimes referred to as the ________ ________ countries. *(Pacific Rim)*

SUGGESTED ASSIGNMENTS

1. **Critical Thinking Worksheet (Basic)** Have students complete Critical Thinking Worksheet 66 in the TEACHER'S RESOURCEBANK™.
2. **Review Worksheet (Basic)** Have students complete Review Worksheet 29 in the TEACHER'S RESOURCEBANK™.

Teacher's Notes

For suggested lesson plan, additional teaching strategies, enrichment activities, daily quizzes, and suggested assignments, see pages 773A–773G.

Introducing the Chapter
Display two wall maps, one a map of Asia before 1914 and the other a map of Asia after World War II. If wall maps are not available, have students refer to the maps on pages 615 and 795 in the textbook. Have students compare the two maps. Then ask the following questions: How many nations that were former colonies have gained independence? Which nations were never colonies?

Ask students to suggest challenges that might arise in the new Asian nations. *(Student responses will include: Building an economy, establishing stable governments, and resisting threats from outside powers.)* Ask students to consider how the existence of these new nations might affect the West. *(They might exert cultural influence, provide economic competition, and serve as pawns in the cold war.)*

Chapter Objectives
After studying Chapter 29, students will be able to:

1. Discuss the changes in Chinese economic and foreign policy instituted by the Communist government.
2. Explain the causes and effects of the Great Proletarian Cultural Revolution.
3. Outline the causes and results of the Korean War.
4. Identify the aims of the American occupation of Japan.
5. Describe the social and economic changes that occurred in postwar Japan.

CHAPTER 29

Asian Nations Struggled to Gain Stability

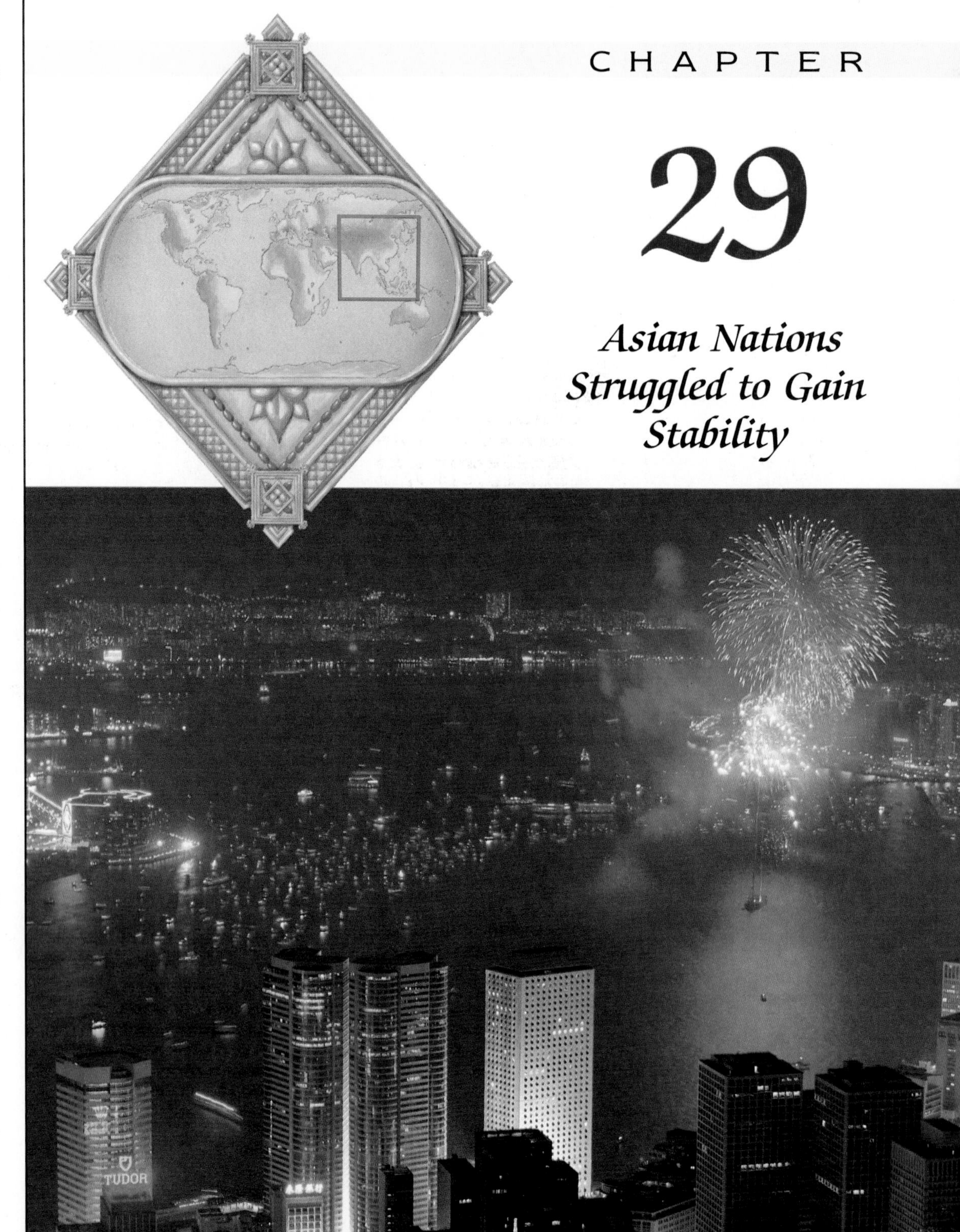

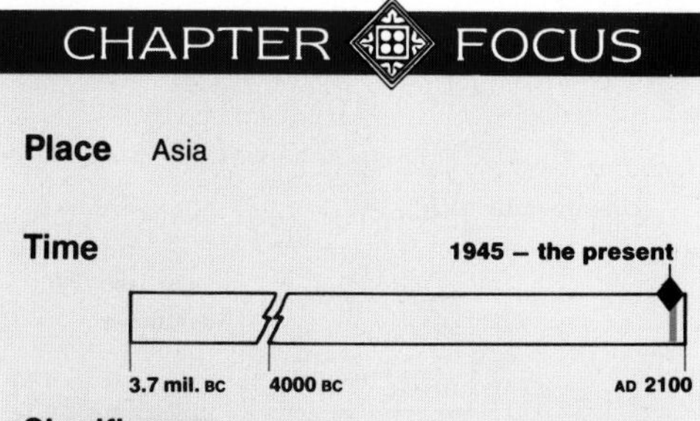

CHAPTER FOCUS

Place Asia

Time 1945 – the present

Significance

The years after World War II saw major political, economic, and social changes in Asia. In China, for example, a Communist government came to power in 1949 after many years of internal struggle. Japan rose out of the ashes of war to become a leading economic power whose influence has extended far beyond Asia.

The movements for self-rule in Asia that had begun decades earlier came to fulfillment in the postwar period. However, this transition from domination to independence was not achieved peacefully. A number of newly independent Asian nations became the focus of armed conflicts arising out of the cold war. Both Korea and Vietnam, for example, saw serious confrontations between Communist and Western nations.

As the 1900s drew to a close, other Asian nations attempted to imitate Japan's "economic miracle." In time, all of these nations began to take an independent, active role in world economic and political affairs.

Terms to Define

non-alignment
mixed economy

People to Identify

Deng Xiaoping
Park Chung Hee
Yasuhiro Nakasone
Indira Gandhi
Benazir Bhutto
Corazon Aquino

Places to Locate

38th parallel
17th parallel

Questions to Guide Your Reading

1 How did the Communists take control and create a new society in China?
2 How did Japan become a leading economic power in the postwar years?
3 By what means did India, Pakistan, and Bangladesh achieve independence?
4 How did the countries of Southeast Asia achieve independence?
5 What impact did the conflict in Vietnam have on other countries in Southeast Asia?
6 In what ways did Asian nations seek security and economic growth?

The hopes and aspirations of all peoples seeking freedom from colonial rulers were eloquently summed up by Jawaharlal Nehru in a speech made on August 14, 1947, announcing Indian independence.

> *"Long years ago we made a tryst [appointment] with destiny, and now the time comes when we shall redeem our pledge, not wholly or in full measure, but very substantially. At the stroke of the midnight hour, when the world sleeps, India will awake to life and freedom. A moment comes, which comes but rarely in history, when we step out from the old to the new, when an age ends, and when the soul of the nation, long suppressed, finds utterance. . . .*
>
> *At the dawn of history India started on her unending quest, and trackless centuries are filled with her striving and the grandeur of her successes and her failures. Through good and ill fortune alike she has never lost sight of that quest or forgotten the ideals which gave her strength. We end today a period of ill fortune and India discovers herself again. The achievement we celebrate today is but a step, an opening of opportunity, to the greater triumphs and achievements that await us. . . ."*

Within 20 years of Nehru's speech, almost every Asian nation had, like India, redeemed the pledge of self-determination.

1 Communists Took Control in China and Created a New Society

During World War II, the Nationalist and Communist Chinese agreed to halt their civil war and form a united front against their common enemy, the Japanese. However, this alliance soon broke down, and the two parties returned to warring with each other. After World War II, the Communists increased their military strength and expanded the territory under their direct control. In time the Communists gained the upper hand in the civil war, and by 1949 they had driven the Nationalists from power.

In 1949 Chiang Kai-shek, the Nationalist leader, fled with his supporters to the island of Taiwan and established a government there (see map,

◀ *Fireworks over Hong Kong's harbor*

6. Trace the development of United States-Japanese relations since 1945.
7. Identify the major social and economic problems facing India.
8. Describe the events that led to the establishment of Bangladesh and Pakistan as two separate countries.
9. Compare the movements toward independence of the countries of Southeast Asia.
10. Discuss the challenges facing the countries of Southeast Asia today.
11. Trace United States involvement in the Vietnamese conflict.
12. Explain how the Vietnam War affected the other countries of Indochina.
13. Discuss the trend toward authoritarian governments in Asia.
14. Describe economic development in Asia.
15. Give examples of Asia's influence on the West.

SECTION 1

Focus/Motivation
Write the following statement on the chalkboard: "The Communist China of today is not wholly a new China" (C. P. Fitzgerald, *The China Giant.* Scott, Foresman). Ask students what they think this statement means. *(The Communists did not so much impose a new system on China as adapt Chinese ways of life to their philosophy.)* Review with the students the traditional ways of life in China that might have been adapted

1A, 1B, 1E, 4I, 5H, a4B, a4C, a4I

to Communist philosophy. *(Answers will include the following: authoritarian rule, a scholarly ruling class, stress on education, fear of foreigners, fear of invasion from the north, and desire to expand to the south.)* Have students reexamine their answers after they have read the section.

Presentation Debating (Average/Group)
Select four students to debate the following: Truman was justified in removing MacArthur from command in Korea. Allow students adequate time before the debate to do further reading and prepare their arguments. Useful sources include R. Leckie's *Conflict: The History of the Korean War* (Avon); William Manchester's *American Caesar* (Little Brown); Cabell Phillips's *The Truman Presidency* (Macmillan); and Dean Acheson's *Korean War* (Norton).

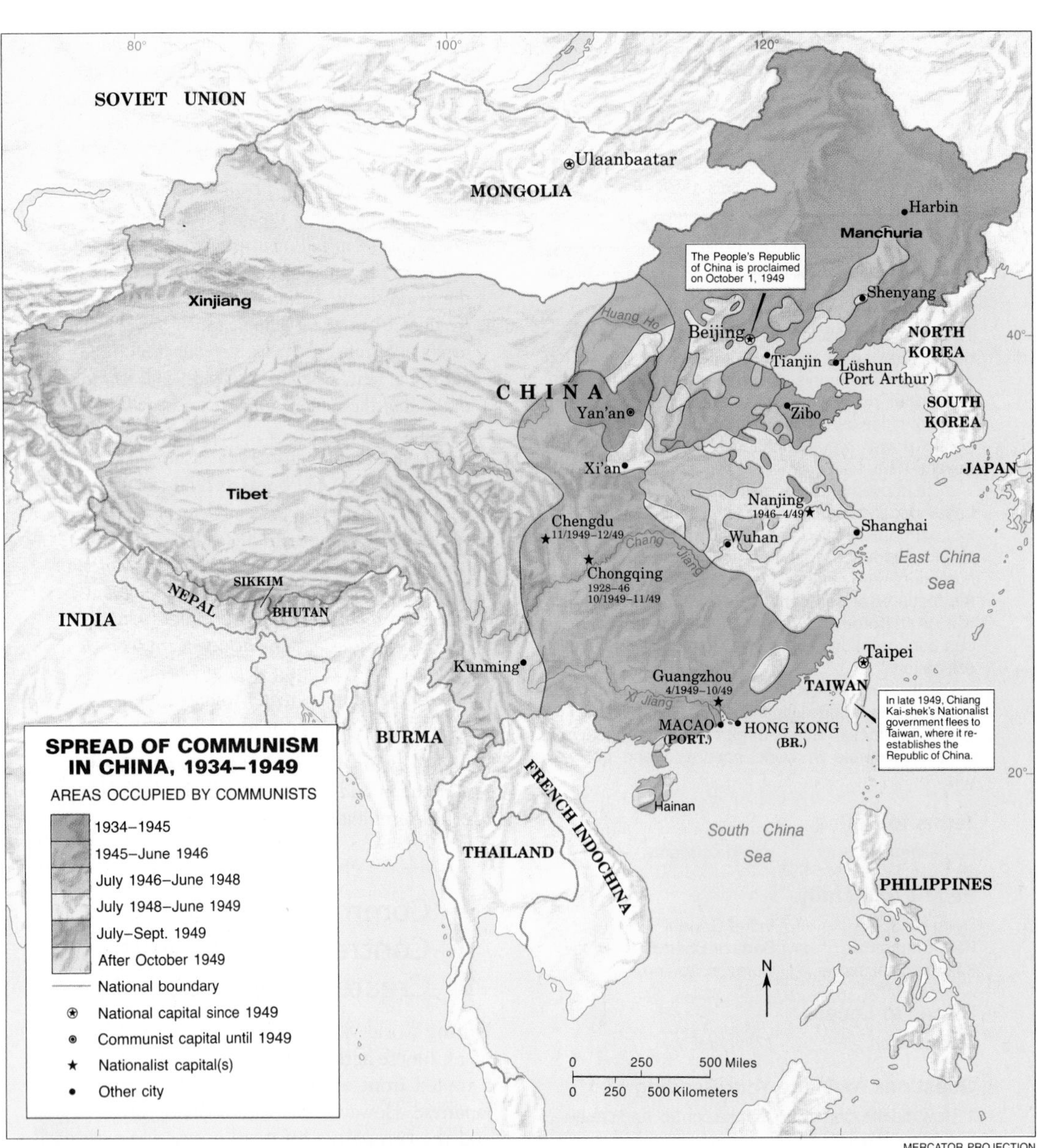

Learning from Maps *In order to protect Taiwan and attack the mainland, the Nationalists fortified small offshore islands. What is the capital of Taiwan?* **Taipei**

this page). On the Chinese mainland, the Communists, led by Mao Zedong, established the People's Republic of China. The United States, which had aided the Nationalists, refused to recognize this new Communist government on the mainland.

The Chinese Economy

The Communists wanted to create a modern, industrialized nation dominated by the Communist Party. To achieve this goal, the Communists first took a political step. Through either election or appointment, they placed Communist Party members in all of the key government and military offices. The new constitution gave executive power to the party's Central Committee and its Politburo, both headed by Mao Zedong.

An overwhelming task faced this new Communist government. China had been devastated by more than 30 years of war. Farms lay destroyed, and industry and transportation had almost ceased to function. The Chinese people had fared little better than their country. Miserably poor, they had been decimated by periodic epidemics and famines.

In 1953 the Communists began the process of rebuilding China by issuing their first Five-Year Plan for economic growth. Although this plan stressed the rapid buildup of heavy industry, it also focused on land reform. Peasants received some land, which they organized into collective farms, while the government operated state farms on much of what remained. The Soviet Union provided part of the capital for the plan, but most of the financing came from China itself.

Despite natural disasters such as droughts and floods, peasant opposition to land reform, and inefficient planning by government officials, the first Five-Year Plan achieved considerable success. Agricultural production increased, and output more than doubled in such heavy industries as coal and steel.

The Great Leap Forward. In 1958 the government announced a second Five-Year Plan, the Great Leap Forward. More ambitious than the first Five-Year Plan, it aimed to speed up economic development while simultaneously developing a completely socialist society.

The Great Leap Forward established huge collective communities, called people's communes, that incorporated agricultural activities and small industries. The largest of these communes had populations in excess of 25,000. Life on a commune bore a strong resemblance to life in the military. Men, women, and children lived in separate dormitories and ate in communal dining halls. People worked long hours in the fields or factories under strict supervision, and everyone received the same pay, regardless of how much he or she produced.

Under the Great Leap Forward, the Chinese government hoped to increase industrial output to the point where it matched that of many Western European countries. To reach this goal, China purchased modern machinery and even complete steel mills, first from the Soviet Union and then from the countries of Western Europe. The government even encouraged the Chinese people to make their own iron and steel in small backyard blast furnaces.

Learning from Pictures *These music students are wearing the red bandanna of the Young Pioneers, a young people's organization open to boys and girls.*

The Great Leap Forward failed dismally. Poor planning by government officials and factory managers brought industry practically to a standstill. In addition, three successive crop failures left millions of people facing severe food shortages. Further, the Chinese people resented the ideas behind the plan. Industrial workers complained bitterly about the long hours they had to work, and the peasants hated communal living. Faced with falling productivity and constant criticism from workers and peasants, the government abandoned the Great Leap Forward in the early 1960s. New policies modified the communes, allowing families to live in their own homes. People still had to work on the communal farmland, but they also had small plots of land on which they could raise their own crops. During the 1960s, under these modified communal arrangements, Chinese agriculture recovered and became moderately successful.

The Four Modernizations. In the late 1970s, the government instituted a new economic development plan, the Four Modernizations, that aimed at improving and updating four important areas of the economy—agriculture, industry, science and technology, and military defense. The plan introduced incentives to increase production. For

777

1B, 1D, 1E, 4I, 5G, 5H, a1C

● The Red Guard even changed the meaning of traffic signals, ordering traffic to move on red and stop on green! Mao excused the excesses of the Red Guard by saying, "To rebel is justified."

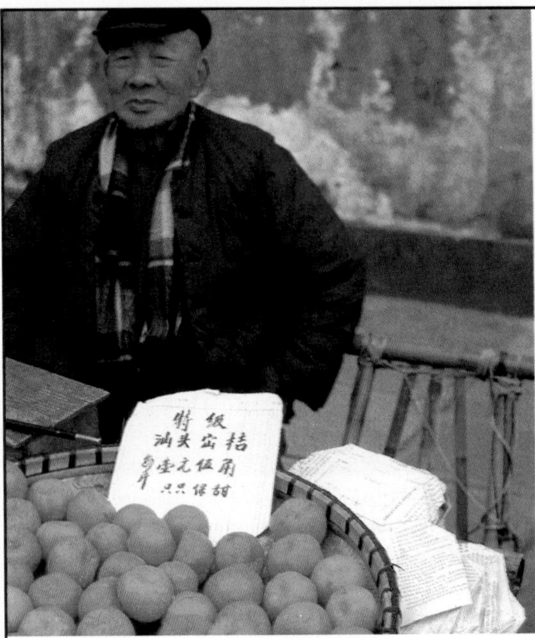

Learning from Pictures *Limited free enterprise is now legal in China. This Chinese merchant sells fruit from his own government-allotted farm plot.*

example, although central planners set production quotas for workers, anything produced above the quotas could be sold for profit. In addition, the Four Modernizations reduced government control of factories and farms and encouraged the import of technology from the West. This new approach certainly helped China become a major industrial power. By the mid-1980s it led the world in coal production, stood second in the production of cement, third in steel, and sixth in petroleum.

The seventh Five-Year Plan (1986–1990) continued this more open approach to the economy. It focused less on industrial growth and more on economic reforms, particularly in the banking and agricultural sectors. In addition, it encouraged a degree of free enterprise. This new direction in Chinese economic policy has resulted in a rising standard of living for the Chinese people. Per capita income, for example, increased more than 14 percent from 1982 to 1983.

Leadership Struggles

Since 1949 officials of the Chinese Communist Party have remained in agreement about the two goals of their revolution: (1) economic development and (2) creation of a classless society. They have often disagreed, however, about the way to achieve these goals. One group believed that economic development had to come first; if necessary, wage incentives should be used to increase production. The other group believed that both goals should be pursued at the same time; if a conflict arose between these goals, social change should take priority over economic issues. This group also believed wage incentives were dangerous, claiming they created inequality and rivalry among workers.

In the early years of Communist rule in China, Liu Shaoqi (LEE•OO SHOW•CHEE) led the advocates of the first point of view. Mao Zedong and his followers advocated the second point of view. In the early 1960s, after the failure of the Great Leap Forward, Liu successfully put his economic development policies into effect. Accusing him of leading China down the "capitalist road," Mao began a concerted effort to destroy Liu's work.

The Cultural Revolution. To this end, in 1966 Mao launched the Great Proletarian Cultural Revolution, a violent attempt at social change. Mao aimed to rid China of the "Four Olds"—old customs, habits, thoughts, and culture—replacing them with a new socialist culture. Mao chose China's young people to lead this revolution. These high school and college students, whom Mao called his "little generals," soon became known as the Red Guard. They went on a rampage throughout China, vandalizing historic buildings, ruining ancient works of art, burning books, and destroying anything they considered part of the "old way." However, they saved their greatest zeal for those people who did not totally comply with Mao's teachings. The Red Guard denounced these people, publicly humiliated them, and sometimes beat, tortured, or even killed them. Those people who survived the Red Guard lost their jobs and their Communist Party membership. Liu himself suffered denunciation and died while in jail.

The Cultural Revolution had a disastrous effect on the Chinese economy. Agricultural and industrial production fell dramatically, and the country's economic development plans suffered a severe setback. In 1969, with the country in a state of chaos, Mao finally called a halt to his experiment in social change. ●

Moderates in control. Upon Mao's death in 1976, a struggle began between Communist moderates and a radical group led by Mao's widow, Qiang

778

The Red Guard had become so powerful that Mao had to use the army to disperse them. Some Red Guard members returned to school, but the vast majority of them were sent to collective farms or factories for "reeducation."

Jing (JEE • AHNG JING). The moderates wanted to return to the policies of Liu Shaoqi, whereas Qiang Jing's group—known as the Gang of Four—wanted to continue the Cultural Revolution and rid China of all vestiges of the past.

In time, the moderates won control of the major party and government offices, and in an attempt to crush the threat posed by the radicals, they placed the Gang of Four on trial for treason. Found guilty, Qiang Jing and her three compatriots received life sentences. The moderates then began to reinstate many of those who had been purged from government offices and the Communist Party during the Cultural Revolution. They even made a reassessment of Mao's ideas and policies, noting that he had made mistakes, specifically in starting the Cultural Revolution. However, the moderates concluded that "his merits are primary and his errors secondary."

By the late 1970s, Deng Xiaoping (DUNG SHOU • PING) had emerged as the leader of the moderates. Although Deng had helped to found the Chinese Communist Party, during the Cultural Revolution he had been denounced as one of the worst "capitalist roaders." As the basis for his Four Modernizations, Deng now used the same ideas that had earned him so much criticism. He also fostered greater openness in social life by encouraging cultural and scientific exchanges with Western countries. In the late 1980s, Deng gave up his government and Communist Party positions, leaving the country in the hands of a younger generation of leaders. Then in the spring of 1989 the government faced a severe challenge as students occupied Tienanmen Square in Beijing to demand democratic reforms. Fearing for the survival of their regime, Chinese leaders declared martial law and ordered the brutal suppression of the demonstrations. Almost 3,000 people were massacred, and 10,000 more were wounded in the crackdown. At the same time, thousands of suspected "counterrevolutionaries" were arrested and executed throughout China. Although martial law was lifted in 1990, the Communist regime continued to suppress human and civil rights.

Foreign Relations

In the early 1950s, the Soviet Union and the People's Republic of China were allies, united by political ideology and common economic interests. However, they soon disagreed, first about the interpretation of Marxism and then over economic policy.

Soviet leaders believed that world communism could be achieved through scientific and economic successes rather than by military conquests. Therefore, they felt that they could live in peaceful coexistence with the West. In the economic realm, the Soviets thought that each Communist country should specialize in those economic activities it did best. Further, the Soviet leaders felt that the Communist nations should integrate their economies under the direction of the most prominent Communist power. Naturally, the Soviet leaders believed that only the Soviet Union was capable of providing such leadership.

Chinese leaders, on the other hand, claimed that Communist nations had an obligation to support "national wars of liberation." In addition, they argued that nations could never live in peaceful coexistence while capitalism existed. In rejecting revolution as the means of social change, the Soviets had abandoned true Marxism, the Chinese said. The Chinese also held that each Communist country should develop its own economy, and that no one country of the Communist bloc should dominate the other countries. They argued that the Soviet model of economic development, which stressed heavy industry, would not work in China with its large agricultural population. The Chinese were not ready to accept the point of view of another government, not even that of the Soviet Union.

At first, the Chinese and the Soviets confined their differences to bitter public speeches and to a struggle for leadership in the Communist bloc and in the developing regions of the world. However, during the 1960s both countries began to station troops along their common border. As a result, a number of clashes occurred on the border, especially in Xinjiang (SHIN • JEE • AHNG), where the Chinese had nuclear facilities.

These border skirmishes helped to bring about a change in Chinese foreign policy. In the past, Mao Zedong and his advisers had made foreign-policy decisions based on which nation they believed represented the greatest threat to China's security. For 20 years, no one doubted that the United States, with military bases in Japan, Taiwan, the Philippines, and Vietnam, posed the most danger to China.

779

1B, 1C, 1D, 1E, 4I, 5C, 5H, a1B, a3B, a3C, a3G, a3I

The Nationalists in Taiwan considered themselves a government in exile. Therefore, all the mainland provinces were represented in the parliament of the Republic of China. Since Taiwan was considered just another province, its representatives were greatly outnumbered by representatives of the mainland.

Learning from Pictures *President Nixon's persistent diplomacy paved the way for the opening of relations with the People's Republic of China. Here the president and Zhou En-lai eat dinner in Shanghai.*

As Chinese-Soviet relations worsened, however, China grew more willing to come to terms with the United States. The first major sign of change came in 1972, when President Richard Nixon visited China. Soon after, the two nations began to permit the exchange of sports teams, journalists, educators, artists, and business leaders. By the mid-1970s, China had opened its doors to American tourists. Finally, in 1979 the United States gave full diplomatic recognition to the People's Republic of China. At the same time, the United States withdrew its recognition of the Nationalist government in Taiwan.

The Nationalists in Taiwan

After the Communists took control of China in 1949, the Chinese Nationalists established themselves on the island of Taiwan, about 100 miles (160 kilometers) from the Chinese mainland. Their government, called the Republic of China, appeared to be democratic. In reality, however, it operated more like a one-party system, with Chiang Kai-shek and other Kuomintang officials having all of the power. The Taiwanese people, who had inhabited the island long before the Nationalists arrived, did not participate much in the government. Nevertheless, the Republic's free enterprise system boosted productivity, and the people enjoyed a relatively high standard of living.

The Republic of China, or Nationalist China, occupied China's permanent seat on the United Nations Security Council for many years. Then, in 1971, the UN expelled the Nationalists and admitted the People's Republic. However, the Nationalists, in anticipation of the UN's move, had already decided to withdraw from the organization.

The United States had given aid to Chiang Kai-shek for many years and had maintained army and navy bases on Taiwan. In agreements reached during President Nixon's visit to the People's Republic, however, the United States promised to withdraw its troops from Taiwan "as soon as tension in the area was reduced."

The renewal of diplomatic ties between the United States and the People's Republic of China dismayed the Taiwanese government. The United States, however, continued to maintain its commercial relations with Taiwan, though it ended diplomatic and military ties.

Diplomatic isolation did not prevent Taiwan from developing into a leading economic power in Asia. Even though it had few natural resources, Taiwan became one of the world's major producers and exporters of manufactured goods. In the 1980s Taiwan's volume of international trade, for example, equaled that of mainland China.

In the political sphere, fundamental changes took place during the 1980s. A native Taiwanese held the presidency and the leadership of the Kuomintang. And Taiwan's leaders encouraged the formation of opposition political parties, promising that future elections would be completely open.

780

1A, 1B, 5B, 5C, a4A, a4B, a4C

● its adherence to free enterprise

The Korean War

Much of the tension between the People's Republic of China and the United States during the 1950s and 1960s grew out of events that took place in Korea after World War II. Agreements made at the end of the war divided Korea at the 38th parallel. The Soviet Union occupied Korea north of this line, while the United States moved troops into the southern part of Korea. The two occupying powers agreed that elections should be held to form a government that would rule the entire country. However, in 1948 the Soviet Union prevented the United Nations commission sent to supervise these elections from entering the north.

Elections held in the south resulted in the creation of the Republic of Korea, known as South Korea, with Syngman Rhee as its president, and the city of Seoul (SOHL) as its capital. At the same time, the Democratic People's Republic, or North Korea, led by Kim Il Sung, was created in the north. The United Nations recognized South Korea as the legal government, while Communist countries recognized only North Korea.

In June 1950 the North Korean army invaded South Korea, quickly taking Seoul. The United Nations Security Council, meeting in emergency session, declared the invasion an unwarranted aggression. It called on UN members to furnish troops and supplies for an army to resist the invasion.

Chinese intervention. Most of the UN troops, as well as their commander, General Douglas MacArthur, came from the United States. In September 1950 MacArthur launched an attack at

Learning from Pictures *Taiwan has developed industries such as shipbuilding. What has contributed to* ● *Taiwan's success as a leading economic power in Asia?*

Learning from Maps *North Korea's farthest advance almost left it in control of the whole peninsula. Which cities did the South control at this time?* Pusan, Taegu

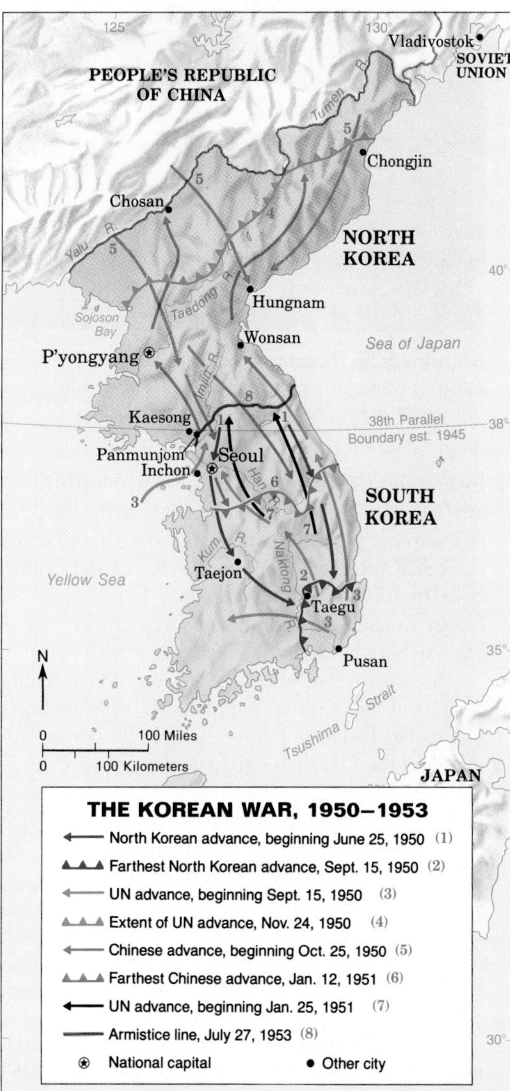

LAMBERT CONFORMAL CONIC PROJECTION

SECTION 1

Closure

Have students discuss the economic changes that have taken place in China since the late 1970s. Ask: How successful has the Four Modernizations program been?

Review Answers

1. ***Great Leap Forward:*** second Chinese Five-Year Plan, aimed at drastically speeding economic development; ***Four Modernizations:*** economic program aimed at improving four important areas of the economy — agriculture, industry, science and technology, and military defense; ***Liu Shaoqi:*** Chinese leader who believed economic development must come before social change; ***Great Proletarian Cultural Revolution:*** Mao's violent attempt at social change; ***Gang of Four:*** Qiang Jiang's group who wanted to continue the Cultural Revolution; ***Deng Xiaoping:*** supporter of Liu, became the most important leader in China in the 1980s; ***Syngman Rhee:*** elected president of South Korea in 1948; ***Park Chung Hee:*** South Korean president, assassinated in 1979; ***Chun Doo Hwan:*** Korean military leader, president from 1979 to 1987

2. ***Taiwan:*** island off coast of south-central China; ***Xinjiang:*** Chinese province on border with the Soviet Union; ***38th Parallel:*** border between North and South Korea; ***Seoul:*** capital

781

1B, 1C, 1D, 1E, 2D, 4I, 5B, 5C, 5H, a1B, a4A

Some people suggested that lack of unity among the opposition parties helped Roh win the election. Opposition leaders, however, charged that the election had been rigged by Roh's supporters.

of South Korea; ***Yalu River:*** border between North Korea and China; ***Panmunjom:*** city close to the border between North and South Korea

3. (a) The reason for the Great Proletarian Cultural Revolution was to rid the Chinese of their attachment to traditional ideas and customs and establish a truly socialist culture. **(b)** The Cultural Revolution had a serious impact on life in China because it devasted the Chinese economy. Production fell drastically, and economic development plans suffered a severe setback.

4. Since the Communist takeover, the Chinese had looked upon the United States as their greatest enemy. After relations soured between China and its ally, the Soviet Union, the Chinese grew more willing to come to terms with the United States. The first sign of change in this policy was the visit of President Nixon to China in 1972. In time, the two countries developed quite close relations.

5. Taiwan suffered from political isolation but enjoyed economic success and began to adopt a more democratic type of government. In South Korea, martial law suppressed civil rights but helped the country to develop economically. Even great pressure from both within and without the country failed to convince Korean leaders to adopt more democratic approaches to government.

Learning from Pictures *Supporters of Roh Tae Woo gather in Seoul for a campaign rally. According to opposition leaders, how did Roh win the election?*

Inchon, on the coast near Seoul. The North Koreans fell back behind their border, with the UN forces in hot pursuit. As the UN troops approached the Yalu River, the border between Korea and China, close to 200,000 Chinese soldiers joined those of North Korea. This combined force quickly drove MacArthur and his army south of the 38th parallel.

A controversy then arose over MacArthur's desire to bomb China's supply bases in Manchuria and to blockade the Chinese coast. President Truman and the UN General Assembly opposed these actions, fearing that they might cause the Soviet Union to come to China's assistance. When MacArthur continued to urge bombing attacks on China, Truman removed him from his post.

Under MacArthur's successor, General Matthew B. Ridgway, the UN forces pushed the Chinese and North Koreans back across the 38th parallel. In July 1951, with the situation at a stalemate, talks to end the hostilities began.

The armistice. After two years of negotiations, the two sides signed an armistice in July 1953 at Panmunjom. It fixed the boundary line between the two Koreas near the 38th parallel. It also established a demilitarized zone of 1.25 miles (2 kilometers) on either side of the boundary. The armistice also called for a peace conference to be held within three months. This conference never took place, however, and no peace treaty was ever signed.

South Korea in the 1980s

Despite South Korea's small size—it is only slightly larger than Indiana—various antagonisms divided the country. These antagonisms—between provinces, between Buddhists and Christians, and between rural and urban people—had existed for years. However, despite those differences, one issue—fear of North Korea—united South Koreans.

After 1953 President Syngman Rhee used this fear to justify moves to increase his power and to curb criticism of his policies. Therefore, although it was established as a democracy in 1948, South Korea virtually became a dictatorship.

Violent protests followed Rhee's election to a fourth term as president in March 1960. He resigned a few weeks later, and for a brief time Korea had a truly democratic government. Then, in 1961 about 250 army officers, led by General Park Chung Hee, staged a coup. For the next 18 years, Park ruled with an iron fist. He introduced a new constitution that reduced the power of the legislature and guaranteed his reelection as president every six years. In addition, he imposed strict censorship on the press and created a powerful secret police force to suppress political opposition. The secret police performed this task by arresting hundreds of dissident political leaders, students, members of the clergy, writers, and labor organizers.

However, President Park also used his power to promote economic development. South Korea's economy, which had grown little during Syngman Rhee's presidency, expanded very rapidly under Park. The most notable developments came in the production of steel and textiles, and the nation's exports of these two products increased dramatically. Because South Korean companies kept wages relatively low and the government held labor unions in check, the country's manufactured goods could be priced to compete successfully in world markets. Today South Korea's economy, based on the free enterprise system, continues to be among the fastest-growing in the world.

782

● In October 1988, under pressure from the opposition and members of his own party, Chun publicly apologized for the mistakes and misdeeds he had committed while in office.

■ The death of Emperor Hirohito in early 1989 led to much discussion about what role his successor should play in Japanese life.

1B, 4I, 5B, a1B, a4A, a4F, a4G, a4H, a4M

Political differences between Park and members of his government led to his assassination in 1979. For a time it appeared that democracy might return to South Korea under a civilian government. But almost immediately a military strongman, Chun Doo Hwan, took control. Chun pledged to end political corruption and to foster real democracy in South Korea. His actions, however, did not match his words. First, he had himself named president. Then he imposed martial law and press censorship and began a campaign of repression against his opponents. The United States, which had maintained a strong military presence in South Korea since the Korean War, strongly objected to Chun's dictatorial policies. He finally ended martial law in 1981 but continued to rule South Korea with an iron hand.

Throughout the 1980s, Chun's opponents continually called for greater political and civil rights. In 1987 a series of particularly violent demonstrations against Chun's government resulted in his resignation. ● Roh Tae Woo, Chun's hand-picked successor, won the election that followed, largely because the opposition could not unite behind a single candidate. Opposition leaders, however, suggested that Roh's election had more to do with ballot-rigging than with their lack of unity.

Like Chun before him, Roh promised democratic reforms. But with the almost constant student demonstrations and the growing calls for reunification with the North, the future of Roh's government and of South Korea itself seem somewhat unclear.

SECTION 1 REVIEW

1. **Identify** Great Leap Forward, Four Modernizations, Liu Shaoqi, Great Proletarian Cultural Revolution, Gang of Four, Deng Xiaoping, Syngman Rhee, Park Chung Hee, Chun Doo Hwan
2. **Locate** Taiwan, Xinjiang, 38th parallel, Seoul, Yalu River, Panmunjom
3. **Determining Cause and Effect** **(a)** What was the reason for the Great Proletarian Cultural Revolution? **(b)** What impact did it have on life in China?
4. **Analyzing Ideas** Why did Chinese foreign policy change in the early 1970s?
5. **Making Comparisons** How do the political changes that took place in Taiwan during the 1980s compare to those that took place in South Korea during the same period?

2 Japan Became an Economic Giant in the Postwar World

After World War II, Japan lost all the territory it had gained during its period of expansion. Its population, now confined to the home islands, faced incredible shortages of food and other necessities. The country desperately needed to increase imports to satisfy the people's needs. But most of the industries that had produced export goods to pay for imports had been damaged or destroyed during the war.

The Occupation of Japan

After the war American troops under the command of General Douglas MacArthur occupied Japan. As supreme commander of the Allied Powers in Japan, MacArthur became the country's virtual ruler. His first task involved the demilitarization of Japan. To this end, he planned to confiscate as reparations the war industries that remained in Japan. But taking factories for reparations would have created the same difficulties in Japan as in Germany. Unless the Allied Powers wished to support them indefinitely, the Japanese had to be given the opportunity to provide for themselves. To do this, however, the Japanese needed to keep their factories and convert them to peacetime activities. The United States, therefore, suggested that the payment of reparations be postponed indefinitely.

MacArthur's second task involved the creation of a non-military and democratic government. Under his supervision the Japanese adopted a new constitution in 1947. The "MacArthur constitution" established Japan as a parliamentary democracy. It called for direct election of the Diet, or parliament, with all adults having the right to vote. The emperor, having renounced his divine status, remained only as a symbol of state. He had little ■ power. Finally, the constitution ended Japan's militarism and limited the country's armed forces to those needed for police purposes.

Postwar Developments

Before World War II, Japan had been the most industrialized of the Asian nations. Although the destruction of many factories and the loss of its

SECTION 2

Focus/Motivation
To stimulate discussion of Japan's economic achievements, ask students to name some Japanese products commonly available in the United States. *(Students might mention automobiles, cameras, electronic equipment, and computers.)* Then ask the following questions: What do these items have in common? *(They are all high-technology products.)* Why do you think Japan has concentrated on producing this type of product? *(Japan has few natural resources and a large population, and it must depend on know-how and efficient production to succeed.)*

Presentation
Presenting an Oral Report (Average/Group)
Organize students into several groups. Assign each group an aspect of Japanese society, such as family life, the position of women in society, the arts, popular entertainment, and so on. Ask the groups to prepare and present oral reports on their assigned topic. Suggest that they use resources in the school and public libraries to complete this assignment.

1B, 1C, 1D, 5B, 5C, 5E, a1B, a1C, a3B, a3C, a3G, a3I

Asian possessions had hurt its economy, Japan made a rapid and impressive recovery after the war.

Economic development. Mechanization and the introduction of new types of seeds and fertilizers had a major impact on Japanese agriculture. Farm output increased dramatically, even though the number of people in the agricultural work force fell. Within a few years, Japan had become practically self-supporting in the production of food.

In the postwar years, Japan also developed efficient industries that made products of high quality. Before the war Japanese goods had been known for their low price and poor quality. Postwar products—photographic, optical, and electronics materials and automobiles—could compete with any in the world in quality as well as price.

Japan entered the 1980s as Asia's leading economic power. Surpassing all others in shipbuilding and electronics manufacturing, it stood as the world's third-ranking industrial nation. However, the country's economic leaders faced a growing problem—where to find markets for a rapidly expanding volume of production.

For many years the United States had been Japan's best customer and principal supplier of raw materials and agricultural products. In this trade relationship, Japan bought more from the United States than the United States purchased from the Japanese. Thus the trade balance favored the United States for many years.

Beginning in the late 1960s, however, the balance of trade swung heavily in favor of Japan. In response, many American politicians pressured their government to limit Japanese imports. They also wanted Japan to remove controls that restricted the number of American imports into Japan. By the late 1980s, the trade imbalance between the two countries had become a major political issue that heightened tensions between the two nations.

Economic and social changes. Postwar economic growth did not benefit everyone in Japan, but it did bring prosperity to a large part of the population. This prosperity led to an increase in consumerism. For example, many families who had lived simply before the war acquired labor-saving household appliances and new automobiles. These better times also brought a better diet and, consequently, a healthier population.

Economic growth, however, did not necessarily lead to an improvement in the quality of life. Rapid industrialization and population growth put land for building at a premium, and prices for land and housing soared. By the mid-1980s many young married couples had no choice but to live with their parents or in tiny apartments in drab high-rise buildings. Industrialization also created another serious problem—environmental pollution. As the decade drew to a close, many Japanese called on their government to pay more attention to improving the quality of life and less to promoting further industrial development.

Postwar economic developments brought about two far-reaching social changes. As more and more women joined the work force, their status in Japanese society began to change. In time they won greater legal, political, and social freedoms. Changing roles within the family and different housing arrangements helped to cause a decline in the emphasis on the family, traditionally the center of all Japanese life. As a result, young people began to make decisions and choices for themselves—on marriage partners and work, for example—that their parents had once made for them.

Political Life and Foreign Relations

The cold war between the Soviet Union and the West led to a reversal of Japan's international position. The MacArthur constitution had limited Japanese armed forces and military production. In addition, the Japanese had signed a treaty agreeing to renounce war as a method of resolving international differences. The Communist victory in China and the stalemate in Korea changed Western policy toward Japan. The Western nations now felt that Japan should be able to defend itself and to aid them in case of war in Asia. These nations, therefore, urged Japan to increase its armed forces.

Fearing a return of the militaristic governments of prewar days, the Japanese had little desire to rearm. They preferred to spend their money building peacetime industries, expanding exports, and raising living standards. As a result, Japan's military expenditures remained at about 1 percent of the GNP. In response to continued pressure from the United States, however, Japan did begin to develop a small, but increasingly powerful, self-defense force.

Japanese political life continued to reflect disagreements over the nation's domestic and foreign policies. The conservative Liberal Democratic

784

History Through the Arts

ARCHITECTURE

Japanese Ceremonial Gate

Although Japan today is a leading modern nation, traditional customs are still very much in evidence. Here we see a ceremonial gate, or *torii,* that has been carefully preserved. Standing in the waters of the Inland Sea, southwest of Hiroshima, the torii greets visitors to the sacred Shinto shrine of Itsukushima. Records of the shrine go back to the year 811, when it was dedicated to the three daughters of the Shinto god Susano. At one time it also enshrined the Japanese god who protected those who fished. In the 1300s the shrine was carefully restored, at great cost, by a samurai ruler and his family.

Today the buildings form a unique architectural complex extending into the sea. The shrine itself is made up of several structures joined together by covered pathways and bridges. One of these buildings, a five-story pagoda built in 1407, contains beautiful treasures of the past. An impressive hall was added by Toyotomi Hideyoshi (see page 463) in the 1600s, and in 1875 this huge torii was completed.

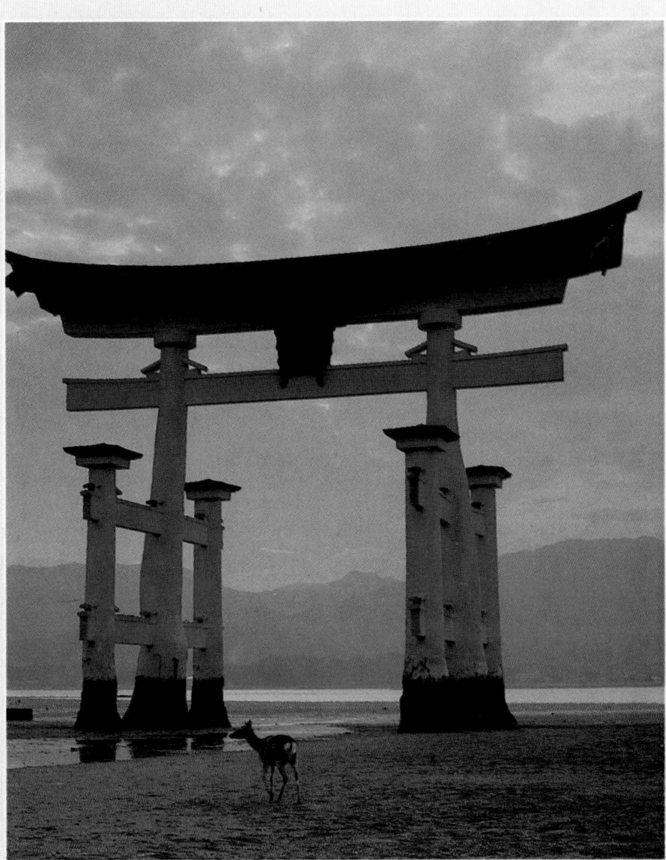

Once each year a favorite Japanese tradition is re-created in front of the torii. On the seventeenth day of the sixth month of the lunar calendar, a colorful water festival takes place, reproducing some of the customs of ancient times through music and dance.

Party controlled the Diet and, therefore, the government. But the Socialist and other opposition parties voiced strong criticism of its policies. These parties also condemned the signing of the security pact with the United States, which was renewed in 1970 and again in 1980. Critics of the government denounced the presence of American military bases on Japanese soil. And they protested the visits of American nuclear-powered vessels to Japanese ports.

Although Japan and the United States continued on friendly terms, United States-Japanese relations came under some stress during the Nixon administration. The reestablishment of contacts between the United States and the People's Republic of China in 1972 dismayed the Japanese because they had not been informed beforehand. The Japanese also resented the new economic pressures put upon them by the United States and other nations during the 1970s.

Since the late 1940s, Japan had been a staunch and unquestioning ally of the United States. By the mid-1980s, however, disagreements over trade and defense policies had complicated United States-Japanese relationships. Many Americans felt apprehensive about the growing trade deficit with Japan, which reached almost $60 billion in 1987. At the same time, many Japanese thought that the time

SECTION 2

Closure

Have students discuss United States-Japanese trade relations. Ask: Should the United States impose quotas on Japanese imports? Why or why not?

Review Answers

1. ***MacArthur constitution:*** constitution, written under General Douglas MacArthur's supervision, adopted by Japan in 1947; ***Diet:*** Japanese parliament established by the MacArthur constitution; ***Yasuhiro Nakasone:*** Japanese prime minister from 1982-1987 who followed pro-American policies

2. If Japanese factories had been taken as reparations, the Allies would have had to support the Japanese indefinitely.

3. In postwar Japan the position of women changed, and they received greater legal, political, and social freedoms. There also was a decline in the emphasis on the family, traditionally the center of Japanese life.

4. The cold war changed Western policy toward Japan. The Allies had wanted Japan to demilitarize completely. However, the Communist takeover in China and the stalemate in Korea convinced Western powers that Japan should be able to defend itself and aid the West in case of war in Asia. Japan, therefore, was urged to increase its armed forces.

1B, 2D, 4E, 4K, 5A, a1C, a4A, a4F, a4G, a4H, a4L, a4M

5. United States-Japanese relations were shaken when President Nixon reestablished relations with the People's Republic of China in 1979 without informing the Japanese beforehand. The Japanese also resented the new economic pressures put upon them by the United States in the 1980s. In response, Japan sought a more independent course in foreign affairs.

SECTION 3

Focus/Motivation
Have students study the map on page 787. Ask them to suggest possible problems that would result from the creation of Pakistan in two parts — East and West. *(Most students will mention the great distance between the two areas.)* Then ask: Do you think these problems would make a separation of the two parts inevitable? Why or why not? What might be gained by a separation? *(Answers will vary.)* Have students review their answers to these questions as they read the section.

Presentation
Comparing Ideas (Average/Group)
Have students prepare in their notebooks a chart of the social, political, and economic problems facing India, Pakistan, and Bangladesh. The chart should include information on religion, language, poverty, illiteracy, population,

had come for Japan to pursue a more independent course in international affairs. However, no serious rift developed between the two countries, due largely to the efforts of Yasuhiro Nakasone (yah • soo • HEE • roh nahk • uh • SOH • neh), Japanese prime minister from 1982 to 1987. Throughout his time in office, Nakasone stressed the benefits both countries could gain from continued close relations.

SECTION 2 REVIEW

1. **Identify** MacArthur constitution, Diet, Yasuhiro Nakasone
2. **Analyzing Ideas** What difficulties would have arisen if Japanese war industries had been taken as reparations?
3. **Classifying Ideas** What two far-reaching social changes were brought about by economic growth after World War II?
4. **Evaluating Ideas** How did the cold war change Japan's international position?
5. **Determining Cause and Effect** What caused strains in Japanese-American relations after 1970?

3 India, Pakistan, and Bangladesh Became Independent Nations

A movement for independence from Great Britain had developed in India after World War I. Indian nationalists continued to make strong demands for immediate independence throughout World War II. Finally, the British Labour Party government, elected in 1945, agreed that India should become independent no later than 1948.

During the independence negotiations, long-standing differences between Hindus and Muslims surfaced. The Muslim League, led by Mohammed Ali Jinnah, felt that its people would be secure only if they had their own state. After much discussion the two sides decided to partition the Indian subcontinent along religious lines (see map, page 787).

The process of partition caused tremendous upheaval and resulted in violence and bloodshed. As the day of independence approached, millions of Hindus and Muslims rushed to cross the borders into their own areas. Violent riots erupted, in which more than 500,000 people died.

The stroke of midnight on August 15, 1947, marked the official birth of the two nations of India and Pakistan. Their first task involved the integration of the princely states. Over the next two years, these states decided which nation to join. Only Kashmir, which had a Hindu ruler and a predominantly Muslim population, joined neither.

India's Government and Leaders

In 1950, India adopted a new constitution that established its government as a federal republic with an elected president and parliament. Although the president was the official head of state, the prime minister and cabinet wielded the power.

Jawaharlal Nehru (NAY • roo), India's first prime minister, served from 1950 until his death in 1964. A wealthy Brahman, Nehru had been educated at Cambridge University in England. On his return to India, he became a lawyer. But after meeting Mahatma Gandhi in 1916, Nehru devoted himself entirely to the independence movement.

Unlike Gandhi, who wanted independent India to return to its traditional way of life, Nehru emphasized modernization. As prime minister, he had five main goals. First, he wanted to unify India by overcoming the dividing forces of religion, language, caste, and regional interests. Next, having seen the religious passions stirred by partition, he wanted India's government to be free of religious interference. Third, he hoped to strengthen and protect democracy in India. With regard to the economy, Nehru intended to follow the example of the Communist countries and develop five-year plans. Finally, in foreign affairs he wanted to follow a policy of **non-alignment,** refusing to ally India with either the United States or the Soviet Union. Nehru's views on this last matter significantly influenced the leaders of other developing nations. In time they, too, adopted a policy of non-alignment.

After Nehru's death, his daughter, Indira Gandhi, became prime minister in 1966 and attempted to carry out his policies. A controversial figure, Indira Gandhi dominated Indian politics for nearly two decades.

In 1971, after Indira Gandhi's reelection as prime minister, her opponents charged that she had rigged the voting. In 1975, when the courts found her guilty, opposition leaders called for her immediate resignation. Gandhi then declared a constitutional state of emergency. The state of

1A, 2D, 4K, 5A, a4B, a4C, a4F

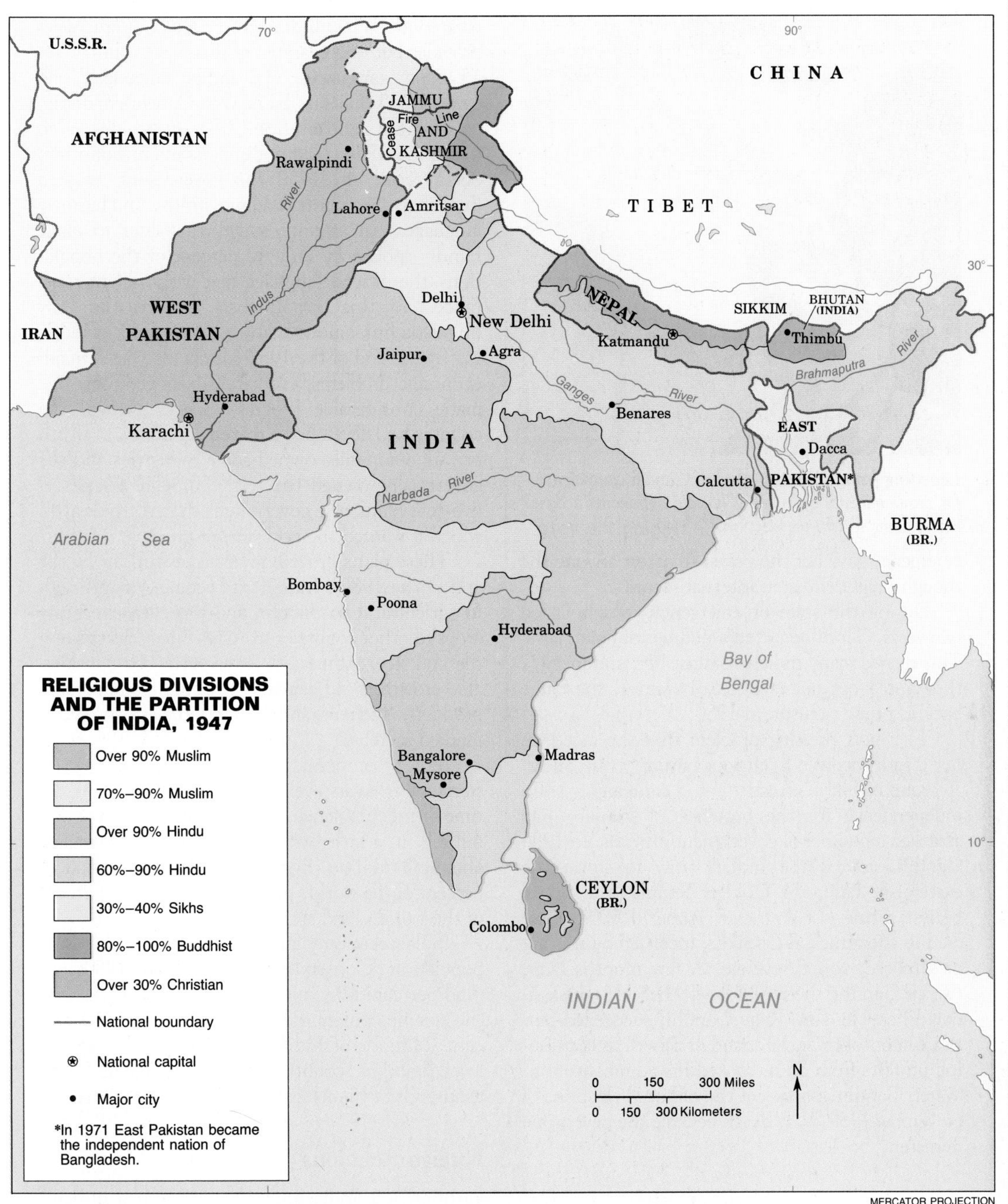

Learning from Maps *The partitioning of India created conflicts between the different religious groups in India. The multi-religious ancient state of Kashmir, which did not want to join India or Pakistan, continues to be a scene of conflict and is a divided state. What two religious groups are fighting for control of Kashmir?* **Muslims and Hindus**

agriculture, industry, and politics. After the chart has been completed, lead a class discussion comparing and contrasting the problems faced by the three countries.

1B, 1C, 2D, 4E, 5A, a1B, a4A

Learning from Pictures *Indira Gandhi campaigns for prime minister of India. What did opponents accuse her of doing to win the elections?* rigging the vote

emergency gave her the power to arrest anyone she thought might threaten internal security.

During the state of emergency, which lasted two years, Gandhi enacted a number of harsh laws. This turned many Indians against her, and in 1977 they voted her out of office. However, she came back as prime minister in 1980.

The most pressing problem that she faced on her return involved a religious minority, the Sikhs. A group of Sikh extremists, in a campaign to win independence for the province of Punjab, had attacked a number of government officials. In 1984 Gandhi ordered the Indian army to storm the extremists' base, the Golden Temple—the Sikhs' holiest shrine—in Amritsar. About 1,000 people died in the attack. The Sikhs, incensed by this act of sacrilege, vowed revenge. A few months later, two of Gandhi's bodyguards—both Sikhs—assassinated her. Her son, Rajiv Gandhi, succeeded her. But rumors of financial scandals as well as continuing protests from Sikhs rocked his administration. When Gandhi's party lost the national elections of November 1989, V. P. Singh became the new prime minister.

Social and Economic Problems

Indians speak with great pride of the social and cultural diversity of their country. But this very diversity, by hindering attempts at unification, has created problems. India's great variety of languages provides but one example of this. The country has 15 major languages, 300 minor languages, and some 3,000 dialects. In newly independent India, government officials from different regions often found that they could not understand one another. As a result, in 1950 the government adopted English as the country's administrative and business language. An attempt some years later to make Hindi—spoken by only 40 percent of the population—the official language met with violent resistance. To this day English remains the only linguistic link among many of the regions of India.

By the end of the 1980s, India also faced major economic problems, even though its economy had made considerable progress. Under Nehru, the country had developed a **mixed economy,** in which private companies owned some industries and the government owned the rest. Through a series of five-year plans, the government charted the way in which it wanted the economy to grow.

These plans proved quite successful, for by the end of the 1980s, India had become self-sufficient in agricultural production and was even exporting crops to other countries in Asia. The country's textile and steel industries also experienced considerable growth. And exports of related manufactured products, such as shirts and bicycles, showed a marked increase.

India's economic problems, in large part, stemmed from its ever-growing population. At the time of independence, the population stood at 350 million. In a little over 40 years it had increased to about 800 million. By the mid-1980s, India had 15 percent of the world's population but only 2 percent of the world's land area.

India's economy failed to grow as rapidly as its population. Consequently, by the late 1980s annual per capita income averaged below $300, and the unemployment rate stood well above 10 percent. Millions of Indians subsisted at the poverty level, and the country's large cities teemed with thousands of homeless people living in the streets.

Foreign Relations

Partition left India and Pakistan with a difficult problem in the northern state of Kashmir (see map, page 787). Kashmir's ruling prince, a Hindu, chose to join India. However, Pakistan claimed Kashmir because 85 percent of its people were Muslim.

788

Sporadic fighting between the two countries continued until 1949, when the United Nations established a cease-fire line. At this point India occupied two-thirds of Kashmir. The cease-fire agreement called for an election in Kashmir to determine the political wishes of the population. However, India prevented that election from ever taking place.

In 1957 India officially annexed part of Kashmir. Pakistan protested, and after sporadic fighting a full-scale war erupted between the two countries in 1965. A year later, the prime ministers of India and Pakistan agreed to withdraw their troops behind the cease-fire line and to negotiate a settlement at a later date. Since that time an uneasy peace has existed between India and Pakistan, but the issue of Kashmir remains unsettled.

In world affairs India tried to cultivate friendships with both the Communist bloc and the West. As a result it soon assumed a leadership role in the non-aligned movement among African and Asian nations. However, India's commitment to non-alignment was strained by tensions with China. In 1959 the Chinese moved into Tibet to put down a revolt. For a long time India had supported the Dalai Lama (dah • LY LAH • muh), Tibet's religious and political leader. After the Chinese attack, the Dalai Lama and some of his followers fled to India, forming a government in exile.

Indian relations with China became even more strained in 1960 with the discovery of a Chinese military base in territory claimed by India. The Indian government declared that the Chinese had unlawfully occupied Indian territory, but the Chinese refused to withdraw. Then, in 1962, the Chinese invaded northeastern India, winning easy victories on their advance toward the Indo-Gangetic Plain. With the Indian army in full retreat, Prime Minister Nehru called on the United States for military assistance. Almost immediately the Chinese declared a cease-fire and withdrew.

During the 1970s India moved further from its non-aligned stance, forging close ties with the Soviet Union. And once again it went to war with Pakistan, this time over independence for Bangladesh.

The Division of Pakistan

At the time of independence, Pakistan consisted of two parts—West Pakistan and East Pakistan—separated by a huge wedge of Indian territory some

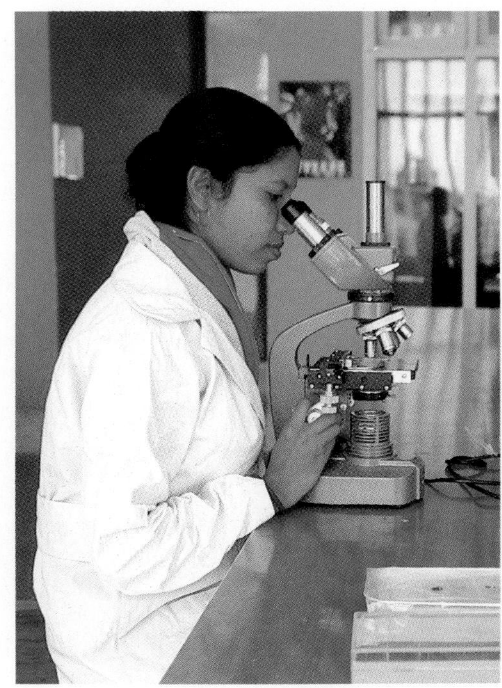

Learning from Pictures *In Bangladesh a research technician works to increase agricultural output.*

1,000 miles (1,600 kilometers) wide. The divided nation faced problems similar to those that plagued India—a rapidly growing population, poverty, illiteracy, and cultural and linguistic differences. In addition, a lack of natural resources and its peculiar geographic situation hindered Pakistan's economic development. Defense expenditures further slowed Pakistan's economic growth.

At first a dominion of the British Commonwealth, Pakistan became a parliamentary republic in 1956. Soon, however, a succession of military leaders took control of the government. General Muhammad Ayub Khan, the first of these, came to power in 1958, vowing to eliminate political corruption and improve the economy. However, opposition to Ayub's government grew as he failed to respond to increasing demands for economic reforms, direct elections, democratic government, and greater autonomy for East Pakistan.

Independence for Bangladesh

Finally, a political scandal forced Ayub Khan to resign in 1969. In the elections held in December

789

SECTION 3

Closure

Point out that India is socially and culturally diverse. Ask: How might the Indian government maintain this diversity yet create a truly unified country?

Review Answers

1. ***non-alignment:*** refusal to ally with either of the superpowers; ***mixed economy:*** economy in which some industries are privately owned and some are government-owned
2. ***Jawaharlal Nehru:*** first prime minister of India after it gained independence; ***Indira Gandhi:*** Nehru's daughter, who dominated Indian politics from 1966 until her assassination in 1984; ***Muhammad Ayub Khan:*** leader of Pakistan forced to resign in 1969; ***Awami League:*** political party dedicated to independence for East Pakistan; ***Muhammad Zia ul-Haq:*** military ruler of Pakistan from 1977 to 1988; ***Benazir Bhutto:*** daughter of Ali Bhutto and first woman to lead Pakistan
3. ***Pakistan:*** located west of India; ***Kashmir:*** province in northern India claimed by both India and Pakistan; ***Tibet:*** northeast of India; ***Bangladesh:*** east of India
4. Nehru's main goals for India included unity, government free of religious interference, economic planning in a socialist pattern, democratic government, and non-alignment in foreign affairs.
5. India's social problems include religious conflicts,

Learning from Pictures *On December 2, 1988, Benazir Bhutto was sworn in as the prime minister of Pakistan, becoming the first woman to govern a Muslim country.*

1970, the Awami League—a political party dedicated to independence for East Pakistan—won many seats in the national assembly. When the central government, fearful of being outvoted, refused to convene the assembly, riots erupted in East Pakistan. The new president, General Agha Muhammad Yahya Khan, sent troops to quell the riots and to arrest the leaders of the Awami League. The situation soon developed into a civil war in which more than 1 million people lost their lives. Another 10 million East Pakistanis fled to safety in India. During the war India came to the aid of the East Pakistani rebels first by sending arms and then by providing troops. Late in 1971 the Pakistani troops surrendered, and a cease-fire was arranged. East Pakistan then became the new nation of Bangladesh.

In 1973 India, Pakistan, and Bangladesh signed a peace settlement. They agreed to an exchange of prisoners of war and the repatriation of people who chose to live either in Bangladesh or in Pakistan. In addition, Pakistan pledged to recognize the independence of Bangladesh.

Bangladesh and Pakistan in the 1980s. Both Bangladesh and Pakistan faced major problems after the division. Bangladesh, ravaged by war, also suffered recurrent famines, epidemics, floods, and devastating tropical storms. The new government proved unequal to the huge task of rebuilding the country, and in the mid-1970s it was toppled by a military coup. Since 1982 General Hussain Muhammad Ershad has ruled the country with an iron fist. Regular batterings from the elements, economic instability, and political unrest make the future of this desperately poor country very uncertain.

For the first half of the 1970s, a civilian government led by Zulfikar Ali Bhutto ruled Pakistan. However, General Muhammad Zia ul-Haq seized control of the government in 1977 and, two years later, had Bhutto executed. Zia imposed martial law, banned political parties, and reformed the legal system so that it more closely followed Islamic teachings. In foreign affairs, although claiming to follow a course of non-alignment, Zia forged strong ties with the United States. And after the Soviet invasion of Afghanistan in 1979, Zia provided refuge and assistance to the Afghan rebel forces.

Zia answered a growing clamor for a return to democratic rule by promising to hold free elections late in 1988. However, in August of that year, Zia was killed when his plane exploded in midair. The

● These included the minister of defense, Juan Ponce Enrile, and the chief of national police, General Fidel Ramos—one of Marcos's relatives.

elections still took place, with Benazir Bhutto, the daughter of Ali Bhutto, emerging as the winner. She became the first woman to serve as head of state of a Muslim nation.

SECTION 3 REVIEW

1. **Define** non-alignment, mixed economy
2. **Identify** Jawaharlal Nehru, Indira Gandhi, Muhammad Ayub Khan, Awami League, Muhammad Zia ul-Haq, Benazir Bhutto
3. **Locate** Pakistan, Kashmir, Tibet, Bangladesh
4. **Understanding Ideas** What were Nehru's five main goals for India?
5. **Classifying Ideas** List the major social and economic problems faced by India.
6. **Analyzing Ideas** What led to the hostility between East and West Pakistan?
7. **Comparing Ideas** How did the foreign policies of India and Pakistan differ during the 1970s?

4 The Countries of Southeast Asia Achieved Independence

Southeast Asia consists of 10 countries: the Philippines, Indonesia, Malaysia, Singapore, Brunei, Vietnam, Cambodia (Kampuchea), Laos, Burma, and Thailand. With the exception of Thailand, all were at one time colonies. After World War II, these countries gained independence. Some did so peacefully, while others resorted to violent means. After achieving independence each began the long and difficult process of political and economic development.

The Philippines

When Spain ceded the Philippines to the United States in 1898, many Filipinos resisted American rule. After a three-year struggle, the United States finally crushed this resistance. However, the American government promised to grant the Filipinos their independence at a later date.

Fulfilling this promise, the United States Congress passed an act granting independence to the Philippines in 1934. But World War II and the Japanese occupation delayed the enactment of independence. Then, on July 4, 1946, the Filipinos proclaimed their country the independent Republic of the Philippines.

After independence the United States maintained military bases in the Philippines. In return it contributed large sums of money to repair war damage and rebuild the Philippine economy. These close ties to the United States led the Philippine government to adopt a strongly pro-Western foreign policy.

In the 1970s Marxist guerrillas began to threaten the peace in the Philippines. A revolt by Muslims, who represented 5 percent of the population, further strained the country's stability. To deal with this internal disorder, President Ferdinand Marcos declared martial law and arrested hundreds of his political opponents. In 1973 Marcos further extended his power by proclaiming a new constitution that gave him an almost unlimited term in office.

Marcos described his government as "constitutional authoritarianism" and promised to "make democracy real." He ended martial law in 1981 and released hundreds of political prisoners. However, the country made little progress toward democracy, and random acts of repression continued. Meanwhile, although Marcos made some reforms, economic conditions in the Philippines worsened.

Opposition to the Marcos regime slowly began to grow. Then, the assassination of opposition leader Benigno Aquino (ah • KEE • noh) in 1983 sparked widespread rioting. Three years later, in 1986, Corazon Aquino, the widow of Benigno Aquino, ran against Marcos in a specially called presidential election. Marcos claimed victory, but when it become obvious that he had rigged the election, the people took to the streets in protest. After a number of army officers shifted their support to Aquino, Marcos fled the country. ●

On taking office Aquino pledged to recover the billions of dollars that she said Marcos and his family had embezzled from the treasury. She also promised to bring an end to the Marxist and Muslim insurrections in the country. But a number of coup attempts and the withdrawal of support by some key politicians have hindered her efforts to attain these goals.

Indonesia

During World War II, the Japanese occupied the East Indies, a group of some 3,000 islands including Sumatra and Java. When the war ended, the

social discrimination, and language differences. India's economy has not grown as fast as its population. Therefore, millions of people live in poverty.
6. First, the central government failed to react to calls for greater autonomy for East Pakistan. Then, when the central government reacted violently to the election victory of the Awami League, riots erupted in East Pakistan.
7. While India developed a pro-Soviet stance because of threats from the Chinese in Tibet, Pakistan developed an anti-Soviet stance and forged close ties with the United States.

SECTION 4

Focus/Motivation
Write on the chalkboard or read to the class the following statement by a captain in the Burmese army:

"We expected so much from independence, and many of us have been disappointed. Ruling ourselves is much tougher than we realized, but we would never admit it publicly even now. We have made lots of mistakes in this country, most of them quite natural, I guess. I do not think we considered thoroughly enough the policies we adopted, the kind of government we set up, or the way we operated it. I don't know too much about the other countries of Southeast Asia, but I have a feeling it is the same there, too."

791

1B, 1E, 4E, 4K, 5A, 5H, a1B, a1C

Ask students to suggest reasons why the newly created governments of Southeast Asia might have had difficulty running their countries. *(Answers will include: Citizens had been subject to colonial rule and were not trained in running a government. A lack of trained business administrators and skilled technicians, combined with a high illiteracy rate, might hold back industrial growth. A large population and dependence on agriculture might hinder economic development.)* As students read the section, they should compare their hypotheses with the information in the textbook.

Presentation Group Project (Average/Group)
Divide the class into groups and assign each group a country discussed in this section. Have the groups further investigate the political and economic developments in their assigned countries in the postwar period. Ask the groups to select representatives to present their findings in oral reports to the class. Then lead a class discussion comparing and contrasting the development of the countries of Southeast Asia. Use the following questions to guide the discussion: What problems do these countries have in common? Which problems are unique to a particular country? How has each nation attempted to solve its problems?

WEAVING

Ikat Cloth

During the last 30 years, in an effort to reduce the tremendous poverty in their countries, Asian governments began to encourage industrialization and economic growth. Many started exporting both manufactured items and handcrafted goods to other areas of the world. Often these goods were sold in stores throughout the United States and Europe.

The woven cloth shown here, from Java, was made by an ancient method of dyeing and weaving known as *ikat*. This technique, more than 1,000 years old, is particularly common in Indonesia and Japan.

The process involves winding the yarn over a frame and then tying the strands at certain points. When the yarn is dyed, the places where the strands are tied together do not absorb color, thus creating a pattern. After the yarn is dyed, it is woven on a loom. The entire process of producing the ikat cloth—from growing the cotton to dyeing the cloth to designing and executing the weaving—is done completely by women.

Decorated textiles such as these have been an important part of Indonesian culture for centuries. Ikat cloths were used to wrap around newborn babies, given as wedding gifts between families, worn as ceremonial costumes, and used as wrappings for the bodies of the dead. Because of the long time needed to produce them and the high quality of the weaving, the cloths became a symbol of wealth.

Dutch, who had administered the East Indies since the 1600s, expected to regain control. However, Achmed Sukarno, a Dutch-trained engineer, led an independence movement against the Dutch. After a year of bitter fighting, the United Nations intervened to secure a cease-fire. Then in 1949, the Netherlands granted independence to the East Indies. The East Indies became the Republic of Indonesia, with Sukarno as its first president.

Indonesia faced problems similar to those of many other newly independent countries. It had few trained civil servants or competent administrators, a high rate of illiteracy, and a chaotic political system. However, the country made some significant gains, especially education and health care. Sukarno also worked to develop a sense of national identity among the Indonesian people.

In the early 1960s, Sukarno became much more authoritarian. In a move that established what he called a "guided democracy," Sukarno dissolved the elected parliament and appointed a new one. This appointed legislature proclaimed him "President for Life" in 1963. During this time Indonesia's problems multiplied. The economy slowed almost to a standstill, and reckless government spending brought the nation close to bankruptcy.

In 1966, taking advantage of a Communist insurrection, General Suharto seized control of the government. As president, Suharto emphasized economic reforms and worked to build closer ties with the West. Using Western aid he began an ambitious industrial development program. He carried this program further with revenues from the state-owned oil industry.

The slump in oil prices in the early 1980s had a devastating effect on the Indonesian economy. Also, a large share of the small amount of oil revenue the government did receive had to be used to pay off foreign debts. As a result, the pace of industrial development in Indonesia again slowed.

In the late 1980s, Suharto's government came under criticism from people both within and outside the country. Many Indonesians complained about the lack of economic progress and the continued mismanagement and corruption of many government officials. And a number of Western countries voiced concern over human rights abuses allegedly committed by the Indonesian military and police forces.

Malaysia, Singapore, and Brunei

In 1963 Malaya, Singapore, Sarawak, and Sabah (North Borneo), which had all become independent from Great Britain, united to form the Federation of Malaysia. The new nation faced difficult problems both externally and internally. To begin with, the Philippines claimed part of Sabah. Also, President Sukarno of Indonesia accused the newly formed Federation of being nothing more than a move by the British to encircle his country. In addition, Sarawak and Sabah had come under heavy attack from Indonesian Communist guerrillas.

Internally, a clash of cultures threatened the Federation. The nation's population consisted of Malays, Chinese, and a small percentage of Indians and other ethnic groups. The majority of the population were Malays; however, Singapore had a large majority of Chinese. Most Malays were uneducated farmers, whereas the Chinese were mainly city dwellers, technically trained and experienced in commerce. Malays controlled the government of the Federation, but the Chinese controlled most of the business and the wealth.

Fearing that the Chinese might increase their political influence, the Malays forced Singapore to secede from the Federation in 1965. Tensions continued to grow between the Malays and the Chinese remaining in Malaysia. Then, in 1969, the tensions exploded in racial riots. Hundreds of people lost their lives before the government declared a state of emergency.

Following these riots, the government began to promote rural development as a means of raising the living standard of Malays. It also increased educational opportunities for Malays and required that the Malay language be used in government-run schools and universities. Thus, by improving the status of the Malay majority, the government hoped to eliminate the educational and economic differences between Malays and other ethnic groups.

Racial tensions erupted once again in the late 1970s with the arrival of thousands of Vietnamese refugees. Since many of these refugees were ethnic Chinese, the Malays feared that the Chinese faction would gain power. As a result, the Malaysian government denied entry to the refugees. Racial friction continued to be Malaysia's major problem as the 1980s drew to a close.

The Republic of Singapore. Singapore, a cluster of one major island and 54 smaller islands, measures less than 240 square miles (620 square kilometers) in area. Since its founding in 1965, Singapore's government has been dominated by one political party—Prime Minister Lee Kwan Yew's People's Action Party. Throughout his time in office, Lee has kept a tight rein on the country, imposing strict controls on labor unions, political activity, and the media.

Singapore prospered as an independent country after it seceded from the Federation of Malaysia. This prosperity grew out of a program of industrial

Learning from Pictures *This view of Singapore shows the city's modern setting. Notice in the foreground the athletic fields showing Western influences.*

SECTION 4

Closure

Have students discuss postwar political developments in Southeast Asia. Ask: What generalization can you make about the type of governments found in Southeast Asia? *(Students will note that most governments in Southeast Asia are authoritarian or military dictatorships.)*

Review Answers

1. ***Ferdinand Marcos:*** president of the Philippines until 1986; ***Corazon Aquino:*** wife of Benigno Aquino, became Philippine president after Marcos fled in 1986; ***Sukarno:*** first president of Indonesia; ***Suharto:*** general who overthrew Sukarno in a coup; ***Lee Kwan Yew:*** prime minister of Singapore since 1965; ***U Nu:*** first premier of independent Burma; ***Ne Win:*** general who seized control in Burma in 1962

2. ***Philippines:*** group of islands in the Pacific southeast of China; ***Sumatra:*** island west of Malaysia; ***Java:*** island southeast of Sumatra; ***Malaysia:*** northern half of Borneo and southern section of Malay peninsula; ***Singapore:*** tip of Malay peninsula; ***Sarawak:*** northwestern section of island of Borneo; ***Brunei:*** small country in northern Borneo; ***Burma:*** east of Bangladesh and India

3. The assassination of Benigno Aquino in 1983 led to widespread rioting in the Philippines. As the 1980s progressed, opposition to Marcos increased.

1B, 4E, 4K, 5A, 5B, 5C, a1B, a3B, a3C, a3G, a3I a4A, a4F, a4H, a4I, a4J, a4K, a4L

• Mention that the Viet Minh was originally formed to resist Vietnam's Japanese occupiers. One task the Viet Minh performed was to provide information on Japanese troop movements to the Office of Strategic Services (OSS), the forerunner of the CIA.

In 1986, Marcos claimed victory over Corazon Aquino in a special presidential election. However, when it became obvious that the election had been rigged, the people took to the streets. After time a number of army generals shifted their support from Marcos to Aquino, and Marcos fled the country.
4. It was a democracy in that there was a parliament. It was guided in that Sukarno appointed that parliament.
5. Singapore had a large majority of Chinese. Although a minority within the Federation as a whole, this ethnic group controlled most of the business and wealth. The Malay majority, fearing the Chinese might increase their political influence, forced Singapore to secede from the Federation in 1965.
6. Ne Win tried to keep Burma neutral. To this end, Win accepted aid from both Communist and Western nations and refused to takes sides in the ongoing East-West conflict.

SECTION 5

Focus/Motivation

Ask students to explain the "domino theory," which many American leaders used to justify United States involvement in the Vietnam War. *(If a country falls to communism, neighboring countries will also fall, like falling dominoes.)* Ask students to think of evidence both supporting and refuting this theory. *(Students may point out*

development that emphasized petroleum refining, textiles, and electronics. By the mid-1980s, Singapore's per capita income, the highest in Southeast Asia, exceeded $6,600. The country's mixed economy of free enterprise and state participation in business helped raise the standard of living for most of its 2.5 million people.

Brunei. The small sultanate of Brunei on the northern coast of Malaysian Borneo decided against joining the Federation of Malaysia. Its leaders feared that it would be overwhelmed by the larger states of Malaya and Singapore. This oil-rich land remained a protectorate of Great Britain until it achieved full independence in 1984.

Burma

Since before World War II, British-held Burma had been strategically important as the starting point of the Burma Road, over which supplies moved to China. Japanese armies invaded Burma in 1942 and held it until 1945. After the war the Burmese did not want the British back, nor did the British try to return. In 1948 Great Britain recognized Burma's independence.

The new nation faced difficulties that included the lack of a strong central government, a scarcity of trained civil servants, tribal and political dissension, and Communist attempts to seize the country. The first premier, U Nu, headed a coalition government that brought the nation some degree of order. This government introduced reforms in land distribution, agriculture, education, and public health.

However, the coalition soon broke into rival factions. As a result, the government—and democracy—did not last long. In 1962 the army, led by General Ne Win, seized control of the government. Ne Win promised to end political dissension, eliminate corruption, and reduce living costs.

In foreign affairs Burma tried to remain neutral. To this end the government accepted help from both Communist and Western nations and refused to take sides in the ongoing East-West conflict. In 1974 a new constitution proclaimed Burma a socialist democratic republic. Under this constitution the country remained neutral and was to seek what it called "the Burmese Way" to socialism.

However, this way led to state-sanctioned brutality and economic ruin. In 1988 student-led violent demonstrations forced Ne Win to resign. But his successors remained unwilling to share power with any other political party. Meanwhile, public order continued to deteriorate. As the 1980s drew to a close, the future of Burma—renamed Myanmar by its new leaders in 1989—looked very unclear.

SECTION 4 REVIEW

1. **Identify** Ferdinand Marcos, Corazon Aquino, Sukarno, Suharto, Lee Kwan Yew, U Nu, Ne Win
2. **Locate** Philippines, Sumatra, Java, Malaysia, Singapore, Sarawak, Brunei, Burma
3. **Classifying Ideas** List the events that led to Corazon Aquino's victory over Ferdinand Marcos in the presidential election in 1986.
4. **Analyzing Ideas** Why do you think Sukarno called the system of government he introduced in the 1960s a "guided democracy"?
5. **Understanding Ideas** Why did Singapore secede from the Federation of Malaysia?
6. **Summarizing Ideas** What approach to foreign affairs did Burmese General Ne Win take?

5 Conflict in Vietnam Affected Other Countries in Southeast Asia

After World War II, some Southeast Asian countries won independence with little or no violence. However, independence movements in Vietnam, Laos, and Cambodia resulted in years of conflict.

The French in Indochina

In the early 1900s, the French became the dominant power in the eastern part of the Indochina Peninsula—an area roughly equivalent to the present-day countries of Vietnam, Laos, and Cambodia (Kampuchea). However, in 1940 after France fell to Germany, the Japanese took control of the area. When the French tried to return after the war, the League for the Independence of Vietnam, a largely Communist group better known as the Viet Minh, resisted them. In order to make a complete break with the French, the League's leader, Ho Chi Minh, declared the country independent on September 2, 1945. But no major governments recognized Ho's declaration, and by the end of 1945 the French had regained control of much of Vietnam. •

Ho hoped to negotiate a quick settlement to the independence question. However, the French

1A, 1B, 4E, 4K, 5A, 5B, a4B, a4C, a4G

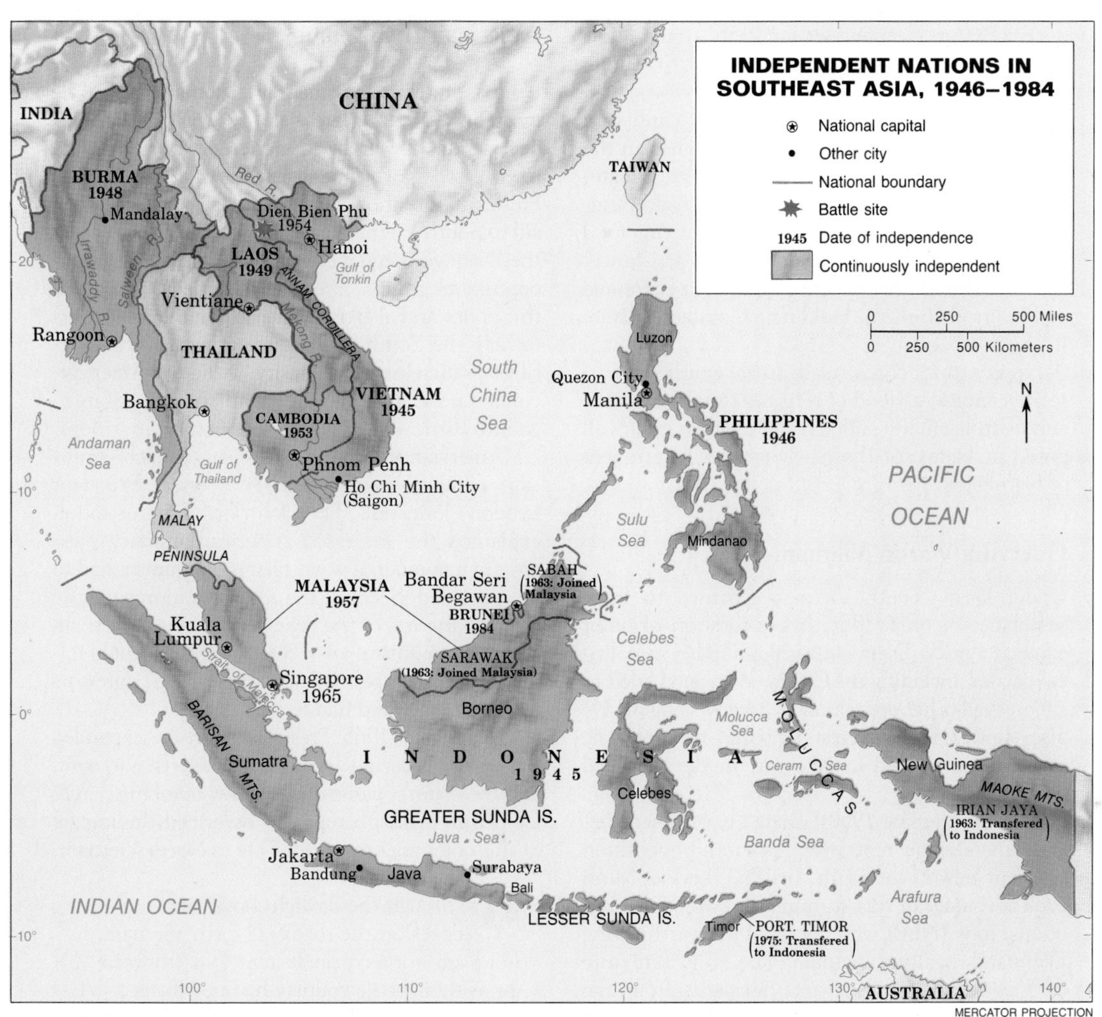

Learning from Maps *Nationalism in Southeast Asia contributed to the formation of dynamic modern countries. Which country is next to the island of Singapore?* **Malaysia**

would agree only to recognize Vietnam as a free state within the French Union, or empire. Ho reluctantly accepted this arrangement. But the situation soon deteriorated, and in 1946 fighting broke out between the French and the Viet Minh in the northern cities of Hanoi and Haiphong.

Against the French the Viet Minh fought what Ho called the "war of the flea." No matter how many "fleas"—Viet Minh soldiers—the French killed, he said, others would take their place and eventually force the French into submission. By the 1950s the French people had grown tired of this costly conflict, which they called "the dirty war." It took a major defeat, the siege of Dien Bien Phu (DYEN BYEN FOO) in May 1954, before the French government agreed. French leaders then quickly indicated their willingness to negotiate an end to the war.

The Geneva Accords, signed in 1954, called for the withdrawal of all foreign troops from the area. They also recognized the independence of Laos and Cambodia and divided Vietnam into two zones at the 17th parallel (see map, page 797). For the time being, Ho Chi Minh would remain in control of the

that a Communist state could serve as a base of operations for invading neighboring countries. However, factors other than foreign involvement, such as popular support, also may be involved in Communist victories.) When students have completed the section, discuss with them whether the events of the last 30 years in Southeast Asia prove or disprove the domino theory.

Presentation
Summarizing Ideas (Average/Group)
Ask students to find out about the current situation in Vietnam, Cambodia (Kampuchea), Laos, or Thailand. Have them read a newspaper every day for a week, summarizing all the news articles concerning their assigned country. At the end of the week, have students share their findings with the rest of the class.

1B, 4E, 4I, 5B, 5G, a1B, a1C

● Mention that the phrase *domino theory* was coined by President Eisenhower in 1954.

north. But an election, set for 1956, would allow the Vietnamese to select a government to reunite the country.

The Geneva Accords left the Viet Minh in a better situation than that of the government in the south. The north had most of Vietnam's raw materials and industries, and it had enough good farmland to become almost self-sufficient in food production. With Chinese and Soviet assistance, the Viet Minh began to consolidate their economic and political strength, building a Communist state in the north.

In contrast, chaos ruled in the south. A war-torn economy, a flood of refugees from the north, and fighting among political and religious groups all posed problems for the newly-formed government of Ngo Dinh Diem (NOH DIN deh • EHM).

Guerrilla War in Vietnam

Under Diem, South Vietnam returned to some semblance of order. But this restoration of order came at a price. Diem outlawed a number of political parties, including the Communists, and tried to suppress all other opposition to his government. He also showed little interest in social or economic reforms and refused to take part in the proposed election of 1956.

During the late 1950s, Diem's government became increasingly repressive. As a result opposition to Diem grew in the south. In 1960 the Viet Minh took advantage of this, forming the National Liberation Front (NLF) with the goal of overthrowing Diem and reuniting Vietnam. The NLF, a mixture of Viet Minh members and dissidents from the south, soon became known as the *Viet Cong,* or Vietnamese Communists.

After undergoing guerrilla training in the north, the Viet Cong infiltrated the rural areas of South Vietnam and began a program of assassinating government officials. And, through a combination of persuasion and terror, they worked to gain either the support or passive acceptance of the South Vietnamese peasants.

Ngo Dinh Diem responded to both internal dissent and Viet Cong guerrilla activity by becoming even more repressive. With conditions in the south growing more and more chaotic, a group of army officers assassinated Diem and took control of the government in 1963. Over the next three years, nine different military groups ruled South Vietnam.

American Involvement

United States involvement in Vietnam began almost unnoticed. It grew slowly, without either a declaration of war by Congress or an announcement by the government to the American people. President Eisenhower sent military and economic aid to South Vietnam and allowed the CIA to assist the Diem government in gathering information on opposition groups. President Kennedy continued this policy and also sent American military advisers to help the South Vietnamese army. As the guerrilla war increased in intensity, so did the American commitment. In time American soldiers began to go into battle along with South Vietnamese troops.

American troop strength began to reach significant numbers in the mid-1960s under President Lyndon Johnson. The Johnson administration explained the increased American military presence in a number of ways. First, communism had to be contained. Second, the administration cited the **domino theory,** or the belief that if South Vietnam fell to communism, all of Southeast Asia would follow. Third, the North Vietnamese were aggressors in the conflict and had to be stopped. ●

In January 1965 President Johnson expanded the war by ordering air attacks on North Vietnam, and the country came under heavy bombing. James Cameron, a British reporter, described the impact of this bombing on everyday life in North Vietnam.

> "Through the daylight hours nothing moves on the roads of North Vietnam, not a car nor a truck. It must look from the air as though the country had no wheeled transport at all. That, of course, is the idea, it is the roads and bridges that are being bombed; it is no longer safe after sunrise to be anywhere near either. . . .
>
> Then the sun goes down and everything starts to move.
>
> At dusk the roads become alive. The engines are started and the convoys grind away through the darkness behind the pinpoints of masked headlamps. There are miles of them, heavy Russian-built trucks, anti-aircraft batteries, all deeply buried under piles of branches and leaves; processions of huge green haystacks. North Vietnam by day is abandoned; by night it thuds and grinds with movement."

796

● Henry Kissinger of the United States and Le Duc Tho of North Vietnam were awarded the Nobel Peace Prize for their work in arranging a cease-fire in the Vietnam War.

■ Vietnamization, and by escalating the war through an invasion of Cambodia and a resumption of the bombing of North Vietnam

1A, 1B, 1C, 4E, 5A, 5B, a1B, a4B, a4C, a4H

At the beginning of 1968, North Vietnamese troops and the Viet Cong launched a major offensive. They overthrew some village governments in South Vietnam and threatened a number of large cities, including Saigon, the capital (see map, this page). However, American and South Vietnamese forces drove back the attackers, inflicting heavy casualties. Even so, the Viet Cong considered this Tet Offensive—named for the Vietnamese New Year celebration—a psychological victory, for many Americans, after seeing television pictures of their embassy in Saigon under direct attack, openly questioned United States involvement in the war.

In March of 1968, President Johnson announced a temporary halt to the bombing of North Vietnam. An agreement with North Vietnam to begin negotiating an end to the war soon followed. However, these peace negotiations, held in Paris, France, quickly became deadlocked.

During 1969, the first year of President Richard Nixon's administration, the number of American troops involved in the Vietnam conflict reached a high of 543,400. But promising to end the war "with honor," President Nixon introduced a policy of "Vietnamization"—preparing the South Vietnamese to take over fighting the war. As a first step in this process, he announced the gradual withdrawal of American troops. Yet, at the same time, he escalated the war. In 1970 he ordered an invasion of neutral Cambodia, long-used by the Viet Cong as a refuge and a supply base. And in 1972 he resumed the bombing of North Vietnam.

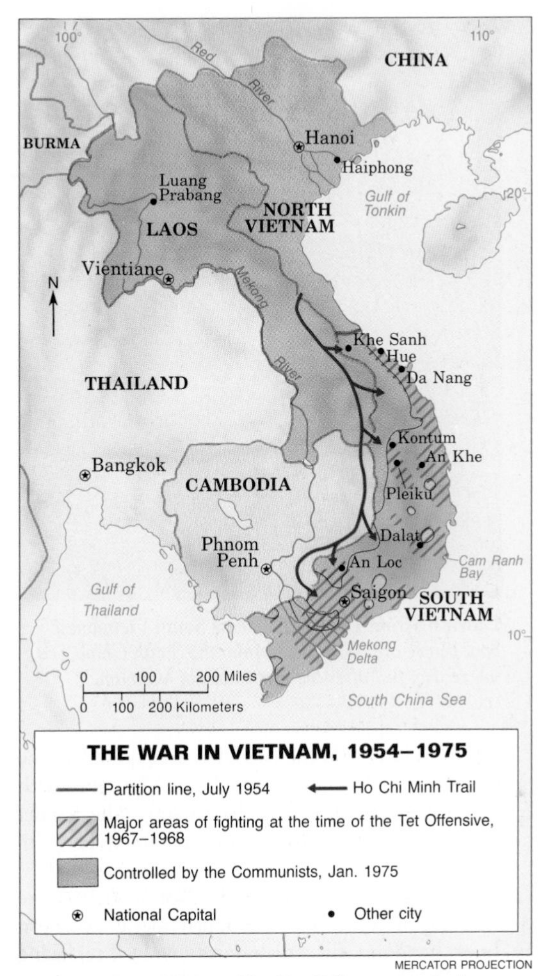

Learning from Maps *The Tet Offensive reached into the heart of South Vietnam. How did President Nixon combat North Vietnam's continued psychological victories?* ■

Ending the War

In 1973 the major parties in the Vietnam War reached an agreement on a cease-fire. Under this ● agreement, known as the Paris Accords, the United States withdrew its remaining troops from South Vietnam. In return the North Vietnamese released American prisoners of war. But in violation of the accords, fighting continued in Vietnam. The South Vietnamese army, without American support, could not hold back the enemy advance, and in April 1975 North Vietnamese troops entered Saigon. Within hours the South Vietnamese government surrendered.

The Vietnam War caused widespread devastation. Civilian and military casualties for both North and South Vietnam numbered more than 5 million. American combat casualties stood at about 58,000 killed and approximately 300,000 wounded. The neighboring countries of Laos and Cambodia did not escape the death and destruction either. Long-standing rivalries among these two countries and Vietnam complicated efforts to recover and rebuild after the war.

A Reunited Vietnam

After the war North Vietnamese officials immediately began to administer all of South Vietnam.

797

4E, 5B, a1B, a1C

● Point out that the ideas behind the Great Proletarian Cultural Revolution in China greatly influenced the Khmer Rouge. They also changed the country's name to Kampuchea.

Learning from Pictures *These South Vietnamese boat people are being towed from the South China Sea, where they fled after the unification of Vietnam.*

Then, in July 1976 the two Vietnams united as one country—the Socialist Republic of Vietnam—with Hanoi, in the north, as the capital. The former southern capital, Saigon, was renamed Ho Chi Minh City.

Even before unification the North Vietnamese had begun to reform the south along northern lines. Economically, this reform involved replacing the South Vietnamese currency with a new national currency, rationing certain consumer goods, and imposing controls on private enterprise. Socially, major educational reforms took place. All schools in the south closed while textbooks underwent revisions and teachers received training in Communist ideology from North Vietnamese advisers. Other changes limited university education to the children of workers and peasant farmers. All students had to spend part of every school year working on farms or in factories.

After the fall of Saigon, more than 6 million South Vietnamese fled their country and became refugees. Some fled because they had worked in the South Vietnamese government or served in the army, and they feared they would be punished by the North Vietnamese. Others left because of the food shortages. By and large, however, most people left because they did not want to live under a Communist government.

Usually these refugees had to pay bribes to government officials just to leave Vietnam. Then they faced a dangerous sea voyage to Malaysia, Thailand, or some other Southeast Asian country. Many of these "boat people," as the refugees became known, died at sea. Those who survived spent long months in crowded camps waiting to obtain permission to settle permanently in another country. Over the years the United States accepted more than 700,000 of these boat people as immigrants.

Cambodia

Cambodia, which had gained independence from France in 1953, attempted to remain neutral in the Vietnam War. The country's leader, Prince Norodom Sihanouk (SEE • hah • nook), found neutrality a difficult path to follow, however. North Vietnamese and Viet Cong troops frequently fled into Cambodia to escape capture, and their chief supply route—the Ho Chi Minh Trail—ran through the eastern part of the country.

In 1970 Lon Nol, a pro-American army general, overthrew Sihanouk in a military coup. Lon Nol promised to take a firmer stand against the Vietnamese Communists who used Cambodia as a refuge.

The Khmer Rouge. While in hiding in Cambodia, the Vietnamese Communists had helped to arm and train a group of Cambodian insurgents called the *Khmer Rouge.* With this assistance, the Khmer Rouge rapidly grew in strength. Sihanouk, who had gone into exile in China, voiced his support for them. In 1975, just a few days before Saigon fell, the Khmer Rouge seized the Cambodian capital, Phnom Penh. They then established a new Communist regime under the leadership of Pol Pot.

This new government evacuated all of Cambodia's cities, sending most residents into the countryside to create new agricultural villages. Lacking tools and farming experience, and without food to tide them over until their first harvest, many of these city people died of starvation. The Khmer ● Rouge also undertook a program to systematically eliminate almost all Cambodia's government officials, army officers, doctors, lawyers, teachers, and

798

READ
WRITE
INTERPRET
CONNECT
THINK

BUILDING HISTORY STUDY SKILLS

Reading About History: Identifying Fallacies in Reasoning

In order to prove a point, an author uses logic, or reasoning. Logic is the process of reaching a conclusion based on the available evidence. We have learned how to identify an author's thesis and evaluate the evidence. One way of determining the strength of an argument is to identify fallacies in the reasoning. A fallacy is an error in the logic. One category of fallacies involves cause and effect. The author has committed a fallacy in reasoning if the conclusion focuses on only one cause or mistakes coincidence for a cause.

Events in history usually have many causes. Thus a conclusion that an event has only one cause oversimplifies history. For example, the statement, "Poverty caused the French Revolution," would be a fallacy in reasoning because it ignores the many other causes.

Another example of a fallacy in reasoning would be the substitution of coincidence as a cause. For example, a Republican president negotiated an end to both the Korean War and the Vietnam War. It is a coincidence and not a cause-and-effect relationship that Republican presidents negotiate successful peace treaties. Some connection must be proven for it to be a cause rather than a coincidence.

How to Identify Fallacies in Reasoning

To identify a fallacy in reasoning, follow these steps.

1. Identify the author's conclusion.
2. Explain the author's reasoning in supporting the conclusion.
3. Identify whether cause-and-effect is involved in the reasoning.
4. Evaluate the use of cause-and-effect. Is only one cause being identified? Is the one cause being used as the sole cause or as the main cause? Is a connection between the cause and the effect being proven?

Developing the Skill

Read the following description of the domino theory in Southeast Asia. Are there any fallacies in the reasoning?

> "You have a row of dominoes set up, you knock over the first one, and what will happen to the last one is that it will go over very quickly. So you have a beginning of a disintegration that would have the most profound influences. . . . If Indochina fell to Communism the Malay Peninsula 'would be scarcely defensible.'"

The main point or conclusion of the domino theory is that if one country falls to the Communists in Southeast Asia, the others will easily fall under their control. It will be an escalating effect because of the country's weaknesses and the Communist buildup of power. The domino theory involves fallacies in reasoning, however. It attributes the ultimate cause of Communist success to only one factor—its success in a neighboring country. It ignores other factors that contribute to the spread of communism. Some of these factors include the economic weaknesses of the country, the political stability, and the extent of nationalism.

Practicing the skill. Reread the steps to identify fallacies in reasoning. Then state how the case of Thailand has provided further evidence that the domino theory involved fallacies in reasoning.

To apply this skill, see Applying History Study Skills on page 805.

United States soldiers in Vietnam

SECTION 5

Closure

Have students discuss the Communist takeover of Vietnam. Ask: Why were the North Vietnamese and the Viet Cong victorious in the Vietnam War?

Review Answers

1. ***domino theory:*** theory that states that if one country falls to communism, other neighboring nations would also fall
2. ***Viet Minh:*** more frequently used name of the League for the Independence of Vietnam; ***Ho Chi Minh:*** Communist leader of the Viet Minh; ***Ngo Dinh Diem:*** South Vietnamese leader who was assassinated in 1963; ***Viet Cong:*** Communist guerrillas in South Vietnam; ***Tet Offensive:*** Viet Cong and North Vietnamese offensive in 1968 during Vietnamese New Year celebration; ***Vietnamization:*** program introduced by President Nixon to prepare the South Vietnamese to take over the war effort; ***Paris Accords:*** 1973 agreement between the United States and North Vietnam that brought a cease-fire to the Vietnam War; ***boat people:*** refugees from South Vietnam who fled by boat and sought asylum in other countries; ***Norodom Sihanouk:*** Cambodian leader who tried to keep his country neutral during the Vietnam War; ***Lon Nol:*** Cambodian military leader who overthrew the Sihanouk government in 1970; ***Khmer Rouge:*** Cambodian

799

1B, 4E, 4I, 5B, a1B, a4A, a4F, a4H, a4I, a4K, a4L, a4M

● Because the meetings between the various Cambodian parties were held in an informal atmosphere, they were referred to as the "cocktail party talks."

insurgents who established a Communist regime in 1975
3. ***Hanoi:*** capital city of North Vietnam; ***Haiphong:*** port city in northern Vietnam; ***Dien Bien Phu:*** northern Vietnam near Laotian border; ***17th parallel:*** border between North and South Vietnam: ***Saigon:*** former capital of South Vietnam, now called Ho Chi Minh City; ***Ho Chi Minh Trail:*** Viet Cong supply route that ran for a thousand miles through Laos, Cambodia, and South Vietnam; ***Phnom Penh:*** capital of Cambodia
4. The Geneva Agreements provided for the division of Vietnam into two zones at the 17th parallel, leaving Ho Chi Minh in charge of the northern zone. The agreements were a victory for the Viet Minh because North Vietnam had most of the industry and minerals and enough good farming land to be almost self-sufficient in food production.
5. After the war a new currency was issued in Vietnam. Many goods were rationed and controls were imposed on private enterprise. School textbooks were revised and teachers retrained. Only children of workers or peasant farmers were allowed to attend universities. All students had to spend part of every school year on a farm or in a factory doing manual labor of some kind.
6. Under Pol Pot, city residents were sent into the countryside to create new agricultural villages. Due to

intellectuals. More than 2 million people met their deaths by execution or starvation in the first three years of Pol Pot's regime. Thousands more fled to makeshift refugee camps in the neighboring country of Thailand.

The Vietnamese invasion. Border disputes and centuries-old rivalries soon brought the Khmer Rouge into conflict with their Vietnamese neighbors. To settle certain territorial questions once and for all, the Vietnamese invaded Cambodia (Kampuchea) in 1978. As the Vietnamese advanced toward Phnom Penh, the Chinese threw their support to the Khmer Rouge. Even so, by early 1979 the Vietnamese had overthrown Pol Pot and had established a pro-Vietnamese government in Phnom Penh.

In the late 1980s, under pressure from the UN, Vietnam withdrew its troops from Cambodia, and China halted military aid to the Khmer Rouge. The ● UN sponsored talks on the future of Cambodia to which all affected parties—the Vietnamese-sponsored government, the Khmer Rouge, and Sihanouk and his followers—were invited.

Laos

Like Cambodia, Laos gained independence from France in 1954. Almost immediately, civil war broke out among the country's political factions. This turmoil continued for the next 20 years.

In the meantime, Laos, although neutral, became increasingly involved in the Vietnam War. The Ho Chi Minh Trail, the Viet Cong's major supply route, wound through the mountain valleys of eastern Laos into Cambodia and South Vietnam. To break this supply line, the United States began bombing the Laotian countryside, causing heavy damage and many civilian casualties.

By 1975 the internal strife in Laos had ended. The Communist faction, the *Pathet Lao,* had set up a Communist regime—the Lao People's Democratic Republic. This new government followed a nonaligned course in the complicated politics of Asia. It accepted aid from both China and the Soviet Union. In addition, it avoided taking sides in the dispute between Vietnam and Cambodia.

Ultimately, however, a nonaligned course proved impossible. Laos had to call on the Vietnamese for help in controlling anti-Communist forces in its northern provinces. In return it allowed Vietnam to station 30,000 troops on Laotian soil. In fact, Vietnam used Laos as the staging area for its invasion of Cambodia. Because of such incidents, relations between Laos and its neighbors continued to be tense throughout the 1980s.

Thailand

Thailand, formerly called Siam, had never been a European colony. During World War II, however, Japan occupied the country. Under Japanese pressure Thailand joined the Axis and declared war on Great Britain and the United States. Later it renounced this alliance and became the first Axis partner admitted to the United Nations.

In the late 1950s, the Thai army took control of the government, establishing a military dictatorship. Strongly pro-Western, this government received military and economic aid from the United States. During the Vietnam War, this close relationship continued. The United States used bases in Thailand as a staging area for bombing raids on North Vietnam, Laos, and Cambodia. In addition, Thai troops fought beside American and South Vietnamese soldiers in Cambodia. When American troops withdrew from Vietnam, many of them were reassigned to bases in Thailand.

Communist victories in Vietnam, Laos, and Cambodia during the mid-1970s forced Thailand to reconsider its relationship with the United States. The Thai government persuaded the Americans to close their military bases in Thailand. It then established diplomatic relationships with China and sought accommodation with the Soviet Union and Vietnam.

SECTION 5 REVIEW

1. **Define** domino theory
2. **Identify** Viet Minh, Ho Chi Minh, Ngo Dinh Diem, Viet Cong, Tet Offensive, Vietnamization, Paris Accords, boat people, Norodom Sihanouk, Lon Nol, Khmer Rouge
3. **Locate** Hanoi, Haiphong, Dien Bien Phu, 17th parallel, Saigon, Ho Chi Minh Trail, Phnom Penh
4. **Analyzing Ideas** Why were the provisions of the Geneva Accords a victory for the Viet Minh?
5. **Classifying Ideas** What changes took place in Vietnam after the war?
6. **Interpreting Ideas** What impact did the Pol Pot regime have on Cambodia (Kampuchea)?
7. **Determining Cause and Effect** How did the Vietnamese invasion of Cambodia affect Thailand's diplomatic relations?

6 Asian Nations Sought Security and Economic Growth

Asia is a region of great diversity containing many nations that differ significantly from one another. However, a closer look at these nations reveals a number of experiences they all have shared.

Political Development

Most of the countries of Asia at one time had been colonies. After independence, most new Asian nations set up representative governments and attempted to build democratic societies. With the passage of time, however, democracy faded in most of Asia. Violent revolutions established Communist governments in China, Vietnam, Cambodia, and Laos. Elsewhere—in the Philippines, Indonesia, and Burma, for example—civil rights came under attack, and authoritarian rule emerged.

By and large, three factors gave rise to this trend toward authoritarianism in Asia. The first factor involved the ethnic and cultural diversity within Asian nations. In India, Malaysia, and the Philippines, for example, age-old antagonisms existed among groups with different heritages or religions. From time to time, these antagonisms erupted into violence. In such cases, government leaders often relied on their military and police forces to maintain domestic peace. To make their work easier, these forces frequently argued for the imposition of strict controls on civil rights. Occasionally, the military forces themselves took over the government when civilian leaders seemed reluctant to impose such controls.

The second factor that helped the development of authoritarianism involved fears about national security. For example, because of the Communist movements on the Indochina Peninsula, leaders in the Philippines, Indonesia, and Thailand feared the spread of revolutionary ideas to their own countries. As a result, these leaders cracked down on leftist groups and granted sweeping powers to the military whenever the slightest signs of Communist influence arose. Similarly, Communist countries feared the anti-Communist policies of the free world. They also feared each other's intentions. For these Communist countries too, fear led to a desire for strong central government and a lack of tolerance for debate and dissent.

The third factor concerned the desire for economic growth. Many Asian leaders perceived

Learning from Pictures *Newly elected Philippine President Corazon Aquino salutes the country's military after a successful revolt against the dictator Ferdinand Marcos.*

lack of experience and tools, many people died. At the same time, almost all government officials, army officers, teachers and intellectuals were systematically and brutally executed. Needless to say, Pol Pot had a devastating impact on Cambodia.

7. During the Vietnam War, Thailand had sided with the United States, and Thai troops had even fought alongside American troops in Vietnam. However, Communist victories in the area caused Thailand to reassess its diplomatic relations. It sought closer ties with Vietnam and other Communist countries in the region.

SECTION 6

Focus/Motivation

Write on the chalkboard the following statement by Rudyard Kipling: "East is East, and West is West, and never the twain shall meet." Call upon students to explain the meaning of the statement. *(Most students will suggest that cultural differences are so great that the peoples of Asia and the West can never understand each other.)* Ask students to provide examples to disprove Kipling's statement. *(Answers will include: The West has influenced the East in such areas as science, technology, clothing, and popular music. The East has influenced the West in art, religion, and philosophy. Japanese economic success has led the West to adopt designs*

1E, 4E, 4I, 5A, 5C, 5H,
a1B, a3B, a3C, a3G, a3I

for manufactured items such as cameras, radios, and automobiles. And some Western business leaders have been influenced by Japanese management ideas.)

Presentation
Researching (Average/Group)
Have each student choose an Asian country and then conduct research on its economy. Students should research the nation's GNP, per capita income, industrial growth rate, population growth rate, major exports, balance of trade, and major occupations. If possible, students should list the number of cars, telephones, radios, and televisions per person in that nation. Have students assemble all their data on a large poster to display in the classroom.

SECTION 6

Closure
Point out that some Asian countries, such as Japan, Taiwan, Singapore, and South Korea, have enjoyed remarkable economic development over the last few years. Have students speculate why these countries have been so successful economically.

Review Answers
1. ***ASEAN:*** Association of Southeast Asian Nations, an economic organization; ***Pacific Rim countries:*** Hong Kong, Japan, South

democratic government as wasteful and inefficient and a hindrance to the speedy development of industrialization policies and programs. Therefore, the desire of these leaders for rapid economic growth contributed to the emergence of authoritarian regimes. To understand this development, it is necessary to examine the issue of economic growth in Asia.

Economic Development

In the late 1980s, roughly 3 billion people, more than half of the total population of the world, lived in Asia. A significant number of Asia's people lived in poverty and suffered its consequences—malnutrition, illiteracy, and sharply reduced life expectancy.

Attempts at economic development. To help create more prosperous and stable societies, in the 1950s most Asian governments began to foster economic development. The approaches of these governments varied. Some used capitalist means, encouraging private enterprise. Others followed socialist principles, with the central government taking control of the economy. Still others pursued a middle course, combining government planning with private enterprise. Whatever the approach, most governments experienced the same result. With a few exceptions, economic development proceeded slowly, if at all.

By and large, most Asian countries experienced slow economic growth because they had little wealth in the first place. Industrialization required huge investments of money in machinery, factories, and distribution networks. Also, the later a country began the process of industrialization, the greater the investment needed to bring that country up to the level of the more developed nations.

In order to get the investment funds they needed, Asian countries depended either on loans or on the export of agricultural goods or natural resources: cocoa, tea, spices, timber, rubber, and copper and other minerals. Throughout most of the 1950s and 1960s, however, the prices of these items in world markets remained relatively low. In addition, periodic economic recessions in the West reduced the demand for the export goods of the Asian nations.

A shortage of experienced managers and trained workers also slowed economic development in much of Asia. To combat this problem, many Asian governments reformed their educational systems and established vocational schools and industrial training programs. But time was needed for these changes to take effect.

Cooperating for development. In the 1970s Asian countries began to find ways of dealing with these and other economic problems. For example, to ensure higher and more stable prices for their exports, many countries combined to form loose economic associations. In addition, Asian countries joined with other developing nations to work for greater concessions from such international loan agencies as the World Bank and the International Monetary Fund (IMF).

Also, Asian countries followed the example of such bodies as the European Community (EC), cooperating to develop common trade and economic policies. For example, the Association of Southeast Asian Nations (ASEAN), although organized in 1967 to combat communism in the region, has concerned itself since the 1970s almost solely with economic matters. Member nations—Brunei, Indonesia, Malaysia, the Philippines, Singapore, and Thailand—have held regular meetings to discuss ways to encourage trade and to handle the problems associated with economic development. Communist nations in Asia have sought similar cooperative agreements by joining the Council for Mutual Economic Assistance, or CMEA (formerly known as COMECON).

Many Asian nations, however, have attempted to spur economic growth through greater government control. Some Asian governments have nationalized certain key industries—oil in Indonesia, for example. By such actions they hoped to ensure the reinvestment of profits in the country's development. Many governments, to prevent interruptions in production, have passed laws limiting the organization of labor unions or prohibiting strikes and other industrial actions. Such authoritarian measures, in some cases, have led to more rapid economic growth but at the expense of individual rights and freedoms.

By the end of the 1980s, economic development in Asia remained a mixed picture. Some countries, such as Japan, South Korea, Singapore, and Taiwan, all strong supporters of free enterprise, have enjoyed remarkable success. However, the economies of the majority of Asian countries are burdened by huge foreign debts. These countries have yet to make any major advances toward significant economic development.

● Automobiles, stereo equipment, televisions, video recorders, computers

Learning from Pictures
An example of Western cultural diffusion is this popular American food franchise found in many Japanese shopping centers. What Asian-made products have dominated world markets?

Asian Cultural Diffusion

For hundreds of years, Asia has influenced the West. The ancient religions, philosophies, and martial arts of China and Japan have long fascinated many Westerners. Exhibits of Asian porcelain, carpets, manuscripts, and other arts and crafts have frequently appeared in prominent Western art galleries. More recently Asia has strongly influenced the buying habits of Western consumers. For example, Asian-made radios, cameras, video equipment, and automobiles, by and large, have dominated world markets over the last decade.

This economic competition from Asia has both alarmed and intrigued Western business leaders. Since the late 1970s, Western economists have traveled throughout Japan trying to discover why Japanese goods compete so well in world markets. Many economists have suggested that the answer lies in the cooperative relationship between management and workers. Others have noted the availability of low-interest business-development loans that enable Japanese companies to buy the latest machinery.

Asian thought also has influenced the West, especially since the end of World War II. For example, Mahatma Gandhi's ideas on nonviolent resistance had a powerful impact on the leaders of the civil rights movement in the United States during the 1960s.

In the late 1800s, the English author Rudyard Kipling wrote, "East is East, and West is West, and never the twain shall meet." He meant that because of the great cultural differences between the two areas, their peoples could never understand one another. For a long time, Kipling's observation appeared correct. Since the early 1970s, however, a greater understanding seems to have developed. As the role played by the Pacific Rim countries—Hong Kong, Japan, South Korea, Singapore, and Taiwan—in the world economy increases, this understanding almost certainly will continue to improve.

SECTION 6 REVIEW

1. **Identify** ASEAN, Pacific Rim countries
2. **Classifying Ideas** List three factors that contributed to the development of authoritarian governments in Asia.
3. **Analyzing Ideas** What problems have Asian nations faced in bringing about industrial development?
4. **Understanding Ideas** How have some Asian nations cooperated to overcome economic problems?
5. **Summarizing Ideas** How have Asian ideas influenced life in the West?

Korea, Singapore, and Taiwan
2. Authoritarian governments developed in Asia because of the need to maintain domestic peace among ethnic and cultural groups, fear of invasion or influence by neighbors, and the desire for speedy solutions to economic problems.
3. Industrialization required large investments in machinery, factories, and distribution networks, but Asian nations lacked the needed capital. In order to get investment funds, they had to depend on loans or sell their raw materials, the value of which depended on world demand. Throughout much of the 1950s and 1960s, demand—and, therefore, prices—for these materials remained low. Another problem was the lack of skilled factory workers and managers.
4. A number of Asian nations established ASEAN, in part, to develop common trade and economic policies. Communist nations in Asia sought similar cooperative agreements by joining COMECON, now called the CMEA.
5. Examples of Asia's influence on the West include judo and other martial arts; manufactured goods such as radios, cameras, and autos; Japanese business practices; and politics, philosophy, and literature.

803

1B, 1D, 1E, 4I, 5A, 5B, 5H, a1B, a1C, a4A, a4E, a4F, a4G, a4H, a4I, a4J, a4K, a4L, a4M

Reteaching

Have students review the Chapter Summary and the appropriate section and questions in the Unit Synthesis. Discuss the concepts until students demonstrate a clear understanding of the material.

Reviewing Important Terms

1. mixed economy;
2. non-alignment;
3. domino theory.

Developing Critical Thinking Skills

1. They put executive power in a committee of the Politburo of the Communist Party. They also initiated a series of five-year plans. Since the late 1970s, the Chinese have allowed some free enterprise.
2. **(a)** MacArthur insisted that Chinese bases in Manchuria be bombed and the coast of China blockaded. Truman opposed such moves. **(b)** When MacArthur continued to advocate these policies, Truman removed him.
3. **(a)** After World War II, Japan developed large and efficient industries that made high quality, competitively-priced products. **(b)** Problems: environmental pollution, scarce land. Benefits: higher standard of living, greater freedom for women. **(c)** Answers will vary.
4. **(a)** industrial weakness, low agricultural production, and over-population **(b)** A series of five-year plans led to industrial development.
5. **(a)**The South Vietnamese government, under Ngo Dinh Diem, became increasingly repressive. Taking advantage of this, the Viet Cong began a guerrilla war to overthrow Diem. **(b)** President Eisenhower sent military and

CHAPTER 29 REVIEW

AD

Year	Event
1946	Filipinos declared independence
1947	Independence of India
1949	Communist takeover of China
1949	Independence of Indonesia
1950–1953	Korean War
1950–1964	Nehru prime minister of India
1954	Geneva Accords
1958	Beginning of Great Leap Forward

Chapter Summary

The following list contains the key concepts you have learned about the nations of Asia between the end of World War II and the present.

1. The period following World War II was a time of conflict and tension for many Asian nations.
2. The victory of Mao Zedong in 1949 brought the Communist Party to power in China. The Chinese Nationalists, led by Chiang Kai-shek, fled to the island of Taiwan off the coast of China.
3. The Communists implemented several plans to modernize their vast nation, while the Nationalists on Taiwan achieved rapid industrialization.
4. Korea was divided after World War II. When Communist North Korea invaded South Korea in 1950, it was repulsed by UN forces, and an armistice was eventually signed.
5. Japan achieved extraordinary economic success in the postwar period and became the most advanced industrial nation in Asia.
6. Japanese society also changed, as women gained recognition of their rights and the family lost its dominant role in daily life.
7. India, under Nehru, adopted a mixed economy but could make few gains because of its constantly growing population.
8. Pakistan faced problems similar to those of India. In addition, Pakistan was separated into two parts. After a civil war, East Pakistan became Bangladesh.
9. In the Philippines, Indonesia, Malaysia, Singapore, and Burma, economic development was fostered by strong central governments. Despite experiencing social problems, these nations began a very gradual process of industrialization.
10. In Southeast Asia, the United States became heavily involved in fighting in Vietnam. North Vietnam conquered South Vietnam and united the nation in the mid-1970s.
11. Vietnam dominated its neighbors, Cambodia and Laos. It also had considerable influence on Thailand. All of these nations struggled with the problems caused by war.
12. The difficulties of economic development led many Asian nations to rely on strong central governments. On the other hand, the Asian nations attempted to promote greater international cooperation.

On a separate sheet of paper, complete the following review exercises.

Reviewing Important Terms

Supply the term that correctly completes each sentence.

1. A _______ _______ is an economic system in which private companies own some industries and the government owns the rest.
2. India followed a policy of _______, refusing to ally itself with either the United States or the Soviet Union.
3. According to the _______ _______, if South Vietnam fell to communism, other nations of Southeast Asia would follow.

Developing Critical Thinking Skills

1. **Summarizing Ideas** What political and economic changes did the Communists bring about in China after they took over the government?
2. **Interpreting Ideas** **(a)** How did President Truman and General MacArthur disagree over the conduct of the Korean War? **(b)** Why did Truman replace MacArthur as commander of the UN forces?
3. **Evaluating Ideas** **(a)** Explain how Japan became the third largest industrial nation in the world. **(b)** What problems and benefits accompanied this rapid growth? **(c)** Do you think the benefits outweighed the problems? Why or why not?
4. **Understanding Ideas** **(a)** What economic problems did India face after achieving independence? **(b)** How did it attempt to solve these problems?
5. **Determining Cause and Effect** **(a)** What were the causes of the Vietnam War? **(b)** How did the United States become involved?
6. **Classifying Ideas** List reasons for past hostilities between the following countries: **(a)** the Soviet Union and China, **(b)** India and Pakistan, **(c)** Pakistan and Bangladesh, **(d)** Singapore and the Federation of Malaysia.
7. **Comparing Ideas** **(a)** How did the Korean War differ from the Vietnam War in terms of causes and results?

804

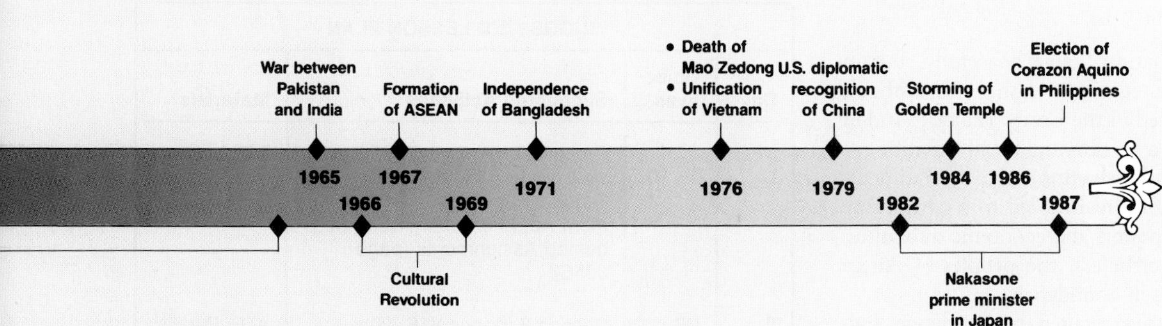

(b) How were the two conflicts similar? **(c)** What roles did the United States and the People's Republic of China play in each of these wars?

8. **Analyzing Primary Sources** Below is the preamble to the Indian constitution. Read this selection and answer the questions that follow.

> "We, the people of India, having solemnly resolved to constitute India into a sovereign democratic republic and to secure to all its citizens: *justice*—social, economic, and political; *liberty* of thought, expression, belief, faith and worship; *equality* of status and of opportunity; and to promote . . . *fraternity* assuring the dignity of the individual and the unity of the nation . . . do hereby adopt, enact, and give to ourselves this Constitution."

(a) What type of government does the constitution promise to the Indian people? **(b)** What ideals does it swear to uphold? **(c)** How do these ideals compare with those stated in the preamble to the United States Constitution?

Relating Geography to History

Turn to the map of Asia on page 776. **(a)** How many miles separate Taiwan and the People's Republic of China? **(b)** How many kilometers? **(c)** Why is Japan in a strategic location for defense of American interests in the Pacific? **(d)** Based on your knowledge of current events, what Asian nations might be most concerned with protecting their borders today? Explain.

Relating Past to Present

1. On a sheet of paper, list evidence that your community has contact with the nations of Asia. For example, observe the cars on a busy street. How many of them are Japanese? Can you buy a shirt made of Indian cotton or a book of Chinese or Japanese poetry? Based on this information, write a short essay discussing Asia's influence on the Western world.
2. Use the *Readers' Guide to Periodical Literature* to find articles on China today. Then prepare a report on how the Communists have changed traditional Chinese society, what economic problems still exist in China, and what life in China is like.

Applying History Study Skills

Before completing this activity, review Building History Study Skills on page 799.

Read the following statement and identify any fallacies in reasoning.

> "Japan's economic growth since World War II took place because the United States helped rebuild the nation's wartorn factories."

Investigating Further

1. **Writing a Report** Use books in your library to gather information on the Vietnam War. One source for your research might be Frances Fitzgerald's *Fire in the Lake* (Little, Brown). Use the information you have found to answer the following questions: **(a)** What were the goals of Ho Chi Minh between 1945 and 1954? **(b)** Why did the peasants support the Viet Cong? **(c)** How did American involvement end? **(d)** What was the final outcome of the war?
2. **Analyzing Literature** One way to gain insight into a culture is to read its literature. Present a short report to the class on one of the following Japanese novels: Yukio Mishima's *Sound of Waves* (Knopf) and *Spring Snow* (Knopf); Junichiro Tanizaki's *Some Prefer Nettles* (Knopf).
3. **Preparing an Oral Report** Unlike most other Asian nations, Japan, Singapore, and Taiwan experienced rapid economic growth after 1945. Using reference materials in your school or public library, gather information on the economic policies that made such development possible. Present your findings to the class in the form of a five minute oral report.
4. **Creating a Chart** Use atlases and encyclopedias in your school or public library to construct a chart comparing the major urban centers of Southeast Asia. Include information on population, places of interest, and major economic activities.

economic aid. President Kennedy sent military advisers. President Johnson increased American troop strength and ordered air attacks on North Vietnam.
6. (a) the interpretation of Marxism and foreign policy; **(b)** long-standing religious hostilities; **(c)** East Pakistan (Bangladesh) demanded greater autonomy. **(d)** The Malays controlled the Federation government, while the Chinese controlled most of the business. The Malays feared the Chinese might gain political influence.
7. (a) The Korean War began with North Korea's attack on South Korea. The war in Vietnam began as a civil war. North and South Korea remained separate, but North and South Vietnam were unified. **(b)** Communist north tried to take over the non-Communist south. **(c)** Both supplied their allies with equipment and troops.
8. (a) a democratic republic; **(b)** justice, liberty, equality, and fraternity; **(c)** The U.S. Constitution mentions: "establish justice, . . . promote the general welfare, and secure the blessings of liberty. . . ."

Relating Geography to History
(a) about 100 miles; **(b)** 160 kilometers; **(c)** its proximity to mainland Asia; **(d)** Clashes have occurred along the borders of China, the Soviet Union, Vietnam, Laos, India, Pakistan, and Cambodia.

Relating Past to Present
1. Answers will vary.
2. Answers will vary.

Applying History Study Skills
Answers may vary.

CHAPTER (pages 806–829)

30 The Nations of Africa and the Middle East Became Independent

(1945 to the present)

CHAPTER OVERVIEW

Independence for most African nations came peacefully, but in some cases war and violence resulted. One of the most difficult transitions to independence occurred in the Congo (Zaire). And in South Africa, apartheid produced a threatening racial situation.

After independence African nations continued to have difficulties. In Nigeria, for example, ethnic rivalries led to a devastating civil war. Intervention by foreign powers and economic difficulties also prevented development. Nevertheless, the peoples of Africa made great strides toward cultural self-confidence.

The nations of the Middle East also secured independence. Iran threw off Soviet and British influence and began a course of modernization. Turkey also resisted Soviet interference and turned to the West for support. A coup in Egypt overthrew the monarchy, and Nasser, the new leader, followed an assertive foreign policy. The creation of Israel led to a war with the Arab nations from which Israel emerged the victor. When Nasser seized the Suez Canal in 1956, Great Britain, France, and Israel invaded Egypt, but worldwide pressure forced them to withdraw.

In 1967, responding to threatening moves by Egypt, Israel swiftly occupied the Sinai Peninsula and other territory in the Six-Day War. In 1973 another Arab-Israeli war occurred. Sadat of Egypt and Begin of Israel signed a peace treaty in 1979, but lasting peace seemed elusive. In Iran the shah was overthrown and an Islamic republic was created.

Great social change occurred in the Middle East after 1945. Cities grew, education expanded significantly, and women's status improved somewhat. At the same time, Islamic fundamentalism became an important force in the Middle East.

SUGGESTED LESSON PLAN

Day	Objectives	Suggested Activities	Materials
1	U7,* C1–2	Introducing the Chapter (page 806–07) Section 1 (pages 807–13), Focus/Motivation (page 807), Presentation (page 808), Closure (page 812), Suggested Teaching Strategies, Enrichment Activities, Daily Quiz, Suggested Assignments (page 805B)	ATE, Pupil's Edition, Teacher's Resource-Bank™
2	U7, C3–5	Section 2 (pages 813–16), Focus/Motivation (page 813), Presentation (page 815), Closure (page 815), Suggested Teaching Strategies, Enrichment Activities, Daily Quiz, Suggested Assignments (page 805C)	ATE, Pupil's Edition, Teacher's Resource-Bank™
3	U7, C6–7	Section 3 (pages 816–20), Focus/Motivation (page 816), Presentation (page 817), Closure (page 819), Suggested Teaching Strategies, Enrichment Activity, Daily Quiz, Suggested Assignments (page 805C)	ATE, Pupil's Edition, Teacher's Resource-Bank™
4	U7, C8–9	Section 4 (pages 820–25), Focus/Motivation (page 821), Presentation (page 821), Closure (page 824), Suggested Teaching Strategies, Enrichment Activities, Daily Quiz, Suggested Assignments (page 805D)	ATE, Pupil's Edition, Teacher's Resource-Bank™
5	U7, C10	Section 5 (pages 825–27), Focus/Motivation (page 825), Presentation (page 826), Closure (page 826), Suggested Teaching Strategies, Enrichment Activities, Daily Quiz, Suggested Assignments (page 805E)	ATE, Pupil's Edition, Teacher's Resource-Bank™
6	U7–9 C1–10	Chapter 30 Form A Test, Reteaching Worksheet, Chapter 30 Form B Test	Teacher's Resource-Bank™ or Workbook and Test Booklet

*C refers to applicable Chapter Objective, U refers to applicable Unit Goal

BOOKS FOR THE TEACHER

Dupuy, Trevor, N. *Elusive Victory: Arab-Israel Wars 1947–1974.* Harper and Row. Examines the strategies used in the wars.

Forbis, William H. *Fall of the Peacock Throne.* Harper & Row. Analyzes the Iranian revolution.

Hallett, Robin. *Africa Since 1875.* University of Chicago Press. Provides a scholarly account of African history.

Horne, Alistair. *A Savage War of Peace: 1954–1962.* Penguin. Explains the Algerian war for independence.

Laquer, Walter. *The Road to Jerusalem: The Origins of the Arab-Israeli Conflict of 1967.* Macmillan. Stresses events leading up to the conflict, conditions in Israel, and United States-Soviet relations.

BOOKS FOR THE STUDENT

Associated Press. *Lightning Out of Israel: The Arab-Israel Conflict.* Associated Press. Gives a journalistic account of the Six-Day War.

Davidson, Margaret. *The Golda Meir Story.* Scribner's. Concentrates on earlier years; highly readable.

Dimbleby, Jonathan. *The Palestinians.* Quartet Books. Includes excellent photographs.

Edmonds, I. G. *Ethiopia: Land of the Conquering Lion of Judah.* Holt, Rinehart and Winston. Provides a general survey written for high school students.

McKown, Robin. *Nkrumah.* Doubleday. Recounts the major events in the life of this African independence leader.

MULTIMEDIA MATERIALS

The Changing Middle East (mp, 25 min.), International Film Foundation. Describes the problems that beset Middle Eastern society, particularly the need for modern technology.

Let My People Go (mp, 54 min.). Films. Depicts the difficulties encountered by the Jews in their long search for a permanent homeland.

Mideast: Economic Development (mp, 18 min.), BFA. Stresses the role of oil in the economy of the Middle East.

World Cultures: Africa (fs), Current Affairs. Surveys present-day issues in Africa. Titles appropriate for Chapter 30: "Tribalism and Nationalism in Black Africa," and "South Africa: The Issue of White Supremacy."

Section 1 (pages 807–813)

African Nations Achieved Independence after World War II

SECTION OVERVIEW

After World War II, independence came rapidly to the nations of SubSaharan Africa. Most African nations achieved independence peacefully, but in some cases war and violence resulted. South Africa remained a troubled country, as apartheid caused considerable unrest and sparked international protests.

SUGGESTED TEACHING STRATEGIES

1. **Preteaching Vocabulary (Basic)** You may wish to preteach the following important vocabulary term: apartheid (*page 812*). Ask students to define apartheid and describe the effect it has on South Africans.
2. **Classifying Ideas (Average/Group)** Put the following lists on the chalkboard or an overhead projector. Have students match each country at the left with its appropriate description at the right.

1. Ghana	**a.** only French colony to choose complete independence
2. Kenya	**b.** nation that came into existence in 1980 after years of guerrilla war
3. Guinea	**c.** first SubSaharan colony to achieve full independence
4. Zaire	**d.** Portuguese colony in which "liberation armies" fought for freedom
5. Angola	**e.** country that experienced the Mau Mau uprising
6. Zimbabwe	**f.** experienced political chaos in the 1960s
7. South Africa	**g.** country that introduced the policy of apartheid

(Answers: 1-c, 2-e, 3-a, 4-f, 5-d, 6-b, 7-g)

ENRICHMENT ACTIVITIES

1. **Presenting an Oral Report (Average/Group)** Interested students might read biographies of African independence leaders and report to the class on how these leaders affected the history of their nations.
2. **Conducting Research (Challenging)** Have interested students select one SubSaharan country to research, basing their research on the following questions: How have topography and climate influenced the development of the country? What has been the country's history since its independence? What is the basis of the country's economy? What are some of the problems that the country faces today? You may wish to have the class make a chart of the information to be put on the bulletin board.

DAILY QUIZ

To assess student understanding of Section 1, give the class the following quiz. (Each item is worth 10 points.)

1. What two African nations were never colonies? *(Liberia and Ethiopia)*
2. (T or F) Second-generation leaders of African independence like Kwame Nkrumah and Jomo Kenyatta demanded immediate independence and equality for all. *(T)*
3. (T or F) The first nationalist African party in Ghana failed miserably in its attempt to gain freedom from Italy. *(F)*
4. In many cases, the second-generation leaders of African independence had been educated in the **a.** West, **b.** East, **c.** native lands, **d.** Soviet Union. *(a)*
5. (T or F) The modern nation of Zaire was formerly a colony of Belgium. *(T)*
6. (T or F) Seeing the results of bloodshed in the Congo and Egypt, the Portuguese quickly freed Angola. *(F)*

7. (T or F) Today Zimbabwe continues to support apartheid, white supremacy, and black subservience. *(F)*
8. Put the following in the correct chronological order **a.** independence of Ghana; **b.** beginnings of apartheid; **c.** World War II. *(c, b, a)*
9. The only former French colony that severed all ties with France was ________. *(Guinea)*
10. ________ ________ is the leader of the African National Congress. *(Nelson Mandela)*

SUGGESTED ASSIGNMENTS

1. **Presenting Oral Reports (Average/Group)** Have students select an African country and find out how its government is trying to promote economic growth. Have students present their findings to the class during the study of Section 2.
2. **Preparing Charts (Basic)** Ask students to prepare a short chart listing the countries of Africa, their former colonial status, and the date of their independence.

Section (pages 813–820)

2 The New African Nations Faced Various Problems

SECTION OVERVIEW

The most pressing need for the new African nations was developing a sense of national unity. In Nigeria a civil war broke out between Biafra and the central government. Intervention by foreign powers complicated the development of national unity. Economic uncertainty also plagued the new nations. Despite these problems, the people of Africa made great strides toward a cultural reawakening.

SUGGESTED TEACHING STRATEGIES

1. **Preteaching Vocabulary (Basic)** You may wish to preteach the following important vocabulary terms: ujamaa *(page 814)*, desertification *(page 815)*. Ask students to detail how erosion can lead to desertification.
2. **Preparing a Bulletin Board Display (Average/Group)** Have students prepare a bulletin-board display on African art. Captions should accompany each picture. Materials can be gathered from magazines such as *Smithsonian*. Some students may want to write to the Afro-American Institute, 833 United Nations Plaza, New York, N.Y. 10017, for a list of artists.

ENRICHMENT ACTIVITIES

1. **Constructing Charts (Average/Group)** Have interested students select a country in Africa. Students are to collect information on their selected country's population, land area, GNP, per capita income, major exports, major imports, literacy rates, type of government, and language. Assemble the data on a large poster or graph to display in the classroom. Useful sources include encyclopedias and almanacs as well as *A Country Study* series (U.S. Government Printing Office).
2. **Preparing an Oral Report (Challenging)** Students may give oral reports on the civil wars in Nigeria and Angola, the overthrow of Haile Selassie in Ethiopia, or the conflict between Ethiopia and Somalia. Students should consult the *Readers' Guide to Periodical Literature* to find articles on the topic. Other sources include I. G. Edmonds's *Ethiopia: Land of the Conquering Lion of Judah* (Holt, Rinehart and Winston); and Herb Boyd's *The Former Portuguese Colonies* (Franklin Watts).

DAILY QUIZ

To assess student understanding of Section 2, give the class the following quiz. (Each item is worth 10 points.)

1. Name one problem new African nations had to solve. *(sense of national unity; economic development; pride in African history)*
2. Name one problem with African national boundaries drawn during the postwar era. *(separation of tribes by boundaries; enemies were grouped together into administrative districts; colonial powers drew boundaries arbitrarily; ethnic rivalries)*
3. (T or F) Nationalist movements in Biafra and the eastern section of Nigeria became symbols of successful integration of two cultures in Egypt. *(F)*
4. Why is the Horn of Africa considered to have a strategic location? *(It overlooks the Red Sea and the Indian Ocean sea lanes to the Persian Gulf.)*
5. How has Nigeria's dependence on oil led to economic difficulties? *(When the world price of oil fell, the economy suffered.)*
6. What Western Hemisphere country provided military aid to the Communists in Angola? *(Cuba)*
7. To spur economic growth, Tanzania organized local, cooperative villages, known as ________. *(ujamaa)*
8. (T or F) After independence most Africans rejected native cultural traditions to become more "modernized." *(F)*
9. (T or F) Swahili enjoyed a rebirth in importance in Tanzania and Kenya as authors developed native literary traditions. *(F)*
10. In 1986 the Nigerian playwright and poet ________ ________ won the Nobel Prize in literature. *(Wole Soyinka)*

SUGGESTED ASSIGNMENTS

1. **Critical Thinking Worksheet (Average/Group)** Have students complete Critical Thinking Worksheet 69 in the TEACHER'S RESOURCEBANK™.
2. **Profile Worksheet (Average/Group)** Have students complete Profile Worksheet 30 in the TEACHER'S RESOURCE-BANK™.

Section (pages 816–820)

3 The Nations of the Middle East Won Their Independence

After World War II, Iran eliminated Soviet and British influence, and Turkey resisted Soviet pressures. The Republic of Israel was proclaimed in 1948, and Israel triumphed over the Arabs in the war that followed. Algeria gained independence from France in 1962 after a long and brutal war. When Egypt under Nasser seized the Suez Canal in 1956, Great Britain, France, and Israel invaded Egypt, but later withdrew.

SUGGESTED TEACHING STRATEGIES

1. **Preteaching Vocabulary (Basic)** You may wish to preteach the following important vocabulary term: kibbutz *(page 818)*. Point out that many American students visit Israel each year to work on a kibbutz.
2. **Identifying People (Basic)** Have students identify the individuals that are described by the following seven statements. The exercise could be presented in the form of a "Who Am I?" class activity.

   a. As prime minister of Iran, I nationalized the British-owned oil company. *(Mussadegh)*
   b. For a time I had to flee Iran, but I returned with the help of the military and the United States. *(Shah Reza Pahlavi)*
   c. I was prime minister of Turkey but was overthrown by the military and executed. *(Menderes)*
   d. I was king of Egypt but was overthrown by a military coup. *(Farouk)*
   e. As ruler of Egypt from 1954 to 1970, I sought to make my country the leader of the Arab world. *(Nasser)*
   f. I became the first president of Israel. *(Weizmann)*
   g. I was a Zionist leader and became the first prime minister of Israel. *(Ben-Gurion)*

ENRICHMENT ACTIVITY

Presenting an Oral Report (Challenging) Have students prepare illustrated oral reports on kibbutz life. They should cover such topics as social structure, education, and government of the kibbutz. Sources include Jonathan Rutland's *Looking at Israel* (Lippincott); and N. B. Kubie's *Israel* (Franklin Watts). Students should also consult the *Readers' Guide to Periodical Literature* for appropriate articles.

DAILY QUIZ

To assess student understanding of Section 3, give the class the following quiz. (Each item is worth 10 points.)

1. (T or F) As World War II ended, Iran effectively reduced Soviet and British influence, nationalized the oil industry, and attained stability under Shah Reza Pahlavi. *(T)*
2. (T or F) Turkey became a member of the Communist bloc after World War II. *(F)*
3. (T or F) The Turkish army intervened in the government in 1960 but later restored civilian rule. *(T)*
4. Which European power did the Egyptians want to eliminate as a force in the Suez? *(Great Britain)*
5. Who led the Egyptians into the modern world between 1954 and 1970? *(Nasser)*
6. Zionists desired to create a homeland for Jews in ______. *(Palestine/Israel)*
7. A kibbutz is **a.** a collective farm, **b.** an Israeli taxi, **c.** a Palestinian refugee settlement, **d.** a neutral zone. *(a)*
8. Algerians won independence from ______ in 1962 after a long and bloody civil war. *(France)*
9. What 1956 crisis in Egypt threatened Europe's oil supply and Israeli independence? *(Suez Crisis)*
10. In 1958 ______ and ______ merged to form the United Arab Republic. *(Egypt, Syria)*

SUGGESTED ASSIGNMENTS

1. **Outlining (Basic)** Have students outline the major events in Israeli history between independence and 1952.
2. **Understanding Current Developments (Average/Group)** Ask students to bring in newspaper and news magazine articles detailing the current status of OPEC. Use the articles as the basis for a class discussion during the study of Section 4.

Section (pages 820–825)

Wars, Oil, and Revolution Changed the Middle East

SECTION OVERVIEW

In the Six-Day War of 1967, Israel defeated the Arabs and gained territory. After a fourth Arab-Israeli war in October 1973, there were intensive efforts to achieve peace in the Middle East. Negotiations between Egypt and Israel led to the signing of a peace treaty in 1979. The formation of OPEC gave the oil-producing nations economic power and bargaining strength. In Iran, revolutionaries overthrew the shah and established an Islamic republic. Relations with the United States were strained when Iranian militants seized American hostages in 1979. An international slump in oil prices in the 1980s created economic problems for OPEC nations.

SUGGESTED TEACHING STRATEGIES

1. **Preteaching Vocabulary (Basic)** You may wish to preteach the following important vocabulary terms: shuttle diplomacy *(page 821)*; terrorism *(page 824)*. Ask: Why would shuttle diplomacy have been impossible 100 years ago? *(Transportation was too slow.)*
2. **Understanding Chronology (Basic)** Put the following events on the chalkboard or an overhead projector. Have students arrange them in chronological order by placing *1* before the event that took place first, *2* before the event that took place second, and so on.

   (4) Sadat became head of Egypt
   (3) Israel captured the Sinai Peninsula, Gaza Strip, Golan Heights, and west bank of Jordan River
   (7) Henry Kissinger began shuttle diplomacy

(1) Union between Egypt and Syria broke up
(8) Sadat visited Israel
(5) Egypt and Syria planned a secret war against Israel
(2) Nasser demanded the removal of UN troops from the border between Egypt and Israel
(6) Israeli troops crossed the Suez Canal and occupied Egyptian land

*3. **Interpreting Visuals: Reading a Special-Purpose Map (Basic)** To reinforce the skill lesson presented on page 823, have students study the map on page R9. Ask: What is the major economic activity in southwestern Australia? *(forestry)*

ENRICHMENT ACTIVITIES

1. **Preparing Charts (Average/Group)** Assign a group of students to prepare a chart showing the distribution of oil resources in the Middle East and throughout the world. Display the chart for the rest of the class, and ask students to draw conclusions based on the chart. Sources include: *World Almanac, Information Please Almanac, Facts on File,* and the *Readers' Guide to Periodical Literature.*
2. **Conducting Research (Challenging)** Assign students to prepare oral or written reports on the following events: the Six-Day War, the October War of 1973, the Camp David Accords, the Iranian revolution, the Iranian hostage crisis, and the Iraq-Iran war. Other students could prepare biographical sketches of Nasser, Sadat, Begin, Meir, Dayan, Shah Reza Pahlavi, and Khomeini. Sources include M. Davidson's *The Golda Meir Story* (Scribner's); A. Dobrins, *A Life for Israel* (Dial); E. Haber's *Menachem Begin: The Legend and the Man* (Delacorte); M. Dayan's *Story of My Life* (William Morrow); and Anwar el-Sadat's *In Search of Identity* (Harper & Row). Students should also consult the *Readers' Guide to Periodical Literature.*

DAILY QUIZ

To assess student understanding of Section 4, give the class the following quiz. (Each item is worth 10 points.)

1. What territories did Israel conquer in the Six-Day War? *(Sinai Peninsula, Gaza Strip, Golan Heights, West Bank)*
2. What do the initials "PLO" stand for? *(Palestine Liberation Organization)*
3. After Nasser died in 1970, _______ _______ -_______ became the new Egyptian leader. *(Anwar el-Sadat)*
4. (T or F) Egypt and Syria attacked Israel in 1973, but made no territorial gains. *(T)*
5. What American Secretary of State used shuttle diplomacy to negotiate a peace settlement between the Israelis and Egyptians and Syrians? *(Kissinger)*
6. Which American president helped Sadat and Begin to develop the Camp David Accords? *(Carter)*
7. Place the following events in correct chronological order: **a.** Camp David Accords, **b.** Six-Day War; **c.** formation of OPEC. *(c, b, a)*
8. What raw material has made the Middle East an important region in terms of world energy supply? *(oil)*
9. What is the organization to which many Middle Eastern countries belong in order to control oil prices? *(OPEC)*
10. The Ayatollah Khomeini led a religious, political, and social revolution against the shah in _______ in 1979. *(Iran)*

SUGGESTED ASSIGNMENTS

1. **Skill Worksheet (Basic)** Have students complete Skill Worksheet 30 in the TEACHER'S RESOURCEBANK™.
2. **Critical Thinking Worksheet (Average/Group)** Have students complete Critical Thinking Worksheet 68 in the TEACHER'S RESOURCEBANK™.

Section 5 (pages 825–827)

A Struggle Between Old and New Ways Plagued the Middle East

SECTION OVERVIEW

The political and economic transformation of the Middle East brought about great social change. Middle-Eastern cities experienced a dramatic rise in population. And the large percentage of young people increased the need for schools and teachers. In general, Middle Eastern societies continued to be male-dominated, but improvements in women's status were made after 1945. As a reaction to this rapid modernization many Muslims turned to Islamic fundamentalism.

SUGGESTED TEACHING STRATEGIES

1. **Preteaching Vocabulary (Basic)** You may wish to preteach the following important vocabulary terms: gross national product, GNP *(page 826)*. Point out that the gross national product is only one of many economic indicators that demonstrate economic growth.
2. **Studying Visuals (Basic)** Have students study the pictures on pages 822 and 827. Based on what they see in these pictures, ask students to give examples of the mixture of traditional and modern life in the Middle East today. What evidence is there of modernization? of the region's strong links with the past? What other generalizations about the Middle East can students make based on these pictures? *(Accept all reasonable answers. Students might say that the oil derrick and modern dress are indications of new wealth and Westernization, while the camel and traditional dress represent old ways.)*

ENRICHMENT ACTIVITIES

1. **Group Project (Average/Group)** In Saudi Arabia and other traditional Middle Eastern countries, women are subject to many restrictions and their opportunities are limited, while in such

countries as Egypt and Israel, there are fewer restrictions on women. A group of students might prepare an illustrated report on women's roles in the Middle East, showing how these roles are changing and examining the great contrasts that exist. Students should consult the *Readers' Guide to Periodical Literature* to find appropriate articles.

2. **Preparing a Chart (Average/Group)** Have students make charts giving figures on population, population per square mile, GNP, and GNP per person for the following countries: Saudi Arabia, Kuwait, Qatar, Iran, Turkey, Israel, Egypt, Libya, United Arab Emirates, and the United States. Students should consult almanacs and encyclopedias to find figures not provided by the textbook. After the charts have been completed, have students make generalizations based on the information they have compiled.

DAILY QUIZ

To assess student understanding of Section 5, give the class the following quiz. (Each item is worth 10 points.)

1. (T or F) The Middle East is about twice the size of the United States. *(T)*
2. List three of the four major languages of the Middle East. *(Hebrew, Arabic, Persian, Turkish)*
3. List three of the four European colonial powers that controlled parts of the Middle East. *(Great Britain, France, Italy, Spain)*
4. (T or F) The Arab League and the United Arab Republic failed to politically unite the Muslim Middle East. *(T)*
5. National wealth is often measured in terms of _______ _______ _______. *(gross national product)*
6. Name two reasons for the growth of Middle Eastern cities. *(migrations from the countryside, high population growth rates)*
7. (T or F) Women have won many rights in the Middle East since 1945. *(T)*
8. (T or F) One of the most dramatic changes in the Middle East is the tremendous decline in those attending school. *(F)*
9. (T or F) Islamic fundamentalists favor more rights and freedoms for women. *(F)*
10. The Muslim leader who became leader of Iran after the ouster of the shah was _______ _______. *(Ayatollah Khomeini)*

SUGGESTED ASSIGNMENTS

1. **Making a Chart (Average/Group)** Have interested students construct a chart for display on the bulletin board. One column of the chart should list traditional ways of living in the Middle East. The other column should list how modernization has affected these traditions.
2. **Review Worksheet (Basic)** Have students complete Review Worksheet 30 in the TEACHER'S RESOURCEBANK™.

For suggested lesson plan, additional teaching strategies, enrichment activities, daily quizzes, and suggested assignments, see pages 805A–805F.

Introducing the Chapter
Have students speculate how World War II might have affected the peoples of Africa and the Middle East. *(Accept all reasonable answers, such as the following: The people of North Africa and the Middle East came in contact with European and American soldiers from whom they may have learned about other ways of life. The demand for raw materials during the war might have given a boost to the colonial economies. European countries might have become less able to control their colonies while focusing on the war and their own recovery from the war.)*

Objectives
After studying Chapter 30, students will be able to:

1. Summarize the methods African nations used to gain independence.
2. Compare the nationalist movements in French and Belgian colonies with those in British colonies.
3. Review the common problems African nations faced.
4. Discuss how the superpower rivalries between the United States and the Soviet Union affected African nationalism.
5. Describe the revival of African culture.
6. Compare the nationalist movements in Iran, Turkey, Egypt, Israel, and Algeria.
7. Outline the causes and effects of the Suez Crisis.
8. Review how the problems of Israel's existence and Palestinian rights

CHAPTER

30

The Nations of Africa and the Middle East Became Independent

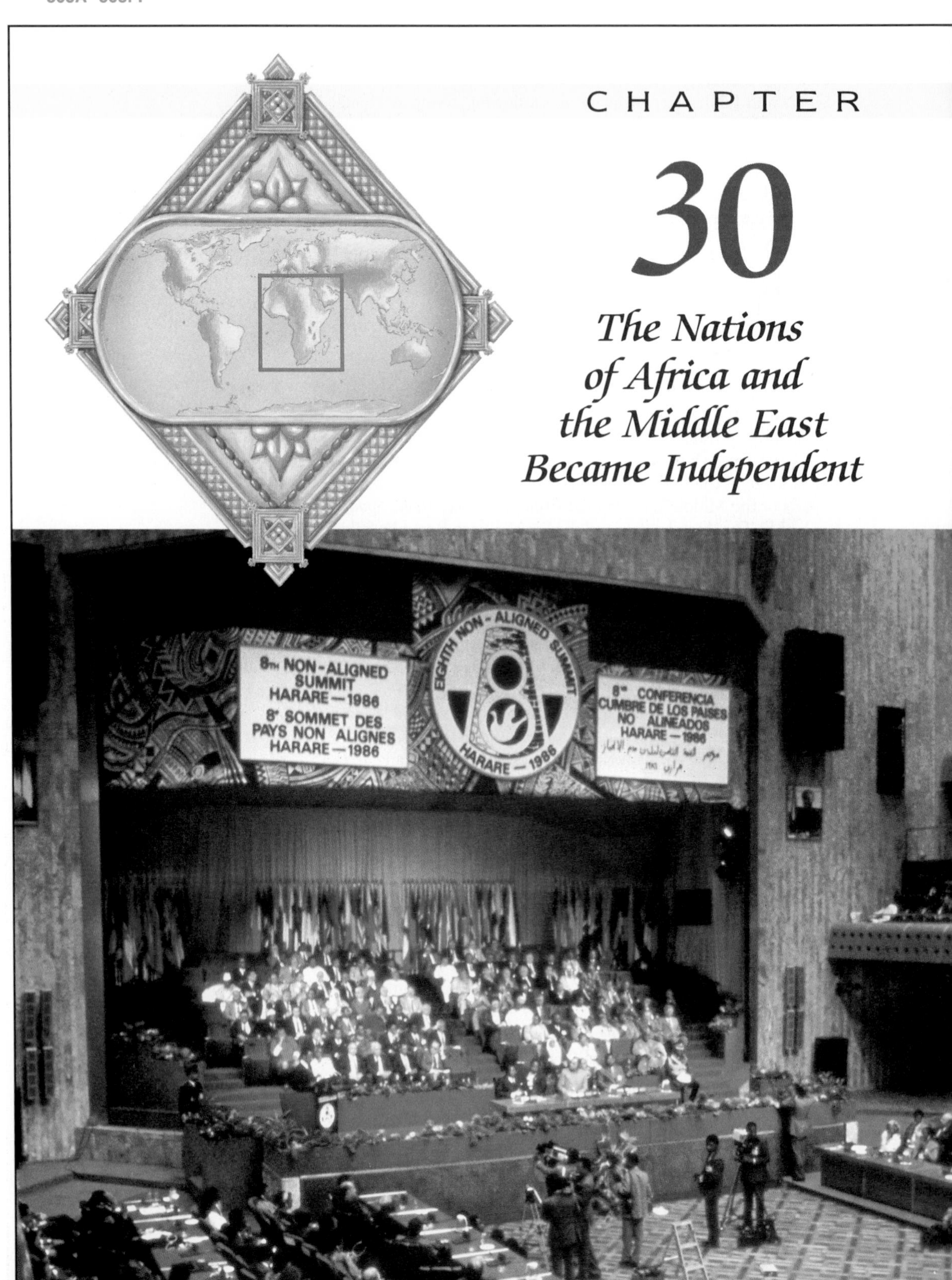

● Discussion topic: How nationalism in postwar Africa compared with nationalism in European countries after the defeat of Napoleon

CHAPTER FOCUS

Place Africa and the Middle East

Time 1945–the present

3.7 mil. BC 4000 BC AD 2100

Significance

One of the most important long-term consequences of World War II was the destruction of the empires of the European nations. In the four decades after the war, more than 1.5 billion people won independence, and the number of nations in the world tripled, mainly as a result of the dissolving of the old European empires. Most of the new nations were located in Africa and the Middle East.

The newly independent nations faced many political, economic, and social problems in their first years of freedom. Politics in these nations usually revolved around one central question: Could the government win the authority it needed to rule? These nations often lacked the proper balance of industry and agriculture necessary for successful economic growth. In addition, many nations lacked an educational base as well as adequate supplies of physicians, teachers, and skilled workers. The ways in which the new nations attacked these problems are as diverse as the nations themselves.

Terms to Define

apartheid	desertification
ujamaa	kibbutz

People to Identify

Jomo Kenyatta	Haile Selassie
Nelson Mandela	Gamal Abdel Nasser
Helen Suzman	Ayatollah Khomeini

Places to Locate

Katanga	Gulf of Aqaba
Biafra	Tehran
Aswan Dam	Beirut

Questions to Guide Your Reading

1 How did African nations achieve independence after 1945?
2 What problems did African nations face after independence?
3 How did the nations of the Middle East secure their independence?
4 How did wars, oil, and revolution transform the Middle East?
5 What conflicts arose between old and new ways in the Middle East?

In 1960 Chief Obafemi Awolowo, a political leader from western Nigeria, reflected on how his newly independent homeland should view human rights.

"I believe that every citizen, however humble and lowly his station in life, has a right to demand from his government the creation of those conditions which will enable him progressively to enjoy, according to civilized standards, the basic necessities of life as well as reasonable comfort and a measure of luxury. In other words, every citizen, regardless of his birth or religion, should be free and reasonably contented. . . .

All men and women should be treated as equal, both as political and economic beings. For this reason all laws, measures, and programs introduced by government must be framed so as to give equal treatment and opportunity to all. . . ."

Awolowo was only one of many African and Middle Eastern leaders who worked to help the people in newly independent nations after 1945.

1 African Nations Achieved Independence After World War II

Momentous changes took place in SubSaharan Africa after World War II. In a relatively short time, from 1946 to 1980, all the African colonies except Namibia (Southwest Africa) achieved independence.

African Nationalism

Although nationalism became a popular force in the postwar world, its roots went back many years. ● In the British colonies of West Africa, the families of African merchants, along with chiefs from the interior, formed an elite, or select, group. These Africans engaged in trade and other business relationships with Europeans. Many received an education in Great Britain. Some worked as missionaries, spreading Christianity in Africa. Others became civil servants.

The members of this elite group became influential representatives of the African point of view. They petitioned the British government in London for constitutional reform. In addition, they started

◀ *The Non-Aligned Nations Conference in Zimbabwe*

affected OPEC's relations with the Western world.
9. List the reasons for and effects of the revolution in Iran.
10. Summarize how modernization and industrialization in the Middle East have conflicted with traditions in the region.

SECTION 1

Focus/Motivation
The following statement was made by an African chief in 1947. Write it on the chalkboard or an overhead projector or read it to the class.

"Only an insignificant minority have any political awareness . . . . It must be realized now and for all time that this articulate minority are destined to rule the country."

Ask students the following questions: How much experience did Africans have in government, according to this chief? *(very little)* Who does the chief think will rule? *(The few who do have political knowledge.)* Ask students to consider whether a government dominated by a few strong leaders can rule justly. *(Accept all reasonable answers. Some students may note that justice under this sort of government relies on the goodwill of its leaders, because the governed do not participate.)*

4E, 4K, 5A, 5B, a1B

● Ask: Why did so many countries of Africa change their colonial names soon after they won their independence?

Presentation Analyzing Maps (Average/Group)
Ask students to compare the map of Africa on page 809 with the map of Africa on page 607. Point out that the map in this chapter shows the independent nations of Africa, while the one in Chapter 23 shows European territories in Africa. Ask: What vestiges of European colonial rule might have been left in Kenya? *(British traditions)* in Mauritania? *(French traditions)* Why might many Africans resent the former colonial powers? *(Answers will vary. Most students will suggest that Africans probably resented being ruled by foreigners.)*

newspapers and organized political associations in their homelands. They accepted the European point of view, however, that it would be many years before Africans were ready for independence.

These nationalists found themselves in a difficult position. As members of a privileged group, they did not feel at ease with their own people and in fact did not seek broad popular support. At the same time, because of their African heritage, they were excluded from European society. Nonetheless, the reforms for which these nationalists fought helped pave the way for nationalism in the postwar era.

A new generation of nationalists gained power after World War II. They were less patient and more determined to obtain equality in the world community. Leaders such as Kwame Nkrumah (en • KROO • mah) in the Gold Coast, Jomo Kenyatta (ken • YAH • tuh) in Kenya, and Nnamdi Azikiwe (ah • zih • KEE • wee) in Nigeria typified this new generation. Unlike earlier leaders, they appealed to the whole population and demanded immediate independence.

The March to Independence

The struggle for national independence in Africa took many forms. Some colonies followed a constitutional process, with popular elections and a peaceful transfer of power. Others, such as Angola, ● Mozambique, and Zimbabwe (formerly Rhodesia), suffered lengthy wars of national liberation. In each case the specific form of the independence effort depended on the particular experience of imperialism in that part of Africa. The following examples demonstrate the various roads to independence.

Ghana. The first SubSaharan colony to achieve independence was in West Africa. In 1957 the British Gold Coast colony became the independent nation of Ghana (see map, page 809). Ghana's leader, Kwame Nkrumah, chose this name to commemorate the ancient African kingdom of Ghana.

Nkrumah had been educated in the United States, where he led the African Students Association. In 1946, when he returned to the Gold Coast colony, the United Gold Coast Convention, a political party of the Westernized elite, invited him to be party secretary. From this post, Nkrumah began to build up a national following based on the slogan "Self-government now." In 1948 he started a newspaper that criticized the British administration and called for civil disobedience.

In 1949 Nkrumah started his own Convention People's Party (CPP). It became the first African political party supported by a large part of the population. The CPP's activities forced the British government to make concessions, and in 1951 it agreed to a national election in the Gold Coast colony. Nkrumah's party won a huge victory, and he formed a government with limited powers under British direction. Nkrumah continued to pressure the British for complete independence, and in 1957 it was finally granted.

Rebellion in Kenya. National parties, inspired by Nkrumah's success, began to appear in other British colonies about the same time. Often, however, they had to face problems very different from Ghana's. For example, in Kenya in East Africa (see map, page 809), white settlers held large tracts of fertile land in the central highlands. Africans were prohibited from owning land in this area. As the African population grew and land shortages became critical after World War II, the exclusion of Africans from the highlands became a source of tension. The Kikuyu (ki • KOO • yoo), Kenya's largest ethnic group, considered this area to be their ancestral homeland.

In the early 1950s, the question of landownership exploded into violence that lasted for several

Learning from Pictures *Although the British jailed Jomo Kenyatta for subversive activities, he later became the first prime minister of an independent Kenya.*

808

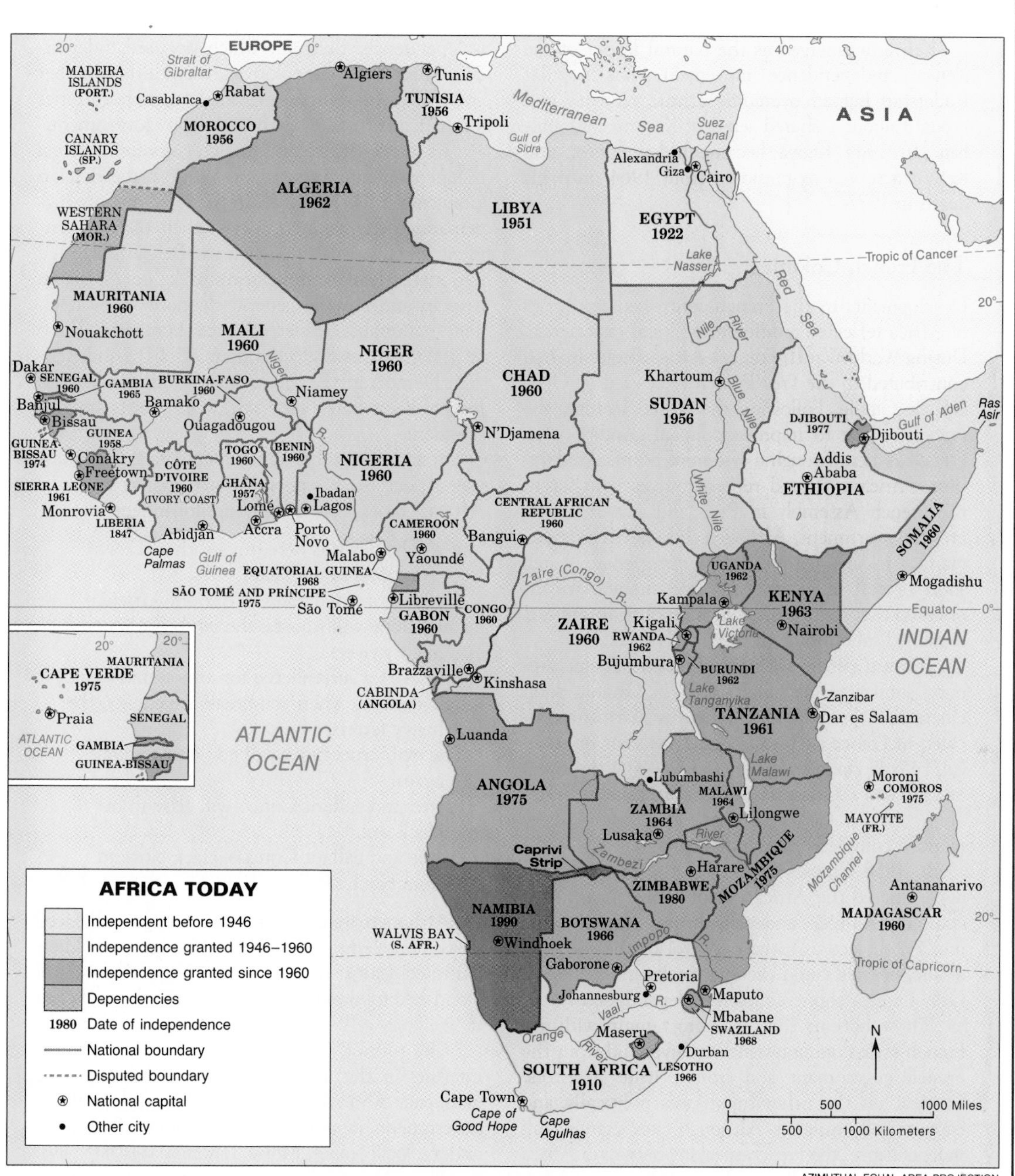

Learning from Maps *The nations of Africa won their independence from European rulers after 1945. What African nations were never colonies?* **Liberia and Ethiopia**

years and took thousands of lives. The British finally succeeded in suppressing the terrorist movement, known as the Mau Mau, that the Kikuyu had formed. Jomo Kenyatta, a Kikuyu leader, was arrested and jailed until 1961. However, the British failed to suppress the demand for independence.

809

Kenyatta emerged as the natural leader of the Kenyan independence movement. His popular leadership helped overcome ethnic rivalries and brought about a shared sense of Kenyan nationalism. In 1963 Kenya became independent, and Kenyatta served as president from 1964 until his death in 1978.

The French Colonies

Developments in the French-controlled territories of Africa reflected a different political experience. During World War II, France's African colonies had contributed to the Free French forces led by General de Gaulle. Following the Allied victory, the French sought to improve political conditions in French Africa through a system of political federation. Africans elected representatives who sat in the French Assembly in Paris and served in the French government. Although this system provided many Africans with political experience, it fell short of real independence. And many Africans resented that their economic and political interests remained subordinate to those of France.

Political parties with broad-based popular support, similar to Nkrumah's CPP in Ghana, soon emerged in French Africa. Led by Africans educated in France such as Léopold Senghor of Senegal, Félix Houphouët-Boigny (oof • WAY-BWAH • nyee) of the Ivory Coast (Côte d'Ivoire), and Sékou Touré (too • RAY) of Guinea, these parties demanded complete independence.

In 1958 Charles de Gaulle, the French president, offered the African colonies a choice. They could remain independent within the French community, subject to French control of their foreign affairs, or they could become totally independent. Only Guinea chose complete independence.

Those nations that chose to remain within a French-style commonwealth received aid from the French government and from private investors. Guinea, on the other hand, was politically and economically isolated. Although later granted full independence, the French-speaking nations of Africa continued to coordinate their economic and foreign policies with France.

The Belgian Congo

Zaire (zah • EER), formerly the Belgian Congo, experienced one of the most difficult transitions to independence. Belgium, which opposed independence because of the colony's great wealth in timber and mineral resources, provided few opportunities for Africans to develop their skills in government.

As in the British and French colonies, a strong independence movement sprang up in the Belgian Congo after World War II. In the 1950s nationalists demanded the right to choose their own government. Finally, in 1960, when the Belgians arrested nationalist leaders and rioting broke out, Belgium gave in and allowed general elections to be held. The nationalist leader, Patrice Lumumba (luh • MUHM • buh), was elected premier of the independent Democratic Republic of the Congo. His rival, Joseph Kasavubu (kah • sah • VOO • boo), became president.

In addition to his political activities, Lumumba was a poet. In his poem "Dawn in the Heart of Africa," he expressed his hopes for independence:

> "The dawn is here, my brother! Dawn!
> Look in our faces,
> A new morning breaks in our old Africa.
> Ours alone will now be the land, the water, mighty rivers
> Poor Africa surrendered for a thousand years.
> The moment when you break the chains, the heavy fetters,
> The evil, cruel times will go never to come again.
> A free and gallant Congo will arise from black soil,
> A free and gallant Congo—black blossom from black seed!"

Although independent, the Congo still faced serious problems. In July 1960, Congolese soldiers mutinied against their Belgian officers. A period of bloodshed followed, during which many people lost their lives.

The turmoil increased and threatened Belgian interests in the mining province of Katanga (see map, page 809). To protect its interests, the Belgian government supported the secession of Katanga under a local leader, Moise Tshombe (SHOM • bay).

The Congo moved rapidly toward complete anarchy. Tshombe's forces in Katanga imprisoned Lumumba. There he was murdered following an alleged escape attempt.

In an attempt to end the bloodshed, the UN Security Council called on Belgium to withdraw its troops from Katanga. It also authorized a UN force

810

to restore order in the Congo. This force, composed mainly of troops from other African nations, was sent into the Congo in the summer of 1960. By the beginning of 1963, Tshombe's army was defeated, and he went into exile.

When UN troops were withdrawn from the Congo in mid-1964, revolts broke out in several provinces. Kasavubu invited Tshombe to return from exile and become premier in a "government of national reconciliation." Although Tshombe accepted, instability continued to plague the young nation, and in 1965 President Kasavubu removed Tshombe from office. Kasavubu himself was then overthrown in a military coup led by Joseph Mobutu, an army general. Mobutu later took the African name Mobutu Sese Seko (SAY • say SAY • koh).

Leadership of the Congo was not clearly established for several years. In 1970 Mobutu was elected president of what became, in the following year, the Republic of Zaire. Zaire gradually began to recover from the political chaos and civil wars of the 1960s.

The Portuguese Colonies

While many African nations were winning their independence, the Portuguese government opposed independence for its colonies. In desperation, African leaders in Angola, Portuguese Guinea, and Mozambique organized "liberation armies" to fight for freedom. In a series of long, bloody wars, they gained control of much of the countryside. However, they failed to dislodge the Portuguese from the major urban centers.

This bloody stalemate continued until 1974, when the military staged a coup in Portugal and announced that Portugal would withdraw from Africa. Within months of the announcement, Portuguese Guinea, Mozambique, and Angola became independent. Only Southern Rhodesia, South Africa, and the trust territory of Namibia remained under minority rule.

Learning from Pictures *United Nations troops arrive in the Congo in 1960. What colonial power controlled Zaire?* **Belgium**

Rhodesia

Developments in the British colony of Rhodesia represented an unusual example of both guerrilla warfare and constitutional change. Rhodesia had a large white population that controlled colonial politics. As in their other colonies, the British supported a policy that gradually would allow the African population to gain the right to vote and that eventually would lead to African majority rule. Within the colony, however, the white government, led by Ian Smith, refused to submit to the British policies.

In 1965 the colony declared its independence—a status that Great Britain and the rest of the world, except for South Africa, refused to recognize. Although the Smith government was isolated internationally, it still refused to meet with African leaders or initiate needed reforms. Consequently, as happened in the neighboring Portuguese colonies, a war of national liberation began. Little success was achieved in the early years of fighting. However, when Angola and Mozambique became independent in 1975, the liberation forces gained a military advantage. They now had countries friendly to their cause in southern Africa.

Under the leadership of Robert Mugabe (moo • GAH • bee) and Joshua Nkomo (en • KOH • moh), the African forces intensified their attacks and succeeded in disrupting the economy of Rhodesia. As the war became increasingly unpopular among the white population, Smith was forced to seek a solution. An arrangement was worked out with moderate African leaders to form a new government under African leadership that would continue to

811

4E, 4K, 5A, a1B, a1C

● The classic — and very graphic — book portraying apartheid is Alan Paton's *Cry! the Beloved Country,* which became the play *Lost in the Stars.*

SECTION 1

Closure

Ask students to define apartheid and detail the problems it has caused for black South Africans. *(It is the policy of racial segregation. Black South Africans are deprived of many rights.)*

Review Answers

1. *apartheid:* South African policy of separation of whites from Africans, Asians, and "coloreds" **2. *Jomo Kenyatta:*** leader of Kenya's independence movement and first president of Kenya; ***CPP:*** Convention People's Party of Ghana; ***Mau Mau:*** terrorist movement of the Kikuyu in Kenya; ***Sékou Touré:*** independence leader of Guinea; ***Joseph Kasavubu:*** first president of the Democratic Republic of the Congo; ***Robert Mugabe:*** elected president of Rhodesia in 1979; ***Bantustans:*** separate tribal states for Africans set up in South Africa; ***Nelson Mandela:*** imprisoned African National Congress leader; ***Helen Suzman:*** white South African member of Parliament who opposes apartheid **3. *Zimbabwe:*** country northeast of South Africa and Botswana; ***Ghana:*** country on northern Atlantic coast near Nigeria; ***Kenya:*** country south of the horn of Africa; ***Zaire:*** country in south central Africa; ***Katanga:*** province of Zaire, formerly part of the Belgian Congo; ***South Africa:*** country on southern tip of Africa

guarantee the privileged economic and social status of whites.

In 1978 Bishop Abel Muzorewa (moo • zuh • RAY • wah) became the new prime minister. However, his new government, which included Ian Smith, did not receive international recognition, and the guerrilla war continued. In 1979 the Muzorewa-Smith government was finally forced to accept a cease-fire and to agree to hold free elections. The elections were to be open to all parties, including the liberation leaders. According to the agreement, the British government would supervise both the cease-fire and the elections. In the elections, held in 1979, Robert Mugabe, considered the most radical of the candidates, won an absolute majority.

In April 1980 Rhodesia became the new nation of Zimbabwe. After years of civil war, Zimbabwe's needs were clear and the government turned its energies to economic recovery. The advance of independence had now reached the borders of the nation of South Africa.

South Africa

South Africa's experience differed from that of any other African nation. It gained independence from Great Britain in 1910 as a white-ruled nation with dominion status. Although linked to Great Britain in foreign affairs, the dominion ruled itself internally as it saw fit. Relying on its resources of gold, diamonds, and cheap labor, South Africa experienced an industrial revolution in the early 1900s. Although industrialization was based on their labor, blacks, who vastly outnumbered whites, were excluded almost totally from the benefits of South Africa's economic success.

● **Apartheid.** Before World War II, English-speaking whites had dominated the government. By custom, non-whites were kept out of better jobs and were segregated socially. In 1948 the Afrikaans-speaking whites, descendants of the original Dutch settlers, came to power in South Africa and passed a series of laws designed to ensure that these customs would not change. This policy, based on the principle of racial separation, became known as **apartheid** (uh • PART • hyt), the Afrikaans word for apartness.

South Africa also extended apartheid to Namibia (Southwest Africa), which it had acquired as a mandate from the League of Nations after World War I. Although the United Nations voted in 1966 to end South Africa's control of Namibia, South Africa ignored the ruling. South Africa's harsh policies led to an increasingly militant nationalist movement in Namibia. Finally, in 1990, South Africa granted Namibia its independence.

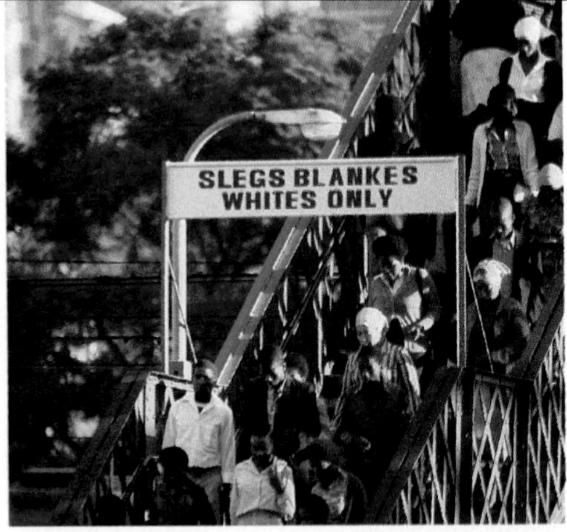

Learning from Pictures *Although the South African government has integrated some facilities, opposition by white extremist political groups has created increasing tensions within the government.*

Within its own territory, South Africa formed separate "tribal states," known as "homelands" or "Bantustans," for Africans. These homelands had no economic resources of their own and were completely dependent on the South African government.

Protests against apartheid. Blacks have protested apartheid since the South African government first adopted the racial policy. One vocal organization is the African National Congress (ANC), which the government banned in 1960. Despite the ban, the ANC has continued to operate from bases in neighboring countries. Although Nelson Mandela, the ANC's leader, was sentenced to life in prison in 1962, other ANC members—particularly Mandela's wife Winnie—have continued to fight apartheid. In addition, black leaders such as Desmond Tutu and Zulu Chief Gatsha Buthelezi (boo • tuh • LAY • zee), as well as an increasing number of white South Africans including Helen Suzman, a member of Parliament, have opposed the government.

In 1976 the South African police brutally crushed a peaceful demonstration by black schoolchildren at Soweto, a black township near Johannesburg. After the Soweto incident, which triggered massive uprisings around the country, many

● Research topic: The current status of apartheid policies and the international response to these policies

■ The boundaries of Nigeria are prime examples of superimposed boundaries: drawn after settlement with no regard for the peoples of the region.

1C, 4K, 5A, a1B, a4A, a4F, a4G, a4I, a4L, a4M

people in South Africa were no longer willing to wait peacefully for change. Thousands of South Africans have since died during the civil unrest.

Faced with growing protests, the South African government relaxed some regulations of apartheid. The government, for example, allowed black unions and interracial marriages. And in 1984 a new constitution went into effect, granting coloreds (people of mixed race) and Asians the right to be represented in the previously all-white Parliament. Blacks, however, were still denied any political participation, and civil strife continued.

In July 1985 the South African government under President P.W. Botha (BOH • tah), faced with the prospect of urban guerrilla warfare, substantially increased its own military and police powers by declaring a state of emergency. As a result the police arrested black union leaders and black nationalists.

In response, many Western nations condemned apartheid and urged Western firms to withdraw investment funds from South Africa. As international pressures increased, the South African government relaxed a few more of apartheid's strict regulations. Then with the election of F.W. de Klerk as state president in September 1989, the pace of change quickened. De Klerk lifted a 30-year ban on antiapartheid rallies and legalized the African National Congress. He also released Nelson Mandela in February 1990 and agreed to meet with him to discuss further reforms. Although de Klerk's actions did not immediately end international economic sanctions, world leaders applauded de Klerk and urged the South Africans to pass further reforms. ●

SECTION 1 REVIEW

1. **Define** apartheid
2. **Identify** Jomo Kenyatta, CPP, Mau Mau, Sékou Touré, Joseph Kasavubu, Robert Mugabe, Bantustans, Nelson Mandela, Helen Suzman
3. **Locate** Zimbabwe, Ghana, Kenya, Zaire, Katanga, South Africa
4. **Interpreting Ideas** How did France deal with its African colonies that wished to be independent?
5. **Summarizing Ideas** What problems did the Belgian Congo experience after achieving independence?
6. **Analyzing Ideas** Why was independence so difficult to achieve in Rhodesia?
7. **Determining Cause and Effect** How has apartheid deprived black South Africans of basic human rights?

2 The New African Nations Faced Various Problems

Having achieved independence, the new nations of Africa still faced many serious problems. Each new nation had to create a sense of national unity among people often divided by differences of language and culture. Many of them had to overcome economic underdevelopment. Finally, a sense of pride in Africa's history and its cultural achievements had to be restored.

National Unity

The most pressing need for each of the new African nations involved developing a sense of national identity among its citizens. This proved to be a difficult task because the boundaries of the new nations were often artificial, drawn by the imperialist powers in the 1800s for their own convenience. In some cases, people of similar racial or cultural backgrounds were separated, while people of different heritages were grouped together.

In addition, colonial administrations had encouraged regional and ethnic differences. In this way they had hoped to discourage the development of national political parties. These ethnic rivalries continued after independence and on occasion led to civil war, as happened in Nigeria.

Nigeria's Civil War

The former British colony of Nigeria gained independence in 1960. The new constitution created a federation of four regions, each of which retained a large degree of local independence. Strong ethnic and regional differences existed in Nigeria, and the government hoped that this loose plan would prevent warfare among the various tribes. The plan, however, did not work. ■

In 1966 the military took over the government, but it could not overcome the tensions created by ethnic and regional distrust. In 1967 the Eastern Region, home of the Ibo-speaking people, seceded from the federation and declared itself the independent Republic of Biafra.

Nigeria plunged into civil war. Throughout the fighting, Nigerian officials maintained that the war with Biafra was a purely domestic problem. They regarded any aid to the Biafrans as interference

4. France offered its colonies a choice: they could remain within the French community, subject to French control of foreign affairs but otherwise independent; or they could sever ties to France and be totally independent.
5. Congolese soldiers mutinied against their Belgian officers and initiated a period of bloodshed. The province of Katanga, with the support of Belgium, seceded from the Congo. The UN intervened, but revolts by small groups broke out again when UN troops withdrew. Political turmoil followed, during which leadership of the country was not clearly established.
6. In Rhodesia the white government refused to jeopardize its privileged position by allowing the African population to vote. A war broke out. Agreement was reached to form a new government under African leadership but with whites' privileges left intact. The war continued until the government was forced to accept a cease-fire and agree to free elections.
7. Hundreds of laws concerning jobs, education, social relations, and intellectual pursuits have governed the lives of nonwhites.

SECTION 2

Focus/Motivation
The following quotation is by the Nigerian novelist Chinua Achebe. Read the quotation aloud, or reproduce copies for the class.

1D, 4K, 5A, 5D, 5L, a1B

● An excellent source for students who want to learn more about Nigeria is "Nigeria Struggles with Boom Times" by Noel Grove on pages 413–44 of the March 1979 issue of *National Geographic.*

"Africans did not hear of culture for the first time from Europeans. Their societies often had great depth and value and beauty. Above all, they had great dignity. Many African peoples all but lost this dignity during the colonial days. It is this dignity that they must now regain . . . .

Let me give one small example to illustrate what I mean by people losing faith in themselves. When I was a schoolboy, it was unheard of to stage Nigerian dances at any of our celebrations. We were told that our dances were heathen. And we came to believe that was true."

Ask students the following questions: What effect did colonialism have on Africans' view of their own culture, according to Achebe? *(The African people lost confidence in the value of their own culture and developed a sense of inferiority.)* How does Achebe view traditional African culture? *(It has beauty and value. Africans need to regain pride in their own culture.)* What specific effects would a new African pride have on African culture? *(Accept all reasonable answers—for example, there might be renewed interest in traditional music, art, and language.)* As students read the section, have them note the ways African cultural pride and self-confidence were reawakened after independence.

in Nigeria's internal affairs. For this reason most African nations refused to recognize Biafra. After 4 years of war and the deaths of about 2 million Biafrans from starvation and disease, Biafra surrendered.

Gradually the Nigerian government restored stability at home and regained a position of leadership in Africa. Nigeria became a respected voice for African interests in the United Nations. Ethnicity and regionalism, however, continued to be sensitive issues in Nigeria.

A democratically elected civilian government returned to Nigeria in 1970. At the same time, the country's oil wealth provided Nigerians with the opportunity to escape the poverty that threatened most other African nations. It also appeared that Nigeria might be the first African nation other than South Africa to achieve a high degree of industrialization.

In the 1980s, however, a drop in the international demand for oil caused Nigeria's oil revenues to fall, and Nigeria's economy suddenly faltered. In late 1983 military officers overthrew the civilian government and boldly introduced new economic measures. As of the late 1980s, however, the Nigerian economy had not recovered, and Nigeria had to borrow from other countries.

Angola and the Horn of Africa

Superpower rivalry complicated the efforts of new African nations to achieve national unity. The problems of the new nations, which included the need for financial and technical assistance, created opportunities for the United States and the Soviet Union to establish their influence in Africa.

When civil war broke out in Angola after independence in 1975, the United States and the Soviet Union rushed arms and support to the rival factions. A Marxist faction aided by Soviet and Cuban troops finally came to power. Cuban troops remained in Angola to ensure the continuation of the regime. Even though the Angolan government continued to rely on Cuban troops in the mid-1980s, it actively sought Western investment in the country.

Soviet-American rivalries were even more complex in the Horn of Africa, a strategic area that includes Ethiopia and Somalia (see map, page 809). The Horn overlooks the Red Sea as well as the Indian Ocean sea lanes to the oil-rich Persian Gulf. It is also an area of relative instability, characterized by frequent border disputes and local independence movements.

When the Ethiopian emperor, Haile Selassie, was overthrown in 1974, a socialist regime came to power. To support the socialist governments in Ethiopia and in nearby Somalia, the Soviet Union provided military aid and advisers. Cuban and East German troops were stationed in Ethiopia. In exchange, Somalia and Ethiopia granted the Soviets rights to local air and naval bases.

Although the Soviet Union gained a temporary advantage, it had provided arms to two traditionally hostile neighbors. When Somalia invaded Ethiopia in 1977, the Soviets supported Ethiopia. Somalia then expelled all Soviet diplomats and advisers and granted rights to a navy base to the United States in exchange for military assistance. This topsy-turvy situation demonstrated that African nations often preferred practical assistance to ideological commitments. This was even more true by the 1980s, when a devastating famine threatened millions of Africans with starvation.

Economic Difficulties

In addition to political challenges, the new African nations faced economic uncertainty. As colonies, they had been part of the economic system of imperialism. In most cases, upon receiving their independence, the new nations lacked the balance between agriculture and industry required for economic growth. Many of them depended on a single crop or mineral resource for most of their income. These products, such as cocoa in Ghana, copper in Zambia and Zaire, or cotton in the Sudan, were subject to large price swings in world markets.

Overcoming dependence on a single resource continued to be one of the greatest challenges facing the nations of Africa in the 1980s. Nations with few resources were unable to escape the cycle of poverty. Zaire, for example, borrowed heavily from international banks to finance its economic expansion. It became the largest debtor nation in SubSaharan Africa.

Tanzania tried a different approach, based on a traditional African social system. It organized local, cooperative villages, known as **ujamaa** (family), to increase productivity and improve standards of living. Unfortunately, most of these villages failed, and economic conditions worsened.

Western nations including the United States have shipped huge amounts of food supplies to the Sahel to save people from starvation. Ask: Is this the long-term solution? Why or why not?

Learning from Pictures *This copper mine is in Lubumbashi, Zaire. Zaire ranks as one of the top producers and exporters of copper and copper products.*

Tanzania was a vivid reminder of the economic problems that African nations still had to overcome.

Among these problems was a constant threat of famine. As the population of Africa continued to expand, many farmers overused the land. To grow more food, farmers planted crops in dry areas or on hills, where fierce winds often stripped away the topsoil. In addition, people in many parts of Africa cut down trees for firewood. As a result of these practices, **desertification,** or the spread of the desert, became common. From 1984 to 1989, for example, the Sahara took over an estimated 250,000 square miles (647,500 square kilometers) of the Sahel, the semiarid plain that stretches across the southern Sahara.

Desertification has created untold miseries for the people of Africa. Only international aid in the form of food supplies has helped people survive widespread famines.

Revival of African Culture

Despite the economic and political disappointments that followed independence, the people of Africa made great strides in one very important area. They experienced a rebirth of cultural self-confidence.

During the colonial era, many Africans lost faith in their own culture as they adopted European attitudes toward Africa. African art and music were considered primitive and crude. Magnificent constructions like Great Zimbabwe, which you read about in Chapter 13, or exquisite artifacts like the bronze masks of Benin, were wrongly attributed to foreign influences. They were thought to be works of ancient Greeks or other people who had been shipwrecked on Africa's shores and had wandered into the interior. The literature of Africa—a treasury of oral traditions including myths, proverbs, and folk tales—was largely unknown to Europeans. Seeing the attitudes of Europeans, most Africans themselves turned away from their history and their cultural heritage.

Not all Africans, however, followed the European example. In East Africa, Swahili poetry and tales continued to be studied as they had been for hundreds of years. The traditions of Swahili were kept alive in the Islamic mosque schools of coastal towns. The written records of this Bantu language go back to the 1600s. The language itself has continued to evolve. James Mbotela's novel, *Uhuru wa Watumwa (Freedom for the Slaves)* (1934), helped give Swahili the modern form from which it continued to grow. Many plays and novels have been written in Swahili, the national language of Tanzania and Kenya.

In West Africa, a new literary tradition developed, using the colonial languages of English and French. Many African authors, especially those from French-speaking areas, first achieved international recognition through works of protest against colonial oppression. In a very intense and personal style, the poems of Léopold Senghor, who later became president of independent Senegal, described the hardships of colonialism. Senghor's works, and the novels of Camara Laye of Cameroon, proudly pointed to the deep, spiritual traditions of Africa and its sense of social community.

In 1986 the Nigerian playwright and poet Wole Soyinka won the Nobel Prize in Literature, becoming the the first African to win the coveted award. Soyinka accepted the award saying: "I don't for a minute consider that the prize is just for me. It's for what I represent. I'm a part of the whole literary tradition of Africa."

These African writers created a new artistic tradition. The result was a remarkable and varied

Presentation
Using News Reports (Average/Group)

Ask students to bring in recent newspaper or magazine articles on events in Africa. Then ask for volunteers to read their articles to the class. Use the articles as the basis for a class discussion on what is going on in African political and social life today.

SECTION 2

Closure

Ask: How have the boundaries drawn by European colonial powers continued to cause problems in Africa? *(The boundaries cut across tribal boundaries and attempt to unite disparate peoples.)*

Review Answers

1. ***ujamaa:*** local, cooperative villages organized to increase productivity and improve standards of living in Tanzania; ***desertification:*** spread of the desert
2. ***Haile Selassie:*** Ethiopian emperor
3. ***Biafra:*** eastern Nigeria
4. Ethnic and regional distrust led to the secession of the eastern region as the Republic of Biafra. Civil war broke out between Biafra and the central government. Biafra received little support, and after great loss of life through war and starvation, it surrendered in 1970.
5. When civil war broke out in Angola in 1975, both the United States and the Soviet Union rushed arms and support to the rival

4E, 4K, 5A, 5C, 5F, a1B, a4A, a4H, a4I, a4L, a4M

● Point out that the United States was attempting to halt the spread of communism into the Middle East when it helped strengthen Iran's monarchy.

factions. To support socialist regimes in Ethiopia and Somalia, the Soviet Union provided military aid and advisors in exchange for naval and air bases in both countries. When Somalia invaded Ethiopia in 1977, the Soviets sided with Ethiopia and were expelled from Somalia. The United States sought use of a naval base in Somalia in return for military assistance.
6. (a) because the entire economy is subject to the ups and downs of the market for that single crop;
(b) Zaire borrowed heavily and soon became the most debt-ridden nation in Sub-Saharan Africa. Tanzania organized local, cooperative villages to increase productivity and improve living standards. Most of these villages failed and economic conditions worsened.
7. A new literary tradition developed and many authors wrote works of protest against colonial and racial oppression. There was a reawakening of interest in African music and a film industry began. African artists employed age-old techniques to make sculptures from wood and copper.

SECTION 3

Focus/Motivation
Put on the chalkboard or read to the class the following quote by Gamal Abdel Nasser of Egypt:

"Within the Arab circle there is a role wandering aimlessly in search of a

Learning from Pictures *Miriam Makeba, a South African singer and composer, sings at a concert dedicated to Nelson Mandela. Her music reaches out to people's sense of human dignity.*

artistic outpouring. Similar achievements were made in reawakening an interest in African music. In addition, a film industry was begun.

In South Africa, themes protesting racial oppression continued to be important. *The Rhythm of Violence,* a play by Lewis Nkosi, and *Down Second Avenue,* an autobiographical novel by Ezekiel Mphalele, were major cultural contributions. They revealed very vividly the difficulty and bitterness of life in South Africa for the black majority.

The creativity of Africa's contemporary literature, music, and films was also seen in sculpture. At workshops in Nigeria, Zimbabwe, and elsewhere, African artists employed age-old techniques to give shape to wood and copper. Others were more clearly influenced by Western art. Throughout Africa, this willingness to mix African and outside influences gave an unusual vitality to the arts. More and more Westerners began to appreciate the achievements of African art. At the same time, Africans themselves found a new pride in their ancient heritage and in Africa's unique contribution to world culture.

SECTION 2 REVIEW

1. **Define** ujamaa, desertification
2. **Identify** Haile Selassie
3. **Locate** Biafra
4. **Determining Cause and Effect** What were the causes and results of the civil war in Nigeria?
5. **Summarizing Ideas** How did the Soviet Union and the United States become politically involved in Angola, Ethiopia, and Somalia?
6. **Interpreting Ideas** **(a)** Explain why dependence on one crop can result in an unstable economy. **(b)** How did Zaire and Tanzania try to improve their economies?
7. **Listing Ideas** List some examples of contemporary African cultural achievements.

3 The Nations of the Middle East Won Their Independence

The Middle East, as it is often defined today, contains the nations of Iran, Israel, Turkey, and the entire Arabic-speaking world. From 1945 to 1962, the nations of the Middle East made great advances in securing independence. Many gained their independence from Western imperial rule. Others, such as Egypt and Iran, were officially independent but were dominated by outsiders. They, too, achieved greater freedom from foreign influence during this period and sought to increase their power within the Middle East.

Iran

At the end of World War II, Great Britain and the Soviet Union still occupied Iran. Although technically a sovereign ruler, the young Shah Muhammad Reza Pahlavi held no power. Iranian leaders wanted to free their country from both Soviet and British influence. With United States support, Iran halted Soviet attempts to gain greater control over the country. ●

In the early 1950s, Iran acted to reduce British influence. The popular Iranian prime minister, Muhammad Mussadegh (MOO • sah • daig), nationalized the British-owned Anglo-Iranian Oil Company in 1951. Mussadegh also led a nationalist struggle against Iranian conservatives who supported the shah and the monarchy.

The struggle within Iran between Mussadegh and the shah reached a showdown in 1953. For a brief time, the shah had to flee Iran. He returned in triumph after the military, supported by the United States, overthrew Mussadegh.

Thereafter, the shah worked to establish his power and to impose rapid modernization upon his country. He relied on close ties with the United States and on his army. By the early 1960s, the shah appeared to be firmly in control.

Turkey

After World War II, Turkey faced Soviet pressure and turned to the West for support. After 1947 Turkey increasingly relied on military and economic aid from the United States, and in 1952 Turkey became a full member of NATO.

At the same time, Turkey moved toward democratic rule. In late 1945 the successor to Kemal Atatürk announced the end of one-party government. The more authoritarian aspects of Atatürk's government were abolished. Free elections were held in May 1950, and the opposition party under Prime Minister Adnan Menderes came to power.

In the late 1950s, the Menderes government lost popularity and began to impose restrictions on its opposition. The Turkish army intervened in 1960, fearing Menderes would eventually destroy some of the reforms Atatürk had instituted. Menderes and many others were arrested, and the former prime minister was later executed. Although the army restored civilian government, the precedent of military intervention in Turkish politics had been established.

Egypt

After 1945 Egyptians were concerned with two foreign issues, both involving Great Britain. The Egyptians wanted to remove the British military base at Suez; they also wanted to eliminate British control over Sudan and to unite that country with Egypt.

The Egyptian ruler, King Farouk, had lost favor with ordinary Egyptians, most of whom lived in extreme poverty and resented the king's extravagance. In addition, Egyptians wanted to speed economic reforms. Egypt was therefore ripe for revolution, and in July 1952, a group of young military officers overthrew the government of King Farouk.

Learning from Pictures *Aswan, Egypt, is one of the most important commercial, mining, and resort cities in the Nile Valley.*

After a power struggle, Gamal Abdel Nasser emerged as Egypt's new leader. From 1954 until his death in 1970, Nasser enjoyed almost complete control in Egypt. He was careful, however, to observe the formalities of democratic rule.

Nasser and his fellow officers represented Egyptians of modest means in revolt against corrupt rulers. The former ruling class had been allied, both commercially and politically, with Great Britain and the West. Thus Nasser's revolution also was characterized as a revolt against the West.

The Nasser government emphasized land reform, industrialization, greater government control over the economy, and the expansion of education. By 1954 Great Britain had agreed to evacuate the Suez base and to allow free elections in Sudan. Sudan, however, chose independence rather than union with Egypt.

Nasser still feared Western influence in the Middle East. He launched Egypt on an assertive foreign policy aimed at dominating the Arabic-speaking world.

Israel and the Arabs

After the Holocaust, which you read about in Chapter 27, the Zionists became more determined to have Palestine as a Jewish homeland. Palestinian Arabs continued to resist what they saw as an

hero. For some reason it seems to me that this role is beckoning to us—to move, to take up its lines, put on its costumes and give it life. Indeed, we are the only ones who can play it. The role is to spark the tremendous latent strengths in the region surrounding us to create a great power, which will then rise up to a level of dignity and undertake a positive part in building the future of mankind."

Ask students to discuss what Nasser's ambitions were, based on this passage. *(Accept all reasonable answers. For example, Nasser believed that the Middle East has great potential for development and a place in world affairs but needs effective leadership. He thought Egypt should provide that leadership.)* At the completion of the chapter, discuss with students the extent to which Nasser's ambitions were realized.

Presentation
Presenting a Newscast (Average/Group)
The entire class can become involved in producing a newscast of the Suez Crisis of 1956. A newscaster should summarize the main events and then ask representatives from Great Britain, France, Israel, Egypt, and the United States for their opinions of the crisis. To find out about public reaction to the incident, students should consult the *Readers' Guide to Periodical Literature* for

4E, 4K, 5A, 5B, a1B

● Many of these immigrants were skilled in the professions and crafts and helped to raise Israel's industrial productivity.

■ Ask: How is a kibbutz like a collective farm in the Soviet Union? How is it different? How is a kibbutz like a farm in the United States? How is it different?

articles written at the time of the crisis. For a detailed account of the fighting, consult T. N. Dupuy's *Elusive Victory: Arab-Israeli Wars 1947–1974* (Harper & Row).

invasion of their homeland. Neighboring Arabs supported the Palestinians.

Great Britain, which held the mandate for Palestine, was never able to obtain an agreement between Zionists and Palestinians. After World War II, Great Britain referred the problem to the UN. In November 1947 the UN voted to partition Palestine into separate Jewish and Arab states with Jerusalem as an international city. When the last British troops left Palestine in May 1948, Zionist leaders proclaimed the Republic of Israel. Chaim Weizmann became its first president and David Ben-Gurion its first prime minister.

The establishment of a Jewish nation infuriated the Palestinian Arabs. As soon as British troops withdrew from the area, armies from neighboring Arab countries moved against Israel.

Although outnumbered by the Arabs, the determined Israelis triumphed. When the war ended in early 1949, Israel had won more territory than it had been allotted in the UN partition plan. The Arab nations accepted a cease-fire, but UN-sponsored efforts to negotiate permanent peace failed. Moreover, some 750,000 Palestinians had been uprooted by the conflict and were living as refugees in neighboring Arab lands. Attempts to work out either the return or resettlement of these Palestinian refugees also failed.

Learning from Pictures *Golda Meir was a Jewish immigrant who came to the United States from Russia. After working for Israeli independence, she moved to the Jewish state, where she later became prime minister.*

From 1949 to 1952, Israel absorbed nearly 600,000 immigrants, almost doubling the Jewish population of the new country. Impressive social ● and economic programs were also developed. Collective farms (the best-known form of which is called the **kibbutz**) proved successful in turning ■ former desert areas into productive land.

Among the Arab nations, only one emerged from the 1948 war with territorial gains. What remained of the proposed Palestinian state was absorbed into Trans-Jordan in 1949. (Trans-Jordan then changed its name to Jordan.) Other Arabs, including many Palestinians, bitterly opposed this action.

Algeria

Most nations of the Middle East had gained independence through limited violence. In Algeria, however, independence came only after a long war.

Algeria was not just a colony but had been legally absorbed into France. In addition, Algeria contained about 1 million French citizens, many from families that had lived in Algeria for several generations. Some families had been there since France had taken over the country in 1830.

There were also French settlers in the neighboring countries of Morocco and Tunisia, although not as many as in Algeria. Moreover, these countries were only French protectorates, not parts of France. France finally gave in to persistent Moroccan and Tunisian nationalist movements and granted independence to both countries in 1956.

In Algeria, however, the French wanted to keep control. An Algerian group called the National Liberation Front (FLN, the initials for its name in French) launched a guerrilla war in 1954. France kept sending in more troops, but the determined FLN could not be crushed. Although bottled up by the strong French army, the FLN won increasing support from all classes of Algerians.

In 1958, as you have read, General de Gaulle became head of the French government. The French in Algeria thought he would push the war there to a successful finish for France. They were disappointed. Slowly, de Gaulle prepared the French to accept Algerian independence.

Talks between the French and the Algerians began in 1961, but the negotiations were long and difficult. Finally, the two sides reached a settlement, and Algeria became independent in July 1962.

● **To emphasize the importance of the Suez Canal to world shipping, ask students to trace on a world map the route that a ship would need to take from the Persian Gulf to Italy if the Suez Canal did not exist. Ask: How would the closing of the Suez Canal affect the world supply of oil?**

The Middle East in World Politics

Soon after the end of World War II, Soviet pressures on Iran, Greece, and Turkey provoked an American-led Western response. American resistance to Soviet efforts in the Middle East, formalized in the Truman Doctrine (see Chapter 28), proved successful in the late 1940s and early 1950s. In general, the West wanted to maintain a strong presence in the Middle East through economic agreements and military bases.

The Soviet Union challenged Western influence in the area by entering into an arms deal with Egypt in 1955. Nasser willingly accepted Soviet arms because he feared continued Western domination more than the possibility of Soviet control. He also had ambitions for Egypt to play a larger role in the Middle East.

The United States and its allies responded to the Soviet-Egyptian arms deal by offering to help finance a major development project—a dam at Aswan on the Nile River. The dam would irrigate new lands for agricultural expansion and also would produce hydroelectric power. It was hoped this would keep Egypt from slipping further into the sphere of Soviet influence. When Nasser later displeased the West, the Aswan Dam offer was abruptly withdrawn. Nasser retaliated by nationalizing the Suez Canal in July 1956.

The Suez Crisis

The nationalization of the Suez Canal posed many problems, including a threat to Europe's oil supply. The industrialized nations of the West depended heavily on oil shipped through the canal from oil fields in the Middle East. In addition, as more Soviet arms poured into Egypt, the West feared increased Soviet influence in the Middle East.

The Egyptian actions especially alarmed Israel. Relations between Israel and the neighboring Arab nations, especially Egypt, had been most unfriendly. Egypt had refused to allow Israeli ships or ships of other countries with cargoes bound for Israel to pass through the Suez Canal.

Egypt's seizure of the canal in 1956 brought tensions to a head. Israel, in a lightning invasion, seized the Gaza Strip—an Egyptian-administered coastal district adjoining Israel's southern border. The Israelis then defeated the Egyptians in the Sinai Peninsula and advanced toward the canal.

Great Britain and France, in a secret agreement with Israel, sent an ultimatum to Egypt. The ultimatum demanded a cease-fire and insisted on temporary British-French occupation of the canal. When Egypt refused, Great Britain and France seized the Mediterranean end of the canal, driving back the Egyptian army. Both sides sank ships in the canal to block it.

The matter was brought before the United Nations. The General Assembly demanded a cease-fire and withdrawal of the invading forces. It also authorized UN forces to patrol the cease-fire line. Great Britain and France, facing pressure from hostile world opinion, withdrew their troops. The Israelis tried to gain Egypt's agreement to their use of the canal, but failed. Then they too withdrew.

In the short war over the Suez Canal, Israel had crippled Nasser's growing military power. Arab fear and distrust of Israel intensified, and a negotiated Arab-Israeli peace became even more remote.

Aftermath of the Suez Crisis

The years 1956 to 1958 brought Soviet influence in the Middle East and Egypt's influence among the Arab nations to a peak. American efforts to rally Middle Eastern nations against further Soviet moves in the Middle East failed. The Soviet Union then agreed to help build the Aswan Dam and developed close ties with other Middle Eastern nations.

Nasser's influence in the Middle East grew to such an extent that an Egyptian-led Arab unity movement, Pan-Arabism, appeared possible. In 1958, partly to coordinate efforts against Israel, Egypt and Syria merged to form the United Arab Republic. Later that year a military coup toppled the pro-Western monarchy in Iraq, the strongest Arab opponent to Nasser's leadership. This event strengthened Nasser even further.

After 1958, however, Nasser's Pan-Arabism policies achieved no more gains. Syria broke away from the United Arab Republic in 1961. In addition, Israel remained strong, despite its isolation.

International politics now settled into a fragile balance. The Middle East was no longer solidly in the Western camp, but the Soviet Union had no major diplomatic triumphs after the 1950s. Indeed, by the end of 1962, no outside power dominated the Middle East, nor was any power within the Middle East likely to do so. The region seemed destined for instability.

SECTION 3

Closure

Ask students to briefly detail the Arab-Israeli conflict that heightened tensions in the Middle East after the creation of Israel. ***(Arabs opposed Israel's existence, and the two sides fought a war.)***

819

1A, 3B, 5A, 5B, 5C, a1B, a4A, a4B, a4C, a4H, a4I, a4M

Review Answers

1. ***kibbutz:*** collective farm in Israel
2. ***Adnan Menderes:*** Turkish prime minister overthrown and executed by the army; ***Farouk:*** Egyptian ruler overthrown by a military coup; ***Gamal Abdel Nasser:*** Egyptian leader from 1954 to 1970; ***Chaim Weizmann:*** first president of Israel; ***David Ben-Gurion:*** first prime minister of Israel; ***FLN:*** National Liberation Front, an Algerian group that conducted guerrilla warfare for independence; ***Pan-Arabism:*** Arab unity movement sponsored by Nasser
3. ***Aswan Dam:*** dam in southern Egypt on Nile
4. Nasser's government emphasized land reform, expansion of education, industrialization, and increased government control over the economy.
5. Algeria was not just a colony but had been legally absorbed into France. Also, Algeria was home to about one million French citizens.
6. **(a)** The United States and its allies offered to help finance the Aswan Dam project, but the offer was abruptly withdrawn when Nasser displeased the West. Nasser retaliated by nationalizing the Suez Canal. **(b)** In a lightning attack, Israel seized the Gaza Strip and defeated the Egyptians in the Sinai Peninsula. Great Britain and France took the Mediterranean end of the canal. Under pressure from hostile world opinion, the invading nations agreed to a cease-fire.

SECTION 3 REVIEW

1. **Define** kibbutz
2. **Identify** Adnan Menderes, Farouk, Gamal Abdel Nasser, Chaim Weizmann, David Ben-Gurion, FLN, Pan-Arabism
3. **Locate** Aswan Dam
4. **Summarizing Ideas** What changes did Nasser's government bring to Egypt?
5. **Interpreting Ideas** Why was Algerian independence difficult for the French to accept?
6. **Determining Cause and Effect** **(a)** What factors led to the Suez crisis of 1956? **(b)** How was it resolved?

4 Wars, Oil, and Revolution Changed the Middle East

By 1962 most of the countries of the Middle East had achieved independence. The remaining British colonies in the Persian Gulf area gained their independence without conflict in the early 1970s. Great power rivalries in the Middle East continued, however, especially between the Soviet Union and the United States. Yet these rivalries were not as intense as they had been between 1945 and 1962. The major issues during the final decades of the 1900s concerned adjustments within the Middle East itself.

The Arab-Israeli Confrontation

After the breakup of the union between Egypt and Syria in 1961, Nasser became more cautious about Pan-Arabism. Yet Egypt's president did not want to forfeit his country's leadership role in the Arabic-speaking world. He therefore faced a difficult choice when tension rose along Israel's border with Syria and Jordan in late 1966. Nasser could support his Arab neighbors at the risk of war with a militarily strong Israel, or he could hold back at the risk of losing his standing as leader of the Arabic-speaking world. Nasser decided to act.

In May 1967 Nasser demanded the withdrawal of UN troops who had been policing the border between Egypt and Israel since the end of the Suez crisis in 1956. Nasser also announced the closing of the Gulf of Aqaba to block Israel's direct sea route to Africa and Asia (see map, this page).

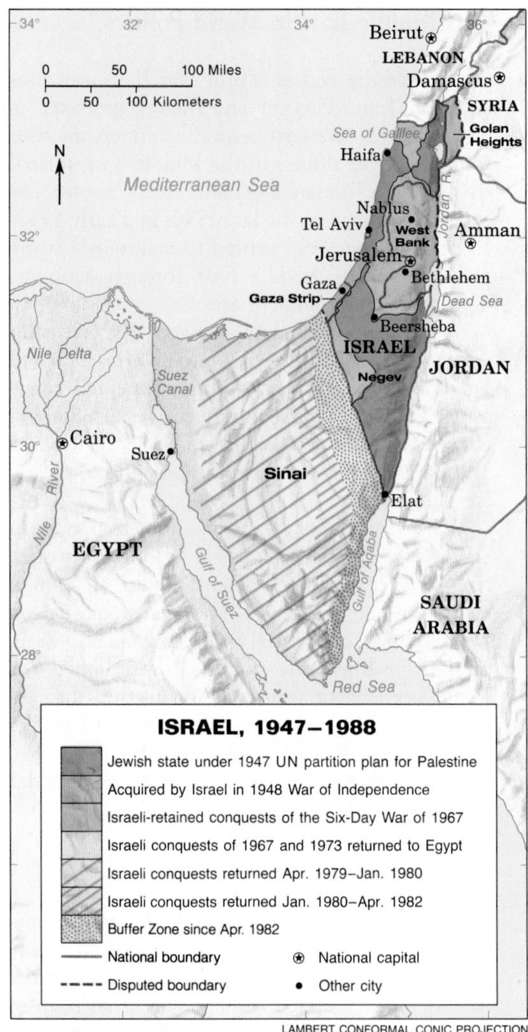

Learning from Maps *Israel has fought many wars to safeguard and expand its borders. What territories did the Israelis win in the Six-Day War?*
Golan Heights, Sinai Peninsula, Gaza Strip, and West Bank

The Six-Day War. Seeing the danger of delay, Israel entered into a lightning war on June 5, 1967. In six days of fighting, Israel captured the Sinai Peninsula and the Gaza Strip from Egypt, seized the Golan Heights from Syria, and took from Jordan the entire west bank of the Jordan River. The so-called "West Bank," part of the original Palestine mandate, had remained in Arab hands after the Arab-Israeli war of 1948. Israel also captured the

STAINED GLASS

Windows in Jerusalem

At the beginning of World War II, almost 16 million Jews lived scattered throughout the world. Then, during the Nazi terrorism that engulfed Europe, as many as 6 million Jews lost their lives. In 1948, when the state of Israel was proclaimed, many Jews went to live there, to join earlier settlers in developing the land.

During the early years when Israel experienced tremendous growth, the Israelis constructed houses, schools, and other facilities for the growing population. One of these was a hospital in the capital, Jerusalem. This brilliantly colored stained-glass window from the hospital's chapel, or synagogue, is called "The Tribe of Joseph." It is one of a series of 12 windows, each devoted to one of Jacob's 12 sons, the founders of the tribes of ancient Israel.

The windows were designed by Marc Chagall, a Russian Jewish artist who fled to France in the 1920s in search of religious and political freedom. There are no figures of human beings in any of these windows because, by Jewish law, images of people are not permitted to appear in synagogues. The artist cleverly used symbols and abstractions of animals, birds, plants, and fish to tell the stories of the Old Testament. An intensely devout man, Chagall conveyed his love for his faith as well as his sense of history in these beautiful windows.

Jordanian section of Jerusalem. Israel then annexed Jerusalem, despite a UN ruling making it an international city.

The Six-Day War, as it came to be called, radically changed Middle Eastern politics. Israel's military superiority over its neighbors was confirmed, but peace remained elusive. The displaced Palestinians no longer expected help from Arab governments to restore them to what had been Palestine. They now relied more on their own guerrilla organization, the Palestine Liberation Organization (PLO) led by Yasir Arafat.

Realizing that they might be drawn into an Arab-Israeli war, the United States and the Soviet Union became interested in arranging a permanent peace settlement in the area. Egypt, Jordan, and Syria wished to regain lost territory. All parties involved had reason to seek a compromise settlement after 1967. However, mutual suspicions and fears doomed many efforts to work out a peace over the next six years.

Egypt Under Sadat

Nasser died in September 1970 and was succeeded by Anwar el-Sadat. Under Sadat's leadership Egypt and Syria secretly planned a war against Israel that began on October 6, 1973. Although the Arabs fought hard, Israeli troops pushed them back and crossed the Suez Canal to occupy Egyptian land. However, the Israelis suffered severe losses during their drive into Egypt.

As had been true after the Six-Day War, all sides had reason to seek a compromise settlement. The United States Secretary of State, Henry Kissinger, began an intensive campaign of **shuttle diplomacy**—moving back and forth from Israel to Egypt to Syria to try to reach an agreement. He eventually achieved two settlements between Israel and Egypt and one between Israel and Syria. Thereafter, the peace initiative ran out of steam. In November 1977, however, Sadat surprised the world. He went to Israel to speak in person to the Israeli Parliament and to Israeli Prime Minister Menachem Begin (BAY • guhn). This was the first time that an Arab leader had visited Israel or even dealt directly with the young nation.

Sadat's action opened a new path of negotiations between Egypt and Israel, which the United States openly supported. Many more months of delicate negotiations were required, aided by the direct intervention of President Jimmy Carter. In September 1978 Carter invited the two leaders to the presidential retreat Camp David, in Maryland. After meetings and negotiations there, Sadat and Begin agreed upon the framework for a peace settlement. The Camp David Accords were followed by a peace treaty that was signed by Israel and Egypt in March 1979.

SECTION 4

Focus/Motivation
Some people believe that if another world war were to start, it would begin in the Middle East. Have students speculate on reasons for this opinion by comparing the Middle East to the Balkans before World War I. *(The major powers of Europe had strong interest in the Balkans, and there was tension among the countries of the area. The Soviet Union and the United States have major interests in the Middle East, and there is great tension between the Israelis and the Arabs.)* Have the students realize that the Soviet Union and the United States are reluctant to send troops to the area because of the danger of war there.

Presentation
Understanding Current Developments (Average/Group)
Ask students to bring in articles from newspapers and news magazines on current events in the Middle East. Use the articles as the basis for a class discussion on the problems that the region is currently facing. Point out that terrorism has constantly plagued the region. Ask: How are foreign governments currently dealing with terrorism?

3B, 5A, 5B, 5D, a1B

● Have students note that the oil-producing countries face the perils of relying on one commodity for the bulk of their prosperity. Ask: What happens when, as in the 1980s, the world price of that commodity declines?

Sadat's actions divided the Arab world. His opponents claimed he had sold out the Palestinians to regain Egyptian territory. His supporters argued that he had started a process that could lead to peace for all, including the Palestinians. Most Israelis supported the peace with Egypt but resisted the idea of a process that might lead to a Palestinian state.

Egypt and Israel had achieved a great breakthrough. Many people doubted, however, whether it would lead to an eventual agreement between the Israelis and the Palestinians—and thus end the Arab-Israeli confrontation. The assassination of Sadat in October 1981 darkened the hopes for peace, and hopes further darkened in 1988 when Egypt's President Hosni Mubarak announced his support for an independent Palestinian state.

Oil and World Energy Needs

The Middle East and the West have dealt with each other over oil since 1901. In that year the shah of Iran (then Persia) granted a concession to a British prospector. Seven years later oil was discovered. Other foreign companies, mainly British and American, later obtained oil concessions from Middle Eastern countries.

With the rising tide of nationalism following World War II, many of the oil-producing countries began to demand more of the profits. Often the companies were willing to grant these demands. In Iran, however, the Anglo-Iranian Oil Company and the government were unable to reach agreement. As a result, the Iranian government nationalized the oil industry. This was a political victory for Iran, but the economic gains it received were less favorable. Because oil glutted the world market, Iran had little economic bargaining power; neither did the other Middle Eastern oil producers.

The Formation of OPEC

Quite rapidly the situation in the oil industry began to change. In 1960 the Latin American nation of Venezuela and the oil-producing nations in the Middle East created the Organization of Petroleum Exporting Countries (OPEC).

As the bargaining agent between the oil companies and oil-consuming industrial nations, OPEC's important advances began in the 1970s. A world oil shortage was by then apparent to everyone.

Learning from Pictures *Throughout the Middle East today, traditional and modern ways exist side by side, as this picture of a camel near an oil rig illustrates.*

During the war with Israel in October 1973, the Arab members of OPEC used their oil as an economic weapon. They drastically cut back production as a means of pressuring Israel and its Western supporters. OPEC's oil embargo caused world oil prices to skyrocket. Although production cutbacks were later eased, it became clear that OPEC had the economic power to fix oil prices.

This power, however, eventually created difficulties as well as benefits for the oil-producing nations of the Middle East. The increases in oil revenues led to rapid and unpredictable social change. Furthermore, the international oil surplus of the 1980s caused many OPEC nations to go into debt. ●

The Iranian Revolution

Throughout the 1960s the Iranian government carried out ambitious modernization programs. These included land distribution to the peasants, a campaign against illiteracy, increased industrialization, and women's liberation. These efforts continued into the 1970s.

822

1A, 5A, a4A, a4B, a4C, a4F, a4G, a4J

● Students might notice that Jordan has no oil or natural gas reserves even though a major petroleum pipeline passes through its territory.

READ
WRITE
● INTERPRET
CONNECT
THINK

BUILDING HISTORY STUDY SKILLS

Interpreting Visuals: Reading a Special-Purpose Map

Historians use many different types of special-purpose maps. A special-purpose map relates data to the geographic setting shown on the map.

How to Read a Special-Purpose Map

To read a special-purpose map, follow these steps.

1. Determine the purpose of the map. Is it designed to give you information on troop movements? resources? land use?
2. Formulate conclusions about the information presented on the map. For example, if the map shows troop movements, can you learn why the troops took the particular routes they did?

Developing the Skill

Study the map of Oil Resources of the Middle East below. The map shows the major oil and natural gas pipelines as well as the major oil and natural gas fields of the countries of the Middle East. The purpose of the map, then, is to show which countries of the Middle East contain major deposits of natural gas and oil. The map also shows how the oil and natural gas are transported to seaports for shipment throughout the world. One conclusion that you can draw from the map is that the Persian Gulf is a vital link in the transport of oil and natural gas throughout the world. Another conclusion you can draw is that P.D.R. Yemen is poorer than its neighbors because it has no oil or natural gas.

Practicing the skill. What other conclusions can you formulate from the information shown on the map of oil resources below? ●

To apply this skill, see Applying History Study Skills on page 829.

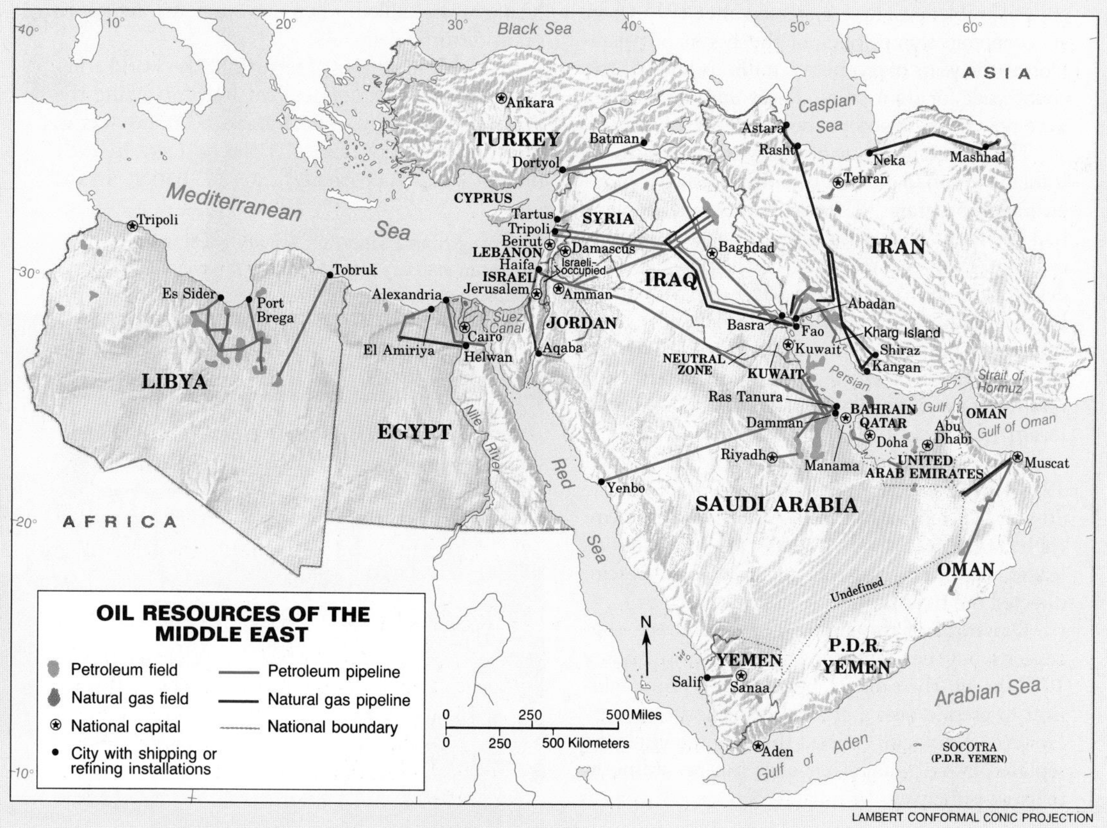

823

3B, 5A, 5B, 5F, a1D

● Point out that terrorism often shocks the world because its victims are usually innocent civilians. Research topic: Other acts of terrorism that have plagued the international community in recent years

SECTION 4

Closure

Ask: What problems continue to plague the Middle East? *(Arab-Israeli confrontation, oil production, revolutions, and terrorism).*

Review Answers

1. ***shuttle diplomacy:*** process in which a negotiator moves back and forth between countries for the purpose of reaching a peace agreement; ***terrorism:*** kidnapping of innocent hostages until ransom demands are met
2. ***PLO:*** Palestinian Liberation Organization; ***Anwar el-Sadat:*** Nasser's successor as president of Egypt: ***Henry Kissinger:*** American secretary of state who tried to negotiate a Middle East peace settlement; ***Menacham Begin:*** former prime minister of Israel; ***Camp David Accords:*** agreement between Sadat and Begin on the framework for a peace settlement; ***Savak:*** Iranian secret police; ***Ayatollah Khomeini:*** religious leader who led the Iranian revolution
3. ***Gulf of Aqaba:*** branch of Red Sea pointing to Israel; ***Qatar:*** peninsula in southern Persian Gulf; ***Bahrain:*** island near Qatar; ***Oman:*** country on eastern Saudi peninsula; ***United Arab Emirates:*** country between Saudi Arabia and Oman; ***Tehran:*** city in northwestern Iran
4. Secretary of State Kissinger used shuttle diplomacy and achieved two settlements—one between Israel and Egypt and

Iran's increasing oil revenues, combined with political changes in surrounding nations, gave Shah Muhammad Reza Pahlavi an opportunity to play a major role in the Middle East. In 1968 Great Britain announced plans to withdraw from the Persian Gulf and to grant independence to Qatar (GUHT • tar), Bahrain, Oman, and the Trucial Sheikdoms (later called the United Arab Emirates). All of these former British colonies were independent nations by 1971. Iran thereafter was the major military power in the Persian Gulf area.

Ties between the shah and the United States were especially close during this period. In addition, since the mid-1960s Iran had enjoyed good relations with the Soviet Union. As a result, the shah's regime appeared strong and stable in the late 1970s. Many Iranians, however, opposed the shah. Some were extremists seeking to establish a Communist state. Others were traditionalists eager to rid the country of Western influences and create a government ruled by religious leaders.

The rapid pace of modernization in Iran had created problems. These increased after 1973 when an economic slump followed the boom oil years. During the years of prosperity, millions had left the countryside for Iran's cities. These uprooted masses were now ready to accept the call for revolution.

The shah failed to win loyalty even from those Iranians who had directly benefited from the modernization programs. Thousands of young Iranians had been sent abroad for higher education at government expense. Yet most of them feared and detested the shah's rule. They felt it was symbolized by the Savak, the hated secret police who were believed responsible for many atrocities. Moreover, the shah tried to keep all power in his hands. As a result, not even his own ministers developed strong loyalty to him.

Riots and mass demonstrations throughout 1978 set the stage for revolution. By this time the 76-year-old religious leader Ayatollah Khomeini (hoh • MAY • nee) had become the revolution's leader. Banished from Iran since 1964, Khomeini directed the fight from exile in France.

Downfall of the shah. The shah made concessions, but they came too late. Finally, in January 1979, he left the country, appointing a prime minister to preside over a gradual transition of power. However, Khomeini insisted that the monarchy be replaced by an Islamic republic, run according to religious principles.

Khomeini returned to Iran in February 1979. Support for the government quickly faded. Leadership within the army was divided, and by mid-February Khomeini's revolution had triumphed. Iranians overwhelmingly voted to establish an Islamic republic, and they elected a president in January 1980. Real power, however, remained with Khomeini.

The hostage crisis. On November 4, 1979, Iranian militants captured the American Embassy in Tehran and seized more than 50 American hostages. The militants were protesting the American decision to let the ailing shah enter the United States for medical treatment. They demanded that the shah be returned to Iran to stand trial. The shah left the United States in December 1979. He died in Egypt in July 1980.

The hostage crisis points out a problem that plagued much of the world in the 1970s and 1980s. Revolutionaries—often frustrated because their demands had not been met—relied on terrorism. **Terrorism** is the kidnapping of innocent people to hold for ransom until demands are met. Often hostages are killed when governments refuse to grant terrorist demands. ●

As with most acts of terrorism, the world community of nations condemned Iran for taking the American hostages. The Iranian economy was in disarray. Even the release of the hostages in 1981 did not ease the problems facing the nation. In the

Learning from Pictures *Iranian militants turned the American embassy compound into a revolutionary headquarters.*

3B, 5A, a1C, a4A, a4F, a4H, a4I

Egypt is an excellent example of the difference between *arithmetic* density and *physiologic* density of population. The arithmetic density in Egypt is only about 126 persons per square mile.

meantime, Iraq had launched an attack against Iran in September 1980 because of a dispute involving a waterway that divides the two countries. The Iran-Iraq War raged until 1988, with both sides suffering heavy casualties.

SECTION 4 REVIEW

1. **Define** shuttle diplomacy, terrorism
2. **Identify** PLO, Anwar el-Sadat, Henry Kissinger, Menachem Begin, Camp David Accords, Savak, Ayatollah Khomeini
3. **Locate** Gulf of Aqaba, Qatar, Bahrain, Oman, United Arab Emirates, Tehran
4. **Summarizing Ideas** Describe the efforts to attain peace in the Middle East after the Arab-Israeli war of October 1973.
5. **Analyzing Ideas** **(a)** How has OPEC demonstrated its power in world affairs? **(b)** Has it succeeded? Explain.
6. **Interpreting Ideas** **(a)** What factors led to the Iranian revolution of 1979? **(b)** Why did Iranian militants seize American hostages in 1979?

5 A Struggle Between Old and New Ways Plagued the Middle East

After 1945 the Middle East changed rapidly. The political and economic transformation of the region brought about great social change as well, resulting in a clash between old and new that still continues.

People and Politics

The Middle East is a vast territory, twice the size of the United States. In the 1980s nearly 270 million people lived in the region, and more than 90 percent were Muslims. Population densities varied widely. Saudi Arabia, for example, more than three times the size of Texas, had only 12 million inhabitants, or only 13.9 persons per square mile. Egypt's Nile Valley, by contrast, averaged almost 3,000 persons per square mile. (A square mile equals 2.59 square kilometers.)

The countries of the Middle East vary in size and importance. Qatar, the size of Delaware, had only about 370,000 inhabitants in 1986. Turkey, somewhat larger than Texas, had about 50 million inhabitants. In fact, just two countries, Egypt and Turkey, contained one-third of the total population of the entire Middle East.

It was not just the size of their populations that made some of the Middle Eastern countries important. The four Persian Gulf states of Kuwait, Qatar, Bahrain, and the United Arab Emirates, for example, contained less than one percent of the Middle East's population. However, they possessed enormous oil wealth and thus had considerable influence.

For centuries, three major languages—Arabic, Persian, and Turkish—have been used throughout the region. With the creation of the state of Israel, Hebrew also has become an important language in the Middle East.

Until modern times the Middle East was not so politically divided. The Ottoman Empire, which lasted until after World War I, controlled most of the Middle East for some 400 years. Only Morocco in the west and Iran in the east escaped Ottoman rule.

The political breakup of the region into separate countries began with Western imperialism. The Middle East, as you have read, was colonized by four different European powers. Great Britain and France divided up most of the area between

Learning from Pictures *Iran's mining of the Persian Gulf and its attacks on neutral shipping forced the United States Navy to escort ships out of the gulf.*

another between Israel and Syria.
5. (a) During the war with Israel in October 1973, the Arab members of OPEC cut back oil production as a means of pressuring Israel and its Western supporters. **(b)** Their oil embargo caused world oil prices to skyrocket. It became clear OPEC had the economic power to fix oil prices.
6. (a) Opposition to the shah came from a number of different groups. The rapid pace of modernization had caused economic problems and political unrest. **(b)** to protest the admission of the shah into the United States for medical treatment

SECTION 5

Focus/Motivation
Have students study pictures in this chapter. Based on what they see in these pictures, ask students to give examples of the mixture of traditional and modern life in the Middle East today. What evidence is there of modernization? *(make a list of items on the chalkboard or an overhead projector)* of the region's strong links with the past? What generalizations about the Middle East can students make based on these pictures? *(Accept all reasonable answers. Students might say that the apartment buildings and various other "modern" conveniences are indications of new wealth and Westernization, while bazaar workers and*

farm laborers carry out ancient occupations.) Discuss why women in revolutionary Iran wear the chador, or veil, a traditional garment of Muslim women. You might also lead the discussion to the particular restrictions on life in certain "hot spots"—i.e., Beirut, Israeli border areas, Afghanistan, Armenia, or other regions where there are armed conflicts or terrorist activities.

Presentation
Seeing Relationships (Average/Group)
Discuss with students the conflict between old values and new traditions that modernization has brought to the Middle East. Ask: Are such conflicts found in the United States? *(Students might suggest that some people oppose rapid modernization but that most favor it.)* Ask students to list advantages and disadvantages of rapid modernization.

SECTION 5

Closure
Ask students to state how Islamic fundamentalism has affected Iran. *(Religious leaders head the government, which is based on strict Islamic principles.)*

Review Answers
1. ***gross national product:*** dollar value of all new, final products produced in a nation each year; ***GNP:*** an abbreviation of gross national product

them. Italy ruled Libya, and Spain controlled part of Morocco. Turkey, Iran, and most of the Arabian Peninsula were never directly colonized. However, they were subjected to persistent economic and military pressures from Europe.

After World War II, there were a number of attempts to create a new political unity in the Middle East. The creation of the Arab League in 1945 was the most important. Egypt, Saudi Arabia, Yemen, Syria, Lebanon, Trans-Jordan, and Iraq formed the league to promote economic and cultural ties among the member nations. Fourteen other Arab nations joined the league after 1945. Nevertheless, in the 1980s the Arab nations remained politically divided, especially on foreign policy.

Unequal Distribution of Resources

Great differences also exist in the distribution of natural resources in the region. As you have read, most of the oil-rich Middle Eastern countries are thinly populated. Only Iran, Iraq, and Algeria have both large populations and large oil resources. By contrast, heavily populated areas such as Turkey, Egypt, Sudan, and Morocco have little oil.

Egypt's great agricultural wealth does not meet the needs of its enormous population. Sudan cannot exploit its agricultural potential because of limited transportation facilities. Other countries, such as Morocco, have a good mix of agricultural and mineral resources. For the entire Middle East, however, only oil is a source of imposing wealth.

Thus, the unequal distribution of natural resources and of population produces difficult economic conditions. The national wealth (what economists call the **gross national product,** or **GNP,** and define as the dollar value of all new, final products produced in a nation each year) in Kuwait, Qatar, and the United Arab Emirates is almost as high as that of the United States. In 1986 the GNP in the United States was more than $16,500 per person per year. In those three tiny Persian Gulf states, the average GNP per person was $16,450. At the other end of the scale, the GNP per person was less than $1,000 in Egypt, Sudan, and Yemen.

Cities and Population Growth

Cities have existed in the Middle East since the dawn of history. Damascus is believed to be the world's oldest continuously occupied city. In 1945 the Middle East already had a significant proportion of its population living in cities. The increase since then has been dramatic.

The population of Cairo, Egypt, was less than 2 million in 1945. It was at least 7 million in 1985. Tehran, the capital of Iran, expanded tenfold in the same period, from 500,000 to 5 million. Baghdad, in Iraq, with a population in 1945 of about 440,000, had more than 3 million inhabitants 40 years later.

In the 1980s nearly half of Lebanon's total population lived in the capital city of Beirut. Israel, often thought of as a land of agricultural pioneers, had a population that was 90 percent urban.

Traditional Middle Eastern cities had narrow, winding streets, bazaars—market streets with rows of tiny shops—and city walls with handsome gates. Although much of this older style has remained, urban growth in recent years has taken the form of high-rise buildings and wide streets.

Before modern times most city dwellers lived in one- or two-story houses hidden behind windowless walls. The few outside windows were heavily shuttered with ornate patterns of metal or wood. Rooms of such city homes opened onto an interior patio. All this assured greater family privacy. In the 1980s more and more people lived in apartment buildings. Also, as industrialization intensified, increasing numbers of people worked in factories and offices.

Much of the growth of Middle Eastern cities was due to migration from the countryside. Much also stemmed from high population growth rates. The population increase was caused both by declining death rates and high birth rates, and the result was a very young population. For example, about one half of Iran's population in 1985 was under the age of 15, while two-thirds was under the age of 30.

Education and Women's Status

The large percentage of young people in the population increased the need for schools and teachers. Middle Eastern countries made great progress in education after 1945. At that time probably fewer than 15 percent of the primary-school-age children were actually in school. In 1980, despite the vast population increase, the average was closer to 65 percent. Several countries, such as Israel, Lebanon, and Tunisia, had almost all primary-school-age children in school.

One of the most visible women in the Middle East has been Anwar el-Sadat's widow, Jehan Raouf Sadat, who has worked extensively to expand the role of women in the Middle East.

Learning from Pictures *While many women in the Middle East wear traditional clothing, others, as in this scene in Kuwait, have adopted Western style clothing.*

The years since 1945 also brought significant expansion in secondary and higher education. Turkey, for example, had more than 240,000 students in colleges and universities in the 1980s. The figure for Egypt was more than 500,000.

The students spent their time on subjects similar to those studied in the West. Many of them trained to become government officials. With the coming of industrialization, there was also a growing need for people with technical skills. Many became mechanics, electricians, and business managers.

Women, too, achieved gains. Only a fraction of the female population received schooling before 1945. After that time the percentage of females in school increased even more rapidly than that of males. Each year more women finished school and took jobs in factories, offices, and in such professions as medicine. A few women entered politics. In general, Middle Eastern societies continued to be male dominated, but improvements in women's status after 1945 were striking.

Religious Nationalism

Many Muslims in the Middle East reacted to the rapid changes by turning to Islamic fundamentalism. This was an attempt to revive the stability and values of the past and was a form of religious nationalism. It was a way for Muslim nations to reject Western influences.

Followers of Islamic fundamentalism differed on leadership and policy, but they agreed in rejecting foreign influences. They wanted to return to traditional Muslim ways. They wished to create religious nations that would apply Islamic law strictly. They opposed such modern trends as women's emancipation.

Ayatollah Khomeini, leader of the Iranian revolution against the shah, was the best-known spokesman of Islamic fundamentalism until his death in 1989. Colonel Muammar al-Qaddafi (kah • DAH • fee), who overthrew the Libyan monarchy in 1969, claimed as well to represent traditional Islamic political values. The religious conservatives of Saudi Arabia were also Muslim fundamentalists, but they opposed both Khomeini and Qaddafi. In the 1970s and 1980s, Muslim and Christian factions in Lebanon engaged in bloody guerrilla warfare. The Lebanese civil war killed thousands of people and destroyed the nation's economy.

Many young people in these countries disliked traditional ways. They rejected outside political influence, but they sought education and were eager to modernize their societies. There was often tension between them and the religious nationalists.

Thus, after 1945 the nations of the Middle East became more industrialized, more urbanized, and better educated. However, the struggle between continuity and change, between old and new, seemed destined to continue.

SECTION 5 REVIEW

1. **Define** gross national product, GNP
2. **Identify** Arab League, bazaars, Muammar al-Qaddafi
3. **Locate** Kuwait, Yemen, Lebanon, Damascus
4. **Summarizing Ideas** **(a)** What changes in education were made in the Middle East after 1945? **(b)** What gains did women in the Middle East achieve?
5. **Determining Cause and Effect** **(a)** Define Islamic fundamentalism. **(b)** Give two examples in the Middle East. **(c)** How has fundamentalism affected relations with the West?

2. ***Arab League:*** loose union of Arab states created in 1945 to promote economic and cultural ties among member nations; ***bazaars:*** market streets with rows of tiny shops; ***Muammar al-Qaddafi:*** army officer who overthrew the Libyan monarchy in 1969
3. ***Kuwait:*** country at western end of Persian Gulf; ***Yemen:*** country on southern tip of Saudi peninsula; ***Lebanon:*** country north of Israel; ***Damascus:*** capital of Syria
4. **(a)** After 1945 average school attendance in primary schools increased dramatically. There was also a significant expansion in secondary and higher education. **(b)** The percentage of females in school after 1945 increased even more rapidly than that of males. Each year more women finished school and took jobs in factories, offices, and professions. A few women entered politics.
5. **(a)** Islamic fundamentalism is an attempt to revive the stability and values of the past and is a form of religious nationalism.
(b) Iran and Libya; **(c)** For the most part, Islamic fundamentalism has caused strains in relations between the West and some Arab nations.

827

Reviewing Important Terms
1. apartheid; **2.** ujamaa; **3.** desertification; **4.** kibbutz; **5.** shuttle diplomacy

Developing Critical Thinking Skills
1. (a) Zimbabwe; **(b)** Ghana; **(c)** Israel; **(d)** Egypt; **(e)** Libya; **(f)** Kenya; **(g)** Egypt; **(h)** Iran; **(i)** Guinea; **(j)** Israel; **(k)** Nigeria.
2. (a) Earlier African leaders formed an elite group, did not seek broad popular support, and believed independence should be gradual. The new generation of nationalists appealed to the entire population and demanded immediate independence. **(b)** Nkrumah led the first political party in Africa to have large popular support. **(c)** Kenyatta's popular leadership helped overcome ethnic rivalries. He served as independent Kenya's first president. **(d)** Mugabe led a guerrilla war against the white-dominated government of Rhodesia.
3. (a) Colonies under the control of France and Great Britain achieved independence with relatively little opposition. **(b)** Belgium gave up the Congo only after rioting broke out. Angola and Mozambique, under Portuguese control, suffered lengthy wars of liberation. **(c)** Neither Great Britain nor France had the economic strength or political backing to maintain its world empire. Belgium was reluctant to grant independence to the Congo because of the colony's great wealth. In the Portuguese colonies, the liberation armies were unable to dislodge colonial forces from the major urban centers.

1B, 3B, 4E, 5A, 5B, a1B, a1C, a4A, a4D, a4E, a4F, a4G, a4H, a4I, a4J, a4K, a4L, a4M

Reteaching
Have students review the Chapter Summary and the appropriate section and questions in the Unit Synthesis. Discuss the concepts until students demonstrate a clear understanding of the material.

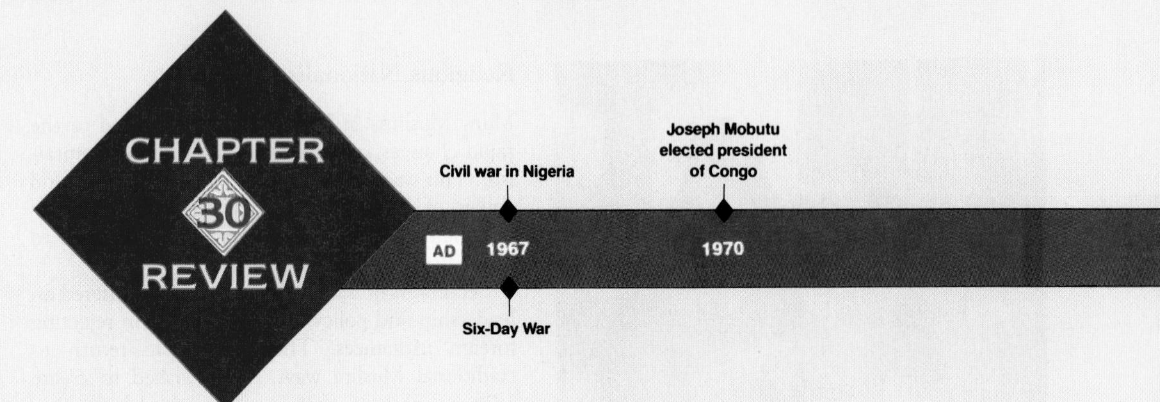

Chapter Summary

The following list contains the key concepts you have learned about Africa and the Middle East since 1945.

1. Independence came rapidly to the African nations after World War II. Most African nations achieved independence peacefully, but a few resorted to violence.
2. Only South Africa resisted any efforts to give the black majority of the population a real voice in their own government. There, the Afrikaans government instituted the apartheid system that separated the races.
3. Africa's new nations faced a number of difficulties. There was often hostility among the groups within a country. This led to a bitter civil war in Nigeria. In Angola the superpowers intervened, as they did in the conflict between Ethiopia and Somalia in the Horn of Africa.
4. Africans also faced economic difficulties and, in the early years of independence, a sense of inferiority about their culture.
5. African cultural achievements gradually gained wide recognition and admiration.
6. Many nations in the Middle East also gained independence after 1945. In addition, nations that were already officially independent were able to reduce foreign influences.
7. A revolution in Iran resulted in the overthrow of the shah and the establishment of an Islamic republic.
8. A continuing problem in the Middle East was the relationship between Israel and its Arab neighbors. Four Arab-Israeli wars were fought between 1948 and 1973. An offer of peace by Egypt led to the signing of a peace treaty in 1979, but the other Arab nations rejected the pact.
9. The nations of the Middle East vary enormously in size, population, and wealth. A number of them gained considerable power as a result of the rise in oil prices in the 1970s.
10. The rapid changes of the period after World War II led to upheaval and a revival of Islamic fundamentalism. The region faced continuing uncertainties and tension in the 1980s.

On a separate sheet of paper, complete the following review exercises.

Reviewing Important Terms

Supply the term that correctly completes each statement

1. The South African policy based on the principle of racial separation became known as ________ , the Afrikaans word for apartness.
2. The Tanzanian local, cooperative villages are known as ________ .
3. Unwise land use patterns have led to ________ , or the spread of the desert in Africa.
4. A collective farm in Israel is known as a ________ .
5. In the 1970s Secretary of State Henry Kissinger began an intensive campaign of ________ ________ , in which he moved back and forth from Israel to Egypt to Syria to try to reach a peace agreement.

Developing Critical Thinking Skills

1. **Classifying Ideas** Name the country of each of the following political and cultural leaders: **(a)** Robert Mugabe, **(b)** Kwame Nkrumah, **(c)** Chaim Weizmann, **(d)** Anwar el-Sadat, **(e)** Muammar al-Qaddafi, **(f)** Jomo Kenyatta, **(g)** Gamal Abdel Nasser, **(h)** Ayatollah Khomeini, **(i)** Sékou Touré, **(j)** Menachem Begin, **(k)** Nnamdi Azikiwe.
2. **Comparing Ideas** **(a)** How did nationalists after 1945 differ from earlier African leaders? How did each of the following contribute to the rise of nationalism in Africa: **(b)** Kwame Nkrumah; **(c)** Jomo Kenyatta; **(d)** Robert Mugabe.
3. **Analyzing Ideas** **(a)** Which African nations achieved independence with relatively little opposition? **(b)** Which did not? **(c)** What reasons might account for these different experiences?
4. **Interpreting Ideas** How did economic problems and ethnic rivalries threaten the stability of many newly independent African nations?
5. **Determining Cause and Effect** **(a)** What were the causes of the Arab-Israeli war of 1948–1949? **(b)** What were the results?
6. **Listing Ideas** What changes occurred in the nations of the Middle East in the years after 1945?
7. **Analyzing a Primary Source** Reread the poem by Patrice Lumumba on page 810. **(a)** What did

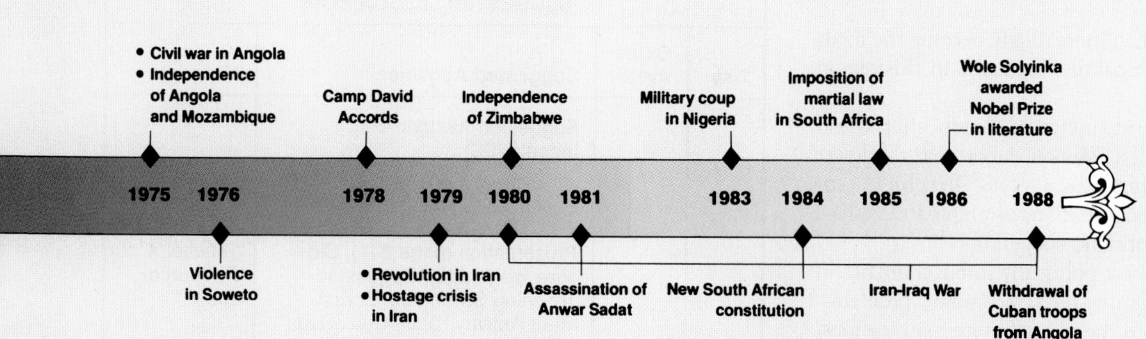

Lumumba mean by the phrase "the dawn is here"? **(b)** To what "evil, cruel times" was he referring? **(c)** Why might this poem appeal to an emerging sense of African nationalism?

Relating Geography to History

Study the map on page 823. **(a)** What nation or nations of the Middle East have no oil or natural gas reserves? **(b)** What problems might the lack of oil and natural gas reserves have for that nation or nations?

Relating Past to Present

1. In the 1980s the situation in the Middle East remained unsettled. In some cases, affairs changed on almost a weekly basis. Using the *Readers' Guide to Periodical Literature,* locate recent articles on events in one of the following nations: Egypt, Israel, Saudi Arabia, Iran, Iraq, Syria, Jordan, or Lebanon. **(a)** How have conditions in this country changed since the printing of this book? **(b)** How have the United States and the Soviet Union responded to these changing conditions in the Middle East?
2. Examine the pictures of African art on pages 296, 300, 301, and 302. Then find examples of present African art in sources such as *National Geographic* or general histories of Africa. Based on evidence in these pictures, support or challenge the following statement: "Modern African art reflects a pride in the cultural achievements of earlier African civilizations."

Applying History Study Skills

Before completing this activity, review Building History Study Skills on page 823.

Study the map entitled "The World: Land Use and Economic Activity" on page R8–R9 and answer the following questions.

1. In what countries outside the Middle East is drilling for oil a major economic activity?
2. How is most of the land on Madagascar used?

Investigating Further

1. **Writing a Report** Prepare a report on the policy of apartheid practiced in the Republic of South Africa. You may consult the *Readers' Guide to Periodical Literature* for articles on this topic. Include in your report answers to the following questions: **(a)** What is the origin and racial makeup of the population in the Republic of South Africa? **(b)** How does the government defend apartheid? **(c)** By what means does the government enforce apartheid? **(d)** How do other African nations react to this racial policy? **(e)** How does the rest of the world react?
2. **Preparing an Oral Report** The novels of Chinua Achebe give Westerners a glimpse into Nigerian society and a changing Africa. Read one of these novels and prepare an oral report on the effects of modernization and the struggle to save or adapt old ways. Possible titles include *Man of the People* (Doubleday), *No Longer at Ease* (Fawcett), and *Things Fall Apart* (Fawcett).
3. **Preparing a Panel Discussion** Prepare a report on the capture of the American Embassy in Tehran and the seizure of more than 50 American hostages by Iranian militants on November 4, 1979. In your report describe the effects of the incident on the Iranians, the hostages, the United States, and the world. Conclude your report by stating the terms of the hostages' release.
4. **Dramatizing History** In recent years the Organization of Petroleum Exporting Countries (OPEC) has become increasingly prominent in world affairs. Work with several of your classmates to find out how OPEC conducts its meetings. Then conduct a mock OPEC meeting in which the ministers discuss how to raise the price of oil and how to enforce their decisions.
5. **Conducting a Debate** Work with several classmates to prepare a debate on the following topic to present to the class:
Resolved: The world community of nations should agree never to meet any terrorist demands.
As you prepare your debate, you might find it useful to research some of the terrorist kidnappings that have taken place in the world in recent years. Possible choices include kidnappings in Lebanon in the late 1980s.

4. In Nigeria ethnic rivalries led to a civil war between Biafra and Nigeria. Economic problems plagued the new African nations because many of them depended on a single crop or mineral resource that was subject to price swings on the world market.
5. (a) Palestinian Arabs were angered by the establishment of a Jewish nation on land they claimed. **(b)** Israel won more territory than it had been allotted in the partition plan.
6. Oil riches brought an improvement in living standards to some people in the Middle East. Many nations experienced rapid urban growth. Educational opportunities were expanded. The status of women greatly improved.
7. (a) Independence had come to the Congo. **(b)** the period of Belgian rule; **(c)** Answers will vary.

Relating Geography to History

(a) P.D.R. Yemen; **(b)** It would not be as wealthy.

Relating Past to Present

1. Answers will vary.
2. Answers will vary.

Applying History Study Skills

1. Canada, the United States, Mexico, Venezuela, Brazil, Argentina, Nigeria, Indonesia, Australia, Great Britain, Netherlands, Romania, Soviet Union, Pakistan, China; **2.** grazing

CHAPTER (pages 830–849)

31 Latin America Became the Focus of World Attention

(1945 TO THE PRESENT)

CHAPTER OVERVIEW

In recent decades Latin America had increasingly become the focus of world attention. However, political developments in this region after World War II were turbulent.

The population of Latin America increased rapidly after World War II, and cities grew dramatically. Women, labor, and the lower class in the cities became important political forces. To achieve economic development, Latin American nations attempted to reduce imports and took steps toward economic cooperation.

Mexico remained one of the most politically stable countries in Latin America, although the country faced economic problems. Many Mexicans had illegally fled to the United States seeking jobs, greatly straining U.S.-Mexican relations.

Revolution in Nicaragua in 1979 brought a Marxist regime to power. However, peace in that country, as well as in many Central American countires, remained elusive. Political and economic problems continued to plague the region.

After a revolution in Cuba, Castro set up a Communist government. In 1962 Soviet aid to Cuba led to a tense confrontation between the United States and the Soviet Union. Castro also attempted to export revolution to other Caribbean nations who continued to experience political, economic, and social unrest.

Many of the countries of South America faced economic problems which contributed to the instability of their governments. Other dilemmas confronting these nations included civilian and military dictatorships, revolutions, and the newest, and most insidious of all dilemmas, the drug trade.

SUGGESTED LESSON PLAN

Day	Objectives	Suggested Activities	Materials
1	U9* C1–3	Introducing the Chapter (pages 830–31) Section 1 (pages 831–36), Focus/Motivation (page 831), Presentation (page 832), Closure (page 835), Suggested Teaching Strategies, Enrichment Activity, Daily Quiz, Suggested Assignments (page 829B)	ATE, Pupil's Edition, Teacher's Resource-Bank™
2	U9, C4	Section 2 (pages 836–40), Focus/Motivation (page 836), Presentation (page 837), Closure (page 839), Suggested Teaching Strategies, Enrichment Activity, Daily Quiz,	ATE, Pupil's Edition, Teacher's Resource-Bank™
		Suggested Assignments (page 829C)	
3	U9, C5–6	Section 3 (pages 841–43), Focus/Motivation (page 841), Presentation (page 841), Closure (page 842), Suggested Teaching Strategies, Enrichment Activity, Daily Quiz, Suggested Assignments (page 829C)	ATE, Pupil's Edition, Teacher's Resource-Bank™
4	U9, C7	Section 4 (pages 844–47), Focus/Motivation (page 844), Presentation (page 844), Closure (page 846), Suggested Teaching Strategies, Enrichment Activity, Daily Quiz, Suggested Assignments (page 829D)	ATE, Pupil's Edition, Teacher's Resource-Bank™
5	U9 C1–7	Chapter 31 Form A Test, Reteaching Worksheet, Chapter 31 Form B Test	Teacher's Resource-Bank™ or Workbook and Test Booklet

*C refers to applicable Chapter Objective, U refers to applicable Unit Goal.

BOOKS FOR THE TEACHER

Abbott, Elizabeth. *Haiti: The Duvaliers and Their Legacy.* McGraw-Hill. Provides inside account of Haiti under the Duvaliers.

Cheney, Glenn Alan. *El Salvador: Country in Crisis.* Franklin Watts. Gives up-to-the minute account of the struggle for power in El Salvador.

Fraser, N., and M. Navarro. *Eva Perón.* Norton. Presents thoroughly researched account of this influential woman.

Gleijeses, Piero. *The Dominican Crisis.* The Johns Hopkins University Press. Gives account of constitutionalists' revolt and U.S. intervention.

MacEoin, Gary. *Revolution Next Door: Latin America in the 1970's.* Holt, Rinehart and Winston. Gives perceptive observations of conditions in Latin America.

BOOKS FOR THE STUDENT

Cook, Fred J. *The Cuban Missile Crisis.* Franklin Watts. Presents an interesting and informative account of the crisis.

Golston, Robert. *The Cuban Revolution.* Bobbs-Merrill. Covers the revolution from the Batista regime to the missile crisis.

O'Shaughnessy, Hugh. *Grenada.* Dodd, Mead & Company. Gives an eyewitness account of the U.S. invasion and the Caribbean history that provoked it.

Rosset, Peter, and John Vandermeer. *Nicaragua: Unfinished Revolution.* Grove Press, Inc. Includes policy statements, articles, and eyewitness accounts of the crisis in Nicaragua.

MULTIMEDIA MATERIALS

Central America: Finding New Ways (mp, 16 min.), Encyclopedia Britannica Educational Corp. Shows the six countries of Central America as a struggling culture steeped in a tradition of extreme poverty.

Cuba and Fidel (mp, 24 min.), Churchill. Depicts the changes in Cuba since Castro's assumption of power.

Cuba: Refugees and the Economy (mp, 25 min.), Gilbert Altschul Prod., Inc. Explores economic and political structure of Cuba, focusing on those who chose to leave.

Latin American Overview (mp, 25 min.), Contemporary Films. Emphasizes U.S. involvement in and problems faced by present Latin American governments.

So That Men Are Free (mp, 27 min.), McGraw-Hill. Shows how the Viconsinos Indians of Peru, with aid from Cornell University, gradually gave up serfdom to become free, capable people.

South America Today (mp, 24 min.), International Films Foundation, Inc. Surveys the political, economic, social, and religious status of the countries of South America.

Section (pages 831–836)

1 Political Conflicts Shook Many Latin American Nations

SECTION OVERVIEW

Following World War II, the countries of Latin America experienced many changes. Among these changes were a rapid growth in the population, the discovery of petroleum products and other resources, and rapid industrialization. All of these factors made Latin America a focus of world attention. However, many of these changes also led to social and political unrest as well as severe economic problems.

SUGGESTED TEACHING STRATEGIES

1. **Preteaching Vocabulary (Basic)** You may wish to preteach the following important vocabulary terms: multinational corporation, import substitution *(page 833)*. Ask students to name any multinational corporations and their chief products. *(Stuents responses may include any of the major oil companies and their products.)*
2. **Classifying Information (Average/Group)** Have each class member write on a sheet of paper what he or she considers the five most important problems facing the countries of Latin America today. Call upon students to read their lists to the class, and then write their responses on the chalkboard or on an overhead projector. When all students have responded, select the five problems most often mentioned and use them as a basis for discussion. The discussion should center on the extent of the problem, solutions that have been tried, and alternatives that students might suggest.

*3. **Making Connections With History: Linking Economics to History (Average/Group)** Have students read an economic fact sheet on any one Latin American nation, and link this economic information to the history of the country.

ENRICHMENT ACTIVITY

Map Project (Average/Group) A group of students can work together to prepare a large illustrated map of Latin America. Students should label each country and develop symbols to show population, natural resources, and industries of each. After the map has been completed, you might use it as a vehicle for class discussion, using the following questions: What are some of the natural resources of Latin America? What are Latin America's major industries? Where are the concentrations of population?

DAILY QUIZ

To assess student understanding of Section 1, give the class the following quiz. (Each item is worth 10 points.)

1. What has been the most important change in Latin America since World War II? *(population growth)*
2. Name one reason for the decline in the death rate in Latin America. *(improved public health measures, improved medical care)*
3. In what area did the population grow the most quickly? suburbs — city — countryside *(city)*
4. (T or F) Immediately after World War II, most Latin American countries permitted almost everyone to vote. *(F)*
5. Name one new group in the electorate that has influenced elections since the 1950s. *(city dwellers, women, laborers)*
6. More than 90 percent of all Latin Americans are of what religion? *(Catholic)*
7. From whom did the Latin American countries hope to receive investment capital to help their economies? *(foreign corporations and manufacturers)*
8. (T or F) Import substitution worked fairly well in all Latin America, especially the larger countries. *(T)*
9. (T or F) Consumer goods like refrigerators and washing machines have suddenly become available to all classes of people in Latin America who can now afford them. *(F)*
10. The Latin American countries generally would place themselves with US — USSR — African and Asian nations — in international relations. *(African and Asian nations)*

SUGGESTED ASSIGNMENTS

1. **Skill Worksheet (Basic)** Have students complete skill worksheet 31 in the TEACHER'S RESOURCEBANK™.
2. **Summarizing Current Events (Basic)** Have each student read a current newspaper article on Latin America. Students are to summarize the article on a sheet of paper, and attach the article to the summary. Call upon students to read their summaries to the class. The articles should serve as the basis for discussion of current events in Latin America.
3. **Research Reports (Challenging)** Have interested students choose a Latin American country and conduct research on its economy. They should research the nation's GNP, per capita income, industrial growth rate, population growth rate, major exports, balance of trade, and major occupations. If possible, students should list the number of cars, phones, radios, and televisions per person in that nation. The students should present the information in the form of a written report.

Section (pages 836–840)

2 Mexico and Central America Set a Different Political Course

SECTION OVERVIEW

Political and economic instability, as well as revolution, have rocked Mexico and the countries of Central America for much of the twentieth century. This region, a commercial and military crossroads for the Western Hemisphere, is of strategic importance to the United States, particularly since the Panama Canal is located there. As a result, the history of these countries has included a series of interventions by the United States. The nations of the Caribbean Basin continue to seek peace and stability but these goals continue to elude them.

SUGGESTED TEACHING STRATEGIES

1. **Preteaching Vocabulary (Basic)** You may wish to preteach the following important vocabulary terms: geopolitical region *(page 836)*; campesino, covert *(page 839)*. Ask the students why nations become involved in covert activities.
2. **Group Discussion (Average/Group)** Divide the class into groups of five. Have each group prepare a list of five suggestions for improving relations between the United States and Nicaragua. Reassemble the class and have students select the five most practical suggestions. Have them discuss possible means by which these suggestions might be carried out.

ENRICHMENT ACTIVITY

Panel Discussion (Challenging) Have an interested group of students present a panel discussion on the question of U.S. aid to the Contra rebels in Nicaragua. One half of the group should present supporting arguments, and the other half should present opposing arguments. Students will need to do further reading before preparing their arguments. Sources include Robert S. Leiken and Barry Rubin's *The Central American Crisis* (Summit Books) and Peter Davis's *Where is Nicaragua?* (Simon and Schuster). They should also consult the *Readers' Guide to Periodical Literature.*

DAILY QUIZ

To assess student understanding of Section 2, give the class the following quiz. (Each item is worth 10 points.)

1. (T or F) The Sandinistas gained control in Nicaragua by promising a mixed economy, nonaligned foreign policy, and pluralism. *(T)*
2. (T or F) According to the immigration law passed by the U.S. Congress in 1986, anyone who hires an illegal alien is subject to a fine of from $10 to $100 for each alien. *(F)*
3. In 1983 President Reagan sent marines to the island of ______ to overthrow a Communist regime. *(Grenada)*
4. The only Latin America country that refused to break relations with Cuba in the 1960s was ______. *(Mexico)*
5. The guerrilla group opposed to the Sandinistas in Nicaragua was called the ______. *(Contras)*
6. The president of Costa Rica who presented a peace proposal in 1987 was ______ ______. *(Oscar Arias)*
7. (T ot F) In the treaty negotiated by the U.S. and Panama, the Panama Canal is to be turned over to Panama by 2000. *(T)*
8. Violence in the country of ______ ______ led to the murder of Archbishop Oscar Romero. *(El Salvador)*
9. (T or F) The campesinos shared in the prosperity in Central America following World War II. *(F)*
10. (T or F) An earthquake in Mexico City in 1985 further strained Mexico's already sagging economy. *(T)*

SUGGESTED ASSIGNMENTS

1. **Preparing an Oral Report (Challenging)** Students might research and prepare an oral report profiling events of the last three decades in Mexico. One source is Charles C. Cumberland's *Mexico: The Struggle for Modernity* (Oxford University Press). Students might also consult the *Readers' Guide to Periodical Literature* to find articles on recent developments in Mexico. Have students present their reports to the class.
2. **Profile Worksheet (Basic)** Have students do Profile Worksheet 31 in the TEACHER'S RESOURCEBANK™.

Section (pages 841–843)

3 Revolution Shook the Islands of the Caribbean

SECTION OVERVIEW

The Cuban revolution of 1959, which brought a Communist government to power only 90 miles from the U.S. shore, has caused continual tension between the United States and Cuba over the past three decades. The Bay of Pigs invasion and the Cuban missile crisis were two of the most serious clashes between the Castro government and the United States.

Seeing the Communist regime in Cuba as a threat to its security, the United States has felt the need to intervene in the affairs of other Caribbean nations. For example, U.S. marines were sent to the Dominican Republic in 1965 to stop a Communist takeover.

SUGGESTED TEACHING STRATEGIES

1. **Preteaching Vocabulary (Basic)** You may wish to preteach the following important vocabulary term: dissident *(page 842)*. Ask students to name another country which has not, until recently, allowed its dissidents to emigrate. *(Students should name the Soviet Union.)*
2. **Making an Outline (Basic)** To better understand the chronological order of events in this section, have students make an outline in their notebooks showing the most important events in recent Caribbean history.

ENRICHMENT ACTIVITY

Book Report (Average/Group) A number of books have been written on the Bay of Pigs invasion. Divide the class into groups to read the book below. Each group might meet on designated days to discuss the book. When the reading has been completed, have each group present a report. The suggested book is Peter Wyden's *Bay of Pigs: The Untold Story* (Simon and Schuster).

DAILY QUIZ

To assess student understanding of Section 3, give the class the following quiz. (Each item is worth 10 points.)

1. Revolutionary leader who was killed leading a guerrilla band in the mountains of Bolivia. *(Ché Guevara)*
2. President Johnson sent 400 marines to the _______ _______ in 1965 to stop a Communist takeover. *(Dominican Republic)*
3. The Caribbean island of _______ _______ is a commonwealth of the United States. *(Puerto Rico)*
4. (T or F) The harsh military rule of the Duvalier family lasted in Haiti for 30 years. *(T)*
5. What country attempted to send missiles to Cuba in 1962? *(Soviet Union)*
6. _______ was the president during the Bay of Pigs invasion. *(Kennedy)*
7. (T or F) All social classes in Cuba were content under Fidel Castro's rule. *(F)*
8. (T or F) The Dominican Republic has one of the most stable governments in the Caribbean. *(T)*
9. The majority of the dissidents who left Cuba in 1980 settled in the _______ _______. *(United States)*
10. (T or F) Recently, Haiti has enjoyed political stability. *(F)*

SUGGESTED ASSIGNMENTS

1. **Critical Thinking Worksheet (Average/Group)** Have students complete Critical Thinking Worksheet 70 in the TEACHER'S RESOURCEBANK™.
2. **Presenting a Talk Show (Challenging)** Have interested students write and present a talk show in which they simulate interviews with Cuban refugees. One source of information is Lorrin Philipson's and Rafael Llerena's *Freedom Flights* (Random House). Students may also check the *Readers' Guide to Periodical Literature* in their school or local library.

Section (pages 844–847)

4 South American Nations Faced New Challenges

SECTION OVERVIEW

The countries of South America underwent enormous change in the postwar period. These changes, which included revolutions, the rise and fall of democracies and dictators, and political and economic reforms, in some cases, have led to an uncertainty about the future.

Unfortunately the drug trade has made significant inroads into some of the countries of South America. This has caused untold damage to these nations, as corruption has permeated law enforcement agencies as well as some local governments.

SUGGESTED TEACHING STRATEGIES

1. **Class Discussion (Average/Group)** You might want to play excerpts from the musical *Evita,* which was based on the life of Eva Perón. Then hold a class discussion of Eva Perón's life and role in Argentine politics. Students should do outside reading on Eva Perón before the discussion. Sources include Donald E. Worcester's *Makers of Latin America* (Dutton) and "We Are Adored, We Are Loved" in *Horizon* magazine (August 1978).
2. **Comparing Ideas (Average/Group)** Interested students might like to work together to construct a chart that shows the similarities and differences between the cultures of any two countries of South America. Have students display the chart on the bulletin board.

ENRICHMENT ACTIVITY

Preparing a Script (Average/Group) The entire class might be involved in the preparation of a script for a "You Are There" program about the overthrow of Salvador Allende. The script should include interviews with people living in Chile who supported the Allende government and those who did not. Also, members of the Allende government, city workers, and members of the military should be interviewed. Students should be able to find sources for the preparation of such a program in their school or local library and by consulting the *Readers' Guide to Periodical Literature.* Select certain students to perform the script for the rest of the class.

DAILY QUIZ

To assess student understanding of Section 4, give the class the following quiz. (Each item is worth 10 points.)

1. The first Marxist government to come to power through peaceful means in the Western Hemisphere did so in the country of ______. *(Chile)*
2. The first woman to become president in the Americas was ______ ______. *(Isabel Perón)*
3. (T or F) The rewards of the "Brazilian Miracle" were reaped mainly by the rich. *(T)*
4. The Peruvian who became Secretary-General of the United Nations in 1982 was ______ ______ ______ ______. *(Javier Pérez de Cuéllar)*
5. The Colombian drug ring was run by the ______ ______. *(Medellín cartel)*
6. (T or F) The Peróns appealed particularly to the working class to gain support. *(T)*
7. By the early 1990s, ______ had a foreign debt of $100 billion, the highest in the world. *(Brazil)*
8. In the 1980s ______ suffered the worst economic depression of the century. *(Peru)*
9. (T or F) The United States did not back the overthrow of Allende. *(F)*
10. (T or F) In 1982 Great Britain defeated Argentina in the Falklands War. *(T)*

SUGGESTED ASSIGNMENTS

1. **Researching Ideas (Challenging)** Assign each class member a country in South America. Students are to research the current type of government in their assigned countries. As a class project, have students construct a large outline map of South America, indicating the type of government of each country in the region. Then ask students what generalizations they can draw, based on this information.
2. **Critical Thinking Worksheet (Average/Group)** Have students complete Critical Thinking Worksheet 71 in the TEACHER'S RESOURCEBANK™.
3. **Review Worksheet (Basic)** Have students complete Review Worksheet 31 in the TEACHER'S RESOURCEBANK™.

Teacher's Notes

For suggested lesson plan, additional teaching strategies, enrichment activities, daily quizzes, and suggested assignments, see pages 829A–829E.

Introducing the Chapter
Have students discuss the possibility of the nations of the Western Hemisphere forming a kind of Common Market. Ask the following questions: What forces might lead to a union of Western Hemisphere nations? *(geography, generally friendly relations, complementary needs)* What forces might interfere with such a union? *(suspicion of United States dominance, ties of Latin American countries with other Third World countries, cultural differences)* Do you think the union would be a good idea? Why or why not? *(Discussion can involve how special trade privileges for members of the union might influence trade with other countries, how United States security might be affected, how the United States might be affected by ready access to such products as Mexican and Venezuelan oil, and how these countries would react to this easy access of the United States to their natural resources.)*

Chapter Objectives
After studying Chapter 31, students will be able to:

1. Summarize the changes over recent decades that have led to political conflict in Latin America.
2. Name three problems Latin American nations face today.
3. Describe industrialization and recent economic developments in Latin America.
4. Outline the political

CHAPTER 31

Latin America Became the Focus of World Attention

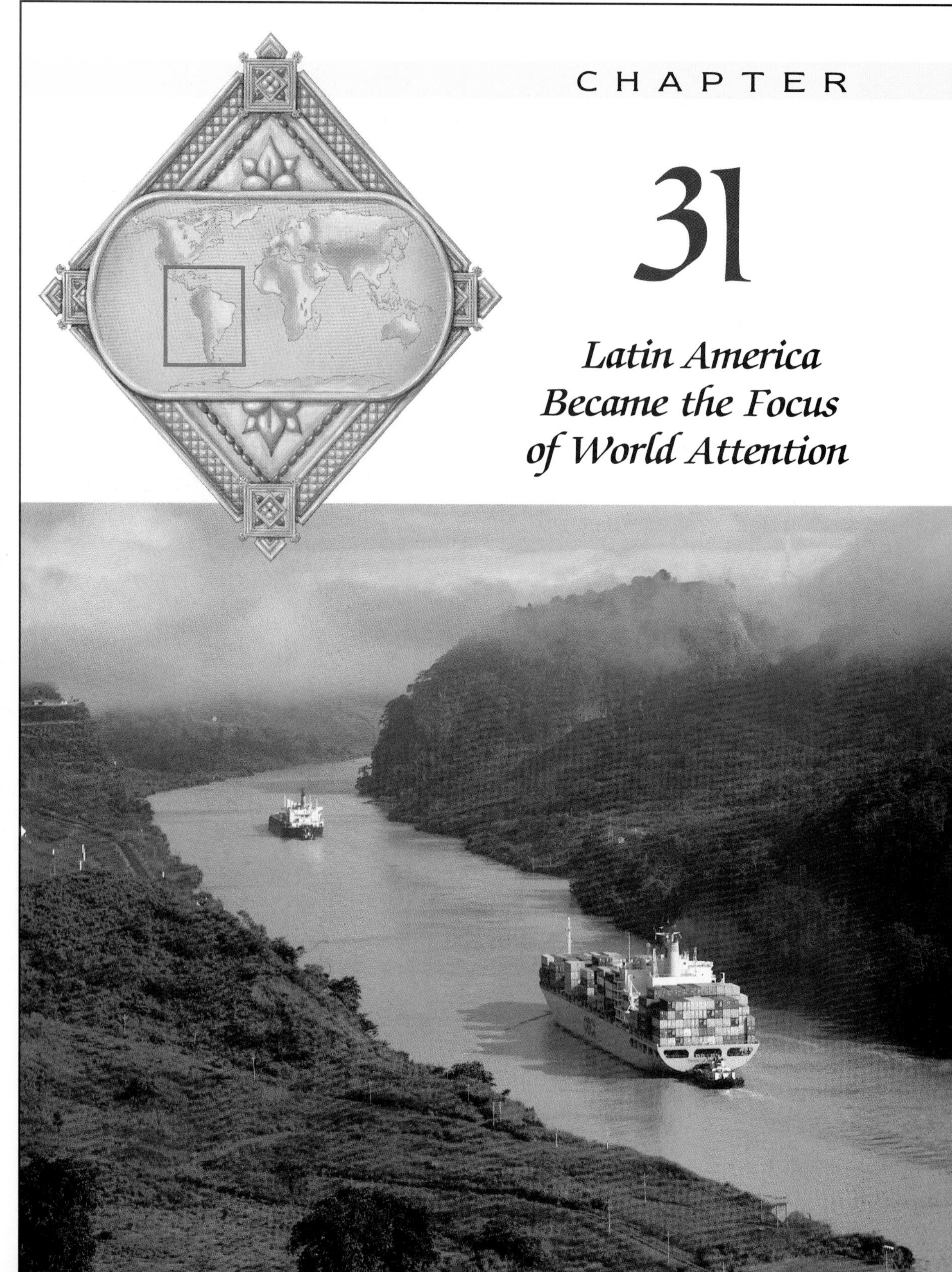

CHAPTER FOCUS

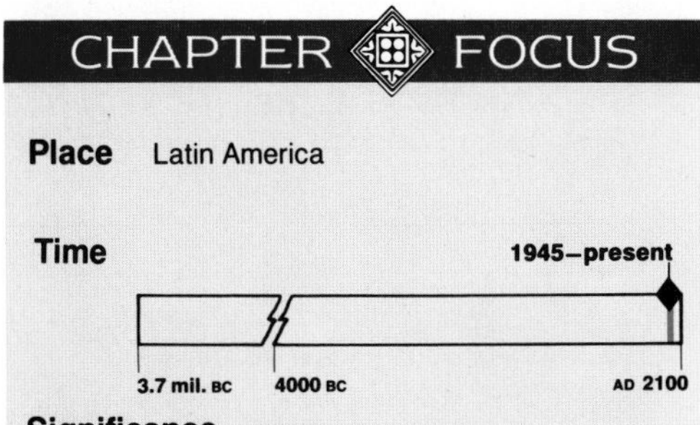

Place Latin America

Time 1945–present

Significance

Sometimes referred to as the "slumbering giant" because of its wealth in human and natural resources, Latin America stands on the threshold of dynamic change and development. Wracked by revolutions and military upheavals, the countries of this region continue to suffer political and economic instability. Nevertheless, the people of this dynamic area of the world persist in working for political, economic, and social progress.

For many years Latin America was overshadowed by the colossus to the north—the United States. The governments and economies of this region, particularly those bordering the Caribbean, depended on the United States. However, this situation is fast changing as the 1900s draw to a close. These developing nations have begun to steer their own courses, often quite different from that which the United States envisions for them. In so doing, the Latin American nations face ever changing challenges.

Terms to Define

multinational corporation	campesino
import substitution	covert
geopolitical region	dissident

People to Identify

Daniel Ortega	Oscar Arias
Manuel Noriega	Fidel Castro

Places to Locate

Guatemala	Panama
Grenada	Cuba
Nicaragua	Dominican Republic
El Salvador	Haiti

Questions to Guide Your Reading

1 What conflicts have plagued Latin America since 1945?
2 What major changes occurred in Mexico, Central America, and the Caribbean islands in recent decades?
3 What type of political and economic system did Castro set up in Cuba?
4 What were some of the upheavals experienced by many of the nations of South America in recent decades?

The death in 1952 of Eva [Evita] Perón, first lady of Argentina, sparked an outpouring of national grief. In Evita, the former actress and radio star, the working class believed they had found their champion. Whether she truly had their interest at heart remains a matter for conjecture. The following is a description of the flamboyant Evita as she declined the nomination for vice president in 1951.

> *"The woman who mounted the steps and looked out upon the frenzied crowd was a far cry from the fledgling first lady of 1946, or the glamour queen of the Rainbow Tour. The blonde curls and gaudy attire had long since given way to what one scholar has called 'the streamlined, eternally classic style which was to be hers—and uniquely hers at that time—until her death.' Her hair was pulled back severely, accentuating the growing gauntness of her features. Tears flooded her eyes. She raised her arms in response to the delirium, and a look of uncertainty clouded her expression."*

Like Argentina, other nations of Latin America have witnessed dramatic changes in governments during the recent chapters of their histories.

1 Political Conflicts Shook Many Latin American Nations

The countries of Latin America underwent enormous changes after World War II. Once relatively unimportant in world affairs and economically backward, Latin America became a focus of world attention. Its growing population, the discovery of vast petroleum deposits and other resources, and its rapid industrialization increased its importance to the rest of the world.

Since achieving independence in the early 1800s, most Latin American societies had followed traditional social and economic patterns. After 1945, however, Latin America seemed to be not merely catching up with the industrialized world, but creating its own patterns.

Rapid Population Growth

The most important change in Latin America after World War II was the sudden surge in population.

◀ ***The Panama Canal Zone***

courses taken by Mexico and Central America since World War II.
5. Describe the revolution and the emergence of Fidel Castro in Cuba, as well as other political events that have shaken the Caribbean region in recent decades.
6. Identify Puerto Rico's unique relationship with the U.S.
7. Outline the events that have occurred in Argentina, Brazil, Chile, Peru, and Colombia in recent decades.

SECTION 1

Focus/Motivation

Write the following quotation by John F. Kennedy on the chalkboard: "Those who make peaceful revolution impossible will make violent revolution inevitable" (John Gunther, *Inside South America,* Harper & Row). Ask students to interpret this quotation. *(Kennedy supported moderate efforts to improve the quality of life for all people. Moderates, he felt, should take such action before radicals succeed in disrupting peace and world order.)* Ask students whether or not they agree with Kennedy's view. Encourage them to support their answers with examples.

When students have completed the section, discuss the quotation again in light of the information they have gained about Latin American countries.

831

1B, 1C, a2J

● Poverty is the ultimate result of this population explosion.
■ In most Latin American cities, about 25 percent of the population live in slums.

Presentation
Interpreting Visual Evidence
(Average/Group)
Have students study the picture on page 832. Ask them to pick out the main evidence of poverty in the photograph *(shanty housing)* and the main evidence of wealth in the photograph *(large modern buildings).* Then lead a class discussion on the problems that might be created when poverty and wealth exist side by side.

In 1940 the population of Latin America totaled about 126 million. By the 1980s its population was estimated to be 398 million.

A decline in the death rate spurred this population explosion. Public health measures, such as insecticides against malaria-carrying mosquitoes, reduced the number of deaths from malaria each year. Most significantly, improved medical care led to a decline in the death rate of children and infants. More children survived their first years of life and went on to adulthood and to parenthood.

Rapid population growth had enormous consequences for Latin America. Birth rates were highest in rural regions, where unequal distribution of land, and in some areas a short supply of it, forced ● more and more people into the cities.

The Growth of Cities

Cities exercised a powerful attraction of their own because they contained a concentration of social services, schools, and popular entertainments. For example, hospitals, universities, and secondary schools were often found only in cities.

The populations of cities grew twice as fast as the general population. In 1940, approximately 16 million Latin Americans lived in various cities of more than 100,000 inhabitants. By 1980, the number had risen to 150 million. Rio de Janeiro, for example, grew from 4.2 million in 1970 to 5.8 million in 1987.

City and national governments had to deal with complex administrative problems. For example, sewer lines, water mains, and electric lines had to be built. Large investments had to be made in road building, public buses, and even subway systems. The heavy machinery and other equipment for all of these building projects could not be found in most Latin American countries. The need to import these items often created a financial burden on the economy.

Many other problems arose in connection with the growth of cities. Most cities faced severe housing shortages. The governments, with so many other new expenses, could not afford to build public housing for the expanded city population. In addition, most of the rural migrants received wages too low to afford any housing. They therefore "squatted" on steep hillsides, tidal flats, and even ■ publicly owned garbage dumps. In the poorest cities of Latin America, as many as half the inhabitants became squatters.

Learning from Pictures *Rio de Janeiro, one of South America's most beautiful cities, constantly struggles to house its growing population.*

The expanded urban population also required a reliable food supply. Until the 1940s commercial agriculture had been designed to supply overseas markets. The supply of food for the cities came from those small farmers who had surpluses to sell. With the growth of cities, however, many Latin American countries needed to import food.

New Political Forces

Most of the constitutions of Latin American countries allowed only literate persons to vote. As they moved to the cities, people were more likely to gain some schooling or learn to read. Thus, the lower class, able to read and therefore to vote, suddenly acquired political importance.

The votes of rural workers had always been controlled by the large landowners, through the bonds of loyalty or fear. These pressures did not exist in the cities. Now, for the first time, politicians had to appeal to a large mass of people to gain votes.

Women had gained the right to vote in a few Latin American countries in the 1930s. However, it was not until the mid-1950s that women were given the right to vote throughout the region. Their votes also increased the electorate.

Labor became another force of political power in postwar Latin America. As employment in factories increased, labor organizing spread and the union movement grew stronger. Governments sensed a danger in allowing unions to grow on their own. Therefore, government leaders followed the policy, begun in the 1930s, of attempting to control the unions. The unions continued to gain strength, however, especially through political parties that supported their interests.

Religion represented another active political force. More than 90 percent of Latin Americans were Catholics. In the past, the Catholic church had espoused conservative ideas in Latin American society and politics. At the same time, the church's concern for the poor and uneducated was an important tradition in many countries. However, following a meeting of the Catholic bishops of the region in 1968, the church's leaders began to take liberal stands on the political issues of welfare and human rights.

The church's strong position on such issues placed it in opposition to government and military leaders and to members of the upper and middle classes. These dominant elements of Latin American society thought of the growing urban class as a danger. They resisted social reforms and the labor movement because they saw them as threats to order and the existing political system.

Learning from Pictures *During Pope John Paul's visit to Chile in 1987, he asked the people to preserve peace but to demand their human rights.*

Problems of Economic Development

During World War II, Latin America had provided vast quantities of raw materials and food to the Allies. After the war Latin American nations found it difficult to stabilize their economies. They continued to supply a few unfinished goods to the industrialized countries. However, demand for their agricultural products and raw materials did not rise fast enough to supply Latin Americans with the income necessary to fund economic growth. Meanwhile the list of goods that Latin America needed to import grew longer.

Most political leaders in Latin America saw economic development as the key to resolving the region's problems. Economic development would provide jobs for the increased population. Industrialization would lessen the country's dependence on foreign sources for vital manufactured goods and would provide consumer goods for everyone. In every country the drive for economic development became a major government project.

Latin American nations invited foreign corporations and manufacturers to establish businesses in their countries in the hope that their investments and technology would help spur industrialization. Since foreign participation would bring in machinery and capital, it seemed to be the cheapest and most rapid way to promote economic development.

Relations between foreign-owned businesses, known as **multinational corporations,** and their host countries developed into a major political issue. Many Latin Americans resented the foreign ownership of important factories. In addition, factory owners often took their profits out of the country rather than reinvesting the funds. Any attempts by the governments to control the flow of profits out of the country proved futile.

Industrialization to Reduce Imports

Between 1956 and 1960, Brazilian leaders continued the economic policy known as **import substitution.** This policy became one of the few political programs on which most Latin Americans could agree. Under import substitution, government officials examined the list of goods that their country imported to find those items that could be produced inside the country. The government would then grant various kinds of favors to encourage manufacturers to produce these items. Tariffs or

833

1D, a1B, a1C, a4A, a4F, a4G, a4M

READ
WRITE
INTERPRET
●CONNECT
THINK

BUILDING HISTORY STUDY SKILLS

Making Connections with History: Linking Economics to History

All societies have access to a limited amount of resources that can be used to produce the goods and services needed to satisfy people's wants. Specifically, at any one time, each society has a given amount of labor, capital, and natural resources. In every society people's wants seem to be greater than all that can possibly be produced. This condition is called "scarcity," and it forms a basic economic problem. Because we cannot have everything we want, we make choices. Much of economics involves how and why institutions, people, and societies make the choices that they do.

"Opportunity cost," another key economic concept, deals with the economic choices that are made in relation to the sacrifices involved. For example, if you are given a choice between going to a play or a rock concert, and you choose the play, the rock concert becomes your opportunity cost since you sacrificed it when you chose the play.

Economic systems determine the manner in which people decide what to produce, how to produce it, and for whom to produce it. These are the basic economic decisions every society must make. They are based upon scarcity and opportunity cost. The economic system of a society affects people's relationships with one another, the kind of government they create, and the history of the society.

How to Link Economics to History

To link economics to history, follow these steps.

1. Identify and define the economic concept being discussed. It is either scarcity, opportunity cost, or an economic system.
2. Describe the effects of the economic concept on government or society.

Developing the Skill

Read the following selection. How does the description of a hacienda in Latin America help us to understand the development of the society there?

> "The hacienda as a society may be described by saying that it was—and is—an economic and social system that seeks to achieve self-sufficiency . . . on a local scale. . . . Each unit expands until it has within its own borders all that it needs—salt from the sea, *panela* (black, unrefined sugar) from its own cane fields, corn, barley, wheat, coconuts, bananas, apples, and pears. All of this depends upon where the hacienda is located. . . . it can run from the seacoast to the mountain top . . . Not all haciendas . . . satisfy this ideal completely, but that is the aim of hacienda organization: to buy nothing; to raise and make everything within the limits of its own boundaries. The big house is built from the timbers found on the land . . . the furniture is made at home. The cloth is woven there from wool shorn off home-grown sheep. The llamas that graze in the hills, the oxen and the horses are raised and broken where they were born. . . . The wooden plow, the wagon, the windmill for the grinding of the corn, or the water mill for the grinding of the cane are all fabricated [made] locally."

The passage is describing an economic system. The decisions about what to produce, how to produce it, and for whom to produce it are made by the owner of the hacienda. The goal of the owner is to make and keep this economic unit self-sufficient and self-governing. The problem of scarcity is solved by the planned use of natural resources. The opportunity cost comes in when the owner makes the choice of what is to be produced on the hacienda.

Practicing the skill. In the free enterprise system of the United States, who answers the three basic economic questions?

To apply this skill, see Applying History Study Skills on page 849.

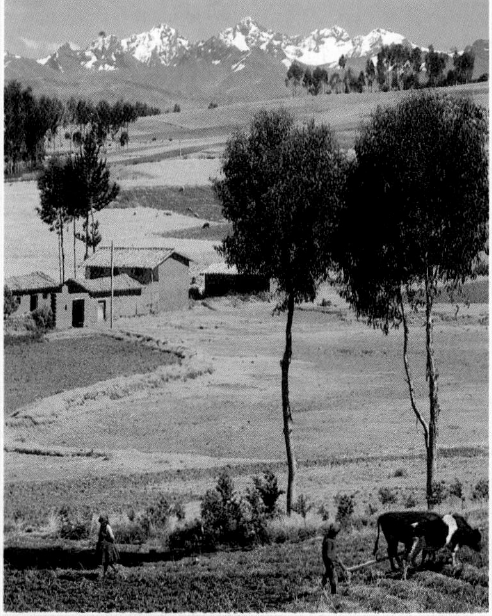

Highland farming near the Andes

834

● steel, heavy machinery, pharmaceuticals, autos

■ In the past two decades, the OAS has been involved with economic development, such as providing industry with capital for investment, improvements in transportation and trade, and easing energy shortages.

Learning from Pictures During the 1980s Mexico's major source of income was crude oil. What products was Mexico producing in the early 1960s? ●

quotas would be set to discourage or prevent importation of similar goods, giving the local industries a chance to develop.

Import substitution worked fairly well in the largest countries—Brazil, Mexico, and Argentina—which had large markets and enough resources to accomplish the task. By the early 1960s, these countries produced steel, heavy machinery, automobiles, pharmaceuticals, and many other consumer goods. These manufactures represented 20 percent of the national output of all goods and services. Some other countries of Latin America, such as Venezuela, Chile, Colombia, Peru, and Uruguay, experienced lesser but significant rates of development.

By the mid-1980s, all the easier substitutions of imports had been made. Many other problems could not be resolved quickly, however. For example, only wealthy people could afford refrigerators, washing machines, and other expensive consumer products. Meanwhile, many people could barely afford to buy enough food or "luxuries" such as toothbrushes and shoes. As a result, in some cases the new factories producing these products ran at half capacity because there was so little demand for their output.

Recent Economic Developments

In the postwar years, Latin American countries attempted new forms of economic association in an effort to lessen dependence on industrialized countries and to cooperate in areas of production, tariffs, and trade. The Andean Pact, enacted in 1969, had some success in meeting these goals. It restricted foreign investment and encouraged both lower tariffs and economic cooperation within Latin America.

Latin American influence also grew in other parts of the world. Trade with the newly independent nations of Africa and Asia increased. The countries of Latin America took leading roles in political and economic world forums, expressing positions closer to those of African and Asian countries than to those of the United States.

Alliances in the Western Hemisphere

During and just after World War II, the nations of the Western Hemisphere entered into several mutual defense pacts. Many leaders viewed such pacts as necessary steps to prevent the spread of communism.

The Organization of American States. Inter-American cooperation went a step further in 1948, when delegates from 21 Western Hemisphere countries met at Bogotá, Colombia, and founded the Organization of American States (OAS). Each member nation sent a representative to a policy-making council. The OAS met regularly at five-year intervals and also in special sessions from time to time. Each member nation agreed to consult the OAS before taking action against another member.

The founding of the OAS represented a continuation of the Good Neighbor policy, through which the United States sought cooperation with its southern neighbors. This ideal, however, proved difficult to achieve. ■

The Alliance for Progress. In 1961 President John F. Kennedy of the United States announced a 10-year program aimed at improving the quality of life in Latin American nations. The "Alliance for Progress" focused on housing, education, sanitation, public services, and tax and land reforms. The United States and 20 Latin American countries participated in the program. The United States alone contributed about $10 billion to the Alliance in the 1960s.

SECTION 1

Closure

Ask students to speculate why organizations such as the OAS and the Alliance for Progress have not achieved their goals of good relations among the nations of the Western Hemisphere.

Review Answers

1. ***multinational corporation:*** foreign-owned business; ***import substitution:*** government policy encouraging the manufacture of items that would otherwise be imported

2. ***OAS:*** Organization of American States founded in 1948 to promote better cooperation among the nations of the Western Hemisphere; ***Alliance for Progress:*** ten-year program started in 1961 that aimed at improving housing, education, sanitation, and public services as well as providing land and tax reform in the Western Hemisphere

3. The growth of Latin American cities resulted in the following: administrative problems, such as providing transportation, water supply, and sewage removal; housing shortages, which led to the rise of slums; and an inadequate food supply.

4. (a) and **(b)** The urban lower classes and women increased the electorate. For the first time, politicians had to appeal to a large mass of people to gain votes. The union movement grew stronger, especially through political

4H, 5J, a1C, a4A, a4F, a4G, a4H, a4L

● All U.S. personnel were pulled out of Grenada in 1985.

parties that represented their interests. The Catholic Church, which in the past had represented conservative ideas, began to take a liberal stand on the political issues of welfare and human rights. The church's new stand placed it in opposition to government, military leaders, and members of the upper and middle classes.
5. (a) Foreign corporations were encouraged to establish businesses in Latin America because it was believed their investments and technology would help get factories started. It also seemed to be the cheapest and most rapid way to promote economic development. **(b)** Latin Americans began to resent foreign ownership of important factories, the influence of foreign-owned companies upon governments through political contributions, and the constant flow of profits out of the country.

SECTION 2

Focus/Motivation
In the 1950s the United States secretly armed a rebel group that overthrew the Guatemalan president. In the 1980s President Reagan believed that the leftist leaders of Nicaragua, the Sandinistas, were trying to topple the government of El Salvador. Therefore, he attempted to send military aid to the anti-Sandinista rebels, or Contras. Although the U.S. Congress voted against aid to the Contras, in what

Despite the large amount of financial assistance provided through the Alliance for Progress, the program failed to achieve most of its goals. Much of the money fell into the hands of corrupt leaders and never reached the poor people for whom it was intended. By the early 1970s, the Alliance for Progress came to an end, mainly because of funding cuts.

SECTION 1 REVIEW

1. **Define** multinational corporation, import substitution
2. **Identify** OAS, Alliance for Progress
3. **Analyzing Ideas** What problems arose as a result of the growth of Latin American cities?
4. **Evaluating Ideas** **(a)** Briefly describe three new political forces that emerged in Latin America in the postwar years. **(b)** Explain the impact of each on this region.
5. **Interpreting Ideas** **(a)** Why were foreign corporations encouraged to establish businesses in Latin America? **(b)** Why did their participation become a political issue?

2 Mexico and Central America Set a Different Political Course

Mexico, Central America, the Caribbean islands, and the countries of South America bordering the Caribbean are called the Caribbean Basin (see map, page 837). This area forms a single **geopolitical region,** one whose members share similar political and geographic features.

The importance of the Caribbean Basin lies in its location as a commercial and military crossroads. The region connects the north-south routes of the hemisphere as well as the routes between the Atlantic and Pacific oceans via the Panama Canal. Although modern aircraft carriers and supertankers cannot pass through the canal, most commercial vessels have no difficulty traversing it. Such heavy traffic in the waterway results in the continued strategic and commercial importance of the canal.

As political instability has rocked the Caribbean Basin in recent years, world attention, particularly that of the United States, has focused on this region.

United States Involvement

In the early 1950s, the United States became heavily involved in Latin American politics. In Guatemala in 1954, for example, the United States intervened to help overthrow a leftist government. The Guatemalan government had passed a land-reform law permitting it to take over and redistribute unused land, much of which was American-owned. Despite international criticism the United States assisted a rebel group that overthrew the Guatemalan president, Jacobo Arbenz.

The United States became even more involved in Latin America in the 1960s, particularly in Cuba (see pages 841–42). Then in 1983 President Reagan, after being asked by neighboring Caribbean countries, sent marines to the island of Grenada to overthrow a Communist regime and replace it with a pro-Western one. The United States also played a complex and controversial role in the internal affairs of Nicaragua and El Salvador. ●

Mexico

Immediately after World War II, Mexico appeared to be one of the most stable countries in Latin

Learning from Pictures *At the Miraflores locks, these ships are raised and lowered from one sea level to another on their way through the Panama Canal.*

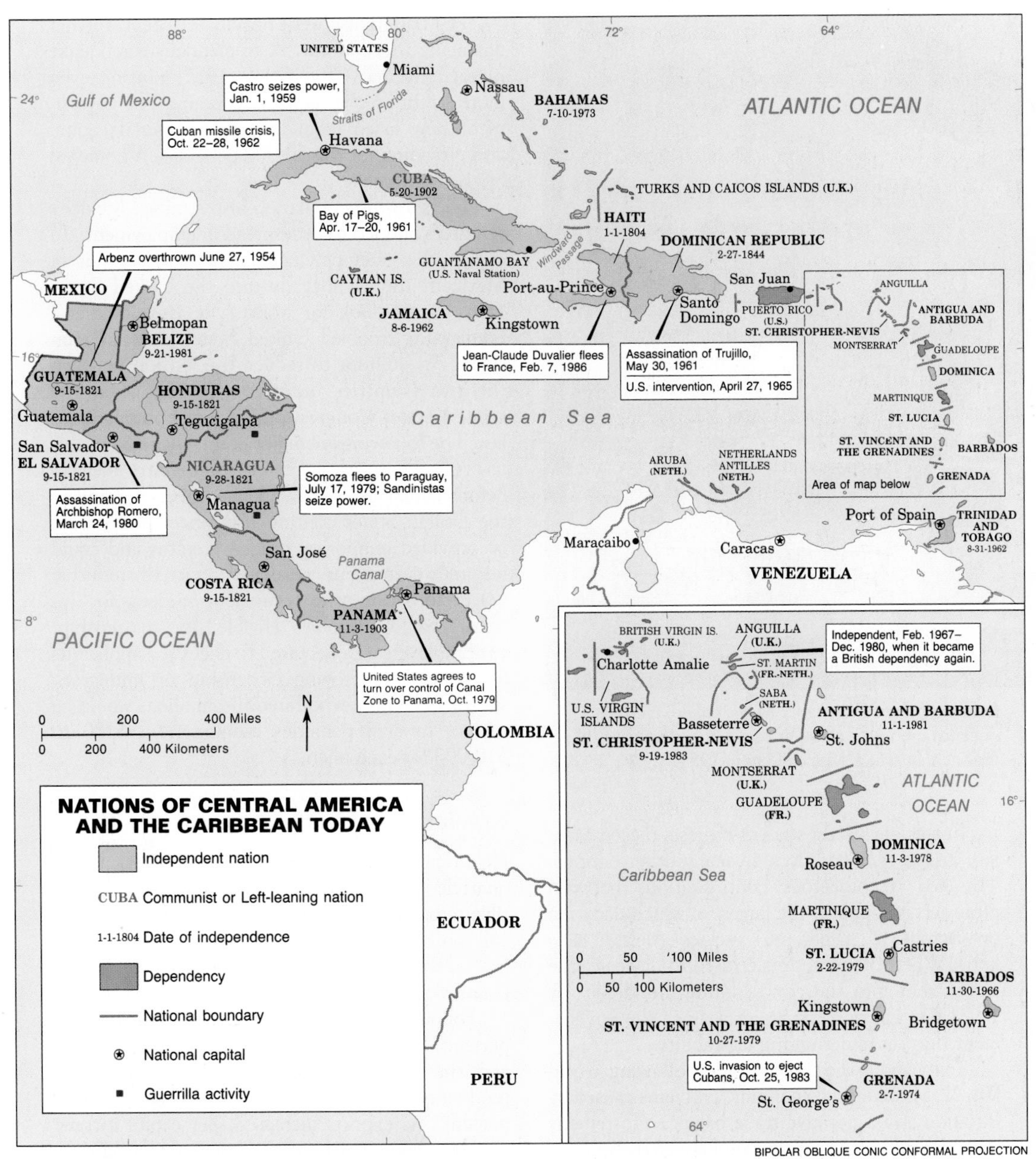

Learning from Maps *Countries of Central America and the Caribbean have confronted many political upheavals. Which countries in the region are Communist?* **Cuba and Nicaragua**

America, functioning smoothly under a presidential system of government. The government swiftly squelched occasional political dissent. At the same time, the government took steps toward establishing a foreign policy that did not necessarily agree with that of the United States. For example, it was the only Latin American country that refused to break relations with Cuba in the early 1960s.

became known as the Iran-Contra scandal, the Contras continued to receive U.S. aid illegally.

In a classroom discussion ask the students what they know about the Iran-Contra scandal. *(Students should be aware that the scandal involved sending illegal aid to the Contras by sources close to President Reagan.)*

Presentation
Classifying Information (Average/Group)

Write the following lists on the chalkboard or an overhead projector and have the students copy them in their notebooks. Then have the students unscramble the words in the first list and match them with the correct description or event in the second list.

1. telcoolta *(Tlateloco)*
2. rsaco meorro *(Oscar Romero)*
3. lunmea roingea *(Manuel Noriega)*
4. iadnel tgoare *(Daniel Ortega)*
5. acrso isara *(Oscar Arias)*

(4) Sandanista leader and president of Nicaragua
(1) site of confrontation between protesters and police in Mexico in 1968
(5) Costa Rican president who presented peace plan for Central America
(3) president of Panama accused by U.S. of helping narcotics dealers
(2) Catholic archbishop killed while saying mass

Learning from Pictures *Mexico and Central America are under constant threat of earthquakes, like the one that struck Mexico City in 1985.*

In the late 1960s, student protests racked Mexico, just as they had done in many other nations. This led to numerous confrontations between protesters and police, the largest of which occurred on October 2, 1968, at Tlateloco (tlahl • TEEL • koh). When the protesters refused to disperse, the troops shot into the crowd, killing hundreds. By 1971 guerrilla activity began against the government, further undermining its stability.

Throughout the three decades following World War II, Mexico faced economic problems caused by inflation and a negative trade balance. To remedy these difficulties, the government lowered the value of the currency several times and cut back its spending.

Mexico's economic picture improved greatly with the discovery of huge oil reserves in the 1970s, and it looked as though the country might finally overcome its economic difficulties. However, by the 1980s the worldwide slump in oil prices had ended the dream of a bright economic future.

The nation also went heavily into debt, further damaging its economy. A tremendous earthquake ravaged Mexico City in late 1985, putting even more strain on the nation's economy. The government now faced rebuilding the shattered capital and providing for the 50,000 persons left homeless by the earthquake.

The growing population also strained Mexico's resources and led to widespread unemployment. To escape this unemployment, tens of thousands of Mexicans slipped illegally into the United States each year to look for work. The issue of illegal immigrants troubled United States-Mexican relations. An attempt to reduce the tension between the two countries occurred in 1986 when the United States Congress passed a new immigration law. The following are major points included in this law: (1) Those who entered the country illegally before January 1, 1982, and had been residing in the United States continuously since then, would be provided temporary residence status and could become permanent residents after 18 months. (2) Persons who were permanent residents for five years would become eligible for citizenship. (3) Employers were required to check job applicants for documents proving citizenship or immigrant status. (4) Those who hired illegal aliens would be subject to civil penalties ranging from $280 to $10,000 for each alien.

Revolution in Central America

Historically the countries of Central America have quarreled with one another and have been susceptible to outside influences. Often one nation would call on a major power, particularly the United States, to intervene in the affairs of a neighboring country.

Following World War II, Central America experienced rapid economic growth. Between 1950 and the late 1970s, the annual gross domestic product of Central America increased at a rate of 5 percent. As exports increased, per capita income doubled. Employment rose as manufacturing doubled. People moved to the cities, and the urban population grew from 15 percent to 43 percent. World prices for major exports such as sugar, coffee, bananas, and cotton soared. Telephone lines, electricity, fertilizers, and pesticides all came into use.

However, while this prosperity continued, only a certain sector of the population benefited. The

838

● The leftist guerrillas have been given aid by Cuba and other socialist nations.

peasants, known as the **campesinos,** did not share in this prosperity. During the 1960s the price of land nearly quadrupled as available arable land decreased. As rents rose, more peasants joined the ranks of a growing class of landless farm workers. These people could not even afford land for subsistence farming.

In addition, earthquakes in Guatemala and Nicaragua in 1972, and killer hurricanes in Honduras in 1974 and Nicaragua in 1988, left many of the poor homeless. Throughout the 1970s and the 1980s, the countries of Central America remained some of the poorest in the world, owing in part to inequality in the distribution of wealth.

A lack of sufficient medical help,* sanitation facilities, and educational services** plagued the countries of Central America. The population increased at an annual rate of 3 percent. In the late 1970s and early 1980s, skyrocketing inflation slowed the economies of the region to a standstill. Faced with these problems, people in El Salvador, Nicaragua, Honduras, and Guatemala began to demand reforms.

The Nicaraguan Revolution

Following the meeting held by the Catholic bishops of Latin America in 1968, the clergy blamed the wealthy for the misery of the poor and no longer supported the military dictatorships so prevalent in this region. Some of the lower-level clergy even joined guerrilla bands fighting the governments. For the first time, the church sided with the peasants against their oppressive rulers.

In addition, a growing class of educated people joined the ranks of those opposing the corrupt dictators. Both of these factors bolstered the revolutionary movement against the corrupt and oppressive dictator Anastasio Somoza in Nicaragua. Almost the entire population rose up against this regime in 1979.

A Marxist-inspired revolutionary organization, the Sandinistas, gained control of the anti-Somoza revolution by promising a mixed economy, nonaligned foreign policy, and pluralism. The Sandinistas took their name from the Nicaraguan guerrilla leader of the 1920s, Augusto Sandino.

*Life expectancy was about 55 years and 1 in 10 infants died.

**Only half the population learned to read.

After taking over the government of Nicaragua, the Sandinistas established close military ties with the Communist governments in Cuba and the Soviet Union. A guerrilla group, called the Contras, attempted to overthrow the Sandinista government with monetary and military aid from the United States. However, fearing a situation similar to that which had occurred in Vietnam in the 1960s and 1970s, the United States Congress voted to stop all aid to the Contras. This led to **covert** or undercover military and financial aid being given to the Contras by men close to President Reagan. Known as the Iran-Contra Scandal, this became a political embarrassment to the president when a few of the people involved were questioned by a congressional investigating committee in 1987 and brought to trial in 1989.

Plunged into a civil war and faced with severe economic problems, the Sandinista leader and Nicaraguan president, Daniel Ortega, looked for ways to come to terms with the Contra rebels. Despite his efforts, however, solving this problem proved impossible to achieve throughout the 1980s.

El Salvador

The Central American country of El Salvador, located adjacent to Nicaragua (see map, page 837), was ruled either by wealthy civilians or military dictatorships from the 1940s to the late 1970s. Guerrilla groups began to form in the 1970s in order to fight the inequities imposed by the government. These organizations managed to mobilize tens of thousands of people into antigovernment demonstrations. At first the military government then in power attempted reforms.

José Napoleón Duarte led the reformist challenge and was president through most of the 1980s. But violent collisions between leftist guerrillas and ● government-backed right-wing groups continued to plague the country. This violence led to the murder in 1980 of Oscar Romero, the Catholic archbishop of El Salvador, while he was saying mass, and, three months later, the unprovoked deaths of three American nuns and an American volunteer.

A stable government and economy seemed to be impossible to obtain in El Salvador. A permanent peace appeared to be the only way of bringing stability to the region. But no one seemed to know how to accomplish this task.

SECTION 2

Closure

Read to the class the quotation from Oscar Arias on page 840 in the textbook. Ask the students to make suggestions as to how peace and stability might be achieved in this region. *(Accept all reasonable answers.)*

Review Answers

1. ***geopolitical region:*** area that shares similar political and geographic features; ***campesino:*** name given to Central American peasants; ***covert:*** undercover military and financial aid

2. ***Tlateloco:*** site of Mexican student protests in 1968, where hundreds were killed when police shot into the crowds; ***Daniel Ortega:*** Nicaraguan president; ***José Napoleón Duarte:*** president of El Salvador; ***Manuel Noriega:*** Panamanian dictator; ***Oscar Arias:*** president of Costa Rica who developed a peace plan for Central America

3. ***Grenada:*** island in the Caribbean off coast of South America; ***Mexico:*** country lying on the southern border of the U.S.; ***Nicaragua:*** Central American country south of El Salvador and Honduras and north of Costa Rica; ***El Salvador:*** Central American country south of Guatemala and southwest of Honduras; ***Panama:*** Central American country south of Costa Rica and north of Colombia; ***Costa Rica:*** Central American country

5I, 5J, a4A, a4F, a4G, a4K, a4M

● Costa Rica has a 93% literacy rate and has been called "a small democracy with an enlightened citizenry."
■ for proposing the Central American Peace Plan

south of Nicaragua and north of Panama
4. (a) World prices for major exports such as sugar, coffee, bananas, and cotton soared. New technology such as telephone lines, electricity, fertilizers, and pesticides were introduced into the area. **(b)** The campesinos did not share in this prosperity. During the 1960s the price of land nearly quadrupled as available arable land decreased. As rents rose, more peasants joined the ranks of a growing landless class. These people could not even afford land for subsistence farming.
5. The misery of the poor and the oppression of corrupt dictators encouraged the dissatisfied to develop a revolutionary front.
6. Fearing a situation such as the one that occurred in Vietnam, the U.S. Congress, in 1983, voted to stop all aid to the Contras.

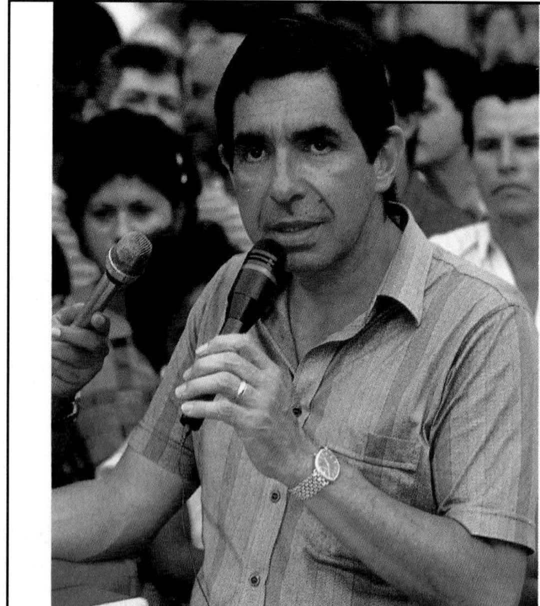

Learning from Pictures *Oscar Arias informally addresses a crowd of supporters in Costa Rica. Why did he win the 1987 Nobel Peace Prize?* ■

Panama

The country of Panama shared the same political and economic fate as its Central American neighbors. The only major difference was that the United States controlled the Panama Canal and 10 miles (16 kilometers) of territory on either side known as the Canal Zone, once part of Panama. American-Panamanian negotiations over control of the canal continued throughout the postwar period. The two nations finally negotiated a treaty, ratified by the United States Senate in 1979, which would gradually turn the canal over to Panama by the year 2000. This treaty caused much controversy in the United States, because many people believed that United States security would be jeopardized when it lost control of the canal.

In the late 1980s, relations between Panama and the United States deteriorated. United States officials accused the Panamanian dictator, General Manuel Noriega, of helping South American narcotics dealers send illegal drugs into the United States. President Reagan attempted to pressure Noriega into resigning and when this failed, cut off all United States military and economic aid to Panama. Then in December 1989, after Panamanian forces killed one American soldier and detained and severely beat another one, President Bush sent a force of 10,000 soldiers to Panama to restore order and capture Noriega. Finally, in January 1990, Noriega, who had gone into hiding, surrendered and was transported to the United States to face trial on drug trafficking charges.

A Peace Proposal for Central America

In August 1987, representatives from throughout Central America met in Guatemala City, Guatemala, for a regional summit conference. At this conference Oscar Arias, the president of Costa Rica, a country with relative economic and political stability, proposed a peace plan for Central America. ● He desperately hoped to seek a solution to the conflicts and violence shaking this region. For this proposal, Arias was given the Nobel Prize for Peace in 1987. The following is an excerpt from a speech given by Arias on the subject of peace in Central America.

> "The democracy in which many American nations live today cannot be consolidated without economic development and social justice. Before any political or economic conditions can be imposed on the democracies of the Americas, there must be a commitment from the Western world to strengthen democracy in all our nations. In the Americas, peace must be democratic, pluralistic, tolerant, and free. While dogmatism and intransigence persist and there is no dialogue, peace will be impossible. Working together for democracy, freedom, and development is working together for peace."

SECTION 2 REVIEW

1. **Define** geopolitical region, campesino, covert
2. **Identify** Tlateloco, Daniel Ortega, José Napoleón Duarte, Manuel Noriega, Oscar Arias
3. **Locate** Grenada, Mexico, Nicaragua, El Salvador, Panama, Costa Rica
4. **Understanding Cause and Effect** **(a)** What caused economic prosperity in Central America in the 1950s and 1960s? **(b)** How did this lead to the establishment of a class of landless poor?
5. **Organizing Ideas** What were two factors that greatly contributed to the revolutionary uprising in Nicaragua?
6. **Analyzing Ideas** Why did the United States Congress vote to discontinue aid to the Contras?

Of the 82 guerrillas who landed with the Castro brothers, only a dozen survived after a detachment of Batista's troops opened fire on them. Fidel, Raúl, Ché, and the other survivors found safety in the jungles of the Sierra Maestras where they set up headquarters.

3 Revolution Shook the Islands of the Caribbean

In 1959 a revolution in Cuba overthrew Fulgencio Batista, the dictator who had held power since 1934. Led by Fidel Castro, the Cuban Revolution was the greatest political upheaval Latin Americans had experienced since the Mexican Revolution of the early 1900s.

Revolution in Cuba

Fidel Castro and his brother Raúl began their campaign to overthrow the Cuban government on July 26, 1953, when they led an assault on an army barracks at Moncada. Although they failed and were captured by Batista's forces, the Castro brothers only spent 11 months in prison. The Castros spent the next few years in exile in Mexico where they trained a group of revolutionaries. They returned to Cuba with a band of 82 men in 1956, and for the next three years the Castro brothers, along with a 27-year-old revolutionary, Ernesto ("Ché") Guevara, conducted guerrilla operations against the Batista government.

By late 1958 Batista lost both public support as well as support from the United States government. He fled to exile in the Dominican Republic on New Year's Eve, and the revolutionaries under Fidel Castro took over the Cuban government.

Cuba under Castro. At first the nations of the world had difficulty determining whether Castro's regime would favor the West or the Communist bloc. However, in a relatively short time the new Cuban government began its swing toward the Soviet bloc, and by the end of 1960, Cuba clearly stood on the path toward communism.

Under Castro's now openly Communist regime, the government proclaimed land reform. The government took over large holdings and nationalized all major firms, seizing United States-owned oil, electric, and telephone companies, and sugar mills and nickel mines.

Castro's Marxist policies led to social unrest in Cuba. The lower class, which made up the majority of the population, supported Castro because his policies guaranteed jobs. Before the revolution unemployment had exceeded 20 percent, and most workers had frequently been unemployed. In addition, Castro's government showed a strong commitment to racial equality in a country where blacks and mulattoes accounted for more than 25 percent of the population. Improvements in welfare, education, and medical care also benefited the lower class.

On the other hand, many of these reforms angered the upper class. The government took over businesses and buildings. Employees ran newspapers that private industry had owned. People formerly associated with the Batista dictatorship fled the island. Increasing numbers of business leaders, landowners, professionals, and technicians also fled.

Learning from Pictures *Many of Castro's revolutionary ideals were challenged by responsible Cuban leaders who wanted a democracy in Cuba. Most of these people became political prisoners or exiles. Those left to enforce Castro's plans were his loyal revolutionary followers.*

SECTION 3

Focus/Motivation
Following the revolution in Cuba in 1959, the Castro government took over much of the privately-owned land as well as privately-owned industries. This caused many wealthy people and professional people to flee Cuba. These refugees brought their abilities and skills to the United States and the other countries where they settled.

Discuss the many contributions of these refugees to American society. Ask students to compare the Cuban immigrants of recent years with the people who were part of the great flow of immigration from Europe in the late 1800s and early 1900s. *(Students may mention that in areas such as Miami, with large Cuban populations, many of the doctors, lawyers, and politicians are Cuban. They may mention that many of these immigrants, just as the immigrants of earlier times, have become Americanized.)*

Presentation
Analyzing Ideas (Average/Group)
Begin a discussion on revolution by asking the students to review the section "Revolution in Cuba" on page 841 in the textbook.

After they have reread this section, ask students what kind of preparations they think would be needed to start a revolution. *(Students should men-*

4I, 5C, 5G

● At a conference of Soviet and American scholars and government officials in 1989, it was learned that 20 atomic warheads had been deployed in Cuba and another 20 were on their way. In addition, American military leaders admitted that a plan to overthrow Castro using United States troops had been strongly considered.

tion such elements as popular support, money, and long-term and contingency plans.) Ask students what would be needed in order for a revolution to succeed. *(Students should mention extreme dedication to a cause, willingness to survive under the most difficult circumstances, and creation of a plan for implementing a government if the revolution succeeds.)*

SECTION 3

Closure

Have students review the major events of this section. Then ask them how the revolution in Cuba has influenced U.S. policy in the Caribbean over the past three decades.

Review Answers

1. *dissident:* person dissatisfied with the government

2. *Fidel Castro:* Communist leader of the revolutionary movement in Cuba that overthrew Batista; ***Ché Guevara:*** Argentinian-born guerrilla leader and close friend of Castro who advocated exporting revolution

3. *Cuba:* Caribbean island south of Florida; ***Dominican Republic:*** eastern half of Caribbean island of Hispaniola, east of Cuba; ***Haiti:*** western half of island of Hispaniola, east of Cuba

4. (a) The Castro government proclaimed land reform, took over large holdings, and nationalized all major firms. **(b)** These

The Bay of Pigs. In 1961 the Cuban government ordered the two American-owned oil refineries on the island to process fuel supplied by the Soviet Union. When the refineries refused, Cuba intervened in their operations. The United States responded by refusing to import sugar from Cuba. Left without a customer for its main product, Cuba offered to supply sugar to the Soviet Union in exchange for arms.

The United States government viewed the relationship between Castro and the Soviets as a threat to American national security. President John Kennedy, elected in 1960, continued President Eisenhower's policy of providing secret assistance to anti-Castro rebels. Accordingly, in 1961 Kennedy approved a landing in Cuba of rebels who had been secretly trained and equipped in the United States. The invasion, which took place at the Bay of Pigs, did not succeed, in part because the expected local uprising did not materialize, in part because the promised United States air cover did not occur, and in part because Castro's forces mounted a strong defense.

The Cuban missile crisis. Fidel Castro feared that the United States would attempt another invasion of Cuba. In 1962 American intelligence services learned that the Soviet Union was sending nuclear missiles to Cuba and building missile sites there. After a tense confrontation, which included the possibility of a nuclear war, Soviet leaders agreed to dismantle the bases and remove the missiles. In return, the United States agreed not to invade Cuba. This agreement allowed Castro's government to continue without further direct interference from the United States

The United States persuaded the Organization of American States to expel Cuba and to join in an economic boycott of the island nation. Cuba thus began a long period of political and economic isolation from its hemispheric neighbors.

Despite his country's isolation, Castro launched a program of exporting Communist revolution to other developing nations, particularly in Latin America and Africa. The Cuban government exported arms, troops, and military advisers to Nicaragua, Angola, and Ethiopia. Ché Guevara instituted as well as implemented this plan. A former Argentine physician, Guevara became a revolutionary when he witnessed the overthrow of President Arbenz of Guatemala in 1954. Ever the revolutionary, Guevara personally led a band of guerrillas in the mountains of Bolivia in 1967, where he was killed by a troop of American-trained Bolivian Rangers.

Economic and social difficulties. Castro's lack of success, first in industrializing Cuba and then in attempting to return the economy to dependence on the sugar crop, led to more economic dependence on the Soviet Union by the 1970s. The failure of Cuba's centrally planned command economy and the lack of consumer goods created social unrest in Cuba. In 1980 this dissatisfaction with the government led many Cubans to seek political asylum in other countries. These people first sought refuge at the Peruvian embassy in Havana. When the Castro government realized how many **dissidents,** or people dissatisfied with the government, were among its citizens, it allowed anyone to emigrate provided he or she informed the authorities. The total reached 125,000, and most left Cuba from the port of Mariel in boats provided by Cuban exiles in Miami. However, not only did Castro rid Cuba of the dissidents but he also opened the gates of prisons and mental hospitals forcing criminals and mentally ill people onto boats that carried other refugees to the United States.

By the late 1980s, Cuba continued Ché Guevara's policy of exporting revolution. Close political and economic ties with the Soviet Union also continued, making it as dependent on the Soviets as it had once been on the United States.

Learning from Pictures *During the Mariel boatlift, Cuban refugees are towed to safety by a United States Coast Guard vessel.*

Puerto Rico

Puerto Rico had been administered since 1898 from Washington, D.C. (see Chapter 23). In the early 1930s, Puerto Ricans under the leadership of Luis Muñoz Marín (mah • REEN) began to lobby for increased autonomy from the United States. In the 1940s, under pressure from Marín and the United Nations, the United States permitted Puerto Rico to draft a new constitution.

Puerto Rican voters and the United States Congress approved Puerto Rico's new status as a commonwealth in 1952. The Commonwealth of Puerto Rico has enjoyed certain tax advantages. As a result, the Puerto Rican economy developed very quickly over the next two decades. This growth depended on capital from the United States and on access to American markets.

Puerto Rico, however, did not have real self-government. During the 1970s, as economic growth slowed, many Puerto Ricans went to the United States to find jobs. Beginning in the 1980s, those Puerto Ricans who remained at home demanded a new political status—either independence, commonwealth, or statehood.

Other Nations of the Caribbean

Cuba was not the only troubled island nation in Latin America in the 1960s. Many countries experienced a shift toward the left and were disrupted by a series of coups and assassinations.

The Dominican Republic. The Dominican dictator Rafael Trujillo, assassinated in 1961, was succeeded by Juan Bosch, the first president to be democratically elected in that country in 38 years. After a coup toppled Bosch in 1965, his followers, some of whom were Communists, started an uprising to return him to power. To prevent a Communist takeover, President Lyndon Johnson of the United States sent 400 marines to support the Dominican Republic's military regime.

Since 1965 the Dominican Republic has made many economic and political strides. The democratic government established there appeared fairly stable by the late 1980s as did its economy, which relied more on light industry and tourism rather than on sugar alone. A strong middle class and a free press and media emerged, making the Dominican Republic one of the most stable countries in the Caribbean.

Learning from Pictures *Armed troops in the streets of Port-au-Prince, Haiti, patrol the city during the elections of 1987.*

Haiti. In 1986, following 30 years of the harsh and corrupt military rule of the Duvalier family, the impoverished country of Haiti attempted a democratic government. The military regime that first took over the reins of government reluctantly allowed an election to be held in November 1987. However, this election was canceled because of the violence that erupted among the rival political parties. Another election held in January 1988 brought a civilian government to power, but this government lasted less than 6 months. By the late 1980s, the future of democracy in Haiti did not look bright.

SECTION 3 REVIEW

1. **Define** dissident
2. **Identify** Fidel Castro, Ché Guevara
3. **Locate** Cuba, Dominican Republic, Haiti
4. **Understanding Cause and Effect** **(a)** What steps did Castro take to reform the economic structure of Cuba? **(b)** What effect did this have on the upper classes? **(c)** What effect did this have on the lower classes?
5. **Interpreting Ideas** **(a)** Why did the United States get involved in the Bay of Pigs invasion? **(b)** What were the reasons for the failure of the Bay of Pigs invasion?
6. **Summarizing Ideas** What were the results of the Cuban missile crisis?

reforms angered the upper classes as many of their businesses were taken over by the government. As a result, many fled Cuba. **(c)** The lower classes benefited from Castro's policies, which guaranteed employment; favored racial equality; and improved welfare, education, and medical care.
5. (a) The U.S. viewed the relationship between Castro and the Soviets as a threat to American national security. **(b)** Kennedy, fearing the involvement of the U.S. in a major confrontation with the Soviets, reduced air coverage promised to the invasion forces. In addition, local uprisings did not materialize, and Castro's forces mounted a strong defensive action.
6. Soviet leaders agreed to dismantle the bases and remove the missiles. In return, the U.S. agreed not to invade Cuba. This agreement allowed Castro's government to continue without further interference from the U.S.

1B, 5B, a1B, a4A

● vice president

SECTION 4

Focus/Motivation
You might introduce this section by showing the film *Brazil: The Gathering Millions* (60 min., b&w, NET Films). The film explains the social, economic, and religious factors leading to population growth and shows the social impact of this growth on Brazil. After viewing the film, have students discuss the reasons for, and impact of, the population growth in Latin America.

Presentation
Illustrating Ideas (Average/Group)
Divide the class into several small groups and assign each group a country in South America. Have each group use almanacs and encyclopedias to locate the following information: population; yearly birth rate; literacy rate; per capita GNP; and average life expectancy. After students have gathered this information, incorporate it into a large chart on the bulletin board. Have students use the chart to formulate generalizations about life in South America.

4 South American Nations Faced New Challenges

Many of the nations of South America experienced turbulent political development in the decades following World War II. Revolutions swept the continent, leaving very few governments and individuals untouched.

Argentina

General Juan Perón came to power in Argentina in the 1940s claiming to be a defender against foreign interference and a supporter of the labor movement. Elected president by a huge majority in 1946, Perón depended greatly on the advice and assistance of his wife, Eva, also known as Evita, a former film and radio star. Eva Perón had a keen understanding of the political uses of the mass media. By appealing particularly to the working class, the Peróns won the support of the people and created an authoritarian regime that suppressed all political opposition.

During World War II, Argentina had profited from selling beef and wheat to the Allies. The Peróns used these profits to nationalize British-owned railways and utilities. Although the Perón regime controlled inflation, other attempted reforms did not improve the economy. By the early 1950s, Argentina had many economic troubles.

When Eva Perón died of cancer in 1952, her husband's popularity suffered. Trouble between Perón and the Catholic church as well as a bankrupt economy brought an end to his dictatorship. Argentina remained politically divided for the next 18 years.

In 1972 Perón returned from exile and was again elected president. His new wife, Isabel Perón, won election as vice president. When Juan Perón died, his widow became the first woman to be president in the Americas.

Political and economic conditions in Argentina continued to deteriorate in the 1970s. Isabel Perón was overthrown in 1976. The military regime that succeeded her led the country into a costly and disastrous war with Great Britain over claims to the Falkland (or Malvina) Islands in 1982. The British succeeded in winning a decisive victory, which proved humiliating to the Argentines.

Learning from Pictures *Isabel Perón carries out her duties as the president of Argentina. What position did Isabel have before she became president?* ●

The defeat of Argentina in the Falklands War led to the downfall of the military government, and free elections were held in 1983. The civilian government put military and government officials on trial to bring to justice those who had tortured and murdered so many political dissenters during the years of military rule. However, this succeeded in undermining its stability because some members of the military attempted mutinies against military officials siding with the government.

Brazil

Political unrest and economic chaos have marked Brazil from the postwar period to the present. Too often the overthrow of governments took place in an effort to save the economy. An example of this

CONNECTIONS: THEN AND NOW

Sunken Ships

Ships have been an important form of transportation since the earliest times. Unfortunately, as long as there have been ships, there have been shipwrecks. One expert estimates that 40,000 ships had sunk in the Mediterranean even before the birth of Jesus.

Since early times, too, people have tried to recover sunken ships and the objects that went down with them. As early as the 200s B.C., the Greeks were diving for sunken treasure. And today divers in the Caribbean use sophisticated equipment to locate gold from Spanish shipwrecks.

Treasure is not the only object of underwater exploration. Archaeologists are interested in recovering sunken ships and the objects they carried. One of the first expeditions recovered artifacts from a ship that sank off the coast of Turkey around 1200 B.C.

Sunken ships are seldom found intact. Sometimes, however, the hulls have been buried in the sand and preserved. The sunken Roman ships from the naval battle of Actium, fought in 31 B.C., have been found intact. More complete ships are being raised to the surface as special equipment is developed for the work.

Because fresh water preserves better than salt, many sunken ships in lakes are still in prime condition. Two warships that sank in Lake Ontario in 1812 are still intact with their guns on deck.

845

In spite of economic problems, Brazil remains the most industrialized nation in Latin America.

SECTION 4

Closure

Ask students to name some of the major challenges confronting the countries of South America. *(Answers may include: extreme poverty, inflation, drug trade, dictatorships.)*

Review Answers

1. ***Juan Perón:*** authoritarian president of Argentina, overthrown in 1955; he returned from exile and was again elected president in 1973; ***Eva Perón:*** wife of Juan Perón who helped him win popular support; ***Isabel Perón:*** third wife of Perón who became president of Argentina and the first woman president in the Americas; ***Salvador Allende:*** Marxist, elected president of Chile, killed in a military coup; ***Medellín cartel:*** organizers of the Colombian drug trade.
2. The defeat of Argentina in the Falklands War led to the downfall of the military government, and free elections were held in 1983.
3. (a) The "Brazilian Miracle" referred to the rapid growth of the Brazilian economy. **(b)** The military government forced wages to decline by setting low minimum wages and pressuring labor unions. More income was shifted to the managers and owners of businesses, and low-cost loans were made available to businesses. Foreign corporations were again urged to invest in Brazil.
4. (a) Allende's administration quickly nationalized all

problem occurred in the early 1960s when João Goulart (GOO • lahr), with the support of a growing labor movement, became president of Brazil. Goulart's policies increased the income of the lower class at the expense of the upper class. As a result, wealthy Brazilians and foreign companies converted their profits into American dollars and deposited them in banks outside the country.

In an effort to prevent what they thought was a threat to the economy, the army overthrew Goulart in 1964. The military government forced wages down by setting a low minimum wage and by pressuring the labor unions. These policies increased the income of business owners. To encourage productivity, the government also made low-cost loans available to businesses. Foreign corporations were also urged to invest in Brazil.

The economy grew so fast that it was widely hailed as the "Brazilian Miracle." The gains from this miracle, however, went mostly to the rich. In fact, most of the population found themselves somewhat poorer than before, even though they worked longer hours and more family members took jobs. In order to maintain its economic program, the government had to control elections, forbid strikes, and censor television and newspapers. The government also went heavily into debt. By the late 1980s Brazil had a total foreign debt of $100 billion, the highest in the world.

Chile's Elected Revolutionaries

Chile, once the oldest continuing democracy in Latin America, underwent important governmental changes in the 1970s and 1980s. In 1970 an alliance of the Socialist and Communist parties resulted in the election of Salvador Allende (ah • YEN • day). With Allende as president, a Marxist government had come to power through peaceful means, the first to do so in the Western Hemisphere.

Allende's administration nationalized all American-owned copper mines, paying low prices for these valuable assets. The government then implemented an across-the-board wage increase, which raised incomes for people in the lower class. For a time the demand for goods increased, producing a business boom. The upper class, however, feared the changes taking place and stopped investing in the economy. Foreign banks also hesitated to make loans to the government.

Hard-pressed for funds, Allende's treasury printed more money to meet its needs. By 1972 staggering inflation had created hardships for all segments of the population. As the economy worsened, unrest and disillusionment spread.

In September 1973 a revolt backed by the United States broke out. Allende was killed and the army took power. Once in power, the military swiftly eliminated all forms of opposition.

The new military government executed thousands of people. Fearing for their lives, thousands of others fled into exile. The government under the leadership of Augustin Pinochet tightly controlled the press and media and curtailed many civil liberties. However, civil unrest continued to plague the country, and a free election was finally held in 1988. The military lost the election to a civilian government, but because of the way in which the constitution was written, the military actually held power in Chile after the election.

Peru

In the decades following World War II, the government of Peru was run by either military dictators or conservative civilians. However, Peru, like so many other Latin American nations, faced economic crises that included inflation, unemployment, and mounting debt.

Although the Peruvian people took great pride in the election of Javier Pérez de Cuéllar of Peru as Secretary-General of the United Nations in 1982, domestic conditions worsened in Peru in the 1980s. In that decade Peru suffered the worst economic depression of the century. This further weakened democracy as successive governments lost popularity in their attempts to grapple with this economic crisis. In addition, the Communist-inspired guerrillas continued to gain strength, making them one of the strongest revolutionary organizations in Latin America.

The Tragedy of Colombia

The years immediately following World War II were ones of severe civil and political upheaval for the people of Colombia. Rioting followed the assassination of a popular leftist leader, Jorge Eliécer Gaitán, in 1948, leaving thousands dead. The years from 1946 to 1958 saw both military and civilian dictators come to power amid civil and economic strife.

Learning from Pictures *Supporters of a civilian government in Chile rally in preelection demonstrations against further military rule.*

However, by the 1960s Colombia's future appeared brighter under a democratic regime. The economy stabilized, and Colombia became known as one of the models of democracy in Latin America.

Unfortunately, a desire for illegal narcotics increased in Europe and the United States during the late 1960s and early 1970s. The fertile land of Colombia became one of the prime regions for growing the marijuana and coca plants used in making narcotics. The lucrative profits brought by trade in these illegal products led to an increase in their production. Crime soared, as those wishing to control this trade jockeyed for power and position. Medellín, once a flourishing industrial city in Colombia, became headquarters for the Medellín cartel that ran the Colombian drug trade.

The Medellín cartel used assassinations as well as other means of intimidation to gain control of law enforcement agencies. Government officials at higher levels often remained uncorrupted and desperately sought ways to end the stranglehold which the cartel held on the government and the economy. However, officials at lower levels, either bribed or threatened by the drug kings, cooperated with the cartel. By the early 1990s, efforts to curtail this destructive trade continued with varying degrees of success.

SECTION 4 REVIEW

1. **Identify** Juan Perón, Eva Perón, Isabel Perón, Salvador Allende, Medellín cartel
2. **Summarizing Ideas** What was the result of the Falkland War in Argentina?
3. **Analyzing Ideas** **(a)** What was the "Brazilian Miracle"? **(b)** How was it achieved?
4. **Synthesizing Ideas** **(a)** What reforms did Allende attempt to make in Chile? **(b)** Why did the United States aid in the overthrow of the Allende government?
5. **Understanding Cause and Effect** **(a)** What caused the growth of the drug trade in Colombia? **(b)** How did this affect the government and economy of Colombia?

American-owned copper mines, paying low prices for these. The government then implemented an across-the-board wage increase, which raised incomes for people in the lower classes. For a time the demand for goods increased, producing a business boom. The upper classes, however, became fearful of the changes taking place and stopped investing in the economy. Foreign banks also hesitated to make loans to the government. **(b)** The United States feared having another Marxist government in the Western Hemisphere.
5. (a) The fertile land in Colombia made it a prime region for growing marijuana and coca plants used in making narcotics.
(b) The drug trade corrupted the government as officials were either bribed or threatened into cooperating with the drug dealers, and the economy was controlled by the drug kings.

847

Reviewing Important Terms
1. multinational corporation; **2.** Import substitution; **3.** geopolitical region; **4.** campesinos; **5.** covert

Developing Critical Thinking Skills
1. (a) a decline in the death rate, particularly infant mortality; more children survived to go on to adulthood and have children of their own; insecticides that controlled disease-carrying insects; **(b)** a scarcity of land in the rural areas; those with little or no land moved to the cities, which became overcrowded and surrounded by slums; the expansion of cities created a demand for services; the lower classes in the cities began to emerge as a new political force
2. (a) to provide jobs for the increased population; to lessen dependence on foreign sources for manufactured goods; and to provide consumer goods for everyone; **(b)** invited foreign corporations to establish businesses in Latin America; tried import substitution; and attempted new forms of economic association
3. It would remove many of the causes of political upheaval characteristic of the region.
4. (a) overthrow of the Guatemalan president; **(b)** continuation of civil war between the Sandinistas and the Contras; **(c)** the Bay of Pigs invasion; **(d)** the halting of a Communist takeover
5. The peasants suddenly had an ally for their social, economic and political fight for freedom. They felt encouraged by this support from the church.

1A, 5B, 5C, 5I, a4A, a4F, a4G, a4H, a4K, a4L, a4M

Reteaching
Have students review the Chapter Summary and the appropriate section and questions in the Unit Synthesis. Discuss the concepts until students demonstrate a clear understanding of the material.

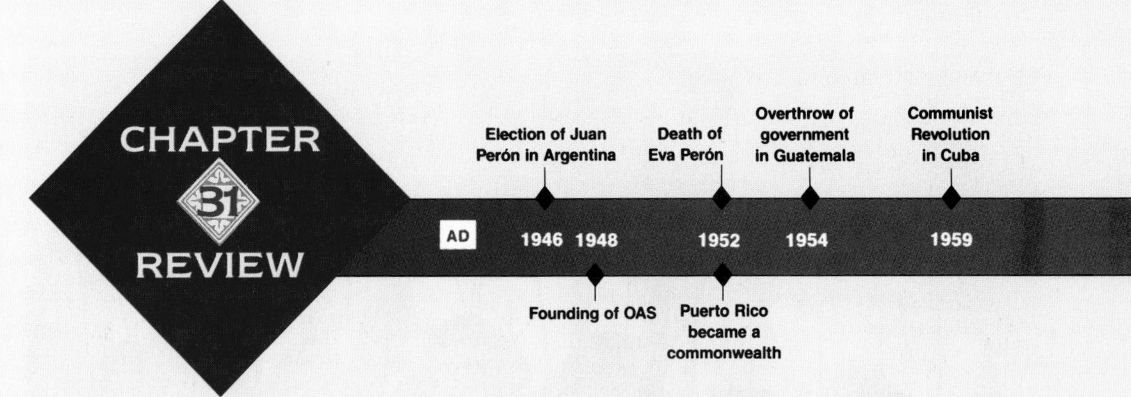

Chapter Summary

The following list contains the key concepts you have learned about the countries of Latin America from the postwar period to the present.

1. The rapid increase in population and growth of the cities changed traditional Latin American society.
2. The lower classes in the cities, women, and labor all emerged as new political forces.
3. The role of foreign-owned corporations in Latin America became a major political issue.
4. Attempts to reduce imports and efforts at economic cooperation were among the steps taken to reduce Latin America's dependence on more developed countries.
5. Organizations such as the OAS and the Alliance for Progress were founded in order to set up security for the Western Hemisphere and to promote better understanding between the United States and Latin America.
6. Revolution in Nicaragua in 1979 brought a Marxist regime to power. A civil war broke out in that country between the Marxist government, run by the Sandinistas, and the antigovernment guerrillas called Contras. The United States aided the Contras until Congress voted against this aid in 1983.
7. Revolution in Cuba in 1959 brought a Communist dictatorship to that country under Fidel Castro. Confrontations with the United States occurred with the Bay of Pigs invasion in 1961 and the Cuban missile crisis in 1962.
8. Both the Dominican Republic and Haiti overthrew dictators. While the Dominican Republic later established a democratic government, Haiti teetered between dictatorship and democracy.
9. In Argentina, Juan Perón established a dictatorship but was ousted in 1952. Although he later returned to power, in 1976 a military regime overthrew the government led by Perón's widow, Isabel.
10. Political unrest and economic chaos have marked Brazil from the postwar period to the present. By the 1990s the country faced a massive foreign debt.
11. Peru faced many problems in the 1980s, while Colombia had to deal with the illegal narcotics trade.

On a separate sheet of paper, complete the following review exercises.

Reviewing Important Terms

Supply the term that correctly completes each statement.

1. A foreign-owned business is called a _______ _______.
2. _______ _______ is an economic policy in which a country encourages the production of goods that the country had been importing.
3. An area with common geographical and political features is called a _______ _______.
4. _______ are peasants in Central America.
5. _______ operations are secret or undercover.

Developing Critical Thinking Skills

1. **Understanding Cause and Effect** **(a)** What were the causes of the population increase in Latin America? **(b)** What were the consequences?
2. **Interpreting Ideas** **(a)** Why did Latin American nations feel that economic development was necessary? **(b)** What efforts did they make to achieve it?
3. **Synthesizing Ideas** How would economic prosperity in Latin America help to establish more political stability?
4. **Understanding Relationships** What were the results of the United States involvement in each of the following: **(a)** Guatemala, **(b)** Nicaragua, **(c)** Cuba, **(d)** Dominican Republic.
5. **Analyzing Ideas** How did the change in the position of the Catholic church after the bishops' conference in 1968 affect the attitude of the peasants with regard to their governments?
6. **Comparing Ideas** **(a)** How were the revolutions in Cuba and Nicaragua different? **(b)** How were they the same?

Relating Geography to History

Turn to the map of Central America and the Caribbean on page 837. **(a)** How many of these nations have Communist governments? **(b)** How

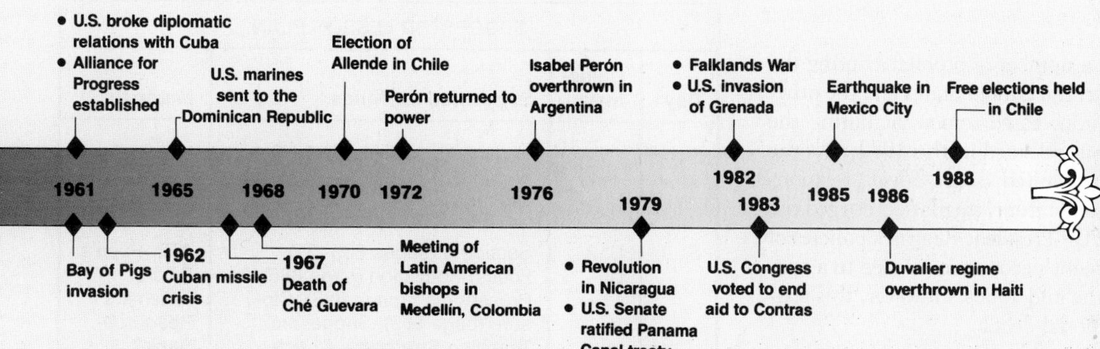

many miles are they from the United States? **(c)** How many kilometers? **(d)** What effect might the presence of Communist governments throughout this region have on United States security?

Relating Past to Present

1. Political affairs in many Latin American countries remained unsettled. Choose one of the Latin American countries and use the *Readers' Guide to Periodical Literature* to find articles on recent developments there. How have changes in Central America affected American foreign policy?
2. For decades many Latin American governments came to power through revolution or coups. Find out how many governments in Latin America today came to power by either a coup or a revolution. Are these governments secure? How many are dictatorships?

Applying History Study Skills

Before completing this activity, review Building History Study Skills on page 834.

Read the following paragraph on what takes place on a hacienda during a revolution. Then answer the questions that follow.

> "What we call social revolutions have all occurred in agricultural countries where the mass of the people lived on what they themselves raised from the soil. In such a society, a revolution is a simple thing. First, you cut off the head of the *hacendado,* then you divide the wheat, corn, and barley stored in the barn and the hacendado's cows, horses, sheep, and chickens. Similarly the plows, digging sticks, and other tools are distributed. The land is taken by the peasants and the revolution is over. What really happens is that the stored consumer goods are divided up among the surrounding peasants, and the limited producers' goods, in the form of seed, animals, tools, and the land itself, fall into the hands of those who have used the tools and animals and worked the land."

1. What economic questions are raised by the passage?
2. How is the problem of scarcity dealt with after a revolution?
3. What does the passage imply might be some of the causes of the revolution?

Investigating Further

1. **Presenting an Oral Report** Although the Brazilian economy grew rapidly in the 1960s and 1970s, many Brazilians still lived in poverty in large slums at the edges of cities. Find out about living conditions in the slums and present an oral report to the class. You might read Carolina de Jesus's *Child of the Dark* (New American Library). Why don't the people of the slums trust the government? How is Carolina different from most people in the slums?
2. **Writing a Report** Select a country in Latin America and prepare a written report on the positive and negative effects of foreign-owned corporations there. You may use the *Readers' Guide to Periodical Literature* to locate articles on this topic. You may wish to select one corporation that operates in a specific Latin American country and prepare a case study detailing the impact that the corporation has had on the citizens of the host country.
3. **Preparing a Chart** Use resources in your school or public library to find the per capita gross national product, the major exports, and the major imports of the following countries: Mexico, Guatemala, El Salvador, Honduras, Belize, Nicaragua, Costa Rica, Panama, Cuba, the Dominican Republic, Haiti, Colombia, Venezuela, Bolivia, Peru, Chile, Brazil, Paraguay, Uruguay, and Argentina. Then assemble the information you have gathered into a chart to display in class.
4. **Preparing a Panel Discussion** The nations of Latin America face many problems typical of developing nations in the world today. Work with a group of your classmates to find more information on how these nations are dealing with the problems of low rates of economic growth, high rates of unemployment and population growth, and burgeoning foreign debts. Then use the information you have collected to prepare a panel discussion detailing possible solutions to the problems.

6. (a) Cuba: uprisings and intervention by the U.S. were unsuccessful in toppling the Castro government; Nicaragua: U.S.-backed Contra rebels have plunged the country into civil war. **(b)** Both had much popular support; both set up Communist governments which antagonized the U.S.

Relating Geography to History

(a) two—Cuba and Nicaragua **(b)** Cuba—90 miles; Nicaragua—about 600 miles **(c)** Cuba—145 kilometers; Nicaragua—about 966 kilometers **(d)** It might jeopardize U.S. security as the U.S. could lose free access to the Panama Canal, which is vitally important to U.S. security.

Relating Past to Present

1. Answers may vary.
2. Answers may vary.

Applying History Study Skills

1. Is the economic system of the hacienda sufficient to meet the needs of the peasants living there? Are the peasants on the hacienda able to live on what they produce? When economic conditions become so difficult for the peasants, how will they react?
2. The land and all that is on it and that it produces are divided among the peasants.
3. The revolution may have been caused by an unequal distribution of wealth. The *hacendado* probably made all of the important economic decisions, paid his workers poorly, and kept them at a subsistence level.

849

CHAPTER (pages 850–873)

32 Challenges Faced the Superpowers in the Modern Era

(1968 to the present)

CHAPTER OVERVIEW

The world's leading powers faced a number of problems during the 1970s and 1980s. Tensions between the United States and the other great superpower, the Soviet Union, eased somewhat during the period of détente in the 1970s, but resumed in the 1980s. As the 1980s drew to a close, however, United States-Soviet relations warmed once again. On the economic front, stagflation dogged the United States throughout the 1970s. President Reagan's policies of cutting taxes and limiting government's economic role led to a revival of the American economy in the mid-1980s. However, this revival came at a price — a huge national debt.

Canada faced a serious domestic problem in the strong separatist movement that developed in the province of Quebec. And although Canadian relations with the United States continued to be close, many Canadians feared becoming economically dependent on their southern neighbor. Many of the nations of Western European sought to consolidate the economic gains they had made in the postwar years. Also, a number of nations in southern Europe returned to democracy after being under the yoke of military dictatorships. And European efforts at economic and political cooperation that had begun in the 1950s continued in the 1970s and 1980s.

The Soviet Union underwent major changes in the 1980s as Mikhail Gorbachev attempted to open Soviet society and restructure its political and economic systems. Although Gorbachev's policies met with mixed reviews both within and outside his country, many people believed that such policies provided real hope for the future of the Soviet Union and its satellite nations.

SUGGESTED LESSON PLAN

Day	Objectives	Suggested Activities	Materials
1	U10*, C1–5	Introducing the Chapter (pages 850–51) Section 1 (pages 851–57), Focus/Motivation (page 851), Presentation (page 852), Closure (page 855), Suggested Teaching Strategies, Enrichment Activity, Daily Quiz, Suggested Assignments (page 849B)	ATE, Pupil's Edition, Teacher's Resource-Bank™
2	U11, C6–8	Section 2 (pages 858–65), Focus/Motivation (page 858), Presentation (page 859), Closure (page 863), Suggested Teaching Strategies, Enrichment Activity, Daily Quiz, Suggested Assignments (page 849C)	ATE, Pupil's Edition, Teacher's Resource-Bank™
3	U12, C9–11	Section 3 (pages 865–71), Focus/Motivation (page 865), Presentation (page 866), Closure (page 869), Suggested Teaching Strategies, Enrichment Activity, Daily Quiz, Suggested Assignments (page 849D)	ATE, Pupil's Edition, Teacher's Resource-Bank™
4	U10–12, C1–11	Chapter 32 Form A Test, Reteaching Worksheet, Chapter 32 Form B Test	Teacher's Resource-Bank™ or Workbook and Test Booklet

*C refers to applicable Chapter Objective, U refers to applicable Unit Goal.

BOOKS FOR THE TEACHER

Barzini, Luigi. *The Europeans.* Simon and Schuster. Draws on the author's personal experience. Presents an enthralling view of Europe and its diverse population.

Cracraft, David. *The Soviet Union Today: An Interpretative Guide,* 2nd ed. University of Chicago. Conveys a realistic picture of life in modern Soviet society.

Gorbachev, Mikhail. *Perestroika: New Thinking for Our Country and Our World.* Harper & Row. Offers an insight into the thinking behind the restructuring in the Soviet Union.

Joyce, William W., ed. *Canada in the Classroom.* National Council for Social Studies. Provides background information on Canada and Canadian-United States relations.

Schlesinger, Arthur M. *The Cycles of American History.* Houghton Mifflin. Traces the key themes in American history through a collection of reflective essays.

BOOKS FOR THE STUDENT

Bender, David L., ed. *The Soviet Union: Opposing Viewpoints.* Greenhaven Press. Offers pro and con debates on *glasnost*, the Soviet economy, the Soviet military, and human rights.

Bernards, Neal, and Lynn Hall, eds. *American Foreign Policy: Opposing Viewpoints.* Greenhaven Press. Discusses the major issues of American foreign policy from a variety of viewpoints.

Binyon, Michael. *Life in Russia.* Berkley. Attempts to show the human side of the Communist superpower.

Garfinkel, Bernard. *Margaret Thatcher.* Chelsea House. Traces the life of the British leader from her childhood to her election as prime minister.

Woodward, Bob, and Carl Bernstein. *The Final Days.* Simon and Schuster. Details the events leading up to the resignation of President Richard Nixon in 1974. Recommended for advanced students.

MULTIMEDIA MATERIALS

Europe: Diverse Continent (6 fs), EBE. Examines Europe from a number of perspectives, including the ideas that divide and unite the continent and its contribution to world civilization.

45/85: America and the World Since World War II (vc. 52 min.), ABC News. Creates an informative montage of world history through newsreels, newscasts, interviews, and still photographs. Vol. III (1961–1975) and Vol. IV (1976–1985) are appropriate for use with this chapter.

Inside the Soviet Union (vc. 57 min.), Close-Up Foundation. Views life in the Soviet Union through the eyes of a Russian now living in the United States.

Modern United States History, Unit 3: 1969–1981 (4 fs), Guidance Associates. Traces the important events of the Nixon, Ford, and Carter administrations.

Section 1 (pages 851–857)

The United States Tried to Maintain its World Leadership

SECTION OVERVIEW

The tensions that marked United States-Soviet relations during the 1960s eased with the introduction of the policy of détente in the 1970s. These tensions returned once again in the 1980s, but as the decade drew to a close President Reagan and Premier Gorbachev moved their countries toward a better understanding. The American economy suffered continuing stagflation throughout the 1970s. The 1980s saw a revival in the economy, but the trade deficit and the national debt both grew dramatically in this period.

In Canada, domestic tension was created by the separatist movement in Quebec. And although a free trade agreement was signed between the United States and Canada, many Canadians grew wary of their country's increasing economic dependence on their neighbor to the south.

SUGGESTED TEACHING STRATEGIES

1. **Preteaching Vocabulary (Basic)** You may wish to preteach the following important vocabulary terms: stagflation, trade deficit (*page 853*); détente, dissident (*page 855*). Ask: Why do you think economists were surprised by the advent of the situation known as stagflation?
2. **Analyzing Ideas (Average/Group)** Organize the class into groups of five. Have each group prepare a list of five suggestions for improving relations between the United States and Canada. Reassemble the class, and have students select the five most practical suggestions. Have them discuss possible means by which these suggestions might be put into effect.

ENRICHMENT ACTIVITY

Debating (Average/Group) A group of students might present a debate on the question of independence for Quebec. Students may need to do further reading before preparing their arguments on this issue. Useful sources of information include A. Bernard's *What Does Quebec Want?* (Lorimer); *Canada in Transition* (H. W. Wilson), edited by G. S. McClellan; and Susan M. Trofimenkoff's *The Dream of Nation* (Macmillan). Students should also consult the *Readers' Guide to Periodical Literature.*

DAILY QUIZ

To assess student understanding of Section 1, give the class the following quiz. (Each item is worth 10 points.)

1. What action by President Nixon sparked violent student demonstrations in 1970? *(the invasion of Cambodia by American troops)*
2. Economists called the combination of decreased economic activity and continued price increases ________. *(stagflation)*
3. During the 1980s the United States changed from a predominantly manufacturing economy to a predominantly ________ economy. *(service)*
4. During the late 1980s, the United States had a ________ ________, meaning that it imported more than it exported. *(trade deficit)*
5. Concerns about the safety of ________ ________ reached a peak in 1979 after the accident at Three Mile Island. *(nuclear energy)*
6. (T or F) President Nixon and Soviet leader Brezhnev signed agreements limiting their countries' production and deployment of missiles. *(T)*
7. (T or F) President Carter felt that human rights should not be a factor in the United States' relations with other nations. *(F)*
8. Which two world leaders met at summit meetings at Geneva and Reykjavik in the mid-1980s? *(President Ronald Reagan of the United States and Premier Mikhail Gorbachev of the Soviet Union.)*
9. Which Canadian province was recognized as a "distinct society" within Canada by an amendment to the 1982 constitution? *(Quebec)*
10. What was the major issue of the 1988 general election in Canada? *(the United States-Canada Free Trade Agreement)*

SUGGESTED ASSIGNMENTS

1. **Critical Thinking Worksheet (Basic)** Have students complete Critical Thinking Worksheet 72 in the TEACHER'S RESOURCEBANK™.

2. **Researching (Average/Group)** Organize the class into two groups. Ask one group to investigate the present negotiations between the United States and the Soviet Union aimed at reducing nuclear arms. Have these students present an oral report explaining the history and current status of these negotiations. Ask the other group to prepare a time line of major events in arms control since 1968. Have this group display its time line on the bulletin board. For sources of information on this subject, suggest that students check the *Readers' Guide to Periodical Literature* for appropriate articles.
3. **Writing a Report (Average/Group)** A number of books have been written on the Watergate affair. Organize the class into groups and assign one of the books listed below to each group. Each group might meet on designated days to read and discuss its book. When the reading has been completed, have each group present a written report. Suggested books are Bob Woodward and Carl Bernstein's *All the President's Men* (Warner) and *The Final Days* (Simon and Schuster); Theodore H. White's *Breach of Faith* (Atheneum); Leon Jaworski's *The Right and the Power* (Reader's Digest Press); and John Dean's *Blind Ambition* (Simon and Schuster).

Section (pages 858–865)

2 Western Europe Searched for Stability

SECTION OVERVIEW

During the 1970s and 1980s, many Western European nations attempted to consolidate the economic gains they had made in the years after World War II. Great Britain and West Germany first followed socialist approaches in these efforts, but in the 1980s they switched to more conservative policies. In contrast, France moved from a conservative economic approach to a socialist one. In southern Europe, a number of countries progressed politically from dictatorship to democracy. And the efforts at economic and political unity that had begun in Europe in the early postwar years made great strides forward during the 1970s and 1980s.

SUGGESTED TEACHING STRATEGIES

1. **Preteaching Vocabulary (Basic)** You may wish to preteach the following important vocabulary term: *Ostpolitik (page 860)*. Have students compare *Ostpolitik* with the policy of détente. Ask: What are the similarities and differences between *Ostpolitik* and détente? *(After students have completed their comparison, you might want to point out that many political scientists consider* Ostpolitik *to be the forerunner of détente.)*
2. **Constructing a Chart (Average/Group)** Organize the class into a number of groups. Assign each group a different country in Western Europe. Students should consult almanacs and encyclopedias to find information on the current economic status of their assigned country. Information to be located includes: gross national product (GNP), per capita income, rate of population growth, total amount of exports and imports, inflation rate, and unemployment rate. Remind students that information should be as current as possible. When students have collected the appropriate information, have them work together to develop a chart comparing the economies of the various countries. Have students display their chart on the bulletin board.

ENRICHMENT ACTIVITY

Defending a Point of View (Challenging) Ask students to reread the excerpt from the Helsinki Accords on page 851. Then have interested students prepare arguments supporting one of the two statements below.

A country's respect and protection of human rights should be the only factor the United States considers when deciding the kind of relations to have with that country.

If the United States is to make decisions about its relations with other countries based on one issue, that issue should be its security.

Remind students that their arguments must be supported by facts or other forms of evidence. Have students present their arguments to the rest of the class. You might use these arguments as the basis for a class discussion on what factors the United States government should consider when making decisions on international relations.

DAILY QUIZ

To assess student understanding of Section 2, give the class the following quiz. (Each item is worth 10 points.)

1. What did critics of Margaret Thatcher's government believe her economic policies had created? *(two societies in Great Britain — a prosperous south and an economically depressed north)*
2. Why did the British government send troops to Northern Ireland in 1969? *(to protect the Catholic population from a Protestant backlash)*
3. How did Margaret Thatcher cut off publicity for terrorist groups in Northern Ireland? *(banning direct radio and television statements by members or supporters of terrorist organizations)*
4. Under which president did France become one of the world's leading weapons dealers? *(Georges Pompidou)*
5. (T or F) Under François Mitterrand, France drastically reduced its involvement in foreign affairs. *(F)*
6. Which West German chancellor developed *Ostpolitik*, a policy designed to create better East-West relations? *(Willy Brandt)*
7. (T or F) Portugal returned to democracy through a military coup. *(T)*
8. (T or F) Under Andreas Papandreou Greece improved its relations with the United States and reaffirmed its commitment to NATO. *(F)*
9. What was the name of the agreement that specified ways to improve East-West cooperation, endorsed the use of negotiation to settle differences among nations, and called upon all nations to respect human rights? *(Helsinki Accords)*

10. Which European leader spoke out against the full economic integration of Europe? *(Margaret Thatcher of Great Britain)*

SUGGESTED ASSIGNMENTS

1. **Geography Supplement (Basic)** Have students complete Geography Application Sheet 16, titled *Labor Migration — A Key to Europe's Economic Growth,* in the Geography Supplement of the TEACHER'S RESOURCEBANK™.
2. **Profile Worksheet (Basic)** Have students complete Profile Worksheet 32 in the TEACHER'S RESOURCEBANK™.
3. **Preparing an Oral Report (Average/Group)** Interested students might like to prepare an oral report for presentation to the class on the impact of "the Troubles" on the young people of Northern Ireland. Useful sources of information include Robert Coles's "Ulster's Children: Waiting for the Prince of Peace" (*Atlantic Monthly,* December 1980); Carolyn Meyer's *Voices of Northern Ireland: Growing Up in a Troubled Land* (Gulliver); and Roger Rosenblatt's *Children of War* (Doubleday).

Section 3 (pages 865–871)
Political Challenges Faced the Soviet Union and Eastern Europe

SECTION OVERVIEW

During the 1970s and early 1980s, Soviet leader Leonid Brezhnev kept a tight rein on his own people and the peoples of the satellite nations. At home he clamped down on any form of dissent. Censorship was strict, and human rights were almost nonexistent. Abroad, he kept the satellite nations in line by the threat of the Brezhnev Doctrine. However, people in the satellite nations continued to test Soviet authority. Perhaps the greatest challenge came from the Polish independent trade union movement, Solidarity.

In the mid-1980s the situation in the Soviet Union began to change. The new leader, Mikhail Gorbachev, attempted to liberalize and restructure the whole of Soviet society. His polices met with mixed reactions both inside and outside the Soviet Union. It remains to be seen whether his efforts will be successful in the Soviet Union and whether these policies will be applied in the nations of Eastern Europe.

SUGGESTED TEACHING STRATEGIES

1. **Preteaching Vocabulary (Basic)** You may wish to preteach the following important vocabulary terms: *glasnost (page 866); perestroika (page 867); samizdat (page 868).* Have the students discuss the new policies introduced by Premier Gorbachev. Ask: Which policy do you think would have the greatest impact on day-to-day life in the Soviet Union — *glasnost* or *perestroika?* Explain your answer.
2. **Understanding Chronology (Average/Group)** Have students construct time lines showing the major events in the development of one of the dissident movements in Eastern Europe, such as Charter 77 in Czechoslovakia and Solidarity in Poland. Suggest that students use the *Readers' Guide to Periodical Literature* to find sources of information on this subject.

*3. **Thinking About History: Conducting a Debate (Average/Group)** To reinforce the skill lesson presented on page 869, have students use the information on pages 868–871 on dissent in the satellite nations to write a proposition and, from this, develop and conduct a debate.

ENRICHMENT ACTIVITY

Analyzing Ideas (Challenging) Interested students might like to read some examples of banned Czechoslovakian literature, such as Jiri Grusa's *The Questionnaire* (Aventura); Bohumil Hrabal's *Closely Watched Trains* (Penguin); Ivan Klima's *My Merry Mornings* (Readers International); Milan Kundera's *The Joke* (Penguin); and Josef Skvorecky's *The Cowards* (Ecco). Have students make brief reports on the books they have read. Suggest that they include in their reports why they think the book was banned in Czechoslovakia.

DAILY QUIZ

To assess student understanding of Section 3, give the class the following quiz. (Each item is worth 10 points.)

1. What did the Brezhnev Doctrine state? *(that the Soviet Union had the right to intervene in the affairs of any satellite nation that seemed to be drifting away from communism.)*
2. What brought détente between the United States and the Soviet Union to an end? *(The Soviet invasion of Afghanistan)*
3. What two new policies did Mikhail Gorbachev introduce? (glasnost *and* perestroika)
4. What previous effort at reform did Gorbachev's economic restructuring resemble? *(the Prague Spring)*
5. What did the people of the Baltic republics hope Gorbachev's political restructuring would bring them? *(greater autonomy)*
6. How did writers in Eastern Europe evade government censors? *(by publishing* samizdat *editions of their works.)*
7. What was Charter 77? *(a group of Czechoslovakian artists and intellectuals who signed a charter calling on their government to honor the human rights articles of the Helsinki Accords.)*
8. Who led the strike of Polish shipyard workers that resulted in the foundation of the independent trade union, Solidarity? *(Lech Walesa)*
9. Which Hungarian leader felt that Gorbachev's plans for economic restructuring did not go far enough? *(Karoly Grosz)*
10. Which leader of the Prague Spring expressed support for Gorbachev's reforms? *(Alexander Dubcek)*

SUGGESTED ASSIGNMENTS

1. **Researching (Basic)** Have students use the most recent editions of *Statesman's Yearbook, The World Almanac,* and *Encyclopedia Britannica Yearbook* to find data on the economies of the Soviet Union and the eight Eastern European nations. Have them use this information to construct tables comparing the

economies of these various countries. Columns in the table should be labeled: "GNP," "Personal Income," "Inflation," and "Unemployment." Encourage students to compare their tables with those of other members of the class.

2. **Review Worksheet (Basic)** Have students complete Review Worksheet 32 in the TEACHER'S RESOURCEBANK™.
3. **Critical Thinking Worksheet (Basic)** Have students complete Critical Thinking Worksheet 73 in the TEACHER'S RESOURCEBANK™.
4. **Skill Worksheet (Basic)** Have students complete Skill Worksheet 32 in the TEACHER'S RESOURCEBANK™.

Teacher's Notes

For suggested lesson plan, additional teaching strategies, enrichment activities, daily quizzes, and suggested assignments, see pages 849A-849E.

Introducing the Chapter
Ask students to list countries that they consider close allies, or "friends," of the United States. *(Most students will suggest the Western European nations, Japan, Canada, Mexico, and so on.)* Then ask them to list countries that they consider opponents, or "enemies," of the United States. *(Students' lists probably will include the Soviet Union, some Eastern European countries, Nicaragua, Cuba, and so on.)* Then point out that in the world of diplomacy things are not always what they seem. To protect its own interests, and to preserve world order, the United States has sometimes developed close relations with countries that appear to be "enemies." Mention that in this chapter students will learn more about the changing diplomatic picture of the world.

Chapter Objectives
After studying Chapter 32, students will be able to:

1. Identify the issues that caused political dissent in the United States during the late 1960s and 1970s.
2. Discuss the economic challenges that faced the United States in the 1970s and 1980s.
3. Outline the changes in American foreign policy made during the 1970s and 1980s.
4. Trace the development of the separatist movement in Canada.
5. Explain why the relationship between the

CHAPTER 32

Challenges Faced the Superpowers in the Modern Era

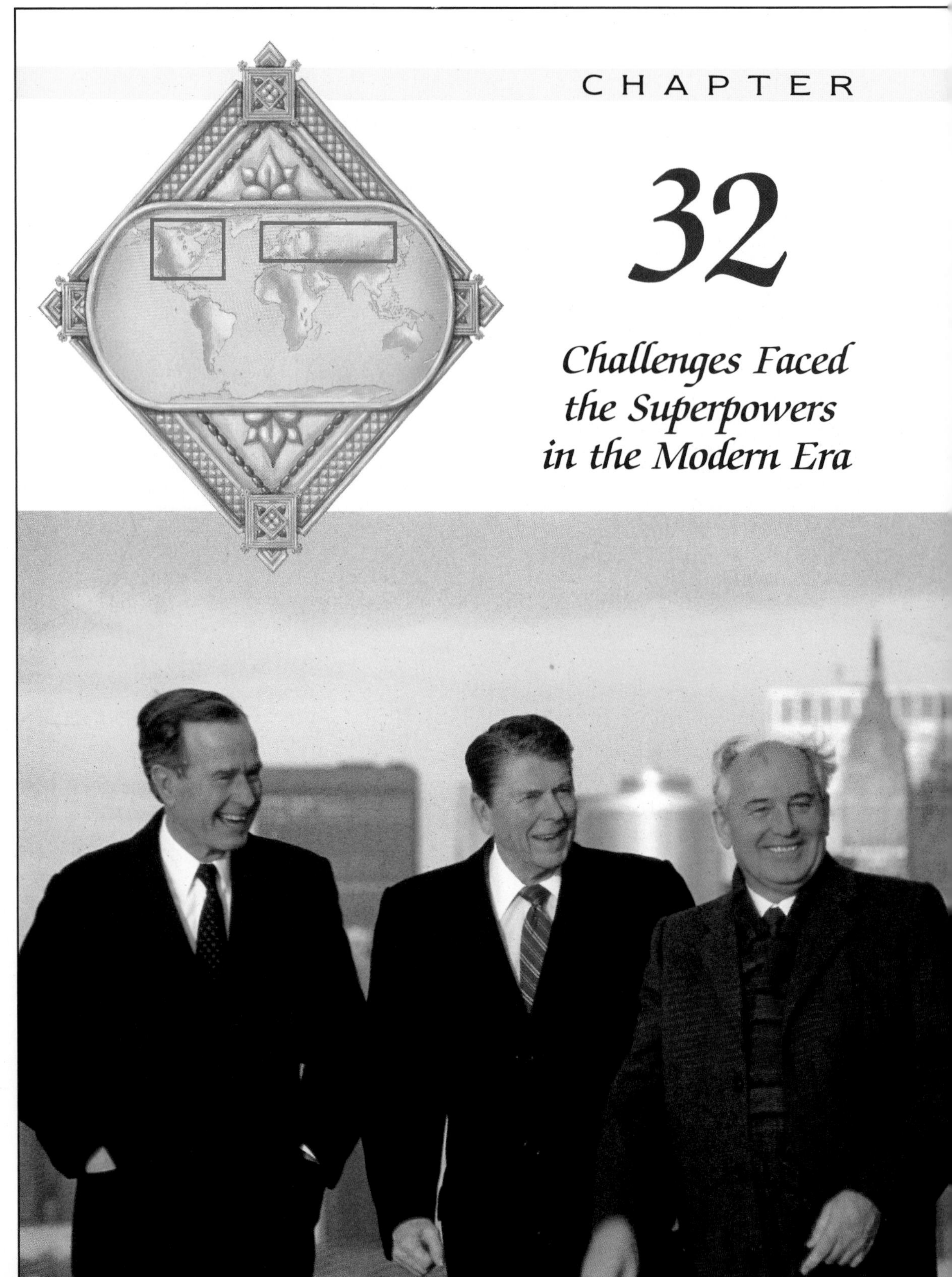

CHAPTER FOCUS

Place North America and Europe

Time 1968–the present

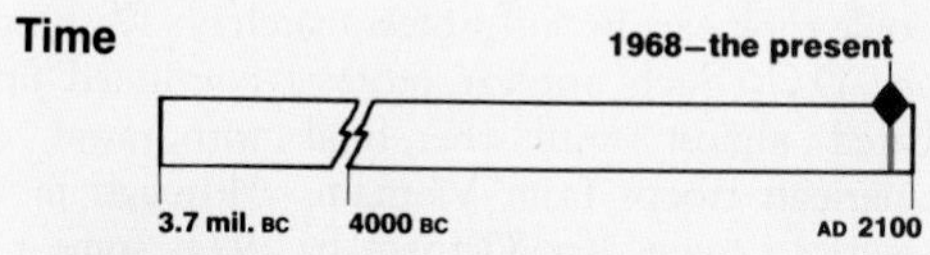

Significance

An economic recession gripped much of the world during the early 1970s and caused major problems for most of the Western nations. After a 10-year struggle, the economies of most of these nations recovered.

During this period the United States worked to maintain its position as a leading nation on the world scene, cementing its already strong ties with Canada and Western Europe and attempting to improve relations with Eastern Europe. Meanwhile, the nations of Western Europe moved toward economic and political unity.

The Soviet Union and Eastern Europe faced major economic and political challenges in the 1970s and 1980s. However, a new Soviet leader attempted to restructure the political and economic organization of his country. Mikhail Gorbachev's new policies and the easing of tensions between East and West seemed to offer new hope for the future.

Terms to Define

stagflation	*Ostpolitik*
trade deficit	*glasnost*
détente	*perestroika*

People to Identify

Gerald Ford	Margaret Thatcher
Jimmy Carter	Willy Brandt
Ronald Reagan	Mikhail Gorbachev
Brian Mulroney	Lech Walesa

Places to Locate

Afghanistan	Armenia
Reykjavik	Latvia
Quebec	Estonia
Azerbaijan	Gdansk

Questions to Guide Your Reading

1 How did the United States maintain its leadership role in world affairs in the 1970s and 1980s?
2 What signs of political and economic stability were evident in Western Europe in the 1970s and 1980s?
3 What political and economic challenges did the Soviet Union and Eastern Europe face as the twentieth century drew to a close?

◀ *A United States-Soviet summit in New York*

On August 1, 1975, in Helsinki, Finland, representatives from 35 nations signed the Final Act of the Conference on Security and Cooperation in Europe. The following excerpt from this document, better known as the Helsinki Accords, describes the participating nations' view of human rights.

> *"The participating States will respect human rights and fundamental freedoms, including the freedom of thought, conscience, religion or belief, for all without distinction as to race, sex, language or religion.*
>
> *They will promote and encourage the effective exercise of civil, political, economic, social, cultural and other rights and freedoms all of which derive from the inherent dignity of the human person and are essential for his free and full development.*
>
> *. . . [T]he participating States will recognize and respect the freedom of the individual to profess and practice, alone or in community with others, religion or belief acting in accordance with the dictates of his own conscience.*
>
> *The participating States on whose territory national minorities exist will respect the right of persons belonging to such minorities to equality before the law, [and] will afford them the full opportunity for the actual enjoyment of human rights and fundamental freedoms."*

In time the human-rights aspect of the Helsinki Accords became a factor in diplomatic relations among nations. As you will read, Soviet violations of the Helsinki Accords led to tensions between the United States and the Soviet Union.

1 The United States Tried to Maintain Its World Leadership

During the 1970s and 1980s, the United States faced a number of problems, including internal political conflicts and several economic reversals. Despite such problems, the country's commitment to its leadership role in world affairs remained strong. Meanwhile, Canada, also confronted with internal political and economic problems, somewhat reluctantly moved toward closer relations with its neighbor to the south.

United States and Canada has been strained in recent years.
6. Describe the changes brought about in Great Britain by Margaret Thatcher's government.
7. Discuss the political and economic changes that have taken place in France and West Germany since the late 1960s.
8. Outline efforts at economic and political cooperation in Europe.
9. Define and explain *glasnost* and *perestroika.*
10. Describe the continuing dissent in the Soviet Union's satellite nations.
11. Discuss how Communist and non-Communist nations have responded to the policies of *glasnost* and *perestroika.*

SECTION 1

Focus/Motivation
Have each student write on a sheet of paper what he or she considers the five most important problems facing the United States today. Call upon students to read their lists to the class, and then write their responses on the chalkboard. When all students have responded, select the five problems most often mentioned and use them as a basis for discussion. The discussion should center on the extent of the problem, solutions that have been tried, and alternative solutions. When students have completed the chapter, have them compare their lists with the problems mentioned in the text.

1B, a2A, a2C, a2D, a2E, a2F, a2J, a2K, a2L

Presentation Constructing a Map (Average/Group)
A group of students can work together to prepare a large illustrated map of Canada. Students should label each province and develop symbols to show the population, natural resources, and industries of each. Students might also include information on climate, and label major cities in each province. After the map has been completed, you might use it as a vehicle for class discussion, posing the following questions: What are Canada's major natural resources? Where are they located? What are Canada's major industries? Where is the majority of the Canadian population concentrated?

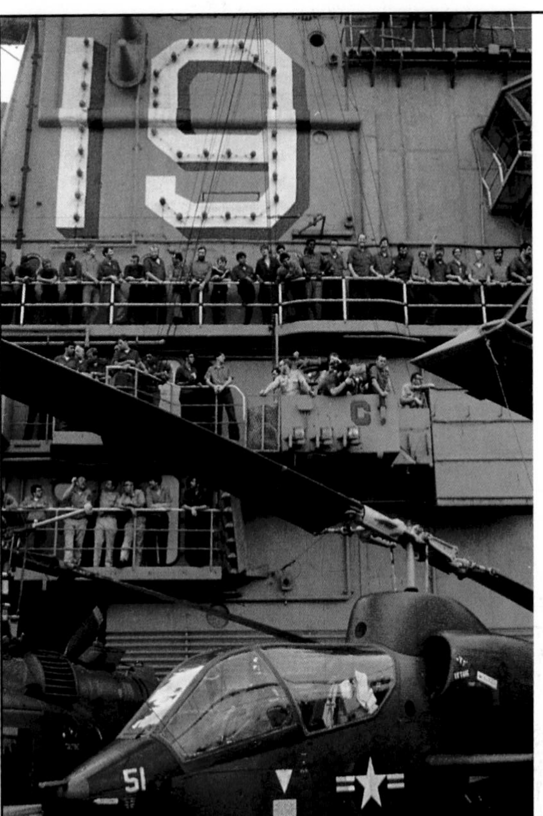

Learning from Pictures *United States naval vessels helped evacuate American and South Vietnamese people when North Vietnam unified the country.*

Ending the Vietnam War

During the presidential campaign of 1968, Richard M. Nixon vowed to end American involvement in the Vietnam War "with honor." As a new decade dawned, the public clamored for the newly elected president to keep this promise.

Antiwar protest. The antiwar movement had begun during the mid-1960s, several years before President Nixon took office. However, its strength grew tremendously during his administration. College students, the movement's most vocal members, regularly staged huge demonstrations against Nixon's war policies on university campuses.

The most violent demonstrations occurred after Nixon's announcement of the American invasion of Cambodia in 1970. In early May four students were shot and killed when the National Guard attempted to break up a protest at Kent State University in Ohio. A few days later, a clash between students and police at Jackson State University in Mississippi led to the deaths of two more students. Almost immediately hundreds of universities across the country closed as students took to the streets to protest these campus shootings. Close to 100,000 people took part in one protest march on Washington, D.C. Such antiwar protests continued unabated almost until the final withdrawal of American troops from Vietnam. Although most American forces left Vietnam by 1973, some remained until the fall of Saigon in 1975.

The impact of the war. The Paris Accords, signed in 1973, finally ended American involvement in the Vietnam War. However, the impact of the war proved long-lasting for the United States. American casualties numbered about 58,000 dead and 150,000 wounded. About 2,500 Americans were listed as missing in action (MIA), and many of them have not been accounted for. In addition to the human toll, the monetary cost of the war, some $160 billion, placed a heavy burden on the American economy. One of the most devastating consequences of the war was the damage it inflicted on the American national identity. Such was the extent of the damage that many Americans, after considering the monetary and human cost of the war, began to doubt the wisdom of the United States playing a major role in world affairs.

The Watergate Scandal

American national identity took another blow from a scandal that brought down the Nixon administration. During the 1972 presidential campaign, burglars had broken into the Democratic Party offices in the Watergate building in Washington, D.C. The burglars had tried to photograph campaign documents and install listening devices in the offices.

In 1973 a Washington newspaper charged that officials of President Nixon's reelection campaign had planned the break-in. The Senate set up a special committee to investigate this charge. During the investigation, evidence verified that members of the White House staff had secretly used illegal funds to conceal the nature of the burglary. Finally, it became clear that President Nixon had known about this cover-up. Impeachment proceedings began in the House of Representatives, but Nixon resigned the presidency before the question of his guilt came to a vote.

1C, 1D, 5D, a1B, a1C, a1D, a2J, a2K, a2L, a3A, a3B, a3H, a3I

● By the late 1980s, the national debt was approaching $3 trillion.
■ Similar changes took place in the economies of other Western industrialized nations — Great Britain, for example — during the 1980s.

Despite Nixon's resignation and his subsequent pardon by President Gerald R. Ford, the Watergate scandal shook the faith of many people in the American political system. Many people began to feel that politicians generally lacked integrity. For them the name *Washington, D.C.*, soon became synonymous with the words "dishonesty" and "corruption." Jimmy Carter, elected in 1976, and Ronald Reagan, elected in 1980, both campaigned for the presidency as outsiders, with no ties to Washington. They vowed to clean up the corruption that had crept into the political system and to restore the faith of Americans in their country's government.

The Economy

During the late 1960s, government spending had skyrocketed as President Johnson tried to finance both his Great Society programs and the Vietnam War. This escalation in government spending, in turn, led to a general increase in prices and a decline in the buying power of the dollar. In the early 1970s, the stability of the American economy became an issue of some concern.

Attempts to stabilize the economy. President Nixon tried to fight the inflation that resulted from the escalation in government spending by cutting federal expenditures and encouraging an increase in interest rates—the cost of borrowing money. However, these measures had little effect on inflation and triggered a recession. Economists gave the name **stagflation** to this unusual combination of decreased economic activity (stagnation) and continued price increases (inflation).

Stagflation plagued the administrations of presidents Ford and Carter. Regardless of the programs they introduced—tight controls on federal spending, tax cuts, and voluntary price and wage freezes—the economic situation showed little improvement.

Then, in 1981 President Ronald Reagan took office, promising to bring the unruly economy under control. A conservative, President Reagan planned to cut many social programs and drastically reduce both government spending and tax rates. With the assistance of Congress, he carried out most of his programs. As a result, by the mid-1980s the rate of inflation had dropped from 13 percent to 4 percent and unemployment from 7 percent to less than 6 percent. Even so, government spending, especially on defense, continued to increase. To cover this increase, the government had to borrow large amounts of money. Consequently, the United States government assumed a huge national debt. ●

Changes in the American economy. For much of the 1900s, the United States had led the world in heavy industry and manufacturing. During the 1970s and 1980s, however, the United States began to lose ground in these areas. American steel companies, shipbuilders, and automakers found it increasingly difficult to compete with their counterparts in Japan, South Korea, and Taiwan, who had more modern factories and much lower labor costs.

As a result, during the 1980s many American steel mills, shipyards, and automobile plants closed, throwing hundreds of thousands of people out of work. This greatly added to the country's unemployment problems and marked a major change in the nature of the American economy. For years manufacturing had dominated economic life in the United States. In the 1980s, however, service-oriented businesses such as financial institutions, retail stores, and restaurants generated the most important economic activity. ■ Some economists worried that the change from a manufacturing economy to a service economy might create problems in the future. They pointed out that although many service jobs commanded high salaries, the majority were low paying. Such jobs, these economists argued, could not support continued economic growth.

In addition to these changes in the American economy, Americans began to buy more and more foreign goods. At the same time, many American businesses found it increasingly difficult to sell their products abroad. This created a **trade deficit**—a situation in which a country imports more than it exports. By the time President George Bush took office in 1989, the trade deficit stood at about $110 billion.

Energy Concerns

One factor that contributed greatly to American economic woes—the OPEC oil embargo of 1973—also caused concern about future energy supplies. The embargo highlighted American dependence on imported oil. This dependence, coupled with the fact that oil, once used, cannot be replaced, forced many Americans to consider alternative energy sources.

853

History Through the Arts

PAINTING

Georgia O'Keeffe

Georgia O'Keeffe, who lived from 1887 to 1986, an American artist, painted this stark and powerful image of a skull set against a blue sky. O'Keeffe lived in New York with her husband, photographer Alfred Stieglitz. Like millions of other Americans, O'Keeffe found the endless variety of the American landscape fascinating and exciting. Each summer she traveled to the desert in the Southwest to paint. It was here that O'Keeffe derived a great source of inspiration for many of her paintings. She wrote, "I brought home the bleached bones as my symbols of the desert. To me they are as beautiful as anything I know."

O'Keeffe's confident style made a clear statement that American artists no longer depended on European influences. She commented about her work, "As I painted along on my cow's skull I thought to myself, I'll make it an American painting. They will not think it great with the red stripes down the sides—Red, White, and Blue—but they will notice it."

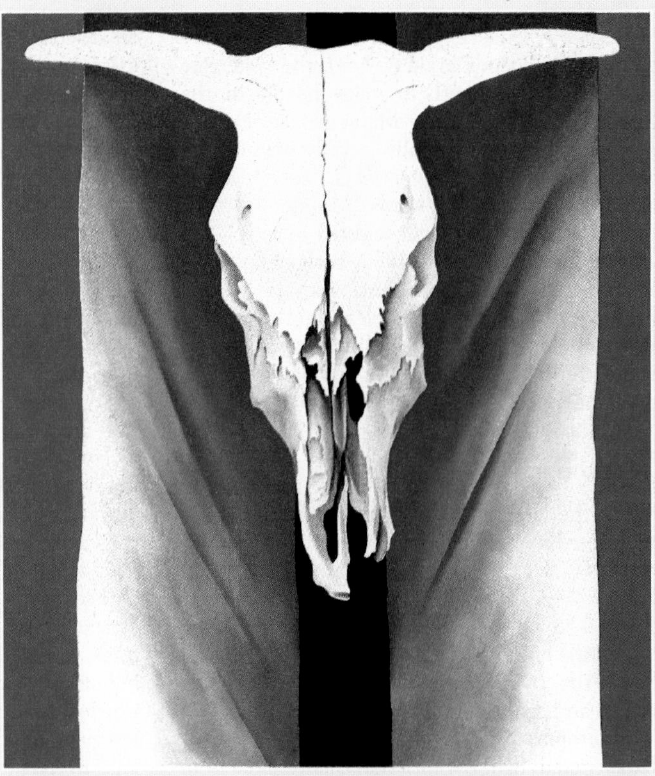

Today the painting hangs in the Metropolitan Museum of Art in New York—for all the world to notice.

Some Americans ruled out the alternative of using other fossil fuels, such as coal and natural gas. Like oil, coal and natural gas are nonrenewable. In addition, the use of coal and natural gas causes major pollution problems. Many people considered nuclear energy to be an economical alternative to fossil fuels. During the 1970s, however, concerns about the safety of nuclear energy began to surface. These concerns peaked in 1979, when an accident at the Three Mile Island nuclear power plant in Pennsylvania released dangerous levels of radioactivity into the air.

In the early 1980s, many people began to protest the use of nuclear power. They advocated the development and use of such renewable energy sources as solar power and wind power. These protesters won few victories against supporters of nuclear power, but their concerns had important effects on American society. In particular, Americans became more aware of the relationship between sensible energy use and a healthy environment.

Changes in Foreign Policy

The United States adopted new approaches to foreign affairs during the 1970s. Intent on easing some of the tension created by the cold war, President Nixon called for better relations with Communist countries. To this end, in 1972 he visited the People's Republic of China. This visit began a period of diplomatic activity that culminated in American recognition of the People's Republic of China in 1979.

Relations with the Soviet Union. President Nixon also made efforts to improve relations with

854

the Soviet Union, and in 1972 he became the first American president to visit that country. During the visit President Nixon and Soviet leader Leonid Brezhnev signed agreements known as the Strategic Arms Limitation Treaties (SALT I). These agreements limited each country's production and deployment of certain missiles. Nixon and Brezhnev also signed several accords relating to environmental, health, and technological cooperation. This improvement in United States–Soviet relations became known as **détente** (day • TAHNT), a French word meaning "an easing of strain."

Presidents Ford and Carter continued the policy of détente throughout much of the 1970s. However, by the end of the decade, strains between the two nations began to show. President Carter, insisting that human rights be made a factor in relations between nations, began to speak out against the way the Soviet government treated **dissidents**—people who opposed Soviet policies. He also criticized Soviet and Cuban intervention in Africa, specifically in the Angolan and Ethiopian civil wars. In response, the Soviets characterized Carter's efforts at peacemaking in the Middle East as interference in other nations' affairs.

The most serious break in the relationship, however, came in 1979, when the Soviet Union invaded Afghanistan to give added support to the Communist regime there. The United States retaliated by rejecting the Strategic Arms Limitation Treaty (SALT II), cutting trade ties with the Soviet Union, and boycotting the 1980 Olympic Games in Moscow.

By the 1980s détente had come to an end. President Reagan, who accused the Soviet Union of encouraging revolution throughout the world, greatly increased defense spending. During the Reagan administration, the United States built up its arsenal of nuclear weapons and provided economic and military assistance to anti-Communist governments. In the next few years, relations between the United States and the Soviet Union deteriorated to such an extent that people began to talk of a new cold war.

In the mid-1980s, however, tension between the two nations eased once again. President Reagan and the new Soviet leader, Mikhail Gorbachev (gawr • bah • CHAWF), held summit meetings in Geneva, Switzerland, in 1985 and in Reykjavik (RAY • kyah • veek), Iceland, in 1986. The two leaders made little, if any, progress on substantive issues at these two meetings. However, when Gorbachev visited Washington, D.C., in 1987, the two countries signed an agreement limiting the deployment of long-range missiles. Although much distrust still remained between the two countries, as the 1980s drew to a close a return to the détente of the 1970s seemed possible.

SECTION 1

Closure

Have the students discuss United States-Canadian trade relations. Ask: Why do you think the United States-Canada Free Trade Agreement of 1988 caused so much dissension among the Canadian people?

Learning from Pictures
The greatest foreign policy achievement for President Carter was the Camp David Accords. Here Anwar el-Sadat (left), President Carter (center), and Menachem Begin (right), sign the agreements.

855

1B, 4I, 5B, 5C, 5D, 5G, 5I, a1C, a1B, a2K, a2L

Review Answers

1. ***stagflation:*** decreased economic activity combined with increased prices; ***trade deficit:*** situation in which a country imports more than it exports; ***détente:*** French word meaning "an easing of strain;" ***dissidents:*** people who opposed Soviet policies

2. ***Gerald Ford:*** president of United States during mid-1970s; ***Jimmy Carter:*** president of United States during late 1970s; ***Ronald Reagan:*** United States president during most of the 1980s; ***SALT I:*** first round of Strategic Arms Limitation Treaties; ***SALT II:*** second Strategic Arms Limitation Treaty, rejected by the United States after the Soviet invasion of Afghanistan; ***Mikhail Gorbachev:*** Soviet leader who attended summit meetings with President Reagan at Geneva and Reykjavik; ***Official Languages Act:*** Canadian legislation that made both English and French official languages of Canada; ***Brian Mulroney:*** Progressive Conservative prime minister of Canada, and strong supporter of Free Trade Agreement of 1988

3. During the 1980s, heavy industry, which had been the mainstay of the American economy since the late 1800s, decreased in importance. Service industries then became the most important economic activity in the United States.

4. Until the early 1970s the consistent aim in foreign

Terrorism and American foreign policy. In 1979 international terrorism became a major influence on American foreign affairs when the Iranians seized the American embassy in Tehran (see Chapter 30). The hostages gained freedom on the day that Ronald Reagan took office in 1981.

Calling the hostage-taking an act of terrorism, Reagan vowed he would never negotiate with terrorists. Rather, he promised to seek them out and make military strikes against them. To this end, in 1986 United States Air Force jets bombed the headquarters of Libyan leader Muammar al-Qaddafi, long suspected by the Reagan administration of financing terrorist acts throughout the world.

Frustration over his government's inability to win freedom for a number of Americans held hostage in Lebanon caused President Reagan to adjust his antiterrorist policy. The hostage-takers, militant Muslims, had strong ties to the Iranian government. An arrangement that would send weapons to Iran—for use in its war with Iraq—in exchange for the release of the hostages was authorized. When this arrangement came to public attention in late 1987, many foreign governments condemned it. Later, after it became known that the proceeds of the arrangement had been secretly diverted to help the cause of the Nicaraguan Contras, some Americans also began to question the wisdom of the Reagan administration's approach to foreign affairs.

An increased role in the world. During President Reagan's administration, the United States began to play a greater part in world affairs. The government sponsored rebel groups fighting against the Communist governments of Angola, Afghanistan, and Nicaragua. Then, in 1983, American troops played an active role in the overthrow of the Marxist government of Grenada, a small island-nation in the Caribbean.

In the Middle East, Reagan sent troops to Lebanon to oversee a cease-fire in that country's long and bloody civil war. He also dispatched a fleet to the Persian Gulf to protect neutral merchant ships from becoming targets in the Iran-Iraq War. But these two moves ended in tragedy. A terrorist attack in Lebanon in 1983 resulted in the deaths of more than 200 American marines. Then in 1988 about 300 Iranian civilians lost their lives when the United States Navy accidentally shot down an Iranian passenger jet.

President Reagan's efforts at diplomacy, however, achieved marked success. His endeavors, in part, helped the peaceful transition from dictatorship to democracy in the Philippines. And, late in his administration, new diplomatic approaches led to better relations with the Soviet Union and other Communist-bloc countries.

Canada

The second largest country in the world, Canada possesses a vast wealth of raw materials. Yet much of its land—especially in the north—is completely unsuitable for habitation. As a result nearly all Canadians live within 200 miles (322 kilometers) of the United States border.

Government and culture. Although Canada's 10 provinces and 2 territories form a federal system much like that of the United States, Canada's provinces have more power than the American

Learning from Pictures *Quebec City is often called the "cradle of French civilization in North America." Notice the signs in the French language.*

● A "French only" law passed by Quebec's parliament required that all public signs, billboards, and store signs in Quebec had to be in French. However, this law was declared unconstitutional in 1988.

■ In 1987 trade transactions between Canada and the state of Michigan alone were worth more than $24 billion.

5B, 5D, a1B, a1C, a2A, a2C, a2D, a2H, a2K, a3A, a4A, a4F, a4H, a4K, a4L

states. For example, the Canadian constitution does not require any of the provinces to abide by future amendments passed by the federal government.

People of two very different cultural backgrounds—those of French descent and those of English descent—make Canada their home. French Canadians, because of their distinct language, Roman Catholic religion, and French-based traditions, have remained culturally separate from the majority of Canadian people. Although a minority in the country as a whole, French Canadians predominate in the province of Quebec, where more than 80 percent of the people speak French as their first language.

Separatism. During the 1960s a French-Canadian separatist movement gathered strength in Quebec. French Canadians sought special recognition of their language and heritage. They also demanded a greater role in both provincial and national governments and protection from discrimination. After Pierre Trudeau (tru • DOH), himself a French Canadian, became prime minister, many of the French Canadians' demands were met. Perhaps their greatest victory came with the passage of the Official Languages Act in 1969. This act made both French and English the official languages of ● Canada.

In 1976 the Quebec Party, which favored the complete separation of Quebec from Canada, gained control of the provincial government. Four years later, in 1980, the party put the separatism issue to the test by holding a referendum.* By a 60-percent majority, the people of Quebec voted to remain part of Canada.

Even so, French Canadians continued to demand special status for Quebec. And Quebec's leaders refused to ratify the 1982 constitution until the federal government offered such recognition. An amended constitution, which accepted Quebec as a "distinct society," finally won the province's support in 1987.

Relations with the United States. For the most part, relations between Canada and the United States have been friendly and productive. The two countries share the longest unguarded border in the world, and they tend to agree on most major international issues. Their closest ties, however, come in the area of trade. For many years each nation has been the other's biggest trading partner. In 1987 alone the value of trade transactions between the two totaled about $150 billion. ■

The relationship between the two countries has come under intermittent strain, however. For example, the two countries have engaged in bitter disputes about fishing rights in the waters of the Pacific Northwest. But by far the greatest strains have resulted from Canadian uneasiness over American involvement in the Canadian economy. Since World War II, Americans have dominated many Canadian companies, either by absorbing them into multinational corporations or by controlling them through large stockholdings.

Canadian uneasiness turned to resentment after the announcement of the United States–Canada Free Trade Agreement in 1988. This agreement proposed the elimination of almost all tariff barriers between the two countries by 1999. Many Canadians characterized the arrangement as a betrayal that would make their country a mere economic colony of the United States. Free trade, they said, would give the United States the opportunity to drain Canada of all its natural resources. Stunned by the furor over the agreement, Prime Minister Brian Mulroney called for a general election. This election, Mulroney said, would serve as a referendum on the free trade issue.

After a bitter campaign, Mulroney's Progressive Conservative Party won a majority of seats in Parliament. However, it received only 44 percent of the popular vote. The election, then, reflected the Canadian uneasiness about the free trade issue.

*A *referendum* is the process in which a measure passed by a legislative body is submitted to the voters for final approval or rejection.

SECTION 1 REVIEW

1. **Define** stagflation, trade deficit, détente, dissidents
2. **Identify** Gerald Ford, Jimmy Carter, Ronald Reagan, SALT I, SALT II, Mikhail Gorbachev, Official Languages Act, Brian Mulroney
3. **Analyzing Ideas** How did the nature of the American economy change in the 1980s?
4. **Understanding Ideas** What changes took place in American foreign policy during the 1970s and 1980s?
5. **Evaluating Ideas** What successes were achieved by the French-Canadian separatist movement?
6. **Classifying Ideas** List the causes of strains in Canadian-American relations.

policy was to resist the ambitions of Communist nations throughout the world. During the 1970s presidents Nixon, Ford, and Carter tried to reduce the tensions between the Communist powers and the United States through détente. During the Reagan administration, tensions between the United States and the Soviet Union were renewed. However, in the late 1980s President Reagan and new Soviet leader Mikhail Gorbachev met to discuss the limitation of nuclear weapons and other foreign policy issues.

5. The Canadian separatists managed to gain many concessions during Pierre Trudeau's administration, especially the recognition of French as one of Canada's official languages. In negotiations on the new Canadian constitution, the separatists also won recognition of Quebec as a "distinct society" within Canada.

6. Fishing rights, American involvement in the Canadian economy through multinational corporate ownership, and the United States-Canada Free Trade Agreement of 1988 all caused strains in the relationship between Canada and the United States.

5D, a1B, a1C

● In the 1987 general election, the Conservative Party won an overwhelming majority of seats in Parliament, yet it received only about 46 percent of the popular vote. In the north of England and in Scotland, the Conservatives received practically no support at all.

SECTION 2

Focus/Motivation
Mention that the North American-European mutual defense pact, the North Atlantic Treaty Organization (NATO), came under attack from people in both Europe and the United States during the 1980s. Have students discuss the following questions: Why is the defense of Europe important to the United States? What do you think might be done to make the funding and decision-making procedures of NATO more equitable?

2 Western Europe Searched for Stability

During the 1970s and 1980s, many countries in Western Europe tried to consolidate the economic gains they had made in the early postwar period. Other countries made political advances, turning from dictatorship to democracy. Although the progress was far from smooth, Western Europe made great strides toward political and economic union.

Great Britain

The period of prosperity that had begun in Great Britain during the 1950s began to fade in the mid-1960s. By the end of the decade, the country faced severe economic problems. Outdated and inefficient factories, low productivity, and worker apathy made it difficult for Great Britain to compete with other industrial nations. As a result, the country's imports soon far outweighed its exports. To help pay for this growth in imports and to finance the expanding number of social programs in its welfare state, the government raised taxes and increased borrowing. These actions, however, put the economy under greater stress. Even the discovery of huge oil deposits in the North Sea off the coast of Great Britain failed to bring relief. By the end of the 1970s, Great Britain, like the United States, staggered under the burden of stagflation.

Learning from Pictures *Margaret Thatcher waves outside the official residence of Great Britain's prime minister at 10 Downing Street.*

Changes under Margaret Thatcher. In 1979, after a decisive victory in a general election, the Conservative Party took control of the British government. The Conservative leader, Margaret Thatcher, became prime minister—the first woman to hold that office. Thatcher charged that Great Britain's government spent too much money on social programs, regulated business and industry too closely, and taxed the people too heavily. She promised to return the country to prosperity by reversing the government's role in the economy.

Over the next few years, Thatcher made huge cuts in social programs. These cuts were so deep that some programs were eliminated. Her opponents argued that her real intention was to completely dismantle the welfare state. Thatcher also passed laws that eased government regulation of business, and she drastically reduced taxes. In addition, she began a program to return most government-owned industries to the private sector.

These policies helped to slash the rate of inflation and to revitalize the economy, especially in southern England. At the same time, however, unemployment grew rapidly in the country's predominantly industrial northern areas, partly as a result of a shift in Great Britain's economy from manufacturing to services. In some older industrial cities, more than 25 percent of the workers were without jobs. Unemployment among young people, unskilled workers, and minority groups ran closer to 50 percent. As the 1980s drew to a close, unemployment in the north began to ease. Even so, critics of Thatcher's government charged that her economic policies had created two societies in Great Britain—one in the prosperous south and another in the economically depressed north. ●

An old conflict. Ireland and the Irish had perplexed successive governments in London practically since the English invasion of Ireland in the

1100s. Most people assumed that the partition of the country in 1922—which created an independent Republic of Ireland in the South and Northern Ireland, which remained part of Great Britain—had solved all problems. Instead, it brought forth new problems. Over the years the Protestant majority in Northern Ireland had gained control of the government and of most of the country's businesses. In contrast, Northern Ireland's Catholic minority had little power and limited political and economic opportunities.

In the late 1960s, Catholics in Northern Ireland began to demonstrate to end discrimination in voting, employment and housing. At first peaceful, these demonstrations soon turned violent. To restore order and to protect the Catholic population from a Protestant backlash, the British government sent troops to Northern Ireland in 1969. Announced as a short-term measure, this stationing of soldiers in Northern Ireland quickly became a permanent policy. By the late 1980s large numbers of British troops remain garrisoned there.

Throughout the 1970s the violence in Northern Ireland escalated as extremists on both sides took advantage of the situation. Assassinations, car bombings, and attacks on British troops became an almost daily occurrence. The most active extremist group was the Irish Republican Army (IRA). Almost entirely Catholic, the IRA wanted to drive the British out of the north and reunite the two Irelands. The IRA took its "war of liberation" far beyond the Irish borders, bombing stores in a number of British cities and attacking British soldiers in other parts of Europe.

Characterizing the activities of both Catholic and Protestant extremists as terrorism, the British government gave the police and the courts in Ireland special powers. The police could detain suspected terrorists without charging them with any offense, and the courts could try without a jury any person charged with terrorist activities. In the late 1980s, the Thatcher administration extended these powers by ending the defendant's right to remain silent in trials in Northern Ireland's courts. Also, Thatcher banned direct radio and television statements by supporters of terrorist organizations. This, she said, would cut off the terrorists' "life-blood"—publicity.

The British government also tried to end the violence in Northern Ireland through political means. The most promising attempt came in 1985 with the Hillsborough Agreement. This gave the Republic of Ireland some participation in the governing of Northern Ireland. In time, however, both Catholics and Protestants denounced the agreement.

By the end of the 1980s, the death toll in what the Northern Irish simply called "the Troubles" stood at more than 2,500. With a peaceful settlement apparently further away than ever and with violence once again beginning to escalate, it seemed likely that this figure would increase.

France

After Charles de Gaulle resigned in 1969, his prime minister, Georges Pompidou (PAHM • pih • doo), replaced him as president. Although the two men had worked together for many years, they viewed France's interests differently. Charles de Gaulle saw France as a major player on the world scene. In contrast, Pompidou felt that France should limit its involvement in foreign affairs and focus instead on domestic issues.

A more realistic approach. Georges Pompidou felt that changes on the international scene had rendered de Gaulle's nationalist approach to foreign affairs impractical. A more realistic strategy, Pompidou believed, would be to seek close, cooperative relations with traditional allies. Therefore, he sought stronger ties with the United States and ended French opposition to British membership in the European Community (EC). Within the EC, Pompidou tried to cooperate with other members rather than to lead them. The one area where Pompidou did take a lead was in arms sales. During his administration France became one of the world's leading weapons dealers.

Pompidou focused on domestic issues for much of his time in office. He introduced a number of social programs that he hoped would ease the problems that had given rise to the political upheavals of the late 1960s. He also embarked on an ambitious plan to renovate much of Paris, France's capital and major tourist attraction. However, an economic crisis, largely brought on by the OPEC oil embargo and price increases in 1973, curtailed many of his plans.

On Pompidou's sudden death in 1974, Valéry Giscard d'Estaing (zhee • SKAHR des • TANG) became president. Like President John F. Kennedy of the

Presentation
Summarizing Ideas (Average/Group)
Have each student select a current newspaper or magazine article on the Common Market or on the economy of any of the Western European countries. Students should read the article, summarize it, and attach the article to the summary. Call upon students to read their summaries in class. Ask the class: What general conclusions can you draw about the current economic situation in Western Europe?

859

4I, 5C, 5D, 5G

● Mitterand's administration was rocked by the revelation that members of the French secret service had been responsible for the 1985 bombing of *Rainbow Warrior,* the flagship of the environmental activist group, Greenpeace, in New Zealand. *Rainbow Warrior* was in the South Pacific to attempt to stop French nuclear tests.

United States, Giscard wanted to take a strong stand in international affairs and encourage social change at home. Giscard continued Pompidou's foreign policies and, in addition, strengthened ties with the Soviet Union, China, and other Communist-bloc countries. On the domestic front, he introduced programs that increased unemployment benefits and health benefits and raised retirement pensions. But economic problems drastically undermined Giscard's plans for social change, making it virtually impossible for him to carry out his programs.

A socialist president. The French electorate, disappointed at Giscard's failure to fulfill his promise of prosperity and social change, chose socialist François Mitterrand (MEE • tehr • ahn) as president in 1981. Mitterrand inherited a country with severe economic problems. For much of the 1970s, France's rate of inflation had averaged above 10 percent. At the same time, budget and trade deficits had grown steadily. And unemployment levels had risen dramatically in the late 1970s.

Mitterrand tried to bolster the fragile economy by nationalizing a number of industries and banks and by increasing taxes on the highest incomes. He also established job-training programs for young people and the unemployed. In addition, he introduced programs to give tax breaks and other assistance to businesses that made special efforts to find work for the long-term unemployed and school dropouts. However, after a major economic reversal in the mid-1980s, Mitterrand dropped most of these policies and adopted a more conservative approach.

Under Mitterrand, France once again took a very active role in foreign affairs. Mitterrand sent French troops to help supervise the cease-fire in the Lebanese civil war. In addition, he provided military assistance to the African nation of Chad—a former French colony—in its border war with Libya. Such actions generally won the approval of the world community. However, not all of Mitterrand's foreign policy measures received such support. His decision to continue nuclear weapons tests in the ● South Pacific was condemned by Australia, New Zealand, and other South Pacific nations. Many nations denounced Mitterrand's readiness to negotiate and make deals with terrorists. However, such negative world opinion did not seem to lessen Mitterrand's popularity among the French people. In 1988 he easily won election to a second term as president.

Learning from Pictures *Connected to West Germany by only one highway and three air corridors, West Berlin stands as a symbol of free enterprise inside East Germany.*

West Germany

By the late 1960s, West Germany had become an economic power in Western Europe. However, it still faced major political problems. Access to West Berlin and relations with East Germany, the Soviet Union, and other Communist countries posed difficult foreign policy challenges. Social Democrat Willy Brandt, who became chancellor in 1969, met these challenges with a new approach.

Ostpolitik. Chancellor Brandt believed that West Germany had to remain firmly allied with Western Europe and the United States. At the same time, however, he felt that tensions between his country and the Eastern bloc had to be reduced. Brandt's efforts at creating better relations between East and West, known as ***Ostpolitik*** (German for "Eastern Policy"), resulted in West German treaties with the Soviet Union and Poland in 1972. *Ostpolitik* eventually led to mutual recognition of East and West Germany in 1973.

In 1974, when it became known that one of his staff members had been spying for East Germany, Brandt resigned. Brandt's finance minister, Helmut Schmidt, replaced him as chancellor. Chancellor Schmidt tried to develop a greater spirit of

860

LINKING GEOGRAPHY TO HISTORY

Looking Beyond Planet Earth

The successful mission of the space shuttle *Discovery* in October 1988 reaffirmed the American commitment to space exploration that had faltered some two years before with the loss of the *Challenger* and its crew of seven. President Ronald Reagan underscored this rekindled commitment when he declared that the United States fully intended to "expand human presence and activity beyond Earth into the solar system."

The National Aeronautics and Space Administration (NASA) has already begun planning journeys to the farthest reaches of the galaxy. The first step involves the construction of a space station named *Freedom* some 220 miles (354 kilometers) above the surface of the earth.

Between 1995 and 1998, 20 shuttle flights are scheduled to carry the parts of the half-million pound station into earth orbit. There astronauts will assemble the space station, which will consist of three laboratories and a housing unit. Once the station is ready for occupancy, crews of 8 astronauts will come aboard for 90-day tours of duty. During these missions, the astronauts will conduct experiments and make observations of the solar system.

All these operations, and many others, constitute the preparation for NASA's ultimate goal—an expedition to our closest planetary neighbor, Mars. This expedition will begin with the assemblying of a huge unmanned cargo ship at the space station *Freedom.* According to NASA's schedule, the cargo ship should depart in 2006 for a nine-month, 34-million mile (54-million kilometer) journey to Mars. About a year later, a second space craft, also assembled at *Freedom* and more than two times larger than the cargo ship, will carry 8 astronauts and embark on a more direct six-month flight to Mars. The two ships will rendezvous in orbit around Mars.

Earth viewed from the space shuttle

Once the docking is completed, 4 astronauts will fly to the surface of Mars for 10 to 20 days of exploration. After collecting rock samples and making scientific observations, the astronauts will return to their spacecraft. They then will begin the long voyage back to earth by way of the space station *Freedom.*

If the Martian mission proves too complex or too expensive, NASA has planned an equally exciting and ambitious voyage to Phobos, one of Mars' two tiny, mysterious moons. A Phobos mission would be similar to the voyage to Mars. It would require two vessels, one a cargo ship, the other a crewed spacecraft. However, the Phobos mission would cost much less. Since the ships would not enter Martian gravity, less fuel would be needed for the return journey. And the ships could be constructed on earth, a far less costly operation than working from *Freedom.*

In the past, historical events and the personalities engaged in them were confined to the surface of the earth. However, NASA's plans ensure that a new history will soon unfold in a new geography—that of the planets that lie in the vastness of space far beyond our own world.

861

4I, 5D, a1B, a1C, a2G, a2K, a4L

Students may suggest that if Ostpolitik had not been adopted, the tensions between the two Germanies would have increased and West Germany would not have signed treaties with the Soviet Union and Poland in 1972.

What If?
Ostpolitik

One outcome of Willy Brandt's policy of Ostpolitik was mutual recognition of East and West Germany. How might relations between the two Germanies have developed if Ostpolitik had not been adopted?

economic and political cooperation among the Western European nations. He also continued Brandt's *Ostpolitik*. However, Schmidt's administration of this policy strained diplomatic relations with the United States.

During much of Schmidt's time in office, West Germany experienced remarkable economic growth, and the West German people enjoyed one of the highest standards of living in the world. In the early 1980s, however, West Germany plunged into an economic recession. For the first time since World War II, West Germans faced the prospect of rising unemployment coupled with rampant inflation.

Christian Democrats regain power. In late 1982, after more than a dozen years out of office, the Christian Democrats regained control of the government. Helmut Kohl, the new chancellor, charged that Schmidt and the Social Democrats had spent West Germany into a recession. Chancellor Kohl promised to return the country to prosperity through policies similar to those followed by Prime Minister Margaret Thatcher in Great Britain and President Ronald Reagan in the United States.

The chancellor also made changes in West German foreign policy. He strongly reaffirmed his government's support for the NATO alliance, which had come under attack from many West Germans in the early 1980s. For example, he backed NATO deployment of American nuclear missiles in West Germany, even though this position sparked huge demonstrations across the country. He also worked to improve relations with the United States. To this end, he supported President Reagan's proposed antimissile program, the Strategic Defense Initiative (SDI). Kohl continued to support the Reagan administration throughout the 1980s.

The Nations of Southern Europe

During the 1970s the four nations of Southern Europe underwent major political changes. Italy, once one of the more stable European nations, experienced almost constant political turmoil. At the same time, Spain, Portugal, and Greece returned to democratic forms of government.

Italy. The world economic recession of the early 1970s hit Italy especially hard. For much of the decade, unemployment levels soared and inflation was rampant. During the same period, the country's political system experienced a great deal of turmoil. No single political party could gain a majority in the Italian parliament, so governments had to be formed through coalitions. Since few of these coalitions lasted very long, little could be done to alleviate the country's severe political and economic problems.

In the late 1970s, a wave of political violence threw the country into a state of chaos. The Red Brigades, a terrorist group, began a series of kidnappings, assassinations, and bombings that continued into the 1980s. Perhaps their bloodiest act was the kidnapping and murder of Aldo Moro, a former prime minister, in 1978.

By the mid-1980s, the police had managed to break the power of the Red Brigades and other terrorist groups, and peace returned to Italy. However, the specter of economic and political turmoil continued to plague the country.

Spain. In 1969 Francisco Franco named Prince Juan Carlos as his successor. On Franco's death in 1975, Juan Carlos became king and immediately set about the task of returning the country to democracy. About 18 months later, in 1977, Spain held its first free elections in more than 40 years. In those elections, moderate political parties led by socialists won the majority of seats in the Cortes, or parliament.

Spain's young democracy faced its first real challenge in 1981. In February of that year, a group of army officers seized the lower house of the Cortes in an attempt to take control of the government. However, their coup failed when the army remained loyal to the king.

By far the greatest challenges that faced the Spanish government in the 1980s concerned the economy and the question of Basque separatism. The Basque region, in the western Pyrenees, has a distinct language and culture, and its people have long sought independence from Spain. In 1980, after the Basque people overwhelmingly voted for home rule, Spain granted the region self-government. However, an extremist Basque separatist group has continued its campaign of violence to win complete independence for the region.

● self-government
■ Andreas Papandreou's father, George, was premier of Greece during the 1960s.

Learning from Pictures *High in the Pyrennes Mountains, Basque villagers maintain their traditional way of life. What did they gain from Spain in 1980?*

Spain's economic problems included a very high rate of unemployment, which in 1985 stood at 22 percent, the highest in Europe. Spanish leaders hoped that membership in the EC, which Spain joined in 1986, would spur economic activity.

Portugal. Ironically, Portugal's return to democracy came about after a military coup. In 1974 army officers led by General Antonio de Spinoza overthrew the dictator Marcello Caetano. Spinoza ● drew up agreements giving independence to Portugal's remaining colonies and then, after calling for democratic elections, resigned. In those elections moderate parties won more than 60 percent of the seats in the parliament. However, the Communist Party also gained in influence.

Throughout the 1970s and 1980s, Portugal's political situation became increasingly volatile, harming the country's economy, the least developed in Western Europe. Portugal's leaders hoped that the economy would improve as a result of the country's acceptance into the EC in 1986.

Greece. "The colonels," the military junta (HOON • tuh) that seized control of the Greek government in 1967, continued their repressive rule until 1974. Discovery of their involvement in an attempted military coup on the island of Cyprus in that year led to their downfall.

Constantine Karamanlis, a former prime minister, took over, named a civilian cabinet, released all political prisoners, and ordered free elections for November 1974. He also called for a referendum on whether to allow the return of King Constantine II. In this election the Greek people rejected the king's return, voting instead to make the country a republic.

Conservatives held power in Greece until 1981, when the Socialist Party, led by Andreas Papandreou (pop • uhn • DRAY • ooh), took control of the government. Papandreou introduced socialist economic policies and moved toward closer ties with Communist-bloc countries. These policy changes caused strains in relations between Greece and the United States in the mid-1980s. The two countries also had major differences of opinion on NATO policies. As the 1980s drew to a close, relations between the two countries remained tense.

Continuing Cooperation ■

The spirit of cooperation among the nations of Western Europe that had developed in the years after World War II continued to grow in the 1970s and 1980s. Formal institutions such as NATO and the EC grew in both strength and numbers, and new steps were taken to ensure the economic, political, and military security of the region. Even though individual nations still had differences of opinion, by the end of the 1980s a real union of European states seemed possible.

The Helsinki Accords. In 1975 representatives of 35 nations, including the United States and the Soviet Union, met in Helsinki, Finland, to discuss the topics of security and cooperation in Europe. These representatives signed an agreement, known as the Helsinki Accords, that specified ways of improving economic and technological cooperation between East and West. The agreement also endorsed the use of peaceful means rather than force in settling differences between nations. Perhaps the most important part of the Helsinki Accords, however, concerned the protection of human rights such as freedom of speech and freedom of worship. All nations, the Accords said, should respect their citizens' basic human rights.

The Helsinki Accords did bring about some improvement in cooperation between East and West. But the Soviet Union and other Eastern-bloc countries largely ignored the human rights aspects of the Accords. This drew strong criticism from the United States and other Western nations. In part, the disagreement over human rights brought about the end of détente between the United States and the Soviet Union in the late 1970s.

SECTION 2

Closure
Have students discuss European economic and political unity. Ask: Do you think the development of a single European market by 1992 is a viable proposition? Why or why not?

Review Answers
1. ***Ostpolitik:*** German word meaning "Eastern Policy," used to describe Chancellor Willy Brandt's foreign policy aimed at reducing tensions between East and West Germany
2. ***Hillsborough Agreement:*** agreement between Great Britain and the Republic of Ireland that gave the Republic some say in the governing of Northern Ireland; ***François Mitterrand:*** socialist president of France during the 1980s; ***Helmut Schmidt:*** chancellor of West Germany during the 1970s; ***Helmut Kohl:*** succeeded Schmidt as chancellor; ***King Juan Carlos:*** king of Spain after Franco's death; ***Andreas Papandreou:*** socialist leader of Greece in the 1980s; ***Helsinki Accords:*** 1975 agreement between 35 nations that set down ways of improving economic and technological cooperation between East and West; ***European Free Trade Association:*** European economic alliance that includes countries not members of the Common Market
3. Margaret Thatcher cut government spending on social programs, passed laws that eased

1A, 5D, a4A, a4B, a4C

government regulation of business, and drastically reduced taxes, while returning most government-owned industries to the private sector.

4. An economic crisis, brought on by the OPEC oil embargo of 1973, curtailed President Pompidou's social programs. Inflation rates above 10 percent, budget and trade deficits, and growing unemployment forced President Giscard d'Estaing to drop many of his social programs.

5. The Social Democrats supported *Ostpolitik*. This resulted in treaties with the Soviet Union and Poland and mutual recognition with East Germany. The Christian Democrats forged closer ties with the West, reaffirming the NATO alliance and support for the placement of American missiles on German soil.

6. Italy experienced almost constant political turmoil, particularly during the early 1970s. Political violence disrupted everyday life. Spain, Portugal, and Greece returned to democratic forms of government. In Spain Juan Carlos became king and held elections, but faced Basque separatism. Portugal suffered a military coup, but then Spinoza held free elections. "The colonels" controlled Greece until involvement in a coup attempt in Cyprus led to their downfall, and first Conservatives and then Socialists took control of the government. Under socialist leader Andreas Papandreou, Greece

Learning from Maps *The CMEA does not include all the Communist nations of Eastern Europe. Which Communist nations do not belong to the Warsaw Pact?* **Albania and Yugoslavia**

freedom of worship. All nations, the Accords said, should respect their citizens' basic human rights.

The Helsinki Accords did bring about some improvement in cooperation between East and West. But the Soviet Union and other Eastern-bloc countries largely ignored the human rights aspects of the Accords. This drew strong criticism from the United States and other Western nations. In part, the disagreement over human rights brought about the end of détente between the United States and the Soviet Union in the late 1970s.

The North Atlantic Treaty Organization. The purpose and policies of the North Atlantic Treaty Organization (NATO) came under close

864

scrutiny during the 1970s, and a number of nations reevaluated their own roles within the alliance. In 1974, in response to the Turkish invasion of Cyprus, Greece withdrew its armed forces from NATO. Although Greece rejoined the alliance in 1980, it continued to question NATO policies.

During the 1980s the alliance came under the heaviest criticism it had experienced since its establishment in 1949. The placement of American nuclear missiles in a number of European countries touched off protests throughout the continent. The Greek government continued to oppose the presence of American troops in Greece. And Spain agreed to remain in the alliance only so long as no American nuclear weapons were placed on Spanish soil. Then the United States Congress threatened to reduce American contributions to NATO unless other members agreed to share the burden of maintaining the alliance.

By the late 1980s, European alliance members readily agreed that they had to share defense costs with the United States. They also discovered that the Warsaw Pact conventional forces far outnumbered those of NATO.

The European Community The 1970s and 1980s saw the European Community, or EC, grow from 6 members to 12. After lengthy negotiations Great Britain finally became a member in 1973. Ireland and Denmark also joined that year. Greece became a full member of the EC in 1981, and five years later Spain and Portugal joined the organization. Six other European nations—Austria, Finland, Iceland, Switzerland, Sweden, and Norway—have formed a separate organization called the European Free Trade Association, or EFTA (see map, page 864).

While the EC grew, it made headway toward setting common practices for its members in taxation, credit, and benefits for workers. It also introduced the European Monetary System, hoping that its members would eventually share one currency. In 1986 the EC predicted that its members would achieve full economic integration by 1992. However, these hopes received a blow in 1988 when British prime minister Margaret Thatcher stated that the dream of a single European market should not be at the expense of individual nations.

Politically, European unity also seemed somewhat elusive. Even so, the EC made important steps toward that goal with the creation of such political structures as the European Parliament and the Council of Ministers. At first, the national parliaments of the various members of the EC selected representatives for the European Parliament. In 1979, however, members of the European Parliament were elected directly by the voters.

For the most part, the parliament served an advisory purpose, but during the 1980s it played a greater role in EC decisions on finance and legislation. The Council of Ministers—consisting of representatives from the 12 member states—made most of the important decisions. By the end of the 1980s, these decisions went beyond EC internal matters. For example, the EC strongly denounced South Africa's policy of apartheid and offered its help in the restructuring process underway in Eastern Europe.

SECTION 2 REVIEW

1. **Define** *Ostpolitik*
2. **Identify** Hillsborough Agreement, François Mitterrand, Helmut Schmidt, Helmut Kohl, King Juan Carlos, Andreas Papandreou, Helsinki Accords, European Free Trade Association
3. **Analyzing Ideas** How did Margaret Thatcher change the British government's role in the economy?
4. **Determining Cause and Effect** What caused the reduction of social programs in France under presidents Pompidou and Giscard d'Estaing?
5. **Contrasting Ideas** What were the differences between the foreign policies of the Social Democrats and those of the Christian Democrats of West Germany?
6. **Classifying Ideas** What major political changes took place in Southern Europe during the 1970s and 1980s?
7. **Evaluating Ideas** What progress did the EC make toward economic unity during the 1970s and 1980s?

3 Political Challenges Faced the Soviet Union and Eastern Europe

During the 1950s and 1960s, the Soviet Union crushed challenges to its authority in a number of satellite nations. However, groups within these satellite nations continued to call for greater freedom and autonomy. Then, in the mid-1980s, a new leader undertook the restructuring and liberalization of the Soviet Union itself.

moved toward closer ties with the Communist-bloc countries.
7. The EC increased membership from 6 to 12 members. It also attempted to set common practices for its members in taxation, credit, and worker benefits, and introduced the European Monetary System.

SECTION 3

Focus/Motivation
Mention that British politician Winston Churchill once referred to the Soviet Union as "a riddle wrapped in a mystery inside an enigma." Ask students to suggest what Churchill meant by this statement. *(Most students will suggest that Churchill was inferring that what went on within the Soviet Union was completely unfathomable by outsiders.)* Then ask students why the Soviet Union was such a mystery to foreigners. *(Most responses will refer to the Soviet government's tight control of the information that is released to the outside world.)* As they read the section, students should consider whether the changes that have taken place in the Soviet Union recently might alter the opinions of people who share Churchill's view.

865

5C, 5D, 5G, a1D, a2K, a3F, a3J

Presentation
Constructing a Chart (Average/Group)
Have students work together to construct a chart of the Soviet government as it operates under the reforms adopted by the Supreme Soviet in December 1988. Suggest that students use newspaper and periodical indexes in the public library to locate sources of information on this subject. Display the completed chart on the bulletin board. It might be useful to lead the class in a discussion of the changes in the Soviet governmental system that the reforms of 1988 brought. Have students refer to a civics book or an encyclopedia for information on the organization of the pre-1988 government.

dissent in the satellite nations. He indicated that nations that strayed from the Soviet line would be dealt with according to the Brezhnev Doctrine. This doctrine gave the Soviet Union the right to intervene in any satellite nation that appeared to be moving away from communism. The Brezhnev Doctrine brought the satellite nations under Soviet control. Although some people continued to call for change, no satellite government attempted reforms as far-reaching as those made during the Prague Spring.

Brezhnev also clamped down on dissent at home. The basic human rights—freedom of speech, of worship, and of movement—were virtually nonexistent. Dissidents, people who criticized the government, usually suffered severe punishment. Some had their union memberships revoked and were thus prevented from working at their chosen careers. Other dissidents, such as the physicist and human rights activist Andrei Sakharov, were sent into internal exile. Still others received harsh prison sentences or were classified as "social misfits" and sent to mental hospitals. In some cases the Soviet government forced them to leave the country. Conversely, it refused to give exit permits to many dissidents, such as Soviet Jews, who wanted to leave the Soviet Union.

While crushing all opposition in both the Soviet Union and the satellite nations, Brezhnev also sought closer ties with the West. He played an active role in détente, or the improvement of Soviet-American relations. He also worked to slow down the arms race. As you have read, he and President Nixon signed SALT I in 1972. In 1979 Brezhnev and President Carter continued this process by signing SALT II. Later that year, however, arms limitation talks and détente came to an abrupt halt with the Soviet invasion of Afghanistan.

Gorbachev takes charge. After Brezhnev's death in 1982, a struggle for leadership began between the "old guard"—people born before the revolution of 1917—and a younger generation of Communist Party members. At first the old guard won control. Yuri Andropov (an • DRO • paf), a former head of the KGB—the Soviet secret police—became the country's leader. In poor health, Andropov held office for less than two years. On Andropov's death Konstantin Chernenko (chur • NEEN • koh), a close associate of Brezhnev, took control. However, Chernenko died just a few months later. The younger generation finally won the struggle in 1985, when Mikhail Gorbachev became leader of the Soviet Union.

A stagnant economy, a costly and bloody war in Afghanistan, and tensions with the West because of a poor human rights record presented the new leader with major problems. Early in 1986 these problems were compounded by an explosion at a nuclear power plant in Chernobyl, near Kiev. Fears about the safety of other nuclear plants undermined the whole of the Soviet Union's energy policy.

To revitalize the Soviet economy and to combat other problems, Gorbachev introduced two new policies. The first, ***glasnost,*** or openness, loosened the reins of censorship and eased the repression of the Brezhnev years. Under *glasnost,* the media had more latitude to report sensitive stories. For example, Soviet journalists gave coverage to the disaster at Chernobyl—a story that in the past the Soviet government would have hidden from its people and the world at large. Also, social scientists began to write studies critical of past leaders, such as Stalin and Brezhnev. Artists and writers were allowed greater freedom of expression, and publishers started to circulate the works of long-banned authors. In addition, many dissidents were freed from exile or prison and allowed to leave or travel outside the Soviet Union. And although the Soviet government still frowned on the practicing of religion, in 1988 it allowed celebrations marking 1,000 years of Christianity in Russia.

With the second new policy, ***perestroika,*** or restructuring, Gorbachev planned to completely overhaul the Soviet political and economic systems. Reforms pushed through by Gorbachev limited the power of the Communist Party, created the new and powerful position of state president, and established a new state legislative body that had broad authority. Gorbachev's political restructuring also limited top government officials' terms of office and called for open and competitive elections.

Gorbachev's economic *perestroika* followed the reforms implemented in Czechoslovakia during the Prague Spring. He shifted many production decisions to on-site farm and factory managers. He also allowed the introduction of free enterprise practices in some areas of the economy. In addition, he tried to create new incentives for increased worker productivity, and he worked to remove corrupt officials from all government economic agencies. Finally, Gorbachev made efforts to shift the emphasis of

For example, in 1987 the works of Boris Pasternak, banned for more than 20 years, were cleared by government censors for publication. However, in 1988 the censors said that the works of Aleksandr Solzhenitsyn would continue to be proscribed.

1E, 5B, 5D, 5G, 5H, a1B, a1C, a1D, a2C

the Soviet economy from heavy industry to the production of consumer goods.

The following statistics illustrate the challenge facing Gorbachev. In 1988 the population of the Soviet Union was about 284 million. Only about 90 million television sets were in use throughout the country. In addition, only about 50,000 personal computers existed in the Soviet Union. Conversely, the population of the United States reached about 248 million in 1988. Most Americans had at least one television set in their homes, and about 30 million Americans owned personal computers.

A reduction in defense spending. Gorbachev realized that this economic shift could be achieved, in part, by cutting back on defense expenditures. For example, in 1987 Gorbachev joined with President Reagan in signing arms treaties that

Learning from Pictures *In Moscow clergy from around the world joined the Russian Orthodox church in celebrating the 1,000th anniversary of Christianity.*

eliminated certain types of nuclear weapons and strictly limited the production of others. Then, in a speech before the United Nations in 1988, Gorbachev announced a plan to reduce Soviet conventional forces. By 1990, he said, the number of troops in the Soviet army would be cut by 500,000 soldiers. The vast majority of Soviet troops and tanks deployed in the satellite nations would return to the Soviet Union. And many troops stationed in Soviet border regions would be pulled back. Most NATO and Warsaw Pact countries applauded this step toward disarmament, although some Western leaders expressed reservations as to its effectiveness.

In addition, Gorbachev acted to end Soviet involvement in Afghanistan, which constituted an incredible drain on the economy. Also, with the Soviet death toll standing at more than 13,000, Gorbachev had begun to doubt the wisdom of continuing the war. Therefore, in 1988 he announced his plan to withdraw the more than 125,000 Soviet troops from Afghanistan. By mid-1989 all Soviet troops had been withdrawn.

Challenges to *glasnost* and *perestroika*. Gorbachev's new policies faced challenges both at home and from abroad.

A direct challenge came from the restlessness among national and ethnic minorities. In part, *glasnost* had helped to bring about this restiveness. The new openness prompted people to express opinions that in the past they would have kept to themselves. For example, in 1988 Christian Armenians, who had lived peacefully in a region of the predominantly Muslim Republic of Azerbaijan (az • uhr • by • JAHN), suddenly demanded that the Republic of Armenia annex their region. Ethnic rioting, which claimed the lives of dozens of people, soon followed. Fearful of further violence, close to 100,000 Armenians fled Azerbaijan. Thousands of these refugees were killed in a massive earthquake that struck Armenia in December 1988.

Throughout 1989 an uneasy truce prevailed between the Azerbaijanis and the Armenians who had remained in Azerbaijan. Then in 1990 ethnic rioting erupted yet again in the beleaguered republic. Hundreds of Armenians were killed. Thousands more fled. Soviet leaders declared a state of emergency and sent in troops. Although the troops restored order, fierce resistance by the Azerbaijanis left many dead. At the same time, Azerbaijani leaders called for secession from the Soviet Union. The

867

Soviets, however, rejected such a possibility, and the troops maintained a strained peace in the republic.

Meanwhile, in the Soviet Baltic republics—Latvia, Lithuania, and Estonia—many people called for greater autonomy. This, they hoped, would come with Gorbachev's political restructuring. However, *perestroika* centralized power in the office of state president. The Baltic peoples felt that *perestroika* had not progressed quickly enough. For them, Gorbachev's pledge of political freedoms and a more open economy seemed little more than empty promises. In an attempt to hasten reform, both Lithuania and Latvia legalized noncommunist political parties and actively called for secession from the Soviet Union in 1990. Although Mikhail Gorbachev admitted that secession might be possible, the Soviets worked to keep them in the U.S.S.R.

The movement to hasten reforms and make the Soviet Union more democratic spread to the capital of Moscow in early 1990. There, Russians took part in demonstrations and demanded democracy. Only a few short years earlier, the army would have crushed such outpourings of discontent. Now, however, the Soviet leaders allowed the demonstrations. Then in February 1990, Mikhail Gorbachev bowed to public pressure and announced that the Soviet Union would allow opposition political parties and would work toward becoming a democracy. Although many Western leaders remained skeptical of such promises, people throughout the world looked for signs that the Soviets would live up to their promises. For their part, the Soviet people themselves remained skeptical. Despite reforms, consumer goods remained in short supply, and few people believed that the Communists would give up either their economic or political power.

The Nations of Eastern Europe

The threat of the Brezhnev Doctrine had prevented any real liberalization in Eastern Europe. However, people throughout the region continued to call for reform.

Continued dissent. During the 1970s the governments of the Eastern European nations followed the Soviet line and imposed harsh, repressive measures to end internal dissent. Even so, many Eastern Europeans continued to voice their opposition to totalitarian rule. Writers skirted government censors by issuing ***samizdat***—a Russian word meaning "self-published"—editions of their work. Exchanging manuscripts, the writers typed about a dozen copies of each, which they then passed on to friends. These friends made more copies and passed those on. In time these *samizdat* editions reached a wide audience.

After the signing of the Helsinki Accords, human rights became a major issue for Eastern European opposition groups. In 1977 a group of about 250 Czechoslovakian artists and intellectuals signed a charter calling on their government to abide by the human rights articles of the Accords. The government quickly branded Charter 77—as the group became known—as a subversive organization and arrested many of its members. Such repression failed to break the spirit of the opposition groups. During the 1980s groups from various countries even began to cooperate in their opposition activities. In 1986, for example, dissidents from Hungary, Czechoslovakia, East Germany, Poland, and Romania jointly issued a statement proclaiming their support for such values as self-government and democracy.

A long period of unrest in Poland that began in 1970 probably posed the greatest threat to communism in Eastern Europe. A few days before Christmas 1970, the Polish government announced huge price increases for food and fuel. About 300 people were killed in the demonstrations and riots that followed.

The atmosphere remained tense in Poland throughout the 1970s. Then, in 1980, a further round of huge price increases was met by a series of strikes. Led by Lech Walesa (vah • WEHN • sah), an unemployed electrician, and a number of shipyard workers, the strikers called for political and economic reforms. In the Gdansk Agreements—named for the Baltic port where the strikes began—the Polish government met many of the strikers' demands, including the right to organize labor unions free of Communist Party control.

The federation of independent trade unions, known as Solidarity, that grew out of the Gdansk Agreements increased in strength during 1981. By the end of the year, membership numbered more than 10 million. Seemingly in a position of power, the leaders of Solidarity called for more concessions from the government. However, in December 1981, under threat of a Soviet invasion, the Polish government imposed martial law, banned Solidarity, and arrested Walesa and other union leaders.

868

1E, 5H, a2G, a3C, a3J, a4A, a4B, a4C, a4F, a4G, a4I, a4J, a4M

READ
WRITE
INTERPRET
CONNECT
●THINK

BUILDING HISTORY STUDY SKILLS

Thinking About History: Conducting a Debate

A debate is a formal competition between two teams to determine which team has greater skill in speaking and reasoning. The two sides publicly dispute an issue in a systematic way, appealing to logic and reason rather than emotion.

How to Conduct a Debate

To conduct a debate, follow these steps.

1. Select the teams. Select two teams, each composed of two or three members, although the size of the team may vary depending on the debate topic or the format used.
2. State the proposition. A proposition is a thesis statement or conclusion that the teams research and then discuss in the debate. The proposition is most often stated as a resolution. For example:
   Resolved: The United States government should cut back on further developing the space program.
   Resolved: The United States government should raise import quotas to correct the trade deficit.
3. Prepare for the debate. Assign the team members research on the proposition. Team members should organize the information into an orderly and logical outline called a brief. Organize the brief on index cards that may be used during the debate.
4. Conduct the debate. The debate itself should consist of two parts separated by an intermission. In the first part–the constructive speeches–each team presents its arguments. Members of each team speak alternately, beginning with the affirmative team. Each constructive speech is limited to eight minutes. Intermission follows. After the intermission, each team refutes the arguments of the opposing team in four-minute speeches called rebuttals.

Developing the Skill

Read the following proposition as well as the constructive speech of the affirmative side and the rebuttal of the negative side.

Resolved: Soviet leader Mikhail Gorbachev's policy of *perestroika,* or moving the Soviet economy away from a command economy and toward a market economy, will have a positive effect on the Soviet Union as well as on world peace.

Affirmative Constructive Speech: Communism, with its strict command economy, was clearly failing in the Soviet Union. The government's plan of putting capital into defense, rather than into the production of consumer goods, led to scarcity of consumer goods and long lines in stores. By introducing the concept of *perestroika,* Gorbachev has taken a revolutionary step toward improving the Soviet economy.

Laws passed in 1987 allow some free enterprise to exist in the Soviet Union. Soviet citizens are now allowed to own small family businesses. New economic incentives have been given to both managers and workers. There is more reliance on the free market mechanism.

The results of all of this will mean that the Soviet people will have an abundance of high-quality consumer goods. As factory managers and workers are paid according to output, the rate of production will rise. As the free market mechanism begins to regulate the economy, competition will develop, further increasing productivity.

Negative Rebuttal: The idea that *perestroika* will benefit the economy of the Soviet Union and thus the world is unrealistic. It is unreasonable to think that the centralized Soviet economy can be converted to a free market economy. The disruption of Soviet life caused by this restructuring will almost certainly be doomed.

So far the cost of restructuring the Soviet economy into one based on consumerism is squeezing the finances of the average person. Prices in the privately owned shops are much higher than they are in the state-owned stores.

Workers are being asked to work harder while seeing little of the promised incentives. Unemployment is looming as factory managers are now allowed to fire employees.

Finally, even if *perestroika* were to succeed, an economically strong Soviet Union would hardly bode well for world peace. On the contrary, if the Soviets had a thriving economy, they might be inclined to once again invest in military defense.

Practicing the skill. From a recent copy of your local newspaper or a news magazine, find an article dealing with a controversial issue. Use this issue to write a proposition and from this, develop and conduct a debate.

To apply this skill, see Applying History Study Skills on page 873.

Perestroika *at work in a farmer's market*

SECTION 3

Closure

Have students discuss Premier Gorbachev's policies of *perestroika* and *glasnost.* Ask: Do you think Premier Gorbachev will succeed in building a truly open society in the Soviet Union? Why or why not?

Review Answers

1. *glasnost:* Russian word meaning "openness," used to describe Premier Gorbachev's policy of loosening censorship and government controls on everyday life in the Soviet Union; ***perestroika:*** Russian word meaning "restructuring," used to describe Gorbachev's efforts to reform the Soviet political and economic systems; ***samizdat:*** Russian word meaning "self-published," used to describe editions put out by banned authors
2. *Andrei Sakharov:* Russian dissident who protested Soviet curtailment of civil rights; ***Charter 77:*** movement founded by 250 Czech artists and intellectuals calling for recognition of human rights in Czechoslovakia; ***Lech Walesa:*** leader of Solidarity trade union in Poland; ***Gdansk Agreements:*** Polish government's concessions to striking workers; recognized workers' right to form unions free of Communist Party control; ***Wojciech Jaruzelski:*** Polish head of state during the 1980s; ***Karoly Grosz:*** Hungarian leader who wanted to expand *perestroika* in his country

3. ***Azerbaijan:*** southern Soviet Union, on the Caspian Sea; ***Armenia:*** southern Soviet Union, west of Azerbaijan; ***Latvia:*** eastern Baltic coast; ***Lithuania:*** eastern Baltic coast, south of Latvia; ***Estonia:*** eastern Baltic coast, north of Latvia
4. Under *glasnost,* the repression of the Brezhnev years was brought to an end. The media had more latitude to report sensitive stories. Social scientists began to write studies critical of past leaders. Artists and writers received greater freedom of expression, and publishers started to print works of long-banned authors. Dissidents received permission to travel outside the Soviet Union, and the government permitted the celebration of a millennium of Christianity in Russia.
5. *Perestroika* completely overhauled the Soviet political system, limiting the power of the Communist Party, creating the powerful position of state president, and establishing a new legislature that had broad authority. It also limited top government officials' terms and called for open and competitive elections.
6. Outdated factories and machinery, products of poor quality, low worker productivity, the imbalanced trade arrangements of CMEA, and huge foreign debt all contributed to economic failures in Eastern Europe.
7. The response has been mixed at best. As to

In 1982, however, Polish leader General Wojciech Jaruzelski (jahr • uhl • ZEHL • skee) lifted martial law and later released Walesa and other union leaders from jail. Demonstrations in support of Solidarity continued through much of the 1980s. After a series of strikes during the summer of 1988, the Polish government once again agreed to discuss political and economic reform with union representatives. The authorities even allowed Walesa to present his case in a debate on national television.

Economic problems. During the late 1970s and 1980s, the economies of the Eastern European nations, in general, began to show signs of fragility. Outdated factories and machinery, products of poor quality, low levels of worker productivity, the imbalanced trade arrangements of CMEA (formerly called COMECON), and a huge foreign debt all contributed to this economic weakness.

Even the "economic miracle" countries of East Germany, Hungary, and Yugoslavia exhibited signs of failure. For example, in Yugoslavia, once one of Eastern Europe's most vigorous economies, industrial output increased only marginally in 1987, and farm output actually fell. The annual rate of inflation reached 150 percent, and unemployment pushed toward 10 percent. Debts owed to other countries proved to be Yugoslavia's most crushing economic problem, however. In 1987, the government had to ask its creditors to reschedule repayment requirements for $19 billion. To combat these growing economic problems, Yugoslavia chose to follow the path taken by most other Eastern European nations. It imposed austerity measures that included huge price increases for food, fuel, and clothing, and tight wage controls.

Responses to *glasnost* and *perestroika*. Most of the Eastern European governments have expressed doubts about *glasnost.* Some have even blamed the policy for problems in their countries. Yugoslavian leaders, for example, have suggested that the resurgence of ethnic and nationalist feelings in their country has resulted from the new openness. However, even though few governments have officially adopted *glasnost,* signs of a new, more open atmosphere have appeared. In 1988 the East German government supported the reopening of a Jewish synagogue in East Berlin that had been closed since the 1930s. The government also relaxed some of its restrictions on other religions. And some observers have suggested that the Polish government's readiness to negotiate with union leaders in 1988 had more to do with *glasnost* than with political need.

It would seem that since the Eastern European nations had so many economic problems, they would have willingly embraced the new policies of Mikhail Gorbachev. However, the response has been mixed at best. The East Germans, who have had a small private sector since World War II and who experimented with *perestroika* in the 1970s, seemed unimpressed. Czechoslovakian leaders, on the other hand, appeared uninterested in economic reform. One reason for this lack of interest was that after the Prague Spring, reform leaders were ousted from the Communist Party. Some governments, however, expressed concern. Most complaints centered on Gorbachev's wish to integrate the economies of the Communist-bloc countries, which would require the Eastern Europeans to adopt all the economic changes the Soviet Union introduced. A number of Eastern Europeans had other problems with *perestroika.* For example, Karoly Grosz, Hungary's leader, felt that the restructuring did not go far enough. Grosz believed that a capitalist approach—if it proved more effective—should be adopted.

Response among dissidents to the new policies also has been mixed. Some have expressed outright disbelief, while others have voiced skepticism. Still others have proclaimed disgust that these policies—essentially their greatest hope of freedom—have come from the Soviet Union, the country that made their dissent necessary. A number of dissidents, however, have thrown their support to the

Learning from Pictures *During Pope John Paul II's visit to Gdansk, Solidarity mounted a huge demonstration.*

new policies, stating that these changes represent an important step toward democracy in Eastern Europe.

In 1987 Alexander Dubcek, the leader of Czechoslovakia during the Prague Spring of 1968, summed up the feelings of these dissidents.

> "Perestroika is indispensable and I support it because I find in it a profound connection with what presented itself to us 20 years ago. Had there been a political leadership in the U.S.S.R. at that time similar to the one today, the military intervention . . . in Czechoslovakia would have been unthinkable."

Effects of *glasnost* and *perestroika.* Throughout 1988 and 1989, Eastern Europeans cited *perestroika* and *glasnost* as they urged more and more government reforms. Poland, the birthplace of Solidarity, led the way by allowing noncommunist political parties to participate in the elections in June 1989. The result was that the Communists shared power with several political parties, particularly Solidarity. In August, the newly elected legislature proclaimed Tadeusz Mazoweiki (maz • oh • VEHT • skee) the first noncommunist prime minister in more than 40 years.

Other Communist regimes soon followed Poland's example. All of these nations followed the same pattern. First, the people took to the streets demanding democratic reforms. Party leaders ignored demands and attempted to crush the fledgling reform movements. In country after country, however, the people refused to be suppressed, and Communist party leaders, desperate to retain some of their powers, agreed to reforms. By early 1990, Hungary, Czechoslovakia, Bulgaria, East Germany, and Romania had promised to allow noncommunist political parties and had set elections for mid-1990.

East Germany and Romania proved two of the most dramatic examples of reform. Before 1989 these two nations had perhaps the most repressive Communist regimes in Europe.

In East Germany, Communist party chief Erich Honecker tried to maintain control. Frustrated by the lack of reform, almost 50,000 East Germans obtained permission to visit Czechoslovakia or Hungary and then fled to West Germany during 1989. Citing ill health, Honecker resigned only to be replaced by Egon Krenz—another Communist. On November 9, 1989, amidst growing protest, Krenz informed the world that East Germany would open its borders at midnight. That night thousands of Berliners gathered at the infamous Berlin Wall. At midnight, people raced to break holes in the wall or to climb over it. In the days that followed, the East German Communists—like those of the rest of Eastern Europe—renounced their monopoly on power, and the two Germanies worked on plans to reunify their nation.

The last nation of the Soviet Bloc to grant reforms was Romania where dictator Nicolae Ceausescu (chow • CHES • koo) ruled ruthlessly. Even there, however, the government could not suppress the will of the people. And by the end of 1989 Ceausescu had been driven from power and executed for treason. The new leaders promptly promised free elections.

By 1990 Western observers had become cautiously optimistic about developments in Eastern Europe. Throughout the region governments had caved in to the demands of citizens who had been deprived of basic human and civil rights for years. Democracy appeared attainable. Troop reductions seemed probable. Although few experts believed that the cold war was indeed over, most hoped that the "Iron Curtain" that had sliced through Europe for more than 40 years was disintegrating.

SECTION 3 REVIEW

1. **Define** *glasnost, perestroika, samizdat*
2. **Identify** Andrei Sakharov, Charter 77, Lech Walesa, Gdansk Agreements, Wojciech Jaruzelski, Karoly Grosz
3. **Locate** Azerbaijan, Armenia, Latvia, Lithuania, Estonia
4. **Analyzing Ideas** What impact did *glasnost* have on Soviet society?
5. **Summarizing Ideas** How did *perestroika* change the political system of the Soviet Union?
6. **Determining Cause and Effect** What factors helped to bring about economic failures in Eastern Europe?
7. **Evaluating Ideas** How did Eastern European governments respond to Mikhail Gorbachev's new policies?

perestroika, the East Germans seemed unimpressed. Czech leaders appeared uninterested in economic reform. Most complaints centered on Gorbachev's wish to integrate the economies of the area, which would require the Eastern Europeans to adopt all the economic changes introduced by the Soviet Union. Hungarians felt the restructuring did not go far enough. Most governments have also expressed doubts about *glasnost.* Yugoslavian leaders have suggested that the resurgence of ethnic and nationalist feelings resulted from the new openness. However, even though few Eastern European governments have officially adopted the policy, signs of a new, open atmosphere have appeared.

871

Reviewing Important Terms
1. Détente; 2. *Ostpolitik;* 3. *glasnost;* 4. *perestroika;* 5. *samizdat*

Developing Critical Thinking Skills
1. **(a)** Recession combined with inflation — a situation known as stagflation — and the shrinking value of the dollar were serious problems in the United States during the 1970s and 1980s. **(b)** The Ford and Carter administrations fought these problems by cutting the federal budget, cutting taxes, and asking for voluntary price and wage freezes. The Reagan administration cut taxes, ended funding for many social programs, and reduced all government spending—at least initially. In addition, President Reagan generally tried to limit the role of government in the economy.
2. Answers will vary.
3. Many Canadians fear that the United States will come to dominate this relationship and that Canada will eventually become completely dependent upon the United States.
4. Brandt's Social Democrats, like Great Britain's Labour Party, developed a more open foreign policy, seeking closer relations with Communist-bloc countries. The Social Democrats and the Labour Party also tried to right what they saw as inequities in society by developing and funding social welfare programs. However, Helmut Kohl's Christian Democrats, like the Conservatives under Margaret Thatcher, reaffirmed ties with the United States, cut government expenses, and limited the role of the government in the economy.

1B, 1E, 4I, 5D, 5E, 5G, 5H, a2C, a2G, a2K, a3A, a3B, a3F, a3J, a4A, a4F, a4G, a4H, a4I, a4J, a4K, a4L

Reteaching
Have students review the Chapter Summary and the appropriate section and questions in the Unit Synthesis. Discuss the concepts until students demonstrate a clear understanding of the material.

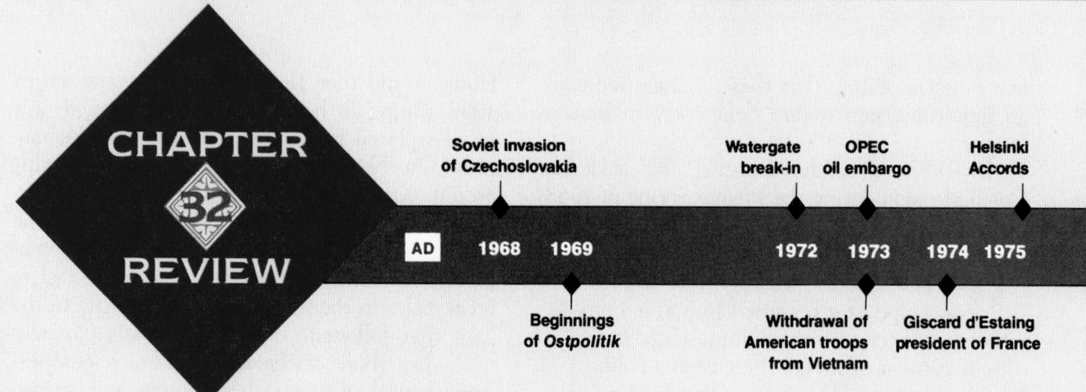

Chapter Summary

The following list contains the key concepts you have learned about North America, Europe, and the Soviet Union from 1968 to the present.

1. The Vietnam War had a long-lasting impact on the United States.
2. Many Americans lost faith in their government when the Watergate scandal became public in 1973.
3. Inflation and unemployment were among the economic problems that plagued the United States throughout the 1970s and into the mid-1980s. During President Reagan's administration these problems were reduced.
4. The nature of the American economy changed significantly during the 1970s and 1980s.
5. Efforts were made to ease tensions between the United States and the Soviet Union during the 1970s. The invasion of Afghanistan by the Soviet Union ended these efforts. However, by the mid-1980s, the two countries once again sought better relations.
6. A separatist movement in Quebec threatened Canadian unity during the 1970s.
7. Canadians were uneasy about their economic relations with the United States.
8. During the 1970s many Western European nations turned to conservative governments to solve their economic problems.
9. A number of nations in southern Europe moved from dictatorships to democracies.
10. The purpose and policies of NATO came under close scrutiny from member nations during the 1970s and 1980s.
11. The EC grew in membership during the 1970s and 1980s and made headway toward organizing Europe into an integrated economic unit.
12. During the 1970s the Soviet Union repressed dissent both at home and in its satellite nations. At the same time, it tried to improve its relations with the West.
13. Mikhail Gorbachev introduced a number of changes in the Soviet Union through the policies of *glasnost* and *perestroika.*
14. The nations of Eastern Europe faced such problems as internal dissent and failing economies during the 1970s and 1980s.

On a separate sheet of paper, complete the following review exercises.

Reviewing Important Terms

Supply the term that correctly completes each statement.

1. ________ is the name given to the improvement in relations between the United States and the Soviet Union during the 1970s.
2. West German chancellor Willy Brandt's efforts to create better relations between East and West became known as ________.
3. Mikhail Gorbachev's policy of ________ loosened the reins of censorship and eased the repression of the Brezhnev years.
4. Through ________, or restructuring, Mikhail Gorbachev planned to overhaul the political and economic systems of the Soviet Union.
5. Eastern European writers skirted government censors by publishing ________ editions of their works.

Developing Critical Thinking Skills

1. **Analyzing Ideas** **(a)** What economic problems faced the United States in the 1970s and 1980s? **(b)** What policies did presidents Ford, Carter, and Reagan use to try to solve these problems?
2. **Explaining Ideas** Some observers have said that American foreign policy has come full circle since the early 1970s. What did they mean by this statement?
3. **Interpreting Ideas** Why do you think many Canadians have expressed concerns about their country's economic relationship with the United States?
4. **Comparing Ideas** What similarities and differences are there between the political changes that took place in Great Britain and those that took place in West Germany during the late 1970s and 1980s?
5. **Understanding Ideas** Why did some members of NATO begin to question that alliance's purpose and policies during the 1970s and 1980s?
6. **Summarizing Ideas** What progress has the EC made toward political unity in Western Europe?
7. **Organizing Ideas** How did *glasnost* and *perestroika* change life in the Soviet Union?

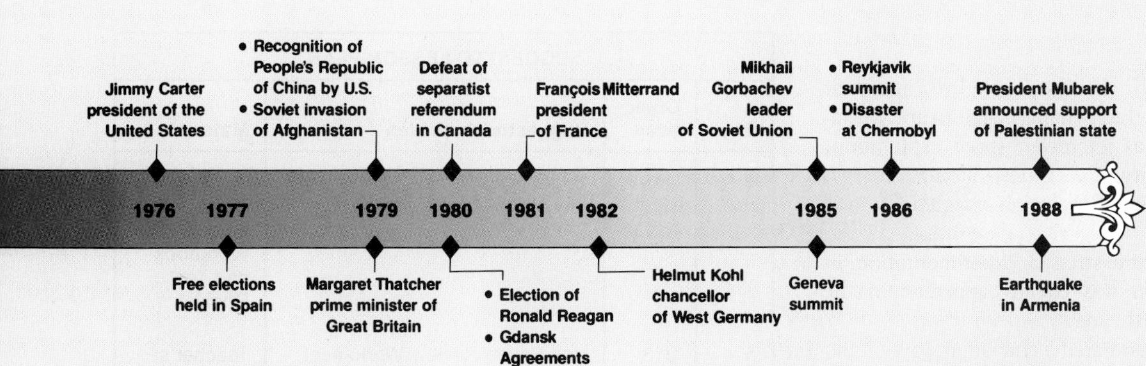

8. **Evaluating Ideas** The Nissan plant in Kentucky below is an example of Japan's economic expansion. Why has it become increasingly difficult for the United States to compete economically with Japan?

Relating Geography to History

Turn to the map on page 864. **(a)** How many nations belong to the EC? **(b)** Where are the majority of EFTA nations located? **(c)** According to the map, how do the EC and CMEA differ? **(d)** In your opinion, what problems does the EC face in building an integrated economy in Europe?

Relating Past to Present

1. Canada's uneasiness about its relationship with the United States is not new. Using information in this textbook and in encyclopedias, trace the development of this feeling among Canadians, describing when these feelings have surfaced in the past.
2. Many political scientists have noted the similarities between the reforms introduced in Czechoslovakia during the Prague Spring and Mikhail Gorbachev's policies of *glasnost* and *perestroika*. **(a)** What similarities do you see between the two? **(b)** Explain your answer.

Applying History Study Skills

Before completing this activity, review Building History Study Skills on page 869.

Conduct a debate by using the following steps and proposition or thesis statement.

Resolved: The nations of Western Europe should achieve political as well as economic unity.

1. Select teams.
2. State the proposition.
3. Prepare for the debate.
4. Conduct the debate.

Investigating Further

1. **Presenting an Oral Report** Relations between Canadians who speak English and Canadians who speak French have occasionally been tense. Prepare a report on the differences between these two cultural groups. Your report should also include a discussion of recent trends toward separatism and away from it. Consult the *Readers' Guide to Periodical Literature* for articles on these topics. Present your report to the rest of the class.
2. **Constructing a Diagram** Use resources in the library to gather information on the relative troop and weapon strengths of the NATO and Warsaw Pact alliances. Then construct a diagram comparing these strengths. Display your diagram on the bulletin board.

5. The installation of American missiles in Western Europe met with opposition from many NATO members. In addition, growing economic success and independence from the United States encouraged a reevaluation of each country's policies and membership in NATO.
6. The EC has successfully encouraged the development of trade, currency regulation, credit, and worker benefits. However, Britain's hesitancy in moving toward a united Europe has stifled attempts at political unity.
7. *Glasnost* encouraged a more critical press and greater openness in artistic expression. *Perestroika* limited the power of the Communist Party, creating a new power base resting in the hands of the president and legislature. It also limited many officials' terms of office.
8. Japan's factories are more modern and it has lower labor costs.

Relating Geography to History

(a) Twelve nations belong to the EC. **(b)** Most of them are in Northern Europe. **(c)** The EC membership is limited to European countries, whereas CMEA has non-European countries as members. **(d)** Answers will vary.

Relating Past to Present

1. Answers will vary.
2. **(a)** and **(b)** Answers will vary.

Applying History Study Skills

If needed, offer students assistance during each stage of the debate.

873

CHAPTER 33 (pages 874–895)
The Modern World Faced the Challenge of Rapid Change

(1945 to the present)

CHAPTER OVERVIEW

In the years following World War II, the way people lived and their attitudes toward the world around them changed significantly. Major technological advances such as jet travel, space exploration, computers, knowledge of heredity and genes, atomic energy, plastics, antibiotics, and the Green Revolution affected life and thought.

Art, literature, and architecture stressed experimentation in ideas and techniques. Innovation was equally apparent in the worlds of music, dance, film, and theater.

The pace of industrialization generated a change in ways of life. The amount of leisure time for the individual increased, creating new interests and new opportunities. The rapid pace of change caused many people to look for anchors of stability, such as religion. People also became more aware of social problems such as hunger and famine, violations of human rights, depletion of natural resources, and destruction of the environment. The social sciences enjoyed a golden age after 1945, as researchers sought greater understanding of social and individual behavior.

SUGGESTED LESSON PLAN

Day	Objectives	Suggested Activities	Materials
1	U13,* C1–2	Introducing The Chapter (pages 874–75) Section 1 (pages 875–84), Focus/Motivation (page 875), Presentation (page 876), Closure (page 884), Suggested Teaching Strategies, Enrichment Activity, Daily Quiz, Suggested Assignments (page 873B)	ATE, Pupil's Edition, Teacher's Resource-Bank™
2	U14, C3–4	Section 2 (pages 884–91), Focus/Motivation (page 885), Presentation (page 886), Closure (page 889), Suggested Teaching Strategies, Enrichment Activity, Daily Quiz, Suggested Assignments (page 873B)	ATE, Pupil's Edition, Teacher's Resource-Bank™
3	U15, C5–6	Section 3 (pages 891–93), Focus/Motivation (page 891), Presentation (page 892), Closure (page 892), Suggested Teaching Strategies, Enrichment Activity, Daily Quiz, Suggested Assignments (page 873C)	ATE, Pupil's Edition, Teacher's Resource-Bank™

*C refers to applicable Chapter Objective, U refers to applicable Unit Goal.

SUGGESTED LESSON PLAN

Day	Objectives	Suggested Activities	Materials
4	U13–15 C1–8	Chapter 33 Form A Test, Reteaching Worksheet, Chapter 33 Form B Test	Teacher's Resource-Bank™ or Workbook and Test Booklet
5	U13–15	Unit Seven Review Worksheet, Unit Seven Test	Teacher's Resource-Bank™ or Test Booklet
6	Unit 5-7 Goals	End of Book Test	Teacher's Resource-Bank™ or Test Booklet

BOOKS FOR THE TEACHER

Friedman, S. D. *Energy: The New Era.* Random House. Examines America's energy policies and prospects for the future.

Hebblethwaite, P. *The Year of Three Popes.* Collins. Presents a penetrating look at two papal conclaves.

Russell, John. *The Meanings of Modern Art.* Harper & Row. Discusses the styles of modern art; includes illustrations.

BOOKS FOR THE STUDENT

Asimov, Isaac. *Change.* Houghton Mifflin. Includes short essays giving glimpses of the future.

Berger, Melvin. *Robots: In Fact and Fiction.* Franklin Watts. Features information on robots in the technical age.

Cartright, E. M., ed. *Apollo Expeditions to the Moon.* NASA. Presents a series of articles on the moon-flight program.

Farb, Peter. *Ecology.* Time-Life. Provides a very informative text.

Rublowsky, John. *Pop Art.* Basic Books. Features the styles and artists of Pop Art; includes photographs.

MULTIMEDIA MATERIALS

Future Shock (mp, 42 min.), McGraw-Hill. Based on the book by Alvin Toffler, this film provides a penetrating look at the superelectronic future.

Leisure Time: The Problem and the Promise (fs), New York Times. Examines the effects of increased leisure time and the changing social patterns it will bring about.

Tragedy and Triumph (World Food) (mp, 28 min.), Journal. Studies the problems of hunger and food production in the modern world.

2000 A.D. (multi-media), Newsweek. Explores the changes that the year 2000 may bring.

Section 1 (pages 875–884) Technological Change Affected Ideas and Behavior

SECTION OVERVIEW

Dramatic changes in technology after 1945 affected all the nations of the world. Some of the most spectacular advances were made in air travel, space exploration, miniaturization, computers, lasers, genetic research, the atom, plastics, antibiotics, and agriculture.

SUGGESTED TEACHING STRATEGIES

1. **Bulletin Board Display (Average/Group)** Have members of the class contribute to a bulletin board display on scientific and technological achievements of the past 35 years.
2. **Determining Results (Basic)** Have students identify specific ways in which each of the advances and developments listed in this section has changed life. *(Accept all reasonable answers.)* You might want to list students' answers on the chalkboard. Then ask students to decide which technological advance has influenced their lives most. Students should support their opinions with facts.

ENRICHMENT ACTIVITY

Panel Discussion (Challenging) At least three of the scientific advances mentioned in the textbook — genetic research, atomic energy, and the Green Revolution — have caused controversy. Divide the class into three groups and have each group hold a panel discussion on one of the three topics. Sources include *Scientific America: Energy and Power, Recombinant DNA,* and *Food and Agriculture,* published by W. H. Freeman; and *The Global 2000 Report to the President,* prepared by the Council on Environmental Quality and the U.S. Department of State. Students should also refer to the *Readers' Guide to Periodical Literature.*

DAILY QUIZ

To assess student understanding of Section 1, give the class the following quiz. (each item is worth 10 points.)

1. Name the jet that made it possible to fly from New York to London in three hours. *(Concorde)*
2. What was Sputnik? *(first Russian satellite)*
3. How did the explosion of *Challenger* affect the American space program *(It temporarily halted space exploration.)*
4. (T or F) Miniaturization led to the development of modern computers. *(T)*
5. What invention provides a highly concentrated, straight and narrow light beam used in medicine, architecture, and construction? *(lasers)*
6. DNA determines ______. *(genetic code, heredity, chromosomes)*
7. What resource is absolutely necessary for the production of plastic? *(Oil)*
8. (T or F) Streptomyacin, penicillin and other anti-bacterial agents are antibiotics. *(T)*
9. (T or F) The agricultural revolution of the 1960s that discovered ways of producing high-yielding seeds was called the "brown revolution." *(F)*
10. (T or F) Technological advances have made consumer goods available to almost everyone in the Western world. *(T)*

SUGGESTED ASSIGNMENTS

1. **Critical Thinking Worksheet (Basic)** Have students complete Critical Thinking Worksheet 74 in the TEACHER'S RESOURCEBANK™.
2. **Profile Worksheet (Basic)** Have students do Profile Worksheet 33 in the TEACHER'S RESOURCEBANK™.

Section 2 (pages 884–891) The Arts and Literature Followed New Directions

SECTION OVERVIEW

A main characteristic of the arts and literature of the post-1945 period was experimentation. Abstract expressionism, pop art, and op art styles of painting emerged. Architects experimented with new styles, materials, and methods of building houses. Music, dance, films, and theater also experienced innovation. Poets and novelists displayed a variety of interests and styles. These new art and literary forms generated enormous popular interest.

SUGGESTED TEACHING STRATEGIES

1. **Learning History Through Art (Average/Group)** Have students study the picture of the Sydney Opera House in the feature on textbook page 887. You might also bring to class pictures of the Guggenheim Museum in New York City and the Transamerica Building in San Francisco. Then have students bring to class pictures of other unusually shaped buildings, perhaps in your own town or in nearby cities. These might be assembled to initiate class discussion or to form a bulletin board display illustrating variety and experimentation in postwar architecture.

2. **Interpreting Music and Art (Average/Group)** This section presents a good opportunity for the art or music teacher to talk to the class about the latest trends in his or her field.

*3. **Making Connections With History: Linking History to Architecture (Average/Group)** Have students find photographs of tropical areas, desert areas, mountain regions, and plains regions. Then have them identify the natural resources early settlers of these regions used to build homes. Ask: How are these early architectural styles characteristic of these regions today?

ENRICHMENT ACTIVITY

Collage (Average/Group) A group of students might prepare a collage for classroom display, illustrating the range of artistic styles of the postwar period. The following styles might be included: abstract expressionism (Jackson Pollock, Willem de Kooning); realism (Andrew Wyeth); surrealism (Salvador Dali); primitive (Grandma Moses); and pop art (Andy Warhol, Roy Lichtenstein).

DAILY QUIZ

To assess student understanding of Section 2, give the class the following quiz. (Each item is worth 10 points.)

1. (T or F) Postwar artists and authors continued to experiment with different forms and styles. *(T)*
2. (T or F) Jackson Pollock, a leading abstract expressionist, concluded that artists should respect recognizable, classical rules established by nineteenth-century artists. *(F)*
3. (T or F) Pop and op art are the same. *(F)*
4. (T or F) John Cage is an example of the new composers who permitted the performers to shape the length, order, and mood of the composition. *(T)*
5. (T or F) George Balanchine continued in the United States the traditions that made Russia a center of ballet. *(T)*
6. What mass medium form included spectacular, multi-million-dollar productions, and also the new socially pertinent, psychologically powerful "New Wave?" *(Film)*
7. (T or F) In the theater, playwrights encouraged actors to try improvisation and spontaneity. *(T)*
8. (T or F) The Beat Generation critiqued society, especially targeting the wealthy and privileged. *(T)*
9. (T or F) Most poets followed strict, traditional rules of meter and rhyme. *(F)*
10. (T or F) Higher average educational levels, increased leisure time, and increased exposure of artistic ideas helped increase interest in the arts. *(T)*

SUGGESTED ASSIGNMENTS

1. **Skill Worksheet (Basic)** Have students complete Skill Worksheet 33 in the TEACHER'S RESOURCEBANK™.
2. **Presenting an Oral Report (Average/Group)** Have students prepare an oral or written report on one of the painters, musicians, dancers, architects, or writers of this period. Reports should include brief biographical sketches and should discuss the individual's major works and achievements. Students should check the card catalog for appropriate sources.
3. **Debating Ideas (Challenging)** Have selected students debate the following topic. Resolved: Crime and violence portrayed on television have an adverse affect on American society. Students may wish to conduct a survey to identify which types of television programs portray the most violence. They also might conduct additional research for their arguments in the public library.

Section 3 (pages 891–893) Patterns of Living Took New Forms

SECTION OVERVIEW

One of the outstanding features of life after 1945 was the speed of change. One result was a greater amount of leisure time, which made possible new interests and opportunities. To cope with rapid change, people turned to religion as a source of stability. Others became concerned about catastrophes in various parts of the world, political repression, and dwindling natural resources. The social sciences contributed a better understanding of change.

SUGGESTED TEACHING STRATEGIES

1. **Applying Historical Knowledge (Average/Group)** Have students imagine that they are historians in the year 3000 exploring the history of their community in the twentieth century. What means might they use to reconstruct the past?
2. **Analyzing Ideas (Average/Group)** Initiate a class discussion about changes in life styles since 1945. Ask the students to consider how career opportunities for women have impacted American society economically, politically, and socially.

ENRICHMENT ACTIVITY

Relating Ideas (Average/Group) Have students look through newspapers and magazines to find pictures that illustrate "traditionalism" in our society — for example, colonial furniture or a Spanish-style church. Students should write a sentence or two describing the traditional features shown in the pictures. After students have written their descriptive sentences, you might want to display the pictures on the bulletin board and discuss the reasons why people turn to ways of the past.

DAILY QUIZ

To assess student understanding of Section 3, give the class the following quiz. (Each item is worth 10 points.)

1. (T or F) The improvement in communications has revolutionized people's life styles. *(T)*

2. (T or F) The new increases in leisure time for people, particularly in the industrial countries, contributed to increased drug use, crime, and divorce. *(T)*
3. (T or F) As leisure time increased, people's participation in organized activities like athletics decreased. *(F)*
4. Name one thing people looked to in order to attain more stability during these times of rapid change. *(religion)*
5. In what religion did Middle Eastern people intensify their interest during the 1970s? *(Islam)*
6. What is the ecumenical movement? *(unity among Christians)*
7. Name two groups or organizations that helped to feed the world's hungry, assisted the impoverished, or aided political prisoners. *(Red Cross, United Nations, Amnesty International, Oxfam)*
8. Who are often the main critics of the political order and of inequities of government in Latin America? *(Catholic Church, priests)*
9. (T or F) The environment is one of the most crucial resources endangered by the changes of the modern era. *(T)*
10. Why study the social sciences, especially history? *(Accept any reasonable answer. Students should mention that it enables them to understand the world they live in.)*

SUGGESTED ASSIGNMENTS

1. **Understanding History Through Art (Average/Group)** Have students select an object or work of art that they think is particularly representative of the modern period and write a feature describing the historical information about our time that this object might reveal to people of the future.
2. **Critical Thinking Worksheet (Basic)** Have students complete Critical Thinking Worksheet 75 in the TEACHER'S RESOURCEBANK™.
3. **Review Worksheet (Basic)** Have students complete Review Worksheet 33 in the TEACHER'S RESOURCEBANK™.

For suggested lesson plan, additional teaching strategies, enrichment activities, daily quizzes, and suggested assignments, see pages 873A-873D.

Introducing the Chapter
To illustrate the interdependence of the countries of the world, bring a chocolate bar to class. Have students imagine that they earn their living by working in a candy factory. Ask the class what ingredients might go into a candy bar. *(sugar, chocolate, nuts, corn syrup, and coconut).* Have students identify where each of these ingredients might be grown or produced. *(Sugar might come from the United States or a Caribbean island. Chocolate might come from cocoa seeds grown in Africa. Nuts might come from Brazil. Corn syrup might be produced from corn grown in the United States; and coconut might come from an island in the South Pacific. In addition, the candy bar is wrapped in a paper wrapper, which might have been produced by a paper company in the Pacific Northwest.)*

Ask students how they might be affected if a drought in the Midwest damaged the corn crop, a revolution took place on a Caribbean island and cut off the sugar supply, or a war broke out in Africa.

You might wish to adapt this activity using items such as a pencil or an article of clothing.

Chapter Objectives
After reading Chapter 33, students will be able to:

1. Discuss how air travel, space exploration, computers and miniaturization

CHAPTER 33

The Modern World Faced the Challenge of Rapid Change

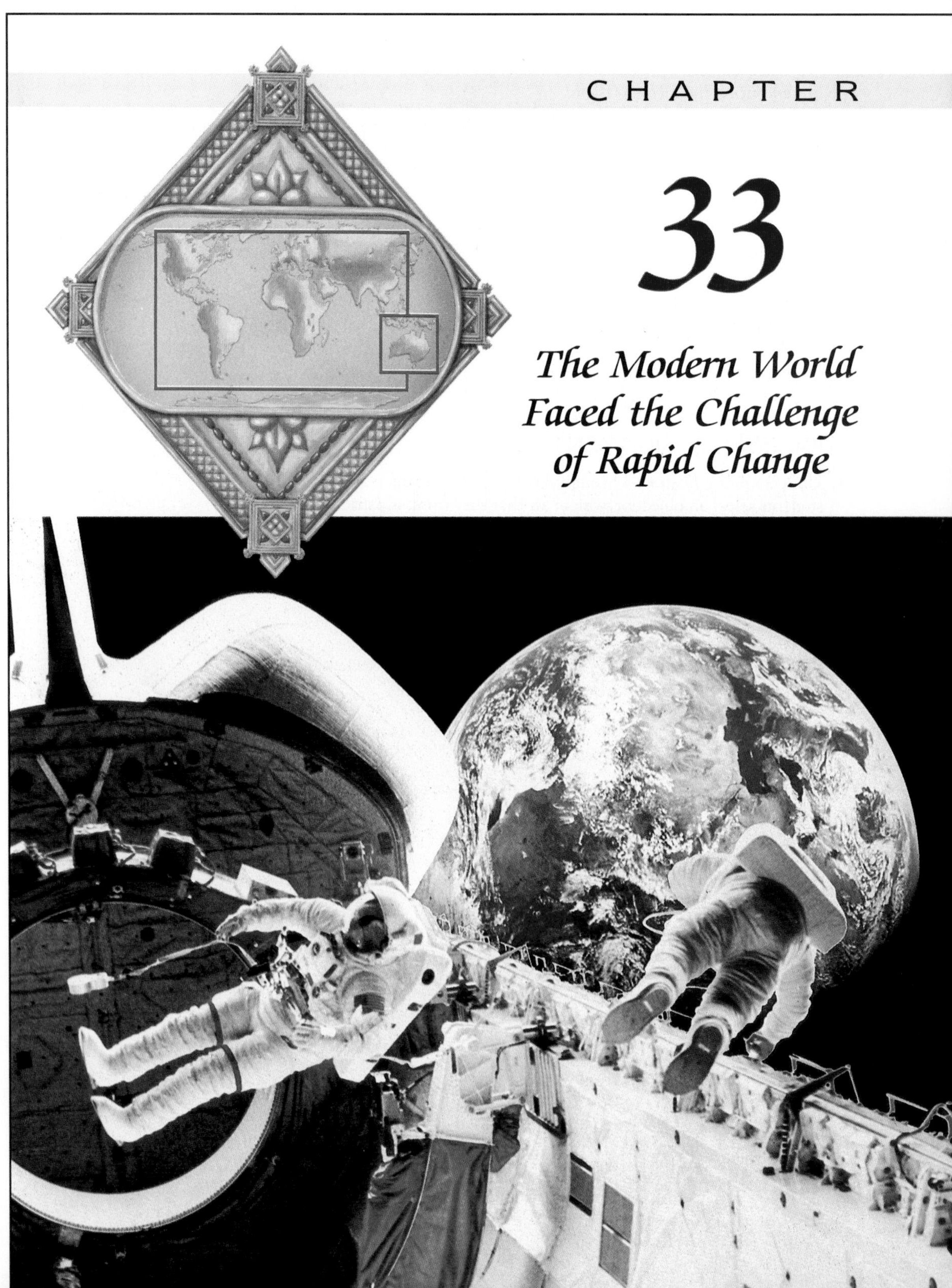

5E, a1C, a3A, a3B, a3G, a3H, a4A, a4F

CHAPTER FOCUS

Place The world and beyond

Time

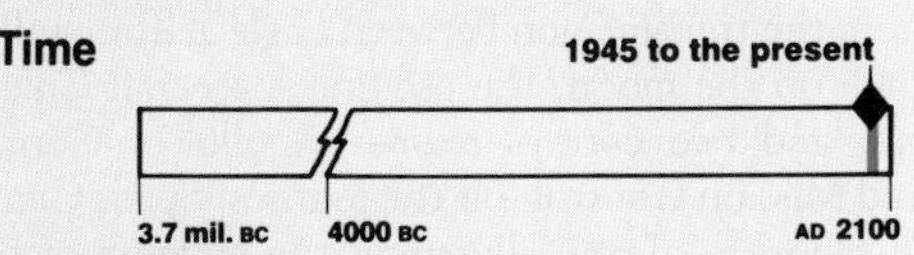

Significance

Vast changes in people's life styles and attitudes about the world marked the years following 1945. The emotional scars of World War II remained, but people rebuilt their lives.

Advances in technology and communication unified the world community. Satellites made it possible for millions of television viewers, otherwise separated by distance and ideas, to witness historic events as they occurred. Although it was an American spacecraft that first achieved a manned lunar landing, astronaut Neil Armstrong represented all people on earth when in 1969 he became the first human being to set foot on the moon.

In the 1970s and 1980s the United States embarked upon an ambitious space exploration program. Television coverage of successful launches became almost routine. Then on January 28, 1986, millions of horrified television viewers watched in disbelief as the space shuttle *Challenger* exploded shortly after lift-off. The crew of seven American astronauts perished, and people all over the world shared the tragedy.

Though people remain separated by geography, cultures, and governments, we are all members of the world community. We laugh and cry. We share some victories and some defeats—we are human beings journeying together on the spaceship *Earth.*

Terms to Define

miniaturization
antibiotics
abstract expressionism
pop art
op art
process art

People to Identify

Neil Armstrong
Steven Spielberg
Ralph Ellison
James Baldwin

Places to Locate

Ethiopia
Marseilles

Questions to Guide Your Reading

1 How did technological change affect ideas and behavior after World War II?
2 What direction did the arts and literature follow after World War II?
3 Why did patterns of living take new forms?

◀ *Shuttle astronauts outside the cargo bay*

Throughout history the lure of the unknown has challenged people's courage, tested their ingenuity, and inspired them to embark upon dangerous quests. Over time many individuals and groups of people have blazed the trail of human progress. Many have come before our time, and many will come after our time. But each era of history has provided unique challenges to the people of the world.

We live in an era of rapid change. Many ideas that existed only in dreams and science fiction 40 years ago have become a reality in the 1980s. Children of the 1940s could only imagine what it would be like to travel in space. Today children can hear the giant engines of the space shuttle roar to life and then watch the massive white spacecraft slice through the clouds in search of new information about the universe beyond.

Other frontiers remain on earth—in science labs where new treatments for disease are discovered; in computerized industries and businesses that bring changes to our lives; and in classrooms, where traditional knowledge and current ideas spark creativity in a new generation that will discover new frontiers and enhance the quality of human life.

1 Technological Change Affected Ideas and Behavior

Dramatic advances in technology after World War II affected all the nations of the world. Although industrialized societies felt the effects most directly, inventions and new devices also brought changes to developing nations.

It would be impossible to list all the discoveries and applications of new ideas that affected the way people thought or lived after 1945. However, a look at some of the most spectacular will illustrate the broad range and sweeping significance of the advances that have taken place in these decades of rapid change.

Air Travel

Improvements in airplanes transformed travel throughout the world. Passenger airliners became larger and faster. In the 1970s the jumbo jet became a common means of transportation. These giant airplanes could easily carry more than 350

have revolutionized communications, medicine, travel, and international relations.
2. Describe the major changes in society brought about by lasers, genetic research, plastics, and other scientific developments.
3. Define abstract expressionism, pop and op art, and tell how they affected painting and sculpture.
4. Compare the ways in which the postwar era influenced architecture, art, music, film, drama, poetry, and novels.
5. Explain why there was a heightened sense of social concern in the postwar years.
6. Outline how the social sciences helped people understand themselves and their culture.

SECTION 1

Focus/Motivation

Often a discovery in one area of knowledge can lead to accomplishments in other fields. Ask students to suggest examples of this process. *(Accept all reasonable answers. For example, space exploration improved communication through satellites; miniaturization led to the development of pocket calculators and portable radios; computers spawned the video market; and lasers opened up new approaches to medicine.)*

5D, 5E, a1C, a3A, a3B, a3G, a3H

Presentation
Analyzing Ideas (Average/Group)
Have students discuss the positive and negative aspects of the space program. Ask: What are the benefits and costs of American space exploration? *(Student responses should include: Benefits—greater knowledge of the universe; "spin-off" products and technological advances, such as teflon, new fuels, and new computer applications; and national pride. Costs—diversion of government funds from equally important programs, development of another area of competition between the superpowers, and the "militarization" of space.)*

passengers. One jumbo jet could carry more cargo in a year than could all the airliners in the world in 1939.

The jumbo jet could also fly much farther and faster than earlier airliners. In 1945 a flight from London to New York took at least 15 hours. This trip had to include a stop because the plane could not fly more than 2,000 miles (3,200 kilometers) without refueling. In 1988 a regular jet airliner could complete the trip in less than six hours. The Concorde, a sleek airliner developed by the British and the French, cuts travel time for the same trip to three hours. New technologies may soon make it possible to fly from Washington, D.C., to Tokyo, Japan, in two hours. Today the world's busiest airports serve millions of passengers each year. Although other means of transportation have also advanced rapidly, air travel has become the most popular and convenient way to reach distant places.

Space Exploration

Although Canada, Japan, and several Western European nations have developed space exploration programs, the United States and the Soviet Union have dominated the "space race." In the 1930s and 1940s, engineers experimented with rockets that could fly at incredible speeds. Both the Soviet and the United States space programs achieved several early successes.

Early successes. The "Space Age" began on October 4, 1957, when the Soviet Union launched *Sputnik 1*, the world's first space satellite, into orbit around the earth. Then in 1961 the Soviets built a rocket with enough power to put a person into orbit around the earth, and Soviet astronaut Yuri Gagarin became the first person to travel in space. The United States responded with its own ambitious program for space exploration.

The United States space program expanded rapidly. In 1957 the United States successfully launched an unmanned rocket into space, and in 1961 Alan Shepard became the first American to travel in space. In 1965 the United States promptly responded to the first Soviet space walk with the first American space walk.

Lunar landing. On July 20, 1969, the United States won the intense race to put the first person on the moon. The Apollo 11 mission transported three American astronauts—Neil Armstrong, Edwin Aldrin, Jr., and Michael Collins—to the moon aboard the spaceship *Columbia.* While Collins stayed behind on the *Columbia* to help coordinate the mission, Armstrong and Aldrin descended to the surface of the moon aboard the lunar module, the *Eagle.* The following excerpt from the transmission between *Eagle* at Tranquillity Base on the moon, the orbiting spacecraft *Columbia,* and two control teams—Apollo 11 Control and Mission Control—at the Johnson Space Center in Houston, Texas, illustrates the triumph of this historic event.

> "EAGLE: Houston, Tranquillity Base here. The Eagle has landed. . . .
>
> HOUSTON: Roger, Tranquillity. Be advised there are lots of smiling faces in this room and all over the world. . . .
>
> HOUSTON (10:37): Neil, this is Houston, what's your status on hatch opening?
>
> TRANQUILLITY BASE: Everything is go here. . . . We're going to try it. The hatch is coming open (Aldrin). . . .
>
> ARMSTRONG: Okay, Houston, I'm on the porch. . . .
>
> HOUSTON: We're getting a picture on TV. . . .
>
> ARMSTRONG: I'm at the foot of the ladder. . . . The surface appears to be very, very fine-grained. . . . I'm going to step off the LM [lunar module] now.
>
> That's one small step for a man, one giant leap for mankind."

Edwin Aldrin joined Neil Armstrong on the moon's surface and for the next two hours the astronauts took photographs, collected lunar soil and rocks, posted a United States flag, and conducted experiments. About 22 hours after the *Eagle* had landed, the astronauts left the moon and returned to the command module. On July 24, 1969, they returned to earth.

The world watched, listened, and followed the quest for knowledge about space into the 1970s, when the main results of space exploration came from unmanned spacecraft.

Unmanned spacecraft. Following a series of manned moon landings from 1969 to 1972, America's space program shifted its emphasis to unmanned spacecraft that explored farther into our solar system. *Pioneer 10* became the first spacecraft to fly by Jupiter. Then in 1977 and 1978, *Voyager 1*

● By the mid-1980s, the space shuttle program averaged about twelve flights per year.

and *Voyager 2* explored the outer planets and provided new information about their makeup. These "flybys" produced spectacular photographs that led researchers to describe Jupiter's mysterious red spot as a giant hurricane in the planet's atmosphere. Other voyages of unmanned spacecraft produced dramatic photographs of Mercury and Venus and of Saturn's majestic rings. Spacecraft also mapped the volcanic peaks and treacherous canyons of Mars. They even landed on the "red planet" in a futile search for life.

Both the United States and the Soviet Union have launched satellites into orbit around the earth. These satellites are divided into three classifications—communications, earth survey, and navigation.

Communication satellites have made 24-hour-a-day global communications possible. Earth survey satellites monitor the weather. Orbiting cameras enable meteorologists to more accurately predict and track life-threatening storm systems. These satellites also offer new ways to improve maps of the world. Navigation satellites enhance ocean and aircraft navigation systems.

New frontiers in space. The 1980s brought even greater American and Soviet successes in space. A new phase of space exploration began in 1981 with the launch of the first American space ● shuttle, *Columbia*. By 1986 these reusable shuttles, which contained elements of both the traditional space capsule and the airplane, had completed two dozen successful missions. Everyone thought that the launch of the *Challenger* and its crew of seven on January 28, 1986, would be another routine success. However, 73 seconds after lift-off the shuttle exploded in a huge ball of flame. The expected single vapor trail separated into two erratic paths in a crystal-clear sky as the rocket boosters broke away. People watching the launch at the space center or on television gasped in horror. The *Challenger* and its crew were lost. The disaster halted America's manned exploration of space for 32 months.

Learning from Pictures *The voyage of* Columbia *paved the way for astronauts to conduct medical experiments in the weightless environment of space.*

Then in September 1988 Americans returned to space. Again the world watched—and waited. An excerpt from the cover story in the October 10, 1988, issue of *Time* magazine describes the event.

> "As the countdown clock flashed out the number of seconds until lift-off, the eyes of an entire nation focused on Launch Pad 39-B and the gleaming white shuttle *Discovery,* flanked by its two solid rocket boosters and clinging to the side of the giant, rust-colored external fuel tank. . . .
>
> Finally, spectators joined in the last 15 seconds of countdown, the engines ignited and the shuttle rose majestically from the pad, carrying its crew of five veteran astronauts. Over the space center's loudspeakers came the triumphant announcement: 'Americans return to space, as *Discovery* clears the tower.' But the cheers were muted as the crowd—many with clenched fists, gritted teeth and teary eyes—nervously watched the spacecraft rise on its pillar of flame, then begin its roll out over the Atlantic. . . . *Discovery* passed the 73-second mark. . . . A smattering of applause and cheers grew into a chorus near the two-minute mark, when the spacecraft successfully jettisoned its two spent solid rocket boosters. But experienced space observers did not relax until *Discovery* shut down its three main engines 6 1/2 minutes later, shucked off its external fuel tank, then slipped safely into orbit 180 miles [290 kilometers] above the earth."

In November 1988 the Soviet Union successfully launched an unmanned space shuttle. Manned flights of the Soviet shuttle followed shortly thereafter. The Soviet shuttle appears to be very similar to the American version. However, the Soviet orbiter is powered by a huge disposable rocket rather than the three reusable main engines that propel the United States shuttle.

The successful exploration of space has been hindered by sporadic failures. But the triumphant successes and the benefits of those accomplishments will have far-reaching effects upon the people of the earth. For example, *Spacelab,* a joint venture of the United States and several Western European nations, was launched from a space shuttle in 1983. The laboratory includes facilities for scientists to perform experiments in industry, medicine, astronomy, and many other fields of study. The shuttle carries *Spacelab* and the scientists into space and then returns them to earth, where the lab is readied for its next mission.

The exploration and the conquest of space have already produced significant opportunities and remarkable products for people on earth. The future holds promises for greater opportunities and even more extensive benefits for humankind.

Miniaturization

Rockets can lift only limited amounts of weight. Therefore, to be sent into space, equipment had to be made as light and as compact as possible. An important consequence of space exploration was the invention of ways of making machines, especially electrical equipment, smaller. This process is called **miniaturization.**

The most significant device that resulted from the process of miniaturization is the transistor. This tiny electronic device, invented in 1948, can do the work done previously by a much larger vacuum tube. Entire electronic circuits, consisting of numerous transistors, can fit into smaller spaces and use less electricity than a single vacuum tube.

Miniaturization made possible dozens of new products that affect the lives and leisure activities of people throughout the world. Portable radios, pocket calculators, digital watches, compact tape recorders, and automatic cameras were developed. Initially, these products were expensive and not widely available. However, costs decreased as technology became more advanced and the demand for such products increased. Today many types of electronic products have become common household items. The manufacture of these products has created huge industries and thousands of jobs.

Computers

The most remarkable product of miniaturization was the modern computer. In the 1600s the French scientist Blaise Pascal invented a machine that could perform arithmetical calculations. The idea intrigued scientists and engineers over the next 300 years. However, the necessary machinery was too large and cumbersome to have many practical applications.

In the 1950s scientists developed smaller machines capable of storing and processing information

878

1D, 5D, 5E, a1C, a3A, a3B, a3G, a3H

● Class Activity: Have students list specific uses of computers and discuss how computers impact society.

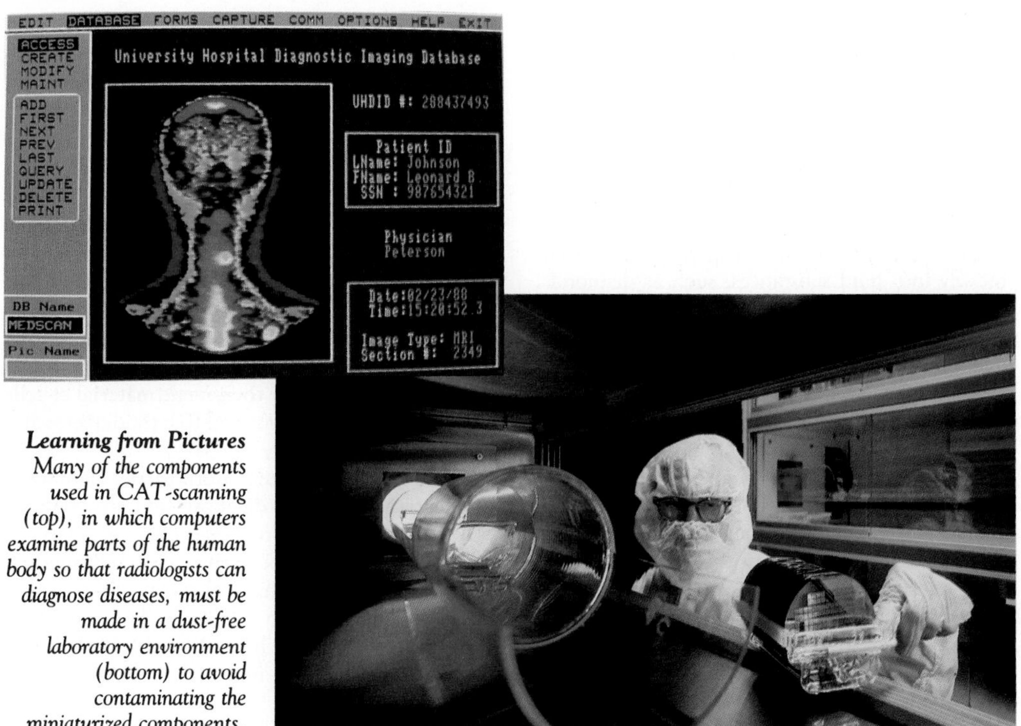

Learning from Pictures *Many of the components used in CAT-scanning (top), in which computers examine parts of the human body so that radiologists can diagnose diseases, must be made in a dust-free laboratory environment (bottom) to avoid contaminating the miniaturized components.*

quickly. These computers rapidly made an impact on society and were improved from year to year. They operated more and more quickly and efficiently, while requiring a smaller and smaller amount of space to store gigantic amounts of information.

By the mid-1980s computers performed a multitude of functions. They guided the flights of spacecraft and recorded every airline reservation in the world. Computers also created significant changes in medicine, enabling doctors to diagnose diseases and treat patients more effectively than ever before. A complex machine called the CAT scanner now allows doctors and technicians to view cross sections of all parts of the human body. As a result, many medical problems that would have required extensive exploratory surgery even a few years ago can now be diagnosed with little or no discomfort to the patient. Other computers can detect a broad ● range of diseases in their earliest and most treatable stages.

In other fields computers draw maps, keep accounts, and print newspapers. Computers also control the flow of fuel to a car's engine and solve complex mathematical questions. Machines with artificial intelligence can now resolve problems in every field that would have been considered impossible 40 years ago.

Computers affect the everyday lives of people in their homes, schools and businesses. Personal computers that play games as well as help families with educational tasks have become as popular as videocassette recorders and compact discs. Businesses use computers to control all types of financial and administrative activities. Computers can even be hooked up to an automobile engine to diagnose specific malfunctions. The range of computer-controlled activities is almost unlimited.

Lasers

In 1960 scientists invented a device called a laser. The laser can store energy and release it all at once in an intense beam of light. This beam remains straight, narrow, and very concentrated, even after it has traveled millions of miles. The laser's uses are extraordinarily varied—a perfect example of the combination of scientific discovery and engineering applications. Surgeons use lasers to weld damaged

879

5D, 5E, a1C, a3A, a3B, a3G, a3H

In the early 1900s, the average life expectancy was about 45 years of age; by the 1980s the average life expectancy had risen to about 73 years of age.

tissue in the eye, to burn away skin growths, and to repair decayed parts of teeth. A laser procedure that produces no heat allows doctors to clear clogged arteries from the heart by cutting through blockages and vaporizing them without damaging the artery walls. For many people, this procedure has become an alternative to heart bypass surgery.

Lasers help engineers make tunnels and pipelines straight. They enable manufacturers to cut precisely into hard substances, such as diamonds. Lasers also transmit radio, television, and telephone signals. They make it possible to show three-dimensional pictures on a television or film screen. Thus one invention has significantly affected dozens of activities and people from many walks of life.

Genetic Research

In 1962 the Nobel Prize for medicine, the most prestigious scientific award in the world, was given to an American, James D. Watson, and two British scientists, Maurice Wilkins and Francis Crick, who had discovered the structure of DNA (deoxyribonucleic acid) during the 1950s. DNA is an essential component of genes—the small units of chromosomes that convey characteristics, such as color of hair and eyes, from parent to child. By understanding DNA, one can understand how a gene is structured—what scientists call the "genetic code."

By unraveling the genetic code, the DNA experimenters came closer to explaining how different life forms are created. This breakthrough made possible new research into viruses, bacteria, human cells, and diseases such as cancer. Scientists could now reproduce life forms in the laboratory and achieve major advances in treating illness.

Recently scientists have deciphered a second genetic code that directs the synthesis of proteins inside cells. This new discovery will also shed light on some inherited disorders caused by malfunctions in the second code. It completely changes our understanding of the nature of what the molecule does within the cell and allows developments thought impossible only five years ago. Genetic engineers can now alter the genetic material of cells to make specific proteins used to treat diabetes and heart disease.

The genetic engineers' work carries significant implications for future diagnosis and treatment of other diseases. Rapid progress is being made in the treatment of cancer. Scientists have also successfully transplanted the major elements of the human immune defense system into mice. This technique may lead to important breakthroughs in the study of AIDS, the common name for acquired immune deficiency syndrome.

AIDS erupted in the United States in the late 1970s and early 1980s. Since that time it has claimed the lives of approximately 44,000 Americans and is expected to claim millions of lives worldwide over the next few years. Unfortunately, there are no known medicines to cure the disease

Learning from Pictures *In order to study atoms, this engineer is operating a particle accelerator that smashes them.*

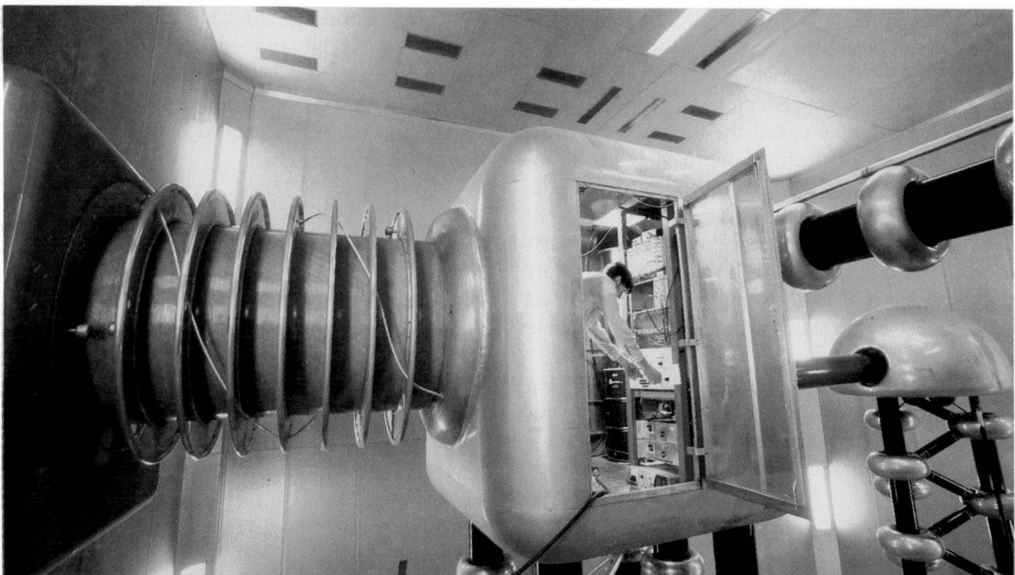

1C, 5D, 5E, a1C, a3A, a3B, a3E, a3G, a3H

● Discussion Topic: Have students discuss the advantages and disadvantages of nuclear power plants.

and no vaccines to prevent it. However, treatments have been developed and their effectiveness is being studied over a period of time.

AIDS is not inherited genetically. It is acquired through sexual contact and contaminated needles, usually associated with intravenous drug use. Babies can acquire the AIDS virus before birth from infected mothers. Ultimately the breakthrough in genetic engineering may lead to a cure for AIDS. Until that time local and national education programs continue to teach and warn people of all ages about the causes and effects of the disease.

The Atom

Just as biologists were able to probe inside the cell, physical scientists became more knowledgeable about the smallest of nature's building blocks, the atom. With increasingly powerful instruments, scientists could examine the tiny particles within the atom. They soon learned how to use the energy released when the structure of the atom is altered.

Atomic energy was first used to build more powerful bombs. Later it was used to develop efficient generators to produce electricity for a burgeoning population. Whenever atomic energy is tapped, dangerous radiation, known as radioactivity, is released. When carefully controlled, radioactivity can have extremely beneficial medical uses—for example, in the treatment of cancer. Even peaceful uses, however, have their dangers. Extensive uncontrolled exposure to radioactivity can alter genes and kill life forms. Thus the advances in understanding the atom offered both benefits and dangers. ●

Plastics

The first synthetic substances—substances that do not occur in nature—were developed by chemists in laboratories in the 1800s. A few of these substances began to have wide applications. For example, celluloid was used to make movie films, and Bakelite was used for electrical equipment. It was not until after 1945, however, that these substances, called plastics, began to appear in every area of life. By the mid-1960s, for example, there was more synthetic rubber than natural rubber in the world.

Plastics became an essential part of daily existence. They completely altered the appearance as well as the manufacture of most of the things people use every day, from toothbrushes to telephones. Synthetic fibers were woven into easy-care fabrics for clothing and upholstery.

Many plastics are made from petroleum products. The availability—and price—of plastics, therefore, depends on the unpredictable nature of international oil prices.

Antibiotics

In 1928 Alexander Fleming discovered penicillin, noting that it stopped the growth of many types of disease-carrying bacteria. Thus it could help cure illnesses caused by those bacteria. In the years after Fleming's discovery, other substances were found to have similar effects. Streptomycin, which was discovered in 1944, attacked bacteria that could resist penicillin. Substances that kill bacteria are called **antibiotics,** and after 1945 they transformed the fight against disease. They cured certain illnesses, such as tuberculosis, that previously had no cure, and they lessened the risk of infection following surgery. The use of antibiotics also improved the health of animals used for food. Although some bacteria came to resist antibiotics, these medicines became essential in reducing sicknesses and preventing contamination of food.

The "Green Revolution"

Through intensive research, scientists in the 1960s developed seeds that yielded much more rice and wheat than ever before. The use of better fertilizers and advances in irrigation techniques further improved the new seeds.

The ability to feed large numbers of people became increasingly critical as the world's population grew to about 5 billion by 1988. Unfortunately, most of the fastest-growing countries are also the poorest and the least able to provide food both for their own people and for export. In the 1980s, for example, Ethiopia, a mountainous nation in northeastern Africa, was unable to cope with a long period of drought and famine that plagued the country. Millions of people starved to death.

Ethiopia's plight concerned people from many other nations of the world. Food supplies eventually became available; but for many Ethiopians, especially children, the help came too late. Ethiopian leaders are now directing their efforts toward long-range agricultural development that will help replenish the soil and produce more food.

Text continues on page 884.

881

PERSPECTIVES: LEGACIES OF THE PAST

The history of fortifications began with prehistoric people. Cowering in caves or behind rocks or trees, early people hid from their enemies. Their two purposes were to protect themselves from attack and position themselves to strike back against the enemy. Throughout history, fortresses have met such needs.

Of course, different circumstances produced different kinds of fortresses. Wealthy societies such as the Roman Empire and modern France built very elaborate walls. Poor societies such as those of northern Europe in the early Middle Ages dug ditches around their towns.

As societies grew stronger, so did their fortifications. Earthen walls or wooden stockades were replaced by masonry. The Egyptians, the Assyrians, and the early Greeks all built walled cities. Some walls were built across open country to protect farmlands. A wall 50 miles (80 kilometers) long was built about 800 B.C. to safeguard the ancient city of Babylon and its surrounding territory against the hostile Medes.

The Roman Empire protected its frontiers with walls. Hadrian's Wall stretched for 73 miles (117 km) across northern England to shelter Roman territory from the "savages" of Scotland. Another Roman wall system (the *Limes*) stretched from the Rhine to the Danube. About 250 B.C. the Chinese, another wealthy society, built the largest wall of all, the Great Wall of China, to keep out the Huns.

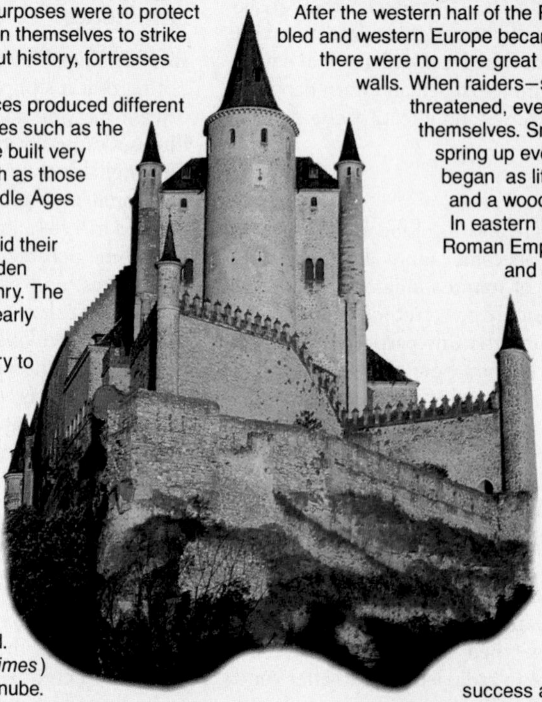

After the western half of the Roman Empire crumbled and western Europe became a poor, rural land, there were no more great nations to build great walls. When raiders—such as the Vikings—threatened, everyone had to fend for themselves. Small castles began to spring up everywhere. They often began as little more than a ditch and a wooden stockade.

In eastern Europe, however, the Roman Empire remained strong, and so did the fortresses. Constantinople was surrounded by a massive system of walls. Attacking Arabs found it impossible to penetrate such mighty defenses.

The invention of gunpowder and siege cannon seemed to spell the end of walled cities. By 1350 attackers were using cannons with success against the castles of French nobles. In 1453 Constantinople's walls,

882

Great Fortifications

which had stood against attack for 1,000 years, tumbled under the fire of Turkish artillery.

But fortresses did not vanish. The 1500s and 1600s brought a new kind of walled city. Bastions were built jutting from the main wall. From them defenders could fire on attackers from several directions.

In the 1800s and 1900s, reinforced concrete made fortifications stronger than ever before in history. Many cities were now protected by rings of steel and concrete forts armed with heavy artillery. But the attackers soon learned how to cope with these new defenses. In the attack on Russia's Pacific stronghold of Port Arthur, Japan's General Nogi wasted 15,000 lives in futile infantry assaults before he found the key to success in his 280-millimeter howitzers. These giant guns could fire shells upward so that they descended on Port Arthur's defenders at a steep and deadly angle.

In 1914 the Germans opened their way through Belgium in the same way. They crushed the massive defenses at the city of Liege with huge howitzers. This was in World War I—the same war that saw a return to the most basic fortification, the ditch. The killing power of modern weapons—especially the machine gun—forced soldiers to dig trenches. By Christmas of 1914, an unbroken line of trenches extended on both sides of the French-German front from the English Channel to Switzerland. In the end, the deadly stalemate of trench warfare broke only when Germany's forces cracked from exhaustion.

The 1900s also brought the greatest failure in fortifications—the Maginot Line. This was an "impregnable" defense system built by the French in the 1930s along the German border. The Maginot Line consisted of gun emplacements, underground fortresses, and miles of tunnels. The Germans, instead of attacking this formidable bulwark, simply went around it through Belgium. There they captured the fort at Eban Emael, the strongest fortress in Europe and the key to the Belgian defenses, with glider troops in a few hours. Thus the two strongest fortifications in the world, believed to be impenetrable, were overcome as though they hardly existed.

Some fortified cities in World War II held out for months, even years. But at the war's conclusion, atomic bombs on Hiroshima and Nagasaki showed that today no wall is strong enough or trench deep enough.

Great fortifications are relics of the past.

Photos *Page 882: Alcazar castle (top), Walled City of Carcassone (bottom); Page 883: Walls of Jericho (top left), Gibraltar (center); Masada (bottom)*

883

1B, 5D, 5F, a1C, a1B, a3A, a3B, a4A, a4F, a4H, a4K, a4L

SECTION 1

Closure

Ask students to discuss how computers affect their daily lives.

Review Answers

1. ***miniaturization:*** making electrical equipment smaller; ***antibiotics:*** substances that stop the growth of disease-carrying bacteria
2. ***Yuri Gagarin:*** first man to travel in space; ***Alan Shepard:*** first American in space; ***Neil Armstrong:*** first man on the moon; ***Discovery:*** American space shuttle that completed the first mission into space after the *Challenger* explosion; ***Spacelab:*** joint space venture of the United States and several Western European nations; ***DNA:*** deoxyribonucleic acid—the small units of chromosomes that convey characteristics from parent to child; ***genetic code:*** determines the structure of a gene; ***radioactivity:*** radiation released when atomic energy is produced; ***synthetic substances:*** substances that do not occur in nature; ***Green Revolution:*** scientific research effort that improved agricultural production
3. ***Ethiopia:*** northeastern Africa
4. Portable radios, pocket calculators, digital watches, compact tape recorders, and automatic cameras were all made possible by miniaturization.
5. **(a)** The programs initially took on the character of a "space race" to conquer the moon's surface and

Commercial Applications of Technology

Since 1945 technological advances have virtually transformed the world. Devices such as telephones, radios, refrigerators, and cameras had been known before 1945. However, only after 1945 were they manufactured cheaply enough to be bought by millions of people. These products are more common in the industrialized nations, but they have also had an enormous impact on the developing nations of the world.

What was so remarkable in the period after 1945 was the widespread application of these modern products. Entire new industries, such as television and computer manufacturing, sprang up. Millions of people were employed in new kinds of jobs, and world markets flourished as nations imported and exported the products of the new technological age. What appears to be almost unbelievable advancement of such technology may be only the beginning of future technological developments.

SECTION 1 REVIEW

1. **Define** miniaturization, antibiotics
2. **Identify** Yuri Gagarin, Alan Shepard, Neil Armstrong, *Discovery, Spacelab,* DNA, genetic code, radioactivity, synthetic substances, Green Revolution
3. **Locate** Ethiopia
4. **Summarizing Ideas** Give examples of new products made possible by miniaturization.
5. **Comparing Ideas** **(a)** How are the space exploration programs of the United States and the Soviet Union similar? **(b)** How are they different?
6. **Classifying Ideas** List three technological advances that have taken place since 1945. Explain the importance of each.
7. **Analyzing Ideas** How can technology be both a benefit and a burden? Give an example.

2 The Arts and Literature Followed New Directions

Two trends became particularly noticeable in the arts and in literature after 1945. One was the commitment to experimentation, which had been evident since the early 1900s. The other was the enormous popular interest in artistic and intellectual developments.

Painting and Sculpture

After 1945 New York City became one of the liveliest centers of new ideas and painting styles. The dominant style of painting was **abstract expressionism.**

The leading abstract expressionist was an American, Jackson Pollock. Pollock believed that the form, colors, and shapes of a painting constituted its most important features. A painting did not have to show recognizable objects; therefore, it was abstract. At the same time, it had to reflect the nature of the artist who was expressing feelings or ideas in paint.

Pollock chose to express himself by randomly dripping different colors of paint onto the surface of a canvas spread out on the floor. When the paint dried, his painting was finished.

Other abstract expressionists used different techniques. Mark Rothko, also an American, created large areas of rich colors. The colors blurred into one another, creating a dazzling effect.

In the 1950s painters moved away from abstract expressionism to experiment in other ways. It was no longer possible to speak of one dominant style. In Great Britain and the United States, a number of artists returned to showing reality—but a special kind of reality. Developing a style called **pop art,** these artists chose as their subjects popular objects such as soup cans, pictures from comic books, or flags.

Experimentation could also be seen in the sculpture of the period. The American sculptor Louise Nevelson, for example, created monumental designs out of "found" objects, such as wooden boxes.

New styles of painting arose in the 1960s. One small group concentrated on **op art**—the use of optical effects. These artists rejected reality as the subject of paintings, instead using brilliant colors and shapes. Another group, the "hard-edge" school, produced bright stripes and slabs of color with well-defined edges.

The 1970s and 1980s saw a return to realism in paintings of scenes, objects, and people. Experiments continued, however, and all styles seemed acceptable in the art world.

Although the earlier art styles remained popular and many classic works of art increased in value, during the 1970s and 1980s many people also came

Discussion Topic: Have students discuss how emphasis on conservation of natural resources has led to changes in architecture.

to appreciate folk art, the work of talented but not necessarily professionally trained painters, sculptors, and craftspeople. Folk art has been popular in many nations of the world for centuries. Because it reflects everyday life and often portrays social, political, or religious views of people who live in a particular place, it is a source of information as well as enjoyment.

The modern age has led artists to incorporate views from outer space and futuristic technology into their work. In the 1980s the title "artist" has come to include photographers, filmmakers, ceramists, glassblowers, and electricians. The artist's materials range from the traditional canvas, paint, marble and bronze to materials such as plastic and scrap metal. Modern art forms may be welded, wired, glued, sewn, or lighted. Today some artists even construct and paint images from sand or create artistic patterns in plowed fields. Skywriting has also become increasingly popular, especially in urban areas.

Current art trends also include **process art** and **conceptual art.** Both of these art trends reduce the emphasis on isolated art objects and focus instead on the arrangement of "environments" composed of both objects and people. Process artists believe that the process of creating the art is more important than the actual art object. Conceptual art carries this idea one step further with the claim that creative thought is more important than either the process or the product created.

Architecture

The search for new ideas and techniques dominated architecture, as it had since the invention of the skyscraper in the early 1900s. Since 1945 materials have changed almost yearly.

One popular new material was rough-cast concrete. This mixture contains pebbles and creates a grainy, rough finish. A pioneer in the use of this technique was French architect Charles-Édouard Jeanneret, known as Le Corbusier (luh kor • BUEZ • yay), one of the most influential architects of the century. Between 1946 and 1952, Le Corbusier built an enormous apartment complex in Marseilles, France, using rough-cast concrete.

The opposite effect, smoothness and polish, also interested architects. They created this smoother look mainly by using huge walls of glass. Le Corbusier himself took this approach when he designed the headquarters of the United Nations in New York City. One of the UN buildings has two enormous walls of glass, with narrow walls of solid concrete at each end. The Lever House in New York City, completed in 1952, set the pattern for a

Learning from Pictures The skylines of the world's cities, such as Dallas, have changed dramatically with modern architectural innovations.

prepare ballistic technology for defense purposes. However, both countries developed technological capabilities for communications and weather purposes. **(b)** The Soviets have emphasized a spacelab-type station development, while the U.S. has developed the space shuttle. Most recently the Soviets have also developed a shuttle.
6. Answers will vary. Possible responses include: improvements in air travel transformed transportation; rockets made space travel and satellites possible; miniaturization made dozens of new products possible; computers store and process information quickly and compactly; lasers are used in medicine, engineering and industry; atomic energy is used to build more powerful bombs and generate electricity; plastics are used in almost every part of daily life.
7. Accept all reasonable answers.

SECTION 2

Focus/Motivation
To set the stage for a discussion of new directions in art and literature, briefly review the social changes that occurred in the United States during the 1960s. Then ask the students to discuss how art and literature often reflect other changes in society.

1B, 5F, a3A, a4A, a4B, a4C, a4F, a4G, a4H, a4J

Presentation
Analyzing Ideas (Average/Group)
Ask students to explain why people become interested in paintings and art objects as investments. *(Students may suggest that because original pieces of art are limited and become more difficult to acquire, they appreciate in value.)*

READ
WRITE
INTERPRET
● CONNECT
THINK

BUILDING HISTORY STUDY SKILLS

Making Connections with History: Linking Architecture to History

Architecture often reflects the values of a culture. The skyscraper is both the triumphant symbol of, and at the same time, an unwelcome intruder into, the city. It shatters scale and steals light, yet it suggests the personality of the city of which it is a part. It has also made the city's character a reflection of its own quality. For example, the Sears Tower in Chicago and the Empire State Building in New York City are the symbols of these metropolitan areas just as the Cathedral of Notre Dame is a symbol of Paris. Linking architecture to history helps historians explain how the environment affects a society, determine the individual's reaction to the environment, and visualize the society's values.

How to Link Architecture to History

To link architecture to history, follow these steps.

1. Establish the historical context of the architecture.
2. Identify the society that built the structure.
3. Identify the major characteristics of the architecture.
4. Describe characteristics of the environment.
5. Relate the environmental characteristics to the historical context.
6. Identify the values expressed by linking the historical context and the environmental characteristics.

Developing the Skill

Analyzing the skyscraper's architecture helps you link architecture to modern history. The skyscraper has become the symbol of the twentieth-century American city. It defines life in the metropolis.

Skyscrapers began to rise above 40 stories by 1910. These towering symbols of urbanization housed more than offices—they also included stores and restaurants. Their lobbies became so large that they became gathering places. The massive arcades became a city within a city.

One example of the skyscraper is the Woolworth Building in New York City. Completed in 1913, it gracefully extends 792 feet (241 meters) above the ground. Although the building is perceived as a sheer tower, its base consists of a 29-story U-shaped mass. Rising from the center front of the structure is a square tower that culminates in an ornate crown at the top. The vertical lines of the base shoot up into the tower, melding the upper and lower masses together.

The architecture of a particular society also reveals more than cultural values—it reveals information about the economic characteristics of a society. For example, an impressive building is a symbol of a successful corporation. The visual effect of massive buildings suggests corporate glory and represents human ability and technical achievement. In the modern age, skyscrapers have become the cathedrals of commerce.

Practicing the skill. Select several books from the library that include photographs of buildings in foreign cities. Then write a brief explanation of the architecture's correlation to the culture and history of that country.

To apply this skill, see Applying History Study Skills on page 895.

Woolworth Building

History Through the Arts

ARCHITECTURE

Sydney Opera House

Like a ship with its sails set for the future, the Opera House dominates the harbor in Sydney, Australia. Built on a peninsula, the building consists of a series of concrete shells that house a center for the performing arts.

Despite its geographical isolation from continental Europe, Australia has maintained a strong British heritage. After World War II, however, many European refugees settled in the island continent. They have helped to make the nation's culture more international.

Thus, when the Australian government decided to build a center to celebrate the arts, it sponsored a worldwide competition to choose an architect. Joern Utzon, a Dane, was the winner. His building rests on a high platform, and the shells rise more than 200 feet (60 meters) above ground level. Utzon's structure contains four theaters—a concert hall, an opera theater, a drama theater, and a chamber music and film hall—each acoustically perfect for the type of performance it holds. Completed in 1973, the Sydney Opera House is among the most recognizable buildings in the world and is considered to be a masterpiece of modern architecture.

wave of skyscrapers sheathed in glass and supported on the inside by steel and reinforced concrete.

Architects also experimented with new ways of building houses. Some houses were cast in concrete in standard units and then shipped to the building site. Others made use of new plastic materials.

New shapes appeared in architectural designs. Notable among these unusually shaped buildings is the group of concrete shells that make up the Sydney Opera House in Australia. The spiral-shaped form of the Guggenheim Museum in New York City was designed by the American architect Frank Lloyd Wright, a leader in the use of unconventional shapes.

In the 1970s and 1980s, architectural designs assumed more contemporary lines. The rapid development of new engineering techniques prompted the construction of domed stadiums such as the Astrodome in Houston, Texas. Graceful contemporary lines also appeared in buildings erected for the Summer Olympic Games in Los Angeles, California, in 1984, and in Seoul, South Korea, in 1988. Other distinctive buildings were constructed for the winter Olympic Games in Sarajevo, Yugoslavia, in 1984 and in Calgary, Canada, in 1988.

Architectural designs of the 1980s emphasized spaciousness and employed innovative features. Some modern homes combined attractive and practical design with solar energy or other devices to save fuel. Many cities had buildings with unique designs, large expanses of glass, or gleaming mirrored tiles that reflected light.

Amid all these new ideas and techniques, no single design or method of building has dominated architecture in the years after 1945. Experimentation has led to a wide variety in architectural styles since World War II.

Music and Dance

Experimentation has been equally apparent in the world of music. New uses of instruments, rhythm, harmony, and melody were introduced. Some composers, however, did write traditional types of music. The British composer Benjamin Britten, for example, wrote operas. The Russian composer

887

Learning from Pictures *Even before Mikhail Gorbachev initiated* glasnost, *Soviet youths jammed rock and roll concerts.*

Dmitry Shostakovich (shahs • tuh • KOH • vich) wrote symphonies divided into four distinct movements, which had been the standard form since the late 1700s.

After 1945 new kinds of sound entered the world of serious music. Experimenters found that computers could produce sounds. Innovative composers wrote pieces for special machines known as synthesizers or for combinations of traditional instruments and synthesizers.

Composers also began to write music that gave performers a major role in determining how a piece would sound. The composer might provide a few notes and some instructions. Then the performer could decide the order, length, and mood of a composition. The pioneer of this method was an American composer, John Cage.

The determination to break new ground, to leave the past behind, was especially obvious in popular music. During the 1950s a form of music known as rock and roll was created in the United States. It had a heavy, accented beat and a simple, repetitive melody. A number of different styles, with such names as folk rock, hard rock, punk rock, and disco, soon developed.

Another form of popular music, country and western music, usually consisted of sentimental ballads. Black* musicians developed such styles as soul music and rhythm and blues.

These musical forms spread rapidly throughout the world, especially among teenagers. A new song quickly became as familiar to the young in Indonesia as in Indiana. The most successful performers became world famous. These individuals and groups toured extensively, and their concerts were sometimes broadcast throughout the world by satellites.

The world of dance also followed new directions after 1945. Artists who had left Russia after its revolution were especially influential in ballet. The greatest of these artists was George Balanchine. He continued in the United States the traditions that had made Russia such an influential center of ballet in the 1800s and 1900s. In the 1960s and 1970s, young ballet stars who came from the Soviet Union to make their careers in the West joined Balanchine.

After 1945 the freer and looser forms of modern dance influenced ballet. An American, Martha Graham, was the most influential teacher of modern dance. She collaborated with ballet dancers in trying to combine the two forms. The use of more modern music to accompany the dancers forced performance changes. As in all the performing arts, the tendency was to leave uniformity

*In the mid-1980s, there was a growing movement to use the name African Americans instead of Black Americans.

888

● Point out that the film industry, like television, is a business and is affected by the law of supply and demand.

behind, to experiment, and to allow more individual expression.

Film

Traditional subjects—adventure stories, comedies, and social dramas—dominated most filmmaking after 1945. Spectacular productions, costing millions of dollars, continued to be popular. Other films, however, made efforts to break free of traditional restrictions. In the 1940s and 1950s, a group of Italian directors produced shattering attacks on social and political injustice. French filmmakers known as the "New Wave" created experimental movies in the 1950s and 1960s. They rejected traditional storytelling techniques and created instead a mysterious and powerful atmosphere in their films. Japanese director Akira Kurosawa's films used violence and psychological insight to create startling new effects.

Technical mastery was particularly evident in American films. A number of directors turned their attention to themes about ordinary people or how outside influences affected the pattern of family life. For example, Steven Spielberg became famous for producing films such as *E. T.—The Extraterrestrial* and *Back to the Future.* By the 1980s filmmaking had become a major art form around the world.

Drama

In the theater, too, important new techniques developed. In East Germany the company founded by playwright Bertolt Brecht staged plays with an emphasis on artificiality. The members of the audience were not to be drawn in but were to be constantly reminded that they were watching a play. In Great Britain traditional forms of Asian drama influenced theatrical productions. Greater emphasis was placed on the actors' spontaneous reactions. Performers were encouraged to improvise, and thus to create something new each night. In South Africa a black theater group emerged from the black-liberation movement. In a presentation called *Asinamali,* which in Zulu means "We have no money," black actors portrayed prisoners of the South African apartheid regime.

Perhaps the most powerful new vision of the modern age was the biting social commentary of the playwrights of the so-called theater of the absurd. Its leaders were Samuel Beckett and Eugène Ionesco, an Irishman and a Romanian, respectively, who lived in France.

Beckett's most famous play, *Waiting for Godot* (1956), is a long, apparently aimless dialogue between two tramps. It portrays a bleak world in which human beings have great difficulty communicating. The play has no real plot and makes no attempt to bring out the character of the two tramps. Bewilderment and absurdity run throughout Beckett's works. These qualities are apparent also in the plays of Ionesco, such as *Rhinoceros* and *The Bald Soprano.*

More realistic but no less biting attacks on modern society were apparent in the works of other playwrights of this period. The most notable of these dramatists were John Osborne, an Englishman, and Arthur Miller, an American. Miller's powerful dramas explored human weaknesses and the tensions in families. Another American, Tennessee Williams, looked at similar themes in the society of the American South.

Social analysis and comment even entered the boisterous world of American musical theater. To some, the most remarkable musical of the post-1945 period was *West Side Story.* It recounted the struggles between rival gangs of New York teenagers. Leonard Bernstein, the noted composer and conductor, wrote the score.

In 1988 Andrew Lloyd Webber directed *The Phantom of the Opera,* a mystery about a ghost's love for a lady singer at the Paris Opera. The plot develops as a young nobleman rekindles his boyhood interest in the singer but notices that she is under a strange influence. As the story unfolds, the nobleman discovers the presence of the phantom in the opera, and the audience learns the phantom's identity.

Poetry and Novels

The aim of these playwrights was to take a stand against the comfortable assumptions of an ever more complicated world. Society's most prosperous citizens and their values were the target of another group of writers, the so-called Beat Generation. These poets and novelists, most of them living in San Francisco and New York City, began writing in the 1950s. They attacked the commercialism they saw in America. They thought writing should be completely spontaneous, and they rejected the traditional forms of the novel and the poem.

SECTION 2

Closure
Ask students to discuss the ways that popular music reflects American society in the 1980s.

Review Answers
1. ***abstract expressionism:*** style of painting that did not show recognizable objects but reflected the nature of the artist; ***pop art:*** style of painting in which popular objects were the subjects; ***op art:*** use of optical effects in art; ***process art:*** arrangement of environments of objects and people that emphasizes the creating as more important than the result; ***conceptual art:*** emphasis on the creative thought processes as more important than the actual product or act of creating
2. ***Louise Nevelson:*** American sculptor who created designs out of "found" objects; ***Le Corbusier:*** architect who emphasized glass walls and built United Nations building; ***Benjamin Britten:*** British composer who wrote operas and other music; ***George Balanchine:*** Russian ballet dancer and choreographer who continued the Russian tradition in the U.S.; ***Martha Graham:*** influential American teacher of modern dance; ***Steven Spielberg:*** film director who focused on ordinary people in cities and changing patterns in family life; ***Arthur Miller:*** playwright who portrayed human weaknesses and family tensions;

1B, 5D,5F, a1A, a1C, a3A, a3D

● Discussion Topic: Have students list changes in education in the last decade and discuss how these changes reflect changes in society.

Beat Generation: writers of the 1950s who attacked commercialism and rejected traditional literary forms; ***Ralph Ellison:*** black writer who explored with anger the life of blacks; ***James Baldwin:*** black American writer who wrote about the lives of blacks in the U.S.
3. ***Marseilles:*** city in southern France, on the Mediterranean coast
4. One of the new characteristics of architecture was the use of rough-cast concrete. Another was the use of huge walls of glass. Architects also experimented with new ways of building houses. Some were cast in concrete in standard units and then shipped to the site, while others were made of new plastic materials. There were also experiments with unusual shapes.
5. Innovative composers wrote pieces for synthesizers or for combinations of traditional instruments and machines. Some composers allowed the performer to decide the order, the length, and the mood of a composition. Popular music also broke new ground.
6. A group of Italian directors produced attacks on social and political injustice. "New Wave" French filmmakers rejected traditional story-telling techniques. The Japanese director Akira Kurosawa produced films that used violence

Protest was a major theme of the leading writers of the postwar years. The most powerful black American writers were Ralph Ellison and James Baldwin. Each explored, with dismay and anger, the life of a black person in the United States. Nigerian novelist Chinua Achebe examined the effects of colonial rule on his native land. The leading German novelists, Günter Grass and Heinrich Böll, explored Hitler's impact on Germany. Boris Pasternak and Alexander Solzhenitsyn wrote savage descriptions of the repressions of the Soviet system.

Another major theme of postwar literature was escape from an increasingly hostile and confusing world. Writers like the American Kurt Vonnegut, Jr., created fantasies about imaginary worlds. They used these fantasies to suggest alternatives to what they saw as the brutality and uncaring behavior of the times.

Prominent Latin American writers chose a similar approach. Octavio Paz, a Mexican poet, contrasted the savagery and the civilized grace of his country's history in surrealistic, dreamlike poems. The Colombian Gabriel García Márquez and the Mexican Carlos Castaneda wrote mystical novels that move puzzlingly through time. Castaneda implied that ordinary people cannot achieve profound levels of wisdom.

Not all writers and poets emphasized protest or disturbing uncertainties. Some, like the American poet Wallace Stevens, enjoyed the traditional poetic function of celebrating nature. Many of his poems try to capture the lushness of the tropics. Another American poet, Marianne Moore, urged poets to be genuine and useful, and to write about topics ordinary people could understand. Attacking snobbery, she cited business documents and school books as acceptable subjects for her poetry. She liked to quote from magazines in her poems, and she wrote one poem to celebrate her favorite baseball team, the Brooklyn Dodgers.

The variety of the interests and styles of poets and novelists was astonishing. Never before had so many books been published. During 1987 in the United States alone, more than 7,500 titles in fiction, poetry, and drama were published.

The Audience for the Arts

The excitement of postwar artistic and literary activity generated enormous public appeal,

Learning from Pictures *This audience in Buenos Aires, Argentina, enjoys an opera at the Colón Theater.*

particularly in the United States. Between 1950 and 1988, Americans spent more than half a billion dollars to construct new museums and art centers. More Americans paid to go to museums, concerts, operas, ballets, or theaters each year than those who paid to attend sporting events.

Throughout the world, more people are completing the equivalent of a high school education, and more people are going to college. People have ● more time for leisure activities, particularly in industrialized countries. Television exposes more people to more kinds of cultural activities. TV brings music, dramatizations of books, plays, and movies to millions of people at home. Many people continue to seek similar entertainment outside the home. Thus education, extra leisure time, and a new awareness have combined to give the arts and literature greater support than they have ever enjoyed before.

Point out that many people had to be trained for new jobs as machinery performed tasks formerly done by people. The unemployment that resulted is called technological unemployment.

1B, 3B, 5B, 5D, 5F, a1A, a1C, a1D, a3A, a3D, a4A, a4F, a4H, a4J, a4K

SECTION 2 REVIEW

1. **Define** abstract expressionism, pop art, op art, process art, conceptual art
2. **Identify** Louise Nevelson, Le Corbusier, Benjamin Britten, George Balanchine, Martha Graham, Steven Spielberg, Arthur Miller, Beat Generation, Ralph Ellison, James Baldwin
3. **Locate** Marseilles
4. **Summarizing Ideas** Describe changes in architectural styles and building materials since 1945.
5. **Interpreting Ideas** What new kinds of sounds were heard in the music of the postwar period?
6. **Analyzing Ideas** Using specific examples, describe how film and theater reflected new techniques and themes.
7. **Classifying Ideas** List three authors of different nationalities who wrote works that protested conditions in their native countries.

3 Patterns of Living Took New Forms

As opportunities multiplied and the pace of life speeded up in industrialized nations, the way people spent their lives changed drastically. Change in developing nations was less dramatic, but there, too, the quickening pace was narrowing the gap between old and new ways of life.

Life Styles

In the decades that followed World War II, women entered the work force as never before. In the 1980s women have had more occupational opportunities than at any other time in history. Today busy families juggle work schedules and responsibilities at home in order to enjoy the rewards of careers and a higher standard of living than their parents and grandparents experienced.

Another feature of life after 1945 that set it apart from life in earlier periods was the speed with which things happened. Illnesses that once would have required months of recovery were cured in a few days with new medicines of the 1980s. A worker might live many miles away from a job, but because of expressways and other improvements related to transportation, he or she could travel from home to work in less than an hour. After work, people could relax at home and watch live coverage of sports events on television. If a person wanted a quick meal, he or she could go to a so-called fast-food restaurant and get almost any kind of food in less than a minute.

An important result of these changes, especially in developed nations, was a greater amount of leisure time. However, people sometimes experienced a restlessness and uncertainty about the best way to spend their time. The use of drugs, the number of crimes committed, and the rate of divorce all increased markedly. Despite these problems, additional leisure time also made possible the pursuit of new interests and opportunities.

Another factor that increased leisure time in developed nations was the shortening of the working year as machines took over more work. Families took vacation trips for granted, especially as travel became cheaper and easier. Even in developing nations, television and movies brought news and entertainment to remote villages.

As a result of rapidly changing life styles after 1945, attitudes and behavior changed rapidly. But it was far from clear what the long-term consequences of advanced technology and more leisure time would be.

The Search for Stability

Amid rapid changes, people looked for anchors of stability. Many renewed their commitment to religion.

In the developing nations, a major response to technological progress was a return to traditional beliefs. For example, the 1970s saw a strengthening of Islam in the Middle East accompanied in many cases by a rejection of non-Muslim ideas and developments.

In Western countries, Christian revivalism had an impact, perhaps for similar reasons. The religious renewal among Christians took a number of forms. In 1962 Pope John XXIII, then head of the Catholic church, called a special council to the Vatican. The effects of the council, which came to be known as Vatican II, were wide reaching. The council modernized the Roman Catholic religious service. It also condemned anti-Semitism and called for reconciliation among all Christian churches.

The worldwide movement, which sought unity among Christians, made some progress after the

and psychological insight. American directors turned their attention to ordinary people. In the theater, Brecht put on plays that aimed not to draw in the audience, but to remind them they were watching a play. Absurdity characterized the works of Beckett and Ionesco. Miller and Williams explored human weaknesses and the tensions in American families. **7.** Student answers should include three of the following: Americans Ralph Ellison and James Baldwin explored the lives of black people in the U.S. The Nigerian novelist Chinua Achebe examined the bitter effects of colonial rule on his native land. The German novelists Günter Grass and Heinrich Böll explored the impact of Hitler on Germany. Boris Pasternak and Aleksandr Solzhenitsyn wrote of the repression of the Soviet system.

SECTION 3

Focus/Motivation

To illustrate the amount of change in today's world, develop with students a list of the changes that have occurred in your community in the last few years. *(For example, old buildings torn down; new buildings constructed; people moving in and out of the community; a growth or decline in traffic).* Then ask students what changes they foresee in the next few years. What effect will these changes have on daily life? *(Accept all reasonable answers.)*

1B, 1C, 1E, 5D, 5F, 5G, 5H, 5I, a1C, a3A

● Point out to students the rise of the Evangelical Movement and its influence upon society and politics.

Presentation
Interpreting Ideas (Average/Group)
Ask students to discuss the changes in life styles in the decades that followed World War II and to evaluate how these changes affected families. *(Students may focus on innovations in education, transportation, and entertainment, in addition to changes in the home due to wives and mothers working).*

SECTION 3

Closure
Have the students discuss the lessons of history. Ask them to speculate what people living one hundred years from now may learn from reading about world history of the 1980s.

Review Answers
1. ***Vatican II:*** council called by Pope John XXIII in 1962 that had wide-reaching effects; ***Red Cross:*** organization devoted to relief work after disasters; ***Amnesty International:*** organization that tried to help political prisoners all over the world; ***Oxfam:*** organization devoted to relieving famine **2.** With leisure time there sometimes came a restlessness and uncertainty about the best way to spend one's time. The use of drugs, the number of crimes committed, and the rate of divorce all increased. However, additional leisure time made possible new interests and

1960s and remains a vital concern among Christians today.

Social Concerns

Another feature of the world after 1945 was the heightened sense of social concern. In earlier ages, one nation cared little about the rights and freedoms of the people in another nation. One country might help a revolution in another country, but the oppression of citizens was usually considered to be an internal problem.

Harsh conditions became more widely noticed after 1945. The Red Cross, founded in 1863, had long been devoted to relief work after disasters, especially war. Now the United Nations established agencies to deal with refugees and hungry children, and to provide medical care. In addition, other new organizations were formed. Amnesty International tried to help political prisoners and mistreated prisoners all over the world. Oxfam devoted itself to relieving famine. After the civil war in Nigeria in the 1960s and the destruction of Cambodia in the 1970s, Oxfam and other organizations fed millions of starving people.

Repressive governments were pressured to ease conditions for their citizens. The Soviet Union, for instance, was urged to give its citizens certain rights—such as the right to emigrate. As a result of these efforts, thousands of Jews, many of whom had been severely treated, were permitted to leave the Soviet Union. Similar pressures were applied to harsh governments in Africa and the Middle East. For example, South Africa was expelled from the United Nations because of its apartheid policy.

In Latin America the criticism was less consistent. The Catholic church became the main force for social change. Priests were often the main critics of governments and the most prominent activists seeking reforms and helping the distressed.

Some concerns went beyond the policies of specific governments. The continuing growth of the world's population, especially in poorer countries, caused worries about food shortages. Another concern was the growing awareness that the world's resources are limited. Oil and such vital metals as copper and chromium appear likely to become more scarce.

Perhaps the most crucial endangered resource was the environment itself. As industries grew, and as developing countries struggled to create their own industries, the air, the oceans, and the earth became polluted by industrial waste products. New international organizations arose to tackle these

Learning from Pictures
Religion continues to be a strong social force in the modern world, as this worship service indicates. ●

1B, 1C, 5F, a1B, a1C, a1D, a4A, a4H, a4L, a4K

● Emphasize that individuals can make the world we live in better if each person is a concerned citizen and an informed voter.

Learning from Pictures *Protesters march to show their opposition to nuclear energy, an issue that requires the serious attention of world leaders.*

problems. They found it difficult to persuade countries to cooperate with one another. However, they were able to make some progress. Nuclear tests in the atmosphere were prohibited, and regulations to protect the seas were set up.

The Lessons of History

The search for answers and the attempt to understand ourselves and the world we live in brings us back to the question with which this book began: Why does anyone bother to study history? Some of the answers that others have come up with over the centuries may have occurred to you by now. For example, history teaches us why some nations gain power while other nations lose it. We learn how decisions made by world leaders and other individuals change history and set precedents for future decisions.

You may have come to realize how and why certain kinds of change take place. Or you may have become able to better understand something that you do or believe, or something that you have observed in current events.

You may have enjoyed studying some periods of history more than others. A story or a primary source reading may have sparked your interest and clarified your understanding of a particular subject. You may have found yourself rooting for the side of justice and visualizing the broad scope of events over time.

To the extent that you have come to better understand the world in which we live and the events that have shaped its vibrant history, you have acted as a historian. You have not just read history; you have become part of it and have discovered why it is important. This insight, more than any of the specific facts or ideas that you may have read about for the first time, has been an essential addition to your education. It has taught you a new way of thinking. In the end, the most vital reason for studying history is that it teaches us how to understand people, events, ideas, particular eras, ourselves, and our place on the time line of history. ●

SECTION 3 REVIEW

1. **Identify** Vatican II, Red Cross, Amnesty International, Oxfam.
2. **Evaluating Ideas** How did increased leisure time affect life styles in the postwar period?
3. **Summarizing Ideas** Discuss religious revivalism in the 1960s, 1970s, and 1980s.
4. **Interpreting Ideas** What progress was made after 1945 in each of the following areas of social concern? **(a)** health? **(b)** human rights? **(c)** the environment?

opportunities.
3. The 1970s saw a strengthening of Islam in the Middle East, in many cases, accompanied by a rejection of non-Muslim ideas and developments. Vatican II modernized the Roman Catholic religious service, condemned anti-Semitism, and called for reconciliation among Christian churches. The ecumenical movement, which sought unity among Christians, made some progress after the 1960s. The ecumenical movement also emphasized social issues and political and economic reforms.
4. (a) The Red Cross continued its disaster relief-work. The United Nations established agencies to deal with refugees, hungry children, and medical care. Oxfam devoted itself to relieving famine. **(b)** Repressured to ease conditions for their citizens. Amnesty International tried to help political and mistreated prisoners. The Soviet ed prisoners. The Soviet Union was urged to allow thousands of Jews to emigrate, and South Africa was expelled from the United Nations because of its policy of apartheid. In addition, many Catholic priests in Latin America became political and social activists. **(c)** New international organizations arose to handle the problems of pollution. Nuclear tests in the atmosphere were banned, and regulations were set up for protection of the seas.

Reviewing Important Terms
1. miniaturization; **2.** synthetic substances; **3.** Antibiotics; **4.** op art; **5.** pop art

Developing Critical Thinking Skills
1. (a) Both countries attempted to launch men to the moon and establish communications and weather satellites. **(b)** Most recently both countries have generally cooperated in space exploration, attempting "fly-bys" of distant planets, developing space shuttles and space lab capabilities.
2. The changes in the arts reflected the absence of absolute standards in society, the drive for experimentation, the influence of technology and science, concern for social issues, and the need for escapism.
3. (a) Atomic energy can be used to develop efficient generators that produce electricity and to treat cancer. **(b)** It can be used to build more powerful bombs. Atomic energy also releases radioactivity, which can alter genes and kill life.
4. (a) Answers will vary. However, students may suggest that the construction of civic centers reflect participation in cultural activities. **(b)** People have more time for leisure activities.
5. (a) and **(b)** The pace and opportunity of life sped up in industrialized nations, and individuals had greater amounts of leisure time. **(c)** Some people accepted change and the available leisure time for self-development and enjoyment. Many people looked for ways to create anchors of stability through

1A, 1B, 5B, 5D, 5F, a1B, a1C, a3A, a4A, a4E, a4F, a4G, a4H, a4I, a4J, a4K, a4L, a4M

Reteaching
Have students review the Chapter Summary and the appropriate section and questions in the Unit Synthesis. Discuss the concepts until students demonstrate a clear understanding of the material.

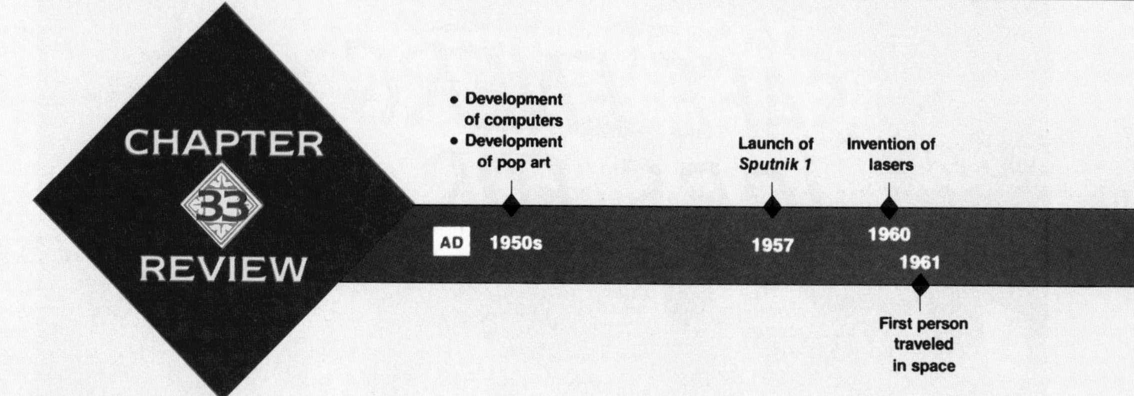

Chapter Summary

The following list contains the key concepts you have learned about the challenges of the modern age.

1. Major technological advances brought about changes in ideas and behavior after 1945. Advances in air travel, space exploration, miniaturization, computers, lasers, knowledge of heredity and genes, understanding of the atom, plastics, antibiotics, and the Green Revolution transformed communications, the understanding of the universe, the processing of information, the products people used every day, economic activities, medicine, and food production.
2. The arts and literature continued the experimentation that had marked their development since the early 1900s. New forms of painting, notably abstract expressionism, pop art, and op art, transformed art.
3. New materials and shapes were created in architecture. Musicians experimented with new kinds of sounds, both in serious compositions and in popular forms. New styles of creativity were also evident in dance and filmmaking. Drama moved in new directions as traditional plays were transformed by the theater of the absurd.
4. Writers all over the world expressed new ideas of protest and escape.
5. All of these cultural activities enjoyed large and growing audiences. More people than ever before went to museums, attended concerts and plays, and bought books.
6. Better education and increased leisure time created more viewers, listeners, and readers than had existed in any previous period.
7. The effects of all these changes on the life styles of ordinary people can be summed up by the word *speed.* Events happened more quickly, and people expected rapid developments. People sought stability amid this rapid change. Some made a renewed commitment to religious beliefs. People of all nations became concerned about political repression and the dwindling of the world's resources.

On a separate sheet of paper, complete the following review exercises.

Reviewing Important Terms

Supply the term that correctly completes each sentence.

1. The process of making machines smaller is called ________.
2. Substances that do not occur in nature are called ________.
3. ________ are medicines used to treat bacterial infections.
4. A painting that does not show recognizable objects is an example of an art style called ________.
5. Paintings of popular objects such as soup cans are examples of an art style called ________ ________.

Developing Critical Thinking Skills

1. **Comparing Ideas** **(a)** How were the early successes of the space exploration programs of the United States and the Soviet Union similar? **(b)** What have the two superpowers accomplished in the space race in the 1980s?
2. **Analyzing Ideas** How did changes in the arts during the modern age reflect changes in society as a whole?
3. **Debating Ideas** **(a)** What are some of the benefits of atomic power? **(b)** What are some of the dangers?
4. **Summarizing Ideas** **(a)** Give evidence to show that more people participate in cultural activities today than ever before. **(b)** What are some of the reasons for this increased participation?
5. **Determining Cause and Effect** **(a)** How did life styles change after World War II? **(b)** What factors account for these changes? **(c)** How did many people come to terms with the new pace of life?
6. **Interpreting Ideas** **(a)** What are some of the many reasons that people study history? **(b)** How can a knowledge of the past help people understand the present?

Relating Geography to History

Select a writer, a composer, or an artist from the United States or a foreign country. Write a short biographical essay; then describe how that person's environment influenced his or her contribution to the arts.

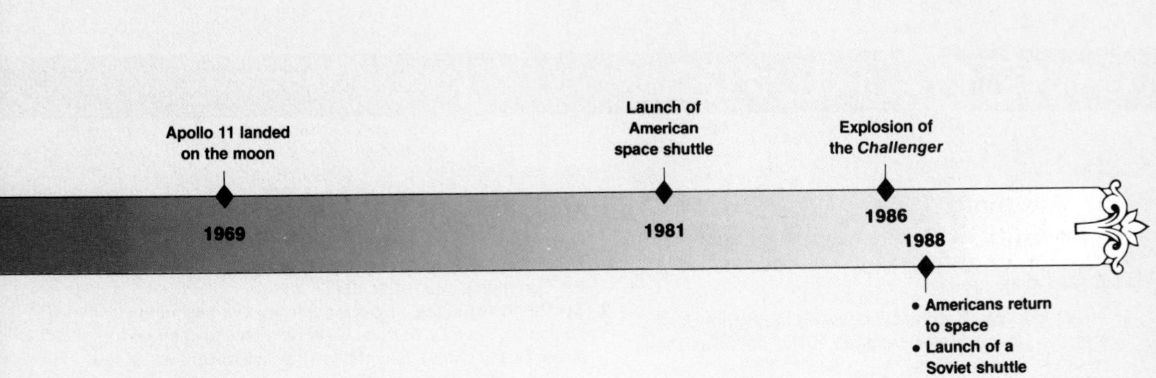

Relating Past to Present

1. **(a)** Turn to the pictures on pages 877 and 879. What technological advances does each photograph illustrate? **(b)** What new industries have developed as a result of these discoveries? **(c)** How have such changes affected your own life?
2. In 1970 Alvin Toffler wrote a book about the effect of rapid change, about people facing the future too soon. Read the passage below from Toffler's *Future Shock,* and then answer the questions that follow.

> "The high velocity [rapid rate] of change can be traced to many factors. Population growth, urbanization, the shifting proportions of young and old—all play their part. Yet technological advance is clearly a critical node [force] in that network of causes; indeed, it may be the node [force] that activates the entire net."

   a. According to Toffler, what factors bring about rapid change?
   b. Which of these factors is most important?
   c. **(1)** Based on what you learned in this chapter and on your knowledge of current events, do you agree with Toffler? **(2)** Why or why not?
3. **(a)** Using a tape recorder, prepare a program of popular music of the 1980s. Then prepare a similar tape for a previous decade. Be sure to have all of the music approved by your teacher. Possible sources of recordings include friends, relatives, and your school or local library. **(b)** What do the tapes reveal about each period? **(c)** How have popular tastes changed? **(d)** How might musical recordings contribute to an understanding of history?

Applying History Study Skills

Before completing this activity, review Building History Study Skills on page 886.

Compare photographs of the medieval cathedral at Salisbury in England and the Trump Tower building in New York City. Then answer the following questions.

1. **(a)** What characteristics of Gothic architecture can you find in the photographs? **(b)** How are these characteristics similar? **(c)** How are they different?
2. Which of the following values do Gothic architecture and medieval society reflect? **(a)** materialism **(b)** human achievement **(c)** God's glory **(d)** power
3. Which values listed in the previous question do skyscraper architecture and modern society reflect?
4. Write a brief essay that compares the cathedral to the skyscraper.

Investigating Further

1. **Preparing a Book Report** Read Aldous Huxley's *Brave New World* (Harper & Row), George Orwell's *Nineteen Eighty-four* (New American Library), or some other book dealing with science fiction or predictions about the future. **(a)** Prepare a book report in which you consider the author's vision of the future. **(b)** What events or changes did Huxley or Orwell fear might take place in the late 1900s? **(c)** Have any of these predictions come true? Explain. **(d)** Using information in this chapter and your knowledge of world affairs, describe how you think the world will look in the year 2020.
2. **Researching Ideas** Use the *Readers' Guide to Periodical Literature* to find articles on the *Voyager* spacecraft. **(a)** What planets did this satellite explore? **(b)** What new moons of other planets did it discover? **(c)** What other new information about the planets did *Voyager* provide? **(d)** You might also want to investigate the plans that the United States has for future space exploration programs.
3. **Writing a Report** The Space Age began in 1957 with the launching of the Soviet satellite *Sputnik.* Using reference materials in your library, prepare a report on why the United States has emerged as the world leader in space exploration. Based on your research, what are some reasons for the success of the United States space program?
4. **Preparing an Oral Presentation** Technological advances have had an impact not only on developed nations but also on developing nations. Select one area of scientific or technological progress, and present information to the class on how advances in this area have changed life in the developing nations of Asia, Africa, and Latin America.

religion and a return to traditional beliefs.
6. (a) Accept all reasonable answers. For example, history teaches us how to think about, and thus how to understand, people, events, ideas, particular ages, and ourselves. **(b)** People understand themselves better by understanding what things happened to them in the past, why these things happened, and why people acted as they did.

Relating Geography to History

Although answers will vary, students should support their opinions with specific examples

Relating Past to Present

1. (a) space exploration and CAT-scanning; **(b)** space and medical industries; **(c)** Accept all reasonable answers.
2. (a) population growth, urbanization, shifting proportions of young and old, and technological advance; **(b)** Accept student opinions that are supported by sound arguments. **(c)** Answers will vary. However, students should support their opinions by giving specific examples.

Applying History Study Skills

1. (a) the immensity of interior space, coupled with the beauty of multicolored light pouring through windows; **(b)** The Trump Tower building is also incredibly large, pointing upward as does the Cathedral. **(c)** The Tower demonstrates man's desire to dominate rather than blend in with nature.
2. (c) God's glory
3. (a), (b), (d)
4. Answers will vary.

Reviewing Concepts

1. satellite; **2.** apartheid; **3.** detente; **4.** *perestroika;*

Applying Critical Thinking Skills

1. The alliance system was set to deter a Soviet drive into Western Europe.
2. In the 1960s Congress passed several civil rights and voting rights acts because of pressure from these leaders.
3. The Korean War began with North Korea's attack on South Korea. The Vietnam War began as a civil war between the South Vietnamese government and the Communists. North and South Korea remained separate at the end of the war. North and South Vietnam were unified into a Communist state.
4. (a) Nkrumah led the first political party in Africa that had a large base of popular support. **(b)** Kenyatta's popular leadership helped overcome ethnic rivalries and and brought about Kenyan nationalism. **(c)** Mugabe led a guerrilla war against the white-dominated government of Rhodesia.
5. Oil brought wealth to some people, many nations experienced rapid growth in the size of cities, educational opportunuties expanded, and the status of women improved.
6. Economic prosperity would cut down on inflation, unemployment, and poverty, all of which cause social and politcal instability.
7. (a) In the 1950s the U.S. secretly armed a rebel group that overthrew the Guatemalan president. **(b)** In the 1980s the U.S. Congress voted to end all aid to the anti-Sandinista rebels in Nicaragua. It was

1B, 5A, 5B, 5C, 5D, 5E, a4A, a4B, a4C, a4D, a4E, a4F, a4G, a4H, a4I, a4J, a4K, a4L

Reteaching

Have students review the Chapter Summary and the appropriate section and questions in the Unit Synthesis. Discuss the concepts until students demonstrate a clear understanding of the material.

UNIT 7 REVIEW

Unit Summary

The following list contains the key concepts you have learned about the challenges that faced the postwar world from 1945 to the present.

1. After World War II, conflicts between the Soviet Union and the United States resulted in the cold war that threatened world peace.
2. When Communist North Korea invaded South Korea in 1950, its troops were repulsed by UN forces, and an armistice was eventually signed.
3. In Southeast Asia, the United States became heavily involved in fighting in Vietnam.
4. Independence came rapidly to the African nations after World War II. Only South Africa resisted any efforts to give the black majority of the population a real voice in their own government.
5. A continuing problem in the Middle East was the hostility between Israel and its Arab neighbors. Four Arab-Israeli wars were fought between 1948 and 1973.
6. A civil war broke out in Nicaragua between the Marxist government, run by the Sandinistas, and the anti-government guerrillas called Contras. The United States assisted the Contras until 1983.
7. Although the Soviet Union's invasion of Afghanistan brought an end to efforts to ease tensions between the Soviet Union and the United States, by the mid-1980s the two countries once again sought better relations.
8. The purpose and policies of NATO came under close scrutiny from member nations during the 1970s and 1980s.
9. After 1945 technological changes transformed communications, the understanding of the universe, the processing of information, the products people used every day, economic activities, medicine, and food production.

On a separate sheet of paper, complete the following review exercises.

Reviewing Concepts

Supply the term that correctly completes each statement.

1. ______ is a term used to describe the Eastern European nations that depend on the Soviet Union.
2. The South African policy based on the principle of racial separation became known as ______, the Afrikaans word for "apartness."
3. ______ is the name given to the improvement in relations between the United States and the Soviet Union during the 1970s.
4. Through ______, or restructuring, Mikhail Gorbachev planned to overhaul the political and economic systems of the Soviet Union.

Applying Critical Thinking Skills

1. **Organizing Ideas** What was the purpose of the alliance systems set up by the Western nations and by the Communist bloc after 1945?
2. **Synthesizing Ideas** How did the work of civil rights leaders such as Dr. Martin Luther King lead to changes in the United States government's policy toward equal rights for all of its citizens?
3. **Comparing Ideas** How did the Korean War and the war in Vietnam differ in terms of causes and results?
4. **Comparing Ideas** How did each of the following contribute to the rise of nationalism in Africa? **(a)** Nkrumah? **(b)** Jomo Kenyatta? **(c)** Mugabe?
5. **Identifying Ideas** What changes occurred in the nations of the Middle East after 1945?
6. **Synthesizing Ideas** How would economic prosperity in Latin America help to establish greater political stability?
7. **Understanding Relationships** What were the results of the United States involvement in each of the following: **(a)** Guatemala, **(b)** Nicaragua, **(c)** Cuba, **(d)** Dominican Republic.
8. **Understanding Ideas** Why did some members of NATO begin to question that alliance's purpose and policies during the 1970s and 1980s?
9. **Interpreting Ideas** **(a)** What are some of the many reasons that people study history? **(b)** How can a knowledge of the past help people understand the present?

Relating Geography to History

Refer to maps in Chapter 27 and Chapter 28. How did the spread of communism affect the map of Europe after the end of World War II?

Writing About History

Write a report that summarizes three major areas of disagreement between the United States and the Soviet Union after 1945. Which was most threatening to world peace? Why?

Further Readings

Fitzgerald, Frances, *Fire in the Lake: The Vietnamese and Americans in Vietnam.* New York: Little, Brown. Describes the Vietnam War.

Gunther, John, *Inside South America.* New York: Harper and Row. Describes South American society and industrial change during the postwar era.

Lee, Harper, *To Kill A Mockingbird.* New York: Harper and Row. Describes the tragedy of prejudice in a small, isolated southern town in the United States after World War II.

1945 to the present

Unit Seven Chronology

Date	Political and Social Developments	Technological and Scientific Advances	Visual Arts and Literature	Religious and Philosophical Thought
1945–1955	Formation of UN **28,*** OAS **31**, NATO **28**, Warsaw Pact **28** Egyptian **30**, Chinese **29**, and Viet Minh **29** revolutions Filipino **29**, Indian **29**, and Israeli **30** independence Nuremburg trials **28** Truman Doctrine and Marshall Plan **28** Berlin blockade **28** Korean conflict **29** *Brown* v. *Bd. of Ed.* **28** Peróns in Argentina **31**	Nuclear power **32** Transistor **33** Computer revolution **33** DNA research **33** Television **33** "Fast food" **33** Increase in leisure time **33**	Education of lower classes **33** Abstract expressionism **33** Britten and Shostakovich **33** Baldwin and Ellison **33** "Beat Generation" **33** Le Corbusier **33** Mark Rothko **33** John Cage **33**	Social analysis and comment by art on society **33**
1956–1965	Suez Crisis **30**, Hungarian revolution **28** Common Market **28, 32** US in Vietnam **29** Berlin Wall **28**, Cuban revolution and missile crisis **31** OPEC **29** Alliance for Progress **31** Martin Luther King and civil rights **28**	St. Lawrence Seaway **28** *Sputnik* **33** Laser technology **33** "Green Revolution" **33** Satellite communication **33** Synthetics and plastics **33**	Black Nationalist prose and poetry **30** Pop and op art **33** Martha Graham **33** French "New Wave" movies **33** Beckett and Ionesco **33** Arthur Miller and Tennessee Williams **33** *West Side Story* **33** Pasternak and Solzhenitsyn **33**	Vatican II **33** Ecumenical movement **33**
1966–1975	SALT **32**, Détente **32**, Soviet invasion of Czechoslovakia **28** Six-Day war **30**, Arab-Israeli War of 1973 **30**, PLO **30** OPEC embargo **32** Watergate **32** Helsinki Accords **32**	Lunar landing **33** Jumbo jets **33** Japanese industrialization **29** Ecology **33**	Chinese Cultural Rev. **29** Leopold Senghor **30** Camara Laye **30** Realism in art **33** George Balanchine **33** Vonnegut and Castaneda **33** *Samizdat* **32**	Islamic fundamentalism **30** Objection to Vietnam War **28, 32** Roman Catholicism as conscience of Latin America **31**
1976–1988	SALT II **32**, Camp David Accords **30** *Perestroika, glasnost* **32** Gorbachev and Reagan summit **32** Assassinations of Sadat **30**, Indira Gandhi **28** Soviets in Afghanistan **30** Southeast Asian independence **29** Solidarity **32**	Three Mile Island **32** Chernobyl **32** *Columbia, Challenger* shuttles **33** Asian economic revolution **29**	Pol Pot executes intellectuals **29** Lewis Nkosi and Ezekiel Mphalele **30** Reassertion of folk art forms **33** Steven Spielberg **33** *Asinamali* **33**	Christian fundamentalism **33** Protests against apartheid **30**

*Indicates chapter in which concept is discussed.

discovered that people close to the president attempted to aid the rebels illegally which greatly embarrassed the Reagan administration. **(c)** In the 1960s the U.S. backed the Bay of Pigs invasion which failed. **(d)** In the 1960s U.S. Marines were sent to the Domincan Republic to keep a Communist-supported regime out of power.

8. Concern over the escalation of the nuclear arms race led many nations to reevaluate their membership in NATO.

9. (a) **History teaches us to think about and to better understand people, events, and ideas of the past and how they relate to the modern world.** **(b)** By studying the past, we learn ways of dealing with circumstances in the present.

Relating Geography to History

Almost all of the eastern half of Europe came under Communist regimes.

Writing About History

Answers will vary.

1B, 1E, 4I, 5B, 5C, 5D, 5G, 5H, 5I, a1C

Focus/Motivation

Ask students to study the maps of Europe on page 763 and page 864. Point out that these maps show postwar military and economic alliances. Ask students how the maps show similarities between politics and economics. *(Most Western nations belong to NATO and the Common Market, while most Communist countries belong to the Warsaw Pact and CMEA.)* Then discuss with students how the ideological differences between the Communist and Western nations affect our lives today.

UNIT SEVEN SYNTHESIS

The World Since 1945

28 Challenges Faced Europe and North America in the Postwar Years

Although the Soviet Union had been part of the Allied Powers in World War II, tensions between the Soviet Union on one side and Western Europe and the United States on the other side mounted after the war. This mutual suspicion and hostility between the Communist and Western nations led to the so-called cold war, which they waged by political and economic means rather than with weapons.

The Postwar Settlement

At the end of the war in Europe, Allied occupation zones were set up in Germany and Austria. Practical arrangements lasted as long as the Allies remained on friendly terms. As the postwar hostility grew, however, decisions by the Allies became more and more difficult to reach. For example, it took 10 years to reach an agreement over Austria, and no final agreement was ever reached on Germany. Instead, the country remained occupied by American, British, French, and Soviet troops. Despite these disagreements, however, the United Nations was founded as an international body dedicated to preserving peace.

The Influence of the Cold War

The problems of the cold war intensified in the late 1940s. Soon after the German surrender, the Soviets set up Communist-controlled governments in Poland, Romania, Bulgaria, and Hungary—known as satellite nations—and made known their intentions to foster communism throughout Europe.

Early in 1947 the United States acted to fight the spread of communism. In March 1947 President Truman, announcing what came to be called the Truman Doctrine, dedicated the United States to helping countries threatened by communism. This policy, referred to as containment, was aimed at "containing," or restricting, the spread of communism.

The United States also instituted the European Recovery Program, often called the Marshall Plan, to help Europe recover from the war. According to the plan, the United States would furnish supplies and funds to help nations rebuild.

Because the nations of Western Europe feared that the Soviets would launch an invasion, they founded the North Atlantic Treaty Organization (NATO), a mutual defense pact. The Soviets responded by founding the Warsaw Pact.

Progress

One of the most outstanding characteristics of postwar Western Europe was its economic and political recovery. In a comparatively short time, Western Europeans had cleared away the rubble of bombed cities, rebuilt roads, rail lines and bridges, and returned their industries to full production.

The nations also made attempts at economic cooperation. In 1957, for example, the European Economic Community (EEC)—usually called the Common Market—was founded.

The Communist Bloc

As the years wore on, people in the satellite nations chafed under Communist rule. In 1956 the Hungarians revolted, and in 1968 the Czechs tried to institute reforms. The Soviets crushed rebels in both countries.

Even though the Communist nations joined to form their own common market, the Council for Mutual Economic Assistance (COMECON or CMEA), living standards in these nations lagged far behind those in the West.

The United States and Canada

For the most part, United States foreign policy during the postwar period revolved around containment. At home, the government consistently aimed to resolve social and political problems and to maintain a flourishing economy.

After World War II, Canada became a vigorous supporter of the United Nations and an important member of NATO. It loaned almost $4 billion to other countries and welcomed thousands of refugees from Europe. Canada also experienced rapid economic growth.

29 Asian Nations Struggled to Gain Stability

The years after World War II saw major political, economic, and social changes in Asia.

China

After World War II the battles between the Nationalists and the Communists in China continued. By 1949 the Communists had forced the Nationalists to set up a government in Taiwan and had taken control of the mainland.

Once in power the Communists worked to set up a Marxist state. Although the Communists did achieve some economic growth, they began to allow some elements of free enterprise into their economy in the 1980s to speed this growth.

Since 1949 officials of the Chinese Communist Party have often disagreed. To combat these arguments, Mao Zedong launched the Great Proletarian Cultural Revolution, a violent attempt at social changes, in 1966. In time, the moderates won control of the major party and government offices and began to reinstate many of those who had been purged from government offices and the Communist Party during the Cultural Revolution.

China's foreign affairs also underwent change. China was first closely aligned with the Soviet Union, but tensions soon cooled this relationship. As Chinese-Soviet relations worsened, China grew more willing to come to terms with the United States, and in 1979 the two nations established diplomatic relations.

Fireworks over Hong Kong

Much of the tension that had separated the People's Republic of China and the United States during the 1950s and 1960s grew out of the Korean War in the 1950s. During that war the Communists had openly aided North Korea's attempts to conquer South Korea. Thanks to intervention by the United Nations, however, the South Koreans remained independent. Today South Korea with its free enterprise system is highly industrialized.

Japan

Although defeated in World War II, Japan has become one of the most industrialized and prosperous nations in the world today. Japan entered the 1980s as Asia's leading economic power. Surpassing all other nations in shipbuilding and electronics manufacturing, it stood as the world's third-ranking industrial nation. However, the country's economic leaders faced a growing problem—where to find markets for a rapidly expanding volume of production. This problem intensified as many nations, including the United States, protested the flooding of their markets with Japanese goods.

India, Pakistan, and Bangladesh

The movement for independence from Great Britain that had begun in India after World War I intensified after World War II. Finally, in 1947, the vast subcontinent was granted independence. However, in doing so the British created fragmented nations by establishing India and East and West Pakistan based upon the Muslim and Hindu populations of each region.

899

Presentation
Making a Chart
(Average/Group)
Write the following headings on the chalkboard or an overhead projector: *China, Japan, Iran,* and *India.* Then ask students to list the significant political and economic developments in each of these countries since 1945. Use the completed charts as the basis of a class discussion on how these countries are meeting the challenges of the late 1900s.

India became the leader of the non-aligned nations—those that steered a middle course between the Communist bloc and the Western powers—and worked to industrialize. By the end of the 1980s, India faced major economic problems even though its economy had made considerable progress. The country's mixed economy, in which private companies owned some industries and the government owed the rest, charted the way in which it wanted the economy to grow in a series of five-year plans.

The nations of Pakistan, divided into two parts separated by a huge wedge of Indian territory some 1,000 miles (1,600 kilometers) wide, proved unworkable. In 1971 the nation divided into Pakistan (formerly West Pakistan) and Bangladesh (formerly East Pakistan).

Both Pakistan and Bangladesh faced daunting problems after the division. Bangladesh, ravaged by war, also suffered recurrent famines, epidemics, floods, and devastating tropical storms. And in Pakistan a military dictatorship ruled until 1988.

Southeast Asia

The Southeast Asian countries of the Philippines, Indonesia, Malaysia, Singapore, Brunei, Vietnam, Cambodia (Kampuchea), Laos, and Burma also won independence after World War II. These nations have all faced varying problems since independence.

Conflict in Vietnam

One of the most troubled countries of the region has been Vietnam which was racked by civil war after its independence. North Vietnam had a Communist government, while South Vietnam had a pro-Western government. After more than 20 years of war, which included direct intervention by the United States, the Communists prevailed and united the country in 1975.

Although reunited, Vietnam faces many problems. The years of war had drained the nation's resources. In addition, many people fled the country.

Vietnam's neighbors also faced problems. When the Communist *Khmer Rouge* captured the government of Cambodia, for example, they tried to impose a Marxist state on the people. In so doing, they murdered thousands of civilians and drained the country of a nation's most important resources—its citizens.

Security and Economic Growth

Most of the countries of Asia at one time had been colonies. After independence, most new Asian nations set up representative governments and attempted to build democratic societies. With the passage of time, however, democracy faded in most of Asia.

In the late 1980s, roughly 3 billion people lived in Asia, more than half of the total population of the world. A significant number of Asia's people lived in poverty and suffered its consequences—malnutrition, illiteracy, and reduced life expectancy.

By and large, most Asian countries experienced slow economic growth because they had little wealth. Industrialization required huge investments of money in machinery for factories and distribution networks. Also, the later a country began the process of industrialization, the greater the investment needed to bring that country up to the level of the more developed nations.

30 The Nations of Africa and the Middle East Became Independent

In the four decades after World War II, more than 1.5 billion people won independence, and the number of nations in the world tripled, mainly because of successful independence movements in old European empires. Most of the new nations were located in Africa and the Middle East.

African Independence

After World War II, a generation of determined nationalists began to work for African independence. Leaders such as Kwame Nkrumah (en • KROO • mah) in the Gold Coast, Jomo Kenyatta in Kenya, and Nnamdi Azikiwe in Nigeria typified this generation. By 1980 all of Africa except Namibia (Southwest Africa) had gained its independence.

All of these new nations except South Africa had black African leaders. In South Africa, however,

1B, 3B, 5A, 5B, 5D, 5F, a1A, a1C

Non-aligned summit

the white minority continued to rule and to segregate the races through its policy of apartheid.

The New African Nations

Having achieved independence, the nations of Africa still faced many serious problems. Each new nation had to create a sense of national unity among peoples often divided by differences of language and culture. Many of them had to overcome economic underdevelopment. Finally, a sense of pride in Africa's history and its cultural achievements had to be restored. Throughout the postwar era, the new nations struggled to achieve these goals, meeting with varying degrees of success.

Independence in the Middle East

Between 1945 and 1962, the nations of the Middle East made great advances in securing independence. Many gained their independence from Western imperial rule. Others, such as Egypt and Iran, were officially independent but were dominated by outsiders. They too achieved greater freedom from foreign influence during this period and also sought to increase their power within the Middle East.

One of the most troublesome problems of the Middle East concerned the creation of the independent nation of Israel in 1948. The Arabs violently opposed the new state, and warfare plagued the region.

Wars, Oil, and Revolution

After 1962 the struggle against colonialism was no longer an issue in the Middle East. Nevertheless, tensions continued to rack the region. The Arab-Israeli confrontation continued despite the signing of the Camp David Accords between Egypt and Israel. Although oil provided income for many Middle Eastern nations, the world oil glut of the 1980s created financial problems. And in Iran a violent revolution toppled the shah and created a government based on Islamic fundamentalism.

Old Versus New

Today political and social fragmentation marks the Middle East. Many nations with different forms of government occupy the region. The unequal distribution of natural resources as well as varying population densities produce difficult economic conditions. Although the nations of this dynamic region are making strides to improve education and to give women more rights, these moves to modernize often conflict with traditional values. And many Muslims in the Middle East have reacted to the rapid changes of the times by turning to Islamic fundamentalism.

31 Latin America Became the Focus of World Attention

The countries of Latin America underwent enormous changes after World War II. Once relatively unimportant in world affairs and economically undeveloped, Latin America became a focus of world attention.

Political Conflicts

The most important change in Latin America after World War II was the sudden surge in population. The governments of Latin America had to provide new services to meet the demands of this growing population. Often economic instability as well as political tensions interfered with the governments' abilities to meet the needs of the populations.

Mexico and Central America

Mexico, Central America, the Caribbean Islands, and the countries of South America bordering the

901

1B, 1E, 4I, 5D, 5G, 5H, 5I, a1C

Closure
Ask: How will space exploration meet the needs of the twenty-first century? *(Students might suggest that exploration will help find new energy sources for our planet.)*

Caribbean are considered part of the Caribbean Basin. The importance of the countries in this region is their location. The Caribbean Basin is considered a commercial and military crossroads in the Western hemisphere. Ships from throughout the world carry goods between the Atlantic and Pacific oceans via the strategic Panama Canal.

As political instability continues to rock the Caribbean Basin, world attention, particularly that of the United States, has focused on this region. Since the early 1950s, the United States has been heavily involved in several countries of the region, including Guatemala, Cuba, Grenada, Nicaragua, and El Salvador.

Mexico, long one of the most stable countries of the region, faced increasing economic and political problems after the 1950s. Although Mexico's economic picture improved greatly with the discovery of huge oil reserves in the 1970s, by the 1980s the worldwide slump in oil prices had burst the dream of a bright economic future.

Communist Revolution

The island nation of Cuba was the site of one of the greatest upheavals in the region. There, in 1959, Fidel Castro led a Communist revolution that toppled long-time dictator Fulgencio Batista. The presence of a Communist government so close to the United States alarmed American leaders. And throughout the postwar era, an uneasy peace typified relations between the two countries.

Cuba was not the only troubled nation in Latin America in the 1960s. Many countries experienced a shift toward the left, being disrupted by a series of coups and assassinations. In the Dominican Republic, the people toppled a dictator and made the first steps toward democracy. The people of Haiti, however, were less successful in their quest for democratic rule. In 1986, an uprising forced the ruling Duvalier family out of the country, but attempts at democratic civilian rule failed.

South America

Revolutions also swept South America after 1945. Argentina, Brazil, Chile, and Peru teetered between dictatorship and democracy, and in Colombia, the growing cocaine traffic threatened to rip the nation apart.

32 Challenges Faced the Superpowers in the Modern Era

After 1968 the struggles between the Western nations and those of the Communist bloc continued as each group encountered new challenges.

The United States

During the 1970s and 1980s, the United States faced a number of problems, including internal political conflicts and several economic reversals. Discontent spurned by United States involvement in Vietnam ended with the withdrawal of American troops in 1973. At the same time, the news that President Richard Nixon had known of plans to break into the Democratic Party offices during the presidential election of 1972 shocked the nation. As the Watergate scandal unfolded, President Nixon resigned.

High inflation rates and unemployment plagued the nation in the 1970s. Both, however, had been brought under control by the 1980s.

Foreign policy also underwent changes, as relations with the Soviet Union deteriorated in the 1970s and then appeared to grow friendlier in the late 1980s. And in the late 1970s, the United States established ties with Communist China.

Challenges also faced Canada in this period. The nation successfully withstood a French-Canadian separatist movement and maintained close, although at times strained, relations with the United States.

U.S.-Soviet summit

Question 1 of the Synthesis Review corresponds to Section 28 of the synthesis, Question 2, to Section 29; Question 3, to Section 30; Question 4, to Section 31; Question 5, to Section 32; Question 6, to Section 33. Question 7 asks students to synthesize information from various sections of the synthesis.

1B, 5D, 5E, 5F, 5I, a1C, a4A, a4F, a4G, a4H, a4I, a4L

Western Europe

Western Europe was plagued by many of the same problems that plagued the United States in the 1970s and the 1980s. The strengthening of the European Community, or EC, and the North Atlantic Treaty Organization, or NATO, encouraged a spirit of cooperation among the various member nations. In 1975 representatives of 35 nations, including the United States and the Soviet Union, signed the Helsinki Accords that set down ways of improving economic and technological cooperation between East and West.

The Soviet Union and Eastern Europe

In the 1970s and early 1980s, the Soviet Union attempted to take a firmer hold on the Eastern-bloc nations, particularly Czechoslovakia and Poland where opposition to the Soviets was widespread. At the same time, Soviet leaders acted to clamp down on dissent at home. When a new leader, Mikhail Gorbachev, took power in 1985, however, Soviet policy changed. Gorbachev instituted the programs of *glasnost* and *perestroika* to lessen political repression and to provide a certain amount of free enterprise in the Communist nation. In foreign policy Gorbachev sought closer ties with the West.

33 The Modern World Faced the Challenge of Rapid Change

Vast changes in how people lived and how they viewed the world marked the years following 1945.

Technological Change

Dramatic advances in technology affected all the nations of the world. Passenger jets transformed travel, and the United States, the Soviet Union, and other nations launched voyages of space exploration. An important consequence of space exploration was the invention of ways of making machines, especially electrical equipment, smaller in a process called miniaturization. The most remarkable product of miniaturization was the modern computer.

During the postwar era, atomic energy was used to build more powerful bombs. It was also used to develop efficient power for generators to produce electricity for a burgeoning population, although the question of safety at nuclear power plants became an issue of deep public concern after accidents at Three Mile Island and Chernobyl.

The Arts and Literature

After 1945 New York became one of the liveliest centers of new ideas and painting styles based upon experimentation. New styles included abstract expressionism, pop art, op art, process art, and conceptual art. Many people also came to appreciate folk art, the work of talented, but not necessarily professionally trained painters, sculptors, and craftspeople. The same search for new ideas and techniques dominated architecture, music, literature, film, and drama.

Patterns of Living

Just as with science and the arts, the postwar period was a time of rapid social change, particularly in Western nations. Women, for example, joined the work force in increasing numbers.

Amid rapid changes, people looked for ways to create anchors of stability. One way was to renew their commitment to religion. At the same time, people throughout the world became increasingly concerned with social issues such as human rights and the environment.

SYNTHESIS REVIEW

1. **Understanding Ideas** How did the United States react to Soviet attempts to spread communism?
2. **Comparing Ideas** How do the economies of Japan and China differ?
3. **Interpreting Ideas** How did oil resources prove to be both advantages and disadvantages for the countries of the Middle East?
4. **Summarizing Ideas** What were the results of the revolution in Cuba?
5. **Analyzing Ideas** Why did Mikhail Gorbachev institute the policies of *glasnost* and *perestroika?*
6. **Seeing Relationships** Why did many people protest nuclear power?
7. **Synthesizing Ideas** How did tensions between the Soviet Union and the United States affect the entire world?

Review Answers

1. The United States helped countries threatened by communism through the policy of containment.
2. Japan has a free enterprise system. China has a Communist system.
3. Although oil provided income for many Middle Eastern nations, the world oil glut of the 1980s created financial problems.
4. Fidel Castro set up a Communist state.
5. to lessen political repression and to provide a certain amount of free enterprise
6. People protested nuclear power because they questioned its safety.
7. Answers will vary. Students might point out that these two countries were so powerful that tensions between them affected the entire world.

REFERENCE SECTION

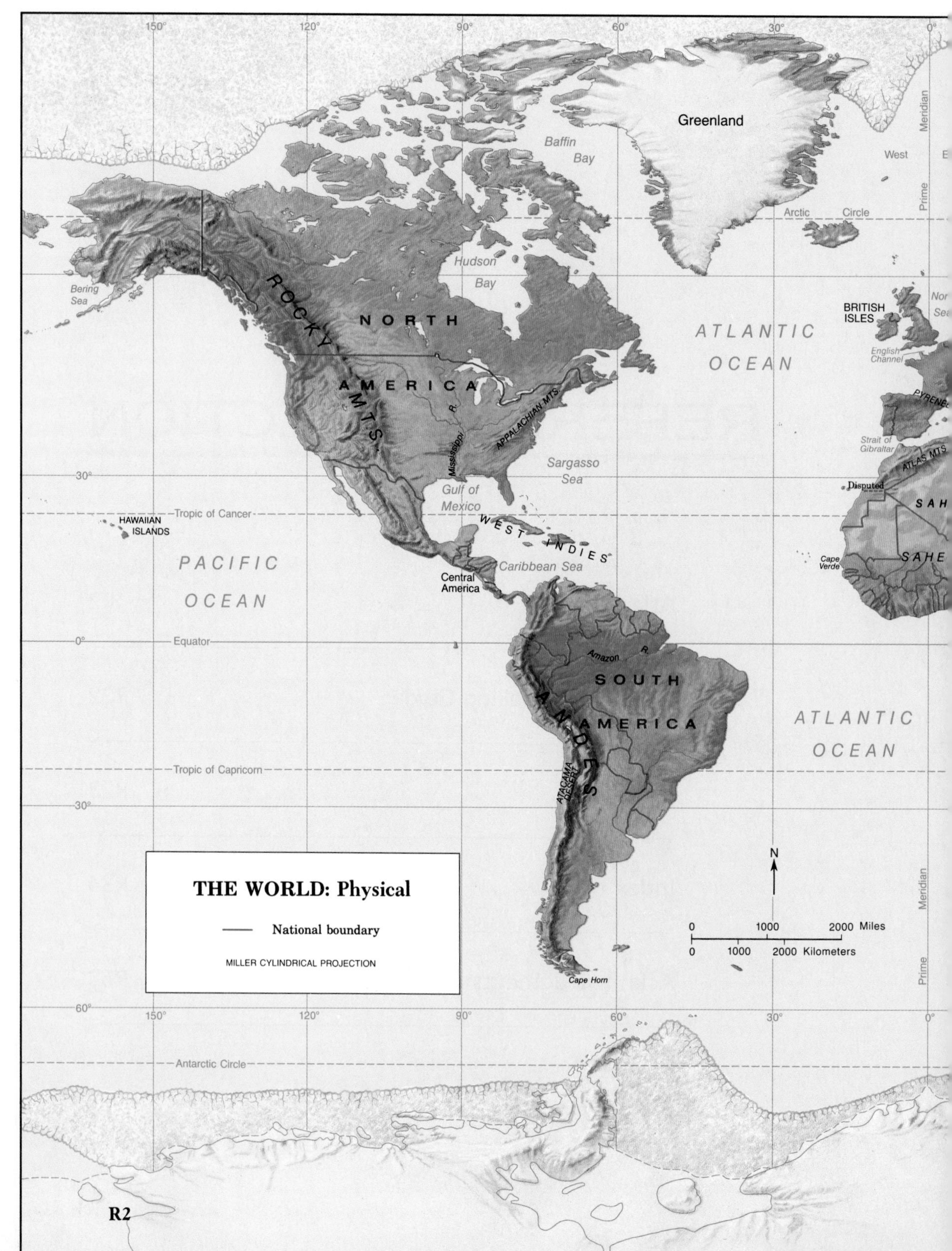
THE WORLD: Physical
National boundary
MILLER CYLINDRICAL PROJECTION
0 1000 2000 Miles
0 1000 2000 Kilometers
N
Greenland
Baffin Bay
Hudson Bay
Bering Sea
ROCKY MTS
NORTH AMERICA
Mississippi R.
APPALACHIAN MTS
Sargasso Sea
Gulf of Mexico
WEST INDIES
Caribbean Sea
Central America
HAWAIIAN ISLANDS
Tropic of Cancer
PACIFIC OCEAN
ATLANTIC OCEAN
BRITISH ISLES
English Channel
Strait of Gibraltar
ATLAS MTS
Disputed
Cape Verde
Arctic Circle
Prime Meridian
West
Equator
Amazon R.
SOUTH AMERICA
ANDES
ATACAMA DESERT
Tropic of Capricorn
Cape Horn
Antarctic Circle
150°
120°
90°
60°
30°
0°

30°
60°
90°
120°
150°
180°
ARCTIC OCEAN
URAL MTS.
Baltic Sea
EUROPE
Danube R.
CARPATHIAN MTS.
Black Sea
CAUCASUS MTS.
Caspian Sea
Mediterranean Sea
ASIA
Disputed
HIMALAYAS
GOBI DESERT
Huang He
Chang Jiang
Ganges R.
Persian G.
Red Sea
Arabian Peninsula
Undefined
NUBIAN DESERT
Arabian Sea
Bay of Bengal
AFRICA
(Congo) R.
Zaire
Sea of Okhotsk
Bering Strait
Bering Sea
60°
30°
East China Sea
South China Sea
PACIFIC OCEAN
Strait of Malacca
Equator
0°
INDIAN OCEAN
INDONESIA
Madagascar
KALAHARI DESERT
Cape of Good Hope
AUSTRALIA
30°
60°
ANTARCTICA

R3

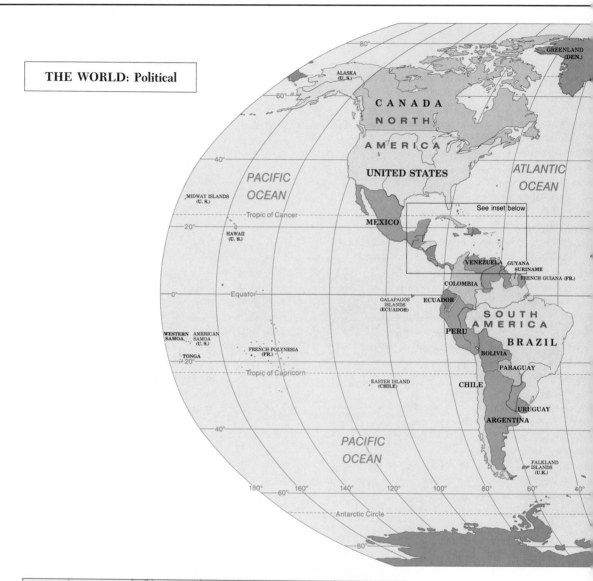

THE WORLD: Political

ALASKA (U. S.)
GREENLAND (DEN.)
CANADA
NORTH AMERICA
UNITED STATES
PACIFIC OCEAN
ATLANTIC OCEAN
MIDWAY ISLANDS (U. S.)
Tropic of Cancer
HAWAII (U. S.)
MEXICO
See inset below
VENEZUELA
GUYANA
SURINAME
FRENCH GUIANA (FR.)
COLOMBIA
Equator
GALAPAGOS ISLANDS (ECUADOR)
ECUADOR
SOUTH AMERICA
PERU
BRAZIL
WESTERN SAMOA
AMERICAN SAMOA (U. S.)
TONGA
FRENCH POLYNESIA (FR.)
Tropic of Capricorn
BOLIVIA
PARAGUAY
EASTER ISLAND (CHILE)
CHILE
URUGUAY
ARGENTINA
PACIFIC OCEAN
FALKLAND ISLANDS (U.K.)
80° 60° 40° 20° 0° 20° 40° 60° 80°
180° 160° 140° 120° 100° 80° 60° 40°
Antarctic Circle

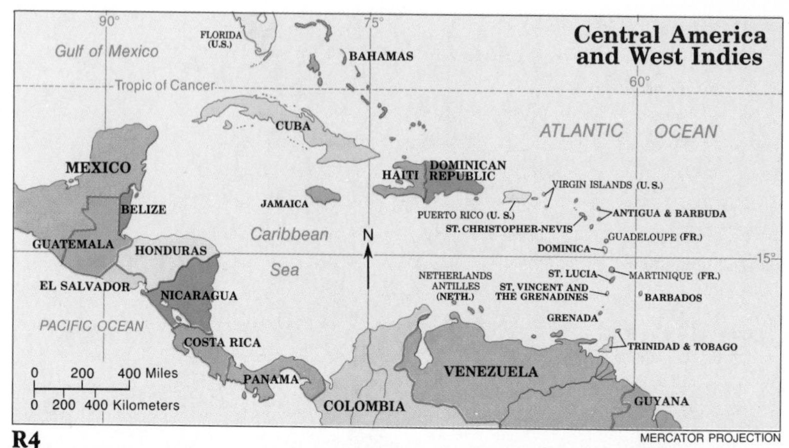

R4

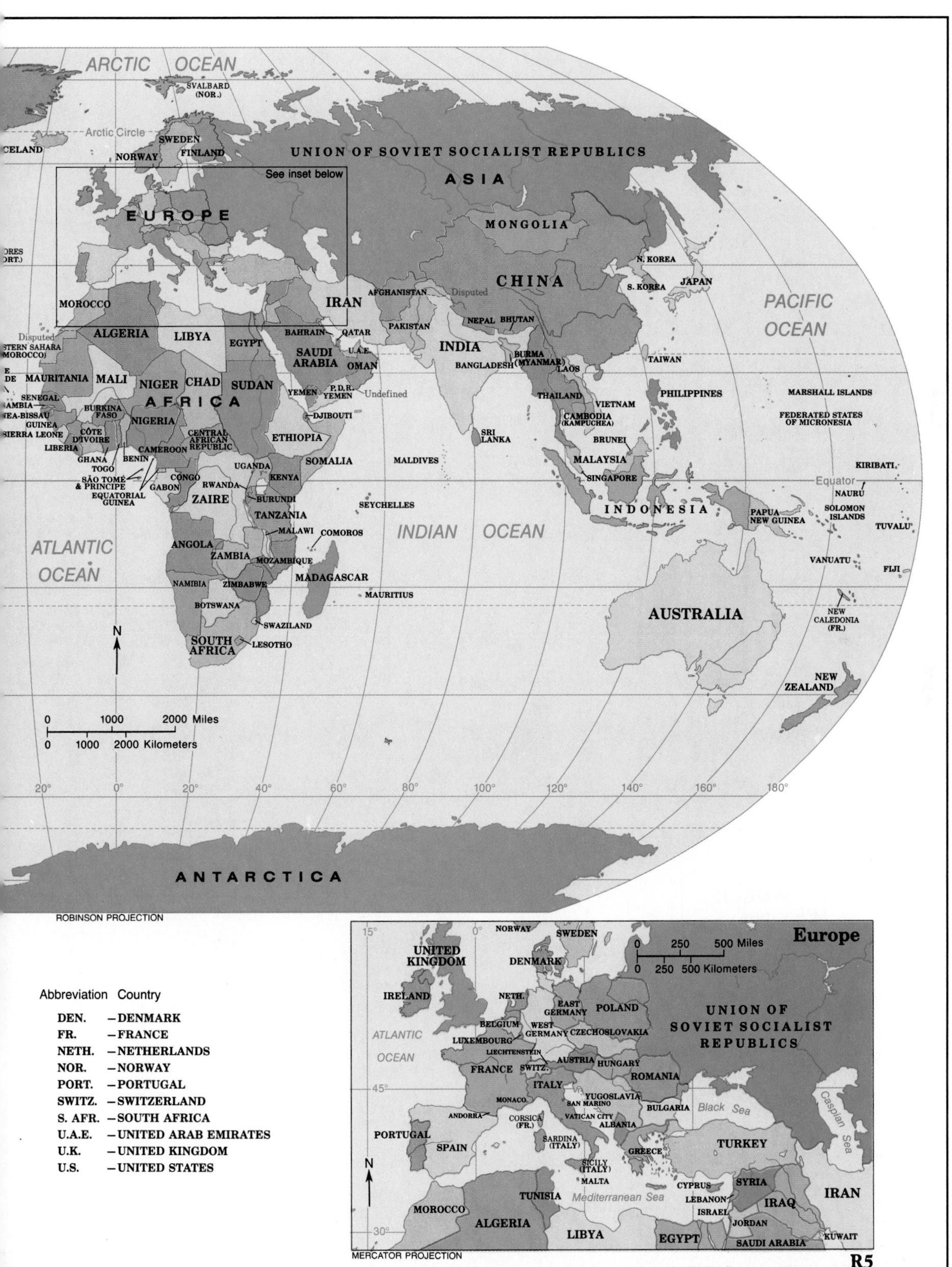
ARCTIC OCEAN
SVALBARD (NOR.)
Arctic Circle
ICELAND
SWEDEN
NORWAY
FINLAND
UNION OF SOVIET SOCIALIST REPUBLICS
See inset below
ASIA
EUROPE
MONGOLIA
N. KOREA
S. KOREA
JAPAN
CHINA
MOROCCO
IRAN
AFGHANISTAN
Disputed
PAKISTAN
NEPAL
BHUTAN
PACIFIC OCEAN
ALGERIA
LIBYA
EGYPT
BAHRAIN
QATAR
SAUDI ARABIA
U.A.E.
OMAN
INDIA
BANGLADESH
BURMA (MYANMAR)
LAOS
TAIWAN
MAURITANIA
MALI
NIGER
CHAD
SUDAN
SENEGAL
AFRICA
YEMEN
P.D.R. YEMEN
Undefined
THAILAND
VIETNAM
PHILIPPINES
MARSHALL ISLANDS
FEDERATED STATES OF MICRONESIA
BURKINA FASO
NIGERIA
GUINEA
SIERRA LEONE
CÔTE D'IVOIRE
LIBERIA
DJIBOUTI
ETHIOPIA
CENTRAL AFRICAN REPUBLIC
CAMEROON
SRI LANKA
CAMBODIA (KAMPUCHEA)
BRUNEI
MALAYSIA
SINGAPORE
GHANA
BENIN
TOGO
SÃO TOMÉ & PRINCIPE
EQUATORIAL GUINEA
GABON
CONGO
RWANDA
ZAIRE
BURUNDI
UGANDA
KENYA
SOMALIA
MALDIVES
KIRIBATI
Equator
NAURU
SEYCHELLES
TANZANIA
INDONESIA
PAPUA NEW GUINEA
SOLOMON ISLANDS
TUVALU
ATLANTIC OCEAN
ANGOLA
MALAWI
COMOROS
INDIAN OCEAN
ZAMBIA
MOZAMBIQUE
MADAGASCAR
VANUATU
FIJI
NAMIBIA
ZIMBABWE
MAURITIUS
BOTSWANA
AUSTRALIA
NEW CALEDONIA (FR.)
SWAZILAND
SOUTH AFRICA
LESOTHO
N
NEW ZEALAND
0 1000 2000 Miles
0 1000 2000 Kilometers
20° 0° 20° 40° 60° 80° 100° 120° 140° 160° 180°
ANTARCTICA
ROBINSON PROJECTION
Europe
15° 0°
NORWAY
SWEDEN
0 250 500 Miles
0 250 500 Kilometers
UNITED KINGDOM
DENMARK
IRELAND
NETH.
EAST GERMANY
POLAND
UNION OF SOVIET SOCIALIST REPUBLICS
BELGIUM
WEST GERMANY
CZECHOSLOVAKIA
ATLANTIC OCEAN
LUXEMBOURG
LIECHTENSTEIN
AUSTRIA
HUNGARY
FRANCE
SWITZ.
ROMANIA
45°
ITALY
MONACO
YUGOSLAVIA
SAN MARINO
BULGARIA
Black Sea
Caspian Sea
ANDORRA
CORSICA (FR.)
VATICAN CITY
ALBANIA
PORTUGAL
SPAIN
SARDINIA (ITALY)
GREECE
TURKEY
N
SICILY (ITALY)
MALTA
CYPRUS
SYRIA
TUNISIA
Mediterranean Sea
LEBANON
IRAQ
IRAN
MOROCCO
ISRAEL
ALGERIA
JORDAN
30°
LIBYA
EGYPT
SAUDI ARABIA
KUWAIT
MERCATOR PROJECTION
R5
Abbreviation Country
DEN. – DENMARK
FR. – FRANCE
NETH. – NETHERLANDS
NOR. – NORWAY
PORT. – PORTUGAL
SWITZ. – SWITZERLAND
S. AFR. – SOUTH AFRICA
U.A.E. – UNITED ARAB EMIRATES
U.K. – UNITED KINGDOM
U.S. – UNITED STATES

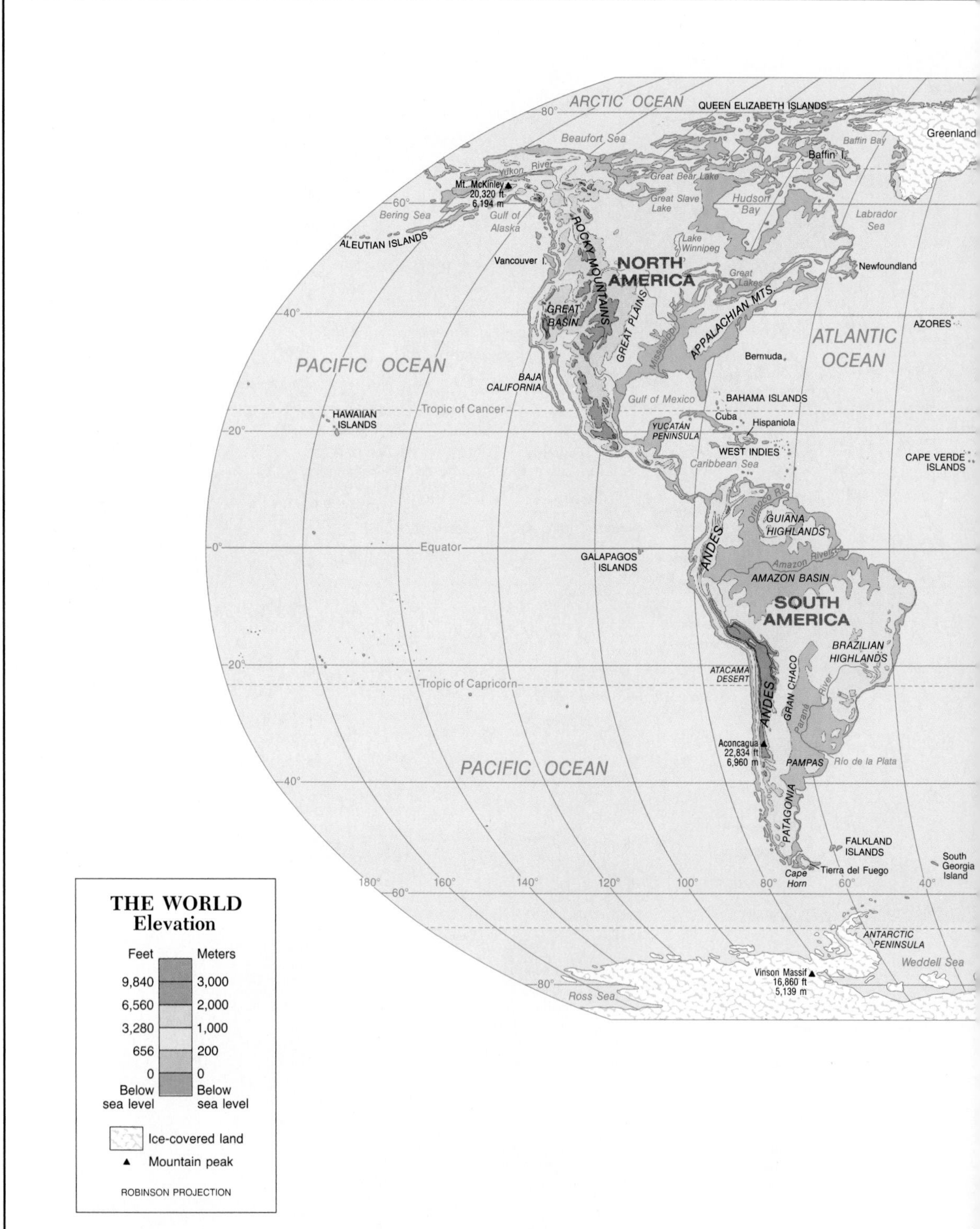

ARCTIC OCEAN
QUEEN ELIZABETH ISLANDS
Greenland
Beaufort Sea
Baffin Bay
Baffin I.
Yukon River
Mt. McKinley
20,320 ft
6,194 m
Great Bear Lake
Great Slave Lake
Hudson Bay
Bering Sea
Gulf of Alaska
Labrador Sea
ALEUTIAN ISLANDS
ROCKY MOUNTAINS
Lake Winnipeg
Vancouver I.
NORTH AMERICA
Great Lakes
Newfoundland
GREAT BASIN
GREAT PLAINS
APPALACHIAN MTS.
Mississippi
AZORES
ATLANTIC OCEAN
PACIFIC OCEAN
Bermuda
BAJA CALIFORNIA
Gulf of Mexico
BAHAMA ISLANDS
HAWAIIAN ISLANDS
Tropic of Cancer
Cuba
Hispaniola
YUCATAN PENINSULA
WEST INDIES
Caribbean Sea
CAPE VERDE ISLANDS
Orinoco R.
GUIANA HIGHLANDS
ANDES
Equator
GALAPAGOS ISLANDS
Amazon River
AMAZON BASIN
SOUTH AMERICA
BRAZILIAN HIGHLANDS
ATACAMA DESERT
Tropic of Capricorn
ANDES
GRAN CHACO
Paraná River
Aconcagua
22,834 ft
6,960 m
PAMPAS
Río de la Plata
PACIFIC OCEAN
PATAGONIA
FALKLAND ISLANDS
South Georgia Island
Cape Horn
Tierra del Fuego
180° 160° 140° 120° 100° 80° 60° 40°
80° 60° 40° 20° 0° 20° 40° 60° 80°
ANTARCTIC PENINSULA
Weddell Sea
Vinson Massif
16,860 ft
5,139 m
Ross Sea
THE WORLD
Elevation
Feet
Meters
9,840
3,000
6,560
2,000
3,280
1,000
656
200
0
0
Below sea level
Below sea level
Ice-covered land
Mountain peak
ROBINSON PROJECTION

R6

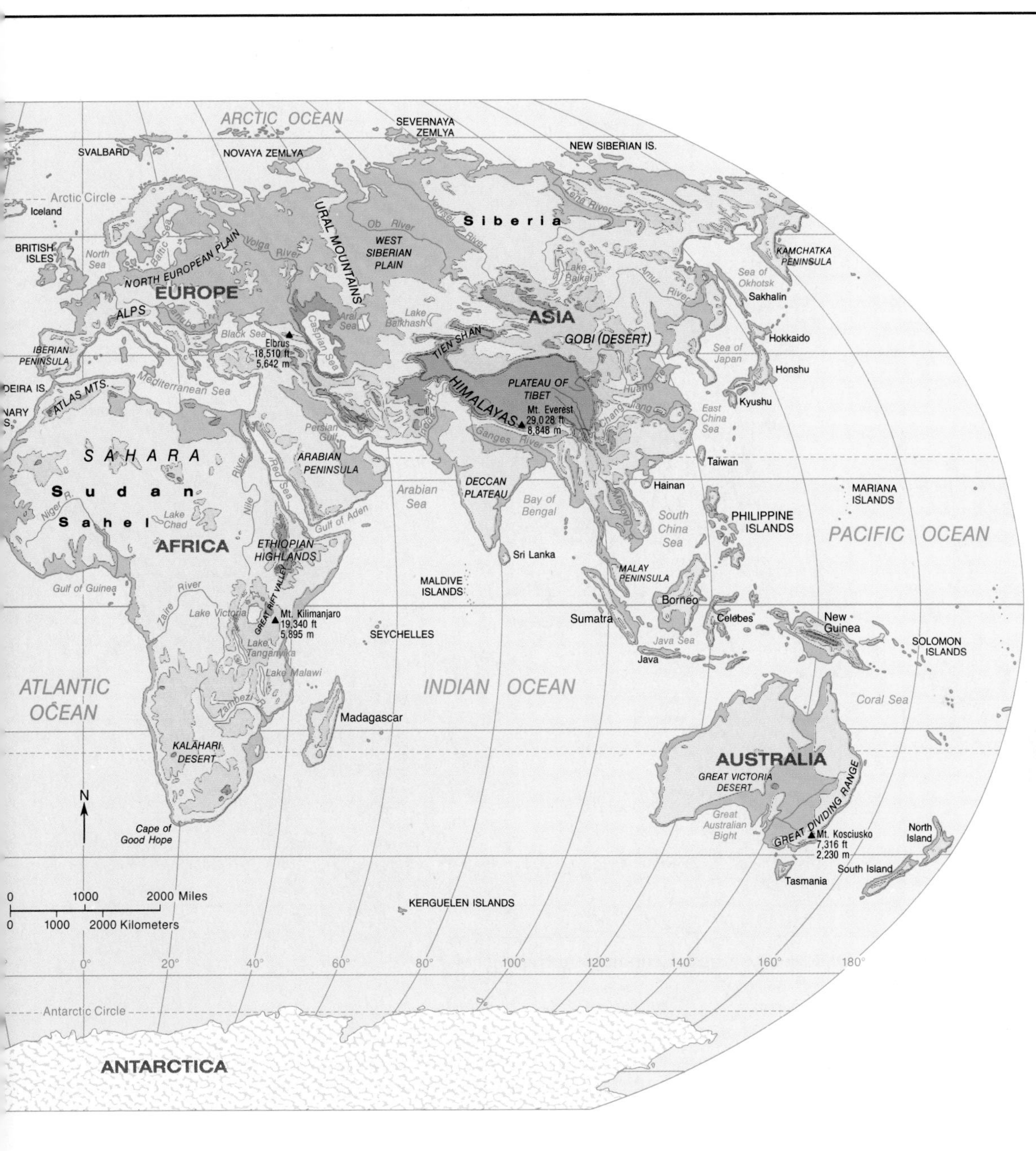

ARCTIC OCEAN
SEVERNAYA ZEMLYA
SVALBARD
NOVAYA ZEMLYA
NEW SIBERIAN IS.
Arctic Circle
Iceland
BRITISH ISLES
North Sea
NORTH EUROPEAN PLAIN
Volga River
URAL MOUNTAINS
Ob River
WEST SIBERIAN PLAIN
Siberia
Lena River
Lake Baikal
Amur River
KAMCHATKA PENINSULA
Sea of Okhotsk
Sakhalin
EUROPE
ALPS
Danube R.
Black Sea
Elbrus 18,510 ft 5,642 m
Caspian Sea
Aral Sea
Lake Balkhash
TIEN SHAN
ASIA
GOBI (DESERT)
Sea of Japan
Hokkaido
Honshu
Kyushu
IBERIAN PENINSULA
Mediterranean Sea
ATLAS MTS.
PLATEAU OF TIBET
HIMALAYAS
Mt. Everest 29,028 ft 8,848 m
Huang
Chang Jiang
East China Sea
Persian Gulf
Ganges River
Taiwan
SAHARA
ARABIAN PENINSULA
Nile River
Red Sea
Arabian Sea
DECCAN PLATEAU
Bay of Bengal
Hainan
MARIANA ISLANDS
Sudan
Sahel
Niger R.
Lake Chad
Gulf of Aden
South China Sea
PHILIPPINE ISLANDS
PACIFIC OCEAN
AFRICA
ETHIOPIAN HIGHLANDS
Sri Lanka
MALAY PENINSULA
Gulf of Guinea
Zaire River
GREAT RIFT VALLEY
MALDIVE ISLANDS
Borneo
Lake Victoria
Mt. Kilimanjaro 19,340 ft 5,895 m
Sumatra
Celebes
New Guinea
Lake Tanganyika
SEYCHELLES
Java Sea
Java
SOLOMON ISLANDS
Lake Malawi
ATLANTIC OCEAN
Zambezi
INDIAN OCEAN
Coral Sea
Madagascar
KALAHARI DESERT
AUSTRALIA
GREAT VICTORIA DESERT
GREAT DIVIDING RANGE
N
Great Australian Bight
Cape of Good Hope
Mt. Kosciusko 7,316 ft 2,230 m
North Island
South Island
Tasmania
0 1000 2000 Miles
0 1000 2000 Kilometers
KERGUELEN ISLANDS
0° 20° 40° 60° 80° 100° 120° 140° 160° 180°
Antarctic Circle
ANTARCTICA

R7

1A

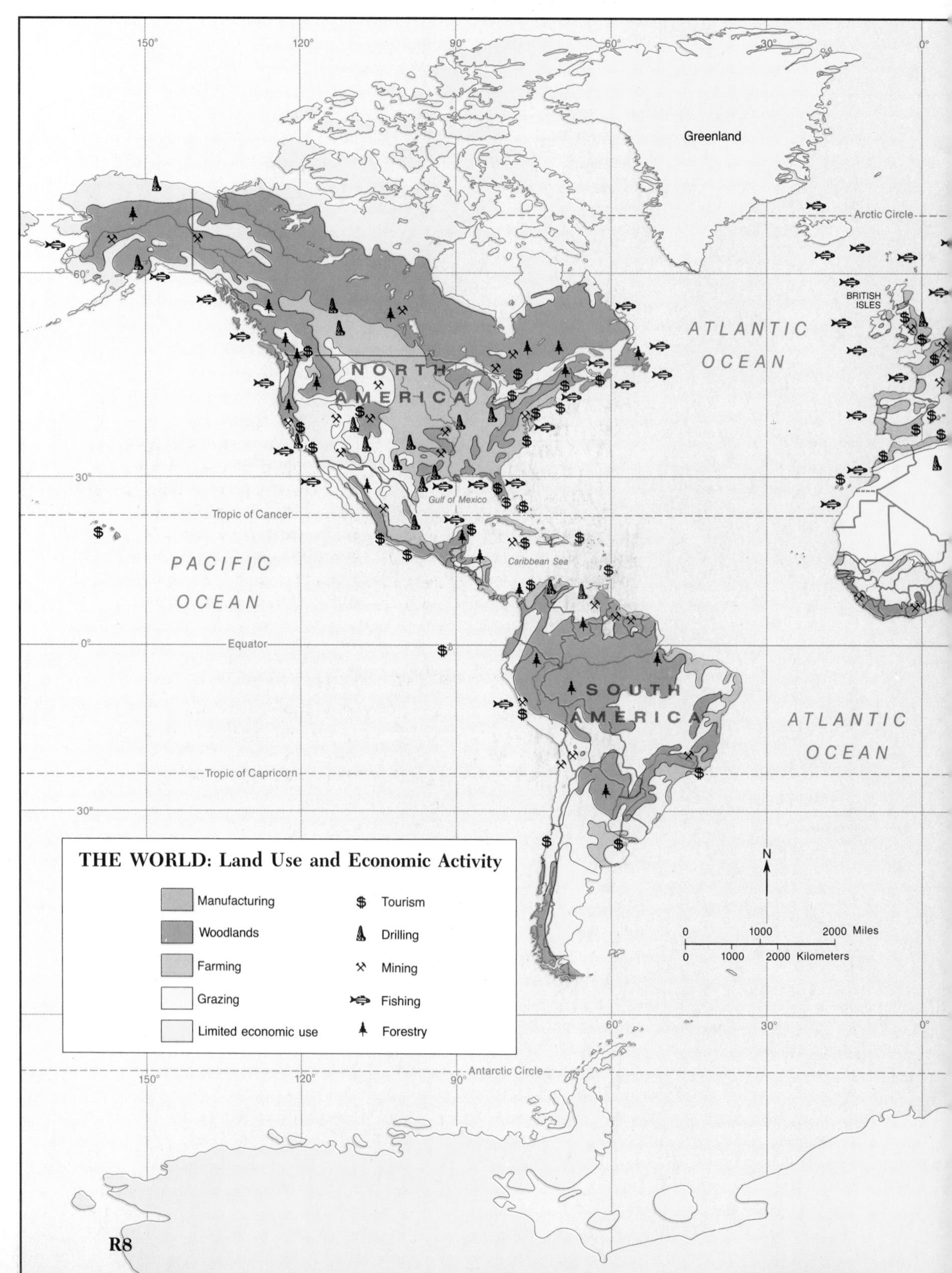

THE WORLD: Land Use and Economic Activity
Manufacturing
Woodlands
Farming
Grazing
Limited economic use
Tourism
Drilling
Mining
Fishing
Forestry
Greenland
NORTH AMERICA
SOUTH AMERICA
ATLANTIC OCEAN
PACIFIC OCEAN
ATLANTIC OCEAN
BRITISH ISLES
Gulf of Mexico
Caribbean Sea
Arctic Circle
Tropic of Cancer
Equator
Tropic of Capricorn
Antarctic Circle
150°
120°
90°
60°
30°
0°
N
0 1000 2000 Miles
0 1000 2000 Kilometers

R8

ARCTIC OCEAN
ASIA
EUROPE
Baltic Sea
Black Sea
Mediterranean Sea
AFRICA
INDIAN OCEAN
PACIFIC OCEAN
INDONESIA
AUSTRALIA
NEW ZEALAND
Madagascar
ANTARCTICA
Tropic of Cancer
Equator
Tropic of Capricorn
Antarctic Circle
30°
60°
90°
120°
150°
180°

R9

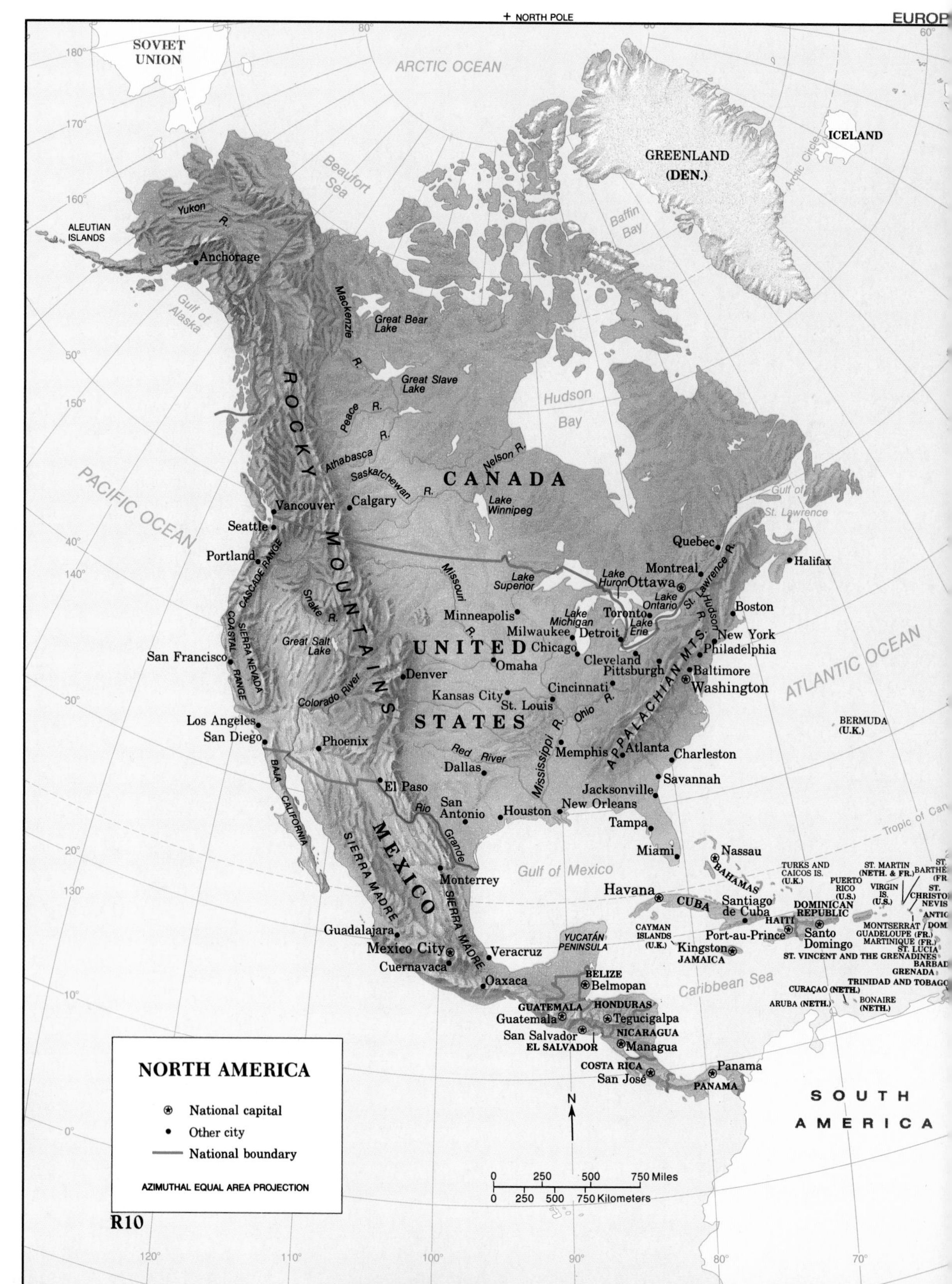
NORTH AMERICA
National capital
Other city
National boundary
AZIMUTHAL EQUAL AREA PROJECTION
R10
NORTH POLE
EUROP
ARCTIC OCEAN
SOVIET UNION
GREENLAND (DEN.)
ICELAND
Arctic Circle
Beaufort Sea
Baffin Bay
ALEUTIAN ISLANDS
Yukon R.
Anchorage
Gulf of Alaska
Mackenzie R.
Great Bear Lake
Great Slave Lake
Hudson Bay
Peace R.
Athabasca R.
Saskatchewan R.
Nelson R.
CANADA
Lake Winnipeg
PACIFIC OCEAN
ROCKY MOUNTAINS
Vancouver
Calgary
Seattle
Portland
CASCADE RANGE
COASTAL RANGE
SIERRA NEVADA
San Francisco
Snake R.
Great Salt Lake
Missouri R.
Lake Superior
Lake Huron
Lake Michigan
Lake Ontario
Lake Erie
Gulf of St. Lawrence
St. Lawrence R.
Hudson R.
Quebec
Montreal
Ottawa
Halifax
Boston
Toronto
Minneapolis
Milwaukee
Detroit
New York
Philadelphia
Chicago
Cleveland
Pittsburgh
Baltimore
Washington
UNITED STATES
Omaha
Denver
Colorado River
Kansas City
St. Louis
Cincinnati
Ohio R.
APPALACHIAN MTS.
ATLANTIC OCEAN
BERMUDA (U.K.)
Los Angeles
San Diego
Phoenix
Mississippi R.
Memphis
Atlanta
Charleston
Red River
Dallas
Savannah
BAJA CALIFORNIA
El Paso
Rio Grande
Jacksonville
San Antonio
Houston
New Orleans
Tampa
Tropic of Cancer
Miami
Nassau
BAHAMAS
MEXICO
SIERRA MADRE
Monterrey
Gulf of Mexico
Havana
CUBA
Santiago de Cuba
TURKS AND CAICOS IS. (U.K.)
PUERTO RICO (U.S.)
ST. MARTIN (NETH. & FR.)
VIRGIN IS. (U.S.)
DOMINICAN REPUBLIC
HAITI
Santo Domingo
Port-au-Prince
CAYMAN ISLANDS (U.K.)
Kingston
JAMAICA
MONTSERRAT / DOM
GUADELOUPE (FR.)
MARTINIQUE (FR.)
ST. LUCIA
ST. VINCENT AND THE GRENADINES
GRENADA
TRINIDAD AND TOBAGO
CURAÇAO (NETH.)
ARUBA (NETH.)
BONAIRE (NETH.)
Caribbean Sea
Guadalajara
Mexico City
Veracruz
Cuernavaca
YUCATÁN PENINSULA
Oaxaca
BELIZE
Belmopan
GUATEMALA
Guatemala
HONDURAS
Tegucigalpa
San Salvador
EL SALVADOR
NICARAGUA
Managua
COSTA RICA
San José
Panama
PANAMA
SOUTH AMERICA
N
0 250 500 750 Miles
0 250 500 750 Kilometers

SOUTH AMERICA
National capital
Other city
National boundary
AZIMUTHAL EQUAL AREA PROJECTION
CARIBBEAN SEA
ATLANTIC OCEAN
PACIFIC OCEAN
VENEZUELA
COLOMBIA
ECUADOR
PERU
BRAZIL
BOLIVIA
PARAGUAY
CHILE
ARGENTINA
URUGUAY
GUYANA
SURINAME
FRENCH GUIANA (FR.)
FALKLAND ISLANDS (U.K.)
SOUTH GEORGIA (U.K.)
TIERRA DEL FUEGO
Cape Horn
PAMPAS
ANDES
Barranquilla
Maracaibo
Caracas
Georgetown
Paramaribo
Cayenne
Medellín
Bogotá
Quito
Guayaquil
Iquitos
Manaus
Fortaleza
Recife
Salvador
Lima
La Paz
Sucre
Brasília
Belo Horizonte
Rio de Janeiro
São Paulo
Asunción
Pôrto Alegre
Córdoba
Rosario
Santiago
Valparaíso
Buenos Aires
Montevideo
Stanley
Magdalena River
Orinoco River
Amazon River
São Francisco River
Paraná River
Paraguay River
Uruguay River
Río de la Plata
Lake Titicaca
Equator
Tropic of Capricorn
N
0 250 500 Miles
0 250 500 Kilometers

EUROPE
National capital
Other city
Canal
National boundary
AZIMUTHAL EQUAL AREA PROJECTION
Reykjavík
ICELAND
Arctic Circle
FAROE IS.
(DEN.)
SHETLAND IS.
(U.K.)
Trondheim
SWEDEN
NORWAY
Bergen
Oslo
Uppsala
Stavanger
Stockholm
Göteborg
Glasgow
Edinburgh
Belfast
UNITED
KINGDOM
DENMARK
North
Sea
Copenhagen
Dublin
IRELAND
Liverpool
Manchester
Baltic
Bornholm
(DEN.)
Kalining
Birmingham
Gdansk
Cardiff
NETHERLANDS
Hamburg
Bristol
Thames R.
London
Bremen
EAST
Amsterdam
The Hague
Berlin
Dover
Rotterdam
GERMANY
Calais
English Channel
Brussels
WEST
GERMANY
BELGIUM
Oder
ATLANTIC
Le Havre
Bonn
Leipzig
Elbe
POLA
Seine
Paris
LUXEMBOURG
Frankfurt
R.
Prague
Krak
OCEAN
Luxembourg
Loire
River
Strasbourg
Stuttgart
CZECHOSLOVAKI
Rhine
Danube
FRANCE
La Rochelle
Dijon
Munich
Zürich
Vienna
Bay of
Biscay
Bern
LIECHTENSTEIN
Geneva
SWITZERLAND
AUSTRIA
Budapest
Bordeaux
Lyon
ALPS
HUNG
Milan
Zagreb
Garonne
Rhône
Venice
Porto
Turin
Po River
Trieste
PYRENEES
Genoa
Belgr
Ebro River
Nice
Marseilles
MONACO
Florence
SAN
MARINO
YUGOSLAV
APENNINES
Sarajevo
ANDORRA
Lisbon
Tagus R.
Madrid
Tiber
PORTUGAL
Barcelona
Corsica
(FR.)
Adriatic Sea
SPAIN
Rome
Valencia
Sardinia
(IT.)
Tiran
ALBA
Seville
Naples
ITALY
BALEARIC ISLANDS
(SP.)
Cádiz
Tyrrhenian
Sea
Strait of Gibraltar
Mediterranean Sea
Ionian
Sea
Palermo
Sicily
AFRICA
R12
MALTA

FINLAND
White Sea
Arkhangelsk
North Dvina River
URAL MOUNTAINS
Lake Ladoga
Helsinki
Leningrad
Gulf of Finland
Tallinn
Gor'kiy
Riga
Moscow
Kuibyshev
Ural River
SOVIET UNION
Vilnius
Minsk
Warsaw
Kiev
Kharkov
Volgograd
Volga River
Dniester River
Don River
CARPATHIAN MTS.
Dnieper R.
Odessa
Sea of Azov
CAUCASUS MTS.
Caspian Sea
ROMANIA
Sevastopol
Bucharest
Danube River
Black Sea
BALKAN MTS.
Sofia
BULGARIA
TURKEY
Istanbul
N
ASIA
Aegean Sea
GREECE
Athens
Crete
0 100 200 300 Miles
0 100 200 300 Kilometers
R13
70°
50°
60°
40°
30°
40°
50°
30°

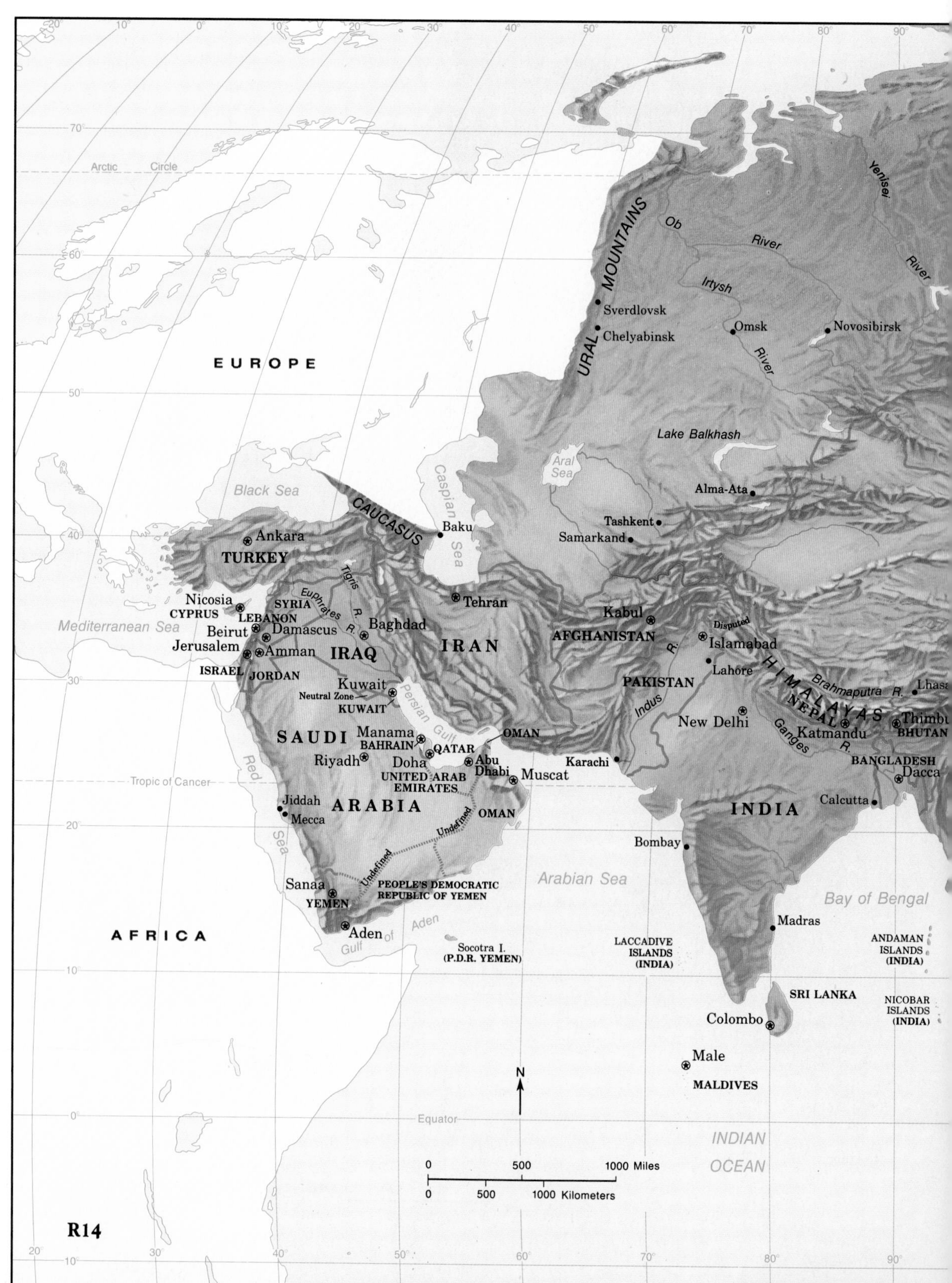
EUROPE
AFRICA
Arctic Circle
Black Sea
Caspian Sea
Mediterranean Sea
Red Sea
Persian Gulf
Arabian Sea
Bay of Bengal
Gulf of Aden
INDIAN OCEAN
Aral Sea
Lake Balkhash
Tropic of Cancer
Equator
URAL MOUNTAINS
CAUCASUS
HIMALAYAS
Ob River
Irtysh River
Yenisei River
Tigris R.
Euphrates R.
Indus R.
Ganges R.
Brahmaputra R.
Sverdlovsk
Chelyabinsk
Omsk
Novosibirsk
Alma-Ata
Tashkent
Samarkand
Baku
Ankara
TURKEY
Nicosia
CYPRUS
SYRIA
LEBANON
Beirut
Damascus
Jerusalem
Amman
ISRAEL
JORDAN
Baghdad
IRAQ
Tehran
IRAN
Kabul
AFGHANISTAN
Disputed
Islamabad
Lahore
PAKISTAN
Kuwait
Neutral Zone
KUWAIT
SAUDI ARABIA
Manama
BAHRAIN
QATAR
Doha
Riyadh
Abu Dhabi
UNITED ARAB EMIRATES
OMAN
Muscat
Karachi
Jiddah
Mecca
Undefined
Sanaa
YEMEN
PEOPLE'S DEMOCRATIC REPUBLIC OF YEMEN
Aden
Socotra I.
(P.D.R. YEMEN)
New Delhi
NEPAL
Katmandu
Thimbu
BHUTAN
Lhasa
BANGLADESH
Dacca
Calcutta
INDIA
Bombay
Madras
LACCADIVE ISLANDS (INDIA)
ANDAMAN ISLANDS (INDIA)
NICOBAR ISLANDS (INDIA)
SRI LANKA
Colombo
Male
MALDIVES
N
0 500 1000 Miles
0 500 1000 Kilometers
R14

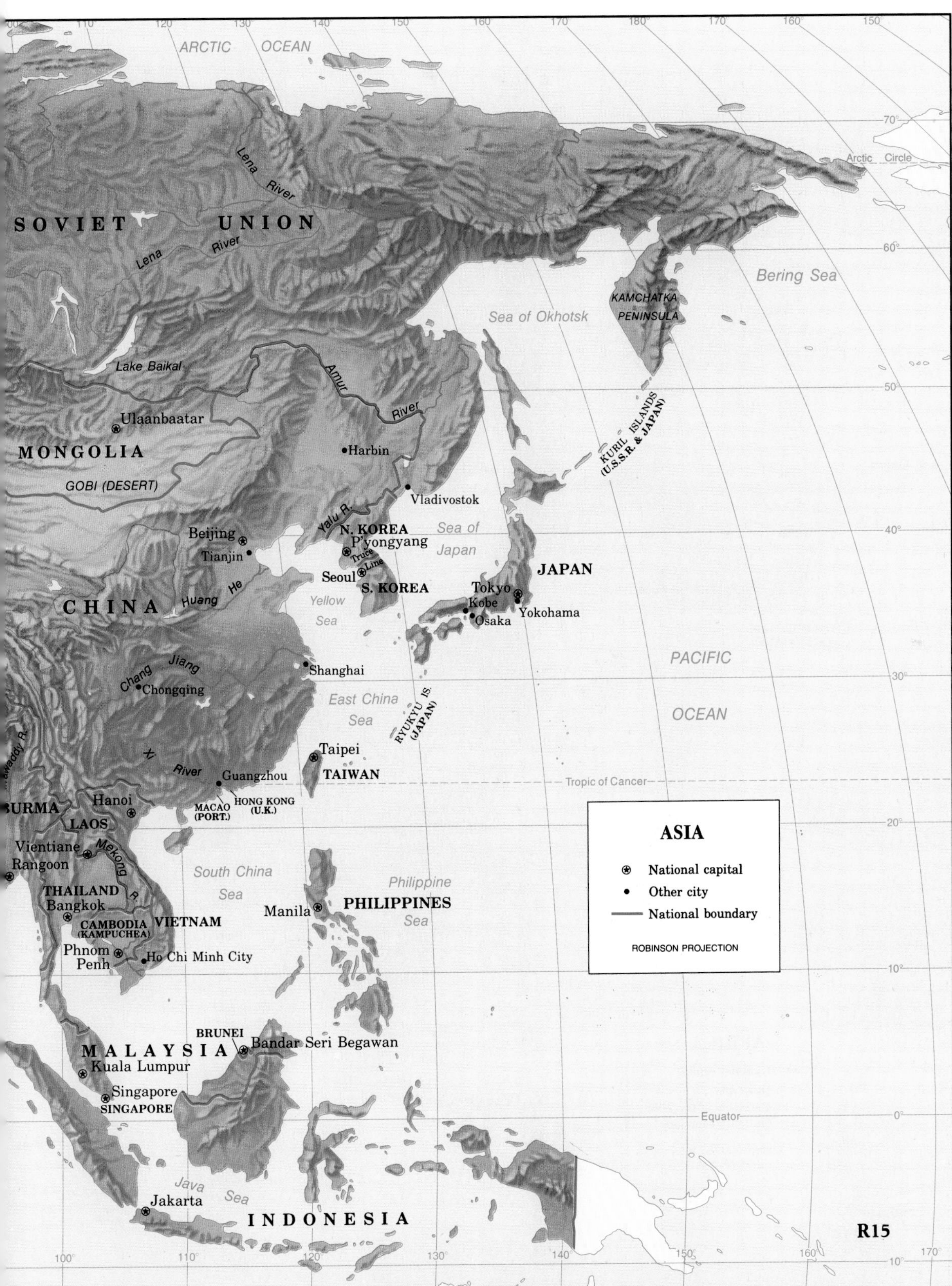
ARCTIC OCEAN
SOVIET UNION
Lena River
Lake Baikal
Amur River
Ulaanbaatar
MONGOLIA
GOBI (DESERT)
Harbin
Vladivostok
Sea of Okhotsk
KAMCHATKA PENINSULA
Bering Sea
Arctic Circle
KURIL ISLANDS (U.S.S.R. & JAPAN)
Yalu R.
N. KOREA
P'yongyang
Truce Line
Seoul
S. KOREA
Sea of Japan
JAPAN
Tokyo
Kobe
Osaka
Yokohama
Beijing
Tianjin
Huang He
CHINA
Yellow Sea
Shanghai
Chang Jiang
Chongqing
East China Sea
RYUKYU IS. (JAPAN)
PACIFIC OCEAN
Xi River
Guangzhou
Taipei
TAIWAN
Tropic of Cancer
MACAO (PORT.)
HONG KONG (U.K.)
Hanoi
BURMA
LAOS
Vientiane
Rangoon
Mekong R.
THAILAND
Bangkok
CAMBODIA (KAMPUCHEA)
VIETNAM
Phnom Penh
Ho Chi Minh City
South China Sea
Philippine Sea
Manila
PHILIPPINES
ASIA
National capital
Other city
National boundary
ROBINSON PROJECTION
BRUNEI
Bandar Seri Begawan
MALAYSIA
Kuala Lumpur
Singapore
SINGAPORE
Equator
Java Sea
Jakarta
INDONESIA
R15

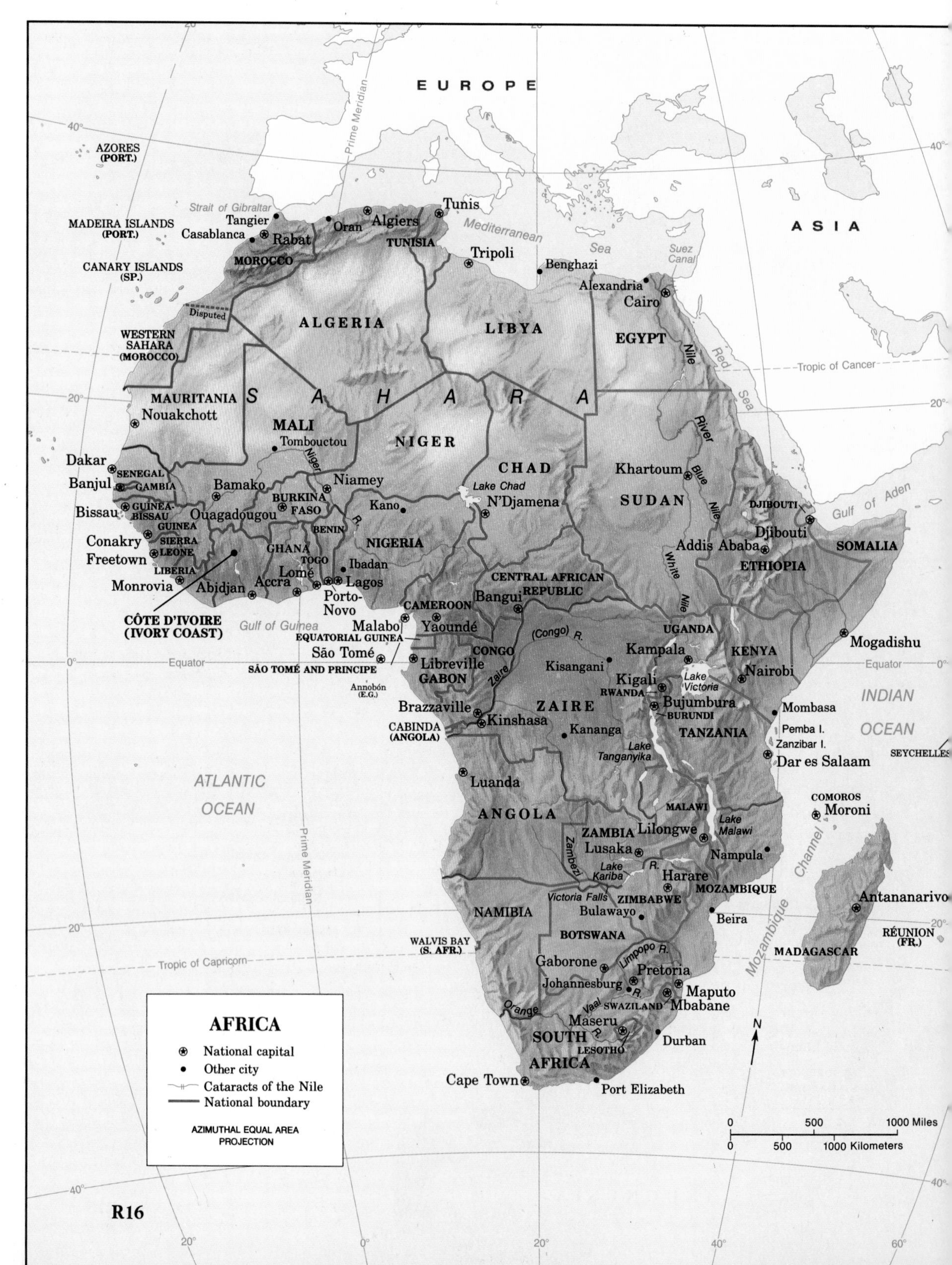

EUROPE
ASIA
AZORES (PORT.)
MADEIRA ISLANDS (PORT.)
CANARY ISLANDS (SP.)
Strait of Gibraltar
Tangier
Casablanca
Rabat
MOROCCO
Oran
Algiers
Tunis
TUNISIA
Mediterranean Sea
Tripoli
Benghazi
Suez Canal
Alexandria
Cairo
Disputed
WESTERN SAHARA (MOROCCO)
ALGERIA
LIBYA
EGYPT
Nile
Red Sea
Tropic of Cancer
MAURITANIA
Nouakchott
S A H A R A
MALI
Tombouctou
NIGER
CHAD
River
Dakar
SENEGAL
Banjul
GAMBIA
Bamako
Niger
Niamey
Lake Chad
N'Djamena
Khartoum
Blue
SUDAN
Nile
DJIBOUTI
Gulf of Aden
Djibouti
Bissau
GUINEA-BISSAU
BURKINA FASO
Ouagadougou
Kano
GUINEA
Conakry
SIERRA LEONE
Freetown
BENIN
NIGERIA
Addis Ababa
SOMALIA
ETHIOPIA
GHANA
TOGO
Ibadan
LIBERIA
Monrovia
Abidjan
Accra
Lomé
Lagos
Porto-Novo
White
CENTRAL AFRICAN REPUBLIC
Bangui
CÔTE D'IVOIRE (IVORY COAST)
Gulf of Guinea
CAMEROON
Malabo
Yaoundé
EQUATORIAL GUINEA
(Congo) R.
UGANDA
Mogadishu
KENYA
São Tomé
SÃO TOMÉ AND PRINCIPE
CONGO
Libreville
GABON
Zaire
Kisangani
Kampala
Equator
Nairobi
Kigali
RWANDA
Lake Victoria
Annobón (E.G.)
Brazzaville
ZAIRE
Bujumbura
BURUNDI
Mombasa
INDIAN OCEAN
Kinshasa
CABINDA (ANGOLA)
Kananga
TANZANIA
Pemba I.
Zanzibar I.
Lake Tanganyika
Dar es Salaam
SEYCHELLES
ATLANTIC OCEAN
Luanda
COMOROS
Moroni
ANGOLA
MALAWI
Lake Malawi
ZAMBIA
Lilongwe
Zambezi
Lusaka
Nampula
Channel
Lake Kariba
R.
Harare
MOZAMBIQUE
Victoria Falls
ZIMBABWE
Antananarivo
NAMIBIA
Bulawayo
Beira
BOTSWANA
RÉUNION (FR.)
WALVIS BAY (S. AFR.)
Limpopo R.
MADAGASCAR
Tropic of Capricorn
Gaborone
Pretoria
Mozambique
Johannesburg
Maputo
Orange
Vaal
SWAZILAND
Mbabane
Maseru
SOUTH AFRICA
LESOTHO
Durban
N
Cape Town
Port Elizabeth
Prime Meridian
AFRICA
National capital
Other city
Cataracts of the Nile
National boundary
AZIMUTHAL EQUAL AREA PROJECTION
0 500 1000 Miles
0 500 1000 Kilometers

R16

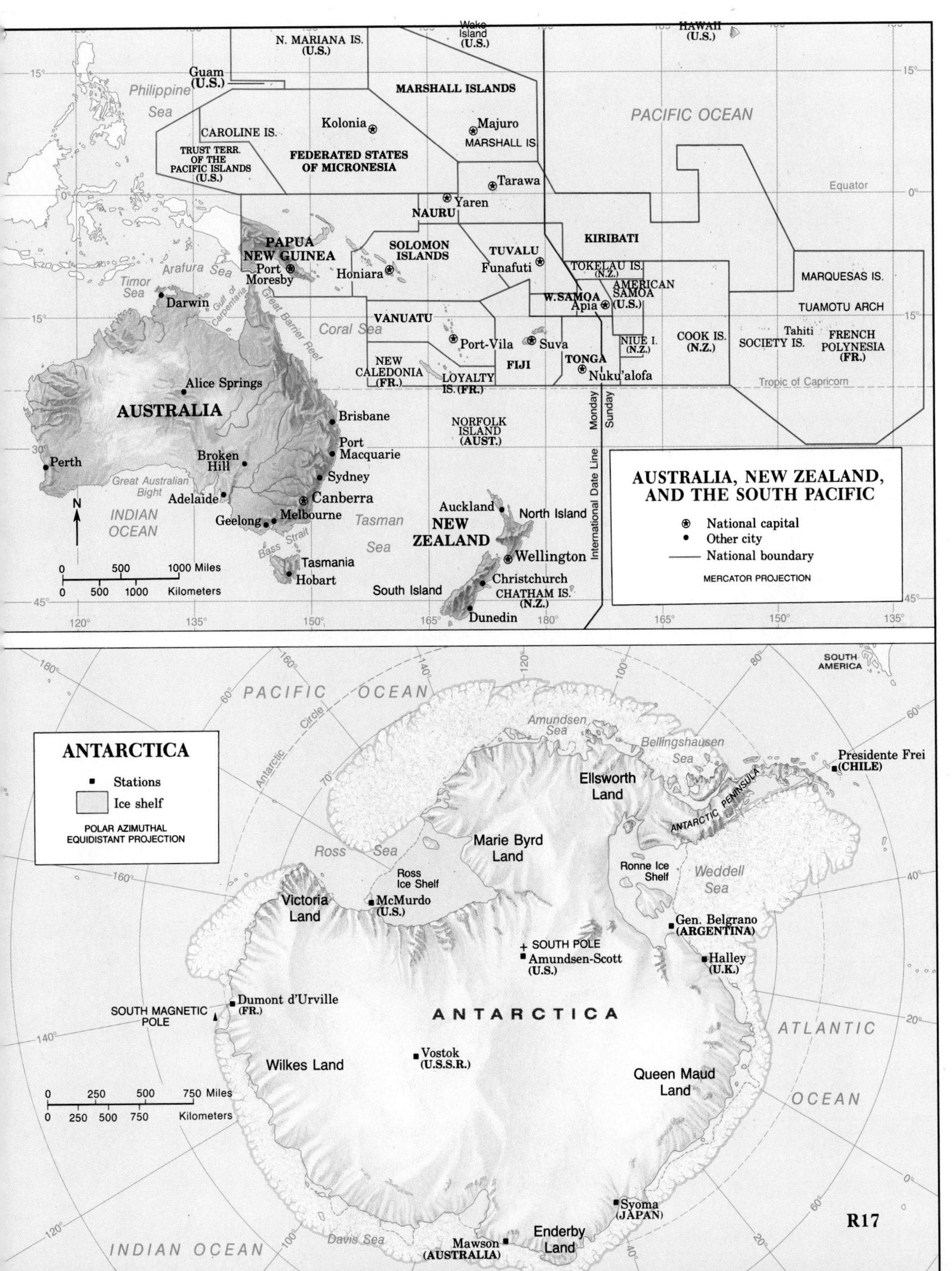
AUSTRALIA, NEW ZEALAND, AND THE SOUTH PACIFIC
National capital
Other city
National boundary
MERCATOR PROJECTION
N. MARIANA IS. (U.S.)
Wake Island (U.S.)
HAWAII (U.S.)
Guam (U.S.)
Philippine Sea
MARSHALL ISLANDS
PACIFIC OCEAN
CAROLINE IS.
Kolonia
Majuro
MARSHALL IS
TRUST TERR. OF THE PACIFIC ISLANDS (U.S.)
FEDERATED STATES OF MICRONESIA
Tarawa
Equator
Yaren
NAURU
KIRIBATI
PAPUA NEW GUINEA
SOLOMON ISLANDS
TUVALU
Port Moresby
Honiara
Funafuti
TOKELAU IS. (N.Z.)
AMERICAN SAMOA (U.S.)
MARQUESAS IS.
Arafura Sea
Timor Sea
W.SAMOA
Apia
TUAMOTU ARCH
Darwin
Gulf of Carpentaria
Great Barrier Reef
VANUATU
Coral Sea
Port-Vila
Suva
NIUE I. (N.Z.)
COOK IS. (N.Z.)
Tahiti
SOCIETY IS.
FRENCH POLYNESIA (FR.)
NEW CALEDONIA (FR.)
FIJI
TONGA
LOYALTY IS. (FR.)
Nuku'alofa
Tropic of Capricorn
Alice Springs
AUSTRALIA
Brisbane
NORFOLK ISLAND (AUST.)
Monday
Sunday
Port Macquarie
Perth
Broken Hill
Sydney
Great Australian Bight
Adelaide
Canberra
Auckland
North Island
International Date Line
INDIAN OCEAN
Geelong
Melbourne
Tasman Sea
NEW ZEALAND
Bass Strait
Wellington
Tasmania
Hobart
Christchurch
CHATHAM IS. (N.Z.)
South Island
Dunedin
0 500 1000 Miles
0 500 1000 Kilometers
ANTARCTICA
Stations
Ice shelf
POLAR AZIMUTHAL EQUIDISTANT PROJECTION
PACIFIC OCEAN
SOUTH AMERICA
Antarctic Circle
Amundsen Sea
Bellingshausen Sea
Presidente Frei (CHILE)
Ellsworth Land
ANTARCTIC PENINSULA
Ross Sea
Marie Byrd Land
Ronne Ice Shelf
Weddell Sea
Ross Ice Shelf
Victoria Land
McMurdo (U.S.)
Gen. Belgrano (ARGENTINA)
SOUTH POLE
Amundsen-Scott (U.S.)
Halley (U.K.)
Dumont d'Urville (FR.)
SOUTH MAGNETIC POLE
ANTARCTICA
ATLANTIC OCEAN
Vostok (U.S.S.R.)
Wilkes Land
Queen Maud Land
0 250 500 750 Miles
0 250 500 750 Kilometers
Syoma (JAPAN)
R17
Enderby Land
Davis Sea
Mawson (AUSTRALIA)
INDIAN OCEAN

1A

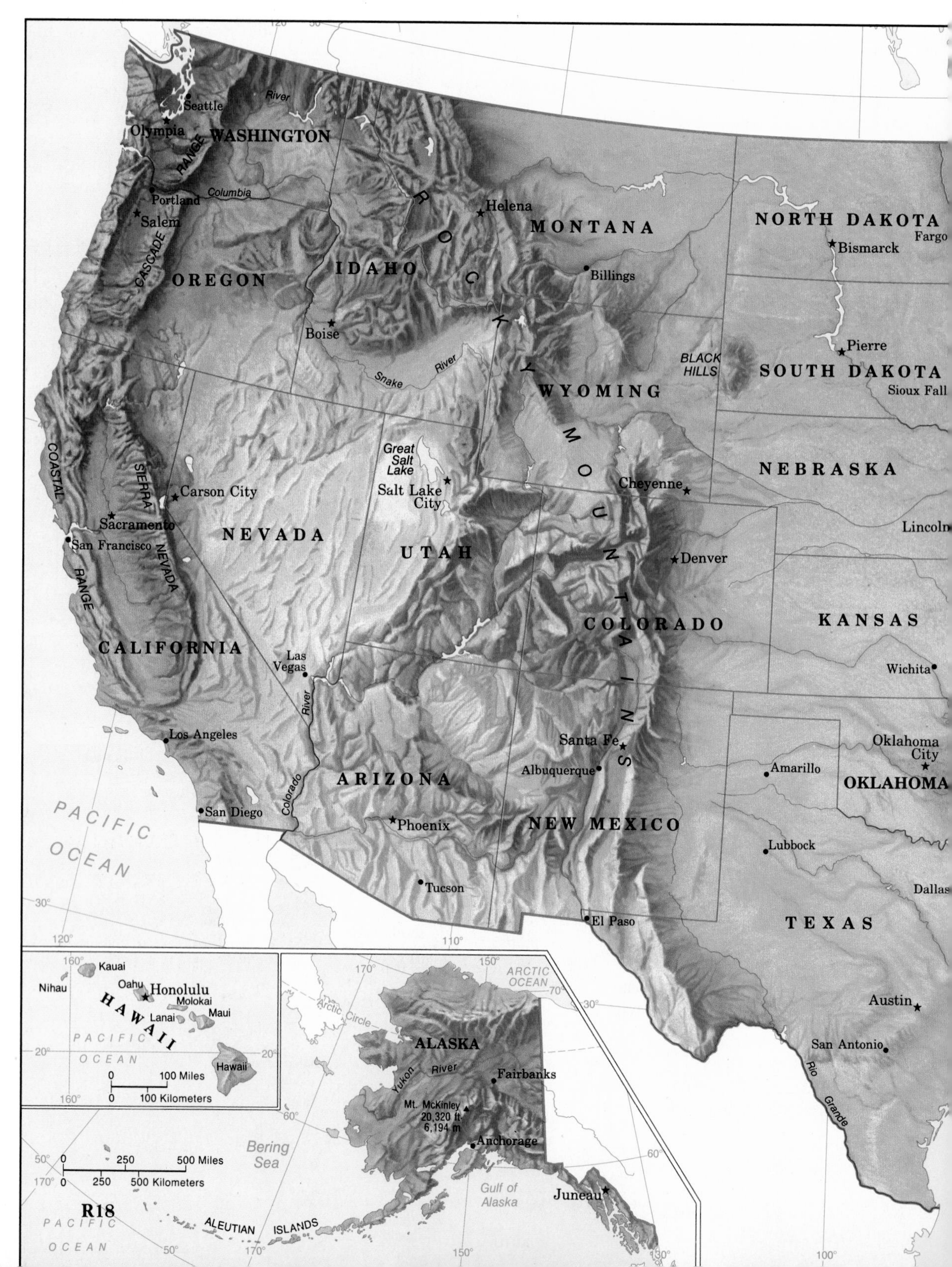

Seattle
River
Olympia
WASHINGTON
RANGE
Portland
Columbia
Salem
CASCADE
OREGON
Helena
MONTANA
ROCKY MOUNTAINS
IDAHO
Billings
NORTH DAKOTA
Fargo
Bismarck
Pierre
SOUTH DAKOTA
Sioux Fall
BLACK HILLS
Boise
Snake River
WYOMING
Great Salt Lake
Salt Lake City
Cheyenne
NEBRASKA
Lincoln
COASTAL RANGE
SIERRA NEVADA
Carson City
Sacramento
San Francisco
NEVADA
UTAH
Denver
COLORADO
KANSAS
Wichita
CALIFORNIA
Las Vegas
River
Colorado
Los Angeles
Santa Fe
Albuquerque
Amarillo
Oklahoma City
OKLAHOMA
ARIZONA
San Diego
Phoenix
NEW MEXICO
Lubbock
PACIFIC OCEAN
Tucson
Dallas
El Paso
TEXAS
Austin
San Antonio
Rio Grande
Kauai
Nihau
Oahu
Honolulu
Molokai
Maui
Lanai
HAWAII
PACIFIC OCEAN
Hawaii
100 Miles
100 Kilometers
ARCTIC OCEAN
Arctic Circle
ALASKA
Yukon River
Fairbanks
Mt. McKinley 20,320 ft 6,194 m
Anchorage
Bering Sea
250
500 Miles
500 Kilometers
Gulf of Alaska
Juneau
R18
ALEUTIAN ISLANDS
PACIFIC OCEAN

THE UNITED STATES
National capital
State capital
Other city
National boundary
State boundary
ALBERS EQUAL AREA PROJECTION
MINNESOTA
WISCONSIN
MICHIGAN
IOWA
ILLINOIS
INDIANA
OHIO
PENNSYLVANIA
NEW YORK
MAINE
VERMONT
NEW HAMPSHIRE
MASSACHUSETTS
RHODE ISLAND
CONNECTICUT
NEW JERSEY
DELAWARE
MARYLAND
WEST VIRGINIA
VIRGINIA
KENTUCKY
MISSOURI
TENNESSEE
NORTH CAROLINA
SOUTH CAROLINA
ARKANSAS
GEORGIA
ALABAMA
MISSISSIPPI
LOUISIANA
FLORIDA
APPALACHIAN MTS.
GREEN MTS.
Duluth
Minneapolis
St. Paul
Milwaukee
Madison
Chicago
Gary
Lansing
Detroit
Des Moines
Omaha
Springfield
Indianapolis
Cincinnati
Columbus
Cleveland
Pittsburgh
Buffalo
Rochester
Albany
Augusta
Montpelier
Concord
Boston
Providence
Hartford
New York
Trenton
Philadelphia
Harrisburg
Wilmington
Dover
Baltimore
Annapolis
Washington
Charleston
Richmond
Norfolk
Frankfort
Louisville
Kansas City
Topeka
St. Louis
Jefferson City
Nashville
Raleigh
Charlotte
Columbia
Charleston
Tulsa
Memphis
Little Rock
Atlanta
Birmingham
Savannah
Montgomery
Jackson
Jacksonville
Tallahassee
Mobile
Baton Rouge
New Orleans
Houston
Orlando
Tampa
Miami
Lake Superior
Lake Michigan
Lake Huron
Lake Ontario
Lake Erie
St. Lawrence River
Hudson River
Mississippi River
Missouri River
Ohio River
Tennessee River
Red River
Chesapeake Bay
ATLANTIC OCEAN
Gulf of Mexico
N
0
250
500 Miles
0
250
500 Kilometers
40°
70°
30°
90°
80°
R19

WASHINGTON
Seattle
Olympia
River
CASCADE RANGE
Columbia
Portland
Salem
OREGON
IDAHO
Boise
Snake River
ROCKY MOUNTAINS
Helena
MONTANA
Billings
NORTH DAKOTA
Bismarck
SOUTH DAKOTA
Pierre
Sioux
BLACK HILLS
WYOMING
Cheyenne
NEBRASKA
Great Salt Lake
Salt Lake City
UTAH
NEVADA
Carson City
COASTAL RANGE
SIERRA NEVADA
Sacramento
San Francisco
CALIFORNIA
Las Vegas
Los Angeles
San Diego
Colorado River
Denver
COLORADO
KANSAS
Wichit
Lin
ARIZONA
Phoenix
Tucson
Santa Fe
Albuquerque
NEW MEXICO
El Paso
Amarillo
Lubbock
OKLAHO
Oklaho
TEXAS
Austin
San Antonio
Rio Grande
PACIFIC OCEAN
30°
120°
110°
Kauai
Nihau
Oahu
Honolulu
Molokai
Lanai
Maui
HAWAII
Hawaii
PACIFIC OCEAN
160°
20°
100 Miles
100 Kilometers
ARCTIC OCEAN
70°
Arctic Circle
ALASKA
Yukon River
Fairbanks
Mt. McKinley 20,320 ft. 6,194 m
Anchorage
Juneau
Bering Sea
Gulf of Alaska
ALEUTIAN ISLANDS
PACIFIC OCEAN
250
500 Miles
250
500 Kilometers
50°
60°
170°
150°
130°
R20
*To understand the relative locations of Alaska and Hawaii as well as the vast distances separating them from the rest of the United States, see the map on page R4.

UNITED STATES*
Elevation
Feet
Meters
13,120
4,000
6,560
2,000
1,640
500
656
200
0
0
Below sea level
Below sea level
National capital
State capital
Other city
National boundary
State boundary
ALBERS EQUAL AREA PROJECTION
MINNESOTA
WISCONSIN
MICHIGAN
IOWA
ILLINOIS
INDIANA
OHIO
MISSOURI
KENTUCKY
TENNESSEE
ARKANSAS
MISSISSIPPI
ALABAMA
GEORGIA
LOUISIANA
FLORIDA
SOUTH CAROLINA
NORTH CAROLINA
VIRGINIA
WEST VIRGINIA
PENNSYLVANIA
NEW YORK
NEW JERSEY
DELAWARE
MARYLAND
CONNECTICUT
RHODE ISLAND
MASSACHUSETTS
VERMONT
NEW HAMPSHIRE
MAINE
APPALACHIAN MTS.
GREEN MTS.
Lake Superior
Lake Michigan
Lake Huron
Lake Erie
Lake Ontario
St. Lawrence River
Hudson River
Mississippi River
Missouri River
Ohio River
Tennessee River
Red River
Chesapeake Bay
ATLANTIC OCEAN
Gulf of Mexico
Duluth
Minneapolis
St. Paul
Milwaukee
Madison
Lansing
Detroit
Chicago
Gary
Des Moines
Omaha
Kansas City
Topeka
Jefferson City
St. Louis
Springfield
Indianapolis
Cincinnati
Louisville
Frankfort
Columbus
Cleveland
Pittsburgh
Charleston
Nashville
Memphis
Tulsa
Little Rock
Birmingham
Atlanta
Jackson
Montgomery
Mobile
Baton Rouge
New Orleans
Houston
Tallahassee
Jacksonville
Savannah
Charleston
Columbia
Charlotte
Raleigh
Richmond
Norfolk
Washington
Annapolis
Baltimore
Dover
Wilmington
Philadelphia
Harrisburg
Trenton
New York
Buffalo
Rochester
Albany
Hartford
Providence
Boston
Concord
Montpelier
Augusta
Orlando
Tampa
Miami
N
0
250
500 Miles
0
250
500 Kilometers
40°
70°
30°
90°
80°

R21

PHONETIC RESPELLING AND PRONUNCIATION GUIDE

Many of the key terms in this textbook have been respelled to help you pronounce them. The following Phonetic Respelling and Pronunciation Guide offers the simplest form of usage and is adapted from *Webster's Ninth New Collegiate Dictionary, Webster's New Geographical Dictionary,* and *Webster's New Biographical Dictionary.* The letter combinations used in the respellings are explained below.

MARK	AS IN	RESPELLING	EXAMPLE
a	alphabet	a	*AL • fuh • bet
ā	Asia	ay	AY • zhuh
ä	cart, top	ah	KAHRT, TAHP
e	let, ten	e	LET, TEN
ē	even, leaf	ee	EE • vuhn, LEEF
i	it, tip, British	i	IT, TIP, BRIT • ish
ī	site, buy, Ohio	y	SYT, BY, oh • HY • oh
	iris	eye	EYE • ris
k	card	k	KARD
ō	over, rainbow	oh	oh • vuhr, RAYN • boh
u̇	book, wood	ooh	BOOHK, WOOHD
ȯ	all, orchid	aw	AWL, AWR • kid
ȯi	foil, coin	oy	FOYL, KOYN
au̇	out	ow	OWT
ə	cup, butter	uh	KUHP, BUHT • uhr
ü	rule, food	oo	ROOL, FOOD
yü	few	yoo	FYOO
zh	vision	zh	VIZH • uhn

*A syllable printed in small capital letters receives heavier emphasis than the other syllables in a word.

PINYIN

Most of the names of Chinese people and Chinese geographical names in this textbook use the Roman alphabet and pronunciation system introduced by the Chinese in the 1950s and in general use since the 1970s. This system, called Pinyin, most accurately reflects the sounds of the Chinese language. The United States government and many newspapers, magazines, and atlases accept and use Pinyin. Both the maps and narrative in this textbook consistently use Pinyin. Some exceptions occur where the names are so well known by their older spellings—using the Wade-Giles system—that the use of Pinyin would confuse rather than help you. Exceptions include Chiang Kai-shek, Kuomintang, Sun Yat-sen, Tibet, Hong Kong, Mongolia, and the word "China" itself.

R22

G•L•O•S•S•A•R•Y

This GLOSSARY contains many of the terms you need to understand as you study world history. After each term there is a brief definition or explanation of the meaning of the term as it is used in world history. The page number in parentheses after each definition refers to the page on which the term is boldfaced in the textbook. A phonetic respelling is provided to help you pronounce many of the terms. (Please refer to the Phonetic Respelling and Pronunciation Guide on page R22.)

The brief definitions in this GLOSSARY do not always provide all the information that you may need to know about these terms. You may find it useful to refer to the page listed in parentheses to read more about the terms.

A

abbot: elected head of a monastery ***(p. 234)***

absolute monarchy: system of government in which the ruler determines policy without consulting either the people or their representatives ***(p. 355)***

abstract expressionism: painting style characterized by forms, colors, and shapes rather than recognizable objects ***(p. 884)***

acropolis: hill or mountain in Greece, together with temples and other public buildings on it ***(p. 106)***

acupuncture: Chinese medicinal practice that involves insertion of needles into designated parts of the body to release energy for healing ***(p. 87)***

adobe: sun-dried brick used to build houses ***(p. 305)***

agora: public meeting place in Greece where all citizens could gather ***(p. 106)***

agriculture: raising crops and livestock for food ***(p. 8)***

almanac: book that predicts the weather and the prospects for growing crops ***(p. 344)***

anarchist: person who believes in the abolition of all governments by force ***(p. 562)***

anarchy: absence of any government at all ***(p. 168)***

animism: ancient religion characterized by belief that spirits inhabited all things ***(p. 52)***

anthropologist: (an • thruh • PAHL • uh • jist) scientist who studies the skeletal remains of early humanlike creatures and people to determine how they looked, how long they lived, and other physical characteristics ***(p. 3)***

antibiotic: substance that stops the growth of bacteria ***(p. 881)***

apartheid: (uh • PART • hyt) official policy of racial separation followed by the South African government after 1948 ***(p. 812)***

appeasement: policy of attempting to preserve peace by yielding to the demands of the aggressor ***(p. 718)***

apprentice: person who went through stages of training and was a candidate for membership in a craft guild ***(p. 257)***

aqueduct: bridgelike structure that carried water from the mountains to the city ***(p. 156)***

arbitration: negotiation for the settlement of a dispute by a party agreed upon by all sides ***(p. 620)***

arch: curved structure over an opening ***(p. 30)***

archaeologist: (ahr • kee • AHL • uh • jist) scientist who excavates ancient settlements and studies artifacts ***(p. 3)***

archon: elected ruler in the early government of Athens ***(p. 114)***

aristocracy: city-state in ancient Greece governed by nobles; today, means a privileged social class ***(p. 110)***

armistice: agreement to stop fighting until a treaty can be drawn up ***(p. 655)***

artifact: human-made material object, for example, a tool, a weapon, or a coin ***(p. 3)***

artisan: skilled craftworker ***(p. 10)***

assimilation: situation in which people of a colony abandoned their local culture and adopted all aspects of another culture ***(p. 609)***

astrolabe: instrument used to calculate latitude ***(p. 356)***

atrocity: brutal crime of war ***(p. 651)***

authoritarian socialism: economic and political system in which the government owns almost all the means of production; communism ***(p. 511)***

autocracy: form of government in which the ruler holds total power ***(p. 78)***

autocrat: one who holds absolute power ***(p. 587)***

B

balance of power: principle of maintaining equilibrium in international politics ***(p. 382)***

barter: exchange of one good or service for another good or service ***(p. 39)***

barter economy: economic system in which goods are exchanged for goods without the use of money ***(p. 255)***

R23

belligerent: warring nation ***(p. 643)***
Bessemer process: way to make steel involving forcing air through molten iron to burn out impurities ***(p. 493)***
biological science: science that deals with living organisms ***(p. 521)***
blitzkrieg: German word for "lightning war" ***(p. 720)***
bourgeoisie: (boorzh • wah • ZEE) city-dwelling middle class in France ***(pp. 425, 510)***
boyar: noble in Kievan society ***(p. 196)***
Brahman: priest in the Vedic religion ***(p. 55)***
broadside: single printed sheet often making fun of a favorite object of humor, such as monks ***(p. 344)***
buffer state: small country located between two hostile powers that often lessens the possibility of conflict between them ***(p. 617)***
burgesses: merchants and professional people from towns and cities in early England ***(p. 397)***
Bushido: (BOOH • shee • doh) samurai code that stressed bravery, loyalty, and honor ***(p. 286)***
business cycle: pattern consisting of alternating periods of prosperity and decline ***(p. 501)***

C

cabinet: leaders of the House of Commons who advised the English monarch ***(p. 407)***
caliph: Islamic word meaning "successor to the prophet" ***(p. 208)***
caliphate: one of three divisions of the Muslim Empire ***(p. 210)***
calligraphy: (kuh • LIG • ruh • fee) artful form of writing originated by the Chinese ***(p. 75)***
campesino: name given to a Central American peasant ***(p. 839)***
canon law: church code of law ***(p. 236)***
capital: wealth earned, saved, or invested in order to produce profits ***(p. 256)***
capitalism: economic system in which private individuals use money that is earned, saved, or invested to produce profits ***(p. 499)***
caravan: group of people traveling over long distances together for safety ***(p. 24)***
cartel: combination of corporations that control an entire industry ***(p. 501)***
caste system: Indian social organization composed of four classes ***(p. 58)***
cavalry: military unit of soldiers on horses ***(p. 34)***
censor: person who registered citizens according to their wealth to determine how much they should pay in taxes ***(p. 146)***
checks and balances: system that prevents any one part of a government from becoming too powerful ***(p. 146)***
chinampa: floating artificial island farmed by Aztecs ***(p. 310)***
chivalry: code of conduct for knights ***(p. 231)***
chora: land outside walls of Greek city-states ***(p. 105)***
citadel: strong central fortress ***(p. 52)***
city-state: form of government developed by the Sumerians; it consisted of a town or city and the surrounding land it controlled ***(p. 29)***
civil service: system that administers the government on a day-to-day basis whose members are usually appointed on the basis of competitive examinations ***(p. 79)***
civilization: highly organized society with complex institutions and attitudes that link a large number of people together ***(p. 3)***
coalition: political groups organized in support of a common cause ***(p. 562)***
cold war: hostility between the Communist and Western nations waged by political and economic means rather than with weapons ***(p. 751)***
collaborator: person willing to assist his or her country's enemies ***(p. 721)***
collective bargaining: process of negotiation between union members and management ***(p. 507)***
collective farm: land pooled into a large farm where people can work together as a group ***(p. 685)***
collegia: (kuh • LEE • jee • uh) workers' trade associations in ancient Rome ***(p. 167)***
colonus: Roman tenant farmer who replaced slaves on large estates ***(p. 157)***
colony: area in which a foreign nation gained total control over another region and its local population ***(p. 602)***
comedy: Greek play mocking ideas and people ***(p. 132)***
command economy: economic system in which government planners make all economic decisions ***(pp. 685, 762)***
commercial capitalism: early phase of capitalism involving merchants who bought, sold, and exchanged goods ***(p. 499)***
Commercial Revolution: changes and developments in the European economy from about 1500 to about 1750 ***(p. 357)***
common law: law based on judges' decisions rather than on a code of statutes ***(p. 242)***
communism: authoritarian socialism ***(p. 511)***
compass: instrument used for navigational purposes showing direction ***(p. 356)***
conceptual art: art trend that claims that creative thought is more important than either the process or the product created ***(p. 885)***

R24

concession: grant of economic rights and privileges in a given area ***(p. 602)***
condominium: situation occurring when two nations rule a third nation as partners ***(p. 602)***
conscription: draft adopted in France that made men from 18 to 45 years of age liable for military service ***(p. 435)***
conservative: person who does not want to change existing conditions ***(p. 433)***
constitution: document outlining the fundamental laws and principles that govern a nation ***(p. 402)***
consul: chief executive in early Rome who ran the government and served as an army commander ***(p. 145)***
consulate: diplomatic office headed by a consul ***(p. 468)***
containment: policy aimed at restricting the spread of communism ***(p. 758)***
contraband: war materials supplied to a belligerent nation by a neutral nation ***(p. 651)***
corporate state: nation in which the major economic activities are organized into syndicates that resemble corporations ***(p. 680)***
corporation: business organization involving the sale of stock to investors but limiting the shareholders' financial responsibility to the amount invested ***(p. 501)***
Counter-Reformation: major effort in the 1530s to create a new, more spiritual outlook in the Catholic church ***(p. 337)***
counterrevolution: fight against the regular French army and the Revolution in the western part of France ***(p. 435)***
coup d'état: (kood • ay • TAH) seizure of power by force ***(p. 439)***
covenant: solemn agreement or promise ***(p. 400)***
covert: term describing undercover military and financial aid to a nation ***(p. 839)***
craft guild: organization of skilled workers engaged in one particular craft ***(p. 257)***
creole: native-born white person who lived in a Latin American colony ***(p. 563)***
crop rotation: alternating crops of different kinds to preserve soil fertility ***(p. 490)***
crucifixion: common Roman method of execution in which the accused was placed on a cross and left to die a slow death from suffocation ***(p. 151)***
Crusade: expedition to regain the Holy Land ***(p. 250)***
cubism: art style that emphasized forms, shapes, and designs ***(p. 668)***
cultural diffusion: spread of culture from one area of the world to another ***(p. 11)***
culture: what humans acquire by living together—language, knowledge, skills, art, literature, and life styles ***(p. 4)***
cuneiform: (kyoo • NEE • uh • fawrm) Sumerian method of writing using a stylus to make combinations of wedge shapes ***(p. 29)***
czar: Russian word for "caesar" or emperor ***(p. 200)***

D

daimyo: (DY • mee • oh) samurai leader who gained the loyalty of the lesser samurai ***(p. 286)***
democracy: government in which all citizens take part and limit the power of rulers ***(p. 110)***
democratic socialism: political system in which the government takes over the means of production peacefully; people retain basic human rights and partial control over economic planning ***(p. 511)***
department: administrative district of France ***(p. 430)***
depression: lowest point of a business cycle ***(p. 501)***
desertification: spread of the desert ***(p. 815)***
détente: (day • TAHNT) era of improved Soviet-American relations ***(p. 855)***
developed nation: nation with a high degree of economic sophistication ***(p. 757)***
developing nation: nation with limited resources and rapid population growth ***(p. 757)***
dharma: Hindu belief in fulfillment of moral duty so that the soul can progress toward deliverance from punishment in the next life ***(p. 58)***
dictator: leader with absolute power ***(p. 146)***
direct democracy: form of government in which all citizens participate directly in making decisions rather than through elected representatives ***(p. 115)***
direct rule: situation that occurs when the imperialist power controls all levels of government and appoints its own officials to govern ***(p. 609)***
dissident: person dissatisfied with the government ***(pp. 842, 855)***
divine right of kings: belief that God ordained certain individuals to govern ***(p. 381)***
division of labor: characteristic of early civilization or later manufacturing process in which different people perform different tasks ***(pp. 9, 499)***
domain: manor land the lord kept for himself; consisted of about one-third of the manor ***(p. 230)***
domestic system: method of production in which work is done in homes rather than in a shop or factory ***(pp. 255, 491)***

R25

domesticate: to tame animals, such as the goat ***(p. 8)***
domino theory: belief that if one nation in a region falls to communism, other nations in the region will also fall to communism ***(p. 796)***
dower: groom's marriage gift to his bride ***(p. 211)***
dowry: money or goods a wife brings to a marriage ***(p. 188)***
drama: play containing action or dialogue and usually involving conflict and emotion ***(p. 131)***
dynasty: family of rulers whose right to rule is hereditary ***(p. 20)***

E

economic boom: sudden increase in prosperity ***(p. 671)***
economic nationalism: policy nations use to try to improve their own economic well-being through protective tariffs and similar restrictions without consideration for other countries ***(p. 671)***
economic sanction: refusal to trade with an offending nation ***(p. 661)***
emigration: movement of people to other lands ***(p. 525)***
émigré: noble who fled France during the Revolution ***(p. 430)***
empire: form of government that unites different territories and peoples under one ruler ***(p. 22)***
enclosure movement: practice of fencing or enclosing common lands into individual holdings ***(p. 490)***
enlightened despotism: system of government in which absolute monarchs ruled according to the principles of the Enlightenment ***(p. 424)***
Enlightenment: belief that people could apply the scientific method and use reason to logically explain human nature ***(p. 421)***
entente: (ahn • TAHNT) friendly understanding or agreement between nations ***(p. 641)***
ephor: one of five rulers or overseers elected by the Assembly in Sparta ***(p. 112)***
epic: long poem describing heroes and great events ***(pp. 58, 106)***
Epic Age: period in the history of India from 1000 B.C. to 500 B.C. ***(p. 57)***
equites: (EK • wuh • teez) class of Roman business people who had great wealth but little political power ***(p. 150)***
ethical monotheism: Jewish form of monotheism that emphasizes proper conduct ***(p. 45)***
evolution: belief that plants and animals developed from common ancestors long ago ***(p. 521)***
excommunication: official act that bars a person from church membership and from taking part in any church ceremonies ***(p. 191)***
executive branch: branch of government that enforces the laws ***(p. 417)***
export: good or service that is sold to another country ***(p. 110)***
extraterritoriality: exemption of foreigners from the laws of the nation where they live or do business ***(p. 461)***

F

factors of production: basic resources necessary for industrialization ***(p. 490)***
factory system: production of goods through use of machines and many workers ***(p. 491)***
fascism: governmental doctrine that relies on dictatorial rule and a totalitarian regime, in which rigid control is maintained by the government through force and censorship ***(p. 679)***
favorable balance of trade: situation that exists when a country sells more goods than it buys from a foreign country ***(p. 359)***
federal system of government: system of government with powers divided between a central, or federal, government and individual states ***(p. 416)***
feudalism: political and military system of local government based on the granting of land in return for loyalty, military assistance, and services ***(p. 228)***
fief: grant of land given by a feudal lord to a vassal ***(p. 228)***
Fourteen Points: President Woodrow Wilson's plan based on the Allies' aims to end World War I ***(p. 654)***
free enterprise: Adam Smith's economic system based on supply, demand, and competition ***(p. 502)***
free trade: practice based on the belief that government should not restrict or interfere in international trade ***(p. 460)***
fresco: wall painting made on wet plaster ***(p. 104)***
functionalism: architectural principle that a building's design should reflect its specific use rather than reflect popular styles ***(p. 670)***

G

galley: type of early European trade ship ***(p. 356)***
general strike: bargaining method in which workers in various industries refuse to work until their demands are met ***(p. 675)***
genetics: study of the ways in which inborn characteristics of plants and animals are inherited by their descendants ***(p. 522)***

R26

gentry: class of Englishmen who owned land and had social position ***(p. 397)***

geocentric theory: theory that earth is at the center of the universe ***(p. 348)***

geopolitical region: area that shares similar political and geographic features ***(p. 836)***

glacier: large, slowly moving mass of snow and ice ***(p. 5)***

glasnost: Soviet policy that loosened censorship and eased the repression of the Brezhnev years ***(p. 866)***

Great Depression: worldwide depression beginning in 1929 ***(p. 672)***

gross national product (GNP): dollar value of all new, finished products produced in a nation in one year ***(p. 826)***

guerrilla warfare: military technique relying on raids by small bands of soldiers ***(p. 374)***

H

habeas corpus: legal right protecting individuals against illegal arrest and imprisonment ***(p. 405)***

hacienda: (hahs • ee • EN • duh) large, self-sufficient farming estate ***(p. 563)***

hegira: (hih • JY • ruh) flight of Muhammad and his followers to Medina in 622; marks the first year of the Muslim calendar ***(p. 206)***

heliocentric theory: theory that the sun is at the center of the universe ***(p. 348)***

Hellenistic culture: culture founded on Greek ideas blended with features from other cultures of the Mediterranean region ***(p. 125)***

helot: (HEL • uht) agricultural worker of Peloponnesus forced to work for the Spartans after the area was conquered ***(p. 111)***

heresy: opinion that conflicts with church doctrine ***(p. 191)***

hieroglyphics: (hy • uhr • GLIF • iks) method of Egyptian writing that uses pictures or symbols to indicate words or sounds ***(p. 19)***

history: record of events since people first developed writing about 5,000 years ago ***(p. 3)***

Holocaust: systematic destruction of European Jews by the Nazis ***(p. 730)***

home rule: self-government ***(p. 547)***

hubris: (HYOO • bruhs) arrogance that doomed character in a Greek play to a tragic fate ***(p. 132)***

humanist: person who stressed dignity of human nature and had appreciation for the arts and for public life ***(p. 326)***

I

Ice Age: time when the Earth had extremely cold weather ***(p. 5)***

icon: Byzantine picture of Jesus, the Virgin Mary, or the saints ***(p. 190)***

iconoclast: Byzantine who believed that the presence of icons constituted idol worship ***(p. 191)***

iconoclastic controversy: argument between the supporters and the opponents of icons ***(p. 191)***

imam: Shiite leader believed to be a direct descendant of Muhammad ***(p. 210)***

imperialism: domination of a powerful nation over the political, economic, and cultural affairs of another nation or region ***(p. 599)***

import: good or service that is bought from another country ***(p. 110)***

import substitution: economic policy in which officials examine the list of goods that a country imports to find those items that could be produced inside the country ***(p. 833)***

impressionist: French artist who painted vivid impressions of people and places as they might appear in a brief glance ***(p. 538)***

indemnity: money for war damages ***(pp. 148, 447)***

indirect rule: British system in which a governor and a council of advisers made colonial laws, but local rulers exerted some authority ***(p. 609)***

indulgence: pardon given in return for repentance or donations to the church ***(p. 333)***

industrial capitalism: phase of the Industrial Revolution in which capitalists were directly involved in producing and manufacturing goods ***(p. 499)***

Industrial Revolution: introduction of industrial technology that changed the way goods were produced ***(p. 489)***

infantry: soldiers trained and equipped to fight on foot ***(p. 133)***

inflation: rise in prices caused by a decrease in the value of the exchange medium ***(pp. 166, 345)***

Inquisition: the search for heretics begun during the mid-1200s ***(p. 237)***

intendant: local administrator of a French province ***(p. 378)***

interdict: church's punishment of an entire region; it involved withholding sacraments ***(p. 236)***

international style: style of architecture that was functional, plain, and severe, using uninterrupted expanses of steel and glass ***(p. 670)***

iron-curtain country: Soviet satellite nation ***(p. 758)***

irrigation: method of supplying water for crops based on using ditches and canals ***(p. 10)***

R27

isolationist: person who believed that Europe's wars were no affair of the United States ***(p. 725)***

J

joint-stock company: business organization that raised money by selling stock, or shares, in the company to investors ***(p. 358)***
journeyman: skilled artisan who worked for a master for wages ***(p. 258)***
judicial branch: branch of government that interprets and applies the laws ***(p. 417)***
jungle: thick growth of plants found on the forest floor in a tropical rain forest ***(p. 294)***
junk: large Chinese ship first built during the Ming period ***(p. 454)***

K

kaiser: (KY • zuhr) title of the German emperor ***(p. 582)***
karma: Hindu belief that the present condition of a person's life reflects what a person did during a previous life ***(p. 58)***
kibbutz: collective farm in Israel ***(p. 818)***
kingdom: term for *monarchy,* an early form of government headed by a king or queen ***(p. 20)***

L

laissez-faire: (le • say-FAYR) belief that government should leave business alone ***(p. 504)***
latifundia: (lat • uh • FUHN • dee • uh) large Roman estates ***(p. 150)***
latitude: distance north or south of the equator ***(p. 356)***
legion: most important military unit of the Roman army; consisted of 4,500 to 6,000 soldiers ***(p. 146)***
legislative branch: branch of government that makes the laws ***(p. 417)***
legitimacy: policy stating that all former ruling families should be restored to their thrones ***(p. 445)***
liberalism: movement that extended the principles of the American and French revolutions; stressed individual rights and the rule of law rather than rule of a monarch ***(pp. 448, 543)***
limited constitutional monarchy: government led by a monarch whose powers were limited by a constitution ***(p. 408)***
linguist: scholar who studies languages ***(p. 295)***
lobbying: policy of trying to get legislators to vote for or against a measure ***(p. 770)***
loess: (LES) extraordinarily fertile soil ***(p. 71)***

M

Magna Carta: English document intended to protect the liberties of nobles ***(p. 240)***
mandate: area to be administered by the government of an advanced nation ***(p. 661)***
Mandate of Heaven: orders ancient Chinese rulers were believed to have received through communication with the spirits ***(p. 73)***
manor: economic unit of the Middle Ages; an estate that included a village ***(p. 229)***
market economy: an economy in which land, labor, and capital are controlled by individuals ***(pp. 256, 762)***
market speculation: risky investment in the stock market in the hope of quick, high profits ***(p. 672)***
martyr: person put to death because he or she refused to renounce certain beliefs ***(p. 164)***
mass production: system of manufacturing large numbers of items that are exactly alike ***(p. 500)***
matrilineal: (ma • truh • LIN • ee • uhl) describes a society in which people trace their ancestry through their mothers rather than through their fathers ***(p. 296)***
mechanization: use of automatic machinery to increase production ***(p. 491)***
medieval: term that describes the period known as the Middle Ages ***(p. 223)***
mercantilism: economic theory stating that there is a fixed amount of wealth in the world and that in order to receive a larger share, one country has to take some wealth away from another country ***(p. 358)***
mercenary: professional soldier paid to serve in a foreign army ***(p. 35)***
merchant guild: organization of merchants ***(p. 257)***
mestizo: person of American Indian and white background ***(p. 563)***
metic: alien or person who was not an Athenian ***(p. 114)***
metropolitan: chief bishop of the Kievan church ***(p. 198)***
Middle Ages: medieval period between ancient times and the modern period ***(p. 223)***
Middle Passage: second stage of the triangular trade system ***(p. 365)***
migrate: to move from place to place ***(p. 5)***
militarism: glorification of armed strength ***(p. 640)***
millet: community of religious minorities within the Ottoman Empire ***(p. 214)***
miniaturization: process of making electronic equipment smaller ***(p. 878)***

R28

miracle play: mystery play; a biblical drama performed in marketplaces ***(p. 260)***
mixed economy: economy characterized by the private ownership of some industries and government ownership of others ***(p. 788)***
mobilize: to organize a nation's resources for combat ***(p. 640)***
moderate: a person who had no extreme views and sided with conservatives or radicals depending on the situation ***(p. 433)***
monarchy: term for *kingdom,* an early form of government headed by a king or queen ***(p. 20)***
monasticism: system of monasteries and convents in which Christians withdrew from the world to lead a life of prayer, fasting, and self-denial ***(p. 234)***
money economy: economic system based on the use of money rather than on barter ***(p. 39)***
monism: Hindu belief that God and human beings are one ***(p. 58)***
monopoly: control of the total production or sale of a good or service by a single firm ***(p. 501)***
monotheism: (MAHN • uh • thee • iz • uhm) belief in one god ***(p. 22)***
monsoon: seasonal wind named for the direction in which it blows or the season in which it occurs ***(p. 51)***
mosaic: picture or design formed by inlaid pieces of stone, glass, or enamel ***(p. 193)***
mosque: Muslim temple ***(p. 207)***
mulatto: person of black and white ancestry ***(p. 563)***
mullah: person learned in Islamic faith and law ***(p. 207)***
multinational corporation: foreign-owned business in a host country ***(p. 833)***
mummification: Egyptian preservation process that involved treating a corpse with various substances ***(p. 27)***
myth: traditional story about the deeds and misdeeds of gods, goddesses, and heroes ***(p. 108)***

N

nationalism: love of one's country rather than love of a native region ***(p. 441)***
nationalize: to put industry under government control or ownership ***(p. 676)***
natural rights: rights to life, liberty, and property ***(p. 405)***
naturalist: person who writes of the ugly and sordid in life, carefully screening emotion and opinion from his or her writings ***(p. 538)***
Neolithic Revolution: shift from food hunting to food production in prehistoric times ***(p. 8)***
95 theses: Luther's protests against indulgences, which he posted on the church door at Wittenberg ***(p. 334)***
nirvana: Buddhist belief of attaining perfect peace by freeing the soul from the endless cycle of reincarnation ***(p. 60)***
nomad: wanderer who travels from place to place in search of food ***(p. 8)***
non-alignment: nation's policy of refusing to ally with either the United States or the Soviet Union ***(p. 786)***

O

oasis: place in the desert where there is irrigation or an underground spring ***(p. 17)***
op art: art style characterized by the use of optical effects ***(p. 884)***
oracle bones: bones used by Chinese priests, who wrote questions on the shoulder bones of cattle or the bottom of tortoise shells and then interpreted answers to the questions from patterns or cracks that developed when the bones were heated ***(p. 75)***
oral tradition: passing of poems, songs, and stories by word of mouth from one generation to another ***(p. 295)***
orator: public speaker ***(p. 134)***
Ostpolitik: German chancellor Brandt's efforts to create better relations between East and West ***(p. 860)***

P

papyrus: reed plant the Egyptians used to make a smooth material to write on ***(p. 19)***
partnership: business owned and controlled by two or more people ***(p. 500)***
passive resistance: civil disobedience; peaceful refusal of citizens to cooperate with their government in order to win concessions from it ***(p. 694)***
pasteurization: process of heating liquids to kill bacteria and prevent fermentation ***(p. 523)***
paterfamilias: (pat • uhr • fuh • MIL • ee • uhs) father of a Roman family; had absolute authority ***(p. 147)***
paternalism: system of governing colonies in much the same way as parents guide their children ***(p. 609)***
patriarch: bishop of administrative centers for the church in the last years of the Roman Empire ***(p. 166)***

R29

patrician: citizen in the ancient Roman aristocracy ***(p. 146)***

patriotism: feeling of loyalty to a country ***(p. 265)***

Pax Romana: period of Roman peace from 27 B.C. to A.D. 180: from the beginning of Augustus' reign until the death of Marcus Aurelius ***(p. 155)***

pedagogue: male slave who taught a young boy manners and went everywhere with him ***(p. 116)***

peninsular: white person who was born in Spain or Portugal but who lived in Latin America ***(p. 563)***

perestroika: Soviet restructuring policy designed to completely overhaul the Soviet political and economic systems ***(p. 866)***

perspective: art technique that involves making distant objects smaller than those in the foreground and arranging them to create the illusion of depth on a flat surface ***(p. 329)***

phalanx: (FAY • langks) military formation composed of 16 rows of soldiers equipped with lances ***(p. 133)***

pharaoh: Egyptian ruler's title ***(p. 20)***

philology: history of words ***(p. 457)***

philosophes: (fee • luh • ZAWFS) thinkers or philosophers of the Enlightenment ***(p. 422)***

philosophy: study of the most fundamental questions of reality and human existence ***(p. 128)***

physical science: science that deals with the inanimate, or nonliving, aspects of nature ***(p. 518)***

planned economy: governmental regulation and direction of natural resources to meet a definite goal ***(p. 674)***

plebeian: (pli • BEE • yuhn) citizen in Rome not of the aristocratic class ***(p. 146)***

plebiscite: (PLEB • uh • syt) procedure used by Napoleon to submit the constitution of his new government to the people for a vote ***(p. 439)***

pogrom: (POH • gruhm) massacre of Jews in Russia ***(p. 589)***

polis: term that in Greece originally meant a fort, but later included the surrounding city ***(p. 105)***

polygamy: marriage to more than one wife ***(p. 64)***

polytheism: (PAHL • i • thee • iz • uhm) belief in many gods ***(p. 22)***

pop art: style used by artists who painted popular objects such as soup cans, pictures from comic books, or flags ***(p. 884)***

pope: title assumed by the patriarch of Rome and head of the Catholic Church; from the Latin word meaning "father" ***(p. 166)***

popular government: idea that people can and should rule themselves and not be ruled by others ***(p. 110)***

popular sovereignty: governmental principle based on just laws and on a government created by and subject to the will of the people ***(p. 423)***

praetor: (PREET • uhr) military commander and judge in ancient Rome ***(p. 146)***

predestination: belief that in the beginning of time God decided who would be saved and who would be damned ***(p. 336)***

prehistory: long period of time before people kept written records ***(p. 3)***

prime minister: chief minister of the cabinet, leader of the government ***(p. 408)***

primogeniture: (pri • moh • JEN • uh • chuhr) French law under which only the eldest son could inherit his father's property ***(pp. 228, 425)***

process art: art style focusing on the arrangement of "environments," composed of objects and people, that emphasize the creation of art as being more important than the actual art ***(p. 885)***

Prohibition: law forbidding the manufacture, sale, and transportation of alcoholic beverages ***(p. 671)***

proletariat: (proh • luh • TAYR • ee • uht) working class ***(p. 510)***

propaganda: ideas, facts, or rumors spread deliberately to further one's cause or to damage an opposing cause ***(p. 648)***

prophet: person who speaks of divinely inspired revelations ***(p. 43)***

protectorate: colony in which the native ruler keeps his title, but officials of the foreign power actually control the region ***(p. 602)***

psychoanalysis: process of revealing and analyzing the unconscious ***(p. 532)***

purge: act of forcing people to leave an organization or an area ***(p. 686)***

Q

quantum theory: Planck's theory that energy can only be released in definite "packages" ***(p. 520)***

queue: (KYOO) single braid that characterized hair style for Chinese men during the Qing dynasty ***(p. 455)***

quipu: (KEE • poo) type of knotted string the Incas used to assist the memory ***(p. 311)***

R

rabbi: Jewish scholar learned in scriptures and in commentaries on religious law ***(p. 162)***

radical: person who wants far-reaching changes ***(p. 433)***

R30

radioactivity: process in which atoms of uranium and radium constantly disintegrate and release energy on their own ***(p. 520)***

radiocarbon dating: technique that allows the age of organic matter to be identified by measuring its rate of decay ***(p. 4)***

rajah: prince who ruled an Aryan city-state ***(p. 57)***

rationalism: characteristic of the Enlightenment; rose from the belief that truth can be arrived at solely by reason ***(p. 421)***

reaction: desire to return to the conditions of an earlier period ***(p.447)***

reactionary: extremist who not only opposes change, but generally would like to turn the clock back to the way things were before ***(p. 447)***

realism: realities of everyday life characterized in literature and art in the mid-1800s ***(p. 536)***

recession: period of temporary business slowdown and increased unemployment ***(p. 769)***

Reformation: religious revolution that split the Christian church in western Europe ***(p. 333)***

regionalism: portrayal of everyday life in different parts of a large country ***(p. 538)***

reincarnation: Hindu belief in transmigration of the soul ***(p. 58)***

Renaissance: movement following the Middle Ages that centered on revival of interest in the classical learning of Greece and Rome ***(p. 325)***

reparation: payment for war damages ***(p. 658)***

representative democracy: form of government in which citizens elect representatives to run the government for them ***(p. 115)***

republic: form of government in which voters elect their leaders ***(p. 145)***

revolution: violent attempt to change a country's government and society ***(p. 395)***

rhetoric: study of oratory, or public speaking ***(p. 117)***

Risorgimento: (ree • sor • jee • MEN • toh) Italian word for "resurgence," used as a name for Italian nationalist movement ***(p. 574)***

romantic movement; romanticism: trend followed by many writers of the early 1800s whose work appealed to sentiment and imagination and dealt with the romance of life—life as it used to be, or ought to be, rather than as it actually was ***(p. 534)***

S

sacrament: special ceremony at which a participant receives the direct favor, or grace, of God to help him or her ward off the consequences of sin ***(p. 233)***

salon: gathering of the social, political, and cultural elite in France ***(p. 423)***

samizdat: Russian word meaning "self-published"; described editions put out by banned authors ***(p. 868)***

samurai: (SAM • uh • ry) Japanese warlord who led local military units ***(p. 286)***

satellite country: nation dependent upon the Soviet Union ***(p. 758)***

savanna: vast area of relatively dry grassland ***(p. 295)***

scholasticism: attempt of medieval philosophers to reconcile faith and reason ***(p. 263)***

scientific method: inquiry method that includes carefully conducted experiments and mathematical calculations to verify the results of the experiments ***(p. 348)***

Scientific Revolution: transformation of thinking during the 1500s caused by experimentation and by questioning traditional opinions ***(p. 347)***

scorched-earth policy: practice of burning or destroying crops and everything else that might be of value to an enemy ***(p. 443)***

scribe: clerk who read or wrote for those who could not ***(p. 26)***

sea dog: English sea captain who was both trader and pirate ***(p. 410)***

secede: to withdraw from a union ***(p. 554)***

sect: society of a few people, usually with a preacher as their leader ***(p. 335)***

sectionalism: rivalry among the various sections of a country ***(p. 554)***

sepoy: (SEE • poy) local troop in India trained and led by a British officer ***(p. 474)***

seppuku: (se • POO • koo) form of ceremonial suicide known as hara-kiri, or "belly-slitting" ***(p. 286)***

serf: person bound to the land ***(p. 230)***

shire: governmental district in early England ***(p. 238)***

shogun: chief officer of the Japanese emperor and the agent of powerful families ***(p. 286)***

shuttle diplomacy: process in which a negotiator moves back and forth between countries for the purpose of reaching a peace agreement ***(p. 821)***

silt: fertile soil carried as sediment in river water ***(pp. 18, 71)***

simony: purchase of a church position during feudal times ***(p. 236)***

social Darwinism: application of Darwin's theory stating that society, like plant and animal worlds, had evolved from lower to higher forms through natural selection. If so-called inferior types were allowed to die out, then society would be made up exclusively of superior people ***(p. 531)***

R31

social science: field of study dealing with economic development, political institutions, history, and relations among people ***(p. 529)***
socialism: political and economic system based on the belief that the means of production should be owned by the government and should be operated for the welfare of all the people ***(p. 507)***
sole proprietorship: business owned and controlled by one person ***(p. 500)***
special theory of relativity: Einstein's theory that no particle of matter can move faster than the speed of light and that motion can be measured only relative to some particular observer ***(p. 520)***
sphere of influence: region where one nation has special economic and political privileges that are recognized by other nations ***(p. 602)***
stagflation: combination of decreased economic activity and continued price increases ***(p. 853)***
standard of living: measure of the quality of life of a people or a country ***(p. 345)***
steppe: vast, grassy plain in eastern Europe ***(p. 196)***
strike: bargaining method involving the refusal of workers to work until their demands have been met ***(p. 506)***
stupa: hemispherical or dome-shaped shrine that held objects associated with Buddha ***(p. 64)***
subsidy: government grant of money ***(p. 359)***
suffrage: voting rights ***(p. 544)***
suffragette: woman who wanted voting rights for all women ***(p. 547)***
sultan: Turkish ruler ***(p. 215)***
summit conference: meeting involving the highest officials of participating nations ***(p. 761)***
surrealism: art movement that attempted to portray and interpret life as if it took place in a dream ***(p. 666)***
suttee: ritual suicide by Indian widows ***(p. 64)***

T

taiga: (TY • guh) forest zone in northern region of Kievan states ***(p. 198)***
tariff: import tax on foreign goods ***(p. 359)***
tax farming: selling the right to collect taxes to private individuals ***(p. 377)***
Ten Commandments: moral laws of the Hebrews revealed to Moses by their god Yahweh ***(p. 42)***
tepee: cone-shaped tent made of buffalo hide ***(p. 306)***
terracing: creating small, flat plots of land by building low walls around the hillsides and filling the space behind them with soil ***(p. 115)***
terrorism: bombings, assassinations, and kidnappings by political groups to force governments to meet their demands ***(pp. 588, 824)***
theocracy: government ruled by the clergy ***(p. 336)***
tithe: church tax collected from Christians in early times that represented one-tenth of their income; today a tithe is a gift to a church that represents one-tenth of a person's income ***(pp. 236, 425)***
totalitarian regime: highly centralized government that allows no opposition and holds total control ***(p. 665)***
trade deficit: situation in which a country imports more than it exports ***(p. 853)***
tragedy: form of Greek drama showing the major character struggling against fate ***(p. 132)***
triangular trade: system through which European merchants shipped goods to Africa in exchange for slaves who were transported to America and sold to plantation owners ***(p. 365)***
tribune: Roman official elected by the Assembly of Tribes ***(p. 146)***
tropical rain forest: vast, forested region receiving more than 100 inches of annual rainfall ***(p. 294)***
troubadour: traveling singer who entertained people during the Middle Ages ***(p. 259)***
tyrant: someone who seizes power by force rather than by inheriting it and rules alone ***(p. 110)***

U

ujamaa: local cooperative village organized to increase productivity and improve standards of living in Tanzania ***(p. 814)***
ultimatum: demand that puts forth the final terms ordered for a settlement ***(p. 643)***
union: association of workers that plans actions and coordinates demands for workers ***(p. 507)***
universal manhood suffrage: the right of every man to vote, regardless of whether he owned property ***(p. 434)***
usury: (YOOZH • uh • ree) policy of charging interest on loans ***(p. 253)***
utilitarianism: belief that the principle of utility, or usefulness, was the standard by which to measure a society and its laws ***(p. 504)***
utopia: an ideal place or society ***(p. 331)***
utopian socialist: person who believes that people can live at peace with each other if they live in small cooperative settlements, owning all of the means of production in common and sharing the products ***(p. 510)***

R32

V

vassal: person granted land from a lord in return for services ***(p. 228)***

vernacular language: "everyday" speech that varies in different places ***(p. 259)***

veto: to refuse to approve a measure ***(p. 145)***

veto power: power to defeat a measure by a single vote ***(p. 755)***

viceroy: representative of the Spanish monarch ***(p. 367)***

W

war of attrition: slow wearing-down process in which each side tries to outlast the other ***(p. 650)***

welfare state: nation in which the government undertakes primary responsibility for the social welfare of its citizens ***(p. 764)***

Western civilization: civilization that evolved in Europe and in recent centuries spread to the Americas ***(p. 101)***

Y

yoga: Hindu religious practice of physical and mental discipline that harmonizes the body with the soul ***(p. 59)***

Z

ziggurat: Sumerian temple built in layers ***(p. 30)***

Zionism: movement to resettle Jews in Palestine ***(p. 692)***

R33

I • N • D • E • X

Page numbers in *italics* that have *c* before them refer to charts, diagrams, or graphs; *f,* to special features; *m,* to maps; *n,* to notes; and *p,* to pictures. The index employs two kinds of cross-references. *See* references lead the reader from a subject term to an alternate term under which page numbers will be found. An example of a *see* reference is

Catholic church. *See* Roman Catholic church

See also references lead the reader from one term, under which page numbers will appear, to another term under which additional information may be found. An example of a *see also* reference is

free enterprise, 502. *See also* laissez-faire

A

R34

R35

R36

C

R37

R38

R39

D

R40

E

R41

R42

R43

G

R44

H

R45

I

R46

J

K

R47

L

R48

M

R49

R50

N

R51

R52

P

R53

R54

Q

R

R55

S

R56

R57

R58

R59

U

R60

X

Y

Z

R62

Copyright © 1985 by National Geographic Society. From "Florence Rises From the Flood" by Joseph Judge in *National Geographic* Magazine, July 1967. Copyright © 1967 by National Geographic Society. From "The Search for Our Ancestors" by Kenneth F. Weaver in *National Geographic* Magazine, November 1985. Copyright © 1985 by National Geographic Society. *Jawaharlal Nehru Memorial Fund:* From "A Tryst with Destiny" in *Jawaharlal Nehru: An Anthology,* edited by Sarvepalli Gopal. © 1980 by Indira Gandhi. *W. W. Norton & Company, Inc.:* From "The Sources of the Cold War" in *On Every Front: The Making of the Cold War* by Thomas G. Paterson. Copyright © 1979 by W. W. Norton & Company, Inc. *Oxford University Press:* "The Origin and Nature of the State" from *Politics* by Aristotle, translated by Benjamin Jowett, in *The Works of Aristotle,* Volume X, edited by W. D. Ross. Published by The Clarendon Press, 1921. From *Documents in the Political History of the European Continent 1815–1939* by G. A. Kertesz. Published by Clarendon Press, 1968. *Penguin Books Ltd.:* From *The Book of the Courtier* by Baldesar Castiglione, translated by George Bull. Copyright © 1967 by George Bull. Published in Penguin Classics. From "The Prologue" in *Geoffrey Chaucer: THE CANTERBURY TALES,* translated by Nevill Coghill. Copyright © 1951, 1958, 1960 by Nevill Coghill. Published in Penguin Classics. From "Pericles' Funeral Oration" in *Thucydides: The Peloponnesian War,* translated by Rex Warner. © 1954 by Rex Warner. Published in Penguin Classics, 1954, 1972. From pp. 102, 105–106 in *Procopius: The Secret History,* translated by G. A. Williamson. Copyright © 1966 by G. A. Williamson. Published in Penguin Classics. From pp. 288–289 by Colonel Thomas Rainsborough in *DIVINE RIGHT AND DEMOCRACY: An Anthology of Political Writing in Stuart England,* edited by David Wootton. Copyright © 1986 by David Wootton. Published in Penguin Classics. *G. P. Putnam's Sons:* From *Personal Narrative of a Pilgrimage to El-Medinah and Meccah* by Richard F. Burton. Published by G. P. Putnam & Co., 1856. *Random House, Inc.:* From p. 244 in *PERÓN: A Biography* by Joseph A. Page. Copyright © 1983 by Joseph A. Page. "Knowing Oneself" by Lao-tzu from *The Wisdom of China and India,* edited by Lin Yutang. Copyright 1942, renewed 1970 by Random House, Inc. *Marian Reiner:* Haiku by Basho in *MORE CRICKET SONGS: Japanese haiku,* translated by Harry Behn. Copyright © 1971 by Harry Behn. All rights reserved. *The Estate of the Late Erich Maria Remarque:* From pp. 189 and 195 in *All Quiet on the Western Front* by Erich Maria Remarque. Copyright 1929, 1930 by Little, Brown and Company; copyright renewed 1957, 1958 by Erich Maria Remarque. All rights reserved. *Rutgers University Press:* From "Speech to the Reichstag" by Otto von Bismarck in *Documents of German History,* edited by Louis L. Snyder. Copyright © 1958 by Rutgers, The State University. *Simon & Schuster, Inc.:* From "They That Turn the Other Cheek" in *I Found No Peace* by Webb Miller. Copyright © 1936, 1963 by Webb Miller. From "The Sinews of Peace: Ex-Prime Minister Churchill Perceives an Iron Curtain" by Winston Churchill in *A Treasury of the World's Great Speeches,* edited by Houston Peterson. Copyright © 1954, 1965 by Simon & Schuster, Inc. *Thames and Hudson Ltd.:* From pp. 74–75 in *Babylon,* Revised Edition, by Joan Oates. © 1979, 1986 by Thames and Hudson Ltd., London. *Time Inc.:* From "The Magic Is Back!" by Leon Jaroff in *Time* Magazine, October 10, 1988. Copyright 1988 by Time Inc. *Time-Life Books Inc.:* Adapted from GREAT AGES OF MAN: *Imperial Rome* by Moses Hadas and the Editors of Time-Life Books. © 1965 by Time-Life Books Inc. *Charles E. Tuttle Co., Inc.:* From p. 15 in *The Code of the Samurai,* translated by A. L. Sadler. Copyright © 1941 by The Japan Foundation. *The University of Chicago Press:* From *Feudal Society* by Marc Bloch, translated by L. A. Manyon. Copyright © 1961 by The University of Chicago. *University of Pennsylvania Press, Philadelphia:* From pp. 15–16 in *History Begins at Sumer* by Samuel Noah Kramer. Copyright © 1981 by the University of Pennsylvania Press. *Viking Penguin, a division of Penguin Books USA, Inc.:* From "The Body Social: Paris During the Hundred Years War" by John of Salsbury in *The Portable Medieval Reader,* edited by James Bruce Ross and Mary Martin McLaughlin. Copyright 1949 by The Viking Press, Inc.; copyright renewed © 1977 by James Bruce Ross and Mary Martin McLaughlin. All rights reserved. From Chapter 9 in *The Grapes of Wrath* by John Steinbeck. Copyright 1939, renewed © 1967 by John Steinbeck. All rights reserved.

Photo Acknowledgements: Positions are shown in abbreviated form as follows: *t*-top, *b*-bottom, *c*-center, *l*-left, *r*-right, *i*-inset.

Key: AR-Art Resource; Bettmann-The Bettmann Archive; Granger-The Granger Collection.

Cover: K. Scholz/H. Armstrong Roberts, Inc.

Title Page: Granger

Front matter: vii *l,* Douglas Mazonowicz/Bruce Coleman, Inc; vii *r,* Ken McVey/After Image; viii *l,* Joe Viesti/Viesti Assoc.; viii *r,* Dallas & John Heaton/Stock, Boston; ix *l,* Dallas & John Heaton/After Image; ix *r,* Naples, Museo Nazionale-SCALA/AR; x *l,* Ken McVey/After Image; x *r,* Granger; xi *tl,* James J. Doro/Berg & Assoc.; xi *bl,* Granger; xi *r,* Granger; xii *l,* Bettmann; xii *r,* G. Otto-Alpha/FPG Int'l.; xiii *l,* Robert Frerck/Odyssey Productions; xiii *r,* Le Mans, Musee Tesse-Giraudon/AR; xiv *tl,* Granger; xiv *bl,* Paris, Carnavalet-Giraudon/AR; xiv *r,* Granger; xv *l,* Paris, Musee d'Orsay-Giraudon/AR; xv *r,* Guildhall Library, London-The Bridgeman Art Library/AR; xvi *l,* Granger; xvi *r,* SEF/AR; xvii *l,* Granger; xvii *r,* Granger; xviii *l,* SCALA/AR; xviii *r,* Granger; xix *l,* AP/Wide World Photos; xix *r,* Michele Grimm/After Image; xx *l,* Lincoln Potter/Gamma-Liaison; xx *r,* Patrick Durand/Sygma Photos; xxi *tl,* Robert Frerck/Odyssey Productions; xxi *bl,* J.L. Atlan/Sygma Photos; xxi *r,* NASA from PHOTRI;
xxvi *t,* Steve Vidler/After Image; xxvi *b,* Walter Frerck/Odyssey Productions;
xxx: *tlc,* SCALA/AR; *trc,* J.M. Giboux/Gamma Liaison; *bl,* Nicholas Foster/The Image Bank; *brc,* Alvin Upitis/Shostal Assoc.; *br,* Picture Archive; *xxxi: tl,* Joe Viesti, Viesti Assoc.; *tr,* Betty Press/Monkmeyer Press Photo Service; *tlc,* Lawrence Manning/Black Star; *trc,* Michael George/Bruce Coleman, Inc.; *br,* Robert Frerck/Odyssey Productions; *blc,* Orion Press-SCALA/AR; *brc,* Joe Viesti/Viesti Assoc.; *bl,* Milt & Joan Mann/Cameramann Int'l.
xxxii: *tl,* NASA; *tr,* Richard Pasley/Stock, Boston; *cr,* Lewis Portnoy/The Stock Market of NY; *bl,* Marc & Evelyn Bernheim/Woodfin Camp & Assoc.; *br,* Bettmann; xxxiii: *tl,* Mel Lindstrom/Tony Stone Worldwide; *tr,* Granger; *cl,* Winn Miller/After Image; *bl,* Granger; *br,* Roger Tully/After Image
xxxiv: *tl,* Picture Archive; *tr,* AR; *cl,* Florence, Pitti Gallery-SCALA/AR; *cr,* Picture Archive; *tc,* Damascus, Nat'l. Museum-Giraudon/AR; *bc,* Giraudon/AR; *bl,* Munich, Residenz Museum/AR; *br,* SCALA/AR; xxxv: *tl,* Camerique/H. Armstrong Roberts, Inc.; *tlc,* James Balog/After Image; *tr,* Dallas & John Heaton/After Image; *cr,* PHOTRI; *c,* Robert Frerck/Odyssey Productions; *bl,* Granger; *bc,* Lee Boltin; *br,* AR.
xxxvi: *tl,* K. Scholz/Shostal Assoc.; *tr,* Jehangir Gazdar/Woodfin Camp & Assoc.; *bl.,* Joe Viesti/Viesti Assoc.; *br,* Chuck Fishman/Woodfin Camp & Assoc.; xxxvii: *tl,* Roland & Sabrina Michaud/Woodfin Camp & Assoc.; *tr* & *cr,* Travelpix/FPG Int'l.; *bl,* Robert Frerck/Woodfin Camp & Assoc.; *br,* Wm. Herbeck/After Image.

Unit I: xl-1, F. Jackson/Bruce Coleman, Inc.; 2, Douglas Mazonowicz/Bruce Coleman, Inc.; 4, Mike Yamashita/Woodfin Camp & Assoc.; 7, Erich Lessing/Magnum Photos; 9*l,* Ara Guler/Magnum Photos; 9*r,* G. Tortoll/Sheridan-Ancient Art & Architecture Collection; 11, Mel Digiacomo/Image Bank; 16, Ken McVey/After Image; 19, Granger; 20, John Launois-Rapho/Black Star; 22, AR; 23, K. Scholz/H. Armstrong Roberts Inc.; 24, ZETA/H. Armstrong Roberts, Inc.; 25*t,* Louvre, Paris/AR; 25*b,* Borromeo/AR; 26, Carlos Sanuvo/Bruce Coleman, Inc.; 29, Lee Boltin Picture Library; 30, Georg Gerster/Comstock; 31, Rev. Schoder/Shostal Assoc.; 37, SEF/AR; 40*t,* Granger; 40*bl,* Cotton Coulson/Woodfin Camp & Assoc.; 40*br,* H. Kingsnorth-Ace/Nawrocki Stock Photo; 41*tl,* Robert B. Pickering/Nawrocki Stock Photo; 41*i,* John Wilson/Nawrocki Stock Photo; 41*b,* All photos Granger except third row left, Nawrocki Stock Photo; 42, Jewish Museum/AR; 44, PHOTRI; 45, A. Himmelreich/FPG; 48, Joe Viesti/Viesti Assoc.; 51, J. Hiebeler/Leo De Wys, Inc.; 52, SCALA/AR; 53, A.R. Khan/Shostal Assoc.; 55, Rome, Museo Nazionale d'Arte Orientale-SCALA/AR; 56, Frank T. Wood/Shostal Assoc.; 59, Three Lions-The Photo Source/Super Stock Int'l; 65*t,* Harold Courlander: Illustration by Enrico Arno From The Tiger's Whisker And Other Tales and Legends From Asia And The Pacific; 65*b,* Culver Pictures; 68, Dallas & John Heaton/Stock, Boston; 72, Cultural Relics Bureau, Beijing, Courtesy Metropolitan Museum of Art; 74*l,* BMFA/Bettmann; 74*c,* Courtesy of the Freer Gallery of Art, Smithsonian Institution, Washington, DC; 74*r,* FOG/Bettmann; 76, Ronald Sheridan Ancient Art & Architecture Collection/AR; 78, Kurt Scholz/Shostal Assoc.; 80, Belzeaux-Rapho/Photo Researchers; 81, Vince Streano/After Image; 83, Paris, Musee Cernuschi-Giraudon/AR; 84, J. Alex Langley/DPI; 85*t,* Joe Viesti/Viesti Assoc.; 85*bl,* Musee Guimet, Cliche Des Musee Nationaux, Paris; 85*br,* Bettmann; 86, Dallas & John Heaton/After Image; 93, Ken McVey/After Image; 95, Joe Viesti/Viesti Assoc.; 97, Dallas & John Heaton/Stock, Boston.

UNIT II: 98–99, Nimatallah/AR; 100, Dallas & John Heaton/ After Image; 103*t.* G.A. Mowat/Taurus Photos; 103*c.* Elisa Leonelli/After Image; 103*b,* Lou Witt/Shostal Assoc.; 104, Heraklion Museum, From Knossos, SCALA/AR; 105*tl,* Museo Nazionale, Athens-SCALA/AR; 105*r,* Athens, National Museum, Dan J. McCoy/Black Star; 105*bl,* Ronald Sheridan/Ancient Art & Architecture Collection; 107, Granger; 109, Nimatallah/AR; 111, William Hubbell/Woodfin Camp & Assoc.; 113, Dan McCoy/Black Star; 114, Uffizi, Florence-SCALA/AR; 116, Vatican Museum, SCALA/AR; 117*t,* Granger; 117*b,* The Louvre, Photo Giraudon Orion Press/AR; 121, J. Paul Kennedy/The Stock Market of NY; 124, Naples, Museo Nazionale, SCALA/AR; 126*i,* K. Benser-Zefa/H. Armstrong Roberts, Inc.; 127, Jan Lukas/AR; 129, Naples, Museo Nazionale, SCALA/AR; 131, Robert Frerck/Odyssey Productions; 132, Ronald Sheridan Ancient Art & Architecture Collection/AR; 133*tl,* Granger; 133*c,* © RMN/Louvre, Paris/AR; 133*r,* The Greek Ministry of Culture & Sciences, Prof. Manolis Andronikos/AR; 135, New York Public Library; 136*tl,* Istanbul, Museo Archeological/AR; 136*tr,* Paris, Louvre-SCALA/AR; 136*b,* Florence, Palace Vecchio-SCALA/AR; 139, Louvre, Paris, Giraudon/AR; 142, Ken McVey/After Image; 147*l,* Naples, Museo Nazionale-SCALA/AR; 147*r,* Rome, Museum of the Roman Civilization, SCALA/AR; 151*t,* Blaine Harrington/The Stock Market of New York; 151*b,* Friedman Damm/Leo De Wys, Inc.; 153, Robert Emmett Bright/Photo Researchers; 154, SCALA/AR; 157, Robert Frerck/Odyssey Productions; 158, Naples, National Museum-SEF/AR; 161, Granger; 163, SCALA/AR; 167, Paris, Louvre-Giraudon/AR; 170, Granger; 172*t,* SCALA/AR; 172*bl,* SCALA/AR; 172*br,* Bruce Hoertel/Gamma-Liaison; 173*tl,* Everett C. Johnson/After Image; 173*tr,* Randy Wells/The Stock Market of NY; 173*bl,* Piotr Kapa/The Stock Market of NY; 173*br,* SCALA/AR; 179, Dallas & John Heaton/After Image; 180, Naples, Museo Nazionale, SCALA/AR; 183, Ken McVey/After Image.

UNIT III: 184–185, Granger; 186, Luis Villota/The Stock Market of NY; 190, Cairo, Coptic Museum-Borromeo/AR; 191, Florence, Museo Del Bargello-SCALA/AR; 192*l,* AR; 192*r,* AR; 193, Erich Lessing/Magnum Culture-Fine Art Archives; 195*t,* Milton & Joan Mann/Cameramann Int'l; 195*c,* F. Grehan/FPG; 195*b,* K. Scholz/H. Armstrong Roberts, Inc.; 198, AR; 199, Granger; 200, K. Scholz/H. Armstrong Roberts, Inc.; 201, Werner H. Muller/Peter Arnold, Inc.; 204, James J. Doro/Berg and Assoc., 207, Robert Azzi/Woodfin Camp & Assoc.; 208, Roland & Sabrina Michaud/Woodfin Camp & Assoc.; 211*r,* Norman A. Thompson/Taurus Photos; 211*i,* Norman A. Thompson/Taurus Photos; 212*l,* Steve Dunwell/The Image Bank; 212*r,* Cairo, Bib. National-Giraudon/AR; 213, Roland & Sabrina Michaud/Woodfin Camp & Assoc.; 214, The Metropolitan Museum of Art, Bequest of Joseph V. McMallan, 1973. (1974.149.18); 217, M. Biber/Photo Researchers; 219, Thomas Rampy/The Image Bank; 222, Granger; 225, Giraudon/AR; 229, Bettmann; 230, Chantilly, Musee Conde-Giraudon/AR; 232, 234, 235, Granger; 237, Giraudon/AR; 240, Granger; 241, Bettmann; 244, Kunsthistorisches Museum, Vienna; 248, Granger; 252, Werner Braun; 252*i,* Bettmann; 254*l,* Culver Pictures; 254*r,* HBJ Photo/Maria Paraskevas; 255, Granger; 256, Josse-SCALA/AR; 258, Granger; 260, Granger; 261, Giraudon/AR; 262, Susan McCartney/Photo Researchers; 262*i,* Shostal Assoc.; 264, Vidler/Leo De Wys, Inc.; 270, Granger; 274, Bettmann; 277, Granger; 279*l,* Granger; 279*r,* Paris, Bibliotheque Nationale-Giraudon/AR; 283, Granger; 285*t,* Steve Vidler/Leo De Wys, Inc.; 285*bl,* Max Tortel/DPI; 285*br,* L.T. Rhodes/Taurus Photos; 287, Granger; 288, Boston Museum of Fine Arts/Bettmann; 292, G. Otto-Alpha/FPG; 296*t,* Lawrence Manning/Black Star; 296*bl,* Sam Emerson/Sygma;

R63

296*br*, Robert Weaver/Gamma Liaison; 296*i*, Granger; 297, Mike Yamashita/Woodfin Camp & Assoc.; 299, Marc & Evelyn Bernheim/Woodfin Camp & Assoc.; 300, Smithsonian Institution, Museum of African Art, Aldo Tution/AR; 301, Granger; 302, Smithsonian Insitution, Museum of African Art-Aldo Tutino/AR; 305*l*, 305*r*, Granger; 306, Ron Sanford/Black Star; 308*t*, Jewish Museum/AR; 308*b*, SCALA/AR; 309*t*, Gay Marche/FPG; 309*c*, Robert Lackenback/Black Star; 309*b*, Paris, Bibl. Palais Bourbon-Giraudon/AR; 310, M.P.L. Fogden/Bruce Coleman, Inc.; 311*l*, Granger; 311*r*, Bettmann; 317, James J. Doro/Berg & Assoc.; 318, Granger; 319,Granger; 320, Bettmann; 321, G. Otto-Alpha/FPG.

Unit IV: 322–323, (c) Musee Nationaux, Paris; 324, Robert Frerck/Odyssey Productions; 327, Musee Des Beaux-Arts De Lille, Jardin Du Musee-Giraudon/AR; 328, SCALA/AR; 329, SCALA/AR; 330, Rome, Gallery Borghese-SCALA/AR; 332, Nuremberg, National Museum-SCALA/AR; 333, Chantilly, Musee Conde-Giraudon/AR; 334, Nuremberg, National Museum-SCALA/AR; 337, Paris, Louvre-Giraudon/AR; 338, SCALA/AR; 339, Granger; 342, Saskia/AR; 343*t*, SCALA/AR; 343*b*, Bob Daemmrich/Stock, Boston; 345, Granger; 346, Uffizi/AR; 348, SCALA/AR; 350, Paris, Louvre-Giraudon/AR; 351, Giraudon/AR; 353, Jan Lukas/AR; 354, Le Mans, Musee Tesse-Giraudon/AR; 356, Frankfort, Stadelsches Kunstinstitat/Joachim Blauel-Artothek; 357, Florence, Museum of Science-SCALA/AR; 358*l*, Frank Lawrence Stevens/Nawrocki Stock Photo; 358*r*, Granger; 362, Granger; 363, Bettmann; 364, 367, Granger; 370, Madrid, Prado-SCALA/AR; 372*t*, Howard Jensen-SCALA/AR; 372*b*, National Geographic Society Photograph, Courtesy U.S. Capitol Historical Society; 373*t*, Giraudon/AR; 373*c*, Granger; 373*b*, Giraudon/AR; 376, Holland, The Hague-SCALA/AR; 377, 379, 380, Granger; 384*t*, Bettmann; 384*b*, Granger; 386, Granger; 388, Martin Van Meytens/AR; 389, Chantilly, Musee. Conde, Chambre De La Reine-Giraudon/AR; 394, 396, 397, 399, Granger; 401, Bettmann; 403, Granger; 404, Granger; 406*t*, J. Paul Kennedy/The Stock Market of NY; 406*b*, Granger; 408, By Courtesy of the Dean and Chapter of Westminster, The Bridgeman Art Library/AR; 409, 410, 411, Granger; 414, Granger; 420, Giraudon/AR; 422, Musee Des Beaux Arts, Rouen-Giraudon/AR; 425, AR; 427, Lauros, Giraudon/AR; 428*t*, Granger; 428*r*, Cesar Vera/Leo De Wys, Inc.; 428*bl*, Baldev/Shostal Associates; 430, 432, 433, 435, 436, Granger; 437, Musees Royaux Des Beaux-Arts De Belgique, Bruxelles; 438, Lieges, Beaux-Arts-SCALA/AR; 441, Giraudon/AR; 445, 448, 452, 457, Granger; 458, Orion Press-SCALA/AR; 459, Granger; 461, Granger; 462, Bettmann; 464, Picture Archive; 466, AR; 467, Picture Archive; 468*l*, 468*r*, The Lowe Art Museum/University of Miami; 469, Istanbul, Library of Topkapi Palace-Giraudon/AR; 471, SEF/AR; 473, Granger; 475, Granger; 481, Robert Frerck/Odyssey Productions; 482, Le Mans, Musee Tesse-Giraudon/AR; 484, Paris, Carnavalet–Giraudon/AR.

Unit V: 486–487, Picture Archive; 488, Paris, Musee D'Orsay-Giraudon/AR; 491, Granger; 492, Granger; 494, Picture Archive; 498, Snark Int'l/AR; 500, Culver Pictures; 502, Granger; 505, Granger; 506, Bettmann; 508*t*, The Bridgeman Art Library/AR; 508*b*, 509*t*, 509*bl*, 509*br*, 510, 511, Granger; 514, Guildhall Library, London-The Bridgeman Art Library/AR; 516, AR; 517, Bettmann; 519*t*, Culver Pictures; 519*bl*, NASA; 519*br*, The Museum of Modern Art Film Stills Archives; 520, Granger; 522, Brown Brothers; 523, Granger; 524, Gernsheim Collection-Harry Ransom Humanities Research Center/The University of Texas at Austin; 525, Culver Pictures; 527, Culver Pictures; 528, SCALA/AR; 529, Winslow Homer, The Croquet Game, 1866, Oil on Canvas, 15.9 × 26.1 CM, Friends of American Art Collection, 1942.35 © 1988 Art Institute of Chicago; 530, Granger; 531, Snark Int'l/AR; 532, Granger; 533, Culver Pictures; 536, 537, Paris, Louvre-SCALA/AR; 538, Mary Cassatt, The Bath, 1891/92, Oil on Canvas, 99.2 × 66.1 CM, Robert Waller Fund, 1910.2, (C) 1988 The Art Institute of Chicago; 539, Giraudon/AR; 542, 545*t*, 545*b*, Granger; 546, Culver Pictures; 548*t*, 548*b*, HBJ Photo; 550*t*, Culver Pictures; 550*b*, 556, 560, Granger; 561, Paris, Carnavalet-Giraudon/AR; 563, Granger; 564, Granger; 566, Bettmann; 567, Granger; 572, 574, SEF/AR; 576, SCALA/AR; 579, Culver Pictures; 581, Granger; 585, Granger; 586, Paris, Bibliotheque Nationale, Estampes-Giraudon/AR; 589, Walters Art Gallery, Baltimore, Courtesy of Robert Forbes Collection; 590, 591, SEF/AR; 595, Granger; 598, Granger; 601, Brown Brothers; 603, SEF/AR; 604, Granger; 609, SEF/AR; 611, Bettmann; 612, Orion Press-SCALA/AR; 614, Orion Press-SCALA/AR; 620, Brown Brothers; 621, Granger; 622, Bettmann; 623, Milton & Joan Mann/Cameramann Int'l; 625, Brown Brothers; 631, Guildhall Library, London-The Bridgeman Art Library/AR; 633, SEF/AR; 635, Granger.

Unit VI: 636–637, The Trustees of the Imperial War Museum, London; 638, Granger; 641, BBC Hulton Picture Library/Bettmann; 643, Granger; 646*t*, Bettmann; 646*bl*, Giraudon/AR; 646*br*, Granger; 647*t*, UPI/Bettmann Newsphotos; 647*c*, SIPA-Press; 647*bl*, George Hall/After Image; 647 *br*, PHOTRI; 649*tr*, Peter Menzel/Stock, Boston; 649*l*, Culver Pictures; 649*br*, Dan McCoy/Rainbow; 652, Brown Brothers; 653, Granger; 655, Snark Int'l/AR; 657, The Trustees of the Imperial War Museum, London; 661, Bettmann; 664, SCALA/AR; 668, The Museum of Modern Art/Film Stills Archive; 669, Bettmann; 670, Western Pennsylvania Conservancy/AR; 673, Bettmann; 674, Photoworld/FPG Int'l; 676, Brown Brothers; 677, Granger; 679, AP/Wide World Photos; 681, UPI/Bettmann Newsphotos; 682, Bettmann; 684, UPI/Bettmann Newsphotos; 686, Bettmann; 690, Granger; 693, UPI/Bettmann Newsphotos; 695, UPI/Bettmann Newsphotos; 697, Bettmann; 701, Collection J. A. F.-Paris/Magnum Photos; 702, SEF/AR; 703, Culver Pictures; 705, Dr. E.R. Degginger, FPSA; 706, 710, AP/Wide World Photos; 714, Seymour/Magnum Photos; 715, Prado, Madrid/AR; 718, AP/Wide World Photos; 719, Franklin D. Roosevelt Library; 721, Granger; 723, Robert Capa/Magnum Photos; 724, Photoworld/FPG Int'l; 728, Galen Rowell/After Image; 731, Franklin D. Roosevelt Library; 734, Culver Pictures; 735, Granger; 736, UPI/Bettmann Newsphoto; 737, UPI/Wide World Photos; 743, Granger; 744, SCALA/AR; 745, Granger; 747, AP/Wide World Photos.

Unit VII: 748–749, E. Streichan/Shostal Assoc.; 750, Tom & Michele Grimm/After Image; 753, Planet News Ltd./Black Star; 754, FPG Int'l; 757, 758, UPI/Bettmann Newsphotos; 760, AP/Wide World Photos; 762, UPI/Bettmann Newsphotos; 765, AP/Wide World Photos; 766, E. Streichan/Shostal Assoc.; 768, AP/Wide World Photos; 770, UPI/Bettmann Newsphoto; 774, Lincoln Potter/Gamma-Liaison; 777, L.S. Williams/H. Armstrong Roberts Inc.; 778, Terry Qing/Alpha-FPG; 780, Magnum Photos; 781, Robin Moyer/Gamma-Liaison; 782, P. Durand/Sygma Photos; 785, Chad Ehlers/Int'l Stock Photo; 788, Baldev/Sygma Photos; 789, John Paul Kay/Peter Arnold, Inc.; 790, Alfred/SIPA-Press; 792, Cooper Hewitt Museum-Smithsonian Institution/AR; 793, Paul Steel/The Stock Market of N. Y.; 798, Magnus Bartlett-Asia Pix/Woodfin Camp & Assoc.; 799, Marilyn Silverstone/Magnum Photos; 801, Sandro Tucci/Gamma-Liaison; 803, Len Berger/Shostal Assoc.; 806, Patrick Durand/Sygma Photos; 808, John Moss/Black Star; 811, Robinson/Black Star; 812, Peter Jordan/Gamma-Liaison; 815, Gamma-Liaison; 816, G. Mendel/Magnum Photos; 817, Rothwell/After Image; 818, Micha Bar-Am/Magnum Photos; 821, Granger; 822, Robert Azzi/Woodfin Camp & Assoc.; 824, Reza/SIPA-Press; 825, Dennis Brack/Black Star; 827, Robert Azzi/Woodfin Camp & Assoc.; 830, Robert Frerck/Odyssey Productions; 832, Stephanie Maze/Woodfin Camp & Assoc.; 833, Montes/SIPA-Press; 834, Robert Frerck/Odyssey Productions; 835, Randy G. Taylor/Sygma Photos; 836, Robert Frerck/Woodfin Camp & Assoc.; 838, T. Campion/Sygma Photos; 840, Bleibtreu/Sygma Photos; 841, Salas-Lockwood/Black Star; 842, Susan Greenwood/Gamma-Liaison; 843, P. Chauvel/Sygma Photos; 844, Besar Cichero Sigha/Black Star; 845*t*, 845*b*, Bill Curtsinger/ Photo Researchers; 847, M. Montecino/Woodfin Camp & Assoc.; 850, J.L. Atlan/Sygma Photos; 852, Nik Wheeler/SIPA-Press; 855, Wally McNamee/Woodfin Camp & Assoc.; 856, Steve Vidler/After Image; 858, Homer Sykes/Woodfin Camp & Assoc.; 860, Dallas & John Heaton/After Image; 861, NASA; 863, Christiana Dittmann/Rainbow; 867, J. Langevin/Sygma Photos; 869, Vauthey/Sygma Photos; 870, Peter Turnely/Black Star; 873, William Strode/Woodfin Camp & Assoc.; 874, NASA From PHOTRI; 877, Orlando Sentinel/Sygma Photos; 879*tl*, Julius Vitali/SIPA-Press; 879*br*, Sepp Seitz/Woodfin Camp & Assoc.; 880, Dan McCoy/Rainbow; 882*t*, 882*b*, Robert Frerck/Odyssey Productions; 883*t*, AR; 883*c*, Robert Frerck/Odyssey Productions; 883*b*, Baron Wolman/After Image; 885, Bill Ross/Woodfin Camp & Assoc.; 886, Berenholtz/The Stock Market of NY; 887, Harvey Lloyd/The Stock Market of NY; 888, Rene Burri/Magnum Photos; 890, Robert Frerck/Odyssey Productions; 892, Henry D. Meyer/Berg & Assoc.; 893, Margaret McCarthy/The Stock Market of NY; 899, Lincoln Potter/Gamma Liaison; 901, Patrick Durand/Sygma Photos; 902, J.L. Atlan/Sygma Photos.

Art Credits: Simon Galkin, pgs. 2, 15, 30, 48, 68, 100, 124, 126, 142, 186, 204, 222, 248, 274, 288, 292, 324, 354, 394, 398, 420, 452, 488, 514, 542, 572, 598, 638, 664, 690, 710, 750, 774, 806, 830, 850, 874.

Maps prepared by R. R. Donnelley & Sons Company Cartographic Services.

R64